CONTENTS

TIME AND SPACE

PREFACE

Having taken up the reins of *Whitaker's Almanack* at the tail end of 2008, I had fully expected to be immersed in a time-honoured process of detailing such important yet relatively uncontroversial matters of record as the composition of parliament and the pay scales of MPs, so nothing had quite prepared me for what lay ahead. Yes, recession had already coiled itself around the UK, squeezing ever tighter and showing no immediate signs of relaxing its grip, but who knew that these dire financial straits would imbue the domestic news story of the year with such a strong sense of moral urgency?

As the saga of MPs' expenses broke, and then broke some more, unfolding an embarrassment of articles over the front pages of *The Daily Telegraph,* it was as if the whole of parliament had been caught fiddling while the UK burned. Each day a further outrage – a 1p phone bill here, a £1,645 floating duck mansion there – was met with growing disbelief. Yet few could wonder at the public outcry. Against a more favourable economic backdrop, perhaps MPs' expenses would have been but a footnote to other events, but this year they seemed to pulse with the same beat, at once symbolising all that was rotten with the economy, local and global, and serving as a focal point of anger for those who were losing jobs, homes and hope, and palpably suffering the fallout firsthand.

As the UK economy languished in the doldrums, bankers proved to be the nation's other favourite blame figures, their unfettered practices having helped to dislodge the country's fiscal system and throw it into disarray. That disarray fermented into discontent, which in turn received concrete expression in the form of the G20 protests on the streets of London and outside the Bank of England (this is the scene depicted in the main image on the front cover). To say it has not been a good year would be an understatement. Key indicators of economic 'health', such as unemployment figures and GDP, take us back not to recent recessions, but plunge us back 80 years, to an economic blight not encountered since the Great Depression. The situation is brought home in the new graphs we've added to introduce this edition's revised and expanded Economic Statistics chapter.

Sadly this year there's been no obvious chink of light, no proverbial silver lining. Yet some solace might be drawn from the fact that the recession has been global (the UK was not alone in its suffering) and an incoming US president arrived with a promise of change. Having galloped to success at the polls in November 2008, Barack Obama seemed equipped to ride the economic storm, albeit propping up the American economy with an unprecedented multibillion-dollar figure. Gordon Brown, however, only just clung on to his premiership when his party attempted to oust him in June. Of course in America there had been no adversary as formidable as the actress best known for her absolutely fabulous turn in a BBC sitcom. Winning public support with more aplomb than the politicians themselves, Joanna Lumley campaigned successfully for Gurkha veterans to have the right to settle in the UK – and received a hero's welcome when she subsequently visited Nepal.

On the international stage, events spiralled. Swine flu swept out from the shutdown on the streets of Mexico City and went on to earn pandemic status, according to the WHO. Protesters flooded the streets of Tehran, demanding democratic change from Iran's clerical rulers. The war in Afghanistan continued, but casualties increased and as the number of British military deaths passed that in Iraq, UK officials faced criticism for not supplying the armed forces with adequate equipment. With Gordon Brown's popularity dipping ever lower, David Cameron looks more like a restless PM-in-waiting than ever. The last date for a general election to take place is 3 June 2010. In the meantime readers can find full details of the 2009 European elections inside this edition: the voting system, lists of all the UK members and UK regional results are in the European Parliament chapter.

On a personal note I am delighted to be joining Whitaker's for its 142nd edition. It is a book I have always admired. Everything in this edition is, as usual, meticulously checked and updated using the most authoritative sources. We are highly appreciative of the thousands of organisations and individuals who go out of their way to respond to our requests for information. I would also like to thank our contributors for their profound subject expertise as well as our in-house team whose unwavering concentration in the face of seemingly boundless facts ensures the whole volume comes together in the form before you now.

Claire Fogg
Editor-in-Chief
September 2009

THE YEAR 2010

CHRONOLOGICAL CYCLES AND ERAS

Dominical Letter	C
Epact	14
Golden Number (Lunar Cycle)	XVI
Julian Period	6723
Roman Indiction	3

	Beginning
Muslim year AH 1431*	18 Dec 2009
Japanese year Heisei 22	1 Jan
Roman year 2763 AUC	14 Jan
Regnal year 59	6 Feb
Chinese year of the Tiger	14 Feb
Sikh new year	14 Mar
Hindu new year (Chaitra)	16 Mar
Indian (Saka) year 1932	22 Mar
Jewish year AM 5771*	9 Sep

* Year begins at sunset on the previous day

RELIGIOUS CALENDARS

CHRISTIAN

Epiphany	6 Jan
Presentation of Christ in the Temple	2 Feb
Ash Wednesday	17 Feb
The Annunciation	25 Mar
Palm Sunday	28 Mar
Maundy Thursday	1 Apr
Good Friday	2 Apr
Easter Day (western churches)	4 Apr
Easter Day (Eastern Orthodox)	4 Apr
Rogation Sunday	9 May
Ascension Day	13 May
Pentecost (Whit Sunday)	23 May
Trinity Sunday	30 May
Corpus Christi	3 June
All Saints' Day	1 Nov
Advent Sunday	28 Nov
Christmas Day	25 Dec

HINDU

Makara Sankranti	14 Jan
Vasant Panchami (Sarasvati Puja)	20 Jan
Mahashivaratri	12 Feb
Holi	28 Feb
Chaitra (Spring new year)	16 Mar
Ramanavami	24 Mar
Raksha Bandhan	24 Aug
Janmashtami	1 Sep
Ganesh Chaturthi, first day	11 Sep
Navaratri festival (Durga Puja), first day	8 Oct
Dasara	17 Oct
Diwali (New Year festival of lights), first day	3 Nov

JEWISH

Purim	28 Feb
Pesach (Passover), first day	30 Mar
Shavuoth (Feast of Weeks), first day	19 May
Rosh Hashanah (Jewish new year)	9 Sep
Yom Kippur (Day of Atonement)	18 Sep
Succoth (Feast of Tabernacles), first day	23 Sep
Hanukkah, first day	2 Dec

MUSLIM

Al-Hijra (Muslim new year)	18 Dec 2009
Ashura	27 Dec 2009
Ramadan, first day	12 Aug
Eid-ul-Fitr	10 Sep
Hajj	15 Nov
Eid-ul-Adha	17 Nov

SIKH

Birthday of Guru Gobind Singh Ji	5 Jan
1 Chet (Sikh new year)	14 Mar
Baisakhi Mela	13 Apr
Birthday of Guru Nanak Dev Ji	14 Apr†
Martyrdom of Guru Arjan Dev Ji	16 Jun
Martyrdom of Guru Tegh Bahadur Ji	24 Nov

† This festival is also currently celebrated according to the lunar calendar

CIVIL CALENDAR

Countess of Wessex's birthday	20 Jan
Accession of the Queen	6 Feb
Duke of York's birthday	19 Feb
St David's Day	1 Mar
Commonwealth Day	8 Mar
Earl of Wessex's birthday	10 Mar
St Patrick's Day	17 Mar
Birthday of the Queen	21 Apr
St George's Day	23 Apr
Europe Day	9 May
Coronation Day	2 Jun
Duke of Edinburgh's birthday	10 Jun
The Queen's Official Birthday	12 Jun
Duchess of Cornwall's birthday	17 Jul
Princess Royal's birthday	15 Aug
Lord Mayor's Day	13 Nov
Prince of Wales' birthday	14 Nov
Remembrance Sunday	14 Nov
Wedding Day of the Queen	20 Nov
St Andrew's Day	30 Nov

LEGAL CALENDAR

LAW TERMS

Hilary Term	11 Jan to 31 Mar
Easter Term	13 Apr to 28 May
Trinity Term	8 Jun to 31 Jul
Michaelmas Term	1 Oct to 21 Dec

QUARTER DAYS	TERM DAYS
England, Wales and Northern Ireland	*Scotland*
Lady – 25 Mar	Candlemas – 28 Feb
Midsummer – 24 Jun	Whitsunday – 28 May
Michaelmas – 29 Sep	Lammas – 28 Aug
Christmas – 25 Dec	Martinmas – 28 Nov

2010

JANUARY

Sunday		3	10	17	24	31
Monday		4	11	18	25	
Tuesday		5	12	19	26	
Wednesday		6	13	20	27	
Thursday		7	14	21	28	
Friday	1	8	15	22	29	
Saturday	2	9	16	23	30	

FEBRUARY

Sunday		7	14	21	28
Monday	1	8	15	22	
Tuesday	2	9	16	23	
Wednesday	3	10	17	24	
Thursday	4	11	18	25	
Friday	5	12	19	26	
Saturday	6	13	20	27	

MARCH

Sunday		7	14	21	28
Monday	1	8	15	22	29
Tuesday	2	9	16	23	30
Wednesday	3	10	17	24	31
Thursday	4	11	18	25	
Friday	5	12	19	26	
Saturday	6	13	20	27	

APRIL

Sunday		4	11	18	25
Monday		5	12	19	26
Tuesday		6	13	20	27
Wednesday		7	14	21	28
Thursday	1	8	15	22	29
Friday	2	9	16	23	30
Saturday	3	10	17	24	

MAY

Sunday		2	9	16	23	30
Monday		3	10	17	24	31
Tuesday		4	11	18	25	
Wednesday		5	12	19	26	
Thursday		6	13	20	27	
Friday		7	14	21	28	
Saturday	1	8	15	22	29	

JUNE

Sunday		6	13	20	27
Monday		7	14	21	28
Tuesday	1	8	15	22	29
Wednesday	2	9	16	23	30
Thursday	3	10	17	24	
Friday	4	11	18	25	
Saturday	5	12	19	26	

JULY

Sunday		4	11	18	25
Monday		5	12	19	26
Tuesday		6	13	20	27
Wednesday		7	14	21	28
Thursday	1	8	15	22	29
Friday	2	9	16	23	30
Saturday	3	10	17	24	31

AUGUST

Sunday	1	8	15	22	29
Monday	2	9	16	23	30
Tuesday	3	10	17	24	31
Wednesday	4	11	18	25	
Thursday	5	12	19	26	
Friday	6	13	20	27	
Saturday	7	14	21	28	

SEPTEMBER

Sunday		5	12	19	26
Monday		6	13	20	27
Tuesday		7	14	21	28
Wednesday	1	8	15	22	29
Thursday	2	9	16	23	30
Friday	3	10	17	24	
Saturday	4	11	18	25	

OCTOBER

Sunday		3	10	17	24	31
Monday		4	11	18	25	
Tuesday		5	12	19	26	
Wednesday		6	13	20	27	
Thursday		7	14	21	28	
Friday	1	8	15	22	29	
Saturday	2	9	16	23	30	

NOVEMBER

Sunday		7	14	21	28
Monday	1	8	15	22	29
Tuesday	2	9	16	23	30
Wednesday	3	10	17	24	
Thursday	4	11	18	25	
Friday	5	12	19	26	
Saturday	6	13	20	27	

DECEMBER

Sunday		5	12	19	26
Monday		6	13	20	27
Tuesday		7	14	21	28
Wednesday	1	8	15	22	29
Thursday	2	9	16	23	30
Friday	3	10	17	24	31
Saturday	4	11	18	25	

PUBLIC HOLIDAYS	*England and Wales*	*Scotland*	*Northern Ireland*
New Year	1 January†	1, 4† January	1 January†
St Patrick's Day	—	—	17 March
*Good Friday	2 April	2 April	2 April
Easter Monday	5 April	—	5 April
Early May	3 May†	3 May	3 May†
Spring	31 May	31 May†	31 May
Battle of the Boyne	—	—	12 July‡
Summer	30 August	2 August	30 August
St Andrew's Day	—	30 Nov§	—
*Christmas	27, 28 December	27, 28 December†	27, 28 December

* In England, Wales and Northern Ireland, Christmas Day and Good Friday are common law holidays

† Subject to royal proclamation

‡ Subject to proclamation by the Secretary of State for Northern Ireland

§ The St Andrew's Day Holiday (Scotland) Bill was approved by parliament on 29 November 2006; it does not oblige employers to change their existing pattern of holidays but provides the legal framework in which the St Andrew's Day bank holiday could be substituted for an existing local holiday from another date in the year

Note: In the Channel Islands, Liberation Day is a bank and public holiday

2011

JANUARY

Sunday		2	9	16	23	30
Monday		3	10	17	24	31
Tuesday		4	11	18	25	
Wednesday		5	12	19	26	
Thursday		6	13	20	27	
Friday		7	14	21	28	
Saturday	1	8	15	22	29	

FEBRUARY

Sunday		6	13	20	27
Monday		7	14	21	28
Tuesday	1	8	15	22	
Wednesday	2	9	16	23	
Thursday	3	10	17	24	
Friday	4	11	18	25	
Saturday	5	12	19	26	

MARCH

Sunday		6	13	20	27
Monday		7	14	21	28
Tuesday	1	8	15	22	29
Wednesday	2	9	16	23	30
Thursday	3	10	17	24	31
Friday	4	11	18	25	
Saturday	5	12	19	26	

APRIL

Sunday		3	10	17	24
Monday		4	11	18	25
Tuesday		5	12	19	26
Wednesday		6	13	20	27
Thursday		7	14	21	28
Friday	1	8	15	22	29
Saturday	2	9	16	23	30

MAY

Sunday	1	8	15	22	29
Monday	2	9	16	23	30
Tuesday	3	10	17	24	31
Wednesday	4	11	18	25	
Thursday	5	12	19	26	
Friday	6	13	20	27	
Saturday	7	14	21	28	

JUNE

Sunday		5	12	19	26
Monday		6	13	20	27
Tuesday		7	14	21	28
Wednesday	1	8	15	22	29
Thursday	2	9	16	23	30
Friday	3	10	17	24	
Saturday	4	11	18	25	

JULY

Sunday		3	10	17	24	31
Monday		4	11	18	25	
Tuesday		5	12	19	26	
Wednesday		6	13	20	27	
Thursday		7	14	21	28	
Friday	1	8	15	22	29	
Saturday	2	9	16	23	30	

AUGUST

Sunday		7	14	21	28
Monday	1	8	15	22	29
Tuesday	2	9	16	23	30
Wednesday	3	10	17	24	31
Thursday	4	11	18	25	
Friday	5	12	19	26	
Saturday	6	13	20	27	

SEPTEMBER

Sunday		4	11	18	25
Monday		5	12	19	26
Tuesday		6	13	20	27
Wednesday		7	14	21	28
Thursday	1	8	15	22	29
Friday	2	9	16	23	30
Saturday	3	10	17	24	

OCTOBER

Sunday		2	9	16	23	30
Monday		3	10	17	24	31
Tuesday		4	11	18	25	
Wednesday		5	12	19	26	
Thursday		6	13	20	27	
Friday		7	14	21	28	
Saturday	1	8	15	22	29	

NOVEMBER

Sunday		6	13	20	27
Monday		7	14	21	28
Tuesday	1	8	15	22	29
Wednesday	2	9	16	23	30
Thursday	3	10	17	24	
Friday	4	11	18	25	
Saturday	5	12	19	26	

DECEMBER

Sunday		4	11	18	25
Monday		5	12	19	26
Tuesday		6	13	20	27
Wednesday		7	14	21	28
Thursday	1	8	15	22	29
Friday	2	9	16	23	30
Saturday	3	10	17	24	31

PUBLIC HOLIDAYS	*England and Wales*	*Scotland*	*Northern Ireland*
New Year	3 January†	3, 4† January	3 January†
St Patrick's Day	—	—	17 March
*Good Friday	22 April	22 April	22 April
Easter Monday	25 April	—	25 April
Early May	2 May†	2 May	2 May†
Spring	30 May	30 May†	30 May
Battle of the Boyne	—	—	12 July‡
Summer	29 August	1 August	29 August
St Andrew's Day	—	30 Nov§	—
*Christmas	26, 27 December	26†, 27 December	26, 27 December

* In England, Wales and Northern Ireland, Christmas Day and Good Friday are common law holidays

† Subject to royal proclamation

‡ Subject to proclamation by the Secretary of State for Northern Ireland

§ The St Andrew's Day Holiday (Scotland) Bill was approved by parliament on 29 November 2006; it does not oblige employers to change their existing pattern of holidays but provides the legal framework in which the St Andrew's Day bank holiday could be substituted for an existing local holiday from another date in the year

Note: In the Channel Islands, Liberation Day is a bank and public holiday

FORTHCOMING EVENTS

* Provisional dates
† Venue not confirmed

JANUARY	
8–17	London Boat Show, Excel, London Docklands
13–17	London Art Fair, Business Design Centre
16–31	London International Mime Festival
*18–31	Celtic Connections Music Festival, Glasgow
19–21	UK Open Dance Championships, Bournemouth International Centre
30–31	RSPB Big Garden Birdwatch
FEBRUARY	
4–7	London Motorcycle Show, Excel, London Docklands
5–21	Leicester Comedy Festival
15–20	Jorvik Viking Festival, Jorvik Viking Centre, York
21	British Academy Film Awards, Royal Opera House, London
26–28	Ceramic Art London, Royal College of Art
27–7 Mar	Bath Literature Festival
MARCH	
4	World Book Day
8	International Women's Day
11–14	Crufts Dog Show, NEC, Birmingham
12–21	National Science and Engineering Week
17–23	BADA Antiques and Fine Art Fair, Duke of York's Square, London
20–28	Oxford Literary Festival
20–5 Apr	Ideal Home Show, Earls Court, London
APRIL	
19–21	London Book Fair, Earls Court, London
22	Earth Day
MAY	
14–16	Battersea Contemporary Art Fair
*Mid-May–31 Aug	Glyndebourne Festival Opera season
25–29	RHS Chelsea Flower Show, Royal Hospital, Chelsea
27–6 Jun	Hay Festival, Hay-on-Wye, Hereford
JUNE	
11–27	Aldeburgh Festival of Music and the Arts, Snape, Suffolk
12	Trooping the Colour, Horse Guards Parade, London
14–22 Aug	Royal Academy of Arts Summer Exhibition, Burlington House, London
*23–27	Glastonbury Festival of Contemporary Performing Arts, Somerset
JULY	
1–11	New Designers Exhibition, Business Design Centre, London
2–17	Cheltenham Music Festival
*3	Pride Parade, London
6–11	RHS Hampton Court Palace Flower Show, Surrey
7–25	Buxton Festival, Derbyshire
9–17	York Early Music Festival
*16–11 Sep	BBC Promenade Concerts, Royal Albert Hall, London
21–25	RHS Flower Show, Tatton Park, Cheshire
*22–31	The Welsh Proms, St David's Hall, Cardiff
23–25	WOMAD Festival, Charlton Park, Wiltshire
*29–1 Aug	Cambridge Folk Festival
*30–8 Aug	Edinburgh Jazz and Blues Festival
31–7 Aug	National Eisteddfod of Wales, Ebbw Vale
AUGUST	
6–28	Edinburgh Military Tattoo, Edinburgh Castle
7–15	Three Choirs Festival, Gloucester
*13–5 Sep	Edinburgh International Festival
*29–30	Notting Hill Carnival, Notting Hill, London
SEPTEMBER	
3–7 Nov	Blackpool Illuminations, Blackpool Promenade
4	Braemar Royal Highland Gathering, Aberdeenshire
*7	Mercury Music Prize
8	International Literacy Day
*9–12	Heritage Open Days, England (nationwide)
*10–12	RHS Wisley Flower Show, RHS Garden, Wisley
13–16	TUC Annual Congress, Manchester
18–22	Liberal Democrat Party Autumn Conference, Liverpool
26–30	Labour Party Conference, Manchester
OCTOBER	
4–8	Conservative Party Conference, Birmingham
9	National Poetry Day
14–17	Frieze Art Fair, Regent's Park, London
Mid-Oct	Booker Prize
Mid-Oct	London Film Festival
Mid-Oct–Jan	Turner Prize Exhibition, Tate Britain, London

NOVEMBER

7	London to Brighton Veteran Car Run
12–14	Classic Motor Show, NEC, Birmingham
13	Lord Mayor's Procession and Show, City of London
Mid-Nov	CBI Annual Conference

SPORTS EVENTS

JANUARY

*10–17	Snooker: Masters, Wembley Arena, London

FEBRUARY

5–7	Badminton: English National Championships, Manchester
6–20 Mar	Rugby Union: Six Nations Championship
7–14	Squash: British National Championships, Manchester
12–28	Winter Olympic Games, Vancouver, Canada
28	Football: League Cup Final, Wembley Stadium, London

APRIL

3	Rowing: Oxford and Cambridge Boat Race, Putney to Mortlake, London
10 Apr	Horse racing: Grand National, Aintree, Liverpool
17–3 May	Snooker: World Championship, Crucible Theatre, Sheffield
25	Athletics: London Marathon, London
25 Apr *or* 3 May	Football: FA Cup Final, Wembley Stadium, London
30 Apr–3 May	Equestrian: Badminton Horse Trials, Badminton
30 Apr–16 May	Cricket: Twenty20 World Cup, West Indies

MAY

1–2	Horse racing: Guineas Festival, Newmarket
†3	Football: FA Women's Cup Final
12–16	Royal Windsor Horse Show, Home Park, Windsor
15	Football: Scottish FA Cup Final, Hampden Park, Glasgow
22	Football: UEFA Champions League Final, Santiago Bernabéu, Madrid
22	Rugby Union: Heineken Cup Final, Stade de France, Paris
29–12 Jun	Motorcycling: TT Races, Isle of Man
*May–Jun	Cricket: England Test and series vs Bangladesh

JUNE

5	Horse racing: The Derby, Epsom Downs
11–11 Jul	Football: World Cup, South Africa
14–19	Golf: British Amateur Golf Championship, Muirfield, Gullane, Scotland
15–19	Horse racing: Royal Ascot
21–4 Jul	Tennis: Wimbledon Championship, All England Lawn Tennis Club, London
30–4 Jul	Rowing: Henley Royal Regatta, Henley-on-Thames

JULY

10–24	Shooting: NRA Imperial Meeting, Bisley Camp, Surrey
15–18	Golf: Open Championship, St Andrews, Fife
15–18	Golf: Women's British Open, Royal Birkdale, Southport, England
*24	Horse racing: King George VI and Queen Elizabeth Diamond Stakes, Ascot
26–1 Aug	Athletics: European Championships, Barcelona
31 Jul–7 Aug	Sailing: Cowes Week, Isle of Wight

AUGUST

*28	Rugby League: Challenge Cup Final, Wembley Stadium, London
*Aug–Sep	Rugby Union: Women's World Cup, England
*Aug–Sep	Cricket: England Test series vs Pakistan

SEPTEMBER

*2–5	Equestrian: Burghley Horse Trials, Stamford, Lincolnshire
8–11	Horse racing: St Leger, Doncaster
30–2 Oct	Horse racing: Cambridgeshire Meeting, Newmarket
Late Sep–Early Oct	Athletics: Great North Run, Newcastle

OCTOBER

3–14	Commonwealth Games, Delhi, India
6–10	Equestrian: Horse of the Year Show, NEC, Birmingham
15–16	Horse racing: Champions Meeting, Newmarket
Early–Mid-Oct	Rugby League: Super League Final, Old Trafford, Manchester

CENTENARIES

2010

1510

17 May Sandro Botticelli, Italian painter, died

1710

4 Jan Giovanni Pergolesi, Italian composer, born
12 Mar Thomas Arne, composer, born
28 Apr Thomas Betterton, actor and dramatist, died

1810

24 Feb Henry Cavendish, physicist and chemist, died
1 Mar Frédéric Chopin, Polish composer and pianist, born
2 Mar Pope Leo XIII, born
8 Jun Robert Schumann, German composer, born
5 Jul Phineas T. Barnum, American impresario, born
10 Aug Camillo Cavour, Italian statesman, born
29 Sep Elizabeth Gaskell, novelist, born

1910

8 Jan Galina Ulanova, Russian ballerina, born
23 Jan Django Reinhardt, Belgian-French guitarist, born
1 Mar David Niven, actor, born
21 Apr Mark Twain, American novelist and satirist, died
6 May Edward VII, king of United Kingdom 1901–10, died
12 May Prof. Dorothy Hodgkin, chemist and Nobel prize winner (1964), born
4 Jun Sir Christopher Cockerell, engineer and inventor of the hovercraft, born
11 Jun Jacques-Yves Cousteau, underwater explorer and filmmaker, born
13 Jun Mary Whitehouse, campaigner, born
23 Jun Jean Anouilh, French playwright, born
12 Jul Charles Stewart Rolls, automobile manufacturer, died
13 Aug Florence Nightingale, founder of trained nursing as a profession, died
26 Aug Mother Teresa, humanitarian and Nobel peace prize winner (1979), born
2 Sep Henri Rousseau, French painter, died
30 Oct Henri Dunant, Swiss founder of the Red Cross and Nobel peace prize winner (1901), died
20 Nov Leo Tolstoy, Russian novelist, died
26 Nov Cyril Cusack, Irish actor, born
19 Dec Jean Genet, French novelist and dramatist, born

2011

1511

30 Jul Giorgio Vasari, Italian painter, architect and writer, born

1711

7 May David Hume, philosopher, born
31 Oct Laura Bassi, Italian physicist, born

1811

31 Mar Robert Bunsen, German chemist, born
11 May Chang and Eng Bunker, conjoined twins from Siam (now Thailand), born
14 Jun Harriet Beecher Stowe, American writer, born
13 Jul Sir George Gilbert Scott, architect, born
18 Jul William Makepeace Thackeray, novelist, born
22 Oct Franz Liszt, Hungarian composer and pianist, born
27 Oct Isaac Singer, American inventor, born
16 Nov John Bright, co-founder of the Anti-Corn Law League, born
21 Nov Heinrich von Kleist, German writer, died
21 Dec Archibald Campbell Tait, Archbishop of Canterbury, born

1911

30 Jan Roy Eldridge, American jazz musician, born
6 Mar Sir Charles Frank, theoretical physicist, born
26 Mar Tennessee Williams, American playwright, born
17 May Maureen O'Sullivan, Irish actor, born
18 May Gustav Mahler, Austrian composer, died
29 May Sir William S. Gilbert, playwright and librettist, died
15 Jun Revd W. V. Awdry, children's writer, born
24 Jun Juan Manuel Fangio, Argentine Formula One racing driver, born
30 Jun Ruskin Spear, painter, born
16 Jul Ginger Rogers, American actor, born
19 Sep Sir William Golding, novelist and Nobel prize winner (1983), born
29 Sep Prof. R. V. Jones, military intelligence scientist, born
29 Oct Joseph Pulitzer, Hungarian-American publisher and journalist, died
12 Nov Revd Dr Chad Varah, founder of the Samaritans, born
5 Dec Wladyslaw Szpilman, Polish pianist and composer, born
30 Dec Jeanette Nolan, American actor, born

THE UNITED KINGDOM

THE UK IN FIGURES

The United Kingdom comprises Great Britain (England, Wales and Scotland) and Northern Ireland. The Isle of Man and the Channel Islands are Crown dependencies with their own legislative systems and are not part of the UK.

ABBREVIATIONS

AAS	*Annual Abstract of Statistics*
ST	*Social Trends*

All data is for the UK unless otherwise stated.

AREA OF THE UNITED KINGDOM

	sq. km	*sq. miles*
United Kingdom	242,495	93,627
England	130,279	50,301
Wales	20,733	8,005
Scotland	77,907	30,080
Northern Ireland	13,576	5,242

Source: ONS – *AAS 2009* (Crown copyright)

POPULATION

The first official census of population in England, Wales and Scotland was taken in 1801 and a census has been taken every ten years since, except in 1941 when there was no census because of war. The last official census in the UK was taken on 29 April 2001 and the next is due in April 2011.

The first official census of population in Ireland was taken in 1841. However, all figures given below refer only to the area which is now Northern Ireland. Figures for Northern Ireland in 1921 and 1931 are estimates based on the censuses taken in 1926 and 1937 respectively.

Estimates of the population of England before 1801, calculated from the number of baptisms, burials and marriages, are:

1570	4,160,221	1670	5,773,646
1600	4,811,718	1700	6,045,008
1630	5,600,517	1750	6,517,035

Further details are available on the Office for National Statistics (ONS) website (W www.statistics.gov.uk)

CENSUS RESULTS *Thousands*

	United Kingdom			England and Wales			Scotland			Northern Ireland		
	Total	*Male*	*Female*	*Total*	*Male*	*Female*	*Total*	*Male*	*Female*	*Total*	*Male*	*Female*
1801	—	—	—	8,893	4,255	4,638	1,608	739	869	—	—	—
1811	13,368	6,368	7,000	10,165	4,874	5,291	1,806	826	980	—	—	—
1821	15,472	7,498	7,974	12,000	5,850	6,150	2,092	983	1,109	—	—	—
1831	17,835	8,647	9,188	13,897	6,771	7,126	2,364	1,114	1,250	—	—	—
1841	20,183	9,819	10,364	15,914	7,778	8,137	2,620	1,242	1,378	1,649	800	849
1851	22,259	10,855	11,404	17,928	8,781	9,146	2,889	1,376	1,513	1,443	698	745
1861	24,525	11,894	12,631	20,066	9,776	10,290	3,062	1,450	1,612	1,396	668	728
1871	27,431	13,309	14,122	22,712	11,059	11,653	3,360	1,603	1,757	1,359	647	712
1881	31,015	15,060	15,955	25,974	12,640	13,335	3,736	1,799	1,936	1,305	621	684
1891	34,264	16,593	17,671	29,003	14,060	14,942	4,026	1,943	2,083	1,236	590	646
1901	38,237	18,492	19,745	32,528	15,729	16,799	4,472	2,174	2,298	1,237	590	647
1911	42,082	20,357	21,725	36,070	17,446	18,625	4,761	2,309	2,452	1,251	603	648
1921	44,027	21,033	22,994	37,887	18,075	19,811	4,882	2,348	2,535	1,258	610	648
1931	46,038	22,060	23,978	39,952	19,133	20,819	4,843	2,326	2,517	1,243	601	642
1951	50,225	24,118	26,107	43,758	21,016	22,742	5,096	2,434	2,662	1,371	668	703
1961	52,709	25,481	27,228	46,105	22,304	23,801	5,179	2,483	2,697	1,425	694	731
1971	55,515	26,952	28,562	48,750	23,683	25,067	5,229	2,515	2,714	1,536	755	781
1981	55,848	27,104	28,742	49,155	23,873	25,281	5,131	2,466	2,664	1,533*	750	783
1991	56,467	27,344	29,123	49,890	24,182	25,707	4,999	2,392	2,607	1,578	769	809
2001	58,789	28,581	30,208	52,042	25,327	26,715	5,062	2,432	2,630	1,685	821	864

* Figure includes 44,500 non-enumerated persons

ISLANDS

	Isle of Man			Jersey			Guernsey†		
	Total	*Male*	*Female*	*Total*	*Male*	*Female*	*Total*	*Male*	*Female*
1901	54,752	25,496	29,256	52,576	23,940	28,636	40,446	19,652	20,794
1921	60,284	27,329	32,955	49,701	22,438	27,263	38,315	18,246	20,069
1951	55,123	25,749	29,464	57,296	27,282	30,014	43,652	21,221	22,431
1971	56,289	26,461	29,828	72,532	35,423	37,109	51,458	24,792	26,666
1991	69,788	33,693	36,095	84,082	40,862	43,220	58,867	28,297	30,570
2001	76,315	37,372	38,943	87,186	42,485	44,701	59,807	29,138	30,669
2006	80,058	39,523	40,535						

† Includes Herm, Jethou and Lithou

Source: ONS – Census Reports (Crown copyright)

RESIDENT POPULATION

UK PROJECTED RESIDENT POPULATION
people, thousands

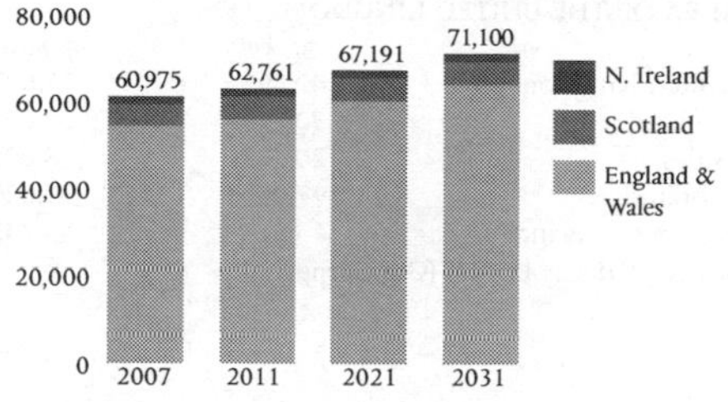

Source: ONS – *AAS 2009* (Crown copyright)

UK PROJECTED RESIDENT POPULATION
by sex, thousands

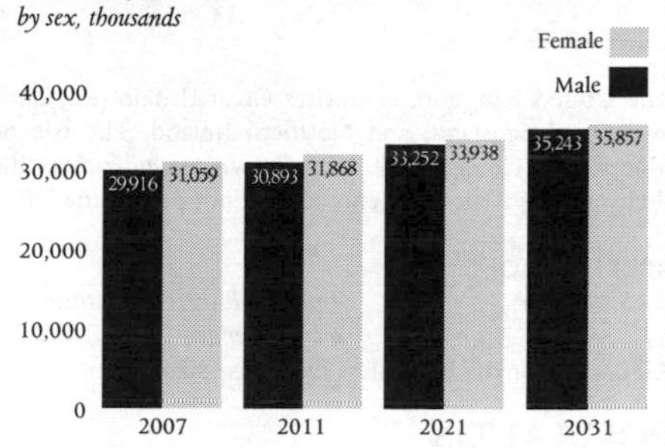

Source: ONS – *AAS 2009* (Crown copyright)

BY AGE AND SEX

	Thousands Male	Female
Under 1	387	368
1–4	1,453	1,383
5–9	1,750	1,674
10–14	1,898	1,806
15–19	2,069	1,947
20–29	4,116	3,990
30–44	6,522	6,620
45–59	5,786	5,942
60–64	1,701	1,782
65–74	2,398	2,660
75–84	1,432	1,992
85+	403	895

Source: ONS – *AAS 2009* (Crown copyright)

BY ETHNIC GROUP

	Thousands
White	
British	49,082
Other	3,127
Mixed	
White and Black Caribbean	229
White and Black African	90
White and Asian	165
Other Mixed	158
Asian	
Indian	1,174
Pakistani	936
Bangladeshi	343
Other Asian	464
Black	
Black Caribbean	633
Black African	774
Black Other	67
Chinese	247
Other	902
ALL*	60,145

* Includes those who did not state their ethnic origin and those in Northern Ireland who stated their ethnicity as white

Source: ONS – *AAS 2009* (Crown copyright)

IMMIGRATION

ACCEPTANCES FOR SETTLEMENT IN THE UK

*Region**	*Number of persons* 2005	2007
Europe: total†	20,810	8,660
Accession States: total	2,180	–
Bulgaria	1,225	–
Remainder of Europe: total	18,630	8,660
Albania	1,015	1,220
Russia	1,795	1,310
Serbia and Montenegro‡	6,805	1,400
Turkey	5,330	2,545
Ukraine	1,195	865
Americas: total	13,905	10,435
Canada	1,215	1,015
Colombia	1,555	590
Jamaica	2,780	2,440
USA	4,350	3,310
Africa: total	54,080	34,050
Angola	1,695	1,590
Dem. Rep. Congo	2,960	2,055
Ghana	2,880	2,560
Kenya	2,690	1,575
Nigeria	5,310	3,965
Sierra Leone	3,420	725
Somalia	8,255	2,845
South Africa	9,385	5,805
Uganda	1,065	530
Zimbabwe	4,520	4,280
Asia: total	83,740	67,955
Indian sub-continent: total	28,990	29,020
Bangladesh	3,085	3,330
India	16,720	14,865
Pakistan	9,185	10,825
Middle East: total	9,395	10,655
Iran	2,055	1,755
Iraq	4,675	7,020
Remainder of Asia: total	45,355	28,280
Afghanistan	9,215	3,165
China§	4,215	3,440
Japan	1,540	925
Malaysia	1,945	1,635
Nepal	3,610	4,155
Philippines	14,710	8,485

Sri Lanka	5,475	2,440
Thailand	1,945	1,605
Oceania: total	6,335	3,615
Australia	3,740	2,215
New Zealand	2,505	1,280
British Overseas Citizens	95	35
Nationality unknown	160	100
ALL NATIONALITIES	179,120	124,855

* Country specified only when the figure for 2005 or 2007 is over 1,000
† Excluding European Economic Area and Swiss nationals
‡ Counted together due to the use of a single (Federal Republic of Yugoslavia) passport
§ Includes Taiwan
Source: ONS – *AAS 2009* (Crown copyright)

BIRTHS

	Live births	*Male*	*Female*	*Birth rate**
United Kingdom	772,200	397,000	376,000	13.8
England and Wales	690,000	354,000	336,000	12.8
Scotland	57,800	30,000	28,000	11.2
Northern Ireland	24,500	13,000	12,000	13.9

* Live births per 1,000 population
Source: ONS – *AAS 2009* (Crown copyright)

FERTILITY RATES

Total fertility rate is the average number of children which would be born to a woman if she experienced the age-specific fertility rates of the period in question throughout her child-bearing life span. The figures for the years 1960–2 are estimates.

	1960–2	*1997*	*2007*
United Kingdom	2.80	1.72	1.90
England and Wales	2.77	1.73	1.92
Scotland	2.98	1.58	1.73
Northern Ireland	3.47	1.93	2.02

Source: ONS – *AAS 2009* (Crown copyright)

TOP TEN BABY NAMES

	1934 Girls	*1934 Boys*	*2007 Girls*	*2007 Boys*
1	Margaret	John	Grace	Jack
2	Jean	Peter	Ruby	Thomas
3	Mary	William	Olivia	Oliver
4	Joan	Brian	Emily	Joshua
5	Patricia	David	Jessica	Harry
6	Sheila	James	Sophie	Charlie
7	Barbara	Michael	Chloe	Daniel
8	Doreen	Ronald	Lily	William
9	June	Kenneth	Ella	James
10	Shirley	George	Amelia	Alfie

Source: ONS (Crown copyright)

LEGAL ABORTIONS

	1997	*2007*
England and Wales	170,145	198,499
Scotland	12,087	13,635

Source: ONS – *AAS 2009* (Crown copyright)

DEATHS

Source: ONS – *AAS 2009* (Crown copyright)

Men	*Deaths*	*Death rate**
United Kingdom	274,883	9.2
England and Wales	240,780	
Scotland	26,895	
Northern Ireland	7,208	
Women		
United Kingdom	299,797	9.7
England and Wales	263,265	
Scotland	29,091	
Northern Ireland	7,441	

* Per 1,000 population

INFANT MORTALITY RATE*

United Kingdom	4.8
England and Wales	4.8
Scotland	4.7
Northern Ireland	4.9

* Deaths of infants under one year of age per 1,000 live births
Source: ONS – *AAS 2009* (Crown copyright)

MARRIAGE AND DIVORCE

	Marriages	*Divorces*
United Kingdom*	270,000	144,220
England and Wales*	231,450	128,534
Scotland	29,866	12,773
Northern Ireland	8,687	2,913

* Provisional figures
Source: ONS – *AAS 2009* (Crown copyright)

HOUSEHOLDS

BY TYPE (GREAT BRITAIN)

Percentages

	1971	*1991*	*2008*
One Person			
Under state pension age	6	11	15
Over state pension age	12	16	15
One family households			
Couple			
No children	27	28	29
1–2 dependent children	26	20	18
3 or more dependent children	9	5	3
Non-dependent children only	8	8	6
Lone parent			
Dependent children	3	6	7
Non-dependent children only	4	4	3
Two or more unrelated adults	4	3	3
Multi-family households	1	1	1
All households (=100%) *(millions)*	18.6	22.4	25.0

Source: ONS – *ST 2009* (Crown copyright)

BY SIZE (GREAT BRITAIN)

Percentages

	1971	*1991*	*2007*
One person	18	27	29
Two people	32	34	35
Three people	19	16	16
Four people	17	16	13
Five people	8	5	5
Six or more people	6	2	2
All households (=100%) *(millions)*	18.6	22.4	25.0
Average household size *(people)*	2.9	2.5	2.4

Source: ONS – *ST 2009* (Crown copyright)

DEPENDENT CHILDREN LIVING IN DIFFERENT FAMILY TYPES
Thousands

	1997	*2005*	*2008*
Married couple	9,570	8,570	8,320
Cohabiting couple	1,000	1,460	1,660
Female lone parent	2,510	2,750	2,810
Male lone parent	230	250	240

Source: ONS – *ST 2009* (Crown copyright)

ADULTS LIVING WITH THEIR PARENTS
Thousands

	2001	*2004*	*2008*
Men			
20–24 years	949	1,054	1,086
25–29 years	454	434	486
30–34 years	208	203	180
Women			
20–24 years	624	675	745
25–29 years	220	201	245
30–34 years	75	89	70

Source: ONS – *ST 2009* (Crown copyright)

MORTGAGES

	1998	*2004*	*2008*
Mortgages* *(thousands)*	10,821	11,515	11,667
Type of mortgage for house purchase† *(percentages)*			
Standard repayment	40	77	60
Endowment	35	5	10
Other‡	22	11	24
Loans in arrears at end-period* *(thousands)*			
By 6–12 months	74	30	72
By 12+ months	35	11	30
Properties repossessed in period	34	8	40

* Estimates cover only members of the Council of Mortgage Lenders, which account for 98 per cent of all outstanding mortgages

† Includes new mortgages advanced by building societies and other major lenders and includes sitting tenants

‡ Includes interest only, PEP/ISA and pension

Source: ONS – *AAS 2009* (Crown copyright)

TYPE OF ACCOMMODATION (GREAT BRITAIN)
Percentages by tenure 2007

	House or bungalow			*Flat or maisonette*	
	Detached	*Semi-detached*	*Terraced*	*Purpose-built*	*Other*
Owner-occupied	30	34	27	7	2
Owned outright	37	34	21	7	1
Owned with mortgage	25	34	31	7	2
Rented from social sector	1	23	31	41	3
Council	1	24	30	43	2
Housing association	2	22	33	39	5
Rented privately	11	22	33	19	15
Furnished	2	14	34	29	22
Unfurnished	15	24	33	16	12
All tenures	23	31	28	15	3

Source: ONS – *AAS 2009* (Crown copyright)

HEALTH

DEATHS BY CAUSE

	England and Wales	Scotland	N. Ireland
Total Deaths	504,052	55,986	14,649
Deaths from natural causes	484,350	53,683	13,876
Certain infectious and parasitic diseases	8,169	949	184
Intestinal infectious diseases	4,225	164	35
Respiratory and other tuberculosis	335	41	10
Meningococcal infection	75	8	3
Viral hepatitis	223	22	4
AIDS (HIV – disease)	256	21	–
Neoplasms	140,080	15,570	3,992
Malignant neoplasms	136,804	15,274	3,870
Malignant neoplasm of trachea, bronchus and lung	29,660	4,115	863
Malignant neoplasm of skin	1,825	164	56
Malignant neoplasm of breast	10,727	1,067	311
Malignant neoplasm of cervix uteri	820	105	16
Malignant neoplasm of prostate	9,230	793	235
Leukaemia	3,935	348	94
Diseases of the blood and blood-forming organs and certain disorders involving the immune mechanism	1,029	111	39
Endocrine, nutritional and metabolic diseases	7,214	980	299
Diabetes mellitus	5,433	726	210
Mental and behavioural disorders	16,582	3,117	514
Vascular and unspecified dementia	14,948	2,446	405
Alcohol abuse	533	321	94
Drug dependence and non-dependent abuse of drugs	781	310	5
Diseases of the nervous system and sense organs	16,375	1,555	588
Meningitis (excluding meningococcal)	164	16	5
Alzheimer's disease	5,697	549	291
Diseases of the circulatory system	170,338	18,579	4,838
Ischaemic heart diseases	79,910	9,343	2,494
Cerebrovascular diseases	46,597	5,333	1,325
Diseases of the respiratory system	68,974	7,362	1,992
Influenza	31	5	1
Pneumonia	28,152	2,444	859
Bronchitis, emphysema and other chronic obstructive pulmonary diseases	23,727	2,901	639
Asthma	1,033	112	28
Diseases of the digestive system	25,670	3,076	711
Gastric and duodenal ulcer	2,833	206	53
Chronic liver disease	6,326	1,080	193
Diseases of the skin and subcutaneous tissue	1,822	131	26
Diseases of the musculo-skeletal system and connective tissue	4,304	395	76
Osteoporosis	1,509	139	12
Diseases of the genito-urinary system	11,301	1,149	381
Complications of pregnancy, childbirth and the puerperium	47	8	–
Certain conditions originating in the perinatal period*	180	157	50
Congenital malformations, deformations and chromosomal abnormalities*	1,235	150	61
Symptoms, signs and abnormal findings not classified elsewhere	11,030	394	125
Senility without mention of psychosis (old age)	9,195	221	95
Sudden infant death syndrome	170	31	4
Deaths from external causes	17,000	2,303	773
All accidents	11,883	1,289	499
Suicide and intentional self-harm	3,165	517	215
Homicide and assault	370†	88	30

* Excludes neonatal deaths (those at age under 28 days): for England and Wales neonatal deaths are included in the total number of deaths but excluded from the cause figures

† This will not be a true figure as registration of homicide and assault deaths in England and Wales is often delayed by adjourned inquests

Source: ONS – *AAS 2009* (Crown copyright)

ALCOHOL CONSUMPTION* BY AGE (GREAT BRITAIN)

Percentages

	16–24	*25–44*	*45–64*	*65+*	*All 16+*
Men					
No units	40	27	24	33	29
Up to 4 units	18	25	33	46	31
4–8 units	12	17	21	14	17
8+ units	30	31	21	7	23
Women					
No units	47	40	40	56	44
Up to 3 units	14	20	25	30	23
3–6 units	14	19	23	12	18
6+ units	25	21	12	2	15

* On at least one day in the previous week. Department of Health guidelines recommend that men should not regularly drink more than three to four units of alcohol per day and women should not regularly drink more than two to three units per day. A unit of alcohol is 8 grams by weight or 10ml by volume of pure alcohol, ie the amount contained in half a pint of ordinary strength beer or lager, a single pub measure of spirits or a small glass of ordinary strength wine

Source: ONS – *ST 2008* (Crown copyright)

NOTIFICATIONS OF INFECTIOUS DISEASES

	2000	*2007*
Measles	2,865	3,869
Mumps	3,367	10,101
Rubella	2,064	1,254
Whooping cough	866	1,203
Scarlet fever	2,544	2,477
Dysentery	1,613	1,383
Food poisoning	98,076	80,889
Typhoid and paratyphoid fevers	205	341
Hepatitis	4,530	5,306
Tuberculosis	7,100	7,461
Malaria	1,166	445

Source: ONS – *AAS 2009* (Crown copyright)

CONSUMPTION OF FRUIT AND VEGETABLES BY AGE (ENGLAND)

	*Average daily portions**
Men	
16–24	3.0
25–34	3.7
35–44	3.5
45–54	3.7
55–64	3.9
65–74	4.0
75+	3.8
Women	
16–24	3.3
25–34	3.9
35–44	4.0
45–54	4.2
55–64	4.5
65–74	4.1
75+	3.6

* The Department of Health recommends that a healthy diet should include at least five portions a day of a variety of fruit and vegetables (excluding potatoes)

Source: ONS – *ST 2008* (Crown copyright)

THE NATIONAL FLAG

The national flag of the United Kingdom is the Union Flag, generally known as the Union Jack.

The Union Flag is a combination of the cross of St George, patron saint of England, the cross of St Andrew, patron saint of Scotland and the cross of St Patrick, patron saint of Ireland.

Cross of St George: cross Gules in a field Argent (red cross on a white ground)

Cross of St Andrew: saltire Argent in a field Azure (white diagonal cross on a blue ground)

Cross of St Patrick: saltire Gules in a field Argent (red diagonal cross on a white ground)

The Union Flag was first introduced in 1606 after the union of the kingdoms of England and Scotland under one sovereign. The cross of St Patrick was added in 1801 after the union of Great Britain and Ireland.

See also Flags of the World colour plates.

FLYING THE UNION FLAG

The correct orientation of the Union Flag when flying is with the broader diagonal band of white uppermost in the hoist (ie near the pole) and the narrower diagonal band of white uppermost in the fly (ie furthest from the pole).

It is the practice to fly the Union Flag daily on some customs houses. In all other cases, the flying of the Union Flag on government buildings is decided by the DCMS at the Queen's command. There is no formal definition of a government building but it is generally accepted to mean a building owned or used by the Crown and predominately occupied or used by civil servants or the Armed Forces. It is now customary for the Union Flag to be flown at Buckingham Palace, Windsor Castle and Sandringham when the Queen is not in residence. Individuals, local authorities and other organisations may fly the Union Flag whenever they wish, subject to compliance with local planning requirements.

FLAGS AT HALF-MAST

Flags are flown at half-mast (ie two-thirds up between the top and bottom of the flagstaff) on the following occasions:

- from the announcement of the death up to the funeral of the sovereign, except on Proclamation Day, when flags are hoisted right up from 11am to sunset
- the funerals of members of the royal family*
- the funerals of foreign rulers*
- the funerals of prime ministers and ex-prime ministers of the UK*
- other occasions by special command of the Queen

On occasions when days for flying flags coincide with days for flying flags at half-mast, the following rules are observed. Flags are flown at full mast:

- although a member of the royal family, or a near relative of the royal family, may be lying dead, unless special commands are received from the Queen to the contrary
- although it may be the day of the funeral of a foreign ruler

If the body of a very distinguished subject is lying at a government office, the flag may fly at half-mast on that office until the body has left (provided it is a day on which the flag would fly) and then the flag is to be hoisted right up. On all other government buildings the flag will fly as usual.

DAYS FOR FLYING FLAGS

On 25 March 2008 the DCMS announced that UK government buildings in England, Scotland and Wales have the freedom to fly the Union Flag at all times, if they wish to do so, and not just on the established days listed below. In addition, on the patron saints' days of Scotland and Wales, the appropriate national flag may be flown alongside the Union Flag on Whitehall government buildings. Flags are hoisted from 8am to sunset.

Countess of Wessex's birthday	20 Jan
Accession of the Queen	6 Feb
Duke of York's birthday	19 Feb
St David's Day (in Wales only)†	1 Mar
Commonwealth Day (2010)	8 Mar
Earl of Wessex's birthday	10 Mar
St Patrick's Day (in Northern Ireland only)‡	17 Mar
Birthday of the Queen	21 Apr
St George's Day (in England only)†	23 Apr
Europe Day†	9 May
Coronation Day	2 Jun
Duke of Edinburgh's birthday	10 Jun
The Queen's Official Birthday (2010)	12 Jun
Duchess of Cornwall's birthday	17 Jul
Princess Royal's birthday	15 Aug
Prince of Wales' birthday	14 Nov
Remembrance Day (2010)	14 Nov
Wedding Day of the Queen	20 Nov
St Andrew's Day (in Scotland only)†	30 Nov
Opening of parliament by the Queen§	
Prorogation of parliament by the Queen§	

THE ROYAL STANDARD

The Royal Standard comprises four quarterings – two for England (three lions passant), one for Scotland¶ (a lion rampant) and one for Ireland (a harp).

The Royal Standard is flown when the Queen is in residence at a royal palace, on transport being used by the Queen for official journeys and from Victoria Tower when the Queen attends parliament. It may also be flown on any building (excluding ecclesiastical buildings) during a visit by the Queen. If the Queen is to be present in a building advice on flag flying can be obtained from the DCMS.

The Royal Standard is never flown at half-mast, even after the death of the Sovereign, as the new monarch immediately succeeds to the throne.

* Subject to special commands from the Queen in each case

† The appropriate national flag, or the European flag, may be flown in addition to the Union Flag, but not in a superior position

‡ Only the Union Flag should be flown

§ Only in the Greater London area, whether or not the Queen performs the ceremony in person

¶ In Scotland a version with two Scottish quarterings is used

THE ROYAL FAMILY

THE SOVEREIGN

ELIZABETH II, by the Grace of God, of the United Kingdom of Great Britain and Northern Ireland and of her other Realms and Territories Queen, Head of the Commonwealth, Defender of the Faith
Her Majesty Elizabeth Alexandra Mary of Windsor, elder daughter of King George VI and of HM Queen Elizabeth the Queen Mother
Born 21 April 1926, at 17 Bruton Street, London W1
Ascended the throne 6 February 1952
Crowned 2 June 1953, at Westminster Abbey
Married 20 November 1947, in Westminster Abbey, HRH the Prince Philip, Duke of Edinburgh
Official residences Buckingham Palace, London SW1A 1AA; Windsor Castle, Berks; Palace of Holyroodhouse, Edinburgh
Private residences Sandringham, Norfolk; Balmoral Castle, Aberdeenshire

HUSBAND OF THE QUEEN

HRH THE PRINCE PHILIP, DUKE OF EDINBURGH, KG, KT, OM, GBE, Royal Victorian Chain, AC, QSO, PC, Ranger of Windsor Park
Born 10 June 1921, son of Prince and Princess Andrew of Greece and Denmark, naturalised a British subject 1947, created Duke of Edinburgh, Earl of Merioneth and Baron Greenwich 1947

CHILDREN OF THE QUEEN

HRH THE PRINCE OF WALES (Prince Charles Philip Arthur George), KG, KT, GCB, OM and Great Master of the Order of the Bath, AK, QSO, PC, ADC(P)
Born 14 November 1948, created Prince of Wales and Earl of Chester 1958, succeeded as Duke of Cornwall, Duke of Rothesay, Earl of Carrick and Baron Renfrew, Lord of the Isles and Great Steward of Scotland 1952
Married (1) 29 July 1981 Lady Diana Frances Spencer (Diana, Princess of Wales (1961–97), youngest daughter of the 8th Earl Spencer and the Hon. Mrs Shand Kydd), marriage dissolved 1996; (2) 9 April 2005 Mrs Camilla Rosemary Parker Bowles, now HRH the Duchess of Cornwall (*born* 17 July 1947, daughter of Major Bruce Shand and the Hon. Mrs Rosalind Shand)
Residences Clarence House, London SW1A 1BA; Highgrove, Doughton, Tetbury, Glos GL8 8TN; Birkhall, Ballater, Aberdeenshire
Issue
1. HRH Prince William of Wales (Prince William Arthur Philip Louis), KG, *born* 21 June 1982
2. HRH Prince Henry of Wales (Prince Henry Charles Albert David), *born* 15 September 1984

HRH THE PRINCESS ROYAL (Princess Anne Elizabeth Alice Louise), KG, KT, GCVO
Born 15 August 1950, declared the Princess Royal 1987
Married (1) 14 November 1973 Captain Mark Anthony Peter Phillips, CVO (*born* 22 September 1948); marriage dissolved 1992; (2) 12 December 1992 Captain Timothy James Hamilton Laurence, MVO, RN (*born* 1 March 1955)
Residence Gatcombe Park, Minchinhampton, Glos GL6 9AT
Issue
1. Peter Mark Andrew Phillips, *born* 15 November 1977, *married* 17 May 2008 Autumn Patricia Kelly
2. Zara Anne Elizabeth Phillips, MBE, *born* 15 May 1981

HRH THE DUKE OF YORK (Prince Andrew Albert Christian Edward), KG, KCVO, ADC(P)
Born 19 February 1960, created Duke of York, Earl of Inverness and Baron Killyleagh 1986
Married 23 July 1986 Sarah Margaret Ferguson, now Sarah, Duchess of York (*born* 15 October 1959, younger daughter of Major Ronald Ferguson and Mrs Hector Barrantes), marriage dissolved 1996
Residence Royal Lodge, Windsor Great Park, Berks
Issue
1. HRH Princess Beatrice of York (Princess Beatrice Elizabeth Mary), *born* 8 August 1988
2. HRH Princess Eugenie of York (Princess Eugenie Victoria Helena), *born* 23 March 1990

HRH THE EARL OF WESSEX (Prince Edward Antony Richard Louis), KG, KCVO
Born 10 March 1964, created Earl of Wessex, Viscount Severn 1999
Married 19 June 1999 Sophie Helen Rhys-Jones, now HRH the Countess of Wessex (*born* 20 January 1965, daughter of Mr and Mrs Christopher Rhys-Jones)
Residence Bagshot Park, Bagshot, Surrey GU19 5HS
Issue
1. Lady Louise Windsor (Louise Alice Elizabeth Mary Mountbatten-Windsor), *born* 8 November 2003
2. Viscount Severn (James Alexander Philip Theo Mountbatten-Windsor), *born* 17 December 2007

NEPHEW AND NIECE OF THE QUEEN

Children of HRH the Princess Margaret, Countess of Snowdon and the Earl of Snowdon (*see* House of Windsor):

DAVID ALBERT CHARLES ARMSTRONG-JONES, VISCOUNT LINLEY, *born* 3 November 1961, *married* 8 October 1993 the Hon. Serena Stanhope, and has issue, Hon. Charles Patrick Inigo Armstrong-Jones, *born* 1 July 1999; Hon. Margarita Elizabeth Alleyne Armstrong-Jones, *born* 14 May 2002

LADY SARAH CHATTO (Sarah Frances Elizabeth), *born* 1 May 1964, *married* 14 July 1994 Daniel Chatto, and has issue, Samuel David Benedict Chatto, *born* 28 July 1996; Arthur Robert Nathaniel Chatto, *born* 5 February 1999

COUSINS OF THE QUEEN

Child of HRH the Duke of Gloucester and HRH Princess Alice, Duchess of Gloucester (*see* House of Windsor):

HRH THE DUKE OF GLOUCESTER (Prince Richard Alexander Walter George), KG, GCVO, Grand Prior of the Order of St John of Jerusalem

Born 26 August 1944
Married 8 July 1972 Birgitte Eva van Deurs, now HRH the Duchess of Gloucester, GCVO (*born* 20 June 1946, daughter of Asger Henriksen and Vivian van Deurs)
Residence Kensington Palace, London W8 4PU
Issue
1. Earl of Ulster (Alexander Patrick Gregers Richard), *born* 24 October 1974 *married* 22 June 2002 Dr Claire Booth, and has issue, Lord Culloden (Xan Richard Anders), *born* 12 March 2007
2. Lady Davina Lewis (Davina Elizabeth Alice Benedikte), *born* 19 November 1977 *married* 31 July 2004 Gary Lewis
3. Lady Rose Gilman (Rose Victoria Birgitte Louise), *born* 1 March 1980 *married* 19 July 2008 George Gilman

Children of HRH the Duke of Kent and Princess Marina, Duchess of Kent (*see* House of Windsor):

HRH THE DUKE OF KENT (Prince Edward George Nicholas Paul Patrick), KG, GCMG, GCVO, ADC(P)
Born 9 October 1935
Married 8 June 1961 Katharine Lucy Mary Worsley, now HRH the Duchess of Kent, GCVO (*born* 22 February 1933, daughter of Sir William Worsley, Bt.)
Residence Wren House, Palace Green, London W8 4PY
Issue
1. Earl of St Andrews (George Philip Nicholas), *born* 26 June 1962, *married* 9 January 1988 Sylvana Tomaselli, and has issue, Baron Downpatrick (Edward Edmund Maximilian George), *born* 2 December 1988; Lady Marina-Charlotte Windsor (Marina-Charlotte Alexandra Katharine Helen), *born* 30 September 1992; Lady Amelia Windsor (Amelia Sophia Theodora Mary Margaret), *born* 24 August 1995
2. Lady Helen Taylor (Helen Marina Lucy), *born* 28 April 1964, *married* 18 July 1992 Timothy Taylor, and has issue, Columbus George Donald Taylor, *born* 6 August 1994; Cassius Edward Taylor, *born* 26 December 1996; Eloise Olivia Katharine Taylor, *born* 3 March 2003; Estella Olga Elizabeth Taylor, *born* 21 December 2004
3. Lord Nicholas Windsor (Nicholas Charles Edward Jonathan), *born* 25 July 1970, *married* 4 November 2006 Paola Doimi de Frankopan, and has issue, Albert Louis Philip Edward Windsor, *born* 22 September 2007

HRH PRINCESS ALEXANDRA, THE HON. LADY OGILVY (Princess Alexandra Helen Elizabeth Olga Christabel), KG, GCVO
Born 25 December 1936
Married 24 April 1963 the Rt. Hon. Sir Angus Ogilvy, KCVO (1928–2004), second son of 12th Earl of Airlie
Residence Thatched House Lodge, Richmond Park, Surrey TW10 5HP
Issue
1. James Robert Bruce Ogilvy, *born* 29 February 1964, *married* 30 July 1988 Julia Rawlinson, and has issue, Flora Alexandra Ogilvy, *born* 15 December 1994; Alexander Charles Ogilvy, *born* 12 November 1996
2. Marina Victoria Alexandra Ogilvy, *born* 31 July 1966, *married* 2 February 1990 Paul Mowatt (marriage dissolved 1997), and has issue, Zenouska May Mowatt, *born* 26 May 1990; Christian Alexander Mowatt, *born* 4 June 1993

HRH PRINCE MICHAEL OF KENT (Prince Michael George Charles Franklin), GCVO
Born 4 July 1942
Married 30 June 1978 Baroness Marie-Christine Agnes Hedwig Ida von Reibnitz, now HRH Princess Michael of Kent (*born* 15 January 1945, daughter of Baron Gunther von Reibnitz)
Residence Kensington Palace, London W8 4PU
Issue
1. Lord Frederick Windsor (Frederick Michael George David Louis), *born* 6 April 1979, *married* 12 September 2009 Sophie Winkleman
2. Lady Gabriella Windsor (Gabriella Marina Alexandra Ophelia), *born* 23 April 1981

ORDER OF SUCCESSION

1	HRH the Prince of Wales
2	HRH Prince William of Wales
3	HRH Prince Henry of Wales
4	HRH the Duke of York
5	HRH Princess Beatrice of York
6	HRH Princess Eugenie of York
7	HRH the Earl of Wessex
8	Viscount Severn
9	Lady Louise Windsor
10	HRH the Princess Royal
11	Peter Phillips
12	Zara Phillips
13	Viscount Linley
14	Hon. Charles Armstrong-Jones
15	Hon. Margarita Armstrong-Jones
16	Lady Sarah Chatto
17	Samuel Chatto
18	Arthur Chatto
19	HRH the Duke of Gloucester
20	Earl of Ulster
21	Lord Culloden
22	Lady Davina Lewis
23	Lady Rose Gilman
24	HRH the Duke of Kent
25	Lady Amelia Windsor
26	Lady Helen Taylor
27	Columbus Taylor
28	Cassius Taylor
29	Eloise Taylor
30	Estella Taylor
31	Lord Frederick Windsor
32	Lady Gabriella Windsor
33	HRH Princess Alexandra, the Hon. Lady Ogilvy
34	James Ogilvy
35	Alexander Ogilvy
36	Flora Ogilvy
37	Marina Ogilvy
38	Christian Mowatt
39	Zenouska Mowatt

HRH Prince Michael of Kent, and the Earl of St Andrews both lost the right of succession to the throne through marriage to a Roman Catholic. Lord Nicholas Windsor, Baron Downpatrick and Lady Marina-Charlotte Windsor renounced their rights to the throne on converting to Roman Catholicism in 2001, 2003 and 2008 respectively. Their children remain in succession provided that they are in communion with the Church of England.

PRIVATE SECRETARIES TO THE ROYAL FAMILY

THE QUEEN
Office: Buckingham Palace, London SW1A 1AA
T 020-7930 4832 W www.royal.gov.uk
Private Secretary to the Queen, Christopher Geidt, CVO, OBE

PRINCE PHILIP, THE DUKE OF EDINBURGH
Office: Buckingham Palace, London SW1A 1AA
T 020-7930 4832
Private Secretary, Brig. Sir Miles Hunt-Davis, KCVO, CBE

THE PRINCE OF WALES AND THE DUCHESS OF CORNWALL
Office: Clarence House, London SW1A 1BA
T 020-7930 4832
Principal Private Secretary, Sir Michael Peat, KCVO

PRINCES WILLIAM AND HENRY OF WALES
Office: Clarence House, London SW1A 1BA
T 020-7930 4832
Private Secretary, James Lowther-Pinkerton, MVO, MBE

THE DUKE OF YORK
Office: Buckingham Palace, London SW1A 1AA
T 020-7930 4832
Private Secretary, Alastair Watson

THE EARL AND COUNTESS OF WESSEX
Office: Bagshot Park, Surrey GU19 5PL
T 01276-707040
Private Secretary, Brig. J. Smedley

THE PRINCESS ROYAL
Office: Buckingham Palace, London SW1A 1AA
T 020-7024 4199
Private Secretary, Capt. N. P. Wright, LVO, RN

THE DUKE AND DUCHESS OF GLOUCESTER
Office: Kensington Palace, London W8 4PU
T 020-7368 1000
Private Secretary, Alistair Wood, MBE

THE DUKE OF KENT
Office: St James's Palace, London SW1A 1BQ
T 020-7930 4872
Private Secretary, N. Adamson, CVO, OBE

THE DUCHESS OF KENT
Office: Wren House, Palace Green, London W8 4PY
T 020-7937 2730
Personal Secretary, Virginia Utley

PRINCE AND PRINCESS MICHAEL OF KENT
Office: Kensington Palace, London W8 4PU
T 020-7938 3519
W www.princemichael.org.uk
Private Secretary, Nicholas Chance, LVO

PRINCESS ALEXANDRA, THE HON. LADY OGILVY
Office: Buckingham Palace, London SW1A 1AA
T 020-7024 4270
Private Secretary, Diane Duke

ROYAL HOUSEHOLD

The PRIVATE SECRETARY is responsible for:

- informing and advising the Queen on constitutional, governmental and political matters in the UK, her other Realms and the wider Commonwealth, including communications with the prime minister and government departments
- organising the Queen's domestic and overseas official programme
- the Queen's speeches, messages, patronage, photographs, portraits and official presents
- communications in connection with the role of the royal family
- dealing with correspondence to the Queen from members of the public
- organising and coordinating royal travel
- coordinating and initiating research to support engagements by members of the royal family

The COMMUNICATIONS AND PRESS SECRETARY is in charge of Buckingham Palace's press office and reports to the private secretary. The press secretary is responsible for:

- developing communications strategies to enhance the public understanding of the role of the monarchy
- briefing the British and international media on the role and duties of the Queen and issues relating to the royal family
- responding to media enquiries
- arranging media facilities in the UK and overseas to support royal functions and engagements
- the management of the royal website

The private secretary is keeper of the royal archives and is responsible for the care of the records of the sovereign and the royal household from previous reigns, preserved in the royal archives at Windsor. As keeper, it is the private secretary's responsibility to ensure the proper management of the records of the present reign with a view to their transfer to the archives as and when appropriate. The private secretary is an *ex officio* trustee of the Royal Collection Trust.

The KEEPER OF THE PRIVY PURSE AND TREASURER to the Queen is responsible for:

- the Queen's Civil List, which is the money paid from the government's Consolidated Fund to meet official expenditure relating to the Queen's duties as head of state and head of the Commonwealth
- through the director of personnel, the planning and management of personnel policy across the royal household, the administration of all its pension schemes and private estates employees, and the allocation of employee and pensioner housing
- information technology systems
- internal audit services
- health and safety; insurance matters
- the privy purse, which is mainly financed by the net income of the Duchy of Lancaster, and meets both official and private expenditure incurred by the Queen
- liaison with other members of the royal family and their households on financial matters
- the Queen's private estates at Sandringham and Balmoral, the Queen's Racing Establishment and the Royal Studs and liaison with the Ascot Authority

- the Home Park at Windsor and liaison with the Crown Estate Commissioners concerning the Home Park and the Great Park at Windsor
- the Royal Philatelic Collection
- administrative aspects of the Military Knights of Windsor
- administration of the Royal Victorian Order, of which the keeper of the privy purse is secretary, Long and Faithful Service Medals, and the Queen's cups, medals and prizes, and policy on commemorative medals

The keeper of the privy purse is one of three royal trustees (in respect of his responsibilities for the Civil List) and is receiver-general of the Duchy of Lancaster and a member of the Duchy's Council.

The keeper of the privy purse is also responsible for property services at occupied royal palaces in England, comprising Buckingham Palace, St James's Palace, Clarence House, Marlborough House Mews, the residential and office areas of Kensington Palace, Windsor Castle and buildings in the Home and Great Parks of Windsor and Hampton Court Mews and Paddocks. The costs of property services for occupied royal palaces are met from a grant-in-aid from the Department for Culture, Media and Sport (DCMS).

The DIRECTOR OF THE PROPERTY SECTION has day-to-day responsibility for the royal household's property section:

- fire safety issues
- repairs and refurbishment of buildings and new buildings work
- utilities and telecommunications
- putting up stages, tents and other work in connection with ceremonial occasions, garden parties and other official functions

The property section is also responsible, on a sub-contract basis from the DCMS, for the maintenance of Marlborough House (which is occupied by the Commonwealth Secretariat).

The keeper of the privy purse also oversees royal communications and information expenditure, which is met from the property services grant-in-aid, and the financial aspects of royal travel, met from a grant-in-aid provided by the Department for Transport.

The keeper of the privy purse is an *ex officio* trustee of the Historic Royal Palaces Trust and the Royal Collection Trust.

The Queen's Civil List and the grants-in-aid for property services and royal travel are provided by the government in return for the net surplus from the Crown Estate and other hereditary revenues.

The MASTER OF THE HOUSEHOLD is responsible for the staff and domestic arrangements at Buckingham Palace, Windsor Castle, the Palace of Holyroodhouse, Balmoral Castle and Sandringham House when the Queen is in residence. These arrangements include:

- the provision of meals for the Queen and other members of the royal family, their guests and royal household employees
- service by liveried staff at meals, receptions and other events
- travel arrangements for employees and the movement of baggage between the royal residences
- cleaning and laundry
- furnishings and the internal decorative appearance of occupied royal palaces in collaboration with the director of the Royal Collection
- liaison with the royalty and diplomatic protection department of the Metropolitan Police concerning security procedures at occupied royal palaces
- the Queen's official entertaining, both at home and overseas, and overseeing aspects of the Queen's private entertaining

The COMPTROLLER, LORD CHAMBERLAIN'S OFFICE is responsible for:

- the organisation of all ceremonial engagements, including state visits to the Queen in the UK, royal weddings and funerals, the state opening of parliament, Guards of Honour at Buckingham Palace, investitures, and the Garter and Thistle ceremonies
- garden parties at Buckingham Palace and the Palace of Holyroodhouse (except for catering and tents)
- the Crown Jewels, which are part of the Royal Collection, when they are in use on state occasions
- coordination of the arrangements for the Queen to be represented at funerals and memorial services and at the arrival and departure of visiting heads of state
- advising on matters of precedence, style and titles, dress, flying of flags, gun salutes, mourning and other ceremonial issues
- supervising the applications from tradesmen for Royal Warrants of Appointment
- advising on the commercial use of royal emblems and contemporary royal photographs
- the ecclesiastical household, the medical household, the body guards and certain ceremonial appointments such as Gentlemen Ushers and Pages of Honour
- the lords in waiting, who represent the Queen on various occasions and escort visiting heads of state during incoming state visits
- the Queen's bargemaster and watermen and the Queen's swans
- the Royal Almonry

The comptroller is also responsible for the Royal Mews, assisted by the CROWN EQUERRY, who has day-to-day responsibility for:

- the provision of carriage processions for the state opening of parliament, state visits, Trooping of the Colour, Royal Ascot, the Garter Ceremony, the Thistle Service, the presentation of credentials to the Queen by incoming foreign ambassadors and high commissioners, and other state and ceremonial occasions
- the provision of chauffeur-driven cars
- coordinating travel arrangements by road in respect of the Queen's official engagements
- supervision and administration of the Royal Mews at Buckingham Palace, Windsor Castle, Hampton Court and the Palace of Holyroodhouse

The comptroller also has overall responsibility for the MARSHAL OF THE DIPLOMATIC CORPS, who is responsible for the relationship between the royal household and the Diplomatic Heads of Mission in London; and the SECRETARY OF THE CENTRAL CHANCERY OF THE ORDERS OF KNIGHTHOOD, who administers the Orders of Chivalry, makes arrangements for investitures and the distribution of

insignia, and ensures the proper public notification of awards through the *London Gazette.*

The DIRECTOR OF THE ROYAL COLLECTION is responsible for:

- the administration and custodial control of the Royal Collection in all royal residences
- the care, display, conservation and restoration of items in the collection
- initiating and assisting research into the collection and publishing catalogues and books on the collection
- making the collection accessible to the public and educating and informing the public about the collection

The Royal Collection, which contains a large number of works of art, is held by the Queen as sovereign in trust for her successors and the nation and is not owned by her as an individual. The administration, conservation and presentation of the Royal Collection are funded by the Royal Collection Trust solely from income from visitors to Windsor Castle, Buckingham Palace and the Palace of Holyroodhouse. The Royal Collection Trust is chaired by the Prince of Wales. The Lord Chamberlain, the private secretary and the keeper of the privy purse are *ex officio* trustees and there are three external trustees appointed by the Queen.

The director of the Royal Collection is also at present the SURVEYOR OF THE QUEEN'S WORKS OF ART and is responsible for pictures and miniatures, the ROYAL LIBRARIAN is responsible for all books, manuscripts, coins and medals, insignia and works of art on paper including the watercolours, prints and drawings in the Print Room at Windsor Castle, and the SURVEYOR OF THE QUEEN'S WORKS OF ART is responsible for furniture, ceramics and the other decorative arts in the collection.

The director of the Royal Collection has overall responsibility for trading activities that fund the Royal Collection Department. These are administered by Royal Collection Enterprises Limited, the trading subsidiary of the Royal Collection Trust. The company, whose chair is the Keeper of the Privy Purse, is responsible for:

- managing access by the public to Windsor Castle (including Frogmore House), Buckingham Palace (including the Royal Mews and the Queen's Gallery) and the Palace of Holyroodhouse
- running shops at each location
- managing the images and intellectual property rights of the Royal Collection

The director of the Royal Collection is also an *ex officio* trustee of the Historic Royal Palaces Trust.

SENIOR MANAGEMENT OF THE ROYAL HOUSEHOLD

Lord Chamberlain, Earl Peel, GCVO, PC

HEADS OF DEPARTMENT

Private Secretary to The Queen, Rt. Hon. Christopher Geidt, CVO, OBE

Keeper of the Privy Purse, Sir Alan Reid, KCVO

Master of the Household, Air Vice-Marshal David Walker, OBE, MVO

Comptroller, Lord Chamberlain's Office, Lt.-Col. Andrew Ford

Director of the Royal Collection, Sir Hugh Roberts, KCVO

NON-EXECUTIVE MEMBERS

Private Secretary to the Duke of Edinburgh, Brig. Sir Miles Hunt-Davis, KCVO, CBE

Private Secretary to the Prince of Wales and the Duchess of Cornwall, Sir Michael Peat, KCVO

THE POET LAUREATE

The post of Poet Laureate was officially established when John Dryden was appointed by royal warrant as Poet Laureate and Historiographer Royal in 1668. The post is attached to the royal household and was originally conferred on the holder for life; in 1999 the length of appointment was changed to a ten-year term. It is customary for the Poet Laureate to write verse to mark events of national importance. The postholder currently receives an honorarium of £5,750 a year.

The Poet Laureate, Carol Ann Duffy, *apptd* 2009

ROYAL SALUTES

ENGLAND

The basic royal salute is 21 rounds with an extra 20 rounds fired at Hyde Park because it is a royal park. At the Tower of London 62 rounds are fired on royal anniversaries (21 plus a further 20 because the Tower is a royal palace and a further 21 'for the City of London') and 41 on other occasions. When the Queen's official birthday coincides with the Duke of Edinburgh's birthday, 124 rounds are fired from the Tower (62 rounds for each birthday). Gun salutes occur on the following royal anniversaries:

- Accession Day
- The Queen's birthday
- Coronation Day
- Duke of Edinburgh's birthday
- The Queen's Official Birthday
- The Prince of Wales' birthday
- State opening of parliament

Gun salutes also occur when parliament is prorogued by the sovereign, on royal births and when a visiting head of state meets the sovereign in London, Windsor or Edinburgh.

In London, salutes are fired at Hyde Park and the Tower of London although on some occasions (state visits, state opening of parliament and the Queen's birthday parade) Green Park is used instead of Hyde Park. Other military saluting stations in England are at Colchester, Dover, Plymouth, Woolwich and York.

Constable of the Royal Palace and Fortress of London, Gen. Sir Richard Dannatt, GCB, CBE, MC

Lieutenant of the Tower of London, Lt.-Gen. Sir Cedric Delves, KBE, DSO

Resident Governor and Keeper of the Jewel House, Maj.-Gen. Keith Cima, CB

Master Gunner of St James's Park, Gen. Sir Alex Harley, KBE, CB

Master Gunner within the Tower, Col. Simon Garrett

SCOTLAND
Royal salutes are authorised at Edinburgh Castle and Stirling Castle. A salute of 21 guns is fired on the following occasions:

- the anniversaries of the birth, accession and coronation of the sovereign
- the anniversary of the birth of the Duke of Edinburgh

A salute of 21 guns is fired in Edinburgh on the occasion of the opening of the general assembly of the Church of Scotland. A salute of 21 guns may also be fired in Edinburgh on the arrival of HM The Queen or a member of the royal family who is a Royal Highness on an official visit.

Military saluting stations are also situated at Cardiff Castle in Wales, Hillsborough Castle in Northern Ireland and in Gibraltar.

ROYAL FINANCES

FUNDING

CIVIL LIST
The Civil List dates back to the late 17th century. It was originally used by the sovereign to supplement hereditary revenues for paying the salaries of judges, ambassadors and other government officers as well as the expenses of the royal household. In 1760, on the accession of George III, it was decided that the Civil List would be provided by parliament to cover all relevant expenditure in return for the king surrendering the hereditary revenues of the Crown (principally the net surplus of the Crown Estate). At that time parliament undertook to pay the salaries of judges, ambassadors etc. In 1831 parliament agreed also to meet the costs of the royal palaces in return for a reduction in the Civil List. Each sovereign has agreed to continue this arrangement. The Civil List now meets the central staff costs and running expenses of the Queen's official household.

Until 1972, the amount of money allocated annually under the Civil List was set for the duration of a reign. The system was then altered to a fixed annual payment for ten years but from 1975 high inflation made an annual review necessary. The system of payments reverted to the practice of a fixed annual payment of £7.9m for a ten year period to 31 December 2000, during this period annual Civil List expenditure reached £6.5m, and a reserve of £35m was established. In order to draw down the reserve, the annual Civil List payment was left at £7.9m for a further ten years to 31 December 2010.

The legislative requirement is for Civil List accounts to be submitted to parliament, in the form of Royal Trustees Reports, at ten-yearly intervals, but from June 2002 accounts have been published annually. The eighth annual accounts for the year ending 31 December 2008 were published in June 2009:

	2007	*2008*
Civil List payment	£7,900,000	£7,900,000
Draw-down from the Civil List reserve	£4,900,000	£6,400,000
Net Receipts	£12,800,000	£14,300,000
Net Civil List Expenditure	(£12,700,000)	(£13,900,000)

PARLIAMENTARY ANNUITIES
The Civil List Acts provide for other members of the royal family to receive parliamentary annuities from government funds to meet the expenses of carrying out their official duties. Since 1993 the Queen has reimbursed all the annuities except those paid to the late Queen Elizabeth the Queen Mother and the Duke of Edinburgh.

The Prince of Wales does not receive a parliamentary annuity. He derives his income from the revenues of the Duchy of Cornwall and these monies meet the official and private expenses of the Prince of Wales and his family (*see* Prince of Wales' Funding).

In 2000 the annual amounts payable to members of the royal family, excluding the Earl of Wessex, were reset at their 1990 levels for the next ten years. The Earl of Wessex had his annuity increased by £45,000 to £141,000 on the occasion of his marriage in 1999.

The annual payments remain as follows until December 2010:

The Duke of Edinburgh	£359,000
The Duke of York	£249,000
The Earl of Wessex	£141,000
The Princess Royal	£228,000
The Duke and Duchess of Gloucester	£175,000
The Duke and Duchess of Kent	£236,000
Princess Alexandra	£225,000
Subtotal	£1,613,000
Refunded to the Treasury by the Queen	(£1,254,000)
TOTAL	£359,000

GRANTS-IN-AID
Grants-in-aid are provided to the royal household annually by the Department for Culture, Media and Sport for property services and communications and information, and by the Department for Transport for royal travel. Property services meets the cost of property maintenance, utilities, telephones and related services at the occupied royal palaces in England (*see* Royal Household section for a list of occupied palaces). Communications and information meets the cost of these services in connection with official royal functions and engagements in England and Scotland. Royal travel meets the cost of official royal travel by air and rail.

GRANTS-IN-AID 2008–9:

	Grant-in-aid voted by parliament	*Total net expenditure*
Property Services	£15,000,000	£15,500,000
Marlborough House Maintenance	£600,000	£400,000
Communications and Information	£500,000	£600,000
Royal Travel	£7,400,000	£6,500,000

THE PRIVY PURSE AND THE DUCHY OF LANCASTER
The funds received by the privy purse pay for official expenses incurred by the Queen as head of state and for some of the Queen's private expenditure. The revenues of the Duchy of Lancaster are the principal source of income for the privy purse. The revenues of the Duchy were retained by George III in 1760 when the hereditary

revenues were surrendered in exchange for the Civil List. The Duchy's affairs are the responsibility of the Duchy Council which reports to the Chancellor of the Duchy of Lancaster, who in turn is accountable directly to the sovereign rather than to parliament. However the chancellor does answer parliamentary questions on matters relating to the Duchy of Lancaster's responsibilities.

THE DUCHY OF LANCASTER, Lancaster Place, London WC2E 7ED
E info@duchyoflancaster.co.uk
W www.duchyoflancaster.co.uk
Chancellor of the Duchy of Lancaster, Rt. Hon. Liam Byrne, MP, *apptd* 2008
Chair of the Council, Lord Shuttleworth
Clerk and Chief Executive, Paul Clarke, FRICS
Receiver-General, Sir Alan Reid, KCVO
Attorney-General, Robert Hildyard, QC

PERSONAL INCOME

The Queen's personal income derives mostly from investments, and is used to meet private expenditure.

EXPENDITURE MET BY GOVERNMENT DEPARTMENTS AND THE CROWN ESTATE 2008–9:

Administration of honours	£600,000
Equerries, orderlies and other personnel	£1,400,000
Maintenance of Holyroodhouse	£1,200,000
State visits to and by the Queen and liaison with the Diplomatic Corps	£400,000
Ceremonial occasions	£200,000
Maintenance of Home Park, Windsor Castle	£600,000
Other	£200,000
Total	£4,600,000

PRINCE OF WALES' FUNDING

The Duchy Estate was created in 1337 by Edward III for his son and heir Prince Edward (the Black Prince) who became the Duke of Cornwall. The Duchy's primary function is to provide an income from its assets for the Prince of Wales. Under a 1337 charter, confirmed by subsequent legislation, the Prince of Wales is not entitled to the proceeds or profit on the sale of Duchy assets but only to the annual income which is generated from these assets. The Duchy is responsible for the sustainable and commercial management of its properties, investment portfolio and approximately 54,521 hectares of land, based mostly in the southwest of England. The Prince of Wales has chosen to use a proportion of his income to meet the cost of his public and charitable work in addition to providing a private source of income. The Duchy also funds the public, charitable and private activities of the Duchess of Cornwall and princes William and Harry. Proceeds from the Duchy are voluntarily subject to income tax.

THE DUCHY OF CORNWALL, 10 Buckingham Gate, London SW1E 6L
T 020-7834 7346 E London@duchyofcornwall.org
W www.duchyofcornwall.org
Lord Warden of the Stannaries, Sir Nicholas Bacon, Bt.
Receiver-General, James Leigh-Pemberton
Attorney-General, Jonathan Crow, QC
Secretary and Keeper of the Records, Bertie Ross

TAXATION

The sovereign is not legally liable to pay income tax or capital gains tax. After income tax was reintroduced in 1842, some income tax was paid voluntarily by the sovereign but over a long period these payments were phased out. In 1992 the Queen offered to pay income and capital gains tax on a voluntary basis from 6 April 1993, and the Prince of Wales offered to pay tax on a voluntary basis on his income from the Duchy of Cornwall (he was already taxed in all other respects).

The main provisions for the Queen and the Prince of Wales to pay tax, set out in a Memorandum of Understanding on Royal Taxation presented to parliament on 11 February 1993, are that the Queen will pay income tax and capital gains tax in respect of her private income and assets, and on the proportion of the income and capital gains of the Privy Purse used for private purposes. Inheritance tax will be paid on the Queen's assets, except for those which pass to the next sovereign, whether automatically or by gift or bequest. The Prince of Wales will pay income tax on income from the Duchy of Cornwall used for private purposes.

The Prince of Wales has confirmed that he intends to pay tax on the same basis following his accession to the throne. Other members of the royal family are subject to tax as for any taxpayer.

MILITARY RANKS AND TITLES

THE QUEEN

ROYAL NAVY
Lord High Admiral of the United Kingdom

ARMY
Colonel-in-Chief
The Life Guards; The Blues and Royals (Royal Horse Guards and 1st Dragoons); The Royal Scots Dragoon Guards (Carabiniers and Greys); The Queen's Royal Lancers; Royal Tank Regiment; Corps of Royal Engineers; Grenadier Guards; Coldstream Guards; Scots Guards; Irish Guards; Welsh Guards; The Royal Regiment of Scotland; The Duke of Lancaster's Regiment (King's, Lancashire and Border); The Royal Welsh; Adjutant General's Corps; The Royal Mercian and Lancastrian Yeomanry; The Governor General's Horse Guards (of Canada); The King's Own Calgary Regiment (Royal Canadian Armoured Corps); Canadian Military Engineers Branch; Royal 22e Regiment (of Canada); Governor General's Foot Guards (of Canada); The Canadian Grenadier Guards; Le Régiment de la Chaudière (of Canada); 2nd Battalion Royal New Brunswick Regiment (North Shore); 48th Highlanders of Canada; The Argyll and Sutherland Highlanders of Canada (Princess Louise's); The Calgary Highlanders; Royal Australian Engineers; Royal Australian Infantry Corps; Royal Australian Army Ordnance Corps; Royal Australian Army Nursing Corps; The Corps of Royal New Zealand Engineers; Royal New Zealand Infantry Regiment; The Malawi Rifles; The Royal Malta Artillery

Affiliated Colonel-in-Chief
The Queen's Gurkha Engineers

Captain-General
Royal Regiment of Artillery; The Honourable Artillery Company; Combined Cadet Force; Royal Regiment of Canadian Artillery; Royal Regiment of Australian Artillery; Royal Regiment of New Zealand Artillery; Royal New Zealand Armoured Corps

Royal Colonel
The Argyll and Sutherland Highlanders, 5th Battalion The Royal Regiment of Scotland

Patron
Royal Army Chaplains' Department

ROYAL AIR FORCE
Air Commodore-in-Chief
Royal Auxiliary Air Force; Royal Air Force Regiment; Air Reserve of Canada; Royal Australian Air Force Reserve; Territorial Air Force (of New Zealand)

Commandant-in-Chief
RAF College, Cranwell

Royal Honorary Air Commodore
RAF Marham; 603 (City of Edinburgh) Squadron Royal Auxiliary Air Force

PRINCE PHILIP, DUKE OF EDINBURGH

ROYAL NAVY
Admiral of the Fleet
Admiral of the Fleet, Royal Australian Navy
Admiral of the Fleet, Royal New Zealand Navy
Admiral of the Royal Canadian Sea Cadets

ROYAL MARINES
Captain-General

ARMY
Field Marshal
Field Marshal, Australian Military Forces
Field Marshal, New Zealand Army
Colonel-in-Chief
The Queen's Royal Hussars (Queen's Own and Royal Irish); The Rifles; Corps of Royal Electrical and Mechanical Engineers; Intelligence Corps; Army Cadet Force Association; The Royal Canadian Regiment; The Royal Hamilton Light Infantry (Wentworth Regiment of Canada); The Cameron Highlanders of Ottawa; The Queen's Own Cameron Highlanders of Canada; The Seaforth Highlanders of Canada; The Royal Canadian Army Cadets; The Royal Australian Corps of Electrical and Mechanical Engineers; The Australian Army Cadet Corps

Colonel
Grenadier Guards

Royal Colonel
The Highlanders, 4th Battalion The Royal Regiment of Scotland

Honorary Colonel
City of Edinburgh University Officers' Training Corps; The Trinidad and Tobago Regiment

Member
Honourable Artillery Company

ROYAL AIR FORCE
Marshal of the Royal Air Force
Marshal of the Royal Australian Air Force
Marshal of the Royal New Zealand Air Force
Air Commodore-in-Chief
Air Training Corps; Royal Canadian Air Cadets

Honorary Air Commodore
RAF Kinloss

THE PRINCE OF WALES

ROYAL NAVY
Admiral
Commodore-in-Chief
Royal Naval Command Plymouth

ARMY
General
Colonel-in-Chief
The Royal Dragoon Guards; The Parachute Regiment; The Royal Gurkha Rifles; Army Air Corps; The Royal Canadian Dragoons; Lord Strathcona's Horse (Royal Canadians); The Royal Regiment of Canada; Royal Winnipeg Rifles; Royal Australian Armoured Corps; The Royal Pacific Islands Regiment; 1st The Queen's Dragoon Guards; The Black Watch (Royal Highland Regiment) of Canada; The Toronto Scottish Regiment (Queen Elizabeth The Queen Mother's Own); The Mercian Regiment

Royal Colonel
The Black Watch, 3rd Battalion The Royal Regiment of Scotland; 51st Highland, 7th Battalion The Royal Regiment of Scotland (Territorial Army)

Colonel
The Welsh Guards

Royal Honorary Colonel
The Queen's Own Yeomanry

ROYAL AIR FORCE
Air Chief Marshal
Honorary Air Commodore
RAF Valley

Air Commodore-in-Chief
Royal New Zealand Air Force

Colonel-in-Chief
Air Reserve Canada

THE DUCHESS OF CORNWALL

ROYAL NAVY
Commodore-in-Chief
Naval Medical Services; Royal Naval Chaplaincy Services

ARMY
Royal Colonel
4th Battalion The Rifles

ROYAL AIR FORCE
Honorary AIr Commodore
RAF Halton; RAF Leeming

PRINCE WILLIAM OF WALES

ROYAL NAVY
Commodore-in-Chief
Scotland Command; Submarines Command

ARMY
Lieutenant
The Blues and Royals (Royal Horse Guards and 1st Dragoons)

ROYAL AIR FORCE
Honorary Air Commandant
RAF Coningsby

PRINCE HENRY OF WALES

ROYAL NAVY
Commodore-in-Chief
Small Ships and Diving Command

ARMY
Lieutenant
The Blues and Royals (Royal Horse Guards and 1st Dragoons)

ROYAL AIR FORCE
Honorary Air Commandant
RAF Honington

THE DUKE OF YORK

ROYAL NAVY
Commander
Admiral of the Marine Society and Sea Cadets
Honorary Captain

ARMY
Colonel-in-Chief
The Royal Irish Regiment (27th (Inniskilling), 83rd, 87th and The Ulster Defence Regiment); 9th/12th Royal Lancers (The Prince of Wales's); The Royal Highland Fusiliers, 2nd Battalion The Royal Regiment of Scotland; The Yorkshire Regiment; Small Arms School Corps; The Queen's York Rangers (First Americans); Royal New Zealand Army Logistics Regiment, The Royal Highland Fusiliers of Canada; The Princess Louise Fusiliers (Canada)

ROYAL AIR FORCE
Honorary Air Commodore
RAF Lossiemouth

THE EARL OF WESSEX

ROYAL NAVY
Commodore-in-Chief
Royal Fleet Auxiliary

Patron
Royal Fleet Auxiliary Association

ARMY
Colonel-in-Chief
Hastings and Prince Edward Regiment; Saskatchewan Dragoons

Royal Colonel
2nd Battalion, The Rifles

Royal Honorary Colonel
Royal Wessex Yeomanry

ROYAL AIR FORCE
Honorary Air Commodore
RAF Waddington

THE COUNTESS OF WESSEX

ARMY
Colonel-in-Chief
Queen Alexandra's Royal Army Nursing Corps; The Lincoln and Welland Regiment; South Alberta Light Horse Regiment

Royal Colonel
5th Battalion, The Rifles

ROYAL AIR FORCE
Honorary Air Commodore
RAF Wittering

THE PRINCESS ROYAL

ROYAL NAVY
Rear-Admiral (Chief Commandant for Women in the Royal Navy)
Commodore-in-Chief
HM Naval Base Portsmouth

ARMY
Colonel-in-Chief
The King's Royal Hussars; Royal Corps of Signals; Royal Logistic Corps; The Royal Army Veterinary Corps; 8th Canadian Hussars (Princess Louise's); Royal Newfoundland Regiment; Canadian Forces Communications and Electronics Branch; The Grey and Simcoe Foresters (Royal Canadian Armoured Corps); The Royal Regina Rifle Regiment; Canadian Forces Medical Branch; Royal Australian Corps of Signals; Royal New Zealand Corps of Signals; Royal New Zealand Nursing Corps

Affiliated Colonel-in-Chief
The Queen's Gurkha Signals; The Queen's Own Gurkha Transport Regiment

Royal Colonel
1st Battalion The Royal Regiment of Scotland; 52nd Lowland, 6th Battalion The Royal Regiment of Scotland

Colonel
The Blues and Royals (Royal Horse Guards and 1st Dragoons)

Honorary Colonel
University of London Officers' Training Corps

Commandant-in-Chief
First Aid Nursing Yeomanry (Princess Royal's Volunteer Corps)

ROYAL AIR FORCE
Honorary Air Commodore
RAF Lyneham; University of London Air Squadron

THE DUKE OF GLOUCESTER

ARMY
Colonel-in-Chief
The Royal Anglian Regiment; Royal Army Medical Corps; Royal New Zealand Army Medical Corps

Deputy Colonel-in-Chief
The Royal Logistic Corps

Royal Colonel
6th Battalion, The Rifles

Honorary Colonel
Royal Monmouthshire Royal Engineers (Militia)

ROYAL AIR FORCE
Honorary Air Marshal
Honorary Air Commodore
RAF Odiham; No. 501 (County of Gloucester) Squadron Royal Auxiliary Air Force

THE DUCHESS OF GLOUCESTER

ARMY
Colonel-in-Chief
Royal Army Dental Corps; Royal Australian Army Educational Corps; Royal New Zealand Army Educational Corps; Canadian Forces Dental Services

Deputy Colonel-in-Chief
Adjutant-General's Corps

Royal Colonel
7th Battalion, The Rifles

Vice-Patron
Adjutant General's Corps Regimental Association

Patron
Royal Army Educational Corps Association; Army Families Federation

THE DUKE OF KENT

ARMY
Field Marshal
Colonel-in-Chief
The Royal Regiment of Fusiliers; Lorne Scots (Peel, Dufferin and Hamilton Regiment)

Deputy Colonel-in-Chief
The Royal Scots Dragoon Guards (Carabiniers and Greys)

Royal Colonel
1st Battalion The Rifles

Colonel
Scots Guards

ROYAL AIR FORCE
Honorary Air Chief Marshal
Honorary Air Commodore
RAF Leuchars

THE DUCHESS OF KENT

ARMY
Deputy Colonel-in-Chief
The Royal Dragoon Guards; Adjutant-General's Corps; The Royal Logistic Corps

PRINCE MICHAEL OF KENT

ROYAL NAVY
Honorary Rear Admiral Royal Naval Reserve

ARMY
Colonel-in-Chief
Essex and Kent Scottish Regiment (Ontario)

ROYAL AIR FORCE
Honorary Air Commodore
RAF Benson

PRINCESS ALEXANDRA, THE HON. LADY OGILVY

ROYAL NAVY
Patron
Queen Alexandra's Royal Naval Nursing Service

ARMY
Colonel-in-Chief
The Queen's Own Rifles of Canada; The Canadian Scottish Regiment (Princess Mary's)

Deputy Colonel-in-Chief
The Queen's Royal Lancers

Royal Colonel
3rd Battalion The Rifles

Royal Honorary Colonel
The Royal Yeomanry

ROYAL AIR FORCE
Patron and Air Chief Commandant
Princess Mary's RAF Nursing Service

Royal Honorary Air Commodore
RAF Cottesmore

KINGS AND QUEENS

ENGLISH KINGS AND QUEENS 927 TO 1603

HOUSES OF CERDIC AND DENMARK

Reign

927–939 ÆTHELSTAN
Son of Edward the Elder, by Ecgwynn, and grandson of Alfred
Acceded to Wessex and Mercia *c.*924, established direct rule over Northumbria 927, effectively creating the Kingdom of England
Reigned 15 years

939–946 EDMUND I
Born 921, son of Edward the Elder, by Eadgifu
Married (1) Ælfgifu (2) Æthelflæd
Killed aged 25, *reigned* 6 years

946–955 EADRED
Son of Edward the Elder, by Eadgifu
Reigned 9 years

955–959 EADWIG
Born before 943, son of Edmund and Ælfgifu
Married Ælfgifu
Reigned 3 years

959–975 EDGAR I
Born 943, son of Edmund and Ælfgifu
Married (1) Æthelflæd (2) Wulfthryth (3) Ælfthryth
Died aged 32, *reigned* 15 years

975–978 EDWARD I (the Martyr)
Born *c.*962, son of Edgar and Æthelflæd
Assassinated aged *c.*16, *reigned* 2 years

978–1016 ÆTHELRED (the Unready)
Born 968/969, son of Edgar and Ælfthryth
Married (1) Ælfgifu (2) Emma, daughter of Richard I, Count of Normandy
1013–14 dispossessed of kingdom by Swegn Forkbeard (King of Denmark 987–1014)
Died aged *c.*47, *reigned* 38 years

1016 (Apr–Nov) EDMUND II (Ironside)
Born before 993, son of Æthelred and Ælfgifu
Married Ealdgyth
Died aged over 23, *reigned* 7 months

1016–1035 CNUT (Canute)
Born *c.*995, son of Swegn Forkbeard, King of Denmark, and Gunhild
Married (1) Ælfgifu (2) Emma, widow of Æthelred the Unready
Gained submission of West Saxons 1015, Northumbrians 1016, Mercia 1016, King of all England after Edmund's death, King of Denmark 1019–35, King of Norway 1028–35
Died aged *c.*40, *reigned* 19 years

1035–1040 HAROLD I (Harefoot)
Born 1016/17, son of Cnut and Ælfgifu
Married Ælfgifu
1035 recognised as regent for himself and his brother Harthacnut; 1037 recognised as king
Died aged *c.*23, *reigned* 4 years

1040–1042 HARTHACNUT (Harthacanute)
Born *c.*1018, son of Cnut and Emma
Titular king of Denmark from 1028
Acknowledged King of England 1035–7 with Harold I as regent; effective king after Harold's death
Died aged *c.*24, *reigned* 2 years

1042–1066 EDWARD II (the Confessor)
Born 1002–5, son of Æthelred the Unready and Emma
Married Eadgyth, daughter of Godwine, Earl of Wessex
Died aged over 60, *reigned* 23 years

1066 (Jan–Oct) HAROLD II (Godwinesson)
Born *c.*1020, son of Godwine, Earl of Wessex, and Gytha
Married (1) Eadgyth (2) Ealdgyth
Killed in battle aged *c.*46, *reigned* 10 months

THE HOUSE OF NORMANDY

1066–1087 WILLIAM I (the Conqueror)
Born 1027/8, son of Robert I, Duke of Normandy; obtained the Crown by conquest
Married Matilda, daughter of Baldwin, Count of Flanders
Died aged *c.*60, *reigned* 20 years

1087–1100 WILLIAM II (Rufus)
Born between 1056 and 1060, third son of William I; succeeded his father in England only
Killed aged *c.*40, *reigned* 12 years

1100–1135 HENRY I (Beauclerk)
Born 1068, fourth son of William I
Married (1) Edith or Matilda, daughter of Malcolm III of Scotland (2) Adela, daughter of Godfrey, Count of Louvain
Died aged 67, *reigned* 35 years

1135–1154 STEPHEN
Born not later than 1100, third son of Adela, daughter of William I, and Stephen, Count of Blois
Married Matilda, daughter of Eustace, Count of Boulogne
1141 (Feb–Nov) held captive by adherents of Matilda, daughter of Henry I, who contested the crown until 1153
Died aged over 53, *reigned* 18 years

THE HOUSE OF ANJOU (PLANTAGENETS)

1154–1189 HENRY II (Curtmantle)
Born 1133, son of Matilda, daughter of Henry I, and Geoffrey, Count of Anjou
Married Eleanor, daughter of William, Duke of Aquitaine, and divorced queen of Louis VII of France
Died aged 56, *reigned* 34 years

1189–1199 RICHARD I (Coeur de Lion)
Born 1157, third son of Henry II
Married Berengaria, daughter of Sancho VI, King of Navarre
Died aged 42, *reigned* 9 years

1199–1216 JOHN (Lackland)
Born 1167, fifth son of Henry II
Married (1) Isabella or Avisa, daughter of William, Earl of Gloucester (divorced) (2) Isabella, daughter of Aymer, Count of Angoulême
Died aged 48, *reigned* 17 years

1216–1272 HENRY III
Born 1207, son of John and Isabella of Angoulême
Married Eleanor, daughter of Raymond, Count of Provence
Died aged 65, *reigned* 56 years

1272–1307 EDWARD I (Longshanks)
Born 1239, eldest son of Henry III
Married (1) Eleanor, daughter of Ferdinand III, King of Castile (2) Margaret, daughter of Philip III of France
Died aged 68, *reigned* 34 years

1307–1327 EDWARD II
Born 1284, eldest surviving son of Edward I and Eleanor
Married Isabella, daughter of Philip IV of France
Deposed Jan 1327, *killed* Sep 1327 aged 43, *reigned* 19 years

1327–1377 EDWARD III
Born 1312, eldest son of Edward II
Married Philippa, daughter of William, Count of Hainault
Died aged 64, *reigned* 50 years

1377–1399 RICHARD II
Born 1367, son of Edward (the Black Prince), eldest son of Edward III
Married (1) Anne, daughter of Emperor Charles IV (2) Isabelle, daughter of Charles VI of France
Deposed Sep 1399, *killed* Feb 1400 aged 33, *reigned* 22 years

THE HOUSE OF LANCASTER

1399–1413 HENRY IV
Born 1366, son of John of Gaunt, fourth son of Edward III, and Blanche, daughter of Henry, Duke of Lancaster
Married (1) Mary, daughter of Humphrey, Earl of Hereford (2) Joan, daughter of Charles, King of Navarre, and widow of John, Duke of Brittany
Died aged *c.*47, *reigned* 13 years

1413–1422 HENRY V
Born 1387, eldest surviving son of Henry IV and Mary
Married Catherine, daughter of Charles VI of France
Died aged 34, *reigned* 9 years

1422–1471 HENRY VI
Born 1421, son of Henry V
Married Margaret, daughter of René, Duke of Anjou and Count of Provence
Deposed Mar 1461, *restored* Oct 1470
Deposed Apr 1471, *killed* May 1471 aged 49, *reigned* 39 years

THE HOUSE OF YORK

1461–1483 EDWARD IV
Born 1442, eldest son of Richard of York (grandson of Edmund, fifth son of Edward III, and son of Anne, great-granddaughter of Lionel, third son of Edward III)
Married Elizabeth Woodville, daughter of Richard, Lord Rivers, and widow of Sir John Grey
Acceded Mar 1461, *deposed* Oct 1470, *restored* Apr 1471
Died aged 40, *reigned* 21 years

1483 (Apr–Jun) EDWARD V
Born 1470, eldest son of Edward IV
Deposed Jun 1483, *died* probably Jul–Sep 1483, aged 12, *reigned* 2 months

1483–1485 RICHARD III
Born 1452, fourth son of Richard of York
Married Anne Neville, daughter of Richard, Earl of Warwick, and widow of Edward, Prince of Wales, son of Henry VI
Killed in battle aged 32, *reigned* 2 years

THE HOUSE OF TUDOR

1485–1509 HENRY VII
Born 1457, son of Margaret Beaufort (great-granddaughter of John of Gaunt, fourth son of Edward III) and Edmund Tudor, Earl of Richmond
Married Elizabeth, daughter of Edward IV
Died aged 52, *reigned* 23 years

1509–1547 HENRY VIII
Born 1491, second son of Henry VII
Married (1) Catherine, daughter of Ferdinand II, King of Aragon, and widow of his elder brother Arthur (divorced) (2) Anne, daughter of Sir Thomas Boleyn (executed) (3) Jane, daughter of Sir John Seymour (died in childbirth) (4) Anne, daughter of John, Duke of Cleves (divorced) (5) Catherine Howard, niece of the Duke of Norfolk (executed) (6) Catherine, daughter of Sir Thomas Parr and widow of Lord Latimer
Died aged 55, *reigned* 37 years

1547–1553 EDWARD VI
Born 1537, son of Henry VIII and Jane Seymour
Died aged 15, *reigned* 6 years

1553 *(6/10–19 Jul) JANE
Born 1537, daughter of Frances (daughter of Mary Tudor, the younger daughter of Henry VII) and Henry Grey, Duke of Suffolk
Married Lord Guildford Dudley, son of the Duke of Northumberland
Deposed Jul 1553, *executed* Feb 1554 aged 16, *reigned* 13/9 days

1553–1558 MARY I
Born 1516, daughter of Henry VIII and Catherine of Aragon
Married Philip II of Spain
Died aged 42, *reigned* 5 years

1558–1603 ELIZABETH I
Born 1533, daughter of Henry VIII and Anne Boleyn
Died aged 69, *reigned* 44 years

* Depending on whether the date of her predecessor's death (6 July) or that of her official proclamation as Queen (10 July) is taken as the beginning of her reign.

BRITISH KINGS AND QUEENS SINCE 1603

THE HOUSE OF STUART

Reign

1603–1625 JAMES I (VI OF SCOTLAND)
Born 1566, son of Mary, Queen of Scots (granddaughter of Margaret Tudor, elder daughter of Henry VII), and Henry Stewart, Lord Darnley
Married Anne, daughter of Frederick II of Denmark
Died aged 58, *reigned* 22 years

1625–1649 CHARLES I
Born 1600, second son of James I
Married Henrietta Maria, daughter of Henry IV of France
Executed 1649 aged 48, *reigned* 23 years

INTERREGNUM 1649–1660

1649–1653 Government by a council of state
1653–1658 Oliver Cromwell, Lord Protector
1658–1659 Richard Cromwell, Lord Protector

Reign

1660–1685 CHARLES II
Born 1630, eldest son of Charles I
Married Catherine, daughter of John IV of Portugal
Died aged 54, *reigned* 24 years

1685–1688 JAMES II (VII OF SCOTLAND)
Born 1633, second son of Charles I
Married (1) Lady Anne Hyde, daughter of Edward, Earl of Clarendon (2) Mary, daughter of Alphonso, Duke of Modena
Reign ended with flight from kingdom Dec 1688
Died 1701 aged 67, *reigned* 3 years

INTERREGNUM

11 Dec 1688 to 12 Feb 1689

Reign

1689–1702 WILLIAM III
Born 1650, son of William II, Prince of Orange, and Mary Stuart, daughter of Charles I
Married Mary, elder daughter of James II
Died aged 51, *reigned* 13 years

and

1689–1694 MARY II
Born 1662, elder daughter of James II and Anne
Died aged 32, *reigned* 5 years

1702–1714 ANNE
Born 1665, younger daughter of James II and Anne
Married Prince George of Denmark, son of Frederick III of Denmark
Died aged 49, *reigned* 12 years

THE HOUSE OF HANOVER

1714–1727 GEORGE I (Elector of Hanover)
Born 1660, son of Sophia (daughter of Frederick, Elector Palatine, and Elizabeth Stuart, daughter of James I) and Ernest Augustus, Elector of Hanover
Married Sophia Dorothea, daughter of George William, Duke of Lüneburg-Celle
Died aged 67, *reigned* 12 years

1727–1760 GEORGE II
Born 1683, son of George I
Married Caroline, daughter of John Frederick, Margrave of Brandenburg-Anspach
Died aged 76, *reigned* 33 years

1760–1820 GEORGE III
Born 1738, son of Frederick, eldest son of George II
Married Charlotte, daughter of Charles Louis, Duke of Mecklenburg-Strelitz
Died aged 81, *reigned* 59 years

REGENCY 1811–1820

Prince of Wales regent owing to the insanity of George III

Reign

1820–1830 GEORGE IV
Born 1762, eldest son of George III
Married Caroline, daughter of Charles, Duke of Brunswick-Wolfenbüttel
Died aged 67, *reigned* 10 years

1830–1837 WILLIAM IV
Born 1765, third son of George III
Married Adelaide, daughter of George, Duke of Saxe-Meiningen
Died aged 71, *reigned* 7 years

1837–1901 VICTORIA
Born 1819, daughter of Edward, fourth son of George III
Married Prince Albert of Saxe-Coburg and Gotha
Died aged 81, *reigned* 63 years

THE HOUSE OF SAXE-COBURG AND GOTHA

1901–1910 EDWARD VII
Born 1841, eldest son of Victoria and Albert
Married Alexandra, daughter of Christian IX of Denmark
Died aged 68, *reigned* 9 years

THE HOUSE OF WINDSOR

1910–1936 GEORGE V
Born 1865, second son of Edward VII
Married Victoria Mary, daughter of Francis, Duke of Teck
Died aged 70, *reigned* 25 years

1936 (20 Jan–11 Dec) EDWARD VIII
Born 1894, eldest son of George V
Married (1937) Mrs Wallis Simpson
Abdicated 1936, *died* 1972 aged 77, *reigned* 10 months

1936–1952 GEORGE VI
Born 1895, second son of George V
Married Lady Elizabeth Bowes-Lyon, daughter of 14th Earl of Strathmore and Kinghorne
Died aged 56, *reigned* 15 years

1952– ELIZABETH II
Born 1926, elder daughter of George VI
Married Philip, son of Prince Andrew of Greece

KINGS AND QUEENS OF SCOTS 1016 TO 1603

Reign

1016–1034 MALCOLM II
*Born c.*954, son of Kenneth II
Acceded to Alba 1005, secured Lothian *c.*1016, obtained Strathclyde for his grandson Duncan *c.*1016, thus reigning over an area approximately the same as that governed by later rulers of Scotland
Died aged *c.*80, *reigned* 18 years

THE HOUSE OF ATHOL

1034–1040 DUNCAN I
Son of Bethoc, daughter of Malcolm II, and Crinan, Mormaer of Atholl
Married a cousin of Siward, Earl of Northumbria
Reigned 5 years

1040–1057 MACBETH
*Born c.*1005, son of a daughter of Malcolm II and Finlaec, Mormaer of Moray
Married Gruoch, granddaughter of Kenneth III
Killed aged *c.*52, *reigned* 17 years

1057–1058 (Aug–Mar) LULACH
*Born c.*1032, son of Gillacomgan, Mormaer of Moray, and Gruoch (and stepson of Macbeth)
Died aged *c.*26, *reigned* 7 months

1058–1093 MALCOLM III (Canmore)
*Born c.*1031, elder son of Duncan I
Married (1) Ingibiorg (2) Margaret (St Margaret), granddaughter of Edmund II of England
Killed in battle aged *c.*62, *reigned* 35 years

1093–1097 DONALD III BÁN
*Born c.*1033, second son of Duncan I
Deposed May 1094, *restored* Nov 1094, *deposed* Oct 1097, *reigned* 3 years

1094 (May–Nov) DUNCAN II
*Born c.*1060, elder son of Malcolm III and Ingibiorg
Married Octreda of Dunbar
Killed aged *c.*34, *reigned* 6 months

1097–1107 EDGAR
*Born c.*1074, second son of Malcolm III and Margaret
Died aged *c.*32, *reigned* 9 years

1107–1124 ALEXANDER I (the Fierce)
*Born c.*1077, fifth son of Malcolm III and Margaret
Married Sybilla, illegitimate daughter of Henry I of England
Died aged *c.*47, *reigned* 17 years

1124–1153 DAVID I (the Saint)
*Born c.*1085, sixth son of Malcolm III and Margaret
Married Matilda, daughter of Waltheof, Earl of Huntingdon
Died aged *c.*68, *reigned* 29 years

1153–1165 MALCOLM IV (the Maiden)
*Born c.*1141, son of Henry, Earl of Huntingdon, second son of David I
Died aged *c.*24, *reigned* 12 years

1165–1214 WILLIAM I (the Lion)
*Born c.*1142, brother of Malcolm IV
Married Ermengarde, daughter of Richard, Viscount of Beaumont
Died aged *c.*72, *reigned* 49 years

1214–1249 ALEXANDER II
Born 1198, son of William I
Married (1) Joan, daughter of John, King of England (2) Marie, daughter of Ingelram de Coucy
Died aged 50, *reigned* 34 years

1249–1286 ALEXANDER III
Born 1241, son of Alexander II and Marie
Married (1) Margaret, daughter of Henry III of England (2) Yolande, daughter of the Count of Dreux
Killed accidentally aged 44, *reigned* 36 years

1286–1290 MARGARET (the Maid of Norway)
Born 1283, daughter of Margaret (daughter of Alexander III) and Eric II of Norway
Died aged 7, *reigned* 4 years

FIRST INTERREGNUM 1290–1292

Throne disputed by 13 competitors. Crown awarded to John Balliol by adjudication of Edward I of England

THE HOUSE OF BALLIOL

Reign

1292–1296 JOHN (Balliol)
*Born c.*1250, son of Dervorguilla, great-great-granddaughter of David I, and John de Balliol
Married Isabella, daughter of John, Earl of Surrey
Abdicated 1296, *died* 1313 aged *c.*63, *reigned* 3 years

SECOND INTERREGNUM 1296–1306

Edward I of England declared John Balliol to have forfeited the throne for contumacy in 1296 and took the government of Scotland into his own hands

THE HOUSE OF BRUCE

Reign

1306–1329 ROBERT I (Bruce)
Born 1274, son of Robert Bruce and Marjorie, countess of Carrick, and great-grandson of the second daughter of David, Earl of Huntingdon, brother of William I
Married (1) Isabella, daughter of Donald, Earl of Mar (2) Elizabeth, daughter of Richard, Earl of Ulster
Died aged 54, *reigned* 23 years

1329–1371 DAVID II
Born 1324, son of Robert I and Elizabeth
Married (1) Joanna, daughter of Edward II of England (2) Margaret Drummond, widow of Sir John Logie (divorced)
Died aged 46, *reigned* 41 years

1332 (Sep–Dec) Edward Balliol, son of John Balliol

1333–1336 Edward Balliol

THE HOUSE OF STEWART

1371–1390 ROBERT II (Stewart)
Born 1316, son of Marjorie (daughter of Robert I) and Walter, High Steward of Scotland
Married (1) Elizabeth, daughter of Sir Robert Mure of Rowallan (2) Euphemia, daughter of Hugh, Earl of Ross
Died aged 74, *reigned* 19 years

1390–1406 ROBERT III
*Born c.*1337, son of Robert II and Elizabeth

	Married Annabella, daughter of Sir John Drummond of Stobhall *Died* aged *c.*69, *reigned* 16 years
1406–1437	JAMES I *Born* 1394, son of Robert III *Married* Joan Beaufort, daughter of John, Earl of Somerset *Assassinated* aged 42, *reigned* 30 years
1437–1460	JAMES II *Born* 1430, son of James I *Married* Mary, daughter of Arnold, Duke of Gueldres *Killed* accidentally aged 29, *reigned* 23 years
1460–1488	JAMES III *Born* 1452, son of James II *Married* Margaret, daughter of Christian I of Denmark *Assassinated* aged 36, *reigned* 27 years
1488–1513	JAMES IV *Born* 1473, son of James III *Married* Margaret Tudor, daughter of Henry VII of England *Killed* in battle aged 40, *reigned* 25 years
1513–1542	JAMES V *Born* 1512, son of James IV *Married* (1) Madeleine, daughter of Francis I of France (2) Mary of Lorraine, daughter of the Duc de Guise *Died* aged 30, *reigned* 29 years
1542–1567	MARY *Born* 1542, daughter of James V and Mary *Married* (1) the Dauphin, afterwards Francis II of France (2) Henry Stewart, Lord Darnley (3) James Hepburn, Earl of Bothwell *Abdicated* 1567, prisoner in England from 1568, *executed* 1587, *reigned* 24 years
1567–1625	JAMES VI (and I of England) *Born* 1566, son of Mary, Queen of Scots, and Henry, Lord Darnley Acceded 1567 to the Scottish throne, *reigned* 58 years Succeeded 1603 to the English throne, so joining the English and Scottish crowns in one person. The two kingdoms remained distinct until 1707 when the parliaments of the kingdoms became conjoined

WELSH SOVEREIGNS AND PRINCES

Wales was ruled by sovereign princes from the earliest times until the death of Llywelyn in 1282. The first English Prince of Wales was the son of Edward I, who was born in Caernarvon town on 25 April 1284. According to a discredited legend, he was presented to the Welsh chieftains as their prince, in fulfilment of a promise that they should have a prince who 'could not speak a word of English' and should be native born. This son, who afterwards became Edward II, was created 'Prince of Wales and Earl of Chester' at the Lincoln Parliament on 7 February 1301.

The title Prince of Wales is borne after individual conferment and is not inherited at birth, though some Princes have been declared and styled Prince of Wales but never formally so created (*s.*). The title was conferred on Prince Charles by the Queen on 26 July 1958. He was invested at Caernarvon on 1 July 1969.

INDEPENDENT PRINCES AD 844 TO 1282

844–878	Rhodri the Great
878–916	Anarawd, son of Rhodri
916–950	Hywel Dda, the Good
950–979	Iago ab Idwal (or Ieuaf)
979–985	Hywel ab Ieuaf, the Bad
985–986	Cadwallon, his brother
986–999	Maredudd ab Owain ap Hywel Dda
999–1008	Cynan ap Hywel ab Ieuaf
1018–1023	Llywelyn ap Seisyll
1023–1039	Iago ab Idwal ap Meurig
1039–1063	Gruffydd ap Llywelyn ap Seisyll
1063–1075	Bleddyn ap Cynfyn
1075–1081	Trahaern ap Caradog
1081–1137	Gruffydd ap Cynan ab Iago
1137–1170	Owain Gwynedd
1170–1194	Dafydd ab Owain Gwynedd
1194–1240	Llywelyn Fawr, the Great
1240–1246	Dafydd ap Llywelyn
1246–1282	Llywelyn ap Gruffydd ap Llywelyn

ENGLISH PRINCES SINCE 1301

1301	Edward (Edward II)
1343	Edward the Black Prince, son of Edward III
1376	Richard (Richard II), son of the Black Prince
1399	Henry of Monmouth (Henry V)
1454	Edward of Westminster, son of Henry VI
1471	Edward of Westminster (Edward V)
1483	Edward, son of Richard III (*d.* 1484)
1489	Arthur Tudor, son of Henry VII
1504	Henry Tudor (Henry VIII)
1610	Henry Stuart, son of James I (*d.* 1612)
1616	Charles Stuart (Charles I)
*c.*1638 (*s.*)	Charles Stuart (Charles II)
1688 (*s.*)	James Francis Edward Stuart (The Old Pretender), son of James II (*d.* 1766)
1714	George Augustus (George II)
1729	Frederick Lewis, son of George II (*d.* 1751)
1751	George William Frederick (George III)
1762	George Augustus Frederick (George IV)
1841	Albert Edward (Edward VII)
1901	George (George V)
1910	Edward (Edward VIII)
1958	Charles, son of Elizabeth II

PRINCESSES ROYAL

The style Princess Royal is conferred at the sovereign's discretion on his or her eldest daughter. It is an honorary title, held for life, and cannot be inherited or passed on. It was first conferred on Princess Mary, daughter of Charles I, in approximately 1642.

*c.*1642	Princess Mary (1631–60), daughter of Charles I
1727	Princess Anne (1709–59), daughter of George II
1766	Princess Charlotte (1766–1828), daughter of George III
1840	Princess Victoria (1840–1901), daughter of Victoria
1905	Princess Louise (1867–1931), daughter of Edward VII
1932	Princess Mary (1897–1965), daughter of George V
1987	Princess Anne (*b.* 1950), daughter of Elizabeth II

THE HOUSE OF WINDSOR

King George V assumed by royal proclamation (17 July 1917) for his House and family, as well as for all descendants in the male line of Queen Victoria who are subjects of these realms, the name of Windsor.

KING GEORGE V
(George Frederick Ernest Albert), second son of King Edward VII *born* 3 June 1865 *married* 6 July 1893 HSH Princess Victoria Mary Augusta Louise Olga Pauline Claudine Agnes of Teck (Queen Mary *born* 26 May 1867 *died* 24 March 1953) *succeeded* to the throne 6 May 1910 *died* 20 January 1936. *Issue*

1. HRH PRINCE EDWARD Albert Christian George Andrew Patrick David *born* 23 June 1894 *succeeded* to the throne as King Edward VIII, 20 January 1936 *abdicated* 11 December 1936 *created* Duke of Windsor 1937 *married* 3 June 1937 Mrs Wallis Simpson (Her Grace The Duchess of Windsor *born* 19 June 1896 *died* 24 April 1986) *died* 28 May 1972

2. HRH PRINCE ALBERT Frederick Arthur George *born* 14 December 1895 *created* Duke of York 1920 *married* 26 April 1923 Lady Elizabeth Bowes-Lyon, youngest daughter of the 14th Earl of Strathmore and Kinghorne (HM Queen Elizabeth the Queen Mother *born* 4 August 1900 *died* 30 March 2002) *succeeded* to the throne as King George VI, 11 December 1936 *died* 6 February 1952. *Issue*
- (1) HRH Princess Elizabeth Alexandra Mary *succeeded* to the throne as Queen Elizabeth II, 6 February 1952 (*see* Royal Family)
- (2) HRH Princess Margaret Rose (later HRH The Princess Margaret, Countess of Snowdon) *born* 21 August 1930 *married* 6 May 1960 Anthony Charles Robert Armstrong-Jones, GCVO *created* Earl of Snowdon 1961 (marriage dissolved 1978) *died* 9 February 2002, having had issue (*see* Royal Family)

3. HRH PRINCESS (Victoria Alexandra Alice) MARY *born* 25 April 1897 *created* Princess Royal 1932 *married* 28 February 1922 Viscount Lascelles, later the 6th Earl of Harewood (1882–1947) *died* 28 March 1965. *Issue*
- (1) George Henry Hubert Lascelles, 7th Earl of Harewood, KBE *born* 7 February 1923 *married* (1) 1949 Maria (Marion) Stein (marriage dissolved 1967) *issue (a)* David Henry George, Viscount Lascelles *born* 1950 *(b)* James Edward *born* 1953 *(c)* (Robert) Jeremy Hugh *born* 1955 (2) 1967 Patricia Tuckwell *issue (d)* Mark Hubert *born* 1964
- (2) Gerald David Lascelles (1924–98) *married* (1) 1952 Angela Dowding (marriage dissolved 1978) *issue (a)* Henry Ulick *born* 1953 (2) 1978 Elizabeth Collingwood (Elizabeth Colvin) *issue (b)* Martin David *born* 1962

4. HRH PRINCE HENRY William Frederick Albert *born* 31 March 1900 *created* Duke of Gloucester, Earl of Ulster and Baron Culloden 1928 *married* 6 November 1935 Lady Alice Christabel Montagu-Douglas-Scott, daughter of the 7th Duke of Buccleuch and Queensberry (HRH Princess Alice, Duchess of Gloucester *born* 25 December 1901 *died* 29 October 2004) *died* 10 June 1974. *Issue*
- (1) HRH Prince William Henry Andrew Frederick *born* 18 December 1941 accidentally *killed* 28 August 1972
- (2) HRH Prince Richard Alexander Walter George (HRH The Duke of Gloucester)

5. HRH PRINCE GEORGE Edward Alexander Edmund *born* 20 December 1902 *created* Duke of Kent, Earl of St Andrews and Baron Downpatrick 1934 *married* 29 November 1934 HRH Princess Marina of Greece and Denmark (*born* 30 November 1906 *died* 27 August 1968) *killed* on active service 25 August 1942. *Issue*
- (1) HRH Prince Edward George Nicholas Paul Patrick (HRH The Duke of Kent)
- (2) HRH Princess Alexandra Helen Elizabeth Olga Christabel (HRH Princess Alexandra, the Hon. Lady Ogilvy)
- (3) HRH Prince Michael George Charles Franklin (HRH Prince Michael of Kent)

6. HRH PRINCE JOHN Charles Francis *born* 12 July 1905 *died* 18 January 1919

DESCENDANTS OF QUEEN VICTORIA

I. HRH Princess Victoria Adelaide Mary Louisa, Princess Royal (1840–1901) *m* Friedrich III (1831–88), German Emperor Mar–Jun 1888

1. HIM Wilhelm II (1859–1941), German Emperor *m* (1) Princess Augusta Victoria of Schleswig-Holstein-Sonderburg-Augustenburg (1858–1921) (2) Princess Hermine of Reuss (1887–1947). *Issue* Wilhelm (1882–1951); Eitel-Friedrich (1883–1942); Adalbert (1884–1948); August Wilhelm (1887–1949); Oskar (1888–1958); Joachim (1890–1920); Viktoria Luise (1892–1980)

2. Charlotte (1860–1919) *m* Bernhard, Duke of Saxe-Meiningen (1851–1928). *Issue* Feodora (1879–1945)

3. Heinrich (1862–1929) *m* Princess Irene of Hesse (*see* III.3). *Issue* Waldemar (1889–1945); Sigismund (1896–1978); Heinrich (1900–4)

4. Sigismund (1864–6)

5. Victoria (1866–1929) *m* (1) Prince Adolf of Schaumburg-Lippe (1859–1916) (2) Alexander Zubkov (1900–36)

6. Waldemar (1868–79)

7. Sophie (1870–1932) *m* Constantine I (1868–1923), King of the Hellenes. *Issue* George II (1890–1947); Alexander I (1893–1920); Helena (1896–1982); Paul I (1901–64); Irene (1904–74); Katherine (Lady Katherine Brandram) (1913–2007)

8. Margarethe (1872–1954) *m* Prince Friedrich Karl of Hesse (1868–1940). *Issue* Friedrich Wilhelm (1893–1916); Maximilian (1894–1914); Philipp (1896–1980); Wolfgang (1896–1989); Richard (1901–69); Christoph (1901–43)

II. HRH Prince Albert Edward (HM KING EDWARD VII) (1841–1910) *succeeded* 22 Jan 1901 *m* HRH Princess Alexandra of Denmark (1844–1925)

1. Albert Victor, Duke of Clarence and Avondale (1864–92)

2. George (HM KING GEORGE V) (1865–1936) (*see* House of Windsor)

3. Louise (1867–1931), Princess Royal *m* 1st Duke of Fife (1849–1912). *Issue* Alexandra (1891–1959); Maud (1893–1945)

4. Victoria (1868–1935)

5. Maud (1869–1938) *m* Prince Carl of Denmark (1872–1957), later King Haakon VII of Norway. *Issue* Olav V (1903–91)

6. Alexander (6–7 Apr 1871)

III. HRH Princess Alice Maud Mary (1843–78) *m* Prince Ludwig (1837–92), Grand Duke of Hesse 1877–92

1. Victoria (1863–1950) *m* Prince Louis of Battenberg (1854–1921), later 1st Marquess of Milford Haven. *Issue* Alice (1885–1969); Louise (1889–1965); George (1892–1938); Louis (1900–79)

2. Elizabeth (1864–1918) *m* Grand Duke Sergius of Russia (1857–1905)

3. Irene (1866–1953) *m* Prince Heinrich of Prussia (*see* I.3)

4. Ernst Ludwig (1868–1937), Grand Duke of Hesse, *m* (1) Princess Victoria Melita of Saxe-Coburg (see IV.3) (2) Princess Eleonore of Solms-Hohensolms-Lich (1871–1937). *Issue* Elizabeth (1895–1903); George, Grand Duke of Hesse (1906–37); Ludwig, Prince of Hesse (1908–68)

5. Frederick William (1870–3)

6. Alix (Tsaritsa of Russia) (1872–1918) *m* Nicholas II, Tsar of All the Russias (1868–1918). *Issue* Grand Duchess Olga (1895–1918); Grand Duchess Tatiana (1897– 1918); Grand Duchess Marie (1899–1918); Grand Duchess Anastasia (1901–18); Alexis, Tsarevich of Russia (1904–18)

7. Marie (1874–8)

IV. HRH Prince Alfred Ernest Albert, Duke of Edinburgh (1844–1900) *succeeded* as Duke of Saxe-Coburg and Gotha 1893 *m* Grand Duchess Marie Alexandrovna of Russia (1853–1920)

QUEEN VICTORIA (Alexandrina Victoria) *b* 1819 *succeeded* 20 Jun 1837 *d* 1901 *m* (Francis) Albert Augustus Charles Emmanuel, Duke of Saxony, Prince of Saxe-Coburg and Gotha (HRH Albert, Prince Consort) (1819–61)

VI. HRH Princess Louise Caroline Alberta (1848–1939) *m* Marquess of Lorne (1845–1914), later 9th Duke of Argyll

VII. HRH Prince Arthur William Patrick Albert, Duke of Connaught (1850–1942) *m* Princess Louisa of Prussia (1860–1917)

1. Margaret (1882–1920) *m* Crown Prince Gustaf Adolf (1882–1973), later King of Sweden. *Issue* Gustaf Adolf, Duke of Västerbotten (1906–47); Count Sigvard Bernadotte (1907–2002); Ingrid (1910–2000); Bertil, Duke of Halland (1912–97); Count Carl Bernadotte (*b* 1916)

2. Arthur (1883–1938) *m* HH Duchess of Fife (1891–1959). *Issue* Alastair Arthur, 2nd Duke of Connaught (1914–43)

3. (Victoria) Patricia (1886–1974) *m* Adm. Hon. Sir Alexander Ramsay (1881–1972). *Issue* Alexander Ramsay of Mar (1919–2000)

VIII. HRH Prince Leopold George Duncan Albert, Duke of Albany (1853–84) *m* Princess Helena of Waldeck (1861–1922)

1. Alice (1883–1981) *m* Prince Alexander of Teck (1874–1957). *Issue* Lady May (1906–94); Rupert, Viscount Trematon (1907–28); Maurice (Mar–Sep 1910)

2. Charles Edward (1884–1954), Duke of Albany until title suspended 1917, Duke of Saxe-Coburg-Gotha, *m* Princess Victoria Adelheid of Schleswig-Holstein-Sonderburg-Glücksburg (1885–1970). *Issue* Johann Leopold (1906–72); Sibylla (1908–72); Dietmar Hubertus (1909–43); Caroline (1912–83); Friedrich Josias (1918–98)

IX. HRH Princess Beatrice Mary Victoria Feodore (1857–1944) *m* Prince Henry of Battenberg (1858–96)

1. Alexander, 1st Marquess of Carisbrooke (1886–1960) *m* Lady Irene Denison (1890–1956). *Issue* Lady Iris Mountbatten (1920–82)

2. Victoria Eugénie (1887–1969) *m* Alfonso XIII, King of Spain (1886–1941). *Issue* Alfonso (1907–38); Jaime (1908–75); Beatriz (1909–2002); Maria (1911–96); Juan (1913–93); Gonzalo (1914–34)

3. Maj. Lord Leopold Mountbatten (1889–1922)

4. Maurice (1891–1914)

1. Alfred, Prince of Saxe-Coburg (1874–99)

2. Marie (1875–1938) *m* Ferdinand (1865–1927), King of Roumania. *Issue* Carol II (1893–1953); Elisabeth (1894–1956); Marie (1900–61); Nicolas (1903–78); Ileana (1909–91); Mircea (1913–16)

3. Victoria Melita (1876–1936) *m* (1) Grand Duke Ernst Ludwig of Hesse (*see* III.4) (2) Grand Duke Kirill of Russia (1876–1938). *Issue* Marie Kirillovna (1907–51); Kira Kirillovna (1909–67); Vladimir Kirillovich (1917–92)

4. Alexandra (1878–1942) *m* Ernst, Prince of Hohenlohe Langenburg (1863–1950). *Issue* Gottfried (1897–1960); Maria (1899–1967); Alexandra (1901–63); Irma (1902–86)

5. Beatrice (1884–1966) *m* Alfonso of Orleans, Infante of Spain (1886–1975). *Issue* Alvaro (1910–97); Alonso (1912–36); Ataulfo (1913–74)

V. HRH Princess Helena Augusta Victoria (1846–1923) *m* Prince Christian of Schleswig-Holstein-Sonderburg-Augustenburg (1831–1917)

1. Christian Victor (1867–1900)

2. Albert (1869–1931), Duke of Schleswig-Holstein

3. Helena (1870–1948)

4. Marie Louise (1872–1956), *m* Prince Aribert of Anhalt (marriage dissolved 1900)

5. Harold (12–20 May 1876)

PRECEDENCE

ENGLAND AND WALES

The Sovereign
The Prince Philip, Duke of Edinburgh
The Prince of Wales
The Sovereign's younger sons
The Sovereign's grandsons
The Sovereign's cousins
Archbishop of Canterbury
Lord High Chancellor
Archbishop of York
The Prime Minister
Lord President of the Council
Speaker of the House of Commons
Lord Speaker
Lord Privy Seal
Ambassadors and High Commissioners
Lord Great Chamberlain
Earl Marshal
Lord Chamberlain of the Household
Lord Steward of the Household
Master of the Horse
Dukes, according to their patent of creation:
1. of England
2. of Scotland
3. of Great Britain
4. of Ireland
5. those created since the Union
Eldest sons of Dukes of the Blood Royal
Marquesses, according to their patent of creation:
1. of England
2. of Scotland
3. of Great Britain
4. of Ireland
5. those created since the Union
Dukes' eldest sons
Earls, according to their patent of creation:
1. of England
2. of Scotland
3. of Great Britain
4. of Ireland
5. those created since the Union
Younger sons of Dukes of Blood Royal
Marquesses' eldest sons
Dukes' younger sons
Viscounts, according to their patent of creation:
1. of England
2. of Scotland
3. of Great Britain
4. of Ireland
5. those created since the Union
Earls' eldest sons
Marquesses' younger sons
Bishop of London
Bishop of Durham
Bishop of Winchester
Other English Diocesan Bishops according to seniority of consecration
Suffragan Bishops, according to seniority of consecration
Secretaries of State, if of the degree of a Baron
Barons, according to their patent of creation:
1. of England
2. of Scotland
3. of Great Britain
4. of Ireland
5. those created since the Union, including Life Barons
Treasurer of the Household
Comptroller of the Household
Vice-Chamberlain of the Household
Secretaries of State under the degree of Baron
Viscounts' eldest sons
Earls' younger sons
Barons' eldest sons
Knights of the Garter
Privy Counsellors
Chancellor of the Exchequer
Chancellor of the Duchy of Lancaster
Justices of the Supreme Court, according to Seniority of appointment
Lord Chief Justice of England and Wales
Master of the Rolls
President of the Queen's Bench Division
President of the Family Division
Chancellor of the High Court
Lords Justices of Appeal, according to seniority of appointment
Judges of the High Court, according to seniority of appointment
Viscounts' younger sons
Barons' younger sons
Sons of Life Peers
Baronets, according to date of patent
Knights of the Thistle
Knights Grand Cross of the Bath
Knights Grand Commanders of the Star of India
Knights Grand Cross of St Michael and St George
Knights Grand Commanders of the Indian Empire
Knights Grand Cross of the Royal Victorian Order
Knights Grand Cross of the British Empire
Knights Commanders of the Bath
Knights Commanders of the Star of India
Knights Commanders of St Michael and St George
Knights Commanders of the Indian Empire
Knights Commanders of the Royal Victorian Order
Knights Commanders of the British Empire
Knights Bachelor
Circuit Judges, according to priority and order of their respective appointments
Companions of the Bath
Companions of the Star of India
Companions of St Michael and St George
Companions of the Indian Empire
Commanders of the Royal Victorian Order
Commanders of the British Empire
Companions of the Distinguished Service Order
Lieutenants of the Royal Victorian Order
Officers of the British Empire
Companions of the Imperial Service Order
Eldest sons of younger sons of peers
Baronets' eldest sons
Eldest sons of knights, in the same order as their fathers
Members of the Royal Victorian Order
Members of the British Empire
Younger sons of baronets
Younger sons of knights, in the same order as their fathers
Esquires
Gentlemen

WOMEN

Women take the same rank as their husbands or as their brothers; but the daughter of a peer marrying a commoner retains her title as Lady or Honourable. Daughters of peers rank next immediately after the wives of their elder brothers, and before their younger brothers' wives. Daughters of peers marrying peers of a lower degree take the same order of precedence as that of their husbands; thus the daughter of a Duke marrying a Baron becomes of the rank of Baroness only, while her sisters married to commoners retain their rank and take precedence over the Baroness. Merely official rank on the husband's part does not give any similar precedence to the wife.

Peeresses in their own right take the same precedence as peers of the same rank, ie from their date of creation.

SCOTLAND

The Sovereign
The Prince Philip, Duke of Edinburgh
The Lord High Commissioner to the General Assembly of the Church of Scotland (while that assembly is sitting)
The Duke of Rothesay (eldest son of the Sovereign)
The Sovereign's younger sons
Grandsons of the Sovereign
The Sovereign's cousins
Lord-Lieutenants
Lord Provosts of cities being *ex-officio* Lord-Lieutenants of those cities during their term of office*
Sheriffs Principal, successively, within their own localities and during holding of office
Lord Chancellor of Great Britain
Moderator of the General Assembly of the Church of Scotland
Keeper of the Great Seal of Scotland (the First Minister)
The Presiding Officer
The Secretary of State for Scotland
Hereditary High Constable of Scotland
Hereditary Master of the Household in Scotland
Dukes, in the same order as in England
Eldest sons of Dukes of the Blood Royal
Marquesses, as in England
Eldest sons of Dukes
Earls, as in England
Younger sons of Dukes of Blood Royal
Eldest sons of Marquesses
Dukes' younger sons
Lord Justice General
Lord Clerk Register
Lord Advocate
The Advocate-General
Lord Justice Clerk
Viscounts, as in England
Eldest sons of Earls
Marquesses' younger sons
Lords of Parliament or Barons, as in England
Eldest sons of Viscounts
Earls' younger sons
Eldest sons of Lords of Parliament or Barons
Knights of the Garter
Knights of the Thistle
Privy Counsellors
Senators of the College of Justice (Lords of Session)
Viscounts' younger sons
Younger sons of Lords of Parliament or Barons
Baronets
Knights Grand Cross and Knights Grand Commanders of orders, as in England
Knights Commanders of orders, as in England
Solicitor-General for Scotland
Lord Lyon King of Arms
Sheriffs Principal, when not within own county
Knights Bachelor
Sheriffs
Companions of Orders, as in England
Commanders of the Royal Victorian Order
Commanders of the British Empire
Companions of the Distinguished Service Order
Lieutenants of the Royal Victorian Order
Officers of the British Empire
Companions of the Imperial Service Order
Eldest sons of younger sons of peers
Eldest sons of baronets
Eldest sons of knights, as in England
Members of the Royal Victorian Order
Members of the British Empire
Baronets' younger sons
Knights' younger sons
Esquires
Gentlemen

* The Lord Provosts of the city districts of Aberdeen, Dundee, Edinburgh and Glasgow are Lord-Lieutenants for those districts *ex officio* and take precedence as such.

THE PEERAGE

ABBREVIATIONS AND SYMBOLS

S.	Scottish title
I.	Irish title
**	hereditary peer remaining in the House of Lords
°	there is no 'of' in the title
b.	born
s.	succeeded
m.	married
w.	widower or widow
M.	minor
†	heir not ascertained at time of going to press
F_	represents forename
S_	represents surname
cr.	created

The rules which govern the creation and succession of peerages are extremely complicated. There are, technically, five separate peerages, the Peerage of England, of Scotland, of Ireland, of Great Britain, and of the United Kingdom. The Peerage of Great Britain dates from 1707 when an Act of Union combined the two kingdoms of England and Scotland and separate peerages were discontinued. The Peerage of the United Kingdom dates from 1801 when Great Britain and Ireland were combined under an Act of Union. Some Scottish peers have received additional peerages of Great Britain or of the United Kingdom since 1707, and some Irish peers additional peerages of the United Kingdom since 1801.

The Peerage of Ireland was not entirely discontinued from 1801 but holders of Irish peerages, whether pre-dating or created subsequent to the Union of 1801, were not entitled to sit in the House of Lords if they had no additional English, Scottish, Great Britain or United Kingdom peerage. However, they are eligible for election to the House of Commons and to vote in parliamentary elections. An Irish peer holding a peerage of a lower grade which enabled him to sit in the House of Lords was introduced there by the title which enabled him to sit, though for all other purposes he was known by his higher title.

In the Peerage of Scotland there is no rank of Baron; the equivalent rank is Lord of Parliament, abbreviated to 'Lord' (the female equivalent is 'Lady').

All peers of England, Scotland, Great Britain or the United Kingdom who are 21 years or over, and of British, Irish or Commonwealth nationality were entitled to sit in the House of Lords until the House of Lords Act 1999, when hereditary peers lost the right to sit. However, section two of the act provided an exception for 90 hereditary peers plus the holders of the office of Earl Marshal and Lord Great Chamberlain to remain as members of the House of Lords for their lifetime or pending further reform. Of the 90 hereditary peers, 75 were elected by the hereditary peers in their political party, or Crossbench grouping, and the remaining 15 by the whole house. Until 7 November 2002 any vacancy arising due to the death of one of the 90 excepted hereditary peers was filled by the runner-up to the original election. From 7 November 2002 any vacancy due to a death has been filled by holding a by-election. By-elections are conducted in accordance with arrangements made by the Clerk of the Parliaments and have to take place within three months of a vacancy occurring. If the vacancy is among the 75, only the excepted hereditary peers in the relevant party or Crossbench grouping are entitled to vote. If the vacancy is among the other 15, the whole house is entitled to vote.

In the list below, peers currently holding one of the 92 hereditary places in the House of Lords are indicated by ** .

In July 2008 proposed further reforms to the House of Lords were presented to parliament in a white paper *An Elected Second Chamber: Further Reform of the House of Lords.*

HEREDITARY WOMEN PEERS

Most hereditary peerages pass on death to the nearest male heir, but there are exceptions, and several are held by women.

A woman peer in her own right retains her title after marriage, and if her husband's rank is the superior she is designated by the two titles jointly, the inferior one second. Her hereditary claim still holds good in spite of any marriage whether higher or lower. No rank held by a woman can confer any title or even precedence upon her husband but the rank of a hereditary woman peer in her own right is inherited by her eldest son (or in some cases daughter).

After the Peerage Act 1963, hereditary women peers in their own right were entitled to sit in the House of Lords, subject to the same qualifications as men, until the House of Lords Act 1999.

LIFE PEERS

Since 1876 non-hereditary or life peerages have been conferred on certain eminent judges to enable the judicial functions of the House of Lords to be carried out. These lords were known as Lords of Appeal in Ordinary or law lords. The judicial role of the House of Lords as the highest appeal court in the UK ended on 30 July 2009 and since 1 October 2009 the UK Supreme Court has assumed jurisdiction on points of law for all civil cases in the UK and all criminal cases in England, Wales and Northern Ireland. Life peers who transferred to the

supreme court as Justices of the Supreme Court are disqualified from sitting or voting in the House of Lords until retirement from the supreme court. On retirement they are able to return to the House of Lords as full members. Newly-appointed Justices of the Supreme Court will no longer automatically be given seats in the House of Lords. (*See also* Law Courts and Offices.)

Justices of the Supreme Court currently disqualified from sitting or voting in the House of Lords until retirement are marked with a '§' in the list of life peerages which follows.

Since 1958 life peerages have been conferred upon distinguished men and women from all walks of life, giving them seats in the House of Lords in the degree of Baron or Baroness. They are addressed in the same way as hereditary lords and barons, and their children have similar courtesy titles.

PEERAGES EXTINCT SINCE THE LAST EDITION

VISCOUNTCY: Ingleby (cr. 1956)
BARONIES: Herschell (cr. 1886); Wilson (cr. 1946)
LIFE PEERAGES: Blaker (cr. 1994); Buxton of Alsa (cr. 1978); Clyde (cr. 1996); Cuckney (cr. 1995); Dahrendorf (cr. 1993); Dean of Harptree (cr. 1993); Dearing (cr. 1998); George (cr. 2004); Gregson (cr. 1975); Hogg of Cumbernauld (cr. 1997); Kingsland (cr. 1994); Lane of Horsell (cr. 1990); Moore of Wolvercote (cr. 1986); Murton of Lindisfarne (cr. 1979); Rees (cr. 1987); Slynn of Hadley (cr. 1992); Thomson of Monifieth (cr. 1977)

DISCLAIMER OF PEERAGES

The Peerage Act 1963 enables peers to disclaim their peerages for life. Peers alive in 1963 could disclaim within twelve months after the passing of the act (31 July 1963); a person subsequently succeeding to a peerage may disclaim within 12 months (one month if an MP) after the date of succession, or of reaching 21, if later. The disclaimer is irrevocable but does not affect the descent of the peerage after the disclaimant's death, and children of a disclaimed peer may, if they wish, retain their precedence and any courtesy titles and styles borne as children of a peer. The disclaimer permitted the disclaimant to sit in the House of Commons if elected as an MP. As the House of Lords Act 1999 removed hereditary peers from the House of Lords, they are now entitled to sit in the House of Commons without having to disclaim their titles.

The following peerages are currently disclaimed:

EARLDOM: Selkirk (1994)
VISCOUNTCY: Stansgate (1963)
BARONIES: Merthyr (1977); Reith (1972); Sanderson of Ayot (1971)
PEERS WHO ARE MINORS (ie under 21 years of age)
EARL: Craven (*b.* 1989)
VISCOUNT: Selby (*b.* 1993)

FORMS OF ADDRESS

Forms of address are given under the style for each individual rank of the peerage. Both formal and social forms of address are given where usage differs; nowadays, the social form is generally preferred to the formal, which increasingly is used only for official documents and on very formal occasions.

ROLL OF THE PEERAGE

Crown Office, House of Lords, London SW1A 0PW

The Roll of the Peerage is kept at the Crown Office and maintained by the Registrar of the Peerage in accordance with the terms of a 2004 royal warrant. The roll records the names of all living life peers and hereditary peers who have proved their succession to the satisfaction of the Lord Chancellor. The Roll of the Peerage is maintained in addition to the Clerk of the Parliaments' register of hereditary peers eligible to stand for election in House of Lords' by-elections.

A person whose name is not entered on the Roll of Peerage can not be addressed or mentioned by the title of a peer in any official document.

Registrar, Ian Denyer, MVO
Assistant Registrar, Grant Bavister

HEREDITARY PEERS

as at 31 August 2009

PEERS OF THE BLOOD ROYAL

Style, His Royal Highness the Duke of _/His Royal Highness the Earl of_
Style of address (formal) May it please your Royal Highness; *(informal)* Sir

Created	*Title, order of succession, name, etc*	*Heir*
	Dukes	
1947	*Edinburgh (1st),* HRH the Prince Philip, Duke of Edinburgh	The Prince of Wales *
1337	*Cornwall,* HRH the Prince of Wales, *s.* 1952	‡
1398 S.	*Rothesay,* HRH the Prince of Wales, *s.* 1952	‡
1986	*York (1st),* Prince Andrew, HRH the Duke of York	None
1928	*Gloucester (2nd),* Prince Richard, HRH the Duke of Gloucester, *s.* 1974	Earl of Ulster
1934	*Kent (2nd),* Prince Edward, HRH the Duke of Kent, *s.* 1942	Earl of St Andrews
	Earl	
1999	*Wessex (1st),* Prince Edward, HRH the Earl of Wessex	Viscount Severn

* In June 1999 Buckingham Palace announced that the current Earl of Wessex will be granted the Dukedom of Edinburgh when the title reverts to the Crown. The title will only revert to the Crown on both the death of the current Duke of Edinburgh and the Prince of Wales' succession as king

‡ The title is held by the sovereign's eldest son from the moment of his birth or the sovereign's accession

DUKES

Coronet, Eight strawberry leaves

Style, His Grace the Duke of _
Envelope (formal), His Grace the Duke of _; *(social),* The Duke of _. *Letter (formal),* My Lord Duke; *(social),* Dear Duke. *Spoken (formal),* Your Grace; *(social),* Duke
Wife's style, Her Grace the Duchess of _
Envelope (formal), Her Grace the Duchess of _; *(social),* The Duchess of _. *Letter (formal),* Dear Madam; *(social),* Dear Duchess. *Spoken,* Duchess
Eldest son's style, Takes his father's second title as a courtesy title (*see* Courtesy Titles)
Younger sons' style, 'Lord' before forename (F_) and surname (S_)
Envelope, Lord F_ S_. *Letter (formal),* My Lord; *(social),* Dear Lord F_. *Spoken (formal),* My Lord; *(social),* Lord F_
Daughters' style, 'Lady' before forename (F_) and surname (S_)
Envelope, Lady F_ S_. *Letter (formal),* Dear Madam; *(social),* Dear Lady F_. *Spoken,* Lady F_

Created	*Title, order of succession, name, etc*	*Heir*
1868 I.	*Abercorn (5th),* James Hamilton, KG, *b.* 1934, *s.* 1979, *m.*	Marquess of Hamilton, *b.* 1969
1701 S.	*Argyll (13th),* Torquhil Ian Campbell, *b.* 1968, *s.* 2001	Marquess of Lorne, *b.* 2004
1703 S.	*Atholl (11th),* John Murray, *b.* 1929, *s.* 1996, *m.*	Marquis of Tullibardine, *b.* 1960
1682	*Beaufort (11th),* David Robert Somerset, *b.* 1928, *s.* 1984, *m.*	Marquess of Worcester, *b.* 1952
1694	*Bedford (15th),* Andrew Ian Henry Russell, *b.* 1962, *s.* 2003, *m.*	Marquess of Tavistock, *b.* 2005
1663 S.	*Buccleuch (10th) and Queensberry (12th) (S. 1684),* Richard Walter John Montagu Douglas Scott, KBE, *b.* 1954, *s.* 2007, *m.*	Earl of Dalkeith, *b.* 1984
1694	*Devonshire (12th),* Peregrine Andrew Morny Cavendish, KCVO, CBE, *b.* 1944, *s.* 2004, *m.*	Marquess of Hartington, *b.* 1969
1900	*Fife (3rd),* James George Alexander Bannerman Carnegie, *b.* 1929, *s.* 1959	Earl of Southesk, *b.* 1961
1675	*Grafton (11th),* Hugh Denis Charles FitzRoy, KG, *b.* 1919, *s.* 1970, *m.*	Earl of Euston, *b.* 1947
1643 S.	*Hamilton (15th) and Brandon (12th) (1711),* Angus Alan Douglas Douglas-Hamilton, *b.* 1938, *s.* 1973 *Premier Peer of Scotland*	Marquis of Douglas and Clydesdale, *b.* 1978
1766 I.	*Leinster (9th),* Maurice FitzGerald, *b.* 1948, *s.* 2004, *m.* *Premier Duke, Marquess and Earl of Ireland*	Lord John F., *b.* 1952

1719	*Manchester (13th),* Alexander Charles David Drogo Montagu, *b.* 1962, *s.* 2002, *m.*	Lord Kimble W. D. M., *b.* 1964
1702	*Marlborough (11th),* John George Vanderbilt Henry Spencer-Churchill, *b.* 1926, *s.* 1972, *m.*	Marquess of Blandford, *b.* 1955
1707 S.	** *Montrose (8th),* James Graham, *b.* 1935, *s.* 1992, *m.*	Marquis of Graham, *b.* 1973
1483	** *Norfolk (18th),* Edward Wiliam Fitzalan-Howard, *b.* 1956, *s.* 2002, *m.* *Premier Duke and Earl Marshal*	Earl of Arundel and Surrey, *b.* 1987
1766	*Northumberland (12th),* Ralph George Algernon Percy, *b.* 1956, *s.* 1995, *m.*	Earl Percy, *b.* 1984
1675	*Richmond (10th) and Gordon (5th) (1876),* Charles Henry Gordon Lennox, *b.* 1929, *s.* 1989, *m.*	Earl of March and Kinrara, *b.* 1955
1707 S.	*Roxburghe (10th),* Guy David Innes-Ker, *b.* 1954, *s.* 1974, *m. Premier Baronet of Scotland*	Marquis of Bowmont and Cessford, *b.* 1981
1703	*Rutland (11th),* David Charles Robert Manners, *b.* 1959, *s.* 1999, *m.*	Marquess of Granby, *b.*1999
1684	*St Albans (14th),* Murray de Vere Beauclerk, *b.* 1939, *s.* 1988, *m.*	Earl of Burford, *b.* 1965
1547	*Somerset (19th),* John Michael Edward Seymour, *b.* 1952, *s.* 1984, *m.*	Lord Seymour, *b.* 1982
1833	*Sutherland (7th),* Francis Ronald Egerton, *b.* 1940, *s.* 2000, *m.*	Marquess of Stafford, *b.* 1975
1814	*Wellington (8th),* Arthur Valerian Wellesley, KG, LVO, OBE, MC, *b.* 1915, *s.* 1972, *m.*	Marquess of Douro, *b.* 1945
1874	*Westminster (6th),* Gerald Cavendish Grosvenor, KG, CB, OBE, *b.* 1951, *s.* 1979, *m.*	Earl Grosvenor, *b.* 1991

MARQUESSES

Coronet, Four strawberry leaves alternating with four silver balls

Style, The Most Hon. the Marquess (of) _ . In Scotland the spelling 'Marquis' is preferred for pre-Union creations
Envelope (formal), The Most Hon. the Marquess of _; *(social),* The Marquess of _. *Letter (formal),* My Lord; *(social),* Dear Lord _. *Spoken (formal),* My Lord; *(social),* Lord _
Wife's style, The Most Hon. the Marchioness (of) _
Envelope (formal), The Most Hon. the Marchioness of _; *(social),* The Marchioness of _. *Letter (formal),* Madam; *(social),* Dear Lady _. *Spoken,* Lady _
Eldest son's style, Takes his father's second title as a courtesy title (*see* Courtesy Titles)
Younger sons' style, 'Lord' before forename and surname, as for Duke's younger sons
Daughters' style, 'Lady' before forename and surname, as for Duke's daughter

Created	*Title, order of succession, name, etc*	*Heir*
1916	*Aberdeen and Temair (7th),* Alexander George Gordon, *b.* 1955, *s.* 2002, *m.*	Earl of Haddo, *b.* 1983
1876	*Abergavenny (6th) and 10th Earl, Abergavenny, 1784,* Christopher George Charles Nevill, *b.* 1955, *s.* 2000, *m.*	To Earldom only, David M. R. N., *b.* 1941
1821	*Ailesbury (8th),* Michael Sidney Cedric Brudenell-Bruce, *b.* 1926, *s.* 1974	Earl of Cardigan, *b.* 1952
1831	*Ailsa (8th),* Archibald Angus Charles Kennedy, *b.* 1956, *s.* 1994	Lord David T. K., *b.* 1958
1815	*Anglesey (7th),* George Charles Henry Victor Paget, *b.* 1922, *s.* 1947, *m.*	Earl of Uxbridge, *b.* 1950
1789	*Bath (7th),* Alexander George Thynn, *b.* 1932, *s.* 1992, *m.*	Viscount Weymouth, *b.* 1974
1826	*Bristol (8th),* Frederick William Augustus Hervey, *b.* 1979, *s.* 1999	Timothy H. H., *b.* 1960
1796	*Bute (7th),* John Colum Crichton-Stuart, *b.* 1958, *s.* 1993, *m.*	Earl of Dumfries, *b.* 1989
1812	° *Camden (6th),* David George Edward Henry Pratt, *b.* 1930, *s.* 1983	Earl of Brecknock, *b.* 1965
1815	** *Cholmondeley (7th),* David George Philip Cholmondeley, KCVO, *b.* 1960, *s.* 1990, *Lord Great Chamberlain*	Charles G. C., *b.* 1959
1816 I.	° *Conyngham (8th),* Henry Vivian Pierpoint Conyngham, *b.* 1951, *s.* 2009, *m.*	Earl of Mount Charles, *b.* 1975
1791 I.	*Donegall (8th),* Arthur Patrick Chichester, *b.* 1952, *s.* 2007, *m.*	Earl of Belfast, *b.*1990
1789 I.	*Downshire (9th),* (Arthur Francis) Nicholas Wills Hill, *b.* 1959, *s.* 2003, *m.*	Earl of Hillsborough, *b.* 1996
1801 I.	*Ely (9th),* Charles John Tottenham, *b.* 1943, *s.* 2006, *m.*	Lord Timothy C. T., *b.* 1948
1801	*Exeter (8th),* (William) Michael Anthony Cecil, *b.* 1935, *s.* 1988, *m.*	Lord Burghley, *b.* 1970

1800 I.	*Headfort (7th),* Thomas Michael Ronald Christopher Taylour, *b.* 1959, *s.* 2005, *m.*	Earl of Bective, *b.* 1989
1793	*Hertford (9th),* Henry Jocelyn Seymour, *b.* 1958, *s.* 1997, *m.*	Earl of Yarmouth, *b.* 1993
1599 S.	*Huntly (13th),* Granville Charles Gomer Gordon, *b.* 1944, *s.* 1987, *m.* *Premier Marquess of Scotland*	Earl of Aboyne, *b.* 1973
1784	*Lansdowne (9th),* Charles Maurice Mercer Nairne Petty-Fitzmaurice, LVO *b.* 1941, *s.* 1999, *m.*	Earl of Kerry, *b.* 1970
1902	*Linlithgow (4th),* Adrian John Charles Hope, *b.* 1946, *s.* 1987, *m.*	Earl of Hopetoun, *b.* 1969
1816 I.	*Londonderry (9th),* Alexander Charles Robert Vane-Tempest-Stewart, *b.* 1937, *s.* 1955, *m.*	Viscount Castlereagh, *b.* 1972
1701 S.	*Lothian (13th),* Michael Andrew Foster Jude Kerr (Michael Ancram), PC, *b.* 1945, *s.* 2004, *m.*	Lord Ralph W. F. J. K., *b.* 1957
1917	*Milford Haven (4th),* George Ivar Louis Mountbatten, *b.* 1961, *s.* 1970, *m.*	Earl of Medina, *b.* 1991
1838	*Normanby (5th),* Constantine Edmund Walter Phipps, *b.* 1954, *s.* 1994, *m.*	Earl of Mulgrave, *b.* 1994
1812	*Northampton (7th),* Spencer Douglas David Compton, *b.* 1946, *s.* 1978, *m.*	Earl Compton, *b.* 1973
1682 S.	*Queensberry (12th),* David Harrington Angus Douglas, *b.* 1929, *s.* 1954	Viscount Drumlanrig, *b.* 1967
1926	*Reading (4th),* Simon Charles Henry Rufus Isaacs, *b.* 1942, *s.* 1980, *m.*	Viscount Erleigh, *b.* 1986
1789	*Salisbury (7th) and Baron Gascoyne-Cecil (life peerage, 1999),* Robert Michael James Gascoyne-Cecil, PC, *b.* 1946, *s.* 2003, *m.*	Viscount Cranborne, *b.* 1970
1800 I.	*Sligo (11th),* Jeremy Ulick Browne, *b.* 1939, *s.* 1991, *m.*	Sebastian U. B., *b.* 1964
1787	° *Townshend (7th),* George John Patrick Dominic Townshend, *b.* 1916, *s.* 1921, *w.*	Viscount Raynham, *b.* 1945
1694 S.	*Tweeddale (14th),* Charles David Montagu Hay, *b.* 1947, *s.* 2005	(Lord) Alistair J. M. H., *b.* 1955
1789 I.	*Waterford (8th),* John Hubert de la Poer Beresford, *b.* 1933, *s.* 1934, *m.*	Earl of Tyrone, *b.* 1958
1551	*Winchester (18th),* Nigel George Paulet, *b.* 1941, *s.* 1968, *m.* *Premier Marquess of England*	Earl of Wiltshire, *b.* 1969
1892	*Zetland (4th),* Lawrence Mark Dundas, *b.* 1937, *s.* 1989, *m.*	Earl of Ronaldshay, *b.* 1965

EARLS

Coronet, Eight silver balls on stalks alternating with eight gold strawberry leaves

Style, The Rt. Hon. the Earl (of) _
Envelope (formal), The Rt. Hon. the Earl (of) _; *(social),* The Earl (of) _. *Letter (formal),* My Lord; *(social),* Dear Lord _. *Spoken (formal),* My Lord; *(social),* Lord _.
Wife's style, The Rt. Hon. the Countess (of) _
Envelope (formal), The Rt. Hon. the Countess (of) _; *(social),* The Countess (of) _. *Letter (formal),* Madam; *(social),* Lady _. *Spoken (formal),* Madam; *(social),* Lady _.
Eldest son's style, Takes his father's second title as a courtesy title (*see* Courtesy Titles)
Younger sons' style, 'The Hon.' before forename and surname, as for Baron's children
Daughters' style, 'Lady' before forename and surname, as for Duke's daughter

Created	*Title, order of succession, name, etc*	*Heir*
1639 S.	*Airlie (13th),* David George Coke Patrick Ogilvy, KT, GCVO, PC, Royal Victorian Chain, *b.* 1926, *s.* 1968, *m.*	Lord Ogilvy, *b.* 1958
1696	*Albemarle (10th),* Rufus Arnold Alexis Keppel, *b.* 1965, *s.* 1979, *m.*	Viscount Bury, *b.* 2003
1952	° *Alexander of Tunis (2nd),* Shane William Desmond Alexander, *b.* 1935, *s.* 1969, *m.*	Hon. Brian J. A., *b.* 1939
1662	*Annandale and Hartfell (11th),* Patrick Andrew Wentworth Hope Johnstone, *b.* 1941, *s.* 1983, *m.* claim established 1985	Lord Johnstone, *b.* 1971
1789 I.	° *Annesley (11th),* Philip Harrison Annesley, *b.* 1927, *s.* 2001, *m.*	Hon. Michael R. A., *b.* 1933
1785 I.	*Antrim (9th),* Alexander Randal Mark McDonnell, *b.* 1935, *s.* 1977, *m.*	Viscount Dunluce, *b.* 1967
1762 I.	** *Arran (9th),* Arthur Desmond Colquhoun Gore, *b.* 1938, *s.* 1983, *m.*	Paul A. G., CMG, CVO, *b.* 1921
1955	° ** *Attlee (3rd),* John Richard Attlee, *b.* 1956, *s.* 1991, *m.*	None
1714	*Aylesford (12th),* Charles Heneage Finch-Knightley, *b.* 1947, *s.* 2008, *m.*	Lord Guernsey, *b.* 1985

1937	** *Baldwin of Bewdley (4th),* Edward Alfred Alexander Baldwin, *b.* 1938, *s.* 1976, *w.*	Viscount Corvedale, *b.* 1973
1922	*Balfour (5th),* Roderick Francis Arthur Balfour, *b.* 1948, *s.* 2003, *m.*	Charles G. Y. B., *b.* 1951
1772	° *Bathurst (8th),* Henry Allen John Bathurst, *b.* 1927, *s.* 1943, *m.*	Lord Apsley, *b.* 1961
1919	° *Beatty (3rd),* David Beatty, *b.* 1946, *s.* 1972, *m.*	Viscount Borodale, *b.* 1973
1797 I.	° *Belmore (8th),* John Armar Lowry-Corry, *b.* 1951, *s.* 1960, *m.*	Viscount Corry, *b.* 1985
1739 I.	*Bessborough (12th),* Myles Fitzhugh Longfield Ponsonby, *b.* 1941, *s.* 2002, *m.*	Viscount Duncannon, *b.* 1974
1815	*Bradford (7th),* Richard Thomas Orlando Bridgeman, *b.* 1947, *s.* 1981, *m.*	Viscount Newport, *b.* 1980
1469	*Buchan (17th),* Malcolm Harry Erskine, *b.* 1930, *s.* 1984, *m.*	Lord Cardross, *b.* 1960
1746	*Buckinghamshire (10th),* (George) Miles Hobart-Hampden, *b.* 1944, *s.* 1983, *m.*	Sir John Hobart, Bt., *b.* 1945
1800	° *Cadogan (8th),* Charles Gerald John Cadogan, *b.* 1937, *s.* 1997, *m.*	Viscount Chelsea, *b.* 1966
1878	° *Cairns (6th),* Simon Dallas Cairns, CVO, CBE, *b.* 1939, *s.* 1989, *m.*	Viscount Garmoyle, *b.* 1965
1455	** *Caithness (20th),* Malcolm Ian Sinclair, PC, *b.* 1948, *s.* 1965, *w.*	Lord Berriedale, *b.* 1981
1800 I.	*Caledon (7th),* Nicholas James Alexander, *b.* 1955, *s.* 1980, *m.*	Viscount Alexander, *b.* 1990
1661	*Carlisle (13th),* George William Beaumont Howard, *b.* 1949, *s.* 1994	Hon. Philip C. W. H., *b.* 1963
1793	*Carnarvon (8th),* George Reginald Oliver Molyneux Herbert, *b.* 1956, *s.* 2001, *m.*	Lord Porchester, *b.* 1992
1748 I.	*Carrick (10th),* David James Theobald Somerset Butler, *b.* 1953, *s.* 1992, *m.*	Viscount Ikerrin, *b.* 1975
1800 I.	° *Castle Stewart (8th),* Arthur Patrick Avondale Stuart, *b.* 1928, *s.* 1961, *m.*	Viscount Stuart, *b.* 1953
1814	°** *Cathcart (7th),* Charles Alan Andrew Cathcart, *b.* 1952, *s.* 1999, *m.*	Lord Greenock, *b.* 1986
1647 I.	*Cavan,* The 12th Earl died in 1988.	†Roger C. Lambart, *b.* 1944
1827	° *Cawdor (7th),* Colin Robert Vaughan Campbell, *b.* 1962, *s.* 1993, *m.*	Viscount Emlyn, *b.* 1998
1801	*Chichester (9th),* John Nicholas Pelham, *b.* 1944, *s.* 1944, *m.*	Richard A. H. P., *b.* 1952
1803 I.	*Clancarty (9th),* Nicholas Power Richard Le Poer Trench, *b.* 1952, *s.* 1995, *m.*	None
1776 I.	*Clanwilliam (7th),* John Herbert Meade, *b.* 1919, *s.* 1989, *w.*	Lord Gillford, *b.* 1960
1776	*Clarendon (8th),* George Edward Laurence Villiers, *b.* 1976, *s.* 2009, *m.*	Lord Hyde, *b.* 2008
1620 I.	*Cork and Orrery (15th),* John Richard Boyle, *b.* 1945, *s.* 2003, *m.*	Viscount Dungarvan, *b.* 1978
1850	*Cottenham (9th),* Mark John Henry Pepys, *b.* 1983, *s.* 2000	Hon. Sam R. P., *b.* 1986
1762 I.	** *Courtown (9th),* James Patrick Montagu Burgoyne Winthrop Stopford, *b.* 1954, *s.* 1975, *m.*	Viscount Stopford, *b.* 1988
1697	*Coventry (13th),* George William Coventry, *b.* 1939, *s.* 2004, *m.*	David D. S. C., *b.* 1973
1857	° *Cowley (7th),* Garret Graham Wellesley, *b.* 1934, *s.* 1975, *w.*	Viscount Dangan, *b.* 1965
1892	*Cranbrook (5th),* Gathorne Gathorne-Hardy, *b.* 1933, *s.* 1978, *m.*	Lord Medway, *b.* 1968
1801 M.	*Craven (9th),* Benjamin Robert Joseph Craven, *b.* 1989, *s.* 1990	Rupert J. E. C., *b.* 1926
1398 S.	*Crawford (29th) and Balcarres (12th) (S. 1651) and Baron Balniel (life peerage, 1974),* Robert Alexander Lindsay, KT, GCVO, PC, *b.* 1927, *s.* 1975, *m. Premier Earl on Union Roll*	Lord Balniel, *b.* 1958
1861	*Cromartie (5th),* John Ruaridh Blunt Grant Mackenzie, *b.* 1948, *s.* 1989, *m.*	Viscount Tarbat, *b.* 1987
1901	*Cromer (4th),* Evelyn Rowland Esmond Baring, *b.* 1946, *s.* 1991, *m.*	Viscount Errington, *b.* 1994
1633 S.	*Dalhousie (17th),* James Hubert Ramsay, *b.* 1948, *s.* 1999, *m., Lord Steward*	Lord Ramsay, *b.* 1981
1725 I.	*Darnley (11th),* Adam Ivo Stuart Bligh, *b.* 1941, *s.* 1980, *m.*	Lord Clifton, *b.* 1968
1711	*Dartmouth (10th),* William Legge, *b.* 1949, *s.* 1997	Hon. Rupert L., *b.* 1951
1761	° *De La Warr (11th),* William Herbrand Sackville, *b.* 1948, *s.* 1988, *m.*	Lord Buckhurst, *b.* 1979
1622	*Denbigh (12th) and Desmond (11th) (I. 1622),* Alexander Stephen Rudolph Feilding, *b.* 1970, *s.* 1995, *m.*	Viscount Feilding, *b.* 2005
1485	*Derby (19th),* Edward Richard William Stanley, *b.* 1962, *s.* 1994, *m.*	Lord Stanley, *b.* 1998
1553	*Devon (18th),* Hugh Rupert Courtenay, *b.* 1942, *s.* 1998, *m.*	Lord Courtenay, *b.* 1975
1800 I.	*Donoughmore (8th),* Richard Michael John Hely-Hutchinson, *b.* 1927, *s.* 1981, *w.*	Viscount Suirdale, *b.* 1952
1661 I.	*Drogheda (12th),* Henry Dermot Ponsonby Moore, *b.* 1937, *s.* 1989, *m.*	Viscount Moore, *b.* 1983
1837	*Ducie (7th),* David Leslie Moreton, *b.* 1951, *s.* 1991, *m.*	Lord Moreton, *b.* 1981
1860	*Dudley (4th),* William Humble David Ward, *b.* 1920, *s.* 1969, *m.*	Viscount Ednam, *b.* 1947
1660 S.	** *Dundee (12th),* Alexander Henry Scrymgeour, *b.* 1949, *s.* 1983, *m.*	Lord Scrymgeour, *b.* 1982
1669 S.	*Dundonald (15th),* Iain Alexander Douglas Blair Cochrane, *b.* 1961, *s.* 1986, *m.*	Lord Cochrane, *b.* 1991
1686 S.	*Dunmore (12th),* Malcolm Kenneth Murray, *b.* 1946, *s.* 1995, *m.*	Hon. Geoffrey C. M., *b.*1949
1822 I.	*Dunraven and Mount-Earl (7th),* Thady Windham Thomas Wyndham-Quin, *b.* 1939, *s.* 1965, *m.*	None

1833	*Durham (7th),* Edward Richard Lambton, *b.* 1961, *s.* 2006, *m.*	Viscount Lambton, *b.* 1985
1837	*Effingham (7th),* David Mowbray Algernon Howard, *b.* 1939, *s.* 1996, *m.*	Lord Howard of Effingham, *b.* 1971
1507 S.	*Eglinton (18th) and Winton (9th) (S. 1600),* Archibald George Montgomerie, *b.* 1939, *s.* 1966, *m.*	Lord Montgomerie, *b.* 1966
1733 I.	*Egmont (12th),* Thomas Frederick Gerald Perceval, *b.* 1934, *s.* 2001, *m.*	Hon. Donald W. P., *b.* 1954
1821	*Eldon (5th),* John Joseph Nicholas Scott, *b.* 1937, *s.* 1976, *m.*	Viscount Encombe, *b.* 1962
1633 S.	*Elgin (11th) and Kincardine (15th) (S. 1647),* Andrew Douglas Alexander Thomas Bruce, KT, *b.* 1924, *s.* 1968, *m.*	Lord Bruce, *b.* 1961
1789 I.	*Enniskillen (7th),* Andrew John Galbraith Cole, *b.* 1942, *s.* 1989, *m.*	Arthur G. C., *b.* 1920
1789 I.	*Erne (6th),* Henry George Victor John Crichton, *b.* 1937, *s.* 1940, *m.*	Viscount Crichton, *b.* 1971
1452 S.	** *Erroll (24th),* Merlin Sereld Victor Gilbert Hay, *b.* 1948, *s.* 1978, *m.* *Hereditary Lord High Constable and Knight Marischal of Scotland*	Lord Hay, *b.* 1984
1661	*Essex (11th),* Frederick Paul de Vere Capell, *b.* 1944, *s.* 2005	William J. C., *b.* 1952
1711	° ** *Ferrers (13th),* Robert Washington Shirley, PC, *b.* 1929, *s.* 1954, *m.*	Viscount Tamworth, *b.* 1952
1789	° *Fortescue (8th),* Charles Hugh Richard Fortescue, *b.* 1951, *s.* 1993, *m.*	John A. F. F., *b.* 1955
1841	*Gainsborough (5th),* Anthony Gerard Edward Noel, *b.* 1923, *s.* 1927, *m.*	Viscount Campden, *b.* 1950
1623 S.	*Galloway (13th),* Randolph Keith Reginald Stewart, *b.* 1928, *s.* 1978, *w.*	Andrew C. S., *b.* 1949
1703 S.	** *Glasgow (10th),* Patrick Robin Archibald Boyle, *b.* 1939, *s.* 1984, *m.*	Viscount of Kelburn, *b.* 1978
1806 I.	*Gosford (7th),* Charles David Nicholas Alexander John Sparrow Acheson, *b.* 1942, *s.* 1966, *m.*	Hon. Patrick B. V. M. A., *b.* 1915
1945	*Gowrie (2nd),* Alexander Patrick Greysteil Hore-Ruthven, PC, *b.* 1939, *s.* 1955, *m.*	Viscount Ruthven of Canberra, *b.* 1964
1684 I.	*Granard (10th),* Peter Arthur Edward Hastings Forbes, *b.* 1957, *s.* 1992, *m.*	Viscount Forbes, *b.* 1981
1833	° *Granville (6th),* Granville George Fergus Leveson-Gower, *b.* 1959, *s.* 1996, *m.*	Lord Leveson, *b.* 1999
1806	° *Grey (6th),* Richard Fleming George Charles Grey, *b.* 1939, *s.* 1963, *m.*	Philip K. G., *b.* 1940
1752	*Guilford (10th),* Piers Edward Brownlow North, *b.* 1971, *s.* 1999, *m.*	Lord North, *b.* 2002
1619	*Haddington (13th),* John George Baillie-Hamilton, *b.* 1941, *s.* 1986, *m.*	Lord Binning, *b.* 1985
1919	° *Haig (3rd),* Alexander Douglas Derrick Haig, *b.* 1961, *s.* 2009, *m.*	None
1944	*Halifax (3rd),* Charles Edward Peter Neil Wood, *b.* 1944, *s.* 1980, *m.*	Lord Irwin, *b.* 1977
1898	*Halsbury (4th),* Adam Edward Giffard, *b.* 1934, *s.* 2000, *m.*	None
1754	*Hardwicke (10th),* Joseph Philip Sebastian Yorke, *b.* 1971, *s.* 1974	Charles E. Y., *b.* 1951
1812	*Harewood (7th),* George Henry Hubert Lascelles, KBE, *b.* 1923, *s.* 1947, *m.*	Viscount Lascelles, *b.* 1950
1742	*Harrington (12th),* Charles Henry Leicester Stanhope, *b.* 1945, *s.* 2009, *m.*	Viscount Petersham, *b.* 1967
1809	*Harrowby (8th),* Dudley Adrian Conroy Ryder, *b.* 1951, *s.* 2007, *m.*	Viscount Sandon, *b.* 1981
1605	** *Home (15th),* David Alexander Cospatrick Douglas-Home, CVO, CBE, *b.* 1943, *s.* 1995, *m.*	Lord Dunglass, *b.* 1987
1821	° ** *Howe (7th),* Frederick Richard Penn Curzon, *b.* 1951, *s.* 1984, *m.*	Viscount Curzon, *b.* 1994
1529	*Huntingdon (16th),* William Edward Robin Hood Hastings Bass, LVO, *b.* 1948, *s.* 1990, *m.*	Hon. Simon A. R. H. H. B., *b.* 1950
1885	*Iddesleigh (5th),* John Stafford Northcote, *b.* 1957, *s.* 2004, *m.*	Viscount St Cyres, *b.* 1985
1756	*Ilchester (10th),* Robin Maurice Fox-Strangways, *b.* 1942, *s.* 2006, *m.*	Lord Stavordale, *b.* 1972
1929	*Inchcape (4th),* (Kenneth) Peter (Lyle) Mackay, *b.* 1943, *s.* 1994, *m.*	Viscount Glenapp, *b.* 1979
1919	*Iveagh (4th),* Arthur Edward Rory Guinness, *b.* 1969, *s.* 1992	Viscount Elveden, *b.* 2003
1925	° *Jellicoe (3rd),* Patrick John Bernard Jellicoe, *b.* 1950, *s.* 2007	Viscount Brocas, *b.* 1970
1697	*Jersey (10th),* George Francis William Child Villiers, *b.* 1976, *s.* 1998 *m.*	Hon. Jamie C. C. V., *b.* 1994
1822 I.	*Kilmorey (6th),* Sir Richard Francis Needham, PC, *b.* 1942, *s.* 1977, *m.*, (does not use title)	Viscount Newry and Mourne, *b.* 1966
1866	*Kimberley (5th),* John Armine Wodehouse, *b.* 1951, *s.* 2002, *m.*	Lord Wodehouse, *b.*1978
1768 I.	*Kingston (12th),* Robert Charles Henry King-Tenison, *b.* 1969, *s.* 2002, *m.*	Viscount Kingsborough, *b.* 2000
1633 S.	*Kinnoull (15th),* Arthur William George Patrick Hay, *b.* 1935, *s.* 1938, *m.*	Viscount Dupplin, *b.* 1962
1677 S.	*Kintore (14th),* James William Falconer Keith, *b.* 1976, *s.* 2004	Lady Iona D. M. G. K., *b.* 1978
1914	° *Kitchener of Khartoum (3rd),* Henry Herbert Kitchener, TD, *b.* 1919, *s.* 1937	None
1624	*Lauderdale (18th),* Ian Maitland, *b.* 1937, *s.* 2008, *m.*	Viscount Maitland, *b.* 1965
1837	*Leicester (7th),* Edward Douglas Coke, *b.* 1936, *s.* 1994, *m.*	Viscount Coke, *b.* 1965
1641 S.	*Leven (14th) and Melville (13th) (S. 1690),* Alexander Robert Leslie Melville, *b.* 1924, *s.* 1947, *m.*	Lord Balgonie, *b.* 1984

1831		*Lichfield (6th),* Thomas William Robert Hugh Anson, *b.* 1978, *s.* 2005	George R. A., *b.* 1960
1803 I.		*Limerick (7th),* Edmund Christopher Pery, *b.* 1963, *s.* 2003, *m.*	Viscount Glentworth, *b.* 1991
1572		*Lincoln (19th),* Robert Edward Fiennes-Clinton, *b.* 1972, *s.* 2001	Hon. William R. F.-C., *b.* 1980
1633 S.	**	*Lindsay (16th),* James Randolph Lindesay-Bethune, *b.* 1955, *s.* 1989, *m.*	Viscount Garnock, *b.* 1990
1626		*Lindsey (14th) and Abingdon (9th) (1682),* Richard Henry Rupert Bertie, *b.* 1931, *s.* 1963, *m.*	Lord Norreys, *b.* 1958
1776 I.		*Lisburne (8th),* John David Malet Vaughan, *b.* 1918, *s.* 1965, *m.*	Viscount Vaughan, *b.* 1945
1822 I.	**	*Listowel (6th),* Francis Michael Hare, *b.* 1964, *s.* 1997, *m.*	Hon. Timothy P. H., *b.* 1966
1905	**	*Liverpool (5th),* Edward Peter Bertram Savile Foljambe, *b.* 1944, *s.* 1969, *m.*	Viscount Hawkesbury, *b.* 1972
1945	°	*Lloyd George of Dwyfor (3rd),* Owen Lloyd George, *b.* 1924, *s.* 1968, *m.*	Viscount Gwynedd, *b.* 1951
1785 I.		*Longford (8th),* Thomas Frank Dermot Pakenham, *b.* 1933, *s.* 2001, *m.*, (does not use title)	Hon. Edward M. P., *b.* 1970
1807		*Lonsdale (8th),* Hugh Clayton Lowther, *b.* 1949, *s.* 2006, *m.*	Hon. William J. L., *b.* 1957
1633 S.		*Loudoun (14th),* Michael Edward Abney-Hastings, *b.* 1942, *s.* 2002, *m.*	Lord Mauchline, *b.* 1974
1838		*Lovelace (5th),* Peter Axel William Locke King, *b.* 1951, *s.* 1964, *m.*	None
1795 I.		*Lucan (7th),* Richard John Bingham, *b.* 1934, *s.* 1964, *m.* (missing since 8 November 1974)	Lord Bingham, *b.* 1967
1880		*Lytton (5th),* John Peter Michael Scawen Lytton, *b.* 1950, *s.* 1985, *m.*	Viscount Knebworth, *b.* 1989
1721		*Macclesfield (9th),* Richard Timothy George Mansfield Parker, *b.* 1943, *s.* 1992, *m.*	Hon. J. David G. P., *b.* 1945
1800		*Malmesbury (7th),* James Carleton Harris, *b.* 1946, *s.* 2000, *m.*	Viscount FitzHarris, *b.* 1970
1776		*Mansfield and Mansfield (8th) (1792),* William David Mungo James Murray, *b.* 1930, *s.* 1971, *m.*	Viscount Stormont, *b.* 1956
1565 S.		*Mar (14th) and Kellie (16th) (S. 1616) and Baron Erskine of Alloa Tower (life peerage, 2000),* James Thorne Erskine, *b.* 1949, *s.* 1994, *m.*	Hon. Alexander D. E., *b.* 1952
1785 I.		*Mayo (11th),* Charles Diarmuidh John Bourke, *b.* 1953, *s.* 2006, *m.*	Lord Naas, *b.* 1985
1627 I.		*Meath (15th),* John Anthony Brabazon, *b.* 1941, *s.* 1998, *m.*	Lord Ardee, *b.* 1977
1766 I.		*Mexborough (8th),* John Christopher George Savile, *b.* 1931, *s.* 1980, *m.*	Viscount Pollington, *b.* 1959
1813		*Minto (7th),* Gilbert Timothy George Lariston Elliot-Murray-Kynynmound, *b.* 1953, *s.* 2005, *m.*	Viscount Melgund, *b.* 1984
1562 S.		*Moray (20th),* Douglas John Moray Stuart, *b.* 1928, *s.* 1974, *m.*	Lord Doune, *b.* 1966
1815		*Morley (6th),* John St Aubyn Parker, KCVO, *b.* 1923, *s.* 1962, *m.*	Viscount Boringdon, *b.* 1956
1458		*Morton (22nd),* John Charles Sholto Douglas, *b.* 1927, *s.* 1976, *m.*	Lord Aberdour, *b.* 1952
1789		*Mount Edgcumbe (8th),* Robert Charles Edgcumbe, *b.* 1939, *s.* 1982	Piers V. E., *b.* 1946
1805	°	*Nelson (10th),* Simon John Horatio Nelson, *b.* 1971, *s.* 2009, *m.*	Viscount Merton, *b.* 1994
1660 S.		*Newburgh (12th),* Don Filippo Giambattista Camillo Francesco Aldo Maria Rospigliosi, *b.* 1942, *s.* 1986, *m.*	Princess Donna Benedetta F. M. R., *b.* 1974
1827 I.		*Norbury (7th),* Richard James Graham-Toler, *b.* 1967, *s.* 2000	None
1806 I.		*Normanton (6th),* Shaun James Christian Welbore Ellis Agar, *b.* 1945, *s.* 1967, *m.*	Viscount Somerton, *b.* 1982
1647 S.	**	*Northesk (14th),* David John MacRae Carnegie, *b.* 1954, *s.* 1994, *m.*	Patrick C. C., *b.* 1940
1801	**	*Onslow (7th),* Michael William Coplestone Dillon Onslow, *b.* 1938, *s.* 1971, *m.*	Viscount Cranley, *b.* 1967
1696 S.		*Orkney (9th),* (Oliver) Peter St John, *b.* 1938, *s.* 1998, *m.*	Viscount Kirkwall, *b.* 1969
1328 I.		*Ormonde and Ossory (I. 1527),* The 25th/18th Earl (7th Marquess) died in 1988	†Viscount Mountgarret *b.* 1961 (*see* that title)
1925		*Oxford and Asquith (2nd),* Julian Edward George Asquith, KCMG, *b.* 1916, *s.* 1928, *w.*	Viscount Asquith, OBE, *b.* 1952
1929	° **	*Peel (3rd),* William James Robert Peel, GCVO, PC, *b.* 1947, *s.* 1969, *m.* *Lord Chamberlain*	Viscount Clanfield, *b.* 1976
1551		*Pembroke (18th) and Montgomery (15th) (1605),* William Alexander Sidney Herbert, *b.* 1978, *s.* 2003, *m.*	Earl of Carnarvon *b.* 1956 (*see* that title)
1605		*Perth (18th),* John Eric Drummond, *b.* 1935, *s.* 2002, *m.*	Viscount Strathallan, *b.* 1965
1905		*Plymouth (3rd),* Other Robert Ivor Windsor-Clive, *b.* 1923, *s.* 1943, *m.*	Viscount Windsor, *b.* 1951
1785		*Portarlington (7th),* George Lionel Yuill Seymour Dawson-Damer, *b.* 1938, *s.* 1959, *m.*	Viscount Carlow, *b.* 1965
1689		*Portland (12th),* Count Timothy Charles Robert Noel Bentinck, *b.* 1953, *s.* 1997, *m.*	Viscount Woodstock, *b.* 1984
1743		*Portsmouth (10th),* Quentin Gerard Carew Wallop, *b.* 1954, *s.* 1984, *m.*	Viscount Lymington, *b.* 1981
1804		*Powis (8th),* John George Herbert, *b.* 1952, *s.* 1993, *m.*	Viscount Clive, *b.* 1979
1765		*Radnor (9th),* William Pleydell-Bouverie, *b.* 1955, *s.* 2008, *m.*	Viscount Folkestone, *b.* 1999
1831 I.		*Ranfurly (7th),* Gerald Françoys Needham Knox, *b.* 1929, *s.* 1988, *m.*	Viscount Northland, *b.* 1957
1771 I.		*Roden (10th),* Robert John Jocelyn, *b.* 1938, *s.* 1993, *m.*	Viscount Jocelyn, *b.* 1989
1801		*Romney (8th),* Julian Charles Marsham, *b.* 1948, *s.* 2004, *m.*	Viscount Marsham, *b.* 1977

1703 S.		*Rosebery (7th),* Neil Archibald Primrose, *b.* 1929, *s.* 1974, *m.*	Lord Dalmeny, *b.* 1967
1806 I.		*Rosse (7th),* William Brendan Parsons, *b.* 1936, *s.* 1979, *m.*	Lord Oxmantown, *b.* 1969.
1801	**	*Rosslyn (7th),* Peter St Clair-Erskine, *b.* 1958, *s.* 1977, *m.*	Lord Loughborough, *b.* 1986
1457 S.		*Rothes (22nd),* James Malcolm David Leslie, *b.* 1958, *s.* 2005, *m.*	Hon. Alexander J. L., *b.* 1962
1861	°	*Russell (6th),* Nicholas Lyulph Russell, *b.* 1968, *s.* 2004	Hon. John F. R., *b.* 1971
1915	°	*St Aldwyn (3rd),* Michael Henry Hicks Beach, *b.* 1950, *s.* 1992, *m.*	Hon. David S. H. B., *b.* 1955
1815		*St Germans (10th),* Peregrine Nicholas Eliot, *b.* 1941, *s.* 1988	Lord Eliot, *b.* 2004
1660	**	*Sandwich (11th),* John Edward Hollister Montagu, *b.* 1943, *s.* 1995, *m.*	Viscount Hinchingbrooke, *b.* 1969
1690		*Scarbrough (13th),* Richard Osbert Lumley, *b.* 1973, *s.* 2004	Hon. Thomas H. L., *b.* 1980
1701 S.		*Seafield (13th),* Ian Derek Francis Ogilvie-Grant, *b.* 1939, *s.* 1969, *m.*	Viscount Reidhaven, *b.* 1963
1882	**	*Selborne (4th),* John Roundell Palmer, KBE, *b.* 1940, *s.* 1971, *m.*	Viscount Wolmer, *b.* 1971
1646 S.		*Selkirk,* Disclaimed for life 1994. (*see* Lord Selkirk of Douglas, Life Peers)	Master of Selkirk, *b.* 1978
1672		*Shaftesbury (12th),* Nicholas Edmund Anthony Ashley-Cooper, *b.* 1979, *s.* 2005	None
1756 I.		*Shannon (9th),* Richard Bentinck Boyle, *b.* 1924, *s.* 1963	Viscount Boyle, *b.* 1960
1442	**	*Shrewsbury and Waterford (22nd) (I. 1446),* Charles Henry John Benedict Crofton Chetwynd Chetwynd-Talbot, *b.* 1952, *s.* 1980, *m. Premier Earl of England and Ireland*	Viscount Ingestre, *b.* 1978
1961		*Snowdon (1st) and Baron Armstrong-Jones (life peerage, 1999),* Antony Charles Robert Armstrong-Jones, GCVO, *b.* 1930, *m.*	Viscount Linley, *b.* 1961
1765	°	*Spencer (9th),* Charles Edward Maurice Spencer, *b.* 1964, *s.* 1992, *m.*	Viscount Althorp, *b.* 1994
1703 S.	**	*Stair (14th),* John David James Dalrymple, *b.* 1961, *s.* 1996, *m.*	Hon. David H. D., *b.* 1963
1984		*Stockton (2nd),* Alexander Daniel Alan Macmillan, MEP, *b.* 1943, *s.* 1986, *m.*	Viscount Macmillan of Ovenden, *b.* 1974
1821		*Stradbroke (6th),* Robert Keith Rous, *b.* 1937, *s.* 1983, *m.*	Viscount Dunwich, *b.* 1961
1847		*Strafford (8th),* Thomas Edmund Byng, *b.* 1936, *s.* 1984, *m.*	Viscount Enfield, *b.* 1964
1606 S.		*Strathmore and Kinghorne (18th) (S. 1677),* Michael Fergus Bowes Lyon, *b.* 1957, *s.* 1987, *m.*	Lord Glamis, *b.* 1986
1603		*Suffolk (21st) and Berkshire (14th) (1626),* Michael John James George Robert Howard, *b.* 1935, *s.* 1941, *m.*	Viscount Andover, *b.* 1974
1955		*Swinton (3rd),* Nicholas John Cunliffe-Lister, *b.* 1939, *s.* 2006, *m.*	Lord Masham *b.* 1970
1714		*Tankerville (10th),* Peter Grey Bennet, *b.* 1956, *s.* 1980	Adrian G. B., *b.* 1958
1822	°	*Temple of Stowe (8th),* (Walter) Grenville Algernon Temple-Gore-Langton, *b.* 1924, *s.* 1988, *m.*	Lord Langton, *b.* 1955
1815		*Verulam (7th),* John Duncan Grimston, *b.* 1951, *s.* 1973, *m.*	Viscount Grimston, *b.* 1978
1729	°	*Waldegrave (13th),* James Sherbrooke Waldegrave, *b.* 1940, *s.* 1995, *m.*	Viscount Chewton, *b.* 1986
1759		*Warwick (9th) and Brooke (9th) (1746),* Guy David Greville, *b.* 1957, *s.* 1996, *m.*	Lord Brooke, *b.* 1982
1633 S.		*Wemyss (13th) and March (9th),* James Donald Charteris, *b.* 1948, *s.* 2008, *m.*	Lord Elcho, *b.* 1984
1621 I.		*Westmeath (13th),* William Anthony Nugent, *b.* 1928, *s.* 1971, *m.*	Hon. Sean C. W. N., *b.* 1965
1624		*Westmorland (16th),* Anthony David Francis Henry Fane, *b.* 1951, *s.* 1993, *m.*	Hon. Harry St C. F., *b.* 1953
1876		*Wharncliffe (5th),* Richard Alan Montagu Stuart Wortley, *b.* 1953, *s.* 1987, *m.*	Viscount Carlton, *b.* 1980
1801		*Wilton (8th),* Francis Egerton Grosvenor, *b.* 1934, *s.* 1999, *m.*	Viscount Grey de Wilton, *b.*1959
1628		*Winchilsea (17th) and Nottingham (12th) (1681),* Daniel James Hatfield Finch Hatton, *b.* 1967, *s.* 1999, *m.*	Viscount Maidstone, *b.* 1998
1766	°	*Winterton (8th),* (Donald) David Turnour, *b.* 1943, *s.* 1991, *m.*	Robert C. T., *b.* 1950
1956		*Woolton (3rd),* Simon Frederick Marquis, *b.* 1958, *s.* 1969, *m.*	None
1837		*Yarborough (8th),* Charles John Pelham, *b.* 1963, *s.* 1991, *m.*	Lord Worsley, *b.* 1990

COUNTESSES IN THEIR OWN RIGHT

Style, The Rt. Hon. the Countess (of) _
Envelope (formal), The Rt. Hon. the Countess (of) _; *(social),* The Countess (of) _. *Letter (formal),* Madam; *(social),* Lady _. *Spoken (formal),* Madam; *(social),* Lady _.
Husband, Untitled
Children's style, As for children of an Earl

Created	*Title, order of succession, name, etc*	*Heir*
1643 S.	*Dysart (12th in line),* Katherine Grant of Rothiemurchus, *b.* 1918, *s.* 2003 *w.*	Lord Huntingtower, *b.* 1946
c.1115 S.	** *Mar (31st in line),* Margaret of Mar, *b.* 1940, *s.* 1975, *m.* Premier Earldom of Scotland	Mistress of Mar, *b.* 1963
1947	° *Mountbatten of Burma (2nd in line),* Patricia Edwina Victoria Knatchbull, CBE, *b.* 1924, *s.* 1979, *w.*	Lord Romsey, (*also* Lord Brabourne (8th) *see* that title)
c.1235 S.	*Sutherland (24th in line),* Elizabeth Millicent Sutherland, *b.* 1921, *s.* 1963, *w.*	Lord Strathnaver, *b.* 1947

VISCOUNTS

Coronet, Sixteen silver balls

Style, The Rt. Hon. the Viscount _
Envelope (formal), The Rt. Hon. the Viscount _; *(social),* The Viscount _. *Letter (formal),* My Lord; *(social),* Dear Lord _. *Spoken,* Lord _.
Wife's style, The Rt. Hon. the Viscountess _
Envelope (formal), The Rt. Hon. the Viscountess _; *(social),* The Viscountess _. *Letter (formal),* Madam; *(social),* Dear Lady _. *Spoken,* Lady _.
Children's style, 'The Hon.' before forename and surname, as for Baron's children
In Scotland, the heir apparent to a Viscount may be styled 'The Master of _ (title of peer)'

Created	*Title, order of succession, name, etc*	*Heir*
1945	*Addison (4th),* William Matthew Wand Addison, *b.* 1945, *s.* 1992, *m.*	Hon. Paul W. A., *b.* 1973
1946	*Alanbrooke (3rd),* Alan Victor Harold Brooke, *b.* 1932, *s.* 1972	None
1919	** *Allenby (3rd),* Lt.-Col. Michael Jaffray Hynman Allenby, *b.* 1931, *s.* 1984, *m.*	Hon. Henry J. H. A., *b.* 1968
1911	*Allendale (4th),* Wentworth Peter Ismay Beaumont, *b.* 1948, *s.* 2002, *m.*	Hon. Wentworth A. I. B., *b.* 1979
1642 S.	*of Arbuthnott (16th),* John Campbell Arbuthnott, KT, CBE, DSC, *b.* 1924, *s.* 1966, *m.*	Master of Arbuthnott, *b.* 1950
1751 I.	*Ashbrook (11th),* Michael Llowarch Warburton Flower, *b.* 1935, *s.* 1995, *m.*	Hon. Rowland F. W. F., *b.* 1975
1917	** *Astor (4th),* William Waldorf Astor, *b.* 1951, *s.* 1966, *m.*	Hon. William W. A., *b.* 1979
1781 I.	*Bangor (8th),* William Maxwell David Ward, *b.* 1948, *s.* 1993, *m.*	Hon. E. Nicholas W., *b.* 1953
1925	*Bearsted (5th),* Nicholas Alan Samuel, *b.* 1950, *s.* 1996, *m.*	Hon. Harry R. S., *b.* 1988
1963	*Blakenham (2nd),* Michael John Hare, *b.* 1938, *s.* 1982, *m.*	Hon. Caspar J. H., *b.* 1972
1935	*Bledisloe (4th),* Rupert Edward Ludlow Bathurst, *b.* 1964, *s.* 2009, *m.*	Hon. Benjamin B., *b.* 2004
1712	*Bolingbroke (7th) and St John (8th) (1716),* Kenneth Oliver Musgrave St John, *b.* 1927, *s.* 1974	Hon. Henry F. St J., *b.* 1957
1960	*Boyd of Merton (2nd),* Simon Donald Rupert Neville Lennox-Boyd, *b.* 1939, *s.* 1983, *m.*	Hon. Benjamin A. L.-B., *b.* 1964
1717 I.	*Boyne (11th),* Gustavus Michael Stucley Hamilton-Russell, *b.* 1965, *s.* 1995, *m.*	Hon. Gustavus A. E. H.-R., *b.* 1999
1929	*Brentford (4th),* Crispin William Joynson-Hicks, *b.* 1933, *s.* 1983, *m.*	Hon. Paul W. J.-H., *b.* 1971
1929	** *Bridgeman (3rd),* Robin John Orlando Bridgeman, *b.* 1930, *s.* 1982, *m.*	Hon. Luke R. O. B., *b.* 1971

1868	*Bridport (4th) and 7th Duke, Bronte in Sicily, 1799,* Alexander Nelson Hood, *b.* 1948, *s.* 1969, *m.*	Hon. Peregrine A. N. H., *b.* 1974
1952	** *Brookeborough (3rd),* Alan Henry Brooke, *b.* 1952, *s.* 1987, *m.*	Hon. Christopher A. B., *b.* 1954
1933	*Buckmaster (4th),* Adrian Charles Buckmaster, *b.* 1949, *s.* 2007, *m.*	Hon. Andrew N. B., *b.* 1980
1939	*Caldecote (3rd),* Piers James Hampden Inskip, *b.* 1947, *s.* 1999, *m.*	Hon. Thomas J. H. I., *b.* 1985
1941	*Camrose (4th),* Adrian Michael Berry, *b.* 1937, *s.* 2001, *m.*	Hon. Jonathan W. B., *b.* 1970
1954	*Chandos (3rd) and Baron Lyttelton of Aldershot (life peerage, 2000),* Thomas Orlando Lyttelton, *b.* 1953, *s.* 1980, *m.*	Hon. Oliver A. L., *b.* 1986
1665 I.	*Charlemont (15th),* John Dodd Caulfeild, *b.* 1966, *s.* 2001, *m.*	Hon. Shane A. C., *b.* 1996
1921	*Chelmsford (4th)* Frederic Corin Piers Thesiger, *b.* 1962, *s.* 1999, *m.*	Hon. Frederic T. *b.* 2006
1717 I.	*Chetwynd (10th),* Adam Richard John Casson Chetwynd, *b.* 1935, *s.* 1965, *m.*	Hon. Adam D. C., *b.* 1969
1911	*Chilston (4th),* Alastair George Akers-Douglas, *b.* 1946, *s.* 1982, *m.*	Hon. Oliver I. A.-D., *b.* 1973
1902	*Churchill (3rd) and 5th UK Baron Churchill (1815),* Victor George Spencer, *b.* 1934, *s.* 1973	To Barony only, Richard H. R. S., *b.* 1926
1718	*Cobham (12th),* Christopher Charles Lyttelton, *b.* 1947, *s.* 2006, *m.*	Hon. Oliver C. L., *b.* 1976
1902	** *Colville of Culross (4th),* John Mark Alexander Colville, QC, *b.* 1933, *s.* 1945, *m.*	Master of Colville, *b.* 1959
1826	*Combermere (6th),* Thomas Robert Wellington Stapleton-Cotton, *b.* 1969, *s.* 2000	Hon. David P. D. S.-C., *b.* 1932
1917	*Cowdray (4th),* Michael Orlando Weetman Pearson, *b.* 1944, *s.* 1995, *m.*	Hon. Peregrine J. D. P., *b.* 1994
1927	** *Craigavon (3rd),* Janric Fraser Craig, *b.* 1944, *s.* 1974	None
1943	*Daventry (4th),* James Edward FitzRoy Newdegate, *b.* 1960, *s.* 2000, *m.*	Hon. Humphrey J. F. N., *b.* 1995
1937	*Davidson (2nd),* John Andrew Davidson, *b.* 1928, *s.* 1970, *m.*	Hon. Malcolm W. M. D., *b.* 1934
1956	*De L'Isle (2nd),* Philip John Algernon Sidney, MBE, *b.* 1945, *s.* 1991, *m.*	Hon. Philip W. E. S., *b.* 1985
1776 I.	*De Vesci (7th),* Thomas Eustace Vesey, *b.* 1955, *s.* 1983, *m.*	Hon. Oliver I. V., *b.* 1991
1917	*Devonport (3rd),* Terence Kearley, *b.* 1944, *s.* 1973	Chester D. H. K., *b.* 1932
1964	*Dilhorne (2nd),* John Mervyn Manningham-Buller, *b.* 1932, *s.* 1980, *m.*	Hon. James E. M.-B., *b.* 1956
1622 I.	*Dillon (22nd),* Henry Benedict Charles Dillon, *b.* 1973, *s.* 1982	Hon. Richard A. L. D., *b.* 1948
1785 I.	*Doneraile (10th),* Richard Allen St Leger, *b.* 1946, *s.* 1983, *m.*	Hon. Nathaniel W. R. St J. St L., *b.* 1971
1680 I.	*Downe (12th),* Richard Henry Dawnay, *b.* 1967, *s.* 2002	Thomas P. D., *b.* 1978
1959	*Dunrossil (3rd),* Andrew William Reginald Morrison, *b.* 1953, *s.* 2000, *m.*	Hon. Callum A. B. M., *b.* 1994
1964	** *Eccles (2nd),* John Dawson Eccles, CBE, *b.* 1931, *s.* 1999, *m.*	Hon. William D. E., *b.* 1960
1897	*Esher (5th),* Christopher Lionel Baliol Brett, *b.* 1936, *s.* 2004, *m.*	Hon. Matthew C. A. B., *b.* 1963
1816	*Exmouth (10th),* Paul Edward Pellew, *b.* 1940, *s.* 1970, *m.*	Hon. Edward F. P., *b.* 1978
1620 S.	** *of Falkland (15th),* Lucius Edward William Plantagenet Cary, *b.* 1935, *s.* 1984, *m. Premier Scottish Viscount on the Roll*	Master of Falkland, *b.* 1963
1720	*Falmouth (9th),* George Hugh Boscawen, *b.* 1919, *s.* 1962, *w.*	Hon. Evelyn A. H. B., *b.* 1955
1720 I.	*Gage (8th),* (Henry) Nicolas Gage, *b.* 1934, *s.* 1993, *m.*	Hon. Henry W. G., *b.* 1975
1727 I.	*Galway (12th),* George Rupert Monckton-Arundell, *b.* 1922, *s.* 1980, *m.*	Hon. J. Philip M., *b.* 1952
1478 I.	*Gormanston (17th),* Jenico Nicholas Dudley Preston, *b.* 1939, *s.* 1940, *m. Premier Viscount of Ireland*	Hon. Jenico F. T. P., *b.* 1974
1816 I.	*Gort (9th),* Foley Robert Standish Prendergast Vereker, *b.* 1951, *s.* 1995, *m.*	Hon. Robert F. P. V., *b.* 1993
1900	** *Goschen (4th),* Giles John Harry Goschen, *b.* 1965, *s.* 1977, *m.*	Hon. Alexander J. E. G., *b.* 2001
1849	*Gough (5th),* Shane Hugh Maryon Gough, *b.* 1941, *s.* 1951	None
1929	*Hailsham (3rd),* Douglas Martin Hogg, PC, QC, MP, *b.* 1945, *s.* 2001, *m.*	Hon. Quintin J. N. M. H., *b.* 1973
1891	*Hambleden (4th),* William Herbert Smith, *b.* 1930, *s.* 1948, *m.*	Hon. William H. B. S., *b.* 1955
1884	*Hampden (7th),* Francis Anthony Brand, *b.* 1970, *s.* 2008, *m.*	Hon. Lucian A. B., *b.* 2005
1936	*Hanworth (3rd),* David Stephen Geoffrey Pollock, *b.* 1946, *s.* 1996, *m.*	Harold W. C. P., *b.* 1988
1791 I.	*Harberton (11th),* Henry Robert Pomeroy, *b.* 1958, *s.* 2004, *m.*	Hon. Patrick C. P., b. 1995
1846	*Hardinge (7th),* Andrew Hartland Hardinge, *b.* 1960, *s.* 2004, *m.*	Hon. Thomas H. de M. H., *b.* 1993
1791 I.	*Hawarden (9th),* (Robert) Connan Wyndham Leslie Maude, *b.* 1961, *s.* 1991, *m.*	Hon. Varian J. C. E. M., *b.* 1997
1960	*Head (2nd),* Richard Antony Head, *b.* 1937, *s.* 1983, *m.*	Hon. Henry J. H., *b.* 1980
1550	*Hereford (19th),* Charles Robin De Bohun Devereux, *b.* 1975, *s.* 2004, *Premier Viscount of England*	Hon. Edward M. de B. D., *b.* 1977
1842	*Hill (9th),* Peter David Raymond Charles Clegg-Hill, *b.* 1945, *s.* 2003	Hon. Michael C. D. C.-H., *b.* 1988

1796	*Hood (8th)*, Henry Lyttleton Alexander Hood, *b.* 1958, *s.* 1999, *m.*	Hon. Archibald L. S. H., *b.* 1993
1945	*Kemsley (3rd)*, Richard Gomer Berry, *b.* 1951, *s.* 1999, *m.*	Hon. Luke G. B., *b.* 1998
1911	*Knollys (3rd)*, David Francis Dudley Knollys, *b.* 1931, *s.* 1966, *m.*	Hon. Patrick N. M. K., *b.* 1962
1895	*Knutsford (6th)*, Michael Holland-Hibbert, *b.* 1926, *s.* 1986, *m.*	Hon. Henry T. H.-H., *b.* 1959
1954	*Leathers (3rd)*, Christopher Graeme Leathers, *b.* 1941, *s.* 1996, *m.*	Hon. James F. L., *b.* 1969
1781 I.	*Lifford (9th)*, (Edward) James Wingfield Hewitt, *b.* 1949, *s.* 1987, *m.*	Hon. James T. W. H., *b.* 1979
1921	*Long (4th)*, Richard Gerard Long, CBE, *b.* 1929, *s.* 1967, *m.*	Hon. James R. L., *b.* 1960
1957	*Mackintosh of Halifax (3rd)*, (John) Clive Mackintosh, *b.* 1958, *s.* 1980, *m.*	Hon. Thomas H. G. M., *b.* 1985
1955	*Malvern (3rd)*, Ashley Kevin Godfrey Huggins, *b.* 1949, *s.* 1978	Hon. M. James H., *b.* 1928
1945	*Marchwood (3rd)*, David George Staveley Penny, *b.* 1936, *s.* 1979, *w.*	Hon. Peter G. W. P., *b.* 1965
1942	*Margesson (2nd)*, Francis Vere Hampden Margesson, *b.* 1922, *s.* 1965, *m.*	Capt. Hon. Richard F. D. M., *b.* 1960
1660 I.	*Massereene (14th) and Ferrard (7th) (I. 1797)*, John David Clotworthy Whyte-Melville Foster Skeffington, *b.* 1940, *s.* 1992, *m.*	Hon. Charles J. C. W.-M. F. S., *b.* 1973
1802	*Melville (9th)*, Robert David Ross Dundas, *b.* 1937, *s.* 1971, *m.*	Hon. Robert H. K. D., *b.* 1984
1916	*Mersey (5th)*, Edward John Hallam Bigham, *b.* 1966, *s.* 2006, *m.*	Hon. David E. H. B., *b.* 1938
1717 I.	*Midleton (12th)*, Alan Henry Brodrick, *b.* 1949, *s.* 1988, *m.*	Hon. Ashley R. B., *b.* 1980
1962	*Mills (3rd)*, Christopher Philip Roger Mills, *b.* 1956, *s.* 1988, *m.*	None
1716 I.	*Molesworth (12th)*, Robert Bysse Kelham Molesworth, *b.* 1959, *s.* 1997	Hon. William J. C. M., *b.* 1960
1801 I.	*Monck (7th)*, Charles Stanley Monck, *b.* 1953, *s.* 1982 (Does not use title)	Hon. George S. M., *b.* 1957
1957	*Monckton of Brenchley (3rd)*, Christopher Walter Monckton, *b.* 1952, *s.* 2006, *m.*	Hon. Timothy D. R. M., *b.* 1955
1946	** *Montgomery of Alamein (2nd)*, David Bernard Montgomery, CBE, *b.* 1928, *s.* 1976, *m.*	Hon. Henry D. M., *b.* 1954
1550 I.	*Mountgarret (18th)*, Piers James Richard Butler, *b.* 1961, *s.* 2004	Hon. Edmund H. R. B., *b.* 1962
1952	*Norwich (2nd)*, John Julius Cooper, CVO, *b.* 1929, *s.* 1954, *m.*	Hon. Jason C. D. B. C., *b.* 1959
1651 S.	*of Oxfuird (14th)*, Ian Arthur Alexander Makgill, *b.* 1969, *s.* 2003	Hon. Robert E. G. M., *b.* 1969
1873	*Portman (10th)*, Christopher Edward Berkeley Portman, *b.* 1958, *s.* 1999, *m.*	Hon. Luke O. B. P., *b.* 1984
1743 I.	*Powerscourt (10th)*, Mervyn Niall Wingfield, *b.* 1935, *s.* 1973, *m.*	Hon. Mervyn A. W., *b.* 1963
1900	*Ridley (4th)*, Matthew White Ridley, KG, GCVO, TD, *b.* 1925, *s.* 1964, *w.*	Hon. Matthew W. R., *b.* 1958
1960	*Rochdale (2nd)*, St John Durival Kemp, *b.* 1938, *s.* 1993, *m.*	Hon. Jonathan H. D. K., *b.* 1961
1919	*Rothermere (4th)*, (Harold) Jonathan Esmond Vere Harmsworth, *b.* 1967, *s.* 1998, *m.*	Hon. Vere R. J. H. H., *b.* 1994
1937	*Runciman of Doxford (3rd)*, Walter Garrison Runciman (Garry), CBE, *b.* 1934, *s.* 1989, *m.*	Hon. David W. R., *b.* 1967
1918	*St Davids (4th)*, Rhodri Colwyn Philipps, *b.* 1966, *s.* 2009, *m.*	Hon. Roland A. J. E. P., *b.* 1970
1801	*St Vincent (8th)*, Edward Robert James Jervis, *b.* 1951, *s.* 2006, *m.*	Hon. James R. A. J., *b.* 1982
1937	*Samuel (3rd)*, David Herbert Samuel, OBE, PHD, *b.* 1922, *s.* 1978, *m.*	Hon. Dan J. S., *b.* 1925
1911	*Scarsdale (4th)*, Peter Ghislain Nathaniel Curzon, *b.* 1949, *s.* 2000, *m.*	Hon. David J. N. C., *b.* 1958
1905 M.	*Selby (6th)*, Christopher Rolf Thomas Gully, *b.* 1993, *s.* 2001	Hon. (James) Edward H. G. G., *b.* 1945
1805	*Sidmouth (8th)*, Jeremy Francis Addington, *b.* 1947, *s.* 2005, *w.*	Hon. Steffan A., *b.* 1966
1940	** *Simon (3rd)*, Jan David Simon, *b.* 1940, *s.* 1993, *m.*	None
1960	** *Slim (2nd)*, John Douglas Slim, OBE, *b.* 1927, *s.* 1970, *m.*	Hon. Mark W. R. S., *b.* 1960
1954	*Soulbury (3rd)*, Peter Edward Ramsbotham, GCMG, GCVO, *b.* 1919, *s.* 2004, *m.* (Does not use title)	Hon. Oliver P. R., *b.* 1943
1776 I.	*Southwell (7th)*, Pyers Anthony Joseph Southwell, *b.* 1930, *s.* 1960, *m.*	Hon. Richard A. P. S., *b.* 1956
1942	*Stansgate*, Anthony Neil Wedgwood Benn, *b.* 1925, *s.* 1960, *w.* Disclaimed for life 1963.	Stephen M. W. B., *b.* 1951
1959	*Stuart of Findhorn (3rd)*, James Dominic Stuart, *b.* 1948, *s.* 1999, *m.*	Hon. Andrew M. S., *b.* 1957
1957	** *Tenby (3rd)*, William Lloyd George, *b.* 1927, *s.* 1983, *m.*	Hon. Timothy H. G. L. G., *b.* 1962
1952	*Thurso (3rd)*, John Archibald Sinclair, *b.* 1953, *s.* 1995, *m.*	Hon. James A. R. S., *b.* 1984
1721	*Torrington (11th)*, Timothy Howard St George Byng, *b.* 1943, *s.* 1961, *m.*	Colin H. C.-B., *b.* 1960
1936	** *Trenchard (3rd)*, Hugh Trenchard, *b.* 1951, *s.* 1987, *m.*	Hon. Alexander T. T., *b.* 1978
1921	** *Ullswater (2nd)*, Nicholas James Christopher Lowther, PC, LVO, *b.* 1942, *s.* 1949, *m.*	Hon. Benjamin J. L., *b.* 1975
1622 I.	*Valentia (16th)*, Frances William Dighton Annesley, *b.* 1959, *s.* 2005, *m.*	Hon. Peter J. A., *b.* 1967
1952	** *Waverley (3rd)*, John Desmond Forbes Anderson, *b.* 1949, *s.* 1990	Hon. Forbes A. R. A., *b.* 1996

1938	*Weir (3rd),* William Kenneth James Weir, *b.* 1933, *s.* 1975, *m.*	Hon. James W. H. W., *b.* 1965
1918	*Wimborne (4th),* Ivor Mervyn Vigors Guest, *b.* 1968, *s.* 1993	Hon. Julien J. G., *b.* 1945
1923	*Younger of Leckie (5th),* James Edward George Younger, *b.* 1955, *s.* 2003, *m.*	Hon. Alexander W. G. Y., *b.* 1993

BARONS/LORDS

Coronet, Six silver balls

Style, The Rt. Hon. the Lord _
Envelope (formal), The Rt. Hon. Lord _; *(social),* The Lord _. *Letter (formal),* My Lord; *(social),* Dear Lord _. *Spoken,* Lord _.
In the Peerage of Scotland there is no rank of Baron; the equivalent rank is Lord of Parliament and Scottish peers should always be styled 'Lord', never 'Baron'.
Wife's style, The Rt. Hon. the Lady _
Envelope (formal), The Rt. Hon. Lady _; *(social),* The Lady _. *Letter (formal),* My Lady; *(social),* Dear Lady _. *Spoken,* Lady _
Children's style, 'The Hon.' before forename (F_) and surname (S_)
Envelope, The Hon. F_ S_. *Letter,* Dear Mr/Miss/Mrs S_. *Spoken,* Mr/Miss/Mrs S_
In Scotland, the heir apparent to a Lord may be styled 'The Master of _ (title of peer)'

Created	*Title, order of succession, name, etc*	*Heir*
1911	*Aberconway (4th),* (Henry) Charles McLaren, *b.* 1948, *s.* 2003, *m.*	Hon. Charles S. M., *b.* 1984
1873	** *Aberdare (5th),* Alastair John Lyndhurst Bruce, *b.* 1947, *s.* 2005, *m.*	Hon. Hector M. N. B., *b.* 1974
1835	*Abinger (9th),* James Harry Scarlett, *b.* 1959, *s.* 2002, *m.*	Hon. Peter R. S., *b.* 1961
1869	*Acton (4th) and Acton of Bridgnorth (life peerage, 2000),* Richard Gerald Lyon-Dalberg-Acton, *b.* 1941, *s.* 1989, *m.*	Hon. John C. F. H. L.-D.-A., *b.* 1966
1887	** *Addington (6th),* Dominic Bryce Hubbard, *b.* 1963, *s.* 1982	Hon. Michael W. L. H., *b.* 1965
1896	*Aldenham (6th) and Hunsdon of Hunsdon (4th) (1923),* Vicary Tyser Gibbs, *b.* 1948, *s.* 1986, *m.*	Hon. Humphrey W. F. G., *b.* 1989
1962	*Aldington (2nd),* Charles Harold Stuart Low, *b.* 1948, *s.* 2000, *m.*	Hon. Philip T. A. L., *b.* 1990
1945	*Altrincham (3rd),* Anthony Ulick David Dundas Grigg, *b.* 1934, *s.* 2001, *m.*	Hon. (Edward) Sebastian G., *b.* 1965
1929	*Alvingham (2nd),* Maj.-Gen. Robert Guy Eardley Yerburgh, CBE, *b.* 1926, *s.* 1955, *m.*	Capt. Hon. Robert R. G. Y., *b.* 1956
1892	*Amherst of Hackney (5th),* Hugh William Amherst Cecil, *b.* 1968, *s.* 2009, *m.*	Hon. Jack W. A. C., *b.* 2001
1881	** *Ampthill (4th),* Geoffrey Denis Erskine Russell, CBE, PC *b.* 1921, *s.* 1973	Hon. David W. E. R., *b.* 1947
1947	*Amwell (3rd),* Keith Norman Montague, *b.* 1943, *s.* 1990, *m.*	Hon. Ian K. M., *b.* 1973
1863	*Annaly (6th),* Luke Richard White, *b.* 1954, *s.* 1990, *m.*	Hon. Luke H. W., *b.* 1990
1885	*Ashbourne (4th),* Edward Barry Greynville Gibson, *b.* 1933, *s.* 1983, *m.*	Hon. Edward C. d'O. G., *b.* 1967
1835	*Ashburton (7th),* John Francis Harcourt Baring, KG, KCVO, *b.* 1928, *s.* 1991, *m.*	Hon. Mark F. R. B., *b.* 1958
1892	*Ashcombe (4th),* Henry Edward Cubitt, *b.* 1924, *s.* 1962, *m.*	Mark E. C., *b.* 1964
1911	*Ashton of Hyde (4th),* Thomas Henry Ashton, *b.* 1958, *s.* 2008, *m.*	Hon. John F. A., *b.* 1966
1800 I.	*Ashtown (7th),* Nigel Clive Crosby Trench, KCMG, *b.* 1916, *s.* 1990, *m.*	Hon. Roderick N. G. T., *b.* 1944
1956	** *Astor of Hever (3rd),* John Jacob Astor, *b.* 1946, *s.* 1984, *m.*	Hon. Charles G. J. A., *b.* 1990
1789 I.	*Auckland (10th) and Auckland (10th) (1793),* Robert Ian Burnard Eden, *b.* 1962, *s.* 1997, *m.*	Henry V. E., *b.* 1958
1313	*Audley,* Barony in abeyance between three co-heiresses since 1997	
1900	** *Avebury (4th),* Eric Reginald Lubbock, *b.* 1928, *s.* 1971, *m.*	Hon. Lyulph A. J. L., *b.* 1954
1718 I.	*Aylmer (14th),* (Anthony) Julian Aylmer, *b.* 1951, *s.* 2006, *m.*	Hon. Michael H. A., *b.* 1991
1929	*Baden-Powell (3rd),* Robert Crause Baden-Powell, *b.* 1936, *s.* 1962, *m.*	Hon. David M. B.-P., *b.* 1940
1780	*Bagot (10th),* (Charles Hugh) Shaun Bagot, *b.* 1944, *s.* 2001, *m.*	Richard C. V. B., *b.* 1941
1953	*Baillieu (3rd),* James William Latham Baillieu, *b.* 1950, *s.* 1973, *m.*	Hon. Robert L. B., *b.* 1979
1607 S.	*Balfour of Burleigh (8th),* Robert Bruce, *b.* 1927, *s.* 1967, *m.*	Hon. Victoria B., *b.* 1973
1945	*Balfour of Inchrye (2nd),* Ian Balfour, *b.* 1924, *s.* 1988, *w.*	None
1924	*Banbury of Southam (3rd),* Charles William Banbury, *b.* 1953, *s.* 1981, *m.*	None
1698	*Barnard (11th),* Harry John Neville Vane, TD, *b.* 1923, *s.* 1964	Hon. Henry F. C. V., *b.* 1959

1887	*Basing (6th)*, Stuart Anthony Whitfield Sclater-Booth, *b.* 1969, *s.* 2007, *m.*	Hon. Luke W. S.-B., *b.* 2000
1917	*Beaverbrook (3rd)*, Maxwell William Humphrey Aitken, *b.* 1951, *s.* 1985, *m.*	Hon. Maxwell F. A., *b.* 1977
1647 S.	*Belhaven and Stenton (13th)*, Robert Anthony Carmichael Hamilton, *b.* 1927, *s.* 1961, *m.*	Master of Belhaven, *b.* 1953
1848 I.	*Bellew (7th)*, James Bryan Bellew, *b.* 1920, *s.* 1981, *w.*	Hon. Bryan E. B., *b.* 1943
1856	*Belper (5th)*, Richard Henry Strutt, *b.* 1941, *s.* 1999, *m.*	Hon. Michael H. S., *b.* 1969
1421	*Berkeley (18th) and Gueterbock (life peerage, 2000)*, Anthony Fitzhardinge Gueterbock, OBE, *b.* 1939, *s.* 1992, *m.*	Hon. Thomas F. G., *b.* 1969
1922	*Bethell (5th)*, James Nicholas Bethell, *b.* 1967, *s.* 2007, *m.*	Hon. Jacob N. D. B., *b.* 200–
1938	*Bicester (3rd)*, Angus Edward Vivian Smith, *b.* 1932, *s.* 1968	Hugh C. V. S., *b.* 1934
1903	*Biddulph (5th)*, (Anthony) Nicholas Colin Maitland Biddulph, *b.* 1959, *s.* 1988, *m.*	Hon. Robert J. M. B., *b.* 1994
1938	*Birdwood (3rd)*, Mark William Ogilvie Birdwood, *b.* 1938, *s.* 1962, *m.*	None
1958	*Birkett (2nd)*, Michael Birkett, *b.* 1929, *s.* 1962, *w.*	Hon. Thomas B., *b.* 1982
1907	*Blyth (5th)*, James Audley Ian Blyth, *b.* 1970, *s.* 2009, *m.*	Hon. Hugo A. J. B., *b.* 2006
1797	*Bolton (8th)*, Harry Algar Nigel Orde-Powlett, *b.* 1954, *s.* 2001, *m.*	Hon. Thomas O.-P., *b.* 1979
1452 S.	*Borthwick (24th)*, John Hugh Borthwick, *b.* 1940, *s.* 1996, *m.*	Hon. James H. A. B. of Glengelt, *b.* 1940
1922	*Borwick (5th)*, (Geoffrey Robert) James Borwick, *b.* 1955, *s.* 2007, *m.*	Hon. Edwin D. W. B., *b.* 1984
1761	*Boston (11th)*, George William Eustace Boteler Irby, *b.* 1971, *s.* 2007, *m.*	Hon. Thomas W. G. B. I., *b.* 1999
1942	** *Brabazon of Tara (3rd)*, Ivon Anthony Moore-Brabazon, *b.* 1946, *s.* 1974, *m.*	Hon. Benjamin R. M.-B., *b.* 1983
1880	*Brabourne (8th)*, Norton Louis Philip Knatchbull, *b.* 1947, *s.* 2005, *m.* (*also* Lord Romsey heir to Countess Mountbatten of Burma, *see* that title)	Hon. Nicholas L. C. N. K., *b.* 1981
1925	*Bradbury (3rd)*, John Bradbury, *b.* 1940, *s.* 1994, *m.*	Hon. John B., *b.* 1973
1962	*Brain (2nd)*, Christopher Langdon Brain, *b.* 1926, *s.* 1966, *m.*	Hon. Michael C. B., *b.* 1928
1938	*Brassey of Apethorpe (3rd)*, David Henry Brassey, OBE, *b.* 1932, *s.* 1967, *m.*	Hon. Edward B., *b.* 1964
1788	*Braybrooke (10th)*, Robin Henry Charles Neville, *b.* 1932, *s.* 1990, *m.*	Richard R. N., *b.* 1977
1957	** *Bridges (2nd)*, Thomas Edward Bridges, GCMG, *b.* 1927, *s.* 1969, *m.*	Hon. Mark T. B., *b.* 1954
1945	*Broadbridge (4th)*, Martin Hugh Broadbridge, *b.* 1929, *s.* 2000, *w.*	Hon. Richard J. M. B., *b.* 1959
1933	*Brocket (3rd)*, Charles Ronald George Nall-Cain, *b.* 1952, *s.* 1967, *w.*	Hon. Alexander C. C. N.-C., *b.* 1984
1860	** *Brougham and Vaux (5th)*, Michael John Brougham, CBE, *b.* 1938, *s.* 1967	Hon. Charles W. B., *b.* 1971
1776	*Brownlow (7th)*, Edward John Peregrine Cust, *b.* 1936, *s.* 1978, *m.*	Hon. Peregrine E. Q. C., *b.* 1974
1942	*Bruntisfield (3rd)*, Michael John Victor Warrender, *b.* 1949, *s.* 2007, *m.*	Hon. John M. P. C. W., *b.* 1996
1950	*Burden (4th)*, Fraser William Elsworth Burden, *b.* 1964, *s.* 2000, *m.*	Hon. Ian S. B., *b.* 1967
1529	*Burgh (8th)*, (Alexander) Gregory Disney Leith, *b.* 1958, *s.* 2001, *m.*	Hon. Alexander J. S. L., *b.* 1986
1903	*Burnham (7th)*, Harry Frederick Alan Lawson, *b.* 1968, *s.* 2005	None
1897	*Burton (3rd)*, Michael Evan Victor Baillie, *b.* 1924, *s.* 1962, *m.*	Hon. Evan M. R. B., *b.* 1949
1643	*Byron (13th)*, Robert James Byron, *b.* 1950, *s.* 1989, *m.*	Hon. Charles R. G. B., *b.* 1990
1937	*Cadman (3rd)*, John Anthony Cadman, *b.* 1938, *s.* 1966, *m.*	Hon. Nicholas A. J. C., *b.* 1977
1945	*Calverley (3rd)*, Charles Rodney Muff, *b.* 1946, *s.* 1971, *m.*	Hon. Jonathan E. M., *b.* 1975
1383	*Camoys (7th)*, (Ralph) Thomas Campion George Sherman Stonor, GCVO, PC, *b.* 1940, *s.* 1976, *m.*	Hon. R. William R. T. S., *b.* 1974
1715 I.	*Carbery (11th)*, Peter Ralfe Harrington Evans-Freke, *b.* 1920, *s.* 1970, *w.*	Hon. Michael P. E.-F., *b.* 1942
1834 I.	*Carew (7th) and Carew (7th) (1838)*, Patrick Thomas Conolly-Carew, *b.* 1938, *s.* 1994, *m.*	Hon. William P. C.-C., *b.* 1973
1916	*Carnock (5th)*, Adam Nicolson, *b.* 1957, *s.* 2008, *m.*	Hon. Thomas N., *b.* 1984
1796 I.	*Carrington (6th) and Carrington (6th) (1797) and Carington of Upton (life peerage, 1999)*, Peter Alexander Rupert Carington, KG, GCMG, CH, MC, PC, *b.* 1919, *s.* 1938, *w.*	Hon. Rupert F. J. C., *b.* 1948
1812 I.	*Castlemaine (8th)*, Roland Thomas John Handcock, MBE, *b.* 1943, *s.* 1973, *m.*	Hon. Ronan M. E. H., *b.* 1989
1936	*Catto (3rd)*, Innes Gordon Catto, *b.* 1950, *s.* 2001, *m.*	Hon. Alexander G. C., *b.* 1952
1918	*Cawley (4th)*, John Francis Cawley, *b.* 1946, *s.* 2001, *m.*	Hon. William R. H. C., *b.* 1981
1858	*Chesham (7th)*, Charles Gray Compton Cavendish, *b.* 1974, *s.* 2009, *m.*	Hon. Oliver N.B.C., *b.* 2007
1945	*Chetwode (2nd)*, Philip Chetwode, *b.* 1937, *s.* 1950, *m.*	Hon. Roger C., *b.* 1968
1945	** *Chorley (2nd)*, Roger Richard Edward Chorley, *b.* 1930, *s.* 1978, *m.*	Hon. Nicholas R. D. C., *b.* 1966
1858	*Churston (5th)*, John Francis Yarde-Buller, *b.* 1934, *s.* 1991, *m.*	Hon. Benjamin F. A. Y.-B., *b.* 1974

1800 I.	*Clanmorris (8th),* Simon John Ward Bingham, *b.* 1937, *s.* 1988, *m.*	Robert D. de B. B., *b.* 1942
1672	*Clifford of Chudleigh (14th),* Thomas Hugh Clifford, *b.* 1948, *s.* 1988, *m.*	Hon. Alexander T. H. C., *b.* 1985
1299	*Clinton (22nd),* Gerard Nevile Mark Fane Trefusis, *b.* 1934, *s.* 1965, *m.*	Hon. Charles P. R. F. T., *b.* 1962
1955	*Clitheroe (2nd),* Ralph John Assheton, *b.* 1929, *s.* 1984, *m.*	Hon. Ralph C. A., *b.* 1962
1919	*Clwyd (4th),* (John) Murray Roberts, *b.* 1971, *s.* 2006	Hon. Jeremy T. R., *b.* 1973
1948	*Clydesmuir (3rd),* David Ronald Colville, *b.* 1949, *s.* 1996, *m.*	Hon. Richard C., *b.* 1980
1960	** *Cobbold (2nd),* David Antony Fromanteel Lytton Cobbold, *b.* 1937, *s.* 1987, *m.*	Hon. Henry F. L. C., *b.* 1962
1919	*Cochrane of Cults (4th),* (Ralph Henry) Vere Cochrane, *b.* 1926, *s.* 1990, *m.*	Hon. Thomas H. V. C., *b.* 1957
1954	*Coleraine (2nd),* (James) Martin (Bonar) Law, *b.* 1931, *s.* 1980, *m.*	Hon. James P. B. L., *b.* 1975
1873	*Coleridge (5th),* William Duke Coleridge, *b.* 1937, *s.* 1984, *m.*	Hon. James D. C., *b.* 1967
1946	*Colgrain (4th),* Alastair Colin Leckie Campbell, *b.* 1951, *s.* 2008, *m.*	Hon. Thomas C. D. C., *b.* 1984
1917	** *Colwyn (3rd),* (Ian) Anthony Hamilton-Smith, CBE, *b.* 1942, *s.* 1966, *m.*	Hon. Craig P. H.-S., *b.* 1968
1956	*Colyton (2nd),* Alisdair John Munro Hopkinson, *b.* 1958, *s.* 1996, *m.*	Hon. James P. M. H., *b.* 1983
1841	*Congleton (8th),* Christopher Patrick Parnell, *b.* 1930, *s.* 1967, *m.*	Hon. John P. C. P., *b.* 1959
1927	*Cornwallis (3rd),* Fiennes Neil Wykeham Cornwallis, OBE, *b.* 1921, *s.* 1982, *m.*	Hon. F. W. Jeremy C., *b.* 1946
1874	*Cottesloe (5th),*John Tapling Fremantle, *b.* 1927, *s.* 1994, *m.*	Hon. Thomas F. H. F., *b.* 1966
1929	*Craigmyle (4th),* Thomas Columba Shaw, *b.* 1960, *s.* 1998, *m.*	Hon. Alexander F. S., *b.* 1988
1899	*Cranworth (3rd),* Philip Bertram Gurdon, *b.* 1940, *s.* 1964, *m.*	Hon. Sacha W. R. G., *b.* 1970
1959	** *Crathorne (2nd),* Charles James Dugdale, *b.* 1939, *s.* 1977, *m.*	Hon. Thomas A. J. D., *b.* 1977
1892	*Crawshaw (5th),* David Gerald Brooks, *b.* 1934, *s.* 1997, *m.*	Hon. John P. B., *b.* 1938
1940	*Croft (3rd),* Bernard William Henry Page Croft, *b.* 1949, *s.* 1997, *m.*	None
1797 I.	*Crofton (8th),* Edward Harry Piers Crofton, *b.* 1988, *s.* 2007	Hon. Charles M. G. C., *b.* 1988
1375	*Cromwell (7th),* Godfrey John Bewicke-Copley, *b.* 1960, *s.* 1982, *m.*	Hon. David G. B.-C., *b.* 1997
1947	*Crook (3rd),* Robert Douglas Edwin Crook, *b.* 1955, *s.* 2001, *m.*	Hon. Matthew R. C., *b.* 1990
1920	*Cullen of Ashbourne (3rd),* Edmund Willoughby Marsham Cokayne, *b.* 1916, *s.* 2000, *w.*	(Hon.) John O'B. M. C., *b.*1920
1914	*Cunliffe (3rd),* Roger Cunliffe, *b.* 1932, *s.* 1963, *m.*	Hon. Henry C., *b.* 1962
1332	*Darcy de Knayth (19th),* Caspar David Ingrams, *b.* 1962, *s.* 2008, *m.*	Hon. Thomas R. I., *b.* 1999
1927	*Daresbury (4th),* Peter Gilbert Greenall, *b.* 1953, *s.* 1996, *m.*	Hon. Thomas E. G., *b.* 1984
1924	*Darling (3rd),* (Robert) Julian Henry Darling, *b.* 1944, *s.* 2003, *m.*	Hon. Robert J. C. D., *b.* 1972
1946	*Darwen (3rd),* Roger Michael Davies, *b.* 1938, *s.* 1988, *m.*	Hon. Paul D., *b.* 1962
1932	*Davies (3rd),* David Davies, *b.* 1940, *s.* 1944, *m.*	Hon. David D. D., *b.* 1975
1812 I.	*Decies (7th),* Marcus Hugh Tristram de la Poer Beresford, *b.* 1948, *s.* 1992, *m.*	Hon. Robert M. D. de la P. B., *b.* 1988
1299	*de Clifford (27th),* John Edward Southwell Russell, *b.* 1928, *s.* 1982, *m.*	Hon. William S. R., *b.* 1930
1851	*De Freyne (7th),* Francis Arthur John French, *b.* 1927, *s.* 1935, *m.*	Hon. Fulke C. A. J. F., *b.* 1957
1821	*Delamere (5th),* Hugh George Cholmondeley, *b.* 1934, *s.* 1979, *m*	Hon. Thomas P. G. C., *b.* 1968
1838	** *de Mauley (7th),* Rupert Charles Ponsonby, *b.* 1957, *s.* 2002, *m.*	Ashley G. P., *b.* 1959
1937	** *Denham (2nd),* Bertram Stanley Mitford Bowyer, KBE, PC, *b.* 1927, *s.* 1948, *m.*	Hon. Richard G. G. B., *b.* 1959
1834	*Denman (5th),* Charles Spencer Denman, CBE, MC, TD, *b.* 1916, *s.* 1971, *w.*	Hon. Richard T. S. D., *b.* 1946
1887	*De Ramsey (4th),* John Ailwyn Fellowes, *b.* 1942, *s.* 1993, *m.*	Hon. Freddie J. F., *b.* 1978
1264	*de Ros (28th),* Peter Trevor Maxwell, *b.* 1958, *s.* 1983, *m. Premier Baron of England*	Hon. Finbar J. M., *b.* 1988
1881	*Derwent (5th),* Robin Evelyn Leo Vanden-Bempde-Johnstone, LVO, *b.* 1930, *s.* 1986, *m.*	Hon. Francis P. H. V.-B.-J., *b.* 1965
1831	*de Saumarez (7th),* Eric Douglas Saumarez, *b.* 1956, *s.* 1991, *m.*	Hon. Victor T. S., *b.* 1956
1910	*de Villiers (4th),* Alexander Charles de Villiers, *b.* 1940, *s.* 2001, *m.*	None
1930	*Dickinson (2nd),* Richard Clavering Hyett Dickinson, *b.* 1926, *s.* 1943, *m.*	Hon. Martin H. D., *b.* 1961
1620 I.	*Digby (12th) and Digby (5th) (1765),* Edward Henry Kenelm Digby, KCVO, *b.* 1924, *s.* 1964, *m.*	Hon. Henry N. K. D., *b.* 1954
1615	*Dormer (17th),* Geoffrey Henry Dormer, *b.* 1920, *s.* 1995, *m.*	Hon. William R. D., *b.* 1960
1943	*Dowding (3rd),* Piers Hugh Tremenheere Dowding, *b.* 1948, *s.* 1992	Hon. Mark D. J. D., *b.* 1949
1439	*Dudley (15th),* Jim Anthony Hill Wallace, *b.* 1930, *s.* 2002, *m.*	Hon. Jeremy W. G. W., *b.* 1964
1800 I.	*Dufferin and Clandeboye (11th),* John Francis Blackwood, *b.* 1944, *s.* 1991 (claim to the peerage not yet established), *m.*	*Hon.* Francis S. B., *b.* 1979
1929	*Dulverton (3rd),* (Gilbert) Michael Hamilton Wills, *b.* 1944, *s.* 1992, *m.*	Hon. Robert A. H. W., *b.* 1983
1800 I.	*Dunalley (7th),* Henry Francis Cornelius Prittie, *b.* 1948, *s.* 1992, *m.*	Hon. Joel H. P., *b.* 1981
1324 I.	*Dunboyne (29th),* John Fitzwalter Butler, *b.* 1951, *s.* 2004, *m.*	Hon. Richard P. T. B., *b.* 1983
1892	*Dunleath (6th),* Brian Henry Mulholland, *b.* 1950, *s.* 1997, *m.*	Hon. Andrew H. M., *b.* 1981
1439 I.	*Dunsany (20th),* Edward John Carlos Plunkett, *b.* 1939, *s.* 1999, *m.*	Hon. Randal P., *b.* 1983

1780		*Dynevor (10th)*, Hugo Griffith Uryan Rhys, *b.* 1966, *s.* 2008	Robert D. A. R., *b.* 1963
1963		*Egremont (2nd) and Leconfield (7th) (1859)*, John Max Henry Scawen Wyndham, *b.* 1948, *s.* 1972, *m.*	Hon. George R. V. W., *b.* 1983
1643		*Elibank (14th)*, Alan D'Ardis Erskine-Murray, *b.* 1923, *s.* 1973, *w.*	Master of Elibank, *b.* 1964
1802		*Ellenborough (8th)*, Richard Edward Cecil Law, *b.* 1926, *s.* 1945, *m.*	Maj. Hon. Rupert E. H. L., *b.* 1955
1509 S.		*Elphinstone (19th) and Elphinstone (5th) (1885)*, Alexander Mountstuart Elphinstone, *b.* 1980, *s.* 1994, *m.*	Hon. Angus J. E., *b.* 1982
1934	**	*Elton (2nd)*, Rodney Elton, TD, *b.* 1930, *s.* 1973, *m.*	Hon. Edward P. E., *b.* 1966
1627 S.		*Fairfax of Cameron (14th)*, Nicholas John Albert Fairfax, *b.* 1956, *s.* 1964, *m.*	Hon. Edward N. T. F., *b.* 1984
1961		*Fairhaven (3rd)*, Ailwyn Henry George Broughton, *b.* 1936, *s.* 1973, *m.*	Maj. Hon. James H. A. B., *b.* 1963
1916		*Faringdon (3rd)*, Charles Michael Henderson, KCVO, *b.* 1937, *s.* 1977, *m.*	Hon. James H. H., *b.* 1961
1756 I.		*Farnham (13th)*, Simon Kenlis Maxwell, *b.* 1933, *s.* 2001, *m.*	Hon. Robin S. M., *b.* 1965
1856 I.		*Fermoy (6th)*, Patrick Maurice Burke Roche, *b.* 1967, *s.* 1984, *m.*	Hon. E. Hugh B. R., *b.* 1972
1826		*Feversham (7th)*, Jasper Orlando Slingsby Duncombe, *b.* 1968, *s.* 2009	Hon. Jake B. D., *b.* 1972
1798 I.		*ffrench (8th)*, Robuck John Peter Charles Mario ffrench, *b.* 1956, *s.* 1986, *m.*	Hon. John C. M. J. F. ff., *b.* 1928
1909		*Fisher (3rd)*, John Vavasseur Fisher, DSC, *b.* 1921, *s.* 1955, *m.*	Hon. Patrick V. F., *b.* 1953
1295		*Fitzwalter (22nd)*, Julian Brook Plumptre, *b.* 1952, *s.* 2004, *m.*	Hon. Edward B. P., *b.* 1989
1776		*Foley (8th)*, Adrian Gerald Foley, *b.* 1923, *s.* 1927, *m.*	Hon. Thomas H. F., *b.* 1961
1445		*Forbes (22nd)*, Nigel Ivan Forbes, KBE, *b.* 1918, *s.* 1953, *m. Premier Lord of Scotland*	Master of Forbes, *b.* 1946
1821		*Forester (9th)*, Charles Richard George Weld-Forester, *b.* 1975, *s.* 2004,	Wolstan W. W.-F., *b.* 1941
1922		*Forres (4th)*, Alastair Stephen Grant Williamson, *b.* 1946, *s.* 1978, *m.*	Hon. George A. M. W., *b.* 1972
1917		*Forteviot (4th)*, John James Evelyn Dewar, *b.* 1938, *s.* 1993, *w.*	Hon. Alexander J. E. D., *b.* 1971
1951	**	*Freyberg (3rd)*, Valerian Bernard Freyberg, *b.* 1970, *s.* 1993	Hon. Joseph J. F., *b.* 2007
1917		*Gainford (3rd)*, Joseph Edward Pease, *b.* 1921, *s.* 1971, *m.*	Hon. George P., *b.* 1926
1818 I.		*Garvagh (5th)*, (Alexander Leopold Ivor) George Canning, *b.* 1920, *s.* 1956, *m.*	Hon. Spencer G. S. de R. C., *b.* 1953
1942	**	*Geddes (3rd)*, Euan Michael Ross Geddes, *b.* 1937, *s.* 1975, *m.*	Hon. James G. N. G., *b.* 1969
1876		*Gerard (5th)*, Anthony Robert Hugo Gerard, *b.* 1949, *s.* 1992, *m.*	Hon. Rupert B. C. G., *b.* 1981
1824		*Gifford (6th)*, Anthony Maurice Gifford, *b.* 1940, *s.* 1961, *m.*	Hon. Thomas A. G., *b.* 1967
1917		*Gisborough (3rd)*, Thomas Richard John Long Chaloner, *b.* 1927, *s.* 1951, *m.*	Hon. T. Peregrine L. C., *b.* 1961
1960		*Gladwyn (2nd)*, Miles Alvery Gladwyn Jebb, *b.* 1930, *s.* 1996	None
1899		*Glanusk (5th)*, Christopher Russell Bailey, *b.* 1942, *s.* 1997, *m.*	Hon. Charles H. B., *b.* 1976
1918	**	*Glenarthur (4th)*, Simon Mark Arthur, *b.* 1944, *s.* 1976, *m.*	Hon. Edward A. A., *b.* 1973
1911		*Glenconner (3rd)*, Colin Christopher Paget Tennant, *b.* 1926, *s.* 1983, *m.*	Cody C. E. T., *b.* 1994
1964		*Glendevon (2nd)*, Julian John Somerset Hope, *b.* 1950, *s.* 1996	Hon. Jonathan C. H., *b.* 1952
1922		*Glendyne (4th)*, John, *b.* 1960, *s.* 2008	None
1939	**	*Glentoran (3rd)*, (Thomas) Robin (Valerian) Dixon, CBE, *b.* 1935, *s.* 1995, *m.*	Hon. Daniel G. D., *b.* 1959
1909		*Gorell (5th)*, John Picton Gorell Barnes, *b.* 1959, *s.* 2007, *m.*	Hon. Oliver G. B., *b.* 1993
1953	**	*Grantchester (3rd)*, Christopher John Suenson-Taylor, *b.* 1951, *s.* 1995, *m.*	Hon. Jesse D. S.-T., *b.* 1977
1782		*Grantley (8th)*, Richard William Brinsley Norton, *b.* 1956, *s.* 1995	Hon. Francis J. H. N., *b.* 1960
1794 I.		*Graves (10th)*, Timothy Evelyn Graves, *b.* 1960, *s.* 2002	None
1445 S.		*Gray (23rd)*, Andrew Godfrey Diarmid Stuart Campbell-Gray, *b.* 1964, *s.* 2003, *m.*	Master of Gray, *b.* 1996
1950		*Greenhill (3rd)*, Malcolm Greenhill, *b.* 1924, *s.* 1989	None
1927	**	*Greenway (4th)*, Ambrose Charles Drexel Greenway, *b.* 1941, *s.* 1975, *m.*	Hon. Nigel. P. G., *b.* 1944
1902		*Grenfell (3rd) and Grenfell of Kilvey (life peerage, 2000)*, Julian Pascoe Francis St Leger Grenfell, *b.* 1935, *s.* 1976, *m.*	Francis P. J. G., *b.* 1938
1944		*Gretton (4th)*, John Lysander Gretton, *b.* 1975, *s.* 1989	Hon. John F. B. G., *b.* 2008
1397		*Grey of Codnor (6th)*, Richard Henry Cornwall-Legh, *b.* 1936, *s.* 1996, *m.*	Hon. Richard S. C. C.-L., *b.* 1976
1955		*Gridley (3rd)*, Richard David Arnold Gridley, *b.* 1956, *s.* 1996, *m.*	Peter A. C. G., *b.* 1940
1964		*Grimston of Westbury (3rd)*, Robert John Sylvester Grimston, *b.* 1951, *s.* 2003, *m.*	Hon. Gerald C. W. G., *b.* 1953
1886		*Grimthorpe (5th)*, Edward John Beckett, *b.* 1954, *s.* 2003, *m.*	Hon. Harry M. B., *b.* 1993
1945		*Hacking (3rd)*, Douglas David Hacking, *b.* 1938, *s.* 1971, *m.*	Hon. Douglas F. H., *b.* 1968
1950		*Haden-Guest (5th)*, Christopher Haden-Guest, *b.* 1948, *s.* 1996, *m.*	Hon. Nicholas H.-G., *b.* 1951

1886		*Hamilton of Dalzell (5th),* Gavin Goulburn Hamilton, *b.* 1968, *s.* 2006, *m.*	Hon. Robert P. H., *b.* 1971
1874		*Hampton (7th),* John Humphrey Arnott Pakington, *b.* 1964, *s.* 2003, *m.*	Hon. Charles R. C. P., *b.* 2005
1939		*Hankey (3rd),* Donald Robin Alers Hankey, *b.* 1938, *s.* 1996, *m.*	Hon. Alexander M. A. H., *b.* 1947
1958		*Harding of Petherton (2nd),* John Charles Harding, *b.* 1928, *s.* 1989, *m.*	Hon. William A. J. H., *b.* 1969
1910		*Hardinge of Penshurst (4th),* Julian Alexander Hardinge, *b.* 1945, *s.* 1997	Hon. Hugh F. H., *b.* 1948
1876		*Harlech (6th),* Francis David Ormsby-Gore, *b.* 1954, *s.* 1985, *m.*	Hon. Jasset D. C. O.-G., *b.* 1986
1939		*Harmsworth (3rd),* Thomas Harold Raymond Harmsworth, *b.* 1939, *s.* 1990, *m.*	Hon. Dominic M. E. H., *b.* 1973
1815		*Harris (8th),* Anthony Harris, *b.* 1942, *s.* 1996, *m.*	Rear-Adm. Michael G. T. H., *b.* 1941
1954		*Harvey of Tasburgh (2nd),* Peter Charles Oliver Harvey, *b.* 1921, *s.* 1968, *w.*	Charles J. G. H., *b.* 1951
1295		*Hastings (23rd),* Delaval Thomas Harold Astley, *b.* 1960, *s.* 2007, *m.*	Hon. Jacob A. A., *b.* 1991
1835		*Hatherton (8th),* Edward Charles Littleton, *b.* 1950, *s.* 1985, *m.*	Hon. Thomas E. L., *b.* 1977
1776		*Hawke (11th),* Edward George Hawke, TD, *b.* 1950, *s.* 1992, *m.*	Hon. William M. T. H., *b.* 1995
1927		*Hayter (4th),* George William Michael Chubb, *b.* 1943, *s.* 2003, *m.*	Hon. Thomas F. F. C., *b.*1986
1945		*Hazlerigg (3rd),* Arthur Grey Hazlerigg, *b.* 1951, *s.* 2002, *m.*	Hon. Arthur W. G. H. *b.* 1987
1943		*Hemingford (3rd),* (Dennis) Nicholas Herbert, *b.* 1934, *s.* 1982, *m.*	Hon. Christopher D. C. H., *b.* 1973
1906		*Hemphill (5th),* Peter Patrick Fitzroy Martyn Martyn-Hemphill, *b.* 1928, *s.* 1957, *m.*	Hon. Charles A. M. M.-H., *b.* 1954
1799 I.	**	*Henley (8th) and Northington (6th) (1885),* Oliver Michael Robert Eden, *b.* 1953, *s.* 1977, *m.*	Hon. John W. O. E., *b.* 1988
1800 I.		*Henniker (9th) and Hartismere (6th) (1866),* Mark Ian Philip Chandos Henniker-Major, *b.* 1947, *s.* 2004, *m.*	Hon. Edward G. M. H.-M., *b.* 1985
1461		*Herbert (19th),* David John Seyfried Herbert, *b.* 1952, *s.* 2002, *m.*	Hon. Oliver R. S. H., *b.* 1976
1935		*Hesketh (3rd),* Thomas Alexander Fermor-Hesketh, KBE, PC, *b.* 1950, *s.* 1955, *m.*	Hon. Frederick H. F.-H., *b.* 1988
1828		*Heytesbury (7th),* James William Holmes à Court, *b.* 1967, *s.* 2004, *m.*	Peter M. H.. H. à. C., *b.* 1968
1886		*Hindlip (6th),* Charles Henry Allsopp, *b.* 1940, *s.* 1993, *m.*	Hon. Henry W. A., *b.* 1973
1950		*Hives (3rd),* Matthew Peter Hives, *b.* 1971, *s.* 1997	Hon. Michael B. H., *b.* 1926
1912		*Hollenden (4th),* Ian Hampden Hope-Morley, *b.* 1946, *s.* 1999, *m*	Hon. Edward H.-M., *b.* 1981
1897		*Holm Patrick (4th),* Hans James David Hamilton, *b.* 1955, *s.* 1991, *m.*	Hon. Ion H. J. H., *b.* 1956
1797 I.		*Hotham (8th),* Henry Durand Hotham, *b.* 1940, *s.* 1967, *m.*	Hon. William B. H., *b.* 1972
1881		*Hothfield (6th),* Anthony Charles Sackville Tufton, *b.* 1939, *s.* 1991, *m.*	Hon. William S. T., *b.* 1977
1930		*Howard of Penrith (3rd),* Philip Esme Howard, *b.* 1945, *s.* 1999, *m.*	Hon. Thomas Philip H., *b.* 1974
1960		*Howick of Glendale (2nd),* Charles Evelyn Baring, *b.* 1937, *s.* 1973, *m.*	Hon. David E. C. B., *b.* 1975
1796 I.		*Huntingfield (7th),* Joshua Charles Vanneck, *b.* 1954, *s.* 1994, *m.*	Hon. Gerard C. A. V., *b.* 1985
1866	**	*Hylton (5th),* Raymond Hervey Jolliffe, *b.* 1932, *s.* 1967, *m.*	Hon. William H. M. J., *b.* 1967
1933		*Iliffe (3rd),* Robert Peter Richard Iliffe, *b.* 1944, *s.* 1996, *m.*	Hon. Edward R. I., *b.* 1968
1543 I.		*Inchiquin (18th),* Conor Myles John O'Brien, *b.* 1943, *s.* 1982, *m.*	Conor J. A. O'B., *b.* 1952
1962		*Inchyra (2nd),* Robert Charles Reneke Hoyer Millar, *b.* 1935, *s.* 1989, *m.*	Hon. C. James C. H. M., *b.* 1962
1964	**	*Inglewood (2nd),* (William) Richard Fletcher-Vane, *b.* 1951, *s.* 1989, *m.*	Hon. Henry W. F. F.-V., *b.* 1990
1919		*Inverforth (4th),* Andrew Peter Weir, *b.* 1966, *s.* 1982	Hon. Benjamin A. W., *b.* 1997
1941		*Ironside (2nd),* Edmund Oslac Ironside, *b.* 1924, *s.* 1959, *m*	Hon. Charles E. G. I., *b.* 1956
1952		*Jeffreys (3rd),* Christopher Henry Mark Jeffreys, *b.* 1957, *s.* 1986, *m.*	Hon. Arthur M. H. J., *b.* 1989
1906		*Joicey (5th),* James Michael Joicey, *b.* 1953, *s.* 1993, *m.*	Hon. William J. J., *b.* 1990
1937		*Kenilworth (4th),* (John) Randle Siddeley, *b.* 1954, *s.* 1981, *m.*	Hon. William R. J. S., *b.* 1992
1935		*Kennet (3rd),* William Aldus Thoby Young, *b.* 1957, *s.* 2009, *m.*	Hon. Archibald W. K. Y., *b.* 1992
1776 I.		*Kensington (8th) and Kensington (5th) (1886),* Hugh Ivor Edwardes, *b.* 1933, *s.* 1981, *m.*	Hon. W. Owen A. E., *b.* 1964
1951		*Kenswood (2nd),* John Michael Howard Whitfield, *b.* 1930, *s.* 1963, *m.*	Hon. Michael C. W., *b.* 1955
1788		*Kenyon (6th),* Lloyd Tyrell-Kenyon, *b.* 1947, *s.* 1993, *m.*	Hon. Lloyd N. T.-K., *b.* 1972
1947		*Kershaw (4th),* Edward John Kershaw, *b.* 1936, *s.* 1962, *m.*	Hon. John C. E. K., *b.* 1971
1943		*Keyes (3rd),* Charles William Packe Keyes, *b.* 1951, *s.* 2005, *m.*	Hon. (Leopold R.) J. K., *b.* 1956
1909		*Kilbracken (4th),* Christopher John Godley, *b.* 1945, *s.* 2006, *m.*	Hon. James J. G., *b.* 1972
1900		*Killanin (4th),* (George) Redmond Fitzpatrick Morris, *b.* 1947, *s.* 1999, *m.*	Hon. Luke M. G. M., *b.* 1975
1943		*Killearn (3rd),* Victor Miles George Aldous Lampson, *b.* 1941, *s.* 1996, *m.*	Hon. Miles H. M. L., *b.* 1977
1789 I.		*Kilmaine (7th),* John David Henry Browne, *b.* 1948, *s.* 1978, *m.*	Hon. John F. S. B., *b.* 1983

1831	*Kilmarnock (8th),* Dr Robin Jordan Boyd, *b.* 1941, *s.* 2009, *m.*	Hon. Simon J. B., *b.* 1978
1941	*Kindersley (3rd),* Robert Hugh Molesworth Kindersley, *b.* 1929, *s.* 1976, *m.*	Hon. Rupert J. M. K., *b.* 1955
1223 I.	*Kingsale (36th),* Nevinson Mark de Courcy, *b.* 1958, *s.* 2005, *m., Premier Baron of Ireland*	Joseph K. C. de C., *b.* 1955
1902	*Kinross (5th),* Christopher Patrick Balfour, *b.* 1949, *s.* 1985, *m.*	Hon. Alan I. B., *b.* 1978
1951	*Kirkwood (3rd),* David Harvie Kirkwood, PHD, *b.* 1931, *s.* 1970, *m.*	Hon. James S. K., *b.* 1937
1800 I.	*Langford (9th),* Col. Geoffrey Alexander Rowley-Conwy, OBE, *b.* 1912, *s.* 1953, *m.*	Hon. Owain G. R.-C., *b.* 1958
1942	*Latham (2nd),* Dominic Charles Latham, *b.* 1954, *s.* 1970	Anthony M. L., *b.* 1954
1431	*Latymer (9th),* Crispin James Alan Nevill Money-Coutts, *b.* 1955, *s.* 2003, *m.*	Hon. Drummond W. T. M.-C., *b.* 1986
1869	*Lawrence (5th),* David John Downer Lawrence, *b.* 1937, *s.* 1968	None
1947	*Layton (3rd),* Geoffrey Michael Layton, *b.* 1947, *s.* 1989, *m.*	Hon. David L., *b.* 1914
1839	*Leigh (6th),* Christopher Dudley Piers Leigh, *b.* 1960, *s.* 2003, *m.*	Hon. Rupert D. L., *b.* 1994
1962	*Leighton of St Mellons (3rd),* Robert William Henry Leighton Seager, *b.* 1955, *s.* 1998	Hon. Simon J. L. S., *b.* 1957
1797	*Lilford (8th),* Mark Vernon Powys, *b.* 1975, *s.* 2005	Robert C. L. P., *b.* 1930
1945	*Lindsay of Birker (3rd),* James Francis Lindsay, *b.* 1945, *s.* 1994, *m.*	Alexander S. L., *b.* 1940
1758 I.	*Lisle (9th),* (John) Nicholas Geoffrey Lysaght, *b.* 1960, *s.* 2003	Hon. David J. L., *b.* 1963
1850	*Londesborough (9th),* Richard John Denison, *b.* 1959, *s.* 1968, *m.*	Hon. James F. D., *b.* 1990
1541 I.	*Louth (16th),* Otway Michael James Oliver Plunkett, *b.* 1929, *s.* 1950, *m.*	Hon. Jonathan O. P., *b.* 1952
1458 S.	*Lovat (16th) and Lovat (5th),* Simon Fraser, *b.* 1977, *s.* 1995	Hon. Jack F., *b.* 1984
1946	*Lucas of Chilworth (3rd),* Simon William Lucas, *b.* 1957, *s.* 2001, *m.*	Hon. John R. M. L., *b.* 1995
1663	** *Lucas (11th) and Dingwall (14th) (S. 1609),* Ralph Matthew Palmer, *b.* 1951, *s.* 1991	Hon. Lewis E. P., *b.* 1987
1929	** *Luke (3rd),* Arthur Charles St John Lawson-Johnston, *b.* 1933, *s.* 1996, *m.*	Hon. Ian J. St J. L.-J., *b.* 1963
1914	** *Lyell (3rd),* Charles Lyell, *b.* 1939, *s.* 1943	None
1859	*Lyveden (7th),* Jack Leslie Vernon, *b.* 1938, *s.* 1999, *m.*	Hon. Colin R. V., *b.* 1967
1959	*MacAndrew (3rd),* Christopher Anthony Colin MacAndrew, *b.* 1945, *s.* 1989, *m.*	Hon. Oliver C. J. M., *b.* 1983
1776 I.	*Macdonald (8th),* Godfrey James Macdonald of Macdonald, *b.* 1947, *s.* 1970, *m.*	Hon. Godfrey E. H. T. M., *b.* 1982
1937	*McGowan (4th),* Harry John Charles McGowan, *b.* 1971, *s.* 2003, *m.*	Hon. Dominic J. W. McG., *b.* 1951
1922	*Maclay (3rd),* Joseph Paton Maclay, *b.* 1942, *s.* 1969, *m.*	Hon. Joseph P. M., *b.* 1977
1955	*McNair (3rd),* Duncan James McNair, *b.* 1947, *s.* 1989, *m.*	Hon. William S. A. M., *b.* 1958
1951	*Macpherson of Drumochter (3rd),* James Anthony Macpherson, *b.* 1978, *s.* 2008	None
1937	** *Mancroft (3rd),* Benjamin Lloyd Stormont Mancroft, *b.* 1957, *s.* 1987, *m.*	Hon. Arthur L. S. M., *b.* 1995
1807	*Manners (6th),* John Hugh Robert Manners, *b.* 1956, *s.* 2008	Hon. Richard N. M., *b.* 1924
1922	*Manton (4th),* Miles Ronald Marcus Watson, *b.* 1958, *s.* 2003, *m.*	Hon. Thomas N. C. D. W., *b.* 1985
1908	*Marchamley (4th),* William Francis Whiteley, *b.* 1968, *s.* 1994	None
1964	*Margadale (3rd),* Alastair John Morrison, *b.* 1958, *s.* 2003, *m.*	Hon. Declan J. M., *b.* 1993
1961	*Marks of Broughton (3rd),* Simon Richard Marks, *b.* 1950, *s.* 1998, *m.*	Hon. Michael M., *b.* 1989
1964	*Martonmere (2nd),* John Stephen Robinson, *b.* 1963, *s.* 1989	Hon. James I. R., *b.* 2003
1776 I.	*Massy (10th),* David Hamon Somerset Massy, *b.* 1947, *s.* 1995	Hon. John H. M., *b.* 1950
1935	*May (4th),* Jasper Bertram St John May, *b.* 1965, *s.* 2006	None
1928	*Melchett (4th),* Peter Robert Henry Mond, *b.* 1948, *s.* 1973	None
1925	*Merrivale (4th),* Derek John Philip Duke, *b.* 1948, *s.* 2007, *m.*	Hon. Thomas D., *b.* 1980
1911	*Merthyr,* Trevor Oswin Lewis, CBE, *b.* 1935, *s.* 1977, *m.* Disclaimed for life 1977	David T. L., *b.* 1977
1919	*Meston (3rd),* James Meston, *b.* 1950, *s.* 1984, *m.*	Hon. Thomas J. D. M., *b.* 1977
1838	** *Methuen (7th),* Robert Alexander Holt Methuen, *b.* 1931, *s.* 1994, *m.*	James P. A. M.-C., *b.* 1952
1711	*Middleton (12th),* (Digby) Michael Godfrey John Willoughby, MC, *b.* 1921, *s.* 1970	Hon. Michael C. J. W., *b.* 1948
1939	*Milford (4th),* Guy Wogan Philipps, *b.* 1961, *s.* 1999, *m.*	Hon. Archie S. P., *b.* 1997
1933	*Milne (3rd),* George Alexander Milne, *b.* 1941, *s.* 2005	Hon. Iain C. L. M., *b.* 1949
1951	*Milner of Leeds (3rd),* Richard James Milner, *b.* 1959, *s.* 2003, *m.*	None
1947	*Milverton (2nd), Revd* Fraser Arthur Richard Richards, *b.* 1930, *s.* 1978, *m.*	Hon. Michael H. R., *b.* 1936
1873	*Moncreiff (6th),* Rhoderick Harry Wellwood Moncreiff, *b.* 1954, *s.* 2002, *m.*	Hon. Harry J. W. M., *b.* 1986

1884		*Monk Bretton (3rd),* John Charles Dodson, *b.* 1924, *s.* 1933, *m.*	Hon. Christopher M. D., *b.* 1958
1885		*Monkswell (5th),* Gerard Collier, *b.* 1947, *s.* 1984, *m.*	Hon. James A. C., *b.* 1977
1728	**	*Monson (11th),* John Monson, *b.* 1932, *s.* 1958, *m.*	Hon. Nicholas J. M., *b.* 1955
1885	**	*Montagu of Beaulieu (3rd),* Edward John Barrington Douglas-Scott-Montagu, *b.* 1926, *s.* 1929, *m.*	Hon. Ralph D.-S.-M., *b.* 1961
1839		*Monteagle of Brandon (6th),* Gerald Spring Rice, *b.* 1926, *s.* 1946, *m.*	Hon. Charles J. S. R., *b.* 1953
1943	**	*Moran (2nd),* (Richard) John (McMoran) Wilson, KCMG, *b.* 1924, *s.* 1977, *m.*	Hon. James M. W., *b.* 1952
1918		*Morris (3rd),* Michael David Morris, *b.* 1937, *s.* 1975, *m.*	Hon. Thomas A. S. M., *b.* 1982
1950		*Morris of Kenwood (3rd),* Jonathan David Morris, *b.* 1968, *s.* 2004, *m.*	Hon. Benjamin J. M., *b.* 1998
1831		*Mostyn (6th),* Llewellyn Roger Lloyd-Mostyn, *b.* 1948, *s.* 2000, *m.*	Hon. Gregory P. R. L.-M., *b.* 1984
1933		*Mottistone (4th),* David Peter Seely, CBE, *b.* 1920, *s.* 1966, *m.*	Hon. Peter J. P. S., *b.* 1949
1945		*Mountevans (3rd),* Edward Patrick Broke Evans, *b.* 1943, *s.* 1974, *m.*	Hon. Jeffrey de C. R. E., *b.* 1948
1283		*Mowbray (27th), Segrave (28th) (1295) and Stourton (24th) (1448),* Edward William Stephen Stourton, *b.* 1953, *s.* 2006, *m.*	Hon. James C. P. S., *b.* 1991
1932		*Moyne (3rd),* Jonathan Bryan Guinness, *b.* 1930, *s.* 1992, *m.*	Hon. Jasper J. R. G., *b.* 1954
1929	**	*Moynihan (4th),* Colin Berkeley Moynihan, *b.* 1955, *s.* 1997, *m.*	Hon. Nicholas E. B. M., *b.* 1994
1781 I.		*Muskerry (9th),* Robert Fitzmaurice Deane, *b.* 1948, *s.* 1988, *m.*	Hon. Jonathan F. D., *b.* 1986
1627 S.		*Napier (14th) and Ettrick (5th) (1872),* Francis Nigel Napier, KCVO, *b.* 1930, *s.* 1954, *m.*	Master of Napier, *b.* 1962
1868		*Napier of Magdala (6th),* Robert Alan Napier, *b.* 1940, *s.* 1987, *m.*	Hon. James R. N., *b.* 1966
1940		*Nathan (3rd),* Rupert Harry Bernard Nathan, *b.* 1957, *s.* 2007, *m.*	None
1960		*Nelson of Stafford (4th),* Alistair William Henry Nelson, *b.* 1973, *s.* 2006	Hon. James J. N., *b.* 1947
1959		*Netherthorpe (3rd),* James Frederick Turner, *b.* 1964, *s.* 1982, *m.*	Hon. Andrew J. E. T., *b.* 1993
1946		*Newall (2nd),* Francis Storer Eaton Newall, *b.* 1930, *s.* 1963, *m.*	Hon. Richard H. E. N., *b.* 1961
1776 I.		*Newborough (8th),* Robert Vaughan Wynn, *b.* 1949, *s.* 1998, *m.*	Hon. Charles H. R. W., *b.* 1923
1892		*Newton (5th),* Richard Thomas Legh, *b.* 1950, *s.* 1992, *m.*	Hon. Piers R. L., *b.* 1979
1930		*Noel-Buxton (3rd),* Martin Connal Noel-Buxton, *b.* 1940, *s.* 1980, *m.*	Hon. Charles C. N.-B., *b.* 1975
1957		*Norrie (2nd),* (George) Willoughby Moke Norrie, *b.* 1936, *s.* 1977, *m.*	Hon. Mark W. J. N., *b.* 1972
1884	**	*Northbourne (5th),* Christopher George Walter James, *b.* 1926, *s.* 1982, *m.*	Hon. Charles W. H. J., *b.* 1960
1866	**	*Northbrook (6th),* Francis Thomas Baring, *b.* 1954, *s.* 1990, *m.*	To the Baronetcy, Peter B. *b.* 1939
1878		*Norton (8th),* James Nigel Arden Adderley, *b.* 1947, *s.* 1993, *m.*	Hon. Edward J. A. A., *b.* 1982
1906		*Nunburnholme (6th),* Stephen Charles Wilson, *b.* 1973, *s.* 2000	Hon. David M. W., *b.* 1954
1950		*Ogmore (3rd),* Morgan Rees-Williams, *b.* 1937, *s.* 2004, *m.*	Hon. Tudor D. R.-W., *b.* 1991
1870		*O'Hagan (4th),* Charles Towneley Strachey, *b.* 1945, *s.* 1961	Hon. Richard T. S., *b.* 1950
1868		*O'Neill (4th),* Raymond Arthur Clanaboy O'Neill, KCVO, TD, *b.* 1933, *s.* 1944, *m.*	Hon. Shane S. C. O'N., *b.* 1965
1836 I.		*Oranmore and Browne (5th) and Mereworth (3rd) (1926),* Dominick Geoffrey Thomas Browne, *b.* 1929, *s.* 2002	Hon. Martin M. D. B., *b.* 1931
1933	**	*Palmer (4th),* Adrian Bailie Nottage Palmer, *b.* 1951, *s.* 1990, *m.*	Hon. Hugo B. R. P., *b.* 1980
1914		*Parmoor (5th),* Michael Leonard Seddon Cripps, *b.* 1942, *s.* 2008, *m.*	Hon. Henry W. A. C., *b.* 1976
1937		*Pender (3rd),* John Willoughby Denison-Pender, *b.* 1933, *s.* 1965, *m.*	Hon. Henry J. R. D.-P., *b.* 1968
1866		*Penrhyn (7th),* Simon Douglas-Pennant, *b.* 1938, *s.* 2003, *m.*	Hon. Edward S. D.-P., *b.* 1966
1603		*Petre (18th),* John Patrick Lionel Petre, *b.* 1942, *s.* 1989, *m.*	Hon. Dominic W. P., *b.* 1966
1918		*Phillimore (5th),* Francis Stephen Phillimore, *b.* 1944, *s.* 1994, *m.*	Hon. Tristan A. S. P., *b.* 1977
1945		*Piercy (3rd),* James William Piercy, *b.* 1946, *s.* 1981	Hon. Mark E. P. P., *b.* 1953
1827		*Plunket (8th),* Robin Rathmore Plunket, *b.* 1925, *s.* 1975, *m.*	Hon. Shaun A. F. S. P., *b.* 1931
1831		*Poltimore (7th),* Mark Coplestone Bampfylde, *b.* 1957, *s.* 1978, *m.*	Hon. Henry A. W. B., *b.* 1985
1690 S.		*Polwarth (11th),* Andrew Walter Hepburne-Scott, *b.* 1947, *s.* 2005, *m.*	Master of Polwarth, *b.* 1973
1930		*Ponsonby of Shulbrede (4th) and Ponsonby of Roehampton (life peerage, 2000),* Frederick Matthew Thomas Ponsonby, *b.* 1958, *s.* 1990	None
1958		*Poole (2nd),* David Charles Poole, *b.* 1945, *s.* 1993, *m.*	Hon. Oliver J. P., *b.* 1972
1852		*Raglan (5th),* FitzRoy John Somerset, *b.* 1927, *s.* 1964	Hon. Geoffrey S., *b.* 1932
1932		*Rankeillour (5th),* Michael Richard Hope, *b.* 1940, *s.* 2005, *m.*	James F. H., *b.* 1968
1953		*Rathcavan (3rd),* Hugh Detmar Torrens O'Neill, *b.* 1939, *s.* 1994, *m.*	Hon. François H. N. O'N., *b.* 1984
1916		*Rathcreedan (3rd),* Christopher John Norton, *b.* 1949, *s.* 1990, *m.*	Hon. Adam G. N., *b.* 1952
1868 I.		*Rathdonnell (5th),* Thomas Benjamin McClintock-Bunbury, *b.* 1938, *s.* 1959, *m.*	Hon. William L. M.-B., *b.* 1966
1911		*Ravensdale (3rd),* Nicholas Mosley, MC, *b.* 1923, *s.* 1966, *m.*	Hon. Shaun N. M., *b.* 1949

1821	*Ravensworth (9th),* Thomas Arthur Hamish Liddell, *b.* 1954, *s.* 2004, *m.*	Hon. Henry A. T. L., *b.* 1987
1821	*Rayleigh (6th),* John Gerald Strutt, *b.* 1960, *s.* 1988, *m.*	Hon. John F. S., *b.* 1993
1937	** *Rea (3rd),* John Nicolas Rea, MD, *b.* 1928, *s.* 1981, *m.*	Hon. Matthew J. R., *b.* 1956
1628 S.	** *Reay (14th),* Hugh William Mackay, *b.* 1937, *s.* 1963, *m.*	Master of Reay, *b.* 1965
1902	*Redesdale (6th) and Mitford (life peerage 2000),* Rupert Bertram Mitford, *b.* 1967, *s.* 1991, *m.*	Hon. Bertram D. M., *b.* 2000
1940	*Reith,* Christopher John Reith, *b.* 1928, *s.* 1971, *m.* Disclaimed for life 1972.	Hon. James H. J. R., *b.* 1971
1928	*Remnant (3rd),* James Wogan Remnant, CVO, *b.* 1930, *s.* 1967, *m.*	Hon. Philip J. R., *b.* 1954
1806 I.	*Rendlesham (9th),* Charles William Brooke Thellusson, *b.* 1954, *s.* 1999, *m.*	Hon. Peter R. T., *b.* 1920
1933	*Rennell (4th),* James Roderick David Tremayne Rodd, *b.* 1978, *s.* 2006	None
1964	*Renwick (2nd),* Harry Andrew Renwick, *b.* 1935, *s.* 1973, *m.*	Hon. Robert J. R., *b.* 1966
1885	*Revelstoke (6th),* James Cecil Baring, *b.* 1938, *s.* 2003, *m.*	Hon. Alexander R. B., *b.* 1970
1905	*Ritchie of Dundee (6th),* Charles Rupert Rendall Ritchie, *b.* 1958, *s.* 2008, *m.*	Hon. Sebastian R., *b.* 2004
1935	*Riverdale (3rd),* Anthony Robert Balfour, *b.* 1960, *s.* 1998	Arthur M. B., *b.* 1938
1961	*Robertson of Oakridge (3rd),* William Brian Elworthy Robertson, *b.* 1975, *s.* 2009, *m.*	None
1938	*Roborough (3rd),* Henry Massey Lopes, *b.* 1940, *s.* 1992, *m.*	Hon. Massey J. H. L., *b.* 1969
1931	*Rochester (2nd),* Foster Charles Lowry Lamb, *b.* 1916, *s.* 1955, *w.*	Hon. David C. L., *b.* 1944
1934	*Rockley (3rd),* James Hugh Cecil, *b.* 1934, *s.* 1976, *m.*	Hon. Anthony R. C., *b.* 1961
1782	*Rodney (10th),* George Brydges Rodney, *b.* 1953, *s.* 1992, *m.*	Hon. John G. B. R., *b.* 1999
1651 S.	*Rollo (14th) and Dunning (5th) (1869),* David Eric Howard Rollo, *b.* 1943, *s.* 1997, *m.*	Master of Rollo, *b.* 1972
1959	*Rootes (3rd),* Nicholas Geoffrey Rootes, *b.* 1951, *s.* 1992, *m.*	William B. R., *b.* 1944
1796 I.	*Rossmore (7th) and Rossmore (6th) (1838),* William Warner Westenra, *b.* 1931, *s.* 1958, *m.*	Hon. Benedict W. W., *b.* 1983
1939	** *Rotherwick (3rd),* (Herbert) Robin Cayzer, *b.* 1954, *s.* 1996, *m.*	Hon. H. Robin C., *b.* 1989
1885	*Rothschild (4th),* (Nathaniel Charles) Jacob Rothschild, OM, GBE, *b.* 1936, *s.* 1990, *m.*	Hon. Nathaniel P. V. J. R., *b.* 1971
1911	*Rowallan (4th),* John Polson Cameron Corbett, *b.* 1947, *s.* 1993	Hon. Jason W. P. C. C., *b.* 1972
1947	*Rugby (3rd),* Robert Charles Maffey, *b.* 1951, *s.* 1990, *m.*	Hon. Timothy J. H. M., *b.* 1975
1919	*Russell of Liverpool (3rd),* Simon Gordon Jared Russell, *b.* 1952, *s.* 1981, *m.*	Hon. Edward C. S. R., *b.* 1985
1876	*Sackville (7th),* Robert Bertrand Sackville-West, *b.* 1958, *s.* 2004, *m.*	Hon. Arthur S-W., *b.* 2000
1964	*St Helens (2nd),* Richard Francis Hughes-Young, *b.* 1945, *s.* 1980, *m.*	Hon. Henry T. H.-Y., *b.* 1986
1559	** *St John of Bletso (21st),* Anthony Tudor St John, *b.* 1957, *s.* 1978, *m.*	Hon. Oliver B. St J., *b.* 1995
1887	*St Levan (4th),* John Francis Arthur St Aubyn, DSC, *b.* 1919, *s.* 1978, *w.*	James P. S. St. A., *b.* 1950
1885	*St Oswald (6th),* Charles Rowland Andrew Winn, *b.* 1959, *s.* 1999, *m.*	Hon. Rowland C. S. H. W., *b.* 1986
1960	*Sanderson of Ayot (2nd),* Alan Lindsay Sanderson, *b.* 1931, *s.* 1971, *m.* Disclaimed for life 1971.	Hon. Michael S., *b.* 1959
1945	*Sandford (3rd),* James John Mowbray Edmondson, *b.* 1949, *s.* 2009, *m.*	Hon. Devon J. E., *b.* 1986
1871	*Sandhurst (6th),* Guy Rees John Mansfield, *b.* 1949, *s.* 2002, *m.*	Hon. Edward J. M., *b.* 1982
1802	*Sandys (7th),* Richard Michael Oliver Hill, *b.* 1931, *s.* 1961, *m.*	The Marquess of Downshire
1888	*Savile (4th),* John Anthony Thornhill Lumley-Savile, *b.* 1947, *s.* 2008, *m.*	James G. A. L-S., *b.* 1975
1447	*Saye and Sele (21st),* Nathaniel Thomas Allen Fiennes, *b.* 1920, *s.* 1968, *m.*	Hon. Martin G. F., *b.* 1961
1826	*Seaford (6th),* Colin Humphrey Felton Ellis, *b.* 1946, *s.* 1999, *m.*	Hon. Benjamin F. T. E., *b.* 1976
1932	** *Selsdon (3rd),* Malcolm McEacharn Mitchell-Thomson, *b.* 1937, *s.* 1963, *m.*	Hon. Callum M. M. M.-T., *b.* 1969
1489 S.	*Sempill (21st),* James William Stuart Whitemore Sempill, *b.* 1949, *s.* 1995, *m.*	Master of Sempill, *b.* 1979
1916	*Shaughnessy (5th),* Charles George Patrick Shaughnessy, *b.* 1955, *s.* 2007, *m.*	David J. S., *b.* 1957
1946	*Shepherd (3rd),* Graham George Shepherd, *b.* 1949, *s.* 2001, *m.*	Hon. Patrick M. S., *b.* 19–
1964	*Sherfield (3rd),* Dwight William Makins, *b.* 1951, *s.* 2006, *m.*	None
1902	*Shuttleworth (5th),* Charles Geoffrey Nicholas Kay-Shuttleworth, *b.* 1948, *s.* 1975, *m.*	Hon. Thomas E. K.-S., *b.* 1976
1950	*Silkin (3rd),* Christopher Lewis Silkin, *b.* 1947, *s.* 2001. Disclaimed for life 2001	Rory L. S., *b.* 1954
1963	*Silsoe (3rd),* Simon Rupert Trustram Eve *b.* 1966, *s.* 2005	Hon. Peter N. T. E., *b.* 1930
1947	*Simon of Wythenshawe (3rd),* Matthew Simon, *b.* 1955, *s.* 2002	Martin S., *b.* 1944
1449 S.	*Sinclair (18th),* Matthew Murray Kennedy St Clair *b.* 1968, *s.* 2004, *m.*	Hugh A. C. St C., *b.* 1957

1957	*Sinclair of Cleeve (3rd),* John Lawrence Robert Sinclair, *b.* 1953, *s.* 1985	None
1919	*Sinha (6th),* Arup Kumar Sinha, *b.* 1966, *s.* 1999	Hon. Dilip K. S., *b.* 1967
1828	** *Skelmersdale (7th),* Roger Bootle-Wilbraham, *b.* 1945, *s.* 1973, *m.*	Hon. Andrew B.-W., *b.* 1977
1916	*Somerleyton (3rd),* Savile William Francis Crossley, GCVO, *b.* 1928, *s.* 1959, *m.*	Hon. Hugh F. S. C., *b.* 1971
1784	*Somers (9th),* Philip Sebastian Somers Cocks, *b.* 1948, *s.* 1995	Alan B. C., *b.* 1930
1780	*Southampton (6th),* Charles James FitzRoy, *b.* 1928, *s.* 1989, *m.*	Hon. Edward C. F., *b.* 1955
1959	*Spens (4th),* Patrick Nathaniel George Spens, *b.* 1968, *s.* 2001, *m.*	Hon. Peter L. S., *b.* 2000
1640	*Stafford (15th),* Francis Melfort William Fitzherbert, *b.* 1954, *s.* 1986, *m.*	Hon. Benjamin J. B. F., *b.* 1983
1938	*Stamp (4th),* Trevor Charles Bosworth Stamp, MD, *b.* 1935, *s.* 1987, *m.*	Hon. Nicholas C. T. S., *b.* 1978
1839	*Stanley of Alderley (8th), Sheffield (8th) (I. 1738) and Eddisbury (7th) (1848),* Thomas Henry Oliver Stanley, *b.* 1927, *s.* 1971, *m.*	Hon. Richard O. S., *b.* 1956
1318	** *Strabolgi (11th),* David Montague de Burgh Kenworthy, *b.* 1914, *s.* 1953, *m.*	Andrew D. W. K., *b.* 1967
1954	*Strang (2nd),* Colin Strang, *b.* 1922, *s.* 1978, *m.*	None
1628	*Strange (17th),* Adam Humphrey Drummond of Megginch, *b.* 1953, *s.* 2005 *m.*	Hon. John A. H. D. of M. *b.* 1992
1955	*Strathalmond (3rd),* William Roberton Fraser, *b.* 1947, *s.* 1976, *m.*	Hon. William G. F., *b.* 1976
1936	*Strathcarron (3rd),* Ian David Patrick Macpherson, *b.* 1949, *s.* 2006, *m.*	Hon. Rory D. A. M., *b.* 1982
1955	** *Strathclyde (2nd),* Thomas Galloway Dunlop du Roy de Blicquy Galbraith, PC, *b.* 1960, *s.* 1985, *m.*	Hon. Charles W. du R. de B. G., *b.* 1962
1900	*Strathcona and Mount Royal (4th),* Donald Euan Palmer Howard, *b.* 1923, *s.* 1959, *m.*	Hon. D. Alexander S. H., *b.* 1961
1836	*Stratheden (6th) and Campbell (6th) (1841),* Donald Campbell, *b.* 1934, *s.* 1987, *m.*	Hon. David A. C., *b.* 1963
1884	*Strathspey (6th),* James Patrick Trevor Grant of Grant, *b.* 1943, *s.* 1992, *m.*	Hon. Michael P. F. G., *b.* 1953
1838	*Sudeley (7th),* Merlin Charles Sainthill Hanbury-Tracy, *b.* 1939, *s.* 1941	D. Andrew J. H.-T., *b.* 1928
1786	*Suffield (11th),* Anthony Philip Harbord-Hamond, MC, *b.* 1922, *s.* 1951, *w.*	Hon. Charles A. A. H.-H., *b.* 1953
1893	*Swansea (5th),* Richard Anthony Hussey Vivian, *b.* 1957, *s.* 2005, *m.*	Hon. James H. H. V., *b.* 1999
1907	*Swaythling (5th),* Charles Edgar Samuel Montagu, *b.* 1954, *s.* 1998, *m.*	Hon. Anthony T. S. M., *b.* 1931
1919	** *Swinfen (3rd),* Roger Mynors Swinfen Eady, *b.* 1938, *s.* 1977, *m.*	Hon. Charles R. P. S. E., *b.* 1971
1935	*Sysonby (3rd),* John Frederick Ponsonby, *b.* 1945, *s.* 1956	None
1831 I.	*Talbot of Malahide (10th),* Reginald John Richard Arundell, *b.* 1931, *s.* 1987, *m.*	Hon. Richard J. T. A., *b.* 1957
1946	*Tedder (3rd),* Robin John Tedder, *b.* 1955, *s.* 1994, *m.*	Hon. Benjamin J. T., *b.* 1985
1884	*Tennyson (6th),* David Harold Alexander Tennyson, *b.* 1960, *s.* 2006	Alan J. D. T., *b.* 1965
1918	*Terrington (6th),* Christopher Richard James Woodhouse, MB, *b.* 1946, *s.* 2001, *m.*	Hon. Jack H. L. W., *b.* 1978
1940	*Teviot (2nd),* Charles John Kerr, *b.* 1934, *s.* 1968, *m.*	Hon. Charles R. K., *b.* 1971
1616	*Teynham (20th),* John Christopher Ingham Roper-Curzon, *b.* 1928, *s.* 1972, *m.*	Hon. David J. H. I. R.-C., *b.* 1965
1964	*Thomson of Fleet (3rd),* David Kenneth Roy Thomson, *b.* 1957, *s.* 2006, *m.*	Hon. Benjamin T., *b.* 2006
1792	*Thurlow (8th),* Francis Edward Hovell-Thurlow-Cumming-Bruce, KCMG, *b.* 1912, *s.* 1971, *w.*	Hon. Roualeyn R. H.-T.-C.-B., *b.* 1952
1876	*Tollemache (5th),* Timothy John Edward Tollemache, *b.* 1939, *s.* 1975, *m.*	Hon. Edward J. H. T., *b.* 1976
1564 S.	*Torphichen (15th),* James Andrew Douglas Sandilands, *b.* 1946, *s.* 1975, *m.*	Robert P. S., *b.* 1950
1947	** *Trefgarne (2nd),* David Garro Trefgarne, PC, *b.* 1941, *s.* 1960, *m.*	Hon. George G. T., *b.* 1970
1921	*Trevethin (4th) and Oaksey (2nd) (1947),* John Geoffrey Tristram Lawrence, OBE, *b.* 1929, *s.* 1971, *m.*	Hon. Patrick J. T. L., *b.* 1960
1880	*Trevor (5th),* Marke Charles Hill-Trevor, *b.* 1970, *s.* 1997, *m.*	Hon. Iain R. H.-T., *b.* 1971
1461 I.	*Trimlestown (21st),* Raymond Charles Barnewall, *b.* 1930, *s.* 1997	None
1940	*Tryon (3rd),* Anthony George Merrik Tryon, *b.* 1940, *s.* 1976	Hon. Charles G. B. T., *b.* 1976
1935	*Tweedsmuir (4th),* John William de l'Aigle (Toby) Buchan, *b.* 1950, *s.* 2008, *m.*	Hon. John A. G. B., *b.* 1986
1523	*Vaux of Harrowden (11th),* Anthony William Gilbey, *b.* 1940, *s.* 2002, *m.*	Hon. Richard H. G. G., *b.*1965
1800 I.	*Ventry (8th),* Andrew Wesley Daubeny de Moleyns, *b.* 1943, *s.* 1987, *m.*	Hon. Francis W. D. de M., *b.* 1965
1762	*Vernon (11th),* Anthony William Vernon-Harcourt, *b.* 1939, *s.* 2000, *m.*	Hon. Simon A. V-H., *b.* 1969
1922	*Vestey (3rd),* Samuel George Armstrong Vestey, KCVO, *b.* 1941, *s.* 1954, *m.*	Hon. William G. V., *b.* 1983

1841	*Vivian (7th),* Charles Crespigny Hussey Vivian, *b.* 1966, *s.* 2004	Hon. Victor A. R. B. V., *b.* 1940
1934	*Wakehurst (3rd),* (John) Christopher Loder, *b.* 1925, *s.* 1970, *m.*	Hon. Timothy W. L., *b.* 1958
1723	** *Walpole (10th) and Walpole of Wolterton (8th) (1756),* Robert Horatio Walpole, *b.* 1938, *s.* 1989, *m.*	Hon. Jonathan R. H. W., *b.* 1967
1780	*Walsingham (9th),* John de Grey, MC, *b.* 1925, *s.* 1965, *m.*	Hon. Robert de. G., *b.* 1969
1936	*Wardington (3rd),* William Simon Pease, *b.* 1925, *s.* 2005, *m.*	None
1792 I.	*Waterpark (7th),* Frederick Caryll Philip Cavendish, *b.* 1926, *s.* 1948, *m.*	Hon. Roderick A. C., *b.* 1959
1942	*Wedgwood (4th),* Piers Anthony Weymouth Wedgwood, *b.* 1954, *s.* 1970, *m.*	Antony J. W., *b.* 1944
1861	*Westbury (6th),* Richard Nicholas Bethell, MBE, *b.* 1950, *s.* 2001, *m.*	Hon. Alexander B., *b.* 1986
1944	*Westwood (3rd),* (William) Gavin Westwood, *b.* 1944, *s.* 1991, *m.*	Hon. W. Fergus W., *b.* 1972
1544/5	*Wharton (12th),* Myles Christopher David Robertson, *b.* 1964, *s.* 2000, *m.*	Hon. Christopher J. R., *b.* 1969
1935	*Wigram (2nd),* (George) Neville (Clive) Wigram, MC, *b.* 1915, *s.* 1960, *w.*	Maj. Hon. Andrew F. C. W., *b.* 1949
1491	** *Willoughby de Broke (21st),* Leopold David Verney, *b.* 1938, *s.* 1986, *m.*	Hon. Rupert G. V., *b.* 1966
1937	*Windlesham (3rd) and Hennessy (life peerage, 1999),* David James George Hennessy, CVO, PC, *b.* 1932, *s.* 1962, *w.*	Hon. James R. H., *b.* 1968
1951	*Wise (2nd),* John Clayton Wise, *b.* 1923, *s.* 1968, *m.*	Hon. Christopher J. C. W., *b.* 1949
1869	*Wolverton (7th),* Christopher Richard Glyn, *b.* 1938, *s.* 1988	Miles J. G., *b.* 1966
1928	*Wraxall (3rd),* Eustace Hubert Beilby Gibbs, KCVO, CMG, *b.* 1929, *s.* 2001, *m.*	Hon. Anthony H. G., *b.* 1958
1915	*Wrenbury (3rd),* Revd John Burton Buckley, *b.* 1927, *s.* 1940, *m.*	Hon. William E. B., *b.* 1966
1838	*Wrottesley (6th),* Clifton Hugh Lancelot de Verdon Wrottesley, *b.* 1968, *s.* 1977, *m.*	Hon. Victor E. F. de V. W., *b.* 2004
1829	*Wynford (9th),* John Philip Robert Best, *b.* 1950, *s.* 2002, *m.*	Hon. Harry R. F. B., *b.* 1987
1308	*Zouche (18th),* James Assheton Frankland, *b.* 1943, *s.* 1965, *m.*	Hon. William T. A. F., *b.* 1984

BARONESSES/LADIES IN THEIR OWN RIGHT

Style, The Rt. Hon. the Lady _ , *or* The Rt. Hon. the Baroness _ , according to her preference. Either style may be used, except in the case of Scottish titles (indicated by S.), which are not baronies (*see* page 44) and whose holders are always addressed as Lady.

Envelope, may be addressed in same way as a Baron's wife or, if she prefers *(formal),* The Rt. Hon. the Baroness _; *(social),* The Baroness _. Otherwise as for a Baron's wife

Husband, Untitled

Children's style, As for children of a Baron

Created	*Title, order of succession, name, etc*	*Heir*
1664	*Arlington,* Jennifer Jane Forwood, *b.* 1939, *s.* 1999, *w.* Title called out of abeyance 1999	Hon. Patrick J. D. F., *b.* 1967
1455	*Berners (16th),* Pamela Vivien Kirkham, *b.* 1929, *s.* 1995, *m.*	Hon. Rupert W. T. K., *b.* 1953
1529	*Braye (8th),* Mary Penelope Aubrey-Fletcher, *b.* 1941, *s.* 1985, *m.*	Two co-heirs
1321	*Dacre (27th),* Rachel Leila Douglas-Home, *b.* 1929, *s.* 1970, *w.*	Hon. James T. A. D.-H., *b.* 1952
1490 S.	*Herries of Terregles (14th),* Anne Elizabeth Fitzalan-Howard, *b.* 1938, *s.* 1975, *w.*	Lady Mary Mumford, *b.* 1940
1597	*Howard de Walden (10th),* Mary Hazel Caridwen Czernin, *b.* 1935, *s.* 2004, *m.* Title called out of abeyance 2004	Hon. Peter J. J. C. *b.* 1966
1602 S.	*Kinloss (12th),* Beatrice Mary Grenville Freeman-Grenville, *b.* 1922, *s.* 1944, *w.*	Master of Kinloss, *b.* 1953
1445 S.	** *Saltoun (20th),* Flora Marjory Fraser, *b.* 1930, *s.* 1979, *w.*	Hon. Katharine I. M. I. F., *b.* 1957
1313	*Willoughby de Eresby (27th),* (Nancy) Jane Marie Heathcote-Drummond-Willoughby, *b.* 1934, *s.* 1983	Two co-heirs

LIFE PEERS

Style, The Rt. Hon. the Lord _ /The Rt. Hon. the Lady _ , *or* The Rt. Hon. the Baroness _ , according to her preference
Envelope (formal), The Rt. Hon. Lord _/Lady_/ Baroness_; *(social),* The Lord _/Lady_/Baroness_
Letter (formal), My Lord/Lady; *(social),* Dear Lord/ Lady _. *Spoken,* Lord/Lady _
Wife's style, The Rt. Hon. the Lady _
Husband, Untitled
Children's style, 'The Hon.' before forename (F_) and surname (S_)
Envelope, The Hon. F_ S_. *Letter,* Dear Mr/Miss/Mrs S_. *Spoken,* Mr/Miss/Mrs S_

NEW LIFE PEERAGES

1 September 2008 to 31 August 2009:
Susan Catherine Campbell, CBE; Stephen Andrew Carter, CBE; Sir Anthony Peter Clarke, PC; Sir Lawrence Antony Collins, PC; Evan Mervyn Davies, CBE; David Anthony Freud; Sir Igor Judge, PC; Sir Brian Francis Kerr, PC; Lady Glenys Elizabeth Kinnock; Peter Benjamin Mandelson, PC; Michael Martin, PC; Paul Myners, CBE; Dame Nuala Patricia O'Loan, DBE; David Philip Pannick, QC; Sir Jonathan Henry Sacks; Sir Alan Michael Sugar

SYMBOLS
* Hereditary peer who has been granted a life peerage. For further details, please refer to the Hereditary Peers section. For example, life peer *Balniel* can be found under his hereditary title *Earl of Crawford and Balcarres*
§ Justices of the Supreme Court currently disqualified from sitting or voting in the House of Lords until they retire from the supreme court. For further information see Law Courts and Offices
† Title not confirmed at time of going to press

CREATED UNDER THE APPELLATE JURISDICTION ACT 1876 (AS AMENDED)

BARONS
Created
2004 §*Brown of Eaton-under-Heywood,* Simon Denis Brown, PC, *b.* 1937, *m.*
1991 *Browne-Wilkinson,* Nicolas Christopher Henry Browne-Wilkinson, PC, *b.* 1930, *m.*
2004 *Carswell,* Robert Douglas Carswell, PC, *b.* 1934, *m.*
2009 §*Collins of Mapesbury,* Lawrence Antony Collins, PC, *b.* 1941
1986 *Goff of Chieveley,* Robert Lionel Archibald Goff, PC, *b.* 1926, *m.*
1985 *Griffiths,* (William) Hugh Griffiths, MC, PC, *b.* 1923, *m.*
1995 *Hoffmann,* Leonard Hubert Hoffmann, PC, *b.* 1934, *m.*
1997 *Hutton,* (James) Brian (Edward) Hutton, PC, *b.* 1931, *m.*
2009 §*Kerr of Tonaghmore,* Brian Francis Kerr, PC, *b.* 1948, *m.*
1993 *Lloyd of Berwick,* Anthony John Leslie Lloyd, PC, *b.* 1929, *m.*
2005 §*Mance,* Jonathan Hugh Mance, PC, *b.* 1943, *m.*
1998 *Millett,* Peter Julian Millett, PC, *b.* 1932, *m.*
1992 *Mustill,* Michael John Mustill, PC, *b.* 1931, *m.*
2007 *Neuberger of Abbotsbury,* David Edmond Neuberger, PC, *b.* 1948, *m., Master of the Rolls*
1994 *Nicholls of Birkenhead,* Donald James Nicholls, PC, *b.* 1933, *m.*
1999 §*Phillips of Worth Matravers,* Nicholas Addison Phillips, b. 1938, *m.*
1997 §*Saville of Newdigate,* Mark Oliver Saville, PC, *b.* 1936, *m.*
2000 *Scott of Foscote,* Richard Rashleigh Folliott Scott, PC, *b.* 1934, *m.*
1995 *Steyn,* Johan van Zyl Steyn, PC, *b.* 1932, *m.*
1982 *Templeman,* Sydney William Templeman, MBE, PC, *b.* 1920, *w.*
2003 §*Walker of Gestingthorpe,* Robert Walker, PC, *b.* 1938, *m.*
1992 *Woolf,* Harry Kenneth Woolf, PC, *b.* 1933, *m.*

BARONESSES
2004 §*Hale of Richmond,* Brenda Marjorie Hale, DBE, PC, *b.* 1945, *m.*

CREATED UNDER THE LIFE PEERAGES ACT 1958

BARONS
Created
2000 **Acton of Bridgnorth,* Lord Acton, *b.* 1941, *m.* (*see* Hereditary Peers)
2001 *Adebowale,* Victor Olufemi Adebowale, CBE, *b.* 1962
2005 *Adonis,* Andrew Adonis, PC, *b.* 1963, *m.*
1998 *Ahmed,* Nazir Ahmed, *b.* 1957, *m.*
1996 *Alderdice,* John Thomas Alderdice, *b.* 1955, *m.*
1998 *Alli,* Waheed Alli, *b.* 1964
2004 *Alliance,* David Alliance, CBE, *b.* 1932
1997 *Alton of Liverpool,* David Patrick Paul Alton, *b.* 1951, *m.*
2005 *Anderson of Swansea,* Donald Anderson, PC, *b.* 1939, *m.*
1992 *Archer of Sandwell,* Peter Kingsley Archer, PC, QC, *b.* 1926, *m.*
1992 *Archer of Weston-super-Mare,* Jeffrey Howard Archer, *b.* 1940, *m.*
1988 *Armstrong of Ilminster,* Robert Temple Armstrong, GCB, CVO, *b.* 1927, *m.*
1999 **Armstrong-Jones,* Earl of Snowdon, GCVO, *b.* 1930, *m.* (*see* Hereditary Peers)
2000 *Ashcroft,* Michael Anthony Ashcroft, KCMG,
2001 *Ashdown of Norton-sub-Hamdon,* Jeremy John Durham (Paddy) Ashdown, GCMG, KBE, PC, *b.* 1941, *m.*
1992 *Ashley of Stoke,* Jack Ashley, CH, PC, *b.* 1922, *w.*

1993 *Attenborough,* Richard Samuel Attenborough, CBE, *b.* 1923, *m.*
1998 *Bach,* William Stephen Goulden Bach, *b.* 1946, *m.*
1997 *Bagri,* Raj Kumar Bagri, CBE, *b.* 1930, *m.*
1997 *Baker of Dorking,* Kenneth Wilfred Baker, CH, PC, *b.* 1934, *m.*
2004 *Ballyedmond,* Dr Edward Haughey, OBE, *b.* 1944, *m.*
1974 **Balniel,* The Earl of Crawford and Balcarres, *b.* 1927, *m.* (*see* Hereditary Peers)
1992 *Barber of Tewkesbury,* Derek Coates Barber, *b.* 1918, *m.*
1983 *Barnett,* Joel Barnett, PC, *b.* 1923, *m.*
1997 *Bassam of Brighton,* (John) Steven Bassam, PC, *b.* 1953
2008 *Bates,* Michael Walton Bates, *b.* 1961
1998 *Bell,* Timothy John Leigh Bell, *b.* 1941, *m.*
2000 *Bernstein of Craigweil,* Alexander Bernstein, *b.* 1936, *m.*
2001 *Best,* Richard Stuart Best, OBE, *b.* 1945, *m.*
2007 *Bew,* Prof. Paul Anthony Elliott Bew, *b.* 1950, *m.*
2001 *Bhatia,* Amirali Alibhai Bhatia, OBE, *b.* 1932, *m.*
2004 *Bhattacharyya,* Prof. (Sushantha) Kumar Bhattacharyya, CBE *b.* 1932, *m.*
2006 *Bilimoria,* Karan Faridoon Bilimoria, CBE, *b.* 1961, *m.*
2005 *Bilston,* Dennis Turner, *b.* 1942, *m.*
1996 *Bingham of Cornhill,* Thomas Henry Bingham, KG, PC, *b.* 1933, *m.*
2000 *Birt,* John Francis Hodgess Birt, *b.* 1944, *m.*
2001 *Black of Crossharbour,* Conrad Moffat Black, OC, PC, *b.* 1944, *m.*
1997 *Blackwell,* Norman Roy Blackwell, *b.* 1952, *m.*
1995 *Blyth of Rowington,* James Blyth, *b.* 1940, *m.*
1996 *Borrie,* Gordon Johnson Borrie, QC, *b.* 1931, *m.*
1976 *Boston of Faversham,* Terence George Boston, QC, *b.* 1930, *m.*
1996 *Bowness,* Peter Spencer Bowness, CBE, *b.* 1943, *m.*
2003 *Boyce,* Michael Boyce, GCB, OBE, *b.* 1943
2006 *Boyd of Duncansby,* Colin David Boyd, PC, *b.* 1953, *m.*
2006 *Bradley,* Keith John Charles Bradley, PC, *b.* 1950, *m.*
1999 *Bradshaw,* William Peter Bradshaw, *b.* 1936, *m.*
1998 *Bragg,* Melvyn Bragg, *b.* 1939, *m.*
1987 *Bramall,* Edwin Noel Westby Bramall, KG, GCB, OBE, MC, *b.* 1923, *m.*
2000 *Brennan,* Daniel Joseph Brennan, QC, *b.* 1942, *m.*
1999 *Brett,* William Henry Brett, *b.* 1942, *m.*
1976 *Briggs,* Asa Briggs, FBA, *b.* 1921, *m.*
2000 *Brittan of Spennithorne,* Leon Brittan, PC, QC, *b.* 1939, *m.*
2004 *Broers,* Prof. Alec (Nigel) Broers, *b.* 1938, *m.*
1997 *Brooke of Alverthorpe,* Clive Brooke, *b.* 1942, *m.*
2001 *Brooke of Sutton Mandeville,* Peter Leonard Brooke, CH, PC, *b.* 1934, *m.*
1998 *Brookman,* David Keith Brookman, *b.* 1937, *m.*
1979 *Brooks of Tremorfa,* John Edward Brooks, *b.* 1927, *m.*
2006 *Browne of Belmont,* Wallace Hamilton Browne, *b.* 1947
2001 *Browne of Madingley,* Edmund John Phillip Browne, *b.* 1948
2006 *Burnett,* John Patrick Aubone Burnett, *b.* 1945, *m.*
1998 *Burns,* Terence Burns, GCB, *b.* 1944, *m.*
1998 *Butler of Brockwell,* (Frederick Edward) Robin Butler, KG, GCB, CVO, PC, *b.* 1938, *m.*
2004 *Cameron of Dillington,* Ewen (James Hanning) Cameron, *b.* 1949, *m.*
1984 *Cameron of Lochbroom,* Kenneth John Cameron, PC, *b.* 1931, *m.*
1981 *Campbell of Alloway,* Alan Robertson Campbell, QC, *b.* 1917, *m.*
2001 *Campbell-Savours,* Dale Norman Campbell-Savours, *b.* 1943, *m.*
2002 *Carey of Clifton,* Rt. Revd George Leonard Carey, PC, *b.* 1935, *m.*
1999 **Carington of Upton,* Lord Carrington, GCMG, *b.* 1919, *m.* (*see* Hereditary Peers)
1999 *Carlile of Berriew,* Alexander Charles Carlile, QC, *b.* 1948, *m.*
1975 *Carr of Hadley,* (Leonard) Robert Carr, PC, *b.* 1916, *m.*
2008 *Carter of Barnes,* Stephen Andrew Carter, CBE, *b.* 1964, *m.*
2004 *Carter of Coles,* Patrick Robert Carter, *b.* 1946, *m.*
1990 *Cavendish of Furness,* (Richard) Hugh Cavendish, *b.* 1941, *m.*
1996 *Chadlington,* Peter Selwyn Gummer, *b.* 1942, *m.*
1964 *Chalfont,* (Alun) Arthur Gwynne Jones, OBE, MC, PC, *b.* 1919, *w.*
2005 *Chidgey,* David William George Chidgey, *b.* 1942, *m.*
1987 *Chilver,* (Amos) Henry Chilver, FRS, FRENG, *b.* 1926, *m.*
1977 *Chitnis,* Pratap Chidamber Chitnis, *b.* 1936, *m.*
1998 *Christopher,* Anthony Martin Grosvenor Christopher, CBE, *b.* 1925, *m.*
2001 *Clark of Windermere,* David George Clark, PC, PHD, *b.* 1939, *m.*
1998 *Clarke of Hampstead,* Anthony James Clarke, CBE, *b.* 1932, *m.*
2009 §*Clarke of Stone-Cum-Ebony,* Anthony Peter Clarke, PC, *b.* 1943, *m.*
1998 *Clement-Jones,* Timothy Francis Clement-Jones, CBE, *b.* 1949, *m.*
1990 *Clinton-Davis,* Stanley Clinton Clinton-Davis, PC, *b.* 1928, *m.*
2000 *Coe,* Sebastian Newbold Coe, KBE, *b.* 1956, *m.*
2001 *Condon,* Paul Leslie Condon, QPM, *m.*
1997 *Cope of Berkeley,* John Ambrose Cope, PC, *b.* 1937, *m.*
2001 *Corbett of Castle Vale,* Robin Corbett, *b.* 1933, *m.*
2006 *Cotter,* Brian Joseph Michael Cotter, *b.* 1938, *m.*
1991 *Craig of Radley,* David Brownrigg Craig, GCB, OBE, *b.* 1929, *m.*
1987 *Crickhowell,* (Roger) Nicholas Edwards, PC, *b.* 1934, *m.*
2006 *Crisp,* (Edmund) Nigel (Ramsay) Crisp, KCB, *b.* 1952, *m.*
1978 *Croham,* Douglas Albert Vivian Allen, GCB, *b.* 1917, *w.*
2003 *Cullen of Whitekirk,* William Douglas Cullen, KT, PC, *b.* 1935, *m.*
2005 *Cunningham of Felling,* John Anderson Cunningham, PC, *b.* 1939, *m.*
1996 *Currie of Marylebone,* David Anthony Currie, *b.* 1946, *m.*
2007 *Darzi of Denham,* Ara Warkes Darzi, KBE, *b.* 1960, *m.*
2006 *Davidson of Glen Clova,* Neil Forbes Davidson, QC, *b.* 1950, *m.*

2009 *Davies of Abersoch,* Evan Mervyn Davies, CBE, *b.* 1952, *m.*
1997 *Davies of Coity,* (David) Garfield Davies, CBE, *b.* 1935, *m.*
1997 *Davies of Oldham,* Bryan Davies, PC, *b.* 1939, *m.*
2006 *Dear,* Geoffrey (James) Dear, QPM, *b.* 1937, *m.*
1991 *Desai,* Prof. Meghnad Jagdishchandra Desai, PHD, *b.* 1940, *m.*
1997 *Dholakia,* Navnit Dholakia, OBE, *b.* 1937, *m.*
1997 *Dixon,* Donald Dixon, PC, *b.* 1929, *m.*
1993 *Dixon-Smith,* Robert William Dixon-Smith, *b.* 1934, *m.*
1985 *Donoughue,* Bernard Donoughue, DPHIL, *b.* 1934
2004 *Drayson,* Paul Rudd Drayson, PC, *b.* 1960, *m.*
1994 *Dubs,* Alfred Dubs, *b.* 1932, *m.*
2004 *Dykes,* Hugh John Maxwell Dykes, *b.* 1939, *m.*
1995 *Eames,* Robert Henry Alexander Eames, OM, PHD, *b.* 1937, *m.*
1992 *Eatwell,* John Leonard Eatwell, PHD, *b.* 1945
1983 *Eden of Winton,* John Benedict Eden, PC, *b.* 1925, *m.*
1999 *Elder,* Thomas Murray Elder, *b.* 1950
1992 *Elis-Thomas,* Dafydd Elis Elis-Thomas, PC, *b.* 1946, *m.*
1985 *Elliott of Morpeth,* Robert William Elliott, *b.* 1920, *m.*
1981 *Elystan-Morgan,* Dafydd Elystan Elystan-Morgan, *b.* 1932, *w.*
2000 **Erskine of Alloa Tower,* Earl of Mar and Kellie, *b.* 1949, *m.* (*see* Hereditary Peers)
1997 *Evans of Parkside,* John Evans, *b.* 1930, *m.*
2000 *Evans of Temple Guiting,* Matthew Evans, CBE, *b.* 1941, *m.*
1998 *Evans of Watford,* David Charles Evans, *b.* 1942, *m.*
1983 *Ezra,* Derek Ezra, MBE, *b.* 1919, *m.*
1997 *Falconer of Thoroton,* Charles Leslie Falconer, QC, *b.* 1951, *m.*
1999 *Faulkner of Worcester,* Richard Oliver Faulkner, *b.* 1946, *m.*
2001 *Fearn, Ronald Cyril Fearn, OBE, b. 1931, m*
1996 *Feldman,* Basil Feldman, *b.* 1926, *m.*
1999 *Fellowes,* Robert Fellowes, GCB, GCVO, PC, *b.* 1941, *m.*
1999 *Filkin,* David Geoffrey Nigel Filkin, CBE, *b.* 1944
1979 *Flowers,* Brian Hilton Flowers, FRS, *b.* 1924, *m.*
1999 *Forsyth of Drumlean,* Michael Bruce Forsyth, *b.* 1954, *m.*
2005 *Foster of Bishop Auckland,* Derek Foster, PC, *b.* 1937, *m.*
1999 *Foster of Thames Bank,* Norman Robert Foster, OM, *b.* 1935, *m.*
2005 *Foulkes of Cumnock,* George Foulkes, PC, *b.* 1942, *m.*
2001 *Fowler,* (Peter) Norman Fowler, PC, *b.* 1938, *m.*
1989 *Fraser of Carmyllie,* Peter Lovat Fraser, PC, QC, *b.* 1945, *m.*
1997 *Freeman,* Roger Norman Freeman, PC, *b.* 1942, *m.*
2009 *Freud,* David Anthony Freud, *b.* 1950 *m.*
2000 *Fyfe of Fairfield,* George Lennox Fyfe, *b.* 1941, *m.*
1997 *Garel-Jones,* (William Armand) Thomas Tristan Garel-Jones, PC, *b.* 1941, *m.*
1999* *Gascoyne-Cecil,* The Marquess of Salisbury, PC , *b.* 1946, *m.* (*see* Hereditary Peers)
1999 *Gavron,* Robert Gavron, CBE, *b.* 1930, *m.*
2004 *Giddens,* Prof. Anthony Giddens, *b.* 1938, *m.*
1997 *Gilbert,* John William Gilbert, PC, PHD, *b.* 1927, *m.*
1977 *Glenamara,* Edward Watson Short, CH, PC, *b.* 1912, *m.*
1999 *Goldsmith,* Peter Henry Goldsmith, QC, *b.* 1950, *m.*
1997 *Goodhart,* William Howard Goodhart, QC, *b.* 1933, *m.*
2005 *Goodlad,* Alastair Robertson Goodlad, KCMG, *b.* 1943, *m.*
1997 *Gordon of Strathblane,* James Stuart Gordon, CBE, *b.* 1936, *m.*
2004 *Gould of Brookwood,* Philip Gould *b.* 1950 *m.*
1999 *Grabiner,* Anthony Stephen Grabiner, QC, *b.* 1945, *m.*
1983 *Graham of Edmonton,* (Thomas) Edward Graham, *b.* 1925, *m.*
2000 *Greaves,* Anthony Robert Greaves, *b.* 1942, *m.*
2000 **Grenfell of Kilvey,* Lord Grenfell, *b.* 1935, *m.* (*see* Hereditary Peers)
2004 *Griffiths of Burry Port,* Revd Dr Leslie John Griffiths, *b.* 1942, *m.*
1991 *Griffiths of Fforestfach,* Brian Griffiths, *b.* 1941, *m.*
2001 *Grocott,* Bruce Joseph Grocott, PC, *b.* 1940, *m.*
2000 **Gueterbock,* Lord Berkley, OBE, *b.* 1939, *m.* (*see* Hereditary Peers)
2000 *Guthrie of Craigiebank,* Charles Ronald Llewelyn Guthrie, GCB, LVO, OBE *b.* 1938, *m.*
1995 *Habgood,* Rt. Revd John Stapylton Habgood, PC, PHD, *b.* 1927, *m.*
2007 *Hameed,* Dr Khalid Hameed, *b.* 1941, *m.*
2005 *Hamilton of Epsom,* Archibald Gavin Hamilton, PC, *b.* 1941, *m.*
2001 *Hannay of Chiswick,* David Hugh Alexander Hannay, GCMG, CH, *b.* 1935, *m.*
1998 *Hanningfield,* Paul Edward Winston White, *b.* 1940
1997 *Hardie,* Andrew Rutherford Hardie, QC, PC, *b.* 1946, *m.*
2006 *Harries of Pentregarth,* Rt. Revd Richard Douglas Harries, *b.* 1936, *m.*
1998 *Harris of Haringey,* (Jonathan) Toby Harris, *b.* 1953, *m.*
1996 *Harris of Peckham,* Philip Charles Harris, *b.* 1942, *m.*
1999 *Harrison,* Lyndon Henry Arthur Harrison, *b.* 1947, *m.*
2004 *Hart of Chilton,* Garry Richard Rushby Hart, *b.* 1940, *m.*
1993 *Haskel,* Simon Haskel, *b.* 1934, *m.*
1998 *Haskins,* Christopher Robin Haskins, *b.* 1937, *m.*
2005 *Hastings of Scarisbrick,* Michael John Hastings, CBE, *b.* 1958, *m.*
1997 *Hattersley,* Roy Sidney George Hattersley, PC, *b.* 1932, *m.*
2004 *Haworth,* Alan Robert Haworth, *b.* 1948, *m.*
1992 *Hayhoe,* Bernard John (Barney) Hayhoe, PC, *b.* 1925, *m.*
1992 *Healey,* Denis Winston Healey, CH, MBE, PC, *b.* 1917, *m.*
1999 **Hennessey,* Lord Windlesham, cvo, *b.* 1932, *m.* (*see* Hereditary Peers)

2001 *Heseltine,* Michael Ray Dibdin Heseltine, CH, PC, *b.* 1933, *m.*
1997 *Higgins,* Terence Langley Higgins, KBE, PC, *b.* 1928, *m.*
2000 *Hodgson of Astley Abbotts,* Robin Granville Hodgson, CBE, *b.* 1942, *m.*
1991 *Hollick,* Clive Richard Hollick, *b.* 1945, *m.*
1979 *Hooson,* (Hugh) Emlyn Hooson, QC, *b.* 1925, *m.*
2005 *Hope of Thornes,* Rt. Revd David Michael Hope, KCVO, PC, *b.* 1940
1995 §*Hope of Craighead,* (James Arthur) David Hope, PC, *b.* 1938, *m.*
2004 *Howard of Rising,* Greville Patrick Charles Howard, *b.* 1941, *m.*
2005 *Howarth of Newport,* Alan Thomas Howarth, CBE, PC, *b.* 1944
1992 *Howe of Aberavon,* (Richard Edward) Geoffrey Howe, CH, PC, QC, *b.* 1926, *m.*
1997 *Howell of Guildford,* David Arthur Russell Howell, PC, *b.* 1936, *m.*
1978 *Howie of Troon,* William Howie, *b.* 1924, *w.*
1997 *Hoyle,* (Eric) Douglas Harvey Hoyle, *b.* 1930, *w.*
1997 *Hughes of Woodside,* Robert Hughes, *b.* 1932, *m.*
2000 *Hunt of Chesterton,* Julian Charles Roland Hunt, CBE, *b.* 1941, *m.*
1997 *Hunt of Kings Heath,* Philip Alexander Hunt, OBE, PC, *b.* 1949, *m.*
1997 *Hunt of Wirral,* David James Fletcher Hunt, MBE, PC, *b.* 1942, *m.*
1997 *Hurd of Westwell,* Douglas Richard Hurd, CH, CBE, PC, *b.* 1930, *w.*
1978 *Hutchinson of Lullington,* Jeremy Nicolas Hutchinson, QC, *b.* 1915, *w.*
1999 *Imbert,* Peter Michael Imbert, CVO, QPM, *b.* 1933, *m.*
1997 *Inge,* Peter Anthony Inge, KG, GCB, PC, *b.* 1935, *m.*
1987 *Irvine of Lairg,* Alexander Andrew Mackay Irvine, PC, QC, *b.* 1940, *m.*
1997 *Jacobs,* (David) Anthony Jacobs, *b.* 1931, *m.*
2006 *James of Blackheath,* David Noel James, CBE, *b.* 1937, *m.*
1997 *Janner of Braunstone,* Greville Ewan Janner, QC, *b.* 1928, *w.*
2007 *Janvrin,* Robin Berry Janvrin, GCB, GCVO, PC, *b.* 1946, *m.*
2006 *Jay of Ewelme,* Michael (Hastings) Jay, GCMG, *b.* 1946, *m.*
1987 *Jenkin of Roding,* (Charles) Patrick (Fleeming) Jenkin, PC, *b.* 1926, *m.*
2000 *Joffe,* Joel Goodman Joffe, CBE, *b.* 1932, *m.*
2001 *Jones,* (Stephen) Barry Jones, *b.* 1937, *m.*
2007 *Jones of Birmingham,* Digby Marritt Jones, *b.* 1955, *m.*
2005, *Jones of Cheltenham,* Nigel David Jones, *b.* 1948, *m.*
1997 *Jopling,* (Thomas) Michael Jopling, PC, *b.* 1930, *m.*
2000 *Jordan,* William Brian Jordan, CBE, *b.* 1936, *m.*
1991 *Judd,* Frank Ashcroft Judd, *b.* 1935, *m.*
2008 *Judge,* Igor Judge, PC, *b.* 1941, *m., Lord Chief Justice of England and Wales*
2004 *Kalms,* Harold Stanley Kalms, *b.* 1931, *m.*
2004 *Kerr of Kinlochard,* John (Olav) Kerr, GCMG, *b.* 1942, *m.*
2001 *Kilclooney,* John David Taylor, PC (NI), *b.* 1937, *m.*
1996 *Kilpatrick of Kincraig,* Robert Kilpatrick, CBE, *b.* 1926, *m.*
1985 *Kimball,* Marcus Richard Kimball, *b.* 1928, *m.*
2001 *King of Bridgwater,* Thomas Jeremy King, CH, PC, *b.* 1933, *m.*
1999 *King of West Bromwich,* Tarsem King, *b.* 1937
1993 *Kingsdown,* Robert (Robin) Leigh-Pemberton, KG, PC, *b.* 1927, *m.*
2005 *Kinnock,* Neil Gordon Kinnock, PC, *b.* 1942, *m.*
1999 *Kirkham,* Graham Kirkham, *b.* 1944, *m.*
1975 *Kirkhill,* John Farquharson Smith, *b.* 1930, *m.*
2005 *Kirkwood of Kirkhope,* Archibald Johnstone Kirkwood, *b.* 1946, *m.*
2007 *Krebs,* Prof. John (Richard) Krebs, FRS, *b.* 1945, *m.*
1987 *Knights,* Philip Douglas Knights, CBE, QPM, *b.* 1920, *m.*
2004 *Laidlaw,* Irvine Alan Stewart Laidlaw, *b.* 1942, *m.*
1991 *Laing of Dunphail,* Hector Laing, *b.* 1923, *m.*
1999 *Laird,* John Dunn Laird, *b.* 1944, *m.*
1998 *Laming,* (William) Herbert Laming, CBE, *b.* 1936, *m.*
1998 *Lamont of Lerwick,* Norman Stewart Hughson Lamont, PC, *b.* 1942, *m.*
1997 *Lang of Monkton,* Ian Bruce Lang, PC, *b.* 1940, *m.*
1992 *Lawson of Blaby,* Nigel Lawson, PC, *b.* 1932, *m.*
2000 *Layard,* Peter Richard Grenville Layard, *b.* 1934, *m.*
1999 *Lea of Crondall,* David Edward Lea, OBE, *b.* 1937
2006 *Leach of Fairford,* Charles Guy Rodney Leach, *b.* 1934, *m.*
2006 *Lee of Trafford,* John Robert Louis Lee, *b.* 1942, *m.*
2004 *Leitch,* Alexander Park Leitch, *b.* 1947, *m.*
1993 *Lester of Herne Hill,* Anthony Paul Lester, QC, *b.* 1936, *m.*
1997 *Levene of Portsoken,* Peter Keith Levene, KBE, *b.* 1941, *m.*
1997 *Levy,* Michael Abraham Levy, *b.* 1944, *m.*
1989 *Lewis of Newnham,* Jack Lewis, FRS, *b.* 1928, *m.*
1999 *Lipsey,* David Lawrence Lipsey, *b.* 1948, *m.*
2001 *Livsey of Talgarth,* Richard Arthur Lloyd Livsey, CBE, *b.* 1935, *m.*
1997 *Lloyd-Webber,* Andrew Lloyd Webber, *b.* 1948, *m.*
1997 *Lofthouse of Pontefract,* Geoffrey Lofthouse, *b.* 1925, *w.*
2006 *Low of Dalston,* Prof. Colin Mackenzie Low, CBE, *b.* 1942, *m.*
2000 *Luce,* Richard Napier Luce, KG, GCVO, PC, *b.* 1936, *m.*
2005 *Lyell of Markyate,* Nicholas Walter Lyell, PC, QC, *b.* 1938, *m.*
2000 **Lyttleton of Aldershot,* The Viscount Chandos, *b.* 1953, *m.* (*see* Hereditary Peers)
1984 *McAlpine of West Green,* (Robert) Alistair McAlpine, *b.* 1942, *m.*
1988 *Macaulay of Bragar,* Donald Macaulay, QC, *b.* 1933, *m.*
1975 *McCarthy,* William Edward John McCarthy, DPHIL, *b.* 1925, *m.*
1976 *McCluskey,* John Herbert McCluskey, *b.* 1929, *m.*

1989 *McColl of Dulwich,* Ian McColl, CBE, FRCS, FRCSE, *b.* 1933, *m.*
1998 *Macdonald of Tradeston,* Angus John Macdonald, CBE, *b.* 1940, *m.*
1991 *Macfarlane of Bearsden,* Norman Somerville Macfarlane, KT, FRSE, *b.* 1926, *m.*
2001 *MacGregor of Pulham Market,* John Roddick Russell MacGregor, CBE, PC, *b.* 1937, *m.*
1982 *McIntosh of Haringey,* Andrew Robert McIntosh, *b.* 1933, *w.*
1979 *Mackay of Clashfern,* James Peter Hymers Mackay, KT, PC, FRSE, *b.* 1927, *m.*
1995 *Mackay of Drumadoon,* Donald Sage Mackay, PC, *b.* 1946, *m.*
2004 *McKenzie of Luton,* William David McKenzie, *b.* 1946, *m.*
1999 *Mackenzie of Culkein,* Hector Uisdean MacKenzie, *b.* 1940
1998 *Mackenzie of Framwellgate,* Brian Mackenzie, OBE, *b.* 1943, *m.*
1974 *Mackie of Benshie,* George Yull Mackie, CBE, DSO, DFC, *b.* 1919, *m.*
1996 *MacLaurin of Knebworth,* Ian Charter MacLaurin, *b.* 1937, *m.*
2001 *Maclennon of Rogart,* Robert Adam Ross Maclennan, PC, *b.* 1936, *m.*
1995 *McNally,* Tom McNally, PC, *b.* 1943, *m.*
2001 *Maginnis of Drumglass,* Kenneth Wiggins Maginnis, *b.* 1938, *m.*
2007 *Malloch-Brown,* George Mark Malloch Brown, KCMG, PC, *b.* 1953, *m.*
2008 *Mandelson,* Peter Benjamin Mandelson, PC, *b.* 1953
2006 *Marland,* Jonathan Peter Marland, *b.* 1956, *m.*
1991 *Marlesford,* Mark Shuldham Schreiber, *b.* 1931, *m.*
1981 *Marsh,* Richard William Marsh, PC, *b.* 1928, *m.*
1998 *Marshall of Knightsbridge,* Colin Marsh Marshall, *b.* 1933, *m.*
2009 *Martin of Springburn,* Michael Martin, PC, *b.* 1945, *m.*
1987 *Mason of Barnsley,* Roy Mason, PC, *b.* 1924, *m.*
2005 *Mawhinney,* Brian Stanley Mawhinney, PC, *b.* 1940, *m.*
2007 *Mawson,* Revd Andrew Mawson, OBE, *b.* 1954, *m.*
2004 *Maxton,* John Alston Maxton, *b.* 1936, *m.*
2001 *May of Oxford,* Robert McCredie May, OM, *b.* 1936, *m.*
1997 *Mayhew of Twysden,* Patrick Barnabas Burke Mayhew, QC, PC, *b.* 1929, *m.*
2000 *Mitchell,* Parry Andrew Mitchell, *b.* 1943, *m.*
2000 **Mitford,* Lord Redesdale, *b.* 1967, *m.* (*see* Hereditary Peers)
2008 *Mogg,* John (Frederick) Mogg, KCMG, *b.* 1943 *m.*
1997 *Molyneaux of Killead,* James Henry Molyneaux, KBE, PC, *b.* 1920
2005 *Moonie,* Dr. Lewis George Moonie, *b.* 1947, *m.*
1992 *Moore of Lower Marsh,* John Edward Michael Moore, PC, *b.* 1937, *w.*
2000 *Morgan,* Kenneth Owen Morgan, *b.* 1934, *m.*
2001 *Morris of Aberavon,* John Morris, KG, QC, *b.* 1931, *m.*
2006 *Morris of Handsworth,* William Manuel Morris, *b.* 1938, *m.*
1997 *Morris of Manchester,* Alfred Morris, PC, *b.* 1928, *m.*
2006 *Morrow,* Maurice George Morrow, *m.*
2001 *Moser,* Claus Adolf Moser, KCB, CBE, *b.* 1922, *m.*
2008 *Myners,* Paul Myners, CBE, *b.* 1948, *m.*
1997 *Naseby,* Michael Wolfgang Laurence Morris, PC, *b.* 1936, *m.*
1997 *Neill of Bladen,* (Francis) Patrick Neill, QC, *b.* 1926, *m.*
1997 *Newby,* Richard Mark Newby, OBE, *b.* 1953, *m.*
1997 *Newton of Braintree,* Antony Harold Newton, OBE, PC, *b.* 1937, *m.*
1994 *Nickson,* David Wigley Nickson, KBE, FRSE, *b.* 1929, *m.*
1975 *Northfield,* (William) Donald Chapman, *b.* 1923
1998 *Norton of Louth,* Philip Norton, *b.* 1951
2000 *Oakeshott of Seagrove Bay,* Matthew Alan Oakeshott, *b.* 1947, *m.*
2005 *O'Neill of Clackmannan,* Martin John O'Neill, *b.* 1945, *m.*
2001 *Ouseley,* Herman George Ouseley, *b.* 1945, *m.*
1992 *Owen,* David Anthony Llewellyn Owen, CH, PC, *b.* 1938, *m.*
1999 *Oxburgh,* Ernest Ronald Oxburgh, KBE, FRS, PHD, *b.* 1934, *m.*
1991 *Palumbo,* Peter Garth Palumbo, *b.* 1935, *m.*
2008 *Pannick,* David Philip Pannick, QC, *b.* 1956, *m.*
2000 *Parekh,* Bhikhu Chhotalal Parekh, *b.* 1935, *m.*
1992 *Parkinson,* Cecil Edward Parkinson, PC, *b.* 1931, *m.*
1999 *Patel,* Narendra Babubhai Patel, *b.* 1938
2000 *Patel of Blackburn,* Adam Hafejee Patel, *b.* 1940
2006 *Patel of Bradford,* Prof. Kamlesh Kumar Patel, OBE, *b.* 1960 *m.*
2005 *Patten of Barnes,* Christopher Francis Patten, CH, PC, *b.* 1944, *m.*
1997 *Patten,* John Haggitt Charles Patten, PC, *b.* 1945, *m.*
1996 *Paul,* Swraj Paul, PC, *b.* 1931, *m.*
1990 *Pearson of Rannoch,* Malcolm Everard MacLaren Pearson, *b.* 1942, *m.*
2001 *Pendry,* Thomas Pendry, *b.* 1934, *m.*
1987 *Peston,* Maurice Harry Peston, *b.* 1931, *m.*
1998 *Phillips of Sudbury,* Andrew Wyndham Phillips, OBE, *b.* 1939, *m.*
1996 *Pilkington of Oxenford,* Revd Canon Peter Pilkington, *b.* 1933, *w.*
1992 *Plant of Highfield,* Prof. Raymond Plant, PHD, *b.* 1945, *m.*
1987 *Plumb,* (Charles) Henry Plumb, *b.* 1925, *m.*
1981 *Plummer of St Marylebone,* (Arthur) Desmond (Herne) Plummer, TD, *b.* 1914, *m.*
2000 **Ponsonby of Roehampton,* Lord Ponsonby of Shulbrede, *b.* 1958 (*see* Hereditary Peers)
2000 *Powell of Bayswater,* Charles David Powell, KCMG, *b.* 1941
1987 *Prior,* James Michael Leathes Prior, PC, *b.* 1927, *m.*
1982 *Prys-Davies,* Gwilym Prys Prys-Davies, *b.* 1923, *m.*
1997 *Puttnam,* David Terence Puttnam, CBE, *b.* 1941, *m.*
1982 *Quinton,* Anthony Meredith Quinton, FBA, *b.* 1925, *m.*
1994 *Quirk,* Prof. (Charles) Randolph Quirk, CBE, FBA, *b.* 1920, *m.*
2001 *Radice,* Giles Heneage Radice, PC, *b.* 1936
2005 *Ramsbotham,* Gen. David John Ramsbotham, GCB, CBE, *b.* 1934, *m.*

2004 *Rana,* Dr Diljit Singh Rana, MBE, *b.* 1938, *m.*
1997 *Randall of St Budeaux,* Stuart Jeffrey Randall, *b.* 1938, *m.*
1997 *Razzall,* (Edward) Timothy Razzall, CBE, *b.* 1943, *m.*
2005 *Rees of Ludlow,* Prof. Martin John Rees, OM, *b.* 1942, *m.*
1988 *Rees-Mogg,* William Rees-Mogg, *b.* 1928, *m.*
1991 *Renfrew of Kaimsthorn,* (Andrew) Colin Renfrew, FBA, *b.* 1937, *m.*
1999 *Rennard,* Christopher John Rennard, MBE, *b.* 1960
1997 *Renton of Mount Harry,* (Ronald) Timothy Renton, PC, *b.* 1932, *m.*
1997 *Renwick of Clifton,* Robin William Renwick, KCMG, *b.* 1937, *m.*
1990 *Richard,* Ivor Seward Richard, PC, QC, *b.* 1932, *m.*
1983 *Richardson of Duntisbourne,* Gordon William Humphreys Richardson, KG, MBE, TD, PC, *b.* 1915, *w.*
1992 *Rix,* Brian Norman Roger Rix, CBE, *b.* 1924, *m.*
2004 *Roberts of Llandudno,* Revd John Roger Roberts, *b.* 1935, *m.*
1997 *Roberts of Conwy,* (Ieuan) Wyn (Pritchard) Roberts, PC, *b.* 1930, *m.*
1999 *Robertson of Port Ellen,* George Islay MacNeill Robertson, KT, GCMG, PC, *b.* 1946, *m.*
1992 §*Rodger of Earlsferry,* Alan Ferguson Rodger, PC, QC, FBA, *b.* 1944
1992 *Rodgers of Quarry Bank,* William Thomas Rodgers, PC, *b.* 1928, *w.*
1999 *Rogan,* Dennis Robert David Rogan, *b.* 1942, *m.*
1996 *Rogers of Riverside,* Richard George Rogers, CH, RA, RIBA, *b.* 1933, *m.*
2001 *Rooker,* Jeffrey William Rooker, PC, *b.* 1941, *m.*
2000 *Roper,* John Francis Hodgess Roper, PC, *b.* 1935, *m.*
2004 *Rosser,* Richard Andrew Rosser, *b.* 1944, *m.*
2006 *Rowe-Beddoe,* David (Sydney) Rowe-Beddoe, *b.* 1937, *m.*
2004 *Rowlands,* Edward Rowlands, CBE, *b.* 1940, *m.*
1997 *Ryder of Wensum,* Richard Andrew Ryder, OBE, PC, *b.* 1949, *m.*
1996 *Saatchi,* Maurice Saatchi, *b.* 1946, *m.*
2009 ‡*Sacks,* Chief Rabbi Dr Jonathan Henry Sacks, *b.* 1948, *m.*
1989 *Sainsbury of Preston Candover,* John Davan Sainsbury, KG, *b.* 1927, *m.*
1997 *Sainsbury of Turville,* David John Sainsbury, *b.* 1940, *m.*
1987 *St John of Fawsley,* Norman Antony Francis St John-Stevas, PC, *b.* 1929
1997 *Sandberg,* Michael Graham Ruddock Sandberg, CBE, *b.* 1927, *m.*
1985 *Sanderson of Bowden,* Charles Russell Sanderson, *b.* 1933, *m.*
1998 *Sawyer,* Lawrence (Tom) Sawyer, *b.* 1943
1997 *Selkirk of Douglas,* James Alexander Douglas-Hamilton, MSP, PC, QC, *b.* 1942, *m.*
1996 *Sewel,* John Buttifant Sewel, CBE, *b.* 1946
1999 *Sharman,* Colin Morven Sharman, OBE, *b.* 1943, *m.*
1994 *Shaw of Northstead,* Michael Norman Shaw, *b.* 1920, *m.*
2006 *Sheikh,* Mohamed Iltaf Sheikh, *b.* 1941, *m.*
2001 *Sheldon,* Robert Edward Sheldon, PC, *b.* 1923, *m.*
1994 *Sheppard of Didgemere,* Allan John George Sheppard, KCVO, *b.* 1932, *m.*
2000 *Shutt of Greetland,* David Trevor Shutt, OBE, PC, *b.* 1942
1997 *Simon of Highbury,* David Alec Gwyn Simon, CBE, *b.* 1939, *m.*
1997 *Simpson of Dunkeld,* George Simpson, *b.* 1942, *m.*
1991 *Skidelsky,* Robert Jacob Alexander Skidelsky, DPHIL, *b.* 1939, *m.*
1997 *Smith of Clifton,* Trevor Arthur Smith, *b.* 1937, *m.*
2005 *Smith of Finsbury,* Christopher Robert Smith, PC, *b.* 1951
2008 *Smith of Kelvin,* Robert (Haldane) Smith, *b.* 1944, *m.*
1999 *Smith of Leigh,* Peter Richard Charles Smith, *b.* 1945, *m.*
2004 *Snape,* Peter Charles Snape, *b.* 1942
2005 *Soley,* Clive Stafford Soley, *b.* 1939
1990 *Soulsby of Swaffham Prior,* Ernest Jackson Lawson Soulsby, PHD, *b.* 1926, *m.*
1997 *Steel of Aikwood,* David Martin Scott Steel, KT, KBE, PC, *b.* 1938, *m.*
2004 *Steinberg,* Leonard Steinberg, *b.* 1936
1991 *Sterling of Plaistow,* Jeffrey Maurice Sterling, GCVO, CBE, *b.* 1934, *m.*
2007 *Stern of Brentford,* Nicholas Herbert Stern, *b.* 1946, *m.*
2005 *Stevens of Kirkwhelpington,* John Arthur Stevens, *b.* 1942, *m.*
1987 *Stevens of Ludgate,* David Robert Stevens, *b.* 1936, *m.*
1999 *Stevenson of Coddenham,* Henry Dennistoun Stevenson, CBE, *b.* 1945, *m.*
1992 *Stewartby,* (Bernard Harold) Ian (Halley) Stewart, RD, PC, FBA, FRSE, *b.* 1935, *m.*
1983 *Stoddart of Swindon,* David Leonard Stoddart, *b.* 1926, *m.*
1997 *Stone of Blackheath,* Andrew Zelig Stone, *b.* 1942, *m.*
2009 *Sugar,* Alan Michael Sugar, *b.* 1947, *m.*
2001 *Sutherland of Houndwood,* Stewart Ross Sutherland, KT, *b.* 1941, *m.*
1971 *Tanlaw,* Simon Brooke Mackay, *b.* 1934, *m.*
1996 *Taverne,* Dick Taverne, QC, *b.* 1928, *m.*
1978 *Taylor of Blackburn,* Thomas Taylor, CBE, *b.* 1929, *m.*
2006 *Taylor of Holbeach,* John Derek Taylor, CBE, *b.* 1943, *m.*
1996 *Taylor of Warwick,* John David Beckett Taylor, *b.* 1952, *m.*
1992 *Tebbit,* Norman Beresford Tebbit, CH, PC, *b.* 1931, *m.*
2001 *Temple-Morris,* Peter Temple-Morris, *b.* 1938, *m.*
2006 *Teverson,* Robin Teverson, *b.* 1952, *m.*
1996 *Thomas of Gresford,* Donald Martin Thomas, OBE, QC, *b.* 1937, *m.*
1997 *Thomas of Macclesfield,* Terence James Thomas, CBE, *b.* 1937, *m.*
1981 *Thomas of Swynnerton,* Hugh Swynnerton Thomas, *b.* 1931, *m.*
1990 *Tombs,* Francis Leonard Tombs, FENG, *b.* 1924, *w.*
1998 *Tomlinson,* John Edward Tomlinson, *b.* 1939
1994 *Tope,* Graham Norman Tope, CBE, *b.* 1943, *m.*
1981 *Tordoff,* Geoffrey Johnson Tordoff, *b.* 1928, *m.*

2004 *Triesman,* David Maxim Triesman, *b.* 1943
2006 *Trimble,* William David Trimble, PC, *b.* 1944, *m.*
2004 *Truscott,* Dr Peter Derek Truscott, *b.* 1959, *m.*
1993 *Tugendhat,* Christopher Samuel Tugendhat, *b.* 1937, *m.*
2004 *Tunnicliffe,* Denis Tunnicliffe, CBE, *b.* 1943, *m.*
2000 *Turnberg,* Leslie Arnold Turnberg, MD, *b.* 1934, *m.*
2005 *Turnbull,* Andrew Turnbull, KCB, CVO, *b.* 1945, *m.*
2005 *Turner of Ecchinswell,* (Jonathan) Adair Turner, *b.* 1955, *m.*
2005 *Tyler,* Paul Archer Tyler, CBE, *b.* 1941, *m.*
2004 *Vallance of Tummel,* Iain (David Thomas) Vallance, *b.* 1943, *m.*
1996 *Vincent of Coleshill,* Richard Frederick Vincent, GBE, KCB, DSO, *b.* 1931, *m.*
1985 *Vinson,* Nigel Vinson, LVO, *b.* 1931, *m.*
1990 *Waddington,* David Charles Waddington, GCVO, PC, QC, *b.* 1929, *m.*
1990 *Wade of Chorlton,* (William) Oulton Wade, *b.* 1932, *m.*
1992 *Wakeham,* John Wakeham, PC, *b.* 1932, *m.*
1999 *Waldegrave of North Hill,* William Arthur Waldegrave, PC, *b.* 1946, *m.*
2007 *Walker of Aldringham,* Michael John Dawson Walker, GCB, CMG, CBE, *b.* 1944, *m.*
1992 *Walker of Worcester,* Peter Edward Walker, MBE, PC, *b.* 1932, *m.*
1995 *Wallace of Saltaire,* William John Lawrence Wallace, PHD, *b.* 1941, *m.*
2007 *Wallace of Tankerness,* James Robert Wallace, PC, QC, *b.* 1954, *m.*
1989 *Walton of Detchant,* John Nicholas Walton, TD, FRCP, *b.* 1922, *w.*
1998 *Warner,* Norman Reginald Warner, PC, *b.* 1940, *m.*
1997 *Watson of Invergowrie,* Michael Goodall Watson, *b.* 1949, *m.*
1999 *Watson of Richmond,* Alan John Watson, CBE, *b.* 1941, *m.*
1977 *Wedderburn of Charlton,* (Kenneth) William Wedderburn, FBA, QC, *b.* 1927, *m.*
1976 *Weidenfeld,* (Arthur) George Weidenfeld, *b.* 1919, *m.*
2007 *West of Spithead,* Adm. Alan William John West, GCB, DSC, *b.* 1948, *m.*
1996 *Whitty,* John Lawrence (Larry) Whitty, *b.* 1943, *m.*
1985 *Williams of Elvel,* Charles Cuthbert Powell Williams, CBE, *b.* 1933, *m.*
1999 *Williamson of Horton,* David (Francis) Williamson, GCMG, CB, PC, *b.* 1934, *m.*
2002 *Wilson of Dinton,* Richard Thomas James Wilson, GCB, *b.* 1942, *m.*
1992 *Wilson of Tillyorn,* David Clive Wilson, KT, GCMG, PHD, *b.* 1935, *m.*
1995 *Winston,* Robert Maurice Lipson Winston, FRCOG, *b.* 1940, *m.*
1985 *Wolfson,* Leonard Gordon Wolfson, *b.* 1927, *m.*
1991 *Wolfson of Sunningdale,* David Wolfson, *b.* 1935, *m.*
1999 *Woolmer of Leeds,* Kenneth John Woolmer, *b.* 1940, *m.*
1994 *Wright of Richmond,* Patrick Richard Henry Wright, GCMG, *b.* 1931, *m.*
2004 *Young of Norwood Green,* Anthony (Ian) Young, *b.* 1942, *m.*
1984 *Young of Graffham,* David Ivor Young, PC, *b.* 1932, *m.*

BARONESSES

Created

2005 *Adams of Craigielea,* Katherine Patricia Irene Adams, *b.* 1947, *w.*
1997 *Amos,* Valerie Ann Amos, *b.* 1954
2007 *Afshar,* Prof. Haleh Afshar, OBE, , *b.* 1944, *m.*
2000 *Andrews,* Elizabeth Kay Andrews, OBE, *b.* 1943, *m.*
1996 *Anelay of St Johns,* Joyce Anne Anelay, DBE, PC, *b.* 1947, *m.*
1999 *Ashton of Upholland,* Catherine Margaret Ashton, PC, *b.* 1956, *m.*
1999 *Barker,* Elizabeth Jean Barker, *b.* 1961
2000 *Billingham,* Angela Theodora Billingham, DPHIL, *b.* 1939, *w.*
1987 *Blackstone,* Tessa Ann Vosper Blackstone, PHD, *b.* 1942
1999 *Blood,* May Blood, MBE, *b.* 1938
2000 *Boothroyd,* Betty Boothroyd, OM, PC, *b.* 1929
2004 *Bonham-Carter of Yarnbury,* Jane Bonham Carter, *b.* 1957, *w.*
2005 *Bottomley of Nettlestone,* Virginia Hilda Brunette Maxwell Bottomley, PC, *b.* 1948, *m.*
1998 *Buscombe,* Peta Jane Buscombe, *b.* 1954, *m.*
2006 *Butler-Sloss,* (Ann) Elizabeth (Oldfield) Butler-Sloss, GBE, PC *b.* 1933, *m.*
1996 *Byford,* Hazel Byford, DBE, *b.* 1941, *m.*
2008 *Campbell of Loughborough,* Susan Catherine Campbell, CBE, *b.* 1948
2007 *Campbell of Surbiton,* Jane Susan Campbell, DBE, *b.* 1959, *m.*
1982 *Carnegy of Lour,* Elizabeth Patricia Carnegy of Lour, *b.* 1925
1992 *Chalker of Wallasey,* Lynda Chalker, PC, *b.* 1942, *m.*
2004 *Chapman,* Nicola Jane Chapman, *b.* 1961
2005 *Clark of Calton,* Dr Lynda Margaret Clark, QC, *b.* 1949
2000 *Cohen of Pimlico,* Janet Cohen, *b.* 1940, *m.*
2005 *Corston,* Jean Ann Corston, PC, *b.* 1942, *w.*
2007 *Coussins,* Jean Coussins, *b.* 1950
1982 *Cox,* Caroline Anne Cox, *b.* 1937, *m.*
1998 *Crawley,* Christine Mary Crawley, *b.* 1950, *m.*
1990 *Cumberlege,* Julia Frances Cumberlege, CBE, *b.* 1943, *m.*
1978 *David,* Nora Ratcliff David, *b.* 1913, *w.*
1993 *Dean of Thornton-le-Fylde,* Brenda Dean, PC, *b.* 1943, *m.*
2005 *Deech,* Ruth Lynn Deech, DBE, *b.* 1943, *m.*
1974 *Delacourt-Smith of Alteryn,* Margaret Rosalind Delacourt-Smith, *b.* 1916, *m.*
2004 *D'Souza,* Dr Frances Gertrude Claire D'Souza, CMG, PC, *b.* 1944, *m.*
1990 *Dunn,* Lydia Selina Dunn, DBE, *b.* 1940, *m.*
1990 *Eccles of Moulton,* Diana Catherine Eccles, *b.* 1933, *m.*
1972 *Elles,* Diana Louie Elles, *b.* 1921, *m.*
1997 *Emerton,* Audrey Caroline Emerton, DBE, *b.* 1935
1974 *Falkender,* Marcia Matilda Falkender, CBE, *b.* 1932
2004 *Falkner of Margravine,* Kishwer Falkner, *b.* 1955, *m.*

1994 *Farrington of Ribbleton,* Josephine Farrington, *b.* 1940, *m.*
2001 *Finlay of Llandaff,* Ilora Gillian Finlay, *b.* 1949, *m.*
1990 *Flather,* Shreela Flather, *m.*
1997 *Fookes,* Janet Evelyn Fookes, DBE, *b.* 1936
2006 *Ford,* Margaret Anne Ford, *b.* 1957, *m.*
2005 *Fritchie,* Irene Tordoff Fritchie, DBE, *b.* 1942, *m.*
1999 *Gale,* Anita Gale, *b.* 1940
2007 *Garden of Frognal,* Susan Elizabeth Garden, *b.* 1944, *m.*
1981 *Gardner of Parkes,* (Rachel) Trixie (Anne) Gardner, *b.* 1927, *w.*
2000 *Gibson of Market Rasen,* Anne Gibson, OBE, *b.* 1940, *m.*
2001 *Golding,* Llinos Golding, *b.* 1933, *m.*
1998 *Goudie,* Mary Teresa Goudie, *b.* 1946, *m.*
1993 *Gould of Potternewton,* Joyce Brenda Gould, *b.* 1932, *m.*
2001 *Greenfield,* Susan Adele Greenfield, CBE, *b.* 1950, *m.*
2000 *Greengross,* Sally Ralea Greengross, OBE, *b.* 1935, *m.*
1991 *Hamwee,* Sally Rachel Hamwee, *b.* 1947
1999 *Hanham,* Joan Brownlow Hanham, CBE, *b.* 1939, *m.*
1999 *Harris of Richmond,* Angela Felicity Harris, *b.* 1944
1996 *Hayman,* Helene Valerie Hayman, PC, *b.* 1949, *m.*
2004 *Henig,* Ruth Beatrice Henig, CBE, *b.* 1943, *m.*
1991 *Hilton of Eggardon,* Jennifer Hilton, QPM, *b.* 1936
1995 *Hogg,* Sarah Elizabeth Mary Hogg, *b.* 1946, *m.*
1990 *Hollis of Heigham,* Patricia Lesley Hollis, DPHIL, *b.* 1941, *m.*
1985 *Hooper,* Gloria Dorothy Hooper, CMG, *b.* 1939
2001 *Howarth of Breckland,* Valerie Georgina Howarth, OBE, *b.* 1940
2001 *Howe of Idlicote,* Elspeth Rosamond Morton Howe, CBE, *b.* 1932, *m.*
1999 *Howells of St Davids,* Rosalind Patricia-Anne Howells, *b.* 1931, *m.*
1991 *James of Holland Park,* Phyllis Dorothy White (P. D. James), OBE, *b.* 1920, *w.*
1992 *Jay of Paddington,* Margaret Ann Jay, PC, *b.* 1939, *m.*
2006 *Jones of Whitchurch,* Margaret Beryl Jones, *b.* 1955
1997 *Kennedy of the Shaws,* Helena Ann Kennedy, QC, *b.* 1950, *m.*
2006 *Kingsmill,* Denise Patricia Byrne Kingsmill, CBE, *b.* 1947, *m.*
2009 *Kinnock of Holyhead,* Glenys Elizabeth Kinnock, *b.* 1944, *m.*
1997 *Knight of Collingtree,* (Joan Christabel) Jill Knight, DBE, *b.* 1927, *w.*
1997 *Linklater of Butterstone,* Veronica Linklater, *b.* 1943, *m.*
1978 *Lockwood,* Betty Lockwood, *b.* 1924, *w.*
1997 *Ludford,* Sarah Ann Ludford, *b.* 1951
2004 *McDonagh,* Margaret Josephine McDonagh
1979 *McFarlane of Llandaff,* Jean Kennedy McFarlane, *b.* 1926
1999 *McIntosh of Hudnall,* Genista Mary McIntosh, *b.* 1946
1997 *Maddock,* Diana Margaret Maddock, *b.* 1945, *m.*
2008 *Manningham-Buller,* Elizabeth (Lydia) Manningham-Buller, DCB, *b.* 1948, *m.*
1991 *Mallalieu,* Ann Mallalieu, QC, *b.* 1945, *m.*
1970 *Masham of Ilton,* Susan Lilian Primrose Cunliffe-Lister, *b.* 1935, *w.*
1999 *Massey of Darwen,* Doreen Elizabeth Massey, *b.* 1938, *m.*
2006 *Meacher,* Molly Christine Meacher, *b.* 1940, *m.*
1998 *Miller of Chilthorne Domer,* Susan Elizabeth Miller, *b.* 1954
1993 *Miller of Hendon,* Doreen Miller, MBE, *b.* 1933, *m.*
2004 *Morgan of Drefelin,* Delyth Jane Morgan, *b.* 1961, *m.*
2001 *Morgan of Huyton,* Sally Morgan, *b.* 1959, *m.*
2004 *Morris of Bolton,* Patricia Morris, OBE, *b.* 1953
2005 *Morris of Yardley,* Estelle Morris, PC, *b.* 1952
2004 *Murphy,* Elaine Murphy, *b.* 1947, *m.*
2004 *Neuberger,* Rabbi Julia (Babette Sarah) Neuberger, DBE, *b.* 1950, *m.*
2007 *Neville-Jones,* (Lilian) Pauline Neville-Jones, DCMG, *b.* 1939
1997 *Nicholson of Winterbourne,* Emma Harriet Nicholson, MEP, *b.* 1941, *m.*
1982 *Nicol,* Olive Mary Wendy Nicol, *b.* 1923, *m.*
2000 *Noakes,* Shiela Valerie Masters, DBE, *b.* 1949, *m.*
2000 *Northover,* Lindsay Patricia Granshaw, *b.* 1954
1991 *O'Cathain,* Detta O'Cathain, OBE, *b.* 1938, *m.*
2009 ‡*O'Loan,* Nuala Patricia, DBE, *b.* 1951, *m.*
1999 *O'Neill of Bengarve,* Onora Sylvia O'Neill, CBE, PHD, *b.* 1941
1989 *Oppenheim-Barnes,* Sally Oppenheim-Barnes, PC, *b.* 1930, *m.*
2006 *Paisley of St George's,* Eileen Emily Paisley, *m.*
1990 *Park of Monmouth,* Daphne Margaret Sybil Désirée Park, CMG, OBE, *b.* 1921
1991 *Perry of Southwark,* Pauline Perry, *b.* 1931, *m.*
1997 *Pitkeathley,* Jill Elizabeth Pitkeathley, OBE, *b.* 1940
1981 *Platt of Writtle,* Beryl Catherine Platt, CBE, FENG, *b.* 1923, *m.*
1999 *Prashar,* Usha Kumari Prashar, CBE, *b.* 1948, *m.*
2004 *Prosser,* Margaret Theresa Prosser, OBE, *b.* 1937
2006 *Quin,* Joyce Gwendoline Quin, PC *b.* 1944
1996 *Ramsay of Cartvale,* Margaret Mildred (Meta) Ramsay, *b.* 1936
1994 *Rawlings,* Patricia Elizabeth Rawlings, *b.* 1939
1997 *Rendell of Babergh,* Ruth Barbara Rendell, CBE, *b.* 1930, *m.*
1998 *Richardson of Calow,* Kathleen Margaret Richardson, OBE, *b.* 1938, *m.*
2004 *Royall of Blaisdon,* Janet Anne Royall, *b.* 1955, *m.*
1997 *Scotland of Asthal,* Patricia Janet Scotland, QC, *b.* 1955, *m.*
2000 *Scott of Needham Market,* Rosalind Carol Scott, *b.* 1957
1991 *Seccombe,* Joan Anna Dalziel Seccombe, DBE, *b.* 1930, *m.*
1998 *Sharp of Guildford,* Margaret Lucy Sharp, *b.* 1938, *m.*
1973 *Sharples,* Pamela Sharples, *b.* 1923, *m.*
2005 *Shephard of Northwold,* Gillian Patricia Shephard, PC, *b.* 1940, *m.*
1995 *Smith of Gilmorehill,* Elizabeth Margaret Smith, *b.* 1940, *w.*
1999 *Stern,* Vivien Helen Stern, CBE, *b.* 1941

1996 *Symons of Vernham Dean,* Elizabeth Conway Symons, *b.* 1951
2005 *Taylor of Bolton,* Winifred Ann Taylor, PC *b.* 1947, *m.*
1992 *Thatcher,* Margaret Hilda Thatcher, KG, OM, PC, FRS, *b.* 1925, *w.*
1994 *Thomas of Walliswood,* Susan Petronella Thomas, OBE, *b.* 1935, *m.*
2006 *Thomas of Winchester,* Celia Marjorie Thomas, MBE, *b.* 1945
1998 *Thornton,* (Dorothea) Glenys Thornton, *b.* 1952, *m.*
2005 *Tonge,* Dr. Jennifer Louise Tonge, *b.* 1941, *m.*
1980 *Trumpington,* Jean Alys Barker, DCVO, PC, *b.* 1922, *w.*
1985 *Turner of Camden,* Muriel Winifred Turner, *b.* 1927, *m.*
1998 *Uddin,* Manzila Pola Uddin, *b.* 1959, *m.*
2007 *Vadera,* Shriti Vadera, PC
2005 *Valentine,* Josephine Clare Valentine
2006 *Verma,* Sandip Verma, *b.* 1959, *m.*
2004 *Wall of New Barnet,* Margaret Mary Wall, *b.* 1941, *m.*
2000 *Walmsley,* Joan Margaret Walmsley, *b.* 1943
1985 *Warnock,* Helen Mary Warnock, DBE, *b.* 1924, *w.*
2007 *Warsi,* Sayeeda Hussain Warsi, *b.* 1971
1999 *Warwick of Undercliffe,* Diana Mary Warwick, *b.* 1945, *m.*
1999 *Whitaker,* Janet Alison Whitaker, *b.* 1936
1996 *Wilcox,* Judith Ann Wilcox, *b.* 1940, *w.*
1999 *Wilkins,* Rosalie Catherine Wilkins, *b.* 1946
1993 *Williams of Crosby,* Shirley Vivien Teresa Brittain Williams, PC, *b.* 1930, *w.*
2004 *Young of Hornsey,* Prof. Margaret Omolola Young, OBE, *b.* 1951, *m.*
1997 *Young of Old Scone,* Barbara Scott Young, *b.* 1948

LORDS SPIRITUAL

The Lords Spiritual are the Archbishops of Canterbury and York and 24 diocesan bishops of the Church of England. The Bishops of London, Durham and Winchester always have seats in the House of Lords; the other 21 seats are filled by the remaining diocesan bishops in order of seniority. The Bishop of Sodor and Man and the Bishop of Gibraltar are not eligible to sit in the House of Lords.

ARCHBISHOPS

Style, The Most Revd and Rt. Hon. the Lord Archbishop of_
Addressed as Archbishop *or* Your Grace

INTRODUCED TO HOUSE OF LORDS

2003 *Canterbury* (104th), Rowan Douglas Williams, PC, DPHIL, *b.* 1950, *m., cons.* 1992, *elected* 2002
2005 *York* (97th), John Mugabi Tucker Sentamu, PC, PHD, *b.* 1949, *m., cons.* 1996, *elected* 2005, *trans.* 2005

BISHOPS

Style, The Rt. Revd the Lord Bishop of _
Addressed as My Lord
elected date of confirmation as diocesan bishop

INTRODUCED TO HOUSE OF LORDS
(as at 31 August 2009)

1996 *London* (132nd), Richard John Carew Chartres, KCVO, PC, *b.* 1947, *m., cons.* 1992, *elected* 1995
2003 *Durham* (71st), Nicholas Thomas Wright, DPHIL, *b.* 1948, *m., cons.* 2003, *elected* 2003
1996 *Winchester* (96th), Michael Charles Scott-Joynt, *b.* 1943, *m., cons.* 1987, *elected* 1995
1997 *Southwark* (9th), Thomas Frederick Butler, *b.* 1940, *m., cons.* 1985, *elected* 1991, *trans.* 1998
1997 *Manchester* (11th), Nigel Simeon McCulloch, *b.* 1942, *m., cons.* 1986, *elected* 1992, *trans.* 2002
1998 *Salisbury* (77th), David Staffurth Stancliffe, *b.* 1942, *m., cons.* 1993, *elected* 1993
1999 *Portsmouth* (8th), Kenneth William Stevenson, *b.* 1949, *m., cons.* 1995, *elected* 1995
2001 *Chester* (40th), Peter Robert Forster, PHD, *m., b.* 1950, *cons.* 1996, *elected* 1996
2003 *Newcastle* (11th), (John) Martin Wharton, *b.* 1944, *m., cons.* 1992, *elected* 1997
2003 *Liverpool* (7th), James Stuart Jones, *b.* 1948, *m., cons.* 1994, *elected* 1998
2003 *Leicester* (6th), Timothy John Stevens, *b.* 1946, *m., cons.* 1995, *elected* 1999
2004 *Norwich* (71st), Graham Richard James, *b.* 1951, *m., cons.* 1993, *elected* 1999
2005 *Exeter* (70th), Michael Lawrence Langrish, *b.* 1946, *m., cons.* 1993, *elected* 2000
2006 *Ripon and Leeds* (12th), John Richard Packer, *b.* 1946, *m., cons.* 1996, *elected* 2000
2007 *Ely* (68th), Dr Anthony John Russell, *b.* 1943, *m., cons.* 1988, *elected* 2000
2008 *Chichester* (102nd), John William Hind, *b.* 1945, *m., cons.* 1991, *elected* 2001
2008 *Lincoln* (71st), Dr John Charles Saxbee, *b.* 1946, *m., cons.* 1994, *elected* 2001
2008 *Bath and Wells* (77th), Peter Bryan Price, *b.* 1944, *m., cons.* 1997, *elected* 2002
2009 *Bradford* (9th), David Charles James, *b.* 1945, *m., cons.* 1998, *elected* 2002
2009 *Wakefield* (12th), Stephen George Platten, *b.* 1947, *m., cons.* 2003, *elected* 2003
2009 *Bristol* (55th), Michael Arthur Hill, *b.* 1947, *m., cons.* 1998, *elected* 2003
2009 *Lichfield* (98th), Jonathan Michael Gledhill, *b.* 1949, *m., cons.* 1996, *elected* 2003
2009 *Blackburn* (8th), Nicholas Stewart Reade, *b.* 1946, *cons.* 2004, *elected* 2004
2009 *Hereford* (104th), Anthony Martin Priddis, *b.* 1948, *cons.* 1996, *elected* 2004

BISHOPS AWAITING SEATS, in order of seniority
(as at 31 August 2009)

Gloucester (40th), Michael Francis Perham, *b.* 1947, *m., cons.* 2004, *elected* 2004
Guildford (9th), Christopher John Hill, *b.* 1945, *m., cons.* 1996, *elected* 2004
Derby (7th), Alastair Llewellyn John Redfern, *b.* 1948, *m., cons.* 1997, *elected* 2005
Birmingham (9th), David Andrew Urquhart, *b.* 1952, *cons.* 2000, *elected* 2006
Oxford (42nd), John Lawrence Pritchard, *b.* 1948, *m., cons.* 2002 *elected* 2007
St Edmundsbury and Ipswich (10th), (William) Nigel Stock, *b.* 1950, *m., cons.* 2000, *elected* 2007
Worcester (113th), John Geoffrey Inge, PHD, *b.* 1955, *m., cons.* 2003, *elected* 2007
Coventry (9th), Christopher John Cocksworth, PHD, *b.* 1959, *m., cons.* 2008, *elected* 2008
Truro (15th), Timothy Martin Thornton, *b.* 1957, *m., cons.* 2001, *elected* 2008
Sheffield (7th), Stephen John Lindsey Croft, *b.* 1957, *m., cons.* 2009, *elected* 2009
St Albans (10th), Alan Gregory Clayton Smith, *b.* 1957, *cons.* 2001, *elected* 2009
Carlisle (66th), James Newcome, *b.* 1953, *m., cons.* 2002, *elected* 2009
Southwell and Nottingham (11th), Paul Butler, *b.* 1955, *m., cons.* 2004, *elected* 2009
Rochester (107th), vacant
Chelmsford (10th), vacant
Peterborough (38th), vacant

COURTESY TITLES AND PEERS' SURNAMES

COURTESY TITLES

The heir apparent to a Duke, Marquess or Earl uses the highest of his father's other titles as a courtesy title. For example, the Marquess of Blandford is heir to the Dukedom of Marlborough, and Viscount Amberley to the Earldom of Russell. Titles of second heirs (when in use) are also given, and the courtesy title of the father of a second heir is indicated by * eg Earl of Mornington, eldest son of *Marquess of Douro.

The holder of a courtesy title is not styled 'the Most Hon.' or 'the Rt. Hon.', and in correspondence 'the' is omitted before the title. The heir apparent to a Scottish title may use the title 'Master'.

MARQUESSES

*Blandford – *Marlborough, D.*
Bowmont and Cessford – *Roxburghe, D.*
Douglas and Clydesdale – *Hamilton, D.*
*Douro – *Wellington, D.*
Graham – *Montrose, D.*
*Hamilton – *Abercorn, D.*
Hartington – *Devonshire, D.*
Lorne – *Argyll, D.*
Stafford – *Sutherland, D.*
Tavistock – *Bedford, D.*
Tullibardine – *Atholl, D.*
*Worcester – *Beaufort, D.*

EARLS

Aboyne – *Huntly, M.*
Arundel and Surrey – *Norfolk, D.*
Bective – *Headfort, M.*
Belfast – *Donegall, M.*
Brecknock – *Camden, M.*
Burford – *St Albans, D.*
*Cardigan – *Ailesbury, M.*
Compton – *Northampton, M.*
*Dalkeith – *Buccleuch, D.*
Dumfries – *Bute, M.*
*Euston – *Grafton, D.*
Glamorgan – **Worcester, M.*
Grosvenor – *Westminster, D.*
Haddo – *Aberdeen and Temair, M.*
Hillsborough – *Downshire, M.*
Hopetoun – *Linlithgow, M.*
Kerry – *Lansdowne, M.*
March and Kinrara – *Richmond, D.*
Medina – *Milford Haven, M.*
*Mount Charles – *Conyngham, M.*
Mornington – **Douro, M.*
Mulgrave – *Normanby, M.*
Percy – *Northumberland, D.*
Ronaldshay – *Zetland, M.*
*St Andrews – *Kent, D.*
*Southesk – *Fife, D.*
Sunderland – **Blandford, M.*
*Tyrone – *Waterford, M.*
Ulster – *Gloucester, D.*
*Uxbridge – *Anglesey, M.*
Wiltshire – *Winchester, M.*
Yarmouth – *Hertford, M.*

VISCOUNTS

Alexander – *Caledon, E.*
Althorp – *Spencer, E.*
Andover – *Suffolk and Berkshire, E.*
Asquith – *Oxford and Asquith, E.*
Boringdon – *Morley, E.*
Borodale – *Beatty, E.*
Boyle – *Shannon, E.*
Brocas – *Jellicoe, E.*
Bury – *Albermarle, E.*
Campden – *Gainsborough, E.*
Carlow – *Portarlington, E.*
Carlton – *Wharncliffe, E.*
Castlereagh – *Londonderry, M.*
Chelsea – *Cadogan, E.*
Chewton – *Waldegrave, E.*
Clanfield – *Peel, E.*
Clive – *Powis, E.*
Coke – *Leicester, E.*
Corry – *Belmore, E.*
Corvedale – *Baldwin of Bewdley, E.*
Cranborne – *Salisbury, M.*
Cranley – *Onslow, E.*
Crichton – *Erne, E.*
Curzon – *Howe, E.*
Dangan – *Cowley, E.*
Drumlanrig – *Queensberry, M.*
Duncannon – *Bessborough, E.*
Dungarvan – *Cork and Orrery, E.*
Dunluce – *Antrim, E.*
Dunwich – *Stradbroke, E.*
Dupplin – *Kinnoull, E.*
Ednam – *Dudley, E.*
Elveden – *Iveagh, E.*
Emlyn – *Cawdor, E*
Encombe – *Eldon, E.*
Enfield – *Strafford, E.*
Erleigh – *Reading, M.*
Errington – *Cromer, E.*
Feilding – *Denbigh and Desmond, E.*
FitzHarris – *Malmesbury, E.*
Folkestone – *Radnor, E.*
Forbes – *Granard, E.*
Garmoyle – *Cairns, E.*
Garnock – *Lindsay, E.*
Glenapp – *Inchcape, E.*
Glentworth – *Limerick, E.*
Grey de Wilton – *Wilton, E.*
Grimstone – *Verulam, E.*
Gwynedd – *Lloyd George of Dwyfor, E.*
Hawkesbury – *Liverpool, E.*
Hinchingbrooke – *Sandwich, E.*
Ikerrin – *Carrick, E.*
Ingestre – *Shrewsbury, E.*
Ipswich – **Euston, E.*
Jocelyn – *Roden, E.*
Kelburn – *Glasgow, E.*
Kingsborough – *Kingston, E.*
Kirkwall – *Orkney, E.*
Knebworth – *Lytton, E.*
Lambton – *Durham, E.*
Lascelles – *Harewood, E.*
Linley – *Snowdon, E.*
Lymington – *Portsmouth, E.*
Macmillan of Ovenden – *Stockton, E.*
Maidstone – *Winchilsea, E*
Maitland – *Lauderdale, E.*
Mandeville – *Manchester, D.*
Marsham – *Romney, E.*
Melgund – *Minto, E.*
Merton – *Nelson, E.*
Moore – *Drogheda, E.*
Newport – *Bradford, E.*
Northland – *Ranfurly, E*
Newry and Mourne – *Kilmorey, E.*
Petersham – *Harrington, E.*
Pollington – *Mexborough, E*
Raynham – *Townshend, M.*
Reidhaven – *Seafield, E.*
Ruthven of Canberra – *Gowrie, E.*
St Cyres – *Iddesleigh, E.*
Sandon – *Harrowby, E.*
Savernake – **Cardigan, E.*
Severn – *Wessex, E.*
Somerton – *Normanton, E.*
Stopford – *Courtown, E.*
Stormont – *Mansfield, E.*
Strabane – **Hamilton, M.*
Strathallan – *Perth, E.*
Stuart – *Castle Stewart, E.*
Suirdale – *Donoughmore, E.*
Tamworth – *Ferrers, E.*
Tarbat – *Cromartie, E.*
Vaughan – *Lisburne, E.*
Weymouth – *Bath, M.*
Windsor – *Plymouth, E.*
Wolmer – *Selborne, E.*
Woodstock – *Portland, E.*

BARONS (LORDS)

Aberdour – *Morton, E.*
Apsley – *Bathurst, E.*
Ardee – *Meath, E.*
Balgonie – *Leven and Melville, E.*
Balniel – *Crawford and Balcarres, E.*
Berriedale – *Caithness, E.*
Bingham – *Lucan, E.*
Binning – *Haddington, E.*
Brooke – *Warwick, E.*
Bruce – *Elgin, E.*
Burghley – *Exeter, M.*
Cardross – *Buchan, E.*
Carnegie – **Southesk, E.*
Clifton – *Darnley, E.*
Cochrane – *Dundonald, E.*
Courtenay – *Devon, E.*
Dalmeny – *Rosebery, E.*
Doune – *Moray, E.*
Downpatrick – **St Andrews, E.*
Dunglass – *Home, E.*
Elcho – *Wemyss and March, E.*
Eliot – *St Germans, E.*
Formartine – **Haddo, E.*
Gillford – *Clanwilliam, E.*
Glamis – *Strathmore, E.*
Greenock – *Cathcart, E.*
Guernsey – *Aylesford, E.*
Hay – *Erroll, E.*
Howard of Effingham – *Effingham, E.*
Huntingtower – *Dysart, C.*

Irwin – *Halifax, E.*
Johnstone – *Annandale and Hartfell, E.*
Langton – *Temple of Stowe, E.*
La Poer – **Tyrone, E.*
Leveson – *Granville, E*
Loughborough – *Rosslyn, E.*
Masham – *Swinton, E.*
Mauchline – *Loudoun, C.*
Medway – *Cranbrook, E.*
Montgomerie – *Eglinton and Winton, E.*
Moreton – *Ducie, E.*
Naas – *Mayo, E.*
Norreys – *Lindsey and Abingdon, E.*
North – *Guilford, E.*
Ogilvy – *Airlie, E.*
Oxmantown – *Rosse, E.*
Paget de Beaudesert – **Uxbridge, E.*
Porchester – *Carnarvon, E.*
Ramsay – *Dalhousie, E.*
Romsey – *Mountbatten of Burma, C.*
Scrymgeour – *Dundee, E.*
Seymour – *Somerset, D.*
Stanley – *Derby, E.*
Stavordale – *Ilchester, E.*
Strathnaver – *Sutherland, C.*
Wodehouse – *Kimberley, E.*
Worsley – *Yarborough, E.*

PEERS' SURNAMES

The following symbols indicate the rank of the peer holding each title:

C. Countess
D. Duke
E. Earl
M. Marquess
V. Viscount
* Life Peer

Where no designation is given, the title is that of a hereditary Baron or Baroness.

Abney-Hastings – *Loudoun, C.*
Acheson – *Gosford, E.*
Adams – *A. of Craigielea**
Adderley – *Norton*
Addington – *Sidmouth, V.*
Adebowale – *A. of Thornes**
Agar – *Normanton, E.*
Aitken – *Beaverbrook*
Akers-Douglas – *Chilston, V.*
Alexander – *A. of Tunis, E.*
Alexander – *Caledon, E.*
Allen – *Croham**
Allsopp – *Hindlip*
Alton – *A. of Liverpool**
Anderson – *A. of Swansea**
Anderson – *Waverley, V.*
Anelay – *A. of St Johns**
Annesley – *Valentia, V.*
Anson – *Lichfield, E.*
Archer – *A. of Sandwell**
Archer – *A. of Weston-super-Mare**
Armstrong – *A. of Ilminster**
Armstrong-Jones – *Snowdon, E.*
Arthur – *Glenarthur*
Arundell – *Talbot of Malahide*
Ashdown – *A. of Norton-sub-Hamdon**
Ashley – *A. of Stoke**
Ashley-Cooper – *Shaftesbury, E.*
Ashton – *A. of Hyde*
Ashton – *A. of Upholland**
Asquith – *Oxford and Asquith, E.*
Assheton – *Clitheroe*
Astley – *Hastings*
Astor – *A. of Hever*
Aubrey-Fletcher – *Braye*
Bailey – *Glanusk*
Baillie – *Burton*
Baillie Hamilton – *Haddington, E.*
Baker – *B. of Dorking**
Baldwin – *B. of Bewdley, E.*
Balfour – *B. of Inchrye*
Balfour – *Kinross*
Balfour – *Riverdale*
Bampfylde – *Poltimore*
Banbury – *B. of Southam*
Barber – *B. of Tewkesbury**
Baring – *Ashburton*
Baring – *Cromer, E.*
Baring – *Howick of Glendale*
Baring – *Northbrook*
Baring – *Revelstoke*
Barker – *Trumpington**
Barnes – *Gorell*
Barnewall – *Trimlestown*
Bassam – *B. of Brighton**
Bathurst – *Bledisloe, V.*
Beauclerk – *St Albans, D.*
Beaumont – *Allendale, V.*
Beckett – *Grimthorpe*
Benn – *Stansgate, V.*
Bennet – *Tankerville, E.*
Bentinck – *Portland, E.*
Beresford – *Decies*
Beresford – *Waterford, M.*
Bernstein – *B. of Craigweil**
Berry – *Camrose, V.*
Berry – *Kemsley, V.*
Bertie – *Lindsey, E.*
Best – *Wynford*
Bethell – *Westbury*
Bewicke-Copley – *Cromwell*
Bigham – *Mersey, V.*
Bingham – *B. of Cornhill**
Bingham – *Clanmorris*
Bingham – *Lucan, E.*
Black – *B. of Crossharbour**
Bligh – *Darnley, E.*
Blyth – *B. of Rowington**
Bonham Carter – *B.-C. of Yarnbury**
Bootle-Wilbraham – *Skelmersdale*
Boscawen – *Falmouth, V.*
Boston – *B. of Faversham**
Bottomley – *B. of Nettlestone**
Bourke – *Mayo, E.*
Bowes Lyon – *Strathmore, E.*
Bowyer – *Denham*
Boyd – *Kilmarnock*
Boyd – *B. of Duncansby**
Boyle – *Cork and Orrery, E.*
Boyle – *Glasgow, E.*
Boyle – *Shannon, E.*
Brabazon – *Meath, E.*
Brand – *Hampden, V.*
Brassey – *B. of Apethorpe*
Brett – *Esher, V.*
Bridgeman – *Bradford, E.*
Brittan – *B. of Spennithorne**
Brodrick – *Midleton, V.*
Brooke – *Alanbrooke, V.*
Brooke – *B. of Alverthorpe**
Brooke – *Brookeborough, V.*
Brooke – *B. of Sutton Mandeville**
Brooks – *B. of Tremorfa**
Brooks – *Crawshaw*
Brougham – *Brougham and Vaux*
Broughton – *Fairhaven*
Brown – *B. of Eaton-under-Heywood**
Browne – *B. of Belmont**
Browne – *B. of Madingley**
Browne – *Kilmaine*
Browne – *Oranmore and Browne*
Browne – *Sligo, M.*
Bruce – *Aberdare*
Bruce – *Balfour of Burleigh*
Bruce – *Elgin and Kincardine, E.*
Brudenell-Bruce – *Ailesbury, M.*
Buchan – *Tweedsmuir*
Buckley – *Wrenbury*
Butler – *B. of Brockwell**
Butler – *Carrick, E.*
Butler – *Dunboyne*
Butler – *Mountgarret, V.*
Byng – *Strafford, E.*
Byng – *Torrington, V.*
Cambell-Savours – *C.-S. of Allerdale**
Cameron – *C. of Dillington**
Cameron – *C. of Lochbroom**
Campbell – *Argyll, D.*
Campbell – *C. of Alloway**
Campbell – *C. of Loughborough**
Campbell – *C. of Surbiton**
Campbell – *Cawdor, E.*
Campbell – *Colgrain*
Campbell – *Stratheden and Campbell*
Campbell-Gray – *Gray*
Canning – *Garvagh*
Capell – *Essex, E.*
Carey – *C. of Clifton**
Carington – *Carrington*
Carlisle – *C. of Berriew**
Carnegie – *Fife, D.*
Carnegie – *Northesk, E.*
Carr – *C. of Hadley**
Carter – *C. of Barnes**
Carter – *C. of Coles**
Cary – *Falkland, V.*
Caulfeild – *Charlemont, V.*
Cavendish – *C. of Furness**
Cavendish – *Chesham*
Cavendish – *Devonshire, D.*
Cavendish – *Waterpark*
Cayzer – *Rotherwick*
Cecil – *Amherst of Hackney*
Cecil – *Exeter, M.*
Cecil – *Rockley*
Chalker – *C. of Wallasey**
Chaloner – *Gisborough*
Chapman – *C. of Leeds**
Chapman – *Northfield**
Charteris – *Wemyss and March, E.*
Chetwynd-Talbot – *Shrewsbury, E.*
Chichester – *Donegall, M.*
Child Villiers – *Jersey, E.*
Cholmondeley – *Delamere*
Chubb – *Hayter*

Clark – *C. of Calton**
Clarke – *C. of Hampstead**
Clarke – *C. of Stone-Cum-Ebony**
Clegg-Hill – *Hill, V.*
Clifford – *C. of Chudleigh*
Cochrane – *C. of Cults*
Cochrane – *Dundonald, E.*
Cocks – *Somers*
Cohen – *C. of Pimlico**
Cokayne – *Cullen of Ashbourne*
Coke – *Leicester, E.*
Cole – *Enniskillen, E.*
Collier – *Monkswell*
Collins – *C. of Mapesbury**
Colville – *Clydesmuir*
Colville – *C. of Culross, V.*
Compton – *Northampton, M.*
Conolly-Carew – *Carew*
Cooper – *Norwich, V*
Cope – *C. of Berkeley**
Corbett – *C. of Castle Vale**.
Corbett – *Rowallan*
Cornwall-Leigh – *Grey of Condor*
Courtenay – *Devon, E.*
Craig – *C. of Radley**
Craig – *Craigavon, V.*
Crichton – *Erne, E.*
Crichton-Stuart – *Bute, M.*
Cripps – *Parmoor*
Crossley – *Somerleyton*
Cubitt – *Ashcombe*
Cunliffe-Lister – *Masham of Ilton**
Cunliffe-Lister – *Swinton, E.*
Cunningham – *C. of Felling**
Currie – *C. of Marylebone**
Curzon – *Howe, E.*
Curzon – *Scarsdale, V.*
Cust – *Brownlow*
Czernin – *Howard de Walden*
Dalrymple – *Stair, E.*
Darzi – *D. of Denham**
Daubeny de Moleyns – *Ventry*
Davidson – *D. of Glen Clova**
Davies – *D. of Abersoch**
Davies – *D. of Coity**
Davies – *Darwen*
Davies – *D. of Oldham**
Dawnay – *Downe, V.*
Dawson-Damer – *Portarlington, E.*
Dean – *D. of Thornton-le-Fylde**
Deane – *Muskerry*
de Courcy – *Kingsale*
de Grey – *Walsingham*
Delacourt-Smith – *Delacourt Smith of Alteryn**
Denison – *Londesborough*
Denison-Pender – *Pender*
Devereux – *Hereford, V.*
Dewar – *Forteviot*
Dixon – *Glentoran*
Dodson – *Monk Bretton*
Douglas – *Morton, E.*
Douglas – *Queensberry, M.*
Douglas-Hamilton – *Hamilton, D.*
Douglas-Hamilton – *Selkirk, E.*
Douglas-Hamilton – *Selkirk of Douglas**
Douglas-Home – *Dacre*
Douglas-Home – *Home, E.*
Douglas-Pennant – *Penrhyn*
Douglas-Scott-Montagu – *Montagu of Beaulieu*
Drummond – *Perth, E.*
Drummond of Megginch – *Strange*
Dugdale – *Crathorne*
Duke – *Merrivale*
Duncombe – *Feversham*
Dundas – *Melville, V.*
Dundas – *Zetland, M.*
Eady – *Swinfen*
Eccles – *E. of Moulton**
Eden – *Auckland*
Eden – *E. of Winton**
Eden – *Henley*
Edgcumbe – *Mount Edgcumbe, E.*
Edmondson – *Sandford*
Edwardes – *Kensington*
Edwards – *Crickhowell**
Egerton – *Sutherland, D.*
Eliot – *St Germans, E.*
Elliott – *E. of Morpeth**
Elliot-Murray-Kynynmound – *Minto, E.*
Ellis – *Seaford*
Erskine – *Buchan, E.*
Erskine – *Mar and Kellie, E.*
Erskine-Murray – *Elibank*
Evans – *E. of Parkside**
Evans – *E. of Temple Guiting**
Evans – *E. of Watford**
Evans – *Mountevans*
Evans-Freke – *Carbery*
Eve – *Silsoe*
Fairfax – *F. of Cameron*
Falconer – *F. of Thoroton**
Falkner – *F. of Margravine**
Fane – *Westmorland, E.*
Farrington – *F. of Ribbleton**
Faulkner – *F. of Worcester**
Fearn – *F. of Southport**
Feilding – *Denbigh and Desmond, E.*
Felton – *Seaford*
Fellowes – *De Ramsey*
Fermor-Hesketh – *Hesketh*
Fiennes – *Saye and Sele*
Fiennes-Clinton – *Lincoln, E.*
Finch Hatton – *Winchilsea, E.*
Finch-Knightley – *Aylesford, E.*
Finlay – *F. of Llandaff**
Fitzalan-Howard – *Herries of Terregles*
Fitzalan-Howard – *Norfolk, D.*
FitzGerald – *Leinster, D.*
Fitzherbert – *Stafford*
FitzRoy – *Grafton, D.*
FitzRoy – *Southampton*
FitzRoy Newdegate – *Daventry, V.*
Fletcher-Vane – *Inglewood*
Flower – *Ashbrook, V.*
Foljambe – *Liverpool, E.*
Forbes – *Granard, E*
Forsyth – *F. of Drumlean**
Forwood – *Arlington*
Foster – *F. of Thames Bank**
Foulkes – *F. of Cumnock**
Fowler – *F. of Sutton Caulfield**
Fox-Strangways – *Ilchester, E.*
Frankland – *Zouche*
Fraser – *F. of Carmyllie**
Fraser – *F. of Kilmorack**
Fraser – *Lovat*
Fraser – *Saltoun*
Fraser – *Strathalmond*
Freeman-Grenville – *Kinloss*
Fremantle – *Cottesloe*
French – *De Freyne*
Fyfe – *F. of Fairfield**
Galbraith – *Strathclyde*
Garden – *G. of Frognal**
Gardner – *G. of Parkes**
Gascoyne-Cecil – *M. of Salisbury**
Gathorne-Hardy – *Cranbrook, E.*
Gibbs – *Aldenham*
Gibbs – *Wraxall*
Gibson – *Ashbourne*
Gibson – *G. of Market Rasen**
Giffard – *Halsbury, E.*
Gilbey – *Vaux of Harrowden*
Glyn – *Wolverton*
Godley – *Kilbracken*
Goff – *G. of Chieveley**
Golding – *G. of Newcastle-under-Lyme**
Gordon – *Aberdeen, M.*
Gordon – *G. of Strathblane**
Gordon – *Huntly, M.*
Gordon Lennox – *Richmond, D.*
Gore – *Arran, E.*
Gould – *G. of Brookwood**
Gould – *G. of Potternewton**
Graham – *G. of Edmonton**
Graham – *Montrose, D.*
Graham-Toler – *Norbury, E.*
Granshaw – *Northover**
Grant of Grant – *Strathspey*
Grant of Rothiemurchus – *Dysart, C.*
Granville – *G. of Eye**
Greenall – *Daresbury*
Greville – *Warwick, E.*
Griffiths – *G. of Burry Port**
Griffiths – *G. of Fforestfach**
Grigg – *Altrincham*
Grimston – *G. of Westbury*
Grimston – *Verulam, E.*
Grosvenor – *Westminster, D.*
Grosvenor – *Wilton and Ebury, E*
Guest – *Wimborne, V*
Gueterbock – *Berkeley*
Guinness – *Iveagh, E.*
Guinness – *Moyne*
Gully – *Selby, V.*
Gummer – *Chadlington**
Gurdon – *Cranworth*
Guthrie – *G. of Craigiebank**
Gwynne Jones – *Chalfont**
Hale – *H. of Richmond**
Hamilton – *Abercorn, D.*
Hamilton – *Belhaven and Stenton*
Hamilton – *H. of Dalzell*
Hamilton – *H. of Epsom**
Hamilton – *Holm Patrick*
Hamilton-Russell – *Boyne, V.*
Hamilton-Smith – *Colwyn*
Hanbury-Tracy – *Sudeley*
Handcock – *Castlemaine*
Hannay – *H. of Chiswick**
Harbord-Hamond – *Suffield*
Harding – *H. of Petherton*
Hardinge – *H. of Penshurst*
Hare – *Blakenham, V.*
Hare – *Listowel, E.*
Harmsworth – *Rothermere, V.*
Harries – *H. of Pentregarth**
Harris – *H. of Haringey**
Harris – *H. of Peckham**

Harris – *H. of Richmond**
Harris – *Malmesbury, E.*
Hart – *H. of Chilton**
Harvey – *H. of Tasburgh*
Hastings – *H. of Scarisbrick**
Hastings Bass – *Huntingdon, E.*
Haughey – *Ballyedmond**
Hay – *Erroll, E.*
Hay – *Kinnoull, E.*
Hay – *Tweeddale, M.*
Heathcote-Drummond-Willoughby – *Willoughby de Eresby*
Hely-Hutchinson – *Donoughmore, E.*
Henderson – *Faringdon*
Hennessy – *Windlesham*
Henniker-Major – *Henniker*
Hepburne-Scott – *Polwarth*
Herbert – *Carnarvon, E.*
Herbert – *Hemingford*
Herbert – *Pembroke, E.*
Herbert – *Powis, E.*
Hervey – *Bristol, M.*
Heseltine – *H. of Thenford**
Hewitt – *Lifford, V.*
Hicks Beach – *St Aldwyn, E.*
Hill – *Downshire, M.*
Hill – *Sandys*
Hill-Trevor – *Trevor*
Hilton – *H. of Eggardon**
Hobart-Hampden – *Buckinghamshire, E.*
Hodgson – *H. of Astley Abbotts**
Hogg – *Hailsham, V.*
Holland-Hibbert – *Knutsford, V.*
Hollis – *H. of Heigham**
Holmes à Court – *Heytesbury*
Hood – *Bridport, V.*
Hope – *Glendevon*
Hope – *H. of Craighead**
Hope – *H. of Thornes**
Hope – *Linlithgow, M.*
Hope – *Rankeillour*
Hope Johnstone – *Annandale and Hartfell, E.*
Hope-Morley – *Hollenden*
Hopkinson – *Colyton*
Hore Ruthven – *Gowrie, E.*
Hovell-Thurlow-Cumming-Bruce – *Thurlow*
Howard – *Carlisle, E.*
Howard – *Effingham, E.*
Howard – *H. of Penrith*
Howard – *H. of Rising**
Howard – *Strathcona*
Howard – *Suffolk and Berkshire, E.*
Howarth – *H. of Breckland**
Howarth – *H. of Newport**
Howe – *H. of Aberavon**
Howe – *H. of Idlicote**
Howell – *H. of Guildford**
Howells – *H. of St. Davids**
Howie – *H. of Troon**
Hubbard – *Addington*
Huggins – *Malvern, V.*
Hughes – *H. of Woodside**
Hughes-Young – *St Helens*
Hunt – *H. of Chesterton**
Hunt – *H. of Kings Heath**
Hunt – *H. of Wirral**
Hurd – *H. of Westwell**
Hutchinson – *H. of Lullington**
Ingrams – *Darcy de Knayth*
Innes-Ker – *Roxburghe, D.*
Inskip – *Caldecote, V.*
Irby – *Boston*
Irvine – *I. of Lairg**
Isaacs – *Reading, M.*
James – *J. of Blackheath**
James – *J. of Holland Park**
James – *Northbourne*
Janner – *J. of Braunstone**
Jay – *J. of Ewelme**
Jay – *J. of Paddington**
Jebb – *Gladwyn*
Jenkin – *J. of Roding**
Jervis – *St Vincent, V.*
Jocelyn – *Roden, E.*
Jolliffe – *Hylton*
Jones – *J. of Birmingham**
Jones – *J. of Cheltenham**
Jones – *J. of Deeside**
Jones – *J. of Whitchurch**
Joynson-Hicks – *Brentford, V.*
Kay-Shuttleworth – *Shuttleworth*
Kearley – *Devonport, V.*
Keith – *Kintore, E.*
Kemp – *Rochdale, V.*
Kennedy – *Ailsa, M*
Kennedy – *K. of the Shaws**
Kenworthy – *Strabolgi*
Keppel – *Albemarle, E.*
Kerr – *K. of Kinlochard**
Kerr – *K. of Tonaghmore**
Kerr – *Lothian, M.*
Kerr – *Teviot*
Kilpatrick – *K. of Kincraig**
King – *Lovelace, E.*
King – *K. of West Bromwich**
King-Tenison – *Kingston, E.*
Kinnock – *K. of Holyhead**
Kirkham – *Berners*
Kirkwood – *K. of Kirkhope**
Kitchener – *K. of Khartoum, E.*
Knatchbull – *Brabourne*
Knatchbull – *Mountbatten of Burma, C.*
Knight – *K. of Collingtree**
Knox – *Ranfurly, E.*
Laing – *L. of Dunphail**
Lamb – *Rochester*
Lambton – *Durham, E.*
Lamont – *L. of Lerwick**
Lampson – *Killearn*
Lang – *L. of Monkton**
Lascelles – *Harewood, E.*
Law – *Coleraine*
Law – *Ellenborough*
Lawrence – *Trevethin and Oaksey*
Lawson – *Burnham*
Lawson – *L. of Blaby**
Lawson-Johnston – *Luke*
Lea – *L. of Crondall**
Leach – *L. of Fairford**
Lee – *L. of Trafford**
Legge – *Dartmouth, E.*
Legh – *Grey of Codnor*
Legh – *Newton*
Leigh-Pemberton – *Kingsdown**
Leith – *Burgh*
Lennox-Boyd – *Boyd of Merton, V.*
Le Poer Trench – *Clancarty, E.*
Leslie – *Rothes, E.*
Leslie Melville – *Leven and Melville, E.*
Lester – *L. of Herne Hill**
Levene – *L. of Portsoken**
Leveson-Gower – *Granville, E.*
Lewis – *L. of Newnham**
Lewis – *Merthyr*
Liddell – *Ravensworth*
Lindesay-Bethune – *Lindsay, E.*
Lindsay – *Crawford, E.*
Lindsay – *L. of Birker*
Linklater – *L. of Butterstone**
Littleton – *Hatherton*
Lloyd – *L. of Berwick**
Lloyd George – *Lloyd George of Dwyfor, E.*
Lloyd George – *Tenby, V.*
Lloyd-Mostyn – *Mostyn*
Loder – *Wakehurst*
Lofthouse – *L. of Pontefract**
Lopes – *Roborough*
Lour – *Carneggy of Lour**
Low – *Aldington*
Low – *L. of Dalston**
Lowry-Corry – *Belmore, E.*
Lowther – *Lonsdale, E.*
Lowther – *Ullswater, V.*
Lubbock – *Avebury*
Lucas – *L. of Chilworth*
Lumley – *Scarbrough, E.*
Lumley-Savile – *Savile*
Lyell – *L. of Markyate**
Lyon-Dalberg-Acton – *Acton*
Lysaght – *Lisle*
Lyttelton – *Chandos, V.*
Lyttelton – *Cobham, V.*
Lytton Cobbold – *Cobbold*
McAlpine – *M. of West Green**
Macaulay – *M. of Bragar**
McClintock-Bunbury – *Rathdonnell*
McColl – *M. of Dulwich**
Macdonald – *M. of Tradeston**
McDonnell – *Antrim, E.*
Macfarlane – *M. of Bearsden**
McFarlane – *M. of Llandaff**
MacGregor – *M. of Pulham Market**
McIntosh – *M. of Haringey**
McIntosh – *M. of Hudnall**
McKenzie – *M. of Luton**
Mackay – *Inchcape, E.*
Mackay – *M. of Clashfern**
Mackay – *M. of Drumadoon**
Mackay – *Reay*
Mackay – *Tanlaw**
MacKenzie – *M. of Culkein**
MacKenzie – *M. of Framwellgate**
Mackenzie – *Cromartie, E.*
Mackie – *M. of Benshie**
Mackintosh – *M. of Halifax, V.*
McLaren – *Aberconway*
*MacLaurin – M. of Knebworth**
MacLennan – *M. of Rogart**
Macmillan – *Stockton, E.*
Macpherson – *M. of Drumochter*
Macpherson – *Strathcarron*
Maffey – *Rugby*
Maginnis – *M. of Drumglass**
Maitland – *Lauderdale, E.*
Makgill – *Oxfuird, V.*
Makins – *Sherfield*
Manners – *Rutland, D.*
Manningham-Buller – *Dilhorne, V.*
Mansfield – *Sandhurst*
Marks – *M. of Broughton*

Marquis – _Woolton, E._
Marshall – _M. of Knightsbridge_*
Marsham – _Romney, E._
Martin – _M. of Springburn_*
Martyn-Hemphill – _Hemphill_
Mason – _M. of Barnsley_*
Massey – _M. of Darwen_*
Masters – _Noakes_*
Maude – _Hawarden, V._
Maxwell – _de Ros_
Maxwell – _Farnham_
May – _M. of Oxford_*
Mayhew – _M. of Twysden_*
Meade – _Clanwilliam, E._
Mercer Nairne Petty-Fitzmaurice – _Lansdowne, M._
Millar – _Inchyra_
Miller – _M. of Chiltorne Domer_*
Miller – _M. of Hendon_*
Milner – _M. of Leeds_
Mitchell-Thomson – _Selsdon_
Mitford – _Redesdale_
Molyneaux – _M. of Killead_*
Monckton – _M. of Brenchley, V._
Monckton-Arundell – _Galway, V._
Mond – _Melchett_
Money-Coutts – _Latymer_
Montagu – _Manchester, D._
Montagu – _Sandwich, E._
Montagu – _Swaythling_
Montagu Douglas Scott – _Buccleuch, D._
Montagu Stuart Wortley – _Wharncliffe, E._
Montague – _Amwell_
Montgomerie – _Eglinton, E._
Montgomery – _M. of Alamein, V._
Moore – _Drogheda, E._
Moore – _M. of Lower Marsh_*
Moore-Brabazon – _Brabazon of Tara_
Moreton – _Ducie, E_
Morgan – _M. of Drefelin_*
Morgan – _M. of Huyton_*
Morris – _Killanin_
Morris – _M. of Aberavon_*
Morris – _M. of Bolton_*
Morris – _M. of Handsworth_*
Morris – _M. of Manchester_*
Morris – _M. of Kenwood_
Morris – _M. of Yardley_*
Morris – _Naseby_*
Morrison – _Dunrossil, V._
Morrison – _Margadale_
Moser – _M. of Regents Park_*
Mosley – _Ravensdale_
Mountbatten – _Milford Haven, M._
Muff – _Calverley_
Mulholland – _Dunleath_
Murray – _Atholl, D._
Murray – _Dunmore, E._
Murray – _Mansfield and Mansfield, E._
Nall-Cain – _Brocket_
Napier – _Napier and Ettrick_
Napier – _N. of Magdala_
Needham – _Kilmorey, E._
Neill – _N. of Bladen_*
Nelson – _N. of Stafford_
Neuberger – _N. of Abbotsbury_*
Nevill – _Abergavenny, M._
Neville – _Braybrooke_
Newton – _N. of Braintree_*
Nicholls – _N. of Birkenhead_*
Nicolson – _Carnock_
Nicholson – _N. of Winterboune_*
Nivison – _Glendyne_
Noel – _Gainsborough, E._
North – _Guilford, E._
Northcote – _Iddesleigh, E._
Norton – _Grantley_
Norton – _N. of Louth_*
Norton – _Rathcreedan_
Nugent – _Westmeath, E._
Oakeshott – _O. of Seagrove Bay_*
O'Brien – _Inchiquin_
Ogilvie-Grant – _Seafield, E._
Ogilvy – _Airlie, E._
O'Neill – _O'N. of Bengarve_*
O'Neill – _O'N. of Clackmannan_*
O'Neill – _Rathcavan_
Orde-Powlett – _Bolton_
Ormsby-Gore – _Harlech_
Ouseley – _O. of Peckham Rye_*
Paget – _Anglesey, M._
Paisley – _P. of St George's_*
Pakenham – _Longford, E._
Pakington – _Hampton_
Palmer – _Lucas and Dingwall_
Palmer – _Selborne, E._
Park – _P. of Monmouth_*
Parker – _Macclesfield, E._
Parker – _Morley, E._
Parnell – _Congleton_
Parsons – _Rosse, E._
Patel – _P. of Blackburn_*
Patel – _P. of Bradford_*
Patten – _P. of Barnes_*
Paulet – _Winchester, M._
Pearson – _Cowdray, V._
Pearson – _P. of Rannoch_*
Pease – _Gainford_
Pease – _Wardington_
Pelham – _Chichester, E._
Pelham – _Yarborough, E._
Pellew – _Exmouth, V_
Pendry – _P. of Stalybridge_*.
Penny – _Marchwood, V._
Pepys – _Cottenham, E._
Perceval – _Egmont, E._
Percy – _Northumberland, D._
Perry – _P. of Southwark_*
Pery – _Limerick, E._
Philipps – _Milford_
Philipps – _St Davids, V._
Phillips – _P. of Sudbury_*
Phillips – _P. of Worth Matravers_*
Phipps – _Normanby, M._
Pilkington – _P. of Oxenford_*
Plant – _P. of Highfield_*
Platt – _P. of Writtle_*
Pleydell-Bouverie – _Radnor, E._
Plummer – _P. of St Marylebone_*
Plumptre – _Fitzwalter_
Plunkett – _Dunsany_
Plunkett – _Louth_
Pollock – _Hanworth, V._
Pomeroy – _Harberton, V._
Ponsonby – _Bessborough, E._
Ponsonby – _de Mauley_
Ponsonby – _P. of Shulbrede_
Ponsonby – _Sysonby_
Powell – _P. of Bayswater_*
Powys – _Lilford_
Pratt – _Camden, M._
Preston – _Gormanston, V._
Primrose – _Rosebery, E._
Prittie – _Dunalley_
Ramsay – _Dalhousie, E._
Ramsay – _R. of Cartvale_*
Ramsbotham – _Soulbury, V._
Randall – _R. of St. Budeaux_*
Rees – _R. of Ludlow_*
Rees-Williams – _Ogmore_
Rendell – _R. of Babergh_*
Renfrew – _R. of Kaimsthorn_*
Renton – _R. of Mount Harry_*
Renwick – _R. of Clifton_*
Rhys – _Dynevor_
Richards – _Milverton_
Richardson – _R. of Calow_*
Richardson – _R. of Duntisbourne_*
Ritchie – _R. of Dundee_
Roberts – _Clwyd_
Roberts – _R. of Conway_*
Roberts – _R. of Llandudno_*
Robertson – _R. of Oakridge_
Robertson – _R. of Port Ellen_*
Robertson – _Wharton_
Robinson – _Martonmere_
Roche – _Fermoy_
Rodd – _Rennell_
Rodger – _R. of Earlsferry_*
Rodgers – _R. of Quarry Bank_*
Rogers – _R. of Riverside_*
Roper-Curzon – _Teynham_
Rospigliosi – _Newburgh, E._
Rous – _Stradbroke, E._
Rowley-Conwy – _Langford_
Royall – _R. of Blaisdon_*
Runciman – _R. of Doxford, V._
Russell – _Ampthill_
Russell – _Bedford, D._
Russell – _de Clifford_
Russell – _R. of Liverpool_
Ryder – _Harrowby, E._
Ryder – _R. of Wensum_*
Sackville – _De La Warr, E._
Sackville-West – _Sackville_
Sainsbury – _S. of Preston Candover_*
Sainsbury – _S. of Turville_*
St Aubyn – _St Levan_
St Clair – _Sinclair_
St Clair-Erskine – _Rosslyn, E._
St John – _Bolingbroke and St John, V._
St John – _St John of Blesto_
St John-Stevas – _St John of Fawsley_*
St Leger – _Doneraile, V._
Samuel – _Bearsted, V._
Sanderson – _S. of Ayot_
Sanderson – _S. of Bowden_*
Sandilands – _Torphichen_
Saumarez – _De Saumarez_
Savile – _Mexborough, E._
Saville – _S. of Newdigate_*
Scarlett – _Abinger_
Schreiber – _Marlesford_*
Sclater-Booth – _Basing_
Scotland – _S. of Asthal_*
Scott – _Eldon, E_
Scott – _S. of Foscotte_*
Scott – _S. of Needham Market_*.
Scrymgeour – _Dundee, E._
Seager – _Leighton of St Mellons_
Seely – _Mottistone_
Seymour – _Hertford, M._
Seymour – _Somerset, D._
Sharp – _S. of Guildford_*
Shaw – _Craigmyle_
Shaw – _S. of Northstead_*
Shephard – _S. of Northwood_*

Sheppard – _S. of Didgemere_*
Shirley – _Ferrers, E._
Short – _Glenamara_*
Shutt – _S. of Greetland_*
Siddeley – _Kenilworth_
Sidney – _De L'Isle, V._
Simon – _S. of Highbury_*
Simon – _S. of Wythenshawe_
Simpson – _S. of Dunkeld_*
Sinclair – _Caithness, E._
Sinclair – _S. of Cleeve_
Sinclair – _Thurso, V._
Skeffington – _Massereene, V._
Smith – _Bicester_
Smith – _Hambleden, V._
Smith – _Kirkhill_*
Smith – _S. of Clifton_*
Smith – _Smith of Finsbury_*
Smith – _S. of Gilmorehill_*
Smith – _S. of Kelvin_*
Smith – _S. of Leigh_*
Somerset – _Beaufort, D._
Somerset – _Raglan_
Soulsby – _S. of Swaffham Prior_*
Spencer – _Churchill, V._
Spencer-Churchill – _Marlborough, D._
Spring Rice – _Monteagle of Brandon_
Stanhope – _Harrington, E._
Stanley – _Derby, E._
Stanley – _of Alderley and Sheffield_
Stapleton-Cotton – _Combermere, V._
Steel – _S. of Aikwood_*
Sterling – _S. of Plaistow_*
Stern – _S. of Brentford_*
Stevens – _S. of Kirkwhelpington_*
Stevens – _S. of Ludgate_*
Stevenson – _S. of Coddenham_*
Stewart – _Galloway, E._
Stewart – _Stewartby_*
Stoddart – _S. of Swindon_*
Stone – _S. of Blackheath_*
Stonor – _Camoys_
Stopford – _Courtown, E._
Stourton – _Mowbray_
Strachey – _O'Hagan_
Strutt – _Belper_
Strutt – _Rayleigh_
Stuart – _Castle Stewart, E._
Stuart – _Moray, E._
Stuart – _S. of Findhorn, V._
Suenson-Taylor – _Grantchester_
Sutherland – _S. of Houndwood_*
Symons – _S. of Vernham Dean_*
Taylor – _Kilclooney_*
Taylor – _T. of Blackburn_*
Taylor – _T. of Bolton_*
Taylor – _T. of Holbeach_*
Taylor – _T. of Warwick_*
Taylour – _Headfort, M._
Temple-Gore-Langton – _Temple of Stowe, E_
Temple-Morris – _Temple-Morris of Llandaff_*
Tennant – _Glenconner_
Thellusson – _Rendlesham_
Thesiger – _Chelmsford, V._
Thomas – _T. of Gresford_*
Thomas – _T. of Macclesfield_*
Thomas – _T. of Swynnerton_*
Thomas – _T. of Walliswood_*
Thomas – _T. of Winchester_*
Thomson – _T. of Fleet_
Thynn – _Bath, M._
Tottenham – _Ely, M._
Trefusis – _Clinton_
Trench – _Ashtown_
Tufton – _Hothfield_
Turner – _Bilston_*
Turner – _Netherthorpe_
Turner – _T. of Camden_*
Turner – _T. of Ecchinswell_*
Turnour – _Winterton, E._
Tyrell-Kenyon – _Kenyon_
Vanden-Bempde-Johnstone – _Derwent_
Vane – _Barnard_
Vane-Tempest-Stewart – _Londonderry, M._
Vanneck – _Huntingfield_
Vaughan – _Lisburne, E._
Vereker – _Gort, V._
Verney – _Willoughby de Broke_
Vernon – _Lyveden_
Vesey – _De Vesci, V._
Villiers – _Clarendon, E._
Vincent – _V. of Coleshill_*
Vivian – _Swansea_
Wade – _W. of Chorlton_*
Waldegrave – _W. of North Hill_*
Walker – _W. of Aldringham_*
Walker – _W. of Gestingthorpe_*
Walker – _W. of Worcester_*
Wall – _W. of New Barnett_*
Wallace – _Dudley_
Wallace – _W. of Saltaire_*
Wallace – _W. of Tankerness_*
Wallace – _W. of Tummel_*
Wallop – _Portsmouth, E._
Walton – _W. of Detchant_*
Ward – _Bangor, V._
Ward – _Dudley, E._
Warrender – _Bruntisfield_
Warwick – _W. of Undercliffe_*
Watson – _W. of Invergowrie_*
Watson – _Manton_
Watson – _W. of Richmond_*
Webber – _Lloyd-Webber_*
Wedderburn – _W. of Charlton_*
Weir – _Inverforth_
Weld-Forester – _Forester_
Wellesley – _Cowley, E._
Wellesley – _Wellington, D._
West – _W. of Spithead_*
Westenra – _Rossmore_
White – _Annaly_
White – _Hanningfield_*
Whiteley – _Marchamley_
Whitfield – _Kenswood_
Williams – _W. of Crosby_*
Williams – _W. of Elve_*
Williamson – _Forres_
Williamson – _W. of Horton_*
Willoughby – _Middleton_
Wills – _Dulverton_
Wilson – _Moran_
Wilson – _Nunburnholme_
Wilson – _W. of Dinton_*
Wilson – _W. of Tillyorn_*
Windsor – _Gloucester, D._
Windsor – _Kent, D._
Windsor-Clive – _Plymouth, E._
Wingfield – _Powerscourt, V._
Winn – _St Oswald_
Wodehouse – _Kimberley, E._
Wolfson – _W. of Sunningdale_*
Wood – _Halifax, E._
Woodhouse – _Terrington_
Woolmer – _W. of Leeds_*
Wright – _W. of Richmond_*
Wyndham – _Egremont and Leconfield_
Wyndham-Quin – _Dunraven, E._
Wynn – _Newborough_
Yarde-Buller – _Churston_
Yerburgh – _Alvingham_
Yorke – _Hardwicke, E._
Young – _Kennet_
Young – _Y. of Graffham_*
Young – _Y. of Hornsey_*
Young – _Y. of Norwood Green_*
Young – _Y. of Old Scone_*
Younger – _Y. of Leckie, V._

ORDERS OF CHIVALRY

THE MOST NOBLE ORDER OF THE GARTER (1348)

KG
Ribbon, Blue
Motto, Honi soit qui mal y pense
(Shame on him who thinks evil of it)

The number of Knights and Lady Companions is limited to 24

SOVEREIGN OF THE ORDER
The Queen

LADIES OF THE ORDER
HRH The Princess Royal, 1994
HRH Princess Alexandra, The Hon. Lady Ogilvy, 2003

ROYAL KNIGHTS
HRH The Prince Philip, Duke of Edinburgh, 1947
HRH The Prince of Wales, 1958
HRH The Duke of Kent, 1985
HRH The Duke of Gloucester, 1997
HRH The Duke of York, 2006
HRH The Earl of Wessex, 2006
HRH Prince William of Wales, 2008

EXTRA KNIGHT COMPANIONS AND LADIES
Grand Duke Jean of Luxembourg, 1972
HM The Queen of Denmark, 1979
HM The King of Sweden, 1983
HM The King of Spain, 1988
HM The Queen of the Netherlands, 1989
HIM The Emperor of Japan, 1998
HM The King of Norway, 2001

KNIGHTS AND LADY COMPANIONS
Duke of Grafton, 1976
Lord Richardson of Duntisbourne, 1983
Lord Carrington, 1985
Duke of Wellington, 1990
Lord Bramall, 1990
Viscount Ridley, 1992
Lord Sainsbury of Preston Candover, 1992
Lord Ashburton, 1994
Lord Kingsdown, 1994
Sir Ninian Stephen, 1994
Baroness Thatcher, 1995
Sir Timothy Colman, 1996
Duke of Abercorn, 1999
Sir William Gladstone, 1999
Lord Inge, 2001
Sir Anthony Acland, 2001
Duke of Westminster, 2003
Lord Butler of Brockwell, 2003
Lord Morris of Aberavon, 2003
Lady Soames, 2005
Lord Bingham of Cornhill, 2005
Sir John Major, 2005
Lord Luce, 2008
Sir Thomas Dunne, 2008

Prelate, Bishop of Winchester
Chancellor, Lord Carrington, KG, GCMG, CH, MC
Register, Dean of Windsor
Garter King of Arms, Peter Gwynn-Jones, CVO
Gentleman Usher of the Black Rod, Lt.-Gen. Sir Frederick Viggers, KCB, CMG, MBE
Secretary, Patric Dickinson, LVO

THE MOST ANCIENT AND MOST NOBLE ORDER OF THE THISTLE (REVIVED 1687)

KT
Ribbon, Green
Motto, Nemo me impune lacessit
(No one provokes me with impunity)

The number of Knights and Ladies of the Thistle is limited to 16

SOVEREIGN OF THE ORDER
The Queen

ROYAL LADY OF THE ORDER
HRH The Princess Royal, 2000

ROYAL KNIGHTS
HRH The Prince Philip, Duke of Edinburgh, 1952
HRH The Prince of Wales, Duke of Rothesay, 1977

KNIGHTS AND LADIES
Earl of Elgin and Kincardine, 1981
Earl of Airlie, 1985
Viscount of Arbuthnott, 1996
Earl of Crawford and Balcarres, 1996
Lady Marion Fraser, 1996
Lord Macfarlane of Bearsden, 1996
Lord Mackay of Clashfern, 1997
Lord Wilson of Tillyorn, 2000
Lord Sutherland of Houndwood, 2002
Sir Eric Anderson, 2002
Lord Steel of Aikwood, 2004
Lord Robertson of Port Ellen, 2004
Lord Cullen of Whitekirk, 2007
Sir Garth Morrison, 2007

Chancellor, Earl of Airlie, KT, GCVO, PC
Dean, Very Revd Gilleasbuig Macmillan, CVO
Secretary and Lord Lyon King of Arms, David Sellar
Gentleman Usher of the Green Rod, Rear Adm. Christopher Layman, CB, DSO, LVO

THE MOST HONOURABLE ORDER OF THE BATH (1725)

GCB *Military* GCB *Civil*

GCB	Knight (or Dame) Grand Cross
KCB	Knight Commander
DCB	Dame Commander
CB	Companion

Ribbon, Crimson
Motto, Tria juncta in uno
(Three joined in one)

Remodelled 1815, and enlarged many times since. The order is divided into civil and military divisions. Women became eligible for the order from 1 January 1971.

THE SOVEREIGN

GREAT MASTER AND FIRST OR PRINCIPAL KNIGHT GRAND CROSS
HRH The Prince of Wales, KG, KT, GCB, OM

Dean of the Order, Dean of Westminster
Bath King of Arms, Adm. Lord Boyce, GCB, OBE
Registrar and Secretary, Rear-Adm. Iain Henderson, CB, CBE
Genealogist, Peter Gwynn-Jones, CVO
Gentleman Usher of the Scarlet Rod, Maj.-Gen. Charles Vyvyan, CB, CBE
Deputy Secretary, Secretary of the Central Chancery of the Orders of Knighthood
Chancery, Central Chancery of the Orders of Knighthood, St James's Palace, London SW1A 1BH

THE ORDER OF MERIT (1902)

OM *Military* OM *Civil*

OM
Ribbon, Blue and crimson

This order is designed as a special distinction for eminent men and women without conferring a knighthood upon them. The order is limited in numbers to 24, with the addition of foreign honorary members.

THE SOVEREIGN

HRH The Prince Philip, Duke of Edinburgh, 1968
Revd Prof. Owen Chadwick, KBE, 1983
Sir Andrew Huxley, 1983
Dr Frederick Sanger, 1986
Baroness Thatcher, 1990
Dame Joan Sutherland, 1991
Sir Michael Atiyah, 1992
Lucian Freud, 1993
Sir Aaron Klug, 1995
Lord Foster of Thames Bank, 1997
Sir James Black, 2000
Sir Anthony Caro, 2000
Prof. Sir Roger Penrose, 2000
Sir Tom Stoppard, 2000
HRH The Prince of Wales, 2002
Lord May of Oxford, 2002
Lord Rothschild, 2002
Sir David Attenborough, 2005
Baroness Boothroyd, 2005
Sir Michael Howard, 2005
Sir Timothy Berners-Lee, KBE, 2007
Lord Eames, 2007
Lord Rees of Ludlow, 2007
Rt. Hon. Jean Chrétien, QC, 2009

Honorary Member, Nelson Mandela, 1995

Secretary and Registrar, Lord Fellowes, GCB, GCVO, PC, QSO
Chancery, Central Chancery of the Orders of Knighthood, St James's Palace, London SW1A 1BH

THE MOST DISTINGUISHED ORDER OF ST MICHAEL AND ST GEORGE (1818)

GCMG KCMG

GCMG	Knight (or Dame) Grand Cross
KCMG	Knight Commander
DCMG	Dame Commander
CMG	Companion

Ribbon, Saxon blue, with scarlet centre
Motto, Auspicium melioris aevi *(Token of a better age)*

THE SOVEREIGN

GRAND MASTER
HRH The Duke of Kent, KG, GCMG, GCVO, ADC

Prelate, Rt. Revd David Urquhart
Chancellor, Sir Christopher Mallaby, GCMG, GCVO
Secretary, Permanent Under-Secretary of State at the Foreign and Commonwealth Office and Head of the Diplomatic Service
Registrar, Lord Wilson of Tillyorn, KT, GCMG
King of Arms, Sir Jeremy Greenstock, GCMG
Gentleman Usher of the Blue Rod, Sir Anthony Figgis, KCVO, CMG
Dean, Dean of St Paul's
Deputy Secretary, Secretary of the Central Chancery of the Orders of Knighthood
Chancery, Central Chancery of the Orders of Knighthood, St James's Palace, London SW1A 1BH

THE MOST EMINENT ORDER OF THE INDIAN EMPIRE (1878)

GCIE	Knight Grand Commander
KCIE	Knight Commander
CIE	Companion

Ribbon, Imperial purple
Motto, Imperatricis auspiciis *(Under the auspices of the Empress)*

THE SOVEREIGN

Registrar, Secretary of the Central Chancery of the Orders of Knighthood
No conferments have been made since 1947

HH Maharaja Shriraj Sahib of Halvad Dhrangadhara, 1947

THE IMPERIAL ORDER OF THE CROWN OF INDIA (1877) FOR LADIES

CI

Badge, the royal cipher of Queen Victoria in jewels within an oval, surmounted by an heraldic crown and attached to a bow of light blue watered ribbon, edged white

The honour does not confer any rank or title upon the recipient

No conferments have been made since 1947

HM The Queen, 1947

THE ROYAL VICTORIAN ORDER (1896)

GCVO KCVO

GCVO	Knight or Dame Grand Cross
KCVO	Knight Commander
DCVO	Dame Commander
CVO	Commander
LVO	Lieutenant
MVO	Member

Ribbon, Blue, with red and white edges
Motto, Victoria

THE SOVEREIGN
GRAND MASTER
HRH The Princess Royal

Chancellor, Lord Chamberlain
Secretary, Keeper of the Privy Purse
Registrar, Secretary of the Central Chancery of the Orders of Knighthood
Chaplain, Chaplain of the Queen's Chapel of the Savoy
Hon. Genealogist, D. H. B. Chesshyre, CVO

THE MOST EXCELLENT ORDER OF THE BRITISH EMPIRE (1917)

GBE KBE

The order was divided into military and civil divisions in December 1918

GBE	Knight or Dame Grand Cross
KBE	Knight Commander
DBE	Dame Commander
CBE	Commander
OBE	Officer
MBE	Member

Ribbon, Rose pink edged with pearl grey with vertical pearl stripe in centre (military division); without vertical pearl stripe (civil division)
Motto, For God and the Empire

THE SOVEREIGN

GRAND MASTER
HRH The Prince Philip, Duke of Edinburgh, KG, KT, OM, GBE, PC

Prelate, Bishop of London
King of Arms, Air Chief Marshal Sir Patrick Hine, GCB, GBE
Registrar, Secretary of the Central Chancery of the Orders of Knighthood
Secretary, Secretary of the Cabinet and Head of the Home Civil Service
Dean, Dean of St Paul's
Gentleman Usher of the Purple Rod, Sir Alexander Michael Graham, GBE, DCL
Chancery, Central Chancery of the Orders of Knighthood, St James's Palace, London SW1A 1BH

ORDER OF THE COMPANIONS OF HONOUR (1917)

CH

Ribbon, Carmine, with gold edges
This order consists of one class only and carries with it no title. The number of awards is limited to 65 (excluding honorary members).

Anthony, Rt. Hon. John, 1981
Ashley of Stoke, Lord, 1975
Attenborough, Sir David, 1995
Baker, Dame Janet, 1993
Baker of Dorking, Lord, 1992
Birtwistle, Sir Harrison, 2000
Brenner, Sydney, 1986
Brook, Peter, 1998
Brooke of Sutton Mandeville, Lord, 1992
Carrington, Lord, 1983
Christie, Sir George, 2001
Davis, Sir Colin, 2001
De Chastelain, Gen. John, 1999
Dench, Dame Judi, 2005
Fraser, Rt. Hon. Malcolm, 1977
Freud, Lucian, 1983
Glenamara, Lord, 1976
Hamilton, Richard, 1999
Hannay of Chiswick, Lord, 2003
Hawking, Prof. Stephen, 1989
Healey, Lord, 1979
Heseltine, Lord, 1997
Hobsbawm, Prof. Eric, 1998
Hockney, David, 1997
Hodgkin, Sir Howard, 2002
Howard, Sir Michael, 2002
Howe of Aberavon, Lord, 1996
Hurd of Westwell, Lord, 1995
King of Bridgewater, Lord, 1992
Lessing, Doris, 1999
Lovelock, Prof. James, 2002
McKellen, Sir Ian Murray, 2008
McKenzie, Prof. Dan Peter, 2003
MacKerras, Sir Charles, 2003
Mahon, Sir Denis, 2002
Major, Rt. Hon. Sir John, 1998
Owen, Lord, 1994
Patten, Rt. Hon. Lord, 1997
Pawson, Prof. Anthony James, 2006
Riley, Bridget, 1998
Rogers of Riverside, Lord, 2008
Sanger, Dr. Frederick, 1981
Somare, Rt. Hon. Sir Michael, 1978
Talboys, Rt. Hon. Sir Brian, 1981
Tebbit, Lord, 1987

Honorary Members, Lee Kuan Yew, 1970, Prof. Amartya Sen, 2000; Bernard Haitink, 2002
Secretary and Registrar, Secretary of the Central Chancery of the Orders of Knighthood

THE DISTINGUISHED SERVICE ORDER (1886)

DSO

Ribbon, Red, with blue edges

Bestowed in recognition of especial services in action of commissioned officers in the Navy, Army and Royal Air Force and (since 1942) Mercantile Marine. The members are Companions only. A bar may be awarded for any additional act of service.

THE IMPERIAL SERVICE ORDER (1902)

ISO

Ribbon, Crimson, with blue centre

Appointment as companion of this order is open to members of the civil services whose eligibility is determined by the grade they hold. The order consists of the sovereign and companions to a number not exceeding 1,900, of whom 1,300 may belong to the home civil services and 600 to overseas civil services. The then prime minister announced in March 1993 that he would make no further recommendations for appointments to the order.

Secretary, Secretary of the Cabinet and Head of the Home Civil Service
Registrar, Secretary of the Central Chancery of the Orders of Knighthood

THE ROYAL VICTORIAN CHAIN (1902)

It confers no precedence on its holders

HM THE QUEEN

HM The King of Thailand, 1960
HM The Queen of Denmark, 1974
HM The King of Sweden, 1975
HM The Queen of the Netherlands, 1982
Gen. Antonio Eanes, 1985
HM The King of Spain, 1986
Dr Richard von Weizsäcker, 1992
HM The King of Norway, 1994
Earl of Airlie, 1997
Rt. Revd and Rt. Hon. Lord Carey of Clifton, 2002
HRH Prince Philip, Duke of Edinburgh, 2007
HM The King of Saudi Arabia, 2007

BARONETAGE AND KNIGHTAGE

BARONETS

Style, 'Sir' before forename and surname, followed by 'Bt'.
Envelope, Sir F_ S_, Bt. *Letter (formal),* Dear Sir; *(social),* Dear Sir F_. *Spoken,* Sir F_
Wife's style, 'Lady' followed by surname
Envelope, Lady S_. *Letter (formal),* Dear Madam; *(social),* Dear Lady S_. *Spoken,* Lady S_
Style of Baronetess, 'Dame' before forename and surname, followed by 'Btss.' (*see also* Dames)

There are five different creations of baronetcies: Baronets of England (creations dating from 1611); Baronets of Ireland (creations dating from 1619); Baronets of Scotland or Nova Scotia (creations dating from 1625); Baronets of Great Britain (creations after the Act of Union 1707 which combined the kingdoms of England and Scotland); and Baronets of the United Kingdom (creations after the union of Great Britain and Ireland in 1801).

Badge of Baronets of the United Kingdom

Badge of Baronets of Nova Scotia

Badge of Ulster

The patent of creation limits the destination of a baronetcy, usually to male descendants of the first baronet, although special remainders allow the baronetcy to pass, if the male issue of sons fail, to the male issue of daughters of the first baronet. In the case of baronetcies of Scotland or Nova Scotia, a special remainder of 'heirs male and of tailzie' allows the baronetcy to descend to heirs general, including women. There are four existing Scottish baronets with such a remainder.

The Official Roll of the Baronetage is kept at the Crown Office and maintained by the Registrar and Assistant Registrar of the Baronetage. Anyone who considers that he or she is entitled to be entered on the roll may apply through the Crown Office to prove their succession. Every person succeeding to a baronetcy must exhibit proofs of succession to the Lord Chancellor. A person whose name is not entered on the official roll will not be addressed or mentioned by the title of baronet or baronetess in any official document, nor will he or she be accorded precedence as a baronet of baronetess.

BARONETCIES EXTINCT SINCE THE LAST EDITION
Macara (cr. 1911); Wakeman (cr. 1828)

OFFICIAL ROLL OF THE BARONETAGE, Crown Office, House of Lords, London SW1A 0PW T 020-7219 2632
Registrar, Ian Denyer, MVO
Assistant Registrar, Grant Bavister

KNIGHTS

Style, 'Sir' before forename and surname, followed by appropriate post-nominal initials if a Knight Grand Cross, Knight Grand Commander or Knight Commander
Envelope, Sir F_ S_. *Letter (formal),* Dear Sir; *(social),* Dear Sir F_. *Spoken,* Sir F_
Wife's style, 'Lady' followed by surname
'*Envelope,* Lady S_. *Letter (formal),* Dear Madam; *(social),* Dear Lady S_. *Spoken,* Lady S_

The prefix 'Sir' is not used by knights who are clerics of the Church of England, who do not receive the accolade. Their wives are entitled to precedence as the wife of a knight but not to the style of 'Lady'.

ORDERS OF KNIGHTHOOD
Knight Grand Cross, Knight Grand Commander, and Knight Commander are the higher classes of the Orders of Chivalry (*see* Orders of Chivalry). Honorary knighthoods of these orders may be conferred on men who are citizens of countries of which the Queen is not head of state. As a rule, the prefix 'Sir' is not used by honorary knights.

KNIGHTS BACHELOR

The Knights Bachelor do not constitute a royal order, but comprise the surviving representation of the ancient state orders of knighthood. The Register of Knights Bachelor, instituted by James I in the 17th century, lapsed, and in 1908 a voluntary association under the title of the Society of Knights (now the Imperial Society of Knights Bachelor) was formed with the primary objectives of continuing the various registers dating from 1257 and obtaining the uniform registration of every created Knight Bachelor. In 1926 a design for a badge to be worn by Knights Bachelor was approved and adopted; in 1974 a neck badge and miniature were added.

THE IMPERIAL SOCIETY OF KNIGHTS BACHELOR, 1 Throgmorton Avenue, London EC2N 2BY
Knight Principal, Sir Robert Balchin
Prelate, Rt. Revd and Rt. Hon. Bishop of London
Registrar, Sir Paul Judge
Hon. Treasurer, Sir Colin Berry
Clerk to the Council, Richard Jenkins, LVO, TD

LIST OF BARONETS AND KNIGHTS *as at 31 August 2009*

†	Not registered on the Official Roll of the Baronetage at the time of going to press
( )	The date of creation of the baronetcy is given in parentheses
I	Baronet of Ireland
NS	Baronet of Nova Scotia
S	Baronet of Scotland

A full entry in italic type indicates that the recipient of a knighthood died during the year in which the honour was conferred. The name is included for purposes of record. Peers are not included in this list.

Aaronson, Sir Michael John, Kt., CBE
Abbott, *Adm.* Sir Peter Charles, GBE, KCB
Abdy, Sir Valentine Robert Duff, Bt. (1850)
Acheson, *Prof.* Sir (Ernest) Donald, KBE
Ackers-Jones, Sir David, KBE, CMG
Ackroyd, Sir Timothy Robert Whyte, Bt. (1956)
Acland, Sir Antony Arthur, KG, GCMG, GCVO
Acland, *Lt.-Col.* Sir (Christopher) Guy (Dyke), Bt. (1890), MVO
Acland, Sir John Dyke, Bt. (1644)
Adam, Sir Kenneth Hugo, Kt., OBE
Adams, Sir Geoffrey Doyne, KCMG
Adams, Sir William James, KCMG
Adsetts, Sir William Norman, Kt., OBE
Adye, Sir John Anthony, KCMG
Aga Khan IV, HH Prince Karim, KBE
Agnew, Sir Crispin Hamlyn, Bt. (S. 1629)
Agnew, Sir John Keith, Bt. (1895)
Agnew, Sir Rudolph Ion Joseph, Kt.
Agnew-Somerville, Sir Quentin Charles Somerville, Bt. (1957)
Ah Koy, Sir James Michael, KBE
Aikens, *Rt. Hon.* Sir Richard John Pearson, Kt.
†Ainsworth, Sir Anthony Thomas Hugh, Bt. (1916)
Aird, *Capt.* Sir Alastair Sturgis, GCVO
Aird, Sir (George) John, Bt. (1901)
Airy, *Maj.-Gen.* Sir Christopher John, KCVO, CBE
Aitchison, Sir Charles Walter de Lancey, Bt. (1938)
Ajegbo, Sir Keith Onyema, Kt., OBE
Akenhead, *Hon.* Sir Robert, Kt.
Alberti, *Prof.* Sir Kurt George Matthew Mayer, Kt.
Albu, Sir George, Bt. (1912)
Alcock, *Air Chief Marshal* Sir (Robert James) Michael, GCB, KBE
Aldous, *Rt. Hon.* Sir William, Kt.
Alexander, Sir Charles Gundry, Bt. (1945)
Alexander, Sir Douglas, Bt. (1921)
Allen, *Prof.* Sir Geoffrey, Kt., PHD, FRS
Allen, Sir John Derek, Kt., CBE
Allen, Sir Mark John Spurgeon, Kt., CMG
Allen, *Hon.* Sir Peter Austin Philip Jermyn, Kt.
Allen, Sir Thomas Boaz, Kt., CBE
Allen, *Hon.* Sir William Clifford, KCMG
Allen, Sir William Guilford, Kt.
Alleyne, Sir George Allanmoore Ogarren, Kt.
Alleyne, *Revd* John Olpherts Campbell, Bt. (1769)
Allinson, Sir (Walter) Leonard, KCVO, CMG
Alliott, *Hon.* Sir John Downes, Kt.
Allison, *Air Chief Marshal* Sir John Shakespeare, KCB, CBE
Ambo, *Rt. Revd* George, KBE
Amet, *Hon.* Sir Arnold Karibone, Kt.
Amory, Sir Ian Heathcoat, Bt. (1874)
Anderson, *Dr* Sir James Iain Walker, Kt., CBE
Anderson, Sir John Anthony, KBE
Anderson, Sir Leith Reinsford Steven, Kt., CBE
Anderson, *Vice-Adm.* Sir Neil Dudley, KBE, CB
Anderson, *Prof.* Sir Roy Malcolm, Kt.
Anderson, Sir (William) Eric Kinloch, KT.
Anderson, *Prof.* Sir (William) Ferguson, Kt., OBE
Anderton, Sir (Cyril) James, Kt., CBE, QPM
Andrew, Sir Robert John, KCB
Andrews, Sir Derek Henry, KCB, CBE
Andrews, Sir Ian Charles Franklin, Kt., CBE, TD
Angus, Sir Michael Richardson, Kt.
Annesley, Sir Hugh Norman, Kt., QPM
Anson, *Vice-Adm.* Sir Edward Rosebery, KCB
Anson, Sir John, KCB
Anson, *Rear-Adm.* Sir Peter, Bt. CB (1831)
Anstruther, Sir Sebastian Paten Campbell, Bt. (S. 1694)
†Anstruther, Sir Tobias Alexander Campbell, Bt. (1798)
Anstruther-Gough-Calthorpe, Sir Euan Hamilton, Bt. (1929)
Antrobus, Sir Edward Philip, Bt. (1815)
Appleyard, Sir Leonard Vincent, KCMG
Appleyard, Sir Raymond Kenelm, KBE
Arbib, Sir Martyn, Kt.
Arbuthnot, Sir Keith Robert Charles, Bt. (1823)
Arbuthnot, Sir William Reierson, Bt. (1964)
Arbuthnott, *Prof.* Sir John Peebles, Kt., PHD, FRSE
†Archdale, Sir Nicholas Edward, Bt. (1928)
Arculus, Sir Ronald, KCMG, KCVO
Arculus, Sir Thomas David Guy, Kt.
Armitage, *Air Chief Marshal* Sir Michael John, KCB, CBE
Armour, *Prof.* Sir James, Kt., CBE
Armstrong, Sir Christopher John Edmund Stuart, Bt. (1841), MBE
Armstrong, Sir Patrick John, Kt., CBE
Armstrong, Sir Richard, Kt., CBE
Armytage, Sir John Martin, Bt. (1738)
Arnold, *Hon.* Sir Richard David, Kt.
Arnold, Sir Thomas Richard, Kt.
Arnott, Sir Alexander John Maxwell, Bt. (1896)
Arrindell, Sir Clement Athelston, GCMG, GCVO, QC
Arthur, Sir Gavyn Farr, Kt.
Arthur, *Lt.-Gen.* Sir (John) Norman Stewart, KCB, CVO
Arthur, Sir Michael Anthony, KCMG
Arthur, Sir Stephen John, Bt. (1841)
Arulkumaran, *Prof.* Sir Sabaratnam, Kt.
Asbridge, Sir Jonathan Elliott, Kt.
Ash, *Prof.* Sir Eric Albert, Kt., CBE, FRS, FRENG
Ashburnham, Sir James Fleetwood, Bt. (1661)
Ashmore, *Admiral of the Fleet* Sir Edward Beckwith, GCB, DSC
Ashworth, *Dr* Sir John Michael, Kt.
Aske, Sir Robert John Bingham, Bt. (1922)
Askew, Sir Bryan, Kt.
Asscher, Prof. Sir (Adolf) William, Kt., MD, FRCP
Astill, *Hon.* Sir Michael John, Kt.
Astley-Cooper, Sir Alexander Paston, Bt. (1821)
Aston, Sir Harold George, Kt., CBE
Astwood, *Hon.* Sir James Rufus, KBE
Atcherley, Sir Harold Winter, Kt.
Atiyah, Sir Michael Francis, Kt., OM, PHD, FRS
Atkins, *Rt. Hon.* Sir Robert James, Kt.
Atkinson, *Prof.* Sir Anthony Barnes, Kt.
Atkinson, *Air Marshal* Sir David William, KBE
Atkinson, Sir Frederick John, KCB
Atkinson, Sir John Alexander, KCB, DFC
Atkinson, Sir Robert, Kt., DSC, FRENG

Atkinson, Sir William Samuel, Kt.
Atopare, Sir Sailas, GCMG
Attenborough, Sir David Frederick, Kt., OM, CH, CVO, CBE, FRS
Aubrey-Fletcher, Sir Henry Egerton, Bt. (1782)
Audland, Sir Christopher John, KCMG
Augier, *Prof.* Sir Fitz-Roy Richard, Kt.
Auld, *Rt. Hon.* Sir Robin Ernest, Kt.
Austin, Sir Anthony Leonard, Bt. (1894)
Austin, *Air Marshal* Sir Roger Mark, KCB, AFC
Austen-Smith, *Air Marshal* Sir Roy David, KBE, CB, CVO, DFC
Avei, Sir Moi, KBE
Axford, Sir William Ian, Kt.
Ayckbourn, Sir Alan, Kt., CBE
Aykroyd, Sir James Alexander Frederic, Bt. (1929)
Aykroyd, Sir Michael David, Bt. (1920)
Aylmer, Sir Richard John, Bt. (I. 1622)
Aynsley-Green, *Prof.* Sir Albert, Kt.
Bacha, Sir Bhinod, Kt., CMG
Backhouse, Sir Alfred James Stott, Bt. (1901)
Bacon, Sir Nicholas Hickman Ponsonby, Bt. (1611 and 1627), *Premier Baronet of England*
Bacon, Sir Sidney Charles, Kt., CB, FRENG.
Baddeley, Sir John Wolsey Beresford, Bt. (1922)
Badge, Sir Peter Gilmour Noto, Kt.
Baer, Sir Jack Mervyn Frank, Kt.
Bagge, Sir (John) Jeremy Picton, Bt. (1867)
Bagnall, *Air Chief Marshal* Sir Anthony, GBE, KCB
Bailey, Sir Alan Marshall, KCB
Bailey, Sir Brian Harry, Kt., OBE
Bailey, Sir John Bilsland, KCB
†Bailey, Sir John Richard, Bt. (1919)
Bailey, Sir Richard John, Kt., CBE
Bailhache, Sir Philip Martin, Kt.
Baillie, Sir Adrian Louis, Bt. (1823)
Bain, *Prof.* Sir George Sayers, Kt.
Baird, Sir Charles William Stuart, Bt. (1809)
†Baird, Sir James Andrew Gardiner, Bt. (S. 1695)
Baird, *Air Marshal* Sir John Alexander, KBE
Baird, *Vice-Adm.* Sir Thomas Henry Eustace, KCB
Bairsto, *Air Marshal* Sir Peter Edward, KBE, CB
Baker, Sir Bryan William, Kt.
Baker, *Prof.* Sir John Hamilton, Kt., QC
Baker, Sir John William, Kt., CBE
Baker, *Rt. Hon.* Sir (Thomas) Scott (Gillespie), Kt.
Balchin, Sir Robert George Alexander, Kt.
Balderstone, Sir James Schofield, Kt.
Baldwin, *Prof.* Sir Jack Edward, Kt., FRS
Baldwin, Sir Peter Robert, KCB
Ball, *Air Marshal* Sir Alfred Henry Wynne, KCB, DSO, DFC
Ball, Sir Christopher John Elinger, Kt.
Ball, *Prof.* Sir John Macleod, Kt.
Ball, Sir Richard Bentley, Bt. (1911)
Ball, *Prof.* Sir Robert James, Kt., PHD
Ballantyne, *Dr* Sir Frederick Nathaniel, GCMG
Bamford, Sir Anthony Paul, Kt.
Band, *Adm.* Sir Jonathon, GCB
Banham, Sir John Michael Middlecott, Kt.
Bannerman, Sir David Gordon, Bt., OBE (S. 1682)
Bannister, Sir Roger Gilbert, Kt., CBE, DM, FRCP
Barber, Sir Michael Bayldon, Kt.
Barber, Sir (Thomas) David, Bt. (1960)
Barbour, *Very Revd* Robert Alexander Stewart, KCVO, MC
Barclay, Sir Colville Herbert Sanford, Bt. (S. 1668)
Barclay, Sir David Rowat, Kt.
Barclay, Sir Frederick Hugh, Kt.
Barclay, Sir Peter Maurice, Kt., CBE
Barder, Sir Brian Leon, KCMG
Baring, Sir John Francis, Bt. (1911)
Barker, Sir Colin, Kt.
Barker, *Hon.* Sir (Richard) Ian, Kt.
Barling, *Hon.* Sir Gerald Edward, Kt.
Barlow, Sir Christopher Hilaro, Bt. (1803)
Barlow, Sir Frank, Kt., CBE
Barlow, Sir (George) William, Kt., FRENG
Barlow, Sir James Alan, Bt. (1902)
Barlow, Sir John Kemp, Bt. (1907)
Barnard, Sir Joseph Brian, Kt.
Barnes, *The Most Revd.* Brian James, KBE
Barnes, Sir (James) David (Francis), Kt., CBE
Barnes, Sir Kenneth, KCB
Barnewall, Sir Reginald Robert, Bt. (I. 1623)
Baron, Sir Thomas, Kt., CBE
Barran, Sir John Napoleon Ruthven, Bt. (1895)
Barratt, Sir Lawrence Arthur, Kt.
Barratt, Sir Richard Stanley, Kt., CBE, QPM
Barrett, Sir Stephen Jeremy, KCMG
Barrett-Lennard, Sir Peter John, Bt. (1801)
Barrington, Sir Benjamin, Bt. (1831)
Barrington, Sir Nicholas John, KCMG, CVO
Barrington-Ward, *Rt. Revd* Simon, KCMG
Barron, Sir Donald James, Kt.
Barrow, Sir Anthony John Grenfell, Bt. (1835)
Barry, Sir (Lawrence) Edward (Anthony Tress), Bt. (1899)
Barter, Sir Peter Leslie Charles, Kt., OBE
†Bartlett, Sir Andrew Alan, Bt. (1913)
Barttelot, *Col.* Sir Brian Walter de Stopham, Bt. (1875), OBE
Bate, Sir David Lindsay, KBE
†Bates, Sir James Geoffrey, Bt. (1880)
Bates, Sir Richard Dawson Hoult, Bt. (1937)
Bateson, *Prof.* Sir Patrick, Kt.
Bather, Sir John Knollys, KCVO
Batho, Sir Peter Ghislain, Bt. (1928)
Bathurst, *Admiral of the Fleet* Sir (David) Benjamin, GCB
Batten, Sir John Charles, KCVO
Battersby, *Prof.* Sir Alan Rushton, Kt., FRS
Battishill, Sir Anthony Michael William, GCB
Baulcombe, *Prof.* Sir David Charles, Kt., FRS
Baxendell, Sir Peter Brian, Kt., CBE, FRENG
Bayly, *Prof.* Sir Christopher Alan, Kt.
Bayne, Sir Nicholas Peter, KCMG
Baynes, Sir Christopher Rory, Bt. (1801)
Bazley, Sir Thomas John Sebastian, Bt. (1869)
Beach, *Gen.* Sir (William Gerald) Hugh, GBE, KCB, MC
Beache, *Hon.* Sir Vincent Ian, KCMG
Beale, *Lt.-Gen.* Sir Peter John, KBE, FRCP
Beamish, Sir Adrian John, KCMG
Bean, *Hon.* Sir David Michael, Kt
Beaumont, *Capt.* the Hon. Sir (Edward) Nicholas (Canning), KCVO
Beaumont, Sir George (Howland Francis), Bt. (1661)
Beatson, *Hon.* Sir Jack, Kt.
Beavis, *Air Chief Marshal* Sir Michael Gordon, KCB, CBE, AFC
Beck, Sir Edgar Philip, Kt.
Beckett, Sir Richard Gervase, Bt. (1921), QC
Beckett, Sir Terence Norman, KBE, FRENG
Beckwith, Sir John Lionel, Kt., CBE
Bedser, Sir Alec Victor, Kt., CBE
Beecham, Sir Jeremy Hugh, Kt.
Beecham, Sir John Stratford Roland, Bt. (1914)
Beetham, *Marshal of the Royal Air Force* Sir Michael James, GCB, CBE, DFC, AFC
Beevor, Sir Thomas Agnew, Bt. (1784)
Beith, *Rt. Hon.* Sir Alan James, Kt.
Beldam, *Rt. Hon.* Sir (Alexander) Roy (Asplan), Kt.
Belich, Sir James, Kt.
Bell, Sir Brian Ernest, KBE
Bell, Sir David Charles Maurice, Kt.
Bell, *Prof.* Sir John Irving, Kt.
Bell, Sir John Lowthian, Bt. (1885)
Bell, *Prof.* Sir Peter Robert Frank, Kt.
Bell, *Hon.* Sir Rodger, Kt.
Bell, Sir Stuart, Kt.
Bellamy, *Hon.* Sir Christopher William, Kt.

Bellingham, Sir Anthony Edward Norman, Bt. (1796)
Bender, Sir Brian Geoffrey, KCB
Benn, Sir (James) Jonathan, Bt. (1914)
Bennett, *Air Vice-Marshal* Sir Erik Peter, KBE, CB
Bennett, *Hon.* Sir Hugh Peter Derwyn, Kt.
Bennett, *Gen.* Sir Phillip Harvey, KBE, DSO
Bennett, Sir Richard Rodney, Kt., CBE
Bennett, Sir Ronald Wilfrid Murdoch, Bt. (1929)
Benson, Sir Christopher John, Kt.
Benyon, Sir William Richard, Kt.
Beresford, Sir (Alexander) Paul, Kt.
Beresford-Peirse, Sir Henry Grant de la Poer, Bt. (1814)
Berghuser, *Hon.* Sir Eric, Kt., MBE
Beringer, *Prof.* Sir John Evelyn, Kt., CBE
Berman, Sir Franklin Delow, KCMG
Berners-Lee, Sir Timothy John, OM, KBE, FRS
Bernard, Sir Dallas Edmund, Bt. (1954)
Bernstein, Sir Howard, Kt.
Berney, Sir Julian Reedham Stuart, Bt. (1620)
Berridge, *Prof.* Sir Michael John, Kt., FRS
Berriman, Sir David, Kt.
Berry, *Prof.* Sir Colin Leonard, Kt., FRCPATH
Berry, *Prof.* Sir Michael Victor, Kt., FRS
Berthoud, Sir Martin Seymour, KCVO, CMG
Best, Sir Richard Radford, KCVO, CBE
Best-Shaw, Sir John Michael Robert, Bt. (1665)
Bethel, Sir Baltron Benjamin, KCMG
Bett, Sir Michael, Kt., CBE
Bettison, Sir Norman George, Kt., QPM
Bevan, Sir Martyn Evan Evans, Bt. (1958)
Bevan, Sir Nicolas, Kt., CB
Bevan, Sir Timothy Hugh, Kt.
Beverley, *Lt.-Gen.* Sir Henry York La Roche, KCB, OBE, RM
Bibby, Sir Michael James, Bt. (1959)
Bichard, Sir Michael George, KCB
Bickersteth, *Rt. Revd* John Monier, KCVO
Biddulph, Sir Ian D'Olier, Bt. (1664)
Bidwell, Sir Hugh Charles Philip, GBE
Biggam, Sir Robin Adair, Kt.
Biggs, Sir Norman Paris, Kt.
Bilas, Sir Angmai Simon, Kt., OBE
Billière, *Gen.* Sir Peter Edgar de la Cour de la, KCB, KBE, DSO, MC
Bindman, Sir Geoffrey Lionel, Kt.
Bingham, *Hon.* Sir Eardley Max, Kt.
Birch, Sir John Allan, KCVO, CMG
Birch, Sir Roger, Kt., CBE, QPM
Bird, Sir Richard Geoffrey Chapman, Bt. (1922)
Birkin, Sir John Christian William, Bt. (1905)
Birkin, Sir (John) Derek, Kt., TD
Birkmyre, Sir James, Bt. (1921)
Birrell, Sir James Drake, Kt.
Birtwistle, Sir Harrison, Kt., CH
Bischoff, Sir Winfried Franz Wilhelm, Kt.
Bishop, Sir Michael David, Kt., CBE
Bisson, *Rt. Hon.* Sir Gordon Ellis, Kt.
Black, Sir James Whyte, Kt., OM, FRCP, FRS
Black, *Adm.* Sir (John) Jeremy, GBE, KCB, DSO
Black, Sir Robert David, Bt. (1922)
Blackburn, *Vice-Adm.* Sir David Anthony James, KCVO, CB
Blackburne, *Hon.* Sir William Anthony, Kt.
Blackett, Sir Hugh Francis, Bt. (1673)
Blackham, *Vice-Adm.* Sir Jeremy Joe, KCB
Blackman, Sir Frank Milton, KCVO, OBE
Blair, *Lt.-Gen.* Sir Chandos, KCVO, OBE, MC
†Blair, Sir Patrick David Hunter, Bt. (1786)
Blair, *Hon.* Sir William James Lynton, Kt.
Blair, Sir Ian Warwick, Kt., QPM
Blake, Sir Alfred Lapthorn, KCVO, MC
Blake, Sir Francis Michael, Bt. (1907)
Blake, *Hon.* Sir Nicholas John Gorrod, Kt.
Blake, Sir Peter Thomas, Kt., CBE
Blake, Sir Anthony Teilo Bruce, Bt. (I. 1622)
Blaker, Sir John, Bt. (1919)
Blakiston, Sir Ferguson Arthur James, Bt. (1763)
Blanch, Sir Malcolm, KCVO
Bland, Sir (Francis) Christopher (Buchan), Kt.
Bland, *Lt.-Col.* Sir Simon Claud Michael, KCVO
Blank, Sir Maurice Victor, Kt.
Blatherwick, Sir David Elliott Spiby, KCMG, OBE
Blelloch, Sir John Nial Henderson, KCB
Blennerhassett, Sir (Marmaduke) Adrian Francis William, Bt. (1809)
Blewitt, *Maj.* Sir Shane Gabriel Basil, GCVO
Blofeld, *Hon.* Sir John Christopher Calthorpe, Kt.
Blois, Sir Charles Nicholas Gervase, Bt. (1686)
Blom-Cooper, Sir Louis Jacques, Kt., QC
Blomefield, Sir Thomas Charles Peregrine, Bt. (1807)
Bloomfield, Sir Kenneth Percy, KCB
Blundell, Sir Thomas Leon, Kt., FRS
Blunden, Sir George, Kt.
Blunden, Sir Philip Overington, Bt. (I. 1766)
Blunt, Sir David Richard Reginald Harvey, Bt. (1720)
Blyth, Sir Charles (Chay), Kt., CBE, BEM
Boardman, *Prof.* Sir John, Kt., FSA, FBA
Bodey, *Hon.* Sir David Roderick Lessiter, Kt.
Bodmer, Sir Walter Fred, Kt., PHD, FRS
Body, Sir Richard Bernard Frank Stewart, Kt.
Bogan, Sir Nagora, KBE
Boileau, Sir Guy (Francis), Bt. (1838)
Boles, Sir Jeremy John Fortescue, Bt. (1922)
Boles, Sir John Dennis, Kt., MBE
Bolt, *Air Marshal* Sir Richard Bruce, KBE, CB, DFC, AFC
Bona, Sir Kina, KBE
Bonallack, Sir Michael Francis, Kt., OBE
Bond, Sir John Reginald Hartnell, Kt.
Bond, *Prof.* Sir Michael Richard, Kt., FRCPSYCH, FRCPGLAS, FRCSE
Bone, *Prof.* Sir James Drummond, Kt., FRSE
Bone, Sir Roger Bridgland, KCMG
Bonfield, Sir Peter Leahy, Kt., CBE, FRENG
Bonham, *Maj.* Sir Antony Lionel Thomas, Bt. (1852)
Bonington, Sir Christian John Storey, Kt., CBE
Bonsall, Sir Arthur Wilfred, KCMG, CBE
Bonsor, Sir Nicholas Cosmo, Bt. (1925)
Boord, Sir Nicolas John Charles, Bt. (1896)
Boorman, *Lt.-Gen.* Sir Derek, KCB
Booth, Sir Christopher Charles, Kt., MD, FRCP
Booth, Sir Clive, Kt.
Booth, Sir Douglas Allen, Bt. (1916)
Booth, Sir Gordon, KCMG, CVO
Boothby, Sir Brooke Charles, Bt. (1660)
Bore, Sir Albert, Kt.
Boreel, Sir Stephan Gerard, Bt. (1645)
Borthwick, Sir Anthony Thomas, Bt. (1908)
Borysiewicz, *Prof.* Sir Leszek Krzysztof, Kt.
Bossom, *Hon.* Sir Clive, Bt. (1953)
Boswell, *Lt.-Gen.* Sir Alexander Crawford Simpson, KCB, CBE
Bosworth, Sir Neville Bruce Alfred, Kt., CBE
Botham, Sir Ian Terence, Kt., OBE
Bottoms, *Prof.* Sir Anthony Edward, Kt.
Bottomley, Sir James Reginald Alfred, KCMG
Boughey, Sir John George Fletcher, Bt. (1798)
Boulton, Sir Clifford John, GCB
Boulton, Sir William Whytehead, Bt. (1944), CBE, TD
Bouraga, Sir Phillip, KBE

Bourn, Sir John Bryant, KCB
Bowater, Sir Euan David Vansittart, Bt. (1939)
†Bowater, Sir Michael Patrick, Bt. (1914)
Bowden, Sir Andrew, Kt., MBE
Bowden, Sir Nicholas Richard, Bt. (1915)
Bowen, Sir Barry Manfield, KCMG
Bowen, Sir Geoffrey Fraser, Kt.
Bowen, Sir Mark Edward Mortimer, Bt. (1921)
Bowes Lyon, Sir Simon Alexander, KCVO
†Bowlby, Sir Richard Peregrine Longstaff, Bt. (1923)
Bowman, Sir Edwin Geoffrey, KCB
Bowman, Sir Jeffery Haverstock, Kt.
Bowman-Shaw, Sir (George) Neville, Kt.
Bowness, Sir Alan, Kt., CBE
Bowyer-Smyth, Sir Thomas Weyland, Bt. (1661)
Boyce, Sir Graham Hugh, KCMG
Boyce, Sir Robert Charles Leslie, Bt. (1952)
Boyd, Sir Alexander Walter, Bt. (1916)
Boyd, Sir John Dixon Iklé, KCMG
Boyd, *Prof.* Sir Robert David Hugh, Kt.
Boyd-Carpenter, Sir (Marsom) Henry, KCVO
Boyd-Carpenter, *Lt.-Gen. Hon.* Sir Thomas Patrick John, KBE
Boyle, Sir Stephen Gurney, Bt. (1904)
Boyson, *Rt. Hon.* Sir Rhodes, Kt.
Brabham, Sir John Arthur, Kt., OBE
Bracewell-Smith, Sir Charles, Bt. (1947)
Bradbeer, Sir John Derek Richardson, Kt., OBE, TD
Bradfield, *Dr* Sir John Richard Grenfell, Kt., CBE
Bradford, Sir Edward Alexander Slade, Bt. (1902)
Brady, *Prof.* Sir John Michael, Kt., FRS
Braithwaite, *Rt. Hon.* Sir Nicholas Alexander, Kt., OBE
Braithwaite, Sir Rodric Quentin, GCMG
Bramley, *Prof.* Sir Paul Anthony, Kt.
Branson, Sir Richard Charles Nicholas, Kt.
Bratza, *Hon.* Sir Nicolas Dušan, Kt.
Breckenridge, *Prof.* Sir Alasdair Muir, Kt., CBE
Brennan, *Hon.* Sir (Francis) Gerard, KBE
Brenton, Sir Anthony Russell, KCMG
Brewer, Sir David William, Kt., CMG
Brierley, Sir Ronald Alfred, Kt.
Briggs, *Hon.* Sir Michael Townley Featherstone, Kt.
Brighouse, *Prof.* Sir Timothy Robert Peter, Kt.
Bright, Sir Graham Frank James, Kt.
Bright, Sir Keith, Kt.
Brigstocke, *Adm.* Sir John Richard, KCB
Brinckman, Sir Theodore George Roderick, Bt. (1831)
†Brisco, Sir Campbell Howard, Bt. (1782)
Briscoe, Sir Brian Anthony, Kt.
Briscoe, Sir John Geoffrey James, Bt. (1910)
Brittan, Sir Samuel, Kt.
†Broadbent, Sir Andrew George, Bt. (1893)
Broadbent, Sir Richard John, KCB
Brocklebank, Sir Aubrey Thomas, Bt. (1885)
Brodie, Sir Benjamin David Ross, Bt. (1834)
Brodie-Hall, Sir Laurence Charles, Kt., AO, CMG
Brooke, Sir Rodney George, Kt., CBE
Brooking, Sir Trevor, Kt., CBE
Bromhead, Sir John Desmond Gonville, Bt. (1806)
Bromley, Sir Michael Roger, KBE
Bromley, Sir Rupert Charles, Bt. (1757)
Brook, *Prof.* Sir Richard John, Kt. OBE
†Brooke, Sir Alistair Weston, Bt. (1919)
Brooke, Sir Francis George Windham, Bt. (1903)
Brooke, *Rt. Hon.* Sir Henry, Kt.
Brooke, Sir (Richard) David Christopher, Bt. (1662)
Brooking, Sir Trevor David, Kt., CBE
Brooks, Sir Timothy Gerald Martin, KCVO
Brooksbank, Sir (Edward) Nicholas, Bt. (1919)
Broomfield, Sir Nigel Hugh Robert Allen, KCMG
†Broughton, Sir David Delves, Bt. (1661)
Broun, Sir Wayne Hercules, Bt. (S. 1686)
Brown, Sir (Austen) Patrick, KCB
Brown, *Adm.* Sir Brian Thomas, KCB, CBE
Brown, Sir David, Kt.
Brown, *Hon.* Sir Douglas Dunlop, Kt.
Brown, Sir George Francis Richmond, Bt. (1863)
Brown, Sir Mervyn, KCMG, OBE
Brown, Sir Peter Randolph, Kt.
Brown, *Rt. Hon.* Sir Stephen, GBE
Brown, Sir Stephen David Reid, KCVO
Browne, Sir Nicholas Walker, KBE, CMG
Brownlie, *Prof.* Sir Ian, Kt., CBE, QC
Brownrigg, Sir Nicholas (Gawen), Bt. (1816)
Browse, *Prof.* Sir Norman Leslie, Kt., MD, FRCS
Bruce, Sir (Francis) Michael Ian, Bt. (S. 1628)
Bruce-Clifton, Sir Hervey James Hugh, Bt. (1804)
Bruce-Gardner, Sir Robert Henry, Bt. (1945)
Brunner, Sir Hugo Laurence Joseph, KCVO
Brunner, Sir John Henry Kilian, Bt. (1895)
Brunton, Sir Gordon Charles, Kt.
†Brunton, Sir James Lauder, Bt. (1908)
Bryan, Sir Arthur, Kt.
Buchan-Hepburn, Sir John Alastair Trant Kidd, Bt. (1815)
Buchanan, Sir Andrew George, Bt. (1878)
Buchanan, *Vice-Adm.* Sir Peter William, KBE
Buchanan, Sir Robert Wilson (Robin), Kt.
Buchanan-Jardine, *Maj.* Sir (Andrew) Rupert (John), Bt. (1885), MC
Buckland, Sir Ross, Kt.
Buckley, Sir Michael Sidney, Kt.
Buckley, *Lt.-Cdr.* Sir (Peter) Richard, KCVO
Buckley, *Hon.* Sir Roger John, Kt.
Buckworth-Herne-Soame, Sir Charles John, Bt. (1697)
Budd, Sir Alan Peter, Kt.
Budd, Sir Colin Richard, KCMG
Bull, Sir George Jeffrey, Kt.
Bull, Sir Simeon George, Bt. (1922)
Bullock, Sir Stephen Michael, Kt.
Bultin, Sir Bato, Kt., MBE
Bunbury, Sir Michael William, Bt. (1681), KCVO
Bunyard, Sir Robert Sidney, Kt., CBE, QPM
Burbidge, Sir Peter Dudley, Bt. (1916)
Burden, Sir Anthony Thomas, Kt., QPM
Burdett, Sir Savile Aylmer, Bt. (1665)
Burgen, Sir Arnold Stanley Vincent, Kt., FRS
Burgess, *Gen.* Sir Edward Arthur, KCB, OBE
Burgess, Sir (Joseph) Stuart, Kt., CBE, PHD, FRSC
Burgh, Sir John Charles, KCMG, CB
Burke, Sir James Stanley Gilbert, Bt. (I. 1797)
Burke, Sir (Thomas) Kerry, Kt.
Burnell-Nugent, *Vice-Adm.* Sir James Michael, KCB, CBE, ADC
Burnet, Sir James William Alexander (Sir Alastair Burnet), Kt.
Burnett, *Air Chief Marshal* Sir Brian Kenyon, GCB, DFC, AFC
Burnett, Sir Charles David, Bt., (1913)
Burnett, *Hon.* Sir Ian Duncan, Kt.
Burnett, Sir Walter John, Kt.
Burney, Sir Nigel Dennistoun, Bt. (1921)
Burns, Sir (Robert) Andrew, KCMG
Burnton, *Rt. Hon.* Sir Stanley Jeffrey, Kt.
†Burrell, Sir Charles Raymond, Bt. (1774)
Burridge, *Air Chief Marshal* Sir Brian Kevin, KCB, CBE, ADC
Burston, Sir Samuel Gerald Wood, Kt., OBE
Burt, Sir Peter Alexander, Kt.

Burton, Sir Carlisle Archibald, Kt., OBE
Burton, Sir George Vernon Kennedy, Kt., CBE
Burton, *Lt.-Gen.* Sir Edmund Fortescue Gerard, KBE
Burton, Sir Graham Stuart, KCMG
Burton, *Hon.* Sir Michael John, Kt.
Burton, Sir Michael St Edmund, KCVO, CMG
Bush, *Adm.* Sir John Fitzroy Duyland, GCB, DSC
Butler, *Hon.* Sir Arlington Griffith, KCMG
Butler, Sir Michael Dacres, GCMG
Butler, Sir (Reginald) Michael (Thomas), Bt. (1922)
Butler, Sir Percy James, Kt., CBE
Butler, *Hon.* Sir Richard Clive, Kt.
Butler, Sir Richard Pierce, Bt. (1628)
Butter, *Maj.* Sir David Henry, KCVO, MC
Butterfield, *Hon.* Sir Alexander Neil Logie, Kt.
Butterfill, Sir John Valentine, Kt.
Buxton, Sir Jocelyn Charles Roden, Bt. (1840)
Buxton, *Rt. Hon.* Sir Richard Joseph, Kt.
Buzzard, Sir Anthony Farquhar, Bt. (1929)
Byatt, Sir Hugh Campbell, KCVO, CMG
Byatt, Sir Ian Charles Rayner, Kt.
Byford, Sir Lawrence, Kt., CBE, QPM
Byron, *Rt. Hon.* Sir Charles Michael Dennis, Kt.
†Cable-Alexander, Sir Patrick Desmond William, Bt. (1809)
Cadbury, Sir (George) Adrian (Hayhurst), Kt.
Cadbury, Sir (Nicholas) Dominic, Kt.
Cadogan, *Prof.* Sir John Ivan George, Kt., CBE, FRS, FRSE
Cahn, Sir Albert Jonas, Bt. (1934)
Cahn, Sir Andrew Thomas, KCMG
Cain, Sir Henry Edney Conrad, Kt.
Caine, Sir Michael (Maurice Micklewhite), Kt., CBE
Caines, Sir John, KCB
Caldwell, Sir Edward George, KCB
Callaghan, Sir William Henry, Kt.
Callan, Sir Ivan Roy, KCVO, CMG
Calman, *Prof.* Sir Kenneth Charles, KCB, MD, FRCP, FRCS, FRSE
Calne, *Prof.* Sir Roy Yorke, Kt., FRS
Calvert-Smith, Sir David, Kt., QC
Cameron, Sir Hugh Roy Graham, Kt., QPM
Campbell, *Prof.* Sir Colin Murray, Kt.
Campbell, Sir Ian Tofts, Kt., CBE, VRD
Campbell, Sir Ilay Mark, Bt. (1808)
Campbell, Sir James Alexander Moffat Bain, Bt. (S. 1668)
Campbell, Sir Lachlan Philip Kemeys, Bt. (1815)
Campbell, Sir Roderick Duncan Hamilton, Bt. (1831)
Campbell, Sir Robin Auchinbreck, Bt. (S. 1628)
Campbell, *Rt. Hon.* Sir Walter Menzies, Kt., CBE, QC
Campbell, *Rt. Hon.* Sir William Anthony, Kt.
Campbell-Orde, Sir John Alexander, Bt. (1790)
Cannadine, *Prof.* Sir David Nicholas, Kt.
†Carden, Sir Christopher Robert, Bt. (1887)
†Carden, Sir John Craven, Bt. (I. 1787)
Carew, Sir Rivers Verain, Bt. (1661)
Carey, Sir de Vic Graham, Kt.
Carey, Sir Peter Willoughby, GCB
Carleton-Smith, *Maj.-Gen.* Sir Michael Edward, Kt., CBE
Carlisle, Sir James Beethoven, GCMG
Carlisle, Sir John Michael, Kt.
Carlisle, Sir Kenneth Melville, Kt.
Carnegie, *Lt.-Gen.* Sir Robin Macdonald, KCB, OBE
Carnegie, Sir Roderick Howard, Kt.
Carnwath, *Rt. Hon.* Sir Robert John Anderson, Kt., CVO
Caro, Sir Anthony Alfred, Kt., OM, CBE
Carr, Sir (Albert) Raymond (Maillard), Kt.
Carr, Sir Peter Derek, Kt., CBE
Carr, *Very Revd Dr* Arthur Wesley, KCVO
Carr-Ellison, *Col.* Sir Ralph Harry, KCVO, TD
Carrick, *Hon.* Sir John Leslie, KCMG
Carrick, Sir Roger John, KCMG, LVO
Carruthers, Sir Ian James, Kt., OBE
Carsberg, *Prof.* Sir Bryan Victor, Kt.
Carter, *Prof.* Sir David Craig, Kt., FRCSE, FRCSGLAS, FRCPE
Carter, Sir John Alexander, Kt.
Carter, Sir John Gordon Thomas, Kt.
Carter, Sir Philip David, Kt., CBE
Carter, Sir Richard Henry Alwyn, Kt.
Cartledge, Sir Bryan George, KCMG
Cary, Sir Roger Hugh, Bt. (1955)
Casey, *Rt. Hon.* Sir Maurice Eugene, Kt.
Cash, Sir Andrew John, Kt., OBE
Cass, Sir Geoffrey Arthur, Kt.
Cassel, Sir Timothy Felix Harold, Bt. (1920)
Cassels, Sir John Seton, Kt., CB
Cassels, *Adm.* Sir Simon Alastair Cassillis, KCB, CBE
Cassidi, *Adm.* Sir (Arthur) Desmond, GCB
Castell, Sir William Martin, Kt.
Castledine, *Prof.* Sir George, Kt.
Catherwood, Sir (Henry) Frederick (Ross), Kt.
Catto, *Prof.* Sir Graeme Robertson Dawson, Kt.
Cave, Sir John Charles, Bt. (1896)
Cave-Browne-Cave, Sir Robert, Bt. (1641)
Cayley, Sir Digby William David, Bt. (1661)
Cayzer, Sir James Arthur, Bt. (1904)
Cazalet, *Hon.* Sir Edward Stephen, Kt.
Cazalet, Sir Peter Grenville, Kt.
Cecil, *Rear-Adm.* Sir (Oswald) Nigel Amherst, KBE, CB
Chadwick, *Rt. Hon.* Sir John Murray, Kt.
Chadwick, Sir Joshua Kenneth Burton, Bt. (1935)
Chadwick, *Revd Prof.* (William) Owen, OM, KBE, FBA
Chadwyck-Healey, Sir Charles Edward, Bt. (1919)
Chakrabarti, Sir Sumantra, KCB
Chalmers, Sir Iain Geoffrey, Kt.
Chalmers, Sir Neil Robert, Kt.
Chalstrey, Sir (Leonard) John, Kt., MD, FRCS
Chan, *Rt. Hon.* Sir Julius, GCMG, KBE
Chan, Sir Thomas Kok, Kt., OBE
Chance, Sir (George) Jeremy ffolliott, Bt. (1900)
Chandler, Sir Colin Michael, Kt.
Chandler, Sir Geoffrey, Kt., CBE
Chantler, *Prof.* Sir Cyril, Kt., MD, FRCP
Chaplin, Sir Malcolm Hilbery, Kt., CBE
Chapman, Sir David Robert Macgowan, Bt. (1958)
Chapman, Sir George Alan, Kt.
Chapman, Sir Sidney Brookes, Kt., MP
Chapple, *Field Marshal* Sir John Lyon, GCB, CBE
Charles, *Hon.* Sir Arthur William Hessin, Kt.
Charlton, Sir Robert (Bobby), Kt., CBE
Charnley, Sir (William) John, Kt., CB, FRENG
Chartres, *Rt. Revd and Rt. Hon.* Richard John Carew, KCVO
Chataway, *Rt. Hon.* Sir Christopher, Kt.
Chatfield, Sir John Freeman, Kt., CBE
†Chaytor, Sir Bruce Gordon, Bt. (1831)
Checketts, *Sqn. Ldr.* Sir David John, KCVO
Checkland, Sir Michael, Kt.
Cheshire, *Air Chief Marshal* Sir John Anthony, KBE, CB
Chessells, Sir Arthur David (Tim), Kt.
†Chetwynd, Sir Robin John Talbot, Bt. (1795)
Cheyne, Sir Patrick John Lister, Bt. (1908)
Chichester, Sir James Henry Edward, Bt. (1641)
Chichester-Clark, Sir Robin, Kt.
Chilcot, *Rt. Hon.* Sir John Anthony, GCB
Child, Sir (Coles John) Jeremy, Bt. (1919)
Chilwell, *Hon.* Sir Muir Fitzherbert, Kt.
Chinn, Sir Trevor Edwin, Kt., CVO

Chipperfield, Sir Geoffrey Howes, KCB
Chisholm, Sir John Alexander Raymond, Kt., FRENG
Chitty, Sir Thomas Willes, Bt. (1924)
Cholmeley, Sir Hugh John Frederick Sebastian, Bt. (1806)
Chow, Sir Chung Kong, Kt.
Chow, Sir Henry Francis, Kt., OBE
Christie, Sir George William Langham, Kt., CH
Christie, Sir William, Kt., MBE
Christopher, Sir Duncan Robin Carmichael, KBE, CMG
Chung, Sir Sze-yuen, GBE, FRENG
Clark, Sir Francis Drake, Bt. (1886)
Clark, Sir John Arnold, Kt.
Clark, Sir Jonathan George, Bt. (1917)
Clark, Sir Robert Anthony, Kt., DSC
Clark, Sir Terence Joseph, KBE, CMG, CVO
Clarke, Sir (Charles Mansfield) Tobias, Bt. (1831)
Clarke, *Hon.* Sir Christopher Simon Courtenay Stephenson, Kt.
Clarke, Sir Christopher James, Kt., OBE
Clarke, *Hon.* Sir David Clive, Kt.
Clarke, Sir Ellis Emmanuel Innocent, GCMG
Clarke, Sir Jonathan Dennis, Kt.
Clarke, Sir Robert Cyril, Kt.
†Clarke, Sir Rupert Grant Alexander, Bt. (1882)
Clay, Sir Edward, KCMG
Clay, Sir Richard Henry, Bt. (1841)
Clayton, Sir David Robert, Bt. (1732)
Cleaver, Sir Anthony Brian, Kt.
Clementi, Sir David Cecil, Kt.
Cleminson, Sir James Arnold Stacey, KBE, MC
Clerk, Sir Robert Maxwell, Bt. (1679), OBE
Clerke, Sir John Edward Longueville, Bt. (1660)
Clifford, Sir Roger Joseph, Bt. (1887)
Clifford, Sir Timothy Peter Plint, Kt.
Clothier, Sir Cecil Montacute, KCB, QC
Clucas, Sir Kenneth Henry, KCB
Coates, Sir Anthony Robert Milnes, Bt. (1911)
Coates, Sir David Frederick Charlton, Bt. (1921)
Coats, Sir Alastair Francis Stuart, Bt. (1905)
Coats, Sir William David, Kt.
Cochrane, Sir (Henry) Marc (Sursock), Bt. (1903)
Cockburn, Sir John Elliot, Bt. (S. 1671)
Cockburn-Campbell, Sir Alexander Thomas, Bt. (1821)
Cockshaw, Sir Alan, Kt., FRENG
†Codrington, Sir Christopher George Wayne, Bt. (1876)
†Codrington, Sir Giles Peter, Bt. (1721)
Coghill, Sir Patrick Kendal Farley, Bt. (1778)
Coghlin, *Rt. Hon.* Sir Patrick, Kt.
Cohen, Sir Edward, Kt.
Cohen, Sir Ivor Harold, Kt., CBE, TD
Cohen, *Prof.* Sir Philip, Kt., PHD, FRS
Cohen, Sir Ronald, Kt.
Cole, Sir (Robert) William, Kt.
Coleman, Sir Robert John, KCMG
Coleridge, *Hon.* Sir Paul James Duke, Kt.
Coles, Sir (Arthur) John, GCMG
Colfox, Sir (William) John, Bt. (1939)
Collett, Sir Christopher, GBE
Collett, Sir Ian Seymour, Bt. (1934)
Collins, Sir Alan Stanley, KCVO, CMG
Collins, *Hon.* Sir Andrew David, Kt.
Collins, Sir Bryan Thomas Alfred, Kt., OBE, QFSM
Collins, Sir John Alexander, Kt
Collins, Sir Kenneth Darlingston, Kt.
Collyear, Sir John Gowen, Kt.
Colman, *Hon.* Sir Anthony David, Kt.
Colman, Sir Michael Jeremiah, Bt. (1907)
Colman, Sir Timothy, KG
†Colquhoun of Luss, Sir Malcolm Rory, Bt. (1786)
Colt, Sir Edward William Dutton, Bt. (1694)
Colthurst, Sir Charles St John, Bt. (1744)
Conant, Sir John Ernest Michael, Bt. (1954)
Connell, *Hon.* Sir Michael Bryan, Kt.
Connery, Sir Sean, Kt.
Connor, Sir William Joseph, Kt.
Conran, Sir Terence Orby, Kt.
Cons, *Hon.* Sir Derek, Kt.
Constantinou, Sir Georkios, Kt., OBE
Conway, *Prof.* Sir Gordon Richard, KCMG, FRS
Cook, Sir Christopher Wymondham Rayner Herbert, Bt. (1886)
Cook, *Prof.* Sir Peter Frederic Chester, Kt.
Cooke, *Col.* Sir David William Perceval, Bt. (1661)
Cooke, Sir Howard Felix Hanlan, GCMG, GCVO
Cooke, *Hon.* Sir Jeremy Lionel, Kt.
Cooke, *Prof.* Sir Ronald Urwick, Kt.
Cooksey, Sir David James Scott, GBE
Cooper, *Gen.* Sir George Leslie Conroy, GCB, MC
Cooper, Sir Henry, Kt.
Cooper, Sir Richard Adrian, Bt. (1905)
Cooper, *Maj.-Gen.* Sir Simon Christie, GCVO
Cooper, Sir William Daniel Charles, Bt. (1863)
Coote, Sir Christopher John, Bt. (I. 1621), *Premier Baronet of Ireland*
Copas, *Most Revd* Virgil, KBE
Copisarow, Sir Alcon Charles, Kt.
Corbett, *Maj.-Gen.* Sir Robert John Swan, KCVO, CB
Cordy-Simpson, *Lt.-Gen.* Sir Roderick Alexander, KBE, CB
Corfield, Sir Kenneth George, Kt., FRENG
Cormack, Sir Patrick Thomas, Kt.
Corness, Sir Colin Ross, Kt.
Cornforth, Sir John Warcup, Kt., CBE, DPHIL, FRS
Corry, Sir James Michael, Bt. (1885)
Cortazzi, Sir (Henry Arthur) Hugh, GCMG
Cory, Sir (Clinton Charles) Donald, Bt. (1919)
Cory-Wright, Sir Richard Michael, Bt. (1903)
Cossons, Sir Neil, Kt., OBE
Cotter, Sir Patrick Laurence Delaval, Bt. (I. 1763)
Cotterell, Sir John Henry Geers, Bt. (1805)
Cottrell, Sir Alan Howard, Kt., PHD, FRS, FRENG
†Cotts, Sir Richard Crichton Mitchell, Bt. (1921)
Coulson, *Hon.* Sir Peter David William, Kt.
Couper, Sir James George, Bt. (1841)
Courtenay, Sir Thomas Daniel, Kt.
Cousins, *Air Chief Marshal* Sir David, KCB, AFC
Coville, *Air Marshal* Sir Christopher Charles Cotton, KCB
Cowan, *Gen.* Sir Samuel, KCB, CBE
Coward, *Vice-Adm.* Sir John Francis, KCB, DSO
Cowen, *Rt. Hon. Prof.* Sir Zelman, GCMG, GCVO
Cowie, Sir Thomas (Tom), Kt., OBE
Cowper-Coles, Sir Sherard Louis, KCMG, LVO
Cox, Sir Alan George, Kt., CBE
Cox, *Prof.* Sir David Roxbee, Kt.
Cox, Sir George Edwin, Kt.
Cradock, *Rt. Hon.* Sir Percy, GCMG
Craft, *Prof.* Sir Alan William, Kt.
Craig, Sir (Albert) James (Macqueen), GCMG
Craig-Cooper, Sir (Frederick Howard) Michael, Kt., CBE, TD
Crane, *Hon.* Sir Peter Francis, Kt.
Crane, *Prof.* Sir Peter Robert, Kt.
Cranston, *Hon.* Sir Ross Frederick, Kt.
Craufurd, Sir Robert James, Bt. (1781)
Craven, Sir John Anthony, Kt.
Craven, Sir Philip Lee, Kt., MBE
Crawford, *Prof.* Sir Frederick William, Kt., FRENG
Crawford, Sir Robert William Kenneth, Kt. CBE
Crawley-Boevey, Sir Thomas Michael Blake, Bt. (1784)
Crew, Sir (Michael) Edward, Kt., QPM
Crewe, *Prof.* Sir Ivor Martin, Kt.
Cresswell, *Hon.* Sir Peter John, Kt.
Crichton-Brown, Sir Robert, KCMG, CBE, TD
Crisp, Sir John Charles, Bt. (1913)
Critchett, Sir Charles George Montague, Bt. (1908)

Crockett, Sir Andrew Duncan, Kt.
Croft, Sir Owen Glendower, Bt. (1671)
Croft, Sir Thomas Stephen Hutton, Bt. (1818)
†Crofton, Sir Hugh Denis, Bt. (1801)
Crofton, *Prof.* Sir John Wenman, Kt.
†Crofton, Sir Julian Malby, Bt. (1838)
Crombie, Sir Alexander, Kt.
Crompton, Sir Dan, Kt., CBE, QPM
Crosby, Sir James Robert, Kt.
Crossland, *Prof.* Sir Bernard, Kt., CBE, FRENG
Crossley, Sir Sloan Nicholas, Bt. (1909)
Crowe, Sir Brian Lee, KCMG
Cruickshank, Sir Donald Gordon, Kt.
Cruthers, Sir James Winter, Kt.
Cubbon, Sir Brian Crossland, GCB
Cubie, *Dr* Sir Andrew, Kt., CBE
Cubitt, Sir Hugh Guy, Kt., CBE
Cullen, Sir (Edward) John, Kt., FRENG
Culme-Seymour, Sir Michael Patrick, Bt. (1809)
Culpin, Sir Robert Paul, Kt.
Cummins, Sir Michael John Austin, Kt.
Cunliffe, *Prof.* Sir Barrington, Kt., CBE
Cunliffe, Sir David Ellis, Bt. (1759)
Cunliffe-Owen, Sir Hugo Dudley, Bt. (1920)
Cunningham, *Lt.-Gen.* Sir Hugh Patrick, KBE
Cunningham, Sir Roger Keith, Kt., CBE
Cunynghame, Sir Andrew David Francis, Bt. (S. 1702)
†Currie, Sir Donald Scott, Bt. (1847)
Curry, Sir Donald Thomas Younger, Kt., CBE
Curtain, Sir Michael, KBE
Curtis, Sir Barry John, Kt.
Curtis, *Hon.* Sir Richard Herbert, Kt.
Curtis, Sir William Peter, Bt. (1802)
Curtiss, *Air Marshal* Sir John Bagot, KCB, KBE
Curwen, Sir Christopher Keith, KCMG
Cuschieri, *Prof.* Sir Alfred, Kt.
Dain, Sir David John Michael, KCVO
Dales, Sir Richard Nigel, KCVO
†Dalrymple-Hay, Sir Malcolm John Robert, Bt. (1798)
†Dalrymple-White, Sir Jan Hew, Bt. (1926)
Dalton, *Vice-Adm.* Sir Geoffrey Thomas James Oliver, KCB
Dalton, Sir Richard John, KCMG
Dalton, *Air Chief Marshal* Sir Stephen Gary George, KCB
Dalyell, Sir Tam (Thomas), Bt. (NS 1685)
Daniel, Sir John Sagar, Kt., DSC
Dankworth, Sir John, Kt., CBE
Dannatt, *Gen.* Sir (Francis) Richard, GCB, CBE, MC
Darell, Sir Jeffrey Lionel, Bt. (1795), MC
Darling, Sir Clifford, GCVO
Darrington, Sir Michael John, Kt.
Darroch, Sir Nigel Kim, KCMG
Dasgupta, *Prof.* Sir Partha Sarathi, Kt.
†Dashwood, Sir Edward John Francis, Bt. (1707), *Premier Baronet of Great Britain*
Dashwood, Sir Richard James, Bt. (1684)
Daunt, Sir Timothy Lewis Achilles, KCMG
Davenport-Handley, Sir David John, Kt., OBE
David, Sir Jean Marc, Kt., CBE, QC
David, *His Hon.* Sir Robin (Robert) Daniel George, Kt.
Davies, Sir Alan Seymour, Kt.
Davies, Sir (Charles) Noel, Kt.
Davies, *Prof.* Sir David Evan Naughton, Kt., CBE, FRS, FRENG
Davies, *Hon.* Sir (David Herbert) Mervyn, Kt., MC, TD
Davies, Sir David John, Kt.
Davies, Sir Frank John, Kt., CBE
Davies, *Prof.* Sir Graeme John, Kt., FRENG
Davies, Sir John Howard, Kt.
Davies, Sir John Michael, KCB
Davies, *Vice-Adm.* Sir Lancelot Richard Bell, KBE
Davies, Sir Peter Maxwell, Kt., CBE
Davies, Sir Rhys Everson, Kt., QC
Davis, Sir Andrew Frank, Kt., CBE
Davis, Sir Colin Rex, Kt., CH, CBE
Davis, Sir Crispin Henry Lamert, Kt.
Davis, Sir John Gilbert, Bt. (1946)
Davis, *Hon.* Sir Nigel Anthony Lambert, Kt.
Davis, Sir Peter John, Kt.
Davis-Goff, Sir Robert (William), Bt. (1905)
Davison, *Rt. Hon.* Sir Ronald Keith, GBE, CMG
†Davson, Sir George Trenchard Simon, Bt. (1927)
Dawanincura, Sir John Norbert, Kt., OBE
Dawbarn, Sir Simon Yelverton, KCVO, CMG
Dawson, *Hon.* Sir Daryl Michael, KBE, CB
Dawson, Sir Hugh Michael Trevor, Bt. (1920)
Dawtry, Sir Alan (Graham), Kt., CBE, TD
Day, Sir Derek Malcolm, KCMG
Day, *Air Chief Marshal* Sir John Romney, KCB, OBE, ADC
Day, Sir (Judson) Graham, Kt.
Day, Sir Michael John, Kt., OBE
Day, Sir Simon James, Kt.
Deane, *Hon.* Sir William Patrick, KBE
Dearlove, Sir Richard Billing, KCMG, OBE
de Bellaigue, Sir Geoffrey, GCVO
†Debenham, Sir Thomas Adam, Bt. (1931)
de Deney, Sir Geoffrey Ivor, KCVO
Deeny, *Hon.* Sir Donnell Justin Patrick, Kt.
De Halpert, *Rear-Adm.* Sir Jeremy Michael, KCVO, CB
de Hoghton, Sir (Richard) Bernard (Cuthbert), Bt. (1611)
De la Bère, Sir Cameron, Bt. (1953)
de la Rue, Sir Andrew George Ilay, Bt. (1898)
De Silva, Sir George Desmond Lorenz, Kt., QC
Dellow, Sir John Albert, Kt., CBE
Delves, *Lt.-Gen.* Sir Cedric Norman George, KBE
Denholm, Sir John Ferguson (Ian), Kt., CBE
Denison-Smith, *Lt.-Gen.* Sir Anthony Arthur, KBE
Denny, Sir Anthony Coningham de Waltham, Bt. (I. 1782)
Denny, Sir Charles Alistair Maurice, Bt. (1913)
Derbyshire, Sir Andrew George, Kt.
Derham, Sir Peter John, Kt.
de Trafford, Sir Dermot Humphrey, Bt. (1841)
Deverell, *Gen.* Sir John Freegard, KCB, OBE
Devesi, Sir Baddeley, GCMG, GCVO
De Ville, Sir Harold Godfrey Oscar, Kt., CBE
Devitt, Sir James Hugh Thomas, Bt. (1916)
de Waal, Sir (Constant Henrik) Henry, KCB, QC
Dewey, Sir Anthony Hugh, Bt. (1917)
De Witt, Sir Ronald Wayne, Kt.
Dhenin, *Air Marshal* Sir Geoffrey Howard, KBE, AFC, GM, MD
Dhrangadhara, HH Maharaja Shriraj Sahib of Halvad, KCIE
Dick-Lauder, Sir Piers Robert, Bt. (S. 1690)
Dickinson, Sir Harold Herbert, Kt.
Dilke, Sir Charles John Wentworth, Bt. (1862)
Dillwyn-Venables-Llewelyn, Sir John Michael, Bt. (1890)
Dixon, Sir Jeremy, Kt.
Dixon, Sir Jonathan Mark, Bt. (1919)
Dixon, Sir Peter John Bellett, Kt.
Djanogly, Sir Harry Ari Simon, Kt., CBE
Dobson, *Vice-Adm.* Sir David Stuart, KBE
Dodds, Sir Ralph Jordan, Bt. (1964)
Dollery, Sir Colin Terence, Kt.
Don-Wauchope, Sir Roger (Hamilton), Bt. (S. 1667)
Donald, Sir Alan Ewen, KCMG
Donald, *Air Marshal* Sir John George, KBE
Donaldson, *Prof.* Sir Liam Joseph, Kt.
Donne, *Hon.* Sir Gaven John, KBE
Donne, Sir John Christopher, Kt.
Donnelly, Sir Joseph Brian, KBE, CMG
Dorey, Sir Graham Martyn, Kt.
Dorman, Sir Philip Henry Keppel, Bt. (1923)
Doughty, Sir William Roland, Kt.

Douglas, *Prof.* Sir Neil James, Kt.
Douglas, *Hon.* Sir Roger Owen, Kt.
Dover, *Prof.* Sir Kenneth James, Kt., DLITT, FBA, FRSE
Dowell, Sir Anthony James, Kt., CBE
Dowling, Sir Robert, Kt.
Downey, Sir Gordon Stanley, KCB
Downs, Sir Diarmuid, Kt., CBE, FRENG
Downward, *Maj.-Gen.* Sir Peter Aldcroft, KCVO, CB, DSO, DFC
Dowson, Sir Philip Manning, Kt., CBE, PRA
Doyle, Sir Reginald Derek Henry, Kt., CBE
D'Oyly, Sir Hadley Gregory Bt. (1663)
Drake, *Hon.* Sir (Frederick) Maurice, Kt., DFC
Drewry, *Lt.-Gen.* Sir Christopher Francis, KCB, CBE
Drinkwater, Sir John Muir, Kt., QC
Driver, Sir Eric William, Kt.
Drury, Sir (Victor William) Michael, Kt., OBE
Dryden, Sir John Stephen Gyles, Bt. (1733 and 1795)
du Cann, *Rt. Hon.* Sir Edward Dillon Lott, KBE
†Duckworth, Sir James Edward Dyce, Bt. (1909)
du Cros, Sir Claude Philip Arthur Mallet, Bt. (1916)
Dudley-Williams, Sir Alastair Edgcumbe James, Bt. (1964)
Duff, *Prof.* Sir Gordon William, Kt.
Duff-Gordon, Sir Andrew Cosmo Lewis, Bt. (1813)
Duffell, *Lt.-Gen.* Sir Peter Royson, KCB, CBE, MC
Duffy, Sir (Albert) (Edward) Patrick, Kt., PHD
Dugdale, Sir William Stratford, Bt. (1936), MC
Duggin, Sir Thomas Joseph, Kt.
Dummett, *Prof.* Sir Michael Anthony Eardley, Kt., FBA
Dunbar, Sir Archibald Ranulph, Bt. (S. 1700)
Dunbar, Sir Robert Drummond Cospatrick, Bt. (S. 1698)
Dunbar, Sir James Michael, Bt. (S. 1694)
Dunbar of Hempriggs, Sir Richard Francis, Bt. (S. 1706)
Dunbar-Nasmith, *Prof.* Sir James Duncan, Kt., CBE
Duncan, Sir James Blair, Kt.
Dunlop, Sir Thomas, Bt. (1916)
Dunn, *Rt. Hon.* Sir Robin Horace Walford, Kt., MC
Dunne, Sir Thomas Raymond, KG, KCVO
Dunning, Sir Simon William Patrick, Bt. (1930)
Dunnington-Jefferson, Sir Mervyn Stewart, Bt. (1958)
Dunstan, *Lt.-Gen.* Sir Donald Beaumont, KBE, CB
Dunt, *Vice-Adm.* Sir John Hugh, KCB
Duntze, Sir Daniel Evans Bt. (1774)
Dupre, Sir Tumun, Kt., MBE
Dupree, Sir (Thomas William James) David, Bt. (1921)
Durand, Sir Edward Alan Christopher David Percy, Bt. (1892)
Durant, Sir (Robert) Anthony (Bevis), Kt.
Durie, Sir David Robert Campbell, KCMG
Durrant, Sir William Alexander Estridge, Bt. (1784)
Duthie, *Prof.* Sir Herbert Livingston, Kt.
Duthie, Sir Robert Grieve (Robin), Kt., CBE
Dwyer, Sir Joseph Anthony, Kt.
Dyke, Sir David William Hart, Bt. (1677)
Dymock, *Vice-Adm.* Sir Anthony Knox, KBE, CB
Dyson, Sir James, Kt., CBE
Dyson, *Rt. Hon.* Sir John Anthony, Kt.
Eady, *Hon.* Sir David, Kt.
Eardley-Wilmot, Sir Michael John Assheton, Bt. (1821)
Earle, Sir (Hardman) George (Algernon), Bt. (1869)
Easton, Sir Robert William Simpson, Kt., CBE
Eaton, *Adm.* Sir Kenneth John, GBE, KCB
Eberle, *Adm.* Sir James Henry Fuller, GCB
Ebrahim, Sir (Mahomed) Currimbhoy, Bt. (1910)
Eckersley, Sir Donald Payze, Kt., OBE
Eddington, Sir Roderick Ian, Kt.
Edge, *Capt.* Sir (Philip) Malcolm, KCVO
†Edge, Sir William, Bt. (1937)
Edmonstone, Sir Archibald Bruce Charles, Bt. (1774)
Edward, *Rt. Hon.* Sir David Alexander Ogilvy, KCMG
Edwardes, Sir Michael Owen, Kt.
Edwards, Sir Christopher John Churchill, Bt. (1866)
Edwards, *Prof.* Sir Christopher Richard Watkin, Kt.
Edwards, Sir Llewellyn Roy, Kt.
Edwards, Sir Robert Paul, Kt.
Edwards, *Prof.* Sir Samuel Frederick, Kt., FRS
†Edwards-Moss, Sir David John, Bt. (1868)
Egan, Sir John Leopold, Kt.
Ehrman, Sir William Geoffrey, KCMG
Eichelbaum, *Rt. Hon.* Sir Thomas, GBE
Elder, Sir Mark Philip, Kt., CBE
Eldon, Sir Stewart Graham, KCMG, OBE
Elias, *Rt. Hon.* Sir Patrick, Kt.
Eliott of Stobs, Sir Charles Joseph Alexander, Bt. (S. 1666)
Elliot, Sir Gerald Henry, Kt.
Elliott, Sir Clive Christopher Hugh, Bt. (1917)
Elliott, Sir David Murray, KCMG, CB
Elliott, *Prof.* Sir John Huxtable, Kt., FBA
Elliott, Sir Randal Forbes, KBE
Elliott, *Prof.* Sir Roger James, Kt., FRS
Elphinstone, Sir John, Bt. (S. 1701)
Elphinstone, Sir John Howard Main, Bt. (1816)
Elton, Sir Arnold, Kt., CBE
Elton, Sir Charles Abraham Grierson, Bt. (1717)
Elton, Sir Leslie, Kt.
Elvidge, Sir John, KCB
Elwes, *Dr* Sir Henry William, KCVO
Elwes, Sir Jeremy Vernon, Kt., CBE
Elwood, Sir Brian George Conway, Kt., CBE
Elworthy, *Air Cdre. Hon.* Sir Timothy Charles, KCVO, CBE
Empey, Sir Reginald Norman Morgan, Kt., OBE
Enderby, *Prof.* Sir John Edwin, Kt. CBE, FRS
Engle, Sir George Lawrence Jose, KCB, QC
English, Sir Terence Alexander Hawthorne, KBE, FRCS
Ennals, Sir Paul Martin, Kt., CBE
Epstein, *Prof.* Sir (Michael) Anthony, Kt., CBE, FRS
Errington, *Col.* Sir Geoffrey Frederick, Bt. (1963), OBE
Errington, Sir Lancelot, KCB
Erskine, Sir (Thomas) Peter Neil, Bt. (1821)
Erskine-Hill, Sir Alexander Rodger, Bt. (1945)
Esmonde, Sir Thomas Francis Grattan, Bt. (I. 1629)
Esplen, Sir John Graham, Bt. (1921)
Essenhigh, *Adm.* Sir Nigel Richard, GCB
Etherton, *Rt. Hon.* Sir Terence Michael Elkan Barnet, Kt.
Evans, Sir Anthony Adney, Bt. (1920)
Evans, *Rt. Hon.* Sir Anthony Howell Meurig, Kt., RD
Evans, *Prof.* Sir Christopher Thomas, Kt., OBE
Evans, *Air Chief Marshal* Sir David George, GCB, CBE
Evans, *Hon.* Sir David Roderick, Kt.
Evans, Sir Harold Matthew, Kt.
Evans, *Hon.* Sir Haydn Tudor, Kt.
Evans, *Prof.* Sir John Grimley, Kt., FRCP
Evans, Sir John Stanley, Kt., QPM
Evans, *Prof.* Sir Martin John, Kt., FRS
Evans, Sir Richard Harry, Kt., CBE
Evans, Sir Richard Mark, KCMG, KCVO
Evans, Sir Robert, Kt., CBE, FRENG
Evans-Lombe, *Hon.* Sir Edward Christopher, Kt.
†Evans-Tipping, Sir David Gwynne, Bt. (1913)
Eveleigh, *Rt. Hon.* Sir Edward Walter, Kt., ERD
Everard, Sir Robin Charles, Bt. (1911)

Every, Sir Henry John Michael, Bt. (1641)
Ewans, Sir Martin Kenneth, KCMG
Ewart, Sir William Michael, Bt. (1887)
Ewbank, *Hon.* Sir Anthony Bruce, Kt.
Eyre, Sir Reginald Edwin, Kt.
Eyre, Sir Richard Charles Hastings, Kt., CBE
Fagge, Sir John Christopher Frederick, Bt. (1660)
Fairbairn, Sir (James) Brooke, Bt. (1869)
Fairlie-Cuninghame, Sir Robert Henry, Bt. (S. 1630)
Fairweather, Sir Patrick Stanislaus, KCMG
Faldo, Sir Nicholas Alexander, Kt., MBE
†Falkiner, Sir Benjamin Simon Patrick, Bt. (I. 1778)
Fall, Sir Brian James Proetel, GCVO, KCMG
Falle, Sir Samuel, KCMG, KCVO, DSC
Fang, *Prof.* Sir Harry, Kt., CBE
Fareed, Sir Djamil Sheik, Kt.
Farmer, Sir Thomas, Kt., CVO, CBE
Farquhar, Sir Michael Fitzroy Henry, Bt. (1796)
Farquharson, *Rt. Hon.* Sir Donald Henry, Kt.
Farrell, Sir Terence, Kt., CBE
Farrer, Sir (Charles) Matthew, GCVO
Farrington, Sir Henry William, Bt. (1818)
Fat, Sir (Maxime) Edouard (Lim Man) Lim, Kt.
Faulkner, Sir (James) Dennis (Compton), Kt., CBE, VRD
Fay, Sir (Humphrey) Michael Gerard, Kt.
Fayrer, Sir John Lang Macpherson, Bt. (1896)
Feachem, *Prof.* Sir Richard George Andrew, KBE
Fean, Sir Thomas Vincent, KCVO
Feilden, Sir Henry Wemyss, Bt., (1846)
Fell, Sir David, KCB
Fender, Sir Brian Edward Frederick, Kt., CMG, PHD
Fenn, Sir Nicholas Maxted, GCMG
Fennell, *Hon.* Sir (John) Desmond Augustine, Kt., OBE
Fennessy, Sir Edward, Kt., CBE
Fenwick, Sir Leonard Raymond, Kt., CBE
Fergus, Sir Howard Archibald, KBE
Ferguson, Sir Alexander Chapman, Kt., CBE
Ferguson-Davie, Sir Michael, Bt. (1847)
Fergusson of Kilkerran, Sir Charles, Bt. (S. 1703)
Fergusson, Sir Ewan Alastair John, GCMG, GCVO
Fermor, Sir Patrick Michael Leigh, Kt., DSO, OBE
Feroze, Sir Rustam Moolan, Kt., FRCS
Fersht, *Prof.* Sir Alan Roy, Kt., FRS
Ferris, *Hon.* Sir Francis Mursell, Kt., TD
ffolkes, Sir Robert Francis Alexander, Bt. (1774), OBE
Field, Sir Malcolm David, Kt.
Field, *Hon.* Sir Richard Alan, Kt.
Fielding, Sir Colin Cunningham, Kt., CB
Fielding, Sir Leslie, KCMG
Fields, Sir Allan Clifford, KCMG
Fieldsend, *Hon.* Sir John Charles Rowell, KBE
Fiennes, Sir Ranulph Twisleton-Wykeham, Bt. (1916), OBE
Figg, Sir Leonard Clifford William, KCMG
Figgis, Sir Anthony St John Howard, KCVO, CMG
Finch, Sir Robert Gerard, Kt.
Finlay, Sir David Ronald James Bell, Bt. (1964)
Finlayson, Sir Garet Orlando, KCMG, OBE
Finney, Sir Thomas, Kt., OBE
†Fison, Sir Charles William, Bt. (1905)
†Fitzgerald, *Revd* Daniel Patrick, Bt. (1903)
FitzGerald, Sir Adrian James Andrew, Bt. (1880)
FitzHerbert, Sir Richard Ranulph, Bt. (1784)
Fitzpatrick, *Air Marshal* Sir John Bernard, KBE, CB
Flanagan, Sir Ronald, GBE
Flaux, *Hon.* Sir Julian Martin, Kt.
Floissac, *Hon.* Sir Vincent Frederick, Kt., CMG, OBE
Floud, *Prof.* Sir Roderick Castle, Kt.
Floyd, *Hon.* Sir Christopher David, Kt.
Floyd, Sir Giles Henry Charles, Bt. (1816)
Foley, *Lt.-Gen.* Sir John Paul, KCB, OBE, MC
Follett, *Prof.* Sir Brian Keith, Kt., FRS
Foot, Sir Geoffrey James, Kt.
Foots, Sir James William, Kt.
†Forbes, Sir James Thomas Stewart, Bt. (1823)
Forbes, *Adm.* Sir Ian Andrew, KCB, CBE
Forbes, *Vice-Adm.* Sir John Morrison, KCB
Forbes, *Hon.* Sir Thayne John, Kt.
†Forbes Adam, Revd Stephen Timothy Beilby, Bt. (1917)
Forbes-Leith, Sir George Ian David, Bt. (1923)
Forbes of Craigievar, Sir Andrew Iain Ochoncar, Bt. (S. 1630)
Ford, Sir Andrew Russell, Bt. (1929)
Ford, Sir David Robert, KBE, LVO
Ford, *Prof.* Sir Hugh, Kt., FRS, FRENG
Ford, Sir John Archibald, KCMG, MC
Ford, *Gen.* Sir Robert Cyril, GCB, CBE
Foreman, Sir Philip Frank, Kt., CBE, FRENG
Forestier-Walker, Sir Michael Leolin, Bt. (1835)
Forman, Sir John Denis, Kt., OBE
Forrest, *Prof.* Sir (Andrew) Patrick (McEwen), Kt.
Forte, Hon. Sir Rocco John Vincent, Kt.
Forwood, Sir Peter Noel, Bt. (1895)
Foskett, *Hon.* Sir David Robert, Kt.
Foster, Sir Andrew William, Kt.
Foster, *Prof.* Sir Christopher David, Kt.
†Foster, Sir Saxby Gregory, Bt. (1930)
Foulkes, Sir Arthur Alexander, KCMG
Foulkes, Sir Nigel Gordon, Kt.
Fountain, *Hon.* Sir Cyril Stanley Smith, Kt.
Fowke, Sir David Frederick Gustavus, Bt. (1814)
Fowler, Sir (Edward) Michael Coulson, Kt.
Fox, Sir Christopher, Kt., QPM
Fox, Sir Paul Leonard, Kt., CBE
France, Sir Christopher Walter, GCB
Francis, Sir Horace William Alexander, Kt., CBE, FRENG
Frank, Sir Robert Andrew, Bt. (1920)
Franklin, Sir Michael David Milroy, KCB, CMG
Fraser, Sir Alasdair MacLeod, Kt.
Fraser, Sir Charles Annand, KCVO
Fraser, *Gen.* Sir David William, GCB, OBE
Fraser, Sir Iain Michael Duncan, Bt. (1943)
Fraser, Sir James Murdo, KBE
Fraser, Sir William Kerr, GCB
Frayling, *Prof.* Sir Christopher John, Kt.
Frederick, Sir Christopher St John, Bt. (1723)
Freedman, *Rt. Hon. Prof.* Sir Lawrence David, KCMG, CBE
Freeland, Sir John Redvers, KCMG
Freeman, Sir James Robin, Bt. (1945)
Freer, *Air Chief Marshal* Sir Robert William George, GBE, KCB
French, *Air Marshal* Sir Joseph Charles, KCB, CBE
Frere, *Vice-Adm.* Sir Richard Tobias, KCB
Fretwell, Sir (Major) John (Emsley), GCMG
Friend *Prof.* Sir Richard Henry, Kt.
Froggatt, Sir Leslie Trevor, Kt.
Froggatt, Sir Peter, Kt.
Frossard, Sir Charles Keith, KBE
Frost, Sir David Paradine, Kt., OBE
Fry, Sir Graham Holbrook, KCMG
Fry, Sir Peter Derek, Kt.
Fry, *Lt.-Gen.* Sir Robert Allan, KCB, CBE
Fulford, *Hon.* Sir Adrian Bruce, Kt.
Fuller, Sir James Henry Fleetwood, Bt. (1910)
Fuller, *Hon.* Sir John Bryan Munro, Kt.
Fulton, *Lt.-Gen.* Sir Robert Henry Gervase, KBE

Furness, Sir Stephen Roberts, Bt. (1913)
Gage, *Rt. Hon.* Sir William Marcus, Kt., QC
Gains, Sir John Christopher, Kt.
Gainsford, Sir Ian Derek, Kt.
Galsworthy, Sir Anthony Charles, KCMG
Galway, Sir James, Kt., OBE
Gamble, Sir David Hugh Norman, Bt. (1897)
Gambon, Sir Michael John, Kt., CBE
Gammell, Sir William Benjamin Bowring, Kt.
Gardiner, Sir John Eliot, Kt., CBE
Gardner, *Prof.* Sir Richard Lavenham, Kt.
Gardner, Sir Roy Alan, Kt.
Garland, *Hon.* Sir Patrick Neville, Kt.
Garland, *Hon.* Sir Ransley Victor, KBE
Garner, Sir Anthony Stuart, Kt.
Garnett, *Adm.* Sir Ian David Graham, KCB
Garnier, *Rear-Adm.* Sir John, KCVO, CBE
Garrard, Sir David Eardley, Kt.
Garrett, Sir Anthony Peter, Kt., CBE
Garrick, Sir Ronald, Kt., CBE, FRENG
Garthwaite, Sir (William) Mark (Charles), Bt. (1919)
Gaskell, Sir Richard Kennedy Harvey, Kt.
Geno, Sir Makena Viora, KBE
Gent, Sir Christopher Charles, Kt.
George, Sir Arthur Thomas, Kt.
George, *Prof.* Sir Charles Frederick, MD, FRCP
George, Sir Richard William, Kt., CVO
Gerken, *Vice-Adm.* Sir Robert William Frank, KCB, CBE
Gershon, Sir Peter Oliver, Kt., CBE
Gethin, Sir Richard Joseph St Lawrence, Bt. (I. 1665)
Ghurburrun, Sir Rabindrah, Kt.
Gibb, Sir Francis Ross (Frank), Kt., CBE, FRENG
Gibbings, Sir Peter Walter, Kt.
Gibbons, Sir (John) David, KBE
Gibbons, Sir William Edward Doran, Bt. (1752)
Gibbs, *Hon.* Sir Richard John Hedley, Kt.
Gibbs, Sir Roger Geoffrey, Kt.
†Gibson, *Revd* Christopher Herbert, Bt. (1931)
Gibson, Sir Ian, Kt., CBE
Gibson, *Rt. Hon.* Sir Peter Leslie, Kt.
Gibson-Craig-Carmichael, Sir David Peter William, Bt. (S. 1702 and 1831)
Gieve, Sir Edward John Watson, KCB
Giffard, Sir (Charles) Sydney (Rycroft), KCMG
Gilbart-Denham, *Lt.-Col.* Sir Seymour Vivian, KCVO
Gilbert, *Air Chief Marshal* Sir Joseph Alfred, KCB, CBE
Gilbert, *Rt. Hon.* Sir Martin John, Kt., CBE
†Gilbey, Sir Walter Gavin, Bt. (1893)
Gill, Sir Anthony Keith, Kt.
Gill, Sir Arthur Benjamin Norman, Kt., CBE
Gillam, Sir Patrick John, Kt.
Gillen, *Hon.* Sir John de Winter, Kt.
†Gillett, Sir Nicholas Danvers Penrose, Bt. (1959)
Gillinson, Sir Clive Daniel, Kt., CBE
Gilmour, Sir John, Bt. (1897)
Gina, Sir Lloyd Maepeza, KBE
Gingell, *Air Chief Marshal* Sir John, GBE, KCB, KCVO
Giordano, Sir Richard Vincent, KBE
Girolami, Sir Paul, Kt.
Girvan, *Rt. Hon.* Sir (Frederick) Paul, Kt.
Gladstone, Sir (Erskine) William, Bt. (1846), KG
Glean, Sir Carlyle Arnold, GCMG
Glenn, Sir (Joseph Robert) Archibald, Kt., OBE
Glidewell, *Rt. Hon.* Sir Iain Derek Laing, Kt.
Glover, Sir Victor Joseph Patrick, Kt.
Glyn, Sir Richard Lindsay, Bt. (1759 and 1800)
Gobbo, Sir James Augustine, Kt., AC
Goldberg, *Prof.* Sir David Paul Brandes, Kt.
Goldring, *Rt. Hon.* Sir John Bernard, Kt.
Gomersall, Sir Stephen John, KCMG
Gonsalves-Sabola, *Hon.* Sir Joaquim Claudino, Kt
Gooch, Sir Miles Peter, Bt. (1866)
Gooch, Sir Arthur Brian Sherlock Heywood, Bt. (1746)
Good, Sir John James Griffen, Kt. CBE
Goodall, Sir (Arthur) David Saunders, GCMG
Goodall, *Air Marshal* Sir Roderick Harvey, KBE, CB, AFC
Goode, Prof. Sir Royston Miles, Kt., CBE, QC
Goodenough, Sir Anthony Michael, KCMG
Goodenough, Sir William McLernon, Bt. (1943)
Goodhart, Sir Philip Carter, Kt.
Goodhart, Sir Robert Anthony Gordon, Bt. (1911)
Goodison, Sir Nicholas Proctor, Kt.
Goodman, Sir Patrick Ledger, Kt., CBE
Goodson, Sir Mark Weston Lassam, Bt. (1922)
Goodwin, Sir Frederick, KBE
Goodwin, Sir Frederick Anderson, Kt.
Goodwin, Sir Matthew Dean, Kt., CBE
Goody, *Prof.* Sir John Rankine, Kt.
†Goold, Sir George William, Bt. (1801)
Gordon, Sir Donald, Kt.
Gordon, Sir Gerald Henry, Kt., CBE, QC
Gordon, Sir Robert James, Bt. (S. 1706)
Gordon-Cumming, Sir Alexander Penrose, Bt. (1804)
†Gore, Sir Nigel Hugh St George, Bt. (I. 1622)
Gore-Booth, Sir Josslyn Henry Robert, Bt. (I. 1760)
Goring, Sir William Burton Nigel, Bt. (1627)
Gorman, Sir John Reginald, Kt., CVO, CBE, MC
Gorst, Sir John Michael, Kt.
Goschen, Sir (Edward) Alexander, Bt. (1916)
Gosling, Sir (Frederick) Donald, KCVO
Goswell, Sir Brian Lawrence, Kt.
Gough, Sir Charles Brandon, Kt.
Goulden, Sir (Peter) John, GCMG
Goulding, Sir Marrack Irvine, KCMG
Goulding, Sir (William) Lingard Walter, Bt. (1904)
Gourlay, *Gen.* Sir (Basil) Ian (Spencer), KCB, OBE, MC, RM
Gourlay, Sir Simon Alexander, Kt.
Gow, *Gen.* Sir (James) Michael, GCB
Gowans, Sir James Learmonth, Kt., CBE, FRCP, FRS
Gozney, Sir Richard Hugh Turton, KCMG
†Graaff, Sir David de Villiers, Bt. (1911)
Grabham, Sir Anthony Henry, Kt.
Graham, *Dr* Sir Albert Cecil, Kt.
Graham, Sir Alexander Michael, GBE
Graham, Sir James Bellingham, Bt. (1662)
Graham, Sir James Fergus Surtees, Bt. (1783)
Graham, Sir James Thompson, Kt., CMG
Graham, Sir John Alexander Noble, Bt. (1906), GCMG
Graham, Sir John Alistair, Kt.
Graham, Sir John Moodie, Bt. (1964)
Graham, Sir Norman William, Kt., CB
Graham, Sir Peter, KCB, QC
Graham, *Lt.-Gen.* Sir Peter Walter, KCB, CBE
†Graham, Sir Ralph Stuart, Bt. (1629)
Graham-Moon, Sir Peter Wilfred Giles, Bt. (1855)
Graham-Smith, *Prof.* Sir Francis, Kt.
Grant, Sir Archibald, Bt. (S. 1705)
Grant, Sir Clifford, Kt.
Grant, Sir (John) Anthony, Kt.
Grant, Sir John Douglas Kelso, KCMG
Grant, Sir Patrick Alexander Benedict, Bt. (S. 1688)
Grant, Sir Paul Joseph Patrick, Kt.
Grant, *Lt.-Gen.* Sir Scott Carnegie, KCB
Grant-Suttie, Sir James Edward, Bt. (S. 1702)

Granville-Chapman, *Lt.-Gen.* Sir Timothy John, GBE, KCB, ADC
Gratton-Bellew, Sir Henry Charles, Bt. (1838)
Gray, *Hon* Sir Charles Anthony St John, Kt.
Gray, Sir Charles Ireland, Kt., CBE
Gray, *Prof.* Sir Denis John Pereira, Kt., OBE, FRCGP
Gray, Sir John Archibald Browne, Kt., SCD, FRS
Gray, *Dr.* Sir John Armstrong Muir, Kt., CBE
Gray, *Lt.-Gen.* Sir Michael Stuart, KCB, OBE
Gray, Sir Robert McDowall (Robin), Kt.
Gray, Sir William Hume, Bt. (1917)
Graydon, *Air Chief Marshal* Sir Michael James, GCB, CBE
Grayson, Sir Jeremy Brian Vincent Harrington, Bt. (1922)
Green, Sir Allan David, KCB, QC
Green, Sir Andrew Fleming, KCMG
Green, Sir Edward Patrick Lycett, Bt. (1886)
Green, Sir Gregory David, KCMG
Green, *Hon.* Sir Guy Stephen Montague, KBE
Green, Sir Kenneth, Kt.
Green, *Prof.* Sir Malcolm, Kt.
Green, Sir Owen Whitley, Kt.
Green, Sir Philip Green, Kt.
Green-Price, Sir Robert John, Bt. (1874)
Greenaway, Sir John Michael Burdick, Bt. (1933)
Greenbury, Sir Richard, Kt.
Greener, Sir Anthony Armitage, Kt.
Greengross, Sir Alan David, Kt.
Greenstock, Sir Jeremy Quentin, GCMG
Greenwell, Sir Edward Bernard, Bt. (1906)
Greenwood, *Prof.* Sir Christopher John, Kt., CMG
Gregson, Sir Peter Lewis, GCB
Greig, Sir (Henry Louis) Carron, KCVO, CBE
Grey, Sir Anthony Dysart, Bt. (1814)
†Grey-Egerton, Sir David Boswell, Bt. (1617), CB, OBE, MC
Grierson, Sir Ronald Hugh, Kt.
Griffiths, Sir Eldon Wylie, Kt.
Grigson, *Hon.* Sir Geoffrey Douglas, Kt.
Grimshaw, Sir Nicholas Thomas, Kt., CBE
Grimwade, Sir Andrew Sheppard, Kt., CBE
Grinstead, Sir Stanley Gordon, Kt.
Grose, *Vice-Adm.* Sir Alan, KBE
Gross, *Hon.* Sir Peter Henry, Kt.
Grossart, Sir Angus McFarlane McLeod, Kt., CBE
Grotrian, Sir Philip Christian Brent, Bt. (1934)
Grove, Sir Charles Gerald, Bt. (1874)
Grove, Sir Edmund Frank, KCVO
Grugeon, Sir John Drury, Kt.
Grundy, Sir Mark, Kt.
Guinness, Sir Howard Christian Sheldon, Kt., VRD
Guinness, Sir John Ralph Sidney, Kt., CB
Guinness, Sir Kenelm Ernest Lee, Bt. (1867)
†Guise, Sir Christopher James, Bt. (1783)
Gull, Sir Rupert William Cameron, Bt. (1872)
Gumbs, Sir Emile Rudolph, Kt.
Gunn, Sir Robert Norman, Kt.
†Gunning, Sir Charles Theodore, Bt. (1778)
Gunston, Sir John Wellesley, Bt. (1938)
Gurdon, *Prof.* Sir John Bertrand, Kt., DPHIL, FRS
Guthrie, Sir Malcolm Connop, Bt. (1936)
Haddacks, *Vice-Adm.* Sir Paul Kenneth, KCB
Hadfield, Sir Ronald, Kt., QPM
Hadlee, Sir Richard John, Kt., MBE
Hagart-Alexander, Sir Claud, Bt. (1886)
Hague, *Prof.* Sir Douglas Chalmers, Kt., CBE
Haines, *Prof.* Sir Andrew Paul, Kt.
Haji-Ioannou, Sir Stelios, Kt.
Halberg, Sir Murray Gordon, Kt., MBE
Hall, Sir Basil Brodribb, KCB, MC, TD
Hall, *Prof.* Sir David Michael Baldock, Kt.
Hall, Sir Ernest, Kt., OBE
Hall, Sir Graham Joseph, Kt.
Hall, Sir Iain Robert, Kt.
Hall, Sir (Frederick) John (Frank), Bt. (1923)
Hall, Sir John, Kt.
Hall, Sir John Bernard, Bt. (1919)
Hall, Sir John Douglas Hoste, Bt. (S. 1687)
Hall, HE *Prof.* Sir Kenneth Octavius, GCMG
Hall, Sir Peter Edward, KBE, CMG
Hall, *Prof.* Sir Peter Geoffrey, Kt., FBA
Hall, Sir Peter Reginald Frederick, Kt., CBE
Hall, Sir William Joseph, KCVO
Halpern, Sir Ralph Mark, Kt.
Halsey, *Revd* John Walter Brooke, Bt. (1920)
Halstead, Sir Ronald, Kt., CBE
Hamblen, *Hon.* Sir Nicholas Archibald, Kt.
Hambling, Sir (Herbert) Hugh, Bt. (1924)
Hamilton, Sir Andrew Caradoc, Bt. (S. 1646)
Hamilton, Sir Edward Sydney, Bt. (1776 and 1819)
Hamilton, Sir James Arnot, KCB, MBE, FRENG
Hamilton, Sir Nigel, KCB
Hamilton-Dalrymple, *Maj.* Sir Hew Fleetwood, Bt. (S. 1697), GCVO
Hamilton-Spencer-Smith, Sir John, Bt. (1804)
Hammick, Sir Stephen George, Bt. (1834)
Hammond, Sir Anthony Hilgrove, KCB, QC
Hampel, Sir Ronald Claus, Kt.
Hampson, Sir Stuart, Kt.
Hampton, Sir (Leslie) Geoffrey, Kt.
Hampton, Sir Philip Roy, Kt.
Hanbury-Tenison, Sir Richard, KCVO
Hancock, Sir David John Stowell, KCB
†Hanham, Sir William John Edward, Bt. (1667)
Hankes-Drielsma, Sir Claude Dunbar, KCVO
Hanley, *Rt. Hon.* Sir Jeremy James, KCMG
Hanmer, Sir John Wyndham Edward, Bt. (1774)
Hannam, Sir John Gordon, Kt.
Hanson, Sir (Charles) Rupert (Patrick), Bt. (1918)
Hanson, Sir John Gilbert, KCMG, CBE
Harcourt-Smith, *Air Chief Marshal* Sir David, GBE, KCB, DFC
Hardie Boys, *Rt. Hon.* Sir Michael, GCMG
Harding, Sir George William, KCMG, CVO
Harding, *Marshal of the Royal Air Force* Sir Peter Robin, GCB
Harding, Sir Roy Pollard, Kt., CBE
Hardy, Sir David William, Kt.
Hardy, Sir James Gilbert, Kt., OBE
Hardy, Sir Richard Charles Chandos, Bt. (1876)
Hare, Sir David, Kt., FRSL
Hare, Sir Nicholas Patrick, Bt. (1818)
Haren, *Dr* Sir Patrick Hugh, Kt.
Harford, Sir (John) Timothy, Bt. (1934)
Harington, Sir Nicholas John, Bt (1611)
Harkness, *Very Revd* James, KCVO, CB, OBE
Harland, *Air Marshal* Sir Reginald Edward Wynyard, KBE, CB
Harley, *Gen.* Sir Alexander George Hamilton, KBE, CB
Harman, *Gen.* Sir Jack Wentworth, GCB, OBE, MC
Harman, *Hon.* Sir Jeremiah LeRoy, Kt.
Harman, Sir John Andrew, Kt.
Harmsworth, Sir Hildebrand Harold, Bt. (1922)
Harper, Sir Ewan William, Kt. CBE
Harper, *Prof.* Sir Peter Stanley, Kt., CBE
Harris, *Prof.* Sir Henry, Kt., FRCP, FRCPATH, FRS
Harris, Sir Jack Wolfred Ashford, Bt. (1932)
Harris, *Air Marshal* Sir John Hulme, KCB, CBE
Harris, *Prof.* Sir Martin Best, Kt., CBE

Harris, Sir Michael Frank, Kt.
Harris, Sir Thomas George, KBE, CMG,
Harrison, *Prof.* Sir Brian Howard, Kt.
Harrison, Sir David, Kt., CBE, FRENG
Harrison, *Surgeon Vice-Adm.* Sir John Albert Bews, KBE
Harrison, *Hon.* Sir Michael Guy Vicat, Kt.
Harrison, Sir Michael James Harwood, Bt. (1961)
Harrison, Sir (Robert) Colin, Bt. (1922)
Harrison, Sir Terence, Kt., FRENG
Harrop, Sir Peter John, KCB
Hart, *Hon.* Sir Anthony Ronald, Kt.
Hart, Sir David Michael, Kt., OBE
Hart, Sir Graham Allan, KCB
Hartwell, Sir (Francis) Anthony Charles Peter, Bt. (1805)
Harvey, Sir Charles Richard Musgrave, Bt. (1933)
Harvie, Sir John Smith, Kt., CBE
Harvie-Watt, Sir James, Bt. (1945)
Haselhurst, *Rt. Hon.* Sir Alan Gordon Barraclough, Kt.
Haskard, Sir Cosmo Dugal Patrick Thomas, KCMG, MBE
Hastie, *Cdre* Sir Robert Cameron, KCVO, CBE, RD
Hastings, Sir Max Macdonald, Kt.
Hastings, *Dr* Sir William George, Kt., CBE
Hatter, Sir Maurice, Kt.
Havelock-Allan, Sir (Anthony) Mark David, Bt. (1858)
Hawkes, Sir John Garry, Kt., CBE
Hawkins, Sir Richard Caesar, Bt. (1778)
†Hawley, Sir Henry Nicholas, Bt. (1795)
Haworth, Sir Philip, Bt. (1911)
Hawthorne, *Prof.* Sir William Rede, Kt., CBE, SCD, FRS, FRENG
Hay, Sir David Russell, Kt., CBE, FRCP, MD
Hay, Sir Hamish Grenfell, Kt.
Hay, Sir John Erroll Audley, Bt. (S. 1663)
†Hay, Sir Ronald Frederick Hamilton, Bt. (S. 1703)
Hayes, Sir Brian, Kt., CBE, QPM
Hayes, Sir Brian David, GCB
Hayman-Joyce, *Lt.-Gen.* Sir Robert John, KCB, CBE
Hayter, Sir Paul David Grenville, KCB, LVO
Hayward, Sir Anthony William Byrd, Kt.
Hayward, Sir Jack Arnold, Kt., OBE
Haywood, Sir Harold, KCVO, OBE
Head, Sir Richard Douglas Somerville, Bt. (1838)
Heap, Sir Peter William, KCMG
Heap, *Prof.* Sir Robert Brian, Kt., CBE, FRS
Hearne, Sir Graham James, Kt., CBE
Heathcote, *Brig.* Sir Gilbert Simon, Bt. (1733), CBE
†Heathcote, Sir Timothy Gilbert, Bt. (1733)
Heatley, Sir Peter, Kt., CBE
Hedley, *Hon.* Sir Mark, Kt.
Hegarty, Sir John Kevin, Kt.
Heiser, Sir Terence Michael, GCB
Henderson, Sir Denys Hartley, Kt.
Henderson, *Hon.* Sir Launcelot Dinadan James, Kt.
Henderson, *Maj.* Sir Richard Yates, KCVO
Hendry, *Prof.* Sir David Forbes, Kt.
Hennessy, Sir James Patrick Ivan, KBE, CMG
†Henniker, Sir Adrian Chandos, Bt. (1813)
Henniker-Heaton, Sir Yvo Robert, Bt. (1912)
Henriques, *Hon.* Sir Richard Henry Quixano, Kt.
Henry, *Rt. Hon.* Sir Denis Robert Maurice, Kt.
Henry, *Hon.* Sir Geoffrey Arama, KBE
†Henry, Sir Patrick Denis, Bt. (1923)
Henshaw, Sir David George, Kt.
Hepple, *Prof.* Sir Bob Alexander, Kt.
Herbecq, Sir John Edward, KCB
Herbert, *Adm.* Sir Peter Geoffrey Marshall, KCB, OBE
Heron, Sir Conrad Frederick, KCB, OBE
Heron, Sir Michael Gilbert, Kt.
Heron-Maxwell, Sir Nigel Mellor, Bt. (S. 1683)
Hervey, Sir Roger Blaise Ramsay, KCVO, CMG
Hervey-Bathurst, Sir Frederick John Charles Gordon, Bt. (1818)
Heseltine, *Rt. Hon.* Sir William Frederick Payne, GCB, GCVO
Hewetson, Sir Christopher Raynor, Kt., TD
Hewett, Sir Richard Mark John, Bt. (1813)
Hewitt, Sir (Cyrus) Lenox (Simson), Kt., OBE
Hewitt, Sir Nicholas Charles Joseph, Bt. (1921)
Heygate, Sir Richard John Gage, Bt. (1831)
Heywood, Sir Peter, Bt. (1838)
Hibbert, Sir Jack, KCB
Hickinbottom, *Hon.* Sir Gary Robert, Kt.
Hickman, Sir (Richard) Glenn, Bt. (1903)
Hicks, Sir Robert, Kt.
Hidden, *Hon.* Sir Anthony Brian, Kt.
Hielscher, Sir Leo Arthur, Kt.
Higgins, *Rt. Hon.* Sir Malachy Joseph, Kt.
Higginson, Sir Gordon Robert, Kt., PHD, FRENG
Hill, Sir Arthur Alfred, Kt., CBE
Hill, Sir Brian John, Kt.
Hill, Sir James Frederick, Bt. (1917)
Hill, Sir John Alfred Rowley, Bt. (I. 1779)
Hill, *Vice-Adm.* Sir Robert Charles Finch, KBE, FRENG
Hill-Norton, *Vice-Adm. Hon.* Sir Nicholas John, KCB
Hill-Wood, Sir Samuel Thomas, Bt. (1921)
Hillhouse, Sir (Robert) Russell, KCB
Hills, Sir Graham John, Kt.
Hine, *Air Chief Marshal* Sir Patrick Bardon, GCB, GBE
Hirsch, *Prof.* Sir Peter Bernhard, Kt., PHD., FRS
Hirst, *Rt. Hon.* Sir David Cozens-Hardy, Kt.
Hirst, Sir Michael William, Kt.
Hoare, *Prof.* Sir Charles Anthony Richard, Kt., FRS
Hoare, Sir David John, Bt. (1786)
Hoare, Sir Charles James, Bt. (I. 1784)
Hobart, Sir John Vere, Bt. (1914)
Hobbs, *Maj.-Gen.* Sir Michael Frederick, KCVO, CBE
Hobday, Sir Gordon Ivan, Kt.
Hobhouse, Sir Charles John Spinney, Bt. (1812)
Hobson, Sir Ronald, KCVO
†Hodge, Sir Andrew Rowland, Bt. (1921)
Hodge, Sir James William, KCVO, CMG
Hodgkin, Sir (Gordon) Howard (Eliot), Kt., CH, CBE
Hodgkinson, Sir Michael Stewart, Kt.
Hodgkinson, *Air Chief Marshal* Sir (William) Derek, KCB, CBE, DFC, AFC
Hodgson, Sir Maurice Arthur Eric, Kt., FRENG
Hodson, Sir Michael Robin Adderley, Bt. (I. 1789)
Hogg, Sir Christopher Anthony, Kt.
†Hogg, Sir Piers Michael James, Bt. (1846)
Holcroft, Sir Peter George Culcheth, Bt. (1921)
Holderness, Sir Martin William, Bt. (1920)
Holden, Sir Paul, Bt. (1893)
Holden, Sir John David, Bt. (1919)
Holden-Brown, Sir Derrick, Kt.
Holder, Sir John Henry, Bt. (1898)
Holdgate, Sir Martin Wyatt, Kt., CB, PHD
Holdsworth, Sir (George) Trevor, Kt., CVO
Holland, *Hon.* Sir Alan Douglas, Kt.
Holland, *Hon.* Sir Christopher John, Kt.
Holland, Sir Clifton Vaughan, Kt.
Holland, Sir Geoffrey, KCB
Holland, Sir John Anthony, Kt.
Holland, Sir Philip Welsby, Kt.
Holliday, *Prof.* Sir Frederick George Thomas, Kt., CBE, FRSE
Hollom, Sir Jasper Quintus, KBE
Holloway, *Hon.* Sir Barry Blyth, KBE
Holm, Sir Ian (Holm Cuthbert), Kt., CBE
Holman, *Hon.* Sir (Edward) James, Kt.
Holmes, *Prof.* Sir Frank Wakefield, Kt.
Holmes, Sir John Eaton, GCVO, KBE, CMG

Holmes-Sellors, Sir Patrick John, KCVO
Holroyd, *Air Marshal* Sir Frank Martyn, KBE, CB
Holroyd, Sir Michael De Courcy Fraser, Kt., CBE
Holroyde, *Hon.* Sir Timothy Victor, Kt.
Holt, *Prof.* Sir James Clarke, Kt.
Holt, Sir Michael, Kt., CBE
Home, Sir William Dundas, Bt. (S. 1671)
Honywood, Sir Filmer Courtenay William, Bt. (1660)
†Hood, Sir John Joseph Harold, Bt. (1922)
Hookway, Sir Harry Thurston, Kt.
Hooper, *Rt. Hon.* Sir Anthony, Kt.
Hope, Sir Colin Frederick Newton, Kt.
Hope, Sir Alexander Archibald Douglas, Bt. (S. 1628)
Hope-Dunbar, Sir David, Bt. (S. 1664)
Hopkin, *Prof.* Sir Deian Rhys, Kt.
Hopkin, Sir Royston Oliver, KCMG
Hopkin, Sir (William Aylsham) Bryan, Kt., CBE
Hopkins, Sir Anthony Philip, Kt., CBE
Hopkins, Sir Michael John, Kt., CBE, RA, RIBA
Hopwood, *Prof.* Sir David Alan, Kt., FRS
Hordern, *Rt. Hon.* Sir Peter Maudslay, Kt.
Horlick, *Vice-Adm.* Sir Edwin John, KBE, FRENG
Horlick, Sir James Cunliffe William, Bt. (1914)
Horlock, *Prof.* Sir John Harold, Kt., FRS, FRENG
Horn, *Prof.* Sir Gabriel, Kt., FRS
Horn-Smith, Sir Julian Michael, Kt.
Hornby, Sir Derek Peter, Kt.
Hornby, Sir Simon Michael, Kt.
Horne, Sir Alan Gray Antony, Bt. (1929)
Horne, *Dr* Sir Alistair Allan, Kt. CBE
Horsbrugh-Porter, Sir John Simon, Bt. (1902)
Horsfall, Sir Edward John Wright, Bt. (1909)
†Hort, Sir Andrew Edwin Fenton, Bt. (1767)
Horton, Sir Robert Baynes, Kt.
Hosker, Sir Gerald Albery, KCB, QC
Hoskins, *Prof.* Sir Brian John, Kt. CBE, FRS
Hoskyns, Sir Benedict Leigh, Bt. (1676)
Hoskyns, Sir John Austin Hungerford Leigh, Kt.
Hotung, Sir Joseph Edward, Kt.
Houghton, *Lt.-Gen.* Sir John Nicholas Reynolds, KCB, CBE
Houghton, Sir John Theodore, Kt., CBE, FRS
Houldsworth, Sir Richard Thomas Reginald, Bt. (1887)
Hourston, Sir Gordon Minto, Kt.
House, *Lt.-Gen.* Sir David George, GCB, KCVO, CBE, MC
Houssemayne du Boulay, Sir Roger William, KCVO, CMG
Houstoun-Boswall, Sir (Thomas) Alford, Bt. (1836)
Howard, Sir David Howarth Seymour, Bt. (1955)
Howard, *Prof.* Sir Michael Eliot, Kt., OM, CH, CBE, MC
Howard-Dobson, *Gen.* Sir Patrick John, GCB
Howard-Lawson, Sir John Philip, Bt. (1841)
Howells, Sir Eric Waldo Benjamin, Kt., CBE
Howes, Sir Christopher Kingston, KCVO, CB
Howlett, *Gen.* Sir Geoffrey Hugh Whitby, KBE, MC
Hoy, Sir Christopher Andrew, Kt., MBE
Huggins, *Hon.* Sir Alan Armstrong, Kt.
Hugh-Jones, Sir Wynn Normington, Kt., LVO
Hugh-Smith, Sir Andrew Colin, Kt.
Hughes, *Rt. Hon.* Sir Anthony Philip Gilson, Kt.
Hughes, Sir Thomas Collingwood, Bt. (1773)
Hughes, Sir Trevor Poulton, KCB
†Hughes-Morgan, Sir (Ian) Parry David, Bt. (1925)
Hull, *Prof.* Sir David, Kt.
Hulse, Sir Edward Jeremy Westrow, Bt. (1739)
Hum, Sir Christopher Owen, KCMG
Hunt, Sir John Leonard, Kt.
Hunt, *Adm.* Sir Nicholas John Streynsham, GCB, LVO
Hunt, Sir Rex Masterman, Kt., CMG
Hunt, *Dr* Sir Richard Timothy, Kt.
Hunt-Davis, *Brig.* Sir Miles Garth, KCVO, CBE
Hunter, Sir Alistair John, KCMG
Hunter, *Prof.* Sir Laurence Colvin, Kt., CBE, FRSE
Hunter, *Dr* Sir Philip John, Kt., CBE
Hunter, Sir Thomas Blane, Kt.
Huntington-Whiteley, Sir Hugo Baldwin, Bt. (1918)
Hurn, Sir (Francis) Roger, Kt.
Hurst, Sir Geoffrey Charles, Kt., MBE
Husbands, Sir Clifford Straugh, GCMG
Hutchison, Sir James Colville, Bt. (1956)
Hutchison, *Rt. Hon.* Sir Michael, Kt.
Hutchison, Sir Robert, Bt. (1939)
Hutt, Sir Dexter Walter, Kt.
Huxley, *Prof.* Sir Andrew Fielding, Kt., OM, FRS
Huxtable, *Gen.* Sir Charles Richard, KCB, CBE
Ibbs, Sir (John) Robin, KBE
Imbert-Terry, Sir Michael Edward Stanley, Bt. (1917)
Imray, Sir Colin Henry, KBE, CMG
Ingham, Sir Bernard, Kt.
Ingilby, Sir Thomas Colvin William, Bt. (1866)
Inglis, Sir Brian Scott, Kt.
Inglis of Glencorse, Sir Roderick John, Bt. (S. 1703)
Ingram, Sir James Herbert Charles, Bt. (1893)
Ingram, Sir John Henderson, Kt., CBE
Inkin, Sir Geoffrey David, Kt., OBE
†Innes, Sir David Charles Kenneth Gordon, Bt. (NS 1686)
Innes of Edingight, Sir Malcolm Rognvald, KCVO
Innes, Sir Peter Alexander Berowald, Bt. (S. 1628)
Irvine, Sir Donald Hamilton, Kt., CBE, MD, FRCGP
Irving, *Prof.* Sir Miles Horsfall, Kt., MD, FRCS, FRCSE
Irwin, *Lt.-Gen.* Sir Alistair Stuart Hastings, KCB, CBE
Irwin, *Hon.* Sir Stephen John, Kt.
Isaacs, Sir Jeremy Israel, Kt.
Isham, Sir Ian Vere Gyles, Bt. (1627)
Ivory, Sir Brian Gammell, Kt., CBE
Jack, *Hon.* Sir Alieu Sulayman, Kt.
Jack, Sir David, Kt., CBE, FRS, FRSE
Jack, *Hon.* Sir Raymond Evan, Kt.
Jackling, Sir Roger Tustin, KCB, CBE
Jackson, Sir Barry Trevor, Kt.
Jackson, Sir Kenneth Joseph, Kt.
Jackson, *Gen.* Sir Michael David, GCB, CBE
Jackson, Sir Michael Roland, Bt. (1902)
Jackson, Sir Nicholas Fane St George, Bt. (1913)
Jackson, Sir Keith Arnold, Bt. (1815)
Jackson, *Hon.* Sir Rupert Matthew, Kt.
Jackson, Sir (William) Roland Cedric, Bt. (1869)
Jacob, *Rt. Hon.* Sir Robert Raphael Hayim (Robin), Kt.
Jacobi, Sir Derek George, Kt., CBE
Jacobi, *Dr* Sir James Edward, Kt., OBE
Jacobs, Sir Cecil Albert, Kt., CBE
Jacobs, *Rt. Hon.* Sir Francis Geoffrey, KCMG, QC
Jacobs, *Hon.* Sir Kenneth Sydney, KBE
Jacomb, Sir Martin Wakefield, Kt.
Jaffray, Sir William Otho, Bt. (1892)
Jagger, Sir Michael Philip, Kt.
James, Sir Cynlais Morgan, KCMG
James, Sir Jeffrey Russell, KBE
James, Sir John Nigel Courtenay, KCVO, CBE
James, Sir Stanislaus Anthony, GCMG, OBE
Jamieson, *Air Marshal* Sir David Ewan, KBE, CB
Jansen, Sir Ross Malcolm, KBE
Jardine of Applegirth, Sir William Murray, Bt. (S. 1672)
Jardine, Sir Andrew Colin Douglas, Bt. (1916)
Jarman, *Prof.* Sir Brian, Kt., OBE
Jarratt, Sir Alexander Anthony, Kt., CB

Jarvis, Sir Gordon Ronald, Kt.
Jawara, *Hon.* Sir Dawda Kairaba, Kt.
Jay, Sir Antony Rupert, Kt., CVO
Jeewoolall, Sir Ramesh, Kt.
Jefferson, Sir George Rowland, Kt., CBE, FRENG
Jeffrey, Sir William Alexander, KCB
Jeffreys, *Prof.* Sir Alec John, Kt., FRS
Jeffries, *Hon.* Sir John Francis, Kt.
Jehangir, Sir Cowasji, Bt. (1908)
†Jejeebhoy, Sir Jehangir, Bt. (1857)
Jenkins, Sir Brian Garton, GBE
Jenkins, Sir Elgar Spencer, Kt., OBE
Jenkins, Sir James Christopher, KCB, QC
Jenkins, Sir Michael Nicholas Howard, Kt., OBE
Jenkins, Sir Michael Romilly Heald, KCMG
Jenkins, Sir Simon, Kt.
Jenkinson, Sir John Banks, Bt. (1661)
Jenks, Sir (Richard) Peter, Bt. (1932)
Jenner, *Air Marshal* Sir Timothy Ivo, KCB
Jennings, Sir John Southwood, Kt., CBE, FRSE
Jennings, Sir Peter Neville Wake, Kt., CVO
Jephcott, Sir Neil Welbourn, Bt. (1962)
Jessel, Sir Charles John, Bt. (1883)
Jewkes, Sir Gordon Wesley, KCMG
Job, Sir Peter James Denton, Kt.
John, Sir David Glyndwr, KCMG
John, Sir Elton Hercules (Reginald Kenneth Dwight), Kt., CBE
Johns, *Vice-Adm.* Sir Adrian James, KCB, CBE, ADC
Johns, *Air Chief Marshal* Sir Richard Edward, GCB, KCVO, CBE
Johnson, Sir Colpoys Guy, Bt. (1755)
Johnson, *Gen.* Sir Garry Dene, KCB, OBE, MC
Johnson, Sir John Rodney, KCMG
†Johnson, Sir Patrick Eliot, Bt. (1818)
Johnson, *Hon.* Sir Robert Lionel, Kt.
Johnson, Sir Vassel Godfrey, Kt., CBE
Johnson-Ferguson, Sir Ian Edward, Bt. (1906)
Johnston, *Lt.-Gen.* Sir Maurice Robert, KCB, CVO, OBE
Johnston, Sir Thomas Alexander, Bt. (S. 1626)
Johnston, Sir William Ian Ridley, Kt., CBE, QPM
Johnstone, Sir Geoffrey Adams Dinwiddie, KCMG
Johnstone, Sir (George) Richard Douglas, Bt. (S. 1700)
Johnstone, Sir (John) Raymond, Kt., CBE
Jolliffe, Sir Anthony Stuart, GBE
Jolly, Sir Arthur Richard, KCMG
Jonas, Sir John Peter, Kt., CBE
Jones, Sir Alan Jeffrey, Kt.
Jones, Sir David Charles, Kt., CBE
Jones, Sir Harry George, Kt., CBE
Jones, Sir John Francis, Kt.
Jones, Sir Keith Stephen, Kt.
Jones, Sir Kenneth Lloyd, Kt., QPM
Jones, Sir Lyndon, Kt.
Jones, Sir (Owen) Trevor, Kt.
Jones, Sir Richard Anthony Lloyd, KCB
Jones, Sir Robert Edward, Kt.
Jones, Sir Roger Spencer, Kt., OBE
Jones, Sir Simon Warley Frederick Benton, Bt. (1919)
†Joseph, *Hon.* Sir James Samuel, Bt. (1943)
Jowell, *Prof.* Sir Roger Mark, Kt. CBE
Jowitt, *Hon.* Sir Edwin Frank, Kt.
Judge, Sir Paul Rupert, Kt.
Jugnauth, *Rt. Hon.* Sir Anerood, KCMG
Jungius, *Vice-Adm.* Sir James George, KBE
Kaberry, *Hon.* Sir Christopher Donald, Bt. (1960)
Kadoorie, *Hon.* Sir Michael David, Kt.
Kakaraya, Sir Pato, KBE
Kamit, Sir Leonard Wilson, Kt., CBE
Kan Yuet-Keung, Sir, GBE
Kapi, *Hon.* Sir Mari, KCMG, CBE
Kaputin, Sir John Rumet, KBE, CMG
Kaufman, *Rt. Hon.* Sir Gerald Bernard, Kt.
Kavali, Sir Thomas, Kt., OBE
Kay, *Prof.* Sir Andrew Watt, Kt.
Kay, *Rt. Hon.* Sir Maurice Ralph, Kt.
Kaye, Sir Paul Henry Gordon, Bt. (1923)
Keane, Sir Richard Michael, Bt. (1801)
Kearney, *Hon.* Sir William John Francis, Kt., CBE
Keegan, Sir John Desmond Patrick, Kt., OBE
Keene, *Rt. Hon.* Sir David Wolfe, Kt.
Keith, *Hon.* Sir Brian Richard, Kt.
Keith, *Prof.* Sir James, KBE
†Kellett, Sir Stanley Charles, Bt. (1801)
Kelly, Sir Christopher William, KCB
Kelly, Sir David Robert Corbett, Kt., CBE
Kemakeza, Sir Allan, Kt.
Kemball, *Air Marshal* Sir (Richard) John, KCB, CBE
Kemp-Welch, Sir John, Kt.
Kenilorea, *Rt. Hon.* Sir Peter, KBE
Kennaway, Sir John Lawrence, Bt. (1791)
Kennedy, Sir Francis, KCMG, CBE
Kennedy, *Hon.* Sir Ian Alexander, Kt.
Kennedy, *Prof.* Sir Ian McColl, Kt.
Kennedy, Sir Ludovic Henry Coverley, Kt.
†Kennedy, Sir Michael Edward, Bt., (1836)
Kennedy, *Rt. Hon.* Sir Paul Joseph Morrow, Kt.
Kennedy, *Air Chief Marshal* Sir Thomas Lawrie, GCB, AFC
Kenny, Sir Anthony John Patrick, Kt., DPHIL, DLITT, FBA
Kenny, *Gen.* Sir Brian Leslie Graham, GCB, CBE
Kentridge, Sir Sydney Woolf, KCMG, QC
Kenyon, Sir Nicholas Roger, Kt., CBE
Keogh, *Prof.* Sir Bruce Edward, KBE
Kermode, Sir (John) Frank, Kt., FBA
Kerr, *Adm.* Sir John Beverley, GCB
Kerry, Sir Michael James, KCB, QC
Kershaw, *Prof.* Sir Ian, Kt.
Kerslake, Sir Robert Walker, Kt.
Keswick, Sir Henry Neville Lindley, Kt.
Keswick, Sir John Chippendale Lindley, Kt.
Kevau, *Prof.* Sir Isi Henao, Kt., CBE
Kikau, *Ratu* Sir Jone Latianara, KBE
Kimber, Sir Timothy Roy Henry, Bt. (1904)
King, *Prof.* Sir David Anthony, Kt., FRS
King, Sir John Christopher, Bt. (1888)
King, *Vice-Adm.* Sir Norman Ross Dutton, KBE
King, *Hon.* Sir Timothy Roger Alan, Kt.
King, Sir Wayne Alexander, Bt. (1815)
Kingman, *Prof.* Sir John Frank Charles, Kt., FRS
Kingsland, Sir Richard, Kt., CBE, DFC
Kingsley, Sir Ben, Kt.
Kinloch, Sir David, Bt. (S. 1686)
Kinloch, Sir David Oliphant, Bt. (1873)
Kipalan, Sir Albert, Kt.
Kirkpatrick, Sir Ivone Elliott, Bt. (S. 1685)
Kirkwood, *Hon.* Sir Andrew Tristram Hammett, Kt.
Kiszely, *Lt.-Gen.* Sir John Panton, KCB, MC
Kitchin, *Hon.* Sir David James Tyson, Kt.
Kitson, *Gen.* Sir Frank Edward, GBE, KCB, MC
Kitson, Sir Timothy Peter Geoffrey, Kt.
Kleinwort, Sir Richard Drake, Bt. (1909)
Klug, Sir Aaron, Kt., OM
Knight, Sir Harold Murray, KBE, DSC
Knight, Sir Kenneth John, Kt., CBE, QFSM
Knight, *Air Chief Marshal* Sir Michael William Patrick, KCB, AFC
Knight, *Prof.* Sir Peter, Kt.
†Knill, Sir Thomas John Pugin Bartholomew, Bt. (1893)
Knowles, Sir Charles Francis, Bt. (1765)
Knowles, Sir Durward Randolph, Kt., OBE
Knowles, Sir Nigel Graham, Kt.
Knox, Sir David Laidlaw, Kt.
Knox, *Hon.* Sir John Leonard, Kt.
Knox-Johnston, Sir William Robert Patrick (Sir Robin), Kt., CBE, RD

Koraea, Sir Thomas, Kt.
Kornberg, *Prof.* Sir Hans Leo, Kt., DSC, SCD, PHD, FRS
Korowi, Sir Wiwa, GCMG
Kroto, *Prof.* Sir Harold Walter, Kt., FRS
Kulukundis, Sir Elias George (Eddie), Kt., OBE
Kurongku, *Most Revd* Peter, KBE
Kwok-Po Li, *Dr* Sir David, Kt., OBE
Lachmann, *Prof.* Sir Peter Julius, Kt.
Lacon, Sir Edmund Vere, Bt. (1818)
Lacy, Sir Patrick Brian Finucane, Bt. (1921)
Lacy, Sir John Trend, Kt., CBE
Laidlaw, Sir Christopher Charles Fraser, Kt.
Laing, Sir (John) Martin (Kirby), Kt., CBE
Laird, Sir Gavin Harry, Kt., CBE
Lake, Sir (Atwell) Graham, Bt. (1711)
Lakin, Sir Michael, Bt. (1909)
Lamb, Sir Albert Thomas, KBE, CMG, DFC
Lamb, *Lt.-Gen.* Sir Graeme Cameron Maxwell, KBE, CMG, DSO
Lambert, Sir John Henry, KCVO, CMG
†Lambert, Sir Peter John Biddulph, Bt. (1711)
Lampl, Sir Frank William, Kt.
Lampl, Sir Peter, Kt., OBE
Lamport, Sir Stephen Mark Jeffrey, KCVO
Landale, Sir David William Neil, KCVO
Landau, Sir Dennis Marcus, Kt.
Lander, Sir Stephen James, KCB
Lane, Prof. Sir David Philip, Kt.
Langham, Sir John Stephen, Bt. (1660)
Langlands, Sir Robert Alan, Kt.
Langley, *Hon.* Sir Gordon Julian Hugh, Kt.
Langrishe, Sir James Hercules, Bt. (I. 1777)
Langstaff, *Hon.* Sir Brian Frederick James, Kt.
Lankester, Sir Timothy Patrick, KCB
Lapli, Sir John Ini, GCMG
Large, Sir Andrew McLeod Brooks, Kt.
Latasi, *Rt. Hon.* Sir Kamuta, KCMG, OBE
Latham, *Rt. Hon.* Sir David Nicholas Ramsey, Kt.
Latham, Sir Michael Anthony, Kt.
Latham, Sir Richard Thomas Paul, Bt. (1919)
Latimer, Sir (Courtenay) Robert, Kt., CBE
Latimer, Sir Graham Stanley, KBE
Latour-Adrien, *Hon.* Sir Maurice, Kt.
Laughton, Sir Anthony Seymour, Kt.
Laurie, Sir Robert Bayley Emilius, Bt. (1834)
Lauterpacht, Sir Elihu, Kt., CBE, QC
Lauti, *Rt. Hon.* Sir Toaripi, GCMG
Lawes, Sir (John) Michael Bennet, Bt. (1882)
Lawler, Sir Peter James, Kt., OBE
Lawrence, Sir Clive Wyndham, Bt. (1906)
Lawrence, Sir Henry Peter, Bt. (1858)
Lawrence, Sir Ivan John, Kt., QC
Lawrence, Sir John Patrick Grosvenor, Kt., CBE
Lawrence, Sir William Fettiplace, Bt. (1867)
Lawrence-Jones, Sir Christopher, Bt. (1831)
Laws, *Rt. Hon.* Sir John Grant McKenzie, Kt.
Lawson, Sir Charles John Patrick, Bt. (1900)
Lawson, *Gen.* Sir Richard George, KCB, DSO, OBE
Lawson-Tancred, Sir Henry, Bt. (1662)
Lawton, *Prof.* Sir John Hartley, Kt., CBE, FRS
Layard, *Adm.* Sir Michael Henry Gordon, KCB, CBE
Lea, *Vice-Adm.* Sir John Stuart Crosbie, KBE
Lea, Sir Thomas William, Bt. (1892)
Leach, *Admiral of the Fleet* Sir Henry Conyers, GCB
Leahy, Sir Daniel Joseph, Kt.
Leahy, Sir John Henry Gladstone, KCMG
Leahy, Sir Terence Patrick, Kt.
Learmont, *Gen.* Sir John Hartley, KCB, CBE
Leaver, Sir Christopher, GBE
Le Bailly, *Vice-Adm.* Sir Louis Edward Stewart Holland, KBE, CB
Le Cheminant, *Air Chief Marshal* Sir Peter de Lacey, GBE, KCB, DFC
Lechmere, Sir Reginald Anthony Hungerford, Bt. (1818)
Ledger, Sir Philip Stevens, Kt., CBE, FRSE
Lee, Sir Christopher Frank Carandini, Kt., CBE
Lee, *Brig.* Sir Leonard Henry, Kt., CBE
Lee, Sir Quo-wei, Kt., CBE
Leeds, Sir Christopher Anthony, Bt. (1812)
Lees, Sir David Bryan, Kt.
Lees, Sir Thomas Edward, Bt. (1897)
Lees, Sir Thomas Harcourt Ivor, Bt. (1804)
Lees, Sir (William) Antony Clare, Bt. (1937)
Leese, Sir Richard Charles, Kt., CBE
le Fleming, Sir David Kelland, Bt. (1705)
Legard, Sir Charles Thomas, Bt. (1660)
Legg, Sir Thomas Stuart, KCB, QC
Leggatt, *Rt. Hon.* Sir Andrew Peter, Kt.
Leggatt, Sir Hugh Frank John, Kt.
Leggett, *Prof.* Sir Anthony James, KBE
Leigh, Sir Geoffrey Norman, Kt.
Leigh, Sir Richard Henry, Bt. (1918)
Leighton, Sir Michael John Bryan, Bt. (1693)
Leitch, Sir George, KCB, OBE
Leith-Buchanan, Sir Gordon Kelly McNicol, Bt. (1775)
Le Marchant, Sir Francis Arthur, Bt. (1841)
Lennox-Boyd, The Hon. Sir Mark Alexander, Kt.
Leon, Sir John Ronald, Bt. (1911)
Leonard, *Rt. Revd Monsignor* and *Rt. Hon.* Graham Douglas, KCVO
Lepping, Sir George Geria Dennis, GCMG, MBE
Le Quesne, Sir (John) Godfray, Kt., QC
Lee-Steere, Sir Ernest Henry, KBE
Leslie, Sir John Norman Ide, Bt. (1876)
Lester, Sir James Theodore, Kt.
Lethbridge, Sir Thomas Periam Hector Noel, Bt. (1804)
Lever, Sir Jeremy Frederick, KCMG, QC
Lever, Sir Paul, KCMG
Lever, Sir (Tresham) Christopher Arthur Lindsay, Bt. (1911)
Leveson, *Rt. Hon.* Sir Brian Henry, Kt.
Levine, Sir Montague Bernard, Kt.
Levinge, Sir Richard George Robin, Bt. (I. 1704)
Lewinton, Sir Christopher, Kt.
Lewis, Sir David Thomas Rowell, Kt.
Lewis, Sir John Anthony, Kt., OBE
Lewis, Sir Leigh Warren, KCB
Lewis, Sir Terence Murray, Kt., OBE, GM, QPM
Lewison, *Hon.* Sir Kim Martin Jordan, Kt.
Ley, Sir Ian Francis, Bt. (1905)
Li, Sir Ka-Shing, KBE
Lickiss, Sir Michael Gillam, Kt.
Liddington, Sir Bruce, Kt.
Liggins, *Prof.* Sir Graham Collingwood, Kt., CBE, FRS
Lightman, *Hon.* Sir Gavin Anthony, Kt.
Lighton, Sir Thomas Hamilton, Bt. (I. 1791)
Likierman, *Prof.* Sir John Andrew, Kt.
Lilleyman, *Prof.* Sir John Stuart, Kt.
Limon, Sir Donald William, KCB
Linacre, Sir (John) Gordon (Seymour), Kt., CBE, AFC, DFM
Lindop, Sir Norman, Kt.
Lindsay, *Hon.* Sir John Edmund Frederic, Kt.
†Lindsay, Sir James Martin Evelyn, Bt. (1962)
†Lindsay-Hogg, Sir Michael Edward, Bt. (1905)
Lipton, Sir Stuart Anthony, Kt.
Lipworth, Sir (Maurice) Sydney, Kt.
Lister-Kaye, Sir John Phillip Lister, Bt. (1812)
Lithgow, Sir William James, Bt. (1925)
Little, *Most Revd* Thomas Francis, KBE
Littler, Sir (James) Geoffrey, KCB

†Llewellyn, Sir Roderic Victor, Bt. (1922)
Llewellyn-Smith, *Prof.* Sir Christopher Hubert, Kt.
Lloyd, *Prof.* Sir Geoffrey Ernest Richard, Kt., FBA
Lloyd, Sir Nicholas Markley, Kt.
Lloyd, *Rt. Hon.* Sir Peter Robert Cable, Kt.
Lloyd, Sir Richard Ernest Butler, Bt. (1960)
Lloyd, *Hon.* Sir Timothy Andrew Wigram, Kt.
Lloyd-Edwards, *Capt.* Sir Norman, KCVO, RD
Lloyd-Hughes, Sir Trevor Denby, Kt.
Lloyd Jones, Sir David, Kt.
Lloyd-Jones, Sir (Peter) Hugh (Jefferd), Kt.
Loader, Air Marshal Sir Clive Robert, KCB, OBE
Lobo, Sir Rogerio Hyndman, Kt., CBE
Lockhead, Sir Moir, Kt., OBE
†Loder, Sir Edmund Jeune, Bt. (1887)
Logan, Sir David Brian Carleton, KCMG
Logan, Sir Donald Arthur, KCMG
Lokoloko, Sir Tore, GCMG, GCVO, OBE
Longmore, *Rt. Hon.* Sir Andrew Centlivres, Kt.
Loram, *Vice-Adm.* Sir David Anning, KCB, CVO
Lord, Sir Michael Nicholson, Kt.
Lorimer, Sir (Thomas) Desmond, Kt.
Los, *Hon.* Sir Kubulan, Kt., CBE
Loughran, Sir Gerald Finbar, KCB
Louisy, *Rt. Hon.* Sir Allan Fitzgerald Laurent, KCMG
Lovell, Sir (Alfred Charles) Bernard, Kt., OBE, FRS
Lovelock, Sir Douglas Arthur, KCB
Lovill, Sir John Roger, Kt., CBE
Lowe, *Air Chief Marshal* Sir Douglas Charles, GCB, DFC, AFC
Lowe, Sir Frank Budge, Kt.
Lowe, Sir Thomas William Gordon, Bt. (1918)
Lowson, Sir Ian Patrick, Bt. (1951)
Lowther, *Col.* Sir Charles Douglas, Bt. (1824)
Lowther, Sir John Luke, KCVO, CBE
Loyd, Sir Julian St John, KCVO
Lu, Sir Tseng Chi, Kt.
Lucas, *Prof.* Sir Colin Renshaw, Kt.
Lucas, Sir Thomas Edward, Bt. (1887)
Lucas-Tooth, Sir (Hugh) John, Bt. (1920)
Lumsden, Sir David James, Kt.
Lushington, Sir John Richard Castleman, Bt. (1791)
Lyall Grant, Sir Mark Justin, KCMG
Lygo, *Adm.* Sir Raymond Derek, KCB
Lyle, Sir Gavin Archibald, Bt. (1929)
Lynch-Blosse, *Capt.* Sir Richard Hely, Bt. (1622)
Lynch-Robinson, Sir Dominick Christopher, Bt. (1920)
Lyne, *Rt. Hon.* Sir Roderic Michael John, KBE, CMG
Lyons, Sir John, Kt.
Lyons, Sir Michael Thomas, Kt.
McAllister, Sir Ian Gerald, Kt., CBE
McAlpine, Sir William Hepburn, Bt. (1918)
Macara, Sir Alexander Wiseman, Kt., FRCP, FRCGP
McCaffrey, Sir Thomas Daniel, Kt.
McCallum, Sir Donald Murdo, Kt., CBE, FRENG
McCamley, Sir Graham Edward, KBE
McCarthy, Sir Callum, Kt.
McCartney, Sir (James) Paul, Kt., MBE
Macartney, Sir John Ralph, Bt. (I. 1799)
McClay, *Dr* Sir Allen James, Kt., CBE
McClement, *Vice-Admiral* Sir Timothy Pentreath, KCB, OBE
McClintock, Sir Eric Paul, Kt.
McCloskey, *Hon.* Sir John Bernard, Kt.
McColl, Sir Colin Hugh Verel, KCMG
McColl, *Gen.* Sir John Chalmers, KCB, CBE, DSO
McCollum, *Rt. Hon.* Sir William, Kt.
McCombe, *Hon.* Sir Richard George Bramwell, Kt.
McConnell, Sir Robert Shean, Bt. (1900)
MacCormac, Sir Richard Cornelius, Kt., CBE
†McCowan, Sir David William, Bt. (1934)
McCullough, *Hon.* Sir (Iain) Charles (Robert), Kt.
MacDermott, *Rt. Hon.* Sir John Clarke, Kt.
Macdonald, Sir Alasdair Uist, Kt., CBE
Macdonald, Sir Kenneth Carmichael, KCB
Macdonald, Sir Kenneth Donald John, Kt., QC
Mcdonald, Sir Trevor, Kt., OBE
Macdonald of Sleat, Sir Ian Godfrey Bosville, Bt. (S. 1625)
McDowell, Sir Eric Wallace, Kt., CBE
MacDuff, *Hon.* Sir Alistair Geoffrey, Kt.
Mace, *Lt.-Gen.* Sir John Airth, KBE, CB
McEwen, Sir John Roderick Hugh, Bt. (1953)
McFarland, Sir John Talbot, Bt. (1914)
MacFarlane, *Prof.* Sir Alistair George James, Kt., CBE, FRS
McFarlane, Sir Andrew Ewart, Kt.
Macfarlane, Sir (David) Neil, Kt.
McFarlane, Sir Ian, Kt.
McGrath, Sir Brian Henry, GCVO
Macgregor, Sir Ian Grant, Bt. (1828)
McGregor, Sir James David, Kt., OBE
MacGregor of MacGregor, Sir Malcolm Gregor Charles, Bt. (1795)
McGrigor, Sir James Angus Rhoderick Neil, Bt. (1831)
McIntosh, Sir Neil William David, Kt., CBE
McIntosh, Sir Ronald Robert Duncan, KCB
McIntyre, Sir Donald Conroy, Kt., CBE
McIntyre, Sir Meredith Alister, Kt.
Mackay, *Hon.* Sir Colin Crichton, Kt.
MacKay, *Prof.* Sir Donald Iain, Kt.
MacKay, Sir Francis Henry, Kt.
McKay, Sir Neil Stuart, Kt., CB
McKay, Sir William Robert, KCB
Mackay-Dick, *Maj.-Gen.* Sir Iain Charles, KCVO, MBE
Mackechnie, Sir Alistair John, Kt.
McKellen, Sir Ian Murray, Kt., CH, CBE
Mackenzie, Sir (James William) Guy, Bt. (1890)
Mackenzie, *Gen.* Sir Jeremy John George, GCB, OBE
†Mackenzie, Sir Peter Douglas, Bt. (S. 1673)
†Mackenzie, Sir Roderick McQuhae, Bt. (S. 1703)
Mackerras, Sir (Alan) Charles (MacLaurin), Kt., CH, CBE
Mackeson, Sir Rupert Henry, Bt. (1954)
McKillop, Sir Thomas Fulton Wilson, Kt.
McKinnon, *Rt. Hon.* Sir Donald Charles, Kt.
McKinnon, Sir James, Kt.
McKinnon, *Hon.* Sir Stuart Neil, Kt.
Mackintosh, Sir Cameron Anthony, Kt.
Mackworth, Sir Digby (John), Bt. (1776)
McLaren, Sir Robin John Taylor, KCMG
McLaughlin, Sir Richard, Kt.
Maclean of Dunconnell, Sir Charles Edward, Bt. (1957)
Maclean, Sir Donald Og Grant, Kt.
Maclean, Sir Lachlan Hector Charles, Bt. (NS 1631)
Maclean, Sir Murdo, Kt.
McLeod, Sir Charles Henry, Bt. (1925)
MacLeod, Sir (John) Maxwell Norman, Bt. (1924)
Macleod, Sir (Nathaniel William) Hamish, KBE
McLintock, Sir Michael William, Bt. (1934)
Maclure, Sir John Robert Spencer, Bt. (1898)
McMahon, Sir Brian Patrick, Bt. (1817)
McMahon, Sir Christopher William, Kt.
McMaster, Sir Brian John, Kt., CBE
McMichael, *Prof.* Sir Andrew James, Kt., FRS
Macmillan, Sir (Alexander McGregor) Graham, Kt.

MacMillan, *Lt.-Gen.* Sir John Richard Alexander, KCB, CBE
McMullin, *Rt. Hon.* Sir Duncan Wallace, Kt.
McMurtry, Sir David, Kt., CBE
Macnaghten, Sir Malcolm Francis, Bt. (1836)
McNair-Wilson, Sir Patrick Michael Ernest David, Kt.
McNamara, *Air Chief Marshal* Sir Neville Patrick, KBE
Macnaughton, *Prof.* Sir Malcolm Campbell, Kt.
McNee, Sir David Blackstock, Kt., QPM
McNulty, Sir (Robert William) Roy, Kt., CBE
MacPhail, Sir Bruce Dugald, Kt.
MacPherson, Sir Nicholas, KCB
Macpherson, Sir Ronald Thomas Steward (Tommy), CBE, MC, TD
Macpherson of Cluny, *Hon.* Sir William Alan, Kt., TD
McQuarrie, Sir Albert, Kt.
MacRae, Sir (Alastair) Christopher (Donald Summerhayes), KCMG
Macready, Sir Nevil John Wilfrid, Bt. (1923)
MacSween, *Prof.* Sir Roderick Norman McIver, Kt.
Mactaggart, Sir John Auld, Bt. (1938)
McWilliam, Sir Michael Douglas, KCMG
McWilliams, Sir Francis, GBE
Madden, Sir David Christopher Andrew, KCMG
†Madden, Sir Charles Jonathan, Bt. (1919)
Maddison, *Hon.* Sir David George, Kt.
Madejski, Sir John Robert, Kt., OBE
Madel, Sir (William) David, Kt.
Magee, Sir Ian Bernard Vaughan, Kt., CB
Magnus, Sir Laurence Henry Philip, Bt. (1917)
Mahon, Sir (John) Denis, Kt., CH, CBE
Mahon, Sir William Walter, Bt. (1819)
Maiden, Sir Colin James, Kt., DPHIL
Maini, *Prof.* Sir Ravinder Nath, Kt.
Maino, Sir Charles, KBE
†Maitland, Sir Charles Alexander, Bt. (1818)
Maitland, Sir Donald James Dundas, GCMG, OBE
Major, *Rt. Hon.* Sir John, KG, CH
Malbon, *Vice-Adm.* Sir Fabian Michael, KBE
Malcolm, Sir James William Thomas Alexander, Bt. (S. 1665)
Malet, Sir Harry Douglas St Lo, Bt. (1791)
Mallaby, Sir Christopher Leslie George, GCMG, GCVO
Mallet, Sir William George, GCMG, CBE
Mallick, *Prof.* Sir Netar Prakash, Kt.
Mallinson, Sir William James, Bt. (1935)
Malpas, Sir Robert, Kt., CBE
Mancham, Sir James Richard Marie, KBE
†Mander, Sir (Charles) Nicholas, Bt. (1911)
Manduell, Sir John, Kt., CBE
Mann, *Hon.* Sir George Anthony, Kt.
Mann, *Rt. Revd* Michael Ashley, KCVO
Mann, Sir Rupert Edward, Bt. (1905)
Manning, Sir David Geoffrey, GCMG, CVO
Mano, Sir Koitaga, Kt., MBE
Mansel, Sir Philip, Bt. (1622)
Mansfield, *Prof.* Sir Peter, Kt.
Mantell, *Rt. Hon.* Sir Charles Barrie Knight, Kt.
Manuella, Sir Tulaga, GCMG, MBE
Manzie, Sir (Andrew) Gordon, KCB
Margetson, Sir John William Denys, KCMG
Margetts, Sir Robert John, Kt., CBE
Mark, Sir Robert, GBE
Markesinis, *Prof.* Sir Basil Spyridonos, Kt. QC
Markham, *Prof.* Sir Alexander Fred, Kt.
Markham, Sir (Arthur) David, Bt. (1911)
Marling, Sir Charles William Somerset, Bt. (1882)
Marmot, Prof. Sir Michael Gideon, Kt.
Marr, Sir Leslie Lynn, Bt. (1919)
Marriner, Sir Neville, Kt., CBE
†Marsden, Sir Simon Neville Llewelyn, Bt. (1924)
Marsh, *Prof.* Sir John Stanley, Kt., CBE
Marshall, Sir Denis Alfred, Kt.
Marshall, *Prof.* Sir (Oshley) Roy, Kt., CBE
Marshall, Sir Peter Harold Reginald, KCMG
Martin, Sir Clive Haydon, Kt., OBE
Martin, Sir George Henry, Kt., CBE
Martin, *Vice-Adm.* Sir John Edward Ludgate, KCB, DSC
Martin, *Prof.* Sir Laurence Woodward, Kt.
Martin, Sir (Robert) Bruce, Kt., QC
Marychurch, Sir Peter Harvey, KCMG
Masefield, Sir Charles Beech Gordon, Kt.
Mason, *Hon.* Sir Anthony Frank, KBE
Mason, Sir (Basil) John, Kt., CB, DSC, FRS
Mason, *Prof.* Sir David Kean, Kt., CBE
Mason, Sir Gordon Charles, Kt., OBE
Mason, Sir John Peter, Kt., CBE
Mason, Sir Peter James, KBE
Mason, *Prof.* Sir Ronald, KCB, FRS
Massey, *Vice-Adm.* Sir Alan, KCB, CBE, ADC
Massie, Sir Herbert William, Kt., CBE
Matane, HE Sir Paulias Nguna, GCMG, OBE
Mathers, Sir Robert William, Kt.
Matheson of Matheson, Sir Fergus John, Bt. (1882)
Mathewson, Sir George Ross, Kt., CBE, PHD, FRSE
Matthews, Sir Terence Hedley, Kt., OBE
Maud, *Hon.* Sir Humphrey John Hamilton, KCMG
Maughan, Sir Deryck, Kt.
Mawer, Sir Philip John Courtney, Kt.
Maxwell, Sir Michael Eustace George, Bt. (S. 1681)
Maxwell-Hyslop, Sir Robert John (Robin), Kt.
Maxwell-Scott, Sir Dominic James, Bt. (1642)
May, *Rt. Hon.* Sir Anthony Tristram Kenneth, Kt.
Mayhew-Sanders, Sir John Reynolds, Kt.
Maynard, *Hon.* Sir Clement Travelyan, Kt.
Meadow, *Prof.* Sir (Samuel) Roy, Kt., FRCP, FRCPE
Medlycott, Sir Mervyn Tregonwell, Bt. (1808)
Meeran, *His Hon.* Sir Goolam Hoosen Kader, Kt.
Meldrum, Sir Graham, Kt., CBE, QFSM
Melhuish, Sir Michael Ramsay, KBE, CMG
Mellon, Sir James, KCMG
Melmoth, Sir Graham John, Kt.
Melville, *Prof.* Sir David, Kt., CBE
Merifield, Sir Anthony James, KCVO, CB
†Meyer, Sir (Anthony) Ashley Frank, Bt. (1910)
Meyer, Sir Christopher John Rome, KCMG
Meyjes, Sir Richard Anthony, Kt.
†Meyrick, Sir Timothy Thomas Charlton, Bt. (1880)
Miakwe, *Hon.* Sir Akepa, KBE
Michael, Sir Duncan, Kt.
Michael, *Dr* Sir Jonathan, Kt.
Michael, Sir Peter Colin, Kt., CBE
Michels, Sir David Michael Charles, Kt.
Middleton, Sir John Maxwell, Kt.
Middleton, Sir Peter Edward, GCB
Miers, Sir (Henry) David Alastair Capel, KBE, CMG
Milbank, Sir Anthony Frederick, Bt. (1882)
Milborne-Swinnerton-Pilkington, Sir Thomas Henry, Bt. (S. 1635)
Milburn, Sir Anthony Rupert, Bt. (1905)
Miles, Sir Peter Tremayne, KCVO
Miles, Sir William Napier Maurice, Bt. (1859)
Millais, Sir Geoffrey Richard Everett, Bt. (1885)
Millard, Sir Guy Elwin, KCMG, CVO
Miller, Sir Albert Joel, KCMG, MVO, MBE, QPM, CPM

Miller, Sir Donald John, Kt., FRSE, FRENG
Miller, *Air Marshal* Sir Graham Anthony, KBE
Miller, Sir Harry Holmes, Bt. (1705)
Miller, Sir Hilary Duppa (Hal), Kt.
Miller, Sir Jonathan Wolfe, Kt., CBE
Miller, Sir Peter North, Kt.
Miller, Sir Robin Robert William, Kt.
Miller, Sir Ronald Andrew Baird, Kt., CBE
Miller of Glenlee, Sir Stephen William Macdonald, Bt. (1788)
Mills, Sir Ian, Kt.
Mills, Sir Keith, Kt.
Mills, Sir Peter Frederick Leighton, Bt. (1921)
Milman, Sir David Patrick, Bt. (1800)
Milne, Sir John Drummond, Kt.
Milne-Watson, Sir Andrew Michael, Bt. (1937)
Milner, Sir Timothy William Lycett, Bt. (1717)
Milton, Sir Simon, Kt.
Milton-Thompson, *Surgeon Vice-Adm.* Sir Godfrey James, KBE
Mirrlees, *Prof.* Sir James Alexander, Kt., FBA
Mitchell, Sir David Bower, Kt.
Mitchell, *Rt. Hon.* Sir James FitzAllen, KCMG
Mitchell, *Very Revd* Patrick Reynolds, KCVO
Mitchell, *Hon.* Sir Stephen George, Kt.
Mitting, *Hon.* Sir John Edward, Kt.
Moate, Sir Roger Denis, Kt.
Moberly, Sir Patrick Hamilton, KCMG
Moffat, Sir Brian Scott, Kt., OBE
Moffat, *Lt.-Gen.* Sir (William) Cameron, KBE
Moir, Sir Christopher Ernest, Bt. (1916)
†Molesworth-St Aubyn, Sir William, Bt. (1689)
†Molony, Sir Thomas Desmond, Bt. (1925)
Monck, Sir Nicholas Jeremy, KCB
Money-Coutts, Sir David Burdett, KCVO
Montagu, Sir Nicholas Lionel John, KCB
Montagu-Pollock, Sir Giles Hampden, Bt. (1872)
Montague, Sir Adrian Alastair, Kt., CBE
Montague-Browne, Sir Anthony Arthur Duncan, KCMG, CBE, DFC
Montgomery, Sir (Basil Henry) David, Bt. (1801), CVO
Montgomery, Sir (William) Fergus, Kt.
Montgomery-Cuninghame, Sir John Christopher Foggo, Bt. (NS 1672)
Moody-Stuart, Sir Mark, KCMG
Moollan, Sir Abdool Hamid Adam, Kt.
Moollan, *Hon.* Sir Cassam (Ismael), Kt.
†Moon, Sir Roger, Bt. (1887)
Moorcroft, Sir William, Kt.
Moore, *Most Revd* Desmond Charles, KBE
Moore, Sir Francis Thomas, Kt.
Moore, Sir John Michael, KCVO, CB, DSC
Moore, *Vice Adm.* Sir Michael Antony Claës, KBE, LVO
Moore, *Prof.* Sir Norman Winfrid, Bt. (1919)
Moore, Sir Patrick Alfred Caldwell, Kt., CBE
Moore, Sir Patrick William Eisdell, Kt., OBE
Moore, Sir Roger George, KBE
Moore, Sir William Roger Clotworthy, Bt. (1932), TD
Moore-Bick, *Rt. Hon.* Sir Martin James, Kt.
Moores, Sir Peter, Kt., CBE
Moran, *Air Marshal* Sir Christopher Hugh, KCB, OBE, MVO
Morauta, Sir Mekere, KCMG
Mordaunt, Sir Richard Nigel Charles, Bt. (1611)
Moreton, Sir John Oscar, KCMG, KCVO, MC
Morgan, *Vice-Adm.* Sir Charles Christopher, KBE
Morgan, *Hon.* Sir Charles Declan, Kt.
Morgan, Sir Graham, Kt.
Morgan, Sir John Albert Leigh, KCMG
Morgan, *Hon.* Sir Paul Hyacinth, Kt.
Morgan-Giles, *Rear-Adm.* Sir Morgan Charles, Kt., DSO, OBE, GM
Morison, *Hon.* Sir Thomas Richard Atkin, Kt.
Morland, *Hon.* Sir Michael, Kt.
Morland, Sir Robert Kenelm, Kt.
Morpeth, Sir Douglas Spottiswoode, Kt., TD
†Morris, Sir Allan Lindsay, Bt. (1806)
Morris, *Air Marshal* Sir Arnold Alec, KBE, CB
Morris, Sir Derek James, Kt.
Morris, Sir Keith Elliot Hedley, KBE, CMG
Morris, *Prof.* Sir Peter John, Kt.
Morris, Sir Trefor Alfred, Kt., CBE, QPM
Morris, *Very Revd* William James, KCVO
Morrison, Sir (Alexander) Fraser, Kt., CBE
Morrison, Sir Howard Leslie, Kt., OBE
Morrison, Sir Kenneth Duncan, Kt., CBE
Morrison, Sir (William) Garth, KT, CBE
Morrison-Bell, Sir William Hollin Dayrell, Bt. (1905)
Morrison-Low, Sir James Richard, Bt. (1908)
Morritt, *Rt. Hon.* Sir (Robert) Andrew, Kt., CVO
Morse, Sir Christopher Jeremy, KCMG
Moseley, Sir George Walker, KCB
Moses, *Rt. Hon.* Sir Alan George, Kt.
Moses, *Very Revd* Dr John Henry, KCVO
Moss, Sir David Joseph, KCVO, CMG
Moss, Sir Stephen Alan, Kt.
Moss, Sir Stirling Craufurd, Kt., OBE
Mostyn, Sir William Basil John, Bt. (1670)
Motion, Sir Andrew, Kt.
Mott, Sir John Harmer, Bt. (1930)
Mottram, Sir Richard Clive, GCB
†Mount, Sir (William Robert) Ferdinand, Bt. (1921)
†Mountain, Sir Edward Brian Stanford, Bt. (1922)
Mountfield, Sir Robin, KCB
Mowbray, Sir John Robert, Bt. (1880)
Moylan, *Hon.* Sir Andrew John Gregory, Kt.
Muir, Sir Laurence Macdonald, Kt.
†Muir, Sir Richard James Kay, Bt. (1892)
Muir-Mackenzie, Sir Alexander Alwyne Henry Charles Brinton, Bt. (1805)
Mulcahy, Sir Geoffrey John, Kt.
Mullens, *Lt.-Gen.* Sir Anthony Richard Guy, KCB, OBE
Mummery, *Rt. Hon.* Sir John Frank, Kt.
Munby, *Hon.* Sir James Lawrence, Kt.
Munn, Sir James, Kt., OBE
Munro, Sir Alan Gordon, KCMG
†Munro, Sir Ian Kenneth, Bt. (S. 1634)
Munro, Sir Alasdair Thomas Ian, Bt. (1825)
Muria, *Hon.* Sir Gilbert John Baptist, Kt.
Murray, Sir David Edward, Kt.
Murray, *Rt. Hon.* Sir Donald Bruce, Kt.
Murray, *Prof.* Sir Kenneth, Kt.
Murray, Sir Nigel Andrew Digby, Bt. (S. 1628)
Murray, Sir Patrick Ian Keith, Bt. (S. 1673)
†Murray, Sir Rowland William, Bt. (S. 1630)
Musgrave, Sir Christopher John Shane, Bt. (1782)
Musgrave, Sir Christopher Patrick Charles, Bt. (1611)
Myers, Sir Philip Alan, Kt., OBE, QPM
Myers, *Prof.* Sir Rupert Horace, KBE
Mynors, Sir Richard Baskerville, Bt. (1964)
Naipaul, Sir Vidiadhar Surajprasad, Kt.
Nairn, Sir Michael, Bt. (1904)
Nairne, *Rt. Hon.* Sir Patrick Dalmahoy, GCB, MC
Naish, Sir (Charles) David, Kt.
Nalau, Sir Jerry Kasip, KBE
Nall, Sir Edward William Joseph Bt. (1954)
Namaliu, *Rt. Hon.* Sir Rabbie Langanai, KCMG

†Napier, Sir Charles Joseph, Bt. (1867)
Napier, Sir John Archibald Lennox, Bt. (S. 1627)
Napier, Sir Oliver John, Kt.
Naylor, Sir Robert, Kt.
Naylor-Leyland, Sir Philip Vyvyan, Bt. (1895)
Neal, Sir Eric James, Kt., CVO
Neale, Sir Gerrard Anthony, Kt.
Neave, Sir Paul Arundell, Bt. (1795)
Neill, *Rt. Hon.* Sir Brian Thomas, Kt.
Neill, Sir (James) Hugh, KCVO, CBE, TD
†Nelson, Sir Jamie Charles Vernon Hope, Bt. (1912)
Nelson, *Hon.* Sir Robert Franklyn, Kt.
Neubert, Sir Michael John, Kt.
New, *Maj.-Gen.* Sir Laurence Anthony Wallis, Kt., CB, CBE
Newall, Sir Paul Henry, Kt., TD
Newby, *Prof.* Sir Howard Joseph, Kt., CBE
Newington, Sir Michael John, KCMG
Newman, Sir Francis Hugh Cecil, Bt. (1912)
Newman, Sir Geoffrey Robert, Bt. (1836)
Newman, *Hon.* Sir George Michael, Kt.
Newman, Sir Kenneth Leslie, GBE, QPM
Newman, *Vice-Adm.* Sir Roy Thomas, KCB
Newman Taylor, *Prof.* Sir Anthony John, Kt., CBE
Newsam, Sir Peter Anthony, Kt.
†Newson-Smith, Sir Peter Frank Graham, Bt. (1944)
Newton, Sir (Charles) Wilfred, Kt., CBE
†Newton, *Revd* George Peter Howgill, Bt. (1900)
†Newton, Sir John Garnar, Bt. (1924)
Ngata, Sir Henare Kohere, KBE
Nice, Sir Geoffrey, Kt., QC
Nicol, *Hon.* Sir Andrew George Lindsay, Kt.
Nichol, Sir Duncan Kirkbride, Kt., CBE
Nicholas, Sir David, Kt., CBE
Nicholas, Sir John William, KCVO, CMG
Nicholls, Sir Nigel Hamilton, KCVO, CBE
Nichols, Sir Richard Everard, Kt.
Nicholson, Sir Bryan Hubert, GBE, Kt.
†Nicholson, Sir Charles Christian, Bt. (1912)
Nicholson, *Rt. Hon.* Sir Michael, Kt.
Nicholson, Sir Paul Douglas, Kt.
Nicholson, Sir Robin Buchanan, Kt., PHD, FRS, FRENG
Nicoll, Sir William, KCMG
Nightingale, Sir Charles Manners Gamaliel, Bt. (1628)
Nixon, Sir Simon Michael Christopher, Bt. (1906)
Noble, Sir David Brunel, Bt. (1902)
Noble, Sir Iain Andrew, Bt., OBE (1923)
Nombri, Sir Joseph Karl, Kt., ISO, BEM
Noon, Sir Gulam Kaderbhoy, Kt., MBE
Norman, Sir Arthur Gordon, KBE, DFC
Norman, Sir Mark Annesley, Bt. (1915)
Norman, Sir Ronald, Kt., OBE
Norman, Sir Torquil Patrick Alexander, Kt., CBE
Normington, Sir David John, KCB
Norrington, Sir Roger Arthur Carver, Kt., CBE
Norris, *Hon.* Sir Alastair Hubert, Kt.
Norriss, Air Marshal Sir Peter Coulson, KBE, CB, AFC
North, Sir Peter Machin, Kt., CBE, QC, DCL, FBA
North, Sir Thomas Lindsay, Kt.
North, Sir (William) Jonathan (Frederick), Bt. (1920)
Norton-Griffiths, Sir John, Bt. (1922)
Nossal, Sir Gustav Joseph Victor, Kt., CBE
Nott, *Rt. Hon.* Sir John William Frederic, KCB
Nourse, *Rt. Hon.* Sir Martin Charles, Kt.
Nugent, Sir John Edwin Lavallin, Bt. (I. 1795)
†Nugent, Sir Christopher George Ridley, Bt. (1806)
†Nugent, Sir (Walter) Richard Middleton, Bt. (1831)
Nunn, Sir Trevor Robert, Kt., CBE
Nunneley, Sir Charles Kenneth Roylance, Kt.
Nursaw, Sir James, KCB, QC
Nurse, Sir Paul Maxime, Kt.
†Nuttall, Sir Harry, Bt. (1922)
Nutting, Sir John Grenfell, Bt. (1903), QC
Oakeley, Sir John Digby Atholl, Bt. (1790)
Oakes, Sir Christopher, Bt. (1939)
†Oakshott, Hon. Sir Michael Arthur John, Bt. (1959)
Oates, Sir Thomas, Kt., CMG, OBE
O'Brien, Sir Frederick William Fitzgerald, Kt.
O'Brien, Sir Richard, Kt., DSO, MC
O'Brien, Sir Timothy John, Bt. (1849)
O'Brien, *Adm.* Sir William Donough, KCB, DSC
O'Connell, Sir Bernard, Kt.
O'Connell, Sir Maurice James Donagh MacCarthy, Bt. (1869)
O'Dea, Sir Patrick Jerad, KCVO
Odell, Sir Stanley John, Kt.
Odgers, Sir Graeme David William, Kt.
O'Donnell, Sir Augustine Thomas, KCB
O'Donnell, Sir Christopher John, Kt.
O'Donoghue, *Lt.-Gen.* Sir Kevin, KCB, CBE
O'Dowd, Sir David Joseph, Kt., CBE, QPM
Ogden, *Dr* Sir Peter James, Kt.
Ogden, Sir Robert, Kt., CBE
Ogilvy, Sir Francis Gilbert Arthur, Bt. (S. 1626)
Ogilvy-Wedderburn, Sir Andrew John Alexander, Bt. (1803)
Ognall, *Hon.* Sir Harry Henry, Kt.
Ohlson, Sir Brian Eric Christopher, Bt. (1920)
Oldham, *Dr* Sir John, Kt., OBE
Oliver, Sir James Michael Yorrick, Kt.
Oliver, Sir Stephen John Lindsay, Kt., QC
O'Loghlen, Sir Colman Michael, Bt. (1838)
Olver, Sir Stephen John Linley, KBE, CMG
Omand, Sir David Bruce, GCB
O'Nions, Prof. Sir Robert Keith, Kt., FRS, PHD
Ondaatje, Sir Christopher, Kt., CBE
Onslow, Sir John Roger Wilmot, Bt. (1797)
Oppenheimer, Sir Michael Bernard Grenville, Bt. (1921)
Oppenshaw, Sir Charles Peter Lawford, Kt., QC
Orde, Sir Hugh Stephen Roden, Kt., OBE
O'Regan, *Dr* Sir Stephen Gerard (Tipene), Kt.
O'Reilly, Sir Anthony John Francis, Kt.
O'Reilly, *Prof.* Sir John James, Kt.
Orr, Sir John, Kt., OBE
Orr-Ewing, Sir (Alistair) Simon, Bt. (1963)
Orr-Ewing, Sir Archibald Donald, Bt. (1886)
Osborn, Sir John Holbrook, Kt.
Osborn, Sir Richard Henry Danvers, Bt. (1662)
Osborne, Sir Peter George, Bt. (I. 1629)
O'Shea, *Prof.* Sir Timothy Michael Martin, Kt.
Osmotherly, Sir Edward Benjamin Crofton, Kt., CB
O'Sullevan, Sir Peter John, Kt., CBE
Oswald, *Admiral of the Fleet* Sir (John) Julian Robertson, GCB
Oswald, Sir (William Richard) Michael, KCVO
Otton, Sir Geoffrey John, KCB
Otton, *Rt. Hon.* Sir Philip Howard, Kt.
Oulton, Sir Antony Derek Maxwell, GCB, QC
Ouseley, *Hon.* Sir Brian Walter, Kt.
Outram, Sir Alan James, Bt. (1858)
Owen, Sir Geoffrey, Kt.
Owen, *Hon.* Sir John Arthur Dalziel, Kt.
Owen, *Hon.* Sir Robert Michael, Kt.
Owen-Jones, Sir Lindsay Harwood, KBE
Packer, Sir Richard John, KCB
Paget, Sir Julian Tolver, Bt. (1871), CVO

Paget, Sir Richard Herbert, Bt. (1886)
Paine, Sir Christopher Hammon, Kt., FRCP, FRCR
Pakenham, *Hon.* Sir Michael Aiden, KBE, CMG
Palin, *Air Chief Marshal* Sir Roger Hewlett, KCB, OBE
Palliser, *Rt. Hon.* Sir (Arthur) Michael, GCMG
Palmer, Sir Albert Rocky, Kt.
Palmer, Sir (Charles) Mark, Bt. (1886)
Palmer, Sir Geoffrey Christopher John, Bt. (1660)
Palmer, *Rt. Hon.* Sir Geoffrey Winston Russell, KCMG
Palmer, Sir John Edward Somerset, Bt. (1791)
Palmer, *Maj.-Gen.* Sir (Joseph) Michael, KCVO
Palmer, Sir Reginald Oswald, GCMG, MBE
Parbo, Sir Arvi Hillar, Kt.
Park, *Hon.* Sir Andrew Edward Wilson, Kt.
Parker, Sir Alan William, Kt., CBE
Parker, Sir Eric Wilson, Kt.
Parker, *Rt. Hon.* Sir Jonathan Frederic, Kt.
Parker, *Maj.* Sir Michael John, KCVO, CBE
Parker, *Lt.-Gen.* Sir Nicholas Ralph, KCB, CBE
Parker, Sir Richard (William) Hyde, Bt. (1681)
Parker, *Rt. Hon.* Sir Roger Jocelyn, Kt.
Parker, Sir (Thomas) John, Kt.
Parker, Sir William Peter Brian, Bt. (1844)
Parkes, Sir Edward Walter, Kt., FRENG
Parkinson, Sir Michael, Kt., CBE
Parry, Sir Emyr Jones, GCMG
Parry-Evans, *Air Chief Marshal* Sir David, GCB, CBE
Parsons, Sir John Christopher, KCVO
Parsons, Sir Richard Edmund (Clement Fownes), KCMG
Partridge, Sir Michael John Anthony, KCB
Partridge, Sir Nicholas Wyndham, Kt., OBE
Pascoe, *Gen.* Sir Robert Alan, KCB, MBE
Pasley, Sir Robert Killigrew Sabine, Bt. (1794)
Paston-Bedingfeld, *Capt.* Sir Edmund George Felix, Bt. (1661)
Paterson, Sir Dennis Craig, Kt.
Patey, Sir William Charters, KCMG
Patnick, Sir (Cyril) Irvine, Kt., OBE
Patten, *Rt. Hon.* Sir Nicholas John, Kt.
Pattie, *Rt. Hon.* Sir Geoffrey Edwin, Kt.
Pattison, *Prof.* Sir John Ridley, Kt., DM, FRCPATH
Pattullo, Sir (David) Bruce, Kt., CBE
Pauncefort-Duncombe, Sir Philip Digby, Bt. (1859)
Payne, Sir Norman John, Kt., CBE, FRENG
Peach, Sir Leonard Harry, Kt.
Peach, *Air Marshal* Sir Stuart William, KCB, CBE
Peacock, *Prof.* Sir Alan Turner, Kt., DSC
Pearce, Sir (Daniel Norton) Idris, Kt., CBE, TD
Pearse, Sir Brian Gerald, Kt.
Pearson, Sir Francis Nicholas Fraser, Bt. (1964)
Pearson, *Gen.* Sir Thomas Cecil Hook, KCB, CBE, DSO
Peart, *Prof.* Sir William Stanley, Kt., MD, FRS
Pease, Sir (Alfred) Vincent, Bt. (1882)
Pease, Sir Richard Thorn, Bt. (1920)
Peat, Sir Gerrard Charles, KCVO
Peat, Sir Michael Charles Gerrard, KCVO
Peckham, *Prof.* Sir Michael John, Kt.
Pedelty, Sir Mervyn Kay, Kt.
Peek, *Vice-Adm.* Sir Richard Innes, KBE, CB, DSC
Peek, Sir Richard Grenville, Bt. (1874)
Peirse, *Air Vice-Marshal* Sir Richard Charles Fairfax, KCVO, CB
Pelgen, Sir Harry Friedrich, Kt., MBE
Peliza, Sir Robert John, KBE, ED
Pelly, Sir Richard John, Bt. (1840)
Pemberton, Sir Francis Wingate William, Kt., CBE
Pendry, *Prof.* Sir John Brian, Kt., FRS
Penrose, *Prof.* Sir Roger, Kt., OM, FRS
Penry-Davey, *Hon.* Sir David Herbert, Kt.
Pepper, *Dr.* Sir David Edwin, KCMG
Pepper, *Prof.* Sir Michael, Kt.
Perowne, *Vice-Adm.* Sir James Francis, KBE
Perring, Sir John Raymond, Bt. (1963)
Perris, Sir David (Arthur), Kt., MBE
Perry, Sir David Howard, KCB
Perry, Sir Michael Sydney, GBE
Pervez, Sir Mohammed Anwar, Kt., OBE
Peters, *Prof.* Sir David Keith, Kt., FRCP
Peterson, Sir Christopher Matthew, Kt., CBE, TD
†Petit, Sir Jehangir, Bt. (1890)
Peto, Sir Henry George Morton, Bt. (1855)
†Peto, Sir Henry Christopher Morton Bampfylde, Bt. (1927)
Peto, *Prof.* Sir Richard, Kt., FRS
Petrie, Sir Peter Charles, Bt. (1918), CMG
Pettigrew, Sir Russell Hilton, Kt.
Pettit, Sir Daniel Eric Arthur, Kt.
Pettitt, Sir Dennis, Kt.
†Philipson-Stow, Sir (Robert) Matthew, Bt. (1907)
Phillips, Sir Fred Albert, Kt., CVO
Phillips, Sir (Gerald) Hayden, GCB
Phillips, Sir John David, Kt., QPM
Phillips, Sir Jonathan, KCB
Phillips, Sir Peter John, Kt., OBE
Phillips, Sir Robin Francis, Bt. (1912)
Phillis, Sir Robert Weston, Kt.
Pickard, Sir (John) Michael, Kt.
Pickthorn, Sir James Francis Mann, Bt. (1959)
Pidgeon, Sir John Allan Stewart, Kt.
†Piers, Sir James Desmond, Bt. (I. 1661)
Piggott-Brown, Sir William Brian, Bt. (1903)
Pigot, Sir George Hugh, Bt. (1764)
Pigott, *Lt.-Gen.* Sir Anthony David, KCB, CBE
Pigott, Sir Berkeley Henry Sebastian, Bt. (1808)
Pike, *Lt.-Gen.* Sir Hew William Royston, KCB, DSO, MBE
Pike, Sir Michael Edmund, KCVO, CMG
Pike, Sir Philip Ernest Housden, Kt., QC
Pilditch, Sir Richard Edward, Bt. (1929)
Pile, Sir Frederick Devereux, Bt. (1900), MC
Pill, *Rt. Hon.* Sir Malcolm Thomas, Kt.
Pilling, Sir Joseph Grant, KCB
Pinsent, Sir Christopher Roy, Bt. (1938)
Pinsent, Sir Matthew Clive, Kt., CBE
Pitakaka, Sir Moses Puibangara, GCMG
Pitcher, Sir Desmond Henry, Kt.
Pitchers, *Hon.* Sir Christopher (John), Kt.
Pitchford, *Hon.* Sir Christopher John, Kt.
Pitman, Sir Brian Ivor, Kt.
Pitoi, Sir Sere, Kt., CBE
Pitt, Sir Michael Edward, Kt.
Plastow, Sir David Arnold Stuart, Kt.
Platt, Sir Harold Grant, Kt.
Platt, Sir Martin Philip, Bt. (1959)
Pledger, *Air Chief Marshal* Sir Malcolm David, KCB, OBE, AFC
Plender, *Hon.* Sir Richard Owen, Kt.
Plumbly, Sir Derek John, KCMG
Pogo, *Most Revd.* Ellison Leslie, KBE
Pohai, Sir Timothy, Kt., MBE
Pole, Sir (John) Richard (Walter Reginald) Carew, Bt. (1628)
Pole, Sir Peter Van Notten, Bt. (1791)
Polkinghorne, *Revd Canon* John Charlton, KBE, FRS
Pollard, Sir Charles, Kt.
†Pollen, Sir Richard John Hungerford, Bt. (1795)
Pollock, Sir George Frederick, Bt. (1866)
Ponder, *Prof.* Sir Bruce Anthony John, Kt.
Ponsonby, Sir Ashley Charles Gibbs, Bt., KCVO, MC (1956)
Poore, Sir Roger Ricardo, Bt. (1795)
Pope, Sir Joseph Albert, Kt., DSC, PHD
Popplewell, *Hon.* Sir Oliver Bury, Kt.

†Porritt, Sir Jonathon Espie, Bt. (1963)
Portal, Sir Jonathan Francis, Bt. (1901)
Porter, *Rt. Hon.* Sir Robert Wilson, Kt., PC (NI)
Potter, *Rt. Hon.* Sir Mark Howard, Kt.
Potts, *Hon.* Sir Francis Humphrey, Kt.
Pound, Sir John David, Bt. (1905)
Povey, Sir Keith, Kt., QPM
Powell, Sir John Christopher, Kt.
Powell, Sir Nicholas Folliott Douglas, Bt. (1897)
Power, Sir Alastair John Cecil, Bt. (1924)
Power, *Hon.* Sir Noel Plunkett, Kt.
Prance, *Prof.* Sir Ghillean Tolmie, Kt., FRS
Pratchett, Sir Terence David John, Kt., OBE
Prendergast, Sir (Walter) Kieran, KCVO, CMG
Prescott, Sir Mark, Bt. (1938)
†Preston, Sir Philip Charles Henry Hulton, Bt. (1815)
Prevost, Sir Christopher Gerald, Bt. (1805)
Price, Sir David Ernest Campbell, Kt.
Price, Sir Francis Caradoc Rose, Bt. (1815)
Price, Sir Frank Leslie, Kt.
Prickett, *Air Chief Marshal* Sir Thomas Other, KCB, DSO, DFC
Prideaux, Sir Humphrey Povah Treverbian, Kt., OBE
Priestly, Sir Julian Gordon, KCMG
†Primrose, Sir John Ure, Bt. (1903)
Pringle, *Air Marshal* Sir Charles Norman Seton, KBE, FRENG
Pringle, *Hon.* Sir John Kenneth, Kt.
Pringle, *Lt.-Gen.* Sir Steuart (Robert), Bt. (S. 1683), KCB
Pritchard, Sir Neil, KCMG
†Prichard-Jones, Sir David John Walter, Bt. (1910)
Proby, Sir William Henry, Bt. (1952)
Proctor-Beauchamp, Sir Christopher Radstock, Bt. (1745)
Prosser, Sir David John, Kt.
Prosser, Sir Ian Maurice Gray, Kt.
Pryke, Sir Christopher Dudley, Bt. (1926)
Puapua, *Rt. Hon.* Sir Tomasi, GCMG, KBE
Pugh, Sir Idwal Vaughan, KCB
Pumphrey, Sir (John) Laurence, KCMG
Purves, Sir William, Kt., CBE, DSO
Purvis, *Vice-Adm.* Sir Neville, KCB
Quan, Sir Henry (Francis), KBE
Quicke, Sir John Godolphin, Kt., CBE
Quigley, Sir (William) George (Henry), Kt., CB, PHD
Quilter, Sir Anthony Raymond Leopold Cuthbert, Bt. (1897)
Quinton, Sir James Grand, Kt.
Radcliffe, Sir Sebastian Everard, Bt. (1813)
Radda, *Prof.* Sir George Karoly, Kt., CBE, FRS
Rae, Sir William, Kt., QPM
Raeburn, Sir Michael Edward Norman, Bt. (1923)
Raikes, *Vice-Adm.* Sir Iwan Geoffrey, KCB, CBE, DSC
Raison, *Rt. Hon.* Sir Timothy Hugh Francis, Kt.
Rake, Sir Michael Derek Vaughan, Kt.
Ralli, Sir Godfrey Victor, Bt., TD (1912)
Ramdanee, Sir Mookteswar Baboolall Kailash, Kt.
Ramphal, Sir Shridath Surendranath, GCMG
Ramphul, Sir Baalkhristna, Kt.
Ramphul, Sir Indurduth, Kt.
Ramsay, Sir Alexander William Burnett, Bt. (1806)
Ramsay, Sir Allan John (Hepple), KBE, CMG
Ramsay-Fairfax-Lucy, Sir Edmund John William Hugh, Bt. (1836)
Ramsden, Sir John Charles Josslyn, Bt. (1689)
Ramsey, *Dr* Sir Frank Cuthbert, KCMG
Ramsey, *Hon.* Sir Vivian Arthur, Kt.
Rankin, Sir Ian Niall, Bt. (1898)
Rasch, Sir Simon Anthony Carne, Bt. (1903)
Rashleigh, Sir Richard Harry, Bt. (1831)
Ratford, Sir David John Edward, KCMG, CVO
Rattee, *Hon.* Sir Donald Keith, Kt.
Rattle, Sir Simon Dennis, Kt., CBE
Rawlins, *Surgeon Vice-Adm.* Sir John Stuart Pepys, KBE
Rawlins, *Prof.* Sir Michael David, Kt., FRCP, FRCPED
Rawlinson, Sir Anthony Henry John, Bt. (1891)
Rea, *Prof.* Sir Desmond, Kt., OBE
Read, *Air Marshal* Sir Charles Frederick, KBE, CB, DFC, AFC
Read, *Prof.* Sir David John, Kt.
Read, Sir John Emms, Kt.
†Reade, Sir Kenneth Ray, Bt. (1661)
Reardon-Smith, Sir (William) Antony (John), Bt. (1920)
Reay, *Lt.-Gen.* Sir (Hubert) Alan John, KBE
Redgrave, *Maj.-Gen.* Sir Roy Michael Frederick, KBE, MC
Redgrave, Sir Steven Geoffrey, Kt., CBE
†Redmayne, Sir Giles Martin, Bt. (1964)
Redwood, Sir Peter Boverton, Bt. (1911)
Reece, Sir Charles Hugh, Kt.
Reedie, Sir Craig Collins, Kt., CBE
Rees, Sir David Allan, Kt., PHD, DSC, FRS
Rees, Sir Richard Ellis Meuric, Kt., CBE
Reeve, Sir Anthony, KCMG, KCVO
Reeves, *Most Revd* Paul Alfred, GCMG, GCVO
Reffell, *Adm.* Sir Derek Roy, KCB
Refshauge, *Maj.-Gen.* Sir William Dudley, Kt., CBE
Reid, Sir Alexander James, Bt. (1897)
Reid, Sir Hugh, Bt. (1922)
Reid, Sir (Philip) Alan, KCVO
Reid, Sir Robert Paul, Kt.
Reid, Sir William Kennedy, KCB
Reiher, Sir Frederick Bernard Carl, KBE, CMG
Reilly, *Lt.-Gen.* Sir Jeremy Calcott, KCB, DSO
Renals, Sir Stanley, Bt. (1895)
Renouf, Sir Clement William Bailey, Kt.
Renshaw, Sir John David Bine, Bt. (1903)
Renwick, Sir Richard Eustace, Bt. (1921)
Reporter, Sir Shapoor Ardeshirji, KBE
Reynolds, Sir David James, Bt. (1923)
Reynolds, Sir Peter William John, Kt., CBE
Rhodes, Sir John Christopher Douglas, Bt. (1919)
Ribeiro, Bernard Francisco, Kt., CBE
Rice, *Prof.* Sir Charles Duncan, Kt.
Rice, *Maj.-Gen.* Sir Desmond Hind Garrett, KCVO, CBE
Rice, Sir Timothy Miles Bindon, Kt.
Richard, Sir Cliff, Kt., OBE
Richards, Sir Brian Mansel, Kt., CBE, PHD
Richards, *Hon.* Sir David Anthony Stewart, Kt.
Richards, Sir David Gerald, Kt.
Richards, *Lt.-Gen.* Sir David, Julian, KCB, CBE, DSO
Richards, Sir Francis Neville, KCMG, CVO
Richards, Sir Rex Edward, Kt., DSC, FRS
Richards, *Rt. Hon.* Sir Stephen Price, Kt.
Richardson, Sir Anthony Lewis, Bt. (1924)
Richardson, *Rt. Hon.* Sir Ivor Lloyd Morgan, Kt.
Richardson, *Lt.-Gen.* Sir Robert Francis, KCB, CVO, CBE
Richardson, Sir Thomas Legh, KCMG
Richardson-Bunbury, Sir (Richard David) Michael, Bt. (I. 1787)
Richmond, Sir David Frank, KBE, CMG
Richmond, *Prof.* Sir Mark Henry, Kt., FRS
Ricketts, Sir Stephen Tristram, Bt. (1828)
Ricks, *Prof.* Sir Christopher Bruce, Kt.
Riddell, Sir John Charles Buchanan, Bt. (S. 1628), CVO
Ridley, Sir Adam (Nicholas), Kt.
Ridley, Sir Michael Kershaw, KCVO
Rifkind, *Rt. Hon.* Sir Malcolm Leslie, KCMG
Rigby, Sir Anthony John, Bt. (1929)

Rigby, Sir Peter, Kt.
Rimer, *Hon.* Sir Colin Percy Farquharson, Kt.
Ripley, Sir William Hugh, Bt. (1880)
Risk, Sir Thomas Neilson, Kt.
Ritako, Sir Thomas Baha, Kt., MBE
Ritblat, Sir John Henry, Kt.
Rivett-Carnac, Sir Miles James, Bt. (1836)
Rix, *Rt. Hon.* Sir Bernard Anthony, Kt.
Robati, Sir Pupuke, KBE
Robb, Sir John Weddell, Kt.
Roberts, *Hon.* Sir Denys Tudor Emil, KBE,
Roberts, Sir Derek Harry, Kt., CBE, FRS, FRENG
Roberts, *Prof.* Sir Edward Adam, KCMG
Roberts, Sir Gilbert Howland Rookehurst, Bt. (1809)
Roberts, Sir Hugh Ashley, KCVO
Roberts, Sir Ivor Anthony, KCMG
Roberts, *Dr* Sir Richard John, Kt.
Roberts, *Maj.-Gen.* Sir Sebastian John Lechmere, KCVO, OBE
Roberts, Sir Samuel, Bt. (1919)
Roberts, Sir William James Denby, Bt. (1909)
Robins, Sir Ralph Harry, Kt., FRENG
†Robinson, Sir Christopher Philipse, Bt. (1854)
Robinson, Sir Gerrard Jude, Kt.
Robinson, Sir Ian, Kt.
Robinson, Sir John James Michael Laud, Bt. (1660)
Robinson, *Dr* Sir Kenneth, Kt.
Robinson, Sir Wilfred Henry Frederick, Bt. (1908)
Robson, Sir John Adam, KCMG
Robson, Sir Stephen Arthur, Kt., CB
Roch, *Rt. Hon.* Sir John Ormond, Kt.
Roche, Sir David O'Grady, Bt. (1838)
Roche, Sir Henry John, Kt.
Rodgers, Sir (Andrew) Piers (Wingate Aikin-Sneath), Bt. (1964)
Rodley, *Prof.* Sir Nigel, KBE
Rodrigues, Sir Alberto Maria, Kt., CBE, ED
Rogers, *Air Chief Marshal* Sir John Robson, KCB, CBE
Rogers, Sir Peter, Kt.
Ropner, Sir John Bruce Woollacott, Bt. (1952)
Ropner, Sir Robert Clinton, Bt. (1904)
Rose, Sir Arthur James, Kt., CBE
Rose, *Rt. Hon.* Sir Christopher Dudley Roger, Kt.
Rose, Sir Clive Martin, GCMG
Rose, Sir David Lancaster, Bt. (1874)
Rose, *Gen.* Sir (Hugh) Michael, KCB, CBE, DSO, QGM
Rose, Sir John Edward Victor, Kt.
Rose, Sir Julian Day, Bt. (1872 and 1909)
Rose, Sir Stuart Alan Ransom, Kt.
Rosenthal, Sir Norman Leon, Kt.
Ross, *Maj.* Sir Andrew Charles Paterson, Bt. (1960)
Ross, *Lt.-Gen.* Sir Robert Jeremy, KCB, OBE
Ross, *Lt.-Col.* Sir Walter Hugh Malcolm, GCVO, OBE
Rossi, Sir Hugh Alexis Louis, Kt.
Rothschild, Sir Evelyn Robert Adrian de, Kt.
Rove, *Revd* Ikan, KBE
Rowe, *Rear-Adm.* Sir Patrick Barton, KCVO, CBE
Rowe-Ham, Sir David Kenneth, GBE
Rowland, Sir (John) David, Kt.
Rowland, Sir Geoffrey Robert, Kt.
Rowlands, Sir David, KCB
Rowley, Sir Richard Charles, Bt. (1836)
Rowling, Sir John Reginald, Kt.
Rowlinson, *Prof.* Sir John Shipley, Kt., FRS
Royce, *Hon.* Sir Roger John, Kt.
Royden, Sir Christopher John, Bt. (1905)
Rudd, Sir (Anthony) Nigel (Russell), Kt.
Rudge, Sir Alan Walter, Kt., CBE, FRS
Rugge-Price, Sir James Keith Peter, Bt. (1804)
Ruggles-Brise, Sir Timothy Edward, Bt. (1935)
Rumbold, Sir Henry John Sebastian, Bt. (1779)
Runchorelal, Sir (Udayan) Chinubhai Madhowlal, Bt. (1913)
Rusby, *Vice-Adm.* Sir Cameron, KCB, LVO
Rushdie, Sir (Ahmed) Salman, Kt.
†Russell, Sir (Arthur) Mervyn, Bt. (1812)
Russell, Sir Charles Dominic, Bt. (1916)
Russell, Sir George, Kt., CBE
Russell, Sir Muir, KCB
Rutter, *Prof.* Sir Michael Llewellyn, Kt., CBE, MD, FRS
Ryan, Sir Derek Gerald, Bt. (1919)
Rycroft, Sir Richard John, Bt. (1784)
Ryder, *Hon.* Sir Ernest Nigel Ryder, Kt., TD
Ryrie, Sir William Sinclair, KCB
Sacranie, Sir Iqbal Abdul Karim Mussa, Kt., OBE
Sainsbury, *Rt. Hon.* Sir Timothy Alan Davan, Kt.
St Clair-Ford, Sir James Anson, Bt. (1793)
St George, Sir John Avenel Bligh, Bt. (I. 1766)
St John-Mildmay, Sir Walter John Hugh, Bt. (1772)
Sainty, Sir John Christopher, KCB
Sales, *Hon.* Sir Philip James, Kt.
Salisbury, Sir Robert William, Kt.
Salt, Sir Patrick MacDonnell, Bt. (1869)
Salt, Sir (Thomas) Michael John, Bt. (1899)
†Salusbury-Trelawny, Sir John William Richard, Bt. (1628)
Sampson, Sir Colin, Kt., CBE, QPM
Samuel, Sir John Michael Glen, Bt. (1898)
Samuelson, Sir (Bernard) Michael (Francis), Bt. (1884)
Samuelson, Sir Sydney Wylie, Kt., CBE
Samworth, Sir David Chetwode, Kt., CBE
Sanders, Sir Robert Tait, KBE, CMG
Sanders, Sir Ronald Michael, KCMG
Sanderson, Sir Frank Linton, Bt. (1920)
Sands, Sir Roger Blakemore, KCB
Sarei, Sir Alexis Holyweek, Kt., CBE
Sargent, Sir William Desmond, Kt., CBE
Sassoon, Sir James Meyer, Kt.
Satchwell, Sir Kevin Joseph, Kt.
Saunders, *Hon.* Sir John Henry Boulton, Kt.
Savile, Sir James Wilson Vincent, Kt., OBE
Savill, *Prof.* Sir John Stewart, Kt.
Savory, Sir Michael Berry, Kt.
Sawers, Sir Robert John, KCMG
Saxby, *Prof.* Sir Robin Keith, Kt.
Scarlett, Sir John McLeod, KCMG, OBE
Scheele, Sir Nicholas Vernon, KCMG
Schiemann, *Rt. Hon.* Sir Konrad Hermann Theodor, Kt.
Scholar, Sir Michael Charles, KCB
Scholey, Sir David Gerald, Kt., CBE
Scholey, Sir Robert, Kt., CBE, FRENG
Scholtens, Sir James Henry, KCVO
Schreier, Sir Bernard, Kt.
Schubert, Sir Sydney, Kt.
Scipio, Sir Hudson Rupert, Kt.
Scoon, Sir Paul, GCMG, GCVO, OBE
Scott, Sir Anthony Percy, Bt. (1913)
Scott, Sir David Aubrey, GCMG
Scott, *Prof.* Sir George Peter, Kt.
Scott, Sir James Jervoise, Bt. (1962)
Scott, Sir Kenneth Bertram Adam, KCVO, CMG
Scott, Sir Oliver Christopher Anderson, Bt. (1909)
Scott, *Prof.* Sir Philip John, KBE
Scott, Sir Ridley, Kt.
Scott, Sir Robert David Hillyer, Kt.
Scott, Sir Walter John, Bt. (1907)
Scott-Lee, Sir Paul Joseph, Kt., QPM
Seale, Sir Clarence David, Kt.
Seale, Sir John Henry, Bt. (1838)
Seaman, Sir Keith Douglas, KCVO, OBE
Sebastian, Sir Cuthbert Montraville, GCMG, OBE
†Sebright, Sir Rufus Hugo Giles, Bt. (1626)
Seccombe, Sir (William) Vernon Stephen, Kt.
Seconde, Sir Reginald Louis, KCMG, CVO
Sedley, *Rt. Hon.* Sir Stephen John, Kt.
Seely, Sir Nigel Edward, Bt. (1896)
Seeto, Sir Ling James, Kt., MBE
Seeyave, Sir Rene Sow Choung, Kt., CBE
Seligman, Sir Peter Wendel, Kt., CBE
Semple, Sir John Laughlin, KCB

Sergeant, Sir Patrick, Kt.
Serota, Sir Nicholas Andrew, Kt.
†Seton, Sir Charles Wallace, Bt. (S. 1683)
Seton, Sir Iain Bruce, Bt. (S. 1663)
Severne, *Air Vice-Marshal* Sir John de Milt, KCVO, OBE, AFC
Shaffer, Sir Peter Levin, Kt., CBE
Shakerley, Sir Geoffrey Adam, Bt. (1838)
Shakespeare, Sir Thomas William, Bt. (1942)
Sharp, Sir Adrian, Bt. (1922)
Sharp, Sir Leslie, Kt., QPM
Sharp, Sir Sheridan Christopher Robin, Bt. (1920)
Sharples, Sir James, Kt., QPM
Shattock, Sir Gordon, Kt.
Shaw, Sir Brian Piers, Kt.
Shaw, Sir (Charles) Barry, Kt., CB, QC
Shaw, Sir Charles De Vere, Bt. (1821)
Shaw, *Prof.* Sir John Calman, Kt., CBE
Shaw, Sir Neil McGowan, Kt.
Shaw, Sir Roy, Kt.
Shaw, Sir Run Run, Kt., CBE
Shaw-Stewart, Sir Ludovic Houston, Bt. (S. 1667)
Shearing, Sir George Albert, Kt. OBE
Shebbeare, Sir Thomas Andrew, KCVO
Sheehy, Sir Patrick, Kt.
Sheffield, Sir Reginald Adrian Berkeley, Bt. (1755)
Shehadie, Sir Nicholas Michael, Kt., OBE
Sheil, *Rt. Hon.* Sir John, Kt.
Sheinwald, Sir Nigel Elton, KCMG
Shelley, Sir John Richard, Bt. (1611)
Shepherd, Sir Colin Ryley, Kt.
Shepherd, Sir John Alan, KCVO, CMG
Sher, Sir Antony, KBE
Sherbourne, Sir Stephen Ashley, Kt., CBE
Sherston-Baker, Sir Robert George Humphrey, Bt. (1796)
Shiffner, Sir Henry David, Bt. (1818)
Silber, *Hon.* Sir Stephen Robert, Kt.
Shinwell, Sir (Maurice) Adrian, Kt.
Shock, Sir Maurice, Kt.
Short, Sir Apenera Pera, KBE
Shortridge, Sir Jon Deacon, KCB
Shuckburgh, Sir Rupert Charles Gerald, Bt. (1660)
Sieff, *Hon.* Sir David, Kt.
Silber, *Rt. Hon.* Sir Stephen Robert, Kt.
Simeon, Sir Richard Edmund Barrington, Bt. (1815)
Simmonds, *Rt. Hon. Dr* Sir Kennedy Alphonse, KCMG
Simmons, *Air Marshal* Sir Michael George, KCB, AFC
Simmons, Sir Stanley Clifford, Kt.
Simms, Sir Neville Ian, Kt., FRENG
Simon, *Hon.* Sir Peregrine Charles Hugh, Kt.
Simonet, Sir Louis Marcel Pierre, Kt., CBE
Simpson, *Dr* Sir Peter Jeffery, Kt.
Sims, Sir Roger Edward, Kt.
Sinclair, Sir Clive Marles, Kt.
Sinclair, Sir Ian McTaggart, KCMG, QC
Sinclair, Sir Patrick Robert Richard, Bt. (S. 1704)
Sinclair, Sir Robert John, Kt.
Sinclair-Lockhart, Sir Simon John Edward Francis, Bt. (S. 1636)
Sinden, Sir Donald Alfred, Kt., CBE
Singer, *Hon.* Sir Jan Peter, Kt.
Singh, Sir Pritpal, Kt.
Singleton, Sir Roger, Kt., CBE
Sione, Sir Tomu Malaefone, GCMG, OBE
†Sitwell, Sir George Reresby Sacheverell, Bt. (1808)
Skeggs, Sir Clifford George, Kt.
Skehel, Sir John James, Kt., FRS
Skingsley, *Air Chief Marshal* Sir Anthony Gerald, GBE, KCB
Skinner, Sir (Thomas) Keith (Hewitt), Bt. (1912)
Skipwith, Sir Patrick Alexander d'Estoteville, Bt. (1622)
Slack, Sir William Willatt, KCVO, FRCS
Slade, Sir Benjamin Julian Alfred, Bt. (1831)
Slade, *Rt. Hon.* Sir Christopher John, Kt.
Slaney, *Prof.* Sir Geoffrey, KBE
Slater, *Adm.* Sir John (Jock) Cunningham Kirkwood, GCB, LVO
Sleight, Sir Richard, Bt. (1920)
Sloan, Sir Andrew Kirkpatrick, Kt., QPM
Sloman, Sir Albert Edward, Kt., CBE
Smart, Sir Jack, Kt., CBE
Smiley, *Lt.-Col.* Sir John Philip, Bt. (1903)
Smith, Sir Alan, Kt., CBE, DFC
Smith, *Hon.* Sir Andrew Charles, Kt.
Smith, Sir Andrew Thomas, Bt. (1897)
†Smith, Sir Robert Christopher Sydney Winwood, Bt. (1809)
Smith, *Prof.* Sir Colin Stansfield, Kt., CBE
Smith, Sir Cyril, Kt., MBE
Smith, *Prof.* Sir David Cecil, Kt., FRS
Smith, Sir David Iser, KCVO
Smith, Sir Dudley (Gordon), Kt.
Smith, *Prof.* Sir Eric Brian, Kt., PHD
Smith, Sir Geoffrey Johnson, Kt.
Smith, Sir John Alfred, Kt., QPM
Smith, Sir Joseph William Grenville, Kt.
Smith, Sir Kevin, Kt., CBE
Smith, Sir Michael John Llewellyn, KCVO, CMG
Smith, Sir (Norman) Brian, Kt., CBE, PHD
Smith, Sir Paul Brierley, Kt., CBE
Smith, *Hon.* Sir Peter (Winston), Kt.
Smith, Sir Robert Courtney, Kt., CBE
Smith, Sir Robert Hill, Bt. (1945)
Smith, *Gen.* Sir Rupert Anthony, KCB, DSO, OBE, QGM
Smith-Dodsworth, Sir John Christopher, Bt. (1784)
Smith-Gordon, Sir (Lionel) Eldred (Peter), Bt. (1838)
Smith-Marriott, Sir Hugh Cavendish, Bt. (1774)
Smurfit, *Dr.* Sir Michael William Joseph, KBE
Smyth, Sir Timothy John, Bt. (1955)
Snyder, Sir Michael John, Kt.
Soar, *Vice-Adm.* Sir Trevor Alan, KCB, OBE
Sobers, Sir Garfield St Auburn, Kt.
Solomon, Sir Harry, Kt.
Somare, *Rt. Hon.* Sir Michael Thomas, GCMG, CH
Somerville, *Brig.* Sir John Nicholas, Kt., CBE
Sorrell, Sir John William, Kt., CBE
Sorrell, Sir Martin Stuart, Kt.
Soulsby, Sir Peter Alfred, Kt.
Soutar, *Air Marshal* Sir Charles John Williamson, KBE
Southby, Sir John Richard Bilbe, Bt. (1937)
Southern, *Prof.* Sir Edwin Mellor, Kt.
Southgate, Sir Colin Grieve, Kt.
Southgate, Sir William David, Kt.
Southward, *Dr* Sir Nigel Ralph, KCVO
Sowrey, *Air Marshal* Sir Frederick Beresford, KCB, CBE, AFC
Sparrow, Sir John, Kt.
Spearman, Sir Alexander Young Richard Mainwaring, Bt. (1840)
Spedding, *Prof.* Sir Colin Raymond William, Kt., CBE
Speed, Sir (Herbert) Keith, Kt., RD
Speelman, Sir Cornelis Jacob, Bt. (1686)
Speight, *Hon.* Sir Graham Davies, Kt.
Spencer, Sir Derek Harold, Kt., QC
Spencer, *Vice-Adm.* Sir Peter, KCB
Spencer-Nairn, Sir Robert Arnold, Bt. (1933)
Spicer, Sir James Wilton, Kt.
Spicer, Sir Nicholas Adrian Albert, Bt. (1906)
Spicer, Sir (William) Michael Hardy, Kt.
Spiers, Sir Donald Maurice, Kt., CB, TD
Spooner, Sir James Douglas, Kt.
Spratt, *Col.* Sir Greville Douglas, GBE, TD
Spring, Sir Dryden Thomas, Kt.
Squire, *Air Chief Marshal* Sir Peter Ted, GCB, DFC, AFC, ADC
Stadlen, *Hon.* Sir Nicholas Felix, Kt.
Stagg, Sir Charles Richard Vernon, KCMG
Stainton, Sir (John) Ross, Kt., CBE
Staite, Sir Richard John, Kt., OBE
Stamer, Sir (Lovelace) Anthony, Bt. (1809)
Stanhope, *Adm.* Sir Mark, KCB, OBE
Stanier, Sir Beville Douglas, Bt. (1917)
Stanley, *Rt. Hon.* Sir John Paul, Kt., MP

Staples, Sir Richard Molesworth, Bt. (I. 1628)
Starkey, Sir John Philip, Bt. (1935)
Staughton, *Rt. Hon.* Sir Christopher Stephen Thomas Jonathan Thayer, Kt.
Stear, *Air Chief Marshal* Sir Michael James Douglas, KCB, CBE
Steel, *Hon.* Sir David William, Kt.
Steer, Sir Alan William, Kt.
Stephen, *Rt. Hon.* Sir Ninian Martin, KG, GCMG, GCVO, KBE
Stephens, Sir (Edwin) Barrie, Kt.
Stephens, Sir William Benjamin Synge, Kt.
Stephenson, Sir Henry Upton, Bt. (1936)
Stephenson, Sir Paul Robert, Kt., QPM
Sternberg, Sir Sigmund, Kt.
Stevens, Sir Jocelyn Edward Greville, Kt., CVO
Stevenson, Sir Simpson, Kt.
Stewart, Sir Alan d'Arcy, Bt. (I. 1623)
Stewart, Sir Brian John, Kt., CBE
Stewart, Sir David James Henderson, Bt. (1957)
Stewart, Sir David John Christopher, Bt. (1803)
Stewart, Sir James Douglas, Kt.
Stewart, Sir James Moray, KCB
Stewart, Sir (John) Simon (Watson), Bt. (1920)
Stewart, Sir John Young, Kt., OBE
Stewart, *Lt.-Col.* Sir Robert Christie, KCVO, CBE, TD
Stewart, Sir Robin Alastair, Bt. (1960)
Stewart, *Prof.* Sir William Duncan Paterson, Kt., FRS, FRSE
Stewart-Clark, Sir John, Bt. (1918)
Stewart-Richardson, Sir Simon Alaisdair, Bt. (S. 1630)
Stewart-Wilson, *Lt.-Col.* Sir Blair Aubyn, KCVO
Stibbon, *Gen.* Sir John James, KCB, OBE
Stirling, Sir Alexander John Dickson, KBE, CMG
Stirling, Sir Angus Duncan Aeneas, Kt.
Stirling-Hamilton, Sir Malcolm William Bruce, Bt. (S. 1673)
Stirling of Garden, *Col.* Sir James, KCVO, CBE, TD
Stirrup, *Air Chief Marshal* Sir Graham Eric (Jock), GCB, AFC, ADC
Stockdale, Sir Thomas Minshull, Bt. (1960)
Stoddart, *Prof.* Sir James Fraser, Kt.
Stoker, *Prof.* Sir Michael George Parke, Kt., CBE, FRCP, FRS, FRSE
Stonhouse, *Revd* Michael Philip, Bt. (1628 and 1670)
Stonor, *Air Marshal* Sir Thomas Henry, KCB
Stoppard, Sir Thomas, Kt., OM, CBE
Storey, *Hon.* Sir Richard, Bt., CBE (1960)
Stothard, Sir Peter Michael, Kt.
Stott, Sir Adrian George Ellingham, Bt. (1920)
Stoute, Sir Michael Ronald, Kt.
Stowe, Sir Kenneth Ronald, GCB, CVO
Stracey, Sir John Simon, Bt. (1818)
Strachan, Sir Curtis Victor, Kt., CVO
Strachey, Sir Charles, Bt. (1801)
Straker, Sir Louis Hilton, KCMG
Strang Steel, Sir (Fiennes) Michael, Bt. (1938)
Street, *Hon.* Sir Laurence Whistler, KCMG
Streeton, Sir Terence George, KBE, CMG
Strickland-Constable, Sir Frederic, Bt. (1641)
Stringer, Sir Donald Edgar, Kt., CBE
Stringer, Sir Howard, Kt.
Strong, Sir Roy Colin, Kt., PHD, FSA
Stronge, Sir James Anselan Maxwell, Bt. (1803)
Stuart, Sir James Keith, Kt.
Stuart, Sir Kenneth Lamonte, Kt.
†Stuart, Sir Phillip Luttrell, Bt. (1660)
†Stuart-Forbes, Sir William Daniel, Bt. (S. 1626)
†Stuart-Menteth, Sir Charles Greaves, Bt. (1838)
Stuart-Paul, *Air Marshal* Sir Ronald Ian, KBE
Stuart-Smith, *Rt. Hon.* Sir Murray, Kt.
Stubbs, Sir William Hamilton, Kt., PHD
Stucley, *Lt.* Sir Hugh George Coplestone Bampfylde, Bt. (1859)
Studd, Sir Edward Fairfax, Bt. (1929)
Studholme, Sir Henry William, Bt. (1956)
Sturridge, Sir Nicholas Anthony, KCVO
Stuttard, Sir John Boothman, Kt.
†Style, Sir William Frederick, Bt. (1627)
Sullivan, *Rt. Hon.* Sir Jeremy Mirth, Kt.
Sullivan, Sir Richard Arthur, Bt. (1804)
Sulston, Sir John Edward, Kt.
Sumner, *Hon.* Sir Christopher John, Kt.
Sunderland, Sir John Michael, Kt.
Sutherland, Sir John Brewer, Bt. (1921)
Sutherland, Sir William George MacKenzie, Kt.
Sutton, *Air Marshal* Sir John Matthias Dobson, KCB
Sutton, Sir Richard Lexington, Bt. (1772)
Swaffield, Sir James Chesebrough, Kt., CBE, RD
Swaine, Sir John Joseph, Kt., CBE
Swan, Sir Conrad Marshall John Fisher, KCVO, PHD
Swan, Sir John William David, KBE
Swann, Sir Michael Christopher, Bt. (1906), TD
Sweeney, Sir George, Kt.
Sweeney, *Hon.* Sir Nigel Hamilton, Kt.
Sweeting, *Prof.* Sir Martin Nicholas, Kt., OBE, FRS
Sweetnam, Sir (David) Rodney, KCVO, CBE, FRCS
Swinburn, *Lt.-Gen.* Sir Richard Hull, KCB
Swinnerton-Dyer, *Prof.* Sir (Henry) Peter (Francis), Bt. (1678), KBE, FRS
Swinton, *Maj.-Gen.* Sir John, KCVO, OBE
Swire, Sir Adrian Christopher, Kt.
Swire, Sir John Anthony, Kt., CBE
Sykes, Sir David Michael, Bt. (1921)
Sykes, Sir Francis John Badcock, Bt. (1781)
Sykes, Sir Hugh Ridley, Kt.
Sykes, *Prof.* Sir (Malcolm) Keith, Kt.
Sykes, Sir Richard, Kt.
Sykes, Sir Tatton Christopher Mark, Bt. (1783)
Symons, *Vice-Adm.* Sir Patrick Jeremy, KBE
Synge, Sir Robert Carson, Bt. (1801)
Synnott, Sir Hilary Nicholas Hugh, KCMG
Talboys, *Rt. Hon.* Sir Brian Edward, CH, KCB
Tang, Sir David Wing-cheung, KBE
Tapps-Gervis-Meyrick, Sir George Christopher Cadafael, Bt. (1791)
Tapsell, Sir Peter Hannay Bailey, Kt., MP
Tate, Sir (Henry) Saxon, Bt. (1898)
Taureka, *Dr* Sir Reubeh, KBE
Tauvasa, Sir Joseph James, KBE
Tavare, Sir John, Kt., CBE
Tavener, *Prof.* Sir John Kenneth, Kt.
Taylor, Sir (Arthur) Godfrey, Kt.
Taylor, Sir Cyril Julian Hebden, GBE
Taylor, Sir Edward Macmillan (Teddy), Kt.
Taylor, Sir Hugh Henderson, KCB
Taylor, *Rt. Revd* John Bernard, KCVO
Taylor, *Dr* Sir John Michael, Kt., OBE
Taylor, *Prof.* Sir Martin John, Kt., FRS
Taylor, Sir Nicholas Richard Stuart, Bt. (1917)
Taylor, *Prof.* Sir William, Kt., CBE
Taylor, Sir William George, Kt.
Teagle, *Vice-Adm.* Sir Somerford Francis, KBE
Teare, *Hon.* Sir Nigel John Martin, Kt.
Teasdale, *Prof.* Sir Graham Michael, Kt.
Tebbit, Sir Donald Claude, GCMG
Tebbit, Sir Kevin Reginald, KCB, CMG
Telito, *HE Revd* Filoimea, GCMG, MBE
Temple, *Prof.* Sir John Graham, Kt.
†Temple, Sir Richard, Bt. (1876)
Temu, *Hon. Dr* Sir Puka, KBE, CMG
Tennant, Sir Anthony John, Kt.
Tennyson-D'Eyncourt, Sir Mark Gervais, Bt. (1930)

Terry, *Air Marshal* Sir Colin George, KBE, CB
Terry, *Air Chief Marshal* Sir Peter David George, GCB, AFC
Thatcher, Sir Mark, Bt. (1990)
Thomas, Sir David John Godfrey, Bt. (1694)
Thomas, Sir Derek Morison David, KCMG
Thomas, Sir Gilbert Stanley, Kt., OBE
Thomas, Sir Jeremy Cashel, KCMG
Thomas, Sir (John) Alan, Kt.
Thomas, *Prof.* Sir John Meurig, Kt., FRS
Thomas, Sir Keith Vivian, Kt.
Thomas, *Dr* Sir Leton Felix, KCMG, CBE
Thomas, Sir Philip Lloyd, KCVO, CMG
Thomas, Sir Quentin Jeremy, Kt., CB
Thomas, *Rt. Hon.* Sir Roger John Laugharne, Kt.
Thomas, *Hon.* Sir Swinton Barclay, Kt.
Thomas, Sir William Michael, Bt. (1919)
Thomas, Sir (William) Michael (Marsh), Bt. (1918)
Thompson, Sir Christopher Peile, Bt. (1890)
Thompson, Sir Clive Malcolm, Kt.
Thompson, Sir David Albert, KCMG
Thompson, Sir Gilbert Williamson, Kt., OBE
Thompson, *Prof.* Sir Michael Warwick, Kt., DSC
Thompson, Sir Nicholas Annesley, Bt. (1963)
Thompson, Sir Nigel Cooper, KCMG, CBE
Thompson, Sir Paul Anthony, Bt. (1963)
Thompson, Sir Peter Anthony, Kt.
Thompson, *Dr* Sir Richard Paul Hepworth, KCVO
Thompson, Sir Thomas d'Eyncourt John, Bt. (1806)
Thomson, Sir (Frederick Douglas) David, Bt. (1929)
Thomson, Sir John Adam, GCMG
Thomson, Sir Mark Wilfrid Home, Bt. (1925)
Thomson, Sir Thomas James, Kt., CBE, FRCP
Thorn, Sir John Samuel, Kt., OBE
Thorne, Sir Neil Gordon, Kt., OBE, TD
Thornton, *Air Marshal* Sir Barry Michael, KCB
Thornton, Sir (George) Malcolm, Kt.
Thornton, Sir Peter Eustace, KCB
Thornton, Sir Richard Eustace, KCVO, OBE
†Thorold, Sir (Anthony) Oliver, Bt. (1642)
Thorpe, *Rt. Hon.* Sir Mathew Alexander, Kt.
Thurecht, Sir Ramon Richard, Kt., OBE
Thwaites, Sir Bryan, Kt., PHD
Tickell, Sir Crispin Charles Cervantes, GCMG, KCVO
Tidmarsh, Sir James Napier, KCVO, MBE
Tikaram, Sir Moti, KBE
Tilt, Sir Robin Richard, Kt.
Tiltman, Sir John Hessell, KCVO
Timmins, *Col.* Sir John Bradford, KCVO, OBE, TD
Tims, Sir Michael David, KCVO
Tindle, Sir Ray Stanley, Kt., CBE
Tirvengadum, Sir Harry Krishnan, Kt.
Tjoeng, Sir James Neng, KBE
Tod, *Vice-Adm.* Sir Jonathan James Richard, KCB, CBE
Todd, *Prof.* Sir David, Kt., CBE
Todd, Sir Ian Pelham, KBE, FRCS
Tollemache, Sir Lyonel Humphry John, Bt. (1793)
Tomkys, Sir (William) Roger, KCMG
Tomlinson, *Prof.* Sir Bernard Evans, Kt., CBE
Tomlinson, Sir John Rowland, Kt., CBE
Tomlinson, Sir Michael John, Kt., CBE
Tomlinson, *Hon.* Sir Stephen Miles, Kt.
Tooke, *Prof.* Sir John Edward, Kt.
Tooley, Sir John, Kt.
ToRobert, Sir Henry Thomas, KBE
Torpy, *Air Marshal* Sir Glenn Lester, GCB, CBE, DSO
Torry, Sir Peter James, GCVO, KCMG
Tory, Sir Geofroy William, KCMG
Touche, Sir Anthony George, Bt. (1920)
Touche, Sir Rodney Gordon, Bt. (1962)
Toulson, *Rt. Hon.* Sir Roger Grenfell, Kt.
Tovadek, Sir Martin, Kt. CMG
Tovey, Sir Brian John Maynard, KCMG
ToVue, Sir Ronald, Kt., OBE
Towneley, Sir Simon Peter Edmund Cosmo William, KCVO
Townsend, Sir Cyril David, Kt.
Traill, Sir Alan Towers, GBE
Treacher, *Adm.* Sir John Devereux, KCB
Treacy, *Hon.* Sir Colman Maurice, Kt.
Treacy, *Hon.* Sir (James Mary) Seamus, Kt.
Treitel, *Prof.* Sir Guenter Heinz, Kt., FBA, QC
Trescowthick, Sir Donald Henry, KBE
Trevelyan, Sir Geoffrey Washington, Bt. (1662 and 1874)
Trezise, Sir Kenneth Bruce, Kt., OBE
Trippier, Sir David Austin, Kt., RD
Tritton, Sir Anthony John Ernest, Bt. (1905)
Trollope, Sir Anthony Simon, Bt. (1642)
Trotman-Dickenson, Sir Aubrey Fiennes, Kt.
Trotter, Sir Neville Guthrie, Kt.
Trotter, Sir Ronald Ramsay, Kt.
Troubridge, Sir Thomas Richard, Bt. (1799)
Trousdell, *Lt.-Gen.* Sir Philip Charles Cornwallis, KBE, CB
Truscott, Sir Ralph Eric Nicholson, Bt. (1909)
Tsang, Sir Donald Yam-keun, KBE
Tuamure-Maoate, *Dr* Sir Terepai, KBE
Tuck, Sir Bruce Adolph Reginald, Bt. (1910)
Tucker, *Hon.* Sir Richard Howard, Kt.
Tuckey, *Rt. Hon.* Sir Simon Lane, Kt.
Tugendhat, *Hon.* Sir Michael George, Kt.
Tuita, Sir Mariano Kelesimalefo, KBE
Tuite, Sir Christopher Hugh, Bt. (1622), PHD
Tuivaga, Sir Timoci Uluiburotu, Kt.
Tully, Sir William Mark, KBE
Tupper, Sir Charles Hibbert, Bt. (1888)
Turbott, Sir Ian Graham, Kt., CMG, CVO
Turing, Sir John Dermot, Bt. (S. 1638)
Turner, Sir Colin William Carstairs, Kt., CBE, DFC
Turner, *Hon.* Sir Michael John, Kt.
Turnquest, Sir Orville Alton, GCMG, QC
Tusa, Sir John, Kt.
Tweedie, *Prof.* Sir David Philip, Kt.
Tyree, Sir (Alfred) William, Kt., OBE
Tyrwhitt, Sir Reginald Thomas Newman, Bt. (1919)
Underhill, *Hon.* Sir Nicholas Edward, Kt.
Underwood, *Prof.* Sir James Cressee Elphinstone, Kt.
Unwin, Sir (James) Brian, KCB
Ure, Sir John Burns, KCMG, LVO
Urquhart, Sir Brian Edward, KCMG, MBE
Urwick, Sir Alan Bedford, KCVO, CMG
Usher, Sir Andrew John, Bt. (1899)
Utting, Sir William Benjamin, Kt., CB
Vardy, Sir Peter, Kt.
Varney, Sir David Robert, Kt.
Vasquez, Sir Alfred Joseph, Kt., CBE, QC
Vassar-Smith, Sir John Rathbone, Bt. (1917)
Vavasour, Sir Eric Michael Joseph Marmaduke, Bt. (1828)
Veness, Sir David, Kt., CBE, QPM
Venner, Sir Kenneth Dwight Vincent, KBE
Vereker, Sir John Michael Medlicott, KCB
†Verney, Sir John Sebastian, Bt. (1946)
Verney, *Hon.* Sir Lawrence John, Kt., TD
†Verney, Sir Edmund Ralph, Bt. (1818)
Vernon, Sir James William, Bt. (1914)
Vernon, Sir (William) Michael, Kt.

Vestey, Sir Paul Edmund, Bt. (1921)
Vickers, *Prof.* Sir Brian William, Kt.
Vickers, Sir John Stuart, Kt.
Vickers, *Lt.-Gen.* Sir Richard Maurice Hilton, KCB, CVO, OBE
Viggers, *Lt-Gen.* Sir Frederick Richard, KCB, CMG, MBE
Viggers, Sir Peter John, Kt.
Vincent, Sir William Percy Maxwell, Bt. (1936)
Vineall, Sir Anthony John Patrick, Kt.
Vines, Sir William Joshua, Kt., CMG
von Schramek, Sir Eric Emil, Kt.
†Vyvyan, Sir Ralph Ferrers Alexander, Bt. (1645)
Wade-Gery, Sir Robert Lucian, KCMG, KCVO
Waena, Sir Nathaniel Rahumaea, GCMG
Waine, *Rt. Revd* John, KCVO
Waite, *Rt. Hon.* Sir John Douglas, Kt.
Waka, Sir Lucas Joseph, Kt., OBE
Wake, Sir Hereward, Bt. (1621), MC
Wakefield, Sir (Edward) Humphry (Tyrell), Bt. (1962)
Wakefield, Sir Norman Edward, Kt.
Wakefield, Sir Peter George Arthur, KBE, CMG
Wakeford, Sir Geoffrey Michael Montgomery, Kt., OBE
Wakeham, *Prof.* Sir William Arnot, Kt.
Wakeley, Sir John Cecil Nicholson, Bt. (1952), FRCS
Wald, *Prof.* Sir Nicholas John, Kt.
Wales, Sir Robert Andrew, Kt.
Waley-Cohen, Sir Stephen Harry, Bt. (1961)
Walford, Sir Christopher Rupert, Kt.
Walker, *Gen.* Sir Antony Kenneth Frederick, KCB
†Walker, Sir Christopher Robert Baldwin, Bt. (1856)
Walker, Sir David Alan, Kt.
Walker, Sir Harold Berners, KCMG
Walker, Sir John Ernest, Kt., DPHIL, FRS
Walker, *Air Marshal* Sir John Robert, KCB, CBE, AFC
Walker, Sir Miles Rawstron, Kt., CBE
Walker, Sir Patrick Jeremy, KCB
Walker, *Hon.* Sir Paul James, Kt.
Walker, Sir Rodney Myerscough, Kt.
Walker, Sir Roy Edward, Bt. (1906)
Walker, *Hon.* Sir Timothy Edward, Kt.
Walker, Sir Victor Stewart Heron, Bt. (1868)
Walker-Okeover, Sir Andrew Peter Monro, Bt. (1886)
Walker-Smith, Sir John Jonah, Bt. (1960)
Wall, Sir (John) Stephen, GCMG, LVO
Wall, *Rt. Hon.* Sir Nicholas Peter Rathbone, Kt.
Wall, *Gen.* Sir Peter Anthony, KCB, CBE
Wall, Sir Robert William, Kt., OBE
Wallace, *Lt.-Gen.* Sir Christopher Brooke Quentin, KBE
Wallace, *Prof.* David James, Kt., CBE, FRS
Wallace, Sir Ian James, Kt., CBE
Waller, *Rt. Hon.* Sir (George) Mark, Kt.
Waller, Sir John Michael, Bt. (I. 1780)
Wallis, Sir Peter Gordon, KCVO
Wallis, Sir Timothy William, Kt.
Walmsley, *Vice-Adm.* Sir Robert, KCB
Walport, *Dr* Sir Mark Jeremy, Kt.
†Walsham, Sir Timothy John, Bt. (1831)
Walters, Sir Dennis Murray, Kt., MBE
Walters, Sir Frederick Donald, Kt.
Walters, Sir Peter Ingram, Kt.
Walters, Sir Roger Talbot, KBE, FRIBA
Wamiri, Sir Akapite, KBE
Wan, Sir Wamp, Kt., MBE
Wanless, Sir Derek, Kt.
Ward, *Rt. Hon.* Sir Alan Hylton, Kt.
Ward, Sir Austin, Kt., QC
Ward, Sir John Devereux, Kt., CBE
Ward, *Prof.* Sir John MacQueen, Kt., CBE
Ward, Sir Joseph James Laffey, Bt. (1911)
Ward, Sir Timothy James, Kt.
Wardale, Sir Geoffrey Charles, KCB
Wardlaw, Sir Henry Justin, Bt. (NS. 1631)
Waring, Sir (Alfred) Holburt, Bt. (1935)
Warmington, Sir Rupert Marshall, Bt. (1908)
Warner, Sir (Edward Courtenay) Henry, Bt. (1910)
Warner, *Prof.* Sir Frederick Edward, Kt., FRS, FRENG
Warner, Sir Gerald Chierici, KCMG
Warren, Sir (Frederick) Miles, KBE
Warren, Sir Kenneth Robin, Kt.
Warren, Sir Nicholas Roger, Kt.
Wass, Sir Douglas William Gretton, GCB
Waterhouse, *Hon.* Sir Ronald Gough, GBE
Waterlow, Sir Christopher Rupert, Bt. (1873)
Waterlow, Sir (James) Gerard, Bt. (1930)
Waters, *Gen.* Sir (Charles) John, GCB, CBE
Waters, Sir (Thomas) Neil (Morris), Kt.
Waterworth, Sir Alan William, KCVO
Wates, Sir Christopher Stephen, Kt.
Watson, Sir Bruce Dunstan, Kt.
Watson, *Prof.* Sir David John, Kt., PHD
Watson, Sir (James) Andrew, Bt. (1866)
Watson, *Vice-Adm.* Sir Philip Alexander, KBE, LVO
Watson, Sir Ronald Matthew, Kt., CBE
Watson, Sir Simon Conran Hamilton, Bt. (1895)
Watt, *Gen.* Sir Charles Redmond, KCB, KCVO, CBE, ADC
Watt, *Surgeon Vice-Adm.* Sir James, KBE, FRCS
Watts, Sir John Augustus Fitzroy, KCMG, CBE
Watts, Sir Philip Beverley, KCMG
Weatherall, *Prof.* Sir David John, Kt., FRS
Weatherall, *Vice-Adm.* Sir James Lamb, KCVO, KBE
Weatherup, *Hon.* Sir Ronald Eccles, Kt.
Webb, *Prof.* Sir Adrian Leonard, Kt.
Webb-Carter, *Gen.* Sir Evelyn John, KCVO, OBE
Webster, *Vice-Adm.* Sir John Morrison, KCB
Wedgwood, Sir (Hugo) Martin, Bt. (1942)
Weekes, Sir Everton DeCourcey, KCMG, OBE
Weinberg, Sir Mark Aubrey, Kt.
Weir, *Hon.* Sir Reginald George, Kt.
Weir, Sir Roderick Bignell, Kt.
Welby, Sir (Richard) Bruno Gregory, Bt. (1801)
Welch, Sir John Reader, Bt. (1957)
Weldon, Sir Anthony William, Bt. (I. 1723)
Weller, Sir Arthur Burton, Kt., CBE
Wellings, Sir Jack Alfred, Kt., CBE
†Wells, Sir Christopher Charles, Bt. (1944)
Wells, Sir John Julius, Kt.
Wells, Sir William Henry Weston, Kt., FRICS
Wesker, Sir Arnold, Kt.
Westbrook, Sir Neil Gowanloch, Kt., CBE
Westmacott, Sir Peter John, KCMG
Weston, Sir Michael Charles Swift, KCMG, CVO
Weston, Sir (Philip) John, KCMG
Whalen, Sir Geoffrey Henry, Kt., CBE
Wheeler, Sir Harry Anthony, Kt., OBE
Wheeler, *Rt. Hon.* Sir John Daniel, Kt.
Wheeler, Sir John Frederick, Bt. (1920)
Wheeler, *Gen.* Sir Roger Neil, GCB, CBE
Wheeler-Booth, Sir Michael Addison John, KCB
Wheler, Sir Trevor Woodford, Bt. (1660)
Whitaker, Sir John James Ingham (Jack), Bt. (1936)
Whitchurch, Sir Graeme Ian, Kt., OBE
White, *Prof.* Sir Christopher John, Kt., CVO
White, Sir Christopher Robert Meadows, Bt. (1937)
White, Sir David (David Jason), Kt., OBE
White, Sir David Harry, Kt.
White, *Hon.* Sir Frank John, Kt.
White, Sir George Stanley James, Bt. (1904)

White, *Adm.* Sir Hugo Moresby, GCB, CBE
White, *Hon.* Sir John Charles, Kt., MBE
White, Sir John Woolmer, Bt. (1922)
White, Sir Nicholas Peter Archibald, Bt. (1802)
White, *Adm.* Sir Peter, GBE
White, Sir Willard Wentworth, Kt., CBE
Whitehead, Sir John Stainton, GCMG, CVO
Whitehead, Sir Philip Henry Rathbone, Bt. (1889)
Whiteley, *Gen.* Sir Peter John Frederick, GCB, OBE, RM
Whitfield, Sir William, Kt., CBE
Whitmore, Sir Clive Anthony, GCB, CVO
Whitmore, Sir John Henry Douglas, Bt. (1954)
Whitney, Sir Raymond William, Kt., OBE
Whitson, Sir Keith Roderick, Kt.
Wickerson, Sir John Michael, Kt.
Wicks, Sir Nigel Leonard, GCB, CVO, CBE
†Wigan, Sir Michael Iain, Bt. (1898)
Wiggin, Sir Alfred William (Jerry), Kt., TD
†Wiggin, Sir Charles Rupert John, Bt. (1892)
†Wigram, Sir John Woolmore, Bt. (1805)
Wilbraham, Sir Richard Baker, Bt. (1776)
Wiles, *Prof.* Sir Andrew John, KBE
Wilkes, *Prof.* Sir Maurice Vincent, Kt.
Wilkes, *Gen.* Sir Michael John, KCB, CBE
Wilkie, *Hon.* Sir Alan Fraser, Kt.
Wilkinson, Sir (David) Graham (Brook) Bt. (1941)
Wilkinson, *Prof.* Sir Denys Haigh, Kt., FRS
Willcocks, Sir David Valentine, Kt., CBE, MC
Willcocks, *Lt.-Gen.* Sir Michael Alan, KCB, CVO
Williams, Sir Arthur Dennis Pitt, Kt.
Williams, Sir (Arthur) Gareth Ludovic Emrys Rhys, Bt. (1918)
Williams, *Prof.* Sir Bruce Rodda, KBE
Williams, Sir Charles Othniel, Kt.
Williams, Sir Daniel Charles, GCMG, QC
Williams, *Adm.* Sir David, GCB
Williams, *Prof.* Sir David Glyndwr Tudor, Kt.
Williams, Sir David Innes, Kt.
Williams, Sir David Reeve, Kt., CBE
Williams, *Hon.* Sir Denys Ambrose, KCMG
Williams, Sir Donald Mark, Bt. (1866)
Williams, *Prof.* Sir (Edward) Dillwyn, Kt., FRCP
Williams, Sir Francis Owen Garbett, Kt., CBE
Williams, *Hon.* Sir (John) Griffith, Kt.
Williams, Sir (Lawrence) Hugh, Bt. (1798)
Williams, Sir Osmond, Bt. (1909), MC
Williams, Sir Peter Michael, Kt.
Williams, Sir (Robert) Philip Nathaniel, Bt. (1915)
Williams, Sir Robin Philip, Bt. (1953)
Williams, *Prof.* Sir Roger, Kt.
Williams, Sir (William) Maxwell (Harries), Kt.
Williams, *Hon.* Sir Wyn Lewis
Williams-Bulkeley, Sir Richard Thomas, Bt. (1661)
Williams-Wynn, Sir David Watkin, Bt. (1688)
Williamson, Sir George Malcolm, Kt.
Williamson, *Marshal of the Royal Air Force* Sir Keith Alec, GCB, AFC
Williamson, Sir Robert Brian, Kt., CBE
†Willink, Sir Edward Daniel, Bt. (1957)
Wills, Sir David James Vernon, Bt. (1923)
Wills, Sir David Seton, Bt. (1904)
Wilmot, Sir David, Kt., QPM
Wilmot, Sir Henry Robert, Bt. (1759)
Wilmut, *Prof.* Sir Ian, Kt., OBE
Wilsey, *Gen.* Sir John Finlay Willasey, GCB, CBE
Wilshaw, Sir Michael, Kt.
Wilson, *Prof.* Sir Alan Geoffrey, Kt.
Wilson, Sir Anthony, Kt.
Wilson, *Vice-Adm.* Sir Barry Nigel, KCB
Wilson, Sir David, Bt. (1920)
Wilson, Sir David Mackenzie, Kt.
Wilson, Sir James William Douglas, Bt. (1906)
Wilson, *Brig.* Sir Mathew John Anthony, Bt. (1874), OBE, MC
Wilson, *Rt. Hon.* Sir Nicholas Allan Roy, Kt.
Wilson, Sir Robert Peter, KCMG
Wilson, *Air Chief Marshal* Sir (Ronald) Andrew (Fellowes), KCB, AFC
Wilton, Sir (Arthur) John, KCMG, KCVO, MC
Wingate, *Capt.* Sir Miles Buckley, KCVO
Winkley, Sir David Ross, Kt.
Winnington, Sir Anthony Edward, Bt. (1755)
Winship, Sir Peter James Joseph, Kt., CBE
Winter, *Dr* Sir Gregory Winter, Kt., CBE
Winterton, Sir Nicholas Raymond, Kt.
Wisdom, Sir Norman, Kt., OBE
Wiseman, Sir John William, Bt. (1628)
Wolfendale, *Prof.* Sir Arnold Whittaker, Kt., FRS
Wolseley, Sir Charles Garnet Richard Mark, Bt. (1628)
†Wolseley, Sir James Douglas, Bt. (I. 1745)
†Wombell, Sir George Philip Frederick, Bt. (1778)
Womersley, Sir Peter John Walter, Bt. (1945)
Woo, Sir Leo Joseph, Kt.
Woo, Sir Po-Shing, Kt.
Wood, Sir Andrew Marley, GCMG
Wood, Sir Anthony John Page, Bt. (1837)
Wood, Sir Ian Clark, Kt., CBE
Wood, *Hon.* Sir John Kember, Kt., MC
Wood, Sir Martin Francis, Kt., OBE
Wood, Sir Michael Charles, KCMG
Wood, *Hon.* Sir Roderic Lionel James, Kt.
Wood, Sir William Alan, KCVO, CB
Woodard, *Rear Adm.* Sir Robert Nathaniel, KCVO
Woodcock, Sir John, Kt., CBE, QPM
Woodhead, *Vice-Adm.* Sir (Anthony) Peter, KCB
Woodhouse, *Rt. Hon.* Sir (Arthur) Owen, KBE, DSC
Woodroffe, *Most Revd* George Cuthbert Manning, KBE
Woods, Sir Robert Kynnersley, Kt., CBE
Woodward, *Hon.* Sir (Albert) Edward, Kt., OBE
Woodward, Sir Clive Ronald, Kt., OBE
Woodward, *Adm.* Sir John Forster, GBE, KCB
Woodward, Sir Thomas Jones (Tom Jones), Kt., OBE
Worsley, *Gen.* Sir Richard Edward, GCB, OBE
Worsley, Sir (William) Marcus (John), Bt. (1838)
Worsthorne, Sir Peregrine Gerard, Kt.
Wratten, *Air Chief Marshal* Sir William John, GBE, CB, AFC
Wraxall, Sir Charles Frederick Lascelles, Bt. (1813)
Wrey, Sir George Richard Bourchier, Bt. (1628)
Wrigglesworth, Sir Ian William, Kt.
Wright, Sir Allan Frederick, KBE
Wright, Sir David John, GCMG, LVO
Wright, *Hon.* Sir (John) Michael, Kt.
Wright, Sir (John) Oliver, GCMG, GCVO, DSC
Wright, *Prof.* Sir Nicholas Alcwyn, Kt.
Wright, Sir Peter Robert, Kt., CBE
Wright, *Air Marshal* Sir Robert Alfred, KBE, AFC
Wright, Sir Stephen John Leadbetter, KCMG
Wrightson, Sir Charles Mark Garmondsway, Bt. (1900)
Wrigley, *Prof.* Sir Edward Anthony (Sir Tony), Kt., PHD, PBA
Wrixon-Becher, Sir John William Michael, Bt. (1831)
Wroughton, Sir Philip Lavallin, KCVO
Wu, Sir Gordon Ying Sheung, KCMG
Yacoub, *Prof.* Sir Magdi Habib, Kt., FRCS

Yaki, Sir Roy, KBE
Yang, *Hon.* Sir Ti Liang, Kt.
Yapp, Sir Stanley Graham, Kt.
Yardley, Sir David Charles Miller, Kt., LLD
Yarrow, Sir Eric Grant, Bt. (1916), MBE
Yocklunn, Sir John (Soong Chung), KCVO
Yoo Foo, Sir (François) Henri, Kt.
Young, Sir Brian Walter Mark, Kt.
Young, Sir Colville Norbert, GCMG, MBE
Young, Sir Dennis Charles, KCMG
Young, *Rt. Hon.* Sir George Samuel Knatchbull, Bt. (1813)
Young, Sir Jimmy Leslie Ronald, Kt., CBE
Young, Sir John Kenyon Roe, Bt. (1821)
Young, Sir John Robertson, GCMG
Young, Sir Leslie Clarence, Kt., CBE
Young, Sir Nicholas Charles, Kt.
Young, Sir Robin Urquhart, KCB
Young, Sir Roger William, Kt.
Young, Sir Stephen Stewart Templeton, Bt. (1945)
Young, Sir William Neil, Bt. (1769)
Younger, Sir Julian William Richard, Bt. (1911)
Yuwi, Sir Matiabe, KBE
Zeeman, *Prof.* Sir (Erik) Christopher, Kt., FRS
Zissman, Sir Bernard Philip, Kt.
Zochonis, Sir John Basil, Kt.
Zunz, Sir Gerhard Jacob (Jack), Kt., FRENG
Zurenuoc, Sir Zibang, KBE

BARONETESS

Maxwell Macdonald (formerly Stirling-Maxwell), Dame Ann, Btss. (NS 1682)

THE ORDER OF ST JOHN

THE MOST VENERABLE ORDER OF THE HOSPITAL OF ST JOHN OF JERUSALEM (1888)

GCStJ	Bailiff/Dame Grand Cross
KStJ	Knight of Justice/Grace
DStJ	Dame of Justice/Grace
CStJ	Commander
OstJ	Officer
SBStJ	Serving Brother
SSStJ	Serving Sister

Motto, Pro Fide, Pro Utilitate Hominum

The Order of St John, founded in the early 12th century in Jerusalem, was a religious order with a particular duty to care for the sick. In Britain the order was dissolved by Henry VIII in 1540 but the British branch was revived in the early 19th century. The branch was not accepted by the Grand Magistracy of the Order in Rome but its search for a role in the tradition of the hospitallers led to the founding of the St John Ambulance Association in 1877 and later the St John Ambulance Brigade; in 1882 the St John Ophthalmic Hospital was founded in Jerusalem. A royal charter was granted in 1888 establishing the Order of St John as a British Order of Chivalry with the sovereign as its head.

Since October 1999 the whole order worldwide has been governed by a Grand Council which includes a representative from each of the eight priories (England, Scotland, Wales, South Africa, New Zealand, Canada, Australia and the USA). In addition there are also two commanderies in Northern Ireland and Western Australia. There are also branches in about 30 other Commonwealth countries. Apart from the St John Ambulance Foundation, the Order is also responsible for the Jerusalem Eye Hospital. Admission to the order is usually conferred in recognition of service to either one of these institutions. Membership does not confer any rank, style, title or precedence on a recipient.

SOVEREIGN HEAD OF THE ORDER
HM The Queen

GRAND PRIOR
HRH The Duke of Gloucester, KG, GCVO

Lord Prior, Prof. Anthony Mellows, OBE, TD
Prelate, Rt. Revd John Nicholls
Deputy Lord Prior, Capt. Sir Norman Lloyd-Edwards, KCVO, RD, RNR
Sub Prior, Prof. Villis Marshall, AC
Secretary General, Rear-Adm. Andrew Gough, CB
Headquarters, 3 Charterhouse Mews, London EC1M 6BB
T 020-7251 3292

DAMES

DAMES GRAND CROSS AND DAMES COMMANDERS

Style, 'Dame' before forename and surname, followed by appropriate post-nominal initials. Where such an award is made to a lady already in possession of a higher title, the appropriate initials follow her name
Envelope, Dame F_ S_, followed by appropriate post-nominal letters. *Letter (formal),* Dear Madam; *(social),* Dear Dame F_. *Spoken,* Dame F_
Husband, Untitled

Dame Grand Cross and Dame Commander are the higher classes for women of the Order of the Bath, the Order of St Michael and St George, the Royal Victorian Order, and the Order of the British Empire. Dames Grand Cross rank after the wives of Baronets and before the wives of Knights Grand Cross. Dames Commanders rank after the wives of Knights Grand Cross and before the wives of Knights Commanders.

Honorary Dames Commanders may be conferred on women who are citizens of countries of which the Queen is not head of state.

LIST OF DAMES
As at 31 August 2009

Women peers in their own right and life peers are not included in this list. Female members of the royal family are not included in this list; details of the orders they hold can be found within the Royal Family section.

If a dame has a double barrelled or hyphenated surname, she is listed under the first element of the name. *A full entry in italic type* indicates that the recipient of an honour died during the year in which the honour was conferred. The name is included for the purposes of record.

Abaijah, Dame Josephine, DBE
Abramsky, Dame Jennifer Gita, DBE
Airlie, The Countess of, DCVO
Albemarle, The Countess of, DBE
Allen, *Prof.* Dame Ingrid Victoria, DBE
Andrews, Dame Julie, DBE
Anglesey, The Marchioness of, DBE
Anson, Lady (Elizabeth Audrey), DBE
Anstee, Dame Margaret Joan, DCMG
Arden, *Rt. Hon.* Dame Mary Howarth (Mrs Mance), DBE
Atkins, Dame Eileen, DBE
Bainbridge, Dame Beryl, DBE
Baker, Dame Janet Abbott (Mrs Shelley), CH, DBE
Bakewell, Dame Joan Dawson, DBE
Barbour, Dame Margaret (Mrs Ash), DBE
Baron, *Hon.* Dame Florence Jacqueline, DBE
Barrow, Dame Jocelyn Anita (Mrs Downer), DBE
Barstow, Dame Josephine Clare (Mrs Anderson), DBE
Bassey, Dame Shirley, DBE
Beasley, *Prof.* Dame Christine Joan, DBE
Beaurepaire, Dame Beryl Edith, DBE
Beer, *Prof.* Dame Gillian Patricia Kempster, DBE, FBA
Bergquist, *Prof.* Dame Patricia Rose, DBE
Bevan, Dame Yasmin, DBE
Bewley, Dame Beulah Rosemary, DBE
Bibby, Dame Enid, DBE
Black, *Prof.* Dame Carol Mary, DBE
Black, *Hon.* Dame Jill Margaret, DBE
Blackadder, Dame Elizabeth Violet, DBE
Blaize, Dame Venetia Ursula, DBE
Blaxland, Dame Helen Frances, DBE
Blume, Dame Hilary Sharon Braverman, DBE
Booth, *Hon.* Dame Margaret Myfanwy Wood, DBE
Bowtell, Dame Ann Elizabeth, DCB
Boyd, Dame Vivienne Myra, DBE
Brain, Dame Margaret Anne (Mrs Wheeler), DBE
Brennan, Dame Maureen, DBE
Bridges, Dame Mary Patricia, DBE
Brindley, Dame Lynne Janie, DBE
Brittan, Dame Diana (Lady Brittan of Spennithorne), DBE
Browne, Lady Moyra Blanche Madeleine, DBE
Buckland, Dame Yvonne Helen Elaine, DBE
Burnell, *Prof.* Dame Susan Jocelyn Bell, DBE
Burslem, Dame Alexandra Vivien, DBE
Byatt, Dame Antonia Susan, DBE, FRSL
Bynoe, Dame Hilda Louisa, DBE
Caldicott, Dame Fiona, DBE, FRCP, FRCPSYCH
Cameron, *Prof.* Dame Averil Millicent, DBE
Campbell-Preston, Dame Frances Olivia, DCVO
Cartwright, Dame Silvia Rose, DBE
Clark, *Prof.* Dame Jill MacLeod, DBE
Clark, *Prof.* Dame (Margaret) June, DBE, PHD
Clayton, Dame Barbara Evelyn (Mrs Klyne), DBE
Cleverdon, Dame Julia Charity, DCVO, CBE
Collarbone, Dame Patricia, DBE
Contreras, *Prof.* Dame Marcela, DBE
Corsar, *Hon.* Dame Mary Drummond, DBE
Coward, Dame Pamela Sarah, DBE
Cox, *Hon.* Dame Laura Mary, DBE
Davies, *Prof.* Dame Kay Elizabeth, DBE
Davies, *Prof.* Dame Sally Claire, DBE
Davies, Dame Wendy Patricia, DBE
Davis, Dame Karlene Cecile, DBE
Dawson, *Prof.* Dame Sandra Jane Noble, DBE
Dell, Dame Miriam Patricia, DBE
Dench, Dame Judith Olivia (Mrs Williams), CH, DBE
Descartes, Dame Marie Selipha Sesenne, DBE, BEM
Devonshire, The Duchess of, DCVO
Digby, Lady, DBE
Dobbs, *Hon.* Dame Linda Penelope, DBE
Docherty, Dame Jacqueline, DBE
Dowling, *Prof.* Dame Ann Patricia, DBE
Duffield, Dame Vivien Louise, DBE
Dumont, Dame Ivy Leona, DCMG
Dunnell, Dame Karen, DCB
Dyche, Dame Rachael Mary, DBE
Elcoat, Dame Catherine Elizabeth, DBE
Ellison, Dame Jill, DBE
Else, Dame Jean, DBE
Engel, Dame Pauline Frances (Sister Pauline Engel), DBE
Esteve-Coll, Dame Elizabeth Anne Loosemore, DBE
Evans, Dame Anne Elizabeth Jane, DBE
Evans, Dame Madeline Glynne Dervel, DBE, CMG

Evison, Dame Helen June Patricia, DBE
Fenner, Dame Peggy Edith, DBE
Fielding, Dame Pauline, DBE
Finch, *Prof.* Dame Janet Valerie, DBE
Forgan, Dame Elizabeth Anne Lucy, DBE
Furse, Dame Clara Hedwig Frances, DBE
Fradd, Dame Elizabeth, DBE
Fraser, Dame Dorothy Rita, DBE
Friend, Dame Phyllis Muriel, DBE
Fry, Dame Margaret Louise, DBE
Gallagher, Dame Monica Josephine, DBE
Ghosh, Dame Helen Frances, DCB
Glen-Haig, Dame Mary Alison, DBE
Glenn, *Prof.* Dame Hazel Gillian, DBE
Glennie, *Dr* Dame Evelyn Elizabeth Ann, DBE
Gloster, *Hon.* Dame Elisabeth (Lady Popplewell), DBE
Glover, Dame Audrey Frances, DBE, CMG
Goodall, *Dr* Dame (Valerie) Jane, DBE
Goodman, Dame Barbara, DBE
Gordon, Dame Minita Elmira, GCMG, GCVO
Gordon, *Hon.* Dame Pamela Felicity, DBE
Gow, Dame Jane Elizabeth (Mrs Whiteley), DBE
Grafton, The Duchess of, GCVO
Grant, Dame Mavis, DBE
Green, Dame Pauline, DBE
Grey, Dame Beryl Elizabeth (Mrs Svenson), DBE
Grey-Thompson, Dame Tanni Carys Davina, DBE
Griffiths, Dame Anne, DCVO
Grimthorpe, The Lady, DCVO
Guilfoyle, Dame Margaret Georgina Constance, DBE
Guthardt, *Revd Dr* Dame Phyllis Myra, DBE
Hakin, *Dr* Dame Barbara Ann, DBE
Hall, *Prof.* Dame Wendy, DBE
Hallett, *Rt. Hon.* Dame Heather Carol, DBE
Harbison, Dame Joan Irene, DBE
Harper, Dame Elizabeth Margaret Way, DBE
Harris, Lady Pauline, DBE
Hassan, Dame Anna Patricia Lucy, DBE
Hay, Dame Barbara Logan, DCMG, MBE
Hedley-Miller, Dame Mary Elizabeth, DCVO, CB
Henderson, Dame Fiona Douglas, DCVO
Hercus, *Hon.* Dame (Margaret) Ann, DCMG
Higgins, *Prof.* Dame Joan Margaret, DBE
Higgins, *Prof.* Dame Julia Stretton, DBE, FRS
Higgins, *Prof.* Dame Rosalyn, DBE, QC
Hill, *Air Cdre* Dame Felicity Barbara, DBE
Hine, Dame Deirdre Joan, DBE, FRCP
Hodgson, Dame Patricia Anne, DBE
Hogg, *Hon.* Dame Mary Claire (Mrs Koops), DBE
Hollows, Dame Sharon, DBE
Holmes, Dame Kelly, DBE
Holroyd, Lady Margaret, DBE
Holt, Dame Denise Mary, DCMG
Hoodless, Dame Elisabeth Anne, DBE
Hufton, *Prof.* Dame Olwen, DBE
Husband, *Prof.* Dame Janet Elizabeth Siarey, DBE
Hussey, Dame Susan Katharine (Lady Hussey of North Bradley), DCVO
Hutton, Dame Deirdre Mary, DBE
Imison, Dame Tamsyn, DBE
Isaacs, Dame Albertha Madeline, DBE
James, Dame Naomi Christine (Mrs Haythorne), DBE
Jenkins, Dame (Mary) Jennifer (Lady Jenkins of Hillhead), DBE
Johnson, *Prof.* Dame Louise Napier, DBE, FRS
Jonas, Dame Judith Mayhew
Jones, Dame Gwyneth (Mrs Haberfeld-Jones), DBE
Jordan, *Prof.* Dame Carole, DBE
Keegan, Dame Elizabeth Mary, DBE
Keegan, Dame Geraldine Mary Marcella, DBE
Kekedo, Dame Rosalina Violet, DBE
Kelleher, Dame Joan, DBE
Kellett-Bowman, Dame (Mary) Elaine, DBE
Kelly, Dame Barbara Mary, DBE
Kelly, Dame Lorna May Boreland, DBE
Kershaw, Dame Janet Elizabeth Murray (Dame Betty), DBE
Kettlewell, *Comdt.* Dame Marion Mildred, DBE
Kidu, Lady, DBE
King, *Hon.* Dame Eleanor Warwick, DBE
Kinnair, Dame Donna, DBE
Kirby, Dame Carolyn Emma, DBE
Kirby, Dame Georgina Kamiria, DBE
Kramer, *Prof.* Dame Leonie Judith, DBE
Laine, Dame Cleo (Clementine) Dinah (Lady Dankworth), DBE
Lake-Tack, *HE* Dame Louise Agnetha, GCMG
Lamb, Dame Dawn Ruth, DBE
Leather, Dame Susan Catherine, DBE
Leslie, Dame Ann Elizabeth Mary, DBE
Lewis, Dame Edna Leofrida (Lady Lewis), DBE
Lott, Dame Felicity Ann Emwhyla (Mrs Woolf), DBE
Louisy, Dame (Calliopa) Pearlette, GCMG
Lynn, Dame Vera (Mrs Lewis), DBE
MacArthur, Dame Ellen Patricia, DBE
Macdonald, Dame Mary Beaton, DBE
McDonald, Dame Mavis, DCB
Mackinnon, Dame (Una) Patricia, DBE
Macmillan of Ovenden, Katharine, Viscountess, DBE
Macur, *Hon.* Dame Julia Wendy, DBE
Mayhew, Dame Judith, DBE
Major, Dame Malvina Lorraine (Mrs Fleming), DBE
Major, Dame Norma Christina Elizabeth, DBE
Marsh, Dame Mary Elizabeth, DBE
Mason, Dame Monica Margaret, DBE
Mellor, Dame Julie Thérèse Mellor, DBE
Metge, *Dr* Dame (Alice) Joan, DBE
Middleton, Dame Elaine Madoline, DCMG, MBE
Mills, Dame Barbara Jean Lyon, DBE, QC
Mirren, Dame Helen, DBE
Moores, Dame Yvonne, DBE
Morgan, *Dr* Dame Gillian Margaret, DBE
Morrison, *Hon.* Dame Mary Anne, DCVO
Muirhead, Dame Lorna Elizabeth Fox, DBE
Muldoon, Lady Thea Dale, DBE, QSO
Mullally, *Revd* Dame Sarah Elisabeth, DBE
Mumford, Lady Mary Katharine, DCVO
Murdoch, Dame Elisabeth Joy, DBE
Nelson, *Prof.* Dame Janet Laughland, DBE
Neville, Dame Elizabeth, DBE, QPM
Ogilvie, Dame Bridget Margaret, DBE, PHD, DSC
Oliver, Dame Gillian Frances, DBE
Ollerenshaw, Dame Kathleen Mary, DBE, DPHIL
Owers, Dame Anne Elizabeth (Mrs Cook), DBE
Oxenbury, Dame Shirley Anne, DBE
Park, Dame Merle Florence (Mrs Bloch), DBE
Parker, *Hon.* Dame Judith Mary Frances, DBE
Partridge, *Prof.* Dame Linda, DBE
Pauffley, *Hon.* Dame Anna Evelyn Hamilton, DBE
Penhaligon, Dame Annette (Mrs Egerton), DBE
Perkins, Dame Mary Lesley, DBE
Peters, Dame Mary Elizabeth, DBE
Pindling, Lady (Marguerite M.), DCMG
Platt, Dame Denise, DBE
Plowright, Dame Joan Ann, DBE
Polak, *Prof.* Dame Julia Margaret, DBE

Poole, Dame Avril Anne Barker, DBE
Porter, Dame Shirley (Lady Porter), DBE
Powell, Dame Sally Ann Vickers, DBE
Prendergast, Dame Simone Ruth, DBE
Price, Dame Margaret Berenice, DBE
Proudman, *Hon.* Dame Sonia Rosemary Susan, DBE
Pugh, *Dr* Dame Gillian Mary, DBE
Purves, Dame Daphne Helen, DBE
Quinn, Dame Sheila Margaret Imelda, DBE
Rafferty, *Hon.* Dame Anne Judith, DBE
Rawson, *Prof.* Dame Jessica Mary, DBE
Rebuck, Dame Gail Ruth, DBE
Rees, *Prof.* Dame Lesley Howard, DBE
Reeves, Dame Helen May, DBE
Reynolds, Dame Fiona Claire, DBE
Richardson, Dame Mary, DBE
Ridsdale, Dame Victoire Evelyn Patricia (Lady Ridsdale), DBE
Rigg, Dame Diana, DBE
Rimington, Dame Stella, DCB
Ritterman, Dame Janet, DBE
Roberts, Dame Jane Elisabeth, DBE
Robins, Dame Ruth Laura, DBE
Robottom, Dame Marlene, DBE
Roe, Dame Marion Audrey, DBE
Roe, Dame Raigh Edith, DBE
Ronson, Dame Gail, DBE
Rothwell, *Prof.* Dame Nancy Jane, DBE
Rumbold, *Rt. Hon.* Dame Angela Claire Rosemary, DBE
Runciman of Doxford, The Viscountess, DBE
Russell, *Dr* Dame Philippa Margaret, DBE
Salas, Dame Margaret Laurence, DBE
Salmond, *Prof.* Dame Mary Anne, DBE
Savill, Dame Rosalind Joy, DBE
Sawyer, *Hon.* Dame Joan Augusta, DBE
Scardino, Dame Marjorie, DBE
Scott, Dame Catherine Margaret (Mrs Denton), DBE
Seward, Dame Margaret Helen Elizabeth, DBE
Sharp, *Hon.* Dame Victoria Madeleine, DBE
Shedrick, *Dr* Dame Daphne Marjorie, DBE
Shirley, Dame Stephanie, DBE
Shovelton, Dame Helena, DBE
Sibley, Dame Antoinette (Mrs Corbett), DBE
Silver, *Dr* Dame Ruth Muldoon, DBE
Slade, *Hon.* Dame Elizabeth Ann, DBE
Smith, Dame Dela, DBE
Smith, *Rt. Hon.* Dame Janet Hilary (Mrs Mathieson), DBE
Smith, *Hon.* Dame Jennifer Meredith, DBE
Smith, Dame Margaret Natalie (Maggie) (Mrs Cross), DBE
Soames, Lady Mary, KG, DBE
Southgate, *Prof.* Dame Lesley Jill, DBE
Spencer, Dame Rosemary Jane, DCMG
Steel, *Hon.* Dame (Anne) Heather (Mrs Beattie), DBE
Stocking, Dame Barbara Mary, DBE
Strachan, Dame Valerie Patricia Marie, DCB
Strathern, *Prof.* Dame Anne Marilyn, DBE
Street, Dame Susan Ruth, DCB
Stringer, *Prof.* Dame Joan Kathleen, DBE
Sutherland, Dame Joan (Mrs Bonynge), OM, DBE
Sutherland, Dame Veronica Evelyn, DBE, CMG
Swift, *Hon.* Dame Caroline Jane (Mrs Openshaw), DBE, QC
Symmonds, Dame Olga Patricia, DBE
Tanner, *Dr* Dame Mary Elizabeth, DBE
Taylor, Dame Elizabeth, DBE
Taylor, Dame Meg, DBE
Te Kanawa, Dame Kiri Janette, DBE
Thomas, *Prof.* Dame Jean Olwen, DBE
Thomas, Dame Maureen Elizabeth (Lady Thomas), DBE
Tinson, Dame Sue, DBE
Tizard, Dame Catherine Anne, GCMG, GCVO, DBE
Tokiel, Dame Rosa, DBE
Trotter, Dame Janet Olive, DBE
Turner-Warwick, Dame Margaret Elizabeth Harvey, DBE, FRCP, FRCPED
Uchida, Dame Mitsuko, DBE
Uprichard, Dame Mary Elizabeth, DBE
Varley, Dame Joan Fleetwood, DBE
Wagner, Dame Gillian Mary Millicent (Lady Wagner), DBE
Wall, Dame (Alice) Anne, (Mrs Michael Wall), DCVO
Wallis, Dame Sheila Ann, DBE
Warburton, Dame Anne Marion, DCVO, CMG
Waterhouse, Dame Rachel Elizabeth, DBE, PHD
Waterman, *Dr* Dame Fanny, DBE
Webb, *Prof.* Dame Patricia, DBE
Weir, Dame Gillian Constance (Mrs Phelps), DBE
Weller, Dame Rita, DBE
Weston, Dame Margaret Kate, DBE
Westwood, Dame Vivienne Isabel, DBE
Wheldon, Dame Juliet Louise, DCB, QC
Williams, Dame Josephine, DBE
Wilson, Dame Jacqueline, DBE
Wilson-Barnett, *Prof.* Dame Jenifer, DBE
Winstone, Dame Dorothy Gertrude, DBE, CMG
Wong Yick-ming, Dame Rosanna, DBE

DECORATIONS AND MEDALS

PRINCIPAL DECORATIONS AND MEDALS

IN ORDER OF WEAR

VICTORIA CROSS (VC), 1856 (*see* below)
GEORGE CROSS (GC), 1940 (*see* below)

BRITISH ORDERS OF KNIGHTHOOD (*see also* Orders of Chivalry)
Order of the Garter
Order of the Thistle
Order of St Patrick
Order of the Bath
Order of Merit
Order of the Star of India
Order of St Michael and George
Order of the Indian Empire
Order of the Crown of India
Royal Victorian Order (Classes I, II and III)
Order of the British Empire (Classes I, II and III)
Order of the Companions of Honour
Distinguished Service Order
Royal Victorian Order (Class IV)
Order of the British Empire (Class IV)
Imperial Service Order
Royal Victorian Order (Class V)
Order of the British Empire (Class V)

BARONET'S BADGE

KNIGHT BACHELOR'S BADGE

INDIAN ORDER OF MERIT (MILITARY)

DECORATIONS
Conspicuous Gallantry Cross (CGC), 1995
Royal Red Cross Class I (RRC), 1883
Distinguished Service Cross (DSC), 1914
Military Cross (MC), December 1914
Distinguished Flying Cross (DFC), 1918
Air Force Cross (AFC), 1918
Royal Red Cross Class II (ARRC)
Order of British India
Kaisar-i-Hind Medal
Order of St John

MEDALS FOR GALLANTRY AND DISTINGUISHED CONDUCT
Union of South Africa Queen's Medal for Bravery, in Gold
Distinguished Conduct Medal (DCM), 1854
Conspicuous Gallantry Medal (CGM), 1874
Conspicuous Gallantry Medal (Flying)
George Medal (GM), 1940
Queen's Police Medal for Gallantry
Queen's Fire Service Medal for Gallantry
Royal West African Frontier Force Distinguished Conduct Medal
King's African Rifles Distinguished Conduct Medal
Indian Distinguished Service Medal
Union of South Africa Queen's Medal for Bravery, in Silver
Distinguished Service Medal (DSM), 1914
Military Medal (MM), 1916
Distinguished Flying Medal (DFM), 1918
Air Force Medal (AFM)
Constabulary Medal (Ireland)
Medal for Saving Life at Sea (Sea Gallantry Medal)
Indian Order of Merit (Civil)
Indian Police Medal for Gallantry
Ceylon Police Medal for Gallantry
Sierra Leone Police Medal for Gallantry
Sierra Leone Fire Brigades Medal for Gallantry
Colonial Police Medal for Gallantry (CPM)
Queen's Gallantry Medal (QGM), 1974
Royal Victorian Medal (RVM), Gold, Silver and Bronze
British Empire Medal (BEM)
Canada Medal
Queen's Police Medal for Distinguished Service (QPM)
Queen's Fire Service Medal for Distinguished Service (QFSM)
Queen's Volunteer Reserves Medal
Queen's Medal for Chiefs

CAMPAIGN MEDALS AND STARS
Including authorised United Nations, European Community/Union and North Atlantic Treaty Organisation medals (in order of date of campaign for which awarded)

POLAR MEDALS (in order of date)

IMPERIAL SERVICE MEDAL

POLICE MEDALS FOR VALUABLE SERVICE
Indian Police Medal for Meritorious Service
Ceylon Police Medal for Merit
Sierra Leone Police Medal for Meritorious Service
Sierra Leone Fire Brigades Medal for Meritorious Service
Colonial Police Medal for Meritorious Service

BADGE OF HONOUR

JUBILEE, CORONATION AND DURBAR MEDALS
Queen Victoria, King Edward VII, King George V, King George VI, Queen Elizabeth II, Visit Commemoration and Long and Faithful Service Medals

EFFICIENCY AND LONG SERVICE DECORATIONS AND MEDALS
Medal for Meritorious Service
Accumulated Campaign Service Medal
Medal for Long Service and Good Conduct (Military)
Naval Long Service and Good Conduct Medal
Medal for Meritorious Service (Royal Navy 1918–28)
Indian Long Service and Good Conduct Medal
Indian Meritorious Service Medal
Royal Marines Meritorious Service Medal (1849–1947)
Royal Air Force Meritorious Service Medal (1918–1928)
Royal Air Force Long Service and Good Conduct Medal
Medal for Long Service and Good Conduct (Ulster Defence Regiment)
Indian Long Service and Good Conduct Medal
Royal West African Frontier Force Long Service and Good Conduct Medal

AN

Almanack

For the Year of Our Lord

2010

ESTABLISHED 1868

BY

JOSEPH WHITAKER, FSA

CONTAINING AN ACCOUNT OF THE

ASTRONOMICAL AND OTHER PHENOMENA

AND

A vast Amount of INFORMATION respecting the GOVERNMENT, FINANCES, POPULATION, COMMERCE, and GENERAL STATISTICS of the various Nations of the WORLD with an INDEX containing nearly 7,500 References

LONDON

OFFICE: 36 SOHO SQUARE

LONDON W1D 3QY

The traditional design of the title page for Whitaker's Almanack which has appeared in each edition since 1868

WHITAKER'S CONCISE ALMANACK
2010

A & C Black Publishers Ltd
36 Soho Square, London W1D 3QY

Whitaker's Almanack published annually since 1868

STANDARD EDITION
Cloth covers
978–1–4081–1364–6

CONCISE EDITION
Paperback
978–1–4081–1361–5

NORTH AMERICAN EDITION
Hardback
978–1–4144–7523–3/1–4144–7523–3
Gale, Cengage Learning

JACKET PHOTOGRAPHS
1. Riot police clash with protesters during an anti-G20 demonstration near the Bank of England in London, 1 April 2009. © Ben Stansall/AFP/Getty Images
2. A broker reacts at the Frankfurt Stock Exchange in September 2008. © Daniel Roland/AP/Press Association Images
3. Michael Jackson performs in Los Angeles, November 1988. © Ron Wolfson/Landov/Press Association Images
4. British number one tennis player Andy Murray during a 2009 Wimbledon Championships match against Spain's Juan Carlos Ferrero. © EMPICS Sport
5. A mass rally in Tehran's Azadi Square by supporters of opposition Iranian presidential candidate Mir Hossein Mousavi, protesting against the election result, in June 2009. © Ben Curtis/AP/Press Association Images
6. The 47 million-year-old *Darwinius masillae* (or 'Ida') fossil, which some believe to be our earliest ancestor. © University of Oslo/PA Wire/Press Association Images
7. Prime Minister Gordon Brown during a visit to Sherburn in Elmet, North Yorkshire, as part of a regional tour in July 2009. © John Giles/PA Wire/Press Association Images

Typeset in the UK by RefineCatch Ltd, Bungay, Suffolk NR35 1EF

Printed in the UK by CPI William Clowes, Beccles, Suffolk NR34 7TL

Whitaker's Almanack was compiled with the assistance of: Christian Research; Press Asssociation and the UK Hydrographic Office.

This book is produced using paper that is made from wood grown in managed, sustainable forests. It is natural, renewable and recyclable. The logging and manufacturing processes conform to the environmental regulations of the country of origin.

A CIP catalogue record for this book is available from the British Library.

EDITORIAL STAFF
Publisher (Yearbooks) and Editor-in-Chief: Claire Fogg
Deputy Editor: Ruth Northey
UK Project Editor: Clare Slaven
Editorial Assistants: Ruth Craven (UK), Ross Fulton (International)

CONTRIBUTORS (where not listed)
Gordon Taylor (Astronomy); Elizabeth Holmes (Education); Karen Harries-Rees (Environment); V. P. Kanitkar (Hindu Calendar); Clive Longhurst (Insurance); Duncan Murray, Chris Priestley (Legal Notes) and Jill Papworth (Taxation)

WHITAKER'S CONCISE ALMANACK

2010

A & C BLACK

LONDON

Royal Sierra Leone Military Forces Long Service and Good Conduct Medal
King's African Rifles and Long Service and Good Conduct Medal
Indian Meritorious Service Medal
Police Long Service and Good Conduct Medal
Fire Brigade Long Service and Good Conduct Medal
African Police Medal for Meritorious Service
Royal Canadian Mounted Police Long Service Medal
Ceylon Police Long Service Medal
Ceylon Fire Services Long Service Medal
Sierra Leone Police Long Service Medal
Colonial Police Long Service Medal
Sierra Leone Fire Brigades Long Service Medal
Mauritius Police Long Service and Good Conduct Medal
Mauritius Fire Services Long Service and Good Conduct Medal
Mauritius Prisons Service Long Service and Good Conduct Medal
Colonial Fire Brigades Long Service Medal
Colonial Prison Service Medal
Hong Kong Disciplined Services Medal
Army Emergency Reserve Decoration (ERD)
Volunteer Officers' Decoration (VD)
Volunteer Long Service Medal
Volunteer Officers' Decoration (for India and the Colonies)
Volunteer Long Service Medal (for India and the Colonies)
Colonial Auxiliary Forces Officers' Decoration
Colonial Auxiliary Forces Long Service Medal
Medal for Good Shooting (Naval)
Militia Long Service Medal
Imperial Yeomanry Long Service Medal
Territorial Decoration (TD), 1908
Ceylon Armed Services Long Service Medal
Efficiency Decoration (ED)
Territorial Efficiency Medal
Efficiency Medal
Special Reserve Long Service and Good Conduct Medal
Decoration for Officers of the Royal Navy Reserve (RD), 1910
Decoration for Officers of the Royal Naval Volunteer Reserve (VRD)
Royal Naval Reserve Long Service and Good Conduct Medal
Royal Naval Volunteer Reserve Long Service and Good Conduct Medal
Royal Naval Auxiliary Sick Berth Reserve Long Service and Good Conduct Medal
Royal Fleet Reserve Long Service and Good Conduct Medal
Royal Naval Wireless Auxiliary Reserve Long Service and Good Conduct Medal
Royal Naval Auxiliary Service Medal
Air Efficiency Award (AE), 1942
Volunteer Reserves Service Medal
Ulster Defence Regiment Medal
Northern Ireland Home Service Medal
Queen's Medal (for Champion Shots of the RN and RM)
Queen's Medal (for Champion Shots of the New Zealand Naval Forces)
Queen's Medal (for Champion Shots in the Military Forces)
Queen's Medal (for Champion Shots of the Air Forces)
Cadet Forces Medal, 1950
Coastguard Auxiliary Service Long Service Medal
Special Constabulary Long Service Medal
Canadian Forces Decoration
Royal Observer Corps Medal
Civil Defence Long Service Medal
Ambulance Service (Emergency Duties) Long Service and Good Conduct Medal
Royal Fleet Auxiliary Service Medal Rhodesia Medal
Royal Ulster Constabulary Service Medal
Northern Ireland Prison Service Medal
Union of South Africa Commemoration Medal
Indian Independence Medal
Pakistan Medal
Ceylon Armed Services Inauguration Medal
Ceylon Police Independence Medal (1948)
Sierra Leone Independence Medal
Jamaica Independence Medal
Uganda Independence Medal
Malawi Independence Medal
Fiji Independence Medal
Papua New Guinea Independence Medal
Solomon Islands Independence Medal
Service Medal of the Order of St John
Badge of the Order of the League of Mercy
Voluntary Medical Service Medal (1932)
Women's Royal Voluntary Service Medal
South African Medal for War Services
Colonial Special Constabulary Medal

HONORARY MEMBERSHIP OF COMMONWEALTH ORDERS

OTHER COMMONWEALTH MEMBERS' ORDERS, DECORATIONS AND MEDALS

FOREIGN ORDERS

FOREIGN DECORATIONS

FOREIGN MEDALS

THE VICTORIA CROSS (1856)

FOR CONSPICUOUS BRAVERY

VC

Ribbon, Crimson, for all Services (until 1918 it was blue for the Royal Navy)

Instituted on 29 January 1856, the Victoria Cross was awarded retrospectively to 1854, the first being held by Lt. C. D. Lucas, RN, for bravery in the Baltic Sea on 21 June 1854 (gazetted 24 February 1857). The first 62 crosses were presented by Queen Victoria in Hyde Park, London, on 26 June 1857.

The Victoria Cross is worn before all other decorations, on the left breast, and consists of a cross-pattée of bronze, 3.8cm in diameter, with the royal crown surmounted by a lion in the centre, and beneath there is the inscription *For Valour*. Holders of the VC currently receive a tax-free annuity of £1,500, irrespective of need or other conditions. In 1911, the right to receive the cross was extended to Indian soldiers, and in 1920 to matrons, sisters and nurses, the staff of the nursing services and other services pertaining to hospitals and nursing, and to civilians of either sex regularly or temporarily under the orders, direction or supervision of the naval, military, or air forces of the crown.

SURVIVING RECIPIENTS OF THE VICTORIA CROSS
as at 31 August 2009

Apiata, *Cpl.* B. H. (New Zealand Special Air Service) 2004 *Afghanistan*
Beharry, *Pte.* J. G. (Princess of Wales's Royal Regiment) 2005 *Iraq*
Cruickshank, *Flt. Lt.* J. A. (RAFVR) 1944 *World War*
Donaldson, *Trooper* M. G. S. (Australian Special Air Service) 2008 *Afghanistan*
Lachhiman Gurung, *Havildar* (8th Gurkha Rifles) 1945 *World War*
Payne, *WO* K., DSC (USA) (Australian Army Training Team) 1969 *Vietnam*
Rambahadur Limbu, *Capt.*, MVO (10th Princess Mary's Gurkha Rifles) 1965 *Sarawak*
Speakman-Pitts, *Sgt.* W. (Black Watch, attached KOSB) 1951 *Korea*
Tulbahadur Pun, *Lt.* (6th Gurkha Rifles) 1944 *World War*

THE GEORGE CROSS (1940)
FOR GALLANTRY

GC

Ribbon, Dark blue, threaded through a bar adorned with laurel leaves
Instituted 24 September 1940 (with amendments, 3 November 1942)

The George Cross is worn before all other decorations (except the VC) on the left breast (when worn by a woman it may be worn on the left shoulder from a ribbon of the same width and colour fashioned into a bow). It consists of a plain silver cross with four equal limbs, the cross having in the centre a circular medallion bearing a design showing St George and the Dragon. The inscription *For Gallantry* appears round the medallion and in the angle of each limb of the cross is the royal cypher 'G VI' forming a circle concentric with the medallion. The reverse is plain and bears the name of the recipient and the date of the award. The cross is suspended by a ring from a bar adorned with laurel leaves on dark blue ribbon 3.8cm wide.

The cross is intended primarily for civilians; awards to the fighting services are confined to actions for which purely military honours are not normally granted. It is awarded only for acts of the greatest heroism or of the most conspicuous courage in circumstances of extreme danger. From 1 April 1965, holders of the cross have received a tax-free annuity, which is currently £1,500. The cross has twice been awarded collectively rather than to an individual: to Malta (1942) and the Royal Ulster Constabulary (1999).

In October 1971 all surviving holders of the Albert Medal and the Edward Medal exchanged those decorations for the George Cross.

SURVIVING RECIPIENTS OF THE GEORGE CROSS
as at 31 August 2009

If the recipient originally received the Albert Medal (AM) or the Edward Medal (EM), this is indicated by the initials in parentheses.

Archer, *Col.* B. S. T., GC, OBE, ERD, 1941
Bamford, J., GC, 1952
Beaton, J., GC, CVO, 1974
Butson, *Lt.-Col.* A. R. C., GC, CD, MD (AM), 1948
Croucher, *Lance Cpl.* M., GC, 2008
Finney, *Trooper* C., GC, 2003
Flintoff, H. H., GC (EM), 1944
Gledhill, A. J., GC, 1967
Gregson, J. S., GC (AM), 1943
Johnson, *WO1 (SSM)* B., GC, 1990
Kinne, D. G., GC, 1954
Lowe, A. R., GC (AM), 1949
Norton, *Maj.* P. A., GC, 2006
Pratt, M. K., GC, 1978
Purves, Mrs M., GC (AM), 1949
Raweng, Awang anak, GC, 1951
Stevens, H. W., GC, 1958
Walker, C., GC, 1972
Walker, C. H., GC (AM), 1942
Wooding, E. A., GC (AM), 1945

CHIEFS OF CLANS IN SCOTLAND

Only chiefs of whole Names or Clans are included, except certain special instances (marked *) who, though not chiefs of a whole Name, were or are for some reason (eg the Macdonald forfeiture) independent. Under decision (*Campbell-Gray*, 1950) that a bearer of a 'double or triple-barrelled' surname cannot be held chief of a part of such, several others cannot be included in the list at present.

THE ROYAL HOUSE: HM The Queen

AGNEW: Sir Crispin Agnew of Lochnaw, Bt., QC
ANSTRUTHER: Tobias Anstruther of Anstruther and Balcaskie
ARBUTHNOTT: Viscount of Arbuthnott, KT, CBE, DSC
BANNERMAN: Sir David Bannerman of Elsick, Bt.
BARCLAY: Peter C. Barclay of Towie Barclay and of that Ilk
BORTHWICK: Lord Borthwick
BOYLE: Earl of Glasgow
BRODIE: Alexander Brodie of Brodie
BROUN OF COLSTOUN: Sir Wayne Broun of Colstoun, Bt.
BRUCE: Earl of Elgin and Kincardine, KT
BUCHAN: David Buchan of Auchmacoy
BURNETT: J. C. A. Burnett of Leys
CAMERON: Donald Cameron of Lochiel
CAMPBELL: Duke of Argyll
CARMICHAEL: Richard Carmichael of Carmichael
CARNEGIE: Duke of Fife
CATHCART: Earl Cathcart
CHARTERIS: Earl of Wemyss and March
CLAN CHATTAN: K. Mackintosh of Clan Chattan
CHISHOLM: Hamish Chisholm of Chisholm *(The Chisholm)*
COCHRANE: Earl of Dundonald
COLQUHOUN: Sir Malcolm Rory Colquhoun of Luss, Bt.
CRANSTOUN: David Cranstoun of that Ilk
CUMMING: Sir Alastair Cumming of Altyre, Bt.
DARROCH: Capt. Duncan Darroch of Gourock
DAVIDSON: Alister Davidson of Davidston
DEWAR: Michael Dewar of that Ilk and Vogrie
DRUMMOND: Earl of Perth
DUNBAR: Sir James Dunbar of Mochrum, Bt.
DUNDAS: David Dundas of Dundas
DURIE: Andrew Durie of Durie, CBE
ELIOTT: Mrs Margaret Eliott of Redheugh
ERSKINE: Earl of Mar and Kellie
FARQUHARSON: Capt. A. Farquharson of Invercauld, MC
FERGUSSON: Sir Charles Fergusson of Kilkerran, Bt.
FORBES: Lord Forbes, KBE
FORSYTH: Alistair Forsyth of that Ilk
FRASER: Lady Saltoun
*FRASER (OF LOVAT): Lord Lovat
GAYRE: R. Gayre of Gayre and Nigg
GORDON: Marquess of Huntly
GRAHAM: Duke of Montrose
GRANT: Lord Strathspey
GUTHRIE: Alexander Guthrie of Guthrie
HAIG: Earl Haig, OBE
HALDANE: Martin Haldane of Gleneagles
HANNAY: David Hannay of Kirkdale and of that Ilk
HAY: Earl of Erroll
HENDERSON: Alistair Henderson of Fordell
HUNTER: Pauline Hunter of Hunterston
IRVINE OF DRUM: David Irvine of Drum
JARDINE: Sir William Jardine of Applegirth, Bt.
JOHNSTONE: Earl of Annandale and Hartfell
KEITH: Earl of Kintore
KENNEDY: Marquess of Ailsa
KERR: Marquess of Lothian, PC
KINCAID: Madam Arabella Kincaid of Kincaid
LAMONT: Revd Peter Lamont of that Ilk
LEASK: Jonathan Leask of that Ilk
LENNOX: Edward Lennox of that Ilk
LESLIE: Earl of Rothes
LINDSAY: Earl of Crawford and Balcarres, KT, GCVO, PC
LIVINGSTONE (or MACLEA): Niall Livingstone of the Bachuil
LOCKHART: Angus Lockhart of the Lee
LUMSDEN: Gillem Lumsden of that Ilk and Blanerne
MACALESTER: William St J. McAlester of Loup and Kennox
MACARTHUR; John MacArthur of that Ilk
MCBAIN: J. H. McBain of McBain
MACDONALD: Lord Macdonald *(The Macdonald of Macdonald)*
*MACDONALD OF CLANRANALD: Ranald Macdonald of Clanranald
*MACDONALD OF KEPPOCH: Ranald MacDonald of Keppoch
*MACDONALD OF SLEAT (CLAN HUSTEAIN): Sir Ian Macdonald of Sleat, Bt.
*MACDONELL OF GLENGARRY: Ranald MacDonell of Glengarry
MACDOUGALL: Morag MacDougall of MacDougall
MACDOWALL: Fergus Macdowall of Garthland
MACGREGOR: Sir Malcolm MacGregor of MacGregor, Bt.
MACINTYRE: Donald MacIntyre of Glenoe
MACKAY: Lord Reay
MACKENZIE: Earl of Cromartie
MACKINNON: Anne Mackinnon of Mackinnon
MACKINTOSH: John Mackintosh of Mackintosh *(The Mackintosh of Mackintosh)*
MACLACHLAN: Euan MacLachlan of MacLachlan
MACLAREN: Donald MacLaren of MacLaren and Achleskine
MACLEAN: Hon. Sir Lachlan Maclean of Duart, Bt., CVO
MACLENNAN: Ruaraidh MacLennan of MacLennan
MACLEOD: Hugh MacLeod of MacLeod
MACMILLAN: George MacMillan of MacMillan
MACNAB: J. C. Macnab of Macnab *(The Macnab)*
MACNAGHTEN: Sir Malcolm Macnaghten of Macnaghten and Dundarave, Bt.
MACNEACAIL: John Macneacail of Macneacail and Scorrybreac
MACNEIL OF BARRA: Ian Macneil of Barra *(The Macneil of Barra)*

MACPHERSON: Hon. Sir William Macpherson of Cluny, TD
MACTAVISH: Steven MacTavish of Dunardry
MACTHOMAS: Andrew MacThomas of Finegand
MAITLAND: Earl of Lauderdale
MAKGILL: Viscount of Oxfuird
MALCOLM (MACCALLUM): Robin N. L. Malcolm of Poltalloch
MAR: Countess of Mar
MARJORIBANKS: Andrew Marjoribanks of that Ilk
MATHESON: Maj. Sir Fergus Matheson of Matheson, Bt.
MENZIES: David Menzies of Menzies
MOFFAT: Madam Moffat of that Ilk
MONCREIFFE: Hon. Peregrine Moncreiffe of that Ilk
MONTGOMERIE: Earl of Eglinton and Winton
MORRISON: Dr Iain Morrison of Ruchdi
MUNRO: Hector Munro of Foulis
MURRAY: Duke of Atholl
NESBITT (or NISBET): Mark Nesbitt of that Ilk
OGILVY: Earl of Airlie, KT, GCVO, PC
OLIPHANT: Richard Oliphant of that Ilk
RAMSAY: Earl of Dalhousie
RIDDELL: Sir John Riddell of Riddell, Bt., KCVO
ROBERTSON: Alexander Robertson of Struan *(Struan-Robertson)*
ROLLO: Lord Rollo
ROSE: Miss Elizabeth Rose of Kilravock
ROSS: David Ross of that Ilk and Balnagowan
RUTHVEN: Earl of Gowrie, PC
SCOTT: Duke of Buccleuch and Queensberry, KBE
SCRYMGEOUR: Earl of Dundee
SEMPILL: Lord Sempill
SHAW: John Shaw of Tordarroch
SINCLAIR: Earl of Caithness
SKENE: Danus Skene of Skene
STIRLING: Fraser Stirling of Cader
STRANGE: Maj. Timothy Strange of Balcaskie
SUTHERLAND: Countess of Sutherland
SWINTON: John Swinton of that Ilk
TROTTER: Alexander Trotter of Mortonhall
URQUHART: Kenneth Urquhart of Urquhart
WALLACE: Ian Wallace of that Ilk
WEDDERBURN: Master of Dundee
WEMYSS: Michael Wemyss of that Ilk

THE PRIVY COUNCIL

The sovereign in council, or Privy Council, was the chief source of executive power until the system of cabinet government developed in the 18th century. Now the Privy Council's main functions are to advise the sovereign and to exercise its own statutory responsibilities independent of the sovereign in council.

Membership of the Privy Council is automatic upon appointment to certain government and judicial positions in the UK, eg cabinet ministers must be Privy Counsellors and are sworn in on first assuming office. Membership is also accorded by the Queen to eminent people in the UK and independent countries of the Commonwealth of which she is Queen, on the recommendation of the prime minister. Membership of the council is retained for life, except for very occasional removals.

The administrative functions of the Privy Council are carried out by the Privy Council Office under the direction of the president of the council, who is always a member of the cabinet. (*See also* Parliament)
President of the Council, Rt. Hon. Lord Mandelson

Clerk of the Council, Judith Simpson
Style The Right (or Rt.) Hon._
*Envelope, The Right (or Rt.) Hon. F_ S_*
*Letter, Dear Mr/Miss/Mrs S_*
*Spoken, Mr/Miss/Mrs S_*
It is incorrect to use the letters PC after the name in conjunction with the prefix The Rt. Hon., unless the Privy Counsellor is a peer below the rank of Marquess and so is styled The Rt. Hon. because of his/her rank.

MEMBERS *as at August 2009*

HRH The Duke of Edinburgh, 1951
HRH The Prince of Wales, 1977

Abernethy, *Hon.* Lord (Alastair Cameron), 2005
Adonis, Lord, 2009
Aikens, Sir Richard, 2008
Ainsworth, Robert, 2005
Airlie, Earl of, 1984
Aldous, Sir William, 1995
Alebua, Ezekiel, 1988
Alexander, Douglas, 2005
Amos, Baroness, 2003
Ampthill, Lord, 1995
Ancram, Michael, 1996
Anderson of Swansea, Lord, 2000
Anelay of St Johns, Baroness, 2009
Angiolini, Elish, 2006
Anthony, Douglas, 1971
Arbuthnot, James, 1998
Archer of Sandwell, Lord, 1977
Arden, Dame Mary, 2000
Armstrong, Hilary, 1999
Arthur, *Hon.* Owen, 1995
Ashdown of Norton-sub-Hamdon, Lord, 1989
Ashley of Stoke, Lord, 1979
Ashton of Upholland, Baroness, 2006
Atkins, Sir Robert, 1995
Auld, Sir Robin, 1995
Baker, Sir Thomas, 2002
Baker of Dorking, Lord, 1984
Balls, Ed, 2007
Barnett, Lord, 1975
Barron, Kevin, 2001
Bassam of Brighton, Lord, 2009
Battle, John, 2002
Beckett, Margaret, 1993
Beith, Sir Alan, 1992
Beldam, Sir Roy, 1989
Benn, Anthony, 1964
Benn, Hilary, 2003
Bercow, John, 2009
Bingham of Cornhill, Lord, 1986
Birch, William, 1992
Bisson, Sir Gordon, 1987
Blackstone, Baroness, 2001
Blair, Anthony, 1994
Blanchard, Peter, 1998
Blears, Hazel, 2005
Blunkett, David, 1997
Boateng, Paul, 1999
Bolger, James, 1991
Booth, Albert, 1976
Boothroyd, Baroness, 1992
Boscawen, *Hon.* Robert, 1992
Bottomley of Nettlestone, Baroness, 1992
Boyd of Duncansby, Lord, 2000
Boyson, Sir Rhodes, 1987
Bradley, Lord, 2001
Bradshaw, Ben, 2009
Brathwaite, Sir Nicholas, 1991
Brittan of Spennithorne, Lord, 1981
Brooke, Sir Henry, 1996
Brooke of Sutton Mandeville, Lord, 1988
Brown, Gordon, 1996
Brown, Nicholas, 1997
Brown, Sir Stephen, 1983
Brown of Eaton-under-Heywood, Lord, 1992
Browne, Desmond, 2005
Browne-Wilkinson, Lord, 1983
Bruce, Malcolm, 2006
Burnham, Andy, 2007
Burnton, Sir Stanley, 2008
Butler of Brockwell, Lord, 2004
Butler-Sloss, Baroness, 1988
Buxton, Sir Richard, 1997
Byers, Stephen, 1998
Byrne, Liam, 2008
Byron, Sir Dennis, 2004
Caborn, Richard, 1999
Caithness, Earl of, 1990
Cameron, David, 2005
Cameron of Lochbroom, Lord, 1984
Camoys, Lord, 1997
Campbell, Sir Walter Menzies, 1999
Campbell, Sir William, 1999
Canterbury, Archbishop of, 2002
Carey of Clifton, Lord, 1991
Carloway, *Hon.* Lord (Colin Sutherland), 2008
Carnwath, Sir Robert, 2002
Carr of Hadley, Lord, 1963
Carrington, Lord, 1959
Carswell, Lord, 1993
Casey, Sir Maurice, 1986
Chadwick, Sir John, 1997
Chalfont, Lord, 1964
Chalker of Wallasey, Baroness, 1987
Chan, Sir Julius, 1981
Chataway, Sir Christopher, 1970
Chilcot, Sir John, 2004
Christie, Perry, 2004
Clark of Windermere, Lord, 1997
Clark, Helen, 1990
Clarke, Charles, 2001
Clarke, Kenneth, 1984
Clarke, *Hon.* Lord (Matthew Clarke), 2008
Clarke, Thomas, 1997
Clarke of Stone-Cum-Ebony, Lord, 1998
Clegg, Nicholas, 2008
Clinton-Davis, Lord, 1998
Clwyd, Ann, 2004
Coghlin, Sir Patrick, 2009
Collins of Mapesbury, Lord, 2007
Cooper, Yvette, 2007
Cope of Berkeley, Lord, 1988
Corston, Baroness, 2003
Cosgrove, *Hon.* Lady (Hazel Cosgrove), 2003
Coulsfield, *Hon.* Lord (John Coulsfield), 2000
Cowen, Sir Zelman, 1981
Cradock, Sir Percy, 1993
Crawford and Balcarres, Earl of, 1972
Creech, *Hon.* Wyatt, 1999
Crickhowell, Lord, 1979
Cullen of Whitekirk, Lord, 1997
Cunningham of Felling, Lord, 1993
Curry, David, 1996
Darling, Alistair, 1997
Darzi of Denham, Lord, 2009
Davies, Denzil, 1978
Davies, Ronald, 1997
Davies of Oldham, Lord, 2006
Davis, David, 1997
Davis, Terence, 1999
Davison, Sir Ronald, 1978
de la Bastide, Michael, 2004
Dean of Thornton-le-Fylde, Baroness, 1998
Denham, John, 2000
Denham, Lord, 1981
Dixon, Lord, 1996
Dobson, Frank, 1997
Donaldson, Jeffrey, 2007
Dorrell, Stephen, 1994
Drayson, Lord, 2008
D'Souza, Baroness, 2009
du Cann, Sir Edward, 1964
Duncan Smith, Iain, 2001
Dunn, Sir Robin, 1980
Dyson, Sir John, 2001
Eassie, *Hon.* Lord (Ronald Mackay), 2006

East, Paul, 1998
Eden of Winton, Lord, 1972
Edward, Sir David, 2005
Eggar, Timothy, 1995
Eichelbaum, Sir Thomas, 1989
Elias, Sir Patrick, 2009
Elias, *Hon.* Dame, Sian, 1999
Elis-Thomas, Lord, 2004
Esquivel, Manuel, 1986
Etherton, Sir Terence, 2008
Evans, Sir Anthony, 1992
Eveleigh, Sir Edward, 1977
Falconer of Thoroton, Lord, 2003
Farquharson, Sir Donald, 1989
Fellowes, Lord, 1990
Ferrers, Earl, 1982
Field, Frank, 1997
Flint, Caroline, 2008
Floissac, Sir Vincent, 1992
Foot, Michael, 1974
Forsyth of Drumlean, Lord, 1995
Foster of Bishop Auckland, Lord, 1993
Foulkes of Cumnock, Lord, 2002
Fowler, Lord, 1979
Fraser, Malcolm, 1976
Fraser of Carmyllie, Lord, 1989
Freedman, Sir Lawrence, 2009
Freeman, John, 1966
Freeman, Lord, 1993
Gage, Sir William, 2004
Garel-Jones, Lord, 1992
Gault, Thomas, 1992
Geidt, Christopher, 2007
George, Bruce, 2000
Gibson, Sir Peter, 1993
Gilbert, Lord, 1978
Gilbert, Sir Martin, 2009
Gill, *Hon.* Lord (Brian Gill), 2002
Girvan, Sir (Frederick) Paul, 2007
Glenamara, Lord, 1964
Glidewell, Sir Iain, 1985
Goff of Chieveley, Lord, 1982
Goggins, Paul, 2009
Goldring, Sir John, 2008
Goldsmith, Lord, 2002
Goodlad, Lord, 1992
Gowrie, Earl of, 1984
Graham, Sir Douglas, 1998
Graham of Edmonton, Lord, 1998
Griffiths, Lord, 1980
Grocott, Lord, 2002
Gummer, John, 1985
Habgood, Rt. Revd Lord, 1983
Hague, William, 1995
Hain, Peter, 2001
Hale of Richmond, Baroness, 1999
Hallett, Dame Heather, 2005
Hamilton, *Hon.* Lord (Arthur Hamilton), 2002
Hamilton of Epsom, Lord, 1991
Hanley, Sir Jeremy, 1994
Hanson, David, 2007
Hardie, Lord, 1997
Hardie Boys, Sir Michael, 1989
Harman, Harriet, 1997
Harrison, Walter, 1977
Haselhurst, Sir Alan, 1999
Hattersley, Lord, 1975
Hayhoe, Lord, 1985
Hayman, Baroness, 2000
Healey, John, 2008
Healey, Lord, 1964
Heathcoat-Amory, David, 1996
Henry, Sir Denis, 1993
Henry, John, 1996
Heseltine, Lord, 1979
Heseltine, Sir William, 1986
Hesketh, Lord, 1991
Hewitt, Patricia, 2001
Higgins, Lord, 1979
Higgins, Sir Malachy, 2007
Hill, Keith, 2003
Hirst, Sir David, 1992
Hodge, Margaret, 2003
Hoffmann, Lord, 1992
Hogg, *Hon.* Douglas, 1992
Hollis of Heigham, Baroness, 1999
Hoon, Geoffrey, 1999
Hooper, Sir Anthony, 2004
Hope of Craighead, Lord, 1989
Hope of Thornes, Lord, 1991
Hordern, Sir Peter, 1993
Howard, Michael, 1990
Howarth, George, 2005
Howarth of Newport, Lord, 2000
Howe of Aberavon, Lord, 1972
Howell of Guildford, Lord, 1979
Howells, Kim, 2009
Hughes, Sir Anthony, 2006
Hughes, Beverley, 2004
Hunt, Jonathon, 1989
Hunt of Kings Heath, Lord, 2009
Hunt of Wirral, Lord, 1990
Hurd of Westwell, Lord, 1982
Hutchison, Sir Michael, 1995
Hutton, Lord, 1988
Hutton, John, 2001
Inge, Lord, 2004
Ingraham, Hubert, 1993
Ingram, Adam, 1999
Irvine of Lairg, Lord, 1997
Jack, Michael, 1997
Jacob, Sir Robert, 2004
Jacobs, Francis, 2005
Janvrin, Lord, 1998
Jay of Paddington, Baroness, 1998
Jenkin of Roding, Lord, 1973
Johnson, Alan, 2003
Johnson Smith, Sir Geoffrey, 1996
Jones, Lord, 1999
Jopling, Lord, 1979
Jowell, Tessa, 1998
Judge, Lord, 1996
Jugnauth, Sir Anerood, 1987
Kaufman, Sir Gerald, 1978
Kay, Sir Maurice, 2004
Keene, Sir David, 2000
Keith, Sir Kenneth, 1998
Kelly, Ruth, 2004
Kenilorea, Sir Peter, 1979
Kennedy, Charles, 1999
Kennedy, Jane, 2003
Kennedy, Sir Paul, 1992
Kerr of Tonaghmore, Lord, 2004
Khan, Sadiq, 2009
King of Bridgwater, Lord, 1979
Kingarth, *Hon.* Lord (Derek Emslie), 2006
Kingsdown, Lord, 1987
Kinnock, Lord, 1983
Kirkwood, *Hon.* Lord (Ian Kirkwood), 2000
Knight, Gregory, 1995
Knight, James, 2008
Lammy, David, 2008
Lamont of Lerwick, Lord, 1986
Lang of Monkton, Lord, 1990
Latasi, Sir Kamuta, 1996
Latham, Sir David, 2000
Lauti, Sir Toaripi, 1979
Laws, Sir John, 1999
Lawson of Blaby, Lord, 1981
Leggatt, Sir Andrew, 1990
Leonard, Rt. Revd Graham, 1981
Letwin, Oliver, 2002
Leveson, Sir Brian, 2006
Liddell, Helen, 1998
Lilley, Peter, 1990
Lloyd of Berwick, Lord, 1984
Lloyd, Sir Peter, 1994
Lloyd, Sir Timothy, 2005
London, Bishop of, 1995
Longmore, Sir Andrew, 2001
Louisy, Sir Allan, 1981
Luce, Lord, 1986
Lyell of Markyate, Lord, 1990
Lyne, Sir Roderic, 2009
McAvoy, Thomas, 2003
McCartney, Ian, 1999
McCollum, Sir Liam, 1997
McConnell, Jack, 2001
MacDermott, Sir John, 1987
Macdonald of Tradeston, Lord, 1999
McFadden, Patrick, 2008
McFall, John, 2004
MacGregor of Pulham Market, Lord, 1985
McGuire, Anne, 2008
McIntosh of Haringey, Lord, 2002
Mackay, Andrew, 1998
McKay, Sir Ian, 1992
Mackay of Clashfern, Lord, 1979
Mackay of Drumadoon, Lord, 1996
McKinnon, Sir Donald, 1992
Maclean, David, 1995
Maclean, *Hon.* Lord (Ranald MacLean), 2001
McLeish, Henry, 2000
Maclennan of Rogart, Lord, 1997
McLoughlin, Patrick, 2005
McMullin, Sir Duncan, 1980
McNally, Lord, 2005
McNulty, Anthony, 2007
MacShane, Denis, 2005
Major, Sir John, 1987
Malloch-Brown, Lord, 2007
Mance, Lord, 1999
Mandelson, Lord, 1998
Mantell, Sir Charles, 1997
Marnoch, *Hon.* Lord (Michael Marnoch), 2001
Marsh, Lord, 1966
Martin of Springburn, Lord, 2000
Mason of Barnsley, Lord, 1968
Mates, Michael, 2004
Maude, *Hon.* Francis, 1992
Mawhinney, Lord, 1994
May, Sir Anthony, 1998
May, Theresa, 2003
Mayhew of Twysden, Lord, 1986
Meacher, Michael, 1997
Mellor, David, 1990
Michael, Alun, 1998
Milburn, Alan, 1998
Miliband, David, 2005
Miliband, Ed, 2007
Millan, Bruce, 1975
Millett, Lord, 1994
Mitchell, Sir James, 1985
Mitchell, Dr Keith, 2004
Molyneaux of Killead, Lord, 1983
Moore, Michael, 1990
Moore of Lower Marsh, Lord, 1986
Moore-Bick, Sir Martin, 2005
Morgan, Rhodri, 2000
Morley, Elliot, 2007
Morris, Charles, 1978
Morris of Aberavon, Lord, 1970
Morris of Manchester, Lord, 1979
Morris of Yardley, Baroness, 1999
Morritt, Sir Robert, 1994
Moses, Sir Alan, 2005
Moyle, Roland, 1978
Mummery, Sir John, 1996
Murphy, Paul, 1999
Murray, *Hon.* Lord (Ronald Murray), 1974

Murray, Sir Donald, 1989
Musa, Wilbert, 2005
Mustill, Lord, 1985
Nairne, Sir Patrick, 1982
Namaliu, Sir Rabbie, 1989
Naseby, Lord, 1994
Needham, Sir Richard, 1994
Neill, Sir Brian, 1985
Neuberger of Abbotsbury, Lord, 2004
Newton of Braintree, Lord, 1988
Nicholls of Birkenhead, Lord, 1995
Nicholson, Sir Michael, 1995
Nimmo Smith, *Hon.* Lord (William Nimmo Smith), 2005
Nott, Sir John, 1979
Nourse, Sir Martin, 1985
O'Brien, Mike, 2009
O'Donnell, Turlough, 1979
Oppenheim-Barnes, Baroness, 1979
Osborne, *Hon.* Lord (Kenneth Osborne), 2001
Otton, Sir Philip, 1995
Owen, Lord, 1976
Paeniu, Bikenibeu, 1991
Paisley, Dr Ian, 2005
Palliser, Sir Michael, 1983
Palmer, Sir Geoffrey, 1986
Parker, Sir Jonathan, 2000
Parker, Sir Roger, 1983
Parkinson, Lord, 1981
Paton, *Hon.* Lady (Ann Paton), 2007
Patten, Lord, 1990
Patten, Sir Nicholas, 2009
Patten of Barnes, Lord, 1989
Patterson, Percival, 1993
Pattie, Sir Geoffrey, 1987
Paul, Lord, 2009
Peel, Earl, 2006
Pendry, Lord, 2000
Penrose, *Hon.* Lord (George Penrose), 2000
Peters, Winston, 1998
Philip, *Hon.* Lord (Alexander Philip), 2005
Phillips of Worth Matravers, Lord, 1995
Pill, Sir Malcolm, 1995
Portillo, Michael, 1992
Potter, Sir Mark, 1996
Prescott, John, 1994
Price, George, 1982
Primarolo, Dawn, 2002
Prior, Lord, 1970
Prosser, *Hon.* Lord (William Prosser), 2000
Puapua, Sir Tomasi, 1982
Purnell, James, 2007
Quin, Baroness, 1998
Radice, Lord, 1999
Raison, Sir Timothy, 1982
Ramsden, James, 1963
Raynsford, Nick, 2001
Redwood, John, 1993
Reed, Lord, 2008
Reid, George, 2004
Reid, John, 1998
Renton of Mount Harry, Lord, 1989
Richard, Lord, 1993
Richards, Sir Stephen, 2005
Richardson, Sir Ivor, 1978
Richardson of Duntisbourne, Lord, 1976
Rifkind, Sir Malcolm, 1986
Rimer, Sir Colin, 2007
Rix, Sir Bernard, 2000
Roberts of Conwy, Lord, 1991
Robertson of Port Ellen, Lord, 1997
Robinson, Peter, 2007
Roch, Sir John, 1993
Rodger of Earlsferry, Lord, 1992
Rodgers of Quarry Bank, Lord, 1975
Rooker, Lord, 1999
Roper, Lord, 2005
Rose, Sir Christopher, 1992
Ross, *Hon.* Lord (Donald MacArthur), 1985
Royall, Baroness, 2008
Rumbold, Dame Angela, 1991
Ryan, Joan, 2007
Ryder of Wensum, Lord, 1990
Sainsbury, Sir Timothy, 1992
St John of Fawsley, Lord, 1979
Salisbury, Marquess of, 1994
Salmond, Alex, 2007
Sandiford, Erskine, 1989
Saville of Newdigate, Lord, 1994
Sawyer, Dame Joan, 2004
Schiemann, Sir Konrad, 1995
Scotland of Asthal, Baroness, 2001
Scott of Foscote, Lord, 1991
Seaga, Edward, 1981
Sedley, Sir Stephen, 1999
Selkirk of Douglas, Lord, 1996
Sheldon, Lord, 1977
Shephard of Northwold, Baroness, 1992
Sheil, Sir John, 2005
Shipley, Jennifer, 1998
Short, Clare, 1997
Shutt of Greetland, Lord, 2009
Simmonds, Kennedy Sir, 1984
Sinclair, Ian, 1977
Slade, Sir Christopher, 1982
Smith, Andrew, 1997
Smith, Angela, 2009
Smith, Dame Janet, 2002
Smith, Jacqueline, 2003
Smith of Finsbury, Lord, 1997
Somare, Sir Michael, 1977
Spellar, John, 2001
Stanley, Sir John, 1984
Staughton, Sir Christopher, 1988
Steel of Aikwood, Lord, 1977
Stephen, Sir Ninian, 1979
Stewartby, Lord, 1989
Steyn, Lord, 1992
Strang, Gavin, 1997
Strathclyde, Lord, 1995
Straw, Jack, 1997
Stuart-Smith, Sir Murray, 1988
Sullivan, Sir Jeremy, 2009
Sutherland, *Hon.* Lord (Ranald Sutherland), 2000
Symons of Vernham Dean, Baroness, 2001
Talboys, Sir Brian, 1977
Taylor of Bolton, Baroness, 1997
Tebbit, Lord, 1981
Templeman, Lord, 1978
Thatcher, Baroness, 1970
Thomas, Edmund, 1996
Thomas, Sir Roger, 2003
Thomas, Sir Swinton, 1994
Thorpe, Jeremy, 1967
Thorpe, Sir Matthew, 1995
Timms, Stephen, 2006
Tipping, Andrew, 1998
Tizard, Robert, 1986
Touhig, Don, 2006
Toulson, Sir Roger, 2007
Trefgarne, Lord, 1989
Trimble, Lord, 1997
Trumpington, Baroness, 1992
Tuckey, Sir Simon, 1998
Ullswater, Viscount, 1994
Upton, Simon, 1999
Vadera, Baroness, 2009
Vaz, Keith, 2006
Waddington, Lord, 1987
Waite, Sir John, 1993
Wakeham, Lord, 1983
Waldegrave of North Hill, Lord, 1990
Walker of Gestingthorpe, Lord, 1997
Walker of Worcester, Lord, 1970
Wall, Sir Nicholas, 2004
Wallace of Tankerness, Lord, 2000
Waller, Sir Mark, 1996
Ward, Sir Alan, 1995
Warner, Lord, 2006
Wheatley, *Hon.* Lord (John Wheatley), 2007
Wheeler, Sir John, 1993
Whitty, Lord, 2005
Wicks, Malcolm, 2008
Widdecombe, Ann, 1997
Wigley, Dafydd, 1997
Williams, Alan, 1977
Williams of Crosby, Baroness, 1974
Williamson of Horton, Lord, 2007
Wills, Michael, 2008
Wilson, Brian, 2003
Wilson, Sir Nicholas, 2005
Windlesham, Lord, 1973
Winterton, Rosie, 2006
Wingti, Paias, 1987
Withers, Reginald, 1977
Woodhouse, Sir Owen, 1974
Woodward, Shaun, 2007
Woolf, Lord, 1986
York, Archbishop of, 2005
Young, Sir George, 1993
Young of Graffham, Lord, 1984
Zacca, Edward, 1992

PRIVY COUNCIL OF NORTHERN IRELAND

The Privy Council of Northern Ireland had responsibilities in Northern Ireland similar to those of the Privy Council in Great Britain until the Northern Ireland Act 1974. Membership of the Privy Council of Northern Ireland is retained for life. Since the Northern Ireland Constitution Act 1973 no further appointments have been made. The postnominal initials PC (NI) are used to differentiate its members from those of the Privy Council.

MEMBERS *as at August 2009*
Bailie, Robin, 1971
Bleakley, David, 1971
Craig, William, 1963
Dobson, John, 1969
Kilclooney, Lord, 1970
Kirk, Herbert, 1962
Porter, Sir Robert, 1969

PARLIAMENT

The United Kingdom constitution is not contained in any single document but has evolved over time, formed partly by statute, partly by common law and partly by convention. A constitutional monarchy, the United Kingdom is governed by ministers of the crown in the name of the sovereign, who is head both of the state and of the government.

The organs of government are the legislature (parliament), the executive and the judiciary. The executive consists of HM government (the cabinet and other ministers), government departments and local authorities (*see* Government Departments, Public Bodies and Local Government sections). The judiciary (*see* Law Courts and Offices section) pronounces on the law, both written and unwritten, interprets statutes and is responsible for the enforcement of the law; the judiciary is independent of both the legislature and the executive.

THE MONARCHY

The sovereign personifies the state and is, in law, an integral part of the legislature, head of the executive, head of the judiciary, commander-in-chief of all armed forces of the crown and supreme governor of the Church of England. The seat of the monarchy is in the United Kingdom. In the Channel Islands and the Isle of Man, which are crown dependencies, the sovereign is represented by a lieutenant-governor. In the member states of the Commonwealth of which the sovereign is head of state, her representative is a governor-general; in UK overseas territories the sovereign is usually represented by a governor, who is responsible to the British government.

Although in practice the powers of the monarchy are now very limited, and restricted mainly to the advisory and ceremonial, there are important acts of government which require the participation of the sovereign. These include summoning, proroguing and dissolving parliament, giving royal assent to bills passed by parliament, appointing important office-holders, eg government ministers, judges, bishops and governors, conferring peerages, knighthoods and other honours, and granting pardon to a person wrongly convicted of a crime. The sovereign appoints the prime minister; by convention this office is held by the leader of the political party which enjoys, or can secure, a majority of votes in the House of Commons. In international affairs the sovereign as head of state has the power to declare war and make peace, to recognise foreign states and governments, to conclude treaties and to annex or cede territory. However, as the sovereign entrusts executive power to ministers of the crown and acts on the advice of her ministers, which she cannot ignore, royal prerogative powers are in practice exercised by ministers, who are responsible to parliament.

Ministerial responsibility does not diminish the sovereign's importance to the smooth working of government. She holds meetings of the Privy Council (*see* below), gives audiences to her ministers and other officials at home and overseas, receives accounts of cabinet decisions, reads dispatches and signs state papers; she must be informed and consulted on every aspect of national life; and she must show complete impartiality.

COUNSELLORS OF STATE

In the event of the sovereign's absence abroad, it is necessary to appoint counsellors of state under letters patent to carry out the chief functions of the monarch, including the holding of Privy Councils and giving royal assent to acts passed by parliament. The normal procedure is to appoint as counsellors three or four members of the royal family among those remaining in the UK.

In the event of the sovereign on accession being under the age of 18 years, or at any time unavailable or incapacitated by infirmity of mind or body for the performance of the royal functions, provision is made for a regency.

THE PRIVY COUNCIL

The sovereign in council, or Privy Council, was the chief source of executive power until the system of cabinet government developed. Its main function today is to advise the sovereign on the approval of various statutory functions and acts of the royal prerogative. These powers are exercised through orders in council and royal proclamations, approved by the Queen at meetings of the Privy Council. The council is also able to exercise a number of statutory duties without approval from the sovereign, including powers of supervision over the registering bodies for the medical and allied professions. These duties are exercised through orders in council.

Although appointment as a privy counsellor is for life, only those who are currently government ministers are involved in the day-to-day business of the council. A full council is summoned only on the death of the sovereign or when the sovereign announces his or her intention to marry. (For a full list of privy counsellors, *see* the Privy Council section.)

There are a number of advisory Privy Council committees whose meetings the sovereign does not attend. Some are prerogative committees, such as those dealing with legislative matters submitted by the legislatures of the Channel Islands and the Isle of Man or with applications for charters of incorporation; and some are provided for by statute, eg those for the universities of Oxford and Cambridge and the Scottish universities.

The Judicial Committee of the Privy Council is the court of final appeal from courts of the UK dependencies, courts of independent Commonwealth countries which have retained the right of appeal and courts of the Channel Islands and the Isle of Man.

It also has certain jurisdiction within the United Kingdom, the most important of which is that it is the court of final appeal for 'devolution issues', ie issues as to the legal competences and functions of the legislative and executive authorities established in Scotland, Wales and Northern Ireland by the devolution legislation of 1998.

The committee is composed of privy counsellors who hold, or have held, high judicial office, although usually only three or five hear each case.

Administrative work is carried out by the Privy Council

Office under the direction of the Lord President of the Council, a cabinet minister.

PARLIAMENT

Parliament is the supreme law-making authority and can legislate for the UK as a whole or for any parts of it separately (the Channel Islands and the Isle of Man are crown dependencies and not part of the UK). The main functions of parliament are to pass laws, to provide (by voting taxation) the means of carrying on the work of government and to scrutinise government policy and administration, particularly proposals for expenditure. International treaties and agreements are by custom presented to parliament before ratification.

Parliament emerged during the late 13th and early 14th centuries. The officers of the king's household and the king's judges were the nucleus of early parliaments, joined by such ecclesiastical and lay magnates as the king might summon to form a prototype 'House of Lords', and occasionally by the knights of the shires, burgesses and proctors of the lower clergy. By the end of Edward III's reign a 'House of Commons' was beginning to appear; the first known Speaker was elected in 1377.

Parliamentary procedure is based on custom and precedent, partly formulated in the standing orders of both houses of parliament, and each house has the right to control its own internal proceedings and to commit for contempt. The system of debate in the two houses is similar; when a motion has been moved, the Speaker proposes the question as the subject of a debate. Members speak from wherever they have been sitting. Questions are decided by a vote on a simple majority. Draft legislation is introduced, in either house, as a bill. Bills can be introduced by a government minister or a private member, but in practice the majority of bills which become law are introduced by the government. To become law, a bill must be passed by each house (for parliamentary stages, *see* Parliamentary Information) and then sent to the sovereign for the royal assent, after which it becomes an act of parliament.

Proceedings of both houses are public, except on extremely rare occasions. The minutes (called *Votes and Proceedings in the Commons* and *Minutes of Proceedings in the Lords*) and the speeches (*The Official Report of Parliamentary Debates,* Hansard) are published daily. Proceedings are also recorded for transmission on radio and television and stored in the Parliamentary Recording Unit before transfer to the National Sound Archive. Television cameras have been allowed into the House of Lords since 1985 and into the House of Commons since 1989; committee meetings may also be televised.

By the Parliament Act of 1911, the maximum duration of a parliament is five years (if not previously dissolved), the term being reckoned from the date given on the writs for the new parliament. The maximum life has been prolonged by legislation in such rare circumstances as the two world wars (31 January 1911 to 25 November 1918; 26 November 1935 to 15 June 1945). Dissolution and writs for a general election are ordered by the sovereign on the advice of the prime minister. The life of a parliament is divided into sessions, usually of one year in length, beginning and ending most often in October or November.

DEVOLUTION

The Scottish parliament and the National Assembly for Wales have legislative power over all devolved matters, ie matters not reserved to Westminster or otherwise outside its powers. The Northern Ireland Assembly has legislative authority in the fields previously administered by the Northern Ireland departments. The assembly was suspended in October 2002 and dissolved in April 2003, before being reinstated on 8 May 2007. For further information, *see* the Regional Government section.

THE HOUSE OF LORDS

London SW1A 0PW
T 020-7219 3000 Information Office 020-7219 3107
E hlinfo@parliament.uk W www.parliament.uk

The House of Lords is the second chamber, or 'Upper House', of the UK's bicameral parliament. Until the beginning of the 20th century, the House of Lords had considerable power, being able to veto any bill submitted to it by the House of Commons. Today the main functions of the House of Lords are to contribute to the legislative process, to act as a check on the government, and to provide a forum of independent expertise. Its judicial role as final court of appeal ends in 2009 as a result of the establishment of a new UK supreme court (*see* Law Courts and Offices section).

The House of Lords has a number of select committees. Some relate to the internal affairs of the house – such as its management and administration – while others carry out important investigative work on matters of public interest. The main areas of work are: Europe, science, the economy, the constitution and communications. House of Lords investigative committees look at broader issues and do not mirror government departments as the select committees in the House of Commons do.

On 12 June 2003 the government announced reforms of the judicial function and the role of the Lord Chancellor as a judge and Speaker of the House of Lords. In 2006 the position of Lord Chancellor was significantly altered by the Constitutional Reform Act 2005. The office holder is no longer speaker of the House of Lords nor head of the judiciary in England and Wales, but remains a cabinet minister (the Lord Chancellor and Secretary of State for Justice), currently in the House of Commons. The function of speaker of the House of Lords was devolved to the newly created post of Lord Speaker. The Rt. Hon. Baroness Hayman was elected as the first Lord Speaker by the house on 4 July 2006.

Members of the House of Lords comprise life peers created under the Life Peerages Act 1958, 92 hereditary peers under the House of Lords Act 1999 and Lords of Appeal in Ordinary, ie law lords, under the Appellate Jurisdiction Act 1876. The Archbishops of Canterbury and York, the Bishops of London, Durham and Winchester, and the 21 senior diocesan bishops of the Church of England are also members.

The House of Lords Act provides for 90 elected hereditary peers to remain in the House of Lords until longer-term reform of the House has been carried out; 42 Conservative, 28 crossbench, three Liberal Democrat and two Labour. Elections for each of the party groups and the crossbenches were held in October and November 1999. Fifteen office holders were elected by the whole house. Two hereditary peers with royal duties, the Earl Marshal and the Lord Great Chamberlain, are also members.

Peers are disqualified from sitting in the house if they are:

- aliens, ie any peer who is not a British citizen, a Commonwealth citizen (under the British Nationality Act 1981) or a citizen of the Republic of Ireland
- under the age of 21
- undischarged bankrupts or, in Scotland, those whose estate is sequestered
- convicted of treason

Bishops retire at the age of 70 and cease to be members of the house at that time.

Members who do not wish to attend sittings of the House of Lords may apply for leave of absence for the duration of a parliament.

Members of the House of Lords are unpaid but are entitled to allowances for attendance at sittings of the house. The daily maxima, between 1 August 2008 and 31 July 2009, were £174 for overnight subsistence, £86.50 for day subsistence and incidental travel, and £75 for office costs.

COMPOSITION *as at 21 July 2009*

Archbishops and bishops	26
Life peers under the Appellate Jurisdiction Act 1876	23
Life peers under the Life Peerages Act 1958	598
Peers under the House of Lords Act 1999	92
Total	739

STATE OF THE PARTIES *as at 21 July 2009**

Conservative	193
Labour	215
Liberal Democrat	71
Crossbench	202
Archbishops and bishops	26
Other	17
Total	724

* Excluding 12 peers on leave of absence, two who are suspended and one disqualified as an MEP

HOUSE OF LORDS PAY BANDS

Staff are placed in the following pay bands according to their level of responsibility and taking account of other factors such as experience and marketability.

Judicial group 4	£165,900
Senior band 3	£97,852–£139,974
Senior band 2	£79,433–£129,729
Senior band 1A	£66,771–£108,806
Senior band 1	£57,561–£96,477
Band A1	£56,049–£71,210
Band A2	£46,604–£58,916

OFFICERS AND OFFICIALS

The house is presided over by the Lord Speaker, whose powers differ from those of the Speaker of the House of Commons. The Lord Speaker has no power to maintain order because the House of Lords is self-regulating.

A panel of deputy speakers is appointed by Royal Commission. The first deputy speaker is the Chair of Committees, appointed at the beginning of each session, who is a salaried officer of the house. He or she takes the chair when the whole house is in committee and in some select committees. He or she is assisted by a panel of deputy chairs, headed by the salaried Principal Deputy Chair of Committees, who is also chair of the European Communities Committee of the house.

The Clerk of the Parliaments is the accounting officer and the chief permanent official responsible for the administration of the house. The Gentleman Usher of the Black Rod is responsible for security and other services and also has royal duties as secretary to the Lord Great Chamberlain.

Lord Speaker (£108,253), Rt. Hon. Baroness Hayman
Chair of Committees (£84,524), Lord Brabazon of Tara
Principal Deputy Chair of Committees (£79,076), Lord Roper
Clerk of the Parliaments (Judicial Group 4), M. G. Pownall
Clerk Assistant (Senior Band 3), D. R. Beamish, LLM
Reading Clerk and Clerk of the Overseas Office (Senior Band 2), Dr R. H. Walters, DPHIL
Clerk of the Committees (Senior Band 2), E. C. Ollard
Director of Facilities (Senior Band 2), C. V. Woodall
Finance Director (Senior Band 1A), Dr F. P. Tudor
Head of Human Resources (Senior Band 1A), S. P. Burton
Clerk of the Judicial Office and Registrar of Lords Interests (Senior Band 1A), B. P. Keith
Director of Information Services and Librarian (Senior Band 2), Dr E. Hallam Smith
Clerk of Public and Private Bill Office and Examiner of Petitions for Private Bills in the House of Lords (Senior Band 1A), T. V. Mohan
Editor of the Official Report (Senior Band 1), A. S. Nicholls
Clerk of the Records (Senior Band 1), Dr C. Shenton
Deputy Finance Director and Head of Finance (Senior Band 1), J. P. Smith
Director of Public Information (Band A1), Miss M. L. Morgan
Counsel to the Chairman of Committees (Senior Band 2), M. Thomas
Second Counsel to the Chairman of Committees (Senior Band 2), Dr C. S. Kerse, CB
Legal Adviser to the Human Rights Committee (Senior Band 2), M. Hunt
Change Manager (Senior Band 1), Mrs M. E. Ollard
Clerk of the Journals (Senior Band 1), C. Johnson
Clerk of the European Union Committee (Senior Band 1A), A. Makower
Clerks of Select Committees (Senior Band 1), Ms C. Salmon Percival; Ms C. K. Mawson
Gentleman Usher of the Black Rod and Serjeant-at-Arms (Senior Band 2), Lt.-Gen. Sir Frederick Viggers, KCB, CMG, MBE
Yeoman Usher of the Black Rod and Deputy Serjeant-at-Arms (Band A2), Brig. H. D. C. Duncan, MBE

LORD GREAT CHAMBERLAIN'S OFFICE

Lord Great Chamberlain, Marquess of Cholmondeley
Secretary to the Lord Great Chamberlain, Lt.-Gen. Sir Frederick Viggers, KCB, CMG, MBE

SELECT COMMITTEES

The main House of Lords select committees, as at June 2009, are as follows:

Communications Committee – Chair, Lord Fowler; *Clerks,* Susan Michell, Ralph Publicover
Constitution Committee – Chair, Lord Goodlad; *Clerk,* Anna Murphy
Delegated Powers and Regulatory Reform – Chair, Lord Goodhart; *Clerk,* Jake Vaughan
Economic Affairs – Chair, Lord Vallance of Tummel; *Clerk,* Bill Sinton
European Union – Chair, Lord Roper; *Clerk,* A. Makower
European Union – Sub-committees:
A (Economic and Financial Affairs and International Trade) – Chair, Baroness Cohen of Pimlico; *Clerk,* Robert Whiteway

B (Internal Market) – *Chair,* Lord Freeman; *Clerk,* James Whittle
C (Foreign Affairs, Defence and Development Policy) – *Chair,* Lord Teverson; *Clerk,* Kathryn Colvin
D (Agriculture and the Environment) – *Chair,* Lord Sewel; *Clerk,* Julia Labeta
E (Law and Institutions) – *Chair,* Lord Mance; *Clerk,* John Turner
F (Home Affairs) – *Chair,* Lord Joplin; *Clerk,* Michael Collon
G (Social and Consumer Affairs) – *Chair,* Baroness Howarth of Breckland; *Clerk,* Kate Meanwell
Information Committee – *Chair,* Lord Renton of Mount Harry; *Clerk,* Richard McLean
Committee for Privileges – *Chair,* Lord Brabazon of Tara; *Clerks,* Dr Christopher Johnson, Brendan Keith
Science and Technology – *Chair,* Lord Sutherland of Houndwood; *Clerk,* Christine Salmon Percival
I – *Chair,* Lord Krebs; *Clerk,* Antony Willott
II – *Chair,* Lord Patel; *Clerk,* Christine Salmon Percival
Human Rights Joint Committee – *Chair,* Andrew Dismore, MP; *Lords Clerk,* Rebecca Neal
Merits of Statutory Instruments Committee – *Chair,* Lord Filkin; *Clerk,* Jake Vaughan

THE HOUSE OF COMMONS

London SW1A 0AA
T 020-7219 3000
Information Office 020-7219 4272
Forthcoming business 020-7219 5532
E hcinfo@parliament.uk W www.parliament.uk

The members of the House of Commons are elected by universal adult suffrage. For electoral purposes, the United Kingdom is divided into constituencies, each of which returns one member to the House of Commons, the member being the candidate who obtains the largest number of votes cast in the constituency. To ensure equitable representation, the four Boundary Commissions keep constituency boundaries under review and recommend any redistribution of seats which may seem necessary because of population movements etc. The number of seats was raised to 640 in 1945, reduced to 625 in 1948, and subsequently rose to 630 in 1955, 635 in 1970, 650 in 1983, 651 in 1992 and 659 in 1997, before falling to 646 in 2005. Of the present 646 seats, there are 529 for England, 40 for Wales, 59 for Scotland and 18 for Northern Ireland.

ELECTIONS

Elections are by secret ballot, each elector casting one vote; voting is not compulsory. For entitlement to vote in parliamentary elections, *see* Legal Notes section. When a seat becomes vacant between general elections, a by-election is held.

British subjects and citizens of the Irish Republic can stand for election as MPs provided they are 21 or over and not subject to disqualification. Those disqualified from sitting in the house include:

- undischarged bankrupts
- people sentenced to more than one year's imprisonment
- members of the House of Lords (but hereditary peers not sitting in the Lords are eligible)
- holders of certain offices listed in the House of Commons Disqualification Act 1975, eg members of the judiciary, civil service, regular armed forces, police forces, some local government officers and some members of public corporations and government commissions

A candidate does not require any party backing but his or her nomination for election must be supported by the signatures of ten people registered in the constituency. A candidate must also deposit £500 with the returning officer, which is forfeit if the candidate does not receive more than 5 per cent of the votes cast. All election expenses at a general election, except the candidate's personal expenses, are subject to a statutory limit of £7,150, plus five pence for each elector in a borough constituency or seven pence for each elector in a county constituency.

See pages 138–183 for an alphabetical list of MPs, results of the last general election in 2005 and results of by-elections since the general election.

STATE OF THE PARTIES *as at 24 July 2009**

Party	*Seats*
Labour	349
Conservative	193
Liberal Democrats	63
Democratic Unionist Party	9
Scottish National Party	7
Independent	5
Sinn Fein (have not taken their seats)	5
Plaid Cymru	3
Social Democratic Labour Party	3
Independent Conservative	1
Independent Labour	1
Respect	1
Ulster Unionist	1
The Speaker and three Deputy Speakers	4
Total	646

* Working majority of 62; 349 Labour MPs less 287 of all other parties (excluding the speaker, deputy speakers and Sinn Fein)

BUSINESS

The week's business of the house is outlined each Thursday by the leader of the house, after consultation between the chief government whip and the chief opposition whip. A quarter to a third of the time will be taken up by the government's legislative programme and the rest by other business. As a rule, bills likely to raise political controversy are introduced in the Commons before going on to the Lords, and the Commons claims exclusive control in respect of national taxation and expenditure. Bills such as the finance bill, which imposes taxation, and the consolidated fund bills, which authorise expenditure, must begin in the Commons. A bill of which the financial provisions are subsidiary may begin in the Lords; and the Commons may waive its rights in regard to Lords' amendments affecting finance.

The Commons has a public register of MPs' financial and certain other interests; this is published annually as a House of Commons paper. Members must also disclose any relevant financial interest or benefit in a matter before the house when taking part in a debate, in certain other proceedings of the house, or in consultations with other MPs, with ministers or with civil servants.

MEMBERS' PAY AND ALLOWANCES

Since 1911 members of the House of Commons have received salary payments; facilities for free travel were introduced in 1924. Salary rates for the last 30 years are as follows:

1979 Jun	£9,450	1995 Jan	£33,189
1980 Jun	11,750	1996 Jan	34,085
1981 Jun	13,950	1996 Jul	43,000
1982 Jun	14,910	1997 Apr	43,860
1983 Jun	15,308	1998 Apr	45,066
1984 Jan	16,106	1999 Apr	47,008
1985 Jan	16,904	2000 Apr	48,371
1986 Jan	17,702	2001 Apr	49,822
1987 Jan	18,500	2002 Apr	55,118
1988 Jan	22,548	2003 Apr	56,358
1989 Jan	24,107	2004 Apr	57,485
1990 Jan	26,701	2005 Apr	59,095
1991 Jan	28,970	2006 Apr	59,686
1992 Jan	30,854	2007 Apr	61,181
1993 Jan	30,854	2008 Apr	63,291
1994 Jan	31,687	2009 Apr	64,766

In 1969 MPs were granted an annual allowance for secretarial and research expenses, revised in July 2001. Members receive administrative and office expenditure (£22,393), a staffing allowance (up to £103,812) and a communications allowance (£10,400).

Since 1972 MPs were able to claim reimbursement for the additional cost of staying overnight away from their main residence while on parliamentary business; this is known as the personal additional accommodation expenditure allowance and from April 2009 was £24,222 per year.

Members of staff who are paid out of the allowances can benefit from a sum not exceeding 10 per cent of their gross salary which is paid into the Portcullis Pension Plan. This sum comes from a central budget.

MEMBERS' PENSIONS

Pension arrangements for MPs were first introduced in 1964. Under the Parliamentary Contributory Pension Fund (PCPF), MPs receive a pension on retirement based upon their salary in their final year, and upon their number of years' service as an MP. Members may pay a contribution rate of 10 per cent or 6 per cent and build up a pension of 2.5 per cent or 2 per cent of salary for each year of service. Pensions are normally payable at age 65; upon retirement at 65, the pension payable is subject to a maximum of 66.6 per cent of salary, inclusive of pensions from employment or self-employment prior to becoming an MP. There are provisions in place for: early retirement for those MPs who cease to serve between the ages of 50 (55 from 6 April 2010) and 65; MPs of any age who retire due to ill health; and pensions for widows/widowers of MPs. All pensions are index-linked. There is an Exchequer contribution to ensure that shortfalls are made up; currently 8.7 per cent of an MP's salary for 15 years from 2006/7.

The House of Commons Members' Fund provides for annual or lump sum grants to ex-MPs, their widows or widowers, and children of those who either ceased to serve as an MP prior to the PCPF being established or who are experiencing hardship. Members contribute £24 a year and the Exchequer £215,000 a year to the fund.

HOUSE OF COMMONS PAY BANDS

Staff are placed in the following Senior Civil Service pay bands. These pay bands apply to the most senior staff in departments and agencies.

Pay Band 1	£58,200–£117,800
Pay Band 1A	£67,600–£128,900
Pay Band 2	£82,900–£162,500
Pay Band 3	£101,500–£208,100

OFFICERS AND OFFICIALS

The House of Commons is presided over by the Speaker, who has considerable powers to maintain order. A deputy speaker, called the chairman of ways and means, and two deputy chairs may preside over sittings of the House of Commons; they are elected by the house, and, like the Speaker, neither speak nor vote other than in their official capacity.

The staff of the house are employed by a commission chaired by the Speaker. The heads of the six House of Commons departments are permanent officers of the house, not MPs. The Clerk of the House is the principal adviser to the Speaker on the privileges and procedures of the house, the conduct of the business of the house, and committees. The Serjeant-at-Arms is responsible for security and ceremonial functions of the house.

Speaker (£144,520)*, Rt. Hon. John Bercow, MP (Buckingham)
Chairman of Ways and Means (£106,136), Sir Alan Haselhurst, MP (Saffron Walden)
First Deputy Chairman of Ways and Means (£101,126), Sylvia Heal, MP (Halesowen and Rowley Regis)
Second Deputy Chairman of Ways and Means (£101,126), Sir Michael Lord, MP (Suffolk Central and Ipswich North)
Parliamentary Commissioner for Standards in Public Life, John Lyon, CB

* Salaries in brackets are the maximum available. Ministers have opted not to take a pay rise for 2009–10 and remain on 2008–9 salaries.

OFFICES OF THE SPEAKER AND CHAIRMAN OF WAYS AND MEANS

Speaker's Secretary, A. Sinclair
Chaplain to the Speaker, Revd Canon R. Wright
Secretary to the Chairman of Ways and Means, J. Whatley

DEPARTMENT OF CHAMBER AND COMMITTEE SERVICES

Clerk of the House of Commons, Dr M. R. Jack

OFFICE OF THE CHIEF EXECUTIVE

Head of Office, Ms P. Helme
Director of Internal Audit, P. Dillon-Robinson

CLERK ASSISTANT'S DIRECTORATE

Clerk Assistant, D. G. Millar
Principal Clerks
Table Office, Ms J. Sharpe
Journals, A. R. Kennon
Overseas Office, M. Hutton

VOTE OFFICE

Deliverer of the Vote, Ms C. Fogarty
Deputy Deliverers of the Vote, O. B. T. Sweeney *(Parliamentary)*; Ms J. Pitt *(Production)*

COMMITTEE DIRECTORATE

Clerk of Committees, D. Natzler
Principal Clerk and Deputy Head of Committee Office, R. W. G. Wilson
Clerk of Domestic Committees/Secretary to the Commission, D. J. Gerhold
Select Committees, P. A. Evans; C. J. Poyser
Head of Scrutiny Unit, M. Hamlyn
Director of Broadcasting, T. Jeffes

LEGISLATION DIRECTORATE
Clerk of Legislation, R. J. Rogers

Principal Clerks
Delegated Legislation, S. J. Patrick
Bills, L. Laurence-Smyth
National Parliament Office (Brussels), Ms L. Davidson
Ways and Means Office, M. Clark

OFFICIAL REPORT DIRECTORATE
Editor, Miss L. Sutherland
Deputy Editors, Ms V. Widgery; A. Newton

SERJEANT-AT-ARMS DIRECTORATE
Serjeant-at-Arms, Mrs J. Pay
Deputy Serjeant-at-Arms, M. Naworynsky
Assistant Serjeant-at-Arms, L. Ward

LEGAL SERVICES OFFICE
Speaker's Counsel and Head of Legal Services Office, M. Carpenter
Counsel for European Legislation, P. Hardy
Counsel for Legislation, Peter Davis
Deputy Counsel, P. Brooksbank; Ms C. Cogger; Ms M. Forbes
Assistant Counsel, G. Beck; Ms. V. Daly; Ms H. Emes

DEPARTMENT OF INFORMATION SERVICES
Director-General and Librarian, J. Pullinger
Directors, R. Clements *(Service Delivery);* Prof. D. Cope *(Parliamentary Office of Science and Technology);* Ms B. McInnes *(Departmental Services);* B. Morgan *(Research);* R. Twigger *(Information Services);* Ms A. Walker *(Public Information);* S. Wise *(Information Management);* Ms H. Wood *(SPIRE Programme)*
Heads of Sections, C. Barclay; Mrs D. Clark; R. Cracknell, T. Edmonds; Ms O. Gay; Mrs C. Gillie; M. Hay; V. Launert; S. McGinness; Mrs K. Marke; Ms C. Meredith; Ms V. Miller; T. O'Leary; Ms P. J. Strickland
Media and Communications Adviser, Ms E. Parratt
Parliamentary Outreach Officer, Ms C. Cowan
Visitor and Information Manager, C. Weeds

DEPARTMENT OF RESOURCES
Director-General of Resources, A. J. Walker
Director of Business Management and Development, Ms J. Rissen
Director of Operations, T. M. Bird
Director of Human Resource Management, Mrs H. Bryson
Director of Finance Policy, C. Ridley
Director, Commercial, vacant
Head of Occupational Health, Safety and Welfare Service, Dr M. McDougall

DEPARTMENT OF FACILITIES
Director-General, J. Borley
Business Management Director, vacant
Parliamentary Director of Estates, M. Barlex
Director of Accommodation Services, J. Robertson
Director of Facilities Finance, P. Collins
Executive Officer, M. Trott
Head of Human Resources and Development, J. van den Broek

CATERING AND RETAIL SERVICES DIRECTORATE
Director of Catering Services, Mrs S. Harrison
Catering Operations Manager (Outbuildings), Ms D. Herd
Food and Beverage Operations Manager, Palace of Westminster, R. Gibbs
Executive Chef, M. Hill
Retail Manager, Mrs M. DeSouza

PARLIAMENTARY INFORMATION AND COMMUNICATION TECHNOLOGY (ICT)
Director of Parliamentary ICT, Ms J. Miller
Director of Technology Directorate, I. Montgomery
Director of Operations and Members Services, M. Taylor
Director of Resources, Ms E. Honer
Director of Programmes and Project Development, R. Ware

NATIONAL AUDIT OFFICE
157–197 Buckingham Palace Road, London SW1W 9SP
T 020-7798 7000
E enquiries@nao.gsi.gov.uk W www.nao.org.uk

The National Audit Office came into existence under the National Audit Act 1983 to replace and continue the work of the former Exchequer and Audit Department. The act reinforced the office's total financial and operational independence from the government and brought its head, the Comptroller and Auditor-General, into a closer relationship with parliament as an officer of the House of Commons.

The National Audit Office provides independent information, advice and assurance to parliament and the public about all aspects of the financial operations of government departments and many other bodies receiving public funds. It does this by examining and certifying the accounts of these organisations. It also regularly publishes reports to parliament on the results of its value for money investigations of the economy (the efficiency and effectiveness with which public resources have been used). The National Audit Office is also the auditor by agreement of the accounts of certain international and other organisations. In addition, the office authorises the issue of public funds to government departments.

Comptroller and Auditor-General, Amyas Morse
Private Secretary, Janey Sacoto
Assistant Auditors-General, Gabrielle Cohen; Ed Humpherson; Wendy Kenway-Smith; Caroline Mawhood; Jim Rickleton; Martin Sinclair; Michael Whitehouse

SELECT COMMITTEES
The more significant committees, as at June 2009, are:

DEPARTMENTAL COMMITTEES
Business and Enterprise – Chair, Peter Luff, MP; *Clerk,* Eve Samson
Children, Schools and Families – Chair, Barry Sheerman, MP; *Clerk,* Kenneth Fox
Communities and Local Government – Chair, Dr Phyllis Starkey, MP; *Clerk,* Huw Yardley
Culture, Media and Sport – Chair, John Whittingdale, MP; *Clerk,* Tracey Garratty
Defence – Chair, Rt. Hon. James Arbuthnot, MP; *Clerk,* Mike Hennessy
Energy and Climate Change – Chair, Elliot Morley, MP; *Clerk,* Tom Goldsmith
Environment, Food and Rural Affairs – Chair, Rt. Hon. Michael Jack, MP; *Clerk,* Richard Cooke
Foreign Affairs – Chair, Mike Gapes, MP; *Clerk,* Dr Robin James
Health – Chair, Rt. Hon. Kevin Barron, MP; *Clerk,* Dr David Harrison
Home Affairs – Chair, Rt. Hon. Keith Vaz, MP; *Clerk,* Elizabeth Flood
Innovation, Universities, Science and Skills – Chair, Phil Willis, MP; *Clerk,* Sarah Davies

International Development – Chair, Rt. Hon. Malcolm Bruce, MP; *Clerk,* Carol Oxborough
Justice – Chair, Rt. Hon. Sir Alan Beith, MP; *Clerk,* Fergus Reid
Northern Ireland Affairs – Chair, Sir Patrick Cormack, MP; *Clerk,* David Weir
Scottish Affairs – Chair, Mohammad Sarwar, MP; *Clerk,* Nerys Welfoot
Transport – Chair, Louise Ellman, MP; *Clerk,* Annette Toft
Treasury – Chair, Rt. Hon. John McFall, MP; *Clerk,* Dr John Benger
Welsh Affairs – Chair, Dr Hywel Francis, MP; *Clerk,* Dr Sue Griffiths
Work and Pensions – Chair, Terry Rooney, MP; *Clerk,* James Rhys

NON-DEPARTMENTAL COMMITTEES
Arms Export Controls – Chair, Roger Berry, MP; *Clerk,* Nerys Welfoot
Environmental Audit – Chair, Tim Yeo, MP; *Clerk,* Gordon Clarke
European Scrutiny – Chair, Michael Connarty, MP; *Clerk,* Alistair Doherty
Finance and Services – Chair, Sir Stuart Bell, MP; *Clerk,* Dorian Gerhold
Human Rights (Joint Committee) – Chair, Andrew Dismore, MP; *Clerks,* Dr Mark Egan, Rebecca Neal
Modernisation of the House of Commons – Chair, Rt. Hon. Harriet Harman, QC, MP; *Clerk,* David Natzler
Procedure – Chair, Rt. Hon. Greg Knight, MP; *Clerk,* Dr Lynn Gardner
Public Accounts – Chair, Edward Leigh, MP; *Clerk,* Mark Etherton
Public Administration – Chair, Dr Tony Wright, MP; *Clerk,* Steven Mark
Regulatory Reform – Chair, Andrew Miller, MP; *Clerk,* John Whatley
Standards and Privileges – Chair, Rt. Hon. Sir George Young, Bt., MP; *Clerk,* Steve Priestley
Statutory Instruments (Joint Committee) – Chair, Rt. Hon. David Maclean, MP; *Clerk,* John Whatley

DOMESTIC COMMITTEE
Administration – Chair, Frank Doran, MP; *Clerk,* Kate Emms

OTHER COMMITTEES (CABINET OFFICE)
Intelligence and Security (Cabinet Office) – Chair, Rt. Hon. Margaret Beckett, MP; *Clerk,* Emma-Louise Avery

PARLIAMENTARY INFORMATION

The following is a short glossary of aspects of the work of parliament. Unless otherwise stated, references are to House of Commons procedures.

BILL – Proposed legislation is termed a bill. The stages of a public bill (for private bills, *see* below) in the House of Commons are as follows:

First reading: This stage merely constitutes an order to have the bill printed.
Second reading: The debate on the principles of the bill.
Committee stage: The detailed examination of a bill, clause by clause. In most cases this takes place in a public bill committee, or the whole house may act as a committee. Public bill committees may take evidence before embarking on detailed scrutiny of the bill. Very rarely, a bill may be examined by a select committee.
Report stage: Detailed review of a bill as amended in committee, on the floor of the house.
Third reading: Final debate on a bill.

Public bills go through the same stages in the House of Lords, but with important differences: the committee stage is taken in committee of the whole house or in a grand committee, in which any peer may participate. There are no time limits, and no selection of amendments can be made at third reading.

A bill may start in either house, and has to pass through both houses to become law. Both houses have to agree the final text of a bill, so that amendments made by the second house are then considered in the originating house, and if not agreed, sent back or themselves amended, until agreement is reached.

CHILTERN HUNDREDS – A nominal office of profit under the crown, the acceptance of which requires an MP to vacate his/her seat. The Manor of Northstead is similar. These are the only means by which an MP may resign.

CONSOLIDATED FUND BILL – A bill to authorise issue of money to maintain government services. The bill is dealt with without debate.

EARLY DAY MOTION – A motion put on the notice paper by an MP without, in general, the real prospect of its being debated. Such motions are expressions of back-bench opinion.

FATHER OF THE HOUSE – The MP whose continuous service in the House of Commons is the longest. The present Father of the House is the Rt. Hon. Alan Williams, MP.

GRAND COMMITTEES – There are three grand committees in the House of Commons, one each for Northern Ireland, Scotland and Wales; they consider matters relating specifically to that country. In the House of Lords, bills may be sent to a grand committee instead of a committee of the whole house (*see also* Bill).

HOURS OF MEETING – The House of Commons normally meets on Mondays and Tuesdays at 2.30pm, Wednesdays at 11.30am, Thursdays at 10.30am and some Fridays at 9.30am. (*See also* Westminster Hall Sittings, below.) The House of Lords normally meets at 2.30pm Mondays and Tuesdays, 3pm on Wednesdays and at 11am on Thursdays. The House of Lords often sits on Fridays at 11am.

LEADER OF THE OPPOSITION – In 1937 the office of leader of the opposition was recognised and a salary was assigned to the post. Since April 2009 this has been £138,383 (including a parliamentary salary of £64,766). The present leader of the opposition is the Rt. Hon. David Cameron, MP.

THE LORD CHANCELLOR – The office of Lord High Chancellor of Great Britain was significantly altered by the Constitutional Reform Act 2005. Previously, the Lord Chancellor was (*ex officio*) the Speaker of the House of Lords, and took part in debates and voted in divisions in the House of Lords. The Department for Constitutional Affairs was created in 2003, which became the Ministry of Justice in 2007, incorporating most of the responsibilities of the Lord Chancellor's department. The role of Speaker has been transferred to the newly created post of Lord Speaker. The Constitutional Reform Act 2005 also brought to an end the Lord Chancellor's role as head of the judiciary. A new Judicial Appointments Commission was created in April 2006, and a new supreme court (separate from the House of Lords) is being established (scheduled to open in 2009).

THE LORD SPEAKER – The first Lord Speaker of the House of Lords, the Rt. Hon. Baroness Hayman, took up office on 4 July 2006. Unlike in the case of the Lord Chancellor, the Lord Speaker is independent of the government and elected by members of the House of Lords rather than appointed by the prime minister. Although the Lord Speaker's primary role is to preside over proceedings in the House of Lords, she does not have the same powers as the speaker of the House of Commons. For example, the Lord Speaker is not responsible for maintaining order during debates, as this is the responsibility of the house as a whole. The Lord Speaker sits in the Lords on one of the woolsacks, which are couches covered in red cloth and stuffed with wool.

THE LORD GREAT CHAMBERLAIN – The Lord Great Chamberlain is a Great Officer of State, the office being hereditary since the grant of Henry I to the family of De Vere, Earls of Oxford. It is now a joint hereditary office rotating on the death of the sovereign between the Cholmondeley, Carington and Ancaster families.

The Lord Great Chamberlain, currently the Marquess of Cholmondeley, is responsible for the royal apartments in the Palace of Westminster, the Royal Gallery, the administration of the Chapel of St Mary Undercroft and, in conjunction with the Lord Speaker and the Speaker of the House of Commons, Westminster Hall. The Lord Great Chamberlain has the right to perform specific services at a coronation, he carries out ceremonial duties in the Palace of Westminster when the sovereign visits the palace and has particular responsibility for the internal administrative arrangements within the House of Lords for state openings of parliament.

OPPOSITION DAY – A day on which the topic for debate is chosen by the opposition. There are 20 such days in a normal session. On 17 days, subjects are chosen by the leader of the opposition; on the remaining three days by the leader of the next largest opposition party.

PARLIAMENT ACTS 1911 AND 1949 – Under these acts, bills may become law without the consent of the Lords, though the House of Lords has the power to delay a public bill for a parliamentary session.

PRIME MINISTER'S QUESTIONS – The prime minister answers questions from 12 to 12.30pm on Wednesdays.

PRIVATE BILL – A bill promoted by a body or an individual to give powers additional to, or in conflict with, the general law, and to which a special procedure applies to enable people affected to object.

PRIVATE MEMBER'S BILL – A public bill promoted by an MP or peer who is not a member of the government.

PRIVATE NOTICE QUESTION – A question adjudged of urgent importance on submission to the Speaker (in the Lords, the Lord Speaker), answered at the end of oral questions.

PRIVILEGE – The House of Commons has rights and immunities to protect it from obstruction in carrying out its duties. These are known as parliamentary privilege and enable Members of Parliament to debate freely. The most important privilege is that of freedom of speech. MPs cannot be prosecuted for sedition or sued for libel or slander over anything said during proceedings in the house. This enables them to raise in the house questions affecting the public good which might be difficult to raise outside owing to the possibility of being sued. The House of Lords has similar privileges.

QUESTION TIME – Oral questions are answered by ministers in the Commons from 2.30 to 3.30pm on Mondays and Tuesdays, 11.30am to 12.30pm on Wednesdays, and 10.30 to 11.30am on Thursdays. Questions are also taken at the start of the Lords sittings, with a daily limit of four oral questions.

ROYAL ASSENT – The royal assent is signified by letters patent to such bills and measures as have passed both Houses of Parliament (or bills which have been passed under the Parliament Acts 1911 and 1949). The sovereign has not given royal assent in person since 1854. On occasion, for instance in the prorogation of parliament, royal assent may be pronounced to the two houses by Lords Commissioners. More usually royal assent is notified to each house sitting separately in accordance with the Royal Assent Act 1967. The old French formulae for royal assent are then endorsed on the acts by the Clerk of the Parliaments.

The power to withhold assent resides with the sovereign but has not been exercised in the UK since 1707.

SELECT COMMITTEES – Consisting usually of 10 to 15 members of all parties, select committees are a means used by both houses in order to investigate certain matters.

Most select committees in the House of Commons are tied to departments: each committee investigates subjects within a government department's remit. There are other select committees dealing with matters such as public accounts (ie the spending by the government of money voted by parliament) and European legislation, and also committees advising on procedures and domestic administration of the house. Major select committees usually take evidence in public; their evidence and reports are published on the parliament website and in hard copy by TSO (The Stationery Office). House of Commons select committees are reconstituted after a general election.

In the House of Lords, select committees do not mirror government departments but cover broader issues. There is a select committee on the European Union (EU), which has seven sub-committees dealing with specific areas of EU policy, which appoints sub-committees to deal with specific subjects, a select committee on science and technology, a select committee on economic affairs and also one on the constitution. There is also a select committee on delegated powers and regulatory reform and one on the merits of statutory instruments. In addition, *ad hoc* select committees have been set up from time to time to investigate specific subjects. There are also joint committees of the two houses, eg the committees on statutory instruments and on human rights.

THE SPEAKER – The Speaker of the House of Commons is the spokesperson and chair of the Chamber. He or she is elected by the house at the beginning of each parliament or when the previous Speaker retires or dies. The Speaker neither speaks in debates nor votes in divisions except when the voting is equal.

VACANT SEATS – When a vacancy occurs in the House of Commons during a session of parliament, the writ for the by-election is moved by a whip of the party to which the member whose seat has been vacated belonged. If the house is in recess, the Speaker can issue a warrant for a writ, should two members certify to him that a seat is vacant.

WESTMINSTER HALL SITTINGS – Following a report by the Modernisation of the House of Commons Select Committee, the Commons decided in May 1999 to set up a second debating forum. It is known as 'Westminster Hall' and sittings are in the Grand Committee Room on Tuesdays and Wednesdays from 9.30 to 11.30am and from 2 to 4.30pm, and Thursdays from 2.30 to 5.30pm. Sittings will be open to the public at the times indicated.

WHIPS – In order to secure the attendance of members of a particular party in parliament, particularly on the occasion of an important vote, whips (originally known as 'whippers-in') are appointed. The written appeal or circular letter issued by them is also known as a 'whip', its urgency being denoted by the number of times it is underlined. Failure to respond to a three-line whip is tantamount in the Commons to secession (at any rate temporarily) from the party. Whips are provided with office accommodation in both houses, and government and some opposition whips receive salaries from public funds.

HOUSE OF COMMONS INFORMATION OFFICE
Norman Shaw Building (North), London SW1A 2TT
T 020-7219 4272
E hcinfo@parliament.uk W www.parliament.uk

PARLIAMENTARY ARCHIVES
Houses of Parliament, London SW1A 0PW
T 020-7219 3074
E archives@parliament.uk W www.parliament.uk/archives

Since 1497, the records of parliament have been kept within the Palace of Westminster. They are in the custody of the Clerk of the Parliaments. In 1946 the House of Lords Record Office, which became the Parliamentary Archives in 2006, was established to supervise their preservation and their availability to the public. Some three million documents are preserved, including acts of parliament from 1497, journals of the House of Lords from 1510, minutes and committee proceedings from 1610, and papers laid before parliament from 1531. Among the records are the Petition of Right, the death warrant of Charles I, the Declaration of Breda, and the Bill of Rights. Records are made available through a public search room.
Clerk of the Records, Dr Caroline Shenton

GOVERNMENT OFFICE

The government is the body of ministers responsible for the administration of national affairs, determining policy and introducing into parliament any legislation necessary to give effect to government policy. The majority of ministers are members of the House of Commons but members of the House of Lords, or of neither house, may also hold ministerial responsibility. The prime minister is, by current convention, always a member of the House of Commons.

THE PRIME MINISTER

The office of prime minister, which had been in existence for nearly 200 years, was officially recognised in 1905 and its holder was granted a place in the table of precedence. The prime minister, by tradition also First Lord of the Treasury and Minister for the Civil Service, is appointed by the sovereign and is usually the leader of the party which enjoys, or can secure, a majority in the House of Commons. Other ministers are appointed by the sovereign on the recommendation of the prime minister, who also allocates functions among ministers and has the power to obtain their resignation or dismissal individually.

The prime minister informs the sovereign on state and political matters, advises on the dissolution of parliament, and makes recommendations for important crown appointments, ie the award of honours, etc.

As the chair of cabinet meetings and leader of a political party, the prime minister is responsible for translating party policy into government activity. As leader of the government, the prime minister is responsible to parliament and to the electorate for the policies and their implementation.

The prime minister also represents the nation in international affairs, eg summit conferences.

THE CABINET

The cabinet developed during the 18th century as an inner committee of the Privy Council, which was the chief source of executive power until that time. The cabinet is composed of about 20 ministers chosen by the prime minister, usually the heads of government departments (generally known as secretaries of state unless they have a special title, eg Chancellor of the Exchequer), the leaders of the two houses of parliament, and the holders of various traditional offices.

The cabinet's functions are the final determination of policy, control of government and coordination of government departments. The exercise of its functions is dependent upon enjoying majority support in the House of Commons. Cabinet meetings are held in private, taking place once or twice a week during parliamentary sittings and less often during a recess. Proceedings are confidential, the members being bound by their oath as privy counsellors not to disclose information about the proceedings.

The convention of collective responsibility means that the cabinet acts unanimously even when cabinet ministers do not all agree on a subject. The policies of departmental ministers must be consistent with the policies of the government as a whole, and once the government's policy has been decided, each minister is expected to support it or resign.

The convention of ministerial responsibility holds a minister, as the political head of his or her department, accountable to parliament for the department's work. Departmental ministers usually decide all matters within their responsibility, although on matters of political importance they normally consult their colleagues collectively. A decision by a departmental minister is binding on the government as a whole.

POLITICAL PARTIES

Before the reign of William and Mary the principal officers of state were chosen by and were responsible to the sovereign alone, and not to parliament or the nation at large. Such officers acted sometimes in concert with one another but more often independently, and the fall of one did not, of necessity, involve that of others, although all were liable to be dismissed at any moment.

In 1693 the Earl of Sunderland recommended to William III the advisability of selecting a ministry from the political party which enjoyed a majority in the House of Commons, and the first united ministry was drawn in 1696 from the Whigs, to which party the king owed his throne. This group became known as the 'Junto' and was regarded with suspicion as a novelty in the political life of the nation, being a small section meeting in secret apart from the main body of ministers. It may be regarded as the forerunner of the cabinet and in the course of time it led to the establishment of the principle of joint responsibility of ministers, so that internal disagreement caused a change of personnel or resignation of the whole body of ministers.

The accession of George I, who was unfamiliar with the English language, led to a disinclination on the part of the sovereign to preside at meetings of his ministers and caused the emergence of a prime minister, a position first acquired by Robert Walpole in 1721 and retained by him without interruption for 20 years and 326 days.

DEVELOPMENT OF PARTIES

In 1828 the Whigs became known as Liberals, a name originally given by opponents to imply laxity of principles, but gradually accepted by the party to indicate its claim to be pioneers and champions of political reform and progressive legislation. In 1861 a Liberal Registration Association was founded and Liberal Associations became widespread. In 1877 a National Liberal Federation was formed, with its headquarters in London. The Liberal Party was in power for long periods during the second half of the 19th century and for several years during the first quarter of the 20th century, but after a split in the party in 1931, the numbers elected remained small. In 1988, a majority of the Liberals agreed on a merger with the Social Democratic Party under the title Social and Liberal Democrats; since 1989 they have been known as the Liberal Democrats. A minority continue separately as the Liberal Party.

Soon after the change from Whig to Liberal, the Tory Party became known as Conservative, a name believed to have been invented by John Wilson Croker in 1830 and to have been generally adopted around the time of the passing of the Reform Act of 1832 – to indicate that the preservation of national institutions was the leading principle of the party. After the Home Rule crisis of 1886 the dissentient Liberals entered into a compact with the Conservatives, under which the latter undertook not to contest their seats, but a separate Liberal Unionist organisation was maintained until 1912, when it was united with the Conservatives.

Labour candidates for parliament made their first appearance at the general election of 1892, when there were 27 standing as Labour or Liberal-Labour. In 1900 the Labour Representation Committee (LRC) was set up in order to establish a distinct Labour group in parliament, with its own whips, its own policy, and a readiness to cooperate with any party which might be engaged in promoting legislation in the direct interests of labour. In 1906 the LRC became known as the Labour Party.

The Council for Social Democracy was announced by four former Labour cabinet ministers in January 1981 and in March 1981 the Social Democratic Party (SDP) was launched. Later that year the SDP and the Liberal Party formed an electoral alliance. In 1988 a majority of the SDP agreed on a merger with the Liberal Party but a minority continued as a separate party under the SDP title. In 1990 it was decided to wind up the party organisation and its three sitting MPs were known as independent social democrats. None were returned at the 1992 general election.

Plaid Cymru was founded in 1926 to provide an independent political voice for Wales and to campaign for self-government in Wales.

The Scottish National Party was founded in 1934 to campaign for independence for Scotland.

The Social Democratic and Labour Party was founded in 1970, emerging from the civil rights movement of the 1960s, with the aim of promoting reform, reconciliation and partnership across the sectarian divide in Northern Ireland, and of opposing violence from any quarter.

The Democratic Unionist Party was founded in 1971 to resist moves by the Ulster Unionist Party which were considered a threat to the Union. Its aim is to maintain Northern Ireland as an integral part of the UK.

The Ulster Unionist Council first met formally in 1905. Its objectives are to maintain Northern Ireland as an integral part of the UK and to promote the aims of the Ulster Unionist Party.

Sinn Fein first emerged in the 1900s as a federation of nationalist clubs. It is a left-wing republican and labour party that seeks to end British governance in Ireland and achieve a 32-county republic.

GOVERNMENT AND OPPOSITION

The government is formed by the party which wins the largest number of seats in the House of Commons at a general election, or which has the support of a majority of members in the House of Commons. By tradition, the leader of the majority party is asked by the sovereign to form a government, while the largest minority party becomes the official opposition with its own leader and a shadow cabinet. Leaders of the government and opposition sit on the front benches of the Commons with their supporters (the back-benchers) sitting behind them.

FINANCIAL SUPPORT

Financial support for opposition parties in the House of Commons was introduced in 1975 and is commonly known as Short Money, after Edward Short, the leader of the house at that time, who introduced the scheme. Short Money allocation for 2009–10 is:

Conservative	£4,104,970
Liberal Democrats	£1,749,385
Plaid Cymru	£68,176
SNP	£145,333
SDLP	£61,118
Democratic Unionists	£163,987

A specific allocation for the leader of the opposition's office was introduced in April 1999 and has been set at £652,936 for the years 2009–10

Financial support for opposition parties in the House of Lords was introduced in 1996 and is commonly known as Cranborne Money.

The parties included here are those with MPs sitting in the House of Commons in the present parliament.

CONSERVATIVE PARTY

Conservative Campaign Headquarters, 30 Millbank, London SW1P 4DP
T 020-7222 9000
E theconservativeparty@conservatives.com
W www.conservatives.com

SHADOW CABINET *as at June 2009*

Leader of the Opposition, Rt. Hon. David Cameron, MP
Senior Member and Secretary of State for Foreign Affairs, Rt. Hon. William Hague, MP
Chancellor of the Exchequer and General Election Campaign Coordinator, George Osborne, MP
Secretary of State for Home Affairs, Chris Grayling, MP
Party Chair, Eric Pickles, MP
Chair of Policy Review and of Conservative Research Department, Rt. Hon. Oliver Letwin, MP
Minister for the Cabinet Office and Chancellor of the Duchy of Lancaster, Rt. Hon. Francis Maude, MP

Secretary of State for Business, Enterprise and Regulatory Reform, Rt. Hon. Kenneth Clarke, MP
Secretary of State for Children, Schools and Families, Michael Gove, MP
Secretary of State for Communities and Local Government, Caroline Spelman, MP
Minister for Community Cohesion, Baroness Warsi, MP
Secretary of State for Culture, Media and Sport, Jeremy Hunt, MP
Secretary of State for Defence, Dr Liam Fox, MP
Secretary of State for Energy and Climate Change, Greg Clark, MP
Secretary of State for Environment, Food and Rural Affairs, Nick Herbert, MP
**Minister for Europe,* Mark Francois, MP
Secretary of State for Health, Andrew Lansley, CBE, MP
**Minister for Housing,* Grant Shapps, MP
Secretary of State for Innovation, Universities and Skills, David Willetts, MP
Secretary of State for International Development, Andrew Mitchell, MP
Secretary of State for Justice, Dominic Grieve, MP
Leader in the House of Commons, Alan Duncan, MP
Leader in the House of Lords, Rt. Hon. Lord Strathclyde
Secretary of State for Northern Ireland, Owen Paterson, MP
Secretary of State for Scotland, David Mundell, MP
**Minister for Security and National Security Adviser to the Leader of the Opposition,* Baroness Neville-Jones, DCMG
Secretary of State for Transport, Theresa Villiers, MP
Chief Secretary to the Treasury, Philip Hammond, MP
Secretary of State for Wales, Cheryl Gillan, MP
Secretary of State for Work and Pensions and Minister for Women, Rt. Hon. Theresa May, MP

CONSERVATIVE WHIPS
House of Lords, Baroness Anelay of St Johns, DBE
House of Commons, Rt. Hon. Patrick McLoughlin, MP
*Attends Cabinet meetings but is not a Cabinet member

LABOUR PARTY

39 Victoria Street, London SW1H 0HA
T 0870-590 0200 W www.labour.org.uk
Parliamentary Party Leader, Rt. Hon. Gordon Brown, MP
Deputy Party Leader, Leader in the Commons and Party Chair, Rt. Hon. Harriet Harman, QC, MP
Leader in the Lords, Rt. Hon. Baroness Royall of Blaisdon
General Secretary, Ray Collins
General Secretary, Welsh Labour, Chris Roberts
General Secretary, Scottish Labour Party, Colin Smyth

LIBERAL DEMOCRATS

4 Cowley Street, London SW1P 3NB
T 020-7222 7999
E info@libdems.org.uk W www.libdems.org.uk
President, Baroness Ros Scott
Hon. Treasurer, Lord Razzall
Chief Executive, Lord Rennard
Parliamentary Party Leader, Rt. Hon. Nick Clegg, MP
Leader in the Lords, Rt. Hon. Lord McNally
Leader in the Commons, David Heath, MP

LIBERAL DEMOCRAT SPOKESMEN *as at May 2009*
Deputy Leader and Shadow Chancellor of the Exchequer, Dr Vincent Cable, MP
Attorney-General, Lord Thomas of Gresford
Business, Enterprise and Regulatory Reform, John Thurso, MP
Cabinet Office, Jenny Willott, MP
Chair of the Manifesto Group and Chief of Staff, Danny Alexander, MP
Children, Schools and Families, David Laws, MP
Communities and Local Government, Julia Goldsworthy, MP
Culture, Media and Sport, Don Foster, MP
Defence, Nick Harvey, MP
Environment, Food and Rural Affairs, Tim Farrow, MP
Foreign and Commonwealth Affairs, Ed Davey, MP
Health, Norman Lamb, MP
Home Affairs, Tom Brake, MP
Housing, Sarah Teather, MP
Innovation, Universities and Skills, Stephen Williams, MP
International Development, Mike Moore, MP
Justice, David Howarth, MP
Scotland and Northern Ireland, Alistair Carmichael, MP
Solicitor-General, David Howarth, MP
Transport, Norman Baker, MP
Treasury, Dr Vincent Cable, MP
Wales, Roger Williams, MP
Work and Pensions, Steve Webb, MP
Chair of the Parliamentary Party, Lorely Burt, MP
Chair of Campaigns and Communications, Ed Davey, MP
Parliamentary Private Secretary to the Leader, Mark Hunter, MP

LIBERAL DEMOCRAT CHIEF WHIPS
House of Lords, Lord Shutt of Greetland
House of Commons, Paul Burstow, MP

NORTHERN IRELAND DEMOCRATIC UNIONIST PARTY

91 Dundela Avenue, Belfast BT4 3BU
T 028-9052 1323
E info@dup.org.uk W www.dup.org.uk
Parliamentary Party Leader, Peter Robinson, MP, MLA
Deputy Leader, Nigel Dodds, MP, MLA
Chair, Lord Morrow, MLA
Hon. Treasurer, Gregory Campbell, MP, MLA
Party Secretary, Michelle McIlveen, MLA

PLAID CYMRU – THE PARTY OF WALES

Ty Gwynfor, Marine Chambers, Anson Court, Atlantic Wharf, Caerdydd CF10 4AL
T 029-2047 2272 E post@plaidcymru.org
W www.plaidcymru.org
Party Leader, Ieuan Wyn Jones, AM
Party President, Dafydd Iwan
Party Vice-President, Jill Evans, MEP
Parliamentary Group Leader, Elfyn Llwyd
Chief Executive, Dr Gwenllian Lansdown

RESPECT – THE UNITY COALITION

PO Box 64078, London E1W 9BJ
T 0871-234 1696 E info@respectparty.org
W www.therespectparty.net
Party Leader, Cllr Salma Yaqoob
Chair, Dr Kay Phillips
Vice-Chair, Abdul Khaliq Mian
National Secretary, Clive Searle

SCOTTISH NATIONAL PARTY

3 Jackson's Entry, Edinburgh EH8 8PJ
T 0131-525 8900
E snp.hq@snp.org W www.snp.org
Westminster Parliamentary Party Leader, Angus Robertson, MP

Westminster Parliamentary Party Chief Whip, Stewart Hosie, MP
Scottish Parliamentary Party Leader, Alex Salmond, MSP
Scottish Parliamentary Party Chief Whip, Brian Adam, MSP
National Treasurer, Cllr Colin Beattie
National Secretary, Dr Duncan Ross
Chief Executive, Peter Murrell

SINN FEIN

53 Falls Road, Belfast BT12 4PD
T 028-9022 3000
E sfadmin@eircom.net W www.sinnfein.ie
Party President, Gerry Adams, MP, MLA
Vice-President, Mary Lou McDonald, MEP
Chair, Declan Kearney
General Secretary, Dawn Doyle

SOCIAL DEMOCRATIC AND LABOUR PARTY

121 Ormeau Road, Belfast BT7 1SH
T 028-9024 7700
E info@sdlp.ie W www.sdlp.ie
Parliamentary Party Leader, Mark Durkan, MP, MLA
Deputy Leader, Dr Alasdair McDonnell, MP, MLA
Party Whip, Pat Ramsey, MLA
Chair, Joe Byrne
Treasurer, Peter McEvoy
General Secretary, Gerry Cosgrove

ULSTER UNIONIST PARTY

First Floor, 174 Albertbridge Road, Belfast BT5 4GS
T 028-9046 3200
E uup@uup.org W www.uup.org
Party Leader, Sir Reg Empey, OBE, MLA
Deputy Leader, Cllr Danny Kennedy, MLA
Party Chairman, David Campbell, CBE
Hon. Treasurer, Cllr Mark Cosgrove
Vice-Chair, Terry Wright

MEMBERS OF PARLIAMENT as at 1 September 2009

* New MP
† Previously MP in another seat
‡ Previously MP for another party

Abbott, Diane (*b.* 1953) *Lab., Hackney North & Stoke Newington,* Maj. 7,427
Adams, Gerry (*b.* 1948) *SF, Belfast West,* Maj. 19,315
***Afriyie**, Adam (*b.* 1965) *C., Windsor,* Maj. 10,292
Ainger, Nick (*b.* 1949) *Lab., Carmarthen West & Pembrokeshire South,* Maj. 1,910
Ainsworth, Peter (*b.* 1956) *C., Surrey East,* Maj. 15,921
Ainsworth, Rt. Hon. Robert (*b.* 1952) *Lab., Coventry North East,* Maj. 14,222
***Alexander**, Danny (*b.* 1972) *LD, Inverness, Nairn, Badenoch & Strathspey,* Maj. 4,148
Alexander, Rt. Hon. Douglas (*b.* 1967) *Lab., Paisley & Renfrewshire South,* Maj. 13,232
Allen, Graham (*b.* 1953) *Lab., Nottingham North,* Maj. 12,171
Amess, David (*b.* 1952) *C., Southend West,* Maj. 8,959
Ancram, Rt. Hon. Michael (*b.* 1945) *C., Devizes,* Maj. 13,194
***Anderson**, David (*b.* 1953) *Lab., Blaydon,* Maj. 5,335
Anderson, Janet (*b.* 1949) *Lab., Rossendale & Darwen,* Maj. 3,676
Arbuthnot, Rt. Hon. James (*b.* 1952) *C., Hampshire North East,* Maj. 12,549
Armstrong, Rt. Hon. Hilary (*b.* 1945) *Lab., Durham North West,* Maj. 13,443
Atkins, Charlotte (*b.* 1950) *Lab., Staffordshire Moorlands,* Maj. 2,438
Atkinson, Peter (*b.* 1943) *C., Hexham,* Maj. 5,020
***Austin**, Ian (*b.* 1965) *Lab., Dudley North,* Maj. 5,432
Austin, John (*b.* 1944) *Lab., Erith & Thamesmead,* Maj. 11,500
Bacon, Richard (*b.* 1962) *C., Norfolk South,* Maj. 8,782
Bailey, Adrian (*b.* 1945) *Lab. (Co-op), West Bromwich West,* Maj. 10,894
Baird, Vera, QC (*b.* 1950) *Lab., Redcar,* Maj. 12,116
Baker, Norman (*b.* 1957) *LD, Lewes,* Maj. 8,474
Baldry, Tony (*b.* 1950) *C., Banbury,* Maj. 10,797
***Balls**, Rt. Hon. Ed (*b.* 1967) *Lab. (Co-op), Normanton,* Maj. 10,002
***Banks**, Gordon (*b.* 1955) *Lab., Ochil & Perthshire South,* Maj. 688
Barker, Gregory (*b.* 1966) *C., Bexhill & Battle,* Maj. 13,449
***Barlow**, Celia (*b.* 1955) *Lab., Hove,* Maj. 420
Baron, John (*b.* 1959) *C., Billericay,* Maj. 11,206
Barrett, John (*b.* 1954) *LD, Edinburgh West,* Maj. 13,600
Barron, Rt. Hon. Kevin (*b.* 1946) *Lab., Rother Valley,* Maj. 14,224
Battle, Rt. Hon. John (*b.* 1951) *Lab., Leeds West,* Maj. 12,810
Bayley, Hugh (*b.* 1952) *Lab., York, City of,* Maj. 10,472
Beckett, Rt. Hon. Margaret (*b.* 1943) *Lab., Derby South,* Maj. 5,657
Begg, Anne (*b.* 1955) *Lab., Aberdeen South,* Maj. 1,348
Beith, Rt. Hon. Sir Alan (*b.* 1943) *LD, Berwick-upon-Tweed,* Maj. 8,632
Bell, Sir Stuart (*b.* 1938) *Lab., Middlesbrough,* Maj. 12,567
Bellingham, Henry (*b.* 1955) *C., Norfolk North West,* Maj. 9,180
Benn, Rt. Hon. Hilary (*b.* 1953) *Lab., Leeds Central,* Maj. 11,866
Benton, Joe (*b.* 1933) *Lab., Bootle,* Maj. 16,357
***Benyon**, Richard (*b.* 1960) *C., Newbury,* Maj. 3,460
Bercow, John (*b.* 1963) *The Speaker, Buckingham,* Maj. 18,129
Beresford, Sir Paul (*b.* 1946) *C., Mole Valley,* Maj. 11,997
Berry, Dr Roger (*b.* 1948) *Lab., Kingswood,* Maj. 7,873
Betts, Clive (*b.* 1950) *Lab., Sheffield Attercliffe,* Maj. 15,967
***Binley**, Brian (*b.* 1942) *C., Northampton South,* Maj. 4,419
Blackman, Liz (*b.* 1949) *Lab., Erewash,* Maj. 7,084
***Blackman-Woods**, Dr Roberta (*b.* 1957) *Lab., Durham, City of,* Maj. 3,274
Blears, Rt. Hon. Hazel (*b.* 1956) *Lab., Salford,* Maj. 7,945
Blizzard, Bob (*b.* 1950) *Lab., Waveney,* Maj. 5,915
Blunkett, Rt. Hon. David (*b.* 1947) *Lab., Sheffield Brightside,* Maj. 13,644
Blunt, Crispin (*b.* 1960) *C., Reigate,* Maj. 10,988
***Bone**, Peter (*b.* 1952) *C., Wellingborough,* Maj. 687
Borrow, David (*b.* 1952) *Lab., Ribble South,* Maj. 2,184
Boswell, Tim (*b.* 1942) *C., Daventry,* Maj. 14,686
Bottomley, Peter (*b.* 1944) *C., Worthing West,* Maj. 9,379
Bradshaw, Ben (*b.* 1960) *Lab., Exeter,* Maj. 7,665
Brady, Graham (*b.* 1967) *C., Altrincham & Sale West,* Maj. 7,159
Brake, Tom (*b.* 1962) *LD, Carshalton & Wallington,* Maj. 1,068
Brazier, Julian (*b.* 1953) *C., Canterbury,* Maj. 7,471
Breed, Colin (*b.* 1947) *LD, Cornwall South East,* Maj. 6,507
Brennan, Kevin (*b.* 1959) *Lab., Cardiff West,* Maj. 8,167
***Brokenshire**, James (*b.* 1968) *C., Hornchurch,* Maj. 480
Brooke, Annette (*b.* 1947) *LD, Dorset Mid & Poole North,* Maj. 5,482
Brown, Rt. Hon. Gordon (*b.* 1951) *Lab., Kirkcaldy & Cowdenbeath,* Maj. 18,216
***Brown**, Lyn (*b.* 1960) *Lab., West Ham,* Maj. 9,801
Brown, Rt. Hon. Nicholas (*b.* 1950) *Lab., Newcastle upon Tyne East & Wallsend,* Maj. 7,565
Brown, Russell (*b.* 1951) *Lab., Dumfries & Galloway,* Maj. 2,922
Browne, Rt. Hon. Desmond (*b.* 1952) *Lab., Kilmarnock & Loudoun,* Maj. 8,703
***Browne**, Jeremy (*b.* 1970) *LD, Taunton,* Maj. 573
Browning, Angela (*b.* 1946) *C., Tiverton & Honiton,* Maj. 11,051
Bruce, Rt. Hon. Malcolm (*b.* 1944) *LD, Gordon,* Maj. 11,026
Bryant, Chris (*b.* 1962) *Lab., Rhondda,* Maj. 16,242
Buck, Karen (*b.* 1958) *Lab., Regent's Park & Kensington North,* Maj. 6,131
Burden, Richard (*b.* 1954) *Lab., Birmingham Northfield,* Maj. 6,454
Burgon, Colin (*b.* 1948) *Lab., Elmet,* Maj. 4,528
Burnham, Rt. Hon. Andy (*b.* 1970) *Lab., Leigh,* Maj. 17,272
Burns, Simon (*b.* 1952) *C., Chelmsford West,* Maj. 9,620
***Burrowes**, David (*b.* 1969) *C., Enfield Southgate,* Maj. 1,747
Burstow, Paul (*b.* 1962) *LD, Sutton & Cheam,* Maj. 2,846
Burt, Alistair (*b.* 1955) *C., Bedfordshire North East,* Maj. 12,251
***Burt**, Lorely (*b.* 1957) *LD, Solihull,* Maj. 279
***Butler**, Dawn (*b.* 1969) *Lab., Brent South,* Maj. 11,326
Butterfill, Sir John (*b.* 1941) *C., Bournemouth West,* Maj. 4,031

Byers, Rt. Hon. Stephen (*b.* 1953) *Lab., Tyneside North,* Maj. 15,037
Byrne, Liam (*b.* 1970) *Lab., Birmingham Hodge Hill,* Maj. 5,449
Cable, Dr Vincent (*b.* 1943) *LD, Twickenham,* Maj. 9,965
Caborn, Rt. Hon. Richard (*b.* 1943) *Lab., Sheffield Central,* Maj. 7,055
Cairns, David (*b.* 1966) *Lab., Inverclyde,* Maj. 11,259
Cameron, Rt. Hon. David (*b.* 1966) *C., Witney,* Maj. 14,156
Campbell, Alan (*b.* 1957) *Lab., Tynemouth,* Maj. 4,143
Campbell, Gregory (*b.* 1953) *DUP, Londonderry East,* Maj. 7,727
Campbell, Rt. Hon. Sir Menzies (*b.* 1941) *LD, Fife North East,* Maj. 12,571
Campbell, Ronnie (*b.* 1943) *Lab., Blyth Valley,* Maj. 8,527
Carmichael, Alistair (*b.* 1965) *LD, Orkney & Shetland,* Maj. 6,627
*__Carswell__, Douglas (*b.* 1971) *C., Harwich,* Maj. 920
Cash, Bill (*b.* 1940) *C., Stone,* Maj. 9,089
Caton, Martin (*b.* 1951) *Lab., Gower,* Maj. 6,703
Cawsey, Ian (*b.* 1960) *Lab., Brigg & Goole,* Maj. 2,894
Challen, Colin (*b.* 1953) *Lab., Morley & Rothwell,* Maj. 12,343
Chapman, Ben (*b.* 1940) *Lab., Wirral South,* Maj. 3,724
Chaytor, David (*b.* 1949) *Lab., Bury North,* Maj. 2,926
Chope, Christopher (*b.* 1947) *C., Christchurch,* Maj. 15,559
Clapham, Michael (*b.* 1943) *Lab., Barnsley West & Penistone,* Maj. 11,314
Clappison, James (*b.* 1956) *C., Hertsmere,* Maj. 11,093
*__Clark__, Greg (*b.* 1967) *C., Tunbridge Wells,* Maj. 9,988
*__Clark__, Katy (*b.* 1967) *Lab., Ayrshire North & Arran,* Maj. 11,296
Clark, Paul (*b.* 1957) *Lab., Gillingham,* Maj. 254
Clarke, Rt. Hon. Charles (*b.* 1950) *Lab., Norwich South,* Maj. 3,653
Clarke, Rt. Hon. Kenneth (*b.* 1940) *C., Rushcliffe,* Maj. 12,974
Clarke, Rt. Hon. Thomas (*b.* 1941) *Lab., Coatbridge, Chryston & Bellshill,* Maj. 19,519
*__Clegg__, Rt. Hon. Nick (*b.* 1967) *LD, Sheffield Hallam,* Maj. 8,682
Clelland, David (*b.* 1943) *Lab., Tyne Bridge,* Maj. 10,400
Clifton-Brown, Geoffrey (*b.* 1953) *C., Cotswold,* Maj. 9,688
Clwyd, Rt. Hon. Ann (*b.* 1937) *Lab., Cynon Valley,* Maj. 13,259
Coaker, Vernon (*b.* 1953) *Lab., Gedling,* Maj. 3,811
Coffey, Ann (*b.* 1946) *Lab., Stockport,* Maj. 9,163
Cohen, Harry (*b.* 1949) *Lab., Leyton & Wanstead,* Maj. 6,857
Connarty, Michael (*b.* 1947) *Lab., Linlithgow & Falkirk East,* Maj. 11,202
‡**Conway**, Derek (*b.* 1953) *Ind. C., Old Bexley & Sidcup,* Maj. 9,920
Cook, Frank (*b.* 1935) *Lab., Stockton North,* Maj. 12,437
*__Cooper__, Rosie (*b.* 1950) *Lab., Lancashire West,* Maj. 6,084
Cooper, Rt. Hon. Yvette (*b.* 1969) *Lab., Pontefract & Castleford,* Maj. 15,246
Corbyn, Jeremy (*b.* 1949) *Lab., Islington North,* Maj. 6,716
Cormack, Sir Patrick (*b.* 1939) *C., Staffordshire South,* Maj. 8,847
Cousins, Jim (*b.* 1944) *Lab., Newcastle upon Tyne Central,* Maj. 3,982
*__Cox__, Geoffrey (*b.* 1960) *C., Devon West & Torridge,* Maj. 3,236
*__Crabb__, Stephen (*b.* 1973) *C., Preseli Pembrokeshire,* Maj. 607
Crausby, David (*b.* 1946) *Lab., Bolton North East,* Maj. 4,103
*__Creagh__, Mary (*b.* 1967) *Lab., Wakefield,* Maj. 5,154
Cruddas, Jonathan (*b.* 1965) *Lab., Dagenham,* Maj. 7,605
Cryer, Ann (*b.* 1939) *Lab., Keighley,* Maj. 4,852
Cummings, John (*b.* 1943) *Lab., Easington,* Maj. 18,636
Cunningham, Jim (*b.* 1941) *Lab., Coventry South,* Maj. 6,255
Cunningham, Tony (*b.* 1952) *Lab., Workington,* Maj. 6,895
Curry, Rt. Hon. David (*b.* 1944) *C., Skipton & Ripon,* Maj. 11,620
Curtis-Thomas, Claire (*b.* 1958) *Lab., Crosby,* Maj. 5,840
Darling, Rt. Hon. Alistair (*b.* 1953) *Lab., Edinburgh South West,* Maj. 7,242
Davey, Edward (*b.* 1965) *LD, Kingston & Surbiton,* Maj. 8,966
David, Wayne (*b.* 1957) *Lab., Caerphilly,* Maj. 15,359
Davidson, Ian (*b.* 1950) *Lab. (Co-op), Glasgow South West,* Maj. 13,896
*__Davies__, Dai (*b.* 1959) *Ind., Blaenau Gwent,* Maj. 2,484
*__Davies__, David (*b.* 1970) *C., Monmouth,* Maj. 4,527
*__Davies__, Philip (*b.* 1972) *C., Shipley,* Maj. 422
‡**Davies**, Quentin (*b.* 1944) *Lab., Grantham & Stamford,* Maj. 7,445
Davis, Rt. Hon. David (*b.* 1948) *C., Haltemprice & Howden,* Maj. 15,355
Dean, Janet (*b.* 1949) *Lab., Burton,* Maj. 1,421
Denham, Rt. Hon. John (*b.* 1953) *Lab., Southampton Itchen,* Maj. 9,302
*__Devine__, Jim (*b.* 1953) *Lab., Livingston,* Maj. 2,680
Dhanda, Parmjit (*b.* 1971) *Lab., Gloucester,* Maj. 4,271
Dismore, Andrew (*b.* 1954) *Lab., Hendon,* Maj. 2,699
Djanogly, Jonathan (*b.* 1965) *C., Huntingdon,* Maj. 12,847
Dobbin, Jim (*b.* 1941) *Lab. (Co-op), Heywood & Middleton,* Maj. 11,083
Dobson, Rt. Hon. Frank (*b.* 1940) *Lab., Holborn & St Pancras,* Maj. 4,787
Dodds, Nigel (*b.* 1958) *DUP, Belfast North,* Maj. 5,188
Doherty, Pat (*b.* 1945) *SF, Tyrone West,* Maj. 5,005
‡**Donaldson**, Rt. Hon. Jeffrey (*b.* 1962) *DUP, Lagan Valley,* Maj. 14,117
Donohoe, Brian (*b.* 1948) *Lab., Ayrshire Central,* Maj. 10,423
Doran, Frank (*b.* 1949) *Lab., Aberdeen North,* Maj. 6,795
Dorrell, Rt. Hon. Stephen (*b.* 1952) *C., Charnwood,* Maj. 8,809
*__Dorries__, Nadine (*b.* 1958) *C., Bedfordshire Mid,* Maj. 11,355
Dowd, Jim (*b.* 1951) *Lab., Lewisham West,* Maj. 9,932
Drew, David (*b.* 1952) *Lab. (Co-op), Stroud,* Maj. 350
*__Duddridge__, James (*b.* 1971) *C., Rochford & Southend East,* Maj. 5,494
Duncan, Alan (*b.* 1957) *C., Rutland & Melton,* Maj. 12,930
Duncan Smith, Rt. Hon. Iain (*b.* 1954) *C., Chingford & Woodford Green,* Maj. 10,641
*__Dunne__, Philip (*b.* 1958) *C., Ludlow,* Maj. 2,027
*__Durkan__, Mark (*b.* 1960) *SDLP, Foyle,* Maj. 5,957
Eagle, Angela (*b.* 1961) *Lab., Wallasey,* Maj. 9,109
Eagle, Maria (*b.* 1961) *Lab., Liverpool Garston,* Maj. 7,193

Efford, Clive (*b.* 1958) *Lab., Eltham,* Maj. 3,276
Ellman, Louise (*b.* 1945) *Lab. (Co-op), Liverpool Riverside,* Maj. 10,214
***Ellwood**, Tobias (*b.* 1966) *C., Bournemouth East,* Maj. 5,244
***Engel**, Natascha (*b.* 1967) *Lab., Derbyshire North East,* Maj. 10,065
Ennis, Jeff (*b.* 1952) *Lab., Barnsley East & Mexborough,* Maj. 14,125
Etherington, Bill (*b.* 1941) *Lab., Sunderland North,* Maj. 9,995
Evans, Nigel (*b.* 1957) *C., Ribble Valley,* Maj. 14,171
†**Evennett**, David (*b.* 1949) *C., Bexleyheath & Crayford,* Maj. 4,551
Fabricant, Michael (*b.* 1950) *C., Lichfield,* Maj. 7,080
Fallon, Michael (*b.* 1952) *C., Sevenoaks,* Maj. 12,970
Farrelly, Paul (*b.* 1962) *Lab., Newcastle-under-Lyme,* Maj. 8,108
***Farron**, Tim (*b.* 1970) *LD, Westmorland & Lonsdale,* Maj. 267
***Featherstone**, Lynne (*b.* 1951) *LD, Hornsey & Wood Green,* Maj. 2,395
Field, Rt. Hon. Frank (*b.* 1942) *Lab., Birkenhead,* Maj. 12,934
Field, Mark (*b.* 1934) *C., Cities of London & Westminster,* Maj. 8,095
Fisher, Mark (*b.* 1944) *Lab., Stoke-on-Trent Central,* Maj. 9,774
Fitzpatrick, Jim (*b.* 1952) *Lab., Poplar & Canning Town,* Maj. 7,129
***Flello**, Robert (*b.* 1966) *Lab., Stoke-on-Trent South,* Maj. 8,681
Flint, Rt. Hon. Caroline (*b.* 1961) *Lab., Don Valley,* Maj. 8,598
Flynn, Paul (*b.* 1935) *Lab., Newport West,* Maj. 5,458
Follett, Barbara (*b.* 1942) *Lab., Stevenage,* Maj. 3,139
Foster, Don (*b.* 1947) *LD, Bath,* Maj. 4,638
Foster, Michael Jabez (*b.* 1946) *Lab., Hastings & Rye,* Maj. 2,026
Foster, Michael (*b.* 1963) *Lab., Worcester,* Maj. 3,144
Fox, Dr Liam (*b.* 1961) *C., Woodspring,* Maj. 6,016
Francis, Dr Hywel (*b.* 1946) *Lab., Aberavon,* Maj. 13,937
Francois, Mark (*b.* 1965) *C., Rayleigh,* Maj. 14,726
†**Fraser**, Christopher (*b.* 1962) *C., Norfolk South West,* Maj. 10,086
Gale, Roger (*b.* 1943) *C., Thanet North,* Maj. 7,634
†‡**Galloway**, George (*b.* 1954) *Respect, Bethnal Green & Bow,* Maj. 823
Gapes, Mike (*b.* 1952) *Lab. (Co-op), Ilford South,* Maj. 9,228
Gardiner, Barry (*b.* 1957) *Lab., Brent North,* Maj. 5,641
Garnier, Edward (*b.* 1952) *C., Harborough,* Maj. 3,892
***Gauke**, David (*b.* 1971) *C., Hertfordshire South West,* Maj. 8,473
George, Andrew (*b.* 1958) *LD, St Ives,* Maj. 11,609
George, Rt. Hon. Bruce (*b.* 1942) *Lab., Walsall South,* Maj. 7,946
Gerrard, Neil (*b.* 1942) *Lab., Walthamstow,* Maj. 7,993
Gibb, Nick (*b.* 1960) *C., Bognor Regis & Littlehampton,* Maj. 7,822
Gidley, Sandra (*b.* 1957) *LD, Romsey,* Maj. 125
Gildernew, Michelle (*b.* 1970) *SF, Fermanagh & South Tyrone,* Maj. 4,582
Gillan, Cheryl (*b.* 1952) *C., Chesham & Amersham,* Maj. 13,798
Gilroy, Linda (*b.* 1949) *Lab. (Co-op), Plymouth Sutton,* Maj. 4,109
Godsiff, Roger (*b.* 1946) *Lab., Birmingham Sparkbrook & Small Heath,* Maj. 3,289
Goggins, Paul (*b.* 1953) *Lab., Wythenshawe & Sale East,* Maj. 10,827
***Goldsworthy**, Julia (*b.* 1978) *LD, Falmouth & Camborne,* Maj. 1,886
***Goodman**, Helen (*b.* 1958) *Lab., Bishop Auckland,* Maj. 10,047
Goodman, Paul (*b.* 1960) *C., Wycombe,* Maj. 7,051
***Goodwill**, Robert (*b.* 1956) *C., Scarborough & Whitby,* Maj. 1,245
***Gove**, Michael (*b.* 1967) *C., Surrey Heath,* Maj. 10,845
Gray, James (*b.* 1954) *C., Wiltshire North,* Maj. 5,303
Grayling, Chris (*b.* 1962) *C., Epsom & Ewell,* Maj. 16,447
Green, Damian (*b.* 1956) *C., Ashford,* Maj. 13,298
***Greening**, Justine (*b.* 1969) *C., Putney,* Maj. 1,766
Greenway, John (*b.* 1946) *C., Ryedale,* Maj. 10,469
Grieve, Dominic (*b.* 1956) *C., Beaconsfield,* Maj. 15,253
***Griffith**, Nia (*b.* 1956) *Lab., Llanelli,* Maj. 7,234
Griffiths, Nigel (*b.* 1955) *Lab., Edinburgh South,* Maj. 405
Grogan, John (*b.* 1961) *Lab., Selby,* Maj. 467
Gummer, Rt. Hon. John (*b.* 1939) *C., Suffolk Coastal,* Maj. 9,685
***Gwynne**, Andrew (*b.* 1974) *Lab., Denton & Reddish,* Maj. 13,498
Hague, Rt. Hon. William (*b.* 1961) *C., Richmond (Yorks),* Maj. 17,807
Hain, Rt. Hon. Peter (*b.* 1950) *Lab., Neath,* Maj. 12,710
Hall, Mike (*b.* 1952) *Lab., Weaver Vale,* Maj. 6,855
Hall, Patrick (*b.* 1951) *Lab., Bedford,* Maj. 3,383
Hamilton, David (*b.* 1950) *Lab., Midlothian,* Maj. 7,265
Hamilton, Fabian (*b.* 1955) *Lab., Leeds North East,* Maj. 5,262
Hammond, Philip (*b.* 1955) *C., Runnymede & Weybridge,* Maj. 12,349
***Hammond**, Stephen (*b.* 1962) *C., Wimbledon,* Maj. 2,301
Hancock, Mike (*b.* 1946) *LD, Portsmouth South,* Maj. 3,362
***Hands**, Greg (*b.* 1965) *C., Hammersmith & Fulham,* Maj. 5,029
Hanson, Rt. Hon. David (*b.* 1957) *Lab., Delyn,* Maj. 6,644
Harman, Rt. Hon. Harriet (*b.* 1950) *Lab., Camberwell & Peckham,* Maj. 13,483
***Harper**, Mark (*b.* 1970) *C., Forest of Dean,* Maj. 2,049
Harris, Dr Evan (*b.* 1965) *LD, Oxford West & Abingdon,* Maj. 7,683
Harris, Tom (*b.* 1964) *Lab., Glasgow South,* Maj. 10,832
Harvey, Nick (*b.* 1961) *LD, Devon North,* Maj. 4,972
Haselhurst, Rt. Hon. Sir Alan (*b.* 1937) *C., Deputy Speaker, Saffron Walden,* Maj. 13,008
Havard, Dai (*b.* 1949) *Lab., Merthyr Tydfil & Rhymney,* Maj. 13,934
Hayes, John (*b.* 1958) *C., South Holland & The Deepings,* Maj. 15,780
Heal, Sylvia (*b.* 1942) *Lab., Deputy Speaker, Halesowen & Rowley Regis,* Maj. 4,337
Heald, Oliver (*b.* 1954) *C., Hertfordshire North East,* Maj. 9,138
Healey, Rt. Hon. John (*b.* 1960) *Lab., Wentworth,* Maj. 15,056
Heath, David (*b.* 1954) *LD, Somerton & Frome,* Maj. 812
Heathcoat-Amory, Rt. Hon. David (*b.* 1949) *C., Wells,* Maj. 3,040
***Hemming**, John (*b.* 1960) *LD, Birmingham Yardley,* Maj. 2,672

Henderson, Doug (*b.* 1949) *Lab., Newcastle upon Tyne North,* Maj. 7,023
Hendrick, Mark (*b.* 1958) *Lab. (Co-op), Preston,* Maj. 9,407
Hendry, Charles (*b.* 1959) *C., Wealden,* Maj. 15,921
Hepburn, Stephen (*b.* 1959) *Lab., Jarrow,* Maj. 13,904
Heppell, John (*b.* 1948) *Lab., Nottingham East,* Maj. 6,939
***Herbert**, Nick (*b.* 1963) *C., Arundel & South Downs,* Maj. 11,309
Hermon, Lady Sylvia (*b.* 1956) *UUP, Down North,* Maj. 4,944
Hesford, Stephen (*b.* 1957) *Lab., Wirral West,* Maj. 1,097
Hewitt, Rt. Hon. Patricia (*b.* 1948) *Lab., Leicester West,* Maj. 9,070
Heyes, David (*b.* 1946) *Lab., Ashton-under-Lyne,* Maj. 13,952
Hill, Rt. Hon. Keith (*b.* 1943) *Lab., Streatham,* Maj. 7,466
***Hillier**, Meg (*b.* 1969) *Lab. (Co-op), Hackney South & Shoreditch,* Maj. 10,204
Hoban, Mark (*b.* 1964) *C., Fareham,* Maj. 11,702
Hodge, Rt. Hon. Margaret (*b.* 1944) *Lab., Barking,* Maj. 8,883
***Hodgson**, Sharon (*b.* 1966) *Lab., Gateshead East & Washington West,* Maj. 13,407
Hoey, Kate (*b.* 1946) *Lab., Vauxhall,* Maj. 9,977
Hogg, Rt. Hon. Douglas (*b.* 1945) *C., Sleaford & North Hykeham,* Maj. 12,705
***Hollobone**, Philip (*b.* 1964) *C., Kettering,* Maj. 3,301
***Holloway**, Adam (*b.* 1965) *C., Gravesham,* Maj. 654
Holmes, Paul (*b.* 1957) *LD, Chesterfield,* Maj. 3,045
Hood, Jimmy (*b.* 1948) *Lab., Lanark & Hamilton East,* Maj. 11,947
Hoon, Rt. Hon. Geoff (*b.* 1953) *Lab., Ashfield,* Maj. 10,213
Hope, Phil (*b.* 1955) *Lab. (Co-op), Corby,* Maj. 1,517
Hopkins, Kelvin (*b.* 1941) *Lab., Luton North,* Maj. 6,487
Horam, John (*b.* 1939) *C., Orpington,* Maj. 4,947
***Horwood**, Martin (*b.* 1962) *LD, Cheltenham,* Maj. 2,303
***Hosie**, Stewart (*b.* 1963) *SNP, Dundee East,* Maj. 383
Howard, Rt. Hon. Michael (*b.* 1941) *C., Folkestone & Hythe,* Maj. 11,680
***Howarth**, David (*b.* 1958) *LD, Cambridge,* Maj. 4,339
Howarth, Rt. Hon. George (*b.* 1949) *Lab., Knowsley North & Sefton East,* Maj. 16,269
Howarth, Gerald (*b.* 1947) *C., Aldershot,* Maj. 5,334
***Howell**, John (*b.* 1955) *C., Henley,* Maj. 10,116
Howells, Rt. Hon. Dr Kim (*b.* 1946) *Lab., Pontypridd,* Maj. 13,191
Hoyle, Lindsay (*b.* 1957) *Lab., Chorley,* Maj. 7,625
Hughes, Rt. Hon. Beverley (*b.* 1950) *Lab., Stretford & Urmston,* Maj. 7,851
Hughes, Simon (*b.* 1951) *LD, Southwark North & Bermondsey,* Maj. 5,406
***Huhne**, Chris (*b.* 1954) *LD, Eastleigh,* Maj. 568
Humble, Joan (*b.* 1951) *Lab., Blackpool North & Fleetwood,* Maj. 5,062
***Hunt**, Jeremy (*b.* 1966) *C., Surrey South West,* Maj. 5,711
***Hunter**, Mark (*b.* 1957) *LD, Cheadle,* Maj. 3,657
***Hurd**, Nick (*b.* 1962) *C., Ruislip-Northwood,* Maj. 8,910
Hutton, Rt. Hon. John (*b.* 1955) *Lab., Barrow & Furness,* Maj. 6,037
Iddon, Dr Brian (*b.* 1940) *Lab., Bolton South East,* Maj. 11,638
Illsley, Eric (*b.* 1955) *Lab., Barnsley Central,* Maj. 12,732
Ingram, Rt. Hon. Adam (*b.* 1947) *Lab., East Kilbride, Strathaven & Lesmahagow,* Maj. 14,723
Irranca-Davies, Huw (*b.* 1963) *Lab., Ogmore,* Maj. 13,703
Jack, Rt. Hon. Michael (*b.* 1946) *C., Fylde,* Maj. 12,459
Jackson, Glenda (*b.* 1936) *Lab., Hampstead & Highgate,* Maj. 3,729
***Jackson**, Stewart (*b.* 1965) *C., Peterborough,* Maj. 2,740
***James**, Sian (*b.* 1959) *Lab., Swansea East,* Maj. 11,249
Jenkin, Bernard (*b.* 1959) *C., Essex North,* Maj. 10,903
Jenkins, Brian (*b.* 1942) *Lab., Tamworth,* Maj. 2,569
Johnson, Rt. Hon. Alan (*b.* 1950) *Lab., Hull West & Hessle,* Maj. 9,450
***Johnson**, Diana (*b.* 1966) *Lab., Hull North,* Maj. 7,351
***Jones**, David (*b.* 1952) *C., Clwyd West,* Maj. 133
Jones, Helen (*b.* 1954) *Lab., Warrington North,* Maj. 12,204
Jones, Kevan (*b.* 1964) *Lab., Durham North,* Maj. 16,781
Jones, Dr Lynne (*b.* 1951) *Lab., Birmingham Selly Oak,* Maj. 8,851
Jones, Martyn (*b.* 1947) *Lab., Clwyd South,* Maj. 6,348
Jowell, Rt. Hon. Tessa (*b.* 1947) *Lab., Dulwich & West Norwood,* Maj. 8,807
Joyce, Eric (*b.* 1960) *Lab., Falkirk,* Maj. 13,475
Kaufman, Rt. Hon. Sir Gerald (*b.* 1930) *Lab., Manchester Gorton,* Maj. 5,808
***Kawczynski**, Daniel (*b.* 1972) *C., Shrewsbury & Atcham,* Maj. 1,808
Keeble, Sally (*b.* 1951) *Lab., Northampton North,* Maj. 3,960
***Keeley**, Barbara (*b.* 1952) *Lab., Worsley,* Maj. 9,368
Keen, Alan (*b.* 1937) *Lab. (Co-op), Feltham & Heston,* Maj. 6,820
Keen, Ann (*b.* 1948) *Lab., Brentford & Isleworth,* Maj. 4,411
Keetch, Paul (*b.* 1961) *LD, Hereford,* Maj. 962
Kelly, Rt. Hon. Ruth (*b.* 1968) *Lab., Bolton West,* Maj. 2,064
Kemp, Fraser (*b.* 1958) *Lab., Houghton & Washington East,* Maj. 16,065
Kennedy, Rt. Hon. Charles (*b.* 1959) *LD, Ross, Skye & Lochaber,* Maj. 14,249
Kennedy, Rt. Hon. Jane (*b.* 1958) *Lab., Liverpool Wavertree,* Maj. 5,173
Key, Robert (*b.* 1945) *C., Salisbury,* Maj. 11,142
***Khan**, Rt. Hon. Sadiq (*b.* 1970) *Lab., Tooting,* Maj. 5,381
Kidney, David (*b.* 1955) *Lab., Stafford,* Maj. 2,121
Kilfoyle, Peter (*b.* 1946) *Lab., Liverpool Walton,* Maj. 15,957
Kirkbride, Julie (*b.* 1960) *C., Bromsgrove,* Maj. 10,080
Knight, Rt. Hon. Greg (*b.* 1949) *C., Yorkshire East,* Maj. 6,283
Knight, Jim (*b.* 1965) *Lab., Dorset South,* Maj. 1,812
***Kramer**, Susan (*b.* 1950) *LD, Richmond Park,* Maj. 3,731
Kumar, Dr Ashok (*b.* 1956) *Lab., Middlesbrough South & Cleveland East,* Maj. 8,000
Ladyman, Dr Stephen (*b.* 1952) *Lab., Thanet South,* Maj. 664
Laing, Eleanor (*b.* 1958) *C., Epping Forest,* Maj. 14,358
Lait, Jacqui (*b.* 1947) *C., Beckenham,* Maj. 8,401
Lamb, Norman (*b.* 1957) *LD, Norfolk North,* Maj. 10,606
Lammy, Rt. Hon. David (*b.* 1972) *Lab., Tottenham,* Maj. 13,034
***Lancaster**, Mark (*b.* 1970) *C., Milton Keynes North East,* Maj. 1,665
Lansley, Andrew (*b.* 1956) *C., Cambridgeshire South,* Maj. 8,001
Laws, David (*b.* 1965) *LD, Yeovil,* Maj. 8,562

Laxton, Bob (*b.* 1944) *Lab., Derby North,* Maj. 3,757
Lazarowicz, Mark (*b.* 1953) *Lab. (Co-op), Edinburgh North & Leith,* Maj. 2,153
***Leech**, John (*b.* 1971) *LD, Manchester Withington,* Maj. 667
Leigh, Edward (*b.* 1950) *C., Gainsborough,* Maj. 8,003
Lepper, David (*b.* 1945) *Lab. (Co-op), Brighton Pavilion,* Maj. 5,030
Letwin, Rt. Hon. Oliver (*b.* 1956) *C., Dorset West,* Maj. 2,461
Levitt, Tom (*b.* 1954) *Lab., High Peak,* Maj. 735
Lewis, Ivan (*b.* 1967) *Lab., Bury South,* Maj. 8,912
Lewis, Dr Julian (*b.* 1951) *C., New Forest East,* Maj. 6,551
Liddell-Grainger, Ian (*b.* 1959) *C., Bridgwater,* Maj. 8,469
Lidington, David (*b.* 1956) *C., Aylesbury,* Maj. 11,065
Lilley, Rt. Hon. Peter (*b.* 1943) *C., Hitchin & Harpenden,* Maj. 11,393
Linton, Martin (*b.* 1944) *Lab., Battersea,* Maj. 163
Lloyd, Tony (*b.* 1950) *Lab., Manchester Central,* Maj. 9,776
Llwyd, Elfyn (*b.* 1951) *PC, Meirionnydd Nant Conwy,* Maj. 6,614
Lord, Sir Michael (*b.* 1938) *C., Deputy Speaker, Suffolk Central & Ipswich North,* Maj. 7,856
Loughton, Tim (*b.* 1962) *C., Worthing East & Shoreham,* Maj. 8,183
Love, Andy (*b.* 1949) *Lab. (Co-op), Edmonton,* Maj. 8,075
Lucas, Ian (*b.* 1960) *Lab., Wrexham,* Maj. 6,819
Luff, Peter (*b.* 1955) *C., Worcestershire Mid,* Maj. 13,327
McAvoy, Rt. Hon. Thomas (*b.* 1943) *Lab. (Co-op), Rutherglen & Hamilton West,* Maj. 16,112
McCabe, Stephen (*b.* 1955) *Lab., Birmingham Hall Green,* Maj. 5,714
McCafferty, Christine (*b.* 1945) *Lab., Calder Valley,* Maj. 1,367
***McCarthy**, Kerry (*b.* 1965) *Lab., Bristol East,* Maj. 8,621
***McCarthy-Fry**, Sarah (*b.* 1955) *Lab. (Co-op), Portsmouth North,* Maj. 1,139
McCartney, Rt. Hon. Ian (*b.* 1951) *Lab., Makerfield,* Maj. 18,149
†McCrea, Revd Dr William (*b.* 1948) *DUP, Antrim South,* Maj. 3,448
McDonagh, Siobhain (*b.* 1960) *Lab., Mitcham & Morden,* Maj. 12,560
***McDonnell**, Dr Alasdair (*b.* 1949) *SDLP, Belfast South,* Maj. 1,235
McDonnell, John (*b.* 1951) *Lab., Hayes & Harlington,* Maj. 10,847
***McFadden**, Rt. Hon. Pat (*b.* 1965) *Lab., Wolverhampton South East,* Maj. 10,495
McFall, Rt. Hon. John (*b.* 1944) *Lab. (Co-op), Dunbartonshire West,* Maj. 12,553
***McGovern**, James (*b.* 1956) *Lab., Dundee West,* Maj. 5,379
McGrady, Edward (*b.* 1935) *SDLP, Down South,* Maj. 9,140
McGuinness, Martin (*b.* 1950) *SF, Ulster Mid,* Maj. 10,976
McGuire, Rt. Hon. Anne (*b.* 1949) *Lab., Stirling,* Maj. 4,767
McIntosh, Anne (*b.* 1954) *C., Vale of York,* Maj. 13,712
McIsaac, Shona (*b.* 1960) *Lab., Cleethorpes,* Maj. 2,642
Mackay, Rt. Hon. Andrew (*b.* 1949) *C., Bracknell,* Maj. 12,036
McKechin, Ann (*b.* 1961) *Lab., Glasgow North,* Maj. 3,338
McKenna, Rosemary (*b.* 1941) *Lab., Cumbernauld, Kilsyth & Kirkintilloch East,* Maj. 11,562
Mackinlay, Andrew (*b.* 1949) *Lab., Thurrock,* Maj. 6,375
Maclean, Rt. Hon. David (*b.* 1953) *C., Penrith & The Border,* Maj. 11,904
McLoughlin, Rt. Hon. Patrick (*b.* 1957) *C., Derbyshire West,* Maj. 10,753
***MacNeil**, Angus (*b.* 1970) *SNP, Na h-Eileanan an Iar,* Maj. 1,441
McNulty, Rt. Hon. Tony (*b.* 1958) *Lab., Harrow East,* Maj. 4,730
MacShane, Rt. Hon. Denis (*b.* 1948) *Lab., Rotherham,* Maj. 10,681
Mactaggart, Fiona (*b.* 1953) *Lab., Slough,* Maj. 7,851
Mahmood, Khalid (*b.* 1961) *Lab., Birmingham Perry Barr,* Maj. 7,948
***Main**, Anne (*b.* 1957) *C., St Albans,* Maj. 1,361
***Malik**, Shahid (*b.* 1967) *Lab., Dewsbury,* Maj. 4,615
Malins, Humfrey (*b.* 1945) *C., Woking,* Maj. 6,612
Mallaber, Judith (*b.* 1951) *Lab., Amber Valley,* Maj. 5,275
Mann, John (*b.* 1960) *Lab., Bassetlaw,* Maj. 10,837
Maples, John (*b.* 1943) *C., Stratford-upon-Avon,* Maj. 12,184
Marris, Rob (*b.* 1955) *Lab., Wolverhampton South West,* Maj. 2,879
Marsden, Gordon (*b.* 1953) *Lab., Blackpool South,* Maj. 7,922
Marshall-Andrews, Bob (*b.* 1944) *Lab., Medway,* Maj. 213
Martlew, Eric (*b.* 1949) *Lab., Carlisle,* Maj. 5,695
***Mason**, John (*b.* 1957) *SNP, Glasgow East,* Maj. 365
Mates, Rt. Hon. Michael (*b.* 1934) *C., Hampshire East,* Maj. 5,509
Maude, Rt. Hon. Francis (*b.* 1953) *C., Horsham,* Maj. 12,627
May, Rt. Hon. Theresa (*b.* 1956) *C., Maidenhead,* Maj. 6,231
Meacher, Rt. Hon. Michael (*b.* 1939) *Lab., Oldham West & Royton,* Maj. 10,454
Meale, Alan (*b.* 1949) *Lab., Mansfield,* Maj. 11,365
Mercer, Patrick (*b.* 1956) *C., Newark,* Maj. 6,464
Merron, Gillian (*b.* 1959) *Lab., Lincoln,* Maj. 4,614
Michael, Rt. Hon. Alun (*b.* 1943) *Lab. (Co-op), Cardiff South & Penarth,* Maj. 9,237
Milburn, Rt. Hon. Alan (*b.* 1958) *Lab., Darlington,* Maj. 10,404
Miliband, Rt. Hon. David (*b.* 1966) *Lab., South Shields,* Maj. 12,312
***Miliband**, Rt. Hon. Edward (*b.* 1969) *Lab., Doncaster North,* Maj. 12,656
Miller, Andrew (*b.* 1949) *Lab., Ellesmere Port & Neston,* Maj. 6,486
***Miller**, Maria (*b.* 1964) *C., Basingstoke,* Maj. 4,680
***Milton**, Anne (*b.* 1955) *C., Guildford,* Maj. 347
Mitchell, Andrew (*b.* 1956) *C., Sutton Coldfield,* Maj. 12,283
Mitchell, Austin (*b.* 1934) *Lab., Great Grimsby,* Maj. 7,654
Moffat, Anne (*b.* 1958) *Lab., East Lothian,* Maj. 7,620
Moffatt, Laura (*b.* 1954) *Lab., Crawley,* Maj. 37
Mole, Chris (*b.* 1958) *Lab., Ipswich,* Maj. 5,332
***Moon**, Madeleine (*b.* 1950) *Lab., Bridgend,* Maj. 6,523
Moore, Michael (*b.* 1965) *LD, Berwickshire, Roxburgh & Selkirk,* Maj. 5,901
Moran, Margaret (*b.* 1955) *Lab., Luton South,* Maj. 5,650
***Morden**, Jessica (*b.* 1968) *Lab., Newport East,* Maj. 6,838
Morgan, Julie (*b.* 1944) *Lab., Cardiff North,* Maj. 1,146

Morley, Rt. Hon. Elliot (*b.* 1952) *Lab., Scunthorpe,* Maj. 8,963
Moss, Malcolm (*b.* 1943) *C., Cambridgeshire North East,* Maj. 8,901
Mountford, Kali (*b.* 1954) *Lab., Colne Valley,* Maj. 1,501
Mudie, George (*b.* 1945) *Lab., Leeds East,* Maj. 11,578
***Mulholland**, Greg (*b.* 1970) *LD, Leeds North West,* Maj. 1,877
Mullin, Chris (*b.* 1947) *Lab., Sunderland South,* Maj. 11,059
***Mundell**, David (*b.* 1962) *C., Dumfriesshire, Clydesdale & Tweeddale,* Maj. 1,738
Munn, Meg (*b.* 1959) *Lab. (Co-op), Sheffield Heeley,* Maj. 11,370
***Murphy**, Conor (*b.* 1963) *SF, Newry & Armagh,* Maj. 8,195
Murphy, Denis (*b.* 1948) *Lab., Wansbeck,* Maj. 10,581
Murphy, Rt. Hon. Jim (*b.* 1967) *Lab., Renfrewshire East,* Maj. 6,657
Murphy, Rt. Hon. Paul (*b.* 1948) *Lab., Torfaen,* Maj. 14,791
Murrison, Dr Andrew (*b.* 1961) *C., Westbury,* Maj. 5,349
Naysmith, Dr Doug (*b.* 1941) *Lab. (Co-op), Bristol North West,* Maj. 8,962
***Neill**, Bob (*b.* 1952) *C., Bromley & Chislehurst,* Maj. 633
***Newmark**, Brooks (*b.* 1958) *C., Braintree,* Maj. 3,893
Norris, Dan (*b.* 1960) *Lab., Wansdyke,* Maj. 1,839
Oaten, Mark (*b.* 1964) *LD, Winchester,* Maj. 7,476
O'Brien, Mike (*b.* 1954) *Lab., Warwickshire North,* Maj. 7,553
O'Brien, Stephen (*b.* 1957) *C., Eddisbury,* Maj. 6,195
O'Hara, Eddie (*b.* 1937) *Lab., Knowsley South,* Maj. 17,688
Olner, Bill (*b.* 1942) *Lab., Nuneaton,* Maj. 2,280
Opik, Lembit (*b.* 1965) *LD, Montgomeryshire,* Maj. 7,173
Osborne, George (*b.* 1971) *C., Tatton,* Maj. 11,731
Osborne, Sandra (*b.* 1956) *Lab., Ayr, Carrick & Cumnock,* Maj. 9,997
Ottaway, Richard (*b.* 1945) *C., Croydon South,* Maj. 13,528
Owen, Albert (*b.* 1960) *Lab., Ynys Mon,* Maj. 1,242
Paice, James (*b.* 1949) *C., Cambridgeshire South East,* Maj. 8,624
Paisley, Revd Rt. Hon. Ian (*b.* 1926) *DUP, Antrim North,* Maj. 17,965
Palmer, Dr Nick (*b.* 1950) *Lab., Broxtowe,* Maj. 2,296
Paterson, Owen (*b.* 1956) *C., Shropshire North,* Maj. 11,020
Pearson, Ian (*b.* 1959) *Lab., Dudley South,* Maj. 4,244
***Pelling**, Andrew (*b.* 1959) *C., Croydon Central,* Maj. 75
***Penning**, Michael (*b.* 1957) *C., Hemel Hempstead,* Maj. 499
***Penrose**, John (*b.* 1964) *C., Weston-Super-Mare,* Maj. 2,079
Pickles, Eric (*b.* 1952) *C., Brentwood & Ongar,* Maj. 11,612
Plaskitt, James (*b.* 1954) *Lab., Warwick & Leamington,* Maj. 266
Pope, Greg (*b.* 1960) *Lab., Hyndburn,* Maj. 5,587
Pound, Stephen (*b.* 1948) *Lab., Ealing North,* Maj. 7,059
Prentice, Bridget (*b.* 1952) *Lab., Lewisham East,* Maj. 6,751
Prentice, Gordon (*b.* 1951) *Lab., Pendle,* Maj. 2,180
Prescott, Rt. Hon. John (*b.* 1938) *Lab., Hull East,* Maj. 11,747
Price, Adam (*b.* 1968) *PC, Carmarthen East & Dinefwr,* Maj. 6,718
Primarolo, Rt. Hon. Dawn (*b.* 1954) *Lab., Bristol South,* Maj. 11,142
Prisk, Mark (*b.* 1962) *C., Hertford & Stortford,* Maj. 13,097
***Pritchard**, Mark (*b.* 1966) *C., The Wrekin,* Maj. 942
Prosser, Gwyn (*b.* 1943) *Lab., Dover,* Maj. 4,941
Pugh, Dr John (*b.* 1948) *LD, Southport,* Maj. 3,838
Purchase, Ken (*b.* 1939) *Lab. (Co-op), Wolverhampton North East,* Maj. 8,156
Purnell, Rt. Hon. James (*b.* 1970) *Lab., Stalybridge & Hyde,* Maj. 8,348
Rammell, Bill (*b.* 1959) *Lab., Harlow,* Maj. 97
Randall, John (*b.* 1955) *C., Uxbridge,* Maj. 6,171
Raynsford, Rt. Hon. Nick (*b.* 1945) *Lab., Greenwich & Woolwich,* Maj. 10,146
Redwood, Rt. Hon. John (*b.* 1951) *C., Wokingham,* Maj. 7,240
Reed, Andy (*b.* 1964) *Lab. (Co-op), Loughborough,* Maj. 1,996
***Reed**, Jamie (*b.* 1973) *Lab., Copeland,* Maj. 6,320
Reid, Alan (*b.* 1954) *LD, Argyll & Bute,* Maj. 5,636
Reid, Rt. Hon. Dr John (*b.* 1947) *Lab., Airdrie & Shotts,* Maj. 14,084
***Rennie**, Willie (*b.* 1967) *LD, Dunfermline & Fife West,* Maj. 1,800
†**Rifkind**, Rt. Hon. Sir Malcolm (*b.* 1946) *C., Kensington & Chelsea,* Maj. 12,418
***Riordan**, Linda (*b.* 1953) *Lab. (Co-op), Halifax,* Maj. 3,417
Robathan, Andrew (*b.* 1951) *C., Blaby,* Maj. 7,873
Robertson, Angus (*b.* 1969) *SNP, Moray,* Maj. 5,676
Robertson, Hugh (*b.* 1962) *C., Faversham & Kent Mid,* Maj. 8,720
Robertson, John (*b.* 1952) *Lab., Glasgow North West,* Maj. 10,093
Robertson, Laurence (*b.* 1958) *C., Tewkesbury,* Maj. 9,892
Robinson, Geoffrey (*b.* 1938) *Lab., Coventry North West,* Maj. 9,315
Robinson, Iris (*b.* 1949) *DUP, Strangford,* Maj. 13,049
Robinson, Rt. Hon. Peter (*b.* 1948) *DUP, Belfast East,* Maj. 5,877
***Rogerson**, Dan (*b.* 1975) *LD, Cornwall North,* Maj. 3,076
Rooney, Terry (*b.* 1950) *Lab., Bradford North,* Maj. 3,511
Rosindell, Andrew (*b.* 1966) *C., Romford,* Maj. 11,589
***Rowen**, Paul (*b.* 1955) *LD, Rochdale,* Maj. 442
Roy, Frank (*b.* 1958) *Lab., Motherwell & Wishaw,* Maj. 15,222
***Roy**, Lindsay (*b.* 1949) *Lab., Glenrothes,* Maj. 6,737
Ruane, Christopher (*b.* 1958) *Lab., Vale of Clwyd,* Maj. 4,669
Ruddock, Joan (*b.* 1943) *Lab., Lewisham Deptford,* Maj. 11,811
Ruffley, David (*b.* 1962) *C., Bury St Edmunds,* Maj. 9,930
Russell, Bob (*b.* 1946) *LD, Colchester,* Maj. 6,277
Russell, Christine (*b.* 1945) *Lab., Chester, City of,* Maj. 915
Ryan, Rt. Hon. Joan (*b.* 1955) *Lab., Enfield North,* Maj. 1,920
Salmond, Rt. Hon. Alex (*b.* 1954) *SNP, Banff & Buchan,* Maj. 11,837
Salter, Martin (*b.* 1954) *Lab., Reading West,* Maj. 4,682
Sanders, Adrian (*b.* 1959) *LD, Torbay,* Maj. 2,029
Sarwar, Mohammad (*b.* 1952) *Lab., Glasgow Central,* Maj. 8,531
***Scott**, Lee (*b.* 1956) *C., Ilford North,* Maj. 1,653

*__Seabeck__, Alison (*b.* 1954) *Lab., Plymouth Devonport,* Maj. 8,103
__Selous__, Andrew (*b.* 1962) *C., Bedfordshire South West,* Maj. 8,277
*__Shapps__, Grant (*b.* 1968) *C., Welwyn Hatfield,* Maj. 5,946
*__Sharma__, Virendra (*b.* 1947) *Lab., Ealing Southall,* Maj. 5,070
__Shaw__, Jonathan (*b.* 1966) *Lab., Chatham & Aylesford,* Maj. 2,332
__Sheerman__, Barry (*b.* 1940) *Lab. (Co-op), Huddersfield,* Maj. 8,351
__Shepherd__, Richard (*b.* 1942) *C., Aldridge-Brownhills,* Maj. 5,507
__Sheridan__, James (*b.* 1952) *Lab., Paisley & Renfrewshire North,* Maj. 11,001
‡__Short__, Rt. Hon. Clare (*b.* 1946) *Ind. Lab., Birmingham Ladywood,* Maj. 6,801
__Simmonds__, Mark (*b.* 1964) *C., Boston & Skegness,* Maj. 5,907
__Simon__, Sion (*b.* 1969) *Lab., Birmingham Erdington,* Maj. 9,575
__Simpson__, Alan (*b.* 1948) *Lab., Nottingham South,* Maj. 7,486
*__Simpson__, David (*b.* 1959) *DUP, Upper Bann,* Maj. 5,298
__Simpson__, Keith (*b.* 1949) *C., Norfolk Mid,* Maj. 7,560
__Singh__, Marsha (*b.* 1954) *Lab., Bradford West,* Maj. 3,026
__Skinner__, Dennis (*b.* 1932) *Lab., Bolsover,* Maj. 18,437
*__Slaughter__, Andrew (*b.* 1960) *Lab., Ealing, Acton & Shepherd's Bush,* Maj. 5,520
__Smith__, Rt. Hon. Andrew (*b.* 1951) *Lab., Oxford East,* Maj. 963
*__Smith__, Angela C. (*b.* 1961) *Lab., Sheffield Hillsborough,* Maj. 11,243
__Smith__, Angela E. (*b.* 1959) *Lab. (Co-op), Basildon,* Maj. 3,142
__Smith__, Chloe (*b.* 1982) *C., Norwich North,* Maj. 7,348
__Smith__, Geraldine (*b.* 1961) *Lab., Morecambe & Lunesdale,* Maj. 4,768
__Smith__, Rt. Hon. Jacqui (*b.* 1962) *Lab., Redditch,* Maj. 2,716
__Smith__, John (*b.* 1951) *Lab., Vale of Glamorgan,* Maj. 1,808
__Smith__, Sir Robert (*b.* 1958) *LD, Aberdeenshire West & Kincardine,* Maj. 7,471
*__Snelgrove__, Anne (*b.* 1957) *Lab., Swindon South,* Maj. 1,353
__Soames__, Hon. Nicholas (*b.* 1948) *C., Sussex Mid,* Maj. 5,890
*__Soulsby__, Sir Peter (*b.* 1948) *Lab., Leicester South,* Maj. 3,717
__Southworth__, Helen (*b.* 1956) *Lab., Warrington South,* Maj. 3,515
__Spellar__, Rt. Hon. John (*b.* 1947) *Lab., Warley,* Maj. 10,147
__Spelman__, Caroline (*b.* 1958) *C., Meriden,* Maj. 7,009
__Spicer__, Sir Michael (*b.* 1943) *C., Worcestershire West,* Maj. 2,475
‡__Spink__, Dr Robert (*b.* 1948) *Ind., Castle Point,* Maj. 8,201
__Spring__, Richard (*b.* 1946) *C., Suffolk West,* Maj. 8,909
__Stanley__, Rt. Hon. Sir John (*b.* 1942) *C., Tonbridge & Malling,* Maj. 13,352
__Starkey__, Dr Phyllis (*b.* 1947) *Lab., Milton Keynes South West,* Maj. 4,010
__Steen__, Anthony (*b.* 1939) *C., Totnes,* Maj. 1,947
__Stewart__, Ian (*b.* 1950) *Lab., Eccles,* Maj. 12,886
__Stoate__, Dr Howard (*b.* 1954) *Lab., Dartford,* Maj. 706
__Strang__, Rt. Hon. Gavin (*b.* 1943) *Lab., Edinburgh East,* Maj. 6,202
__Straw__, Rt. Hon. Jack (*b.* 1946) *Lab., Blackburn,* Maj. 8,009
__Streeter__, Gary (*b.* 1955) *C., Devon South West,* Maj. 10,141
__Stringer__, Graham (*b.* 1950) *Lab., Manchester Blackley,* Maj. 12,027
__Stuart__, Gisela (*b.* 1955) *Lab., Birmingham Edgbaston,* Maj. 2,349
*__Stuart__, Graham (*b.* 1962) *C., Beverley & Holderness,* Maj. 2,580
__Stunell__, Andrew (*b.* 1942) *LD, Hazel Grove,* Maj. 7,748
__Sutcliffe__, Gerry (*b.* 1953) *Lab., Bradford South,* Maj. 9,167
__Swayne__, Desmond (*b.* 1956) *C., New Forest West,* Maj. 17,285
*__Swinson__, Jo (*b.* 1980) *LD, Dunbartonshire East,* Maj. 4,061
__Swire__, Hugo (*b.* 1959) *C., Devon East,* Maj. 7,936
__Syms__, Robert (*b.* 1956) *C., Poole,* Maj. 5,988
__Tami__, Mark (*b.* 1963) *Lab., Alyn & Deeside,* Maj. 8,378
__Tapsell__, Sir Peter (*b.* 1930) *C., Louth & Horncastle,* Maj. 9,896
__Taylor__, Dari (*b.* 1944) *Lab., Stockton South,* Maj. 6,139
__Taylor__, David (*b.* 1946) *Lab. (Co-op), Leicestershire North West,* Maj. 4,477
__Taylor__, Ian (*b.* 1945) *C., Esher & Walton,* Maj. 7,727
__Taylor__, Matthew (*b.* 1963) *LD, Truro & St Austell,* Maj. 7,403
__Taylor__, Dr Richard (*b.* 1935) *Ind., Wyre Forest,* Maj. 5,250
__Teather__, Sarah (*b.* 1974) *LD, Brent East,* Maj. 2,712
__Thomas__, Gareth (*b.* 1967) *Lab. (Co-op), Harrow West,* Maj. 2,028
*__Thornberry__, Emily (*b.* 1960) *Lab., Islington South & Finsbury,* Maj. 484
__Thurso__, John (*b.* 1953) *LD, Caithness, Sutherland & Easter Ross,* Maj. 8,168
__Timms__, Rt. Hon. Stephen (*b.* 1955) *Lab., East Ham,* Maj. 13,155
*__Timpson__, Edward (*b.* 1973) *C., Crewe & Nantwich,* Maj. 7,860
__Tipping__, Paddy (*b.* 1949) *Lab., Sherwood,* Maj. 6,652
__Todd__, Mark (*b.* 1954) *Lab., Derbyshire South,* Maj. 4,495
__Touhig__, Rt. Hon. Don (*b.* 1947) *Lab. (Co-op), Islwyn,* Maj. 15,740
__Tredinnick__, David (*b.* 1950) *C., Bosworth,* Maj. 5,319
__Trickett__, Jon (*b.* 1950) *Lab., Hemsworth,* Maj. 13,481
__Truswell__, Paul (*b.* 1955) *Lab., Pudsey,* Maj. 5,870
__Turner__, Andrew (*b.* 1953) *C., Isle of Wight,* Maj. 12,978
__Turner__, Dr Desmond (*b.* 1939) *Lab., Brighton Kemptown,* Maj. 2,737
__Turner__, Neil (*b.* 1945) *Lab., Wigan,* Maj. 11,767
__Twigg__, Derek (*b.* 1959) *Lab., Halton,* Maj. 14,606
__Tyrie__, Andrew (*b.* 1957) *C., Chichester,* Maj. 10,860
*__Ussher__, Kitty (*b.* 1971) *Lab., Burnley,* Maj. 5,778
*__Vaizey__, Ed (*b.* 1969) *C., Wantage,* Maj. 8,017
*__Vara__, Shailesh (*b.* 1960) *C., Cambridgeshire North West,* Maj. 9,833
__Vaz__, Rt. Hon. Keith (*b.* 1956) *Lab., Leicester East,* Maj. 15,876
__Viggers__, Sir Peter (*b.* 1938) *C., Gosport,* Maj. 5,730
*__Villiers__, Theresa (*b.* 1968) *C., Chipping Barnet,* Maj. 5,960
__Vis__, Dr Rudi (*b.* 1941) *Lab., Finchley & Golders Green,* Maj. 741

*__Walker__, Charles (*b.* 1967) *C., Broxbourne,* Maj. 11,509
*__Wallace__, Ben (*b.* 1970) *C., Lancaster & Wyre,* Maj. 4,171
Walley, Joan (*b.* 1949) *Lab., Stoke-on-Trent North,* Maj. 10,036
Walter, Robert (*b.* 1948) *C., Dorset North,* Maj. 2,244
*__Waltho__, Lynda (*b.* 1960) *Lab., Stourbridge,* Maj. 407
Ward, Claire (*b.* 1972) *Lab., Watford,* Maj. 1,148
Wareing, Robert (*b.* 1930) *Lab., Liverpool West Derby,* Maj. 15,225
Waterson, Nigel (*b.* 1950) *C., Eastbourne,* Maj. 1,124
Watkinson, Angela (*b.* 1941) *C., Upminster,* Maj. 6,042
Watson, Tom (*b.* 1967) *Lab., West Bromwich East,* Maj. 11,652
Watts, Dave (*b.* 1951) *Lab., St Helens North,* Maj. 13,962
Webb, Prof. Steve (*b.* 1965) *LD, Northavon,* Maj. 11,033
Weir, Michael (*b.* 1957) *SNP, Angus,* Maj. 1,601
Whitehead, Dr Alan (*b.* 1950) *Lab., Southampton Test,* Maj. 7,018
Whittingdale, John (*b.* 1959) *C., Maldon & Chelmsford East,* Maj. 12,573
Wicks, Malcolm (*b.* 1947) *Lab., Croydon North,* Maj. 13,888
Widdecombe, Rt. Hon. Ann (*b.* 1947) *C., Maidstone & The Weald,* Maj. 14,856
Wiggin, Bill (*b.* 1966) *C., Leominster,* Maj. 13,187
Willetts, David (*b.* 1956) *C., Havant,* Maj. 6,508
Williams, Rt. Hon. Alan (*b.* 1930) *Lab., Swansea West,* Maj. 4,269
Williams, Betty (*b.* 1944) *Lab., Conwy,* Maj. 3,081
Williams, Hywel (*b.* 1953) *PC, Caernarfon,* Maj. 5,209
*__Williams__, Mark (*b.* 1966) *LD, Ceredigion,* Maj. 219
Williams, Roger (*b.* 1948) *LD, Brecon & Radnorshire,* Maj. 3,905
*__Williams__, Stephen (*b.* 1966) *LD, Bristol West,* Maj. 5,128
Willis, Phil (*b.* 1941) *LD, Harrogate & Knaresborough,* Maj. 10,429
*__Willott__, Jenny (*b.* 1974) *LD, Cardiff Central,* Maj. 5,593
Wills, Rt. Hon. Michael (*b.* 1952) *Lab., Swindon North,* Maj. 2,571
Wilshire, David (*b.* 1943) *C., Spelthorne,* Maj. 9,936
Wilson, Phil (*b.* 1959) *Lab., Sedgefield,* Maj. 6,956
*__Wilson__, Rob (*b.* 1965) *C., Reading East,* Maj. 475
*__Wilson__, Sammy (*b.* 1953) *DUP, Antrim East,* Maj. 7,304
Winnick, David (*b.* 1933) *Lab., Walsall North,* Maj. 6,640
Winterton, Lady Ann (*b.* 1941) *C., Congleton,* Maj. 8,246
Winterton, Sir Nicholas (*b.* 1938) *C., Macclesfield,* Maj. 9,401
Winterton, Rt. Hon. Rosie (*b.* 1958) *Lab., Doncaster Central,* Maj. 9,802
Wishart, Peter (*b.* 1962) *SNP, Perth & Perthshire North,* Maj. 1,521
Wood, Mike (*b.* 1946) *Lab., Batley & Spen,* Maj. 5,788
Woodward, Rt. Hon. Shaun (*b.* 1958) *Lab., St Helens South,* Maj. 9,309
Woolas, Phil (*b.* 1959) *Lab., Oldham East & Saddleworth,* Maj. 3,590
Wright, Anthony (*b.* 1954) *Lab., Great Yarmouth,* Maj. 3,055
Wright, David (*b.* 1967) *Lab., Telford,* Maj. 5,406
Wright, Iain (*b.* 1972) *Lab., Hartlepool,* Maj. 7,478
*__Wright__, Jeremy (*b.* 1972) *C., Rugby & Kenilworth,* Maj. 1,556
Wright, Dr Tony (*b.* 1948) *Lab., Cannock Chase,* Maj. 9,227
Wyatt, Derek (*b.* 1949) *Lab., Sittingbourne & Sheppey,* Maj. 79
Yeo, Tim (*b.* 1945) *C., Suffolk South,* Maj. 6,606
Young, Rt. Hon. Sir George (*b.* 1941) *C., Hampshire North West,* Maj. 13,264
Younger-Ross, Richard (*b.* 1953) *LD, Teignbridge,* Maj. 6,215

GENERAL ELECTION RESULTS

The results of voting in each parliamentary division at the general election of 5 May 2005 are given below. *See also* By-elections.

SCOTTISH BOUNDARY CHANGES

The number of Scottish constituencies was reduced from 72 to 59 for the 2005 general election, bringing the average electorate of each constituency in line with that of England.

For the majority of constituencies where a boundary change has taken place, it is not appropriate to make a straight comparison between the results of 2001 and 2005. The seat of Dundee East, for example, comprises 80 per cent of the old Dundee East constituency and 30 per cent of the old Angus constituency; it cannot therefore be described as a simple gain for the Scottish National Party from Labour. The term 'notional' used here refers to a theoretical set of results, published by Professors Rallings and Thrasher of Plymouth University, that estimates the way each new constituency might have voted in the 2001 general election.

KEY

* New MP
† Previously MP in another seat
‡ Previously MP for another party
§ Notional result; *see* explanation of Scottish boundary changes
E. Electorate T. Turnout

Abbreviations

AFC	Alliance for Change
Alliance	Alliance
AP	Alternative Party
Baths	Save the Bristol North Baths Party
Bean	New Millennium Bean
BMG	Blair Must Go Party
BNP	British National Party
BPP	British Public Party
Bridges	Build Duddon and Morecambe Bridges
Burnley	Burnley First Independent
C.	Conservative
CAP	Community Action Party
CG	Community Group
CL	Communist League
Clause 28	Clause 28 Children's Protection Christian Democrats
Comm.	Communist Party
Comm. Brit.	Communist Party of Britain
Community	Community
CP	Civilisation Party
CPA	Christian Peoples Alliance
Croydon	Croydon Pensions Alliance
Currency	Virtue Currency Cognitive Appraisal Party
Cut Tax	Cut Tax on Diesel and Petrol
DDTP	Death, Dungeons & Taxes Party
Dem. Lab.	Democratic Labour Party
Dem. Soc. All.	Democratic Socialist Alliance – People Before Profit
DUP	Democratic Unionist Party
EDP	English Democratic Party
EPP	English Parliamentary Party
Elvis	Church of the Militant Elvis Party
Eng. Dem.	English Democrats Party
Eng. Ind.	English Independence Party
FF	familiesfirst.uk.net
Fit	Fit Party For Integrity And Trust
Forum	Open-Forum
FP	Freedom Party
Free Scot.	Free Scotland Party
FWP	Forward Wales Party
GBB	Get Britain Back Party
Good	Common Good
Green	Green
Green Soc.	Alliance for Green Socialism
Honesty	Demanding Honesty in Politics and Whitehall
Ind.	Independent
Ind. Green	Independent Green Voice
Ind. Pr. Lab.	Independent Progressive Labour
IP	Imperial Party
Iraq	Iraq War, Not in My Name
IWCA	Independent Working Class Association
IZB	Islam Zinda Baad Platform
JP	Justice Party
KHHC	Kidderminster Hospital and Health Concern
Lab.	Labour
Lab. (Co-op)	Labour (Cooperative)
LCA	Legalise Cannabis Alliance
LD	Liberal Democrat
Lib.	Liberal
Local	Local Community Party
Loony	Monster Raving Loony Party
Masts	Removal of Tetra Masts in Cornwall
MC	The Millenium Council
Meb. Ker.	Mebyon Kernow
MNP	Motorcycle News Party
NACVP	Newcastle Academy with Christian Values Party
NEP	New England Party
NF	National Front
Northern	Northern Progress for You
OCV	Operation Christian Vote
OFD	Organisation of Free Democrats
Online	Seeks a Worldwide Online Participatory Directory
Paisley	Pride in Paisley Party
PC	Plaid Cymru
PDP	Progressive Democratic Party
PHF	People of Horsham First
Power	Max Power Party
PPN-V	Peace Party, Non-Violence, Justice, Environment
PPS	Pensioners Party Scotland
Progress	Peace and Progress Party
Protest	Protest Vote Party
PRTYP	Personality and Rational Thinking? Yes! Party
Publican	Publican Party – Free to Smoke (Pubs)
RA	Residents Association
R & R Loony	Rock & Roll Loony Party
Respect	Respect – the Unity Coalition
RP	The Resolutionist Party
St Albans	St Albans Party
Scot. Green	Scottish Green Party
Scot. Ind.	Scottish Independence Party
Scot. Senior	Scottish Senior Citizens Party
Scot. U.	Scottish Unionist
SDLP	Social Democratic and Labour Party
Senior	Senior Citizens Party
SF	Sinn Fein
Silent	Silent Majority Party
SNH	Safeguard the National Health Service
SNP	Scottish National Party
Soc. All.	Socialist Alliance
Soc. Alt.	Socialist Alternative Party
Socialist	Socialist
Soc. Lab.	Socialist Labour Party
Soc. Unity	Socialist Unity Network
SOS	SOS! Voters Against Overdevelopment of Northampton
Speaker	The Speaker
SSCUP	Scottish Senior Citizens Unity Party
SSP	Scottish Socialist Party
Tele.	telepathicpartnership.com
TEPK	Tigers Eye the Party for Kids
Third	Third Way
TP	Their Party
UKC	UK Community Issues Party
UKIP	UK Independence Party
UK Path	UK Pathfinders
UKPP	UK Pensioners Party
UUP	Ulster Unionist Party
Veritas	Veritas
Vote Dream	Vote for Yourself Rainbow Dream Ticket
Wessex Reg.	Wessex Regionalist
Work	The People's Choice Making Politicians Work
WP	Workers' Party
WRP	Workers' Revolutionary Party
XPP	Xtraordinary People Party
YPB	Your Party (Banbury)

PARLIAMENTARY CONSTITUENCIES AS AT 5 MAY 2005 GENERAL ELECTION

UK Turnout
E. 44,245,939 T. 27,148,510 (61.4%)

ENGLAND

ALDERSHOT
E. 78,553 T. 48,141 (61.28%) C. hold
Gerald Howarth, C. 20,572
Adrian Collett, LD 15,238
Howard Linsley, Lab. 9,895
Derek Rumsey, UKIP 1,182
Gary Cowd, Eng. Dem. 701
Howling Lord Hope, Loony 553
C. maj. 5,334 (11.08%)
1.74% swing C. to LD
(2001: C. maj. 6,564 (14.49%))

ALDRIDGE-BROWNHILLS
E. 61,761 T. 39,556 (64.05%) C. hold
Richard Shepherd, C. 18,744
Jon Phillips, Lab. 13,237
Roy Sheward, LD 4,862
William Vaughan, BNP 1,620
Graham Eardley, UKIP 1,093
C. maj. 5,507 (13.92%)
1.98% swing Lab. to C.
(2001: C. maj. 3,768 (9.97%))

ALTRINCHAM & SALE WEST
E. 67,247 T. 44,310 (65.89%) C. hold
Graham Brady, C. 20,569
John Stockton, Lab. 13,410
Ian Chappell, LD 9,595
Gary Peart, UKIP 736
C. maj. 7,159 (16.16%)
4.70% swing Lab. to C.
(2001: C. maj. 2,941 (6.75%))

AMBER VALLEY
E. 75,376 T. 47,391 (62.87%) Lab. hold
Judy Mallaber, Lab. 21,593
Gillian Shaw, C. 16,318
Kate Smith, LD 6,225
Paul Snell, BNP 1,243
Alexander Stevenson, Veritas 1,224
Hugh Price, UKIP 788
Lab. maj. 5,275 (11.13%)
2.55% swing Lab. to C.
(2001: Lab. maj. 7,227 (16.24%))

ARUNDEL & SOUTH DOWNS
E. 72,535 T. 49,690 (68.50%) C. hold
*Nick Herbert, C. 24,752
Derek Deedman, LD 13,443
Sharon Whitlam, Lab. 8,482
Andrew Moffat, UKIP 2,700
Mark Stack, Protest 313
C. maj. 11,309 (22.76%)
3.55% swing C. to LD
(2001: C. maj. 13,704 (29.86%))

ASHFIELD
E. 73,403 T. 42,051 (57.29%) Lab. hold
Rt. Hon. Geoff Hoon, Lab. 20,433
Giles Inglis-Jones, C. 10,220
Wendy Johnson, LD 5,829
Roy Adkins, Ind. 2,292
Kathryn Allsop, Ind. 1,900
Sarah Hemstock, Veritas 1,108
Eddie Grenfell, Ind. 269
Lab. maj. 10,213 (24.29%)
4.72% swing Lab. to C.
(2001: Lab. maj. 13,268 (33.72%))

ASHFORD
E. 79,493 T. 51,685 (65.02%) C. hold
Damian Green, C. 26,651
Valerie Whitaker, Lab. 13,353
Chris Took, LD 8,308
Richard Boden, Green 1,753
Bernard Stroud, UKIP 1,620
C. maj. 13,298 (25.73%)
5.19% swing Lab. to C.
(2001: C. maj. 7,359 (15.35%))

ASHTON UNDER LYNE
E. 72,000 T. 36,967 (51.34%) Lab. hold
David Heyes, Lab. 21,211
Graeme Brown, C. 7,259
Les Jones, LD 5,108
Anthony Jones, BNP 2,051
Dr John Whittaker, UKIP 768
Jack Crossfield, Local 570
Lab. maj. 13,952 (37.74%)
2.82% swing Lab. to C.
(2001: Lab. maj. 15,518 (43.39%))

AYLESBURY
E. 82,428 T. 51,458 (62.43%) C. hold
David Lidington, C. 25,252
Peter Jones, LD 14,187
Mohammed Khaliel, Lab. 9,540
Christopher Adams, UKIP 2,479
C. maj. 11,065 (21.50%)
0.56% swing LD to C.
(2001: C. maj. 10,009 (20.39%))

BANBURY
E. 87,168 T. 56,209 (64.48%) C. hold
Tony Baldry, C. 26,382
Les Sibley, Lab. 15,585
Zoe Patrick, LD 10,076
Alyson Duckmanton, Green 1,590
Dianna Heimann, UKIP 1,241
James Starkey, NF 918
Christopher Rowe, YPB 417
C. maj. 10,797 (19.21%)
4.54% swing Lab. to C.
(2001: C. maj. 5,219 (10.13%))

BARKING
E. 57,658 T. 28,906 (50.13%) Lab. hold
Rt. Hon. Margaret Hodge, Lab. 13,826
Keith Prince, C. 4,943
Richard Barnbrook, BNP 4,916
Toby Wickenden, LD 3,211
Terry Jones, UKIP 803
Laurie Cleeland, Green 618
Demetrious Panton, Ind. 530
Michael Saxby, WRP 59
Lab. maj. 8,883 (30.73%)
3.61% swing Lab. to C.
(2001: Lab. maj. 9,534 (37.94%))

BARNSLEY CENTRAL
E. 60,592 T. 28,615 (47.23%) Lab. hold
Eric Illsley, Lab. 17,478
Miles Crompton, LD 4,746
Peter Morel, C. 3,813
Geoff Broadley, BNP 1,403
Donald Wood, Ind. 1,175
Lab. maj. 12,732 (44.49%)
5.22% swing Lab. to LD
(2001: Lab. maj. 15,130 (54.93%))

BARNSLEY EAST & MEXBOROUGH
E. 66,941 T. 33,026 (49.34%) Lab. hold
Jeff Ennis, Lab. 20,779
Sharron Brook, LD 6,654
Carolyn Abbott, C. 4,853
Terence Robinson, Soc. Lab. 740
Lab. maj. 14,125 (42.77%)
4.44% swing Lab. to LD
(2001: Lab. maj. 16,789 (51.64%))

BARNSLEY WEST & PENISTONE
E. 66,985 T. 36,852 (55.02%) Lab. hold
Michael Clapham, Lab. 20,372
Clive Watkinson, C. 9,058
Alison Brelsford, LD 7,422
Lab. maj. 11,314 (30.70%)
2.52% swing Lab. to C.
(2001: Lab. maj. 12,352 (35.74%))

BARROW & FURNESS
E. 61,883 T. 36,493 (58.97%) Lab. hold
Rt. Hon. John Hutton, Lab. 17,360
Bill Dorman, C. 11,323
Barry Rabone, LD 6,130
Alan Beach, UKIP 758
Timothy Bell, Bridges 409
Brian Greaves, Veritas 306
Helene Young, Ind. 207
Lab. maj. 6,037 (16.54%)
4.40% swing Lab. to C.
(2001: Lab. maj. 9,889 (25.34%))

BASILDON
E. 73,912 T. 43,141 (58.37%)
Lab. (Co-op) hold
Angela Smith, Lab. (Co-op) 18,720
Aaron Powell, C. 15,578
Martin Thompson, LD 4,473
Emma Colgate, BNP 2,055
Alix Blythe, UKIP 1,143
Vikki Copping, Green 662
Kim Gandy, Eng. Dem. 510
Lab. (Co-op) maj. 3,142 (7.28%)
5.82% swing Lab. (Co-op) to C.
(2001: Lab. (Co-op) maj. 7,738 (18.93%))

BASINGSTOKE
E. 76,404 T. 48,123 (62.98%) C. gain
*Maria Miller, C. 19,955
Paul Harvey, Lab. 15,275
Jen Smith, LD 9,952
Peter Effer, UKIP 1,044
Darren Shirley, Green 928
Roger Robertson, BNP 821
Roger Macnair, MC 148
C. maj. 4,680 (9.73%)
3.95% swing Lab. to C.
(C. gain because previous MP defected to DUP in 2004)
(2001: C. maj. 880 (1.83%))

BASSETLAW
E. 69,389 T. 40,342 (58.14%) Lab. hold
John Mann, Lab. 22,847
Jonathan Sheppard, C. 12,010
David Dobbie, LD 5,485
Lab. maj. 10,837 (26.86%)
0.90% swing C. to Lab.
(2001: Lab. maj. 9,748 (25.06%))

BATH
E. 66,824 T. 45,836 (68.59%) LD hold

Don Foster, LD	20,101
Sian Dawson, C.	15,463
Harriet Ajderian, Lab.	6,773
Eric Lucas, Green	2,494
Richard Crowder, UKIP	770
Patrick Cobbe, Ind.	177
Graham Walker, Ind.	58

LD maj. 4,638 (10.12%)
5.63% swing LD to C.
(2001: LD maj. 9,894 (21.37%))

BATLEY & SPEN
E. 62,948 T. 39,208 (62.29%) Lab. hold

Mike Wood, Lab.	17,974
Robert Light, C.	12,186
Neil Bentley, LD	5,731
Colin Auty, BNP	2,668
Clive Lord, Green	649

Lab. maj. 5,788 (14.76%)
0.81% swing C. to Lab.
(2001: Lab. maj. 5,064 (13.14%))

BATTERSEA
E. 69,548 T. 41,049 (59.02%) Lab. hold

Martin Linton, Lab.	16,569
Dominic Schofield, C.	16,406
Norsheen Bhatti, LD	6,006
Hugo Charlton, Green	1,735
Terence Jones, UKIP	333

Lab. maj. 163 (0.40%)
6.67% swing Lab. to C.
(2001: Lab. maj. 5,053 (13.73%))

BEACONSFIELD
E. 68,083 T. 43,523 (63.93%) C. hold

Dominic Grieve, C.	24,126
Peter Chapman, LD	8,873
Alex Sobel, Lab.	8,422
John Fagan, UKIP	2,102

C. maj. 15,253 (35.05%)
1.96% swing LD to C.
(2001: C. maj. 13,065 (31.07%))

BECKENHAM
E. 74,738 T. 48,964 (65.51%) C. hold

Jacqui Lait, C.	22,183
Liam Curran, Lab.	13,782
Jef Foulger, LD	10,862
James Cartwright, UKIP	1,301
Roderick Reed, Ind.	836

C. maj. 8,401 (17.16%)
3.14% swing Lab. to C.
(2001: C. maj. 4,959 (10.88%))

BEDFORD
E. 70,629 T. 42,072 (59.57%) Lab. hold

Patrick Hall, Lab.	17,557
Richard Fuller, C.	14,174
Michael Headley, LD	9,063
Peter Conquest, UKIP	995
John McCready, Ind.	283

Lab. maj. 3,383 (8.04%)
3.57% swing Lab. to C.
(2001: Lab. maj. 6,157 (15.17%))

BEDFORDSHIRE MID
E. 73,768 T. 50,420 (68.35%) C. hold

*Nadine Dorries, C.	23,345
Mark Chapman, LD	11,990
Martin Lindsay, Lab.	11,351
Richard Joselyn, UKIP	1,372
Ben Foley, Green	1,292
Howard Martin, Veritas	769
Saqhib Ali, Ind.	301

C. maj. 11,355 (22.52%)
2.55% swing C. to LD
(2001: C. maj. 8,066 (17.29%))

BEDFORDSHIRE NORTH EAST
E. 72,757 T. 49,505 (68.04%) C. hold

Alistair Burt, C.	24,725
Keith White, Lab.	12,474
Stephen Rutherford, LD	10,320
James May, UKIP	1,986

C. maj. 12,251 (24.75%)
2.9% swing Lab. to C.
(2001: C. maj. 8,577 (18.96%))

BEDFORDSHIRE SOUTH WEST
E. 74,096 T. 45,814 (61.83%) C. hold

Andrew Selous, C.	22,114
Joyce Still, Lab.	13,837
Andy Strange, LD	7,723
Tom Wise, UKIP	1,923
Kenson Gurney, Forum	217

C. maj. 8,277 (18.07%)
8.15% swing Lab. to C.
(2001: C. maj. 776 (1.77%))

BERWICK-UPON-TWEED
E. 56,944 T. 36,090 (63.38%) LD hold

Rt. Hon. Alan Beith, LD	19,052
Mike Elliott, C.	10,420
Glen Reynolds, Lab.	6,618

LD maj. 8,632 (23.92%)
0.31% swing C. to LD
(2001: LD maj. 8,458 (23.30%))

BETHNAL GREEN & BOW
E. 85,950 T. 44,007 (51.20%)
Respect gain

†‡George Galloway, Respect	15,801
Oona King, Lab.	14,978
Shahagir Bakth Faruk, C.	6,244
Syed Nurul Islam Dulu, LD	4,928
John Foster, Green	1,950
Ejiro Etefia, AFC	68
Celia Pugh, CL	38

Respect maj. 823 (1.87%)
26.20% swing Lab. to Respect
(2001: Lab. maj. 10,057 (26.14%))

BEVERLEY & HOLDERNESS
E. 77,460 T. 50,202 (64.81%) C. hold

*Graham Stuart, C.	20,434
George McManus, Lab.	17,854
Brian Willie, LD	9,578
Oliver Marriott, UKIP	2,336

C. maj. 2,580 (5.14%)
1.73% swing Lab. to C.
(2001: C. maj. 781 (1.68%))

BEXHILL & BATTLE
E. 69,676 T. 46,834 (67.22%) C. hold

Greg Barker, C.	24,629
Mary Varrall, LD	11,180
Michael Jones, Lab.	8,457
Anthony Smith, UKIP	2,568

C. maj. 13,449 (28.72%)
2.63% swing LD to C.
(2001: C. maj. 10,503 (23.45%))

BEXLEYHEATH & CRAYFORD
E. 65,025 T. 42,580 (65.48%) C. gain

†David Evennett, C.	19,722
Nigel Beard, Lab.	15,171
David Raval, LD	5,144
John Dunford, UKIP	1,302
Jay Lee, BNP	1,241

C. maj. 4,551 (10.69%)
7.17% swing Lab. to C.
(2001: Lab. maj. 1,472 (3.65%))

BILLERICAY
E. 79,537 T. 48,858 (61.43%) C. hold

John Baron, C.	25,487
Anneliese Dodds, Lab.	14,281
Mike Hibbs, LD	6,471
Bryn Robinson, BNP	1,435
Seantino Callaghan, UKIP	1,184

C. maj. 11,206 (22.94%)
5.97% swing Lab. to C.
(2001: C. maj. 5,013 (10.99%))

BIRKENHEAD
E. 57,097 T. 27,786 (48.66%) Lab. hold

Rt. Hon. Frank Field, Lab.	18,059
Stuart Kelly, LD	5,125
Howard Morton, C.	4,602

Lab. maj. 12,934 (46.55%)
5.54% swing Lab. to LD
(2001: Lab. maj. 15,591 (53.82%))

BIRMINGHAM EDGBASTON
E. 64,893 T. 37,631 (57.99%) Lab. hold

Gisela Stuart, Lab.	16,465
Deirdre Alden, C.	14,116
Mike Dixon, LD	5,185
Peter Beck, Green	1,116
Stephen White, UKIP	749

Lab. maj. 2,349 (6.24%)
3.10% swing Lab. to C.
(2001: Lab. maj. 4,698 (12.45%))

BIRMINGHAM ERDINGTON
E. 64,951 T. 31,746 (48.88%) Lab. hold

Sion Simon, Lab.	16,810
Victoria Elvidge, C.	7,235
Jerry Evans, LD	5,027
Sharon Ebanks, BNP	1,512
Rannal Hepburn, UKIP	746
Terry Williams, NF	416

Lab. maj. 9,575 (30.16%)
1.20% swing Lab. to C.
(2001: Lab. maj. 9,962 (32.55%))

BIRMINGHAM HALL GREEN
E. 57,222 T. 34,536 (60.35%) Lab. hold

Stephen McCabe, Lab.	16,304
Eddie Hughes, C.	10,590
Roger Harmer, LD	6,682
David Melhuish, UKIP	960

Lab. maj. 5,714 (16.55%)
1.77% swing Lab. to C.
(2001: Lab. maj. 6,648 (20.09%))

BIRMINGHAM HODGE HILL
E. 53,903 T. 28,417 (52.72%) Lab. hold

Liam Byrne, Lab.	13,822
Nicola Davies, LD	8,373
Deborah Thomas, C.	3,768
Denis Adams, BNP	1,445
Adrian Duffen, UKIP	680
Azmat Begg, Progress	329

Lab. maj. 5,449 (19.18%)
18.29% swing Lab. to LD
(2004 July by-election: Lab. maj. 460 (2.25%))
(2001: Lab. maj. 11,618 (43.90%))

BIRMINGHAM LADYWOOD
E. 70,977 T. 33,246 (46.84%) Lab. hold
Rt. Hon. Clare Short, Lab. 17,262
Ayoub Khan, LD 10,461
Philippa Stroud, C. 3,515
Lynette Nazemi-Afshar, UKIP 2,008
Lab. maj. 6,801 (20.46%)
20.11% swing Lab. to LD
(2001: Lab. maj. 18,143 (57.61%))

BIRMINGHAM NORTHFIELD
E. 54,868 T. 31,056 (56.60%) Lab. hold
Richard Burden, Lab. 15,419
Vicky Ford, C. 8,965
Trevor Sword, LD 4,171
Mark Cattell, BNP 1,278
Gillian Chant, UKIP 641
Richard Rodgers, Good 428
Louise Houldey, Soc. Alt. 120
Francis Sweeney, WRP 34
Lab. maj. 6,454 (20.78%)
2.81% swing Lab. to C.
(2001: Lab. maj. 7,798 (26.40%))

BIRMINGHAM PERRY BARR
E. 70,126 T. 38,911 (55.49%) Lab. hold
Khalid Mahmood, Lab. 18,269
Jon Hunt, LD 10,321
Naweed Khan, C. 6,513
Dr Mohammad Naseem, Respect 2,173
Rajinder Clair, Soc. Lab. 890
Bimla Balu, UKIP 745
Lab. maj. 7,948 (20.43%)
1.61% swing Lab. to LD
(2001: Lab. maj. 8,753 (23.39%))

BIRMINGHAM SELLY OAK
E. 70,162 T. 41,740 (59.49%) Lab. hold
Dr Lynne Jones, Lab. 19,226
Joe Tildesley, C. 10,375
Richard Brighton, LD 9,591
Barney Smith, Green 1,581
Ronan Burnett, UKIP 967
Lab. maj. 8,851 (21.21%)
2.29% swing Lab. to C.
(2001: Lab. maj. 10,339 (25.78%))

BIRMINGHAM SPARKBROOK & SMALL HEATH
E. 73,721 T. 38,192 (51.81%) Lab. hold
Roger Godsiff, Lab. 13,787
Salma Yaqoob, Respect 10,498
Talib Hussain, LD 7,727
Sameer Mirza, C. 3,480
Jennifer Brookes, UKIP 1,342
Ian Jamieson, Green 855
Abdul Chaudhary, Ind. 503
Lab. maj. 3,289 (8.61%)
24.4% swing Lab. to Respect
(2001: Lab. maj. 16,246 (44.33%))

BIRMINGHAM YARDLEY
E. 50,975 T. 29,431 (57.74%) LD gain
*John Hemming, LD 13,648
Jayne Innes, Lab. 10,976
Paul Uppal, C. 2,970
Robert Purcell, BNP 1,523
Mohammed Yaqub, UKIP 314
LD maj. 2,672 (9.08%)
8.83% swing Lab. to LD
(2001: Lab. maj. 2,578 (8.59%))

BISHOP AUCKLAND
E. 67,534 T. 38,128 (56.46%) Lab. hold
*Helen Goodman, Lab. 19,065
Chris Foote-Wood, LD 9,018
Richard Bell, C. 8,736
Margaret Hopson, UKIP 1,309
Lab. maj. 10,047 (26.35%)
8.36% swing Lab. to LD
(2001: Lab. maj. 13,926 (36.12%))

BLABY
E. 75,444 T. 49,388 (65.46%) C. hold
Andrew Robathan, C. 22,487
David Morgan, Lab. 14,614
Jeff Stephenson, LD 9,382
Michael Robinson, BNP 1,704
Delroy Young, UKIP 1,201
C. maj. 7,873 (15.94%)
1.45% swing Lab. to C.
(2001: C. maj. 6,209 (13.03%))

BLACKBURN
E. 73,494 T. 41,805 (56.88%) Lab. hold
Rt. Hon. Jack Straw, Lab. 17,562
Imtiaz Ameen, C. 9,553
Tony Melia, LD 8,608
Nicholas Holt, BNP 2,263
Craig Murray, Ind. 2,082
Dorothy Baxter, UKIP 954
Graham Carter, Green 783
Lab. maj. 8,009 (19.16%)
1.90% swing Lab. to C.
(2001: Lab. maj. 9,249 (22.85%))

BLACKPOOL NORTH & FLEETWOOD
E. 74,975 T. 43,290 (57.74%) Lab. hold
Joan Humble, Lab. 20,620
Gavin Williamson, C. 15,558
Steven Bate, LD 5,533
Roy Hopwood, UKIP 1,579
Lab. maj. 5,062 (11.69%)
0.87% swing Lab. to C.
(2001: Lab. maj. 5,721 (13.44%))

BLACKPOOL SOUTH
E. 73,529 T. 38,342 (52.15%) Lab. hold
Gordon Marsden, Lab. 19,375
Michael Winstanley, C. 11,453
Doreen Holt, LD 5,552
Roy Goodwin, BNP 1,113
John Porter, UKIP 849
Lab. maj. 7,922 (20.66%)
0.32% swing Lab. to C.
(2001: Lab. maj. 8,262 (21.30%))

BLAYDON
E. 62,413 T. 39,053 (62.57%) Lab. hold
*David Anderson, Lab. 20,120
Peter Maughan, LD 14,785
Dorothy Luckhurst, C. 3,129
Norman Endacott, UKIP 1,019
Lab. maj. 5,335 (13.66%)
3.70% swing Lab. to LD
(2001: Lab. maj. 7,809 (21.06%))

BLYTH VALLEY
E. 63,640 T. 35,773 (56.21%) Lab. hold
Ronnie Campbell, Lab. 19,659
Jeffrey Reid, LD 11,132
Michael Windridge, C. 4,982
Lab. maj. 8,527 (23.84%)
5.72% swing Lab. to LD
(2001: Lab. maj. 12,188 (35.28%))

BOGNOR REGIS & LITTLEHAMPTON
E. 65,591 T. 40,747 (62.12%) C. hold
Nick Gibb, C. 18,183
George O'Neill, Lab. 10,361
Simon McDougall, LD 8,927
Adrian Lithgow, UKIP 3,276
C. maj. 7,822 (19.20%)
2.36% swing Lab. to C.
(2001: C. maj. 5,643 (14.48%))

BOLSOVER
E. 67,568 T. 38,699 (57.27%) Lab. hold
Dennis Skinner, Lab. 25,217
Denise Hawksworth, LD 6,780
Hasan Imam, C. 6,702
Lab. maj. 18,437 (47.64%)
4.53% swing Lab. to LD
(2001: Lab. maj. 18,777 (49.06%))

BOLTON NORTH EAST
E. 67,394 T. 36,911 (54.77%) Lab. hold
David Crausby, Lab. 16,874
Paul Brierley, C. 12,771
Adam Killeya, LD 6,044
Kevin Epsom, UKIP 640
Alan Ainscow, Veritas 375
Lynne Lowe, Soc. Lab. 207
Lab. maj. 4,103 (11.12%)
5.25% swing Lab. to C.
(2001: Lab. maj. 8,422 (21.62%))

BOLTON SOUTH EAST
E. 63,697 T. 31,850 (50.00%) Lab. hold
Dr Brian Iddon, Lab. 18,129
Deborah Dunleavy, C. 6,491
Frank Harasiwka, LD 6,047
Florence Bates, UKIP 840
David Jones, Veritas 343
Lab. maj. 11,638 (36.54%)
0.57% swing Lab. to C.
(2001: Lab. maj. 12,871 (37.69%))

BOLTON WEST
E. 63,836 T. 40,543 (63.51%) Lab. hold
Rt. Hon. Ruth Kelly, Lab. 17,239
Philip Allott, C. 15,175
Tim Perkins, LD 7,241
Marjorie Ford, UKIP 524
Michael Ford, Veritas 290
Kate Griggs, XPP 74
Lab. maj. 2,064 (5.09%)
4.15% swing Lab. to C.
(2001: Lab. maj. 5,518 (13.39%))

BOOTLE
E. 53,700 T. 25,622 (47.71%) Lab. hold
Joe Benton, Lab. 19,345
Chris Newby, LD 2,988
Wafik Moustafa, C. 1,580
Paul Nuttall, UKIP 1,054
Peter Glover, Soc. Alt. 655
Lab. maj. 16,357 (63.84%)
2.59% swing Lab. to LD
(2001: Lab. maj. 19,043 (69.01%))

BOSTON & SKEGNESS
E. 71,212 T. 41,869 (58.79%) C. hold
Mark Simmonds, C. 19,329
Paul Kenny, Lab. 13,422
Dr Richard Horsnell, UKIP 4,024
Alan Riley, LD 3,649
Wendy Russell, BNP 1,025
Marcus Petz, Green 420
C. maj. 5,907 (14.11%)
6.42% swing Lab. to C.
(2001: C. maj. 515 (1.28%))

BOSWORTH
E. 71,596 T. 47,499 (66.34%) C. hold
David Tredinnick, C. 20,212
Rupert Herd, Lab. 14,893
James Moore, LD 10,528
Denis Walker, UKIP 1,866
C. maj. 5,319 (11.20%)
3.07% swing Lab. to C.
(2001: C. maj. 2,280 (5.05%))

BOURNEMOUTH EAST
E. 63,426 T. 37,599 (59.28%) C. hold
*Tobias Ellwood, C. 16,925
Andrew Garratt, LD 11,681
David Stokes, Lab. 7,191
Thomas Collier, UKIP 1,802
C. maj. 5,244 (13.95%)
2.18% swing LD to C.
(2001: C. maj. 3,434 (9.59%))

BOURNEMOUTH WEST
E. 63,658 T. 33,924 (53.29%) C. hold
Sir John Butterfill, C. 14,057
Richard Renaut, LD 10,026
Dafydd Williams, Lab. 7,824
Michael Maclaire-Hillier, UKIP 2,017
C. maj. 4,031 (11.88%)
2.90% swing C. to LD
(2001: C. maj. 4,718 (14.02%))

BRACKNELL
E. 80,657 T. 51,141 (63.41%) C. hold
Rt. Hon. Andrew Mackay, C. 25,412
Janet Keene, Lab. 13,376
Lee Glendon, LD 10,128
Vincent Pearson, UKIP 1,818
Dominica Roberts, Ind. 407
C. maj. 12,036 (23.53%)
4.95% swing Lab. to C.
(2001: C. maj. 6,713 (13.64%))

BRADFORD NORTH
E. 64,515 T. 34,397 (53.32%) Lab. hold
Terry Rooney, Lab. 14,622
David Ward, LD 11,111
Teck Khong, C. 5,569
Lynda Cromie, BNP 2,061
Steve Schofield, Green 560
Umit Yildiz, Respect 474
Lab. maj. 3,511 (10.21%)
9.88% swing Lab. to LD
(2001: Lab. maj. 8,969 (25.61%))

BRADFORD SOUTH
E. 67,576 T. 36,605 (54.17%) Lab. hold
Gerry Sutcliffe, Lab. 17,954
Geraldine Carter, C. 8,787
Mike Doyle, LD 5,334
Dr James Lewthwaite, BNP 2,862
Derek Curtis, Green 695
Jason Smith, UKIP 552
Therese Muchewicz, Veritas 421
Lab. maj. 9,167 (25.04%)
1.23% swing Lab. to C.
(2001: Lab. maj. 9,662 (27.50%))

BRADFORD WEST
E. 67,356 T. 36,369 (54.00%) Lab. hold
Marsha Singh, Lab. 14,570
Haroon Rashid, C. 11,544
Mukhtar Ali, LD 6,620
Paul Cromie, BNP 2,525
Parvez Darr, Green 1,110
Lab. maj. 3,026 (8.32%)
1.27% swing Lab. to C.
(2001: Lab. maj. 4,165 (10.85%))

BRAINTREE
E. 80,458 T. 53,055 (65.94%) C. gain
*Brooks Newmark, C. 23,597
Alan Hurst, Lab. 19,704
Peter Turner, LD 7,037
James Abbott, Green 1,308
Roger Lord, UKIP 1,181
Buster Michael Nolan, Ind. 228
C. maj. 3,893 (7.34%)
4.02% swing Lab. to C.
(2001: Lab. maj. 358 (0.71%))

BRENT EAST
E. 56,227 T. 31,068 (55.25%) LD hold
Sarah Teather, LD 14,764
Yasmin Qureshi, Lab. 12,052
Kwasi Kwarteng, C. 3,193
Shahrar Ali, Green 905
Michelle Weininger, Ind. 115
Rainbow George Weiss, Vote Dream 39
LD maj. 2,712 (8.73%)
30.68% swing Lab. to LD
(2003 Sept. by-election: LD maj. 1,118 (5.36%))
(2001: Lab. maj. 13,047 (45.00%))

BRENT NORTH
E. 60,148 T. 35,682 (59.32%) Lab. hold
Barry Gardiner, Lab. 17,420
Bob Blackman, C. 11,779
Havard Hughes, LD 5,672
Babar Ahmad, Progress 685
Rainbow George Weiss, Vote Dream 126
Lab. maj. 5,641 (15.81%)
7.13% swing Lab. to C.
(2001: Lab. maj. 10,205 (30.07%))

BRENT SOUTH
E. 56,508 T. 29,764 (52.67%) Lab. hold
*Dawn Butler, Lab. 17,501
James Allie, LD 6,175
Rishi Saha, C. 4,485
Rowan Langley, Green 957
Shaun Wallace, Ind. 297
Rocky Fernandez, Ind. 288
Rainbow George Weiss, Vote Dream 61
Lab. maj. 11,326 (38.05%)
12.20% swing Lab. to LD
(2001: Lab. maj. 17,380 (60.69%))

BRENTFORD & ISLEWORTH
E. 84,366 T. 46,017 (54.54%) Lab. hold
Ann Keen, Lab. 18,329
Alexander Northcote, C. 13,918
Andrew Dakers, LD 10,477
John Hunt, Green 1,652
Phillip Andrews, Community 1,118
Michael Stoneman, NF 523
Lab. maj. 4,411 (9.59%)
6.80% swing Lab. to C.
(2001: Lab. maj. 10,318 (23.18%))

BRENTWOOD & ONGAR
E. 64,496 T. 44,145 (68.45%) C. hold
Eric Pickles, C. 23,609
Gavin Stollar, LD 11,997
John Adams, Lab. 6,579
Stuart Gulleford, UKIP 1,805
Anthony Appleton, Ind. 155
C. maj. 11,612 (26.30%)
1.91% swing LD to C.
(2001: C. maj. 2,821 (6.48%))

BRIDGWATER
E. 75,790 T. 48,109 (63.48%) C. hold
Ian Liddell-Grainger, C. 21,240
Matthew Burchell, Lab. 12,771
James Main, LD 10,940
Ray Weinstein, UKIP 1,767
Charlie Graham, Green 1,391
C. maj. 8,469 (17.60%)
1.96% swing Lab. to C.
(2001: C. maj. 4,987 (10.42%))

BRIGG & GOOLE
E. 67,364 T. 42,578 (63.21%) Lab. hold
Ian Cawsey, Lab. 19,257
Matthew Bean, C. 16,363
Gary Johnson, LD 5,690
Stephen Martin, UKIP 1,268
Lab. maj. 2,894 (6.80%)
1.43% swing Lab. to C.
(2001: Lab. maj. 3,961 (9.65%))

BRIGHTON KEMPTOWN
E. 65,985 T. 39,719 (60.19%) Lab. hold
Dr Desmond Turner, Lab. 15,858
Judith Symes, C. 13,121
Marina Pepper, LD 6,560
Simon Williams, Green 2,800
Dr James Chamberlain-Webber, UKIP 758
Caroline O'Reilly, PPN-V 172
John McLeod, Soc. Lab. 163
Elaine Cook, Ind. 127
Phil Clarke, Soc. Alt. 113
Gene Dobbs, Ind. 47
Lab. maj. 2,737 (6.89%)
2.83% swing Lab. to C.
(2001: Lab. maj. 4,922 (12.56%))

BRIGHTON PAVILION
E. 68,087 T. 43,578 (64.00%) Lab. (Co-op) hold
David Lepper, Lab. (Co-op) 15,427
Mike Weatherley, C. 10,397
Keith Taylor, Green 9,571
Hazel Thorpe, LD 7,171
Kimberley Crisp-Comotto, UKIP 508
Tony Greenstein, Green Soc. 188
Ian Fyvie, Soc. Lab. 152
Christopher Rooke, Ind. 122
Keith Jago, Ind. 42
Lab. (Co-op) maj. 5,030 (11.55%)
6.06% swing Lab. (Co-op) to C.
(2001: Lab. (Co-op) maj. 9,643 (23.68%))

BRISTOL EAST
E. 68,096 T. 41,720 (61.27%) Lab. hold
*Kerry McCarthy, Lab. 19,152
Philip James, LD 10,531
Julia Manning, C. 8,787
Arjuna Krishna-Das, Green 1,586
Jean Smith, UKIP 1,132
Paulette North, Respect 532
Lab. maj. 8,621 (20.66%)
8.59% swing Lab. to LD
(2001: Lab. maj. 13,392 (33.20%))

BRISTOL NORTH WEST
E. 77,703 T. 47,492 (61.12%) Lab. (Co-op) hold
Dr Doug Naysmith, Lab. (Co-op) 22,192
Alastair Watson, C. 13,230
Bob Hoyle, LD 9,545
Christopher Lees, UKIP 1,132
Michael Blundell, EDP 828
Graeme Jones, Soc. Alt. 565
Lab. (Co-op) maj. 8,962 (18.87%)
2.28% swing Lab. (Co-op) to C.
(2001: Lab. (Co-op) maj. 11,087 (23.74%))

BRISTOL SOUTH
E. 70,835 T. 42,328 (59.76%) Lab. hold
Rt. Hon. Dawn Primarolo, Lab. 20,778
Kay Barnard, LD 9,636
Graham Hill, C. 8,466
Charlie Bolton, Green 2,127
Mark Dent, UKIP 1,321
Lab. maj. 11,142 (26.32%)
7.86% swing Lab. to LD
(2001: Lab. maj. 14,181 (34.61%))

BRISTOL WEST
E. 81,382 T. 57,396 (70.53%) LD gain
*Stephen Williams, LD 21,987
Valerie Davey, Lab. 16,859
David Martin, C. 15,429
Justin Quinnell, Green 2,163
Simon Muir, UKIP 439
Bernard Kennedy, Soc. Lab. 329
Doug Reid, Baths 190
LD maj. 5,128 (8.93%)
8.44% swing Lab. to LD
(2001: Lab. maj. 4,426 (7.95%))

BROMLEY & CHISLEHURST
E. 71,173 T. 46,137 (64.82%) C. hold
Rt. Hon. Eric Forth, C. 23,583
Rachel Reeves, Lab. 10,241
Peter Brooks, LD 9,368
David Hooper, UKIP 1,475
Ann Garrett, Green 1,470
C. maj. 13,342 (28.92%)
4.01% swing Lab. to C.
(2001: C. maj. 9,037 (20.90%))

BROMSGROVE
E. 70,762 T. 47,810 (67.56%) C. hold
Julie Kirkbride, C. 24,387
David Jones, Lab. 14,307
Sue Haswell, LD 7,197
Paul Buckingham, UKIP 1,919
C. maj. 10,080 (21.08%)
1.63% swing Lab. to C.
(2001: C. maj. 8,138 (17.81%))

BROXBOURNE
E. 68,106 T. 40,628 (59.65%) C. hold
*Charles Walker, C. 21,878
Jamie Bolden, Lab. 10,369
Andrew Porrer, LD 4,973
Dr Andrew Emerson, BNP 1,929
Martin Harvey, UKIP 1,479
C. maj. 11,509 (28.33%)
2.28% swing Lab. to C.
(2001: C. maj. 8,993 (23.76%))

BROXTOWE
E. 71,121 T. 48,806 (68.62%) Lab. hold
Dr Nick Palmer, Lab. 20,457
Bob Seely, C. 18,161
David Watts, LD 7,837
Paul Anderson, Green 896
Patricia Wolfe, UKIP 695
Damian Hockney, Veritas 590
Mark Gregory, Ind. 170
Lab. maj. 2,296 (4.70%)
3.64% swing Lab. to C.
(2001: Lab. maj. 5,873 (11.98%))

BUCKINGHAM
E. 70,265 T. 48,307 (68.75%) C. hold
John Bercow, C. 27,748
David Greene, Lab. 9,619
Luke Croydon, LD 9,508
David Williams, UKIP 1,432
C. maj. 18,129 (37.53%)
4.05% swing Lab. to C.
(2001: C. maj. 13,325 (29.43%))

BURNLEY
E. 65,869 T. 38,983 (59.18%) Lab. hold
*Kitty Ussher, Lab. 14,999
Gordon Birtwistle, LD 9,221
Harry Brooks, Burnley 5,786
Yousuf Miah, C. 4,206
Len Starr, BNP 4,003
Dr Jeff Slater, Ind. 392
Robert McDowell, UKIP 376
Lab. maj. 5,778 (14.82%)
9.15% swing Lab. to LD
(2001: Lab. maj. 10,498 (28.46%))

BURTON
E. 78,556 T. 47,882 (60.95%) Lab. hold
Janet Dean, Lab. 19,701
Adrian Pepper, C. 18,280
Sandra Johnson, LD 6,236
Julie Russell, BNP 1,840
Philip Lancaster, UKIP 913
Brian Buxton, Veritas 912
Lab. maj. 1,421 (2.97%)
3.73% swing Lab. to C.
(2001: Lab. maj. 4,849 (10.44%))

BURY NORTH
E. 72,268 T. 44,439 (61.49%) Lab. hold
David Chaytor, Lab. 19,130
David Nuttall, C. 16,204
Wilf Davison, LD 6,514
Stewart Clough, BNP 1,790
Philip Silver, UKIP 476
Ryan O'Neill, Soc. Lab. 172
Ian Upton, Veritas 153
Lab. maj. 2,926 (6.58%)
4.00% swing Lab. to C.
(2001: Lab. maj. 6,532 (14.58%))

BURY SOUTH
E. 66,898 T. 39,154 (58.53%) Lab. hold
Ivan Lewis, Lab. 19,741
Alex Williams, C. 10,829
Victor D'Albert, LD 6,968
Jim Greenhalgh, UKIP 1,059
Yvonne Hossack, Ind. 557
Lab. maj. 8,912 (22.76%)
4.77% swing Lab. to C.
(2001: Lab. maj. 12,772 (32.30%))

BURY ST EDMUNDS
E. 79,658 T. 52,619 (66.06%) C. hold
David Ruffley, C. 24,332
David Monaghan, Lab. 14,402
David Chappell, LD 10,423
Dr John Howlett, UKIP 1,859
Graham Manning, Green 1,603
C. maj. 9,930 (18.87%)
6.95% swing Lab. to C.
(2001: C. maj. 2,503 (4.98%))

CALDER VALLEY
E. 71,325 T. 47,770 (66.98%) Lab. hold
Christine McCafferty, Lab. 18,426
Liz Truss, C. 17,059
Liz Ingleton, LD 9,027
John Gregory, BNP 1,887
Paul Palmer, Green 1,371
Lab. maj. 1,367 (2.86%)
1.83% swing Lab. to C.
(2001: Lab. maj. 3,094 (6.52%))

CAMBERWELL & PECKHAM
E. 55,739 T. 28,991 (52.01%) Lab. hold
Rt. Hon. Harriet Harman, Lab. 18,933
Richard Porter, LD 5,450
Jessica Lee, C. 2,841
Paul Ingram, Green 1,172
Derek Penhallow, UKIP 350
Margaret Sharkey, Soc. Lab. 132
Sanjay Kulkarni, WRP 113
Lab. maj. 13,483 (46.51%)
4.88% swing Lab. to LD
(2001: Lab. maj. 14,123 (56.26%))

CAMBRIDGE
E. 70,154 T. 43,569 (62.10%) LD gain
*David Howarth, LD 19,152
Anne Campbell, Lab. 14,813
Ian Lyon, C. 7,193
Martin Lucas Smith, Green 1,245
Helene Davies, UKIP 569
Tom Woodcock, Respect 477
Suzon Forscey-Moore, Ind. 60
Graham Wilkinson, Ind. 60
LD maj. 4,339 (9.96%)
14.99% swing Lab. to LD
(2001: Lab. maj. 8,579 (20.03%))

CAMBRIDGESHIRE NORTH EAST
E. 85,079 T. 50,877 (59.80%) C. hold
Malcolm Moss, C. 24,181
Ffinlo Costain, Lab. 15,280
Alan Dean, LD 8,693
Leonard Baynes, UKIP 2,723
C. maj. 8,901 (17.50%)
2.12% swing Lab. to C.
(2001: C. maj. 6,373 (13.26%))

CAMBRIDGESHIRE NORTH WEST
E. 79,694 T. 49,092 (61.60%) C. hold
*Shailesh Vara, C. 22,504
Ayfer Orhan, Lab. 12,671
John Souter, LD 11,232
Robert Brown, UKIP 2,685
C. maj. 9,833 (20.03%)
0.80% swing Lab. to C.
(2001: C. maj. 8,101 (18.43%))

CAMBRIDGESHIRE SOUTH
E. 77,022 T. 52,648 (68.35%) C. hold
Andrew Lansley, C. 23,676
Andrew Dickson, LD 15,675
Sandra Wilson, Lab. 10,189
Robin Page, UKIP 1,556
Simon Saggers, Green 1,552
C. maj. 8,001 (15.20%)
1.09% swing C. to LD
(2001: C. maj. 8,403 (17.38%))

CAMBRIDGESHIRE SOUTH EAST
E. 85,901 T. 56,060 (65.26%) C. hold
James Paice, C. 26,374
Jonathan Chatfield, LD 17,750
Fiona Ross, Lab. 11,936
C. maj. 8,624 (15.38%)
0.97% swing C. to LD
(2001: C. maj. 8,990 (17.33%))

CANNOCK CHASE
E. 75,194 T. 43,155 (57.39%) Lab. hold
Dr Tony Wright, Lab. 22,139
Ian Collard, C. 12,912
Jenny Pinkett, LD 5,934
Roy Jenkins, UKIP 2,170
Lab. maj. 9,227 (21.38%)
2.34% swing Lab. to C.
(2001: Lab. maj. 10,704 (26.07%))

CANTERBURY
E. 72,046 T. 47,587 (66.05%) C. hold
Julian Brazier, C. 21,113
Alex Hilton, Lab. 13,642
Jenny Barnard-Langston, LD 10,059
Geoff Meaden, Green 1,521
John Moore, UKIP 926
Rocky van de Benderskum, LCA 326
C. maj. 7,471 (15.70%)
5.56% swing Lab. to C.
(2001: C. maj. 2,069 (4.58%))

CARLISLE
E. 59,508 T. 35,394 (59.48%) Lab. hold
Eric Martlew, Lab. 17,019
Mike Mitchelson, C. 11,324
Steven Tweedie, LD 5,916
Steven Cochrane, UKIP 792
Lezley Gibson, LCA 343
Lab. maj. 5,695 (16.09%)
0.12% swing Lab. to C.
(2001: Lab. maj. 5,702 (16.33%))

CARSHALTON & WALLINGTON
E. 67,844 T. 43,061 (63.47%) LD hold
Tom Brake, LD 17,357
Ken Andrew, C. 16,289
Andrew Theobald, Lab. 7,396
Francis Day, UKIP 1,111
Bob Steel, Green 908
LD maj. 1,068 (2.48%)
4.36% swing LD to C.
(2001: LD maj. 4,547 (11.20%))

CASTLE POINT
E. 69,480 T. 45,802 (65.92%) C. hold
Dr Robert Spink, C. 22,118
Luke Akehurst, Lab. 13,917
James Sandbach, LD 4,719
Neil Hamper, UKIP 3,431
Irene Willis, Green 1,617
C. maj. 8,201 (17.91%)
7.71% swing Lab. to C.
(2001: C. maj. 985 (2.48%))

CHARNWOOD
E. 76,274 T. 50,616 (66.36%) C. hold
Rt. Hon. Stephen Dorrell, C. 23,571
Richard Robinson, Lab. 14,762
Sue King, LD 9,057
Andrew Holders, BNP 1,737
Jamie Bye, UKIP 1,489
C. maj. 8,809 (17.40%)
0.68% swing Lab. to C.
(2001: C. maj. 7,739 (16.03%))

CHATHAM & AYLESFORD
E. 70,515 T. 42,080 (59.68%) Lab. hold
Jonathan Shaw, Lab. 18,387
Anne Jobson, C. 16,055
Debra Enever, LD 5,744
Jeffrey King, UKIP 1,226
Michael Russell, Eng. Dem. 668
Lab. maj. 2,332 (5.54%)
2.69% swing Lab. to C.
(2001: Lab. maj. 4,340 (10.92%))

CHEADLE
E. 68,123 T. 47,437 (69.63%) LD hold
Patsy Calton, LD 23,189
Stephen Day, C. 19,169
Martin Miller, Lab. 4,169
Vincent Cavanagh, UKIP 489
Richard Chadfield, BNP 421
LD maj. 4,020 (8.47%)
4.20% swing C. to LD
(2001: LD maj. 33 (0.08%))

CHELMSFORD WEST
E. 82,489 T. 51,052 (61.89%) C. hold
Simon Burns, C. 22,946
Stephen Robinson, LD 13,326
Russell Kennedy, Lab. 13,236
Kenneth Wedon, UKIP 1,544
C. maj. 9,620 (18.84%)
0.18% swing C. to LD
(2001: C. maj. 6,261 (13.01%))

CHELTENHAM
E. 71,541 T. 43,621 (60.97%) LD hold
*Martin Horwood, LD 18,122
Dr Vanessa Gearson, C. 15,819
Christopher Evans, Lab. 4,988
Dr Robert Hodges, Ind. 2,651
Keith Bessant, Green 908
Niall Warry, UKIP 608
Dancing Ken Hanks, Loony 525
LD maj. 2,303 (5.28%)
3.64% swing LD to C.
(2001: LD maj. 5,255 (12.56%))

CHESHAM & AMERSHAM
E. 69,217 T. 47,097 (68.04%) C. hold
Cheryl Gillan, C. 25,619
John Ford, LD 11,821
Rupa Huq, Lab. 6,610
Nick Wilkins, Green 1,656
David Samuel-Camps, UKIP 1,391
C. maj. 13,798 (29.30%)
1.53% swing LD to C.
(2001: C. maj. 11,882 (26.24%))

CHESTER, CITY OF
E. 69,785 T. 44,903 (64.34%) Lab. hold
Christine Russell, Lab. 17,458
Paul Offer, C. 16,543
Mia Jones, LD 9,818
Allan Weddell, UKIP 776
Ed Abrams, Eng. Dem. 308
Lab. maj. 915 (2.04%)
6.66% swing Lab. to C.
(2001: Lab. maj. 6,894 (15.36%))

CHESTERFIELD
E. 74,007 T. 44,121 (59.62%) LD hold
Paul Holmes, LD 20,875
Simon Rich, Lab. 17,830
Mark Kreling, C. 3,605
Christopher Brady, UKIP 997
Ian Jerram, Eng. Dem. 814
LD maj. 3,045 (6.90%)
0.54% swing Lab. to LD
(2001: LD maj. 2,586 (5.82%))

CHICHESTER
E. 78,645 T. 52,401 (66.63%) C. hold
Andrew Tyrie, C. 25,302
Alan Hilliar, LD 14,442
Jonathan Austin, Lab. 9,632
Douglas Denny, UKIP 3,025
C. maj. 10,860 (20.72%)
1.09% swing C. to LD
(2001: C. maj. 11,355 (22.93%))

CHINGFORD & WOODFORD GREEN
E. 61,386 T. 38,648 (62.96%) C. hold
Rt. Hon. Iain Duncan Smith, C. 20,555
Simon Wright, Lab. 9,914
John Beanse, LD 6,832
Michael McGough, UKIP 1,078
Barry White, Ind. 269
C. maj. 10,641 (27.53%)
6.35% swing Lab. to C.
(2001: C. maj. 5,487 (14.84%))

CHIPPING BARNET
E. 66,143 T. 42,381 (64.07%) C. hold
*Theresa Villiers, C. 19,744
Pauline Coakley-Webb, Lab. 13,784
Sean Hooker, LD 6,671
Audrey Poppy, Green 1,199
Victor Kaye, UKIP 924
Rainbow George Weiss, Vote Dream 59
C. maj. 5,960 (14.06%)
3.85% swing Lab. to C.
(2001: C. maj. 2,701 (6.36%))

CHORLEY
E. 78,838 T. 49,569 (62.87%) Lab. hold
Lindsay Hoyle, Lab. 25,131
Simon Mallett, C. 17,506
Alexander Wilson-Fletcher, LD 6,932
Lab. maj. 7,625 (15.38%)
1.11% swing Lab. to C.
(2001: Lab. maj. 8,444 (17.61%))

CHRISTCHURCH
E. 74,109 T. 51,565 (69.58%) C. hold
Christopher Chope, C. 28,208
Leslie Coman, LD 12,649
Jim King, Lab. 8,051
David Hughes, UKIP 2,657
C. maj. 15,559 (30.17%)
1.42% swing LD to C.
(2001: C. maj. 13,544 (27.32%))

CITIES OF LONDON & WESTMINSTER
E. 72,577 T. 36,487 (50.27%) C. hold
Mark Field, C. 17,260
Hywel Lloyd, Lab. 9,165
Marie-Louise Rossi, LD 7,306
Tristan Smith, Green 1,544
Colin Merton, UKIP 399
Brian Haw, Ind. 298
Jill McLachlan, CPA 246
David Harris, Veritas 218
Cass Jean-Claude Cass-Horne, Ind. 51
C. maj. 8,095 (22.19%)
4.47% swing Lab. to C.
(2001: C. maj. 4,499 (13.24%))

CLEETHORPES
E. 70,746 T. 43,589 (61.61%) Lab. hold
Shona McIsaac, Lab. 18,889
Martin Vickers, C. 16,247
Geoff Lowis, LD 6,437
Bill Hardie, UKIP 2,016
Lab. maj. 2,642 (6.06%)
3.59% swing Lab. to C.
(2001: Lab. maj. 5,620 (13.25%))

COLCHESTER
E. 79,010 T. 44,899 (56.83%) LD hold
Bob Russell, LD 21,145
Kevin Bentley, C. 14,868
Laura Bruni, Lab. 8,886
LD maj. 6,277 (13.98%)
0.64% swing C. to LD
(2001: LD maj. 5,553 (12.70%))

COLNE VALLEY
E. 74,121 T. 48,920 (66.00%) Lab. hold
Kali Mountford, Lab. 17,536
Maggie Throup, C. 16,035
Elisabeth Wilson, LD 11,822
Barry Fowler, BNP 1,430
Lesley Hedges, Green 1,295
Helen Martinek, Veritas 543
Ian Mumford, Loony 259
Lab. maj. 1,501 (3.07%)
3.40% swing Lab. to C.
(2001: Lab. maj. 4,639 (9.87%))

CONGLETON
E. 72,770 T. 46,682 (64.15%) C. hold
Lady Ann Winterton, C. 21,189
Nicholas Milton, Lab. 12,943
Eleanor Key, LD 12,550
C. maj. 8,246 (17.66%)
0.92% swing Lab. to C.
(2001: C. maj. 7,134 (15.82%))

COPELAND
E. 54,206 T. 33,757 (62.28%) Lab. hold
*Jamie Reed, Lab. 17,033
Chris Whiteside, C. 10,713
Frank Hollowell, LD 3,880
Edward Caley-Knowles, UKIP 735
Brian Earley, Ind. 734
Alan Mossop, Eng. Dem. 662
Lab. maj. 6,320 (18.72%)
2.22% swing C. to Lab.
(2001: Lab. maj. 4,964 (14.28%))

CORBY
E. 73,000 T. 48,527 (66.48%) Lab. (Co-op) hold
Phil Hope, Lab. (Co-op) 20,913
Andrew Griffith, C. 19,396
David Radcliffe, LD 6,184
Ian Gillman, UKIP 1,278
Steve Carey, Soc. Lab. 499
John Morris, Ind. 257
Lab. (Co-op) maj. 1,517 (3.13%)
4.47% swing Lab. (Co-op) to C.
(2001: Lab. (Co-op) maj. 5,700 (12.07%))

CORNWALL NORTH
E. 86,841 T. 55,982 (64.46%) LD hold
*Dan Rogerson, LD 23,842
Mark Formosa, C. 20,766
David Acton, Lab. 6,636
David Campbell-Bannerman, UKIP 3,063
Dick Cole, Meb. Ker. 1,351
Alan Eastwood, Veritas 324
LD maj. 3,076 (5.49%)
6.36% swing LD to C.
(2001: LD maj. 9,832 (18.21%))

CORNWALL SOUTH EAST
E. 80,704 T. 53,455 (66.24%) LD hold
Colin Breed, LD 24,986
Ashley Gray, C. 18,479
Colin Binley, Lab. 6,069
David Lucas, UKIP 2,693
Graham Sandercock, Meb. Ker. 769
Anne Assheton-Salton, Veritas 459
LD maj. 6,507 (12.17%)
0.89% swing C. to LD
(2001: LD maj. 5,375 (10.39%))

COTSWOLD
E. 71,039 T. 47,351 (66.65%) C. hold
Geoffrey Clifton-Brown, C. 23,326
Philip Beckerlegge, LD 13,638
Mark Dempsey, Lab. 8,457
Richard Buckley, UKIP 1,538
James Derieg, Ind. 392
C. maj. 9,688 (20.46%)
2.80% swing C. to LD
(2001: C. maj. 11,983 (26.06%))

COVENTRY NORTH EAST
E. 70,225 T. 37,195 (52.97%) Lab. hold
Rt. Hon. Robert Ainsworth, Lab. 21,178
Jaswant Singh Birdi, C. 6,956
Russell Field, LD 6,123
Dave Nellist, Soc. Alt. 1,874
Paul Southeran, UKIP 1,064
Lab. maj. 14,222 (38.24%)
2.02% swing Lab. to C.
(2001: Lab. maj. 15,751 (42.27%))

COVENTRY NORTH WEST
E. 73,180 T. 43,438 (59.36%) Lab. hold
Geoffrey Robinson, Lab. 20,942
Brian Connell, C. 11,627
Iona Anderson, LD 7,932
David Clarke, BNP 1,556
Sandra List, UKIP 766
Nicola Downes, Soc. Alt. 615
Lab. maj. 9,315 (21.44%)
2.06% swing Lab. to C.
(2001: Lab. maj. 10,874 (25.56%))

COVENTRY SOUTH
E. 68,884 T. 40,685 (59.06%) Lab. hold
Jim Cunningham, Lab. 18,649
Heather Wheeler, C. 12,394
Vincent McKee, LD 7,228
Rob Windsor, Soc. Alt. 1,097
William Brown, UKIP 829
Irene Rogers, Ind. 344
James Rooney, FF 144
Lab. maj. 6,255 (15.37%)
2.64% swing Lab. to C.
(2001: Lab. maj. 8,279 (20.65%))

CRAWLEY
E. 71,911 T. 41,973 (58.37%) Lab. hold
Laura Moffatt, Lab. 16,411
Henry Smith, C. 16,374
Rupert Sheard, LD 6,503
Richard Trower, BNP 1,277
Ronald Walters, UKIP 935
Robin Burnham, Dem. Soc. All. 263
Arshad Khan, JP 210
Lab. maj. 37 (0.09%)
8.52% swing Lab. to C.
(2001: Lab. maj. 6,770 (17.13%))

CREWE & NANTWICH
E. 72,472 T. 43,485 (60.00%) Lab. hold
Gwyneth Dunwoody, Lab. 21,240
Eveleigh Moore-Dutton, C. 14,162
Paul Roberts, LD 8,083
Lab. maj. 7,078 (16.28%)
3.78% swing Lab. to C.
(2001: Lab. maj. 9,906 (23.84%))

CROSBY
E. 54,255 T. 36,194 (66.71%) Lab. hold
Claire Curtis-Thomas, Lab. 17,463
Debi Jones, C. 11,623
Jim Murray, LD 6,298
Dr John Whittaker, UKIP 454
Geoffrey Bottoms, Comm. Brit. 199
David Braid, Clause 28 157
Lab. maj. 5,840 (16.14%)
3.26% swing Lab. to C.
(2001: Lab. maj. 8,353 (22.66%))

CROYDON CENTRAL
E. 80,825 T. 48,957 (60.57%) C. gain
*Andrew Pelling, C. 19,974
Geraint Davies, Lab. 19,899
Jeremy Hargreaves, LD 6,384
Ian Edwards, UKIP 1,066
Bernice Golberg, Green 1,036
Marianne Bowness, Veritas 304
John Cartwright, Loony 193
Janet Stearn, Work 101
C. maj. 75 (0.15%)
4.42% swing Lab. to C.
(2001: Lab. maj. 3,984 (8.69%))

CROYDON NORTH
E. 83,796 T. 43,847 (52.33%) Lab. hold
Malcolm Wicks, Lab. 23,555
Tariq Ahmad, C. 9,667
Adrian Gee-Turner, LD 7,560
Shasha Khan, Green 1,248
Henry Pearce, UKIP 770
Peter Gibson, Croydon 394
Winston McKenzie, Veritas 324
Farhan Rasheed, Ind. 197
Michelle Chambers, Work 132
Lab. maj. 13,888 (31.67%)
4.29% swing Lab. to C.
(2001: Lab. maj. 16,858 (40.25%))

CROYDON SOUTH
E. 76,872 T. 48,897 (63.61%) C. hold
Richard Ottaway, C. 25,320
Paul Smith, Lab. 11,792
Sandra Lawman, LD 10,049
James Feisenberger, UKIP 1,054
Graham Dare, Veritas 497
Mark Samuel, Work 185
C. maj. 13,528 (27.67%)
4.18% swing Lab. to C.
(2001: C. maj. 8,697 (19.30%))

DAGENHAM
E. 60,141 T. 30,841 (51.28%) Lab. hold
Jonathan Cruddas, Lab. 15,446
Michael White, C. 7,841
James Kempton, LD 3,106
Lawrence Rustem, BNP 2,870
Gerard Batten, UKIP 1,578
Lab. maj. 7,605 (24.66%)
3.43% swing Lab. to C.
(2001: Lab. maj. 8,693 (31.52%))

DARLINGTON
E. 65,281 T. 39,388 (60.34%) Lab. hold
Rt. Hon. Alan Milburn, Lab. 20,643
Anthony Frieze, C. 10,239
Robert Adamson, LD 7,269
John Hoodless, UKIP 730
Dai Davies, Veritas 507
Lab. maj. 10,404 (26.41%)
0.19% swing C. to Lab.
(2001: Lab. maj. 9,529 (23.38%))

DARTFORD
E. 74,028 T. 46,779 (63.19%) Lab. hold
Dr Howard Stoate, Lab. 19,909
Gareth Johnson, C. 19,203
Peter Bucklitsch, LD 5,036
Mark Croucher, UKIP 1,407
Michael Tibby, NEP 1,224
Lab. maj. 706 (1.51%)
2.94% swing Lab. to C.
(2001: Lab. maj. 3,306 (7.39%))

DAVENTRY
E. 88,758 T. 60,439 (68.09%) C. hold
Tim Boswell, C. 31,206
Andrew Hammond, Lab. 16,520
Hannah Saul, LD 9,964
Barry Mahoney, UKIP 1,927
Barrie Wilkins, Veritas 822
C. maj. 14,686 (24.30%)
3.64% swing Lab. to C.
(2001: C. maj. 9,649 (17.02%))

DENTON & REDDISH
E. 68,267 T. 35,442 (51.92%) Lab. hold
*Andrew Gwynne, Lab. 20,340
Alex Story, C. 6,842
Allison Seabourne, LD 5,814
John Edgar, BNP 1,326
Gerald Price, UKIP 1,120
Lab. maj. 13,498 (38.08%)
3.77% swing Lab. to C.
(2001: Lab. maj. 15,330 (45.63%))

DERBY NORTH
E. 68,173 T. 43,818 (64.27%) Lab. hold
Bob Laxton, Lab. 19,272
Richard Aitken-Davies, C. 15,515
Jeremy Beckett, LD 7,209
Martin Bardoe, Veritas 958
Michelle Medgyesy, UKIP 864
Lab. maj. 3,757 (8.57%)
3.64% swing Lab. to C.
(2001: Lab. maj. 6,982 (15.85%))

DERBY SOUTH
E. 70,397 T. 43,373 (61.61%) Lab. hold
Rt. Hon. Margaret Beckett, Lab. 19,683
Lucy Care, LD 14,026
David Brackenbury, C. 8,211
David Black, UKIP 845
Frank Leeming, Veritas 608
Lab. maj. 5,657 (13.04%)
12.05% swing Lab. to LD
(2001: Lab. maj. 13,855 (32.16%))

DERBYSHIRE NORTH EAST
E. 70,981 T. 43,434 (61.19%) Lab. hold
*Natascha Engel, Lab. 21,416
Dominic Johnson, C. 11,351
Tom Snowdon, LD 8,812
Kenneth Perkins, UKIP 1,855
Lab. maj. 10,065 (23.17%)
2.96% swing Lab. to C.
(2001: Lab. maj. 12,258 (29.10%))

DERBYSHIRE SOUTH
E. 85,049 T. 55,820 (65.63%) Lab. hold
Mark Todd, Lab. 24,823
Simon Spencer, C. 20,328
Deborah Newton-Cook, LD 7,600
David Joines, BNP 1,797
Edward Spalton, Veritas 1,272
Lab. maj. 4,495 (8.05%)
3.53% swing Lab. to C.
(2001: Lab. maj. 7,851 (15.11%))

DERBYSHIRE WEST
E. 73,865 T. 51,143 (69.24%) C. hold
Patrick McLoughlin, C. 24,378
David Menon, Lab. 13,625
Ray Dring, LD 11,408
Michael Cruddas, UKIP 1,322
Nick Delves, Loony 405
Martin Kyslun, Ind. 5
C. maj. 10,753 (21.03%)
3.23% swing Lab. to C.
(2001: C. maj. 7,370 (14.57%))

DEVIZES
E. 86,168 T. 56,146 (65.16%) C. hold
Rt. Hon. Michael Ancram, C. 27,253
Fiona Hornby, LD 14,059
Sharon Charity, Lab. 12,519
Alan Wood, UKIP 2,315
C. maj. 13,194 (23.50%)
0.84% swing C. to LD
(2001: C. maj. 11,896 (22.34%))

DEVON EAST
E. 71,000 T. 49,247 (69.36%) C. hold
Hugo Swire, C. 23,075
Tim Dumper, LD 15,139
James Court, Lab. 7,598
Colin McNamee, UKIP 3,035
Christopher Way, Ind. 400
C. maj. 7,936 (16.11%)
0.51% swing C. to LD
(2001: C. maj. 8,195 (17.13%))

DEVON NORTH
E. 76,203 T. 51,930 (68.15%) LD hold
Nick Harvey, LD 23,840
Orlando Fraser, C. 18,868
Mark Cann, Lab. 4,656
John Browne, UKIP 2,740
Richard Knight, Green 1,826
LD maj. 4,972 (9.57%)
1.76% swing C. to LD
(2001: LD maj. 2,984 (6.06%))

DEVON SOUTH WEST
E. 71,307 T. 48,885 (68.56%) C. hold
Gary Streeter, C. 21,906
Judy Evans, LD 11,765
Christopher Mavin, Lab. 11,545
Hugh Williams, UKIP 3,669
C. maj. 10,141 (20.74%)
3.86% swing C. to LD
(2001: C. maj. 7,144 (15.23%))

DEVON WEST & TORRIDGE
E. 83,489 T. 58,584 (70.17%) C. gain
*Geoffrey Cox, C. 25,013
David Walter, LD 21,777
Rebecca Richards, Lab. 6,001
Matthew Jackson, UKIP 3,790
Peter Christie, Green 2,003
C. maj. 3,236 (5.52%)
3.83% swing LD to C.
(2001: LD maj. 1,194 (2.14%))

DEWSBURY
E. 62,243 T. 38,595 (62.01%) Lab. hold
*Shahid Malik, Lab. 15,807
Sayeeda Warsi, C. 11,192
Kingsley Hill, LD 5,624
David Exley, BNP 5,066
Brenda Smithson, Green 593
Alan Girvan, Ind. 313
Lab. maj. 4,615 (11.96%)
4.18% swing Lab. to C.
(2001: Lab. maj. 7,449 (20.32%))

DON VALLEY
E. 66,993 T. 36,864 (55.03%) Lab. hold
Caroline Flint, Lab. 19,418
Adam Duguid, C. 10,820
Stewart Arnold, LD 6,626
Lab. maj. 8,598 (23.32%)
1.33% swing Lab. to C.
(2001: Lab. maj. 9,520 (25.99%))

DONCASTER CENTRAL
E. 65,731 T. 34,351 (52.26%) Lab. hold
Rosie Winterton, Lab. 17,617
Patrick Wilson, LD 7,815
Stefan Kerner, C. 6,489
John Wilkinson, BNP 1,239
Alan Simmons, UKIP 1,191
Lab. maj. 9,802 (28.53%)
8.80% swing Lab. to LD
(2001: Lab. maj. 11,999 (35.39%))

DONCASTER NORTH
E. 61,741 T. 31,578 (51.15%) Lab. hold
*Ed Miliband, Lab. 17,531
Martin Drake, C. 4,875
Doug Pickett, LD 3,800
Martin Williams, CG 2,365
Lee Hagan, BNP 1,506
Robert Nixon, UKIP 940
Michael Cassidy, Eng. Dem. 561
Lab. maj. 12,656 (40.08%)
4.17% swing Lab. to C.
(2001: Lab. maj. 15,187 (48.42%))

DORSET MID & POOLE NORTH
E. 65,924 T. 45,159 (68.50%) LD hold
Annette Brooke, LD 22,000
Simon Hayes, C. 16,518
Philip Murray, Lab. 5,221
Avril King, UKIP 1,420
LD maj. 5,482 (12.14%)
5.63% swing C. to LD
(2001: LD maj. 384 (0.88%))

DORSET NORTH
E. 74,286 T. 52,815 (71.10%) C. hold
Robert Walter, C. 23,714
Emily Gasson, LD 21,470
John Yarwood, Lab. 4,596
Richard Frampton Hobbs, UKIP 1,918
Ralph Arliss, Green 1,117
C. maj. 2,244 (4.25%)
1.85% swing C. to LD
(2001: C. maj. 3,797 (7.94%))

DORSET SOUTH
E. 70,668 T. 48,584 (68.75%) Lab. hold
Jim Knight, Lab. 20,231
Ed Matts, C. 18,419
Graham Oakes, LD 7,647
Hugh Chalker, UKIP 1,571
Vic Hamilton, LCA 282
Bernard Parkes, Respect 219
Andrew Kirkwood, PRTYP 107
Colin Bex, Wessex Reg. 83
David Marchesi, Soc. Lab. 25
Lab. maj. 1,812 (3.73%)
1.70% swing C. to Lab.
(2001: Lab. maj. 153 (0.34%))

DORSET WEST
E. 69,764 T. 53,225 (76.29%) C. hold
Rt. Hon. Oliver Letwin, C. 24,763
Justine McGuinness, LD 22,302
Dave Roberts, Lab. 4,124
Linda Guest, UKIP 1,084
Susan Greene, Green 952
C. maj. 2,461 (4.62%)
0.89% swing LD to C.
(2001: C. maj. 1,414 (2.85%))

DOVER
E. 70,884 T. 47,884 (67.55%) Lab. hold
Gwyn Prosser, Lab. 21,680
Paul Watkins, C. 16,739
Antony Hook, LD 7,607
Mike Wiltshire, UKIP 1,252
Vic Matcham, Ind. 606
Lab. maj. 4,941 (10.32%)
0.62% swing Lab. to C.
(2001: Lab. maj. 5,199 (11.56%))

DUDLEY NORTH
E. 68,766 T. 41,408 (60.22%) Lab. hold
*Ian Austin, Lab. 18,306
Ian Hillas, C. 12,874
Gerry Lewis, LD 4,257
Simon Darby, BNP 4,022
Malcolm Davis, UKIP 1,949
Lab. maj. 5,432 (13.12%)
2.26% swing Lab. to C.
(2001: Lab. maj. 6,800 (17.63%))

DUDLEY SOUTH
E. 65,228 T. 39,276 (60.21%) Lab. hold
Ian Pearson, Lab. 17,800
Marco Longhi, C. 13,556
Jonathan Bramall, LD 4,808
John Salvage, BNP 1,841
Andrew Benion, UKIP 1,271
Lab. maj. 4,244 (10.81%)
3.98% swing Lab. to C.
(2001: Lab. maj. 6,817 (18.76%))

DULWICH & WEST NORWOOD
E. 72,232 T. 41,989 (58.13%) Lab. hold
Rt. Hon. Tessa Jowell, Lab. 19,059
Jonathan Mitchell, LD 10,252
Kim Humphreys, C. 9,200
Jenny Jones, Green 2,741
Ralph Atkinson, UKIP 290
David Heather, Veritas 241
Amanda Rose, Soc. Lab. 149
Judy Weleminsky, Fit 57
Lab. maj. 8,807 (20.97%)
9.37% swing Lab. to LD
(2001: Lab. maj. 12,310 (32.19%))

DURHAM NORTH
E. 67,506 T. 37,341 (55.32%) Lab. hold
Kevan Jones, Lab. 23,932
Philip Latham, LD 7,151
Mark Watson, C. 6,258
Lab. maj. 16,781 (44.94%)
4.12% swing Lab. to LD
(2001: Lab. maj. 18,683 (48.44%))

DURHAM NORTH WEST
E. 68,130 T. 39,509 (57.99%) Lab. hold
Rt. Hon. Hilary Armstrong, Lab. 21,312
Alan Ord, LD 7,869
Jamie Devlin, C. 6,463
Watts Stelling, Ind. 3,865
Lab. maj. 13,443 (34.03%)
6.80% swing Lab. to LD
(2001: Lab. maj. 16,333 (41.64%))

DURHAM, CITY OF
E. 71,441 T. 44,364 (62.10%) Lab. hold
*Dr Roberta Blackman-Woods, Lab. 20,928
Carol Woods, LD 17,654
Ben Rogers, C. 4,179
Anthony Martin, Veritas 1,603
Lab. maj. 3,274 (7.38%)
12.51% swing Lab. to LD
(2001: Lab. maj. 13,441 (32.40%))

EALING ACTON & SHEPHERD'S BUSH
E. 70,454 T. 39,623 (56.24%) Lab. hold
*Andrew Slaughter, Lab. 16,579
Jonathan Gough, C. 11,059
Gary Malcolm, LD 9,986
Geoff Burgess, Green 1,999
Lab. maj. 5,520 (13.93%)
7.54% swing Lab. to C.
(2001: Lab. maj. 10,789 (29.00%))

EALING NORTH
E. 78,298 T. 46,507 (59.40%) Lab. hold
Stephen Pound, Lab. 20,956
Roger Curtis, C. 13,897
Francesco Fruzza, LD 9,148
Alan Outten, Green 1,319
Robin Lambert, UKIP 692
David Malindine, Veritas 495
Lab. maj. 7,059 (15.18%)
5.58% swing Lab. to C.
(2001: Lab. maj. 11,837 (26.33%))

EALING SOUTHALL
E. 83,738 T. 47,045 (56.18%) Lab. hold
Piara Khabra, Lab. 22,937
Nigel Bakhai, LD 11,497
Mark Nicholson, C. 10,147
Sarah Edwards, Green 2,175
Malkiat Bilku, WRP 289
Lab. maj. 11,440 (24.32%)
6.59% swing Lab. to LD
(2001: Lab. maj. 13,683 (29.22%))

EASINGTON
E. 61,084 T. 31,855 (52.15%) Lab. hold
John Cummings, Lab. 22,733
Christopher Ord, LD 4,097
Lucille Nicholson, C. 3,400
Ian McDonald, BNP 1,042
Dave Robinson, Soc. Lab. 583
Lab. maj. 18,636 (58.50%)
4.00% swing Lab. to LD
(2001: Lab. maj. 21,949 (66.49%))

EAST HAM
E. 78,104 T. 39,569 (50.66%) Lab. hold
Stephen Timms, Lab. 21,326
Abdul Khaliq Mian, Respect 8,171
Sarah Macken, C. 5,196
Ann Haigh, LD 4,296
David Bamber, CPA 580
Lab. maj. 13,155 (33.25%)
19.95% swing Lab. to Respect
(2001: Lab. maj. 21,032 (56.42%))

EASTBOURNE
E. 74,628 T. 48,392 (64.84%) C. hold
Nigel Waterson, C. 21,033
Stephen Lloyd, LD 19,909
Andrew Jones, Lab. 5,268
Andrew Meggs, UKIP 1,233
Clive Gross, Green 949
C. maj. 1,124 (2.32%)
1.24% swing C. to LD
(2001: C. maj. 2,154 (4.81%))

EASTLEIGH
E. 76,844 T. 49,771 (64.77%) LD hold
*Christopher Huhne, LD 19,216
Conor Burns, C. 18,648
Chris Watt, Lab. 10,238
Christopher Murphy, UKIP 1,669
LD maj. 568 (1.14%)
2.64% swing LD to C.
(2001: LD maj. 3,058 (6.43%))

ECCLES
E. 69,006 T. 34,632 (50.19%) Lab. hold
Ian Stewart, Lab. 19,702
Thelma Matuk, C. 6,816
Jane Brophy, LD 6,429
Peter Reeve, UKIP 1,685
Lab. maj. 12,886 (37.21%)
3.29% swing Lab. to C.
(2001: Lab. maj. 14,528 (43.78%))

EDDISBURY
E. 72,249 T. 45,674 (63.22%) C. hold
Stephen O'Brien, C. 21,181
Mark Green, Lab. 14,986
Joanne Crotty, LD 8,182
Steve Roxborough, UKIP 1,325
C. maj. 6,195 (13.56%)
1.64% swing Lab. to C.
(2001: C. maj. 4,568 (10.29%))

EDMONTON
E. 58,764 T. 34,703 (59.05%) Lab. (Co-op) hold
Andy Love, Lab. (Co-op) 18,456
Lionel Zetter, C. 10,381
Dr Iarla Kilbane-Dawe, LD 4,162
Nina Armstrong, Green 889
Gwyneth Rolph, UKIP 815
Lab. (Co-op) maj. 8,075 (23.27%)
2.42% swing Lab. (Co-op) to C.
(2001: Lab. (Co-op) maj. 9,772 (28.10%))

ELLESMERE PORT & NESTON
E. 68,249 T. 42,069 (61.64%) Lab. hold

Andrew Miller, Lab.	20,371
Myles Hogg, C.	13,885
Steve Cooke, LD	6,607
Henry Crocker, UKIP	1,206

Lab. maj. 6,486 (15.42%)
5.37% swing Lab. to C.
(2001: Lab. maj. 10,861 (26.15%))

ELMET
E. 68,514 T. 47,146 (68.81%) Lab. hold

Colin Burgon, Lab.	22,260
Andrew Millard, C.	17,732
Madeleine Kirk, LD	5,923
Tracy Andrews, BNP	1,231

Lab. maj. 4,528 (9.60%)
0.26% swing C. to Lab.
(2001: Lab. maj. 4,171 (9.08%))

ELTHAM
E. 57,236 T. 35,305 (61.68%) Lab. hold

Clive Efford, Lab.	15,381
Spencer Drury, C.	12,105
Ian Gerrard, LD	5,669
Jeremy Elms, UKIP	1,024
Barry Roberts, BNP	979
Andrew Graham, Ind.	147

Lab. maj. 3,276 (9.28%)
5.71% swing Lab. to C.
(2001: Lab. maj. 6,996 (20.70%))

ENFIELD NORTH
E. 66,460 T. 40,749 (61.31%) Lab. hold

Joan Ryan, Lab.	18,055
Nick de Bois, C.	16,135
Simon Radford, LD	4,642
Terence Farr, BNP	1,004
Gary Robbens, UKIP	750
Patrick Burns, Ind.	163

Lab. maj. 1,920 (4.71%)
0.63% swing Lab. to C.
(2001: Lab. maj. 2,291 (6.01%))

ENFIELD SOUTHGATE
E. 63,613 T. 42,210 (66.35%) C. gain

*David Burrowes, C.	18,830
Stephen Twigg, Lab.	17,083
Ziz Kakoulakis, LD	4,724
Trevor Doughty, Green	1,083
Brian Hall, UKIP	490

C. maj. 1,747 (4.14%)
8.69% swing Lab. to C.
(2001: Lab. maj. 5,546 (13.23%))

EPPING FOREST
E. 72,776 T. 44,860 (61.64%) C. hold

Eleanor Laing, C.	23,783
Bambos Charalambous, Lab.	9,425
Michael Heavens, LD	8,279
Julian Leppert, BNP	1,728
Andrew Smith, UKIP	1,014
Robin Tilbrook, Eng. Dem.	631

C. maj. 14,358 (32.01%)
6.07% swing Lab. to C.
(2001: C. maj. 8,426 (19.87%))

EPSOM & EWELL
E. 75,515 T. 49,879 (66.05%) C. hold

Chris Grayling, C.	27,146
Jonathan Lees, LD	10,699
Charles Mansell, Lab.	10,265
Peter Kefford, UKIP	1,769

C. maj. 16,447 (32.97%)
3.50% swing LD to C.
(2001: C. maj. 10,080 (21.61%))

EREWASH
E. 78,376 T. 50,553 (64.50%) Lab. hold

Liz Blackman, Lab.	22,472
David Simmonds, C.	15,388
Martin Garnett, LD	7,073
Robert Kilroy-Silk, Veritas	2,957
Sadie Graham, BNP	1,319
Geoffrey Kingscott, UKIP	941
R. U. Seerius, Loony	287
David Bishop, Elvis	116

Lab. maj. 7,084 (14.01%)
0.13% swing Lab. to C.
(2001: Lab. maj. 6,932 (14.26%))

ERITH & THAMESMEAD
E. 72,058 T. 37,651 (52.25%) Lab. hold

John Austin, Lab.	20,483
Chris Bromby, C.	8,983
Steven Toole, LD	5,088
Brian Ravenscroft, BNP	1,620
Barrie Thomas, UKIP	1,477

Lab. maj. 11,500 (30.54%)
1.47% swing Lab. to C.
(2001: Lab. maj. 11,167 (33.48%))

ESHER & WALTON
E. 76,926 T. 47,878 (62.24%) C. hold

Ian Taylor, C.	21,882
Mark Marsh, LD	14,155
Richard Taylor, Lab.	9,309
Bernard Collignon, UKIP	1,582
Chinners Chinnery, Loony	608
Richard Cutler, Soc. Lab.	342

C. maj. 7,727 (16.14%)
5.17% swing C. to LD
(2001: C. maj. 11,538 (25.34%))

ESSEX NORTH
E. 73,037 T. 47,959 (65.66%) C. hold

Bernard Jenkin, C.	22,811
Elizabeth Hughes, Lab.	11,908
James Raven, LD	9,831
Christopher Fox, Green	1,718
George Curtis, UKIP	1,691

C. maj. 10,903 (22.73%)
3.37% swing Lab. to C.
(2001: C. maj. 7,186 (15.99%))

EXETER
E. 84,964 T. 55,068 (64.81%) Lab. hold

Ben Bradshaw, Lab.	22,619
Peter Cox, C.	14,954
Jon Underwood, LD	11,340
Margaret Danks, Lib.	2,214
Tim Brenan, Green	1,896
Mark Fitzgeorge-Parker, UKIP	1,854
John Stuart, Ind.	191

Lab. maj. 7,665 (13.92%)
4.21% swing Lab. to C.
(2001: Lab. maj. 11,759 (22.35%))

FALMOUTH & CAMBORNE
E. 71,509 T. 48,015 (67.15%) LD gain

*Julia Goldsworthy, LD	16,747
Candy Atherton, Lab.	14,861
Ashley Crossley, C.	12,644
Michael Mahon, UKIP	1,820
David Mudd, Ind.	961
Paul Holmes, Lib.	423
Hilda Wasley, Meb. Ker.	370
Peter Gifford, Veritas	128
Richard Smith, Masts	61

LD maj. 1,886 (3.93%)
9.52% swing Lab. to LD
(2001: Lab. maj. 4,527 (9.67%))

FAREHAM
E. 72,599 T. 48,576 (66.91%) C. hold

Mark Hoban, C.	24,151
James Carr, Lab.	12,449
Richard De Ste-Croix, LD	10,551
Peter Mason-Apps, UKIP	1,425

C. maj. 11,702 (24.09%)
4.33% swing Lab. to C.
(2001: C. maj. 7,009 (15.42%))

FAVERSHAM & KENT MID
E. 66,411 T. 43,626 (65.69%) C. hold

Hugh Robertson, C.	21,690
Andrew Bradstock, Lab.	12,970
David Naghi, LD	7,204
Robert Thompson, UKIP	1,152
Norman Davidson, Loony	610

C. maj. 8,720 (19.99%)
4.90% swing Lab. to C.
(2001: C. maj. 4,183 (10.19%))

FELTHAM & HESTON
E. 75,391 T. 37,282 (49.45%)
Lab. (Co-op) hold

Alan Keen, Lab. (Co-op)	17,741
Mark Bowen, C.	10,921
Satnam Kaur Khalsa, LD	6,177
Graham Kemp, NF	975
Elizabeth Anstis, Green	815
Leon Mullett, UKIP	612
Warwick Prachar, Ind.	41

Lab. (Co-op) maj. 6,820 (18.29%)
8.35% swing Lab. (Co-op) to C.
(2001: Lab. (Co-op) maj. 12,657 (34.99%))

FINCHLEY & GOLDERS GREEN
E. 69,808 T. 43,214 (61.90%) Lab. hold

Dr Rudi Vis, Lab.	17,487
Andrew Mennear, C.	16,746
Sue Garden, LD	7,282
Noel Lynch, Green	1,136
Jeremy Jacobs, UKIP	453
Rainbow George Weiss, Vote Dream	110

Lab. maj. 741 (1.71%)
3.40% swing Lab. to C.
(2001: Lab. maj. 3,716 (8.51%))

FOLKESTONE & HYTHE
E. 70,914 T. 48,503 (68.40%) C. hold

Rt. Hon. Michael Howard, C.	26,161
Peter Carroll, LD	14,481
Maureen Tomison, Lab.	6,053
Dr Hazel Dawe, Green	688
Petrina Holdsworth, UKIP	619
Lord Toby Jug, Loony	175
Rodney Hylton-Potts, GBB	153
Grahame Leon-Smith, Senior	151
Sylvia Dunn, Progress	22

C. maj. 11,680 (24.08%)
5.60% swing LD to C.
(2001: C. maj. 5,907 (12.88%))

FOREST OF DEAN
E. 67,225 T. 47,640 (70.87%) C. gain

*Mark Harper, C.	19,474
Isabel Owen, Lab.	17,425
Christopher Coleman, LD	8,185
Patricia Hill, UKIP	1,140
Stephen Tweedie, Green	991
Anthony Reeve, Ind.	300
Gerald Morgan, EPP	125

C. maj. 2,049 (4.30%)
4.45% swing Lab. to C.
(2001: Lab. maj. 2,049 (4.59%))

FYLDE
E. 75,703 T. 45,510 (60.12%) C. hold
Rt. Hon. Michael Jack, C. 24,287
William Parbury, Lab. 11,828
Bill Winlow, LD 7,748
Tim Akeroyd, Lib. 1,647
C. maj. 12,459 (27.38%)
2.95% swing Lab. to C.
(2001: C. maj. 9,610 (21.48%))

GAINSBOROUGH
E. 70,733 T. 45,681 (64.58%) C. hold
Edward Leigh, C. 20,040
Adrian Heath, LD 12,037
John Knight, Lab. 11,744
Steven Pearson, UKIP 1,860
C. maj. 8,003 (17.52%)
1.02% swing C. to LD
(2001: C. maj. 8,071 (19.07%))

GATESHEAD EAST & WASHINGTON WEST
E. 61,421 T. 34,668 (56.44%) Lab. hold
*Sharon Hodgson, Lab. 20,997
Frank Hindle, LD 7,590
Lee Martin, C. 4,812
Jim Batty, UKIP 1,269
Lab. maj. 13,407 (38.67%)
7.29% swing Lab. to LD
(2001: Lab. maj. 17,904 (53.26%))

GEDLING
E. 68,917 T. 44,069 (63.95%) Lab. hold
Vernon Coaker, Lab. 20,329
Anna Soubry, C. 16,518
Raymond Poynter, LD 6,070
Alan Margerison, UKIP 741
Deborah Johnson, Veritas 411
Lab. maj. 3,811 (8.65%)
2.06% swing Lab. to C.
(2001: Lab. maj. 5,598 (12.78%))

GILLINGHAM
E. 72,223 T. 45,167 (62.54%) Lab. hold
Paul Clark, Lab. 18,621
Tim Butcher, C. 18,367
Andrew Stamp, LD 6,734
Craig MacKinlay, UKIP 1,191
Gordon Bryan, Ind. 254
Lab. maj. 254 (0.56%)
2.41% swing Lab. to C.
(2001: Lab. maj. 2,272 (5.38%))

GLOUCESTER
E. 82,500 T. 51,803 (62.79%) Lab. hold
Parmjit Dhanda, Lab. 23,138
Paul James, C. 18,867
Jeremy Hilton, LD 7,825
Gary Phipps, UKIP 1,116
Bryan Meloy, Green 857
Lab. maj. 4,271 (8.24%)
0.10% swing C. to Lab.
(2001: Lab. maj. 3,880 (8.05%))

GOSPORT
E. 71,119 T. 43,034 (60.51%) C. hold
Peter Viggers, C. 19,268
Richard Williams, Lab. 13,538
Roger Roberts, LD 7,145
John Bowles, UKIP 1,825
Andrea Smith, Green 1,258
C. maj. 5,730 (13.32%)
3.36% swing Lab. to C.
(2001: C. maj. 2,621 (6.59%))

GRANTHAM & STAMFORD
E. 74,074 T. 47,147 (63.65%) C. hold
Quentin Davies, C. 22,109
Ian Selby, Lab. 14,664
Patrick O'Connor, LD 7,838
Stuart Rising, UKIP 1,498
Benedict Brown, Eng. Dem. 774
John Andrews, OFD 264
C. maj. 7,445 (15.79%)
3.02% swing Lab. to C.
(2001: C. maj. 4,518 (9.76%))

GRAVESHAM
E. 68,705 T. 45,179 (65.76%) C. gain
*Adam Holloway, C. 19,739
Chris Pond, Lab. 19,085
Bruce Parmenter, LD 4,851
Geoff Coates, UKIP 850
Christopher Nickerson, Eng. Ind. 654
C. maj. 654 (1.45%)
6.29% swing Lab. to C.
(2001: Lab. maj. 4,862 (11.14%))

GREAT GRIMSBY
E. 63,711 T. 32,964 (51.74%) Lab. hold
Austin Mitchell, Lab. 15,512
Giles Taylor, C. 7,858
Andrew de Freitas, LD 6,356
Stephen Fyfe, BNP 1,338
Martin Grant, UKIP 1,239
David Brooks, Green 661
Lab. maj. 7,654 (23.22%)
5.78% swing Lab. to C.
(2001: Lab. maj. 11,484 (34.78%))

GREAT YARMOUTH
E. 68,887 T. 41,378 (60.07%) Lab. hold
Anthony Wright, Lab. 18,850
Mark Fox, C. 15,795
Stephen Newton, LD 4,585
Bertie Poole, UKIP 1,759
Michael Skipper, LCA 389
Lab. maj. 3,055 (7.38%)
1.96% swing Lab. to C.
(2001: Lab. maj. 4,564 (11.31%))

GREENWICH & WOOLWICH
E. 64,033 T. 35,615 (55.62%) Lab. hold
Rt. Hon. Nick Raynsford, Lab. 17,527
Christopher Le Breton, LD 7,381
Alistair Craig, C. 7,142
David Sharman, Green 1,579
Garry Bushell, Eng. Dem. 1,216
Stanley Gain, UKIP 709
Puvarani Nagalingam, Ind. 61
Lab. maj. 10,146 (28.49%)
8.21% swing Lab. to LD
(2001: Lab. maj. 13,433 (41.29%))

GUILDFORD
E. 75,566 T. 51,631 (68.33%) C. gain
*Anne Milton, C. 22,595
Sue Doughty, LD 22,248
Karen Landles, Lab. 5,054
John Pletts, Green 811
Martin Haslam, UKIP 645
John Morris, PPN-V 166
Victoria Lavin, Ind. 112
C. maj. 347 (0.67%)
0.90% swing LD to C.
(2001: LD maj. 538 (1.12%))

HACKNEY NORTH & STOKE NEWINGTON
E. 59,260 T. 29,380 (49.58%) Lab. hold
Diane Abbott, Lab. 14,268
James Blanchard, LD 6,841
Ertan Hurer, C. 4,218
Mischa Borris, Green 2,907
David Vail, Ind. 602
Nusrat Sen, Soc. Lab. 296
Nigel Barrow, Loony 248
Lab. maj. 7,427 (25.28%)
10.84% swing Lab. to LD
(2001: Lab. maj. 13,651 (46.09%))

HACKNEY SOUTH & SHOREDITCH
E. 64,818 T. 32,237 (49.73%) Lab. (Co-op) hold
*Meg Hillier, Lab. (Co-op) 17,048
Gavin Baylis, LD 6,844
John Moss, C. 4,524
Ipemndoh dan Iyan, Green 1,779
Dean Ryan, Respect 1,437
Benjamin Rae, Lib. 313
Monty Goldman, Comm. 200
Jonty Leff, WRP 92
Lab. (Co-op) maj. 10,204 (31.65%)
8.97% swing Lab. (Co-op) to LD
(2001: Lab. (Co-op) maj. 15,049 (49.59%))

HALESOWEN & ROWLEY REGIS
E. 65,748 T. 41,327 (62.86%) Lab. hold
Sylvia Heal, Lab. 19,243
Les Jones, C. 14,906
Martin Turner, LD 5,204
Nikki Sinclaire, UKIP 1,974
Lab. maj. 4,337 (10.49%)
4.12% swing Lab. to C.
(2001: Lab. maj. 7,359 (18.74%))

HALIFAX
E. 64,861 T. 39,659 (61.14%) Lab. (Co-op) hold
*Linda Riordan, Lab. (Co-op) 16,579
Kris Hopkins, C. 13,162
Michael Taylor, LD 7,100
Geoff Wallace, BNP 2,627
Thomas Holmes, NF 191
Lab. (Co-op) maj. 3,417 (8.62%)
3.28% swing Lab. (Co-op) to C.
(2001: Lab. (Co-op) maj. 6,129 (15.17%))

HALTEMPRICE & HOWDEN
E. 68,471 T. 48,029 (70.15%) C. hold
Rt. Hon. David Davis, C. 22,792
Jon Neal, LD 17,676
Edward Hart, Lab. 6,104
Jonathan Mainprize, BNP 798
Philip Lane, UKIP 659
C. maj. 5,116 (10.65%)
3.16% swing LD to C.
(2001: C. maj. 1,903 (4.33%))

HALTON
E. 64,379 T. 34,183 (53.10%) Lab. hold
Derek Twigg, Lab. 21,460
Colin Bloom, C. 6,854
Roger Barlow, LD 5,869
Lab. maj. 14,606 (42.73%)
3.92% swing Lab. to C.
(2001: Lab. maj. 17,428 (50.56%))

HAMMERSMITH & FULHAM
E. 79,082 T. 49,327 (62.37%) C. gain
*Greg Hands, C. 22,407
Melanie Smallman, Lab. 17,378
Alan Bullion, LD 7,116
Fiona Harrold, Green 1,933
Giles Fisher, UKIP 493
C. maj. 5,029 (10.20%)
7.35% swing Lab. to C.
(2001: Lab. maj. 2,015 (4.51%))

HAMPSHIRE EAST
E. 79,801 T. 53,139 (66.59%) C. hold
Rt. Hon. Michael Mates, C. 24,273
Ruth Bright, LD 18,764
Marjory Broughton, Lab. 8,519
David Samuel, UKIP 1,583
C. maj. 5,509 (10.37%)
3.66% swing C. to LD
(2001: C. maj. 8,890 (17.68%))

HAMPSHIRE NORTH EAST
E. 72,939 T. 47,287 (64.83%) C. hold
Rt. Hon. James Arbuthnot, C. 25,407
Adam Carew, LD 12,858
Kevin McGrath, Lab. 7,630
Paul Birch, UKIP 1,392
C. maj. 12,549 (26.54%)
1.81% swing C. to LD
(2001: C. maj. 13,257 (30.17%))

HAMPSHIRE NORTH WEST
E. 79,763 T. 51,265 (64.27%) C. hold
Rt. Hon. Sir George Young, C. 26,005
Martin Tod, LD 12,741
Michael Mumford, Lab. 10,594
Peter Sumner, UKIP 1,925
C. maj. 13,264 (25.87%)
1.50% swing C. to LD
(2001: C. maj. 12,009 (24.69%))

HAMPSTEAD & HIGHGATE
E. 68,737 T. 38,173 (55.53%) Lab. hold
Glenda Jackson, Lab. 14,615
Piers Wauchope, C. 10,886
Ed Fordham, LD 10,293
Sian Berry, Green 2,013
Magnus Nielsen, UKIP 275
Rainbow George Weiss, Vote Dream 91
Lab. maj. 3,729 (9.77%)
6.24% swing Lab. to C.
(2001: Lab. maj. 7,876 (22.24%))

HARBOROUGH
E. 74,583 T. 47,922 (64.25%) C. hold
Edward Garnier, C. 20,536
Jill Hope, LD 16,644
Peter Evans, Lab. 9,222
Marietta King, UKIP 1,520
C. maj. 3,892 (8.12%)
1.60% swing C. to LD
(2001: C. maj. 5,252 (11.31%))

HARLOW
E. 63,500 T. 39,733 (62.57%) Lab. hold
Bill Rammell, Lab. 16,453
Robert Halfon, C. 16,356
Lorna Spenceley, LD 5,002
John Felgate, UKIP 981
Anthony Bennett, Veritas 941
Lab. maj. 97 (0.24%)
6.39% swing Lab. to C.
(2001: Lab. maj. 5,228 (13.03%))

HARROGATE & KNARESBOROUGH
E. 65,622 T. 42,858 (65.31%) LD hold
Phil Willis, LD 24,113
Maggie Punyer, C. 13,684
Lorraine Ferris, Lab. 3,627
Chris Royston, UKIP 845
Colin Banner, BNP 466
John Allman, AFC 123
LD maj. 10,429 (24.33%)
1.68% swing C. to LD
(2001: LD maj. 8,845 (20.97%))

HARROW EAST
E. 84,033 T. 50,823 (60.48%) Lab. hold
Tony McNulty, Lab. 23,445
David Ashton, C. 18,715
Pash Nandhra, LD 7,747
Paul Cronin, UKIP 916
Lab. maj. 4,730 (9.31%)
6.92% swing Lab. to C.
(2001: Lab. maj. 11,124 (23.14%))

HARROW WEST
E. 74,228 T. 47,759 (64.34%)
Lab. (Co-op) hold
Gareth Thomas, Lab. (Co-op) 20,298
Mike Freer, C. 18,270
Christopher Noyce, LD 8,188
Janice Cronin, UKIP 576
Berjis Daver, Ind. 427
Lab. (Co-op) maj. 2,028 (4.25%)
4.48% swing Lab. (Co-op) to C.
(2001: Lab. (Co-op) maj. 6,156 (13.20%))

HARTLEPOOL
E. 68,776 T. 35,436 (51.52%) Lab. hold
Iain Wright, Lab. 18,251
Jody Dunn, LD 10,773
Amanda Vigar, C. 4,058
George Springer, UKIP 1,256
Frank Harrison, Soc. Lab. 373
Iris Ryder, Green 288
John Hobbs, Ind. 275
Sausage Supremo Headbanger, Loony 162
Lab. maj. 7,478 (21.10%)
11.51% swing Lab. to LD
(2004 Sept. by-election: Lab. maj. 2,033 (6.48%))
(2001: Lab. maj. 14,571 (38.29%))

HARWICH
E. 80,474 T. 50,408 (62.64%) C. gain
*Douglas Carswell, C. 21,235
Ivan Henderson, Lab. 20,315
Keith Tully, LD 5,913
Jeffrey Titford, UKIP 2,314
John Tipple, Respect 477
Christopher Humphrey, Ind. 154
C. maj. 920 (1.83%)
3.61% swing Lab. to C.
(2001: Lab. maj. 2,596 (5.40%))

HASTINGS & RYE
E. 72,765 T. 43,004 (59.10%) Lab. hold
Michael Foster, Lab. 18,107
Mark Coote, C. 16,081
Richard Stevens, LD 6,479
Terry Grant, UKIP 1,098
Sally Phillips, Green 1,032
John Ord-Clarke, Loony 207
Lab. maj. 2,026 (4.71%)
2.87% swing Lab. to C.
(2001: Lab. maj. 4,308 (10.45%))

HAVANT
E. 68,545 T. 41,351 (60.33%) C. hold
David Willetts, C. 18,370
Sarah Bogle, Lab. 11,862
Alex Bentley, LD 8,358
Timothy Dawes, Green 1,006
Steve Harris, UKIP 998
Ian Johnson, BNP 562
Russell Thomas, Veritas 195
C. maj. 6,508 (15.74%)
2.67% swing Lab. to C.
(2001: C. maj. 4,207 (10.40%))

HAYES & HARLINGTON
E. 57,493 T. 32,389 (56.34%) Lab. hold
John McDonnell, Lab. 19,009
Richard Worrall, C. 8,162
Jon Ball, LD 3,174
Tony Hazel, BNP 830
Martin Haley, UKIP 552
Brian Outten, Green 442
Paul Goddard, Ind. 220
Lab. maj. 10,847 (33.49%)
4.03% swing Lab. to C.
(2001: Lab. maj. 13,466 (41.56%))

HAZEL GROVE
E. 64,376 T. 39,117 (60.76%) LD hold
Andrew Stunell, LD 19,355
Alan White, C. 11,607
Andrew Graystone, Lab. 6,834
Keith Ryan, UKIP 1,321
LD maj. 7,748 (19.81%)
1.06% swing LD to C.
(2001: LD maj. 8,435 (21.92%))

HEMEL HEMPSTEAD
E. 73,095 T. 47,108 (64.45%) C. gain
*Michael Penning, C. 19,000
Tony McWalter, Lab. (Co-op) 18,501
Dr Richard Grayson, LD 8,089
Barry Newton, UKIP 1,518
C. maj. 499 (1.06%)
4.61% swing Lab. (Co-op) to C.
(2001: Lab. (Co-op) maj. 3,742 (8.16%))

HEMSWORTH
E. 67,339 T. 36,792 (54.64%) Lab. hold
Jon Trickett, Lab. 21,630
Jonathan Mortimer, C. 8,149
David Hall-Matthews, LD 5,766
John Burdon, Veritas 1,247
Lab. maj. 13,481 (36.64%)
3.87% swing Lab. to C.
(2001: Lab. maj. 15,636 (44.39%))

HENDON
E. 71,764 T. 41,839 (58.30%) Lab. hold
Andrew Dismore, Lab. 18,596
Dr Richard Evans, C. 15,897
Nahid Boethe, LD 5,831
David Williams, Green 754
Melvyn Smallman, UKIP 637
Rainbow George Weiss, Vote Dream 68
Michael Stewart, PDP 56
Lab. maj. 2,699 (6.45%)
5.85% swing Lab. to C.
(2001: Lab. maj. 7,417 (18.16%))

HENLEY
E. 68,538 T. 46,537 (67.90%) C. hold
Boris Johnson, C. 24,894
David Turner, LD 12,101
Kaleem Saeed, Lab. 6,862
Mark Stevenson, Green 1,518
Delphine Gray-Fisk, UKIP 1,162
C. maj. 12,793 (27.49%)
4.22% swing LD to C.
(2001: C. maj. 8,458 (19.05%))

HEREFORD
E. 71,813 T. 46,894 (65.30%) LD hold
Paul Keetch, LD 20,285
Virginia Taylor, C. 19,323
Tom Calver, Lab. 4,800
Brian Lunt, Green 1,052
Christopher Kingsley, UKIP 1,030
Peter Morton, Ind. 404
LD maj. 962 (2.05%)
0.06% swing LD to C.
(2001: LD maj. 968 (2.17%))

HERTFORD & STORTFORD
E. 73,394 T. 49,692 (67.71%) C. hold
Mark Prisk, C. 25,074
Richard Henry, Lab. 11,977
James Lucas, LD 9,129
Peter Hart, Green 1,914
David Sodey, UKIP 1,026
Debbie Le May, Veritas 572
C. maj. 13,097 (26.36%)
7.24% swing Lab. to C.
(2001: C. maj. 5,603 (11.88%))

HERTFORDSHIRE NORTH EAST
E. 72,190 T. 47,374 (65.62%) C. hold
Oliver Heald, C. 22,402
Andrew Harrop, Lab. 13,264
Iain Coleman, LD 10,147
David Hitchman, UKIP 1,561
C. maj. 9,138 (19.29%)
3.79% swing Lab. to C.
(2001: C. maj. 3,444 (7.71%))

HERTFORDSHIRE SOUTH WEST
E. 73,170 T. 50,088 (68.45%) C. hold
*David Gauke, C. 23,494
Ed Featherstone, LD 15,021
Kerron Cross, Lab. 10,466
Colin Rodden, UKIP 1,107
C. maj. 8,473 (16.92%)
0.54% swing C. to LD
(2001: C. maj. 8,181 (17.31%))

HERTSMERE
E. 67,572 T. 42,572 (63.00%) C. hold
James Clappison, C. 22,665
Kelly Tebb, Lab. 11,572
Jonathan Davies, LD 7,817
James Dry, Soc. Lab. 518
C. maj. 11,093 (26.06%)
7.12% swing Lab. to C.
(2001: C. maj. 4,902 (11.81%))

HEXHAM
E. 60,374 T. 41,513 (68.76%) C. hold
Peter Atkinson, C. 17,605
Kevin Graham, Lab. 12,585
Andrew Duffield, LD 10,673
Ian Riddell, Eng. Dem. 521
Thomas Davison, IP 129
C. maj. 5,020 (12.09%)
3.06% swing Lab. to C.
(2001: C. maj. 2,529 (5.96%))

HEYWOOD & MIDDLETON
E. 71,510 T. 39,053 (54.61%) Lab. (Co-op) hold
Jim Dobbin, Lab. (Co-op) 19,438
Stephen Pathmarajah, C. 8,355
Crea Lavin, LD 7,261
Gary Aronsson, BNP 1,855
Phil Burke, Lib. 1,377
Dr John Whittaker, UKIP 767
Lab. (Co-op) maj. 11,083 (28.38%)
0.86% swing Lab. (Co-op) to C.
(2001: Lab. (Co-op) maj. 11,670 (30.09%))

HIGH PEAK
E. 75,275 T. 49,989 (66.41%) Lab. hold
Tom Levitt, Lab. 19,809
Andrew Bingham, C. 19,074
Marc Godwin, LD 10,000
Michael Schwartz, UKIP 1,106
Lab. maj. 735 (1.47%)
3.93% swing Lab. to C.
(2001: Lab. maj. 4,489 (9.33%))

HITCHIN & HARPENDEN
E. 67,207 T. 47,387 (70.51%) C. hold
Rt. Hon. Peter Lilley, C. 23,627
Hannah Hedges, LD 12,234
Paul Orrett, Lab. 10,499
John Saunders, UKIP 828
Peter Rigby, Ind. 199
C. maj. 11,393 (24.04%)
2.66% swing C. to LD
(2001: C. maj. 6,663 (14.83%))

HOLBORN & ST PANCRAS
E. 68,237 T. 34,359 (50.35%) Lab. hold
Rt. Hon. Frank Dobson, Lab. 14,857
Jill Fraser, LD 10,070
Margot James, C. 6,482
Adrian Oliver, Green 2,798
Rainbow George Weiss, Vote Dream 152
Lab. maj. 4,787 (13.93%)
10.98% swing Lab. to LD
(2001: Lab. maj. 11,175 (35.90%))

HORNCHURCH
E. 59,773 T. 38,169 (63.86%) C. gain
*James Brokenshire, C. 16,355
John Cryer, Lab. 15,875
Nat Green, LD 2,894
Ian Moore, BNP 1,313
Lawrence Webb, UKIP 1,033
Malvin Brown, RA 395
Graham Williamson, Third 304
C. maj. 480 (1.26%)
2.71% swing Lab. to C.
(2001: Lab. maj. 1,482 (4.17%))

HORNSEY & WOOD GREEN
E. 76,621 T. 47,330 (61.77%) LD gain
*Lynne Featherstone, LD 20,512
Barbara Roche, Lab. 18,117
Peter Forrest, C. 6,014
Jayne Forbes, Green 2,377
Roy Freshwater, UKIP 310
LD maj. 2,395 (5.06%)
14.57% swing Lab. to LD
(2001: Lab. maj. 10,614 (24.09%))

HORSHAM
E. 80,974 T. 54,495 (67.30%) C. hold
Rt. Hon. Francis Maude, C. 27,240
Rosie Sharpley, LD 14,613
Rehman Chishti, Lab. 9,320
Hugo Miller, UKIP 2,552
Jim Duggan, Ind. 416
Martin Jeremiah, PHF 354
C. maj. 12,627 (23.17%)
1.87% swing C. to LD
(2001: C. maj. 13,666 (26.92%))

HOUGHTON & WASHINGTON EAST
E. 67,089 T. 34,694 (51.71%) Lab. hold
Fraser Kemp, Lab. 22,310
Mark Greenfield, LD 6,245
Anthony Devenish, C. 4,772
John Richardson, BNP 1,367
Lab. maj. 16,065 (46.30%)
7.20% swing Lab. to LD
(2001: Lab. maj. 19,818 (58.91%))

HOVE
E. 69,939 T. 44,796 (64.05%) Lab. hold
*Celia Barlow, Lab. 16,786
Nicholas Boles, C. 16,366
Paul Elgood, LD 8,002
Anthea Ballam, Green 2,575
Stuart Bower, UKIP 575
Paddy O'Keeffe, Respect 268
Bob Dobbs, Ind. 95
Richard Franklin, Silent 78
Brian Ralfe, Ind. 51
Lab. maj. 420 (0.94%)
3.31% swing Lab. to C.
(2001: Lab. maj. 3,171 (7.55%))

HUDDERSFIELD
E. 61,723 T. 34,940 (56.61%) Lab. (Co-op) hold
Barry Sheerman, Lab. (Co-op) 16,341
Emma Bone, LD 7,990
David Meacock, C. 7,597
Julie Stewart-Turner, Green 1,651
Karl Hanson, BNP 1,036
Theresa Quarmby, Ind. 325
Lab. (Co-op) maj. 8,351 (23.90%)
7.18% swing Lab. (Co-op) to LD
(2001: Lab. (Co-op) maj. 10,046 (28.39%))

HULL EAST
E. 65,407 T. 31,022 (47.43%) Lab. hold
Rt. Hon. John Prescott, Lab. 17,609
Andy Sloan, LD 5,862
Katy Lindsay, C. 4,038
Alan Siddle, BNP 1,022
Janet Toker, Lib. 1,018
Graham Morris, Veritas 750
Ronald Noon, Ind. 334
Linda Muir, Soc. Lab. 207
Carl Wagner, LCA 182
Lab. maj. 11,747 (37.87%)
5.88% swing Lab. to LD
(2001: Lab. maj. 15,325 (49.64%))

HULL NORTH
E. 62,590 T. 29,584 (47.27%) Lab. hold
*Diana Johnson, Lab. 15,364
Denis Healy, LD 8,013
Lydia Rivlin, C. 3,822
Martin Deane, Green 858
Brian Wainwright, BNP 766
Tineke Robinson, Veritas 389
Christopher Veasey, Northern 193
Carl Wagner, LCA 179
Lab. maj. 7,351 (24.85%)
6.30% swing Lab. to LD
(2001: Lab. maj. 10,721 (37.44%))

HULL WEST & HESSLE
E. 61,494 T. 27,818 (45.24%) Lab. hold
Rt. Hon. Alan Johnson, Lab. 15,305
David Nolan, LD 5,855
Karen Woods, C. 5,769
Stephen Wallis, Veritas 889
Lab. maj. 9,450 (33.97%)
4.66% swing Lab. to LD
(2001: Lab. maj. 10,951 (37.87%))

HUNTINGDON
E. 83,843 T. 52,418 (62.52%) C. hold
Jonathan Djanogly, C. 26,646
Julian Huppert, LD 13,799
Stephen Sartain, Lab. 9,821
Derek Norman, UKIP 2,152
C. maj. 12,847 (24.51%)
0.78% swing C. to LD
(2001: C. maj. 12,792 (26.06%))

HYNDBURN
E. 67,086 T. 39,449 (58.80%) Lab. hold
Greg Pope, Lab. 18,136
James Mawdsley, C. 12,549
Bill Greene, LD 5,577
Christian Jackson, BNP 2,444
Dr John Whittaker, UKIP 743
Lab. maj. 5,587 (14.16%)
3.66% swing Lab. to C.
(2001: Lab. maj. 8,219 (21.49%))

ILFORD NORTH
E. 70,718 T. 43,000 (60.80%) C. gain
*Lee Scott, C. 18,781
Linda Perham, Lab. 17,128
Mark Gayler, LD 5,896
Andrew Cross, UKIP 902
Martin Levin, Ind. 293
C. maj. 1,653 (3.84%)
4.55% swing Lab. to C.
(2001: Lab. maj. 2,115 (5.26%))

ILFORD SOUTH
E. 79,639 T. 42,693 (53.61%)
Lab. (Co-op) hold
Mike Gapes, Lab. (Co-op) 20,856
Stephen Metcalfe, C. 11,628
Matthew Lake, LD 8,761
Kashif Rana, BPP 763
Colin Taylor, UKIP 685
Lab. (Co-op) maj. 9,228 (21.61%)
6.14% swing Lab. (Co-op) to C.
(2001: Lab. (Co-op) maj. 13,997 (33.90%))

IPSWICH
E. 68,825 T. 41,878 (60.85%) Lab. hold
Chris Mole, Lab. 18,336
Paul West, C. 13,004
Richard Atkins, LD 8,464
Alison West, UKIP 1,134
Jervis Kay, Eng. Dem. 641
Sally Wainman, Ind. 299
Lab. maj. 5,332 (12.73%)
4.03% swing Lab. to C.
(2001 Nov. by-election: Lab. maj. 4,087 (14.91%))
(2001: Lab. maj. 8,081 (20.79%))

ISLE OF WIGHT
E. 109,046 T. 66,843 (61.30%) C. hold
Andrew Turner, C. 32,717
Anthony Rowlands, LD 19,739
Mark Chiverton, Lab. 11,484
Michael Tarrant, UKIP 2,352
Edward Corby, Ind. 551
C. maj. 12,978 (19.42%)
7.48% swing LD to C.
(2001: C. maj. 2,826 (4.45%))

ISLINGTON NORTH
E. 58,427 T. 31,494 (53.90%) Lab. hold
Jeremy Corbyn, Lab. 16,118
Laura Willoughby, LD 9,402
Nicola Talbot, C. 3,740
Jon Nott, Green 2,234
Lab. maj. 6,716 (21.32%)
10.78% swing Lab. to LD
(2001: Lab. maj. 12,958 (42.88%))

ISLINGTON SOUTH & FINSBURY
E. 57,748 T. 30,961 (53.61%) Lab. hold
*Emily Thornberry, Lab. 12,345
Bridget Fox, LD 11,861
Melanie McLean, C. 4,594
James Humphries, Green 1,471
Patricia Theophanides, UKIP 470
Andy the Hat Gardner, Loony 189
Chris Gidden, Ind. 31
Lab. maj. 484 (1.56%)
12.12% swing Lab. to LD
(2001: Lab. maj. 7,280 (25.81%))

JARROW
E. 61,814 T. 33,978 (54.97%) Lab. hold
Stephen Hepburn, Lab. 20,554
Bill Schardt, LD 6,650
Linkson Jack, C. 4,807
Alan Badger, UKIP 1,567
Roger Nettleship, SNH 400
Lab. maj. 13,904 (40.92%)
5.06% swing Lab. to LD
(2001: Lab. maj. 17,595 (51.03%))

KEIGHLEY
E. 68,229 T. 46,312 (67.88%) Lab. hold
Ann Cryer, Lab. 20,720
Karl Poulsen, C. 15,868
Nader Fekri, LD 5,484
Nick Griffin, BNP 4,240
Lab. maj. 4,852 (10.48%)
0.62% swing C. to Lab.
(2001: Lab. maj. 4,005 (9.24%))

KENSINGTON & CHELSEA
E. 62,662 T. 31,336 (50.01%) C. hold
†Rt. Hon. Sir Malcolm Rifkind, C. 18,144
Jennifer Kingsley, LD 5,726
Catherine Atkinson, Lab. 5,521
Julia Stephenson, Green 1,342
Mildred Eilorat, UKIP 395
Alfred Bovill, Ind. 107
Eddie Adams, Green Soc. 101
C. maj. 12,418 (39.63%)
0.46% swing LD to C.
(2001: C. maj. 8,771 (31.28%))

KETTERING
E. 81,887 T. 55,646 (67.95%) C. gain
*Philip Hollobone, C. 25,401
Phil Sawford, Lab. 22,100
Roger Aron, LD 6,882
Rosemarie Clark, UKIP 1,263
C. maj. 3,301 (5.93%)
3.58% swing Lab. to C.
(2001: Lab. maj. 665 (1.24%))

KINGSTON & SURBITON
E. 72,671 T. 49,750 (68.46%) LD hold
Edward Davey, LD 25,397
Kevin Davis, C. 16,431
Nick Parrott, Lab. 6,553
Barry Thornton, UKIP 657
John Hayball, Soc. Lab. 366
David Henson, Veritas 200
Rainbow George Weiss, Vote Dream 146
LD maj. 8,966 (18.02%)
6.95% swing LD to C.
(2001: LD maj. 15,676 (31.93%))

KINGSWOOD
E. 84,400 T. 56,311 (66.72%) Lab. hold
Dr Roger Berry, Lab. 26,491
Owen Inskip, C. 18,618
Geoff Brewer, LD 9,089
John Knight, UKIP 1,444
David Burnside, Ind. 669
Lab. maj. 7,873 (13.98%)
6.26% swing Lab. to C.
(2001: Lab. maj. 13,962 (26.51%))

KNOWSLEY NORTH & SEFTON EAST
E. 70,403 T. 37,053 (52.63%) Lab. hold
George Howarth, Lab. 23,461
Flo Clucas, LD 7,192
Naman Purewal, C. 5,064
Michael McDermott, BNP 872
Stephen Whatham, Soc. Lab. 464
Lab. maj. 16,269 (43.91%)
4.52% swing Lab. to LD
(2001: Lab. maj. 18,927 (50.45%))

KNOWSLEY SOUTH
E. 70,726 T. 36,444 (51.53%) Lab. hold
Eddie O'Hara, Lab. 24,820
David Smithson, LD 7,132
Andrea Leadsom, C. 4,492
Lab. maj. 17,688 (48.53%)
4.86% swing Lab. to LD
(2001: Lab. maj. 21,316 (58.26%))

LANCASHIRE WEST
E. 74,777 T. 43,155 (57.71%) Lab. hold

*Rosie Cooper, Lab.	20,746
Alf Doran, C.	14,662
Richard Kemp, LD	6,059
Alan Freeman, UKIP	871
Stephen Garrett, Eng. Dem.	525
David Braid, Clause 28	292

Lab. maj. 6,084 (14.10%)
4.17% swing Lab. to C.
(2001: Lab. maj. 9,643 (22.44%))

LANCASTER & WYRE
E. 80,739 T. 52,061 (64.48%) C. gain

*Ben Wallace, C.	22,266
Anne Sacks, Lab.	18,095
Stuart Langhorn, LD	8,453
Jon Barry, Green	2,278
John Mander, UKIP	969

C. maj. 4,171 (8.01%)
4.47% swing Lab. to C.
(2001: Lab. maj. 481 (0.92%))

LEEDS CENTRAL
E. 62,939 T. 29,186 (46.37%) Lab. hold

Rt. Hon. Hilary Benn, Lab.	17,526
Ruth Coleman, LD	5,660
Brian Cattell, C.	3,865
Mark Collett, BNP	1,201
Peter Sewards, UKIP	494
Mick Dear, Ind.	189
Oluwole Taiwo, Ind.	126
Julian Fitzgerald, AFC	125

Lab. maj. 11,866 (40.66%)
6.53% swing Lab. to LD
(2001: Lab. maj. 14,381 (52.67%))

LEEDS EAST
E. 54,691 T. 30,077 (54.99%) Lab. hold

George Mudie, Lab.	17,799
Andrew Tear, LD	6,221
Dominic Ponniah, C.	5,557
Peter Socrates, Ind.	500

Lab. maj. 11,578 (38.49%)
5.48% swing Lab. to LD
(2001: Lab. maj. 12,643 (43.51%))

LEEDS NORTH EAST
E. 63,304 T. 41,467 (65.50%) Lab. hold

Fabian Hamilton, Lab.	18,632
Matthew Lobley, C.	13,370
Jonathan Brown, LD	8,427
Celia Foote, Green Soc.	1,038

Lab. maj. 5,262 (12.69%)
2.57% swing Lab. to C.
(2001: Lab. maj. 7,089 (17.82%))

LEEDS NORTH WEST
E. 71,644 T. 44,711 (62.41%) LD gain

*Greg Mulholland, LD	16,612
Judith Blake, Lab.	14,735
George Lee, C.	11,510
Martin Hemingway, Green	1,128
Adrian Knowles, Eng. Dem.	545
Jeannie Sutton, Green Soc.	181

LD maj. 1,877 (4.20%)
9.59% swing Lab. to LD
(2001: Lab. maj. 5,236 (12.33%))

LEEDS WEST
E. 62,882 T. 33,718 (53.62%) Lab. hold

Rt. Hon. John Battle, Lab.	18,704
Darren Finlay, LD	5,894
Tim Metcalfe, C.	4,807
David Blackburn, Green	2,519
Julie Day, BNP	1,166
David Sewards, UKIP	628

Lab. maj. 12,810 (37.99%)
6.85% swing Lab. to LD
(2001: Lab. maj. 14,935 (46.54%))

LEICESTER EAST
E. 66,383 T. 41,306 (62.22%) Lab. hold

Keith Vaz, Lab.	24,015
Suella Fernandes, C.	8,139
Susan Cooper, LD	7,052
Colin Brown, Veritas	1,666
Valerie Smalley, Soc. Lab.	434

Lab. maj. 15,876 (38.44%)
2.69% swing C. to Lab.
(2001: Lab. maj. 13,442 (33.06%))

LEICESTER SOUTH
E. 72,310 T. 42,411 (58.65%) Lab. gain

*Sir Peter Soulsby, Lab.	16,688
Parmjit Singh Gill, LD	12,971
Martin McElwee, C.	7,549
Yvonne Ridley, Respect	2,720
Matthew Follett, Green	1,379
Ken Roseblade, Veritas	573
Dave Roberts, Soc. Lab.	315
Paul Lord, Ind.	216

Lab. maj. 3,717 (8.76%)
14.26% swing Lab. to LD
(2004 July by-election: LD maj.1,654 (5.62%))
(2001: Lab. maj. 13,243 (31.43%))

LEICESTER WEST
E. 62,389 T. 33,224 (53.25%) Lab. hold

Rt. Hon. Patricia Hewitt, Lab.	17,184
Sarah Richardson, C.	8,114
Zuffar Haq, LD	5,803
Geoff Forse, Green	1,571
Steve Score, Soc. Alt.	552

Lab. maj. 9,070 (27.30%)
0.86% swing Lab. to C.
(2001: Lab. maj. 9,639 (29.02%))

LEICESTERSHIRE NORTH WEST
E. 70,519 T. 47,140 (66.85%) Lab. (Co-op) hold

David Taylor, Lab. (Co-op)	21,449
Nicola Le Page, C.	16,972
Rod Keyes, LD	5,682
John Blunt, UKIP	1,563
Clive Potter, BNP	1,474

Lab. (Co-op) maj. 4,477 (9.50%)
4.31% swing Lab. (Co-op) to C.
(2001: Lab. (Co-op) maj. 8,157 (18.12%))

LEIGH
E. 72,473 T. 36,488 (50.35%) Lab. hold

Andy Burnham, Lab.	23,097
Laurance Wedderburn, C.	5,825
Dave Crowther, LD	4,962
Ian Franzen, CAP	2,189
Thomas Hampson, LCA	415

Lab. maj. 17,272 (47.34%)
0.49% swing C. to Lab.
(2001: Lab. maj. 16,362 (46.35%))

LEOMINSTER
E. 70,587 T. 48,793 (69.12%) C. hold

Bill Wiggin, C.	25,407
Caroline Williams, LD	12,220
Paul Bell, Lab.	7,424
Felicity Norman, Green	2,191
Peter Venables, UKIP	1,551

C. maj. 13,187 (27.03%)
2.42% swing LD to C.
(2001: C. maj. 10,367 (22.19%))

LEWES
E. 67,073 T. 46,552 (69.40%) LD hold

Norman Baker, LD	24,376
Rory Love, C.	15,902
Richard Black, Lab.	4,169
Susan Murray, Green	1,071
John Petley, UKIP	1,034

LD maj. 8,474 (18.20%)
1.58% swing LD to C.
(2001: LD maj. 9,710 (21.37%))

LEWISHAM DEPTFORD
E. 59,018 T. 30,393 (51.50%) Lab. hold

Joan Ruddock, Lab.	16,902
Columba Blango, LD	5,091
James Cartlidge, C.	3,773
Darren Johnson, Green	3,367
Ian Page, Soc. Alt.	742
Dr David Holland, UKIP	518

Lab. maj. 11,811 (38.86%)
7.21% swing Lab. to LD
(2001: Lab. maj. 15,293 (52.54%))

LEWISHAM EAST
E. 59,135 T. 31,127 (52.64%) Lab. hold

Bridget Prentice, Lab.	14,263
James Cleverly, C.	7,512
Richard Thomas, LD	6,787
Anna Baker, Green	1,243
Arnold Tarling, UKIP	697
Bernard Franklin, NF	625

Lab. maj. 6,751 (21.69%)
4.12% swing Lab. to C.
(2001: Lab. maj. 8,959 (29.82%))

LEWISHAM WEST
E. 58,349 T. 31,923 (54.71%) Lab. hold

Jim Dowd, Lab.	16,611
Alex Feakes, LD	6,679
Evett McAnuff, C.	6,396
Nick Long, Green	1,464
Jens Winton, UKIP	773

Lab. maj. 9,932 (31.11%)
8.25% swing Lab. to LD
(2001: Lab. maj. 11,920 (38.68%))

LEYTON & WANSTEAD
E. 60,444 T. 33,272 (55.05%) Lab. hold

Harry Cohen, Lab.	15,234
Meher Khan, LD	8,377
Julien Foster, C.	7,393
Ashley Gunstock, Green	1,522
Nick Jones, UKIP	591
Marc Robertson, Ind.	155

Lab. maj. 6,857 (20.61%)
10.71% swing Lab. to LD
(2001: Lab. maj. 12,904 (38.27%))

LICHFIELD
E. 65,565 T. 43,744 (66.72%) C. hold

Michael Fabricant, C.	21,274
Nigel Gardner, Lab.	14,194
Ian Jackson, LD	6,804
Malcolm McKenzie, UKIP	1,472

C. maj. 7,080 (16.19%)
2.78% swing Lab. to C.
(2001: C. maj. 4,426 (10.62%))

LINCOLN
E. 65,203 T. 36,857 (56.53%) Lab. hold
Gillian Merron, Lab. 16,724
Karl McCartney, C. 12,110
Lisa Gabriel, LD 6,715
Nicholas Smith, UKIP 1,308
Lab. maj. 4,614 (12.52%)
5.08% swing Lab. to C.
(2001: Lab. maj. 8,420 (22.68%))

LIVERPOOL GARSTON
E. 63,669 T. 34,974 (54.93%) Lab. hold
Maria Eagle, Lab. 18,900
Paula Keaveney, LD 11,707
Amber Rudd, C. 3,424
Kevin Kearney, UKIP 780
David Oatley, WRP 163
Lab. maj. 7,193 (20.57%)
8.85% swing Lab. to LD
(2001: Lab. maj. 12,494 (38.27%))

LIVERPOOL RIVERSIDE
E. 75,171 T. 31,191 (41.49%)
Lab. (Co-op) hold
Louise Ellman, Lab. (Co-op) 17,951
Richard Marbrow, LD 7,737
Gabrielle Howatson, C. 2,843
Peter Cranie, Green 1,707
Beth Marshall, Soc. Lab. 498
Ann Irving, UKIP 455
Lab. (Co-op) maj. 10,214 (32.75%)
10.98% swing Lab. (Co-op) to LD
(2001: Lab. (Co-op) maj. 13,950 (54.70%))

LIVERPOOL WALTON
E. 62,044 T. 27,930 (45.02%) Lab. hold
Peter Kilfoyle, Lab. 20,322
Kiron Reid, LD 4,365
Sharon Buckle, C. 1,655
Joseph Moran, UKIP 1,108
Daniel Wood, Lib. 480
Lab. maj. 15,957 (57.13%)
3.05% swing Lab. to LD
(2001: Lab. maj. 17,996 (63.24%))

LIVERPOOL WAVERTREE
E. 69,189 T. 35,171 (50.83%) Lab. hold
Rt. Hon. Jane Kennedy, Lab. 18,441
Colin Eldridge, LD 13,268
Jason Steen, C. 2,331
Mark Bill, UKIP 660
Gary Theys, Soc. Lab. 244
Paul Filby, Dem. Soc. All. 227
Lab. maj. 5,173 (14.71%)
11.81% swing Lab. to LD
(2001: Lab. maj. 12,319 (38.33%))

LIVERPOOL WEST DERBY
E. 64,591 T. 30,464 (47.16%) Lab. hold
Robert Wareing, Lab. 19,140
Patrick Maloney, LD 3,915
Steve Radford, Lib. 3,606
Peter Garrett, C. 2,567
Kai Andersen, Soc. Lab. 698
Peter Baden, UKIP 538
Lab. maj. 15,225 (49.98%)
2.66% swing Lab. to LD
(2001: Lab. maj. 15,853 (51.29%))

LOUGHBOROUGH
E. 72,351 T. 46,140 (63.77%)
Lab. (Co-op) hold
Andy Reed, Lab. (Co-op) 19,098
Nicky Morgan, C. 17,102
Graeme Smith, LD 8,258
Bernard Sherratt, UKIP 1,094
John McVay, Veritas 588
Lab. (Co-op) maj. 1,996 (4.33%)
5.04% swing Lab. (Co-op) to C.
(2001: Lab. (Co-op) maj. 6,378 (14.41%))

LOUTH & HORNCASTLE
E. 75,313 T. 46,683 (61.99%) C. hold
Sir Peter Tapsell, C. 21,744
Frank Hodgkiss, Lab. 11,848
Fiona Martin, LD 9,480
Christopher Pain, UKIP 3,611
C. maj. 9,896 (21.20%)
2.10% swing Lab. to C.
(2001: C. maj. 7,554 (16.99%))

LUDLOW
E. 64,572 T. 46,540 (72.07%) C. gain
*Philip Dunne, C. 20,979
Matthew Green, LD 18,952
Nigel Knowles, Lab. 4,974
Jim Gaffney, Green 852
Michael Zuckerman, UKIP 783
C. maj. 2,027 (4.36%)
4.07% swing LD to C.
(2001: LD maj. 1,630 (3.78%))

LUTON NORTH
E. 68,175 T. 39,122 (57.38%) Lab. hold
Kelvin Hopkins, Lab. 19,062
Hannah Hall, C. 12,575
Linda Jack, LD 6,081
Colin Brown, UKIP 1,255
Kayson Gurney, Forum 149
Lab. maj. 6,487 (16.58%)
4.46% swing Lab. to C.
(2001: Lab. maj. 9,977 (25.50%))

LUTON SOUTH
E. 71,949 T. 38,918 (54.09%) Lab. hold
Margaret Moran, Lab. 16,610
Richard Stay, C. 10,960
Qurban Hussain, LD 8,778
Charles Lawman, UKIP 957
Marc Scheimann, Green 790
Mohammed Ilyas, Respect 725
Arthur Lynn, WRP 98
Lab. maj. 5,650 (14.52%)
5.62% swing Lab. to C.
(2001: Lab. maj. 10,133 (25.75%))

MACCLESFIELD
E. 72,267 T. 45,621 (63.13%) C. hold
Sir Nicholas Winterton, C. 22,628
Stephen Carter, Lab. 13,227
Catherine O'Brien, LD 8,918
John Scott, Veritas 848
C. maj. 9,401 (20.61%)
2.41% swing Lab. to C.
(2001: C. maj. 7,200 (15.79%))

MAIDENHEAD
E. 63,978 T. 45,850 (71.67%) C. hold
Rt. Hon. Theresa May, C. 23,312
Kathryn Newbound, LD 17,081
Janet Pritchard, Lab. 4,144
Tim Rait, BNP 704
Douglas Lewis, UKIP 609
C. maj. 6,231 (13.59%)
3.00% swing LD to C.
(2001: C. maj. 3,284 (7.58%))

MAIDSTONE & THE WEALD
E. 74,054 T. 48,755 (65.84%) C. hold
Rt. Hon. Ann Widdecombe, C. 25,670
Beth Breeze, Lab. 10,814
Mark Corney, LD 10,808
Anthony Robertson, UKIP 1,463
C. maj. 14,856 (30.47%)
3.92% swing Lab. to C.
(2001: C. maj. 10,318 (22.64%))

MAKERFIELD
E. 69,039 T. 35,580 (51.54%) Lab. hold
Rt. Hon. Ian McCartney, Lab. 22,494
Kulveer Ranger, C. 4,345
Trevor Beswick, LD 3,789
Peter Franzen, CAP 2,769
Dennis Shambley, BNP 1,221
Gregory Atherton, UKIP 962
Lab. maj. 18,149 (51.01%)
0.04% swing C. to Lab.
(2001: Lab. maj. 17,750 (50.92%))

MALDON & CHELMSFORD EAST
E. 69,502 T. 46,091 (66.32%) C. hold
John Whittingdale, C. 23,732
Sue Tibballs, Lab. 11,159
Matthew Lambert, LD 9,270
Jesse Pryke, UKIP 1,930
C. maj. 12,573 (27.28%)
4.05% swing Lab. to C.
(2001: C. maj. 8,462 (19.19%))

MANCHESTER BLACKLEY
E. 60,229 T. 27,591 (45.81%) Lab. hold
Graham Stringer, Lab. 17,187
Iain Donaldson, LD 5,160
Amar Ahmed, C. 3,690
Roger Bullock, UKIP 1,554
Lab. maj. 12,027 (43.59%)
6.99% swing Lab. to LD
(2001: Lab. maj. 14,464 (54.53%))

MANCHESTER CENTRAL
E. 69,656 T. 29,264 (42.01%) Lab. hold
Tony Lloyd, Lab. 16,993
Marc Ramsbottom, LD 7,217
Tom Jackson, C. 2,504
Steven Durrant, Green 1,292
Richard Kemp, NF 421
Damien O'Connor, Ind. Pr. Lab. 382
Dr John Whittaker, UKIP 272
Ronald Sinclair, Soc. Lab. 183
Lab. maj. 9,776 (33.41%)
9.80% swing Lab. to LD
(2001: Lab. maj. 13,742 (53.00%))

MANCHESTER GORTON
E. 64,696 T. 29,123 (45.02%) Lab. hold
Rt. Hon. Sir Gerald Kaufman, Lab. 15,480
Qassim Afzal, LD 9,672
Amanda Byrne, C. 2,848
Gregory Beaman, UKIP 783
Dan Waller, WRP 181
Matthew Kay, RP 159
Lab. maj. 5,808 (19.94%)
10.79% swing Lab. to LD
(2001: Lab. maj. 11,304 (41.51%))

MANCHESTER WITHINGTON
E. 67,781 T. 37,458 (55.26%) LD gain
*John Leech, LD 15,872
Rt. Hon. Keith Bradley, Lab. 15,205
Karen Bradley, C. 3,919
Brian Candeland, Green 1,595
Dr Robert Gutfreund-Walmsley, UKIP 424
Ivan Benett, Ind. 243
Yasmin Zalzala, Ind. 153
Richard Reed, TP 47
LD maj. 667 (1.78%)
17.33% swing Lab. to LD
(2001: Lab. maj. 11,524 (32.88%))

MANSFIELD
E. 69,131 T. 38,276 (55.37%) Lab. hold
Alan Meale, Lab. 18,400
Anne Wright, C. 7,035
Stewart Rickersey, Ind. 6,491
Roger Shelley, LD 5,316
Michael Harvey, Veritas 1,034
Lab. maj. 11,365 (29.69%)
0.13% swing Lab. to C.
(2001: Lab. maj. 11,038 (29.95%))

MEDWAY
E. 67,251 T. 41,093 (61.10%) Lab. hold
Bob Marshall-Andrews, Lab. 17,333
Mark Reckless, C. 17,120
Geoffrey Juby, LD 5,152
Robert Oakley, UKIP 1,488
Lab. maj. 213 (0.52%)
4.64% swing Lab. to C.
(2001: Lab. maj. 3,780 (9.79%))

MERIDEN
E. 77,342 T. 46,503 (60.13%) C. hold
Caroline Spelman, C. 22,416
Jim Brown, Lab. 15,407
William Laitinen, LD 7,113
Denis Brookes, UKIP 1,567
C. maj. 7,009 (15.07%)
3.29% swing Lab. to C.
(2001: C. maj. 3,784 (8.49%))

MIDDLESBROUGH
E. 65,924 T. 32,140 (48.75%) Lab. hold
Sir Stuart Bell, Lab. 18,562
Joe Michna, LD 5,995
Caroline Flynn-Macleod, C. 5,263
Ron Armes, BNP 819
Michael Landers, UKIP 768
Jackie Elder, Ind. 503
Derrick Arnott, Ind. 230
Lab. maj. 12,567 (39.10%)
9.03% swing Lab. to LD
(2001: Lab. maj. 16,330 (48.43%))

MIDDLESBROUGH SOUTH & CLEVELAND EAST
E. 71,883 T. 43,696 (60.79%) Lab. hold
Dr Ashok Kumar, Lab. 21,945
Mark Brooks, C. 13,945
Carl Minns, LD 6,049
Geoffrey Groves, BNP 1,099
Charlotte Bull, UKIP 658
Lab. maj. 8,000 (18.31%)
1.47% swing Lab. to C.
(2001: Lab. maj. 9,351 (21.26%))

MILTON KEYNES NORTH EAST
E. 78,758 T. 50,104 (63.62%) C. gain
*Mark Lancaster, C. 19,674
Brian White, Lab. 18,009
Jane Carr, LD 9,789
Michael Phillips, UKIP 1,400
Peter Richardson, Green 1,090
Anant Vyas, Ind. 142
C. maj. 1,665 (3.32%)
3.60% swing Lab. to C.
(2001: Lab. maj. 1,829 (3.88%))

MILTON KEYNES SOUTH WEST
E. 82,228 T. 48,709 (59.24%) Lab. hold
Dr Phyllis Starkey, Lab. 20,862
Iain Stewart, C. 16,852
Neil Stuart, LD 7,909
George Harlock, UKIP 1,750
Alan Francis, Green 1,336
Lab. maj. 4,010 (8.23%)
3.57% swing Lab. to C.
(2001: Lab. maj. 6,978 (15.38%))

MITCHAM & MORDEN
E. 65,172 T. 39,868 (61.17%) Lab. hold
Siobhain McDonagh, Lab. 22,489
Andrew Shellhorn, C. 9,929
Jo Christie-Smith, LD 5,583
Tom Walsh, Green 1,395
Adrian Roberts, Veritas 286
Rathy Alagaratnam, Ind. 186
Lab. maj. 12,560 (31.50%)
2.40% swing Lab. to C.
(2001: Lab. maj. 13,785 (36.31%))

MOLE VALLEY
E. 68,181 T. 49,415 (72.48%) C. hold
Sir Paul Beresford, C. 27,060
Nasser Butt, LD 15,063
Farmida Bi, Lab. 5,310
David Payne, UKIP 1,475
Roger Meekins, Veritas 507
C. maj. 11,997 (24.28%)
1.35% swing LD to C.
(2001: C. maj. 10,153 (21.57%))

MORECAMBE & LUNESDALE
E. 67,775 T. 41,635 (61.43%) Lab. hold
Geraldine Smith, Lab. 20,331
James Airey, C. 15,563
Alex Stone, LD 5,741
Lab. maj. 4,768 (11.45%)
0.39% swing Lab. to C.
(2001: Lab. maj. 5,092 (12.22%))

MORLEY & ROTHWELL
E. 72,248 T. 42,495 (58.82%) Lab. hold
Colin Challen, Lab. 20,570
Nick Vineall, C. 8,227
Stewart Golton, LD 6,819
Robert Finnigan, Ind. 4,608
Chris Beverley, BNP 2,271
Lab. maj. 12,343 (29.05%)
1.20% swing Lab. to C.
(2001: Lab. maj. 12,090 (31.45%))

NEW FOREST EAST
E. 68,633 T. 45,235 (65.91%) C. hold
Dr Julian Lewis, C. 21,975
Brian Dash, LD 15,424
Stephen Roberts, Lab. 5,492
Katy Davies, UKIP 2,344
C. maj. 6,551 (14.48%)
2.70% swing LD to C.
(2001: C. maj. 3,829 (9.08%))

NEW FOREST WEST
E. 69,232 T. 46,067 (66.54%) C. hold
Desmond Swayne, C. 26,004
Murari Kaushik, LD 8,719
Janice Hurne, Lab. 7,590
Brian Lawrence, UKIP 1,917
Janet Richards, Green 1,837
C. maj. 17,285 (37.52%)
3.80% swing LD to C.
(2001: C. maj. 13,191 (29.92%))

NEWARK
E. 72,249 T. 45,696 (63.25%) C. hold
Patrick Mercer, C. 21,946
Jason Reece, Lab. 15,482
Stuart Thompstone, LD 7,276
Charlotte Creasy, UKIP 992
C. maj. 6,464 (14.15%)
2.56% swing Lab. to C.
(2001: C. maj. 4,073 (9.02%))

NEWBURY
E. 75,903 T. 54,673 (72.03%) C. gain
*Richard Benyon, C. 26,771
David Rendel, LD 23,311
Oscar Van Nooijen, Lab. 3,239
David McMahon, UKIP 857
Nicholas Cornish, Ind. 409
Barrie Singleton, Ind. 86
C. maj. 3,460 (6.33%)
5.54% swing LD to C.
(2001: LD maj. 2,415 (4.75%))

NEWCASTLE-UNDER-LYME
E. 68,414 T. 39,788 (58.16%) Lab. hold
Paul Farrelly, Lab. 18,053
Jeremy Lefroy, C. 9,945
Trevor Johnson, LD 7,528
David Nixon, UKIP 1,436
John Dawson, BNP 1,390
Prof. Andrew Dobson, Green 918
Marian Harvey-Lover, Veritas 518
Lab. maj. 8,108 (20.38%)
2.72% swing Lab. to C.
(2001: Lab. maj. 9,986 (25.82%))

NEWCASTLE UPON TYNE CENTRAL
E. 62,734 T. 35,920 (57.26%) Lab. hold
Jim Cousins, Lab. 16,211
Greg Stone, LD 12,229
Wendy Morton, C. 5,749
Joe Hulm, Green 1,254
Clive Harding, NACVP 477
Lab. maj. 3,982 (11.09%)
11.10% swing Lab. to LD
(2001: Lab. maj. 11,605 (33.28%))

NEWCASTLE UPON TYNE EAST & WALLSEND
E. 56,900 T. 31,678 (55.67%) Lab. hold
Rt. Hon. Nick Brown, Lab. 17,462
David Ord, LD 9,897
Norma Dias, C. 3,532
William Hopwood, Soc. Alt. 582
Martin Levy, Comm. Brit. 205
Lab. maj. 7,565 (23.88%)
9.81% swing Lab. to LD
(2001: Lab. maj. 14,223 (43.50%))

NEWCASTLE UPON TYNE NORTH
E. 64,599 T. 38,444 (59.51%) Lab. hold
Doug Henderson, Lab. 19,224
Ron Beadle, LD 12,201
Neil Hudson, C. 6,022
Roland Wood, NF 997
Lab. maj. 7,023 (18.27%)
11.22% swing Lab. to LD
(2001: Lab. maj. 14,450 (39.73%))

NORFOLK MID
E. 81,738 T. 54,734 (66.96%) C. hold
Keith Simpson, C. 23,564
Daniel Zeichner, Lab. 16,004
Vivienne Clifford-Jackson, LD 12,988
Simon Fletcher, UKIP 2,178
C. maj. 7,560 (13.81%)
2.57% swing Lab. to C.
(2001: C. maj. 4,562 (8.68%))

NORFOLK NORTH
E. 80,784 T. 58,965 (72.99%) LD hold
Norman Lamb, LD 31,515
Iain Dale, C. 20,909
Philip Harris, Lab. 5,447
Stuart Agnew, UKIP 978
Justin Appleyard, Ind. 116
LD maj. 10,606 (17.99%)
8.56% swing C. to LD
(2001: LD maj. 483 (0.86%))

NORFOLK NORTH WEST
E. 82,171 T. 50,649 (61.64%) C. hold
Henry Bellingham, C. 25,471
Damien Welfare, Lab. 16,291
Simon Higginson, LD 7,026
Michael Stone, UKIP 1,861
C. maj. 9,180 (18.12%)
5.66% swing Lab. to C.
(2001: C. maj. 3,485 (6.81%))

NORFOLK SOUTH
E. 85,896 T. 58,974 (68.66%) C. hold
Richard Bacon, C. 26,399
Dr Ian Mack, LD 17,617
John Morgan, Lab. 13,262
Philip Tye, UKIP 1,696
C. maj. 8,782 (14.89%)
1.28% swing LD to C.
(2001: C. maj. 6,893 (12.32%))

NORFOLK SOUTH WEST
E. 88,260 T. 55,127 (62.46%) C. hold
†Christopher Fraser, C. 25,881
Charmaine Morgan, Lab. 15,795
April Pond, LD 10,207
Delia Hall, UKIP 2,738
Kim Hayes, Ind. 506
C. maj. 10,086 (18.30%)
0.30% swing Lab. to C.
(2001: C. maj. 9,366 (17.69%))

NORMANTON
E. 65,129 T. 37,424 (57.46%) Lab. (Co-op) hold
*Ed Balls, Lab. (Co-op) 19,161
Andrew Percy, C. 9,159
Simone Butterworth, LD 6,357
John Aveyard, BNP 1,967
Mark Harrop, Ind. 780
Lab. (Co-op) maj. 10,002 (26.73%)
1.18% swing Lab. (Co-op) to C.
(2001: Lab. (Co-op) maj. 9,937 (29.09%))

NORTHAMPTON NORTH
E. 73,926 T. 42,048 (56.88%) Lab. hold
Sally Keeble, Lab. 16,905
Damian Collins, C. 12,945
Andrew Simpson, LD 10,317
John Howsam, UKIP 1,050
Paul Withrington, SOS 495
Andrew Otchie, CPA 336
Lab. maj. 3,960 (9.42%)
4.80% swing Lab. to C.
(2001: Lab. maj. 7,893 (19.02%))

NORTHAMPTON SOUTH
E. 89,722 T. 54,481 (60.72%) C. gain
*Brian Binley, C. 23,818
Tony Clarke, Lab. 19,399
Kevin Barron, LD 8,327
Derek Clark, UKIP 1,032
Anthony Green, Veritas 508
John Harrisson, SOS 437
John Percival, Loony 354
Fitzy Fitzpatrick, Ind. 346
Tim Webb, CPA 260
C. maj. 4,419 (8.11%)
4.92% swing Lab. to C.
(2001: Lab. maj. 885 (1.73%))

NORTHAVON
E. 81,800 T. 59,056 (72.20%) LD hold
Prof. Steve Webb, LD 30,872
Chris Butt, C. 19,839
Patricia Gardener, Lab. 6,277
Adrian Blake, UKIP 1,032
Alan Pinder, Green 922
Thomas Beacham, Ind. 114
LD maj. 11,033 (18.68%)
0.48% swing C. to LD
(2001: LD maj. 9,877 (17.71%))

NORWICH NORTH
E. 76,992 T. 47,033 (61.09%) Lab. hold
Dr Ian Gibson, Lab. 21,097
James Tumbridge, C. 15,638
Robin Whitmore, LD 7,616
Adrian Holmes, Green 1,252
John Youles, UKIP 1,122
Bill Holden, Ind. 308
Lab. maj. 5,459 (11.61%)
0.62% swing Lab. to C.
(2001: Lab. maj. 5,863 (12.85%))

NORWICH SOUTH
E. 70,409 T. 42,190 (59.92%) Lab. hold
Rt. Hon. Charles Clarke, Lab. 15,904
Andrew Aalders-Dunthorne, LD 12,251
Antony Little, C. 9,567
Adrian Ramsay, Green 3,101
Vandra Ahlstrom, UKIP 597
Christine Constable, Eng. Dem. 466
Don Barnard, LCA 219
Roger Blackwell, WRP 85
Lab. maj. 3,653 (8.66%)
7.09% swing Lab. to LD
(2001: Lab. maj. 8,816 (20.70%))

NOTTINGHAM EAST
E. 60,634 T. 30,091 (49.63%) Lab. hold
John Heppell, Lab. 13,787
Issan Ghazni, LD 6,848
Jim Thornton, C. 6,826
Ashley Baxter, Green 1,517
Anthony Ellwood, UKIP 740
Pete Ratcliff, Soc. Unity 373
Lab. maj. 6,939 (23.06%)
11.44% swing Lab. to LD
(2001: Lab. maj. 10,320 (34.71%))

NOTTINGHAM NORTH
E. 61,894 T. 30,383 (49.09%) Lab. hold
Graham Allen, Lab. 17,842
Priti Patel, C. 5,671
Tim Ball, LD 5,190
Irena Marriott, UKIP 1,680
Lab. maj. 12,171 (40.06%)
0.34% swing Lab. to C.
(2001: Lab. maj. 12,240 (40.74%))

NOTTINGHAM SOUTH
E. 68,921 T. 34,840 (50.55%) Lab. hold
Alan Simpson, Lab. 16,506
Sudesh Mattu, C. 9,020
Tony Sutton, LD 7,961
Ken Browne, UKIP 1,353
Lab. maj. 7,486 (21.49%)
2.90% swing Lab. to C.
(2001: Lab. maj. 9,989 (27.29%))

NUNEATON
E. 73,440 T. 45,280 (61.66%) Lab. hold
Bill Olner, Lab. 19,945
Mark Pawsey, C. 17,665
Ali Asghar, LD 5,884
Keith Tyson, UKIP 1,786
Lab. maj. 2,280 (5.04%)
6.18% swing Lab. to C.
(2001: Lab. maj. 7,535 (17.40%))

OLD BEXLEY & SIDCUP
E. 68,227 T. 44,572 (65.33%) C. hold
Derek Conway, C. 22,191
Gavin Moore, Lab. 12,271
Nickolas O'Hare, LD 6,564
Michael Barnbrook, UKIP 2,015
Claire Sayers, BNP 1,227
Gregory Peters, Ind. 304
C. maj. 9,920 (22.26%)
7.16% swing Lab. to C.
(2001: C. maj. 3,345 (7.94%))

OLDHAM EAST & SADDLEWORTH
E. 75,680 T. 43,367 (57.30%) Lab. hold
Phil Woolas, Lab. 17,968
Tony Dawson, LD 14,378
Keith Chapman, C. 7,901
Michael Treacy, BNP 2,109
Valerie Nield, UKIP 873
Philip O'Grady, Ind. 138
Lab. maj. 3,590 (8.28%)
1.14% swing LD to Lab.
(2001: Lab. maj. 2,726 (6.00%))

OLDHAM WEST & ROYTON
E. 70,496 T. 37,562 (53.28%) Lab. hold
Rt. Hon. Michael Meacher, Lab. 18,452
Sean Moore, C. 7,998
Stuart Bodsworth, LD 7,519
Anita Corbett, BNP 2,606
David Short, UKIP 987
Lab. maj. 10,454 (27.83%)
2.81% swing Lab. to C.
(2001: Lab. maj. 13,365 (33.44%))

ORPINGTON
E. 78,276 T. 54,734 (69.92%) C. hold
John Horam, C. 26,718
Chris Maines, LD 21,771
Emily Bird, Lab. 4,914
Mick Greenhough, UKIP 1,331
C. maj. 4,947 (9.04%)
4.25% swing LD to C.
(2001: C. maj. 269 (0.53%))

OXFORD EAST
E. 72,234 T. 41,790 (57.85%) Lab. hold
Rt. Hon. Andrew Smith, Lab. 15,405
Steve Goddard, LD 14,442
Virginia Morris, C. 6,992
Jacob Sanders, Green 1,813
Honest Blair, Ind. 1,485
Maurice Leen, IWCA 892
Peter Gardner, UKIP 715
Pat Mylvaganam, Ind. 46
Lab. maj. 963 (2.30%)
11.83% swing Lab. to LD
(2001: Lab. maj. 10,344 (25.96%))

OXFORD WEST & ABINGDON
E. 80,195 T. 52,600 (65.59%) LD hold
Dr Evan Harris, LD 24,336
Amanda McLean, C. 16,653
Antonia Bance, Lab. 8,725
Tom Lines, Green 2,091
Marcus Watney, UKIP 795
LD maj. 7,683 (14.61%)
1.60% swing LD to C.
(2001: LD maj. 9,185 (17.81%))

PENDLE
E. 64,917 T. 41,132 (63.36%) Lab. hold
Gordon Prentice, Lab. 15,250
Jane Ellison, C. 13,070
Shazad Anwar, LD 9,528
Thomas Boocock, BNP 2,547
Graham Cannon, UKIP 737
Lab. maj. 2,180 (5.30%)
2.73% swing Lab. to C.
(2001: Lab. maj. 4,275 (10.76%))

PENRITH & THE BORDER
E. 70,922 T. 46,882 (66.10%) C. hold
Rt. Hon. David Maclean, C. 24,046
Geyve Walker, LD 12,142
Michael Boaden, Lab. 8,958
William Robinson, UKIP 1,187
Mark Gibson, LCA 549
C. maj. 11,904 (25.39%)
3.89% swing C. to LD
(2001: C. maj. 14,677 (33.17%))

PETERBOROUGH
E. 67,499 T. 41,204 (61.04%) C. gain
*Stewart Jackson, C. 17,364
Rt. Hon. Helen Clark, Lab. 14,624
Nick Sandford, LD 6,876
Mary Herdman, UKIP 1,242
Terry Blackham, NF 931
Marc Potter, MNP 167
C. maj. 2,740 (6.65%)
6.91% swing Lab. to C.
(2001: Lab. maj. 2,854 (7.17%))

PLYMOUTH DEVONPORT
E. 72,848 T. 42,013 (57.67%) Lab. hold
*Alison Seabeck, Lab. 18,612
Richard Cuming, C. 10,509
Judith Jolly, LD 8,000
Bill Wakeham, UKIP 3,324
Keith Greene, Ind. 747
Robert Hawkins, Soc. Lab. 445
Tony Staunton, Respect 376
Lab. maj. 8,103 (19.29%)
5.98% swing Lab. to C.
(2001: Lab. maj. 13,033 (31.24%))

PLYMOUTH SUTTON
E. 67,202 T. 38,192 (56.83%)
Lab. (Co-op) hold
Linda Gilroy, Lab. (Co-op) 15,497
Oliver Colvile, C. 11,388
Karen Gillard, LD 8,685
Robert Cumming, UKIP 2,392
Rob Hawkins, Soc. Lab. 230
Lab. (Co-op) maj. 4,109 (10.76%)
4.24% swing Lab. (Co-op) to C.
(2001: Lab. (Co-op) maj. 7,517 (19.24%))

PONTEFRACT & CASTLEFORD
E. 61,871 T. 32,947 (53.25%) Lab. hold
Yvette Cooper, Lab. 20,973
Simon Jones, C. 5,727
Wesley Paxton, LD 3,942
Suzy Cass, BNP 1,835
Bob Hague, Green Soc. 470
Lab. maj. 15,246 (46.27%)
2.95% swing Lab. to C.
(2001: Lab. maj. 16,378 (52.17%))

POOLE
E. 64,178 T. 40,513 (63.13%) C. hold
Robert Syms, C. 17,571
Mike Plummer, LD 11,583
Darren Brown, Lab. 9,376
John Barnes, UKIP 1,436
Peter Pirnie, BNP 547
C. maj. 5,988 (14.78%)
2.42% swing C. to LD
(2001: C. maj. 7,166 (18.27%))

POPLAR & CANNING TOWN
E. 81,544 T. 39,010 (47.84%) Lab. hold
Jim Fitzpatrick, Lab. 15,628
Tim Archer, C. 8,499
Oliur Rahman, Respect 6,573
Janet Ludlow, LD 5,420
Terry McGrenera, Green 955
Aminul Hoque, Ind. 815
Tony Smith, Veritas 650
Simeon Ademolake, CPA 470
Lab. maj. 7,129 (18.27%)
11.55% swing Lab. to C.
(2001: Lab. maj. 14,104 (41.35%))

PORTSMOUTH NORTH
E. 62,884 T. 37,717 (59.98%)
Lab. (Co-op) hold
*Sarah McCarthy-Fry, Lab. (Co-op) 15,412
Penny Mordaunt, C. 14,273
Gary Lawson, LD 6,684
Mike Smith, UKIP 1,348
Lab. (Co-op) maj. 1,139 (3.02%)
5.45% swing Lab. (Co-op) to C.
(2001: Lab. (Co-op) maj. 5,134 (13.93%))

PORTSMOUTH SOUTH
E. 70,969 T. 40,374 (56.89%) LD hold
Mike Hancock, LD 17,047
Caroline Dinenage, C. 13,685
Mark Button, Lab. 8,714
Dennis Pierson, UKIP 928
LD maj. 3,362 (8.33%)
3.60% swing LD to C.
(2001: LD maj. 6,094 (15.54%))

PRESTON
E. 63,351 T. 34,081 (53.80%)
Lab. (Co-op) hold
Mark Hendrick, Lab. (Co-op) 17,210
Fiona Bryce, C. 7,803
William Parkinson, LD 5,701
Michael Lavalette, Respect 2,318
Ellen Boardman, UKIP 1,049
Lab. (Co-op) maj. 9,407 (27.60%)
3.22% swing Lab. (Co-op) to C.
(2001: Lab. (Co-op) maj. 12,268 (34.04%))

PUDSEY
E. 70,411 T. 46,444 (65.96%) Lab. hold
Paul Truswell, Lab. 21,261
Pamela Singleton, C. 15,391
James Keeley, LD 8,551
David Daniel, UKIP 1,241
Lab. maj. 5,870 (12.64%)
0.09% swing C. to Lab.
(2001: Lab. maj. 5,626 (12.45%))

PUTNEY
E. 61,498 T. 36,574 (59.47%) C. gain
*Justine Greening, C. 15,497
Tony Colman, Lab. 13,731
Jeremy Ambache, LD 5,965
Keith Magnum, Green 993
Anthony Gahan, UKIP 388
C. maj. 1,766 (4.83%)
6.46% swing Lab. to C.
(2001: Lab. maj. 2,771 (8.09%))

RAYLEIGH
E. 71,996 T. 46,193 (64.16%) C. hold
Mark Francois, C. 25,609
Julian Ware-Lane, Lab. 10,883
Sid Cumberland, LD 7,406
Janet Davies, UKIP 2,295
C. maj. 14,726 (31.88%)
6.25% swing Lab. to C.
(2001: C. maj. 8,290 (19.38%))

READING EAST
E. 72,806 T. 43,912 (60.31%) C. gain
*Rob Wilson, C. 15,557
Tony Page, Lab. 15,082
Prof. John Howson, LD 10,619
Rob White, Green 1,548
David Lamb, UKIP 849
Jan Lloyd, Ind. 135
Rex Hora, Ind. 122
C. maj. 475 (1.08%)
6.95% swing Lab. to C.
(2001: Lab. maj. 5,588 (12.81%))

READING WEST
E. 69,011 T. 42,103 (61.01%) Lab. hold
Martin Salter, Lab. 18,940
Ewan Cameron, C. 14,258
Denise Gaines, LD 6,663
Peter Williams, UKIP 1,180
Adrian Windisch, Green 921
Dave Boyle, Veritas 141
Lab. maj. 4,682 (11.12%)
4.98% swing Lab. to C.
(2001: Lab. maj. 8,849 (21.08%))

REDCAR
E. 66,947 T. 38,861 (58.05%) Lab. hold
Vera Baird, Lab. 19,968
Ian Swales, LD 7,852
Jonathan Lehrle, C. 6,954
Christopher McGlade, Ind. 2,379
Andrew Harris, BNP 985
Edward Walker, UKIP 564
John Taylor, Soc. Lab. 159
Lab. maj. 12,116 (31.18%)
8.25% swing Lab. to LD
(2001: Lab. maj. 13,443 (35.19%))

REDDITCH
E. 64,121 T. 40,291 (62.84%) Lab. hold
Rt. Hon. Jacqui Smith, Lab. 18,012
Karen Lumley, C. 15,296
Nigel Hicks, LD 5,602
John Ison, UKIP 1,381
Lab. maj. 2,716 (6.74%)
0.02% swing C. to Lab.
(2001: Lab. maj. 2,484 (6.71%))

REGENT'S PARK & KENSINGTON NORTH
E. 78,975 T. 40,680 (51.51%) Lab. hold
Karen Buck, Lab. 18,196
Jeremy Bradshaw, C. 12,065
Rabi Martins, LD 7,569
Dr Paul Miller, Green 1,985
Pamela Perrin, UKIP 456
Rezouk Boufas, CP 227
Abby Dharamsey, Ind. 182
Lab. maj. 6,131 (15.07%)
6.32% swing Lab. to C.
(2001: Lab. maj. 10,266 (27.71%))

REIGATE
E. 65,719 T. 42,605 (64.83%) C. hold
Crispin Blunt, C. 20,884
Jane Kulka, LD 9,896
Sam Townend, Lab. 8,896
Jeremy Wraith, UKIP 1,921
Harold Green, EDP 600
Michael Selby, Ind. 408
C. maj. 10,988 (25.79%)
0.46% swing C. to LD
(2001: C. maj. 8,025 (20.33%))

RIBBLE SOUTH
E. 75,357 T. 47,511 (63.05%) Lab. hold
David Borrow, Lab. 20,428
Lorraine Fullbrook, C. 18,244
Mark Alcock, LD 7,634
Kenneth Jones, UKIP 1,205
Lab. maj. 2,184 (4.60%)
1.82% swing Lab. to C.
(2001: Lab. maj. 3,792 (8.22%))

RIBBLE VALLEY
E. 75,692 T. 49,766 (65.75%) C. hold
Nigel Evans, C. 25,834
Julie Young, LD 11,663
Jack Davenport, Lab. 10,924
Kevin Henry, UKIP 1,345
C. maj. 14,171 (28.48%)
2.81% swing LD to C.
(2001: C. maj. 11,238 (22.85%))

RICHMOND (YORKS)
E. 69,521 T. 45,200 (65.02%) C. hold
Rt. Hon. William Hague, C. 26,722
Neil Foster, Lab. 8,915
Jacquie Bell, LD 7,982
Leslie Rowe, Green 1,581
C. maj. 17,807 (39.40%)
1.17% swing Lab. to C.
(2001: C. maj. 16,319 (37.06%))

RICHMOND PARK
E. 70,555 T. 51,374 (72.81%) LD hold
*Susan Kramer, LD 24,011
Marco Forgione, C. 20,280
James Butler, Lab. 4,768
James Page, Green 1,379
Peter Dul, UKIP 458
Peter Flower, CPA 288
Margaret Harrison, Ind. 83
Rainbow George Weiss, Vote Dream 63
Richard Meacock, Ind. 44
LD maj. 3,731 (7.26%)
1.42% swing LD to C.
(2001: LD maj. 4,964 (10.10%))

ROCHDALE
E. 69,894 T. 40,836 (58.43%) LD gain
*Paul Rowen, LD 16,787
Lorna Fitzsimons, Lab. 16,345
Khalid Hussain, C. 4,270
Derek Adams, BNP 1,773
Dr John Whittaker, UKIP 499
Samir Chatterjee, Green 448
Mohammed Salim, IZB 361
Carl Faulkner, Veritas 353
LD maj. 442 (1.08%)
7.72% swing Lab. to LD
(2001: Lab. maj. 5,655 (14.35%))

ROCHFORD & SOUTHEND EAST
E. 71,186 T. 39,462 (55.44%) C. hold
*James Duddridge, C. 17,874
Fred Grindrod, Lab. 12,380
Graham Longley, LD 5,967
John Croft, UKIP 1,913
Andrew Vaughan, Green 1,328
C. maj. 5,494 (13.92%)
2.43% swing C. to Lab.
(2001: C. maj. 7,034 (18.78%))

ROMFORD
E. 58,571 T. 36,482 (62.29%) C. hold
Andrew Rosindell, C. 21,560
Margaret Mullane, Lab. 9,971
Geoffrey Seeff, LD 3,066
John McCaffrey, BNP 1,088
Terry Murray, UKIP 797
C. maj. 11,589 (31.77%)
7.51% swing Lab. to C.
(2001: C. maj. 5,977 (16.74%))

ROMSEY
E. 72,177 T. 50,311 (69.71%) LD hold
Sandra Gidley, LD 22,465
Caroline Nokes, C. 22,340
Matthew Stevens, Lab. 4,430
Michael Wigley, UKIP 1,076
LD maj. 125 (0.25%)
2.32% swing LD to C.
(2001: LD maj. 2,370 (4.89%))

ROSSENDALE & DARWEN
E. 72,207 T. 44,437 (61.54%) Lab. hold
Janet Anderson, Lab. 19,073
Nigel Adams, C. 15,397
Mike Carr, LD 6,670
Anthony Wentworth, BNP 1,736
Graeme McIver, Green 821
David Duthie, UKIP 740
Lab. maj. 3,676 (8.27%)
1.85% swing Lab. to C.
(2001: Lab. maj. 5,223 (12.63%))

ROTHER VALLEY
E. 67,973 T. 39,495 (58.10%) Lab. hold
Rt. Hon. Kevin Barron, Lab. 21,871
Colin Phillips, C. 7,647
Phillip Bristow, LD 6,272
Nicholas Cass, BNP 2,020
Gordon Brown, UKIP 1,685
Lab. maj. 14,224 (36.01%)
2.21% swing Lab. to C.
(2001: Lab. maj. 14,882 (40.44%))

ROTHERHAM
E. 54,410 T. 29,978 (55.10%) Lab. hold
Rt. Hon. Denis MacShane, Lab. 15,840
Timothy Gordon, LD 5,159
Lee Rotherham, C. 4,966
Marlene Guest, BNP 1,986
David Cutts, UKIP 1,122
Richard Penycate, Green 905
Lab. maj. 10,681 (35.63%)
8.83% swing Lab. to LD
(2001: Lab. maj. 13,077 (44.55%))

RUGBY & KENILWORTH
E. 83,303 T. 56,949 (68.36%) C. gain
*Jeremy Wright, C. 23,447
Andy King, Lab. 21,891
Richard Allanach, LD 10,143
John Thurley, UKIP 911
Brian Hadland, Ind. 299
Lillian Pallikaropoulos, Ind. 258
C. maj. 1,556 (2.73%)
4.04% swing Lab. to C.
(2001: Lab. maj. 2,877 (5.35%))

RUISLIP-NORTHWOOD
E. 60,774 T. 39,670 (65.27%) C. hold
*Nick Hurd, C. 18,939
Mike Cox, LD 10,029
Ashley Riley, Lab. 8,323
Graham Lee, Green 892
Ian Edward, NF 841
Roland Courtenay, UKIP 646
C. maj. 8,910 (22.46%)
3.49% swing C. to LD
(2001: C. maj. 7,537 (20.29%))

RUNNYMEDE & WEYBRIDGE
E. 74,172 T. 43,524 (58.68%) C. hold
Philip Hammond, C. 22,366
Paul Greenwood, Lab. 10,017
Henry Bolton, LD 7,771
Anthony Micklethwait, UKIP 1,719
Charles Gilman, Green 1,180
Mad Crab Collett, Loony 358
Katrina Osman, UKC 113
C. maj. 12,349 (28.37%)
4.33% swing Lab. to C.
(2001: C. maj. 8,360 (19.70%))

RUSHCLIFFE
E. 79,913 T. 56,311 (70.47%) C. hold
Rt. Hon. Kenneth Clarke, C. 27,899
Edward Gamble, Lab. 14,925
Karrar Khan, LD 9,813
Simon Anthony, Green 1,692
Matthew Faithfull, UKIP 1,358
Daniel Moss, Veritas 624
C. maj. 12,974 (23.04%)
4.76% swing Lab. to C.
(2001: C. maj. 7,357 (13.51%))

RUTLAND & MELTON
E. 75,823 T. 49,284 (65.00%) C. hold
Alan Duncan, C. 25,237
Linda Arnold, Lab. 12,307
Grahame Hudson, LD 9,153
Peter Baker, UKIP 1,554
Duncan Shelley, Veritas 696
Helen Pender, Ind. 337
C. maj. 12,930 (26.24%)
3.97% swing Lab. to C.
(2001: C. maj. 8,612 (18.30%))

RYEDALE
E. 67,770 T. 44,120 (65.10%) C. hold
John Greenway, C. 21,251
Gordon Beever, LD 10,782
Paul Blanchard, Lab. 9,148
Stephen Feaster, UKIP 1,522
John Clarke, Lib. 1,417
C. maj. 10,469 (23.73%)
6.31% swing LD to C.
(2001: C. maj. 4,875 (11.11%))

SAFFRON WALDEN
E. 77,600 T. 53,020 (68.32%) C. hold
Rt. Hon. Sir Alan Haselhurst, C. 27,263
Elfreda Tealby-Watson, LD 14,255
Swatantra Nandanwar, Lab. 8,755
Raymond Tyler, UKIP 1,412
Raymond Brown, Eng. Dem. 860
Trevor Hackett, Veritas 475
C. maj. 13,008 (24.53%)
0.27% swing LD to C.
(2001: C. maj. 12,004 (23.99%))

ST ALBANS
E. 64,595 T. 45,462 (70.38%) C. gain
*Anne Main, C. 16,953
Kerry Pollard, Lab. 15,592
Michael Green, LD 11,561
Richard Evans, UKIP 707
Janet Girsman, St Albans 430
Mark Reynolds, Ind. 219
C. maj. 1,361 (2.99%)
6.60% swing Lab. to C.
(2001: Lab. maj. 4,466 (10.21%))

ST HELENS NORTH
E. 69,834 T. 39,271 (56.23%) Lab. hold
Dave Watts, Lab. 22,329
John Beirne, LD 8,367
Paul Oakley, C. 7,410
Sylvia Hall, UKIP 1,165
Lab. maj. 13,962 (35.55%)
3.99% swing Lab. to LD
(2001: Lab. maj. 15,901 (42.29%))

ST HELENS SOUTH
E. 65,441 T. 35,473 (54.21%) Lab. hold
Shaun Woodward, Lab. 19,345
Brian Spencer, LD 10,036
Una Riley, C. 4,602
Malcolm Nightingale, UKIP 847
Michael Perry, Soc. Lab. 643
Lab. maj. 9,309 (26.24%)
0.17% swing Lab. to LD
(2001: Lab. maj. 8,985 (26.58%))

ST IVES
E. 74,716 T. 50,417 (67.48%) LD hold
Andrew George, LD 25,577
Christian Mitchell, C. 13,968
Michael Dooley, Lab. 6,583
Michael Faulkner, UKIP 2,551
Katrina Slack, Green 1,738
LD maj. 11,609 (23.03%)
1.31% swing C. to LD
(2001: LD maj. 10,053 (20.41%))

SALFORD
E. 53,294 T. 22,600 (42.41%) Lab. hold
Rt. Hon. Hazel Blears, Lab. 13,007
Norman Owen, LD 5,062
Laetitia Cash, C. 3,440
Lisa Duffy, UKIP 1,091
Lab. maj. 7,945 (35.15%)
6.88% swing Lab. to LD
(2001: Lab. maj. 11,012 (48.91%))

SALISBURY
E. 80,385 T. 54,322 (67.58%) C. hold
Robert Key, C. 25,961
Richard Denton-White, LD 14,819
Clare Moody, Lab. 9,457
Frances Howard, UKIP 2,290
Hamish Soutar, Green 1,555
John Holme, Ind. 240
C. maj. 11,142 (20.51%)
1.98% swing LD to C.
(2001: C. maj. 8,703 (16.54%))

SCARBOROUGH & WHITBY
E. 73,806 T. 46,912 (63.56%) C. gain
*Robert Goodwill, C. 19,248
Lawrence Quinn, Lab. 18,003
Tania Exley-Moore, LD 7,495
Jonathan Dixon, Green 1,214
Paul Abbott, UKIP 952
C. maj. 1,245 (2.65%)
5.10% swing Lab. to C.
(2001: Lab. maj. 3,585 (7.54%))

SCUNTHORPE
E. 62,669 T. 32,664 (52.12%) Lab. hold
Elliot Morley, Lab. 17,355
Julian Sturdy, C. 8,392
Neil Poole, LD 5,556
David Baxendale, UKIP 1,361
Lab. maj. 8,963 (27.44%)
1.70% swing Lab. to C.
(2001: Lab. maj. 10,372 (30.83%))

SEDGEFIELD
E. 66,666 T. 41,483 (62.23%) Lab. hold
Rt. Hon. Tony Blair, Lab. 24,429
Grp Capt Al Lockwood, C. 5,972
Robert Browne, LD 4,935
Reg Keys, Ind. 4,252
William Brown, UKIP 646
Mark Farrell, NF 253
Fiona Luckhurst-Matthews, Veritas 218
Berony Abraham, Ind. 209
Boney Maroncy, Loony 157
Jonathan Cockburn, BMG 103
Terry Pattinson, Senior 97
Cherri Gilham, UKPP 82
Helen John, Ind. 68
John Barker, Ind. 45
Julian Brennan, Ind. 17
Lab. maj. 18,457 (44.49%)
0.25% swing C. to Lab.
(2001: Lab. maj. 17,713 (44.00%))

SELBY
E. 78,111 T. 52,549 (67.27%) Lab. hold
John Grogan, Lab. 22,623
Mark Menzies, C. 22,156
Ian Cuthbertson, LD 7,770
Lab. maj. 467 (0.89%)
1.68% swing Lab. to C.
(2001: Lab. maj. 2,138 (4.25%))

SEVENOAKS
E. 65,109 T. 43,298 (66.50%) C. hold
Michael Fallon, C. 22,437
Ben Abbotts, LD 9,467
Tim Stanley, Lab. 9,101
Robert Dobson, UKIP 1,309
John Marshall, Eng. Dem. 751
Mark Ellis, UK Path 233
C. maj. 12,970 (29.96%)
1.09% swing LD to C.
(2001: C. maj. 10,154 (23.83%))

SHEFFIELD ATTERCLIFFE
E. 67,815 T. 37,019 (54.59%) Lab. hold
Clive Betts, Lab. 22,250
Kevin Moore, LD 6,283
Tracy Critchlow, C. 5,329
Jonathan Arnott, UKIP 1,680
Beverley Jones, BNP 1,477
Lab. maj. 15,967 (43.13%)
5.22% swing Lab. to LD
(2001: Lab. maj. 18,844 (52.60%))

SHEFFIELD BRIGHTSIDE
E. 51,379 T. 24,629 (47.94%) Lab. hold
Rt. Hon. David Blunkett, Lab. 16,876
Jonathan Harston, LD 3,232
Tim Clark, C. 2,205
Christopher Hartigan, BNP 1,537
Judith Clarke, UKIP 779
Lab. maj. 13,644 (55.40%)
6.37% swing Lab. to LD
(2001: Lab. maj. 17,049 (66.72%))

SHEFFIELD CENTRAL
E. 59,862 T. 29,985 (50.09%) Lab. hold
Rt. Hon. Richard Caborn, Lab. 14,950
Ali Qadar, LD 7,895
Samantha George, C. 3,094
Bernard Little, Green 1,808
Maxine Bowler, Respect 1,284
Mark Payne, BNP 539
Charlotte Arnott, UKIP 413
Lab. maj. 7,055 (23.53%)
9.09% swing Lab. to LD
(2001: Lab. maj. 12,544 (41.72%))

SHEFFIELD HALLAM
E. 59,606 T. 40,427 (67.82%) LD hold
*Nick Clegg, LD 20,710
Spencer Pitfield, C. 12,028
Mahroof Hussain, Lab. 5,110
Rob Cole, Green 1,331
Sid Cordle, CPA 441
Nigel James, UKIP 438
Ian Senior, BNP 369
LD maj. 8,682 (21.48%)
1.48% swing LD to C.
(2001: LD maj. 9,347 (24.44%))

SHEFFIELD HEELEY
E. 59,748 T. 34,093 (57.06%)
Lab. (Co-op) hold
Meg Munn, Lab. (Co-op) 18,405
Colin Ross, LD 7,035
Aster Crawshaw, C. 4,987
John Beatson, BNP 1,314
Rob Unwin, Green 1,312
Mark Suter, UKIP 775
Mark Dunnell, Soc. Alt. 265
Lab. (Co-op) maj. 11,370 (33.35%)
0.47% swing Lab. (Co-op) to LD
(2001: Lab. (Co-op) maj. 11,704
(34.28%))

SHEFFIELD HILLSBOROUGH
E. 75,706 T. 45,884 (60.61%) Lab. hold
*Angela Smith, Lab. 23,477
John Commons, LD 12,234
Jackie Doyle-Price, C. 6,890
David Wright, BNP 2,010
Maurice Patterson, UKIP 1,273
Lab. maj. 11,243 (24.50%)
4.87% swing Lab. to LD
(2001: Lab. maj. 14,569 (34.25%))

SHERWOOD
E. 75,913 T. 47,117 (62.07%) Lab. hold
Paddy Tipping, Lab. 22,824
Bruce Laughton, C. 16,172
Peter Harris, LD 6,384
Moritz Dawkins, UKIP 1,737
Lab. maj. 6,652 (14.12%)
3.15% swing Lab. to C.
(2001: Lab. maj. 9,373 (20.42%))

SHIPLEY
E. 69,575 T. 47,666 (68.51%) C. gain
*Philip Davies, C. 18,608
Christopher Leslie, Lab. 18,186
John Briggs, LD 7,018
Tom Linden, BNP 2,000
Quentin Deakin, Green 1,665
David Crabtree, Iraq 189
C. maj. 422 (0.89%)
1.99% swing Lab. to C.
(2001: Lab. maj. 1,428 (3.10%))

SHREWSBURY & ATCHAM
E. 73,193 T. 50,296 (68.72%) C. gain
*Daniel Kawczynski, C. 18,960
Michael Ion, Lab. 17,152
Richard Burt, LD 11,487
Peter Lewis, UKIP 1,349
Emma Bullard, Green 1,138
James Gollins, Ind. 126
Nigel Harris, Online 84
C. maj. 1,808 (3.59%)
5.38% swing Lab. to C.
(2001: Lab. maj. 3,579 (7.17%))

SHROPSHIRE NORTH
E. 73,477 T. 46,510 (63.30%) C. hold
Owen Paterson, C. 23,061
Sandra Samuels, Lab. 12,041
Steven Bourne, LD 9,175
Ian Smith, UKIP 2,233
C. maj. 11,020 (23.69%)
5.14% swing Lab. to C.
(2001: C. maj. 6,241 (13.42%))

SITTINGBOURNE & SHEPPEY
E. 62,950 T. 40,803 (64.82%) Lab. hold
Derek Wyatt, Lab. 17,051
Gordon Henderson, C. 16,972
Jane Nelson, LD 5,183
Stephen Dean, UKIP 926
Mad MikeYoung, R & R Loony 479
David Cassidy, Veritas 192
Lab. maj. 79 (0.19%)
4.54% swing Lab. to C.
(2001: Lab. maj. 3,509 (9.27%))

SKIPTON & RIPON
E. 76,485 T. 50,521 (66.05%) C. hold
Rt. Hon. David Curry, C. 25,100
Paul English, LD 13,480
Paul Baptie, Lab. 9,393
Ian Bannister, UKIP 2,274
Robert Leakey, Currency 274
C. maj. 11,620 (23.00%)
1.66% swing C. to LD
(2001: C. maj. 12,930 (26.32%))

SLEAFORD & NORTH HYKEHAM
E. 79,612 T. 53,397 (67.07%) C. hold
Rt. Hon. Douglas Hogg, C. 26,855
Katrina Bull, Lab. 14,150
David Harding-Price, LD 9,710
Guy Croft, UKIP 2,682
C. maj. 12,705 (23.79%)
3.05% swing Lab. to C.
(2001: C. maj. 8,622 (17.70%))

SLOUGH
E. 71,595 T. 37,095 (51.81%) Lab. hold
Fiona Mactaggart, Lab. 17,517
Sheila Gunn, C. 9,666
Thomas McCann, LD 5,739
Ajaz Khan, Respect 1,632
Geoff Howard, UKIP 1,415
David Wood, Green 759
Paul Janik, Ind. 367
Lab. maj. 7,851 (21.16%)
5.45% swing Lab. to C.
(2001: Lab. maj. 12,508 (32.07%))

SOLIHULL
E. 77,910 T. 52,313 (67.15%) LD gain
*Lorely Burt, LD 20,896
John Taylor, C. 20,617
Rory Vaughan, Lab. 8,058
Diane Carr, BNP 1,752
Andrew Moore, UKIP 990
LD maj. 279 (0.53%)
10.01% swing C. to LD
(2001: C. maj. 9,407 (19.49%))

SOMERTON & FROME
E. 77,806 T. 54,102 (69.53%) LD hold
David Heath, LD 23,759
Clive Allen, C. 22,947
Joseph Pestell, Lab. 5,865
William Lukins, UKIP 1,047
Carleton Beaman, Veritas 484
LD maj. 812 (1.50%)
0.12% swing C. to LD
(2001: LD maj. 668 (1.27%))

SOUTH HOLLAND & THE DEEPINGS
E. 77,453 T. 48,249 (62.29%) C. hold
John Hayes, C. 27,544
Linda Woodings, Lab. 11,764
Steve Jarvis, LD 6,244
Jamie Corney, UKIP 1,950
Paul Poll, Ind. 747
C. maj. 15,780 (32.71%)
4.34% swing Lab. to C.
(2001: C. maj. 11,099 (24.02%))

SOUTH SHIELDS
E. 59,403 T. 30,206 (50.85%) Lab. hold
Rt. Hon. David Miliband, Lab. 18,269
Stephen Psallidas, LD 5,957
Richard Lewis, C. 5,207
Nader Afshari-Naderi, Ind. 773
Lab. maj. 12,312 (40.76%)
2.78% swing Lab. to LD
(2001: Lab. maj. 14,090 (46.28%))

SOUTHAMPTON ITCHEN
E. 78,818 T. 43,225 (54.84%) Lab. hold
Rt. Hon. John Denham, Lab. 20,871
Flick Drummond, C. 11,569
David Goodall, LD 9,162
Kim Rose, UKIP 1,623
Lab. maj. 9,302 (21.52%)
2.80% swing Lab. to C.
(2001: Lab. maj. 11,223 (27.13%))

SOUTHAMPTON TEST
E. 72,833 T. 41,783 (57.37%) Lab. hold
Dr Alan Whitehead, Lab. 17,845
Stephen MacLoughlin, C. 10,827
Steve Sollitt, LD 10,368
John Spottiswoode, Green 1,482
Peter Day, UKIP 1,261
Lab. maj. 7,018 (16.80%)
5.08% swing Lab. to C.
(2001: Lab. maj. 11,207 (26.96%))

SOUTHEND WEST
E. 64,915 T. 39,830 (61.36%) C. hold
David Amess, C. 18,408
Peter Wexham, LD 9,449
Jan Etienne, Lab. 9,072
Carole Sampson, UKIP 1,349
Dr Marimuthu Velmurugan, Ind. 745
Jeremy Moss, Eng. Dem. 701
Dan Anslow, Power 106
C. maj. 8,959 (22.49%)
0.55% swing LD to C.
(2001: C. maj. 7,941 (21.25%))

SOUTHPORT
E. 67,977 T. 41,201 (60.61%) LD hold
Dr John Pugh, LD 19,093
Mark Bigley, C. 15,255
Paul Brant, Lab. 5,277
Terry Durrance, UKIP 749
Bill Givens, YPB 589
Harry Forster, Veritas 238
LD maj. 3,838 (9.32%)
1.00% swing C. to LD
(2001: LD maj. 3,007 (7.31%))

SOUTHWARK NORTH & BERMONDSEY
E. 77,084 T. 37,959 (49.24%) LD hold
Simon Hughes, LD 17,874
Kirsty McNeill, Lab. 12,468
David Branch, C. 4,752
Storm Poorun, Green 1,137
Linda Robson, UKIP 791
Paul Winnett, NF 704
Simi Lawanson, CPA 233
LD maj. 5,406 (14.24%)
5.94% swing LD to Lab.
(2001: LD maj. 9,632 (26.13%))

SPELTHORNE
E. 69,650 T. 42,829 (61.49%) C. hold
David Wilshire, C. 21,620
Keith Dibble, Lab. 11,684
Simon James, LD 7,318
Christopher Browne, UKIP 1,968
Caroline Schwark, UKC 239
C. maj. 9,936 (23.20%)
7.70% swing Lab. to C.
(2001: C. maj. 3,262 (7.80%))

STAFFORD
E. 70,359 T. 45,554 (64.75%) Lab. hold
David Kidney, Lab. 19,889
David Chambers, C. 17,768
Barry Stamp, LD 6,390
Frederick Goode, UKIP 1,507
Lab. maj. 2,121 (4.66%)
3.34% swing Lab. to C.
(2001: Lab. maj. 5,032 (11.34%))

STAFFORDSHIRE MOORLANDS
E. 69,136 T. 44,253 (64.01%) Lab. hold
Charlotte Atkins, Lab. 18,126
Marcus Hayes, C. 15,688
John Fisher, LD 6,927
Steve Povey, UKIP 3,512
Lab. maj. 2,438 (5.51%)
4.09% swing Lab. to C.
(2001: Lab. maj. 5,838 (13.69%))

STAFFORDSHIRE SOUTH
Deferred until 23 June 2005 due to the death of the Liberal Democrat candidate during the general election campaign (*see* by-elections)

STALYBRIDGE & HYDE
E. 66,013 T. 35,314 (53.50%) Lab. hold
James Purnell, Lab. 17,535
Lisa Boardman, C. 9,187
Viv Bingham, LD 5,532
Nigel Byrne, BNP 1,399
Mike Smee, Green 1,088
Dr John Whittaker, UKIP 573
Lab. maj. 8,348 (23.64%)
2.00% swing Lab. to C.
(2001: Lab. maj. 8,859 (27.64%))

STEVENAGE
E. 66,889 T. 41,934 (62.69%) Lab. hold
Barbara Follett, Lab. 18,003
George Freeman, C. 14,864
Julia Davies, LD 7,610
Victoria Peebles, UKIP 1,305
Antal Losonczi, Ind. 152
Lab. maj. 3,139 (7.49%)
6.35% swing Lab. to C.
(2001: Lab. maj. 8,566 (20.18%))

STOCKPORT
E. 65,593 T. 35,771 (54.53%) Lab. hold
Ann Coffey, Lab. 18,069
Elizabeth Berridge, C. 8,906
Lyn-Su Floodgate, LD 7,832
Richard Simpson, UKIP 964
Lab. maj. 9,163 (25.62%)
3.54% swing Lab. to C.
(2001: Lab. maj. 11,569 (32.70%))

STOCKTON NORTH
E. 63,271 T. 36,428 (57.57%) Lab. hold
Frank Cook, Lab. 20,012
Harriett Baldwin, C. 7,575
Neil Hughes, LD 6,869
Kevin Hughes, BNP 986
Gordon Parkin, UKIP 986
Lab. maj. 12,437 (34.14%)
3.60% swing Lab. to C.
(2001: Lab. maj. 14,647 (41.34%))

STOCKTON SOUTH
E. 71,286 T. 44,923 (63.02%) Lab. hold
Dari Taylor, Lab. 21,480
James Gaddas, C. 15,341
Mike Barker, LD 7,171
Sandra Allison, UKIP 931
Lab. maj. 6,139 (13.67%)
3.44% swing Lab. to C.
(2001: Lab. maj. 9,086 (20.55%))

STOKE-ON-TRENT CENTRAL
E. 57,643 T. 27,907 (48.41%) Lab. hold
Mark Fisher, Lab. 14,760
John Redfern, LD 4,986
Esther Baroudy, C. 4,823
Michael Coleman, BNP 2,178
Joseph Bonfiglio, UKIP 914
Jim Cessford, Soc. Alt. 246
Lab. maj. 9,774 (35.02%)
5.50% swing Lab. to LD
(2001: Lab. maj. 11,845 (41.86%))

STOKE-ON-TRENT NORTH
E. 58,422 T. 30,760 (52.65%) Lab. hold
Joan Walley, Lab. 16,191
Benjamin Browning, C. 6,155
Henry Jebb, LD 4,561
Spencer Cartlidge, BNP 2,132
Eileen Braithwaite, UKIP 696
Ian Taylor, Veritas 689
Harry Chesters, Ind. 336
Lab. maj. 10,036 (32.63%)
3.25% swing Lab. to C.
(2001: Lab. maj. 11,784 (39.13%))

STOKE-ON-TRENT SOUTH
E. 70,612 T. 37,820 (53.56%) Lab. hold
*Robert Flello, Lab. 17,727
Mark Deaville, C. 9,046
Andrew Martin, LD 5,894
Mark Leat, BNP 3,305
Neville Benson, UKIP 1,043
Grant Allen, Veritas 805
Lab. maj. 8,681 (22.95%)
3.08% swing Lab. to C.
(2001: Lab. maj. 10,489 (29.11%))

STONE
E. 70,359 T. 47,036 (66.85%) C. hold
Bill Cash, C. 22,733
Mark Davis, Lab. 13,644
Peter Stevens, LD 9,111
Michael Nattrass, UKIP 1,548
C. maj. 9,089 (19.32%)
3.05% swing Lab. to C.
(2001: C. maj. 6,036 (13.22%))

STOURBRIDGE
E. 64,479 T. 41,708 (64.68%) Lab. hold
*Lynda Waltho, Lab. 17,089
Diana Coad, C. 16,682
Chris Bramall, LD 6,850
Daniel Pui Chai Mau, UKIP 1,087
Lab. maj. 407 (0.98%)
4.29% swing Lab. to C.
(2001: Lab. maj. 3,812 (9.55%))

STRATFORD-UPON-AVON
E. 84,591 T. 58,240 (68.85%) C. hold
John Maples, C. 28,652
Dr Susan Juned, LD 16,468
Rachel Blackmore, Lab. (Co-op) 10,145
Harry Cottam, UKIP 1,621
Mick Davies, Green 1,354
C. maj. 12,184 (20.92%)
0.29% swing C. to LD
(2001: C. maj. 11,802 (21.49%))

STREATHAM
E. 79,193 T. 40,615 (51.29%) Lab. hold
Rt. Hon. Keith Hill, Lab. 18,950
Darren Sanders, LD 11,484
James Sproule, C. 7,238
Shane Collins, Green 2,245
Trevor Gittings, UKIP 396
William Colvill, WRP 127
Philippa Stone, Ind. 100
Robert West, Ind. 40
Sarah Acheng, Ind. 35
Lab. maj. 7,466 (18.38%)
10.09% swing Lab. to LD
(2001: Lab. maj. 14,270 (38.57%))

STRETFORD & URMSTON
E. 61,979 T. 38,101 (61.47%) Lab. hold
Rt. Hon. Beverley Hughes, Lab. 19,417
Damian Hinds, C. 11,566
Faraz Bhatti, LD 5,323
Mark Krantz, Respect 950
Michael McManus, UKIP 845
Lab. maj. 7,851 (20.61%)
6.71% swing Lab. to C.
(2001: Lab. maj. 13,239 (33.97%))

STROUD
E. 79,748 T. 56,875 (71.32%) Lab. (Co-op) hold
David Drew, Lab. (Co-op) 22,527
Neil Carmichael, C. 22,177
Peter Hirst, LD 8,026
Martin Whiteside, Green 3,056
Edward Noble, UKIP 1,089
Lab. (Co-op) maj. 350 (0.62%)
4.26% swing Lab. (Co-op) to C.
(2001: Lab. (Co-op) maj. 5,039 (9.13%))

SUFFOLK CENTRAL & IPSWICH NORTH
E. 76,271 T. 50,866 (66.69%) C. hold
Sir Michael Lord, C. 22,333
Neil MacDonald, Lab. 14,477
Andrew Houseley, LD 10,709
John West, UKIP 1,754
Martin Wolfe, Green 1,593
C. maj. 7,856 (15.44%)
4.04% swing Lab. to C.
(2001: C. maj. 3,469 (7.36%))

SUFFOLK COASTAL
E. 77,423 T. 52,557 (67.88%) C. hold
Rt. Hon. John Gummer, C. 23,415
David Rowe, Lab. 13,730
David Young, LD 11,637
Richard Curtis, UKIP 2,020
Paul Whitlow, Green 1,755
C. maj. 9,685 (18.43%)
4.92% swing Lab. to C.
(2001: C. maj. 4,326 (8.58%))

SUFFOLK SOUTH
E. 70,237 T. 48,707 (69.35%) C. hold
Tim Yeo, C. 20,471
Kathy Pollard, LD 13,865
Kevin Craig, Lab. 11,917
James Carver, UKIP 2,454
C. maj. 6,606 (13.56%)
1.45% swing C. to LD
(2001: C. maj. 5,081 (11.22%))

SUFFOLK WEST
E. 72,856 T. 44,205 (60.67%) C. hold
Richard Spring, C. 21,682
Michael Jefferys, Lab. 12,773
Adrian Graves, LD 7,573
Ian Smith, UKIP 2,177
C. maj. 8,909 (20.15%)
5.02% swing Lab. to C.
(2001: C. maj. 4,295 (10.12%))

SUNDERLAND NORTH
E. 58,146 T. 28,913 (49.72%) Lab. hold
Bill Etherington, Lab. 15,719
Stephen Daughton, C. 5,724
James Hollern, LD 4,277
Neil Herron, Ind. 2,057
Debra Hiles, BNP 1,136
Lab. maj. 9,995 (34.57%)
5.11% swing Lab. to C.
(2001: Lab. maj. 13,354 (44.78%))

SUNDERLAND SOUTH
E. 62,256 T. 30,712 (49.33%) Lab. hold
Chris Mullin, Lab. 17,982
Robert Oliver, C. 6,923
Gareth Kane, LD 4,492
David Guynan, BNP 1,166
Rosalyn Warner, Loony 149
Lab. maj. 11,059 (36.01%)
3.91% swing Lab. to C.
(2001: Lab. maj. 13,667 (43.82%))

SURREY EAST
E. 73,948 T. 49,253 (66.60%) C. hold
Peter Ainsworth, C. 27,659
Jeremy Pursehouse, LD 11,738
James Bridge, Lab. 7,288
Tony Stone, UKIP 2,158
Winston Matthews, LCA 410
C. maj. 15,921 (32.32%)
2.13% swing LD to C.
(2001: C. maj. 13,203 (28.06%))

SURREY HEATH
E. 76,090 T. 47,858 (62.90%) C. hold
*Michael Gove, C. 24,642
Rosalyn Harper, LD 13,797
Chris Lowe, Lab. 7,989
Steve Smith, UKIP 1,430
C. maj. 10,845 (22.66%)
0.66% swing C. to LD
(2001: C. maj. 10,819 (23.99%))

SURREY SOUTH WEST
E. 72,977 T. 52,409 (71.82%) C. hold
*Jeremy Hunt, C. 26,420
Simon Cordon, LD 20,709
Thomas Sleigh, Lab. 4,150
Timothy Clark, UKIP 958
Glenn Platt, Veritas 172
C. maj. 5,711 (10.90%)
4.58% swing LD to C.
(2001: C. maj. 861 (1.74%))

SUSSEX MID
E. 72,114 T. 49,494 (68.63%) C. hold
Hon. Nicholas Soames, C. 23,765
Serena Tierney, LD 17,875
Robert Fromant, Lab. 6,280
Harold Piggott, UKIP 1,574
C. maj. 5,890 (11.90%)
1.58% swing C. to LD
(2001: C. maj. 6,898 (15.05%))

SUTTON & CHEAM
E. 63,319 T. 41,932 (66.22%) LD hold
Paul Burstow, LD 19,768
Richard Willis, C. 16,922
Anand Shukla, Lab. 4,954
Rainbow George Weiss, Vote Dream 288
LD maj. 2,846 (6.79%)
2.02% swing LD to C.
(2001: LD maj. 4,304 (10.84%))

SUTTON COLDFIELD
E. 72,995 T. 46,318 (63.45%) C. hold
Andrew Mitchell, C. 24,308
Robert Pocock, Lab. 12,025
Craig Drury, LD 7,710
Stephen Shorrock, UKIP 2,275
C. maj. 12,283 (26.52%)
1.63% swing Lab. to C.
(2001: C. maj. 10,104 (23.25%))

SWINDON NORTH
E. 73,636 T. 44,885 (60.96%) Lab. hold
Michael Wills, Lab. 19,612
Justin Tomlinson, C. 17,041
Mike Evemy, LD 6,831
Robert Tingey, UKIP 998
Andy Newman, Soc. Unity 208
Ernest Reynolds, Ind. 195
Lab. maj. 2,571 (5.73%)
6.71% swing Lab. to C.
(2001: Lab. maj. 8,105 (19.15%))

SWINDON SOUTH
E. 72,267 T. 43,472 (60.15%) Lab. hold
*Anne Snelgrove, Lab. 17,534
Robert Buckland, C. 16,181
Sue Stebbing, LD 7,322
Bill Hughes, Green 1,234
Stephen Halden, UKIP 955
Alan Hayward, Ind. 193
John Williams, Ind. 53
Lab. maj. 1,353 (3.11%)
6.90% swing Lab. to C.
(2001: Lab. maj. 7,341 (16.92%))

TAMWORTH
E. 71,675 T. 43,740 (61.03%) Lab. hold
Brian Jenkins, Lab. 18,801
Christopher Pincher, C. 16,232
Phillip Bennion, LD 6,175
Patrick Eston, Veritas 1,320
Tom Simpson, UKIP 1,212
Lab. maj. 2,569 (5.87%)
2.78% swing Lab. to C.
(2001: Lab. maj. 4,598 (11.42%))

TATTON
E. 64,140 T. 41,414 (64.57%) C. hold
George Osborne, C. 21,447
Justin Madders, Lab. 9,716
Ainsley Arnold, LD 9,016
Diane Bowler, UKIP 996
Michael Gibson, Ind. 239
C. maj. 11,731 (28.33%)
3.73% swing Lab. to C.
(2001: C. maj. 8,611 (20.86%))

TAUNTON
E. 85,466 T. 59,528 (69.65%) LD gain
*Jeremy Browne, LD 25,764
Adrian Flook, C. 25,191
Andrew Govier, Lab. 7,132
Helen Miles, UKIP 1,441
LD maj. 573 (0.96%)
0.69% swing C. to LD
(2001: C. maj. 235 (0.43%))

TEIGNBRIDGE
E. 88,674 T. 60,898 (68.68%) LD hold
Richard Younger-Ross, LD 27,808
Stanley Johnson, C. 21,593
Chris Sherwood, Lab. 6,931
Trevor Colman, UKIP 3,881
Reginald Wills, Lib. 685
LD maj. 6,215 (10.21%)
2.56% swing C. to LD
(2001: LD maj. 3,011 (5.08%))

TELFORD
E. 59,277 T. 34,206 (57.71%) Lab. hold
David Wright, Lab. 16,506
Stella Kyriazis, C. 11,100
Ian Jenkins, LD 4,941
Tom McCartney, UKIP 1,659
Lab. maj. 5,406 (15.80%)
5.67% swing Lab. to C.
(2001: Lab. maj. 8,383 (27.15%))

TEWKESBURY
E. 72,145 T. 45,453 (63.00%) C. hold
Laurence Robertson, C. 22,339
Alistair Cameron, LD 12,447
Charles Mannan, Lab. 9,179
Robert Rendell, Green 1,488
C. maj. 9,892 (21.76%)
0.96% swing LD to C.
(2001: C. maj. 8,663 (19.17%))

THANET NORTH
E. 72,734 T. 43,732 (60.13%) C. hold
Roger Gale, C. 21,699
Iris Johnston, Lab. 14,065
Mark Barnard, LD 6,279
Timothy Stocks, UKIP 1,689
C. maj. 7,634 (17.46%)
0.79% swing Lab. to C.
(2001: C. maj. 6,650 (15.88%))

THANET SOUTH
E. 63,436 T. 41,242 (65.01%) Lab. hold
Dr Stephen Ladyman, Lab. 16,660
Mark MacGregor, C. 15,996
Guy Voizey, LD 5,431
Nigel Farage, UKIP 2,079
Howard Green, Green 888
Maude Kinsella, Ind. 188
Lab. maj. 664 (1.61%)
1.47% swing Lab. to C.
(2001: Lab. maj. 1,792 (4.54%))

THURROCK
E. 79,545 T. 43,692 (54.93%) Lab. hold
Andrew Mackinlay, Lab. 20,636
Garry Hague, C. 14,261
Earnshaw Palmer, LD 4,770
Nick Geri, BNP 2,526
Carol Jackson, UKIP 1,499
Lab. maj. 6,375 (14.59%)
6.08% swing Lab. to C.
(2001: Lab. maj. 9,997 (26.76%))

TIVERTON & HONITON
E. 83,375 T. 58,168 (69.77%) C. hold
Angela Browning, C. 27,838
David Nation, LD 16,787
Fiona Bentley, Lab. 7,944
Robert Edwards, UKIP 2,499
Roy Collins, Lib. 1,701
Colin Matthews, Green 1,399
C. maj. 11,051 (19.00%)
3.87% swing LD to C.
(2001: C. maj. 6,284 (11.26%))

TONBRIDGE & MALLING
E. 68,444 T. 46,063 (67.30%) C. hold
Rt. Hon. Sir John Stanley, C. 24,357
Victoria Hayman, Lab. 11,005
John Barstow, LD 8,980
David Waller, UKIP 1,721
C. maj. 13,352 (28.99%)
4.77% swing Lab. to C.
(2001: C. maj. 8,250 (19.44%))

TOOTING
E. 70,504 T. 41,568 (58.96%) Lab. hold
*Sadiq Khan, Lab. 17,914
James Bethell, C. 12,533
Stephanie Dearden, LD 8,110
Siobhan Vitelli, Green 1,695
Ali Zaidi, Respect 700
Strachan McDonald, UKIP 424
Ian Perkin, Ind. 192
Lab. maj. 5,381 (12.95%)
7.36% swing Lab. to C.
(2001: Lab. maj. 10,400 (27.67%))

TORBAY
E. 76,474 T. 47,303 (61.86%) LD hold
Adrian Sanders, LD 19,317
Marcus Wood, C. 17,288
David Pedrick-Friend, Lab. 6,972
Graham Booth, UKIP 3,726
LD maj. 2,029 (4.29%)
4.91% swing LD to C.
(2001: LD maj. 6,708 (14.10%))

TOTNES
E. 74,744 T. 50,575 (67.66%) C. hold
Anthony Steen, C. 21,112
Michael Treleaven, LD 19,165
Valerie Burns, Lab. 6,185
Roger Knapman, UKIP 3,914
Michael Thompson, Ind. 199
C. maj. 1,947 (3.85%)
1.73% swing C. to LD
(2001: C. maj. 3,597 (7.30%))

TOTTENHAM
E. 66,231 T. 31,664 (47.81%) Lab. hold
David Lammy, Lab. 18,343
Wayne Hoban, LD 5,309
William MacDougall, C. 4,278
Janet Alder, Respect 2,014
Pete McAskie, Green 1,457
Jaamit Durrani, Soc. Lab. 263
Lab. maj. 13,034 (41.16%)
8.39% swing Lab. to LD
(2001: Lab. maj. 16,916 (53.53%))

TRURO & ST AUSTELL
E. 80,256 T. 51,564 (64.25%) LD hold
Matthew Taylor, LD 24,089
Dr Fiona Kemp, C. 16,686
Dr Charlotte Mackenzie, Lab. 6,991
David Noakes, UKIP 2,736
Conan Jenkin, Meb. Ker. 1,062
LD maj. 7,403 (14.36%)
0.84% swing LD to C.
(2001: LD maj. 8,065 (16.04%))

TUNBRIDGE WELLS
E. 64,630 T. 42,482 (65.73%) C. hold
*Greg Clark, C. 21,083
Laura Murphy, LD 11,095
Jacqui Jedrzejewski, Lab. 8,736
Victor Webb, UKIP 1,568
C. maj. 9,988 (23.51%)
0.35% swing C. to LD
(2001: C. maj. 9,730 (24.20%))

TWICKENHAM
E. 72,015 T. 51,687 (71.77%) LD hold
Dr Vincent Cable, LD 26,696
Paul Maynard, C. 16,731
Brian Whitington, Lab. 5,868
Henry Gower, Green 1,445
Douglas Orchard, UKIP 766
Brian Gilbert, Ind. 117
Rainbow George Weiss, Vote Dream 64
LD maj. 9,965 (19.28%)
1.98% swing C. to LD
(2001: LD maj. 7,655 (15.33%))

TYNE BRIDGE
E. 53,565 T. 26,383 (49.25%) Lab. hold
David Clelland, Lab. 16,151
Chris Boyle, LD 5,751
Tom Fairhead, C. 2,962
Kevin Scott, BNP 1,072
Jill Russell, Respect 447
Lab. maj. 10,400 (39.42%)
9.35% swing Lab. to LD
(2001: Lab. maj. 14,889 (57.19%))

TYNEMOUTH
E. 64,023 T. 42,859 (66.94%) Lab. hold
Alan Campbell, Lab. 20,143
Michael McIntyre, C. 16,000
Colin Finlay, LD 6,716
Lab. maj. 4,143 (9.67%)
5.05% swing Lab. to C.
(2001: Lab. maj. 8,678 (19.77%))

TYNESIDE NORTH
E. 64,634 T. 36,939 (57.15%) Lab. hold
Rt. Hon. Stephen Byers, Lab. 22,882
Duncan McLellan, C. 7,845
Gillian Ferguson, LD 6,212
Lab. maj. 15,037 (40.71%)
7.09% swing Lab. to C.
(2001: Lab. maj. 20,668 (55.01%))

UPMINSTER
E. 55,075 T. 34,676 (62.96%) C. hold
Angela Watkinson, C. 16,820
Keith Darvill, Lab. 10,778
Peter Truesdale, LD 3,128
Ronald Ower, RA 1,455
Chris Roberts, BNP 1,173
Alan Hindle, UKIP 701
Melanie Collins, Green 543
David Durant, Third 78
C. maj. 6,042 (17.42%)
6.88% swing Lab. to C.
(2001: C. maj. 1,241 (3.67%))

UXBRIDGE
E. 57,878 T. 34,378 (59.40%) C. hold
John Randall, C. 16,840
Rod Marshall, Lab. 10,669
Dr Tariq Mahmood, LD 4,544
Cliff Le May, BNP 763
Stephen Young, Green 725
Robert Kerby, UKIP 553
Peter Shaw, NF 284
C. maj. 6,171 (17.95%)
5.84% swing Lab. to C.
(2001: C. maj. 2,098 (6.28%))

VALE OF YORK
E. 76,000 T. 50,378 (66.29%) C. hold
Anne McIntosh, C. 26,025
David Scott, Lab. 12,313
Jeremy Wilcock, LD 12,040
C. maj. 13,712 (27.22%)
0.70% swing Lab. to C.
(2001: C. maj. 12,517 (25.81%))

VAUXHALL
E. 79,637 T. 37,353 (46.90%) Lab. hold
Kate Hoey, Lab. 19,744
Charles Anglin, LD 9,767
Edward Heckels, C. 5,405
Tim Summers, Green 1,705
Robert McWhirter, UKIP 271
Daniel Lambert, Socialist 240
Janus Polenceus, Eng. Dem. 221
Lab. maj. 9,977 (26.71%)
6.14% swing Lab. to LD
(2001: Lab. maj. 13,018 (38.99%))

WAKEFIELD
E. 73,118 T. 43,381 (59.33%) Lab. hold
*Mary Creagh, Lab. 18,802
Alec Shelbrooke, C. 13,648
David Ridgway, LD 7,063
Grant Rowe, BNP 1,328
Derek Hardcastle, Green 1,297
John Upex, UKIP 467
Paul McEnhill, Eng. Dem. 356
Mick Griffiths, Soc. Alt. 319
Linda Sheridan, Soc. Lab. 101
Lab. maj. 5,154 (11.88%)
3.70% swing Lab. to C.
(2001: Lab. maj. 7,954 (19.28%))

WALLASEY
E. 63,764 T. 36,671 (57.51%) Lab. hold
Angela Eagle, Lab. 20,085
Leah Fraser, C. 10,976
Joanna Pemberton, LD 4,770
Philip Griffiths, UKIP 840
Lab. maj. 9,109 (24.84%)
4.02% swing Lab. to C.
(2001: Lab. maj. 12,276 (32.87%))

WALSALL NORTH
E. 63,268 T. 33,428 (52.84%) Lab. hold
David Winnick, Lab. 15,990
Ian Lucas, C. 9,350
Douglas Taylor, LD 4,144
William Locke, BNP 1,992
Anthony Lenton, UKIP 1,182
Peter Smith, Dem. Lab. 770
Lab. maj. 6,640 (19.86%)
4.60% swing Lab. to C.
(2001: Lab. maj. 9,391 (29.06%))

WALSALL SOUTH
E. 60,370 T. 35,315 (58.50%) Lab. hold
Rt. Hon. Bruce George, Lab. 17,633
Kabir Sabar, C. 9,687
Mohamed Hanif Asmal, LD 3,240
Derek Bennett, UKIP 1,833
Kevin Smith, BNP 1,776
Nadia Fazal, Respect 1,146
Lab. maj. 7,946 (22.50%)
2.98% swing Lab. to C.
(2001: Lab. maj. 9,931 (28.46%))

WALTHAMSTOW
E. 63,079 T. 34,444 (54.60%) Lab. hold
Neil Gerrard, Lab. 17,323
Farid Ahmed, LD 9,330
Jane Wright, C. 6,254
Robert Brock, UKIP 810
Nancy Taaffe, Soc. Alt. 727
Lab. maj. 7,993 (23.21%)
12.18% swing Lab. to LD
(2001: Lab. maj. 15,181 (44.09%))

WANSBECK
E. 63,096 T. 36,809 (58.34%) Lab. hold
Denis Murphy, Lab. 20,315
Simon Reed, LD 9,734
Ginny Scrope, C. 5,515
Dr Nic Best, Green 1,245
Lab. maj. 10,581 (28.75%)
3.13% swing Lab. to LD
(2001: Lab. maj. 13,101 (35.01%))

WANSDYKE
E. 70,359 T. 50,933 (72.39%) Lab. hold
Dan Norris, Lab. 20,686
Chris Watt, C. 18,847
Gail Coleshill, LD 10,050
Peter Sandell, UKIP 1,129
Geoffrey Parkes, Ind. 221
Lab. maj. 1,839 (3.61%)
3.86% swing Lab. to C.
(2001: Lab. maj. 5,113 (10.42%))

WANTAGE
E. 76,156 T. 51,931 (68.19%) C. hold
*Ed Vaizey, C. 22,354
Andrew Crawford, LD 14,337
Mark McDonald, Lab. 12,464
Adam Twine, Green 1,332
Nikolai Tolstoy-Miloslavsky, UKIP 798
Gerald Lambourne, Eng. Dem. 646
C. maj. 8,017 (15.44%)
1.92% swing LD to C.
(2001: C. maj. 5,600 (11.40%))

WARLEY
E. 56,171 T. 32,087 (57.12%) Lab. hold
Rt. Hon. John Spellar, Lab. 17,462
Karen Bissell, C. 7,315
Tony Ferguson, LD 4,277
Simon Smith, BNP 1,761
Malcolm Connigale, Soc. Lab. 637
David Matthews, UKIP 635
Lab. maj. 10,147 (31.62%)
3.05% swing Lab. to C.
(2001: Lab. maj. 11,850 (37.72%))

WARRINGTON NORTH
E. 73,352 T. 40,418 (55.10%) Lab. hold
Helen Jones, Lab. 21,632
Andrew Ferryman, C. 9,428
Peter Walker, LD 7,699
John Kirkham, UKIP 1,086
Mike Hughes, CAP 573
Lab. maj. 12,204 (30.19%)
4.38% swing Lab. to C.
(2001: Lab. maj. 15,156 (38.95%))

WARRINGTON SOUTH
E. 75,724 T. 46,797 (61.80%) Lab. hold
Helen Southworth, Lab. 18,972
Fiona Bruce, C. 15,457
Ian Marks, LD 11,111
Gerald Kelley, UKIP 804
Paul Kennedy, Ind. 453
Lab. maj. 3,515 (7.51%)
4.37% swing Lab. to C.
(2001: Lab. maj. 7,387 (16.24%))

WARWICK & LEAMINGTON
E. 81,205 T. 54,784 (67.46%) Lab. hold
James Plaskitt, Lab. 22,238
Chris White, C. 21,972
Linda Forbes, LD 8,119
Ian Davison, Green 1,534
Greville Warwick, UKIP 921
Lab. maj. 266 (0.49%)
5.32% swing Lab. to C.
(2001: Lab. maj. 5,953 (11.12%))

WARWICKSHIRE NORTH
E. 75,435 T. 46,939 (62.22%) Lab. hold
Mike O'Brien, Lab. 22,561
Ian Gibb, C. 15,008
Jerry Roodhouse, LD 6,212
Michaela Mackenzie, BNP 1,910
Iain Campbell, UKIP 1,248
Lab. maj. 7,553 (16.09%)
2.81% swing Lab. to C.
(2001: Lab. maj. 9,639 (21.71%))

WATFORD
E. 76,280 T. 49,394 (64.75%) Lab. hold
Claire Ward, Lab. 16,575
Sal Brinton, LD 15,427
Ali Miraj, C. 14,634
Steve Rackett, Green 1,466
Kenneth Wight, UKIP 1,292
Lab. maj. 1,148 (2.32%)
12.75% swing Lab. to LD
(2001: Lab. maj. 5,555 (11.98%))

WAVENEY
E. 77,138 T. 49,653 (64.37%) Lab. hold
Bob Blizzard, Lab. 22,505
Peter Aldous, C. 16,590
Nick Bromley, LD 7,497
Brian Aylett, UKIP 1,861
Graham Elliott, Green 1,200
Lab. maj. 5,915 (11.91%)
3.11% swing Lab. to C.
(2001: Lab. maj. 8,553 (18.13%))

WEALDEN
E. 82,261 T. 55,653 (67.65%) C. hold
Charles Hendry, C. 28,975
Christopher Wigley, LD 13,054
Dudley Rose, Lab. 9,360
Julian Salmon, Green 2,150
Keith Riddle, UKIP 2,114
C. maj. 15,921 (28.61%)
1.25% swing LD to C.
(2001: C. maj. 13,772 (26.11%))

WEAVER VALE
E. 69,072 T. 39,420 (57.07%) Lab. hold
Mike Hall, Lab. 18,759
Jonathan Mackie, C. 11,904
Nigel Griffiths, LD 7,723
Brenda Swinscoe, UKIP 1,034
Lab. maj. 6,855 (17.39%)
3.58% swing Lab. to C.
(2001: Lab. maj. 9,637 (24.54%))

WELLINGBOROUGH
E. 79,679 T. 53,005 (66.52%) C. gain
*Peter Bone, C. 22,674
Paul Stinchcombe, Lab. 21,987
Richard Church, LD 6,147
James Wrench, UKIP 1,214
Nicholas Alex, Veritas 749
Andy Dickson, Soc. Lab. 234
C. maj. 687 (1.30%)
2.96% swing Lab. to C.
(2001: Lab. maj. 2,355 (4.62%))

WELLS
E. 77,842 T. 52,965 (68.04%) C. hold
Rt. Hon. David Heathcoat-Amory, C. 23,071
Tessa Munt, LD 20,031
Dan Whittle, Lab. 8,288
Steven Reed, UKIP 1,575
C. maj. 3,040 (5.74%)
0.15% swing LD to C.
(2001: C. maj. 2,796 (5.45%))

WELWYN HATFIELD
E. 65,617 T. 44,716 (68.15%) C. gain
*Grant Shapps, C. 22,172
Melanie Johnson, Lab. 16,226
Sara Bedford, LD 6,318
C. maj. 5,946 (13.30%)
8.05% swing Lab. to C.
(2001: Lab. maj. 1,196 (2.79%))

WENTWORTH
E. 63,561 T. 35,596 (56.00%) Lab. hold
John Healey, Lab. 21,225
Mark Hughes, C. 6,169
Keith Orrell, LD 4,800
Jonathan Pygott, BNP 1,798
John Wilkinson, UKIP 1,604
Lab. maj. 15,056 (42.30%)
3.20% swing Lab. to C.
(2001: Lab. maj. 16,449 (48.70%))

WEST BROMWICH EAST
E. 60,565 T. 35,512 (58.63%) Lab. hold
Tom Watson, Lab. 19,741
Rosemary Bromwich, C. 8,089
Ian Garrett, LD 4,386
Carl Butler, BNP 2,329
Steven Grey, UKIP 607
Judith Sambrook, Soc. Lab. 200
Margaret Macklin, Ind. 160
Lab. maj. 11,652 (32.81%)
1.46% swing C. to Lab.
(2001: Lab. maj. 9,763 (29.89%))

WEST BROMWICH WEST
E. 66,752 T. 34,917 (52.31%) Lab. (Co-op) hold
Adrian Bailey, Lab. (Co-op) 18,951
Mimi Harker, C. 8,057
Martyn Smith, LD 3,583
James Lloyd, BNP 3,456
Kevin Walker, UKIP 870
Lab. (Co-op) maj. 10,894 (31.20%)
2.23% swing Lab. (Co-op) to C.
(2001: Lab. (Co-op) maj. 11,355 (35.66%))

WEST HAM
E. 62,184 T. 30,966 (49.80%) Lab. hold
*Lyn Brown, Lab. 15,840
Lindsey German, Respect 6,039
Chris Whitbread, C. 3,618
Alexandra Sugden, LD 3,364
Jane Lithgow, Green 894
Stephen Hammond, CPA 437
Henry Mayhew, UKIP 409
Generoso Alcantara, Veritas 365
Lab. maj. 9,801 (31.65%)
19.12% swing Lab. to Respect
(2001: Lab. maj. 15,645 (53.45%))

WESTBURY
E. 83,039 T. 55,604 (66.96%) C. hold
Dr Andrew Murrison, C. 24,749
Duncan Hames, LD 19,400
Phil Gibby, Lab. 9,640
Lincoln Williams, UKIP 1,815
C. maj. 5,349 (9.62%)
0.42% swing C. to LD
(2001: C. maj. 5,294 (10.46%))

WESTMORLAND & LONSDALE
E. 69,363 T. 49,636 (71.56%) LD gain
*Tim Farron, LD 22,569
Tim Collins, C. 22,302
John Reardon, Lab. 3,796
Robert Gibson, UKIP 660
Anthony Kemp, Ind. 309
LD maj. 267 (0.54%)
3.55% swing C. to LD
(2001: C. maj. 3,147 (6.57%))

WESTON-SUPER-MARE
E. 74,900 T. 49,095 (65.55%) C. gain
*John Penrose, C. 19,804
Brian Cotter, LD 17,725
Damien Egan, Lab. 9,169
Paul Spencer, UKIP 1,207
Clive Courtney, BNP 778
William Human, Ind. 225
Paul Hemingway-Arnold, Honesty 187
C. maj. 2,079 (4.23%)
2.48% swing LD to C.
(2001: LD maj. 338 (0.72%))

WIGAN
E. 64,267 T. 34,278 (53.34%) Lab. hold
Neil Turner, Lab. 18,901
John Coombes, C. 7,134
Denise Capstick, LD 6,051
Dr John Whittaker, UKIP 1,166
Kevin Williams, CAP 1,026
Lab. maj. 11,767 (34.33%)
3.29% swing Lab. to C.
(2001: Lab. maj. 13,743 (40.91%))

WILTSHIRE NORTH
E. 80,896 T. 56,061 (69.30%) C. hold
James Gray, C. 26,282
Paul Fox, LD 20,979
David Nash, Lab. 6,794
Neil Dowdney, UKIP 1,428
Philip Allnatt, Ind. 578
C. maj. 5,303 (9.46%)
1.07% swing LD to C.
(2001: C. maj. 3,878 (7.32%))

WIMBLEDON
E. 63,714 T. 43,404 (68.12%) C. gain
*Stephen Hammond, C. 17,886
Roger Casale, Lab. 15,585
Stephen Gee, LD 7,868
Giles Barrow, Green 1,374
Andrew Mills, UKIP 408
Christopher Coverdale, Ind. 211
Alastair Wilson, TEPK 50
Rainbow George Weiss, Vote Dream 22
C. maj. 2,301 (5.30%)
7.20% swing Lab. to C.
(2001: Lab. maj. 3,744 (9.11%))

WINCHESTER
E. 85,810 T. 61,658 (71.85%) LD hold
Mark Oaten, LD 31,225
George Hollingbery, C. 23,749
Patrick Davies, Lab. 4,782
Dr David Abbott, UKIP 1,321
Arthur Uther Pendragon, Ind. 581
LD maj. 7,476 (12.12%)
2.08% swing LD to C.
(2001: LD maj. 9,634 (16.29%))

WINDSOR
E. 68,290 T. 43,693 (63.98%) C. hold
*Adam Afriyie, C. 21,646
Antony Wood, LD 11,354
Mark Muller, Lab. 8,339
David Black, UKIP 1,098
Derek Wall, Green 1,074
Peter Hooper, Ind. 182
C. maj. 10,292 (23.56%)
1.22% swing LD to C.
(2001: C. maj. 8,889 (21.11%))

WIRRAL SOUTH
E. 58,834 T. 39,704 (67.48%) Lab. hold
Ben Chapman, Lab. 16,892
Carl Cross, C. 13,168
Simon Holbrook, LD 8,568
David Scott, UKIP 616
Laurence Jones, Ind. 460
Lab. maj. 3,724 (9.38%)
1.65% swing Lab. to C.
(2001: Lab. maj. 5,049 (12.68%))

WIRRAL WEST
E. 61,050 T. 41,233 (67.54%) Lab. hold
Stephen Hesford, Lab. 17,543
Esther McVey, C. 16,446
Jeff Clarke, LD 6,652
John Moore, UKIP 429
Roger Taylor, AP 163
Lab. maj. 1,097 (2.66%)
3.65% swing Lab. to C.
(2001: Lab. maj. 4,035 (9.97%))

WITNEY
E. 78,053 T. 53,869 (69.02%) C. hold
David Cameron, C. 26,571
Liz Leffman, LD 12,415
Tony Gray, Lab. 11,845
Richard Dossett-Davies, Green 1,682
Paul Wesson, UKIP 1,356
C. maj. 14,156 (26.28%)
0.79% swing LD to C.
(2001: C. maj. 7,973 (16.20%))

WOKING
E. 72,676 T. 46,045 (63.36%) C. hold
Humfrey Malins, C. 21,838
Anne Lee, LD 15,226
Ellie Blagbrough, Lab. 7,507
Matthew Davies, UKIP 1,324
Michael Osman, UKC 150
C. maj. 6,612 (14.36%)
0.70% swing C. to LD
(2001: C. maj. 6,759 (15.75%))

WOKINGHAM
E. 68,614 T. 46,072 (67.15%) C. hold
Rt. Hon. John Redwood, C. 22,174
Prue Bray, LD 14,934
David Black, Lab. 6,991
Frank Carstairs, UKIP 994
Top Cat Owen, Loony 569
Richard Colborne, BNP 376
Michael Hall, Tele. 34
C. maj. 7,240 (15.71%)
1.02% swing LD to C.
(2001: C. maj. 5,994 (13.67%))

WOLVERHAMPTON NORTH EAST
E. 60,595 T. 32,956 (54.39%)
Lab. (Co-op) hold
Ken Purchase, Lab. (Co-op) 17,948
Alexandra Robson, C. 9,792
David Jack, LD 3,845
Lydia Simpson, UKIP 1,371
Lab. (Co-op) maj. 8,156 (24.75%)
3.45% swing Lab. (Co-op) to C.
(2001: Lab. (Co-op) maj. 9,965 (31.64%))

WOLVERHAMPTON SOUTH EAST
E. 54,047 T. 28,251 (52.27%) Lab. hold
*Pat McFadden, Lab. 16,790
James Fairbairn, C. 6,295
David Murray, LD 3,682
Kevin Simmons, UKIP 1,484
Lab. maj. 10,495 (37.15%)
4.26% swing Lab. to C.
(2001: Lab. (Co-op) maj. 12,464 (45.66%))

WOLVERHAMPTON SOUTH WEST
E. 67,096 T. 41,679 (62.12%) Lab. hold
Rob Marris, Lab. 18,489
Sandy Verma, C. 15,610
Colin Ross, LD 5,568
Douglas Hope, UKIP 1,029
Edward Mullins, BNP 983
Lab. maj. 2,879 (6.91%)
0.81% swing Lab. to C.
(2001: Lab. maj. 3,487 (8.53%))

WOODSPRING
E. 71,662 T. 51,618 (72.03%) C. hold
Dr Liam Fox, C. 21,587
Mike Bell, LD 15,571
Chanel Stevens, Lab. 11,249
Rebecca Lewis, Green 1,309
Anthony Butcher, UKIP 1,269
Michael Howson, BNP 633
C. maj. 6,016 (11.65%)
3.90% swing C. to LD
(2001: C. maj. 8,798 (18.04%))

WORCESTER
E. 72,384 T. 46,388 (64.09%) Lab. hold
Michael Foster, Lab. 19,421
Margaret Harper, C. 16,277
Mary Dhonau, LD 7,557
Richard Chamings, UKIP 1,113
Martin Roberts, BNP 980
Chris Lennard, Green 921
Prudence Dowson, Ind. 119
Lab. maj. 3,144 (6.78%)
3.13% swing Lab. to C.
(2001: Lab. maj. 5,766 (13.04%))

WORCESTERSHIRE MID
E. 71,546 T. 48,127 (67.27%) C. hold
Peter Luff, C. 24,783
Matt Gregson, Lab. 11,456
Margaret Rowley, LD 9,796
Tony Eaves, UKIP 2,092
C. maj. 13,327 (27.69%)
2.01% swing Lab. to C.
(2001: C. maj. 10,627 (23.67%))

WORCESTERSHIRE WEST
E. 66,999 T. 47,077 (70.27%) C. hold
Sir Michael Spicer, C. 20,959
Tom Wells, LD 18,484
Qamar Bhatti, Lab. 4,945
Caroline Bovey, UKIP 1,590
Malcolm Victory, Green 1,099
C. maj. 2,475 (5.26%)
3.37% swing C. to LD
(2001: C. maj. 5,374 (11.99%))

WORKINGTON
E. 61,441 T. 39,737 (64.68%) Lab. hold
Tony Cunningham, Lab. 19,554
Judith Pattinson, C. 12,659
Kate Clarkson, LD 5,815
Mark Richardson, UKIP 1,328
John Peacock, LCA 381
Lab. maj. 6,895 (17.35%)
4.30% swing Lab. to C.
(2001: Lab. maj. 10,850 (25.94%))

WORSLEY
E. 69,534 T. 36,946 (53.13%) Lab. hold
*Barbara Keeley, Lab. 18,859
Graham Evans, C. 9,491
Richard Clayton, LD 6,902
Bernard Gill, UKIP 1,694
Lab. maj. 9,368 (25.36%)
3.99% swing Lab. to C.
(2001: Lab. maj. 11,787 (33.33%))

WORTHING EAST & SHOREHAM
E. 72,302 T. 44,543 (61.61%) C. hold
Tim Loughton, C. 19,548
Daniel Yates, Lab. 11,365
James Doyle, LD 10,844
Richard Jelf, UKIP 2,109
Chris Baldwin, LCA 677
C. maj. 8,183 (18.37%)
2.06% swing Lab. to C.
(2001: C. maj. 6,139 (14.25%))

WORTHING WEST
E. 71,780 T. 44,941 (62.61%) C. hold
Peter Bottomley, C. 21,383
Claire Potter, LD 12,004
Antony Bignell, Lab. 8,630
Timothy Cross, UKIP 2,374
Chris Baldwin, LCA 550
C. maj. 9,379 (20.87%)
0.02% swing C. to LD
(2001: C. maj. 9,037 (20.91%))

WREKIN, THE
E. 67,291 T. 45,054 (66.95%) C. gain
*Mark Pritchard, C. 18,899
Peter Bradley, Lab. 17,957
Bill Tomlinson, LD 6,608
Bruce Lawson, UKIP 1,590
C. maj. 942 (2.09%)
5.37% swing Lab. to C.
(2001: Lab. maj. 3,587 (8.65%))

WYCOMBE
E. 71,464 T. 44,427 (62.17%) C. hold
Paul Goodman, C. 20,331
Julia Wassell, Lab. 13,280
James Oates, LD 8,780
Robert Davis, UKIP 1,735
David Fitton, Ind. 301
C. maj. 7,051 (15.87%)
4.41% swing Lab. to C.
(2001: C. maj. 3,168 (7.04%))

WYRE FOREST
E. 73,192 T. 46,987 (64.20%)
KHHC hold
Dr Richard Taylor, KHHC 18,739
Mark Garnier, C. 13,489
Marc Bayliss, Lab. 10,716
Fran Oborski, Lib. 2,666
Rustie Lee, UKIP 1,074
Bert Priest, Loony 303
KHHC maj. 5,250 (11.17%)
13.92% swing KHHC to C.
(2001: KHHC maj. 17,630 (35.93%))

WYTHENSHAWE & SALE EAST
E. 71,766 T. 36,184 (50.42%) Lab. hold
Paul Goggins, Lab. 18,878
Jane Meehan, C. 8,051
Alison Firth, LD 7,766
William Ford, UKIP 1,120
Lynn Worthington, Soc. Alt. 369
Lab. maj. 10,827 (29.92%)
3.02% swing Lab. to C.
(2001: Lab. maj. 12,608 (35.97%))

YEOVIL
E. 77,668 T. 49,913 (64.26%) LD hold
David Laws, LD 25,658
Ian Jenkins, C. 17,096
Colin Rolfe, Lab. 5,256
Graham Livings, UKIP 1,903
LD maj. 8,562 (17.15%)
4.50% swing C. to LD
(2001: LD maj. 3,928 (8.16%))

YORK, CITY OF
E. 75,555 T. 46,597 (61.67%) Lab. hold
Hugh Bayley, Lab. 21,836
Clive Booth, C. 11,364
Andrew Waller, LD 10,166
Andy D'Agorne, Green 2,113
Richard Jackson, UKIP 832
Ken Curran, Ind. 121
Damien Fleck, DDTP 93
Andrew Hinkles, Ind. 72
Lab. maj. 10,472 (22.47%)
3.12% swing Lab. to C.
(2001: Lab. maj. 13,779 (28.72%))

YORKSHIRE EAST
E. 76,648 T. 46,925 (61.22%) C. hold
Rt. Hon. Greg Knight, C. 21,215
Emma Hoddinott, Lab. 14,932
Jim Wastling, LD 9,075
Christopher Tresidder, UKIP 1,703
C. maj. 6,283 (13.39%)
1.29% swing Lab. to C.
(2001: C. maj. 4,682 (10.81%))

WALES

ABERAVON
E. 51,080 T. 30,104 (58.94%) Lab. hold
Dr Hywel Francis, Lab. 18,077
Claire Waller, LD 4,140
Philip Evans, PC 3,545
Annunziata Rees-Mogg, C. 3,064
Walter Wright, Veritas 768
Miranda La Vey, Green 510
Lab. maj. 13,937 (46.30%)
3.57% swing Lab. to LD
(2001: Lab. maj. 16,108 (53.36%))

ALYN & DEESIDE
E. 58,939 T. 35,496 (60.22%) Lab. hold
Mark Tami, Lab. 17,331
Lynne Hale, C. 8,953
Paul Brighton, LD 6,174
Richard Coombs, PC 1,320
William Crawford, UKIP 918
Klaus Armstrong-Braun, FWP 378
Judith Kilshaw, Ind. 215
Glyn Davies, Comm Brit 207
Lab. maj. 8,378 (23.60%)
1.22% swing Lab. to C.
(2001: Lab. maj. 9,222 (26.04%))

BLAENAU GWENT
E. 53,301 T. 35,251 (66.14%) Ind. gain
*Peter Law, Ind. 20,505
Maggie Jones, Lab. 11,384
Brian Thomas, LD 1,511
John Price, PC 843
Dr Phillip Lee, C. 816
Peter Osborne, UKIP 192
Ind. maj. 9,121 (25.87%)
43.38% swing Lab. to Ind.
(2001: Lab. maj. 19,313 (60.88%))

BRECON & RADNORSHIRE
E. 55,171 T. 38,341 (69.49%) LD hold
Roger Williams, LD 17,182
Andrew Davies, C. 13,277
Leighton Veale, Lab. 5,755
Mabon ap Gwynfor, PC 1,404
Elizabeth Phillips, UKIP 723
LD maj. 3,905 (10.18%)
4.09% swing C. to LD
(2001: LD maj. 751 (2.00%))

BRIDGEND
E. 63,936 T. 37,859 (59.21%) Lab. hold
*Madeleine Moon, Lab. 16,410
Helen Baker, C. 9,887
Paul Warren, LD 7,949
Gareth Clubb, PC 2,527
Jonathan Spink, Green 595
Kunnathur Rajan, UKIP 491
Lab. maj. 6,523 (17.23%)
4.96% swing Lab. to C.
(2001: Lab. maj. 10,045 (27.15%))

CAERNARFON
E. 46,393 T. 27,999 (60.35%) PC hold
Hywel Williams, PC 12,747
Martin Eaglestone, Lab. 7,538
Melfyn ab Owain, LD 3,508
Guy Opperman, C. 3,483
Elwyn Williams, UKIP 723
PC maj. 5,209 (18.60%)
3.26% swing Lab. to PC
(2001: PC maj. 3,511 (12.08%))

CAERPHILLY
E. 66,939 T. 39,229 (58.60%) Lab. hold
Wayne David, Lab. 22,190
Lindsay Whittle, PC 6,831
Stephen Watson, C. 5,711
Ashgar Ali, LD 3,861
Graeme Beard, FWP 636
Lab. maj. 15,359 (39.15%)
1.00% swing PC to Lab.
(2001: Lab. maj. 14,425 (37.15%))

CARDIFF CENTRAL
E. 61,001 T. 36,132 (59.23%) LD gain
*Jenny Willott, LD 17,991
Jon Owen Jones, Lab. (Co-op) 12,398
Gotz Mohindra, C. 3,339
Richard Grigg, PC 1,271
Raja Gul Raiz, Respect 386
Frank Hughes, UKIP 383
Anne Savoury, Ind. 168
Captain Beany, Bean 159
Catherine Taylor-Dawson, Vote Dream 37
LD maj. 5,593 (15.48%)
8.69% swing Lab. (Co-op) to LD
(2001: Lab. (Co-op) maj. 659 (1.89%))

CARDIFF NORTH
E. 64,341 T. 45,360 (70.50%) Lab. hold
Julie Morgan, Lab. 17,707
Jonathan Morgan, C. 16,561
John Dixon, LD 8,483
John Rowlands, PC 1,936
Don Hulston, UKIP 534
Alison Hobbs, FWP 138
Catherine Taylor-Dawson, Vote Dream 1
Lab. maj. 1,146 (2.53%)
5.87% swing Lab. to C.
(2001: Lab. maj. 6,165 (14.26%))

CARDIFF SOUTH & PENARTH
E. 65,710 T. 36,912 (56.17%) Lab. (Co-op) hold
Rt. Hon. Alun Michael, Lab. (Co-op) 17,447
Victoria Green, C. 8,210
Gavin Cox, LD 7,529
Jason Toby, PC 2,023
John Matthews, Green 729
Jennifer Tuttle, UKIP 522
Dave Bartlett, Soc. Alt. 269
Andrew Taylor, Ind. 104
Catherine Taylor-Dawson, Vote Dream 79
Lab. (Co-op) maj. 9,237 (25.02%)
4.67% swing Lab. (Co-op) to C.
(2001: Lab. (Co-op) maj. 12,287 (34.37%))

CARDIFF WEST
E. 59,847 T. 34,561 (57.75%) Lab. hold
Kevin Brennan, Lab. 15,729
Simon Baker, C. 7,562
Alison Goldsworthy, LD 6,060
Neil McEvoy, PC 4,316
Joe Callan, UKIP 727
Catherine Taylor-Dawson, Vote Dream 167
Lab. maj. 8,167 (23.63%)
4.79% swing Lab. to C.
(2001: Lab. maj. 11,321 (33.22%))

CARMARTHEN EAST & DINEFWR
E. 53,484 T. 38,291 (71.59%) PC hold
Adam Price, PC 17,561
Ross Hendry, Lab. 10,843
Suzy Davies, C. 5,235
Juliana Hughes, LD 3,719
Mike Squires, UKIP 661
Sid Whitworth, LCA 272
PC maj. 6,718 (17.54%)
5.37% swing Lab. to PC
(2001: PC maj. 2,590 (6.81%))

CARMARTHEN WEST & PEMBROKESHIRE SOUTH
E. 56,245 T. 37,863 (67.32%) Lab. hold
Nick Ainger, Lab. 13,953
David Morris, C. 12,043
John Dixon, PC 5,582
John Allen, LD 5,399
Josie MacDonald, UKIP 545
Alex Daszak, LCA 237
Nick Turner, Ind. 104
Lab. maj. 1,910 (5.04%)
3.62% swing Lab. to C.
(2001: Lab. maj. 4,538 (12.29%))

CEREDIGION
E. 53,493 T. 35,947 (67.20%) LD gain
*Mark Williams, LD 13,130
Simon Thomas, PC 12,911
John Harrison, C. 4,455
Alun Davies, Lab. 4,337
Dave Bradney, Green 846
Iain Sheldon, Veritas 268
LD maj. 219 (0.61%)
6.00% swing PC to LD
(2001: PC maj. 3,944 (11.40%))

CLWYD SOUTH
E. 52,353 T. 32,931 (62.90%) Lab. hold
Martyn Jones, Lab. 14,808
Tom Biggins, C. 8,460
Deric Burnham, LD 5,105
Mark Strong, PC 3,111
Alwyn Humphreys, FWP 803
Nick Powell, UKIP 644
Lab. maj. 6,348 (19.28%)
3.64% swing Lab. to C.
(2001: Lab. maj. 8,898 (26.56%))

CLWYD WEST
E. 55,642 T. 35,614 (64.01%) C. gain
*David Jones, C. 12,909
Gareth Thomas, Lab. 12,776
Frank Taylor, LD 4,723
Eilian Williams, PC 3,874
Warwick Nicholson, UKIP 512
Jimmy James, Ind. 507
Patrick Keenan, Soc. Lab. 313
C. maj. 133 (0.37%)
1.80% swing Lab. to C.
(2001: Lab. maj. 1,115 (3.22%))

CONWY
E. 53,987 T. 33,657 (62.34%) Lab. hold
Betty Williams, Lab. 12,479
Guto Bebb, C. 9,398
Gareth Roberts, LD 6,723
Paul Rowlinson, PC 3,730
Jim Killock, Green 512
David Lloyd Jones, Soc. Lab. 324
Kenneth Khambatta, UKIP 298
Tim Evans, LCA 193
Lab. maj. 3,081 (9.15%)
4.47% swing Lab. to C.
(2001: Lab. maj. 6,219 (18.10%))

CYNON VALLEY
E. 45,369 T. 26,647 (58.73%) Lab. hold
Rt. Hon. Ann Clwyd, Lab. 17,074
Geraint Benney, PC 3,815
Margaret Phelps, LD 2,991
Antonia Dunn, C. 2,062
Susan Davies, UKIP 705
Lab. maj. 13,259 (49.76%)
0.77% swing PC to Lab.
(2001: Lab. maj. 12,998 (48.22%))

DELYN
E. 52,766 T. 34,004 (64.44%) Lab. hold
David Hanson, Lab. 15,540
John Bell, C. 8,896
Tudor Jones, LD 6,089
Phil Thomas, PC 2,524
May Crawford, UKIP 533
Nigel Williams, Ind. 422
Lab. maj. 6,644 (19.54%)
2.65% swing Lab. to C.
(2001: Lab. maj. 8,605 (24.84%))

GOWER
E. 60,925 T. 39,542 (64.90%) Lab. hold
Martin Caton, Lab. 16,786
Mike Murray, C. 10,083
Nick Tregoning, LD 7,291
Sian Caiach, PC 3,089
Richard Lewis, UKIP 1,264
Rhodri Griffiths, Green 1,029
Lab. maj. 6,703 (16.95%)
1.42% swing Lab. to C.
(2001: Lab. maj. 7,395 (19.80%))

ISLWYN
E. 50,595 T. 30,865 (61.00%) Lab. (Co-op) hold
Don Touhig, Lab. (Co-op) 19,687
Jim Criddle, PC 3,947
Lee Dillon, LD 3,873
Phillip Howells, C. 3,358
Lab. (Co-op) maj. 15,740 (51.00%)
0.67% swing PC to Lab. (Co-op)
(2001: Lab. (Co-op) maj. 15,309 (48.31%))

LLANELLI
E. 55,678 T. 35,344 (63.48%) Lab. hold
*Nia Griffith, Lab. 16,592
Neil Baker, PC 9,358
Adrian Phillips, C. 4,844
Ken Rees, LD 4,550
Lab. maj. 7,234 (20.47%)
1.39% swing PC to Lab.
(2001: Lab. maj. 6,403 (17.69%))

MEIRIONNYDD NANT CONWY
E. 33,443 T. 20,640 (61.72%) PC hold
Elfyn Llwyd, PC 10,597
Rhodri Jones, Lab. 3,983
Dan Munford, C. 3,402
Adrian Fawcett, LD 2,192
Francis Wykes, UKIP 466
PC maj. 6,614 (32.04%)
2.53% swing Lab. to PC
(2001: PC maj. 5,684 (26.98%))

MERTHYR TYDFIL & RHYMNEY
E. 54,579 T. 29,976 (54.92%) Lab. hold

Dai Havard, Lab.	18,129
Ceirion Rees, LD	4,195
Noel Turner, PC	2,972
Roger Berry, C.	2,680
Neil Greer, FWP	1,030
Gwyn Parry, UKIP	699
Ina Marsden, Soc. Lab.	271

Lab. maj. 13,934 (46.48%)
3.88% swing Lab. to LD
(2001: Lab. maj. 14,923 (47.10%))

MONMOUTH
E. 63,093 T. 45,653 (72.36%) C. gain

*David Davies, C.	21,396
Huw Edwards, Lab.	16,869
Phil Hobson, LD	5,852
Jonathan Clark, PC	993
John Bufton, UKIP	543

C. maj. 4,527 (9.92%)
5.39% swing Lab. to C.
(2001: Lab. maj. 384 (0.86%))

MONTGOMERYSHIRE
E. 46,766 T. 30,097 (64.36%) LD hold

Lembit Opik, LD	15,419
Simon Baynes, C.	8,246
David Tinline, Lab.	3,454
Ellen ap Gwynn, PC	2,078
Clive Easton, UKIP	900

LD maj. 7,173 (23.83%)
1.16% swing C. to LD
(2001: LD maj. 6,234 (21.51%))

NEATH
E. 57,607 T. 35,817 (62.17%) Lab. hold

Rt. Hon. Peter Hain, Lab.	18,835
Geraint Owen, PC	6,125
Sheila Waye, LD	5,112
Harri Lloyd Davies, C.	4,136
Susan Jay, Green	658
Gerry Brienza, Ind.	360
Pat Tabram, LCA	334
Heather Falconer, Respect	257

Lab. maj. 12,710 (35.49%)
3.41% swing Lab. to PC
(2001: Lab. maj. 14,816 (42.31%))

NEWPORT EAST
E. 54,956 T. 31,825 (57.91%) Lab. hold

*Jessica Morden, Lab.	14,389
Ed Townsend, LD	7,551
Matthew Collings, C.	7,459
Mohammad Asghar, PC	1,221
Roger Thomas, UKIP	945
Liz Screen, Soc. Lab.	260

Lab. maj. 6,838 (21.49%)
9.60% swing Lab. to LD
(2001: Lab. maj. 9,874 (31.56%))

NEWPORT WEST
E. 60,287 T. 35,732 (59.27%) Lab. hold

Paul Flynn, Lab.	16,021
Dr William Morgan, C.	10,563
Nigel Flanagan, LD	6,398
Tony Salkeld, PC	1,278
Hugh Moelwyn Hughes, UKIP	848
Peter Varley, Green	540
Saeid Arjomand, Ind.	84

Lab. maj. 5,458 (15.27%)
5.63% swing Lab. to C.
(2001: Lab. maj. 9,304 (26.54%))

OGMORE
E. 52,349 T. 30,278 (57.84%) Lab. hold

Huw Irranca-Davies, Lab.	18,295
Jackie Radford, LD	4,592
Dr Norma Lloyd-Nesling, C.	4,243
John Williams, PC	3,148

Lab. maj. 13,703 (45.26%)
2.01% swing Lab. to LD
(2002 Feb. by-election: Lab maj. 5,721 (31.13%))
(2001: Lab. maj. 14,574 (48.02%))

PONTYPRIDD
E. 65,074 T. 39,634 (60.91%) Lab. hold

Dr Kim Howells, Lab.	20,919
Mike Powell, LD	7,728
Quentin Gwynne Edwards, C.	5,321
Julie Richards, PC	4,420
David Bevan, UKIP	1,013
Robert Griffiths, Comm.	233

Lab. maj. 13,191 (33.28%)
7.91% swing Lab. to LD
(2001: Lab. maj. 17,684 (46.16%))

PRESELI PEMBROKESHIRE
E. 55,502 T. 38,587 (69.52%) C. gain

*Stephen Crabb, C.	14,106
Sue Hayman, Lab.	13,499
Dewi Smith, LD	4,963
Matt Mathias, PC	4,752
James Carver, UKIP	498
Molly Scott-Cato, Green	494
Trish Bowen, Soc. Lab.	275

C. maj. 607 (1.57%)
4.79% swing Lab. to C.
(2001: Lab. maj. 2,946 (8.01%))

RHONDDA
E. 51,041 T. 31,148 (61.03%) Lab. hold

Chris Bryant, Lab.	21,198
Layton Percy Jones, PC	4,956
Karen Roberts, LD	3,264
Paul Stuart-Smith, C.	1,730

Lab. maj. 16,242 (52.14%)
2.48% swing PC to Lab.
(2001: Lab. maj. 16,047 (47.19%))

SWANSEA EAST
E. 58,813 T. 30,834 (52.43%) Lab. hold

*Sian James, Lab.	17,457
Robert Speht, LD	6,208
Ellenor Bland, C.	3,103
Carolyn Shan Couch, PC	2,129
Kevin Holloway, BNP	770
Timothy Jenkins, UKIP	674
Tony Young, Green	493

Lab. maj. 11,249 (36.48%)
9.27% swing Lab. to LD
(2001: Lab. maj. 16,148 (53.70%))

SWANSEA WEST
E. 57,946 T. 33,086 (57.10%) Lab. hold

Rt. Hon. Alan Williams, Lab.	13,833
Rene Kinzett, LD	9,564
Mohammed Abdel-Haq, C.	5,285
Harri Roberts, PC	2,150
Martyn Shrewsbury, Green	738
Martyn Ford, UKIP	609
Yvonne Holley, Veritas	401
Robert Williams, Soc. Alt.	288
Steve Pank, LCA	218

Lab. maj. 4,269 (12.90%)
9.64% swing Lab. to LD
(2001: Lab. maj. 9,550 (29.75%))

TORFAEN
E. 60,669 T. 35,979 (59.30%) Lab. hold

Rt. Hon. Paul Murphy, Lab.	20,472
Nick Ramsay, C.	5,681
Veronica Watkins, LD	5,678
Aneurin Preece, PC	2,242
David Rowlands, UKIP	1,145
Richard Turner-Thomas, Ind.	761

Lab. maj. 14,791 (41.11%)
2.54% swing Lab. to C.
(2001: Lab. maj. 16,280 (46.19%))

VALE OF CLWYD
E. 51,982 T. 32,313 (62.16%) Lab. hold

Christopher Ruane, Lab.	14,875
Felicity Elphick, C.	10,206
Elizabeth Jewkes, LD	3,820
Mark Jones, PC	2,309
Mark Young, Ind.	442
Edna Khambatta, UKIP	375
Jeff Ditchfield, LCA	286

Lab. maj. 4,669 (14.45%)
1.68% swing Lab. to C.
(2001: Lab. maj. 5,761 (17.81%))

VALE OF GLAMORGAN
E. 68,657 T. 47,324 (68.93%) Lab. hold

John Smith, Lab.	19,481
Alun Cairns, C.	17,673
Mark Hooper, LD	6,140
Barry Shaw, PC	2,423
Richard Suchorzewski, UKIP	840
Karl-James Langford, Lib.	605
Paul Mules, Soc. Lab.	162

Lab. maj. 1,808 (3.82%)
3.29% swing Lab. to C.
(2001: Lab. maj. 4,700 (10.40%))

WREXHAM
E. 48,016 T. 30,385 (63.28%) Lab. hold

Ian Lucas, Lab.	13,993
Tom Rippeth, LD	7,174
Dr Therese Coffey, C.	6,079
Sion Owen, PC	1,744
John Walker, BNP	919
Janet Williams, FWP	476

Lab. maj. 6,819 (22.44%)
6.72% swing Lab. to LD
(2001: Lab. maj. 9,188 (30.58%))

YNYS MON
E. 52,512 T. 35,462 (67.53%) Lab. hold

Albert Owen, Lab.	12,278
Eurig Wyn, PC	11,036
Peter Rogers, Ind.	5,216
James Roach, C.	3,915
Sarah Green, LD	2,418
Elaine Gill, UKIP	367
Tim Evans, LCA	232

Lab. maj. 1,242 (3.50%)
0.58% swing PC to Lab.
(2001: Lab. maj. 800 (2.35%))

SCOTLAND

ABERDEEN NORTH
E. 65,714 T. 36,634 (55.75%) Lab. win
Frank Doran, Lab. 15,557
Steve Delaney, LD 8,762
Kevin Stewart, SNP 8,168
David Anderson, C. 3,456
John Connon, SSP 691
Lab. maj. 6,795 (18.55%)
§ 9.25% swing Lab. to LD
(§ 2001 Lab. maj. 9,294 (23.66%))

ABERDEEN SOUTH
E. 67,012 T. 41,621 (62.11%) Lab. win
Anne Begg, Lab. 15,272
Vicki Harris, LD 13,924
Stewart Whyte, C. 7,134
Maureen Watt, SNP 4,120
Rhonda Reekie, Scot. Green 768
Donald Munro, SSP 403
Lab. maj. 1,348 (3.24%)
§ 3.13% swing Lab. to LD
(§ 2001 Lab. maj. 3,931 (9.49%))

ABERDEENSHIRE WEST & KINCARDINE
E. 65,548 T. 41,648 (63.54%) LD win
Sir Robert Smith, LD 19,285
Alex Johnstone, C. 11,814
James Barrowman, Lab. 5,470
Caroline Little, SNP 4,700
Lorna Grant, SSP 379
LD maj. 7,471 (17.94%)
§ 2.25% swing C. to LD
(§ 2001 LD maj. 5,146 (13.44%))

AIRDRIE & SHOTTS
E. 61,955 T. 33,158 (53.52%) Lab. win
Rt. Hon. Dr John Reid, Lab. 19,568
Malcolm Balfour, SNP 5,484
Helen Watt, LD 3,792
Stuart Cottis, C. 3,271
Fraser Coats, SSP 706
Joseph Rowan, Scot. Ind. 337
Lab. maj. 14,084 (42.48%)
§ 1.51% swing SNP to Lab.
(§ 2001 Lab. maj. 13,545 (39.46%))

ANGUS
E. 63,093 T. 38,186 (60.52%) SNP win
Mike Weir, SNP 12,840
Sandy Bushby, C. 11,280
Douglas Bradley, Lab. 6,850
Scott Rennie, LD 6,660
Alan Manley, SSP 556
SNP maj. 1,601 (4.20%)
§ 1.34% swing C. to SNP
(§ 2001 SNP maj. 532 (1.52%))

ARGYLL & BUTE
E. 67,325 T. 43,229 (64.21%) LD win
Alan Reid, LD 15,786
James McGrigor, C. 10,150
Carolyn Manson, Lab. 9,696
Isobel Strong, SNP 6,716
Deirdre Henderson, SSP 881
LD maj. 5,636 (13.04%)
§ 1.94% swing C. to LD
(§ 2001 LD maj. 3,832 (9.16%))

AYR, CARRICK & CUMNOCK
E. 73,448 T. 45,048 (61.33%) Lab. win
Sandra Osborne, Lab. 20,433
Mark Jones, C. 10,436
Colin Waugh, LD 6,341
Charles Brodie, SNP 5,932
Donald Sharp, SSCUP 592
Murray Steele, SSP 554
James McDaid, Soc. Lab. 395
Bryan McCormack, UKIP 365
Lab. maj. 9,997 (22.19%)
§ 2.18% swing Lab. to C.
(§ 2001 Lab. maj. 12,387 (26.56%))

AYRSHIRE CENTRAL
E. 68,643 T. 42,871 (62.46%) Lab. win
Brian Donohoe, Lab. 19,905
Garry Clark, C. 9,482
Iain Kennedy, LD 6,881
Jahangir Hanif, SNP 4,969
Denise Morton, SSP 820
Robert Cochrane, Soc. Lab. 468
Jim Groves, UKIP 346
Lab. maj. 10,423 (24.31%)
§ 0.68% swing C. to Lab.
(§ 2001 Lab. maj. 9,772 (22.96%))

AYRSHIRE NORTH & ARRAN
E. 72,986 T. 44,205 (60.57%) Lab. win
*Katy Clark, Lab. 19,417
Stewart Connell, C. 8,121
Tony Gurney, SNP 7,938
George White, LD 7,264
Colin Turbett, SSP 780
John Pursley, UKIP 382
Louise McDaid, Soc. Lab. 303
Lab. maj. 11,296 (25.55%)
§ 2.68% swing Lab. to C.
(§ 2001 Lab. maj. 12,140 (27.33%))

BANFF & BUCHAN
E. 65,570 T. 37,216 (56.76%) SNP win
Alex Salmond, SNP 19,044
Sandy Wallace, C. 7,207
Eleanor Anderson, LD 4,952
Rami Okasha, Lab. 4,476
Victor Ross, OCV 683
Kathleen Kemp, UKIP 442
Steve Will, SSP 412
SNP maj. 11,837 (31.81%)
§ 2.22% swing C. to SNP
(§ 2001 SNP maj. 9,744 (27.37%))

BERWICKSHIRE, ROXBURGH & SELKIRK
E. 71,702 T. 45,300 (63.30%) LD win
Michael Moore, LD 18,993
John Lamont, C. 13,092
Sam Held, Lab. 7,206
Aileen Orr, SNP 3,885
John Hein, Lib. 916
Graeme McIver, SSP 695
Peter Neilson, UKIP 601
LD maj. 5,901 (13.00%)
§ 5.90% swing LD to C.
(§ 2001 LD maj. 10,770 (24.80%))

CAITHNESS, SUTHERLAND & EASTER ROSS
E. 46,837 T. 27,663 (59.06%) LD win
John Thurso, LD 13,957
Alan Jamieson, Lab. 5,789
Karen Shirron, SNP 3,686
Angus Ross, C. 2,835
Gordon Campbell, Ind. 848
Luke Ivory, SSP 548
LD maj. 8,168 (29.53%)
§ 7.60% swing Lab. to LD
(§ 2001 LD maj. 4,078 (14.33%))

COATBRIDGE, CHRYSTON & BELLSHILL
E. 67,385 T. 38,344 (56.90%) Lab. win
Rt. Hon. Thomas Clarke, Lab. 24,725
Duncan Ross, SNP 5,206
Rodney Ackland, LD 4,605
Lindsay Paterson, C. 2,775
Joan Kinloch, SSP 1,033
Lab. maj. 19,519 (50.90%)
§ 1.82% swing Lab. to SNP
(§ 2001 Lab. maj. 22,092 (54.55%))

CUMBERNAULD, KILSYTH & KIRKINTILLOCH EAST
E. 64,748 T. 39,088 (60.37%) Lab. win
Rosemary McKenna, Lab. 20,251
James Hepburn, SNP 8,689
Hugh O'Donnell, LD 5,817
James Boswell, C. 2,718
Willie O'Neill, SSP 1,141
Patrick Elliott, OCV 472
Lab. maj. 11,562 (29.58%)
§ 1.11% swing Lab. to SNP
(§ 2001 Lab. maj. 12,667 (31.79%))

DUMFRIES & GALLOWAY
E. 74,273 T. 50,891 (68.52%) Lab. win
Russell Brown, Lab. 20,924
Peter Duncan, C. 18,002
Douglas Henderson, SNP 6,182
Keith Legg, LD 4,259
John Schofield, Scot. Green 745
John Dennis, SSP 497
Mark Smith, OCV 282
Lab. maj. 2,922 (5.74%)
§ 2.73% swing C. to Lab.
(§ 2001 Lab. maj. 141 (0.28%))

DUMFRIESSHIRE, CLYDESDALE & TWEEDDALE
E. 66,045 T. 44,616 (67.55%) C. win
*David Mundell, C. 16,141
Sean Marshall, Lab. 14,403
Patsy Kenton, LD 9,046
Andrew Wood, SNP 4,075
Sarah MacTavish, SSP 521
Tony Lee, UKIP 430
C. maj. 1,738 (3.90%)
§ 7.98% swing Lab. to C.
(§ 2001 Lab. maj. 5,254 (12.06%))

DUNBARTONSHIRE EAST
E. 64,763 T. 46,724 (72.15%) LD win
*Jo Swinson, LD 19,533
John Lyons, Lab. 15,472
David Jack, C. 7,708
Chris Sagan, SNP 2,716
Stuart Callison, Scot. Green 876
Pamela Page, SSP 419
LD maj. 4,061 (8.69%)
§ 7.49% swing Lab. to LD
(§ 2001 Lab. maj. 2,601 (6.29%))

DUNBARTONSHIRE WEST
E. 67,805 T. 41,589 (61.34%) Lab. (Co-op) win
Rt. Hon. John McFall, Lab. (Co-op) 21,600
Tom Chalmers, SNP 9,047
Niall Walker, LD 5,999
Campbell Murdoch, C. 2,679
Les Robertson, SSP 1,708
Bryan Maher, UKIP 354
Marlon Dawson, OCV 202
Lab. (Co-op) maj. 12,553 (30.18%)
§ 4.65% swing Lab. (Co-op) to SNP
(§ 2001 Lab. (Co-op) maj. 18,169 (39.49%))

DUNDEE EAST
E. 63,335 T. 39,540 (62.43%) SNP win
*Stewart Hosie, SNP 14,708
Iain Luke, Lab. 14,325
Christopher Bustin, C. 5,061
Clive Sneddon, LD 4,498
Harvey Duke, SSP 537
Donald Low, UKIP 292
David Allison, Ind. 119
SNP maj. 383 (0.97%)
§ 1.13% swing Lab. to SNP
(§ 2001 Lab. maj. 496 (1.29%))

DUNDEE WEST
E. 65,857 T. 36,936 (56.09%) Lab. win
*James McGovern, Lab. 16,468
Joe Fitzpatrick, SNP 11,089
Nykoma Garry, LD 5,323
Christopher McKinlay, C. 3,062
Jim McFarlane, SSP 994
Lab. maj. 5,379 (14.56%)
§ 3.99% swing Lab. to SNP
(§ 2001 Lab. maj. 8,410 (22.54%))

DUNFERMLINE & FIFE WEST
E. 70,775 T. 42,394 (59.90%) Lab. win
Rachel Squire, Lab. 20,111
David Herbert, LD 8,549
Douglas Chapman, SNP 8,026
Roger Smillie, C. 4,376
Susan Archibald, SSP 689
Ian Borland, UKIP 643
Lab. maj. 11,562 (27.27%)
§ 6.47% swing Lab. to LD
(§ 2001 Lab. maj. 14,845 (36.64%))

EAST KILBRIDE, STRATHAVEN & LESMAHAGOW
E. 75,132 T. 47,733 (63.53%) Lab. win
Rt. Hon. Adam Ingram, Lab. 23,264
Douglas Edwards, SNP 8,541
John Oswald, LD 7,904
Tony Lewis, C. 4,776
Kirsten Robb, Scot. Green 1,575
Rose Gentle, Ind. 1,513
John Houston, Ind. 160
Lab. maj. 14,723 (30.84%)
§ 0.78% swing SNP to Lab.
(§ 2001 Lab. maj. 13,999 (29.29%))

EAST LOTHIAN
E. 70,989 T. 45,776 (64.48%) Lab. win
Anne Picking, Lab. 18,983
Chris Butler, LD 11,363
William Stevenson, C. 7,315
Paul McLennan, SNP 5,995
Michael Collie, Scot. Green 1,132
Gary Galbraith, SSP 504
Eric Robb, UKIP 306
William Thompson, OCV 178
Lab. maj. 7,620 (16.65%)
§ 7.54% swing Lab. to LD
(§ 2001 Lab. maj. 14,011 (31.73%))

EDINBURGH EAST
E. 64,826 T. 39,709 (61.25%) Lab. win
Rt. Hon. Gavin Strang, Lab. 15,899
Gordon Mackenzie, LD 9,697
Stefan Tymkewycz, SNP 6,760
Mev Brown, C. 4,093
Cara Gillespie, Scot. Green 2,266
Catriona Grant, SSP 868
Brett Harris, DDTP 89
Peter Clifford, Ind. 37
Lab. maj. 6,202 (15.62%)
§ 8.47% swing Lab. to LD
(§ 2001 Lab. maj. 12,808 (32.56%))

EDINBURGH NORTH & LEITH
E. 68,038 T. 42,640 (62.67%) Lab. (Co-op) win
Mark Lazarowicz, Lab. (Co-op) 14,597
Mike Crockart, LD 12,444
Iain Whyte, C. 7,969
Davie Hutchison, SNP 4,344
Mark Sydenham, Scot. Green 2,482
Bill Scott, SSP 804
Lab. (Co-op) maj. 2,153 (5.05%)
§ 8.26% swing Lab. (Co-op) to LD
(§ 2001 Lab. (Co-op) maj. 8,688 (21.56%))

EDINBURGH SOUTH
E. 60,993 T. 42,698 (70.00%) Lab. win
Nigel Griffiths, Lab. 14,188
Marilyne MacLaren, LD 13,783
Gavin Brown, C. 10,291
Graham Sutherland, SNP 2,635
Dr Steve Burgess, Scot. Green 1,387
Morag Robertson, SSP 414
Lab. maj. 405 (0.95%)
§ 6.50% swing Lab. to LD
(§ 2001 Lab. maj. 5,785 (13.95%))

EDINBURGH SOUTH WEST
E. 67,135 T. 43,926 (65.43%) Lab. win
Rt. Hon. Alistair Darling, Lab. 17,476
Gordon Buchan, C. 10,234
Simon Clark, LD 9,252
Nick Elliott-Cannon, SNP 4,654
John Blair-Fish, Scot. Green 1,520
Pat Smith, SSP 585
William Boys, UKIP 205
Lab. maj. 7,242 (16.49%)
§ 0.71% swing Lab. to C.
(§ 2001 Lab. maj. 7,951 (17.91%))

EDINBURGH WEST
E. 65,741 T. 45,265 (68.85%) LD win
John Barrett, LD 22,417
David Brogan, C. 8,817
Navraj Singh Ghaleigh, Lab. 8,433
Sheena Cleland, SNP 4,124
Ailsa Spindler, Scot. Green 964
Gary Clark, SSP 510
LD maj. 13,600 (30.05%)
§ 6.71% swing C. to LD
(§ 2001 LD maj. 5,320 (11.86%))

FALKIRK
E. 76,784 T. 45,750 (59.58%) Lab. win
Eric Joyce, Lab. 23,264
Laura Love, SNP 9,789
Callum Chomczuk, LD 7,321
David Potts, C. 4,538
Danny Quinlan, SSP 838
Lab. maj. 13,475 (29.45%)
§ 0.36% swing Lab. to SNP
(§ 2001 Lab. maj. 13,555 (30.17%))

FIFE NORTH EAST
E. 62,057 T. 38,556 (62.13%) LD win
Rt. Hon. Sir Menzies Campbell, LD 20,088
Mike Scott-Hayward, C. 7,517
Anthony King, Lab. 4,920
Rod Campbell, SNP 4,011
Jim Park, Scot. Green 1,071
Dr Duncan Pickard, UKIP 533
Jack Ferguson, SSP 416
LD maj. 12,571 (32.60%)
§ 3.20% swing C. to LD
(§ 2001 LD maj. 9,686 (26.20%))

GLASGOW CENTRAL
E. 64,053 T. 28,037 (43.77%) Lab. win
Mohammad Sarwar, Lab. 13,518
Isabel Nelson, LD 4,987
Bill Kidd, SNP 4,148
Richard Sullivan, C. 1,757
Gordon Masterton, Scot. Green 1,372
Marie Gordon, SSP 1,110
Walter Hamilton, BNP 671
Ian Johnson, Soc. Lab. 255
Thomas Greig, OCV 139
Elinor McKenzie, Comm. Brit. 80
Lab. maj. 8,531 (30.43%)
§ 7.36% swing Lab. to LD
(§ 2001 Lab. maj. 9,382 (33.82%))

GLASGOW EAST
E. 64,130 T. 30,939 (48.24%) Lab. win
David Marshall, Lab. 18,775
Lachlan McNeill, SNP 5,268
David Jackson, LD 3,665
Carl Thomson, C. 2,135
George Savage, SSP 1,096
Lab. maj. 13,507 (43.66%)
§ 1.48% swing Lab. to SNP
(§ 2001 Lab. maj. 15,238 (46.62%))

GLASGOW NORTH
E. 55,419 T. 27,921 (50.38%) Lab. win
Ann McKechin, Lab. 11,001
Amy Rodger, LD 7,663
Kenneth McLean, SNP 3,614
Brian Pope, C. 2,441
Martin Bartos, Scot. Green 2,135
Nick Tarlton, SSP 1,067
Lab. maj. 3,338 (11.96%)
§ 8.70% swing Lab. to LD
(§ 2001 Lab. maj. 8,023 (29.36%))

GLASGOW NORTH EAST
E. 62,042 T. 28,418 (45.80%) Speaker win
Rt. Hon. Michael Martin, Speaker 15,153
John McLaughlin, SNP 5,019
Doris Kelly, Soc. Lab. 4,036
Graham Campbell, SSP 1,402
Daniel Houston, Scot. U. 1,266
Scott McLean, BNP 920
Joe Chambers, Ind. 622
Speaker maj. 10,134 (35.66%)
§ 6.62% swing Speaker to SNP
(§ 2001 Speaker maj. 15,203 (48.90%))

GLASGOW NORTH WEST
E. 61,880 T. 34,061 (55.04%) Lab. win
John Robertson, Lab. 16,748
Paul Graham, LD 6,655
Graeme Hendry, SNP 4,676
Murray Roxburgh, C. 3,262
Martha Wardrop, Scot. Green 1,333
Anthea Irwin, SSP 1,108
Colin Muir, Soc. Lab. 279
Lab. maj. 10,093 (29.63%)
§ 6.80% swing Lab. to LD
(§ 2001 Lab. maj. 13,231 (38.83%))

GLASGOW SOUTH
E. 68,837 T. 38,431 (55.83%) Lab. win
Tom Harris, Lab. 18,153
Arthur Sanderson, LD 7,321
Finlay MacLean, SNP 4,860
Dr Janette McAlpine, C. 4,836
Kay Allan, Scot. Green 1,692
Ronnie Stevenson, SSP 1,303
Dorothy Entwistle, Soc. Lab. 266
Lab. maj. 10,832 (28.19%)
§ 4.93% swing Lab. to LD
(§ 2001 Lab. maj. 13,042 (33.15%))

GLASGOW SOUTH WEST
E. 62,005 T. 30,977 (49.96%) Lab. (Co-op) win
Ian Davidson, Lab. (Co-op) 18,653
James Dornan, SNP 4,757
Katy Gordon, LD 3,593
Scott Brady, C. 1,786
Keith Baldassara, SSP 1,666
Alistair McConnachie, Ind. Green 379
Violet Shaw, Soc. Lab. 143
Lab. (Co-op) maj. 13,896 (44.86%)
§ 0.22% swing SNP to Lab. (Co-op)
(§ 2001 Lab. (Co-op) maj. 14,687 (44.42%))

GLENROTHES
E. 66,563 T. 37,366 (56.14%) Lab. win
John MacDougall, Lab. 19,395
John Beare, SNP 8,731
Elizabeth Riches, LD 4,728
Belinda Don, C. 2,651
George Rodger, PPS 716
Morag Balfour, SSP 705
Paul Smith, UKIP 440
Lab. maj. 10,664 (28.54%)
§ 2.71% swing Lab. to SNP
(§ 2001 Lab. maj. 12,988 (33.95%))

GORDON
E. 71,925 T. 44,438 (61.78%) LD win
Malcolm Bruce, LD 20,008
Iain Brotchie, Lab. 8,982
Philip Atkinson, C. 7,842
Joanna Strathdee, SNP 7,098
Tommy Paterson, SSP 508
LD maj. 11,026 (24.81%)
§ 3.73% swing Lab. to LD
(§ 2001 LD maj. 6,845 (17.36%))

INVERCLYDE
E. 59,291 T. 36,098 (60.88%) Lab. win
David Cairns, Lab. 18,318
Stuart McMillan, SNP 7,059
Douglas Herbison, LD 6,123
Gordon Fraser, C. 3,692
David Landels, SSP 906
Lab. maj. 11,259 (31.19%)
§ 2.51% swing Lab. to SNP
(§ 2001 Lab. maj. 11,314 (29.06%))

INVERNESS, NAIRN, BADENOCH & STRATHSPEY
E. 69,636 T. 44,255 (63.55%) LD win
*Danny Alexander, LD 17,830
David Stewart, Lab. 13,682
David Thompson, SNP 5,992
Robert Rowantree, C. 4,579
Donnie MacLeod, Scot. Green 1,065
Donald Lawson, Publican 678
George MacDonald, SSP 429
LD maj. 4,148 (9.37%)
§ 6.01% swing Lab. to LD
(§ 2001 Lab. maj. 1,134 (2.65%))

KILMARNOCK & LOUDOUN
E. 72,851 T. 44,383 (60.92%) Lab. win
Rt. Hon. Desmond Browne, Lab. 20,976
Daniel Coffey, SNP 12,273
Gary Smith, C. 5,026
Kevin Lang, LD 4,945
Hugh Kerr, SSP 833
Ronnie Robertson, UKIP 330
Lab. maj. 8,703 (19.61%)
§ 5.45% swing Lab. to SNP
(§ 2001 Lab. maj. 13,621 (30.51%))

KIRKCALDY & COWDENBEATH
E. 71,606 T. 41,796 (58.37%) Lab. win
Rt. Hon. Gordon Brown, Lab. 24,278
Alan Bath, SNP 6,062
Alex Cole-Hamilton, LD 5,450
Stuart Randall, C. 4,308
Steve West, SSP 666
Peter Adams, UKIP 516
James Parker, Scot. Senior 425
Elizabeth Kwantes, Ind. 47
Pat Sargent, Ind. 44
Lab. maj. 18,216 (43.58%)
§ 1.84% swing SNP to Lab.
(§ 2001 Lab. maj. 16,238 (39.91%))

LANARK & HAMILTON EAST
E. 73,736 T. 43,589 (59.11%) Lab. win
Jimmy Hood, Lab. 20,072
Fraser Grieve, LD 8,125
John Wilson, SNP 7,746
Robert Pettigrew, C. 5,576
Dennis Reilly, SSP 802
Donald Mackay, UKIP 437
Duncan McFarlane, Ind. 416
Robin Mawhinney, OCV 415
Lab. maj. 11,947 (27.41%)
§ 5.89% swing Lab. to LD
(§ 2001 Lab. maj. 12,861 (28.59%))

LINLITHGOW & FALKIRK EAST
E. 76,739 T. 46,389 (60.45%) Lab. win
Michael Connarty, Lab. 22,121
Gordon Guthrie, SNP 10,919
Stephen Glenn, LD 7,100
Michael Veitch, C. 5,486
Ally Hendry, SSP 763
Lab. maj. 11,202 (24.15%)
§ 1.16% swing Lab. to SNP
(§ 2001 Lab. maj. 11,796 (26.46%))

LIVINGSTON
E. 76,353 T. 44,337 (58.07%) Lab. win
Rt. Hon. Robin Cook, Lab. 22,657
Angela Constance, SNP 9,560
Charles Dundas, LD 6,832
Alison Ross, C. 4,499
Steven Nimmo, SSP 789
Lab. maj. 13,097 (29.54%)
§ 1.17% swing Lab. to SNP
(§ 2001 Lab. maj. 13,638 (31.88%))

MIDLOTHIAN
E. 60,644 T. 37,704 (62.17%) Lab. win
David Hamilton, Lab. 17,153
Fred Mackintosh, LD 9,888
Colin Beattie, SNP 6,400
Iain McGill, C. 3,537
Norman Gilfillan, SSP 726
Lab. maj. 7,265 (19.27%)
§ 6.98% swing Lab. to LD
(§ 2001 Lab. maj. 12,017 (31.29%))

MORAY
E. 66,463 T. 38,793 (58.37%) SNP win
Angus Robertson, SNP 14,196
Jamie Halcro-Johnston, C. 8,520
Kevin Hutchens, Lab. 7,919
Linda Gorn, LD 7,460
Norma Anderson, SSP 698
SNP maj. 5,676 (14.63%)
§ 4.07% swing C. to SNP
(§ 2001 SNP maj. 1,852 (5.06%))

MOTHERWELL & WISHAW
E. 66,987 T. 37,109 (55.40%) Lab. win
Frank Roy, Lab. 21,327
Ian MacQuarrie, SNP 6,105
Conor Snowden, LD 4,464
Peter Finnie, C. 3,440
Gregor MacEwan, SSP 1,019
Dallas Carter, Free Scot. 384
Coral Thompson, OCV 370
Lab. maj. 15,222 (41.02%)
§ 2.35% swing SNP to Lab.
(§ 2001 Lab. maj. 13,778 (36.33%))

NA H-EILEANAN AN IAR
E. 21,576 T. 13,836 (64.13%) SNP gain
*Angus MacNeil, SNP 6,213
Calum MacDonald, Lab. 4,772
Dr Jean Davis, LD 1,096
James Hargreaves, OCV 1,048
Andy Maciver, C. 610
Joanne Telfer, SSP 97
SNP maj. 1,441 (10.41%)
9.29% swing Lab. to SNP
(2001: Lab. maj. 1,074 (8.16%))

OCHIL & PERTHSHIRE SOUTH
E. 70,731 T. 46,697 (66.02%) Lab. win
*Gordon Banks, Lab. 14,645
Annabelle Ewing, SNP 13,957
Elizabeth Smith, C. 10,021
Catherine Whittingham, LD 6,218
George Baxter, Scot. Green 978
Iain Campbell, SSP 420
David Bushby, UKIP 275
Maitland Kelly, Free Scot. 183
Lab. maj. 688 (1.47%)
§ 0.18% swing Lab. to SNP
(§ 2001 Lab. maj. 821 (1.83%))

ORKNEY & SHETLAND
E. 33,048 T. 17,742 (53.69%) LD hold
Alistair Carmichael, LD 9,138
Richard Meade, Lab. 2,511
Frank Nairn, C. 2,357
John Mowat, SNP 1,833
John Aberdein, SSP 992
Scott Dyble, UKIP 424
Paul Cruickshank, LCA 311
Brian Nugent, Free Scot. 176
LD maj. 6,627 (37.35%)
8.29% swing Lab. to LD
(2001: LD maj. 3,475 (20.77%))

PAISLEY & RENFREWSHIRE NORTH
E. 63,076 T. 40,885 (64.82%) Lab. win
James Sheridan, Lab. 18,697
Bill Wilson, SNP 7,696
Lewis Hutton, LD 7,464
Philip Lardner, C. 5,566
Angela McGregor, SSP 646
Katharine McGavigan, Soc. Lab. 444
John Pearson, UKIP 372
Lab. maj. 11,001 (26.91%)
§ 1.34% swing Lab. to SNP
(§ 2001 Lab. maj. 12,417 (29.58%))

PAISLEY & RENFREWSHIRE SOUTH
E. 60,181 T. 37,860 (62.91%) Lab. win
Douglas Alexander, Lab. 19,904
Eileen McCartin, LD 6,672
Andrew Doig, SNP 6,653
Thomas Begg, C. 3,188
Iain Hogg, SSP 789
Gordon Matthew, Paisley 381
Robert Rodgers, Ind. 166
Howard Broadbent, Soc. Lab. 107
Lab. maj. 13,232 (34.95%)
§ 6.24% swing Lab. to LD
(§ 2001 Lab. maj. 13,968 (36.10%))

PERTH & PERTHSHIRE NORTH
E. 70,895 T. 45,930 (64.79%) SNP win
Peter Wishart, SNP 15,469
Douglas Taylor, C. 13,948
Doug Maughan, Lab. 8,601
Gordon Campbell, LD 7,403
Philip Stott, SSP 509
SNP maj. 1,521 (3.31%)
§ 3.85% swing SNP to C.
(§ 2001 SNP maj. 5,020 (11.01%))

RENFREWSHIRE EAST
E. 65,714 T. 47,405 (72.14%) Lab. hold
Jim Murphy, Lab. 20,815
Richard Cook, C. 14,158
Dr Gordon Macdonald, LD 8,659
Osama Bhutta, SNP 3,245
Ian Henderson, SSP 528
Lab. maj. 6,657 (14.04%)
2.43% swing Lab. to C.
(2001: Lab. maj. 9,141 (18.90%))

ROSS, SKYE & LOCHABER
E. 50,507 T. 32,538 (64.42%) LD win
Rt. Hon. Charles Kennedy, LD 19,100
Christine Conniff, Lab. 4,851
John Hodgson, C. 3,275
Mhairi Will, SNP 3,119
David Jardine, Scot. Green 1,097
Phillip Anderson, UKIP 500
Anne Macleod, SSP 412
Morris Grant, Ind. 184
LD maj. 14,249 (43.79%)
§ 11.27% swing Lab. to LD
(§ 2001 LD maj. 6,567 (21.26%))

RUTHERGLEN & HAMILTON WEST
E. 73,998 T. 43,261 (58.46%)
Lab. (Co-op) win
Rt. Hon. Thomas McAvoy, Lab. (Co-op) 24,054
Ian Robertson, LD 7,942
Margaret Park, SNP 6,023
Peter Crerar, C. 3,621
Bill Bonnar, SSP 1,164
Janice Murdoch, UKIP 457
Lab. (Co-op) maj. 16,112 (37.24%)
§ 5.37% swing Lab. (Co-op) to LD
(§ 2001 Lab. (Co-op) maj. 18,504 (44.42%))

STIRLING
E. 64,554 T. 43,691 (67.68%) Lab. win
Anne McGuire, Lab. 15,729
Stephen Kerr, C. 10,962
Kelvin Holdsworth, LD 9,052
Frances McGlinchey, SNP 5,503
Duncan Illingworth, Scot. Green 1,302
Rowland Sheret, SSP 458
James McDonald, Ind. 261
Michael Willis, OCV 215
Matthew Desmond, UKIP 209
Lab. maj. 4,767 (10.91%)
§ 4.18% swing Lab. to C.
(§ 2001 Lab. maj. 8,303 (19.28%))

NORTHERN IRELAND

ANTRIM EAST
E. 58,335 T. 31,767 (54.46%)
DUP gain
*Sammy Wilson, DUP 15,766
Roy Beggs, UUP 8,462
Sean Neeson, Alliance 4,869
Danny O'Connor, SDLP 1,695
James McKeown, SF 828
David Kerr, Vote Dream 147
DUP maj. 7,304 (22.99%)
11.67% swing UUP to DUP
(2001: UUP maj. 128 (0.36%))

ANTRIM NORTH
E. 74,450 T. 45,926 (61.69%)
DUP hold
Revd Ian Paisley, DUP 25,156
Philip McGuigan, SF 7,191
Rodney McCune, UUP 6,637
Sean Farren, SDLP 5,585
Jayne Dunlop, Alliance 1,357
DUP maj. 17,965 (39.12%)
0.47% swing DUP to SF
(2001: DUP maj. 14,224 (28.90%))

ANTRIM SOUTH
E. 66,931 T. 37,957 (56.71%)
DUP gain
†Revd William McCrea, DUP 14,507
David Burnside, UUP 11,059
Noreen McClelland, SDLP 4,706
Henry Cushinan, SF 4,407
David Ford, Alliance 3,278
DUP maj. 3,448 (9.08%)
5.69% swing UUP to DUP
(2001: UUP maj. 1,011 (2.29%))

BELFAST EAST
E. 53,176 T. 30,831 (57.98%)
DUP hold
Peter Robinson, DUP 15,152
Sir Reg Empey, UUP 9,275
Naomi Long, Alliance 3,746
Deborah Devenny, SF 1,029
Mary Muldoon, SDLP 844
Alan Greer, C. 434
Joe Bell, WP 179
Lynda Gilby, Vote Dream 172
DUP maj. 5,877 (19.06%)
0.13% swing DUP to UUP
(2001: DUP maj. 7,117 (19.32%))

BELFAST NORTH
E. 52,853 T. 30,540 (57.78%)
DUP hold
Nigel Dodds, DUP 13,935
Gerry Kelly, SF 8,747
Alban Maginness, SDLP 4,950
Fred Cobain, UUP 2,154
Marjorie Hawkins, Alliance 438
Marcella Delaney, WP 165
Lynda Gilby, Vote Dream 151
DUP maj. 5,188 (16.99%)
0.69% swing SF to DUP
(2001: DUP maj. 6,387 (15.60%))

BELFAST SOUTH
E. 52,668 T. 32,028 (60.81%)
SDLP gain
*Dr Alasdair McDonnell, SDLP 10,339
James Spratt, DUP 9,104
Michael McGimpsey, UUP 7,263
Alex Maskey, SF 2,882
Geraldine Rice, Alliance 2,012
Lynda Gilby, Vote Dream 235
Paddy Lynn, WP 193
SDLP maj. 1,235 (3.86%)
11.91% swing UUP to SDLP
(2001: UUP maj. 5,399 (14.23%))

BELFAST WEST
E. 53,831 T. 34,545 (64.17%) SF hold
Gerry Adams, SF 24,348
Alex Attwood, SDLP 5,033
Diane Dodds, DUP 3,652
Chris McGimpsey, UUP 779
John Lowry, WP 432
Lynda Gilby, Vote Dream 154
Liam Kennedy, Ind. 147
SF maj. 19,315 (55.91%)
4.36% swing SDLP to SF
(2001: SF maj. 19,342 (47.20%))

DOWN NORTH
E. 59,748 T. 32,290 (54.04%)
UUP hold

Lady Sylvia Hermon, UUP	16,268
Peter Weir, DUP	11,324
David Alderdice, Alliance	2,451
Liam Logan, SDLP	1,009
Julian Robertson, C.	822
Christopher Carter, Ind.	211
Janet McCrory, SF	205

UUP maj. 4,944 (15.31%)
20.35% swing UUP to DUP
(2001: UUP maj. 7,324 (19.69%))

DOWN SOUTH
E. 73,668 T. 48,177 (65.40%)
SDLP hold

Edward McGrady, SDLP	21,557
Caitriona Ruane, SF	12,417
Jim Wells, DUP	8,815
Dermot Nesbitt, UUP	4,775
Julian Crozier, Alliance	613

SDLP maj. 9,140 (18.97%)
3.82% swing SDLP to SF
(2001: SDLP maj. 13,858 (26.61%))

FERMANAGH & SOUTH TYRONE
E. 67,174 T. 48,793 (72.64%) SF hold

Michelle Gildernew, SF	18,638
Arlene Foster, DUP	14,056
Tom Elliott, UUP	8,869
Tommy Gallagher, SDLP	7,230

SF maj. 4,582 (9.39%)
12.35% swing SF to DUP
(2001: SF maj. 53 (0.10%))

FOYLE
E. 69,207 T. 45,609 (65.90%)
SDLP hold

*Mark Durkan, SDLP	21,119
Mitchel McLaughlin, SF	15,162
William Hay, DUP	6,557
Eammon McCann, Soc EA	1,649
Earl Storey, UUP	1,091
Ben Reel, Vote Dream	31

SDLP maj. 5,957 (13.06%)
5.28% swing SDLP to SF
(2001: SDLP maj. 11,550 (23.63%))

LAGAN VALLEY
E. 70,742 T. 42,572 (60.18%)
DUP gain

‡Jeffrey Donaldson, DUP	23,289
Basil McCrea, UUP	9,172
Seamus Close, Alliance	4,316
Paul Butler, SF	3,197
Patricia Lewsley, SDLP	2,598

DUP maj. 14,117 (33.16%)
38.13% swing UUP to DUP
(2001: UUP maj. 18,342 (39.93%))

LONDONDERRY EAST
E. 58,861 T. 35,504 (60.32%)
DUP hold

Gregory Campbell, DUP	15,225
David McClarty, UUP	7,498
John Dallat, SDLP	6,077
Billy Leonard, SF	5,709
Yvonne Boyle, Alliance	924
Malcolm Samuel, Ind.	71

DUP maj. 7,727 (21.76%)
8.50% swing UUP to DUP
(2001: DUP maj. 1,901 (4.77%))

NEWRY & ARMAGH
E. 72,448 T. 50,696 (69.98%) SF gain

*Conor Murphy, SF	20,965
Dominic Bradley, SDLP	12,770
Paul Berry, DUP	9,311
Danny Kennedy, UUP	7,025
Gerry Markey, Ind.	625

SF maj. 8,195 (16.16%)
11.30% swing SDLP to SF
(2001: SDLP maj. 3,575 (6.43%))

STRANGFORD
E. 69,040 T. 37,032 (53.64%)
DUP hold

Iris Robinson, DUP	20,921
Gareth McGimpsey, UUP	7,872
Kieran McCarthy, Alliance	3,332
Joe Boyle, SDLP	2,496
Terry Dick, C.	1,462
Dermot Kennedy, SF	949

DUP maj. 13,049 (35.24%)
16.34% swing UUP to DUP
(2001: DUP maj. 1,110 (2.57%))

TYRONE WEST
E. 60,286 T. 43,487 (72.13%) SF hold

Pat Doherty, SF	16,910
Dr Kieran Deeny, Ind.	11,905
Thomas Buchanan, DUP	7,742
Eugene McMenamin, SDLP	3,949
Derek Hussey, UUP	2,981

SF maj. 5,005 (11.51%)
14.65% swing SF to Ind.
(2001: SF maj. 5,040 (10.39%))

ULSTER MID
E. 62,666 T. 45,426 (72.49%) SF hold

Martin McGuinness, SF	21,641
Ian McCrea, DUP	10,665
Patsy McGlone, SDLP	7,922
Billy Armstrong, UUP	4,853
Francis Donnelly, WP	345

SF maj. 10,976 (24.16%)
2.12% swing DUP to SF
(2001: SF maj. 9,953 (19.93%))

UPPER BANN
E. 72,402 T. 44,422 (61.35%)
DUP gain

*David Simpson, DUP	16,679
David Trimble, UUP	11,381
John O'Dowd, SF	9,305
Dolores Kelly, SDLP	5,747
Alan Castle, Alliance	955
Tom French, WP	355

DUP maj. 5,298 (11.93%)
7.98% swing UUP to DUP
(2001: UUP maj. 2,058 (4.03%))

BY-ELECTIONS 2005–9

Abbreviations of parties standing in the 2005–9 by-elections (*see also* General Election Results):

Com.	The Common Good
FPP	The Fur Play Party
Honest	Put An Honest Man Into Parliament
Libertarian	Libertarian Party
MGB	Independent (Miss Great Britain) Party
Money	Money Reform Party
NOTA	None of the Above Party
SCP	Scottish Christian Party (formerly Operation Christian Vote)
SPGB	Socialist Party of Great Britain
Tolls	Abolish Forth Bridge Tolls Party

BLAENAU GWENT
29 June 2006
E. 52,508 T. 27,165 (51.73%) Ind. hold

*Dai Davis, Ind.	12,543
Owen Smith, Lab.	10,059
Steffan Lewis, PC	1,755
Amy Kitcher, LD	1,477
Margrit Williams, C.	1,013
Alan Hope, Loony	318

Ind maj. 2,484 (9.14%)
8.37% swing Ind. to Lab.
(2005: Ind. maj. 9,121 (25.81%))

BROMLEY & CHISLEHURST
29 June 2006
E. 71,818 T. 29,052 (40.45%) C. hold

*Bob Neill, C.	11,621
Ben Abbotts, LD	10,988
Nigel Farage, UKIP	2,347
Rachel Reeves, Lab.	1,925
Anne Garrett, Green	811
Paul Winnett, NF	476
John Hemming-Clarke, Ind.	442
Stevens Uncles, Eng. Dem.	212
John Cartwright, Loony	132
Nick Hadziannis, Ind.	65
Anne Belsey, Money	33

C. maj. 633 (2.18%)
14.32% swing C. to LD
(2005: C. maj. 13,342 (28.92%))

CHEADLE
14 July 2005
E. 68,051 T. 37,567 (55.20%) LD hold

*Mark Hunter, LD	19,593
Stephen Day, C.	15,936
Martin Miller, Lab.	1,739
Leslie Leggett, Veritas	218
John Allman, AFC	81

LD maj. 3,657 (9.73%)
0.63% swing C. to LD
(2005: LD maj. 4,020 (8.47%))

CREWE & NANTWICH
22 May 2008
E. 71,963 T. 41,856 (58.16%) C. gain

Edward Timpson, C.	20,539
Tamsin Dunwoody, Lab.	12,679
Elizabeth Shenton, LD	6,040
Mike Nattrass, UKIP	922
Robert Smith, Green	359
David Roberts, Eng. Dem.	275
The Flying Brick, Loony	236
Mark Walklate, Ind.	217
Paul Thorogood, Cut Tax	118
Gemma Garrett, MGB	113

C. maj. 7,860 (18.9%)
17.6% swing Lab. to C.
(2005: Lab maj. 7,078 (16.28%))

DUNFERMLINE & FIFE WEST
9 February 2006
E. 71,017 T. 34,578 (48.69%) LD gain

*Willie Rennie, LD	12,391
Catherine Stihler, Lab.	10,591
Douglas Chapman, SNP	7,261
Carrie Ruxton, C.	2,702
John McAllion, SSP	537
James Hargreaves, SCP	411
Thomas Minogue, Tolls	374
Ian Borland, UKIP	208
Dick Rodgers, Good	103

LD maj. 1,800 (5.21%)
16.24% swing Lab. to LD
(2005: Lab maj. 11,562 (27.27%))

EALING SOUTHALL
19 July 2007
E. 85,423 T. 36,618 (42.87%) Lab. hold

*Virendra Sharma, Lab.	15,188
Nigel Bakhai, LD	10,118
Tony Lit, C.	8,230
Sarah Edwards, Green	1,135
Salvinder Dhillon, Respect	588
Dr Kunnathur Rajan, UKIP	285
Yaqub Masih, Christian Party	280
Jasdev Rai, Ind.	275
John Cartwright, Loony	188
Sati Chaggar, Eng. Dem.	152
Gulbash Singh, Ind.	92
Kuldeep Grewal, Ind.	87

Lab. maj. 5,070 (13.85%)
5.24% swing Lab. to LD
(2005: Lab. maj. 11,440 (24.32%))

GLASGOW EAST
24 July 2008
E. 62,051 T. 26,174 (42.18%) SNP gain

John Mason, SNP	11,277
Margaret Curran, Lab.	10,912
Davena Rankin, C.	1,639
Ian Robertson, LD	915
Frances Curran, SSP	555
Tricia McLeish, Solidarity	512
Eileen Duke, Green	232
Chris Creighton, Ind.	67
Hamish Howett, Choice	65

SNP maj. 365 (1.39%)
22.53% swing Lab. to SNP
(2005: Lab. maj. 13,507 (43.66%))

GLENROTHES
6 November 2008
E. 69,155 T. 36,195 (52.34%) Lab. hold

Lindsay Roy, Lab.	19,946
Peter Grant, SNP	13,209
Maurice Golden, C.	1,381
Harry Wills, LD	947
Jim Parker, SSCUP	296
Morag Balfour, SSP	212
Kris Seunarine, UKIP	117
Louise McLeary, Solidarity	87

4.96% swing Lab. to SNP
(2005: Lab. maj. 10,664 (28.54%))

HALTEMPRICE AND HOWDEN*
10 July 2008
E. 70,266 T. 23,911 (34.03%) C. hold

David Davis, C.	17,113
Shan Oakes, Green	1,758
Joanne Robinson, Eng. Dem.	1,714
Tess Culnane, NF	544
Gemma Garrett, MGB	521
Jill Saward, Ind.	492
Mad Cow-Girl, Loony	412
Walter Sweeney, Ind.	238
David Craig, Ind.	135
David Pinder, New Party	135
David Icke, ND	110

C. maj. 15,355 (64.22%)
(2005 election, C. maj. 5,116 (10.65%))
* candidates that received less than 100 votes have not been included

HENLEY
26 June 2008
E. 69,086 T. 34,761 (50.32%) C. hold

John Howell, C.	19,796
Stephen Kearney, LD	9,690
Mark Stevenson, Green	1,321
Timothy Rait, BNP	1,243
Richard McKenzie, Lab.	1,066
Chris Adams, UKIP	843
Bananaman Owen, Loony	242
Derek Allpass, Eng. Dem.	157
Amanda Harrington, MGB	128
Dick Rodgers, Com.	121
Louise Cole, MGB	91
Harry Bear, FPP	73

C. maj. 10,116 (56.95%)
0.81% swing LD to C.
(2005: C. maj. 12,793 (27.49%))

LIVINGSTON
29 September 2005
E. 76,376 T. 29,477 (38.59%) Lab. hold

*Jim Devine, Lab.	12,319
Angela Constance, SNP	9,639
Charles Dundas, LD	4,362
Gordon Lindhurst, C.	1,993
David Robertson, Green	529
Steven Nimmo, SSP	407
Peter Adams, UKIP	108
Melville Brown, Ind.	55
John Allman, AFC	33
Brian Gardner, SPGB	32

Lab. maj. 2,680 (9.09%)
10.22% swing Lab. to SNP
(2005: Lab. maj. 13,097 (29.54%))

NORWICH NORTH
23 July 2009

E. 75,124 T. 34,377 (46.76%)	C. gain
Chloe Smith, C.	13,591
Chris Ostrowski, Lab.	6,243
April Pond, LD	4,803
Glenn Tingle, UKIP	4,068
Rupert Read, Green	3,350
Craig Murray, Honest	953
Robert West, BNP	941
Bill Holden, Ind.	166
Howling Laud, Loony	144
Anne Fryatt, NOTA	59
Thomas Burridge, Libertarian	36
Peter Baggs, Ind.	23

C. maj. 7,348 (21.37%)
16.49% swing Lab. to C.
(2005: Lab. maj. 5,459 (11.61%))

SEDGEFIELD
19 July 2007

E. 67,339 T. 27,980 (41.55%)	Lab. hold
*Phil Wilson, Lab.	12,528
Greg Stone, LD	5,572
Graham Robb, C.	4,082
Andrew Spence, BNP	2,494
Paul Gittins, Ind.	1,885
Toby Horton, UKIP	536
Chris Haine, Green	348
Stephen Gash, Eng. Dem.	177
Tim Grainger, Christian Party	177
Alan Hope, Loony	129
Norman Scarth, Anti-Crime Party	34

Lab. maj. 6,956 (24.86%)
11.06% swing Lab. to LD
(2005: Lab. maj. 18,457 (44.49%))

STAFFORDSHIRE SOUTH
23 June 2005

E. 68,763 T. 25,635 (37.28%)	C. hold
Sir Patrick Cormack, C.	13,343
Paul Kalinauckas, Lab.	4,496
Jo Crotty, LD	3,540
Malcolm Hurst, UKIP	2,675
Garry Bushell, Eng. Dem.	643
Kate Spohrer, Green	437
Adrian Davies, FP	434
The Revd David Braid, Clause 28	67

C. maj. 8,847 (34.51%)
9.10% swing Lab. to C.
(2001: C. maj. 6,881 (16.31%))

THE GOVERNMENT

as at 1 September 2009

THE CABINET

Prime Minister, First Lord of the Treasury and Minister for the Civil Service
Rt. Hon. Gordon Brown, MP (since June 2007)
Chancellor of the Exchequer
Rt. Hon. Alistair Darling, MP (since June 2007)
Chief Secretary to the Treasury
Rt. Hon. Liam Byrne, MP (since June 2009)
Leader of the House of Commons and Lord Privy Seal, Deputy Leader and Chair of the Labour Party, and Minister for Women and Equalities
Rt. Hon. Harriet Harman, QC, MP (since June 2007)
Leader of the House of Lords (since October 2008) *and Chancellor of the Duchy of Lancaster* (since June 2009)
Rt. Hon. Baroness Royall of Blaisdon
Minister for the Cabinet Office (since June 2009), *Minister for the Olympics and Paymaster General* (since June 2007)
Rt. Hon. Tessa Jowell, MP
Secretary of State for Business, Innovation and Skills, First Secretary and Lord President of the Council
Rt. Hon. Lord Mandelson (since June 2009)
Secretary of State for Children, Schools and Families
Rt. Hon. Ed Balls, MP (since June 2007)
Secretary of State for Communities and Local Government
Rt. Hon. John Denham, MP (since June 2009)
Secretary of State for Culture, Media and Sport
Rt. Hon. Ben Bradshaw, MP (since June 2009)
Secretary of State for Defence (since June 2009)
Rt. Hon. Bob Ainsworth, MP
Secretary of State for Energy and Climate Change
Rt. Hon. Edward Miliband, MP (since October 2008)
Secretary of State for Environment, Food and Rural Affairs
Rt. Hon. Hilary Benn, MP (since June 2007)
Secretary of State for Foreign and Commonwealth Affairs
Rt. Hon. David Miliband, MP (since June 2007)
Secretary of State for Health
Rt. Hon. Andy Burnham, MP (since June 2009)
Secretary of State for the Home Department
Rt. Hon. Alan Johnson, MP (since June 2009)
Secretary of State for International Development
Rt. Hon. Douglas Alexander, MP (since June 2007)
Secretary of State for Justice and Lord Chancellor
Rt. Hon. Jack Straw, MP (since June 2007)
Secretary of State for Northern Ireland
Rt. Hon. Shaun Woodward, MP (since June 2007)
Secretary of State for Scotland
Rt. Hon. Jim Murphy, MP (since June 2009)
Secretary of State for Transport
Rt. Hon. Lord Adonis (since June 2009)
Secretary of State for Wales
Rt. Hon. Peter Hain, MP (since June 2009)
Secretary of State for Work and Pensions
Rt. Hon. Yvette Cooper, MP (since June 2009)

The Attorney-General (Rt. Hon. Baroness Scotland of Asthal, QC)*, the Minister of State for Housing (Rt. Hon. John Healey, MP), the Minister of State for Africa, Asia and the UN (vacant), the Minister of State for Business, Innovation and Skills (Rt. Hon Pat McFadden, MP), the Minister of State for Children, Young People and Families (Rt. Hon. Dawn Primarolo, MP)*, the Minister of State for Employment and Welfare Reform (Rt. Hon. Jim Knight, MP), the Minister of State for Regional Economic Development and Coordination (Rt. Hon. Rosie Winterton, MP)*, the Minister of State for Science and Innovation (Rt. Hon. Lord Drayson), the Minister of State for Transport (Rt. Hon. Sadiq Khan, MP)*, the Parliamentary Private Secretaries to the Prime Minister (Anne Snelgrove, MP; Jon Trickett, MP), the Chief Whip in the House of Commons (Parliamentary Secretary to the Treasury) and Minister for the North East (Rt. Hon. Nicholas Brown, MP), and the Chief Whip in the House of Lords and Captain of the Gentlemen-at-Arms (Lord Bassam of Brighton) attend cabinet meetings although they are not members of the cabinet.

* Only attends cabinet meetings when ministerial responsibilities are on the agenda

LAW OFFICERS

Attorney-General
Rt. Hon. Baroness Scotland of Asthal, QC (since June 2007)
Solicitor-General
Vera Baird, QC, MP (since June 2007)
Advocate-General for Scotland
Lord Davidson of Glen Clova, QC (since May 2006)

MINISTERS OF STATE

Business, Innovation and Skills
Kevin Brennan, MP*
Lord Davies of Abersoch†
Rt. Hon. Lord Drayson‡
Rt. Hon. David Lammy, MP
Rt. Hon. Pat McFadden, MP
Rt. Hon. Rosie Winterton, MP§
Cabinet Office
Rt. Hon. Tessa Jowell, MP
Rt. Hon. Angela E. Smith, MP
Children, Schools and Families
Vernon Coaker, MP
Rt. Hon. Dawn Primarolo, MP
Communities and Local Government
Rt. Hon. John Healey, MP
Defence
Bill Rammell, MP
Energy and Climate Change
Lord Hunt of Kings Heath
Joan Ruddock, MP
Environment, Food and Rural Affairs
Jim Fitzpatrick, MP
Equalities Office
Maria Eagle, MP¶
Rt. Hon. Harriet Harman, QC, MP
Foreign and Commonwealth Office
Baroness Kinnock of Holyhead
Ivan Lewis, MP
Health
Phil Hope, MP
Rt. Hon. Mike O'Brien, MP
Gillian Merron, MP

Home Office
Rt. Hon. David Hanson, MP
Phil Woolas, MP**
International Development
Gareth Thomas, MP
Justice
Rt. Hon. Michael Wills, MP
Northern Ireland Office
Rt. Hon. Paul Goggins, MP
Transport
Rt. Hon. Sadiq Khan, MP
Work and Pensions
Angela Eagle, MP
Rt. Hon. Jim Knight, MP

* Also works in the Department for Children, Schools and Families
† Also works in the Foreign and Commonwealth Office
‡ Also works in the Ministry of Defence
§ Also works in the Department for Communities and Local Government
¶ Also works in the Ministry of Justice
** Also works in HM Treasury

UNDER-SECRETARIES OF STATE

Business, Innovation and Skills
Ian Lucas, MP
Rt. Hon. Stephen Timms, MP
Baroness Vadera*
Lord Young of Norwood Green
Children, Schools and Families
Diana R. Johnson, MP
Baroness Morgan of Drefelin
Iain Wright, MP
Communities and Local Government
Ian Austin, MP
Lord McKenzie of Luton†
Shahid Malik, MP
Culture, Media and Sport
Barbara Follett, MP
Siôn Simon, MP
Gerry Sutcliffe, MP
Defence
Quentin Davies, MP
Kevan Jones, MP
Rt. Hon. Baroness Taylor of Bolton‡
Energy and Climate Change
David Kidney, MP
Environment, Food and Rural Affairs
Lord Davies of Oldham
Huw Irranca-Davies, MP
Dan Norris, MP
Equalities Office
Michael J. Foster, MP
Foreign and Commonwealth Office
Chris Bryant, MP
Health
Ann Keen, MP
Home Office
Lord Brett
Alan Campbell, MP
Lord West of Spithead
International Development
Michael Foster, MP
Justice
Lord Bach
Bridget Prentice, MP
Claire Ward, MP
Scotland Office
Ann McKechin, MP
Transport
Paul Clark, MP
Chris Mole, MP
Wales Office
Wayne David, MP
Work and Pensions
Helen Goodman, MP
Jonathan Shaw, MP

* Also works in the Cabinet Office
† Also works in the Department for Work and Pensions
‡ Also works in the Foreign and Commonwealth Office

OTHER MINISTERS

Parliamentary Private Secretaries to the Prime Minister
Anne Snelgrove, MP; Jon Trickett, MP
Cabinet Office
Rt. Hon. Tessa Jowell, MP *(Paymaster-General)*
Baroness Vadera *(Parliamentary Secretary)*
Leader of the Commons
Harriet Harman, QC, MP *(Lord Privy Seal, Labour Party Chair and Minister for Women and Equalities)*
Barbara Keeley, MP *(Parliamentary Secretary and Deputy Leader of the Commons)*
Treasury
Rt. Hon. Stephen Timms, MP *(Financial Secretary)*
Ian Pearson, MP *(Economic Secretary)*
Sarah McCarthy-Fry, MP *(Exchequer Secretary)*

GOVERNMENT WHIPS

HOUSE OF LORDS

Captain of the Honourable Corps of the Gentlemen-at-Arms (Chief Whip)
Lord Bassam of Brighton
Captain of the Queen's Bodyguard of the Yeomen of the Guard (Deputy Chief Whip)
Rt. Hon. Lord Davies of Oldham
Lords-in-Waiting
Lord Brett
Lord Faulkner of Worcester
Lord Tunnicliffe
Lord Young of Norwood Green
Baronesses-in-Waiting
Baroness Crawley
Baroness Farrington of Ribbleton
Baroness Thornton

HOUSE OF COMMONS

Parliamentary Secretary to the Treasury (Chief Whip)
Rt. Hon. Nicholas Brown, MP
Treasurer of HM Household (Deputy Chief Whip)
Rt. Hon. Thomas McAvoy, MP
Comptroller of HM Household
Rt. Hon. John Spellar, MP
Vice-Chamberlain of HM Household
Helen Jones, MP
Lords Commissioners of HM Treasury
Bob Blizzard, MP; Tony Cunningham, MP; Stephen McCabe, MP; Frank Roy, MP; Dave Watts, MP
Assistant Whips
Lyn Brown, MP; Dawn Butler, MP; Mary Creagh, MP; John Heppell, MP; Sharon Hodgson, MP; Kerry McCarthy, MP; George Mudie, MP; Mark Tami, MP; David Wright, MP

GOVERNMENT DEPARTMENTS

THE CIVIL SERVICE

Under the Next Steps programme, launched in 1988, many semi-autonomous executive agencies were established to carry out much of the work of the civil service. Executive agencies operate within a framework set by the responsible minister which specifies policies, objectives and available resources. All executive agencies are set annual performance targets by their minister. Each agency has a chief executive, who is responsible for the day-to-day operations of the agency and who is accountable to the minister for the use of resources and for meeting the agency's targets. The minister accounts to parliament for the work of the agency. Nearly 75 per cent of civil servants now work in executive agencies. In April 2009 there were 522,890 permanent civil servants, down from about 537,000 in June 2005.

The Senior Civil Service was created in 1996 and on 1 April 2009 comprised 4,750 staff from permanent secretary to the former grade 5 level, including all agency chief executives. All government departments and executive agencies are now responsible for their own pay and grading systems for civil servants outside the Senior Civil Service.

SALARIES 2009–10

MINISTERIAL SALARIES *from 1 April 2009*

Ministers who are members of the House of Commons receive a parliamentary salary of £64,766 in addition to their ministerial salary.

Prime minister	£132,923
Cabinet minister (Commons)	£79,754
Cabinet minister (Lords)	£108,253
Minister of state (Commons)	£41,370
Minister of state (Lords)	£84,524
Parliamentary under-secretary (Commons)	£31,401
Parliamentary under-secretary (Lords)	£73,617

SPECIAL ADVISERS' SALARIES *from 1 April 2009*

Special advisers to government ministers are paid out of public funds; their salaries are negotiated individually, but are usually in the range of £40,352 to £106,864.

CIVIL SERVICE SALARIES *from 1 April 2009*

Senior Civil Servants	
Permanent secretary	£141,800–£279,300
Band 3	£101,500–£208,100
Band 2	£82,900–£162,500
Band 1A	£67,600–£128,900
Band 1	£58,200–£117,800

Staff are placed in pay bands according to their level of responsibility and taking account of other factors such as experience and marketability. Movement within and between bands is based on performance. Following the delegation of responsibility for pay and grading to government departments and agencies from 1 April 1996, it is no longer possible to show service-wide pay rates for staff outside the Senior Civil Service.

GOVERNMENT DEPARTMENTS

For more information on government departments, *see* W www.cabinetoffice.gov.uk/ministerial_responsibilities.aspx

ATTORNEY-GENERAL'S OFFICE

Attorney-General's Office, 20 Victoria Street, London SW1H 0NF
T 020-7271 2492
E correspondenceunit@attorneygeneral.gsi.gov.uk
W www.attorneygeneral.gov.uk
Attorney-General's Chambers, Royal Courts of Justice, Belfast BT1 3JY
T 028-9054 6082

The law officers of the crown for England and Wales are the Attorney-General and the Solicitor-General. The Attorney-General, assisted by the Solicitor-General, is the chief legal adviser to the government and is also ultimately responsible for all crown litigation. She has overall responsibility for the work of the Law Officers' Departments (the Treasury Solicitor's Department, the Crown Prosecution Service, the Serious Fraud Office, the Revenue and Customs Prosecution Office, the Army Prosecuting Authority, HM Crown Prosecution Service Inspectorate and the Attorney-General's Office). She has a specific statutory duty to superintend the discharge of their duties by the Director of Public Prosecutions (who heads the Crown Prosecution Service) and the Director of the Serious Fraud Office. The Director of Public Prosecutions for Northern Ireland and the Crown Solicitor for Northern Ireland are also responsible to the Attorney-General for the performance of their functions. The Attorney-General has specific responsibilities for the enforcement of the criminal law and also performs certain public interest functions, eg protecting charities and appealing unduly lenient sentences. She also deals with questions of law arising in bills and with issues of legal policy.

Attorney-General, Rt. Hon. Baroness Scotland, QC
Private Secretary, W. Hart
Solicitor-General, V. Baird, QC, MP
Director-General, J. Jones
Director, Criminal Law, S. Patten

DEPARTMENT FOR BUSINESS, INNOVATION AND SKILLS

1 Victoria Street, London SW1H 0ET
T 020-7215 5000 E enquiries@bis.gsi.gov.uk
W www.bis.gov.uk

The Department for Business, Innovation and Skills (BIS) was established in June 2009 by merging the Department for Business, Enterprise and Regulatory Reform and the Department for Innovation, Universities and Skills. It aims to build Britain's capabilities to compete in the global economy. The merger brought together expertise in enterprise, innovation, and world-class science and research. Among other roles, the department advocates the needs of business across government; promotes an enterprise environment; invests in the development of the higher education system; invests in the UK's science base; invests in skills through the further education system, aims to expand the number of apprenticeships; collaborates with regional development agencies to build economic growth in England; and encourages innovation in the UK.

Secretary of State for Business, Innovation and Skills, Rt. Hon. Lord Mandelson
Principal Private Secretary, Richard Abel
Senior Private Secretary, Bryan Payne
Private Secretaries, Duncan Buchanan; Paul McCaffrey
Special Advisers, Stephen Adams; Patrick Loughran; Geoffrey Norris
Minister of State, Rt. Hon. Pat McFadden, MP *(Business, Innovation and Skills)*
Private Secretary, Kate Hall
Special Adviser, Matt Cooke
Minister of State, Rt. Hon. Lord Drayson *(Science and Innovation)**
Private Secretary, Julian MacCormack
Minister of State, Rt. Hon. David Lammy, MP *(Higher Education and Intellectual Property)*
Private Secretary, Rob Kettell
Minister of State, Rt. Hon. Rosie Winterton, MP *(Regional Economic Development and Coordination)*†
Private Secretary, Alan Dick
Minister of State, Lord Davies of Abersoch, CBE *(Trade, Investment and Business)*‡
Private Secretary, Katie Melville
Minister of State, Kevin Brennan, MP *(Further Education, Skills, Apprenticeships and Consumer Affairs)*§
Private Secretary, Kellie Hurst
Parliamentary Under-Secretary of State, Ian Lucas, MP *(Business and Regulatory Reform)*
Private Secretary, Chris Maskell
Parliamentary Under-Secretary of State, Baroness Vadera *(Economic Competitiveness, Small Business and Enterprise)*ℭ
Private Secretary, Anjli Mehta
Parliamentary Under-Secretary of State, Lord Young of Norwood Green *(Postal Affairs and Employment Relations)*
Private Secretary, Amy Jordan
Parliamentary Under-Secretary of State, Stephen Timms, MP
Permanent Secretary, Simon Fraser
Private Secretary, Alesha De-Freitas
Head of Parliamentary Unit, Ian Webster

* Jointly with the Ministry of Defence
† Jointly with the Department for Communities and Local Government
‡ Jointly with the Foreign and Commonwealth Office
§ Jointly with the Department for Children, Schools and Families
ℭ Jointly with the Cabinet Office

MANAGEMENT BOARD
Chair, Simon Fraser *(Permanent Secretary of State)*
Members, John Alty *(Fair Markets Group)*; Andrew Cahn *(UK Trade and Investment)*; Hilary Douglas *(Chief Operating Officer)*; John Edwards *(Finance)*; Jitinder Kohli *(Better Regulation Executive)*; Vicky Pryce *(Economics)*; Philip Rutnam *(Enterprise and Business)*; Rachel Sandby-Thomas *(Legal Services)*
Non-Executive Members, Arnoud De Meyer; Roger Urwin; Dr Brian Woods-Scawen

BETTER REGULATION EXECUTIVE
1 Victoria Street, London SW1 0ET
T 020-7215 5000 W www.betterregulation.gov.uk

The Better Regulation Executive works with businesses and across government to minimise bureaucracy by reducing and simplifying regulation from the public, private and voluntary sectors. It challenges new legislation and simplifies, improves or removes existing legislation.
Chair, vacant
Chief Executive, Jitinder Kohli

SHAREHOLDER EXECUTIVE
1 Victoria Street, London SW1H 0ET
T 020-7215 3909
W www.shareholderexecutive.gov.uk

The Shareholder Executive was established in September 2003 to improve the government's performance as a shareholder in government-owned businesses and to provide a source of corporate finance expertise within government; currently the executive's remit covers 26 businesses.
Chair, Philip Remnant
Chief Executive, Stephen Lovegrove

CABINET OFFICE

70 Whitehall, London SW1A 2AS
Switchboard 020-7276 3000 T 020-7276 1234
W www.cabinet-office.gov.uk

The Cabinet Office, alongside the Treasury, sits at the centre of the government. It has three core functions: to support the prime minister in defining and delivering the government's objectives; to support the cabinet in ensuring the coherence, quality and delivery of policy and operations across departments; and strengthening the Civil Service's capabilities in terms of organisation, leadership and skills. The department is headed by the Minister for the Cabinet Office.
Prime Minister, First Lord of the Treasury and Minister for the Civil Service, Rt. Hon. Gordon Brown, MP
Principal Private Secretary to the Prime Minister, James Bowler
Minister for the Cabinet Office, the Olympics and London and Paymaster General, Tessa Jowell, MP
Parliamentary Private Secretary, Lindsay Roy, MP
Principal Private Secretary, Patrick White
Private Secretary, John Tucker
Minister of State, Angela E. Smith, MP
Private Secretary, Philip Lloyd
Parliamentary Secretary, Baroness Vadera
Private Secretary, Lisa Hine
Secretary of the Cabinet and Head of the Home Civil Service, Sir Gus O'Donnell, KCB
Principal Private Secretary, Jennifer Hepker
Private Secretary, Sharmin Joarder
Assistant Private Secretary, Jackie Fraser *(Diary)*
Permanent Secretary, Sir Richard Mottram, GCB *(Intelligence, Security and Resilience)*

The CORPORATE SERVICES GROUP comprises the Business Support Group, Cabinet Office Management, and the Change Team. It was established to provide overall technology leadership in three key areas of government: the transformation of public services for the benefit of citizens, businesses, taxpayers and front-line staff; the efficiency of the corporate services and infrastructure of government organisations; and the steps necessary to achieve the effective delivery of technology for government.

BUSINESS SUPPORT GROUP
Kirkland House, 22–26 Whitehall, London SW1A 2WH
T 020-7276 0530
Director-General, Strategic Finance and Operations, Roger Marsh

CABINET OFFICE HUMAN RESOURCES
Admiralty Arch South, The Mall, London SW1A 2WH
T 020-7276 6200
Director, Janette Durbin

CABINET OFFICE MANAGEMENT
Admiralty Arch, The Mall, London SW1A 2WH
T 020-7276 3090
Director-General, Transformational Government and Cabinet Office Management, Alexis Cleveland

FINANCIAL AND ESTATE MANAGEMENT
Kirkland House, 22–26 Whitehall, London SW1A 2WH
T 020-7276 6150
Director, Jerry Page

GOVERNANCE AND CHANGE
Kirkland House, 22–26 Whitehall, London SW1A 2WH
T 020-7276 2160
Director, Sarah Cox

KNOWLEDGE AND INFORMATION MANAGEMENT
Admiralty Arch, The Mall, London SW1A 2WH
T 020-7276 6324
Head of Knowledge and Information Management, Roger Smethurst

OFFICE OF HER MAJESTY'S GOVERNMENT CHIEF INFORMATION OFFICER
1 Horse Guards Road, London SW1A 2HQ
T 020-7276 3248
HM Government Chief Information Officer, John Suffolk

The CIVIL SERVICE CAPABILITY GROUP comprises Cabinet Office Shared Services and Leadership, Civil Service Performance and Review, Talent Management, Workforce. The group is responsible for recruiting and developing staff and raising the capability of HR management throughout the civil service.
Head of CSCG, Gill Rider

CABINET OFFICE SHARED SERVICES
Admiralty Arch, The Mall, London SW1A 2WH
T 020-7276 2088
Director, Janet Wilkes

CIVIL SERVICE PERFORMANCE AND REVIEW
Admiralty Arch, The Mall, London SW1A 2WH
T 020-7270 1516
Director, Brian Etheridge

LEADERSHIP AND TALENT MANAGEMENT
Admiralty Arch, The Mall, London SW1A 2WH
T 020-7276 1171
Director, Helen Dudley

WORKFORCE
Admiralty Arch, The Mall, London SW1A 2WH
T 020-7276 1559
Director, Dusty Amroliwala

The DOMESTIC POLICY GROUP comprises the Economic and Domestic Affairs Secretariat, the European and Global Issues Secretariat, the Honours and Appointments Secretariat, the Office of the Third Sector, the Social Exclusion Task Force and the Strategy Unit.

ECONOMIC AND DOMESTIC AFFAIRS SECRETARIAT
Cabinet Office, 70 Whitehall, London SW1A 2WH
T 020-7276 0240
Director-General, Paul Britton, CB

EUROPEAN AND GLOBAL ISSUES SECRETARIAT
70 Whitehall, London SW1A 2WH
T 020-7930 4433
Prime Minister's Adviser on International and European Policy, Jon Cunliffe, CB

HONOURS AND APPOINTMENTS SECRETARIAT
Ground Floor, Admiralty Arch, The Mall, London SW1A 2WH
T 020-7276 2777
Ceremonial Officer, Denis Brennan

OFFICE OF THE THIRD SECTOR
Second Floor, Admiralty Arch, South Side, The Mall, London SW1A 2WH
T 020-7276 6026
Director-General, Campbell Robb

SOCIAL EXCLUSION TASK FORCE
Admiralty Arch, The Mall, London SW1A 2WH
T 020-7276 2323
Director, Naomi Eisenstadt, CB

STRATEGY UNIT
Admiralty Arch, The Mall, London SW1A 2WH
T 020-7276 1881 W www.cabinetoffice.gov.uk/strategy
Director, Gareth Davies

The COMMUNICATION AND INFORMATION GROUP comprises Cabinet Office Communications and Government Communication.

CABINET OFFICE COMMUNICATIONS
22 Whitehall, London SW1A 2WH
T 020-7276 0079/2002
Director, Jenny Grey

GOVERNMENT COMMUNICATION
26 Whitehall, London SW1A 2WH
T 020-7276 2712 W www.comms.gov.uk
Permanent Secretary, Matt Tee

INTELLIGENCE, SECURITY AND RESILIENCE GROUP
70 Whitehall, London SW1A 2AS
W www.intelligence.gov.uk
The Prime Minister's Security Adviser and Head of Intelligence, Security and Resilience, Robert Hannigan

CIVIL CONTINGENCIES SECRETARIAT
22 Whitehall, London SW1A 2WH
T 020-7276 5061
Director, Bruce Mann

COUNTER TERRORISM AND CRISIS MANAGEMENT TEAM
70 Whitehall, London SW1A 2AS
Deputy Director, vacant

DIRECTORATE OF SECURITY AND INTELLIGENCE
26 Whitehall, London SW1A 2WH
Director, Chris Wright

EMERGENCY PLANNING COLLEGE
The Hawkhills, Easingwold, York YO61 3EG
T 01347-825006 W www.epcollege.gov.uk
Chief Executive, Michael Charlton-Weedy

FOREIGN AND DEFENCE POLICY SECRETARIAT
Cabinet Office, 70 Whitehall, London SW1A 2AS
T 020-7930 4433
Prime Minister's Foreign Policy Adviser and Head of Secretariat, Simon McDonald, CMG

JOINT INTELLIGENCE ORGANISATION
70 Whitehall, London SW1A 2AS
W www.intelligence.gov.uk
Chair of the Joint Intelligence Committee and Head of Intelligence Assessment, Alex Allan

NATIONAL SECURITY SECRETARIAT
70 Whitehall, London SW1A 2AS
T 020-7276 0255
Director, William Nye

PRIME MINISTER'S OFFICE
10 Downing Street, London SW1A 2AA
T 020-7930-4433
W www.number-10.gov.uk
Prime Minister, Rt. Hon Gordon Brown, MP
Parliamentary Private Secretaries, Anne Snelgrove, MP; Jon Trickett, MP
Permanent Secretary, Jeremy Heywood, CB, CVO
Principal Private Secretary, James Bowler
Director of Communications and the Prime Minister's Spokesman, Michael Ellam
Deputy Chief of Staff, Gavin Kelly
Director of Political Strategy, David Muir
Director of Government Relations, Sue Nye
Head of Policy Unit, Dan Corry
Advisers to the Prime Minister on Political Press Issues, Michael Dugher; John Woodcock
Head of International Economic Affairs, European and G8 Sherpa, Jon Cunliffe, CB
Head of Foreign and Defence Policy, Simon McDonald, CMG

CROSS GOVERNMENT UNITS in the Cabinet Office comprises the Committee on Standards in Public Life (*see* Public Bodies section), Independent Offices and the Office of the Parliamentary Counsel.

INDEPENDENT OFFICES

OFFICE OF THE COMMISSIONER FOR PUBLIC APPOINTMENTS (OCPA)
3rd Floor, 35 Great Smith Street, London SW1P 3BQ
T 020-7276 2625 E ocpa@gtnet.gov.uk
W www.publicappointmentscommissioner.org

The Commissioner for Public Appointments is responsible for monitoring, regulating and reporting on ministerial appointments to public bodies. The commissioner can investigate complaints about the way in which appointments were made or applicants treated.
Commissioner for Public Appointments, Janet Gaymer, CBE, QC
Secretary to the Commissioner and Head of the Independent Offices, Dr Richard Jarvis

OFFICE OF THE CIVIL SERVICE COMMISSIONERS (OCSC)
35 Great Smith Street, London SW1P 3BQ
T 020-7276 2617 W www.civilservicecommissioners.org

The Civil Service Commissioners are the custodians of the principle of selection on merit by fair and open competition; they publish a recruitment code and audit departments' and agencies' performance against it. When the most senior posts are opened to people from outside the service, the commissioners normally chair the recruitment process.
First Commissioner, Janet Paraskeva
Commissioners (part-time), Sir Michael Aaronson, CBE; Mark Addison; John MacAuslan; Dame Alexander Burslem, DBE; Janet Gaymer, CBE, QC; Prof. Christine Hallett; Ms Mary Jo Jacobi; Bernard Knight; Sir Neil McIntosh; Ms Elizabeth McMeikan; Anthea Millett, CBE; Ms Stella Pantelides; Ranjit Sondhi; Libby Watkins

OFFICE OF THE PARLIAMENTARY COUNSEL
36 Whitehall, London SW1A 2AY
T 020-7210 2588 W www.parliamentary-counsel.gov.uk
First Parliamentary Counsel, Stephen Laws, CB
Chief Executive, Jim Barron, CBE

INTELLIGENCE AND SECURITY COMMITTEE SECRETARIAT
70 Whitehall, London SW1A 2AS
T 020-7276 1215 W www.cabinetoffice.gov.uk/intelligence
Head of Management Unit, Emma-Louise Avery

INTERNAL AUDIT SERVICE
4th Floor, Ashdown House, 123 Victoria Street, London SW1E 6DE
T 020-7944 6521
Head, Steve Simmonds

DEPARTMENT FOR CHILDREN, SCHOOLS AND FAMILIES
Sanctuary Buildings, Great Smith Street, London SW1P 3BT
Castle View House, East Lane, Runcorn WA7 2GJ
Mowden Hall, Staindrop Road, Darlington DL3 9BG
Moorfoot, Sheffield S1 4PQ
T 0870-001 2345 Public Enquiries 0870-000 2288
E info@dcsf.gsi.gov.uk W www.dcsf.gov.uk

The Department for Children, Schools and Families (DCSF) was established in June 2007 in place of the Department for Education and Skills (DfES), in order to achieve better integrated children's services and improved educational standards; higher education and lifelong learning directorates moved to the Department for Innovation, Universities and Skills (now the Department for Business, Innovation and Skills).

The DCSF is responsible for everything affecting children and young people under the age of 19, including schools and relevant services. The department's objectives are to increase the number of children reaching expected standards; help children out of poverty; and re-engage disaffected young people. It also aims to respond to factors affecting children and families, such as demographic and socio-economic change, developing technology and increasing global competition.
Secretary of State for Children, Schools and Families, Rt. Hon. Ed Balls, MP
Principal Private Secretary, Sinead O'Sullivan
Deputy Principal Private Secretary, Emma Cottrell
Private Secretaries, Sophie Taylor; Peter Walsh
Special Advisers, Francine Bates; Alex Belardinelli
Parliamentary Private Secretary, Andrew Gwynne, MP
Minister of State, Vernon Coaker, MP *(Schools and Learners)*
Private Secretary, Caroline Cane
Parliamentary Private Secretary, Phil Wilson, MP

Minister of State, Rt. Hon. Dawn Primarolo, MP *(Children, Young People and Families)*
Private Secretary, David Curtis
Parliamentary Private Secretary, vacant
Parliamentary Under-Secretary of State, Diana Johnson, MP *(Schools)*
Private Secretary, Philip Carr
Parliamentary Under-Secretary of State, Baroness Morgan of Drefelin *(Children, Young People and Families)*
Private Secretary, Nichola Vasey
Parliamentary Under-Secretary of State, Iain Wright, MP *(14–19 Reform and Apprenticeships)*
Private Secretary, Caroline Kaegler
Parliamentary Clerk, Helen Heyden
Spokesperson in the House of Lords, Baroness Delyth Morgan
Permanent Secretary, David Bell
Private Secretary, Bernie Serieux

MANAGEMENT BOARD
Chair, David Bell *(Permanent Secretary of State)*
Members, Philip Augar; Jon Coles *(Schools)*; Michael Hearty *(Corporate Services)*; Tom Jeffery *(Children and Families)*; Katherine Kerswell; Lesley Longstone *(Young People)*; Caroline Wright *(Communications)*

DEPARTMENT FOR COMMUNITIES AND LOCAL GOVERNMENT

Eland House, London SW1E 5DU
T 020-7944 4400 W www.communities.gov.uk

The Department for Communities and Local Government (CLG) was formed in May 2006 with a remit to promote community cohesion and prevent extremism, as well as responsibility for housing, urban regeneration and planning. It unites the communities and civil renewal functions previously undertaken by the Home Office, with responsibility for regeneration, neighbourhood renewal and local government (previously held by the Office of the Deputy Prime Minister, which was abolished following a cabinet reshuffle in May 2006).

The CLG also has responsibility for equality policy on race and faith (functions that were previously split between several government departments).

Secretary of State for Communities and Local Government, John Denham, MP
Private Secretary, Nick Dexter
Parliamentary Private Secretary, Natascha Engel, MP
Minister of State, Rt. Hon. John Healey, MP *(Housing)*
Private Secretary, Mark Livesey
Parliamentary Private Secretary, Clive Efford, MP
Minister of State, Rosie Winterton, MP
Private Secretary, Fakruz Zaman
Parliamentary Private Secretary, vacant
Parliamentary Under-Secretary of State, Shahid Malik, MP
Private Secretary, Alistair Macdonald
Parliamentary Under-Secretary of State, Ian Austin, MP
Private Secretary, Stella Michael
Parliamentary Under-Secretary of State, Lord McKenzie of Luton
Private Secretary, Lee Burge
Permanent Secretary, Peter Housden
Private Secretary, Jenan Hasan
Chief Scientist, Prof. Michael Kelly

MANAGEMENT BOARD
Chair, Peter Housden *(Permanent Secretary of State)*
Members, Lindsay Bell *(Local Government and Regeneration) (acting)*; Christina Bienkowska *(Strategy and Performance)*; Mike Falvey *(HR and Transformational Change)*; Debbie Hewitt; Richard McCarthy *(Housing and Planning)*; Joe Montgomery *(Regions and Communities)*; Hunada Nouss *(Finance and Corporate Service Delivery)*; David Rossington *(Communities Group) (acting)*; Rob Vincent; Sarah Weir; Dame Jo Williams

DEPARTMENT FOR CULTURE, MEDIA AND SPORT

2–4 Cockspur Street, London SW1Y 5DH
T 020-7211 6200 F 020-7211 6032
E enquiries@culture.gov.uk W www.culture.gov.uk

The Department for Culture, Media and Sport (DCMS) was established in July 1997 and aims to improve the quality of life for all those in the UK through cultural and sporting activities while championing the tourism, creative and leisure industries. It is responsible for government policy relating to the arts, sport, the National Lottery, tourism, libraries, museums and galleries, broadcasting, creative industries – including film and the music industry – press freedom and regulation, licensing, gambling and the historic environment.

The department is also responsible for 54 public bodies that help deliver the department's strategic aims and objectives, the 2012 Olympic Games and Paralympic Games, the listing of historic buildings and scheduling of ancient monuments, the export licensing of cultural goods, and the management of the Government Art Collection and the Royal Parks (its sole executive agency). It has the responsibility for humanitarian assistance in the event of a disaster, as well as for the organisation of the annual Remembrance Day ceremony at the Cenotaph. In May 2005 the DCMS assumed responsibility for fashion design, advertising and the arts market from the then Department for Trade and Industry – now the Department for Business, Innovation and Skills – which it also works jointly with on design issues (including sponsorship of the Design Council) and on relations with the computer games and publishing industries.

Secretary of State for Culture, Media and Sport, Rt. Hon Ben Bradshaw, MP
Principal Private Secretary, Rita Patel
Special Advisers, Phil French; Lenny Shallcross
Parliamentary Private Secretary, Mary Creagh, MP
Parliamentary Under-Secretary of State, Rt. Hon. Barbara Follett, MP *(Culture and Tourism)*
Private Secretary, Ruth Evans
Parliamentary Private Secretary, Derek Wyatt, MP
Parliamentary Under-Secretary of State, Gerry Sutcliffe, MP *(Sport)*
Private Secretary, Graeme Brown
Parliamentary Under-Secretary of State, Siôn Simon, MP *(Creative Industries)*
Private Secretary, Leonie Philips
Permanent Secretary, Jonathan Stephens
Private Secretary, Lizzie West

MANAGEMENT BOARD
Chair, Jonathan Stephens *(Permanent Secretary of State)*
Members, Jeremy Beeton *(Government Olympic Executive)*; David Roe *(Corporate Services)*; Andrew Ramsay, CB *(Partnerships and Programmes)*

MINISTRY OF DEFENCE

see Defence section

DEPARTMENT OF ENERGY AND CLIMATE CHANGE

3 Whitehall Place, London SW1A 2HD
T 0300-060 4000 E enquiries@decc.gsi.gov.uk
W www.decc.gov.uk

The Department of Energy and Climate Change was formed in 2008. The department combined much of the climate change group, previously part of the Department for Environment, Food and Rural Affairs, with the energy group, previously part of the Department for Business, Enterprise and Regulatory Reform. The department is responsible for all aspects of UK energy policy, and for tackling global climate change on behalf of the UK. DECC's three main objectives are to ensure the UK's energy is secure, affordable and efficient; to bring about the transition to a low-carbon Britain; and to achieve an international agreement on climate change at Copenhagen in December 2009.

Secretary of State for the Department for Energy and Climate Change, Rt. Hon. Ed Miliband, MP
Private Secretary, Ashley Ibbett
Parliamentary Private Secretary, David Hamilton, MP
Minister of State, Joan Ruddock, MP
Private Secretary, Martin Meadows
Parliamentary Private Secretary, Emily Thornberry, MP
Minister of State, Lord Hunt of King's Heath, OBE
Private Secretary, William Farquhar
Parliamentary Private Secretary, Madeleine Moon, MP
Parliamentary Under-Secretary of State, David Kidney, MP
Private Secretary, Emily Veitch

MANAGEMENT BOARD
Permanent Secretary, Moira Wallace
Members, Peter Betts *(Energy and Climate Change International) (acting);* Edmund Hosker *(Corporate Support and Shared Services) (acting);* Phil Wynn Owen *(National Climate Change and Consumer Support);* Willy Rickett *(Energy Markets and Infrastructure)*

DEPARTMENT FOR ENVIRONMENT, FOOD AND RURAL AFFAIRS

Nobel House, 17 Smith Square, London SW1P 3JR
T 020-7238 3000
Helpline 0845-933 5577 F 020-7238 6591
E helpline@defra.gsi.gov.uk W www.defra.gov.uk

The Department for Environment, Food and Rural Affairs (DEFRA) is responsible for government policy on the environment, rural matters, farming and food production; its central aim is sustainable development. In association with the agriculture departments of the Scottish government, the National Assembly for Wales and the Northern Ireland Office, and with the Intervention Board, the department is responsible for negotiations in the EU on the common agricultural and fisheries policies, and for single European market questions relating to its responsibilities. Its remit includes international agricultural and food trade policy.

The department's five strategic priorities are climate change, adaptation and mitigation; sustainable consumption and production; the protection of natural resources and the countryside; sustainable rural communities; and sustainable farming and food, including animal health and welfare. DEFRA is also the lead government department for emergencies in animal and plant diseases, flooding, food and water supply, dealing with the consequences of a chemical, biological, radiological or nuclear incident, and other threats to the environment.

Secretary of State for Environment, Food and Rural Affairs, Rt. Hon. Hilary Benn, MP
Principal Private Secretary, John Kittmer
Private Secretaries, Akeela Bashir; Diane Duffy; Helen Emmett; Peter Featherstone; Dan Hamza-Goodacre; Rhys Jackson; Cathy Miller
Minister of State, Jim Fitzpatrick, MP *(Farming and the Environment)*
Senior Private Secretary, Karen Morgan
Private Secretaries, Amy Ferguson; Emma Prince; Dan Skerten; Samantha Suares
Parliamentary Private Secretary, Dr Ashok Kumar, MP
Parliamentary Under-Secretary of State, Huw Irranca-Davies, MP *(Marine and Natural Environment)*
Senior Private Secretary, Sarah Wardle
Private Secretaries, Rob Davies; William Pryer; Nicole Roberts
Parliamentary Under-Secretary of State, Dan Norris, MP *(Rural Affairs and Environment)*
Senior Private Secretary, Mike Rowe
Private Secretaries, William Boohan; Frances Kirwan; Amelia Munn, Yasmin Nasser
Parliamentary Under-Secretary of State, Lord Davies of Oldham *(House of Lords)*
Senior Private Secretary, Mike Rowe
Private Secretaries, William Boohan; Frances Kirwan; Amelia Munn; Yasmin Nasser
Permanent Secretary, Helen Ghosh
Private Secretary, Helen Fasham

MANAGEMENT BOARD
Chair, Helen Ghosh *(Permanent Secretary of State)*
Members, Gill Aitken *(Law and HR);* Mike Anderson *(Climate Change);* Poul Christensen, Alexis Cleveland; Bill Griffiths, Bill Stow *(Strategy and Evidence);* Peter Unwin *(Environment and Rural);* Prof. Robert Watson *(Chief Scientific Adviser);* Katrina Williams *(Food and Farming)*

FOREIGN AND COMMONWEALTH OFFICE

King Charles Street, London SW1A 2AH
T 020-7008 1500 W www.fco.gov.uk

The Foreign and Commonwealth Office (FCO) provides, through its staff in the UK and through its diplomatic missions abroad, the means of communication between the British government and other governments – and international governmental organisations – on all matters falling within the field of international relations.

It is responsible for alerting the British government to the implications of developments overseas; promoting British interests overseas; protecting British citizens abroad; explaining British policies to, and cultivating relationships with, governments overseas; the discharge of British responsibilities to the overseas territories; entry clearance UK visas (with the Home Office); and promoting British business overseas (jointly with the Department for Business, Innovation and Skills through UK Trade and Investment).

Secretary of State for Foreign and Commonwealth Affairs, Rt. Hon. David Miliband, MP
Principal Private Secretary, Matthew Gould
Special Advisers, Madlin Sadler; Sarah Schaefer
Parliamentary Private Secretary, Dan Norris, MP
Minister of State, Baroness Kinnock of Holyhead *(Europe)*
Private Secretary, Laura Clark
Parliamentary Private Secretary, Derek Wyatt, MP

Minister of State, Ivan Lewis, MP *(Middle East and North Africa, NATO, Terrorism)*
Private Secretary, Lisa Glover
Parliamentary Private Secretary, Doug Henderson, MP
Parliamentary Under-Secretary of State, Chris Bryant, MP
Private Secretary, Anjoum Noorani
Minister of State, Lord Davies of Abersoch, CBE *(Trade and Investment)*
Private Secretary, Debbie Clark
Permanent Under-Secretary of State and Head of HM Diplomatic Service, Sir Peter Ricketts, CMG
Private Secretary, Diane Sheard

MANAGEMENT BOARD
Group Chief Executive, UK Trade and Investment, Andrew Cahn
Members, James Bevan *(Change and Delivery);* Nick Baird *(Europe and Globalisation);* Alistair Johnson; Mariot Leslie *(Defence/Intelligence);* Keith Luck *(Finance);* Mark Lyall Grant *(Political);* Tony Mather *(Chief Information Officer);* Alison Platt

GOVERNMENT EQUALITIES OFFICE

Eland House, Bressenden Place, London SW1E 5DU
T 020-7944 0601 E enquiries@geo.gsi.gov.uk
W www.equalities.gov.uk

The Government Equalities Office (GEO) was created in July 2007. The GEO is responsible for the government's overall strategy on equality. Its work includes leading the development of a more integrated approach on equality across government; sponsoring the Equality and Human Rights Commission and Women's National Commission; taking forward the Minister for Women's priorities; taking forward work on the equality bill and supporting the work of the National Equality Panel. The department is responsible for leading policy on gender equality and sexual orientation, and for integrating work on disability, age, race and religion or belief into the overall equality framework.

Minister for Women and Equality, Rt. Hon. Harriet Harman, QC, MP *(Lord Privy Seal, Leader of the House of Commons and Labour Party Chair)*
Private Secretary, Lise-Anne Boissiere
Parliamentary Private Secretary, Nia Griffith, MP
Minister of State, Maria Eagle, MP
Private Secretary (at Ministry of Justice), Dileeni Daniel-Selvaratnam
Solicitor-General, Vera Baird, QC, MP
Parliamentary Under-Secretary of State, Michael Foster, MP
Private Secretary, Jack Feintuck

SENIOR MANAGEMENT TEAM
Director-General, Jonathan Rees
Policy Director, Janice Shersby
Director, Corporate Services, Chris Bull
Deputy Director, Discrimination Law, Melanie Field
Deputy Director, Gender Equality Policy and Inclusion, Helene Reardon-Bond
Deputy Director, Strategy, Alison Pritchard
Non-Executive Directors, Peter Bungard; Judy McKnight; Janet Soo-Chung

DEPARTMENT OF HEALTH

Richmond House, 79 Whitehall, London SW1A 2NS
T 020-7210 3000
W www.dh.gov.uk

The Department of Health is responsible for the provision of the National Health Service (NHS) in England and for social care. The department's aims are to support, protect, promote and improve the nation's health; to secure the provision of comprehensive, high-quality care for all those who need it, regardless of their ability to pay, where they live or their age; and to provide responsive adult social care for those who lack the support they need.

The Department of Health is responsible for setting health and social care policy in England. The department's work sets standards and drives modernisation across all areas of the NHS, social care and public health.

Secretary of State for Health, Rt. Hon. Andy Burnham, MP
Principal Private Secretary, Maeve Walsh
Parliamentary Private Secretary, Phil Wilson, MP
Minister of State, Rt. Hon. Mike O'Brien, MP, QC *(Health Services)*
Private Secretary, Elizabeth Gunnion
Parliamentary Private Secretary, James Cunningham, MP
Minister of State, Gillian Merron, MP *(Public Health)*
Private Secretary, Sarah Kirby
Parliamentary Private Secretary, Linda Waltho
Minister of State, Phil Hope, MP *(Care Services)*
Private Secretary, Ian Ellis
Parliamentary Under-Secretary of State, Ann Keen, MP *(Health Services)*
Private Secretary, Jeff Porter
Parliamentary Clerk, Tim Elms

MANAGEMENT BOARD
Chair, Hugh Taylor, CB (*Permanent Secretary of State)*
Members, Julie Baddeley; David Behan, CBE *(Social Care, Local Government and Care Partnerships);* Prof. Sir Liam Donaldson, KB *(Chief Medical Officer);* Richard Douglas, CB *(Finance and Operations);* Derek Myers; David Nicholson, CBE *(Chief Executive, NHS);* Mike Wheeler

NATIONAL CLINICAL DIRECTORS
Cancer, Prof. Mike Richards, CBE
Children, Young People and Community Services, Dr Sheila Shribman
Community Pharmacy, Jonathan Mason
Diabetes, Dr Rowan Hillson, MBE
Diagnostic Kidney Services, Dr Donal J. O'Donoghue
Emergency Access, Prof. Sir George Alberti
Equality and Human Rights, Surinder Sharma
Health and Work, Prof. Dame Carol Black
Heart Disease and Stroke, Prof. Roger Boyle, CBE
Hospital Pharmacy, Martin Stephens
Imaging, Dr Erika Denton
Learning Disabilities, Scott Watkin *(co-national director);* Anne Williams
Mental Health, Prof. Louis Appleby, CBE
Older People's Services, vacant
Pandemic Influenza Preparedness, Prof. Lindsey Davies
Patients and the Public, Joan Saddler, OBE
Primary Care, Dr David Colin-Thome
Service Reconfiguration, Prof. Sir George Alberti
Transplantation, Chris J. Rudge
Trauma Care, Prof. Keith Willett
Widening Participation in Learning, Prof. Bob Fryer, CBE

SOLICITOR'S OFFICE*
Solicitor, Richard Heaton
Director of DWP Legal Services, Greer Kerrigan, CB
Director of DH Legal Services, Frances Logan

* Also the solicitor's office for the Department for Work and Pensions

SPECIAL HEALTH AUTHORITIES
Care Quality Commission
W www.cqc.org.uk
Health Protection Agency
W www.hpa.org.uk
National Blood Service
W www.blood.co.uk
National Clinical Assessment Service
W www.ncas.npsa.nhs.uk
National Institute for Health and Clinical Excellence
W www.nice.org.uk
National Treatment Agency for Substance Misuse
W www.nta.nhs.uk
National Patient Safety Agency
W www.npsa.nhs.uk
NHS Appointments Commission
W www.appointments.org.uk
NHS Business Services Authority
W www.nhsbsa.nhs.uk
NHS Litigation Authority
W www.nhsla.com
UK Transplant
W www.uktransplant.org.uk

HOME OFFICE

2 Marsham Street, London SW1P 4DF
T 020-7035 4848 E public.enquiries@homeoffice.gsi.gov.uk
W www.homeoffice.gov.uk

The Home Office deals with those internal affairs in England and Wales which have not been assigned to other government departments. The Secretary of State for the Home Department is the link between the Queen and the public, and exercises certain powers on her behalf, including that of the royal pardon.

The Home Office aims to build a safe, just and tolerant society and to maintain and enhance public security and protection; to support and mobilise communities so that they are able to shape policy and improvement for their locality, overcome nuisance and anti-social behaviour, maintain and enhance social cohesion and enjoy their homes and public spaces peacefully; to deliver departmental policies and responsibilities fairly, effectively and efficiently; and to make the best use of resources. These objectives reflect the priorities of the government and the home secretary in areas of crime, citizenship and communities, namely to reduce crime and the fear of crime through visible, responsive and accountable policing; to reduce organised and international crime; to combat terrorism and other threats to national security; to ensure the effective delivery of justice; to reduce re-offending and protect the public; to reduce the availability and abuse of dangerous drugs; to regulate entry to, and settlement in, the UK in the interests of sustainable growth and social inclusion; and to support strong, active communities in which people of all races and backgrounds are valued and participate on equal terms.

The Home Office delivers these aims through the immigration services, its agencies and non-departmental public bodies, and by working with partners in private, public and voluntary sectors, individuals and communities. The home secretary is also the link between the UK government and the governments of the Channel Islands and the Isle of Man.

Secretary of State for the Home Department, Rt. Hon. Alan Johnson, MP
Principal Private Secretary, Richard Westlake
Assistant Private Secretary, Gareth Edwards
Special Advisers, Mario Dunn; Clare Montagu
Strategic Communications Adviser, Jo Revill
Minister of State, Rt. Hon. David Hanson, MP *(Security, Counter-Terrorism and Policing Reform)*
Private Secretary, Laura Ratcliffe
Minister of State, Phil Woolas, MP *(Borders)*
Private Secretary, Michael MacMillan
Parliamentary Under-Secretary of State, Lord West of Spithead, GCB, DSC *(Security and Counter-Terrorism)*
Private Secretary, Tom Hartley
Parliamentary Under-Secretary of State, Alan Campbell, MP *(Crime Reduction)*
Private Secretary, Paul Daly
Parliamentary Under-Secretary of State, Lord Brett *(Identity)*
Private Secretary (acting), Neil Roberts
Permanent Secretary of State, Sir David Normington, KCB
Private Secretary, Rachel Hopcroft

MANAGEMENT BOARD
Chair, Sir David Normington, KCB *(Permanent Secretary of State)*
Members, Derrick Anderson; Yasmin Diamond *(Communications);* Charles Farr *(Office for Security and Counter Terrorism);* James Hall *(Identity and Passport Service);* John Heywood; Lin Homer, CB *(UK Border Agency);* Helen Kilpatrick *(Financial and Commercial);* Peter Makeham, CB *(Strategy and Reform);* Stephen Rimmer *(Crime and Policing Group);* Kevin White, CB *(Human Resources)*

OFFICE FOR CRIMINAL JUSTICE REFORM
Chief Executive, Sharon White
Directors, Arwa'a Abdulla *(Policy and Process);* Helen Judge *(Strategy, Policy and Resources);* Catherine Lee *(Delivery and Communications)*
Note: The OCJR is a cross-departmental organisation, also reporting to the Ministry of Justice and the Office of the Attorney-General

DEPARTMENT FOR INTERNATIONAL DEVELOPMENT

1 Palace Street, London SW1 5HE
T 020-7023 0000
Abercrombie House, Eaglesham Road, East Kilbride, Glasgow G75 8EA
T 01355-844000
Public Enquiries 0845-300 4100
E enquiry@dfid.gov.uk W www.dfid.gov.uk

The Department for International Development (DFID) is responsible for promoting sustainable development and reducing poverty. The central focus of the government's policy, based on the 1997, 2000 and 2006 white papers on international development, is a commitment to the internationally agreed Millennium Development Goals, to be achieved by 2015. These seek to eradicate extreme poverty and hunger; achieve universal primary education; promote gender equality and empower women; reduce child mortality; improve maternal health; combat HIV/AIDS, malaria and other diseases; ensure environmental sustainability; and encourage a global partnership for development.

DFID's assistance is concentrated in the poorest countries of sub-Saharan Africa and Asia, but also contributes to poverty reduction and sustainable development in middle-income countries, including those in Latin America and Eastern Europe. The department works in partnership with governments committed to the

Millennium Development Goals, and with the private sector and the research community. It also works with multilateral institutions, including the World Bank, United Nations agencies and the European Commission. The department has headquarters in London and East Kilbride, offices in many developing countries, and staff based in British embassies and high commissions around the world.

Secretary of State for International Development, Rt. Hon. Douglas Alexander, MP
Principal Private Secretary, Matt Baugh
Private Secretary, Kate Joseph
Special Adviser, Richard Darlington
Parliamentary Private Secretary, Russell Brown, MP
Parliamentary Clerk, Jo Smith
Minister of State, Gareth R. Thomas, MP
Private Secretary, Alasdair Wardhaugh
Parliamentary Under-Secretary of State, Mike Foster, MP
Private Secretary, Greg Hicks
House of Lords Spokesperson, Baroness Amos
Liaison Peer, Baroness Whitaker
Whips, Bob Blizzard, MP *(Commons);* Baroness Royall *(Lords)*
Permanent Secretary, Minouche Shafik

MANAGEMENT BOARD

Members, Martin Dinham *(International);* Helen Ghosh; Bill Griffiths; Sue Owen *(Corporate Performance);* Mark Lowcock *(Country Programmes);* Andrew Steer *(Policy and Research)*

CDC GROUP

Cardinal Place, 80 Victoria Street SW1E 5JL
T 020-7963 4700 E enquiries@cdcgroup.com
W www.cdcgroup.com

Founded in 1948, CDC is a government-owned fund of funds that provides capital to invest through third-party fund managers in private equity funds focused on emerging economies; it covers countries in Africa, Asia and Latin America. CDC is a public limited company with the Department for International Development as its 100 per cent shareholder.

Chair, Richard Gillingwater, CBE
Chief Executive, Richard Laing

MINISTRY OF JUSTICE

102 Petty France, London SW1P 9AJ
T 020-3334 3555 E general.queries@justice.gsi.gov.uk
W www.justice.gov.uk

The Ministry of Justice (MoJ) was established in May 2007 and the responsibilities of the Department for Constitutional Affairs (DCA) were transferred to it. The MoJ's priorities are to protect the public; reduce reoffending; promote and provide access to justice; engender confidence in the justice system; uphold people's human rights, alongside their information and democratic rights; and to safeguard and modernise the constitution.

The MoJ incorporates the National Offender Management Service, which includes HM Prison Service and the National Probation Service, and the Office for Criminal Justice Reform (a cross-departmental organisation also reporting to the Home Office and the Office of the Attorney-General). In April 2006 the largest central government tribunals were incorporated into the MoJ (then, the DCA) as the Tribunals Service (*see* Tribunals section). The remit of the Lord Chancellor was also altered: he continues to be the government minister responsible to parliament for the judiciary and the courts system, but is no longer the head of the judiciary. The Lord Chief Justice has taken on the role of head of the judiciary and now performs many of the judicial functions formerly undertaken by the Lord Chancellor.

The MoJ established an independent Judicial Appointments Commission and related bodies, and retains its association with several associated departments, non-departmental public bodies and executive agencies, including the Northern Ireland Court Service, Her Majesty's Land Registry, the National Archives, the Legal Service Commission, and the Public Guardianship Office. The administrative functions of the Scotland Office and the Wales Office transferred to the MoJ in June 2003. Responsibilities for the maintenance of the relationship between Westminster and the devolved administrations in Edinburgh and Cardiff remain with the Secretary of State for Scotland and the Secretary of State for Wales respectively.

Secretary of State for Justice and Lord Chancellor, Rt. Hon. Jack Straw, MP
Principal Private Secretary, Alison Blackburne
Special Advisers, Mark Davies; Declan McHugh
Parliamentary Private Secretary, Mike Hall, MP
Minister of State, Michael Wills, MP
Private Secretary, Warren Seddon
Parliamentary Private Secretary, Stephen Hesford, MP
Minister of State, Maria Eagle, MP
Private Secretary, Dileeni Daniel-Selvaratnam
Parliamentary Under-Secretary of State, Lord Bach
Private Secretary, Hugo Deadman
Parliamentary Under-Secretary of State, Bridget Prentice, MP
Private Secretary, Peter Spence
Parliamentary Under-Secretary of State, Claire Ward, MP
Private Secretary, Phil Lawley
Permanent Secretary, Suma Chakrabarti
Private Secretary, Hannah Davenport
Parliamentary Clerk, Ann Nixon

CORPORATE MANAGEMENT BOARD

Chair, Suma Chakrabarti *(Permanent Secretary of State)*
Members, Anne Bulford; Rowena Collins-Rice *(Democracy, Constitution and Law, Chief Legal Advisor);* Carolyn Downs *(Corporate Performance, Deputy Permanent Secretary);* Helen Edwards, CBE *(Criminal Justice);* Andy Good *(Corporate Human Resources);* Peter Handcock, CBE *(Access to Justice);* David MacLeod; Marco Pierleoni *(Finance & Commercial);* Jonathan Slater *(Business Transformation);* Phil Wheatley *(National Offender Management Service)*

NORTHERN IRELAND OFFICE

11 Millbank, London SW1P 4PN
T 020-7210 3000
Castle Buildings, Stormont, Belfast BT4 3SG
T 028-9052 0700 E mail@nio.gov.uk
W www.nio.gov.uk

The Northern Ireland Office was established in 1972, when the Northern Ireland (Temporary Provisions) Act transferred the legislative and executive powers of the Northern Ireland parliament and government to the UK parliament and a secretary of state.

The Northern Ireland Office is responsible primarily for security issues, law and order and prisons, and for matters relating to the political and constitutional future of the province. It also deals with international issues as they affect Northern Ireland.

Under the terms of the 1998 Good Friday Agreement, power was devolved to the Northern Ireland Assembly in 1999. The assembly took on responsibility for the relevant areas of work previously undertaken by the departments of the Northern Ireland Office, covering agriculture and rural development, the environment, regional development, social development, education, higher education, training and employment, enterprise, trade and investment, culture, arts and leisure, health, social services, public safety and finance and personnel. In October 2002 the Northern Ireland Assembly was suspended and Northern Ireland returned to direct rule, but despite repeated setbacks, devolution was restored on 8 May 2007. For further details, *see* Regional Government section.

Secretary of State for Northern Ireland, Rt. Hon. Shaun Woodward, MP
Parliamentary Private Secretary, Rob Marris, MP
Minister of State, Paul Goggins, MP
Permanent Secretary, Sir Jonathan Phillips
Head of the Northern Ireland Civil Service, Bruce Robinson

NORTHERN IRELAND INFORMATION SERVICE
Castle Buildings, Stormont Estate, Belfast BT4 3SG
T 028-9052 0700

OFFICE OF THE ADVOCATE-GENERAL FOR SCOTLAND

Dover House, Whitehall, London SW1A 2AU
T 020-7270 6713
Office of the Solicitor to the Advocate-General, Victoria Quay, Leith, Edinburgh EH6 6QQ
T 0131-244 1635
E privateoffice@advocategeneral.gsi.gov.uk
W www.oag.gov.uk

The Advocate-General for Scotland is one of the three law officers of the crown, alongside the Attorney-General and the Solicitor-General for England and Wales. He is the legal adviser to the UK government on Scottish law and is supported by staff in the Office of the Advocate-General for Scotland. The office is divided into the Legal Secretariat, based mainly in London, and the Office of the Solicitor to the Advocate-General, based in Edinburgh.

The post was created as a consequence of the constitutional changes set out in the Scotland Act 1998, which created a devolved Scottish parliament. The Lord Advocate and the Solicitor-General for Scotland then became part of the Scottish government and the Advocate-General took over their previous role as legal adviser to the government on Scots law. *See also* Regional Government section and Ministry of Justice.

Advocate-General for Scotland, Lord Davidson of Glen Clova, QC
Private Secretary, Susan Cook

OFFICE OF THE LEADER OF THE HOUSE OF COMMONS

26 Whitehall, London SW1A 2WH
T 020-7276 1005
E leader@commonsleader.x.gsi.gov.uk
W www.commonsleader.gov.uk

The Office of the Leader of the House of Commons is responsible for the arrangement of government business in the House of Commons and for planning and supervising the government's legislative programme. The Leader of the House of Commons upholds the rights and privileges of the house and acts as a spokesperson for the government as a whole.

The leader reports regularly to the cabinet on parliamentary business and the legislative programme. In her capacity as leader of the house, she is a member of the Public Accounts Commission and of the House of Commons Commission. She also chairs the cabinet committee on the legislative programme. As Lord Privy Seal, she is chair of the board of trustees of the Chevening Estate.

The Deputy Leader of the House of Commons supports the leader in handling the government's business in the house. She is responsible for monitoring MPs' and peers' correspondence and is a member of several committees.

Leader of the House of Commons and Lord Privy Seal, Rt. Hon. Harriet Harman, QC, MP
Principal Private Secretary, Matilda Quiney
Private Secretaries, Lise-Anne Boissiere; Mike Winter
Deputy Leader of the House of Commons, Barbara Keeley, MP
Private Secretary, Kate Wilson

PRIVY COUNCIL OFFICE

2 Carlton Gardens, London SW1Y 5AA
T 020-7747 5310 E pcosecretariat@pco.x.gsi.gov.uk
W www.privy-council.gov.uk

The primary function of the office is to act as the secretariat to the Privy Council. It is responsible for the arrangements leading to the making of all royal proclamations and orders in council; for certain formalities connected with ministerial changes; for considering applications for the granting (or amendment) of royal charters; for the scrutiny and approval of by-laws and statutes of chartered institutions and of the governing instruments of universities and colleges; for approving use of the word 'university' in a company name; and for the appointment of high sheriffs and many crown and Privy Council appointments to governing bodies. Under the relevant acts, the office is responsible for the approval of certain regulations and rules made by the governing bodies of the medical and certain allied professions.

The Lord President of the Council is the ministerial head of the office and presides at meetings of the Privy Council, is a member of the cabinet and Leader of the House of Lords. She has no departmental portfolio but is a member of several cabinet committees, and supports the Lord Chancellor in his responsibility for the House of Lords reform. She is the Lords' spokesperson on equality and human rights issues, and is responsible to the prime minister for the organisation of government business in the house as well as repeating in the House of Lords statements made by the prime minister in the House of Commons. She also gives guidance to the house on matters of order and procedure. The Clerk of the Council is the administrative head of the Privy Council office.

Lord President of the Council (and Leader of the House of Lords), Lord Mandelson, PC
Clerk of the Council, Judith Simpson
Head of Secretariat and Senior Clerk, Ceri King
Senior Clerks, Christopher Berry; Meriel McCullagh
Registrar of the Judicial Committee, Mary MacDonald

SCOTLAND OFFICE

Dover House, Whitehall, London SW1A 2AU
T 020-7270 6754
1 Melville Crescent, Edinburgh EH3 7HW
T 0131-244 9010
E scottish.secretary@scotland.gsi.gov.uk
W www.scotlandoffice.gov.uk

The Scotland Office is the department of the Secretary of State for Scotland which represents Scottish interests within the UK government in matters reserved to the UK parliament. The Secretary of State for Scotland also exercises certain specific functions in relation to devolution, including those provided for in the Scotland Act 1998; maintains the stability of the devolution settlement for Scotland; and pays grants to the Scottish Consolidated Fund and manages other financial transactions.

Reserved matters include the constitution, foreign affairs, defence, international development, the civil service, financial and economic matters, national security, immigration and nationality, misuse of drugs, trade and industry, various aspects of energy regulation (eg coal, electricity, oil, gas and nuclear energy), various aspects of transport, social security, employment, abortion, genetics, surrogacy, medicines, broadcasting and equal opportunities. Devolved matters include health and social work, education and training, local government and housing, justice and police, agriculture, forestry, fisheries, the environment, tourism, sports, heritage, economic development and internal transport. *See also* Regional Government section and Ministry of Justice.

Secretary of State for Scotland, Jim Murphy, MP
Private Secretary, Kate Richards
Parliamentary Private Secretary, Russell Brown, MP
Parliamentary Under-Secretary of State, Ann McKechin, MP
Private Secretary, Barbara Reid
Spokesperson in the House of Lords, Lord Davidson of Glen Clova

DEPARTMENT FOR TRANSPORT

Great Minster House, 76 Marsham Street, London SW1P 4DR
T 020-7944 8300 W www.dft.gov.uk

The Department for Transport (DfT) was established in May 2002 following the de-merger of the Department of Transport, Local Government and the Regions. The department's role is to oversee the delivery of a reliable, safe and secure transport system; to determine overall transport strategy and to manage relationships with the local, regional and private sector partners that deliver that strategy. Its main responsibilities are aviation, freight, health and safety, integrated and local transport, London Underground, maritime, mobility and inclusion, railways, roads and road safety, shipping and vehicles.

The department's work is focused on the following objectives: supporting national economic competitiveness and growth by delivering reliable and efficient transport networks; reducing transport's emissions of carbon dioxide and other greenhouse gases; reducing the risk of death, injury or illness arising from transport and promoting travel modes that are beneficial to health; promoting equality of opportunity for all citizens; improving quality of life for transport users and non-transport users; and promoting a healthy natural environment. The department funds the provision and maintenance of infrastructure, subsidises services and fares on social grounds and sets regulatory standards, especially for safety, accessibility and environmental impact.

Secretary of State for Transport, Lord Andrew Adonis
Principal Private Secretary, Tim Figures
Minister of State, Rt. Hon. Sadiq Khan, MP
Private Secretary, Peter Lee
Parliamentary Under-Secretary of State, Chris Mole, MP
Private Secretary, Stephen Hennigan
Parliamentary Under-Secretary of State, Paul Clark, MP
Private Secretary, Audy Utchanah
Permanent Secretary, Robert Devereux
Private Secretary, Victoria Robb

MANAGEMENT BOARD
Chair, Robert Devereux *(Permanent Secretary of State)*
Members, Brian Collins *(Chief Scientific Adviser);* Alan Cook; Sally Davis; Steve Gooding *(Motoring and Freight Services);* Richard Hatfield *(International Networks and Environment);* Bronwyn Hill *(City and Regional Networks Group);* David Hipple *(Corporate Support Functions);* Mike Mitchell *(National Networks);* Christopher Muttukumaru *(Legal Adviser);* Ed Smith

HM TREASURY

1 Horse Guards Road, London SW1A 2HQ
T 020-7270 4558 F 020-7270 4861
E public.enquiries@hm-treasury.gov.uk
W www.hm-treasury.gov.uk

HM Treasury is the country's economics and finance ministry, and is responsible for formulating and implementing the government's financial and economic policy. It aims to raise the rate of sustainable growth, boost prosperity, and provide the conditions necessary for universal economic and employment opportunities. The Office of the Lord High Treasurer has been continuously in commission for over 200 years. The Lord High Commissioners of HM Treasury are the First Lord of the Treasury (who is also the prime minister), the Chancellor of the Exchequer and five junior lords. This board of commissioners is assisted at present by the chief secretary, the parliamentary secretary (who is also the government chief whip in the House of Commons), the financial secretary, the economic secretary and the exchequer secretary. The prime minister as first lord is not primarily concerned with the day-to-day aspects of Treasury business; neither are the parliamentary secretary and the junior lords as government whips. Treasury business is managed by the Chancellor of the Exchequer and the other Treasury ministers, assisted by the permanent secretary.

The chief secretary is responsible for public expenditure, including spending reviews and strategic planning; in-year control; public sector pay and pensions; efficiency in public services; capital investment; and public service delivery and performance. He also has responsibility for the Treasury's interest in devolution, assists the Chancellor of the Exchequer where necessary on international and European issues, and oversees the integration of the tax and benefit system.

The financial secretary is the departmental minister for HM Revenue and Customs and the Valuation Office Agency and has strategic oversight of the UK tax system as a whole. She is the lead minister on European and international tax issues, and her responsibilities include the Finance Bill, the voluntary sector and charities, childcare issues and tax credits.

The exchequer secretary is a title only used occasionally, normally when the post of paymaster-general is allocated to a minister outside of the Treasury (as it is at present; Rt. Hon. Tessa Jowell, MP was appointed paymaster-general as Olympic minister within the Cabinet Office in June 2007). Her responsibilities include enterprise and productivity; competition and better regulation; science, innovation and skills policy; regional economic policy and environmental issues.

The economic secretary's responsibilities include financial services policy, including tax issues; personal savings policy; foreign exchange reserves and debt

management policy; stamp duty land tax and real estate investment trusts; and EMU preparations.
Prime Minister and First Lord of the Treasury, Rt. Hon. Gordon Brown, MP
Chancellor of the Exchequer, Rt. Hon. Alistair Darling, MP
Principal Private Secretary, Dan Rosenfield
Private Secretaries, Sophie Dean; Gemma Timms
Parliamentary Private Secretary, Ann Coffey, MP
Special Advisers, Catherine Macleod; Sam White
Council of Economic Advisers, Torsten Henricson-Bell; Andrew Maugham; Geoffrey Spence
Chief Secretary to the Treasury, Rt. Hon. Liam Byrne, MP
Private Secretary, Giles Thomson
Parliamentary Private Secretary, vacant
Financial Secretary to the Treasury, Rt. Hon. Stephen Timms, MP
Private Secretary, Cerys Morgan
Parliamentary Private Secretary, vacant
Exchequer Secretary to the Treasury, Sarah McCarthy-Fry, MP
Private Secretary, Pedro Wrobel
Economic Secretary to the Treasury, Ian Pearson, MP
Private Secretary, Simon Whitfield
Minister of State (with responsibility for revenue protection at the border), Phil Woolas, MP
Financial Services Secretary, Paul Myners, CBE
Permanent Secretary to the Treasury, Nick Macpherson
Private Secretary, Amber Batool
Parliamentary Secretary to the Treasury and Government Chief Whip, Rt. Hon. Nicholas Brown, MP
Parliamentary Private Secretary, vacant
Lords Commissioners of HM Treasury (Whips), Bob Blizzard, MP; Tony Cunningham, MP; Stephen McCabe, MP; Frank Roy, MP; Dave Watts, MP
Assistant Whips, Lyn Brown, MP; Dawn Butler, MP; Mary Creagh, MP; John Heppell, MP, Sharon Hodgson, MP; Kerry McCarthy, MP; George Mudie, MP; Mark Tami, MP; David Wright, MP

MANAGEMENT BOARD
Chair, Nick Macpherson *(Permanent Secretary of State)*
Members, Andrew Hudson *(Public Services and Growth);* Mark Neale *(Budget, Tax and Welfare);* Stephen Pickford and Tom Scholar *(International and Finance);* Dave Ramsden *(Macroeconomic and Fiscal Policy);* Ray Shostak *(Director General, Performance Management);* Nigel Smith *(Office of Government Commerce)*

OFFICE OF GOVERNMENT COMMERCE (OGC)
Rosebery Court, St Andrews Business Park, Norwich, Norfolk NR7 0HS
T 0845-000 4999 E servicedesk@ogc.gsi.gov.uk
W www.ogc.gov.uk
The Office of Government Commerce was set up in April 2000. It is responsible for increasing the government's value for money by improving standards and capability in procurement, for example by commodities buying, delivering major capital projects, and maximising the effective use of government spending and a £30bn property estate.
Chief Executive, Nigel Smith

BUYING SOLUTIONS
5th Floor, Royal Liver Building, Pier Head, Liverpool L3 1PE
T 0845-410 2222 E info@buyingsolutions.gov.uk
W www.buyingsolutions.gov.uk
The agency provides a professional procurement service to government departments and other public bodies. It was established in 2001 and is an executive agency of the Office of Government Commerce in the Treasury.
Chief Executive, Alison Littley

THE PRIME MINISTER'S DELIVERY UNIT
1 Horse Guards Road, London SW1A 2HQ
T 020-7270 5867
E PMDUBusinessCo-ordinationteam@hm-treasury.x.gsi.gov.uk
W www.hm-treasury.gov.uk
The Prime Minister's Delivery Unit was established in June 2001. Its role is to help the government to deliver improved and more efficient public services. The unit reports jointly to the prime minister and the chancellor, and works closely with Number 10, the Cabinet Office and other departments on the critical priorities and actions needed to strengthen delivery across government.
Head of Unit, Ray Shostak, CBE

WALES OFFICE
Gwydyr House, Whitehall, London SW1A 2NP
T 020-7270 0534
E walesoffice@walesoffice.gsi.gov.uk
W www.walesoffice.gov.uk
The Wales Office was established in 1999 when most of the powers of the Welsh Office were handed over to the National Assembly for Wales. It is the department of the Secretary of State for Wales, who is the key government figure liaising with the devolved government in Wales and who represents Welsh interests in the cabinet and parliament. The secretary of state has the right to attend and speak at sessions of the National Assembly (and must consult the assembly on the government's legislative programme). *See also* Regional Government section and Ministry of Justice.
Secretary of State for Wales, Rt. Hon. Peter Hain, MP
Principal Private Secretary, Simon Morris
Parliamentary Under-Secretary, Wayne David, MP
Director of Office, Alan Cogbill

DEPARTMENT FOR WORK AND PENSIONS
Caxton House, Tothill Street, London SW1H 9NA
T 020-7962 8000 E enquiries@dwp.gsi.gov.uk
W www.dwp.gov.uk
The Department for Work and Pensions was formed in June 2001 from parts of the former Department of Social Security, the Department for Education and Employment and the Employment Service. The department helps unemployed people of working age into work, helps employers to fill their vacancies and provides financial support to people unable to help themselves, through back-to-work programmes. The department also administers the child support system, social security benefits and the social fund. In addition, the department has reciprocal social security arrangements with other countries.
Secretary of State for Work and Pensions, Rt. Hon. Yvette Cooper, MP
Principal Private Secretary, John Oliver
Private Secretaries, Melanie Hogger; Katherine Newall; James Rose; Phill Wells
Special Advisers, Will McDonald; Ellie Wilcox
Minister of State, Rt. Hon. Jim Knight, MP *(Employment and Welfare Reform)*
Private Secretary, Sarah Ormerod
Parliamentary Private Secretary, Liz Blackman, MP
Assistant Private Secretaries, Lynn Eccles; Andrew Logan; Rachel Radice; James Stephens
Minister of State, Angela Eagle, MP *(Pensions and the Ageing Society)*

Private Secretary, Michael Dynan-Oakley
Assistant Private Secretaries, Emily Holdup; Holly Riley
Parliamentary Under-Secretary of State, Helen Goodman, MP
Private Secretaries, Glen Brown; Jonathan Forster; Gill Hartlet
Parliamentary Under-Secretary of State, Jonathan Shaw, MP
Private Secretary, Michael Hewson
Assistant Private Secretaries, Lucy Fletcher; Helen Hutchings
Minister of State, Jonathan Shaw, MP *(Disabled People, Minister for the South East)*
Private Secretary, Katie Miles
Assistant Private Secretaries, Helen McDaniel; David Miller *(for the South East)*; James Rogers
Permanent Secretary, Leigh Lewis
Private Secretaries, Olmer Slocombe; Judith Tunstall; Lucy Wyatt

PENSIONS CLIENT DIRECTORATE
Director-General, vacant

GROUP FINANCE DIRECTORATE
Director-General, John Codling

CORPORATE INFORMATION TECHNOLOGY
Director-General, Joe Harley

HUMAN RESOURCES GROUP
Director-General, Chris Last

HEALTH, WORK AND WELLBEING DIRECTORATE
Director, Chief Medical Adviser, Chief Scientist, Dr Bill Gunnyeon

LEGAL GROUP
Director-General, Richard Heaton

COMMUNICATIONS NETWORK
Director, Sue Garrard

EQUALITY GROUP
Director-General, Adam Sharples

WORK WELFARE GROUP
Director-General, Sue Owen

EXECUTIVE AGENCIES

Executive agencies are well-defined business units that carry out services with a clear focus on delivering specific outputs within a framework of accountability to ministers. They can be set up or disbanded without legislation, and they are organisationally independent from the department they are answerable to. In the following list the agencies are shown in the accounts of their sponsor departments. Legally they act on behalf of the relevant secretary of state. Their chief executives also perform the role of accounting officers, which means they are responsible for the money spent by their organisations. Staff employed by agencies are civil servants.

CABINET OFFICE

COI (CENTRAL OFFICE OF INFORMATION)
Hercules Road, London SE1 7DU
T 020-7928 2345 F 020-7928 5037
W www.coi.gov.uk

The COI is the principal agency within government for the provision and procurement of marketing and communications services. Administrative responsibility for the COI rests with the minister for the Cabinet Office.
Chief Executive, M. Lund
Deputy Chief Executive, P. Buchanan

MANAGEMENT BOARD
Members, Ms A. Butler; M. Cross; I. Hamilton; G. Hooper; H. Lederer; Ms E. Lochhead; N. Martinson; A. Wade; Mrs S. Whetton

ATTORNEY-GENERAL'S OFFICE

NATIONAL FRAUD AUTHORITY
PO Box 64170, London WC1A 9BP
T 020-3356 1000 W www.attorneygeneral.gov.uk/nfa

The National Fraud Authority (NFA) was established on 1 October 2008 to increase protection for the UK economy from the harm caused by fraud. It works with private, public and third sector organisations to initiate, coordinate and communicate counter-fraud activity across the economy. The authority's priorities are to tackle the key fraud threats to the UK, and to act effectively to pursue fraudsters and hold them to account. The NFA is also working to improve the support available to fraud victims and to build the UK's capability to share and act on knowledge about fraud, both nationally and internationally.
Chief Executive, Dr Bernard Herdan, CB

TREASURY SOLICITOR'S DEPARTMENT
1 Kemble Street, London WC2B 4TS
T 020-7210 3000
E thetreasurysolicitor@tsol.gsi.gov.uk
W www.tsol.gov.uk

The Treasury Solicitor's Department, which became an executive agency in 1996, provides legal services for many government departments and is answerable to the Attorney-General. Those departments without their own lawyers are provided with legal advice, and both they and other departments are provided with litigation services. The Treasury Solicitor is also the Queen's Proctor, and is responsible for collecting ownerless goods *(bona vacantia)* on behalf of the crown.
HM Procurator-General and Treasury Solicitor (Permanent Secretary), Paul Jenkins

BONA VACANTIA DIVISION
Head of Division, Zane Denton

CABINET OFFICE AND CENTRAL ADVISORY DIVISION
Head of Division, vacant

DEPARTMENT OF CULTURE, MEDIA AND SPORT DIVISION
Legal Adviser, Patrick Kilgarriff

DEPARTMENT FOR CHILDREN, SCHOOLS AND FAMILIES DIVISION
Legal Adviser, Claire Johnston

EUROPEAN DIVISION
Head of Division, Paul Berman

HM TREASURY ADVISORY DIVISION
Legal Adviser, Stephen Parker

LITIGATION GROUP
Head of Division, Hugh Giles

DEPARTMENT FOR BUSINESS, INNOVATION AND SKILLS

COMPANIES HOUSE

Crown Way, Cardiff CF14 3UZ
T 0303-123 4500
E enquiries@companieshouse.gov.uk
W www.companieshouse.gov.uk

Companies House incorporates companies, registers company documents and provides company information.
Registrar of Companies for England and Wales, Gareth Jones
Registrar of Companies for Scotland, Dorothy Blair

THE INSOLVENCY SERVICE

21 Bloomsbury Street, London WC1B 3QW
Insolvency Enquiry Line 0845-602 9848
Redundancy Enquiry Line 0845-145 0004
W www.insolvency.gov.uk

The role of the service includes administration and investigation of the affairs of bankrupts, partners and companies in compulsory liquidation; dealing with the disqualification of directors in all corporate failures; authorising and regulating the insolvency profession; providing banking and investment services for bankruptcy and liquidation estate funds; assessing and paying statutory entitlement to redundancy payments when an employer cannot, or will not, pay its employees; and advising ministers on insolvency, redundancy and related issues.
Inspector-General and Chief Executive, Stephen Speed
Deputy Chief Executive, Graham Horne
Deputy Inspectors-General, Les Cramp;
Inspector of Companies and Head of Investigation and Enforcement Services, Robert Burns

INTELLECTUAL PROPERTY OFFICE

Concept House, Cardiff Road, Newport NP10 8QQ
T 0845-950 0505 E enquiries@ipo.gov.uk
W www.ipo.gov.uk

The Intellectual Property Office, formerly known as the Patent Office, was established in 1990 and became a trading fund in 1991. The office is responsible for intellectual property (IP) policy and operation in the UK, and aims to educate business, researchers and the public about the IP system; facilitate the appropriate protection and use of rights; design and provide commercial services to assist business use of the IP system; and create a domestic and international legal and political framework, which balances the interests of rights holders with the need for open competition and free markets.
Comptroller-General and Chief Executive, Ian Fletcher

NATIONAL MEASUREMENT OFFICE

Stanton Avenue, Teddington, Middx TW11 0JZ
T 020-8943 7272 E info@nmo.gov.uk
W www.nmo.bis.gov.uk

The National Measurement Office (NMO) was created in April 2009, merging the functions of the National Weights and Measures Laboratory and the National Measurement System. NMO is responsible for all aspects of the national measurement system and provides a legal metrology infrastructure necessary to facilitate fair competition, support innovation, promote international trade and protect consumers, health and the environment.
Chief Executive, Peter Mason

DEPARTMENT FOR COMMUNITIES AND LOCAL GOVERNMENT

FIRE SERVICE COLLEGE

Moreton-in-Marsh, Gloucestershire GL56 0RH
T 01608-650831 E enquiries@fireservicecollege.ac.uk
W www.fireservicecollege.ac.uk

The Fire Service College provides fire-related training, both practical and theoretical, consultancy, and library and information services to the UK fire and rescue service, other UK public sector organisations, the private sector, and the international market.
Chief Executive (acting), Sally Sheen

ORDNANCE SURVEY

Romsey Road, Southampton SO16 4GU
T 0845-605 0505
E customerservices@ordnancesurvey.co.uk
W www.ordnancesurvey.co.uk

Ordnance Survey is the national mapping agency for Great Britain. It is a government department and executive agency operating as a trading fund since 1999.
Director-General and Chief Executive, Vanessa Lawrence, CB

PLANNING INSPECTORATE

Temple Quay House, 2 The Square, Temple Quay, Bristol BS1 6PN
T 0117-372 6372
E enquiries@planning-inspectorate.gsi.gov.uk
Crown Buildings, Cathays Park, Cardiff CF10 3NQ
T 029-2082 3866 E wales@planning-inspectorate.gsi.gov.uk
W www.planning-inspectorate.gov.uk

The main work of the inspectorate consists of the processing of planning and enforcement appeals, and holding examinations into local development plans and regional spatial strategies. It also deals with appeals against the decisions of local authorities on planning applications; appeals against local authority enforcement notices; listed building consent appeals; advertisement appeals; rights of way cases, and cases arising from the Environmental Protection and Water acts, the Transport and Works Act 1992 and other highways legislation.
Chief Executive, Katrine Sporle

THE QUEEN ELIZABETH II CONFERENCE CENTRE

Broad Sanctuary, London SW1P 3EE
T 020-7222 5000 F 020-7798 4200
E info@qeiicc.co.uk W www.qeiicc.co.uk

The centre provides secure conference facilities for national and international government and private sector use.
Chief Executive, Ernest Vincent

DEPARTMENT FOR CULTURE, MEDIA AND SPORT

THE ROYAL PARKS

The Old Police House, Hyde Park, London W2 2UH
T 020-7298 2000 E hq@royalparks.gsi.gov.uk
W www.royalparks.org.uk

Royal Parks is responsible for maintaining and developing over 2,000 hectares (5,000 acres) of urban parkland contained within the eight royal parks in London: Bushy Park (with the Longford river); Green Park; Greenwich Park; Hyde Park; Kensington Gardens; Regent's Park (with Primrose Hill); Richmond Park and St James's Park.
Chief Executive, Mark Camley

DEPARTMENT FOR ENVIRONMENT, FOOD AND RURAL AFFAIRS

ANIMAL HEALTH
Corporate Centre, Block C, Government Buildings, Whittington Road, Worcester WR5 2LQ
T 01905-763355
E corporate-office@animalhealth.gsi.gov.uk
W www.defra.gov.uk/animalhealth
Animal Health is an executive agency that also works on behalf of the Welsh Assembly Government, the Scottish government and the Food Standards Agency. It is the government's delivery agent for ensuring the health and welfare of farmed animals. It is also responsible for the prevention, detection and management of diseases in animals. Animal Health's main responsibilities include protecting the welfare of farmed animals; the eradication of endemic disease; import and export certification; animal by-product regulation; and preparedness for managing exotic animal diseases. Animal Health is also reponsible for licensing the trade in endangered species for conservation purposes; for ensuring that eggs are correctly labelled and there is compliance with marketing conditions; and for monitoring the standard of hygiene in relation to the nation's raw milk supply.
Chief Executive, Catherine Brown

CENTRE FOR ENVIRONMENT, FISHERIES AND AQUACULTURE SCIENCE (CEFAS)
Pakefield Road, Lowestoft, Suffolk NR33 0HT
T 01502-562244 W www.cefas.co.uk
Established in April 1997, the agency provides research and consultancy services in fisheries science and management, aquaculture, fish health and hygiene, environmental impact assessment, and environmental quality assessment.
Chief Executive, Richard Judge

FOOD AND ENVIRONMENT RESEARCH AGENCY
Sand Hutton, York YO41 1LZ
T 01904-462000 F 01904-462111
E info@fera.gsi.gov.uk W www.fera.defra.gov.uk
The Food and Environment Research Agency was formed on 1 April 2009 from the merger of the Central Science Laboratory, the Government Contamination Service, and DEFRA's Plant Health division and Plant Varieties office. The agency's purpose is to support and develop a sustainable food chain, a healthy natural environment, and to protect the community from biological and chemical risks. It does this by providing evidence, analysis and professional advice to the government, international organisations and the private sector. The agency brings together expertise in policy issues, particularly relating to seed, plant and bee health; inspection services necessary to ensure protection for seeds, crops and horticulture; multi-disciplinary science to rapidly diagnose threats, evaluate risk and inform policy in food and environmental areas; and in responding to and recovering from unforeseen or emergency situations.
Chief Executive, Adrian Belton

MARINE AND FISHERIES AGENCY
Ergon House, Area 4A, Horseferry Road, London SW1P 2AL
T 020-7270 8326 E info@mfa.gsi.gov.uk
W www.mfa.gov.uk
The Marine and Fisheries Agency was established in October 2005 to coordinate for the first time the service delivery, inspection and enforcement of activities provided by the government to the fishing industry and other marine stakeholders in England and Wales.
Chief Executive, Nigel Gooding

RURAL PAYMENTS AGENCY
Kings House, 33 Kings Road, Reading RG1 3BU
T 0845-603 7777
E enquiries@rpa.gsi.gov.uk W www.rpa.gov.uk
The RPA was established in 2001. It is the single paying agency responsible for Common Agricultural Policy (CAP) schemes in England and for certain schemes throughout the UK; it intends to deliver over £2bn of payments to farmers and traders per year.
Chief Executive, Tony Cooper
Chief Operating Officer (interim), Steve Pearce

VETERINARY LABORATORIES AGENCY
Woodham Lane, New Haw, Addlestone, Surrey KT15 3NB
T 01932-341111
E enquiries@vla.defra.gov.uk W www.vla.gov.uk
The Veterinary Laboratories Agency is a regional network of 16 veterinary laboratories and two surveillance centres, which provides all sectors of the animal health industry with animal disease surveillance, diagnostic services and veterinary scientific research.
Chief Executive, Prof. S. P. Borriello

VETERINARY MEDICINES DIRECTORATE
Woodham Lane, New Haw, Addlestone, Surrey KT15 3LS
T 01932-336911 E postmaster@vmd.defra.gsi.gov.uk
W www.vmd.gov.uk
The Veterinary Medicines Directorate is responsible for all aspects of the authorisation and control of veterinary medicines, including post-authorisation surveillance of residues in animals and animal products. It is also responsible for the development and enforcement of legislation concerning veterinary medicines and the provision of policy advice to ministers.
Chief Executive, Steve Dean

FOREIGN AND COMMONWEALTH OFFICE

FCO SERVICES
Hanslope Park, Milton Keynes MK19 7BH
T 01908-515789 E fco.services@fco.gov.uk
W www.fcoservices.gov.uk
FCO Services was established as an executive agency in April 2006 and became a trading fund in April 2008. It delivers a combination of secure IT, estates and logistical services to the FCO in the UK and at its missions overseas and to other UK government departments and public bodies. Its customers also include other governments and international institutions with whom the UK has close links.
Chief Executive, Chris Moxey

CORPS OF QUEEN'S MESSENGERS
Support Group, Foreign and Commonwealth Office, London SW1A 2AH
T 020-7008 2779
The Corps of Queen's Messengers, couriers of confidential and important documents, was transferred to FCO Services in 2006.
Chief Executive, Chris Moxey
Superintendent of the Corps of Queen's Messengers, Sqn. Ldr. J. S. Frizzell
Queen's Messengers, S. J. Addy; P. B. G. Allen; R. G. Allen;

Maj. A. N. D. Bols; Maj. S. Cambridge; J. Coates; A. Dingle; S. Harrop; J. A. Hatfield; Sqn. Ldr. P. J. Hearn; Sqn. Ldr. A. M. Hill; W. Lisle; Maj. K. J. Rowbottom; B. S. Thorpe; R. T. Wilson

WILTON PARK CONFERENCE CENTRE
Wiston House, Steyning, W. Sussex BN44 3DZ
T 01903-815020 E admin@wiltonpark.org.uk
W www.wiltonpark.org.uk
Wilton Park organises international affairs conferences and is hired out to government departments and commercial users.
Chief Executive, Richard Burge

DEPARTMENT OF HEALTH

MEDICINES AND HEALTHCARE PRODUCTS REGULATORY AGENCY (MHRA)
Market Towers, 1 Nine Elms Lane, London SW8 5NQ
T 020-7084 2000 E info@mhra.gsi.gov.uk
W www.mhra.gov.uk
The MHRA is responsible for protecting and promoting public and patient safety by ensuring that medicines, healthcare products and medical equipment meet appropriate standards of safety, quality, performance and effectiveness, and are used safely.
Chair, Prof. Sir Alasdair Breckenridge, CBE
Chief Executive, Prof. Kent Woods

NHS PURCHASING AND SUPPLY AGENCY
Premier House, 60 Caversham Road, Reading RG1 7EB
T 0118-980 8600 E pasa@pasa.nhs.uk
W www.pasa.nhs.uk
The agency was established in April 2000 and is responsible for ensuring that the NHS makes the most effective use of its resources by getting the best value for money possible when purchasing goods and services. The agency advises ministers and government on policy and the strategic direction of procurement across the NHS.
Chief Operating Officer, John Cooper

HOME OFFICE

CRIMINAL RECORDS BUREAU
PO Box 110, Liverpool L69 3EF
T 0870-909 0811 W www.crb.gov.uk
The Criminal Records Bureau was launched in March 2002 and provides access to criminal record information to enable organisations in the public, private and voluntary sectors to make safer recruitment decisions by identifying candidates who may be unsuitable for certain work – especially that which involves children or vulnerable adults.
Chief Executive (interim), Steve Long

IDENTITY AND PASSPORT SERVICE
Globe House, 89 Eccleston Square, London SW1V 1PN
T Passport Advice Line 0300-222 0000, General Register Office 0845-603 7788
E hqenquiries@ips.gsi.gov.uk W www.ips.gov.uk
The Identity and Passport Service was established in April 2006 and incorporates the UK Passport Service and the General Register Office. The role of the UK Passport Service is to provide passport services and, from late 2009 onwards, it is scheduled to begin the issue of identity cards for British and foreign nationals resident in the UK (as part of the National Identity Scheme). The General Register Office is responsible for overseeing the system of civil registration in England and Wales, which involves administering the marriage laws; securing an effective system for the registration of births, adoptions, civil partnerships, marriages and deaths; maintaining an archive of births, civil partnerships, marriages and deaths; maintaining the adopted children's register, adoption contact register and other registers; and supplying certificates from the registers and the archives for research or family history purposes.
Chief Executive and Registrar-General, James Hall

UK BORDER AGENCY
Lunar House, 40 Wellesley Road, Croydon, Surrey CR9 2BY
T 0870 606 7766 E ukbapublicenquiries@ukba.gsi.gov.uk
W www.ukba.homeoffice.gov.uk
The UK Border Agency was established in April 2008 and became an executive agency of the Home Office in April 2009. The agency brings together the work previously carried out by the Border and Immigration Agency, customs detection work at the border from HM Revenue and Customs, and UK visa services from the Foreign and Commonwealth Office. Its three objectives are to protect the border and the UK's national interests; to tackle border tax fraud, smuggling and immigration crime; and to implement fast and fair decisions.
Chief Executive, Lin Homer
Board Members, Jonathan Sedgwick (Deputy Chief Execcutive); Roger Baker; James Bevan; Brodie Clark; Matthew Coats; Joe Dugdale; Mike Eland; Tamara Finkelstein; Mike Hawker; Justin Holliday; Martin Peach; David Wood; Barbara Woodward

MINISTRY OF JUSTICE

HER MAJESTY'S COURTS SERVICE
see Law Courts and Offices section

LAND REGISTRY
Lincoln's Inn Fields, London WC2A 3PH
T 020-7917 8888
E propertyinformationteam@landregistry.gsi.gov.uk
W www.landregistry.gov.uk
The registration of title to land was first introduced in England and Wales by the Land Registry Act 1862. Land Registry maintains and develops the Land Register for England and Wales, and is an executive agency and trading fund responsible to the Secretary of State for Justice. The Land Register has been open to public inspection since 1990.
Chief Land Registrar and Chief Executive, Peter Collis, CB

NATIONAL ARCHIVES
Kew, Richmond, Surrey TW9 4DU
T 020-8876 3444
W www.nationalarchives.gov.uk
The National Archives, a government department and an executive agency reporting to the Secretary of State for Justice, was formed in April 2003 by bringing together the Public Record Office (founded in 1838) and the Historical Manuscripts Commission (founded in 1869).

The National Archives leads on record management policy with government, and provides access to government records at its sites in Kew and Islington and through digital resources available online. The National Archives also oversees information and archive management across the UK, setting standards and providing advice and support to raise the standards of information management. OPSI – with its copyright, legislation and official publishing roles – has operated from within the National Archives since October 2006.

The organisation administers the UK's public records system under the Public Records Acts of 1958 and 1967. The records it holds span 900 years – from the Domesday Book to the latest government papers to be released – and fill more than 160km (100 miles) of shelving.
Chief Executive, Ms Natalie Ceeney

OFFICE OF PUBLIC SECTOR INFORMATION
102 Petty France, London SW1H 9AJ
T 01603-723011 W www.opsi.gov.uk
The Office of Public Sector Information (OPSI) operates from within the National Archives as of October 2006, after previously being attached to the Cabinet Office. It is responsible for policy in relation to access and re-use of UK public sector information. The legal and statutory responsibilities of Her Majesty's Stationery Office (HMSO), in relation to statutory publishing and the management of crown copyright, operate from within the OPSI's wider remit.
Director/Controller, Carol Tullo

NATIONAL OFFENDER MANAGEMENT SERVICE
see Prison Service section

OFFICE OF THE PUBLIC GUARDIAN
PO Box 15118, Birmingham B16 6GX
T 0845-330 2900
E customerservices@publicguardian.gsi.gov.uk
W www.publicguardian.gov.uk
The Office of the Public Guardian was established on 1 October 2007, in place of the Public Guardianship Office. It is responsible for providing services that support the financial, property, health and welfare matters of people lacking in the mental capacity to make decisions in a particular area. Capacity is assessed in accordance with the requirements set out in the Mental Capacity Act 2005.
Chief Executive and Public Guardian Designate, Martin John

TRIBUNALS SERVICE
see Tribunals section

NORTHERN IRELAND OFFICE

COMPENSATION AGENCY
Royston House, 34 Upper Queen Street, Belfast BT1 6FD
T 028-9024 9944 E comp-agency@nics.gov.uk
W www.compensationni.gov.uk
The Compensation Agency supports the victims of violent crime by providing compensation to those who sustain loss as a result of actions taken under emergency provisions legislation.
Chief Executive, Robert Crawford

FORENSIC SCIENCE NORTHERN IRELAND
151 Belfast Road, Carrickfergus, Co. Antrim BT38 8PL
T 028-9036 1888 E forensic.science@fsni.gov.uk
W www.fsni.gov.uk
Forensic Science Northern Ireland aims to enhance the delivery of justice by providing scientific support and advice for the police and the legal profession, and training and analytical support for pathologists.
Chief Executive, Stanley Brown

NORTHERN IRELAND PRISON SERVICE
see Prison Service section

YOUTH JUSTICE AGENCY
Corporate Headquarters, 41–43 Waring Street, Belfast BT1 2DY
T 028-9031 6400 E info@yjani.gov.uk
W www.youthjusticeagencyni.gov.uk
The Youth Justice Agency aims to prevent children committing criminal offences through provision of community-based services, youth conferencing services, attendance centres and secure custody.
Chief Executive, Bill Lockhart, OBE

DEPARTMENT FOR TRANSPORT

DRIVER AND VEHICLE LICENSING AGENCY (DVLA)
Longview Road, Swansea SA6 7JL
T 01792-782341 W www.dvla.gov.uk
The agency was established as an executive agency in 1990 and became a trading fund in 2004. It is responsible for registering and licensing drivers and vehicles, and for collection and enforcement of vehicle excise duty (some £4.9bn annually). The DVLA also maintains records of all those who are entitled to drive various types of vehicle (currently around 43 million people), all vehicles entitled to travel on public roads (currently 32 million), and drivers' endorsements, disqualifications and medical conditions.
Chief Executive, Noel Shanahan

DRIVING STANDARDS AGENCY
The Axis Building, 112 Upper Parliament Street, Nottingham NG1 6LP
T 0115-936 6666 E customer.services@dsa.gsi.gov.uk
W www.dsa.gov.uk
The agency is responsible for carrying out theory and practical driving tests for car drivers, motorcyclists, bus and lorry drivers, and for maintaining the registers of approved driving instructors and large goods vehicle instructors. It also supervises Compulsory Basic Training (CBT) for learner motorcyclists. There are two area offices, which manage over 400 practical driving test centres across Britain.
Chief Executive, Rosemary Thew

GOVERNMENT CAR AND DESPATCH AGENCY
46 Ponton Road, London SW8 5AX
T 020-7217 3837 E info@gcda.gsi.gov.uk
W www.dft.gov.uk/gcda
The agency provides secure transport and mail distribution to government and the public sector.
Chief Executive, Roy Burke

HIGHWAYS AGENCY
123 Buckingham Palace Road, London SW1W 9HA
T 0845-955 6575 Information Line 0845-750 4030
E ha_info@highways.gsi.gov.uk W www.highways.gov.uk
The Highways agency is responsible for operating, maintaining and improving England's 7,050km (4,406 miles) of motorways and trunk roads – known as the strategic road network – on behalf of the Secretary of State for Transport.
Chief Executive, Graham Dalton

MARITIME AND COASTGUARD AGENCY
Spring Place, 105 Commercial Road, Southampton SO15 1EG
T 023-8032 9100
W www.mcga.gov.uk
The agency's aims are to prevent loss of life, continuously

improve maritime safety and protect the marine environment.
Chief Executive, Peter Cardy
Chief Coastguard, Rod Johnson

VEHICLE CERTIFICATION AGENCY
1 Eastgate Office Centre, Eastgate Road, Bristol BS5 6XX
T 0117-952 4235 W www.vca.gov.uk
The agency is the UK authority responsible for ensuring that vehicles and vehicle parts have been designed and constructed to meet internationally agreed standards of safety and environmental protection.
Chief Executive, P. Markwick

VEHICLE AND OPERATOR SERVICES AGENCY
Berkeley House, Croydon Street, Bristol BS5 0DA
T 0117-954 3211
Enquiry Line 0300-123 9000
E enquiries@vosa.gov.uk W www.vosa.gov.uk
The Vehicle and Operator Services Agency was formed in April 2003 from the merger of the Vehicle Inspectorate and the Traffic Area Network. The agency works with the independent traffic commissioners to improve road safety and the environment; safeguard fair competition by promoting and enforcing compliance with commercial operator licensing requirements; process applications for licences to operate lorries and buses; register bus services; operate and administer testing schemes for all vehicles, including the supervision of the MOT testing scheme; enforce the law on vehicles to ensure that they comply with legal standards and regulations; enforce drivers' hours and licensing requirements; provide training and advice for commercial operators; and investigate vehicle accidents, defects and recalls.
Chief Executive (interim), Alastair Peoples

HM TREASURY

NATIONAL SAVINGS AND INVESTMENTS
375 Kensington High Street, London W14 8SD
T 0845-964 5000 W www.nsandi.com
NS&I (National Savings and Investments) came into being in 1861 when the Palmerston government set up the Post Office Savings Bank, a savings scheme which aimed to encourage ordinary wage earners 'to provide for themselves against adversity and ill health'. NS&I was established as a government department in 1969. It became an executive agency of the Treasury in 1996 and is responsible for the design, marketing and administration of savings and investment products for personal savers and investors. It has almost 27 million customers with over £94bn invested. *See also* Banking and Finance.
Chief Executive, Jane Platt

ROYAL MINT
PO Box 500, Llantrisant, Pontyclun CF72 8YT
T 01443-222111
W www.royalmint.com
The Royal Mint has operated as a trading fund since 1975, and was established as an executive agency in 1990.

The prime responsibility of the Royal Mint is the provision of United Kingdom coinage, but it actively competes in world markets for a share of the available circulating coin business and about half of the coins and blanks it produces annually are exported. It also manufactures special proof and uncirculated quality coins in gold, silver and other metals; military and civil decorations and medals; commemorative and prize medals; and royal and official seals.
Master of the Mint, Chancellor of the Exchequer *(ex officio)*
Chief Executive, A. Stafford

UK DEBT MANAGEMENT OFFICE
Eastcheap Court, 11 Philpot Lane, London EC3M 8UD
T 0845-357 6500
W www.dmo.gov.uk
The UK Debt Management Office (DMO) was launched as an executive agency of HM Treasury in April 1998. The Chancellor of the Exchequer determines the policy and financial framework within which the DMO operates, but delegates operational decisions on debt and cash management and the day-to-day running of the office to the chief executive. The DMO's remit is to carry out the government's debt management policy of minimising financing costs over the long term, and to minimise the cost of offsetting the government's net cash flows over time, while operating at a level of risk approved by ministers in both cases. The DMO is also responsible for providing loans to local authorities through the Public Works Loan Board, for managing the assets of certain public sector bodies through the Commissioners for the Reduction of the National Debt, and for administering the operational delivery of the government's Credit Guarantee Scheme.
Chief Executive, Robert Stheeman

DEPARTMENT FOR WORK AND PENSIONS

CHILD SUPPORT AGENCY (CSA)
PO Box 55, Brierly Hill, West Midlands DY5 1YL
T 0845-713 3133 W www.csa.gov.uk
The CSA was set up in April 1993. It is responsible for the administration of the Child Support Act and for the assessment, collection and enforcement of maintenance payments. Government plans to establish a new organisation, the Child Maintenance and Enforcement Commission (CMEC), were outlined in the Child Maintenance White Paper; the new organisation will take over responsibility for the Child Support Agency's work in stages over a number of years from 2008.
Chief Executive of CSA and CMEC, Stephen Geraghty

JOBCENTRE PLUS
First Floor, Steel City House, West Street, Sheffield S1 2GQ
T 0845-606 0234 W www.jobcentreplus.gov.uk
Jobcentre Plus was formed in April 2002 following the merger of the Employment Service and some parts of the Benefits Agency. The agency administers claims for, and payment of, social security benefits to help people gain employment or improve their prospects for work, as well as helping employers to fill their vacancies.
Chief Executive (acting), Mel Groves

THE PENSION, DISABILITY AND CARERS SERVICE
Room 204, Richmond House, 79 Whitehall, London SW1A 2NS
T DCS 0800-882200, Pension Service 0845-606 0265
W www.thepensionservice.gov.uk, www.dwp.gov.uk/dcs
The Pension, Disability and Carers Service was formed in 2008 from the Pension Service and the Disability and Carers Service (DCS). The agency serves over 15 million customers in Great Britain and abroad and it employs over

16,000 staff. The service administers benefits including disability living allowance, state pension and winter fuel payments.
Chief Executive, Terry Moran, CB

NON-MINISTERIAL GOVERNMENT DEPARTMENTS

Non-ministerial government departments are part of central government but are not headed by a minister and are not funded by a sponsor department. They are created to implement specific legislation, but do not have the ability to change it. Departments may have links to a minister, but the minister is not responsible for the department's overall performance. Staff employed by non-ministerial departments are civil servants.

CHARITY COMMISSION

PO Box 1227, Liverpool L69 3UG
T 0845-300 0218
W www.charitycommission.gov.uk

The Charity Commission for England and Wales is the government department whose aim is to give the public confidence in the integrity of charities. It also carries out the functions of the registration, monitoring and support of charities and the investigation of alleged wrongdoing. The commission maintains a computerised register of nearly 190,000 charities. It is accountable to the courts and, for its efficiency, to the home secretary. There are eight board members appointed by the Home Office for a fixed term and the commission has offices in London, Liverpool, Taunton and Newport.
Chair, Dame Suzi Leather
Chief Executive, Andrew Hind

CROWN ESTATE

16 New Burlington Place, London W1S 2HX
T 020-7851 5000 F 020-7851 5128
W www.thecrownestate.co.uk

The Crown Estate is valued at £7.3bn, and includes substantial blocks of urban property, primarily in London, almost 146,000 hectares (360,000 acres) of rural land, almost half of the foreshore, and the sea bed out to the 12 nautical mile territorial limit throughout the UK. The Crown Estate is part of the hereditary possessions of the sovereign 'in right of the crown', managed under the provisions of the Crown Estate Act 1961. The Crown Estate has a duty to maintain and enhance the capital value of estate and the income obtained from it. Under the terms of the act, the Crown Estate pays its revenue surplus to the Treasury every year.
Chair, Ian Grant, CBE
Chief Executive, Roger Bright

CROWN PROSECUTION SERVICE

50 Ludgate Hill, London EC4M 7EX
T 020-7796 8000 E enquiries@cps.gsi.gov.uk
W www.cps.gov.uk

The Crown Prosecution Service (CPS) is the independent body responsible for prosecuting people in England and Wales. The CPS was established as a result of the Prosecution of Offences Act 1985. It works closely with the police to advise on lines of inquiry and to decide on appropriate charges and other disposals in all but minor cases. *See also* Law Courts and Offices.
Director of Public Prosecutions, Keir Starmer, QC
Chief Executive, Peter Lewis

EXPORT CREDITS GUARANTEE DEPARTMENT (ECGD)

PO Box 2200, 2 Exchange Tower, Harbour Exchange Square, London E14 9GS
T 020-7512 7887 E help@ecgd.gsi.gov.uk
W www.ecgd.gov.uk

ECGD is the UK's official export credit agency and was established in 1919. A separate government department reporting to the Secretary of State for Business, Innovation and Skills, it has 90 years' experience of working closely with exporters, project sponsors, banks and buyers to help UK exporters of capital equipment and project-related goods and services. ECGD does this by providing help in arranging finance packages for buyers of UK goods by guaranteeing bank loans; insurance against non-payment to UK exporters; and overseas investment insurance – a facility that gives UK investors up to 15 years' insurance against political risks such as war, expropriation and restrictions on remittances.
Chief Executive and Accounting Officer, P. Crawford
Non-Executive Chair, G. Pimlott

FOOD STANDARDS AGENCY

Aviation House, 125 Kingsway, London WC2B 6NH
T 020-7276 8829
E helpline@foodstandards.gsi.gov.uk
W www.food.gov.uk, www.eatwell.gov.uk

The FSA was established in April 2000 to protect public health from risks arising in connection with the consumption of food, and otherwise to protect the interests of consumers in relation to food. The agency has the general function of developing policy in these areas and provides information and advice to the government, other public bodies and consumers. It also sets standards for and monitors food law enforcement by local authorities. The agency is a UK-wide non-ministerial government body, led by a board which has been appointed to act in the public interest. It has executive offices in Scotland, Wales and Northern Ireland. It is advised by advisory committees on food safety matters of special interest to each of these areas.
Chair, Lord Rooker
Deputy Chair, Dr Ian Reynolds
Chief Executive, Tim Smith

FOOD STANDARDS AGENCY NORTHERN IRELAND, 10C Clarendon Road, Belfast BT1 3BG
T 028-9041 7700 E infofsani@foodstandards.gsi.gov.uk

FOOD STANDARDS AGENCY SCOTLAND, St Magnus House, 6th Floor, 25 Guild Street, Aberdeen AB11 6NJ
T 01224-285100 E scotland@foodstandards.gsi.gov.uk

FOOD STANDARDS AGENCY WALES, 11th Floor, Southgate House, Wood Street, Cardiff CF10 1EW
T 029-2067 8999 E wales@foodstandards.gsi.gov.uk

MEAT HYGIENE SERVICE

Kings Pool, Peasholme Green, York YO1 7PR
T 01904-455501
E mhs.enquiries@mhs.gov.uk

The Meat Hygiene Service was launched in April 1995 as an agency of the former Ministry of Agriculture, Fisheries and Food, and became an executive agency of the Food Standards Agency in April 2000. It protects public health and animal welfare at slaughter through veterinary supervision and meat inspection in approved fresh meat establishments in Great Britain.
Chief Executive, Steve McGrath

FORESTRY COMMISSION

Silvan House, 231 Corstorphine Road, Edinburgh EH12 7AT
T 0131-334 0303 E enquiries@forestry.gsi.gov.uk
W www.forestry.gov.uk

The Forestry Commission is the government department responsible for forestry policy in Great Britain. It reports directly to forestry ministers (ie the Secretary of State for Environment, Food and Rural Affairs, the Scottish ministers and the National Assembly for Wales), to whom it is responsible for advice on forestry policy and for the implementation of that policy.

The commission's principal objectives are to protect Britain's forests and woodlands; expand Britain's forest area; enhance the economic value of forest resources; conserve and improve the biodiversity, landscape and cultural heritage of forests and woodlands; develop opportunities for woodland recreation; and increase public understanding of, and community participation in, forestry.

Chair (part-time), Rt. Hon. Lord Clark of Windermere
Director-General and Deputy Chair, T. Rollinson

FORESTRY COMMISSION ENGLAND, Great Eastern House, Tenison Road, Cambridge CB1 2DU T 01223-314546
FORESTRY COMMISSION SCOTLAND, Silvan House, 231 Corstorphine Road, Edinburgh EH12 7AT T 0131-334 0303
FORESTRY COMMISSION WALES, Victoria Terrace, Aberystwyth, Ceredigion SY23 2DQ T 0845-604 0845
NORTHERN RESEARCH STATION, Roslin, Midlothian EH25 9SY T 0131-445 2176

FOREST ENTERPRISE

Forest Enterprise England, 620 Bristol Business Park, Coldharbour Lane, Bristol BS16 1EJ
T 0117-906 6000
Forest Enterprise Scotland, 1 Highlander Way, Inverness Business and Retail Park, Inverness IV2 7GB
T 01463-232811

Forest Enterprise was established as an executive agency of the Forestry Commission in 1996 to manage the UK's forest estate; it ceased to exist as a single executive agency in March 2003, when three new agencies were created – one each for England, Wales and Scotland. Forest Enterprise Wales has since been wound up, with its responsibilities reabsorbed by the Forestry Commission.

The agencies in England and Scotland take their direction from their respective country governments but their basic remit is to provide environmental, social and economic benefits from the forests they manage.

Chief Executives, Simon Hodgson *(England);* Dr Hugh Insley *(Scotland)*

FOREST RESEARCH

Alice Holt Lodge, Farnham, Surrey GU10 4LH
T 01420-22255
E research.info@forestry.gsi.gov.uk
W www.forestresearch.gov.uk

Forest Research is also an executive agency of the Forestry Commission. Its objectives are to inform and support forestry's contribution to the development and delivery of the policies of the government and devolved administrations; to provide research, development and monitoring services relevant to UK forestry interests; and to transfer knowledge actively and appropriately.

Chief Executive, Dr James Pendlebury
Research Director, Dr Peter Freer-Smith

GOVERNMENT ACTUARY'S DEPARTMENT

Finlaison House, 15–17 Furnival Street, London EC4A 1AB
T 020-7211 2601
E enquiries@gad.gov.uk W www.gad.gov.uk

The Government Actuary's Department was established in 1919 and provides a consulting service to government departments, the public sector, and overseas governments. The actuaries advise on social security schemes and superannuation arrangements in the public sector at home and abroad, on population and other statistical studies, and on supervision of insurance companies and pension funds.

Government Actuary, T. J. Llanwarne
Deputy Government Actuary, vacant
Chief Actuaries, E. I. Battersby; I. A. Boonin; H. Duckers; D. J. Hughes; S. R. Humphrey; K. Kneller; M. Lunnon

HM REVENUE AND CUSTOMS

Board of HM Revenue and Customs, 100 Parliament Street, London SW1A 2BQ
T 020-7147 0000 W www.hmrc.gov.uk

HMRC was formed following the integration of the Inland Revenue and HM Customs and Excise, which was made formal by parliament in April 2005. It administers, and advises the Chancellor of the Exchequer on, any matters connected with the following areas: income, corporation, capital gains, inheritance, insurance premium, stamp, land and petroleum revenue taxes; environmental taxes (climate change and aggregates levy, landfill tax); value added tax (VAT); customs duties and frontier protection; excise duties; National Insurance; tax credits, child benefit and the Child Trust Fund; enforcement of the minimum wage; and recovery of student loan repayments.

Chair, Mike Clasper

VALUATION OFFICE AGENCY

Wingate House, 93–107 Shaftesbury Avenue, London W1D 5BU
T 0300-050 1700 E customerservices@voa.gsi.gov.uk
W www.voa.gov.uk

Established in 1991, the Valuation Office is an executive agency of HM Revenue and Customs. It is responsible for compiling and maintaining the business rating and council tax valuation lists for England and Wales; valuing property throughout Great Britain for the purposes of taxes administered by the Inland Revenue; providing statutory and non-statutory property valuation services in England, Wales and Scotland; and giving policy advice to ministers on property valuation matters. In April 2009 the VOA assumed responsibility for the functions of The Rent Service, which provided a rental valuation service to local authorities in England, and fair rent determinations for landlords and tenants.

Chief Executive (acting), David Park

NATIONAL SCHOOL OF GOVERNMENT

Sunningdale Park, Larch Avenue, Ascot, Berks SL5 0QE
T 01344-634000
E customer.services@nationalschool.gsi.gov.uk
W www.nationalschool.gov.uk

The National School of Government is the learning and development partner of the UK Civil Service. It became a separate non-ministerial department on 1 January 2007. It is run by public servants for public servants, and aims to improve services for citizens by using learning and development to raise the bar for public services.

Principal and Chief Executive, Rod Clark

OFFICE OF FAIR TRADING (OFT)

Fleetbank House, 2–6 Salisbury Square, London EC4Y 8JX
T 020-7211 8000
E enquiries@oft.gsi.gov.uk W www.oft.gov.uk

The OFT is a non-ministerial government department established by statute in 1973, and it is the UK's consumer and competition authority. It encourages businesses to comply with competition and consumer law and to improve their trading practices through self-regulation. It acts decisively to stop hardcore or flagrant offenders, studies markets and recommends action where required, and empowers consumers with the knowledge and skills to make informed choices.

Chair, Philip Collins
Chief Executive Officer, John Fingleton

OFFICE OF GAS AND ELECTRICITY MARKETS (OFGEM)

9 Millbank, London SW1P 3GE
T 020-7901 7295 E consumeraffairs@ofgem.gov.uk
W www.ofgem.gov.uk

OFGEM is the regulator for Britain's gas and electricity industries. Its role is to protect and advance the interests of consumers by promoting competition where possible, and through regulation only where necessary. OFGEM operates under the direction and governance of the Gas and Electricity Markets Authority, which makes all major decisions and sets policy priorities for OFGEM. OFGEM's powers are provided for under the Gas Act 1986 and the Electricity Act 1989, as amended by the Utilities Act 2000. It also has enforcement powers under the Competition Act 1998 and the Enterprise Act 2002.

Chair, Lord Mogg, KCMG
Chief Executive, Alistair Buchanan

OFFICE OF RAIL REGULATION

1 Kemble Street, London WC2B 4AN
T 020-7282 2000 E contact.cct@orr.gsi.gov.uk
W www.rail-reg.gov.uk

The Office of the Rail Regulator was set up under the Railways Act 1993. It became the ORR in July 2004, under the provisions of the Railways and Transport Safety Act 2003. On 1 April 2006, in addition to its role as economic regulator, the ORR became the health and safety regulator for the rail industry. This transfer of responsibility from the Health and Safety Executive was given effect under the Railways Act 2005. The board and chair are appointed by the Secretary of State for Transport. The ORR's key roles are to ensure that Network Rail, the owner and operator of the national railway infrastructure (the track and signalling), manages the network efficiently and in a way that meets the needs of its users; to encourage continuous improvement in health and safety performance while securing compliance with relevant health and safety law, including taking enforcement action as necessary; and to develop policy and enhance relevant railway health and safety legislation. It is also responsible for licensing operators of railway assets, setting the terms for access by operators to the network and other railway facilities, and enforcing competition law in the rail sector.

Chair, Anna Walker
Chief Executive, Bill Emery

OFFICE FOR STANDARDS IN EDUCATION, CHILDREN'S SERVICES AND SKILLS (OFSTED)

Royal Exchange Buildings, St Ann's Square, Manchester M2 7LA
T 0845-404040 E enquiries@ofsted.gov.uk
W www.ofsted.gov.uk

OFSTED was established under the Education (Schools Act) 1992 and was relaunched on 1 April 2007 with a wider remit, bringing together four formerly separate inspectorates. It works to raise standards in services through the inspection and regulation of care for children and young people, and inspects education and training for children of all ages. *See also* The Education System.

HM Chief Inspector, Christine Gilbert, CBE
Chair, Zenna Atkins

POSTAL SERVICES COMMISSION (POSTCOMM)

Hercules House, 6 Hercules Road, London SE1 7DB
T 020-7593 2100 E info@psc.gov.uk
W www.psc.gov.uk

Postcomm is an independent regulator set up by the Postal Services Act 2000 to secure the universal postal service, improve postal services by introducing competition to the UK postal market, licence postal operators dealing with mail costing less than £1 to deliver, and ensure that postal operators, including Royal Mail, meet the needs of their customers throughout the UK. Postcomm also monitors – and reports to the Department for Business, Innovation and Skills – on the network of post offices in the UK.

Chair, Nigel Stapleton
Chief Executive, Tim Brown

REVENUE AND CUSTOMS PROSECUTIONS OFFICE (RCPO)

New Kings Beam House, 22 Upper Ground, London SE1 9BT
T 020-7147 7500 E enquiries@rcpo.gsi.gov.uk
W www.rcpo.gov.uk

The Revenue and Customs Prosecutions Office (RCPO) prosecutes major drug trafficking and tax fraud cases in the UK, currently at a rate of around 1,300 each year. It is an independent prosecuting authority and handles cases from HM Revenue and Customs and the Serious Organised Crime Agency. Prior to the establishment of the RCPO in April 2005, criminal prosecutions were handled separately by Customs and Excise and Inland Revenue Lawyers. The RCPO's director is appointed by the attorney-general.

Director, David Green, QC

SECURITY AND INTELLIGENCE SERVICES

GOVERNMENT COMMUNICATIONS HEADQUARTERS (GCHQ)

Hubble Road, Cheltenham GL51 0EX
T 01242-221491 E pressoffice@gchq.gsi.gov.uk
W www.gchq.gov.uk

GCHQ produces signals intelligence in support of national security and the UK's economic wellbeing, and in the prevention or detection of serious crime. Additionally, GCHQ's Information Assurance arm, CESG, is the national technical authority for information assurance, and provides advice and assistance to government departments, the armed forces and other national infrastructure bodies on the security of their communications and information systems. GCHQ was

placed on a statutory footing by the Intelligence Services Act 1994 and is headed by a director who is directly accountable to the foreign secretary.
Director, Iain Lobban

SECRET INTELLIGENCE SERVICE (MI6)
PO Box 1300, London SE1 1BD
W www.mi6.gov.uk
The Secret Intelligence Service produces secret intelligence in support of the government's security, defence, foreign and economic policies. It was placed on a statutory footing by the Intelligence Services Act 1994 and is headed by a chief, known as 'C', who is directly accountable to the foreign secretary.
Chief, Sir John Sawers

SECURITY SERVICE (MI5)
PO Box 3255, London SW1P 1AE
T 020-7930 9000
W www.mi5.gov.uk
The Security Service is responsible for security intelligence work against covertly organised threats to the UK. These include terrorism, espionage and the proliferation of weapons of mass destruction. The Security Service also provides security advice to a wide range of organisations to help reduce vulnerability to threats from individuals, groups or countries hostile to UK interests. The home secretary has parliamentary accountability for the Security Service.
Director-General, Jonathan Evans

SERIOUS FRAUD OFFICE
Elm House, 10–16 Elm Street, London WC1X 0BJ
T 020-7239 7272
E public.enquiries@sfo.gsi.gov.uk
W www.sfo.gov.uk
The Serious Fraud Office is an independent government department that investigates and prosecutes serious or complex fraud. It is part of the UK Criminal Justice System. The office is headed by a director who is appointed by and accountable to the Attorney-General, and has jurisdiction over England, Wales and Northern Ireland but not Scotland, the Isle of Man or the Channel Islands.
Director, Richard Alderman

UK STATISTICS AUTHORITY
Statistics House, Tredegar Park, Newport, Gwent NP10 8XG
T 0845 604 1857 E authority.enquiries@statistics.gov.uk
W www.statisticsauthority.gov.uk
The UK Statistics Authority was established on 1 April 2008 by the Statistics and Registration Service Act 2007 as an independent body operating at arm's length from the government. Its overall objective is to promote and safeguard the production and publication of official statistics and ensure their quality and comprehensiveness. The authority's main functions are the oversight of the Office for National Statistics (ONS); monitoring and reporting on all UK official statistics; and independent assessment of official statistics.

MANAGEMENT BOARD
Chair, Sir Michael Scholar, KCB
Board Members, Lord Rowe-Beddoe *(Deputy Chair, ONS);* Richard Alldritt *(Head of Assessment);* Partha Dasgupta; Jil Matheson *(National Statistician);* Moira Gibb; Prof. Sir Roger Jowell, CBE *(Deputy Chair, Official Statistics);* Steve Newman *(Director of Finance, ONS);* Prof. Steve Nickell; Prof. David Rhind

OFFICE FOR NATIONAL STATISTICS (ONS)
Cardiff Road, Newport NP10 8XG
T 0845-601 3034 E info@statistics.gov.uk
W www.statistics.gov.uk
The ONS was created in 1996 by the merger of the Central Statistical Office and the Office of Population Censuses and Surveys. On 1 April 2008 it became the executive office of the UK Statistics Authority. As part of these changes, the office's responsibility for the General Register Office transferred to the Identity and Passport Service of the Home Office.

The ONS is responsible for preparing, interpreting and publishing key statistics on the government, economy and society of the UK. Its key responsibilities include the provision of population estimates and projections and statistics on health and other demographic matters in England and Wales; the production of the UK National Accounts and other economic indicators; the organisation of population censuses in England and Wales and surveys for government departments and public bodies.
National Statistician and Director of ONS, Jil Matheson

UK TRADE AND INVESTMENT
Kingsgate House, 66–74 Victoria Street, London SW1E 6SW
T 020-7215 8000 W www.uktradeinvest.gov.uk
UK Trade and Investment is a government organisation that helps UK-based companies succeed in international markets. It assists overseas companies to bring high quality investment to the UK economy.
Chief Executive, Andrew Cahn

WATER SERVICES REGULATION AUTHORITY (OFWAT)
Centre City Tower, 7 Hill Street, Birmingham B5 4UA
T 0121-625 1300 E enquiries@ofwat.gsi.gov.uk
W www.ofwat.gov.uk
OFWAT succeeded the director-general of Water Services on 1 April 2006. It is the independent economic regulator of the water and sewerage companies in England and Wales. It is responsible for ensuring that the water industry in England and Wales provides customers with a good quality and efficient service at a fair price. OFWAT's main duties are to ensure that the companies can finance and carry out the functions specified in the Water Industry Act 1991 and to protect the interests of water customers, by promoting value and safeguarding future water and sewerage services.
Chair, Philip Fletcher
Chief Executive, Regina Finn

PUBLIC BODIES

The following section is a listing of public bodies and selected other civil service organisations.

Whereas executive agencies are either part of a government department or are one in their own right (*see* Government Departments section), public bodies carry out their functions to a greater or lesser extent at arm's length from central government. Ministers are ultimately responsible to parliament for the activities of the public bodies sponsored by their department and in almost all cases (except where there is separate statutory provision) ministers make the appointments to their boards. Departments are responsible for funding and ensuring good governance of their public bodies.

The term 'public body' is a general one which includes public corporations, such as the BBC; NHS bodies; and non-departmental public bodies (NDPBs). There were 790 NDPBs sponsored by UK government departments as at 31 March 2008. This figure is made up of 198 executive NDPBs, 410 advisory NDPBs, 33 tribunal NDPBs and 149 independent monitoring boards. The following is not a complete list of these organisations.

ADJUDICATOR'S OFFICE

8th Floor, Euston Tower, 286 Euston Road, London NW1 3US
T 020-7667 1832 W www.adjudicatorsoffice.gov.uk

The Adjudicator's Office investigates complaints about the way HM Revenue and Customs, the Valuation Office Agency, the Office of the Public Guardian and the Insolvency Service have handled a person's affairs.
The Adjudicator, Judy Clements, OBE

ADMINISTRATIVE JUSTICE AND TRIBUNALS COUNCIL

81 Chancery Lane, London WC2A 1BQ
T 020-7855 5200 E enquiries@ajtc.gsi.gov.uk
W www.ajtc.gov.uk

The Administrative Justice and Tribunals Council (AJTC) is a permanent standing advisory body set up under the Tribunals, Courts and Enforcement Act. It consists of 15 members appointed by the Lord Chancellor, Scottish and Welsh ministers. It has Scottish and Welsh Committees which discharge its responsibilities in their respective territories. The Parliamentary Ombudsman is an *ex officio* member of the council and of its Scottish and Welsh Committees.

The principal functions of the AJTC are to keep the administrative justice system under review; keep under review and report on the constitution and working of listed tribunals; and keep under review and report on the constitution and working of statutory inquiries. It is consulted by and advises government departments on a wide range of subjects relating to adjudicative procedures.
Chair, Richard Thomas, CBE
Members, The Parliamentary Ombudsman *(ex officio)*, Jodi Berg; Alice Brown; Prof. Andrew Coyle; Sue Davis, CBE; Penny Letts, OBE; Prof. Alistair MacLeary; Bronwyn McKenna; Bernard Quoroll; Prof. Genevra Richardson, CBE; Dr Jonathan Spencer, CB; Dr Adrian V. Stokes, OBE; Pat Thomas, CBE; Brian Thompson; Prof. Sir Adrian Webb

WELSH COMMITTEE OF THE ADMINISTRATIVE JUSTICE AND TRIBUNALS COUNCIL

81 Chancery Lane, London WC2A 1BQ
T 020-7855 5200
E enquiries@ajtc.gsi.gov.uk
Chair, Prof. Sir Adrian Webb
Members, The Public Services Ombudsman for Wales *(ex officio)*; Bob Chapman; Gareth Lewis; Rhian Williams-Flew

SCOTTISH COMMITTEE OF THE ADMINISTRATIVE JUSTICE AND TRIBUNALS COUNCIL

George House, 126 George Street, Edinburgh EH2 4HH
T 0131-271 4300 W www.ajtc.gov.uk
Chair, Prof. A. MacLeary
Members, The Parliamentary Commissioner for Administration *(ex officio)*; The Scottish Public Services Ombudsman *(ex officio)*; Prof. Andrew Coyle; Richard Henderson; Eileen MacDonald; Michael Menlowe; Michael Scanlan

ADVISORY, CONCILIATION AND ARBITRATION SERVICE (ACAS)

22nd Floor, Euston Tower, 286 Euston Road, London NW1 3JJ
T 020-7210 3613 Helpline 0845-747 4747
W www.acas.org.uk

The Advisory, Conciliation and Arbitration Service was set up under the Employment Protection Act 1975 (the provisions now being found in the Trade Union and Labour Relations (Consolidation) Act 1992).

ACAS is funded by the Department for Business, Innovation and Skills. A council sets its strategic direction, policies and priorities, and makes sure the agreed strategic objectives and targets are met. It consists of a chair and 11 employer, trade union and independent members, appointed by the Secretary of State for Business, Innovation and Skills. ACAS aims to improve organisations and working life through better employment relations, to provide up-to-date information, independent advice and high-quality training, and to work with employers and employees to solve problems and improve performance.

ACAS has 13 regional offices in Birmingham, Bury St Edmunds, Bristol, Cardiff, Fleet, Glasgow, Leeds, Liverpool, London, Manchester, Newcastle upon Tyne, Nottingham and Paddock Wood.
Chair, Ed Sweeney
Chief Executive, John Taylor

ADVISORY COUNCIL ON NATIONAL RECORDS AND ARCHIVES

The National Archives, Kew, Surrey TW9 4DU
T 020-8392 5377
W www.nationalarchives.gov.uk/advisorycouncil

The Advisory Council on National Records and Archives advises the Lord Chancellor on all matters relating to the preservation, use of, and access to historical manuscripts, records and archives of all kinds. The council meets four times a year, and its main task is to consider requests for the extended closure of public records, or from departments that want to keep records. The council encompasses the statutory Advisory Council on Public Records and the Advisory Council on Historical Manuscripts.
Chair, Lord Neuberger of Abbotsbury *(Master of the Rolls)*

AGRICULTURE AND HORTICULTURE DEVELOPMENT BOARD

Stoneleigh Park, Kenilworth, Warwickshire CV8 2TL
T 02476-692051 E info@ahdb.org.uk W www.ahdb.org.uk

The Agriculture and Horticulture Development Board (AHDB) was established under the Agriculture and Horticulture development Board Order 2008 and became operational on 1 April 2008. AHDB raises levies via six sector organisations – cereals and oilseeds (HGCA), beef and lamb (EBLEX), horticulture (HDC), milk (DairyCo), pigs (BPEX), and potatoes (Potato Council) – the funds raised by each organisation are used for the benefit of that specific sector. The AHDB board consists of ten members; the chairs for each of the six sector organisations, and four independent members.
Chairman, John Bridge
Independent members, Chris Bones; John Bridge; Lorraine Clinton; Clare Dodgson
Sector members, Tim Bennett (DairyCo); Neil Bragg (HDC); John Cross (EBLEX); Stewart Houston (BPEX); Allan Stevenson (Potato Council); Jonathan Tipples (HGCA)
Chief Executive, Kevin Roberts

ANCIENT MONUMENTS ADVISORY BOARD FOR WALES (CADW)

Plas Carew, Unit 5–7 Cefn Coed, Parc Nantgarw, Cardiff CF15 7QQ
T 01443-336000 E cadw@wales.gsi.gov.uk
W www.cadw.wales.gov.uk

The Ancient Monuments Advisory Board for Wales advises the Welsh Assembly Government on its statutory functions in respect of ancient monuments.
Chair, Richard Brewer
Members, Prof. Miranda Aldhouse-Green, FSA; Prof. Nancy Edwards; Prof. Ralph Griffiths, DLITT; John Hilling; Christopher Musson, MBE, FSA; Dr Emma Plunkett Dillon; Dr Anthony Ward; Prof. Alasdair Whittle, FBA, DPHIL

ARCHITECTURE AND DESIGN SCOTLAND

Bakehouse Close, 146 Canongate, Edinburgh EH8 8DD
T 0131-556 6699 E info@ads.org.uk
W www.ads.org.uk

Architecture and Design Scotland (A+DS) was established in 2005 by the Scottish government as the national champion for good architecture, urban design and planning in the built environment; it works with a wide range of organisations at national, regional and local levels. A+DS also assumed the independent design review and advisory role of the Royal Fine Art Commission for Scotland.
Chair, Raymond Young, CBE
Chief Executive, Sebastian Tombs

ARMED FORCES' PAY REVIEW BODY

6th Floor, Kingsgate House, 66–74 Victoria Street, London SW1E 6SW
T 020-7215 8859 W www.ome.uk.com

The Armed Forces' Pay Review Body was appointed in 1971. It advises the prime minister and the Secretary of State for Defence on the pay and allowances of members of naval, military and air forces of the crown.
Chair, Prof. David Greenaway
Members, Robert Burgin; Mary Carter; Very Revd. Dr Graham Forbes, CBE; Alison Gallico; Dr Peter Knight, CBE; Prof. Derek Leslie; John Steele; Air Vice-Marshall Ian Stewart (retd), CB

ARTS COUNCIL ENGLAND

14 Great Peter Street, London SW1P 3NQ
T 0845-300 6200
E enquiries@artscouncil.org.uk
W www.artscouncil.org.uk

Arts Council England is the national development agency for the arts in England, distributing public money from government and the National Lottery. Between 2008 and 2011 Arts Council England plans to invest £1.3bn of public funds in 888 arts organisations in England. Further Arts Council grants are awarded to individuals, arts organisations, national touring and other people who use the arts in their work.

In 2002, the Arts Council of England and nine regional arts boards joined together to form a single development organisation for the arts. The governing council's members and chair are appointed by the Secretary of State for Culture, Media and Sport usually for a term of four years, and meet approximately five times a year.
Chair, Dame Liz Forgan
Members, Diran Adebayo; Janet Barnes; Tom Bloxham, MBE; Andrew Brewerton; Kentake Chinyelu-Hope; Felicity Harvest; Lady Hollick; Keith Khan; Sir Brian McMaster, CBE; Francois Matarasso; Elsie Owusu, OBE; Alice Rawsthorn; Dr Tom Shakespeare; Prof. Stuart Timperley; Dorothy Wilson
Chief Executive, Alan Davey

ARTS COUNCIL OF NORTHERN IRELAND

77 Malone Road, Belfast BT9 6AQ
T 028-9038 5200 E info@artscouncil-ni.org
W www.artscouncil-ni.org

The Arts Council of Northern Ireland is the prime distributor of government funds in support of the arts in Northern Ireland. It is funded by the Department of Culture, Arts and Leisure and from National Lottery funds.
Chair, Rosemary Kelly
Members, Eithne Benson; Kate Bond; Damien Coyle *(Vice-Chair)*; Raymond Fullerton; David Irvine; Anthony Kennedy; Bill Montgomery; Ian Montgomery; Sharon O'Connor; Joseph Rice; Paul Seawright; Brian Sore; Peter Spratt; Janine Walker
Chief Executive, Roisin McDonough

ARTS COUNCIL OF WALES

Bute Place, Cardiff CF10 5AL
T 0845-873 4900 E feedback@artswales.org.uk
W www.artswales.org.uk

The Arts Council of Wales was established in 1994 by royal charter and is the development body for the arts in Wales. It funds arts organisations with funding from the National Assembly for Wales and is the distributor of National Lottery funds to the arts in Wales. The grant for 2007–8 was £29.73m from the National Assembly and £9.85m from the National Lottery.
Chair, Prof. Dai Smith
Members, Simon Dancey; Maggie Hampton; John Metcalf; Robin Morrison; Christopher O'Neil; Dr Ian J. Rees; Clive Sefia; Ruth Till, MBE; David Vokes; Debbie Wilcox; Rhiannon Wyn Hughes, MBE
Chief Executive, Nick Capaldi

AUDIT COMMISSION

1st Floor, Millbank Tower, London SW1P 4HQ
T 0844-798 1212
E enquiries@audit-commission.gov.uk
W www.audit-commission.gov.uk

The Audit Commission was set up in 1983 and is an independent body responsible for ensuring that public money is spent economically, efficiently and effectively, to achieve high-quality local services for the public. Its remit covers around 11,000 bodies in England, which between them spend more than £200bn of public money each year. Its work covers local government, health, criminal justice organisations and public services.

The commission has a chair, a deputy chair and a board of up to 20 commissioners who are appointed by the Department for Communities and Local Government following consultation with key stakeholders.
Chair, Michael O'Higgins
Deputy Chair, Bahrat Shah
Commissioners, Lord Adebowale; Steve Bundred; Jim Coulter; Dr Jennifer Dixon; Sheila Drew Smith; Cllr Stephen Houghton; Sir Thomas Legg; Dame Denise Platt; Raj Rajagopal; Jenny Watson; Cllr Chris White
Chief Executive, Steve Bundred

AUDIT SCOTLAND

110 George Street, Edinburgh EH2 4LH
T 0845-146 1010 E info@auditscotland.gov.uk
W www.audit-scotland.gov.uk

Audit Scotland was set up in 2000 to provide services to the Accounts Commission and the Auditor General for Scotland. Together they help to ensure that public sector bodies in Scotland are held accountable for the proper, efficient and effective use of public funds.

Audit Scotland's work covers about 200 bodies including local authorities; police forces and fire rescue services; health boards; further education colleges; Scottish Water; the Scottish government; executive agencies such as the Prison Service and non-departmental public bodies such as Scottish Enterprise.

Audit Scotland carries out financial and regularity audits to ensure that public sector bodies adhere to the highest standards of financial management and governance. It also performs audits to ensure that these bodies achieve the best value for money. All of Audit Scotland's work in connection with local authorities, fire and police boards is carried out for the Accounts Commission; its other work is undertaken for the Auditor-General.
Auditor-General, R. W. Black
Chair of the Accounts Commission, J. Baillie

BANK OF ENGLAND

Threadneedle Street, London EC2R 8AH
T 020-7601 4444 E enquiries@bankofengland.co.uk
W www.bankofengland.co.uk

The Bank of England was incorporated in 1694 under royal charter. It was nationalised in 1946 under the Bank of England Act of that year which gave HM Treasury statutory powers over the bank. It is the banker of the government and it manages the issue of banknotes. Since 1998 it has been operationally independent and its Monetary Policy Committee has been responsible for setting short-term interest rates to meet the government's inflation target. Its responsibility for banking supervision was transferred to the Financial Services Authority in the same year. As the central reserve bank of the country, the Bank of England keeps the accounts of British banks, and of most overseas central banks; the larger banks and building societies are required to maintain with it a proportion of their cash resources. The bank's core purposes are monetary stability and financial stability. The Banking Act 2009 increased the responsibilities of the bank, including giving the bank a new financial stability objective and creating a special resolution regime for dealing with failing banks.
Governor, M. A. King
Deputy Governors, Charles Bean; Paul Tucker
Court of Directors, B. Barber; Roger Carr; Antonio Horta-Osorio; Sir David Lees; Susan Rice; Mark Tucker; Lord Adair Turner; Harrison Young
Monetary Policy Committee, The Governor; the Deputy Governors; Mrs K. Barker; Prof. Tim Besley; D. Blanchflower; Spencer Dale; Paul Fisher; Dr Andrew Sentance
Adviser to the Governor, Graham Nicholson
Chief Cashier and Executive Director, Banking Services, A. Bailey
The Auditor, S. Brown

BIG LOTTERY FUND

1 Plough Place, London EC4A 1DE
T 020-7211 1800 Advice Line 0845-410 2030
E general.enquiries@biglotteryfund.org.uk
W www.biglotteryfund.org.uk

The Big Lottery Fund was launched in 2004, merging the New Opportunities Fund and the Lottery Charities Board (Community Fund). The fund is responsible for giving out half of the money for good causes raised by the National Lottery. The money is distributed to charitable, benevolent and philanthropic organisations in the voluntary and community sectors, as well as health, education and environmental projects. The Big Lottery Fund also assumed the Millennium Commission's role of supporting large-scale regenerative projects.
Chair, Prof. Sir Clive Booth
Vice-Chair, Anna Southall
Regional Chairs, Sanjay Dighe *(England)*; Breidge Gadd, CBE *(Northern Ireland)*; Alison Magee *(Scotland)*; Huw Vaughan *(Wales)*
General Members, Judith Donovan, CBE; Roland Doven, MBE; John Gartside, OBE; Rajay Naik; Albert Tucker; Diana Whitworth

Chief Executive, Peter Wanless
Directors, Walter Rader *(Northern Ireland)*; Dharmendra Kanani *(Scotland)*; Ceri Doyle *(Wales)*

BOUNDARY COMMISSIONS

ENGLAND
5th Floor, Clive House, 70 Petty France, London SW1H 9EX
T 020-7189 3716 E information@justice.gsi.gov.uk
W www.statistics.gov.uk/pbc/
Deputy Chair, Hon. Mr Justice Sales

WALES
1st Floor, Caradog House, 1–6 St Andrews Place, Cardiff CF10 3BE
T 029-2039 5031 E bcomm.wales@wales.gsi.gov.uk
W www.bcomm-wales.gov.uk
Deputy Chair, Hon. Justice Lloyd Jones

SCOTLAND
3 Drumsheugh Gardens, Edinburgh EH3 7QJ
T 0131-538 7510 F 0131-538 7511
E secretariat@scottishboundaries.gov.uk
W www.bcomm-scotland.gov.uk
Deputy Chair, Hon. Lord Woolman

NORTHERN IRELAND
Forestview, Purdy's Lane, Newtownbreda, Belfast BT8 7AR
T 028-9069 4800 E bcni@belfast.org.uk
W www.boundarycommission.org.uk
Deputy Chair, Hon. Mr Justice McLaughlin

The commissions, established in 1944, are constituted under the Parliamentary Constituencies Act 1986 (as amended). The Speaker of the House of Commons is *ex officio* chair of all four commissions in the UK. Each of the four commissions is required by law to keep the parliamentary constituencies in their part of the UK under review (in the case of the Scottish Commission this includes constituencies for the Scottish parliament). The latest Boundary Commission report for England was laid before parliament in February 2007, and the proposals outlined will take effect at the next general election. The latest report from Northern Ireland was published in May 2006, from Wales in January 2005 and the most recent Scottish report on Westminster constituencies was completed in December 2004.

BRITISH BROADCASTING CORPORATION (BBC)

Television Centre, Wood Lane, London W12 7RJ
T 020-8743 8000 BBC Information Line 0870-010 0222
W www.bbc.co.uk

The BBC was incorporated under royal charter in 1926 as successor to the British Broadcasting Company Ltd. The BBC's current charter, which came into force on 1 January 2007 and extends to 31 December 2016, recognises the BBC's editorial independence and sets out its public purposes. The BBC Trust was formed under the new charter and replaces the Board of Governors; it sets the strategic direction of the BBC and has a duty to represent the interests of licence fee payers. The chair, vice-chair and other trustees are appointed by the Queen-in-Council. The BBC is financed by revenue from receiving licences for the home services and by grant-in-aid from parliament for the World Service (radio). *See also* Broadcasting.

BBC TRUST MEMBERS
Chair, Sir Michael Lyons
Vice-Chair, Chitra Bharucha
National Trustees, Alison Hastings *(England)*; Rotha Johnston *(Northern Ireland)*; Janet Lewis-Jones *(Wales)*; Jeremy Peat *(Scotland)*
Trustees, Diane Coyle; Anthony Fry; Patricia Hodgson; David Liddiment; Mehmuda Mian; Richard Tait

EXECUTIVE BOARD
Director-General and Chair, Mark Thompson
Deputy Director-General, Mark Byford
Directors, Tim Davie *(Audio and Music)*; Jana Bennett *(Vision)*; Sharon Baylay *(Marketing, Communications and Audiences)*; Erik Huggers *(Future Media and Technology)*; Lucy Adams *(People)*; Zarin Patel *(Chief Financial Officer)*
Chief Executive, BBC Worldwide, John Smith
Chief Operating Officer, Caroline Thomson
Senior Independent Director, Marcus Agius
Non-Executive Directors, Val Gooding, CBE; Dr Mike Lynch, OBE; David Robbie; Dr Samir Shah, OBE; Robert Webb, QC

STATION CONTROLLERS
BBC1, Jay Hunt
BBC2, Janice Hadlow
BBC3, Danny Cohen
BBC4, Richard Klein
BBC News Channel, Kevin Bakhurst
BBC Parliament, Peter Knowles
BBC Northern Ireland, Peter Johnston
BBC Scotland, Ken MacQuarrie
BBC Wales, Menna Richards
Radio 1, 1Xtra, Asian Network and Switch, Andy Parfitt
Radio 2 and 6 Music, Bob Shennan
Radio 3, Roger Wright
Radio 4, Mark Damazer
Radio 5 Live, Adrian Van Klaveren

BRITISH COUNCIL

Bridgewater House, 58 Whitworth Street, Manchester M1 6BB
T 0161-957 7000 E general.enquiries@britishcouncil.org
W www.britishcouncil.org

The British Council was established in 1934, incorporated by royal charter in 1940 and granted a supplemental charter in 1993. It is an independent, non political organisation which promotes Britain abroad and is the UK's international organisation for educational and cultural relations. The British Council is represented in 216 towns and cities in 109 countries. Grant-in-aid received from the Foreign and Commonwealth Office in 2007–8 was £189m.
Chair, Lord Kinnock, PC
Chief Executive, Martin Davidson, CMG

BRITISH FILM INSTITUTE (BFI)

21 Stephen Street, London W1T 1LN
T 020-7255 1444 W www.bfi.org.uk

The BFI, established in 1933, offers opportunities for people throughout the UK to experience, learn and discover more about the world of film and moving image culture. It incorporates the BFI National Archive, the BFI National Library, a range of DVD releases, publications and educational materials (including the monthly *Sight and Sound* magazine), BFI Southbank, BFI Distribution,

the annual BFI London Film Festival as well as the BFI London Lesbian and Gay Film Festival, and the BFI IMAX cinema, and provides advice and support for regional cinemas and film festivals across the UK.
Chair, Greg Dyke
Director, Amanda Nevill

BRITISH LIBRARY

96 Euston Road, London NW1 2DB
T 020-7412 7676 E visitor-services@bl.uk
W www.bl.uk

The British Library was established in 1973. It is the UK's national library and occupies a key position in the library and information network. It aims to serve scholarship, research, industry, commerce and all other major users of information. Its services are based on a collection of 150 million separate items, including books, journals, manuscripts, maps, stamps, music, patents, newspapers and sound recordings in all written and spoken languages. The library is now based at three sites: London (St Pancras and Colindale) and Boston Spa, W. Yorks. The library's sponsoring department is the Department for Culture, Media and Sport.

Access to the reading rooms at St Pancras is limited to holders of a British Library reader's pass; information about eligibility is available from the reader admissions office. The exhibition galleries and public areas are open to all, free of charge.

BRITISH LIBRARY BOARD
Chair, Sir Colin Lucas
Chief Executive and Deputy Chair, Mrs L. Brindley
Members, Ms D. Airey; R. S. Broadhurst, CBE; Prof. R. Burgess; Sir K. Calman; Lord Fellowes; Ms S. Forbes, CBE; Prof. W. Hall, CBE; Ms E. Mackay, CB; Prof. K. McLuskie; M. Semple, OBE

SCHOLARSHIP AND COLLECTIONS
Americas Collections, T 020-7412 7743
Asia, Pacific and Africa Collections, T 020-7412 7873
British and Irish Collections, T 020-7412 7538
British Library Newspapers, Colindale Avenue, London NW9 5HE T 020-7412 7353
British Library Sound Archive, T 020-7412 7676
Early Printed Collections, T 020-7412 7564
Map Library, T 020-7412 7702
Music Library, T 020-7412 7772
Philatelic Collections, T 020-7412 7635
Reader Information, T 020-7412 7676
West European Collections, T 020-7412 7572

OPERATIONS AND SERVICES
Permission Clearance, T 020-7412 7755
Research Services, T 020-7412 7903

SCIENCE, TECHNOLOGY AND INNOVATION
Business, T 020-7412 7454
National Preservation Office, T 020-7412 7612
Patents, T 020-7412 7919
Science and Technology, T 020-7412 7494/7288
Social Science, Law and Official Publications, T 020-7412 7536

BRITISH LIBRARY, BOSTON SPA
Boston Spa, Wetherby, W. Yorks LS23 7BQ
T 01937-546060

BRITISH MUSEUM

Great Russell Street, London WC1B 3DG
T 020-7323 8000
E information@britishmuseum.org
W www.britishmuseum.org

The British Museum houses the national collection of antiquities, ethnography, coins and paper money, medals, prints and drawings. The British Museum may be said to date from 1753, when parliament approved the holding of a public lottery to raise funds for the purchase of the collections of Sir Hans Sloane and the Harleian manuscripts, and for their proper housing and maintenance. The building (Montagu House) was opened in 1759. The existing buildings were erected between 1823 and the present day, and the original collection has increased to its current dimensions by gifts and purchases. Total government grant-in-aid for 2008–9 was £43m.

BOARD OF TRUSTEES
Appointed by the Sovereign, HRH The Duke of Gloucester, KG, GCVO
Appointed by the Prime Minister, Chief Emeka Anyaoku; Karen Armstrong; Lord Broers; Sir Ronald Cohen; Prof. Sir Barry Cunliffe, CBE; Francis Finlay; Niall FitzGerald, KBE *(Chair)*; Dame Liz Forgan, OBE; Val Gooding, OBE; Bonnie Greer; Penny Hughes; George Iacobescu, CBE; Baroness Kennedy; Richard Lambert; Dr David Norgrove; Lord Stern
Appointed by the Trustees of the British Museum, Stephen Green; Lord Powell of Bayswater, KCMG
Appointed by the Royal Society, Dr Olga Kennard; Ms Edmee P. Leventis
Appointed by the Royal Academy, Antony Gormley, OBE
Appointed by the British Academy, Prof. Sir Christopher Bayly

OFFICERS
Director, Neil MacGregor
Deputy Director, Dr Andrew Burnett
Director of Public Engagement, Joanna Mackle
Director of Administration, Chris Yates
Director of Visitor and Building Services, Stephen Gill
Heads of Departments, Xerxes Mazda *(Education)*; Zoe Hancock *(Planning and Projects)*; Carolyn Young *(Membership Development)*; Hannah Boulton *(Press and Marketing)*

KEEPERS
Keeper of Africa, Oceania and the Americas, Jonathan King
Keeper of Ancient Egypt and Sudan, Vivian Davies
Keeper of of Asia, Jan Stuart
Keeper of Coins and Medals, Joe Cribb
Keeper of Greece and Rome, J. Lesley Fitton
Keeper of the Middle East, John Curtis
Keeper of Prehistory and Europe, Jonathan Williams
Keeper of Prints and Drawings, Antony Griffiths
Conservation and Scientific Research, David Saunders

BRITISH PHARMACOPOEIA COMMISSION

Market Towers, 1 Nine Elms Lane, London SW8 5NQ
T 020-7084 2561 E bpcom@mhra.gsi.gov.uk
W www.pharmacopoeia.gov.uk

The British Pharmacopoeia Commission sets standards for medicinal products used in human and veterinary medicines and is responsible for publication of the *British*

Pharmacopoeia (a publicly available statement of the standard that a product must meet throughout its shelf-life), the *British Pharmacopoeia (Veterinary)* and the *British Approved Names*. It has 16 members, including two lay members, who are appointed by the Appointments Commission (the body responsible for appointments to all of the Medicines Act advisory bodies).
Chair, Prof. A. D. Woolfson
Vice-Chair, V'lain Fenton-May
Secretary and Scientific Director, Dr M. G. Lee

BRITISH STANDARDS INSTITUTION

389 Chiswick High Road, London W4 4AL
T 020-8996 9001 E cservices@bsigroup.com
W www.bsi-global.com

British Standards – a part of the BSI Group – was the world's first national standards-making body, established in 1901, and is the recognised national standards body in the UK for the preparation, publication and marketing of national standards, both for products and for the service sector. About 90 per cent of its standards work is internationally linked. British Standards are issued for voluntary adoption, though in some cases compliance with a British Standard is required by legislation. Industrial and consumer products and services certified as complying with the relevant British Standard and operating an assessed quality management system are eligible to carry BSI's certification trade mark, known as the 'Kitemark'.
Chair, Sir David John, KCMG
Chief Executive, Howard Kerr

BRITISH WATERWAYS

64 Clarendon Road, Watford WD17 1DA
T 01923-201120
E enquiries.hq@britishwaterways.co.uk
W www.britishwaterways.co.uk

British Waterways conserves and manages the network of over 3,540km (2,200 miles) of canals and rivers in England, Scotland and Wales. Its sponsoring departments are the Department for Environment, Food and Rural Affairs in England and Wales, and the Enterprise, Transport and Lifelong Learning Department in Scotland.

Its responsibilities include maintaining the waterways and structures on and around them; looking after wildlife and the waterway environment; and ensuring that canals and rivers are safe and enjoyable places to visit
Chair, Tony Hales
Vice-Chair, Richard Bowker
Chief Executive, Robin Evans, FRICS

CARE QUALITY COMMISSION

Finsbury Tower, 103–105 Bunhill Row, London EC1Y 8TG
T 0300-061 6161 E enquiries@cqc.org.uk
W www.cqc.org.uk

The Care Quality Commission (CQC) was established on 1 April 2009, bringing together the work of the Healthcare Commission, the Mental Health Act Commission and the Commission for Social Care Inspection. CQC is the independent regulator of health and adult social care in England, including those provided by the NHS, local authorities, private companies and voluntary organisations. Its main functions are to register health and social care providers; monitor and inspect all health and social care; enforce standards and to implement fines, public warnings or closures if these are not met; to review services regularly; and to report findings publicly.
Chair, Barbara Young
Chief Executive, Cynthia Bower
Board, Prof. Deirdre Kelly; Martin Marshall; Olu Olasode; Kay Sheldon; Jo Williams

CENTRAL ARBITRATION COMMITTEE

PO Box 51547, London NW1 3JJ
T 020-7904 2300 E enquiries@cac.gov.uk
W www.cac.gov.uk

The Central Arbitration Committee (CAC) is a permanent independent body with statutory powers whose main function is to adjudicate on applications relating to the statutory recognition and de-recognition of trade unions for collective bargaining purposes, where such recognition or de-recognition cannot be agreed voluntarily. In addition, the CAC has a statutory role in determining disputes between trade unions and employers over the disclosure of information for collective bargaining purposes, and in resolving applications and complaints under the information and consultation regulations, and performs a similar role in relation to the legislation on the European Works Council, European companies, European cooperative societies and cross-border mergers. The CAC also provides voluntary arbitration in industrial disputes.

The committee consists of a chair and 10 deputy chairs, 28 members experienced as representatives of employers and 25 members experienced as representatives of workers. Members of the committee are appointed by the Secretary of State for Business, Innovation and Skills after consulting ACAS.
Chair, Sir Michael Burton
Chief Executive, Graeme Charles

CERTIFICATION OFFICE FOR TRADE UNIONS AND EMPLOYERS' ASSOCIATIONS

Euston Tower, 286 Euston Road, London NW1 3JJ
T 020-7210 3734 E info@certoffice.org
W www.certoffice.org

The Certification Office is an independent statutory authority. The certification officer is appointed by the Secretary of State for Business, Innovation and Skills and is responsible for maintaining a list of trade unions and employers' associations; ensuring compliance with statutory requirements; keeping annual returns from trade unions and employers' associations available for public inspection; determining complaints concerning trade union elections, certain ballots and certain breaches of trade union rules; for ensuring observance of statutory requirements governing mergers between trade unions and employers' associations; for overseeing the political funds and finances of trade unions and employers' associations; and for certifying the independence of trade unions.
Certification Officer, David Cockburn

SCOTLAND
69A George Street, Edinburgh EH2 2JG
T 0131-220 7660
Assistant Certification Officer for Scotland, Christine Stuart

CHURCH COMMISSIONERS

Church House, Great Smith Street, London SW1P 3AZ
T 020-7898 1000 E commissioners.enquiry@c-of-e.org
W www.cofe.anglican.org/about/churchcommissioners

The Church Commissioners were established in 1948 by the amalgamation of Queen Anne's Bounty (established 1704) and the Ecclesiastical Commissioners (established 1836). They are responsible for the management of some of the Church of England's assets, the income from which is predominantly used to help pay for the stipend and pension of the clergy and to support the church's work throughout the country. The commissioners own UK and global company shares, over 45,000ha (112,000 acres) of agricultural land, a residential estate in central London, and commercial property across Great Britain, plus an interest in overseas property via managed funds. They also carry out administrative duties in connection with pastoral reorganisation and closed churches.

The commissioners are: the Archbishops of Canterbury and of York; four bishops, three clergy and four lay persons elected by the respective houses of the General Synod; two deans elected by all the deans; three persons nominated by the Queen; three persons nominated by the Archbishops of Canterbury and York; three persons nominated by the archbishops after consultation with others including the Lord Mayors of London and York and the vice-chancellors of the universities of Oxford and Cambridge; the First Lord of the Treasury; the Lord President of the Council; the home secretary; the Secretary of State for Culture, Media and Sport; and the Speakers of the House of Commons and the House of Lords.

CHURCH ESTATES COMMISSIONERS
First, A. Whittam Smith
Second, Sir Stuart Bell, MP
Third, T. E. H. Walker

OFFICERS
Secretary, A. C. Brown

ASSISTANT SECRETARIES
Chief Surveyor, J. Cannon
Chief Investments Manager, M. Chaloner
Pastoral and Redundant Churches, P. Lewis
Official Solicitor, S. Slack

COAL AUTHORITY

200 Lichfield Lane, Mansfield, Notts NG18 4RG
T 01623-637000 E thecoalauthority@coal.gov.uk
W www.coal.gov.uk

The Coal Authority was established under the Coal Industry Act 1994 to manage certain functions previously undertaken by British Coal, including ownership of unworked coal. It is responsible for licensing coal mining operations and for providing information on coal reserves and past and future coal mining. It settles subsidence damage claims which are not the responsibility of licensed coal mining operators. It deals with the management and disposal of property, and with surface hazards such as abandoned coal mine entries.
Chair, Dr Helen Mounsey
Chief Executive, Philip Lawrence

COMMISSION FOR ARCHITECTURE AND THE BUILT ENVIRONMENT (CABE)

1 Kemble Street, London WC2B 4AN
T 020-7070 6700 E info@cabe.org.uk
W www.cabe.org.uk

CABE was established in 1999 and is responsible for promoting the importance of high-quality architecture and urban design, and for encouraging the understanding of architecture through educational and regional initiatives. The commission offers free advice to local authorities, public sector clients and others embarking on building projects of any size or purpose. CABE has a board of 16 commissioners, appointed by the Secretary of State for Culture, Media and Sport for a maximum of two four-year terms.
Chair, John Sorrell, CBE
Chief Executive, Richard Simmons

COMMISSION FOR INTEGRATED TRANSPORT (CFIT)

2nd Floor, 55 Victoria Street, London SW1H 0EU
T 020-7944 8131 E cfit@dft.gsi.gov.uk
W www.cfit.gov.uk

The CfIT was established in June 1999. Its role is to provide independent expert advice to the government in order to achieve a transport system that supports sustainable development. The CfIT also encourages best practice among local authorities and delivery agencies, and assesses both the impact of new technology on future policy options and transport policy initiatives from outside the UK. Members of the commission are appointed by the transport secretary.
Chair, Peter Hendy, CBE
Vice-Chair, David Leeder
Vice-Chair, Dr Lynn Sloman

COMMISSION FOR RURAL COMMUNITIES

John Dower House, Crescent Place, Cheltenham GL50 3RA
T 01242-521381 E info@ruralcommunities.gov.uk
W www.ruralcommunities.gov.uk

The Commission for Rural Communities was established in October 2006; it was formerly an operating division of the now-defunct Countryside Agency. It is a statutory body under the Natural Environment and Rural Communities Act 2006 and it aims to provide well-informed, independent advice to government and to ensure that policies reflect the needs of people living and working in rural England, with a particular focus on tackling disadvantage. Its three key roles are to be a rural advocate, an expert adviser and an independent watchdog. The commission is funded by an annual grant from the Department for Environment, Food and Rural Affairs and commissioners are appointed by the secretary of state.
Chair and Rural Advocate, Dr Stuart Burgess
Commissioners, Prof. Sheena Asthana; Richard Burge; Richard Childs, QPM; Dr Jim Cox, OBE; Elinor Goodman; John Mills, CBE; Howard Petch, CBE; Sue Prince, OBE; Rachel Purchase; Prof. Mark Shucksmith, OBE; Prof. Michael Winter, OBE
Chief Executive, Sarah McAdam

COMMITTEE ON STANDARDS IN PUBLIC LIFE

35 Great Smith Street, London SW1P 3BQ
T 020-7276 2595 E standards@evidence.x.gsi.gov.uk
W www.public-standards.org.uk

The Committee on Standards in Public Life was set up in October 1994. It is a standing body whose chair and members are appointed by the prime minister; three members are nominated by the leaders of the three main political parties. The committee's remit is to examine concerns about standards of conduct of all holders of public office, including arrangements relating to financial and commercial activities, and to make recommendations as to any changes in present arrangements which might be required to ensure the highest standards of propriety in public life. It is also charged with reviewing issues in relation to the funding of political parties. The committee does not investigate individual allegations of misconduct.

Chair, Sir Christopher Kelly, KCB
Members, Lloyd Clarke, QPM; Oliver Heald, MP; Baroness Maddock; Rt. Hon. Alun Michael, MP; Sir Derek Morris, CBE; Dame Denise Platt, CBE; David Prince, CBE; Dr Elizabeth Vallance; Dr Brian Woods-Scawen, CBE

COMMONWEALTH WAR GRAVES COMMISSION

2 Marlow Road, Maidenhead, Berks SL6 7DX
T 01628-634221 E casualty.enq@cwgc.org
W www.cwgc.org

The Commonwealth War Graves Commission (formerly Imperial War Graves Commission) was founded by royal charter in 1917. It is responsible for the commemoration of around 1.7 million members of the forces of the Commonwealth who lost their lives in the two world wars. More than one million graves are maintained in 23,274 burial grounds throughout the world. Over three-quarters of a million men and women who have no known grave or who were cremated are commemorated by name on memorials built by the commission.

The funds of the commission are derived from the six participating governments, ie the UK, Canada, Australia, New Zealand, South Africa and India.

President, HRH The Duke of Kent, KG, GCMG, GCVO, ADC
Chair, Secretary of State for Defence (UK)
Vice-Chair, Adm. Sir Ian Garnett, KCB
Members, High Commissioners in London for Australia, Canada, South Africa, New Zealand and India; Air Chief Marshal Sir Joe French, KCB, CBE; Ian Henderson, CBE, FRICS; Lt.-Gen. Sir Alistair Irwin, KCB, CBE; Sara Jones, CBE; Alan Meale, MP; Keith Simpson, MP; Prof. Hew Strachan, FRSE; Sir Rob Young, GCMG
Director-General and Secretary to the Commission, R. E. Kellaway, CBE
Deputy Director-General, T. V. Reeves
Legal Adviser and Solicitor, G. C. Reddie

COMPETITION COMMISSION

Victoria House, Southampton Row, London WC1B 4AD
T 020-7271 0100 E info@cc.gsi.gov.uk
W www.competition-commission.org.uk

The commission was established in 1948 as the Monopolies and Restrictive Practices Commission (later the Monopolies and Mergers Commission); it became the Competition Commission in April 1999 under the Competition Act 1998. The commission conducts in-depth inquiries into mergers, markets, and the regulation of major industries. Every inquiry the commission undertakes is in response to a reference made to it by another authority, usually the Office of Fair Trading. The commission has no power to conduct inquiries on its own initiative. The Enterprise Act 2002 introduced a new regime for the assessment of mergers and markets in the UK – in most related investigations the commission is responsible for making decisions on the competition questions and for making and implementing decisions on appropriate remedies.

The commission has a full-time chair and three deputy chairs. There are usually around 40 part-time commission members, who usually carry out investigations in groups of four or five after appointment by the chair. All are appointed by the Secretary of State for Business, Innovation and Skills for eight-year terms.

Chair, Peter Freeman
Deputy Chairs, Christopher Clarke; Dr Peter Davis; Diana Guy
Non-Executive Directors, Tony Foster; Dame Patricia Hodgson, DBE
Chief Executive and Secretary, David Saunders

COMPETITION SERVICE

Victoria House, Bloomsbury Place, London WC1A 2EB
T 020-7979 7979 E info@catribunal.org.uk
W www.catribunal.org.uk

The Enterprise Act 2002 created the Competition Service, a corporate body and executive non-departmental public body whose purpose is to fund and provide support services to the Competition Appeal Tribunal (CAT). Support services include everything necessary to facilitate the carrying out by CAT of its statutory functions such as administrative staff, accommodation and office equipment.

Director, Operations, Jeremy Straker
Members, Sir Gerald Barling (President, CAT); Janet Rubin (chair and external member)
Registrar (CAT), Charles Dhanowa, OBE

CONSUMER COUNCIL FOR WATER

Victoria Square House, Victoria Square, Birmingham B2 4AJ
T 0121-345 1000 E enquiries@ccwater.org.uk
W www.ccwater.org.uk

The Consumer Council for Water was established in 2005 under the Water Act 2003 to represent consumers' interests in respect of price, service and value for money from their water and sewerage services, and to investigate complaints from customers about their water company. There are four regional committees in England and one in Wales.

Chair, Dame Yve Buckland, DBE

CONSUMER FOCUS

4th Floor, Artillery House, Artillery Row, London SW1P 1RT
T 020-7799 7900 E contact@consumerfocus.org.uk
W www.consumerfocus.org.uk

Consumer Focus was formed from the merger of Energywatch, Postwatch and the National Consumer Council, and began operations in October 2008. The organisation works for the interests of consumers in private and public sectors throughout England, Scotland and Wales (and for postal services in Northern Ireland). Consumer Focus has legislative powers, including the right to investigate any complaint if it is of wider interest; the right to open up information from providers; the power to conduct research and the ability to make an official super-complaint about failing services. Consumer Focus is a non-departmental public body of the Department for Business, Innovation and Skills.

Chair, Larry Whitty
Chief Executive, Ed Mayo

CORPORATION OF TRINITY HOUSE

Trinity House, Tower Hill, London EC3N 4DH
T 020-7481 6900 E enquiries@thls.org
W www.trinityhouse.co.uk

The Corporation of Trinity House is the General Lighthouse Authority for England, Wales and the Channel Islands, and was granted its first charter by Henry VIII in 1514. Its remit is to assist the safe passage of a variety of vessels through some of the busiest sea-lanes in the world; it does this by deploying and maintaining approximately 600 aids to navigation, ranging from lighthouses to a satellite navigation service. The corporation also has certain statutory jurisdiction over aids to navigation maintained by local harbour authorities and is responsible for marking or dispersing wrecks dangerous to navigation, except those occurring within port limits or wrecks of HM ships.

The statutory duties of Trinity House are funded by the General Lighthouse Fund, which is provided from light dues levied on ships calling at ports of the UK and the Republic of Ireland. The corporation is a deep-sea pilotage authority, authorised by the Secretary of State for Transport to license deep-sea pilots. In addition Trinity House is a charitable organisation that maintains a number of retirement homes for mariners and their dependants, funds a four-year training scheme for those seeking a career in the merchant navy, and also dispenses grants to a wide range of maritime charities. The charity work is wholly funded by its own activities.

The corporation is controlled by a board of Elder Brethren; a separate board controls the Lighthouse Service. The Elder Brethren also act as nautical assessors in marine cases in the Admiralty Division of the High Court.

ELDER BRETHREN

Master, HRH The Prince Philip, Duke of Edinburgh, KG, KT, PC
Deputy Master, Rear-Adm. Sir Jeremy De Halpert, KCVO, CB
Wardens, Capt. Duncan Glass *(Rental)*; Capt. Nigel Pryke *(Nether)*
Elder Brethren, HRH The Prince of Wales, KG, KT, GCB; HRH The Duke of York, KG, KCVO, ADC; HRH The Princess Royal, KG, KT, GCVO; Capt. Roger Barker; Adm. Lord Boyce, GCB, OBE; Lord Browne of Madingley; Viscount Cobham; Capt. John Burton-Hall, RD; Lord Carrington, KG, GCMG, CH, PC; Capt. Sir Malcolm Edge, KCVO; Capt. Ian Gibb; Lord Greenway; Lord Mackay of Clashfern, KT, PC; Capt. Peter Mason, CBE; Cdre. Peter Melson, CBE, RN; Capt. David Orr; Douglas Potter; Capt. Derek Richards, RD, RNR; Cdr. Sir Miles Rivett-Carnac, RN; Lord Robertson of Port Ellen, KT, GCMG, PC; Rear-Adm. Sir Patrick Rowe, KCVO, CBE; Cdre. Jim Scorer; Sir Brian Shaw; Simon Sherrard; Adm. Sir Jock Slater, GCB, LVO; Capt. David Smith, OBE, RN; Cdre. David Squire, CBE, RFA; Cdre. Lord Sterling of Plaistow, CBE, GCVO, RNR; Capt. Colin Stewart, LVO; Sir Adrian Swire, AE; Capt. Sir Miles Wingate, KCVO; Capt. Thomas Woodfield, OBE; Capt. Richard Woodman

OFFICERS

Secretary, Graham Hockley
Director of Finance, Jerry Wedge
Director of Operations, Cdre. Jim Scorer
Director of Navigation, Capt. Roger Barker

COUNTRYSIDE COUNCIL FOR WALES/CYNGOR CEFN GWLAD CYMRU

Maes-y-Ffynnon, Penrhosgarnedd, Bangor, Gwynedd LL57 2DW
T 0845-130 6229 E enquiries@ccw.gov.uk
W www.ccw.gov.uk

The Countryside Council for Wales is the government's statutory adviser on sustaining natural beauty, wildlife and the opportunity for outdoor enjoyment in Wales and its inshore waters. It is funded by the National Assembly for Wales and accountable to the First Secretary, who appoints its members.

Chair, John Lloyd Jones, OBE
Chief Executive, Roger Thomas

COVENT GARDEN MARKET AUTHORITY

Covent House, New Covent Garden Market, London SW8 5NX
T 020-7720 2211 E info@cgma.gov.uk
W www.newcoventgardenmarket.com

The Covent Garden Market Authority is constituted under the Covent Garden Market Acts 1961 to 1977, the board being appointed by the Department of Environment, Food and Rural Affairs. The authority owns and operates the 22.7ha (56 acre) New Covent Garden Markets (fruit, vegetables, flowers), which have been trading at the site since 1974.

Chair (part-time), Rt. Hon. Baroness Dean of Thornton-le-Fylde
Chief Executive, Jan Lloyd

CRIMINAL CASES REVIEW COMMISSION

Alpha Tower, Suffolk Street Queensway, Birmingham B1 1TT
T 0121-633 1800 E info@ccrc.x.gsi.gov.uk
W www.ccrc.gov.uk

The Criminal Cases Review Commission is an independent body set up under the Criminal Appeal Act 1995. It is a non-departmental public body reporting to parliament via the Lord Chancellor and Secretary of State for Justice. It is responsible for investigating possible miscarriages of justice in England, Wales and Northern Ireland, and deciding whether or not to refer cases back to an appeal court. Membership of the commission is by royal appointment; the senior executive staff are appointed by the commission.

Chair, Richard Foster, CBE
Members, M. Allen; Ms P. Barrett; M. Emerton; J. England; Ms J. Goulding; D. Jessel; A. MacGregor, QC; I. Nicholl; E. Smith; J. Weeden
Principal Director, C. Albert

CRIMINAL INJURIES COMPENSATION AUTHORITY (CICA)

Tay House, 300 Bath Street, Glasgow G2 4LN
T 0800-358 3601 E enquiries@cica.gsi.gov.uk
W www.cica.gov.uk

CICA is the government body responsible for administering the Criminal Injuries Compensation Scheme in England, Scotland and Wales (separate arrangements apply in Northern Ireland). CICA deals with every aspect of applications for compensation under the 1996, 2001 and 2008 Criminal Injuries Compensation Schemes. There is a separate avenue of appeal to the Tribunals Service – Criminal Injuries Compensation (*see* Tribunals section).
Chief Executive, Carole Oatway

CROFTERS COMMISSION

Castle Wynd, Inverness IV2 3EQ
T 01463-663450
E info@crofterscommission.org.uk
W www.crofterscommission.org.uk

The Crofters Commission, established in 1955 under the Crofters (Scotland) Act, is a government-funded organisation tasked with overseeing crofting legislation. It works with communities to regulate crofting and advises Scottish ministers on crofting matters. The commission administers the Crofting Counties Agricultural Grants Scheme and the Crofters' Cattle Improvement Scheme. It also provides a free enquiry service.
Convenor, Drew Ratter
Chief Executive, Nick Reiter

DEER COMMISSION FOR SCOTLAND

Great Glen House, Leachkin Road, Inverness IV3 8NW
T 01463-725000 E enquiries@dcs.gov.uk
W www.dcs.gov.uk

The Deer Commission for Scotland has the general functions of furthering the conservation and control of deer in Scotland. It has the statutory duty, with powers, to prevent damage to agriculture, forestry and the habitat by deer. It is funded by the Scottish government.
Chair (part-time), Prof. J. Milne, MBE
Chief Executive, N. Halfhide

DESIGN COUNCIL

34 Bow Street, London WC2E 7DL
T 020-7420 5200 E info@designcouncil.org.uk
W www.designcouncil.org.uk

The Design Council is a campaigning organisation which works with partners in business, education and government to promote the effective use of good design; its aim is to make businesses more competitive and public services more effective. It is a registered charity with a royal charter and is funded jointly by grant-in-aid from the Department for Business, Innovation and Skills and the Department for Culture, Media and Sport; the secretaries of state of these two departments appoint the chair and members of the council.
Chair, Sir Michael Bichard
Chief Executive, David Kester

ENGLISH HERITAGE (HISTORIC BUILDINGS AND MONUMENTS COMMISSION FOR ENGLAND)

1 Waterhouse Square, 138–142 Holborn, London EC1N 2ST
T 020-7973 3000
W www.english-heritage.org.uk

English Heritage was established under the National Heritage Act 1983. On 1 April 1999 it merged with the Royal Commission on the Historical Monuments of England to become the new lead body for England's historic environment. It is sponsored by the Department for Culture, Media and Sport and its duties are to carry out and sponsor archaeological, architectural and scientific surveys and research designed to increase the understanding of England's past and its changing condition; to identify buildings, monuments and landscapes for protection whilst also offering expert advice, skills and grants to conserve these sites; to encourage town planners to make imaginative re-use of historic buildings to aid regeneration of the centres of cities, towns and villages; to manage and curate selected sites; and to curate and make publicly accessible the National Monuments Record, whose records of over one million historic sites and buildings, and extensive collections of photographs, maps, drawings and reports, constitute the central database and archive of England's historic environment.
Chair, Baroness Andrews, OBE
Commissioners, Lynda Addison, OBE; Maria Adebowale; Joyce Bridges, CBE; Prof. David Cannadine, DPHIL, LITT D, FBA; Manish Chande; Prof. Sir Barry Cunliffe, CBE; Gilly Drummond; Michael Jolly, CBE; Jane Kennedy; Earl of Leicester, CBE; Chris Wilkinson, OBE; Elizabeth Williamson, FSA
Chief Executive, Dr Simon Thurley

CUSTOMER SERVICES DEPARTMENT, PO Box 569, Swindon SN2 2YP T 0870-333 1181 E customers@english-heritage.org.uk
NATIONAL MONUMENTS RECORD CENTRE, Kemble Drive, Swindon SN2 2GZ T 01793-414600

ENVIRONMENT AGENCY

Rio House, Waterside Drive, Aztec West, Almondsbury, Bristol BS32 4UD
T 0870-850 6506
E enquiries@environment-agency.gov.uk
W www.environment-agency.gov.uk

The Environment Agency was established in 1996 under the Environment Act 1995 and is a non-departmental public body sponsored by the Department for Environment, Food and Rural Affairs and the National Assembly for Wales – around 60 per cent of the agency's funding is from the government, with the rest raised from various charging schemes. The agency is responsible for pollution prevention and control in England and Wales, and for the management and use of water resources, including flood defences, fisheries and navigation. It has head offices in London and Bristol, and eight regional offices.

THE BOARD
Chair, Lord Smith of Finsbury
Members, James Braithwaite, CBE; Andrew Brown; Peter Bye; John Edmonds; Prof. Ruth Hall; Richard Percy; Dr Lyndon Stanton; Cllr Kay Twitchen, OBE; Dr Malcolm Smith; Lady Warner, OBE; Lord Whitty
Chief Executive (acting), Paul Leinster

EQUALITY AND HUMAN RIGHTS COMMISSION

Arndale House, The Arndale Centre, Manchester M4 3AQ
T 0161-829 8100 E info@equalityhumanrights.com
W www.equalityhumanrights.com

The Equality and Human Rights Commission (EHRC) is a statutory body, established under the Equality Act 2006 and launched in October 2007. It inherited the responsibilities of the Commission for Racial Equality, the Disability Rights Commission and the Equal Opportunities Commission. The EHRC's purpose is to reduce inequality, eliminate discrimination, strengthen relations between people, and promote and protect human rights. It enforces equality legislation on age, disability and health, gender, race, religion and belief, sexual orientation or transgender status, and encourages compliance with the Human Rights Act 1998 throughout England, Wales and Scotland. For information on how to contact the helpline, visit the EHRC website.

Chair, Trevor Phillips
Deputy Chair, Baroness Prosser, OBE
Commissioners, Morag Alexander; Kay Allen; Kay Carberry, CBE; Jeannie Drake, CBE; Joel Edwards; Baroness Greengross, OBE; Ziauddin Sardar; Maeve Sherlock, OBE; Ben Summerskill (until December 2009); Dr Neil Wooding
Chief Executive (interim), Neil Kinghan

EQUALITY COMMISSION FOR NORTHERN IRELAND

Equality House, 7–9 Shaftesbury Square, Belfast BT2 7DP
T 028-9050 0600 Textphone 028-9050 0589
E information@equalityni.org W www.equalityni.org

The Equality Commission was set up in 1999 under the Northern Ireland Act 1998 and is responsible for promoting equality, keeping the relevant legislation under review, eliminating discrimination on the grounds of race, disability, sexual orientation, gender, religion and political opinion and for overseeing the statutory duty on public authorities to promote equality of opportunity.

Chief Commissioner, Bob Collins
Deputy Chief Commissioner, Jane Morrice
Chief Executive, Evelyn Collins, CBE

FOREIGN COMPENSATION COMMISSION (FCC)

Old Admiralty Building, London SW1A 2PA
T 020-7008 1321 E fcc@fco.gov.uk
W http://foi.fco.gov.uk/en/access-information/Ndpbs/fcc

The FCC was set up by the Foreign Compensation Act 1950 primarily to distribute, under orders in council, funds received from other governments in accordance with agreements to pay compensation for expropriated British property and other losses sustained by British nationals. The FCC carries out both judicial and administrative functions, including the adjudication of claims by applicants and the investment and management of compensation funds. There are no active compensation programmes at present.

Chair, Dr John Barker

GAMBLING COMMISSION

Victoria Square House, Victoria Square, Birmingham B2 4BP
T 0121-230 6666
E info@gamblingcommission.gov.uk
W www.gamblingcommission.gov.uk

The Gambling Commission was established under the Gambling Act 2005, and took over the role previously occupied by the Gaming Board for Great Britain in regulating and licensing all commercial gambling – apart from spread betting and the National Lottery – ie casinos, bingo, betting, remote gambling, gaming machines and lotteries. It also advises local and central government on related issues, and is responsible for the protection of children and the vulnerable from being exploited or harmed by gambling. The commission is sponsored by the Department for Culture, Media and Sport, with its work funded mainly by licence fees paid by the gambling industry.

Chair, Brian Pomeroy
Chief Executive, Jenny Williams

GOVERNMENT OFFICES FOR THE ENGLISH REGIONS

The Government Office Network consists of nine regional offices in cities across England, and their corporate centre, the GO Network and central services. The nine Government Offices for the Regions (GOs) are the primary means by which a wide range of government policies are delivered in the English regions. The Government Offices bring together the activities and interests of 12 'sponsor' government departments: the Department for Communities and Local Government; the Department for Business, Innovation and Skills; the Department for Children, Schools and Families; the Department of Energy and Climate Change; the Department for Environment, Food and Rural Affairs; the Home Office; the Department for Culture, Media and Sport; the Department for Work and Pensions; the Department for Transport; the Department of Health; the Cabinet Office; and the Ministry of Justice. GOs offer experience and expertise to the departments in the development of policy and in the way that policies are best implemented.

GOs contribute to a diverse range of tasks including regenerating communities, fighting crime, tackling housing needs, improving public health, raising standards in education and skills, tackling countryside issues, and reducing unemployment and responding to large scale wide impact incidents. GOs also manage significant spending programmes on behalf of the departments, including a number of European funds.

GOVERNMENT OFFICE NETWORK CENTRE AND SERVICES

4th Floor, Eland House, Bressenden Place, London SW1E 5DU
T 020-7944 0702 W www.gos.gov.uk

Director-General, Joe Montgomery
Director, Brian Hackland
Deputy Directors, Stuart MacDonald *(Business Development)*; Vince Brady *(Human Resources)*; Julian Bowrey *(Strategy and Performance)*

EAST MIDLANDS
The Belgrave Centre, Stanley Place, Talbot Street, Nottingham NG1 5GG
T 0115-971 9971
E enquiries@goem.gsi.gov.uk
W www.goem.gov.uk
Regional Director, Jonathan Lindley

EAST OF ENGLAND
Eastbrook, Shaftesbury Road, Cambridge CB2 2DF
T 01223-372500
W www.go-east.gov.uk
Regional Director, Paul Pugh

LONDON
Riverwalk House, 157–161 Millbank, London SW1P 4RR
T 020-7217 3111
W www.gos.gov.uk/gol
Regional Director, Chris Hayes

NORTH EAST
Citygate, Gallowgate, Newcastle upon Tyne NE1 4WH
T 0191-201 3300
W www.go-ne.gov.uk
Regional Director, Jonathan Blackie

NORTH WEST
City Tower, Piccadilly Plaza, Manchester M1 4BE
T 0161-952 4000
W www.go-nw.gov.uk
Regional Director, Liz Meek

SOUTH EAST
Bridge House, 1 Walnut Tree Close, Guildford GU1 4GA
T 01483-882002
W www.go-se.gov.uk
Regional Director, Colin Byrne

SOUTH WEST
2 Rivergate, Temple Quay, Bristol BS1 6EH
T 0117-900 1700
W www.gosw.gov.uk
Regional Director, Jon Bright

WEST MIDLANDS
5 St Phillips Place, Colmore Row, Birmingham B3 2PW
T 0121-352 5050
E enquiries.team@gowm.gsi.gov.uk
W www.go-wm.gov.uk
Regional Director, Trudi Elliot

YORKSHIRE AND THE HUMBER
Lateral, 8 City Walk, Leeds LS11 9AT
T 0113-341 3000
E yhenquiries@goyh.gsi.gov.uk
W www.goyh.gov.uk
Regional Director, Felicity Everiss

HEALTH AND SAFETY EXECUTIVE

London, Rose Court, 2 Southwark Bridge, London SE1 9HS
Liverpool, Redgrave Court, Merton Road, Bootle, Merseyside L20 7HS
T 0845-345 0055 E hse.infoline@connaught.plc.uk
W www.hse.gov.uk

The Health and Safety Commission (HSC) and the Health and Safety Executive (HSE) merged on 1 April 2008 to form a single national regulatory body responsible for promoting the cause of better health and safety at work.

HSE regulates all industrial and commercial sectors except operations in the air and at sea. This includes agriculture, construction, manufacturing, services, transport, mines, offshore oil and gas, nuclear, quarries and major hazard sites in chemicals and petrochemicals.

HSE is responsible for developing and enforcing health and safety law, providing guidance and advice, commissioning research, inspection including accident and ill-health investigation, developing standards and licensing or approving some work activities such as nuclear power and asbestos removal. HSE is a government agency sponsored by the Department for Work and Pensions.

Chair, Judith Hackitt, CBE
Board Members, Sandy Blair; Danny Carrigan; Robin Dahlberg; Judith Donovan; David Gartside; Sayeed Khan; Hugh Robertson; Elizabeth Snape; John Spanswick
Chief Executive, Geoffrey Podger

HEALTH PROTECTION AGENCY (HPA)

7th Floor, Holborn Gate, 330 High Holborn, London WC1V 7PP
T 020-7759 2700 E hpa.enquiries@hpa.org.uk
W www.hpa.org.uk

The HPA was set up in 2003 and is responsible for providing an integrated approach to protecting public health through the provision of support and advice to the NHS, local authorities, emergency services, other NDPBs, the Department of Health and the devolved administrations.

The HPA works at local, regional, national and international levels to reduce the impact of infectious diseases and reduce exposure to chemicals, radiation and poisons, as well as ensure a rapid response when hazards occur. The HPA provides services in Northern Ireland and works closely with the devolved administrations, so that there is a coordinated response to incidents, trends and outbreaks on a national level. Research and development projects conducted by HPA scientists are primarily concerned with new methods of treating illness and assessing exposure to chemicals or radiation.

Chair, Dr David Heymann
Board Members, Dr Barbara Bannister, FRCP; James T. Brown; Michael Carroll; Prof. Charles Easmon, CBE, FMEDSCI; Helen Froud; Prof. William Gelletly, OBE; Martin Hindle; Dr Rosemary Leonard, MBE; Prof. Alan Maryon-Davis, FRCP; Dr Vanessa Mayatt; Deborah Oakley; Prof. Debby Reynolds
Chief Executive, Justin McCracken

HER MAJESTY'S OFFICERS OF ARMS

COLLEGE OF ARMS (HERALDS' COLLEGE)
Queen Victoria Street, London EC4V 4BT
T 020-7248 2762
E enquiries@college-of-arms.gov.uk
W www.college-of-arms.gov.uk

The Sovereign's Officers of Arms (Kings, Heralds and Pursuivants of Arms) were first incorporated by Richard III in 1484. The powers vested by the crown in the Earl Marshal (the Duke of Norfolk) with regard to state ceremonial are largely exercised through the college. The college is also the official repository of the arms and pedigrees of English, Welsh, Northern Irish and Commonwealth (except Canadian) families and their descendants, and its records include official copies of the records of the Ulster King of Arms, the originals of which remain in Dublin. The 13 officers of the college specialise in genealogical and heraldic work for their respective clients.

Arms have long been, and still are, granted by letters patent from the Kings of Arms. A right to arms can only be established by the registration in the official records of the College of Arms of a pedigree showing direct male line descent from an ancestor already appearing therein as being entitled to arms, or by making application through the College of Arms for a grant of arms. Grants are made to corporations as well as to individuals.

Earl Marshal, Duke of Norfolk

KINGS OF ARMS

Garter, P. L. Gwynn-Jones, CVO, FSA
Clarenceux, D. H. B. Chesshyre, CVO, FSA
Norroy and Ulster, T. Woodcock, LVO, FSA

HERALDS

Richmond (and Earl Marshal's Secretary), P. L. Dickinson, LVO
York, H. E. Paston-Bedingfeld
Chester, T. H. S. Duke
Lancaster, R. J. B. Noel
Windsor (and Registrar), W. G. Hunt, TD
Somerset, D. V. White

PURSUIVANTS

Rouge Dragon, C. E. A. Cheesman
Bluemantle, M. P. D. O'Donoghue

COURT OF THE LORD LYON

HM New Register House, Edinburgh EH1 3YT
T 0131-556 7255
W www.lyon-court.com

Her Majesty's Officers of Arms in Scotland perform ceremonial duties and in addition may be consulted by members of the public on heraldic and genealogical matters in a professional capacity.

KING OF ARMS

Lord Lyon King of Arms, David Sellar, FSA SCOT, FRHISTS

HERALDS

Albany, J. A. Spens, MVO, RD, WS
Rothesay, Sir Crispin Agnew of Lochnaw, Bt., QC
Ross, C. J. Burnett, FSA SCOT

PURSUIVANTS

Carrick, Mrs C. G. W. Roads, MVO, FSA SCOT
Unicorn, The Hon. Adam Bruce, WS

EXTRAORDINARY OFFICERS

Orkney Herald Extraordinary, Sir Malcolm Innes of Edingight, KCVO, WS
Angus Herald Extraordinary, R. O. Blair, CVO, WS
Islay Herald Extraordinary, Alastair Campbell of Airds

HERALD PAINTER

Herald Painter, Mrs Y. Holton

HIGHLANDS AND ISLANDS ENTERPRISE

Cowan House, Inverness Retail and Business Park, Inverness IV2 7GF T 01463-234171
E info@hient.co.uk
W www.hie.co.uk

Highlands and Islands Enterprise (HIE) was set up under the Enterprise and New Towns (Scotland) Act 1991. Its role is to deliver community and economic development in line with the Scottish government economic strategy. It focuses on helping high growth businesses, improving regional competitiveness and strengthening communities. HIE's budget for 2009–10 is £85.4m.

Chair, W. Roe
Chief Executive, J. R. S. Cumming, CBE

HISTORIC ROYAL PALACES

Apartment 39A, Hampton Court Palace, Surrey KT8 9AU
T 0844-482 7777 E operators@hrp.org.uk
W www.hrp.org.uk

Historic Royal Palaces was established in 1998 as a royal charter body with charitable status and is contracted by the Secretary of State for Culture, Media and Sport to manage the palaces on her behalf. The palaces – the Tower of London, Hampton Court Palace, the Banqueting House, Kensington Palace and Kew Palace – are owned by the Queen on behalf of the nation.

The organisation is governed by a board comprising a chair and ten non-executive trustees. The chief executive is accountable to the board of trustees and ultimately to parliament. Historic Royal Palaces receives no funding from the government or the crown.

TRUSTEES

Chair, Charles Mackay
Appointed by the Queen, Sir Trevor McDonald, OBE; Sir Adrian Montague, CBE; Sir Alan Reid, KCVO; Sir Hugh Roberts, KCVO, FSA
Appointed by the Secretary of State, Sophie Andreae; Dawn Austwick, OBE; Sue Farr; John Hamer; Malcolm Reading
Ex officio, Gen. Sir Roger Wheeler, GCB, CBE *(Constable of the Tower of London)*

OFFICERS

Chief Executive, Michael Day
Resident Governor, HM Tower of London, Maj.-Gen. Keith Cima, CB

HOMES AND COMMUNITIES AGENCY

110 Buckingham Palace Road, Victoria, London SW1W 9SA
T 0300-1234 500 E mail@homesandcommunities.co.uk
W www.homesandcommunities.co.uk

The Homes and Communities Agency (HCA) was formed in December 2008 as the national housing regeneration agency for England. It is a non-departmental public body sponsored by the Department for Communities and Local Government. The HCA aims to create thriving communities and affordable homes by providing funding for affordable housing and bringing land back into productive use; it also strives to improve quality of life by raising standards for the physical and social environment. For 2008–11 the HCA has a budget of £17.3bn, of which £8.4bn will be invested in affordable homes for rent and sale through the National Affordable Housing Programme.

Chair, Robert Napier
Chief Executive, Bob Kerslake

HORSERACE TOTALISATOR BOARD

Westgate House, Tote Park, Chapel Lane, Wigan WN3 4HS
T 0800-666100 E customercare@totesport.com
W www.totesport.com

The Horserace Totalisator Board (the Tote) operates totalisators on approved racecourses in Great Britain, provides on and off-course cash and credit offices, telephone betting and a website. It was established in 1928 (then the Racecourse Betting Control Board) and renamed following the Betting Levy Act 1961. With the Horserace Totalisator and Betting Levy Board Act 1972, the Tote was empowered to operate as a bookmaker, offering bets at fixed odds on any sporting event, and under the Horserace Totalisator Board Act 1997 to take bets on any event, except the National Lottery. It retains exclusivity over pools' betting on British horseracing. The chair and members of the board are appointed by the Secretary of State for Culture, Media and Sport.
Chair, Mike Smith
Chief Executive, Trevor Beaumont

HUMAN FERTILISATION AND EMBRYOLOGY AUTHORITY (HFEA)

21 Bloomsbury Street, London WC1B 3HF
T 020-7291 8200 E admin@hfea.gov.uk
W www.hfea.gov.uk

The HFEA was established in 1991 under the Human Fertilisation and Embryology Act 1990. It is the UK's independent regulator tasked with overseeing safe and appropriate practice in fertility treatment and embryo research, including licensing and monitoring centres carrying out IVF, artificial insemination and human embryo research. HFEA also provides a range of detailed information for patients, professionals and government, and maintains a formal register of information about donors, fertility treatments and children born as a result of those treatments.
Chair, Prof. Lisa Jardine, CBE
Chief Executive (interim), Alan Doran

HUMAN GENETICS COMMISSION

Area 605, Wellington House, 133–155 Waterloo Road, London SE1 8UG
T 020-7972 4351 E hgc@dh.gsi.gov.uk
W www.hgc.gov.uk

The Human Genetics Commission was established in 1999, subsuming three previous advisory committees. Its remit is to give ministers strategic advice on how developments in human genetics will impact on people and healthcare, focusing in particular on the social and ethical implications.
Chair, Prof. Jonathan Montgomery
Members, Prof. Tim Aitman; Prof. Thomas Baldwin; Prof. Angus Clarke; Prof. Sarah Cunningham-Burley; Dr Paul Darragh; Dr Paul Debenham; Nicola Drury; Dr Frances Flinter; Ros Gardner; Prof. John Harris; Michael Harrison; Alastair Kent; Dr Anneke Lucassen; Dr Duncan McHale; Dr Alice Maynard; Dr Lola Oni; Dr Rosalind Skinner; Sir John Sulston (vice-chair); Dr Anita Thomas

HUMAN TISSUE AUTHORITY (HTA)

Second Floor, Finlaison House, 15–17 Furnival Street, London EC4A 1AB
T 020-7211 3400 E enquiries@hta.gov.uk
W www.hta.gov.uk

The HTA was established on 1 April 2005 under the Human Tissue Act 2004, and is sponsored and part-funded by the Department of Health. Its role is to inform the public and Secretary of State for Health about issues within its remit, which include the import, export, storage and use of human bodies and tissue for scheduled purposes, and disposal of human tissue following its use in medical treatment or for scheduled purposes. The HTA is the competent authority under the EU tissues and cells directive for regulating human tissue banking for transplant services.

The HTA also supersedes and extends the role that was previously performed by the now-defunct Unrelated Live Transplant Regulatory Authority (ULTRA) in setting out the circumstances in which live 'transplantable material' (from both related and unrelated donors) will be allowed.
Chair, Shirley Harrison
Chief Executive, Adrian McNeil

IMPERIAL WAR MUSEUM

Lambeth Road, London SE1 6HZ
T 020-7416 5320 E mail@iwm.org.uk
W www.iwm.org.uk

The museum, founded in 1917, illustrates and records all aspects of the two world wars and other military operations involving Britain and the Commonwealth since 1914. It was opened in its present home, formerly Bethlem Royal Hospital, in 1936. The museum is a multi-branch organisation that also includes the Churchill Museum and Cabinet War Rooms in Whitehall; HMS *Belfast* in the Pool of London; Imperial War Museum Duxford in Cambridgeshire; and Imperial War Museum North in Trafford, Manchester.

The total projected grant-in-aid (including grants for special projects) for 2009–10 is £24.16m.

OFFICERS

Chair of Trustees, Air Chief Marshal Sir Peter Squire, GCB, DFC, AFC, DSc
Director-General, Diane Lees
Directors, Richard Ashton *(Imperial War Museum Duxford)*; Jon Card *(Secretary, Finance)*; Sue Coleman *(Development)*; Jim Forrester *(Imperial War Museum North)*; Angela Godwin *(Public Services)*, Brad King *(HMS Belfast)*; Phil Reed *(Churchill Museum and Cabinet War Rooms)*; Alan Stoneman *(Corporate Services)*; Mark Whitmore *(Collections)*

INDEPENDENT REVIEW SERVICE FOR THE SOCIAL FUND

4th Floor, Centre City Podium, 5 Hill Street, Birmingham B5 4UB
T 0121-606 2100 E sfc@irs-review.org.uk
W www.irs-review.org.uk

The Social Fund Commissioner is appointed by the Secretary of State for Work and Pensions. The commissioner appoints Social Fund Inspectors, who provide an independent review for customers dissatisfied with decisions made in Jobcentre Plus offices throughout England, Scotland and Wales regarding the grants and loans available from the Discretionary Social Fund.
Social Fund Commissioner, Sir Richard Tilt

INDEPENDENT SAFEGUARDING AUTHORITY

PO Box 181, Darlington, DL1 9FA
T 0300-123 1111 E info@vbs-info.org.uk
W www.isa-gov.org.uk

The Independent Safeguarding Authority (ISA) was created in 2008 to help prevent unsuitable people working with children and vulnerable adults in England, Wales and Northern Ireland. It assumed full responsibility for decisions to bar individuals from working with vulnerable people in January 2009. ISA works in partnership with the Criminal Records Bureau to assess each person who wants to work or volunteer with vulnerable people on a case-by-case basis. Once the scheme has been fully rolled out, employers who work with vulnerable people will only be allowed to recruit those who are ISA registered. ISA is a non-departmental public body sponsored by the Home Office.
Chair, Sir Roger Singleton, CBE
Chief Executive, Adrian McAllister

INDUSTRIAL INJURIES ADVISORY COUNCIL

Second Floor, Caxton House, Tothill Street, London SW1H 9NA
T 020-7449 5618 E iiac@dwp.gsi.gov.uk
W www.iiac.org.uk

The Industrial Injuries Advisory Council was established under the National Insurance (Industrial Injuries) Act 1946, which came into effect on 5 July 1948. Statutory provisions governing its work are set out in section 171–173 of the Social Security Administration Act 1992. The council consists of 16 members appointed by the Secretary of State for Work and Pensions, and has three roles: to consider and advise on matters relating to industrial injuries benefit or its administration referred to it by the secretary of state for the Department for Social Development in Northern Ireland; to consider and provide advice on any draft regulations the secretary of state proposes to make on industrial injuries benefit or its administration; and to advise on any other matter relating to industrial injuries benefit or its administration.
Chair, Prof. Keith Palmer

INFORMATION COMMISSIONER'S OFFICE

Wycliffe House, Water Lane, Wilmslow, Cheshire SK9 5AF
T 0845-630 6060 E mail@ico.gsi.gov.uk
W www.ico.gov.uk

The Information Commissioner's Office is sponsored by the Ministry of Justice and oversees and enforces the Freedom of Information Act 2000 and the Data Protection Act 1998, with the objective of promoting public access to official information and protecting personal information.

The Data Protection Act 1998 sets out rules for the processing of personal information and applies to records held on computers and some paper files. It works in two ways: it dictates that those who record and use personal information (data controllers) must be open about how the information is used and must follow the eight principles of 'good information handling', and it gives individuals certain rights to access their personal information.

The Freedom of Information Act 2000 is designed to help end the culture of unnecessary secrecy and open up the inner workings of the public sector to citizens and businesses. Under the Freedom of Information Act, public authorities must produce a publication scheme that sets out what information the public authority is obliged to publish by law.

The Information Commissioner's Office also enforces and oversees the environmental information regulations, and the privacy and electronic communications regulations.

The Information Commissioner reports annually to parliament on the performance of his functions under the acts and has obligations to assess breaches of the acts.
Information Commissioner, Richard Thomas

JOINT NATURE CONSERVATION COMMITTEE

Monkstone House, City Road, Peterborough PE1 1JY
T 01733-562626 E communications@jncc.gov.uk
W www.jncc.gov.uk

The committee was established under the Environmental Protection Act 1990 and was reconstituted by the Natural Environment and Rural Communities Act 2006. It advises the government and others on UK and international nature conservation issues and disseminates knowledge on these subjects. It establishes common standards for the monitoring of nature conservation and research, and provides guidance to Natural England, Scottish Natural Heritage, the Council for Nature Conservation and the Countryside, and the Countryside Council for Wales.
Chair, Dr Peter Bridgewater
Deputy Chair, Prof. Lynda Warren

LAW COMMISSION

Steel House, 11 Tothill Street, London SW1H 9LJ
T 020-3334 0200
E chief.executive@lawcommission.gsi.gov.uk
W www.lawcom.gov.uk

The Law Commission was set up under the Law Commissions Act 1965, to make proposals to the government for the examination of the law in England and Wales and for its revision where it is unsuited for modern requirements, obscure, or otherwise unsatisfactory. It recommends to the Lord Chancellor programmes for the examination of different branches of the law and suggests whether the examination should be carried out by the commission itself or by some other body. The commission is also responsible for the preparation of Consolidation and Statute Law (Repeals) Bills.
Chair, Hon. Mr Justice Etherton
Commissioners, E. J. Cooke; David Hertzell; Dr Jeremy Horder; Kenneth Parker, QC
Chief Executive, Mark Ormerod

LEARNING AND SKILLS COUNCIL (LSC)

Cheylesmore House, Quinton Road, Coventry CV1 2WT
T 0870-900 6800 E info@lsc.gov.uk
W www.lsc.gov.uk

The LSC was established in 2001 to replace the Further Education Funding and the Training and Enterprise Councils. It is a non-departmental public body responsible for the planning and funding of post-16 education in colleges, schools and training providers. Its remit is to ensure that high-quality post-16 provision is available to meet the needs of employers, individuals and communities. The LSC operates through a national office

based in Coventry and also through local departments, which work to promote the equality of opportunity in the workplace; its budget for 2008–9 was £11.6bn.
Chair, Chris Banks, CBE
Chief Executive, Mark Haysom, CBE

LEGAL SERVICES COMMISSION

4 Abbey Orchard Street, London SW1P 2BS
T 020-7783 7000
W www.legalservices.gov.uk, www.communitylegaladvice.org.uk

The Legal Services Commission was created under the Access to Justice Act 1999 and replaced the Legal Aid Board in April 2000. It is a non-departmental public body which is sponsored by the Ministry of Justice.

The commission is responsible for two schemes. The Community Legal Service funds the delivery of civil legal and advice services, identifies priorities and unmet needs, and develops suppliers and services to meet those needs. The Criminal Defence Service provides free legal advice and representation for people involved in criminal investigations or proceedings.

The commission produces free information leaflets which are available from solicitors' and advisory offices, and from the commission's website.
Chief Executive, Carolyn Regan
Chair, Sir Bill Callaghan

MUSEUM OF LONDON

150 London Wall, London EC2Y 5HN
T 020 7001 9844
E info@museumoflondon.org.uk
W www.museumoflondon.org.uk

The Museum of London illustrates the history of London from prehistoric times to the present day. It opened in 1976 and is based on the amalgamation of the former Guildhall Museum and London Museum. The museum is controlled by a board of governors, appointed (ten each) by the prime minister and the City of London. The museum is currently funded by grants from the Greater London Authority and the City of London. The lower galleries of the museum are closed for refurbishment until spring 2010. The total grant-in-aid for 2008–9 was £14m.
Chair of Board of Governors, Michael Cassidy, CBE
Director, Prof. Jack Lohman

MUSEUMS, LIBRARIES AND ARCHIVES COUNCIL (MLA)

1st Floor, Grosvenor House, 14 Bennetts Hill, Birmingham B2 5RS
T 0121-345 7300 **E** info@mla.gov.uk
W www.mla.gov.uk

The MLA was launched in April 2000 and is the lead strategic agency for museums, libraries and archives. It is a non-departmental public body sponsored by the Department for Culture, Media and Sport. The MLA replaced the Museums and Galleries Commission (MGC) and the Library and Information Commission (LIC).
Chair, Andrew Motion
Board Members, Geoffrey Bond, OBE; Nick Dodd; Yinnon Ezra, MBE; Helen Forde; John Hicks; Sir Geoffrey Holland; Glen Lawes; Robert Wand
Chief Executive, Roy Clare

NATIONAL ARMY MUSEUM

Royal Hospital Road, London SW3 4HT
T 020-7730 0717
E info@national-army-museum.ac.uk
W www.national-army-museum.ac.uk

The National Army Museum was established by royal charter in 1960, and covers the history of five centuries of the British Army. It chronicles the campaigns and battles fought over this time as well as the social history and development of the Army, and its impact on Britain, Europe and the world. The museum houses a wide array of artefacts, paintings, photographs, uniforms and equipment.
Chair, General Sir Jack Deverell, KCB, OBE
Director, Dr Alan J. Guy

NATIONAL ENDOWMENT FOR SCIENCE, TECHNOLOGY AND THE ARTS (NESTA)

1 Plough Place, London EC4A 1DE
T 020-7438 2500 **E** nesta@nesta.org.uk
W www.nesta.org.uk

NESTA was established under the National Lottery Act 1998 with a £200m endowment from the proceeds of the National Lottery. Its endowment is presently over £300m. NESTA invests in early-stage companies, informs and shapes policy, and delivers practical programmes to enable others to solve future challenges.
Chair, Chris Powell
Chief Executive, Jonathan Kestenbaum

NATIONAL GALLERIES OF SCOTLAND

The Dean Gallery, 73 Belford Road, Edinburgh EH4 3DS
T 0131-624 6200 **E** enquiries@nationalgalleries.org
W www.nationalgalleries.org

The National Galleries of Scotland comprise the National Gallery of Scotland, the Scottish National Portrait Gallery, the Scottish National Gallery of Modern Art, the Dean Gallery and the Royal Scottish Academy Building. There are also partner galleries at Paxton House, Berwickshire, and Duff House, Banffshire. Total government grant-in-aid for 2009–10 was forecast at £12.41m.

TRUSTEES
Chair, Ben Thomson
Trustees, Ian Barr; Anne Bonnar; Richard Burns; Herbert Coutts, MBE; James Dawney; Marc Ellington; James Knox; Ray Macfarlane; Alasdair Morton; Prof. Richard Thomson; Dr Ruth Wishart

OFFICERS
Director-General, John Leighton
Directors, M. Clarke *(National Gallery of Scotland)*; Dr Simon Groom *(Scottish National Gallery of Modern Art and Dean Gallery)*; J. Holloway *(Scottish National Portrait Gallery)*

NATIONAL GALLERY

Trafalgar Square, London WC2N 5DN
T 020-7747 2885 **E** information@ng-london.org.uk
W www.nationalgallery.org.uk

The National Gallery, which houses a permanent collection of western European painting from the 13th to the 20th century, was founded in 1824, following a parliamentary grant of £60,000 for the purchase and exhibition of the Angerstein collection of pictures. The present site was first occupied in 1838; an extension to the north of the building with a public entrance in Orange Street was opened in 1975; the Sainsbury wing was opened in 1991; and the Getty Entrance opened off Trafalgar Square at the east end of the main building in 2004. Total government grant-in-aid for 2009–10 is £27.29m.

BOARD OF TRUSTEES
Chair, M. Getty
Trustees, S. Burke; G. Dalal; Prof. D. Ekserdjian; J. Fenton; Lady Heseltine; Prof. Dame J. Higgins; M. Hintze; Lord Kerr of Kinlochard; P. Lankester; J. Lessore; Lady Normanby; H. Rothschild; C. Thomson

OFFICERS
Director, Dr N. Penny
Director of Collections, Dr S. Foister
Director of Public Affairs and Development, S. Ward
Director of Conservation, M. H. Wyld, CBE
Director of Education, Information and Access, Jillian Barker
Director of Scientific Research, Dr A. Roy
Senior Curator, D. Jaffé

NATIONAL HERITAGE MEMORIAL FUND

7 Holbein Place, London SW1W 8NR
T 020-7591 6000 E enquire@hlf.org.uk
W www.nhmf.org.uk

The National Heritage Memorial Fund was set up under the National Heritage Act 1980 in memory of people who have given their lives for the United Kingdom. The fund provides grants to organisations based in the UK, mainly so they can buy items of outstanding interest and of importance to the national heritage. These must either be at risk or have a memorial character. The fund is administered by a chair and 14 trustees who are appointed by the prime minister.

The National Heritage Memorial Fund receives an annual grant from the Department for Culture, Media and Sport. Under the the National Lottery etc Act 1993 the trustees of the fund became responsible for the distribution of funds for both the National Heritage Memorial Fund and the Heritage Lottery Fund.
Chair, Jenny Abramsky
Head, Eilish McGuinness

NATIONAL LIBRARY OF SCOTLAND

George IV Bridge, Edinburgh EH1 1EW
T 0131-623 3700 E enquiries@nls.uk
W www.nls.uk

The library, which was founded as the Advocates' Library in 1682, became the National Library of Scotland (NLS) in 1925. It is funded by the Scottish government. It contains about 14 million books and pamphlets, two million maps, 25,000 newspaper and magazine titles and 100,000 manuscripts, including the John Murray Archive. It has an unrivalled Scottish collection as well as online catalogues and digital resources which can be accessed through the NLS website.

Material can be consulted in the reading rooms, which are open to anyone with a valid reader's ticket.
Chair of the Trustees, Prof. Michael Anderson, OBE, FBA, FRSE
National Librarian and Secretary to the Trustees, M. Wade
Directors, C. Newton *(Collections and Research)*; D. Campbell *(Corporate Services)*; A. Miller *(Customer Services)*; T. Wishart *(Development and External Relations)*

NATIONAL LIBRARY OF WALES/LLYFRGELL GENEDLAETHOL CYMRU

Aberystwyth SY23 3BU
T 01970-632800
E holi@llgc.org.uk W www.llgc.org.uk

The National Library of Wales was founded by royal charter in 1907, and is funded by the National Assembly for Wales. It contains about five million printed books, 40,000 manuscripts, four million deeds and documents, numerous maps, prints and drawings, and a sound and moving image collection. It specialises in manuscripts and books relating to Wales and the Celtic peoples. It is the repository for pre-1858 Welsh probate records, manorial records and tithe documents, and certain legal records. Admission is by reader's ticket to the reading rooms but entry to the exhibition programme is free.
President, Rt Hon. Dafydd Wigley
Heads of Departments, G. Jenkins *(Collection Services)*; M. W. Mainwaring *(Corporate Services)*; R. Arwel Jones *(Public Services)*
Librarian, A. M. W. Green

NATIONAL LOTTERY COMMISSION

101 Wigmore Street, London W1U 1QU
T 020-7016 3400 E publicaffairs@natlotcomm.gov.uk
W www.natlotcomm.gov.uk

The National Lottery Commission replaced the Office of the National Lottery (OFLOT) in 1999 under the National Lottery Act 1998. The commission is responsible for the granting, varying and enforcing of licences to run the National Lottery. It also runs the competition to award the next licence. Its duties are to ensure that the National Lottery is run with all due propriety, that the interests of players are protected, and, subject to these two objectives, that returns to the good causes are maximised. The commission does not have a role in the distribution of funds to good causes, this is undertaken by 16 distributors, visit W www.lotteryfunding.org.uk for further information. Gaming and lotteries in the UK are officially regulated and may only be run by licensed operators or in licensed premises.

The Department for Culture, Media and Sport (DCMS) is responsible for gaming and lottery policy and laws. Empowered by the National Lottery Act 1993 (as amended), the DCMS directs the National Lottery Commission, who in turn regulates Camelot, the lottery operator. Camelot, a private company wholly owned by five shareholders, was granted a third licence to run the Lottery from 1 February 2009 for ten years.
Chair, Anne Wright, CBE
Chief Executive, Mark Harris

NATIONAL MARITIME MUSEUM

Park Row, Greenwich, London SE10 9NF
T 020-8858 4422
W www.nmm.ac.uk

Established in 1934, the National Maritime Museum provides information on the maritime history of Great

Britain and is the largest institution of its kind in the world, with over two million items in its collections related to seafaring, navigation and astronomy. The museum is in three groups of buildings in Greenwich Park: the main building, the Queen's House (built by Inigo Jones, 1616–35) and the Royal Observatory, Greenwich (including Christopher Wren's Flamsteed House). In 2007 a £16m project opened a new astronomy centre and planetarium (now the only public planetarium in London) at the Royal Observatory.

Director, Kevin Fewster
Chair, Lord Sterling of Plaistow, GCVO, CBE

NATIONAL MUSEUMS AND GALLERIES NORTHERN IRELAND

Botanic Gardens, Belfast BT9 5AB
T 0845-608 0000 **E** info@nmni.com
W www.nmni.com

The organisation of National Museums and Galleries of Northern Ireland was established under the Museums and Galleries (Northern Ireland) Order in 1998 and includes the Ulster Museum with Armagh Museum, the Ulster Folk and Transport Museum, the Ulster American Folk Park and W5 at Odyssey (a wholly owned subsidiary).

Legislation requires National Museums and Galleries of Northern Ireland's board of trustees to care for, preserve and add to the collections; ensure that the collections are exhibited to the public; ensure that the significance of the collections is interpreted; and promote the awareness, appreciation and understanding of the public in relation to art, history and science, to the culture and way of life of the people and to the migration and settlement of people.

Chair, Dan Harvey, OBE
Trustees, Linda Beers; Lt-Col. (retd) Reginald Harvey Bicker, OBE; Neil Bodger; Pat Carvill; Dame Geraldine Keegan; Joe Kelly; Dr Richard Browne McMinn, OBE; David Moore; Wendy Osborne, OBE; Anne Peoples; Thomas Shaw, CBE; Dr Brian Scott; Dr Alastair Walker
Chief Executive, Tim Cooke

NATIONAL MUSEUMS LIVERPOOL

127 Dale Street, Liverpool L2 2JH
T 0151-207 0001
W www.liverpoolmuseums.org.uk

The board of trustees of the National Museums Liverpool (formerly National Museums and Galleries on Merseyside) is responsible for World Museum Liverpool, the Merseyside Maritime Museum, the Lady Lever Art Gallery, the Walker Art Gallery, Sudley House, the National Conservation Centre, the International Slavery Museum and the Museum of Liverpool. Total government grant-in-aid for 2008–9 was £19.5m.

Chair of the Board of Trustees, Prof. P. Redmond, CBE
Director, Dr D. Fleming
Director of Art Galleries, R. King
Executive Director of Collections Management, World Museum Liverpool, J. Millard
Director, Merseyside Maritime Museum (interim), R. Mulhearn
Director of Urban History, Museum of Liverpool, J. Dugdale
Director of Collections Management, National Conservation Centre, S. A. Yates
Head of International Slavery Museum, Dr R. Benjamin

NATIONAL MUSEUMS SCOTLAND

Chambers Street, Edinburgh EH1 1JF
T 0131-225 7534 **E** info@nms.ac.uk **W** www.nms.ac.uk

National Museums Scotland (NMS) provides advice, expertise and support to the museums community across Scotland, and undertakes fieldwork that often involves collaboration at local, national and international levels. NMS comprises the National Museum of Scotland, the National War Museum, the National Museum of Rural Life, the National Museum of Flight, the National Museum of Costume and the National Museums Collection Centre. Its collections represent more than two centuries of collecting and include Scottish and classical archaeology, decorative and applied arts, world cultures and social history and science, technology and the natural world. Total grant-in-aid funding from the Scottish government for 2008–9 was £21.078m.

Up to 15 trustees can be appointed by the Minister for Culture, External Affairs and the Constitution for a term of four years, and may serve a second term.

Chair, Sir Angus Grossart, CBE, LLD, DLITT
Trustees, Dr Isabel F. Bruce, OBE; James Fiddes, OBE, FRICS; Dr Anna Gregor, CBE, FRCR, FRCP; Lesley Hart, MBE; Andrew Holmes; Michael Kirwan, FCA; Prof. Michael Lynch, FRSE, FSA SCOT; Neena Mahal; Prof. Malcolm McLeod, CBE, FRSE; Prof. Stuart Monro, OBE; Ian Ritchie, CBE, FRENG, FRSE; Sir John Ward, CBE, FRSE, FRSA; Iain Watt
Director, Dr Gordon Rintoul

NATIONAL MUSEUM WALES – AMGUEDDFA CYMRU

Cathays Park, Cardiff CF10 3NP
T 029-2039 7951 **E** post@museumwales.ac.uk
W www.museumwales.ac.uk

National Museum Wales – Amgueddfa Cymru aims to provide a complete illustration of the geology, mineralogy, zoology, botany, ethnography, archaeology, art, history and special industries of Wales. It is comprised of the National Museum Cardiff; St Fagans National History Museum; Big Pit – National Coal Museum, Blaenafon; the National Roman Legion Museum, Caerleon; the National Slate Museum, Llanberis; the National Wool Museum, Dre-fach Felindre; and the National Waterfront Museum, Swansea. Total funding from the Welsh Assembly government for 2008–9 was £24.5m.

President, Paul E. Loveluck, CBE
Vice-President, Elisabeth Elias
Director-General, Michael Houlihan
Trustees, Carole-Anne Davies; Dr Haydn Edwards; Miriam Hazel Griffiths; Dr Iolo ap Gwynn; Prof. Colin L. Jones, OBE; Emeritus Prof. Richard G. W. Jones; Prof. J. W. Last, CBE; Christina Macaulay; Peter W. Morgan; Prof. Jonathan Osmond; Gareth Williams; H. R. C. Williams; Dr Brian Willott, CB; Rhiannon Wyn Hughes, MBE

NATIONAL PORTRAIT GALLERY

St Martin's Place, London WC2H 0HE
T 020-7312 2463
W www.npg.org.uk

The National Portrait Gallery was formed after a grant was made in 1856 to form a gallery of the portraits of the most eminent persons in British history. The present building was opened in 1896 and the Ondaatje Wing (including a new Balcony Gallery, Tudor Gallery, IT Gallery, lecture theatre and roof-top restaurant) opened in May 2000. There are three regional partnerships displaying portraits at Montacute House, Beningbrough Hall and Bodelwyddan Castle. Total government grant-in-aid for 2008–9 was £7.693m.

BOARD OF TRUSTEES
Chair, Prof. David Cannadine, FBA, FRSL
Trustees, Zeinab Badawi; Sir Nicholas Blake, QC; Dr Augustus Casely-Hayford; Marchioness of Douro, OBE; Amelia Fawcett, CBE; Sir Nicholas Grimshaw, CBE, PRA; Rt. Hon. Lord Janvrin, GCB, GCVO, QSO; Prof. Ludmilla Jordanova; David Mach, RA; Sir Christopher Ondaatje, CBE, OC; Rt. Hon. Baroness Royall of Blaisdon; Prof. Sara Selwood; Marina Warner, CBE, FBA
Director, Sandy Nairne

NATURAL ENGLAND

1 East Parade, Sheffield S1 2ET
T 0845-600 3078 E enquiries@naturalengland.org.uk
W www.naturalengland.org.uk

Natural England was established on 1 October 2006 after the Natural Environment and Rural Communities Act received royal assent in March 2006. It is the government's advisor on the natural environment, providing practical advice, grounded in science, on how best to safeguard England's natural wealth. The organisation's remit is to ensure sustainable stewardship of the land and sea and to ensure England's environment can adapt and survive for future generations. Natural England works with farmers and land managers; business and industry; planners and developers; national, regional and local government; interest groups and local communities to help them improve their local environment.
Chief Executive, Dr Helen Phillips

NATURAL HISTORY MUSEUM

Cromwell Road, London SW7 5BD
T 020-7942 5000 W www.nhm.ac.uk

The Natural History Museum originates from the natural history departments of the British Museum, which grew extensively during the 19th century; in 1860 it was agreed that the natural history collections should be separated from the British Museum's collections of books, manuscripts and antiquities. Part of the site of the 1862 International Exhibition in South Kensington was acquired for the new museum, and the museum opened to the public in 1881. In 1963 the Natural History Museum became completely independent with its own board of trustees. The Natural History Museum at Tring, bequeathed by the second Lord Rothschild, has formed part of the museum since 1937. The Geological Museum merged with the Natural History Museum in 1985. In September 2009 the Natural History Museum opened the Darwin Centre, which contains public galleries, scientific research areas and space for 22 million zoological specimens, 17 million insect specimens and three million botanical specimens. Total government grant-in-aid for 2009–10 is £51.05m.

BOARD OF TRUSTEES
Chair, Oliver Stocken
Trustees, Daniel Alexander; QC, Prof. Sir Roy Anderson, FRS; Louise Charlton; Prof. David Drewry; Prof. Dianne Edwards, CBE, FRS; Prof Alex Halliday, FRS; Ian J. Henderson, CBE, FRICS; Dr Derek Langslow, CBE; Prof. Jacquie McGlade; Prof Georgina Mace, CBE, FRS; Sir David Omand, GCB, KCB

SENIOR STAFF
Director, Dr Michael Dixon
Director of Estates and Services, David Sanders
Director of Finance and Administration, Neil Greenwood
Director of Human Resources, Paul Brereton
Director, Natural History Museum at Tring, Teresa Wild
Director of Public Engagement Group, Sharon Ament
Director of Science, Richard Lane
Head of Audit and Review, David Thorpe
Head of Library and Information Services, Graham Higley
Keeper of Botany, Dr Johannes Vogel
Keeper of Entomology, Dr Malcolm Scoble
Keeper of Mineralogy, Dr Andy Fleet
Keeper of Palaeontology, Prof. Norman MacLeod
Keeper of Zoology, Prof. Phil Rainbow
Museum Manager, Ian Jenkinson

NHS PAY REVIEW BODY

6th Floor, Kingsgate House, 66–74 Victoria Street, London SW1E 6SW
T 020-7215 4453 W www.ome.uk.com

The Review Body for Nurses and Allied Health Professions was set up in 1983, and following the Agenda for Change in 2004 the body changed its name to the Review Body for Nursing and Other Health Professions. It was renamed the NHS Pay Review Body in July 2007 to recognise its broader staff remit. It advises the prime minister and the Secretary of State for Health, and ministers of the Scottish government, Welsh Assembly and Northern Ireland Assembly on the remuneration of all staff employed in the NHS paid under the agenda for change, with the exception of doctors, dentists and a few senior managers. The review body covers over 1.3 million staff in the UK.
Chair, Prof. Gillian Morris
Members, Philip Ashmore; Prof. David Blackaby; Lucinda Bolton; Prof. Richard Disney; John Galbraith; Graham Jagger; Wilma MacPherson, CBE; Ian McKay; Prof. Alan Manning; Sharon Whitlam

NORTHERN IRELAND HUMAN RIGHTS COMMISSION

Temple Court, 39 North Street, Belfast BT1 1NA
T 028-9024 3987 Textphone 028-9024 9066
E information@nihrc.org W www.nihrc.org

The Northern Ireland Human Rights Commission was set up in March 1999. Its main functions are to keep under review the law and practice relating to human rights in Northern Ireland, to advise the government and to promote an awareness of human rights in Northern Ireland. It can also take cases to court. The members of the commission are appointed by the Secretary of State for Northern Ireland.
Chief Commissioner, Prof. Monica McWilliams
Commissioners, Jonathan Bell; Thomas Duncan; Prof. Colin Harvey; Alan Henry; Ann Hope; Colin Larkin; Eamonn O'Neill; Geraldine Rice; Lady Daphne Trimble
Chief Executive, Peter O'Neill

NORTHERN LIGHTHOUSE BOARD

84 George Street, Edinburgh EH2 3DA
T 0131-473 3100
E enquiries@nlb.org.uk W www.nlb.org.uk

The Northern Lighthouse Board is the general lighthouse authority for Scotland and the Isle of Man and owes its origin to an act of parliament passed in 1786. At present there are 19 commissioners who operate under the Merchant Shipping Act 1995.

The commissioners control 209 lighthouses, many lighted and unlighted buoys, a DGPS (differential global positioning system) station and an ELORAN (long-range navigation) system. *See also* Transport.

Chair, Sir Andrew Cubie, CBE, FRSE
Commissioners, Lord Advocate; Solicitor-General for Scotland; Lord Provosts of Edinburgh, Glasgow and Aberdeen; Convener of Highland Council; Convener of Argyll and Bute Council; Sheriffs-Principal of North Strathclyde, Tayside, Central and Fife, Grampian, Highlands and Islands, South Strathclyde, Dumfries and Galloway, Lothians and Borders and Glasgow and Strathkelvin; Capt. Mike Close; Robert Quayle; John Ross, CBE; Capt. George Sutherland; Alistair Whyte
Chief Executive, Roger Lockwood, CB

OFFICE OF COMMUNICATIONS (OFCOM)

Riverside House, 2A Southwark Bridge Road, London SE1 9HA
T 0300-123 3000 E contact@ofcom.org.uk
W www.ofcom.org.uk

OFCOM was established in 2003 under the Office of Communications Act 2002 as the independent regulator and competition authority for the UK communications industries with responsibility for television, radio, telecommunications and wireless communications services.

Chief Executive, Ed Richards
Chair, Colette Bowe
Deputy Chair, Philip Graf, CBE
Board Members, Millie Banerjee, CBE; Tim Gardham; Stuart McIntosh; Peter Phillips; Mike McTighe

OFFICE OF MANPOWER ECONOMICS (OME)

6th Floor, Kingsgate House, 66–74 Victoria Street, London SW1E 6SW
T 020-7215 8253 W www.ome.uk.com

The OME was set up in 1971. It is an independent non-statutory organisation which is responsible for servicing independent review bodies which advise on the pay of various public service groups, the Police Negotiating Board and the Police Advisory Board for England and Wales. The OME is also responsible for servicing *ad hoc* bodies of inquiry and for undertaking research into pay and associated matters as requested by the government.

OME Director, Ian Jones
Director, NHS Pay Review Body Secretariat, Research and Analysis Group and OME Deputy Director, Margaret McEvoy *Director, Armed Forces' and Prison Service Secretariats,* Christine Haworth
Director, Doctors and Dentists and Senior Salaries Secretariats, Keith Masson
Director, School Teachers', Police Negotiating Board and Police Advisory Board for England and Wales Secretariats, Chris Dee

PARADES COMMISSION

Windsor House, 9–15 Bedford Street, Belfast BT2 7EL
T 028-9089 5900
E info@paradescommission.org
W www.paradescommission.org

The Parades Commission was set up under the Public Processions (Northern Ireland) Act 1998. Its function is to encourage and facilitate local accommodation of contentious parades; where this is not possible, the commission is empowered to make legal determinations about such parades, which may include imposing conditions on aspects of the notified parade (such as restrictions on routes/areas and exclusion of certain groups with a record of bad behaviour).

The chair and members are appointed by the Secretary of State for Northern Ireland; the membership must, as far as is practicable, be representative of the community in Northern Ireland.

Chair, Rena Shepherd
Vice-Chair, Anne Monaghan
Members, Kelly Andrews; Dr Joe Hendron; Vilma Patterson, MBE; Alison Scott-McKinley

PAROLE BOARD FOR ENGLAND AND WALES

Grenadier House, 99–105 Horseferry Road, London SW1P 2DX
T 0845-251 2220 E info@paroleboard.gov.uk
W www.paroleboard.gov.uk

The Parole Board was established under the Criminal Justice Act 1967 and became an independent executive non-departmental public body under the Criminal Justice and Public Order Act 1994. It is the body that protects the public by making risk assessments about prisoners to decide who may safely be released into the community and who must remain in, or be returned to, custody. Board decisions are taken at two main types of panels of up to of three members: 'paper panels' for the majority of cases, or oral hearings for decisions concerning prisoners serving life or indeterminate sentences for public protection.

Chair, Rt. Hon. Sir David Latham
Chief Executive, Linda Lennon, CBE

PAROLE BOARD FOR SCOTLAND

Saughton House, Broomhouse Drive, Edinburgh EH11 3XD
T 0131-244 8373
E paroleboardforscotlandexecutive@scotland.gsi.gov.uk
W www.scottishparoleboard.gov.uk

The board directs and advises the Scottish ministers on the release of prisoners on licence, and related matters.

Chair, Prof. A. Cameron
Vice-Chair, Ms K. McQuillan

PENSION PROTECTION FUND (PPF)

Knollys House, 17 Addiscombe Road, Croydon CR0 6SR
T 0845-600 2541 E information@ppf.gsi.gov.uk
W www.pensionprotectionfund.org.uk

The PPF became operational in 2005. It was established to pay compensation to members of eligible defined-benefit pension schemes where a qualifying insolvency event in relation to the employer occurs and

where there is a lack of sufficient assets in the pension scheme. The PPF is also responsible for the Fraud Compensation Fund (which provides compensation to occupational pension schemes that suffer a loss that can be attributed to dishonesty). The chair and board of the PPF are appointed by, and accountable to, the Secretary of State for Work and Pensions, and are responsible for paying compensation, calculating annual levies (which help fund the PPF), and setting and overseeing investment strategy.
Chair, Lawrence Churchill
Chief Executive, Alan Rubenstein

PENSIONS REGULATOR

Napier House, Trafalgar Place, Brighton BN1 4DW
T 0870-606 3636
E customersupport@thepensionsregulator.gov.uk
W www.thepensionsregulator.gov.uk

The Pensions Regulator was established in 2005 as the regulator of work-based pension schemes in the UK, replacing the Occupational Pensions Regulatory Authority (OPRA). It aims to protect the benefits of occupational and personal pension scheme members by working with trustees, employers, pension providers and advisors. The regulator's work focuses on encouraging better management and administration of schemes, ensuring that final salary schemes have a sensible funding plan, and encouraging money purchase schemes to provide members with the information they need to make informed choices about their pension fund. The Pensions Act gave the regulator a range of powers which can be used to protect scheme members, but a strong emphasis is placed on educating and enabling those responsible for managing pension schemes, and powers are used as a last resort. The regulator offers two free online resources to help trustees and employers understand their role, duties and obligations.
Chair, David Norgrove
Chief Executive, Tony Hobman

POLICE ADVISORY BOARD FOR ENGLAND AND WALES

6th Floor, Kingsgate House, 66–74 Victoria Street, London SW1E 6SW
T 020-7215 8101 W www.ome.uk.com

The Police Advisory Board for England and Wales was established in 1965 and provides advice to the home secretary on general questions affecting the police in England and Wales. It also considers draft regulations which the secretary of state proposes to make with respect to matters other than hours of duty, leave, pay and allowances or the issue, use and return of police clothing, personal equipment and other effects.
Independent Chair, John Randall
Independent Deputy Chair, Prof. Gillian Morris

POLICE NEGOTIATING BOARD (PNB)

6th Floor, Kingsgate House, 66–74 Victoria Street, London SW1E 6SW
T 020-7215 8101 W www.ome.uk.com

The PNB was established in 1980 to negotiate pay, allowances, hours of duty, leave and pensions of United Kingdom police officers and to make recommendations on these matters to the Secretary of State for Home Affairs, Northern Ireland secretary, and Scottish ministers.
Independent Chair, John Randall
Independent Deputy Chair, Prof. Gillian Morris

PRISON SERVICE PAY REVIEW BODY

6th Floor, Kingsgate House, 66–74 Victoria Street, London SW1E 6SW
T 020-7215 8369 W www.ome.uk.com

The Prison Service Pay Review Body was set up in 2001. It makes independent recommendations on the pay of prison governors, operational managers, prison officers and related grades for the Prison Service in England and Wales and for the Northern Ireland Prison Service.
Chair, Jerry Cope
Members, Dr Henrietta Campbell; Richard Childs, QPM; Bronwen Mary Curtis, CBE; John Davies, OBE; David Lebrecht; Joseph Magee; Dr Peter Riach

REGIONAL DEVELOPMENT AGENCIES

Broadway House, Tothill Street, London SW1H 9NQ
T 020-7222 8180
W www.englandsrdas.com

Regional Development Agencies (RDAs) were established to help the English regions improve their relative economic performance and reduce social and economic disparities within and between regions. Their five statutory objectives are to further economic development and regeneration; to promote business efficiency and competitiveness; to promote employment; to enhance the development and application of skills relevant to employment; and to contribute to sustainable development. There are nine RDAs in England, and they are financed through a single fund provided by contributing government departments (BIS, DCSF, DEFRA and DCMS). In 2008–9 the RDA's budget was £2.19bn, in 2009–10 it is £2.25bn.

RDA REGIONS

NORTH WEST: PO Box 37, Renaissance House, Centre Park, Warrington WA1 1QN T 01925-400100 *Chair,* Bryan Gray, MBE
YORKSHIRE: Victoria House, 2 Victoria Place, Leeds LS11 5AE T 0113-394 9600 *Chair,* Terry Hodgkinson
NORTH EAST: Stella House, Goldcrest Way, Newburn Riverside, Newcastle upon Tyne NE15 8NY T 0191-229 6200 *Chair,* Margaret Fay
WEST MIDLANDS: 3 Priestley Wharf, Holt Street, Aston Science Park, Birmingham B7 4BN T 0121-380 3500 *Chair,* Sir Roy McNulty
EAST MIDLANDS: Apex Court, City Link, Nottingham NG2 4LA T 0115-988 8300 *Chair,* Dr Bryan Jackson
EAST OF ENGLAND: The Business Centre, Station Road, Histon, Cambridge CB4 9LQ T 01223-713900 *Chair,* Richard Ellis
SOUTH WEST: Sterling House, Dix's Field, Exeter EX1 1QA T 01392-214747 *Chair,* Sir Harry Studholme
LONDON: Palestra, 197 Blackfriars Road, London SE1 8AA T 020-7593 8700 *Chair,* Harvey McGrath
SOUTH EAST: Cross Lanes, Guildford GU1 1YA T 01483-484200 *Chair,* Jim Brathwaite

REGISTRAR OF PUBLIC LENDING RIGHT

Richard House, Sorbonne Close, Stockton on Tees TS17 6DA
T 01642-604699 E authorservices@plr.uk.com
W www.plr.uk.com

Under the Public Lending Right system, in operation since 1983, payment is made from public funds to authors whose books are lent out from public libraries. Payment is made once a year and the amount each author receives is proportionate to the number of times (established from a sample) that each registered book has been lent out during the previous year. The registrar of PLR, who is appointed by the Secretary of State for Culture, Media and Sport, compiles the register of authors and books. Authors resident in all European Economic Area countries are eligible to apply. (The term 'author' covers writers, illustrators, translators, and some editors/compilers.)

A payment of 5.98 pence was made in 2008–9 for each estimated loan of a registered book, up to a top limit of £6,600 for the books of any one registered author; the money for loans above this level is used to augment the remaining PLR payments. In 2009 the sum of £6.63m was paid out to 23,773 registered authors and assignees as the annual payment of PLR.

Registrar, Dr J. G. Parker

REVIEW BODY ON DOCTORS' AND DENTISTS' REMUNERATION

6th Floor, Kingsgate House, 66–74 Victoria Street, London SW1E 6SW
T 020-7215 8407 W www.ome.uk.com

The Review Body on Doctors' and Dentists' Remuneration was set up in 1971. It advises the prime minister, first ministers in Scotland, Wales and Northern Ireland, and the Ministers for Health, in England, Scotland, Wales and Northern Ireland on the remuneration of doctors and dentists taking any part in the National Health Service.

Chair, Ron Amy, OBE
Members, Katrina Easterling; David Grafton; Sally Smedley; Prof. Alasdair Smith; Prof. Steve Thompson; David Williamson

ROYAL AIR FORCE MUSEUM

Grahame Park Way, London NW9 5LL
T 020-8205 2266 E london@rafmuseum.org
W www.rafmuseum.org

The museum has two sites, one at the former airfield at Hendon and the second at Cosford, in the West Midlands, both of which illustrate the development of aviation from before the Wright brothers to the present-day RAF with over 100 aircraft, as well as artefacts, aviation memorabilia, fine art and photographs. Total government grant-in-aid for 2007–8, provided by the Ministry of Defence, was £7.02m.

Director-General, Dr M. A. Fopp

ROYAL BOTANIC GARDEN EDINBURGH

20A Inverleith Row, Edinburgh EH3 5LR
T 0131-552 7171 W www.rbge.org.uk

The Royal Botanic Garden Edinburgh (RBGE) originated as the Physic Garden, established in 1670 beside the Palace of Holyroodhouse. The garden moved to its present 28-hectare site at Inverleith, Edinburgh, in 1821. There are also three regional gardens: Benmore Botanic Garden, near Dunoon, Argyll; Logan Botanic Garden, near Stranraer, Wigtownshire; and Dawyck Botanic Garden, near Stobo, Peeblesshire. Since 1986 RBGE has been administered by a board of trustees established under the National Heritage (Scotland) Act 1985. It receives an annual grant from the Scottish government's Rural and Environmental Research and Analysis Directorate.

The RBGE is an international centre for scientific research on plant diversity and for horticulture education and conservation. It has an extensive library, a herbarium with almost three million preserved plant specimens, and over 15,000 species in the living collections.

Chair of the Board of Trustees, Sir George Mathewson, CBE, LLD, FRSE
Regius Keeper, Prof. Stephen Blackmore, FRSE

ROYAL BOTANIC GARDENS (RBG) KEW

Richmond, Surrey TW9 3AB
T 020-8332 5655
Wakehurst Place, Ardingly, W. Sussex RH17 6TN
T 01444-89000
E info@kew.org W www.kew.org

The Royal Botanic Gardens (RBG) Kew were originally laid out as a private garden for Kew House for George III's mother, Princess Augusta, in 1759. The gardens were much enlarged in the 19th century, notably by the inclusion of the grounds of the former Richmond Lodge. In 1965 the garden at Wakehurst Place was acquired; it is owned by the National Trust and managed by RBG Kew. Under the National Heritage Act 1983 a board of trustees was set up to administer the gardens, which in 1984 became an independent body supported by grant-in-aid from the Department of Environment, Food and Rural Affairs.

The functions of RBG Kew are to carry out research into plant sciences, to disseminate knowledge about plants and to provide the public with the opportunity to gain knowledge and enjoyment from the gardens' collections. There are extensive national reference collections of living and preserved plants and a comprehensive library and archive. The main emphasis is on plant conservation and biodiversity; Wakehurst Place houses the Millennium Seed Bank, which is the largest *ex situ* conservation project ever conceived – its aim is to acquire seed from 25 per cent of Earth's wild plant species by 2020.

BOARD OF TRUSTEES
Chair, Lord Selborne
Members, Marcus Agius; Tanya Burman; Andrew Cahn; Richard Deverell; Prof. Jonathan Drori, CBE; Prof. Charles Godfray; Dr Sandy Harrison; Richard Lapthorne, CBE; Prof. Sir William Stewart
Director, Prof. Stephen Hopper

ROYAL COMMISSION ON ENVIRONMENTAL POLLUTION

Room 108, 55 Whitehall, c/o 3–8 Whitehall Place, London SW1A 2HH
T 020-7270 8159 E enquiries@rcep.org.uk
W www.rcep.org.uk

The commission was set up in 1970 to advise on national and international matters concerning the pollution of the environment. The commission's advice is mainly in the form of reports which are the outcome of studies, the most recent of which relates to the urban environment. Members are appointed by the Queen on the advice of the prime minister.

Chair, Prof. Sir John Lawton, CBE, FRS

Members, Prof. Nicholas Cumpsty; Prof. Michael H. Depledge; Dr I. Graham-Bryce, CBE, FRSE; Prof. J. Jowell, QC; Prof. Maria Lee; Prof. Peter Liss; Prof. Gordon Mackerron; Prof. Peter Matthews; Prof. Judith Petts; Prof. S. Rayner; Prof. Michael Roberts; Prof. Joanne Scott; Prof. Lynda Warren

ROYAL COMMISSION ON THE ANCIENT AND HISTORICAL MONUMENTS OF SCOTLAND

John Sinclair House, 16 Bernard Terrace, Edinburgh EH8 9NX
T 0131-662 1456 E info@rcahms.gov.uk
W www.rcahms.gov.uk

The Royal Commission on the Ancient and Historical Monuments of Scotland (RCAHMS) was established by a royal warrant in 1908, which was revised in 1992, and is appointed to provide for the collecting, recording and interpretation of information on the architectural, industrial, archaeological and maritime heritage of Scotland, to give a picture of the human influence on Scotland's places from the earliest times to the present day. It is funded by the Scottish government. More than 14.5 million items, including photographs, maps, drawings and documents, are available through the search room, and online databases provide access to over 100,000 images and information on 280,000 buildings and sites. RCAHMS also looks after Scotland's national collection of historical aerial photography as well as the Aerial Reconnaissance archive of international wartime photography .

Chair, Prof. John Hume, OBE, FSA SCOT
Commissioners, Kate Byrne; Mark Hopton, FSA SCOT; Prof. John Hunter, FSA, FSA SCOT; Prof. Angus Macdonald, FSA SCOT; Gordon Masterton; Prof. Christopher Morris, FSA, FRSE, FRSA; Dr Jane Murray, FSA SCOT; Dr Stana Nenadic, FSA SCOT; Elspeth Reid
Chief Executive, Diana Murray, FSA, FSA SCOT

ROYAL COMMISSION ON THE ANCIENT AND HISTORICAL MONUMENTS OF WALES

Crown Building, Plas Crug, Aberystwyth SY23 1NJ
T 01970-621200 E nmr.wales@rcahmw.gov.uk
W www.rcahmw.gov.uk

The Royal Commission was established in 1908 and is currently empowered by a royal warrant of 2001 to survey, record, publish and maintain a database of ancient, historical and maritime sites and structures, and landscapes, in Wales. The commission is funded by the National Assembly for Wales and is also responsible for the National Monuments Record of Wales, which is open daily for public reference and has a public enquiry service. The commission is responsible for supplying archaeological information to Ordnance Survey, for the coordination of archaeological aerial photography in Wales, and for sponsorship of the regional Sites and Monuments Records.

Chair, Dr Eurwyn William, FSA
Vice-Chair, Dr Llinos Smith, FRHISTS
Commissioners, Prof. Antony D. Carr, FSA, FRHISTS; Mrs A. Eastham; Neil Harries; John W. Lloyd, CB; Jonathan Matthews Hudson; John Newman, FSA; Henry Owen-John; Mark Redknap; Prof. C. M. Williams, FRHISTS

ROYAL MAIL GROUP

100 Victoria Embankment, London EC4Y 0HQ
T 020-7250 2888 W www.royalmailgroup.com

Crown services for the carriage of government dispatches were set up in about 1516. The conveyance of public correspondence began in 1635 and the mail service was made a parliamentary responsibility with the setting up of a Post Office in 1657. Telegraphs came under Post Office control in 1870 and the Post Office Telephone Service began in 1880. The National Girobank service of the Post Office began in 1968. The Post Office ceased to be a government department in 1969 when responsibility for the running of the postal, telecommunications, giro and remittance services was transferred to a public authority of the same name.

The British Telecommunications Act 1981 separated the functions of the Post Office, making it solely responsible for postal services and Girobank. Girobank was privatised in 1990. The Postal Services Act 2000 turned the Post Office into a wholly owned public limited company establishing a regulatory regime under the Postal Service Commission. The Post Office Group changed its name to Consignia plc in March 2001 when its new corporate structure took effect; in November 2002 the name was changed to Royal Mail Group plc. As of 1 January 2006 the UK postal service market was fully liberalised, and any licensed operator is now able to deliver mail to businesses and residential customers.

Royal Mail processes and delivers over 75 million letters, packets and parcels to 28 million addresses every day; 24 million customers are served in the 11,500 Post Office branches. The Royal Mail Group directly employs around 176,000 people in the UK.

The chair, chief executive and members of the board are appointed by the Secretary of State for Business, Innovation and Skills but responsibility for the running of Royal Mail Group as a whole rests with the board in its corporate capacity.

BOARD
Chair, Donald Brydon, CBE
Chief Executive (Royal Mail Group), Adam Crozier
Managing Director, Alan Cook, CBE *(Post Office Ltd)*
Members, Ian Duncan *(Group Finance Director)*; Mark Higson *(Managing Director, Royal Mail Letters)*
Non-Executive Directors, Andrew Carr-Locke; Lord Currie; Richard Handover, CBE; Baroness Prosser, OBE
Company Secretary, Jonathan Evans, OBE

ROYAL NAVAL MUSEUM

HM Naval Base (PP66), Portsmouth PO1 3NH
T 023-9272 7562 E info@royalnavalmuseum.org
W www.royalnavalmuseum.org

The Royal Naval Museum is a non-departmental public body sponsored by the Ministry of Defence, and is a registered charity governed by a board of trustees. It is located in Portsmouth Historic Dockyard alongside Nelson's flagship, HMS *Victory*, and is housed in three buildings offering exhibitions on the Navy from the 18th century onwards. The museum aims to provide an effective and accessible repository for the heritage of the Navy, and to raise public awareness, and encourage scholarship and research into, the history and achievements of the Royal Navy.

Chair, Adm. Sir Peter Abbott, GBE, KCB

SCHOOL TEACHERS' REVIEW BODY

6th Floor, Kingsgate House, 66–74 Victoria Street, London SW1E 6SW
T 020-7215 8314 W www.ome.uk.com

The School Teachers' Review Body was set up under the School Teachers' Pay and Conditions Act 1991. It is required to examine and report on such matters relating to the statutory conditions of employment of school teachers in England and Wales as may be referred to it by the education secretary.

Chair, Dr Anne Wright
Members, Jennifer Board; Monojit Chatterji; Peter Dolton; Dewi Jones; Elizabeth Kidd; Esmond Lindop; Stella Pantelides; Bruce Warman; Anne Watts, CBE

SCIENCE MUSEUM

Exhibition Road, London SW7 2DD
T 0870-870 4868 E sciencem@sciencemuseum.org.uk
W www.sciencemuseum.org.uk

The Science Museum, part of the National Museum of Science & Industry (NMSI), houses the national collections of science, technology, industry and medicine. The museum began as the science collection of the South Kensington Museum and first opened in 1857. In 1883 it acquired the collections of the Patent Museum and in 1909 the science collections were transferred to the new Science Museum, leaving the art collections with the Victoria and Albert Museum. The Wellcome Wing was opened in July 2000.

Some of the museum's larger objects, ranging across aircraft, agricultural machinery, computing, mechanical engineering, and road and rail transport collections, are at Science Museum Swindon, Wilts. The NMSI also incorporates the National Railway Museum, York, the National Media Museum, Bradford, and Locomotion: the National Railway Museum at Shildon.

Total government grant-in-aid for 2008–9 is £39.0m.

Chair, Rt. Hon. Lord Waldegrave of North Hill
Trustees, Lady Chisholm; Sir Ron U. Cooke; Howard Covington; Prof. Dame Anne Dowling, FRENG; Lord Faulkner of Worcester; Dr Douglas Gurr; Lord Rees of Ludlow, FRS; Prof. Averil Macdonald; Sir Howard Newby, CBE; Dr Gill Samuels, CBE; Prof. Simon J. Schaffer; Dr Maggie Semple, OBE; Dr Tony Sewell; Martin G. Smith; Prof. Roderick A. Smith, FRENG; Janet Street-Porter; Christopher Swinson, OBE; Sir William Wells; Michael G. Wilson, OBE
Director of NMSI, Molly Jackson
Director of Science Museum, Prof. Chris Rapley, CBE
Director of National Media Museum, Colin Philpott
Director of National Railway Museum, Andrew Scott, CBE

SCOTTISH ARTS COUNCIL

12 Manor Place, Edinburgh EH3 7DD
T 0131-226 6051 E help.desk@scottisharts.org.uk
W www.scottisharts.org.uk

The Scottish Arts Council is the main arts development agency in Scotland. It is a non-departmental public body, accountable to the Scottish government. The Scottish Arts Council invests funds from the Scottish government and National Lottery and works with partners to support and develop artistic excellence and creativity throughout Scotland. The Scottish government have proposed the creation of a new body, Creative Scotland, that will inherit the existing functions and resources of the Scottish Arts Council and Scottish Screen. It is anticipated that legislation to establish the new statutory organisation will be passed in 2010.

Chair, Richard Holloway
Members, Dinah Caine; Donald Emslie; Steven Grimmond; Charles Lovatt; Ray Macfarlane *(Deputy Chair)*; Barbara McKissack; Jim McSharry; John Mulgrew; Rab Noakes; Ben Twist
Chief Executive, Jim Tough

SCOTTISH CRIMINAL CASES REVIEW COMMISSION

5th Floor, Portland House, 17 Renfield Street, Glasgow G2 5AH
T 0141-270 7030 E info@sccrc.org.uk
W www.sccrc.org.uk

The commission is a non-departmental public body, funded by the Scottish Government Criminal Justice Directorate, and established in April 1999. It assumed the role previously performed by the Secretary of State for Scotland to consider alleged miscarriages of justice in Scotland and refer cases meeting the relevant criteria to the high court for determination. Members are appointed by the Queen on the recommendation of the First Minister; senior executive staff are appointed by the commission.

Chair, Jean Couper, CBE
Members, Gerrard Bann; David Belfall; Graham Bell, QC; Prof. Brian Caddy; Stewart Campbell; Prof. George Irving, CBE; Gerard McClay; Christopher Shead
Chief Executive, Gerard Sinclair

SCOTTISH ENTERPRISE

Atrium Court, 50 Waterloo Street, Glasgow G2 6HQ
T 0141-248 2700 E enquiries@scotent.co.uk
W www.scottish-enterprise.com

Scottish Enterprise was established in 1991 and its purpose is to stimulate the sustainable growth of Scotland's economy. It is funded by the Scottish government and is responsible to the Scottish ministers. Working in partnership with the private and public sectors, Scottish Enterprise aims to further the development of Scotland's economy by helping ambitious and innovative businesses grow and become more successful. Scottish Enterprise is particularly interested in industries with competitive advantage in Scotland, including energy; life sciences; tourism; financial services; food and drink; and digital markets and enabling technologies.

Chair, Crawford Gillies
Chief Executive, Jack Perry

SCOTTISH ENVIRONMENT PROTECTION AGENCY (SEPA)

Erskine Court, Castle Business Park, Stirling FK9 4TR
T 01786-457700 Hotline 0800-807060
E info@sepa.org.uk W www.sepa.org.uk

SEPA was established in 1996 and is the public body responsible for environmental protection in Scotland. It regulates potential pollution to land, air and water; the storage, transport and disposal of controlled waste; and the safekeeping and disposal of radioactive materials. It does this within a complex legislative framework of acts of parliament, EC directives and regulations, granting licences to operations of industrial processes

and waste disposal. SEPA also operates Floodline (T 0845-988 1188), a public service providing information on the possible risk of flooding 24 hours a day, 365 days a year.
Chair, David Sigsworth
Chief Executive, Campbell Gemmell
Directors, Colin Bayes *(Environmental Regulation and Improvement)*; Calum MacDonald *(Environmental and Organisational Development)*; James Curran *(Environmental Science)*

SCOTTISH LAW COMMISSION

140 Causewayside, Edinburgh EH9 1PR
T 0131-668 2131 E info@scotlawcom.gov.uk
W www.scotlawcom.gov.uk

The Scottish Law Commission, established in 1965, keeps the law in Scotland under review and makes proposals for its development and reform. It is responsible to the Scottish ministers through the Scottish Government Justice Department.
Chair (part-time), Hon. Lord Drummond Young
Chief Executive, M. McMillan
Commissioners, Prof. G. L. Gretton; P. Layden, QC, TDC; J. Tyre, QC

SCOTTISH LEGAL AID BOARD

44 Drumsheugh Gardens, Edinburgh EH3 7SW
T 0131-226 7061 Helpline 0845-122 8686
E general@slab.org.uk W www.slab.org.uk

The Scottish Legal Aid Board was set up under the Legal Aid (Scotland) Act 1986 to manage legal aid in Scotland. It reports to the Scottish government. Board members are appointed by Scottish ministers.
Chair, Iain A. Robertson, CBE
Members, Graham Bell, QC; Les Campbell; Joseph Hughes; Denise Loney; Paul McBride, QC; Susan McPhee; Ellen Morton; David Nicol; Elaine Rosie; Sheriff Kenneth Ross; Graham Watson
Chief Executive, Lindsay Montgomery

SCOTTISH NATURAL HERITAGE (SNH)

Great Glen House, Leachkin Road, Inverness IV3 8NW
T 01463-725000 E enquiries@snh.gov.uk
W www.snh.org.uk

SNH was established in 1992 under the Natural Heritage (Scotland) Act 1991. It provides advice on nature conservation to all those whose activities affect wildlife, landforms and features of geological interest in Scotland, and seeks to develop and improve facilities for the enjoyment and understanding of the Scottish countryside. It is funded by the Scottish government.
Chair, Andrew Thin
Chief Executive, I. Jardine
Chief Scientific Adviser, C. Galbraith
Directors of Operations, J. Thomson *(Strategy and Communications)*; S. Davies *(North)*; R. Fairley *(South)*
Director of Corporate Services, J. Moore

SCOTTISH PRISONS COMPLAINTS COMMISSION

Government Buildings, Broomhouse Drive, Edinburgh EH11 3XD
T 0131-244 8423 E spcc@scotland.gsi.gov.uk

The commission was established in 1994. It is an independent body to which prisoners in Scottish prisons can make applications in relation to any matter where they have failed to obtain satisfaction from the Scottish Prison Service's internal grievance procedures. Clinical judgements made by medical officers, matters which are the subject of legal proceedings and matters relating to sentence, conviction, parole, and life licence decision-making are excluded from the commission's jurisdiction. The commissioner is appointed by the Scottish ministers.
Commissioner (interim), Carolyn Girvan

SEAFISH INDUSTRY AUTHORITY

18 Logie Mill, Logie Green Road, Edinburgh EH7 4HS
T 0131-558 3331 E seafish@seafish.co.uk
W www.seafish.org

Established under the Fisheries Act 1981, the authority on seafood works with all sectors of the UK seafood industry to satisfy consumers, raise standards, improve efficiency and secure a sustainable and profitable future. Services range from research and development, economic consulting, market research and training and accreditation through to account management and legislative advice for the seafood industry. It is sponsored by the four UK fisheries departments, which appoint the board, and is funded by a levy on seafood.
Chair, Charles Howeson
Chief Executive, John Rutherford

SENIOR SALARIES REVIEW BODY

6th Floor, Kingsgate House, 66–74 Victoria Street, London SW1E 6SW
T 020-7215 8276 W www.ome.uk.com

The Senior Salaries Review Body (formerly the Top Salaries Review Body) was set up in 1971 to advise the prime minister on the remuneration of the judiciary, senior civil servants and senior officers of the armed forces. In 1993 its remit was extended to cover the pay, pensions and allowances of MPs, ministers and others whose pay is determined by the Ministerial and Other Salaries Act 1975, and also the allowances of peers. If asked, it advises on the pay of officers and members of the devolved parliament and assemblies.
Chair, Bill Cockburn, CBE, TD
Members, Richard Disney; Martin Fish; Prof. David Greenaway; Michael Langley; David Metcalf; Sir Peter North, CBE, QC; Christopher Stephens; Bruce Warman; Paul Williams

SERIOUS ORGANISED CRIME AGENCY (SOCA)

PO Box 8000, London SE11 5EN
T 0370-496 7622 W www.soca.gov.uk

SOCA was established in April 2006. It took over the functions of the National Criminal Intelligence Service and the National Crime Squad, as well as the role of HM Revenue and Customs in investigating drug trafficking and related criminal finance, and some of the functions of the UK Immigration Service in dealing with organised immigration crime. Its remit is to prevent and detect serious organised crime and to gather, store, analyse and disseminate information on crime. SOCA is also tasked with providing support to law enforcement partners. The Assets Recovery Agency merged with SOCA on 1 April 2008.

The Secretary of State for Home Affairs appoints the chair and director-general, may set SOCA strategies and will judge the success of its efforts. Grant-in-aid is provided by the Home Office and for 2008–9 was set provisionally at £442m in resource funding.
Chair, Sir Stephen Lander
Director-General, Bill Hughes
Directors, David Bolt *(Intelligence)*; Malcolm Cornberg *(Corporate Services)*; Paul Evans *(Intervention)*; Trevor Pearce *(Enforcement)*
Non-Executive Directors, Peter Clarke; Elizabeth France; Susan Garrard; Janet Paraskeva; Francis Plowden

STUDENT LOANS COMPANY LTD

100 Bothwell Street, Glasgow G2 7JD
T 0141-306 2000 W www.slc.co.uk

The Student Loans Company is wholly owned by the government. It processes and administers financial assistance for undergraduates who have secured a place at university or college, under the Student Loans Scheme (established in 1990) and the Income Contingent Loans Scheme (established in 1998). From 2008–9 support payments to students totalled £6.2bn, of which £2.9bn was in maintenance loans and £1bn was in maintenance grants. As at the end of the year the company had over 3.6 million borrowers.
Chair, John Goodfellow
Chief Executive, Ralph Seymour-Jackson

TATE BRITAIN

Millbank, London SW1P 4RG
T 020-7887 8888 E visiting.britain@tate.org.uk
W www.tate.org.uk/britain

Tate Britain displays the national collection of British art from 1500 to the present day – with special attention and dedicated space given to Blake, Turner and Constable. The gallery opened in 1897, the cost of building (£80,000) being defrayed by Sir Henry Tate, who also contributed the nucleus of the present collection. The Turner wing was opened in 1910, and further galleries and a new sculpture hall followed in 1937. In 1979 a further extension was built, and the Clore Gallery was opened in 1987. The Centenary Development was opened in 2001.

There are four Tate galleries: Tate Britain and Tate Modern in London, Tate Liverpool and Tate St Ives; the entire Tate collection is available to view online.

BOARD OF TRUSTEES
Chair, Lord Browne of Madingley
Trustees, Helen Alexander; Tom Bloxham; Sir Howard Davies; Jeremy Deller; David Ekserdjian; Anish Kapoor; Patricia Lankester; Elisabeth Murdoch; Franck Petitgas; Monisha Shah

OFFICERS
Director, Sir Nicholas Serota
Director, Tate Britain, Dr Stephen Deuchar
Director, Tate Liverpool, Dr Christoph Grunenberg
Director, Tate Modern, Vicente Todoli
Artistic Director, Tate St Ives, Martin Clark
Executive Director, Tate St Ives, Mark Osterfield

TATE MODERN

Bankside, London SE1 9TG
T 020-7887 8888 E visiting.modern@tate.org.uk
W www.tate.org.uk/modern

Opened in May 2000, Tate Modern displays the Tate collection of international modern art dating from 1900 to the present day. It includes works by Dalí, Picasso, Matisse and Warhol as well as many contemporary works. It is housed in the former Bankside Power Station in London, which was redesigned by the Swiss architects Herzog and de Meuron.
Director, Vicente Todoli

TENANT SERVICES AUTHORITY

Maple House, 149 Tottenham Court Road, London W1T 7BN
T 0845-230 7000 E enquiries@tsa.gsx.gov.uk
W www.tenantservicesauthority.org

The Tenant Services Authority (TSA) was established on 1 December 2008 as the regulator for affordable housing. It took over the regulatory powers of the Housing Corporation. The TSA's main aim is to raise the standards of services for tenants. Subject to parliamentary approval, from spring 2010 the TSA will become responsible for all affordable housing in England, whether it is provided by local authorities, housing associations or arm's-length management organisations.
Chair, Anthony Mayer
Chief Executive, Peter Marsh

TOURISM BODIES

Visit Britain, Visit Scotland, Visit Wales and the Northern Ireland Tourist Board are responsible for developing and marketing the tourist industry in their respective regions. Visit Wales is not listed here as it is part of the Welsh Assembly government, within the Department for Heritage, and not a public body.

VISIT BRITAIN
1 Palace Street, Victoria SW1E 5HE T 020-8846 9000
E thames.tower@visitbritain.com W www.visitbritain.com
Chair, Christopher Rodrigues, CBE
Chief Executive, Sandie Dawe, MBE

VISIT SCOTLAND
94 Ocean Drive, Leith, Edinburgh EH6 6JH T 0131-472 2222
E info@visitscotland.com W www.visitscotland.com
Chair, Peter Lederer, CBE
Chief Executive, Philip Riddle, OBE

NORTHERN IRELAND TOURIST BOARD
St Anne's Court, 59 North Street, Belfast BT1 1NB
T 028-9023 1221
E info@nitb.com W www.discovernorthernireland.com
Chair, Howard Hastings
Chief Executive, Alan Clarke

TRAINING AND DEVELOPMENT AGENCY

151 Buckingham Palace Road, London SW1W 9SZ
T 020-7023 8000 E corporatecomms@tda.gov.uk
W www.tda.gov.uk, www.teach.gov.uk

The Training and Development Agency (TDA) was launched in September 2005 and took on the role, and expanded the remit of, the Teacher Training Agency. The

TDA aims to attract able and committed people to teaching, concentrating specifically on subjects where teachers are in short supply; provide schools and their staff with good information on training and development opportunities; and ensure that new teachers enter schools with appropriate skills and knowledge, through working closely with providers of initial teacher training.
Chief Executive, Graham Holley

TRANSPORT FOR LONDON (TFL)

Windsor House, 42–50 Victoria Street, London SW1H 0TL
T 020-7222 5600
E enquire@tfl.gov.uk W www.tfl.gov.uk

TfL was formed in July 2000 as a functional body of the Greater London Authority and is responsible for the capital's transport system. Its role is to implement the Mayor of London's transport strategy and manage the transport services across London for which the mayor has responsibility.

As a result, TfL is responsible for London's buses, London Underground, London Overground, the Docklands Light Railway (DLR) and the management of Croydon Tramlink, London River Services and Victoria Coach Station. It also runs the London Transport Museum; manages the Congestion Charging scheme and Low Emission Zone; regulates the city's taxis and private hire trade; maintains 580km of main roads and all of London's traffic lights; coordinates schemes for people with impaired mobility; runs Dial-a-Ride and the London boroughs taxi card scheme; and promotes walking and cycling initiatives.
Chair, Boris Johnson
Commissioner, Peter Hendy

UK ATOMIC ENERGY AUTHORITY

The Manor Court, Chilton, Oxon OX11 0RN
T 01235-431810
W www.ukaea.org.uk

The UK Atomic Energy Authority (UKAEA) was established by the Atomic Energy Authority Act 1954 and took over responsibility for the research and development of the civil nuclear power programme. The UKAEA is responsible for leading the development of the Harwell Science and Innovation Campus, and for corporate governance and the provision of relevant services. The UKAEA also undertakes the UK's contribution to the international fusion programme and manages the world's leading fusion research project. UKAEA is part of the UKAEA group, which includes a commercial arm responsible for the safe management of nuclear sites on behalf of the Nuclear Decommissioning Authority, and site licence companies that undertake the decommissioning of nuclear sites.
Chair, Lady Barbara Judge
Chief Executive, Norman Harrison

UK FILM COUNCIL

10 Little Portland Street, London W1W 7JG
T 020-7861 7861
E info@ukfilmcouncil.org.uk W www.ukfilmcouncil.org.uk

The council was created in April 2000 by the Department for Culture, Media and Sport. The council's board is comprised of 15 directors and has been established as a private company limited by guarantee, with an intention to move it to a statutory basis at a later stage. It invests grant-in-aid and National Lottery funds in film development and production, training, international development and export promotion, distribution and exhibition, and education.

The Office of the British Film Commissioner (formerly UK Film Council International) is part of the same organisation, and was originally established in 1991. Its remit is to attract inward investment by promoting the UK as an international production centre to the film and television industries and encouraging the use of British locations, services, facilities and personnel.
Chair, Tim Bevan, CBE
Chief Executive, John Woodward
British Film Commissioner, Colin Brown

UNITED KINGDOM SPORTS COUNCIL (UK SPORT)

40 Bernard Street, London WC1N 1ST
T 020-7211 5100
E info@uksport.gov.uk W www.uksport.gov.uk

UK Sport was established by royal charter in 1996 and is accountable to parliament through the Department for Culture, Media and Sport. Its role is to lead the UK to sporting excellence by supporting winning athletes, world-class events, world-class standards and ethically fair and drug-free sport. UK Sport is responsible for managing and distributing public investment and is a statutory distributor of funds raised by the National Lottery. Government grant-in-aid for 2008–9 was £72.2m and national lottery funding was £49.8m.
Chair, Baroness Sue Campbell, CBE
Chief Executive, John Steele

VICTORIA AND ALBERT MUSEUM

Cromwell Road, London SW7 2RL
T 020-7942 2000 W www.vam.ac.uk

The Victoria and Albert Museum (V&A) is the national museum of fine and applied art and design. It descends directly from the Museum of Manufactures, which opened in Marlborough House in 1852 after the Great Exhibition of 1851. The museum was moved in 1857 to become part of the South Kensington Museum. It was renamed the Victoria and Albert Museum in 1899. It also houses the National Art Library and Print Room.

The museum administers the V&A Museum of Childhood at Bethnal Green, which was opened in 1872; the building is the most important surviving example of the type of glass and iron construction used by Paxton for the Great Exhibition. Total government grant-in-aid for 2009–10 is £44.76m.
Chair, Paul Ruddock
Trustees, D. Adjaye, OBE; E. Davies, OBE; T. Dixon, OBE; Prof. Sir C. Frayling; Ms B. Jackson, CBE; Prof. L. Jardine, CBE; S. McGuckin; Ms E. O' Connor; Ms M. Ogundehin; Rt. Hon. Sir T. Sainsbury; Dame M. Scardino, DBE; S. Shah, OBE; R. Stefanowski; Dr P. Thompson
Director of the V&A, M. Jones

WALLACE COLLECTION

Hertford House, Manchester Square, London W1U 3BN
T 020-7563 9500 E enquiries@wallacecollection.org
W www.wallacecollection.org

The Wallace Collection was bequeathed to the nation by the widow of Sir Richard Wallace, in 1897, and Hertford House was subsequently acquired by the government. The collection contains works by Titian and Rembrandt, and includes porcelain, furniture and an array of arms and armour. Total government grant-in-aid for 2008–9 was estimated at £4.23m.

Director, Rosalind Savill

WOMEN'S NATIONAL COMMISSION

Eland House, Bressenden Place, London SW1E 5DU
T 020-7944 0585 E wnc@communities.gsi.gov.uk
W www.thewnc.org.uk

The Women's National Commission was established in 1969 as an independent advisory committee to the government. It is an umbrella organisation representing women and women's organisations in the UK. Its remit is to ensure that the informed opinions of women are given their due weight in the deliberations of the government and in public debate on matters of public interest, including those of special interest to women. The commission is an advisory NDPB sponsored by the Government Equalities Office.

Chair, Baroness Gould of Potternewton
Director, Barbara-Ann Collins
Deputy Director (Corporate), Daniel Barrow
Deputy Director (Policy), Susan Green

REGIONAL GOVERNMENT

LONDON

GREATER LONDON AUTHORITY (GLA)

City Hall, The Queen's Walk, London SE1 2AA
T 020-7983 4100 E mayor@london.gov.uk
W www.london.gov.uk

On 7 May 1998 London voted in favour of the formation of the Greater London Authority (GLA). The first elections to the GLA took place on 4 May 2000 and the new authority took over its responsibilities on 3 July 2000. In July 2002 the GLA moved to one of London's most spectacular buildings, newly built on a brownfield site on the south bank of the Thames, adjacent to Tower Bridge. The third and most recent election to the GLA took place on 1 May 2008.

The structure and objectives of the GLA stem from its eight main areas of responsibility. These are transport, policing, fire and emergency planning, economic development, planning, culture and health. There are four functional bodies that coordinate these functions and report to the GLA: the London Development Agency (LDA), the London Fire and Emergency Planning Authority (LFEPA), the Metropolitan Police Authority (MPA) and Transport for London (TfL). The GLA also absorbed a number of other London bodies, such as the London Ecology Unit and the London Research Centre.

The GLA consists of a directly elected mayor, the Mayor of London, and a separately elected assembly, the London Assembly. The mayor has the key role of decision making, with the assembly performing the tasks of regulating and scrutinising these decisions, and investigating issues of importance to Londoners. In addition, the GLA has around 600 permanent staff to support the activities of the mayor and the assembly, which are overseen by a head of paid service. The mayor may appoint two political advisers and not more than ten other members of staff, though he does not necessarily exercise this power, but he may not appoint the chief executive, the monitoring officer or the chief finance officer. These must be appointed jointly by the assembly and the mayor.

Every aspect of the assembly and its activities must be open to public scrutiny and therefore accountable. The assembly holds the mayor to account through scrutiny of his strategies, decisions and actions. This is carried out by direct questioning at assembly meetings and by conducting detailed investigations in committee.

People's Question Time gives Londoners the chance to question the mayor and the London Assembly about plans, priorities and policies for London. The statutory event is held twice a year in different parts of London.

The role of the mayor can be broken down into a number of key areas:

- to represent and promote London at home and abroad and speak up for Londoners
- to devise strategies and plans to tackle London-wide issues, such as crime, transport, housing and planning, environment, accountability, business and skills, public services, society and culture, local government and the Olympic and Paralympic Games, sport and health; and to set budgets for TfL, the LDA, the MPA and the LFEPA.
- The mayor is chair of TfL and MPA and has the power to appoint members to their boards and those of the LDA; he also makes appointments to the police and fire authorities.
- With London's successful bid to host the 2012 Olympic and Paralympic Games, the previous mayor was the signatory to the contract with the International Olympic Committee undertaking that the games would be delivered.

The role of the assembly can be broken down into a number of key areas:

- to check on and balance the mayor
- to scrutinise the mayor
- to have the power to amend the mayor's budget by a majority of two-thirds
- to have the power to summon the mayor, senior staff of the Authority and functional bodies
- to investigate issues of London-wide significance and make proposals to appropriate stakeholders
- to provide the deputy mayor and the members serving on the police, fire and emergency planning authorities with advice

Mayor, Boris Johnson
Deputy Mayors, Richard Barnes (Statutory Deputy Mayor); Kit Malthouse (Policing); Sir Simon Milton (Policy and Planning)
Chair of the London Assembly, Darren Johnson
Deputy Chair of the Assembly, Jennette Arnold

ELECTIONS AND THE VOTING SYSTEMS

The assembly is elected every four years at the same time as the mayor, and consists of 25 members. There is one member from each of the 14 GLA constituencies topped up with 11 London members who are representatives of political parties or individuals standing as independent candidates. The last election was on 1 May 2008.

Two distinct voting systems are used to appoint the existing mayor and the assembly. The mayor is elected using the supplementary vote system (SVS). With SVS, electors have two votes: one to give a first choice for mayor and one to give a second choice. Electors can only have one effective vote and so cannot vote twice for the same candidate. If one candidate gets more than half of all the first-choice votes, he or she becomes mayor. If no candidate gets more than half of the first-choice votes, the two candidates with the most first-choice votes remain in the election and all the other candidates drop out. The second-choice votes on the ballot papers of the candidates who drop out are then counted. Where these second-choice votes are for the two remaining candidates they are added to the first-choice votes these candidates already have. The candidate with the most first- and second-choice votes combined becomes the Mayor of London.

The assembly is appointed using the additional member system (AMS). Under AMS, electors have two votes. The first vote is for a constituency candidate. The second vote is for a party list or individual candidate contesting the London-wide assembly seats. The 14 constituency members are elected under the first-past-the-post system, the same system used in general and local elections. Electors vote for one candidate and the candidate with the most votes wins. The additional (London) members are drawn from party lists or are independent candidates who stand as London members; they are chosen using a form of proportional representation.

The Greater London Returning Officer (GLRO) is the independent official responsible for running the election in London. He is supported in this by returning officers in each of the 14 London constituencies.

GLRO, Leo Boland

TRANSPORT FOR LONDON (TFL)

TfL is the integrated body responsible for London's transport system. Its role is to implement the mayor's transport strategy for London and manage transport services across the capital for which the mayor has responsibility. TfL is directed by a management board whose members are chosen for their understanding of transport matters and are appointed by the mayor, who chairs the board. TfL's role is:

- to manage the London Underground, buses, Croydon Tramlink and the Docklands Light Railway (DLR)
- to manage a network of main roads and all of London's traffic lights
- to regulate taxis and minicabs
- to run the London River Services, Victoria Coach Station and London's Transport Museum
- to help to coordinate the Dial-a-Ride and Taxicard schemes for door-to-door services for transport users with mobility problems
- to manage the North London railway (since autumn 2007)

The London Borough Councils maintain the role of highway and traffic authorities for 95 per cent of London's roads. A £5 congestion charge for motorists driving into central London between the hours of 7am and 6.30pm, Monday to Friday (excluding public holidays) was introduced on 17 February 2003, and was subsequently raised to £8 on 4 July 2005. On 19 February 2007, the charge zone roughly doubled in size after a westward expansion (although this is due to be abolished in spring 2010), and the time zone changed to finish earlier at 6pm.

TfL introduced a low emission zone for London on 4 February 2008. It consisted of a £200 daily charge for polluting vehicles that entered the zone, which covered most of Greater London. Lorries over 12 tonnes that did not meet emissions standards were the first to be affected. Charges for vehicles exceeding three-and-a-half tonnes and buses and coaches exceeding five tonnes began on 7 July 2008; tougher emissions standards will be introduced in January 2012. Proposed additional charges, to apply to minibuses and vans from October 2010, have been suspended subject to public consultation.

Transport Commissioner for London, Peter Hendy

LONDON DEVELOPMENT AGENCY (LDA)

The LDA promotes economic development and regeneration. It is one of the nine regional development agencies set up around the country to perform this task. It is run by a board of 14 members appointed by the mayor. The key aspects of the LDA's role are:

- to further the economic development and regeneration of London
- to promote business efficiency, investment and competitiveness
- to promote employment
- to enhance the skills of local people
- to contribute to sustainable development

The London boroughs retain powers to promote economic development in their local areas.

Chair, Harvey McGrath

THE ENVIRONMENT

The mayor is required to formulate strategies to tackle London's environmental issues including the quality of water, air and land; the use of energy and London's contribution to climate change targets; groundwater levels and traffic emissions; and municipal waste management.

METROPOLITAN POLICE AUTHORITY (MPA)

This body, which oversees the policing of London, consists of 23 members; 12 from the assembly and 11 independents. One of the independents is appointed directly by the home secretary. The role of the MPA is:

- to monitor and scrutinise the Metropolitan Police Service
- to maintain an efficient and effective police force
- to secure best value in the delivery of policing services
- to publish an annual policing plan
- to set police targets and monitor performance
- to be part of the appointment, discipline and removal of senior officers
- to be responsible for the police budget

The boundaries of the metropolitan police districts have been changed to be consistent with the 32 London boroughs. Areas beyond the GLA remit have been incorporated into the Surrey, Hertfordshire and Essex police areas. The City of London has its own police force.

Chair, Boris Johnson

LONDON FIRE AND EMERGENCY PLANNING AUTHORITY (LFEPA)

In July 2000 the London Fire and Civil Defence Authority became the London Fire and Emergency Planning Authority. It consists of 17 members, eight drawn from the assembly, seven from the London boroughs and two mayoral appointees. The role of the LFEPA is:

- to set the strategy for the provision of fire services
- to ensure that the fire brigade can meet all the normal requirements efficiently
- to ensure that effective arrangements are made for the fire brigade to receive emergency calls and deal with them promptly
- to ensure members of the fire brigade are properly trained and equipped
- to ensure that information useful to the development of the fire brigades is gathered
- to ensure arrangements for advice and guidance on fire protection are made

Chair, Brian Coleman, FRSA

SALARIES *as at June 2009*	
Mayor	£143,911
Deputy Mayors	
Richard Barnes	£95,141
Kit Malthouse	£52,910
Sir Simon Milton	£127,784
Chair of the Assembly	£63,468
Assembly Members	£52,910
Assembly Members who are also MPs	£17,636

LONDON ASSEMBLY COMMITTEES
Chair, Audit Panel, Roger Evans
Chair, Budget and Performance Committee, John Biggs
Chair, Business Management and Administration Committee, Jennette Arnold
Chair, Confirmation Hearings Committee, various
Chair, Economic Development, Culture, Sport and Tourism Committee, Dee Doocey
Chair, Environment Committee, Murad Qureshi
Chair, Health and Public Services Committee, James Cleverly
Chair, Planning and Housing Committee, Jenny Jones
Chair, Standards Committee, Clare Lloyd-Jones
Chair, Transport Committee, Caroline Pidgeon

GLA ORGANISATIONAL STRUCTURE

Following a reorganisation of the GLA, the structure below was expected to be in place by October 2009

STRATEGIC MANAGEMENT AND DELIVERY
Private Office
External Affairs
Public Liaison
Public Affairs
Press
Marketing and Events

COMMUNITIES AND INTELLIGENCE
Health and Communities
Economic and Business Policy
Intelligence
Community Safety and Policing Liaison

DEVELOPMENT AND ENVIRONMENT
Planning
Housing
Transport and Environment

LONDON 2012
Resources
Finance
Legal
Squares and Building Management
HR
Technology

ASSEMBLY SECRETARIAT
Scrutiny and Investigation
Committee and Member Services
Elections and Special Projects
External Relations

LONDON ASSEMBLY MEMBERS

as at 1 July 2009

Arbour, Tony, *C., South West,* Maj. 26,928
Arnold, Jennette, *Lab., North East,* Maj. 28,437
Bacon, Gareth, *C., London List*
Barnbrook, Richard, *BNP, London List*
Barnes, Richard, *C., Ealing and Hillingdon,* Maj. 28,638
Biggs, John, *Lab., City and East,* Maj. 31,553
Boff, Andrew, *C., London List*
Borwick, Victoria, *C., London List*
Cleverly, James, *C., Bexley and Bromley,* Maj. 75,237
Coleman, Brian, *C., Barnet and Camden,* Maj. 19,693
Doocey, Dee, *LD, London List*
Duvall, Len, *Lab., Greenwich and Lewisham,* Maj. 16,134
Evans, Roger, *C., Havering and Redbridge,* Maj. 43,025
Gavron, Nicky, *Lab., London List*
Johnson, Darren, *Green, London List*
Jones, Jenny, *Green, London List*
McCartney, Joanne, *Lab., Enfield and Haringey,* Maj. 1,402
Malthouse, Kit, *C., West Central,* Maj. 51,381
O'Connell, Stephen, *C., Croydon and Sutton,* Maj. 42,665
Pidgeon, Caroline, *LD, London List*
Qureshi, Murad, *Lab., London List*
Shah, Navin, *Lab., Brent and Harrow,* Maj. 1,649
Shawcross, Valerie, *Lab., Lambeth and Southwark,* Maj. 23,648
Tracey, Richard, *C., Merton and Wandsworth,* Maj. 26,293
Tuffrey, Michael, *LD, London List*

STATE OF THE PARTIES *as at 1 July 2009*

Party	*Seats*
Conservative (C.)	11
Labour (Lab.)	8
Liberal Democrats (LD)	3
Green	2
British National Party (BNP)	1

MAYORAL ELECTION RESULTS

as at 1 May 2008

E. 5,419,913 T. 45.33%

Change in turnout from 2004: + 8.38%
Good votes: 1st choice 2,415,952 (98.32%); 2nd choice 2,004,078 (82.94%)
Rejected votes: 1st choice 41,032 (1.67%); 2nd choice 412,054 (17.05%)

First	*Party*	*Votes*	*%*
Boris Johnson	C.	1,043,761	42.48
Ken Livingstone	Lab.	893,877	36.38
Brian Paddick	LD	236,685	9.63
Sian Berry	Green	77,374	3.15
Richard Barnbrook	BNP	69,710	2.84
Alan Craig	CPA	39,249	1.60
Gerard Batten	UKIP	24,222	0.91
Lindsey German	Left List	16,796	0.68
Matt O'Connor	Eng. Dem.	10,695	0.44
Winston McKenzie	Ind.	5,389	0.22

Second	*Party*	*Votes*	*%*
Brian Paddick	LD	641,412	26.11
Sian Berry	Green	331,727	13.50
Ken Livingstone	Lab.	303,198	12.34
Boris Johnson	C.	257,792	10.49
Richard Barnbrook	BNP	128,609	5.23
Gerard Batten	UKIP	113,651	4.63
Alan Craig	CPA	80,140	3.26
Matt O'Connor	Eng. Dem.	73,538	2.99
Winston McKenzie	Ind.	38,954	1.59
Lindsey German	Left List	35,057	1.43

LONDON ASSEMBLY ELECTION RESULTS

As at 1 May 2008

E. Electorate T. Turnout

See General Election Results for a list of party abbreviations

CONSTITUENCIES

E. 5,419,913 T. 45.28%

BARNET AND CAMDEN

E. 376,818 T. 47.77%

Brian Coleman, C.	72,659
Nicky Gavron, Lab.	52,966
Nick Russell, LD	22,213
Miranda Dunn, Green	16,782
Magnus Nielsen, UKIP	3,678
Clement Adebayo, CPA	3,536
David Stevens, Eng. Dem.	2,146
Dave Hoefling, Left List	2,074
Graham Dare, Veritas	510

C. majority 19,693

BEXLEY AND BROMLEY

E. 407,003 T. 49.85%

James Cleverly, C.	105,162
Alex Heslop, Lab.	29,925
Tom Papworth, LD,	21,244
Paul Winnett, NF	11,288
Ann Garrett, Green	9,261
Mick Greenhough, UKIP	8,021
John Hemming-Clark, Ind.	6,684
Miranda Suit, CPA	4,408
Steven Uncles, Eng. Dem.	2,907
David Davis, Left List	1,050

C. majority 75,237

BRENT AND HARROW

E. 367,337 T. 43.10%

Navin Shah, Lab.	57,716
Bob Blackman, C.	56,067
James Allie, LD	19,299
Shahrar Ali, Green	10,129
Zena Sherman, CPA	4,180
Sunita Webb, UKIP	3,021
Pat McManus, Left List	2,287
Arvind Tailor, Eng. Dem.	2,150

Lab. majority 1,649

CITY AND EAST

E. 470,863 T. 39.79%

John Biggs, Lab.	63,635
Philip Briscoe, C.	32,082
Hanif Abdulmuhit, Respect	26,760
Robert Bailey, BNP	18,020
Rajonuddin Jalal, LD	13,724
Heather Finlay, Green	11,478
Thomas Conquest, CPA	7,306
Michael McGough, UKIP	3,078
Graham Kemp, NF	2,350
Michael Gavan, Left List	2,274
John Griffiths, Eng. Dem.	2,048
Julie Crawford, Ind.	701

Lab. majority 31,553

CROYDON AND SUTTON

E. 360,221 T. 48.99%

Stephen O'Connell, C.	76,477
Shafi Khan, Lab.	33,812
Abigail Lock, LD	32,335
David Pickles, UKIP	9,440
Shasha Khan, Green	8,969
David Campanale, CPA	6,910
Richard Castle, Eng. Dem.	4,186
Zana Hussain, Left List	1,361

C. majority 42,665

EALING AND HILLINGDON

E. 401,671 T. 44.05%

Richard Barnes, C.	74,710
Ranjit Dheer, Lab.	46,072
Nigel Bakhai, LD	18,004
Sarah Edwards, Green	12,606
Ian Edward, NF	7,939
Mary Boyle, CPA	5,100
Lynnda Robson, UKIP	4,465
Salvinder Dhillon, Left List	2,390
Sati Chaggar, Eng. Dem.	1,853

C. majority 28,638

ENFIELD AND HARINGEY

E. 351,536 T. 46.04%

Joanne McCartney, Lab.	52,665
Matthew Laban, C.	51,263
Monica Whyte, LD	23,550
Pete McAskie, Green	12,473
Segun Johnson, CPA	5,779
Sait Akgul, Left List	5,639
Brian Hall, UKIP	4,682
Teresa Cannon, Eng. Dem.	2,282

Lab. majority 1,402

GREENWICH AND LEWISHAM

E. 347,252 T. 42.98%

Len Duvall, Lab.	53,174
Andy Jennings, C.	37,040
Brian Robson, LD	18,174
Susan Luxton, Green	15,607
Tess Culnane, NF	8,509
Stephen Hammond, CPA	5,079
Arnold Tarling, UKIP	3,910
Jennifer Jones, Left List	2,045
Johanna Munilla, Eng. Dem.	1,716
Chris Flood, Soc. Alt.	1,587

Lab. majority 16,134

HAVERING AND REDBRIDGE

E. 369,407 T. 45.46%

Roger Evans, C.	78,493
Balvinder Saund, Lab.	35,468
Farrukh Islam, LD	12,443
Lawrence Webb, UKIP	12,203
Ashley Gunstock, Green	9,126
Leo Brookes, Eng. Dem.	6,487
Paula Warren, CPA	5,533
Dr Peter Thorogood, Ind.	3,450
Carole Vincent, Left List	1,473

C. majority 43,025

LAMBETH AND SOUTHWARK
E. 395,202 T. 42.09%

Valerie Shawcross, Lab.	60,601
Caroline Pidgeon, LD	36,953
Shirley Houghton, C.	32,835
Shane Collins, Green	18,011
Geoffrey Macharia, CPA	4,432
Jens Winton, UKIP	3,012
Katt Young, Left List	1,956
Janus Polenceus, Eng. Dem.	1,867
Jasmijn De Boo, Animals Count	1,828
Daniel Lambert, Socialist	1,588

Lab. majority 23,648

MERTON AND WANDSWORTH
E. 362,542 T. 47.16%
NORTH EAST

Richard Tracey, C.	75,103
Leonie Cooper, Lab.	48,810
Shas Sheehan, LD	17,187
Roy Vickery, Green	14,124
Strachan McDonald, UKIP	4,286
Ellen Greco, CPA	4,053
Steve Scott, Eng. Dem.	2,160
Kris Stewart, Left List	1,714

C. majority 26,293

NORTH EAST
E. 451,787 T. 43.80%

Jennette Arnold, Lab.	73,551
Alexander Ellis, C.	45,114
Meral Ece, LD	28,973
Aled Fisher, Green	28,845
Unjum Mirza, Left List	6,019
Nicholas Jones, UKIP	5,349
Maxine Hargreaves, CPA	5,323
John Dodds, Eng. Dem.	3,637

Lab. majority 28,437

SOUTH WEST
E. 415,092 T. 46.15%

Tony Arbour, C.	76,913
Stephen Knight, LD	49,985
Ansuya Sodha, Lab.	30,190
John Hunt, Green	12,774
Andrew Cripps, NF	4,754
Peter Dul, UKIP	3,779
Sue May, CPA	3,718
Andrew Constantine, Free England Party	2,908
Roger Cooper, Eng. Dem.	1,874
Tansy Hoskins, Left List	1,526

C. majority 26,928

WEST CENTRAL
E. 343,182 T. 48.48%

Kit Malthouse, C.	86,651
Murad Qureshi, Lab.	35,270
Julia Stephenson, Green	16,874
Merlene Emerson, LD	15,934
Paul Wiffen, UKIP	3,060
Alex Vaughan, Eng. Dem.	1,858
Explo Nani-Kofi, Left List	1,630
Abby Dharamsey, Ind.	962

C. majority 51,381

TOP-UP MEMBERS

BRITISH NATIONAL PARTY
Richard Barnbrook

CONSERVATIVE
Andrew Boff
Victoria Borwick
Gareth Bacon

GREEN PARTY
Darren Johnson
Jenny Jones

LABOUR
Nicky Gavron
Murad Qureshi

LIBERAL DEMOCRAT
Dee Doocey
Caroline Pidgeon
Michael Tuffrey

WALES

WELSH ASSEMBLY GOVERNMENT

Cathays Park, Cardiff CF10 3NQ
T 0845-010 3300 W http://wales.gov.uk

The Welsh Assembly Government is comprised of the first minister, deputy first minister, Welsh ministers, the counsel general (the chief legal adviser), and the deputy Welsh ministers. The 60 assembly members delegate their executive powers, including the implementation of policies and legislation, to the first minister – who is elected by the whole assembly and is therefore usually the leader of the largest political party. In turn, the first minister delegates responsibility for delivering the executive functions to Welsh ministers, who together form the cabinet.

The Welsh Assembly Government has responsibility over the following devolved areas: agriculture, fisheries, forestry and rural development; ancient monuments and historic buildings; culture; economic development; education and training; environment; fire and rescue services; food; health and health services; highways and transport; housing; local government; public administration; social welfare; sport and recreation; tourism; town and county planning; water and flood defence; and the Welsh language.

First Minister for Wales, Rt. Hon. Rhodri Morgan, AM
Deputy First Minister for Wales, and Minister for the Economy and Transport, Ieuan Wyn Jones, AM
Minister for Children, Education, Lifelong Learning and Skills, Jane Hutt, AM
Minister for Environment, Sustainability and Housing, Jane Davidson, AM
Minister for Finance and Public Service Delivery, Andrew Davies, AM
Minister for Health and Social Services, Edwina Hart, MBE, AM
Minister for Heritage, Alun Ffred Jones, AM
Minister for Rural Affairs, Elin Jones, AM
Minister for Social Justice and Local Government, Dr Brian Gibbons, AM
Deputy Minister for Housing, Jocelyn Davies, AM
Deputy Minister for Regeneration, Leighton Andrews, AM
Deputy Minister for Skills, John Griffiths, AM
Deputy Minister for Social Services, Gwenda Thomas, AM
Counsel General and Leader of the House, Carwyn Jones, AM
Clerk to the Assembly and Chief Executive of Assembly Commission, Claire Clancy

MANAGEMENT BOARD

Permanent Secretary, Dame Gillian Morgan
Director General, Children, Education, Lifelong Learning and Skills, David Hawker
Director General, Economy and Transport, Gareth Hall
Director General, Finance, Christine Daws
Director General, Health and Social Services, Paul Williams
Director General, People, Places and Corporate Services, Bernard Galton
Director General, Public Service and Local Government Delivery, Emyr Roberts
Director General, Sustainable Futures, Clive Bates
Non-Executive Directors, Kathryn Bishop; Elan Cross Stephens; James Turner

DEPARTMENTS

Children, Education, Lifelong Learning and Skills
Constitutional Affairs, Equality and Communication
Corporate Information and Services
Economy and Transport
Environment, Sustainability and Housing
Finance
Health and Social Services
Heritage
Human Resources
Legal Services
Public Health and Health Professions
Public Services and Performance
Rural Affairs
Social Justice and Local Government

EXECUTIVE AGENCIES

CADW – Welsh Historic Monuments

ASSEMBLY COMMITTEES

Audit
Business
Children and Young People
Communities and Culture
Enterprise and Learning
Equality of Opportunity
European and External Affairs
Finance
Health, Wellbeing and Local Government
Petitions
Scrutiny of First Minister
Standards of Conduct
Sustainability

ASSEMBLY COMMISSION

The Assembly Commission was created under the Government of Wales Act 2006. It is a corporate body which has responsibility for the provision of property, staff and services to support Assembly members. The commission is made up of three directorates, the Assembly Business directorate, the Legal Services directorate and the directorate of the Chief Operating Officer; all three are supported by a corporate unit and accountable to the chief executive. Membership of the Assembly Commission includes a presiding officer and four assembly members, with not more than one member (other than the presiding officer) from the same political group.

Presiding Officer, Lord Dafydd Elis-Thomas, PC, AM
Members, Lorraine Barrett, Peter Black; Chris Franks; William Graham
Chief Executive, Clare Clancy

NATIONAL ASSEMBLY FOR WALES

Cardiff Bay, Cardiff CF99 1NA
T 0845-010 5500 W www.assemblywales.org

In July 1997 the government announced plans to establish a National Assembly for Wales. In a referendum in September 1997 about 50 per cent of the electorate voted, of whom 50.3 per cent voted in favour of the assembly. Elections are held every four years and the first elections took place on 6 May 1999, the second on 1 May 2003 and the third on 3 May 2007.

Welsh Assembly members are elected using the additional member system. Voters are given two votes, one for a constituency member and one for a regional member. The constituency members are elected under the first-past-the-post system, also used to elect constituency members to the London Assembly. Four regional members in each of the five constituencies are then chosen from party lists or independent candidates using a form of proportional representation.

Until 2007 the National Assembly for Wales had responsibility in Wales for ministerial functions relating to health and personal social services; education; the Welsh language, arts and culture; local government; housing; water and sewerage; environmental protection; sport; agriculture and fisheries; forestry; land use, including town and country planning and conservation; roads; tourism; and European Union matters.

The Government of Wales Act 2006 introduced a radical change to the functions and status of the National Assembly for Wales. With effect from 25 May 2007 the act formally separated the National Assembly for Wales (the legislature – made up of 60 elected assembly members) and the Welsh Assembly Government (the executive – comprising the first minister, Welsh ministers, deputy Welsh ministers and the counsel general). It also made changes to the electoral process: candidates are no longer permitted to stand for both a constituency and a regional list. The act enabled the National Assembly for Wales to formulate its own legislation (assembly measures) on devolved matters such as health, education, social services and local government; the assembly is given legislative competence (the legal authority to pass measures) on a case-by-case basis by the UK parliament.

The National Assembly for Wales also scrutinises and monitors the Welsh Assembly Government. It meets in the Senedd debating chamber. The 60 assembly members examine and approve assembly measures and approve certain items of subordinate legislation; approve budgets for the Welsh Assembly Government's programmes; hold Welsh ministers to account; and analyse and debate their decisions and policies.

Presiding Officer, Lord Dafydd Elis-Thomas, PC, AM

SALARIES *2008–9*	
First Minister*	£78,575
Minister/Presiding Officer*	£40,759
Deputy Minister/Deputy Presiding Officer*	£25,637
Assembly Members (AM)†	£51,899

* Also receives the assembly member salary

† Reduced by two-thirds if the member is already an MP or an MEP

MEMBERS OF THE NATIONAL ASSEMBLY FOR WALES

as at 4 June 2009

Andrews, Leighton, *Lab., Rhondda,* Maj. 6,215
Asghar, Mohammad, *PC, South Wales East region*
Barrett, Lorraine Jayne, *Lab., Cardiff S. and Penarth,* Maj. 2,754
Bates, Michael, *LD, Montgomeryshire,* Maj. 1,979
Black, Peter, *LD, South Wales West region*
Bourne, Prof. Nicholas, *C., Mid and West Wales region*
Burnham, Eleanor, *LD, North Wales region*
Burns, Angela, *C., Carmarthen West and South Pembrokeshire,* Maj. 98
Butler, Rosemary Janet Mair, *Lab., Newport W.,* Maj. 1,401
Cairns, Alun, *C., South Wales West region*
Chapman, Christine, *Lab., Cynon Valley,* Maj. 5,623
Cuthbert, Jeffrey, *Lab., Caerphilly,* Maj. 2,287
Davidson, Jane Elizabeth, *Lab., Pontypridd,* Maj. 3,347
Davies, Alun, *Lab., Mid and West Wales region*
Davies, Andrew David, *Lab., Swansea West,* Maj. 1,511
Davies, Andrew Robert, *C., South Wales Central region*
Davies, Jocelyn, *PC, South Wales East region*
Davies, Paul, *C., Preseli Pembrokeshire,* Maj. 3,205
Elis-Thomas, Lord Dafydd, *PC, Dwyfor Meirionnydd,* Maj. 8,868
Evans, Nerys, *PC, Mid and West Wales region*
Franks, Christopher, *PC, South Wales Central region*
German, Michael, *LD, South Wales East region*
Gibbons, Brian, *Lab., Aberavon,* Maj. 6,571
Graham, William, *C., South Wales East region*
Gregory, Janice, *Lab., Ogmore,* Maj. 7,900
Griffiths, Albert John, *Lab., Newport East,* Maj. 875
Griffiths, Lesley, *Lab., Wrexham,* Maj. 1,250
Hart, Edwina, *Lab., Gower,* Maj. 1,192
Hutt, Jane, *Lab., Vale of Glamorgan,* Maj. 83
Isherwood, Mark, *C., North Wales region*
James, Irene, *Lab., Islwyn,* Maj. 2,218
Jenkins, Bethan, *PC, South Wales West region*
Jones, Alun Ffred, *PC, Arfon,* Maj. 5,018
Jones, Carwyn Howell, *Lab., Bridgend,* Maj. 2,556
Jones, Elin, *PC, Ceredigion,* Maj. 3,955
Jones, Gareth, *PC, Aberconwy,* Maj. 1,693
Jones, Helen Mary, *PC, Llanelli,* Maj. 3,884
Jones, Margaret Ann (Ann), *Lab., Vale of Clwyd,* Maj. 92
Law, Trish, *Ind., Blaenau Gwent,* Maj. 5,357
Lewis, Huw, *Lab., Merthyr Tydfil and Rhymney,* Maj. 4,581
Lloyd, Dr David, *PC, South Wales West region*
Lloyd, Val, *Lab., Swansea East,* Maj. 4,961
Melding, David, *C., South Wales Central region*
Mewies, Sandra Elaine, *Lab., Delyn,* Maj. 511
Millar, Darren, *C., Clwyd West,* Maj. 1,596
Morgan, Hywel Rhodri, *Lab., Cardiff West,* Maj. 3,698
Morgan, Jonathan, *C., Cardiff North,* Maj. 4,844
Neagle, Lynne, *Lab., Torfaen,* Maj. 5,396
Ramsay, Nicholas, *C., Monmouth,* Maj. 8,469
Randerson, Jennifer Elizabeth, *LD, Cardiff C.,* Maj. 6,565
Ryder, Janet, *PC, North Wales region*
Sargeant, Carl, *Lab., Alyn and Deeside,* Maj. 3,362
Sinclair, Karen, *Lab., Clwyd South,* Maj. 1,119
Thomas, Gwenda, *Lab., Neath,* Maj. 1,944
Thomas, Rhodri, *PC, Carmarthen East and Dinefwr,* Maj. 8,469
Watson, Joyce, *Lab., Mid and West Wales region*
Williams, Brynle, *C., North Wales region*
Williams, Kirsty, *LD, Brecon and Radnorshire,* Maj. 5,354
Wood, Leanne, *PC, South Wales Central region*
Wyn Jones, Ieuan, *PC, Ynys Mon,* Maj. 4,392

STATE OF THE PARTIES *as at 4 June 2009*

	Constituency AMs	*Regional AMs*	*AM total*
Labour (Lab.)	23*	2	25*
Plaid Cymru (PC)	6*	8	14*
Conservative (C.)	5	7	12
Liberal Democrats (LD)	3	3	6
Others	1	0	1
The Presiding Officer	1	0	1
The Deputy Presiding Officer	1	0	1
Total	40	20	60

* Excludes the presiding officer (PC) and deputy presiding officer (Lab.), who have no party allegiance while in post

NATIONAL ASSEMBLY ELECTION RESULTS

As at 3 May 2007
E. Electorate T. Turnout
See General Election Results for a list of party abbreviations

CONSTITUENCIES

E. 2,248,122 T. 43.5%

ABERAVON (S. WALES WEST)
E. 51,536 T. 20,528 (39.83%)

Brian Gibbons, Lab.	10,129
Linet Purcell, PC	3,558
Andrew Tutton, Neath Port Talbot Ratepayers Association	2,561
Daisy Meyland-Smith, C.	1,990
Claire Waller, LD	1,450
Captain Beany, Bean	840

Lab. majority 6,571 (32.01%)
4.82% swing Lab. to PC

ALYN AND DEESIDE (WALES N.)
E. 59,355 T. 21,095 (35.54%)

Carl Sargeant, Lab.	8,196
Will Gallagher, C.	4,834
Dennis Hutchinson, Ind.	3,241
Paul Brighton, LD	2,091
Dafydd Passe, PC	1,398
William Crawford, UKIP	1,335

Lab. majority 3,362 (15.94%)
3.66% swing Lab. to C.

BLAENAU GWENT (S. WALES EAST)
E. 52,816 T. 23,518 (44.53%)

Trish Law, Ind.	12,722
Keren Bender, Lab.	7,365
Gareth Lewis, LD	1,351
Natasha Asghar, PC	1,129
Bob Hayward, C.	951

Ind. majority 5,357 (22.78%)
46.5% swing Lab. to Ind.

BRECON AND RADNORSHIRE (WALES MID AND W.)
E. 55,428 T. 28,748 (51.87%)

Kirsty Williams, LD	15,006
Suzy Davies, C.	9,652
Neil Stone, Lab.	2,514
Arwel Lloyd, PC	1,576

LD majority 5,354 (18.62%)
0.58% swing LD to C.

BRIDGEND (S. WALES WEST)
E. 59,550 T. 24,552 (41.23%)

Carwyn Jones, Lab.	9,889
Emma Greenow, C.	7,333
Paul Warren, LD	3,730
Nicholas Thomas, PC	3,600

Lab. majority 2,556 (10.41%)
0.71% swing Lab. to C.

CAERNARFON (WALES N.)
E. 39,891 T. 19,573 (49.07%)

Alun Ffred Jones, PC	10,260
Martin Eaglestone, Lab.	5,242
Gerry Frobisher, C.	1,858
Mel ab Owain, LD	1,424
Elwyn Williams, UKIP	789

PC majority 5,018 (25.64%)
3.43% swing Lab. to PC

CAERPHILLY (S. WALES EAST)
E. 62,046 T. 26,922 (43.39%)

Jeff Cuthbert, Lab.	8,937
Lindsay Whittle, PC	7,000
Ron Davies, Ind.	6,071
Richard Foley, C.	3,227
Huw Price, LD	1,687

Lab. majority 1,937 (7.19%)
5.07% swing Lab. to PC

CARDIFF CENTRAL (S. WALES CENTRAL)
E. 62,202 T. 22,397 (36.01%)

Jenny Randerson, LD	11,462
Sue Lent, Lab.	4,897
Andrew Murphy, C.	3,137
Thomas Whitfield, PC	1,855
Frank Hughes, UKIP	1,046

LD majority 6,565 (29.31%)
2.71% swing LD to Lab.

CARDIFF NORTH (S. WALES CENTRAL)
E. 65,687 T. 33,702 (51.31%)
C. majority 4,844 (14.37%)
8.16% swing Lab. to C.

Jonathan Morgan, C.	15,253
Sophie Howe, Lab.	10,409
Ed Bridges, LD	4,287
Wyn Jones, PC	2,491
Dai Llewellyn, UKIP	1,262

CARDIFF SOUTH AND PENARTH (S. WALES CENTRAL)
E. 71,312 T. 26,728 (37.48%)

Lorraine Barrett, Lab.	10,106
Karen Robson, C.	7,352
Dominic Hannigan, LD	5,445
Jason Toby, PC	3,825

Lab. majority 2,754 (10.30%)
4.22% swing Lab. to C.

CARDIFF WEST (S. WALES CENTRAL)
E. 64,588 T. 26,889 (41.63%)

Rhodri Morgan, Lab.	10,390
Craig Williams, C.	6,692
Neil McEvoy, PC	5,719
Alison Goldsworthy, LD	4,088

Lab. majority 3,698 (13.75%)
8.77% swing Lab. to C.

CARMARTHEN EAST AND DINEFWR (WALES MID AND W.)
E. 52,528 T. 29,269 (55.72%)

Rhodri Glyn Thomas, PC	15,655
Kevin Madge, Lab.	7,186
Henrietta Hensher, C.	4,676
Ian Walton, LD	1,752

PC majority 8,469 (28.94%)
5.85% swing Lab. to PC

CARMARTHEN WEST AND SOUTH PEMBROKESHIRE (WALES MID AND W.)
E. 57,477 T. 28,568 (49.70%)

Angela Burns, C.	8,590
Christine Gwyther, Lab.	8,492
John Dixon, PC	8,340
John Gossage, LD	1,806
Malcolm Calver, Ind.	1,340

C. majority 98 (0.34%)
7.45% swing Lab. to C.

CEREDIGION (WALES MID AND W.)
E. 54,071 T. 30,108 (55.68%)

Elin Jones, PC	14,818
John Davies, LD	10,863
Trefor Jones, C.	2,369
Linda Grace, Lab.	1,530
Emyr Morgan, Ind.	528

PC majority 3,955 (13.14%)
2.20% swing PC to LD

CLWYD SOUTH (WALES N.)
E. 51,865 T. 19,498 (37.59%)

Karen Sinclair, Lab.	6,838
John Bell, C.	5,719
Nia Davies, PC	3,894
Frank Biggs, LD	1,838
David Rowlands, UKIP	1,209

Lab. majority 1,119 (5.74%)
6.04% swing Lab. to C.

CLWYD WEST (WALES N.)
E. 57,312 T. 26,205 (45.72%)

Darren Millar, C.	8,905
Alun Pugh, Lab.	7,309
Philip Edwards, PC	7,162
Simon Croft, LD	1,705
Warwick Nicholson, UKIP	1,124

C. majority 1,596 (6.09%)
4.13% swing Lab. to C.

CONWY (WALES N.)
E. 44,143 T. 20,699 (46.89%)

Gareth Jones, PC	7,983
Dylan Jones-Evans, C.	6,290
Denise Idris Jones, Lab.	4,508
Euron Hughes, LD	1,918

PC majority 1,693 (8.18%)
2.86% swing C. to PC

CYNON VALLEY (S. WALES CENTRAL)
E. 50,846 T. 19,517 (38.38%)

Christine Chapman, Lab.	11,058
Liz Walters, PC	5,435
Neill John, C.	2,024
Margaret Phelps, LD	1,000

Lab. majority 5,623 (28.81%)
7.16% swing Lab. to PC

DELYN (WALES N.)
E. 52,733 T. 21,668 (41.09%)

Sandy Mewies, Lab.	7,506
Antoinette Sandbach, C.	6,996
Meg Ellis, PC	3,179
Ian Matthews, LD	2,669
Derek Bigg, UKIP	1,318

Lab. majority 510 (2.35%)
3.63% swing Lab. to C.

GOWER (S. WALES WEST)
E. 61,520 T. 27,545 (44.77%)
Lab. majority 1,192 (4.33%)

Edwina Hart, Lab.	9,406
Byron Davis, C.	8,214
Darren Price, PC	5,106
Nick Tregoning, LD	2,924
Alex Lewis, UKIP	1,895

9.84% swing Lab. to C.

ISLWYN (S. WALES EAST)
E. 54,795 T. 23,564 (43.00%)

Irene James, Lab.	8,883
Kevin Etheridge, Ind.	6,665
Allan Pritchard, PC	5,084
Paul Williams, C.	1,797
Mark Maguire, LD	1,135

Lab. majority 2,218 (9.41%)
23.3% swing Lab. to Ind.

LLANELLI (WALES MID AND W.)
E. 56,154 T. 27,602 (49.15%)

Helen Mary Jones, PC	13,839
Catherine Thomas, Lab.	9,955
Andrew Morgan, C.	2,757
Jeremy Townsend, LD	1,051

PC majority 3,884 (14.07%)
7.08% swing Lab. to PC

MEIRIONNYDD NANT CONWY (WALES MID AND W.)
E. 46,718 T. 22,122 (47.35%)

Dafydd Elis-Thomas, PC	13,201
Mike Wood, C.	4,333
David Phillips, Lab.	2,749
Steve Churchman, LD	1,839

PC majority 8,868 (40.09%)
1.57% swing PC to C.

MERTHYR TYDFIL AND RHYMNEY (S. WALES EAST)
E. 54,025 T. 21,028 (38.92%)

Huw Lewis, Lab.	7,776
Amy Kitcher, LD	3,195
Clive Tovey, Ind.	2,622
Glyndwr Jones, PC	2,519
Jeff Edwards, Ind.	1,950
Giles Howard, C.	1,151
Jock Greer, Ind.	844
Vivienne Hadley, Ind.	809
Richard Williams, Ind.	162

Lab. majority 4,581 (21.79%)
15.77% swing Lab. to LD

MONMOUTH (S. WALES EAST)
E. 63,000 T. 29,565 (46.93%)

Nick Ramsay, C.	15,389
Richard Clark, Lab.	6,920
Jacqui Sullivan, LD	4,359
Jonathan Clark, PC	2,093
Ed Abrams, Eng. Dem.	804

C. majority 8,469 (28.65%)
0.99% swing C. to Lab.

MONTGOMERYSHIRE (WALES MID AND W.)
E. 48,377 T. 22,300 (46.10%)

Mick Bates, LD	8,704
Don Munford, C.	6,725
David Thomas, PC	3,076
Charles Lawson, UKIP	2,251
Rachel Maycock, Lab.	1,544

LD majority 1,979 (8.87%)
1.18% swing LD to C.

NEATH (S. WALES WEST)
E. 57,952 T. 25,200 (43.48%)

Gwenda Thomas, Lab.	10,934
Alun Llewelyn, PC	8,990
Andrew Sivertsen, C.	2,956
Sheila Waye, LD	2,320

Lab. majority 1,944 (7.71%)
7.29% swing Lab. to PC

NEWPORT EAST (S. WALES EAST)
E. 53,060 T. 19,906 (37.52%)

John Griffiths, Lab.	6,395
Ed Townsend, LD	5,520
Peter Fox, C.	4,512
Trefor Puw, PC	1,696
James Harris, Ind.	1,354
Mike Blundell, Eng. Dem.	429

Lab. majority 875 (4.40%)
12.00% swing Lab. to LD

NEWPORT WEST (S. WALES EAST)
E. 58,981 T. 23,659 (40.11%)

Rosemary Butler, Lab.	9,582
Matthew Evans, C.	8,181
Nigel Flanagan, LD	2,813
Brian Hancock, PC	2,449
Andrew Constantine, Eng. Dem.	634

Lab. majority 1,401 (5.92%)
5.79% swing Lab. to C.

OGMORE (S. WALES WEST)
E. 56,973 T. 22,766 (39.96%)

Janice Gregory, Lab.	11,761
Sian Caiach, PC	3,861
Norma Lloyd-Nesling, C.	2,663
Steve Smith, Ind.	2,337
Martin Plant, LD	2,144

Lab. majority 7,900 (34.70%)
2.65% swing Lab. to PC

PONTYPRIDD (S. WALES CENTRAL)
E. 57,512 T. 23,501 (40.86%)

Jane Davidson, Lab.	9,836
Michael Powell, LD	6,449
Richard Grigg, PC	4,181
Janice Charles, C.	3,035

Lab. majority 3,387 (14.41%)
11.08% swing Lab. to LD

PRESELI PEMBROKESHIRE (WALES MID AND W.)
E. 56,435 T. 28,720 (50.89%)

Paul Davies, C.	11,086
Tamsin Dunwoody, Lab.	7,881
John Osmond, PC	7,101
Hywel Davies, LD	2,652

C. majority 3,205 (11.16%)
8.52% swing Lab. to C.

RHONDDA (S. WALES CENTRAL)
E. 52,478 T. 22,107 (42.13%)

Leighton Andrews, Lab.	12,875
Jill Evans, PC	6,660
Karen Roberts, LD	1,441
Howard Parsons, C.	1,131

Lab. majority 6,215 (28.11%)
3.23% swing Lab. to PC

SWANSEA EAST (S. WALES WEST)
E. 59,186 T. 20,717 (35.00%)

Val Lloyd, Lab.	8,590
Helen Clarke, LD	3,629
Danny Bowles, PC	3,218
Bob Dowdle, C.	2,025
David Robinson, Ind.	1,618
Ray Welsby, Ind. Welsby	1,177
Gary Evans, Ind. Evans	460

Lab. majority 4,961 (23.95%)
0.49% swing LD to Lab.

SWANSEA WEST (S. WALES WEST)
E. 61,469 T. 22,879 (37.22%)

Andrew Davies, Lab.	7,393
Peter May, LD	5,882
Harri Davies, C.	4,379
Ian Titherington, PC	3,583
Richard Lewis, UKIP	1,642

Lab. majority 1,511 (6.60%)
5.75% swing Lab. to LD

TORFAEN (S. WALES EAST)
E. 62,592 T. 23,215 (37.09%)

Lynne Neagle, Lab.	9,921
Graham Smith, C.	4,525
Ian Williams, Ind.	3,348
Rhys ab Elis, PC	2,762
Patrick Legge, LD	2,659

Lab. majority 5,396 (23.24%)
6.18% swing Lab. to C.

VALE OF CLWYD (WALES N.)
E. 55,234 T. 22,275 (40.33%)

Ann Jones, Lab.	8,104
Matt Wright, C.	8,012
Mark Jones, PC	3,884
Mark Young, LD	2,273

Lab. majority 92 (0.41%)
7.40% swing Lab. to C.

VALE OF GLAMORGAN (S. WALES CENTRAL)
E. 68,856 T. 33,686 (48.92%)

Jane Hutt, Lab.	11,515
Gordon Kemp, C.	11,432
Barry Shaw, PC	4,671
Mark Hooper, LD	3,758
Kevin Mahoney, UKIP	2,310

Lab. majority 83 (0.25%)
4.02% swing Lab. to C.

WREXHAM (WALES N.)
E. 50,759 T. 19,567 (38.55%)

Lesley Griffiths, Lab.	5,633
John Marek, Ind.	4,383
Felicity Elphick, C.	3,372
Bruce Roberts, LD	3,268
Sion Aled Owen, PC	1,878
Peter Lewis, UKIP	1,033

Lab. majority 1,250 (6.39%)
6.0% swing Ind. to Lab.

YNYS MON (WALES N.)
E. 51,814 T. 26,820 (51.76%)

Ieuan Wyn Jones, PC	10,653
Peter Rogers, Ind.	6,261
Jonathan Austin, Lab.	4,681
James Roach, C.	3,480
Mandi Abrahams, LD	912
Francis Wykes, UKIP	833

PC majority 4,392 (16.38%)
10.5% swing PC to Ind.

REGIONS
E. 2,248,122 T. 43.4%

MID AND WEST WALES
E. 427,188 T. 216,957 (50.79%)

PC	67,258	(31.00%)
C.	49,606	(22.86%)
Lab.	39,979	(18.43%)
LD	28,790	(13.27%)
Green	8,768	(4.04%)
UKIP	8,191	(3.78%)
BNP	6,389	(2.94%)
Soc. Lab.	2,196	(1.01%)
Ind.	1,598	(0.74%)
Welsh Christian Party	1,493	(0.69%)
Ind. Evans	1,108	(0.51%)
Comm. Brit.	666	(0.31%)
Veritas	502	(0.23%)
CPA	413	(0.19%)

PC majority 17,652 (8.14%)
1.16% swing PC to C. (2003 PC majority 5,423)

ADDITIONAL MEMBERS
Nick Bourne, *C.* — Joyce Watson, *Lab.*
Alun Davies, *Lab.* — Nerys Evans, *PC*

NORTH WALES
E. 463,106 T. 196,442 (42.42%)

Lab.	51,831	(26.38%)
PC	50,558	(25.74%)
C.	50,266	(25.59%)
LD	15,275	(7.78%)
BNP	9,986	(5.08%)
UKIP	8,015	(4.08%)
Green	5,660	(2.88%)
Soc. Lab.	2,209	(1.12%)
Welsh Christian Party	1,300	(0.66%)
Comm. Brit.	700	(0.36%)
CPA	642	(0.33%)

Lab. majority 1,273 (0.65%)
4.72% swing Lab. to PC (2003 Lab. majority 13,610)

ADDITIONAL MEMBERS
Brynle Williams, *C.* — Eleanor Burnham, *LD*
Mark Isherwood, *C.* — Janet Ryder, *PC*

SOUTH WALES CENTRAL
E. 493,481 T. 208,294 (42.21%)

Lab.	70,799	(33.99%)
C.	45,147	(21.67%)
PC	32,207	(15.46%)
LD	29,262	(14.05%)
BNP	7,889	(3.79%)
Green	7,831	(3.76%)
UKIP	7,645	(3.67%)
Welsh Christian Party	1,987	(0.95%)
Soc. Lab.	1,744	(0.84%)
Respect	1,079	(0.52%)
Soc. Alt.	838	(0.40%)
Comm. Brit.	817	(0.39%)
CPA	757	(0.36%)
Socialist Equality Party	292	(0.14%)

Lab. majority 25,652 (12.32%)
5.16% swing Lab. to C. (2003 Lab. majority 40,965)

ADDITIONAL MEMBERS
David Melding, *C.* — Leanne Wood, *PC*
Andrew Davies, *C.* — Chris Franks, *PC*

SOUTH WALES EAST
E. 461,315 T. 190,064 (41.20%)

Lab.	67,998	(35.78%)
C.	37,935	(19.96%)
PC	25,915	(13.63%)
LD	20,947	(11.02%)
BNP	8,940	(4.70%)
UKIP	8,725	(4.59%)
Green	5,414	(2.85%)
Ind.	4,876	(2.57%)
Soc. Lab.	3,693	(1.94%)
Welsh Christian Party	2,498	(1.31%)
Eng. Dem.	1,655	(0.87%)
Comm. Brit.	979	(0.52%)
CPA	489	(0.26%)

Lab. majority 30,063 (15.82%)
4.55% swing Lab. to C. (2003 Lab. majority 42,291)

ADDITIONAL MEMBERS
William Graham, *C.* — Jocelyn Davies, *PC*
Michael German, *LD* — Mohammed Asghar, *PC*

SOUTH WALES WEST
E. 408,186 T. 163,127 (39.96%)

Lab.	58,347	(35.77%)
PC	28,819	(17.67%)
C.	26,199	(16.06%)
LD	20,226	(12.40%)
BNP	8,993	(5.51%)
Green	6,130	(3.76%)
UKIP	5,914	(3.63%)
Soc. Lab.	2,367	(1.45%)
Welsh Christian Party	1,685	(1.03%)
Ind. James	1,186	(0.73%)
Soc. Alt.	1,027	(0.63%)
Respect	713	(0.44%)
Ind.	582	(0.36%)
Comm. Brit.	546	(0.33%)
CPA	393	(0.24%)

Lab. majority 29,528 (18.10%)
2.87% swing Lab. to PC (2003 Lab. majority 33,267)

ADDITIONAL MEMBERS
Alun Cairns, *C.* — Bethan Jenkins, *PC*
Peter Black, *LD* — Dai Lloyd, *PC*

SCOTLAND

SCOTTISH GOVERNMENT

St Andrew's House, Regent Road, Edinburgh EH1 3DG
T 0845-774 1741 Enquiry Line 0131-556 8400
E ceu@scotland.gsi.gov.uk
W www.scotland.gov.uk

The Scottish government is the devolved government for Scotland. It is responsible for most of the issues of day-to-day concern to the people of Scotland, including health, education, justice, rural affairs and transport, and manages an annual budget of over £30bn.

The government was known as the Scottish executive when it was established in 1999, following the first elections to the Scottish parliament. The current administration was formed after elections in May 2007.

The government is led by a first minister who is nominated by the parliament and in turn appoints the other Scottish ministers who make up the cabinet.

Civil servants in Scotland are accountable to Scottish ministers, who are themselves accountable to the Scottish parliament.

CABINET

First Minister, Rt. Hon. Alex Salmond, MSP
Minister for Culture, External Affairs and Constitution, Mike Russell, MSP
Minister for Parliamentary Business, Bruce Crawford, MSP
Deputy First Minister and Cabinet Secretary for Health and Wellbeing, Nicola Sturgeon, MSP
Minister for Housing and Communities, Alex Neil, MSP
Minister for Public Health and Sport, Shona Robison, MSP
Cabinet Secretary for Education and Lifelong Learning, Fiona Hyslop, MSP
Minister for Children and Early Years, Adam Ingram, MSP
Minister for Schools and Skills, Keith Brown, MSP
Cabinet Secretary for Finance and Sustainable Growth, John Swinney, MSP
Minister for Enterprise, Energy and Tourism, Jim Mather, MSP
Minister for Transport, Infrastructure and Climate Change, Stewart Stevenson, MSP
Cabinet Secretary for Justice, Kenny MacAskill, MSP
Minister for Community Safety, Fergus Ewing, MSP
Cabinet Secretary for Rural Affairs and the Environment, Richard Lochhead, MSP
Minister for Environment, Roseanna Cunningham, MSP

LAW OFFICERS

Lord Advocate, Elish Angiolini, QC
Solicitor-General for Scotland, Frank Mulholland, QC

STRATEGIC BOARD

Permanent Secretary, Sir John Elvidge, KCB
Director-General, Economy, and Chief Economic Adviser, Dr Andrew Goudie
Director-General, Education, Philip Rycroft
Director-General, Environment, Richard Wakeford
Director-General, Finance and Corporate Services, Stella Manzie, CBE
Director-General, Health, and Chief Executive of NHS Scotland, Dr Kevin Woods
Director-General, Justice and Communities, Robert Gordon, CB
Non-Executive Directors, Prof. William Bound; David Fisher; Heather Logan

CHANGE AND CORPORATE SERVICES

Saughton House, Broomhouse Drive, Edinburgh EH11 3XD
Director of Change and Corporate Services, Paul Gray

ECONOMY DEPARTMENT

Victoria Quay, Edinburgh EH6 6QQ
Directorates: Built Environment; Culture, External Affairs and Tourism; DG Coordination – Economy, Business Management and Support; Inspectorate of Prosecution in Scotland; Office of the Chief Economic Adviser; Public Sector Simplification; Public Service Reform; Scottish Development International; Transport
Director-General and Chief Economic Adviser, Dr Andrew Goudie

EXECUTIVE AGENCIES

General Register Office of Scotland
Historic Scotland
National Archives of Scotland
Registers of Scotland
Scottish Water
Transport Scotland
Water Industry Commission

EDUCATION DEPARTMENT

Victoria Quay, Edinburgh EH6 6QQ
Directorates: Business, Enterprise and Energy; Children, Young People and Social Care; DG Coordination – Education; General Group; Lifelong Learning; Office of the Chief Scientific Adviser; Schools
Director-General, Philip Rycroft

EXECUTIVE AGENCIES

HM Inspectorate of Education
Social Work Inspection Agency
Student Awards Agency for Scotland

ENVIRONMENT DEPARTMENT

Victoria Quay, Edinburgh EH6 6QQ
Directorates: Climate Change and Water Industry; DG Coordination – Business Management and Support and Environment; Environmental Quality; Greener Scotland; Marine; On the Ground; Rural; Rural and Environment Research and Analysis; Rural Payments and Inspections; State Veterinary Service
Director-General, Richard Wakeford

EXECUTIVE AGENCIES

Cairngorms National Park Authority
Crofters Commission
Deer Commission Scotland
Loch Lomond and Trossach National Park Authority
Royal Botanic Gardens
Scottish Agricultural Wages Board
Scottish Environmental Protection Agency
Scottish Natural Heritage

HEALTH DEPARTMENT

St Andrew's House, Regent Road, Edinburgh EH1 3DG
Directorates: Chief Medical Officer; Chief Nursing Officer; DG Coordination: Health; Health Delivery; Health Finance; Health Workforce; Healthcare Policy and Strategy; E Health; Equalities, Social Inclusion and Sport; Primary and Community Care; Public Health and Health Improvement; Scottish Academy for Health Policy and Management
Director-General and Chief Executive of NHS Scotland, Dr Kevin Woods

EXECUTIVE AGENCIES
Mental Health Tribunal (Scotland)
Scottish Commission for the Regulation of Care

JUSTICE AND COMMUNITIES DEPARTMENT
St Andrew's House, Regent Road, Edinburgh EH1 3DG
Directorates: Constitution, Law and Courts; Courts; Criminal Justice; DG Coordination – Justice and Communities; Housing and Regeneration; Judicial Appointments Board for Scotland; Office of the Scottish Parliamentary Counsel; Planning and Environmental Appeals; Police and Community Safety; Scottish Government Legal Directorate; Scottish Prisons Complaints Commissioner; SGLD Group A; SGLD Group B; SGLD Group C
Director-General, Robert Gordon, CB

EXECUTIVE AGENCIES
Accountant in Bankruptcy
HM Inspectorate of Constabulary
HMC Inspectorate of Fire Rescue Service
HMC Inspectorate of Prisons
Office of Scottish Charity Regulator
Parole Board for Scotland
Risk Management Authority
Scottish Charity Appeals Panel
Scottish Court Service
Scottish Housing Regulator
Scottish Prison Service

CROWN OFFICE AND PROCURATOR FISCAL SERVICE
29 Chambers Street, Edinburgh EH1 1LD
T 0844-561 2000
Chief Executive and Crown Agent, Norman McFadyen

OFFICE OF THE PERMANENT SECRETARY
St Andrew's House, Regent Road, Edinburgh EH1 3DG
T 0131-244 4028
Permanent Secretary, Sir John Elvidge, KCB

AUDIT SCOTLAND
110 George Street, Edinburgh EH2 4LH
T 0845-146 1010
W www.audit-scotland.gov.uk
Auditor-General, Robert W. Black
Accounts Commission Chair, John Baillie

SCOTTISH PARLIAMENT

Edinburgh EH99 1SP
T 0131-348 5000 Textphone 0800-092 7100
E sp.info@scottish.parliament.uk
W www.scottish.parliament.uk

In July 1997 the government announced plans to establish a Scottish parliament. In a referendum on 11 September 1997 about 60 per cent of the electorate voted. Of those who voted, 74.3 per cent voted in favour of the parliament and 63.5 per cent in favour of it having tax-raising powers. Elections are held every four years. The first elections were held on 6 May 1999, when around 59 per cent of the electorate voted. The first meeting was held on 12 May 1999 and the Scottish parliament was officially opened on 1 July 1999 at the Assembly Hall, Edinburgh. A new building to house parliament was opened, in the presence of the Queen, at Holyrood on 9 October 2004. On 3 May 2007 the third elections to the Scottish parliament took place.

The Scottish parliament has 129 members (including the presiding officer), comprising 73 constituency members and 56 additional regional members, mainly from party lists. It can introduce primary legislation and has the power to raise or lower the basic rate of income tax by up to three pence in the pound. Members of the Scottish Parliament are elected using the additional member system, the same system used to elect London Assembly and Welsh Assembly members.

The areas for which the Scottish parliament is responsible include: education, health, law, environment, economic development, local government, housing, police, fire services, planning, financial assistance to industry, tourism, some transport, heritage and the arts, agriculture, forestry and food standards.

SALARIES *as at 1 April 2009*	
First Minister*	£82,094
Cabinet Secretaries*	£42,588
Lord Advocate*	£55,638
Solicitor-General for Scotland*	£40,233
Ministers*	£26,676
MSPs†	£56,671
Presiding Officer*	£42,588
Deputy Presiding Officer*	£26,676

* In addition to the MSP salary
† Reduced by two-thirds if the member is already an MP or an MEP

MEMBERS OF THE SCOTTISH PARLIAMENT

as at 26 May 2009
Adam, Brian, *SNP, Aberdeen North,* Maj. 3,749
Aitken, Bill, *C., Glasgow region*
Alexander, Wendy, *Lab., Paisley North,* Maj. 5,113
Allan, Alasdair, *SNP, Western Isles,* Maj. 687
Baillie, Jackie, *Lab., Dumbarton,* Maj. 1,611
Baker, Claire, *Lab., Mid Scotland and Fife region*
Baker, Richard, *Lab., North East Scotland region*
Boyack, Sarah, *Lab., Edinburgh Central,* Maj. 1,193
Brankin, Rhona, *Lab., Midlothian,* Maj. 1,702
Brocklebank, Ted, *C., Mid Scotland and Fife region*
Brown, Gavin, *C., Lothians region*
Brown, Keith, *SNP, Ochil,* Maj. 490
Brown, Robert E., *LD, Glasgow region*
Brownlee, Derek, *C., South of Scotland region*
Butler, Bill, *Lab., Glasgow Anniesland,* Maj. 4,306
Campbell, Aileen, *SNP, South of Scotland region*
Carlaw, Jackson, *C., West of Scotland region*
Chisholm, Malcolm, *Lab., Edinburgh North and Leith,* Maj. 2,444
Coffey, Willie, *SNP, Kilmarnock and Loudon,* Maj. 1,342
Constance, Angela, *SNP, Livingston,* Maj. 870
Craigie, Cathie, *Lab., Cumbernauld and Kilsyth,* Maj. 2,079
Crawford, Bruce, *SNP, Stirling,* Maj. 620
Cunningham, Roseanna, *SNP, Perth,* Maj. 2,495
Curran, Margaret, *Lab., Glasgow Baillieston,* Maj. 3,934
Don, Nigel, *SNP, North East Scotland region*
Doris, Bob, *SNP, Glasgow region*
Eadie, Helen, *Lab., Dunfermline East,* Maj. 3,993
Ewing, Fergus, *SNP, Inverness East, Nairn and Lochaber,* Maj. 5,471
Fabiani, Linda, *SNP, Central Scotland region*
Ferguson, Patricia, *Lab., Glasgow Maryhill,* Maj. 2,310
Fergusson, Alex, *C., Galloway and Upper Nithsdale,* Maj. 3,333

Finnie, Ross, *LD, West of Scotland region*
FitzPatrick, Joe, *SNP, Dundee West,* Maj. 1,946
Foulkes, George, *Lab., Lothians region*
Fraser, Murdo, *C., Mid Scotland and Fife region*
Gibson, Kenneth, *SNP, Cunninghame North,* Maj. 48
Gibson, Rob, *SNP, Highlands and Islands region*
Gillon, Karen, *Lab., Clydesdale,* Maj. 2,893
Glen, Marlyn, *Lab., North East Scotland region*
Godman, Trish, *Lab., Renfrewshire West,* Maj. 2,178
Goldie, Annabel, *C., West of Scotland region*
Gordon, Charlie, *Lab., Glasgow Cathcart,* Maj. 2,189
Grahame, Christine, *SNP, South of Scotland region*
Grant, Rhoda, *Lab., Highlands and Islands region*
Gray, Iain, *Lab., East Lothian,* Maj. 2,448
Harper, Robin, *Scot. Green, Lothians region*
Harvie, Christopher, *SNP, Mid Scotland and Fife region*
Harvie, Patrick, *Scot. Green, Glasgow region*
Henry, Hugh, *Lab., Paisley South,* Maj. 4,230
Hepburn, Jamie, *SNP, Central Scotland region*
Hume, Jim, *LD, South of Scotland region*
Hyslop, Fiona, *SNP, Lothians region*
Ingram, Adam, *SNP, South of Scotland region*
Jamieson, Cathy, *Lab., Carrick, Cumnock and Doon Valley,* Maj. 3,986
Johnstone, Alex, *C., North East Scotland region*
Kelly, James, *Lab., Glasgow Rutherglen,* Maj. 4,393
Kerr, Andy, *Lab., East Kilbride,* Maj. 1,972
Kidd, Bill, *SNP, Glasgow region*
Lamont, Johann, *Lab., Glasgow Pollok,* Maj. 4,393
Lamont, John, *C., Roxburgh and Berwickshire,* Maj. 1,985
Livingstone, Marilyn, *Lab., Kirkcaldy,* Maj. 2,622
Lochhead, Richard, *SNP, Moray,* Maj. 7,924
MacAskill, Kenny, *SNP, Edinburgh East and Musselburgh,* Maj. 1,382
Macdonald, Lewis, *Lab., Aberdeen Central,* Maj. 382
MacDonald, Margo, *Ind., Lothians region*
Macintosh, Kenneth, *Lab., Eastwood,* Maj. 913
McArthur, Liam, *LD, Orkney,* Maj. 2,476
McAveety, Frank, *Lab., Glasgow Shettleston,* Maj. 2,881
McCabe, Tom, *Lab., Hamilton South,* Maj. 3,652
McConnell, Jack, *Lab., Motherwell and Wishaw,* Maj. 5,938
McGrigor, Jamie, *C., Highlands and Islands region*
McInnes, Alison, *LD, North East Scotland region*
McKee, Ian, *SNP, Lothians region*
McKelvie, Christina, *SNP, Central Scotland region*
***McLaughlin**, Anne, *SNP, Glasgow*
McLetchie, David, *C., Edinburgh Pentlands,* Maj. 4,525
McMahon, Michael, *Lab., Hamilton North and Bellshill,* Maj. 4,865
McMillan, Stuart, *SNP, West of Scotland region*
McNeil, Duncan, *Lab., Greenock and Inverclyde,* Maj. 3,024
McNeill, Pauline, *Lab., Glasgow Kelvin,* Maj. 1,207
McNulty, Des, *Lab., Clydebank and Milngavie,* Maj. 3,179
Martin, Paul, *Lab., Glasgow Springburn,* Maj. 5,095
Marwick, Tricia, *SNP, Central Fife,* Maj. 1,166
Mather, Jim, *SNP, Argyll and Bute,* Maj. 815
Matheson, Michael, *SNP, Falkirk West,* Maj. 776
Maxwell, Stewart, *SNP, West of Scotland region*
Milne, Nanette, *C., North East Scotland region*
Mitchell, Margaret, *C., Central Scotland region*
Morgan, Alasdair, *SNP, South of Scotland region*
Mulligan, Mary, *Lab., Linlithgow,* Maj. 1,150
Munro, John F., *LD, Ross, Skye and Inverness West,* Maj. 3,486
Murray, Elaine, *Lab., Dumfries,* Maj. 2,839
Neil, Alex, *SNP, Central Scotland region*
O'Donnell, Hugh, *LD, Central Scotland region*
Oldfather, Irene, *Lab., Cunninghame South,* Maj. 2,168
Park, John, *Lab., Mid Scotland and Fife region*
Paterson, Gil, *SNP, West of Scotland region*
Peacock, Peter, *Lab., Highlands and Islands region*
Peattie, Cathy, *Lab., Falkirk East,* Maj. 1,872
Pringle, Michael, *LD, Edinburgh South,* Maj. 1,929
Purvis, Jeremy, *LD, Tweeddale, Ettrick and Lauderdale,* Maj. 598
Robison, Shona, *SNP, Dundee East,* Maj. 4,524
Rumbles, Mike, *LD, Aberdeenshire West and Kincardine,* Maj. 5,170
Russell, Michael, *SNP, South of Scotland region*
Salmond, Alex, *SNP, Gordon,* Maj. 2062
Scanlon, Mary, *C., Highlands and Islands region*
Scott, John, *C., Ayr,* Maj. 3,906
Scott, Tavish, *LD, Shetland,* Maj. 4,909
Simpson, Richard, *Lab., Mid Scotland and Fife region*
Smith, Elaine, *Lab., Coatbridge and Chryston,* Maj. 4,510
Smith, Elizabeth, *C., Mid Scotland and Fife region*
Smith, Iain, *LD, Fife North East,* Maj. 5,016
Smith, Margaret, *LD, Edinburgh West,* Maj. 5,886
†Somerville, Shirley-Anne, *SNP, Lothians region*
Stephen, Nicol, *LD, Aberdeen South,* Maj. 2,732
Stevenson, Stewart, *SNP, Banff and Buchan,* Maj. 10,530
Stewart, David, *Lab., Highlands and Islands region*
Stone, Jamie, *LD, Caithness, Sutherland and Easter Ross,* Maj. 2,323
Sturgeon, Nicola, *SNP, Glasgow Govan,* Maj. 744
Swinney, John, *SNP, North Tayside,* Maj. 7,584
Thompson, Dave, *SNP, Highlands and Islands region*
Tolson, Jim, *LD, Dunfermline West,* Maj. 476
Watt, Maureen, *SNP, North East Scotland region*
Welsh, Andrew, *SNP, Angus,* Maj. 8,243
White, Sandra, *SNP, Glasgow region*
Whitefield, Karen, *Lab., Airdrie and Shotts,* Maj. 1,446
Whitton, David, *Lab., Strathkelvin and Bearsden,* Maj. 3,388
Wilson, Bill, *SNP, West of Scotland region*
Wilson, John, *SNP, Central Scotland region*

* Bashir Ahmad died on 6 February 2009 and was replaced by Anne McLaughlin on 9 February 2009

† Stefan Tymkewycz stepped down after his election to the Scottish parliament and was replaced by Shirley-Anne Somerville on 31 August 2007

STATE OF THE PARTIES *as at 26 May 2009*

	Constituency MSPs	*Regional MSPs*	*Total*
Scottish National Party (SNP)	21	26	47
Scottish Labour Party (Lab.)	37	9	46
Scottish Conservative and Unionist Party (C.)	3	13	16
Scottish Liberal Democrats (LD)	11	5	16
Scottish Green Party (Scot. Green)	0	2	2
Independent (Ind.)	0	1	1
Presiding Officer‡	1	0	1
Total	73	56	129

‡ The presiding officer was elected as a constituency member for the Conservatives but has no party allegiance while in post

The Presiding Officer, Alex Fergusson, MSP
Deputy Presiding Officers, Trish Godman, MSP *(Lab.)*; Alasdair Morgan, MSP *(SNP)*

SCOTTISH PARLIAMENT ELECTION RESULTS

as at 3 May 2007
E. Electorate T. Turnout
See General Election Results for a list of party abbreviations

CONSTITUENCIES
E. 3,899,472 T. 51.7%

ABERDEEN CENTRAL
(Scotland North East Region)
E. 46,588 T. 21,120 (45.33%)

Lewis Macdonald, Lab.	7,232
Karen Shirron, SNP	6,850
John Stewart, LD	4,693
Andrew Jones, C.	2,345

Lab. majority 382 (1.81%)
2.06% swing Lab. to SNP

ABERDEEN NORTH
(Scotland North East Region)
E. 51,507 T. 24,891 (48.33%)

Brian Adam, SNP	11,406
Elaine Thomson, Lab.	7,657
Steve Delaney, LD	3,836
Carol Garvie, C.	1,992

SNP majority 3,749 (15.06%)
6.62% swing Lab. to SNP

ABERDEEN SOUTH
(Scotland North East Region)
E. 56,700 T. 29,885 (52.71%)

Nicol Stephen, LD	10,843
Maureen Watt, SNP	8,111
Rami Okasha, Lab.	5,499
David Davidson, C.	5,432

LD majority 2,732 (9.14%)
11.21% swing LD to SNP

ABERDEENSHIRE WEST AND KINCARDINE
(Scotland North East Region)
E. 65,233 T. 34,823 (53.38%)

Mike Rumbles, LD	14,314
Dennis Robertson, SNP	9,144
Stewart Whyte, C.	8,604
James Noble, Lab.	2,761

LD majority 5,170 (14.85%)
8.48% swing LD to SNP

AIRDRIE AND SHOTTS
(Scotland Central Region)
E. 57,660 T. 27,160 (47.10%)

Karen Whitefield, Lab.	11,907
Sophia Coyle, SNP	10,461
Iain McGill, C.	2,370
Robert Gorrie, LD	1,452
Mev Brown, Scottish Voice	970

Lab. majority 1,446 (5.32%)
15.23% swing Lab. to SNP

ANGUS
(Scotland North East Region)
E. 61,362 T. 31,960 (52.08%)

Andrew Welsh, SNP	15,686
Alex Johnstone, C.	7,443
Doug Bradley, Lab.	5,032
Scott Rennie, LD	3,799

SNP majority 8,243 (25.79%)
1.67% swing C. to SNP

ARGYLL AND BUTE
(Highlands and Islands Region)
E. 48,846 T. 28,792 (58.94%)

Jim Mather, SNP	9,944
George Lyon, LD	9,129
Jamie McGrigor, C.	5,571
Mary Galbraith, Lab.	4,148

SNP majority 815 (2.83%)
9.17% swing LD to SNP

AYR
(Scotland South Region)
E. 55,034 T. 31,025 (56.37%)

John Scott, C.	12,619
John Duncan, Lab.	8,713
Iain White, SNP	7,952
Stuart Ritchie, LD	1,741

C. majority 3,906 (12.59%)
3.30% swing Lab. to C.

BANFF AND BUCHAN
(Scotland North East Region)
E. 56,324 T. 27,285 (48.44%)

Stewart Stevenson, SNP	16,031
Geordie Burnett-Stuart, C.	5,501
Kay Barnett, Lab.	3,136
Alison McInnes, LD	2,617

SNP majority 10,530 (38.59%)
3.30% swing C. to SNP

CAITHNESS, SUTHERLAND AND EASTER ROSS
(Highlands and Islands Region)
E. 41,789 T. 22,334 (53.44%)
LD majority 2,323 (10.40%)
4.38% swing LD to SNP

Jamie Stone, LD	8,981
Rob Gibson, SNP	6,658
John McKendrick, Lab.	3,152
Donald MacDonald, C.	2,586
Gordon Campbell, Ind.	957

CARRICK, CUMNOCK AND DOON VALLEY
(Scotland South Region)
E. 65,166 T. 33,785 (51.84%)

Cathy Jamieson, Lab.	14,350
Adam Ingram, SNP	10,364
Tony Lewis, C.	6,729
Paul McGreal, LD	1,409
Hugh Hill, Ind.	809
Ray Barry, Equal Parenting Alliance	124

Lab. majority 3,986 (11.80%)
9.61% swing Lab. to SNP

CLYDEBANK AND MILNGAVIE
(Scotland West Region)
E. 48,700 T. 26,765 (54.96%)

Des McNulty, Lab.	11,617
Gil Paterson, SNP	8,438
Murray Roxburgh, C.	3,544
Ashay Ghai, LD	3,166

Lab. majority 3,179 (11.88%)
2.61% swing Lab. to SNP

CLYDESDALE
(Scotland South Region)
E. 66,011 T. 33,332 (50.49%)

Karen Gillon, Lab.	13,835
Aileen Campbell, SNP	10,942
Colin McGavigan, C.	5,604
Fraser Grieve, LD	2,951

Lab. majority 2,893 (8.68%)
5.94% swing Lab. to SNP

COATBRIDGE AND CHRYSTON
(Scotland Central Region)
E. 54,423 T. 25,725 (47.27%)

Elaine Smith, Lab.	11,860
Frances McGlinchey, SNP	7,350
Ross Thomson, C.	2,305
Julie McAnulty, Ind.	1,843
Doreen Nisbet, LD	1,519
Gaille McCann, Scottish Voice	848

Lab. majority 4,510 (17.53%)
9.19% swing Lab. to SNP

CUMBERNAULD AND KILSYTH
(Scotland Central Region)
E. 49,197 T. 26,382 (53.63%)

Cathie Craigie, Lab.	12,672
Jamie Hepburn, SNP	10,593
Hugh O'Donnell, LD	1,670
Anne Harding, C.	1,447

Lab. majority 2,079 (7.88%)
2.87% swing SNP to Lab.

CUNNINGHAME NORTH
(Scotland West Region)
E. 55,925 T. 30,241 (54.07%)

Kenneth Gibson, SNP	9,295
Allan Wilson, Lab.	9,247
Philip Lardner, C.	5,466
Campbell Martin, Ind.	4,423
Lewis Hutton, LD	1,810

SNP majority 48 (0.16%)
5.99% swing Lab. to SNP

CUNNINGHAME SOUTH
(Scotland South Region)
E. 49,969 T. 23,422 (46.87%)

Irene Oldfather, Lab.	10,270
Duncan Ross, SNP	8,102
Pat McPhee, C.	3,073
Iain Dale, LD	1,977

Lab. majority 2,168 (9.26%)
8.71% swing Lab. to SNP

DUMBARTON
(Scotland West Region)
E. 54,023 T. 30,054 (55.63%)

Jackie Baillie, Lab.	11,635
Graeme McCormick, SNP	10,024
Brian Pope, C.	4,701
Alex Mackie, LD	3,385
John Black, Scottish Jacobite Party	309

Lab. majority 1,611 (5.36%)
8.79% swing Lab. to SNP

DUMFRIES
(Scotland South Region)
E. 53,518 T. 33,419 (62.44%)

Elaine Murray, Lab.	13,707
Murray Tosh, C.	10,868
Michael Russell, SNP	6,306
Lynne Hume, LD	2,538

Lab. majority 2,839 (8.50%)
2.54% swing C. to Lab.

DUNDEE EAST
(Scotland North East Region)
E. 53,804 T. 26,869 (49.94%)

Shona Robison, SNP	13,314
Iain Luke, Lab.	8,790
Chris Bustin, C.	2,976
Clive Sneddon, LD	1,789

SNP majority 4,524 (16.84%)
8.25% swing Lab. to SNP

DUNDEE WEST
(Scotland North East Region)
E. 49,711 T. 24,268 (48.82%)

Joe Fitzpatrick, SNP	10,955
Jill Shimi, Lab.	9,009
Michael Charlton, LD	2,517
Belinda Don, C.	1,787

SNP majority 1,946 (8.02%)
6.14% swing Lab. to SNP

DUNFERMLINE EAST
(Scotland Mid and Fife Region)
E. 51,115 T. 24,568 (48.06%)

Helen Eadie, Lab.	10,995
Ewan Dow, SNP	7,002
Graeme Brown, C.	3,718
Karen Utting, LD	2,853

Lab. majority 3,993 (16.25%)
7.62% swing Lab. to SNP

DUNFERMLINE WEST
(Scotland Mid and Fife Region)
E. 56,953 T. 29,525 (51.84%)

Jim Tolson, LD	9,952
Scott Barrie, Lab.	9,476
Len Woods, SNP	7,296
Peter Lyburn, C.	2,363
Susan Archibald, Scottish Voice	438

LD majority 476 (1.61%)
10.77% swing Lab. to LD

EAST KILBRIDE
(Scotland Central Region)
E. 66,935 T. 35,902 (53.64%)

Andy Kerr, Lab.	15,334
Linda Fabiani, SNP	13,362
Graham Simpson, C.	4,114
David Clark, LD	3,092

Lab. majority 1,972 (5.49%)
5.00% swing Lab. to SNP

EAST LOTHIAN
(Scotland South Region)
E. 61,378 T. 34,471 (56.16%)

Iain Gray, Lab.	12,219
Andrew Sharp, SNP	9,771
Judy Hayman, LD	6,249
Bill Stevenson, C.	6,232

Lab. majority 2,448 (7.10%)
10.08% swing Lab. to SNP

EASTWOOD
(Scotland West Region)
E. 67,347 T. 42,187 (62.64%)

Ken Macintosh, Lab.	15,099
Jackson Carlaw, C.	14,186
Stewart Maxwell, SNP	7,972
Gordon MacDonald, LD	3,603
Frank McGhee, Ind.	1,327

Lab. majority 913 (2.16%)
3.68% swing Lab. to C.

EDINBURGH CENTRAL
(Lothians Region)
E. 55,953 T. 29,396 (52.54%)

Sarah Boyack, Lab.	9,155
Siobhan Mathers, LD	7,962
Shirley-Anne Somerville, SNP	7,496
Fiona Houston, C.	4,783

Lab. majority 1,193 (4.06%)
2.73% swing Lab. to LD

EDINBURGH EAST AND MUSSELBURGH
(Lothians Region)
E. 56,578 T. 29,967 (52.97%)

Kenny MacAskill, SNP	11,209
Norman Murray, Lab.	9,827
Gillian Cole-Hamilton, LD	5,473
Christine Wright, C.	3,458

SNP majority 1,382 (4.61%)
12.91% swing Lab. to SNP

EDINBURGH NORTH AND LEITH
(Lothians Region)
E. 60,340 T. 31,685 (52.51%)

Malcolm Chisholm, Lab.	11,020
Mike Crockart, LD	8,576
Davie Hutchison, SNP	8,044
Iain Whyte, C.	4,045

Lab. majority 2,444 (7.71%)
6.92% swing Lab. to LD

EDINBURGH PENTLANDS
(Lothians Region)
E. 57,891 T. 34,377 (59.38%)

David McLetchie, C.	12,927
Sheila Gilmore, Lab.	8,402
Ian McKee, SNP	8,234
Simon Clark, LD	4,814

C. majority 4,525 (13.16%)
3.42% swing Lab. to C.

EDINBURGH SOUTH
(Lothians Region)
E. 57,621 T. 32,573 (56.53%)

Mike Pringle, LD	11,398
Donald Anderson, Lab.	9,469
Robert Holland, SNP	6,117
Gavin Brown, C.	5,589

LD majority 1,929 (5.92%)
2.71% swing Lab. to LD

EDINBURGH WEST
(Lothians Region)
E. 59,814 T. 34,752 (58.10%)

Margaret Smith, LD	13,677
Sheena Cleland, SNP	7,791
Gordon Lindhurst, C.	7,361
Richard Meade, Lab.	5,343
John Wilson, Ind.	580

LD majority 5,886 (16.94%)
7.00% swing LD to SNP

FALKIRK EAST
(Scotland Central Region)
E. 57,663 T. 30,333 (52.60%)

Cathy Peattie, Lab.	13,184
Annabelle Ewing, SNP	11,312
Scott Campbell, C.	3,701
Natalie Maver, LD	2,136

Lab. majority 1,872 (6.17%)
9.00% swing Lab. to SNP

FALKIRK WEST
(Scotland Central Region)
E. 56,254 T. 28,785 (51.17%)

Michael Matheson, SNP	12,068
Dennis Goldie, Lab.	11,292
Stephen O'Rourke, C.	2,887
Callum Chomczuk, LD	2,538

SNP majority 776 (2.70%)
1.13% swing Lab. to SNP

FIFE CENTRAL
(Scotland Mid and Fife Region)
E. 58,215 T. 26,965 (46.32%)

Tricia Marwick, SNP	11,920
Christine May, Lab.	10,754
Elizabeth Riches, LD	2,288
Maurice Golden, C.	2,003

SNP majority 1,166 (4.32%)
7.56% swing Lab. to SNP

FIFE NORTH EAST
(Scotland Mid and Fife Region)
E. 61,078 T. 31,552 (51.66%)

Iain Smith, LD	13,307
Ted Brocklebank, C.	8,291
Roderick Campbell, SNP	6,735
Kenny Young, Lab.	2,557
Tony Campbell, Ind.	662

LD majority 5,016 (15.90%)
0.68% swing LD to C.

GALLOWAY AND UPPER NITHSDALE
(Scotland South Region)
E. 52,583 T. 30,318 (57.66%)

Alex Fergusson, C.	13,387
Alasdair Morgan, SNP	10,054
Stephen Hodgson, Lab.	4,935
Alastair Cooper, LD	1,631
Sandy Richardson, Ind.	311

C. majority 3,333 (10.99%)
5.33% swing SNP to C.

GLASGOW ANNIESLAND
(Glasgow Region)
E. 48,344 T. 22,139 (45.79%)

Bill Butler, Lab.	10,483
Bill Kidd, SNP	6,177
Bill Aitken, C.	3,154
Danica Gilland, LD	2,325

Lab. majority 4,306 (19.45%)
4.38% swing Lab. to SNP

GLASGOW BAILLIESTON
(Glasgow Region)
E. 44,367 T. 17,272 (38.93%)

Margaret Curran, Lab.	9,141
Lachie McNeill, SNP	5,207
Richard Sullivan, C.	1,276
David Jackson, LD	1,060
George Hargreaves, Scottish Christian Party	588

Lab. majority 3,934 (22.78%)
5.52% swing Lab. to SNP

GLASGOW CATHCART
(Glasgow Region)
E. 47,822 T. 21,657 (45.29%)

Charlie Gordon, Lab.	8,476
James Dornan, SNP	6,287
David Smith, Ind.	2,911
Davena Rankin, C.	2,324
Shabnum Mustapha, LD	1,659

Lab. majority 2,189 (10.11%)
6.40% swing Lab. to SNP

GLASGOW GOVAN
(Glasgow Region)
E. 47,405 T. 21,521 (45.40%)

Nicola Sturgeon, SNP	9,010
Gordon Jackson, Lab.	8,266
Chris Young, LD	1,091
Martyn McIntyre, C.	1,680
Asif Nasir, Ind.	423
Elinor McKenzie, Comm. Brit.	251

SNP majority 744 (3.46%)
4.65% swing Lab. to SNP

GLASGOW KELVIN
(Glasgow Region)
E. 55,096 T. 23,500 (42.65%)

Pauline McNeill, Lab.	7,875
Sandra White, SNP	6,668
Martin Bartos, Green	2,971
Katy Gordon, LD	2,843
Brian Cooklin, C.	1,943
Niall Walker, Ind.	744
Isobel Macleod, Scottish Christian Party	456

Lab. majority 1,207 (5.14%)
4.88% swing Lab. to SNP

GLASGOW MARYHILL
(Glasgow Region)
E. 46,060 T. 16,564 (35.96%)

Patricia Ferguson, Lab.	7,955
Bob Doris, SNP	5,645
Kenn Elder, LD	1,936
Heather MacLeod, C.	1,028

Lab. majority 2,310 (13.95%)
7.74% swing Lab. to SNP

GLASGOW POLLOK
(Glasgow Region)
E. 47,189 T. 19,416 (41.15%)

Johann Lamont, Lab.	10,456
Chris Stephens, SNP	6,063
Gerald Michaluk, C.	1,460
Christine Gilmore, LD	1,437

Lab. majority 4,393 (22.63%)
0.85% swing Lab. to SNP

GLASGOW RUTHERGLEN
(Glasgow Region)
E. 50,005 T. 24,252 (48.50%)

James Kelly, Lab.	10,237
Margaret Park, SNP	5,857
Robert Brown, LD	5,516
Christina Harcus, C.	2,094
Tom Greig, Scottish Christian Party	548

Lab. majority 4,380 (18.06%)
6.43% swing Lab. to SNP

GLASGOW SHETTLESTON
(Glasgow Region)
E. 44,278 T. 14,801 (33.43%)

Frank McAveety, Lab.	7,574
John McLaughlin, SNP	4,693
Ross Renton, LD	1,182
William MacNair, C.	946
Bob Graham, Scottish Christian Party	406

Lab. majority 2,881 (19.46%)
9.45% swing Lab. to SNP

GLASGOW SPRINGBURN
(Glasgow Region)
E. 47,021 T. 17,612 (37.46%)

Paul Martin, Lab.	10,024
Anne McLaughlin, SNP	4,929
Katy McCloskey, LD	1,108
Gordon Wilson, C.	1,067
David Johnston, Scottish Christian Party	404

Lab. majority 5,095 (28.93%)
7.09% swing Lab. to SNP

GORDON
(Scotland North East Region)
E. 65,431 T. 35,363 (54.05%)

Alex Salmond, SNP	14,650
Nora Radcliffe, LD	12,588
Nanette Milne, C.	5,348
Neil Cardwell, Lab.	2,276
Donald Marr, Ind.	199
Dave Mathers, Ind.	185
Bob Ingram, Scottish Enterprise Party	117

SNP majority 2,062 (5.83%)
10.66% swing LD to SNP

GREENOCK AND INVERCLYDE
(Scotland West Region)
E. 44,646 T. 23,105 (51.75%)

Duncan McNeil, Lab.	10,035
Stuart McMillan, SNP	7,011
Ross Finnie, LD	3,893
Charles Ferguson, C.	2,166

Lab. majority 3,024 (13.09%)
6.37% swing Lab. to SNP

HAMILTON NORTH AND BELLSHILL
(Scotland Central Region)
E. 53,854 T. 25,366 (47.10%)

Michael McMahon, Lab.	12,334
Alex Neil, SNP	7,469
James Callander, C.	2,835
Douglas Herbison, LD	1,726
Joe Gorman, Scottish Voice	571
Gordon Weir, Ind.	431

Lab. majority 4,865 (19.18%)
6.75% swing Lab. to SNP

HAMILTON SOUTH
(Scotland Central Region)
E. 48,838 T. 23,211 (47.53%)

Tom McCabe, Lab.	10,280
Christina McKelvie, SNP	6,628
Margaret Mitchell, C.	2,929
Michael McGlynn, Ind.	1,764
John Oswald, LD	1,610

Lab. majority 3,652 (15.73%)
3.89% swing Lab. to SNP

INVERNESS EAST, NAIRN AND LOCHABER
(Highlands and Islands Region)
E. 71,609 T. 39,609 (55.31%)

Fergus Ewing, SNP	16,443
Craig Harrow, LD	10,972
Linda Stewart, Lab.	7,559
Jamie Halcro-Johnston, C.	4,635

SNP majority 5,471 (13.81%)
0.48% swing SNP to LD

KILMARNOCK AND LOUDOUN
(Scotland Central Region)
E. 60,753 T. 33,435 (55.03%)

Willie Coffey, SNP	14,297
Margaret Jamieson, Lab.	12,955
Janette McAlpine, C.	4,127
Ron Aitken, LD	2,056

SNP majority 1,342 (4.01%)
3.93% swing Lab. to SNP

KIRKCALDY
(Scotland Mid and Fife Region)
E. 50,761 T. 24,195 (47.66%)

Marilyn Livingstone, Lab.	10,627
Chris Harvie, SNP	8,005
Alice Soper, LD	3,361
David Potts, C.	2,202

Lab. majority 2,622 (10.84%)
5.58% swing Lab. to SNP

LINLITHGOW
(Lothians Region)
E. 56,175 T. 29,637 (52.76%)

Mary Mulligan, Lab.	12,715
Fiona Hyslop, SNP	11,565
Donald Cameron, C.	3,125
Martin Oliver, LD	2,232

Lab. majority 1,150 (3.88%)
1.62% swing Lab. to SNP

LIVINGSTON
(Lothians Region)
E. 66,348 T. 33,224 (50.08%)

Angela Constance, SNP	13,159
Bristow Muldoon, Lab.	12,289
Ernie Walker, Action to Save St John's Hospital	2,814
David Brown, C.	2,804
Evan Bell, LD	2,158

SNP majority 870 (2.62%)
7.31% swing Lab. to SNP

MIDLOTHIAN
(Lothians Region)
E. 48,395 T. 25,111 (51.89%)

Rhona Brankin, Lab.	10,671
Colin Beattie, SNP	8,969
Ross Laird, LD	2,704
P. J. Lewis, C.	2,269
George McCleery, Had Enough Party	498

Lab. majority 1,702 (6.78%)
8.37% swing Lab. to SNP

MORAY
(Highlands and Islands Region)
E. 60,959 T. 30,274 (49.66%)

Richard Lochhead, SNP	15,045
Mary Scanlon, C.	7,121
Lee Butcher, Lab.	4,580
Dominique Rommel, LD	3,528

SNP majority 7,924 (26.17%)
3.24% swing C. to SNP

MOTHERWELL AND WISHAW
(Scotland Central Region)
E. 53,875 T. 26,150 (48.54%)

Jack McConnell, Lab.	12,574
Marion Fellows, SNP	6,636
Diane Huddleston, C.	1,990
John Swinburne, SSCUP	1,702
Stuart Douglas, LD	1,570
Tom Selfridge, Scottish Christian Party	1,491
Richard Leat, Anti-Trident Party	187

Lab. majority 5,938 (22.71%)
6.88% swing Lab. to SNP

OCHIL
(Scotland Mid and Fife Region)
E. 58,104 T. 31,553 (54.30%)

Keith Brown, SNP	12,147
Brian Fearon, Lab.	11,657
George Murray, C.	4,284
Lorraine Caddell, LD	3,465

SNP majority 490 (1.55%)
0.29% swing Lab. to SNP

ORKNEY
(Highlands and Islands Region)
E. 16,195 T. 8,653 (53.43%)

Liam McArthur, LD	4,113
John Mowat, SNP	1,637
Helen Gardiner, C.	1,632
Iain MacDonald, Lab.	1,134
Barrie Johnson, Ind.	137

LD majority 2,476 (28.61%)
1.95% swing LD to SNP

PAISLEY NORTH
(Scotland West Region)
E. 44,081 T. 23,206 (52.64%)

Wendy Alexander, Lab.	12,111
Andy Doig, SNP	6,998
Malcolm MacAskill, C.	1,721
Angela McGarrigle, LD	1,570
Iain Hogg, SSP	525
John Plott, Ind.	281

Lab. majority 5,113 (22.03%)
1.31% swing SNP to Lab.

PAISLEY SOUTH
(Scotland West Region)
E. 49,175 T. 25,527 (51.91%)

Hugh Henry, Lab.	12,123
Fiona McLeod, SNP	7,893
Eileen McCartin, LD	3,434
Tom Begg, C.	2,077

Lab. majority 4,230 (16.57%)
3.38% swing SNP to Lab.

PERTH
(Scotland and Mid Fife Region)
E. 62,220 T. 34,862 (56.03%)

Roseanna Cunningham, SNP	13,751
Liz Smith, C.	11,256
Peter Barrett, LD	4,767
Doug Maughan, Lab.	4,513
Jim Fairlie, Free Scot.	575

SNP majority 2,495 (7.16%)
2.43% swing C. to SNP

RENFREWSHIRE WEST
(Scotland West Region)
E. 50,787 T. 29,129 (57.36%)

Trish Godman, Lab.	10,467
Annabel Goldie, C.	8,289
Bill Wilson, SNP	8,167
Simon Hutton, LD	2,206

Lab. majority 2,178 (7.48%)
1.22% swing Lab. to C.

ROSS, SKYE AND INVERNESS WEST
(Highlands and Islands Region)
E. 59,237 T. 31,719 (53.55%)

John Farquhar Munro, LD	13,501
Dave Thompson, SNP	10,015
Maureen Macmillan, Lab.	4,789
John Hodgson, C.	3,122
Iain Brodie, Scottish Enterprise Party	292

LD majority 3,486 (10.99%)
6.32% swing LD to SNP

ROXBURGH AND BERWICKSHIRE
(Scotland South Region)
E. 47,862 T. 25,680 (53.65%)

John Lamont, C.	10,556
Euan Robson, LD	8,571
Aileen Orr, SNP	4,127
Mary Lockhart, Lab.	2,108
Jesse Rae, No Description	318

C. majority 1,985 (7.73%)
9.40% swing LD to C.

SHETLAND
(Highlands and Islands Region)
E. 17,108 T. 9,795 (57.25%)

Tavish Scott, LD	6,531
Val Simpson, SNP	1,622
Mark Jones, C.	972
Scott Burnett, Lab.	670

LD majority 4,909 (50.12%)
11.99% swing SNP to LD

STIRLING
(Scotland and Mid Fife Region)
E. 52,864 T. 32,625 (61.71%)

Bruce Crawford, SNP	10,447
Sylvia Jackson, Lab.	9,827
Bob Dalrymple, C.	8,081
Alex Cole-Hamilton, LD	3,693
Liz Law, Peace Party	577

SNP majority 620 (1.90%)
9.41% swing Lab. to SNP

STRATHKELVIN AND BEARSDEN
(Scotland West Region)
E. 60,389 T. 36,595 (60.60%)

David Whitton, Lab.	11,396
Robin Easton, SNP	8,008
Jean Turner, Ind.	6,742
Stephanie Fraser, C.	5,178
Cathy McInnes, LD	4,658
Bob Handyside, Scottish Christian Party	613

Lab. majority 3,388 (9.26%)
3.91% swing Lab. to SNP

TAYSIDE NORTH
(Scotland Mid and Fife Region)
E. 62,133 T. 35,396 (56.97%)

John Swinney, SNP	18,281
Murdo Fraser, C.	10,697
Michael Marna, Lab.	3,243
James Taylor, LD	3,175

SNP majority 7,584 (21.43%)
3.96% swing C. to SNP

TWEEDDALE, ETTRICK AND LAUDERDALE
(Scotland South Region)
E. 53,588 T. 30,327 (56.59%)

Jeremy Purvis, LD	10,656
Christine Grahame, SNP	10,058
Derek Brownlee, C.	5,594
Catherine Maxwell-Stuart, Lab.	4,019

LD majority 598 (1.97%)
0.02% swing LD to SNP

WESTERN ISLES
(Highlands and Islands Region)
E. 22,051 T. 13,625 (61.79%)

Alasdair Allan, SNP	6,354
Alasdair Morrison, Lab.	5,667
Ruaraidh Ferguson, LD	852
Dave Petrie, C.	752

SNP majority 687 (5.04%)
5.43% swing Lab. to SNP

REGIONS
E. 3,899,472 T. 52.4%

GLASGOW
E. 477,587 T. 206,618 (43.26%)

Lab.	78,838	(38.16%)
SNP	55,832	(27.02%)
LD	14,767	(7.15%)
C.	13,781	(6.67%)
Green	10,759	(5.21%)
Solidarity	8,525	(4.13%)
BNP	3,865	(1.87%)
SSCUP	3,703	(1.79%)
Scottish Christian Party	2,991	(1.45%)
Soc. Lab.	2,680	(1.30%)
CPA	2,626	(1.27%)
SSP	2,579	(1.25%)
Scottish Unionist Party	1,612	(0.78%)
Publican Party Smoking-Room in Pubs	952	(0.46%)
Ind. Shoaib	582	(0.28%)
Ind. Green	496	(0.24%)
UKIP	405	(0.20%)
Scottish Voice	389	(0.19%)
Ind. Nasir	317	(0.15%)
Scotland Against Crooked Lawyers	293	(0.14%)
Ind.	286	(0.14%)
Comm. Brit.	260	(0.13%)
Nine Per Cent Growth Party	80	(0.04%)

Lab. majority 23,006 (11.13%)
4.75% swing Lab. to SNP (2003 Lab. majority 42,146)

ADDITIONAL MEMBERS
Bill Aitken, *C.*
Robert Brown, *LD*
Bashir Ahmad, *SNP*
Sandra White, *SNP*
Bob Doris, *SNP*
Bill Kidd, *SNP*
Patrick Harvie, *Green*

HIGHLANDS AND ISLANDS
E. 337,794 T. 185,773 (55.00%)

SNP	63,979	(34.44%)
LD	37,001	(19.92%)
Lab.	32,952	(17.74%)
C.	23,334	(12.56%)
Green	8,602	(4.63%)
Scottish Christian Party	6,332	(3.41%)
SSCUP	3,841	(2.07%)
BNP	2,152	(1.16%)
Solidarity	1,833	(0.99%)
UKIP	1,287	(0.69%)
Soc. Lab.	1,027	(0.55%)
SSP	973	(0.52%)
Publican Party Smoking-Room in Pubs	914	(0.49%)
CPA	885	(0.48%)
Scottish Voice	450	(0.24%)
Scottish Enterprise Party	211	(0.11%)

SNP majority 26,978 (14.52%)
4.94% swing LD to SNP (2003 SNP majority 1,892)

ADDITIONAL MEMBERS
Mary Scanlon, *C.*
Jamie McGrigor, *C.*
Peter Peacock, *Lab.*
Rhoda Grant, *Lab.*
David Stewart, *Lab.*
Rob Gibson, *SNP*
Dave Thompson, *SNP*

LOTHIANS
E. 519,115 T. 287,039 (55.29%)

SNP	76,019	(26.48%)
Lab.	75,495	(26.30%)
C.	37,548	(13.08%)
LD	36,571	(12.74%)
Green	20,147	(7.02%)
Ind.	19,256	(6.71%)
SSCUP	4,176	(1.45%)
Solidarity	2,998	(1.04%)
BNP	2,637	(0.92%)
Soc. Lab.	2,190	(0.76%)
Scottish Christian Party	2,002	(0.70%)
SSP	1,994	(0.69%)
Publican Party Smoking-Room in Pubs	1,230	(0.43%)
Witchery Tour Party	867	(0.30%)
CPA	848	(0.30%)
UKIP	834	(0.29%)
Had Enough Party	670	(0.23%)
Scottish Voice	661	(0.23%)
Scotland Against Crooked Lawyers	322	(0.11%)
Ind. Scott	189	(0.07%)
Scottish Enterprise Party	183	(0.06%)
Ind. Wilson	129	(0.04%)
Ind. Thorp	73	(0.03%)

SNP majority 524 (0.18%)
4.22% swing Lab. to SNP (2003 Lab. majority 21,960)

ADDITIONAL MEMBERS
Gavin Brown, *C.*
George Foulkes, *Lab.*
Fiona Hyslop, *SNP*
Ian McKee, *SNP*
Stefan Tymkewycz, *SNP*
Robin Harper, *Green*
Margo MacDonald, *Ind.*

SCOTLAND CENTRAL
E. 559,452 T. 284,512 (50.86%)

Lab.	112,596	(39.58%)
SNP	89,210	(31.36%)
C.	24,253	(8.52%)
LD	14,648	(5.15%)
Green	7,204	(2.53%)
SSCUP	7,060	(2.48%)
Scottish Christian Party	5,575	(1.96%)
Solidarity	5,012	(1.76%)
CPA	4,617	(1.62%)
BNP	4,125	(1.45%)
Soc. Lab.	2,303	(0.81%)
SSP	2,188	(0.77%)
Scottish Voice	1,955	(0.69%)
Scottish Unionist Party	1,544	(0.54%)
Publican Party Smoking-Room in Pubs	1,500	(0.53%)
UKIP	722	(0.25%)

Lab. majority 23,386 (8.22%)
4.83% swing Lab. to SNP (2003 Lab. majority 47,044)

ADDITIONAL MEMBERS
Margaret Mitchell, *C.*
Hugh O'Donnell, *LD*
Alex Neil, *SNP*
Linda Fabiani, *SNP*
Jamie Hepburn, *SNP*
Christina McKelvie, *SNP*
John Wilson, *SNP*

SCOTLAND MID AND FIFE
E. 513,443 T. 273,083 (53.19%)

SNP	90,090 (32.99%)
Lab.	71,922 (26.34%)
C.	44,341 (16.24%)
LD	36,195 (13.25%)
Green	10,318 (3.78%)
SSCUP	5,523 (2.02%)
BNP	2,620 (0.96%)
Solidarity	2,468 (0.90%)
Scottish Christian Party	1,698 (0.62%)
UKIP	1,587 (0.58%)
Soc. Lab.	1,523 (0.56%)
Publican Party Smoking-Room in Pubs	1,309 (0.48%)
SSP	1,116 (0.41%)
Scottish Voice	919 (0.34%)
CPA	790 (0.29%)
Free Scotland Party	664 (0.24%)

SNP majority 18,168 (6.65%)
4.45% swing Lab. to SNP (2003 Lab. majority 5,608)

ADDITIONAL MEMBERS
Murdo Fraser, *C.*
Liz Smith, *C.*
Ted Brocklebank, *C.*
John Park, *Lab.*
Claire Baker, *Lab.*
Richard Simpson, *Lab.*
Chris Harvie, *SNP*

SCOTLAND NORTH EAST
E. 506,660 T. 256,282 (50.58%)

SNP	105,265 (41.07%)
Lab.	52,125 (20.34%)
LD	40,934 (15.97%)
C.	37,666 (14.70%)
Green	8,148 (3.18%)
BNP	2,764 (1.08%)
Solidarity	2,004 (0.78%)
Scottish Christian Party	1,895 (0.74%)
CPA	1,173 (0.46%)
SSP	1,051 (0.41%)
UKIP	1,045 (0.41%)
SSCUP	930 (0.36%)
Scottish Voice	569 (0.22%)
Soc. Lab.	491 (0.19%)
Scottish Enterprise Party	222 (0.09%)

SNP majority 53,140 (20.73%)
6.82% swing Lab. to SNP (2003 SNP majority 17,274)

ADDITIONAL MEMBERS
Alex Johnstone, *C.*
Nanette Milne, *C.*
Richard Baker, *Lab.*
Marlyn Glen, *Lab.*
Alison McInnes, *LD*
Maureen Watt, *SNP*
Nigel Don, *SNP*

SCOTLAND SOUTH
E. 514,105 T. 276,910 (53.86%)

Lab.	79,762 (28.80%)
SNP	77,053 (27.83%)
C.	62,475 (22.56%)
LD	28,040 (10.13%)
Green	9,254 (3.34%)
SSCUP	5,335 (1.93%)
Solidarity	3,433 (1.24%)
BNP	3,212 (1.16%)
Scottish Christian Party	2,353 (0.85%)
Soc. Lab.	1,633 (0.59%)
UKIP	1,429 (0.52%)
SSP	1,114 (0.40%)
CPA	839 (0.30%)
Scottish Voice	490 (0.18%)
Ind.	488 (0.18%)

Lab. majority 2,709 (0.98%)
5.32% swing Lab. to SNP (2003 Lab. majority 15,128)

ADDITIONAL MEMBERS
Derek Brownlee, *C.*
Jim Hume, *LD*
Christine Grahame, *SNP*
Michael Russell, *SNP*
Adam Ingram, *SNP*
Alasdair Morgan, *SNP*
Aileen Campbell, *SNP*

SCOTLAND WEST
E. 475,073 T. 268,179 (56.45%)

Lab.	91,725 (34.20%)
SNP	75,953 (28.32%)
C.	40,637 (15.15%)
LD	22,515 (8.40%)
Green	8,152 (3.04%)
SSCUP	5,231 (1.95%)
Solidarity	4,774 (1.78%)
Scottish Christian Party	3,729 (1.39%)
BNP	3,241 (1.21%)
CPA	3,027 (1.13%)
Save Our NHS Group	2,682 (1.00%)
SSP	1,716 (0.64%)
Soc. Lab.	1,557 (0.58%)
Scottish Unionist Party	1,245 (0.46%)
UKIP	888 (0.33%)
Scottish Voice	522 (0.19%)
Scottish Jacobite Party	446 (0.17%)
Socialist Equality Party	139 (0.05%)

Lab. majority 15,772 (5.88%)
2.70% swing Lab. to SNP (2003 Lab. majority 12,351)

ADDITIONAL MEMBERS
Annabel Goldie, *C.*
Jackson Carlaw, *C.*
Ross Finnie, *LD*
Stewart Maxwell, *SNP*
Gil Paterson, *SNP*
Bill Wilson, *SNP*
Stuart McMillan, *SNP*

NORTHERN IRELAND

NORTHERN IRELAND EXECUTIVE

Stormont Castle, Stormont, Belfast BT4 3TT
T 028-9052 0700
W www.northernireland.gov.uk

The first minister and deputy first minister head the executive committee of ministers and, acting jointly, determine the total number of ministers in the executive. First and deputy first ministers are elected by Northern Ireland assembly members through a formula of parallel consent that requires a majority of designated unionists, a majority of designated nationalists and a majority of the whole assembly to vote in favour. The parties elected to the assembly select ministerial portfolios in proportion to party strengths using the d'Hondt nominating procedure.

The executive committee includes five DUP ministers, four SF ministers, two Ulster Unionist members, one Social Democratic and Labour Party minister alongside the first minister Peter Robinson, MLA of the DUP and the deputy first minister, Martin McGuinness, MLA, of SF.

EXECUTIVE COMMITTEE

First Minister, Rt. Hon. Peter Robinson, MP, MLA
Deputy First Minister, Martin McGuinness, MP, MLA
Junior Ministers, Gerry Kelly, MLA; Rt. Hon. Jeffrey Donaldson, MP, MLA
Minister for Agriculture and Rural Development, Michelle Gildernew, MP, MLA
Minister for Culture, Arts and Leisure, Gregory Campbell, MP, MLA
Minister for Education, Caitriona Ruane, MLA
Minister for Employment and Learning, Sir Reg Empey, MLA
Minister for Enterprise, Trade and Investment, Arlene Foster, MLA
Minister for Environment, Sammy Wilson, MP, MLA
Minister for Finance and Personnel, Nigel Dodds, OBE, MP, MLA
Minister for Health, Social Services and Public Safety, Michael McGimpsey, MLA
Minister for Regional Development, Conor Murphy, MP, MLA
Minister for Social Development, Margaret Ritchie, MLA

OFFICE OF THE FIRST MINISTER AND DEPUTY FIRST MINISTER

Stormont Castle, Stormont, Belfast BT4 3TT
T 028-9052 8400 W www.ofmdfmni.gov.uk

DEPARTMENT OF AGRICULTURE AND RURAL DEVELOPMENT

Dundonald House, Upper Newtownards Road, Belfast BT4 3SB
T 028-9052 4420 W www.dardni.gov.uk

EXECUTIVE AGENCIES
Forest Service
Rivers Agency

DEPARTMENT OF CULTURE, ARTS AND LEISURE

Causeway Exchange, 1–7 Bedford Street, Belfast BT1 7FB
T 028-9025 8825 W www.dcalni.gov.uk

EXECUTIVE AGENCY
Public Record Office of Northern Ireland

DEPARTMENT OF EDUCATION

Rathgael House, Balloo Road, Bangor, Co. Down BT19 7PR
T 028-9127 9279 W www.deni.gov.uk

DEPARTMENT FOR EMPLOYMENT AND LEARNING

Adelaide House, 39–49 Adelaide Street, Belfast BT2 8FD
T 028-9025 7777 W www.delni.gov.uk

DEPARTMENT OF ENTERPRISE, TRADE AND INVESTMENT

Netherleigh, Massey Avenue, Belfast BT4 2JP T 028-9052 9900
W www.detini.gov.uk

EXECUTIVE AGENCIES
General Consumer Council for Northern Ireland
Health and Safety Executive
Invest Northern Ireland
Northern Ireland Tourist Board

DEPARTMENT OF THE ENVIRONMENT

Clarence Court, 10–18 Adelaide Street, Belfast BT2 8GB
T 028-9054 0540 W www.doeni.gov.uk

EXECUTIVE AGENCIES
Driver and Vehicle Agency (Northern Ireland)
Environment and Heritage Service
Planning Service

DEPARTMENT OF FINANCE AND PERSONNEL

Rathgael House, Balloo Road, Bangor BT19 7PR
T 028-9185 8111 W www.dfpni.gov.uk

EXECUTIVE AGENCIES
Northern Ireland Statistics and Research Agency (Incorporates Land Registers of Northern Ireland and Ordnance Survey of Northern Ireland)
Land and Property Services

DEPARTMENT OF HEALTH, SOCIAL SERVICES AND PUBLIC SAFETY

Castle Buildings, Stormont, Belfast BT4 3SJ T 028-9052 0500
W www.dhsspsni.gov.uk

EXECUTIVE AGENCY
Northern Ireland Health and Social Services Estate Agency

DEPARTMENT FOR REGIONAL DEVELOPMENT

Clarence Court, 10–18 Adelaide Street, Belfast BT2 8GB
T 028-9054 0540 W www.drdni.gov.uk

EXECUTIVE AGENCY
Roads Agency

DEPARTMENT FOR SOCIAL DEVELOPMENT

Lighthouse Building, 1 Cromac Place, Gasworks Business Park, Ormeau Road, Belfast BT7 2JB T 028-9082 9028
W www.dsdni.gov.uk

EXECUTIVE AGENCY
Northern Ireland Housing Executive

NORTHERN IRELAND AUDIT OFFICE

106 University Street, Belfast BT7 1EU
T 028-9025 1000
E info@niauditoffice.gov.uk W www.niauditoffice.gov.uk
Comptroller and Auditor-General for Northern Ireland, J. M. Dowdall, CB

NORTHERN IRELAND AUTHORITY FOR UTILITY REGULATION
Queens House, 14 Queen Street, Belfast BT1 6ER
T 028-9031 1575
W www.niaur.gov.uk
Chair, Prof. Peter Matthews

NORTHERN IRELAND ASSEMBLY

Parliament Buildings, Stormont, Belfast BT4 3XX
T 028-9052 1333
W www.niassembly.gov.uk

The Northern Ireland Assembly was established as a result of the Belfast Agreement (also known as the Good Friday Agreement) in April 1998. The agreement was endorsed through a referendum held in May 1998 and subsequently given legal force through the Northern Ireland Act 1998.

The Northern Ireland Assembly has full legislative and executive authority for all matters that are the responsibility of the government's Northern Ireland departments – known as transferred matters. Excepted and reserved matters are defined in schedules 2 and 3 of the Northern Ireland Act 1998 and remain the responsibility of UK parliament.

The first assembly election occurred on 25 June 1998 and the 108 members elected met for the first time on 1 July 1998. Members of the Northern Ireland Assembly are elected by the single transferable vote system from 18 constituencies – six per constituency. Under the single transferable vote system every voter has a single vote that can be transferred from one candidate to another. Voters number their candidates in order of preference. Where candidates reach their quota of votes and are elected, surplus votes are transferred to other candidates according to the next preference on each voter's ballot slip. The candidate in each round with the fewest votes is eliminated and their surplus votes are redistributed according to the voter's next preference. The process is repeated until the required number of members are elected.

On 29 November 1999 the assembly appointed ten ministers as well as the chairs and deputy chairs for the ten statutory departmental committees. Devolution of powers to the Northern Ireland Assembly occurred on 2 December 1999, following several delays concerned with Sinn Fein's inclusion in the executive while Irish Republican Army (IRA) weapons were yet to be decommissioned.

Since the devolution of powers, the assembly has been suspended by the Secretary of State for Northern Ireland on four occasions. The first was between 11 February and 30 May 2000, with two 24-hour suspensions on 10 August and 22 September 2001 – all owing to a lack of progress in decommissioning. The final suspension took place on 14 October 2002 after unionists walked out of the executive following a police raid on Sinn Fein's office investigating alleged intelligence gathering.

The assembly was formally dissolved in April 2003 in anticipation of an election, which eventually took place on 26 November 2003. The results of the election changed the balance of power between the political parties, with an increase in the number of seats held by the Democratic Unionist Party (DUP) and Sinn Fein (SF), so that they became the largest parties. The assembly was restored to a state of suspension following the November election while political parties engaged in a review of the Belfast Agreement aimed at fully restoring the devolved institutions.

In July 2005 the leadership of the IRA formally ordered an end to its armed campaign; it authorised a representative to engage with the Independent International Commission on Decommissioning in order to verifiably put the arms beyond use. On 26 September 2005 General John de Chastelain, the chair of the commission, along with two independent church witnesses confirmed that the IRA's entire arsenal of weapons had been decommissioned.

Following the passing of the Northern Ireland Act 2006 the secretary of state created a non-legislative fixed-term assembly, whose membership consisted of the 108 members elected in the 2003 election. It first met on 15 May 2006 with the remit of making preparations for the restoration of devolved government; its discussions informed the next round of talks called by the British and Irish governments held at St Andrews. The St Andrews agreement of 13 October 2006 led to the establishment of the transitional assembly.

The Northern Ireland (St Andrews Agreement) Act 2006 set out a timetable to restore devolution, and also set the date for the third election to the assembly as 7 March 2007. The DUP and SF again had the largest number of Members of the Legislative Assembly (MLAs) elected, and although the initial restoration deadline of 26 March was missed, the leaders of the DUP and SF (Revd Dr Ian Paisley, MP, MLA and Gerry Adams, MLA, respectively) took part in a historic meeting and made a joint commitment to establish an executive committee in the assembly to which devolved powers were restored on 8 May 2007.

SALARIES *as at May 2009*

Assembly Member	£43,101

NORTHERN IRELAND ASSEMBLY MEMBERS

as at May 2009

Adams, Gerry, *SF, West Belfast*
Anderson, Martina, *SF, Foyle*
Armstrong, Billy, *UUP, Mid Ulster*
Attwood, Alex, *SDLP, West Belfast*
Beggs, Roy, *UUP, East Antrim*
Boylan, Cathal, *SF, Newry and Armagh*
Bradley, Dominic, *SDLP, Newry and Armagh*
Bradley, Mary, *SDLP, Foyle*
Bradley, P. J., *SDLP, South Down*
Brady, Mickey, *SF, Newry and Armagh*
Bresland, Allan, *DUP, West Tyrone*
Brolly, Francie, *SF, East Londonderry*
Browne of Belmont, Lord, *DUP, East Belfast*
Buchanan, Thomas, *DUP, West Tyrone*
Burns, Thomas, *SDLP, South Antrim*
Butler, Paul, *SF, Lagan Valley*
Campbell, Gregory, *DUP, East Londonderry*
Clarke, Trevor, *DUP, South Antrim*
Clarke, Willie, *SF, South Down*
Cobain, Fred, *UUP, North Belfast*
Coulter, Revd Dr Robert, *UUP, North Antrim*
Craig, Jonathan, *DUP, Lagan Valley*
Cree, Leslie, *UUP, North Down*
Dallat, John, *SDLP, East Londonderry*
Deeny, Dr Kieran, *Ind., West Tyrone*
Dodds, Nigel, *DUP, North Belfast*
Doherty, Pat, *SF, West Tyrone*
Donaldson, Jeffrey, *DUP, Lagan Valley*
Durkan, Mark, *SDLP, Foyle*
Easton, Alex, *DUP, North Down*

Elliot, Tom, *UUP, Fermanagh and South Tyrone*
Empey, Sir Reg, *UUP, East Belfast*
Farry, Stephen, *All., North Down*
Ford, David, *All., South Antrim*
Foster, Arlene, *DUP, Fermanagh and South Tyrone*
Gallagher, Tommy, *SDLP, Fermanagh and South Tyrone*
Gardiner, Samuel, *UUP, Upper Bann*
Gildernew, Michelle, *SF, Fermanagh and South Tyrone*
Hamilton, Simon, *DUP, Strangford*
Hanna, Carmel, *SDLP, South Belfast*
Hay, William, *DUP, Foyle*
Hilditch, David, *DUP, East Antrim*
Irwin, William, *DUP, Newry and Armagh*
Kelly, Dolores, *SDLP, Upper Bann*
Kelly, Gerry, *SF, North Belfast*
Kennedy, Danny, *UUP, Newry and Armagh*
***Kinahan**, Danny, *UUP, South Antrim*
Lo, Anna, *All., South Belfast*
Long, Naomi, *All., East Belfast*
Lunn, Trevor, *All., Lagan Valley*
Maginness, Alban, *SDLP, North Belfast*
Maskey, Alex, *SF, South Belfast*
Maskey, Paul, *SF, West Belfast*
McCallister, John, *UUP, South Down*
McCann, Fra, *SF, West Belfast*
McCann, Jennifer, *SF, West Belfast*
McCarthy, Kieran, *All., Strangford*
McCartney, Raymond, *SF, Foyle*
McCausland, Nelson, *DUP, North Belfast*
McClarty, David, *UUP, East Londonderry*
McCrea, Basil, *UUP, Lagan Valley*
McCrea, Ian, *DUP, Mid Ulster*
McCrea, Dr William, *DUP, South Antrim*
McDonnell, Dr Alasdair, *SDLP, South Belfast*
McElduff, Barry, *SF, West Tyrone*
McFarland, Alan, *UUP, North Down*
McGill, Claire, *SF, West Tyrone*
McGimpsey, Michael, *UUP, South Belfast*
McGlone, Patsy, *SDLP, Mid Ulster*
McGuinness, Martin, *SF, Mid Ulster*
†**McHugh**, Gerry, *Ind., Fermanagh and South Tyrone*
McIlveen, Michelle, *DUP, Strangford*
McKay, Daithi, *SF, North Antrim*
McLaughlin, Mitchel, *SF, South Antrim*
McNarry, David, *UUP, Strangford*
McQuillan, Adrian, *DUP, East Londonderry*
Molloy, Francie, *SF, Mid Ulster*
Morrow, Lord, *DUP, Fermanagh and South Tyrone*
Moutray, Stephen, *DUP, Upper Bann*
Murphy, Conor, *SF, Newry and Armagh*
Neeson, Sean, *All., East Antrim*
Newton, Robin, *DUP, East Belfast*
Ni Chuilín, Caral, *SF, North Belfast*
O'Dowd, John, *SF, Upper Bann*
O'Loan, Declan, *SDLP, North Antrim*
O'Neill, Michelle, *SF, Mid Ulster*
Paisley, Revd Dr Ian, PC, *DUP, North Antrim*
Paisley, Ian Jr, *DUP, North Antrim*
Poots, Edwin, *DUP, Lagan Valley*
Purvis, Dawn, *PUP, East Belfast*
Ramsey, Pat, *SDLP, Foyle*
Ramsey, Sue, *SF, West Belfast*
Ritchie, Margaret, *SDLP, South Down*
Robinson, George, *DUP, East Londonderry*
Robinson, Iris, *DUP, Strangford*
Robinson, Ken, *UUP, East Antrim*
Robinson, Peter, *DUP, East Belfast*
‡**Ross**, Alastair, *DUP, East Antrim*
Ruane, Caitriona, *SF, South Down*
Savage, George, *UUP, Upper Bann*
Shannon, Jim, *DUP, Strangford*
Simpson, David, *DUP, Upper Bann*
Spratt, Jimmy, *DUP, South Belfast*
Storey, Mervyn, *DUP, North Antrim*
Weir, Peter, *DUP, North Down*
Wells, Jim, *DUP, South Down*
Wilson, Brian, *Green, North Down*
Wilson, Sammy, *DUP, East Antrim*

* David Burnside resigned with effect from 1 June 2009 and was replaced by Danny Kinahan with effect from 9 June 2009
† Gerry McHugh resigned from Sinn Fein on 30 November 2007 and now sits as an independent member
‡ George Dawson died on 7 May 2007 and was replaced by Alastair Ross, whose appointment was notified by the Chief Electoral Officer with effect from 14 May 2007

STATE OF THE PARTIES *as at May 2009*

Party	*Seats*
Democratic Unionist Party (DUP)	36
Sinn Fein (SF)	27
Ulster Unionist Party (UUP)	18
Social Democratic and Labour Party (SDLP)	16
Alliance Party (Alliance)	7
Independent (Ind.)	2
Progressive Unionist Party (PUP)	1
Green Party	1

NORTHERN IRELAND ASSEMBLY ELECTION RESULTS

as at 7 March 2007
E. 1,107,904 T. 62.3%

E. Electorate T. Turnout
First = first-preference votes
Final = final total for that candidate, after all necessary transfers of lower-preference votes
R. = round
* = eliminated last
See General Election Results for a list of party abbreviations

ANTRIM EAST
E. 56,666 T. 30,293 (53.46%)

	First	*Final*	*Elected (R.)*
Sammy Wilson, DUP	6,755	6,755	First (1)
George Dawson, DUP	4,167	4,777	Second (2)
Sean Neeson, Alliance	3,114	5,191	Fourth (10)
Roy Beggs, UUP	3,076	5,115	Fifth (12)
David Hilditch, DUP	2,732	4,587	Third (3)
Ken Robinson, UUP	1,881	4,195	Sixth (13)
*Danny O'Connor, SDLP	1,769	3,298	
Stewart Dickson, Alliance	1,624		
Mark Dunn, UUP	1,617		
Oliver McMullan, SF	1,168		
Tom Robinson, UK Unionist Party	731		
Mark Bailey, Green	612		
John Anderson, Ind.	398		
Tim Lewis, C.	395		

ANTRIM NORTH
E. 72,814 T. 44,655 (61.33%)

	First	*Final*	*Elected (R.)*
Revd Ian Paisley , DUP	7,716	7,716	First (1)
Daithi McKay, SF	7,065	7,065	Second (1)

Ian Paisley Jr, DUP	6,106	7,264	Third (2)
Mervyn Storey, DUP	5,171	6,924	Fifth (8)
Revd Robert Coulter, UUP	5,047	6,579	Fourth (7)
Declan O'Loan, SDLP	3,281	6,498	Sixth (10)
*Deirdre Nelson, DUP	2,740	4,092	
Orla Black, SDLP	2,129		
Lyle Cubitt, UK Unionist Party	1,848		
Robert Swann, UUP	1,281		
Jayne Dunlop, Alliance	1,254		
Paul McGlinchey, Ind.	383		
James Gregg, Ind.	310		

ANTRIM SOUTH
E. 65,654 T. 38,481 (58.61%)

	First	*Final*	*Elected (R.)*
Mitchel McLaughlin, SF	6,313	6,313	First (1)
Revd William McCrea, DUP	6,023	6,023	Second (1)
David Ford, Alliance	5,007	5,495	Third (5)
David Burnside, UUP	4,507	6,926	Fourth (7)
Trevor Clarke, DUP	4,302	5,544	Fifth (8)
*Mel Lucas, DUP	2,840	4,429	
Thomas Burns, SDLP	2,721	5,396	Sixth (8)
Danny Kinahan, UUP	2,391		
Noreen McClelland, SDLP	1,526		
Stephen Nicholl, UUP	927		
Robert McCartney, UK Unionist Party	893		
Pete Whitcroft, Green	507		
Stephen O'Brien, C.	129		
Marcella Delaney, WP	89		

BELFAST EAST
E. 49,757 T. 29,873 (60.04%)

	First	*Final*	*Elected (R.)*
Peter Robinson, DUP	5,635	5,635	First (1)
Naomi Long, Alliance	5,585	5,585	Second (1)
Sir Reg Empey, UUP	4,139	4,620	Third (3)
Lord Wallace Browne, DUP	3,185	3,734	Fifth (10)
Dawn Purvis, Progressive Unionist Party	3,045	4,208	Fourth (10)
Robin Newton, DUP	2,335	3,517	Sixth (10)
*Michael Copeland, UUP	1,557	2,999	
Niall O'Donnghaile, SF	1,055		
Jim Rodgers, UUP	820		
Mary Muldoon, SDLP	816		
Steve Agnew, Green	653		
Glyn Chambers, C.	427		
Thomas Black, Socialist Party	225		
Joe Bell, WP	107		
Rainbow George, Make Politicians History	47		

BELFAST NORTH
E. 49,372 T. 30,067 (60.90%)

	First	*Final*	*Elected (R.)*
Nigel Dodds, DUP	6,973	6,973	First (1)
Gerry Kelly, SF	5,414	5,414	Second (1)
Caral Ni Chuilin, SF	3,680	4,587	Third (3)
Fred Cobain, UUP	2,498	3,967	Fifth (10)
Nelson McCausland, DUP	2,462	3,818	Sixth (10)
Alban Maginness, SDLP	2,212	4,830	Fourth (9)
Pat Convery, SDLP	1,868		
*William Humphrey, DUP	1,673	3,327	
Raymond McCord, Ind.	1,320		
Peter Emerson, Green	590		
Tommy McCullough, Alliance	486		
Robert McCartney, UK Unionist Party	360		
John Lavery, WP	139		
Rainbow George, Make Politicians History	40		

BELFAST SOUTH
E. 48,923 T. 30,533 (62.41%)

	First	*Final*	*Elected (R.)*
Jimmy Spratt, DUP	4,762	4,762	First (1)
Dr Alasdair McDonnell, SDLP	4,379	4,379	Second (1)
Alex Maskey, SF	3,996	4,167	Sixth (10)
Anna Lo, Alliance	3,829	4,415	Third (8)
Carmel Hanna, SDLP	3,748	4,262	Fifth (10)
Michael McGimpsey, UUP	2,647	4,927	Fourth (10)
*Christopher Stalford, DUP	2,035	3,275	
Dr Esmond Birnie, UUP	1,804		
Bob Stoker, UUP	1,122		
Brenda Cooke, Green	737		
Andrew Park, Progressive Unionist Party	410		
David Hoey, UK Unionist Party	298		
Jim Barbour, Socialist Party	248		
Paddy Lynn, WP	123		
Roger Lomas, C.	108		
Rainbow George, Make Politicians History	66		
Charles Smyth, Pro-Capitalism	22		
Geoffrey Wilson, Ind.	10		

BELFAST WEST
E. 50,792 T. 34,238 (67.41%)

	First	*Final*	*Elected (R.)*
Gerry Adams, SF	6,029	6,029	First (1)
Sue Ramsey, SF	4,715	5,267	Second (2)
Paul Maskey, SF	4,368	5,075	Third (6)
Jennifer McCann, SF	4,265	4,849	Fourth (6)
Fra McCann, SF	4,254	4,647	Sixth (6)
*Diane Dodds, DUP	3,661	4,166	
Alex Attwood, SDLP	3,036	4,779	Fifth (6)
Margaret Walsh, SDLP	1,074		
Sean Mitchell, People Before Profit	774		
Louis West, UUP	558		
John Lowry, WP	434		
Geraldine Taylor, Republican Sinn Fein	427		
Dan McGuinness, Alliance	127		
Rainbow George, Make Politicians History	68		

DOWN NORTH
E. 57,525 T. 30,930 (53.77%)

	First	*Final*	*Elected (R.)*
Alex Easton, DUP	4,946	4,946	First (1)
Peter Weir, DUP	3,376	4,380	Fifth (10)
Stephen Farry, Alliance	3,131	4,466	Second (8)
Leslie Cree, UUP	2,937	4,687	Third (10)
Brian Wilson, Green	2,839	4,572	Fourth (10)
Alan McFarland, UUP	2,245	3,986	Sixth (10)
*Alan Graham, DUP	2,147	3,255	
Marion Smith, UUP	2,098		
Robert McCartney, UK Unionist Party	1,806		
Brian Rowan, Ind.	1,194		
Alan Chambers, Ind.	1,129		
Liam Logan, SDLP	1,115		
James Leslie, C.	864		
Deaglan Page, SF	390		
Elaine Martin, Progressive Unionist Party	367		
Chris Carter, Ind.	123		

DOWN SOUTH
E. 71,704 T. 46,623 (65.02%)

	First	*Final*	*Elected (R.)*
Catriona Ruane, SF	6,334	6,676	First (7)
Margaret Ritchie, SDLP	5,838	6,945	Third (8)
P. J. Bradley, SDLP	5,652	6,650	Fourth (9)
Jim Wells, DUP	5,542	8,463	Fifth (10)
Willie Clarke, SF	5,138	7,382	Second (8)
John McCallister, UUP	4,447	7,721	Sixth (11)
*Michael Carr, SDLP	2,972	3,883	
Eamonn McConvey, SF	2,662		
William Burns, DUP	2,611		
Ciaran Mussen, Green	1,622		
Henry Reilly, UKIP	1,229		
David Griffin, Alliance	691		
Martin Cunningham, Ind.	434		
Nelson Wharton, UK Unionist Party	424		
Peter Bowles, C.	391		
Malachi Curran, Lab.	123		

FERMANAGH AND SOUTH TYRONE
E. 65,826 T. 46,845 (71.16%)

	First	*Final*	*Elected (R.)*
Arlene Foster, DUP	7,138	7,138	First (1)
Michelle Gildernew, SF	7,026	7,026	Second (1)
Tom Elliott, UUP	6,603	6,680	Third (2)
Gerry McHugh, SF	5,103	5,777	Sixth (8)
*Sean Lynch, SF	4,704	5,188	
Lord Morrow, DUP	4,700	7,014	Fifth (8)
Tommy Gallagher, SDLP	4,440	6,640	Fourth (7)
Kenny Donaldson, UUP	2,531		
Vincent Currie, SDLP	2,043		
Gerry McGeough, Ind.	814		
Allan Leonard, Alliance	521		
Michael McManus, Republican Sinn Fein	431		
Robert McCartney, UK Unionist Party	388		

FOYLE
E. 64,889 T. 41,455 (63.89%)

	First	*Final*	*Elected (R.)*
William Hay, DUP	6,960	6,960	First (1)
Mark Durkan, SDLP	6,401	6,401	Second (1)
Martina Anderson, SF	5,414	5,972	Third (6)
Raymond McCartney, SF	4,321	7,275	Fourth (8)
Pat Ramsey, SDLP	3,242	5,396	Fifth (10)
Lynn Fleming, SF	2,914		
Mary Bradley, SDLP	2,891	4,419	Sixth (10)
*Helen Quigley, SDLP	2,648	4,314	
Eamonn McCann, Socialist Environmental Alliance	2,045		
Peggy O'Hara, Ind.	1,789		
Peter Munce, UUP	1,755		
Adele Corry, Green	359		
Yvonne Boyle, Alliance	224		
Willie Frazer, Ind.	73		

LAGAN VALLEY
E. 70,101 T. 42,058 (60.00%)

	First	*Final*	*Elected (R.)*
Jeffrey Donaldson, DUP	9,793	9,793	First (1)
Paul Butler, SF	5,098	6,387	Second (6)
Basil McCrea, UUP	4,031	6,712	Third (7)
Trevor Lunn, Alliance	3,765	6,264	Fourth (7)
Jonathan Craig, DUP	3,471	6,147	Fifth (8)
Edwin Poots, DUP	3,457	5,386	Sixth (9)
*Paul Givan, DUP	3,377	4,728	
Marietta Farrell, SDLP	2,839		
Billy Bell, UUP	2,599		
Ronnie Crawford, UUP	1,147		
Michael Rogan, Green	922		
Robert McCartney, UK Unionist Party	853		
Neil Johnston, C.	387		
John Magee, WP	83		

LONDONDERRY EAST
E. 56,104 T. 34,180 (60.92%)

	First	*Final*	*Elected (R.)*
Gregory Campbell, DUP	6,845	6,845	First (1)
Francie Brolly, SF	4,476	5,003	Third (7)
George Robinson, DUP	3,991	4,869	Second (5)
David McClarty, UUP	2,875	4,409	Fifth (9)
Adrian McQuillan, DUP	2,650	4,074	Sixth (9)
John Dallat, SDLP	2,638	6,380	Fourth (8)
Billy Leonard, SF	2,321		
*Norman Hillis, UUP	2,054	3,195	
Orla Beattie, SDLP	1,797		
Barney Fitzpatrick, Alliance	1,401		
Edwin Stevenson, UUP	1,338		
Leslie Cubitt, UK Unionist Party	549		
Phillippe Moison, Green	521		
Michael McGonigle, Republican Sinn Fein	393		
Victor Christie, Ind.	73		

NEWRY AND ARMAGH

E. 70,823 T. 50,165 (70.83%)

	First	*Final*	*Elected (R.)*
Conor Murphy, SF	7,437	7,437	First (1)
Cathal Boylan, SF	7,105	7,105	Second (1)
Danny Kennedy, UUP	6,517	7,653	Fifth (5)
William Irwin, DUP	6,418	8,008	Fourth (5)
Mickey Brady, SF	6,337	7,514	Third (4)
Dominic Bradley, SDLP	5,318	6,311	Sixth (7)
*Sharon Haughey, SDLP	4,500	5,368	
Paul Berry, Ind.	2,317		
Davy Hyland, Ind.	2,188		
Willie Frazer, Ind.	605		
Arthur Morgan, Green	599		
Maire Hendron, Alliance	278		

STRANGFORD

E. 66,648 T. 36,340 (54.53%)

	First	*Final*	*Elected (R.)*
Iris Robinson, DUP	5,917	5,917	First (1)
Jim Shannon, DUP	4,788	5,178	Second (6)
Kieran McCarthy, Alliance	4,085	5,207	Third (9)
Simon Hamilton, DUP	3,889	4,998	Fifth (13)
David McNarry, UUP	3,709	6,036	Fourth (10)
Michelle McIlveen, DUP	3,468	4,579	Sixth (13)
*Joe Boyle, SDLP	3,068	4,548	
Angus Carson, UUP	2,128		
Dermot Kennedy, SF	1,089		
George Ennis, UK Unionist Party	872		
Stephanie Sim, Green	868		
Michael Henderson, UUP	675		
David Gregg, Ind.	650		
Bob Little, C.	508		
Cedric Wilson, Ind.	305		

TYRONE WEST

E. 58,367 T. 41,839 (71.68%)

	First	*Final*	*Elected (R.)*
Barry McElduff, SF	6,971	6,971	First (1)
Pat Doherty, SF	6,709	6,709	Second (1)
Clare McGill, SF	4,757	6,217	Third (3)
Tom Buchanan, DUP	4,625	6,208	Fourth (6)
Allan Bresland, DUP	4,244	5,543	Sixth (7)
Dr Kieran Deeny, Ind.	3,778	5,616	Fifth (7)
Derek Hussey, UUP	3,686		
*Josephine Deehan, SDLP	2,689	5,186	
Eugene McMenamin, SDLP	2,272		
Seamus Shiels, SDLP	1,057		
Joe O'Neill, Republican Sinn Fein	448		
Robert McCartney, UK Unionist Party	220		

ULSTER MID

E. 61,223 T. 44,728 (73.06%)

	First	*Final*	*Elected (R.)*
Martin McGuinness, SF	8,065	8,065	First (1)
Ian McCrea, DUP	7,608	7,608	Second (1)
Francie Molloy, SF	6,597	6,597	Third (1)
Michelle O'Neill, SF	6,432	6,432	Fourth (1)
Patsy McGlone, SDLP	4,976	6,430	Fifth (5)
Billy Armstrong, UUP	4,781	6,355	Sixth (7)
*Kate Lagan, SDLP	2,759	3,531	
Walter Millar, UK Unionist Party	1,210		
Ann Forde, DUP	1,021		
Brendan McLaughlin, Republican Sinn Fein	437		
Margaret Marshall, Alliance	221		
Harry Hutchinson, Ind.	170		

UPPER BANN

E. 70,716 T. 43,235 (61.14%)

	First	*Final*	*Elected (R.)*
John O'Dowd, SF	7,733	7,733	First (1)
David Simpson, DUP	6,828	6,828	Second (1)
Samuel Gardiner, UUP	5,135	7,265	Fourth (9)
Dolores Kelly, SDLP	4,689	6,191	Third (8)
Stephen Moutray, DUP	3,663	7,550	Fifth (11)
*Dessie Ward, SF	3,118	4,732	
Junior McCrum, DUP	2,975		
George Savage, UUP	2,167	5,998	Sixth (12)
Arnold Hatch, UUP	1,815		
David Calvert, No Description	1,332		
Helen Corry, Green	1,156		
Sheila McQuaid, Alliance	798		
Pat McAleenan, SDLP	761		
Barry Toman, Republican Sinn Fein	386		
David Fry, C.	248		
Suzanne Peeples, Ind.	78		

EUROPEAN PARLIAMENT

European parliament elections take place at five-yearly intervals; the first direct elections to the parliament were held in 1979. In mainland Britain, members of the European parliament (MEPs) were elected in all constituencies on a first-past-the-post basis until 1999, when a regional system of proportional representation was introduced; in Northern Ireland three MEPs have been elected by the single transferable vote system of proportional representation since 1979. From 1979 to 1994 the number of seats held by the UK in the European parliament was 81, which increased to 87 in the 1994 election, decreased to 78 following EU enlargement in 2004, and decreased to 72 for the 2009 election (England 59, Wales 4, Scotland 6, Northern Ireland 3) as a result of Bulgaria and Romania joining the EU in 2007.

At the 2009 European parliament elections all UK MEPs were elected under a 'closed-list' regional system of proportional representation, with England being divided into nine regions and Scotland, Wales and Northern Ireland each constituting a region. Since June 2004 residents of Gibraltar vote in the South West region. Parties submitted a list of candidates for each region in their own order of preference. Voters voted for a party or an independent candidate, and the first seat in each region was allocated to the party or candidate with the highest number of votes. The rest of the seats in each region were then allocated broadly in proportion to each party's share of the vote. Each region returned the following number of members: East Midlands, 5; Eastern, 7; London, 8; North East, 3; North West, 8; South East, 10; South West, 6; West Midlands, 6; Yorkshire and the Humber, 6; Wales, 4; Northern Ireland, 3; Scotland, 6.

If a vacancy occurs due to the resignation or death of an MEP, it is filled by the next available person on that party's list. If an independent MEP resigns or dies, a by-election is held. Where an MEP leaves the party on whose list he/she was elected, there is no requirement to resign and he/she can remain in office until the next election.

British subjects and nationals of member states of the European Union are eligible for election to the European parliament provided they are 21 or over and not subject to disqualification. Since 1994, eligible citizens have had the right to vote in elections to the European parliament in the UK as long as they are entered on the electoral register.

In July 2009 a new MEP statute introduced the same salary for all MEPs (€91,980), fixed at a rate of 38.5 per cent of the basic salary of a European court of justice judge. Previously MEPs received a salary set at the level of the national parliamentary salary of their country.

The next elections to the European parliament will take place in 2014. For further information visit the UK's European Parliament website (W www.europarl.org.uk).

UK MEMBERS *as at June 2009*

* Denotes membership of the last European parliament
† Previously sat as a member of UUP

Agnew, John (b. 1949), *UKIP, Eastern*
Andreasen, Marta (b. 1954), *UKIP, South East*
***Ashworth**, Richard (b. 1947), *C., South East*
***Atkins**, Rt. Hon. Sir Robert (b. 1946), *C., North West*
***Batten**, Gerard (b. 1972), *UKIP, London*
Bearder, Catherine (b. 1949) *LD, South East*
***Bloom**, Godfrey (b. 1949), *UKIP, Yorkshire and the Humber*
***Bowles**, Sharon M. (b. 1953), *LD, South East*
***Bradbourn**, Philip, OBE (b. 1951), *C., West Midlands*
Brons, Andrew (b. 1947), *BNP, Yorkshire and the Humber*
Bufton, John (b. 1962), *UKIP, Wales*
***Callanan**, Martin (b. 1961), *C., North East*
Campbell Bannerman, David (b. 1960), *UKIP, Eastern*
***Cashman**, Michael (b. 1950), *Lab., West Midlands*
***Chichester**, Giles B. (b. 1946), *C., South West*
***Clark**, Derek (b. 1933), *UKIP, East Midlands*
Colman, Trevor (b. 1941), *UKIP, South West*
Dartmouth, Earl of (b. 1949), *UKIP, South West*
***Davies**, Christopher G. (b. 1954), *LD, North West*
***de Brún**, Bairbre (b. 1954), *SF, Northern Ireland*
***Deva**, Niranjan J. A. (Nirj), FRSA (b. 1948), *C., South East*
Dodds, Diane (b. 1958), *DUP, Northern Ireland*
***Duff**, Andrew N. (b. 1950), *LD, Eastern*
***Elles**, James E. M. (b. 1949), *C., South East*
***Evans**, Jillian R. (b. 1959), *PC, Wales*
***Farage**, Nigel P. (b. 1964), *UKIP, South East*
Ford, Vicky (b. 1945), *C., Eastern*
Foster, Jacqueline (b. 1947), *C., North West*
Fox, Ashley (b. 1969), *C., South West*
Girling, Julie (b. 1956), *C., South West*
Griffin, Nick (b. 1959), *BNP, North West*
***Hall**, Fiona (b. 1955), *LD, North East*
***Hannan**, Daniel J. (b. 1971), *C., South East*
***Harbour**, Malcolm (b. 1947), *C., West Midlands*
***Helmer**, Roger (b. 1944), *C., East Midlands*
***Honeyball**, Mary (b. 1952), *Lab., London*
***Howitt**, Richard (b. 1961), *Lab., Eastern*
***Hudghton**, Ian (b. 1951), *SNP, Scotland*
***Hughes**, Stephen (b. 1952), *Lab., North East*
***Kamall**, Syed S. (b. 1967), *C., London*
***Karim**, Sajjad (b. 1970), *C., North West*
***Kirkhope**, Timothy J. R. (b. 1945), *C., Yorkshire and the Humber*
***Lambert**, Jean D. (b. 1950), *Green, London*
***Lucas**, Dr Caroline (b. 1960), *Green, South East*
***Ludford**, Baroness (b. 1951), *LD, London*
***Lynne**, Elizabeth (b. 1948), *LD, West Midlands*
Lyon, George (b. 1956), *LD, Scotland*
***McAvan**, Linda (b. 1962), *Lab., Yorkshire and the Humber*
***McCarthy**, Arlene (b. 1960), *Lab., North West*
McClarkin, Emma (b. 1978), *C., East Midlands*
***McMillan-Scott**, Edward H. C. (b. 1949), *C., Yorkshire and the Humber*
***Martin**, David W. (b. 1954), *Lab., Scotland*
***Moraes**, Claude (b. 1965), *Lab., London*
***Nattrass**, Mike (b. 1945), *UKIP, West Midlands*
***Newton Dunn**, William F. (Bill) (b. 1941), *LD, East Midlands*
***†Nicholson**, James (b. 1945), *UCUNF, Northern Ireland*
Nuttall, Paul (b. 1976), *UKIP, North West*
***Simpson**, Brian (b. 1953), *Lab., North West*
Sinclaire, Nikki (b. 1968), *UKIP, West Midlands*
***Skinner**, Peter W. (b. 1959), *Lab., South East*

***Smith**, Alyn (b. 1973), *SNP, Scotland*
***Stevenson**, Struan (b. 1948), *C., Scotland*
***Stihler**, Catherine D. (b. 1973), *Lab., Scotland*
***Sturdy**, Robert W. (b. 1944), *C., Eastern*
Swinburne, Kay (b. 1968), *C., Wales*
***Tannock**, Dr Charles (b. 1957), *C., London*
***Van Orden**, Geoffrey (b. 1945), *C., Eastern*
Vaughan, Derek (b. 1961), *Lab., Wales*
***Wallis**, Diana (b. 1954), *LD, Yorkshire and the Humber*
***Watson**, Graham R. (b. 1956), *LD, South West*
***Willmott**, Glenis (b. 1951), *Lab., East Midlands*
Yannakoudakis, Marina (b. 1956), *C., London*

UK REGIONS *as at June 2009 Election*

Abbreviations

AC	Animals Count
ChP	Christian Party
JT	Jury Team
Libertas	Libertas
No2EU	No2EU Yes to Democracy
Peace	Peace Party
Pensioners	Pensioners Party
Roman	Roman Party
SGB	Socialist Party of Great Britain
SLP	Socialist Labour Party
SSP	Scottish Socialist Party
TUV	Traditional Unionist Voice
UCUNF	Ulster Conservatives and Unionists – New Force
UKF	United Kingdom First
YD	Wai D (Your Decision)
Yes2EU	YES2EUROPE

For other abbreviations, *see* UK General Election Results. For detailed information on which areas of the country are covered by a particular region, please contact the Home Office.

E. 44,173,690 T. 34.48%

EASTERN

(Bedfordshire, Cambridgeshire, Essex, Hertfordshire, Luton, Norfolk, Peterborough, Southend-on-Sea, Suffolk, Thurrock)

E. 4,252,669	T. 38.0%
C.	500,331 (31.2%)
UKIP	313,921 (19.6%)
LD	221,235 (13.8%)
Lab.	167,833 (10.5%)
Green	141,016 (8.8%)
BNP	97,013 (6.1%)
UKF	38,185 (2.4%)
Eng. Dem.	32,211 (2.0%)
CPA	24,646 (1.5%)
No2EU	13,939 (0.9%)
SLP	13,599 (0.8%)
AC	13,201 (0.8%)
Libertas	9,940 (0.6%)
Ind.	9,916 (0.6%)
JT	6,354 (0.4%)
C. majority	186,410

(June 2004, C. maj. 169,366)

MEMBERS ELECTED
1. *G. Van Orden, *C.* 2. D. Campbell Bannerman, *UKIP* 3. *R. Sturdy, *C.* 4. *A. Duff, *LD* 5. *R. Howitt, *Lab.* 6. V. Ford, *C.* 7. J. Agnew, *UKIP*

EAST MIDLANDS

(Derby, Derbyshire, Leicester, Leicestershire, Lincolnshire, Northamptonshire, Nottingham, Nottinghamshire, Rutland)

E. 3,312,944	T. 37.51%
C.	370,275 (30.2%)
Lab.	206,945 (16.9%)
UKIP	201,984 (16.4%)
LD	151,428 (12.3%)
BNP	106,319 (8.7%)
Green	83,939 (6.8%)
Eng. Dem.	28,498 (2.3%)
UKF	20,561 (1.7%)
CPA	17,907 (1.5%)
SLP	13,590 (1.1%)
No2EU	11,375 (0.9%)
Libertas	7,882 (0.6%)
JT	7,362 (0.6%)
C. majority	204,243

(June 2004, C. maj. 4,864)

MEMBERS ELECTED
1. *R. Helmer, *C.* 2.*G. Willmott, *Lab.* 3. *D. Clark, *UKIP* 4. E. McClarkin, *C.* 5. *W. Newton Dunn, *LD*

LONDON

E. 5,257,624	T. 33.53%
C.	479,037 (27.4%)
Lab.	372,590 (21.3%)
LD	240,156 (13.7%)
Green	190,589 (10.9%)
UKIP	188,440 (10.8%)
BNP	86,420 (4.9%)
CPA	51,336 (2.9%)
Ind	50,014 (2.9%)
Eng. Dem.	24,477 (1.4%)
No2EU	17,758 (1.0%)
SLP	15,306 (0.9%)
Libertas	8,444 (0.5%)
JT	7,284 (0.4%)
Ind, SC	4,918 (0.3%)
SGB	4,050 (0.2%)
Yes2EU	3,384 (0.2%)
Ind.	3,248 (0.2%)
Ind.	1,972 (0.1%)
Ind.	1,603 (0.1%)
C. majority	106,447

(June 2004, C. maj. 38,357)

MEMBERS ELECTED
1. *C. Tannock, *C.* 2. *C. Moraes, *Lab.* 3. *Baroness Ludford, *LD* 4. *S. Kamall, *C.* 5. *J. Lambert, *Green* 6. *G. Batten, *UKIP* 7. *M. Honeyball, *Lab.* 8. M. Yannakoudakis, *C.*

NORTH EAST

(Co. Durham, Darlington, Hartlepool, Middlesbrough, Northumberland, Redcar and Cleveland, Stockton-on-Tees, Tyne and Wear)

E. 1,939,709	T. 30.50%
Lab.	147,338 (25.0%)
C.	116,911 (19.8%)
LD	103,644 (17.6%)
UKIP	90,700 (15.4%)
BNP	52,700 (8.9%)
Green	34,081 (5.8%)
Eng. Dem.	13,007 (2.2%)
SLP	10,238 (1.7%)
No2EU	8,066 (1.4%)
CPA	7,263 (1.2%)
Libertas	3,010 (0.5%)
JT	2,904 (0.5%)
Lab. majority	30,427

(June 2004, Lab. maj. 121,088)

MEMBERS ELECTED
1. *S. Hughes, *Lab.* 2. *M. Callanan, *C.* 3. *Ms F. Hall, *LD*

NORTHERN IRELAND

(Northern Ireland forms a three-member seat with a single transferable vote system)

E. 1,141,979	T. 42.81%
	1st Pref. Votes
Bairbre de Brún, *SF*	126,184 (26.0%)
Diane Dodds, *DUP*	88,346 (18.2%)
Jim Nicholson, *UCUNF*	82,893 (17.1%)
Alban Maginness, *SDLP*	78,489 (16.2%)
Jim Allister, *TUV*	66,197 (13.7%)
Ian James Parsley, *Alliance*	26,699 (5.5%)
Steven Agnew, *Green*	15,764 (3.3%)

MEMBERS ELECTED
1. *B. de Brún, *SF* 2. *‡J. Nicholson, *UCUNF* 3. D. Dodds, *DUP*

NORTH WEST

(Blackburn-with-Darwen, Blackpool, Cheshire, Cumbria, Greater Manchester, Halton, Lancashire, Merseyside, Warrington)

E. 1,651,825	T. 31.90%
C.	423,174 (25.6%)
Lab.	336,831 (20.4%)
UKIP	261,740 (15.8%)
LD	235,639 (14.3%)
BNP	132,094 (8.0%)
Green	127,133 (7.7%)
Eng. Dem.	40,027 (2.4%)
SLP	26,224 (1.6%)
CPA	25,999 (1.6%)
No2EU	23,580 (1.4%)
JT	8,783 (0.5%)
Libertas	6,980 (0.4%)
Ind.	3,621 (0.2%)
C. majority	86,343

(June 2004, Lab. maj. 66,942)

MEMBERS ELECTED
1. *Sir R. Atkins, *C.* 2. A. McCarthy, *Lab.* 3. P. Nuttall, *UKIP* 4. *C. Davies, *LD* 5. *S. Karim, *C.* 6. *B. Simpson, *Lab.* 7. J. Foster, *C.* 8. N. Griffin, *BNP*

SCOTLAND

E. 3,873,163	T. 28.60%
SNP	321,007 (29.1%)
Lab.	229,853 (20.8%)
C.	185,794 (16.8%)
LD	127,038 (11.5%)
Green	80,442 (7.3%)
UKIP	57,788 (5.2%)
BNP	27,174 (2.5%)
SLP	22,135 (2.0%)
CPA	16,738 (1.5%)
SSP	10,404 (0.9%)
Ind.	10,189 (0.9%)
No2EU	9,693 (0.9%)
JT	6,257 (0.6%)
SNP majority	91,154

(June 2004, Lab. maj. 79,360)

MEMBERS ELECTED
1. *I. Hudghton, *SNP* 2. *D. Martin, *Lab.* 3. *S. Stevenson, *C.* 4. *A. Smith, *SNP* 5. G. Lyon, *LD* 6. *C. Stihler, *Lab.*

SOUTH EAST

(Bracknell Forest, Brighton and Hove, Buckinghamshire, East Sussex, Hampshire, Isle of Wight, Kent, Medway, Milton Keynes, Newbury, Oxfordshire, Portsmouth, Reading, Slough, Southampton, Surrey, West Sussex, Windsor and Maidenhead, Wokingham)

E. 6,231,875	T. 38.19%
C.	812,288 (34.8%)
UKIP	440,002 (18.8%)
LD	330,340 (14.1%)
Green	271,506 (11.6%)
Lab.	192,592 (8.2%)
BNP	101,769 (4.4%)
Eng. Dem.	52,526 (2.2%)
CPA	35,712 (1.5%)
No2EU	21,455 (0.9%)
Libertas	16,767 (0.7%)
SLP	15,484 (0.7%)
UKF	15,261 (0.7%)
JT	14,172 (0.6%)
Peace Party	9,534 (0.4%)
Roman Party	5,450 (0.2%)
C. majority	372,286

(June 2004, C. maj. 345,259)

MEMBERS ELECTED
1. *D. Hannan, *C.* 2. *N. Farage, *UKIP* 3. *R. Ashworth, *C.* 4. *S. Bowles, *LD* 5. *Dr C. Lucas, *Green* 6. *N. Deva, *C.* 7. M. Andreasen, *UKIP* 8. *J. Elles, *C.* 9. *P. Skinner, *Lab.* 10. C. Bearder, *LD*

SOUTH WEST

(Bath and North East Somerset, Bournemouth, Bristol, Cornwall, Devon, Dorset, Gloucestershire, North Somerset, Plymouth, Poole, Somerset, South Gloucestershire, Swindon, Torbay, Wiltshire, Isles of Scilly, Gibraltar)

E. 3,998,479	T. 39.04%
C.	468,472 (30.2%)
UKIP	341,845 (22.1%)
LD	266,253 (17.2%)
Green	144,179 (9.3%)
Labour	118,716 (7.7%)
BNP	60,889 (3.9%)
Pensioners	37,785 (2.4%)
Eng. Dem.	25,313 (1.6%)
CPA	21,329 (1.4%)
Meb. Ker.	14,922 (1.0%)
SLP	10,033 (0.6%)
No2EU	9,741 (0.6%)
Ind.	8,971 (0.6%)
Libertas	7,292 (0.5%)
FPFT	7,151 (0.5%)
JT	5,758 (0.4%)
YD	789 (0.1%)
C. majority	126,627

(June 2004, C. maj. 130,587)

MEMBERS ELECTED
1. *G. Chichester, *C.* 2. T. Colman, *UKIP* 3. *G. Watson, *LD* 4. J. McCulloch Girling, *C.* 5. W. Dartmouth, *UKIP* 6. A. Peter Fox, *C.*

WALES

E. 2,251,968	T. 30.50%
C.	145,193 (21.2%)
Lab.	138,852 (20.3%)
PC	126,702 (18.5%)
UKIP	87,585 (12.8%)
LD	73,082 (10.7%)
Green	38,160 (5.6%)
BNP	37,114 (5.4%)
ChP	13,037 (1.9%)
SLP	12,402 (1.8%)
No2EU	8,600 (1.3%)
JT	3,793 (0.6%)
C. majority	6,341

(June 2004, Lab. maj. 120,039)

MEMBERS ELECTED
1. K. Swinburne, *C.* 2. D. Vaughan. *Lab.* 3. *J. Evans, *PC* 4. J. Bufton, *UKIP*

WEST MIDLANDS

(Herefordshire, Shropshire, Staffordshire, Stoke-on-Trent, Telford and Wrekin, Warwickshire, West Midlands Metropolitan area, Worcestershire)

E. 4,056,370	T. 35.07%
C.	396,487 (28.1%)
UKIP	300,471 (21.3%)
Lab.	240,201 (17.0%)
LD	170,246 (12.0%)
BNP	121,967 (8.6%)
Green	88,244 (6.2%)
Eng. Dem.	32,455 (2.3%)
CPA	18,784 (1.3%)
SLP	14,724 (1.0%)
No2EU	13,415 (0.9%)
JT	8,721 (0.6%)
Libertas	6,961 (0.5%)
C. majority	96,016

(June 2004, C. maj. 56,324)

MEMBERS ELECTED
1. *P. Bradbourn, *C.* 2. *M. Nattrass, *UKIP* 3. *M. Cashman, *Lab.* 4. *M. Harbour, *C.* 5. *L. Lynne, *LD* 6. N. Sinclaire, *UKIP*

YORKSHIRE AND THE HUMBER

(East Riding of Yorkshire, Kingston-upon-Hull, North East Lincolnshire, North Lincolnshire, North Yorkshire, South Yorkshire, West Yorkshire, York)

E. 3,792,415	T. 32.51%
C.	299,802 (24.5%)
Lab.	230,009 (18.8%)
UKIP	213,750 (17.4%)
LD	161,552 (13.2%)
BNP	120,139 (9.8%)
Green	104,456 (8.5%)
Eng. Dem.	31,287 (2.6%)
SLP	19,380 (1.6%)
CPA	16,742 (1.4%)
No2EU	15,614 (1.3%)
JT	7,181 (0.6%)
Libertas	6,268 (0.5%)
C. majority	69,793

(June 1999, Lab. maj. 25,844)

MEMBERS ELECTED
1. *E. McMillan-Scott, *C.* 2. *L. McAvan, *Lab.* 3. *G. Bloom, *UKIP* 4. *D. Wallis, *LD* 5. *T. Kirkhope, *C.* 6. A. Brons, *BNP*

LOCAL GOVERNMENT

Major changes in local government were introduced in England and Wales in 1974 and in Scotland in 1975 by the Local Government Act 1972 and the Local Government (Scotland) Act 1973. Further significant alterations were made in England by the Local Government Acts of 1985, 1992 and 2000.

The structure in England was based on two tiers of local authorities (county councils and district councils) in the non-metropolitan areas; and a single tier of metropolitan councils in the six metropolitan areas of England and London borough councils in London.

Following reviews of the structure of local government in England by the Local Government Commission (now the Boundary Commission for England), 46 unitary (all-purpose) authorities were created between April 1995 and April 1998 to cover certain areas in the non-metropolitan counties. The remaining county areas continue to have two tiers of local authorities. The county and district councils in the Isle of Wight were replaced by a single unitary authority on 1 April 1995; the former counties of Avon, Cleveland, Humberside and Berkshire were replaced by unitary authorities; and Hereford and Worcester was replaced by a new county council for Worcestershire (with district councils) and a unitary authority for Herefordshire. On 1 April 2009 the county areas of Cornwall, Durham, Northumberland, Shropshire and Wiltshire were given unitary status and two new unitary authorities were created for Bedfordshire (Bedford and Central Bedfordshire) and Cheshire (Cheshire East and Cheshire West & Chester) replacing the two-tier county/district system in these areas.

The Local Government (Wales) Act 1994 and the Local Government etc (Scotland) Act 1994 abolished the two-tier structure in Wales and Scotland with effect from 1 April 1996, replacing it with a single tier of unitary authorities.

ELECTIONS

Local elections are normally held on the first Thursday in May. Generally, all British subjects, citizens of the Republic of Ireland, Commonwealth and other European Union citizens who are 18 years or over and resident on the qualifying date in the area for which the election is being held, are entitled to vote at local government elections. A register of electors is prepared and published annually by local electoral registration officers.

A returning officer has the overall responsibility for an election. Voting takes place at polling stations, arranged by the local authority and under the supervision of a presiding officer specially appointed for the purpose. Candidates, who are subject to various statutory qualifications and disqualifications designed to ensure that they are suitable to hold office, must be nominated by electors for the electoral area concerned.

In England, the Boundary Committee for England, part of the Electoral Commission, is responsible for carrying out periodic reviews of electoral arrangements, to consider whether the boundaries of wards or divisions within a local authority need to be altered to take account of changes in electorate; structural reviews, to consider whether a single, unitary authority should be establised in an area instead of an existing two-tier system; and administrative boundary reviews of district or county authorities.

The Local Government Boundary Commission for Wales, the Boundary Commission for Scotland and the Boundary Commission for Northern Ireland are responsible for reviewing the electoral arrangements and boundaries of local authorities within their respective regions.

The Local Government Act 2000 provided for the secretary of state to change the frequency and phasing of elections.

THE BOUNDARY COMMITTEE FOR ENGLAND, Trevelyan House, Great Peter Street, London SW1P 2HW
T 020-7271 0500 **E** info@boundarycommittee.org.uk
W www.boundarycommittee.org.uk

LOCAL GOVERNMENT BOUNDARY COMMISSION FOR WALES, Caradog House, 1–6 St Andrew's Place, Cardiff CF10 3BE **T** 029-2039 5031
E lgbc.wales@wales.gsi.gov.uk **W** www.lgbc-wales.gov.uk

THE BOUNDARY COMMISSION FOR SCOTLAND, 3 Drumsheugh Gardens, Edinburgh EH3 7QJ
T 0131-538 7510 **E** enquiries@scottishboundaries.gov.uk
W www.lgbc-scotland.gov.uk

THE BOUNDARY COMMISSION FOR NORTHERN IRELAND, Forestview, Purdy's Lane, Newtownbreda, Belfast BT8 7AR **T** 020 9069 4800 **E** bcni@belfast.org.uk
W www.boundarycommission.org.uk

INTERNAL ORGANISATION

The council as a whole is the final decision-making body within any authority. Councils are free to a great extent to make their own internal organisational arrangements. The Local Government Act, given royal assent on 28 July 2000, allows councils to adopt one of three broad categories of a new constitution which include a separate executive.

These three categories are:

- A directly elected mayor with a cabinet selected by that mayor
- A cabinet, either elected by the council or appointed by its leader
- A directly elected mayor and council manager

Normally, questions of policy are settled by the full council, while the administration of the various services is the responsibility of committees of councillors. Day-to-day decisions are delegated to the council's officers, who act within the policies laid down by the councillors.

FINANCE

Local government in England, Wales and Scotland is financed from four sources: the council tax, non-domestic rates, government grants and income from fees and charges for services.

COUNCIL TAX

Under the Local Government Finance Act 1992, from 1 April 1993 the council tax replaced the community charge (which had been introduced in April 1989 in Scotland and April 1990 in England and Wales in place of domestic rates).

The council tax is a local tax levied by each local council. Liability for the council tax bill usually falls on the owner-occupier or tenant of a dwelling which is their sole or main residence. Council tax bills may be reduced because of the personal circumstances of people resident in a property, and there are discounts in the case of dwellings occupied by fewer than two adults.

In England, unitary and metropolitan authorities are responsible for collecting their own council tax from which the police authorities claim their share. In areas where there are two tiers of local authority, each county, district and police authority sets its own council tax rate, the district authorities collect the combined council tax and the county councils and police authorities claim their share from the district councils' collection funds. In Wales, each unitary authority and each police authority sets its own council tax rate. The unitary authorities collect the combined council tax and the police authorities claim their share from the funds. In Scotland, each local authority sets its own rate of council tax.

The tax relates to the value of the dwelling. In England and Scotland each dwelling is placed in one of eight valuation bands, ranging from A to H, based on the property's estimated market value as at 1 April 1991. In Wales there are nine bands, ranging from A to I, based on the estimated market value of property as at 1 April 2003.

The valuation bands and ranges of values in England, Wales and Scotland are:

England

A	Up to £40,000	E	£88,001–£120,000
B	£40,001–£52,000	F	£120,001–£160,000
C	£52,001–£68,000	G	£160,001–£320,000
D	£68,001–£88,000	H	Over £320,001

Wales

A	Up to £44,000	F	£162,001–£223,000
B	£44,001–£65,000	G	£223,001–£324,000
C	£65,001–£91,000	H	£324,001–£424,000
D	£91,001–£123,000	I	Over £424,001
E	£123,001–£162,000		

Scotland

A	Up to £27,000	E	£58,001–£80,000
B	£27,001–£35,000	F	£80,001–£106,000
C	£35,001–£45,000	G	£106,001–£212,000
D	£45,001–£58,000	H	Over £212,001

The council tax within a local area varies between the different bands according to proportions laid down by law. The charge attributable to each band as a proportion of the Band D charge set by the council is approximately:

A	67%	F	144%
B	78%	G	167%
C	89%	H	200%
D	100%	I	233%*
E	122%		

* Wales only

The average Band D council tax bill for each authority area is given in the tables on the following pages. There may be variations from the given figure within each district council area because of different parish or community precepts being levied.

NON-DOMESTIC RATES

Non-domestic (business) rates are collected by billing authorities; these are the district councils in those areas of England with two tiers of local government and unitary authorities in other parts of England, in Wales and in Scotland. In respect of England and Wales, the Local Government Finance Act 1988 provides for liability for rates to be assessed on the basis of a poundage (multiplier) tax on the rateable value of property (hereditaments). Separate multipliers are set by the Department for Communities and Local Government (CLG) in England, the Welsh Assembly government and the Scottish government. Rates are collected by the billing authority for the area where a property is located. Rate income collected by billing authorities is paid into a national non-domestic rating (NNDR) pool and redistributed to individual authorities on the basis of the adult population figure as prescribed by CLG, the Welsh Assembly government or the Scottish government. The rates pools are maintained separately in England, Wales and Scotland. Actual payment of rates in certain cases is subject to transitional arrangements, to phase in the larger increases and reductions in rates resulting from the effects of the latest revaluation.

Rateable values for the 2005 rating lists came into effect on 1 April 2005. They are derived from the rental value of property as at 1 April 2003 and determined on certain statutory assumptions by the Valuation Office Agency in England and Wales, and by local area assessors in Scotland. New property which is added to the list, and significant changes to existing property, necessitate amendments to the rateable value on the same basis. Rating lists (valuation rolls in Scotland) remain in force until the next general revaluation. Such revaluations take place every five years, the next being in 2010.

Certain types of property are exempt from rates, eg agricultural land and buildings, certain businesses and some places of public religious worship. Charities and other non-profit-making organisations may receive full or partial relief. Empty commercial property in England and Wales is exempt from business rates for the first three months that the property is vacant (six months for an industrial property), after which full business rates are normally payable.* In Scotland an empty commercial property is exempt from business rates for the first three months and entitled to a 50 per cent discount thereafter, except for some types of premises, such as factories, which are entirely exempt.

* Empty property with a rateable value of less than £15,000 is exempt from business rates until 31 March 2010

GOVERNMENT GRANTS

In addition to specific grants in support of revenue expenditure on particular services, central government pays a revenue support grant to local authorities. This grant is paid to each local authority so that if each authority spends at the level of its standard spending assessment, all authorities in the same class can set broadly the same council tax.

COMPLAINTS

ENGLAND

In England the Local Government Ombudsman investigates complaints of injustice arising from maladministration by local authorities and certain other bodies. The Local Government Ombudsman will not usually consider a complaint unless the local authority concerned has had an opportunity to investigate and reply to a complainant.

The Local Government Act 2000 established a standards board, now called Standards for England, and an independent tribunal known as the Adjudication Panel for England. Standards for England's main task is to ensure that standards of ethical conduct are maintained and to investigate any allegations that councillors have breached the council's code of conduct. At the end of the investigation, the case may be referred to either the relevant local authority's standards committee or the Adjudication Panel, which has a number of sanctions at its disposal, up to and including the disqualification of a member from holding office for five years. Unlike the ombudsmen, Standards for England does not deal with issues of corporate maladministration nor seek to secure financial recompense for complainants.

THE ADJUDICATION PANEL FOR ENGLAND, Tribunal Service, York House, 31–36 York Place, Leeds LS1 2ED
T 0113-389 6086
E AP-enquiries@tribunals.gsi.gov.uk
W www.adjudicationpanel.tribunals.gov.uk

LOCAL GOVERNMENT OMBUDSMAN, PO Box 4771, Coventry CV4 0EH T 0300-061 0614 E advice@lgo.org.uk
W www.lgo.org.uk
Ombudsmen, Tony Redmond, Anne Seex, Jerry White

STANDARDS FOR ENGLAND, 4th Floor, Griffin House, 40 Lever Street, Manchester M1 1BB T 0161-817 5300
E enquiries@standardsboard.gov.uk
W www.standardsforengland.gov.uk

WALES

The office of Public Services Ombudsman for Wales came into force on 1 April 2006 incorporating the functions of the Local Government Ombudsman for Wales.

PUBLIC SERVICES OMBUDSMAN FOR WALES, 1 Ffordd yr Hen Gae, Pencoed CF35 5LJ
T 01656-641150 E ask@ombudsman-wales.org.uk
W www.ombudsman-wales.org.uk
Ombudsman, Peter Tyndall

SCOTLAND

The Scottish Public Services Ombudsman is responsible for complaints regarding the maladaministration of local government in Scotland.

SCOTTISH PUBLIC SERVICES OMBUDSMAN, Freepost EH641, Edinburgh EH3 0BR T 0800-377 7330
E ask@spso.org.uk W www.spso.org.uk
Ombudsman, Jim Martin

NORTHERN IRELAND

The Northern Ireland Commissioner for Complaints fulfils a similar function in Northern Ireland, investigating complaints about local authorities and certain public bodies. Complaints are made to the relevant local authority in the first instance but may also be made directly to the Commissioner.

NORTHERN IRELAND COMMISSIONER FOR COMPLAINTS, Freepost BEL 1478, Belfast BT1 6LR
T 0800-343424 E ombudsman@ni-ombudsman.org.uk
W www.ni-ombudsman.org.uk
Northern Ireland Commissioner for Complaints, Tom Frawley, CBE

THE QUEEN'S REPRESENTATIVES

The lord-lieutenant of a county is the permanent local representative of the Crown in that county. The appointment of lord-lieutenants is now regulated by the Lieutenancies Act 1997. They are appointed by the sovereign on the recommendation of the prime minister. The retirement age is 75. The office of lord-lieutenant dates from 1551, and its holder was originally responsible for maintaining order and for local defence in the county. The duties of the post include attending on royalty during official visits to the county, performing certain duties in connection with the armed forces (and in particular the reserve forces), and making presentations of honours and awards on behalf of the Crown. In England, Wales and Northern Ireland, the lord-lieutenant usually also holds the office of *Custos Rotulorum.* As such, he or she acts as head of the county's commission of the peace (which recommends the appointment of magistrates).

The office of sheriff (from the Old English shire-reeve) of a county was created in the tenth century. The sheriff was the special nominee of the sovereign, and the office reached the peak of its influence under the Norman kings. The Provisions of Oxford (1258) laid down a yearly tenure of office. Since the mid-16th century the office has been purely civil, with military duties taken over by the lord lieutenant of the county. The sheriff (commonly known as 'high sheriff') attends on royalty during official visits to the county, acts as the returning officer during parliamentary elections in county constituencies, attends the opening ceremony when a high court judge goes on circuit, executes high court writs, and appoints under-sheriffs to act as deputies. The appointments and duties of the sheriffs in England and Wales are laid down by the Sheriffs Act 1887.

The serving high sheriff submits a list of names of possible future sheriffs to a tribunal which chooses three names to put to the sovereign. The tribunal nominates the high sheriff annually on 12 November and the sovereign picks the name of the sheriff to succeed in the following year. The term of office runs from 25 March to the following 24 March (the civil and legal year before 1752). No person may be chosen twice in three years if there is any other suitable person in the county.

CIVIC DIGNITIES

District councils in England and local councils in Wales may petition for a royal charter granting borough or 'city' status to the council.

In England and Wales the chair of a borough or county borough council may be called a mayor, and the chair of a city council may be called a lord mayor if lord mayoralty has been conferred on that city. Parish councils in England and community councils in Wales may call themselves 'town councils', in which case their chair is the town mayor.

In Scotland the chair of a local council may be known as a convenor; a provost is the mayoral equivalent. The chair of the councils for the cities of Aberdeen, Dundee, Edinburgh and Glasgow are lord provosts.

ENGLAND

In April 2009 five county councils were given unitary status, abolishing the two-tier district/county system within these areas, and a further four unitary authorities were created from the division of the county areas of Bedfordshire and Cheshire. There are now 27 counties; divided into 201 districts, 55 unitary authorities (plus the Isles of Scilly) and 36 metropolitan boroughs.

The populations of most of the unitary authorities are in the range of 100,000 to 300,000. The district councils have populations broadly in the range of 60,000 to 100,000; some, however, have larger populations, because of the need to avoid dividing large towns, and some in mainly rural areas have smaller populations.

The main conurbations outside Greater London – Tyne and Wear, West Midlands, Merseyside, Greater Manchester, West Yorkshire and South Yorkshire – are divided into 36 metropolitan boroughs, most of which have a population of over 200,000.

There are also about 8,700 town and parish councils with a population coverage of around 17 million.

ELECTIONS

For districts, counties and for about 8,000 parishes, there are elected councils, consisting of directly elected councillors. The councillors elect one of their number as chair annually.

In general, councils can have whole council elections, elections by thirds or elections by halves. However all metropolitan authorities must hold elections by thirds. The electoral cycle of any new unitary authority is specified in the appropriate statutory order under which it is established.

FUNCTIONS

In areas with a two-tier system of local governance, functions are divided between the district and county authorities, with those functions affecting the larger area or population generally being the responsibility of the county council. A few functions continue to be exercised over the larger area by joint bodies, made up of councillors from each authority within the area.

Generally the allocation of functions is as follows:

County councils: education; strategic planning; traffic, transport and highways; fire service; consumer protection; refuse disposal; smallholdings; social care; libraries

District councils: local planning; housing; highways (maintenance of certain urban roads and off-street car parks); building regulations; environmental health; refuse collection; cemeteries and crematoria; collection of council tax and non-domestic rates

Unitary and metropolitan councils: their functions are all those listed above, except that the fire service is exercised by a joint body

Concurrently by county and district councils: recreation (parks, playing fields, swimming pools); museums; encouragement of the arts, tourism and industry

PARISH COUNCILLS

Parish or town councils are the most local tier of government in England. There are currently around 10,000 parishes in England, of which around 8,700 have councils served by approximately 70,000 councillors. Since 15 February 2008 local councils have been able to create new parish councils without seeking approval from the government. Around 80 per cent of parish councils represent populations of less than 2,500; parishes with no parish council can be grouped with neighbouring parishes under a common parish council. A parish council comprises at least five members, the number being fixed by the district council. Elections are held every four years, at the time of the election of the district councillor for the ward including the parish. Full parish councils must be formed for those parishes with more than 999 electors – below this number, parish meetings comprising the electors of the parish must be held at least twice a year.

Parish council functions include: allotments; encouragement of arts and crafts; community halls, recreational facilities (eg open spaces, swimming pools), cemeteries and crematoria; and many minor functions. They must also be given an opportunity to comment on planning applications. They may, like county and district councils, spend limited sums for the general benefit of the parish. They levy a precept on the district councils for their funds. Parish precepts for 2009–10 totalled £340m, an increase of 5.8 per cent on 2008–9.

REGIONAL ASSEMBLIES

Eight voluntary regional chambers were established for the East Midlands, the East of England, the North East, the North West, the South East, the South West, the West Midlands and Yorkshire and the Humber under the Regional Development Agencies Act 1998. The chambers operated within the same boundaries as the Regional Development Agencies. The Regional Assemblies (Preparations) Act received royal assent on 8 May 2003, giving the chambers responsibility to act as regional planning bodies and to receive direct funding from central government for fulfilling this role.

The government's *Sub-national Review of Economic Development and Regeneration* (July 2007) contained a number of recommendations for organising infrastructure at regional and local levels. In particular, regional assemblies were to be abolished by 2010, with responsibility for regional planning being passed to the regional development agencies. Local authorities will have a new statutory duty to assess local economic conditions and have a stronger role in the area's economic development.

FINANCE

The local government budget requirement (including parish precepts) for 2009–10 is £54bn; of this £25.6bn is to be raised through council tax, £19.5bn from redistributed business rates, £4.5bn from revenue support grant and £4.3bn from police grant.

In England, the average council tax per dwelling for 2009–10 is £1,175, up from £1,146 in 2008–9, an increase of 2.6 per cent. The average council tax bill for a Band D dwelling (occupied by two adults, including parish precepts) for 2009–10 is £1,414, an average increase of 3 per cent from 2008–9. The average Band D council tax is £1,453 in shire areas, £1,372 in metropolitan areas and £1,308 in London. Since 2006–7 the London figure has included a levy to fund the 2012 Olympic Games which equates to a £20 a year increase on a Band D council tax.

The provisional amount estimated to be raised from national non-domestic rates from central and local lists is £19.5bn. The non-domestic rating multiplier for England for 2009–10 is 48.5p (48.1p for small businesses). The City of London is able to set a different multiplier from the rest of England; for 2009–10 this is 48.9p (48.5p for small businesses).

Under the Local Government and Housing Act 1989, local authorities have four main ways of paying for capital expenditure: borrowing and other forms of extended credit; capital grants from central government towards some types of capital expenditure; 'usable' capital receipts from the sale of land, houses and other assets; and revenue.

The amount of capital expenditure which a local authority can finance by borrowing (or other forms of credit) is effectively limited by the credit approvals issued to it by central government. Most credit approvals can be used for any kind of local authority capital expenditure; these are known as basic credit approvals. Others (supplementary credit approvals) can be used only for the kind of expenditure specified in the approval, and so are often given to fund particular projects or services.

Local authorities can use all capital receipts from the sale of property or assets for capital spending, except in the case of sales of council houses. Generally, the 'usable' part of a local authority's capital receipts consists of 25 per cent of receipts from the sale of council houses and 50 per cent of other housing assets such as shops or vacant land. The balance has to be set aside as provision for repaying debt and meeting other credit liabilities.

EXPENDITURE

Local authority budgeted net expenditure for 2008–9 is:

Service	*£ million*
Education	41,474
Highways and transport	6,099
Social care	19,460
Housing (excluding HRA)	2,483
Cultural, environment and planning	10,355
Police	12,245
Fire and rescue	2,364
Courts	69
Central services	3,704
Mandatory rent allowances	9,075
Mandatory rent rebates	671
Rent rebates granted to HRA tenants	3,757
Other services	320
Net current expenditure	112,077
Capital financing	3,572
Capital expenditure charged to revenue account	1,225
Council tax benefit	3,468
Discretionary non-domestic rate relief	28
Bad debt provision	35
Flood defence payments to Environment Agency	29
Pensions interest cost and expected return on pensions assets	3,782
Less interest receipts	(1,264)
Less specific grants outside AEF	(19,816)
Gross revenue expenditure	103,136
Less specific grants inside AEF	(42,123)
Less area based grant	2,725
Net revenue expenditure	58,288
Less appropriations from pensions reserves	(4,704)
Less appropriations from other revenue reserves	(1,194)
Less adjustments	(13)
BUDGET REQUIREMENT	52,403

HRA = Housing Revenue Account
AEF = aggregate external finance

LONDON

The Greater London Council was abolished in 1986 and London was divided into 32 borough councils, which have a status similar to the metropolitan borough councils in the rest of England, and the City of London Corporation.

In March 1998 the government announced proposals for a Greater London Authority (GLA) covering the area of the 32 London boroughs and the City of London, which would comprise a directly elected mayor and a 25-member assembly. A referendum was held in London on 7 May 1998; the turnout was approximately 34 per cent and 72 per cent of electors voted in favour of the GLA. A London mayor was elected on 4 May 2000 and the Authority assumed its responsibilities on 3 July 2000. (*see also* Regional Government)

The GLA is responsible for transport, economic development, strategic planning, culture, health, the environment, the police and fire and emergency planning. The separately elected assembly scrutinises the mayor's activities and approves plans and budgets. There are 14 constituency assembly members, each representing a separate area of London (each constituency is made up of two or three complete London boroughs). Eleven additional members, making up the total assembly complement of 25 members, are elected on a London-wide basis, either as independents or from party political lists on the basis of proportional representation.

LONDON BOROUGH COUNCILS

The London boroughs have whole council elections every four years, in the year immediately following the county council election year. The most recent elections took place on 4 May 2006.

The borough councils have responsibility for the following functions: building regulations, cemeteries and crematoria, consumer protection, education, youth employment, environmental health, electoral registration, food, drugs, housing, leisure services, libraries, local planning, local roads, museums, parking, recreation (parks, playing fields, swimming pools), refuse collection and street cleaning, social services, town planning, and traffic management.

CITY OF LONDON CORPORATION

The City of London Corporation is the local authority for the City of London. Its legal definition is the 'Mayor and Commonalty and Citizens of the City of London'. It is governed by the court of common council, which consists of the lord mayor, 25 other aldermen and 100 common councilmen. The lord mayor and two sheriffs are nominated annually by the City guilds (the livery companies) and elected by the court of aldermen. Aldermen and councilmen are elected from the 25 wards into which the City is divided; councilmen must stand for re-election annually. The council is a legislative assembly, and there are no political parties.

The corporation has the same functions as the London borough councils. In addition, it runs the City of London Police; is the health authority for the Port of London; has health control of animal imports throughout Greater London, including at Heathrow airport; owns and manages public open spaces throughout Greater London; runs the central criminal court; and runs Billingsgate, Smithfield and Spitalfields markets.

THE CITY GUILDS (LIVERY COMPANIES)
The livery companies of the City of London grew out of early medieval religious fraternities and began to emerge as trade and craft guilds, retaining their religious aspect, in the 12th century. From the early 14th century, only members of the trade and craft guilds could call themselves citizens of the City of London. The guilds began to be called livery companies, because of the distinctive livery worn by the most prosperous guild members on ceremonial occasions, in the late 15th century.

By the early 19th century the power of the companies within their trades had begun to wane, but those wearing the livery of a company continued to play an important role in the government of the City of London. Liverymen still have the right to nominate the lord mayor and sheriffs, and most members of the court of common council are liverymen.

WALES

The Local Government (Wales) Act 1994 abolished the two-tier structure of eight county and 37 district councils which had existed since 1974, and replaced it, from 1 April 1996, with 22 unitary authorities. The new authorities were elected in May 1995. Each unitary authority inherited all the functions of the previous county and district councils, except fire services (which are provided by three combined fire authorities, composed of representatives from the unitary authorities) and national parks (which are the responsibility of three independent national park authorities).

COMMUNITY COUNCILS
In Wales community councils are the equivalent of parishes in England. Unlike England, where many areas are not in any parish, communities have been established for the whole of Wales, approximately 865 communities in all. Community meetings may be convened as and when desired.

Community or town councils exist in 736 of the communities and further councils may be established at the request of a community meeting. Community councils have broadly the same range of powers as English parish councils. Community councillors are elected for a term of four years.

ELECTIONS
Elections take place every four years; the last elections took place in May 2008.

FINANCE
Total budgeted revenue expenditure for 2009–10 is £7.3bn, an increase of 4.6 per cent on 2008–9. Total budget requirement, which excludes expenditure financed by specific and special government grants and any use of reserves, is £5.6bn. This comprises revenue support grant of £3.2bn, support from the national non-domestic rate pool of £894m, police grant of £236m and £1.2bn to be raised through council tax. The non-domestic rating multiplier for Wales for 2009–10 is 48.9p. The average band D council tax levied in Wales for 2009–10 is £1,086, comprising unitary authorities £894, police authorities £168 and community councils £24.

EXPENDITURE
Local authority budgeted net revenue expenditure for 2009–10 is:

Service	*£ million*
Education	2,484
Social services	1,371
Council fund housing, including housing benefit	841
Local environmental services	410
Roads and transport	317
Libraries, culture, heritage, sport and recreation	270
Planning, economic and community development	117
Council tax collection	31
Debt financing costs: counties	319
Central administrative and other revenue expenditure	309
Police	675
Fire	146
National parks	16
Gross revenue expenditure	7,305
Less specific and special government grants	(1,682)
Net revenue expenditure	5,623
Less appropriations from reserves	(63)
BUDGET REQUIREMENT	5,560

SCOTLAND

The Local Government etc (Scotland) Act 1994 abolished the two-tier structure of nine regional and 53 district councils which had existed since 1975 and replaced it, from 1 April 1996, with 29 unitary authorities on the mainland; the three islands councils remained. The new authorities were elected in April 1995.

In July 1999 the Scottish parliament assumed responsibility for legislation on local government. The government had established a commission on local government and the Scottish parliament (the McIntosh Commission) to make recommendations on the relationship between local authorities and the Scottish parliament and on increasing local authorities' accountability.

The local government in Scotland bill was introduced to the Scottish parliament in May 2002. The bill focused on three integrated core elements:

- A power for local authorities to promote and improve the well-being of their area and/or persons in it
- Statutory underpinning for community planning through the introduction of a duty on local authorities and key partners, including police, health boards and enterprise agencies
- A duty to secure best value

ELECTIONS
The unitary authorities consist of directly elected councillors. The Scottish Local Government (Elections) Act 2002 moved elections from a three-year to a four-year cycle; the last elections took place in May 2007.

FUNCTIONS
The functions of the councils and islands councils are: education; social work; strategic planning; the provision of infrastructure such as roads; consumer protection; flood prevention; coast protection; valuation and rating; the police and fire services; civil defence; electoral registration; public transport; registration of births, deaths and marriages; housing; leisure and recreation;

development and building control; environmental health; licensing; allotments; public conveniences; and the administration of district courts.

COMMUNITY COUNCILS
Scottish community councils differ from those in England and Wales. Their purpose as defined in statute is to ascertain and express the views of the communities they represent, and to take in the interests of their communities such action as appears to be expedient or practicable. Around 1,200 community councils have been established under schemes drawn up by local authorities in Scotland.

FINANCE
Budgeted total revenue support for 2009–10 is £10.8bn, comprising £7.6bn general revenue funding, non-domestic rate income of £2.2bn and ring-fenced grants of £757m. The non-domestic rate multiplier or poundage for 2009–10 is 48.1p. All non-domestic properties in with a rateable value of £15,000 or less may be eligible for non-domestic rates relief of up to 100 per cent. The average band D council tax for 2009–10 is £1,149.

EXPENDITURE
The 2009–10 net expenditure budget estimates for local authorities in Scotland were:

Service	*£ million*
Education	4,798
Cultural and related services	630
Social work services	2,776
Police	1,129
Roads and transport	509
Environmental services	670
Fire	328
Planning and development services	236
Other	1,771
TOTAL	12,848

NORTHERN IRELAND

For the purpose of local government Northern Ireland has a system of 26 single-tier district councils.

ELECTIONS
Council members are elected for periods of four years at a time on the principle of proportional representation.

FUNCTIONS
The district councils have three main roles. These are:

Executive: responsibility for a wide range of local services including building regulations; community services; consumer protection; cultural facilities; environmental health; miscellaneous licensing and registration provisions, including dog control; litter prevention; recreational and social facilities; refuse collection and disposal; street cleaning; and tourist development

Representative: nominating representatives to sit as members of the various statutory bodies responsible for the administration of regional services such as drainage, education, fire, health and personal social services, housing, and libraries

Consultative: acting as the medium through which the views of local people are expressed on the operation in their area of other regional services – notably conservation (including water supply and sewerage services), planning and roads – provided by those departments of central government which have an obligation, statutory or otherwise, to consult the district councils about proposals affecting their areas

FINANCE
Local government in Northern Ireland is funded by a system of rates. The ratepayer receives a combined tax bill consisting of the regional rate and the district rate, which is set by each district council. The regional and district rates are both collected by the Land and Property Services Agency (formerly the Rate Collection Agency). The product of the district rates is paid over to each council whilst the product of the regional rate supports expenditure by the departments of the executive and assembly.

Since April 2007 domestic rates bills have been based on the capital value of a property, rather than the rental value. The capital value is defined as the price the property might reasonably be expected to realise had it been sold on the open market on 1 January 2005. Non-domestic rates bills are based on 2001 rental values.

Rate bills are calculated by multiplying the property's net annual rental value (NAV) (in the case of non-domestic property), or capital value (in the case of domestic property), by the regional and district rate poundages respectively.

For 2009–10 the overall average domestic poundage is 0.6575p compared to 0.6424p in 2008–9. The overall average non-domestic rate poundage in 2009–10 is 52.35p compared to 51.21p in 2008–9.

POLITICAL COMPOSITION OF LOCAL COUNCILS

as at June 2009

Abbreviations

All.	Alliance
BNP	British National Party
C.	Conservative
DUP	Democratic Unionist Party
Green	Green
Ind.	Independent
Ind. Un.	Independent Unionist
Lab.	Labour
LD	Liberal Democrat
Lib.	Liberal
O.	Other
PC	Plaid Cymru
R	Residents Associations/Ratepayers
SD	Social Democrat
SDLP	Social Democratic and Labour Party
SF	Sinn Fein
SNP	Scottish National Party
Soc.	Socialist
UUP	Ulster Unionist Party
v.	Vacant

Total number of seats is given in parentheses after council name.

ENGLAND

COUNTY COUNCILS

Buckinghamshire (57)	C. 46; LD 11
Cambridgeshire (69)	C. 42; LD 23; Lab. 2; Green 1; v. 1
Cumbria (84)	C. 38; Lab. 24; LD 16; Ind. 5; SD 1
Derbyshire (64)	C. 33; Lab. 21; LD 8; Ind. 1; v. 1
Devon (62)	C. 41; LD 14; Lab. 4; Ind. 3; Green 1
Dorset (45)	C. 28; LD 16; Ind. 1
East Sussex (49)	C. 29; LD 13; Lab. 4; Ind. 3
Essex (75)	C. 60; LD 12; Ind. 2; Lab. 1
Gloucestershire (63)	C. 42; LD 13; Lab. 4; O. 2; Green 1; Ind. 1
Hampshire (78)	C. 51; LD 25; Lab. 1; O. 1
Hertfordshire (77)	C. 56; LD 16; Lab. 3; BNP 1; Green 1
Kent (84)	C. 74; LD 7; Lab. 2; Ind. 1
Lancashire (84)	C. 51; Lab. 16; LD 10; Ind. 3; Green 2; BNP 1; O. 1
Leicestershire (55)	C. 36; LD 14; Lab. 4; BNP 1
Lincolnshire (77)	C. 60; Ind. 8; LD 5; Lab. 4
Norfolk (84)	C. 60; LD 13; Green 7; Lab. 3; O. 1
North Yorkshire (72)	C. 48; Ind. 11; LD 11; Lab. 1; Lib. 1
Northamptonshire (73)	C. 56; LD 9; Lab. 6; Ind. 2
Nottinghamshire (67)	C. 35; Lab. 13; Ind. 9; LD 9; O. 1
Oxfordshire (74)	C. 52; LD 10; Lab. 9; Green 2; Ind. 1
Somerset (58)	C. 35; LD 21; Lab. 2
Staffordshire (62)	C. 49; LD 4; O. 4; Lab. 3; Ind. 2
Suffolk (75)	C. 55; LD 11; Lab. 4; Green 2; Ind. 2; O. 1
Surrey (80)	C. 56; LD 13; R 9; Lab. 1; Ind. 1
Warwickshire (62)	C. 38; LD 12; Lab. 11; Ind. 1
West Sussex (71)	C. 48; LD 21; Lab. 2
Worcestershire (57)	C. 42; LD 8; Lab. 3; O. 3; Lib. 1

DISTRICT COUNCILS

Adur (29)	C. 26; R 2; LD 1
Allerdale (56)	Lab. 21; C. 19; Ind. 11; LD 4; v. 1
Amber Valley (45)	C. 29; Lab. 13; BNP 2; v. 1
Arun (56)	C. 42; LD 9; Lab. 3; Ind. 2
Ashfield (33)	LD 12; Lab. 8; Ind. 7; C. 3; O. 2; v. 1
Ashford (43)	C. 28; LD 8; O. 3; Ind. 2; Lab. 2
Aylesbury Vale (59)	C. 37; LD 21; Ind. 1
Babergh (43)	C. 19; LD 16; Ind. 7; O. 1
Barrow-in-Furness (36)	C. 17; Lab. 8; Ind. 4; Soc. 4; O. 2; LD 1
Basildon (42)	C. 28; Lab. 11; LD 3
Basingstoke and Deane (60)	C. 33; LD 14; Lab. 9; Ind. 2; O. 2
Bassetlaw (48)	C. 30; Lab. 16; Ind. 2
Blaby (39)	C. 27; LD 7; Lab. 4; Ind. 1
Bolsover (37)	Lab. 27; Ind. 7; R 2; O. 1
Boston (32)	O. 22; C. 6; Ind. 3; BNP 1
Braintree (60)	C. 42; Lab. 9; R 5; Green 2; LD 1; Ind. 1
Breckland (54)	C. 48; Lab. 3; O. 3
Brentwood (37)	C. 28; LD 6; Lab. 2 ; Ind. 1
Broadland (47)	C. 34; LD 10; Ind. 3
Bromsgrove (39)	C. 26; Lab. 6; R 6; Ind. 1
Broxbourne (38)	C. 35; Lab. 3
Broxtowe (44)	C. 16; LD 14; Lab. 12; Ind. 1; v. 1
Burnley (45)	LD 22; Lab. 12; C. 6; BNP 4; Ind. 1
Cambridge (42)	LD 28; Lab. 11; C. 1; Green 1; Ind. 1
Cannock Chase (41)	Lab. 15; LD 14; C. 12
Canterbury (50)	C. 29; LD 18; Lab. 2; Ind. 1
Carlisle (52)	Lab. 23; C. 21; LD 7; Ind. 1
Castle Point (41)	C. 25; Ind. 15 ; Lab. 1
Charnwood (52)	C. 32; Lab. 13; LD 5; BNP 1; Ind. 1
Chelmsford (57)	C. 31; LD 26
Cheltenham (39)	LD 19; C. 17; O. 3
Cherwell (50)	C. 44; LD 4; Lab. 2
Chesterfield (48)	LD 38; Lab. 10
Chichester (48)	C. 33; LD 11; Ind. 4
Chiltern (40)	C. 30; LD 9; Ind. 1
Chorley (47)	C. 27; Lab. 15; LD 3; Ind. 2
Christchurch (24)	C. 17; Ind. 3; LD 3; v. 1
Colchester (60)	C. 27; LD 23; Lab. 7; Ind. 3
Copeland (51)	Lab. 31; C. 18; Ind. 2
Corby (29)	Lab. 16; C. 8; LD 5
Cotswolds (44)	C. 37; LD 5; Ind. 2
Craven (30)	C. 15; Ind. 10; LD 5;
Crawley (37)	C. 26; Lab. 9; LD 2
Dacorum (51)	C. 44; LD 5; Lab. 2
Dartford (44)	C. 26; Lab. 12; R 6
Daventry (38)	C. 34; LD 2; Lab. 1; v. 1

Derbyshire Dales (39)	C. 26; LD 8; Lab. 3; Ind. 1; v. 1
Dover (45)	C. 28; Lab. 15; LD 2
East Cambridgeshire (39)	C. 24; LD 13; Ind. 2
East Devon (59)	C. 40; LD 11; Ind. 8
East Dorset (36)	C. 25; LD 11
East Hampshire (44)	C. 30; LD 13; Ind. 1
East Hertfordshire (50)	C. 42; Ind. 4; LD 4
East Lindsey (60)	C. 27; O. 20; Lab. 7; Ind. 3; LD 3
East Northamptonshire (40)	C. 38; Ind. 2
East Staffordshire (39)	C. 24; Lab. 12; LD 2; Ind. 1
Eastbourne (27)	LD 20; C. 7
Eastleigh (44)	LD 38; C. 4; Lab. 2
Eden (38)	O. 18; C. 13; LD 5; Ind. 2
Elmbridge (60)	C. 32; R 21; LD 7
Epping Forest (58)	C. 35; LD 9; R 6; BNP 4; Ind. 3; Lab. 1
Epsom and Ewell (38)	R 23; LD 10; C. 4; Lab. 1
Erewash (51)	C. 27; Lab. 19; Ind. 2; LD 2; v. 1
Exeter (40)	LD 13; C. 12; Lab. 11; Lib. 4
Fareham (31)	C. 22; LD 9
Fenland (40)	C. 39; Ind. 1
Forest Heath (27)	C. 20; LD 4; O. 2; Ind. 1
Forest of Dean (48)	C. 24; Ind. 13; Lab. 8; LD 2; v. 1
Fylde (51)	C. 29; Ind. 14; R 3; O. 3; LD 2
Gedling (50)	C. 28; Lab. 9; LD 9; Ind. 4
Gloucester (36)	C. 17; LD 11; Lab. 8
Gosport (34)	C. 16; LD 13; Lab. 4; Ind. 1
Gravesham (44)	C. 27; Lab. 17
Great Yarmouth (39)	C. 24; Lab. 15
Guildford (48)	C. 27; LD 21
Hambleton (44)	C. 39; Ind. 3; LD 2
Harborough (37)	C. 26; LD 11
Harlow (33)	C. 18; LD 9; Lab. 6
Harrogate (54)	C. 28; LD 19; Ind. 6; v. 1
Hart (35)	C. 17; LD 10; O. 6; Ind. 2
Hastings (32)	C. 15; Lab 13; LD 3; Ind. 1
Havant (38)	C. 32; Lab 3; LD 3
Hertsmere (39)	C. 29; LD 7; Lab. 3
High Peak (43)	C. 25; Lab. 9; LD 5; Ind. 4
Hinckley and Bosworth (34)	LD 19; C. 12; Lab. 2; Ind. 1
Horsham (44)	C. 30; LD 12; Ind. 2
Huntingdonshire (52)	C. 38; LD 11; Ind. 2; v. 1
Hyndburn (35)	C. 17; Lab. 12; Ind. 5; v. 1
Ipswich (48)	Lab. 21; C. 19; LD 8
Kettering (36)	C. 28; Lab. 6; Ind. 2
King's Lynn and West Norfolk (62)	C. 52; Lab 4; LD 4; Ind. 2
Lancaster (60)	Ind. 19; Lab. 13; Green 12; C. 11; LD 5
Lewes (41)	LD 21; C. 18; Ind. 2
Lichfield (56)	C. 43; Lab. 5; LD 4; Ind. 3; v. 1
Lincoln City (33)	C. 18; Lab. 14; LD 1
Maidstone (55)	C. 29; LD 21; Ind. 5;
Maldon (31)	C. 27; Ind. 4;
Malvern Hills (38)	C. 29; LD 5; Ind. 3; Green 1
Mansfield (46)	Ind. 28; Lab. 13; LD 4; C. 1
Melton (28)	C. 20; Ind. 5; Lab. 3
Mendip (47)	C. 24; LD 21; Ind. 2
Mid Devon (42)	C. 17; Ind. 15; LD 10
Mid Suffolk (40)	C. 25; LD 10; Ind. 5
Mid Sussex (54)	C. 30; LD 23; Lab. 1
Mole Valley (41)	C. 22; LD 14; Ind. 3; O. 2
New Forest (60)	C. 46; LD 14
Newark and Sherwood (46)	C. 26; Ind. 9; Lab. 7; LD 4
Newcastle-under-Lyme (60)	C. 24; LD 19; Lab. 12; O. 5
North Devon (43)	C. 23; LD 17; Ind. 3
North Dorset (33)	C. 17; LD 13; Ind. 3
North East Derbyshire (53)	Lab. 28; C. 10; LD 9; Ind. 6
North Hertfordshire (49)	C. 32; LD 9; Lab. 8
North Kesteven (43)	C. 25; Ind. 14; LD 3; v. 1
North Norfolk (48)	LD 30; C. 16; Ind. 1; v. 1
North Warwickshire (35)	C. 20; Lab. 15
North West Leicestershire (38)	C. 27; Lab. 5; LD 3; BNP 2; Ind. 1
Northampton (47)	LD 26; C. 15; Lab. 5; Ind. 1
Norwich (39)	Lab. 15; Green 13; LD 6; C. 5
Nuneaton and Bedworth (34)	C. 18; Lab. 14; BNP 2
Oadby and Wigston (26)	LD 21; C. 5
Oxford (48)	Lab. 23; LD 16; Green 7; O. 2
Pendle (49)	LD 19; C. 16; Lab. 11; BNP 2; Ind. 1
Preston (57)	Lab. 24; C. 21; LD 9; Ind. 3
Purbeck (24)	C. 11; LD 11; Ind. 2
Redditch (29)	C. 15; Lab. 10; LD 3; BNP 1
Reigate and Banstead (51)	C. 39; R 6; LD 3; Ind. 2; Lab. 1
Ribble Valley (40)	C. 30; LD 9; Ind. 1
Richmondshire (34)	C. 18; O. 10; LD 6
Rochford (39)	C. 33; LD 5; Ind. 1
Rossendale (36)	C. 21; Lab. 11; LD 3; O. 1
Rother (38)	C. 28; LD 8; Ind. 2
Rugby (48)	C. 27; Lab. 11; LD 10
Runnymede (42)	C. 36; Ind. 6
Rushcliffe (50)	C. 34; LD 11; Green 2; Lab. 2; Ind. 1
Rushmoor (42)	C. 29; LD 8; Lab. 5
Ryedale (30)	C. 14; LD 7; Ind. 5; Lib. 2; R 1; v. 1
St Albans (58)	LD 30; C. 22; Lab. 5; Ind. 1
St Edmundsbury (45)	C. 36; O. 4; LD 3; Lab. 2
Scarborough (50)	C. 21; Ind. 16; LD 6; Lab. 3; Green 2; v. 2
Sedgemoor (50)	C. 36; Lab. 11; LD 3
Selby (41)	C. 30; Lab. 9; Ind. 2
Sevenoaks (54)	C. 41; LD 7; Lab. 4; Ind. 1; BNP 1
Shepway (46)	C. 37; LD 6; O. 2; Ind. 1
South Bucks (40)	C. 36; Ind. 2; LD 2
South Cambridgeshire (57)	C. 31; LD 16; Ind. 9; Lab. 1
South Derbyshire (36)	C. 21; Lab. 13; Ind. 2
South Hams (40)	C. 28; LD 9; Ind. 2; O. 1
South Holland (37)	C. 25; Ind. 11; O. 1
South Kesteven (58)	C. 35; Ind. 15; LD 6; Lab. 2
South Lakeland (51)	LD 36; C. 14; Lab. 1
South Norfolk (46)	C. 39; LD 7
South Northamptonshire (42)	C. 35; Ind. 7
South Oxfordshire (48)	C. 38; LD 6; Ind. 2; Lab. 1; R 1
South Ribble (55)	C. 44; Lab. 9; Ind. 1; LD 1
South Somerset (60)	LD 38; C. 17; Ind. 5
South Staffordshire (49)	C. 42; Ind. 5; Lab. 1; LD 1
Spelthorne (39)	C. 31; LD 8
Stafford (59)	C. 41; Lab. 12; LD 6

Staffordshire Moorlands (56)	C. 29; Ind. 16. LD 6; Lab. 5
Stevenage (39)	Lab. 30; C. 5; LD 3; Ind. 1
Stratford-on-Avon (52)	C. 32; LD 18; Ind. 2
Stroud (51)	C. 31; Lab. 7; Green 6; LD 5; Ind. 1; O. 1
Suffolk Coastal (55)	C. 45; LD 9; Lab. 1
Surrey Heath (40)	C. 30; LD 7; Lab. 2; Ind. 1
Swale (47)	C. 28; Lab. 10; LD 5; Ind. 4
Tamworth (30)	C. 24; Lab. 5; Ind. 1
Tandridge (42)	C. 33; LD 8; Ind. 1
Taunton Deane (56)	LD 26; C. 25; Ind. 4; Lab. 1
Teignbridge (46)	LD 20; C. 19; Ind. 7
Tendring (60)	C. 27; O. 12; Lab. 6; LD 6; R. 5; Ind. 4
Test Valley (48)	C. 33; LD 15
Tewkesbury (38)	C. 19; LD 16; Ind. 3
Thanet (56)	C. 34; Lab. 19; Ind. 3
Three Rivers (48)	LD 31; C. 12; Lab. 4; BNP 1
Tonbridge and Malling (53)	C. 46; LD 7
Torridge (36)	C. 14; Ind. 12; LD 5; Lib. 4; v. 1
Tunbridge Wells (48)	C. 44; LD 4
Uttlesford (44)	C. 27; LD 14; Ind. 3
Vale of White Horse (51)	LD 33; C. 18
Warwick (46)	C. 24; Lab. 9; LD 9; Ind. 4
Watford (37)	LD 27; C. 4; Green 3; Lab. 3
Waveney (48)	C. 30; Lab. 12; LD 3; Ind. 2; Green 1
Waverley (57)	C. 51; Ind. 3; LD 3
Wealden (55)	C. 33; LD 13; O. 6; Green 2; Ind. 1
Wellingborough (36)	C. 29; Lab. 4; Ind. 2; v. 1
Welwyn and Hatfield (48)	C. 38; Lab. 7; LD 3
West Devon (31)	C. 13; O. 9; LD 7; Ind. 2
West Dorset (48)	C. 28; LD 14; Ind. 6
West Lancashire (54)	C. 35; Lab. 18; Ind. 1
West Lindsey (37)	C. 21; LD 14; Ind. 2
West Oxfordshire (49)	C. 40; LD 6; Ind. 2; Lab. 1
West Somerset (31)	Ind. 17; C. 13; v. 1
Weymouth and Portland (36)	C. 19; LD 10; Lab. 4; Ind. 3
Winchester (57)	C. 29; LD 24; Ind. 3; Lab. 1
Woking (36)	C. 19; LD 17
Worcester (35)	C. 17; Lab. 13; LD 3; Ind. 2
Worthing (37)	C. 25; LD 12
Wychavon (45)	C. 35; LD 9; v. 1
Wycombe (60)	C. 49; LD 7; Lab. 2; Ind. 2
Wyre (55)	C. 46; Lab. 8; Lib. 1
Wyre Forest (42)	C. 21; Ind. 12; Lib. 5; Lab. 2; LD 2

LONDON BOROUGH COUNCILS

Barking and Dagenham (51)	Lab. 36; BNP 12; C. 2; Ind. 1
Barnet (63)	C. 37; Lab. 20; LD 6
Bexley (63)	C. 54; Lab. 8; Ind. 1
Brent (63)	LD 27; Lab. 21; C. 15
Bromley (60)	C. 49; LD 7; Lab. 4
Camden (54)	LD 24; Lab. 15; C. 12; Green 3
Croydon (70)	C. 43; Lab. 26; Ind. 1
Ealing (69)	C. 43; Lab. 23; LD 3
Enfield (63)	C. 33; Lab. 28; O. 2
Greenwich (51)	Lab. 36; C. 13; LD 2
Hackney (57)	Lab. 45; C. 9; LD 2; Green 1
Hammersmith and Fulham (46)	C. 33; LD 13
Haringey (57)	Lab. 31; LD 26; C. 1
Harrow (63)	C. 35; Lab. 24; Ind. 2; LD 2
Havering (54)	C. 33; R 15; Lab. 2; BNP 1; LD 1
Hillingdon (65)	C. 45; Lab. 17; LD 2; Ind. 1
Hounslow (60)	C. 24; Lab. 24; O. 6; Ind. 3; LD 3
Islington (48)	Lab. 23; LD 23; Green 1; Ind. 1
Kensington and Chelsea (54)	C. 45; Lab. 9
Kingston upon Thames (48)	LD 25; C. 21; Ind. 1; Lab. 1
Lambeth (63)	Lab. 38; LD 18; C. 6; Green 1
Lewisham (55)	Lab. 27; LD 17; Green 6; C. 3; Soc. 2
Merton (60)	C. 29; Lab. 27; R 3; Ind. 1
Newham (60)	Lab. 54; O. 4; Ind. 2
Redbridge (63)	C. 30; Lab. 17; LD 11; Ind. 4; BNP 1
Richmond upon Thames (54)	LD 35; C. 18; Ind. 1
Southwark (63)	Lab. 29; LD 27; C. 6; Green 1
Sutton (54)	LD 31; C. 20; Ind. 1; O. 1; v. 1
Tower Hamlets (51)	Lab. 33; C. 8; O. 6; LD 4
Waltham Forest (60)	Lab. 25; LD 20; C. 15
Wandsworth (60)	C. 51; Lab. 9
Westminster (60)	C. 49; Lab. 11

METROPOLITAN BOROUGHS

Barnsley (63)	Lab. 32; Ind. 22; C. 6; O. 2; LD 1
Birmingham (120)	C. 49; Lab. 36; LD 32; O. 3
Bolton (60)	Lab. 28; C. 23; LD 9
Bradford (90)	C. 37; Lab. 35; LD 13; Green 3; BNP 2
Bury (51)	C. 26; Lab. 16; LD 9
Calderdale (51)	C. 21; LD 16; Lab. 8; Ind. 4; BNP 1; O. 1
Coventry (54)	C. 27; Lab. 24; Soc. 2; LD 1
Doncaster (64)	Lab. 25; Ind. 12; LD 11; C. 9; O. 7
Dudley (72)	C. 43; Lab. 26; LD 2; O. 1
Gateshead (66)	Lab. 41; LD 24; Lib. 1
Kirklees (69)	Lab. 22; C. 21; LD 19; Green 4; Ind. 2; BNP 1
Knowsley (63)	Lab. 47; LD 16
Leeds (99)	Lab. 42; LD 25; C. 23; Ind. 5; Green 3; BNP 1
Liverpool (90)	LD 46; Lab 39; Lib. 3; Green 2
Manchester (96)	Lab. 62; LD 33; C. 1
Newcastle-upon-Tyne (78)	LD 50; Lab. 28
North Tyneside (60)	C. 31; Lab. 21; LD 8
Oldham (60)	LD. 30; Lab. 22; C. 7; Ind. 1
Rochdale (60)	LD 33; Lab. 18; C. 8; Ind. 1
Rotherham (63)	Lab. 49; C. 10; Ind. 2; BNP 1; O. 1
St Helens (48)	Lab. 23; LD 18; C. 6; v. 1
Salford (60)	Lab. 36; C. 13; LD 9; Ind. 2
Sandwell (72)	Lab. 49; C. 14; LD 5; BNP 2; Ind. 2
Sefton (66)	LD 28; Lab. 21; C. 17
Sheffield (84)	LD 44; Lab. 36; Green 3; Ind. 1
Solihull (51)	C. 26; LD 18; Lab. 5; BNP 1; Green 1
South Tyneside (54)	Lab. 31; Ind. 12; O. 5; C. 3; LD 3
Stockport (63)	LD 36; Lab. 12; C. 10; R 3; Ind. 1; v. 1

Sunderland (75)	Lab. 48; C. 22; Ind. 4; LD 1
Tameside (57)	Lab. 43; C. 10; Ind. 3; v.1
Trafford (63)	C. 39; Lab. 19; LD 5
Wakefield (63)	Lab. 32; C. 23; Ind. 6; LD 2
Walsall (60)	C. 34; Lab. 17; LD 6; Ind. 2; O. 1
Wigan (75)	Lab. 41; C. 11; Ind. 10; O. 9; LD 4
Wirral (66)	C. 25; Lab. 20; LD 20; O. 1
Wolverhampton (60)	Lab. 28; C. 27; LD 5

UNITARY COUNCILS

Bath and North East Somerset (65)	C. 31; LD 26; Lab. 5; Ind. 2; O. 1
Bedford (36)	LD 13; C. 9; Ind. 7; Lab. 7
Blackburn with Darwen (64)	Lab. 27; C. 18; LD 13; O. 5; Ind. 1
Blackpool (42)	C. 27; Lab. 12; LD 3
Bournemouth (54)	C. 39; LD 7; Ind. 5; Lab. 3
Bracknell Forest (42)	C. 39; Lab. 3
Brighton and Hove (54)	C. 25; Lab. 13; Green 12; LD 2; Ind. 1; v. 1
Bristol (70)	LD 36; C. 17; Lab 16; Green 1
Central Bedfordshire (66)	C. 54; LD 11; Ind. 1
Cheshire East (81)	C. 59; LD 12; Lab. 6; Ind. 4
Cheshire West and Chester (72)	C. 53; Lab. 13; LD 4; Ind. 2
Cornwall (123)	C. 50; LD 38; Ind. 32 O. 3
Darlington (53)	Lab. 29; C. 18; LD 6
Derby (51)	LD 19; C. 15; Lab. 15; Ind. 2
Durham (126)	Lab. 68; LD 27; Ind. 21; C. 10
East Riding of Yorkshire (67)	C. 46; LD 12; Ind. 4; Lab. 3; SD 1; O. 1
Halton (56)	Lab. 33; LD 14; C. 9
Hartlepool (48)	Lab. 23; Ind. 12; LD 6; C. 5; O. 2
Herefordshire (58)	C. 31; Ind. 14; LD 9; Lab. 2 Green 1; O. 1
Isles of Scilly (21)*	O. 21
Isle of Wight (40)	C. 24; Ind. 10; LD 5; Lab. 1
Kingston-upon-Hull (59)	LD 34; Lab. 20; O. 3; C. 2
Leicester (54)	Lab. 37; C. 8; LD 6; Green 2; Ind. 1
Luton (48)	Lab. 26; LD 17; C. 5
Medway (55)	C. 33; Lab. 13; LD 8; Ind. 1
Middlesbrough (49)	Lab. 28; Ind. 13; C. 6; Green 1; LD 1
Milton Keynes (51)	LD 21; C. 20; Lab. 10
North East Lincolnshire (42)	LD 19; C. 16; Lab. 5; Ind. 2
North Lincolnshire (43)	Lab. 22; C. 18; Ind. 2; LD 1
North Somerset (61)	C. 46; Ind. 6; LD 5; Lab. 3; Green 1
Northumberland (67)	LD 26; C. 19; Lab. 17; Ind. 5
Nottingham (55)	Lab. 42; C. 7; LD 6
Peterborough (57)	C. 43; Ind. 9; LD 3; Lab. 2
Plymouth (57)	C. 37; Lab. 18; Ind. 2
Poole (42)	C. 23; LD 17; Ind. 2
Portsmouth (42)	LD 23; C. 17; Lab. 2
Reading (46)	Lab. 19; C. 18; LD 8; Ind. 1
Redcar and Cleveland (59)	Lab. 25; LD 15; C. 11; Ind. 7
Rutland (26)	C. 19; Ind. 5; LD 2
Shropshire (74)	C. 54; LD 11; Lab. 7; Ind. 2
Slough (41)	Lab. 22; C. 7; Ind. 6; LD 3; Lib. 3
South Gloucestershire (70)	C. 33; LD 28; Lab. 9
Southampton (48)	C. 26; Lab. 14; LD 8
Southend-on-Sea (51)	C. 27; LD 11; Ind. 7; Lab. 6
Stockton-on-Tees (56)	Lab. 22; Ind. 15; C. 13; LD 5; v. 1
Stoke-on-Trent (60)	Ind. 25; Lab. 13; BNP 9; C. 6; LD 5; O. 2
Swindon (59)	C. 43; Lab. 12; LD 3; Ind. 1
Telford and Wrekin (54)	C. 25; Lab. 18; Ind. 4; O. 4; LD 3
Thurrock (49)	C. 23; Lab. 23; Ind. 2; BNP 1
Torbay (37)	C. 24; LD 9; Ind. 4
Warrington (57)	LD 28; Lab. 22; C. 7
West Berkshire (52)	C. 36; LD 16
Wiltshire (98)	C. 62; LD 24; Ind. 7; O. 3; Lab. 2
Windsor and Maidenhead (57)	C. 36; LD 16; R 5
Wokingham (54)	C. 44; LD 10
York (47)	LD 20; Lab. 18; C. 7; Green 2

* Thirteen councillors are elected by the residents of the isle of St Mary's and two councillors each are elected by the residents of the four other islands (Bryher, St Agnes, St Martins and Tresco)

WALES

Blaenau Gwent (42)	Ind. 19; Lab. 15; O. 6; LD 2
Bridgend (54)	Lab. 26; Ind. 14; LD 7; C. 6; PC 1
Caerphilly (73)	Lab. 32; PC 32; Ind. 9
Cardiff (75)	LD 35; C. 17; Lab. 13; PC 7; Ind. 3
Carmarthenshire (74)	Ind. 30; PC 30; Lab. 11; LD 1; O. 2
Ceredigion (42)	PC 20; Ind. 12; LD 9; Lab. 1
Conwy (59)	C. 22; Ind. 13; PC 13; Lab. 7; LD 4
Denbighshire (47)	C. 18; Ind. 11; PC 8; Lab. 7; O. 3
Flintshire (70)	Ind. 26; Lab. 22; LD 12; C. 9; PC 1
Gwynedd (75)	PC 35; Ind. 18; O. 13; LD 5; Lab. 4
Merthyr Tydfil (33)	Ind. 19; Lab. 10; LD 4;
Monmouthshire (43)	C. 28; Lab. 6; LD 5; Ind. 2; PC 2
Neath Port Talbot (64)	Lab. 37; PC 11; Ind. 6; LD 4; O. 3; SD 3
Newport (50)	Lab. 22; C. 17; LD 9; Ind. 1; PC 1
Pembrokeshire (60)	Ind. 39; O. 6; C. 5; Lab. 5; PC 5
Powys (73)	O. 44; LD 15; C. 9; Lab. 4; Ind. 1
Rhondda Cynon Taff (75)	Lab. 45; PC 20; Ind. 6; LD 3; C. 1
Swansea (72)	Lab. 30; LD 24; Ind. 13; C. 4; PC 1
Torfaen (44)	Lab. 18; Ind. 13; C. 5; O. 3; PC 3; LD 2
Vale of Glamorgan (47)	C. 25; Lab. 13; PC 6; Ind. 3
Wrexham (52)	O. 28; Lab. 11; C. 5; Ind. 4; PC 4
Ynys Mon (Isle of Anglesey) (40)	Ind. 20; PC 8; Lab. 5; O. 3; C. 2; LD 2

SCOTLAND

Aberdeen (43)	LD 15; SNP 13; Lab. 10; C. 4; Ind. 1
Aberdeenshire (68)	LD 24; SNP 20; C. 13; Ind. 11
Angus (29)	O. 15; SNP 13; Ind. 1
Argyll and Bute (36)	Ind. 17; SNP 10; LD 6; C. 3
Clackmannanshire (18)	Lab. 8; SNP 7; C. 1; Ind. 1; LD 1
Dumfries and Galloway (47)	C. 18; Lab. 14; SNP 10; LD 3; Ind. 2
Dundee (29)	SNP 14; Lab. 8; C. 3; Ind. 2; LD 2
East Ayrshire (32)	Lab. 14; SNP 14; C. 3; Ind. 1
East Dunbartonshire (24)	SNP 8; Lab. 6; C. 5; LD 3; Ind. 2
East Lothian (23)	Lab. 7; SNP 7; LD 6; C. 2; Ind. 1
East Renfrewshire (20)	C. 7; Lab. 7; SNP 3; Ind. 2; LD 1
Edinburgh (58)	LD 17; Lab. 15; SNP 12; C. 11; Green 3
Eilean Siar (Western Isles) (31)	Ind. 25; SNP 4; Lab. 2
Falkirk (32)	Lab. 14; SNP 13; Ind. 3; C. 2
Fife (78)	Lab. 24; SNP 22; LD 21; Ind. 7; C. 4
Glasgow (79)	Lab. 46; SNP 21; Green 5; LD 5; C. 1; Ind. 1
Highland (80)	Ind. 29; LD 22; SNP 17; Lab. 7; O. 5
Inverclyde (20)	Lab. 8; SNP 5; LD 4; Ind. 2; C. 1
Midlothian (18)	Lab. 10; SNP 6; LD 2
Moray (26)	Ind. 11; SNP 10; C. 3; Lab. 2
North Ayrshire (30)	Lab. 12; SNP 8; Ind. 5; C. 3; LD 2
North Lanarkshire (70)	Lab. 41; SNP 22; Ind. 5; C. 1; LD 1
Orkney Islands (21)	Ind. 21
Perth and Kinross (41)	SNP 18; C. 11; LD 7; Lab. 3; Ind. 2
Renfrewshire (40)	SNP 17; Lab. 16; LD 4; C. 2; Ind. 1
Scottish Borders (34)	C. 11; LD 10; SNP 6; Ind. 5; O. 2
Shetland Islands (22)	Ind. 22
South Ayrshire (30)	C. 12; SNP 8; Lab. 7; Ind. 3
South Lanarkshire (67)	Lab. 31; SNP 26; C. 7; Ind. 3
Stirling (22)	Lab. 8; SNP 7; C. 4; LD 3
West Dunbartonshire (22)	SNP 9; Lab. 8; Ind. 4; Soc. 1
West Lothian (32)	Lab. 14; SNP 13; O. 3; C. 1; Ind. 1

NORTHERN IRELAND

Antrim (19)	DUP 5; UUP 5; SF 3; All. 2; SDLP 2; Ind. 1; O. 1
Ards (23)	DUP 11; UUP 6; All. 3; Ind. 2; SDLP 1
Armagh City (22)	SDLP 6; DUP 5; SF 5; UUP 5; Ind. Un. 1
Ballymena (24)	DUP 8; O. 6; UUP 4; Ind. 2; SDLP 2; C. 1; SF 1
Ballymoney (16)	DUP 6; SF 3; SDLP 2; UUP 2; Ind. Un. 1; O. 1; v. 1
Banbridge (17)	DUP 6; UUP 5; SDLP 3; All. 1; O. 1; SF 1
Belfast (51)	DUP 15; SF 14; SDLP 8; UUP 7; All. 4; O. 2; Ind. 1
Carrickfergus (17)	DUP 9; All. 3; UUP 3; Ind. 2
Castlereagh (23)	DUP 12; All. 4; UUP 4; SDLP 2; O. 1
Coleraine (22)	DUP 8; UUP 8; SDLP 3; All. 1; Ind. 1; SF 1
Cookstown (16)	SDLP 5; SF 5; DUP 3; UUP 3
Craigavon (26)	DUP 8; SF 6; UUP 6; Ind. 3; SDLP 3
Derry City (30)	SDLP 14; SF 10; DUP 5; UUP 1
Down (23)	SDLP 10; SF 5; UUP 3; DUP 2; C. 1; Green 1; Ind. Un. 1
Dungannon and South Tyrone (22)	SF 8; UUP 5; DUP 4; SDLP 4; Ind. 1
Fermanagh (23)	SF 7; SDLP 5; UUP 5; DUP 4; Ind. 2
Larne (15)	DUP 4; UUP 4; All. 2; Ind. 2; SDLP 2; O. 1
Limavady (15)	SF 6; SDLP 3; DUP 2; O. 2; UUP 2
Lisburn (30)	DUP 12; UUP 7; SF 4; All. 3; SDLP 3; O. 1
Magherafelt (16)	SF 6; DUP 4; O. 2; SDLP 2; UUP 2
Moyle (15)	SF 4; DUP 3; Ind. 3; SDLP 3; UUP 2
Newry and Mourne (30)	SF 12; SDLP 9; DUP 2; Ind. 2; UUP 2; Green 1; Ind. Un. 1; O. 1
Newtownabbey (25)	DUP 12; UUP 6; All. 3; Ind. 1; O. 1; SDLP 1; SF 1
North Down (25)	DUP 8; UUP 8; All. 6; Ind. 2; Green 1
Omagh (21)	SF 10; DUP 3; SDLP 3; UUP 3; Ind. 2
Strabane (16)	SF 8; DUP 3; SDLP 2; UUP 2; Ind. 1

ENGLAND

The region of England lies between 55° 46′ and 49° 57′ 30″ N. latitude (from a few miles north of the mouth of the Tweed to the Lizard), and between 1° 46′ E. and 5° 43′ W. longitude (from Lowestoft to Land's End). England is bounded on the north by the Cheviot Hills; on the south by the English Channel; on the east by the Straits of Dover (Pas de Calais) and the North Sea; and on the west by the Atlantic Ocean, Wales and the Irish Sea. It has a total area of 130,432 sq. km (50,360 sq. miles): land 130,279 sq. km (50,301 sq. miles); inland water 153 sq. km (59 sq. miles).

POPULATION

The population at the 2001 census was 49,138,831. The average density of the population in 2001 was 377 persons per sq. km (976 per sq. mile).

FLAG

The flag of England is the cross of St George, a red cross on a white field (cross gules in a field argent). The cross of St George, the patron saint of England, has been used since the 13th century.

RELIEF

There is a marked division between the upland and lowland areas of England. In the extreme north the Cheviot Hills (highest point, the Cheviot, 815m/2,674ft) form a natural boundary with Scotland. Running south from the Cheviots, though divided from them by the Tyne Gap, is the Pennine range (highest point, Cross Fell, 893m/2,930ft), the main orological feature of the country. The Pennines culminate in the Peak District of Derbyshire (Kinder Scout, 636m/2,088ft). West of the Pennines are the Cumbrian mountains, which include Scafell Pike (978m/3,210ft), the highest peak in England, and to the east are the Yorkshire Moors, their highest point being Urra Moor (454m/1,490ft).

In the west, the foothills of the Welsh mountains extend into the bordering English counties of Shropshire (the Wrekin, 407m/1,334ft; Long Mynd, 516m/1,694ft) and Hereford and Worcester (the Malvern Hills – Worcestershire Beacon, 425m/1,394ft). Extensive areas of highland and moorland are also to be found in the south-western peninsula formed by Somerset, Devon and Cornwall, principally Exmoor (Dunkery Beacon, 519m/1,704ft), Dartmoor (High Willhays, 621m/2,038ft) and Bodmin Moor (Brown Willy, 420m/1,377ft). Ranges of low, undulating hills run across the south of the country, including the Cotswolds in the Midlands and south-west, the Chilterns to the north of London, and the North (Kent) and South (Sussex) Downs of the south-east coastal areas.

The lowlands of England lie in the Vale of York, East Anglia and the area around the Wash. The lowest-lying are the Cambridgeshire Fens in the valleys of the Great Ouse and the river Nene, which are below sea-level in places. Since the 17th century extensive drainage has brought much of the Fens under cultivation. The North Sea coast between the Thames and the Humber, low-lying and formed of sand and shingle for the most part, is subject to erosion and defences against further incursion have been built along many stretches.

HYDROGRAPHY

The Severn is the longest river in Great Britain, rising in the north-eastern slopes of Plynlimon (Wales) and entering England in Shropshire, with a total length of 354km (220 miles) from its source to its outflow into the Bristol Channel, where it receives the Bristol Avon on the east and the Wye on the west; its other tributaries are the Vyrnwy, Tern, Stour, Teme and Upper (or Warwickshire) Avon. The Severn is tidal below Gloucester, and a high bore or tidal wave sometimes reverses the flow as high as Tewkesbury (21.75km/13.5 miles above Gloucester). The scenery of the greater part of the river is very picturesque, and the Severn is a noted salmon river, with some of its tributaries being famous for trout. Navigation is assisted by the Gloucester and Berkeley Ship Canal (26km/16.25 miles), which admits vessels of 350 tons to Gloucester. The Severn Tunnel was begun in 1873 and completed in 1886 at a cost of £2m and after many difficulties caused by flooding. It is 7km (4 miles 628 yards) in length (of which 3.67km/2.25 miles are under the river). The Severn road bridge between Haysgate, Gwent, and Almondsbury, Glos, with a centre span of 988m (3,240ft), was opened in 1966.

The longest river wholly in England is the Thames, with a total length of 346km (215 miles) from its source in the Cotswold hills to the Nore, and is navigable by ocean-going ships to London Bridge. The Thames is tidal to Teddington (111km/69 miles from its mouth) and forms county boundaries almost throughout its course; on its banks are situated London, Windsor Castle, Eton College and Oxford University. Of the remaining English rivers, those flowing into the North Sea are the Tyne, Wear, Tees, Ouse and Trent from the Pennine Range, the Great Ouse (257km/160 miles), which rises in Northamptonshire, and the Orwell and Stour from the hills of East Anglia. Flowing into the English Channel are the Sussex Ouse from the Weald, the Itchen from the Hampshire Hills, and the Axe, Teign, Dart, Tamar and Exe from the Devonian hills. Flowing into the Irish Sea are the Mersey, Ribble and Eden from the western slopes of the Pennines and the Derwent from the Cumbrian mountains.

The English Lakes, notable for their picturesque scenery and poetic associations, lie in Cumbria's Lake District; the largest are Windermere (14.7 sq. km/5.7 sq. miles), Ullswater (8.8 sq. km/3.4 sq. miles) and Derwent Water (5.3 sq. km/2.0 sq. miles).

ISLANDS

The Isle of Wight is separated from Hampshire by the Solent. The capital, Newport, stands at the head of the estuary of the Medina, and Cowes (at the mouth) is the chief port. Other centres are Ryde, Sandown, Shanklin, Ventnor, Freshwater, Yarmouth, Totland Bay, Seaview and Bembridge.

Lundy (the name is derived from the Old Norse for 'puffin island'), 18km (11 miles) north-west of Hartland Point, Devon, is around 5km (3 miles) long and almost 1km (half a mile) wide on average, with a total area of around 452 hectares (1,116 acres), and a population of around 18. It became the property of the National Trust in 1969 and is now principally a bird sanctuary.

The Isles of Scilly comprise around 140 islands and

skerries (total area, 10 sq. km/6 sq. miles) situated 45 km (28 miles) south-west of Land's End in Cornwall. Only five are inhabited: St Mary's, St Agnes, Bryher, Tresco and St Martin's. The population at the 2001 census was 2,153. The entire group has been designated an Area of Outstanding Natural Beauty because of its unique flora and fauna. Tourism and the winter/spring flower trade for the home market form the basis of the economy of the islands. The island group is a recognised rural development area.

EARLY HISTORY

Archaeological evidence suggests that England has been inhabited since at least the Palaeolithic period, though the extent of the various Palaeolithic cultures was dependent upon the degree of glaciation. The succeeding Neolithic and Bronze Age cultures have left abundant remains throughout the country; the best-known of these are the henges and stone circles of Stonehenge (ten miles north of Salisbury, Wilts) and Avebury (Wilts), both of which are believed to have been of religious significance. In the latter part of the Bronze Age the Goidels, a people of the Celtic race, invaded the country and brought with them Celtic civilisation and dialects; as a result place names in England bear witness to the spread of the invasion across the whole region.

THE ROMAN CONQUEST

The Roman conquest of Gaul (57–50 BC) brought Britain into close contact with Roman civilisation, but although Julius Caesar raided the south of Britain in 55 and 54 BC, conquest was not undertaken until nearly 100 years later. In AD 43 the Emperor Claudius dispatched Aulus Plautius, with a well-equipped force of 40,000, and himself followed with reinforcements in the same year. Success was delayed by the resistance of Caratacus (Caractacus), the British leader from AD 48–51, who was finally captured and sent to Rome, and by a great revolt in AD 61 led by Boudicca (Boadicea), Queen of the Iceni, but the south of Britain was secured by AD 70, and Wales and the area north to the Tyne by about AD 80.

In AD 122, the Emperor Hadrian visited Britain and built a continuous rampart, since known as Hadrian's Wall, from Wallsend to Bowness (Tyne to Solway). The work was entrusted by the Emperor Hadrian to Aulus Platorius Nepos, legate of Britain from AD 122 to 126, and it was intended to form the northern frontier of the Roman Empire.

The Romans administered Britain as a province under a governor, with a well-defined system of local government, each Roman municipality ruling itself and its surrounding territory, while London was the centre of the road system and the seat of the financial officials of the Province of Britain. Colchester, Lincoln, York, Gloucester and St Albans stand on the sites of five Roman municipalities, and Wroxeter, Caerleon, Chester, Lincoln and York were at various times the sites of legionary fortresses. Well-preserved Roman towns have been uncovered at or near Silchester *(Calleva Atrebatum)*, ten miles south of Reading, Wroxeter *(Viroconium Cornoviorum)*, near Shrewsbury, and St Albans *(Verulamium)* in Hertfordshire.

Four main groups of roads radiated from London, and a fifth (the Fosse) ran obliquely from Lincoln through Leicester, Cirencester and Bath to Exeter. Of the four groups radiating from London, one ran south-east to Canterbury and the coast of Kent, a second to Silchester and thence to parts of western Britain and south Wales, a third (later known as Watling Street) ran through St Albans to Chester, with various branches, and the fourth reached Colchester, Lincoln, York and the eastern counties.

In the fourth century Britain was subjected to raids along the east coast by Saxon pirates, which led to the establishment of a system of coastal defences from the Wash to Southampton Water, with forts at Brancaster, Burgh Castle (Yarmouth), Walton (Felixstowe), Bradwell, Reculver, Richborough, Dover, Lympne, Pevensey and Porchester (Portsmouth). The Irish (Scoti) and Picts in the north were also becoming more aggressive and from around AD 350 incursions became more frequent and more formidable. As the Roman Empire came increasingly under attack towards the end of the fourth century, many troops were removed from Britain for service in other parts of the empire. The island was eventually cut off from Rome by the Teutonic conquest of Gaul, and with the withdrawal of the last Roman garrison early in the fifth century, the Romano-British were left to themselves.

SAXON SETTLEMENT

According to legend, the British King Vortigern called in the Saxons to defend his lands against the Picts. The Saxon chieftains Hengist and Horsa landed at Ebbsfleet, Kent, and established themselves in the Isle of Thanet, but the events during the one-and-a-half centuries between the final break with Rome and the re-establishment of Christianity are unclear. However, it would appear that over the course of this period the raids turned into large-scale settlement by invaders traditionally known as Angles (England north of the Wash and East Anglia), Saxons (Essex and southern England) and Jutes (Kent and the Weald), which pushed the Romano-British into the mountainous areas of the north and west. Celtic culture outside Wales and Cornwall survives only in topographical names. Various kingdoms established at this time attempted to claim overlordship of the whole country, hegemony finally being achieved by Wessex (with the capital at Winchester) in the ninth century. This century also saw the beginning of raids by the Vikings (Danes), which were resisted by Alfred the Great (871–899), who fixed a limit on the advance of Danish settlement by the Treaty of Wedmore (878), giving them the area north and east of Watling Street on the condition that they adopt Christianity.

In the tenth century the kings of Wessex recovered the whole of England from the Danes, but subsequent rulers were unable to resist a second wave of invaders. England paid tribute *(Danegeld)* for many years, and was invaded in 1013 by the Danes and ruled by Danish kings (including Cnut) from 1016 until 1042, when Edward the Confessor was recalled from exile in Normandy. On Edward's death in 1066 Harold Godwinson (brother-in-law of Edward and son of Earl Godwin of Wessex) was chosen to be King of England. After defeating (at Stamford Bridge, Yorkshire, 25 September 1066) an invading army under Harald Hadraada, King of Norway (aided by the outlawed Earl Tostig of Northumbria, Harold's brother), Harold was himself defeated at the Battle of Hastings on 14 October 1066, and the Norman conquest secured the throne of England for Duke William of Normandy, a cousin of Edward the Confessor.

CHRISTIANITY

Christianity reached the Roman province of Britain from Gaul in the third century (or possibly earlier). Alban, traditionally Britain's first martyr, was put to death as a

Christian during the persecution of Diocletian (22 June 303) at his native town *Verulamium,* and the Bishops of *Londinium, Eboracum* (York), and *Lindum* (Lincoln) attended the Council of Arles in 314. However, the Anglo-Saxon invasions submerged the Christian religion in England until the sixth century: conversion was undertaken in the north from 563 by Celtic missionaries from Ireland led by St Columba, and in the south by a mission sent from Rome in 597 which was led by St Augustine, who became the first archbishop of Canterbury. England appears to have been converted again by the end of the seventh century and followed, after the Council of Whitby in 663, the practices of the Roman Church, which brought the kingdom into the mainstream of European thought and culture.

PRINCIPAL CITIES

There are 50 cities in England and space constraints prevent us from including profiles of them all. Below is a selection of England's principal cities with the date on which city status was conferred in parenthesis. Other cities are: Chichester (pre-1900), Derby (1977), Ely (pre-1900), Exeter (pre-1900), Gloucester (pre-1900), Hereford (pre-1900), Lancaster (1937), Lichfield (pre-1900), London (pre-1900), Peterborough (pre-1900), Plymouth (1928), Portsmouth (1926), Preston (2002), Ripon (pre-1900), Salford (1926), Sunderland (1992), Truro (pre-1900), Wakefield (pre-1900), Wells (pre-1900), Westminster (pre-1900), Wolverhampton (2000) and Worcester (pre-1900).

Certain cities have also been granted a lord mayoralty – this grant confers no additional powers or functions and is purely honorific. Cities with lord mayors are: Birmingham, Bradford, Bristol, Canterbury, Chester, Coventry, Exeter, Kingston-upon-Hull, Leeds, Leicester, Liverpool, London, Manchester, Newcastle-upon-Tyne, Norwich, Nottingham, Oxford, Plymouth, Portsmouth, Sheffield, Stoke-on-Trent, Westminster and York.

BATH (PRE-1900)

Bath stands on the River Avon between the Cotswold Hills to the north and the Mendips to the south. In the early 18th century, Bath became England's premier spa town where the rich and celebrated members of fashionable society gathered to 'take the waters' and enjoy the town's theatres and concert rooms. During this period the architect John Wood laid the foundations for a new Georgian city to be built using the honey coloured stone for which Bath is famous today.

Contemporary Bath is a thriving tourist destination and remains a leading cultural, religious and historical centre with many art galleries and historic sites including the Pump Room (1790); the Royal Crescent (1767); the Circus (1754); the 18th-century Assembly Rooms (housing the Museum of Costume); Pulteney Bridge (1771); the Guildhall and the Abbey, now over 500 years old, which is built on the site of a Saxon monastery. In 2006 the Bath Thermae Spa was completed and the hot springs re-opened to the public for the first time since 1978; combining five historic spa buildings with contemporary architecture, it is the only spa in the UK to utilise naturally occurring thermal waters.

BIRMINGHAM (PRE-1900)

Birmingham is Britain's second largest city, with a population of over one million. The generally accepted derivation of 'Birmingham' is the *ham* (dwelling-place) of the *ing* (family) of *Beorma,* presumed to have been Saxon. During the Industrial Revolution the town grew into a major manufacturing centre and in 1889 was granted city status.

Recent developments include Millennium Point, which houses Thinktank, the Birmingham science museum, and Brindleyplace, a development of shops, offices and leisure facilities on a former industrial site clustered around canals. In 2003 the Bullring shopping centre was officially opened as part of the city's urban regeneration programme.

The principal buildings are the Town Hall (1834–50), the Council House (1879), Victoria Law Courts (1891), the University of Birmingham (1906–9), the 13th-century Church of St Martin-in-the-Bull-Ring (rebuilt 1873), the cathedral (formerly St Philip's Church) (1711), the Roman Catholic cathedral of St Chad (1839–41), the Assay Office (1773), the Rotunda (1964) and the National Exhibition Centre (1976). There is also the Birmingham Museum and Art Gallery which was founded in 1885 and is home to a collection of Pre-Raphaelite paintings.

BRADFORD (PRE-1900)

During the Industrial Revolution of the 18th and 19th centuries Bradford expanded rapidly, largely as a result of the thriving wool industry.

Bradford city centre has a host of buildings with historical and cultural interest, including City Hall, with its 19th-century Lord Mayor's rooms and Victorian law court; Bradford Cathedral; the Priestley, a theatre and arts centre originally established as the Bradford Civic Playhouse by J. B. Priestley and friends; the National Media Museum which houses seven floors of interactive displays and three cinemas; Piece Hall Yard which incorporates the Bradford Club, a Victorian Gothic style building dating from 1837, and the Peace Museum.

BRIGHTON AND HOVE (2000)

Brighton and Hove is situated on the south coast of England, around 96 km (60 miles) south of London. Originally a fishing village called Brighthelmstone, it was transformed into a fashionable seaside resort in the 18th century when Dr Richard Russell popularised the benefits of his 'sea-water cure'; as one of the closest beaches to London, Brighton began to attract wealthy visitors. One of these was the Prince Regent (the future King George IV), who first visited in 1783 and became so fond of the city that in 1807 he bought the former farmhouse he had been renting, and gradually turned it into Brighton's most recognisable building, the Royal Pavilion. The Pavilion is renowned for its Indo-Saracenic exterior, featuring minarets and an enormous central dome designed by John Nash, combined with the lavish chinoiserie of Frederick Crace's and Robert Jones' interiors.

Brighton and Hove's Regency heritage can also be seen in the numerous elegant squares and crescents designed by Amon Wilds and Augustin Busby that dominate the seafront.

Brighton and Hove is once again a fashionable resort, known for its cafe culture, lively nightlife and thriving gay scene.

BRISTOL (PRE-1900)

Bristol was a royal borough before the Norman conquest. The earliest form of the name is *Bricgstow.*

The principal buildings include the 12th-century Cathedral with Norman chapter house and gateway; the

14th-century Church of St Mary Redcliffe; Wesley's Chapel, Broadmead; the Merchant Venturers' Almshouses; the Council House (1956); the Guildhall; the Exchange (erected from the designs of John Wood in 1743); Cabot Tower; the University and Clifton College. The Roman Catholic cathedral at Clifton was opened in 1973.

The Clifton Suspension Bridge, with a span of 214m (702ft) over the Avon, was projected by Isambard Kingdom Brunel in 1836 but was not completed until 1864. Brunel's SS *Great Britain,* the first ocean-going propeller-driven ship, now forms a museum at the Western Dockyard, from where she was originally launched in 1843. The docks themselves have been extensively restored and redeveloped; the 19th-century two-storey former tea warehouse is now the Arnolfini centre for contemporary arts, and an 18th-century sail loft houses the Architecture Centre. Behind the baroque-domed facade of the former 'E' Shed are shops, cafes, restaurants and the Watershed Media Centre, and on Princes Wharf 1950s transit sheds, which formerly housed the Industrial Museum, are being renovated and converted into the new Museum of Bristol, due to open in 2011.

CAMBRIDGE (1951)

Cambridge, a settlement far older than its ancient university, lies on the River Cam (or Granta). The city is a county town and regional headquarters. Its industries include technology research and development, and biotechnology. Among its open spaces are Jesus Green, Sheep's Green, Coe Fen, Parker's Piece, Christ's Pieces, the University Botanic Garden, and the 'Backs' – lawns and gardens through which the Cam winds behind the principal line of college buildings. Historical sites east of the Cam include King's Parade, Great St Mary's Church, Gibbs' Senate House and King's College Chapel.

University and college buildings provide the outstanding features of Cambridge's architecture but several churches (especially St Benet's, the oldest building in the city, and Holy Sepulchre or the Round Church) are also notable. The Guildhall (1937) stands on a site, of which at least part has held municipal buildings since 1224.

CANTERBURY (PRE-1900)

Canterbury, seat of the Archbishop of Canterbury, the primate of the Church of England, dates back to prehistoric times. It was the Roman *Durovernum Cantiacorum* and the Saxon *Cant-wara-byrig* (stronghold of the men of Kent). It was here in 597 that St Augustine began the conversion of the English to Christianity, when Ethelbert, King of Kent, was baptised.

Of the Benedictine St Augustine's Abbey, burial place of the Jutish Kings of Kent, only ruins remain. St Martin's Church, on the eastern outskirts of the city, is stated by Bede to have been the place of worship of Queen Bertha, the Christian wife of King Ethelbert, before the advent of St Augustine.

In 1170 the rivalry of Church and State culminated in the murder in Canterbury Cathedral, by Henry II's knights, of Archbishop Thomas Becket. His shrine became a great centre of pilgrimage, as described in Chaucer's *Canterbury Tales.* After the Reformation pilgrimages ceased, but the prosperity of the city was strengthened by an influx of Huguenot refugees, who introduced weaving. The poet and playwright Christopher Marlowe was born and raised in Canterbury (the city is home to the 1,000-seat Marlowe Theatre) and there are also literary associations with Defoe, Dickens, Joseph Conrad and Somerset Maugham.

The cathedral, its architecture ranging from the 11th to the 15th centuries, is famous worldwide. Visitors are attracted particularly to the Martyrdom, the Black Prince's Tomb, the Warriors' Chapel and the many examples of medieval stained glass.

The medieval city walls are built on Roman foundations and the 14th-century West Gate is one of the finest buildings of its kind in the country.

The Canterbury Arts Festival takes place at a variety of venues throughout the city each autumn.

CARLISLE (PRE-1900)

Carlisle is situated at the confluence of the rivers Eden and Caldew, 497km (309 miles) north-west of London and around 16km (10 miles) from the Scottish border. It was granted a charter in 1158.

The city stands at the western end of Hadrian's Wall and dates from the original Roman settlement of *Luguvalium.* Granted to Scotland in the tenth century, Carlisle is not included in the Domesday Book. William Rufus reclaimed the area in 1092 and the castle and city walls were built to guard Carlisle and the western border; the citadel is a Tudor addition to protect the south of the city. Border disputes were common until the problem of the Debateable Lands was settled in 1552. During the Civil War the city remained Royalist; in 1745 Carlisle was besieged for the last time by the Young Pretender (Bonnie Prince Charlie).

The cathedral, originally a 12th-century Augustinian priory, was enlarged in the 13th and 14th centuries after the diocese was created in 1133. To the south is a restored tithe barn and nearby the 18th-century church of St Cuthbert, the third to stand on a site dating from the seventh century.

Carlisle is the major shopping, commercial and agricultural centre for the area, and industries include the manufacture of metal goods, biscuits and textiles. However, the largest employer is the services sector, most notably in central and local government, retailing and transport. The city occupies an important position at the centre of a network of major roads, as a stage on the main west coast rail services, and with its own airport at Crosby-on-Eden.

CHESTER (PRE-1900)

Chester is situated on the River Dee. Its recorded history dates from the first century when the Romans founded the fortress of *Deva.* The city's name is derived from the Latin *castra* (a camp or encampment). During the Middle Ages, Chester was the principal port of north-west England but declined with the silting of the Dee estuary and competition from Liverpool. The city was also an important military centre, notably during Edward I's Welsh campaigns and the Elizabethan Irish campaigns. During the Civil War, Chester supported the King and was besieged from 1643 to 1646. Chester's first charter was granted *c.*1175 and the city was incorporated in 1506. The office of sheriff is the earliest created in the country (1120s), and in 1992 the mayor was granted the title of Lord Mayor, who also enjoys the title 'Admiral of the Dee'.

The city's architectural features include the city walls (an almost complete two-mile circuit), the unique 13th-century Rows (covered galleries above the street-level shops), the Victorian Gothic Town Hall (1869), the castle (rebuilt 1788 and 1822) and numerous half-timbered buildings. The cathedral was a Benedictine abbey until the Dissolution of the Monasteries.

Remaining monastic buildings include the chapter house, refectory and cloisters and there is a modern free-standing bell tower. The Norman church of St John the Baptist was a cathedral church in the early Middle Ages.

COVENTRY (PRE-1900)

Coventry is an important industrial centre, producing vehicles, machine tools, agricultural machinery, man-made fibres, aerospace components and telecommunications equipment. New investment has come from financial services, power transmission, professional services, leisure and education.

The city owes its beginning to Leofric, Earl of Mercia, and his wife Godiva who, in 1043, founded a Benedictine monastery. The guildhall of St Mary and three of the city's churches date from the 14th and 15th centuries, and 16th-century almshouses can still be seen. Coventry's first cathedral was destroyed during the Reformation, its second in the 1940 blitz (the walls and spire remain) and the new cathedral designed by Sir Basil Spence, consecrated in 1962, now draws numerous visitors.

Coventry is the home of the University of Warwick, Coventry University, Coventry Transport Museum, which specialises in British road transport, and the Skydome Arena.

DURHAM (PRE-1900)

The city of Durham is a major tourist attraction and its prominent Norman cathedral and castle are set high on a wooded peninsula overlooking the River Wear. The cathedral was founded as a shrine for the body of St Cuthbert in 995. The present building dates from 1093 and among its many treasures is the tomb of the Venerable Bede (673–735). Durham's prince bishops had unique powers up to 1836, being lay rulers as well as religious leaders. As a palatinate, Durham could have its own army, nobility, coinage and courts. The castle was the main seat of the prince bishops for nearly 800 years; it is now used as a college by the University of Durham. The university, founded in the early 19th century on the initiative of Bishop William Van Mildert, is England's third oldest.

Among other buildings of interest is the Guildhall in the Market Place which dates from the 14th century. Annual events include Durham's regatta in June (claimed to be the oldest rowing event in Britain) and the annual Gala (formerly Durham Miners' Gala) in July.

KINGSTON-UPON-HULL (PRE-1900)

Hull (officially Kingston-upon-Hull, so named by Edward I) lies at the junction of the River Hull with the Humber, 35km (22 miles) from the North Sea. It is one of the major seaports of the UK. The port provides a wide range of cargo services, including ro-ro and container traffic, and handles an estimated million passengers annually on daily sailings to Rotterdam and Zeebrugge. There is a variety of manufacturing and service industries. City status was accorded in 1897 and the office of mayor raised to the dignity of Lord Mayor in 1914.

The city, restored after heavy air raid damage during the Second World War, has good educational facilities with both the University of Hull and a campus of the University of Lincoln being within its boundaries. Hull is home to the world's only submarium, The Deep, a £45.5m project which opened in 2002, and the Kingston Communications Stadium, with a seating capacity for 25,000, which was also completed in 2002.

Tourism is a growing industry; the old town area has been renovated and includes museums, a marina and a shopping complex. Just west of the city is the Humber Bridge, a suspension bridge, opened in 1981, which crosses the Humber Estuary.

LEEDS (PRE-1900)

Leeds, situated in the lower Aire Valley, is a junction for road, rail, canal and air services and an important commercial centre. It was first incorporated by Charles I in 1626. The earliest forms of the name are *Loidis* or *Ledes,* the origins of which are obscure.

The principal buildings are the Civic Hall (1933), the Town Hall (1858), the Municipal Buildings and Art Gallery (1884) with the Henry Moore Gallery (1982), the Corn Exchange (1863) and the University. The parish church (St Peter's) was rebuilt in 1841; the 17th-century St John's Church has a fine interior with a famous English Renaissance screen; the last remaining 18th-century church in the city is Holy Trinity in Boar Lane (1727). Kirkstall Abbey (about three miles from the centre of the city), founded by Henry de Lacy in 1152, is one of the most complete examples of a Cistercian house now remaining. Temple Newsam, birthplace of Lord Darnley and largely rebuilt by Sir Arthur Ingram *c.*1620, was acquired by the council in 1922. Adel Church, about five miles from the centre of the city, is a fine Norman structure. The Royal Armouries Museum forms part of a group of museums, including the Tower of London, which house the national collection of antique arms and armour.

LEICESTER (1919)

Leicester is situated in central England. The city was an important Roman settlement and also one of the five Viking boroughs of Danelaw. In 1485 Richard III was buried in Leicester following his death at the nearby Battle of Bosworth. In 1589 Queen Elizabeth I granted a charter to the city and the ancient title was confirmed by letters patent in 1919.

The textile industry was responsible for Leicester's early expansion and the city still maintains a strong manufacturing base. Cotton mills and factories are now undergoing extensive regeneration and are being converted into offices, apartments, bars and restaurants. The principal buildings include the two universities (the University of Leicester and De Montfort University), as well as the Town Hall, the 13th-century Guildhall, De Montfort Hall, Leicester Cathedral, the Jewry Wall (the UK's highest standing Roman wall), St Nicholas Church and St Mary de Castro church. The motte and Great Hall of Leicester can be seen from the castle gardens, situated next to the River Soar.

Leicester is now one of the UK's most ethnically diverse cities – home to the only Jain temple in the West and hosting the country's second-largest Caribbean carnival.

LINCOLN (PRE-1900)

Situated 64km (40 miles) inland on the River Witham, Lincoln derives its name from a contraction of *Lindum Colonia,* the settlement founded in AD 48 by the Romans to command the crossing of Ermine Street and Fosse Way. Sections of the third-century Roman city wall can be seen, including an extant gateway (Newport Arch), and excavations have discovered traces of a sewerage system unique in Britain. The Romans also drained the surrounding fenland and created a canal system, laying the foundations of Lincoln's agricultural prosperity and also the city's importance in the medieval wool trade as a port and staple town.

As one of the five boroughs of Danelaw, Lincoln was an important trading centre in the ninth and tenth centuries and prosperity from the wool trade lasted until the 14th century. This wealth enabled local merchants to build parish churches, of which three survive, and there are also remains of a 12th-century Jewish community (Jew's House and Court, Aaron's House). However, the removal of the staple to Boston in 1369 heralded a decline, from which the city only recovered fully in the 19th century, when improved fen drainage made Lincoln agriculturally important. Improved canal and rail links led to industrial development, mainly in the manufacture of machinery, components and engineering products.

The castle was built shortly after the Norman Conquest and is unusual in having two mounds; on one motte stands a keep (Lucy's Tower) added in the 12th century. It currently houses one of the four surviving copies of the Magna Carta. The cathedral was begun *c.*1073 when the first Norman bishop moved the see of Lindsey to Lincoln, but was mostly destroyed by fire and earthquake in the 12th century. Rebuilding was begun by St Hugh and completed over a century later. Other notable architectural features are the 12th-century High Bridge, the oldest in Britain still to carry buildings, and the Guildhall, situated above the 15th-century Stonebow gateway.

LIVERPOOL (PRE-1900)

Liverpool, on the north bank of the river Mersey, 5km (3 miles) from the Irish Sea, is the United Kingdom's foremost port for Atlantic trade. Tunnels link Liverpool with Birkenhead and Wallasey.

There are 2,100 acres of dockland on both sides of the river and the Gladstone and Royal Seaforth Docks can accommodate tanker-sized vessels. Liverpool Free Port was opened in 1984.

Liverpool was created a free borough in 1207 and a city in 1880. From the early 18th century it expanded rapidly with the growth of industrialisation and the transatlantic slave trade. Surviving buildings from this period include the Bluecoat Chambers (1717, formerly the Bluecoat School), the Town Hall (1754, rebuilt to the original design 1795), and buildings in Rodney Street, Canning Street and the suburbs. Notable from the 19th and 20th centuries are the Anglican cathedral, built from the designs of Sir Giles Gilbert Scott (the foundation stone was laid in 1904, but the building was only completed in 1980); the Catholic Metropolitan Cathedral (designed by Sir Frederick Gibberd, consecrated 1967) and St George's Hall (1842), regarded as one of the finest modern examples of classical architecture. The refurbished Albert Dock (designed by Jesse Hartley) contains the Merseyside Maritime Museum, the International Slavery Museum and the Tate Liverpool art gallery.

In 1852 an act was passed establishing a public library, museum and art gallery; as a result Liverpool had one of the first public libraries in the country. The Brown, Picton and Hornby libraries form one of the country's major collections. The Victoria Building of Liverpool University; the Royal Liver, Cunard and Mersey Docks & Harbour Company buildings at the Pier Head; the Municipal Buildings and the Philharmonic Hall are other examples of the city's fine architecture.

Six areas of Liverpool's maritime mercantile city were designated as UNESCO World Heritage Sites in 2004, and Liverpool was elected as the European Capital of Culture for 2008.

MANCHESTER (PRE-1900)

Manchester (the *Mamucium* of the Romans, who occupied it in AD 79) is a commercial and industrial centre engaged in the engineering, chemical, clothing, food processing and textile industries and in education. Banking, insurance and a growing leisure industry are among its prime commercial activities. The city is connected with the sea by the Manchester Ship Canal, opened in 1894, 57km (35.5 miles) long, and accommodating ships up to 15,000 tons.

The principal buildings are the Town Hall, erected in 1877 from the designs of Alfred Waterhouse, with a large extension of 1938; the Royal Exchange (1869, enlarged 1921); the Central Library (1934); Heaton Hall; the 17th-century Chetham Library; the Rylands Library (1900), which includes the Althorp collection; the university precinct; the 15th-century cathedral (formerly the parish church); the Manchester Central conference and exhibition centre and the Bridgewater Hall (1996) concert venue. Manchester is the home of the Hallé Orchestra, the Royal Northern College of Music, the Royal Exchange Theatre and numerous public art galleries.

To accommodate the Commonwealth Games held in the city in 2002, new sports facilities were built including a stadium, swimming pool complex and the National Cycling Centre.

The town received its first charter of incorporation in 1838 and was created a city in 1853.

NEWCASTLE UPON TYNE (PRE-1900)

Newcastle upon Tyne, on the north bank of the River Tyne, is 13km (8 miles) from the North Sea. A cathedral and university city, it is the administrative, commercial and cultural centre for north-east England and the principal port. It is an important manufacturing centre with a wide variety of industries.

The principal buildings include the Castle Keep (12th century), Black Gate (13th century), Blackfriars (13th century), West Walls (13th century), St Nicholas's Cathedral (15th century, fine lantern tower), St Andrew's Church (12th–14th century), St John's (14th–15th century), All Saints (1786 by Stephenson), St Mary's Roman Catholic Cathedral (1844), Trinity House (17th century), Sandhill (16th-century houses), Guildhall (Georgian), Grey Street (1834–9), Central Station (1846–50), Laing Art Gallery (1904), University of Newcastle Physics Building (1962) and Medical Building (1985), Civic Centre (1963) and the Central Library (1969). Open spaces include the Town Moor (927 acres) and Jesmond Dene. Numerous bridges span the Tyne at Newcastle, including the Tyne Bridge (1928) and the tilting Millennium Bridge (2001) – which links the city with Gateshead to the south.

The city's name is derived from the 'new castle' (1080) erected as a defence against the Scots. In 1400 it was made a county, and in 1882 a city.

NORWICH (PRE-1900)

Norwich grew from an early Anglo-Saxon settlement near the confluence of the rivers Yare and Wensum, and now serves as the provincial capital for the predominantly agricultural region of East Anglia. The name is thought to relate to the most northerly of a group of Anglo-Saxon villages or *wics*. The city's first known charter was granted in 1158 by Henry II.

Norwich serves its surrounding area as a market town and commercial centre, with banking and insurance prominent among the city's businesses. From the 14th century until the Industrial Revolution, Norwich was the regional centre of the woollen industry, but now the biggest single industry is financial services and principal trades are engineering, printing, shoemaking, the production of chemicals and clothing, food processing and technology. Norwich is accessible to seagoing vessels by means of the River Yare, entered at Great Yarmouth, 32km (20 miles) to the east.

Among many historic buildings are the cathedral (completed in the 12th century and surmounted by a 15th-century spire 96m (315ft) in height); the keep of the Norman castle (now a museum and art gallery); the 15th-century flint-walled Guildhall; some thirty medieval parish churches; St Andrew's and Blackfriars' Halls; the Tudor houses preserved in Elm Hill and the Georgian Assembly House. The University of East Anglia is on the city's western boundary.

NOTTINGHAM (PRE-1900)

Nottingham stands on the River Trent. *Snotingaham* or *Notingeham,* literally the homestead of the people of Snot, is the Anglo-Saxon name for the Celtic settlement of *Tigguocobauc,* or the house of caves. In 878, Nottingham became one of the five boroughs of Danelaw. William the Conqueror ordered the construction of Nottingham Castle, while the town itself developed rapidly under Norman rule. Its laws and rights were later formally recognised by Henry II's charter in 1155. The castle became a favoured residence of King John. In 1642 King Charles I raised his personal standard at Nottingham Castle at the start of the Civil War.

Nottingham is home to Notts County FC (the world's oldest football league side), Nottingham Forest FC, Nottingham Racecourse, Trent Bridge cricket ground and the National Watersports Centre. The principal industries include textiles, pharmaceuticals, food manufacturing, engineering and telecommunications. There are two universities within the city boundaries.

Architecturally, Nottingham has a wealth of notable buildings, particularly those designed in the Victorian era by T. C. Hine and Watson Fothergill. The city council owns the castle, of Norman origin but restored in 1878, Wollaton Hall (1580–8), Newstead Abbey (once home of Lord Byron), the Guildhall (1888) and Council House (1929). St Mary's, St Peter's and St Nicholas' churches are of interest, as is the Roman Catholic cathedral (Pugin, 1842–4). Nottingham was granted city status in 1897.

OXFORD (PRE-1900)

Oxford is a university city, an important industrial centre and a market town. Industry played a minor part in Oxford until the motor industry was established in 1912.

Oxford is known for its architecture, its oldest specimens being the reputedly Saxon tower of St Michael's Church, the remains of the Norman castle and city walls, and the Norman church at Iffley. It also has many Gothic buildings, such as the Divinity Schools, the Old Library at Merton College, William of Wykeham's New College, Magdalen and Christ Church colleges and many other college buildings. Later centuries are represented by the Laudian quadrangle at St John's College, the Renaissance Sheldonian Theatre by Wren, Trinity College Chapel, All Saints Church, Hawksmoor's mock-Gothic at All Souls College, and the 18th-century Queen's College. In addition to individual buildings, High Street and Radcliffe Square both form interesting architectural compositions. Most of the colleges have gardens, those of Magdalen, New College, St John's and Worcester being the largest.

The Oxford University Museum of Natural History, renowned for its spectacular neo-gothic architecture, houses the university's scientific collections of zoological, entomological and geological specimens and is attached to the neighbouring Pitt Rivers Museum which houses ethnographic and archaeological objects from around the world. The Ashmolean is the city's museum of art and archaeology and Modern Art Oxford hosts a programme of contemporary art exhibitions.

ST ALBANS (PRE-1900)

The origins of St Albans, situated on the River Ver, stem from the Roman town of *Verulamium.* Named after the first Christian martyr in Britain, who was executed there, St Albans has developed around the Norman abbey and cathedral church (consecrated 1115), built partly of materials from the old Roman city. The museums house Iron Age and Roman artefacts and the Roman theatre, unique in Britain, has a stage as opposed to an amphitheatre. Archaeological excavations in the city centre have revealed evidence of pre-Roman, Saxon and medieval occupation.

The town's significance grew to the extent that it was a signatory and venue for the drafting of the Magna Carta. It was also the scene of riots during the Peasants' Revolt, the French King John was imprisoned there after the Battle of Poitiers, and heavy fighting took place there during the Wars of the Roses.

Previously controlled by the Abbot, the town achieved a charter in 1553 and city status in 1877. The street market, first established in 1553, is still an important feature of the city, as are many hotels and inns, surviving from the days when St Albans was an important coach stop. Tourist attractions include historic churches and houses and a 15th-century clock tower.

The city is now home to a wide range of businesses, with special emphasis on information and legal services, and is home to the Royal National Rose Society.

SALISBURY (PRE-1900)

The history of Salisbury centres around the cathedral and cathedral close. The city evolved from an Iron Age camp a mile to the north of its current position which was strengthened by the Romans and called *Serviodunum.* The Normans built a castle and cathedral on the site and renamed it Sarum. In 1220 Bishop Richard Poore and the architect Elias de Derham decided to build a new Gothic style cathedral. The cathedral was completed 38 years later and a community known as New Sarum, now called Salisbury, grew around it. Originally the cathedral had a squat tower; the 123m (404ft) spire that makes the cathedral the tallest medieval structure in the world was added *c.*1315. A walled close with houses for the clergy was built around the cathedral; the Medieval Hall still stands today, alongside buildings dating from the 13th to the 20th century, including some designed by Sir Christopher Wren.

A prosperous wool and cloth trade allowed Salisbury to flourish until the 17th century. When the wool trade declined new crafts were established including cutlery, leather and basket work, saddlery, lacemaking, joinery and malting. By 1750 it had become an important road junction and coaching centre and in the Victorian era the railways enabled a new age of expansion and prosperity. Today Salisbury is a thriving tourist centre.

SHEFFIELD (PRE-1900)
Sheffield is situated at the junction of the Sheaf, Porter, Rivelin and Loxley valleys with the River Don and was created a city in 1893. Though its cutlery, silverware and plate have long been famous, Sheffield has other and now more important industries: special and alloy steels, engineering, tool-making, medical equipment and media-related industries (in its new cultural industries quarter). Sheffield has two universities and is an important research centre.

The parish church of St Peter and St Paul, founded in the 12th century, became the cathedral church of the Diocese of Sheffield in 1914. The Roman Catholic Cathedral Church of St Marie (founded 1847) was created a cathedral for the new diocese of Hallam in 1980. Parts of the present building date from *c.*1435. The principal buildings are the Town Hall (1897), the Cutlers' Hall (1832), City Hall (1932), Graves Art Gallery (1934), Mappin Art Gallery, the Crucible Theatre and the restored Lyceum theatre, which dates from 1897 and was reopened in 1990. Three major sporting and entertainment venues were opened between 1990 and 1991: Sheffield Arena, Don Valley Stadium and Pond's Forge. The Millennium Galleries opened in 2001.

SOUTHAMPTON (1964)
Southampton is a major seaport on the south coast of England, situated between the mouths of the Test and Itchen rivers. Southampton's natural deep-water harbour has made the area an important settlement since the Romans built the first port (known as *Clausentum*) in the first century, and Southampton's port has witnessed several important departures, including those of King Henry V in 1415 for the Battle of Agincourt, RMS *Titanic* in 1912, and the *Mayflower* in 1620.

The city's strategic importance, not only as a seaport but also as a centre for aircraft production, meant that it was heavily bombed during the Second World War; however, many historically significant structures remain, including the Wool House, dating from 1417 and now used as the Maritime Museum; parts of the Norman city walls which are among the most complete in the UK; the Bargate, which was originally the main gateway into the city; God's House Tower, now the Museum of Archaeology; St Michael's, the city's oldest church; and the Tudor Merchants Hall.

Home to the National Oceanography Centre, the international Southampton Boat Show and some of the country's principal watersports venues, Southampton's coastal setting and maritime history remain its main focus, but it also features extensive parks and a thriving entertainment scene.

STOKE-ON-TRENT (1925)
Stoke-on-Trent, standing on the River Trent and familiarly known as 'the potteries', is the main centre of employment for the population of north Staffordshire. The city is the largest clayware producer in the world (china, earthenware, sanitary goods, refractories, bricks and tiles) and also has a wide range of other manufacturing industries, including steel, chemicals, engineering and tyres. Extensive reconstruction has been carried out in recent years.

The city was formed by the federation of the separate municipal authorities of Tunstall, Burslem, Hanley, Stoke, Fenton, and Longton in 1910 and received its city status in 1925.

WINCHESTER (PRE-1900)
Winchester, the ancient capital of England, is situated on the River Itchen. The city is rich in architecture of all types, especially notable is the cathedral. Built in 1079–93 the cathedral exhibits examples of Norman, early English and Perpendicular styles and is the burial place of author Jane Austen. Winchester College, founded in 1382, is one of the country's most famous public schools, and the original building (1393) remains largely unaltered. St Cross Hospital, another great medieval foundation, lies one mile south of the city. The almshouses were founded in 1136 by Bishop Henry de Blois, and Cardinal Henry Beaufort added a new almshouse of 'Noble Poverty' in 1446. The chapel and dwellings are of great architectural interest, and visitors may still receive the 'Wayfarer's Dole' of bread and ale.

Excavations have done much to clarify the origins and development of Winchester. Part of the forum and several of the streets from the Roman town have been discovered. Excavations in the Cathedral Close have uncovered the entire site of the Anglo-Saxon cathedral (known as the Old Minster) and parts of the New Minster which was built by Alfred's son, Edward the Elder, and is the burial place of the Alfredian dynasty. The original burial place of St Swithun, before his remains were translated to a site in the present cathedral, was also uncovered.

Excavations in other parts of the city have thrown much light on Norman Winchester, notably on the site of the Royal Castle (adjacent to which the new Law Courts have been built) and in the grounds of Wolvesey Castle, where the great house built by Bishops Giffard and Henry de Blois in the 12th century has been uncovered. The Great Hall, built by Henry III between 1222 and 1236, survives and houses the Arthurian Round Table.

YORK (PRE-1900)
The city of York is an archiepiscopal seat. Its recorded history dates from AD 71, when the Roman Ninth Legion established a base under Petilius Cerealis that would later become the fortress of *Eburacum,* or *Eboracum.* In Anglo-Saxon times the city was the royal and ecclesiastical centre of Northumbria, and after capture by a Viking army in AD 866 it became the capital of the Viking kingdom of Jorvik. By the 14th century the city had become a great mercantile centre, mainly because of its control of the wool trade, and was used as the chief base against the Scots. Under the Tudors its fortunes declined, although Henry VIII made it the headquarters of the Council of the North. Excavations on many sites, including Coppergate, have greatly expanded knowledge of Roman, Viking and medieval urban life.

With its development as a railway centre in the 19th century the commercial life of York expanded, and today the city is home to the award-winning National Railway Museum. The principal industries are the manufacture of chocolate, scientific instruments and sugar.

The city is rich in examples of architecture of all periods. The earliest church was built in AD 627 and, from the 12th to 15th centuries, the present Minster was built in a succession of styles. Other examples within the city are the medieval city walls and gateways, churches and guildhalls. Domestic architecture includes the Georgian mansions of The Mount, Micklegate and Bootham.

LORD-LIEUTENANTS AND HIGH SHERIFFS

Area	*Lord-Lieutenant*	*High Sheriff (2009–10)*
Bedfordshire	S. Whitbread	Cynthia Gresham
Berkshire	Hon. Mary Bayliss	Dr Christina Hill Williams
Bristol	Mary Prior, MBE	Dr Timothy Chambers
Buckinghamshire	Sir Henry Aubrey-Fletcher	Allan Westray
Cambridgeshire	Hugh Duberly, CBE	Lady De Ramsey
Cheshire	W. Bromley-Davenport	William Fergusson
Cornwall	Lady Mary Holborow	Iain Mackie
Cumbria	J. Cropper	Elizabeth Thornely
Derbyshire	William Tucker	Sir Henry Every, Bt.
Devon	Eric Dancer, CBE	Edward Fursdon
Dorset	Valerie Pitt-Rivers	Victoria McDonaugh
Durham	Sir Paul Nicholson	Alasdair MacConachie, OBE
East Riding of Yorkshire	Hon. Susan Cunliffe-Lister	Patrick Farnsworth
East Sussex	Peter Field	William Shelford
Essex	Lord Petre	Rupert Gosling
Gloucestershire	Sir Henry Elwes KCVO	Anne Chambers
Greater London	Sir David Brewer, CMG	Andrew Morgan
Greater Manchester	Warren Smith	Christian Wewer
Hampshire	Mrs M. Fagan	Dr Clare Bartlett
Herefordshire	Countess of Darnley	Hon. Gilbert Greenall, CBE
Hertfordshire	Countess of Verulam	Jane Wentworth-Stanley
Isle of Wight	Maj.-Gen. Martin White, CB, CBE	Gabrielle Edwards
Kent	Allan Willett, CMG	Jane Rogers
Lancashire	Lord Shuttleworth	Caroline Reynolds
Leicestershire	Lady Gretton	Maurice Thompson
Lincolnshire	Anthony Worth	Lady Sarah McCorquodale
Merseyside	Dame Lorna Fox Muirhead, DBE	David McDonnell
Norfolk	Richard Jewson	Robert Carter
North Yorkshire	Lord Crathorne	Francesca Horsfield
Northamptonshire	Lady Juliet Townsend, LVO	Susan Fenwick
Northumberland	Duchess of Northumberland	John Blackett-Ord
Nottinghamshire	Sir Andrew Buchanan, Bt.	John Rowen
Oxfordshire	Tim Stevenson, OBE	Charles Dick
Rutland	Dr Laurence Howard, OBE	Elizabeth Mills
Shropshire	A. Heber-Percy	Anna Turner
Somerset	Lady Gass	John Alvis, MBE
South Yorkshire	David Moody	Helena Muller
Staffordshire	J. Hawley, TD	Richard Haszard
Suffolk	Lord Tollemache	James Buckle
Surrey	Mrs S. Goad	Lady Elizabeth Toulson, CBE
Tyne and Wear	N. Sherlock, OBE	Gavin Black
Warwickshire	M. Dunne	Lady Kilmaine
West Midlands	Paul Sabapathy, CBE	Paul Bassi
West Sussex	Susan Pyper	Simon Knight
West Yorkshire	Dr Ingrid Roscoe	Jeremy Burton
Wiltshire	John Bush, OBE	Robert Floyd
Worcestershire	M. Brinton	Hon. Gilbert Greenall, CBE

COUNTY COUNCILS

Council & Administrative Headquarters	*Telephone*	*Population**	*Council Tax†*	*Chief Executive*
Buckinghamshire, Aylesbury	01296-395000	490,600	£1,057	Chris Williams
Cambridgeshire, Cambridge	0345-045 5222	597,400	£1,017	Mark Lloyd
Cumbria, Carlisle	01228-606060	496,900	£1,140	Jill Stannard *(acting)*
Derbyshire, Matlock	01629-580000	758,200	£1,061	Nick Hodgson
Devon, Exeter	01392-382000	750,100	£1,095	Phil Norrey
Dorset, Dorchester	01305-221000	406,800	£1,135	David Jenkins
East Sussex, Lewes	01273-481000	508,300	£1,127	Cheryl Miller, CBE
Essex, Chelmsford	0845-743 0430	1,376,400	£1,067	Joanna Killian
Gloucestershire, Gloucester	01452-425000	582,600	£1,066	Peter Bungard
Hampshire, Winchester	01962-841841	1,276,800	£1,018	Andrew Smith
Hertfordshire, Hertford	01992-555555	1,066,100	£1,119	Caroline Tapster
Kent, Maidstone	01622-671411	1,394,700	£1,026	Peter Gilroy, OBE
Lancashire, Preston	0545-053 0000	1,168,100	£1,108	Ged Fitzgerald
Leicestershire, Leicester	0116-232 3232	641,000	£1,037	John Sinnott
Lincolnshire, Lincoln	01522-552222	692,800	£1,040	Tony McArdle
Norfolk, Norwich	0844-800 8020	840,700	£1,124	David White
North Yorkshire, Northallerton	01609-780780	595,500	£1,027	John Marsden
Northamptonshire, Northampton	01604-236236	678,300	£993	Katherine Kerswell
Nottinghamshire, Nottingham	0115-982 3823	771,900	£1,193	Nick Burrows
Oxfordshire, Oxford	01865-792422	635,500	£1,131	Joanna Simons
Somerset, Taunton	0845-345 9166	522,800	£1,027	Alan Jones
Staffordshire, Stafford	01785-223121	825,800	£1,010	Ron Hilton
Suffolk, Ipswich	0845-606 6067	709,400	£1,100	Andrea Hill
Surrey, Kingston upon Thames	0845-600 9009	1,098,200	£1,089	David McNulty
Warwickshire, Warwick	01926-410410	526,700	£1,128	Jim Graham
West Sussex, Chichester	01243-777100	776,300	£1,134	Mark Hammond
Worcestershire, Worcester	01905-763763	555,400	£1,014	Trish Haines

* *Source:* The Office of National Statistics – *Mid-2007 Population Estimates* (Crown copyright)

† Average 2009–10 Band D council tax in the county area exclusive of precepts for fire and police authorities. County councils claim their share of the combined council tax from the collection funds of the district authorities into whose area they fall. Average Band D council tax bills for the billing authority are given on the following pages

…RICT COUNCILS

District Council	*Telephone*	*Population**	*Council Tax*†	*Chief Executive*
Adur	01273-263000	60,600	£1,549	Ian Lowrie
Allerdale	01900-702702	94,500	£1,503	Harry Dyke *(acting)*
Amber Valley	01773-570222	120,400	£1,472	Peter Carney
Arun	01903-737500	146,400	£1,483	Ian Sumnall
Ashfield	01623-450000	115,900	£1,583	Philip Marshall *(acting)*
Ashford	01233-637311	112,500	£1,378	Paul Naylor *(acting)*
Aylesbury Vale	01296-585858	174,100	£1,463	Andrew Grant
Babergh	01473-822801	86,700	£1,453	Patricia Rockall
Barrow-in-Furness	01229-816300	71,800	£1,535	Tom Campbell
Basildon	01268-533333	169,800	£1,515	Bala Mahendran
Basingstoke and Deane	01256-844844	160,100	£1,338	Tony Curtis
Bassetlaw	01909-533533	111,700	£1,587	David Hunter
Blaby	0116-275 0555	92,900	£1,458	Sandra Whiles
Bolsover	01246-240000	74,200	£1,539	Wesley Lumley
Boston	01205-314200	58,400	£1,394	Michael Gallagher
Braintree	01376-552525	140,900	£1,449	Allan Reid
Breckland	01362-695333	129,900	£1,429	Trevor Holden
Brentwood	01277-312500	71,600	£1,436	Joanna Killian
Broadland	01603-431133	123,000	£1,475	Colin Bland
Bromsgrove	01527-873232	92,300	£1,464	Kevin Dicks
Broxbourne	01992-785555	89,500	£1,375	Mike Walker
Broxtowe	0115-917 7777	110,900	£1,592	Ruth Hyde
Burnley	01282-425011	87,500	£1,567	Steve Rumbelow
CAMBRIDGE	01223-457000	120,000	£1,401	Antoinette Jackson
Cannock Chase	01543-462621	94,400	£1,458	Stephen Brown
CANTERBURY	01227-862000	148,000	£1,412	Colin Carmichael
CARLISLE	01228-817000	103,500	£1,530	Maggie Mooney
Castle Point	01268-882200	89,200	£1,491	David Marchant
Charnwood	01509-263151	164,800	£1,424	Geoffrey Parker *(acting)*
Chelmsford	01245-606606	164,500	£1,449	Steve Packham
Cheltenham	01242-262626	112,300	£1,446	Andrew North
Cherwell	01295-252535	137,600	£1,483	Mary Harpley
Chesterfield	01246-345345	100,600	£1,435	Huw Bowen
Chichester	01243-785166	109,400	£1,438	John Marsland
Chiltern	01494-729000	90,800	£1,474	Alan Goodrum
Chorley	01257-515151	104,100	£1,509	Donna Hall
Christchurch	01202-495000	45,400	£1,536	Michael Turvey
Colchester	01206-282222	175,500	£1,445	Adrian Pritchard
Copeland	0845-054 8600	70,400	£1,521	Liam Murphy
Corby	01536-464000	55,200	£1,355	Chris Mallender
Cotswold	01285-623000	83,000	£1,452	David Neudegg
Craven	01756-700600	56,000	£1,480	Paul Shevlin
Crawley	01293-438000	100,100	£1,454	Lee Harris
Dacorum	01442-228000	138,600	£1,437	Daniel Zammit
Dartford	01322-343434	90,600	£1,409	Graham Harris
Daventry	01327-871100	79,100	£1,363	Ian Vincent
Derbyshire Dales	01629-761100	70,200	£1,510	David Wheatcroft
Dover	01304-821199	106,700	£1,426	Nadeem Aziz
East Cambridgeshire	01353-665555	81,000	£1,418	John Hill
East Devon	01395-516551	132,300	£1,460	Mark Williams
East Dorset	01202-886201	85,800	£1,588	David McIntosh
East Hampshire	01730-266551	111,000	£1,402	Daphne Gardner *(acting)*
East Hertfordshire	01279-655261	134,000	£1,477	Anne Freimanis
East Lindsey	01507-601111	140,100	£1,352	Nigel Howells
East Northamptonshire	01832-742000	85,400	£1,362	David Oliver
East Staffordshire	01283-508000	108,300	£1,459	Andy O'Brien
Eastbourne	01323-410000	95,600	£1,561	Martin Ray
Eastleigh	023-8068 8000	120,100	£1,403	Bernie Topham
Eden	01768-817817	51,900	£1,517	Kevin Douglas
Elmbridge	01372-474474	131,000	£1,486	Robert Moran

District Council	*Telephone*	*Population**	*Council Tax†*	*Chief Executive*
Epping Forest	01992-564000	123,300	£1,460	Peter Haywood
Epsom and Ewell	01372-732000	70,900	£1,445	Frances Rutter *(acting)*
Erewash	0115-907 2244	110,700	£1,460	Jeremy Jaroszek
EXETER	01392-277888	122,400	£1,433	Philip Bostock
Fareham	01329-236100	109,500	£1,361	Peter Grimwood
Fenland	01354-654321	91,400	£1,495	Tim Pilsbury
Forest Heath	01638-719000	63,200	£1,458	David Burnip
Forest of Dean	01594-810000	81,900	£1,466	Sue Pangbourne *(acting)*
Fylde	01253-658658	76,400	£1,508	Phillip Woodward
Gedling	0115-901 3901	111,700	£1,564	Peter Murdock
GLOUCESTER	01452-522232	114,500	£1,441	Julian Wain
Gosport	023-9258 4242	79,200	£1,423	Ian Lycett
Gravesham	01474-337000	97,700	£1,395	Glyn Thomson
Great Yarmouth	01493-856100	93,900	£1,462	Richard Packham
Guildford	01483-505050	134,400	£1,450	David Hill
Hambleton	0845-121 1555	86,900	£1,404	Peter Simpson
Harborough	01858-828282	82,300	£1,455	Sue Smith
Harlow	01279-446655	78,300	£1,511	Malcolm Morley
Harrogate	01423-500600	158,800	£1,516	Wallace Sampson
Hart	01252-622122	89,900	£1,425	Geoff Bonner
Hastings	0845-274 1066	86,200	£1,574	Roy Mawford
Havant	023-9247 4174	116,900	£1,413	Sandy Hopkins
Hertsmere	020-8207 2277	97,000	£1,442	Donald Graham
High Peak	0845-129 7777	92,800	£1,477	Simon Baker
Hinckley and Bosworth	01455-238141	104,400	£1,402	Steve Atkinson
Horsham	01403-215100	129,900	£1,443	Tom Crowley
Huntingdonshire	01480-388388	167,700	£1,427	David Monks
Hyndburn	01254-388111	82,000	£1,544	David Welsby
Ipswich	01473-432000	121,000	£1,563	James Hehir
Kettering	01536-410333	89,500	£1,379	David Cook, MBE
King's Lynn and West Norfolk	01553-616200	143,500	£1,461	Ray Harding
LANCASTER	01524-582000	143,500	£1,510	Mark Cullinan
Lewes	01273-471600	94,500	£1,598	John Crawford
Lichfield	01543-308000	97,500	£1,422	Nina Dawes
LINCOLN	01522-881188	87,800	£1,444	Andrew Taylor
Maidstone	01622-602000	144,200	£1,459	David Petford
Maldon	01621-854477	62,400	£1,465	Steve Watson
Malvern Hills	01684-862151	74,300	£1,441	Chris Bocock
Mansfield	01623-463463	100,100	£1,596	Ruth Marlow
Melton	01664-502502	49,200	£1,450	Lynn Aisbett
Mendip	01749-648999	109,100	£1,452	David Thomson
Mid Devon	01884-255255	75,900	£1,522	Gerald Hirsch
Mid Suffolk	01449-720711	93,800	£1,454	Andrew Good
Mid Sussex	01444-458166	130,300	£1,468	John Jory
Mole Valley	01306-885001	81,200	£1,441	Darren Mepham
New Forest	023-8028 5000	174,700	£1,437	David Yates
Newark and Sherwood	01636-650000	112,600	£1,638	Andrew Muter
Newcastle-under-Lyme	01782-717717	124,300	£1,430	Mark Barrow
North Devon	01271-327711	92,100	£1,513	M. Mansell; S. Pitcher
North Dorset	01258-454111	67,600	£1,537	Elizabeth Goodall
North East Derbyshire	01246-231111	98,000	£1,529	Mike Goodwin
North Hertfordshire	01462-474000	122,500	£1,482	John Campbell
North Kesteven	01529-414155	104,800	£1,406	Ian Fytche
North Norfolk	01263-513811	100,800	£1,477	Philip Burton
North Warwickshire	01827-715341	62,200	£1,545	Jeremy Hutchinson
North West Leicestershire	01530-454545	90,400	£1,471	Christine Fisher
Northampton	01604-837837	202,800	£1,398	David Kennedy
NORWICH	0344-980 3333	132,200	£1,530	Laura McGillivray
Nuneaton and Bedworth	02476-376376	121,200	£1,501	Christine Kerr
Oadby and Wigston	0116-288 8961	56,800	£1,453	Mark Hall
OXFORD	01865-249811	151,000	£1,543	Peter Sloman
Pendle	01282-661661	90,000	£1,567	Stephen Barnes
PRESTON	01772-906900	131,900	£1,568	Lorraine Norris
Purbeck	01929-556561	45,800	£1,577	Steve Mackenzie
Redditch	01527-64252	79,600	£1,463	Kevin Dicks *(acting)*
Reigate and Banstead	01737-276000	132,300	£1,485	Nigel Clifford
Ribble Valley	01200-425111	58,300	£1,467	Marshal Scott

District Council	*Telephone*	*Population**	*Council Tax†*	*Chief Executive*
Richmondshire	01748-829100	51,400	£1,496	Peter Simpson
Rochford	01702-546366	82,200	£1,487	Paul Warren
Rossendale	01706-217777	67,000	£1,569	Helen Lockwood *(acting)*
Rother	01424-787999	88,200	£1,546	Derek Stevens
Rugby	01788-533533	91,000	£1,487	Simon Warren
Runnymede	01932-838383	82,600	£1,419	Paul Turrell
Rushcliffe	0115-981 9911	109,000	£1,585	Allen Graham
Rushmoor	01252-398398	89,400	£1,401	Andrew Lloyd
Ryedale	01653-600666	53,300	£1,495	Janet Waggott
ST ALBANS	01727-866100	132,300	£1,468	Daniel Goodwin
St Edmundsbury	01284-763233	102,900	£1,463	Geoff Rivers
Scarborough	01723-232323	108,400	£1,510	Jim Dillon
Sedgemoor	0845-408 2540	112,200	£1,423	Mr Kerry Rickards
Selby	01757-705101	80,800	£1,487	Martin Connor
Sevenoaks	01732-227000	114,300	£1,466	Robin Hales
Shepway	01303-853000	100,100	£1,500	Alistair Stewart
South Bucks	01895-837200	64,300	£1,455	Chris Furness
South Cambridgeshire	08450-450500	137,300	£1,411	Greg Harlock
South Derbyshire	01283-221000	91,200	£1,453	Frank McArdle
South Hams	01803-861234	83,500	£1,481	David Incoll
South Holland	01775-761161	82,600	£1,393	Terry Huggins
South Kesteven	01476-406080	131,100	£1,375	Beverly Agass *(acting)*
South Lakeland	01539-733333	104,900	£1,522	Peter Ridgway
South Norfolk	01508-533633	117,300	£1,499	Sandra Dinneen
South Northamptonshire	01327-322322	90,300	£1,400	Jean Morgan
South Oxfordshire	01491-823000	128,400	£1,471	David Buckle
South Ribble	01772-421491	106,700	£1,523	Jean Hunter
South Somerset	01935-462462	157,800	£1,463	Philip Dolan
South Staffordshire	01902-696000	106,300	£1,388	Steve Winterflood
Spelthorne	01784-451499	90,900	£1,454	Roberto Tambini
Stafford	01785-619000	124,000	£1,413	Ian Thompson
Staffordshire Moorlands	01538 483483	95,400	£1,428	Simon Baker
Stevenage	01438-242242	79,400	£1,450	Nick Parry
Stratford-on-Avon	01789-267575	117,800	£1,477	Paul Lankester
Stroud	01453-766321	110,700	£1,496	David Hagg
Suffolk Coastal	01394-383789	124,400	£1,441	Stephen Baker
Surrey Heath	01276-707100	83,300	£1,485	Michael Willis
Swale	01795-417330	130,300	£1,398	Abdool Kara
Tamworth	01827-709709	75,600	£1,394	David Weatherley
Tandridge	01883-722000	82,500	£1,487	Stephen Weigel
Taunton Deane	01823-356356	108,200	£1,400	Penny James
Teignbridge	01626-361101	126,800	£1,498	Nicola Bulbeck
Tendring	01255-686868	146,200	£1,436	John Hawkins
Test Valley	01264-368000	114,700	£1,366	Roger Tetstall
Tewkesbury	01684-295010	79,200	£1,396	Michael Dawson
Thanet	01843-577000	129,200	£1,445	Richard Samuel
Three Rivers	01923-776611	86,400	£1,455	Dr Steven Halls
Tonbridge and Malling	01732-844522	115,700	£1,430	David Hughes
Torridge	01237-428700	65,000	£1,487	John van de Laarschot
Tunbridge Wells	01892-526121	105,600	£1,401	Sheila Wheeler
Uttlesford	01799-510510	72,500	£1,459	John Mitchell
Vale of White Horse	01235-520202	117,000	£1,447	David Buckle
Warwick	01926-450000	134,600	£1,463	Chris Elliott
Watford	01923-226400	79,700	£1,515	Manny Lewis
Waveney	01502-562111	117,300	£1,410	Stephen Baker
Waverley	01483-523333	117,800	£1,485	Mary Orton
Wealden	01323-443322	143,800	£1,587	Charles Lant
Wellingborough	01933-229777	75,900	£1,324	Lyn Martin-Bennison
Welwyn & Hatfield	01707-357000	106,700	£1,498	Michel Saminaden
West Devon	01822-813600	52,100	£1,549	David Incoll
West Dorset	01305-251010	97,100	£1,552	David Clarke
West Lancashire	01695-577177	109,800	£1,510	William Taylor
West Lindsey	01427-676676	88,000	£1,440	Duncan Sharkey
West Oxfordshire	01993-861000	101,600	£1,415	David Neudegg
West Somerset	01643-703704	35,400	£1,434	Adrian Dyer
Weymouth and Portland	01305-838000	65,100	£1,629	Tom Grainger
WINCHESTER	01962-840222	111,300	£1,405	Simon Eden

District Council	*Telephone*	*Population**	*Council Tax†*	*Chief Executive*
Woking	01483-755855	91,400	£1,486	Ray Morgan, OBE
WORCESTER	01905-723471	93,700	£1,420	vacant
Worthing	01903-239999	99,600	£1,479	Ian Lowrie
Wychavon	01386-565000	117,100	£1,405	Jack Hegarty
Wycombe	01494-461000	161,400	£1,429	Karen Satterford
Wyre	01253-891000	110,900	£1,495	Jim Corry
Wyre Forest	01562-732928	98,600	£1,465	Walter Delin

* *Source:* ONS – *Mid-2007 Population Estimates* (Crown copyright)
† Average Band D council tax bill for 2009–10
Councils in CAPITAL LETTERS have city status

METROPOLITAN BOROUGH COUNCILS

Metropolitan Borough Councils	*Telephone*	*Population**	*Council Tax†*	*Chief Executive*
Barnsley	01226-770770	224,600	£1,364	Philip Coppard
BIRMINGHAM	0121-303 9944	1,010,200	£1,238	Stephen Hughes
Bolton	01204-333333	262,300	£1,388	Sean Harriss
BRADFORD	01274-432001	497,400	£1,269	Tony Reeves
Bury	0161-253 5000	183,300	£1,404	Mark Sanders
Calderdale	01422-357257	200,100	£1,425	Owen Williams
COVENTRY	024-7683 3333	306,700	£1,438	Martin Reeves
Doncaster	01302-734444	291,100	£1,278	Paul Hart
Dudley	01384-812345	305,400	£1,254	John Pollychronakis
Gateshead	0191-433 3000	190,500	£1,570	Roger Kelly
Kirklees	01484-221000	401,000	£1,377	Rob Vincent
Knowsley	0151-489 6000	150,900	£1,416	Sheena Ramsey
LEEDS	0113-222 4444	761,100	£1,280	Paul Rogerson
LIVERPOOL	0151-233 3000	435,500	£1,511	Colin Hilton
MANCHESTER	0161-234 5000	458,100	£1,316	Sir Howard Bernstein
NEWCASTLE UPON TYNE	0191-232 8520	271,600	£1,490	Barry Rowland *(acting)*
North Tyneside	0191-643 5991	196,000	£1,450	Andrew Kerr
Oldham	0161-911 3000	219,500	£1,518	Charlie Parker
Rochdale	01706-647474	206,100	£1,426	Roger Ellis
Rotherham	01709-382121	253,400	£1,412	vacant
St Helens	01744-456000	177,400	£1,352	Carole Hudson
SALFORD	0161-794 4711	219,200	£1,512	Barbara Spicer
Sandwell	0121-569 2200	287,500	£1,309	Allison Fraser
Sefton	0151-922 4040	276,200	£1,448	Margaret Carney
SHEFFIELD	0114-272 6444	530,300	£1,455	John Mothersole
Solihull	0121-704 6000	203,600	£1,308	Mark Rogers
South Tyneside	0191-427 1717	151,000	£1,410	Irene Lucas
Stockport	0161-480 4949	280,900	£1,506	John Schultz
SUNDERLAND	0191-520 5555	280,300	£1,328	Dave Smith
Tameside	0161-342 8355	214,400	£1,333	Steven Pleasant
Trafford	0161-912 1212	212,800	£1,272	vacant
WAKEFIELD	01924-306090	321,600	£1,274	Joanne Roney, OBE
Walsall	01922-650000	254,500	£1,478	Paul Sheehan
Wigan	01942-244991	305,600	£1,344	Joyce Redfearn
Wirral	0151-606 2000	310,200	£1,440	Stephen Maddox
WOLVERHAMPTON	01902-556556	236,000	£1,462	vacant

* *Source:* ONS – *Mid-2007 Population Estimates* (Crown copyright)
† Average Band D council tax bill for 2009–10
Councils in CAPITAL LETTERS have city status

UNITARY COUNCILS

Unitary Councils	*Telephone*	*Population**	*Council Tax*†	*Chief Executive*
Bath and North East Somerset	01225-477000	178,300	£1,423	John Everitt
Bedford	01234-267422	154,900	£1,527	Philip Simpkins
Blackburn with Darwen	01254-585585	140,900	£1,449	Graham Burgess
Blackpool	01253-477477	142,500	£1,473	Steve Weaver
Bournemouth	01202-451451	163,200	£1,453	Pam Donnellan
Bracknell Forest	01344-352000	113,500	£1,329	Timothy Wheadon
BRIGHTON AND HOVE	01273-290000	253,500	£1,447	Alex Bailey *(acting)*
BRISTOL	0117-922 2000	416,400	£1,533	Jan Ormondroyd
Central Bedfordshire	0300-300 8000	252,100	£1,596	Richard Carr
Cheshire East	0300-123 5500	360,800	£1,420	Erika Wenzel
Cheshire West and Chester	0300-123 8123	328,100	£1,448	Steve Robinson
Cornwall	0300-123 4100	529,500	£1,411	Kevin Lavery
Darlington	01325-380651	100,000	£1,386	Ada Burns
DERBY	01332-293111	237,900	£1,327	Adam Wilkinson
DURHAM	0300-123 7070	504,900	£1,567	George Garlick
East Riding of Yorkshire	01482-887700	333,000	£1,477	Nigel Pearson
Halton	0151-424 2061	119,500	£1,323	David Parr
Hartlepool	01429-266522	91,400	£1,629	Paul Walker
Herefordshire	01432-260000	178,400	£1,455	Chris Bull
Isle of Wight	01983-821000	139,500	£1,424	Steve Beynon
Isles of Scilly‡	01720-422537	2,100	£1,135	Philip Hygate
KINGSTON-UPON-HULL	01482-609100	257,000	£1,336	Mr Kim Ryley
LEICESTER	0116-254 9922	292,600	£1,381	Sheila Lock
Luton	01582-546000	188,800	£1,344	Kevin Crompton
Medway	01634-333333	252,200	£1,296	Neil Davies
Middlesbrough	01642-245432	138,700	£1,475	Ian Parker
Milton Keynes	01908-691691	228,400	£1,360	David Hill
North East Lincolnshire	01472-313131	158,400	£1,498	Tony Hunter
North Lincolnshire	01724-296296	159,400	£1,512	Simon Driver
North Somerset	01934-888888	204,700	£1,392	Graham Turner
Northumberland	01670-533000	310,600	£1,445	Steve Stewart
NOTTINGHAM	0115-915 5555	288,700	£1,515	Jane Todd
PETERBOROUGH	01733-747474	163,300	£1,296	Gillian Beasley
PLYMOUTH	01752-668000	250,700	£1,428	Barry Keel
Poole	01202-633633	138,100	£1,406	John McBride
PORTSMOUTH	023-9282 2251	197,700	£1,352	David Williams
Reading	0118-939 0900	143,700	£1,467	Michael Coughlin
Redcar and Cleveland	0164-277 4774	139,400	£1,516	Amanda Skelton
Rutland	01572-722577	38,400	£1,656	Helen Briggs
Shropshire	0345-678 9000	290,900	£1,472	Sheila Healy *(acting)*
Slough	01753-475111	120,100	£1,341	Ruth Bagley
South Gloucestershire	01454-868686	256,500	£1,489	Amanda Deeks
SOUTHAMPTON	023-8022 3855	231,200	£1,411	Brad Roynon
Southend-on-Sea	01702-215000	162,000	£1,281	Robert Tinlin
Stockton-on-Tees	01642-393939	190,200	£1,451	Neil Schneider
STOKE-ON-TRENT	01782-234567	239,000	£1,350	Chris Harman *(acting)*
Swindon	01793-463000	189,500	£1,366	Gavin Jones
Telford and Wrekin	01952-202100	161,700	£1,391	Victor Brownless *(acting)*
Thurrock	01375-652652	150,000	£1,266	Bob Coomber *(acting)*
Torbay	01803-201201	134,200	£1,450	Elizabeth Raikes
Warrington	01925-444400	195,200	£1,336	Diana Terris
West Berkshire	01635-42400	150,700	£1,472	Nick Carter
Wiltshire	0300-456 0100	452,600	£1,475	Dr. Keith Robinson
Windsor and Maidenhead	01628-683800	141,000	£1,277	Ian Trenholm
Wokingham	0118-974 6000	156,600	£1,435	Susan Law
YORK	01904-613161	193,300	£1,331	Kersten England

* *Source:* ONS – *Mid-2007 Population Estimates* (Crown copyright)
† Average Band D council tax bill for 2009–10
‡ Under the Isles of Scilly Clause the council has additional functions to other unitary authorities
Councils in CAPITAL LETTERS have city status

MAP OF COUNCILS IN ENGLAND

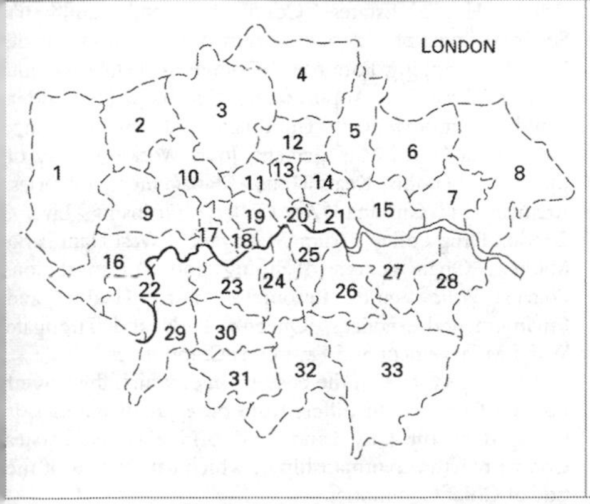

1 Hillingdon
2 Harrow
3 Barnet
4 Enfield
5 Waltham Forest
6 Redbridge
7 Barking and Dagenham
8 Havering
9 Ealing
10 Brent
11 Camden
12 Haringey
13 Islington
14 Hackney
15 Newham
16 Hounslow
17 Hammersmith and Fulham
18 Kensington and Chelsea
19 City of Westminster
20 City of London
21 Tower Hamlets
22 Richmond upon Thames
23 Wandsworth
24 Lambeth
25 Southwark
26 Lewisham
27 Greenwich
28 Bexley
29 Kingston upon Thames
30 Merton
31 Sutton
32 Croydon
33 Bromley

LONDON

THE CITY OF LONDON CORPORATION

The City of London is the historic centre at the heart of London known as 'the square mile' around which the vast metropolis has grown over the centuries. The City's residential population is roughly 9,000 and in addition, around a third of a million people work in the City. The civic government is carried on by the City of London Corporation through the court of Common Council.

The City is an international financial and business centre, generating about £30bn a year for the British economy. It includes the head offices of the principal banks, insurance companies and mercantile houses, in addition to buildings ranging from the historic Roman Wall and the 15th-century Guildhall, to the massive splendour of St Paul's Cathedral and the architectural beauty of Wren's spires.

The City of London was described by Tacitus in AD 62 as 'a busy emporium for trade and traders'. Under the Romans it became an important administration centre and hub of the road system. Little is known of London in Saxon times, when it formed part of the kingdom of the East Saxons. In 886 Alfred recovered London from the Danes and reconstituted it a burgh under his son-in-law. In 1066 the citizens submitted to William the Conqueror who in 1067 granted them a charter, which is still preserved, establishing them in the rights and privileges they had hitherto enjoyed.

THE MAYORALTY

The mayoralty was probably established about 1189, the first mayor being Henry Fitz Ailwyn who filled the office for 23 years and was succeeded by Fitz Alan (1212–14). A new charter was granted by King John in 1215, directing the mayor to be chosen annually, which has been done ever since, though in early times the same individual often held the office more than once. A familiar instance is that of 'Whittington, thrice Lord Mayor of London' (in reality four times, 1397, 1398, 1406, 1419); and many modern cases have occurred. The earliest instance of the phrase 'lord mayor' in English is in 1414. It was used more generally in the latter part of the 15th century and became invariable from 1535 onwards. At Michaelmas the liverymen in Common Hall choose two aldermen who have served the office of sheriff for presentation to the Court of Aldermen, and one is chosen to be lord mayor for the following mayoral year.

LORD MAYOR'S DAY

The lord mayor of London was previously elected on the feast of St Simon and St Jude (28 October), and from the time of Edward I, at least, was presented to the King or to the Barons of the Exchequer on the following day, unless that day was a Sunday. The day of election was altered to 16 October in 1346, and after some further changes was fixed for Michaelmas Day in 1546, but the ceremonies of admittance and swearing-in of the lord mayor continued to take place on 28 and 29 October respectively until 1751. In 1752, at the reform of the calendar, the lord mayor was continued in office until 8 November, the 'new style' equivalent of 28 October. The lord mayor is now presented to the lord chief justice at the royal courts of justice on the second Saturday in November to make the final declaration of office, having been sworn in at Guildhall on the preceding day. The procession to the royal courts of justice is popularly known as the Lord Mayor's Show.

REPRESENTATIVES

Aldermen are mentioned in the 11th century and their office is of Saxon origin. They were elected annually between 1377 and 1394, when an act of parliament of Richard II directed them to be chosen for life.

The Common Council was, at an early date, substituted for a popular assembly called the *Folkmote*. At first only two representatives were sent from each ward, but now each of the City's 25 wards is represented by an alderman and at least two Common Councilmen (the number depending on the size of the ward).

OFFICERS

Sheriffs were Saxon officers; their predecessors were the *wic-reeves* and *portreeves* of London and Middlesex. At first they were officers of the Crown, and were named by the Barons of the Exchequer; but Henry I (in 1132) gave the citizens permission to choose their own Sheriffs, and the annual election of Sheriffs became fully operative under King John's charter of 1199. The citizens lost this privilege, as far as the election of the Sheriff of Middlesex was concerned, by the Local Government Act 1888; but the liverymen continue to choose two Sheriffs of the City of London, who are appointed on Midsummer Day and take office at Michaelmas.

The office of Chamberlain is an ancient one, the first contemporary record of which is 1237. The town clerk (or Common Clerk) is first mentioned in 1274.

ACTIVITIES

The work of the City of London Corporation is assigned to a number of committees which present reports to the Court of Common Council. These committees are: Barbican Centre; Barbican Residential; Board of Governors of the City of London Freeman's School, the City of London School, the City of London School for Girls, the Guildhall School of Music and Drama and the Museum of London; City Bridge Trust; City Lands and Bridge House Estates; Community and Children's Services; Court of Alderman; Court of Common Council; Education; Epping Forest and Commons; Establishment; Finance; Freedom Applications; Gresham (city side); Guildhall Improvement; Guildhall Yard East Building; Hampstead Heath Management; Joint Working Party of the Three Schools; Keats House Management; Libraries, Archives and Guildhall Art Gallery; Licensing; Livery; London Drug Policy Forum; Managers of West Ham Park; Markets; Open Spaces; Planning and Transportation; Police; Policy and Resources; Port Health and Environmental Services; Queen's Park and Highgate Wood Management and Standards Committees.

The City's estate, in the possession of which the City of London Corporation differs from other municipalities, is managed by the City Lands and Bridge House Estates Committee, the chairmanship of which carries with it the title of Chief Commoner.

The Honourable the Irish Society, which manages the City Corporation's estates in Ulster, consists of a governor and five other aldermen, the recorder, and 19 Common Councilmen, of whom one is elected deputy governor.

THE LORD MAYOR 2009–10
The Rt. Hon. the Lord Mayor, Nicholas Anstee*
Private Secretary, William Campbell
* Provisional at time of going to press

THE SHERIFFS 2009–10
Peter Cook; Alderman David Wootton (Langbourn)

OFFICERS, ETC
Town Clerk, Chris Duffield
Chamberlain, Chris Bilsland
Chief Commoner (2009), William B. Fraser OBE
Clerk, The Honourable the Irish Society, C. Fisher

THE ALDERMEN
with office held and date of appointment to that office

Name and Ward	*CC*	*Ald.*	*Shff*	*Lord Mayor*
Lord Levene of Portsoken, KBE, *Aldgate*	1983	1984	1995	1998
Sir David Howard, Bt., *Cornhill*	1972	1986	1997	2000
Sir Michael Oliver, *Bishopsgate*	1980	1987	1997	2001
Sir Robert Finch, *Coleman Street*	–	1992	1999	2003
Sir Michael Savory, *Bread Street*	1980	1996	2001	2004
Sir David Brewer, *Bassishaw*	1992	1996	2002	2005
Sir John Stuttard, *Lime Street*	–	2001	2005	2006
Sir David Lewis, *Broad Street*	–	2001	2006	2007
Sir Ian Luder, *Castle Baynard*	1998	2005	2007	2008

All the above have passed the Civic Chair

Dr Andrew Parmley, *Vintry*	1992	2001	
Simon Walsh, *Farringdon Wt.*	1989	2000	
Robert Hall, *Farringdon Wn.*	1995	2002	
Alison Gowman, *Dowgate*	1991	2002	
Gordon Haines, *Queenhithe*	–	2004	
Roger Gifford, *Cordwainer*	–	2004	2008
David Mauleverer, *Walbrook*	–	2005	2001
Michael Bear, *Portsoken*	2003	2005	2007
David Wootton, *Langbourn*	2002	2005	
Alan Yarrow, *Bridge*	–	2007	
Jeffrey Evans, *Cheap*	–	2007	
Sir Paul Judge, *Tower*	–	2007	
Fiona Woolf, CBE, *Candlewick*	–	2007	
John White, TD, *Billingsgate*	–	2008	
David Graves, *Cripplegate*	–	2008	

THE COMMON COUNCIL
Deputy: each Common Councilman so described serves as deputy to the alderman of her/his ward.

Abrahams, G. C. (2000)	*Farringdon Wt.*
Absalom, J. D. (1994)	*Farringdon Wt.*
Ayers, K. E. (1996)	*Bassishaw*
Bain-Stewart, A. (2005)	*Farringdon Wn.*
Barker, *Deputy* J. A., OBE (1981)	*Cripplegate*
Barrow, D. (2007)	*Aldgate*
Bennett, *Deputy* J. A. (2005)	*Broad Street*
Bird, J. L., OBE (1977)	*Tower*
Boleat, M. J. (2002)	*Cordwainer*
Bradshaw, D. J. (1991)	*Cripplegate Wn.*
Burleigh, I. B. (2005)	*Portsoken*
Cassidy, *Deputy* M. J., CBE (1989)	*Coleman Street*
Catt, R. M. (2004)	*Castle Baynard*
Cenci Di Bello, Mrs P. J. (2004)	*Farringdon Wn.*
Chadwick, R. A. H. (1994)	*Tower*
Challis, N. K. (2005)	*Castle Baynard*
Chapman, J. D. (2006)	*Langbourn*
Cohen, *Deputy* Mrs C. M., OBE (1986)	*Lime Street*
Cotgrove, D. (1991)	*Lime Street*
Cressey, N. (2009)	*Portsoken*
Currie, *Deputy* Miss S. E. M. (1985)	*Cripplegate Wt.*
Davies, P.S. (2009)	*Broad Street*
Day, M. J. (2005)	*Bishopsgate*
Dove, W. H., MBE (1993)	*Bishopsgate*
Duckworth, S. D. (2000)	*Bishopsgate*
Dudley, Revd Dr M. R. (2002)	*Aldersgate*
Duffield, R. W. (2004)	*Farringdon Wn.*
Dunphy, P. G. (2009)	*Cornhill*
Eskenzi, *Deputy* A. N., CBE (1970)	*Farringdon Wn.*
Eve, *Deputy* R. A. (1980)	*Cheap*
Everett, K. M. (1984)	*Candlewick*
Farr, M. C. (1998)	*Walbrook*
Farrow, *Deputy* M. W. W. (1996)	*Farringdon Wt.*
Fernandes, S. A. (2009)	*Coleman Street*
Fraser, S. J. (1993)	*Coleman Street*
Fraser, *Deputy* W. B., OBE (1981)	*Vintry*
Fredericks, M. B. (2008)	*Tower*
Galloway, *Deputy* A. D., OBE (1981)	*Bishopsgate*
Gillon, G. M. F. (1995)	*Cordwainer*
Ginsburg, *Deputy* S. (1990)	*Bishopsgate*
Graves, A. C. (1985)	*Bishopsgate*
Haines, *Deputy* Revd S. D. (2005)	*Cornhill*
Halliday, *Deputy* Mrs P. A., OBE (1992)	*Walbrook*
Hardwick, Dr P. B. (1987)	*Aldgate*
Harris, B. N. (2004)	*Bridge*
Henderson-Begg, M. (1977)	*Coleman Street*
Hoffman, T. D. D. (2002)	*Vintry*
Hudson, M. (2007)	*Castle Baynard*
Hughes-Penney, R. C. (2004)	*Farringdon Wn.*
Hunt, W. G., TD (2004)	*Castle Baynard*
James, Clare (2008)	*Farringdon Wn.*
Jones, *Deputy* H. L. M. (2004)	*Portsoken*
King, *Deputy* A. J. N. (1999)	*Queenhithe*
Knowles, *Deputy* S. K., MBE (1984)	*Candlewick*
Lawrence, *Deputy* G. A. (2002)	*Farringdon Wt.*
Leck, P. (1998)	*Aldersgate*
Littlechild, V. (2009)	*Cripplegate*
Llewelyn-Davies, A. (2009)	*Billingsgate*
Lodge, O. W., TD (2009)	*Bread Street*
Lord, C. E. (2009)	*Farringdon Wt.*
McGuinness, *Deputy* C. S. (1997)	*Castle Baynard*
Malins, J. H., QC (1981)	*Farringdon Wt.*
Martinelli, *Deputy* P. J. (2009)	*Farringdon Wt.*
Mayhew, J. P. (1996)	*Aldersgate*
Mead, Mrs W. (1997)	*Farringdon Wt.*
Merrett, R. A. (2009)	*Bassishaw*
Mooney, B. D. F. (1998)	*Queenhithe*
Moore, G. W. (2009)	*Cripplegate*
Morris, H. F. (2008)	*Aldgate*
Moys, Mrs S. D. (2001)	*Aldgate*
Nash, *Deputy* Mrs J. C., OBE (1983)	*Aldersgate*
Newman, Mrs P. B., CBE (1989)	*Aldersgate*
Owen, *Deputy* Mrs J., MBE (1975)	*Langbourn*
Owen-Ward, J. R. (1983)	*Bridge*
Page, M. (2002)	*Farringdon Wn.*
Pembroke, *Deputy* Mrs A. M. F. (1978)	*Cheap*

Pollard, J. H. G. (2002)	*Dowgate*
Priest, H. J. S. (2009)	*Castle Baynard*
Pulman, *Deputy* G. A. G. (1983)	*Tower*
Punter, C. (1993)	*Cripplegate Wn.*
Quilter, S. D. (1998)	*Cripplegate Wt.*
Regan, *Deputy* R. D. (1998)	*Farringdon Wn.*
Regis, D. (2009)	*Portsoken*
Richardson, M. C. (2009)	*Coleman Street*
Robinson, Mrs D. C. (1989)	*Bishopsgate*
Rogula, E. (2008)	*Lime Street*
Scott, J. G. S. (1999)	*Broad Street*
Seaton, I. (2009)	*Bassishaw*
Sherlock, *Deputy* M. R. C. (1992)	*Dowgate*
Shilson, *Deputy*, G. R. E., DPHIL (2009)	*Bread Street*
Simons, J. L. (2004)	*Castle Baynard*
Snyder, *Deputy* Sir Michael (1986)	*Cordwainer*
Spanner, J. H., TD (2001)	*Farringdon Wt.*
Starling, Mrs A. J. (2006)	*Cripplegate Wt.*
Thompson, D. J. (2004)	*Aldgate*
Tomlinson, J. (2004)	*Cripplegate Wt.*
Tumbridge, J. R. (2009)	*Tower*
Twogood, M. (2004)	*Farringdon Wt.*
Welbank, *Deputy* M. (2005)	*Billingsgate*
Willoughby, *Deputy* P. J. (1985)	*Bishopsgate*

THE CITY GUILDS (LIVERY COMPANIES)

The constitution of the livery companies has been unchanged for centuries. There are three ranks of membership: freemen, liverymen and assistants. A person can become a freeman by patrimony (through a parent having been a freeman); by servitude (through having served an apprenticeship to a freeman); or by redemption (by purchase).

Election to the livery is the prerogative of the company, who can elect any of its freemen as liverymen. Assistants are usually elected from the livery and form a Court of Assistants which is the governing body of the company. The master (in some companies called the prime warden) is elected annually from the assistants.

The register for 2009–10 lists 24,835 liverymen of the guilds entitled to vote at elections at Common Hall.

The order of precedence, omitting extinct companies, is given in parentheses after the name of each company in the list below. In certain companies the election of Master or Prime Warden for the year does not take place until the autumn. In such cases the master or prime warden for 2008–9, rather than 2009–10, is given.

THE TWELVE GREAT COMPANIES
In order of civic precedence

MERCERS *(1). Hall,* Mercers' Hall, Ironmonger Lane, London EC2V 8HE *Livery,* 350. *Clerk,* Menna McGregor *Master,* Bill Scarborough

GROCERS *(2). Hall,* Grocers' Hall, Princes Street, London EC2R 8AD *Livery,* 333. *Clerk,* Brig. Robert Pridham, OBE *Master,* Andrew Dalton

DRAPERS *(3). Hall,* Drapers' Hall, Throgmorton Avenue, London EC2N 2DQ *Livery,* 310. *Clerk,* Rear-Adm. Alastair Ross, CB, CBE *Master,* David Addis

FISHMONGERS *(4). Hall,* Fishmongers' Hall, London Bridge, London EC4R 9EL *Livery,* 358. *Clerk,* Nigel Cox *Prime Warden,* Andrew Smith

GOLDSMITHS *(5). Hall,* Goldsmiths' Hall, Foster Lane, London EC2V 6BN *Livery,* 285. *Clerk,* Richard Melly *Prime Warden,* Rupert Hambro

MERCHANT TAYLORS *(6/7). Hall,* Merchant Taylors' Hall, 30 Threadneedle Street, London EC2R 8JB *Livery,* 285. *Clerk,* Rear-Adm. Nicholas Harris, CB, MBE *Master,* Christopher Hare

SKINNERS *(6/7). Hall,* Skinners' Hall, 8 Dowgate Hill, London EC4R 2SP *Livery,* 400. *Clerk,* Maj.-Gen. Brian Plummer, CBE *Master,* Jonathan Minter, CBE

HABERDASHERS *(8). Hall,* Haberdashers' Hall, 18 West Smithfield, London EC1A 9HQ *Livery,* 302. *Clerk,* Rear-Adm. Richard Phillips, CB *Master,* G. Pulman, QC

SALTERS *(9). Hall,* Salters' Hall, 4 Fore Street, London EC2Y 5DE *Livery,* 163. *Clerk,* Capt. David Morris, RN *Master,* Richard Callingham

IRONMONGERS *(10). Hall,* Ironmongers' Hall, 1 Shaftesbury Place, London EC2Y 8AA *Livery,* 133. *Clerk,* Col. Hamon Massey *Master,* H. Charnaud

VINTNERS *(11). Hall,* Vintners' Hall, Upper Thames Street, London EC4V 3BG *Livery,* 312. *Clerk,* Brig. Michael Smyth, OBE *Master,* Sam Dow

CLOTHWORKERS *(12). Hall,* Clothworkers' Hall, Dunster Court, Mincing Lane, London EC3R 7AH *Livery,* 228. *Clerk,* Andrew Blessley *Master,* Neil Foster

OTHER CITY GUILDS
In alphabetical order

ACTUARIES *(91).* 3rd Floor Cheapside House, 138 Cheapside, London EC2V 6BW *Livery,* 232. *Clerk,* David Johnson *Master,* Adrian Waddingham

AIR PILOTS AND AIR NAVIGATORS *(81). Hall,* Cobham House, 9 Warwick Court, Gray's Inn, London WC1R 5DJ *Livery,* 570. *Clerk,* Paul Tacon *Grand Master,* HRH The Duke of York, KG, KCVO, ADC(P) *Master,* Rear-Adm. Colin Cooke-Priest, CB, CVO

APOTHECARIES *(58). Hall,* Apothecaries' Hall, 14 Black Friars Lane, London EC4V 6EJ *Livery,* 1,271. *Clerk,* A. Wallington-Smith *Master,* Prof. T Beedham

ARBITRATORS *(93).* 13 Hall Gardens, Colney Heath, St Albans, Herts AL4 0QF *Livery,* 175. *Clerk,* Gaye Duffy *Master,* Chris Dancaster

ARMOURERS AND BRASIERS *(22). Hall,* Armourers' Hall, 81 Coleman Street, London EC2R 5BJ *Livery,* 123. *Clerk,* Cdre Christopher Waite *Master,* David Chapman

BAKERS *(19). Hall,* Bakers' Hall, 9 Harp Lane, London EC3R 6DP *Livery,* 350. *Clerk,* John Tompkins *Master,* David Powell

BARBERS *(17). Hall,* Barber-Surgeons' Hall, Monkwell Square, Wood Street, London EC2Y 5BL *Livery,* 220. *Clerk,* Col. Peter Durrant, MBE *Master,* Dr J. Bolton, FRCPSYCH

BASKETMAKERS *(52).* Doric House, 108 Garstang Road West, Poulton le Fylde, Lancs FY6 7SN *Livery,* 300. *Clerk,* Roger de Pilkyngton *Prime Warden,* Michael Stemp

BLACKSMITHS *(40).* 48 Upwood Road, London SE12 8AN *Livery,* 235. *Clerk,* Christopher Jeal *Prime Warden,* Sir David Brewer, CMG

BOWYERS *(38).* 5 Archer House, Vicarage Crescent, London SW11 3LF *Livery,* 91. *Clerk,* Richard Wilkinson *Master,* Peter Harrow

BREWERS *(14). Hall,* Brewers' Hall, Aldermanbury Square, London EC2V 7HR *Livery,* 180. *Clerk,* Brig. David Ross, CBE *Master,* Tony Mair

BRODERERS *(48).* Ember House, 35–37 Creek Road, East Molesey, Surrey KT8 9BE *Livery,* 129. *Clerk,* Peter Crouch *Master,* Charles Gotto

BUILDERS MERCHANTS *(88).* 4 College Hill,

London EC4R 2RB *Livery,* 193. *Clerk,* T. Statham *Master,* Kenneth Pepperrell

BUTCHERS *(24). Hall,* Butchers' Hall, 87 Bartholomew Close, London EC1A 7EB *Livery,* 633. *Clerk,* Cdre Anthony Morrow, CVO *Master,* Brian Wheatley

CARMEN *(77).* Five Kings House, 1 Queen Street Place, London EC4R 1QS *Livery,* 500. *Clerk,* Walter Gill *Master,* Brian Wadsworth

CARPENTERS *(26). Hall,* Carpenters' Hall, 1 Throgmorton Avenue, London EC2N 2JJ *Livery,* 196. *Clerk,* Brig. Tim Gregson, MBE *Master,* Revd Dr W. Povey

CHARTERED ACCOUNTANTS *(86).* The Rustlings, Valley Close, Studham, Dunstable LU6 2QN *Livery,* 332. *Clerk,* Clifford Bygrave *Master,* Graham Ward

CHARTERED ARCHITECTS *(98).* 82A Muswell Hill Road, London N10 3JR *Livery,* 150. *Clerk,* David Cole-Adams *Master,* Roger France

CHARTERED SECRETARIES AND ADMINISTRATORS *(87).* 3rd Floor, Saddlers' House, 40 Gutter Lane, London EC2V 6BR *Livery,* 277. *Clerk,* Col. Michael Dudding, OBE, TD *Master,* Deputy Robin Eve

CHARTERED SURVEYORS *(85).* 75 Meadway Drive, Horsell, Woking, Surrey GU21 4TF *Livery,* 345. *Clerk,* Amanda Jackson *Master,* Laurence Johnstone

CLOCKMAKERS *(61).* Salters' Hall, 4 Fore Street, London EC2Y 5DE *Livery,* 285. *Clerk,* Joe Buxton *Master,* Cdr Peter Linstead-Smith, OBE

COACHMAKERS AND COACH-HARNESS MAKERS *(72).* 48 Aldernay Street, London SW1V 4EX *Livery,* 400. *Clerk,* Lt.-Col. Peter Henderson, OBE *Master,* Dr Stephen Hammerton

CONSTRUCTORS *(99).* Forge Farmhouse, Glassenbury, Cranbrook, Kent TN17 2QE *Livery,* 160. *Clerk,* Tim Nicholson *Master,* Dr Christine Rigden

COOKS *(35).* Coombe Ridge, Thursley Road, Churt, Farnham, Surrey GU10 2LQ *Livery,* 75. *Clerk,* Michael Thatcher, LLB *Master,* Graham Craddock

COOPERS *(36). Hall,* Coopers' Hall, 13 Devonshire Square, London EC2M 4TH *Livery,* 260. *Clerk,* Lt.-Col. Adrian Carroll *Master,* George Prescott, QC

CORDWAINERS *(27).* Clothworkers' Hall, Dunster Court, Mincing Lane, London EC3R 7AH *Livery,* 168. *Clerk,* John Miller *Master,* Mark Shaw

CURRIERS *(29).* Hedgerley, 10 The Leaze, Ashton Keynes, Wiltshire SN6 6PE *Livery,* 93. *Clerk,* Gp Capt. David Moss *Master,* William Moberly

CUTLERS *(18). Hall,* Cutlers' Hall, Warwick Lane, London EC4M 7BR *Livery,* 100. *Clerk,* J. Allen *Master,* M. Pocock

DISTILLERS *(69).* 1 The Sanctuary, Westminster, London SW1P 3JT *Livery,* 260. *Clerk,* Edward Macey-Dare *Master,* Simon Leschallas

DYERS *(13). Hall,* Dyers' Hall, 10 Dowgate Hill, London EC4R 2ST *Livery,* 136. *Clerk,* Russell Vaizey *Prime Warden,* A. Burdon-Cooper

ENGINEERS *(94).* Wax Chandlers' Hall, 6 Gresham Street, London EC2V 7AD *Livery,* 330. *Clerk,* Air Vice-Marshal Graham Skinner, CBE *Master,* Christopher Price, OBE, FRENG

ENVIRONMENTAL CLEANERS *(97).* 121 Hacton Lane, Upminster, Essex RM14 2NL *Livery,* 280. *Clerk,* Neil Morley *Master,* Jack Amos

FAN MAKERS *(76).* Skinners' Hall, 8 Dowgate Hill, London EC4R 2SP *Livery,* 202. *Clerk,* Keith Patterson *Master,* Prof. J. Salter

FARMERS *(80). Hall,* The Farmers' and Fletchers' Hall, 3 Cloth Street, London EC1A 7LD *Livery,* 300. *Clerk,* Col. David King, OBE *Master,* J Courtney

FARRIERS *(55).* 19 Queen Street, Chipperfield, Kings Langley, Herts WD4 9BT *Livery,* 330. *Clerk,* Charlotte Clifford *Master,* Reg Howe

FELTMAKERS *(63).* Post Cottage, Greywell, Hook, Hants RG29 1DA *Livery,* 173. *Clerk,* Maj. J. Coombs *Master,* Susan Wood

FIREFIGHTERS *(103).* The Insurance Hall, 20 Aldermanbury, London EC2V 7HY *Livery,* 80. *Clerk,* Martin Bonham *Master,* Geoffrey Morgan

FLETCHERS *(39). Hall,* The Farmers' and Fletchers' Hall, 3 Cloth Street, London EC1A 7LD *Livery,* 143. *Clerk,* Capt. Michael Johnson, RN *Master,* Capt. A. Poulter, OBE

FOUNDERS *(33). Hall,* Founders' Hall, 1 Cloth Fair, London EC1A 7JQ *Livery,* 175. *Clerk,* A. Gillett *Master,* Dr T. Rollason

FRAMEWORK KNITTERS *(64).* 86 Park Drive, Upminster, Essex RM14 3AS *Livery,* 215. *Clerk,* Alan Clark *Master,* Jeremy Beachell

FRUITERERS *(45).* Chapelstones, 84 High Street, Codford St Mary, Warminster BA12 0ND *Livery,* 283. *Clerk,* Lt.-Col. L. French *Master,* Alan French

FUELLERS *(95).* 26 Merrick Square, London SE1 4JB *Livery,* 135. *Clerk,* Sir Anthony Reardon Smith, Bt. *Master,* Michael Husband

FURNITURE MAKERS *(83). Hall,* Furniture Makers' Hall, 12 Austin Friars, London EC2N 2HE *Livery,* 225. *Clerk,* Charles Kerrigan *Master,* Peter Kelsey

GARDENERS *(66).* 25 Luke Street, London EC2A 4AR *Livery,* 285. *Clerk,* Cdr Robert Woolgar, OBE *Master,* Louise Robinson

GIRDLERS *(23). Hall,* Girdlers' Hall, Basinghall Avenue, London EC2V 5DD *Livery,* 80. *Clerk,* Brig. I. Rees *Master,* Michael Keene

GLASS SELLERS *(71).* 57 Witley Court, Coram Street, London WC1N 1HD *Livery,* 230. *Clerk,* Col. Audrey Smith *Master,* Robin Arculus

GLAZIERS AND PAINTERS OF GLASS *(53). Hall,* Glaziers' Hall, 9 Montague Close, London SE1 9DD *Livery,* 292. *Clerk,* Alex Galloway, CVO *Master,* Alderman Sir John Stuttard

GLOVERS *(62).* 17 Tite Street, London SW3 4JR *Livery,* 250. *Clerk,* C. Blackshaw *Master,* O. Holmes

GOLD AND SILVER WYRE DRAWERS *(74).* 9A Prince of Wales Mansions, Prince of Wales Drive, London SW11 4BG *Livery,* 305. *Clerk,* Cdr. R. House, RN *Master,* Timothy Waller

GUNMAKERS *(73).* The Proof House, 48–50 Commercial Road, London E1 1LP *Livery,* 350. *Clerk,* Col. William Chesshyre *Master,* Brig. Paul Cort

HACKNEY CARRIAGE DRIVERS *(104).* 25 The Grove, Parkfield, Latimer, Bucks HP5 1UE *Livery,* 102. *Clerk,* Mary Whitworth *Master,* Michael Davies

HORNERS *(54).* St. Stephen's House, Hide Place, London SW1P 4NJ *Livery,* 225. *Clerk,* Raymond Layard *Master,* David Spofforth

INFORMATION TECHNOLOGISTS *(100). Hall,* Information Technologists' Hall, 39A Bartholomew Close, London EC1A 7JN *Livery,* 301. *Clerk,* Michael Grant *Master,* Charles Hughes

INNHOLDERS *(32). Hall,* Innholders' Hall, 30 College Street, London EC4R 2RH *Livery,* 154. *Clerk,* Dougal Bulger *Master,* Alderman Sir Robert Finch

INSURERS *(92).* The Hall, 20 Aldermanbury, London EC2V 7HY *Livery,* 380. *Clerk,* L. Walters *Master,* Graeme King

INTERNATIONAL BANKERS *(106).* 12 Austin Friars, London EC2N 2HE *Livery,* 152. *Clerk,* Wg Cdr Tim Woods, BEM *Master,* Robert Wigley

JOINERS AND CEILERS *(41)*. 75 Meadway Drive, Horsell, Woking, Surrey GU21 4TF *Livery*, 128. *Clerk*, Amanda Jackson *Master*, H. de Sausmarez

LAUNDERERS *(89)*. *Hall*, Launderers' Hall, 9 Montague Close, London Bridge, London SE1 9DD *Livery*, 240. *Clerk*, Mrs J. Polek *Master*, Murray Simpson

LEATHERSELLERS *(15)*. *Hall*, Leathersellers' Hall, 15 St Helen's Place, London EC3A 6DQ *Livery*, 150. *Clerk*, David Santa-Olalla *Master*, Charles Barrow

LIGHTMONGERS *(96)*. Crown Wharf, 11A Coldharbour, Blackwall Reach, London E14 9NS *Livery*, 180. *Clerk*, Derek Wheatley *Master*, Hugh Ogus

LORINERS *(57)*. Hampton House, High Street, East Grinstead, West Sussex RH19 3AW *Livery*, 411. *Clerk*, Peter Lusty *Master*, Elisabeth Hobeday

MAKERS OF PLAYING CARDS *(75)*. 256 St David's Square, London E14 3WE *Livery*, 138. *Clerk*, David Barrett *Master*, Brian Porritt

MANAGEMENT CONSULTANTS *(105)*. Skinners' Hall, 8 Dowgate Hill, London EC4R 2SP *Livery*, 177. *Clerk*, Leslie Johnson *Master*, Prof. Bob Garratt

MARKETORS *(90)*. 5a Nottingham Mansions, Nottingham Street, Marylebone, London W1U 5EN *Livery*, 267. *Clerk*, Mrs Adele Thorpe *Master*, Venetia Howes

MASONS *(30)*. 22 Cannon Hill, Southgate, London N14 6LG *Livery*, 160. *Clerk*, Heather Rowell *Master*, Adrian Sarson

MASTER MARINERS *(78)*. *Hall*, HQS Wellington, Temple Stairs, Victoria Embankment, London WC2R 2PN *Livery*, 197. *Clerk*, Cdre Angus Menzies, RN *Master*, Capt. Malcolm Parrott, RFA

MUSICIANS *(50)*. 6th Floor, 2 London Wall Building, London EC2M 5PP *Livery*, 385. *Clerk*, Margaret Alford *Master*, Maurice Summerfield

NEEDLEMAKERS *(65)*. PO Box 3682, Windsor, Berkshire SL4 3WR *Livery*, 200. *Clerk*, Philip Grant *Master*, Malcolm Samuels

PAINTER-STAINERS *(28)*. *Hall*, Painters' Hall, 9 Little Trinity Lane, London EC4V 2AD *Livery*, 320. *Clerk*, Christopher Twyman *Master*, Richard Martin

PATTENMAKERS *(70)*. 3 The High Street, Sutton Valence, Kent ME17 3AG *Livery*, 200. *Clerk*, Col. R. Murfin, TD *Master*, Helen Auty

PAVIORS *(56)*. 3 Ridgemount Gardens, Enfield, Middx EN2 8QL *Livery*, 280. *Clerk*, John White *Master*, Andrew Panter

PEWTERERS *(16)*. *Hall*, Pewterers' Hall, Oat Lane, London EC2V 7DE *Livery*, 80. *Clerk*, Capt. Paddy Watson, RN *Master*, Christopher Peacock

PLAISTERERS *(46)*. *Hall*, Plaisterers' Hall, 1 London Wall, London EC2Y 5JU *Livery*, 210. *Clerk*, Hilary Machtus *Master*, Robert Dalrymple

PLUMBERS *(31)*. Wax Chandlers' Hall, 6 Gresham Street, London EC2V 7AD *Livery*, 360. *Clerk*, Lt.-Col. Anthony Paterson-Fox *Master*, David Hamilton

POULTERS *(34)*. The Old Butchers, Station Road, Groombridge, Kent TN3 9QX *Livery*, 208. *Clerk*, Gwen Butcher *Master*, David Bridges

SADDLERS *(25)*. *Hall*, Saddlers' Hall, 40 Gutter Lane, London EC2V 6BR *Livery*, 75. *Clerk*, Col. N. Lithgow, CBE *Master*, D. Chandler

SCIENTIFIC INSTRUMENT MAKERS *(84)*. 9 Montague Close, London SE1 9DD *Livery*, 185. *Clerk*, Neville Watson *Master*, H. Tee, CBE

SCRIVENERS *(44)*. HQS Wellington, Temple Stairs, Victoria Embankment, London WC2R 2PN *Livery*, 200. *Clerk*, Paul Elliott *Master*, Leslie Brace

SECURITY PROFESSIONALS *(108)*. WIllowcroft, Old Forest Road, Winnersh, Wokingham, Berkshire RG41 1HY *Livery*, 150. *Clerk*, Bill Clark *Master*, Stephen Parsons

SHIPWRIGHTS *(59)*. Ironmongers Hall, Shaftesbury Place, London EC2Y 8AA *Livery*, 446. *Clerk*, Capt. Nigel Williams, RN *Permanent Master*, HRH The Duke of Edinburgh, KG, KT, OM *Prime Warden*, Graham Clarke

SOLICITORS *(79)*. 4 College Hill, London EC4R 2RB *Livery*, 350. *Clerk*, Neil Cameron *Master*, Alderman Sir David Lewis

SPECTACLE MAKERS *(60)*. Apothecaries' Hall, Black Friars Lane, London EC4V 6EL *Livery*, 390. *Clerk*, Lt.-Col. John Salmon, OBE *Master*, Dr John Shilling, FRCS

STATIONERS AND NEWSPAPER MAKERS *(47)*. *Hall*, Stationers' Hall, Ave Maria Lane, London EC4M 7DD *Livery*, 476. *Clerk*, Brig. Denzil Sharp, AFC *Master*, Richard Brewster

TALLOW CHANDLERS *(21)*. *Hall*, Tallow Chandlers' Hall, 4 Dowgate Hill, London EC4R 2SH *Livery*, 179. *Clerk*, Brig. R. Wilde, CBE *Master*, Ian Bowden

TAX ADVISERS *(107)*. 191 West End Road, Ruislip, Middx HA4 6LD *Freemen*, 135. *Clerk*, Paul Herbage *Master*, Nicholas Woolf

TIN PLATE WORKERS (ALIAS WIRE WORKERS) *(67)*. Highbanks, Ferry Road, Surlingham, Norwich, Norfolk NR14 7AR *Livery*, 220. *Clerk*, Michael Henderson-Begg *Master*, Andrew Hill

TOBACCO PIPE MAKERS AND TOBACCO BLENDERS *(82)*. Green Meadow, Steep, Hants GU32 1AE *Livery*, 150. *Clerk*, Barbara Hines *Master*, J. Alexander, CBE

TURNERS *(51)*. 182 Temple Chambers, Temple Avenue, London EC4Y 0HP *Livery*, 183. *Clerk*, Edward Windsor Clive *Master*, C Roberts, CB

TYLERS AND BRICKLAYERS *(37)*. 30 Shelley Avenue, Tiptree CO5 0SF *Livery*, 155. *Clerk*, Barry Blumson *Master*, Julyan Gordon

UPHOLDERS *(49)*. Hall in the Wood, 46 Quail Gardens, Selsdon Vale, Croydon CR2 8TF *Livery*, 213. *Clerk*, Jean Cody *Master*, Michael Gilham

WATER CONSERVATORS *(102)*. The Lark, 2 Bell Lane, Worlington, Bury St Edmunds, Suffolk IP28 8SE *Livery*, 210. *Clerk*, Ralph Riley *Master*, Rear-Adm. Bob Mark

WAX CHANDLERS *(20)*. *Hall*, Wax Chandlers' Hall, 6 Gresham Street, London EC2V 7AD *Livery*, 130. *Clerk*, Georgina Brown *Master*, Hon. Dr Colin Kolbert

WEAVERS *(42)*. Saddlers' House, Gutter Lane, London EC2V 6BR *Livery*, 125. *Clerk*, John Snowdon *Upper Bailiff*, John Hodges

WHEELWRIGHTS *(68)*. 7 Glengall Road, Bexleyheath, Kent DA7 4AL *Livery*, 221. *Clerk*, Brian François *Master*, Richard Proctor

WOOLMEN *(43)*. The Old Post Office, 56 Lower Way, Great Brickhill, Bucks MK17 9AG *Livery*, 141. *Clerk*, Gillian Wilson *Master*, Elizabeth Peacock

WORLD TRADERS *(101)*. 13 Hall Gardens, Colney Heath, St. Albans, Herts AL4 0QF *Livery*, 208. *Clerk*, Mrs Gaye Duffy *Master*, Michael Wren

PARISH CLERKS *(No Livery*)*. Acreholt, 33 Medstead Road, Beech, Alton, Hants GU34 4AD *Members*, 95. *Clerk*, Lt.-Col. Brian Coombes *Master*, E. Roberts

WATERMEN AND LIGHTERMEN *(No Livery*)*. *Hall*, Watermen's Hall, 16 St Mary-at-Hill, London EC3R 8EF *Craft Owning Freemen*, 408. *Clerk*, Colin Middlemiss *Master*, David Gordon

* Parish Clerks and Watermen and Lightermen have requested to remain with no livery

LONDON BOROUGH COUNCILS

Council	*Telephone*	*Population**	*Council Tax†*	*Chief Executive*
Barking and Dagenham	020-8592 4500	166,900	£1,326	Robert Whiteman
Barnet	020-8359 2000	329,700	£1,423	Nick Walkley
Bexley	020-8303 7777	221,100	£1,427	Will Tuckley
Brent	020-8937 1234	270,000	£1,369	Gareth Daniel
Bromley	020-8464 3333	300,700	£1,289	Doug Patterson
Camden	020-7278 4444	231,900	£1,332	Moira Gibb, CBE
CITY OF LONDON CORPORATION	020-7606 3030	8,000	£943	Chris Duffield
Croydon	020-8726 6000	339,500	£1,448	Jon Rouse
Ealing	020-8825 5000	305,300	£1,370	Darra Singh
Enfield	020-8379 1000	285,100	£1,410	Rob Leak
Greenwich	020-8854 8888	223,100	£1,291	Mary Ney
Hackney	020-8356 5000	209,700	£1,308	Tim Shields
Hammersmith and Fulham	020-8748 3020	172,500	£1,147	Geoff Alltimes
Haringey	020-8489 0000	224,700	£1,494	Dr Ita O'Donovan
Harrow	020-8863 5611	214,600	£1,496	Michael Lockwood
Havering	01708-434343	228,400	£1,511	Cheryl Coppell
Hillingdon	01895-250111	250,700	£1,423	Hugh Dunnachie
Hounslow	020-8583 2000	220,600	£1,400	Mark Gilks
Islington	020-7527 2000	187,800	£1,272	John Foster
Kensington and Chelsea	020-7937 5464	178,600	£1,092	Derek Myers
Kingston upon Thames	020-8547 5757	157,900	£1,631	Bruce McDonald
Lambeth	020-7926 1000	273,200	£1,235	Derrick Anderson
Lewisham	020-8314 6000	258,500	£1,352	Barry Quirk, CBE
Merton	020-8543 2222	199,300	£1,432	Ged Curran
Newham	020-8430 2000	249,600	£1,255	Joe Duckworth
Redbridge	020-8554 5000	254,400	£1,405	Roger Hampson
Richmond upon Thames	020-8891 1411	180,000	£1,597	Gillian Norton
Southwark	020 7525 5000	274,400	£1,222	Nicola Stanton
Sutton	020-8770 5000	185,900	£1,451	Paul Martin
Tower Hamlets	020-7364 5000	215,300	£1,195	Dr. Kevan Collins *(acting)*
Waltham Forest	020-8496 3000	222,300	£1,462	Andrew Kilburn
Wandsworth	020-8871 6000	281,800	£687	Gerald Jones
WESTMINSTER	020-7641 6000	234,100	£688	Mike More

* *Source:* ONS – *Mid-2007 Population Estimates* (Crown copyright)
† Average Band D council tax bill for 2009–10
Councils in CAPITAL LETTERS have city status

WALES

Cymru

The principality of Wales (Cymru) occupies the extreme west of the central southern portion of the island of Great Britain, with a total area of 20,778 sq. km (8,022 sq. miles): land 20,733 sq. km (8,005 sq. miles); inland water 45 sq. km (17 sq. miles). It is bordered in the north by the Irish Sea, in the south by the Bristol Channel, in the east by the English counties of Cheshire West and Chester, Shropshire, Herefordshire and Gloucestershire, and in the west by St George's Channel.

Across the Menai Straits is Ynys Mon (Isle of Anglesey) (715 sq. km/276 sq. miles), communication with which is facilitated by the Menai Suspension Bridge (305m/1,000ft long) built by Telford in 1826, and by the Britannia Bridge (351m/1,151ft), a two-tier road and rail truss arch design, rebuilt in 1972 after a fire destroyed the original tubular railway bridge built by Stephenson in 1850. Holyhead harbour, on Holy Isle (north-west of Anglesey), provides ferry services to Dublin (113km/70 miles).

POPULATION

The population at the 2001 census was 2,903,085 (men 1,403,782; women 1,499,303). The average density of population in 2001 was 140 persons per sq. km (362 per sq. mile).

RELIEF

Wales is a country of extensive tracts of high plateau and shorter stretches of mountain ranges deeply dissected by river valleys. Lower-lying ground is largely confined to the coastal belt and the lower parts of the valleys. The highest mountains are those of Snowdonia in the north west (Snowdon, 1,085m/3,559ft), Berwyn (Aran Fawddwy, 906m/2,971ft), Cader Idris (Pen y Gadair, 892m/2,928ft), Dyfed (Plynlimon, 752m/2,467ft), and the Black Mountains, Brecon Beacons and Black Forest ranges in the south-east (Pen y Fan, 886m/2,906ft; Waun Fâch, 811m/2,660ft; Carmarthen Van, 802m/2,630ft).

HYDROGRAPHY

The principal river in Wales is the Severn, which flows from the slopes of Plynlimon to the English border. The Wye (209km/130 miles) also rises in the slopes of Plynlimon. The Usk (90km/56 miles) flows into the Bristol Channel through Gwent. The Dee (113km/70 miles) rises in Bala Lake and flows through the Vale of Llangollen, where an aqueduct (built by Telford in 1805) carries the Pontcysyllte branch of the Shropshire Union Canal across the valley. The estuary of the Dee is the navigable portion, it is 23km (14 miles) in length and about 8km (5 miles) in breadth. The Towy (109km/68 miles), Teifi (80km/50 miles), Taff (64km/40 miles), Dovey (48km/30 miles), Taf (40km/25 miles) and Conway (39km/24 miles) are wholly Welsh rivers.

The largest natural lake is Bala (Llyn Tegid) in Gwynedd, nearly 7km (4 miles) long and 1.6km (1 mile) wide. Lake Vyrnwy is an artificial reservoir, about the size of Bala, it forms the water supply of Liverpool; Birmingham's water is supplied from reservoirs in the Elan and Claerwen valleys.

WELSH LANGUAGE

According to the 2001 census results, the percentage of people aged three years and over who are able to speak Welsh is:

Blaenau Gwent	9.1	Neath Port Talbot	17.8
Bridgend	10.6	Newport	9.6
Caerphilly	10.9	Pembrokeshire	21.5
Cardiff	10.9	Powys	20.8
Carmarthenshire	50.1	Rhondda Cynon Taf	12.3
Ceredigion	51.8	Swansea	13.2
Conwy	29.2	Torfaen	10.7
Denbighshire	26.1	Vale of Glamorgan	11.1
Flintshire	14.1	Wrexham	14.4
Gwynedd	68.7	Ynys Mon (Isle of Anglesey)	59.8
Merthyr Tydfil	10.0		
Monmouthshire	9.0	*Total in Wales*	20.5

FLAG

The flag of Wales, the Red Dragon (Y Ddraig Goch), is a red dragon on a field divided white over green (per fess argent and vert a dragon passant gules). The flag was augmented in 1953 by a royal badge on a shield encircled with a riband bearing the words *Ddraig Goch Ddyry Cychwyn* and imperially crowned, but this augmented flag is rarely used.

EARLY HISTORY

The earliest inhabitants of whom there is any record appear to have been subdued or exterminated by the Goidels (a people of Celtic race) in the Bronze Age. A further invasion of Celtic Brythons and Belgae followed in the ensuing Iron Age. The Roman conquest of southern Britain and Wales was for some time successfully opposed by Caratacus (Caractacus or Caradog), chieftain of the Catuvellauni and son of Cunobelinus (Cymbeline). South-east Wales was subjugated and the legionary fortress at Caerleon-on-Usk established by around AD 75–7; the conquest of Wales was completed by Agricola around AD 78. Communications were opened up by the construction of military roads from Chester to Caerleon-on-Usk and Caerwent, and from Chester to Conwy (and thence to Carmarthen and Neath). Christianity was introduced in the fourth century, during the Roman occupation.

ANGLO-SAXON ATTACKS

The Anglo-Saxon invaders of southern Britain drove the Celts into the mountain stronghold of Wales, and into Strathclyde (Cumberland and south-west Scotland) and Cornwall, giving them the name of *Waelisc* (Welsh), meaning 'foreign'. The West Saxons' victory of Deorham (AD 577) isolated Wales from Cornwall and the battle of Chester (AD 613) cut off communication with Strathclyde and northern Britain. In the eighth century the boundaries of the Welsh were further restricted by the annexations of Offa, King of Mercia, and counter-attacks were largely prevented by the construction of an artificial boundary from the Dee to the Wye (Offa's Dyke).

In the ninth century Rhodri Mawr (844–878) united the country and successfully resisted further incursions of the Saxons by land and raids of Norse and Danish pirates by sea, but at his death his three provinces of Gwynedd (north), Powys (central) and Deheubarth (south) were divided among his three sons, Anarawd, Mervyn and Cadell. Cadell's son Hywel Dda ruled a large part of Wales and codified its laws but the provinces were not united again until the rule of Llewelyn ap Seisyllt (husband of the heiress of Gwynedd) from 1018 to 1023.

THE NORMAN CONQUEST

After the Norman conquest of England, William I created palatine counties along the Welsh frontier, and the Norman barons began to make encroachments into Welsh territory. The Welsh princes recovered many of their losses during the civil wars of Stephen's reign (1135–54), and in the early 13th century Owen Gruffydd, prince of Gwynedd, was the dominant figure in Wales. Under Llywelyn ap Iorwerth (1194–1240) the Welsh united in powerful resistance to English incursions and Llywelyn's privileges and *de facto* independence were recognised in the Magna Carta. His grandson, Llywelyn ap Gruffydd, was the last native prince; he was killed in 1282 during hostilities between the Welsh and English, allowing Edward I of England to establish his authority over the country. On 7 February 1301, Edward of Caernarvon, son of Edward I, was created Prince of Wales, a title subsequently borne by the eldest son of the sovereign.

Strong Welsh national feeling continued, expressed in the early 15th century in the rising led by Owain Glyndwr, but the situation was altered by the accession to the English throne in 1485 of Henry VII of the Welsh House of Tudor. Wales was politically annexed by England under the Act of Union of 1535, which extended English laws to the principality and gave it parliamentary representation for the first time.

EISTEDDFOD

The Welsh are a distinct nation, with a language and literature of their own; the national bardic festival (Eisteddfod), instituted by Prince Rhys ap Griffith in 1176, is still held annually.

PRINCIPAL CITIES

There are five cities in Wales (with date city status conferred): Bangor (pre-1900), Cardiff (1905), Newport (2002), St David's (1994) and Swansea (1969).

Cardiff and Swansea have also been granted Lord Mayoralities.

CARDIFF

Cardiff, at the mouth of the rivers Taff, Rhymney and Ely, is the capital city of Wales and at the 2001 census had a population of 305,353. The city has changed dramatically in recent years following the regeneration of Cardiff Bay and construction of a barrage, which has created a permanent freshwater lake and waterfront for the city. As the capital city, Cardiff is home to the National Assembly for Wales and is a major administrative, retail, business and cultural centre.

The city is home to many fine buildings including the City Hall, Cardiff Castle, Llandaff Cathedral, the National Museum of Wales, university buildings, law courts and the Temple of Peace and Health. The Millennium Stadium opened in 1999 and has hosted FA Cup finals and other high-profile English football matches since 2001.

SWANSEA

Swansea *(Abertawe)* is a seaport with a population of 223,293 at the 2001 census. The Gower peninsula was brought within the city boundary under local government reform in 1974.

The principal buildings are the Norman Castle (rebuilt *c.*1330), the Royal Institution of South Wales, founded in 1835 (including library), the University of Wales Swansea at Singleton and the Guildhall, containing Frank Brangwyn's British Empire panels. The Dylan Thomas Centre, formerly the old Guildhall, was restored in 1995. More recent buildings include the County Hall, the Maritime Quarter Marina, the Wales National Pool and the National Waterfront Museum.

Swansea was chartered by the Earl of Warwick (1158–84), and further charters were granted by King John, Henry III, Edward II, Edward III and James II, Oliver Cromwell and the Marcher Lord William de Breos. It was formally invested with city status in 1969 by HRH The Prince of Wales.

LORD-LIEUTENANTS AND HIGH SHERIFFS

Area	*Lord-Lieutenant*	*High Sheriff (2009–10)*
Clwyd	T. Jones, CBE	Henry Robertson
Dyfed	Hon. Robin Lewis, OBE	Gareth Rowlands
Gwent	S. Boyle	Stephen Hughes
Gwynedd	His Hon. Huw Daniel	Trevor Corbett
Mid Glamorgan	Kate Thomas, CVO	John Tal-Williams, MBE
Powys	Hon. Mrs E. Legge-Bourke, LVO	David Lloyd
S. Glamorgan	Dr Peter Beck, MD, FRCP	Prof. Anthony Hazell
W. Glamorgan	D. Byron Lewis	Dr Ronald John

LOCAL COUNCILS

Council	*Administrative Headquarters*	*Telephone*	*Population**	*Council Tax†*	*Chief Executive*
Blaenau Gwent	Ebbw Vale	01495-350555	69,200	£1,325	Robin Morrison
Bridgend	Bridgend	01656-643643	133,900	£1,184	Dr Jo Farrar
Caerphilly	Hengoed	01443-815588	171,800	£1,057	Stuart Rosser
CARDIFF	Cardiff	029-2087 2000	321,000	£1,028	Byron Davies
Carmarthenshire	Carmarthen	01267-234567	179,500	£1,111	Mark James
Ceredigion	Aberaeron	01545-570881	77,800	£1,067	Bronwen Morgan
Conwy	Conwy	01492-574000	111,700	£1,007	Byron Davies
Denbighshire	Ruthin	01824-706000	97,000	£1,201	Ian Miller
Flintshire	Mold	01352-752121	150,500	£1,080	Colin Everett
Gwynedd	Caernarfon	01766-771000	118,400	£1,148	Harry Thomas
Merthyr Tydfil	Merthyr Tydfil	01685-725000	55,600	£1,252	Alistair Neill
Monmouthshire	Cwmbran	01633-644644	88,200	£1,145	Paul Matthews
Neath Port Talbot	Port Talbot	01639-763333	137,400	£1,292	vacant
NEWPORT	Newport	01633-656656	140,200	£921	Tracey Lee
Pembrokeshire	Haverfordwest	01437-764551	117,900	£864	Bryn Parry-Jones
Powys	Llandrindod Wells	01597-826000	132,000	£1,057	Jeremy Patterson *(acting)*
Rhondda Cynon Taff	Tonypandy	01443-424000	233,700	£1,214	Keith Griffiths
SWANSEA	Swansea	01792-636000	228,100	£1,073	Paul Smith
Torfaen	Pontypool	01495-762200	91,100	£1,108	Alison Ward
Vale of Glamorgan	Barry	01446-700111	124,000	£1,043	John Maitland-Evans
Wrexham	Wrexham	01978-292000	131,900	£1,069	Isobel Garner
Ynys Mon (Isle of Anglesey)	Ynys Mon	01248-750057	69,000	£1,013	Richard Jones *(acting)*

* *Source:* ONS – *Mid-2007 Population Estimates* (Crown copyright)
† Average Band D council tax bill 2009–10
Councils in CAPITAL LETTERS have city status

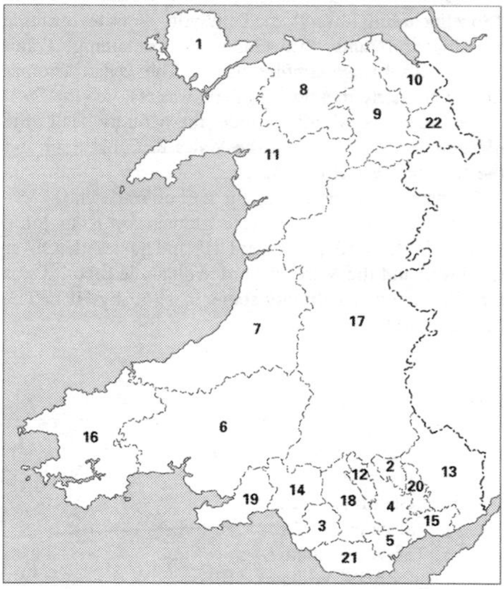

Key	*Council*	*Key*	*Council*
1	Anglesey (Ynys Mon)	12	Merthyr Tydfil
2	Blaenau Gwent	13	Monmouthshire
3	Bridgend	14	Neath Port Talbot
4	Caerphilly	15	Newport
5	Cardiff	16	Pembrokeshire
6	Carmarthenshire	17	Powys
7	Ceredigion	18	Rhondda, Cynon, Taff
8	Conwy	19	Swansea
9	Denbighshire	20	Torfaen
10	Flintshire	21	Vale of Glamorgan
11	Gwynedd	22	Wrexham

SCOTLAND

Scotland occupies the northern portion of the main island of Great Britain and includes the Inner and Outer Hebrides, Orkney, Shetland and many other islands. It lies between 60° 51′ 30″ and 54° 38′ N. latitude and between 1° 45′ 32″ and 6° 14′ W. longitude, with England to the south, the Atlantic Ocean on the north and west, and the North Sea on the east.

The greatest length of the mainland (Cape Wrath to the Mull of Galloway) is 441km (274 miles), and the greatest breadth (Buchan Ness to Applecross) is 248km (154 miles). The customary measurement of the island of Great Britain is from the site of John o' Groats house, near Duncansby Head, Caithness, to Land's End, Cornwall, a total distance of 970km (603 miles) in a straight line and approximately 1,448km (900 miles) by road.

The total area of Scotland is 78,807 sq. km (30,427 sq. miles): land 77,907 sq. km (30,080 sq. miles), inland water 900 sq. km (347 sq. miles).

POPULATION

The population at the 2001 census was 5,062,011 (men 2,432,494; women 2,629,517). The average density of the population in 2001 was 64 persons per sq. km (166 per sq. mile).

RELIEF

There are three natural orographic divisions of Scotland. The southern uplands have their highest points in Merrick (843m/2,766ft), Rhinns of Kells (814m/2,669ft) and Cairnsmuir of Carsphairn (797m/2,614ft), in the west; and the Tweedsmuir Hills in the east (Broad Law 840m/2,756ft; Dollar Law 817m/2,682ft; Hartfell 808m/2,651ft).

The central lowlands, formed by the valleys of the Clyde, Forth and Tay, divide the southern uplands from the northern Highlands, which extend almost from the extreme north of the mainland to the central lowlands, and are divided into a northern and a southern system by the Great Glen.

The Grampian Mountains, which entirely cover the southern Highland area, include in the west Ben Nevis (1,343m/4,406ft), the highest point in the British Isles, and in the east the Cairngorm Mountains (Ben Macdui 1,309m/4,296ft; Braeriach 1,295m/4,248ft; Cairn Gorm 1,245m/4,084ft). The north-western Highland area contains the mountains of Wester and Easter Ross (Carn Eige 1,183m/3,880ft; Sgurr na Lapaich 1,151m/3,775ft).

Created, like the central lowlands, by a major geological fault, the Great Glen (97km/60 miles long) runs between Inverness and Fort William, and contains Loch Ness, Loch Oich and Loch Lochy. These are linked to each other and to the north-east and south-west coasts of Scotland by the Caledonian Canal, providing a navigable passage between the Moray Firth and the Inner Hebrides.

HYDROGRAPHY

The western coast is fragmented by peninsulas and islands, and indented by fjords (sea-lochs), the longest of which is Loch Fyne (68km/42 miles long) in Argyll. Although the east coast tends to be less fractured and lower, there are several great drowned inlets (firths), eg Firth of Forth, Firth of Tay and Moray Firth, as well as the Firth of Clyde in the west.

The lochs are the principal hydrographic feature. The largest in Scotland and in Britain is Loch Lomond (70 sq. km/27 sq. miles), in the Grampian valleys and the longest and deepest is Loch Ness (39km/24 miles long and 244m/800ft deep), in the Great Glen.

The longest river is the Tay (188km/117 miles), noted for its salmon. It flows into the North Sea, with Dundee on the estuary, which is spanned by the Tay Bridge (3,136m/10,289ft) opened in 1887 and the Tay Road Bridge (2,245m/7,365ft) opened in 1966. Other noted salmon rivers are the Dee (145km/90 miles) which flows into the North Sea at Aberdeen, and the Spey (177km/110 miles), the swiftest flowing river in the British Isles, which flows into Moray Firth. The Tweed, which gave its name to the woollen cloth produced along its banks, marks in the lower stretches of its 154km (96 mile) course the border between Scotland and England.

The most important river commercially is the Clyde (171km/106 miles), formed by the junction of the Daer and Portrail water, which flows through the city of Glasgow to the Firth of Clyde. During its course it passes over the picturesque Falls of Clyde, Bonnington Linn (9m/30ft), Corra Linn (26m/84ft), Dundaff Linn (3m/10ft) and Stonebyres Linn (24m/80ft), above and below Lanark. The Forth (106km/66 miles), upon which stands Edinburgh, the capital, is spanned by the Forth Railway Bridge (1890), which is 1,625m (5,330ft) long, and the Forth Road Bridge (1964), which has a total length of 1,876m (6,156ft) (over water) and a single span of 914m (3,000ft).

The highest waterfall in Scotland, and the British Isles, is Eas a'Chùal Aluinn with a total height of 201m (658ft), which falls from Glas Bheinn in Sutherland. The Falls of Glomach, on a head-stream of the Elchaig in Wester Ross, have a drop of 113m (370ft).

GAELIC LANGUAGE

According to the 2001 census, 1.2 per cent of the population of Scotland, mainly in Eilean Siar (Western Isles), were able to speak the Scottish form of Gaelic.

LOWLAND SCOTTISH LANGUAGE

Several regional lowland Scottish dialects, known variously as Scots, Scotch, Lallans or Doric, are widely spoken. The General Register Office (Scotland) estimated in 1996 that 1.5 million people, or 30 per cent of the population, are Scots speakers. A question on Scots was not included in the 2001 census.

FLAG

The flag of Scotland is known as the Saltire. It is a white diagonal cross on a blue field (saltire argent in a field azure) and represents St Andrew, the patron saint of Scotland.

THE SCOTTISH ISLANDS

ORKNEY

The Orkney Islands (total area 972 sq. km/376 sq. miles) lie about ten km (six miles) north of the mainland, separated from it by the Pentland Firth. Of the 90 islands and islets (holms and skerries) in the group, about one-third are inhabited.

The total population at the 2001 census was 19,245; the 2001 populations of the islands shown here include those of smaller islands forming part of the same council district.

Mainland, 15,339	Rousay, 267
Burray, 357	Sanday, 478
Eday, 121	Shapinsay, 300
Flotta, 81	South Ronaldsay, 854
Hoy, 392	Stronsay, 358
North Ronaldsay, 70	Westray, 563
Papa Westray, 65	

The islands are rich in prehistoric and Scandinavian remains, the most notable being the Stone Age village of Skara Brae, the burial chamber of Maes Howe, the many brochs (towers) and the 12th-century St Magnus Cathedral. Scapa Flow, between the Mainland and Hoy, was the war station of the British Grand Fleet from 1914 to 1919 and the scene of the scuttling of the surrendered German High Seas Fleet (21 June 1919).

Most of the islands are low-lying and fertile, and farming (principally beef cattle) is the main industry. Flotta, to the south of Scapa Flow, is the site of the oil terminal for the Piper, Claymore and Tartan fields in the North Sea.

The capital is Kirkwall (population 6,206) situated on Mainland.

SHETLAND

The Shetland Islands have a total area of 1,427 sq. km (551 sq. miles) and a population at the 2001 census of 21,988. They lie about 80km (50 miles) north of the Orkneys, with Fair Isle about half way between the two groups. Out Stack, off Muckle Flugga, 1.6km (one mile) north of Unst, is the most northerly part of the British Isles (60° 51′ 30″ N. lat.).

There are over 100 islands, of which 16 are inhabited. Populations at the 2001 census were:

Mainland, 17,575	Muckle Roe, 104
Bressay, 384	Trondra, 133
East Burra, 66	Unst, 720
Fair Isle, 69	West Burra, 784
Fetlar, 86	Whalsay, 1,034
Housay, 76	Yell, 957

Shetland's many archaeological sites include Jarlshof, Mousa and Clickhimin, and its long connection with Scandinavia has resulted in a strong Norse influence on its placenames and dialect.

Industries include fishing, knitwear and farming. In addition to the fishing fleet there are fish processing factories, and the traditional handknitting of Fair Isle and Unst is now supplemented with machine-knitted garments. Farming is mainly crofting, with sheep being raised on the moorland and hills of the islands. Latterly the islands have become a centre of the North Sea oil industry, with pipelines from the Brent and Ninian fields running to the terminal at Sullom Voe, the largest of its kind in Europe.

The capital is Lerwick (population 6,830) situated on Mainland. Lerwick is the main centre for supply services for offshore oil exploration and development.

THE HEBRIDES

Until the late 13th century the Hebrides included other Scottish islands in the Firth of Clyde, the peninsula of Kintyre (Argyll), the Isle of Man, and the (Irish) Isle of Rathlin. The origin of the name is probably the Greek *Eboudai,* latinised as *Hebudes* by Pliny, and corrupted to its present form. The Norwegian name *Sudreyjar* (Southern Islands) was latinised as *Sodorenses,* a name that survives in the Anglican bishopric of Sodor and Man.

There are over 500 islands and islets, of which about 100 are inhabited, though mountainous terrain and extensive peat bogs mean that only a fraction of the total area is under cultivation. Stone, Bronze and Iron Age settlement has left many remains, including those at Callanish on Lewis, and Norse colonisation influenced language, customs and placenames. Occupations include farming (mostly crofting and stock-raising), fishing and the manufacture of tweeds and other woollens. Tourism is also an important part of the economy.

The Inner Hebrides lie off the west coast of Scotland and are relatively close to the mainland. The largest and best-known is Skye (area 1,665 sq. km/643 sq. miles; pop. 9,251; chief town, Portree), which contains the Cuillin Hills (Sgurr Alasdair 993m/3,257ft); Bla Bheinn (928m/3,046ft); the Storr (719m/2,358ft) and the Red Hills (Beinn na Caillich 732m/2,403ft). Other islands in the Highland council area include Raasay (pop. 194), Rum, Eigg (pop. 131) and Muck.

Further south the Inner Hebridean islands include Arran (pop. 5,058) containing Goat Fell (874m/2,868ft); Coll and Tiree (pop. 934); Colonsay and Oronsay (pop. 113); Easdale (pop. 58); Gigha (pop. 110); Islay (area 608 sq. km/235 sq. miles; pop. 3,457); Jura (area 414 sq. km/160 sq. miles; pop. 188) with a range of hills culminating in the Paps of Jura (Beinn-an-Oir, 785m/2,576ft, and Beinn Chaolais, 755m/2,477ft); Lismore (pop. 146); Luing (pop. 220); and Mull (area 950 sq. km/367 sq. miles; pop. 2,696; chief town Tobermory) containing Ben More (967m/3,171ft).

The Outer Hebrides, separated from the mainland by the Minch, now form the Eilean Siar (Western Isles) council area (area 2,897 sq. km/1,119 sq. miles; pop. 26,502). The main islands are Lewis with Harris (area 1,994 sq. km/770 sq. miles, pop. 19,918), whose chief town, Stornoway, is the administrative headquarters; North Uist (pop. 1,320); South Uist (pop. 1,818); Benbecula (pop. 1,249) and Barra (pop. 1,078). Other inhabited islands include Bernera (233), Berneray (136), Eriskay (133), Grimsay (201), Scalpay (322) and Vatersay (94).

EARLY HISTORY

There is evidence of human settlement in Scotland dating from the third millennium BC, the earliest settlers being Mesolithic hunters and fishermen. Early in the second millennium BC, New Stone Age farmers began to cultivate crops and rear livestock; their settlements were on the west coast and in the north, and included Skara Brae and Maeshowe (Orkney). Settlement by the early Bronze Age 'Beaker Folk', so-called from the shape of their drinking vessels, in eastern Scotland dates from about 1800 BC. Further settlement is believed to have occurred from 700 BC onwards, as tribes were displaced from further south by new incursions from the Continent and the Roman invasions from AD 43.

Julius Agricola, the Roman governor of Britain AD 77–84, extended the Roman conquests in Britain by advancing into Caledonia, culminating with a victory at Mons Graupius, probably in AD 84; he was recalled to Rome shortly afterwards and his forward policy was not pursued. Hadrian's Wall, mostly completed by AD 30, marked the northern frontier of the Roman empire except for the period between about AD 144 and 190 when the frontier moved north to the Forth-Clyde isthmus and a turf wall, the Antonine Wall, was manned.

After the Roman withdrawal from Britain, there were centuries of warfare between the Picts, Scots, Britons, Angles and Vikings. The Picts, generally accepted to be descended from the indigenous Iron Age people of northern Scotland, occupied the area north of the Forth. The Scots, a Gaelic-speaking people of northern Ireland, colonised the area of Argyll and Bute (the kingdom of Dalriada) in the fifth century AD and then expanded eastwards and northwards. The Britons, speaking a Brythonic Celtic language, colonised Scotland from the south from the first century BC; they lost control of south-eastern Scotland (incorporated into the kingdom of Northumbria) to the Angles in the early seventh century but retained Strathclyde (south-western Scotland and Cumbria). Viking raids from the late eighth century were followed by Norse settlement in the western and northern isles, Argyll, Caithness and Sutherland from the mid-ninth century onwards.

UNIFICATION

The union of the areas which now comprise Scotland began in AD 843 when Kenneth mac Alpin, king of the Scots from *c.*834, also became king of the Picts, joining the two lands to form the kingdom of Alba (comprising Scotland north of a line between the Forth and Clyde rivers). Lothian, the eastern part of the area between the Forth and the Tweed, seems to have been leased to Kenneth II of Alba (reigned 971–995) by Edgar of England *c.*973, and Scottish possession was confirmed by Malcolm II's victory over a Northumbrian army at Carham *c.*1016. At about this time Malcolm II (reigned 1005–34) placed his grandson Duncan on the throne of the British kingdom of Strathclyde, bringing under Scots rule virtually all of what is now Scotland.

The Norse possessions were incorporated into the kingdom of Scotland from the 12th century onwards. An uprising in the mid-12th century drove the Norse from most of mainland Argyll. The Hebrides were ceded to Scotland by the treaty of Perth in 1266 after a Norwegian expedition in 1263 failed to maintain Norse authority over the islands. Orkney and Shetland fell to Scotland in 1468–9 as a pledge for the unpaid dowry of Margaret of Denmark, wife of James III, although Danish claims of suzerainty were relinquished only with the marriage of Anne of Denmark to James VI in 1590.

From the 11th century, there were frequent wars between Scotland and England over territory and the extent of England's political influence. The failure of the Scottish royal line with the death of Margaret of Norway in 1290 led to disputes over the throne which were resolved by the adjudication of Edward I of England. He awarded the throne to John Balliol in 1292 but Balliol's refusal to be a puppet king led to war. Balliol surrendered to Edward I in 1296 and Edward attempted to rule Scotland himself. Resistance to Scotland's loss of independence was led by William Wallace, who defeated the English at Stirling Bridge (1297), and Robert Bruce, crowned in 1306, who held most of Scotland by 1311 and routed Edward II's army at Bannockburn (1314). England recognised the independence of Scotland in the treaty of Northampton in 1328. Subsequent clashes include the disastrous battle of Flodden (1513) in which James IV and many of his nobles fell.

THE UNION

In 1603 James VI of Scotland succeeded Elizabeth I on the throne of England (his mother, Mary Queen of Scots, was the great-granddaughter of Henry VII), his successors reigning as sovereigns of Great Britain. Political union of the two countries did not occur until 1707.

THE JACOBITE REVOLTS

After the abdication (by flight) in 1688 of James VII and II, the crown devolved upon William III (grandson of Charles I) and Mary II (elder daughter of James VII and II). In 1689 Graham of Claverhouse roused the Highlands on behalf of James VII and II, but died after a military success at Killiecrankie.

After the death of Anne (younger daughter of James VII and II), the throne devolved upon George I (great-grandson of James VI and I). In 1715, armed risings on behalf of James Stuart (the Old Pretender, son of James VII and II) led to the indecisive battle of Sheriffmuir, and the Jacobite movement died down until 1745, when Charles Stuart (the Young Pretender) defeated the Royalist troops at Prestonpans and advanced to Derby (1746). From Derby, the adherents of 'James VIII and III' (the title claimed for his father by Charles Stuart) fell back on the defensive and were finally crushed at Culloden (16 April 1746) by an army led by by the Duke of Cumberland, son of George II.

PRINCIPAL CITIES

ABERDEEN

Aberdeen, 209km (130 miles) north-east of Edinburgh, received its charter as a Royal Burgh in 1124. Scotland's third largest city, Aberdeen lies between two rivers, the Dee and the Don, facing the North Sea; the city has a strong maritime history and is today a major centre for offshore oil exploration and production. It is also an ancient university town and distinguished research centre. Other industries include engineering, food processing, textiles, paper manufacturing and chemicals.

Places of interest include King's College, St Machar's Cathedral, Brig o' Balgownie, Duthie Park and Winter Gardens, Hazlehead Park, the Kirk of St Nicholas, Mercat Cross, Marischal College and Marischal Museum, Provost Skene's House, Aberdeen Art Gallery, Gordon Highlanders Museum, Satrosphere Science Centre, and Aberdeen Maritime Museum.

DUNDEE

The Royal Burgh of Dundee is situated on the north bank of the Tay estuary. The city's port and dock installations are important to the offshore oil industry and the airport also provides servicing facilities. Principal industries include textiles, biotechnology and digital media, lasers, printing, tyre manufacture, food processing, engineering and tourism.

The unique City Churches – three churches under one roof, together with the 15th-century St Mary's Tower – are the most prominent architectural feature. Dundee is home to two historic ships: the Dundee-built RRS *Discovery* which took Capt. Scott to the Antarctic lies alongside Discovery Quay, and the frigate *Unicorn,* the only British-built wooden warship still afloat, is moored in Victoria Dock. Places of interest include Mills Public Observatory, the Tay road and rail bridges, Dundee Contemporary Arts centre, McManus Galleries, Claypotts Castle, Broughty Castle, Verdant Works (textile heritage centre) and the Sensation Science Centre.

EDINBURGH

Edinburgh is the capital city and seat of government in Scotland. The new Scottish parliament building designed by Enric Miralles was completed in 2004 and is open to visitors. The city is built on a group of hills and both the old and new towns are inscribed on the UNESCO World Cultural and Natural Heritage List for their cultural significance.

Other places of interest include the castle, which houses the Stone of Scone and also includes St Margaret's Chapel, the oldest building in Edinburgh, and near it, the Scottish National War Memorial; the Palace of Holyroodhouse, the Queen's official residence in Scotland; Parliament House, the present seat of the judicature; Princes Street; three universities (Edinburgh, Heriot-Watt, Napier); St Giles' Cathedral; St Mary's (Scottish Episcopal) Cathedral (Sir George Gilbert Scott); the General Register House (Robert Adam); the National and Signet libraries; the National Gallery of Scotland; the Royal Scottish Academy; the Scottish National Portrait Gallery and the Edinburgh International Conference Centre.

GLASGOW

Glasgow, a Royal Burgh, is Scotland's largest city and its principal commercial and industrial centre. The city occupies the north and south banks of the Clyde, formerly one of the chief commercial estuaries in the world. The main industries include engineering, electronics, finance, chemicals and printing. The city is also a key tourist and conference destination.

The chief buildings are the 13th-century Gothic cathedral, the university (Sir George Gilbert Scott), the City Chambers, the Royal Concert Hall, St Mungo Museum of Religious Life and Art, Pollok House, the School of Art (Charles Rennie Mackintosh), Kelvingrove Art Gallery and Museum, the Gallery of Modern Art, the Burrell Collection museum and the Mitchell Library. The city is home to the Royal Scottish National Orchestra, Scottish Opera, Scottish Ballet and BBC Scotland and Scottish Television (STV).

INVERNESS

Inverness was granted city status in 2000. The city's name is derived from the Gaelic for 'the mouth of the Ness', referring to the river on which it lies. Inverness is recorded as being at the junction of the old trade routes since AD 565. Today the city is the main administrative centre for the north of Scotland and is the capital of the Highlands. Tourism is one of the city's main industries.

Among the city's most notable buildings is Abertarff House, built in 1593 and the oldest secular building remaining in Inverness. Balnain House, built as a town house in 1726, is a fine example of early Georgian architecture. The Old High Church, on St Michael's Mount, is the original parish church of Inverness and is built on the site of the earliest Christian church in the city. Parts of the church date back to the 14th century.

Stirling was granted city status in 2002. Aberdeen, Dundee, Edinburgh and Glasgow have also been granted Lord Mayoralty/Lord Provostship.

LORD-LIEUTENANTS

Title	*Name*
Aberdeen City*	Lord Provost Peter Stephen
Aberdeenshire	A. Farquharson, OBE
Angus	Mrs G. Osborne
Argyll and Bute	K. Mackinnon
Ayrshire and Arran	John Duncan, QPM
Banffshire	Clare Russell
Berwickshire	Maj. A. Trotter
Caithness	Miss M. Dunnett
Clackmannan	Mrs S. Cruickshank
Dumfries	Jean Tulloch
Dunbartonshire	Rear-Adm. Alexander Gregory, OBE
Dundee City*	Lord Provost John Letford
East Lothian	W. Garth Morrison, CBE
Edinburgh City*	Rt. Hon. Lord Provost George Grubb
Eilean Siar (Western Isles)	A. Matheson, OBE
Fife	Mrs C. Dean
Glasgow City*	Rt. Hon. Lord Provost Robert Winter
Inverness	Donald Angus Cameron of Lochiel
Kincardineshire	Carol Kinghorn
Lanarkshire	G. Cox, MBE
Midlothian	Patrick Prenter, CBE
Moray	Grenville Shaw Johnston, OBE, TD
Nairn	Ewen Brodie of Lethan
Orkney	Dr Anthony Trickett, MBE
Perth and Kinross	Brig. Melville Jameson, CBE
Renfrewshire	Guy Clark
Ross and Cromarty	Janet Bowen
Roxburgh, Ettrick and Lauderdale	Hon. Capt. Gerald Maitland-Carew
Shetland	J. Scott
Stirling and Falkirk	Mrs M. McLachlan
Sutherland	Dr Monica Maitland Main
The Stewartry of Kirkcudbright	Lt.-Col. Sir Malcolm Walter Hugh Ross, GCVO, OBE
Tweeddale	Capt. D. Younger
West Lothian	Mrs I. Brydie, MBE
Wigtown	Marion Brewis

* The Lord Provosts of the four cities of Aberdeen, Dundee, Edinburgh and Glasgow are Lord-Lieutenants *ex officio* for those districts

LOCAL COUNCILS

Council	*Administrative Headquarters*	*Telephone*	*Population**	*Council Tax*†	*Chief Executive*
ABERDEEN	Aberdeen	01224-522000	209,300	£1,230	Sue Bruce
Aberdeenshire	Aberdeen	01467-620981	239,200	£1,141	Colin McKenzie
Angus	Forfar	0845-277 7778	109,900	£1,072	David Sawers
Argyll and Bute	Lochgilphead	01546-602127	91,400	£1,178	Sally Loudon
Clackmannanshire	Alloa	01259-452000	49,900	£1,148	Angela Leitch
Dumfries and Galloway	Dumfries	01387-260000	148,300	£1,049	Gavin Stevenson
DUNDEE	Dundee	01382-434000	142,200	£1,211	Alex Stephen
East Ayrshire	Kilmarnock	01563-576000	119,600	£1,189	Fiona Lees
East Dunbartonshire	Kirkintilloch	0845-045 4510	104,900	£1,142	Gerry Cornes
East Lothian	Haddington	01620-827827	94,400	£1,118	Alan Blackie
East Renfrewshire	Giffnock	0141-577 3000	89,300	£1,126	Lorraine McMillan
EDINBURGH	Edinburgh	0131-200 2000	468,100	£1,169	Tom Aitchison, CBE
Eilean Siar (Western Isles)	Stornoway	01851-703773	26,300	£1,024	Malcolm Burr
Falkirk	Falkirk	01324-506070	150,700	£1,070	Mary Pitcaithly, OBE
Fife	Glenrothes	0845-555555	360,500	£1,118	Ronnie Hinds
GLASGOW	Glasgow	0141-287 2000	581,900	£1,213	George Black
Highland	Inverness	01463-702000	217,400	£1,163	Alistair Dodds
Inverclyde	Greenock	01475-717171	81,100	£1,198	John Mundell
Midlothian	Dalkeith	0131-270 7500	79,500	£1,210	Kenneth Lawrie
Moray	Elgin	01343-543451	86,900	£1,135	Alastair Keddie
North Ayrshire	Irvine	0845-603 0590	135,800	£1,152	Elma Murray
North Lanarkshire	Motherwell	01698-302222	324,700	£1,098	Gavin Whitefield
Orkney	Kirkwall	01856-873535	19,900	£1,037	Alistair Buchan
Perth and Kinross	Perth	01738-475000	142,100	£1,158	Bernadette Malone
Renfrewshire	Paisley	0141-842 5000	169,600	£1,165	David Martin
Scottish Borders	Melrose	01835-824000	111,400	£1,084	David Hume
Shetland	Lerwick	01595-693535	22,000	£1,053	David Clark
South Ayrshire	Ayr	01292-612000	111,700	£1,154	David Anderson
South Lanarkshire	Hamilton	01698-454444	309,500	£1,101	Archie Strang
STIRLING	Stirling	0845-277 7000	88,200	£1,209	Bob Jack
West Dunbartonshire	Dumbarton	01389-737000	91,100	£1,163	David McMillan
West Lothian	Livingston	01506-775000	167,800	£1,128	Alex Linkston

* *Source:* ONS – *Mid-2007 Population Estimates* (Crown copyright)
† Average Band D council tax bill 2009–10
Councils in CAPITAL LETTERS have city status

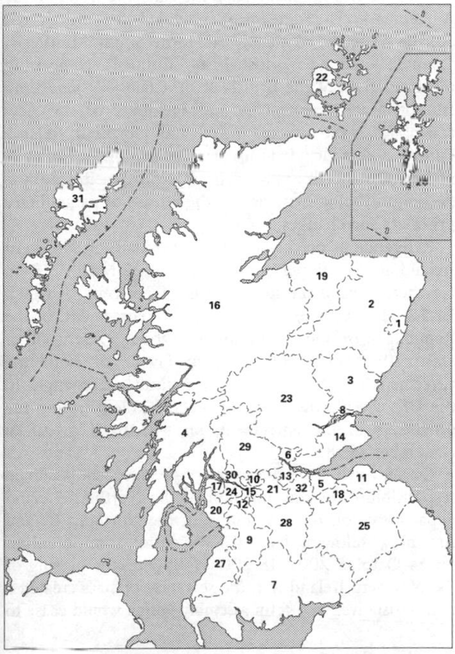

Key	*Council*	*Key*	*Council*
1	Aberdeen City	18	Midlothian
2	Aberdeenshire	19	Moray
3	Angus	20	North Ayrshire
4	Argyll and Bute	21	North Lanarkshire
5	City of Edinburgh	22	Orkney
6	Clackmannanshire	23	Perth and Kinross
7	Dumfries and Galloway	24	Renfrewshire
8	Dundee City	25	Scottish Borders
9	East Ayrshire	26	Shetland
10	East Dunbartonshire	27	South Ayrshire
11	East Lothian	28	South Lanarkshire
12	East Renfrewshire	29	Stirling
13	Falkirk	30	West Dunbartonshire
14	Fife	31	Western Isles (Eilean Siar)
15	Glasgow City	32	West Lothian
16	Highland		
17	Inverclyde		

NORTHERN IRELAND

Northern Ireland has a total area of 14,149 sq. km (5,463 sq. miles): land, 13,576 sq. km (5,242 sq. miles); inland water, 573 sq. km (221 sq. miles).

The population of Northern Ireland at the 2001 census was 1,685,267 (men 821,449; women 863,818). The average density of population in 2001 was 119 persons per sq. km (308 per sq. mile).

At the 2001 census, the number of persons in the various religious denominations (expressed as percentages of the total population) were: Catholic, 40.26; Presbyterian, 20.69; Church of Ireland, 15.30; Methodist Church in Ireland, 3.51; other Christian (including Christian related) 6.07; other religions and philosophies, 0.3; no religion or religion not stated, 13.88.

FLAG

The official national flag of Northern Ireland is the Union Flag.

PRINCIPAL CITIES

In addition to Belfast and Londonderry, three other places in Northern Ireland have been granted city status: Armagh (1994), Lisburn (2002) and Newry (2002).

BELFAST

Belfast, the administrative centre of Northern Ireland, is situated at the mouth of the River Lagan at its entrance to Belfast Lough. The city grew to be a great industrial centre, owing to its easy access by sea to Scottish coal and iron.

The principal buildings are of a relatively young age and include the parliament buildings at Stormont, the City Hall, Waterfront Hall, the Law Courts, the Public Library and the Museum and Art Gallery.

Belfast received its first charter of incorporation in 1613 and was created a city in 1888; the title of lord mayor was conferred in 1892.

LONDONDERRY

Londonderry (originally Derry) is situated on the River Foyle, and has important associations with the City of London. The Irish Society was created by the City of London in 1610, and under its royal charter of 1613 it fortified the city and was for a long time closely associated with its administration. Because of this connection the city was incorporated in 1613 under the new name of Londonderry.

The city is famous for the great siege of 1688–9, when for 105 days the town held out against the forces of James II. The city walls are still intact and form a circuit of 1.6 km (one mile) around the old city.

Interesting buildings are the Protestant cathedral of St Columb's (1633) and the Guildhall, reconstructed in 1912 and containing a number of beautiful stained glass windows, many of which were presented by the livery companies of London.

CONSTITUTIONAL HISTORY

Northern Ireland is subject to the same fundamental constitutional provisions which apply to the rest of the United Kingdom. It had its own parliament and government from 1921 to 1972, but after increasing civil unrest the Northern Ireland (Temporary Provisions) Act 1972 transferred the legislative and executive powers of the Northern Ireland parliament and government to the UK parliament and a secretary of state. The Northern Ireland Constitution Act 1973 provided for devolution in Northern Ireland through an assembly and executive, but a power-sharing executive formed by the Northern Ireland political parties in January 1974 collapsed in May 1974. Following the collapse of the power-sharing executive Northern Ireland returned to direct rule governance under the provisions of the Northern Ireland Act 1974, placing the Northern Ireland department under the direction and control of the Northern Ireland secretary.

In December 1993 the British and Irish governments published the Joint Declaration complementing their political talks, and making clear that any settlement would need to be founded on principles of democracy and consent. The declaration also stated that all democratically mandated parties could be involved in political talks as long as they permanently renounced paramilitary violence.

On 12 January 1998 the British and Irish governments issued a joint document, *Propositions on Heads of Agreement,* proposing the establishment of various new cross-border bodies; further proposals were presented on 27 January. A draft peace settlement was issued by the talks' chairman, US Senator George Mitchell, on 6 April 1998 but was rejected by the Unionists the following day. On 10 April agreement was reached between the British and Irish governments and the eight Northern Ireland political parties still involved in the talks (the Good Friday Agreement). The agreement provided for an elected Northern Ireland Assembly, a North/South Ministerial Council, and a British-Irish Council comprising representatives of the British, Irish, Channel Islands and Isle of Man governments and members of the new assemblies for Scotland, Wales and Northern Ireland. Further points included the abandonment of the Republic of Ireland's constitutional claim to Northern Ireland; the decommissioning of weapons; the release of paramilitary prisoners and changes in policing.

Referendums on the agreement were held in Northern Ireland and the Republic of Ireland on 22 May 1998. In Northern Ireland the turnout was 81 per cent, of which 71.12 per cent voted in favour of the agreement. In the Republic of Ireland, the turnout was about 55 per cent, of which 94.4 per cent voted in favour of both the agreement and the necessary constitutional change. In the UK, the Northern Ireland Act 1998, enshrining the provisions of the agreement, received royal assent in November 1998.

On 28 April 2003 the secretary of state again assumed responsibility for the direction of the Northern Ireland departments on the dissolution of the Northern Ireland Assembly, following its initial suspension from midnight on 14 October 2002. In 2006, following the passing of the Northern Ireland Act, the secretary of state created a non-legislative fixed-term assembly which would cease to operate either when the political parties agreed to restore devolution, or on 24 November 2006 (whichever occurred first). In October 2006 a timetable to restore devolution was drawn up (St Andrews Agreement) and a transitional Northern Ireland Assembly was formed on 24 November. The transitional assembly was dissolved in January 2007 in preparation for elections to be held on 7 March; following the elections a power-sharing executive was formed and the new 108-member Northern Ireland Assembly became operational on 8 May 2007.

See also Regional Government.

FINANCE

Northern Ireland's expenditure is funded through the Northern Ireland Consolidated Fund (NICF). Up until devolution on 2 December 1999, the NICF was largely financed by Northern Ireland's attributed share of UK taxation and supplemented by a grant-in-aid. From devolution, these separate elements have been subsumed into a single block grant. The Northern Ireland Departmental Expenditure Limit for 2009–10 was set at £9,990m.

LORD-LIEUTENANTS AND HIGH SHERIFFS

County	*Lord-Lieutenant*	*Sheriff (2009)*
Antrim	Joan Christie	Nigel Dobbs
Armagh	The Earl of Caledon	Dr Gerard Millar
Belfast City	Lady Carswell, OBE	Francis McCoubrey
Down	Sir William Hall KCVO	Lady Augusta Nicholson
Fermanagh	The Earl of Erne	Helen Wood, MBE
Londonderry	Denis Desmond, CBE	David Henderson
Londonderry City	Dr Donal Keegan, OBE	Ian Crowe
Tyrone	The Duke of Abercorn, KG	Dr Brendan O'Hare

LOCAL COUNCILS

Council	*County Area*	*Map Key*	*Telephone*	*Population**	*Chief Executive*
Antrim	Down	1	028-9446 3113	52,600	David McCammick
Ards	Down	2	028-9182 4000	77,100	Ashley Boreland
ARMAGH	Armagh	3	028-3752 9600	57,700	John Briggs
Ballymena	Antrim	4	028-2566 0300	62,100	Anne Donaghy
Ballymoney	Antrim	5	028-2766 0200	29,700	John Dempsey
Banbridge	Down	6	028-4066 0600	46,400	Liam Hannaway
BELFAST	Antrim & Down	7	028-9032 0202	267,500	Peter McNaney
Carrickfergus	Antrim	8	028-9335 8000	40,000	Alan Cardwell
Castlereagh	Down	9	028-9046 4500	65,600	Adrian Donaldson, MBE
Coleraine	Londonderry	10	028-7034 7034	56,800	Roger Wilson
Cookstown	Tyrone	11	028-8676 2205	35,400	Michael McGuckin
Craigavon	Armagh	12	028-3831 2400	88,800	Michael Docherty *(acting)*
DERRY	Londonderry	13	028-7136 5151	108,500	Valerie Watts
Down	Down	14	028-4461 0800	69,200	John McGrillen
Dungannon & South Tyrone	Tyrone	15	028-8772 0300	54,300	Alan Burke/Iain Frazer *(acting)*
Fermanagh	Fermanagh	16	028-6632 5050	61,300	Rodney Connor
Larne	Antrim	17	028-2827 2313	31,300	Geraldine McGahey
Limavady	Londonderry	18	028-7772 2226	34,400	Liam Flanigan
LISBURN	Antrim	19	028-9250 9250	113,500	Norman Davidson
Magherafelt	Londonderry	20	028-7939 7979	43,100	John McLaughlin
Moyle	Antrim	21	028-2076 2225	16,700	Richard Lewis
NEWRY & Mourne	Down & Armagh	22	028-3031 3031	95,500	Thomas McCall
Newtownabbey	Antrim	23	028-9034 0000	81,700	Norman Dunn
North Down	Down	24	028-9127 0371	78,700	Trevor Polley
Omagh	Tyrone	25	028 8224 5321	51,500	Daniel McSorley
Strabane	Tyrone	26	028-7138 2204	39,400	Philip Faithfull

* *Source:* ONS – *Mid-2007 Population Estimates* (Crown copyright)

Councils in CAPITAL LETTERS have city status

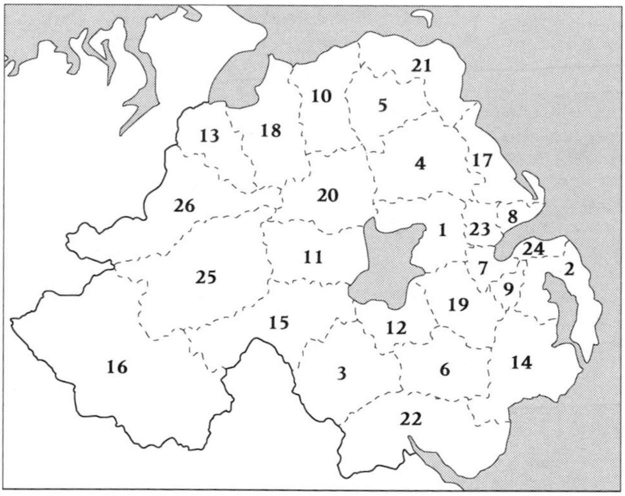

THE ISLE OF MAN

Ellan Vannin

The Isle of Man is an island situated in the Irish Sea, at latitude 54° 3′–54° 25′ N. and longitude 4° 18′–4° 47′ W., nearly equidistant from England, Scotland and Ireland. Although the early inhabitants were of Celtic origin, the Isle of Man was part of the Norwegian Kingdom of the Hebrides until 1266, when this was ceded to Scotland. Subsequently granted to the Stanleys (Earls of Derby) in the 15th century and later to the Dukes of Atholl, it was brought under the administration of the Crown in 1765. The island forms the bishopric of Sodor and Man.

The total land area is 572 sq. km (221 sq. miles). The 2006 census showed a resident population of 80,058 (men, 39,523; women, 40,535). The main language in use is English. Around 1,550 people are able to speak the Manx Gaelic language.

CAPITAL – ΨDouglas; population, 26,218 (2006). ΨCastletown (3,109) is the ancient capital; the other towns are ΨPeel (4,280) and ΨRamsey (7,309)

FLAG – A red flag charged with three conjoined armoured legs in white and gold

NATIONAL DAY – 5 July (Tynwald Day)

GOVERNMENT

The Isle of Man is a self-governing Crown dependency, with its own parliamentary, legal and administrative system. The British government is responsible for international relations and defence. Under the UK Act of Accession, Protocol 3, the island's relationship with the European Union is limited to trade alone and does not extend to financial aid. The Lieutenant-Governor is the Queen's personal representative on the island.

The legislature, Tynwald, is the oldest parliament in the world in continuous existence. It has two branches: the Legislative Council and the House of Keys. The council consists of the President of Tynwald, the Bishop of Sodor and Man, the Attorney-General (who does not have a vote) and eight members elected by the House of Keys. The House of Keys has 24 members, elected by universal adult suffrage. The branches sit separately to consider legislation and sit together, as Tynwald Court, for most other parliamentary purposes.

The presiding officer of Tynwald Court is the President of Tynwald, elected by the members, who also presides over sittings of the Legislative Council. The presiding officer of the House of Keys is the Speaker, who is elected by members of the house.

The principal members of the Manx government are the chief minister and nine departmental ministers, who comprise the Council of Ministers.

Lieutenant-Governor, HE Vice-Adm. Sir Paul Haddacks, KCB
President of Tynwald, Hon. Noel Cringle
Speaker, House of Keys, Hon. Steve Rodan, SHK
The First Deemster and Clerk of the Rolls, Michael Kerruish
Clerk of Tynwald, Secretary to the House of Keys and Counsel to the Speaker, Roger Phillips
Clerk of the Legislative Council and Deputy Clerk of Tynwald, Jonathan King
Attorney-General, W. Corlett, QC
Chief Minister, Hon. Tony Brown, MHK
Chief Secretary, Mrs M. Williams

ECONOMY

Most of the income generated in the island is earned in the services sector with financial and professional services accounting for just over half of the national income. Tourism and manufacturing are also major generators of income whilst the island's other traditional industries of agriculture and fishing now play a smaller role in the economy. Under the terms of protocol 3, the island has tariff-free access to EU markets for its goods.

In May 2009 the island's unemployment rate was 2.1 per cent and inflation (RPI) was −0.2 per cent.

FINANCE

The budget for 2009–10 provides for net revenue expenditure of £572.1m. The principal sources of government revenue are taxes on income and expenditure. Income tax is payable at a rate of 10 per cent on the first £10,500 of taxable income for single resident individuals and 18 per cent on the balance, after personal allowances of £9,200. These bands are doubled for married couples. The rate of income tax for trading companies is zero per cent except for income from banking and land and property, which is taxed at 10 per cent. By agreement with the British government, the island keeps most of its rates of indirect taxation (VAT and duties) the same as those in the UK. However, VAT on tourist accommodation, property, repairs and renovations is charged at 5 per cent. A reciprocal agreement on national insurance benefits and pensions exists between the governments of the Isle of Man and the UK. Taxes are also charged on property (rates), but these are comparatively low.

The major government expenditure items are health, social security, social services and education, which account for 59 per cent of the government budget. The island makes an annual contribution to the UK for defence and other external services.

The island has a special relationship with the European Union and neither contributes money to nor receives funds from the EU budget.

Ψ = sea port

THE CHANNEL ISLANDS

The Channel Islands, situated off the north-west coast of France (at a distance of 16km (10 miles) at their closest point), are the only portions of the Dukedom of Normandy still belonging to the Crown, to which they have been attached since the Norman Conquest of 1066. They were the only British territory to come under German occupation during the Second World War, following invasion on 30 June and 1 July 1940. The islands were relieved by British forces on 9 May 1945, and 9 May (Liberation Day) is now observed as a bank and public holiday.

The islands consist of Jersey (11,630ha/28,717 acres), Guernsey (6,340ha/15,654 acres), and the dependencies of Guernsey: Alderney (795ha/1,962 acres), Brecqhou (30ha/74 acres), Great Sark (419ha/1,035 acres), Little Sark (97ha/239 acres), Herm (130ha/320 acres), Jethou (18ha/44 acres) and Lihou (15ha/38 acres) – a total of 19,474ha/48,083 acres, or 194 sq. km/75 sq. miles. The 2001 census showed the population of Jersey as 87,186; Guernsey, 59,807 and Alderney, 2,294. Sark did not complete the same census but a recent informal census gave its population figure as 591. The official languages are English and French. In country districts of Jersey and Guernsey and throughout Sark a Norman-French *patois* is also in use, though to a lesser extent.

GOVERNMENT

The islands are Crown dependencies with their own legislative assemblies (the States in Jersey and Alderney, the States of Deliberation in Guernsey and the Chief Pleas in Sark), systems of local administration and law, and their own courts. Acts passed by the States require the sanction of the Queen-in-council. The UK government is responsible for defence and international relations. The Channel Islands are not part of the European Union but, under protocol 3, have trading rights with the free movement of goods within the EU.

In both Jersey and Guernsey bailiwicks the Lieutenant-Governor and Commander-in-Chief, who is appointed by the Crown, is the personal representative of the Queen and the channel of communication between the Crown (via the Privy Council) and the island's government.

The head of government in both Jersey and Guernsey is the Chief Minister. Jersey has a ministerial system of government; the executive comprises the Council of Ministers and consists of a chief minister and nine other ministers. The ministers are assisted by up to 13 assistant ministers. Members of the States who are not in the executive are able to sit on a number of scrutiny panels and the Public Accounts Committee to examine the policy of the executive and hold ministers to account. Guernsey has a consensus form of government. There are ten States departments with mandated responsibilities, each department is constituted of a minister and four members of the States. Each of the ministers has a seat on the Policy Council which is presided over by the Chief Minister. There are also five specialist committees, each led by a chair, responsible for scrutinising policy, finance and legislation, parliamentary procedural matters and public sector pay negotiations.

Justice is administered by the royal courts of Jersey and Guernsey, each consisting of the bailiff and 12 elected jurats. The bailiffs of Jersey and Guernsey, appointed by the Crown, are presidents of the states and of the royal courts of their respective islands.

Each bailiwick constitutes a deanery under the jurisdiction of the Bishop of Winchester.

ECONOMY

A mild climate and good soil have led to the development of intensive systems of agriculture and horticulture, which form a significant part of the economy. Equally important are earnings from tourism and banking and finance: the low rates of income and corporation tax and the absence of death duties make the islands an important offshore financial centre. In addition, there is no VAT or equivalent tax in Guernsey and only small goods and services tax in Jersey (set at 3 per cent for three years from 6 May 2008).

Principal exports are agricultural produce and flowers; imports are chiefly machinery, manufactured goods, food, fuel and chemicals. Trade with the UK is regarded as internal.

British currency is legal tender in the Channel Islands but each bailiwick issues its own coins and notes (*see* Currency section). They also issue their own postage stamps; UK stamps are not valid.

JERSEY

Lieutenant-Governor and Commander-in-Chief of Jersey, HE Lt.-Gen. Andrew Peter Ridgway, CB, CBE, *apptd* 2006
Secretary and ADC, Lt.-Col. A. Woodrow, OBE, MC
Bailiff of Jersey, Michael St J. Birt QC
Deputy Bailiff, vacant
Attorney-General, W. Bailhache, QC
Receiver-General, P. Lewin
Solicitor-General, Timothy Le Cocq, QC
Greffier of the States, M. de la Haye
States Treasurer, I. Black
Chief Minister, Senator T. Le Sueur

FINANCE

	2007	*2008**
Revenue income	£764,293,000	£872,075,000
Revenue expenditure	£691,143,000	£814,690,000
Capital expenditure	£52,393,000	£71,168,000

* The States of Jersey Treasury moved to new accounting standards in 2008 so these figures are not comparable with 2007 figures

CHIEF TOWN – ΨSt Helier, on the south coast
FLAG – A white field charged with a red saltire cross, and the arms of Jersey in the upper centre

GUERNSEY AND DEPENDENCIES

Lieutenant-Governor and Commander-in-Chief of the Bailiwick of Guernsey and its Dependencies, HE Vice-Adm. Sir Fabian Malbon, KBE, *apptd* 2005
Presiding Officer, Bailiff Sir Geoffrey Rowland
Deputy Presiding Officer, Richard Collas

HM Procureur and Receiver-General, Howard Roberts, QC
HM Comptroller, vacant

GUERNSEY
Chief Minister, Deputy Lyndon Trott
Chief Executive, Mike Brown

FINANCE

	2007	*2008*
Revenue	£365,004,000	£348,775,000
Expenditure	£294,481,000	£296,641,000

CHIEF TOWNS – ΨSt Peter Port, on the east coast of Guernsey; St Anne on Alderney
FLAG – White, bearing a red cross of St George, with a gold cross of Normandy overall in the centre

ALDERNEY
President of the States, Sir Norman Browse, OBE
Chief Executive, David Jeremiah, OBE, QC
Greffier, Sarah Kelly

SARK
Sark was the last European territory to abolish feudal parliamentary representation. Elections for a democratic legislative assembly took place in December 2008, with the *conseillers* taking their seats in the newly constituted Chief Pleas in January 2009.
Seigneur of Sark, John Beaumont, OBE
Seneschal, Lt.-Col. R Guille, MBE
Greffier, Trevor Hamon

OTHER DEPENDENCIES
Herm and Lihou are owned by the States of Guernsey; Herm is leased, Lithou is uninhabited. Jethou is leased by the Crown to the States of Guernsey and is sub-let by the States. Brecqhou is within the legislative and judicial territory of Sark.

Ψ = seaport

LAW COURTS AND OFFICES

HIERARCHY OF ENGLISH COURTS

Court	*Courts it binds*	*Courts it follows*
European court of justice	The court making the preliminary reference	None
Supreme court	All English courts	None
Court of appeal	Divisional courts High court Crown court County courts Magistrates' courts	Supreme court
Divisional Courts	High court Crown court County courts Magistrates' courts	Supreme court Court of appeal
High Court	County courts Magistrates' courts	Supreme court Court of appeal Divisional courts
Crown court	None	Supreme court
County courts	None	Court of appeal
Magistrates' courts	None	Divisional courts High court

JUDICATURE OF ENGLAND AND WALES

The legal system in England and Wales is divided into criminal law and civil law. Criminal law is concerned with acts harmful to the community and the rules laid down by the state for the benefit of citizens, whereas civil law governs the relationships and transactions between individuals. Administrative law is a kind of civil law usually concerning the interaction of individuals and the state, and most cases are heard in tribunals specific to the subject (*see* Tribunals section). Scotland and Northern Ireland possess legal systems that differ from the system in England and Wales in law, judicial procedure and court structure, but retain the distinction between criminal and civil law.

The supreme court of the United Kingdom is the highest judicial authority; it replaced the House of Lords in its judicial capacity on 1 October 2009. It is the ultimate court of appeal for all courts in Great Britain and Northern Ireland (except criminal courts in Scotland) for all cases except those concerning the interpretation and application of European Community law, including preliminary rulings requested by British courts and tribunals, which are decided by the European court of justice (*see* European Union section). The UK supreme court also assumed jurisdiction in relation to devolution matters under the Scotland Act 1998, the Northern Ireland Act 1988 and the Government of Wales Act 2006; these powers were transferred from the Judicial Committee of the Privy Council. Ten of the twelve Lords of Appeal in Ordinary from the House of Lords transferred to the 12-member supreme court when it came into operation (at the same time one law lord retired and another was appointed Master of the Rolls). All new justices of the supreme court will be appointed by an independent UK Supreme Court Appointments Commission, and will not be members of the House of Lords. The eleventh justice of the supreme court was appointed through the appointments commission on 20 April 2009, and the twelfth appointment had not been made at the time of going to press.

Under the provisions of the Criminal Appeal Act 1995, a commission was set up to direct and supervise investigations into possible miscarriages of justice and to refer cases to the appeal courts on the grounds of conviction and sentence; these functions were formerly the responsibility of the home secretary.

SENIOR COURTS OF ENGLAND AND WALES

The senior courts of England and Wales (until September 2009 known as the supreme court of judicature of England and Wales) comprise the high court, the crown court and the court of appeal. The President of the Courts of England and Wales, a new title given to the Lord Chief Justice under the Constitutional Reform Act 2005, is the head of the judiciary.

The high court was created in 1875 and combined many previously separate courts. Sittings are held at the royal courts of justice in London or at about 120 district registries outside the capital. It is the superior civil court and is split into three divisions – the chancery division, the Queen's bench division and the family division – each of which is further divided. The chancery division is headed by the Chancellor of the High Court and is concerned mainly with equity, trusts, tax and bankruptcy, while also including two specialist courts, the patents court and the companies court. The Queen's bench division (QBD) is the largest of the three divisions, and is headed by its own president, who is also Head of Criminal Justice. It deals with common law (ie tort, contract, debt and personal injuries), some tax law, eg VAT tribunal appeals, and encompasses the admiralty court and the commercial court. The QBD also administers the technology and construction court. The family division was created in 1970 and is headed by its own president, who is also Head of Family Justice, and hears cases concerning divorce, access to and custody of children, and other family matters. The divisional court of the high court sits in the family and chancery divisions, and hears appeals from the magistrates' courts and county courts.

The crown court was set up in 1972 and sits at 77 centres throughout England and Wales. It deals with more serious (indictable) criminal offences, which are triable before a judge and jury, including treason, murder, rape, kidnapping, armed robbery and Official Secrets Act offences. It also handles cases transferred from the magistrates' courts where the magistrate decides his or her own power of sentence is inadequate, or where someone appeals against a magistrate's decision, or in a case that is triable 'either way' where the accused has chosen a jury trial. The crown court centres are divided into three tiers: high court judges, and sometimes circuit judges and recorders (part-time circuit judges), sit in first-tier centres and deal with the most serious (Class 1) criminal offences (eg murder, treason) and with some civil high court cases; the second-tier centres are presided over by high court judges, circuit judges or recorders and deal with Class 2 criminal offences (eg rape, manslaughter); third-tier courts deal with Class 3 criminal offences, with circuit judges or recorders presiding.

The court of appeal hears appeals against both fact and law, and was last restructured in 1966 when it replaced the court of criminal appeal. It is split into the civil division (which hears appeals from the high court, tribunals and in certain cases, the county courts) and the criminal division (which hears appeals from the crown court). Cases are heard by Lord Justices of Appeal if deemed suitable for reconsideration.

The Constitutional Reform Act 2005 instigated several key changes to the judiciary in England and Wales. These included the establishment of an independent supreme court, which opened in October 2009; the reform of the post of Lord Chancellor, transferring its judicial functions to the President of the Courts of England and Wales; a duty on government ministers to uphold the independence of the judiciary by barring them from trying to influence judicial decisions through any special access to judges; the formation of a fully transparent and independent Judicial Appointments Commission that is responsible for selecting candidates to recommend for judicial appointment to the Secretary of State for Justice; and the creation of the post of Judicial Appointments and Conduct Ombudsman.

CRIMINAL CASES

In criminal matters the decision to prosecute (in the majority of cases) rests with the Crown Prosecution Service (CPS), which is the independent prosecuting body in England and Wales. The CPS is headed by the director of public prosecutions, who works under the superintendence of the Attorney-General. Certain categories of offence continue to require the Attorney-General's consent for prosecution.

Most minor criminal cases (summary offences) are dealt with in magistrates' courts, usually by a bench of three unpaid lay magistrates (justices of the peace) sitting without a jury and assisted on points of law and procedure by a legally trained clerk. There were 29,270 justices of the peace as at 1 April 2009. In busier courts a full-time, salaried and legally qualified district judge (magistrates' court) – formerly known as a stipendiary judge – presides alone. There were 145 district judges (magistrates' courts) as at 1 August 2009. Magistrates' courts oversee the completion of 95 per cent of all criminal cases. Magistrates' courts also house some family proceedings courts (which deal with relationship breakdown and childcare cases) and youth courts. Cases of medium seriousness (known as 'offences triable either way') where the defendant pleads not guilty can be heard in the crown court for a trial by jury, if the defendant so chooses. Preliminary proceedings in a serious case to decide whether there is evidence to justify committal for trial in the crown court are dealt with in the magistrates' courts.

The 77 centres that the crown court sits in are divided into seven regions; a case is presided over by high court judges, circuit judges or recorders. There are around 1,400 recorders; they must sit a minimum of 15 days per year and are usually subject to a maximum of 30. A jury is present in all trials that are contested.

Appeals from magistrates' courts against sentence or conviction are made to the crown court, and appeals upon a point of law are made to the high court, which may ultimately be appealed to the supreme court. Appeals from the crown court, either against sentence or conviction, are made to the court of appeal (criminal division), presided over by the Lord Chief Justice. Again, these appeals may be brought to the supreme court if a point of law is contested, and if the house considers it is of sufficient importance.

CIVIL CASES

Most minor civil cases – including contract, tort (especially personal injuries), property, divorce and other family matters, bankruptcy etc – are dealt with by the county courts, of which there are 216 (*see* the Court Service website, W www.hmcourts-service.gov.uk, for further details). Cases are heard by circuit judges, recorders or district judges. For cases involving small claims (with certain exceptions, where the amount claimed is £5,000 or less) there are informal and simplified procedures designed to enable parties to present their cases themselves without recourse to lawyers. Where there are financial limits on county court jurisdiction, claims that exceed those limits may be tried in the county courts with the consent of the parties, subject to the court's agreement, or in certain circumstances on transfer from the high court. Outside London, bankruptcy proceedings can be heard in designated county courts. Magistrates' courts also deal with certain classes of civil case and committees of magistrates license public houses, clubs and betting shops. For the implementation of the Children Act 1989, a new structure of hearing centres was set up in 1991 for family proceedings cases, involving magistrates' courts (family proceedings courts), divorce county courts, family hearing centres and care centres.

Appeals in certain family matters heard in the family proceedings courts go to the family division of the high court. Appeals against decisions made in magistrates' courts are heard in the crown court. Appeals from county courts may be heard in the court of appeal (civil division), presided over by the Master of the Rolls, and may go on to the supreme court.

CORONERS' COURTS
The coroners' courts investigate violent and unnatural deaths or sudden deaths where the cause is unknown. Doctors, the police, various public authorities or members of the public may bring cases before a local coroner (a senior lawyer or doctor), in order to determine whether further criminal investigation is necessary. Where a death is sudden and the cause is unknown, the coroner may order a post-mortem examination to determine the cause of death rather than hold an inquest in court. An inquest must be held however if a person died in a violent or unnatural way, or died in prison or other unusual circumstances. If the coroner suspects murder, manslaughter or infanticide, he or she must summon a jury.

SUPREME COURT OF THE UNITED KINGDOM

President of the Supreme Court (£214,165), Rt. Hon. Lord Phillips of Worth Matravers, *born* 1938, *apptd* 2008
Deputy President of the Supreme Court, Rt. Hon. Lord Hope of Craighead, *born* 1938, *apptd* 1996

JUSTICES OF THE SUPREME COURT *as at 1 October 2009* (each £206,857)
Style, The Rt. Hon. Lord/Lady–

Rt. Hon. Lord Saville of Newdigate, *born* 1936, *apptd* 1997
Rt. Hon. Lord Rodger of Earlsferry, *born* 1944, *apptd* 2001
Rt. Hon. Lord Walker of Gestingthorpe, *born* 1938, *apptd* 2002
Rt. Hon. Lady Hale of Richmond, *born* 1945, *apptd* 2004
Rt. Hon. Lord Brown of Eaton-under-Heywood, *born* 1937, *apptd* 2004
Rt. Hon. Lord Mance, *born* 1943, *apptd* 2005
Rt. Hon. Lord Collins of Mapesbury, *born* 1941, *apptd* 2009
Rt. Hon. Lord Kerr of Tonaghmore, *born* 1948, *apptd* 2009
Rt. Hon. Lord Clarke of Stone-cum-Ebony, *born* 1943, *apptd* 2009

UNITED KINGDOM SUPREME COURT
Parliament Square, London SW1P 3BD T 020-7960 1900
Chief Executive, Jenny Rowe

SENIOR JUDICIARY OF ENGLAND AND WALES

Lord Chief Justice of England and Wales (£239,845), Rt. Hon. Lord Judge, *born* 1941, *apptd* 2008
Master of the Rolls and Head of Civil Justice (£214,165), Rt. Hon. Lord Neuberger of Abbotsbury, *born* 1948, *apptd* 2009
President of the Queen's Bench Division (£206,857), Sir Anthony May, *born* 1940, *apptd* 2008
President of the Family Division and Head of Family Justice (£206,857), Rt. Hon. Sir Mark Potter, *born* 1937, *apptd* 2005
Chancellor of the High Court (£206,857), Rt. Hon. Sir Andrew Morritt, CVO, *born* 1938, *apptd* 2000

SENIOR COURTS OF ENGLAND AND WALES

COURT OF APPEAL
Master of the Rolls (£214,165), Rt. Hon. Lord Neuberger of Abbotsbury, *born* 1948, *apptd* 2009
Secretary, Ms J. Sears
Clerk, Grahame Lister

LORD JUSTICES OF APPEAL *as at 1 September 2009* (each £196,707)

Style, The Rt. Hon. Lord/Lady Justice [surname]
Rt. Hon. Sir Malcolm Pill, *born* 1938, *apptd* 1995
Rt. Hon. Sir Alan Ward, *born* 1938, *apptd* 1995
Rt. Hon. Sir Mathew Thorpe, *born* 1938, *apptd* 1995
Rt. Hon. Sir George Waller, *born* 1940, *apptd* 1996
Rt. Hon. Sir John Mummery, *born* 1938, *apptd* 1996
Rt. Hon. Sir John Laws, *born* 1945, *apptd* 1999
Rt. Hon. Sir Stephen Sedley, *born* 1939, *apptd* 1999
Rt. Hon. Sir Bernard Rix, *born* 1944, *apptd* 2000
Rt. Hon. Dame Mary Arden, DBE, *born* 1947, *apptd* 2000
Rt. Hon. Sir David Keene, *born* 1941, *apptd* 2000
Rt. Hon. Sir John Dyson, *born* 1943, *apptd* 2001
Rt. Hon. Sir Andrew Longmore, *born* 1944, *apptd* 2001
Rt. Hon. Sir Robert Carnwath, CVO, *born* 1945, *apptd* 2002
Rt. Hon. Sir Scott Baker, *born* 1937, *apptd* 2002
Rt. Hon. Dame Janet Smith, DBE, *born* 1940, *apptd* 2002
Rt. Hon. Sir Roger Thomas, *born* 1947, *apptd* 2003
Rt. Hon. Sir Robin Jacob, *born* 1941, *apptd* 2003
Rt. Hon. Sir Nicholas Wall, *born* 1945, *apptd* 2004
Rt. Hon. Sir Maurice Kay, *born* 1942, *apptd* 2004
Rt. Hon. Sir Anthony Hooper, *born* 1937, *apptd* 2004
Rt. Hon. Sir Timothy Lloyd, *born* 1946, *apptd* 2005
Rt. Hon. Sir Martin Moore-Bick, *born* 1948, *apptd* 2005
Rt. Hon. Sir Nicholas Wilson, *born* 1945, *apptd* 2005
Rt. Hon. Sir Alan Moses, *born* 1945, *apptd* 2005
Rt. Hon. Sir Stephen Richards, *born* 1950, *apptd* 2005
Rt. Hon. Dame Heather Hallett, DBE, *born* 1949, *apptd* 2005
Rt. Hon. Sir Anthony Hughes, *born* 1948, *apptd* 2006
Rt. Hon. Sir Brian Leveson, *born* 1949, *apptd* 2006
Rt. Hon. Sir Roger Toulson, *born* 1946, *apptd* 2007
Rt. Hon. Sir Colin Rimer, *born* 1944, *apptd* 2007
Rt. Hon. Sir Stanley Burnton, *born* 1942, *apptd* 2007
Rt. Hon. Sir Terrence Etherton, *born* 1951, *apptd* 2008
Rt. Hon. Sir Rupert Jackson, *born* 1948, *apptd* 2008
Rt. Hon. Sir John Goldring, *born* 1944, *apptd* 2008
Rt. Hon. Sir Richard Aikens, *born* 1948, *apptd* 2008
Rt. Hon. Sir Jeremy Sullivan, *born* 1945, *apptd* 2009
Rt. Hon. Sir Patrick Elias, *born* 1947, *apptd* 2009
Rt. Hon. Sir Nicholas Patten, *born* 1950, *apptd* 2009
Ex Officio Judges, Lord Chief Justice of England and Wales; Master of the Rolls; President of the Queen's Bench Division; President of the Family Division; and Chancellor of the High Court

COURT OF APPEAL (CIVIL DIVISION)
Vice-President, Rt. Hon. Sir Mark Waller

COURT OF APPEAL (CRIMINAL DIVISION)
Vice-President, Rt. Hon. Sir Anthony Hughes
Judges, Lord Chief Justice of England and Wales; Master of the Rolls; Lord Justices of Appeal; and Judges of the High Court of Justice

COURTS-MARTIAL APPEAL COURT
Judges, Lord Chief Justice of England and Wales; Master of the Rolls; Lord Justices of Appeal; and Judges of the High Court of Justice

HIGH COURT OF JUSTICE

CHANCERY DIVISION
Chancellor of the High Court (£206,857), Rt. Hon. Sir Andrew Morritt, CVO, *born* 1938, *apptd* 2000
Secretary, Ms E. Harbert
Clerk, Sheila Glasgow

JUDGES *as at 1 September 2009* (each £172,753)
Style, The Hon. Mr/Mrs Justice [surname]

Hon. Sir William Blackburne, *born* 1944, *apptd* 1993
Hon. Sir Peter Smith, *born* 1952, *apptd* 2002
Hon. Sir Kim Lewison, *born* 1952, *apptd* 2003
Hon. Sir David Richards, *born* 1951, *apptd* 2003
Hon. Sir George Mann, *born* 1951, *apptd* 2004
Hon. Sir Nicholas Warren, *born* 1949, *apptd* 2005
Hon. Sir David Kitchin, *born* 1955, *apptd* 2005
Hon. Sir Michael Briggs, *born* 1954, *apptd* 2006
Hon. Sir Launcelot Henderson, *born* 1951, *apptd* 2006
Hon. Sir Paul Morgan, *born* 1952, *apptd* 2007
Hon. Sir Alastair Norris, *born* 1950, *apptd* 2007
Hon. Sir Gerald Barling, *born* 1949, *apptd* 2007
Hon. Sir Christopher Floyd, *born* 1951, *apptd* 2007
Hon. Sir Philip Sales, *born* 1962, *apptd* 2008
Hon. Dame Sonia Proudman, DBE, *born* 1949, *apptd* 2008
Hon. Sir Richard Arnold, *born* 1961, *apptd* 2008

The Chancery Division also includes three specialist courts: the companies court, the patents court and the bankruptcy court.

QUEEN'S BENCH DIVISION
Lord Chief Justice of England and Wales (£239,845), Rt. Hon. Lord Igor Judge, *born* 1941, *apptd* 2008
Secretary, Michèle Souris
Clerk, Linda Francis
President (£206,857), Rt. Hon. Sir Anthony May, *born* 1940, *apptd* 2008
Vice-President (£196,707), Rt. Hon. Sir Roger Thomas, *born* 1947, *apptd* 2008

JUDGES *as at 1 September 2009* (each £172,753)
Style, The Hon. Mr/Mrs Justice [surname]

Hon. Sir Stuart McKinnon, *born* 1938, *apptd* 1988
Hon. Sir Andrew Collins, *born* 1942, *apptd* 1994
Hon. Sir Alexander Butterfield, *born* 1942, *apptd* 1995
Hon. Sir David Eady, *born* 1943, *apptd* 1997
Hon. Sir David Penry-Davey, *born* 1942, *apptd* 1997
Hon. Sir David Steel, *born* 1943, *apptd* 1998
Hon. Sir Nicolas Bratza, *born* 1945, *apptd* 1998
Hon. Sir Michael Burton, *born* 1946, *apptd* 1998
Hon. Sir Stephen Silber, *born* 1944, *apptd* 1999
Hon. Dame Anne Rafferty, DBE, *born* 1950, *apptd* 2000
Hon. Sir Richard Henriques, *born* 1943, *apptd* 2000
Hon. Sir Stephen Tomlinson, *born* 1952, *apptd* 2000
Hon. Sir Andrew Smith, *born* 1947, *apptd* 2000
Hon. Sir Christopher Pitchford, *born* 1947, *apptd* 2000
Hon. Sir Duncan Ouseley, *born* 1950, *apptd* 2000
Hon. Sir Richard McCombe, *born* 1952, *apptd* 2001
Hon. Sir Raymond Jack, *born* 1942, *apptd* 2001
Hon. Sir Robert Owen, *born* 1944, *apptd* 2001
Hon. Sir Colin Mackay, *born* 1943, *apptd* 2001
Hon. Sir John Mitting, *born* 1947, *apptd* 2001
Hon. Sir Roderick Evans, *born* 1946, *apptd* 2001
Hon. Sir Nigel Davis, *born* 1951, *apptd* 2001
Hon. Sir Peter Gross, *born* 1952, *apptd* 2001
Hon. Sir Brian Keith, *born* 1944, *apptd* 2001
Hon. Sir Jeremy Cooke, *born* 1949, *apptd* 2001
Hon. Sir Richard Field, *born* 1947, *apptd* 2002
Hon. Sir Colman Treacy, *born* 1949, *apptd* 2002
Hon. Sir Peregrine Simon, *born* 1950, *apptd* 2002
Hon. Sir Roger Royce, *born* 1944, *apptd* 2002
Hon. Dame Laura Cox, DBE, *born* 1951, *apptd* 2002
Hon. Sir Adrian Fulford, *born* 1953, *apptd* 2002
Hon. Sir Jack Beatson, *born* 1948, *apptd* 2003
Hon. Sir Michael Tugendhat, *born* 1944, *apptd* 2003
Hon. Sir David Clarke, *born* 1942, *apptd* 2003
Hon. Dame Elizabeth Gloster, DBE, *born* 1949, *apptd* 2004
Hon. Sir David Bean, *born* 1954, *apptd* 2004
Hon. Sir Alan Wilkie, *born* 1947, *apptd* 2004
Hon. Dame Linda Dobbs, DBE, *born* 1951, *apptd* 2004
Hon. Sir Paul Walker, *born* 1954, *apptd* 2004
Hon. Sir David Calvert-Smith, *born* 1945, *apptd* 2005
Hon. Sir Christopher Clarke, *born* 1947, *apptd* 2005
Hon. Sir Charles Openshaw, *born* 1947, *apptd* 2005
Hon. Dame Caroline Swift, DBE, *born* 1955, *apptd* 2005
Hon. Sir Brian Langstaff, *born* 1948, *apptd* 2005
Hon. Sir David Jones, *born* 1952, *apptd* 2005
Hon. Sir Vivian Ramsey, *born* 1950, *apptd* 2005
Hon. Sir Nicholas Underhill, *born* 1952, *apptd* 2006
Hon. Sir Stephen Irwin, *born* 1953, *apptd* 2006
Hon. Sir Nigel Teare, *born* 1952, *apptd* 2006
Hon. Sir Griffith Williams, *born* 1944, *apptd* 2007
Hon. Sir Wyn Williams, *born* 1951, *apptd* 2007
Hon. Sir Timothy King, *born* 1946, *apptd* 2007
Hon. Sir John Saunders, *born* 1959, *apptd* 2007
Hon. Sir Julian Flaux, *born* 1955, *apptd* 2007
Hon. Sir Nicholas Stadlen, *born* 1950, *apptd* 2007
Hon. Sir Robert Akenhead, *born* 1949, *apptd* 2007
Hon. Sir David Foskett, *born* 1949, *apptd* 2007
Hon. Sir Nicholas Blake, *born* 1949, *apptd* 2007
Hon. Sir Ross Cranston, *born* 1948, *apptd* 2007
Hon. Sir Peter Coulson, *born* 1958, *apptd* 2008
Hon. Sir David Maddison, *born* 1947, *apptd* 2008
Hon. Sir Richard Plender, *born* 1945, *apptd* 2008
Hon. Sir William Blair, *born* 1950, *apptd* 2008
Hon. Sir Alistair MacDuff, *born* 1945, *apptd* 2008
Hon. Sir Ian Burnett, *born* 1958, *apptd* 2008
Hon. Sir Nigel Sweeney, *born* 1954, *apptd* 2008
Hon. Dame Elizabeth Slade, DBE, *born* 1949, *apptd* 2008
Hon. Sir Nicholas Hamblen, *born* 1957, *apptd* 2008
Hon. Sir Gary Hickinbottom, *born* 1955, *apptd* 2009
Hon. Sir Timothy Holroyde, *born* 1955, *apptd* 2009
Hon. Dame Victoria Sharp, DBE, *born* 1956, *apptd* 2009
Hon. Sir Andrew Nicol, *born* 1951, *apptd* 2009

The Queen's Bench Division also includes three specialist courts – the commercial court, the admiralty court and the administration court – and administers the technology and construction court.

FAMILY DIVISION
President (£206,857), Rt. Hon. Sir Mark Potter, *born* 1937, *apptd* 2005
Secretary, Mrs S. Leung
Clerk, John Curtis

JUDGES *as at 1 September 2009* (each £172,753)
Style, The Hon. Mr/Mrs Justice [surname]

Hon. Sir Jan Singer, *born* 1944, *apptd* 1993
Hon. Sir Hugh Bennett, *born* 1943, *apptd* 1995

Hon. Sir Edward Holman, *born* 1947, *apptd* 1995
Hon. Dame Mary Hogg, DBE, *born* 1947, *apptd* 1995
Hon. Sir Arthur Charles, *born* 1948, *apptd* 1998
Hon. Sir David Bodey, *born* 1947, *apptd* 1999
Hon. Dame Jill Black, DBE, *born* 1954, *apptd* 1999
Hon. Sir James Munby, *born* 1948, *apptd* 2000
Hon. Sir Paul Coleridge, *born* 1949, *apptd* 2000
Hon. Sir Mark Hedley, *born* 1946, *apptd* 2002
Hon. Dame Anna Pauffley, DBE, *born* 1956, *apptd* 2003
Hon. Sir Roderic Wood, *born* 1951, *apptd* 2004
Hon. Dame Florence Baron, DBE, *born* 1952, *apptd* 2004
Hon. Sir Ernest Ryder, *born* 1957, *apptd* 2004
Hon. Sir Andrew McFarlane, *born* 1954, *apptd* 2005
Hon. Dame Julia Macur, DBE, *born* 1957, *apptd* 2005
Hon. Sir Andrew Moylan, *born* 1953, *apptd* 2007
Hon. Dame Eleanor King, DBE, *born* 1957, *apptd* 2008
Hon. Dame Judith Parker, DBE, *born* 1950, *apptd* 2008

DEPARTMENTS AND OFFICES OF THE SENIOR COURTS OF ENGLAND AND WALES

Royal Courts of Justice, London WC2A 2LL
T 020-7947 6000

DIRECTOR'S OFFICE

T 020-7947 6159
Director, D. Thompson
Area Directors, L. Ladlow *(Court of Appeal)*; S. Fash *(High Court Group)*; H. Smith *(Probate Service)*
Managers, K. Richardson *(Finance)*; A. Monsarrat *(Regional Change and Performance)*

ADMIRALTY, COMMERCIAL AND LONDON MERCANTILE COURT

T 020-7947 6112
Registrar (£102,921), J. Kay, QC
Admiralty Marshal and Court Manager, K. Houghton

BANKRUPTCY COURT REGISTRY

T 020-7947 6441
Chief Registrar (£128,296), S. Baister
Bankruptcy Registrars (£102,921), C. Derrett; G. W. Jaques; W. Nicholls; J. A. Simmonds
Court Manager, P. O'Brien

CENTRAL OFFICE OF THE SENIOR COURTS

Senior Master (QBD), and Queen's Remembrancer (£128,296), S. D. Whitaker
Masters of the Senior Courts (QBD) (£102,921), P. G. A. Eyre; B. J. F. Fontaine; I. H. Foster; H. J. Leslie; G. H. Rose; B. Yoxall
Court Manager, Michael Parker

CHANCERY CHAMBERS

T 020-7947 6754
Chief Master (£128,296), J. Winegarten
Masters of the Senior Courts (£102,921, T. J. Bowles; N. W. Bragge; J. A. Moncaster; N. S. Price; P. R. Teverson
Court Manager, P. O'Brien

COURT OF APPEAL CIVIL DIVISION

T 020-7947 6916
Area Director (£102,921), L. Ladlow
Court Manager, Kim Langan

COURT OF APPEAL CRIMINAL DIVISION

T 020-7947 6011
Registrar (£102,921), R. A. Venne
Deputy Registrar, Mrs L. G. Knapman
Court Manager, Miss C. Brownbill

ADMINISTRATIVE COURT OFFICE

T 020-7947 6655
Master of the Crown Office, and Queen's Coroner and Attorney (£102,921), R. A. Venne
Head of Crown Office, Mrs L. G. Knapman

EXAMINERS OF THE COURT

Empowered to take examination of witnesses in all divisions of the High Court.
Examiners, M. W. M. Chism; A. G. Dyer; A. W. Hughes; Mrs G. M. Keene; R. M. Planterose

COSTS OFFICE

T 020-7947 6423
Senior Costs Judge (£128,296), P. T. Hurst
Masters of the Senior Courts (£102,921), C. D. N. Campbell; A. Gordon-Saker; P. Haworth; J. E. O'Hare; P. R. Rogers; J. Simons; C. C. Wright
Court Manager, Helene Newman

COURT OF PROTECTION

11th Floor, Archway Towers, 2 Junction Road, London N19 5SZ
T 0845-330 2900
Senior Judge (£128,296), D. Lush

COURT OF PROTECTION VISITORS

Office of the Public Guardian, PO Box 15118, Birmingham B16 6GX T 0845-330 2900

The Mental Capacity Act 2005 came into force on 1 October 2007, and it makes provision for two panels of court of protection visitors (special visitors or general visitors).

ELECTION PETITIONS OFFICE

Room E19, Royal Courts of Justice, London WC2A 2LL
T 020-7947 7529

The office accepts petitions and deals with all matters relating to the questioning of parliamentary, European parliament and local government elections, and with applications for relief under the 'representation of the people' legislation.
Prescribed Officer (£128,296), Senior Master, S. D. Whitaker
Chief Clerk, M. Parker

OFFICIAL RECEIVERS' DEPARTMENT

21 Bloomsbury Street, London WC1B 3QW
T 020-7637 1110
Chief Executive (Insolvency Service), S. Speed
Head of Service, L. Gramp
Deputy Chief Executive, G. Horn

OFFICE OF THE OFFICIAL SOLICITOR'S AND PUBLIC TRUSTEE

81 Chancery Lane, London WC2A 1DD
T 020-7911 7127
Official Solicitor to the Senior Courts, A. Pitblado
Deputy Official Solicitor, M. Maughan
Public Trustee, N. Crew

PRINCIPAL REGISTRY (FAMILY DIVISION)

First Avenue House, 42–49 High Holborn, London WC1V 6NP
T 020-7947 6000
Senior District Judge (£128,296), P. Waller
District Judges (£102,921), Mrs A. Aitken; A. R. S. Bassett-Cross; M. C. Berry; Ms S. M. Bowman;

Ms H. C. Bradley; Ms P. Cushing; Ms K. E. Green; P. Greene; R. Harper; Ms H. MacGregor; K. Malik; C. Million; Ms C. Reid; Ms L. D. Roberts; R. Robinson; M. Segal; Ms S. Walker; K. J. White
Area Director, London Civil and Family, L. Stririati
Head of Operations, London Family, J. Miller

PROBATE SERVICE
Thomas More Building, 8th Floor, Royal Courts of Justice, Strand, London WC2A 2LL
T 020-7947 6000
Area *Director,* H. Smith

DISTRICT PROBATE REGISTRARS
Probate Manager of London, T. Constantinou
Birmingham District, P. Walbeoff
Brighton District, S. Catt
Bristol District, R. Joyce
Ipswich District, H. Whitby
Leeds District, A. Parry
Liverpool District, K. Clark-Rimmer
Manchester District, K. Murphy
Newcastle District, M. C. Riley
Oxford District, R. D'Costa
Wales District, P. Curran
Winchester District, A. Butler

JUDGE ADVOCATES

The Judge Advocate-General is the officer in supreme control of the courts martial in the armed forces; historically, the role was shared by the Judge Advocate of the Fleet for the Royal Navy and the Judge Advocate-General for the Army and Royal Air Force. However, in 2004 the functions of the Judge Advocate of the Fleet were largely delegated to the Judge Advocate-General. The two offices were amalgamated in 2008 under the Armed Forces Act 2006, and the role of Judge Advocate of the Fleet was completely transferred to the Judge Advocate-General.

OFFICE OF THE JUDGE ADVOCATE-GENERAL OF THE FORCES
81 Chancery Lane, London WC2A IBQ
T 020-7218 8095
Judge Advocate-General (£138,548), His Hon. Judge Blackett
Vice-Judge Advocate-General (£120,785), Michael Hunter
Judge Advocates (£106,921)*, J. F. T. Bayliss; C. R. Burn; J. P. Camp; M. R. Elsom; R. D. Hill; A. J. B. McGrigor; R. C. C. Seymour
Style for Judge Advocates, Judge Advocate [surname]

* Salary includes £2,000 London salary lead and a London allowance of £2,000

HIGH COURT AND CROWN COURT CENTRES

First-tier centres deal with both civil and criminal cases and are served by high court and circuit judges. Second-tier centres deal with criminal cases only and are served by high court and circuit judges. Third-tier centres deal with criminal cases only and are served only by circuit judges.

LONDON REGION
First-tier – None
Second-tier – Central Criminal Court
Third-tier – Blackfriars, Croydon, Harrow, Inner London, Isleworth, Kingston upon Thames, Snaresbrook, Southwark, Wood Green, Woolwich
Regional Director, Kevin Pogson, 2nd Floor, Rose Court, 2 Southwark Bridge, London SE1 9HS T 020-7921 2010
Area Directors, Dave Weston *(Crime, Central and South);* Sandra Aston *(Crime, North East and West);* Luigi Strinati *(Family and Civil)*

The high court in Greater London sits at the Royal Courts of Justice.

MIDLAND REGION
First-tier – Birmingham, Lincoln, Nottingham, Stafford, Warwick
Second-tier – Leicester, Northampton, Shrewsbury, Worcester, Wolverhampton
Third-tier – Coventry, Derby, Hereford, Stoke-on-Trent
Regional Director, Alan Eccles, PO Box 11772, 6th Floor, Temple Court, Bull Street, Birmingham B4 6WF T 0121-250 6162
Area Directors, Kelvin Launchbury *(Birmingham, Coventry, Solihull and Warwickshire);* Peter Hammersley *(Black Country, Staffordshire and West Mercia);* Mark Swales *(Derbyshire and Nottinghamshire);* Richard Redgrave *(Leicestershire and Rutland, Lincolnshire and Northamptonshire)*

NORTH-EAST REGION
First-tier – Leeds, Newcastle upon Tyne, Sheffield, Teesside
Second-tier – Bradford, York
Third-tier – Doncaster, Durham, Kingston-upon-Hull, Great Grimsby
Regional Director, S. Caven, 11th Floor, West Riding House, Albion Street, Leeds LS1 5AA T 0113-251 1200
Area Directors, Sheila Proudlock *(Cleveland, Durham and Northumbria);* Paul Bradley *(South Yorkshire and Humber);* Dyfed Foulkes *(North and West Yorkshire)*

NORTH WEST REGION
First-tier – Carlisle, Chester, Liverpool, Manchester (Crown Square), Preston
Third-tier – Barrow-in-Furness, Bolton, Burnley, Knutsford, Lancaster, Manchester (Minshull Street), Warrington
Regional Director, Richard Knott, PO Box 4237, Manchester M60 1TE T 0161-240 5800
Area Directors, Geoffrey Appleton *(Cheshire and Merseyside);* Gill Hague *(Cumbria and Lancashire);* John Foley *(Greater Manchester)*

SOUTH-EAST REGION
First-tier – Cambridge, Chelmsford, Lewes, Norwich, Oxford
Second-tier – Ipswich, Luton, Maidstone, Reading, St Albans
Third-tier – Aylesbury, Basildon, Canterbury, Chichester, Croydon, Guildford, King's Lynn, Peterborough, Southend
Regional Director, Keith Budgen, 3rd Floor, Rose Court, 2 Southwark Bridge, London SE1 9HS T 020-7921 2061
Area Directors, Mark Littlewood *(Bedfordshire, Essex and Hertfordshire);* Pauline Cornford *(Norfolk, Suffolk and Cambridgeshire);* Julia Eeles *(Sussex, Surrey and Kent);* Jonathan Lane *(Thames Valley)*

SOUTH-WEST REGION
First-tier – Bristol, Exeter, Truro, Winchester
Second-tier – Dorchester & Weymouth, Gloucester, Plymouth
Third-tier – Barnstaple, Bournemouth, Newport (IoW), Portsmouth, Salisbury, Southampton, Swindon, Taunton

Regional Director, Peter Risk, Spectrum, 3rd Floor, Svitea, Bond Street, Bristol BS1 3LG T 0117-300 6238
Area Directors, Rod White *(Avon and Somerset);* David Gentry *(Devon and Cornwall);* Rod Brummitt *(Dorset, Gloucestershire and Wiltshire);* Simon Townley *(Hampshire and Isle of Wight)*

WALES REGION
First-tier – Caernarfon, Cardiff, Merthyr Tydfil, Mold, Swansea
Second-tier – Carmarthen, Newport, Welshpool
Third-tier – Dolgellau, Haverfordwest
Regional Director, Miss C. Pillman, Churchill House, Churchill Way, Cardiff CF10 2HH T 029-2067 8302
Area Directors, Stephen Whale (acting) *(Mid and West Wales);* Howard Lloyd *(North Wales);* Alan Davies *(South-East Wales)*

CIRCUIT JUDGES

Circuit judges are barristers of at least seven years' standing or recorders of at least five years' standing. Circuit judges serve in the county courts and the crown court.
Style, His/Her Hon. Judge [surname]
Senior Presiding Judge, Rt. Hon. Lord Justice Leveson
Senior Circuit Judges, each £138,548
Circuit Judges at the Central Criminal Court, London (Old Bailey Judges), each £138,548
Circuit Judges, each £128,296

LONDON AND SOUTH-EAST REGION
Presiding Judges, Hon. Mr Justice Bean; Hon. Mr Justice Calvert-Smith; Hon. Mr Justice Cooke; Hon. Mr Justice Saunders

MIDLAND REGION
Presiding Judges, Hon. Mrs Justice Macur, DBE; Hon. Mr Justice Treacy

NORTH-EAST REGION
Presiding Judges, Hon. Mr Justice Openshaw; Hon. Mr Justice Wilkie

NORTH-WEST REGION
Presiding Judges, Hon. Mr Justice David Clarke; Hon. Mr Justice Irwin

SOUTH-WEST REGION
Presiding Judges, Hon. Mr Justice Field; Hon. Mr Justice Royce

WALES REGION
Presiding Judges, Hon. Mr Justice Lloyd Jones; Hon. Mr Justice Davis

DISTRICT JUDGES

District judges, formerly known as registrars of the court, are solicitors of at least seven years' standing and serve in county courts.
District Judges (each £102,921)

DISTRICT JUDGES (MAGISTRATES' COURTS)

District judges (magistrates' courts), formerly known as stipendiary magistrates, must be barristers or solicitors of at least seven years' standing (including at least two years' experience as a deputy district judge), and serve in magistrates' courts. All former provincial and metropolitan stipendiary magistrates can serve nationally within any district.
District Judges each £105,400 (salary includes £4,000 inner London weighting)

CROWN PROSECUTION SERVICE

50 Ludgate Hill, London EC4M 7EX
T 020-7796 8000 E enquiries@cps.gsi.gov.uk
W www.cps.gov.uk

The Crown Prosecution Service (CPS) is responsible for prosecuting cases investigated by the police in England and Wales, with the exception of cases conducted by the Serious Fraud Office and certain minor offences.

The CPS is headed by the director of public prosecutions (DPP), who works under the superintendence of the attorney-general. The service comprises a headquarters and 43 areas (including two head offices in London and York), with each area corresponding to a police area in England and Wales. Each area is headed by a chief crown prosecutor supported by an area business manager.

Director of Public Prosecutions, Keir Starmer, QC
Chief Executive, Peter Lewis
Directors, Mike Kennedy *(Business Development);* David Jones *(Business Information Systems);* Sue Hemming *(Counter-Terrorism);* Dale Simon *(Equality and Diversity);* John Graham *(Finance);* Ros McCool *(Human Resources);* Alison Saunders *(Organised Crime);* Roger Daw *(Policy);* Alison Levitt *(Principal Legal Adviser);* Simon Clements *(Special Crime)*
Head of Strategic Communications, P. Teare

CPS AREAS ENGLAND
CPS DIRECT, 6th Floor, United House, Piccadilly, York YO1 9PQ T 01904-545400
Chief Crown Prosecutor, Martin Goldman
AVON AND SOMERSET, 2nd Floor, Froomsgate House, Rupert Street, Bristol BS1 2QJ T 0117-930 2800
Chief Crown Prosecutor, Barry Hughes
BEDFORDSHIRE, Sceptre House, 7–9 Castle Street, Luton LU1 3AJ T 01582-816600
Chief Crown Prosecutor, Richard Newcombe
CAMBRIDGESHIRE, Justinian House, Spitfire Close, Ermine Business Park, Huntingdon, Cambs PE29 6XY T 01480-825200
Chief Crown Prosecutor, Richard Crowley
CHESHIRE, 2nd Floor, Windsor House, Pepper Street, Chester CH1 1TD T 01244-408600
Chief Crown Prosecutor, Ian Rushton
CLEVELAND,1 Hudson Quay, The Halyard, Middlehaven, Middlesbrough TS3 6RT T 01642-204500
Chief Crown Prosecutor, Gerry Wareham
CUMBRIA, 1st Floor, Stocklund House, Castle Street, Carlisle CA3 8SY T 01228-882900
Chief Crown Prosecutor, Claire Lindley
DERBYSHIRE, 7th Floor, St Peter's House, Gower Street, Derby DE1 1SB T 01332-614000
Chief Crown Prosecutor, Brian Gunn
DEVON AND CORNWALL, Hawkins House, Pynes Hill, Rydon Lane, Exeter EX2 5SS T 01392-288000
Chief Crown Prosecutor, Tracy Easton
DORSET, Ground Floor, Oxford House, Oxford Road, Bournemouth BH8 8HA T 01202-498700
Chief Crown Prosecutor, Kate Brown
DURHAM, Elvet House, Hallgarth Street, Durham DH1 3AT T 0191-383 5800
Chief Crown Prosecutor, Chris Enzor

ESSEX, County House, 100 New London Road, Chelmsford CM2 0RG T 01245-455800
Chief Crown Prosecutor, Ken Caley

GLOUCESTERSHIRE, 2 Kimbrose Way, Gloucester GL1 2DB T 01452-872400
Chief Crown Prosecutor, Adrian Foster

GREATER MANCHESTER, PO Box 237, 5th Floor, Sunlight House, Quay Street, Manchester M60 3PS T 0161-827 4700
Chief Crown Prosecutor, John Holt

HAMPSHIRE AND ISLE OF WIGHT, 3rd Floor, Black Horse House, 8–10 Leigh Road, Eastleigh, Hants SO50 9FH T 023-8067 3800
Chief Crown Prosecutor, Nick Hawkins

HERTFORDSHIRE, Queen's House, 58 Victoria Street, St Albans, Herts AL1 3HZ T 01727-798700
Chief Crown Prosecutor, David Robinson

HUMBERSIDE, Citadel House, 58 High Street, Kingston-upon-Hull HU1 1QD T 01482-621000
Chief Crown Prosecutor, Barbara Petchey

KENT, Priory Gate, 29 Union Street, Maidstone ME14 1PT T 01622-356300
Chief Crown Prosecutor, Roger Coe-Salazar

LANCASHIRE, 2nd Floor Podium, Unicentre, Lord's Walk, Preston PR1 1QH T 01772-208100
Chief Crown Prosecutor, Robert Marshall

LEICESTERSHIRE, Princes Court, 34 York Road, Leicester LE1 5TU T 0116-204 6700
Chief Crown Prosecutor, Kate Carty

LINCOLNSHIRE, Crosstrend House, 10A Newport, Lincoln LN1 3DF T 01522-585900
Chief Crown Prosecutor, Jaswant Narwal

LONDON, 7th Floor, CPS HQ, 50 Ludgate Hill, London, EC4M 7EX T 020-7796 8000
Chief Crown Prosecutor, Dru Sharpling

MERSEYSIDE, 7th Floor (South), Royal Liver Building, Pier Head, Liverpool L3 1HN T 0151-239 6400
Chief Crown Prosecutor, Paul Whittaker

NORFOLK, Carmelite House, St James Court, Whitefriars, Norwich NR3 1SL T 01603 693000
Chief Crown Prosecutor, Andrew Baxter

NORTH YORKSHIRE, Athena House, Kettlestring Lane, Clifton Moor, York YO30 4XF T 01904-731700
Chief Crown Prosecutor, Robert Turnbull

NORTHAMPTONSHIRE, Beaumont House, Cliftonville, Northampton NN1 5BE T 01604-823600
Chief Crown Prosecutor, Grace Ononiwu

NORTHUMBRIA, St Ann's Quay, 122 Quayside, Newcastle upon Tyne NE1 3BD T 0191-260 4200
Chief Crown Prosecutor, Wendy Williams

NOTTINGHAMSHIRE, 2 King Edward Court, King Edward Street, Nottingham NG1 1EL T 0115-852 3300
Chief Crown Prosecutor, Judith Walker

SOUTH YORKSHIRE, Greenfield House, 32 Scotland Street, Sheffield S3 7DQ T 0114-229 8600
Chief Crown Prosecutor (acting), Peter Mann

STAFFORDSHIRE, Building 3, Etruria Valley Office Village, Etruria, Stoke-on-Trent ST1 5RU T 01782-664560
Chief Crown Prosecutor, vacant

SUFFOLK, 9th Floor, St Vincent's House, 1 Cutler Street, Ipswich IP1 1UL T 01473-282100
Chief Crown Prosecutor, Paula Abrahams

SURREY, Gateway, Power Close, Guildford, Surrey GU1 1EJ T 01483-468200
Chief Crown Prosecutor, Portia Ragnauth

SUSSEX, City Gates, 185 Dyke Road, Brighton BN3 1TL T 01273-765600
Chief Crown Prosecutor, Sarah Jane Gallagher

THAMES VALLEY, Eaton Court, 112 Oxford Road, Reading RG1 7LL T 0118-915 3600
Chief Crown Prosecutor, Baljit Ubhey

WARWICKSHIRE, Rossmore House, 10 Newbold Terrace, Leamington Spa CV32 4EA T 01926-455000
Chief Crown Prosecutor, Nigel Gumley

WEST MERCIA, Artillery House, Heritage Way, Droitwich, Worcester WR9 8YB T 01905-825000
Chief Crown Prosecutor, Colin Chapman

WEST MIDLANDS, Colmore Gate, 2 Colmore Row, Birmingham B3 2QA T 0121-262 1300
Chief Crown Prosecutor, Harry Ireland

WEST YORKSHIRE, Oxford House, Oxford Row, Leeds LS1 3BE T 0113-290 2700
Chief Crown Prosecutor, Neil Franklin

WILTSHIRE, 2nd Floor, Fox Talbot House, Bellinger Close, Malmesbury Road, Chippenham SN15 1BN T 01249-766100
Chief Crown Prosecutor, Karen Harrold

CPS AREAS WALES

DYFED POWYS, Heol Penlanffos, Tanerdy, Carmarthen, Dyfed SA31 2EZ T 01267-242100
Chief Crown Prosecutor, Jim Brisbane

GWENT, Vantage Point, Ty Coch Way, Cwmbran NP44 7XX T 01633-261100
Chief Crown Prosecutor, David Archer

NORTH WALES, Bromfield House, Ellice Way, Wrexham LL13 7YW T 01978-346000
Chief Crown Prosecutor, Ed Beltrami

SOUTH WALES, 20th Floor, Capital House, Greyfriars Road, Cardiff CF10 3PL T 029-2080 3905
Chief Crown Prosecutor, Christopher Woolley

HER MAJESTY'S COURTS SERVICE

4th Floor, 102 Petty France, London SW1H 9AJ
T 0845-456 8770
E customerserviceshq@hmcourts-service.gsi.gov.uk
W www.hmcourts-service.gov.uk

Her Majesty's Courts Service (HMCS) was launched on 1 April 2005, bringing together the Magistrates' Courts Service and the Court Service into a single organisation. It is responsible for managing magistrates' courts, the probate service, the crown court and county courts in England and Wales. It is also responsible for managing the royal courts of justice, where the majority of high court and court of appeal cases are heard. HMCS is an executive agency of the Ministry of Justice.
Chief Executive, Mrs Chris Mayer, CBE

JUDICIAL APPOINTMENTS COMMISSION

Steel House, 11 Tothill Street, London SW1H 9LJ
T 020-3334 0453 E enquiries@jac.gsi.gov.uk
W www.judicialappointments.gov.uk

The Judicial Appointments Commission was established as an independent non-departmental public body in April 2006 by the Constitutional Reform Act 2005. Its role is to select judicial office holders independently of government (a responsibility previously held by the Lord Chancellor). It has a statutory duty to encourage diversity in the range of persons available for selection and is sponsored by the Ministry of Justice and accountable to parliament through the Lord Chancellor. It is made up of 15 commissioners, including a chair.
Chair, Baroness Prashar, CBE

Commissioners, Mrs Justice Black, DBE; Dame Boreland-Kelly, DBE, FRSA; Dame Prof. Hazel Genn, DBE; Rt. Hon. Lady Justice Hallett, DBE; Sir Geoffrey Inkin, OBE; Her Hon. Judge Kirkham; Edward Nally; Sara Nathan; Charles Newman; His Hon. Judge Pearl; Francis Plowden; Harriet Spicer; Jonathan Sumption, OBE, QC; Rt. Hon. Lord Justice Toulson
Chief Executive, Clare Pelham

DIRECTORATE OF JUDICIAL OFFICES

The Directorate of Judicial Offices for England and Wales (DJO) was established in April 2006 following the implementation of the Constitutional Reform Act 2005, and incorporates the Judicial Office, the Judicial Communications Office and the Judicial Studies Board. It provides the Lord Chief Justice, the judicial executive board, the judges council, and some senior judges with the support they need to fulfil the new responsibilities which transferred to the judiciary in April 2006. Although part of the directorate is based at the royal courts of justice (which is managed by HM Courts Service), the directorate works independently from government departments and agencies.

CHIEF EXECUTIVE'S OFFICE

T 020-7947 7960
Chief Executive Officer, Anne Sharp
Personal Secretary, Sarah Welfoot

JUDICIAL OFFICE

T 020-7073 4858
Head, Jonathan Creer
Secretary to the Judges' Council, Barbara Flaxman

JUDICIAL COMMUNICATIONS OFFICE

T 020-7947 7836
Head of Judicial Communications, Mike Wicksteed
Chief Public Information Officer, Peter Farr *(Public Communications)*
Head of Corporate Communications, Jane Holman

JUDICIAL STUDIES BOARD

Steel House, 11 Tothill Street, London SW1H 9LJ
T 020-7217 4708 W www.jsboard.co.uk
Executive Directors, Judith Killick; Maggy Pigott
Director of Studies, His Hon. Judge Phillips, CBE
Heads, Mark Shore *(Corporate Services);* Judith Lennard *(Judicial Training);* Lynne McGechie *(Training Advice);* Helen Baker *(Tribunals/ETAC/International);* Terry Hunter *(Magistrates' Courts Training)*

JUDICIAL COMMITTEE OF THE PRIVY COUNCIL

The Judicial Committee of the Privy Council is the final court of appeal for the United Kingdom overseas territories (*see* UK Overseas Territories section), crown dependencies and those independent Commonwealth countries which have retained this avenue of appeal (Antigua and Barbuda, Bahamas, Barbados, Belize, Brunei, Cook Islands and Niue, Dominica, Grenada, Jamaica, Kiribati, Mauritius, St Christopher and Nevis, St Lucia, St Vincent and the Grenadines, Trinidad and Tobago, and Tuvalu) and the sovereign base areas of Akrotiri and Dhekelia in Cyprus. The committee also hears appeals against pastoral schemes under the Pastoral Measure 1983, and deals with appeals from veterinary disciplinary bodies.

Until October 2009, the Judicial Committee of the Privy Council was the final arbiter in disputes as to the legal competence of matters done or proposed by the devolved legislative and executive authorities in Scotland, Wales and Northern Ireland. This is now the responsibility of the new UK Supreme Court.

In 2008 the Judicial Committee dealt with a total of 58 appeals and 46 petitions for special leave to appeal.

The members of the Judicial Committee are the justices of the supreme court, and Privy Counsellors who hold or have held high judicial office in the United Kingdom or in certain designated courts of Commonwealth countries from which appeals are taken to committee.

JUDICIAL COMMITTEE OF THE PRIVY COUNCIL

Parliament Square, London SW1A 2AJ T 020-7960 1500
Registrar of the Privy Council, Mary Macdonald
Group Manager, Jackie Lindsay

SCOTTISH JUDICATURE

Scotland has a legal system separate from, and differing greatly from, the English legal system in enacted law, judicial procedure and the structure of courts.

In Scotland the system of public prosecution is headed by the Lord Advocate and is independent of the police, who have no say in the decision to prosecute. The Lord Advocate, discharging his functions through the Crown Office in Edinburgh, is responsible for prosecutions in the high court, sheriff courts and district courts. Prosecutions in the high court are prepared by the Crown Office and conducted in court by one of the law officers, by an advocate-depute, or by a solicitor advocate. In the inferior courts the decision to prosecute is made and prosecution is preferred by procurators fiscal, who are lawyers and full-time civil servants subject to the directions of the Crown Office. A permanent legally qualified civil servant, known as the crown agent, is responsible for the running of the Crown Office and the organisation of the Procurator Fiscal Service, of which he or she is the head.

Scotland is divided into six sheriffdoms, each with a full-time sheriff principal. The sheriffdoms are further divided into sheriff court districts, each of which has a legally qualified resident sheriff or sheriffs, who are the judges of the court.

In criminal cases sheriffs principal and sheriffs have the same powers; sitting with a jury of 15 members, they may try more serious cases on indictment, or, sitting alone, may try lesser cases under summary procedure. Minor summary offences are dealt with in district courts which are administered by the district and the islands local government authorities and presided over by lay justices of the peace (of whom some 500 regularly sit in court) and, in Glasgow only, by stipendiary magistrates. Juvenile offenders (children under 16) may be brought before an informal children's hearing comprising three local lay people. The superior criminal court is the high court of justiciary which is both a trial and an appeal court. Cases on indictment are tried by a high court judge, sitting with a jury of 15, in Edinburgh and on circuit in other towns. Appeals from the lower courts against conviction or sentence are also heard by the high court, which sits as an appeal court only in Edinburgh. There is no further appeal to the supreme court in criminal cases.

In civil cases the jurisdiction of the sheriff court extends to most kinds of action. Appeals against decisions of the sheriff may be made to the sheriff principal and thence to the court of session, or direct to the court of session, which sits only in Edinburgh. The court of session is divided into the inner and the outer house. The outer house is a court of first instance in which cases are heard by judges sitting singly, sometimes with a jury of 12. The inner house, itself subdivided into two divisions of equal status, is mainly an appeal court. Appeals may be made to the inner house from the outer house as well as from the sheriff court. An appeal may be made from the inner house to the supreme court.

The judges of the court of session are the same as those of the high court of justiciary, with the Lord President of the court of session also holding the office of Lord Justice General in the high court. Senators of the College of Justice are Lords Commissioners of Justiciary as well as judges of the court of session. On appointment, a senator takes a judicial title, which is retained for life. Although styled The Hon./Rt. Hon. Lord, the senator is not a peer, although some judges are peers in their own right.

The office of coroner does not exist in Scotland. The local procurator fiscal inquires privately into sudden or suspicious deaths and may report findings to the crown agent. In some cases a fatal accident inquiry may be held before the sheriff.

COURT OF SESSION AND HIGH COURT OF JUSTICIARY

The Lord President and Lord Justice General (£214,165), Rt. Hon. Lord Hamilton, *born* 1942, *apptd* 2005
Private Secretary, A. Maxwell

INNER HOUSE
Lords of Session (each £196,707)

FIRST DIVISION
The Lord President

Rt. Hon. Lord Nimmo Smith (William Nimmo Smith), *born* 1942, *apptd* 1996
Rt. Hon. Lord Kingarth (Derek Emslie), *born* 1945, *apptd* 1997
Rt. Hon. Lord Eassie (Ronald Mackay), *born* 1945, *apptd* 2008
Rt. Hon. Lord Reed (Robert Reed), *born* 1956, *apptd* 2008

SECOND DIVISION
Lord Justice Clerk (£206,857), Rt. Hon. Lord Gill (Brian Gill), *born* 1942, *apptd* 2001
Rt. Hon. Lord Osborne (Kenneth Osborne), *born* 1937, *apptd* 1990
Rt. Hon. Lord Wheatley (John Wheatley), *born* 1941, *apptd* 2000
Rt. Hon. Lady Paton (Ann Paton), *born* 1952, *apptd* 2000
Rt. Hon. Lord Carloway (Colin Sutherland), *born* 1954, *apptd* 2008
Rt. Hon. Lord Clarke (Matthew Clarke), *born* 1947, *apptd* 2008

OUTER HOUSE
Lords of Session (each £172,753)
Rt. Hon. Lord Hardie (Andrew Hardie), *born* 1946, *apptd* 2000
Rt. Hon. Lord Mackay of Drumadoon (Donald Mackay), *born* 1946, *apptd* 2000
Hon. Lord McEwan (Robin McEwan), *born* 1943, *apptd* 2000
Hon. Lord Menzies (Duncan Menzies), *born* 1953, *apptd* 2001
Hon. Lord Drummond Young (James Drummond Young), *born* 1950, *apptd* 2001
Hon. Lord Emslie (Nigel Emslie), *born* 1947, *apptd* 2001
Hon. Lady Smith (Anne Smith), *born* 1955, *apptd* 2001
Hon. Lord Brodie (Philip Brodie), *born* 1950, *apptd* 2002
Hon. Lord Bracadale (Alastair Campbell), *born* 1949, *apptd* 2003
Hon. Lady Dorrian (Leona Dorrian), *born* 1959, *apptd* 2005
Hon. Lord Hodge (Patrick Hodge), *born* 1953, *apptd* 2005
Hon. Lord Macphail (Iain Macphail), *born* 1938, *apptd* 2005
Hon. Lord Glennie (Angus Glennie), *born* 1950, *apptd* 2005
Hon. Lord Kinclaven (Alexander F. Wylie), *born* 1951, *apptd* 2005
Hon. Lady Clark of Calton (Lynda Clark), *born* 1946, *apptd* 2006
Hon. Lord Turnbull (Alan Turnbull), *born* 1958, *apptd* 2006
Hon. Lord Brailsford (Sidney Brailsford), *born* 1954, *apptd* 2006
Hon. Lord Uist (Roderick Macdonald), *born* 1951, *apptd* 2006
Hon. Lord Malcolm (Colin M. Campbell), *born* 1953, *apptd* 2007
Hon. Lord Matthews (Hugh Matthews), *born* 1953, *apptd* 2007
Hon. Lord Woolman (Stephen Woolman), *born* 1953, *apptd* 2008
Hon. Lord Pentland (Paul Cullen), *born* 1957, *apptd* 2008
Hon. Lord Bannatyne (Iain Peebles), *born* 1954, *apptd* 2008
Hon. Lady Stacey (Valerie E. Stacey), *born* 1954, *apptd* 2009

COURT OF SESSION AND HIGH COURT OF JUSTICIARY
Parliament House, Parliament Square, Edinburgh EH1 1HQ
T 0131-225 2595
Principal Clerk of Session and Justiciary, Graheme Marwick
Deputy Principal Clerk of Justiciary, G. Prentice
Deputy Principal Clerk of Session and Principal Extractor, R. Cockburn
Depute in Charge of Offices of Court, Y. Anderson
Keeper of the Rolls, A. Moffat
Depute Clerks of Session and Justiciary, J. Atkinson; D. Bruton; D. Cullen; L. Curran; W. Dunn; P. Fiddes; A. Finlayson; C. Fyffe; R. Jenkins; T. Kell; L. McLachlan; D. MacLeod; R. MacPherson; A. McArdle; L. MacNamara, I. Martin, N. McGinley; A. McKay; D. Morrison; R. Newlands; R. Philips; C. Reid; C. Richardson; C. Scott; R. Sinclair; K. Todd; P. Weir

SHERIFF COURT OF CHANCERY
27 Chambers Street, Edinburgh EH1 1LB
T 0131-225 2525

The court deals with service of heirs and completion of title in relation to heritable property.
Sheriff Principal, Edward F. Bowen, QC

HM COMMISSARY OFFICE
27 Chambers Street, Edinburgh EH1 1LB
T 0131-225 2525

The office is responsible for issuing confirmation, a legal document entitling a person to execute a deceased person's will, and other related matters.
Commissary Clerk, David Fyfe

SCOTTISH LAND COURT
126 George Street, Edinburgh EH2 4HH
T 0131-271 4360

The court deals with disputes relating to agricultural and crofting land in Scotland.
Chair (£138,548), Hon. Lord McGhie (James McGhie), QC
Members, D. J. Houston; A. Macdonald *(part-time)*; J. A. Smith *(part-time)*
Principal Clerk, K. H. R. Graham, WS
Deputy Principal Clerk, M. I. E. Steel

SCOTTISH GOVERNMENT, CONSTITUTION, LAW AND COURTS DIRECTORATE
Legal System Division, Room 2W, St Andrew's House, Edinburgh EH1 3DG
T 0131-244 2698

The Courts Directorate is responsible for the appointment of judges and sheriffs to meet the needs of the business of the supreme and sheriffs court in Scotland. It is also responsible for the efficient administration of a number of specialist courts and tribunals.
Deputy Director, C. McKay

JUDICIAL APPOINTMENTS BOARD FOR SCOTLAND
38–39 Drumsheugh Gardens, Edinburgh EH3 7SW
T 0131-528 5101

The board's remit is to provide the first minister with a list of candidates recommended for appointment to the posts of senator of the court of session, sheriff principal, sheriff and part-time sheriff.
Chair, Sir Muir Russell, KCB, FRSE

SCOTTISH COURT SERVICE
Hayweight House, 23 Lauriston Street, Edinburgh EH3 9DQ
T 0131-229 9200 W www.scotcourts.gov.uk

The Scottish Court Service is an executive agency within the Scottish Government Justice Department. It is responsible to the Scottish ministers for the provision of staff, courthouses and associated services for the supreme and sheriff courts.
Chief Executive, Eleanor Emberson

SHERIFFDOMS

SALARIES	
Sheriff Principal	£138,548
Sheriff	£128,296

GLASGOW AND STRATHKELVIN
Sheriff Principal, James A. Taylor

GRAMPIAN, HIGHLAND AND ISLANDS
Sheriff Principal, Sir Stephen S. T. Young, Bt., QC

LOTHIAN AND BORDERS
Sheriff Principal, E. F. Bowen, QC

NORTH STRATHCLYDE
Sheriff Principal, B. A. Kerr, QC

SOUTH STRATHCLYDE, DUMFRIES AND GALLOWAY
Sheriff Principal, B. A. Lockhart

TAYSIDE, CENTRAL AND FIFE
Sheriff Principal, R. A. Dunlop, QC

JUSTICE OF THE PEACE AND STIPENDIARY MAGISTRATES COURT

GLASGOW
R. B. Christie, *apptd* 1985; A. Findlay, *apptd* 2008; Ms J. Kerr, *apptd* 2008; Mrs J. A. M. MacLean, *apptd* 1990

CROWN OFFICE AND PROCURATOR FISCAL SERVICE

CROWN OFFICE
25 Chambers Street, Edinburgh EH1 1LA
T 0131-226 2626 W www.crownoffice.gov.uk
Crown Agent, Norman McFadyen
Deputy Crown Agent, John Dunn

PROCURATORS FISCAL

SALARIES	
Area Fiscals	£57,300–£160,000
District Procurator Fiscal	£46,920–£116,000

GRAMPIAN AREA
Area Procurator Fiscal, Mrs A. Currie *(Aberdeen)*

HIGHLAND AND ISLANDS AREA
Area Procurator Fiscal, A. Laing *(Inverness)*

LANARKSHIRE AREA
Area Procurator Fiscal, Ms J. Cameron *(Hamilton)*

CENTRAL AREA
Area Procurator Fiscal, Ms M. MacLeod *(Stirling)*

TAYSIDE AREA
Area Procurator Fiscal, T. Dysart *(Dundee)*

FIFE AREA
Area Procurator Fiscal, C. Ritchie *(Kirkcaldy)*

LOTHIAN AND BORDERS AREA
Area Procurator Fiscal, Ms M. McLaughlin *(Edinburgh)*

AYRSHIRE AREA
Area Procurator Fiscal, Mrs G. Watt *(Kilmarnock)*

ARGYLL AND CLYDE AREA
Area Procurator Fiscal, J. Watt *(Paisley)*

DUMFRIES AND GALLOWAY AREA
Area Procurator Fiscal, Ms R. McQuaid *(Dumfries)*

GLASGOW AREA
Area Procurator Fiscal, Ms L. Thomson *(Glasgow)*

COURT OF THE LORD LYON

HM New Register House, Edinburgh EH1 3YT
T 0131-556 7255
W www.lyon-court.com

The Court of the Lord Lyon is the Scottish Court of Chivalry (including the genealogical jurisdiction of the *Ri-Sennachie* of Scotland's Celtic kings). The Lord Lyon King of Arms has jurisdiction, subject to appeal to the Court of Session and the House of Lords, in questions of heraldry and the right to bear arms. The court also administers the Public Register of All Arms and Bearings and the Public Register of All Genealogies in Scotland. Pedigrees are established by decrees of Lyon Court and by letters patent. As Royal Commissioner in Armory, the Lord Lyon grants patents of arms to virtuous and well-deserving Scots and to petitioners (personal or corporate) in the Queen's overseas realms of Scottish connection, and also issues birthbrieves. For information on Her Majesty's Officers of Arms in Scotland, *see* the Court of the Lord Lyon in the Public Bodies section.

Lord Lyon King of Arms, David Sellar, FSA SCOT, FRHISTS
Lyon Clerk and Keeper of the Records, Mrs C. G. W. Roads, MVO, FSA SCOT
Procurator Fiscal, vacant
Macer, H. M. Love

NORTHERN IRELAND JUDICATURE

In Northern Ireland the legal system and the structure of courts closely resemble those of England and Wales; there are, however, often differences in enacted law.

The supreme court of judicature of Northern Ireland comprises the court of appeal, the high court of justice and the crown court. The practice and procedure of these courts is similar to that in England. The superior civil court is the high court of justice, from which an appeal lies to the Northern Ireland court of appeal; the supreme court is the final civil appeal court.

The crown court, served by high court and county court judges, deals with criminal trials on indictment. Cases are heard before a judge and, except those involving offences specified under emergency legislation, a jury. Appeals from the crown court against conviction or sentence are heard by the Northern Ireland court of appeal; the supreme court is the final court of appeal.

The decision to prosecute in cases tried on indictment and in summary cases of a serious nature rests in Northern Ireland with the director of public prosecutions, who is responsible to the attorney-general. Minor summary offences are prosecuted by the police.

Minor criminal offences are dealt with in magistrates' courts by a legally qualified resident magistrate and, where an offender is under the age of 17, by juvenile courts each consisting of a resident magistrate and two lay members specially qualified to deal with juveniles (at least one of whom must be a woman). On 1 July 2009 there were 764 justices of the peace in Northern Ireland. Appeals from magistrates' courts are heard by the county court, or by the court of appeal on a point of law or an issue as to jurisdiction.

Magistrates' courts in Northern Ireland can deal with certain classes of civil case but most minor civil cases are dealt with in county courts. Judgments of all civil courts are enforceable through a centralised procedure administered by the Enforcement of Judgments Office.

SUPREME COURT OF JUDICATURE

The Royal Courts of Justice, Belfast BT1 3JF
T 028-9023 5111

Lord Chief Justice of Northern Ireland (£214,165), Rt. Hon. Sir Declan Morgan, *born* 1952, *apptd* 2009
Principal Secretary, S. T. A. Rogers

LORD JUSTICES OF APPEAL (£196,707)
Style, The Rt. Hon. Lord Justice [surname]

Rt. Hon. Sir Malachy Higgins, *born* 1944, *apptd* 2007
Rt. Hon. Sir Paul Girvan, *born* 1948, *apptd* 2007
Rt. Hon. Sir Patrick Coghlin, *born* 1945, *apptd* 2008

PUISNE JUDGES (£172,753)
Style, The Hon. Mr Justice [surname]

Hon. Sir John Gillen, *born* 1947, *apptd* 1998
Hon. Sir Richard McLaughlin, *born* 1947, *apptd* 1999
Hon. Sir Ronald Weatherup, *born* 1947, *apptd* 2001
Hon. Sir Reginald Weir, *born* 1947, *apptd* 2003
Hon. Sir Donnell Deeny, *born* 1950, *apptd* 2004
Hon. Sir Anthony Hart, *born* 1946, *apptd* 2005
Hon. Sir Seamus Treacy, *born* 1956, *apptd* 2007
Hon. Sir William Benjamin Synge Stephens, *born* 1954, *apptd* 2007
Hon. Sir Bernard McCloskey, *born* 1956, *apptd* 2008

MASTERS OF THE SUPREME COURT (£102,921)
Master, Queen's Bench and Appeals, C. J. McCorry
Master, Office of Care and Protection, H. Wells
Master, Chancery and Probate, R. A. Ellison
Master, Matrimonial, C. W. G. Redpath
Master, Queen's Bench and Matrimonial, E. Bell
Master, Taxing Office, J. Baillie
Master, Bankruptcy, F. Kelly

OFFICIAL SOLICITOR
Official Solicitor to the Supreme Court of Northern Ireland, Miss B. M. Donnelly

COUNTY COURTS

JUDGES (£128,296)
Style, His/Her Hon. Judge [surname]

Judge Babington; Judge Finnegan; Judge Gibson, QC; Her Hon. Judge Kennedy; Judge Lockie; Judge Loughran; Judge Lynch; Judge McFarland; Judge McKay, QC; Judge McReynolds; Judge Markey, QC; Judge Martin *(Chief Social Security and Child Support Commissioner)*; Judge Miller, QC; Judge Philpott, QC; Judge Rodgers; Judge Smyth, QC

RECORDERS
Belfast (£149,632), Judge Burgess
Londonderry (£128,296), Judge Marrinan, QC

MAGISTRATES' COURTS

DISTRICT JUDGES (MAGISTRATES' COURTS) (£102,921)
There are 20 resident magistrates in Northern Ireland.

NORTHERN IRELAND COURT SERVICE
Windsor House, Bedford Street, Belfast BT2 7LT
T 028-9032 8594 W www.courtsni.gov.uk
Director, D. A. Laver

CROWN SOLICITOR'S OFFICE
PO Box 410, Royal Courts of Justice, Belfast BT1 3JY
T 028-9054 6047
Crown Solicitor, J. Conn

PUBLIC PROSECUTION SERVICE
93 Chichester Street, Belfast BT1 3TR
T 028-9054 2444 W www.ppsni.gov.uk
Director of Public Prosecutions, James Hamilton

TRIBUNALS

THE TRIBUNALS SERVICE

5th Floor, 102 Petty France, London SW1H 9AJ
T 0845-600 0877 W www.tribunals.gov.uk

The Tribunals Service, launched in April 2006, is an executive agency within the Ministry of Justice that provides common administrative support to central government tribunals (plus the Adjudicator to HM Land Registry and the Gender Recognition Panel, which are not technically tribunals). The service also aims to deliver greater consistency in practice and procedure, to ensure tribunals are manifestly independent from those whose decisions are being reviewed, and to provide increased access to information for the public.

A new two-tier tribunal system was established on 3 November 2008 as a result of radical reform under the Tribunals, Courts and Enforcement Act 2007. The Tribunals Service now operates a First-tier Tribunal and an Upper Tribunal, both of which are split into chambers. The chambers group together individual tribunals (now also known as 'jurisdictions') which deal with similar work or require similar skills. Cases start in the First-tier Tribunal and there is a right of appeal to the Upper Tribunal. Some tribunals transferred to the new two-tier system immediately and most tribunals are expected to transfer into it by the end of 2010. The exception is employment tribunals, which will remain outside this structure. The Act also allowed legally qualified tribunal chairmen and adjudicators to swear the judicial oath and become judges.

Senior President, Lord Justice Carnwath
Deputy Senior President, Mr Justice Walker
Chief Executive, Kevin Sadler

FIRST-TIER TRIBUNAL

The main function of the First-tier Tribunal is to hear appeals by citizens against decisions of the government. Appeals are heard by a panel made up of one judge and two non-legal members who are specialists in their field. Judges are appointed by the Lord Chancellor; other members are appointed by the Secretary of State relevant to the tribunal (or jurisdiction) in question. Most of the tribunals administered by central government are expected to become part of the First-tier Tribunal, with new chambers being created as this happens.

GENERAL REGULATORY CHAMBER

The General Regulatory Chamber was to be established in September 2009, subject to parliamentary approval. Intended to bring together individual tribunals that hear appeals on regulatory issues, the chamber replaces the Charity Tribunal, the Consumer Credit Appeals Tribunal, the Estate Agents Appeals Panel, and some functions of the Transport Tribunal. The Information, Gambling Appeals, Claims Management, Adjudication Panel for England, and Immigration Services tribunals are scheduled to join the chamber in January 2010.

IMMIGRATION SERVICES TRIBUNAL

7th Floor, Victory House, 30–34 Kingsway, London WC2B 6EX
T 020-3077 5860 E imset@tribunals.gsi.gov.uk
W www.immigrationservicestribunal.gov.uk

The Immigration Services tribunal is an independent judicial body established in 2000 to provide a forum in which appeals against decisions of the Immigration Services Commissioner and complaints made by the Immigration Services Commissioner can be heard and determined. The cases exclusively concern people providing advice and representation services in connection with immigration matters.

The tribunal forms part of the Ministry of Justice. There is a president, who is the judicial head; other judicial members, who must be legally qualified; lay members, who must have substantial experience in immigration services or in the law and procedure relating to immigration; and a secretary, who is responsible for administration. The tribunal can sit anywhere in the UK.

Subject to parliamentary approval, the Immigration Services tribunal is scheduled to join the first-tier General Regulatory Chamber in January 2010.

President, His Hon. Judge the Lord Parmoor

INFORMATION TRIBUNAL

Arnhem House Support Centre, PO Box 6987, Leicester LE1 6ZX
T 0845-6000 877 E informationtribunal@tribunals.gsi.gov.uk
W www.informationtribunal.gov.uk

The Information tribunal determines appeals against notices issued by the Information Commissioner. The chair and deputy chair are appointed by the Lord Chancellor and must be legally qualified. Lay members are appointed by the Lord Chancellor to represent the interests of data users or data subjects. A tribunal consists of a chair and deputy chair sitting with two of the lay members. The tribunal is scheduled to join the first-tier General Regulatory Chamber in January 2010.

Chair, Prof. John Angel

HEALTH, EDUCATION AND SOCIAL CARE CHAMBER

President, His Hon. Judge Sycamore

CARE STANDARDS

18 Pocock Street, London SE1 0BW
T 020-7960 0660 E cst@tribunals.gsi.gov.uk
W www.carestandardstribunal.gov.uk

The tribunal was established under the Protection of Children Act 1999 and considers appeals in relation to decisions made about the inclusion of individuals' names on the list of those considered unsuitable to work with children or vulnerable adults, restrictions from teaching and employment in schools/further education institutions, and the registration of independent schools. It also deals with general registration decisions made about care homes, children's homes, childcare providers, nurses' agencies, social workers, residential family centres, independent hospitals and fostering agencies. The tribunal's principal judge appoints the panels for each case.

Principal judge, His Hon. Judge Pearl

FAMILY HEALTH SERVICES APPEAL AUTHORITY
York House, York Place, Leeds LS1 2ED
T 0113-389 6061 W www.fhsaa.tribunals.gov.uk

The Family Health Services Appeal Authority (FHSAA) is independent of the Department of Health and considers appeals against the decisions of primary care trusts (PCTs), including appeals by GPs, dentists, pharmacists and opticians regarding action taken against them. The president allocates appeals and applications to panels normally consisting of a legal chair, a professional member and a lay member. The FHSAA's president and members are appointed by the Lord Chancellor. The FHSAA is expected to transfer to the first-tier Health, Education and Social Care Chamber.
President, Paul Kelly

MENTAL HEALTH
Secretariat: PO Box 8793, 5th Floor, Leicester LE1 8BN
T 0845-233 2022 W www.mhrt.org.uk

The tribunal is an independent judicial body which reviews the cases of patients compulsorily detained under the provisions of the Mental Health Act 1983 (amended by the Mental Health Act 2007). It has the power to discharge the patient, to recommend leave of absence, to recommend supervised community treatment, or to recommend transfer to another hospital. Judges are appointed by the Lord Chancellor, and non-legal members are appointed by the Secretary of State for Health or the Secretary of State for Wales. Each case is heard by three members including a judge and a medical specialist. There are separate mental health tribunals in Wales and Scotland.

SPECIAL EDUCATIONAL NEEDS AND DISABILITY
Ground Floor, Mowden Hall, Staindrop Road DL3 9BG
T 0870-241 2555 E sendistqueries@tribunals.gsi.gov.uk
W www.sendist.gov.uk

The Special Educational Needs and Disability tribunal considers parents' appeals against the decisions of local authorities (LAs) about children's special educational needs if parents cannot reach agreement with the LA. It also considers claims of disability discrimination in schools.
Principal judge, vacant

SOCIAL ENTITLEMENT CHAMBER
President, His Hon. Judge Martin

ASYLUM SUPPORT
Christopher Wren House, 113 High Street, Croydon CR0 1QG
T 020-8588 2500 Freephone 0800-389 7913
W www.asylum-support-tribunal.gov.uk

Asylum Support deals with appeals against decisions made by the UK Border Agency (UKBA). The UKBA decides whether asylum seekers and their dependants meet the test of destitution according to the Immigration and Asylum Act 1999, and determines what support, such as money or accommodation, should be provided. Asylum Support can only consider appeals against a refusal or termination of support, and can ask the Home Secretary to reconsider the matter, substitute the original decision with the tribunal's decision, or dismiss the appeal.
Principal judge, Sehba Storey

CRIMINAL INJURIES COMPENSATION
Head Office, Wellington House, 134–136 Wellington Street, Glasgow G2 2XL T 0141-354 8555
Judicial Review Enquiries, 11th Floor, Cardinal Tower, Farringdon Road, London EC1M 3HS T 020-7549 4600
E enquiries-cicap@tribunals.gsi.gov.uk W www.cicap.gov.uk

The Criminal Injuries Compensation tribunal (previously known as the Criminal Injuries Compensation Appeals Panel) determines appeals against review decisions made by the Criminal Injuries Compensation Authority on applications for compensation made by victims of violent crime. It only considers appeals on claims made on or after 1 April 1996 under the Criminal Injuries Compensation Scheme.
Principal Judge, Roger Goodier

SOCIAL SECURITY AND CHILD SUPPORT
4th Floor, Fox Court, 14 Grays Inn Road, London WC1X 8HN
T 020-3206 0640 W www.appeals-service.gov.uk

The Social Security and Child Support tribunal (SSCS) arranges and hears appeals on a range of decisions made by the Department for Work and Pensions, HM Revenue and Customs, and local authorities. Appeals considered include those concerned with income support, jobseeker's allowance, child support, child tax credit, retirement pensions, housing benefit, council tax benefit, disability living allowance, vaccine damage, tax credits and compensation recovery.

The tribunal is headed by the president of the Social Entitlement Chamber. The SSCS also contains an executive agency responsible for the administration of appeals, headed by the chief executive of the Tribunals Service.

TAX CHAMBER
45 Bedford Square, London WC1B 3DN
T 0845-223 8080 E taxappeals@tribunals.gsi.gov.uk
W www.tribunals.gov.uk/tax

The Tax Chamber, established on 1 April 2009, replaced four separate tax tribunals, the General Commissioners of Income Tax, the Special Commissioners, the VAT and Duties Tribunals, and section 706 tribunals. The chamber hears most appeals against decisions of Her Majesty's Revenue and Customs in relation to tax. The chamber listens to appeals about income tax; corporation tax; capital gains tax; inheritance tax; national insurance contributions; and VAT or duties, and appeals can be made by individuals or organisations, single taxpayers or large multinational companies. Appeals are heard by legally qualified judges, non-legally qualified expert members or a mix of the two. The chamber has jurisdiction throughout the UK.
President (acting), His Hon. Sir Stephen Oliver, QC

WAR PENSIONS AND ARMED FORCES COMPENSATION CHAMBER
5th Floor, Fox Court, 14 Gray's Inn Road, London WC1X 8HN
T 020-3206 0705 E pensions.appeal@tribunals.gsi.gov.uk
W www.pensionsappealtribunals.gov.uk

The War Pensions and Armed Forces Compensation Chamber holds the War Pensions and Armed Forces Compensation tribunal (previously known as Pensions Appeals), which has existed in some form since the War Pensions Act 1919. It hears appeals from ex-servicemen

or women who have had their claims for a war pension rejected by the Secretary of State for Defence. The tribunal considers appeals under the war pensions scheme for injuries that occurred before 5 April 2005, and under the armed forces compensation scheme for injuries after that date. Under the war pensions scheme the tribunal decides on entitlement to a war pension, the percentage at which the War Pensions Agency has assessed a disablement and whether an allowance is justified (eg for mobility needs). Under the armed forces compensation scheme it judges entitlement to an award and the amount of the award. The tribunal's jurisdiction covers England and Wales.
President, Judge Bano

PENSIONS APPEAL TRIBUNALS FOR SCOTLAND
126 George street, Edinburgh EH2 4HH
T 0131-271 4340 E info@patscotland.org.uk
W www.patscotland.org.uk
President, C. M. McEachran, QC

UPPER TRIBUNAL

The Upper Tribunal deals with appeals from, and enforcement of, decisions taken by the First-tier Tribunal. It has also assumed some of the supervisory powers of the courts to deal with the actions of tribunals, government departments and some other public authorities. All the decision-makers of the Upper Tribunal are judges or expert members sitting in a panel chaired by a judge, and are specialists in the areas of law they handle. Over time their decisions are expected to build comprehensive case law for each area covered by the tribunals.

ADMINISTRATIVE APPEALS CHAMBER
1st Floor, Procession House, 55 Ludgate Hill, London EC4M 7JW
T 020-7029 9850 E adminappeals@tribunals.gsi.gov.uk
W www.administrativeappeals.tribunals.gov.uk

The Administrative Appeals Chamber took over the work of the Social Security, Child Support and Pensions Appeal Commissioners, which dealt with appeals from what are now the Social Entitlement Chamber, and the War Pensions and Armed Forces Compensation Chamber. It also deals with appeals from the Health, Education and Social Care Chamber of the First-tier Tribunal, Forfeiture Act references and appeals in cases about safeguarding vulnerable groups. The Upper Tribunal in Northern Ireland deals with appeals from the Pensions Appeal Tribunal for Northern Ireland. There are 16 full-time judges and 17 deputy judges who sit part-time. Judges normally sit on their own to hear cases and most of their cases are decided without oral hearings.
President, Mr Justice Walker

OFFICE OF THE SOCIAL SECURITY COMMISSIONERS AND CHILD SUPPORT COMMISSIONERS FOR NORTHERN IRELAND
Headline Building, 10–14 Victoria Street, Belfast BT1 3GG
T 028-9072 8731
E socialsecuritycommissioners@courtsni.gov.uk
W www.courtsni.gov.uk

The role of Northern Ireland Social Security Commissioners and Child Support Commissioners is similar to that of the Administrative Appeals Chamber in England, Wales and Scotland; they also have jurisdiction to deal with questions arising under the Forfeiture (Northern Ireland) Order 1982. The commissioners are not part of the Tribunals Service. There are two commissioners for Northern Ireland.
Chief Commissioner, His Hon. Judge Martin, QC
Commissioner, Dr Kenneth Mullan

FINANCE AND TAX CHAMBER
45 Bedford Square, London WC1B 3DN
T 020-7612 9700 E financeandtaxappeals@tribunals.gsi.gov.uk
W www.tribunals.gov.uk/financeandtax

The Finance and Tax Chamber decides applications for permissions to appeal and appeals on point of law from decisions of the Tax Chamber in the first-tier. The judiciary consists of high court judges and specialist tax judiciary, and the tribunal has jurisdiction throughout the UK.
President, Mr Justice Warren

LANDS CHAMBER
43–45 Bedford Square, London WC1B 3AS
T 020-7612 9710 E lands@tribunals.gsi.gov.uk
W www.landstribunal.gov.uk

The Lands tribunal determines questions relating to the valuation of land, rating appeals from valuation tribunals, appeals from leasehold valuation tribunals and residential property tribunals, the discharge or modification of restrictive covenants, and compulsory purchase compensation. The tribunal may also arbitrate under references by consent. Cases are usually heard by a single member but they may sometimes be heard by two or three members.
President, G. R. Bartlett, QC

LANDS TRIBUNAL FOR SCOTLAND
George House, 126 George Street, Edinburgh EH2 4HH
T 0131-271 4350 E mailbox@lands-tribunal-scotland.org.uk
W www.lands-tribunal-scotland.org.uk

The Lands Tribunal for Scotland has much the same remit as the tribunal for England and Wales but also covers questions relating to tenants' rights to buy their homes under the Housing (Scotland) Act 1987. It is not part of the Tribunals Service. The president is appointed by the Lord President of the Court of Session.
President, Hon. Lord McGhie, QC

EMPLOYMENT TRIBUNALS

ENGLAND AND WALES
3rd Floor, Alexandra House, 14–22 The Parsonage, Manchester M3 2JA
T 0845-795 9775 W www.employmenttribunals.gov.uk

Employment Tribunals for England and Wales sit in 12 regions. The tribunals deal with matters of employment law, redundancy, dismissal, contract disputes, sexual, racial and disability discrimination and related areas of dispute which may arise in the workplace. A public register of judgments is held at 100 Southgate Street, Bury St Edmunds, Suffolk IP33 2AQ.

Chairs, who may be full-time or part-time, are legally qualified. They, along with the tribunal members, are appointed by the Ministry of Justice.
President, David John Latham

SCOTLAND
Central Office, Eagle Building, 215 Bothwell Street, Glasgow G2 7TS
T 0141-204 0730

Tribunals in Scotland have the same remit as those in England and Wales. Chairs are appointed by the Lord President of the Court of Session and lay members by the Secretary of State for Trade and Industry.
President, Colin Milne

EMPLOYMENT APPEAL TRIBUNAL

London Office: Audit House, 58 Victoria Embankment, London EC4Y 0DS
T 020-7273 1041 E londoneat@tribunals.gsi.gov.uk
Edinburgh Office: 52 Melville Street, Edinburgh EH3 7HF
T 0131-225 3963
W www.employmentappeals.gov.uk

The Employment Appeal Tribunal hears appeals (on points of law only) arising from decisions made by employment tribunals. Hearings are conducted by a judge, either alone or accompanied by two lay members who have practical experience in employment relations. Administrative support is provided by the Tribunals Service.
President, Hon. Mr Justice Underhill
Registrar, Pauline Donleavy

ASYLUM AND IMMIGRATION TRIBUNAL

PO Box 6987, Leicester LE1 6ZX
T 0845-600 0877 E customer.service@tribunals.gsi.gov.uk
W www.ait.gov.uk

The Asylum and Immigration Tribunal (AIT) hears appeals against decisions made by the Home Office; its powers are derived from the Immigration and Asylum Act 1999. Immigration judges are appointed by the Lord Chancellor and hear appeals against decisions to: refuse asylum under the Refugee Convention; refuse entry into the UK, refuse to issue or extend a visa; deport a person from the UK; or deprive a person of UK citizenship. An appeal against a decision will go before a hearing, where the appellant, his/her representative and a representative from the Home Office will attend before an immigration judge (or panel, sometimes including non-legal members) who will make a determination on whether the appeal should be allowed or dismissed. In certain circumstances, either side may apply for a reconsideration of the determination. Depending on how the appeal was heard (by a single immigration judge or by a panel) will dictate where any applications for reconsideration will be lodged. In early 2010 the AIT will be replaced by specialist asylum and immigration chambers in the First-tier and Upper Tribunals.
President, Hon. Mr Justice Hodge, OBE

FINANCIAL SERVICES AND MARKETS TRIBUNAL

45 Bedford Square, London WC1B 3DN
T 020-7612 9700 E fs&mt@tribunals.gsi.gov.uk
W www.tribunals.gov.uk/finance

The Financial Services and Markets Tribunal hears cases arising from decisions issued by the Financial Services Authority against financial service providers, including banks, clearing houses, stockbrokers and mortgage advisers. The president, a panel of legally qualified chairs and a panel of lay members are all appointed by the Lord Chancellor.
President, His Hon. Sir Stephen Oliver, QC

SPECIAL IMMIGRATION APPEALS COMMISSION

Procession House, 55 Ludgate Hill, London EC4M 7JW
T 0845-600 0877 E siac.poacoffice@tribunals.gsi.gov.uk
W www.siac.tribunals.gov.uk

The commission was set up under the Special Immigration Appeals Commission Act 1997. Its main function is to consider appeals against orders for deportations in cases which involve, in the main, considerations of national security or the public interest. The commission also hears appeals against decisions to deprive persons of citizenship status. Members are appointed by the Lord Chancellor.
Chair, Hon. Mr Justice Mitting

TRANSPORT TRIBUNAL

7th Floor, Victory House, 30–34 Kingsway, London WC2B 6EX
T 020-3077 5860 E transport@tribunals.gsi.gov.uk
W www.transporttribunal.gov.uk

The Transport Tribunal has three jurisdictions: it hears appeals against decisions made by Traffic Commissioners at public inquiries, appeals against decisions of the Registrar of Approved Driving Instructors and is able to resolve disputes under the Postal Services Act 2000. The tribunal consists of a legally qualified president, other judicial members, and lay members. The president and legal members are appointed by the Lord Chancellor and the lay members by the transport secretary. Members of the Transport Tribunal also act as the London Service Permit Appeals Panel. Appeals from decisions made by the Driving Standards Agency are scheduled to transfer to the jurisdiction of the first tier General Regulatory Chamber in September 2009.
President, H. B. H. Carlisle, QC

INDEPENDENT TRIBUNALS

The following tribunals are not administered by the Tribunals Service.

AGRICULTURAL LAND TRIBUNALS

c/o DEFRA, Nobel House, 17 Smith Square, London SW1P 3JR
T 0845-933 5577 E helpline@defra.gsi.gov.uk
W www.defra.gov.uk/farm/working/index.htm

Agricultural Land Tribunals settle disputes and other issues between agricultural landlords and tenants under the Agricultural Holdings Act 1986, and drainage disputes between neighbours under the Land Drainage Act 1991.

There are seven tribunals covering England and one covering Wales. For each tribunal the Lord Chancellor appoints a chair and one or more deputies (barristers or solicitors of at least seven years' standing). The Lord Chancellor also appoints lay members to three statutory panels: the 'landowners' panel, the 'farmers' panel and the 'drainage' panel.

Each tribunal is an independent statutory body with jurisdiction only within its own geographical area. A separate tribunal is constituted for each case, and consists of a chair and two lay members nominated by the chair.
Chairs (England), Shirley Evans; His Hon. John Machin; George Newsom; Paul de la Piquerie; His Hon. Robert Taylor; Nigel Thomas; Martin Wood
Chair (Wales), James Buxton

CIVIL AVIATION AUTHORITY

CAA House, 45–59 Kingsway, London WC2B 6TE
T 020-7453 6162 E legal@caa.co.uk
W www.caa.co.uk

The Civil Aviation Authority (CAA) does not have a separate tribunal department as such, but for certain purposes the CAA must conform to tribunal requirements. For example, to deal with appeals against the refusal or revocation of aviation licences and certificates issued by the CAA, and the allocation of routes outside of the EU to airlines.

The chair and four non-executive members who may sit on panels for tribunal purposes are appointed by the Secretary of State for Transport.
Chair, Dame Deirdre Hutton, DBE

COMMONS COMMISSIONERS

Area 3C, Nobel House, 17 Smith Square, London SW1P 3JR
T 020-7238 4492 E commons.commissioners@defra.gsi.gov.uk

The Commons Commissioners are responsible for deciding disputes about boundaries, ownership or rights for common land arising under the Commons Registration Act 1965. They also enquire into the ownership of unclaimed common land and village greens. Commissioners must be barristers or solicitors of at least seven years' standing and are appointed by the Lord Chancellor. The work of the Commissioners is due to end in 2009–10.
Chief Commons Commissioner, Edward Cousins

COMPETITION APPEAL TRIBUNAL

Victoria House, Bloomsbury Place, London WC1A 2EB
T 020-7979 7979 E info@catribunal.org.uk
W www.catribunal.org.uk

The Competition Appeal Tribunal (CAT) is a specialist tribunal established to hear certain cases in the sphere of UK competition and economic regulatory law. It hears appeals against decisions of the Office of Fair Trading (OFT) and their sectoral regulators, and also decisions of the OFT, Secretary of State for Trade and Industry and Competition Commission. The CAT also has jurisdiction to award damages in respect of infringements of EC or UK competition law and to hear appeals against decisions of OFCOM.

Cases are heard before a panel consisting of three members: either the president or a member of the panel of chairmen and two ordinary members. The members of the panel of chairmen are judges of the Chancery Division of the high court and other senior lawyers. The ordinary members have expertise in law and/or related fields. The president and chairmen are appointed by the Lord Chancellor; the ordinary members are appointed by the secretary of state.
President, Hon. Mr Justice Barling

COPYRIGHT TRIBUNAL

Room 2G31, Concept House, Cardiff Road, Newport NP10 9FU
T 01633-811035 E copyright.tribunal@ipo.gov.uk
W www.ipo.gov.uk/copy/tribunal

The Copyright Tribunal resolves disputes over the terms and conditions of licences offered by, or licensing schemes operated by, collective licensing bodies in the copyright and related rights area. Its decisions are appealable to the high court on points of law only.

The chair and two deputy chairs are appointed by the Lord Chancellor. Up to eight ordinary members are appointed by the Secretary of State for Trade and Industry. The tribunal operates on a panel basis and its members have wide expertise in business, public administration and the professions.
Chair, His Hon. Judge Fysh, QC

INDUSTRIAL TRIBUNALS AND THE FAIR EMPLOYMENT TRIBUNAL (NORTHERN IRELAND)

Killymeal House, 2 Cromac Quay, Ormeau Road, Belfast BT7 2JD
T 028-9032 7666 E mail@employmenttribunalsni.org
W www.employmenttribunalsni.co.uk

The industrial tribunal system in Northern Ireland was set up in 1965 and has a similar remit to the employment tribunals in the rest of the UK. There is also a Fair Employment Tribunal, which hears and determines individual cases of alleged religious or political discrimination in employment. Employers can appeal to the Fair Employment Tribunal if they consider the directions of the Equality Commission to be unreasonable, inappropriate or unnecessary, and the Equality Commission can make application to the tribunal for the enforcement of undertakings or directions with which an employer has not complied.

The president, vice-president and chairs of the Industrial Tribunal and the Fair Employment Tribunal are appointed by the Lord Chancellor. The panel members to both the industrial tribunals and the Fair Employment Tribunal were appointed by the Department for Employment and Learning, but any future appointments will be made through a full public appointment process.
President of the Industrial Tribunals and the Fair Employment Tribunal, Eileen McBride

INVESTIGATORY POWERS TRIBUNAL

PO Box 33220, London SW1H 9ZQ
T 020-7035 3711 W www.ipt-uk.com

The Investigatory Powers Tribunal replaced the Interception of Communications Tribunal, the Intelligence Services Tribunal, the Security Services Tribunal and the complaints function of the commissioner appointed under the Police Act 1997.

The Regulation of Investigatory Powers Act 2000 (RIPA) provides for a tribunal made up of senior members of the legal profession, independent of the government and appointed by the Queen, to consider all complaints against the intelligence services and those against public authorities in respect of powers covered by RIPA; and to consider proceedings brought under section 7 of the Human Rights Act 1998 against the intelligence services and law enforcement agencies in respect of these powers.
President, Rt. Hon. Lord Justice Mummery

NATIONAL HEALTH SERVICE TRIBUNAL (SCOTLAND)

Fyfe Ireland LLP, 6 Blythswood Square, Glasgow G2 4AD
T 0141-222 2216

The Scottish National Health Service Tribunal considers representations that the continued inclusion of a family health service practitioner (eg a doctor, dentist, optometrist or pharmacist) on a health board's list would

be prejudicial to the efficiency of the service concerned, by virtue either of fraudulent practices or unsatisfactory personal or professional conduct. If this is established, the tribunal has the power to disqualify practitioners from working in the NHS family health services. The tribunal sits when required and is composed of a chair, one lay member, and one practitioner member drawn from a representative professional panel. The chair is appointed by the Lord President of the Court of Session, and the lay member and the members of the professional panel are appointed by the Scottish ministers.
Chair, J. Michael D. Graham

RESIDENTIAL PROPERTY TRIBUNAL SERVICE

10 Alfred Place, London WC1E 7LR
T 020-7446 7700 **E** rptscorporateunit@communities.gsi.gov.uk
W www.rpts.gov.uk

The Residential Property Tribunal Service provides members to sit on panels for the Rent Assessment Committees, Residential Property Tribunals and Leasehold Valuation Tribunals, and serves the private-rented and leasehold property market in England by resolving disputes between leaseholders, tenants and landlords. The president and chair are appointed by the Lord Chancellor and other members are appointed by the Department for Communities and Local Government and the Ministry of Justice.
Senior President, Siobhan McGrath

SOLICITORS' DISCIPLINARY TRIBUNAL

3rd Floor, Gate House, 1 Farringdon Street, London EC4M 7NS
T 020-7329 4808 **E** enquiries@solicitorsdt.com
W www.solicitorstribunal.org.uk

The Solicitors' Disciplinary Tribunal is an independent statutory body whose members are appointed by the Master of the Rolls. The tribunal considers applications made to it alleging either professional misconduct and/or a breach of the statutory rules by which solicitors are bound against an individually named solicitor, former solicitor, registered foreign lawyer, or solicitor's clerk. The tribunal has around 30 members, two thirds are solicitor members and one third are lay members. The president, solicitor members and lay members are remunerated by the Ministry of Justice.
President, A. Isaacs

SOLICITORS' DISCIPLINE TRIBUNAL (SCOTTISH)

Unit 3.5, The Granary Business Centre, Coal Road, Cupar, Fife KY15 5YQ
T 01334-659088 **W** www.ssdt.org.uk

The Scottish Solicitors' Discipline Tribunal is an independent statutory body with a panel of 25 members, 13 of whom are solicitors; members are appointed by the Lord President of the Court of Session. Its principal function is to consider complaints of misconduct against solicitors in Scotland.
Chair, A. Cockburn

TRAFFIC PENALTY TRIBUNAL

Barlow House, Minshull Street, Manchester M1 3DZ
T 0161-242 5252 **E** info@trafficpenaltytribunal.gov.uk
W www.trafficpenaltytribunal.gov.uk

The Traffic Penalty Tribunal considers appeals from motorists against penalty charge notices issued by Civil Enforcement Authorities in England and Wales (outside London) under the Road Traffic Act 1991 and the Traffic Management Act 2004, and considers appeals against bus lane contraventions in England (outside London). Parking adjudicators are appointed with the express consent of the Lord Chancellor and must be lawyers of five years' standing. Cases are decided by a single adjudicator, either in a postal, telephone or a personal hearing.
Head of Service, Louise Hutchinson

VALUATION TRIBUNAL SERVICE

2nd Floor, Black Lion House, 45 Whitechapel Road, London E1 1DU
T 020-7426 3900 **W** www.valuation-tribunals.gov.uk

The Valuation Tribunal Service (VTS) was created as a corporate body by the Local Government Act 2003, and is responsible for providing or arranging the services required for the operation of the valuation tribunal for England. The VTS board is comprised of a chair and members appointed by the secretary of state. The VTS is funded by the Department for Communities and Local Government.
Chair, VTS Board, Anne Galbraith, OBE

VALUATION TRIBUNAL FOR ENGLAND

President's Office, 2nd Floor, Black Lion House, 45 Whitechapel Road, London E1 1DU
T 020 7246 3900 **W** www.valuation-tribunals.gov.uk

The Valuation Tribunal for England (VTE) came into being on 1 October 2009, replacing 56 valuation tribunals in England. Provision for the VTE was made in the Local Government and Public Involvement in Health Act 2007. The Valuation Tribunal for England hears appeals concerning council tax and non-domestic rating and land drainage rates. A separate tribunal is constituted for each hearing, and consists of a chair and two or three other members. A clerk, who is a paid employee of the VTS, is present to advise on points of procedure and law. The national president is the judicial head of a volunteer membership. Members will in future be appointed by the Judicial Appointments Commission.
President, Prof. Graham Zellick

VALUATION TRIBUNAL SERVICE FOR WALES

Governing Council of VTSW, Dinerth Road, Rhos on Sea, Colwyn Bay LL28 4UL
T 01492-546610 **E** northwales.vt@vto.gsx.gov.uk

The Valuation Tribunal Service for Wales (VTSW) was created under the Valuation Tribunals (Wales) Regulations 2005, and is responsible for providing or arranging the services required for the operation of the four tribunals in Wales. The governing council of the VTSW is comprised of four regional presidents, one of whom is elected director together with one member who is appointed by the National Assembly for Wales. The VTSW tribunals hear appeals concerning council tax and non-domestic rating, and land drainage rates in Wales. An individual tribunal, supported by a clerk, is constituted for each hearing and is normally serviced by three members, one of whom also chairs.
Chief Executive, Simon Hill

OMBUDSMAN SERVICES

The following section is a listing of selected ombudsman services. Ombudsmen are a free, independent and impartial means of resolving certain disputes outside of the courts. These disputes are, in the majority of cases, concerned with whether something has been badly or unfairly handled (for example due to delay, neglect, inefficiency or failure to follow proper procedures). Most ombudsman schemes are established by statute; they cover various public and private bodies and generally examine matters only after the relevant body has been given a reasonable opportunity to deal with the complaint.

After conducting an investigation an ombudsman will usually issue a written report, which normally suggests a resolution to the dispute and often includes recommendations concerning the improvement of procedures.

BRITISH AND IRISH OMBUDSMAN ASSOCIATION (BIOA)

PO Box 308, Twickenham TW1 9BE
T 020-8894 9272 E secretary@bioa.org.uk
W www.bioa.org.uk

The BIOA was established in 1994 and exists to provide information for the public about ombudsmen and other complaint-handling services. An ombudsman scheme must meet four conditions to attain BIOA membership – independence from the organisations the ombudsman has the power to investigate, fairness, effectiveness and public accountability. Membership is open to ombudsmen schemes from the UK, Ireland, the Channel Islands, the Isle of Man and British overseas territories.

The following is a selection of organisations that are members of the BIOA.
Chair, Emily O'Reilly
Secretary, Ian Pattison

FINANCIAL OMBUDSMAN SERVICE

South Quay Plaza, 183 Marsh Wall, London E14 9SR
T 020-7964 1000
E complaint.info@financial-ombudsman.org.uk
W www.financial-ombudsman.org.uk

The Financial Ombudsman Service settles individual disputes between businesses providing financial services and their customers. The service deals with around a million enquiries every year and settles over 100,000 disputes. The service examines complaints about most financial matters, including banking, insurance, mortgages, pensions, savings, loans and credit cards. *See also* Banking and Finance.
Chief Ombudsman, Walter Merricks, CBE
Chair, Sir Christopher Kelly, KCB

HOUSING OMBUDSMAN SERVICE

81 Aldwych, London WC2B 4HN
T 020-7421 3800 E info@housing-ombudsman.org.uk
W www.housing-ombudsman.org.uk

The Housing Ombudsman Service, established in 1997, deals with complaints and disputes involving tenants and housing associations and social landlords, certain private sector landlords and managing agents. The ombudsman has a statutory jurisdiction over all registered social landlords in England. Private and other landlords can join the service on a voluntary basis. Complaints from council/local authority tenants have to be made to the Local Government Ombudsman.
Ombudsman, Dr Mike Biles
Deputy Ombudsman, Rafael Runco

INDEPENDENT POLICE COMPLAINTS COMMISSION (IPCC)

90 High Holborn, London WC1V 6BH
T 0845-300 2002 E enquiries@ipcc.gsi.gov.uk
W www.ipcc.gov.uk

The IPCC succeeded the Police Complaints Authority in 2004. It was established under the Police Reform Act 2002. The IPCC has teams of investigators headed by directors in each of its regions to assist with the supervision and management of some police investigations. They also carry out independent investigations into serious incidents or allegations of misconduct by persons serving with the police. The IPCC decides on appeals against complaints investigated by the police service. It also has responsibility for investigating complaints of serious incidents, including death or injury, made against staff of HM Revenue and Customs, the Serious Organised Crime Agency and the United Kingdom Border Agency. The 12 commissioners of the IPCC must not previously have worked for the police.
Chair, Nick Hardwick
Deputy Chairs, Deborah Glass; Len Jackson
Chief Executive, Jane Furniss

LOCAL GOVERNMENT OMBUDSMAN

Advice Team, PO Box 4771, Coventry CV4 0EH
T 0300-061 0614 W www.lgo.org.uk

The Local Government Ombudsman deals with complaints of injustice arising from maladministration by local authorities and certain other bodies.

There are three ombudsmen in England, each with responsibility for different regions; they aim to provide satisfactory redress for complainants and better administration for the authorities. The ombudsmen investigate complaints about most council matters, including housing, planning, education, social care, consumer protection, drainage and council tax. *See also* Local Government.
Local Government Ombudsmen, Tony Redmond; Anne Seex; Jerry White

NORTHERN IRELAND OMBUDSMAN

Progressive House, 33 Wellington Place, Belfast BT1 6HN
T 028-9023 3821 E ombudsman@ni-ombudsman.org.uk
W www.ni-ombudsman.org.uk

The ombudsman (also known as the Assembly Ombudsman for Northern Ireland and the Northern Ireland Commissioner for Complaints) is appointed under

legislation with powers to investigate complaints by people claiming to have sustained injustice arising from action taken by a Northern Ireland government department, or any other public body within his remit. The ombudsman can investigate all local councils, education and library boards, health and social services boards and trusts, as well as all government departments and their agencies. As commissioner for complaints, the ombudsman can investigate complaints about doctors, dentists, pharmacists, optometrists and other healthcare professionals.
Ombudsman, Dr Tom Frawley, CBE
Deputy Ombudsman, Marie Anderson

OFFICE OF THE LEGAL SERVICES OMBUDSMAN

3rd Floor, Sunlight House, Quay Street, Manchester M3 3JZ
T 0161-839 7262, 0845-601 0794 **E** lso@olso.gsi.gov.uk
W www.olso.org

The Legal Services Ombudsman oversees the handling of complaints against solicitors, barristers, licensed conveyancers, legal executives, patent attorneys and trademark attorneys by their professional bodies. A complainant must first complain to the relevant professional body before raising the matter with the ombudsman, who will then investigate the way the complaint was dealt with. The ombudsman is independent of the legal profession and her services are free of charge, although she is unable to give legal advice.
Ombudsman, Zahida Manzoor, CBE
Operations Manager, Gavin Brown

OFFICE OF THE PENSIONS OMBUDSMAN

6th Floor, 11 Belgrave Road, London SW1V 1RB
T 020-7630 2200 **E** enquiries@pensions-ombudsman.org.uk
W www.pensions-ombudsman.org.uk

The Pensions Ombudsman is appointed by the Secretary of State for Work and Pensions, under the Pension Schemes Act 1993 as amended by the Pensions Act 1995. He investigates and decides complaints and disputes about the way that personal and occupational pension schemes are run. As the Ombudsman for the Board of the Pension Protection Fund, he can deal with disputes about the decisions made by the board or the actions of their staff. He also deals with appeals against decisions made by the scheme manager under the Financial Assistance Scheme.
Pensions Ombudsman, Tony King

PARLIAMENTARY AND HEALTH SERVICE OMBUDSMAN

Millbank Tower, Millbank, London SW1P 4QP
T 0345-015 4033 **E** phso.enquiries@ombudsman.org.uk
W www.ombudsman.org.uk

The Parliamentary Ombudsman (also known as the Parliamentary Commissioner for Administration) is independent of government and is an officer of parliament. She is responsible for investigating complaints referred to her by MPs from members of the public who claim to have sustained injustice in consequence of maladministration by or on behalf of government departments and certain non-departmental public bodies. In 1999 an additional 158 public bodies were brought within the jurisdiction of the Parliamentary Ombudsman. Certain types of action by government departments or bodies are excluded from investigation.

The Health Service Ombudsman for England is responsible for investigating complaints against National Health Service authorities and trusts that are not dealt with by those authorities to the satisfaction of the complainant. Complaints can be referred directly by the member of the public who claims to have sustained injustice or hardship in consequence of the failure in a service provided by a relevant body. The ombudsman's jurisdiction now covers complaints about family doctors, dentists, pharmacists and opticians, and complaints about actions resulting from clinical judgement.

The Health Service Ombudsman is also responsible for investigating complaints that information has been wrongly refused under the Code of Practice on Openness in the National Health Service 1995. The parliamentary and the health offices are presently held by the same person.
Parliamentary Ombudsman and Health Service Ombudsman, Ms A. Abraham
Deputy Ombudsman, Ms K. Hudson

PROPERTY OMBUDSMAN

Beckett House, 4 Bridge Street, Salisbury, Wiltshire SP1 2LX
T 01722-333306 **E** admin@tpos.co.uk
W www.tpos.co.uk

The Property Ombudsman service was established in 1998 and provides a service for dealing with disputes between estate agents and consumers who are actual or potential buyers or sellers of residential property, or residential letting agents, in the UK.

Complaints that the ombudsman considers include allegations of unfair treatment, maladministration and infringement of legal rights. The ombudsman's role is to resolve these complaints in full and final settlement and, where appropriate, make an award of financial compensation.
Ombudsman, Christopher Hamer

PUBLIC SERVICES OMBUDSMAN FOR WALES

1 Ffordd yr Hen Gae, Pencoed CF35 5LJ
T 01656-641150 **E** ask@ombudsman-wales.org.uk
W www.ombudsman-wales.org.uk

The office of Public Services Ombudsman for Wales was established, with effect from 1 April 2006, by the Public Services Ombudsman (Wales) Act 2005. The ombudsman, who is appointed by the Queen, investigates complaints of injustice caused by maladministration or service failure by the National Assembly for Wales Commission (and public bodies sponsored by the assembly); Welsh Assembly Government; National Health Service bodies, including GPs, family health service providers and hospitals; registered social landlords; local authorities, including community councils; fire and rescue authorities; police authorities; national park authorities; and countryside and environmental organisations. Free leaflets explaining the process of making a complaint are available from the ombudsman's office.
Ombudsman, Peter Tyndall

REMOVALS INDUSTRY OMBUDSMAN SCHEME

PO Box 771 Tring, Hertfordshire HP23 5XB
T 01442-891736 **E** removalombudsman@btconnect.com
W www.removalsombudsman.org.uk

The Removals Industry Ombudsman Scheme was established to resolve disputes between removal companies that are members of the scheme and their clients, both domestic and commercial. The ombudsman investigates complaints such as breaches of contract, unprofessional conduct, delays, or breaches in the code of practice.
Ombudsman, Shelley Radice

SCOTTISH PUBLIC SERVICES OMBUDSMAN

Freepost EH641, Edinburgh EH3 0BR
T 0800-377 7330 **E** ask@spso.org.uk
W www.spso.org.uk

The Scottish Public Services Ombudsman (SPSO) was established in 2002. The ombudsman investigates complaints about Scottish government departments and agencies, councils, housing associations, the National Health Service (NHS), the Scottish Parliamentary Corporate Body and most other public bodies. The public bodies that the SPSO may consider investigating are contained in a list outlined in the Scottish Public Services Ombudsman Act 2002. The ombudsman's remit was extended in 2005 to cover Scotland's further education colleges and higher education institutions. Complaints considered by the ombudsman include complaints about poor service, failure to provide a service and administrative failure.
Scottish Public Services Ombudsman, Jim Martin

THE OMBUDSMAN SERVICE LTD

Wilderspool Park, Greenalls Avenue, Warrington WA4 6HL
W www.tosl.org.uk

The Ombudsman Service Limited (TOSL) is a not-for-profit private limited company that administers three ombudsman services – the Energy Ombudsman, Otelo (the Office of the Telecommunications Ombudsman) and the Surveyors Ombudsman Service.

The Energy Ombudsman resolves disputes between domestic and small business customers and their gas and electricity companies.

Otelo deals with complaints from consumers concerning public communications providers (any company that provides an electronic communications network or service to members of the public or small businesses).

The Surveyors Ombudsman Service investigates complaints made about the service provided by chartered surveyors and estate agents, for example a breach of legal obligations, avoidable delays, discourtesy or incompetence.
Chair, Peter Holland, CBE
Chief Ombudsman, Lewis Shand Smith
Ombudsmen, Elizabeth France, CBE *(Surveyors)*; Dr Richard Sills *(Energy)*; Andrew Walker *(Otelo)*

ENERGY OMBUDSMAN

PO Box 966, Warrington WA4 9DF
T 0330-440 1624
E enquiries@energy-ombudsman.org.uk
W www.energy-ombudsman.org.uk

OTELO

PO Box 730, Warrington WA4 6WU
T 0300-440 1614
E enquiries@otelo.org.uk **W** www.otelo.org.uk

SURVEYORS OMBUDSMAN SERVICE

PO Box 1021, Warrington WA4 9FE
T 0300-440 1635
E enquiries@surveyors-ombudsman.org.uk
W www.surveyors-ombudsman.org.uk

WATERWAYS OMBUDSMAN

PO Box 35, York YO60 6WW
T 01347-879075 **E** enquiries@waterways-ombudsman.org
W www.waterways-ombudsman.org

The Waterways Ombudsman considers complaints of maladministration or unfairness made against British Waterways or its subsidiaries, including British Waterways Marinas Limited. Complaints concerning the waterways responsibilities of the Environment Agency should be directed to the Parliamentary and Health Service Ombudsman.
Ombudsman, Hilary Bainbridge

THE POLICE SERVICE

There are 52 police forces in the United Kingdom: 43 in England and Wales, including the Metropolitan Police and the City of London Police, eight in Scotland and the Police Service of Northern Ireland. Most forces' areas are coterminous with one or more local authority areas. The Isle of Man, States of Jersey and Guernsey have their own forces responsible for policing in their respective islands and bailiwicks. The Serious Organised Crime Agency (SOCA) is responsible for the investigation of national and international serious organised crime.

Police authorities are independent bodies, responsible for the supervision of local policing. There are 43 police authorities in England and Wales, plus an additional one for British Transport Police. Most police authorities have 17 members, comprising nine local councillors and eight independent members, of whom at least one must be a magistrate. Authorities which are responsible for larger areas may have more members, such as the Metropolitan Police Authority which has 23 members: 12 drawn from the London Assembly, 10 independent members and one magistrate. The Corporation of London acts as the police authority for the City of London Police. In Scotland, six of the forces are maintained by joint police boards, made up of local councillors from each council in the force area; the other two constabularies (Dumfries & Galloway and Fife) are directly administered by their respective councils. The Northern Ireland Policing Board is an independent public body consisting of 19 political and independent members.

Police forces in England, Scotland and Wales are financed by central and local government grants and a precept on the council tax. The Police Service of Northern Ireland is wholly funded by central government. The police authorities, subject to the approval of the home secretary (in England and Wales), the Northern Ireland secretary and to regulations, are responsible for appointing the Chief Constable. In England and Wales the latter are responsible for the force's budget, levying the precept on the council tax, publishing annual policing plans and reports, setting local objectives, monitoring performance targets and appointing or dismissing senior officers. In Scotland the police authorities are responsible for setting the force's budget, providing the resources necessary to police the area adequately and appointing officers of the rank of Assistant Chief Constable and above. In Northern Ireland, the Northern Ireland Policing Board exercises similar functions.

The home secretary, the Northern Ireland secretary and the Scottish government are responsible for the organisation, administration and operation of the police service. They regulate police ranks, discipline, hours of duty and pay and allowances. All police forces are subject to inspection by HM Inspectors of Constabulary, who report to the home secretary, Scottish government or the Northern Ireland secretary.

COMPLAINTS

The Independent Police Complaints Commission (IPCC) was established under the Police Reform Act 2002 and became operational on 1 April 2004. The IPCC is responsible for carrying out independent investigations into serious incidents or allegations of misconduct by those serving with the police in England and Wales, HM Revenue and Customs, the Serious Organised Crime Agency (SOCA) and the UK Border Agency. It has the power to initiate, undertake and oversee investigations and is also responsible for the way complaints are handled by local police forces. Complaints regarding local operational issues or quality of service should be made directly to the Chief Constable of the police force concerned or to the local police authority.

If a complaint is relatively minor, the police force will attempt to resolve it internally and an official investigation might not be required. In more serious cases the IPCC or police force may refer the case to the Crown Prosecution Service, which will decide whether to bring criminal charges against the officer(s) involved. An officer who is dismissed, required to resign or reduced in rank, whether as a result of a complaint or not, can appeal to a police appeals tribunal established by the relevant police authority.

Under the Police, Public Order and Criminal Justice (Scotland) Act 2006, which came into force on 1 April 2007, the Police Complaints Commissioner for Scotland is responsible for providing independent scrutiny of the way Scottish police forces, authorities and policing agencies handle complaints from the public. The commissioner also has the power to direct police forces to re-examine any complaints which are not considered to have been dealt with satisfactorily. If there is a suggestion of criminal activity, the complaint is investigated by a procurator fiscal.

The Police Ombudsman for Northern Ireland provides an independent police complaints system for Northern Ireland, dealing with all stages of the complaints procedure. Complaints that cannot be resolved informally are investigated and the ombudsman recommends a suitable course of action to the Chief Constable of the Police Service of Northern Ireland or the Northern Ireland Policing Board based on the investigation's findings. The ombudsman may recommend that a police officer be prosecuted, but the decision to prosecute a police officer rests with the Director of Public Prosecutions.

INDEPENDENT POLICE COMPLAINTS COMMISSION, 5th Floor, 90 High Holborn, London WC1V 6BH **T** 0845-300 2002 **E** enquiries@ipcc.gsi.gov.uk **W** www.ipcc.gov.uk

POLICE COMPLAINTS COMMISSIONER FOR SCOTLAND, PO Box 26300, Hamilton, ML3 3AR **T** 0808-178 5577 **E** enquiries@pcc-scotland.org **W** www.pcc-scotland.org
Police Complaints Commissioner for Scotland, Jim Martin

POLICE OMBUDSMAN FOR NORTHERN IRELAND, New Cathedral Buildings, St Anne's Square, 11 Church Street, Belfast BT1 1PG **T** 028-9082 8600 **E** info@policeombudsman.org **W** www.policeombudsman.org
Police Ombudsman, Al Hutchinson

POLICE SERVICES

FORENSIC SCIENCE SERVICE

Headquarters: Trident Court, 2920 Solihull Parkway, Birmingham Business Park, Birmingham B37 7YN
T 0121-329 5200 W www.forensic.gov.uk

The Forensic Science Service (FSS) is a government-owned company which is independent from the police service. It provides forensic science and technology services to police forces in England and Wales and other law enforcement agencies such as the Crown Prosecution Service, SOCA, MoD Police and Guarding Agency, British Transport Police and HM Revenue and Customs. Services are also available to defence lawyers and commercial companies. The FSS primarily covers England and Wales but can provide services worldwide.
Chair, Bill Griffiths

NATIONAL EXTREMISM TACTICAL COORDINATION UNIT

PO Box 525, Huntingdon PE29 9AL
T 01480-425091 E mailbox@netcu.pnn.police.uk
W www.netcu.org.uk

The National Extremism Tactical Coordination Unit (NETCU) provides the police service of England and Wales and other law enforcement agencies with tactical advice and guidance on policing domestic extremism and associated criminality. The unit also supports organisations and companies that are the targets of domestic extremism campaigns. NETCU is funded by the Home Office, is accountable to the National Coordinator for Domestic Extremism and forms part of the Association of Chief Police Officers' Terrorism and Allied Matters business unit.
National Coordinator for Domestic Extremism, Anton Setchell

NATIONAL POLICING IMPROVEMENT AGENCY

4th Floor, 10–18 Victoria Street, London SW1H 0NN
T 020-7147 8200 W www.npia.police.uk

Established under the Police and Justice Act 2006 the National Policing Improvement Agency (NPIA) is a non-departmental public body sponsored and funded by the Home Office, with its executive leadership drawn from the police service.The NPIA is owned and governed by the board which comprises representatives of the Association of Chief Police Officers, the Association of Police Authorities and the Home Office, in addition to the chair, chief executive and two independent members. The board is responsible for agreeing the budget and setting the objectives for the NPIA.

The NPIA's remit is to ensure that agreed programmes of reforms are implemented and good practice is applied throughout the police service. It is responsible for the procurement and deployment of information and communications technology systems to support and improve policing and works actively with police forces to develop a wide range of learning and professional development programmes. The NPIA is charged with improving policing in England and Wales but it is also connected to policing bodies in Scotland and Northern Ireland and collaborates with them on some initiatives.
Chief Executive, Peter Neyroud, QPM
Chair, Peter Holland, CBE

NPIA MISSING PERSONS BUREAU

Foxley Hall, Bramshill, Hook, Hampshire RG27 0JW
T 01256-602979
E missingpersonsbureau@npia.pnn.police.uk
W www.missingpersons.police.uk

The NPIA Missing Persons Bureau was launched in April 2008 within the National Policing Improvement Agency. The NPIA Missing Persons Bureau acts as the centre for the exchange of information connected with the search for missing persons nationally and internationally alongside the police and other related organisations. The unit focuses on cross-matching missing persons with unidentified persons or bodies by maintaining records, including a dental index of ante-mortem chartings of long-term missing persons and post-mortem chartings from unidentified bodies. The bureau also manages the missing children website (W www.missingkids.co.uk) and coordinates the child rescue alert services.

Information is supplied and collected for all persons who have been missing in the UK for over three days (or less where police deem appropriate), foreign nationals reported missing in the UK, UK nationals reported missing abroad and all unidentified bodies and persons found within the UK.

SERIOUS ORGANISED CRIME AGENCY

PO Box 8000, London SE11 5EN T 0370-496 7622
W www.soca.gov.uk

The Serious Organised Crime Agency (SOCA) is an executive non-departmental public body sponsored by, but operationally independent from, the Home Office. The agency was formed in April 2006 from the amalgamation of the National Crime Squad, National Criminal Intelligence Service, the part of HM Revenue and Customs responsible for dealing with drug trafficking and associated criminal finance and the part of the UK Immigration Service responsible for dealing with organised immigration crime. In April 2008 the Assests Recovery Agency merged with SOCA.

SOCA broadly aims to apportion around 40 per cent of its operational effort in tackling primarily Class A drugs trafficking, around 25 per cent of its capabilities towards organised immigration crime, 10 per cent on individual and private sector fraud and 15 per cent to deal with other organised crime. SOCA works closely with other law enforcement agencies and organisations and the remaining 10 per cent of its capabilities is specifically set aside for assisting its law enforcement partners in achieving their objectives.
Chair, Sir Stephen Lander, KCB
Director-General, William Hughes, QPM

POLICE FORCES

ENGLAND*

Force	*Telephone*	*Strength†*	*Chief Constable*
Avon and Somerset	0845-456 7000	3,401	C. Port
Bedfordshire	01234-841212	1,230	Gillian Parker, QPM
Cambridgeshire	0845-456 4564	1,397	Julie Spence, OBE
Cheshire	01244-350000	2,292	D. Whatton
Cleveland	01642-326326	1,727	Sean Price, QPM
Cumbria	0845-330 0247	1,262	Craig Mackey, QPM
Derbyshire	0845-123 3333	2,072	M. Creedon
Devon and Cornwall	0845-277 7444	3,555	Stephen Otter, QPM
Dorset	01202-222222	1,490	M. Baker, QPM
Durham	0345-606 0365	1,609	T. Stoddart, QPM
Essex	0300-333 4444	3,516	R. Baker, QPM
Gloucestershire	0845-090 1234	1,385	Dr Timothy Brain, OBE, QPM
Greater Manchester	0161-872 5050	8,119	Peter Fahy, QPM
Hampshire	0845-045 4545	3,848	Alex Marshall
Hertfordshire	01707-354000	2,151	Frank Whiteley, QPM
Humberside	0845-606 0222	2,140	Tim Hollis, QPM
Kent	01622-690690	3,724	Michael Fuller, QPM
Lancashire	01772-614444	3,630	Stephen Finnigan, QPM
Leicestershire	0116-222 2222	2,300	Matt Baggott, CBE, QPM
Lincolnshire	01522-532222	956	R. Crompton
Merseyside	0151-709 6010	4,504	B. Hogan-Howe, QPM
North Yorkshire	0845-606 0247	1,481	Grahame Maxwell
Norfolk	0845-456 4567	1,664	Ian McPherson, QPM
Northamptonshire	0845-370 0700	1,347	Peter Maddison
Northumbria	01661-872555	4,034	M. Craik, QPM
Nottinghamshire	0115-967 0900	2,368	J. Hodson, QPM
South Yorkshire	0114-220 2020	3,124	M. Hughes, QPM
Staffordshire	0300-123 4455	2,297	Chris Sims, OBE
Suffolk	01473-613500	1,359	Simon Ash
Surrey	0845-125 2222	2,011	Mark Rowley
Sussex	0845-607 0999	3,124	Martin Richards
Thames Valley	0845-850 5505	4,280	Sara Thornton, QPM
Warwickshire	01926-415000	1,028	Keith Bristow, QPM
West Mercia	0300-333 3000	2,495	Paul West, QPM
West Midlands	0845-113 5000	8,682	Sir Paul Scott-Lee, QPM
West Yorkshire	01924-375222	5,892	Sir Norman Bettison
Wiltshire	0845-408 7000	1,217	Brian Moore, QPM
WALES			
Dyfed-Powys	0845-330 2000	1,196	Ian Arundale
Gwent	01633-838111	1,492	M. Giannasi
North Wales	0845-607 1001	1,576	R. Brunstrom, QPM
South Wales	01656-655555	3,242	Barbara Wilding, CBE, QPM
SCOTLAND			
Central Scotland	01786-456000	827	Kevin Smith
Dumfries and Galloway	0845-600 5701	525	Patrick Shearer, QPM
Fife	0845-600 5702	1,073	Norma Graham, QPM
Grampian	0845-600 5700	1,467	Colin McKerracher, CBE, QPM
Lothian and Borders	0131-311 3131	2,864	David Strang, QPM
Northern	01463-715555	732	Ian Latimer
Strathclyde	0141-532 2000	7,400	Stephen House, QPM
Tayside	0845-600 5705	1,164	Kevin Mathieson
NORTHERN IRELAND			
Police Service of NI	0845-600 8000	7,909	Sir Hugh Orde, OBE
ISLANDS			
Isle of Man	01624-631212	236	Mike Langdon, QPM
States of Jersey	01534-612612	246	Graham Power, QPM
Guernsey	01481-725111	177	G. Le Page, QPM

* For the City of London Police and the Metropolitan Police Service *see* London Forces

† Size of force as at February 2009

Source: R. Hazell & Co. *Police and Constabulary Almanac 2009*

LONDON FORCES

CITY OF LONDON POLICE

37 Wood Street, London EC2P 2NQ **T** 020-7601 2222
W www.cityoflondon.police.uk
Strength (February 2009), 825

Though small, the City of London has one of the most important financial centres in the world and the force has particular expertise in areas such as fraud investigation. The force has a wholly elected police authority, the police committee of the Corporation of London, which appoints the commissioner.
Commissioner, Mike Bowron, QPM
Assistant Commissioner, Frank Armstrong
Commander, Patrick Rice

METROPOLITAN POLICE SERVICE

New Scotland Yard, 8–10 Broadway, London SW1H 0BG
T 020-7230 1212 **W** www.met.police.uk
Strength (February 2009), 30,674
Commissioner, Sir Paul Stephenson, QPM
Deputy Commissioner (acting), Tim Godwin, OBE, QPM

The Metropolitan Police Service is divided into four main areas for operational purposes:

TERRITORIAL POLICING
Most of the day-to-day policing of London is carried out by 33 borough operational command units; 32 command units operate within the same boundaries as the London borough councils, plus there is an additional unit which is responsible for policing Heathrow airport.
Assistant Commissioner (acting), Rose Fitzpatrick

SPECIALIST CRIME DIRECTORATE
The Specialist Crime Directorate's main areas of focus are dismantling criminal networks of all levels, from neighbourhood street gangs to sophisticated international operations, and seizing their assets; safeguarding children and young people from physical, sexual and emotional abuse; and the investigation and prevention of homicide.
Assistant Commissioner (acting), Janet Williams

SPECIALIST OPERATIONS
Specialist Operations is divided into three commands:
- *Counter Terrorism Command* is responsible for the prevention and disruption of terrorist activity, domestic extremism and related offences both within London and nationally, providing an explosives disposal and chemical, biological, radiological and nuclear capability within London, assisting the security services in fulfilling their roles and providing a single point of contact for international partners in counter-terrorism matters
- *Protection Command* is responsible for the protection and security of high-profile persons; key public figures, including the royal family; official delegations in the UK and overseas; and others where it is in the national interest or intelligence suggests protection is necessary. It is also responsible for protecting royal residences and embassies, providing residential protection for visiting heads of state, heads of government and foreign ministers and advising the diplomatic community on security
- *Protective Security Command* works in conjunction with authorities at the Houses of Parliament to provide security for peers, MPs, employees and visitors to the palace of Westminster. It is also responsible for policing Heathrow and London City airports

Assistant Commissioner, John Yates, QPM

CENTRAL OPERATIONS
Central Operations consists of a number of specialised units with a broad range of policing functions which provide an integrated, community-focused service to London. Central Operations also has the remit for delivering the security arrangements for the 2012 London Olympic Games.
Assistant Commissioner (acting), Chris Allison

SPECIALIST FORCES

BRITISH TRANSPORT POLICE

25–27 Camden Road, London NW1 9LN **T** 020-7830 8800
W www.btp.police.uk
Strength (February 2009), 2,835

British Transport Police is the national police force for the railways in England, Wales and Scotland, including the London Underground system, Docklands Light Railway, Glasgow Subway, Midland Metro Tram system and Croydon Tramlink. The chief constable reports to the British Transport Police Authority. The members of the authority are appointed by the transport secretary and include representatives from the rail industry as well as independent members. Officers are paid the same as other police forces.
Chief Constable, Ian Johnston, CBE, QPM
Deputy Chief Constable, Andy Trotter, OBE, QPM

CIVIL NUCLEAR CONSTABULARY

Building F6, Culham Science Centre, Abingdon,
Oxfordshire OX14 3DB **T** 01235-466606 **W** www.cnc.police.uk
Strength (March 2009), 867

The Civil Nuclear Constabulary (CNC) operates under the strategic direction of the Department of Energy and Climate Change. The CNC is a specialised armed force whose role is the protection of civil nuclear sites and nuclear materials. The constabulary is responsible for policing UK civil nuclear industry facilities and for escorting nuclear material between establishments within the UK and worldwide.
Chief Constable, Richard Thompson
Deputy Chief Constable, John Sampson

MINISTRY OF DEFENCE POLICE

Ministry of Defence Police and Guarding Agency, Wethersfield, Braintree, Essex CM7 4AZ **T** 01371-854000
Strength (March 2009), 3,551

Part of the Ministry of Defence Police and Guarding Agency, the Ministry of Defence Police is a statutory civil police force with particular responsibility for the security and policing of the MoD environment. It contributes to the physical protection of property and personnel within its jurisdiction and provides a comprehensive police service to the MoD as a whole.
Chief Constable/Chief Executive, Stephen Love
Deputy Chief Constable, G. McAuley

THE SPECIAL CONSTABULARY

The Special Constabulary is a force of trained volunteers who support and work with their local police force usually for a minimum of four hours a week (the

Metropolitan Police Special Constabulary usually asks for a minimum commitment of eight hours a week). Special Constables are thoroughly grounded in the basic aspects of police work, such as self-defence, powers of arrest, common crimes and preparing evidence for court, before they can begin to carry out any police duties. Once they have completed their training, they have the same powers as a regular officer and wear a similar uniform. Information on the Special Constabulary can be found on the National Policing Improvement Agency website (W www.npia.police.uk).

RATES OF PAY

London weighting of £2,220 per annum (from 1 July 2009) is awarded to all police officers working in London irrespective of their ranks and in addition to the salaries listed below:

BASIC RATES OF PAY *from 1 September 2009*

Chief Constables of Greater Manchester, Strathclyde and West Midlands*	£173,994–£176,943
Chief Constable*	£123,858–£165,147
Deputy Chief Constable*	£106,167–£135,660
Assistant Chief Constable and Commanders*	£88,470–£103,218
Chief Superintendent	£72,543–£76,680
Superintendent Range 2†	£69,558–£74,022
Superintendent	£60,750–£70,779
Inspector‡§	£50,502 (£52,515)–£52,578 (£54,588)
Chief Inspector‡§	£45,624 (£47,625)–£49,488 (£51,504)
Sergeant‡	£35,610–£40,020
Constable‡	£22,680–£35,610
Metropolitan Police	
Commissioner	£253,620
Deputy Commissioner	£209,382
City of London Police	
Commissioner	£156,900
Assistant Commissioner	£129,414
Police Service of Northern Ireland	
Chief Constable	£188,736
Deputy Chief Constable	£153,348

* Chief Officers may receive a bonus of at least 5 per cent of pensionable pay if their performance is deemed exceptional

† For Superintendents who were not given the rank of Chief Superintendent on its re-introduction on 1 January 2002

‡ Officers who have been on the highest available salary for one year have access to a competence-related threshold payment of £1,182 per annum

§ London salary in parentheses (applicable only to officers in the Metropolitan and City of London police forces)

STAFF ASSOCIATIONS

Police officers are not permitted to join a trade union or to take strike action. All ranks have their own staff associations.

ASSOCIATION OF CHIEF POLICE OFFICERS OF ENGLAND, WALES AND NORTHERN IRELAND, 10 Victoria Street, London SW1H 0NN T 020-7084 8950
Secretary, T. Flaherty

ENGLAND AND WALES

POLICE FEDERATION OF ENGLAND AND WALES, Federation House, Highbury Drive, Leatherhead, Surrey KT22 7UY T 01372-352000 W www.polfed.org E gensec@polfed.org
General Secretary, Ian Rennie

POLICE SUPERINTENDENTS' ASSOCIATION OF ENGLAND AND WALES, 67A Reading Road, Pangbourne, Reading RG8 7JD T 0118-984 4005 E enquiries@policesupers.com W www.policesupers.com
National Secretary, Chief Supt. Patrick Stayt

SCOTLAND

ASSOCIATION OF CHIEF POLICE OFFICERS IN SCOTLAND, 26 Holland Street, Glasgow G2 4NH T 0141-435 1230 W www.acpos.police.uk
General Secretary, vacant

ASSOCIATION OF SCOTTISH POLICE SUPERINTENDENTS, *Secretariat,* 173 Pitt Street, Glasgow G2 4JS T 0141-221 5796 E secretariat@scottishpolicesupers.org.uk W www.scottishpolicesupers.org.uk
General Secretary, Carol Forfar

SCOTTISH POLICE FEDERATION, 5 Woodside Place, Glasgow G3 7QF T 0141-332 5234 W www.spf.org.uk
General Secretary and Treasurer, Calum Steele

NORTHERN IRELAND

POLICE FEDERATION FOR NORTHERN IRELAND, 77–79 Garnerville Road, Belfast BT4 2NX T 028-9076 4200 E office.pfni@btconnect.com W www.policefed-ni.org.uk
Secretary, Stevie McCann

SUPERINTENDENTS' ASSOCIATION OF NORTHERN IRELAND, PSNI College, Garnerville Road, Belfast BT4 2NX T 028-9092 2201 E mail@psani.org W www.psani.org
Secretary (interim), Wesley Wilson, QPM

THE PRISON SERVICE

The prison services in the United Kingdom are the responsibility of the Secretary of State for Justice, the Scottish Government Justice Department and the Secretary of State for Northern Ireland. The chief directors-general (chief executive in Scotland, director in Northern Ireland), officers of the Prison Service, the Scottish Prison Service and the Northern Ireland Prison Service are responsible for the day-to-day running of the system.

There are 140 prison establishments in England and Wales, 16 in Scotland and three in Northern Ireland. Convicted prisoners are classified according to their assessed security risk and are housed in establishments appropriate to that level of security. There are no open prisons in Northern Ireland. Female prisoners are housed in women's establishments or in separate wings of mixed prisons. Remand prisoners are, where possible, housed separately from convicted prisoners. Offenders under the age of 21 are usually detained in a Young Offender Institution, which may be a separate establishment or part of a prison. Appellant and failed asylum seekers are held in Immigration Removal Centres, or in separate units of other prisons.

Eleven prisons are now run by the private sector in England and Wales, and in England, Wales and Scotland all escort services have been contracted out to private companies. In Scotland, two prisons (Kilmarnock and Addiewell) were built and financed by the private sector and are being operated by private contractors.

There are independent prison inspectorates in England, Wales and Scotland which report annually on conditions and the treatment of prisoners. The Chief Inspector of Criminal Justice in Northern Ireland and HM Chief Inspector of Prisons for England and Wales perform an inspectorate role for prisons in Northern Ireland. Every prison establishment also has an independent monitoring board made up of local volunteers.

Any prisoner whose complaint is not satisfied by the internal complaints procedures may complain to the prisons ombudsman for England and Wales, the Scottish Prisons Complaints Commission or the prisoner ombudsman for Northern Ireland.

The 11 private sector prisons in England and Wales are the direct responsibility of the chief executive of the National Offender Management Service (NOMS). NOMS was created in January 2004, in order to integrate prisons and probation into a system whereby end-to-end management of offenders is provided; this is expected to reduce re-offending and cut the growth rate of the prison population. In May 2007 NOMS was amalgamated into the Ministry of Justice; in 2008 it was restructured with responsibilities for running HM Prison Service, overseeing the contracts of privately run prisons, managing probation performance and creating probation trusts. The prisons and probation inspectors, the prisons ombudsman and the independent monitoring boards report to the home secretary and to the secretary of state in Northern Ireland.

PRISON STATISTICS

PRISON POPULATION (UK)
as at April 2009
The projected 'high scenario' prison population for 2015 in England and Wales is 95,800; the 'low scenario' is 83,400.

PRISON POPULATION (UK) *as at April 2009*

	Remand	*Sentenced*	*Other*
ENGLAND AND WALES			
Male	12,314	64,720	1,477
Female	762	3,466	55
Total	13,076	68,186	1,532
SCOTLAND*			
Male	1,429	5,381	—
Female	114	230	—
Total	1,543	5,611	—
N. IRELAND			
Male	462	959	6
Female	22	24	—
Total	484	983	6
UK TOTAL	15,103	74,780	1,538

* Figures for Scotland are as at 30 June 2007
Sources: Home Office; Scottish Prison Service; Northern Ireland Prison Service

PRISON CAPACITY (ENGLAND AND WALES)
as at 5 June 2009

Male prisoners	78,519
Female prisoners	4,279
Number of prisoners held in police cells under Operation Safeguard and in court cells*	0
Total	82,798
Useable operational capacity	84,838
Number under home detention curfew supervision	2,599

* No places are currently activated under Operation Safeguard

SENTENCED PRISON POPULATION BY SEX AND OFFENCE (ENGLAND AND WALES)
as at April 2009

	Male	*Female*
Violence against the person	19,002	859
Sexual offences	7,831	52
Burglary	7,554	212
Robbery	8,563	335
Theft, handling	3,061	425
Fraud and forgery	1,664	279
Drugs offences	9,789	891
Motoring offences	1,117	22
Other offences	5,746	358
Offence not recorded	295	23
*Total**	64,622	3,456

* Figures do not include civil (non-criminal) prisoners or fine defaulters
Source: Home Office – *Research Development Statistics*

SENTENCED POPULATION BY LENGTH OF SENTENCE (ENGLAND AND WALES)
as at April 2009

	Adults	*Young offenders*
Less than 12 months	5,893	1,740
12 months to less than 4 years	19,105	4,626
4 years to less than life	22,526	1,863
Life	11,595	730
*Total**	59,119	8,959

* Figures do not include civil (non-criminal) prisoners or fine defaulters
Source: Home Office – *Research Development Statistics*

AVERAGE DAILY SENTENCED POPULATION BY LENGTH OF SENTENCE 2008–9 (SCOTLAND)

	Adults	*Young offenders*
Less than 4 years	2,692	496
4 years or over (including life)	2,776	192
Total	5,468	688

Source: Scottish Prison Service – *Annual Report and Accounts 2008–9*

SELF-INFLICTED DEATHS IN PRISON APRIL 2008 – APRIL 2009 (ENGLAND AND WALES)

Men	61
Women	2
Total	63
Rate per 100,000 prisoners in custody	76.0

Source: NOMS, Safer Custody and Offender Policy Group

THE PRISON SERVICES

HM PRISON SERVICE

Cleland House, Page Street, London SW1P 4LN
T 0870-000 1397 E public.enquiries@hmps.gsi.gov.uk
W www.hmprisonservice.gov.uk

HM Prison Service became part of the National Offender Management Service on 1 April 2008 as part of the reorganisation of the Ministry of Justice.

SALARIES
from 1 April 2009

Senior Manager A	£62,515–£82,071
Senior Manager B	£58,165–£79,661
Senior Manager C	£55,060–£71,740
*Senior Manager D	£41,715–£60,433
Manager E	£31,210–£45,568
Manager F	£27,690–£38,654
Manager G	£24,235–£31,822

* Salary for new entrants and promotees from 22 July 2009; excludes the Required Hours Addition of £5,474

THE NATIONAL OFFENDER MANAGEMENT SERVICE BOARD
Director-General (SCS), Phil Wheatley, CB
Chief Operating Officer (SCS), Michael Spurr
Director of Estate Capacity, John Aspinall
Director of Commissioning Operational Policy (SCS), Ian Poree
Director of Finance and Performance (SCS), Ann Beasley
Director of High Security Prisons (SCS), Danny McAllister
Director of Human Resources (SCS), Robin Wilkinson
Director of Offender Health (SCS), Richard Bradshaw
Board Secretary and Head of Secretariat (SMB), Ken Everett
Legal Adviser, Andrew Dodsworth
Media Relations, Debbie Kirby
Race Equality Adviser, Matt Wotton

DIRECTORS OF OFFENDER MANAGEMENT
Beverley Shears *(East Midlands);* Trevor Williams *(East of England);* Digby Griffith *(London);* Phil Copple *(North-East);* Caroline Marsh *(North-West);* Roger Hill *(South East);* Colin Allars *(South-West);* Yvonne Thomas *(Wales);* Gill Mortlock *(West Midlands);* Steve Wagstaffe *(Yorkshire and Humberside)*

OPERATING COSTS OF PRISON SERVICE IN ENGLAND AND WALES 2008–9

Staff costs	£2,527,161,000
Other operating costs	£2,801,631,000
Operating income	(£384,423,000)
Net operating costs for the year	£4,944,369,000

Source: HM Prison Service – *Annual Report and Accounts 2008–9*

SCOTTISH PRISON SERVICE (SPS)

Calton House, 5 Redheughs Rigg, Edinburgh EH12 9HW
T 0131-244 8747 E gaolinfo@sps.pnn.gov.uk
W www.sps.gov.uk

SALARIES 2009–10
Senior managers in the Scottish Prison Service, including governors and deputy governors of prisons, are paid across three pay bands:

Band I	£53,319–£66,426
Band H	£42,322–£55,041
Band G	£33,326–£45,766

SPS BOARD
Chief Executive, Mike Ewart
Directors, Alastair Merrill *(Corporate Services);* Willie Pretswell *(Finance and Business Services);* Dr Andrew Fraser *(Health and Care);* Stephen Swan *(Human Resources);* Eric Murch *(Partnerships and Commissioning);* Rona Sweeney *(Prisons)*
Non-Executive Directors, Allan Burns; Rachel Gwyon; Harry McGuigan; Jane Martin; Susan Matheson; Bill Morton; Zoe Van Zwanenberg

OPERATING COSTS OF SCOTTISH PRISON SERVICE 2008–9

Total income	£2,400,000
Total expenditure	£311,656,000
Staff costs	£135,936,000
Running costs	£145,927,000
Other current expenditure	£29,793,000
Operating cost	£309,256,000
Cost of capital charges	£22,248,000
Interest payable and similar charges	£18,000
Interest receivable	(£1,000)
Net operating cost	£331,521,000

Source: Scottish Prison Service – *Annual Report and Accounts 2008–9*

NORTHERN IRELAND PRISON SERVICE

Dundonald House, Upper Newtownards Road, Belfast BT4 3SU
T 028-9052 2922 E info@niprisonservice.gov.uk
W www.niprisonservice.gov.uk

SALARIES 2008–9

Governor 1	£71,465–£77,018
Governor 2	£64,996–£69,009
Governor 3	£56,242–£60,010
Governor 4	£48,910–£52,974
Governor 5	£42,962–£48,184

SENIOR STAFF

Director, Robin Masefield, CBE
Deputy Directors, Mark McGuckin *(Finance and Personnel);* Max Murray *(Operations);* vacant *(Services)*

OPERATING COSTS OF NORTHERN IRELAND PRISON SERVICE 2008–9

Staff costs	£92,420,000
Net running costs	£23,290,000
Depreciation	£11,292,000
Finance charges	£7,616,000
Impairment of fixed assets	£0
Operating expenditure	£134,618,000
Other current expenditure	£4,702,000
Net operating costs for the year	£139,320,000

Source: Northern Ireland Prison Service – *Annual Report and Accounts 2008–9*

PRISON ESTABLISHMENTS

as at April 2009

ENGLAND AND WALES

Prison	*Address*	*Prisoners*	*Governor/Director*
ACKLINGTON	Northumberland NE65 9XF	934	Mick Lees
ALBANY	Isle of Wight PO30 5RS	557	Barry Greenbury
ALTCOURSE (private prison)	Liverpool L9 7LH	1,271	John McLaughlin
†‡ASHFIELD (private prison)	Bristol BS16 9QJ	360	Wendy Sinclair
ASHWELL	Leics LE15 7LF	184	Ian Thomas *(acting)*
*‡ASKHAM GRANGE	York YO23 3FT	109	vacant
‡AYLESBURY	Bucks HP20 1EH	436	David Kennedy
BEDFORD	Bedford MK40 1HG	460	Frank Flynn
BELMARSH	London SE28 0EB	871	Phil Wragg
BIRMINGHAM	Birmingham B18 4AS	1,437	James Shanley
BLANTYRE HOUSE	Kent TN17 2NH	115	Jim Carmichael
BLUNDESTON	Suffolk NR32 5BG	516	Sue Doolan
†‡BRINSFORD	Wolverhampton WV10 7PY	531	Pete Knapton
‡BRISTOL	Bristol BS7 8PS	610	Kenny Brown
‡BRIXTON	London SW2 5XF	752	Paul McDowell
*BRONZEFIELD (private prison)	Middlesex TW15 3JZ	423	Helga Swidenbank
BUCKLEY HALL	Lancs OL12 9DP	379	Mick Regan
BULLINGDON	PO Box 50, Oxon OX25 1WD	1,076	Andy Lattimore
‡BULLWOOD HALL	Essex SS5 4TE	227	Paul Wailen
CAMP HILL	Isle of Wight PO30 5PB	560	Barry Greenbury
CANTERBURY	Kent CT1 1PJ	310	Chris Bartlett
†CARDIFF	Cardiff CF24 0UG	812	Sian West
‡CASTINGTON	Northumberland NE65 9XG	369	Alex Tait
CHANNINGS WOOD	Devon TQ12 6DW	724	Jeannine Hendrick
‡CHELMSFORD	Essex CM2 6LQ	682	Rob Davis
COLDINGLEY	Surrey GU24 9EX	505	John Robinson
‡COOKHAM WOOD	Kent ME1 3LU	78	Helen Rinaldi
DARTMOOR	Devon PL20 6RR	626	Tony Corcoran
‡DEERBOLT	Co. Durham DL12 9BG	443	Jenny Mooney
‡DONCASTER (private prison)	Doncaster DN5 8UX	1,129	Brian Anderson
†DORCHESTER	Dorset DT1 1JD	236	Serena Watts
DOVEGATE (private prison)	Staffs ST14 8XR	848	Wyn Jones
§DOVER	Kent CT17 9DR	292	Andy Bell
*DOWNVIEW	Surrey SM2 5PD	345	Ian Murray
*‡DRAKE HALL	Staffs ST21 6LQ	260	Bridie Oaks-Richards
DURHAM	Durham DH1 3HU	925	Alan Tallentire
*‡EAST SUTTON PARK	Kent ME17 3DF	92	Jim Carmichael
*‡EASTWOOD PARK	Glos GL12 8DB	333	Tim Beeston
EDMUNDS HILL	Suffolk CB8 9YN	367	Kevin Reilly
ELMLEY	Kent ME12 4DZ	945	Ed Tullet
ERLESTOKE	Wilts SN10 5TU	467	Andy Rogers
EVERTHORPE	E. Yorks HU15 1RB	657	Susan Morrison
†‡EXETER	Devon EX4 4EX	528	Mark Flinton
FEATHERSTONE	Wolverhampton WV10 7PU	684	Simon Cartwright
†‡FELTHAM	Middx TW13 4ND	622	Cathy Robinson
FORD	W. Sussex BN18 0BX	554	Sharon Williams
‡FOREST BANK (private prison)	Manchester M27 8FB	1,144	Trevor Short
*FOSTON HALL	Derby DE65 5DN	241	Grey Riley-Smith
FRANKLAND	Durham DH1 5YD	728	Dave Thompson
FULL SUTTON	York YO41 1PS	582	Steve Tilley
GARTH	Preston PR26 8NE	821	Terry Williams
GARTREE	Leics LE16 7RP	683	Susan Howard
†‡GLEN PARVA	Leicester LE18 4TN	781	Nigel Smith
†‡GLOUCESTER	Gloucester GL1 2JN	302	Mike Bolton
GRENDON	Bucks HP18 0TL	502	Dr Peter Bennett
‡GUYS MARSH	Dorset SP7 0AH	567	Julia Killick
§HASLAR	Hampshire PO12 2AW	143	Vicky Baker
HAVERIGG	Cumbria LA18 4NA	613	Martin Farquhar
HEWELL	Worcs B97 6QS	1,402	Alison Perry
HIGH DOWN	Surrey SM2 5PJ	1,014	Peter Dawson
HIGHPOINT	Suffolk CB8 9YG	921	Dave Taylor
†‡HINDLEY	Lancs WN2 5TH	211	Ray Hill

Prison	*Address*	*Prisoners*	*Governor/Director*
‡HOLLESLEY BAY	Suffolk IP12 3JW	337	Declan Moore
*‡HOLLOWAY	London N7 0NU	435	Sue Saunders
HOLME HOUSE	Stockton-on-Tees TS18 2QU	969	Matt Spencer
‡HULL	Hull HU9 5LS	1,016	Paul Foweather
‡HUNTERCOMBE	Oxon RG9 5SB	291	Kevin Leggett
KENNET	Merseyside L31 1HX	344	Derek Harrison
KINGSTON	Portsmouth PO3 6AS	173	Ian Telfer
KIRKHAM	Lancs PR4 2RN	586	John Hewitson
KIRKLEVINGTON GRANGE	Cleveland TS15 9PA	266	Alan Richer
LANCASTER	Lancaster LA1 1YL	227	Peter Francis
†‡LANCASTER FARMS	Lancaster LA1 3QZ	506	Steve Lawrence
LATCHMERE HOUSE	Surrey TW10 5HH	198	Phil Taylor
LEEDS	Leeds LS12 2TJ	1,125	Rob Kellet
LEICESTER	Leicester LE2 7AJ	335	Alison Clarke
‡LEWES	E. Sussex BN7 1EA	639	Eoin McLennan-Murray
LEYHILL	Glos GL12 8BT	496	Mick Bell
LINCOLN	Lincoln LN2 4BD	680	Michael Wood
§LINDHOLME	Doncaster DN7 6EE	1,109	Paul Kempster
LITTLEHEY	Cambs PE28 0SR	713	Danny Spencer
LIVERPOOL	Liverpool L9 3DF	1,303	Alan Brown
LONG LARTIN	Worcs WR11 8TZ	431	Ferdie Parker
*‡LOW NEWTON	Durham DH1 5YA	284	Paddy Fox
LOWDHAM GRANGE (private prison)	Notts NG14 7DA	693	John Biggin
MAIDSTONE	Kent ME14 1UZ	525	Steve O'Connell
MANCHESTER	Manchester M60 9AH	1,218	Richard Vince
‡MOORLAND CLOSED	Doncaster DN7 6BW	769	Tom Wheatley
‡MOORLAND OPEN	Doncaster DN7 6EL	245	Tom Wheatley
*MORTON HALL	Lincoln LN6 9PT	347	Jamie Bennett
THE MOUNT	Herts HP3 0NZ	763	Damian Evans
*‡NEW HALL	W. Yorks WF4 4XX	373	Gareth Sands
NORTH SEA CAMP	Lincs PE22 0QX	308	Graham Batchford
‡NORTHALLERTON	N. Yorks DL6 1NW	179	Norman Griffin
‡NORWICH	Norfolk NR1 4LU	521	Paul Baker
NOTTINGHAM	Nottingham NG5 3AG	550	Peter Wright
‡ONLEY	Warks CV23 8AP	649	John O'Sullivan
†‡PARC (private prison)	Bridgend, S. Wales CF35 6AR	1,199	Janet Wallsgrove
PARKHURST	Isle of Wight PO30 5NX	494	Barry Greenbury
‡PENTONVILLE	London N7 8TT	1,083	Nick Leader
*†PETERBOROUGH (private prison)	Peterborough PE3 7PD	607	Mike Conway
‡PORTLAND	Dorset DT5 1DL	598	Steve Holland
‡PRESCOED	Monmouthshire NP4 0TB	419	David Ward
PRESTON	Lancs PR1 5AB	741	Paul Holland
RANBY	Notts DN22 8EU	1,064	Louise Taylor
†‡READING	Berks RG1 3HY	247	Pauline Bryant
RISLEY	Cheshire WA3 6BP	1,074	Bob McColm
‡ROCHESTER	Kent ME1 3QS	590	John Wilson
RYE HILL (private prison)	Warks CV23 8SZ	655	Cathy James
*SEND	Surrey GU23 7LJ	268	Ian Murray
SHEPTON MALLET	Somerset BA4 5LU	188	Nick Evans
‡SHREWSBURY	Shropshire SY1 2HR	300	Gerry Hendry
SPRING HILL	Bucks HP18 0TL	502	Dr Peter Bennett
STAFFORD	Stafford ST16 3AW	734	Peter Small
STANDFORD HILL	Kent ME12 4AA	441	Andy Hudson
STOCKEN	Leics LE15 7RD	804	Steve Turner
‡STOKE HEATH	Shropshire TF9 2JL	563	Teresa Clarke
*‡STYAL	Cheshire SK9 4HR	436	Steve Hall
SUDBURY	Derbys DE6 5HW	577	Ken Kan
SWALESIDE	Kent ME12 4AX	826	Kieron Taylor
†‡SWANSEA	Swansea SA1 3SR	420	Andrea Whitfield
‡SWINFEN HALL	Staffs WS14 9QS	619	Tom Watson
‡THORN CROSS	Cheshire WA4 4RL	288	Sue Brown
USK	Monmouthshire NP15 1XP	419	David Ward
THE VERNE	Dorset DT5 1EQ	582	Denise Hodder
WAKEFIELD	West Yorks WF2 9AG	731	Jacqui Tilley
WANDSWORTH	London SW18 3HS	1,637	Ian Mulholland
‡WARREN HILL	Suffolk IP12 3JW	203	Roger Plant

Prison	Address	Prisoners	Governor/Director
WAYLAND	Norfolk IP25 6RL	1,000	Richard Booty
WEALSTUN	W. Yorks LS23 7AZ	518	Norma Harrington
WELLINGBOROUGH	Northants NN8 2NH	638	Peter Siddons
‡WERRINGTON	Stoke-on-Trent ST9 0DX	128	John Huntingdon
‡WETHERBY	W. Yorks LS22 5ED	381	Will Styles
WHATTON	Nottingham NG13 9FQ	833	Lynn Saunders
WHITEMOOR	Cambs PE15 0PR	446	Steve Rodford
WINCHESTER	Winchester SO22 5DF	686	Claudia Sturt
WOLDS (private prison)	E. Yorks HU15 2JZ	381	Dave McDonnell
WOODHILL	Bucks MK4 4DA	823	Luke Serjeant
WORMWOOD SCRUBS	London W12 0AE	1,273	Phil Taylor
WYMOTT	Preston PR26 8LW	1,067	Paul Norbury

SCOTLAND

Prison	Address	Prisoners	Governor/Director
ABERDEEN	Aberdeen AB11 8FN	231	Audrey Mooney
ADDIEWELL(private prison)	West Lothian EH55 8GA	702	Audrey Park
†BARLINNIE	Glasgow G33 2QX	1,466	Bill McKinlay
CASTLE HUNTLY	Dundee DD2 5HL	298 (with Noranside)	Mike Inglis
*†‡CORNTON VALE	Stirling FK9 5NU	398	Teresa Medhurst
†DUMFRIES	Dumfries DG2 9AX	179	Martyn Bettel
†EDINBURGH	Edinburgh EH11 3LN	913	Nigel Ironside
GLENOCHIL	Tullibody FK10 3AD	662	Dan Gunn
†‡GREENOCK	Greenock PA16 9AH	267	Malcolm McLennan
*†INVERNESS	Inverness IV2 3HH	151	David Abernethy
†‡KILMARNOCK (private prison)	Kilmarnock KA1 5AA	548	Scott McNairn
NORANSIDE	Angus DD8 3QY	298 (with Castle Huntly)	Mike Inglis
†PERTH	Perth PH2 8AT	712	Kate Donegan
PETERHEAD	Aberdeenshire AB42 2YY	305	Michael Stoney
†‡POLMONT	Falkirk FK2 0AB	712	Derek McGill
SHOTTS	Lanarkshire ML7 4LE	539	Ian Gunn

NORTHERN IRELAND

Prison	Address	Prisoners	Governor/Director
*†‡HYDEBANK WOOD	Belfast BT8 8NA	223	Austin Treacy
†§MAGHABERRY	Co. Antrim BT28 2NF	839	Steve Rodford
MAGILLIGAN	Co. Londonderry BT49 0LR	411	Tom Woods

PRISON ESTABLISHMENTS KEY
* Women's establishment or establishment with units for women
† Remand Centre or establishment with units for remand prisoners
‡ Young Offender Institution or establishment with units for young offenders
§ Immigration Removal Centre or establishment with units for immigration detainees

DEFENCE

The armed forces of the United Kingdom comprise the Royal Navy, the Army and the Royal Air Force (RAF). The Queen is Commander-in-Chief of all the armed forces. The Secretary of State for Defence is responsible for the formulation and content of defence policy and for providing the means by which it is conducted. The formal legal basis for the conduct of defence in the UK rests on a range of powers vested by statute and letters patent in the Defence Council, chaired by the Secretary of State for Defence. Beneath the ministers lies the top management of the Ministry of Defence (MoD), headed jointly by the Permanent Secretary and the Chief of Defence Staff. The Permanent Secretary is the government's principal civilian adviser on defence and has the primary responsibility for policy, finance, management and administration. He is also personally accountable to parliament for the expenditure of all public money allocated to defence purposes. The Chief of the Defence Staff is the professional head of the armed forces in the UK and the principal military adviser to the secretary of state and the government.

The Defence Board is the executive of the Defence Council. Chaired by the Permanent Secretary, it acts as the main executive board of the Ministry of Defence, providing senior level leadership and strategic management of defence.

The Central Staff, headed by the Vice-Chief of the Defence Staff and the Second Permanent Under-Secretary of State, is the policy core of the department. Defence Equipment and Support, headed by the Chief of Defence Materiel, is responsible for purchasing defence equipment and providing logistical support to the armed forces.

A permanent Joint Headquarters for the conduct of joint operations was set up at Northwood in 1996. The Joint Headquarters connects the policy and strategic functions of the MoD head office with the conduct of operations and is intended to strengthen the policy/executive division.

The UK pursues its defence and security policies through its membership of NATO (to which most of its armed forces are committed), the European Union, the Organisation for Security and Cooperation in Europe and the UN (*see* International Organisations section).

STRENGTH OF THE ARMED FORCES

	Royal Navy	*Army*	*RAF*	*All Services*
1975 strength	76,200	167,100	95,000	338,300
1990 strength	63,210	152,810	89,680	305,700
2001 strength	42,420	109,530	53,700	205,650
2002 strength	41,630	110,050	53,000	204,680
2003 strength	41,550	112,130	53,240	206,920
2004 strength	40,880	112,750	53,390	207,020
2005 strength	39,940	109,290	51,870	201,100
2006 strength	39,390	107,730	48,730	195,850
2007 strength	38,860	106,170*	45,370	190,400*
2008 strength	38,570*	105,090*	43,390*	187,060*
2009 strength	38,340*	106,460*	43,570*	188,370*

* Provisional figures

Source: MoD Defence Analytical Services Agency *National Statistics* (Crown copyright)

SERVICE PERSONNEL BY RANK AND GENDER*

	Officers		*Other ranks*	
	Males	*Females*	*Males*	*Females*
All services	27,860	3,830	142,660	14,020
Royal Navy	6,700	720	27,980	2,950
Army	12,880	1,620	85,260	6,700
RAF	8,280	1,490	29,420	4,380

* Provisional figures

Source: MoD Defence Analytical Services Agency *National Statistics* (Crown copyright)

UK regular forces include trained and untrained personnel and nursing services, but exclude Gurkhas, full-time reserve service personnel, mobilised reservists and naval activated reservists. As at 1 April 2009 these groups provisionally numbered:

All Gurkhas	3,860
Full-time reserve service	2,100
Mobilised reservists	
Army	1,450
RAF	200
Naval activated reservists	230

Source: MoD Defence Analytical Services Agency *National Statistics* (Crown copyright)

CIVILIAN PERSONNEL

1993 level	159,600
2000 level	121,300
2001 level	118,200
2002 level	110,100
2003 level	107,600
2004 level	108,990
2005 level	107,680
2006 level	102,970
2007 level	95,790
2008 level	88,690
2009 level	85,730

Source: MoD Defence Analytical Services Agency *National Statistics* (Crown copyright)

UK REGULAR FORCES: DEATHS

In 2008 there were a total of 137 deaths among the UK regular armed forces, of which 40 were serving in the Royal Navy and Royal Marines, 79 in the Army and 18 in the RAF. The largest single cause of death was as a result of hostile action (killed in action and died of wounds), which accounted for 52 deaths (38 per cent of the total) in 2008. Land transport accidents accounted for 27 deaths (20 per cent) and other accidents accounted for a further 19 deaths (14 per cent). Suicides accounted for two deaths or 1 per cent of the total.

NUMBER OF DEATHS AND MORTALITY RATES

	1999	2002	2005	2007	2008
Total number	142	147	160	204	137
Royal Navy	26	26	27	27	40
Army	84	94	93	145	79
RAF	32	27	40	32	18
Mortality rates per thousand					
Tri-service rate	0.66	0.72	0.79	1.05	0.72
Navy	0.60	0.67	0.69	0.69	1.08
Army	0.74	0.83	0.83	1.29	0.72
RAF	0.49	0.52	0.71	0.69	0.33

Source: MoD Defence Analytical Services Agency *National Statistics* (Crown copyright)

NUCLEAR FORCES

The Vanguard Class SSBN (ship submersible ballistic nuclear) provides the UK's strategic nuclear deterrent. Each Vanguard Class submarine is capable of carrying 16 Trident D5 missiles equipped with nuclear warheads.

There is a ballistic missile early warning system station at RAF Fylingdales in North Yorkshire.

ARMS CONTROL

The 1990 Conventional Armed Forces in Europe (CFE) Treaty, which commits all NATO and former Warsaw Pact members to limiting their holdings of five major classes of conventional weapons, has been adapted to reflect the changed geo-strategic environment and negotiations continue for its implementation. The Open Skies Treaty, which the UK signed in 1992 and entered into force in 2002, allows for the overflight of states parties by other states parties using unarmed observation aircraft.

The UN Convention on Certain Conventional Weapons (as amended 2001), which bans or restricts the use of specific types of weapons that are considered to cause unnecessary or unjustifiable suffering to combatants, or to affect civilians indiscriminately, was ratified by the UK in 1995. In 1968 the UK signed and ratified the Nuclear Non-Proliferation Treaty, which came into force in 1970 and was indefinitely and unconditionally extended in 1995. In 1996 the UK signed the Comprehensive Nuclear Test Ban Treaty and ratified it in 1998. The UK is a party to the 1972 Biological and Toxin Weapons Convention, which provides for a worldwide ban on biological weapons, and the 1993 Chemical Weapons Convention, which came into force in 1997 and provides for a verifiable worldwide ban on chemical weapons.

DEFENCE BUDGET DEPARTMENTAL EXPENDITURE LIMITS (DEL) *(£ billion)*

	Resource budget	*Capital budget*	*Total DEL*
2007–8 (outturn)	35.7	7.9	43.6
2008–9 (estimate)	37.9	8.6	46.5
2009–10 (projection)	38.7	9.1	47.8

Source: HM Treasury – *Budget 2009* (Crown copyright)

MINISTRY OF DEFENCE

Main Building, Whitehall, London SW1A 2HB
T 020-7218 9000 W www.mod.uk

Secretary of State for Defence, Rt. Hon. Bob Ainsworth, MP
Private Secretary, Will Jessett
Special Advisers, Alaina McDonald; Andy Bagnall
Parliamentary Private Secretary, vacant
Minister of State for the Armed Forces, Bill Rammell, MP
Private Secretary, Caroline Pusey
Parliamentary Private Secretary, Dave Anderson, MP
Minister of State for Strategic Defence Acquisition Reform, Rt. Hon. Lord Drayson
Private Secretary, Jonathan Ware
Parliamentary Under-Secretary of State and Minister for Defence Equipment and Support, Quentin Davies, MP
Private Secretary, Dr Glenn Kelly
Parliamentary Under-Secretary of State and Minister for International Defence and Security, Rt. Hon. Baroness Taylor of Bolton
Private Secretary, Mark Selfridge
Parliamentary Under-Secretary of State for Defence and Minister for Veterans, Kevan Jones, MP
Private Secretary, Alan Nisbett

CHIEFS OF STAFF

Chief of the Defence Staff, Air Chief Marshal Sir Jock Stirrup, GCB, AFC, ADC
Vice Chief of the Defence Staff, Gen. Sir Nick Houghton, KCB, CBE
Chief of the Naval Staff and First Sea Lord, Adm. Sir Mark Stanhope, KCB, OBE, ADC
Assistant Chief of the Naval Staff, Rear-Adm. Philip Jones
Chief of the General Staff, Gen. Sir David Richards, KCB, CBE, DSO
Assistant Chief of the General Staff, Maj.-Gen. James Bucknell
Chief of the Air Staff, Air Chief Marshal Sir Stephen Dalton, KCB, ADC
Assistant Chief of the Air Staff, Air Vice-Marshal T. Anderson, CB, DSO

SENIOR OFFICIALS

Permanent Under-Secretary of State, Sir Bill Jeffrey, KCB
Second Permanent Under-Secretary of State, Ursula Brennan
Chief of Defence Materiel, Gen. Sir Kevin O'Donoghue, KCB, CBE
Chief Scientific Adviser, Prof. Mark Welland, FRS, FRENG
Director-General Finance, John Thompson

THE DEFENCE COUNCIL

The Defence Council is the senior committee of the MoD, and was established by royal prerogative under letters patent in April 1964. The letters patent confer on the Defence Council the command over all of the armed forces and charge the council with such matters relating to the administration of the armed forces as the Secretary of State for Defence should direct them to execute. It is chaired by the Secretary of State for Defence and consists of the Secretary of State for Defence, the Minister of State for the Armed Forces, the Parliamentary Under-Secretary of State and Minister of State for Defence Equipment and Support, the Parliamentary Under-Secretary of State and Minister for International Defence and Security, the Parliamentary Under-Secretary of State for Defence and the Minister for Veterans, the Chief of Defence Staff, the Permanent Under-Secretary of State, the Chief of the Naval Staff and First Sea Lord, the Chief of the General Staff, the Chief of the Air Staff, the Vice-Chief of the Defence Staff, the Chief of Defence Materiel, the Chief Scientific Adviser, the Second Permanent Under-Secretary of State and the Director-General Finance.

CENTRAL STAFF

Vice-Chief of the Defence Staff, Gen. Sir Nick Houghton, KCB, CBE
Second Permanent Under-Secretary of State, Ursula Brennan

PERMANENT JOINT HQ
Chief of Joint Operations, Air Vice-Marshal Sir Stuart Peach, KCB, CBE
Chief of Staff (Operations), Rear-Adm. George Zambellas, DSC
Chief of Staff (Joint Warfare Development), Maj.-Gen. R. Porter, MBE

FLEET COMMAND
Commander-in-Chief Fleet, Adm. Sir Trevor Soar, KCB, OBE
Deputy Commander-in-Chief Fleet, Vice-Adm. Richard Ibbotson, CB, DSC

NAVAL HOME COMMAND
Second Sea Lord and Commander-in-Chief Naval Home Command, Adm. Alan Massey, CBE, ADC
Chief of Staff to Second Sea Lord and Commander-in-Chief Naval Home Command, Rear-Adm. Charles Montgomery, CBE

LAND COMMAND
Commander-in-Chief Land Forces, Gen. Sir Peter Wall, KCB, CBE
Chief of Staff Land Forces, Maj.-Gen. Mark Poffley, OBE

ADJUTANT-GENERAL'S COMMAND
Adjutant-General, Lt.-Gen. W. Rollo, CBE
Deputy Adjutant-General and Director-General Service Conditions (Army), Maj.-Gen. A. Gregory

AIR COMMAND
Commander-in-Chief Air Command, Air Chief Marshal Chris Moran, OBE, MVO
Deputy Commander-in-Chief Operations, Air Marshal Iain McNicoll, CB, CBE
Deputy Commander-in-Chief Personnel, Air Marshal Simon Bryant, CBE

DEFENCE EQUIPMENT AND SUPPORT
Chief of Defence Materiel, Gen. Sir Kevin O'Donoghue, KCB, CBE
Chief Operating Officer, Dr Andrew Tyler
Chief of Corporate Services, T. Flesher
Chief of Materiel (Fleet), Vice-Adm. Andy Matthews, OBE
Chief of Materiel (Land), Lt.-Gen. Gary Coward, CB, OBE
Chief of Materiel (Air), Air Marshal Kevin Leeson, CBE

EXECUTIVE AGENCIES

DEFENCE SCIENCE AND TECHNOLOGY LABORATORY
Porton Down, Salisbury, Wiltshire SP4 0JQ **T** 01980-613121
E centralenquiries@dstl.gov.uk **W** www.dstl.gov.uk
Chief Executive, Dr Frances Saunders

DEFENCE STORAGE AND DISTRIBUTION AGENCY
Building C16, C Site, Bicester, Oxon OX25 1LP **T** 01869-256128
Chief Executive, Neil Firth

DEFENCE SUPPORT GROUP
Building 203, Monxton Road, Andover, Hampshire SP11 8HT
T 01264-383295 **E** info@dsg.mod.uk
Chief Executive, Archie Hughes

DEFENCE VETTING AGENCY
Building 107, Imphal Barracks, Fulford Road, York YO10 4AS
T 01904–662644 **E** dvacustomersupport@land.mod.uk
Chief Executive, Jacky Ridley

MET OFFICE
Fitzroy Road, Exeter, Devon EX1 3PB **T** 0870-900 0100
E enquiries@metoffice.gov.uk **W** www.metoffice.gov.uk
Chief Executive, John Hirst

MINISTRY OF DEFENCE POLICE AND GUARDING AGENCY
Weathersfield, Braintree, Essex CM7 4AZ **T** 01371-854751
E corpcomms@mdpga.mod.uk
Chief Constable, Stephen Love

PEOPLE, PAY AND PENSIONS AGENCY
J Block Foxhill, Combe Down, Bath BA1 5AB **T** 0800-345 7772
E peopleservices@pppa.mod.uk
Chief Executive, David Ball

SERVICE CHILDREN'S EDUCATION
HQ SCE, Wegberg Military Complex, BFPO 40 **T** (+49) (2161) 908 2294 **E** info@sceschools.com **W** www.sceschools.com
Chief Executive, David Wadsworth

SERVICE PERSONNEL AND VETERANS AGENCY (SPVA)
Norcross, Blackpool FY5 3WP **T** 0800-169 2277 (veterans' enquiries) **E** veterans.help@spva.gsi.gov.uk
W www.veterans-uk.info
Chief Executive, Kathy Barnes

UK HYDROGRAPHIC OFFICE
Admiralty Way, Taunton, Somerset TA1 2DN **T** 01823-337900
E helpdesk@ukho.gov.uk **W** www.ukho.gov.uk
Chief Executive, Mike Robinson

ARMED FORCES TRAINING AND RECRUITMENT

In April 2006 the MoD removed agency status from the three armed forces training agencies which now function as an integral part of their respective service.

Flag Officer Sea Training (FOST) is responsible for all Royal Navy and Royal Fleet Auxiliary training. FOST's International Defence Training provides the focal point for all aspects of naval training. Training is divided into five streams: Naval Core Training (responsible for new entry, command, leadership and management training); Royal Marine; Submarine; Surface and Aviation.

The Army Recruiting and Training Division (ARTD) is responsible for the four key areas of army training: soldier initial training, at the School of Infantry or at one of the army's four other facilities; officer initial training at the Royal Military Academy Sandhurst; trade training at one of the army's specialist facilities; and resettlement training for those about to leave the army. Trade training facilities include: the Armour Centre; the Defence College of Logistics and Personnel Administration; the Royal School of Artillery; the Royal School of Military Engineering and the School of Army Aviation.

The Royal Air Force No. 22 (Training) Group exists to recruit RAF personnel and provide trained specialist personnel to the armed forces as a whole, such as providing the army air corps with trained helicopter pilots. The group is split into eight areas: RAF College Cranwell and Director of Recruiting; the Directorate of Flying Training (DFT); the Directorate of Joint Technical Training (DJTT); the Air Cadet Organisation (ACO); Core Headquarters; the Defence College of Aeronautical Engineering (DCAE); the Defence College of Communications and Information Systems (DCCIS) and the Defence College of Electro-Mechanical Engineering (DCEME).

USEFUL WEBSITES
W www.rncom.mod.uk
W www.army.mod.uk
W www.raf.mod.uk

THE ROYAL NAVY

LORD HIGH ADMIRAL OF THE UNITED KINGDOM
HM The Queen

ADMIRALS OF THE FLEET
HRH The Prince Philip, Duke of Edinburgh, KG, KT, OM, GBE, AC, QSO, PC, *apptd* 1953
Sir Edward Ashmore, GCB, DSC, *apptd* 1977
Sir Henry Leach, GCB, *apptd* 1982
Sir Julian Oswald, GCB, *apptd* 1993
Sir Benjamin Bathurst, GCB, *apptd* 1995

ADMIRALS
(Former Chiefs or Vice Chiefs of Defence Staff and First Sea Lords who remain on the active list)
Slater, Sir Jock, GCB, LVO, *apptd* 1991
Boyce, Lord, GCB, OBE, *apptd* 1995
Abbott, Sir Peter, GBE, KCB, *apptd* 1995
Essenhigh, Sir Nigel, GCB, *apptd* 1998
West of Spithead, Lord, GCB, DSC, *apptd* 2000
Band, Sir Jonathon, GCB, *apptd* 2002

ADMIRALS
HRH The Prince of Wales, KG, KT, GCB, OM, AK, QSO, PC, ADC
Stanhope, Sir Mark, KCB, OBE, ADC *(First Sea Lord and Chief of Naval Staff)*
Soar, Sir Trevor, KCB, OBE *(Commander-in-Chief Fleet)*

VICE-ADMIRALS
Laurence, Timothy, CB, MVO *(Chief Executive Defence Estates)*
Wilkinson, Peter *(Deputy Chief of Defence Staff (Personnel))*
Massey, Sir Alan, KCB, CBE, ADC *(Second Sea Lord and Commander-in-Chief Naval Home Command)*
Ibbotson, Richard, CB, DSC *(Deputy Commander-in-Chief Fleet, Chief of Staff Navy Command HQ and Chief Naval Warfare Officer)*
Lambert, Paul, CB *(Deputy Chief of Defence Staff (Equipment Capability))*
Matthews, Andrew, CB *(Chief of Materiel (Fleet) and Chief of Fleet Support to the Navy Board)*
Cooling, Robert *(Chief of Staff to the Supreme Allied Commander Transformation)*

REAR-ADMIRALS
HRH The Princess Royal, KG, KT, GCVO *(Chief Commandant for Women in the Royal Navy)*
Zambellas, George, DSC *(Chief of Staff (Operations), Permanent Joint HQ)*
Hussain, Amjad *(Capability Manager (Precision Attack) and Controller of the Navy)*
Moncrieff, Ian *(National Hydrographer and Deputy Chief Executive UK Hydrographic Office)*
Johnstone-Burt, (Charles) Anthony, OBE *(Cdr Joint Helicopter Command)*
Snow, Christopher *(Flag Officer Sea Training and Rear-Adm. Surface Ships (Head of Fighting Arm))*
Love, Robert, OBE *(Director Ships and Chief Naval Engineering Officer)*
Montgomery, Charles, CBE *(Naval Secretary and Chief of Staff (Personnel))*
Richards, Alan *(Assistant Chief of Defence Staff (Strategy and Plans))*
Charlier, Simon *(Chief of Staff (Aviation), Rear-Adm. Fleet Air Arm (Head of Fighting Arm))*
Jones, Philip *(Assistant Chief of Naval Staff)*
Lister, Simon, OBE *(Director Submarines)*
Alabaster, Martin *(Flag Officer Scotland, Northern England and Northern Ireland and Flag Officer Reserve Forces)*
Lloyd, Stephen *(Chief Strategic Systems Executive)*
Anderson, Mark *(Cdr (Operations) and Rear-Adm. Submarines (Head of Fighting Arm))*
Corder, Ian *(Deputy Cdr Striking Force NATO)*
Williams, Simon, OBE *(Senior Directing Staff (Navy), Royal College of Defence Studies)*
Hudson, Peter, CBE *(Cdr UK Maritime Forces)*
Williams, Bruce, CBE *(Chief of Staff to the Maritime Component Command Naples and Senior Naval Representative Naples)*

SURGEON REAR-ADMIRALS
Raffaelli, Philip, QHP, FRCP *(Director Strategic Change)*
Jarvis, Lionel, QHS *(Assistant Chief of Defence Staff (Health))*

ROYAL MARINES

CAPTAIN-GENERAL
HRH The Prince Philip, Duke of Edinburgh, KG, KT, OM, GBE, AC, QSO, PC

LIEUTENANT-GENERAL
Dutton, James, CBE *(Deputy Cdr International Security and Assistance Force and Senior British Military Representative, Afghanistan)*

MAJOR-GENERALS
Robison, Garry *(Chief of Staff (Capability))*
Thomas, Jeremy, DSO *(Assistant Chief of Defence Staff (Intelligence Capability))*
Salmon, Andrew, OBE *(Cdr UK Amphibious Forces and Commandant General Royal Marines)*
Capewell, David, OBE *(Deputy Cdr NATO Rapid Deployment Corps, Italy)*
Mason, Jeffrey, MBE *(Assistant Chief of Defence Staff (Logistic Operations))*

The Royal Marines were formed in 1664 and are part of the Naval Service. Their primary purpose is to conduct amphibious and land warfare. The principal operational units are:

- Three Commando Brigade, an amphibious all arms brigade trained to operate in arduous environments (a core element of the UK's Joint Rapid Reaction Force). The commando units each have a strength of around 700 and are based in Taunton (40 Commando), Plymouth (42 Commando) and Arbroath (45 Commando)
- Fleet Protection Group, responsible for a wide range of tasks worldwide in support of the Royal Navy. The group is over 500 strong and is based at HM Naval Base Clyde on the west coast of Scotland
- Assault Group, which has its headquarters located in Devonport, Plymouth is responsible for ten landing craft training squadron at Poole, Dorset and 11 amphibious trials and training squadron at Instow, Devon

The Royal Marines also provide detachments for warships and land-based naval parties as required.

ROYAL MARINES RESERVES (RMR)

The Royal Marines Reserve is a commando-trained volunteer force with the principal role, when mobilised, of supporting the Royal Marines. The RMR consists of approximately 600 trained ranks who are distributed between the five RMR centres in the UK. Approximately 10 per cent of the RMR are working with the regular corps on long-term attachments within all of the Royal Marines regular units.

OTHER PARTS OF THE NAVAL SERVICE

FLEET AIR ARM

The Fleet Air Arm (FAA) provides the Royal Navy with a multi-role aviation combat capability able to operate autonomously at short notice worldwide in all environments, over the sea and land. The FAA numbers some 6,200 people, which comprises 11.5 per cent of the total Royal Naval strength. It operates some 200 combat aircraft and more than 50 support/training aircraft.

ROYAL FLEET AUXILIARY SERVICE (RFA)

The Royal Fleet Auxiliary Service is a civilian-manned flotilla of 16 ships. Its primary role is to supply the Royal Navy and host nations while at sea with fuel, ammunition, food and spares, enabling them to maintain operations away from their home ports. It also provides amphibious support and secure sea transport for military units and their equipment. The ships routinely support and embark Royal Naval Air Squadrons.

ROYAL NAVAL RESERVE (RNR)

The Royal Naval Reserve is an integral part of the Naval Service. It comprises up to 3,250 men and women who volunteer to train in their spare time to enable the Royal Navy to meet its operational commitments, at times of crisis or war.

The broad training requirements are set by the Royal Navy organisations responsible for the operational tasking of the respective branches; for most branches, training is conducted at one of the 13 RNR units across the UK. Basic training is provided at HMS Raleigh, Torpoint in Cornwall for ratings and at the Britannia Royal Naval College, Dartmouth in Devon for officers; both these and most other RNR courses are of two weeks duration or less.

QUEEN ALEXANDRA'S ROYAL NAVAL NURSING SERVICE

The first nursing sisters were appointed to naval hospitals in 1884 and the Queen Alexandra's Royal Naval Nursing Service (QARNNS) gained its current title in 1902. Nursing ratings were introduced in 1960 and men were integrated into the service in 1982; QARNNS recruits qualified nurses as both officers and ratings, and student nurse training can be undertaken in the service.

Patron, HRH Princess Alexandra, the Hon. Lady Ogilvy, KG, GCVO

Director of Naval Nursing Services and Matron-in-Chief, Capt. H. Allkins, QARNNS

HM FLEET

as at 1 June 2009

Submarines	
Vanguard Class	Vanguard, Vengeance, Victorious, Vigilant
Swiftsure Class	Sceptre
Trafalgar Class	Talent, Tireless, Torbay, Trafalgar, Trenchant, Triumph, Turbulent
Aircraft Carriers	Ark Royal, Illustrious, Invincible*
Amphibious Assault Ships	Ocean, Albion, Bulwark
Destroyers	
Type 42 Batch 2	Liverpool, Nottingham
Type 42 Batch 3	Edinburgh, Gloucester, Manchester, York
Frigates	
Type 22	Campbeltown, Chatham, Cornwall, Cumberland
Type 23	Argyll, Iron Duke, Kent, Lancaster, Monmouth, Montrose, Northumberland, Portland, Richmond, St Albans, Somerset, Sutherland, Westminster
Minehunters	
Hunt Class	Atherstone, Brocklesby, Cattistock, Chiddingfold, Hurworth, Ledbury, Middleton, Quorn
Sandown Class	Bangor, Blyth, Grimsby, Pembroke, Penzance, Ramsey, Shoreham, Walney
Patrol Class	
Archer Class P2000 Training Boats	Archer, Biter, Blazer, Charger, Dasher, Example, Exploit, Explorer, Express, Puncher, Pursuer, Raider, Ranger, Smiter, Tracker, Trumpeter
Gibraltar Squadron 16m Fast Patrol Class	Sabre, Scimitar
River Class Patrol Vessels	Mersey, Severn, Tyne, Clyde
Survey Vessels	
Ice Patrol Ship	Endurance
Ocean Survey Vessel	Scott
Coastal Survey Vessels	Gleaner, Roebuck
Multi-Role Survey Vessels	Echo, Enterprise

* HMS Invincible is currently being held at very low readiness

ROYAL FLEET AUXILIARY

Landing Ship Dock (Auxiliary)	RFA Cardigan Bay, RFA Mounts Bay, RFA Largs Bay, RFA Lyme Bay
Wave Class	RFA Wave Knight, RFA Wave Ruler
Rover Class	RFA Black Rover, RFA Gold Rover
Leaf Class	RFA Orangeleaf, RFA Bayleaf
Fort Class	RFA Fort Austin, RFA Fort George, RFA Fort Rosalie, RFA Fort Victoria
Forward Repair Ship	RFA Diligence
Joint Casualty Treatment Ship/Maritime Afloat Training Capability	RFA Argus

THE ARMY

THE QUEEN

FIELD MARSHALS
HRH The Prince Philip, Duke of Edinburgh, KG, KT, OM, GBE, AC, QSO, PC, *apptd* 1953
Lord Bramall, KG, GCB, OBE, MC, *apptd* 1982
Lord Vincent of Coleshill, GBE, KCB, DSO, *apptd* 1991
Sir John Chapple, GCB, CBE, *apptd* 1992
HRH The Duke of Kent, KG, GCMG, GCVO, ADC, *apptd* 1993
Lord Inge, KG, GCB *apptd* 1994

FORMER CHIEFS OF STAFF
Gen. Lord Guthrie of Craigiebank, GCB, LVO, OBE, *apptd* 1994
Gen. Sir Roger Wheeler, GCB, CBE, *apptd* 1997
Gen. Lord Walker of Aldringham, GCB, CMG, CBE, *apptd* 2000
Gen. Sir Mike Jackson, GCB, CBE, DSO, *apptd* 2003
Gen. Sir Timothy Granville-Chapman, GBE, KCB, *apptd* 2005
Gen. Sir Richard Dannatt, GCB, CBE, MC, *apptd* 2006

GENERALS
O'Donoghue, Sir Kevin, KCB, CBE *(Chief of Defence Materiel, Defence Equipment and Support and Master General of Logistics)*
HRH The Prince of Wales, KG, KT, GCB, OM, AK, QSO, PC, ADC
McColl, Sir John, KCB, CBE, DSO *(Deputy Supreme Allied Cdr Europe)*
Richards, Sir David, KCB, CBE, DSO, ADC *(Chief of the General Staff)*
Houghton, Sir Nicholas, KCB, CBE *(Vice Chief of Defence Staff)*
Wall, Sir Peter, KCB, CBE *(Commander-in-Chief Land Forces)*

LIEUTENANT-GENERALS
Parker, Sir Nick, KCB, CBE *(Deputy Cdr International Stabilisation and Assistance Force, Afghanistan)*
Lillywhite, L., CB, MBE, QHS *(Surgeon General)*
Applegate, R., OBE *(Defence Career Partner)*
Leakey, A., CMG, CBE *(Director-General European Union Military Staff)*
Baxter, R., CBE *(Deputy Chief of the Defence Staff (Health))*
Rollo, W., CBE *(Adjutant-General)*
Shirreff, A., CBE *(Cdr Allied Rapid Reaction Corps)*
Graham, A., CBE *(Director Defence Academy)*
Bill, D., CB *(UK Military Representative to NATO and the European Union)*
Brown, C., CBE *(Iraq Compendium Study Team Leader)*
Mayall, S. *(Deputy Chief of Defence Staff (Operations))*
White-Spunner, B., CBE *(Cdr Field Army)*
Coward, G., CB, OBE *(Chief of Materiel (Land), Defence Equipment and Support and Quartermaster General)*
Mans, M., CBE *(Cdr Regional Forces)*

MAJOR-GENERALS
Howell, D., CB, OBE *(Director-General Army Legal Services)*
Roberts, Sir Sebastian, KCVO, OBE *(Senior Army Member, Royal College of Defence Studies)*
Whitley, A., CMG, CBE *(Senior British Loan Service Officer, Oman)*
Wilson, C., CB, CBE *(Director Battlespace Manoeuvre and Master General of the Ordnance)*
Newton, P., CBE *(Assistant Chief of Defence Staff (Concepts and Doctrine))*
Gregory, A. *(Director-General Personnel)*
Melvin, R., OBE *(Senior Army Member, Royal College of Defence Studies)*
Bucknall, J., CBE *(Assistant Chief of the General Staff)*
Binns, G., CBE, DSO, MC *(Commandant Joint Services Command and Staff College)*
von Bertele, M., OBE, QHP *(Director-General Army Medical Services)*
Macklin, A. *(Armoured Fighting Vehicles Group Leader, Defence Equipment and Support)*
Berragan, G. *(Director-General Army Recruiting and Training)*
Shaw, J., CBE *(Assistant Chief of Defence Staff (International Security Policy))*
Lalor, S., TD *(Assistant Chief of the Defence Staff (Reserves and Cadets))*
Sykes, R. *(Defence Services Secretary)*
Page, J., CB, OBE *(MoD)*
Moore, W., CBE *(Defence Career Partner)*
Cubitt, W., CBE *(GOC London District and Maj.-Gen. Commanding The Household Division)*
Rutherford-Jones, D. *(Military Secretary)*
Rutledge, M., OBE *(GOC 5th Division)*
Brealey, B. *(GOC Theatre Troops)*
Bradshaw, A., CB, OBE *(GOC 1st (UK) Armoured Division)*
Inshaw, T. *(Director Training and Education)*
Kennett, A., CBE *(Director-General Land Warfare)*
Caplin, N. *(GOC UK Support Command, Germany)*
Robbins, Ven. S., QHC *(Chaplain General to HM Land Forces)*
Barrons, R., CBE *(Chief of Staff HQ Allied Reaction Corps)*
Dale, I., CBE *(Director Land Equipment, Defence Equipment and Support)*
Porter, R., MBE *(Chief of Staff (Joint Warfare Development), Permanent Joint HQ, UK)*
Gordon, J., CBE *(Cdr British Forces Cyprus and Administrator of the Sovereign Base Areas of Akrotiri and Dhekelia)*
Deverell, C., MBE *(Director-General Logistics, Supply and Equipment, HQ Land Forces)*
Kirkland, R., CBE *(GOC 4th Division)*
Carter, N., CBE *(GOC 6th (UK) Division)*
Poffley, M., OBE *(Chief of Staff HQ Land Forces)*
Andrews, S., CBE *(Director Strategic Change, Defence Medical Services)*
Mackay, A, CBE *(GOC 2nd Division)*
Foster, A., MBE *(Deputy Force Cdr UK Mission, Congo)*
Everard, J., CBE *(GOC 3rd (UK) Division)*
Marriot, P., CBE *(Commandant Royal Military Academy Sandhurst)*

CONSTITUTION OF THE ARMY

The army consists of the Regular Army, the Regular Reserve and the Territorial Army (TA). It is commanded by the Chief of the General Staff, who is the professional Head of Service and Chair of the Executive Committee of the Army Board, which provides overall strategic policy and direction to the commands. These are: Land Command, which comprises the Field Army, Regional Forces and the Joint Helicopter Command; and the

Adjutant-General's Command, responsible for army personnel matters and education and training. The army is divided into functional arms and services, sub-divided into regiments and corps (listed below in order of precedence). The first phase of a major reform programme known as the Future Army Structure (FAS) was completed during 2008. The FAS incorporates changes in tactical doctrine, organisational structure, personnel terms and conditions of service and the introduction of new equipment. Under the first phase, the infantry was re-structured into large multi-battalion regiments, which involved amalgamations and changes in title for some regiments.

Members of the public can write for general information to Headquarters Adjutant General Secretariat, Trenchard Lines, Upavon, Wiltshire SN9 6BE. All enquiries with regard to records of serving personnel (Regular and Territorial Army) should be directed to The Army Personnel Centre Help Desk, Kentigern House, 65 Brown Street, Glasgow G2 8EX T 0141-224 2023/3303. Enquirers should note that the Army is governed in the release of personal information by various Acts of Parliament.

ORDER OF PRECEDENCE OF CORPS AND REGIMENTS OF THE BRITISH ARMY

ARMS

HOUSEHOLD CAVALRY
The Life Guards
The Blues and Royals (Royal Horse Guards and 1st Dragoons)

ROYAL HORSE ARTILLERY
(when on parade, the Royal Horse Artillery take precedence over the Household Cavalry)

ROYAL ARMOURED CORPS
1st the Queen's Dragoon Guards
The Royal Scots Dragoon Guards (Carabiniers and Greys)
The Royal Dragoon Guards
The Queen's Royal Hussars (The Queen's Own and Royal Irish)
9th/12th Royal Lancers (Prince of Wales')
The King's Royal Hussars
The Light Dragoons
The Queen's Royal Lancers
1st Royal Tank Regiment
2nd Royal Tank Regiment

ROYAL REGIMENT OF ARTILLERY
(with the exception of the Royal Horse Artillery (*see* above))

CORPS OF ROYAL ENGINEERS

ROYAL CORPS OF SIGNALS

REGIMENTS OF FOOT GUARDS
Grenadier Guards
Coldstream Guards
Scots Guards
Irish Guards
Welsh Guards

REGIMENTS OF INFANTRY
The Royal Regiment of Scotland
The Princess of Wales' Royal Regiment (Queen and Royal Hampshire's)
The Duke of Lancaster's Regiment (King's, Lancashire and Border)
The Royal Regiment of Fusiliers
The Royal Anglian Regiment
The Rifles
The Yorkshire Regiment
The Mercian Regiment
The Royal Welsh
The Royal Irish Regiment
The Parachute Regiment
The Royal Gurkha Rifles

SPECIAL AIR SERVICE

ARMY AIR CORPS

SERVICES

ROYAL ARMY CHAPLAINS' DEPARTMENT
THE ROYAL LOGISTIC CORPS
ROYAL ARMY MEDICAL CORPS
CORPS OF ROYAL ELECTRICAL AND MECHANICAL ENGINEERS
ADJUTANT-GENERAL'S CORPS
ROYAL ARMY VETERINARY CORPS
SMALL ARMS SCHOOL CORPS
ROYAL ARMY DENTAL CORPS
INTELLIGENCE CORPS
ARMY PHYSICAL TRAINING CORPS
QUEEN ALEXANDRA'S ROYAL ARMY NURSING CORPS
CORPS OF ARMY MUSIC
THE ROYAL MONMOUTHSHIRE ROYAL ENGINEERS (MILITIA) (TA)
THE HONOURABLE ARTILLERY COMPANY (TA)
REST OF THE TERRITORIAL ARMY (TA)

ARMY EQUIPMENT

Tanks	386
Challenger 2	386
Reconnaissance vehicles	475
Fuchs	11
Sabre	137
Scimitar	327
Reconnaissance aircraft	3
Armoured Infantry Fighting Vehicle	575
Armoured Personnel Carrier	2,718
Combat Personnel Vehicle	100
Jackal	100
Artillery pieces	877
Anti-tank missile	800+
Helicopters	299
Attack	166
Apache	67
Lynx	99
Observation	133
Gazelle	133
Unmanned aerial vehicle*	192+
Surface-to-air missile	339+
Land radar	157
Miscellaneous boats/craft	4
Amphibious craft	4
Logistics and support vehicles	6

* 2008 figure
Source: Military Balance 2009

THE TERRITORIAL ARMY (TA)

The Territorial Army is part of the UK's reserve land forces and provides support to the regular army at home and overseas. The TA is divided into three types of unit: national, regional, and sponsored. TA soldiers serving in regional units complete a minimum of 27 days training a year, comprising some evenings, weekends and an annual two-week camp. National units normally specialise in a specific role or trade, such as logistics, IT, communications or medical services. Members of national units have a lower level of training commitment and complete 19 days training a year. Sponsored reserves are individuals who will serve, as members of the workforce of a company contracted to the MoD, in a military capacity and have agreed to accept a reserve liability to be called up for active service in a crisis. As at 1 February 2009 the TA's total strength was around 35,900.

QUEEN ALEXANDRA'S ROYAL ARMY NURSING CORPS

The Queen Alexandra's Royal Army Nursing Corps (QARANC) was founded in 1902 as Queen Alexandra's Imperial Military Nursing Service and gained its present title in 1949. The QARANC has trained nurses for the register since 1950 and also trains and employs health care assistants to Level 2 NVQ, with the option to train to Level 3. The corps recruits qualified nurses as officers and other ranks and in 1992 male nurses already serving in the army were transferred to the QARANC.

Colonel-in-Chief, HRH The Countess of Wessex
Colonels Commandant, Col. Rosemary Kennedy, TD; Col. Bridget McEvilly, CBE

THE ROYAL AIR FORCE

THE QUEEN

MARSHAL OF THE ROYAL AIR FORCE
HRH The Prince Philip, Duke of Edinburgh, KG, KT, OM, GBE, AC, QSO, PC, *apptd* 1953

FORMER CHIEFS OF THE AIR STAFF

MARSHALS OF THE ROYAL AIR FORCE
Sir Michael Beetham, GCB, CBE, DFC, AFC, *apptd* 1982
Sir Keith Williamson, GCB, AFC, *apptd* 1985
Lord Craig of Radley, GCB, OBE, *apptd* 1988

AIR CHIEF MARSHALS
Sir Michael Graydon, GCB, CBE, *apptd* 1991
Sir Richard Johns, GCB, KCVO, OBE, *apptd* 1994
Sir Peter Squire, GCB, DFC, AFC *apptd* 1999
Sir Glenn Torpy, GCB, CBE, DSO *apptd* 2006

AIR RANK LIST

AIR CHIEF MARSHALS
Stirrup, Sir Jock, GCB, AFC, ADC *(Chief of the Defence Staff)*
HRH The Prince of Wales, KG, KT, GCB, OM, AK, QSO, PC, ADC
Dalton, Sir Stephen, KCB, ADC *(Chief of the Air Staff)*
Moran, Sir Christopher, KCB, OBE, MVO, ADC *(Commander-in-Chief, Air Command)*

AIR MARSHALS
Peach, Sir Stuart, KCB, CBE *(Chief of Joint Operations)*
McNicoll, I., CB, CBE *(Deputy Commander-in-Chief Operations, Air Command)*
Walker, D., CBE, AFC *(Deputy Cdr Allied Air Component Command, Ramstein)*
Nickols, C., CBE *(Chief of Defence Intelligence)*
Ruddock, P., CBE *(Director-General Saudi Arabia Armed Forces Project)*
Harper, C., CBE *(Deputy Commander Allied Joint Force Command, Brunssum)*
Bryant, S., CBE *(Deputy Commander-in-Chief Personnel and Air Member for Personnel, Air Command)*
Leeson, K., CBE *(Chief of Materiel (Air)/Air Member for Materiel)*

AIR VICE-MARSHALS
Ness, C., CB *(Director Haddon-Cave Review)*
Walker, D., OBE, MVO *(Master of the Royal Household)*
Mills, Revd P., QHC *(Director RAF Chaplaincy Services)*
Pulford, A., CBE *(Assistant Chief of Defence Staff (Operations))*
Allan, R., OBE *(Director Information Systems and Services)*
Anderson, T., CB, DSO *(Assistant Chief of the Air Staff)*
Kurth, N., CBE *(Chief of Staff (Support) Air Command)*
Garwood, R., CBE, DFC *(Chief of Staff (Operations) Air Command)*
Bollom, S. *(Director Combat (Air) Defence Equipment and Support)*
Wiles, M., CBE *(Director Joint Support Chain, Defence Equipment and Support)*
Dixon, C., OBE *(Director Information Superiority/Air Member for Equipment Capability)*
Evans, C., QHP *(Cdr Joint Medical Command)*
Hillier, S., CBE, DFC *(Air Officer Commanding No. 2 Group)*
Harwood, M., CBE *(Head of the British Defence Staff, USA and Defence Attaché)*
Bagwell, G., CBE *(Air Officer Commanding No. 1 Group)*
Stacey, G., MBE *(Senior British Military Adviser, HQ USA Central Command)*
Lloyd, M. *(Chief of Staff Personnel and Air Secretary)*
Irvine, L. *(Director RAF Legal Services)*
North, B., OBE *(Air Officer Commanding, No. 22 Group/Chief of Staff Training)*
Lamonte, J. *(Chief of Staff Strategy, Policy and Plans, Air Command)*
Bates, B., CBE *(Senior Directing Staff (Air), Royal College of Defence Studies)*
Young, J., OBE *(Director Defence Support Review)*

CONSTITUTION OF THE RAF

The RAF consists of a single command, Air Command, based at RAF High Wycombe. RAF Air Command was formed on 1 April 2007 from the amalgamation of Strike Command and Personnel and Training Command.

Air Command consists of three groups, each organised around specific operational duties. No. 1 Group is the coordinating organisation for the tactical fast-jet forces responsible for attack, offensive support and air defence operations. No. 2 Group provides air combat support including air transport and air to air refuelling; intelligence surveillance; targeting and reconnaissance; and force protection. No. 22 (Training) Group recruits personnel and provides trained specialist personnel to the RAF, as well as to the Royal Navy and the Army (*see also* Armed Forces Training and Recruitment).

RAF EQUIPMENT

Aircraft	
BAe 125	6
BAe 146	2
Dominie	9
Firefly	38
Globemaster	6
Harrier	68
Hawk	112
Hercules	43
Islander	2
Nimrod	18
Sentinel	5
Sentry	7
Super King Air (leased)	7
Tornado	209
Tristar	9
Tucano	95
Tutor	99
Typhoon	57
VC10	16
Helicopters	
Chinook	40
Griffin	16
Merlin	28
Puma	43
Sea King	25
Squirrel	31

Source: Military Balance 2009

ROYAL AUXILIARY AIR FORCE

The Auxiliary Air Force was formed in 1924 to train an elite corps of civilians to serve their country in flying squadrons in their spare time. In 1947 the force was awarded the prefix 'royal' in recognition of its distinguished war service and the Sovereign's Colour for the Royal Auxiliary Air Force (RAuxAF) was presented in 1989. The RAuxAF continues to recruit civilians who undertake military training in their spare time to support the Royal Air Force in times of emergency or war.

Air Commodore-in-Chief, HM The Queen

Honorary Inspector-General Royal Auxiliary Air Force, Air Marshal Ian McFadyen, CB, OBE

Inspector Royal Auxiliary Air Force, Gp Capt. Gary Bunkell, QVRM, AE, ADC

PRINCESS MARY'S ROYAL AIR FORCE NURSING SERVICE

The Princess Mary's Royal Air Force Nursing Service (PMRAFNS) was formed on 1 June 1918 as the Royal Air Force Nursing Service. In June 1923, His Majesty King George V gave his royal assent for the Royal Air Force Nursing Service to be known as the Princess Mary's Royal Air Force Nursing Service. Men were integrated into the PMRAFNS in 1980.

Patron and Air Chief Commandant, HRH Princess Alexandra, The Hon. Lady Ogilvy, KG, GCVO

Director of Nursing Services and Matron-in-Chief, Gp Capt. Jacqueline Gross

SERVICE SALARIES

The following rates of pay apply from 1 April 2009.

The pay rates shown are for army personnel. The rates also apply to personnel of equivalent rank and pay band in the other services (*see* below for table of relative ranks).

Rank	*Annual salary*
SECOND LIEUTENANT	£24,132.60
LIEUTENANT	
On appointment	£29,006.40
After 1 year in rank	£29,773.44
After 2 years in rank	£30,536.04
After 3 years in rank	£31,294.92
After 4 years in rank	£32,061.72
CAPTAIN	
On appointment	£37,172.52
After 1 year in rank	£38,168.28
After 2 years in rank	£39,175.80
After 3 years in rank	£40,187.64
After 4 years in rank	£41,187.36
After 5 years in rank	£42,194.88
After 6 years in rank	£43,194.60
After 7 years in rank	£43,704.48
After 8 years in rank	£44,206.32
MAJOR	
On appointment	£46,824.00
After 1 year in rank	£47,980.32
After 2 years in rank	£49,128.36
After 3 years in rank	£50,292.60
After 4 years in rank	£51,444.96
After 5 years in rank	£52,609.20
After 6 years in rank	£53,765.40
After 7 years in rank	£54,917.52
After 8 years in rank	£56,077.92
LIEUTENANT-COLONEL	
On appointment	£65,717.16
After 1 year in rank	£66,588.48
After 2 years in rank	£67,451.52
After 3 years in rank	£68,314.92
After 4 years in rank	£69,178.08
After 5 years in rank	£73,151.04
After 6 years in rank	£74,126.40
After 7 years in rank	£75,110.88
After 8 years in rank	£76,095.24
COLONEL	
On appointment	£79,716.12
After 1 year in rank	£80,707.08
After 2 years in rank	£81,701.88
After 3 years in rank	£82,692.84
After 4 years in rank	£83,683.80
After 5 years in rank	£84,674.52
After 6 years in rank	£85,665.48
After 7 years in rank	£86,660.40
After 8 years in rank	£87,655.20
BRIGADIER	
On appointment	£95,127.60
After 1 year in rank	£96,090.72
After 2 years in rank	£97,053.72
After 3 years in rank	£98,012.76
After 4 years in rank	£98,983.80

PAY SYSTEM FOR SENIOR MILITARY OFFICERS

Revised pay rates effective from 1 April 2009 for all military officers of 2* rank and above (excluding medical and dental officers).

MAJOR-GENERAL (2*)	*Annual salary*
Scale 1	£103,872.96
Scale 2	£105,399.96
Scale 3	£107,420.04
Scale 4	£109,830.96
Scale 5	£112,244.04
Scale 6	£114,654.96
Scale 7	£117,065.04
LIEUTENANT-GENERAL (3*)	
Scale 1	£122,094.96
Scale 2	£129,669.00
Scale 3	£137,243.04
Scale 4	£142,029.96
Scale 5	£146,820.96
Scale 6	£151,608.96
Scale 7	n/a
GENERAL (4*)	
Scale 1	£162,212.04
Scale 2	£165,444.96
Scale 3	£168,753.96
Scale 4	£172,130.04
Scale 5	£175,571.04
Scale 6	£179,084.04
Scale 7	n/a

Field Marshal – appointments to this rank will not usually be made in peacetime. The salary for holders of the rank is equivalent to the salary of a 5-star General, a salary created only in times of war. In peacetime, the equivalent rank to Field Marshal is the Chief of the Defence Staff. From 1 April 2009, the annual salary range for the Chief of the Defence Staff is £233,157.00–£247,427.04.

OFFICERS COMMISSIONED FROM THE SENIOR RANKS

Rank	*Annual salary*
Level 15	£49,686.48
Level 14	£49,361.40
Level 13	£49,020.12
Level 12	£48,357.60
Level 11	£47,699.16
Level 10	£47,032.68
Level 9	£46,370.16
Level 8	£45,707.88
Level 7*	£44,880.84
Level 6	£44,370.96
Level 5	£43,853.04
Level 4†	£42,829.20
Level 3	£42,319.32
Level 2	£41,797.44
Level 1‡	£40,777.80

* Officers commissioned from the ranks with more than 15 years' service enter on level 7

† Officers commissioned from the ranks with between 12 and 15 years' service enter on level 4

‡ Officers commissioned from the ranks with less than 12 years' service enter on level 1

SOLDIERS' SALARIES

Under the Pay 2000 scheme, personnel are paid in either a high or low band in accordance with how their trade has been allocated to those bands at each rank. Pay is based on trade and rank, not on individual appointment, or in response to temporary changes in role.

Rates of pay effective from 1 April 2009 are:

Rank	*Lower Band*	*Higher Band*
PRIVATE		
Level 1	£16,681.20	£16,681.20
Level 2	£17,142.96	£17,982.00
Level 3	£17,604.60	£19,852.92
Level 4	£19,146.24	£21,346.44
LANCE CORPORAL (levels 5–7 also applicable to Privates)		
Level 5	£20,178.00	£23,602.68
Level 6	£21,021.24	£24,750.96
Level 7	£21,920.52	£25,886.88
Level 8	£22,924.08	£27,051.36
Level 9	£23,755.20	£28,372.08
CORPORAL		
Level 1	£25,886.88	£27,051.36
Level 2	£27,051.36	£28,372.08
Level 3	£28,372.08	£29,761.20
Level 4	£28,589.04	£30,455.64
Level 5	£28,813.80	£31,190.52
Level 6	£29,042.76	£31,836.96
Level 7	£29,255.40	£32,531.64
SERGEANT		
Level 1	£29,424.00	£32,113.92
Level 2	£30,194.88	£32,945.04
Level 3	£30,953.64	£33,780.00
Level 4	£31,266.72	£34,205.64
Level 5	£32,081.76	£34,872.12
Level 6	£33,189.72	£35,538.48
Level 7	£33,442.80	£36,204.84
STAFF SERGEANT		
Level 1	£32,571.72	£36,228.96
Level 2	£32,997.12	£37,104.24
Level 3	£34,069.08	£37,991.40
Level 4	£34,868.04	£38,870.64
WARRANT OFFICER II (levels 5–7 also applicable to Staff Sergeants)		
Level 5	£35,341.68	£39,753.96
Level 6	£36,939.72	£40,633.20
Level 7	£37,505.64	£41,219.40
Level 8	£37,991.40	£41,805.48
Level 9	£38,850.60	£42,403.80
WARRANT OFFICER I		
Level 1	£37,842.84	£41,255.28
Level 2	£38,577.60	£42,066.36
Level 3	£39,356.40	£42,789.12
Level 4	£40,135.32	£43,575.96
Level 5	£40,918.08	£44,354.88
Level 6	£42,066.36	£45,145,68
Level 7	£43,254.84	£45,836.40

RELATIVE RANK – ARMED FORCES

Royal Navy	*Army*	*Royal Air Force*
1 Admiral of the Fleet	1 Field Marshal	1 Marshal of the RAF
2 Admiral (Adm.)	2 General (Gen.)	2 Air Chief Marshal
3 Vice-Admiral (Vice-Adm.)	3 Lieutenant-General (Lt.-Gen.)	3 Air Marshal
4 Rear-Admiral (Rear-Adm.)	4 Major-General (Maj.-Gen.)	4 Air Vice-Marshal
5 Commodore (Cdre)	5 Brigadier (Brig.)	5 Air Commodore (Air Cdre)
6 Captain (Capt.)	6 Colonel (Col.)	6 Group Captain (Gp Capt.)
7 Commander (Cdr)	7 Lieutenant-Colonel (Lt.-Col.)	7 Wing Commander (Wg Cdr)
8 Lieutenant-Commander (Lt.-Cdr)	8 Major (Maj.)	8 Squadron Leader (Sqn Ldr)
9 Lieutenant (Lt.)	9 Captain (Capt.)	9 Flight Lieutenant (Flt Lt)
10 Sub-Lieutenant (Sub-Lt.)	10 Lieutenant (Lt.)	10 Flying Officer (FO)
11 Midshipman	11 Second Lieutenant (2nd Lt.)	11 Pilot Officer (PO)

SERVICE RETIRED PAY

On compulsory retirement

Those who leave the services having served at least five years, but not long enough to qualify for the appropriate immediate pension, now qualify for a preserved pension and terminal grant, both of which are payable at age 60. The tax-free resettlement grants shown below are payable on release to those who qualify for a preserved pension and who have completed nine years' service from age 21 (officers) or 12 years from age 18 (other ranks).

The annual rates for army personnel are given. The rates also apply to personnel of equivalent rank in the other services, including the nursing services.

OFFICERS

Applicable to officers who give full pay service on the active list on or after 31 March 2009. Pensionable earnings for senior officers (*) is defined as the total amount of basic pay received during the year ending on the day prior to retirement, or the amount of basic pay received during any 12-month period within 3 years prior to retirement, whichever is the higher. Figures for senior officers are percentage rates of pensionable earnings on final salary arrangements on or after 31 March 2009.

No. of years reckonable service	*Capt. and below*	*Major*	*Lt.-Col.*	*Colonel*	*Brigadier*	*Major-General**	*Lieutenant-General**	*General**
16	£12,310	£14,662	£19,224	£23,285	£27,660	—	—	—
17	£12,878	£15,358	£20,206	£24,353	£28,739	—	—	—
18	£13,445	£16,055	£21,188	£25,421	£29,817	—	—	—
19	£14,013	£16,751	£22,171	£26,490	£30,895	—	—	—
20	£14,580	£17,448	£23,153	£27,558	£31,974	—	—	—
21	£15,147	£18,144	£24,135	£28,626	£33,052	—	—	—
22	£15,715	£18,840	£25,118	£29,694	£34,131	—	—	—
23	£16,282	£19,537	£26,100	£30,762	£35,209	—	—	—
24	£16,850	£20,233	£27,083	£31,831	£36,287	38.5%	—	—
25	£17,417	£20,930	£28,065	£32,899	£37,366	39.7%	—	—
26	£17,984	£21,626	£29,047	£33,967	£38,444	40.8%	—	—
27	£18,552	£22,323	£30,030	£35,035	£39,522	42.0%	42.0%	—
28	£19,119	£23,019	£31,012	£36,104	£40,601	43.1%	43.1%	—
29	£19,687	£23,716	£31,994	£37,172	£41,679	44.3%	44.3%	—
30	£20,254	£24,412	£32,977	£38,240	£42,758	45.4%	45.4%	45.4%
31	£20,821	£25,108	£33,959	£39,308	£43,836	46.6%	46.6%	46.6%
32	£21,389	£25,805	£34,941	£40,376	£44,914	47.7%	47.7%	47.7%
33	£21,956	£26,501	£35,924	£41,445	£45,993	48.9%	48.9%	48.9%
34	£22,524	£27,198	£36,906	£42,513	£47,071	50.0%	50.0%	50.0%

WARRANT OFFICERS, NCOS AND PRIVATES

(Applicable to soldiers who give full pay service on or after 31 March 2009)

No. of years reckonable service	*Below Corporal*	*Corporal*	*Sergeant*	*Staff Sergeant*	*Warrant Officer Level II*	*Warrant Officer Level I*
22	£7,285	£9,398	£10,303	£11,737	£12,530	£13,324
23	£7,540	£9,726	£10,663	£12,146	£12,968	£13,789
24	£7,794	£10,054	£11,023	£12,556	£13,405	£14,254
25	£8,048	£10,382	£11,382	£12,966	£13,842	£14,719
26	£8,303	£10,710	£11,742	£13,375	£14,280	£15,184
27	£8,557	£11,038	£12,102	£13,785	£14,717	£15,649
28	£8,811	£11,366	£12,461	£14,195	£15,154	£16,114
29	£9,065	£11,694	£12,821	£14,604	£15,592	£16,579
30	£9,320	£12,022	£13,180	£15,014	£16,029	£17,044
31	£9,574	£12,350	£13,540	£15,424	£16,467	£17,510
32	£9,828	£12,678	£13,900	£15,833	£16,904	£17,975
33	£10,083	£13,006	£14,259	£16,243	£17,341	£18,440
34	£10,337	£13,334	£14,619	£16,653	£17,779	£18,905
35	£10,591	£13,662	£14,979	£17,062	£18,216	£19,370
36	£10,845	£13,990	£15,338	£17,472	£18,653	£19,835
37	£11,100	£14,318	£15,698	£17,882	£19,091	£20,300

GRANTS AND GRATUITIES

Terminal grants are in each case three times the rate of retired pay or pension. There are special rates of retired pay for certain other ranks not shown above. Lower rates are payable in cases of voluntary retirement.

A gratuity of £4,190 is payable for officers with short service commissions for each year completed. Resettlement grants are £14,398 for officers and £9,841 for other ranks.

THE EDUCATION SYSTEM

Responsibility for education in England lies with the Secretaries of State for Children, Schools and Families (DCSF) and Business, Innovation and Skills (BIS); in Wales, with Welsh ministers; in Scotland, with Scottish ministers; and in Northern Ireland with the education minister and the minister for employment and learning.

EXPENDITURE

Most education expenditure is incurred by local authorities, who direct funding on to schools, children's centres and other educational institutions according to their own spending plans or in accordance with conditions of grant funding. Expenditure for higher and further education in England and Scotland is met by the respective funding agencies; in Wales it is provided directly to post-16 providers.

The bulk of direct expenditure by BIS, the Welsh Assembly Government and the Scottish government is directed towards supporting post-16 education. Funding for higher education in universities and colleges is channelled through the Higher Education Funding Councils (HEFCs). Funding for research is distributed partly through the HEFCs and partly through Research Councils. Funding for further education, sixth form provision, work based learning and adult and community education is channelled through the funding councils for that sector, but in Wales is provided directly to post-16 providers through the Welsh Assembly Government's Department for Children, Education, Lifelong Learning and Skills (DCELLS). In addition, BIS currently funds student support for students who normally live in England and the Welsh Assembly Government is responsible for student support in Wales for students who normally live in Wales. The DCSF is responsible for the City Technology Colleges, the City College for the Technology of the Arts, and pays grants under the specialist schools programme in England. In Northern Ireland funding for higher and further education is provided by the Department for Employment and Learning. This department is also responsible for the provision of funding for student support.

LOCAL EDUCATION ADMINISTRATION

In England and Wales the school education service is administered by local authorities, which have day-to-day responsibility for providing state primary and secondary education and special schools. They are also responsible for securing early years education and special education for pupils in their area which can be in maintained and special schools or in non-local authority maintained schools and other settings. Local authorities share with the appropriate funding bodies (in Wales with the Assembly Government) the duty to provide adult education to meet local needs.

Unlike other services, where local authorities are financed largely from council tax, since 2006–7 revenue funding for schools is provided through the Dedicated Schools Grant from the DCSF to each local authority.

Responsibility for commissioning education and training provision for 16 to 19-year-olds is to be transferred from the Learning and Skills Council (LSC) to local authorities. This will mean more local accountability and allow local authorities to take a more integrated approach to the delivery of services to young people. It is hoped that education and training providers will develop a collaborative approach, responding to the needs of both learners and employers.

Capital funding is provided to schools and authorities through a combination of devolved, targeted and strategic programmes including the Building Schools for the Future and Academies programmes.

Authority-maintained schools usually manage their own budgets: the local authority allocates funds to schools, largely on the basis of pupil numbers, and the schools' governing bodies are responsible for overseeing spending and for most aspects of staffing, including appointments and dismissals. Local authorities have intervention powers to add additional governors, take back control of a school's budget or apply to the secretary of state to replace the governing body of a school with an interim executive board when a school is placed under special measures, is judged to require significant improvement or is causing concern and has not complied with a warning notice from the authority.

Funding support for statutory age school education in Wales is provided to local authorities through the revenue support grant – the block grant for the Welsh Assembly Government supports local authorities to deliver a wide range of services.

In Scotland there are three categories of school: publicly funded, grant aided and independent. The vast majority are publicly funded and the duty of providing education locally in Scotland rests with the education authorities. They are responsible for the construction of buildings, the employment of teachers and other staff, and the provision of equipment and materials.

Devolved school management is in place for all primary, secondary and special schools. From August 2007, parent councils replaced school boards. The new councils are designed to make parents more involved in their child's education.

Scotland has primary, secondary and special schools, of which there are 392 state-funded faith schools: 388 Catholic, one Jewish and three Episcopalian.

Education, with the exception of further and higher education, is administered locally in Northern Ireland by five education and library boards (ELBs), which fund controlled and maintained schools and whose costs are met in full by the Northern Ireland Executive. All grant-aided schools include elected parents and teachers on their boards of governors. All schools and colleges of further education have full responsibility for their own budgets, including staffing costs.

EDUCATION IN FIGURES

EXPENDITURE

UK EXPENDITURE ON EDUCATION AND TRAINING
(£m)

	2007–8 outturn	*2008–9 est*
Under-fives	4,425	4,708
Primary schools	21,381	22,421
Secondary schools	23,459	24,224
Post-secondary non-tertiary education	8,547	8,827

Tertiary education	11,675	12,342
Training	2,413	2,888
Other education and training	6,198	7,377
Total	78,098	82,787

Source: PESA 2009

UK MANAGED EXPENDITURE ON EDUCATION *(percentage of GDP)*

	2006–7 outturn	*2007–8 outturn*	*2008–9 est*
Education	5.4	5.5	5.8

Source: PESA 2009

UK MANAGED EXPENDITURE ON EDUCATION (REAL TERMS) *(£bn)*

1999–2000	51.3	2004–5	70.2
2000–1	55.2	2005–6	73.6
2001–2	60.2	2006–7	75.0
2002–3	62.3	2007–8	78.1
2003–4	67.6	2008–9 (est)	80.8

Source: PESA 2009

UK EXPENDITURE BY THE GOVERNMENT AND LOCAL AUTHORITIES (2007–8) *(£m)*

Local authorities	
Current	45,104
Capital	4,627
Total	49,731
Central government	
Current	26,065
Capital	2,670
Total	28,735
All public authorities	
Current	71,169
Capital	7,297
TOTAL	78,466

Source: PESA 2009

SCHOOLS AND PUPILS

PRE-SCHOOL EDUCATION (2008) *(percentage)*

	Public sector	*Private and voluntary*	*Total*
UK	64	35	99
England	62	39	101
Wales	86	—	86
Scotland	70	26	96
Northern Ireland	57	14	72

UK SCHOOLS BY CATEGORY (2007–8)

	England	*Wales*
Maintained nursery schools	447	28
Maintained primary and secondary schools	20,500	1,731
Community	12,590	1,456
Voluntary aided	4,266	163
Voluntary controlled	2,636	100
Foundation	1,008	12
Pupil referral units	455	51
Maintained special schools	933	44
Non-maintained special schools	72	—
City Technology Colleges and City Colleges for the Technology of the Arts	5	—
Academies	83	—
Independent schools	2,327	66
Total	24,882	1,920

Scotland	
Publicly funded schools	2,722
Primary	2,153
Secondary	376
Special	193
Independent	154
Primary	59
Secondary	54
Special	41
Total	2,905
Northern Ireland	
Grant-aided mainstream	
Nursery*	98
Primary	868
Secondary	226
grammar	69
other	157
Non-maintained mainstream	17
Special (maintained)	45†
Total	1,254

* Excludes voluntary and private pre-school education centres
† Figure includes two hospital schools

UK PUPILS IN THE MAINTAINED SECTOR (2007–8)

Nursery pupils	151,100
Primary pupils	4,891,900
Secondary pupils	3,953,400
Pupils in special schools	100,100
Pupils in pupil referral units	16,700
Total	9,113,300

SPECIAL NEEDS PUPILS (2007–8)

	Pupils with special educational needs	*Percentage of all pupils*
England	223,600	2.8
Wales	14,900	3.1
Scotland*	10,300	1.2
Northern Ireland	13,000	3.9
Total	261,800	2.7

* For Scotland, pupils with a record of needs or a coordinated support plan, including some who also had an individualised educational programme (IEP)

TEACHERS

FULL-TIME QUALIFIED TEACHERS (2006–7 est) *(thousands)*

	E&W	*Scotland*	*NI*	*UK*
Maintained nursery and primary schools	178.0	22.4	7.6	207.0
Maintained secondary schools	200.4	24.2	9.8	234.4
Non-maintained mainstream schools	55.9	2.7	0.1	58.7
All special schools	17.7	2.1	0.7	20.5
Total	450.9	51.4	18.2	520.6

UK PRIMARY SCHOOL PUPIL-TEACHER RATIOS*

	England	*Wales*	*Scotland*	*NI*
2005–6	22.0	19.8	17.1	20.5
2006–7	21.8	19.9	16.3	20.8
2007–8	21.6	19.9	16.0	20.6

* The average size of classes 'as taught' was 25.8 in 2007–8 (Figures refer to 'all classes' rather than 'one-teacher classes' only)

UK SECONDARY SCHOOLS (2007–8)

	England	*Wales*	*Scotland*	*NI*
No. of pupils	3,289,000	206,900	309,500	149,900
Average class size	20.9	20.2	—	—
Pupil-teacher ratio	16.5	16.6	12.0	14.5

POST-16 AND HIGHER EDUCATION

POST-16 STUDENTS (2006–7)

	Full-time	*Part-time*
UK	1,046,600	2,593,600
England	928,200	1,988,200
Wales	43,600	189,200
Scotland*	47,000	304,300
Northern Ireland	27,800	111,900

* Enrolments, not head count

HIGHER EDUCATION STUDENTS* (2007–8)

	Part-time	*Full-time*	*Total*
HE students	–	–	2,306,105
Postgraduate students	252,755	248,380	501,135
Undergraduate students	572,965	1,232,005	1,804,970

* includes UK, EU and non-EU students

Source: HESA 2009

UK HIGHER EDUCATION QUALIFICATIONS AWARDED (2007–8)

	Full-time	*Part-time*
First degrees	297,235	37,655
Postgraduate research	15,420	4,050
Postgraduate taught	97,950	62,635
PGCE	24,015	4,045
Other graduate	54,380	79,070
Total	489,005	187,455

Source: HESA 2009

UK HIGHER EDUCATION INCOME BY SOURCE (2007–8)

	£ thousand	*Percentage of total*
Funding council grants	8,507,989	36.3
Tuition fees, education grants and contracts	6,253,998	26.7
Research grants and contracts	3,721,881	15.9
Endowment and investment	507,791	2.2
Other	4,447,967	19.0
Total	23,439,626	100

Source: HESA 2009

UK HIGHER EDUCATION EXPENDITURE (2007–8)

	£ thousand	*Percentage of total*
Staff costs	13,135,202	57.4
Other operating expenses	8,276,341	36.2
Depreciation	1,187,706	5.2
Interest payable	285,730	1.2
Total	22,884,979	100

Source: HESA 2009

Statistics are published by each of the home education departments and the Higher Education Statistics Agency (HESA) through press notices, bulletins and statistical volumes. These can be found on the following websites:

ENGLAND W www.dcsf.gov.uk, www.bis.gov.uk
WALES W www.wales.gov.uk
SCOTLAND W www.scotland.gov.uk
NORTHERN IRELAND W www.deni.gov.uk
HESA W www.hesa.ac.uk

THE INSPECTORATE

ENGLAND

The Office for Standards in Education, Children's Services and Skills (OFSTED) was created on 1 April 2007. It has responsibility for the regulatory and inspection activities of the former Office for Standards in Education; inspection of adult learning and training formerly undertaken by the Adult Learning Inspectorate; the regulation and inspection of children's social care formerly undertaken by the Commission for Social Care Inspection; and the inspection of the Children and Family Court Advisory and Support Service formerly undertaken by Her Majesty's Inspectorate of Court Administration.

OFSTED is a non-ministerial government department whose executive head is Her Majesty's Chief Inspector of Education, Children's Services and Skills (HMCI). OFSTED is responsible for the registration and inspection of childcare, arrangements for social care and support of children and young people, and the inspection of all maintained and some independent schools. It is also responsible for the inspection of further education, all publicly funded adult education and training and some privately funded training provision, and the inspection of teacher training.

The inspection of the Children and Family Court Advisory and Support Service (CAFCASS) is also undertaken by OFSTED. Joint area reviews and annual performance assessments of local children's services provision continue to be led by OFSTED. The post of the Children's Rights Director (CRD) transferred to OFSTED from the Commission for Social Care Inspection on 1 April 2007.

The Education and Inspections Act that established the new OFSTED requires the inspectorate to promote improvement in the public services it inspects and regulates; ensure that these services focus on the interests of children, parents, learners and employers; and ensure that these services are efficient and effective. The act also established a board to provide strategic oversight of OFSTED. The non-executive board has a duty to have regard to the views of service users as well as a statutory purpose to encourage improvement.

WALES

HM Inspectorate for Education and Training in Wales (Estyn: Arolygiaeth Ei Mawrhydi dros Addysg a Hyfforddiant yng Nghymru) is responsible for inspecting early years provision in the non-maintained sector, primary schools, secondary schools, special schools (including independent special schools), pupil referral units, independent schools, further education, youth support services, local education authorities, initial teacher training, work-based learning, Careers Wales companies, the education, guidance and training elements of Workstep programmes and adult community-based learning. Its remit from the Welsh ministers also includes providing advice on a wide range of education and training matters.

SCOTLAND

HM Inspectorate of Education (HMIE) is an executive agency of the Scottish government. HM Inspectors (HMIs) inspect or review and report on education in primary, secondary and special schools, further education institutions (under contract to the Scottish Further and Higher Education Funding Council), initial teacher education, community learning, care and welfare of pupils, the education functions of local authorities, prison education, children's services and in other contexts as necessary. They work in collaboration with the Care Commission in integrated inspection of pre-school education centres and residential schools, with Audit Scotland on the inspection of education authorities and on behalf of the Scottish Further and Higher Education Funding Council in the review of Scotland's 43 further education colleges.

The HMIs work in teams alongside lay members (who are volunteer members of the public) and associate assessors (who are practising teachers or senior educationalists seconded for the inspection). HMIE is led by the senior chief inspector, supported by six chief inspectors (five of whom head inspectorates) and twelve assistant chief inspectors. The Scottish Further and Higher Education Funding Council has a duty to ensure that provision is made for accessing and enhancing the quality of higher education provided and works on this with the Quality Assurance Agency for Higher Education (QAA).

NORTHERN IRELAND

Inspection is carried out in Northern Ireland by the Education and Training Inspectorate, which provides inspection services for the Department of Education Northern Ireland, the Department for Employment and Learning and the Department of Culture, Arts and Leisure. Schools are currently inspected once every five to seven years. In further education and training, survey inspections are carried out at least once every four years. In addition each educational institution is visited on a regular basis by a district inspector. The inspectorate provides evidence-based advice to ministers and departments to assist in the formulation of policies in education, training and youth.

SCHOOLS

Full-time education is compulsory in Great Britain for all children between five and 16 years (for pupils in England who started secondary school in 2008 the compulsory age will be 17) and between four and 16 years in Northern Ireland. About 94 per cent of children in the United Kingdom receive free education from public funds and the rest attend fee-charging schools or are educated at home. Provision is being increased for pre-school children and many pupils remain at school after the minimum leaving age. No fees are charged in any publicly maintained school in England, Wales and Scotland. In Northern Ireland, fees may be charged in voluntary schools and are paid by pupils in preparatory departments of grammar schools, but pupils admitted to the secondary departments of grammar schools, unless they come from outside Northern Ireland, do not pay fees. Students under 19 years of age attending courses at further education colleges are not charged course fees.

ENGLAND AND WALES

There are two main types of school in England and Wales: schools maintained by the state, which charge no fees; and independent schools, which charge fees. Schools maintained by the state, with the exception of the academies and city technology colleges, which exist in England alone, are maintained by local authorities. Schools maintained by the state are classified as community, voluntary or foundation schools. Community schools are owned by local authorities and wholly funded by them (although sixth forms have separate funding arrangements). They are non-denominational and provide primary and secondary education. Schools in the voluntary category provide primary and secondary education and many have a particular religious ethos. Although the school buildings are in many cases provided by the voluntary body (known as the foundation), the authority financially maintains them.

There are two subdivisions in the voluntary category: *voluntary controlled* and *voluntary aided*. In the case of voluntary controlled schools, the authority bears all the costs. In voluntary aided schools, the governing body is responsible for capital expenditure on the buildings, perimeter walls and fences, playgrounds, furniture fixtures and fittings (including ICT), and the Secretary of State for Children, Schools and Families may pay a capital grant of up to 90 per cent of approved capital expenditure. The local authority is responsible for capital work to playing fields and for all revenue funding. Sixth forms have separate funding arrangements. The arrangements in Wales are similar but the rate of grant support is 85 per cent.

Foundation schools provide primary and secondary education. They can have a religious character, although most do not. They are funded by the local authority, and by the relevant funding bodies in respect of sixth form provision, although the land and buildings will be owned by a foundation or by the governors. The government's policy in England is to encourage community and voluntary controlled schools to become self-governing as foundation schools. The government is also encouraging schools to acquire foundations (known as trusts) as a means of forming permanent relationships with external partners.

Local authorities are required to provide the schools that they maintain with a delegated budget to cover their running costs. Authorities can retain funding of various centrally provided services, including transport and some special educational needs. The authority acts as admission authority for most community and some voluntary schools.

Academies (England only) are all-ability independent state schools set up and managed by independent sponsors, separate from local authority control. They are funded by the government at a level comparable to other local schools. No fees are paid by parents. There are currently 133 academies open (June 2009) with a further 70 projected to open in September 2009 and January 2010. Sponsors come from a wide range of backgrounds: universities, individual philanthropists, businesses, the charitable sector, high performing state schools and colleges, existing private schools, educational foundations and the faith communities.

City Technology Colleges (CTCs) and *City Colleges for the Technology of the Arts (CCTAs)* are found in England only, and are state-aided but independent of local authorities. Their aim is to widen the choice of secondary education in disadvantaged urban areas and to teach a broad curriculum with an emphasis on science, technology, business understanding and arts technologies. Capital costs are shared by government and business sponsors, and running costs are covered by a per capita grant from the DCSF. To date 12 of the 14 CTCs have converted to academies.

Trust schools are foundation schools supported by a charitable foundation that shares the school's aspirations for their pupils and can support them in continuing improvement. As foundation schools they employ their own staff and set their own admissions arrangements. The trust holds the school's land and building and appoints governors. Trust schools remain part of their local authority's group of maintained schools. The trust allows schools to build long-term relationships with partners such as businesses, charities, universities and other schools to help raise standards and widen opportunities for pupils. As of June 2009 there were almost 180 operating trust schools and over 370 schools working towards trust status.

SCHOOL MANAGEMENT INITIATIVES

Federations involve two or more schools in England combining their governing bodies. Alternatively, schools might choose to have statutory collaborative governance arrangements involving a joint committee(s) to the governing bodies of two or more schools. This collaboration could entail sharing the curriculum, teaching resources, staff, ICT facilities, sports facilities or budgets. Federations can involve a mix of primary and secondary schools, whereas joint governance committees can also involve FE colleges.

All publicly maintained schools have a *governing body*, usually made up of a number of parent and local community representatives, governors appointed by the authority if the school is local authority-maintained, the headteacher and other staff. Voluntary schools and some foundation schools have foundation governors who are generally appointed to protect the ethos of the school. Governing bodies are responsible for the overall conduct and policies of schools including their academic aims and objectives.

The *Specialist Schools Programme* is open to all maintained secondary schools in England, including special schools with secondary age pupils, that wish to develop a curriculum specialism in one of ten areas: arts, business and enterprise, engineering, humanities, languages, mathematics and computing, music, science, sport, and technology. A new specialism for Special Educational Needs (SEN) was also introduced in 2005. Specialist schools receive additional recurrent funding to support the targets within their plan. This is currently calculated at a rate of £129 per pupil per annum. In addition, they receive a one-off capital grant of £100,000 supplemented by sponsorship, to improve facilities. Specialist schools are expected to include sponsors, local businesses and/or employers on their governing bodies. In June 2009 there were around 3,038 designated specialist schools, representing over 93 per cent of England's total number of secondary schools. Re-designation to the programme is reviewed at the time the school has OFSTED section 5 inspections, usually every three years. At this point, schools which meet certain prescribed criteria are also invited to take on extra roles under the High Performing Specialist School strand of the programme. The Specialist Schools Programme is currently being reviewed.

Independent/State School Partnerships were launched in 1998 to encourage good practice for the benefit of both sectors. In the first nine years of the scheme more than 330 projects received joint funding of around £10m. In May 2008 the tenth round of partnerships was announced with 24 partnerships receiving over £4m over the next three years. The latest round has focused on support for gifted and talented young people, with activities centred on an increasing attainment in science, maths and modern foreign languages at GCSE, A-level and degree level, particularly from communities where aspirations are low.

The Leading Edge Partnership Programme is available to specialist schools which meet the High Performing Specialist Schools (HPSS) criteria. The programme is designed to enable groups of schools to work together to improve results at key stages 3 and 4, particularly among the lowest attaining pupils in the partnership. Schools in the programme are expected to develop solutions to challenges facing the education system and partnerships are expected to engage in opportunities to share practice, and learn from others through national events. There are currently over 200 such partnerships.

Sure Start Children's Centres in England are intended to increase the availability of childcare in disadvantaged areas; improve health, education and emotional development for young children; support parents and help them to take up job or training opportunities. There are over 3,000 centres providing integrated services for under-fives, with the goal of opening another 500 by 2010. Sure Start's remit is confined to the under-fives.

SCOTLAND

Education authority schools (known as publicly funded schools) are financed by local government, partly through revenue support grants from central government, and partly from local taxation. Devolved management from the local authority to the school is in place for more than 88 per cent of all school-level expenditure. There are seven grant-aided special schools and one grant-aided mainstream school. They are managed by boards and receive grants direct from the Scottish government. Independent schools charge fees, receive no direct grant and are required to be registered with Scottish ministers and, like other schools, are subject to inspection by HMIE.

NORTHERN IRELAND

Controlled schools are managed by the education and library boards (ELBs) through boards of governors consisting of representatives of transferors (mainly the Protestant churches), parents, teachers and the ELB. Within the controlled sector there is a small number of integrated schools. There are also grant maintained integrated schools which are funded directly by the Department of Education.

Voluntary maintained schools are managed by boards of governors consisting of members nominated by trustees (mainly Roman Catholic) with representatives of teachers, parents and the ELB. Voluntary schools receive grants towards capital costs and running costs in whole or in part. A majority are entitled to capital grants at 100 per cent. Voluntary non-maintained schools are mainly voluntary grammar schools managed by boards of governors consisting of representatives of parents, teachers and, in most cases, the Department of Education and the ELB, as well as those appointed as provided in each school's scheme of management. Integrated schools exist to educate Protestant and Roman Catholic children, as well as those of other faiths and no faith, together. Latest figures show that there are currently 59 integrated schools, comprising 20 integrated second level colleges and 39 integrated primary schools.

There are a number of Irish-language schools and units, and in June 2009 there were 25 freestanding Irish-medium schools (24 of which received recurrent funding from the department) and 11 Irish-medium units attached to schools in the English language sector. Of the 24 schools, 23 are Irish-medium primary schools. There are also four Irish-medium nursery units.

THE STATE SYSTEM

PRE-SCHOOL EDUCATION

Pre-school education is for children from 3 to 5 years of age. It is not compulsory, parents can take as little or as much of their entitlement as they choose, although a free place is available for every 3- and 4-year-old whose parents want one. In England all 3- and 4-year-olds are entitled to 12.5 hours a week of free early education over 38 weeks of the year. Children are eligible from 1 January, 1 April or 1 September, following their third birthday. From September 2010 the free early education entitlement will increase from 12.5 to 15 hours a week. From this time, free early education will be more flexible as parents will be able to use their weekly entitlement for longer periods over a minimum of three days. Free places are funded by local authorities and are delivered by a range of providers in the maintained and non-maintained sectors – nursery schools; nursery classes in primary schools; private schools; private day nurseries; voluntary playgroups; pre-schools and registered childminders. In order to receive funding, providers should be working towards the early learning goals and other features of the Early Years Foundation Stage curriculum; they should be inspected on a regular basis by education inspectors appointed by OFSTED and meet any conditions set by the local authority.

Since September 2008 the foundation stage curriculum, Birth to Three Matters, and relevant elements of the national daycare standards will be consolidated into the Early Years Foundation Stage (EYFS). This is a single framework for the development, learning and care of all children in early years settings. The latest available data (January 2009) shows that around 95 per cent of 3-year-olds and virtually all 4-year-olds in England were receiving at least some free early education.

In Wales, a free part-time education place in a maintained school or funded non-maintained setting is available for each child from the term following their third birthday. Non-maintained settings which are funded by local authorities to provide education are regularly inspected by the Care and Social Services Inspectorate for Wales and Estyn. Since September 2008 the foundation phase framework for children's learning for 3 to 7-year-olds in Wales has been introduced on a four-year rolling programme.

In Scotland, councils have a duty to provide a pre-school education for all 3 and 4-year-olds whose parents request one. In August 2007, the legal duty for provision increased to 475 hours of free pre-school education a year, although local authorities have the power to provide more if they choose. Most provision is delivered in daily 2.5 hour sessions, but alternative arrangements are possible. In Northern Ireland children who have reached the age of 4 on or before 1 July will start primary school at the beginning of the following September. In Northern Ireland approximately 30 per cent of pre-school education takes place in voluntary/private sector playgroups funded by the Department of Education.

PRIMARY EDUCATION

Primary education begins at 5 years in Great Britain and 4 years in Northern Ireland. In England, Wales and Northern Ireland pupils generally transfer to secondary school at 11 years; in Scotland they generally transfer at age 12.

Primary schools consist mainly of infant schools for children aged 5 to 7, junior schools for those aged 7 to 11, and combined junior and infant schools for both age groups. First schools in some parts of England cater for ages 5 to 10 as the first stage of a three-tier system of first, middle and secondary schools. Unlike England, Scotland has only primary schools.

MIDDLE SCHOOLS

Middle schools take children from first schools, mostly in England, cover varying age ranges between 8 and 14 and usually lead on to comprehensive upper schools.

SECONDARY EDUCATION

Secondary schools are for children aged 11 to 16 and for those who choose to stay on to 18. At 16, many students prefer to move on to tertiary or sixth form colleges or into further education colleges or work-based training. Most secondary schools in England, Wales and Scotland are co-educational. The largest secondary schools have over 1,500 pupils and around 60 per cent of pupils in the United Kingdom are in schools which take over 1,000 pupils.

In England and Wales the main types of maintained secondary schools are comprehensive schools, whose admission arrangements are without reference to ability or aptitude; deemed middle schools (in England), for children aged between eight and 14 years who then move on to senior comprehensive schools at 12, 13 or 14; and (in England) grammar schools, with selective intake, providing an academic course from 11 to 16–18 years.

In Scotland all pupils in education authority secondary schools attend schools with a comprehensive intake. Most of these schools provide a full range of courses appropriate to all levels of ability from first to sixth year.

In Northern Ireland the process of selection (in 2008 the Transfer Test replaced the 11-plus examination for September 2009 admissions to secondary school) has been controversial. Following the restoration of the Northern Ireland Assembly, the minister for education proposed a phased ending of academic selection over a three-year period. However, these proposals did not attract the necessary level of support to become law. Post-primary transfer arrangements for September 2010 admissions will now be unregulated, informed by guidance from the Department of Education.

From 2013 the new post-primary arrangements will guarantee all pupils access to a much wider range of courses, with a minimum of 24 courses at key stage 4, and 27 at post-16. At least one third of the courses on offer will be general (academic) in nature, and at least one third will be (applied vocational/professional/technical). Legislation has been made to give effect to these changes and to enable schools to enter into collaborative arrangements with other schools, FE colleges or other providers.

SPECIAL EDUCATION

Wherever appropriate, taking parents' wishes into account, children with special educational needs are educated in ordinary schools, which are required to publish their policy for pupils with such needs. Schools and local authorities in England and Wales and Education and Library Boards (ELBs) in Northern Ireland are required to identify and secure provision for children with special educational needs and to involve the parents in decisions.

In Scotland, school placing is a matter of agreement between education authorities and parents. Parents have the right to say which school they want their child to attend, and a right of appeal where their wishes are not being met. Legislation passed by the Scottish parliament in 2004 reformed the then system of special educational needs, replacing it with a broader system which focuses on all children who, for whatever reasons, need additional support. Most special schools are managed and paid for by local authorities. However, there are independent special schools, managed by voluntary organisations whose costs are met mainly from fees charged to local authorities for children placed there. There are seven special schools which receive a grant from the Scottish government to partly cover costs.

In Northern Ireland both controlled and maintained special schools are funded by local ELBs and have partially delegated budgets. ELBs can also fund places in a small number of local independent schools, recognised by the Department of Education as providers of special education. Parents can use the Dispute Avoidance and Resolution Service and have a right of appeal to the Special Educational Needs and Disability Tribunal where their wishes are not being met.

In England and Wales maintained special schools are run by education authorities which pay all the costs of maintenance. All maintained schools must have a delegated budget. Non-maintained special schools are run by voluntary bodies; they may receive grants from central government for capital expenditure and for equipment but their current expenditure is met primarily from the fees charged to education authorities for pupils placed in the schools. Some independent schools provide education wholly or mainly for children with special educational needs.

Of all the pupils with statements of special educational needs in 2008–9, 55.6 per cent were educated in mainstream schools.

ELECTIVE HOME EDUCATION

In England and Wales parents have the responsibility for their children's education, which they can fulfil either by sending children to school or, in a minority of cases, by educating at home. The education must be efficient and full-time, and suitable to the child's age, ability and aptitude and to any special educational needs the child may have. Parents have no legal obligation to notify the local authority that a child is being educated at home, but where a child is taken out of school, they must notify the school that they are taking full responsibility for the child's education so that the child's name can be deleted from the school register. It is then the school's duty to report this to the local authority. For children in special schools, parents must seek the consent of the local authority before taking steps to educate them outside the school system. In Northern Ireland, Education and Library Boards determine whether home education provision is appropriate. Although home education is also legal in Scotland, different laws and guidance apply from those in England and Wales. There are no official figures on the numbers of pupils educated outside school.

THE CURRICULUM

ENGLAND

The national curriculum was introduced in England from 1988 for the period of compulsory schooling from 5 to 16. It is mandatory in all maintained schools. Following a review in 1999, a revised curriculum was introduced in schools from September 2000 extending the curriculum to include the foundation stage for children aged 3 to 5.

Since September 2008 the Early Years Foundation Stage (EYFS) has been mandatory for all schools and nurseries in OFSTED-registered settings attended by children aged under 5. The EYFS brings together the existing national standards for daycare and childminding, Birth to Three Matters and curriculum guidance for the foundation stage.

The Childcare Act 2006 provides for the EYFS learning and development requirement to comprise three elements: the early learning goals, educational programmes and assessment arrangements. It sets out six areas covered by the early learning goals and educational programmes:

- Personal, social and emotional development
- Communication, language and literacy
- Problem solving, reasoning and numeracy
- Knowledge and understanding of the world
- Physical development
- Creative development

The Education Act 2002 extended the national curriculum to include the foundation stage. This act also established a single national assessment system called the foundation stage profile.

At key stages 1 and 2, the statutory subjects in the national curriculum are:

Core subjects	*Foundation subjects*
English	Design and Technology
Mathematics	Information and Communication Technology
Science	History
	Geography
	Art and Design
	Music
	Physical Education

In April 2009, the Government accepted Sir Jim Rose's proposals for a new primary curriculum, incorporating six areas of learning, to be introduced from September 2011.

A revised secondary curriculum began being implemented from September 2008. At key stage 3 (11 to 14-year-olds) a modern foreign language and citizenship are introduced. At key stage 4 (14 to 16-year-olds) pupils are required to continue to study the core subjects, plus physical education, information and communication technology and citizenship. Careers and sex education are statutory subjects for all secondary pupils and work-related learning is compulsory for all pupils at key stage 4. In addition, schools must provide access for each key stage 4 pupil to a minimum of one course in the arts (art and design, music, dance, drama and media arts), one course in the humanities (history and geography), at least one modern foreign language and design and technology. Other subjects, such as classical languages, are taught when the resources of individual schools permit. Religious education must be taught across all key stages. Parents have the right to withdraw their children from religious and sex education classes.

Statutory assessment takes place at the end of the EYFS and national tests and tasks take place in English and mathematics at the end of key stage 1 (7-year-olds), with the addition of science at the end of key stage 2 (11-year-olds). At key stage 1 the results of tasks and tests are not reported but are used to underpin teachers' overall assessment of pupils. At key stages 2 and 3 separate teacher assessments of pupils' progress are made. In Key Stage 2 this is set alongside the test results. At key stage 4, the GCSE and vocational equivalents are the main form of assessment.

Each year the DCSF in England publishes four sets of achievement and attainment tables showing performance measures for every school and local authority based on results at key stage 2, GCSE, A-level and equivalent qualifications.

The Qualifications and Curriculum Development Agency (QCDA) is a non-departmental public body that was established by the Education Act 1997 (formerly known as QCA – the Qualifications and Curriculum Authority). It is governed by a board whose members are appointed by the Secretary of State for Children, Schools and Families. The QCDA performs a wide range of functions in England, including monitoring and advising on the curriculum for young people of compulsory school age and developing and delivering high quality national curriculum tests as well as supervising the delivery of and modernisation of GCSE and A-level examination, associated assessments and tests. The QCDA also has a statutory responsibility for regulating qualifications offered in schools, colleges and workplaces, a role that has now passed on an interim basis to the Office of the Qualifications and Examinations Regulator (OFQUAL) pending legislation to set up a permanent independent regulator.

Since April 2008 the Office of the Qualifications and Examinations Regulator, known as OFQUAL, has been responsible for ensuring that standards are maintained in all 14–19 qualifications and that different qualifications are more easily comparable. The government intends OFQUAL to become the sole regulator of 14–19 qualifications, but until this legislation is passed, it operates as part of QCA. Afterwards, the regulator will be accountable to parliament rather than to government ministers.

WALES

Wales has introduced a distinctive Foundation Phase curriculum for 3 to 7-year-olds. Full implementation began for 3-year-olds from September 2008 and for 4-year-olds from September 2009. It will replace Key Stage 1 for 5-year-olds in 2010 and 6-year-olds in 2011. The national curriculum continues for 7 to 16-year-olds. Originally it was broadly similar to that of England, with separate and distinctive characteristics for Wales reflected in the programmes of study where appropriate. From September 2008 a revised school curriculum was implemented, consisting of the National Curriculum subjects together with frameworks for personal and social education, careers, religious education and for skills. Welsh is compulsory for pupils at all key stages, either as a first or as a second language.

In July 2003, it was announced that statutory testing would be removed for pupils in Wales at the end of key stage 2 from 2004–5 and for key stage 3 from 2005–6. Statutory teacher assessment remains and is being strengthened by moderation and accreditation arrangements. It is the only form of statutory assessment from key stages 1 to 3. Similarly, the Foundation Phase will be subject to statutory teacher assessment.

The Department for Children, Education, Lifelong Learning and Skills, within the Welsh Assembly Government, was created following a merger in 2006.

SCOTLAND

The management and delivery of the curriculum in Scotland is not prescribed by statute but is the responsibility of education authorities and individual schools. Advice and guidance are provided by the Scottish government and Learning and Teaching Scotland, which also has a developmental role. Those bodies have produced guidelines on the structure of the curriculum. There are also guidelines on assessment across the whole curriculum and on reporting to parents.

National assessments for reading, writing and mathematics may be used as part of a range of evidence that teachers consider to arrive at judgements about pupils' levels of attainment. National assessments are carried out by the school when the teacher judges that a pupil has completed a level. Assessment for 5 to 14-year-olds is done at six levels (A–F) and most pupils are expected to move from one level to the next at roughly 18-month to two-year intervals.

Provision is also made for teaching in Gaelic in many parts of Scotland and the number of pupils, from nursery to secondary, in Gaelic-medium education is growing.

For 15 to 18-year-olds, national qualifications, a unified framework of courses and awards, was introduced in 1999. The Scottish Qualifications Authority awards, the certificates.

Scotland is pursuing its biggest education reform for a generation in the shape of a major review of all aspects of the curriculum. *Curriculum for Excellence* – which aims to provide more professional autonomy for teachers, greater choice and opportunity for pupils and a single coherent curriculum for all children and young people aged 3 to 18 – will be implemented from 2010.

NORTHERN IRELAND

A revised statutory curriculum is being introduced on a phased basis from September 2007 to June 2010. The revised curriculum is less prescriptive in content to give schools greater flexibility to shape their teaching. It has a greater emphasis on developing skills, including the cross-curricular skills of communication, using mathematics and using ICT, along with thinking skills such as creativity, teamwork and problem solving. It also has a new area – known as personal development at primary level and learning for life and work at post-primary level – which includes employability, citizenship and personal development, to better prepare young people for all aspects of life and work. In addition to religious education, the revised curriculum is made up of areas of learning as set out below:

Primary	*Post-Primary*
The arts	Learning for life and work
Language and literacy	The arts
Mathematics and numeracy	Language and literacy
Personal development and mutual understanding	Mathematics and numeracy
	Modern languages
Physical education	Physical education
The world around us	Science and technology
	Environment and society

Key changes include the introduction of the new key stage known as the foundation stage, which covers years one and two of primary school. This is to allow a more appropriate learning style for the youngest pupils and to ease the transition from pre-school. At key stage 4, the statutory requirements have been significantly reduced in order to provide greater choice and flexibility for pupils. This will be counterbalanced by the entitlement framework, intended to be in place by 2013, which will guarantee pupils access to a wider range of academic and professional courses.

Revised assessment arrangements are also being introduced to support the revised curriculum. Diagnostic assessment of pupils in years four to seven in literacy and numeracy will be carried out in the autumn term and will help teachers identify any particular strengths or weaknesses and inform teaching throughout the year. In the summer term, teachers will assess pupils in the cross-curricular skills of communication, using mathematics and ICT, with reference to levels of progression, mapped to industry-recognised functional skills standards. This information will be reported to parents using a new pupil profile, which provides a standardised format for the annual school report to parents and will include information on a pupil's progress in the skills and areas of learning, their interests and strengths, and any focus for development. Pupils at key stage 4 and beyond will continue to be assessed through public examinations, including GCSEs and A-levels.

The Council for the Curriculum, Examinations and Assessment (CCEA) is a unique educational body in the UK in that it combines the three functions of a curriculum advisory body, an awarding body and a qualifications regulatory body. It monitors and advises the Department of Education on all matters relating to the curriculum, assessment arrangements and examinations in grant-aided schools. It conducts GCSE, A- and AS level examinations, pupil assessment at key stages 1, 2 and 3 and administers the transfer procedure tests. It also ensures that qualifications offered by awarding bodies in Northern Ireland are of an appropriate quality and standard.

INTERNATIONAL PRIMARY CURRICULUM

The International Primary Curriculum (IPC) is a comprehensive curriculum designed to improve learning and develop international awareness. The 420 schools in the UK which use the IPC are still required to follow the national curriculum but use the IPC as a tool to improve teaching and learning.

PUBLIC EXAMINATIONS AND QUALIFICATIONS

ENGLAND, WALES AND NORTHERN IRELAND

In 1988 a single system of examinations, the General Certificate of Secondary Education (GCSE) – usually taken after five years of secondary education – was introduced. The GCSE is the main method of assessing the performance of pupils on a subject-specific basis. The structure of the examination reflects national curriculum requirements where applicable. Although most GCSEs are in academic subects, some cover vocational areas such as business, engineering health and social care, ICT, leisure and tourism, and manufacturing.

GCSE specifications are based on subject criteria covering course objectives, content and assessment methods; differentiated assessment (ie different papers or questions for different ranges of ability) and grade-related criteria (ie grades awarded on absolute rather than relative performance). The GCSE certificates are awarded on an eight-point scale, from A* to G. All GCSE specifications, assessments and grading procedures are monitored by qualification regulators for England, Wales and Northern Ireland (Ofqual, DCELLS and CCEA) to ensure that they conform to the national criteria.

Students are increasingly encouraged to continue their education post-16. For those who do so, in addition to the vocational qualifications outlined below, there are GCE (General Certificate of Education), AS (Advanced Subsidiary) and A (Advanced) levels. Since September 2005 A-levels have also been available in a range of vocational areas – often termed applied A-levels.

A-level courses usually last two years and have traditionally provided the foundation for entry to higher education. AS-level was introduced in September 2000; it represents the first half of a full A-level and is assessed accordingly. The A-level qualification most commonly consists of four units (two AS units and two A2 units). (Music and sciences have six units and they remain as three AS and three A2 units). Students who go on to complete the full A-level will be assessed on their attainment in all four (or six) units, which may be taken either in stages or at the end of the course. A-levels and AS-levels are marked on a six-point scale from A to E. An A* grade will be introduced to the grading of A-levels in 2010 to reward the most exceptional students.

An extended project was introduced in September 2008. It is a single piece of work requiring a high degree of planning, preparation, research and and autonomous working. Projects differ by subject and require research skills to explore a subject independently and in depth. It is accredited as half an A level.

VOCATIONAL QUALIFICATIONS

There are two broad categories of vocational qualifications: National Vocational Qualifications (NVQs), which demonstrate competence in a specific occupation (or aspect of an occupation), and vocationally related qualifications, which usually give a broader, more general preparation for an industry or wider occupational area. All vocational qualifications are based upon national occupational standards, which are designed by employers. Vocational qualifications are accredited into the national qualifications framework by the QCA at nine levels:

- Entry level
- Level 1 – Foundation Skills
- Level 2 – Operative/Semi-skilled
- Level 3 – Technician/Craft/Skilled/Supervisory
- Level 4 – Technical/Middle Management
- Level 5 – Chartered/Professional/Senior Management
- Level 6 – Knowledge Based Professionals
- Level 7 – High Level Specialist Professional/Senior Professionals
- Level 8 – Leading Experts/Practitioners

WELSH BACCALAUREATE

The Welsh Baccalaureate (WBQ) adds an extra dimension to the subjects already available for 14 to 19-year-olds in Wales. It combines a compulsory core, which incorporates personal development skills, with options from existing qualifications to make one wider award. The WBQ can be studied in English or Welsh, or a combination of the two. Following positive evaluation of pilots, the Welsh Baccalaureate is being rolled out across the 14 to 19 age range at Advanced, Intermediate and Foundation levels. As at September 2009 there are

30,000 learners following WBQ courses at 168 centres in Wales.

KEY SKILLS QUALIFICATIONS
The Key Skills (Core Skills in Scotland) qualifications were introduced in six skills areas and at four levels in September 2000. Key Skills are mandatory as part of the core of the WBQ, feature in Modern Apprenticeship frameworks, and are a key component of the 14–19 Learning Core. The two main principles informing Key Skills are the ability to apply the skills in a variety of contexts, and their use to develop effective learning strategies. From September 2010, Functional Skills will replace Key Skills qualifications in England, while Essential Skills will replace them in Wales.

SCOTLAND

Scotland has its own system of public examinations, and in 1999 a new system of national qualifications was introduced. Five levels of study are offered: Access, Intermediate 1, Intermediate 2, Higher and Advanced Higher. The Higher course and Advanced Higher course are direct replacements for the old SCE Higher grade and the Certificate of Sixth Year Studies respectively. National qualifications are included on the Scottish Credit and Qualifications Framework (SCQF) (*see* below), with Access equating to levels 1 to 3, Intermediate 1 to level 4, Intermediate 2 to level 5, Higher to level 6 and Advanced Higher to level 7.

Skills for Work courses are available at Access 3, Intermediate 1 and 2 and Higher level. These are practical courses designed to be an equivalent option to an existing qualification, such as Standard Grade, to help young people develop skills and knowledge in broad vocational areas, core skills, an understanding of the workplace, positive attitudes to learning and employability skills.

National courses consist of blocks of study called national units. A unit usually consists of around 40 hours of study and there are three units in a course. Unit awards demonstrate that a learner has achieved competence in a particular area of study. National course awards are graded by external assessment, which consists of an examination, coursework or performance, or a combination of two or more of these. National course awards also require candidates to pass all unit assessments of the course. A typical national course external assessment requires candidates to demonstrate long-term retention of knowledge, high levels of problem solving, integration of knowledge across a whole course and an ability to apply knowledge and skills in novel situations. The range of subjects has been expanded to include vocational qualifications.

A number of schools use the new national qualifications system for pupils in their fourth year of secondary education, but the majority of this lower age group still take the traditional Standard Grade examinations at the end of a two-year course.

In June 2009, plans were announced for the next generation of National Qualifications, including National 4 and 5 (to replace Standard Grade General and Credit and Intermediate 1 and 2) and new National Literacy and National Numeracy awards (at SCQF levels 3–5). Access, Higher and Advanced Highers will remain but be reviewed in keeping with *Curriculum for Excellence*. The literacy and numeracy awards will be available from 2012–13, with the other and revised qualifications available from 2013–14 onwards.

INTERNATIONAL BACCALAUREATE

The International Baccalaureate (IB) offers three educational programmes for a worldwide community of schools. Founded in 1968, the IB currently works with 2,638 schools and more than 719,000 students in 139 countries.

POST-16 EDUCATION

The proportion of 16 to 18-year-olds in education or training has risen steadily over the last seven years. In 2008 the proportion of 16 to 18-year-olds participating in learning reached 79.7 per cent, the highest recorded. This increase is linked to the September Guarantee, which offered a place in learning to all young people completing compulsory education in the current or previous year.

ENGLAND

The further education (FE) system provides a wide range of education and training opportunities for individuals from age 14 upwards and employers. Learning opportunities are provided at all levels from basic skills to higher education. The central policy aim is to build a further education system that provides the skills the economy needs to sustain quality of life and to contribute to the UK's international standing. The goal is to lead the world in skills development – with virtually all young people staying on in education and training to age 19, and half progressing to higher education; all adults having the support they need to improve their skills throughout life; and all employers seeing skills as key to their success.

In March 2006 the reform strategy *Further Education: Raising Skills, Improving Life Chances* was launched; it set out a programme of changes to deliver the above aims. Key aspects include:

- a new economic mission for FE
- providers of learning and skills to specialise to supply world class services
- an enhanced role for employers and learners in shaping development
- new entitlements to learning and support for those who most need it – free tuition for first level 3 for 19 to 25-year-olds and learner accounts for adults on level 3 programmes
- a new strategy for raising quality, with intervention to eliminate poor quality provision
- public funding focused on delivery priorities
- less bureaucracy along with more autonomy for effective providers

The English FE system includes independent providers (voluntary and private sector) who offer a range of work-based and personal and community learning. Personal and community development learning takes place in a wide range of settings usually delivered via local authorities. Post-16 education and training (excluding Higher Education) in England is funded through the Learning and Skills Council (LSC).

WORK-BASED LEARNING
Apprenticeships are a way for learners to get practical experience while gaining nationally recognised qualifications. The LSC in England and the Welsh Assembly Government in Wales contribute towards the cost of the training and assessment. Apprenticeships normally last between one and three years (four in Wales) and there are two levels: apprenticeships and advanced

apprenticeships at levels 2 and 3 respectively. Both of these lead to:

- National Vocational Qualifications (NVQs)
- Key Skills qualifications – transferable work-related skills such as IT and communication and problem solving
- Technical certificates – vocationally related qualifications that provide the basic knowledge of the NVQ

In England in 2007–8, 225,000 young people started an apprenticeship.

> The government published *World Class Apprenticeships* in January 2008. This strategy sets out a major series of reforms over the next few years to strengthen and radically expand the programme, including establishing a new national apprenticeship service to run the programme in England.
>
> Supporting these plans is the Apprenticeships, Skills, Children and Learning Bill, which was published in July 2008 and is expected to receive Royal Assent in autumn 2009.

Diplomas are new qualifications designed to give young people an alternative to traditional learning. Combining theoretical and applied learning, they aim to provide a method that ensures that young people are both educated and employable. Pupils completing diplomas should have functional skills in English, Maths and ICT, and be able to apply these in work situations. Diploma Development Partnerships (DDPs) have been established to explore content development. These DDPs, led by Sector Skills Councils and including employers, higher education, school and college and awarding body representatives, specify the content of the diplomas. Awarding bodies will then develop the qualifications. Content for the first five diplomas (ICT, health and social care, engineering, creative and media, and construction and the built environment) became available for teaching in September 2008. In 2009 business administration and finance, hair and beauty, hospitality and catering, land-based and environmental, and manufacturing were available for teaching. Among the diplomas to be added in 2010–11 are public services, sport and active leisure, travel and tourism, science, and humanities and social sciences. A new statutory entitlement will be in place for all 14 to 19-year-olds from September 2013.

WALES

In Wales, the aims and makeup of the FE system are similar to those outlined for England, although, as the education portfolio is devolved to the Welsh Assembly, the policy documents vary. Current thinking is outlined in *Skills That Work for Wales,* which was published in July 2008 and is the Welsh response to the *Leitch Review of Skills in the UK*. The document sets out new approaches to funding; the transformation of the learning network; business support; and integrated skills and employment services delivered through a partnership between the Assembly Government and the Department for Work and Pensions.

SCOTLAND

Since autumn 2005, the Scottish Further and Higher Education Funding Council has been the statutory body responsible for funding Scotland's 43 further education colleges. The Scottish Qualifications Authority (SQA) is the statutory awarding body for qualifications in the national education and training system. It is both the main awarding body for qualifications for work including Scottish Vocational Qualifications (SVQs) and is also their accrediting body. The SQA is by statute required clearly to separate its awarding and accrediting functions.

There are three main qualification 'families' in Scottish further education: national qualifications; Higher national qualifications (HNC and HND); and SVQs. In addition to Standard Grade qualifications, national qualifications are available at five levels. Another feature of the qualifications system is the Scottish Group Award (SGA). SGAs are built up unit by unit and allow credit transfer from other qualifications (such as Standard Grade or SVQ), providing a further option, especially for adult learners. SVQs are competence-based qualifications suitable for teaching in the workplace, but they can also be taken in further education colleges. The Scottish Credit and Qualifications Framework includes qualifications across academic and vocational sectors. It comprises 12 levels, covering all mainstream qualifications from Access level in national qualifications to postgraduate qualifications, and including SVQs. In the academic year 2007–8 there were 489,610 student enrolments on vocational and non-vocational courses in further education colleges. Of this total, higher education courses accounted for 27 per cent of college activity, measured by full-time equivalents.

NORTHERN IRELAND

All further education colleges are independent corporate bodies like their counterparts in the rest of the UK. Responsibility for the sector lies with the Department for Employment and Learning (DELNI), which funds the colleges directly. The colleges own their own property, are responsible for their own services and employ their own staff. The governing bodies of the colleges must include at least 50 per cent membership from those who are engaged or employed in business, industry or any profession.

In August 2007 Northern Ireland's 16 further education colleges merged into six new area-based colleges. In 2007–8 there were 142,100 professional and technical enrolments across the six Northern Ireland FE colleges. Of these, 29,213 were full-time and 112,887 part-time. The majority of full-time enrolments are in the 16–19 age group, while most part-time students are over 19.

LEARNER SUPPORT

The *Education Maintenance Allowance* (EMA) is an income assessed allowance that supports 16 to 19-year-olds learning in England. EMA consists of a weekly allowance of up to £30, which is payable to those from households with an income of up to £30,810 who participate in learning with a recognised provider. In addition to the weekly payment, learners in receipt of EMA can receive bonus payments if they meet the terms of their learning agreement. In Wales, EMA consists of a weekly allowance of up to £30, plus periodic bonus payments, and is available to learners from low-income households who stay on in school or college.

Care2Learn (C2L) is available in England to enable young parents under the age of 20 to return to learning after having a baby. The scheme is not income assessed and will pay up to £160 per week (£175 in London) to cover the costs of childcare.

Parents aged 20 and over, who are attending a school sixth form or sixth form college may be eligible for support from the *Sixth Form College Childcare* scheme. This is an income assessed scheme that enables parents to return to learning by covering the costs of childcare at the same rates as C2L.

For adults (19 and over) in England similar discretionary learner support funds are available for the most disadvantaged students with the greatest need. These provide financial help with the costs of childcare, books, equipment and transport and residential funding. Funds are administered by colleges and other providers.

The *adult learning grant* (ALG) provides low-skilled, low-income adults with support for the costs of learning. Up to £30 per week is paid during term time to adults (aged 19 and above) who are studying full time for their first full level 2 (5 GCSEs or equivalent) or first full level 3 qualification (2 A-levels or equivalent). ALG is administered by the LSC and is available throughout England.

Dance and Drama Awards (DaDA) are national scholarships funded by the LSC. They offer greatly reduced tuition fees and help with living and learning costs at a number of high-quality private DaDA providers in England. DaDA aim to ensure that access to training is based on potential to succeed in the profession and not ability to pay.

Residential Bursaries are available from 50 specialist residential colleges that offer courses not readily accessible elsewhere like agriculture, horticulture and art and design. Funding is allocated directly to the colleges by the LSC.

Residential Support Scheme provides financial support for accommodation costs to those students who need to study away from home. Students apply for funding and support is awarded following a household income assessment.

Discretionary Learner Support Funds are available to help students of age 16 and over with the costs associated with further education. They are distributed by the college and targeted at those in greatest need.

For students over 18 in the UK who choose to fund their course themselves, *career development loans* are available from three high street banks. Loans of between £300 and £8,000 can be used to pay for the costs of vocational training courses. Interest on the loan is paid by the LSC while the student is completing the course. Eligible Welsh-domiciled students aged 19 years or over on further education courses, whether full-time or part-time (subject to a minimum contact requirement), receive a means-tested non-repayable assembly learning grant. Discretionary financial contingency funds are also available to all students suffering hardship and are administered by the institutions themselves. In addition, individual learning accounts are available in Wales, which provide adults with means-tested support of up to £200 to undertake a wide range of learning. Eligible Scottish-domiciled further education students can apply to their college for discretionary support in the form of bursaries. These can include allowances for maintenance, travel, study, dependants and additional support needs.

In Northern Ireland the following arrangements are in place for students in further education:

- *FE Awards* – non-refundable assistance administered by the Western Education and Library Board (WELB)
- *FE Support Funds* (discretionary) – financial help for students who are inhibited by financial consideration from accessing and participating in FE colleges

For more information on FE awards, *see* the DEL website.

TEACHERS

ENGLAND AND WALES

All qualified teachers working in maintained primary, special and secondary schools, non-maintained special schools and pupil referral units are required to register with the General Teaching Council for England (GTCE) or the General Teaching Council for Wales (GTCW).

All new entrants to the teaching profession in maintained primary and secondary schools are required to be graduates and to have qualified teacher status (QTS). QTS is achieved by successfully completing a course of initial teacher training, traditionally either a Bachelor of Education (BEd) degree, BA with QTS, BSc with QTS or the Postgraduate Certificate of Education (PGCE). New entrants are statutorily required to serve a three term (full-time, pro rata part-time) induction period during which they will have a structured programme of support. All initial teacher training has a strong element of practical school-based work, with student teachers spending significant periods of their training in the classroom.

In addition to the traditional routes, various employment-based routes to QTS have been developed. The Graduate Teacher Programme (GTP) is designed for mature, well-qualified people who can quickly take on teaching responsibilities and who need to earn a living while they train. Trainees are paid a salary and undergo up to a year of school-based training. The Registered Teacher Programme (RTP) is designed for people without a degree or formal teaching qualification but with at least two years of higher education; entrants are paid a salary and complete a degree while undergoing training for up to two years. Since 2008 the RTP has only operated in England. Employment-based training routes account for about 15 per cent of all teacher training places in England; in Wales the GTP forms around 3 per cent of the total.

Teachers in further education (FE) are not required to have QTS, though roughly half have a teaching qualification and most have industrial, commercial or professional experience. Since July 2002, all new entrants to FE teaching in Wales are required to have, or to be working towards, a specified FE teaching qualification. A qualification for aspiring headteachers, the National Professional Qualification for Headship (NPQH), has been introduced. The National College for School Leadership administers this qualification and others and acts as a focus for development and support. In Wales, the NPQH and other headship programmes are administered by the Welsh Assembly Government.

Eligible trainees on postgraduate initial teacher training (ITT) courses in England are entitled to a tax-free training bursary. In 2009–10 those training as teachers of mathematics, science, ICT, design and technology, modern languages, religious education and music each receive £9,000. For all other secondary subjects the allowance is £6,000 and for primary it is £4,000.

In Wales the bursaries are £2,200 (primary), £4,200 (secondary) and £7,200 (designated secondary priority subjects, *see* above, including Welsh). A tuition fee grant of £1,940 is also available for those who reside in Wales. Newly qualified teachers with a PGCE may also be eligible for a taxable 'golden hello' payment worth £5,000 (mathematics and science) or £2,500 (all other priority subjects). Details are available at W www.teach.gov.uk/funding and www.teachertrainingwales.org/financial.htm

In Wales a similar scheme operates for those undertaking the full-time PGCE (FE) or PGCE (PcET). Eligible students receive a bursary of £6,000 (£7,000 for mathematics and science courses since September 2005), paid in instalments while studying. In England, other training awards may be available through the secondary shortage subject scheme (SSSS). This is an additional, means-tested hardship fund from the Training and Development Agency for Schools. The subjects currently included are: design and technology, geography, information technology, mathematics, modern languages, music, religious education and science.

In Wales, placement grants supported by the Higher Education Funding Council for Wales (HEFCW) provide £1,200 per funded student on undergraduate priority courses – the same subjects that attract the £4,200 and £7,200 training grants – and £700 to students on other undergraduate courses.

The Training and Development Agency for Schools (TDA) is the body responsible for attracting quality people to initial teacher training (ITT), funding universities, colleges and schools and for helping schools develop and train their staff. The TDA administers a returners' programme for qualified teachers who wish to refresh their skills before returning to the profession. Participants are entitled to a bursary of up to £150 a week to a total of £1,500 and additional childcare support. The TDA supports the sharing of good practice in teacher training, encourages schools to offer placements for trainee teachers, and funds training and assessment for higher level teaching assistant (HLTA) status. For more information about the TDA *see* W www.tda.gov.uk.

In Wales, accreditation and funding of ITT is undertaken by the HEFCW. Its role also includes commissioning research to improve the standards of teachers and teacher training; working with Estyn (Her Majesty's Inspectorate for Education and Training in Wales) to ensure these universities meet Welsh Assembly Government standards; setting trainee recruitment targets for each provider, to reflect the Welsh Assembly Government's overall national targets; and promoting best practice and supporting ITT providers' development strategies with funding.

The General Teaching Council for England (GTCE) acts as a disciplinary body dealing with cases of misconduct and incompetence in England and hears appeal hearings for registered teachers who have failed their induction year (*see also* Professional Education). The separate General Teaching Council for Wales (GTCW) fulfils a similar role in Wales.

The Specialist Teacher Assistant scheme provides trained support to qualified teachers in the teaching of reading, writing and arithmetic to young pupils.

SCOTLAND

The General Teaching Council for Scotland (GTCS) advises central government on matters relating to teacher supply and the professional suitability of all teacher training courses. It is also the body responsible for disciplinary procedures in cases of professional misconduct. All teachers in maintained schools must be registered with the GTCS. Only graduates are accepted as entrants to the profession; primary school teachers undertake either a four-year vocational degree course or a one-year postgraduate course, while teachers of academic subjects in secondary schools undertake the latter. There is also a combined degree sometimes known as a concurrent degree.

The Scottish Qualification for Headship has been introduced for aspiring headteachers. Universities with specialist education departments provide both in-service and pre-service training for teachers. The universities are funded by the Scottish Higher Education Funding Council, which also sets intake levels for teacher education courses in line with guidance provided by the Scottish government.

NORTHERN IRELAND

All new entrants to teaching in grant-aided schools are graduates and hold an approved teaching qualification. A fully integrated programme of Initial Teacher Education (ITE), induction and early professional development as well as the Professional Qualification for Headship programme, is in place in Northern Ireland. ITE is provided by Queen's University, Belfast, University of Ulster, Stranmillis University College, St Mary's University College and the Open University (NI). The university colleges are concerned with teacher education mainly for the primary school sector and the universities mainly for the post-primary sector. The General Teaching Council for Northern Ireland (GTCNI) advises government on professional issues, maintains a register of qualified teachers and acts as a disciplinary body.

SALARIES

Qualified teachers in England and Wales, other than the leadership group (which includes headteachers, deputy headteachers and advanced skills teachers) are paid on a six-point main pay scale. Teachers who demonstrate exceptional ability have the opportunity to be assessed against national standards and moving to the three point upper scale. An 'Excellent Teacher' scheme has been available to schools since September 2006. This allows eligible teachers to access a 'spot' salary There are teaching and learning responsibility payments for specific posts, special needs work and recruitment and retention factors which may be awarded at the discretion of the relevant body, ie the governing body or the local authority. The advanced skills teacher grade was introduced to enhance prospects in the classroom for the most able teachers. Experienced teachers are assessed against national standards to move on to the upper pay scale, after which they receive performance-related pay increases. There is a statutory superannuation scheme. Teachers working in the London area are paid on separate pay scales. As at September 2009, salary scales for teachers in England and Wales are:

Headteacher	£41,426–£102,734
Excellent teachers	£38,804–£50,918
Advanced skills teacher	£36,618–£55,669
Classroom teacher (upper pay scale)	£33,412–£35,929
Classroom teacher (main pay scale)	£21,102–£30,842
Associate teachers	£15,461–£24,453
Inner London	
Headteacher	£48,353–£109,658
Excellent teachers	£47,188–£59,302
Advanced skills teacher	£43,538–£62,596
Classroom teacher (upper pay scale)	£40,288–£43,692
Classroom teacher (main pay scale)	£26,000–£35,568
Associate teachers	£19,445–£28,434

Teachers in Scotland are paid on a seven-point scale. The entry point is for newly qualified teachers undertaking their probationary year. Movement from the probationary point is dependent on achieving the standard for full registration. Additional allowances are payable under a range of circumstances, such as distant islands and remote schools. As at 1 April 2009, salary scales for teachers in Scotland were:

Headteacher/deputy headteacher	£41,298–£80,607
Principal teacher	£36,411–£46,992
Chartered teacher	£34,428–£40,941
Main grade	£20,937–£33,399

Teachers in Northern Ireland have broadly similar pay and working conditions as teachers in England and Wales, although negotiated through separate local negotiating machinery. There is some variation to reflect local circumstances: for example, Northern Ireland does not have an advanced skills teacher grade nor an excellent teachers scheme. As at September 2008, salary scales for teachers in Northern Ireland are:

Principal	£40,494–£100,424
Vice-Principal	from £35,794
Classroom teacher	£20,627–£35,121

Classroom teachers who take on teaching and learning responsibilities outside of their normal classroom duties may be awarded one of five teaching allowances ranging from £1,764 to £11,381 per annum on top of their basic pay. As in England and Wales, schools in Northern Ireland can also award allowances for recruitment and retention purposes and for the teaching of pupils with special educational needs.

HIGHER EDUCATION

The term higher education is used to describe education above A-level, Higher and Advanced Higher Grade and their equivalent, which is provided in universities, colleges of higher education and in some FE colleges.

The main purposes of higher education are:

- to enable people to develop their capabilities and fulfil their potential, both personally and at work
- to advance knowledge and understanding through scholarship and research
- to contribute to an economically successful and culturally diverse nation

The government provides strategic direction to higher education in line with its policy commitments. Advice to government on matters relating to higher education and its use of funds is provided by the separate Higher Education Funding Councils for England and Wales, in Scotland by the Scottish Further and Higher Education Funding Council and in Northern Ireland by the Department for Employment and Learning. The former receive a block grant from central government which they allocate to the universities and colleges. In Northern Ireland the grant is allocated directly to institutions by the Department for Employment and Learning.

The Scottish Further and Higher Education Funding Council funds 20 institutions of higher education. There are 15 universities including the Open University in Scotland and there are also two specialist art colleges, a conservatoire, an agricultural college and the UHI Millennium Institute in the Highlands and Islands. The universities are broadly managed as described above and the remaining colleges are managed by independent governing bodies which include representatives of industrial, commercial, professional and educational interests.

In Northern Ireland higher education is provided in six regional further education colleges, the two universities and the two university colleges. These institutions offer a range of courses, including first and postgraduate degrees, PGCEs, undergraduate diplomas and certificates, foundation degrees, Higher National Diplomas and professional qualifications.

TYPES OF HIGHER EDUCATION INSTITUTION

The Further and Higher Education Act 1992 and parallel legislation in Scotland removed the distinction between higher education provided by the universities and that provided in England, Scotland and Wales by the former polytechnics and colleges of higher education. It allowed all polytechnics, and other higher education institutions which satisfy the necessary criteria, to award their own taught course and research degrees and to adopt the title of university. All the polytechnics and some colleges of higher education have since done so. The change of name does not affect the legal constitution of the institutions.

There are now 109 universities in the UK, up from the 48 which existed prior to the Further and Higher Education Acts 1992. Of the 109 total, 90 are in England (including the University of London, which has a federal structure), 3 in Wales, 14 in Scotland (including the Open University) and 2 in Northern Ireland.

GOVERNANCE OF UNIVERSITIES AND COLLEGES

The pre-1992 universities each have their own system of internal governance but broad similarities exist. They are run by a council which is the executive governing body and is responsible for all the affairs of the university including appointments, promotions and bidding for and allocation of financial resources. At least half the members of the council are drawn from outside the university. Many of the council's functions are carried out through committees. The senate reports to the council and deals primarily with academic issues. It consists of the council and members elected from within the university. The 1992 Act, and the Education Reform Act 1988, set out the system of governance for universities which were formerly polytechnics or other higher education institutions and for the colleges of higher education. Each institution has an instrument and articles of government that are approved by the Privy Council. These post-1992 institutions are run by boards of governors, which are responsible for the mission, finances and all appointments. Much of the board's business is delegated to committees. In particular, there is usually an academic board that deals with all matters relating to teaching and research. Most of the newest universities to be created were originally established by trust deed and have become incorporated as companies limited by guarantee. Their memorandum and articles of association incorporate the instrument and articles of government and are subject to Privy Council approval.

OPEN UNIVERSITY AND THE UNIVERSITY FOR INDUSTRY

The non-residential Open University provides a modular programme of courses throughout the UK and internationally, leading to first and higher degrees, diplomas and certificates. Students are taught through distance learning, using written and audio-visual materials and the internet, supported by tutorials and short residential courses. No qualifications are needed for entry at undergraduate level. In 2006–7 the Open University received £212.1m in public funding and there was a total of 164,000 undergraduate students, 18,000 postgraduate students and a further 32,000 students on programmes at other institutions validated by the university. More than 675,000 degrees, certificates and diplomas have been awarded since the university's first students started to study in 1971. Research across a wide range of disciplines feeds directly into the university's teaching. The university has five Centres of Research Excellence – in citizenship, identities and governance; comparative criminological research; computing; education and educational technology; and earth, planetary, space and astronomical research. In addition, it carries out internationally recognised research in geography, design, art history, music, history, literature, pure mathematics, statistics, materials engineering and biological sciences. The university's open content initative is making educational resources freely available on the internet, with learning support and collaboration tools to connect students and educators.

- the Open University is the UK's largest university, teaching 35 per cent of all part-time undergraduate students in the UK each year
- 44 per cent of new OU undergraduate students in the UK have fewer than two A-levels
- the median age of new undergraduate level students is 32

The University for Industry (Ufi) Ltd operates learndirect and is the largest government-backed e-learning organisation in the world. Ufi aims to boost people's employability, by helping them to gain skills and qualifications, as well as improve organisations' productivity and competitiveness. Through the national network of more than 840 learndirect centres in England and Wales, Ufi provides access and support to a range of services from taster activities to e-learning courses which are linked to qualifications. Information and courses are also available for people who have been made redundant or who are at risk of redundancy. Since its launch in 2000, more than 2.65 million people have taken over 6.8 million learndirect courses.

ACADEMIC STAFF

Each university and college appoints its own academic staff. The Universities and Colleges Employers Association (UCEA) is the employers' association for subscribing universities and other higher education institutions in the UK. It provides a framework within which representatives of institutions receive guidance and discuss salaries, conditions of service, employee relations and all matters connected with the employment of staff and employees. The services of the UCEA include collective bargaining and an annual salary survey. Academic staff in higher education require no formal teaching qualification; however all new teaching staff are now expected to obtain a teaching qualification which meeets the requirements of the new professional standards. The Higher Education Academy leads, supports and informs the professional development and recognition of staff in higher education as well as promoting good practice and providing information, advice and resources; it has developed a professional standards framework in consulation with the sector. The Leadership Foundation for Higher Education provides a dedicated service of support and advice on leadership, governance and management for all the UK's higher education institutions.

In the academic year 2007–8 there were 174,945 academic staff in all higher education institutions in the UK, of which 116,495 were full-time.

As a result of the national framework agreement, staff working in higher education should be, since August 2006, paid on a single national pay scale, which is used as the basis for locally negotiated pay and grading structures. The framework sought to unify pay arrangements as well as address concerns about equal pay. Since October 2008 the 51-point national pay spine has ranged from £12,773 to £53,943. Negotiations for the annual pay increase took place in summer 2009.

COURSES

In the UK all universities and some colleges award their own degrees and other qualifications and may act as awarding and validating bodies for colleges. The power to award degrees is regulated by law and it is an offence to purport to award a UK degree unless authorised to do so. The Quality Assurance Agency for Higher Education advises government on applications for degree-awarding powers.

The Quality Assurance Agency for Higher Education (QAA) was established in 1997 and is an independent public body funded by subscriptions from UK universities and colleges of higher education, and through contracts with the main higher education funding bodies. Its principal role is to safeguard the standards of higher education qualifications and encourage improvements in quality where possible. It does this by working with universities and colleges to define standards for higher education, through a framework known as the academic infrastructure, which includes subject benchmark statements and a code of practice. QAA also carries out reviews of higher education institutions against these standards and publishes their outcomes. It advises governments on applications for the grant of degree awarding powers, university title or designation as a higher education institution. QAA is governed by a board, which has overall responsibility for the conduct and strategic direction. The board has 15 members.

Facilities exist for full-time and part-time study, day release, sandwich or block release. Credit accumulation and transfer systems allow a student to achieve a final qualification by accumulating credits for courses of study successfully achieved, or even professional experience, over a period of time.

Higher education courses comprise: first degree and postgraduate (including research) degrees, there is also a variety of Higher Education Diplomas and Certificates, often studied part-time in Higher Education (DipHE); BTEC Higher National Diplomas (HND) and Higher National Certificates (HNC); and preparation for professional examinations.

The Foundation Degree, launched in 2001, is a two-year vocational higher education qualification, co-designed by employers, which forms either a self-contained qualification or a basis for further study leading to an honours degree or further professional qualifications.

Undergraduate courses lead to the title of Bachelor – Bachelor of Arts (BA) and Bachelor of Science (BSc) being the most common – except in certain Scottish universities where Master is sometimes used for a first degree in arts subjects. For a higher degree the titles are Master of Arts (MA), Master of Science (MSc) and the research degrees of Master of Philosophy (MPhil) and Doctor of Philosophy (PhD or, at a few universities, DPhil).

Most undergraduate courses at universities and colleges of higher education run for three years, but some take four years or longer. Postgraduate studies vary in length.

Post-experience short courses form a significant part of higher education provision, reflecting the demand for professional and technical training. An increasing proportion of these courses are co-funded by students and employers.

ADMISSIONS

The government's target is to increase participation in higher education to 50 per cent of 18 to 30-year-olds by 2010. Institutions suffer financial penalties if the number of students laid down for them by the funding councils is exceeded, but the individual university or college decides which students to accept. The formal entry requirements to most degree courses are two or more A-levels at grade E or above (or equivalent), and to HND courses one A-level (or equivalent). In practice, most offers of places require qualifications in excess of this, higher requirements usually reflecting the popularity of a course or institution. These requirements do not, however, exclude applications from students with a variety of non-GCSE qualifications or unquantified experience and skills.

For admission to a degree, DipHE or HND, potential students apply through UCAS, the organisation responsible for managing applications to higher education courses in the UK. UCAS operates an online application system and provides services to applicants, advisory services, schools, colleges and universities and facilitates and promotes access to higher education. Application services exist across a range of subject areas and for UK universities and colleges. More than 500,000 people wanting to study at a university or college of higher education use the service each year and 100,000 of them use the specialist services: the Graduate Teacher Training Registry (GTTR) and the Conservatoires UK Admissions Service (CUKAS). The Open University conducts its own admissions. Details of initial teacher training courses in Scotland can be obtained from those universities offering such courses, from Universities Scotland, and from the website created by the Scottish government to promote teaching: W www.teachinginscotland.com.

For admission as a postgraduate student, universities and colleges normally require a good first degree in a subject related to the proposed course of study or research. Applications can be made to individual institutions, except for teaching and social work. There is also now an alternative to applying to postgraduate courses; UKPASS is an online application service created by UCAS. It was set up in 2007 following demand from the higher education sector to have a centralised admissions service that would not only help institutions to monitor their applicants but would also enable them to get to know more about this particular group, which is the fastest growing sector of the UK higher education marketplace.

FEES AND GRANTS

FEES FOR FULL-TIME STUDENTS IN 2009–10

The Higher Education Act 2004 introduced variable tuition fees for full-time higher education courses at English and Welsh institutions, and these came into effect for courses starting in September 2006 or later. In Northern Ireland variable tuition fees were introduced under the Higher Education (Northern Ireland) Order 2005. Fees are capped at £3,000 subject only to inflationary increases until 2010. In the academic year 2007–8 the maximum an institution could charge new students was £3,070 a year. This rose to £3,145 in 2008–9 and £3,225 in 2009–10.

From September 2006 no student – no matter when they started – has had to pay tuition fees before they start their course or while they are studying as student loans for tuition fees are available (*see* below).

Welsh Higher Education institutions also charge fees (up to £3,225 in 2009–10). Students who normally live in Wales (and EU students) and who study at a university or college in Wales are entitled to a fee grant up to a maximum of £1,940.

ENGLAND

For those starting a full-time higher education course in 2009–10, the main types of financial help are:

- maintenance grant or a special support grant* – up to £2,906
- student loan for tuition fees to cover fees in full – up to £3,225
- student loan for maintenance – up to £4,950 if living away from home, or more if studying in London (though the maximum amount is reduced if in receipt of a maintenance grant)
- bursary from the university or college being attended

* The special support grant replaces the maintenance grant for full-time students who claim income-related benefits

REPAYMENT OF STUDENT LOANS

Repayment of both student loans for maintenance and student loans for tuition fees does not start until the April after the student has left their course and is earning more than £15,000 a year. Repayments are calculated at 9 per cent of income over the threshold of £15,000, so someone earning £18,000 would pay back around £22 a month. If income falls below the threshold, repayments cease until income rises above it again. Those who pay tax through PAYE have repayments deducted from their salaries, while the self-employed make repayments through their tax returns.

PART-TIME HIGHER EDUCATION STUDENTS

Part-time higher education students on courses in England may be entitled to a grant towards their fees, and a grant towards their course costs. This help does not have to be repaid, and entitlement to the fee grant and the course grant depends on the student's income and that of their husband, wife or partner. Students who already have a degree cannot usually apply for this support.

In 2009–10 a grant for fees of up to £1,210 is available. If fees are less than this amount, the maximum amount that can be applied for is the cost of the fees. If the fees are more than this amount, the individual applying for them will need to make up the difference. In 2009–10 the maximum grant to help with the cost of books, travel and other expenses is £260. Part-time students with disabilities may be eligible for disabled students allowances.

WALES

From 2009, students who started after 2006 and 2007 have been charged a deferred flexible fee of up to £3,225. However, students who normally live in Wales and study at a university or college in Wales can apply for a fee grant of up to £1,940 a year which does not have to be repaid. This tuition fee grant is available regardless of family income and is paid directly to the place of study. Since September 2006 eligible full-time undergraduate students who live in Wales have not had to pay fees before starting their course or while they are studying. Instead, a student loan for fees can be taken out, which does not have to be repaid until the course is finished and earnings are over £15,000 a year.

It was announced in March 2009 that the following will apply for Welsh students entering higher education in 2010–11:

- students from low income households will be able to apply for an assembly learning grant of up to £5,000
- the household income threshold for a partial assembly learning grant will rise to £50,000
- there will be no tuition fee grant
- an enhanced tuition fee loan will enable full-time undergraduates to defer payment of fees
- all new Welsh domiciled students who take out a maintenance loan from academic year 2010–11 will receive up to £1,500 debt relief when they start repayment

Welsh students entering higher education in the academic year 2009–10 are not affected by the above. For 2009 starters the assembly learning grant is worth up to £2,906. Continuing students are entitled to the same student finance arrangements as in previous years (including a tuition fee grant if studying in Wales), although continuing students taking out new maintenance loans from 2010–11 may be eligible for debt relief.

Students who normally live in Wales but choose to study elsewhere in the UK will be charged fees according to the fee regime of the country in which they study and that set by the institution. Student Finance Wales will provide a loan to defer this fee but students who live in Wales and are studying elsewhere in the UK will not be entitled to the fee grant.

Fee levels in Wales are the same for students who normally live elsewhere in the UK and began studying in Wales in the academic year 2006–7. However, these students are not eligible to receive Student Finance Wales services but will instead receive support from their home country. The Welsh national bursary began in Wales in the academic year 2007–8. Eligible students, regardless of where they live in the UK will receive a means tested bursary of a minimum around £310, which will be additional to other support received and will not be offset by any reductions in other forms of support.

SCOTLAND

The arrangements for Scottish students in Scotland from 2009 are as follows:

Tuition fees – contributions have been abolished for all eligible full-time Scottish domiciled and EU students studying in Scotland.

Student loans – living cost support is mainly provided through a means-tested student loan. An additional loan of £590 is available to young students from low-income backgrounds.

Bursaries – the young students' bursary (YSB) is available to young students from low-income backgrounds. It is non-repayable and reduces the level of debt which eligible students accrue during a course of study. In 2009–10 the maximum annual support provided through YSB is £2,575.

SUPPLEMENTARY GRANTS

Depending on eligibility, students in Scotland may also receive: the adult dependants grant; the lone parents grant; childcare fund support; travel costs and the disabled students allowance (consisting of the basic allowance, the special equipment allowance and non-medical personal help). Students who are experiencing particular financial difficulty can apply for assistance from their institution's discretionary funds.

NORTHERN IRELAND

The arrangements for Northern Ireland are very similar to those for England with these differences:

- the maintenance grant is worth up to £3,406
- the higher education bursary is up to £2,000
- the access to learning fund is known as the support fund in Northern Ireland and is allocated by central government directly to the institution

POSTGRADUATE AWARDS

In general, postgraduate students do not qualify for mandatory support (including student loans and tuition fee assistance). An exception to this is the PGCE.

Awards for postgraduate courses are the responsibility of the Research Councils, depending on the field of study. Research Councils are independent bodies and make their own decisions about expenditure on postgraduate support according to the resources available to them. The fact that a course lies within its remit does not oblige the Research Councils to support every or indeed any student applying for awards.

It is for institutions to decide the level of their fees. The government is raising the levels of award available to postgraduates under the competitive merit-based system provided by the Research Councils: the minimum PhD stipend will be £13,290 in 2009–10.

Targeted support is also available to meet particular needs: postgraduate students can apply through their colleges for discretionary help from the access to learning fund. Disabled students allowances are also available to eligible students undertaking postgraduate study.

There is support available to students in Scotland for postgraduate study through the Postgraduate Students' Allowances Scheme (PSAS), which is administered by the Student Awards Agency for Scotland (SAAS). Eligible students can apply for an award consisting of a means tested maintenance grant and payment of tuition fees. Courses supported under PSAS are generally nine-month-long, taught postgraduate diploma courses on largely vocational subjects. Awards from PSAS are discretionary, not mandatory, so there is no guarantee of an award at postgraduate level.

There is support available to students who wish to pursue postgraduate study in Northern Ireland (at either Queen's University of Belfast or University of Ulster). All students should apply to the university for an application form. Students should apply for a place on the course and for an award. As there are always more applicants than awards, not all applicants who secure a place on the courses will be successful in obtaining an award. *See also* Research Councils.

LIFELONG LEARNING

In the UK, the duty of securing adult and continuing education leading to academic or vocational qualifications is statutory. The Learning and Skills Council (LSC) in England, the Welsh Assembly Government and the Scottish Funding Council are responsible for and fund those courses which take place in their sector and lead to academic and vocational qualifications, prepare students to undertake further or higher education courses, or confer basic skills; the Higher Education Funding Councils fund advanced courses of continuing education. Local authorities have the power, although not the duty, to provide those courses which do not fall within the remit of the funding bodies. In Northern Ireland the Department for Employment and Learning is responsible for the funding of the statutory further education sector.

From April 2010 the LSC will be replaced: 16–19 funding will transfer to local authorities supported by a new Young People's Learning Agency, and for adults a Skills Funding Agency (SFA) will be created.

There are currently 16 National Skills Academies in various stages of development. These provide a network of specialist training and skills provision for sectors and businesses of all sizes and are employer led, funded and designed. The Train to Gain scheme provides employers with free and subsidised training for their employees. In January 2009, a £140m package for 35,000 additional apprenticeship places was announced, helping to strengthen the country's competitiveness and extend opportunities to people facing redundancy. In 2007–8, 225,000 people started apprenticeships.

The Apprenticeships, Skills, Children and Learning Bill proposes that new duties be placed on local authorities to secure suitable education and training for the children and young people in juvenile custody in their authority.

Of the many voluntary bodies providing adult education, the biggest is the Workers' Educational Association (WEA), which operates throughout England and Scotland to provide over 104,000 courses each year, reaching more than 110,000 adults. The WEA is a charity supported by funding from the LSC in England, and by the Scottish government and local authorities in Scotland. Similar but separate organisations operate in Wales: Coleg Harlech WEA (covering North Wales) and WEA South Wales. The National Institute of Adult Continuing Education, has a broad remit to promote lifelong learning opportunities for adults.

Wales operates a range of programmes to support skills development, including the Workforce Development Programme, a flexible system of grants to meet part of the cost of training employees, an employers' pledge in association with Basic Skills Cymru, and the Wales Union Learning Fund. The new Wales skills strategy, Skills that Work for Wales, has been implemented since autumn 2008. Advice on its implementation, and on skills, employment and business development more generally, will be provided by the Wales Employment and Skills Board, the Chair of which is also a member of the UK Commission on Employment and Skills.

NIACE Dysgu Cymru, the Welsh committee, receives financial support from the Welsh Assembly and support in kind from local authorities, and advises government, voluntary bodies and education providers on adult continuing education and training matters in Wales. In Scotland, policy responsibility for community learning and development lies with Learning Connections and the Directorate General for Education of the Scottish government. Individual learning accounts (ILAs) are a Scottish government scheme that can pay for a wide range of learning activities with a variety of registered providers, including colleges and universities. ILA Scotland funding can be used by eligible learns to cover, either wholly or in part, the fee costs of learning. In Northern Ireland, responsibility for lifelong learning lies with the Department for Employment and Learning.

CONTACTS

APPRENTICESHIPS T 0800-015 0600
W www.apprenticeships.co.uk

COUNCIL FOR THE CURRICULUM EXAMINATIONS AND ASSESSMENT (NORTHERN IRELAND) T 028-9026 1200
W www.ccea.org.uk

DEPARTMENT FOR BUSINESS, INNOVATION AND SKILLS (ENGLAND) T 020-7215 5555
W www.bis.gov.uk

DEPARTMENT FOR CHILDREN, SCHOOLS AND FAMILIES (ENGLAND) T 0870-000 2288
W www.dcsf.gov.uk

DEPARTMENT FOR EMPLOYMENT AND LEARNING NORTHERN IRELAND T 028-9025 7777
W www.delni.gov.uk

DEPARTMENT OF EDUCATION NORTHERN IRELAND T 028-9127 9279 W www.deni.gov.uk

DIPLOMAS T 0870-000 2288 W www.dfes.gov.uk/14-19

EDUCATION DEPARTMENT, SCOTTISH GOVERNMENT T 0845-345 4745
W www.teachinginscotland.com

EDUCATION OTHERWISE T 0870-730 0074
W www.education-otherwise.org

EDUCATION AND TRAINING INSPECTORATE (NORTHERN IRELAND) T 028-9127 9726
W www.etini.gov.uk

EUROPEAN SOCIAL FUND W www.esf.gov.uk

GENERAL TEACHING COUNCIL FOR ENGLAND
T 0370-001 0308 W www.gtce.org.uk

GENERAL TEACHING COUNCIL FOR NORTHERN IRELAND T 028-9033 3390 W www.gtcni.org.uk

GENERAL TEACHING COUNCIL FOR SCOTLAND
T 0131-314 6000 W www.gtcs.org.uk

GENERAL TEACHING COUNCIL FOR WALES
T 029-2055 0350 W www.gtcw.org.uk

HER MAJESTY'S CHIEF INSPECTOR OF EDUCATION AND TRAINING IN WALES
T 029-2044 6446 W www.estyn.gov.uk

HER MAJESTY'S INSPECTORATE OF EDUCATION IN SCOTLAND T 01506-600200 W www.hmie.gov.uk

HIGHER EDUCATION ACADEMY T 01904-717500
W www.heacademy.ac.uk

HIGHER EDUCATION FUNDING COUNCIL FOR ENGLAND T 0117-931 7317 W www.hefce.ac.uk

HIGHER EDUCATION FUNDING COUNCIL FOR WALES T 029-2076 1861 W www.hefcw.ac.uk

HIGHER EDUCATION STATISTICS AGENCY
T 01242-255577 W www.hesa.ac.uk

HOME EDUCATION ADVISORY SERVICE
T 01707-371854 W www.heas.org.uk

INTERNATIONAL BACCALAUREATE ORGANISATION T (+41) (22) 791 7740 W www.ibo.org

LEARNING AND SKILLS COUNCIL (ENGLAND)
T 0845-019 4170 W www.lsc.gov.uk

LEARNING AND TEACHING SCOTLAND
T 0870-010 0297 W www.ltscotland.org.uk

NATIONAL INSTITUTE OF ADULT CONTINUING EDUCATION T 0116-204 4200 W www.niace.org.uk
OFFICE FOR STANDARDS IN EDUCATION, CHILDREN'S SERVICES AND SKILLS (ENGLAND) T 0845-640 4045 W www.ofsted.gov.uk
OFFICE OF THE QUALIFICATIONS AND EXAMINATIONS REGULATOR T 0300-303 3344 W www.ofqual.gov.uk
OPEN UNIVERSITY T 0870-333 4340 W www.open.ac.uk
PROFESSIONAL QUALIFICATION FOR HEADSHIP (NORTHERN IRELAND) T 028-9061 8121 W www.rtuni.org
QUALITY ASSURANCE AGENCY T 0141-572 3420 W www.qaa.ac.uk
QUALIFICATIONS AND CURRICULUM DEVELOPMENT AGENCY T 020-7509 5556 W www.qcda.gov.uk
SCOTTISH FUNDING COUNCIL T 0131-313 6500 W www.sfc.ac.uk
SCOTTISH GOVERNMENT T 0845-774 1741 W www.scotland.gov.uk
SCOTTISH QUALIFICATION FOR HEADSHIP T 0131-651 6179 W www.sqh.ed.ac.uk
SCOTTISH QUALIFICATIONS AUTHORITY T 0845-279 1000 W www.sqa.org.uk
STUDENT AWARDS AGENCY FOR SCOTLAND T 0845-111 1711 W www.student-support-saas.gov.uk
STUDENT FINANCE ENGLAND T 0845-300 5090
STUDENT FINANCE WALES T 0845-602 8845 W www.studentfinancewales.co.uk
SURE START T 0870-000 2288 W www.surestart.gov.uk
TRAINING AND DEVELOPMENT AGENCY FOR SCHOOLS T 020-7023 8001 W www.tda.gov.uk
UCAS T 0871-468 0468 W www.ucas.com
UNIVERSITIES AND COLLEGES EMPLOYERS ASSOCIATION T 020-7383 2444 W www.ucea.ac.uk
UNIVERSITY FOR INDUSTRY T 0114-291 5000 W www.ufi.com
WELSH ASSEMBLY T 0845-010 5500 W www.wales.gov.uk
WORKERS' EDUCATION ASSOCIATION T 020-7426 3450 W www.wea.org.uk

UNIVERSITIES

The following is a list of universities, which are those institutions that have been granted degree-awarding powers by either a royal charter or an act of parliament, or have been granted permission to use the word 'university' (or 'university college') by the Privy Council. There are other recognised bodies in the UK with degree-awarding powers, as well as institutions offering courses leading to a degree from a recognised body. Further information is available at W www.bis.gov.uk

Student numbers represent the number of undergraduate and postgraduate students based on information available at May 2009.

Variable tuition fees or 'top-up fees' were introduced for students starting courses in the 2006–7 academic year. Each university can now choose how much to charge students for tuition, up to a maximum of £3,225 for the 2009–10 academic year in England, Wales and Northern Ireland and £1,820 in Scotland (£2,895 for medicine). Students who started their course before 2006–7 are still charged according to the old system. For more information on tuition fees and student loans, *see* the Education System section.

Whether the fees apply varies depending on where the student is from. English and Northern Irish students pay top-up fees wherever they study in the UK; Welsh students pay variable fees in England, Scotland and Northern Ireland, but are entitled to a partial tuition fee grant if they remain in Wales or attend a course that is not available at any Welsh university; Scottish students do not pay fees in Scotland but pay variable tuition fees in England, Wales and Northern Ireland. EU students pay fees as if they came from the country they are studying in (ie the lowest amount) and international students pay their university's international fees, which are typically much higher than variable fees.

RESEARCH ASSESSMENT EXERCISE

The research assessment exercise (RAE) gives a rating to each university department or specialist college put forward for evaluation, based on the quality of its research. It enables the higher education funding bodies to distribute public funds for research selectively on the basis of quality. Institutions conducting the best research receive a larger proportion of the available grant so that the infrastructure for the top level of research in the UK is protected and developed. The table below shows the top five universities or specialist colleges for each discipline based on the mean average ranking of the overall quality of their research. The next RAE is due at the end of 2012.

Subject	*Universities or university colleges*
Anthropology	LSE (1), SOAS (1), Cambridge (3), Roehampton (4), UCL (5)
Archaeology	Durham (1), Reading (2), Cambridge (3), Liverpool (3), Oxford (3)
Biological sciences	Institute of Cancer Research (1), Oxford (1), Manchester (3), Sheffield (3), Dundee (5), RHUL (5)
Business and management	London Business School (1), Imperial (2), Cambridge (3), Cardiff (4), King's (5), Oxford (5), Warwick (5), Lancaster (5), LSE (5), Bath (5)
Chemistry	Cambridge (1), Nottingham (2), Oxford (3), Bristol (4), Edinburgh (4), St Andrews (4)
Classics	Cambridge (1), Oxford (2), UCL (3), Durham (4), King's (4), Warwick (4)
Communication and media studies	Westminster (1), East Anglia (2), Goldsmiths (3), LSE (3), Cardiff (5)
Computer science	Cambridge (1), Edinburgh (2), Imperial (2), Southampton (2), Manchester (5), Oxford (5), UCL (5)
Dentistry	Manchester (1), Queen Mary (2), King's (3), Sheffield (4), Bristol (5), Cardiff (5)
Drama and performing arts	Queen Mary (1), St Andrews (2), Manchester (3), Warwick (4), Bristol (5), King's (5)
Economics	LSE (1), UCL (2), Essex (3), Oxford (3), Warwick (3)
Engineering (civil)	Imperial (1), Swansea (2), Cardiff (3), Newcastle (4), Nottingham (4)
Engineering (electronic)	Leeds (1), Bangor (2), Manchester (2), Surrey (2), Imperial (5)
Engineering (general)	Cambridge (1), Oxford (2), Nottingham (3), Leeds (3), Imperial (5), Swansea (5)
English	York (1), Edinburgh (2), Manchester (2), Queen Mary (2), Exeter (5), Nottingham (5), Oxford (5)
French	Oxford (1), King's (2), Warwick (2), Aberdeen (4), Cambridge (4), St Andrews (4)
Geography	Bristol (1), Cambridge (1), Durham (1), Oxford (1), Queen Mary (1)
German, Dutch and Scandinavian	Oxford (1), Cambridge (2), Durham (2), King's (2), Leeds (2), RHUL (2), St Andrews (2), UCL (2)
History	Imperial (1), Essex (2), Kent (2), Liverpool (2), Oxford (2), Warwick (2)
Law	LSE (1), UCL (2), Oxford (3), Durham (4), Nottingham (4)
Mathematics (applied)	Cambridge (1), Oxford (1), Bristol (3), Bath (4), Portsmouth (4), St Andrews (4)
Mathematics (pure)	Imperial (1), Warwick (2), Oxford (3), Cambridge (4), Bristol (5), Edinburgh (5), Heriot-Watt (5)

Subject	*Universities or university colleges*
Mathematics (statistics)	Oxford (1), Cambridge (2), Imperial (3), Bristol (4), Warwick (4)
Music	RHUL (1), Birmingham (2), Manchester (2), Cambridge (4), King's (4), Sheffield (4), Southampton (4)
Nursing and Midwifery	Manchester (1), Southampton (2), Ulster (3), York (4), City (5)
Philosophy	UCL (1), St Andrews (1), King's (2), Reading (2), Sheffield (2)
Physics	Lancaster (1), Bath (2), Cambridge (2), Nottingham (2), St Andrews (2)
Politics	Essex (1), Sheffield (1), Aberystwyth (3), Oxford (4), LSE (5)
Pre-clinical studies	Oxford (1), Manchester (2), UCL (2), Queen Mary (4), Bristol (5), King's (5)
Psychology	Cambridge (1), Oxford (2), Birmingham (3), UCL (4), Birkbeck (5), Cardiff (5)
Sociology	Essex (1), Goldsmiths (1), Lancaster (1), Manchester (1), York (1)
Sports-related subjects	Birmingham (1), Loughborough (1), Bristol (3), Liverpool John Moores (4), Stirling (5)
Theology and religious studies	Durham (1), Aberdeen (2), Cambridge (3), Oxford (3), UCL (3)

UG = undergraduate PG = postgraduate

UNIVERSITY OF ABERDEEN (1495)
King's College, Aberdeen AB24 3FX **T** 01224-272000
W www.abdn.ac.uk
Students: 10,395 UG; 5,650 PG
Chancellor, Lord Wilson of Tillyorn, KT, GCMG, FRSE
Principal and Vice-Chancellor, Prof. C. Duncan Rice, FRSE
Academic Registrar, Dr Gillian Macintosh

UNIVERSITY OF ABERTAY DUNDEE (1994)
Bell Street, Dundee DD1 1HG **T** 01382-308000
W www.abertay.ac.uk
Students: 3,525 UG; 608 PG
Chancellor, Lord Airlie, PC, KT, GCVO
Vice-Chancellor, Prof. Bernard King, CBE
Academic Registrar, Dr Colin Fraser

ANGLIA RUSKIN UNIVERSITY (1992)
Rivermead Campus, Bishop Hall Lane, Chelmsford, Essex CM1 1SQ **T** 0845-271 3333 **W** www.anglia.ac.uk
Students: 16,700 UG; 2,305 PG
Chancellor, Lord Ashcroft, KCMG
Vice-Chancellor, Prof. Michael Thorne, FRSA
The Secretary and Clerk, Stephen Bennett

UNIVERSITY OF THE ARTS LONDON (Formerly The London Institute (1986), University of the Arts London was formed in 2004)
65 Davies Street, London W1K 5DA **T** 020-7514 6000
W www.arts.ac.uk
Students: 10,322 UG; 2,297 PG
Chancellor, Lord Stevenson, CBE
Rector, Sir Michael Bichard, KCB
University Secretary, Martin Prince

COLLEGES

CAMBERWELL COLLEGE OF ARTS (1898)
Peckham Road, London SE5 8UF **T** 020-7514 6302
W www.camberwell.arts.ac.uk
Head of College, Chris Wainwright

CENTRAL SAINT MARTINS COLLEGE OF ART & DESIGN (1854)
Southampton Row, London WC1B 4AP **T** 020-7514 7022
W www.csm.arts.ac.uk
Head of College, Jane Rapley, OBE

CHELSEA COLLEGE OF ART & DESIGN (1895)
Millbank, London SW1P 4RJ **T** 020-7514 7751
W www.chelsea.arts.ac.uk
Head of College, Chris Wainwright

LONDON COLLEGE OF COMMUNICATION (1894)
Elephant & Castle, London SE1 6SB **T** 020-7514 6500
W www.lcc.arts.ac.uk
Head of College, Sandra Kemp

LONDON COLLEGE OF FASHION (1963)
20 John Princes Street, London W1G 0BJ **T** 020-7514 7500
W www.fashion.arts.ac.uk
Head of College, Dr Frances Corner

WIMBLEDON COLLEGE OF ART (1930)
Merton Hall Road, London SW19 3QA **T** 020-7514 9641
W www.wimbledon.arts.ac.uk
Head of College, Chris Wainwright

ASTON UNIVERSITY (1966)
Aston Triangle, Birmingham B4 7ET **T** 0121-204 3000
W www.aston.ac.uk
Students: 7,155 UG; 2,415 PG
Chancellor, Sir Michael Bett, CBE
Vice-Chancellor, Prof. Julia King, CBE, FRENG, FRSA
Chief Operating Officer, Richard Middleton

UNIVERSITY OF BATH (1966)
Bath BA2 7AY **T** 01225-388388 **W** www.bath.ac.uk
Students: 9,460 UG; 3,758 PG
Chancellor, Lord Tugendhat
Vice-Chancellor, Prof. Glynis Breakwell, FRSA
University Secretary, Mark Humphriss

BATH SPA UNIVERSITY (2005)
Newton Park, Newton St Loe, Bath BA2 9BN
T 01225-875875 **W** www.bathspa.ac.uk
Students: 5,492 UG; 2,084 PG
Vice-Chancellor, Prof. Frank Morgan
Academic Registrar, Christopher Ellicott

UNIVERSITY OF BEDFORDSHIRE (1993)
Park Square, Luton LU1 3JU **T** 01582-734111
W www.beds.ac.uk
Students: 10,250 UG; 5,641 PG
Chancellor, Sir Robin Biggam
Vice-Chancellor, Prof. Les Ebdon
Registrar, Prof. Jim Franklin

UNIVERSITY OF BIRMINGHAM (1900)
Edgbaston, Birmingham B15 2TT **T** 0121-414 3344
W www.bham.ac.uk

Students: 18,547 UG; 10,670 PG
Chancellor, Sir Dominic Cadbury
Vice-Chancellor, Prof. David Eastwood
Registrar and Secretary, Mr Lee Sanders

BIRMINGHAM CITY UNIVERSITY (1992)
Perry Barr, Birmingham B42 2SU T 0121-331 5000
W www.bcu.ac.uk
Students: 19,760 UG; 3,485 PG
Chancellor, Lord Mayor of Birmingham, Chauhdry Rashid
Vice-Chancellor, Prof. David H. Tidmarsh
Secretary and Registrar, Maxine Penlington

UNIVERSITY OF BOLTON (2005)
Deane Road, Bolton BL3 5AB T 01204-903903
W www.bolton.ac.uk
Students: 9,455 UG; 2,241 PG
Vice-Chancellor and Chief Executive, Dr George Holmes
Deputy Vice Chancellor, Dr Peter Marsh
Director of Marketing and Communications, Dr Nigel Hill

BOURNEMOUTH UNIVERSITY (1992)
Fern Barrow, Poole, Dorset BH12 5BB T 01202-524111
W www.bournemouth.ac.uk
Students: 15,595 UG; 2,280 PG
Chancellor, Lord Phillips of Worth Matravers, PC, QC
Vice-Chancellor, Prof. Paul Curran
Registrar, Noel Richardson

UNIVERSITY OF BRADFORD (1966)
Bradford, W. Yorks BD7 1DP T 01274-232323
W www.brad.ac.uk
Students: 8,924 UG; 2,778 PG
Chancellor, Imran Khan
Vice-Chancellor, Prof. Mark Cleary
Registrar, Adrian Pearce

UNIVERSITY OF BRIGHTON (1992)
Mithras House, Lewes Road, Brighton BN2 4AT
T 01273-600900 W www.bton.ac.uk
Students: 16,637 UG; 3,832 PG
Chairman, Lord Mogg
Vice-Chancellor, Prof. Julian Crampton
Registrar, Mrs Carol Burns

UNIVERSITY OF BRISTOL (1909)
Senate House, Tyndall Avenue, Bristol BS8 1TH
T 0117-928 9000 W www.bristol.ac.uk
Students: 12,516 UG; 5,144 PG
Chancellor, Baroness Hale of Richmond, DBE, PC
Vice Chancellor, Prof. Eric Thomas
Registrar, Derek Pretty

BRUNEL UNIVERSITY (1966)
Uxbridge, Middx UB8 3PH T 01895-274000
W www.brunel.ac.uk
Students: 10,405 UG; 3,860 PG
Chancellor, Lord Wakeham, PC
Vice-Chancellor and Principal, Prof. Chris Jenks, FRSA
Secretary and Registrar, Susan Lapworth

UNIVERSITY OF BUCKINGHAM (1983)
Buckingham MK18 1EG T 01280-814080
W www.buckingham.ac.uk
Students: 714 UG; 296 PG
Chancellor, Sir Martin Jacomb
Vice-Chancellor, Dr Terence Kealey
Registrar, Prof. Len Evans

BUCKINGHAMSHIRE NEW UNIVERSITY (2007)
High Wycombe Campus, Queen Alexander Road, High Wycombe HP11 2JZ T 0800-0565 660 W www.bucks.ac.uk
Students: 5,427 UG; 449 PG
Vice-Chancellor, Prof. Ruth Farwell
Registrar, Hilary Garland

UNIVERSITY OF CAMBRIDGE (1209)
The Old Schools, Trinity Lane, Cambridge CB2 1TN
T 01223-337733 W www.cam.ac.uk
Students: 11,608 UG; 6,216 PG
Chancellor, HRH The Prince Philip, Duke of Edinburgh, KG, KT, OM, GBE, PC, FRS
Vice-Chancellor, Prof. Alison Richard (Newnham)
High Steward, Dame Bridget Ogilvie, DBE, FRS (Girton)
Chancellor, HRH The Prince Philip, Duke of Edinburgh, KG, KT, OM, GBE, PC, FRS
Vice-Chancellor, Prof. Alison Richard (Newnham)
High Steward, Dame Bridget Ogilvie, DBE, FRS (Girton)
Deputy High Steward, vacant
Commissary, Lord Mackay of Clashfern, KT, PC, FRSE (Trinity)
Pro-Vice-Chancellors, Prof. A. D. Cliff (Christ's); Prof. I. M. Leslie (Christ's); Dr K. B. Pretty (Homerton); Prof. J. M. Rallison (Trinity); Prof. S. J. Young (Emmanuel)
Proctors, Revd J. L. Caddick (Emmanuel); Revd L. A. Yates (St John's)
Orator, Dr R. Thompson (Selwyn)
Registrary, Dr J. W. Nicholls (Emmanuel)
Librarian, Mrs A. E. Jarvis (Wolfson)
Director of the Fitzwilliam Museum, Dr T. Potts (Clare)
Academic Secretary, G. P. Allen (Wolfson)
Director of Finance, A. M. Reid (Wolfson)

COLLEGES AND HALLS *with dates of foundation*
CHRIST'S (1505)
Master, Prof. Frank Kelly, FRS
CHURCHILL (1960)
Master, Prof. Sir David Wallace, CBE, FRS
CLARE (1326)
Master, Prof. A. J. Badger
CLARE HALL (1966)
President, Prof. Sir Martin Harris
CORPUS CHRISTI (1352)
Master, Mr S. Laing
DARWIN (1964)
Master, Prof. W. A. Brown, CBE
DOWNING (1800)
Master, Prof. B. J. Everitt, FRS
EMMANUEL (1584)
Master, Lord Wilson of Dinton, GCB
FITZWILLIAM (1966)
Master, Prof. R. D. Lethbridge
GIRTON (1869)
Mistress, Prof. S. J. Smith, FBA
GONVILLE AND CAIUS (1348)
Master, Sir Christopher Hum, KCMG
HOMERTON (1824)
Principal, Dr K. B. Pretty
HUGHES HALL (1985)
President, Mrs S. Squire
JESUS (1496)
Master, Prof. R. Mair, FRS, FRENG
KING'S (1441)
Provost, Prof. T. R. Harrison
LUCY CAVENDISH (1965)
President, Prof J. Todd

MAGDALENE (1542)
Master, Mr D. D. Robinson
MURRAY EDWARDS (1954)
President, Dr J. Barnes
NEWNHAM (1871)
Principal, Dame Patricia Hodgson, DBE
PEMBROKE (1347)
Master, Sir Richard Dearlove, KCMG, OBE
PETERHOUSE (1284)
Master, Prof. A. K. Dixon
QUEENS' (1448)
President, Prof. Lord Eatwell
ROBINSON (1977)
Warden, Prof. A. D. Yates
ST CATHARINE'S (1473)
Master, Prof. Dame Jean Thomas, DBE, FRS
ST EDMUND'S (1896)
Master, Prof. J. P. Luzio
ST JOHN'S (1511)
Master, Prof. C. Dobson, FRS
SELWYN (1882)
Master, Prof. R. J. Bowring
SIDNEY SUSSEX (1596)
Master, Prof. A. F. Wallace-Hadrill, OBE
TRINITY (1546)
Master, Prof. Lord Rees of Ludlow, PRS
TRINITY HALL (1350)
Master, Prof. M. J. Daunton, FBA
WOLFSON (1965)
President, Dr G. Johnson

CANTERBURY CHRIST CHURCH UNIVERSITY (2005)
North Holmes Road, Canterbury CT1 1QU **T** 01227-767700
W www.canterbury.ac.uk
Students: 11,835 UG; 3,715 PG
Chancellor, Rt Revd and Rt Hon. Rowan Williams, PC, DPHIL
Vice-Chancellor and Principal, Prof. Michael Wright
Academic Registrar, Lorri Currie

CARDIFF UNIVERSITY (1883)
Cardiff CF10 3XQ **T** 029-2087 4000 **W** www.cardiff.ac.uk
Students: 20,593 UG; 6,213 PG
President, Lord Kinnock, PC
Vice-Chancellor, Dr David Grant, CBE, FRENG

UNIVERSITY OF CENTRAL LANCASHIRE (1992)
Preston PR1 2HE **T** 01772-201201 **W** www.uclan.ac.uk
Students: 27,325 UG; 3,925 PG
Chancellor, Sir Richard Evans, CBE
Vice-Chancellor, Dr Malcolm McVicar

UNIVERSITY OF CHESTER (2005)
Parkgate Road, Chester CH1 4BJ **T** 01244-511000
W www.chester.ac.uk
Students: 6,873 UG; 3,485 PG
Chancellor, His Grace, The Duke of Westminster, KG, OBE, DL
Vice-Chancellor, Canon Prof. Tim Wheeler, DL
Director of Registry Services, Mr Jonathan Moores

UNIVERSITY OF CHICHESTER (2005)
Bishop Otter Campus, College Lane, Chichester PO19 6PE
T 01243-816000 **W** www.chiuni.ac.uk
Students: 4,103 UG; 1,346 PG
Vice-Chancellor, Dr Robin Baker
Academic and Student Services Director, Graham Fice

CITY UNIVERSITY (1966)
Northampton Square, London EC1V 0HB **T** 020-7040 5060
W www.city.ac.uk
Students: 14,530 UG; 6,880 PG
Pro-Chancellor, Rt. Hon. the Lord Mayor Ian Luder, BT, DSC
Vice-Chancellor, Prof. Malcolm Gillies

COVENTRY UNIVERSITY (1992)
Priory Street, Coventry CV1 5FB **T** 024-7688 7688
W www.coventry.ac.uk
Students: 15,101 UG; 3,267 PG
Chancellor, Sir John Egan
Vice-Chancellor, Prof. Madeleine Atkins
Academic Registrar and Secretary, Ms Kate Quantrell

DE MONTFORT UNIVERSITY (1992)
The Gateway, Leicester LE1 9BH **T** 08459-454647
W www.dmu.ac.uk
Students: 18,669 UG; 3,748 PG
Chancellor, Lord Alli
Vice-Chancellor, Prof. Philip Tasker
Registrar, Eugene Critchlow

UNIVERSITY OF DERBY (1992)
Kedleston Road, Derby DE22 1GB **T** 01332-590500
W www.derby.ac.uk
Students: 12,978 UG; 3,135 PG
Chancellor, The Duke of Devonshire, CBE
Vice-Chancellor, Prof. John Coyne
Registrar, June Hughes

UNIVERSITY OF DUNDEE (1967)
Nethergate, Dundee DD1 4HN **T** 01382-384000
W www.dundee.ac.uk
Students: 11,070 UG; 5,650 PG
Chancellor, Lord Patel, FRSE
Acting Principal and Vice-Chancellor, Prof. Peter Downes, OBE, FRSE
Secretary, Dr Jim McGeorge

DURHAM UNIVERSITY (1832)
The University Office, Durham DH1 3HP **T** 0191-334 2000
W www.dur.ac.uk
Students: 11,278 UG; 4,251 PG
Chancellor, Bill Bryson
Vice-Chancellor and Warden, Prof. C. F. Higgins, FRSE, FRSA, FMEDSCI
Registrar and Secretary, Carolyn Fowler

COLLEGES
COLLINGWOOD (1972)
Principal, Prof E. Corrigan, FRS
STEPHENSON (2001)
Principal, Prof. A. C. Darnell
GREY
Master, Prof. J. M. Chamberlain, DPHIL
HATFIELD (1846)
Master, Prof. T. P. Burt, DSC
JOHN SNOW (2001)
Principal, Prof. Carolyn Summerbell
JOSEPHINE BUTLER (2006)
Principal, A. Simpson
ST AIDAN'S
Principal (acting), Dr Susan F. Frenk
ST CHAD'S (1904)
Principal, Revd Dr J. P. M. Cassidy

ST CUTHBERT'S SOCIETY (1888)
Principal, Prof. G. Towl
ST HILD AND ST BEDE (1975)
Principal, Prof. C. J. Hutchinson
ST JOHN'S (1909)
Principal, Revd Dr D. Wilkinson
ST MARY'S
Principal, Prof. P. Gilmartin
TREVELYAN (1966)
Principal, Prof. H. M. Evans
UNIVERSITY (1832)
Master, Prof. M. E. Tucker
USHAW
President, Fr. J. Marsland
USTINOV
Principal, Penelope B. Wilson, DPHIL
VAN MILDERT (1965)
Master, Prof. P. O'Meara, DPHIL

UNIVERSITY OF EAST ANGLIA (1963)
Norwich NR4 7TJ **T** 01603-456161 **W** www.uea.ac.uk
Students: 10,988 UG; 3,260 PG
Chancellor, Sir Brandon Gough
Vice-Chancellor, Prof. Edward Acton
Academic Registrar, Brian Summers

UNIVERSITY OF EAST LONDON (1898)
University Way, London E16 2RD **T** 020-8223 3000
W www.uel.ac.uk
Students: 12,969 UG; 4,387 PG
Chancellor, Lord Rix
Vice-Chancellor (acting), Prof. Susan Price
Registrar and Secretary, Alan Ingle

EDGE HILL UNIVERSITY (2006)
St Helens Road, Ormskirk, Lancs L39 4QP **T** 01695-575171
W www.edgehill.ac.uk
Students: 7,750 UG; 10,200 PG
Chancellor, Prof. Tanya Byron
Vice-Chancellor, Dr John Cater
University Secretary, Ian Jones

UNIVERSITY OF EDINBURGH (1583)
Old College, South Bridge, Edinburgh EH8 9YL
T 0131-650 1000 **W** www.ed.ac.uk
Students: 21,419 UG; 3,724 PG
Chancellor, HRH The Prince Philip, Duke of Edinburgh, KG, KT, OM
Principal and Vice-Chancellor, Prof. Sir Timothy O'Shea, FRSE
University Secretary, Melvyn Cornish

EDINBURGH NAPIER UNIVERSITY (1992)
Craighouse Road, Edinburgh EH10 5LG **T** 0845-260 6040
W www.napier.ac.uk
Students: 11,871 UG; 2,133 PG
Chancellor, Tim Waterstone
Vice-Chancellor, Prof. Joan Stringer, CBE
Secretary, Dr Gerry Webber

UNIVERSITY OF ESSEX (1965)
Wivenhoe Park, Colchester CO4 3SQ **T** 01206-873333
W www.essex.ac.uk
Students: 6,376 UG; 2,786 PG
Chancellor, Lord Phillips of Sudbury, OBE
Vice-Chancellor, Prof. Colin Riordan
Academic Registrar, Dr Tony Rich

UNIVERSITY OF EXETER (1955)
The Queen's Drive, Exeter EX4 4QJ **T** 01392-661000
W www.exeter.ac.uk
Students: 11,955 UG; 3,570 PG
Chancellor, Floella Benjamin, OBE
Vice-Chancellor, Prof. Steve Smith
Registrar and Secretary, David Allen

UNIVERSITY OF GLAMORGAN (1992)
Pontypridd CF37 1DL **T** 0800-716925 **W** www.glam.ac.uk
Students: 18,240 UG; 3,256 PG
Chancellor, Lord Morris of Aberavon, KG, PC, QC
Vice-Chancellor, Prof. David Halton
Academic Registrar, William Callaway

UNIVERSITY OF GLASGOW (1451)
Gilbert Scott Building, University Avenue, Glasgow G12 8QQ
T 0141-330 2000 **W** www.gla.ac.uk
Students: 19,405 UG; 3,395 PG
Chancellor, Prof. Sir Kenneth Calman, KCB, MD, FRCS
Vice-Chancellor, Prof. Anton Muscatelli, FRSE
Secretary of Court, David Newall

GLASGOW CALEDONIAN UNIVERSITY (1993)
City Campus, 70 Cowcaddens Road, Glasgow G4 0BA
T 0141-331 3000 **W** www.caledonian.ac.uk
Students: 14,319 UG; 2,595 PG
Chancellor, Lord Macdonald of Tradeston, PC, CBE
Vice-Chancellor and Principal, Prof. Pamela Gillies, FRSA
Registrar, Mr Brendan Ferguson

UNIVERSITY OF GLOUCESTERSHIRE (2001)
The Park, Cheltenham GL50 2RH **T** 01242-714700
W www.glos.ac.uk
Students: 6,700 UG; 1,820 PG
Chancellor, Lord Carey of Clifton, PC
Vice-Chancellor, Prof. Patricia Broadfoot, CBE
Academic Registrar, Julie Thackray

UNIVERSITY OF GREENWICH (1992)
Old Royal Naval College, Park Row, Greenwich, London
SE10 9LS **T** 020-8331 8000 **W** www.gre.ac.uk
Students: 18,412 UG; 6,121 PG
Chancellor, Lord Hart of Chilton
Vice-Chancellor, Baroness Blackstone
Secretary and Registrar, Linda Cording

HERIOT-WATT UNIVERSITY (1966)
Edinburgh EH14 4AS **T** 0131-449 5111 **W** www.hw.ac.uk
Students: 5,708 UG; 1,791 PG
Chancellor, Prof. Anton Muscatelli, CBE, FRCP
Principal and Vice-Chancellor, Prof. Andrew Walker
Registrar, Ms Kathy Patterson

UNIVERSITY OF HERTFORDSHIRE (1992)
College Lane, Hatfield, Herts AL10 9AB **T** 01707-284000
W www.herts.ac.uk
Students: 23,310 UG; 3,905 PG
Chancellor, Marquess of Salisbury, PC
Vice-Chancellor, Prof. Tim Wilson
Registrar, Philip Waters

UNIVERSITY OF HUDDERSFIELD (1992)
Queensgate, Huddersfield HD1 3DH **T** 01484-422288
W www.hud.ac.uk
Students: 14,929 UG; 3,390 PG
Chancellor, Prof. Patrick Stewart, OBE
Vice-Chancellor, Prof. Bob Cryan
University Secretary, Mr A. E. Mears

UNIVERSITY OF HULL (1927)
Cottingham Road, Hull HU6 7RX **T** 01482-346311
W www.hull.ac.uk
Students: 13,639 UG; 2,270 PG
Chancellor, Baroness Bottomley, PC
Vice-Chancellor, Prof. David J. Drewry, FRSA
Registrar and Secretary, Mrs Frances Owen

IMPERIAL COLLEGE LONDON (1907)
South Kensington, London SW7 2AZ **T** 020-7589 5111
W www.imperial.ac.uk
Students: 8,419 UG; 3,900 PG
Rector, Sir Roy Anderson
Senior Principal, Prof. Sir Peter Knight
Academic Registrar, Bob Westaway

KEELE UNIVERSITY (1962)
Keele, Staffs ST5 5BG **T** 01782-732000 **W** www.keele.ac.uk
Students: 9,035 UG; 2,380 PG
Chancellor, Prof. Sir David Weatherall, MD
Vice-Chancellor, Prof. Dame Janet Finch, CBE
Registrar and Secretary, Simon Morris, FRSA

UNIVERSITY OF KENT (1965)
Canterbury, Kent CT2 7NZ **T** 01227-764000
W www.kent.ac.uk
Students: 15,967 UG; 2,197 PG
Chancellor, Prof. Sir Robert Worcester, KBE
Vice-Chancellor, Prof. Julia Goodfellow, CBE
Academic Registrar, Jon Pink

KINGSTON UNIVERSITY (1992)
River House, 53–57 High Street, Kingston upon Thames, Surrey KT1 1LQ **T** 020-8417 9000 **W** www.kingston.ac.uk
Students: 18,034 UG; 3,266 PG
Chancellor, Sir Peter Hall
Vice-Chancellor, Prof. Sir Peter Scott
University Secretary, Donald Beaton

UNIVERSITY OF LANCASTER (1964)
Bailrigg, Lancaster LA1 4YW **T** 01524-65201
W www.lancs.ac.uk
Students: 9,048 UG; 3,592 PG
Chancellor, Sir Christian Bonington, CBE
Vice-Chancellor, Prof. Paul Wellings
Chief Operating Officer, Andrew Neal

UNIVERSITY OF LEEDS (1904)
Leeds LS2 9JT **T** 0113-243 1751 **W** www.leeds.ac.uk
Students: 24,374 UG; 6,931 PG
Chancellor, Lord Bragg, LLD, DLITT, DCL
Vice-Chancellor, Prof. Michael Arthur, DM, FRCP
Secretary, J. Roger Gair

LEEDS METROPOLITAN UNIVERSITY (1992)
Civic Quarter, Leeds LS1 3HE **T** 0113-812 0000
W www.leedsmet.ac.uk
Students: 23,310 UG; 3,905 PG
Chancellor, vacant
Chief Executive (acting), Geoff Hitchins
Registrar, Stephen Denton

UNIVERSITY OF LEICESTER (1957)
University Road, Leicester LE1 7RH **T** 0116-252 2522
W www.le.ac.uk
Students: 10,971 UG; 10,657 PG
Chancellor, Sir Peter Williams, CBE, FRS, FRENG
Vice-Chancellor, Prof. Robert Burgess
Registrar, Dave Hall

UNIVERSITY OF LINCOLN (1992)
Brayford Pool, Lincoln LN6 7TS **T** 01522-882000
W www.lincoln.ac.uk
Students: 8,984 UG; 711 PG
Chancellor, Lord Adebowale
Vice-Chancellor, Prof. David Chiddick
Registrar, Mr Chris Spendlove

UNIVERSITY OF LIVERPOOL (1903)
Liverpool, Merseyside L69 7ZX **T** 0151-794 2000
W www.liv.ac.uk
Students: 13,598 UG; 2,803 PG
Chancellor, Lord Owen, CH, PC, FRCP
Vice-Chancellor, Prof. Sir Howard Newby, FRSA
Chief Operating Officer, Patrick Hackett

LIVERPOOL HOPE UNIVERSITY (2005)
Hope Park, Liverpool L16 9JD **T** 0151-291 3000
W www.hope.ac.uk
Students: 5,665 UG; 1,395 PG
Chancellor, Baroness Cox
Vice-Chancellor, Prof. Gerald Pillay, FRSA
Registrar, Neil McLaughlin Cook

LIVERPOOL JOHN MOORES UNIVERSITY (1992)
Egerton Court, 2 Rodney Street, Liverpool L3 5UX
T 0151-231 2121 **W** www.ljmu.ac.uk
Students: 15,904 UG; 3,965 PG
Chancellor, Dr Brian May, CBE
Vice-Chancellor, Prof. Michael Brown, CBE, DL
Secretary, Alison Wild

UNIVERSITY OF LONDON (1836)
Senate House, Malet Street, London WC1E 7HU
T 020-7862 8000 **W** www.london.ac.uk
Chancellor, HRH the Princess Royal, KG, GCVO, FRS
Vice-Chancellor, Prof. Sir Graeme Davies, FRENG, FRSE
Chair of the Board of Trustees, Dame Jenny Abransky
Director of Administration, Catherine Swarbrick
Chancellor, HRH the Princess Royal, KG, GCVO, FRS
Vice-Chancellor, Prof. Sir Graeme Davies, FRENG, FRSE
Pro-Chancellor, Lord Sutherland of Houndwood, KT, FBA
Director of Administration, Catherine Swarbrick

COLLEGES

BIRKBECK COLLEGE
Malet Street, London WC1E 7HX
Students: 14,150 UG, 3,075 PG
President, Prof J. E. Hobsbawm
Master, Prof. D. Latchman

CENTRAL SCHOOL OF SPEECH AND DRAMA
Embassy Theatre, Eton Avenue, London NW3 3HY
Students: 570 UG; 310 PG
President, Rt. Hon. Peter Mandleson
Principal, Prof. Gavin Henderson, CBE

COURTAULD INSTITUTE OF ART
North Block, Somerset House, Strand, London WC2R 0RN
Students: 160 UG; 280 PG
Director, Dr Deborah Swallow

GOLDSMITHS COLLEGE
Lewisham Way, New Cross, London SE14 6NW
Students, 5,280 UG; 2,215 PG
Warden, Prof. Geoffrey Crossick

HEYTHROP COLLEGE
Kensington Square, London W8 5HQ
Students: 380 UG; 360 PG
Principal, Revd Dr J. McDade, SJ, BD

INSTITUTE OF CANCER RESEARCH
Registered offices, 123 Old Brompton Road, London SW7 3RP
Chief Executive, Prof. P. Rigby

INSTITUTE OF EDUCATION
20 Bedford Way, London WC1H 0AL
Students: 310 UG; 7,075 PG
Director, Prof. G. Whitty

KING'S COLLEGE LONDON (includes Guy's, King's and St Thomas's Schools of Medicine, Dentistry and Biomedical Sciences)
Strand, London WC2R 2LS
Students: 14,110 UG; 6,995 PG
Principal, Prof. R. Trainor

LONDON BUSINESS SCHOOL
Regent's Park, London NW1 4SA
Students: 1,555 PG (postgraduate only)
Dean, Sir Andrew Likierman

LONDON SCHOOL OF ECONOMICS AND POLITICAL SCIENCE
Houghton Street, London WC2A 2AE
Students: 3,920 UG; 5,185 PG
Director, Sir Howard Davies

LONDON SCHOOL OF HYGIENE AND TROPICAL MEDICINE
Keppel Street, London WC1E 7HT
Students: 1,100 PG (postgraduate only)
Dean, Prof. Sir Andrew Haines

QUEEN MARY (incorporating St Bartholomew's and the Royal London School of Medicine and Dentistry)
Mile End Road, London E1 4NS
Students: 10,315 UG; 3,295 PG
Principal, Prof. Simon Gaskell

ROYAL ACADEMY OF MUSIC
Marylebone Road, London NW1 5HT
Students: 320 UG; 410 PG
Principal, Prof. J. Freeman-Attwood

ROYAL HOLLOWAY
Egham Hill, Egham, Surrey TW20 0EX
Students: 6,560 UG; 1,825 PG
Principal, Prof. S. Hill

ROYAL VETERINARY COLLEGE
Royal College Street, London NW1 0TU
Students: 1,430 UG; 365 PG
Principal and Dean, Prof. Q. McKellar

ST GEORGE'S
Cranmer Terrace, London SW17 0RE
Students: 3,705 UG; 455 PG
Principal, Prof. Peter Kopelman, FRCGP

SCHOOL OF ORIENTAL AND AFRICAN STUDIES
Thornhaugh Street, Russell Square, London WC1H 0XG
Students: 2,775 UG; 1,955 PG
Director, Prof. Paul Webley

SCHOOL OF PHARMACY
29–39 Brunswick Square, London WC1N 1AX
Students: 705 UG; 525 PG
Dean, Prof. Anthony Smith

UNIVERSITY COLLEGE LONDON (including UCL Medical School)
Gower Street, London WC1E 6BT
Students: 11,920 UG; 9,070 PG
Provost and President, Prof. Malcolm Grant, CBE

INSTITUTES

UNIVERSITY OF LONDON INSTITUTE IN PARIS
9–11 rue de Constantine, 75340 Paris, Cedex 07
Director, Prof. Andrew Hussey

UNIVERSITY MARINE BIOLOGICAL STATION
Millport, Isle of Cumbrae KA28 0EG
Acting Director, Prof. J. Atkinson

SCHOOL OF ADVANCED STUDY
Senate House, Malet Street, London WC1E 7HU
Dean, Prof. Sir Roderick Floud, FBA

INSTITUTE OF ADVANCED LEGAL STUDIES
Charles Clore House, 17 Russell Square, London WC1B 5DR
Director, Prof. Avrom Sherr

INSTITUTE OF CLASSICAL STUDIES
Senate House, Malet Street, London WC1E 7HU
Director, Prof. M. Edwards

INSTITUTE OF COMMONWEALTH STUDIES
28 Russell Square, London WC1B 5DS
Director, Prof. Philip Murphy

INSTITUTE OF ENGLISH STUDIES
Senate House, Malet Street, London WC1E 7HU
Director, Prof. W. Gould

INSTITUTE OF GERMANIC AND ROMANCE STUDIES
Senate House, Malet Street, London WC1E 7HU
Director, Prof. Naomi Segal

INSTITUTE OF HISTORICAL RESEARCH
Senate House, Malet Street, London WC1E 7HU
Director, Prof. Miles Taylor

INSTITUTE OF MUSICAL RESEARCH
Senate House, Malet Street, London WC1E 7HU
Director, Prof. Katharine Ellis

INSTITUTE OF PHILOSOPHY
Senate House, Malet Street, London WC1E 7HU
Director, Prof. Barry Smith

INSTITUTE FOR THE STUDY OF THE AMERICAS
Senate House, Malet Street, London WC1E 7HU
Director, Prof. Maxine Molyneux

WARBURG INSTITUTE
Woburn Square, London WC1H 0AB
Director, Prof. C. Hope

LONDON METROPOLITAN UNIVERSITY (2002)
31 Jewry Street, London EC3N 2EY **T** 020-7423 0000
W www.londonmet.ac.uk
Students: 20,920 UG; 7,055 PG

Interim Vice-Chancellor and Chief Executive, Alfred Morris
Academic Registrar, Dr Ray Smith

LONDON SOUTH BANK UNIVERSITY (1992)
103 Borough Road, London SE1 0AA T 020-7815 7815
W www.lsbu.ac.uk
Students: 18,524 UG; 5,836 PG
Chancellor, Sir Trevor McDonald, OBE
Vice-Chancellor, Martin Earwicker

LOUGHBOROUGH UNIVERSITY (1966)
Ashby Road, Loughborough, Leics LE11 3TU T 01509-263171
W www.lboro.ac.uk
Students: 11,939 UG; 4,176 PG
Chancellor, Sir John Jennings, CBE, FRSE, PHD
Vice-Chancellor, Prof. Shirley Pearce, CBE
Chief Operating Officer, Will Spinks

UNIVERSITY OF MANCHESTER (2004)
Oxford Road, Manchester M13 9PL T 0161-306 6000
W www.manchester.ac.uk
Students: 26,160 UG; 9,281 PG
Chancellor, Tom Bloxham, MBE
President and Vice-Chancellor, Prof. Alan Gilbert
Registrar and Secretary, Albert McMenemy

MANCHESTER METROPOLITAN UNIVERSITY (1992)
All Saints, Manchester M15 6BH T 0161-247 2000
W www.mmu.ac.uk
Students: 27,115 UG; 6,001 PG
Chancellor, vacant
Vice-Chancellor, Prof. John Brooks, DSC
Registrar, Gwyn Arnold

MIDDLESEX UNIVERSITY (1992)
Hendon Campus, The Burroughs, London NW4 4BT
T 020-8411 5555 W www.mdx.ac.uk
Students: 16,177 UG; 4,139 PG
Chancellor, Lord Sheppard of Didgemere, KT, KCVO
Vice-Chancellor, Prof. Michael Driscoll
Registrar, Colin Davis

UNIVERSITY OF NEWCASTLE UPON TYNE (1963)
6 Kensington Terrace, Newcastle upon Tyne NE1 7RU
T 0191-222 6000 W www.ncl.ac.uk
Students: 14,155 UG; 4,723 PG
Chancellor, Sir Liam Donaldson
Vice-Chancellor, Prof. Chris Brink, FRS, DPHIL
Registrar, Dr John V. Hogan

UNIVERSITY OF NORTHAMPTON (2005)
Park Campus, Boughton Green Road, Northampton NN2 7AL
T 01604-735500 W www.northampton.ac.uk
Students: 9,085 UG; 1,775 PG
Chancellor, Baroness Falkner
Vice-Chancellor, Ann Tate
Registrar, Jane Bunce

NORTHUMBRIA UNIVERSITY AT NEWCASTLE (1992)
Ellison Building, Ellison Place, Newcastle upon Tyne NE1 8ST
T 0191-232 6002 W www.northumbria.ac.uk
Students: 28,864 UG; 5,154 PG
Chancellor, Lord Stevens of Kirkwhelpington, QPM, FRSA
Vice-Chancellor, Prof. Andrew Wathey, FRENG
Registrar, Paul Kelly

UNIVERSITY OF NOTTINGHAM (1948)
King's Meadow Campus, Lenton Lane, Nottingham NG7 2NR
T 0115-951 5151 W www.nottingham.ac.uk
Students: 28,647 UG; 7,038 PG
Chancellor, Prof. Yang Fujia, LITTD
Vice Chancellor, Prof. David Greenaway
Registrar, Dr Paul Greatrix

NOTTINGHAM TRENT UNIVERSITY (1992)
Burton Street, Nottingham NG1 4BU T 0115-941 8418
W www.ntu.ac.uk
Students: 18,409 UG; 5,186 PG
Chancellor, Sir Michael Parkinson
Vice-Chancellor, Prof. Neil Gorman
Registrar, David Samson

OPEN UNIVERSITY (1969)
Walton Hall, Milton Keynes MK7 6AA T 01908-274066
W www.open.ac.uk
Students: 166,530 UG; 15,165 PG
Chancellor, Lord Puttnam
Vice-Chancellor, Prof. Brenda Gourley
Secretary, Fraser Woodburn

UNIVERSITY OF OXFORD (*c.*12th century)
University Offices, Wellington Square, Oxford OX1 2JD
T 01865-270000 W www.ox.ac.uk
Students: 11,734 UG; 8,101 PG
Chancellor, Lord Patten of Barnes, CH, PC (Balliol, St Antony's)
High Steward, Lord Rodger of Earlsferry (Balliol, New, St Hugh's)
Vice-Chancellor, Prof. Andrew Hamilton
Chancellor, Lord Patten of Barnes, CH, PC (Balliol, St Antony's)
High Steward, Lord Rodger of Earlsferry (Balliol, New, St Hugh's)
Vice-Chancellor, Prof. Andrew Hamilton
Pro-Vice-Chancellors, Dame Fiona Caldicott (Somerville); Prof. E. G. McKendrick (Lady Margaret Hall); Prof. A. P. Monaco (Merton); Prof. M. J. Earl (Green Templeton); Prof. I. A. Walmsley (St. Hugh's)
Registrar, Dr J. K. Maxton (University)
Secretary of the Faculties and Academic Registrar, M. D. Sibly (St Anne's)
Public Orator, R. H. A. Jenkyns
Director of University Library Services and Bodley's Librarian, Dr S. E. Thomas (Balliol)
Director of the Ashmolean Museum, Dr C. Brown (Worcester)
Keeper of Archives, S. Bailey
Director of Estates, Ms J. Wood
Director of Finance, G. F. B. Kerr

COLLEGES AND HALLS *with dates of foundation*
ALL SOULS (1438)
Warden, Prof. Sir John Vickers
BALLIOL (1263)
Master, Andrew Graham
BLACKFRIARS (1221)
Regent, Revd Richard Finn
BRASENOSE (1509)
Principal, Prof. Roger Cashmore, FRS
CAMPION HALL (1896)
Master, Revd Dr Peter l'Estrange
CHRIST CHURCH (1546)
Dean, Very Revd Christopher A. Lewis

CORPUS CHRISTI (1517)
President, Sir Tim Lankester, KCB
EXETER (1314)
Rector, Ms Frances Cairncross, CBE
GREEN TEMPLETON (2008)
President, Dr Colin Bundy
HARRIS MANCHESTER (1786)
Principal, Revd Ralph Waller
HERTFORD (1874)
Principal, Dr John Landers
JESUS (1571)
Principal, Lord Krebs, FRS
KEBLE (1868)
Warden, Prof. Averil Cameron, CBE, FBA
KELLOGG (1990)
President, Prof. Jonathan M. Michie
LADY MARGARET HALL (1878)
Principal, Dr Frances Lannon
LINACRE (1962)
Principal, Prof. Paul Slack, FBA
LINCOLN (1427)
Rector, Prof. Paul Langford, FBA
MAGDALEN (1458)
President, Prof. David Clary, FRS
MANSFIELD (1886)
Principal, Dr Diana Walford, FRCP
MERTON (1264)
Warden, Prof. Dame Jessica Rawson, CBE, FBA
NEW COLLEGE (1379)
Warden, Prof. Sir Curtis Price
NUFFIELD (1958)
Warden, Prof. Stephen Nickell, FBA
ORIEL (1326)
Provost, Sir Derek Morris
PEMBROKE (1624)
Master, Giles Henderson, CBE
QUEEN'S (1340)
Provost, Prof. Paul Madden, FRS
REGENT'S PARK (1820)
Principal, Revd Dr Robert Ellis
ST ANNE'S (1952)
Principal, Tim Gardam
ST ANTONY'S (1953)
Warden, Prof. Margaret MacMillan
ST BENET'S HALL (1897)
Master, Revd J. Felix Stephens
ST CATHERINE'S (1963)
Master, Prof. Roger Ainsworth
ST CROSS (1965)
Master, Prof. Andrew Goudie
ST EDMUND HALL (*c.*1278)
Principal, Prof. Keith Gull, CBE, FRS
ST HILDA'S (1893)
Principal, Sheila Forbes, CBE
ST HUGH'S (1886)
Principal, Andrew Dilnot, CBE
ST JOHN'S (1555)
President, Sir Michael Scholar, KCB
ST PETER'S (1929)
Master, Prof. Bernard Silverman, FRS
ST STEPHEN'S HOUSE (1876)
Principal, Revd Dr Robin Ward
SOMERVILLE (1879)
Principal, Dame Fiona Caldicott, DBE, FRCP, FRCPSYCH
TRINITY (1554)
President, Sir Ivor Roberts, KCMG
UNIVERSITY (1249)
Master, Sir Ivor Crewe, GCB, CVO
WADHAM (1610)
Warden, Sir Neil Chalmers, CBE
WOLFSON (1966)
President, Prof. Hermione Lee, FBA, FRSL, CBE
WORCESTER (1714)
Provost, Richard Smethurst
WYCLIFFE HALL (1877)
Principal, Revd Dr Richard Turnbull

OXFORD BROOKES UNIVERSITY (1992)
Gipsy Lane, Oxford OX3 0BP **T** 01865-484848
W www.brookes.ac.uk
Students: 11,489 UG; 4,011 PG
Chancellor, Shami Chakrabarti, CBE
Vice-Chancellor, Prof. Janet Beer
Deputy Vice Chancellor and Registrar, Rex Knight

UNIVERSITY OF PLYMOUTH (1992)
Drake Circus, Plymouth PL4 8AA **T** 01752-600600
W www.plymouth.ac.uk
Students: 27,559 UG; 4,364 PG
Vice-Chancellor and Chief Executive, Prof. Wendy Purcell
Academic Registrar and Secretary, Miss Jane Hopkinson

UNIVERSITY OF PORTSMOUTH (1992)
6–8, Hampshire Terrace, Portsmouth PO1 2RY **T** 023-9284 8484
W www.port.ac.uk
Students: 17,146 UG; 3,503 PG
Chancellor, Sheila Hancock, OBE
Vice-Chancellor, Prof. John Craven
Academic Registrar, Andrew Rees

QUEEN MARGARET UNIVERSITY (2007)
Queen Margaret University Drive, Musselburgh, Edinburgh EH21 6UU **T** 0131-474 0000 **W** www.qmu.ac.uk
Students: 3,218 UG; 410 PG
Chancellor, Sir Tom Farmer, CBE, KCSG
Vice Chancellor, Dr Petra Wend
Academic Registrar, Irene Hynd

QUEEN'S UNIVERSITY BELFAST (1908)
University Road, Belfast BT7 1NN **T** 028-9024 5133
W www.qub.ac.uk
Students: 17,615 UG; 4,610 PG
Chancellor, Kamalesh Sharma
Vice-Chancellor, Prof. Peter Gregson, FRENG
Registrar, James O'Kane

UNIVERSITY OF READING (1926)
Whiteknights, PO Box 217, Reading RG6 6AH **T** 0118-987 5123
W www.reading.ac.uk
Students: 13,057 UG; 4,735 PG
Chancellor, Sir John Madejski, OBE, DL
Vice-Chancellor, Prof. Gordon Marshall, CBE, FBA

ROBERT GORDON UNIVERSITY (1992)
Schoolhill, Aberdeen AB10 1FR **T** 01224-262000
W www.rgu.ac.uk
Students: 9,107 UG; 5,129 PG
Chancellor, Sir Ian Wood, CBE
Vice-Chancellor, Prof. R. Michael Pittilo
Academic Registrar, Hilary Douglas

ROEHAMPTON UNIVERSITY (2004)
Erasmus House, Roehampton Lane, London SW15 5PU
T 020-8392 3000 **W** www.roehampton.ac.uk

Students: 6,396 UG; 2,289 PG
Chancellor, John Simpson, CBE
Vice-Chancellor, Prof. Paul O'Prey
Academic Secretary, Robin Geller

ROYAL COLLEGE OF ART (1967)
Kensington Gore, London SW7 2EU **T** 020-7590 4444
W www.rca.ac.uk
Students: 890 PG
Provost, Sir Terence Conran
Rector and Vice-Provost, Prof. Sir Christopher Frayling
Registrar, Alan Selby

ROYAL COLLEGE OF MUSIC (1882)
Prince Consort Road, London SW7 2BS **T** 020-7589 3643
W www.rcm.ac.uk
Students: 360 UG; 289 PG
President, HRH The Prince of Wales, KG, KT, GCB
Vice-Chancellor, Prof. Colin Lawson, DMUS, FRCM
Director of Operations, Kevin Porter

UNIVERSITY OF ST ANDREWS (1413)
College Gate, St Andrews, Fife KY16 9AJ **T** 01334-476161
W www.st-andrews.ac.uk
Students: 5,952 UG; 1,306 PG
Chancellor, Sir Menzies Campbell, CBE, QC, MP
Principal and Vice-Chancellor, Dr Louise Richardson
Registrar, Lorraine Fraser

UNIVERSITY OF SALFORD (1967)
Salford, Greater Manchester M5 4WT **T** 0161-295 5000
W www.salford.ac.uk
Students: 15,650 UG; 3,530 PG
Chancellor, Prof. Sir Martin Harris
Vice-Chancellor, Prof. Martin Hall
Registrar, Dr Adrian Graves

UNIVERSITY OF SHEFFIELD (1905)
Western Bank, Sheffield S10 2TN **T** 0114-222 2000
W www.sheffield.ac.uk
Students: 18,002 UG; 6,002 PG
Chancellor, Sir Peter Middleton, GCB
Vice-Chancellor, Prof. Keith Burnett, CBE, DPHIL, FRS
Registrar and Secretary, Dr David Fletcher

SHEFFIELD HALLAM UNIVERSITY (1992)
City Campus, Howard Street, Sheffield S1 1WB
T 0114-225 5555 **W** www.shu.ac.uk
Students: 23,537 UG; 7,555 PG
Chancellor, Prof. Lord Winston, DSC, FRCOG, FRCP
Vice-Chancellor, Prof. Philip Jones, LLB, LLM
Secretary and Registrar, Elizabeth Winders

UNIVERSITY OF SOUTHAMPTON (1952)
Building 37, Highfield, Southampton SO17 1BJ
T 023-8059 5000 **W** www.soton.ac.uk
Students: 17,425 UG; 6,340 PG
Chancellor, Sir John Parker
Vice-Chancellor, Prof. Don Nutbeam
Registrar and Chief Operating Officer, Simon Higman

SOUTHAMPTON SOLENT UNIVERSITY (2005)
East Park Terrace, Southampton SO14 0YN **T** 023-8031 9000
W www.solent.ac.uk
Students: 10,780 UG; 740 PG
Chancellor, Admiral the Lord West of Spithead, GCB, DSC
Vice-Chancellor, Prof. Van Gore

STAFFORDSHIRE UNIVERSITY (1992)
Federation House, Stoke-on-Trent, Staffs ST4 2DE
T 01782-294000 **W** www.staffs.ac.uk
Students: 13,704 UG; 5,830 PG
Chancellor, Lord Morris of Handsworth
Vice-Chancellor, Prof. Christine E. King, CBE, FRSA
University Secretary, Ken Sproston

UNIVERSITY OF STIRLING (1967)
Stirling FK9 4LA **T** 01786-473171 **W** www.external.stir.ac.uk
Students: 7,205 UG; 2,600 PG
Chancellor, Dr James Naughtie, OBE
Vice-Chancellor, Prof. Christine Hallett, FRSE
Registrar, Mrs Joanna Morrow

UNIVERSITY OF STRATHCLYDE (1964)
16 Richmond Street, Glasgow G1 1XQ **T** 0141-552 4400
W www.strath.ac.uk
Students: 11,496 UG; 4,924 PG
Chancellor, Rt. Hon. Lord Hope of Craighead, FRSE
Vice-Chancellor, Prof. Jim McDonald, DPHIL, FRSC, FRSE
Secretary, Dr Peter West, OBE

UNIVERSITY OF SUNDERLAND (1992)
Edinburgh Building, Chester Road, Sunderland SR1 3SD
T 0191-515 2000 **W** www.sunderland.ac.uk
Students: 15,045 UG; 2,665 PG
Chancellor, Steve Cram, MBE
Vice-Chancellor, Prof. Peter Fidler
Secretary, Mr John Pacey

UNIVERSITY OF SURREY (1966)
Guildford, Surrey GU2 7XH **T** 01483-300800
W www.surrey.ac.uk
Students: 9,652 UG; 4,789 PG
Chancellor, HRH the Duke of Kent, KG, GCMG, GCVO
Vice-Chancellor, Prof. Christopher Snowden, FRS, FRENG
Registrar, Mr Philip Henry, TD

UNIVERSITY OF SUSSEX (1961)
Sussex House, Falmer, Brighton BN1 9RH **T** 01273-606755
W www.sussex.ac.uk
Students: 9,795 UG; 2,660 PG
Chancellor, Sanjeev Bhaskar, OBE
Vice-Chancellor, Prof. Michael Farthing
Academic Registrar, Dr Philip Harvey

UNIVERSITY OF TEESSIDE (1992)
Middlesbrough, Tees Valley TS1 3BA **T** 01642-218121
W www.tees.ac.uk
Students: 23,538 UG; 2,562 PG
Chancellor, Lord Sawyer
Vice-Chancellor and Chief Executive, Prof. Graham Henderson
University Secretary and Clerk to Governors, Morgan McClintock

THAMES VALLEY UNIVERSITY (1993)
St Mary's Road, Ealing, London W5 5RF **T** 020-8579 5000
W www.tvu.ac.uk
Students: 7,999 UG; 1,037 PG
Chancellor, Lord Bilimoria, CBE
Vice-Chancellor, Prof. Peter John
Registrar, Ann Marie Dalton

UNIVERSITY OF ULSTER (1984)
Cromore Road, Coleraine, Co. Londonderry BT52 1SA
T 0870-040 0700 W www.ulster.ac.uk
Students: 19,130 UG; 4,760 PG
Chancellor, Sir Richard Nichols
Vice-Chancellor, Prof. Richard Barnett
Registrar, Norma Cameron

UNIVERSITY OF WALES (1893)
King Edward VII Avenue, Cathays Park, Cardiff CF10 3NS
T 029-2037 6999 W www.wales.ac.uk
Chancellor, HRH The Prince of Wales, KG, KT, GCB
Senior Vice-Chancellor, Prof. M. Clement, FRSA

ACCREDITED INSTITUTIONS

ABERYSTWYTH UNIVERSITY
Old College, King Street, Aberystwyth SY23 2AX
T 01970-623111
Students: 8,130 UG; 1,735 PG
Vice-Chancellor, Prof. N. G. Lloyd

BANGOR UNIVERSITY
Gwynedd LL57 2DG
T 01248-351151
Students: 8,460 UG; 2,055 PG
Vice-Chancellor, Prof. M. Jones

GLYNDWR UNIVERSITY
Plas Coch, Mold Road, Wrexham LL11 2AW
T 01978-290666
Students: 6,625 UG; 635 PG
Principal, Prof. M. Scott

UNIVERSITY OF WALES INSTITUTE, CARDIFF
Llandaff Centre, Western Avenue, Cardiff CF5 2SG
T 029-2041 6070
Students: 7,465 UG; 2,435 PG
Vice-Chancellor, Prof. A. J. Chapman

UNIVERSITY OF WALES, LAMPETER
Lampeter SA48 7ED
T 01570-422351
Students: 6,890 UG; 995 PG
Vice-Chancellor, Alfred Morris, CBE, DL

UNIVERSITY OF WALES, NEWPORT
Caerleon Campus, Newport NP6 1YG
T 01633-430088
Students: 7,595 UG; 1,525 PG
Vice-Chancellor, Dr P. Noyes

SWANSEA UNIVERSITY
Singleton Park SA2 8PP
T 01792-205678
Students: 11,730 UG; 2,145 PG
Vice-Chancellor, Prof. R. B. Davies

SWANSEA METROPOLITAN UNIVERSITY
Mount Pleasant, Swansea SA1 6ED
T 01792-481000
Students: 4,520 UG; 1,075 PG
Vice-Chancellor, Prof. D. Warner

TRINITY COLLEGE, CARMARTHEN
Carmarthen SA31 3EP
T 01267-676767
Students: 1,980 UG; 245 PG
Vice-Chancellor, Dr M. Hughes

UNIVERSITY OF WARWICK (1965)
Coventry CV4 7AL T 024-7652 3523 W www.warwick.ac.uk
Students: 11,434 UG; 5,300 PG
Chancellor, Richard Lambert
Vice-Chancellor, Prof. Nigel Thrift
Registrar, Jon Baldwin

UNIVERSITY OF WESTMINSTER (1992)
309 Regent Street, London W1B 2UW T 020-7911 5000
W www.westminster.ac.uk
Students: 16,282 UG; 5,996 PG
Chancellor, Lord Paul
Vice-Chancellor and Rector, Prof. Geoffrey Petts
Academic Registrar, Carole Mainstone

UNIVERSITY OF THE WEST OF ENGLAND (1992)
Frenchay Campus, Coldharbour Lane, Bristol BS16 1QY
T 0117-965 6261 W www.uwe.ac.uk
Students: 23,621 UG; 6,128 PG
Chancellor, Rt. Hon. Baroness Elizabeth Butler-Sloss, GBE
Vice-Chancellor, Prof. Steven West, KB, CBE
Registrar, Tessa Harrison

UNIVERSITY OF THE WEST OF SCOTLAND (1992)
Paisley PA1 2BE T 0141-848 3000 W www.uws.ac.uk
Students: 16,415 UG; 1,720 PG
Chancellor, Lord Smith of Kelvin, FSA, KT
Principal and Vice-Chancellor, Prof. Seamus McDaid
Secretary, Kenneth Alexander

UNIVERSITY OF WINCHESTER (2005)
Winchester SO22 4NR T 01962-841515
W www.winchester.ac.uk
Students: 4,329 UG; 984 PG
Chancellor, Mary Fagan
Vice-Chancellor, Prof. Joy Carter
Registrar, Mrs Lyn Black

UNIVERSITY OF WOLVERHAMPTON (1992)
Wulfruna Street, Wolverhampton WV1 1SB T 01902-321000
W www.wlv.ac.uk
Students: 18,828 UG; 4,092 PG
Chancellor, Lord Paul
Vice-Chancellor, Prof. Caroline Gipps
Academic Registrar, Mr Paul Travill

UNIVERSITY OF WORCESTER (2005)
Henwick Grove, Worcester WR2 6AJ T 01905-855000
W www.worcester.ac.uk
Students: 6,175 UG; 1,590 PG
Chancellor, HRH The Duke of Gloucester, KG, GCVO
Vice-Chancellor and Chief Executive, Prof. David Green
Registrar and Secretary, John Ryan

UNIVERSITY OF YORK (1963)
Heslington, York YO10 5DD T 01904-430000
W www.york.ac.uk
Students: 9,564 UG; 3,298 PG
Chancellor, Greg Dyke
Vice-Chancellor, Prof. Brian Cantor, FRENG, FIM, FRMS
Registrar, Dr David Duncan

YORK ST JOHN UNIVERSITY (2006)
Lord Mayor's Walk, York YO31 7EX T 01904-624624
W www.yorksj.ac.uk
Students: 4,950 UG; 744 PG
Chancellor, Most Revd Dr John Sentamu, PC
Vice-Chancellor, Prof. Diane Willcocks
Registrar, Pauline Aldous

PROFESSIONAL EDUCATION

The organisations selected below provide specialist training, conduct examinations or are responsible for maintaining a register of those with professional qualifications in their sector, thereby controlling entry into a profession.

EU RECOGNITION

It is possible for those with professional qualifications obtained in the UK to have these recognised in other European countries. Further information can be obtained from:

EUROPE OPEN UK NARIC, Oriel House, Oriel Road, Cheltenham, Glos GL50 1XP T 0871-226 2850 W www.europeopen.org.uk

ACCOUNTANCY

Salary range for chartered accountants:
Certified £14,500–£25,000 (starting) rising to £29,000–£52,000+ (qualified)
Management £23,000 (starting), £25,000–£57,000 (newly qualified), £62,000–£106,000+ at senior levels
Public finance £28,500–£34,000 (newly qualified) rising to £34,000–£100,000+

Most chartered accountancy trainees are graduates, although some contracts are available to school-leavers. The undergraduate degree is followed by a three-year training contract with an approved employer culminating in professional exams provided by the Institute of Chartered Accountants in England and Wales (ICAEW), the Institute of Chartered Accountants of Scotland (ICAS) or the Institute of Chartered Accountants in Ireland (ICAI). Success in the examination and membership of one of the institutes allows the use of the designation 'chartered accountant' and the letters ACA or CA.

The training route for chartered certified accountants is similar to that of chartered accountants and is taken by students in a range of business sectors and countries. The Association of Chartered Certified Accountants (ACCA) qualification involves up to 14 examinations and a minimum of three years of relevant supervised experience. Chartered certified accountants can use the designatory letters ACCA.

Chartered management accountants focus on accounting for businesses, and most do not work in accountancy practices but in industry, commerce, not-for-profit and public sector organisations. Graduates who have not studied a business or accounting undergraduate degree must gain the Chartered Institute of Management Accountants (CIMA) Certificate in Business Accounting (formerly known as the foundation level) before studying for the CIMA Professional Qualification. The qualification requires three years of practical experience combined with nine examinations and a pass in the Institute's Test of Professional Competence in Management Accounting (TOPCIMA).

Chartered public finance accountants usually work for public bodies, but they can also work in the private sector. To gain chartered public finance accountant status (CPFA), trainees must complete the three parts of the Chartered Institute of Public Finance and Accountancy (CIPFA) Professional Accountancy Qualification (PAQ), which takes approximately three years. The first stage is the certificate level, which leads to affiliate membership of CIPFA, the second is the diploma level which leads to associate membership, and finally completion of the Final Test of Professional Competence leads to full membership of CIPFA.

ASSOCIATION OF CHARTERED CERTIFIED ACCOUNTANTS (ACCA) 29 Lincoln's Inn Fields, London WC2A 3EE T 020-7059 5000 E info@accaglobal.com W www.accaglobal.com
Chief Executive, Helen Brand

CHARTERED INSTITUTE OF MANAGEMENT ACCOUNTANTS (CIMA) 26 Chapter Street, London SW1P 4NP T 020-7663 5441 W www.cimaglobal.com
Chief Executive, Charles Tilley

CHARTERED INSTITUTE OF PUBLIC FINANCE AND ACCOUNTANCY (CIPFA) 3 Robert Street, London WC2N 6RL T 020-7543 5600 E corporate@cipfa.org W www.cipfa.org.uk
Chief Executive, Steve Freer

INSTITUTE OF CHARTERED ACCOUNTANTS IN ENGLAND AND WALES (ICAEW) Chartered Accountants' Hall, PO Box 433, London EC2P 2BJ T 020-7920 8100 W www.icaew.com
Chief Executive, Michael Izza

INSTITUTE OF CHARTERED ACCOUNTANTS IN IRELAND (ICAI) The Linenhall, 32–38 Linenhall Street, Belfast BT2 8BG T 028-9032 1600 E ca@icai.ie W www.icai.ie
Chief Executive, Pat Costello

INSTITUTE OF CHARTERED ACCOUNTANTS OF SCOTLAND (ICAS) CA House, 21 Haymarket Yards, Edinburgh EH12 5BH T 0131-347 0100 E enquiries@icas.org.uk W www.icas.org.uk
Chief Executive, Anton Colella

ACTUARIAL SCIENCE

Salary range: £23,000–£28,000 for graduate trainees; £42,000–£55,000 after qualification; £50,000–£100,000+ for senior roles

Actuaries apply financial and statistical theories to solve business problems. These problems usually involve analysing future financial events in order to assess investment risks for businesses. The UK actuarial profession is controlled by the Institute of Actuaries in London and the Faculty of Actuaries in Edinburgh (operating together as 'the actuarial profession'). The faculty and institute together develop actuarial techniques and set examinations, professional codes and disciplinary standards. UK qualified actuaries may be fellows of either organisation. On average, it takes five years to qualify as an actuary; examinations are held twice a year, and applicants to the profession must also have completed three years of actuarial work experience before gaining fellowship.

The Financial Reporting Council (FRC) is the unified independent regulator for corporate reporting, auditing, actuarial practice, corporate governance and the professionalism of accountants and actuaries. The FRC's

Board for Actuarial Standards sets and maintains technical actuarial standards independently of the profession while the Professional Oversight Board of the FRC oversees the regulation by the actuarial profession of its members. The Accountancy and Actuarial Discipline Board operates an investigation and discipline scheme in relation to members of the profession who raise issues affecting UK public interest.

FACULTY OF ACTUARIES Maclaurin House, 18 Dublin Street, Edinburgh EH1 3PP T 0131-240 1300 E faculty@actuaries.org.uk W www.actuaries.org.uk
Secretary, Richard Maconachie

FINANCIAL REPORTING COUNCIL (FRC) 5th Floor, Aldwych House, 71–91 Aldwych, London WC2B 4HN T 020-7492 2300 W www.frc.org.uk
Chief Executive, Paul Boyle

INSTITUTE OF ACTUARIES Staple Inn Hall, High Holborn, London WC1V 7QJ T 020-7632 2100 E institute@actuaries.org.uk W www.actuaries.org.uk
Chief Executive, Caroline Instance

ARCHITECTURE

Salary range: £17,000–£31,000 during training; newly registered £29,000–£34,000; project architect and senior roles £36,000–£80,000+

It takes a minimum of seven years to become an architect, involving three stages: a three-year first degree, a two-year second degree or diploma and two years of professional experience followed by the successful completion of a professional practice examination.

The Architects Registration Board (ARB) is the independent regulator for the profession. It was set up by an act of parliament in 1997 and is responsible for maintaining the register of UK architects, prescribing qualifications that lead to registration as an architect, investigating complaints about the conduct and competence of architects, and ensuring only those who are registered with ARB offer their services as an architect. It is only following registration with ARB that an architect can apply for chartered membership of the Royal Institute of British Architects (RIBA). RIBA, the UK body for architecture and the architectural profession, received its royal charter in 1837 and validates courses at over 40 UK schools of architecture; it also validates overseas courses. RIBA provides support and training for its members in the form of training, technical services and events and sets standards for the education of architects.

The Chartered Institute of Architectural Technologists is the international qualifying body for chartered architectural technologists (MCIAT) and architectural technicians (TCIAT).

ARCHITECTS REGISTRATION BOARD (ARB) 8 Weymouth Street, London W1W 5BU T 020-7580 5861 E info@arb.org.uk W www.arb.org.uk
Registrar and Chief Executive, Alison Carr

CHARTERED INSTITUTE OF ARCHITECTURAL TECHNOLOGISTS 397 City Road, London EC1V 1NH T 020-7278 2206 E info@ciat.org.uk W www.ciat.org.uk
Chief Executive, Francesca Berriman

ROYAL INSTITUTE OF BRITISH ARCHITECTS (RIBA) 66 Portland Place, London W1B 1AD T 020-7580 5533 E info@inst.riba.org W www.riba.org
Chief Executive, Richard Hastilow, CBE

ENGINEERING

Salary range:
Civil/structural £16,000–£21,000 (graduate); £38,000–£53,000 with experience, rising to £80,000+ in senior posts
Chemical £20,000–£33,000 (graduate); £47,000–£77,000+ (chartered)
Electrical £17,500–£27,000 (graduate); £41,000+ with experience

The Engineering Council UK (ECUK) sets standards of professional competence and ethics for engineers, technologists and technicians, and regulates the profession through the 36 institutions (Licensed Members) listed below who are licensed to put suitably qualified members on the ECUK's Register of Engineers. All candidates for registration as Chartered Engineer, Incorporated Engineer or Engineering Technician must satisfy the competence standards set by ECUK and be members of the appropriate institution. Applicants must show that they have a satisfactory educational base, have undergone approved professional development, and, at interview, must demonstrate their professional competence against specific criteria.

ENGINEERING COUNCIL UK 246 High Holborn, London WC1V 7EX T 020-3206 0500 E info@engc.org.uk W www.engc.org.uk
Chief Executive Officer, Andrew Ramsay

LICENSED MEMBERS

British Computer Society W www.bcs.org.uk
British Institute of Non-destructive Testing W www.bindt.org
Chartered Institution of Building Services Engineers W www.cibse.org
Chartered Institute of Plumbing and Heating Engineers W www.ciphe.org.uk
Chartered Institution of Water and Environmental Management W www.ciwem.org
Energy Institute W www.energyinst.org.uk
Institute of Acoustics W www.ioa.org.uk
Institute of Cast Metals Engineers W www.icme.org.uk
Institute of Healthcare Engineering and Estate Management W www.iheem.org.uk
Institute of Highway Incorporated Engineers W www.ihie.org.uk
Institute of Marine Engineering, Science and Technology W www.imarest.org
Institute of Materials, Minerals and Mining W www.iom3.org
Institute of Measurement and Control W www.instmc.org.uk
Institute of the Motor Industry W www.motor.org.uk
Institute of Physics W www.iop.org
Institute of Physics and Engineering in Medicine W www.ipem.ac.uk
Institution of Agricultural Engineers W www.iagre.org
Institution of Chemical Engineers W www.icheme.org
Institution of Civil Engineers W www.ice.org.uk
Institution of Engineering Designers W www.ied.org.uk
Institution of Engineering and Technology W www.theiet.org
Institution of Fire Engineers W www.ife.org.uk
Insititution of Gas Engineers and Managers W www.igem.org.uk
Institution of Highways and Transportation W www.iht.org
Institution of Lighting Engineers W www.ile.org.uk

Institution of Mechanical Engineers
W www.imeche.org
Institution of Railway Signal Engineers W www.irse.org
Institution of Royal Engineers W www.instre.org
Institution of Structural Engineers W www.istructe.org
Institution of Water Officers W www.iwo.org.uk
Nuclear Institute W www.nuclearinst.com
Royal Aeronautical Society W www.raes.org.uk
Royal Institution of Naval Architects W www.rina.org.uk
Society of Environmental Engineers
W www.environmental.org.uk
Society of Operations Engineers W www.soe.org.uk
Welding Institute W www.twi.co.uk

HEALTHCARE

CHIROPRACTIC

Salary range: £22,000–£25,000 starting salary; with own practice up to £70,000

Chiropractors diagnose and treat conditions caused by problems with joints, ligaments, tendons and nerves of the body. The General Chiropractic Council (GCC) is the independent statutory regulatory body for chiropractors and its role and remit is defined in the Chiropractors Act 1994. The GCC sets the criteria for the recognition of chiropractic degrees and for standards of proficiency and conduct. Details of the institutions offering degree programmes are available on the GCC website (*see* below). It is illegal for anyone in the UK to use the title 'chiropractor' unless registered with the GCC.

The British Chiropractic Association and the Scottish Chiropractic Association are representative bodies for the profession and are sources of further information.

BRITISH CHIROPRACTIC ASSOCIATION 59 Castle Street, Reading RG1 7SN T 0118-950 5950
W www.chiropractic-uk.co.uk
Executive Director, Sue Wakefield

GENERAL CHIROPRACTIC COUNCIL 44 Wicklow Street, London WC1X 9HL T 020-7713 5155
E enquiries@gcc-uk.org W www.gcc-uk.org
Chief Executive, Margaret Coats

SCOTTISH CHIROPRACTIC ASSOCIATION
1 Chisholm Avenue, Bishopton, Renfrewshire PA7 5JH
T 0141-404 0260 E admin@sca-chiropractic.org
W www.sca-chiropractic.org
Administrator, Morag Cairns

DENTISTRY

Salary range: see Health: Employees and Salaries

The General Dental Council (GDC) is the organisation that regulates dental professionals in the United Kingdom. All dentists, dental hygienists, dental therapists, clinical dental technicians and orthodontic therapists must be registered with the GDC to work in the UK.

There are various different routes to qualify for registration as a dentist, including holding a degree from a UK university; completing the GDC's qualifying examination; or holding a relevant European Economic Area or overseas diploma. The GDC's purpose is to protect the public through the regulation of UK dental professionals. It keeps up-to-date registers of dental professionals, works to set standards of dental practice, behaviour and education, and helps to protect patients by hearing complaints and taking action against professionals where necessary.

The British Dental Association is a membership organisation that provides dentists with professional and educational services.

BRITISH DENTAL ASSOCIATION 64 Wimpole Street, London W1G 8YS T 020-7935 0875 E enquiries@bda.org
W www.bda.org
Chief Executive, Peter Ward

GENERAL DENTAL COUNCIL 37 Wimpole Street, London W1G 8DQ T 020-7887 3800
E information@gdc-uk.org W www.gdc-uk.org
Chief Executive, Duncan Rudkin

MEDICINE

Salary range: see Health: Employees and Salaries

The General Medical Council (GMC) sets the standards for basic medical education; this covers undergraduate study (usually five years) and the first year of training after graduation. Subsequent training is regulated by the Postgraduate Medical Education and Training Board (PMETB). The first two years of training after graduation are collectively called the 'foundation programme'.

All doctors must be registered with the GMC, which is responsible for protecting the public. It does this by setting standards for professional practice, overseeing medical education, keeping a register of qualified doctors and taking action where a doctor's fitness to practise is in doubt. Doctors are eligible for full registration upon successful completion of the first year of training after graduation.

Following the foundation programme, many doctors undertake specialist training (provided by the colleges and faculties listed below) to become either a consultant or a GP. Once specialist training has been completed, doctors are awarded the Certificate of Completion of Training (CCT) and are eligible to be placed on either the GMC's specialist register or its GP register. The responsibility for awarding CCTs lies with the PMETB. The GMC and the PMETB are due to merge on 1 April 2010.

GENERAL MEDICAL COUNCIL (GMC) 350 Euston Road, London NW1 3JN T 0845-357 8001
E gmc@gmc-uk.org W www.gmc-uk.org
Chief Executive, Finlay Scott

POSTGRADUATE MEDICAL EDUCATION AND TRAINING BOARD (PMETB) Hercules House, Hercules Road, London SE1 7DU T 020-7160 6100
E info@pmetb.org.uk W www.pmetb.org.uk
Chief Executive, Graham Smith

SOCIETY OF APOTHECARIES OF LONDON Black Friars Lane, London EC4V 6EJ T 020 7236 1189
E clerk@apothecaries.org W www.apothecaries.org
Clerk, A. M. Wallington Smith

SPECIALIST TRAINING COLLEGES AND FACULTIES

College of Emergency Medicine
W www.collemergencymed.ac.uk
Faculty of Pharmaceutical Medicine W www.fpm.org.uk
Faculty of Public Health W www.fphm.org.uk
Royal College of Anaesthetists W www.rcoa.ac.uk
Royal College of General Practitioners W www.rcgp.org.uk
Royal College of Obstetricians and Gynaecologists
W www.rcog.org.uk
Royal College of Opthalmologists W www.rcophth.ac.uk
Royal College of Paediatrics and Child Health
W www.rcpch.ac.uk
Royal College of Pathologists W www.rcpath.org
Royal College of Physicians of London
W www.rcplondon.ac.uk

Royal College of Physicians and Surgeons of Glasgow W www.rcpsg.ac.uk
Royal College of Physicians of Edinburgh W www.rcpe.ac.uk
Royal College of Psychiatrists W www.rcpsych.ac.uk
Royal College of Radiologists W www.rcr.ac.uk
Royal College of Surgeons of Edinburgh W www.rcsed.ac.uk
Royal College of Surgeons of England W www.rcseng.ac.uk

MEDICINE, SUPPLEMENTARY PROFESSIONS

The standard of professional education for arts therapists, biomedical scientists, chiropodists and podiatrists, clinical scientists, dietitians, occupational therapists, operating department practitioners, orthoptists, paramedics, physiotherapists, prosthetists and orthotists, radiographers, and speech and language therapists is regulated by the Health Professions Council (HPC), who only register those practitioners who meet certain standards of training, performance and conduct. Other than biomedical science and clinical science, all the professions listed below are described by the NHS as 'allied health professions'. The HPC currently registers over 170,000 professionals.

HEALTH PROFESSIONS COUNCIL Park House, 184 Kennington Park Road, London SE11 4BU T 020-7582 0866 E info@hpc-uk.org W www.hpc-uk.org
Chief Executive and Registrar, Marc Seale

ART, DRAMA AND MUSIC THERAPIES

Salary range: £23,000 rising to £28,000–£42,000+ in senior posts

An art, drama or music therapist encourages people to express their feelings and emotions through art, such as painting and drawing, drama or music. A postgraduate qualification in the relevant therapy is required. Details of accredited training programmes in the UK can be obtained from the following organisations:

ASSOCIATION OF PROFESSIONAL MUSIC THERAPISTS 24–27 White Lion Street, London N1 9PD T 020-7387 6100 E apmtoffice@aol.com W www.apmt.org
Chair, Stephen Sandford

BRITISH ASSOCIATION OF ART THERAPISTS 24–27 White Lion Street, London N1 9PD T 020-7686 4216 E info@baat.org W www.baat.org
Chief Executive, Val Huet

BRITISH ASSOCIATION OF DRAMA THERAPISTS Waverley, Battledown Approach, Cheltenham, Gloucestershire GL52 6RE T 01242-235 5155 E enquiries@badth.org.uk W www.badth.org.uk
Chair, Madeline Andersen-Warren

BIOMEDICAL SCIENCES

Salary range: £20,000–£60,000+

Biomedical scientists analyse specimens from patients in order to help make diagnoses. Qualifications from higher education establishments and training in medical laboratories are required for membership of the Institute of Biomedical Science, which sets the professional standards of competence for practitioners of biomedical science.

INSTITUTE OF BIOMEDICAL SCIENCE 12 Coldbath Square, London EC1R 5HL T 020-7713 0214 E mail@ibms.org W www.ibms.org
Chief Executive, Alan Potter

CHIROPODY AND PODIATRY

Salary range: £19,500–£37,000

Chiropodists and podiatrists assess, diagnose and treat problems of the lower leg and foot. The Society of Chiropodists and Podiatrists is the professional body and trade union for the profession. Qualifications granted and degrees recognised by the society are approved by the Health Professions Council (HPC). HPC registration is required in order to use the titles chiropodist and podiatrist.

SOCIETY OF CHIROPODISTS AND PODIATRISTS 1 Fellmonger's Path, Tower Bridge Road, London SE1 3LY T 020-7234 8620 E enq@scpod.org W www.feetforlife.org
Chief Executive, Joanna Brown

CLINICAL SCIENCE

Salary range: £23,000–£70,000+

Clinical scientists conduct tests in laboratories in order to diagnose and manage disease. The Association of Clinical Scientists is responsible for setting the criteria for competence of applicants to the HPC's register and to present a Certificate of Attainment to candidates following a successful assessment. This certificate will allow direct registration with the HPC.

ASSOCIATION OF CLINICAL SCIENTISTS c/o Association for Clinical Biochemistry, 130–132 Tooley Street, London SE1 2TU T 020-7940 8960 E info@assclinsci.org W www.assclinsci.org
Chair, Dr Iain Chambers

DIETETICS

Salary range: £20,000–£38,000

Dietitians advise patients on how to improve their health and counter specific health problems through diet. The British Dietetic Association, established in 1936, is the professional association for dietitians. Full membership is open to UK-registered dietitians, who must also be registered with the Health Professions Council.

BRITISH DIETETIC ASSOCIATION 5th Floor, Charles House, 148–149 Great Charles Street Queensway, Birmingham B3 3HT T 0121-200 8080 E info@bda.uk.com W www.bda.uk.com
Chief Executive, Andy Burman

OCCUPATIONAL THERAPY

Salary range: £19,500–£38,000; up to £52,000 in consultancy posts

Occupational therapists work with people who have physical, mental and/or social problems, either from birth or as a result of accident, illness or ageing, and aim to make them as independent as possible. The professional qualification and eligibility for registration may be obtained upon successful completion of a validated course in any of the educational institutions approved by the College of Occupational Therapists, which is the professional body for occupational therapy in the UK. The courses are normally degree-level courses based in higher education institutions.

COLLEGE OF OCCUPATIONAL THERAPISTS 106–114 Borough High Street, London SE1 1LB T 020-7357 6480 W www.cot.org.uk
Chief Executive, Julia Roberts

MENTAL HEALTH

Salary range:
Clinical psychologist £25,000 rising to £30,000–£50,000+ with experience
Counsellor £18,000–£25,000 rising to £30,000+ with experience

Educational psychologist £21,000 rising to £31,000 when chartered and £41,000+ in senior posts
Psychotherapist £19,000–£25,000 (starting) rising to £65,000+ in senior positions

Mental health professionals (other than psychiatrists, who are trained doctors) can work in a range of settings including prisons, schools and hospitals as well as businesses. The UK psychological profession is represented by the British Psychological Society (BPS), which has more than 47,000 members. It accredits qualifications in psychology, and offers support to members through continuing professional development. The Association of Educational Psychologists (AEP) represents the interests of educational psychologists, while the British Association for Counselling and Psychotherapy (BACP) sets educational standards and provides professional support to those psychologists working in psychotherapy or counselling-related roles. The BPS website provides more information on the different specialisations that may be pursued by psychologists.

BRITISH PSYCHOLOGICAL SOCIETY (BPS)
St Andrews House, 48 Princess Road East, Leicester LE1 7DR **T** 0116-254 9568 **E** enquiries@bps.org.uk
W www.bps.org.uk
President, Sue Gardner

ASSOCIATION OF EDUCATIONAL PSYCHOLOGISTS (AEP) 4 The Riverside Centre, Frankland Lane, Durham DH1 5TA **T** 0191-384 9512
W www.aep.org.uk
General Secretary, Charles Ward

BRITISH ASSOCIATION FOR COUNSELLING AND PSYCHOTHERAPY (BACP) BACP House, 15 St John's Business Park, Lutterworth, Leicestershire LE17 4HB
T 01455-883300 **E** bacp@bacp.co.uk **W** www.bacp.co.uk
President, Cary Cooper, CBE

ORTHOPTICS
Salary range: £20,000–£26,000 rising to £29,000–£64,000 in senior posts

Orthoptists undertake the diagnosis and treatment of all types of squint and other anomalies of binocular vision, working in close collaboration with ophthalmologists. The professional body is the British and Irish Orthoptic Society and training is at degree level.

BRITISH AND IRISH ORTHOPTIC SOCIETY Tavistock House North, Tavistock Square, London WC1H 9HX
T 020-7387 7992 **W** www.orthoptics.org.uk
Chair, Rosemary Auld

PARAMEDICAL SERVICES
Salary range: £19,500–£32,000

Paramedics deal with accidents and emergencies, assessing patients and carrying out any specialist treatment and care needed in the first instance. The body that represents ambulance professionals is the British Paramedic Association.

BRITISH PARAMEDIC ASSOCIATION 28 Wilfred Street, Derby DE23 8GF **T** 01332-746356
E exec.bpa@britishparamedic.org
W www.britishparamedic.org
Chief Executive, Roland Furber

PHYSIOTHERAPY
Salary range: £19,500–£25,000 (junior); up to £37,000 (team manager); £36,000–£62,000 (consultant)

Physiotherapists are concerned with movement and function and deal with problems arising from injury, illness and ageing. Full-time three- or four-year degree courses are available at over 30 higher education institutions in the UK. Information about courses leading to state registration is available from the Chartered Society of Physiotherapy.

CHARTERED SOCIETY OF PHYSIOTHERAPY
14 Bedford Row, London WC1R 4ED **T** 020-7306 6666
W www.csp.org.uk
Chief Executive, Phil Gray

PROSTHETICS AND ORTHOTICS
Salary range: £18,000 on qualification, rising to £35,000+ with experience

Prosthetists provide artificial limbs, while orthotists provide devices to support or control a part of the body. It is necessary to obtain an honours degree to become a prosthetist or orthotist. Training is centred at the universities of Salford and Strathclyde.

BRITISH ASSOCIATION OF PROSTHETISTS AND ORTHOTISTS Sir James Clark Building, Abbey Mill Business Centre, Paisley PA1 1TJ **T** 0141-561 7217
E enquiries@bapo.com **W** www.bapo.org
Chair, Steve Mottram

RADIOGRAPHY
Salary range. £20,000–£33,000; £38,000–£64,000 (consultant/management)
In order to practise both diagnostic and therapeutic radiography in the UK, it is necessary to have successfully completed a course of education and training recognised by the Privy Council. Such courses are offered by universities throughout the UK and lead to the award of a degree in radiography. Further information is available from the Society and College of Radiographers.

SOCIETY AND COLLEGE OF RADIOGRAPHERS
207 Providence Square, Mill Street, London SE1 2EW
T 020-7740 7200 **E** info@sor.org **W** www.sor.org
Chief Executive, Richard Evans

SPEECH AND LANGUAGE THERAPY
Salary range. £20,000 rising upwards of £50,000 in senior roles

Speech and language therapists (SLTs) work with people with speech, voice and swallowing problems. The Royal College of Speech and Language Therapists is the professional body for speech and language therapists and support workers. Alongside the Health Professions Council, it accredits education and training courses leading to qualification.

ROYAL COLLEGE OF SPEECH AND LANGUAGE THERAPISTS 2 White Hart Yard, London SE1 1NX
T 020-7378 1200 **E** info@rcslt.org **W** www.rcslt.org
Chief Executive, Kamini Gadhok, MBE

NURSING
Salary range: see Health: Employees and Salaries

In order to practice in the UK all nurses and midwives must be registered with the Nursing and Midwifery Council (NMC). The NMC is a statutory regulatory body that establishes and maintains standards of education, training, conduct and performance for nursing and midwifery. Courses leading to registration are at a minimum of diploma in higher education, although some are offered at degree level and all are a minimum of three years if undertaken full-time. The NMC approves programmes run jointly by higher education institutions with their healthcare service partners who offer clinical placements. The nursing part of the register has four fields of practice: adult, children's, learning disability and mental health nursing. During the first year of a nursing course, the common foundation programme, students have experience of the four fields of practice. In addition those studying to become adult nurses have experience of nursing in relation to medicine, surgery, maternity care and nursing in the home. The NMC also sets standards for programmes leading to registration as a midwife and a range of post-registration courses including specialist practice programmes, nurse prescribing and those for teachers of nursing and midwifery. The NMC has a part of the register for specialist community public health nurses and approves programmes for health visitors, occupational health nurses and school nurses.

The Royal College of Nursing is the largest professional union for nursing in the UK, representing qualified nurses, healthcare assistants and nursing students in the NHS and the private sector.

NURSING AND MIDWIFERY COUNCIL 23 Portland Place, London W1B 1PZ T 020-7333 9333
E advice@nmc-uk.org W www.nmc-uk.org
Chief Executive and Registrar, Kathy George

ROYAL COLLEGE OF NURSING 20 Cavendish Square, London W1G 0RN T 020-740 3333 W www.rcn.org.uk
Chief Executive and General Secretary, Dr Peter Carter

OPTOMETRY AND DISPENSING OPTICS

Salary range:
Optometrist £20,000–£50,000 (up to £73,000 for consultant posts)
Dispensing Optician £20,000–£30,000+

There are various routes to qualification as a dispensing optician. Qualification takes three years in total, and can be completed by combining a distance learning course or day release while working as a trainee under the supervision of a qualified and registered optician. Alternatively, students can do a two-year full-time course followed by one year of supervised practice with a qualified and registered optician. Training must be done at a training establishment approved by the regulatory body – the General Optical Council (GOC). There are six training establishments which are approved by the GOC: the Association of British Dispensing Opticians (ABDO), Anglia Ruskin University, Bradford College, the City and Islington College, City University and Glasgow Caledonian University. All routes are concluded by ABDO examinations, successful completion of which leads to registration with the GOC, which is compulsory for all practising dispensing opticians. After qualifying as a dispensing optician and completing training to fit contact lenses, students have the option to take a career progression course at the University of Bradford that allows them to graduate with a degree in optometry in one calendar year.

Optometrists must obtain an undergraduate optometry degree from one of the eight institutions approved by the GOC (Anglia Ruskin University, Aston University, the University of Bradford, Cardiff University, City University, Glasgow Caledonian University, the University of Manchester and the University of Ulster). Following graduation, trainees must complete a year of supervised salaried training with a registered optometrist after which they must pass a series of assessments set by the College of Optometrists. As with dispensing opticians, optometrists must then register with the GOC in order to practise.

ASSOCIATION OF BRITISH DISPENSING OPTICIANS 199 Gloucester Terrace W2 6LD
T 020-7298 5100 E general@abdo.org.uk
W www.abdo.org.uk
General Secretary, Sir Anthony Garrett, CBE

COLLEGE OF OPTOMETRISTS 41–42 Craven Street, London WC2N 5NG T 020-7839 6000
E optometry@college-optometrists.org
W www.college-optometrists.org
Chief Executive, Bryony Pawinska

GENERAL OPTICAL COUNCIL (GOC) 1 Harley Street, London W1G 8DJ T 020-7580 3898 E goc@optical.org
W www.optical.org
Chief Executive, Dian Taylor

OSTEOPATHY

Salary Range: £16,000–£65,000

Osteopathy is a way of detecting and treating damage in areas of the body such as muscles, ligaments, nerves and joints. Osteopathy is a statutorily self-regulated healthcare profession. The General Osteopathic Council (GOsC) maintains a register of those entitled to practise osteopathy in the UK. It is a criminal offence for anyone to describe themselves as an osteopath unless they are registered with the GOsC.

To gain entry to the register, applicants must hold a recognised qualification from an osteopathic education institute accredited by the GOsC; this involves a four to five year honours degree programme combined with clinical training.

GENERAL OSTEOPATHIC COUNCIL Osteopathy House, 176 Tower Bridge Road, London SE1 3LU
T 020-7357 6655 E info@osteopathy.org.uk
W www.osteopathy.org.uk
Chief Executive and Registrar, Evlynne Gilvarry

PHARMACY

Salary range: £20,000–£60,000+

Pharmacists are involved in the preparation and use of medicines, from the discovery of their active ingredients to their use by patients. Pharmacists also monitor the effects of medicines, both for patient care and for research purposes.

The Royal Pharmaceutical Society of Great Britain (RPSGB) is the regulatory and professional body for pharmacists in England, Scotland and Wales. It has a statutory duty to maintain the registers of pharmacists and pharmacy premises. The Pharmaceutical Society of Northern Ireland (PSNI) performs the same role in Northern Ireland. In order to register, students must complete a four-year degree in pharmacy that is accredited by either the RPSGB or the PSNI followed by one year of pre-registration training at an approved pharmacy, and must then pass an entrance examination. The RPSGB is working towards the demerger of its regulatory and professional roles that would result in the creation of a new General Pharmaceutical Council and a new professional body by 2010.

PHARMACEUTICAL SOCIETY OF NORTHERN IRELAND 73 University Street, Belfast BT7 1HL T 028-9032 6927 E mail@psni.org.uk W www.psni.org.uk
Director, Trevor Patterson

ROYAL PHARMACEUTICAL SOCIETY OF GREAT BRITAIN (RPSGB) 1 Lambeth High Street, London SE1 7JN T 020-7735 9141 E enquiries@rpsgb.org W www.rpsgb.org
Chief Executive and Registrar, Jeremy Holmes

JOURNALISM

Salary range: starting salaries £10,000–£18,000; £23,000+ for established journalists, rising to £50,000+ for senior journalists/editors

The National Council for the Training of Journalists (NCTJ) accredits 42 education providers who run courses for journalists; it also provides professional support to journalists.

The Broadcast Journalism Training Council (BCTJ) is an association of the UK's main broadcast journalism employers and accredits courses in broadcast journalism.

BROADCAST JOURNALISM TRAINING COUNCIL (BJTC) 18 Miller's Close, Rippingale Nr. Bourne, Lincolnshire PE10 0TH T 01778-440025 E sec@bjtc.org.uk W www.bjtc.org.uk
Secretary, Jim Latham

NATIONAL COUNCIL FOR THE TRAINING OF JOURNALISTS (NCTJ) The New Granary, Station Road, Newport, Saffron Walden, Essex CB11 3PL T 01799-544014 E info@nctj.com W www.nctj.com
Chief Executive, Joanne Butcher

INFORMATION MANAGEMENT

Salary range:
Archivist £18,000–£26,000 (starting); £26,000–£40,000+ in senior roles
Information Officer £17,000–£27,000 (starting); £28,000–£44,000+ in senior posts
Librarian £20,000–£25,000 (newly qualified); £45,000+ in senior posts

The Chartered Institute of Library and Information Professionals (CILIP) is the professional body for librarians, information specialists and knowledge managers. CILIP accredits undergraduate and postgraduate librarianship and information courses. The Society of Archivists is the professional body for archivists and record managers. The Association for Information Management provides training and advice on a wide range of topics relevant to the work of information professionals.

ASSOCIATION FOR INFORMATION MANAGEMENT (ASLIB) 207 Davina House, 137–149 Goswell Road, London EC1V 7ET T 020-7253 3349 E furtherinformation@aslib.com W www.aslib.com
Chief Executive, Roger Bowes

CHARTERED INSTITUTE OF LIBRARY AND INFORMATION PROFESSIONALS (CILIP) 7 Ridgmount Street, London WC1E 7AE T 020-7255 0500 E info@cilip.org.uk W www.cilip.org.uk
President, Bob McKee

SOCIETY OF ARCHIVISTS Prioryfield House, 20 Canon Street, Taunton, Somerset TA1 1SW T 01823-327030 E societyofarchivists@archives.org.uk W www.archives.org.uk
Executive Director, John Chambers

LAW

There are three types of practising lawyers: barristers, notaries and solicitors. Solicitors tend to work as a group in firms, and can be approached directly by individuals. They advise on a variety of legal issues and must decide the most appropriate course of action, if any. Notaries have all the powers of a solicitor other than the conduct of litigation. Most of them are primarily concerned with the preparation and authentication of documents for use abroad. Barristers are usually self-employed. If a solicitor believes that a barrister is required, he or she will instruct one on behalf of the client; the client will not have contact with the barrister without the solicitor being present.

When specialist expertise is needed, barristers give opinions on complex matters of law, and when clients require representation in the higher courts (crown courts, the high court, the court of appeal and the supreme court), barristers provide a specialist advocacy service. However, solicitors – who represent their clients in the lower courts such as tribunals, magistrates' courts and county courts – can also apply for advocacy rights in the higher courts instead of briefing a barrister.

THE BAR

Salary range: £70,000–£200,000+

The governing body of the Bar of England and Wales is the General Council of the Bar, also known as the Bar Council. Since January 2006, the regulatory functions of the Bar Council (including regulating the education and training requirements for those wishing to enter the profession) have been undertaken by the Bar Standards Board.

In the first (or 'academic') stage of training, aspiring barristers must obtain a law degree of a good standard (at least second class). Alternatively, a non-law degree (at least second class) followed by a one-year full-time or two-year part-time Graduate Diploma in Law (PgDL).

The second (vocational) stage is the completion of the Bar Vocational Course (BVC), which is available at eight validated institutions in the UK and must be applied for around one year in advance (W www.bvconline.co.uk). All barristers must join one of the four Inns of Court prior to commencing the BVC.

Students are 'called to the Bar' by their Inn after completion of the vocational stage, but cannot practise as a barrister until completion of the third stage, which is called 'pupillage'. Call to the Bar does not entitle a person to practise as a barrister – successful completion of pupillage is now a pre-requisite. Pupillage lasts for two six-month periods: the 'non practising six' and the 'practising six'. The former consists of shadowing an experienced barrister, while the latter involves appearing in court as a barrister.

Admission to the Bar of Northern Ireland is controlled by the Honorable Society of the Inn of Court of Northern Ireland; admission as an Advocate to the Scottish Bar is through the Faculty of Advocates.

BAR STANDARDS BOARD The Bar Council, 289–293 High Holborn, London WC1V 7HZ T 020-7611 1444 E contactus@barstandardsboard.org.uk W www.barstandardsboard.org.uk
Director, Mandie Lavin

FACULTY OF ADVOCATES Parliament House, Edinburgh EH1 1RF T 0131-226 5071 W www.advocates.org.uk
Chief Executive Officer, Tony Parker

GENERAL COUNCIL OF THE BAR 289–293 High Holborn, London WC1V 7HZ T 020-7242 0082 E contactus@barcouncil.org.uk W www.barcouncil.org.uk
Chief Executive, David Hobart

GENERAL COUNCIL OF THE BAR OF NORTHERN IRELAND The Bar Library, 91 Chichester Street, Belfast BT1 3JQ T 028-9056 2349 E chief.executive@barcouncil-ni.org.uk W www.barlibrary.com
Chief Executive, Brendan Garland

HONOURABLE SOCIETY OF THE INN OF COURT OF NORTHERN IRELAND Bar Council Office, The Bar Library, 91 Chichester Street, Belfast BT1 3JQ T 028-9056 2349 W www.actuaries.org.uk
Under-Treasurer, John P. B. Maxwell

THE INNS OF COURT

HONOURABLE SOCIETY OF GRAY'S INN 8 South Square, London WC1R 5ET T 020-7458 7800 W www.graysinn.org.uk
Under-Treasurer, Brig. Anthony Faith, CBE

HONOURABLE SOCIETY OF LINCOLN'S INN Treasury Office, Lincoln's Inn, London WC2A 3TL T 020-7405 1393 E mail@lincolnsinn.org.uk W www.lincolnsinn.org.uk
Under-Treasurer, Col. D. Hills, MBE

HONOURABLE SOCIETY OF THE INNER TEMPLE Inner Temple, London EC4Y 7HL T 020-7797 8250 W www.innertemple.org.uk
Sub-Treasurer, Patrick Maddams

HONOURABLE SOCIETY OF THE MIDDLE TEMPLE Middle Temple Lane, London EC4Y 9AT T 020-7427 4800 E members@middletemple.org.uk W www.middletemple.org.uk
Under-Treasurer, Air Cdre Peter Hilling

NOTARIES PUBLIC

Notaries are qualified lawyers with a postgraduate Cambridge University diploma in notarial practice. Once a potential notary has passed the postgraduate diploma they can petition the Court of Faculties for a 'faculty'. After the faculty is granted, the notary is able to practice; however, for the first two years this must be under the supervision of an experienced notary. The admission and regulation of notaries in England and Wales is a statutory function of the Faculty Office. This jurisdiction was confirmed by the Courts and Legal Services Act 1990. The Notaries Society of England and Wales is the representative body for practising notaries.

THE FACULTY OFFICE, 1 The Sanctuary, Westminster, London SW1P 3JT T 020-7222 5381 W www.facultyoffice.org.uk
Registrar, Peter Beesley

THE NOTARIES SOCIETY OF ENGLAND AND WALES, PO Box 226, Melton Woodbridge IP12 1WX T 01394-380436 E admin@the notariessociety.org.uk W www.thenotariessociety.org.uk
Secretary, Christopher J. Vaughan

SOLICITORS

Salary range: £30,000–£90,000

Graduates from any discipline can train to be a solicitor; however, if the undergraduate degree is not in law, a one-year conversion course (either the Common Professional Examination (CPE) or the Graduate Diploma in Law (GDL)) must be completed. The next stage, and the beginning of the vocational phase, is the Legal Practice Course (LPC), which takes one year and is obligatory for both law and non-law graduates. The LPC provides professional instruction for prospective solicitors and can be completed on a full-time or part-time basis. Trainee solicitors then enter the final stage, which is a paid period of supervised work that lasts two years for full-time contracts. The employer that provides the training contract must be authorised by the Solicitors Regulation Authority (SRA) (the regulatory body of the Law Society of England and Wales), the Law Society of Scotland, or the Law Society of Northern Ireland. The SRA also monitors the training contract to ensure that it provides the trainee with the expertise to qualify as a solicitor.

Conveyancers are specialist property lawyers, dealing with the legal processes involved in transferring buildings, land and associated finances from one owner to another. This was the sole responsibility of solicitors until 1987 but under current legislation it is now possible for others to train as conveyancers.

COUNCIL FOR LICENSED CONVEYANCERS (CLC) 16–17 Glebe Road, Chelmsford, Essex CM1 1QG T 01245-349599 W www.conveyancer.org.uk
Chief Executive, Mr V. Olowe

THE LAW SOCIETY OF ENGLAND AND WALES The Law Society's Hall, 113 Chancery Lane, London WC2A 1PL T 020-7242 1222 E contact@lawsociety.org.uk W www.lawsociety.org.uk
Chief Executive, Des Hudson

LAW SOCIETY OF NORTHERN IRELAND Law Society House, 96 Victoria Street, Belfast BT1 3GN T 028-9023 1614 E info@lawsoc-ni.org W www.lawsoc-ni.org
Chief Executive and Secretary, Alan Hunter

LAW SOCIETY OF SCOTLAND 26 Drumsheugh Gardens, Edinburgh EH3 7YR T 0131-226 7411 E lawscot@lawscot.org.uk W www.lawscot.org.uk
Chief Executive, Lorna Jack

SOLICITORS REGULATION AUTHORITY Ipsley Court, Berrington Close, Redditch, Worcs B98 0TD T 0870-606 2555 E contactcentre@sra.org.uk W www.sra.org.uk
Chair, Peter Williamson

SOCIAL WORK

Salary range: £20,000–£29,000 (starting), rising to £40,000 as an experienced manager; £50,000+ at senior levels

Social workers tend to specialise in either adult or children's services. The General Social Care Council is responsible for setting standards of conduct and practice for social care workers and their employers; regulating the workforce and social work education and training. A degree or postgraduate qualification is needed in order to become a social worker. For more information *see* Social Welfare.

GENERAL SOCIAL CARE COUNCIL (GSCC) Goldings House, 2 Hay's Lane, London SE1 2HB T 020-7397 5100 E info@gscc.org.uk W www.gscc.org.uk
Chief Executive, Mike Wardle

SURVEYING

Salary range: £18,000–£24,000 in junior posts; £32,000+ (chartered); £70,000+ in senior roles

The Royal Institution of Chartered Surveyors (RICS) is the professional body that represents and regulates property professionals including land surveyors, valuers, auctioneers, quantity surveyors and project managers. Entry to the institution, following completion of a

RICS-accredited degree, is through completion of the Assessment of Professional Competence (APC), which involves a period of practical training concluded by a final assessment of competence. Entry as a technical surveyor requires completion of the Assessment of Technical Competence (ATC), which mirrors the format of the APC. The different levels of RICS membership are MRICS (member) or FRICS (fellow) for chartered surveyors, and TechRICS for technical surveyors.

Relevant courses can also be accredited by the Chartered Institute of Building (CIOB), which represents managers working in a range of construction disciplines; CIOB offers four levels of membership to those who satisfy its requirements: FCIOB (fellow), MCIOB (member), ICIOB (incorporated) and ACIOB (associate).

CHARTERED INSTITUTE OF BUILDING Englemere, King's Ride, Ascot SL5 7TB **T** 01344-630700
E reception@ciob.org.uk **W** www.ciob.org.uk
Chief Executive, Chris Blythe

ROYAL INSTITUTION OF CHARTERED SURVEYORS (RICS) RICS Contact Centre, Surveyor Court, Westwood Way, Coventry CV4 8JE **T** 0870-333 1600
E contactrics@rics.org **W** www.rics.org
Chief Executive, Louis Armstrong

TEACHING

(*See also* Education)
Salary range: £20,000–£41,000; headteacher £45,000–£90,000

The General Teaching Councils for England, Northern Ireland, Scotland and Wales maintain registers of qualified teachers in their respective countries, and registration is a legal requirement in order to teach in local authority schools. The Graduate Teacher Training Registry (GTTR) processes applications for entry to postgraduate teaching courses in England, Wales and Scotland.

Further information on how to become a teacher in England and Wales is available on the Training and Development Agency for Schools website (*see* below). Personal advice is available from the Teaching Information Line (**T** 0845-600 0991; **T** 0845-600 0992 for Welsh speakers). Details on courses in Scotland can be obtained from universities and the GTTR. Details of the courses in Northern Ireland can be obtained from individual universities and the Department of Education in Northern Ireland.

The College of Teachers, under the terms of its royal charter, provides professional qualifications and membership to teachers and those involved in education in the UK and overseas.

DEPARTMENT OF EDUCATION NORTHERN IRELAND Rathgael House, Balloo Road, Bangor BT19 7PR
T 028-9127 9279 **E** mail@deni.gov.uk **W** www.deni.gov.uk
Permanent Secretary, Will Haire

GENERAL TEACHING COUNCIL FOR ENGLAND Whittington House, 19–30 Alfred Place, London WC1E 7EA
T 0870-001 0308 **E** info@gtce.org.uk **W** www.gtce.org.uk
Chief Executive, Keith Bartley

GENERAL TEACHING COUNCIL FOR NORTHERN IRELAND 4th Floor, Albany House, 73–75 Great Victoria Street, Belfast BT2 7AF **T** 028-9033 3390
E info@gtcni.org.uk **W** www.gtcni.org.uk
Chairperson, Sally McKee

GENERAL TEACHING COUNCIL FOR SCOTLAND Clerwood House, 96 Clermiston Road, Edinburgh EH12 6UT
T 0131-314 6000 **E** gtcs@gtcs.org.uk **W** www.gtcs.org.uk
Chief Executive, Anthony Finn

GENERAL TEACHING COUNCIL FOR WALES 4th Floor, Southgate House, Wood Street, Cardiff CF10 1EW
T 029-2055 0350 **E** information@gtcw.org.uk
W www.gtcw.org.uk
Chief Executive, Gary Brace

GRADUATE TEACHER TRAINING REGISTRY Rosehill, New Barn Lane, Cheltenham GL52 3LZ
T 0871-468 0469 **E** enquiries@gttr.ac.uk **W** www.gttr.ac.uk
Chief Executive, Anthony McClaran

THE COLLEGE OF TEACHERS Institute of Education, 20 Bedford Way, London WC1H 0AL **T** 020-7911 5536
E enquiries@cot.ac.uk **W** www.cot.ac.uk
President, Prof. Geof Whitty, FRSA

TRAINING AND DEVELOPMENT AGENCY FOR SCHOOLS 151 Buckingham Palace Road, London SW1W 9SZ **T** 020-7023 8001 **W** www.tda.gov.uk
Chief Executive, Graham Holley

VETERINARY MEDICINE

Salary range: veterinary surgeons £30,000–£50,000+

The regulatory body for veterinary surgeons in the UK is the Royal College of Veterinary Surgeons (RCVS), which keeps the register of those entitled to practise veterinary medicine as well as the list of qualified veterinary nurses. Holders of recognised degrees from any of the six UK university veterinary schools or from certain EU or overseas universities are entitled to be registered, and holders of certain other degrees may take a statutory membership examination. The UK's veterinary schools are located at the University of Bristol, the University of Cambridge, the University of Edinburgh, the University of Glasgow, the University of Liverpool and the Royal Veterinary College in London; all veterinary degrees last for five years except that offered at Cambridge, which lasts for six. A new course at the University of Nottingham is undergoing approval in time for its first veterinary graduates in 2011.

The British Veterinary Association is the professional body representing veterinary surgeons. The British Veterinary Nursing Association is the professional body representing veterinary nurses.

BRITISH VETERINARY ASSOCIATION 7 Mansfield Street, London W1G 9NQ **T** 020-7636 6541
E bvahq@bva.co.uk **W** www.bva.co.uk
Secretary General, Henrietta Alderman

BRITISH VETERINARY NURSING ASSOCIATION 82 Greenway Business Centre, Harlow Business Park, Harlow CM19 5QE **T** 01279-408644 **E** bvna@bvna.co.uk
W www.bvna.org.uk

ROYAL COLLEGE OF VETERINARY SURGEONS Belgravia House, 62–64 Horseferry Road, London SW1P 2AF
T 020-7222 2001 **E** admin@rcvs.org.uk **W** www.rcvs.org.uk
Registrar, Jane C. Hern

INDEPENDENT SCHOOLS

Independent schools (non-maintained mainstream schools) charge fees and are owned and managed under special trusts, with profits being used for the benefit of the schools concerned. In 2007–8 there were 2,527 non-maintained mainstream schools in the UK, educating over 628,000 pupils, or around 6 per cent of the total school-age population. The approximate number of pupils at non-maintained mainstream schools in 2007–8 was:

UK	628,400
England	587,100
Wales	9,600
Scotland	30,900
Northern Ireland	800

The Independent Schools Council (ISC), formed in 1974, acts on behalf of the eight independent schools' associations which constitute it. These associations are:

Association of Governing Bodies of Independent Schools (AGBIS)
Council of British International Schools (COBIS)
Girls' Schools Association (GSA)
Headmasters' & Headmistresses' Conference (HMC)
Independent Association of Prep Schools (IAPS)
Independent Schools Association (ISA)
Independent Schools' Bursars Association (ISBA)
Society of Headmasters & Headmistresses of Independent Schools (SHMIS)

There were 514,531 pupils being educated in 1,265 Independent Schools Council (ISC) accredited schools in 2008–9. Most of the schools outside ISC membership are likely to be privately owned. The Independent Schools Inspectorate (ISI) was demerged from ISC with effect from 1 January 2008 and is legally and operationally independent of ISC. ISI works as an accredited inspectorate of schools in ISC membership under a framework agreed with the DCSF. A school must pass an ISI accreditation inspection to qualify for membership of an association within ISC.

In 2008 at GCSE 58.4 per cent of all exams taken by ISC independent school candidates achieved either an A* or A grade (compared to the national average of 21 per cent), and at A-level 76.9 per cent of entries were awarded an A or B grade (national average, 50.8 per cent). In 2008–9 over 133,000 pupils at ISC schools received help with their fees in the form of bursaries and scholarships from the schools. These cost the schools nearly £400m.

INDEPENDENT SCHOOLS COUNCIL
St Vincent House, 30 Orange Street, London WC2H 7HH
T 020-7766 7070 **W** www.isc.co.uk

The list of schools below was compiled from the *Independent Schools Yearbook 2009–10* (ed. Judy Mott, published by A&C Black) which includes schools whose heads are members of one of the ISC's five Heads' Associations. Further details are available online (**W** www.isyb.co.uk).

The fees shown below represent the upper limits payable as at September 2009 for UK pupils who do not qualify for any reduction; scholarships and bursaries are available at many of the schools listed.

School	*Web Address*	*Termly Fees* *Day*	*Board*	*Head*
ENGLAND				
Abbey Gate College, Cheshire	www.abbeygatecollege.co.uk	£3,155	–	Mrs L. Horner
The Abbey School, Berks	www.theabbey.co.uk	£3,840	–	Mrs B. Stanley
Abbots Bromley School for Girls, Staffs	www.abbotsbromley.staffs.sch.uk	£4,500	£7,400	Mrs P. Woodhouse
Abbot's Hill School, Herts	www.abbotshill.herts.sch.uk	£4,440	–	Mrs K. Lewis
Abbotsholme School, Derbys	www.abbotsholme.com	£5,750	£8,440	S. Fairclough
Abingdon School, Oxon	www.abingdon.org.uk	£4,460	£9,150	M. Turner
Ackworth School, W. Yorks	www.ackworthschool.com	£3,736	£6,116	Mrs K. Bell
Aldenham School, Herts	www.aldenham.com	£5,695	£8,279	J. Fowler
Alderley Edge School for Girls, Cheshire	www.aesg.info	£2,856	–	Mrs S. Goff
Alleyn's School, London SE22	www.alleyns.org.uk	£4,479	–	C. Diggory
Amberfield School, N. Yorks	www.amberfield.suffolk.sch.uk	£3,190	–	Mrs L. Ingram
Ampleforth College, N. Yorks	www.college.ampleforth.org.uk	£5,485	£8,815	Rev C. Everitt
Ardingly College, W. Sussex	www.ardingly.com	£6,305	£8,405	P. Green
Arnold School, Lancs	www.arnoldschool.com	£2,847	–	B. Hughes
Ashford School, Kent	www.ashfordschool.co.uk	£4,480	£8,140	M. Buchanan
Ashville College, N. Yorks	www.ashville.co.uk	£3,570	£6,990	A. Fleck
Austin Friars St Monica's Senior School, Cumbria	www.austinfriars.cumbria.sch.uk	£3,538	–	C. Lumb
Bablake School, W. Midlands	www.bablake.com	£2,880	–	J. Watson
Badminton School, Bristol	www.badminton.bristol.sch.uk	£5,860	£8,840	Mrs J. Scarrow
Bancroft's School, Essex	www.bancrofts.org	£3,985	–	Mrs M. Ireland
Barnard Castle School, Durham	www.barnardcastleschool.org.uk	£3,416	£5,989	D. Ewart
Batley Grammar School, W. Yorks	www.batleygrammar.co.uk	£2,857	–	Mrs B. Tullie
Battle Abbey School, E. Sussex	www.battleabbeyschool.com	£4,400	£7,450	R. Clark

Bearwood College, Berks	www.bearwoodcollege.co.uk	£5,044	£8,655	S. Aiano
Bedales School, Hants	www.bedales.org.uk	£7,265	£9,240	K. Budge
Bedford High School for Girls, Beds	www.bedfordhigh.co.uk	£3,661	£6,860	Mrs J. Eldridge
Bedford Modern School, Beds	www.bedmod.co.uk	£3,332	–	S. Smith
Bedford School, Beds	www.bedfordschool.org.uk	£4,938	£7,883	J. Moule
Bedstone College, Shrops	www.bedstone.org	£3,850	£6,985	M. S. Symonds
Beechwood Sacred Heart School, Kent	www.beechwood.org.uk	£4,530	£7,500	N. Beesley
Benenden School, Kent	www.benenden.kent.sch.uk	–	£9,350	Mrs C. Oulton
Berkhamsted School, Herts	www.berkhamstedschool.org.uk	£5,194	£8,264	M. Steed
Bethany School, Kent	www.bethanyschool.org.uk	£4,728	£7,381	N. Dorey
Birkdale School, S. Yorks	www.birkdaleschool.org.uk	£3,312	–	R. Court
Birkenhead School, Merseyside	www.birkenheadschool.co.uk	£2,990	–	D. Clark
Bishop's Stortford College, Herts	www.bishops-stortford-college.herts.sch.uk	£3,720	£6,529	J. Trotman
Blackheath High School, London SE3	www.blackheathhighschool.gdst.net	£3,867	–	Mrs E. Laws
Bloxham School, Oxon	www.bloxhamschool.com	£4,655	£8,505	M. Allbrook
Blundell's School, Devon	www.blundells.org	£5,392	£8,360	I. Davenport
Bolton School Boys' Division, Lancs	www.boltonschool.org/seniorboys	£3,062	–	P. Britton
Bolton School Girls' Division, Lancs	www.boltonschool.org/seniorgirls	£3,062	–	Mrs G. Richards
Bootham School, N. Yorks	www.boothamschool.com	£4,750	–	J. Taylor
Bournemouth Collegiate School, Dorset	www.bournemouthcollegiateschool.co.uk	£2,693	£6,124	Stephen Duckitt
Box Hill School, Surrey	www.boxhillschool.com	£5,000	£7,000	M. Eagers
Bradfield College, Berks	www.bradfieldcollege.org.uk	£7,300	£9,125	P. Roberts
Bradford Girls' Grammar School, W. Yorks	www.bggs.com	£3,511	–	Mrs K. Matthews
Bradford Grammar School, W. Yorks	www.bradfordgrammar.com	£3,262	–	S. Davidson
Brentwood School, Essex	www.brentwoodschool.co.uk	£4,388	£7,822	D. Davies
Brighton and Hove High School, E. Sussex	www.gdst.net/bhhs	£3,100	–	K. Roberts
Brighton College, E. Sussex	www.brightoncollege.net	£5,728	£9,228	R. Cairns
Brigidine School Windsor, Berks	www.brigidine.org.uk	£4,365	–	Mrs E. Robinson
Bristol Grammar School, Bristol	www.bristolgrammarschool.co.uk	£3,444	–	R. MacKinnon
Bromley High School, Kent	www.bromleyhigh.gdst.net	£3,867	–	Mrs L. Duggleby
Bromsgrove School, Worcs	www.bromsgrove-school.co.uk	£4,040	£7,920	C. Edwards
Bruton School for Girls, Somerset	www.brutonschool.co.uk	£4,050	£7,311	J. Burrough
Bryanston School, Dorset	www.bryanston.co.uk	£7,468	£9,220	Ms S. Thomas
Burgess Hill School for Girls, W. Sussex	www.burgesshill-school.com	£4,150	£7,210	Mrs A. Aughwane
Bury Grammar School Boys, Lancs	www.bgsboys.co.uk	£2,669	–	Revd S. Harvey
Bury Grammar School Girls, Lancs	www.bgsg.bury.sch.uk	£2,669	–	Mrs R. Georghiou
Canford School, Dorset	www.canford.com	£6,805	£8,730	J. Lever
Casterton School, Lancs	www.castertonschool.co.uk	£4,703	£7,860	Mrs G. Sykes
Caterham School, Surrey	www.caterhamschool.co.uk	£4,420	£8,247	J. Thomas
Central Newcastle High School,	www.newcastlehigh.gdst.net	£3,100	–	Mrs H. French
Channing School, London N6	www.channing.co.uk	£4,295	–	Mrs B. Elliott
Charterhouse, Surrey	www.charterhouse.org.uk	£7,835	£9,480	Revd J. Witheridge
Cheadle Hulme School, Cheshire	www.cheadlehulmeschool.co.uk	£2,963	–	P. Dixon
Cheltenham College, Glos	www.cheltcoll.gloucs.sch.uk	£7,145	£9,270	J. Richardson
The Cheltenham Ladies' College, Glos	www.cheltladiescollege.org	£5,938	£8,842	Mrs V. Tuck
Chetham's School of Music, Manchester	www.chethams.com	sliding scale	–	Mrs C. Hickman
Chetwynde School, Cumbria	www.chetwynde.co.uk	£2,600	–	Mrs I. Nixon
Chigwell School, Essex	www.chigwell-school.org	£4,680	£6,929	M. Punt
Christ's Hospital, W. Sussex	www.christs-hospital.org.uk	sliding scale		J. Franklin
Churcher's College, Hants	www.churcherscollege.com	£3,580	–	S. Williams
City of London Freemen's School, Surrey	www.clfs.surrey.sch.uk	£4,653	£7,404	P. MacDonald
City of London School, London EC4	www.clsb.org.uk	£4,254	–	D. Levin
City of London School for Girls, London EC2	www.clsg.org.uk	£4,311	–	Miss D. Vernon
Claremont Fan Court School, Surrey	www.claremont-school.co.uk	£4,321	–	Mrs A. Stanley

Clayesmore School, Dorset	www.clayesmore.com	£6,416	£8,769	M. Cooke
Clifton College, Bristol	www.cliftoncollegeuk.com	£5,975	£8,825	M. Moore
Cobham Hall, Kent	www.cobhamhall.com	£5,650	£8,500	P. Mitchell
Cokethorpe School, Oxon	www.cokethorpe.org.uk	£4,625	–	D. Ettinger
Colfe's School, London SE12	www.colfes.com	£4,044	–	R. Russell
Colston's School, Bristol	www.colstons.bristol.sch.uk	£3,240	£6,355	P. Fraser
Combe Bank School, Kent	www.combebank.kent.sch.uk	£4,585	–	Mrs E. Abbotts
Concord College, Shrops	www.concordcollegeuk.com	£3,707	£7,800	N. Hawkins
Cranford House School, Oxon	www.cranford-house.org	£4,130	–	Mrs C. Hamilton
Cranleigh School, Surrey	www.cranleigh.org	£7,195	£8,827	G. Waller
Croydon High School, Surrey	www.gdst.net/croydonhigh	£3,867	–	Mrs Z. Braganza
Culford School, Suffolk	www.culford.co.uk	£4,985	£7,980	J. Johnson-Munday
Dame Alice Harpur School, Beds	www.dahs.co.uk	£3,342	–	Mrs J. Berry
Dame Allan's Boys' School, Tyne and Wear	www.dameallans.co.uk	£2,990	–	Dr J. Hind
Dame Allan's Girls' School, Tyne and Wear	www.dameallans.co.uk	£2,990	–	Dr J. Hind
Dauntsey's School, Wilts	www.dauntseys.org	£4,850	£8,175	S. Roberts
Dean Close School, Glos	www.deanclose.org.uk	£6,340	£8,975	J. Lancashire
Denstone College, Staffs	www.denstonecollege.org	£3,755	£6,539	D. Derbys
Derby High School, Derbys	www.derbyhigh.derby.sch.uk	£2,980	–	C. Callaghan
Dodderhill School, Worcs	www.dodderhill.co.uk	£2,975	–	Mrs J. Mumby
Dover College, Kent	www.dovercollege.org.uk	£3,995	£8,232	S. Jones
d'Overbroeck's College, Oxon	www.doverbroecks.com	£5,785	£8,640	S. Cohen
Downe House, Berks	www.downehouse.net	£6,750	£9,325	Mrs E. McKendrick
Downside, Somerset	www.downside.co.uk	£4,360	£8,047	L. Maidlow Davis
Duke of York's Royal Military School, Kent	www.doyrms.mod.uk	–	£2,555	C. Johnson
Dulwich College, London SE21	www.dulwich.org.uk	£4,524	£9,110	Dr J. Spence
Dunottar School, Surrey	www.dunottar.surrey.sch.uk	£3,865	–	Mrs J. Hellier
Durham High School for Girls, Durham	www.dhsfg.org.uk	£3,100	–	Mrs A. Templeman
Durham School, Durham	www.durhamschool.co.uk	£4,853	£6,930	E. George
Eastbourne College, E. Sussex	www.eastbourne-college.co.uk	£5,545	£8,375	S. Davies
Edgbaston High School, W. Midlands	www.edgbastonhigh.co.uk	£2,908	–	Dr R. Weeks
Ellesmere College, Shrops	www.ellesmere.com	£4,815	£7,830	B. Wignall
Eltham College, London SE9	www.eltham-college.org.uk	£3,990	–	P. Henderson
Emanuel School, London SW11	www.emanuel.org.uk	£4,581	–	M. Hanley-Browne
Epsom College, Surrey	www.epsomcollege.org.uk	£6,240	£9,135	S. Borthwick
Eton College, Berks	www.etoncollege.com	–	£9,617	A. Little
Ewell Castle School, Surrey	www.ewellcastle.co.uk	£3,700	–	A. Tibble
Exeter School, Devon	www.exeterschool.org.uk	£3,190	–	R. Griffin
Farlington School, W. Sussex	www.farlingtonschool.net	£4,322	£6,873	Mrs J. Goyer
Farnborough Hill, Hants	www.farnborough-hill.org.uk	£3,440	–	Mrs S. Buckle
Farringtons School, Kent	www.farringtons.org.uk	£3,740	£7,100	Mrs C. James
Felsted School, Essex	www.felsted.org	£5,983	£7,993	Dr M. Walker
Forest School, London E17	www.forest.org.uk	£4,298	–	Mrs S. Kerr-Dineen
Framlingham College, Suffolk	www.framlingham.suffolk.sch.uk	£4,823	£7,504	P. Taylor
Francis Holland School, London NW1	www.francisholland.org.uk	£4,475	–	Mrs V. Durham
Francis Holland School, London SW11	www.fhs-sw1.org.uk	£4,560	–	Miss S. Pattenden
Frensham Heights, Surrey	www.frensham-heights.org.uk	£5,230	£7,750	A. Fisher
Friends' School, Essex	www.friends.org.uk	£4,565	£7,095	G. Wigley
Fulneck School, W. Yorks	www.fulneckschool.co.uk	£3,255	£5,990	T. Kernohan
Gateways School, W. Yorks	www.gatewayschool.co.uk	£3,171	–	Mrs Y. Wilkinson
Giggleswick School, N. Yorks	www.giggleswickschool.co.uk	£5,775	£8,437	G. Boult
The Godolphin and Latymer School, London W6	www.godolphinandlatymer.com	£4,782	–	Mrs R. Mercer
The Godolphin School, Wilts	www.godolphin.org	£5,300	£7,620	Miss M. Horsburgh
The Grange School, Cheshire	www.grange.org.uk	£2,830	–	C. Jeffery
Greenacre School for Girls, Surrey	www.greenacre.surrey.sch.uk	£3,700	–	Mrs L. Redding
Gresham's School, Norfolk	www.greshams.com	£6,370	£8,295	P. John
Guildford High School, Surrey	www.guildfordhigh.surrey.sch.uk	£4,008	–	Mrs F. Boulton

The Haberdashers' Aske's Boys' School, Herts	www.habsboys.org.uk	£4,499	–	P. Hamilton
Haberdashers' Aske's School for Girls, Herts	www.habsgirls.org.uk	£3,665	–	Mrs E. Radice
Haileybury, Herts	www.haileybury.com	£6,446	£8,583	J. Davies
Halliford School, Middx	www.hallifordschool.co.uk	£3,553	–	P. Cottam
Hampshire Collegiate School, Hants	www.hampshirecs.org.uk	£4,103	£6,789	H. MacDonald
Hampton School, Middx	www.hamptonschool.org.uk	£4,470	–	B. Martin
Harrogate Ladies' College, N. Yorks	www.hlc.org.uk	£4,234	£7,394	G. Hazell
Harrow School, Middx	www.harrowschool.org.uk	–	£9,515	B. Lenon
Headington School, Oxon	www.headington.org	£4,170	£7,995	Mrs A. Coutts
Heathfield School, Berks	www.heathfieldstmarys.com	–	£8,698	Mrs J. Heywood
Heathfield School, Middx	www.heathfield.gdst.net	£3,867	–	Miss C. Juett
Hereford Cathedral School, Herefordshire	www.herefordcs.com	£3,502	–	P. Smith
Hethersett Old Hall School, Norfolk	www.hohs.co.uk	£3,615	£6,750	S. Crump
Highclare School, W. Midlands	www.highclareschool.co.uk	£3,110	–	Mrs M. Viles
Highgate School, London N6	www.highgateschool.org.uk	£4,870	–	A. Pettitt
Hipperholme Grammar School Foundation, W. Yorks	www.hgsf.org.uk	£2,995	–	Dr J. Scarth
Hollygirt School, Notts	www.hollygirt.co.uk	£2,998	–	Mrs P. Hutley
Holy Trinity School, Worcs	www.holytrinity.co.uk	£3,000	–	Graham Hurrell
Hull Collegiate School, E. Yorks	www.hullcollegiateschool.co.uk	£2,970	–	R. Haworth
Hurstpierpoint College, W. Sussex	www.hppc.co.uk	£5,960	£8,125	T. Manly
Hymers College, E. Yorks	www.hymerscollege.co.uk	£2,772	–	D. Elstone
Immanuel College, Herts	www.immanuelcollege.co.uk	£4,150	–	P. Skelker
Ipswich High School, Suffolk	www.ipswichhighschool.co.uk	£3,100	–	Ms E. Purves
Ipswich School, Suffolk	www.ipswich.suffolk.sch.uk	£3,587	£6,384	I. Galbraith
James Allen's Girls' School, London SE22	www.jags.org.uk	£4,210	–	Mrs M. Gibbs
The John Lyon School, Middx	www.johnlyon.org	£4,365	–	Miss K. Haynes
Kelly College, Devon	www.kellycollege.com	£4,600	£8,050	Dr G. Hawley
Kent College, Kent	www.kentcollege.com	£4,847	£8,342	D. Lamper
Kent College Pembury, Kent	www.kent-college.co.uk	£4,984	£8,034	Mrs S. Huang
Kimbolton School, Cambs	www.kimbolton.cambs.sch.uk	£3,870	£6,410	J. Belbin
King Edward VI. High School for Girls, W. Midlands	www.kehs.org.uk	£3,090	–	Miss S. Evans
King Edward VI. School, Hants	www.kes.hants.sch.uk	£3,625	–	A. Thould
King Edward VII. and Queen Mary School, Lancs	www.keqms.co.uk	£2,720	–	R. Karling
King Edward's School, Somerset	www.kesbath.com	£3,540	–	M. Boden
King Edward's School, W. Midlands	www.kes.org.uk	£3,130	–	J. Claughton
King Edward's School, Surrey	www.kesw.surrey.sch.uk	£5,575	£7,760	P. Kerr Fulton-Peebles
King Henry VIII. School, W. Midlands	www.khviii.com	£2,880	–	G. Fisher
King William's College, Isle of Man	www.kwc.im	£5,720	£8,331	Dr S. Welch
Kingham Hill School, Oxon	www.kingham-hill.oxon.sch.uk	£4,700	£7,800	Revd N. Seward
King's College School, London SW19	www.kcs.org.uk	£5,300	–	A. Halls
King's College, Somerset	www.kings-taunton.co.uk	£5,410	£7,990	R. Biggs
King's High School, Warks	www.kingshighwarwick.co.uk	£3,118	–	Mrs E. Surber
King's School, Somerset	www.kingsbruton.com	£5,882	£8,237	I. Wilmshurst
The King's School, Canterbury, Kent	www.kings-school.co.uk	£6,910	£9,350	N. Clements
The King's School, Chester, Cheshire	www.kingschester.co.uk	£3,214	–	C. Ramsey
The King's School, Cambs	www.kingsschoolely.co.uk	£5,310	£7,685	Mrs S. Freestone
The King's School, Glos	www.thekingsschool.co.uk	£4,925	–	A. Macnaughton
The King's School, Macclesfield, Cheshire	www.kingsmac.co.uk	£2,930	–	S. Coyne
King's School, Rochester, Kent	www.kings-school-rochester.co.uk	£3,980	£8,650	Dr I. Walker
The King's School, Tyne and Wear	www.kings-tynemouth.org.uk	£3,093	–	P. Cantwell
The King's School, Worcs	www.ksw.org.uk	£3,502	–	T. Keyes
Kingsley School, Devon	www.kingsleyschoolbideford.co.uk	£3,660	£6,990	A. Waters & S. Nicholson

The Kingsley School, Warks	www.thekingsleyschool.com	£3,285	–	Mrs C. Mannion Watson
Kingston Grammar School, Surrey	www.kgs.org.uk	£4,625	–	C. Baxter
Kingswood School, Somerset	www.kingswood.bath.sch.uk	£3,579	£7,865	S. Morris
Kirkham Grammar School, Lancs	www.kirkhamgrammar.co.uk	£2,830	£5,332	D. Walker
The Lady Eleanor Holles School, Middx	www.lehs.org.uk	£4,400	–	Mrs G. Low
Lancing College, W. Sussex	www.lancingcollege.co.uk	£6,235	£8,925	J. Gillespie
Langley School, Norfolk	www.langleyschool.co.uk	£3,440	£6,995	D. Findlay
Latymer Upper School, London W6	www.latymer-upper.org	£4,600	–	P. Winter
Lavant House, W. Sussex	www.lavanthouse.org.uk	£4,195	£6,600	Mrs K. Bartholomew
The Grammar School at Leeds, W. Yorks	www.gsal.org.uk	£3,291	–	M. Bailey
Leicester Grammar School, Leics	www.leicestergrammar.org.uk	£3,190	–	C. King
Leicester High School for Girls, Leics	www.leicesterhigh.co.uk	£3,000	–	Mrs J. Burns
Leighton Park School, Berks	www.leightonpark.com	£5,560	£8,480	J. Dunston
Leweston School, Dorset	www.leweston.co.uk	£4,940	£7,570	A. Aylward
The Leys School, Cambs	www.thelcys.net	£5,420	£8,220	M. Slater
The Licensed Victuallers' School, Berks	www.lvs.ascot.sch.uk	£4,320	£7,585	G. Best
Lincoln Minster School, Lincs	www.lincolnminsterschool.co.uk	£3,406	£6,446	C. Rickart
Liverpool College, Merseyside	www.liverpoolcollege.org.uk	£3,037	–	H. van Mourik Broekman
Lodge School, Surrey	www.lodgeschool.co.uk	£3,910	–	Miss P. Maynard
Longridge Towers School, Northumberland	www.lts.org.uk	£3,444	£7,226	A. Clemit
Lord Wandsworth College, Hants	www.lordwandsworth.org	£5,837	£8,227	F. Livingstone
Loughborough Grammar School, Leics	www.lesgrammar.org	£3,223	£8,996	P. Fisher
Loughborough High School, Leics	www.leshigh.org	£2,997	–	Miss B. O'Connor
Luckley–Oakfield School, Berks	www.luckley.wokingham.sch.uk	£4,245	£7,233	Miss V. Davis
Magdalen College School, Oxon	www.mcsoxford.org	£4,209	–	T. Hands
Malvern College, Worcs	www.malcol.org	£6,185	£9,658	A. Clark
Malvern St James, Worcs	www.malvernstjames.co.uk	£4,535	£8,960	Mrs Hayes
The Manchester Grammar School,	www.mgs.org	£3,080	–	C. Ray
Manchester High School for Girls,	www.manchesterhigh.co.uk	£2,978	–	Mrs A. Hewitt
Manor House School, Surrey	www.manorhouseschool.org	£4,070	–	Miss Z. Axton
The Marist Senior School, Berks	www.themaristschools.com	£3,300	–	K. McCloskey
Marlborough College, Wilts	www.marlboroughcollege.org	£7,060	£9,415	N. Sampson
Marymount International School, Surrey	www.marymountlondon.com	£5,843	£9,810	Sister Michaeline O'Dwyer
The Maynard School, Devon	www.maynard.co.uk	£3,297	–	Ms B. Hughes
Merchant Taylors' Boys' School, Merseyside	www.merchanttaylors.com	£2,808	–	D. Cook
Merchant Taylors' Girls' School, Merseyside	www.merchanttaylors.com	£2,808	–	Mrs L. Robinson
Merchant Taylors' School, Middx	www.mtsn.org.uk	£4,893	–	S. Wright
Mill Hill School, London NW7	www.millhill.org.uk	£5,206	£8,226	Dr D. Luckett
Millfield, Somerset	www.millfieldschool.com	£6,160	£9,025	C. Considine
Milton Abbey School, Dorset	www.miltonabbey.co.uk	£6,930	£9,240	W. Hughes-D'Aeth
Moira House Girls School, E. Sussex	www.moirahouse.co.uk	£5,705	£7,870	Mrs L. Watson
Monkton Combe Senior School, Somerset	www.monktoncombeschool.com	£5,524	£8,502	R. Backhouse
More House School, London SW1	www.morehouse.org.uk	£4,499	–	R. Carlysle
Moreton Hall, Shrops	www.moretonhall.org	£6,860	£8,510	J. Forster
Mount St Mary's College, Derbys	www.msmcollege.com	£3,456	£6,667	L. McKell
The Mount School, London NW7	www.mountschool.com	£3,510	–	Ms C. Cozens
The Mount School, N. Yorks	www.mountschoolyork.co.uk	£4,465	£6,945	Mrs D. Gant
New Hall School, Essex	www.newhallschool.co.uk	£4,980	£7,480	Mrs K. Jeffrey
Newcastle-under-Lyme School, Staffs	www.nuls.org.uk	£2,891	–	N. Rugg
The Newcastle upon Tyne Church High School, Tyne and Wear	www.churchhigh.com	£3,226	–	Mrs J. Gatenby
North Cestrian Grammar School, Cheshire	www.ncgs.co.uk	£2,565	–	D. Vanstone

North London Collegiate School, Middx	www.nlcs.org.uk	£4,308	–	Mrs B. McCabe
Northampton High School, Northants	www.gdst.net/northamptonhigh	£3,280	–	Mrs S. Dixon
Northamptonshire Grammar School, Northants	www.ngs-school.com	£3,603	–	N. Toone
Northwood College, Middx	www.northwoodcollege.co.uk	£4,000	–	Miss J. Pain
Norwich High School, Norfolk	www.gdst.net/norwich/	£3,100	–	Mrs V. Bidwell
Norwich School, Norfolk	www.norwich-school.org.uk	£3,681	–	J. Hawkins
Notre Dame Senior School, Surrey	www.notredame.co.uk	£3,825	–	Mrs B. Williams
Notting Hill and Ealing High School, London W13	www.nhehs.gdst.net	£3,885	–	Ms L. Hunt
Nottingham Girls' High School, Notts	www.nottinghamgirlshigh.gdst.net	£3,100	–	Mrs S. Gorham
Nottingham High School, Notts	www.nottinghamhigh.co.uk	£3,491	–	K. Fear
Oakham School, Rutland	www.oakham.rutland.sch.uk	£5,065	£8,475	N. Lashbrook
Ockbrook School, Derbys	www.ockbrook.derby.sch.uk	£3,030	£5,605	Mrs A. Steele
Oldham Hulme Grammar Schools, Lancs	www.hulme-grammar.oldham.sch.uk	£2,750	–	Dr P. Neeson
The Oratory School, Berks	www.oratory.co.uk	£6,025	£8,340	C. Dytor
Oswestry School, Shrops	www.oswestryschool.org.uk	£3,995	£6,825	P. Stockdale
Oundle School, Northants	www.oundleschool.org.uk	£5,645	£8,660	C. Bush
Our Lady of Sion School, W. Sussex	www.sionschool.org.uk	£3,140	–	M. Scullion
Our Lady's Abingdon Senior School, Oxon	www.olab.org.uk	£3,328	–	Mrs L. Renwick
Oxford High School, Oxon	www.oxfordhigh.gdst.net	£3,115	–	Miss O. Lusk
Padworth College, Berks	www.padworth.com	£3,250	£7,500	Mrs L. Melhuish
Palmers Green High School, London N21	www.pghs.co.uk	£3,595	–	Mrs C. Edmundson
Pangbourne College, Berks	www.pangbournecollege.com	£5,995	£8,475	T. Garnier
The Perse School for Girls and The Stephen Perse Sixth Form College, Cambs	www.persegirls.com; www.stephenperse.com	£4,385	–	Miss P. Kelleher
The Perse Upper School, Cambs	www.perse.co.uk	£4,286	–	E. Elliott
Peterborough High School, Cambs	www.peterboroughhigh.co.uk	£3,633	£6,731	A. Meadows
Pipers Corner School, Bucks	www.piperscorner.co.uk	£4,070	£6,710	Mrs H. Ness-Gifford
Plymouth College, Devon	www.plymouthcollege.com	£3,870	£7,350	Dr S. Wormleighton
Pocklington School, E. Yorks	www.pocklingtonschool.com	£3,632	£6,502	M. Ronan
Polam Hall School, Durham	www.polamhall.com	£3,595	£6,895	Miss M. Green
Portland Place School, London W1	www.portland-place.co.uk	£4,750	–	R. Walker
The Portsmouth Grammar School, Hants	www.pgs.org.uk	£3,926		J. Priory
Portsmouth High School, Hants	www.gdst.net/portsmouthhigh	£3,100	–	Mrs J. Clough
The Princess Helena College, Herts	www.phc.herts.sch.uk	£5,280	£7,625	Mrs J-A. Duncan
Princethorpe College, Warks	www.wcisf.co.uk	£2,890	–	E. Hester
Prior Park College, Somerset	www.priorparkschools.co.uk	£4,253	£7,669	J. Murphy-O'Connor
Prior's Field, Surrey	www.priorsfieldschool.com	£4,555	£7,365	Mrs J. Rouseblade
The Purcell School, Herts	www.purcell-school.org	£8,018	£10,254	P. Crook
Putney High School, London SW15	www.putneyhigh.gdst.net	£3,885	–	Dr D. Lodge
Queen Anne's School, Berks	www.qas.org.uk	£5,695	£8,395	Mrs J. Harrington
Queen Elizabeth Grammar School, W. Yorks	www.wgsf.org.uk	£3,133	–	M. Gibbons
Queen Elizabeth's Grammar School, Lancs	www.qegs.blackburn.sch.uk	£3,047	–	S. Corns
Queen Elizabeth's Hospital, Bristol	www.qehbristol.co.uk	£3,295	–	S. Holliday
Queen Margaret's School, N. Yorks	www.queenmargaretsschool.co.uk	£4,907	£7,744	Dr P. Silverwood
Queen Mary's School, N. Yorks	www.queenmarys.org	£4,435	£5,775	R. McKenzie Johnston
Queen's College, London, London W1	www.qcl.org.uk	£4,470	–	Mrs F. Ramsey
Queen's College, Somerset	www.queenscollege.org.uk	£4,570	£7,225	C. Alcock
Queen's Gate School, London SW7	www.queensgate.org.uk	£4,650	–	Mrs R. Kamaryc
The Queen's School, Cheshire	www.queens.cheshire.sch.uk	£3,285	–	Mrs C. Buckley
Queenswood, Herts	www.queenswood.org	£6,725	£8,705	Mrs P. Edgar

Radley College, Oxon	www.radley.org.uk	£9,115	–	A. McPhail
Ratcliffe College, Leics	www.ratcliffecollege.com	£4,281	£6,455	G. Lloyd
The Read School, N. Yorks	www.readschool.co.uk	£2,828	£6,061	R. Hadfield
Reading Blue Coat School, Berks	www.blue-coat.reading.sch.uk	£3,950	–	M. Windsor
The Red Maids' School, Bristol	www.redmaids.bristol.sch.uk	£3,135	–	Mrs I. Tobias
Redland High School for Girls, Bristol	www.redlandhigh.com	£3,050	–	Mrs C. Bateson
Reed's School, Surrey	www.reeds.surrey.sch.uk	£5,950	£7,871	D. Jarrett
Reigate Grammar School, Surrey	www.reigategrammar.org	£4,410	–	D. Thomas
Rendcomb College, Glos	www.rendcombcollege.co.uk	£5,853	£7,848	G. Holden
Repton School, Derbys	www.repton.org.uk	£6,460	£8,706	R. Holroyd
Rishworth School, W. Yorks	www.rishworth-school.co.uk	£3,320	£6,435	R. Baker
Roedean School, E. Sussex	www.roedean.co.uk	£5,450	£9,400	Mrs F. King
Rossall School, Lancs	www.rossallschool.org.uk	£3,670	£9,450	Dr S. Winkley
The Royal Grammar School, Surrey	www.rgs-guildford.co.uk	£4,154	–	J. Cox
Royal Grammar School, Tyne and Wear	www.rgs.newcastle.sch.uk	£3,109	–	B. Trafford
RGS. Worcester, Worcs	www.rgsw.org.uk	£3,066	–	A. Rattue
The Royal High School, Bath, Somerset	www.gdst.net/royalhighbath	£3,100	£6,077	J. Graham-Brown
The Royal Hospital School, Suffolk	www.royalhospitalschool.org	£3,735	£6,556	H. Blackett
The Royal Masonic School for Girls, Herts	www.royalmasonic.herts.sch.uk	£4,460	£7,130	Mrs D. Rose
Royal Russell School, Surrey	www.royalrussell.co.uk	£4,430	£8,770	J. Jennings
Royal School Hampstead, London NW3	www.royalschoolhampstead.net	£3,500	£6,900	Ms J. Ebner
The Royal Wolverhampton School, W. Midlands	www.theroyalschool.co.uk	£3,870	£7,695	S. Bailey
Rugby School, Warks	www.rugbyschool.net	£5,655	£9,075	P. Derham
Ryde School with Upper Chine, Isle of Wight	www.rydeschool.org.uk	£3,195	£6,535	Dr N. England
Rye St Antony, Oxon	www.ryestantony.co.uk	£3,675	£6,200	Miss A. Jones
St Albans High School, Herts	www.stahs.org.uk	£3,820	–	Mrs R. Martin
St Albans School, Herts	www.st-albans.herts.sch.uk	£4,230	–	A. Grant
St Andrew's School, Beds	www.standrewsschoolbedford.com	£3,295	–	S. Skehan
Saint Augustine's Priory School, London W5	www.saintaugustinespriory.org.uk	£3,440	–	Mrs F. Gumley-Mason
St Bede's College, Manchester	www.stbedescollege.co.uk	£2,798	–	M. Barber
St Bede's Senior School, E. Sussex	www.stbedesschool.org	£4,975	£8,090	R. Maloney
St Bees School, Cumbria	www.st-bees-school.org	£4,716	£7,946	P. Capes
St Benedict's School, London W5	www.stbenedicts.org.uk	£3,920	–	C. Cleugh
St Catherine's School, Surrey	www.stcatherines.info	£4,392	£7,230	Mrs A. Phillips
St Catherine's School, Middx	www.stcatherineschool.co.uk	£3,505	–	Sister P. Thomas
St Christopher School, Herts	www.stchris.co.uk	£4,680	£8,215	R. Palmer
St Columba's College, Herts	www.stcolumbascollege.org	£3,472	–	D. Buxton
St Dominic's Priory School, Staffs	www.st-dominics.co.uk	£2,955	–	Mrs M. Adamson
St Dominic's School, Staffs	www.stdominicsschool.co.uk	£3,360	–	Mrs S. White
St Dunstan's College, London SE6	www.stdunstans.org.uk	£4,220	–	Mrs J. Davies
St Edmund's College, Herts	www.stedmundscollege.org	£4,560	£7,405	C. Long
St Edmund's School, Kent	www.stedmunds.org.uk	£5,333	£8,300	J. Gladwin
St Edward's, Oxford, Oxon	www.stedwards.oxon.sch.uk	£7,385	£9,230	A. Trotman
St Edward's School, Glos	www.stedwards.co.uk	£3,869	–	A. Nash
Saint Felix School, Suffolk	www.stfelix.co.uk	£4,195	£7,345	D. Ward
St Francis' College, Herts	www.st-francis.herts.sch.uk	£3,595	£7,070	Mrs D. MacGinty
St Gabriel's School, Berks	www.stgabriels.co.uk	£4,100	–	A. Jones
St George's College, Surrey	www.st-georges-college.co.uk	£4,610	–	J. Peake
St George's School, W. Midlands	www.sgse.co.uk	£3,465	–	Miss H. Phillips
St George's School, Berks	www.stgeorges-ascot.org.uk	£5,750	£8,850	Mrs C. Jordan
The School of St Helen and St Katharine, Oxon	www.shsk.org.uk	£3,595	–	Miss R. Edbrooke
St Helen's School for Girls, Middx	www.sthn.co.uk	£4,057	–	Mrs M. Morris
St James Independent School for Senior Boys, Middx	www.stjamesschools.co.uk	£3,830	£5,300	D. Boddy
St James Senior Girls' School, London W14	www.stjamesgirls.co.uk	£3,830	–	Mrs L. Hyde
St John's College, Hants	www.stjohnscollege.co.uk	£2,850	£6,250	N. Thorne
St John's School, Surrey	www.stjohnsleatherhead.co.uk	£5,900	£8,110	N. Haddock
St Joseph's College, Suffolk	www.stjos.co.uk	£3,675	£6,360	Mrs S. Grant

St Joseph's Convent School, Berks	www.st-josephs.reading.sch.uk	£3,500	–	Mrs M. Sheridan
St Lawrence College, Kent	www.slcuk.com	£4,683	£8,129	Revd M. Aitken
St Leonards–Mayfield School, E. Sussex	www.mayfieldgirls.org	£5,095	£7,670	Miss A. Beary
St Margaret's School, Herts	www.stmargaretsbushey.org.uk	£4,220	£7,600	Mrs L. Crighton
St Margaret's School, Devon	www.stmargarets-school.co.uk	£3,110	–	Mrs S. Cooper
St Martha's Senior School, Herts	www.st-marthas.co.uk	£3,100	–	J. Sheridan
Saint Martin's, W. Midlands	www.saintmartins-school.com	£3,230	–	Mrs J. Carwithen
St Mary's School Ascot, Berks	www.st-marys-ascot.co.uk	£6,500	£9,140	Mrs M. Breen
St Mary's Calne, Wilts	www.stmaryscalne.org	£6,750	£9,300	Mrs H. Wright
St Mary's School, Cambs	www.stmaryscambridge.co.uk	£4,040	£8,528	Miss C. Avery
St Mary's School, Essex	www.stmaryscolchester.org.uk	£2,925	–	Mrs H. Vipond
St Mary's College, Merseyside	www.stmaryscrosby.co.uk	£2,787	–	M. Kennedy
St Mary's School, Bucks	www.stmarysschool.co.uk	£3,940	–	Mrs F. Balcombe
St Mary's School, Dorset	www.st-marys-shaftesbury.co.uk	£4,990	£7,260	R. James
St Mary's, Worcs	www.stmarys.org.uk	£3,175	–	Mrs S. Cookson
St Nicholas' School, Hants	www.st-nicholas.hants.sch.uk	£3,480	–	Mrs A. Whatmough
St Paul's Girls' School, London W6	www.spgs.org	£5,434	–	Ms C. Farr
St Paul's School, London SW13	www.stpaulsschool.org.uk	£5,796	£8,591	G. Stephen
St Peter's School York, N. Yorks	www.st-peters.york.sch.uk	£4,561	£7,344	R. Smyth
St Swithun's School, Hants	www.stswithuns.com	£4,800	£7,915	Dr H. Harvey
St Teresa's School, Surrey	www.stteresasschool.com	£4,480	–	Mrs L. Falconer
Scarborough College, N. Yorks	www.scarboroughcollege.co.uk	£3,652	£5,989	J. Lee
Seaford College, W. Sussex	www.seaford.org	£5,075	£7,750	T. Mullins
Sedbergh School, Cumbria	www.sedberghschool.org	£6,250	£8,500	C. Hirst
Sevenoaks School, Kent	www.sevenoaksschool.org	£5,471	£8,774	Mrs C. Ricks
Shebbear College, Devon	www.shebbearcollege.co.uk	£3,280	£6,100	R. Barnes
Sheffield High School, S. Yorks	www.sheffieldhighschool.org.uk	£3,070	–	Mrs V. Dunsford
Sherborne Girls, Dorset	www.sherborne.com	£6,540	£8,995	Mrs J. Dwyer
Sherborne School, Dorset	www.sherborne.org	£7,355	£9,085	S. Eliot
Shiplake College, Oxon	www.shiplake.org.uk	£5,326	£7,896	A. Davies
Shrewsbury High School, Shrops	www.shrewsburyhigh.gdst.net	£3,100	–	Mrs M. Cass
Shrewsbury School, Shrops	www.shrewsbury.org.uk	£6,232	£8,800	J. Goulding
Sibford School, Oxon	www.sibford.oxon.sch.uk	£3,663	£7,117	M. Goodwin
Silcoates School, W. Yorks	www.silcoates.org.uk	£3,727	–	D. Wideman
Sir William Perkins's School, Surrey	www.swps.org.uk	£3,808	–	Mrs S. Cooke
Solihull School, W. Midlands	www.solsch.org.uk	£3,160	–	P. Griffiths
South Hampstead High School, London NW3	www.shhs.gdst.net	£3,867	–	Mrs J. Stephen
Stafford Grammar School, Staffs	www.stafford-grammar.co.uk	£3,007	–	M. Darley
Stamford High School, Lincs	www.ses.lincs.sch.uk	£3,800	£6,936	S. Roberts
Stamford School, Lincs	www.ses.lincs.sch.uk	£3,800	£6,936	S. Roberts
Stanbridge Earls School, Hants	www.stanbridgeearls.co.uk	£5,958	£8,016	G. Link
Stockport Grammar School, Cheshire	www.stockportgrammar.co.uk	£2,847	–	A. Chicken
Stonar School, Wilts	www.stonarschool.com	£4,130	£7,270	Mrs S. Shayler
Stonyhurst College, Lancs	www.stonyhurst.ac.uk	£4,879	£8,345	A. Johnson
Stover School, Devon	www.stover.co.uk	£3,235	£6,750	Mrs S. Bradley
Stowe School, Bucks	www.stowe.co.uk	£6,620	£9,130	A. Wallersteiner
Streatham and Clapham High School, London SW16	www.gdst.net/streathamhigh	£3,867	–	Mrs S. Mitchell
Sunderland High School, Tyne and Wear	www.sunderlandhigh.co.uk	£2,671	–	Dr A. Slater
Surbiton High School, Surrey	www.surbitonhigh.com	£3,851	–	Ms E. Haydon
Sutton High School, Surrey	www.suttonhigh.gdst.net	£3,867	–	S. Callaghan
Sutton Valence School, Kent	www.svs.org.uk	£5,390	£8,525	B. Grindlay
Sydenham High School, London SE26	www.gdst.net/sydenhamhigh	£3,867	–	Mrs K. Pullen
Talbot Heath, Dorset	www.talbotheath.org.uk	£3,360	£5,596	Mrs C. Dipple
Taunton School, Somerset	www.tauntonschool.co.uk	£4,840	£7,830	Dr J. Newton
Teesside High School, Cleveland	www.teessidehigh.co.uk	£3,414	–	T. Packer
Tettenhall College, W. Midlands	www.tettenhallcollege.co.uk	£3,823	£6,708	P. Bodkin
Thetford Grammar School, Norfolk	www.thetgram.norfolk.sch.uk	£3,315	–	G. Price
Thornton College, Bucks	www.thorntoncollege.com	£3,205	£5,250	Miss A. Williams
Thorpe House School, Norfolk	www.thorpehouseschool.com	£2,610	–	Mrs A-M. Sutcliffe
Tonbridge School, Kent	www.tonbridge-school.co.uk	£7,179	£9,662	T. Haynes
Tormead School, Surrey	www.tormeadschool.org.uk	£3,855	–	Mrs S. Marks

Trent College, Notts	www.trentcollege.net	£4,320	£5,400	Mrs G. Dixon
Tring Park School for the Performing Arts, Herts	www.tringpark.com	£6,570	£9,175	S. Anderson
Trinity School, Surrey	www.trinity-school.org	£3,868	–	M. Bishop
Truro High School for Girls, Cornwall	www.trurohigh.co.uk	£3,380	£6,425	Mrs C. Pascoe
Truro School, Cornwall	www.truroschool.com	£3,485	£6,665	P. Smith
Tudor Hall, Oxon	www.tudorhallschool.com	£5,258	£8,090	Miss W. Griffiths
University College School, London NW3	www.ucs.org.uk	£4,960	–	K. Durham
Uppingham School, Rutland	www.uppingham.co.uk	£6,389	£9,125	R. Harman
Wakefield Girls' High School, W. Yorks	www.wgsf.org.uk	£3,133	–	Mrs P. Langham
Walthamstow Hall, Kent	www.walthamstow-hall.co.uk	£4,740	–	Mrs J. Milner
Warminster School, Wilts	www.warminsterschool.org.uk	£4,110	£7,150	M. J. Priestley
Warwick School, Warks	www.warwickschool.org	£3,311	£7,065	E. Halse
Wellingborough School, Northants	www.wellingboroughschool.org	£3,904	–	G. Bowe
Wellington College, Berks	www.wellingtoncollege.org.uk	£6,920	£9,235	Dr A. Seldon
Wellington School, Somerset	www.wellington-school.org.uk	£3,570	£6,366	M. Reader
Wells Cathedral School, Somerset	www.wells-cathedral-school.com	£4,573	£7,643	Mrs E. Cairncross
West Buckland School, Devon	www.westbuckland.devon.sch.uk	£3,690	£6,500	J. Vick
Westfield School, Tyne and Wear	www.westfield.newcastle.sch.uk	£3,217	–	Mrs M. Farndale
Westholme School, Lancs	www.westholmeschool.com	£2,686	–	Mrs L. Croston
Westminster School, London SW1	www.westminster.org.uk	£7,094	£9,448	M. Spurr
Westonbirt, Glos	www.westonbirt.gloucs.sch.uk	£5,845	£8,695	Mrs M. Henderson
Whitgift School, Surrey	www.whitgift.co.uk	£4,422	–	C. Barnett
Wimbledon High School, London SW19	www.wimbledonhigh.gdst.net	£3,885	–	Mrs H. Hanbury
Winchester College, Hants	www.winchestercollege.org	£9,135	£9,615	R. Townsend
Windermere St Anne's School, Cumbria	www.wsaschool.com	£4,318	£7,732	I. Lavender
Wisbech Grammar School, Cambs	www.wgs.cambs.sch.uk	£3,330	–	N. Hammond
Withington Girls' School, Manchester	www.withington.manchester.sch.uk	£3,137	–	Mrs J. Pickering
Woldingham School, Surrey	www.woldinghamschool.co.uk	£5,135	£8,435	Mrs J. Triffitt
Wolverhampton Grammar School, W. Midlands	www.wgs.org.uk	£3,545	–	J. Darby
Woodbridge School, Suffolk	www.woodbridge.suffolk.sch.uk	£4,152	£7,336	S. Cole
Woodhouse Grove School, W. Yorks	www.woodhousegrove.co.uk	£3,310	£6,580	D. Humphreys
Worksop College, Notts	www.worksopcollege.notts.sch.uk	£5,015	£7,400	R. Collard
Worth School, W. Sussex	www.worthschool.co.uk	£6,113	£8,252	G. Carminati
Wrekin College, Shrops	www.wrekincollege.com	£4,770	£7,875	S. Drew
Wychwood School, Oxon	www.wychwood-school.org.uk	£3,555	£5,780	Mrs S. Wingfield Digby
Wycliffe College, Glos	www.wycliffe.co.uk	£5,290	£8,600	Mrs M. Burnet Ward
Wycombe Abbey School, Bucks	www.wycombeabbey.com	£7,050	£9,400	Mrs C. Hall
Wykeham House School, Hants	www.wykehamhouse.com	£3,080	–	Mrs L. Clarke
Yarm School, Cleveland	www.yarmschool.org	£3,310	–	D. Dunn
The Yehudi Menuhin School, Surrey	www.yehudimenuhinschool.co.uk	sliding scale		N. Chisholm

WALES

Christ College, Brecon	www.christcollegebrecon.com	£3,950	£6,945	Mrs E. Taylor
Haberdashers' Monmouth School for Girls, Monmouth	www.habs-monmouth.org	£3,634	£6,665	Mrs H. Davy
Howell's School, Denbigh	www.howells.org	£3,900	£6,300	Miss R. Hodgson
Howell's School Llandaff, Cardiff	www.howells-cardiff.gdst.net	£3,120	–	Mrs S. Davis
Llandovery College, Llandovery	www.llandoverycollege.com	£4,270	£6,313	I. Hunt
Monmouth School, Monmouth	www.habs-monmouth.org	£3,920	£6,665	S. Connors
Rougemont School, Newport	www.rougemontschool.co.uk	£3,168	–	Dr J. Tribbick
Ruthin School, Ruthin	www.ruthinschool.co.uk	£3,675	£6,665	J. Rowlands
Rydal Penrhos School, Colwyn Bay	www.rydal-penrhos.com	£3,965	£8,125	P. Lee-Browne
St David's College, Llandudno	www.stdavidscollege.co.uk	£5,320	£7,900	S. Hay

NORTHERN IRELAND

Bangor Grammar School, Bangor	www.bangorgrammarschool.org.uk	–	–	S. Connolly
Belfast Royal Academy,	www.belfastroyalacademy.com	£47	–	J. Dickson

Campbell College, Belfast	www.campbellcollege.co.uk	£697	£3,422	J. Piggot
Coleraine Academical Institution, Coleraine	www.coleraineai.com	£43	–	Dr D. Carruthers
Foyle and Londonderry College, Londonderry	www.foylenet.org/foyleandlondonderry	£40	–	W. Magill
Methodist College, Belfast	www.methody.org	£47	£2,834	J. Naismith
The Royal Belfast Academical Institution,	www.rbai.org.uk	£258	–	Miss J. Williamson
The Royal School Dungannon, Dungannon	www.royaldungannon.com	£45	£2,128	D. Burnett

SCOTLAND

Dollar Academy, Dollar	www.dollaracademy.org.uk	£3,147	£7,182	J. Robertson
The High School of Dundee,	www.highschoolofdundee.co.uk	£3,162	–	Dr J. Halliday
The Edinburgh Academy,	www.edinburghacademy.org.uk	£3,460	–	M. Longmore
Fettes College, Edinburgh	www.fettes.com	£6,035	£8,288	M. Spens
George Heriot's School, Edinburgh	www.george-heriots.com	£3,034	–	A. Hector
George Watson's College, Edinburgh	www.gwc.org.uk	£3,053	–	G. Edwards
The Glasgow Academy,	www.theglasgowacademy.org.uk	£3,065	–	P. Brodie
The High School of Glasgow,	www.glasgowhigh.com	£3,111	–	C. Mair
Glenalmond College, Perth	www.glenalmondcollege.co.uk	£5,792	£8,494	G. Woods
Hutchesons' Grammar School, Glasgow	www.hutchesons.org	£2,909	–	Dr K. Greig
Kelvinside Academy, Glasgow	www.kelvinsideacademy.org.uk	£3,207	–	Mrs L. Douglas
Kilgraston, Bridge of Earn	www.kilgraston.com	£4,395	£7,495	M. Farmer
Lomond School, Helensburgh	www.lomond-school.org	£2,920	£6,245	S. Mills
Loretto School, Musselburgh	www.loretto.com	£5,735	£8,435	P. Hogan
The Mary Erskine School, Edinburgh	www.esms.edin.sch.uk	£2,914	£5,814	J. Gray
Merchiston Castle School, Edinburgh	www.merchiston.co.uk	£5,820	£8,040	A. Hunter
Morrison's Academy, Crieff	www.morrisonsacademy.org	£3,108	–	G. Pengelley
Robert Gordon's College, Aberdeen	www.rgc.aberdeen.sch.uk	£3,088	–	H. Ouston
St Aloysius' College, Glasgow	www.staloysius.org	£2,802	–	J. Stoer
St Columba's School, Kilmacolm	www.st-columbas.org	£2,967	–	D. Girdwood
St George's School for Girls, Edinburgh	www.st-georges.edin.sch.uk	£3,490	£6,990	Mrs H. Mackie
St Margaret's School for Girls, Aberdeen	www.st-margaret.aberdeen.sch.uk	£3,166	–	Mrs A. Everest
St Margaret's School, Edinburgh	www.st-margarets.edin.sch.uk	£3,274	£6,778	Mrs J. McGhee
Stewart's Melville College, Edinburgh	www.esms.edin.sch.uk	£2,914	£5,814	J. Gray
Strathallan School, Perth	www.strathallan.co.uk	£5,533	£8,154	B. Thompson

CHANNEL ISLANDS

Elizabeth College, Guernsey	www.elizcoll.org	£2,450	–	G. Hartley
The Ladies' College, Guernsey	www.ladiescollege.com	£1,885	–	Ms J. Riches
Victoria College, Jersey	www.vcj.sch.je	£1,390	–	R. Cook

NATIONAL ACADEMIES OF SCHOLARSHIP

The national academies are self-governing bodies whose members are elected as a result of achievement and distinction in the academy's field. Within their discipline, the academies provide advice, support education and exceptional scholars, stimulate debate, promote UK research worldwide and collaborate with international counterparts.

In addition to income from donations, membership contributions, trading and investments, the English academies receive grant-in-aid funding from the science budget, administered by the Department for Business Innovation and Skills.

SCIENCE BUDGET ALLOCATIONS

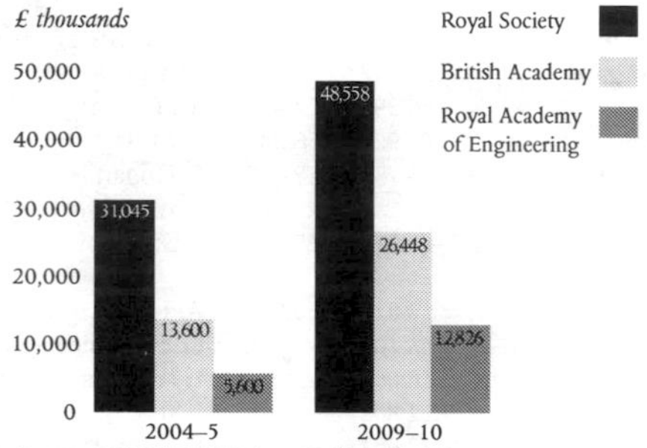

Source: BERR / DIUS Science Budget Allocations

ACADEMY OF MEDICAL SCIENCES (1998)

10 Carlton House Terrace, London SW1Y 5AH
T 020-7969 5288
W www.acmedsci.ac.uk

The Academy of Medical Sciences was established in 1998 to promote advances in medical science and to ensure these are converted into healthcare benefits for society. It campaigns for the development, protection and promotion of careers for academics in the biomedical sciences and encourages good practice in training and development.

The academy is independent and self-governing and receives funding from a variety of sources including the fellowship, charitable donations, government and industry. It was allocated £1.75m from the Department of Health, spread over five years from 2004.

Fellows are elected from a broad range of medical sciences: biomedical, clinical and population based. The academy includes in its remit vetinary medicine, dentistry, nursing, medical law, economics, sociology and ethics. Elections are from nominations put forward by existing fellows.

At June 2009 there were 947 fellows and 26 honorary fellows.

President, Prof. Sir John Bell, FRS, PMedSci
Vice-Presidents, Sir Michael Rutter, CBE, FRS, FMedSci; Prof. Ronald Laskey FRS, FMedSci
Executive Director, Dr Helen Munn

BRITISH ACADEMY (1902)

10 Carlton House Terrace, London SW1Y 5AH
T 020-7969 5200
W www.britac.ac.uk

The British Academy is an independent, self-governing learned society for the promotion of the humanities and social sciences. It supports advanced academic research and is a channel for the government's support of research in those disciplines.

The fellows are scholars who have attained distinction in one of the branches of study that the academy exists to promote. Candidates must be nominated by existing fellows. There are 890 ordinary fellows, 19 honorary fellows and 307 corresponding fellows overseas.

President, Baroness O'Neill, FBA
Chief Executive, Dr R. Jackson

ROYAL ACADEMY OF ENGINEERING (1976

3 Carlton House Terrace, London SW1Y 5DG
T 020-7766 0600
W www.raeng.org.uk

The Royal Academy of Engineering was established as the Fellowship of Engineering in 1976. It was granted a royal charter in 1983 and its present title in 1992. It is an independent, self-governing body whose object is the pursuit, encouragement and maintenance of excellence in the whole field of engineering, in order to promote the advancement of science, art and practice of engineering for the benefit of the public.

Election to the fellowship is by invitation only, from nominations supported by the body of fellows. At May 2009 there were 1,404 fellows. The Duke of Edinburgh is the senior fellow and the Duke of Kent is a royal fellow.

President, Lord Browne of Madingley, FRENG, FRS
Senior Vice-President, Prof. R. J. Mair, FRENG, FRS
Chief Executive, P. D. Greenish, CBE

ROYAL SOCIETY (1660)

6–9 Carlton House Terrace, London SW1Y 5AG
T 020-7451 2500
W www.royalsociety.org

The Royal Society is an independent academy promoting the natural and applied sciences. Founded in 1660, the society has three roles, as the UK academy of science, as a learned society and as a funding agency. It is an independent, self-governing body under a royal charter, promoting and advancing all fields of physical and biological sciences, of mathematics and engineering, medical and agricultural sciences and their application.

Fellows are elected for their contributions to science, both in fundamental research resulting in greater understanding, and also in leading and directing scientific and technological progress in industry and research establishments. A maximum of 44 new fellows, who must be citizens or residents of the British Commonwealth countries or Ireland, may be elected annually.

Up to eight foreign members, who are selected from those not eligible to become fellows because of citizenship or residency, are elected annually for their contributions to science.

One honorary fellow may be elected each year from those not eligible for election as fellows or foreign members. There are approximately 1,400 fellows and foreign members covering all scientific disciplines.
President, Prof. Lord Rees of Ludlow, PRS
Executive Secretary, S. Cox, CVO

ROYAL SOCIETY OF EDINBURGH (1783)

22–26 George Street, Edinburgh EH2 2PQ
T 0131-240 5000
W www.royalsoced.org.uk

The Royal Society of Edinburgh (RSE) is an educational charity and Scotland's National Academy. An independent body with charitable status, its multidisciplinary membership represents a knowledge resource for the people of Scotland. Granted its royal charter in 1783 for the 'advancement of learning and useful knowledge', the society organises conferences, debates and lectures; conducts independent inquiries; facilitates international collaboration and showcases the country's research and development capabilities; provides educational activities for primary and secondary school students and awards prizes and medals. The society also awards over £2m annually to Scotland's top researchers and entrepreneurs working in Scotland.

At May 2009 there were 1,521 fellows.
President, Lord Wilson of Tillyorn, KT, GCMG, PRS
Vice-Presidents, Prof. Tariq Durrani, OBE, FRENG, FRSE, Prof. Hector MacQueen, FRSE, Sir Thomas McKillop, KE, FRSE, Lord Patel, FRSE
General Secretary, Prof. Geoffrey Boulton, OBE, FRS, FRSE

PRIVATELY FUNDED ARTS ACADEMIES

The Royal Academy and the Royal Scottish Academy support the visual arts community in the UK, hold educational events and promote interest in the arts. They are entirely privately funded through contributions by 'friends' (regular donors who receive benefits such as free entry, previews and magazines), bequests, corporate donations and exhibitions.

ROYAL ACADEMY OF ARTS (1768)

Burlington House, Piccadilly, London W1J 0BD
T 020-7300 8000
W www.royalacademy.org.uk

The Royal Academy of Arts is an independent, self-governing society devoted to the encouragement and promotion of the fine arts.

Membership of the academy is limited to 80 academicians, all being painters, engravers, sculptors or architects. Candidates are nominated and elected by the existing academicians. There is also a limited class of honorary academicians, of whom as of May 2009 there were 20.
President, Sir Nicholas Grimshaw, CBE PRA
Secretary and Chief Executive, Charles Saumarez Smith, CBE

ROYAL SCOTTISH ACADEMY (1838)

The Mound, Edinburgh EH2 2EL
T 0131-225 6671
W www.royalscottishacademy.org

Founded in 1826 and granted a Royal Charter in 1838, The Royal Scottish Academy is an independent institution led by prominent Scottish artists and architects. It promotes and supports the visual arts through an ongoing exhibitions programme, related educational events and through a series of awards, bursaries and scholarships for artists at all stages of their careers.

Members are elected from the disciplines of art and architecture and elections are from nominations put forward by the existing membership. At mid-2009 there were 32 honorary members and around 105 members.
President, Prof. Bill Scott, PRSA
Secretary, Arthur Watson, RSA

RESEARCH COUNCILS

The government funds basic and applied civil science research, mostly through seven research councils, which are established under royal charter and supported by the Department for Business, Innovation and Skills (BIS). Research Councils UK is the strategic partnership of these seven councils* (for further information *see* W www.rcuk.ac.uk). The councils support research and training in universities and other higher education and research establishments. The science budget, administered by BIS, contributes to public sector investment in research, with funding from other government departments (including higher education funding) and regional development making up the remaining investment. The councils also receive income for research commissioned by government departments and the private sector, in addition to income from charitable sources. The annual science budget will rise from £3.72bn in 2009–10 to £3.97bn in 2010–11.

GOVERNMENT SCIENCE BUDGET
£ thousand

	2008–9	*2009–10*
Arts and Humanities Research Council	103,492	104,397
Biotechnology and Biological Sciences Research Council	427,000	452,563
Economic and Social Research Council	164,924	170,614
Engineering and Physical Sciences Research Council	795,057	814,528
Medical Research Council	605,538	658,472
Natural Environment Research Council	392,150	408,162
Science and Technology Facilities Council	623,641	630,337
Capital Investment Fund	135,000	184,860
Higher Education Innnovation Fund	85,000	99,000

Source: DIUS – *Science Budget Allocations 2008–9 to 2010–11*

ALCOHOL EDUCATION AND RESEARCH COUNCIL

Eliot House, 10–12 Allington Street, London SW1E 5EH
T 020-7808 7150 F 020-7808 7151 W www.aerc.org.uk

The AERC was established by act of parliament in 1982 to administer the Alcohol Education and Research Fund. The government fund is used in UK education and research projects to develop new ways to help those with drinking problems. The AERC funds up to five research projects of around £50,000 every year and awards a number of small research grants up to a maximum of £5,000. The AERC aims to increase awareness of alcohol issues, to reduce alcohol-related harm and to encourage best practice.
Chief Executive, Mr Dave Roberts
Director, Prof. Ray Hodgson

ARTS AND HUMANITIES RESEARCH COUNCIL*

Whitefriars, Lewins Mead, Bristol BS1 2AE
T 0117-987 6500 F 0117-987 6600 W www.ahrc.ac.uk

Launched in April 2005 as the successor organisation to the Arts and Humanities Research Board, the AHRC provides funding for postgraduate training and research in the arts and humanities. In any one year, the AHRC makes approximately 700 research awards and around 1,500 postgraduate awards. Awards are made after a rigorous peer review process, which ensures the quality of applications.
Chair, Prof. Sir Alan Wilson
Chief Executive, Prof. Philip Esler

BIOTECHNOLOGY AND BIOLOGICAL SCIENCES RESEARCH COUNCIL*

Polaris House, North Star Avenue, Swindon SN2 1UH
T 01793-413201

Established by royal charter in 1994, the BBSRC aims to advance UK expertise on the understanding and exploitation of biological systems. It funds research into how all living organisms function and behave, benefiting the agriculture, food, health, pharmaceutical and chemical sectors. To deliver its mission, the BBSRC supports research and training in universities and research centres throughout the UK, including the institutes listed below.
Chair, Prof. Sir T. Blundell
Chief Executive, Prof. D. Kell

INSTITUTES

BABRAHAM INSTITUTE, Babraham Hall, Babraham, Cambridge CB2 3AT T 01223-496000
Director, Prof. M. Wakelam

GENOME ANALYSIS CENTRE, Norwich Research Park, Colney, Norwich NR4 7UH T 01603-450000
Director, Dr J. Rogers

IAH PIRBRIGHT LABORATORY, Ash Road, Pirbright, Woking, Surrey GU24 0NF T 01483-232441
Head, Dr M. Johnson

INSTITUTE FOR ANIMAL HEALTH, Compton Laboratory, Compton, Newbury, Berks RG20 7NN T 01635-578411
Director, Prof. M. Shirley

INSTITUTE OF FOOD RESEARCH, Norwich Research Park, Colney Lane, Norwich NR4 7UA T 01603-255000
Director, Prof. D. Boxer

JOHN INNES CENTRE, Norwich Research Park, Colney, Norwich NR4 7UH T 01603-450000
Director, Prof. C. Lamb

NORTH WYKE RESEARCH, Okehampton, Devon EX20 2SB T 01837-883500
Head, Prof. L. Firbank

ROTHAMSTED RESEARCH, Rothamsted, Harpenden, Herts AL5 2JQ T 01582-763133
Director, Prof. I. Crute

ECONOMIC AND SOCIAL RESEARCH COUNCIL*

Polaris House, North Star Avenue, Swindon SN2 1UJ
T 01793-413000 E comms@esrc.ac.uk
W www.esrcsocietytoday.ac.uk

The purpose of the ESRC is to promote and support research and postgraduate training in the social sciences. It also provides advice, disseminates knowledge and promotes public understanding in these areas. The ESRC provides core funding to the centres listed below. Further information can be obtained on the ESRC website, including details of centres it funds in collaboration with other research councils.

Chair, Dr Alan Gillespie
Chief Executive, Prof. Ian Diamond

RESEARCH CENTRES

CENTRE FOR ANALYSIS OF RISK AND REGULATION, London School of Economics and Political Science, Houghton Street, London WC2A 2AE T 020-7955 6577
Director, Prof. B. Hutter

CENTRE FOR BUSINESS RELATIONSHIPS, ACCOUNTABILITY, SUSTAINABILITY AND SOCIETY, University of Cardiff, 55 Park Place, Cardiff CF10 3AT T 029-2087 6582
Director, Prof. K. Peattie

CENTRE FOR CHARITABLE GIVING AND PHILANTHROPY, Cass Business School, City University, London EC1H 0HB T 020-7040 0136
Directors, Prof. J. Harrow and Prof. C. Pharoah

CENTRE FOR CLIMATE CHANGE, ECONOMICS AND POLICY, LSE, Houghton Street, London WC2 2AE T 020-7106 1221
Directors, Prof. J. Rees and Prof. A. Gouldson

CENTRE FOR COMPETITION POLICY, University of East Anglia, Norwich NR4 7TJ T 01603-593715
Director, Prof. C. Waddams

CENTRE FOR ECONOMIC LEARNING AND SOCIAL EVOLUTION, University College, Gordon Street, London WC1H 0AN T 020-7679 4565
Director, Prof. M. Armstrong

CENTRE FOR ECONOMIC PERFORMANCE, London School of Economics and Political Science, Houghton Street, London WC2A 2AE T 020-7955 7048
Director, Prof. J. Van Reenen

CENTRE FOR MARKET AND PUBLIC ORGANISATION, University of Bristol, Bristol BS8 1TN T 0117-928 8436
Director, Prof. S. Burgess

CENTRE FOR MICROECONOMIC ANALYSIS OF PUBLIC POLICY, Institute for Fiscal Studies, 7 Ridgmount Street, London WC1E 7AE T 020-7291 4800
Director, Prof. R. Blundell

CENTRE FOR POPULATION CHANGE, School of Social Sciences, University of Southampton SO17 1BJ
Director, Prof. J. Falkingham

CENTRE FOR RESEARCH ON SOCIO-CULTURAL CHANGE, University of Manchester, Manchester M13 9PL T 0161-275 8985
Directors, Prof. M. Savage; Prof. K. Williams

CENTRE FOR SOCIAL, TECHNOLOGICAL AND ENVIRONMENTAL PATHWAYS TO SUSTAINABILITY, Institute of Development Studies, Brighton BN1 9RE T 01273-606261
Director, Prof. M. Leach

CENTRE ON MICRO-SOCIAL CHANGE, University of Essex, Colchester, Essex CO4 3SQ T 01206-872957
Director, Prof. S. Pudney

CENTRE ON MIGRATION, POLICY AND SOCIETY, University of Oxford, Oxford OX2 6QS T 01865-274711
Director, Prof. Michael Keith

CENTRE ON SKILLS, KNOWLEDGE AND ORGANISATIONAL PERFORMANCE, Department of Education, University of Oxford, 15 Norham Gardens, Oxford OX2 6PY T 01865-611030
Director, Mr K. Mayhew

DEAFNESS, COGNITION AND LANGUAGE, 49 Gordon Square, London WC1H OPD T 020-7679 4200
Director, Prof. B. Woll

ELECTRICITY POLICY RESEARCH GROUP, University of Cambridge, Trumpinton Street CB2 1AG T 01223-335246
Director, Prof. D. Newbery

ESRC GENOMICS NETWORK, T 01793-418002
Directors, Prof. Ruth Chadwick; Prof. John Dupré; Prof. David Wield; Prof. Steve Yearley

INTERNATIONAL CENTRE FOR LIFECOURSE STUDIES IN SOCIETY AND HEALTH, UCL Research Department of Epidemiology and Public Health T 020-7679 1708
Director, Prof. M. Bartley

LANGUAGE-BASED AREA STUDIES CENTRES, T 01793-413089
Directors, Dr Robin Azelwood; Dr Richard Berry; Dr Elisabeth Kendall; Prof. Victor King; Dr Frank Pieke

LEARNING AND LIFE CHANCES IN KNOWLEDGE ECONOMIES AND SOCIETIES (LLAKES), Institute of Education, University of London, 20 Bedford Way, London WC1H 0AL T 020-7911 5464
Director, Prof. A. Green

RESEARCH GROUP ON LIFESTYLES, VALUES AND ENVIRONMENT, University of Surrey, Guildford, Surrey GU2 1AG T 01793-413061
Director, Prof. T. Jackson

SPATIAL ECONOMICS RESEARCH CENTRE, LSE, Houghton Street, London WC2A 2AE T 020-7955 6581
Director, Dr Henry Overman

SUSSEX ENERGY GROUP, The Freeman Centre, University of Sussex, Brighton BN1 9QE T 01273-876584
Director, Dr J. Watson

ENGINEERING AND PHYSICAL SCIENCES RESEARCH COUNCIL*

Polaris House, North Star Avenue, Swindon SN2 1ET
T 01793-444000, **Helpline:** 01793-444100
W www.epsrc.ac.uk

The EPSRC is the UK government's main funding agency for research and training in engineering and the physical sciences in universities and other organisations throughout the UK. It also provides advice, disseminates knowledge and promotes public understanding in these areas.

Chair, John Armitt, CBE, FRENG
Chief Executive, Prof. David Delpy, FRS

HEALTH PROTECTION AGENCY

7th Floor, Holborn Gate, 330 High Holborn, London WC1V 7PP
T 020-7759 2700 F 020-7759 2733 E webteam@hpa.org.uk
W www.hpa.org.uk

The Health Protection Agency is a Special Health Authority, established in 2003 (merged with the National Radiological Protection Board in 2005), which gives advice to the public, health authorities and the government. It works to reduce the impact of infectious diseases and exposure to chemicals, poisons and radiation at local, national and regional levels and in emergency situations. The agency researches new ways to combat illness and to assess exposure to chemicals and radiation to determine whether treatment is needed.

Chairman, Sir William Stewart
Chief Executive, Justin McCracken

RESEARCH CENTRES

CENTRE FOR INFECTIONS, 61 Colindale Avenue, London NW9 5EQ T 020-8200 4400
Director, Prof. Peter Borriello

CENTRE FOR EMERGENCY PREPAREDNESS AND RESPONSE Porton Down, Salisbury, SP4 0JG T 01980-612100
Director, Dr Stephen Chatfield

CENTRE FOR RADIATION, CHEMICAL AND ENVIRONMENTAL HAZARDS, Chilton, Didcot OX11 0RQ T 01235-831600
Director, Dr Roger Cox

MEDICAL RESEARCH COUNCIL*

20 Park Crescent, London W1B 1AL T 020-7636 5422
W www.mrc.ac.uk

The purpose of the MRC is to promote medical and related biological research. The council employs its own research staff and funds research by other institutions and individuals, complementing the research resources of the universities and hospitals.

Chair, Sir John Chisholm
Chief Executive, Sir Leszek Borysiewicz
Chair, Neurosciences and Mental Health Board, Prof. C. Kennard
Chair, Molecular and Cellular Medicine Board, Prof. P. Luzio
Chair, Infections and Immunity Board, Prof. D. Smith
Chair, Population and Systems Medicine Board, Prof. S. Holgate

MRC UNITS, CENTRES AND INSTITUTES

Anatomical Neuropharmacology Unit
W mrcanu.pharm.ox.ac.uk
Biostatistics Unit
W www.mrc-bsu.cam.ac.uk
Cambridge Behavioural and Clinical Neuroscience Institute
W www.psychol.cam.ac.uk/bcni
Cancer Cell Unit
W www.hutchison-mrc.cam.ac.uk
Cell Biology Unit
W www.ucl.ac.uk/lmcb
Centre for Developmental and Biomedical Genetics
W cdbg.shef.ac.uk
Centre for Developmental Neurobiology at King's College London
W www.kcl.ac.uk/depsta/biomedical/mrc
Centre for Neurodegenerative Research
W cnr.iop.kcl.ac.uk
Centre for Nutritional Epidemiology in Cancer Prevention and Survival
W www.srl.cam.ac.uk
Centre for Protein Engineering
W www.mrc-cpe.cam.ac.uk
Centre for Regenerative Medicine
W www.scrm.ed.ac.uk
Clinical Sciences Centre
W www.csc.mrc.ac.uk
Clinical Trials Unit
W www.ctu.mrc.ac.uk
Cognition and Brain Sciences Unit
W www.mrc-cbu.cam.ac.uk
Collaborative Centre for Human Nutrition Research
W www.mrc-hnr.cam.ac.uk
Epidemiology Resource Centre
W www.mrc.soton.ac.uk
Epidemiology Unit
W www.mrc-epid.cam.ac.uk
Functional Genomics Unit
W www.mrcfgu.ox.ac.uk
Human Genetics Unit
W www.hgu.mrc.ac.uk
Human Immunology Unit
W www.imm.ox.ac.uk/groups/mrc-hiu
Human Reproductive Sciences Unit
W www.hrsu.mrc.ac.uk
Institute of Hearing Research
W www.ihr.mrc.ac.uk
Laboratories, the Gambia
W www.mrc.gm
Laboratory of Molecular Biology
W www2.mrc-lmb.cam.ac.uk
Mammalian Genetics Unit
W www.mgu.har.mrc.ac.uk
Mitochondrial Biology Unit
W www.mrc-mbu.cam.ac.uk
Molecular Haemotology Unit
W www.imm.ox.ac.uk/groups/mrc_molhaem
MRC/Asthma UK Centre in Allergic Mechanisms of Asthma
W www.asthma-allergy.ac.uk
MRC/Cancer Research UK/BHF Clinical Trial Service Unit & Epidemiological Studies Unit
W www.ctsu.ox.ac.uk
MRC Centre for Causal Analyses in Translational Epidemiology
W www.bristol.ac.uk/caite
MRC Centre of Epidemiology for Child Health
W www.ich.ucl.ac.uk
MRC Centre for Genomics and Global Health
W www.cggh.ox.ac.uk
MRC Centre for Neuromuscular Diseases
W www.cnmd.ac.uk
MRC Centre for Obesity and Related Metabolic Diseases
W www.mrl.ims.cam.ac.uk
MRC Centre for Outbreak Analysis and Modelling
W www1.imperial.ac.uk
MRC Centre for Transplantation
W http://transplantation.kcl.ac.uk
MRC General Practice Research Framework
W www.gprf.mrc.ac.uk
MRC Radiation Oncology and Biology Initiative
W www.rob.ox.ac.uk
MRC/UCL Centre for Medical Molecular Virology
T 020-7504 9343
MRC Unit for Lifelong Health and Ageing
W www.nhsd.mrc.ac.uk
MRC/University of Birmingham Centre for Immune Regulation
W www.bham.ac.uk/mrcbcir
MRC/University of Edinburgh Centre for Inflammation Research
W www.cir.med.ed.ac.uk
MRC/University of Sussex Centre in Genome Damage and Stability
W www.sussex.ac.uk/gdsc

National Institute for Medical Research
W www.nimr.mrc.ac.uk
Prion Unit
W www.prion.ucl.ac.uk
Protein Phosphorylation Unit
W www.dundee.ac.uk/lifesciences/mrcppu
Social and Public Health Sciences Unit
W www.msoc-mrc.gla.ac.uk
Social, Genetic and Developmental Psychiatry Research Centre
W www.iop.kcl.ac.uk/departments
Centre for Stem Cell Biology and Medicine
W www.stemcells.cam.ac.uk
MRC/University of Bristol Centre for Synaptic Plasticity
W www.bris.ac.uk/depts/synaptic
Toxicology Unit
W www.le.ac.uk/mrctox
MRC/UVRIUganda Research Unit on AIDS
T (+256) (41) 320272
Virology Unit
W www.mrcvu.gla.ac.uk

NATIONAL PHYSICAL LABORATORY

Hampton Road, Teddington, Middx TW11 0LW
T 020-8977 3222 F 020-8614 0446 E enquiry@npl.co.uk
W www.npl.co.uk

The National Physical Laboratory (NPL) was established in 1900 and is the UK's national measurement institute. It develops, maintains and disseminates national measurement standards for physical quantities such as mass, length, time, temperature, voltage and force. It also conducts underpinning research on engineering materials and information technology, and disseminates good measurement practice. It is government-owned but contractor-operated.
Managing Director, B. Bowsher

NATURAL ENVIRONMENT RESEARCH COUNCIL*

Polaris House, North Star Avenue, Swindon SN2 1EU
T 01793-411500 W www.nerc.ac.uk

The NERC funds and carries out impartial scientific research in the sciences relating to natural environment. Its work covers the full range of atmospheric, earth, biological, terrestrial and aquatic sciences, from the depths of the oceans to the upper atmosphere. Its mission is to gather and apply knowledge, create understanding and predict the behaviour of the natural environment and its resources.
Chair, Edmund Wallis
Chief Executive, Prof. Alan Thorpe

RESEARCH CENTRES
BRITISH ANTARCTIC SURVEY, High Cross, Madingley Road, Cambridge CB3 0ET T 01223-221400
Director, Prof. Nick Owens
BRITISH GEOLOGICAL SURVEY, Kingsley Dunham Centre, Keyworth, Nottingham NG12 5GG
T 0115-936 3100
Executive Director, Dr John Ludden
BRITISH OCEANOGRAPHIC DATA CENTRE, Joseph Proudman Building, 6 Brownlow Street, Liverpool L3 5DA
T 0151-795 4884
Director, Dr Juan Brown
CENTRE FOR ECOLOGY AND HYDROLOGY, Maclean Building, Benson Lane, Crowmarsh Gifford, Wallingford OX10 8BB T 01491-838800
Director, Prof. Patricia Nuttall, OBE

COLLABORATIVE CENTRES
CENTRE FOR EARTH OBSERVATION INSTRUMENTATION, NERC, Polaris House, North Star Avenue, Swindon SN2 1EU T 01793-411698
Director, Prof. Mick Johnson
CENTRE FOR POPULATION BIOLOGY, Imperial College London, Silwood Park Campus, Ascot SL5 7PY
T 020-7594 2475
Director, Prof. Georgina Mace, FRS
NATIONAL CENTRE FOR ATMOSPHERIC SCIENCE, NERC, Polaris House, North Star Avenue, Swindon SN2 1EU
T 01793-411609
Director, Prof. Stephen Mobbs
NATIONAL CENTRE FOR EARTH OBSERVATION, Department of Meteorology, University of Reading, Building 58, Earley Gate, Reading RG6 6BB
T 0118-3786728
Director, Prof. Alan O'Neill
NATIONAL INSTITUTE FOR ENVIRONMENTAL E-SCIENCE, Department of Earth Sciences, University of Cambridge, Downing Street, Cambridge CB2 3EQ
T 01223-764917
Director, Dr Martin Dove
NATIONAL OCEANOGRAPHY CENTRE, SOUTHAMPTON, University of Southampton, Waterfront Campus, European Way, Southampton SO14 3ZH
T 023-8059 6666
Director, Prof. Ed Hill
PLYMOUTH MARINE LABORATORY, Prospect Place, Plymouth PL1 3DH T 01752-633100
Director, Prof. Steven de Mora
SCOTTISH ASSOCIATION FOR MARINE SCIENCE, Dunstaffnage Marine Laboratory, Oban PA37 1QA
T 01631-559000
Director, Prof. Laurence Mee
SEA MAMMAL RESEARCH UNIT, Gatty Marine Laboratory, University of St Andrews, St Andrews KY16 8LB
T 01334-462630
Director, Prof. Ian Boyd
TYNDALL CENTRE FOR CLIMATE CHANGE RESEARCH, School of Environmental Sciences, University of East Anglia, Norwich, Norfolk NR4 7TJ T 01603-593900
Executive Director, Prof. Kevin Anderson
UK ENERGY RESEARCH CENTRE, 58 Prince's Gate, Exhibition Road, London SW7 2PG T 020-7594 1574
Research Director, Prof. Jim Skea

SCIENCE AND TECHNOLOGY FACILITIES COUNCIL*

Polaris House, North Star Avenue, Swindon SN2 1SZ
T 01793-442000 F 01793-442002 W www.scitech.ac.uk

Formed by royal charter on 1 April 2007, through the merger of the Council for the Central Laboratory of the Research Councils and the Particle Physics and Astronomy Research Council, the STFC is a non-departmental public body reporting to the Department for Business, Innovation and Skills.

The STFC invests in large national and international research facilities, while delivering science, technology and expertise for the UK. The council is involved in research projects including the Diamond Light Source Synchrotron and the Large Hadron Collider, and develops new areas of science and technology. The EPSRC has transferred its responsibility for nuclear physics to the STFC.
Chair, Peter Warry
Chief Executive, Prof. Keith Mason

CHILBOLTON OBSERVATORY, Chilbolton, Stockbridge, Hampshire SO20 6BJ T 01264-860391
DARESBURY LABORATORY, Daresbury Science and Innovation Campus, Warrington WA4 4AD T 01925-603000
RUTHERFORD APPLETON LABORATORY, Harwell Science and Innovation Campus, Didcot OX11 0QX T 01235-445000
UK ASTRONOMY TECHNOLOGY CENTRE, Royal Observatory, Edinburgh, Blackford Hill, Edinburgh EH9 3HJ T 0131-668 8100

RESEARCH AND TECHNOLOGY ORGANISATIONS

Over 30 industrial and technological research bodies are members of the Association of Independent Research and Technology Organisations Limited (AIRTO). Members' activities span a wide range of disciplines from life sciences to engineering. Their work includes basic research, development and design of innovative products or processes, instrumentation testing and certification, and technology and management consultancy. AIRTO publishes a directory to help clients identify the organisations that might be able to assist them. For a full list of members, *see* AIRTO's website.

AIRTO LTD, c/o CAMPDEN BRI, Station Road, Chipping Campden, Glos GL55 6LD T 01386-842247
E airto@campden.co.uk W www.airto.co.uk
President, Prof. R. Brook, OBE, FRENG

HEALTH

NATIONAL HEALTH SERVICE

The National Health Service (NHS) came into being on 5 July 1948 under the National Health Service Act 1946, covering England and Wales and, under separate legislation, Scotland and Northern Ireland. The NHS is now administered by the Secretary of State for Health (in England), the Welsh Assembly Government, the Scottish government and the Secretary of State for Northern Ireland.

The function of the NHS is to provide a comprehensive health service designed to secure improvement in the physical and mental health of the people and to prevent, diagnose and treat illness. It was founded on the principle that treatment should be provided according to clinical need rather than ability to pay, and should be free at the point of delivery.

Hospital, mental, dental, nursing, ophthalmic and ambulance services and facilities for the care of expectant and nursing mothers and young children are provided by the NHS to meet all reasonable requirements. Rehabilitation services such as occupational therapy, physiotherapy, speech therapy and surgical and medical appliances are supplied where appropriate. Specialists and consultants who work in NHS hospitals can also engage in private practice, including the treatment of their private patients in NHS hospitals.

STRUCTURE

The structure of the NHS remained relatively stable for the first 30 years of its existence. In 1974, a three-tier management structure comprising regional health authorities, area health authorities and district management teams was introduced in England, and the NHS became responsible for community health services. In 1979 area health authorities were abolished and district management teams were replaced by district health authorities.

The National Health Service and Community Care Act 1990 provided for more streamlined regional health authorities and district health authorities, and for the establishment of family health services authorities (FHSA) and NHS trusts. The concept of the 'internal market' was introduced into health care, whereby care was provided through NHS contracts where health authorities or boards and GP fundholders (the purchasers) were responsible for buying health care from hospitals, non-fundholding GPs, community services and ambulance services (the providers). The Act also paved the way for the community care reforms, which were introduced in April 1993, and changed the way care is administered for older people, the mentally ill, the physically disabled and people with learning disabilities.

ENGLAND

Regional health authorities in England were abolished in April 1996 and replaced by eight regional offices which, together with the headquarters in Leeds, formed the NHS executive (which has since been merged with the Department of Health). In April 2002, as an interim arrangement, the eight regional offices were replaced by four directorates of health and social care (DHSC). In April 2003, the DHSCs were abolished.

HEALTH AUTHORITIES

In April 1996 the district health authorities and family health service authorities were merged to form 100 unified health authorities (HAs) in England. In April 2002, 28 new health authorities were formed from the existing HAs. In October 2002, as part of the new arrangements set out in the NHS Reform and Health Care Professions Act 2002, these new health authorities were renamed strategic health authorities. The whole of England is now split into 10 strategic health authorities (SHAs) each of which is divided into various types of trusts that take responsibilty for running different NHS services locally. The different types of trusts comprise acute trusts and foundation trusts (which are responsible for the management of NHS hospitals), ambulance trusts, care trusts, mental health trusts and primary care trusts. SHAs are charged with improving and monitoring the performance of the trusts in their area.

PRIMARY CARE TRUSTS

The first 17 primary care trusts (PCTs) became operational on 1 April 2000 and there are now around 150 PCTs in England. PCTs were created to give primary care professionals greater control over how resources are best used to benefit patients. PCTs are free-standing statutory bodies responsible for securing the provision of services and integrating health and social care locally. PCTs receive most of their funding directly from the Department of Health and can use this to purchase hospital and other services from NHS trusts and other healthcare providers. They are also responsible for making payments to independent primary care contractors such as GPs and dentists.

Each PCT is overseen by a board, typically comprising a chair; at least five non-executive directors who are appointed by the Appointments Commission; at least five executive members, including the chief executive, finance director and director of public health; and at least two members of the PCT's professional executive committee (PEC), which is made up of health professionals. Clinical expertise is provided by the PEC with representation from local GPs, nurses, other health professionals and social services. The board concentrates on the overall strategies for the trust and ensures the trust meets its statutory, financial and legal obligations.

ACUTE TRUSTS AND FOUNDATION TRUSTS

Hospitals are managed by acute trusts that are responsible for the quality of hospital health care and for spending funds efficiently. There are around 175 acute NHS trusts and 60 mental health NHS trusts which oversee around 1,600 NHS hospitals and specialist care centres.

First introduced in April 2004, there are now 115 foundation trusts in England. NHS foundation trusts are NHS hospitals, but have their own accountability and governance systems, which function outside of the Department of Health's framework, giving them greater freedom to run their own affairs. NHS foundation trusts treat patients according to NHS principles and standards and are regulated by the Care Quality Commission.

STRATEGIC HEALTH AUTHORITIES

EAST OF ENGLAND, Victoria House, Capital Park, Fulbourn, Cambridge CB21 5XB T 01223-597500 W www.eoe.nhs.uk
Chief Executive, Sir Neil McKay, CB

EAST MIDLANDS, Octavia House, Bostocks Lane, Sandiacre, Nottingham NG10 5QG T 0115-968 4444 W www.eastmidlands.nhs.uk
Chief Executive, Dame Barbara Hakin, DBE

LONDON, 4th Floor Southside, 105 Victoria Street, London SW1E 6QT T 020-7932 3700 W www.london.nhs.uk
Chief Executive, Ruth Carnall, CBE

NORTH EAST, Riverside House, Goldcrest Way, Newcastle upon Tyne NE15 8NY T 0191-210 6400 W www.northeast.nhs.uk
Chief Executive, Ian Dalton

NORTH WEST, Gateway House, Piccadilly South, Manchester M60 7LP T 0161-236 9456 W www.northwest.nhs.uk
Chief Executive, Mike Farrar, CBE

SOUTH CENTRAL, Newbury Business Park, London Road, Newbury, Berks RG14 2PZ T 01635-275500 W www.southcentral.nhs.uk
Chief Executive, Jim Easton

SOUTH EAST, York House, 18–20 Masetts Road, Horley, Surrey RH6 7DE, T 01293-778899 W www.southeastcoast.nhs.uk
Chief Executive, Candy Morris

SOUTH WEST, South West House, Blackbrook Park Avenue, Taunton, Somerset TA1 7PX T 01823-361000 W www.southwest.nhs.uk
Chief Executive, Sir Ian Carruthers, OBE

WEST MIDLANDS, St Chad's Court, 213 Hagley Road, Edgbaston, Birmingham B16 9RG T 0845-155 1022 W www.westmidlands.nhs.uk
Chief Executive, Ian Cumming, OBE

YORKSHIRE AND THE HUMBER, Blenheim House, Duncombe Street, Leeds LS1 4PL T 0113-295 2000 W www.yorkshireandhumber.nhs.uk
Acting Chief Executive, Dame Barbara Hakin, DBE

Contact details for PCTs and other NHS trusts in England can be found on the NHS Choices website (W www.nhs.uk).

WALES

LOCAL HEALTH BOARDS AND COMMUNITY HEALTH COUNCILS

In Wales there were five HAs which replaced the former 17 HAs and FHSAs in April 1996. The HAs set up 22 local health groups (LHGs), coterminous with local authority areas (*see* Local Government section), which began work in April 1999. Originally they advised HAs, but in March 2003 the five HAs were abolished and the LHGs, were renamed local health boards (LHBs) and took up a role similar to PCTs, assuming responsibility for commissioning services and devising strategies for improving health. They also integrate the delivery of primary and community care. Each local health board has a governing body made up of local doctors, a nurse, other health professionals, members of the local authority and voluntary organisations and others to represent the interests of patients. There is also a small executive team to take action on decisions and provide services for the public. There are also 19 community health councils (CHCs).

SPECIALISED SERVICES AND PUBLIC HEALTH

Although LHBs plan and fund most hospital and family health services there are a few specialised services which are overseen at national level. These services are the responsibility of the Health Commission Wales (specialised services), which was set up in April 2003. The National Public Health Service for Wales also gives advice and guidance to LHBs on a range of issues such as communicable disease protection and control as well as childhood immunisation.

NHS TRUSTS AND HOSPITALS

There are nine NHS trusts in Wales, including one all-Wales ambulance trust. Between them, the trusts are responsible for managing 118 hospitals.

REGIONAL OFFICES

There are three regional offices of the Welsh Assembly Government for mid and west Wales, north Wales and south-east Wales. The regional offices support coordination at local level between LHBs, local authorities and NHS trusts. They have a specific role in ensuring that Welsh Assembly Government initiatives are carried out.

Contact details for the LHBs, community health councils, NHS trusts and all other NHS national and local services in Wales are available in the *NHS Wales Directory* on the NHS Wales website (W www.wales.nhs.uk).

SCOTLAND

The Scottish government Health Directorate is responsible both for NHS Scotland and for the development and implementation of health and community care policy. The chief executive of NHS Scotland leads the central management of the NHS, is accountable to ministers for the efficiency and performance of the service and heads the Health Department which oversees the work of the 14 regional health boards. These boards provide strategic management for the entire local NHS system and are responsible for ensuring that services are delivered effectively and efficiently.

In addition to the 14 regional health boards there are a further eight special boards which provide national services, such as the Scottish ambulance service and NHS National Services Scotland which provides national screening programmes, blood transfusion services and monitors communicable diseases.

REGIONAL HEALTH BOARDS

AYRSHIRE AND ARRAN, Eglinton House, Ailsa Hospital, Dalmellington Road, Ayr KA6 6AB T 01292-513600 W www.nhsayrshireandarran.com
Chief Executive, Dr Wai-yin Hatton

BORDERS, Newstead, Melrose TD6 9DA T 01896-826000 W www.nhsborders.org.uk
Chief Executive, John Glennie

DUMFRIES AND GALLOWAY, Mid North, Crichton Hall, Dumfries DG1 4TG T 01387-272702 W www.nhsdg.scot.nhs.uk
Chief Executive, John Burns

FIFE, Hayfield House, Hayfield Road, Kirkcaldy, Fife KY2 5AH T 01592-643355 W www.nhsfife.scot.nhs.uk
Chief Executive, George Brechin

FORTH VALLEY, Carseview House, Castle Business Park, Stirling FK9 4SW T 01786-463031

W www.nhsforthvalley.com
Chief Executive, Fiona Mackenzie
GRAMPIAN, Summerfield House, 2 Eday Road, Aberdeen AB15 6RE T 0845-456 6000 W www.nhsgrampian.org
Chief Executive, Richard Carey
GREATER GLASGOW AND CLYDE, Dalian House, 350 St Vincent Street, Glasgow G3 8YZ T 0141-201 4444 W www.nhsggc.org.uk
Chief Executive, Robert Calderwood
HIGHLAND, Assynt House, Beechwood Park, Inverness IV2 3BW T 01463-717123 W www.nhshighland.scot.nhs.uk
Chief Executive, Dr Roger Gibbins
LANARKSHIRE, 14 Beckford Street, Hamilton, Lanarkshire ML3 0BR T 01698-281313 W www.nhslanarkshire.org.uk
Chief Executive, Tim Davison
LOTHIAN, Deaconess House, 148 Pleasance, Edinburgh EH8 9RS T 0131-536 9000 W www.nhslothian.scot.nhs.uk
Chief Executive, Prof. James Barbour, OBE
ORKNEY, Garden House, New Scapa Road, Kirkwall, Orkney KW15 1BH T 01856-888000 W www.ohb.scot.nhs.uk
Chief Executive, Ian Crozier
SHETLAND, Brevik House, South Road, Lerwick ZE1 0TG T 01595-743063 W www.shb.scot.nhs.uk
Chief Executive, Sandra Laurenson
TAYSIDE, Kings Cross, Clepington Road, Dundee DD3 8EA T 01382-818479 W www.nhstayside.scot.nhs.uk
Chief Executive, Prof. Tony Wells
WESTERN ISLES, 37 South Beach Street, Stornoway, Isle of Lewis HS1 2BB T 01851-702997 W www.wihb.scot.nhs.uk
Chief Executive, Gordon Jamieson

NORTHERN IRELAND

On 1 April 2009 the four health and social services boards in Northern Ireland were replaced by a single health and social care board for the whole of Northern Ireland. The new board together with its local commissioning groups (whose boundaries are subject to review pending the outcome of local government reform) are responsible for improving the health and social wellbeing of people in the area for which they are responsible, planning and commissioning services, and coordinating the delivery of services in a cost-effective manner.

HEALTH AND SOCIAL CARE BOARD, 12–22 Linenhall Street, Belfast BT2 8BS T 028-9032 1313 W www.hscboard.hscni.net
Chief Executive, John Compton

THE NHS PLAN

In July 2000 the government launched the NHS Plan, a ten-year strategy to modernise the health service. In June 2004 it also launched the NHS Improvement Plan, which set out the next stage of NHS reform, moving the focus from access to services towards the broader issues of public health and chronic disease management. The core aims are to sustain increased levels of investment in the NHS and to continue to focus on the improvements outlined in the NHS Plan, while delivering greater levels of choice and information to patients. In July 2004, the Department of Health published *National Standards, Local Action: Health and Social Care Standards and Planning Framework 2005/6–2007/8,* which cut the number of national targets that NHS providers must comply with from 62 to 20. These national targets, which cover areas such as waiting times for accident and emergency treatment, have become national core standards which all providers of care must maintain from April 2005. Alongside this, NHS providers have been given power to set more locally relevant targets.

In June 2008 the Department of Health published *High Quality Care for All,* the final report of the next stage review. The report emphasised that there would be more choice for patients such as care plans for those with long-term conditions and the right for patients to choose care providers, including GPs. The report also stated that there would be increased investment in wellbeing and prevention services. In addition there was to be no new centrally imposed targets, instead service providers would be able to initiate and make changes to improve the quality of care for patients.

FINANCE

The NHS is still funded mainly through general taxation, although in recent years more reliance has been placed on the NHS element of national insurance contributions, patient charges and other sources of income.

The budgeted departmental expenditure limit for the NHS in England was set at £103.6bn for 2009–10. Expenditure for the NHS in Wales, Scotland and Northern Ireland is set by the devolved governments.

PRIVATE FINANCE INITIATIVE

The Private Finance Initiative (PFI) was launched in 1992, and involves the private sector in designing, building, financing and operating new hospitals and primary care premises, which are then leased to the NHS. Partnerships for Health, a public-private venture between the Department of Health and Partnerships UK plc was established in September 2001. Its role was to support the development of NHS Local Improvement Finance Trusts (LIFT) by implementing a standard approach to procurement as well as providing some equity. LIFTs were set up as limited companies with the local NHS Partnerships for Health and the private sector as shareholders to build and refurbish primary care premises, which the schemes own and then rent to GPs on a lease basis (as well as other parties such as chemists, opticians, dentists etc).

At the end of March 2008, 48 LIFT projects, in four waves, had been approved in England; of these, 47 had reached financial close. Forty-two of these schemes now have buildings open to patients. The total capital cost of all LIFT schemes as at 31 March 2008 was £1,341.39m.

EMPLOYEES AND SALARIES

NHS HEALTH SERVICE STAFF (GREAT BRITAIN)
Full-time equivalent

All hospital, community and public health medical staff	92,670
All hospital and community dental staff	3,466
Nursing and midwifery staff	485,289
General medical practitioners	40,634
General dental practitioners	2,301
Ophthalmic medical practitioners	439
Ophthalmic opticians	10,228

Source: ONS – *Annual Abstract of Statistics 2008* (Crown copyright)

SALARIES

Many general practitioners (GPs) are self-employed and hold contracts, either on their own or as part of a partnership, with their local primary care trust. The profit of GPs varies according to the services they provide for their patients and the way they choose to provide these services. The pay range for salaried GPs employed directly by primary care trusts for 2009–10 is £53,249–£80,354, dependent on, among other factors, length of service and experience. Most NHS dentists are self-employed contractors. A contract for dentists was introduced on 1 April 2006 which provides dentists with an annual income in return for carrying out an agreed amount, or units, of work. A salaried dentist employed directly by a PCT earns between £37,344 and £79,875.

BASIC SALARIES FOR HOSPITAL MEDICAL AND DENTAL STAFF*
from 1 April 2009

Consultant (2003 contract)	£74,504–£100,446
Consultant (pre-2003 contract)	£61,859–£80,186
Specialist Registrar	£30,685–£46,246
Speciality Registrar (full)	£29,411–£46,246
Speciality Registrar (fixed term)	£29,411–£38,911
Senior House Officer	£27,523–£38,322
House Officer	£22,190–£24,960

* These figures do not include merit awards, discretionary points or banding supplements

NURSES
From 1 December 2004 the *Agenda for Change* pay system was introduced throughout the UK for all NHS staff with the exception of medical and dental staff, doctors in public health medicine and the community health service. Nurses' salaries are incorporated in the *Agenda for Change* nine pay band structure, which provides additional payments for flexible working such as providing out-of-hours services, working weekends and nights and being 'on-call'.

SALARIES FOR NURSES AND MIDWIVES

Nurse/Midwife Consultant	£37,996–£65,657
Modern Matron	£37,996–£45,596
Nurse advanced/team manager	£29,789–£39,273
Midwife higher level	£29,789–£39,273
Nurse specialist/team leader	£24,831–£33,436
Hospital/Community Midwife	£24,831–£33,436
Registered Nurse/entry level Midwife	£20,710–£26,839

HEALTH SERVICES

PRIMARY CARE

Primary care comprises the services provided by general practitioners, community health centres, pharmacies, dental surgeries and opticians. Primary nursing care includes the work carried out by practice nurses, community nurses, community midwives and health visitors.

PRIMARY MEDICAL SERVICES
In England, primary medical services are the responsibility of primary care trusts (PCT) who contract with healthcare providers – GPs, dentists, pharmacists etc – to provide the service to the NHS.

In Wales, responsibility for primary medical services rests with local health boards (LHB), in Scotland with the 14 regional health boards and in Northern Ireland with the health and social care board.

Any vocationally trained doctor may provide general or personal medical services. GPs may also have private fee-paying patients, but not if that patient is already an NHS patient on that doctor's patient list.

A person who is ordinarily resident in the UK is eligible to register with a GP (or PMS provider) for free primary care treatment. Should a patient have difficulty in registering with a doctor, he or she should contact the local PCT for help. When a person is away from home he/she can still access primary care treatment from a GP if they ask to be treated as a temporary resident. In an emergency any doctor in the service will give treatment and advice.

GPs or PCTs are responsible for the care of their patients 24 hours a day, seven days a week, but can fulfil the terms of their contract by delegating or transferring responsibility for out-of-hours (OOH) care to an accredited provider.

Increasingly, some secondary care services, such as minor operations and consultations, can be provided in a primary care setting. The number of such practitioners is growing.

In addition there are around 93 NHS walk-in centres throughout England. Usually open seven days a week, from early in the morning until late in the evening, they are nurse-led and provide treatment for minor ailments and injuries, health information and self-help advice.

HEALTH COSTS
Some people are exempt from, or entitled to help with, health costs such as prescription charges, ophthalmic and dental costs, and in some cases help towards travel costs to and from hospital.

The following list is intended as a general guide to those who may be entitled to help, or who are exempt from some of the charges relating to the above:

- children under 16 and young people in full-time education who are under 19
- people aged 60 or over
- pregnant women and women who have had a baby in the last 12 months
- people, or their partners, who are in receipt of income support, income-based jobseeker's allowance and/or income-based employment and support allowance
- people in receipt of the pension credit guarantee credit
- diagnosed glaucoma patients, people who have been advised by an ophthalmologist that they are at risk of glaucoma and people aged 40 or over who have an immediate family member who is a diagnosed glaucoma patient
- diagnosed diabetic patients
- NHS in-patients
- NHS out-patients for all prescribed contraceptives, medication given at a hospital, NHS walk-in centre, personally administered by a GP or supplied at a hospital or primary care trust clinic for the treatment of tuberculosis or a sexually transmissable infection
- patients of the Community Dental Service or an out-patient of the NHS Hospital Dental Service
- people registered blind or partially sighted
- people who need complex lenses
- war pensioners whose treatment/prescription is for their accepted disablement and who have a valid exemption certificate
- people who are entitled to, or named on, a valid NHS tax credit exemption or HC2 certificate

People in other circumstances may also be eligible for help; *see* booklet HC12 (England) and HCS2 (Scotland) for further information.

WALES

On 1 April 2007 all prescription charges (including those for medical supports and appliances and wigs) for people living in Wales were abolished. The above guide still applies for NHS dental and optical charges although all people aged under 25 living in Wales are also entitled to free dental examinations.

PHARMACEUTICAL SERVICES

Patients may obtain medicines and appliances under the NHS from any pharmacy whose owner has entered into arrangements with the PCT to provide this service. There are also some suppliers who only provide special appliances. In rural areas, where access to a pharmacy may be difficult, patients may be able to obtain medicines, etc, from a dispensing doctor.

In England, a charge of £7.20 is payable for each item supplied (except for contraceptives for which there is no charge), unless the patient is exempt and the declaration on the back of the prescription form is completed. Prepayment certificates (£28.25 valid for three months, £104.00 valid for a year) may be purchased by those patients not entitled to exemption who require frequent prescriptions.

Since 1 April 2008 prescription charges in Scotland have been different from England; a charge of £4 is payable for each item supplied and prepayment certificates are available for four months (£13) and 12 months (£38).

In Northern Ireland the health minister announced on 1 September 2008 that prescription charges would be abolished from 1 April 2010. From 1 January 2009 prescription charges were reduced from £6.85 to £3 for each indvidual item supplied and prepayment certificates were reduced from £35.85 to £9 for a four-month certificate and from £98.70 to £25 for a 12-month certificate.

In Wales NHS prescription charges were abolished on 1 April 2007.

DENTAL SERVICES

Dentists, like doctors, may take part in the NHS and also have private patients. Dentists are responsible to the local health provider in whose areas they provide services. Patients may go to any dentist who is taking part in the NHS and is willing to accept them. On 1 April 2006 the charging system for NHS dentistry in England and Wales was changed. There is now a three tier payment system based on the individual course of treatment required.

COURSE OF TREATMENT COSTS 2009–10

	England/Wales
Examination, diagnosis, preventive care (A)* (eg x-rays, scale and polish)	£16.50/£12.00
A+ basic additional treatment (eg fillings and extractions)	£45.60/£39.00
A+ all other treatment (eg more complex procedures such as crowns, dentures etc)	£198.00/£177.00

* Urgent and out-of-hours treatment is also charged at this payment tier

The cost of individual treatment plan should be known prior to treatment and some dental practices may require payment in advance. There is no charge for writing a prescription or removing stitches and only one charge is payable for each course of treatment even if more than one visit to the dentist is required. If additional treatment is required within two months of visiting the dentist and this is covered by the course of treatment most recently paid for (eg payment was made for the second tier of treatment but an additional filling is required) then this will be provided free of charge.

SCOTLAND AND NORTHERN IRELAND

Scotland and Northern Ireland have yet to simplify their charging systems. NHS dental patients pay 80 per cent of the cost of the individual items of treatment provided up to a maximum of £384. Patients in Scotland are entitled to free basic and extensive examinations.

GENERAL OPHTHALMIC SERVICES

General ophthalmic services are administered by local health providers. Testing of sight may be carried out by any ophthalmic medical practitioner or ophthalmic optician (optometrist). The optician must give the prescription to the patient, who can take this to any supplier of glasses to have them dispensed. Only registered opticians can supply glasses to children and to people registered as blind or partially sighted.

Free eyesight tests and help towards the cost are available to people in certain circumstances. Help is also available for the purchase of glasses or contact lenses (*see* Health Costs section). In Scotland eye examinations, which include a sight test, are free to all. Help is also available for the purchase of glasses or contact lenses to those entitled to help with health costs in the same way it is available to those in England and Wales.

CHILD HEALTH SERVICES

Pre-school services at GP surgeries or child health clinics provide regular monitoring of children's physical, mental and emotional health and development and advise parents on their children's health and welfare.

NHS DIRECT AND NHS 24

NHS Direct is a 24-hour nurse-led advice telephone service for England and Wales. It provides medical advice as well as directing people to the appropriate part of the NHS for treatment if necessary (T 0845 4647).

NHS 24 provides an equivalent service for Scotland (T 0845-424 2424).

SECONDARY CARE AND OTHER SERVICES

HOSPITALS

NHS hospitals provide acute and specialist care services, treating conditions which normally cannot be dealt with by primary care specialists, and provide for medical emergencies.

NUMBER OF BEDS 2007*

	Average daily available beds	*Average daily occupation of beds*
England	160,297	135,132
Wales	13,600	11,200
Scotland	26,800	21,700
Northern Ireland	7,895	6,513

* Figures for Scotland and Wales are for 2006–7; figures for England are for 2007–8

Sources: Department of Health; ONS; Welsh Assembly Government

HOSPITAL CHARGES

Acute or foundation trusts can provide hospital accommodation in single rooms or small wards, if not required for patients who need privacy for medical reasons. The patient is still an NHS patient, but there may be a charge for these additional facilities. Acute or foundation trusts can charge for certain patient services that are considered to be additional treatments over and above the normal hospital service provision. There is no blanket policy to cover this and each case is considered in the light of the patient's clinical need. However, if an item or service is considered to be an integral part of a patient's treatment by their clinician, then a charge should not be made.

In some NHS hospitals, accommodation and services are available for the treatment of private patients where it does not interfere with care for NHS patients. Income generated by treating private patients is then put back into local NHS services. Private patients undertake to pay the full costs of medical treatment, accommodation, medication and other related services. Charges for private patients are set locally.

WAITING LISTS

England

In July 2004 a target of an 18-week maximum wait, from start time (ie seeing a GP) to treatment, was set to be achieved by the end of 2008. Known as the referral to treatment (RTT) pathway, it means that no patient should now wait more than 18 weeks unless it is clinically appropriate or they choose to do so. Monthly data is published on the NHS 18-weeks website (W www.18weeks.nhs.uk). In June 2009 the number of patients who completed their RTT pathway totalled 320,725; of which 94 per cent were seen within 18 weeks compared with 87 per cent in June 2008.

Wales

In Wales the standards for maximum waiting times are 14 weeks for in-patient or day case treatment and 10 weeks for a first out-patient appointment (excluding child and adolescent mental health services). At the end of June 2009 the number of patients waiting for in-patient or day case treatment totalled 46,458; of which 93 per cent were admitted within the 14-week period compared with 81 per cent in June 2008. The number of patients waiting for a first out-patient appointment totalled 115,876 at the end of June 2009; of which 97 per cent were seen within the ten-week period compared with 73 per cent in June 2008.

Scotland

In Scotland the national standard is for patients to be seen at an out-patient appointment within 15 weeks of referral by their GP or dentist. At the 31 March 2009, 153,875 patients were on the list; of these, just one had been waiting over 15 weeks. In comparison, at the end of March 2008, 162,525 patients were on the list; of which 4,520 had been waiting over 15 weeks.

Northern Ireland

In 2007 the health minister set new targets to ensure that by March 2008 no patient would wait more than 13 weeks for a first out-patient appointment and no more than 21 weeks for in-patient or day case treatment. The total number of people waiting for a first out-patient appointment at the end of March 2009 was 68,942, of these, 241 had been waiting over 13 weeks. The number of people waiting for in-patient treatment at the end of March 2009 was 32,663, of these, 107 had been waiting for more than 21 weeks.

AMBULANCE SERVICE

The NHS provides emergency ambulance services free of charge via the 999 emergency telephone service. Air ambulances, provided through local charities and partially funded by the NHS, are used throughout the UK. They assist with cases where access may be difficult or heavy traffic could hinder road progress. Non-emergency ambulance services are provided free of charge to patients who are deemed to require them on medical grounds.

Since 1 April 2001 all services have had a system of call prioritisation. The prioritisation procedures require all emergency calls to be classified as either immediately life threatening (category A) or other emergency (category B). Services are expected to reach 75 per cent of Category A (life threatening) calls within eight minutes and 95 per cent of category B calls within 19 minutes.

AMBULANCE STAFF 2008

	Total staff	*Number of paramedics*
England	30,518	9,203
Wales	1,413	847
Scotland	3,379	1,269
Northern Ireland	1,038	621*

* Includes emergency medical technicians

Source: ONS – *Annual Abstract of Statistics 2009* (Crown copyright)

BLOOD AND TRANSPLANT SERVICES

There are four national bodies which coordinate the blood donor programme and transplant and related services in the UK. Donors give blood at local centres on a voluntary basis.

NHS BLOOD AND TRANSPLANT, Oak House, Reeds Crescent, Watford, Herts WD24 4QN T 01923-486800 W www.nhsbt.nhs.uk

WELSH BLOOD SERVICE, Ely Valley Road, Talbot Green, Pontyclun CF72 9WB T 01443-622000 W www.welsh-blood.org.uk

SCOTTISH NATIONAL BLOOD TRANSFUSION SERVICE, 21 Ellen's Glen Road, Edinburgh EH17 7QT T 0131-536 5700 W www.scotblood.co.uk

NORTHERN IRELAND BLOOD TRANSFUSION SERVICE, Lisburn Road, Belfast BT9 7TS T 028-9032 1414 W www.nibts.org

HOSPICES

Hospice or palliative care may be available for patients with life-threatening illnesses. It may be provided at the patient's home or in a voluntary or NHS hospice or in hospital, and is intended to ensure the best possible quality of life for the patient during their illness, and to provide help and support to both the patient and the patient's family. The National Council for Palliative Care coordinates NHS and voluntary services in England, Wales and Northern Ireland; the Scottish Partnership for Palliative Care performs the same function in Scotland.

NATIONAL COUNCIL FOR PALLIATIVE CARE, The Fitzpatrick Building, 188–194 York Way, London N7 9AS T 020-7697 1520 W www.ncpc.org.uk

SCOTTISH PARTNERSHIP FOR PALLIATIVE CARE, 1A Cambridge Street, Edinburgh EH1 2DY T 0131-229 0538 W www.palliativecarescotland.org.uk

COMPLAINTS

Firstly, an attempt must be made to resolve the complaint at a local level directly with the healthcare provider concerned. Patient advice and liaison services (PALS) have been established for every NHS and primary care trust in England. PALS are not part of the complaints procedure itself, but can give advice on local complaints procedure, or resolve concerns informally. If the case is not resolved locally or the complainant is not satisfied with the way a local NHS body or practice has dealt with their complaint, they may approach the Health Service Ombudsman in England, the Scottish Public Services Ombudsman, Public Services Ombudsman for Wales or the Commissioner for Complaints in Northern Ireland.

RECIPROCAL ARRANGEMENTS

The European Health Insurance Card (EHIC) allows UK residents access to state-provided healthcare that may become necessary while temporarily travelling in all European Economic Area countries and Switzerland either free of charge or at a reduced cost. A card is free, valid for up to five years and should be obtained before travelling. Applications can be made by telephone (T 0845-606 2030), online (W www.ehic.org.uk) or by post (a form is available from the post office).

The UK also has bilateral agreements with several other countries, including Australia and New Zealand, for the free provision of urgent medical treatment.

European Economic Area nationals visiting the UK and visitors from other countries with which the UK has bilateral health care agreements are entitled to receive emergency health care on the NHS on the same terms as it is available to UK residents.

SOCIAL WELFARE

SOCIAL SERVICES

The Secretary of State for Health (in England), the Welsh Assembly Government, the Scottish government and the Secretary of State for Northern Ireland are responsible, under the Local Authority Social Services Act 1970, for the provision of social services for older people, disabled people, families and children, and those with mental disorders. Personal social services are administered by local authorities according to policies, with standards set by central and devolved government. Each authority has a director and a committee responsible for the social services functions placed upon them. Local authorities provide, enable and commission care after assessing the needs of their population. The private and voluntary sectors also play an important role in the delivery of social services, and an estimated 6 million people in the UK provide substantial regular care for a member of their family.

The Care Quality Commission (CQC) was established in April 2009, bringing together the independent regulation of health, mental health and adult social care. Prior to 1 April 2009 this work was carried out by three separate organisations: the Healthcare Commission, the Mental Health Act Commission and the Commission for Social Care Inspection. The CQC is responsible for the registration of health and social care providers, the monitoring and inspection of all health and adult social care, issuing fines, public warnings or closures if standards are not met and for undertaking regular performance reviews. Since April 2007 the Office for Standards in Education, Children's Services and Skills (OFSTED) has been responsible for inspecting and regulating all care services for children and young people in England. Both OFSTED and CQC collate information on local care services and make this information available to the public.

The Care and Social Services Inspectorate Wales (CSSIW), an operationally independent part of the Welsh Assembly Government, is reponsible for the regulation and inspection of all social care services in Wales and the Scottish Commission for the Regulation of Care (the Care Commission), established in April 2002 under the Regulation of Care (Scotland) Act 2001, is the independent care services regulator for Scotland.

The Department of Health, Social Services and Public Safety is responsible for social care services in Northern Ireland.

CARE QUALITY COMMISSION (CQC), Citygate, Gallowgate, Newcastle upon Tyne NE1 4PA
T 0300-061 6161 E enquiries@cqc.org.uk
W www.cqc.org.uk

OFFICE FOR STANDARDS IN EDUCATION, CHILDREN'S SERVICES AND SKILLS (OFSTED), Royal Exchange Buildings, St Ann's Square, Manchester M2 7LA T 0845-640 4045 E enquiries@ofsted.gov.uk
W www.ofsted.gov.uk

CARE AND SOCIAL SERVICES INSPECTORATE WALES (CSSIW), Cathays Park, Cardiff CF10 3NQ
T 01443-848450 E cssiw@wales.gsi.gov.uk
W www.cssiw.org.uk

SCOTTISH COMMISSION FOR THE REGULATION OF CARE, Compass House, 11 Riverside Drive, Dundee DD1 4NY T 01382-207100
E enquiries@carecommission.com
W www.carecommission.com

DEPARTMENT OF HEALTH, SOCIAL SERVICES AND PUBLIC SAFETY, Castle Buildings, Stormont, Belfast BT4 3SJ T 028-9052 0500 W www.dhsspsni.gov.uk

STAFF

Total Social Services Staff (England)	279,400
Home help service	31,700
Field social workers	40,100
Day care establishments staff	27,300
Residential care staff	46,400

Source: ONS – *Annual Abstract of Statistics 2008* (Crown copyright)

OLDER PEOPLE

Services for older people are designed to enable them to remain living in their own homes for as long as possible. Local authority services include advice, domestic help, meals in the home, alterations to the home to aid mobility, emergency alarm systems, day and/or night attendants, laundry services and the provision of day centres and recreational facilities. Charges may be made for these services. Respite care may also be provided in order to allow carers temporary relief from their responsibilities.

Local authorities and the private sector also provide 'sheltered housing' for older people, sometimes with resident wardens.

If an older person is admitted to a residential home, charges are made according to a means test; if the person cannot afford to pay, the costs are met by the local authority.

DISABLED PEOPLE

Services for disabled people are designed to enable them to remain living in their own homes wherever possible. Local authority services include advice, adaptations to the home, meals in the home, help with personal care, occupational therapy, educational facilities and recreational facilities. Respite care may also be provided in order to allow carers temporary relief from their responsibilities.

Special housing may be available for disabled people who can live independently, and residential accommodation for those who cannot.

FAMILIES AND CHILDREN

Local authorities are required to provide services aimed at safeguarding the welfare of children in need and, wherever possible, allowing them to be brought up by their families. Services include advice, counselling, help in the home and the provision of family centres. Many authorities also provide short-term refuge accommodation for women and children.

DAY CARE

In allocating day care places to children, local authorities give priority to children with special needs, whether in terms of their health, learning abilities or social needs.

Since September 2001 OFSTED has been responsible for the regulation and registration of all early years childcare and education provision in England (previously the responsibility of the local authorities). All day care and childminding services which care for children under eight years of age for more than two hours a day must register with OFSTED and are inspected at least every two years. As at 30 June 2009 there were 95,535 registered childcare providers in England.

CHILD PROTECTION

Children considered to be at risk of physical injury, neglect or sexual abuse are placed on the local authority's child protection register. Local authority social services staff, schools, health visitors and other agencies work together to prevent and detect cases of abuse. In England as at 31 March 2008 there were 29,200 children on child protection registers, of these, 13,400 were at risk of neglect, 3,400 of physical abuse, 2,000 of sexual abuse and 7,900 of emotional abuse. At 31 March 2008 there were 2,320 children on child protection registers in Wales, 2,437 in Scotland and 2,071 in Northern Ireland.

LOCAL AUTHORITY CARE

Local authorities are required to provide accommodation for children who have no parents or guardians or whose parents or guardians are unable or unwilling to care for them. A family proceedings court may also issue a care order where a child is being neglected or abused, or is not attending school; the court must be satisfied that this would positively contribute to the well-being of the child.

The welfare of children in local authority care must be properly safeguarded. Children may be placed with foster families, who receive payments to cover the expenses of caring for the child or children, or in residential care.

Children's homes may be run by the local authority or by the private or voluntary sectors; all homes are subject to inspection procedures. As at 31 March 2007, 81,100 children in the UK were in the care of local authorities, of these, 51,100 were in foster placements and 9,800 were in children's homes.

ADOPTION

Local authorities are required to provide an adoption service, either directly or via approved voluntary societies. In 2007, 5,224 children aged under 18 were entered in the adopted children register in the UK.

PEOPLE WITH LEARNING DISABILITIES

Services for people with learning disabilities are designed to enable them to remain living in the community wherever possible. Local authority services include short-term care, support in the home, the provision of day care centres, and help with other activities outside the home. Residential care is provided for the severely or profoundly disabled.

MENTALLY ILL PEOPLE

Under the care programme approach, mentally ill people should be assessed by specialist services, receive a care plan and a key worker should be appointed for each patient. Regular reviews of the person's progress should be conducted. Local authorities provide help and advice to mentally ill people and their families, and places in day centres and social centres. Social workers can apply for a mentally disturbed person to be compulsorily detained in hospital. Where appropriate, mentally ill people are provided with accommodation in special hospitals, local authority accommodation, or at homes run by private or voluntary organisations. Patients who have been discharged from hospitals may be placed on a supervision register.

NATIONAL INSURANCE

The National Insurance (NI) scheme operates under the Social Security Contributions and Benefits Act 1992 and the Social Security Administration Act 1992, and orders and regulations made thereunder. The scheme is financed by contributions payable by earners, employers and others (*see* below). Money collected under the scheme is used to finance the National Insurance Fund (from which contributory benefits are paid) and to contribute to the cost of the National Health Service.

NATIONAL INSURANCE FUND

Estimated receipts, payments and statement of balances of the National Insurance Fund for 2009–10:

Receipts	*£ million*
Net national insurance contributions	77,040
Compensation from the Consolidated Fund for statutory sick, maternity, paternity and adoption pay recoveries	1,988
Income from investments	2,495
State scheme premiums	78
Other receipts	48
TOTAL RECEIPTS	81,649

Payments	*£ million*
Benefits	
At present rates	71,114
Increase due to proposed rate changes	3,764
Personal and stakeholder pensions contracted-out rebates	2,313
Age-related rebates for contracted-out money purchase schemes	228
Administration costs	1,301
Redundancy fund payments	359
Transfer to Northern Ireland	395
Other payments	64
TOTAL PAYMENTS	79,537

Balances	*£ million*
Opening balance	52,717
Excess of receipts over payments	2,112
BALANCE AT END OF YEAR	54,829

CONTRIBUTIONS

There are six classes of National Insurance contributions (NICs):

Class 1	paid by employees and their employers
Class 1A	paid by employers who provide employees with certain benefits in kind for private use, such as company cars
Class 1B	paid by employers who enter into a pay as you earn (PAYE) settlement agreement with HM Revenue and Customs
Class 2	paid by self-employed people
Class 3	voluntary contributions paid to protect entitlement to the state pension for those who do not pay enough NI contributions in another class
Class 4	paid by the self-employed on their taxable profits over a set limit. These are normally paid by self-employed people in addition to class 2 contributions. Class 4 contributions do not count towards benefits.

The lower and upper earnings limits and the percentage rates referred to below apply from April 2009 to April 2010.

CLASS 1

Class 1 contributions are paid where a person:

- is an employed earner (employee), office holder (eg company director) or employed under a contract of service in Great Britain or Northern Ireland
- is 16 or over and under state pension age
- earns at or above the earnings threshold of £110 per week (including overtime pay, bonus, commission etc, without deduction of superannuation contributions)

Class 1 contributions are made up of primary and secondary contributions. Primary contributions are those paid by the employee and these are deducted from earnings by the employer. Since 6 April 2001 the employee's and employer's earnings thresholds have been the same and are referred to as the earnings threshold. Primary contributions are not paid on earnings below the earnings threshold of £110.00 per week. However, between the lower earnings limit of £95.00 per week and the earnings threshold of £110.00 per week, NI contributions are treated as having been paid to protect the benefit entitlement position of lower earners. Contributions are payable at the rate of 11 per cent on earnings between the earnings threshold and the upper earnings limit of £844.00 per week (9.4 per cent for contracted-out employment). Above the upper earnings limit 1 per cent is payable.

Some married women or widows pay a reduced rate of 4.85 per cent on earnings between the earnings threshold and upper earnings limits and 1 per cent above this. It is no longer possible to elect to pay the reduced rate but those who had reduced liability before 12 May 1977 may retain it for as long as certain conditions are met. *See* leaflet *Married Women Paying Reduced Rate National Insurance Contributions (NICs).*

Secondary contributions are paid by employers of employed earners at the rate of 12.8 per cent on all earnings above the earnings threshold of £110.00 per week. There is no upper earnings limit for employers' contributions. Employers operating contracted-out salary related schemes pay reduced contributions of 9.1 per cent; those with contracted-out money-purchase schemes pay 11.4 per cent. The contracted-out rate applies only to that portion of earnings between the earnings threshold and the upper earnings limit. Employers' contributions below and above those respective limits are assessed at the appropriate not contracted-out rate.

CLASS 2

Class 2 contributions are paid where a person is self-employed and is 16 or over and under state pension age. Contributions are paid at a flat rate of £2.40 per week regardless of the amount earned. However, those with earnings of less than £5,075 a year can apply for small earnings exception, eg exemption from liability to pay class 2 contributions. Those granted exemption from class 2 contributions may pay class 2 or class 3 contributions voluntarily. Self-employed earners (whether or not they pay class 2 contributions) may also be liable to pay class 4 contributions based on profits. There are special rules for those who are concurrently employed and self-employed.

Married women and widows can no longer choose not to pay class 2 contributions but those who elected not to pay class 2 contributions before 12 May 1977 may retain the right for as long as certain conditions are met.

Class 2 contributions are collected by the national insurance contributions department of HM Revenue and Customs (HMRC), by direct debit or quarterly bills.

CLASS 3

Class 3 contributions are voluntary flat-rate contributions of £12.05 per week payable by persons over the age of 16 who would otherwise be unable to qualify for retirement pension and certain other benefits because they have an insufficient record of class 1 or class 2 contributions. This may include those who are not working, those not liable for class 1 or class 2 contributions or those excepted from class 2 contributions. Married women and widows who on or before 11 May 1977 elected not to pay class 1 (full rate) or class 2 contributions cannot pay class 3 contributions while they retain this right. Class 3 contributions are collected by HMRC by quarterly bills or direct debit.

CLASS 4

Self-employed people whose profits and gains are over £5,715 a year pay class 4 contributions in addition to class 2 contributions. This applies to self-employed earners over 16 and under the state pension age. Class 4 contributions are calculated at 8 per cent of annual profits or gains between £5,715 and £43,875 and 1 per cent above. Class 4 contributions are assessed and collected by HMRC. It is possible, in some circumstances, to apply for exceptions from liability to pay class 4 contributions or to have the amount of contribution reduced.

PENSIONS

Many people will qualify for a state pension; however, there are further pension choices available, such as personal and stakeholder pensions. There are also other non-pension savings and investment options. The following section provides background information on existing pension schemes.

STATE PENSION SCHEME

The state pension scheme consists of:

- basic state pension
- additional state pension

People may be able to get both or either when they reach state pension age and meet the qualifying conditions.

The state pension does not have to be claimed at state pension age, people can delay claiming it to earn extra weekly state pension or a lump sum payment.

Basic State Pension

The amount of basic state pension paid is dependent on the number of 'qualifying years' a person has established during their working life. In 2009–10, the full basic state pension is £95.25 a week and the minimum basic state pension is £23.81 a week (*see also* Benefits, State Pension: Categories A and B).

Working Life

Working life is counted from the start of the tax year in which a person reaches 16 to the end of the tax year before the one in which they reach state pension age: for men this is normally 49 years and for women this varies between 44 and 49 years depending on their birth date (*see* State Pension Age).

Qualifying Years

A 'qualifying year' is a tax year in which a person has enough earnings on which they have paid, are treated as having paid, or have been credited with national insurance (NI) contributions (*see* National Insurance Credits section). By state pension age, a person needs to have one qualifying year from NI contributions paid or from NI contributions treated as being paid to be eligible for any basic state pension. From 6 April 2010 a person will also be entitled to a basic state pension based on just one qualifying year of national insurance credits. The number of qualifying years can be reduced if a person qualifies for home responsibilities protection (*see* below).

For people reaching state pension age before 6 April 2010, to get the full rate (100 per cent) basic state pension, a person must normally have qualifying years for about 90 per cent of their working life. To get the minimum basic state pension (25 per cent) a person normally needs ten or 11 qualifying years. From 6 April 2010 a person reaching state pension age will be entitled to a full basic state pension if they have 30 qualifying years.

National Insurance Credits

Those in receipt of carer's allowance, working tax credit (with a disability element), jobseeker's allowance, incapacity benefit, employment support allowance, unemployability supplement, statutory sick pay, statutory maternity pay or statutory adoption pay may have class 1 NI contributions credited to them each week. People may also get credits if they are unemployed and looking for work or too sick to work, even if they have not paid enough contributions to receive benefit. Persons undertaking certain training courses or jury service or who have been wrongly imprisoned for a conviction which is quashed on appeal may also get class 1 NI credits for each week they fulfil certain conditions. Class 1 credits are also available to men for the tax years in which they reach age 60 up to age 64, if they are not liable to pay contributions. Credits for men approaching state pension age will be phased out from 6 April 2010 in line with the increase in women's state pension age and men born after 1954 will no longer receive them. Class 1 NI credits count toward all future contributory benefits. A class 3 NI credit for basic state pension and bereavement benefit purposes is awarded, where required, for each week the working tax credit (without a disability element) has been received. Class 3 credits are also awarded automatically to young people aged 16 to 18 if they have not paid enough contributions to gain a qualifying year. However, for people reaching state pension before 6 April 2010, a state pension will not be paid based on a record of NI credits alone.

State Pension Age

State pension age is:

- 65 for men
- 60 for women born on or before 5 April 1950
- 65 for women born on or after 6 April 1955

Women born between 6 April 1950 and 5 April 1955 will have a state pension age between 60 and 65 depending on their date of birth. Further information can be obtained from the online state pension calculator (W www.thepensionservice.gov.uk/state-pension/age-calculator.asp).

Using the NI Contribution Record of Another Person to Claim a State Pension

Married women who are not entitled to a state pension on their own NI contributions may get a basic state pension calculated using their husband's NI contribution record. A basic state pension may be paid of up to 60 per cent of the husband's entitlement (up to £57.05 a week in 2009–10). From 6 April 2010, married men and civil partners will be able to claim a basic state pension based on their wife or civil partner's NI record if better than one based on their own record and if their wife or civil partner was born after 6 April 1950. A state pension is also payable to widows, widowers, surviving civil partners, and people who are divorced or whose civil partnership has been dissolved, based on their late or ex-spouse's/civil partner's NI contributions.

Non-contributory State Pensions

A non-contributory state pension may be payable to those aged 80 or over who live in England, Scotland or Wales, and have done so for a total of ten years or more for any continuous period in the 20 years after their 60th birthday, if they are not entitled to another category of state pension, or are entitled to one below the rate of £57.05 a week in 2009–10 (*see also* Benefits, State Pension for people aged 80 and over).

Graduated Retirement Benefit

Graduated Retirement Benefit (GRB) is based on the amount of graduated NI contributions paid into the GRB scheme between April 1961 and April 1975 (*see also* Benefits, Graduated Retirement Benefit).

Home Responsibilities Protection

It is possible for people who have a low income or are unable to work because they care for children or a sick or disabled person at home to reduce the number of qualifying years required for basic state pension. This is called home responsibilities protection (HRP) and can be given for any tax year since April 1978; the number of years for which HRP is given is deducted from the number of qualifying years needed. HRP may, in some cases, also qualify the recipient for additional state pension. Since April 2003, HRP has also been available to approved foster carers.

From 6 April 2010 HRP will be replaced by weekly credits for parents and carers. A class 3 NI credit will be given, where required, towards basic state pension and bereavement benefits for spouses and civil partners. An earnings factor credit towards additional state pension will also be awarded. Any years of HRP acquired before 6 April 2010 will be converted to qualifying years of credits for people reaching state pension age after that date, up to a maximum of 22 years for basic state pension purposes.

Additional State Pension

The amount of additional state pension paid depends on the amount of earnings a person has, or is treated as having, between the lower and upper earnings limits (from April 2009, the upper accruals point replaced the upper earnings limit for additional pension) for each complete tax year between 6 April 1978 (when the scheme started) and the tax year before they reach state pension age. The right to additional state pension does not depend on the person's right to basic state pension.

From 1978 to 2002, additional state pension was called the State Earnings-Related Pension Scheme (SERPS). SERPS covered all earnings by employees from 6 April 1978 to 5 April 1997 on which standard rate class 1 NI contributions had been paid, and earnings between 6 April 1997 and 5 April 2002 if the standard rate class 1 NI contributions had been contracted-in.

In 2002, SERPS was reformed through the state second pension, by improving the pension available to low and moderate earners and extending access to certain carers and people with long-term illness or disability. If earnings on which class 1 NI contributions have been paid or can be treated as paid are above the annual NI lower earnings limit (£4,940 for 2009–10) but below the statutory low earnings threshold (£13,900 for 2009–10), the state second pension regards this as earnings of £13,900 and it is treated as equivalent. Certain carers and people with long-term illness and disability will be considered as having earned at the low earnings threshold for each complete tax year since 2002–3 even if they do not work at all, or earn less than the annual NI lower earnings limit.

The amount of additional state pension paid also depends on when a person reaches state pension age; changes phased in from 6 April 1999 mean that pensions are calculated differently from that date.

Inheritance

Men or women widowed before 6 October 2002 can inherit all of their late spouse's SERPS pension. From 6 October 2002, the maximum percentage of SERPS pension that a person can inherit from a late spouse or civil partner depends on their late spouse or civil partner's date of birth:

Maximum SERPS entitlement	*d.o.b (men)*	*d.o.b (women)*
100%	5/10/37 or earlier	5/10/42 or earlier
90%	6/10/37 to 5/10/39	6/10/42 to 5/10/44
80%	6/10/39 to 5/10/41	6/10/44 to 5/10/46
70%	6/10/41 to 5/10/43	6/10/46 to 5/10/48
60%	6/10/43 to 5/10/45	6/10/48 to 5/7/50
50%	6/10/45 or later	6/7/50 or later

The maximum state second pension a person can inherit from a late spouse or civil partner is 50 per cent.

Pension Forecasts

The Pension, Disability and Carers Service provides a state pension forecasting service. A state pension forecast provides an estimate of the current value of an individual's state pension, based on information currently held on their NI record, and an estimate of what it may be worth when they reach state pension age (T 0845-300 0168 W www.direct.gov.uk/pensions).

PRIVATE PENSION SCHEMES

Contracted-Out Appropriate Personal Pension Schemes (including Appropriate Stakeholder Pension Schemes)

Since July 1988 an employee has been able to start a personal pension which, if it meets certain conditions, can be used in place of the additional state pension. These pensions are known as appropriate personal pensions (APPs) and employees who use them in place of the additional state pension are said to be 'contracted-out' of the state scheme.

At the end of the tax year HM Revenue and Customs pays an age-related rebate on contracted-out employees NI contributions together with tax relief on the employee's share of the rebate directly into the scheme to be invested on behalf of the employee. These payments are known as 'minimum contributions'.

Age-related rebates are intended to provide benefits broadly equivalent to those given up in the additional state pension. At retirement, a contracted-out deduction will be made from additional state pension accrued from 6 April 1987 to 5 April 1997.

Contracted-Out Salary-Related (COSR) Scheme

- these schemes (also known as contracted-out defined benefit (DB) schemes) provide a pension related to earnings and the length of pensionable service
- any notional additional state pension built up from 6 April 1978 to 5 April 1997 will be reduced by the amount of guaranteed minimum pension (GMP) accrued during that period (the contracted-out deduction)
- from 6 April 1997 these schemes no longer provide a GMP. Instead, as a condition of contracting out they have to satisfy a reference scheme test to ensure that the benefits provided are at least as good as a prescribed standard
- when someone contracts out of the additional state pension through a COSR scheme, both the scheme member and the employer, pay a reduced rate of NI contributions (known as the contracted-out rebate) to compensate for the additional state pension given up

Contracted-Out Money Purchase (COMP) Scheme

- these schemes (also known as contracted-out defined contribution (DC) schemes) provide a pension based on the value of the fund at retirement, ie the money paid in, along with the investment return
- the part of the COMP fund derived from protected rights (rights made up mainly from the contracted-out rebate and its investment return) is intended to provide benefits broadly equivalent to those given up in the additional state pension

- a contracted-out deduction, which may be more or less than that part of the pension derived from the protected rights, will be made from any notional additional pension built up from 6 April 1988 to 5 April 1997
- as with a COSR scheme, when someone contracts out of the additional state pension through a COMP scheme, both the scheme member and the employer pay a reduced rate of NI contributions (the contracted-out rebate) to compensate for the state pension given up. In addition, at the end of each tax year, HM Revenue and Customs pays an additional age-related rebate direct to the scheme for investment on behalf of the employee

Contracted-Out Mixed Benefit (COMB) Scheme
A mixed benefit scheme is a single scheme with both a salary related section and a money purchase section. Scheme rules set out which section individual employees may join and the circumstances (if any), in which members may move between sections. Each section must satisfy the respective contracting-out conditions for COSR and COMP schemes.

For more information on contracted-out pension schemes *see* the Department for Work and Pensions' leaflet *Contracted-out Pensions* (PM7).

STAKEHOLDER PENSION SCHEMES

Introduced in 2001, stakeholder pensions are available to everyone but are principally for moderate earners who do not have access to a good value company pension scheme. Stakeholder pensions must meet a number of minimum standards to make sure they are flexible, portable and annual management charges are capped. The minimum contribution is £20.

As with personal pensions it is possible to invest up to £3,600 (including tax relief) into stakeholder pensions each year without evidence of earnings. Contributions can be made on someone else's behalf, for example, a non-working partner.

Stakeholder pensions can also be used by employees to contract out of the additional state pension. For more information *see* Contracted-Out Appropriate Personal Pension Schemes (including Appropriate Stakeholder Pension Schemes).

COMPLAINTS

The Pensions Advisory Service provides information and guidance to members of the public, on state, company, personal and stakeholder schemes. They also help any member of the public who has a problem, complaint or dispute with their occupational or personal pensions.

There are two bodies for pension complaints. The Financial Ombudsman Service deals with complaints which predominantly concern the sale and/or marketing of occupational, stakeholder and personal pensions. The Pensions Ombudsman deals with complaints which predominantly concern the management (after sale or marketing) of occupational, stakeholder and personal pensions.

The Pensions Regulator is the UK regulator for work-based pension schemes; it concentrates its resources on schemes where there is the greatest risk to the security of members' benefits, promotes good administration practice for all work-based schemes and works with trustees, employers and professional advisers to put things right when necessary.

WAR PENSIONS AND THE ARMED FORCES COMPENSATION SCHEME

The Service Personnel and Veterans Agency (SPVA) is an executive agency of the Ministry of Defence. SPVA was formed on 1 April 2007 from the former Armed Services Personnel Administration Agency and the Veterans Agency to provide services to both serving personnel and veterans.

SPVA is responsible for the administration of the war pensions scheme and the armed forces compensation scheme (AFCS) to members of the armed forces in respect of disablement or death due to service. There is also a scheme for civilians and civil defence workers in respect of the Second World War, and other schemes for groups such as merchant seamen and Polish armed forces who served under British command during the Second World War. The agency is also responsible for the administration of the armed forces pension scheme, which provides occupational pensions for ex-service personnel (*see* Defence).

THE WAR PENSIONS SCHEME

War disablement pension is awarded for the disabling effects of any injury, wound or disease which was the result of, or was aggravated by, conditions of service in the armed forces prior to 6 April 2005. Claims are only considered once the person has left the armed forces. The amount of pension paid depends on the severity of disablement, which is assessed by comparing the health of the claimant with that of a healthy person of the same age and sex. The person's earning capacity or occupation are not taken into account in this assessment. A pension is awarded if the person has a disablement of 20 per cent or more and a lump sum is usually payable to those with a disablement of less than 20 per cent. No award is made for noise-induced sensorineural hearing loss where the assessment of disablement is less than 20 per cent.

A pension is payable to war widows, widowers and surviving civil partners where the spouse's or civil partner's death was due to, or hastened by, service in the armed forces, prior to 6 April 2005, or where the spouse or civil partner was in receipt of a war disablement pension constant attendance allowance (or would have been if not in hospital) at the time of death. A pension is also payable to widows, widowers or surviving civil partners if the spouse or civil partner was receiving the war disablement pension at the 80 per cent rate or higher in conjunction with unemployability supplement at the time of death. War widows, widowers and surviving civil partners receive a standard rank-related rate, but a lower weekly rate is payable to war widows, widowers and surviving civil partners of personnel of the rank of Major or below who are under the age of 40, without children and capable of maintaining themselves. This is increased to the standard rate at age 40. Allowances are paid for children (in addition to child benefit) and adult dependants. An age allowance is automatically given when the widow, widower or surviving civil partner reaches 65 and increased at ages 70 and 80.

Pensioners living overseas receive the same pension rates as those living in the UK. All war disablement pensions and allowances and pensions for war widows, widowers and surviving civil partners are tax-free in the UK; this does not always apply in overseas countries due to different tax laws.

SUPPLEMENTARY ALLOWANCES
A number of supplementary allowances may be awarded to a war pensioner which are intended to meet various needs which may result from disablement or death and take account of its particular effect on the pensioner, pensioner's spouse or civil partner. The principal supplementary allowances are unemployability supplement, allowance for lowered standard of occupation and constant attendance allowance. Others include exceptionally severe disablement allowance, severe disablement occupational allowance, treatment allowance, mobility supplement, comforts allowance, clothing allowance, age allowance and widow/widower/surviving civil partner's age allowance. Rent and children's allowances are also available on pensions for war widows, widowers and surviving civil partners.

ARMED FORCES COMPENSATION SCHEME
The armed forces compensation scheme (AFCS) became effective on 6 April 2005 and covers all regular (including Gurkhas) and reserve personnel whose injury, ill health or death is caused by service on or after 6 April 2005. Ex-members of the armed forces who served prior to this date or who are in receipt of any pension under the war pensions scheme will continue to receive their pension and any associated benefits in the normal way. The new scheme affects only those who served after 6 April 2005.

The AFCS provides compensation where service in the armed forces is the only or main cause of injury, illness or death. Compensation can also be paid in certain exceptional circumstances to off-duty personnel, for example, to victims of a terrorist attack targeted due to their position in the armed forces. Under the terms of the scheme a lump sum is payable to service or ex-service personnel based on a 15-level tariff, graduated according to the seriousness of the condition. A guaranteed income payment (GIP), payable for life, is received by those who could be expected to experience a serious loss of earning capability. A GIP will also be paid to surviving spouses, civil partners and unmarried partners who meet certain criteria. GIP is calculated by multiplying the pensionable pay of the service person by a factor which depends on the age of the person's last birthday. The younger the person, the higher the factor, because there are more years to normal retirement age.

DEPARTMENT FOR WORK AND PENSIONS BENEFITS
Most benefits are paid in addition to those in receipt of payments under the AFCS and the war pensions scheme, but may be affected by any supplementary allowances in payment. Any state pension for which a war widow, widower or surviving civil partner qualifies for on their own NI contribution record can be paid in addition to monies received under the war pensions scheme.

CLAIMS AND QUESTIONS
Further information on the war pensions scheme, the armed forces compensation scheme and the nearest War Pensioners' Welfare Office can be obtained from the Service Personnel and Veterans Agency by telephone (T 0800-169 2277, if calling from the UK or, if living overseas, T (+44) (125) 386-6043).

SERVICE PERSONNEL AND VETERANS AGENCY,
Norcross, Blackpool FY5 3WP
E veterans.help@spva.gsi.gov.uk W www.veterans-uk.info

TAX CREDITS

Tax credits are administered by HM Revenue and Customs (HMRC) and are awarded for up to 12 months, although they can be adjusted during the year to reflect changes in income or circumstances. Further information regarding the qualifying conditions for tax credits, how to claim and the rates payable is available online on the HMRC website (W www.hmrc.gov.uk/taxcredits).

WORKING TAX CREDIT

Working tax credit is a payment from the government to support people on low incomes. It may be claimed by those aged 25 or over who work at least 30 hours a week; those aged 50 or over who are returning to work after a period on benefits of at least six months; and those aged 16 or over who work at least 16 hours a week and are responsible for a child or young person or have a disability that puts them at a disadvantage of getting a job.

The system makes assumptions based on the national minimum wage and the number of hours worked per week. An annual income of £8,994 represents the 2009–10 income of an adult working 30 hours a week at the national minimum wage: six months at the 2008–9 rate of £5.73 per hour and six months at the rate of £5.80 per hour (national minimum wage from October 2009).

WORKING TAX CREDIT 2009–10

Annual Income/Status	*Tax Credit per annum*
£5,000*	
Single	–
Couple	–
Single adult with a disability	£4,420
£8,994†	
Single	£1,660
Couple	£3,525
Single adult with a disability	£4,195
£10,000	
Single	£1,270
Couple	£3,130
Single adult with a disability	£3,805
£15,000	
Single	–
Couple	£1,180
Single adult with a disability	£1,855

* Those with incomes of £5,000 a year are assumed to work part-time (working between 16 and 30 hours a week)

† Income of £8,994 represents the income of an adult working 30 hours per week at the national minimum wage rate (*see* above for explanation). In families with an income of £8,994 a year or more, at least one adult is assumed to be working 30 or more hours a week

CHILDCARE

In families with children where a lone parent or both partners in a couple work for at least 16 hours a week, or where one partner works and the other is disabled, the family is entitled to the childcare element of working tax credit. This payment can contribute up to 80 per cent of childcare costs up to a maximum of £175 a week for one child and up to £300 a week for two or more children. Families can only claim if they use an approved or registered childcare provider.

CHILD TAX CREDIT

Child tax credit combines all income-related support for children and is paid direct to the main carer. The credit is made up of a main 'family' payment with additional payments for each extra child in the household, for children with a disability and an extra payment for children who are severely disabled. Child tax credit is available to households where:

- there is at least one dependant under 16
- there is at least one dependant under 20 who is in relevant education or training or is registered for work, education or training with an approved body

CHILD TAX CREDIT AND WORKING TAX CREDIT 2009–10 *(£ per year)*

	One Child		Two Children	
Annual Income	*No Childcare*	*Maximum Childcare*	*No Childcare*	*Maximum Childcare*
0	2,780	2,780	5,020	5,020
5,000*	6,535	13,835	8,770	21,285
8,994*	6,310	13,610	8,545	21,060
10,000†	5,915	12,215	8,155	20,670
15,000	3,965	11,265	6,205	18,720
20,000	2,015	9,315	4,255	16,770
25,000	545	7,365	2,305	14,820
30,000	545	5,415	545	12,870
35,000	545	3,465	545	10,920
40,000	545	1,515	545	8,970
45,000	545	545	545	7,020
50,000	545	545	545	5,070
60,000	–	–	–	1.170
65,000	–	–	–	320
70,000	–	–	–	–

* At income levels of £5,000 and £8,994 awards are shown for lone parents. At an income level of £5,000 the award is shown for a lone parent working part-time (between 16 and 30 hours a week). At an income level of £8,994 the award is shown for a lone parent working 30 hours a week

† At an income level of £10,000 awards are shown for two parents working part-time (between 16 and 30 hours per week)

BENEFITS

The following is intended as a general guide to the benefits system. Conditions of entitlement and benefit rates change annually and all prospective claimants should check exact entitlements and rates of benefit directly with their local Jobcentre Plus office, pension centre or online (W www.direct.gov.uk). Leaflets relating to the various benefits and contribution conditions for different benefits are available from local Jobcentre Plus offices.

CONTRIBUTORY BENEFITS

Entitlement to contributory benefits depends on national insurance contribution conditions being satisfied either by the claimant or by someone on the claimant's behalf (depending on the kind of benefit). The class or classes of national insurance contribution relevant to each benefit are:

Jobseeker's allowance (contribution-based)	Class 1
Incapacity benefit	Class 1 or 2
Employment and Support Allowance (contributory)	Class 1 or 2
Widow's benefit and bereavement benefit	Class 1, 2 or 3
State pensions, categories A and B	Class 1, 2 or 3

The system of contribution conditions relates to yearly levels of earnings on which national insurance (NI) contributions have been paid.

JOBSEEKER'S ALLOWANCE

Jobseeker's allowance (JSA) replaced unemployment benefit and income support for unemployed people under state pension age from 7 October 1996. There are two routes of entitlement. Contribution-based JSA is paid at a personal rate (ie additional benefit for dependants is not paid) to those who have made sufficient NI contributions in two particular tax years. Savings and partner's earnings are not taken into account and payment can be made for up to six months. Rates of JSA correspond to income support rates.

Claims are made through Jobcentre Plus. A person wishing to claim JSA must generally be unemployed or working on average less than 16 hours a week, capable of work and available for any work which he or she can reasonably be expected to do, usually for at least 40 hours per week. The claimant must agree and sign a 'jobseeker's agreement', which will set out his or her plans to find work, and must actively seek work. If the claimant refuses work or training the benefit may be sanctioned for between one and 26 weeks.

A person will be sanctioned from JSA for up to 26 weeks if he or she has left a job voluntarily without just cause or through misconduct. In these circumstances, it may be possible to receive hardship payments, particularly where the claimant or the claimant's family is vulnerable, eg if sick or pregnant, or with children or caring responsibilities.

Weekly Rates from April 2009

Person aged 16–24	£50.95
Person aged 25 to state pension age*	£64.30

* Since October 2003 people aged between 60 and state pension age can choose to claim pension credits instead of JSA

INCAPACITY BENEFIT

Employment and support allowance replaced incapacity benefit for new claimants from 27 October 2008. Those claiming incapacity benefit prior to this date will continue to receive it for as long as they qualify, although it is intended that remaining recipients of incapacity benefit will be moved to employment and support allowance by 2013. There are three rates of incapacity benefit:

- short-term lower rate for the first 28 weeks of sickness
- short-term higher rate from weeks 29 to 52
- long-term rate from week 53 onwards

The terminally ill and those entitled to the highest rate care component of disability living allowance are paid the long-term rate after 28 weeks. Incapacity benefit is taxable after 28 weeks.

An age addition payment may be available where incapacity for work commenced before the age of 45. Increases are also available for adult dependants caring for children.

The 'personal capability' assessment is the main test for incapacity benefit claims. Claimants are assessed on their ability to carry out a range of work-related activities and may also be required to attend a medical examination. Incapacity benefit claimants (excluding people who are severely disabled and those who are terminally ill) are invited back for work-focused interviews at intervals of not longer than three years. The interviews do not include medical tests, but if the claimant is due for a medical test around the same time, their local office will aim to schedule both together.

Weekly Rates from April 2009

Short-term incapacity benefit lower rate	
Person under state pension age	£67.75
Person over state pension age	£86.20
Short term incapacity benefit higher rate	
Person under state pension age	£80.15
Person over state pension age	£89.80
Long-term incapacity benefit	
Person under state pension age	£89.80
Person over state pension age	–

EMPLOYMENT AND SUPPORT ALLOWANCE

From 27 October 2008, employment and support allowance (ESA) replaced incapacity benefit and income support paid on the grounds of incapacity or disability. The benefit consists of two strands, contribution-based benefit and income-related benefit, so that people no longer need to make two claims for benefit in order to gain their full entitlement. Contributory ESA is available to those who have limited capability for work but cannot get statutory sick pay from their employer. Those over pensionable age are not entitled to ESA. Apart from those who qualify under the special provisions for people incapacitated in youth, entitlement to contributory ESA is based on a person's NI contribution record. In order to qualify for contributory ESA, two contribution conditions, based on the last three years before the tax year in which benefit is claimed, must be satisfied. The amount of contributory ESA payable may be reduced where the person receives more than a specified amount of occupational or personal pension. Contributory ESA is paid only in respect of the person claiming the benefit – there are no additional amounts for dependants.

At the outset, new claimants are paid a basic allowance (the same rate as jobseeker's allowance) for 13 weeks while their medical condition is assessed and a work capability assessment is conducted. Following the completion of the assessment phase those claimants capable of engaging in work-related activities will receive a work-related activity component on top of the basic rate. The work-related activity component can be subject to sanctions if the claimant does not engage in the conditionality requirements without good reason. The maximum sanction is equal to the value of the work-related activity component of the benefit.

Those with the most severe health conditions or disabilities will receive the support component, which is more than the work-related activity component. Claimants in receipt of the support component are not required to engage in work-related activities, although they can volunteer to do so or undertake permitted work if their condition allows.

Weekly Rates from April 2009

ESA plus work-related activity component	up to £89.80
ESA plus support component	up to £95.15

BEREAVEMENT BENEFITS

Bereavement benefits replaced widow's benefit on 9 April 2001. Those claiming widow's benefit before this date will continue to receive it under the old scheme for as long as they qualify. The new system provides bereavement benefits for widows, widowers and, from 5 December 2005, surviving civil partners (providing that their deceased spouse or civil partner paid NI contributions). The new system offers benefits in three forms:

- *Bereavement payment* – may be received by a man or woman who is under the state pension age at the time of their spouse or civil partner's death, or whose husband, wife or civil partner was not entitled to a category A retirement pension when he or she died. It is a single tax-free lump sum of £2,000 payable immediately on widowhood or loss of a civil partner
- *Widowed parent's allowance* – a taxable benefit payable to the surviving partner if he or she is entitled or treated as entitled to child benefit, or to a widow if she is expecting her husband's baby at the time of his death
- *Bereavement allowance* – a taxable weekly benefit paid for 52 weeks after the spouse or civil partner's death. If aged over 55 and under state pension age the full allowance is payable, if aged between 45 and 54 a percentage of the full rate is paid. A widow, widower or surviving civil partner may receive this allowance if his or her widowed parent's allowance ends before 52 weeks.

It is not possible to receive widowed parent's allowance and bereavement allowance at the same time. Bereavement benefits and widow's benefit, in any form, cease upon remarriage or a new civil partnership or are suspended during a period of cohabitation as partners without being legally married or in a civil partnership.

Weekly Rates from April 2009

Bereavement payment (lump sum)	£2,000
Widowed parent's allowance (or widowed mother's allowance)	£95.25
Bereavement allowance (or widow's pension), full entitlement (aged 55 and over at time of spouse's or civil partner's death)	£95.25

Amount of bereavement allowance (or widow's pension) by age of widow/widower or surviving civil partner at spouse's or civil partner's death:

aged 54	£88.58
aged 53	£81.92
aged 52	£75.25
aged 51	£68.58
aged 50	£61.91
aged 49	£55.25
aged 48	£48.58
aged 47	£41.91
aged 46	£35.24
aged 45	£28.58

STATE PENSION: CATEGORIES A AND B

Category A pension is payable for life to men and women who reach state pension age, who satisfy the contributions conditions and who claim for it. Category B pension is payable for life to married women, widows, widowers and surviving civil partners and is based on their wife, husband or civil partner's contributions. It is payable to a married woman only when both the wife and husband have both reached state pension age and claimed their state pension (from 6 April 2010 it will no longer be a condition that the husband has actually claimed his state pension). From 6 April 2010 a married man and civil partner will be able to qualify for a category B pension from their wife's or civil partner's contributions providing the wife or civil partner were born on or after 6 April 1950. Category B pension is also payable to widows, widowers and surviving civil partners who are bereaved before state pension age if they were previously entitled to widowed parent's allowance or bereavement allowance based on their late spouse's or civil partner's NI contributions. Widows who are bereaved when over state pension age can qualify for a category B pension regardless of the age of their husband when he died, although at present, it is only paid to widowers and civil partners bereaved over state pension age if their wife or civil partner had reached state pension age when they died. Widowers or surviving civil partners who reach state pension age on or after 6 April 2010 will be able to get a category B pension on the same terms as widows.

Where a person is entitled to both a category A and category B pension then they can be combined to give a composite pension, but this cannot be more than the full rate pension. Where a person is entitled to more than one category A or category B pension then only one can be paid. In such cases the person can choose which to get; if no choice is made, the most favourable one is paid.

A person may defer claiming their pension beyond state pension age. In doing so they may earn increments which will increase the weekly amount paid by one per cent per five weeks of deferral (equivalent to 10.4 per cent/year) when they claim their state pension. If a person delays claiming for at least 12 months they are given the option of a one-off taxable lump sum, instead of a pension increase, based on the weekly pension deferred, plus interest of at least 2 per cent above the Bank of England base rate. If a married man defers his category A pension, his wife cannot claim a category B pension on his contributions but she may earn increments on her state pension during this time. A woman can defer her category B pension, and earn increments, even if her husband is claiming his category A pension.

An increase is paid for an adult dependant, providing the dependant's earnings do not exceed £64.30 and the couple are living together. If the couple are not living together an increase is payable if the dependant's earnings are not above £57.05. Provision for children is made through child tax credits. An age addition of 25p per week is payable with a state pension if a pensioner is aged 80 or over.

Since 1989 pensioners have been allowed to have unlimited earnings without affecting their state pension. *See also* Pensions.

Weekly Rates from April 2009	
Category A or B pension for a single person	£23.81–£95.25
Maximum category B pension (married women)	£57.05
Increase for adult dependant	£57.05
Age addition at age 80	£0.25

GRADUATED RETIREMENT BENEFIT

Graduated retirement benefit (GRB) is based on the amount of graduated NI contributions paid into the GRB scheme between April 1961 and April 1975, however, it is still paid in addition to any state pension to those who made the relevant contributions. A person will receive graduated retirement benefit based on their own contributions, even if not entitled to a basic state pension. Widows, widowers and surviving civil partners may inherit half of their deceased spouse's or civil partner's entitlement, but none that the deceased spouse or civil partner may have been eligible for from a former spouse or civil partner. If a person defers making a claim beyond state pension age, they may earn an increase or a one-off lump sum payment in respect of their deferred graduated retirement benefit; calculated in the same way as for category A or B state pension.

NON-CONTRIBUTORY BENEFITS

These benefits are paid from general taxation and are not dependent on NI contributions.

JOBSEEKER'S ALLOWANCE (INCOME-BASED)

Those who do not qualify for contribution-based jobseeker's allowance (JSA(c)), those who have exhausted their entitlement to contribution-based JSA or those for whom contribution-based JSA provides insufficient income may qualify for income-based JSA. The amount paid depends on age, whether they are single or a couple, number of dependants and amount of income and savings. Income-based JSA comprises three parts:

- a personal allowance for the jobseeker and his/her partner*
- premiums for people with special needs
- amounts for housing costs

* Since April 2003, child dependants have been provided for through the child tax credit system

The rules of entitlement are the same as for contribution-based JSA.

If one person in a couple was born after 28 October 1957 and neither person in the couple has responsibility for a child or children, then the couple will have to make a joint claim for JSA if they wish to receive income-based JSA.

Weekly Rates from April 2009	
Person aged 16–24	£50.95
Person aged 25 to state pension age	£64.30
Couple with one or both under 18*	£50.95–£76.90
Couple aged 18 to state pension age	£100.95
Lone parents aged under 18	£50.95
Lone parents aged 18 to state pension age	£64.30

* depending on circumstances

MATERNITY ALLOWANCE

Maternity allowance (MA) is a benefit available for pregnant women who cannot get statutory maternity pay (SMP) from their employer or have been employed/self-employed during or close to their pregnancy. In order to qualify for payment, a woman must have been employed and/or self-employed for at least 26 weeks in the 66 week period up to and including the week before the baby is due (test period). These weeks do not have to be in a row and any part weeks worked will count towards the 26 weeks. She must also have average weekly earning of at least £30 (maternity allowance threshold) over any 13 weeks of the woman's choice within the test period.

Self-employed women who pay class 2 NI contributions or who hold a small earnings exception certificate are deemed to have enough earnings to qualify for MA.

A woman can choose to start receiving MA from the 11th week before the week in which the baby is due (if she stops work before then) up to the day following the day of birth. The exact date MA starts will depend on when the woman stops work to have her baby or if the baby is born before she stops work. However, where the woman is absent from work wholly or partly due to her pregnancy in the four weeks before the week the baby is due to be born, MA will start the day following the first day of absence from work. MA is paid for a maximum of 39 weeks.

The woman may be entitled to get extra payments for her husband, civil partner or someone else who looks after her children.

Weekly Rate from April 2009	
Standard rate	£123.06 or 90 per cent of the woman's average weekly earnings if less than £123.06

CHILD BENEFIT

Child benefit is payable for virtually all children aged under 16 and for those aged 16 and 17 if they are in relevant education or training or are registered for work, education or training with an approved body.

Weekly Rates from April 2009	
Eldest/only child	£20.00
Each subsequent child	£13.20

GUARDIAN'S ALLOWANCE

Guardian's allowance is payable to a person who is bringing up a child or young person because the child's parents have died, or in some circumstances, where only one parent has died. To receive the allowance the person must be in receipt of child benefit for the child or young person, although they do not have to be the child's legal guardian.

Weekly Rate from April 2009	
Each child	£14.10

HEALTH IN PREGNANCY GRANT

A one-off payment of £190 for each pregnancy to all women who meet the residency requirements, irrespective of income, from the 25th week of pregnancy. The grant has to be claimed from HM Revenue and Customs following authorisation by a doctor or midwife.

CARER'S ALLOWANCE

Carer's allowance (CA) is a benefit payable to people who spend at least 35 hours per week caring for a severely disabled person. To qualify for CA a person must be caring for someone in receipt of one of the following benefits:

- attendance allowance
- disability living allowance care component at the middle or highest rate
- constant attendance allowance, paid at not less than the normal maximum rate or basic (full-day) rate, under the industrial injuries or war pension schemes.

Weekly Rate from April 2009	
Carer's allowance	£53.10

SEVERE DISABLEMENT ALLOWANCE

Since April 2001 severe disablement allowance (SDA) has not been available to new claimants. Those claiming SDA before that date will continue to receive it for as long as they qualify.

Weekly Rates from April 2009	
Basic rate	£57.45
Age related addition*:	
Under 40	£15.65
40–49	£9.10
50–59	£5.35

* The age addition applies to the age when incapacity began

ATTENDANCE ALLOWANCE

This may be payable to people aged 65 or over who need help with personal care because they are physically or mentally disabled, and who have needed help for a period of at least six months. Attendance allowance has two rates: the lower rate is for day or night care, and the higher rate is for day and night care. People not expected to live for more than six months because of a progressive disease can receive the highest rate of attendance allowance straight away.

Weekly Rates from April 2009	
Higher rate	£70.35
Lower rate	£47.10

DISABILITY LIVING ALLOWANCE

This may be payable to people aged under 65 who have had personal care and/or mobility needs because of an illness or disability for a period of at least three months and are likely to have those needs for a further six months or more. The allowance has two components: the care component, which has three rates, and the mobility component, which has two rates. The rates depend on the care and mobility needs of the claimant. People not expected to live for more than six months because of a progressive disease will automatically receive the highest rate of the care component.

Weekly Rates from April 2009	
Care component	
Higher rate	£70.35
Middle rate	£47.10
Lowest rate	£18.65
Mobility component	
Higher rate	£49.10
Lower rate	£18.65

STATE PENSION FOR PEOPLE AGED 80 AND OVER

A state pension, also referred to as category D pension, is provided for people aged 80 and over if they are not entitled to another category of pension or are entitled to a state pension that is less than £57.05 a week. The person must also live in Great Britain and have done so for a period of ten years or more in any continuous 20-year period since their 60th birthday.

Weekly Rate from April 2009	
Single person	£57.05

INCOME SUPPORT

Broadly speaking income support is a benefit for those aged 16 and over whose income is below a certain level, work on average less than 16 hours a week and who are:

- bringing up children alone
- registered sick or disabled
- a student who is also a lone parent or disabled
- caring for someone who is sick or elderly

Pension credit replaced income support for people aged 60 or over on 6 October 2003.

Income support is not payable if the claimant, or claimant and partner, have capital or savings in excess of £16,000 – and deductions are made for capital and savings in excess of £6,000. For people permanently in residential care and nursing homes deductions apply for capital in excess of £10,000.

Sums payable depend on fixed allowances laid down by law for people in different circumstances. If both partners are eligible for income support, either may claim it for the couple. People receiving income support may be able to receive housing benefit, help with mortgage or home loan interest and help with healthcare. They may also be eligible for help with exceptional expenses from the Social Fund. Special rates may apply to some people living in residential care or nursing homes.

INCOME SUPPORT PREMIUMS

Income support premiums are extra weekly payments for those with additional needs. People qualifying for more than one premium will normally only receive the highest single premium for which they qualify. However, family premium, disabled child premium, severe disability premium and carer premium are payable in addition to other premiums.

Child tax credit replaced premiums for people with children for all new income support claims from 6 April 2004. People with children who were already in receipt of income support in April 2004 and have not claimed child tax credit may qualify for:

- the family premium if they have at least one child
- the disabled child premium if they have a child who receives disability living allowance or is registered blind
- the enhanced disability child premium if they have a child in receipt of the higher rate disability living allowance care component

Carers may qualify for:

- the carer premium if they or their partner are in receipt of carer's allowance

Long-term sick or disabled people may qualify for:

- the disability premium if they or their partner are receiving certain benefits because they are disabled or cannot work; are registered blind; or if the claimant has

been incapable of work or receiving statutory sick pay for at least 364 days (196 days if the person is terminally ill), including periods of incapacity separated by eight weeks or less
- the severe disability premium if the person lives alone and receives the middle or higher rate of disability living allowance care component and no one receives carer's allowance for caring for that person
- the enhanced disability premium if the person is in receipt of the higher rate disability living allowance care component

People with a partner aged over 60 may qualify for:
- the pensioner premium

WEEKLY RATES OF INCOME SUPPORT
from April 2009

Single person	
aged 16–24	£50.95
aged 25+	£64.30
aged under 18 and a single parent	£50.95
aged 18+ and a single parent	£64.30
Couples	
Both under 18	£50.95
Both under 18, in certain circumstances	£76.90
One under 18, one aged 18-24	£50.95
One under 18, one aged 25+	£64.30
Both aged 18+	£100.95
Dependent children	£56.11
Premiums	
Family premium	£17.30
Disabled child premium	£51.24
Enhanced disability child premium	£20.65
Carer premium	£29.50
Disability premium	
Single person	£27.50
Couples	£39.15
Severe disability premium	£52.85
Enhanced disability premium	
Single person	£13.40
Couples	£19.30
Pensioner premium	£105.70

PENSION CREDIT

Pension credit was introduced on 6 October 2003 and replaced income support for those aged 60 and over.

There are two elements to pension credit:

THE GUARANTEE CREDIT

The guarantee credit guarantees a minimum income of £130.00 for single people and £198.45 for couples, with additional elements for people who have:
- eligible housing costs
- severe disabilities
- caring responsibilities

Income from state pension, private pensions, earnings, working tax credit and certain benefits are taken into account when calculating the guarantee credit. For savings and capital in excess of £6,000 (£10,000 for people living in residential care and nursing homes); £1 for every £500 or part of £500 held is taken into account as income when working out entitlement to pension credit.

People receiving the guarantee credit element of pension credit will be able to receive housing benefit, council tax benefit and help with healthcare costs.

Weekly Rates from April 2009

Additional amount for severe disability	
Single person	£52.85
Couple (one qualifies)	£52.85
Couple (both qualify)	£105.70
Additional amount for carers	£29.50

THE SAVINGS CREDIT

Single people aged 65 or over (and couples where one member is 65 or over) may be entitled to a savings credit which rewards pensioners who have made modest provision towards their retirement. The savings credit is calculated by taking into account any qualifying income above the savings credit threshold. For 2009–10 the threshold is £96.00 for single people and £153.40 for couples. The savings credit gives pensioners a cash addition calculated at 60p for every pound of qualifying income they have between the savings credit threshold and the guarantee credit. After this, the maximum reward will be reduced by 40p for every pound of income above the guarantee level. The maximum savings credit is £20.40 per week (£27.03 a week for couples).

Income that qualifies towards the savings credit includes state pensions, earnings, second pensions and capital above £6,000.

Some people will be entitled to the guarantee credit, some to the savings credit and some to both.

Where only the savings credit is in payment, people need to claim standard housing benefit or council tax benefit. Although local authorities take any savings credit into account in the housing benefit or council tax benefit assessment, for people aged 65 and over housing benefit or council tax benefit is enhanced to ensure that gains in pension credit are not depleted.

HOUSING BENEFIT

Housing benefit is designed to help people with rent (including rent for accommodation in guesthouses, lodgings or hostels). It does not cover mortgage payments. The amount of benefit paid depends on:
- the income of the claimant, and partner if there is one, including earned income, unearned income (any other income including some other benefits) and savings
- number of dependants
- certain extra needs of the claimant, partner or any dependants
- number and gross income of people sharing the home who are not dependent on the claimant
- how much rent is paid

Housing benefit is not payable if the claimant, or claimant and partner, have savings in excess of £16,000. The amount of benefit is affected if savings held exceed £6,000 (£10,000 for people living in residential care and nursing homes). Housing benefit is not paid for meals, fuel or certain service charges that may be included in the rent. Deductions are also made for most non-dependants who live in the same accommodation as the claimant (and their partner).

The maximum amount of benefit (which is not necessarily the same as the amount of rent paid) may be paid where the claimant is in receipt of income support, income-based jobseeker's allowance, the guarantee element of pension credit or where the claimant's income is less than the amount allowed for their needs. Any income over that allowed for their needs will mean that their benefit is reduced.

LOCAL HOUSING ALLOWANCE

Local housing allowance (LHA), which was rolled out nationally from 7 April 2008, is a new way of calculating the rent element of housing benefit based on the area in which a person lives and household size. It affects people in the deregulated private rented sector who make a new claim for housing benefit or existing recipients who move address. LHA ensures that tenants in similar circumstances in the same area receive the same amount of financial support for their housing costs. It does not affect the way a person's income or capital is taken into account. LHA is paid to the tenant rather than the landlord in most circumstances and tenants are able to keep any excess benefit up to a maximum of £15 per week that is over and above the cost of their rent. If their rent is higher than their LHA entitlement they must make up the difference from other sources of income.

COUNCIL TAX BENEFIT

Nearly all the rules which apply to housing benefit apply to council tax benefit, which helps people on low incomes to pay council tax bills. The amount payable depends on how much council tax is paid and who lives with the claimant. The benefit may be available to those receiving income support, income-based jobseeker's allowance, the guarantee element of pension credit or to those whose income is less than that allowed for their needs. Any income over that allowed for their needs will mean that their council tax benefit is reduced. Deductions are made for non-dependants.

The maximum amount that is payable for those living in properties in council tax bands A to E is 100 per cent of the claimant's council tax liability. This also applies to those living in properties in bands F to H who were in receipt of the benefit at 31 March 1998 if they have remained in the same property.

If a person shares a home with one or more adults (not their partner) who are on a low income, it may be possible to claim a second adult rebate. Those who are entitled to both council tax benefit and second adult rebate will be awarded whichever is the greater. Second adult rebate may be claimed by those not in receipt of or eligible for council tax benefit.

THE SOCIAL FUND

REGULATED PAYMENTS

Sure Start Maternity Grant

Sure start maternity grant (SSMG) is a one-off payment of £500 to help people on low incomes pay for essential items for new babies that are expected, born, adopted, the subject of a parental order (following a surrogate birth) or, in certain circumstances, the subject of a residency order. SSMG can be claimed any time from the 29th week of pregnancy up to three months after the birth, adoption or date of parental or residency order. Those eligible are people in receipt of income support, income-based jobseeker's allowance, pension credit, child tax credit at a rate higher than the family element or working tax credit where a disability or severe disability element is in payment.

Funeral Payments

Payable to help cover the necessary cost of burial or cremation, a new burial plot with an exclusive right of burial (where burial is chosen), certain other expenses, and up to £700 for any other funeral expenses, such as the funeral director's fees, the coffin or flowers. Those eligible are people receiving income support, income-based jobseeker's allowance, pension credit, child tax credit at a higher rate than the family element, working tax credit where a disability or severe disability element is in payment, council tax benefit or housing benefit who have good reason for taking responsibility for the funeral expenses. These payments are recoverable from any estate of the deceased.

Cold Weather Payments

A payment of £25.00 when the average temperature is recorded at or forecast to be 0°C or below over seven consecutive days in the qualifying person's area between 1 November 2009 and 1 March 2010. Payments are made to people on pension credit or child tax credit with a disability element, those on income support whose benefit includes a pensioner or disability premium, and those on income-based jobseeker's allowance or employment and support allowance who have a child who is disabled or under the age of five. Payments are made automatically and do not have to be repaid.

Winter Fuel Payments

For 2009–10 the winter fuel payment is up to £250 for households with someone aged 60–79 and up to £400 for households with someone aged 80 or over. The rate paid is based on the person's age and circumstances in the 'qualifying week' between 21 and 27 September 2009. The majority of eligible people are paid automatically before Christmas, although a few need to claim. Payments do not have to be repaid.

Christmas Bonus

The Christmas bonus is a one-off tax-free £10 payment made before Christmas to those people in receipt of a qualifying benefit in the qualifying week.

DISCRETIONARY PAYMENTS

Community Care Grants

These are intended to help people in receipt of income support, income-based jobseeker's allowance or employment and support allowance, pension credit, or payments on account of such benefits (or those likely to receive these benefits within the next six weeks because they are leaving residential or institutional accommodation) to live as independently as possible in the community; ease exceptional pressures on families; care for a prisoner or young offender released on temporary licence; help people set up home as part of a resettlement programme and/or assist with certain travelling expenses. They do not have to be repaid.

Budgeting Loans

These are interest-free loans to people who have been receiving income support, income-based jobseeker's allowance or employment and support allowance, pension credit or payments on account of such benefits for at least 26 weeks, for intermittent expenses that may be difficult to budget for.

Crisis Loans

These are interest-free loans to anyone aged 16 or over, whether receiving benefits or not, who is without resources in an emergency or due to a disaster, where there is no other means of preventing serious damage or serious risk to their or their family members' health or safety.

SAVINGS
Savings over £500 (£1,000 for people aged 60 or over) are taken into account for community care grants and savings of £1,000 (£2,000 for people aged 60 or over) are taken into account for budgeting loans. All savings are taken into account for crisis loans. Savings are not taken into account for sure start maternity grant, funeral payments, cold weather payments, winter fuel payments or the Christmas bonus.

INDUSTRIAL INJURIES AND DISABLEMENT BENEFITS

The Industrial Injuries Scheme, administered under the Social Security Contributions and Benefits Act 1992, provides a range of benefits designed to compensate for disablement resulting from an industrial accident (ie an accident arising out of and in the course of an earner's employment) or from a prescribed disease due to the nature of a person's employment. Those who are self-employed are not covered by this scheme.

INDUSTRIAL INJURIES DISABLEMENT BENEFIT
A person may be able to claim industrial injuries disablement benefit if they are ill or disabled due to an accident or incident that happened at work or in connection with work in England, Scotland or Wales. The amount of benefit awarded depends on the person's age and the degree of disability as assessed by a doctor.

The benefit is payable whether the person works or not and those who are incapable of work are entitled to draw other benefits, such as statutory sick pay or incapacity benefit, in addition to industrial injuries disablement benefit. It may also be possible to claim the following allowances:

- reduced earnings allowance for those who are unable to return to their regular work or work of the same standard and who had their accident (or whose disease started) before 1 October 1990. At state pension age this is converted to retirement allowance
- constant attendance allowance for those with a disablement of 100 per cent who need constant care. There are four rates of allowance depending on how much care the person needs
- exceptionally severe disablement allowance can be claimed in addition to constant care attendance allowance at one of the higher rates for those who need constant care permanently

Weekly Rates of Benefit from April 2009

Degree of disablement	*Aged 18+ or with dependants*	*Aged under 18 with no dependants*
100 per cent	£143.60	£88.05
90	£129.24	£79.25
80	£114.88	£70.44
70	£100.52	£61.64
60	£86.16	£52.83
50	£71.80	£44.03
40	£57.44	£35.22
30	£43.08	£26.42
20	£28.72	£17.61
Unemployability supplement		£88.75
Reduced earnings allowance (maximum)		£57.44
Retirement allowance (maximum)		£14.36
Constant attendance allowance (normal maximum rate)		£57.50
Exceptionally severe disablement allowance		£57.50

OTHER BENEFITS
People who are disabled because of an accident or disease that was the result of work that they did before 5 July 1948 are not entitled to industrial injuries disablement benefit. They may, however, be entitled to payment under the Workmen's Compensation Scheme or the Pneumoconiosis, Byssinosis and Miscellaneous Diseases Benefit Scheme. People who suffer from certain industrial diseases caused by dust, or their dependants, can make a claim for an additional payment under the Pneumoconiosis Act 1979 if they are unable to get damages from the employer who caused or contributed to the disease.

Diffuse Mesothelioma Payment
Since 1 October 2008 any person suffering from the asbestos-related disease, diffuse mesothelioma, who is unable to make a claim under the Pneumoconiosis Act 1979, have not received payment in respect of the disease from an employer, via a civil claim or elsewhere and are not entitled to compensation from a MoD scheme, can claim a one-off lump sum payment. The scheme covers people whose exposure to asbestos occurred in the UK and was not as a result of their work as an employee (ie they lived near a factory using asbestos). The amount paid depends on the age of the person when the disease was diagnosed, or the date of the claim if the diagnosis date is not known. From 1 October 2009 claims must be received within 12 months of the date of diagnosis. If the sufferer has died, their dependants may be able to claim, but must do so within 12 months of the date of death.

CLAIMS AND QUESTIONS

Entitlement to benefit and regulated Social Fund payments is determined by a decision maker on behalf of the Secretary of State for the Department for Work and Pensions. A claimant who is dissatisfied with that decision can ask for an explanation. He or she can dispute the decision by applying to have it revised or, in particular circumstances, superseded. The claimant can go to the Appeals Service where the case will be heard by an independent tribunal. There is a further right of appeal to a social security commissioner against the tribunal's decision but this is on a point of law only and leave to appeal must first be obtained.

Decisions on claims and applications for housing benefit and council tax benefit are made by local authorities. The explanation, dispute and appeals process is the same as for other benefits.

All decisions on applications to the discretionary Social Fund are made by Jobcentre Plus Social Fund decision makers. Applicants can ask for a review of the decision within 28 days of the date on the decision letter. The Social Fund review officer will review the case and there is a further right of review by an independent Social Fund inspector.

EMPLOYER PAYMENTS

STATUTORY MATERNITY PAY
Employers pay statutory maternity pay (SMP) to pregnant women who have been employed by them full or part-time continuously for at least 26 weeks into the 15th week before the week the baby is due, and whose earnings on average at least equal the lower earnings limit applied to NI contributions (£95 a week from April 2009). SMP can be paid for a maximum period of up to 39 weeks. If the qualifying conditions are met women will

receive a payment of 90 per cent of their average earnings for the first six weeks, followed by 33 weeks at £123.06 or 90 per cent of the woman's average weekly earnings if this is less than £123.06. SMP can be paid, at the earliest, 11 weeks before the week in which the baby is due, up to the day following the birth. Women can decide when they wish their maternity leave and pay to start and can work until the baby is born. However, where the woman is absent from work wholly or partly due to her pregnancy in the four weeks before the week the baby is due to be born, SMP will start the day following the first day of absence from work.

Employers are reimbursed for 92 per cent of the SMP they pay. Small employers with annual gross NI payments of £45,000 or less recover 100 per cent of the SMP paid out plus 4.5 per cent in compensation for the secondary NI contributions paid on SMP.

STATUTORY PATERNITY PAY

Employers pay statutory paternity pay (SPP) to employees who are taking leave when a child is born or placed for adoption. To qualify the employee must:

- have responsibility for the child's upbringing
- be the biological father of the child (or the child's adopter), or the spouse/civil partner/partner of the mother or adopter
- have been employed by the same employer for at least 26 weeks ending with the 15th week before the baby is due (or the week in which the adopter is notified of having been matched with a child)
- continue working for the employer up to the child's birth (or placement for adoption)
- have earnings on average at least equal to the lower earnings limit applied to NI contributions (£95 a week from April 2009)

Employees who meet these conditions receive payment of £123.06 or 90 per cent of the employee's average weekly earnings if this is less than £123.06. The employee can choose to be paid for one or two consecutive weeks. The earliest the SPP period can begin is the date of the child's birth or placement for adoption. The SPP period must be completed within eight weeks of that date. SPP is not payable for any week in which the employee works. Employers are reimbursed in the same way as for statutory maternity pay.

STATUTORY ADOPTION PAY

Employers pay statutory adoption pay (SAP) to employees taking adoption leave from their employers. To qualify for SAP the employee must:

- be newly matched with a child by an adoption agency
- have been employed by the same employer for at least 26 weeks ending the week in which they have been notified of being matched with a child
- have earnings at least equal to the lower earnings limit applied to NI contributions (£95 a week from April 2009)

Employees who meet these conditions receive payment of £123.06 or 90 per cent of their average weekly earnings if this is less than £123.06 for up to 39 weeks. The earliest SAP can be paid from is two weeks before the expected date of placement, the latest it can start is the date of the child's placement. Where a couple adopt a child, only one of them may receive SAP, the other may be able to receive statutory paternity pay (SPP) if they meet the eligibility criteria. Employers are reimbursed in the same way as for statutory maternity pay.

STATUTORY SICK PAY

Employers pay statutory sick pay (SSP) for up to a maximum of 28 weeks to any employee incapable of work for four or more consecutive days. Employees must have done some work under their contract of service and have average weekly earnings of at least £95 from April 2009. SSP is a daily payment and is usually paid for the days that an employee would normally work, these days are known a qualifying days. SSP is not paid for the first three qualifying days in a period of sickness. SSP is paid at £79.15 per week and is subject to PAYE and NI contributions. Employees who cannot obtain SSP may be able to claim incapacity benefit. Employers may be able to recover some SSP costs.

THE WATER INDUSTRY

Water services in England and Wales are provided by private companies. In Scotland there is a single authority, Scottish Water, which is answerable to the Scottish government, and in Northern Ireland all services are provided by Northern Ireland Water, a government-owned company. In the UK the water industry provides services to over 24 million properties and has an annual turnover of £8bn. It also manages assets that include over 1,400 water treatment and 9,300 wastewater treatment works, 60 impounding reservoirs, over 6,000 service reservoirs/water towers and over 800,000km of water mains and sewers.

ENGLAND AND WALES

The water industry supplies around 16 billion litres of water a day to domestic and commercial customers and collects and treats more than 10 billion litres of wastewater a day. In quality tests carried out in 2008, the water industry in England and Wales achieved 99.96 per cent compliance with the standards required by the European Drinking Water Directive. In England and Wales the Secretary of State for Environment, Food and Rural Affairs and the National Assembly for Wales have overall responsibility for water policy and oversee environmental standards for the water industry.

Water UK is the industry association that represents all UK water and wastewater service suppliers at national and European level and is funded directly by its members who are the service suppliers for England, Scotland, Wales and Northern Ireland; every member has a seat on the Water UK Council. The statutory consumer representative body for water services is the Consumer Council for Water.

CONSUMER COUNCIL FOR WATER, 1st Floor, Victoria Square House, Victoria Square, Birmingham B2 4AJ
T 0845-039 2837 **W** www.ccwater.org.uk

WATER UK, 1 Queen Anne's Gate, London SW1H 9BT
T 020-7344 1844 **W** www.water.org.uk
Chief Executive, Pamela Taylor

WATER SERVICE COMPANIES

(not a member of Water UK)*

*ALBION WATER LTD, 71 Clarence Road, Teddington, Middlesex TW11 0BN **T** 020-8943 4867
W www.albionwater.co.uk

ANGLIAN WATER SERVICES LTD, Customer Services, PO Box 770, Lincoln LN5 7WX **T** 0845-714 5145
W www.anglianwater.co.uk

BOURNEMOUTH & WEST HAMPSHIRE WATER PLC, George Jessel House, Francis Avenue, Bournemouth, Dorset BH11 8NX **T** 01202-590059
W www.bwhwater.co.uk

BRISTOL WATER PLC, PO Box 218, Bridgwater Road, Bristol BS99 7AU **T** 0117-966 5881
W www.bristolwater.co.uk

CAMBRIDGE WATER PLC, 90 Fulbourn Road, Cambridge CB1 9JN **T** 01223-706050 **W** www.cambridge-water.co.uk

*CHOLDERTON & DISTRICT WATER COMPANY, Estate Office, Cholderton, Salisbury, Wiltshire SP4 0DR
T 01980-629203
W www.choldertonwater.co.uk

DEE VALLEY WATER PLC, Packsaddle, Wrexham Road, Rhostyllen, Wrexham LL14 4EH **T** 01978-846946
W www.deevalleygroup.com

DWR CYMRU (WELSH WATER), Pentwyn Road, Nelson, Treharris, Mid Glamorgan CF46 6LY **T** 0800-052 0145
W www.dwrcymru.co.uk

ESSEX & SUFFOLK WATER PLC (subsidiary of Northumbrian Water Ltd), Hall Street, Chelmsford, Essex CM2 0HH **T** 0845-782 0999 **W** www.eswater.co.uk

NORTHUMBRIAN WATER LTD, Abbey Road, Pity Me, Durham DH1 5FJ **T** 0870-717 1100 **W** www.nwl.co.uk

PORTSMOUTH WATER LTD, PO Box 8, West Street, Havant, Hampshire PO9 1LG **T** 023-9249 9888
W www.portsmouthwater.co.uk

SEVERN TRENT LTD, 2297 Coventry Road, Birmingham B26 3PU **T** 0121-722 4000 **W** www.stwater.co.uk

SOUTH EAST WATER LTD, Rocfort Road, Snodland, Kent ME6 5AH **T** 01903-264444 **W** www.southeastwater.co.uk

SOUTH STAFFORDSHIRE WATER PLC, PO Box 63, Walsall WS2 7PJ **T** 0845-607 0456
W www.south-staffs-water.co.uk

SOUTH WEST WATER LTD, Peninsula House, Rydon Lane, Exeter EX2 7HR **T** 0800-169 1144
W www.southwestwater.co.uk

SOUTHERN WATER, Southern House, Yeoman Road, Worthing, W. Sussex BN13 3NX **T** 0845-278 0845
W www.southernwater.co.uk

SUTTON AND EAST SURREY WATER PLC, London Road, Redhill, Surrey RH1 1LJ **T** 01737-772000
W www.waterplc.com

THAMES WATER UTILITIES LTD, Clearwater Court, Vastern Road, Reading, Berks RG1 8DB **T** 0845-920 0800
W www.thameswater.co.uk

UNITED UTILITIES WATER PLC, Haweswater House, Lingley Mere Business Park, Lingley Green Avenue, Great Sankey, Warrington WA5 3LP **T** 01925-237000
W www.unitedutilities.com

VEOLIA WATER EAST LTD, Mill Hill, Manningtree, Essex CO11 2AZ **T** 0845-148 9288 **W** www.veoliawater.co.uk/east

VEOLIA WATER SOUTHEAST LTD, The Cherry Garden, Cherry Garden Lane, Folkestone, Kent CT19 4QB
T 0845-888 5888 **W** www.veoliawater.co.uk/southeast

VEOLIA WATER THREE VALLEYS (VEOLIA WATER CENTRAL LTD), Tamblin Way, Hatfield, Herts AL10 9EZ
T 0845-782 3333 **W** www.veoliawater.co.uk/central

WESSEX WATER SERVICES LTD, Claverton Down Road, Bath BA2 7WW **T** 01225-526000 **W** wessexwater.co.uk

YORKSHIRE WATER SERVICES LTD, PO Box 52, Bradford BD3 7YD **T** 0845-124 2424
W www.yorkshirewater.com

ISLAND WATER AUTHORITIES

(not members of Water UK)

COUNCIL OF THE ISLES OF SCILLY, Town Hall, St Mary's, Isles of Scilly TR21 0LW **T** 01720-422537
W www.scilly.gov.uk

ISLE OF MAN WATER AUTHORITY, Tromode Road, Douglas, Isle of Man IM2 5PA T 01624-695949 W www.gov.im/water

JERSEY WATER, PO Box 69, Mulcaster House, Westmount Road, St. Helier, Jersey JE4 9PN T 01534-707300 W www.jerseywater.je

STATES OF GUERNSEY WATER BOARD, PO Box 30, South Esplanade, St Peter Port, Guernsey GY1 3AS T 01481-724552 W www.gov.gg

REGULATORY BODIES

The Water Services Regulation Authority (OFWAT) was established under the Water Industry Act 1991 and is the independent economic regulator of the water and sewerage companies in England and Wales. Overall responsibility for water policy and overseeing environmental standards for the water industry lies with DEFRA and the Welsh Assembly. OFWAT's main duties are to ensure that the companies can finance and carry out their statutory functions and to protect the interests of water customers. OFWAT is a non-ministerial government department headed by a board following a change in legislation introduced by the Water Act 2003.

Under the Competition Act 1998, from 1 March 2000 the Competition Appeal Tribunal has heard appeals against the regulator's decisions regarding anti-competitive agreements and abuse of a dominant position in the marketplace. The Water Act 2003 placed a new duty on OFWAT to contribute to the achievement of sustainable development.

The Environment Agency has statutory duties and powers in relation to water resources, pollution control, flood defence, fisheries, recreation, conservation and navigation in England and Wales. They are also responsible for issuing permits, licences, consents and registrations such as industrial licences to extract water and fishing licences.

The Drinking Water Inspectorate (DWI) is the drinking water quality regulator for England and Wales, responsible for assessing the quality of the drinking water supplied by the water companies and investigating any incidents affecting drinking water quality, initiating prosecution where necessary. The DWI also provides scientific advice on drinking water policy issues to DEFRA and the Welsh Assembly.

OFWAT, Centre City Tower, 7 Hill Street, Birmingham B5 4UA T 0121-625 1300 E enquiries@ofwat.gsi.gov.uk W www.ofwat.gov.uk
Chairman, Philip Fletcher, CBE
Chief Executive, Regina Finn

METHODS OF CHARGING

In England and Wales, most domestic customers still pay for domestic water supply and sewerage services through charges based on the rateable value of their property. Overall, companies expect about 37 per cent of household customers in England and Wales to have metered supplies in 2009–10. Industrial and most commercial customers are charged according to consumption.

Under the Water Industry Act 1999, water companies can continue basing their charges on the old rateable value of the property. Domestic customers can continue paying on an unmeasured basis unless they choose to pay according to consumption. After having a meter installed (which is free of charge), a customer can revert to unmeasured charging within 12 months. Domestic, school and hospital customers cannot be disconnected for non-payment.

Price limits for the period 2005–10 were set by OFWAT in December 2004.

The average increase in prices for 2009–10 is 3.4 per cent, which includes inflation of 3 per cent. Average bills for water services range from £92 for Portsmouth Water to £206 for South West Water, with an overall average of £163. The average sewerage bill costs £180, ranging from £117 for Thames water up to £283 for South West Water.

WATER SUPPLY AND CONSUMPTION 2007–8

	Supply		*Consumption*			
	Distribution Input (megalitres/day)	*Total Leakage (megalitres/day)*	*Household (litres/head/day)*		*Non-household (litres/property/day)*	
			Unmetered	*Metered*	*Unmetered*	*Metered*
WATER AND SEWERAGE COMPANIES						
Anglian	1,164.8	210	158	142	595.1	2,799.7
Dwr Cymru	840.2	205	156	123	488.2	2,902.6
Northumbrian	1154.6	135	147	129	801.8	3,503.8
Severn Trent	1,883.3	490	141	115	852.1	2,100.8
South West	434.9	84	154	131	1,231.4	1,517.4
Southern	561.6	83	159	137	782.2	2,264.1
Thames	2,572.0	715	158	144	796.0	2951.9
United Utilities	1,849.4	460	144	116	737.6	2,809.2
Wessex	352.7	72	149	136	3,227.7	2,035.3
Yorkshire	1,279.5	295	150	133	132.0	2,621.9
Total	12,093.0	2,749	—	—	—	—
Average	—	—	151	131	819.8	2,520.8
WATER ONLY COMPANIES						
Total	2,661.8	474	—	—	—	—
Average	—	—	165	141	931.9	2,494.2

Source: OFWAT

SCOTLAND

Overall responsibility for national water policy in Scotland rests with the Scottish ministers. Until the Local Government (Scotland) Act 1994, water supply and sewerage services were local authority responsibilities. The Central Scotland Water Development Board had the function of developing new sources of water supply for the purpose of providing water in bulk to water authorities whose limits of supply were within the board's area. Under the act, three new public water authorities, covering the north, east and west of Scotland respectively, took over the provision of water and sewerage services from April 1996. The Central Scotland Water Development Board was then abolished. The act also established the Scottish Water and Sewerage Customers Council representing consumer interests. It monitored the performance of the authorities; approved charges schemes; investigated complaints; and advised the secretary of state. The Water Industry Act 1999, whose Scottish provisions were accepted by the Scottish government, abolished the Scottish Water and Sewerage Customers Council and replaced it in November 1999 with a Water Industry Commissioner.

The Water Industry (Scotland) Act 2002 resulted from the Scottish government's proposal that a single authority was better placed than three separate authorities to harmonise changes across the Scottish water industry. In 2002 the three existing water authorities (East of Scotland Water, North of Scotland Water and West of Scotland Water) merged to form Scottish Water. Scottish Water is a public sector company, structured and managed like a private company, but remains answerable to the Scottish parliament. Scottish Water is regulated by the Water Industry Commission for Scotland, the Scottish Environment Protection Agency (SEPA), and the Drinking Water Quality Regulator for Scotland. The Water Industry Commissioner is responsible for regulating all aspects of economic and customer service performance, including water and sewerage charges. SEPA is responsible for environmental issues, including controlling pollution and promoting the cleanliness of Scotland's rivers, lochs and coastal waters. Waterwatch Scotland is the consumer representative body for the water industry and the national complaints handling authority for water customers in Scotland.

METHODS OF CHARGING

Scottish Water sets charges for domestic and non-domestic water and sewerage provision through charges schemes which are regulated by the Water Industries Commissioner for Scotland. In February 2004 the harmonisation of all household charges across the country was completed following the merger of the separate authorities under Scottish Water. In June 2009 the Water Industry Commission for Scotland recommended that annual price rises should be kept at 1.5 per cent below the rate of inflation for the next four years. A final decison from Scottish Water and others on the proposal is expected in late 2009.

SCOTTISH ENVIRONMENT PROTECTION AGENCY, Erskine Court, Castle Business Park, Stirling FK9 4TR **T** 01786-457700 **W** www.sepa.org.uk

SCOTTISH WATER, PO Box 8855, Edinburgh EH10 6YQ **T** 0845-601 8855 **W** www.scottishwater.co.uk

WATER INDUSTRY COMMISSION FOR SCOTLAND, Ochil House, Springkerse Business Park, Stirling FK7 7XE **T** 01786-430200 **W** www.watercommission.co.uk

WATERWATCH SCOTLAND, Corporate Office, Forrester Lodge, Inglewood, Alloa FK10 2HU **T** 0845-850 3344 **W** www.waterwatchscotland.org

NORTHERN IRELAND

Formerly an executive agency of the Department for Regional Development, Northern Ireland Water is a government-owned company set up as a result of government reform of water and sewerage services in April 2007. It is responsible for policy and coordination with regard to the supply, distribution and cleanliness of water, and the provision and maintenance of sewerage services. The Northern Ireland Authority for Utility Regulation (NIAUR) is responsible for regulating the water services provided by Northern Ireland Water. The Drinking Water Inspectorate, a unit in the Northern Ireland Environment Agency (NIEA), regulates drinking water quality. Another NIEA unit, the Water Management Unit, has responsibility for the protection of the aquatic environment. The Consumer Council for Northern Ireland is the consumer representative body for water services.

METHODS OF CHARGING

The water and sewerage used by domestic customers in Northern Ireland is currently paid for by the Department for Regional Development, a system which will continue until at least March 2010, after which plans are due to be phased in for each household to pay a direct charge for water services delivered by Northern Ireland Water. Both water and sewerage charges are to have two parts, each consisting of a yearly standing charge of around £55 and a variable charge based on a capital value assessment of the property of the customer or on the amount of water consumed. Bills will be worked out according to the standard tariff (based on house value), reduced tariff (low-income households) or a metered tariff. Non-domestic customers in Northern Ireland became subject to water and sewerage charges and trade effluent charges where applicable in April 2008.

CONSUMER COUNCIL FOR NORTHERN IRELAND, 116 Holywood Road, Belfast BT4 1NY **T** 028-9067 2488 **W** www.consumercouncil.org.uk

NORTHERN IRELAND AUTHORITY FOR UTILITY REGULATION (NIAUR), Queens House, 14 Queen Street, Belfast BT1 6ER **T** 028-9031 1575 **W** www.niaur.gov.uk

NORTHERN IRELAND WATER, PO Box 126, Belfast BT1 9DJ **T** 0845-744 0088 **W** www.niwater.com

ENERGY

The main primary sources of energy in Britain are oil, natural gas, coal, nuclear power and water power. The main secondary sources (ie sources derived from the primary sources) are electricity, coke and smokeless fuels and petroleum products. The Department of Energy and Climate Change (DECC) is responsible for promoting energy efficiency.

INDIGENOUS PRODUCTION OF PRIMARY FUELS
Million tonnes of oil equivalent

	2007	*2008*
Coal	10.7	11.4
Primary oils	83.9	78.6
Natural gas	72.1	69.7
Primary electricity	14.9	13.0
Renewable and waste	4.4	4.4
Total	186.0	176.9

Source: Department of Energy and Climate Change

INLAND ENERGY CONSUMPTION BY PRIMARY FUEL
Million tonnes of oil equivalent, seasonally adjusted

	2007	*2008*
Coal	40.9	37.9
Petroleum	75.6	74.4
Natural gas	90.0	92.9
Nuclear electricity	14.0	11.9
Hydro electricity	0.9	1.1
Net Imports	0.4	0.9
Renewables and waste	4.7	5.3
Total	226.5	224.2

Source: Department of Energy and Climate Change

TRADE IN FUELS AND RELATED MATERIALS (2008)

	Quantity, million tonnes of oil equivalent	*Value £m*
Imports		
Coal and other solid fuel	30.1	3,661
Crude petroleum	57.0	20,538
Petroleum products	28.4	13,256
Natural gas	31.1	6,426
Electricity	1.0	483
Total	147.5	44,364
Exports		
Coal and other solid fuel	0.9	156
Crude petroleum	47.1	16,586
Petroleum products	38.7	14,727
Natural gas	9.8	1,945
Electricity	0.1	110
Total	96.6	33,525

Source: DECC/ONS

OIL

Until the 1960s Britain imported almost all its oil supplies. In 1969 oil was discovered in the Arbroath field in the North Sea. The first oilfield to be brought into production was Argyll in 1975, and since the mid-1970s Britain has been a major producer of crude oil.

Licences for exploration and production are granted to companies by the Department of Energy and Climate Change; the leading British oil companies are BP and Shell. At the end of 2004, 565 seaward production licences and 101 onshore petroleum exploration and development licences had been awarded, and there were a total of 314 offshore oil and gas fields in production. The UK has nine refineries at present producing approximately 82 million tonnes of oil products a year. To date, the UK has produced around 26 billion barrels of oil equivalent (boe). It is estimated that there is between 4 and 12 billion barrels remaining to be produced. Total UK oil production peaked in 1999 and is now declining. Profits from oil production are subject to a special tax regime with different taxes applying depending on the date of approval of each field.

DRILLING ACTIVITY (2008)
by number of wells started

	Offshore	*Onshore*
Exploration	44	9
Appraisal	61	11
Development	170	20

Source: Department of Energy and Climate Change

INDIGENOUS PRODUCTION AND REFINERY RECEIPTS
Thousand tonnes

	2007	*2008*
Indigenous production	76,575	71,665
Crude oil	70,357	65,497
NGLs*	6,218	6,168
Refinery receipts	75,707	75,844

* Natural Gas Liquids: condensates and petroleum gases derived at onshore treatment plants

Source: Department of Energy and Climate Change

DELIVERIES OF PETROLEUM PRODUCTS FOR INLAND CONSUMPTION BY ENERGY USE
Thousand tonnes

	2007	*2008*
Industry	6,218	5,807
Transport	53,541	51,924
Domestic	2,594	2,730
Other	1,376	1,305
Total	63,728	61,766

Source: Department of Energy and Climate Change

COAL

Mines were in private ownership until 1947 when they were nationalised and came under the management of the National Coal Board, later the British Coal Corporation. The corporation held a monopoly on coal production until 1994 when the industry was restructured. Under the Coal Industry Act 1994, the Coal Authority was established to take over ownership of coal reserves and to issue licences to private mining companies. The Coal Authority is also responsible for the physical legacy of mining, eg subsidence damage claims and publishes current data on the coal industry.

The mines owned by the British Coal Corporation were sold as five separate businesses in 1994 and coal production is now undertaken entirely in the private sector. Coal output was around 50 million tonnes a year in 1994 but has since declined to below 17 million tonnes. As at 31 March 2009 there were seven larger and ten small underground mines as well as 35 surface mines in the UK.

The main consumer of coal in the UK is the electricity supply industry. Coal still supplies a third of the UK's electricity needs but as indigenous production has declined, imports have risen to make up the shortfall and now represent around 66 per cent of feedstock, half of which is supplied from Russia.

Following the publication of an energy white paper in 2003 which recognised that a low-carbon economy required the development of cleaner coal technologies, a further energy white paper (published in May 2007) set out the government's international and domestic energy strategy to meet the long-term challenges posed by climate change to ensure secure, clean and affordable energy. Coal's availability, flexibility and reliability compared to other sources mean that it is expected to continue to play an important role in the future generating mix, but there is a need to tackle carbon emissions through the introduction of abatement technologies and, in the long term, the introduction of carbon capture and storage (CCS).

CCS attempts to mitigate the effects of global warming by capturing the carbon dioxide emissions from power stations that burn fossil fuels, preventing the gas from being released into the atmosphere, storing it in underground geological formations.

In April 2009 the government announced that all new combustion power stations would have to be Carbon Capture Ready and outlined proposals for a new regime for coal-fired power stations. On 17 June it published *A Framework for the Development of Clean Coal*. Proposals under consultation include:

- provision for up to four commercial-scale CCS demonstrations in Britain, covering a range of CCS technologies;
- a requirement that any new coal power station in England and Wales demonstrate CCS on a defined area of its capacity;
- a requirement for new coal power stations to retrofit CCS to their full station capacity within five years of CCS being judged technically and economically proven (projected to occur by 2020)

CCS is still in its infancy and only through its successful demonstration and development will it be possible for coal to remain a part of a low-carbon UK energy mix. To environmentalists, CCS remains an expensive and unproven technology with the potential for captured carbon to leak. There are also concerns that investment is being diverted from the development of renewable technologies.

INLAND COAL USE
Thousand tonnes

	2007	*2008*
Fuel producers		
Electricity generators	52,515	47,801
Heat generation	456	458
Coke manufacture	5,933	5,875
Blast furnaces	1,242	1,170
†Other conversion industries	245	317
Final consumption		
Industry	1,862	1,872
Domestic	648	684
Public administration	14	14
Commerce	6	10
Agriculture	4	5

† Mainly recycled products
Source: Department of Energy and Climate Change

COAL PRODUCTION AND FOREIGN TRADE
Thousand tonnes

	2007	*2008*
Deep-mined	7,674	8,096
Opencast	8,866	9,509
Imports	43,365	43,785
Exports	–544	–599
Total supply	62,777*	57,935*
TOTAL	62,932	58,212

* Includes an estimate for slurry and stock change
Source: Department of Energy and Climate Change

GAS

From the late 18th century gas in Britain was produced from coal. In the 1960s town gas began to be produced from oil-based feedstocks using imported oil. In 1965 gas was discovered in the North Sea in the West Sole field, which became the first gasfield in production in 1967, and from the late 1960s natural gas began to replace town gas. From October 1998 Britain was connected to the continental European gas system via a pipeline from Bacton, Norfolk to Zeebrugge, Belgium. Gas is transported through 275,000km of mains pipeline including 6,400km of high-pressure gas pipelines owned and operated in the UK by National Grid Gas plc.

The gas industry in Britain was nationalised in 1949 and operated as the Gas Council. The Gas Council was replaced by the British Gas Corporation in 1972 and the industry became more centralised. The British Gas Corporation was privatised in 1986 as British Gas plc. In 1993 the Monopolies and Mergers Commission found that British Gas's integrated business in Great Britain as a gas trader and the owner of the gas transportation system could operate against the public interest. In February 1997, British Gas demerged its trading arm to become two separate companies, BG plc and Centrica plc. BG Group, as the company is now known, is an international natural gas company whose principal business is finding and developing gas reserves and building gas markets. Its core operations are located in the UK, South America,

Egypt, Trinidad and Tobago, Kazakhstan and India. Centrica runs the trading and services operations under the British Gas brand name in Great Britain. In October 2000 BG demerged its pipeline business, Transco, which became part of Lattice Group, finally merging with the National Grid Group in 2002 to become National Grid Transco plc.

In July 2005 National Grid Transco plc changed its name to National Grid plc and Transco plc became National Grid Gas plc. In the same year National Grid Gas also completed the sale of four of its eight gas distribution networks. The distribution networks transport gas at lower pressures, which eventually supply the consumers such as domestic customers. The Scotland and south-east of England networks were sold to Scotia Gas Networks. The Wales and south-west network was sold to Wales & West Utilities and the network in the north-east to Northern Gas Networks. This was the biggest change in the corporate structure of gas infrastructure since privatisation in 1986.

Competition was gradually introduced into the industrial gas market from 1986. Supply of gas to the domestic market was opened to companies other than British Gas, starting in April 1996 with a pilot project in the West Country and Wales, with the rest of the UK following soon after. Since competition was introduced in domestic retail of gas, around half of Britain's 20 million gas customers have changed their supplier.

Declines in UK indigenous gas production and increasing demand led to the UK becoming a net importer of gas once more in 2004. In 2008, imports accounted for 28 per cent of gas input into the transmission system. Until 2004 the UK was entirely self-sufficient in terms of gas consumption, but it is estimated that by 2020 imported gas may feed up to 80 per cent of UK energy demands. As part of the Energy Act 2008, the government plans to strengthen regulation of the offshore gas supply infrastructure, to allow private sector investment to help maintain UK energy supplies.

BG GROUP PLC, Thames Valley Park, Reading RG6 1PT
T 0118-935 3222 W www.bg-group.com
Chair, Sir Robert Wilson
Chief Executive, Frank Chapman

CENTRICA PLC, Millstream, Maidenhead Road, Windsor, Berkshire SL4 5GD T 01753-494000 W www.centrica.co.uk
Chair, Roger Carr
Chief Executive, Sam Laidlaw

NATIONAL GRID TRANSCO PLC, Lakeside House, The Lakes, Northampton NN4 7HD T 0845-606 6677
W www.nationalgrid.com
Chair, Sir John Parker
Chief Executive, Steve Holliday

UK GAS CONSUMPTION BY INDUSTRY
GWh

	2006	*2007*
Iron and steel industry	8,406	7,337
Other industries	135,411	129,475
Domestic	364,850	349,943
Public administration	48,816	44,589
Agriculture	2,013	1,999
Miscellaneous	18,027	17,323
Total gas consumption	1,036,153	1,045,533

Source: Annual Abstract of Statistics 2009 (Crown copyright)

ELECTRICITY

The first power station in Britain generating electricity for public supply began operating in 1882. In the 1930s a national transmission grid was developed and it was reconstructed and extended in the 1950s and 1960s. Power stations were operated by the Central Electricity Generating Board.

Under the Electricity Act 1989, 12 regional electricity companies, responsible for the distribution of electricity from the national grid to consumers, were formed from the former area electricity boards in England and Wales. Four companies were formed from the Central Electricity Generating Board: three generating companies (National Power plc, Nuclear Electric plc and Powergen plc) and the National Grid Company plc, which owned and operated the transmission system in England and Wales. National Power and Powergen were floated on the stock market in 1991.

National Power was demerged in October 2000 to form two separate companies: International Power plc and Innogy plc, which manages the bulk of National Power's UK assets. Nuclear Electric was split into two parts in 1996 (*see* Nuclear Energy).

The National Grid Company was floated on the stock market in 1995 and formed a new holding company, National Grid Group. National Grid Group completed a merger with Lattice in 2002 to form National Grid Transco, a public limited company (*see* Gas).

Following privatisation, generators and suppliers in England and Wales traded via the Electricity Pool. A competitive wholesale trading market known as NETA (New Electricity Trading Arrangements) replaced the Electricity Pool in March 2001, which was extended to include Scotland via the British Electricity Transmissions and Trading Arrangements (BETTA) in 2005. As part of BETTA, National Grid became the system operator for all transmission. The introduction of competition into the domestic electricity market was completed in May 1999. Since competition was introduced, around half of Britain's 26 million electricity customers have switched their supplier.

In Scotland, three new companies were formed under the Electricity Act 1989: Scottish Power plc and Scottish Hydro-Electric plc, which were responsible for generation, transmission, distribution and supply; and Scottish Nuclear Ltd. Scottish Power and Scottish Hydro-Electric were floated on the stock market in 1991. Scottish Hydro-Electric merged with Southern Electric in 1998 to become Scottish and Southern Energy plc. Scottish Nuclear was incorporated into British Energy in 1996. BETTA opened the Scottish market to the same competition that had applied in England and Wales.

In Northern Ireland, Northern Ireland Electricity plc was set up in 1993 under a 1991 Order in Council. In 1993 it was floated on the stock market and in 1998 it became part of the Viridian Group and is responsible for distribution and supply.

On 30 September 2003 the Electricity Association, the industry's main trade association, was replaced with three separate trade bodies:

ASSOCIATION OF ELECTRICITY PRODUCERS, Charles House, 5–11 Regent Street, London SW1Y 4LR
T 020-7930 9390 W www.aepuk.com

ENERGY NETWORKS ASSOCIATION, 6th floor, Dean Bradley House, 52 Horseferry Road, London SW1P 2AF
T 020-7706 5100 W www.energynetworks.org

ENERGY RETAIL ASSOCIATION, 1 Hobhouse Court, Suffolk Street, London SW1Y 4HH T 020-7104 4150 W www.energy-retail.org.uk

ELECTRICITY GENERATION, SUPPLY AND CONSUMPTION

GWh

	2006	*2007*
Electricity generated		
Conventional thermal and other*	157,382	144,404
Combined cycle gas turbine stations	118,495	139,826
Nuclear stations	75,451	63,028
Hydroelectric stations		
Natural flow	3,693	4,144
Pumped storage	3,853	3,859
Renewables other than hydro	3,386	2,991
Major power producers: total	362,260	358,252
Other generators	36,563	38,205
Electricity used on works: total	19,210	18,087
Electricity supplied (gross)		
Conventional thermal and other*	148,341	136,399
Combined cycle gas turbine stations	116,398	137,561
Nuclear stations	69,237	57,249
Hydroelectric stations		
Natural flow	3,680	4,114
Pumped storage	3,722	3,846
Renewables other than hydro	3,175	2,574
Major power producers: total	344,554	341,742
Other generators total	35,059	36,628
Electricity used in pumping	4,918	5,071
Electricity consumed		
Fuel industries	7,913	8,048
Final users total	345,327	342,552
Industrial sector	118,934	118,340
Domestic sector	116,449	115,050
Other sectors	109,944	109,062
Total	353,239	350,601

* Includes electricity supplied by gas turbines, oil engines and plants producing electricity from renewable resources other than hydro

Source: Annual Abstract of Statistics 2009 (Crown copyright)

GAS AND ELECTRICITY SUPPLIERS

With the gas and electricity markets open, most suppliers offer their customers both services. The majority of gas/electricity companies have become part of larger multi-utility companies, often operating internationally.

As part of measures to reduce the UK's carbon output, the government has outlined plans to introduce 'smart meters' to all UK homes. Smart meters perform the traditional meter function of measuring energy consumption, in addition to more advanced functions such as allowing energy suppliers to communicate directly with their customers and removing the need for meter readings and bill estimates. The meters also allow domestic customers to have direct access to energy consumption information.

The following list comprises a selection of suppliers offering gas and electricity. Organisations in italics are subsidiaries of the companies listed in capital letters directly above.

ENGLAND, SCOTLAND AND WALES

BRITISH GAS/SCOTTISH GAS, PO Box 3055, Eastbourne BN21 9FE T 0800-048 0505 W www.britishgas.co.uk

CE ELECTRIC UK, www.ceelectricuk.com

Northern Electric Distribution Ltd, Manor House, Station Road, New Penshaw, Houghton-le-Spring DH4 7LA T 0845-070 7172

Yorkshire Electricity Distribution, Manor House, Station Road, New Penshaw, Houghton-le-Spring DH4 7LA T 0845-602 4453

CENTRICA PLC, Millstream, Maidenhead Road, Windsor, Berkshire SL4 5GD T 01753-494000 W www.centrica.co.uk

EDF ENERGY, 40 Grosvenor Place, Victoria, London SW1X 7EN T 0800-096 9000 W www.edfenergy.com

E.ON, 6th Floor, 100 Pall Mall, London SW1Y 5NQ T 024-7618 3843 W www.eon-uk.com

NPOWER, Oak House, Bridgwater Road, Warndon, Worcester WR4 9FP T 01793-877777 W www.npower.com

SCOTTISH AND SOUTHERN ENERGY PLC, Inveralmond House, 200 Dunkeld Road, Perth PH1 3AQ T 01738-456000 W www.scottish-southern.co.uk

Scottish Hydro Electric, PO Box 7506, Perth PH1 3QR T 0845-300 2141 W www.hydro.co.uk

Southern Electric, PO Box 7506, Perth PH1 3QR T 0845-744 4555 W www.southern-electric.co.uk

SWALEC, PO Box 7506, Perth PH1 3QR T 0800-052 5252 W www.swalec.co.uk

SCOTTISHPOWER, New Alderton House, Dove Wynd, Bellshill, ML4 3FF T 0845-272 7999 W www.scottishpower.co.uk

NORTHERN IRELAND

VIRIDIAN GROUP PLC, 120 Malone Road, Belfast BT9 5HT T 028-9066 8416 W www.viridiangroup.co.uk

Energia, Energia House, 62 Newforge Lane, Belfast BT9 5NF T 028-9068 5900 W www.viridianenergia.co.uk

Northern Ireland Electricity, 120 Malone Road, Belfast BT9 5HT T 08457-643643 W www.nie.co.uk

REGULATION OF THE GAS AND ELECTRICITY INDUSTRIES

The Office of the Gas and Electricity Markets (OFGEM) regulates the gas and electricity industries in Great Britain. It was formed in 1999 by the merger of the Office of Gas Supply and the Office of Electricity Regulation. OFGEM's overriding aim is to protect and promote the interests of all gas and electricity customers by promoting competition and regulating monopolies. It is governed by an authority and its powers are provided for under the Gas Act 1986, the Electricity Act 1989 and the Utilities Act 2000. Energywatch is the independent gas and electricity watchdog, set up in November 2000 through the Utility Act to protect and promote the interests of gas and electricity consumers. In October 2008 Energywatch merged with Postwatch and the National Consumer Council to form a new advocacy body, Consumer Focus.

CONSUMER FOCUS, 4th Floor, Artillery House, Artillery Row, London SW1P 1RT T 020-7799 7900 W www.consumerfocus.org.uk

THE OFFICE OF THE GAS AND ELECTRCITY MARKETS (OFGEM), 9 Millbank, London SW1 3GE T 020-7901 7000 W www.ofgem.gov.uk

NUCLEAR POWER

Nuclear reactors began to supply electricity to the national grid in 1956; nuclear power is generated in the UK at six magnox reactors, seven advanced gas-cooled reactors (AGR) and one pressurised water reactor (PWR), Sizewell 'B' in Suffolk. In 1989 nuclear stations were withdrawn from privatisation. In 1996 Nuclear Electric Ltd and Scottish Nuclear Ltd became operating subsidiaries of British Energy and the magnox stations were transferred to Nuclear Electric which became Magnox Electric, later part of British Nuclear Fuels Ltd. British Energy manages eight nuclear power stations (seven AGRs and one PWR) and generates around one-fifth of the UK's electricity.

In April 2005 the responsibility for the decommissioning of civil nuclear reactors and other nuclear facilities used in research and development was handed from the UK Atomic Energy Authority (UKAEA) to a new body, the Nuclear Decommissioning Authority (NDA). The NDA is a non-departmental public body, funded mainly by the Department of Energy and Climate Change. Until April 2007, UK Nirex was responsible for the disposal of intermediate and some low-level nuclear waste. After this date Nirex was integrated into the NDA and renamed the Radioactive Waste Management Directorate. The UKAEA now operates on a private contractor basis and is decommissioning the nuclear power stations at Dounreay, Harwell and Winfrith.

In 2008 electricity supplied from nuclear sources was at its lowest proportion since 1981 at 13 per cent. However, the 2008 Energy Bill paved the way for the construction of up to ten new nuclear power stations by 2020. A number of factors have led to government backing for nuclear power: domestic gas supplies are running low; oil and gas prices are high; carbon emissions must be cut to comply with EU legislation and meet global climate change targets; and a number of coal-fired power stations that fail to meet clean air requirements are due to be closed. The government has long foreseen an energy gap in the country's future generating capacity due to the decommissioning of current nuclear stations and the necessity of cutting back on fossil fuels.

Nuclear power has its advantages: reactors emit virtually no carbon dioxide and uranium prices remain relatively steady. However, the advantages of low emissions are countered by the high costs of construction and there are difficulties in disposing of nuclear waste. Currently, the only method is to store it securely until it has slowly decayed to safe levels. Public distrust persists despite the advances in safety technology.

SAFETY AND REGULATION

The Nuclear Safety Directorate of the Health and Safety Executive is the nuclear industry's regulator. Operations at all UK nuclear power stations are governed by a site licence which is issued under the Nuclear Installations Act. The Nuclear Installations Inspectorate (NII) monitors compliance and has the jurisdiction to close down a reactor if the terms of the licence are breached. DECC is responsible for security at all the UK's nuclear power stations, which are policed by the Civil Nuclear Constabulary, a specialised armed force created in April 2005. In February 2009 Magnox Electric Ltd was found guilty of breaking the Radioactive Substances Act 2003: it had left a radioactive leak on a holding tank at the Bradwell-On-Sea plant unchecked for 14 years.

RENEWABLE SOURCES

Renewable sources of energy principally include biofuels, hydro, wind and solar. Renewable sources produced over 5.9 million tonnes of oil equivalent for primary energy usage in 2008; of this, about 4.3 million tonnes was used to generate electricity and 0.8 million tonnes to generate heat. In 2008, the UK generated 5.5 per cent of its total energy production from renewable sources, up by 0.6 per cent from 2007.

The government's principal mechanism for developing renewable energy sources are Non-Fossil Fuel Obligation Renewables Orders. Under the terms of the orders, regional electricity companies are required to buy specified amounts of electricity from non-fossil fuel sources. The Renewables Obligation (RO) aims to increase the contribution of electricity from renewables in the UK, so that 9.1 per cent of licensed UK electricity sales should be from renewable sources eligible for the RO by 2009, and 15.4 per cent should be eligible by 2016. In 2008 renewables accounted for 5.4 per cent of sales on an RO basis, a rise on the 2007 figure of 4.8 per cent.

A renewables obligation has been in place in England and Wales since April 2002 to give incentives to generators to supply progressively higher levels of renewable energy over time. These measures included exempting renewable energy sources from the climate change levy, capital grants, enhanced research funding and regional planning to meet renewables targets. The government approved an EU-wide agreement in March 2007 to generate 20 per cent of energy production from renewable sources by 2020. It has since negotiated down the national share in this target to 15 per cent of energy production by 2020 (and 10 per cent by 2010), a figure many believe optimistic. In July 2009 the government published a Renewable Energy Strategy, which outlines policies that will help the UK to meet the 15 per cent target. Other impediments to the expansion of renewable energy production include planning restrictions, rising raw material prices, and the possible redirection of funds to develop CCS technology and nuclear energy sources. For further information on renewable energy sources *see* The Environment.

RENEWABLE ENERGY SOURCES (2008)

	Percentage
Biofuels and wastes	81.1
Landfill gas	26.7
Sewage gas	4.1
Wood combustion	7.9
Co-firing	9.0
Waste combustion	9.1
Liquid biofuels	14.0
Other biofuels	10.3
Hydro	7.5
Large-scale	6.7
Small-scale	0.8
Wind	10.3
Geothermal and active solar heating	1.0
Total	100

Source: Department of Energy and Climate Change

TRANSPORT

CIVIL AVIATION

Since the privatisation of British Airways in 1987, UK airlines have been operated entirely by the private sector. In 2008, total capacity of British airlines amounted to 53 billion tonne km, of which 41 billion tonne km was on scheduled services. British airlines carried around 131 million passengers, 105 million on scheduled services and 26 million on charter flights. Overall, passenger traffic decreased by 2 per cent. Traffic at the five main London airports decreased by 2 per cent over 2008 and regional airlines also saw a decrease of 2 per cent. Leading British airlines include BMI, British Airways, EasyJet, Monarch, My Travel Airways, Thomas Cook Airlines, Thomson Airways and Virgin Atlantic. Irish airline Ryanair also operates frequent flights from Britain.

There are around 144 licensed civil aerodromes in Britain, with Heathrow and Gatwick handling the highest volume of passengers. BAA plc owns and operates seven major airports: Heathrow, Gatwick, Stansted, Southampton, Glasgow, Edinburgh and Aberdeen, which between them handle about 62 per cent of air passengers and a high percentage of air cargo traffic in Britain. Other airports are controlled by local authorities or private companies.

The Civil Aviation Authority (CAA), an independent statutory body, is responsible for the regulation of UK airlines. This includes economic and airspace regulation, air safety, consumer protection and environmental research and consultancy. All commercial airline companies must be granted an air operator's certificate, which is issued by the CAA to operators meeting the required safety standards. The CAA issues airport safety licences, which must be obtained by any airport used for public transport and training flights. All British-registered aircraft must be granted an airworthiness certificate, and the CAA issues professional licences to pilots, flight crew, ground engineers and air traffic controllers. The CAA also manages the Air Travel Organiser's Licence (ATOL), the UK's principal travel protection scheme. The CAA's costs are met entirely from charges on those whom it regulates; there is no direct government funding of the CAA's work.

The Transport Act, passed by parliament on 29 November 2000, separated the CAA from its subsidiary, National Air Traffic Services (NATS), which provides air traffic control services to aircraft flying in UK airspace and over the eastern part of the North Atlantic. In March 2001 the Airline Group, a consortium of seven UK airlines (British Airways, BMI, Virgin Atlantic, Britannia, Monarch, EasyJet and Airtours), was selected by the government as its strategic partner for NATS. Financial restructuring of NATS was completed in March 2003 with additional equity investment of £65m each from BAA and the government. The new structure enabled NATS to begin a ten-year £1bn investment programme, to increase its flight handling capability from two to three million flights per annum by 2012. NATS is a public private partnership between the Airline Group (a consortium of seven UK airlines) which holds 42 per cent of the shares; NATS staff, who hold 5 per cent; BAA, which holds 4 per cent, and the government, which holds 49 per cent and a golden share. In 2008 NATS handled a total of 2,433,946 flights, a slight decrease of 1.5 per cent against 2007 figures.

AIR PASSENGERS 2008

All UK Airports: Total	235,359,000
Aberdeen (BAA)	3,290,000
Barra (HIAL)*	11,000
Belfast City	2,571,000
Belfast International	5,223,000
Benbecula (HIAL)*	34,000
Biggin Hill†	–
Birmingham	9,577,000
Blackpool	439,000
Bournemouth	1,079,000
Bristol	6,229,000
Cambridge	2,000
Campbeltown (HIAL)*	9,000
Cardiff	1,979,000
City of Derry (Eglinton)	439,000
Coventry	331,000
Doncaster Sheffield	968,000
Dundee	61,000
Durham Tees Valley	645,000
Edinburgh (BAA)	8,992
Exeter	951,000
Gatwick (BAA)	34,162,000
Glasgow (BAA)	8,135,000
Gloucestershire	20,000
Hawarden (Chester)†	–
Heathrow (BAA)	66,907,000
Humberside	424,000
Inverness (HIAL)*	671,000
Islay (HIAL)*	29,000
Isle of Man	754,000
Isles of Scilly (St Mary's)	123,000
Isles of Scilly (Tresco)	37,000
Kent International	12,000
Kirkwall (HIAL)*	138,000
Lands End (St Just)	26,000
Leeds Bradford	2,860,000
Lerwick (Tingwall)	5,000
Liverpool	5,330,000
London City	3,260,000
Luton	10,174,000
Lydd	2,000
Manchester	21,063,000
Newcastle	5,017,000
Newquay	431,000
Norwich	583,000
Nottingham (East Midlands International)	5,616,000
Penzance Heliport	98,000
Plymouth	99,000
Prestwick	2,414,000
Scatsta	243,000
Shoreham	5,000
Southampton (BAA)	1,946,000
Southend	44,000
Stansted (BAA)	22,340,000
Stornoway (HIAL)*	131,000

Sumburgh (HIAL)*	154,000
Tiree (HIAL)*	8,000
Wick (HIAL)*	23,000
Channel Islands Airports: Total	2,582,739
Alderney	77,104
Guernsey	914,603
Jersey	1,591,032

* Highlands and Islands Airports Ltd (HIAL)
† Figure not supplied by airport
Source: Civil Aviation Authority

CAA, CAA House, 45–59 Kingsway, London WC2B 6TE
T 020-7379 7311 W www.caa.co.uk
BAA, 234 Bath Road, Hayes, Middlesex UB3 5AP
T 020-8745 9800 W www.baa.com

Gatwick Airport	T 0870-000 2468
Heathrow Airport	T 0870-000 0123
Southampton Airport	T 0870-040 0009
Stansted Airport	T 0870-000 0303
Aberdeen Airport	T 0870-040 0006
Edinburgh Airport	T 0870-040 0007
Glasgow Airport	T 0870-040 0008

BMI, Donington Hall, Castle Donington, Derby DE74 2SB
T 01332-854000 W www.flybmi.com
BRITISH AIRWAYS, PO Box 365, Waterside, Harmondsworth UB7 0GB T 0844-493 0787
W www.britishairways.com
EASYJET, Hangar 89, London Luton Airport LU2 9PF
T 0871-244 2366 W www.easyjet.com
MONARCH, Prospect House, Prospect Way, London Luton Airport LU2 9NU T 0870-040 5040
W www.flymonarch.com
THOMAS COOK AIRLINES, Thomas Cook Business Park, Coningsby Road, Peterborough PE3 8SB T 0844-855 0515
W www.thomascookairlines.com
THOMSON AIRWAYS, Wigmore House, Wigmore Place, Wigmore Lane, Luton, Bedfordshire LU2 9TN
T 0870-607 6757 W www.thomsonfly.com
VIRGIN ATLANTIC, The Office, Crawley, Sussex RH10 9NU
T 01293-562345 W www.virgin-atlantic.com

RAILWAYS

The railway network in Britain was developed by private companies in the 19th century. In 1948 the main railway companies were nationalised and were run by a public authority, the British Transport Commission. The commission was replaced by the British Railways Board in 1963, operating as British Rail. On 1 April 1994, responsibility for managing the track and railway infrastructure passed to a newly formed company, Railtrack plc. In October 2001 Railtrack was put into administration under the Railways Act 1993 and Ernst and Young was appointed as administrator. In October 2002 Railtrack was taken out of administration and replaced by the not-for-profit company Network Rail. The British Railways Board continued as operator of all train services until 1996–7, when they were sold or franchised to the private sector.

The Strategic Rail Authority (SRA) was created to provide strategic leadership to the rail industry and formally came into being on 1 February 2001 following the passing of the Transport Act 2000. In January 2002 it published its first strategic plan, setting out the strategic priorities for Britain's railways over the next ten years. In addition to its coordinating role, the SRA was responsible for allocating government funding to the railways and awarding and monitoring the franchises for operating rail services.

On 15 July 2004 the transport secretary announced a new structure for the rail industry in the white paper *The Future of Rail*. These proposals were implemented under the Railways Act 2005, which abolished the Strategic Rail Authority, passing most of its functions to the Department for Transport; established the Rail Passengers Council (RPC) as a single national body, dissolving the regional committees; and gave devolved governments in Scotland and Wales more say in decisions at a local level. In addition, responsibility for railway safety regulation was transferred to the Office of Rail Regulation from the Health and Safety Executive.

OFFICE OF RAIL REGULATION

The Office of Rail Regulation (ORR) was established on 5 July 2004 by the Railways and Transport Safety Act 2003, replacing the Office of the Rail Regulator. As the railway industry's economic and safety regulator, the ORR's principal function is to regulate Network Rail's stewardship of the national network. The ORR also licenses operators of railway assets, approves agreements for access by operators to track, stations and light maintenance depots, and enforces domestic competition law. The ORR is led by a board appointed by the Secretary of State for Transport and chaired by Anna Walker.

SERVICES

For privatisation, under the Railways Act 1993, domestic passenger services were divided into 25 train operating units, which were franchised to private sector operators via a competitive tendering process. The train operators formed the Association of Train Operating Companies (ATOC) to act as the official voice of the passenger rail industry and provide its members with a range of services enabling them to comply with conditions imposed on them through their franchise agreements and operating licences.

As at June 2009 there were 29 passenger train operating companies: Arriva Trains Wales, c2c; Chiltern Railways, CrossCountry, East Midlands Trains, Eurostar, First Capital Connect, First Great Western, First Hull Trains, First TransPennine Express, Gatwick Express, Grand Central, Heathrow Connect, Heathrow Express, Island Line Trains (Isle of Wight), London Midland, London Overground, London Underground, Merseyrail, National Express East Anglia, National Express East Coast, Northern Rail, ScotRail, South West Trains, Southeastern, Southern, Stansted Express, Virgin Trains and Wrexham & Shropshire.

Network Rail publishes a national timetable which contains details of rail services operated over the UK network and sea ferry services which provide connections with Ireland, the Isle of Man, the Isle of Wight, the Channel Islands and some European destinations.

The national rail enquiries service offers information about train times and fares for any part of the country, Transport for London (TfL) provides London-specific travel information for all modes of travel and Eurostar provides information for international channel tunnel rail services:

NATIONAL RAIL ENQUIRIES
T 0845-748 4950 W www.nationalrail.co.uk

TRANSPORT FOR LONDON
T 020-7222 1234 W www.tfl.gov.uk
EUROSTAR
T 0870-518 6186 W www.eurostar.com

PASSENGER FOCUS AND LONDON TRAVELWATCH

Passenger Focus is the operating name of the Rail Passengers' Council, a single national consumer body for rail, which is funded by the Department for Transport but whose independence is guaranteed by an act of parliament. Rail Users' Consultative Committees were set up under the Railways Act 1993 to protect the interests of users of the services and facilities provided on Britain's rail network. The Transport Act 2000 changed their name to Rail Passenger Committees (RPCs) and brought the committees under the overall sponsorship of the Strategic Rail Authority. There were eight RPCs nationwide, one for each of the six English regions and one each for Scotland and Wales. Under the Railways Act 2005, the eight regional committees were disbanded in June 2005 and their functions and duties transferred to the Rail Passengers' Council, the Strategic Rail Authority was abolished and sponsorship for the Rail Passengers' Council transferred to the Department for Transport.

Established in July 2000, London TravelWatch is the operating name of the official watchdog organisation representing the interests of transport users in and around the capital. Officially known as the London Transport Users' Committee, it is sponsored and funded by the London Assembly and is independent of the transport operators. London TravelWatch represents users of buses, the Underground, river and rail services in and around London, including Eurostar and Heathrow Express, Croydon Tramlink and the Docklands Light Railway. The interests of pedestrians, cyclists and motorists are also represented, as are those of taxi users.

FREIGHT

Rail freight services are provided by a small number of companies. On privatisation, British Rail's bulk freight operations were sold to English, Welsh and Scottish Railways (EWS). There are currently eight freight operating companies licensed to provide services for moving goods by rail: Advenza, Colas Rail, Direct Rail Services, DB Schenker (formerly EWS), First GBRf (part of the First Group), Fastline, Freightliner Group and Freight Europe. The Department for Transport announced in June 2007 that £44m worth of funding would be awarded via the Rail Environmental Benefit Procurement Scheme over three years in order to encourage the movement of freight on rail that would otherwise be transported by road. In 2007–8 freight moved by rail amounted to 21.2 billion tonne-kilometres.

NETWORK RAIL

Network Rail is responsible for the tracks, bridges, tunnels, level crossings, viaducts and 18 main stations that form Britain's rail network. In addition to providing the timetables for the passenger and freight operators, Network Rail is also responsible for all the signalling and electrical control equipment needed to operate the rail network and for monitoring and reporting performance across the industry.

Network Rail is a private company run as a commercial business; it is directly accountable to its members and regulated by the ORR. The members have similar rights to those of shareholders in a public company except they do not receive dividends or share capital and thereby have no financial or economic interest in Network Rail. All of Network Rail's profits are reinvested into maintaining and upgrading the rail infrastructure.

ASSOCIATION OF TRAIN OPERATING COMPANIES, 3rd Floor, 40 Bernard Street, London WC1N 1BY T 020-7841 8000 W www.atoc.org
LONDON TRAVELWATCH, 6 Middle Street, London EC1A 7JA T 020-7505 9000 W www.londontravelwatch.org.uk
NETWORK RAIL, Kings Place, 90 York Way, London N1 9AG T 020-3356 9595 W www.networkrail.co.uk
OFFICE OF RAIL REGULATION, 1 Kemble Street, London WC2B 4AN T 020-7282 2000 W www.rail-reg.gov.uk
PASSENGER FOCUS, Freepost (RRRE-ETTC-LEEI), PO Box 4257, Manchester M60 3AR T 030-0123 2350 W www.passengerfocus.org.uk

RAIL SAFETY

On 1 April 2006 responsibility for health and safety policy and enforcement on the railways transferred from the Health and Safety Executive to the Office of Rail Regulation (ORR).

In 2008 a total of 28 passengers, railway staff and other members of the public were fatally injured in all rail incidents (excluding trespassers and suicides), compared with 27 in 2007.

ACCIDENTS ON RAILWAYS

	2007	*2008*
Train incident fatalities	5	4
Passengers	1	0
Railway employees	0	0
Others	4	4
Train incident injuries	110	27
Passengers	94	10
Railway staff	12	10
Others	3	7

TRESPASSERS, SUICIDES AND ATTEMPTED SUICIDES 2008

Fatalities	288
Injuries	156

Source: ORR – *National Rail Trends 2008–9 Yearbook*

OTHER RAIL SYSTEMS

Responsibility for the London Underground passed from the government to the Mayor and Transport for London on 15 July 2003, with a public-private partnership (PPP) already in place. Plans for a public-private partnership for London Underground were pushed through by the government in February 2002 despite opposition from the Mayor of London and a range of transport organisations. Under the PPP, long-term contracts with private companies were estimated to enable around £16bn to be invested in renewing and upgrading the Underground's infrastructure over 15 years. Responsibility for stations, trains, operations, signalling and safety remains in the public sector. In 2007–8 there were 1,096 million passenger journeys on the London Underground, an increase of 5.4 per cent on the previous year.

Britain has nine other light rail, tram or underground systems: Blackpool Trams, Croydon Tramlink, Docklands Light Railway (DLR), Glasgow Subway, Manchester

Metrolink, Midland Metro, Nottingham Express Transit (NET), Stagecoach Supertram in Sheffield and Tyne and Wear Metro.

Light rail and metro systems in Great Britain contributed to the growth in public transport, with 201 million passenger journeys in 2007–8, an increase of 4.7 per cent on the previous year. In England there were 187 million passenger journeys in 2007–8, compared with 124 million in 2000–1. The government's ten-year Transport Plan target is to double light rail use in England (measured by number of passenger journeys) by 2010 compared to 2000 levels.

THE CHANNEL TUNNEL

The earliest recorded scheme for a submarine transport connection between Britain and France was in 1802. Tunnelling began simultaneously on both sides of the Channel three times: in 1881, in the early 1970s, and on 1 December 1987, when construction workers bored the first of the three tunnels which form the Channel Tunnel. Engineers 'holed through' the first tunnel (the service tunnel) on 1 December 1990 and tunnelling was completed in June 1991. The tunnel was officially inaugurated by the Queen and President Mitterrand of France on 6 May 1994.

The submarine link comprises two rail tunnels, each carrying trains in one direction, which measure 7.6m (24.93ft) in diameter. Between them lies a smaller service tunnel, measuring 4.8m (15.75ft) in diameter. The service tunnel is linked to the rail tunnels by 130 cross-passages for maintenance and safety purposes. The tunnels are 50km (31 miles) long, 38km (24 miles) of which is under the seabed at an average depth of 40m (132ft). The rail terminals are situated at Folkestone and Calais, and the tunnels go underground at Shakespeare Cliff, Dover, and Sangatte, west of Calais.

RAIL LINKS

The British Channel Tunnel Rail Link route runs from Folkestone to St Pancras station, London, with intermediate stations at Ashford and Ebbsfleet in Kent.

Construction of the rail link was financed by the private sector with a substantial government contribution. A private sector consortium, London and Continental Railways Ltd (LCR), comprising Union Railways and the UK operator of Eurostar, owns the rail link and was responsible for its design and construction. The rail link was constructed in two phases: phase one, from the Channel Tunnel to Fawkham Junction, Kent, began in October 1998 and opened to fare-paying passengers on 28 September 2003; phase two, from Southfleet Junction to St Pancras, was completed in November 2007.

There are direct services from the UK to Calais, Disneyland Paris, Lille and Paris in France and Brussels in Belgium. There are also direct services to Avignon in the south of France between July and September and during the winter months (December to April) to the French Alps. High-speed trains also run from Lille to the south of France.

Eurostar, the high speed passenger train service, connects London with Paris in 2 hours 15 minutes, Brussels in 1 hour 51 minutes and Lille in 1 hour 20 minutes. There are Eurostar terminals at London St Pancras, Ashford and Ebbsfleet in Kent, Paris Gare Du Nord, Brussels-South and Lille in France.

ROADS

HIGHWAY AUTHORITIES

The powers and responsibilities of highway authorities in England and Wales are set out in the Highways Act 1980; for Scotland there is separate legislation.

Responsibility for motorways and other trunk roads in Great Britain rests in England with the Secretary of State for Transport, in Scotland with the Scottish government, and in Wales with the Welsh Assembly Government. The highway authority for non-trunk roads in England, Wales and Scotland is, in general, the local authority in whose area the roads lie. With the establishment of the Greater London Authority in July 2000, Transport for London became the highway authority for roads in London.

In Northern Ireland the Department of Regional Development is the statutory road authority responsible for public roads and their maintenance and construction; the Roads Service executive agency carries out these functions on behalf of the department.

FINANCE

In England all aspects of trunk road and motorway funding are provided directly by the government to the Highways Agency, which operates, maintains and improves a network of motorways and trunk roads around 7,050km (miles) long, on behalf of the secretary of state. Since 2001 the length of the network that the Highways Agency is responsible for has been decreasing due to a policy of de-trunking, which transfers responsibility for non-core roads to local authorities. For the financial year 2009–10 the Highways Agency's total planned expenditure is £7,591m: £1,113m for maintenance, £1,086m for major improvements, £429m for traffic management and technology improvements and the remainder for other programmes and administration costs.

Government support for local authority capital expenditure on roads and other transport infrastructure is provided through grant and credit approvals as part of the Local Transport Plan (LTP). Local authorities bid for resources on the basis of a five-year programme built around delivering integrated transport strategies. As well as covering the structural maintenance of local roads and the construction of major new road schemes, LTP funding also includes smaller-scale safety and traffic management measures with associated improvements for public transport, cyclists and pedestrians.

For the financial year 2009–10, total allocated LTP funding amounted to £1,345m: £693m for formulaic maintenance, £589m for integrated transport measures and £63m for other maintenance.

Total expenditure by the Welsh Assembly Government on trunk roads, motorways, rail, bus and other transport services (including grants to local authorities) in 2008–9 was over £609m. Planned expenditure for 2009–10 is £628m.

Since 1 July 1999 all decisions on Scottish transport expenditure have been devolved to the Scottish government. Total expenditure on motorways and trunk roads in Scotland during 2008–9 was £1,011m (including cost of capital, depreciation and other annually managed expenditure charges). Planned expenditure for 2009–10 is £1,103m.

In Northern Ireland total expenditure by the Roads Service on all roads in 2008–9 was £161.5m, with £144.3m spent on trunk roads and motorways. Planned expenditure for 2009–10 is £179.1m, with £153m allocated for trunk roads and motorways.

The Transport Act 2000 gave English and Welsh local authorities (outside London) powers to introduce road-user charging or workplace parking levy schemes. The act requires that the net revenue raised is used to improve local transport services and facilities for at least ten years. The aim is to reduce congestion and encourage greater use of alternative modes of transport. Schemes developed by local authorities require government approval. The UK's first toll road, the M6 Toll, opened in December 2003 and runs for 43.5km (27 miles) around Birmingham from junction 3a to junction 11a on the M6.

Charging schemes in London are allowed under the 1999 Greater London Authority Act. The Central London Congestion Charge Scheme began on 17 February 2003 (*see also* Regional Government).

ROAD LENGTHS 2007
Kilometres

	England	*Wales*	*Scotland*	*Great Britain*
Motorways	3,011	141	407	3,559
Dual carriageway	6,604	549	783	7,936
Single carriageway	25,671	3,617	9,519	38,807
B roads	19,963	2,982	7,320	30,265
C roads	64,207	9,797	10,419	84,423
Unclassified roads	181,983	16,775	31,131	229,889
Total	301,440	33,861	59,578	394,879

Source: Department for Transport

FREIGHT TRANSPORT BY ROAD (GREAT BRITAIN) 2007

GOODS MOVED	
By mode of working (billion tonne kilometres)	
All modes	161.5
Own account	45.9
Public haulage	115.6
By gross weight of vehicle (billion tonne kilometres)	
All vehicles	161.5
3.5–25 tonnes	15.7
Over 25 tonnes	145.8
GOODS LIFTED	
By mode of working (million tonnes)	
All modes	1,869
Own account	724
Public haulage	1,145
By gross weight of vehicle (million tonnes)	
All vehicles	1,869
3.5–25 tonnes	245
Over 25 tonnes	1,624

Source: Department for Transport

ROAD TRAFFIC BY TYPE OF VEHICLE (GREAT BRITAIN) 2007
Million vehicle kilometres

All motor vehicles	513,000
Cars and taxis	404,100
Motorcycles	5,600
Buses and coaches	5,700
Light vans	68,200
Other goods vehicles	29,400
Pedal cycles	4,200

Source: Department for Transport

BUSES

The majority of bus services outside London are provided on a commercial basis by private operators. Local authorities have powers to subsidise services where needs are not being met by a commercial service.

The Transport Act 2000 outlines a ten-year transport plan intended to promote bus use, through agreements between local authorities and bus operators, and to improve the standard and efficiency of services. Funding for many new services has been made available through the rural bus grants and urban bus challenge schemes. In addition, the Bus Service Operators Grant (BSOG) is paid directly to bus operators by the government and reinburses the major part of the excise duty paid on the fuel used in operating locally registered bus services. In 2007–8 BSOG amounted to £487m.

Since April 2008 people aged 60 and over and disabled people who qualify under the categories listed in the Transport Act 2000 have been able to travel for free on any local bus across England between 9.30am and 11pm Monday to Friday and all day at weekends and bank holidays. Local authorities recompense operators for the reduced fare revenue. A similar scheme operates in Wales, although there is no time restriction. In Scotland, people aged 60 and over and disabled people have been able to travel for free on any local or long-distance bus anywhere in Scotland since April 2006.

In London, Transport for London (TfL) has overall responsibility for setting routes, service standards and fares for the bus network. Almost all routes are competitively tendered to commercial operators.

In Northern Ireland, passenger transport services are provided by Ulsterbus and Metro (formerly Citybus), two wholly owned subsidiaries of the Northern Ireland Transport Holding Company. Along with Northern Ireland Railways, Ulsterbus and Metro operate under the brand name of Translink and are publicly owned. Ulsterbus is responsible for virtually all bus services in Northern Ireland except Belfast city services, which are operated by Metro. People living in Northern Ireland aged 65 and over can travel on buses and trains for free once they have obtained a Senior SmartPass from Translink.

BUS PASSENGER JOURNEYS 2007–8 (GREAT BRITAIN)
No. of journeys (millions)

England	4,530
London	2,090
Wales	122
Scotland	513
Total	5,164

Source: Department for Transport

TAXIS AND PRIVATE HIRE VEHICLES

A taxi is a public transport vehicle with fewer than nine passenger seats, which is licensed to 'ply for hire'. This distinguishes taxis from private hire vehicles which must be booked in advance through an operator. In London, taxis and private hire vehicles are licensed by the Public Carriage Office (PCO), part of TfL. Outside of London, local authorities are responsible for the licensing of taxis and private hire vehicles operational in their respective administrative areas. In 2006–7 there were 73,600 taxis and 130,100 licensed private hire vehicles in England and Wales, of these, 21,600 taxis and 44,400 private hire vehicles were licensed by the PCO in London.

ROAD SAFETY

In March 2000, the government published a new road safety strategy, *Tomorrow's Roads – Safer for Everyone*, which set new casualty reduction targets for 2010. The new targets include a 40 per cent reduction in the overall number of people killed or seriously injured in road accidents, a 50 per cent reduction in the number of children killed or seriously injured and a 10 per cent reduction in the slight casualty rate (per 100 million vehicle kilometres), all compared with the average for 1994–8.

There were 231,000 reported casualties on roads in Great Britain in 2008, 7 per cent less than in 2007. Child casualties overall fell by 8 per cent with 124 child fatalities, a slight increase of 2 per cent compared to 2007 figures. Car user casualties decreased by 8 per cent on the 2007 level to 149,169 and fatalities decreased by 12 per cent to 1,257. Pedestrian casualties were 28,481 in 2008, 6 per cent less than 2007, while pedestrian deaths were 11 per cent lower compared to 2007 at 572. Compared to 2007, pedal cyclist casualties increased by 1 per cent to 16,297, although the number of pedal cyclists killed on British roads decreased by 15 per cent to 115.

ROAD ACCIDENT CASUALTIES 2008

	Fatal	*Serious*	*Slight*	*All Severities*
Average for 1994–8	3,578	44,078	272,272	319,928
England	2,123	22,241	179,772	204,136
Wales	143	1,253	9,789	11,185
Scotland	272	2,535	12,756	15,563
Great Britain	2,538	26,029	202,317	230,884

Source: Department for Transport

ROAD ACCIDENT CASUALTIES

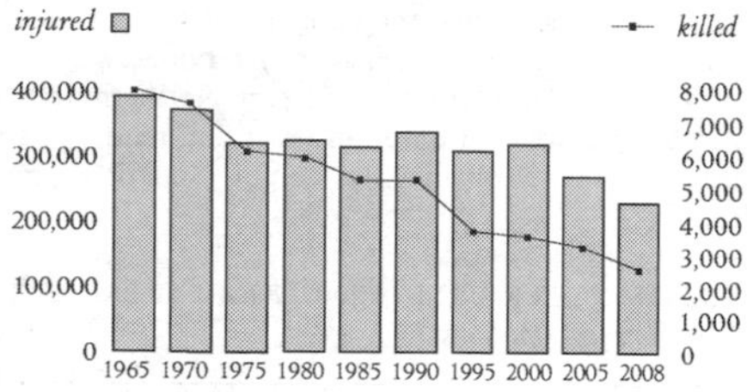

Source: Department for Transport

DRIVING LICENCES

It is necessary to hold a valid full licence in order to drive unaccompanied on public roads in the UK. Learner drivers must obtain a provisional driving licence before starting to learn to drive and must then pass theory and practical tests to obtain a full driving licence.

There are separate tests for driving motorcycles, cars, passenger-carrying vehicles (PCVs) and large goods vehicles (LGVs). Drivers must hold full car entitlement before they can apply for PCV or LGV entitlements.

The Driver and Vehicle Licensing Agency (DVLA) ceased the issue of paper licences in March 2000, but those currently in circulation will remain valid until they expire or the details on them change. The photocard driving licence was introduced to comply with the second EC directive on driving licences. This requires a photograph of the driver to be included on all UK licences issued from July 2001.

To apply for a first photocard driving licence, individuals are required to complete the form *Application for a Driving Licence* (D1).

The minimum age for driving motor cars, light goods vehicles up to 3.5 tonnes and motorcycles is 17 (moped, 16). Since June 1997, drivers who collect six or more penalty points within two years of qualifying lose their licence and are required to take another test. All forms and leaflets including *What You Need to Know About Driving Licences* (D100), are available from post offices, DVLA local offices and online (W www.dvla.gov.uk or W www.direct.gov.uk).

The DVLA is responsible for issuing driving licences, registering and licensing vehicles, and collecting excise duty in Great Britain. Driver and Vehicle Licensing Northern Ireland (DVLNI), part of the Driver and Vehicle Agency (DVA), has similar responsibilities in Northern Ireland.

DRIVING LICENCE FEES

valid from February 2009 to March 2010

Provisional licence	
Car, motorcycle or moped	£50.00
Bus or lorry	Free
After disqualification until passing re-test	Free
Changing a provisional licence to a full licence	Free
Renewal	
Renewing the photo on the licence (must be renewed every 10 years)	£20.00
At age 70 and over	Free
For medical reasons	Free
Bus or lorry licence	Free
After disqualification	£65.00
After disqualification for some drink driving offences†	£90.00
After revocation	£50.00
Replacing a lost or stolen licence	£20.00
Adding an entitlement to a full licence	Free
Removing expired endorsements	
from a photocard licence	£20.00
from a paper licence (while exchanging it for a photocard licence)	£20.00
Exchanging	
a paper licence for a photocard licence	£20.00
a photocard for a photocard licence	£20.00
a full GB licence for a full Northern Ireland licence	Free
a full GB licence for a full EC/EEA or other foreign licence (including Channel Islands and Isle of Man)	Free
a full EC/EEA or other foreign licence (including Channel Islands and Isle of Man) for a full GB licence	£50.00
Change of name or address (existing licence must be surrendered)	Free

† For an alcohol-related offence where the DVLA needed to arrange medical enquiries

DRIVING TESTS

The Driving Standards Agency (DSA) is responsible for carrying out driving tests and approving driving instructors in Great Britain. Driver and Vehicle Testing, part of the Driver and Vehicle Agency, is responsible for testing drivers and vehicles in Northern Ireland.

DRIVING TESTS TAKEN AND PASSED
April 2008–March 2009

	Number Taken	*Percentage Passed*
Practical Test		
Car	1,717,466	45
Motorcycle	105,440	66
Large goods vehicle	64,926	49
Passenger-carrying vehicle	10,325	52
Theory Test		
Car	1,290,776	65
Motorcycle	103,330	80
Large goods vehicle *	14,487	72
Multiple choice†	20,732	79
Hazard perception†	20,582	82
Passenger-carrying vehicle*	3,480	69
Multiple choice†	4,654	78
Hazard perception†	4,697	81

* The combined theory test for large goods vehicles and passenger-carrying vehicles was replaced with two separate tests (hazard perception and multiple choice) from 4 August 2008. The figures are for 1 April to 3 August 2008 and are not comparable with earlier years.
† Figures are from 4 August 2008 to 31 March 2009
Source: DSA

The theory and practical driving tests can be booked with a postal application, online (W www.direct.gov.uk/drivingtest) or by phone (T 0300-200 1122).

DRIVING TEST FEES (WEEKDAY/EVENING* AND WEEKEND)
from April 2009

Theory tests	
Car and motorcycle	£31.00
Bus and lorry	
Multiple choice test	£35.00
Hazard perception test	£15.00
Driver Certificate of Professional Competence (CPC)	£30.00
Practical tests	
Car	£62.00/£75.00
Tractor and other specialist vehicles	£62.00/£75.00
Motorcycle	
Module 1	£10.00/£10.00
Module 2	£70.00/£82.00
Lorry and bus	£115.00/£141.00
Driver Certificate of Professional Competence (CPC)	£55.00/£63.00
Car and trailer	£115.00/£141.00
Extended tests for disqualified drivers	
Car	£124.00/£150.00
Motorcycle	
Module 1	£10.00/£10.00
Module 2	£140.00/£164.00

* After 4.30pm

VEHICLE LICENCES
Registration and first licensing of vehicles is through local offices of the DVLA in Swansea. Local facilities for relicensing are available at any post office which deals with vehicle licensing. Applicants will need to take their vehicle registration document (V5C) or, if this is not available, the applicant must complete form V62. Postal applications can be made to the post offices shown in the V100 booklet, which also provides guidance on registering and licensing vehicles. All forms and booklets are available at post offices, DVLA local offices and online (W www.dvla.gov.uk or W www.direct.gov.uk)

MOTOR VEHICLES LICENSED 2008 (GREAT BRITAIN)

	Thousands
All cars	28,390
Motorcycles	1,291
Light goods vehicles	3,236
Heavy goods vehicles	519
Buses and coaches	180
Other vehicles*	591
Total	34,206

* Includes rear diggers, lift trucks, rollers, ambulances, taxis, three wheelers and agricultural vehicles
Source: Department for Transport

VEHICLE EXCISE DUTY
Details of the present duties chargeable on motor vehicles are available at DVLA local offices, post offices and online (W www.dvla.gov.uk or W www.direct.gov.uk). The Vehicle Excise and Registration Act 1994 provides *inter alia* that any vehicle kept on a public road but not used on roads is chargeable to excise duty as if it were in use. All non-commercial vehicles constructed before 1 January 1973 are exempt from vehicle excise duty. Any vehicle licensed on or after 31 January 1998, not in use and not kept on public roads must be registered as SORN (Statutory Off Road Notification) to be exempted from vehicle excise duty. From 1 January 2004 the registered keeper of a vehicle remains responsible for taxing a vehicle or making a SORN declaration until that liability is formally transferred to a new keeper.

RATES OF DUTY *from May 2009*

	12 months	6 months
Cars (private/light goods) registered before 1 March 2001		
Under 1,549cc	£125.00	£68.75
Over 1,549cc	£190.00	£104.50
Cars (private/light goods) registered on or after 1 March 2001	£185.00	£101.75
Euro 4 light goods vehicles registered between 1 March 2003 and 31 December 2006	£125.00	£68.75
Euro 5 light goods vehicles registered between 1 January 2009 and 31 December 2010	£125.00	£68.75
Motorcycles (with or without sidecar)		
Not over 150cc	£15.00	–
151–400cc	£33.00	–
401–600cc	£48.00	–
600cc+	£66.00	£36.30
Tricycles		
Not over 150cc	£15.00	–
All others	£66.00	£36.30
*Buses**		
Seating 10–17	£165.00	£90.75
Seating 18–36	£220.00	£121.00
Seating 37–61	£330.00	£181.50
Seating 62+	£500.00	£275.00

* Seating capacity includes driver. The 12-month rate for all reduced pollution buses is £165.00 and the 6-month rate is £90.75

RATES OF DUTY

Cars registered on or after 1 March 2001

Band	CO_2 *Emissions (g/km)*	*Petrol and Diesel Car 12 months*	*6 months*	*Alternative Fuel Car 12 months*	*6 months*
A	Up to 100	–	–	–	–
B–C	101–120	£35.00	–	£15.00	–
D–E	121–140	£120.00	£66.00	£100.00	£55.00
F	141–150	£125.00	£68.75	£105.00	£57.75
G	151–165	£150.00	£82.50	£130.00	£71.50
H–I	166–185	£175.00	£96.25	£155.00	£85.25
J–K*	186–225	£215.00	£118.25	£200.00	£110.00
L–M	226–255+	£405.00	£222.75	£390.00	£214.50

* Includes cars that have a CO_2 emission figure over 225g/km but were registered before 23 March 2006

MOT TESTING

Cars, motorcycles, motor caravans, light goods and dual-purpose vehicles more than three years old must be covered by a current MOT test certificate. However, some vehicles (ie minibuses, ambulances and taxis) may require a certificate at one year old. All certificates must be renewed annually. The MOT testing scheme is administered by the Vehicle and Operator Services Agency (VOSA) on behalf of the Secretary of State for Transport.

A fee is payable to MOT testing stations, which must be authorised to carry out tests. The current maximum fees are:

For cars, private hire and public service vehicles, motor caravans, dual purpose vehicles, ambulances and taxis (all up to eight passenger seats)	£54.00
For motorcycles	£29.20
For motorcycles with sidecar	£37.20
For three-wheeled vehicles (up to 450kg unladen weight)	£37.20
*Private passenger vehicles and ambulances with:	
9–12 passenger seats	£56.45 (£63.05)
13–16 passenger seats	£58.65 (£79.30)
16+ passenger seats	£79.45 (£122.65)
Goods vehicles (3,000–3,500kg)	£57.70

* Figures in parentheses include seatbelt installation check

SHIPPING AND PORTS

Sea trade has always played a central role in Britain's economy. By the 17th century Britain had built up a substantial merchant fleet and by the early 20th century it dominated the world shipping industry. Until the late 1990s the size and tonnage of the UK-registered trading fleet had been steadily declining. In December 1998 the government published *British Shipping: Charting a New Course,* which outlined strategies to promote the long-term interests of British shipping. By the end of 2008 the number of ships in the UK-flagged merchant fleet had increased by 79 per cent while gross tonnage had more than quadrupled since 1998. The UK-flagged merchant fleet now constitutes 1.3 per cent of the world merchant fleet in terms of vessels and 1.8 per cent in terms of gross tonnage.

Freight is carried by liner and bulk services, almost all scheduled liner services being containerised. About 95 per cent by weight of Britain's overseas trade is carried by sea; this amounts to 75 per cent of its total value. Passengers and vehicles are carried by roll-on, roll-off ferries, hovercraft, hydrofoils and high-speed catamarans. There were around 45 million ferry passengers in 2008, of whom 23 million travelled internationally.

Lloyd's of London provides the most comprehensive shipping intelligence service in the world. *Lloyd's Shipping Index,* published daily, lists some 25,000 ocean-going vessels and gives the latest known report of each.

PORTS

There are more than 650 ports in Great Britain for which statutory harbour powers have been granted. Of these about 120 are commercially significant ports. In 2008* the largest ports in terms of freight tonnage were Grimsby and Immingham (65.3 million tonnes), London (53.0 million tonnes), Tees and Hartlepool (45.4 million tonnes), Southampton (41.0 million tonnes), Forth (39.1 million tonnes), Milford Haven (35.9 million tonnes), Liverpool (32.2 million tonnes), Felixstowe (25.0 million tonnes), Dover (24.3 million tonnes) and Medway (15.0 million tonnes). Belfast is the principal freight port in Northern Ireland.

Broadly speaking, ports are owned and operated by private companies, local authorities or trusts. The largest operator is Associated British Ports which owns 21 ports. Provisional port traffic results show that 562.5 million tonnes were handled by UK ports in 2008, a decrease of 3.3 per cent on the previous year's figure of 581.5 million tonnes.

* Provisional data

MARINE SAFETY

The Maritime and Coastguard Agency is an executive agency of the Department for Transport. Working closely with the shipping industry and the public, its aims are to:

- reduce accidents and accident-related deaths within UK search and rescue waters and coastline
- reduce accidents and accident-related deaths from UK-registered merchant ships and fishing vessels
- reduce the number of incidents of pollution from shipping activities in the UK pollution control zone

HM Coastguard maintains a 24-hour search and rescue response and coordination capability for the whole of the UK coast and the internationally agreed search and rescue region. HM Coastguard is responsible for mobilising and organising resources in response to people in distress at sea, or at risk of injury or death on the UK's cliffs or shoreline.

Locations hazardous to shipping in coastal waters are marked by lighthouses and other lights and buoys. The lighthouse authorities are the Corporation of Trinity House (for England, Wales and the Channel Islands), the

Northern Lighthouse Board (for Scotland and the Isle of Man), and the Commissioners of Irish Lights (for Northern Ireland and the Republic of Ireland). Trinity House maintains 69 lighthouses, 10 light vessels/floats, 412 buoys, 19 beacons, 48 radar beacons and seven DGPS (Differential Global Positioning System) stations*. The Northern Lighthouse Board maintains 209 lighthouses, 162 buoys, 37 beacons, 27 radar beacons, nine AIS (automatic identification system) stations, four DGPS stations and one LORAN (long-range navigation) station; and Irish Lights looks after 80 lighthouses, 147 buoys, 45 beacons, 22 radar beacons, four AIS stations, three DGPS stations and two LANBYs (large automatic navigational buoy).

Harbour authorities are responsible for pilotage within their harbour areas, and the Ports Act 1991 provides for the transfer of lights and buoys to harbour authorities where these are used for mainly local navigation.

* DGPS is a satellite-based navigation system

UK-OWNED TRADING VESSELS

500 gross tons and over, as at end 2007

Type of vessel	*No.*	*Gross tonnage*
Tankers	143	5,246,000
Bulk carriers	63	2,786,000
Specialised carriers	19	798,000
Fully cellular container	101	4,893,000
Ro-Ro (passenger and cargo)	105	1,445,000
Other general cargo	158	1,070,000
Passenger	23	1,088,000
All vessels	612	17,327,000

Source: Department for Transport

UK SEA PASSENGER MOVEMENTS 2007

Type of journey	*No. of passenger movements**
International	
Ro-Ro Passengers on short sea routes	23,668,000
Passengers on long sea journeys	68,000
Passengers on cruises beginning or ending at UK ports	1,064,000
Domestic†	3,640,000
Total	28,440,000

* Passengers are included at both departure and arrival if their journeys begin and end at a UK seaport

† Between mainland Great Britain, Northern Ireland, Isle of Man, Channel Islands, Orkney and Shetland

Source: Department for Transport

MARINECALL WEATHER FORECAST SERVICE

Marinecall offers a wide range of inshore, offshore and European forecasts from the Met Office which include gale and strong wind warnings, the general situation, wind speed and direction, probability and strength of gusts, developing weather conditions, visibility and sea state. Information is provided by various means including telephone, fax, SMS etc. Marinecall 10-day forecasts contain a 48-hour inshore waters forecast for the coastal area and up to 12 miles offshore, followed by a 1–5 day forecast for the local sea area, 6–10 day national forecast and an outlook for the month ahead. In addition fax forecasts provide an Atlantic surface pressure chart and 24-hour offshore forecast maps. Other services such as area specific, current weather reports and 48-hour forecasts are also available.

MARINECALL 10-DAY FORECAST

	By Phone	By Fax
INSHORE AREA	09068-500+	09065-300+
Cape Wrath – Rattray Head	451	251
Rattray Head – Berwick	452	252
Berwick – Whitby	453	253
Whitby – Gibraltar Point	454	254
Gibraltar Point – North Foreland	455	255
North Foreland – Selsey Bill	456	256
Selsey Bill – Lyme Regis	457	257
Lyme Regis – Hartland Point	458	258
Hartland Point – St David's Head	459	259
St David's Head – Great Ormes Head	460	260
Great Ormes Head – Mull of Galloway	461	261
Mull of Galloway – Mull of Kintyre	462	262
Mull of Kintyre – Ardnamurchan	463	263
Ardnamurchan – Cape Wrath	464	264
Lough Foyle – Carlingford Lough	465	265
Channel Islands	432	–
OFFSHORE AREA		
English Channel	992	270
Southern North Sea	991	271
Irish Sea	954	273
Biscay	953	274
North-west Scotland	955	275
Northern North Sea	985	276

Marinecall by UK landline is charged at 60p per minute and Marinecall by fax at £1.50 per minute. Calls from mobiles may be subject to network operator surcharges. Subscription packages are available.

UK SHIPPING FORECAST AREAS

Weather bulletins for shipping are broadcast daily on BBC Radio 4 at 00h 48m, 05h 20m, 12h 01m and 17h 54m. All transmissions are broadcast on long wave at 1515m (198kHz) and the 00h 48m and 05h 20m transmissions are also broadcast on FM. The bulletins consist of a gale warning summary, general synopsis, sea-area forecasts and coastal station reports. In addition, gale warnings are broadcast at the first available programme break after receipt. If this does not coincide with a news bulletin, the warning is repeated after the next news bulletin. Shipping forecasts and gale warnings are also available online (W www.bbc.co.uk/weather/coast/shipping).

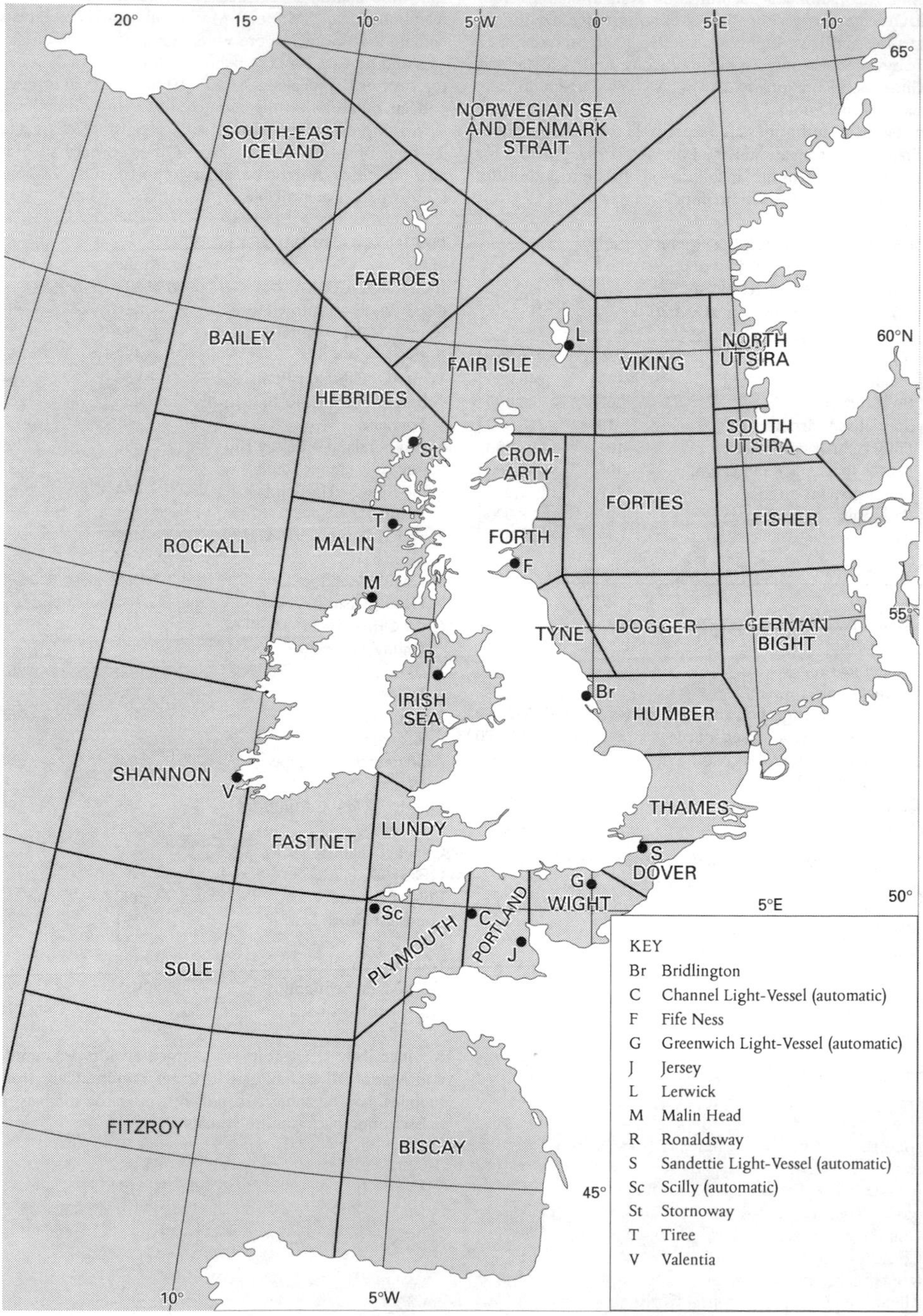

RELIGION IN THE UK

The 2001 census included a voluntary question on religion for the first time (although the question had been included in previous censuses in Northern Ireland); 92 per cent of people chose to answer the question. In the UK, 71.6 per cent of people in Britain identified themselves as Christian (42.1 million people). After Christianity, the next most prevalent faith was Islam with 2.7 per cent describing their religion as Muslim (1.6 million people). The next largest religious groups were Hindus (559,000), followed by Sikhs (336,000), Jews (267,000), Buddhists (152,000) and people from other religions (179,000). Together, these groups accounted for less than 3 per cent of the total UK population. People in Northern Ireland were most likely to say that they identified with a religion (86 per cent) compared with 77 per cent in England and Wales and 67 per cent in Scotland. The English counties with the highest proportion of Christians are Durham, Merseyside and Cumbria, each with 82 per cent or more; in Wales it is Ynys Mon (Isle of Anglesey) (79 per cent). London has the highest proportion of Muslims (8.5 per cent), Hindus (4.1 per cent), Jews (2.1 per cent), Buddhists (0.8 per cent) and people of other religions (0.5 per cent). Around 16 per cent of the UK population stated that they had no religion. The districts with the highest proportions of people with no religion were Norwich, Brighton and Hove and Cambridge, all with over 25 per cent. This category included those who identified themselves as agnostics, atheists, heathens and Jedi Knights.

CENSUS 2001 RESULTS — RELIGIONS IN THE UK

	thousands	*per cent*
Christian	42,079	71.6
Buddhist	152	0.3
Hindu	559	1.0
Jewish	267	0.5
Muslim	1,591	2.7
Sikh	336	0.6
Other religion	179	0.3
All religions	45,163	76.8
No religion	9,104	15.5
Not stated	4,289	7.3
All no religion/not stated	13,626	23.2
TOTAL	58,789	100

Source: Census 2001

INTER-CHURCH AND INTER-FAITH COOPERATION

The main umbrella body for the Christian churches in the UK is Churches Together in Britain and Ireland. There are also ecumenical bodies in each of the constituent countries of the UK: Churches Together in England, Action of Churches Together in Scotland, CYTUN (Churches Together in Wales), and the Irish Council of Churches. The Free Churches Group (formerly the Free Churches Council), which is closely associated with Churches Together in England, represents most of the free churches in England and Wales, and the Evangelical Alliance represents evangelical Christians.

The Inter Faith Network for the United Kingdom promotes cooperation between faiths, and the Council of Christians and Jews works to improve relations between the two religions. Churches Together in Britain and Ireland also has a commission on inter-faith relations.

ACTION OF CHURCHES TOGETHER IN SCOTLAND, Inglewood House, Alloa, Clackmannanshire FK10 2HU T 01259-216980 W www.acts-scotland.org
General Secretary, Brother Stephen Smyth

CHURCHES TOGETHER IN BRITAIN AND IRELAND, 3rd Floor, Bastille Court, 2 Paris Gardens, London SE1 8ND T 020-7654 7254 E info@ctbi.org.uk W www.ctbi.org.uk
General Secretary, Revd Bob Fyffe

CHURCHES TOGETHER IN ENGLAND, 27 Tavistock Square, London WC1H 9HH T 020-7529 8131 E office@cte.org.uk W www.churches-together.net
General Secretary, Revd Dr David Cornick

COUNCIL OF CHRISTIANS AND JEWS, 1st Floor, Camelford House, 87-89 Albert Embankment, London SE1 7TP T 020-7820 0090 E cjrelations@ccj.org.uk W www.ccj.org.uk
Chief Executive, David Gifford

CYTUN (CHURCHES TOGETHER IN WALES), 58 Richmond Road, Cardiff CF24 3UR T 029-2046 4204 E post@cytun.org.uk W www.cytun.org.uk
Chief Executive, Revd Aled Edwards, OBE

EVANGELICAL ALLIANCE, 186 Kennington Park Road, London SE11 4BT T 020-7207 2100 E info@eauk.org W www.eauk.org
General Director, Steve Clifford

FREE CHURCHES GROUP, 27 Tavistock Square, London WC1H 9HH T 020-7529 8131 E freechurch@cte.org.uk
Executive Secretary, Revd Mark Fisher

INTER-FAITH NETWORK FOR THE UK, 8A Lower Grosvenor Place, London SW1W 0EN T 020-7931 7766 E ifnet@interfaith.org.uk W www.interfaith.org.uk
Director, Dr Harriet Crabtree

IRISH COUNCIL OF CHURCHES, Inter-Church Centre, 48 Elmwood Avenue, Belfast BT9 6AZ T 028-9066 3145 E info@irishchurches.org W www.irishchurches.org
General Secretary, Michael Earle

CHRISTIANITY

Christianity is a monotheistic faith based on the person and teachings of Jesus Christ, and all Christian denominations claim his authority. Central to its teaching is the concept of God and his son Jesus Christ, who was crucified and resurrected in order to enable mankind to attain salvation.

The Jewish scriptures predicted the coming of a *Messiah,* an 'anointed one', who would bring salvation. To Christians, Jesus of Nazareth, a Jewish rabbi (teacher) who was born in Palestine, was the promised Messiah. Jesus' birth, teachings, crucifixion and subsequent resurrection are recorded in the *Gospels,* which, together with other scriptures that summarise Christian belief, form the *New Testament.* This, together with the Hebrew scriptures – entitled the *Old Testament* by Christians – makes up the Bible, the sacred texts of Christianity.

BELIEFS

Christians believe that sin distanced mankind from God, and that Jesus was the son of God, sent to redeem mankind from sin by his death. In addition, many believe that Jesus will return again at some future date, triumph over evil and establish a kingdom on earth, thus inaugurating a new age. The Gospel assures Christians that those who believe in Jesus and obey his teachings will be forgiven their sins and will be resurrected from the dead.

PRACTICES

Christian practices vary widely between different Christian churches, but prayer, charity and giving (for the maintenance of the church buildings, for the work of the church, and to those in need) are common to all. In addition, certain days of observance, ie the *Sabbath, Easter* and *Christmas,* are celebrated by most Christians. The Orthodox, Roman Catholic and Anglican churches celebrate many more days of observance, based on saints and significant events in the life of Jesus. The belief in sacraments, physical signs believed to have been ordained by Jesus Christ to symbolise and convey spiritual gifts, varies greatly between Christian denominations; *baptism* and the *Eucharist* are practised by most Christians. Baptism, symbolising repentance and faith in Jesus, is an act marking entry into the Christian community; the Eucharist, the ritual re-enactment of the Last Supper, Jesus' final meal with his disciples, is also practised by most denominations. Other sacraments, such as anointing the sick; the laying on of hands to symbolise the passing on of the office of priesthood or to heal the sick and speaking in tongues, where it is believed that the person is possessed by the Holy Spirit, are less common. In denominations where infant baptism is practised, confirmation (where the person confirms the commitments made on their behalf in infancy) is common. Matrimony and the ordination of priests are also widely believed to be sacraments. Many Protestants regard only baptism and the Eucharist to be sacraments; the Quakers and the Salvation Army reject the use of sacraments.

Most Christians believe that God actively guides the church.

THE EARLY CHURCH

The Apostles were Jesus' first converts and are recognised by Christians as the founders of the Christian community. The new faith spread rapidly throughout the eastern provinces of the Roman Empire. Early Christianity was subjected to great persecution until AD 313, when Emperor Constantine's Edict of Toleration confirmed its right to exist and it was established as the religion of the Roman Empire in AD 381.

The Christian faith was slowly formulated in the first millennium of the Christian era. Between AD 325 and 787 there were seven Oecumenical Councils at which bishops from the entire Christian world assembled to resolve various doctrinal disputes. The estrangement between East and West began after Constantine moved the centre of the Roman Empire from Rome to Constantinople, and it grew after the division of the Roman Empire into eastern and western halves. Linguistic and cultural differences between Greek East and Latin West served to encourage separate ecclesiastical developments which became pronounced in the tenth and early 11th centuries.

Administration of the church was divided between five ancient patriarchates: Rome and all the West, Constantinople (the imperial city – the 'New Rome'), Jerusalem and all of Palestine, Antioch and all the East and Alexandria and all of Africa. Of these, only Rome was in the Latin West and after the schism in 1054, Rome developed a structure of authority centralised on the Papacy, while the Orthodox East maintained the style of localised administration.

Papal authority over the doctrine and jurisdiction of the church in Western Europe was unrivalled after the split with the Eastern Orthodox Church until the Protestant Reformation in the 16th century.

CHRISTIANITY IN BRITAIN

An English church already existed when Pope Gregory sent Augustine to evangelise the English in AD 596. Conflicts between Church and State during the Middle Ages culminated in the Act of Supremacy in 1534, which repudiated papal supremacy and declared King Henry VIII to be the supreme head of the church in England. Since 1559 the English monarch has been termed the Supreme Governor of the Church of England.

In 1560 the jurisdiction of the Roman Catholic Church in Scotland was abolished and the first assembly of the Church of Scotland ratified the Confession of Faith, drawn up by a committee led by John Knox. In 1592 parliament passed an act guaranteeing the liberties of the church and its Presbyterian government. King James VI (James I of England) and later Stuart monarchs attempted to reintroduce episcopacy, but a Presbyterian church was finally restored in 1690 and secured by the Act of Settlement (1690) and the Act of Union (1707).

PORVOO DECLARATION

The Porvoo Declaration was drawn up by representatives of the British and Irish Anglican churches and the Nordic and Baltic Lutheran churches and was approved by the General Synod of the Church of England in July 1995. Churches that approve the declaration regard baptised members of each other's churches as members of their own, and allow free interchange of episcopally ordained ministers within the rules of each church.

NON-CHRISTIAN RELIGIONS AND BELIEFS

BAHA'I FAITH

Mirza Husayn-'Ali, known as *Baha'u'llah* (Glory of God) was born in Iran in 1817 and became a follower of the *Bab,* a religious reformer and prophet who was imprisoned for his beliefs and executed on the grounds of heresy in 1850. Baha'u'llah was himself imprisoned in 1852, and in 1853 he had a vision that he was the 'promised one' foretold by the Bab. He was exiled after his release from prison and eventually arrived in Acre, now in Israel, where he continued to compose the Baha'i sacred scriptures. He died in 1892 and was succeeded by his son, Abdu'l-Baha, as spiritual leader, under whose guidance the faith spread to Europe and North America. He was followed by Shoghi Effendi, his grandson, who translated many of Baha'u'llah's works into English. Upon his death in 1957, a democratic system of leadership was brought into operation.

The Baha'i faith espouses the unity and relativity of religious truth and teaches that there is only one God, whose will has been revealed to mankind by a series of messengers, such as Zoroaster, Abraham, Moses, Buddha, Krishna, Christ, Muhammad, the Bab and Baha'u'llah, who were seen as the founders of separate religions, but whose common purpose was to bring God's message to mankind. It teaches that all races and both sexes are equal and deserving of equal opportunities and treatment, that education is a fundamental right and encourages a fair distribution of wealth. In addition, the faith exhorts mankind to establish a world federal system to promote peace and tolerance.

A feast is held every 19 days, which consists of prayer and readings of Baha'i scriptures, consultation on community business, and social activities. Music, food and beverages usually accompany the proceedings. There is no clergy; each local community elects a local assembly, which coordinates community activities, enrols new members, counsels and assists members in need, and conducts Baha'i marriages and funerals. A national assembly is elected annually by locally elected delegates, and every five years the national spiritual assemblies meet together to elect the Universal House of Justice, the supreme international governing body of the Baha'i Faith. Worldwide there are over 13,000 local spiritual assemblies; there are around five million members residing in about 235 countries, of which 179 have national organisations.

THE BAHA'I OFFICE OF PUBLIC INFORMATION, 27 Rutland Gate, London SW7 1PD **T** 020-7584 2566 **E** opi@bahai.org.uk **W** www.bahai.org.uk
Secretary of the National Spiritual Assembly, Dr Kishan Manocha
Director, Office of Public Information, Robert Weinberg
Director, Diplomatic Relations, Barney Leith

BUDDHISM

Buddhism originated in what is now the Bihar area of northern India in the teachings of Siddhartha Gautama, who became the *Buddha* (Enlightened One). In the Thai or Suriyakati calendar the beginning of the Buddhist era is dated from death of Buddha; the year 2010 is therefore 2553 by the Thai Buddhist reckoning.

Fundamental to Buddhism is the concept of rebirth, whereby each life carries with it the consequences of the conduct of earlier lives (known as the law of *karma*) and this cycle of death and rebirth is broken only when the state of *nirvana* has been reached. Buddhism steers a middle path between belief in personal continuity and the belief that death results in total extinction.

While doctrine does not have a pivotal position in Buddhism, a statement of four 'Noble Truths' is common to all its schools and varieties. These are: suffering is inescapable in even the most fortunate of existences; craving is the root cause of suffering; abandonment of the selfish mindset is the way to end suffering; and bodily and mental discipline, accompanied by the cultivation of wisdom and compassion, provides the spiritual path ('Noble Eightfold Path') to accomplish this. Buddhists deny the idea of a creator and prefer to emphasise the practical aspects of moral and spiritual development.

The schools of Buddhism can be broadly divided into three: *Theravada,* the generally monastic-led tradition practised in Sri Lanka and South-East Asia; *Mahayana,* the philosophical and popular traditions of the Far East; and *Esoteric,* the Tantric-derived traditions found in Tibet and Mongolia and, to a lesser extent, China and Japan. The extensive Theravada scriptures are contained in the *Pali Canon,* which dates in its written form from the first century BC. Mahayana and Esoteric schools have Sanskrit-derived translations of these plus many more additional scriptures as well as exegetical material.

In the East the new and full moons and the lunar quarter days were (and to a certain extent, still are) significant in determining the religious calendar. Most private homes contain a shrine where offerings, worship and other spiritual practices (such as meditation, chanting or mantra recitation) take place on a daily basis. Buddhist festivals vary according to local traditions within the different schools and there is very little uniformity – even in commemorating the birth, enlightenment and death of the Buddha.

There is no governing authority for Buddhism in the UK. Communities representing all schools of Buddhism operate independently. The Buddhist Society was established in 1924; it runs courses, lectures and meditation groups, and publishes books about Buddhism. The Network of Buddhist Organisations was founded in 1993 to promote fellowship and dialogue between Buddhist organisations and to facilitate cooperation in matters of common interest.

There are estimated to be at least 300 million Buddhists worldwide. Of the 152,000 Buddhists in the UK (according to the 2001 census), 60,000 are white British (the majority are converts), 36,000 Chinese, 15,000 Asian and 36,000 'other ethnic'.

THE BUDDHIST SOCIETY, 58 Eccleston Square, London SW1V 1PH **T** 020-7834 5858 **E** info@thebuddhistsociety.org **W** www.thebuddhistsociety.org

FRIENDS OF THE WESTERN BUDDHIST ORDER, The London Buddhist Centre, 51 Roman Road, London E2 0HU **T** 0845-458 4716 **E** info@lbc.org.uk **W** www.fwbo.org

THE NETWORK OF BUDDHIST ORGANISATIONS, 6 Tyne Road, Bishopston, Bristol BS7 8EE **T** 0845-345 8978 **E** secretary@nbo.org.uk **W** www.nbo.org.uk

THE OFFICE OF TIBET, Tibet House, 1 Culworth Street, London NW8 7AF **T** 020-7722 5378 **E** info@tibet.com **W** www.tibet.com
Representative of HH the Dalai Lama, Thubten Samdup

SOKA GAKKAI INTERNATIONAL (UK), Taplow Court Grand Cultural Centre, Taplow, Berkshire SL6 0ER **T** 01628-773163 **W** www.sgi-uk.org

HINDUISM

Hinduism has no historical founder but had become highly developed in India by *c.*2500 BC. Its adherents originally called themselves Aryans; Muslim invaders first called the Aryans 'Hindus' (derived from 'Sindhu', the name of the river Indus) in the eighth century.

Most Hindus hold that *satya* (truthfulness), honesty, sincerity and devotion to God are essential for good living. They believe in one supreme spirit *(Brahman),* and in the transmigration of *atman* (the soul). Most Hindus accept the doctrine of *karma* (consequences of actions), the concept of *samsara* (successive lives) and the possibility of all atmans achieving *moksha* (liberation from samsara) through *jnana* (knowledge), *yoga* (meditation), *karma* (work or action) and *bhakti* (devotion).

Most Hindus offer worship to *murtis* (images of deities) representing different incarnations or aspects of Brahman, and follow their *dharma* (religious and social duty) according to the traditions of their *varna* (social class), *ashrama* (stage in life), *jaiti* (caste) and *kula* (family).

Hinduism's sacred texts are divided into *shruti* ('that which is heard'), including the *Vedas,* and *smriti* ('that which is remembered'), including the *Ramayana,* the *Mahabharata,* the *Puranas* (ancient myths), and the sacred law books. Most Hindus recognise the authority of the *Vedas,* the oldest holy books, and accept the philosophical teachings of the *Upanishads*, the *Vedanta Sutras* and the *Bhagavad-Gita*.

Hindus believe Brahman to be omniscient, omnipotent, limitless and all-pervading. Brahman is usually worshipped in its deity form. Brahma, Vishnu and Shiva are the most important deities or aspects of Brahman worshipped by Hindus; their respective consorts are Saraswati, Lakshmi and Durga or Parvati, also known as Shakti. There are believed to have been ten *avatars* (incarnations) of Vishnu, of whom the most important are Rama and Krishna. Other popular gods are Ganesha, Hanuman and Subrahmanyam. All Hindu gods are seen as aspects of the supreme spirit (Brahman), not as competing deities.

Orthodox Hindus revere all gods and goddesses equally, but there are many denominations, including the Hare-Krishna movement (ISKCon), the Arya Samaj and the Swaminarayan Hindu mission, in which worship is concentrated on one deity. The *guru* (spiritual teacher) is seen as the source of spiritual guidance.

Hinduism does not have a centrally trained and ordained priesthood. The pronouncements of the *shankaracharyas* (heads of monasteries) of Shringeri, Puri, Dwarka and Badrinath are heeded by the orthodox but may be ignored by the various sects.

The commonest form of worship is *puja*, in which water, flowers, food, fruit, incense and light are offered to the deity. Puja may be done either in a home shrine or a *mandir* (temple). Many British Hindus celebrate *samskars* (purification rites), to name a baby, for the sacred thread (an initiation ceremony), marriage and cremation.

The largest communities of Hindus in Britain are in Leicester, London, Birmingham and Bradford, and developed as a result of immigration from India, eastern Africa and Sri Lanka.

There are an estimated 800 million Hindus worldwide; there are around 559,000 adherents, according to the 2001 UK census, and over 140 temples in the UK.

ARYA SAMAJ LONDON, 69A Argyle Road, London W13 0LY **T** 020-8991 1732
E aryasamajlondon@yahoo.co.uk **W** aryasamajlondon.co.uk
General Secretary, Amrit Lal Bhardwaj

BHARATIYA VIDYA BHAVAN, Institute of Indian Art and Culture, 4A Castletown Road, London W14 9HE
T 020-7381 3086 **E** info@bhavan.net **W** www.bhavan.net
Executive Director, Dr M. N. Nandakumara

INTERNATIONAL SOCIETY FOR KRISHNA CONSCIOUSNESS (ISKCON), Bhaktivedanta Manor, Dharam Marg, Hilfield Lane, Aldenham, Watford, Herts WD25 8EZ **T** 01923-851000
E bhaktivendanta.manor@pamho.net
W www.krishnatemple.com
Temple Chair, Sruti Dharma Das

NATIONAL COUNCIL OF HINDU TEMPLES (UK), 1 Hans Close, Stoke, Coventry CV2 4WA **T** 0780-505 4776
E sanjay.jagatia@ntlworld.com **W** www.nchtuk.org
General Secretary, Sanjay Jagatia

SWAMINARAYAN HINDU MISSION (SHRI SWAMINARAYAN MANDIR), 105–119 Brentfield Road, London NW10 8LD **T** 020-8965 2651
E info@mandir.org **W** www.mandir.org

HUMANISM

Humanism traces its roots back to ancient times, with Indian, Chinese, Greek and Roman philosophers expressing Humanist ideas some 2,500 years ago. Confucius, the Chinese philosopher who lived *c.*500 BC, believed that religious observances should be replaced with moral values as the basis of social and political order and that 'the true way' is based on reason and humanity. He also stressed the importance of benevolence and respect for others, and believed that the individual situation should be considered rather than the global application of traditional rules.

Humanists believe that there is no God or other supernatural being, that humans have only one life (Humanists do not believe in an after-life or reincarnation) and that humans can live ethical and fulfilling lives without religious beliefs through a moral code derived from a shared history, personal experience and thought. There are no sacred Humanist texts. Particular emphasis is placed on science as the only reliable source of knowledge of the universe. Many Humanists recognise a need for ceremonies to mark important occasions in life and the British Humanist Association has a network of celebrants who are trained and accredited to conduct baby namings, weddings and funerals. The British Humanist Association's campaigns for a secular society (a society based on freedom of religious or non-religious belief with no privileges for any particular set of beliefs) are based on equality and human rights. The association also campaigns for inclusive schools that meet the needs of all parents and pupils, regardless of their religious or non-religious beliefs.

BRITISH HUMANIST ASSOCIATION, 1 Gower Street, London WC1E 6HD **T** 020-7079 3580 **F** 020-7079 3588
E info@humanism.org.uk **W** www.humanism.org.uk
Chief Executive, Hanne Stinson

ISLAM

Islam (which means 'peace arising from submission to the will of Allah' in Arabic) is a monotheistic religion which was taught in Arabia by the Prophet Muhammad, who was born in Mecca (Al-Makkah) in 570 AD. Islam spread to Egypt, north Africa, Spain and the borders of China in the century following the Prophet's death, and is now the predominant religion in Indonesia, the near and Middle East, northern and parts of western Africa, Pakistan, Bangladesh, Malaysia and some of the former Soviet republics. There are also large Muslim communities in other countries.

For Muslims (adherents of Islam), there is one God *(Allah)*, who holds absolute power. Muslims believe that Allah's commands were revealed to mankind through the prophets, who include Abraham, Moses and Jesus, but that Allah's message was gradually corrupted until revealed finally and in perfect form to Muhammad through the angel *Jibril* (Gabriel) over a period of 23 years. This last, incorruptible message is said to have been recorded in the *Qur'an* (Koran), which contains 114 divisions called *surahs*, each made up of *ayahs* of various lengths, and is held to be the essence of all previous scriptures. The *Ahadith* are the records of the Prophet Muhammad's deeds and sayings (the *Sunnah*) as practised and recounted by his immediate followers. A culture and a system of law and theology gradually developed to form a distinctive Islamic civilisation. Islam makes no distinction between sacred and worldly affairs and provides rules for every aspect of human life. The *Shariah* is the sacred law of Islam based primarily upon prescriptions derived from the *Qur'an* and the *Sunnah* of the Prophet.

The 'five pillars of Islam' are *shahadah* (a declaration of faith in the oneness and supremacy of Allah and the messengership of Muhammad); *salat* (formal prayer, to be performed five times a day facing the *Ka'bah* (the most sacred shrine in the holy city of Mecca)); *zakat* (welfare due, paid annually on all savings at the rate of 2.5 per cent); *sawm* (fasting during the month of Ramadan from dawn until sunset); and *hajj* (pilgrimage to Mecca made once in a lifetime if the believer is financially and physically able). Some Muslims would add *jihad* as the sixth pillar (striving for the cause of good and resistance to evil).

Two main groups developed among Muslims. *Sunni* Muslims accept the legitimacy of Muhammad's first four *caliphs* (successors as head of the Muslim community) and of the authority of the Muslim community as a whole. About 90 per cent of Muslims are Sunni Muslims.

Shi'ites recognise only Muhammad's son-in-law Ali as his rightful successor and the *Imams* (descendants of Ali, not to be confused with *imams,* who are prayer leaders or religious teachers) as the principal legitimate religious authority. The largest group within Shi'ism is *Twelver Shi'ism,* which has been the official school of law and theology in Iran since the 16th century; other subsects include the *Ismailis,* the *Druze* and the *Alawis,* the latter two differing considerably from the main body of Muslims. The *Ibadis* of Oman are neither Sunni nor Shia, deriving from the strictly observant *Khariji* (Seceeders). There is no organised priesthood, but learned men such as imams, *ulama,* and *ayatollahs* are accorded great respect. The *Sufis* are the mystics of Islam. Mosques are centres for worship and teaching and also for social and welfare activities.

Islam was first recorded in western Europe in the eighth century AD when 800 years of Muslim rule began in Spain. Later, Islam spread to eastern Europe. More recently, Muslims came to Europe from Africa, the Middle East and Asia in the late 19th century. Both the Sunni and Shi'a traditions are represented in Britain, but the majority of Muslims in Britain adhere to Sunni Islam. Efforts to establish a representative national body for Muslims in Britain resulted in the founding, in 1997, of the Muslim Council of Britain. In addition, there are many other Muslim organisations in the UK. There are around 1,200 million Muslims worldwide, with nearly two million adherents and about 1,650 mosques in the UK.

IMAMS AND MOSQUES COUNCIL, 20–22 Creffield Road, London W5 3RP T 020-8992 6636 E msraza@muslimcollege.ac.uk
Director, Moulana M. S. Raza

ISLAMIC CULTURAL CENTRE – THE LONDON CENTRAL MOSQUE, 146 Park Road, London NW8 7RG T 020-7725 2213 E info@iccuk.org W www.iccuk.org
Director, Dr Ahmad Al-Dubayan

MUSLIM COUNCIL OF BRITAIN, PO Box 57330, London E1 2WJ T 0845-262 6786 E admin@mcb.org.uk W www.mcb.org.uk
Secretary-General, Dr Muhammad Abdul Bari

MUSLIM WORLD LEAGUE LONDON, 46 Goodge Street, London W1T 4LU T 020-7636 7568
Director, Dr Ahmad Makhoodom

UNION OF MUSLIM ORGANISATIONS OF THE UK AND IRELAND, 109 Campden Hill Road, London W8 7TL T 020-7221 6608
Secretary-General, Dr Syed A. Pasha

JAINISM

Jainism traces its history to Vardhamana Jnatriputra, known as *Tirthankara Mahavira* (the Great Hero) whose traditional dates were 599–527 BC. Jains believe he was the last of a series of 24 *Jinas* (those who overcome all passions and desires) or *Tirthankaras* (those who show a way across the ocean of life) stretching back to remote antiquity. Born to a noble family in north-eastern India (the state of Bihar), he renounced the world for the life of a wandering ascetic and after 12 years of austerity and meditation he attained enlightenment. He then preached his message until, at the age of 72, he left the mortal world and achieved total liberation *(moksha)* from the cycle of death and rebirth.

Jains declare that the Hindu rituals of transferring merit are not acceptable as each living being is responsible for its own actions. They recognise some of the minor deities of the Hindu pantheon, but the supreme objects of worship are the Tirthankaras. The pious Jain does not ask favours from the Tirthankaras, but seeks to emulate their example in his or her own life.

Jains believe that the universe is eternal and self-subsisting, that there is no omnipotent creator God ruling it and the destiny of the individual is in his or her own hands. *Karma,* the fruit of past actions, is believed to determine the place of every living being and rebirth may be in the heavens, on earth as a human, an animal or other lower being, or in the hells. The ultimate goal of existence for Jains is *moksha,* a state of perfect knowledge and tranquility for each individual soul, which can be achieved only by gaining enlightenment.

The Jainist path to liberation is defined by the three jewels: *Samyak Darshan* (right perception), *Samyak Jnana* (right knowledge) and *Samyak Charitra* (right conduct). Of the five fundamental precepts of the Jains, *Ahimsa* (non-injury to any form of being, in any mode: thought, speech or action) is the first and foremost, and was popularised by Gandhi as *Ahimsa paramo dharma* (non-violence is the supreme religion).

The largest population of Jains can be found in India but there are approximately 30,000 Jains in Britain, sizeable communities in North America, East Africa, Australia and smaller groups in many other countries.

INSTITUTE OF JAINOLOGY, Unit 18, Silicon Business Centre, 28 Wadsworth Road, Perivale, Greenford, Middx UB6 7JZ T 020-8997 2300 E enquiries@jainology.org W www.jainology.org
Hon. Secretary, Dr Harshad Sanghrajka

JUDAISM

Judaism is the oldest monotheistic faith. The primary text of Judaism is the Hebrew bible or *Tanakh,* which records how the descendants of Abraham were led by Moses out of their slavery in Egypt to Mount Sinai where God's law *(Torah)* was revealed to them as the chosen people. The *Talmud,* which consists of commentaries on the *Mishnah* (the first text of rabbinical Judaism), is also held to be authoritative, and may be divided into two main categories: the *halakah* (dealing with legal and ritual matters) and the *aggadah* (dealing with theological and ethical matters not directly concerned with the regulation of conduct). The *midrash* comprises rabbinic writings containing biblical interpretations in the spirit of the aggadah. The halakah has become a source of division: orthodox Jews regard Jewish law as derived from God and therefore unalterable; progressive Jews seek to interpret it in the light of contemporary considerations; and conservative Jews aim to maintain most of the traditional rituals but to allow changes in accordance with tradition. Reconstructionist Judaism, a 20th-century movement, regards Judaism as a culture rather than a theological system and accepts all forms of Jewish practice.

The family is the basic unit of Jewish ritual, with the synagogue playing an important role as the centre for public worship and religious study. A synagogue is led by a group of laymen who are elected to office. The Rabbi is primarily a teacher and spiritual guide. The Sabbath is the central religious observance. Most British Jews are descendants of either the *Ashkenazim* of central and eastern Europe or the *Sephardim* of Spain, Portugal and the Middle East.

The Chief Rabbi of the United Hebrew Congregations of the Commonwealth is appointed by a Chief Rabbinate Conference, and is the rabbinical authority of the mainstream Orthodox sector of the Ashkenazi Jewish community, the largest body of which is the United Synagogue. His formal ecclesiastical authority is not recognised by the Reform Synagogues of Great Britain (the largest progressive group), the Union of Liberal and Progressive Synagogues, the Sephardi community or the Assembly of Masorti Synagogues. He is, however, generally recognised both outside the Jewish community and within it as the public religious representative of the totality of British Jewry. The Chief Rabbi is President of the London *Beth Din* (Court of Judgement), a rabbinic court. The *Dayanim* (Assessors) adjudicate in disputes or on matters of Jewish law and tradition; they also oversee dietary law administration, marriage, divorce and issues of personal status.

The Board of Deputies of British Jews, established in 1760, is the representative body of British Jewry. The basis of representation is through the election of deputies by synagogues and communal organisations. It protects and promotes the interests of British Jewry, acts as the central voice of the community and seeks to counter anti-Jewish discrimination and anti-Semitic activities.

There are over 12.5 million Jews worldwide; in the UK there are an estimated 300,000 adherents and almost 400 synagogues.

OFFICE OF THE CHIEF RABBI, Adler House, 735 High Road, London N12 0US T 020-8343 6301 F 020-8343 6310 E info@chiefrabbi.org W www.chiefrabbi.org
Chief Rabbi, Sir Jonathan Sacks

BETH DIN (COURT OF THE CHIEF RABBI), 305 Ballards Lane, London N12 8NP T 020-8343 6270 E info@bethdin.org.uk W www.theus.org.uk
Registrar, David Frei
Dayanim, Rabbi Chanoch Ehrentreu *(Consultant Dayan)*; Menachem Gelley *(Senior Dayan)*; Ivan Binstock; Yonason Abraham; Shmuel Simons

ASSEMBLY OF MASORTI SYNAGOGUES, Alexander House, 3 Shakespeare Road, London N3 1XE T 020-8349 6650 E enquiries@masorti.org.uk W www.masorti.org.uk
Executive Director, Michael Gluckman

BOARD OF DEPUTIES OF BRITISH JEWS, 6 Bloomsbury Square, London WC1A 2LP T 020-7543 5400 F 020-7543 0010 E info@bod.org.uk W www.bod.org.uk
President, Vivian Wineman

FEDERATION OF SYNAGOGUES, 65 Watford Way, London NW4 3AQ T 020-8202 2263 E info@federationofsynagogues.com W www.federationofsynagogues.com
President, Alan Finlay
Chief Executive, Dr Eli Kienwald

LIBERAL JUDAISM, The Montagu Centre, 21 Maple Street, London W1T 4BE T 020-7580 1663 E montagu@liberaljudaism.org W www.liberaljudaism.org
Chief Executive, Rabbi Danny Rich

THE MOVEMENT FOR REFORM JUDAISM, The Sternberg Centre for Judaism, 80 East End Road, London N3 2SY T 020-8349 5640 E admin@reformjudaism.org.uk W www.reformjudaism.org.uk
Head of Movement, Rabbi Dr Tony Bayfield

SPANISH AND PORTUGUESE JEWS' CONGREGATION, 2 Ashworth Road, London W9 1JY T 020-7289 2573 E howardmiller@spsyn.org.uk
Chief Executive, Howard Miller

UNION OF ORTHODOX HEBREW CONGREGATIONS, 140 Stamford Hill, London N16 6QT T 020-8802 6226
President, Rabbi Dovid Frand
Executive Coordinator, Chanoch Kesselman
Secretary, Chayim Schneck

UNITED SYNAGOGUE HEAD OFFICE, Adler House, 735 High Road, London N12 0US T 020-8343 8989 E info@theus.org.uk W www.theus.org.uk
Chief Executive, Jeremy Jacobs

PAGANISM

Paganism draws on the ideas of the Celtic people of pre-Roman Europe and is closely linked to Druidism. The first historical record of Druidry comes from classical Greek and Roman writers of the third century BC, who noted the existence of Druids among a people called the Keltoi who inhabited central and southern Europe. The word druid may derive from the Indo-European 'dreo-vid', meaning 'one who knows the truth'. In practice it was probably understood to mean something like 'wise-one' or 'philosopher-priest'.

Paganism is a pantheistic nature-worshipping religion which incorporates beliefs and ritual practices from ancient times. Pagans place much emphasis on the natural world and the ongoing cycle of life and death is central to their beliefs. Most Pagans believe that they are part of nature and not separate from, or superior to it, and seek to live in a way that minimises harm to the natural environment (the word Pagan derives from the Latin *Paganus,* meaning 'rural'). Paganism strongly emphasises the equality of the sexes, with women playing a prominent role in the modern Pagan movement and goddess worship featuring in most ceremonies. Paganism cannot be defined by any principal beliefs because it is shaped by each individual's experiences.

The Pagan Federation was founded in 1971 to provide information on Paganism, campaigns on issues which affect Paganism and provides support to members of the Pagan community. Within the UK the Pagan Federation is divided into 13 districts each with a district manager, regional and local coordinators. Local meetings are called 'moots' and take place in private homes, pubs or coffee bars. The Pagan Federation publishes a quarterly journal, *Pagan Dawn,* formerly *The Wiccan* (founded in 1968). The federation also publishes other material, arranges members-only and public events and maintains personal contact by letter with individual members and the wider Pagan community. Regional gatherings and conferences are held throughout the year.

THE PAGAN FEDERATION, BM Box 7097, London WC1N 3XX T 0798-603 4387 E secretary@paganfed.org W www.paganfed.org
President, John MacIntyre
Secretary, Lee-Anne Haye

SIKHISM

The Sikh religion dates from the birth of Guru Nanak in the Punjab in 1469. 'Guru' means teacher but in Sikh tradition has come to represent the divine presence of God giving inner spiritual guidance. Nanak's role as the human vessel of the divine guru was passed on to nine successors, the last of whom (Guru Gobind Singh) died in

1708. The immortal guru is now held to reside in the sacred scripture, Guru Granth Sahib, and so to be present in all Sikh gatherings.

Guru Nanak taught that there is one God and that different religions are like different roads leading to the same destination. He condemned religious conflict, ritualism and caste prejudices. The fifth Guru, Guru Arjan Dev, largely compiled the Sikh Holy scripture, a collection of hymns *(gurbani)* known as the *Adi Granth*. It includes the writings of the first five gurus and the ninth guru, and selected writings of Hindu and Muslim saints whose views are in accord with the gurus' teachings. Guru Arjan Dev also built the Golden Temple at Amritsar, the centre of Sikhism. The tenth guru, Guru Gobind Singh, passed on the guruship to the sacred scripture, *Guru Granth Sahib* and founded the *Khalsa*, an order intended to fight against tyranny and injustice. Male initiates to the order added 'Singh' to their given names and women added 'Kaur'. Guru Gobind Singh also made the wearing of five symbols obligatory: *kaccha* (a special undergarment), *kara* (a steel bangle), *kirpan* (a small sword), *kesh* (long unshorn hair, and consequently the wearing of a turban) and *kangha* (a comb). These practices are still compulsory for those Sikhs who are initiated into the Khalsa (the *Amritdharis*). Those who do not seek initiation are known as *Sehajdharis*.

There are no professional priests in Sikhism; anyone with a reasonable proficiency in the Punjabi language can conduct a service. Worship can be offered individually or communally, and in a private house or a *gurdwara* (temple). Sikhs are forbidden to eat meat prepared by ritual slaughter; they are also asked to abstain from smoking, alcohol and other intoxicants. Such abstention is compulsory for the Amritdharis.

There are about 20 million Sikhs worldwide and, according to the 2001 census, there are 336,000 adherents in the UK. Every gurdwara manages its own affairs; there is no central body in the UK. The Sikh Missionary Society provides an information service.

SIKH MISSIONARY SOCIETY UK, 10 Featherstone Road, Southall, Middx UB2 5AA **T** 020-8574 1902
E info@sikhmissionarysociety.org
W www.sikhmissionarysociety.org
Hon. General Secretary, Teja Singh Manget

ZOROASTRIANISM

Zoroastrians are followers of the Iranian prophet Spitaman Zarathushtra (or Zoroaster in its hellenised form) who lived *c.*1200 BC. Zoroastrians were persecuted in Iran following the Arab invasion of Persia in the seventh century AD and a group (who are known as Parsis) migrated to India in the eighth century AD to avoid harassment and persecution. Zarathushtra's words are recorded in five poems called the *Gathas,* which, together with other scriptures, forms the *Avesta.*

Zoroastrianism teaches that there is one God, *Ahura Mazda* (Wise Lord), and that all creation stems ultimately from God; the Gathas teach that human beings have free will, are responsible for their own actions and can choose between good and evil. It is believed that choosing *Asha* (truth or righteousness), with the aid of *Vohu Manah* (good mind), leads to happiness for the individual and society, whereas choosing evil leads to unhappiness and conflict. The *Gathas* also encourage hard work, good deeds and charitable acts. Zoroastrians believe that after death the immortal soul is judged by God, and is then sent to paradise or hell, where it will stay until the end of time to be resurrected for the final judgement.

In Zoroastrian places of worship, an urn containing fire is the central feature; the fire symbolises purity, light and truth and is a visible symbol of the *Fravashi* or *Farohar* (spirit), the presence of Ahura Mazda in every human being. Zoroastrians respect nature and much importance is attached to cultivating land and protecting air, earth and water.

The Zoroastrian Trust Funds of Europe is the main body for Zorastrians in the UK. Founded in 1861 as the Religious Funds of the Zorastrians of Europe, it disseminates information on the Zoroastrian faith, provides a place of worship and maintains separate burial grounds for Zoroastrians. It also holds religious and social functions and provides assistance to Zoroastrians as considered necessary, including the provision of loans and grants to students of Zoroastrianism.

There are approximately 140,000 Zoroastrians worldwide, of which around 7,000 reside in Britain, mainly in London and the South East.

ZOROASTRIAN TRUST FUNDS OF EUROPE, Zoroastrian Centre, 440 Alexandra Avenue, Harrow, Middx HA2 9TL **T** 020-8866 0765 **E** secretary@ztfe.com
W www.ztfe.com
President, Paurushasp B. Jila

CHURCHES

There are two established (ie state) churches in the United Kingdom: the Church of England and the Church of Scotland. There are no established churches in Wales or Northern Ireland, though the Church in Wales, the Scottish Episcopal Church and the Church of Ireland are members of the Anglican Communion.

CHURCH OF ENGLAND

The Church of England is the established (ie national) church in England and is organised locally into dioceses and parishes. It traces its life back to the first coming of Christianity to England. Its position is defined by the ancient creeds of the church and by the 39 Articles of Religion (1571), the Book of Common Prayer (1662) and the Ordinal. The Church of England is thus both catholic and reformed. It is the mother church of the Anglican Communion.

THE ANGLICAN COMMUNION

The Anglican Communion consists of 38 independent provincial or national Christian churches throughout the world, many of which are in Commonwealth countries and originate from missionary activity by the Church of England. Every ten years all the bishops in the Communion meet at the Lambeth Conference, convened by the Archbishop of Canterbury. The conference has no policy-making authority but is an important forum for discussing and forming consensus around issues of common concern. The Anglican Consultative Council was formed following a resolution of the 1968 Lambeth Conference which discerned the need for more frequent and representative contact than was possible through a once-a-decade conference of bishops. The council came into being in 1969 and meets every two to three years to liaise between the member churches and provinces of the Anglican Communion.

There are around 70 million Anglicans organised into 500 dioceses and 64,000 individual congregations worldwide.

STRUCTURE

The Church of England is divided into the two provinces of Canterbury and York, each under an archbishop. The two provinces are subdivided into 44 dioceses.

Legislative provision for the Church of England is made by the General Synod, established in 1970. It also discusses and expresses opinion on any other matter of religious or public interest. The General Synod has 467 members in total, divided between three houses: the House of Bishops, the House of Clergy and the House of Laity. It is presided over jointly by the Archbishops of Canterbury and York and normally meets twice a year. The synod has the power, delegated by parliament, to frame statute law (known as a 'measure') on any matter concerning the Church of England. A measure must be laid before both houses of parliament, who may accept or reject it but cannot amend it. Once accepted the measure is submitted for royal assent and then has the full force of law. In addition to the General Synod, there are synods at diocesan level.

The Archbishops' Council was established in January 1999. Its creation was the result of changes to the Church of England's national structure proposed in 1995 and subsequently approved by the synod and parliament. The council's purpose, set out in the National Institutions Measure 1998, is 'to coordinate, promote and further the work and mission of the Church of England'. It reports to the General Synod. The Archbishops' Council comprises the Archbishops of Canterbury and York, *ex officio,* the prolocutors elected by the convocations of Canterbury and York, the chair and vice-chair of the House of Laity, elected by that house, two bishops, two clergy and two lay persons elected by their respective houses of the General Synod, and up to six persons appointed jointly by the two archbishops with the approval of the General Synod.

There are also a number of national boards, councils and other bodies working on matters such as social responsibility, mission, Christian unity and education which report to the General Synod through the Archbishops' Council.

GENERAL SYNOD OF THE CHURCH OF ENGLAND, Church House, Great Smith Street, London SW1P 3NZ T 020-7898 1000
Joint Presidents, Archbishops of Canterbury and York
HOUSE OF BISHOPS: *Chair,* Archbishop of Canterbury; *Vice-Chair,* Archbishop of York
HOUSE OF CLERGY: *Chairs (alternating),* Ven. Norman Russell; Canon Glyn Webster
HOUSE OF LAITY: *Chair,* Dr Christina Baxter; *Vice-Chair,* Dr Philip Giddings
ARCHBISHOPS' COUNCIL, Church House, Great Smith Street, London SW1P 3NZ T 020-7898 1000
Joint Presidents, Archbishops of Canterbury and York; *Secretary-General,* William Fittall

THE ORDINATION OF WOMEN

The canon making it possible for women to be ordained to the priesthood was promulgated in the General Synod in February 1994 and the first 32 women priests were ordained on 12 March 1994.

MEMBERSHIP

In 2007, 138,900 people were baptised, the Church of England had an electoral roll membership of 1.2 million, and each week about 1.2 million people attended services. As at December 2008 there were over 16,000 churches and places of worship; 354* dignitaries (including bishops, archdeacons and cathedral clergy); 7,521* full-time parochial stipendiary clergy; 340* full-time non parochial stipendiary clergy; 1,580 chaplains etc; 344 lay workers and Church Army evangelists; 7,653 licensed readers and 2,537 readers with permission to officiate and active emeriti; and approximately 4,580 active retired ordained clergy.

* Data excludes the Diocese of Europe

	Full-time Diocesan Clergy 2008		Electoral Roll Membership
	Male	*Female*	*2007*
Bath and Wells	168	40	36,000
Birmingham	123	45	17,500
Blackburn	159	17	34,700
Bradford	85	14	11,300
Bristol	103	29	15,400
Canterbury	113	24	20,600
Carlisle	120	25	20,400
Chelmsford	315	72	45,300
Chester	197	46	42,600
Chichester	273	19	54,100
Coventry	98	18	17,300
Derby	130	25	17,800
Durham	151	38	22,800
Ely	105	37	18,300
Europe	107*	12*	10,300
Exeter	189	34	30,800
Gloucester	108	31	22,100
Guildford	145	30	28,100
Hereford	69	27	17,600
Leicester	105	38	16,400
Lichfield	243	55	44,600
Lincoln	138	35	28,400
Liverpool	162	49	26,800
London	447	67	64,400
Manchester	185	56	32,600
Newcastle	106	32	16,000
Norwich	158	35	19,800
Oxford	286	89	52,700
Peterborough	112	29	18,300
Portsmouth	94	18	16,400
Ripon and Leeds	94	36	15,300
Rochester	185	29	28,500
St Albans	187	65	36,900
St Edmundsbury and Ipswich	114	27	23,300
Salisbury	168	44	40,700
Sheffield	120	37	17,400
Sodor and Man	12	1	2,700
Southwark	268	76	44,800
Southwell and Nottingham	107	43	18,800
Truro	91	18	15,700
Wakefield	113	39	19,800
Winchester	190	21	37,000
Worcester	113	30	19,200
York	183	43	33,000
Total	6,739	1,595	1,173,000

STIPENDS 2009–10†

Archbishop of Canterbury	£70,810
Archbishop of York	£60,690
Bishop of London	£55,630
Other diocesan bishops	£38,440
Suffragan bishops	£31,360
Assistant bishops (full-time)	£30,350
Deans	£31,360
Archdeacons (recommended)	£30,350
Residentiary canons	£24,280‡
Incumbents and clergy of similar status	£22,250‡

* 2007 figures
† For those appointed on or after 1 April 2004, transitional arrangements are in place for those appointed prior to this date.
‡ Adjusted regionally to reflect variations in the cost of living

CANTERBURY

104TH ARCHBISHOP AND PRIMATE OF ALL ENGLAND

Most Revd and Rt. Hon. Rowan Williams, *cons.* 1992, *apptd* 2002; Lambeth Palace, London SE1 7JU
Signs Rowan Cantuar:

BISHOPS SUFFRAGAN

Dover, Rt. Revd Stephen Venner, *cons. 1994, apptd* 1999; Upway, St Martin's Hill, Canterbury, Kent CT1 1PR
Maidstone, Rt. Revd Graham Cray, *cons.* 2001, *apptd* 2001; Bishop's House, Pett Lane, Charing, Ashford, Kent TN27 0DL
Ebbsfleet, Rt. Revd Andrew Burnham, *cons.* 2000, *apptd* 2000 (provincial episcopal visitor); Bishop's House, Dry Sandford, Abingdon, Oxon OX13 6JP
Richborough, Rt. Revd Keith Newton, *cons.* 2002, *apptd* 2002 (provincial episcopal visitor); 6 Mellis Gardens, Woodford Green, Essex IG8 0BH

DEAN

Very Revd Robert Willis, *apptd* 2001

Organist, D. Flood, FRCO, *apptd* 1988

ARCHDEACONS

Canterbury, Ven. Sheila Watson *apptd* 2007
Maidstone, Ven. Philip Down, *apptd* 2002

Vicar-General of Province and Diocese, Chancellor Sheila Cameron, QC
Commissary-General, His Hon. Richard Walker
Joint Registrars of the Province, Canon John Rees; Stephen Slack
Diocesan Registrar and Legal Adviser, Richard Sturt
Diocesan Secretary, Julian Hills, Diocesan House, Lady Wootton's Green, Canterbury CT1 1NQ **T** 01227-459401

YORK

97TH ARCHBISHOP AND PRIMATE OF ENGLAND

Most Revd and Rt. Hon. Dr John Sentamu, *cons.* 1996, *trans.* 2005; Bishopthorpe, York YO23 2GE
Signs Sentamu Ebor:

BISHOPS SUFFRAGAN

Hull, Rt. Revd Richard Frith, *cons.* 1998, *apptd* 1998; Hullen House, Woodfield Lane, Hessle, Hull HU13 0ES
Selby, Rt. Revd Martin Wallace, *cons.* 2003, *apptd* 2003; Bishop's House, Barton le Street, Malton, York YO17 6PL
Whitby vacant

PRINCIPAL EPISCOPAL VISITOR

Rt. Revd Martyn Jarrett (*Bishop Suffragen of Beverley*), *cons.* 1994, *apptd* 2000; 3 North Lane, Roundhay, Leeds LS8 2QJ

DEAN

Very Revd Keith Jones, *apptd* 2004

Director of Music, Robert Sharpe, *apptd* 2008

ARCHDEACONS

Cleveland, Ven. Paul Ferguson, *apptd* 2001
East Riding, Ven. David Butterfield, *apptd* 2006
York, Ven. Richard Seed, *apptd* 1999
Chancellor of the Diocese, His Hon. Judge Peter Collier, QC, *apptd* 2006
Registrar and Legal Secretary, Lionel Lennox
Diocesan Secretary, Peter Warry, Diocesan House, Aviator Court, Clifton Moor, York YO30 4WJ **T** 01904-699500

LONDON *(Canterbury)*

132ND BISHOP

Rt. Revd and Rt. Hon. Richard Chartres, KCVO, *cons.* 1992, *apptd* 1995; The Old Deanery, Dean's Court, London EC4V 5AA
Signs Richard Londin:

AREA BISHOPS

Edmonton, Rt. Revd Peter Wheatley, *cons.* 1999, *apptd* 1999; 27 Thurlow Road, London NW3 5PP
Kensington, Rt. Revd Paul Williams, *cons.* 2009, *apptd* 2008; Dial House, Riverside, Twickenham, Middlesex TW1 3DT
Stepney, Rt. Revd Canon Stephen Oliver, *cons.* 2003, *apptd* 2003; 63 Coborn Road, London E3 2DB
Willesden, Rt. Revd Peter Broadbent, *cons.* 2001, *apptd* 2001; 173 Willesden Lane, London NW6 7YN

BISHOP SUFFRAGAN

Fulham, Rt. Revd John Broadhurst, *cons.* 1996, *apptd* 1996; 26 Canonbury Park South, London N1 2FN

DEAN OF ST PAUL'S

Rt. Revd Graeme Knowles, *apptd* 2007

Organist, Andrew Carwood, *apptd* 2007

ARCHDEACONS

Charing Cross, Ven. Dr William Jacob, *apptd* 1996
Hackney, Ven. Lyle Dennen, *apptd* 1999
Hampstead, Ven. Michael Lawson, *apptd* 1999
London, Ven. David Meara, *apptd* 2009
Middlesex, Ven. Stephen Welch, *apptd* 2006
Northolt, Ven. Rachel Treweek, *apptd* 2006

Chancellor, Nigel Seed, QC, *apptd* 2002
Registrar and Legal Secretary, Paul Morris
Diocesan Secretary, Keith Robinson, London Diocesan House, 36 Causton Street, London SW1P 4AU T 020-7932 1100

DURHAM *(York)*

71ST BISHOP

Rt. Revd Dr N. Thomas Wright, *cons.* 2003, *apptd* 2003; Auckland Castle, Bishop Auckland DL14 7NR
Signs Thomas Dunelm:

BISHOP SUFFRAGAN

Jarrow, Rt. Revd Mark Bryant, *cons.* 2007, *apptd* 2007; Bishop's House, 25 Ivy Lane, Low Fell, Gateshead NE9 6QD

DEAN

Very Revd Michael Sadgrove, *apptd* 2003

Organist, James Lancelot, FRCO, *apptd* 1985

ARCHDEACONS

Auckland, Ven. Nicholas Barker, *apptd* 2007
Durham, Ven. Ian Jagger, *apptd* 2006
Sunderland, Ven. Stuart Bain, *apptd* 2002

Chancellor, The Worshipful Revd Dr Rupert Bursell, QC, *apptd* 1989
Registrar and Legal Secretary, Hilary Monckton-Milnes
Diocesan Secretary, Ian Boothroyd, Diocesan Office, Auckland Castle, Bishop Auckland, Co. Durham DL14 7QJ T 01388-604515

WINCHESTER *(Canterbury)*

96TH BISHOP

Rt. Revd Michael C. Scott-Joynt, *cons.*1987, *trans.* 1995: Wolvesey, Winchester SO23 9ND
Signs Michael Winton:

BISHOPS SUFFRAGAN

Basingstoke, Rt. Revd Trevor Willmott, *cons.* 2002, *apptd* 2002, Bishopswood End, Kingswood Rise, Four Marks, Alton, Hants GU34 5BD
Southampton, vacant

DEAN

Very Revd James Atwell, *apptd* 2005
Dean of Jersey (A Peculiar), Very Revd Robert Key, *apptd* 2005
Dean of Guernsey (A Peculiar), Very Revd Paul Mellor, *apptd* 2003
Director of Music, Andrew Lumsden, *apptd* 2002

ARCHDEACONS

Bournemouth, Ven. Adrian Harbidge, *apptd* 1998
Winchester, Ven. Michael Harley, *apptd* 2009

Chancellor, Christopher Clark, *apptd* 1993
Registrar and Legal Secretary, Peter White
Diocesan Secretary, Andrew Robinson, Old Alresford Place, Alresford, Hants SO24 9DH T 01962-737305

BATH AND WELLS *(Canterbury)*

78TH BISHOP

Rt. Revd Peter Price, *cons.* 1997, *apptd* 2002; The Palace, Wells BA5 2PD
Signs Peter Bath & Wells

BISHOP SUFFRAGAN

Taunton, Rt. Revd Peter Maurice, *cons.* 2006, *apptd* 2006; The Palace, Wells BA5 2PD

DEAN

Very Revd John Clarke, *apptd* 2004

Organist, Matthew Owens, *apptd* 2005

ARCHDEACONS

Bath, Ven. Andrew Piggott, *apptd* 2005
Taunton, Ven. John Reed, *apptd* 1999
Wells, Ven. Nicola Sullivan, *apptd* 2006

Chancellor, Timothy Briden, *apptd* 1993
Registrar and Legal Secretary, Tim Berry
Diocesan Secretary, Nicholas Denison, The Old Deanery, Wells, Somerset BA5 2UG T 01749-670777

BIRMINGHAM *(Canterbury)*

8TH BISHOP

Rt. Revd David Urquhart, *cons.* 2000, *apptd* 2006; Bishop's Croft, Old Church Road, Harborne, Birmingham B17 0BG
Signs David Birmingham:

BISHOP SUFFRAGAN

Aston, Rt. Revd Andrew Watson, *cons.* 2008, *apptd* 2008; 175 Harborne Park Road, Birmingham B17 0BH

DEAN

Very Revd Bob Wilkes, *apptd* 2006

Organist, Marcus Huxley, FRCO, *apptd* 1986

ARCHDEACONS

Aston, Ven. Dr Brian Russell, *apptd* 2005
Birmingham, Ven. Hayward Osborne, *apptd* 2001

Chancellor, His Hon. Judge Martin Cardinal, *apptd* 2005
Registrar and Legal Secretary, Hugh Carslake

Diocesan Secretary, Jim Drennan, 175 Harborne Park Road, Harborne, Birmingham B17 0BH T 0121-426 0400

BLACKBURN *(York)*

8TH BISHOP

Rt. Revd Nicholas Reade, *apptd* 2003, *cons.* March 2004; Bishop's House, Ribchester Road, Blackburn BB1 9EF
Signs Nicholas Blackburn

BISHOPS SUFFRAGAN

Burnley, Rt. Revd John Goddard, *cons.* 2000, *apptd* 2000; Dean House, 449 Padiham Road, Burnley BB12 6TE
Lancaster, Rt. Revd Geoffrey Pearson, *cons.* 2006, *apptd* 2006; The Vicarage, Whinney Brow Lane, Shireshead, Forton, Preston PR3 0AE

DEAN

Very Revd Christopher Armstrong, *apptd* 2001

Organist and Director of Music, Richard Tanner, *apptd* 1998

ARCHDEACONS

Blackburn, Ven. John Hawley, *apptd* 2002
Lancaster, Ven. Peter Ballard, *apptd* 2006

Chancellor, His Hon. Judge John Bullimore, *apptd* 1990
Registrar and Legal Secretary, Thomas Hoyle
Diocesan Secretary, Graeme Pollard, Diocesan Office, Cathedral Close, Blackburn BB1 5AA T 01254-503070

BRADFORD *(York)*

9TH BISHOP

Rt. Revd David James, *apptd* 2002; Bishopscroft, Ashwell Road, Heaton, Bradford BD9 4AU
Signs David Bradford

DEAN

Very Revd Dr David Ison, *apptd* 2005

Organist, Andrew Teague, FRCO, *apptd* 2003

ARCHDEACONS

Bradford, Ven. David Lee, *apptd* 2004
Craven, Ven. Paul Slater, *apptd* 2005

Chancellor, His Hon. Judge John de G. Walford, *apptd* 1999
Registrar and Legal Secretary, Peter Foskett
Diocesan Secretary, Malcolm Halliday, Kadugli House, Elmsley Street, Steeton, Keighley BD20 6SE T 01535-650555

BRISTOL *(Canterbury)*

55TH BISHOP

Rt. Revd Michael Hill, *cons.* 1998, *apptd* 2003; 58A High Street, Winterbourne, Bristol BS36 1JQ
Signs Michael Bristol

BISHOP SUFFRAGAN

Swindon, Rt. Revd Dr Lee Rayfield, *cons.* 2005, *apptd* 2005; Mark House, Field Rise, Swindon, Wiltshire, SN1 4HP

DEAN

Very Revd Robert W. Grimley, *apptd* 1997

Organist and Director of Music, Mark Lee, *apptd* 1998

ARCHDEACONS

Bristol, Ven. Tim McClure, *apptd* 1999
Malmesbury, Ven. Alan Hawker, *apptd* 1998

Chancellor, Dr James Behrens, *apptd* 2005
Registrar and Legal Secretary, Tim Berry
Diocesan Secretary, Lesley Farrall, Diocesan Church House, 23 Great George Street, Bristol BS1 5QZ T 0117-906 0100

CARLISLE *(York)*

66TH BISHOP

Rt. Revd James Newcome, *cons.* 2002, *apptd* 2009; Rose Castle, Dalston, Carlisle CA5 7BZ
Signs James Carlisle:

BISHOP SUFFRAGAN

Penrith, vacant; Holm Croft, Castle Road, Kendal, Cumbria LA9 7AU

DEAN

Very Revd Mark Boyling, *apptd* 2004

Organist, Jeremy Suter, FRCO, *apptd* 1991

ARCHDEACONS

Carlisle, Ven. Kevin Roberts, *apptd* 2009
West Cumberland, Ven. Dr Richard Pratt, *apptd* 2009
Westmorland and Furness, Ven. George Howe, *apptd* 2000

Chancellor, Geoffrey Tattersall, QC, *apptd* 2003
Registrar and Legal Secretary, Jane Lowdon
Diocesan Secretary, Derek Hurton, Church House, West Walls, Carlisle CA3 8UE T 01228-522573

CHELMSFORD *(Canterbury)*

10TH BISHOP

vacant

BISHOPS SUFFRAGAN

Barking, Rt. Revd David Hawkins, *cons.* 2002, *apptd* 2003; Barking Lodge, Verulam Avenue, London, E17 8ES
Bradwell, Rt. Revd Dr Laurence Green, *cons.* 1993, *apptd* 1993; Bishop's House, Orsett Road, Horndon-on-the-Hill, Stanford-le-Hope, Essex SS17 8NS
Colchester, Rt. Revd Christopher Morgan, *cons.* 2001, *apptd* 2001; 1 Fitzwalter Road, Colchester, Essex CO3 3SS

DEAN

Very Revd Peter S. M. Judd, *apptd* 1997

Master of Music, Peter Nardone, *apptd* 2000

ARCHDEACONS

Colchester, Ven. Annette Cooper, *apptd* 2004
Harlow, Ven. Martin Webster, *apptd* 2009
Southend, Ven. David Lowman, *apptd* 2001
West Ham, Ven. Elwin Cockett, *apptd* 2007

Chancellor, George Pulman QC, *apptd* 2001
Registrar and Legal Secretary, Brian Hood
Chief Executive, Steven Webb, 53 New Street, Chelmsford, Essex CM1 1AT T 01245-294400

CHESTER *(York)*

40TH BISHOP

Rt. Revd Peter Forster, PHD, *cons.* 1996, *apptd* 1996; Bishop's House, Abbey Square, Chester CH1 2JD
Signs Peter Cestr:

BISHOPS SUFFRAGAN

Birkenhead, Rt. Revd Keith Sinclair, *cons.* 2007, *apptd* 2007; Bishop's Lodge, 67 Bidston Road, Prenton CH43 6TR

Stockport, Rt. Revd Robert Atwell, *cons.* 2008, *apptd* 2008; Bishop's Lodge, Back Lane, Dunham Town, Altrincham WA14 4SG

DEAN
Very Revd Dr Gordon McPhate, *apptd* 2002

Organist and Director of Music, Philip Rushforth, FRCO, *apptd* 2008

ARCHDEACONS
Chester, Ven. Donald Allister, *apptd* 2002
Macclesfield, Ven. Richard Gillings, *apptd* 1994

Chancellor, His Hon. Judge Turner, QC, *apptd* 1998
Registrar and Legal Secretary, Helen McFall
Diocesan Secretary, Dr John Mason, Church House, Lower Lane, Aldford, Chester CH3 6HP **T** 01244-681973

CHICHESTER *(Canterbury)*
102ND BISHOP
Rt. Revd John Hind, *cons.* 1991, *apptd* 2001; The Palace, Chichester PO19 1PY
Signs John Cicestr:

BISHOPS SUFFRAGAN
Horsham, Rt. Revd Mark Sowerby, *cons.* 2009, *apptd* 2009
Lewes, Rt. Revd Wallace Benn, *cons.* 1997, *apptd* 1997; Bishop's Lodge, 16A Prideaux Road, Eastbourne, E. Sussex BN21 2NB

DEAN
Very Revd Nicholas Frayling, *apptd* 2002

Organist, Sarah Baldock, *apptd* 2007

ARCHDEACONS
Chichester, Ven. Douglas McKittrick, *apptd* 2002
Horsham, Ven. Roger Combes, *apptd* 2003
Lewes and Hastings, Ven. Philip Jones, *apptd* 2005

Chancellor, Mark Hill
Registrar and Legal Secretary, John Stapleton
Diocesan Secretary, Jonathan Prichard, Diocesan Church House, 211 New Church Road, Hove, E. Sussex BN3 4ED **T** 01273-421021

COVENTRY *(Canterbury)*
9TH BISHOP
Rt. Revd Dr Christopher Cocksworth, *cons.* 2008, *apptd* 2008; The Bishop's House, 23 Davenport Road, Coventry CV5 6PW
Signs Christopher Coventry

BISHOP SUFFRAGAN
Warwick, Rt. Revd John Stroyan, *cons.* 2005, *apptd* 2005; Warwick House, 139 Kenilworth Road, Coventry CV4 7AP

DEAN
Very Revd John Irvine, *apptd* 2001

Director of Music, Mr Kerry Beaumont, *apptd* 2006

ARCHDEACONS
Coventry, Ven. Ian Watson, *apptd* 2007
Warwick, vacant

Chancellor, Stephen Eyre, *apptd* 2009
Registrar and Legal Secretary, David Dumbleton
Diocesan Secretary, Simon Lloyd, Cathedral & Diocesan Offices, 1 Hilltop, Coventry CV1 5AB **T** 024-7652 1200

DERBY *(Canterbury)*
7TH BISHOP
Rt. Revd Dr Alastair Redfern, *cons.* 1997, *apptd* 2005; The Bishop's House, 6 King Street, Duffield, Belper, Derbyshire, DE56 4EU
Signs Alastair Derby

BISHOP SUFFRAGAN
Repton, Rt. Revd Humphrey Southern, *cons.* 2007, *apptd* 2007; Repton House, Lea, Matlock, Derbyshire DE4 5JP

DEAN
Very Revd Dr Jeffrey Cuttell, *apptd* 2008

Organist, Peter Gould, *apptd* 1982

ARCHDEACONS
Chesterfield, vacant
Derby, Ven. Dr Christopher Cunliffe, *apptd* 2006

Chancellor, His Hon. Judge John Bullimore, *apptd* 1981
Registrar and Legal Secretary, Mrs Nadine Waldron
Diocesan Secretary, Bob Carey, Derby Church House, Full Street, Derby DE1 3DR **T** 01332-388650

ELY *(Canterbury)*
68TH BISHOP
Rt. Revd Dr Anthony Russell, *cons.* 1988, *apptd* 2000; The Bishop's House, Ely, Cambs CB7 4DW
Signs Anthony Ely

BISHOP SUFFRAGAN
Huntingdon, Rt. Revd David Thomson, DPHIL, *cons.* 2008, *apptd* 2008; 14 Lynn Road, Ely, Cambs CB6 1DA

DEAN
Very Revd Dr Michael Chandler, *apptd* 2003

Director of Music, Paul Trepte, FRCO, *apptd* 1991

ARCHDEACONS
Cambridge, Ven. John Beer, *apptd* 2004
Huntingdon and Wisbech, Ven. Hugh McCurdy, *apptd* 2005

Chancellor, Rt. Hon. Sir William Gage, QC
Registrar, Peter Beesley
Diocesan Secretary, Dr Matthew Lavis, Bishop Woodford House, Barton Road, Ely, Cambs CB7 4DX **T** 01353-652700

EXETER *(Canterbury)*
70TH BISHOP
Rt. Revd Michael Langrish, *cons.* 1993, *apptd* 2000; The Palace, Exeter, EX1 1HY
Signs Michael Exon:

BISHOPS SUFFRAGAN
Crediton, Rt. Revd Robert Evens, *cons.* 2004, *apptd* 2004; 32 The Avenue, Tiverton EX16 4HW
Plymouth, Rt. Revd John Ford, *cons.* 2006, *apptd* 2005; 31 Riverside Walk, Tamerton Foliot, Plymouth PL5 4AQ

DEAN
Very Revd Jonathan Meyrick, *apptd* 2005

Director of Music, Andrew Millington, *apptd* 1999

ARCHDEACONS
Barnstaple, Ven. David Gunn-Johnson, *apptd* 2003
Exeter, Ven. Penny Driver, *apptd* 2006
Plymouth, Ven. Tony Wilds, *apptd* 2001
Totnes, Ven. John Rawlings, *apptd* 2006

Chancellor, Hon. Sir Andrew McFarlane
Registrar and Legal Secretary, M. Follett
Diocesan Secretary, Mark Beedell, The Old Deanery, The Cloisters, Exeter EX1 1HS T 01392-272686

GIBRALTAR IN EUROPE *(Canterbury)*

3RD BISHOP
Rt. Revd Dr Geoffrey Rowell, *cons.* 1994, *apptd* 2001; Bishop's Lodge, Church Road, Worth, Crawley, West Sussex RH10 7RT

BISHOP SUFFRAGAN
In Europe, Rt. Revd David Hamid, *cons.* 2002, *apptd* 2002; 14 Tufton Street, London SW1P 3QZ
Dean, Cathedral Church of the Holy Trinity, Gibraltar, Very Revd Dr John Paddock

Chancellor, Pro-Cathedral of St Paul, Valletta, Malta, Canon Simon Godfrey
Chancellor, Pro-Cathedral of the Holy Trinity, Brussels, Belgium, Canon Dr Robert Innes

ARCHDEACONS
Eastern, Ven. Patrick Curran
North-West Europe, Ven. John de Wit
France, Ven. Kenneth Letts
Gibraltar, Ven. David Sutch
Italy, vacant
Scandinavia and Germany, vacant
Switzerland, vacant

Chancellor, Mark Hill
Registrar and Legal Secretary, Aiden Hargreaves-Smith
Diocesan Secretary, Adrian Mumford, 14 Tufton Street, London SW1P 3QZ T 020-7898 1155

GLOUCESTER *(Canterbury)*

40TH BISHOP
Rt. Revd Michael Perham, *cons.* 2004, *apptd* 2004; Bishopscourt, Pitt Street, Gloucester GL1 2BQ
Signs Michael Gloucestr

BISHOP SUFFRAGAN
Tewkesbury, Rt. Revd John Went, *cons.* 1995, *apptd* 1995; Bishop's House, Staverton, Cheltenham GL51 0TW

DEAN
Very Revd Nicholas Bury, *apptd* 1997

Director of Music, Adrian Partington, *apptd* 2007

ARCHDEACONS
Cheltenham, Ven. Hedley Ringrose, *apptd* 1998
Gloucester, Ven. Geoffrey Sidaway, *apptd* 2000

Chancellor and Vicar-General, June Rodgers, *apptd* 1990
Registrar and Legal Secretary, Chris Peak
Diocesan Secretary, Dr Kevin Brown, Church House, College Green, Gloucester GL1 2LY T 01452-410022

GUILDFORD *(Canterbury)*

9TH BISHOP
Rt. Revd Christopher Hill, *cons.* 1996, *apptd* 2004; Willow Grange, Woking Road, Guildford GU4 7QS
Signs Christopher Guildford

BISHOP SUFFRAGAN
Dorking, Rt. Revd Ian Brackley, *cons.* 1996, *apptd* 1995; Dayspring, 13 Pilgrims Way, Guildford GU4 8AD

DEAN
Very Revd Victor Stock, *apptd* 2002

Organist, Katherine Dienes-Williams, *apptd* 2007

ARCHDEACONS
Dorking, Ven. Julian Henderson, *apptd* 2005
Surrey, Ven. Stuart Beake, *apptd* 2005

Chancellor, Andrew Jordan
Registrar and Legal Secretary, Peter Beesley
Diocesan Secretary, Stephen Marriott, Diocesan House, Quarry Street, Guildford GU1 3AG T 01483-571826

HEREFORD *(Canterbury)*

104TH BISHOP
Rt. Revd Anthony Priddis, *cons.* 1996, *apptd* 2004; The Bishop's House, Hereford HR4 9BN
Signs Anthony Hereford

BISHOP SUFFRAGAN
Ludlow, Rt. Revd Alistair Magowan, *cons.* 2009, *apptd* 2009; Bishop's House, Corvedale Road, Craven Arms, Shropshire SY7 9BT

DEAN
Very Revd Michael Tavinor, *apptd* 2002

Organist, Geraint Bowen, FRCO, *apptd* 2001

ARCHDEACONS
Hereford, Ven. Malcolm Colmer, *apptd* 2005
Ludlow, Rt. Revd Michael Hooper, *apptd* 2002

Chancellor, His Hon. Judge Roger Kaye, QC
Registrar and Legal Secretary, Peter Beesley
Diocesan Secretary, John Clark, The Palace, Hereford HR4 9BL T 01432-373300

LEICESTER *(Canterbury)*

6TH BISHOP
Rt. Revd Timothy Stevens, *cons.* 1995, *apptd* 1999; Bishop's Lodge, 10 Springfield Road, Leicester LE2 3BD
Signs Timothy Leicester

DEAN
Very Revd Vivienne Faull, *apptd* 2000

Director of Music, Jonathan Gregory, *apptd* 1994

ARCHDEACONS
Leicester, Ven. Richard Atkinson, *apptd* 2002
Loughborough, David Newman, *apptd* 2009

Chancellor, Dr James Behrens
Registrar and Legal Secretary, Trevor Kirkman
Diocesan Secretary, Jane Easton, Church House, 3–5 St Martin's East, Leicester LE1 5FX T 0116-248 7400

LICHFIELD *(Canterbury)*

98TH BISHOP
Rt. Revd Jonathan Gledhill *cons.* 1996, *apptd* 2003; Bishop's House, The Close, Lichfield WS13 7LG
Signs Jonathan Lichfield

BISHOPS SUFFRAGAN
Shrewsbury, Rt. Revd Mark Rylands, *cons.* 2009, *apptd* 2009; Athlone House, 66 London Road, Shrewsbury SY2 6PG

Stafford, Rt. Revd A. Gordon Mursell, *cons.* 2005, *apptd* 2005; Ash Garth, 6 Broughton Crescent, Barlaston, Stoke on Trent, ST12 9DD
Wolverhampton, Rt. Revd Clive Gregory, *cons.* 2007, *apptd* 2007; 61 Richmond Road, Wolverhampton WV3 9JH

DEAN
Very Revd Adrian Dorber, *apptd* 2005

Organist, Philip Scriven, *apptd* 2002

ARCHDEACONS
Lichfield, Ven. Christopher Liley, *apptd* 2001
Salop, Ven. John Hall, *apptd* 1998
Stoke-on-Trent, Ven. Godfrey Owen Stone *apptd* 2002
Walsall, vacant

Chancellor, His Hon. Judge Marten Coates
Registrar and Legal Secretary, N. Blackie
Diocesan Secretary, vacant, St Mary's House, The Close, Lichfield, Staffs WS13 7LD T 01543-306030

LINCOLN *(Canterbury)*

71ST BISHOP
Rt. Revd Dr John Saxbee, *cons.* 1994, *apptd* 2002; Bishop's House, Eastgate, Lincoln LN2 1QQ
Signs John Lincoln

BISHOPS SUFFRAGAN
Grantham, Rt. Revd Dr Timothy Ellis, *cons.* 2006, *apptd* 2006; Saxonwell Vicarage, Church Street, Long Bennington, Newark NG23 5ES
Grimsby, Rt. Revd David D. J. Rossdale, *cons.* 2000, *apptd* 2000; Bishop's House, Church Lane, Irby-upon-Humber, Grimsby DN37 7JR

DEAN
Very Revd Philip Buckler, *apptd* 2007

Director of Music, A. Prentice, *apptd* 2003

ARCHDEACONS
Lincoln, Ven. Timothy Barker, *apptd* 2009
Lindsey and Stow, Ven. Jane Sinclair, *apptd* 2007

Chancellor, His Hon. Judge Mark Bishop, QC, *apptd* 2007
Registrar and Legal Secretary, Caroline Mockford, *apptd* 2008
Diocesan Secretary, Max Manin, The Old Palace, Lincoln LN2 1PU T 01522-504050

LIVERPOOL *(York)*

7TH BISHOP
Rt. Revd James Jones, *cons.* 1994, *apptd* 1998; Bishop's Lodge, Woolton Park, Liverpool L25 6DT
Signs James Liverpool

BISHOP SUFFRAGAN
Warrington, vacant

DEAN
Very Revd Justin Welby, *apptd* 2007

Director of Music, David Poulter, *apptd* 2008

ARCHDEACONS
Liverpool, Ven. Richard Panter, *apptd* 2002
Warrington, Ven. Peter Bradley, *apptd* 2001

Chancellor, Hon. Sir Mark Hedley
Registrar and Legal Secretary, Roger Arden
Diocesan Secretary, Mike Eastwood, St James House, 20 St James Street, Liverpool L1 7BY T 0151-709 9722

MANCHESTER *(York)*

11TH BISHOP
Rt. Revd Nigel McCulloch, *cons.* 1986, *apptd* 2002, *trans.* 2002; Bishopscourt, Bury New Road, Manchester M7 4LE
Signs Nigel Manchester

BISHOPS SUFFRAGAN
Bolton, Rt. Revd Christopher Edmondson, *cons.* 2008, *apptd* 2008; Bishop's Lodge, Walkden Road, Worsley, Manchester M28 2WH
Hulme, Rt. Revd Stephen Lowe, *cons.* 1999, *apptd* 1999; 14 Moorgate Avenue, Withington, Manchester M20 1HE
Middleton, Rt. Revd Mark Davies, *cons.* 2008, *apptd* 2008; The Hollies, Manchester Road, Rochdale OL11 3QY

DEAN
Revd Rogers Govender, *apptd* 2006

Organist, Christopher Stokes, *apptd* 1992

ARCHDEACONS
Bolton, Ven. David Bailey, *apptd* 2008
Manchester, Ven. Mark Ashcroft, *apptd* 2009
Rochdale, Cherry Vann, *apptd* 2008

Chancellor, Geoffrey Tattersall, QC
Registrar and Legal Secretary, Jane Monks
Chief Executive, John Beck, Diocesan Church House, 90 Deansgate, Manchester M3 2GH T 0161-828 1400

NEWCASTLE *(York)*

11TH BISHOP
Rt. Revd J. Martin Wharton, *cons.* 1992, *apptd* 1997; Bishop's House, 29 Moor Road South, Gosforth, Newcastle upon Tyne NE3 1PA
Signs Martin Newcastle

ASSISTANT BISHOP
Rt. Revd Paul Richardson, *cons.* 1987, *apptd* 1999

DEAN
Very Revd Christopher C. Dalliston, *apptd* 2003

Director of Music, Michael Stoddart, *apptd* 2009

ARCHDEACONS
Lindisfarne, Ven. Dr Peter Robinson, *apptd* 2008
Northumberland, Ven. Geoffrey Miller, *apptd* 2004

Chancellor, His Hon. Judge David Hodson, *apptd* 2009
Registrar and Legal Secretary, Jane Lowdon
Diocesan Secretary, Philip Davies, Church House, St John's Terrace, North Shields NE29 6HS T 0191-270 4100

NORWICH *(Canterbury)*

71ST BISHOP
Rt. Revd Graham R. James, *cons.* 1993, *apptd* 2000; Bishop's House, Norwich NR3 1SB
Signs Graham Norvic:

BISHOPS SUFFRAGAN
Lynn, Rt. Revd James Langstaff, *cons.* 2004, *apptd* 2004; The Old Vicarage, Castle Acre, King's Lynn PE32 2AA
Thetford, Rt. Revd Alan Winton, PHD, *cons.* 2009, *apptd* 2009; The Red House, 53 Norwich Road, Stoke Holy Cross, Norwich NR14 8AB

DEAN
Very Revd Graham Smith, *apptd* 2004

Master of Music, David Lowe, *apptd* 2007

ARCHDEACONS
Lynn, Ven. John Ashe, *apptd* 2008
Norfolk, Ven. David Hayden, *apptd* 2002
Norwich, Ven. Jan McFarlane, *apptd* 2008

Chancellor, His Hon. Judge Paul Downes, *apptd* 2007
Registrar and Legal Secretary, Stuart Jones
Assistant Diocesan Secretary, David Broom, Diocesan House, 109 Dereham Road, Easton, Norwich, Norfolk NR9 5ES T 01603-880853

OXFORD *(Canterbury)*
42ND BISHOP
Rt. Revd John Pritchard *cons.* 2002, *apptd* 2007; Diocesan Church House, North Hinksey Lane, Oxford OX2 0NB
Signs John Oxon:

AREA BISHOPS
Buckingham, Rt. Revd Dr Alan Wilson *cons.* 2003, *apptd* 2003; Sheridan, Grimms Hill, Great Missenden, Bucks HP16 9BD
Dorchester, Rt. Revd Colin Fletcher, *cons.* 2000, *apptd* 2000; Arran House, Sandy Lane, Yarnton, Oxon OX5 1PB
Reading, Rt. Revd Stephen Cottrell, *cons.* 2004, *apptd* 2004; Bishop's House, Tidmarsh Lane, Tidmarsh, Reading RG8 8HA

DEAN OF CHRIST CHURCH
Very Revd Dr Christopher Lewis, *apptd* 2003

Organist, Dr Stephen Darlington, FRCO, *apptd* 1985

ARCHDEACONS
Berkshire, Ven. Norman Russell, *apptd* 1998
Buckingham, Ven. Karen Gorham, *apptd* 2007
Oxford, Ven. Julian Hubbard, *apptd* 2005

Chancellor, Revd Dr Rupert Bursell, *apptd* 2001
Registrars and Legal Secretaries, Dr F. E. Robson and Revd Canon John Rees
Diocesan Secretary, Rosemary Pearce, Diocesan Church House, North Hinksey, Oxford OX2 0NB T 01865-208202

PETERBOROUGH *(Canterbury)*
38TH BISHOP
vacant

BISHOP SUFFRAGAN
Brixworth, Rt. Revd Frank White, *cons.* 2002, *apptd* 2002; 4 The Avenue, Dallington, Northampton NN1 4RZ

DEAN
Very Revd Charles Taylor, *apptd* 2007

Director of Music, Andrew Reid, *apptd* 2004

ARCHDEACONS
Northampton, Ven. Christine Allsopp, *apptd* 2005
Oakham, Ven. David Painter, *apptd* 2000

Chancellor, David Pittaway, QC, *apptd* 2005
Registrar and Legal Secretary, Revd Canon Raymond Hemingray
Diocesan Secretary, Canon Richard Pestell, Diocesan Office, The Palace, Peterborough PE1 1YB T 01733-887000

PORTSMOUTH *(Canterbury)*
8TH BISHOP
Rt. Revd Dr Kenneth Stevenson, *cons.* 1995, *apptd* 1995; Bishopsgrove, 26 Osborn Road, Fareham, Hants PO16 7DQ
Signs Kenneth Portsmouth

DEAN
Very Revd David Brindley, *apptd* 2002

Organist, David Price, *apptd* 1996

ARCHDEACONS
Isle of Wight, Ven. Caroline Baston, *apptd* 2006
Portsdown, Ven. Trevor Reader, *apptd* 2006
The Meon, Ven. Peter Hancock, *apptd* 1999

Chancellor, C. Clark, QC
Registrar and Legal Secretary, Hilary Tyler
Diocesan Secretary, Wendy Kennedy, Diocesan Offices, 1st Floor, Peninsular House, Wharf Road, Portsmouth PO2 8HB T 023-9289 9664

RIPON AND LEEDS *(York)*
12TH BISHOP
Rt. Revd John Packer, *cons.* 1996, *apptd* 2000; Bishop Mount, Ripon HG4 5DP
Signs John Ripon and Leeds

BISHOP SUFFRAGAN
Knaresborough, Rt. Revd James Bell, *cons.* 2004, *apptd* 2004; Thistledown, Main Street, Exelby, Bedale DL8 2HD

DEAN
Revd Keith Jukes, *apptd* 2007

Director of Music, Andrew Bryden, *apptd* 2003

ARCHDEACONS
Leeds, Ven. Peter Burrows, *apptd* 2005
Richmond, Ven. Janet Henderson, *apptd* 2007

Chancellor, His Hon. Judge Simon Grenfell, *apptd* 1992
Registrars and Legal Secretaries, Nicola Harding; Christopher Tunnard
Diocesan Secretary, Philip Arundel, Diocesan Office, St Mary's Street, Leeds LS9 7DP T 0113-200 0540

ROCHESTER *(Canterbury)*
106TH BISHOP
Rt. Revd Dr Michael Nazir-Ali, *cons.* 1984, *apptd* 1994; Bishopscourt, Rochester ME1 1TS
Signs Michael Roffen:

BISHOP SUFFRAGAN
Tonbridge, Rt. Revd Dr Brian C. Castle, *cons.* 2002, *apptd* 2002; Bishop's Lodge, 48 St Botolph's Road, Sevenoaks TN13 3AG

DEAN
Very Revd Adrian Newman, *apptd* 2004

Director of Music, Scott Farrell, *apptd* 2008

ARCHDEACONS
Bromley, Ven. Paul Wright, *apptd* 2003
Rochester, Ven. Peter Lock, *apptd* 2000
Tonbridge, Ven. Clive Mansell, *apptd* 2002

Chancellor, John Gallagher, *apptd* 2006
Registrar and Legal Secretary, Owen Carew-Jones
Diocesan Secretary, Canon Louise Gilbert, St Nicholas Church, Boley Hill, Rochester ME1 1SL T 01634-560000

ST ALBANS *(Canterbury)*

10TH BISHOP

Rt. Revd Dr Alan Smith, *cons.* 2001, *apptd* 2009, *trans.* 2009; Abbey Gate House, St Albans AL3 4HD
Signs Alan St Albans

BISHOPS SUFFRAGAN

Bedford, Rt. Revd Richard N. Inwood, *cons.* 2003, *apptd* 2003; Bishop's Lodge, Bedford Road, Cardington, Bedford MK44 3SS

Hertford, Rt. Revd Christopher R. J. Foster, *cons.* 2001, *apptd* 2001; Hertford House, Abbey Mill Lane, St Albans AL3 4HE

DEAN

Very Revd Dr Jeffrey John, *apptd* 2004

Organist, Andrew Lucas, *apptd* 1998

ARCHDEACONS

Bedford, Ven. Paul Hughes, *apptd* 2004
Hertford, Ven. Trevor Jones, *apptd* 1997
St Albans, Ven. Jonathan Smith, *apptd* 2008

Chancellor, Roger Kaye, *apptd* 2002
Registrar and Legal Secretary, David Cheetham
Diocesan Secretary, Susan Pope, Holywell Lodge, 41 Holywell Hill, St Albans AL1 1HE T 01727-854532

ST EDMUNDSBURY AND IPSWICH *(Canterbury)*

10TH BISHOP

Rt. Revd Nigel Stock, *cons.* 2000, *apptd* 2007; Bishop's House, 4 Park Road, Ipswich IP1 3ST
Signs Nigel St Edum and Ipswich

BISHOP SUFFRAGAN

Dunwich, Rt. Revd Clive Young, *cons.* 1999, *apptd* 1999; 28 Westerfield Road, Ipswich IP4 2UJ

DEAN

Very Revd Neil Collings, *apptd* 2006

Director of Music, James Thomas, *apptd* 1997

ARCHDEACONS

Ipswich, vacant
Sudbury, Ven. David Brierley, *apptd* 2006
Suffolk, Ven. Dr Judy Hunt, *apptd* 2009

Chancellor, vacant
Registrar and Legal Secretary, James Hall
Diocesan Secretary, Nicholas Edgell, Diocesan Office, St Nicholas Centre, 4 Cutler Street, Ipswich IP1 1UQ T 01473-298500

SALISBURY *(Canterbury)*

77TH BISHOP

Rt. Revd Dr David S. Stancliffe, *cons.* 1993, *apptd* 1993; South Canonry, The Close, Salisbury SP1 2ER
Signs David Sarum

BISHOPS SUFFRAGAN

Ramsbury, Rt. Revd Stephen Conway, *cons.* 2006, *apptd* 2006; Southbroom House, London Road, Devizes, Wiltshire SN10 1LT

Sherborne, Rt. Revd Graham Kings, PHD, *cons.* 2009, *apptd* 2009; Little Bailie, Dullar Lane, Sturminster Marshall, Wimborne, Dorset BH21 4AD

DEAN

Very Revd June Osborne, *apptd* 2004

Organist, David Halls, *apptd* 2005

ARCHDEACONS

Dorset, vacant
Sarum, Ven. Alan Jeans, *apptd* 2003
Sherborne, Ven. Paul Taylor, *apptd* 2004
Wilts, Ven. John Wraw, *apptd* 2004

Chancellor, His Hon. Judge Samuel Wiggs, *apptd* 1997
Registrar and Legal Secretary, Andrew Johnson
Diocesan Secretary, Lucinda Herklots, Church House, Crane Street, Salisbury SP1 2QB T 01722-411922

SHEFFIELD *(York)*

7TH BISHOP

Rt. Revd Steven Croft, PHD, *cons.* 2009, *apptd* 2008; Bishopscroft, Snaithing Lane, Sheffield S10 3LG
Signs Steven Sheffield

BISHOP SUFFRAGAN

Doncaster, Rt. Revd Cyril Guy Ashton, *cons.* 2000, *apptd* 2000; Bishop's House, 3 Farrington Court, Wickersley, Rotherham S66 1JQ

DEAN

Very Revd Peter Bradley, *apptd* 2003

Master of Music, Neil Taylor, *apptd* 1997

ARCHDEACONS

Doncaster, Ven. Robert Fitzharris, *apptd* 2001
Sheffield and Rotherham, Ven. Richard Blackburn, *apptd* 1999

Chancellor, Prof. David McClean, *apptd* 1992
Registrar and Legal Secretary, Andrew Vidler
Diocesan Secretary, Malcolm Fair, Diocesan Church House, 95–99 Effingham Street, Rotherham S65 1BL T 01709-309100

SODOR AND MAN *(York)*

81ST BISHOP

Rt. Revd Robert Paterson, *cons.* 2008, *apptd* 2008; The Bishop's House, The Falls, Tromode Road, Douglas, Isle of Man IM4 4PZ
Signs Robert Sodor and Man

ARCHDEACON OF MAN

Ven. Brian Smith, *apptd* 2005
Vicar-General and Chancellor, Clare Faulds
Registrar, Jonathan Kewley
Diocesan Secretary, D. Robertson, 2 North Shore Road, Ramsey, Isle of Man IM8 3DF T 01624-816538

SOUTHWARK *(Canterbury)*

9TH BISHOP

Rt. Revd Dr Tom F. Butler, *cons.* 1985, *apptd* 1998; Bishop's House, 38 Tooting Bec Gardens, London SW16 1QZ
Signs Thomas Southwark

AREA BISHOPS

Croydon, Rt. Revd Nicholas Baines, *cons.* 2003, *apptd* 2003; St Matthew's House, 100 George Street, Croydon, Surrey CR0 1PE

Kingston upon Thames, Rt. Revd Richard Cheetham, *cons.* 2002, *apptd* 2002; Kingston Episcopal Area Office, St Cecilia's, Sutherland Grove, London SW18 5JR

Woolwich, Rt. Revd Christopher Chessun, *cons.* 2005, *apptd* 2005; Diocesan Office (*see* below)

DEAN
Very Revd Colin B. Slee, OBE, *apptd* 1994

Organist, Peter Wright, FRCO, *apptd* 1989

ARCHDEACONS
Croydon, Ven. Tony Davies, *apptd* 1994
Lambeth, Ven. Christopher Skilton, *apptd* 2003
Lewisham, Ven. Christine Hardman, *apptd* 2001
Reigate, Ven. Daniel Kajumba, *apptd* 2001
Southwark, Ven. Dr Michael Ipgrave, *apptd* 2004
Wandsworth, Ven. Stephen Roberts, *apptd* 2005

Acting Chancellor, Philip Petchey
Registrar and Legal Secretary, Paul Morris
Diocesan Secretary, Simon Parton, Trinity House, 4 Chapel Court, Borough High Street, London SE1 1HW T 020-7939 9400

SOUTHWELL AND NOTTINGHAM *(York)*

11TH BISHOP
Rt. Revd Paul Butler, *cons.* 2004, *apptd* 2009; Bishop's Manor, Southwell NG25 0JR
Signs Paul Southwell

BISHOP SUFFRAGAN
Sherwood, Rt. Revd Anthony Porter, *cons.* 2006, *apptd* 2006; Dunham House, 8 Westgate, Southwell NG25 0JL

DEAN
Very Revd John Guille, *apptd* 2007

Organist, Paul Hale, *apptd* 1989

ARCHDEACONS
Newark, Ven. Nigel Peyton, *apptd* 1999
Nottingham, Ven. Peter Hill, *apptd* 2007

Chancellor, Linda Box, *apptd* 2005
Registrar and Legal Secretary, Christopher Hodson
Diocesan Secretary, Dunham House, Westgate, Southwell, Notts NG25 0JL T 01636-817204

TRURO *(Canterbury)*

15TH BISHOP
Rt. Revd Tim Thornton, *cons.* 2001, *apptd* 2008; Lis Escop, Truro TR3 6QQ
Signs Tim Truro

BISHOP SUFFRAGAN
St Germans, Rt. Revd Royden Screech, *cons.* 2000, *apptd* 2000; 32 Falmouth Road, Truro, Cornwall TR1 2HX

DEAN
Very Revd Dr Christopher Hardwick, *apptd* 2005

Organist and Director of Music, Chris Gray, *apptd* 2008

ARCHDEACONS
Cornwall, Ven. Roger Bush, *apptd* 2006
Bodmin, Ven. Clive Cohen, *apptd* 2000

Chancellor, Timothy Briden, *apptd* 1998
Registrar and Legal Secretary, Martin Follett
Diocesan Secretary, Sheri Sturgess, Diocesan House, Kenwyn, Truro TR1 1JQ T 01872-274351

WAKEFIELD *(York)*

12TH BISHOP
Rt. Revd Stephen Platten, *cons.* 2003, *apptd* 2003; Bishop's Lodge, Woodthorpe Lane, Wakefield WF2 6JL
Signs Stephen Wakefield

BISHOP SUFFRAGAN
Pontefract, Rt. Revd Anthony William Robinson, *cons.* 2003, *apptd* 2002; Pontefract House, 181A Manygates Lane, Wakefield WF2 7DR

DEAN
Very Revd Jonathan Greener, *apptd* 2007

Organist, Jonathan Bielby, FRCO, *apptd* 1972

ARCHDEACONS
Halifax, Ven. Robert Freeman, *apptd* 2003
Pontefract, Peter Townley, *apptd* 2008

Chancellor, Paul Downes, *apptd* 2006
Registrar and Legal Secretaries, Julian Gill; Julia Wilding
Diocesan Secretary, Ashley Ellis, Church House, 1 South Parade, Wakefield WF1 1LP T 01924-371802

WORCESTER *(Canterbury)*

113TH BISHOP
Rt. Revd Dr John Inge, *cons.* 2003, *apptd* 2007; The Bishop's Office, The Old Palace, Deansway, Worcester WR1 2JE
Signs John Wigorn

SUFFRAGAN BISHOP
Dudley, Rt. Revd Dr David S. Walker, *cons.* 2000, *apptd* 2000; The Bishop's House, Bishop's Walk, Cradley Heath B64 7JF

DEAN
Very Revd Peter Atkinson, *apptd* 2006

Organist, Dr Adrian Lucas, *apptd* 1996

ARCHDEACONS
Dudley, Ven. Fred Trethewey, *apptd* 2001
Worcester, Ven. Roger Morris, *apptd* 2008

Chancellor, Charles Mynors, *apptd* 1999
Registrar and Legal Secretary, Michael Huskinson
Diocesan Secretary, Robert Higham, The Old Palace, Deansway, Worcester WR1 2JE T 01905-20537

ROYAL PECULIARS

WESTMINSTER
The Collegiate Church of St Peter
Dean, Very Revd Dr John Hall
Sub Dean and Archdeacon, Canon Robert Wright, *apptd* 2005
Chapter Clerk and Receiver-General, Sir Stephen Lamport, KCVO, Chapter Office, 20 Dean's Yard, London SW1P 3PA
Organist, James O'Donnell, *apptd* 1999
Registrar, Stuart Holmes, MVO
Legal Secretary, Christopher Vyse, *apptd* 2000

WINDSOR
The Queen's Free Chapel of St George within Her Castle of Windsor
Dean, Rt. Revd David Conner, *apptd* 1998
Chapter Clerk, Charlotte Manley, LVO, OBE, *apptd* 2003; Chapter Office, The Cloisters, Windsor Castle, Windsor, Berks SL4 1NJ
Director of Music, Timothy Byram-Wigfield, *apptd* 2004

OTHER ANGLICAN CHURCHES

THE CHURCH IN WALES

The Anglican Church was the established church in Wales from the 16th century until 1920, when the estrangement of the majority of Welsh people from Anglicanism resulted in disestablishment. Since then the Church in Wales has been an autonomous province consisting of six sees. The bishops are elected by an electoral college comprising elected lay and clerical members, who also elect one of the diocesan bishops as Archbishop of Wales.

The legislative body of the Church in Wales is the Governing Body, which has 142 members divided between the three orders of bishops, clergy and laity. Its president is the Archbishop of Wales and it meets twice annually. Its decisions are binding upon all members of the church. The church's property and finances are the responsibility of the Representative Body. There are about 66,720 members of the Church in Wales, with 550 stipendiary clergy and 960 parishes.

THE REPRESENTATIVE BODY OF THE CHURCH IN WALES, 39 Cathedral Road, Cardiff CF11 9XF T 029-2034 8200 *Secretary,* John Shirley

12th ARCHBISHOP OF WALES, Most Revd Dr Barry Morgan (Bishop of Llandaff), *elected* 2003 *Signs* Barry Cambrensis

BISHOPS

Bangor (81st), Rt. Revd Andrew John, *b.* 1964 *cons.* 2008, *elected* 2008; Ty'r Esgob, Upper Garth Road, Bangor, Gwynedd LL57 2SS *Signs* Andrew Bangor. *Stipendiary clergy,* 49

Llandaff (102nd), Most Revd Dr Barry Morgan (*also* Archbishop of Wales), *b.* 1947, *cons.* 1993, *trans.* 1999; Llys Esgob, The Cathedral Green, Llandaff, Cardiff CF5 2YE *Signs* Barry Cambrensis. *Stipendiary clergy,* 143

Monmouth (9th), Rt. Revd Dominic Walker, *b.* 1948, *cons.* 1997, *elected* 2003; Bishopstow, Stow Hill, Newport NP20 4EA *Signs* Dominic Monmouth. *Stipendiary clergy,* 90

St Asaph (76th), Rt. Revd Gregory Cameron, *b.* 1959, *cons.* 2009, *elected* 2009; Esgobty, Upper Denbigh Road, St Asaph, Denbighshire LL17 0TW *Signs* Gregory St Asaph. *Stipendiary clergy,* 102

St David's (128th), Rt. Revd (John) Wyn Evans, *b.* 1946, *cons.* 2008, *elected* 2008; Llys Esgob, Abergwili, Carmarthen SA31 2JG *Signs* Wyn St Davids. *Stipendiary clergy,* 126

Swansea and Brecon (9th), Rt. Revd John Davies, *b.* 1953, *cons.* 2008, *elected* 2008; Ely Tower, Castle Square, Brecon, Powys LD3 9DJ *Signs* John Swansea & Brecon. *Stipendiary clergy,* 71

The stipend for a diocesan bishop of the Church in Wales is £38,264 a year for 2009–10.

SCOTTISH EPISCOPAL CHURCH

The Scottish Episcopal Church was founded after the Act of Settlement (1690) established the presbyterian nature of the Church of Scotland. The Scottish Episcopal Church is a member of the worldwide Anglican Communion. The governing authority is the General Synod, an elected body of 140 members (70 from the clergy and 70 from the laity) which meets once a year. The bishop who convenes and presides at meetings of the General Synod is called the 'primus' and is elected by his fellow bishops.

There are 38,330 members of the Scottish Episcopal Church, seven bishops, 512 serving clergy and around 320 churches and places of worship.

THE GENERAL SYNOD OF THE SCOTTISH EPISCOPAL CHURCH, 21 Grosvenor Crescent, Edinburgh EH12 5EE T 0131-225 6357 W www.scotland-anglican.org *Secretary-General,* John Stuart

PRIMUS OF THE SCOTTISH EPISCOPAL CHURCH, Most Revd David Chillingworth (Bishop of St Andrews, Dunkeld and Dunblane), *elected* 2009

BISHOPS

Aberdeen and Orkney, Rt. Revd Dr Bob Gillies, *b.* 1951, *cons.* 2007, *elected* 2007. *Clergy,* 54

Argyll and the Isles, vacant. *Clergy* 22

Brechin, Rt. Revd Dr John Mantle, *b.* 1946, *cons.* 2005, *elected* 2005. *Clergy,* 35

Edinburgh, Rt. Revd Brian Smith, *b.* 1943, *cons.* 1993, *elected* 2001. *Clergy,* 162

Glasgow and Galloway, vacant. *Clergy,* 99

Moray, Ross and Caithness, Rt. Revd Mark Strange, *b.* 1961, *cons.* 2007, *elected* 2007. *Clergy,* 31

St Andrews, Dunkeld and Dunblane, Most Revd David Chillingworth, *b.* 1951, *cons.* 2005, *elected* 2005. *Clergy,* 86

The minimum stipend of a diocesan bishop of the Scottish Episcopal Church for 2009 is £33,375 (ie 1.5 times the standard clergy stipend of £22,250).

CHURCH OF IRELAND

The Anglican Church was the established church in Ireland from the 16th century but never secured the allegiance of the majority and was disestablished in 1871. The Church of Ireland is divided into the provinces of Armagh and Dublin, each under an archbishop. The provinces are subdivided into 12 dioceses.

The legislative body is the General Synod, which has 660 members in total, divided between the House of Bishops (12 members) and the House of Representatives (216 clergy and 432 laity). The Archbishop of Armagh is elected by the House of Bishops; other episcopal elections are made by an electoral college.

There are around 390,000 members of the Church of Ireland, 275,000 in Northern Ireland and 115,000 in the Republic of Ireland. There are two archbishops, ten bishops and over 500 stipendiary clergy.

CENTRAL OFFICE, Church of Ireland House, Church Avenue, Rathmines, Dublin 6 T (+353) (1) 497 8422 *Chief Officer and Secretary of the Representative Church Body,* D. C. Reardon

PROVINCE OF ARMAGH

Archbishop of Armagh, Primate of all Ireland and Metropolitan, Most Revd Alan Harper, OBE, *b.* 1944, *cons.* 2002, *trans.* 2007. *Clergy,* 55

BISHOPS

Clogher, Rt. Revd Michael Jackson, PHD, DPHIL, *b.* 1956, *cons.* 2002, *apptd* 2002. *Clergy,* 32

Connor, Rt. Revd Alan Abernethy, *b.* 1957, *cons.* 2007, *apptd* 2007. *Clergy,* 106

Derry and Raphoe, Rt. Revd Kenneth Good, *b.* 1952, *cons.* 2002, *apptd* 2002. *Clergy,* 51

Down and Dromore, Rt. Revd Harold Miller, *b.* 1950, *cons.* 1997, *apptd* 1997. *Clergy,* 116

Kilmore, Elphin and Ardagh, Rt. Revd Kenneth Clarke, *b.* 1949, *cons.* 2001, *apptd* 2001. *Clergy,* 21

Tuam, Killala and Achonry, Rt. Revd Richard Henderson, DPHIL, *b.* 1957, *cons.* 1998, *apptd* 1998. *Clergy,* 13

PROVINCE OF DUBLIN

Archbishop of Dublin, Bishop of Glendalough, Primate of Ireland and Metropolitan, Most Revd John Neill, *b.* 1945, *apptd* 2002. *Clergy,* 86

BISHOPS

Cashel and Ossory, Most Revd Michael Burrows, *b.* 1961, *cons.* 2006, *apptd* 2006. *Clergy,* 42

Cork, Cloyne and Ross, Rt. Revd William Colton, *b.* 1960, *cons.* 1999, *apptd* 1999. *Clergy,* 30

Limerick, Killaloe and Ardfert, Rt. Revd Trevor Williams, *b.* 1948, *cons.* 2008. *Clergy,* 19

Meath and Kildare, Most Revd Richard Clarke, PHD, *b.* 1949, *cons.* 1996, *apptd* 1996. *Clergy,* 26

OVERSEAS

PRIMATES

Primate and Presiding Bishop of Aotearoa, New Zealand and Polynesia, Most Revd William Turei

Primate of Australia, Most Revd Phillip Aspinall

Primate of Brazil, Most Revd Maurício Araújo de Andrade

Archbishop of the Province of Burundi, Most Revd Bernard Ntahoturi

Archbishop and Primate of Canada, Most Revd Frederick Hiltz

Archbishop of the Province of Central Africa, vacant

Primate of the Central Region of America, Most Revd Martin de Jesus Barahona

Archbishop of the Province of Congo, Most Revd Dr Dirokpa Fidèle

Primate of the Province of Hong Kong Sheng Kung Hui, Most Revd Paul Kwong

Archbishop of the Province of the Indian Ocean, Most Revd Gerald Ernest

Primate of Japan (Nippon Sei Ko Kai), Most Revd Nathaniel Uematsu

President-Bishop of Jerusalem and the Middle East, Most Revd Dr Mouneer Anis

Archbishop of the Province of Kenya, Most Revd Eliud Wabukala

Archbishop of the Province of Korea, Rt. Revd Soloman Yoon

Archbishop of the Province of Melanesia, Most Revd David Vunagi

Archbishop of Mexico, Most Revd Carlos Touche-Porter

Archbishop of the Province of Myanmar, Most Revd Stephen Oo

Archbishop of the Province of Nigeria, Most Revd Peter Akinola

Archbishop of Papua New Guinea, Most Revd James Ayong

Prime Bishop of the Philippines, Rt. Revd Edward Malecdan

Archbishop of the Province of Rwanda, Most Revd Emmanuel Kolini

Primate of the Province of South East Asia, Most Revd Dr John Chew

Metropolitan of the Province of Southern Africa, Most Revd Thabo Makgoba

Presiding Bishop of the Southern Cone of America, Most Revd Gregory Venables

Archbishop of the Province of the Sudan, Most Revd Daniel Yak

Archbishop of the Province of Tanzania, Most Revd Valentino Mokiwa

Archbishop of the Province of Uganda, Most Revd Henry Orombi

Presiding Bishop and Primate of the USA, Most Revd Katharine Schori

Archbishop of the Province of West Africa, Most Revd Justice Ofei Akrofi

Archbishop of the Province of the West Indies, vacant

OTHER CHURCHES AND EXTRA-PROVINCIAL DIOCESES

Anglican Church of Bermuda, extra-provincial to Canterbury
Bishop, Rt. Revd Patrick White

Church of Ceylon, extra-provincial to Canterbury
Bishop of Colombo, Rt. Revd Duleep de Chickera
Bishop of Kurunagala, Rt. Revd Kumara Illangasinghe

Episcopal Church of Cuba, Rt. Revd Miguel Tamayo *(interim)*

Falkland Islands, extra-provincial to Canterbury
Episcopal Commissary, Rt. Revd Stephen Venner (Bishop of Dover)

Lusitanian Church (Portuguese Episcopal Church), extra-provincial to Canterbury
Bishop, Rt. Revd Fernando Soares

Reformed Episcopal Church of Spain, extra-provincial to Canterbury
Bishop, Rt. Revd Carlos López-Lozano

MODERATION OF CHURCHES IN FULL COMMUNION WITH THE ANGLICAN COMMUNION

Church of Bangladesh, Rt. Revd Paul Sarkar

Church of North India, Most Revd Purely Lyngdoh

Church of South India, Most Revd John Gladstone

Church of Pakistan, Rt. Revd Samuel Azariah

CHURCH OF SCOTLAND

The Church of Scotland is the national church of Scotland. The church is reformed in doctrine, and presbyterian in constitution, ie based on a hierarchy of courts of ministers and elders and, since 1990, of members of a diaconate. At local level the Kirk Session consists of the parish minister and ruling elders. At district level the presbyteries, of which there are 44 in Britain, consist of all the ministers in the district, one ruling elder from each congregation, and those members of the diaconate who qualify for membership. The General Assembly is the supreme authority, and is presided over by a Moderator chosen annually by the Assembly. The sovereign, if not present in person, is represented by a Lord High Commissioner who is appointed each year by the Crown.

The Church of Scotland has around 485,000 members, 966 parish ministers and 1,464 churches. There are about 20 ministers and other personnel working overseas.

Lord High Commissioner (2009–10), Rt. Hon. George Reid

Moderator of the General Assembly (2009–10), Rt. Revd William Hewitt

Principal Clerk, Very Revd Dr F. Macdonald

Depute Clerk, Revd Dr M. MacLean

Procurator, Miss L. Dunlop

Law Agent and Solicitor of the Church, Mrs J. Wilson

Parliamentary Agent, I. McCulloch (*London*)

General Treasurer, I. Grimmond

Secretary, Church and Society Council, Revd Ewan Aitken

CHURCH OFFICE, 121 George Street, Edinburgh EH2 4YN
T 0131-225 5722

PRESBYTERIES AND CLERKS
Aberdeen, Revd George Cowie and Revd John Ferguson
Abernethy, Revd J. MacEwan
Annandale and Eskdale, Revd C. Haston
Angus, Revd M. Goss
Ardrossan, Revd J. Mackay
Argyll, I. Maclagan
Ayr, Revd K. Elliott
Buchan, George Berstan
Caithness, J. Houston
Dumbarton, Revd C. Caskie
Dumfries and Kirkcudbright, Revd G. Savage
Dundee, Revd J. Wilson
Dunfermline, Revd E. Kenny
Dunkeld and Meigle, Revd J. Russell
Duns, P. Johnson
Edinburgh, Revd G. Whyte
England, Revd Scott Brown
Europe, Revd J. Cowie
Falkirk, Revd J. O'Brien
Glasgow, Revd Dr A. Kerr
Gordon, G. Moore
Greenock and Paisley, Revd A. Ward
Hamilton, Revd S. Paterson
Inverness, Revd A. Younger
Irvine and Kilmarnock, Revd C. Brockie
Jedburgh, Revd W. Frank Campbell
Kincardine and Deeside, Revd Hugh Conkey
Kirkcaldy, Rosemary Frew
Lanark, Revd J. Cutler
Lewis, Revd T. Sinclair
Lochaber, Mrs E. Gill
Lochcarron-Skye, Revd A. MacArthur
Lothian, J. McCulloch
Melrose and Peebles, Jack Stewart
Moray, Revd Hugh Smith
Orkney, Revd T. Hunt
Perth, Revd D. Main
Ross, Revd T. McWilliam
St Andrews, Revd J. Redpath
Shetland, Revd C. Greig
Stirling, Dorothy Kinloch
Sutherland, Mrs M. Stobo
Uist, Revd M. Smith
West Lothian, Revd D. Shaw
Wigtown and Stranraer, Revd D. Dutton

The stipends for ministers in the Church of Scotland in 2009 range from £23,139–£30,426, depending on length of service.

ROMAN CATHOLIC CHURCH

The Roman Catholic Church is one worldwide Christian church acknowledging as its head the Bishop of Rome, known as the Pope (Father). He leads a communion of followers of Christ, who believe they continue his presence in the world as servants of faith, hope and love to all society. The Pope is held to be the successor of St Peter and thus invested with the power which was entrusted to St Peter by Jesus Christ. A direct line of succession is therefore claimed from the earliest Christian communities. With the fall of the Roman Empire the Pope also became an important political leader. His territory is now limited to the 0.44 sq. km (0.17 sq. miles) of the Vatican City State, created to provide some independence to the Pope from Italy and other nations.

The Pope exercises spiritual authority over the church with the advice and assistance of the Sacred College of Cardinals, the supreme council of the church. He is also advised by bishops in communion with him, by a group of officers which form the Roman Curia and by his ambassadors, called Apostolic Nuncios, who liaise with the Bishops' Conference in each country.

Those members of the College of Cardinals who are under the age of 80 elect a successor of the Pope following his death. The assembly of the cardinals called to the Vatican for the election of a new Pope is known as the conclave. In complete seclusion the cardinals vote by a secret ballot; a two-thirds majority is necessary before the vote can be accepted as final. When a cardinal receives the necessary number of votes, the Dean of the Sacred College formally asks him if he will accept election and the name by which he wishes to be known. On his acceptance of the office of Supreme Pontiff, the conclave is dissolved and the first Cardinal Deacon announces the election to the assembled crowd in St Peter's Square.

The number of cardinals was fixed at 70 by Pope Sixtus V in 1586 but has been steadily increased since the pontificate of John XXIII and at the end of March 2005 stood at 183, plus one cardinal 'in pectore' (their name kept secret by the Pope for fear of persecution). At the end of March 2005, 117 of the 183 cardinals were cardinal electors, who took part in the election of Pope Benedict XVI, following the death of Pope John Paul II in April 2005.

The Pope has full legislative, judicial and administrative power over the whole church. He is aided in his administration by the curia, which is made up of a number of departments. The Secretariat of State is the central office for carrying out the Pope's instructions and is presided over by the Cardinal Secretary of State. It maintains relations with the departments of the curia, with the episcopate, with the representatives of the Holy See in various countries, governments and private persons. The congregations and pontifical councils are the Pope's ministries and include departments such as the Congregation for the Doctrine of Faith, whose field of competence concerns faith and morals; the Congregation for the Clergy and the Congregation for the Evangelisation of Peoples, the Pontifical Council for the Family and the Pontifical Council for the Promotion of Christian Unity.

The Vatican State does not have diplomatic representatives. The Holy See, composed of the Pope and those who help him in his mission for the church, is recognised by the Conventions of Vienna as an international moral body. The representatives of the Holy See are known as Apostolic Nuncios. Where representation is only to the local churches and not to the government of a country, the papal representative is known as an apostolic delegate. The Roman Catholic Church has an estimated 840 million adherents under the care of some 2,500 diocesan bishops worldwide.

SOVEREIGN PONTIFF
His Holiness Pope Benedict XVI (Joseph Ratzinger), *born* Bavaria, Germany, 16 April 1927; *ordained priest* 1951; *appointed Archbishop* (of Munich), March 1977; *created Cardinal* June 1977; *assumed pontificate* 19 April 2005

SECRETARIAT OF STATE

Secretary of State, HE Cardinal Tarcisio Bertone
First Section (General Affairs), Most Revd Fernando Filoni (Titular Archbishop of Volturno)
Second Section (Relations with Other States), Most Revd Dominique Mamberti (Titular Archbishop of Sagona)

BISHOPS' CONFERENCE

The Catholic Church in England and Wales consists of a total of 22 dioceses. The Bishops' Conference, which coordinates common activity, includes the diocesan bishops, the Apostolic Exarch of the Ukrainians, the Bishop of the Forces and the auxiliary bishops. The conference is headed by the president (Most Revd Vincent Nichols, Archbishop of Westminster) and vice-president (The Most Revd Peter Smith, Archbishop of Cardiff). There are six departments, each with an episcopal chair: the Department for Christian Life and Worship (the Bishop of Leeds), the Department for Dialogue and Unity (the Archbishop of Southwark), the Department for Catholic Education and Formation (the Bishop of Nottingham), the Department for Christian Responsibility and Citizenship (the Archbishop of Cardiff), the Department for International Affairs (the Bishop of Clifton) and the Department for Evangelisation and Catechesis (the Bishop of Arundel and Brighton).

The Bishops' Conference Standing Committee is made up of two directly elected bishops in addition to the Metropolitan Archbishops and chairs from each of the above departments. The committee has general responsibility for continuity of policy between the plenary sessions of the conference, preparing the conference agenda and implementing its decisions.

The administration of the Bishops' Conference is funded by a levy on each diocese, according to income. A general secretariat in London coordinates and supervises the Bishops' Conference administration activities. There are also other agencies and consultative bodies affiliated to the conference.

The Bishops' Conference of Scotland is the permanently constituted assembly of the bishops of Scotland. The conference is headed by the president (HE Cardinal Keith Patrick O'Brien, Archbishop of St. Andrews and Edinburgh). The conference establishes various agencies which have an advisory function in relation to the conference. The more important of these agencies are called commissions and each one has a bishop president who, with the other members of the commissions, are appointed by the conference.

The Irish Catholic Bishops' Conference (also known as the Irish Episcopal Conference) has as its president Cardinal Sean Brady of Armagh. Its membership comprises all 33 of the archbishops and bishops of Ireland. It appoints various commissions and agencies to assist with the work of the Catholic Church in Ireland.

The Catholic Church in the UK has an estimated 915,556 mass attendees, 5,599 priests and 4,583 churches.

Bishops' Conferences secretariats:

ENGLAND AND WALES, 39 Eccleston Square, London SW1V 1BX **T** 020-7630 8220 **F** 020-7901 4821 **E** secretariat@cbcew.org.uk **W** www.catholicchurch.org.uk
General Secretary, Mgr Andrew Summersgill

SCOTLAND, 64 Aitken Street, Airdrie ML6 6LT **T** 01236-764061 **W** www.bpsconfscot.com
General Secretary, Revd Paul Conroy

IRELAND, Columba Centre, Maynooth, County Kildare **T** (+353) (1) 505 3000 **E** info@catholicbishops.ie **W** www.catholicbishops.ie
Secretary, Most Revd William Lee (Bishop of Waterford and Lismore)
Executive Secretary, Revd Eamon Martin

GREAT BRITAIN

APOSTOLIC NUNCIO TO GREAT BRITAIN

Most Revd Faustino Sainz Muñoz, 54 Parkside, London SW19 5NE **T** 020-8944 7189

ENGLAND AND WALES

THE MOST REVD ARCHBISHOPS

Westminster, Vincent Nichols, *cons.* 1992, *apptd* 2009 *Archbishop Emeritus,* Cardinal Cormac Murphy-O'Connor, *cons.* 1977, *elevated* 2001 *Auxiliaries,* George Stack, *cons.* 2001; Bernard Longley *cons.* 2003; Alan Hopes *cons.* 2003; John Arnold *cons.* 2006. *Clergy,* 690. *Archbishop's Residence,* Archbishop's House, Ambrosden Avenue, London SW1P 1QJ **T** 020-7798 9033

Birmingham, vacant *Auxiliaries,* Philip Pargeter, *cons.* 1990; David McGough, *cons.* 2005; William Kenney *(Diocesan Administrator), cons.* 1987. *Clergy,* 446. *Archbishop's Residence,* Archbishop's House, 8 Shadwell Street, Birmingham B4 6EY **T** 0121-236 9090

Cardiff, Peter Smith, *cons.* 1995, *apptd* 2001. *Clergy,* 93. *Archbishop's Residence,* Archbishop's House, 41-43 Cathedral Road, Cardiff CF11 9HD **T** 029 2022 0411

Liverpool, Patrick Kelly, *cons.* 1984, *apptd* 1996 *Auxiliary,* Thomas Williams, *cons.* 2003. *Clergy,* 461. *Diocesan Curia,* Archdiocese of Liverpool, Centre for Evangelisation, Croxteth Drive, Sefton Park, Liverpool L17 1AA **T** 0151-522 1000

Southwark, Kevin McDonald, *cons.* 2001, *apptd* 2003 *Auxiliaries,* John Hine, *cons.* 2001; Patrick Lynch, *cons.* 2006; Paul Hendricks, *cons.* 2006. *Clergy,* 546. *Diocesan Curia,* Archbishop's House, 150 St George's Road, London SE1 6HX **T** 020-7928 5592

THE RT. REVD BISHOPS

Arundel and Brighton, Kieran Conry, *cons.* 2001, *apptd* 2001. *Clergy,* 96. *Diocesan Curia,* Bishop's House, The Upper Drive, Hove, E. Sussex BN3 6NB **T** 01273-506387

Brentwood, Thomas McMahon, *cons.* 1980, *apptd* 1980. *Clergy,* 121. *Bishop's Office,* Cathedral House, Ingrave Road, Brentwood, Essex CM15 8AT **T** 01277-232266

Clifton, Declan Lang, *cons.* 2001, *apptd* 2001. *Clergy,* 251. *Bishop's House,* St Ambrose, North Road, Leigh Woods, Bristol BS8 3PW **T** 0117-973 3072

East Anglia, Michael Evans, *cons* 2003, *apptd* 2003. *Clergy,* 129. *Diocesan Curia,* The White House, 21 Upgate, Poringland, Norwich NR14 7SH **T** 01508-492202

Hallam, John Rawsthorne, *cons.* 1981, *apptd* 1997. *Clergy,* 75. *Bishop's House,* 75 Norfolk Road, Sheffield S2 2SZ **T** 0114-278 7988

Hexham and Newcastle, Seamus Cunningham, *cons.* 2009, *apptd* 2009. *Clergy,* 211. *Diocesan Curia,* Bishop's House, East Denton Hall, 800 West Road, Newcastle upon Tyne NE5 2BJ **T** 0191-228 0003

Lancaster, Michael Campbell, *cons.* 2008, *apptd* 2009. *Clergy,* 170. *Bishop's Office,* The Pastoral Centre, Balmoral Road, Lancaster LA1 3BT **T** 01524-596050

Leeds, Arthur Roche, *cons.* 2001, *apptd* 2004. *Clergy,* 193. *Diocesan Curia,* Hinsley Hall, 62 Headingley Lane, Leeds LS6 2BX **T** 0113-261 8022

Menevia (Wales), Thomas Burns, *cons.* 2002, *apptd* 2008. *Clergy*, 60. *Diocesan Curia*, 27 Convent Street, Swansea SA1 2BX T 01792-644017

Middlesbrough, Terence Drainey, *cons.* 2008, *apptd* 2007. *Clergy*, 99. *Diocesan Curia*, 50A The Avenue, Linthorpe, Middlesbrough TS5 6QT T 01642-850505

Northampton, Peter Doyle, *Clergy*, 178. *Diocesan Curia*, Bishop's House, Marriott Street, Northampton NN2 6AW T 01604-715635

Nottingham, Malcolm McMahon, *cons.* 2000, *apptd* 2000. *Clergy*, 162. *Bishop's House*, 27 Cavendish Road East, The Park, Nottingham NG7 1BB T 0115-947 4786

Plymouth, Christopher Budd, *cons.* 1986, *apptd* 1985. *Clergy*, 130. *Bishop's Residence*, Bishop's House, 31 Wyndham Street West, Plymouth PL1 5RZ T 01752-224414

Portsmouth, Crispian Hollis, *cons.* 1987, *apptd* 1989. *Clergy*, 282. *Bishop's Residence*, Bishop's House, Edinburgh Road, Portsmouth, Hants PO1 3HG T 023-9282 0894

Salford, Terence Brain, *cons.* 1991, *apptd* 1997. *Clergy*, 387. *Diocesan Curia*, 5 Gerald Road, Pendleton, Salford M6 6DL T 0161-736 1421

Shrewsbury, Brian Noble, *cons.* 1995, *apptd* 1995. *Clergy* 141. *Diocesan Curia*, 2 Park Road South, Prenton, Wirral CH43 4UX T 0151-652 9855

Wrexham (Wales), Edwin Regan, *cons.*1994, *apptd* 1994. *Clergy*, 45. *Diocesan Curia*, Bishop's House, Sontley Road, Wrexham LL13 7EW T 01978-262726

SCOTLAND

THE MOST REVD ARCHBISHOPS

St Andrews and Edinburgh, HE Cardinal Keith Patrick O'Brien, *cons.* 1985, *apptd* 1985, *elevated* 2003. *Clergy*, 170. *Diocesan Office*, 100 Strathearn Road, Edinburgh EH9 1BB T 0131-623 8900

Glasgow, Mario Joseph Conti, *cons.* 1977, *apptd* 2002. *Clergy*, 225. *Diocesan Curia*, 196 Clyde Street, Glasgow G1 4JY T 0141-226 5898

THE RT. REVD BISHOPS

Aberdeen, Peter Moran, *cons.* 2003, *apptd* 2003. *Clergy*, 43. *Diocesan Curia*, Bishop's House, 3 Queen's Cross, Aberdeen AB15 4XU T 01224-319154

Argyll and the Isles, Joseph Toal, *cons.* 2008, *apptd* 2008. *Clergy*, 32. *Bishop's House*, Esplanade, Oban, Argyll PA34 5AB T 01631-567436

Dunkeld, Vincent Logan, *cons.* 1981. *Clergy*, 50. *Diocesan Curia*, 24–28 Lawside Road, Dundee DD3 6XY T 01382-225453

Galloway, John Cunningham, *cons.* 2004, *apptd* 2004. *Clergy* 56. *Diocesan Curia*, 8 Corsehill Road, Ayr KA7 2ST T 01292-266750

Motherwell, Joseph Devine, *cons.* 1977, *apptd* 1983. *Clergy*, 123. *Diocesan Curia*, Coursington Road, Motherwell ML1 1PP T 01698-269114

Paisley, Philip Tartaglia, *cons.* 2005, *apptd* 2005. *Clergy*, 83. *Diocesan Curia*, Diocesan Centre, Cathedral Precincts, Incle Street, Paisley PA1 1HR T 0141-847 6130

BISHOPRIC OF THE FORCES

vacant. *Administration*, RC Bishopric of the Forces, Wellington House, St Omer Barracks, Thornhill Road, Aldershot, Hants GU11 2BG T 01252-348234

IRELAND

There is one hierarchy for the whole of Ireland. Several of the dioceses have territory partly in the Republic of Ireland and partly in Northern Ireland.

APOSTOLIC NUNCIO TO IRELAND

HE Most Revd Giuseppe Leanza (Titular Archbishop of Lilybaeum), 183 Navan Road, Dublin 7 T (+353) (1) 838 0577 F (+353) (1) 838 0276

THE MOST REVD ARCHBISHOPS

Armagh, Cardinal Seán Brady (*also* Primate of all Ireland), *cons.* 1995, *apptd* 1996. *Archbishop Emeritus*, HE Cardinal Cahal Daly *cons.* 1967, *elevated* 1991. *Auxiliary Bishop*, Most Revd Gerard Clifford, *cons.* 1991. *Clergy*, 165. *Bishop's Residence*, Ara Coeli, Armagh BT61 7QY T 028-3752 2045

Cashel and Emly, Dermot Clifford, *cons.* 1986, *apptd* 1988. *Clergy*, 103. *Archbishop's House*, Thurles, Co. Tipperary T (+353) (504) 21512

Dublin, Diarmuid Martin, *cons.* 1999, *apptd Coadjutor Archbishop* 2003, *succeeded as Archbishop* 2004. *Emeritus Archbishop*, HE Cardinal Desmond Connell, *cons.* 1988, *elevated* 2001. *Auxiliaries*, Eamonn Walsh, *cons.* 1990; Fiachra O'Ceallaigh, *cons* 1994; Raymond Field, *cons.* 1997. *Clergy*, 994. *Archbishop's House*, Drumcondra, Dublin 9 T (+353) (1) 837 3732

Tuam, Michael Neary, *cons.* 1992, *apptd* 1995. *Clergy*, 141. *Archbishop's House*, Tuam, Co. Galway T (+353) (93) 24166

THE RT. REVD BISHOPS

Achonry, Brendan Kelly, *cons.* 2008, *apptd* 2007. *Clergy*, 53. *Bishop's House*, Edmondstown, Ballaghaderreen, Co. Roscommon T (+353) (94) 986 0021

Ardagh and Clonmacnois, Colm O'Reilly, *cons.* 1983, *apptd* 1983. *Clergy*, 65. *Diocesan Office*, St Michael's, Longford, Co. Longford T (+353) (43) 46432

Clogher, Joseph Duffy, *cons.* 1979, *apptd* 1979. *Clergy*, 74. *Bishop's House*, Monaghan T (+353) (47) 81019

Clonfert, John Kirby, *cons.* 1988 *apptd* 1988. *Clergy*, 40. *Bishop's Residence*, Coorheen, Loughrea, Co. Galway T (+353) (91) 841560

Cloyne, John Magee, *cons.* 1987, *apptd* 1987. *Clergy*, 144. *Diocesan Centre*, Cobh, Co. Cork T (+353) (21) 481 1430

Cork and Ross, John Buckley, *cons.* 1984, *apptd* 1998. *Clergy*, 136. *Diocesan Office*, Cork and Ross Offices, Redemption Road, Cork T (+353) (21) 430 1717

Derry, Seamus Hegarty, *cons.* 1982, *apptd* 1994. *Auxiliary*, Francis Lagan, *cons.* 1988. *Clergy*, 130. *Bishop's House*, St Eugene's Cathedral, Derry BT48 9YG T 028-7126 2302

Down and Connor, Noel Treanor, *cons.* 2008, *apptd* 2008. *Auxiliaries*, Anthony Farquhar, *cons.* 1983; Donal McKeown, *cons.* 2001. *Clergy*, 216. *Bishop's Residence*, Lisbreen, 73 Somerton Road, Belfast, Co. Antrim BT15 4DE T 028-9077 6185

Dromore, John McAreavey, *cons.* 1999, *apptd* 1999. *Clergy*, 43. *Bishop's House*, 44 Armagh Road, Newry, Co. Down BT35 6PN T 028-3026 2444

Elphin, Christopher Jones, *cons.* 1994, *apptd* 1994. *Clergy*, 70. *Bishop's Residence*, St Mary's, Sligo T (+353) (71) 916 2670

Ferns, Denis Brennan, *cons.* 2006, *apptd* 2006. *Clergy*, 122. *Bishop's House*, Summerhill, Wexford T (+353) (53) 912 2177

Galway, Kilmacduagh and Kilfenora, Martin Drennan, *cons.* 1997, *apptd* 2005. *Clergy*, 76. *Bishop's Residence*, Mount Saint Mary's, Taylor's Hill, Galway T (+353) (91) 563566

Kerry, William Murphy, *cons.* 1995, *apptd* 1995. *Clergy*, 124. *Bishop's House*, Killarney, Co. Kerry T (+353) (64) 31168

Kildare and Leighlin, James Moriarty, *cons.* 1991, *apptd* 2002. *Clergy,* 110. *Bishop's House,* Carlow T (+353) (59) 917 6725

Killala, John Fleming, *cons.* 2002, *apptd* 2002. *Clergy,* 54. *Bishop's House,* Ballina, Co. Mayo T (+353) (96) 21518

Killaloe, William Walsh, *cons.* 1994, *apptd* 1994. *Clergy,* 130. *Diocesan Office,* Westbourne, Ennis, Co. Kildare T (+353) (65) 682 8638

Kilmore, Leo O'Reilly, *cons.* 1997, *apptd* 1998. *Clergy,* 90. *Bishop's House,* Cullies, Co. Cavan T (+353) (49) 433 1496

Limerick, Donal Murray, *cons.* 1982, *apptd* 1996. *Clergy,* 109. *Diocesan Office,* Social Service Centre, Henry Street, Limerick T (+353) (61) 315856

Meath, Michael Smith, *cons.* 1984, *apptd* 1990. *Clergy,* 141. *Bishop's House,* Dublin Road, Mullingar, Co. Westmeath T (+353) (44) 934 8841

Ossory, Séamus Freeman, *cons.* 2007, *apptd* 2007. *Clergy,* 79. *Bishop's Residence,* Sion House, Kilkenny T (+353) (56) 776 2448

Raphoe, Philip Boyce, *cons.* 1995, *apptd* 1995. *Clergy,* 82. *Bishop's Residence,* Ard Adhamhnáin, Letterkenny, Co. Donegal T (+353) (74) 912 1208

Waterford and Lismore, William Lee, *cons.* 1993, *apptd* 1993. *Clergy,* 114. *Bishop's House,* John's Hill, Waterford T (+353) (51) 874463

OTHER CHURCHES IN THE UK

AFRICAN AND CARIBBEAN CHURCHES

There are large numbers of African and Caribbean Christian churches or groups in the UK. Some of the larger churches or groups include: the Aladura Churches, the Beneficial Veracious Christ Church, the Cherubim and Seraphim Church, the Christ Embassy, the Deeper Life Bible Church, The Gospel Faith Mission International, Kingsway International Christian Centre, the New Covenant Church, the New Testament Assembly (pentecostal), the Progressive National Baptist Convention, the Redeemed Christian Church of God, the Ruach Ministries and the Universal Prayer Ministries.

The African and Caribbean Evangelical Alliance (ACEA) was established in 1984 to aid the development of black majority churches in the UK. The alliance provides support to churches, organisations and individuals and provides a point of contact for the media and government agencies.

African and Caribbean churches are among the fastest growing and largest churches in the UK. There are estimated to be around 135,000 members of African and Caribbean churches in the UK.

AFRICAN AND CARIBBEAN EVANGELICAL ALLIANCE (ACEA), Whitefield House, 186 Kennington Park Road, London SE11 4BT T 020-7735 7373 E acea@eauk.org W www.acea-uk.org
Chief Executive Officer, Katei Kirby

ASSOCIATED PRESBYTERIAN CHURCHES OF SCOTLAND

The Associated Presbyterian Churches came into being in 1989 as a result of a division within the Free Presbyterian Church of Scotland. The Associated Presbyterian Churches is reformed and evangelistic in nature and emphasises the importance of doctrine based primarily on the Bible and secondly on the Westminster Confession of Faith. There are congregations in Scotland and Canada, with an estimated 300 members, 6 ministers and 11 congregations in Scotland.

ASSOCIATED PRESBYTERIAN CHURCHES OF SCOTLAND, APC Manse, Polvinster Road, Oban PA34 5TN T 01631-567076 E archibald.mcphail@virgin.net W www.apchurches.org
Moderator of Presbytery, Revd Dr Malcolm MacInnes
Clerk of Presbytery, Revd Archibald McPhail

BAPTIST CHURCH

Baptists trace their origins to John Smyth, who in 1609 in Amsterdam reinstituted the baptism of conscious believers as the basis of the fellowship of a gathered church. Members of Smyth's church established the first Baptist church in England in 1612. They came to be known as 'General' Baptists and their theology was Arminian, whereas a later group of Calvinists who adopted the baptism of believers came to be known as 'Particular' Baptists. The two sections of the Baptists were united into one body, the Baptist Union of Great Britain and Ireland, in 1891. In 1988 the title was changed to the Baptist Union of Great Britain.

Baptists emphasise the complete autonomy of the local church, although individual churches are linked in various kinds of associations. There are international bodies (such as the Baptist World Alliance) and national bodies, but some Baptist churches belong to neither. However, in Great Britain the majority of churches and associations belong to the Baptist Union of Great Britain. There are also Baptist Unions in Wales, Scotland and Ireland which are much smaller than the Baptist Union of Great Britain, and there is some overlap of membership.

There are currently around 140,000 members, 2,500 ministers and 2,000 churches associated with the Baptist Union of Great Britain. The Baptist Union of Great Britain is one of the founder members of the European Baptist Federation (1948) and the Baptist World Alliance (1905) which represents around 40 million members worldwide.

In the Baptist Union of Scotland there are 13,365 members, 140 pastors and 172 churches.

In the Baptist Union of Wales (Undeb Bedyddwyr Cymru) there are 14,396 members, 118 pastors and 435 churches, including those in England.

BAPTIST UNION OF GREAT BRITAIN, Baptist House, PO Box 44, 129 Broadway, Didcot, Oxon OX11 8RT T 01235-517700 E info@baptist.org.uk W www.baptist.org.uk
General Secretary, Revd Jonathan Edwards

BAPTIST UNION OF SCOTLAND, 14 Aytoun Road, Glasgow G41 5RT T 0141-423 6169 E director@scottishbaptist.org.uk
General Director, vacant

BAPTIST UNION OF WALES, Y Llwyfan, Trinity College, College Road, Carmarthen SA31 3EQ T 01267-245660 E peter@bedyddwyrcymru.co.uk W www.buw.org.uk
President of the English Assembly (2009–10), Revd Peter Richards
President of the Welsh Assembly (2009–10), Revd Olaf Davies
General Secretary of the Baptist Union of Wales, Revd Peter Thomas

THE BRETHREN

The Brethren was founded in Dublin in 1827–8, it rejected denominationalism and clericalism, and based itself on the structures and practices of the early church. Many groups sprang up; the group at Plymouth became the best known, resulting in the designation by others as the 'Plymouth Brethren'. Early worship had a prescribed form but quickly assumed an unstructured, non-liturgical format.

There are services devoted to worship, usually involving the breaking of bread, and separate preaching meetings. There is no salaried ministry.

A theological dispute led in 1848 to schism between the Open Brethren and the Closed or Exclusive Brethren, each branch later suffering further divisions.

Open Brethren churches are completely independent, but freely cooperate with each other and are run by appointed elders. Exclusive Brethren churches believe in a universal fellowship between congregations. They do not have appointed elders, but use respected members of their congregation to perform certain administrative functions.

The Brethren are established throughout the UK, Ireland, Europe, India, Africa and Australasia. In the UK there are an estimated 71,415 members, 1,268 assembly halls and around 207 full-time workers who are Bible teachers, evangelists and perform administrative functions. There are a number of publishing houses which publish Brethren-related literature. Chapter Two is the main supplier of such literature in the UK and also has a Brethren history archive which is available for use by appointment.

CHAPTER TWO, Conduit Mews, London SE18 7AP
T 020-8316 5389 W www.chaptertwobooks.org.uk

CONGREGATIONAL FEDERATION

The Congregational Federation was founded by members of Congregational churches in England and Wales who did not join the United Reformed Church in 1972. There are also churches in Scotland and France affiliated to the federation. The federation exists to encourage congregations of believers to worship in free assembly, but it has no authority over them and emphasises their right to independence and self-governance.

The federation has 9,151 members, 80 accredited ministers and 295 churches in England, Wales and Scotland.

CONGREGATIONAL FEDERATION, 8 Castle Gate, Nottingham NG1 7AS T 0115-911 1460
E admin@congregational.org.uk
W www.congregational.org.uk
President of the Federation (2009–10), Revd Jill Stephens
General Secretary, Revd M. Heaney

FELLOWSHIP OF INDEPENDENT EVANGELICAL CHURCHES

The Fellowship of Independent Evangelical Churches was founded by Revd E. J. Poole-Connor (1872–1962) in 1922. In 1923 the fellowship published its first register of non-denominational pastors, evangelists and congregations who had accepted the doctrinal basis for the fellowship.

Members of the fellowship have two primary convictions, firstly to defend the evangelical faith, and secondly that evangelicalism is the bond that unites the fellowship, rather than forms of worship or church government.

The Fellowship of Independent Evangelical Churches exists to promote the welfare of non-denominational Bible churches and to give expression to the fundamental doctrines of evangelical Christianity. It supports individual churches by gathering and disseminating information and resources, advising churches on current theological, moral, social and practical issues and seeking to uphold the quality and integrity of church leaders through the Pastors' Association.

More than 490 churches are linked through the fellowship, which has 11 regions covering the whole of the UK. There are more than 330 pastors and approximately 35,000 people worship in fellowship churches every Sunday.

FELLOWSHIP OF INDEPENDENT EVANGELICAL CHURCHES, 39 The Point, Market Harborough, Leics LE16 7QU T 01858-434540 E admin@fiec.org.uk
W www.fiec.org.uk
President (2007–10), Revd Rupert Bentley-Taylor
General Secretary, Richard Underwood

FREE CHURCH OF ENGLAND

The Free Church of England, otherwise called the Reformed Episcopal Church, is an independent church, constituted according to the historic faith, tradition and practice of the Church of England. Its roots lie in the 18th century, but most of its growth took place from the 1840s onwards, as clergy and congregations joined it from the established church in protest against the Oxford Movement. The historic episcopate was conferred on the English church in 1876 through bishops of the Reformed Episcopal Church (which had broken away from the Protestant Episcopal Church in the USA in 1873). A branch of the Reformed Episcopal Church was founded in the UK and this merged with the Free Church of England in 1927 to create the present church.

Worship is according to the *Book of Common Prayer* and some modern liturgy is permissable. Only men are ordained to the orders of deacon, presbyter and bishop.

The Free Church of England has around 1,290 members, 29 congregations and around 44 ministers, now mainly confined to England. It also has a few members in New Zealand and one congregation in St Petersburg, Russia.

THE FREE CHURCH OF ENGLAND, 329 Wolverhampton Road West, Willenhall WV13 2RL
T 01902-607335 W www.fcofe.org.uk
General Secretary, Rt. Revd Paul Hunt

FREE CHURCH OF SCOTLAND

The Free Church of Scotland was formed in 1843 when over 400 ministers withdrew from the Church of Scotland as a result of interference in the internal affairs of the church by the civil authorities. In 1900, all but 26 ministers joined with others to form the United Free Church (most of which rejoined the Church of Scotland in 1929). In 1904 the remaining 26 ministers were recognised by the House of Lords as continuing the Free Church of Scotland.

The church maintains strict adherence to the Westminster Confession of Faith (1648) and accepts the Bible as the sole rule of faith and conduct. Its general assembly meets annually. It also has links with reformed churches overseas. The Free Church of Scotland has about 12,000 members, 90 ministers and 100 congregations.

FREE CHURCH OF SCOTLAND, 15 North Bank Street, The Mound, Edinburgh EH1 2LS T 0131-226 5286
E offices@freechurchofscotland.org.uk
W www.freechurch.org
Chief Administrative Officer, Rod Morrison

FREE PRESBYTERIAN CHURCH OF SCOTLAND

The Free Presbyterian Church of Scotland was formed in 1893 by two ministers of the Free Church of Scotland who refused to accept a Declaratory Act passed by the Free Church General Assembly in 1892. The Free

Presbyterian Church of Scotland is Calvinistic in doctrine and emphasises observance of the Sabbath. It adheres strictly to the Westminster Confession of Faith of 1648.

The church has about 3,000 members in Scotland and about 4,000 in overseas congregations. It has 20 ministers and 50 churches in the UK.

FREE PRESBYTERIAN CHURCH OF SCOTLAND, 133 Woodlands Road, Glasgow G3 6LE T 0141-332 9283
W www.fpchurch.org.uk
Moderator 2009–10, Revd George Hutton
Clerk of the Synod, Revd John MacLeod

HOLY APOSTOLIC CATHOLIC ASSYRIAN CHURCH OF THE EAST

The Holy Apostolic Catholic Assyrian Church of the East traces its beginnings to the middle of the first century. It spread from Upper Mesopotamia throughout the territories of the Persian Empire. The Assyrian Church of the East became theologically separated from the rest of the Christian community following the Council of Ephesus in 431. The church is headed by the Catholicos Patriarch and is episcopal in government. The liturgical language is Syriac (Aramaic). The Assyrian Church of the East and the Roman Catholic Church agreed a common Christological declaration in 1994 and a process of dialogue between the Assyrian Church of the East and the Chaldean Catholic Church, which is in communion with Rome but shares the Syriac liturgy, was instituted in 1996.

The church has about 400,000 members in the Middle East, India, Europe, North America and Australasia. In the UK there are around 7,000 members, three congregations and 15 priests.

The church in Great Britain forms part of the diocese of Europe under Mar Odisho Oraham.

HOLY APOSTOLIC CATHOLIC ASSYRIAN CHURCH OF THE EAST, 66 Montague Road, London W7 3PQ
T 020-8579 7259
Representative in Great Britain, Very Revd Younan Y. Younan

INDEPENDENT METHODIST CHURCHES

The Independent Methodist Churches were formed in 1805 and remained independent when the Methodist Church in Great Britain was formed in 1932. They are mainly concentrated in the industrial areas of the north of England.

The churches are Methodist in doctrine but their organisation is congregational. All the churches are members of the Independent Methodist Connexion of Churches. The controlling body of the Connexion is the Annual Meeting, to which churches send delegates. The Connexional President is elected annually. Between annual meetings the affairs of the Connexion are handled by departmental committees. Ministers are appointed by the churches and trained through the Connexion. The ministry is open to both men and women and is unpaid. There are 1,900 members, 86 ministers and 84 churches in Great Britain.

INDEPENDENT METHODIST RESOURCE CENTRE, Fleet Street, Pemberton, Wigan, WN5 0DS
T 01942-223526 E resourcecentre@imcgb.org.uk
W www.imcgb.org.uk
President, Eric Southwick
General Secretary, William Gabb

LUTHERAN CHURCH

Lutheranism is based on the teachings of Martin Luther, the German leader of the Protestant Reformation. The authority of the scriptures is held to be supreme over church tradition. The teachings of Lutheranism are explained in detail in 16th-century confessional writings, particularly the Augsburg Confession. Lutheranism is one of the largest Protestant denominations and it is particularly strong in northern Europe and the USA. Some Lutheran churches are episcopal, while others have a synodal form of organisation; unity is based on doctrine rather than structure. Most Lutheran churches are members of the Lutheran World Federation, based in Geneva.

Lutheran services in Great Britain are held in 18 languages to serve members of different nationalities. Services usually follow ancient liturgies. English-language congregations are members either of the Lutheran Church in Great Britain or of the Evangelical Lutheran Church of England. The Lutheran Church in Great Britain and other Lutheran churches in Britain are members of the Lutheran Council of Great Britain, which represents them and coordinates their common work.

There are over 70 million Lutherans worldwide; in Great Britain there are about 100,000 members, 50 clergy and 100 congregations.

THE LUTHERAN COUNCIL OF GREAT BRITAIN, 30 Thanet Street, London WC1H 9QH T 020-7554 2900
F 020-7383 3081 E enquiries@lutheran.org.uk
W www.lutheran.org.uk
General Secretary, Revd Thomas Bruch

METHODIST CHURCH

The Methodist movement started in England in 1729 when the Revd John Wesley, an Anglican priest, and his brother Charles met with others in Oxford and resolved to conduct their lives and study by 'rule and method'. In 1739 the Wesleys began evangelistic preaching and the first Methodist chapel was founded in Bristol in the same year. In 1744 the first annual conference was held, at which the Articles of Religion were drawn up. Doctrinal emphases included repentance, faith, the assurance of salvation, social concern and the priesthood of all believers. After John Wesley's death in 1791 the Methodists withdrew from the established church to form the Methodist Church. Methodists gradually drifted into many groups, but in 1932 the Wesleyan Methodist Church, the United Methodist Church and the Primitive Methodist Church united to form the Methodist Church of Great Britain.

The governing body of the Methodist Church is the conference. The conference meets annually in June or July and consists of three parts: the diaconal, ministerial and representative sessions. The Methodist Church is structured as a 'Connexion' of churches, circuits and districts: the circuit is formed from the local churches in a defined area; a number of circuits make up each of the 36 districts which provide the link between the conference and the circuits. There are around 70 million Methodists worldwide; at the last count in 2007 there were 267,257 members, 3,509 ministers, 226 Deacons and 6,402 churches in Great Britain.

THE METHODIST CHURCH OF GREAT BRITAIN, Methodist Church House, 25 Marylebone Road, London NW1 5JR T 020-7486 5502
E helpdesk@methodistchurch.org.uk
W www.methodist.org.uk
President of the Conference (2009–10), Revd David Gamble
Vice-President of the Conference (2009–10), Dr Richard Vautrey

General Secretary and Secretary of the Conference, Revd Dr Martyn Atkins

THE METHODIST CHURCH IN IRELAND
The Methodist Church in Ireland is autonomous but has close links with British Methodism. It has a community roll of 51,843 members, 126 ministers, 235 lay preachers and 224 churches.
1 Fountainville Avenue, Belfast BT9 6AN
T 028-9032 4554 E secretary@irishmethodist.org
W www.irishmethodist.org
President (2009–10) and Secretary, Revd Donald Ker

ORTHODOX CHURCHES

EASTERN ORTHODOX CHURCH
The Eastern (or Byzantine) Orthodox Church is a communion of self-governing Christian churches that recognises the honorary primacy of the Oecumenical Patriarch of Constantinople.

The position of Orthodox Christians is that the faith was fully defined during the period of the Oecumenical Councils. In doctrine it is strongly trinitarian, and stresses the mystery and importance of the sacraments. It is episcopal in government. The structure of the Orthodox Christian year differs from that of western churches.

Orthodox Christians throughout the world are estimated to number about 300 million; there are 300,000 in the UK.

GREEK ORTHODOX CHURCH (PATRIARCHATE OF ANTIOCH)
There are 19 parishes in the UK and Ireland. The Diocese of Western and Central Europe is led by HE Metropolitan John (Yazigi), based in Paris.
St George's Cathedral, 1A Redhill Street, London NW1 4BG
T 020-7383 0403 E fr.s.gholam@antiochgreekorth.co.uk
W www.antiochgreekorth.co.uk
Priest, Fr. Samir Gholam
Antiochian Orthodox Parish, St Botolph's Church, Bishopsgate, London EC2M 3TL T 01223-362933
E aslanharper@clara.co.uk W www.london.antichian.org.uk
Archpriest, Fr. Michael Harper

GREEK ORTHODOX CHURCH (PATRIARCHATE OF CONSTANTINOPLE)
The presence of Greek Orthodox Christians in Britain dates back at least to 1677 when Archbishop Joseph Geogirenes of Samos fled from Turkish persecution and came to London. The present Greek cathedral in Moscow Road, Bayswater, was opened for public worship in 1879 and the Diocese of Thyateira and Great Britain was established in 1922. There are now 120 parishes and other communities (including monasteries) in the UK, served by five bishops, 107 clergy, nine cathedrals and about 94 churches.
The Patriarchate of Constantinople in Great Britain, Thyateira House, 5 Craven Hill, London W2 3EN
T 020-7723 4787 F 020-7224 9301
E mail@thyateira.org.uk W www.thyateira.org.uk
Archbishop, Gregorios of Thyateira and Great Britain

RUSSIAN ORTHODOX CHURCH
The records of Russian Orthodox Church activities in Britain date from the visit to England of Tsar Peter I in the early 18th century. Clergy were sent from Russia to serve the chapel established to minister to the staff of the Imperial Russian Embassy in London.

In 2007, after an 80-year division, the Russian Orthodox Church Outside Russia agreed to become an autonomous part of the Russian Orthodox Church, Patriarchate of Moscow. The reunification agreement was signed by Patriarch Alexy II, 15th Patriarch of Moscow and All Russia and Metropolitan Laurus, leader of the Russian Orthodox Church Outside Russia on 17 May at a ceremony at Christ the Saviour Cathedral in Moscow. Patriarch Alexy II died on 5 December 2008. Metropolitan Kirill of Smolensk and Kaliningrad was enthroned as the 16th Patriarch of Moscow and All Russia on 1 February 2009, having been elected by a secret ballot of clergy on 27 January 2009.

The diocese of Sourozh is the diocese of the Russian Orthodox Church in Great Britain and Ireland and is led by Bishop Elisey of Sourozh.
Diocese of Sourozh, Diocesan Office, Cathedral of the Dormition and All Saints, 67 Ennismore Gardens, London SW7 1NH T 020-7584 0096
W www.sourozh.org
Diocesan Bishop, Rt. Revd Elisey (Ganaba) of Sourozh
Assistant Diocesan Bishop, Most Revd Anatoly (Kuznetsov) of Kerch

SERBIAN ORTHODOX CHURCH (PATRIARCHATE OF SERBIA)
There are around 4,000 members in the UK served by 12 clergy. The UK is part of the Diocese of Great Britain and Scandinavia under Bishop Dositej. The church can be contacted in the UK via the church of St Sava in London.
Serbian Orthodox Church in Great Britain, Saint Sava, 89 Lancaster Road, London W11 1QQ
T 020-7727 8367 E crkva@spclondon.org
W www.spclondon.org
Priest, Very Revd Milun Kostic

OTHER NATIONALITIES
The Patriarchates of Romania and Bulgaria (Diocese of Western Europe) have memberships estimated at 20,000 and 2,000 respectively, while the Georgian Orthodox Church has around 500 members. The Belarusian (membership estimated at 2,400) and Latvian (membership of around 100) Orthodox churches are part of the Patriarchate of Constantinople.

ORIENTAL ORTHODOX CHURCHES
The term 'Oriental Orthodox Churches' is now generally used to describe a group of six ancient eastern churches (Armenian, Coptic, Eritrean, Ethiopian, Indian (Malankara) and Syrian) which rejected the Christological definition of the Council of Chalcedon (AD 451). There are estimated to be around 50 million members worldwide of the Oriental Orthodox Churches and about 20,075 in the UK.

ARMENIAN ORTHODOX CHURCH (PATRIARCHATE OF ETCHMIADZIN)
The Armenian Orthodox Church is led by HH Karekin II, Catholicos of All Armenians. Bishop Nathan Hovhannisian is the Primate of the Armenian Church of Great Britain and President of the Armenian Community and Church Council.
Armenian Church of Great Britain, The Armenian Vicarage, Iverna Gardens, London W8 6TP
T 020-7937 0152 E arajnortaran@aol.com
W www.accc.org.uk
Primate, Bishop Nathan Hovhannisian

COPTIC ORTHODOX CHURCH

The Coptic Orthodox Church is led by HH Pope Shenouda III and is represented in Great Britain by Bishop Angaelos at the Coptic Orthodox Cathedral of St George at the Coptic Orthodox Church Centre. The Coptic Orthodox Church is the largest Oriental Orthodox community in Great Britain.

Coptic Orthodox Church Centre, Shephalbury Manor, Broadhall Way, Stevenage, Herts SG2 8NP
T 01438-745232 E general@copticcentre.com
W www.copticcentre.com
Bishop, Bishop Angaelos

BRITISH ORTHODOX CHURCH

The British Orthodox Church is canonically part of the Coptic Orthodox Patriarchate of Alexandria. As it ministers to British people all its services are in English.

The British Orthodox Church, 10 Heathwood Gardens, Charlton, London SE7 8EP T 020-8854 3090
E boc@nildram.co.uk W www.britishorthodox.org
Metropolitan, Abba Seraphim

INDIAN ORTHODOX CHURCH

The Indian Orthodox Church, also known as the Malankara Orthodox Church, is part of the Diocese of Europe, UK and Canada under Metropolitan HG Dr Mathews Mar Thimotios. The church in the UK can be contacted via Fr Abraham Thomas at St Gregorios Indian Orthodox Church.

Indian Orthodox Church, St Gregorios Indian Orthodox Church, Cranfield Road, Brockley, London SE4 1UF
T 020-8691 9456 E vicar@indian-orthodox.co.uk
W www.indian-orthodox.co.uk
Vicar, Revd Fr Abraham Thomas
Hon. Secretary, Dr Thomas Jacob T 020-8407 0025
E ioclondon@googlemail.com

SYRIAN ORTHODOX CHURCH

The Patriarchate Vicariate of the Syrian Orthodox Church in the United Kingdom is represented by Fr Toma Hazim Dawood.

Syrian Orthodox Church in the UK, 5 Canning Road, Croydon CR0 6QA T 020-8654 7531
E enquiry@syrianorthodoxchurch.net
W www.syrianorthodoxchurch.net
Patriarchal Vicar, Fr Toma Hazim Dawood

PENTECOSTAL CHURCHES

Pentecostalism is inspired by the descent of the Holy Spirit upon the apostles at Pentecost. The movement began in Los Angeles, USA, in 1906 and is characterised by baptism with the Holy Spirit, divine healing, speaking in tongues (glossolalia), and a literal interpretation of the scriptures.

The Pentecostal movement in Britain dates from 1907. Initially, groups of Pentecostalists were led by laymen and did not organise formally. However, in 1915 the Elim Foursquare Gospel Alliance (more usually called the Elim Pentecostal Church) was founded in Ireland by George Jeffreys and currently has about 550 churches, 68,500 adherents and 650 accredited ministers. In 1924 about 70 independent assemblies formed a fellowship, the Assemblies of God in Great Britain and Ireland, which now incorporates around 700 churches and is known as the Assemblies of God Incorporated.

The Apostolic Church grew out of the 1904–5 revivals in South Wales and was established in 1916. The Apostolic Church has around 109 churches, 5,400 adherents and 103 ministers in the UK. The New Testament Church of God was established in England in 1953 and has around 125 congregations, 28,137 members and 320 ministers across England and Wales. In recent years many aspects of Pentecostalism have been adopted by the growing charismatic movement within the Roman Catholic, Protestant and Eastern Orthodox churches. There are about 105 million Pentecostalists worldwide, with about 354,934 adherents in the UK.

THE APOSTOLIC CHURCH, International Administration Offices, PO Box 51298, London SE11 9AJ T 020-7735 5784
E admin@apostolic-church.org
National Leader, Emmanuel Mbakwe

THE ASSEMBLIES OF GOD INCORPORATED, PO Box 7634, Nottingham NG11 6ZY T 0115-921 7272
E info@aog.org.uk W www.aog.org.uk

THE ELIM PENTECOSTAL CHURCH, De Walden House, De Walden Road, West Malvern, Worcestershire WR14 4DF T 0845-302 6750 E info@elimhq.net
W www.elim.org.uk
General Superintendent, Revd John Glass

THE NEW TESTAMENT CHURCH OF GOD, 3 Cheyne Walk, Northampton NN1 5PT T 01604-824222
W www.ntcg.org.uk
Administrative Bishop, Eric Brown

PRESBYTERIAN CHURCH IN IRELAND

The Presbyterian Church in Ireland is reformed in doctrine and presbyterian in constitution. Presbyterianism was established in Ireland as a result of the Ulster plantation in the early 17th century when English and Scottish Protestants mainly settled in the north of Ireland.

There are 21 presbyteries under the chief court known as the general assembly. The general assembly meets annually and is presided over by a moderator who is elected for one year. The ongoing work of the church is undertaken by 15 boards under which there are specialist committees.

There are around 255,557 members of Irish presbyterian churches in the UK and Ireland, forming 549 congregations.

THE PRESBYTERIAN CHURCH IN IRELAND, Church House, Belfast BT1 6DW T 028-9032 2284
E info@presbyterianireland.org
W www.presbyterianireland.org
Moderator (2009–10), Revd Dr Stafford Carson
Clerk of Assembly and General Secretary, Revd Dr Donald Watts

PRESBYTERIAN CHURCH OF WALES

The Presbyterian Church of Wales or Calvinistic Methodist Church of Wales is Calvinistic in doctrine and presbyterian in constitution. It was formed in 1811 when Welsh Calvinists severed the relationship with the established church by ordaining their own ministers. It secured its own confession of faith in 1823 and a Constitutional Deed in 1826, and since 1864 the General Assembly has met annually, presided over by a moderator elected for a year. The doctrine and constitutional structure of the Presbyterian Church of Wales was confirmed by act of parliament in 1931–2.

The Church has 30,000 members, 60 ministers and 714 congregations.

THE PRESBYTERIAN CHURCH OF WALES, Tabernacle Chapel, 81 Merthyr Road, Whitchurch, Cardiff CF14 1DD
T 029-2062 7465 E swyddfa.office@ebcpcw.org.uk
W www.ebcpcw.org.uk
Moderator (2009–10), Revd Gwenda Richards
General Secretary, Revd Ifan Roberts

RELIGIOUS SOCIETY OF FRIENDS (QUAKERS)

Quakerism is a religious denomination which was founded in the 17th century by George Fox and others in an attempt to revive what they saw as the original 'primitive Christianity'. The movement, at first called Friends of the Truth, started in the Midlands, Yorkshire and north-west England, but there are now Quakers all over Britain and in 36 countries around the world. The colony of Pennsylvania, founded by William Penn, was originally Quaker.

Emphasis is placed on the experience of God in daily life rather than on sacraments or religious occasions. There is no church calendar. Worship is largely silent and there are no appointed ministers; the responsibility for conducting a meeting is shared equally among those present. Religious tolerance and social reform have always been important to Quakers, together with a commitment to peace and non-violence in resolving disputes.

There are more than 25,300 'friends' or Quakers in Great Britain. There are about 500 places where Quaker meetings are held, many of them Quaker-owned Friends Meeting Houses. The Britain Yearly Meeting is the name given to the central organisation of Quakers in Britain.

THE RELIGIOUS SOCIETY OF FRIENDS (QUAKERS) IN BRITAIN, Friends House, 173–177 Euston Road, London NW1 2BJ T 020-7663 1000
E enquiries@quaker.org.uk W www.quaker.org.uk
Recording Clerk, Gillian Ashmore

SALVATION ARMY

The Salvation Army is an international Christian organisation working in 117 countries worldwide. As a church and registered charity, the Salvation Army is funded through donations from its members, the general public and, where appropriate, government grants.

The Salvation Army was founded by a Methodist minister, William Booth, in the East End of London in 1865, and now has 709 local church and community centres, 57 residential centres for the homeless, 17 elderly care centres and six substance misuse centres. It also runs a clothing recycling programme, charity shops, a prison visiting service and a family tracing service. In 1878 it adopted a quasi-military command structure intended to inspire and regulate its endeavours and to reflect its view that the church was engaged in spiritual warfare. There are around 50,000 members and 1,500 Salvation Army officers (full-time ministers) in the UK. Salvationists emphasise evangelism and the provision of social welfare.

UK TERRITORIAL HEADQUARTERS, 101 Newington Causeway, London SE1 6BN T 0845-634 0101
E info@salvationarmy.org.uk
W www.salvationarmy.org.uk
UK Territorial Commander, Commissioner John Matear

SEVENTH-DAY ADVENTIST CHURCH

The Seventh-day Adventist Church is a worldwide Christian church marked by its observance of Saturday as the Sabbath. The church also places an emphasis on the imminent second coming of Jesus Christ. Its beliefs and practices are rooted in the Bible and summarised in its '28 fundamental beliefs'.

The denomination grew out of the Millerite movement in the USA during the mid-19th century and was formally established in 1863. The world church is governed by the general conference, with smaller regions administered by divisions, union conferences and local conferences.

The church has a worldwide membership of over 17 million, with a missionary presence in over 200 countries and territories. In the UK and Ireland there are approximately 30,000 members worshipping in 277 churches and companies.

BRITISH UNION CONFERENCE OF SEVENTH-DAY ADVENTISTS, Stanborough Park, Watford WD25 9JZ
T 01923-672251 W www.adventist.org.uk
President, Don McFarlane

THE (SWEDENBORGIAN) NEW CHURCH

The New Church is based on the teachings of the 18th century Swedish scientist and theologian Emanuel Swedenborg (1688–1772), who believed that Jesus Christ appeared to him and instructed him to reveal the spiritual meaning of the Bible. He claimed to have visions of the spiritual world, including heaven and hell, and conversations with angels and spirits. He published several theological works, including descriptions of the spiritual world and a Bible commentary.

The second coming of Jesus Christ is believed to have already taken place and is still taking place, being not an actual physical reappearance of Christ, but rather his return in spirit. It is also believed that concurrent with our life on earth is life in a parallel spiritual world, of which we are usually unconscious until death. There are around 30,000 Swedenborgians worldwide, with 8,470 members, 25 Churches and 11 ministers in the UK.

THE GENERAL CONFERENCE OF THE NEW CHURCH, Swedenborg House, 20 Bloomsbury Way, London WC1A 2TH T 0845-686 0086
E enquiries@generalconference.org.uk
W www.generalconference.org.uk
Chief Executive, Michael Hindley

UNDEB YR ANNIBYNWYR CYMRAEG

Undeb Yr Annibynwyr Cymraeg, the Union of Welsh Independents, was formed in 1872 and is a voluntary association of Welsh Congregational churches and personal members. It is mainly Welsh-speaking. Congregationalism in Wales dates back to 1639 when the first Welsh Congregational church was opened in Gwent. Member churches are traditionally Calvinistic in doctrine, although a wide range of interpretations are permitted, and congregationalist in organisation. Each church has complete independence in the government and administration of its affairs.

The Union has 28,892 members, 98 ministers and 449 member churches.

UNDEB YR ANNIBYNWYR CYMRAEG, 5 Axis Court, Riverside Business Park, Swansea Vale, Swansea SA7 0AJ
T 01792-795888 E undeb@annibynwyr.org
W www.annibynwyr.org
President of the Union (2009–10), Revd Guto Prys ap Gwynfor
General Secretary, Revd Dr Geraint Tudur

UNITED REFORMED CHURCH

The United Reformed Church (URC) was first formed by the union of most of the Congregational churches in England and Wales with the Presbyterian Church of England in 1972. Congregationalism dates from the mid-16th century. It is Calvinistic in doctrine, and its followers form independent self-governing congregations bound under God by covenant, a principle laid down in the writings of Robert Browne (1550–1633). From the late 16th century the movement was driven underground by persecution, but the cause was defended at the

Westminster Assembly in 1643 and the Savoy Declaration of 1658 laid down its principles. Congregational churches formed county associations for mutual support and in 1832 these associations merged to form the Congregational Union of England and Wales.

Presbyterianism in England also dates from the mid 16th century, and was Calvinistic and evangelical in its doctrine. It was governed by a hierarchy of courts.

In the 1960s there was close cooperation locally and nationally between congregational and presbyterian churches. This led to union negotiations and a Scheme of Union, supported by act of parliament in 1972. In 1981 a further unification took place, with the Reformed Association of Churches of Christ becoming part of the URC. In 2000 a third union took place, with the Congregational Union of Scotland. In its basis the United Reformed Church reflects local church initiative and responsibility with a conciliar pattern of oversight.

The United Reformed Church is divided into 13 synods, each with a synod moderator. There are around 1,600 congregations which serve around 75,000 adults and 70,000 children and young people. There are around 750 serving ministers.

The General Assembly is the central body, and comprises around 400 representatives, mainly appointed by the synods, of which half are lay persons and half are ministers. From 2010 the General Assembly will meet biennially to elect two moderators, both lay and ordained, who will then become the public representatives of the URC. This will replace the current arrangement where one lay or ordained moderator is elected annually by the General Assembly. As a transitional arrangement the moderator will remain in office for two years from 2008.

UNITED REFORMED CHURCH, 86 Tavistock Place, London WC1H 9RT T 020-7916 2020 E info@urc.org.uk W www.urc.org.uk
Moderator of the General Assembly (2008–10), Revd John Marsh
General Secretary, Revd Roberta Rominger

WESLEYAN REFORM UNION

The Wesleyan Reform Union was founded by Methodists who left or were expelled from Wesleyan Methodism in 1849 following a period of internal conflict. Its doctrine is conservative evangelical and its organisation is congregational, each church having complete independence in the government and administration of its affairs. The union has around 1,550 members, 18 ministers and 105 churches.

THE WESLEYAN REFORM UNION, Wesleyan Reform Church House, 123 Queen Street, Sheffield S1 2DU T 0114-272 1938 E admin@thewru.co.uk W www.thewru.com
President (2009–10), Stuart Allen
General Secretary, Revd Colin Braithwaite

NON-TRINITARIAN CHURCHES

CHRISTADELPHIAN

Christadelphians believe that the Bible is the word of God and that it reveals both God's dealings with mankind in the past and his plans for the future. These plans centre on the work of Jesus Christ, who it is believed will return to Earth to establish God's kingdom. Christadelphians have existed since the 1850s, beginning in the USA through the work of an Englishman, Dr John Thomas.

THE CHRISTADELPHIAN, 404 Shaftmoor Lane, Hall Green, Birmingham B28 8SZ T 0121-777 6328 E enquiries@thechristadelphian.com W www.thechristadelphian.com

CHURCH OF CHRIST, SCIENTIST

The Church of Christ, Scientist was founded by Mary Baker Eddy in the USA in 1879 to 'reinstate primitive Christianity and its lost element of healing'. Christian Science teaches the need for spiritual regeneration and salvation from sin, but is best known for its reliance on prayer alone in the healing of sickness. Adherents believe that such healing is the result of divine laws, or divine science, and is in direct line with that practised by Jesus Christ (revered, not as God, but as the son of God) and by the early Christian church.

The denomination consists of The First Church of Christ, Scientist, in Boston, Massachusetts, USA ('The Mother Church') and its branch churches in almost 80 countries worldwide. The Bible and Mary Baker Eddy's book, *Science and Health with Key to the Scriptures,* are used for daily spiritual guidance and healing by all members and are read at services; there are no clergy. Those engaged in full-time healing are called Christian Science practitioners, of whom there are 1,500 worldwide. The church also publishes *The Christian Science Monitor.*

No membership figures are available, since Mary Baker Eddy felt that numbers are no measure of spiritual vitality and ruled that such statistics should not be published. There are almost 2,000 branch churches worldwide, including over 100 in the UK.

CHRISTIAN SCIENCE COMMITTEE ON PUBLICATION, Unit T10, Tideway Yard, 125 Mortlake High Street, London SW14 8SN T 020-8150 0245 E londoncs@csps.com W www.christianscience.com
District Manager for the UK and the Republic of Ireland, Tony Lobl

CHURCH OF JESUS CHRIST OF LATTER-DAY SAINTS

The Church of Jesus Christ of Latter-Day Saints (often referred to as 'Mormons') was founded in New York State, USA, in 1830, and came to Britain in 1837. The oldest continuous congregation of the church is in Preston, Lancashire.

Mormons are Christians who claim to belong to the 'restored church' of Jesus Christ. They believe that true Christianity died when the last original apostle died, but that it was given back to the world by God and Christ through Joseph Smith, the church's founder and first president. They accept and use the Bible as scripture, but believe in continuing revelation from God and use additional scriptures, including *The Book of Mormon: Another Testament of Jesus Christ.* The importance of the family is central to the church's beliefs and practices. Church members set aside Monday evenings as family home evenings when Christian family values are taught. Polygamy was formally discontinued in 1890.

The church has no paid ministry: local congregations are headed by a leader chosen from amongst their number. The world governing body, based in Utah, USA, is led by a president, believed to be the chosen prophet, and his two counsellors. There are more than 13 million members worldwide, with over 190,000 adherents and 411 congregations in the UK.

CHURCH OF JESUS CHRIST OF LATTER-DAY SAINTS, British Headquarters, 751 Warwick Road, Solihull, W. Midlands B91 3DQ T 0121-712 1200 W www.lds.org.uk

JEHOVAH'S WITNESSES

The movement now known as Jehovah's Witnesses grew from a Bible study group formed by Charles Taze Russell in 1872 in Pennsylvania, USA. In 1896 it adopted the name of the Watch Tower Bible and Tract Society, and in 1931 its members became known as Jehovah's Witnesses.

Jehovah's (God's) Witnesses believe in the Bible as the word of God, and consider it to be inspired and historically accurate. They take the scriptures literally, except where there are obvious indications that they are figurative or symbolic, and reject the doctrine of the Trinity. Witnesses also believe that the earth will remain forever and that all those approved of by Jehovah will have eternal life on a cleansed and beautified earth; only 144,000 will go to heaven to rule with Christ. They believe that the second coming of Christ began in 1914 and his thousand-year reign on earth is imminent, and that armageddon (a final battle in which evil will be defeated) will precede Christ's rule of peace. They refuse to take part in military service and do not accept blood transfusions.

The nine-member world governing body is based in New York, USA. There is no paid ministry, but each congregation has elders assigned to look after various duties and every Witness is assigned homes to visit in their congregation. There are over 7.1 million Jehovah's Witnesses worldwide, with 132,000 Witnesses in the UK organised into more than 1,500 congregations.

BRITISH ISLES HEADQUARTERS, Watch Tower House, The Ridgeway, London NW7 1RN **T** 020-8906 2211
E opi@uk.jw.org **W** www.watchtower.org

UNITARIAN AND FREE CHRISTIAN CHURCHES

Unitarianism has its historical roots in the Judaeo-Christian tradition but rejects the deity of Christ and the doctrine of the Trinity. It allows the individual to embrace insights from all the world's faiths and philosophies, as there is no fixed creed. It is accepted that beliefs may evolve in the light of personal experience.

Unitarian communities first became established in Poland and Transylvania in the 16th century. The first avowedly Unitarian place of worship in the British Isles opened in London in 1774. The General Assembly of Unitarian and Free Christian Churches came into existence in 1928 as the result of the amalgamation of two earlier organisations.

There are around 5,000 Unitarians in Great Britain and about 76 Unitarian ministers. Nearly 200 self-governing congregations and fellowship groups, including a small number overseas, are members of the General Assembly.

GENERAL ASSEMBLY OF UNITARIAN AND FREE CHRISTIAN CHURCHES, Essex Hall, 1–6 Essex Street, London WC2R 3HY **T** 020-7240 2384
E ga@unitarian.org.uk **W** www.unitarian.org.uk
President (2009–10), Revd Robert Wightman
Vice-President (2009–10), Neville Kenyon

COMMUNICATIONS

POSTAL SERVICES

The Royal Mail Group plc operates Parcelforce Worldwide, General Logistics Systems (GLS), Post Office and Royal Mail. Each working day Royal Mail processes and delivers more than 75 million items to 28 million addresses. The Postal Services Commission (Postcomm), an independent regulator accountable to parliament, oversees postal operations in the UK. It is responsible for the smooth introduction of competition into postal services, and the market was opened to full competition in January 2006. All postal operators, including Royal Mail, are licensed by Postcomm to ensure that the mail they handle is always secure and that they maintain certain standards. In October 2008 Postwatch merged with Energywatch to form Consumer Focus, a new consumer representation and advocacy body. Consumer Focus is responsible for postal services and takes up complaints on behalf of consumers against any licensed provider of postal services.

CONSUMER FOCUS, 4th Floor, Artillery House, Artillery Row, London SW1P 1RT **T** 020 7799 7900 **W** www.consumerfocus.org.uk

POSTCOMM, Hercules House, 6 Hercules Road, London SE1 7DB **T** 020 7593 2100 **W** www.psc.gov.uk

PRICING IN PROPORTION

Since August 2006 Royal Mail has priced mail according to its size as well as its weight. The system is intended to reflect the fact that larger, bulkier items cost more to handle than smaller, lighter ones. There are three basic categories of correspondence:

LETTER

Length up to 240mm, *width* up to 165mm, *thickness* up to 5mm, *weight* up to 100g, eg most cards, postcards and bills

LARGE LETTER

Length up to 353mm, *width* up to 250mm, *thickness* up to 25mm, *weight* up to 750g, eg most A4 documents, CDs and magazines

PACKET

Length over 353mm, *width* over 250mm, *thickness* over 25mm, *weight* over 750g, eg books, clothes, gifts, prints and posters in cylindrical packaging

INLAND POSTAL SERVICES

Below are details of a number of popular postal services along with prices correct as at April 2009.

INLAND POST RATES

Format	*Maximum weight*	*First class*	*Second class*†
Letter*	100g	£0.39	£0.30
Large letter	100g	£0.61	£0.47
	250g	£0.90	£0.76
	500g	£1.24	£1.04
	750g	£1.77	£1.51
Packet	100g	£1.28	£1.08
	250g	£1.62	£1.41
	500g	£2.14	£1.85
	750g	£2.65	£2.24
	1,000g	£3.25	£2.70

* Includes postcards

† First class post is normally delivered on the following working day and second class within three working days

UK PARCEL RATES

Maximum weight	*Standard tariff**
2kg	£4.41
4kg	£7.06
6kg	£9.58
8kg	£11.74
10kg	£12.61
20kg	£14.69

* Standard parcels are normally delivered within three to five working days

OVERSEAS POSTAL SERVICES

Royal Mail divides the world into two zones: **Europe** (Albania, Andorra, Armenia, Austria, Azerbaijan, Azores, Balearic Islands, Belarus, Belgium, Bosnia and Hercegovina, Bulgaria, Canary Islands, Corsica, Croatia, Cyprus, Czech Republic, Denmark, Estonia, Faroe Islands, Finland, France, Georgia, Germany, Gibraltar, Greece, Greenland, Hungary, Iceland, Ireland, Italy, Kazakhstan, Kosovo, Kyrgyzstan, Latvia, Liechtenstein, Lithuania, Luxembourg, Macedonia, Madeira, Malta, Moldova, Monaco, Montenegro, Netherlands, Norway, Poland, Portugal, Romania, Russia, San Marino, Serbia, Slovakia, Slovenia, Spain, Sweden, Switzerland, Tajikistan, Turkey, Turkmenistan, Ukraine, Uzbekistan, Vatican City State) and **Rest of the World** (all countries that are not listed under Europe)

OVERSEAS SURFACE MAIL RATES

Letters

Maximum weight	*Standard tariff*	*Maximum weight*	*Standard tariff*
20g†	£0.54	450g	£4.88
60g	£0.92	500g	£5.39
100g	£1.30	750g	£7.92
150g	£1.83	1,000g	£10.44
200g	£2.34	1,250g	£12.97
250g	£2.86	1,500g	£15.50
300g	£3.36	1,750g	£17.80
350g	£3.86	2,000g	£19.95
400g	£4.38		

* Letters and postcards to Europe are sent by Airmail

† Includes postcards

Small packets and printed papers

Maximum weight	*Standard tariff*	*Maximum weight*	*Standard tariff*
100g	£0.91	450g	£3.06
150g	£1.22	500g	£3.36
200g	£1.53	750g	£4.89
250g	£1.84	1,000g	£6.42
300g	£2.14	1,500g	£9.48
350g	£2.44	2,000g*	£12.17
400g	£2.76		

* Maximum weight. For printed papers only: add £0.26 for each additional 50g up to a maximum weight of 5kg

AIRMAIL LETTERS

Europe:

Maximum weight	*Standard tariff*	*Maximum weight*	*Standard tariff*
20g*	£0.56	300g	£3.89
40g	£0.81	320g	£4.08
60g	£1.05	340g	£4.27
80g	£1.28	360g	£4.46
100g	£1.52	380g	£4.65
120g	£1.77	400g	£4.84
140g	£2.02	420g	£5.03
160g	£2.26	440g	£5.22
180g	£2.51	460g	£5.41
200g	£2.73	480g	£5.60
220g	£2.96	500g	£5.79
240g	£3.19	1,000g	£10.04
260g	£3.43	2,000g	£17.54
280g	£3.65		

* Includes postcards

Rest of the World:

Maximum weight	*Standard tariff*
Postcards	£0.62
20g	£0.90
40g	£1.35
60g	£1.82
80g	£2.31
100g	£2.80
500g	£10.44
1,000g	£17.44
2,000g	£29.94

Note that there are different rates for small packets and printed matter. *See* W www.royalmail.com for further details.

SPECIAL DELIVERY SERVICES

INTERNATIONAL SIGNED FOR AND AIRSURE

Express airmail services (maximum weight 2kg) that include £34 compensation in case of loss or damage. The fee for International Signed For is £3.70 plus airmail postage. The fee for Airsure is £4.50 plus airmail postage.

RECORDED SIGNED FOR

Provides a record of posting and delivery of letters and ensures a signature on delivery. This service is recommended for items of little or no monetary value. All packets must be handed to the post office and a receipt issued as proof of posting. The charge is 75p plus the standard first or second class postage with up to £36 compensation in case of loss or damage.

SPECIAL DELIVERY NEXT DAY

A guaranteed next working day delivery service by 1pm to 99 per cent of the UK for first class letters and packets (maximum item weight is 10kg). Prices start at £4.95. There is also a service that guarantees delivery by 9am (maximum item weight is 2kg). Prices start at £10.85. There is also a Saturday guarantee for mail sent out on a Friday, which costs an additional £2.20 an item.

OTHER SERVICES

BUSINESS SERVICES

A range of postal services are available to businesses including business collection, freepost, business reply services, business packaging for special deliveries, international bulk and sustainable mailing options. Smartstamp allows businesses to print postage directly from a computer using a pre-pay system.

COMPENSATION

Compensation for loss or damage to an item sent varies according to the service used to send the item.

KEEPSAFE

Mail is held for up to two months while the addressee is away and is delivered when the addressee returns. Prices start at £8.95 for 17 days. Perishable items are returned to the sender. Recorded items are held for a week before being returned to the sender, and special delivery items for three weeks beyond the Keepsafe expiry date.

PASSPORT APPLICATIONS

Many post offices process passport applications. To find your nearest post office offering this service and for further information, *see* W www.postoffice.co.uk.

POST OFFICE BOX

A PO Box provides a short and memorable alternative address. Mail is held at a local delivery office until the addressee is ready to collect it. A PO Box costs £51 for six months or £62.85 for a year.

POSTCODE FINDER

Customers can search an online database to find UK postcodes and addresses. For more information *see* W www.postcode.royalmail.com

REDIRECTION

A printed form obtainable from the Post Office or from www.royalmail.com must be signed by the person to whom the letters are to be addressed. A fee is payable for each different surname on the application form. The charges are: one month, £7.65 (abroad via airmail, £15.50); three months, £16.85 (£33.75); six months, £26.00 (£52.05); 12 months, £39.05 (£78.10).

TRACK AND TRACE

An online service for customers to track the progress of items sent using special delivery. It is accessible from www.royalmail.com and www.postoffice.co.uk.

CONTACTS

Parcelforce Worldwide
T 08708-501150 W www.parcelforce.com

Post Office enquiries
T 08457-223344 W www.postoffice.co.uk

Postcode enquiry line
T 0906-302 1222 / 08457-111222

Royal Mail business enquiries
T 08457-950950
Royal Mail general enquiries
T 08457-740740 W www.royalmail.com

TELECOMMUNICATIONS

In 1984 the Telecommunications Act set the framework for a competitive market for telecommunications by abolishing British Telecom's (BT) exclusive right to provide services. The early 1990s saw the market open up and a number of new national public telecommunications operators (PTOs) received licences. This ended the duopoly that had existed in the 1980s when only BT and Mercury had licences to provide fixed line telecoms networks in the UK.

Four EU directives covering framework, authorisation, access and interconnection and universal services were agreed in March 2002 with the aim of further developing a pro-competitive regulatory structure. These directives were provided for in the Communications Act which came into force in July 2003. Under the act, licences are no longer required for providing communications networks or services in the UK. All persons providing such networks and services are subject to 'general conditions of entitlement', which constitute a set of rules they are obliged to observe.

Mobile network technology has improved dramatically since the launch in 1985 of the first-generation 900MHz analogue GSM service (known as TACS), which offered little or no data capability. In 1992 Vodafone launched a new digital global system for mobile communications (GSM) network, usually referred to as 2G or second generation. This technology used digital encoding and allowed voice and low-speed data communications. 2G technology has now been extended, via the enhanced data transfer rate of 2.5G, to 3G or third generation.

RECENT DEVELOPMENTS

The four GSM operators, namely Orange, O2, T-Mobile and Vodafone, were joined in March 2003 by the first 3G operator, '3' (Hutchison 3UK). Orange, T-Mobile and Vodafone all launched their own 3G services in 2004, and O2 in February 2005. 3G offers far greater capability in data transmission and services. The number of 3G subscriptions grew by 4.7 million during 2007, with 17 per cent of mobile users using 3G at the end of the year compared to 11 per cent in 2006.

Technological developments have merged the previously distinct areas of television, internet and telephony. In 2005, operators introduced live streaming television over 3G networks, with deals struck between broadcasters and mobile operators. In May 2005 Orange became the first operator in the UK to launch a mobile television service. Rival operators have since introduced similar services.

The government is also encouraging the use of Wi-Fi (wireless fidelity). Deregulation has allowed public network operators to use certain parts of the spectrum, which are exempt from licensing for wireless LAN (Wi-Fi) type systems. Initially only personal use was permitted in these bands, but this has now been expanded to a full commercial service. Wi-Fi hotspots and zones are found in a wide range of public locations, and 12 city centres now offer continuous Wi-Fi coverage using a network of wireless networks or 'mesh' of 300-metre range Wi-Fi signals.

FIXED LINE COMMUNICATIONS

In the year to December 2007 customers spent £9.3bn on fixed line telephony and there was a slight increase in the number of fixed exchange lines to 33.7 million (from 33.6 million in 2006), mainly resulting from a rise in the number of business lines. BT's share of fixed lines remained high at the end of 2007 at 66 per cent. However, due to local loop unbundling – which enables operators to connect directly to the consumer using BT lines, then add their own equipment to offer broadband and other services – a growing proportion of consumers are buying voice services from an operator other than BT. At the end of 2007, 38 per cent of UK landlines were taking a voice service from an alternative network provider.

The number of residential and small/medium business internet connections reached 18.3 million at the end of 2007, a 1.7 million increase from 2006; of this total, the number of broadband connections grew from 13 million to 15.6 million.

TOTAL TELECOMS CONNECTIONS
millions

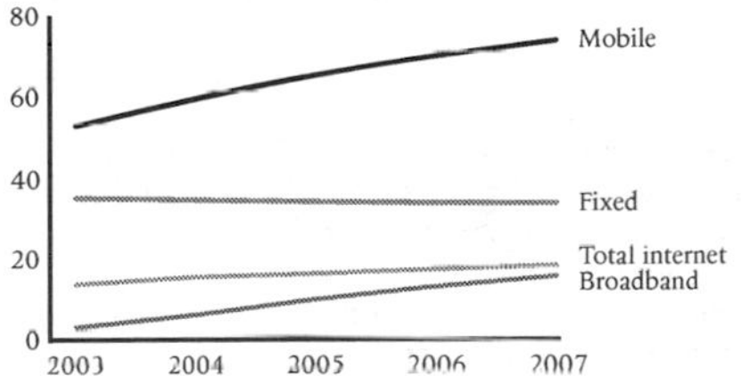

Source: OFCOM *The Communications Market 2008*

MOBILE COMMUNICATIONS

In *The Communications Market 2008* report, UK regulator OFCOM revealed that year-on-year growth in mobile revenues continued during 2007, with income from users totalling £15.1bn and representing 50 per cent of all retail telecoms revenue. At the end of 2007 there were 73.5 million active mobile connections in the UK, equating to approximately 1.25 connections per head of population. This is due to the take-up of devices such as mobile data cards and 3G dongles for business purposes, and by many consumers having more than one phone to take advantage of call rates from different suppliers.

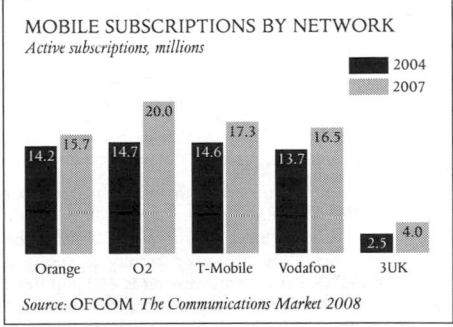

MOBILE SUBSCRIPTIONS BY NETWORK
Active subscriptions, millions

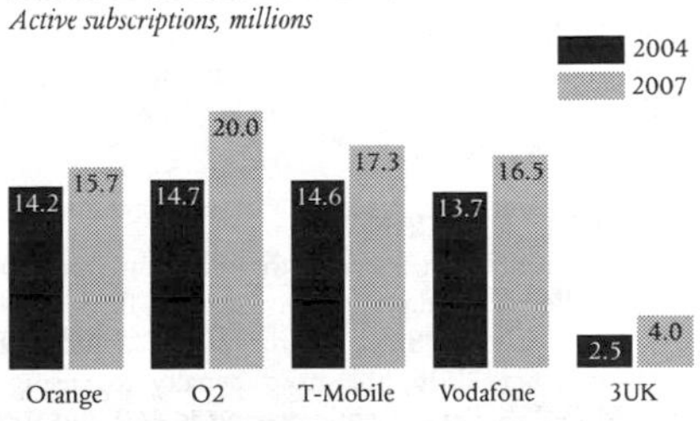

Source: OFCOM *The Communications Market 2008*

With various technologies converging, the structure of the mobile communications industry is becoming increasingly complex, but it can broadly be divided into two types of players: network operators, such as Orange and Vodafone, who own the infrastructure, set tariffs and bill customers, and mobile virtual network operators (MVNOs), who lease network capacity from the operators.

MOBILE SUBSCRIPTIONS

There are two basic types of mobile subscription: contracts and pre-pay or 'pay as you go'. The proportion of contract to pay-as-you-go customers in the UK has remained relatively constant over the last few years. At the end of 2007 there were 26.4 million active contract subscribers and 47.2 million pre-pay customers.

HEALTH

In 1999 the Independent Expert Group on Mobile Phones (IEGMP) was established to examine the possible effects of mobile phones, base stations and transmitters on health. The main findings of the IEGMP's report *Mobile Phones and Health,* published in May 2000, were:

- exposure to radio frequency radiation below guideline levels did not cause adverse health effects to the general population
- the use of mobile phones by drivers of any vehicle can increase the chance of accidents
- the widespread use of mobile phones by children for non-essential calls should be discouraged because if there are unrecognised adverse health effects children may be more vulnerable
- there is no general risk to the health of people living near to base stations on the basis that exposures are expected to be much lower than guidelines set by the International Commission on Non-Ionising Radiation Protection (ICNIRP)

As part of its response to the research recommendations contained in the IEGMP's report, the government set up the Mobile Telecommunications Health and Research (MTHR) programme in 2001 to undertake independent research into the possible health risks from mobile telephone technology. The MTHR programme published its report in September 2007 concluding that neither mobile phones nor base stations have been found to be associated with any biological or adverse health effects. The full report can be found on the MTHR website (W www.mthr.org.uk).

A national measurement programme, to ensure that emissions from mobile phone base stations do not exceed the ICNIRP guideline levels, is overseen by OFCOM and annual audits of these levels can be found on the sitefinder part of its website. The Health Protection Agency is responsible for providing information and advice in relation to the health effects of electromagnetic fields, including those emitted from mobile phones and base stations (W www.hpa.org.uk).

SAFETY WHILE DRIVING

Under legislation that came into effect in December 2003 it is illegal for drivers to use a hand-held mobile phone while driving. Since February 2007, under the Road Safety Act 2006, the fixed penalty for using a hand-held mobile device while driving is £60 and three penalty points. The same fixed penalty can also be issued to a driver for not having proper control of a vehicle while using a hands-free device. If the police or driver chooses to take the case to court rather than issue or accept a fixed penalty notice, the maximum fine is £1,000 for car drivers and £2,500 for drivers of vans, lorries, buses and coaches.

REGULATION

Under the Communications Act 2003, OFCOM is the independent regulator and competition authority for the UK communications industries, with responsibilities across television, radio, telecommunications and wireless communications services. Competition in the communications market is also regulated by the Office of Fair Trading, although OFCOM takes the lead in competition investigations in the UK market. The Competition Appeal Tribunal hears appeals against OFCOM's decisions, and price-related appeals are referred to the Competition Commission.

CONTACTS

DEPARTMENT FOR BUSINESS, INNOVATION AND SKILLS, 1 Victoria Street, London SW1H 0ET
T 020-7215 5000 W www.bis.gov.uk

OFCOM, Riverside House, 2A Southwark Bridge Road, London SE1 9HA T 020-7981 3000 W www.ofcom.org.uk

INTERNATIONAL DIRECT DIALLING

When dialling add two zeros before the IDD code, followed by the area code and the telephone number. Also add two zeros before the IDD code when dialling into the UK unless otherwise indicated.

* No extra zeros should be added
† Varies depending on area and/or carrier
‡ used to dial between Ireland and Northern Ireland; cheaper than using the UK code

	IDD from UK	*IDD to UK*
Afghanistan	93	44
Albania	355	44
Algeria	213	44
American Samoa	1 684	011 44*
Andorra	376	44
Angola	244	44
Anguilla	1 264	011 44*
Antigua and Barbuda	1 268	011 44*
Argentina	54	44
Armenia	374	44
Aruba	297	44
Ascension Island	247	44
Australia	61	11 44
Austria	43	44
Azerbaijan	994	810 44*
Azores	351	44
Bahamas	1 242	011 44*
Bahrain	973	44
Bangladesh	880	44
Barbados	1 246	011 44*
Belarus	375	810 44*
Belgium	32	44
Belize	501	44
Benin	229	44
Bermuda	1 441	011 44*
Bhutan	975	44
Bolivia	591	10 44† 11 44† 12 44† 13 44†
Bosnia and Hercegovina	387	44
Botswana	267	44

Brazil	55	14 44†
		15 44†
		21 44†
		23 44†
		31 44†
British Virgin Islands	1 284	011 44*
Brunei	673	44
Bulgaria	359	44
Burkina Faso	226	44
Burundi	257	44
Cambodia	855	1 44
Cameroon	237	44
Canada	1	011 44*
Cape Verde	238	0 44*
Cayman Islands	1 345	011 44*
Central African Republic	236	19 44*
Chad	235	15 44*
Chile	56	44
China	86	44
Colombia	57	9 44*
The Comoros	269	44
Congo, Dem. Rep. of	243	44
Congo, Rep. of	242	44
Cook Islands	682	44
Costa Rica	506	44
Côte d'Ivoire	225	44
Croatia	385	44
Cuba	53	119 44*
Cyprus	357	44
Czech Rep.	420	44
Denmark	45	44
Djibouti	253	44
Dominica	1 767	011 44*
Dominican Rep.	1 809	011 44*
	1 829	
East Timor	670	44
Ecuador	593	44
Egypt	20	44
El Salvador	503	44
Equatorial Guinea	240	44
Eritrea	291	44
Estonia	372	44
Ethiopia	251	44
Falkland Islands	500	44
Faeroe Islands	298	44
Fiji	679	44
Finland	358	990 44*†
France	33	44
French Guiana	594	44
French Polynesia	689	44
Gabon	241	44
The Gambia	220	44
Georgia	995	810 44*
Germany	49	44
Ghana	233	44
Gibraltar	350	44
Greece	30	44
Greenland	299	44
Grenada	1 473	011 44*
Guadeloupe	590	44
Guam	1 671	011 44*
Guatemala	502	44
Guinea	224	44
Guinea-Bissau	245	44
Guyana	592	1 44
Haiti	509	44
Honduras	504	44
Hong Kong	852	1 44

Hungary	36	44
Iceland	354	44
India	91	44
Indonesia	62	1 44†
		7 44†
Iran	98	44
Iraq	964	44
Ireland	353	44
		048*‡
Israel	972	44†
Italy	39	44
Jamaica	1 876	011 44*
Japan	81	1 44†
		010 44*
		41 44†
		61 44†
Jordan	962	44†
Kazakhstan	7	810 44*
Kenya	254	44
Kiribati	686	44
Korea, Dem. People's Rep. of	850	44
Korea, Republic of	82	1 44†
		2 44†
Kuwait	965	44
Kyrgyzstan	996	44
Laos	856	14 44*
Latvia	371	44
Lebanon	961	44
Lesotho	266	44
Liberia	231	44
Libya	218	44
Liechtenstein	423	44
Lithuania	370	44
Luxembourg	352	44
Macao	853	44
Macedonia	389	44
Madagascar	261	44
Madeira	351	44
Malawi	265	44
Malaysia	60	44
Maldives	960	44
Mali	223	44
Malta	356	44
Marshall Islands	692	011 44*
Martinique	596	44
Mauritania	222	44
Mauritius	230	44
Mayotte	269	10 44*
Mexico	52	44*
Micronesia, Federated States of	691	011 44*
Midway Island	1 808	011 44*
Moldova	373	44
Monaco	377	44
Mongolia	976	1 44
Montenegro	382	44
Montserrat	1 664	011 44*
Morocco	212	44
Mozambique	258	44
Myanmar	95	44
Namibia	264	44
Nauru	674	44
Nepal	977	44
The Netherlands	31	44
Netherlands Antilles	599	44
New Caledonia	687	44

New Zealand	64	44	Slovakia	421	44
Nicaragua	505	44	Slovenia	386	44
Niger	227	44	Solomon Islands	677	44
Nigeria	234	9 44	Somalia	252	44
Niue	683	44	South Africa	27	44
Norfolk Island	672	44	Spain	34	44
Northern Mariana Islands	1 670	011 44*	Sri Lanka	94	44
			Sudan	249	44
Norway	47	44	Suriname	597	44
Oman	968	44	Swaziland	268	44
Pakistan	92	44	Sweden	46	44
Palau	680	011 44*	Switzerland	41	44
Panama	507	44	Syria	963	44
Papua New Guinea	675	05 44*	Taiwan	886	2 44
Paraguay	595	2 44	Tajikistan	992	810 44*
Peru	51	44	Tanzania	255	0 44
The Philippines	63	44	Thailand	66	1 44
Poland	48	44	Togo	228	44
Portugal	351	44	Tokelau	690	44
Puerto Rico	1 787	011 44*	Tonga	676	44
	1 939		Trinidad and Tobago	1 868	011 44*
Qatar	974	44	Tristan de Cunha	290	44
Réunion	262	44	Tunisia	216	44
Romania	40	44	Turkey	90	44
Russia	7	810 44*	Turkmenistan	993	810 44*
Rwanda	250	44	Turks and Caicos Islands	1 649	011 44*
St Christopher and Nevis	1 869	011 44*	Tuvalu	688	44
			Uganda	256	0 44
St Helena	290	44	Ukraine	380	810 44*
St Lucia	1 758	011 44*	United Arab Emirates	971	44
St Pierre and Miquelon	508	44	United States of America	1	011 44*
St Vincent and the Grenadines	1 784	011 44*	Uruguay	598	44
			Uzbekistan	998	810 44*
Samoa	685	0 44*	Vanuatu	678	44
San Marino	378	44	Vatican City State	39	44
Sao Tome and Principe	239	44		379	
Saudi Arabia	966	44	Venezuela	58	44
Senegal	221	44	Vietnam	84	44
Serbia	381	44	Virgin Islands	1 340	011 44*
Seychelles	248	44	Yemen	967	44
Sierra Leone	232	44	Zambia	260	44
Singapore	65	1 44	Zimbabwe	263	44

INTERNET DOMAIN NAMES

Internet top-level domains names are two-letter codes that appear at the end of a website address to identify its country or territory of origin. Websites that use a country code top-level domain must be registered with the individual country or dependent territory. The list below is of active domain names for countries only.

ad	Andorra
ae	United Arab Emirates
af	Afghanistan
ag	Antigua and Barbuda
al	Albania
am	Armenia
ao	Angola
aq	The Antarctic
ar	Argentina
at	Austria
au	Australia
az	Azerbaijan
ba	Bosnia and Hercegovina
bb	Barbados
bd	Bangladesh
be	Belgium
bf	Burkina Faso
bg	Bulgaria
bh	Bahrain
bi	Burundi
bj	Benin
bn	Brunei
bo	Bolivia
br	Brazil
bs	The Bahamas
bt	Bhutan
bw	Botswana
by	Belarus
bz	Belize
ca	Canada
cd	Congo, Dem. Republic of
cf	Central African Republic
cg	Congo, Republic of
ch	Switzerland
ci	Côte d'Ivoire
cl	Chile
cm	Cameroon
cn	China
co	Colombia
cr	Costa Rica
cu	Cuba
cv	Cape Verde
cy	Cyprus
cz	Czech Republic
de	Germany
dj	Djibouti
dk	Denmark
dm	Dominica
do	Dominican Republic
dz	Algeria
ec	Ecuador
ee	Estonia
eg	Egypt
er	Eritrea

s	Spain	lr	Liberia	sa	Saudi Arabia
t	Ethiopia	ls	Lesotho	sb	Solomon Islands
u	European Union	lt	Lithuania	sc	Seychelles
i	Finland	lu	Luxembourg	sd	Sudan
j	Fiji	lv	Latvia	se	Sweden
m	Micronesia, Federated States of	ly	Libya	sg	Singapore
r	France	ma	Morocco	si	Slovenia
ga	Gabon	mc	Monaco	sk	Slovakia
gb	United Kingdom	md	Moldova	sl	Sierra Leone
gd	Grenada	me	Montenegro	sm	San Marino
ge	Georgia	mg	Madagascar	sn	Senegal
gh	Ghana	mh	Marshall Islands	so	Somalia
gm	The Gambia	mk	Macedonia	sr	Suriname
gn	Guinea	ml	Mali	st	São Tomé and Príncipe
gq	Equatorial Guinea	mm	Myanmar	sv	El Salvador
gr	Greece	mn	Mongolia	sy	Syria
gt	Guatemala	mr	Mauritania	sz	Swaziland
gw	Guinea-Bissau	mt	Malta	td	Chad
gy	Guyana	mu	Mauritius	tg	Togo
hn	Honduras	mv	Maldives	th	Thailand
hr	Croatia	mw	Malawi	tj	Tajikistan
ht	Haiti	mx	Mexico	tl	East Timor
hu	Hungary	my	Malaysia	tm	Turkmenistan
d	Indonesia	mz	Mozambique	tn	Tunisia
e	Ireland	na	Namibia	to	Tonga
l	Israel	ne	Niger	tp	East Timor*
n	India	ng	Nigeria	tr	Turkey
q	Iraq	ni	Nicaragua	tt	Trinidad and Tobago
r	Iran	nl	The Netherlands	tv	Tuvalu
s	Iceland	no	Norway	tw	Taiwan
t	Italy	np	Nepal	tz	Tanzania
m	Jamaica	nr	Nauru	ua	Ukraine
o	Jordan	nz	New Zealand	ug	Uganda
p	Japan	om	Oman	uk	United Kingdom
e	Kenya	pa	Panama	us	United States of America
g	Kyrgyzstan	pe	Peru	uy	Uruguay
h	Cambodia	pg	Papua New Guinea	uz	Uzbekistan
i	Kiribati	ph	The Philippines	va	Vatican City State (Holy See)
m	The Comoros	pk	Pakistan	vc	St Vincent and the Grenadines
n	St Christopher and Nevis	pl	Poland	ve	Venezuela
r	Korea, Republic of	pt	Portugal	vn	Vietnam
w	Kuwait	pw	Palau	vu	Vanuatu
z	Kazakhstan	py	Paraguay	ws	Samoa
a	Laos	qa	Qatar	ye	Yemen
b	Lebanon	ro	Romania	za	South Africa
c	St Lucia	rs	Serbia	zm	Zambia
i	Liechtenstein	ru	Russian Federation	zw	Zimbabwe
k	Sri Lanka	rw	Rwanda		

* No new registrations are being accepted for the code .tp, which is active but being phased out in favour of .tl

Note: North Korea has no internet country code top-level domain, but .kp is reserved for the country

THE ENVIRONMENT

The past two decades have witnessed a reduction in the production of chemicals that damage the ozone layer by 95 per cent, the establishment of a greenhouse gas emissions reduction treaty and carbon trading, and the introduction of much legislation. However, there remain persistent and intractable problems. Climate change continues to be a major threat to the planet, according to the United Nations Environment Programme's *Global Environment Outlook (GEO-4)* report, which assessed the current state of the global atmosphere, land, water and biodiversity and evaluated changes since 1987.

There is unequivocal evidence for climate change. Global average temperatures are about 0.7 per cent higher than in the pre-industrial era, while the rate of global average temperature change has increased from 0.1°C per decade over the last 100 years, to 0.16°C in the past decade. The second half of the 20th century was the warmest period in the northern hemisphere for 1,300 years, according to the UN report, *Climate Change 2007: The Physical Science Basis.* Extreme weather events have increased and regional climate patterns are changing. Heat waves and changes in storm tracks and precipitation can now be traced back to climate change caused by human activity.

A best estimate for temperature rise in the 21st century is between 1.8°C and 4°C. A rise of more than 2°C above pre-industrial levels is the danger area where major, irreversible damage becomes far more likely. Sea levels are predicted to rise by 50–100cm by the end of this century. Even the best case scenario would hit low-lying coastal areas, where one in ten people live worldwide. Climate change is Europe's most pressing challenge, with other areas of concern including biodiversity, marine ecosystems, land and water resources, air pollution and health.

Past legislation has worked, according to the European Environment Agency. Water and air have been cleaned up, ozone-depleting substances have been phased out and more waste is recycled. But these environmental success stories are being undermined by changes in personal consumption patterns. Europeans are living longer and more live alone, increasing demand on living space. They travel further and more often and are consuming the planet's natural resources at twice the world's average rate.

Transport is the fastest-growing contributor to greenhouse gas emissions and will continue to be for the foreseeable future. It is one of the few sectors where emissions are still rising rapidly, currently accounting for 22 per cent of total European greenhouse gas emissions. Cars produce about 12 per cent of European Union (EU) carbon dioxide emissions. Between 1990 and 2006, European passenger transport volumes and carbon dioxide emissions from road transport both grew by 26 per cent. From 1990 to 2004, air transport grew by 96 per cent while carbon dioxide emissions rose by 86 per cent and are forecast to continue to grow at 4 to 5 per cent a year. New EU legislation will reduce carbon dioxide emissions from new cars to 130g per kilometre by 2015, with a target of 95g per kilometre by 2020. Average emissions are now around 160g per kilometre. Interest in biofuels, which are made from renewable biological sources, is also increasing. By 2020, 10 per cent of transport fuel must be from renewable sources. Biodiesel is the most common biofuel in Europe, while ethanol is the most common worldwide. Biofuels have numerous benefits, including reducing fossil fuel use, decreasing greenhouse gas emissions and promoting rural development. But there are also downsides including higher prices for food crops such as corn, pressure on farmland biodiversity, soil erosion and deforestation. With these issues in mind, governments prefer and support sustainable biofuel production. Any rewards under the EU fuel rules after 2011 will be given only for biofuels that meet sustainability standards, which use criteria for monitoring land-use change, biodiversity conservation, soil conservation, water use and workers' rights. Twenty per cent of UK biofuels currently meet sustainability standards, which is 10 per cent below the government target.

Attention is turning to individuals and what they can do to reduce their carbon footprint. This is a measure of the amount of carbon dioxide emitted by the fossil fuels burned as part of a person's daily life or, in the case of an organisation, as part of its everyday operations. More than 40 per cent of the UK's carbon dioxide emissions come from people's homes and travel. Households are responsible for 16 per cent of the EU's greenhouse gas emissions with 70 per cent of energy used for home heating, 14 per cent for heating water and 12 per cent for lighting and appliances.

The UK's carbon footprint was 542.6 million tonnes of carbon dioxide in 2007. This means the average Briton's annual carbon footprint is 8.9 tonnes of carbon dioxide, whereas the average American generates 20 tonnes of carbon dioxide each year, compared to the global average of about 4 tonnes. Initiatives targeting individuals include the UK's 'We're in this Together' campaign that aims to provide ideas for changing personal behaviour and practical suggestions to reduce household emissions by one tonne over three years.

UK CO^2 EMISSIONS

By source category, 2007

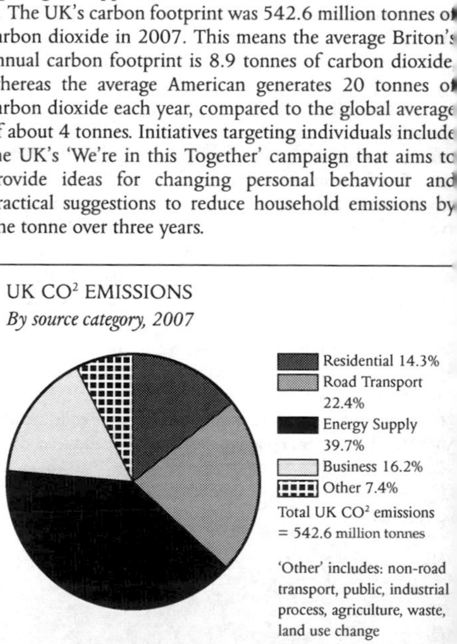

Source: National Atmospheric Emissions Inventory

SELECTED UK TARGETS

CLIMATE CHANGE

- Reduce carbon dioxide emissions to 20 per cent below 1990 levels by 2010, 26 per cent by 2020, and 80 per cent by 2050

- UK to reduce greenhouse gas emissions to 12.5 per cent below 1990 levels by 2008–12
- Carbon dioxide emissions from new cars to be 130g per kilometre by 2015 and 95g per kilometre by 2020

WASTE
- Recycle or compost 40 per cent of household waste by 2010 and 50 per cent by 2020
- Reduce amount of household waste not re-used, recycled or composted from 22.2 million tonnes in 2000 to 12.2 million tonnes by 2020, a reduction of 45 per cent
- Reduce biodegradable municipal waste sent to landfill to 75 per cent of 1995 levels by 2010, 50 per cent by 2013 and 35 per cent by 2020
- Recycle or compost 60 per cent of municipal waste in Scotland by 2020 and 70 per cent by 2025

ENERGY
- Provide 10 per cent of UK electricity from renewable sources by 2010 and 15 per cent by 2020
- Scotland to generate 31 per cent of electricity from renewable sources by 2011, rising to 50 per cent by 2020

EUROPEAN UNION MEASURES

Environmental legislation in the EU is based around the principle that the polluter pays and policies are formulated at the level of international conventions and protocols, European directives, and national legislation and strategies. The interlinked Sixth Environment Action Programme, EU Sustainable Development Strategy and the Cardiff Process (which aims to integrate environmental concerns into other policies) are being developed as a framework for more detailed strategies.

The first environment action programme began in the 1970s and the EU adopted the sixth programme, *Environment 2010: Our Future, Our Choice,* in January 2001. Focusing on the topics of climate change, nature and biodiversity, environment and health, and natural resources and waste, it is the cornerstone of EU policy.

The European Commission (EC) is also using more diverse methods, in particular market-based instruments such as environmental taxes and voluntary measures. These are increasingly being used across Europe. Taxing energy consumption and selling the right to emit greenhouse gases are key ways of tackling climate change, and both follow the 'polluter pays' principle. Items subject to environmental taxes in Europe include plastic bags (Belgium, Ireland and Italy), plastic mineral water bottles (Italy), milk and fruit juice cartons (Norway), tyres (Denmark and Finland), disposable cutlery (Belgium) and paper and cardboard (France).

SUSTAINABLE DEVELOPMENT

The environmental agenda has become part of a wider move to address sustainability that incorporates social, environmental and economic development. During the World Summit on Sustainable Development, held in Johannesburg in 2002, governments agreed on a series of commitments in five priority areas: water and sanitation, energy, health, agriculture and biodiversity. Approved targets and timetables included halving the number of people who lack access to clean water or proper sanitation by 2015, and reducing biodiversity loss by 2010. Following the summit, the United Nations Commission on Sustainable Development agreed its programme for the next 15 years. In addition, 2005–15 has been named as the 'Water for Life' decade.

The EU's latest sustainable development strategy, launched in 2005, focuses on climate change and clean energy; public health threats; social exclusion, demography and migration; management of natural resources; sustainable transport and global poverty and development. These challenges are related and there are multiple links between them, eg the use of renewable energy and climate change, or climate change and poverty.

The UK also has a sustainable development strategy, *Securing the Future,* alongside a framework for sustainable development across the UK, *Our Future – Different Paths,* shared between the government, the devolved administrations and the Northern Ireland Office.

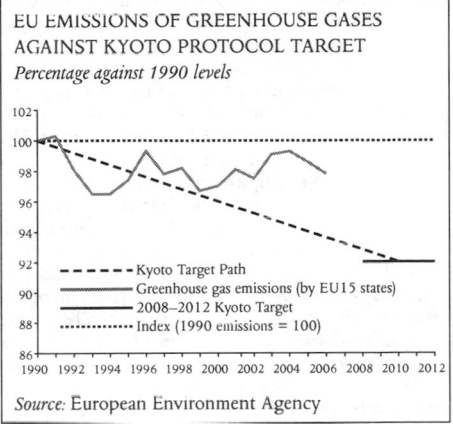

EU EMISSIONS OF GREENHOUSE GASES AGAINST KYOTO PROTOCOL TARGET
Percentage against 1990 levels

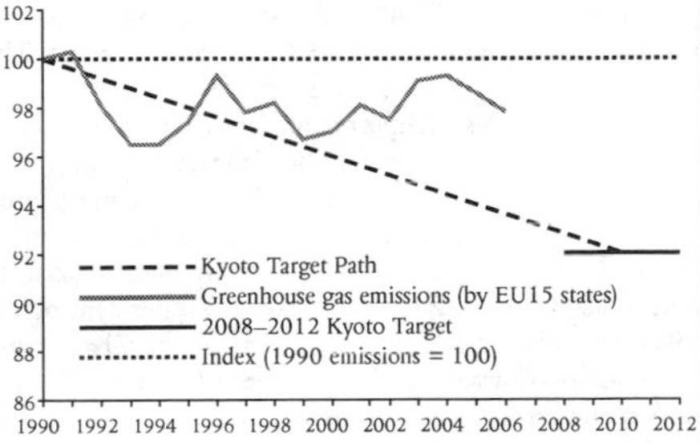

Source: European Environment Agency

CLIMATE CHANGE AND AIR POLLUTION

Temperature in central England has risen by about 1°C since the 1970s, with 2006 being the warmest year on record. Severe wind storms have become more frequent over the past few decades, but are not above those of the 1920s. Sea levels around the UK rose by 1mm a year in the 20th century, although the rate for the 1990s and 2000s is higher.

The government's response to climate change has been driven by the UN framework convention on climate change. This is a binding agreement that aims to reduce the risks of global warming by limiting greenhouse gas emissions. Between 1970 and 2004, global greenhouse gas emissions rose by 70 per cent (24 per cent since 1990) and carbon dioxide emissions grew by 80 per cent (28 per cent since 1990). Progress towards the convention's targets is assessed at regular conferences. At Kyoto in 1997, the Kyoto protocol was adopted. It covers the six main greenhouse gases: carbon dioxide, methane, nitrous oxide, hydrofluorocarbons (HFCs), perfluorocarbons (PFCs) and sulphur hexafluoride. Under the protocol, industrialised countries agreed to a legally binding target of cutting emissions of greenhouse gases by 5.2 per cent below 1990 levels by 2008–12. The protocol came into force in February 2005 after it was ratified by Russia. The USA has not ratified the treaty, while the UK set its own target at a 12.5 per cent reduction on 1990. A post-Kyoto agreement is expected at the Copenhagen conference in December 2009.

The EU wants to limit global warming to less than 2°C above pre-industrial temperatures. To achieve this, global emissions need to peak before 2020 and be reduced to less than 50 per cent of 1990 levels by 2050. The EU has proposed that developed countries as a group cut their greenhouse gas emissions to 30 per cent below 1990 levels by 2020. It also wants developing countries, particularly the big emerging economies, to limit the growth in their collective emissions to 15–30 per cent below 'business as usual' levels by the same deadline. The agreement should also include a framework for action on adaptation to climate change.

In March 2007, the EU heads of state and government agreed a firm target of cutting 20 per cent of the EU's greenhouse gas emissions by 2020, rising to 30 per cent if the USA, Canada and India make similar commitments. Greenhouse gas emissions in the 27 EU member states are decreasing. Between 1990 and 2006, they dropped by 7.7 per cent, although they did rise in Spain, Portugal, Greece and Italy. Current projections indicate that the EU-27 will not meet the 20 per cent target.

Net emissions of carbon dioxide in the UK fell by 12.8 per cent between 1990 and 2007, taking emissions trading into account, and by 8.5 per cent without. The UK brought its energy and climate change polices together at the new Department of Energy and Climate Change in October 2008. The following month, the Climate Change Act, together with an accompanying strategy, set out a framework to move the UK to a low-carbon economy. The UK already had a goal to reduce its carbon dioxide emissions to 20 per cent below 1990 levels by 2010. However, the Climate Change Act proposed two further goals: an interim target of a 26 per cent reduction in carbon dioxide emissions below 1990 levels by 2020 (which is under review) and a legally binding target of an 80 per cent reduction by 2050. The government must also set binding limits on carbon dioxide emissions during five-year budget periods.

Measures to tackle climate change in the UK are also covered by the climate change programme, launched in March 2006. It targets every sector of the economy and includes: a stricter emissions cap for industry; measures to encourage the uptake of biofuels in petrol; tighter building regulations; measures to improve household energy efficiency; a renewed emphasis on encouraging and enabling the general public, businesses and public authorities to help achieve the government's targets; and increased levels of microgeneration.

The UK has a voluntary greenhouse gas emissions trading scheme that allows businesses to buy an emission allowance to meet emission targets, or to sell surplus emission allowances. A new UK-wide emissions trading scheme, the Carbon Reduction Commitment (CRC), starts in April 2010 and is aimed at organisations such as supermarkets and banks. There are no current plans to introduce emissions trading for individuals in the UK, and the idea meets with considerable public resistance. It would entail setting an overall emission cap and dividing emissions rights equally across the population; carbon credits would be surrendered when buying fuel, transport or energy, and any 'excess' credits sold to those who need them. An initial government study concluded that the concept is ahead of its time and would be costly to implement. According to the Environmental Audit Committee, personal carbon trading has the potential to drive greater emissions reductions than green taxation, but making it publicly and politically acceptable will decide its fate.

A mandatory EC emissions trading scheme for carbon dioxide applies at a company level. The companies covered by the ruling account for almost half of the EU's total carbon dioxide emissions. From 2012, airlines will be included in the scheme, covering emissions from all domestic and international flights arriving at, or departing from, an EU airport. Ticket prices are expected to rise by around €40 (£34) for long-haul and €9 (£8) for short-haul return fights. The EU has indicated a willingness to link its trading scheme to those in other countries. It has also begun to place a greater emphasis on adaptation, in particular proposing a framework to strengthen the EU's resilience to cope with the effects of climate change.

WASTE

By 2020 the EU could be generating 45 per cent more waste than in 1995. In the UK the uncoupling of waste growth from economic growth is a key objective along with placing greater emphasis on prevention and reuse, putting less non-municipal waste into landfill and investing in the infrastructure necessary to divert waste from landfill. The principles informing this thinking are: the waste hierarchy of reduce, reuse, recycle, dispose; the 'proximity principle' of disposing of waste close to its generation; and national self-sufficiency.

In 2007 the UK generated about 575kg of municipal waste per person compared with an average across Europe of 522kg, ranging from a low of 294kg per person in the Czech Republic to 801kg in Denmark. The majority of municipal waste across Europe went into landfill (41 per cent), the rest was recycled (22 per cent), incinerated (20 per cent) or composted (17 per cent). In the UK, the proportion of household waste recycled or composted has been increasing steadily, reaching 35 per cent in the year to June 2008 in contrast to 6 per cent in 1995–6. The UK is still behind the Netherlands, Belgium, Austria and Germany, who recycle or compost around 60 per cent of their municipal waste. Bulgaria, however, puts 100 per cent of its municipal waste into landfill, while in Greece it is over 80 per cent.

EU directives help to shape UK policy, particularly in relation to commercial and industrial waste. For instance, the EU's European Integrated Products Policy aims to minimise the environmental impact of a product by looking at all phases of its life-cycle and encouraging each one to improve its environmental performance. A series of directives on packaging waste, vehicles, waste electrical and electronic equipment and batteries is intended to promote greater responsibility for products at the end of their life. The EU is also examining the issue of bio-waste (ie biodegradable garden, kitchen and food waste) which accounts for around one third of municipal waste.

WATER

Climate change alters rainfall patterns in ways that can put pressure on water resources, resulting in many regions having more droughts. The EU flagship water legislation, the Water Framework Directive, takes this into account. Among its policy suggestions is the pricing of water in ways that would encourage efficient water use, thereby addressing water scarcity and drought.

Water strategy in the UK tackles similar issues: the sustainable delivery of secure water supplies; an improved and protected water environment; fair, affordable and cost-reflective water charges; reduced water industry greenhouse gas emissions; and more sustainable and effective management of surface water.

For drinking water, wastewater discharges, rivers, coastal water and bathing water, quality targets are set at both EU and UK level: the aim is to achieve 'good water status' throughout the EU by 2015. The EC has launched an interactive internet tool, WISE (Water Information System for Europe), which provides water data and allows users to monitor water quality in their neighbourhood. In the quality tests for bathing water in 2008, 96 per cent of swimming spots in the UK met the EU directive's minimum requirements, compared to two thirds in 1988, while 64 per cent achieved a newer, tighter standard. This is a marked improvement since the early 1990s, when less than a third of England's beaches met the toughest standards.

ENERGY

Energy used in the home is responsible for 25 per cent of the UK's carbon dioxide emissions. The Climate Change Act 2008 sets out four energy policy goals for the UK: cutting carbon dioxide emissions by 80 per cent by 2050, maintaining reliable energy supplies, promoting competitive energy markets, and ensuring homes are adequately and affordably heated. In terms of renewable energy, the UK target is to increase the contribution of renewables to 10 per cent of electricity by 2010, with a further target (set by the EU) of 15 per cent by 2020.

The EC has also adopted a number of targets. These are to improve energy efficiency by 20 per cent by 2020; increase the level of renewables used in transport fuel to 10 per cent by 2020 (the target was originally just for biofuels); and for 20 per cent of the EU's energy consumption to come from renewables by 2020. In 2006, renewable energy accounted for 7.1 per cent of EU primary energy consumption.

Worldwide, wind energy has the largest share of investment and is growing at 25–30 per cent annually, accounting for 120GW of electricity in 2008. Grid-tied solar photovoltaic technology is growing at 50–60 per cent a year and accounts for 8GW. Developing countries account for more than 40 per cent of existing renewable power capacity, more than 70 per cent of existing solar hot water capacity and 45 per cent of biofuel production.

ALTERNATIVE ENERGY

Gigawatt hours generated

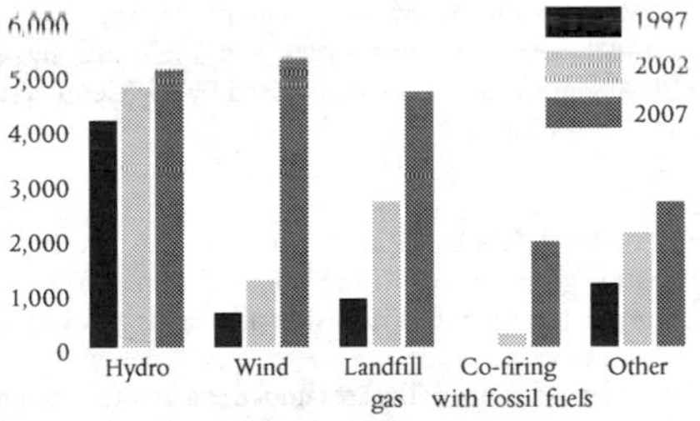

Source: Digest of UK Energy Statistics

The capacity for renewables is increasing and the publication of a UK Renewable Energy Strategy is expected. In 2007, renewables accounted for 5 per cent of electricity generated in the UK, an increase from 4.7 per cent in 2006. Hydropower has traditionally been the UK's largest renewable source and both on- and offshore wind power are popular with power generators. The British Wind Energy Association says that new projects could result in more than 5 million homes being powered by wind in the next few years. According to the Renewable Energy Centre, energy capacity from biofuel and waste will soon overtake hydro generation. A UK bioethanol plant with a capacity matching the largest in the world is scheduled for 2009 and a straw-fired power station in Cambridgeshire generates enough power to heat and light 80,000 homes. Wave and tidal technologies are still at the experimental stage. According to findings from the international scientific congress held in advance of the 2009 Copenhagen climate conference, renewable energy technologies such as wind and photovoltaics, given adequate financial and political support, could supply 40 per cent of the world's electricity by 2050.

ENVIRONMENT AND HEALTH

Particulate matter in the air, noise and ground-level ozone damage the health of thousands of people every year. Environmental pollutants, including pesticides, endocrine disruptors, dioxins and PCBs persist in the environment and not enough is known about their long-term effect on health. There are also concerns about the effects of electromagnetic fields on human health and the potential risks associated with nanotechnology are unclear.

Concerns about pollution's impact on health are addressed by the EU environment and health strategy and its Environment and Health Action Plan 2004–10. The plan outlines an integrated approach involving closer co-operation between the health, environment and research areas. It builds on an assessment of the current baseline knowledge in the areas of: integrated monitoring of dioxins and PCBs, heavy metals and endocrine disrupters; childhood cancer, neurodevelopmental disorders and respiratory health; human biomonitoring, environment and health indicators; and research needs.

A chemicals policy, under which industry has to provide information on the effects of chemicals on human health and the environment, as well as on safe ways of handling them, has also been set up.

CONTACTS

DEPARTMENT OF ENVIRONMENT, FOOD AND RURAL AFFAIRS, Eastbury House, 30–34 Albert Embankment, London SE1 7TL T 0845 933 5577 W www.defra.gov.uk

DEPARTMENT OF ENERGY AND CLIMATE CHANGE, 3 Whitehall Place, London SW1A 2HD T 0300-060 4000 W www.decc.gov.uk

ENVIRONMENT AGENCY, Rio House, Almonsbury, Bristol BS32 4UD T 0870 850 6506 W www.environment-agency.gov.uk

EUROPEAN ENVIRONMENT AGENCY, Kongens Nytorv 6, DK-1050 Copenhagen K, Denmark T +45 3336 7100 W www.eea.europa.eu

ROYAL COMMISSION ON ENVIRONMENTAL POLLUTION, Room 108, 55 Whitehall, London SW1A 2EY T 020-7270 8190 W www.rcep.org.uk

SCOTTISH EXECUTIVE, ENVIRONMENT DIRECTORATE, Victoria Quay, Edinburgh EH6 6QQ T 0131-556 8400 W www.scotland.gov.uk

CONSERVATION AND HERITAGE

NATIONAL PARKS

© Natural England – material is reproduced with the permission of Natural England

ENGLAND AND WALES

There are now eight national parks in England and three in Wales. In addition, the Norfolk and Suffolk Broads are considered to have equivalent status to a national park and the South Downs is due to gain national park status in 2010. Under the provisions of the National Parks and Access to the Countryside Act 1949, as clarified by the Natural Environment and Rural Communities Act 2006, areas designated as national parks have a statutory requirement to conserve and protect scenic landscapes from inappropriate development and to provide access to the land for public enjoyment.

Natural England is the statutory body which has the power to designate national parks in England, and the Countryside Council for Wales is responsible for national parks in Wales. Designations in England are confirmed by the Secretary of State for Environment, Food and Rural Affairs and those in Wales by the Welsh Assembly Government. The designation of a national park does not affect the ownership of the land or remove the rights of the local community. The majority of the land in the national parks is owned by private landowners (74 per cent) or by bodies such as the National Trust (7 per cent) and the Forestry Commission (7 per cent). The national park authorities own only around 2 per cent of the land.

The Environment Act 1995 replaced the existing national park boards and committees with free-standing national park authorities (NPAs). NPAs are the sole local planning authorities for their areas and as such influence land use and development, and deal with planning applications. Their duties include conserving and enhancing the natural beauty, wildlife and cultural heritage of the parks; promoting opportunities for public understanding and enjoyment; and fostering the economic and social well-being of the communities within national parks. The NPAs publish management plans as statements of their policies and appoint their own officers and staff.

The Broads Authority was established under the Norfolk and Suffolk Broads Act 1998 and meets the requirement for the authority to have a navigation function in addition to a regard for the needs of agriculture, forestry and the economic and social interests of those who live or work in the Broads.

MEMBERSHIP

Membership of English NPAs comprises local authority appointees, members directly appointed by the environment secretary of state and members appointed by him after a consultation with local parishes. Under the Natural Environment and Rural Communities Act 2006 every district, county or unitary authority with land in a national park is entitled to appoint at least one member unless it chooses to opt out. The total number of local authority and parish members must exceed the number of national members. Since 1 April 2007 NPAs have between 22 and 30 members.

The Broads Authority has 21 members: nine appointed by the constituent local authorities, two appointed by the Navigation Committee and ten appointed by the Secretary of State. The Secretary of State's appointees include at least three which are appointed after consultation with representatives of boating interests and at least two which are appointed after consultation with representatives of landowning and farming interests.

In Wales two-thirds of NPA members are appointed by the constituent local authorities and one-third by the Welsh Assembly Government, advised by the Countryside Council for Wales.

FUNDING

The English NPAs and the Broads Authority are funded by central government. In the financial year 2009–10 a core grant totalling £47.5m was allocated between the authorities.

In Wales, national parks are funded via a grant from the National Assembly. National park grant for 2009–10 amounted to £11.27m. The three NPAs in Wales receive further funding from relevant local authorities.

All NPAs and the Broads Authority can take advantage of grants from other bodies including lottery and European grants.

The national parks (with date designation confirmed) are:

BRECON BEACONS (1957), Powys (66 per cent)/Carmarthenshire/Rhondda, Cynon and

Taff/Merthyr Tydfil/Blaenau Gwent/Monmouthshire, 1,344 sq. km/519 sq. miles – The park is centred on the Brecon Beacons mountain range, which includes the three highest mountains in southern Britain (Pen y Fan, Corn Du and Cribyn), but also includes the valley of the rivers Usk and Wye, the Black Mountains to the east and the Black Mountain to the west. There are information centres at the national park visitor centre at Libanus (near Brecon), Abergavenny, Llandovery and Pontneddfechan.
National Park Authority, Plas y Ffynnon, Cambrian Way, Brecon, Powys LD3 7HP **T** 01874-624437
E enquiries@breconbeacons.org
W www.breconbeacons.org
Chief Executive, John Cook

BROADS (1989), Norfolk/Suffolk, 305 sq. km/118 sq. miles – The Broads are located between Norwich and Great Yarmouth on the flood plains of the six rivers flowing through the area to the sea. The area is one of fens, winding waterways, woodland and marsh. The 60 or so broads are man-made, and many are connected to the rivers by dykes, providing over 200km of navigable waterways. There are information centres at Beccles, Hoveton, Potter Heigham, Ranworth, Whitlingham and Toad Hole Cottage at How Hill.
Broads Authority, Dragonfly House, 2 Gilders Way, Norwich NR3 1UB **T** 01603-610734
E broads@broads-authority.gov.uk
W www.broads-authority.gov.uk
Chief Executive, Dr John Packman

DARTMOOR (1951), Devon, 953 sq. km/368 sq. miles – The park consists of moorland and rocky granite tors, and is rich in prehistoric remains. There are information centres at Haytor, Newbridge, Princetown (main visitor centre) and Postbridge.
National Park Authority, Parke, Bovey Tracey, Devon TQ13 9JQ **T** 01626-832093 **E** hq@dartmoor-npa.gov.uk
W www.dartmoor-npa.gov.uk
Chief Executive, Kevin Bishop

EXMOOR (1954), Somerset (71 per cent)/Devon, 694 sq. km/268 sq. miles – Exmoor is a moorland plateau inhabited by wild Exmoor ponies and red deer. There are many ancient remains and burial mounds. There are national park centres at Dunster, Dulverton and Lynmouth.
National Park Authority, Exmoor House, Dulverton, Somerset TA22 9HL **T** 01398-323665
E info@exmoor-nationalpark.gov.uk
W www.exmoor-nationalpark.gov.uk
Chief Executive/National Park Officer, Dr Nigel Stone

LAKE DISTRICT (1951), Cumbria, 2,292 sq. km/885 sq. miles – The Lake District includes England's highest mountains (Scafell Pike, Helvellyn and Skiddaw) but it is most famous for its glaciated lakes. There are national park information centres at Bowness Bay, Keswick, Ullswater and a visitor centre at Brockhole, Windermere.
National Park Authority, Murley Moss, Oxenholme Road, Kendal, Cumbria LA9 7RL **T** 01539-724555
E hq@lake-district.gov.uk **W** www.lake-district.gov.uk
National Park Officer, Richard Leafe

NEW FOREST (2005), Hampshire, 570 sq. km/220 sq. miles – The forest has been protected since 1079 when it was declared a royal hunting forest. The area consists of forest, ancient woodland and heathland. Much of the forest is managed by the Forestry Commission, which provides several campsites. The main villages are Brockenhurst, Burley and Lyndhurst, which has a visitor centre.
National Park Authority, South Efford House, Milford Road, Lymington, Hants SO41 0JD **T** 01590-646600
E enquiries@newforestnpa.gov.uk
W www.newforestnpa.gov.uk
Chief Executive, Lindsay Cornish

NORTH YORK MOORS (1952), North Yorkshire (96 per cent)/Redcar and Cleveland, 1,434 sq. km/554 sq. miles – The park consists of woodland and moorland, and includes the Hambleton Hills and the Cleveland Way. There are information centres at Danby and Sutton Bank.
National Park Authority, The Old Vicarage, Bondgate, Helmsley, York YO62 5BP **T** 01439-770657
E info@northyorkmoors-npa.gov.uk **W** www.moors.uk.net
Chief Executive/National Park Officer, Andrew Wilson

NORTHUMBERLAND (1956), Northumberland, 1,048 sq. km/405 sq. miles – The park is an area of hill country stretching from Hadrian's Wall to the Scottish border. There are information centres at Ingram, Once Brewed and Rothbury.
National Park Authority, Eastburn, South Park, Hexham, Northumberland NE46 1BS **T** 01434-605555
E enquiries@nnpa.org.uk
W www.northumberlandnationalpark.org.uk
Chief Executive, Tony Gates

PEAK DISTRICT (1951), Derbyshire (64 per cent)/Staffordshire/South Yorkshire/Cheshire/West Yorkshire/Greater Manchester, 1,437 sq. km/555 sq. miles – The Peak District includes the gritstone moors of the 'Dark Peak' and the limestone dales of the 'White Peak'. There are information centres at Bakewell, Castleton, Edale and Upper Derwent.
National Park Authority, Aldern House, Baslow Road, Bakewell, Derbyshire DE45 1AE **T** 01629-816200
E customer.service@peakdistrict.gov.uk
W www.peakdistrict.gov.uk
Chief Executive, Jim Dixon

PEMBROKESHIRE COAST (1952 and 1995), Pembrokeshire, 621 sq. km/240 sq. miles – The park includes cliffs, moorland and a number of islands, including Skomer and Ramsey. There are information centres in Newport and Tenby and a gallery and visitor centre, Oriel y Parc, in St Davids.
National Park Authority, Llanion Park, Pembroke Dock, Pembrokeshire SA72 6DY **T** 0845-345 7275
E info@pembrokeshirecoast.org.uk **W** www.pcnpa.org.uk
Chief Executive/National Park Officer, Nic Wheeler

SNOWDONIA/ERYRI (1951), Gwynedd/Conwy, 2,176 sq. km/840 sq. miles – Snowdonia is an area of deep valleys and rugged mountains. There are information centres at Aberdyfi, Beddgelert, Betws y Coed, Blaenau Ffestiniog, Dolgellau and Harlech.
National Park Authority, Penrhyndeudraeth, Gwynedd LL48 6LF **T** 01766-770274 **E** parc@snowdonia-npa.gov.uk
W www.snowdonia-npa.gov.uk
Chief Executive, Aneurin Phillips

YORKSHIRE DALES (1954), North Yorkshire (88 per cent)/Cumbria, 1,769 sq. km/683 sq. miles – The Yorkshire Dales is composed primarily of limestone overlaid in places by millstone grit. The three peaks of Ingleborough, Whernside and Pen-y-ghent are within the park. There are information centres at Grassington, Hawes, Aysgarth Falls, Malham and Reeth.
National Park Authority, Yoredale, Bainbridge, Leyburn, N. Yorks DL8 3EL **T** 0870-166 6333
E info@yorkshiredales.org.uk **W** www.yorkshiredales.org.uk
Chief Executive, David Butterworth

THE SOUTH DOWNS
A designation order for a South Downs national park was made by the then Countryside Agency (now Natural England) in December 2002. The proposed boundary was considered in a public inquiry from November 2003 to March 2005. In February 2006 the designation process was postponed following a high court ruling (the 'Meyrick' judgment) regarding part of the 2005 New Forest designation which changed the way in which criteria for national park status had been widely understood. The Department for Environment, Food and Rural Affairs (DEFRA) clarified the national parks legislation through the Natural Environment and Rural Communities Act 2006 and the South Downs designation process was restarted in March 2007. On 31 March 2009 the secretary of state accepted the designation order boundary, subject to decisions on six small boundary additions. The park is unlikely to be formally designated until early 2010. The national park authority is due to be instated in April 2010 and acquire statutory powers in 2011.

THE SOUTH DOWNS, West Sussex/Hampshire, 1,624 sq. km/627 sq. miles – The South Downs contains a diversity of natural habitats, including flower-studded chalk grassland, ancient woodland, flood meadow, lowland heath and rare chalk heathland.
South Downs Joint Committee, Victorian Barn, Victorian Business Centre, Ford Lane, Ford, Arundel, W. Sussex BN18 0EF T 01243-558700 E comms@southdowns-aonb.gov.uk W www.southdowns.gov.uk
South Downs Officer, Martin Beaton

SCOTLAND

On 9 August 2000 the national parks (Scotland) bill received royal assent, giving parliament the ability to create national parks in Scotland. The first two Scottish national parks became operational in 2002 and 2003 respectively. The Act gives Scottish parks wider powers than in England and Wales, including statutory responsibilities for the economy and rural communities. The board of each Scottish NPA consists of 25 members, of which five are directly elected by a postal ballot of the local electorate. The remaining 20 members, ten of which are nominated by the constituent local authorities, are chosen by the Scottish ministers. In Scotland, the national parks are central government bodies and are wholly funded by the Scottish government. Funding for 2009–10 totals £12.7m.

CAIRNGORMS (2003), North-East Scotland, 3,800 sq. km/1,466 sq. miles – The Cairngorms national park is the largest in the UK. It displays a vast collection of landforms, including five of the six highest mountains in the UK. The near natural woodlands contain remnants of the original ancient Caledonian pine forest.
National Park Authority, 14 The Square, Grantown-on-Spey, Morayshire PH26 3HG T 01479-873535 E enquiries@cairngorms.co.uk W www.cairngorms.co.uk
Chief Executive, Jane Hope

LOCH LOMOND AND THE TROSSACHS (2002), Argyll and Bute/Perth and Kinross/Stirling/West Dunbartonshire, 1,865 sq. km/720 sq. miles – The park boundaries encompass lochs, rivers, forests, 20 mountains above 3,000ft including Ben More and a further 20 mountains between 2,500ft and 3,000ft.
National Park Authority, Carrochan, Carrochan Road, Balloch G83 8EG T 01389-722600 E info@lochlomond-trossachs.org W www.lochlomond-trossachs.org
Chief Executive, Fiona Logan

NORTHERN IRELAND

There is a power to designate national parks in Northern Ireland under the Nature Conservation and Amenity Lands Order (Northern Ireland) 1985, but there are currently no national parks in Northern Ireland.

AREAS OF OUTSTANDING NATURAL BEAUTY

ENGLAND AND WALES

Under the National Parks and Access to the Countryside Act 1949, provision was made for the designation of areas of outstanding natural beauty (AONBs). Natural England is responsible for AONBs in England and the Countryside Council for Wales for the Welsh AONBs. Designations in England are confirmed by the Secretary of State for Environment, Food and Rural Affairs and those in Wales by the National Assembly for Wales. The Countryside and Rights of Way (CROW) Act 2000 placed greater responsibility on local authorities to protect AONBs and made it a statutory duty for relevant authorities to produce a management plan for their AONB area. The CROW Act also provided for the creation of conservation boards for larger and more complex AONBs. The first two conservation boards for the Cotswolds and Chilterns AONBs were established in July 2004.

The primary objective of the AONB designation is to conserve and enhance the natural beauty of the area. Where an AONB has a conservation board, it has the additional purpose of increasing public understanding and enjoyment of the special qualities of the area; the board has greater weight should there be a conflict of interests between the two. In addition, the board is also required to foster the economic and social well-being of the local communities but without incurring significant expenditure in doing so. Overall responsibility for AONBs lies with the relevant local authorities or conservation board. To coordinate planning and management responsibilities between local authorities in whose area they fall, AONBs are overseen by a joint advisory committee (or similar body) which includes representatives from the local authorities, landowners, farmers, residents and conservation and recreation groups. Core funding for AONBs is provided by central government through Natural England and the Countryside Council for Wales.

The 40 Areas of Outstanding Natural Beauty (with date designation confirmed) are:

ARNSIDE AND SILVERDALE (1972), Cumbria/Lancashire, 75 sq. km/29 sq. miles
BLACKDOWN HILLS (1991), Devon/Somerset, 370 sq. km/143 sq. miles
CANNOCK CHASE (1958), Staffordshire, 68 sq. km/26 sq. miles
CHICHESTER HARBOUR (1964), Hampshire/West Sussex, 74 sq. km/29 sq. miles
CHILTERNS (1965; extended 1990), Bedfordshire/Buckinghamshire/Herefordshire/Oxfordshire, 833 sq. km/322 sq. miles
CLWYDIAN RANGE (1985), Denbighshire/Flintshire, 157 sq. km/61 sq. miles

CORNWALL (1959; Camel Estuary 1983), 958 sq. km/370 sq. miles
COTSWOLDS (1966; extended 1990), Gloucestershire/Oxfordshire/Warwickshire/Wiltshire/Worcestershire, 2,038 sq. km/787 sq. miles
CRANBORNE CHASE AND WEST WILTSHIRE DOWNS (1983), Dorset/Hampshire/Somerset/Wiltshire, 983 sq. km/380 sq. miles
DEDHAM VALE (1970; extended 1978, 1991), Essex/Suffolk, 90 sq. km/35 sq. miles
DORSET (1959), Dorset/Somerset, 1,129 sq. km/436 sq. miles
EAST DEVON (1963), 268 sq. km/103 sq. miles
EAST HAMPSHIRE (1962), 383 sq. km/148 sq. miles
FOREST OF BOWLAND (1964), Lancashire/North Yorkshire, 802 sq. km/310 sq. miles
GOWER (1956), Swansea, 188 sq. km/73 sq. miles
HIGH WEALD (1983), East Sussex/Kent/Surrey/West Sussex, 1,460 sq. km/564 sq. miles
HOWARDIAN HILLS (1987), North Yorkshire, 204 sq. km/79 sq. miles
ISLE OF WIGHT (1963), 189 sq. km/73 sq. miles
ISLES OF SCILLY (1976), 16 sq. km/6 sq. miles
KENT DOWNS (1968), 878 sq. km/339 sq. miles
LINCOLNSHIRE WOLDS (1973), 558 sq. km/215 sq. miles
LLEYN (1957), Gwynedd, 161 sq. km/62 sq. miles
MALVERN HILLS (1959), Gloucestershire/Worcestershire, 150 sq. km/58 sq. miles
MENDIP HILLS (1972; extended 1989), Somerset, 198 sq. km/76 sq. miles
NIDDERDALE (1994), North Yorkshire, 603 sq. km/233 sq. miles
NORFOLK COAST (1968), 451 sq. km/174 sq. miles
NORTH DEVON (1960), 171 sq. km/66 sq. miles
NORTH PENNINES (1988), Cumbria/Durham/North Yorkshire/Northumberland, 1,983 sq. km/766 sq. miles
NORTH WESSEX DOWNS (1972), Hampshire/Oxfordshire/Wiltshire, 1,730 sq. km/668 sq. miles
NORTHUMBERLAND COAST (1958), 135 sq. km/52 sq. miles
QUANTOCK HILLS (1957), Somerset, 99 sq. km/38 sq. miles
SHROPSHIRE HILLS (1959), 804 sq. km/310 sq. miles
SOLWAY COAST (1964), Cumbria, 115 sq. km/44 sq. miles
SOUTH DEVON (1960), 337 sq. km/130 sq. miles
SUFFOLK COAST AND HEATHS (1970), 403 sq. km/156 sq. miles
SURREY HILLS (1958), 419 sq. km/162 sq. miles
SUSSEX DOWNS (1966), 983 sq. km/379 sq. miles
TAMAR VALLEY (1995), Cornwall/Devon, 195 sq. km/75 sq. miles
WYE VALLEY (1971), Gloucestershire/Herefordshire/Monmouthshire, 326 sq. km/126 sq. miles
YNYS MON (ISLE OF ANGLESEY) (1967), 221 sq. km/85 sq. miles

NORTHERN IRELAND

The Department of the Environment for Northern Ireland, with advice from the Council for Nature Conservation and the Countryside, designates Areas of Outstanding Natural Beauty in Northern Ireland. At present there are nine and these cover a total area of 2,849 sq. km (1,100 sq. miles). Dates given are those of designation.

ANTRIM COAST AND GLENS (1988), Co. Antrim, 706 sq. km/272 sq. miles
BINEVENAGH (2006), Co. Londonderry, 166 sq. km/64 sq. miles
CAUSEWAY COAST (1989), Co. Antrim, 42 sq. km/16 sq. miles
LAGAN VALLEY (1965), Co. Down, 39 sq. km/15 sq. miles
LECALE COAST (1967), Co. Down, 31 sq. km/12 sq. miles
MOURNE (1986), Co. Down, 570 sq. km/220 sq. miles
RING OF GULLION (1991), Co. Armagh, 154 sq. km/59 sq. miles
SPERRIN (1968; extended 2008), Co. Tyrone/Co. Londonderry, 1,182 sq. km/456 sq. miles
STRANGFORD LOUGH (1972), Co. Down, 280 sq. km/108 sq. miles

NATIONAL SCENIC AREAS

In Scotland, national scenic areas have a broadly equivalent status to AONBs. Scottish Natural Heritage recognises areas of national scenic significance. At the end of June 2009 there were 40, covering a land area of 1,020,500 hectares (2,521,710 acres) and a marine area of 357,900 hectares (884,390 acres).

Development within national scenic areas is dealt with by local authorities, who are required to consult Scottish Natural Heritage concerning certain categories of development. Disagreements between Scottish Natural Heritage and local authorities are referred to the Scottish government. Land management uses can also be modified in the interest of scenic conservation.

ASSYNT-COIGACH, Highland, 90,200ha/222,884 acres
BEN NEVIS AND GLEN COE, Highland, 101,600ha/251,053 acres
CAIRNGORM MOUNTAINS, Highland/Aberdeenshire/Moray, 67,200ha/166,051 acres
CUILLIN HILLS, Highland, 21,900ha/54,115 acres
DEESIDE AND LOCHNAGAR, Aberdeenshire, 40,000ha/98,840 acres
DORNOCH FIRTH, Highland, 7,500ha/18,532 acres
EAST STEWARTRY COAST, Dumfries and Galloway, 4,500ha/11,119 acres
EILDON AND LEADERFOOT, Borders, 3,600ha/8,896 acres
FLEET VALLEY, Dumfries and Galloway, 5,300ha/13,096 acres
GLEN AFFRIC, Highland, 19,300ha/47,690 acres
GLEN STRATHFARRAR, Highland, 3,800ha/9,390 acres
HOY AND WEST MAINLAND, Orkney Islands, 14,800ha/36,571 acres
JURA, Argyll and Bute, 21,800ha/53,868 acres
KINTAIL, Highland, 15,500ha/38,300 acres
KNAPDALE, Argyll and Bute, 19,800ha/48,926 acres
KNOYDART, Highland, 39,500ha/97,604 acres
KYLE OF TONGUE, Highland, 18,500ha/45,713 acres
KYLES OF BUTE, Argyll and Bute, 4,400ha/10,872 acres
LOCH NA KEAL, Mull, Argyll and Bute, 12,700ha/31,382 acres

LOCH LOMOND, Argyll and Bute, 27,400ha/67,705 acres
LOCH RANNOCH AND GLEN LYON, Perthshire and Kinross, 48,400ha/119,596 acres
LOCH SHIEL, Highland, 13,400ha/33,111 acres
LOCH TUMMEL, Perthshire and Kinross, 9,200ha/22,733 acres
LYNN OF LORN, Argyll and Bute, 4,800ha/11,861 acres
MORAR, MOIDART AND ARDNAMURCHAN, Highland, 13,500ha/33,358 acres
NITH ESTUARY, Dumfries and Galloway, 9,300ha/22,980 acres
NORTH ARRAN, North Ayrshire, 23,800ha/58,810 acres
NORTH-WEST SUTHERLAND, Highland, 20,500ha/50,655 acres
RIVER EARN, Perthshire and Kinross, 3,000ha/7,413 acres
RIVER TAY, Perthshire and Kinross, 5,600ha/13,838 acres
ST KILDA, Eilean Siar (Western Isles), 900ha/2,224 acres
SCARBA, LUNGA AND THE GARVELLACHS, Argyll and Bute, 1,900ha/4,695 acres
SHETLAND, Shetland Isles, 11,600ha/28,664 acres
SMALL ISLANDS, Highland, 15,500ha/38,300 acres
SOUTH LEWIS, HARRIS AND NORTH UIST, Eilean Siar (Western Isles), 109,600ha/270,822 acres
SOUTH UIST MACHAIR, Eilean Siar (Western Isles), 6,100ha/15,073 acres
THE TROSSACHS, Stirling, 4,600ha/11,367 acres
TROTTERNISH, Highland, 5,000ha/12,355 acres
UPPER TWEEDDALE, Borders, 10,500ha/25,945 acres
WESTER ROSS, Highland, 145,300ha/359,036 acres

THE NATIONAL FOREST

The National Forest is being planted across 517 sq. km (200 sq. miles) of Derbyshire, Leicestershire and Staffordshire. Seven million trees, of mixed species but mainly broadleaved, covering over 5,400 hectares (13,300 acres) have been planted. The aim is to eventually cover about one-third of the designated area.

The project was developed in 1992–5 by the Countryside Commission and is now run by the National Forest Company, which was established in April 1995. The National Forest Company is responsible for the delivery of the government-approved National Forest Strategy and is funded by DEFRA.

NATIONAL FOREST COMPANY, Enterprise Glade, Bath Lane, Moira, Swadlincote, Derbyshire DE12 6BD
T 01283-551211 **E** enquiries@nationalforest.org
W www.nationalforest.org
Chief Executive, Sophie Churchill

SITES OF SPECIAL SCIENTIFIC INTEREST

Site of special scientific interest (SSSI) is a legal notification applied to land in England, Scotland or Wales which Natural England (NE) (formerly English Nature), Scottish Natural Heritage (SNH) or the Countryside Council for Wales (CCW) identifies as being of special interest because of its flora, fauna, geological, geomorphological or physiographical features. In some cases, SSSIs are managed as nature reserves.

NE, SNH and CCW must notify the designation of an SSSI to the local planning authority, every owner/occupier of the land, and the environment secretary, the Scottish ministers or the National Assembly for Wales. Forestry and agricultural departments and a number of other interested parties are also formally notified.

Objections to the notification of an SSSI can be made and ultimately considered at a full meeting of the Council of NE or CCW. In Scotland an objection will be dealt with by the main board of SNH or an appropriate subgroup, depending on the nature of the objection. Unresolved objections on scientific grounds from those with a legal interest in the land must be referred to the Advisory Committee on SSSI.

The protection of these sites depends on the cooperation of individual landowners and occupiers. Owner/occupiers must consult NE, SNH or CCW and gain written consent before they can undertake certain listed activities on the site. Funds are available through management agreements and grants to assist owners and occupiers in conserving sites' interests. Sites can also be protected by management schemes, management notices and other enforcement mechanisms. As a last resort a site can be purchased.

The number and area of SSSIs in Britain as at May 2009 was:

	Number	*Hectares*	*Acres*
England	4,115	1,077,087	2,661,540
Scotland	1,455	1,038,395	2,565,839
Wales	1,025	265,068	655,009

NORTHERN IRELAND

In Northern Ireland 257 Areas of Special Scientific Interest (ASSIs) have been declared by the Department of the Environment for Northern Ireland.

NATIONAL NATURE RESERVES

National nature reserves are defined in the National Parks and Access to the Countryside Act 1949 as modified by the Natural Environment and Rural Communities Act 2006. National nature reserves may be managed solely for the purpose of conservation, or for both the purposes of conservation and recreation, providing this does not compromise the conservation purpose.

Natural England (NE), Scottish Natural Heritage (SNH) or the Countryside Council for Wales (CCW) can declare as a national nature reserve land which is held and managed as a nature reserve under an agreement; land held and managed by NE, SNH or CCW; or land held and managed as a nature reserve by an approved body. NE, SNH or CCW can make by-laws to protect reserves from undesirable activities; these are subject to confirmation by the Secretary of State for Environment, Food and Rural Affairs, the National Assembly for Wales or the Scottish ministers in Scotland.

The number and area of national nature reserves in Britain as at May 2009 was:

	Number	*Hectares*	*Acres*
England	223	95,859	236,873
Scotland	66	137,275	339,202
Wales	69	24,307	60,066

NORTHERN IRELAND

Nature reserves are established and managed by the Department of the Environment for Northern Ireland, with advice from the Council for Nature Conservation and the Countryside. Nature reserves are declared under the Nature Conservation and Amenity Lands (Northern Ireland) order 1985; to date, 47 nature reserves have been declared.

LOCAL NATURE RESERVES

Local nature reserves are defined in the National Parks and Access to the Countryside Act 1949 (as amended by the Natural Environment and Rural Communities Act 2006) as land designated for the study and preservation of flora and fauna, or of geological or physiographical features. Local nature reserves also have a statutory obligation to provide opportunities for the enjoyment of nature or open air recreation, providing this does not compromise the conservation purpose of the reserve. Local authorities in England, Scotland and Wales the power to acquire, declare and manage reserves in consultation with Natural England, Scottish Natural Heritage and the Countryside Council for Wales. There is similar legislation in Northern Ireland where the consulting organisation is the Environment and Heritage Service.

Any organisation, such as water companies, educational trusts, local amenity groups and charitable nature conservation bodies, such as wildlife trusts, may manage local nature reserves, provided that a local authority has a legal interest in the land. This means that the local authority must either own it, lease it or have a management agreement with the landowner.

The number and area of designated local nature reserves in Britain as at May 2009 was:

	Number	*Hectares*	*Acres*
England	1,421	35,373	87,406
Scotland	54	9,953	24,594
Wales	78	5,544	13,699

FOREST RESERVES

The Forestry Commission is the government department responsible for forestry policy throughout Great Britain. Forestry is a devolved matter, with the separate Forestry Commissions for England, Scotland and Wales reporting directly to their appropriate minister. The equivalent body in Northern Ireland is the Forest Service, an agency of the Department of Agriculture and Rural Development for Northern Ireland. The Forestry Commission in each country is led by a director who is also a member of the GB Board of Commissioners. As at March 2009, UK woodland certified by the Foresty Commission (including Forestry Commission-managed woodland) amounted to around 1,283,000 hectares: 347,000 hectares in England, 124,000 hectares in Wales, 746,000 hectares in Scotland and 65,000 hectares in Northern Ireland. For more information, *see* W www.forestry.gov.uk

There are 34 forest nature reserves in Northern Ireland, covering 1,512 hectares (3,736 acres), designated and administered by the Forest Service. There are also 16 national nature reserves on Forest Service-owned property.

MARINE NATURE RESERVES

The Secretary of State for Environment, Food and Rural Affairs, the National Assembly for Wales and the Scottish government have the power to designate marine nature reserves. Natural England, Scottish Natural Heritage and the Countryside Council for Wales select and manage these reserves. Marine nature reserves may be established in Northern Ireland under a 1985 Order.

Marine nature reserves provide protection for marine flora and fauna, and geological and physiographical features on land covered by tidal waters or parts of the sea in or adjacent to the UK. Reserves also provide opportunities for study and research. In June 2009 the Marine and Coastal Access Bill proposed replacing marine nature reserves with a new kind of protected area, marine conservation zones (MCZ), to increase the protection of species and habitats deemed to be of national importance over a wider area. Individual MCZs would have varying levels of protection: some would restrict specific activities, while others would prohibit all damaging activities.

The existing statutory marine nature reserves are:

LUNDY (1986), Bristol Channel
SKOMER (1990), Dyfed
STRANGFORD LOUGH (1995), Northern Ireland

WORLD HERITAGE SITES

The Convention Concerning the Protection of the World Cultural and Natural Heritage was adopted by the United Nations Educational Scientific and Cultural Organisation (UNESCO) in 1972 and ratified by the UK in 1984. As at 16 April 2009 186 states were party to the convention. The convention provides for the identification, protection and conservation of cultural and natural sites of outstanding universal value.

Cultural sites may be:

- sites representing architectural and technological innovation or cultural interchange
- sites of artistic, historic, aesthetic, archaeological, scientific, ethnologic or anthropologic value
- 'cultural landscapes', ie sites whose characteristics are marked by significant interactions between human populations and their natural environment
- exceptional examples of traditional settlement or land- or sea-use; especially those threatened by irreversible change

Natural sites may be:

- those with remarkable physical, biological or geological formations
- those with outstanding universal value from the point of view of science, conservation or natural beauty
- the habitat of threatened species and plants

Governments which are party to the convention nominate sites in their country for inclusion in the World Cultural and Natural Heritage List. Nominations are considered by the World Heritage Committee, an inter-governmental committee composed of 21 representatives of the parties to the convention. The committee is advised by the International Council on Monuments and Sites (ICOMOS), the International Centre for the Study of the Preservation and Restoration of Cultural Property (ICCROM) and the World Conservation Union (IUCN). ICOMOS evaluates and reports on proposed cultural and mixed sites, ICCROM provides expert advice and training on how to conserve and restore cultural property and IUCN provides technical evaluations of natural heritage sites and reports on the state of conservation of listed sites. The Department for Culture, Media and Sport represents the UK government in matters relating to the convention.

A prerequisite for inclusion in the World Heritage List is the existence of an effective legal protection system in the country in which the site is situated and a detailed management plan to ensure the conservation of the site. Inclusion in the list does not confer any greater degree of protection on the site than that offered by the national protection framework.

If a site is considered to be in serious danger of decay or damage, the committee may add it to the World Heritage in Danger List. Sites on this list may benefit from particular attention or emergency measures to allay threats and allow them to retain their world heritage status, or in extreme cases of damage or neglect they may lose their world heritage status completely.

Financial support for the conservation of sites on the World Cultural and Natural Heritage List is provided by the World Heritage Fund, administered by the World Heritage Committee. The fund's income is derived from compulsory and voluntary contributions from the states party to the convention and from private donations.

DESIGNATED SITES

As at 30 June 2009, following the 33rd session of the World Heritage Committee, 890 sites were inscribed on the World Cultural and Natural Heritage List. Of these, 25 are in the United Kingdom and three in British overseas territories; 23 are listed for their cultural significance (†), four for their natural significance (*) and one for both cultural and natural significance. The year in which sites were designated appears in parentheses. In 2005 Hadrian's Wall, a World Heritage Site in its own right since 1987, was joined by the upper German-Raetian Limes to form the first section of a trans-national world heritage site, Frontiers of the Roman Empire.

UNITED KINGDOM

†Bath – the city (1987)
†Blaenarvon industrial landscape, Wales (2000)
†Blenheim Palace and Park, Oxfordshire (1987)
†Canterbury Cathedral, St Augustine's Abbey, St Martin's Church, Kent (1988)
†Castle and town walls of King Edward I, north Wales – Beaumaris, Caernarfon Castle, Conwy Castle, Harlech Castle, Ynys Mon (Isle of Anglesey) (1986)
†Cornwall and west Devon mining landscape (2006)
†Derwent Valley Mills, Derbyshire (2001)
*Dorset and east Devon coast (2001)
†Durham Cathedral and Castle (1986)
†Edinburgh old and new towns (1995)
†Frontiers of the Roman Empire, Hadrian's Wall, northern England (1987, 2005)
*Giant's Causeway and Causeway coast, Co. Antrim (1986)
†Greenwich, London – maritime Greenwich, including the Royal Naval College, Old Royal Observatory, Queen's House, town centre (1997)
†Heart of Neolithic Orkney (1999)
†Ironbridge Gorge, Shropshire – the world's first iron bridge and other early industrial sites (1986)
†Liverpool – six areas of the maritime mercantile city (2004)
†New Lanark, South Lanarkshire, Scotland (2001)
†Pontcysyllte Aqueduct and Canal, Wrexham, Wales (2009)
†Royal Botanic Gardens, Kew (2003)
†*St Kilda, Eilean Siar (Western Isles) (1986)
†Saltaire, West Yorkshire (2001)
†Stonehenge, Avebury and related megalithic sites, Wiltshire (1986)
†Studley Royal Park, Fountains Abbey, St Mary's Church, N. Yorkshire (1986)
†Tower of London (1988)
†Westminster Abbey, Palace of Westminster, St Margaret's Church, London (1987)

BRITISH OVERSEAS TERRITORIES

*Henderson Island, Pitcairn Islands, South Pacific Ocean (1988)
*Gough Island and Inaccessible Island (part of Tristan da Cunha), South Atlantic Ocean (1995)
†St George town and related fortifications, Bermuda (2000)

WORLD HERITAGE CENTRE, UNESCO 7 Place de Fontenoy, 75352 Paris 07 SP, France
W http://whc.unesco.org

CONSERVATION OF WILDLIFE AND HABITATS

The UK is party to a number of international conventions.

BERN CONVENTION

The 1979 Bern Convention on the Conservation of European Wildlife and Natural Habitats came into force in the UK in June 1982. Currently there are 48 contracting parties and a number of other states attend meetings as observers.

The aims are to conserve wild flora and fauna and their natural habitats, especially where this requires the cooperation of several countries, and to promote such cooperation. The convention gives particular emphasis to endangered and vulnerable species.

All parties to the convention must promote national conservation policies and take account of the conservation of wild flora and fauna when setting planning and development policies. Reports on contracting parties' conservation policies must be submitted to the standing committee every four years.

SECRETARIAT OF THE BERN CONVENTION STANDING COMMITTEE, Council of Europe, 67075 Strasbourg-Cedex, France **T** (+33) (3) 8841 2000 **W** www.coe.int

BIODIVERSITY

The UK ratified the Convention on Biological Diversity in June 1994. As at June 2009 there were 191 parties to the convention.

The objectives are the conservation of biological diversity, the sustainable use of its components and the fair and equitable sharing of the benefits arising out of the use of genetic resources. There are seven thematic work programmes addressing agricultural biodiversity, marine and coastal biodiversity and the biodiversity of inland waters, dry and sub-humid lands, islands, mountains and forests. The Conference of the Parties to the Convention on Biological Diversity adopted a supplementary agreement to the convention known as the Cartagena Protocol on Biosafety on 29 January 2000. The protocol seeks to protect biological diversity from potential risks that may be posed by introducing modified living organisms, resulting from biotechnology, into the environment. As at June 2009, 153 countries were party to the protocol; the UK joined on 17 February 2004.

The UK Biodiversity Action Plan (UKBAP) is the UK government's response to the Convention on Biological Diversity and constitutes a record of UK biological resources and a detailed plan for their protection. The list of priority species and habitats under the UKBAP covers 1,150 species and 65 habitats. The UK Biodiversity Partnership Standing Committee guides and supports the UK Biodiversity Partnership in implementing UKBAP; it also coordinates between the four UK country groups which form the partnership and are responsible for implementing UKBAP at a national level. In addition, the UK Biodiversity Partnership includes two support groups: the Biodiversity Research Advisory Group and the Biodiversity Reporting and Information Group.

BIODIVERSITY POLICY UNIT, Zone 1/07, Temple Quay House, 2 The Square, Temple Quay, Bristol BS1 6EB **T** 0845-933 5577 **W** www.ukbap.org.uk

BONN CONVENTION

The 1979 Convention on Conservation of Migratory Species of Wild Animals (also known as CMS or Bonn Convention) came into force in the UK in October 1979. As at 1 March 2009, 111 countries were party to the convention.

It requires the protection of listed endangered migratory species and encourages international agreements covering these and other threatened species. International agreements can range from legally binding treaties to less formal memorandums of understanding.

Six agreements have been concluded to date under the convention. They aim to conserve seals in the Wadden Sea; bat populations in Europe; small cetaceans of the Baltic and North Seas; African-Eurasian migratory waterbirds; cetaceans of the Mediterranean Sea, Black Sea and contiguous Atlantic area; and albatrosses and petrels. A further 17 memorandums of understanding have been agreed for the Siberian crane, slender-billed curlews, marine turtles of the Atlantic coast of Africa, Indian Ocean and South-East Asia, the middle-European population of the great bustard, bukhara deer, aquatic warblers, West African populations of the African elephant, the saiga antelope, cetaceans of the Pacific Islands, dugongs (large marine mammals), Mediterranean monk seals, the ruddy-headed goose, grassland birds, birds of prey, small cetaceans and manatees of West Africa, and high Andean flamingoes.

UNEP/CMS SECRETARIAT, United Nations Premises, Hermann-Ehlers-Str. 10, 53113 Bonn, Germany **T** (+49) (228) 815 2401 **E** secretariat@cms.int **W** www.cms.int

CITES

The 1973 Convention on International Trade in Endangered Species of Wild Fauna and Flora (CITES) is an agreement between governments to ensure that international trade in specimens of wild animals and plants does not threaten their survival. The UK became party to the convention in July 1975 and there are currently 175 member countries. Countries party to the convention ban commercial international trade in an agreed list of endangered species and regulate and monitor trade in other species that might become endangered. The convention accords varying degrees of protection to more than 30,000 species of animals and plants whether they are traded as live specimens or as products derived from them, such as fur coats and dried herbs.

The Conference of the Parties to CITES meets every two to three years to review the convention's implementation. The Wildlife Species Conservation Division at the Department for Environment, Food and Rural Affairs in Bristol (*see* address above) carries out the government's responsibilities under CITES.

CITES SECRETARIAT, International Environment House, Chemin des Anémones, CH-1219 Châtelaine, Geneva, Switzerland **T** (+41) (22) 917 8139/8140 **E** info@cites.org **W** www.cites.org

EUROPEAN WILDLIFE TRADE REGULATION

The Council (EC) Regulation on the Protection of Species of Wild Fauna and Flora by Regulating Trade Therein came into force in the UK on 1 June 1997. It is intended to standardise wildlife trade regulations across Europe and to improve the application of CITES.

RAMSAR CONVENTION

The 1971 Ramsar Convention on Wetlands of International Importance especially as Waterfowl Habitat entered into force in the UK in May 1976. As at June 2009, 159 countries were party to the convention.

The aim of the convention is the conservation and wise use of wetlands and their resources. Governments that are party to the convention must designate wetlands and include wetland conservation considerations in their land-use planning. 1,847 wetland sites, totalling 181 million hectares, have been designated for inclusion in the list of wetlands of international importance. The UK currently has 166 designated sites covering 917,988 hectares. The member countries meet every three years to assess the progress of the convention and the next meeting is scheduled for May 2012.

The UK has set targets under the Ramsar Strategic Plan, 2009–15. Progress towards these is monitored by the UK Ramsar Committee, known as the Joint Working Party. The UK and the Republic of Ireland have established a formal protocol to ensure common monitoring standards for waterbirds in the two countries.

RAMSAR CONVENTION SECRETARIAT, rue Mauverney 28, CH-1196 Gland, Switzerland
T (+41) (22) 999 0170 **W** www.ramsar.org

UK LEGISLATION

The Wildlife and Countryside Act 1981 gives legal protection to a wide range of wild animals and plants. Every five years the statutory nature conservation agencies (Natural England, Countryside Council for Wales and Scottish Natural Heritage) are required to review schedules 5 (animals, other than birds) and 8 (plants) of the Wildlife and Countryside Act 1981. They make recommendations to the Secretary of State for Environment, Food and Rural Affairs, the National Assembly for Wales and the Scottish government for changes to these schedules. The most recent variation of schedule 5 for England came into effect in February 2008 (the fourth quinquennial review recommended no changes to schedule 8, the fifth is currently underway).

Under section 9 of the act it is an offence to kill, injure, take, possess or sell (whether alive or dead) any wild animal included in schedule 5 of the act and to disturb its place of shelter and protection or to destroy that place. However certain species listed on schedule 5 are protected against some, but not all, of these activities.

Under section 13 of the act it is illegal without a licence to pick, uproot, sell or destroy plants listed in schedule 8. Since January 2001, under the Countryside and Rights of Way Act 2000, persons found guilty of an offence under part 1 of the Wildlife and Countryside Act 1981 face a maximum penalty of up to £5,000 and/or up to six months custodial sentence per specimen.

BIRDS

The act lays down a close season for birds (listed on Schedule 2, part 1) from 1 February to 31 August inclusive, each year. Exceptions to these dates are made for:

Capercaillie and (except Scotland) Woodcock – 1 February to 30 September
Snipe – 1 February to 11 August
Birds listed on schedule 2, part 1 (below high water mark) (*see* below) – 21 February to 31 August
Wild duck and wild geese, in or over any area below the high-water mark of ordinary spring tides – 21 February to 31 August
Birds listed on schedule 2, part 1, which may be killed or taken outside the close season are: capercaillie; coot; certain wild duck (gadwall, goldeneye, mallard, pintail, pochard, shoveler, teal, tufted duck, wigeon); certain wild geese (Canada, greylag, pink-footed, white-fronted (in England and Wales only); golden plover; moorhen; snipe; and woodcock.

Section 16 of the 1981 act allows licences to be issued on either an individual or general basis, to allow the killing, taking and sale of certain birds for specified reasons such as public health and safety. All other wild birds are fully protected by law throughout the year.

ANIMALS PROTECTED BY SCHEDULE 5

Adder *(Vipera berus)**
Allis Shad *(Alosa alosa)**
Anemone, Ivell's Sea *(Edwardsia ivelli)*
Anemone, Starlet Sea *(Nematosella vectensis)*
Bat, Horseshoe, all species *(Rhinolophidae)*
Bat, Typical, all species *(Vespertilionidae)*
Beetle *(Hypebaeus flavipes)*
Beetle, Lesser Silver Water *(Hydrochara caraboides)*
Beetle, Mire Pill *(Curimopsis nigrita)**
Beetle, Rainbow Leaf *(Chrysolina cerealis)*
Beetle, Spangled Water *(Graphoderus zonatus)*
Beetle, Stag *(Lucanus cervus)**
Beetle, Violet Click *(Limoniscus violaceus)*
Beetle, Water *(Paracymus aeneus)*
Burbot *(Lota lota)*
Butterfly, Adonis Blue *(Lysandra bellargus)*
Butterfly, Black Hairstreak *(Strymonidia pruni)*
Butterfly, Brown Hairstreak *(Thecla betulae)*
Butterfly, Chalkhill Blue *(Lysandra coridon)*
Butterfly, Chequered Skipper *(Carterocephalus palaemon)*
Butterfly, Duke of Burgundy Fritillary *(Hamearis lucina)*
Butterfly, Glanville Fritillary *(Melitaea cinxia)*
Butterfly, Heath Fritillary *(Mellicta athalia* or *Melitaea athalia)*
Butterfly, High Brown Fritillary *(Argynnis adippe)*
Butterfly, Large Blue *(Maculinea arion)*
Butterfly, Large Copper *(Lycaena dispar)*
Butterfly, Large Heath *(Coenonympha tullia)*
Butterfly, Large Tortoiseshell *(Nymphalis polychloros)*
Butterfly, Lulworth Skipper *(Thymelicus acteon)*
Butterfly, Marsh Fritillary *(Eurodryas aurinia)*
Butterfly, Mountain Ringlet *(Erebia epiphron)*
Butterfly, Northern Brown Argus *(Aricia artaxerxes)*
Butterfly, Pearl-bordered Fritillary *(Boloria euphrosyne)*
Butterfly, Purple Emperor *(Apatura iris)*
Butterfly, Silver Spotted Skipper *(Hesperia comma)*
Butterfly, Silver-studded Blue *(Plebejus argus)*
Butterfly, Small Blue *(Cupido minimus)*
Butterfly, Swallowtail *(Papilio machaon)*
Butterfly, White Letter Hairstreak *(Stymonida w-album)*
Butterfly, Wood White *(Leptidea sinapis)*
Cat, Wild *(Felis silvestris)*
Cicada, New Forest *(Cicadetta montana)*
Crayfish, Atlantic Stream *(Austropotamobius pallipes)**
Cricket, Field *(Gryllus campestris)*
Cricket, Mole *(Gryllotalpa gryllotalpa)*
Damselfly, Southern *(Coenagrion mercuriale)*
Dolphin, all species *(Cetacea)*
Dormouse *(Muscardinus avellanarius)*
Dragonfly, Norfolk Aeshna *(Aeshna isosceles)*

Frog, Common *(Rana temporaria)**
Goby, Couch's *(Gobius couchii)*
Goby, Giant *(Gobius cobitis)*
Grasshopper, Wart-biter *(Decticus verrucivorus)*
Hatchet Shell, Northern *(Thyasira gouldi)*
Hydroid, Marine *(Clavopsella navis)*
Lagoon Snail *(Paludinella littorina)*
Lagoon Snail, De Folin's *(Caecum armoricum)*
Lagoon Worm, Tentacled *(Alkmaria romijni)*
Leech, Medicinal *(Hirudo medicinalis)*
Lizard, Sand *(Lacerta agilis)*
Lizard, Viviparous *(Lacerta vivipara)**
Marten, Pine *(Martes martes)*
Moth, Barberry Carpet *(Pareulype berberata)*
Moth, Black-veined *(Siona lineata* or *Idaea lineata)*
Moth, Essex Emerald *(Thetidia smaragdaria)*
Moth, Fiery Clearwing *(Bembecia chrysidiformis)*
Moth, Fisher's Estuarine *(Gortyna borelii)*
Moth, New Forest Burnet *(Zygaena viciae)*
Moth, Reddish Buff *(Acosmetia caliginosa)*
Moth, Sussex Emerald *(Thalera fimbrialis)*
Mussel, Fan *(Atrina fragilis)**
Mussel, Freshwater Pearl *(Margaritifera margaritifera)*
Newt, Great Crested (or Warty) *(Triturus cristatus)*
Newt, Palmate *(Triturus helveticus)**
Newt, Smooth *(Triturus vulgaris)**
Otter, Common *(Lutra lutra)*
Porpoise, all species *(Cetacea)*
Sandworm, Lagoon *(Armandia cirrhosa)*
Sea Fan, Pink *(Eunicella verrucosa)**
Sea Slug, Lagoon *(Tenellia adspersa)*
Sea-mat, Trembling *(Victorella pavida)*
Seahorse, Short Snouted (England only) *(Hippocampus hippocampus)*
Seahorse, Spiny (England only) *(Hippocampus guttulatus)*
Shad, Twaite *(Alosa fallax)**
Shark, Angel (England only) *(Squatina squatina)**
Shark, Basking *(Cetorhinus maximus)*
Shrimp, Fairy *(Chirocephalus diaphanus)*
Shrimp, Lagoon Sand *(Gammarus insensibilis)*
Shrimp, Tadpole *(Triops cancriformis)*
Slow-worm *(Anguis fragilis)**
Snail, Glutinous *(Myxas glutinosa)*
Snail, Roman (England only) *(Helix pomatia)**
Snail, Sandbowl *(Catinella arenaria)*
Snake, Grass *(Natrix natrix* or *Natrix helvetica)**
Snake, Smooth *(Coronella austriaca)*
Spider, Fen Raft *(Dolomedes plantarius)*
Spider, Ladybird *(Eresus niger)*
Squirrel, Red *(Sciurus vulgaris)*
Sturgeon *(Acipenser sturio)*
Toad, Common *(Bufo bufo)**
Toad, Natterjack *(Bufo calamita)*
Turtle, Marine, all species *(Dermochelyidae* and *Cheloniidae)*
Vendace *(Coregonus albula)*
Vole, Water *(Arvicola terrestris)*
Walrus *(Odobenus rosmarus)*
Whale, all species *(Cetacea)*
Whitefish *(Coregonus lavaretus)*

* These species are protected against some, but not all, of the activities listed under section 9 of the Wildlife and Countryside Act 1981

PLANTS PROTECTED BY SCHEDULE 8

Adder's Tongue, Least *(Ophioglossum lusitanicum)*
Alison, Small *(Alyssum alyssoides)*
Anomodon, Long-leaved *(Anomodon longifolius)*
Beech-lichen, New Forest *(Enterographa elaborata)*
Blackwort *(Southbya nigrella)*
Bluebell *(Hyacinthoides non-scripta)**
Bolete, Royal *(Boletus regius)*
Broomrape, Bedstraw *(Orobanche caryophyllacea)*
Broomrape, Oxtongue *(Orobanche loricata)*
Broomrape, Thistle *(Orobanche reticulata)*
Cabbage, Lundy *(Rhynchosinapis wrightii)*
Calamint, Wood *(Calamintha sylvatica)*
Caloplaca, Snow *(Caloplaca nivalis)*
Catapyrenium, Tree *(Catapyrenium psoromoides)*
Catchfly, Alpine *(Lychnis alpina)*
Catillaria, Laurer's *(Catellaria laureri)*
Centaury, Slender *(Centaurium tenuiflorum)*
Cinquefoil, Rock *(Potentilla rupestris)*
Cladonia, Convoluted *(Cladonia convoluta)*
Cladonia, Upright Mountain *(Cladonia stricta)*
Clary, Meadow *(Salvia pratensis)*
Club-rush, Triangular *(Scirpus triquetrus)*
Colt's-foot, Purple *(Homogyne alpina)*
Cotoneaster, Wild *(Cotoneaster integerrimus)*
Cottongrass, Slender *(Eriophorum gracile)*
Cow-wheat, Field *(Melampyrum arvense)*
Crocus, Sand *(Romulea columnae)*
Crystalwort, Lizard *(Riccia bifurca)*
Cudweed, Broad-leaved *(Filago pyramidata)*
Cudweed, Jersey *(Gnaphalium luteoalbum)*
Cudweed, Red-tipped *(Filago lutescens)*
Cut-grass *(Leersia oryzoides)*
Diapensia *(Diapensia lapponica)*
Dock, Shore *(Rumex rupestris)*
Earwort, Marsh *(Jamesoniella undulifolia)*
Eryngo, Field *(Eryngium campestre)*
Fern, Dickie's Bladder *(Cystopteris dickieana)*
Fern, Killarney *(Trichomanes speciosum)*
Flapwort, Norfolk *(Leiocolea rutheana)*
Fleabane, Alpine *(Erigeron borealis)*
Fleabane, Small *(Pulicaria vulgaris)*
Fleawort, South Stack *(Tephroseris integrifolia ssp maritima)*
Frostwort, Pointed *(Gymnomitrion apiculatum)*
Fungus, Hedgehog *(Hericium erinaceum)*
Galingale, Brown *(Cyperus fuscus)*
Gentian, Alpine *(Gentiana nivalis)*
Gentian, Dune *(Gentianella uliginosa)*
Gentian, Early *(Gentianella anglica)*
Gentian, Fringed *(Gentianella ciliata)*
Gentian, Spring *(Gentiana verna)*
Germander, Cut-leaved *(Teucrium botrys)*
Germander, Water *(Teucrium scordium)*
Gladiolus, Wild *(Gladiolus illyricus)*
Goblin Lights *(Catolechia wahlenbergii)*
Goosefoot, Stinking *(Chenopodium vulvaria)*
Grass-poly *(Lythrum hyssopifolia)*
Grimmia, Blunt-leaved *(Grimmia unicolor)*
Gyalecta, Elm *(Gyalecta ulmi)*
Hare's-ear, Sickle-leaved *(Bupleurum falcatum)*
Hare's-ear, Small *(Bupleurum baldense)*
Hawk's-beard, Stinking *(Crepis foetida)*
Hawkweed, Northroe *(Hieracium northroense)*
Hawkweed, Shetland *(Hieracium zetlandicum)*
Hawkweed, Weak-leaved *(Hieracium attenuatifolium)*
Heath, Blue *(Phyllodoce caerulea)*
Helleborine, Red *(Cephalanthera rubra)*
Helleborine, Young's *(Epipactis youngiana)*
Horsetail, Branched *(Equisetum ramosissimum)*
Hound's-tongue, Green *(Cynoglossum germanicum)*
Knawel, Perennial *(Scleranthus perennis)*
Knotgrass, Sea *(Polygonum maritimum)*
Lady's-slipper *(Cypripedium calceolus)*

Lecanactis, Churchyard *(Lecanactis hemisphaerica)*
Lecanora, Tarn *(Lecanora archariana)*
Lecidea, Copper *(Lecidea inops)*
Leek, Round-headed *(Allium sphaerocephalon)*
Lettuce, Least *(Lactuca saligna)*
Lichen, Arctic Kidney *(Nephroma arcticum)*
Lichen, Ciliate Strap *(Heterodermia leucomelos)*
Lichen, Coralloid Rosette *(Heterodermia propagulifera)*
Lichen, Ear-lobed Dog *(Peltigera lepidophora)*
Lichen, Forked Hair *(Bryoria furcellata)*
Lichen, Golden Hair *(Teloschistes flavicans)*
Lichen, Orange-fruited Elm *(Caloplaca luteoalba)*
Lichen, River Jelly *(Collema dichotomum)*
Lichen, Scaly Breck *(Squamarina lentigera)*
Lichen, Stary Breck *(Buellia asterella)*
Lily, Snowdon *(Lloydia serotina)*
Liverwort *(Petallophyllum ralfsi)*
Liverwort, Lindenberg's Leafy *(Adelanthus lindenbergianus)*
Marsh-mallow, Rough *(Althaea hirsuta)*
Marshwort, Creeping *(Apium repens)*
Milk-parsley, Cambridge *(Selinum carvifolia)*
Moss *(Drepanocladius vernicosus)*
Moss, Alpine Copper *(Mielichoferia mielichoferi)*
Moss, Baltic Bog *(Sphagnum balticum)*
Moss, Blue Dew *(Saelania glaucescens)*
Moss, Blunt-leaved Bristle *(Orthotrichum obtusifolium)*
Moss, Bright Green Cave *(Cyclodictyon laetevirens)*
Moss, Cordate Beard *(Barbula cordata)*
Moss, Cornish Path *(Ditrichum cornubicum)*
Moss, Derbyshire Feather *(Thamnobryum angustifolium)*
Moss, Dune Thread *(Bryum mamillatum)*
Moss, Flamingo *(Desmatodon cernuus)*
Moss, Glaucous Beard *(Barbula glauca)*
Moss, Green Shield *(Buxbaumia viridis)*
Moss, Hair Silk *(Plagiothecium piliferum)*
Moss, Knothole *(Zygodon forsteri)*
Moss, Large Yellow Feather *(Scorpidium turgescens)*
Moss, Millimetre *(Micromitrium tenerum)*
Moss, Multi-fruited River *(Cryphaea lamyana)*
Moss, Nowell's Limestone *(Zygodon gracilis)*
Moss, Polar Feather *(Hygrohypnum polare)*
Moss, Rigid Apple *(Bartramia stricta)*
Moss, Round-leaved Feather *(Rhyncostegium rotundifolium)*
Moss, Schleicher's Thread *(Bryum schleicheri)*
Moss, Slender Green Feather *(Drepanocladus vernicosus)*
Moss, Triangular Pygmy *(Acaulon triquetrum)*
Moss, Vaucher's Feather *(Hypnum vaucheri)*
Mudwort, Welsh *(Limosella austeralis)*
Naiad, Holly-leaved *(Najas marina)*
Naiad, Slender *(Najas flexilis)*
Orache, Stalked *(Halimione pedunculata)*
Orchid, Early Spider *(Ophrys sphegodes)*
Orchid, Fen *(Liparis loeselii)*
Orchid, Ghost *(Epipogium aphyllum)*
Orchid, Lapland Marsh *(Dactylorhiza lapponica)*
Orchid, Late Spider *(Ophrys fuciflora)*
Orchid, Lizard *(Himantoglossum hircinum)*
Orchid, Military *(Orchis militaris)*
Orchid, Monkey *(Orchis simia)*
Pannaria, Caledonia *(Panneria ignobilis)*
Parmelia, New Forest *(Parmelia minarum)*
Parmentaria, Oil Stain *(Parmentaria chilensis)*
Pear, Plymouth *(Pyrus cordata)*
Penny-cress, Perfoliate *(Thlaspi perfoliatum)*
Pennyroyal *(Mentha pulegium)*
Pertusaria, Alpine Moss *(Pertusaria bryontha)*
Petalwort *(Petallophyllum ralfsi)*
Physcia, Southern Grey *(Physcia tribacioides)*
Pigmyweed *(Crassula aquatica)*
Pine, Ground *(Ajuga chamaepitys)*
Pink, Cheddar *(Dianthus gratianopolitanus)*
Pink, Childing *(Petroraghia nanteuilii)*
Pink, Deptford (England and Wales only) *(Dianthus armeria)*
Polypore, Oak *(Buglossoporus pulvinus)*
Pseudocyphellaria, Ragged *(Pseudocyphellaria lacerata)*
Psora, Rusty Alpine *(Psora rubiformis)*
Puffball, Sandy Stilt *(Battarraea phalloides)*
Ragwort, Fen *(Senecio paludosus)*
Ramping-fumitory, Martin's *(Fumaria martinii)*
Rampion, Spiked *(Phyteuma spicatum)*
Restharrow, Small *(Ononis reclinata)*
Rock-cress, Alpine *(Arabis alpina)*
Rock-cress, Bristol *(Arabis stricta)*
Rustwort, Western *(Marsupella profunda)*
Sandwort, Norwegian *(Arenaria norvegica)*
Sandwort, Teesdale *(Minuartia stricta)*
Saxifrage, Drooping *(Saxifraga cernua)*
Saxifrage, Tufted *(Saxifraga cespitosa)*
Saxifrage, Yellow Marsh *(Saxifrage hirulus)*
Solenopsora, Serpentine *(Solenopsora liparina)*
Solomon's-seal, Whorled *(Polygonatum verticillatum)*
Sow-thistle, Alpine *(Cicerbita alpina)*
Spearwort, Adder's-tongue *(Ranunculus ophioglossifolius)*
Speedwell, Fingered *(Veronica triphyllos)*
Speedwell, Spiked *(Veronica spicata)*
Spike-rush, Dwarf *(Eleocharis parvula)*
Star-of-Bethlehem, Early *(Gagea bohemica)*
Starfruit *(Damasonium alisma)*
Stonewort, Bearded *(Chara canescens)*
Stonewort, Foxtail *(Lamprothamnium papulosum)*
Strapwort *(Corrigiola litoralis)*
Sulphur-tresses, Alpine *(Alectoria ochroleuca)*
Threadmoss, Long-leaved *(Bryum neodamense)*
Turpswort *(Geocalyx graveolens)*
Violet, Fen *(Viola persicifolia)*
Viper's-grass *(Scorzonera humilis)*
Water-plantain, Floating *(Luronium natans)*
Water-plantain, Ribbon-leaved *(Alisma gramineum)*
Wood-sedge, Starved *(Carex depauperata)*
Woodsia, Alpine *(Woodsia alpina)*
Woodsia, Oblong *(Woodsia ilvenis)*
Wormwood, Field *(Artemisia campestris)*
Woundwort, Downy *(Stachys germanica)*
Woundwort, Limestone *(Stachys alpina)*
Yellow-rattle, Greater *(Rhinanthus serotinus)*

* Protected against some, but not all, of the activities listed under section 13 of the Wildlife and Countryside Act 1981

HISTORIC BUILDINGS AND MONUMENTS

ENGLAND

Under the Planning (Listed Buildings and Conservation Areas) Act 1990, the Secretary of State for Culture, Media and Sport has a statutory duty to compile lists of buildings or groups of buildings in England which are of special architectural or historic interest. Under the Ancient Monuments and Archaeological Areas Act 1979 as amended by the National Heritage Act 1983, the secretary of state is also responsible for compiling a schedule of ancient monuments. Decisions are taken on the advice of English Heritage. On 1 April 2005 responsibility for the administration of the listing system was transferred from the secretary of state to English Heritage. This marked the start of a programme of changes designed to increase the involvement and awareness of the property owner and make the listing process more straightforward and more accountable.

LISTED BUILDINGS

Listed buildings are classified into Grade I, Grade II* and Grade II. There are currently around 373,800 individual listed buildings in England, of which approximately 92 per cent are Grade II listed. Almost all pre-1700 buildings are listed, as are most buildings of 1700 to 1840. English Heritage carries out thematic surveys of particular types of buildings with a view to making recommendations for listing, and members of the public may propose a building for consideration. The main purpose of listing is to ensure that care is taken in deciding the future of a building. No changes which affect the architectural or historic character of a listed building can be made without listed building consent (in addition to planning permission where relevant). Applications for listed building consent are normally dealt with by the local planning authority, although English Heritage is always consulted about proposals affecting Grade I and Grade II* properties. It is a criminal offence to demolish a listed building, or alter it in such a way as to affect its character, without consent.

SCHEDULED MONUMENTS

There are currently around 22,300 scheduled monuments in England. English Heritage is carrying out a Monuments Protection Programme assessing archaeological sites with a view to making recommendations for scheduling, and members of the public may propose a monument for consideration. All monuments proposed for scheduling are considered to be of national importance. Where buildings are both scheduled and listed, ancient monuments legislation takes precedence. The main purpose of scheduling a monument is to preserve it for the future and to protect it from damage, destruction or any unnecessary interference. Once a monument has been scheduled, scheduled monument consent is required before any works can be carried out. The scope of the control is more extensive and more detailed than that applied to listed buildings, but certain minor works, as detailed in the Ancient Monuments (Class Consents) Order 1994, may be carried out without consent. It is a criminal offence to carry out unauthorised work to scheduled monuments.

WALES

Under the Planning (Listed Buildings and Conservation Areas) Act 1990 and the Ancient Monuments and Archaeological Areas Act 1979, the National Assembly for Wales is responsible for listing buildings and scheduling monuments in Wales on the advice of Cadw (the Welsh Assembly's historic environment division), the Historic Buildings Advisory Council for Wales, the Ancient Monuments Advisory Board for Wales and the Royal Commission on the Ancient and Historical Monuments of Wales (RCAHMW). The criteria for evaluating buildings are similar to those in England and the same listing system is used. There are approximately 29,900 listed buildings and approximately 4,100 scheduled monuments in Wales.

SCOTLAND

Under the Planning (Listed Buildings and Conservation Areas) (Scotland) Act 1997 and the Ancient Monuments and Archaeological Areas Act 1979, Scottish ministers are responsible for listing buildings and scheduling monuments in Scotland on the advice of Historic Scotland, the Historic Environment Advisory Council for Scotland (HEACS) and the Royal Commission on the Ancient and Historical Monuments of Scotland (RCAHMS). The criteria for evaluating buildings are similar to those in England but an A, B, C(S) categorisation is used. There are approximately 47,400 listed buildings and 8,050 scheduled monuments in Scotland.

NORTHERN IRELAND

Under the Planning (Northern Ireland) Order 1991 and the Historic Monuments and Archaeological Objects (Northern Ireland) Order 1995, the Department of the Environment of the Northern Ireland Executive is responsible for listing buildings and scheduling monuments in Northern Ireland on the advice of the Environment and Heritage Service, the Historic Buildings Council for Northern Ireland and the Historic Monuments Council for Northern Ireland. The criteria for evaluating buildings are similar to those in England but an A, B+, B1 and B2 categorisation is used. There are approximately 8,500 listed buildings and 1,802 scheduled monuments in Northern Ireland.

ENGLAND

For more information on English Heritage properties, including those listed below, the official website is www.english-heritage.org.uk
For more information on National Trust properties in England, including those listed below, the official website is www.nationaltrust.org.uk
(EH) English Heritage property
(NT) National Trust property

A LA RONDE (NT), Exmouth, Devon EX8 5BD
T 01395-265514
Unique 16-sided house completed *c.*1796
ALNWICK CASTLE, Alnwick, Northumberland NE66 1NQ
T 01665-510777 W www.alnwickcastle.com
Seat of the Dukes of Northumberland since 1309; Italian Renaissance-style interior; gardens with spectacular water features
ALTHORP, Northants NN7 4HQ T 01604-770107
W www.althorp.com
Spencer family seat; Diana, Princess of Wales memorabilia
ANGLESEY ABBEY (NT), Lode, Cambs CB25 9EJ
T 01223-810080 W www.angleseyabbey.org
House built *c.*1600; houses many paintings and a unique clock collection; gardens and Lode Mill
APSLEY HOUSE (EH), London W1J 7NT T 020-7499 5676
Built by Robert Adam 1771–8, home of the Dukes of Wellington since 1817 and known as 'No. 1 London'; collection of fine and decorative arts
ARUNDEL CASTLE, Arundel, W. Sussex BN18 9AB
T 01903-882173 W www.arundelcastle.org
Castle dating from the Norman Conquest; seat of the Dukes of Norfolk
AVEBURY (NT), Wilts SN8 1RF T 01672-539250
Remains of stone circles constructed 4,000 years ago surrounding the later village of Avebury
BANQUETING HOUSE, Whitehall, London SW1A 2ER
T 0844-482 7777 W www.hrp.org.uk
Designed by Inigo Jones; ceiling paintings by Rubens; site of the execution of Charles I
BASILDON PARK (NT), Reading, Berks RG8 9NR
T 0118-984 3040
Palladian mansion built in 1776–83 by John Carr
BATTLE ABBEY (EH), Battle, E. Sussex TN33 0AD
T 01424-775705
Remains of the abbey founded by William the Conqueror on the site of the Battle of Hastings
BEAULIEU, Brockenhurst, Hants SO42 7ZN T 01590-612345
W www.beaulieu.co.uk
House and gardens; Beaulieu Abbey and exhibition of monastic life; National Motor Museum
BEESTON CASTLE (EH), Cheshire CW6 9TX
T 01829-260464
Built in the 13th century by Ranulf, sixth Earl of Chester
BELTON HOUSE (NT), Grantham, Lincs NG32 2LS
T 01476-566116
17th-century house; formal gardens in landscaped park
BELVOIR CASTLE, Grantham, Lincs NG32 1PE
T 01476-871002 W www.belvoircastle.com
Seat of the Dukes of Rutland; 19th-century Gothic-style castle
BERKELEY CASTLE, Glos GL13 9BQ T 01453-810332
W www.berkeley-castle.com
Completed 1153; site of the murder of Edward II (1327)
BIRDOSWALD FORT (EH), Cumbria CA8 7DD
T 01697-747602
Stretch of Hadrian's Wall with Roman wall fort, turret and milecastle
BLENHEIM PALACE, Woodstock, Oxon OX20 1PX
T 0870-060 2080 W www.blenheimpalace.com
Seat of the Dukes of Marlborough and Winston Churchill's birthplace; designed by Vanbrugh
BLICKLING HALL (NT), Blickling, Norfolk NR11 6NF
T 01263-738030
Jacobean house with state rooms; temple and 18th-century orangery
BODIAM CASTLE (NT), Bodiam, E. Sussex TN32 5UA
T 01580-830196
Well-preserved medieval moated castle built in 1385
BOLSOVER CASTLE (EH), Bolsover, Derbys S44 6PR
T 01246-822844
17th-century buildings on site of medieval castle
BOSCOBEL HOUSE (EH), Bishops Wood, Staffs ST19 9AR
T 01902-850244
Timber-framed 17th-century hunting lodge; refuge of fugitive Charles II
BOUGHTON HOUSE, Kettering, Northants NN14 1BJ
T 01536-515731 W www.boughtonhouse.org.uk
A 17th-century house with French-style additions; home of the Dukes of Buccleuch and Queensbury
BOWOOD HOUSE, Calne, Wilts SN11 0LZ
T 01249-812102 W www.bowood-house.co.uk
An 18th-century house in Capability Brown park, with lake, temple and arboretum
BROADLANDS, Romsey, Hants SO51 9ZD T 01794-505010
W www.broadlands.net
Palladian mansion in Capability Brown park; Mountbatten exhibition
BRONTË PARSONAGE, Haworth, W. Yorks BD22 8DR
T 01535-642323 W www.bronte.org.uk
Home of the Brontë sisters; museum and memorabilia
BUCKFAST ABBEY, Buckfastleigh, Devon TQ11 0EE
T 01364-645550 W www.buckfast.org.uk
Benedictine monastery on medieval foundations
BUCKINGHAM PALACE, London SW1A 1AA
T 020-7766 7300 W www.royal.gov.uk
Purchased by George III in 1761, and the Sovereign's official London residence since 1837; 18 state rooms, including the Throne Room, and Picture Gallery
BUCKLAND ABBEY (NT), Yelverton, Devon PL20 6EY
T 01822-853607
13th-century Cistercian monastery; home of Sir Francis Drake
BURGHLEY HOUSE, Stamford, Lincs PE9 3JY
T 01780-752451 W www.burghley.co.uk
Late Elizabethan house built by William Cecil, first Lord Burghley
CALKE ABBEY (NT), Ticknall, Derbys DE73 7LE
T 01332-863822
Baroque 18th-century mansion
CARISBROOKE CASTLE (EH), Newport, Isle of Wight PO30 1XY T 01983-522107
W www.carisbrookecastlemuseum.org.uk
Norman castle; museum; prison of Charles I 1647–8
CARLISLE CASTLE (EH), Carlisle, Cumbria CA3 8UR
T 01228-591922
Medieval castle; prison of Mary Queen of Scots
CARLYLE'S HOUSE (NT), Chelsea, London SW3 5HL
T 020-7352 7087
Home of Thomas Carlyle

CASTLE ACRE PRIORY (EH), Swaffham, Norfolk PE32 2XD **T** 01760-755394
Remains include 12th-century church and prior's lodgings

CASTLE DROGO (NT), Drewsteignton, Devon EX6 6PB **T** 01647-433306
Granite castle designed by Lutyens

CASTLE HOWARD, N. Yorks YO60 7DA **T** 01653-648444 **W** www.castlehoward.co.uk
Designed by Vanbrugh 1699–1726; mausoleum designed by Hawksmoor

CASTLE RISING CASTLE (EH), King's Lynn, Norfolk PE31 6AH **T** 01553-631330
12th-century keep in a massive earthwork with gatehouse and bridge

CHARLES DARWIN'S HOUSE (EH), Down House, Luxted Road, Downe, Kent BR6 7JT **T** 01689-859119
The family home where Darwin wrote *On the Origin of Species*

CHARTWELL (NT), Westerham, Kent TN16 1PS **T** 01732-866368
Home of Sir Winston Churchill

CHATSWORTH, Bakewell, Derbys DE45 1PP **T** 01246-565300 **W** www.chatsworth.org
Tudor mansion set in magnificent parkland

CHESTERS ROMAN FORT (EH), Chollerford, Northumberland NE46 4EU **T** 01434-681379
Roman cavalry fort built to guard Hadrian's Wall

CHYSAUSTER ANCIENT VILLAGE (EH), Penzance, Cornwall TR20 8XA **T** 07831-757934
Remains of Celtic settlement; eight stone-walled homesteads

CLANDON HOUSE (NT), West Clandon, Guildford, Surrey GU4 7RQ **T** 01483-222482 **W** www.clandonpark.co.uk
18th-century Palladian mansion and gardens, which contain a Maori meeting house, removed from New Zealand in 1892

CLIFFORD'S TOWER (EH), York YO1 9SA **T** 01904-646940
13th-century tower built on a mound; remains of a castle built by William the Conqueror

CLIVEDEN (NT), Taplow, Berks SL6 0JA **T** 01494-755 5562
Former home of the Astors, now a hotel set in garden and woodland

CORBRIDGE ROMAN SITE (EH), Corbridge, Northumberland NE45 5NT **T** 01434-632349
Excavated central area of a Roman town and successive military bases

CORFE CASTLE (NT), Wareham, Dorset BH20 5EZ **T** 01929-481294
Ruined former royal castle dating from the 11th century

CROFT CASTLE (NT), Herefordshire HR6 9PW **T** 01568-780141
Pre-Conquest border castle with Georgian-Gothic interior

DEAL CASTLE (EH), Deal, Kent CT14 7BA **T** 01304-372762
Largest of the coastal defence forts built by Henry VIII

DICKENS HOUSE, Doughty Street, London WC1N 2LX **T** 020-7405 2127 **W** www.dickensmuseum.com
House occupied by Dickens 1837–9; manuscripts, furniture and portraits

DOVE COTTAGE, Grasmere, Cumbria LA22 9SH **T** 01539-435544 **W** www.wordsworth.org.uk
Wordsworth's home 1799–1808; museum

DOVER CASTLE (EH), Dover, Kent CT16 1HU **T** 01304-211067
Castle with Roman, Saxon and Norman features; wartime operations rooms

DR JOHNSON'S HOUSE, Gough Square, London EC4A 3DE **T** 020-7353 3745 **W** www.drjohnsonshouse.org
Home of Samuel Johnson 1748–59

DUNSTANBURGH CASTLE (EH), Craster, nr Alnwick, Northumberland NE66 3TT **T** 01665-576231
14th-century castle ruins on a cliff with a substantial gatehouse-keep

ELTHAM PALACE (EH), Eltham, London SE9 5QE **T** 020-8294 2548
Combines an Art Deco country house and remains of medieval palace set in moated gardens

FARLEIGH HUNGERFORD CASTLE (EH), Somerset BA2 7RS **T** 01225-754026
Late 14th-century castle with two courts; chapel with tomb of Sir Thomas Hungerford

FARNHAM CASTLE KEEP (EH), Farnham, Surrey GA9 0JA **T** 01252-713393
Large 12th-century castle keep with motte and bailey wall

FISHBOURNE ROMAN PALACE, Salthill Road, Fishbourne, Chichester, W. Sussex PO19 3QR **T** 01243-785977 **W** www.sussexpast.co.uk
Excavated Roman palace with largest collection of in-situ mosaics in Britain

FOUNTAINS ABBEY (NT), nr Ripon, N. Yorks HG4 3DY **T** 01765-608888 **W** www.fountainsabbey.org.uk
Deer park; St Mary's Church; ruined Cistercian monastery; Georgian water garden

FRAMLINGHAM CASTLE (EH), Woodbridge, Suffolk IP13 9BP **T** 01728-724189
Castle (*c.*1200) with high curtain walls enclosing an almshouse (1639)

FURNESS ABBEY (EH), Barrow-in-Furness, Cumbria LA13 0PJ **T** 01229-823420
Remains of church and cloister buildings founded in 1123

GLASTONBURY ABBEY, Glastonbury, Somerset BA6 9EL **T** 01458-832267 **W** www.glastonburyabbey.com
Ruins of a 12th-century abbey rebuilt after fire; site of an early Christian settlement

GOODRICH CASTLE (EH), Ross-on-Wye, Herefordshire HR9 6HY **T** 01600-890538
Remains of 13th-century castle with 12th-century keep

GREENWICH, London SE10 9NF **T** 020-8858 4422 **W** www.greenwichwhs.org.uk
Former Royal Observatory (founded 1675) housing the time ball and zero meridian of longitude; the Queen's House, designed for Queen Anne, wife of James I, by Inigo Jones; Painted Hall and Chapel (Old Royal Naval College)

GRIMES GRAVES (EH), Brandon, Norfolk IP26 5DE **T** 01842-810656
Neolithic flint mines; one shaft can be descended

GUILDHALL, London EC2P 2EJ **T** 020-7332 1313 **W** www.cityoflondon.gov.uk
Centre of civic government of the City built *c.*1441; facade built 1788–9

HADDON HALL, Bakewell, Derbys DE45 1LA **T** 01629-812855 **W** www.haddonhall.co.uk
Well-preserved 12th-century manor house

HAILES ABBEY (EH), Cheltenham, Glos GL54 5PB **T** 01242-602398
Ruins of a 13th-century Cistercian monastery

HAM HOUSE (NT), Richmond-upon-Thames, Surrey TW10 7RS T 020-8940 1950
Stuart house with lavish interiors and formal gardens

HAMPTON COURT PALACE, East Molesey, Surrey KT8 9AU T 0844-482 7777 W www.hrp.org.uk
16th-century palace with additions by Wren

HARDWICK HALL (NT), Chesterfield, Derbys S44 5QJ T 01246-850430
Built 1591–7 for Bess of Hardwick

HARDY'S COTTAGE (NT), Higher Bockhampton, Dorset DT2 8QJ T 01305-262366
Birthplace and home of Thomas Hardy

HAREWOOD HOUSE, Harewood, W. Yorks LS17 9LG T 0113-218 1010 W www.harewood.org
18th-century house designed by John Carr and Robert Adam; park by Capability Brown

HATFIELD HOUSE, Hatfield, Herts AL9 5NQ T 01707-287010 W www.hatfield-house.co.uk
Jacobean house built by Robert Cecil; surviving wing of Royal Palace of Hatfield (*c.*1485)

HELMSLEY CASTLE (EH), Helmsley, N. Yorks YO62 5AB T 01439-770442
12th-century keep and curtain wall with 16th-century buildings; spectacular earthwork defences

HEVER CASTLE, nr Edenbridge, Kent TN8 7NG T 01732-865224 W www.hever-castle.co.uk
13th-century double-moated castle; childhood home of Anne Boleyn

HOLKER HALL, Cumbria LA11 7PL T 01539-558328 W www.holker-hall.co.uk
Former home of the Dukes of Devonshire; award-winning gardens

HOLKHAM HALL, Wells-next-the-Sea, Norfolk NR23 1AB T 01328-710227 W www.holkham.co.uk
Palladian mansion; notable fine art collection

HOUSESTEADS ROMAN FORT (EH), Hexham, Northumberland NE47 6NN T 01434-344363
Excavated infantry fort on Hadrian's Wall with museum

HUGHENDEN MANOR (NT), High Wycombe, Bucks HP14 4LA T 01494-755565
Home of Disraeli; small formal garden

JANE AUSTEN'S HOUSE, Chawton, Hants GU34 1SD T 01420-83262 W www.jane-austens-house-museum.org.uk
Jane Austen's home from 1809 to 1817

KEDLESTON HALL (NT), Derbys DE22 5JH T 01332-842191
Classical Palladian mansion built 1759–65; complete Robert Adam interiors

KELMSCOTT MANOR, nr Lechlade, Glos GL7 3HJ T 01367-252486 W www.kelmscottmanor.org.uk
Summer home of William Morris, with products of Morris and Co.

KENILWORTH CASTLE (EH), Kenilworth, Warks CV8 1NE T 01926-852078
Largest castle ruin in England

KENSINGTON PALACE, Kensington Gardens, London W8 4PX T 0870-482 7777 W www.hrp.org.uk
Built in 1605 and enlarged by Wren; birthplace of Queen Victoria; Royal Ceremonial Dress collection

KENWOOD HOUSE (EH), Hampstead Lane, London NW3 7JR T 020-8348 1286
Neo-classical villa housing the Iveagh bequest of paintings and furniture

KEW PALACE, Richmond-upon-Thames, Surrey TW9 3AB T 0870-482 7777 W www.hrp.org.uk
Includes Queen Charlotte's Cottage, used by King George III and family as a summerhouse

KINGSTON LACY (NT), Wimborne Minster, Dorset BH21 4EA T 01202-883402
17th-century house with 19th-century alterations; important art collection

KNEBWORTH HOUSE, Knebworth, Herts SG3 6PY T 01438-812661 W www.knebworthhouse.com
Tudor manor house concealed by 19th-century Gothic decoration; Lutyens gardens

KNOLE (NT), Sevenoaks, Kent TN15 0RP T 01732-450608
House dating from 1456 set in parkland; fine art collection; birthplace of Vita Sackville-West

LAMBETH PALACE, London SE1 7JU T 020-7898 1200 W www.archbishopofcanterbury.org
Official residence of the Archbishop of Canterbury; partly dating from the 12th century

LANERCOST PRIORY (EH), Brampton, Cumbria CA8 2HQ T 01697-73030
The nave of the Augustinian priory church, *c.*1166, is still used; remains of other claustral buildings

LANHYDROCK (NT), Bodmin, Cornwall PL30 5AD T 01208-265950
House dating from the 17th century; 50 rooms, including kitchen and nursery

LEEDS CASTLE, nr Maidstone, Kent ME17 1PL T 01622-765400 W www.leeds-castle.com
Castle dating from the ninth century, on two islands in lake

LEVENS HALL, Kendal, Cumbria LA8 0PD T 01539-560321 W www.levenshall.co.uk
Elizabethan house with unique topiary garden (1694); steam engine collection

LINCOLN CASTLE, Lincoln, Lincs LN1 3AA T 01522-511068 W www.lincolnshire.gov.uk
Built by William the Conqueror in 1068

LINDISFARNE PRIORY (EH), Holy Island, Northumberland TD15 2RX T 01289-389200
Founded in AD 635; re-established in the 12th century as a Benedictine priory, now ruined

LITTLE MORETON HALL (NT), Congleton, Cheshire CW12 4SD T 01260-272018
Timber-framed moated Tudor manor house with knot garden

LONGLEAT HOUSE, Warminster, Wilts BA12 7NW T 01985-844400 W www.longleat.co.uk
Elizabethan house in Italian Renaissance style; safari park

LULLINGSTONE ROMAN VILLA (EH), Eynsford, Kent DA4 0JA T 01322-863467
Large villa occupied for much of the Roman period; fine mosaics

MARBLE HILL HOUSE (EH), Twickenham, Middx TW1 2NL T 020-8892 5115
English Palladian villa with Georgian paintings and furniture

MICHELHAM PRIORY, Hailsham, E. Sussex BN27 3QS T 01323-844224 W www.sussexpast.co.uk
Tudor house built onto an Augustinian priory

MIDDLEHAM CASTLE (EH), Leyburn, N. Yorks DL8 4QJ T 01969-623899
12th-century keep within later fortifications; childhood home of Richard III

MONTACUTE HOUSE (NT), Montacute, Somerset TA15 6XP T 01935-823289
Elizabethan house with National Portrait Gallery collection of portraits from the period

MOUNT GRACE PRIORY (EH), Northallerton, N. Yorks DL6 3JG T 01609-883494
Carthusian priory with remains of monastic buildings

OLD SARUM (EH), Salisbury, Wilts SP1 3SD
T 01722-335398
Earthworks enclosing remains of Norman castle and cathedral

ORFORD CASTLE (EH), Orford, Suffolk IP12 2ND
T 01394-450472
Circular keep of *c.*1170 and remains of coastal defence castle built by Henry II

OSBORNE HOUSE (EH), East Cowes, Isle of Wight PO32 6JX T 01983-200022
Queen Victoria's seaside residence

OSTERLEY PARK (NT), Isleworth, Middx TW7 4RB
T 01494-755566 W www.osterleypark.org.uk
Elizabethan mansion set in parkland

PENDENNIS CASTLE (EH), Falmouth, Cornwall TR11 4LP
T 01326-316594
Well-preserved 16th-century coastal defence castle

PENSHURST PLACE, Penshurst, Kent TN11 8DG
T 01892-870307 W www.penshurstplace.com
House with medieval Baron's Hall and 14th-century gardens

PETWORTH HOUSE (NT), Petworth, W. Sussex GU28 0AE
T 01798-343929
Late 17th-century house set in Capability Brown landscaped deer park

PEVENSEY CASTLE (EH), Pevensey, E. Sussex BN24 5LE
T 01323-762604
Walls of a fourth-century Roman fort; remains of an 11th-century castle

PEVERIL CASTLE (EH), Castleton, Derbys S33 8WQ
T 01433-620613
12th-century castle defended on two sides by precipitous rocks

POLESDEN LACEY (NT), nr Dorking, Surrey RH5 6BD
T 01372-458203
Regency villa remodelled in the Edwardian era; fine paintings and furnishings

PORTCHESTER CASTLE (EH), Portchester, Hants PO16 9QW T 02392-378291
Walls of a late Roman fort enclosing a Norman keep and an Augustinian priory church

POWDERHAM CASTLE, Kenton, Devon EX6 8JQ
T 01626-890243 W www.powderham.co.uk
Medieval castle with 18th- and 19th-century alterations

RABY CASTLE, Staindrop, Co. Durham DL2 3AH
T 01833-660202 W www.rabycastle.com
14th-century castle with walled gardens

RAGLEY HALL, Alcester, Warks B49 5NJ T 01789-762090
W www.ragleyhall.com
17th-century house with gardens, park and lake

RICHBOROUGH ROMAN FORT (EH), Richborough, Kent CT13 9JW T 01304-612013
Landing-site of the Claudian invasion in AD 43

RICHMOND CASTLE (EH), Richmond, N. Yorks DL10 4QW T 01748-822493
12th-century keep with 11th-century curtain wall

RIEVAULX ABBEY (EH), nr Helmsley, N. Yorks YO62 5LB
T 01439-798228
Remains of a Cistercian abbey founded *c.*1132

ROCHESTER CASTLE (EH), Rochester, Kent ME1 1SW
T 01634-402276
11th-century castle partly on the Roman city wall, with a square keep of *c.*1130

ROCKINGHAM CASTLE, Market Harborough, Leics LE16 8TH T 01536-770240 W www.rockinghamcastle.com
Built by William the Conqueror

ROYAL PAVILION, Brighton BN1 1EE T 03000-290900
W www.royalpavilion.org.uk
Palace of George IV, in Chinese style with Indian exterior and Regency gardens

RUFFORD OLD HALL (NT), nr Ormskirk, Lancs L40 1SG
T 01704-821254
16th-century hall with unique screen

ST AUGUSTINE'S ABBEY (EH), Canterbury, Kent CT1 1TF
T 01227-767345
Remains of Benedictine monastery founded AD 597

ST MAWES CASTLE (EH), St Mawes, Cornwall TR2 5DE
T 01326-270526
Coastal defence castle built by Henry VIII

ST MICHAEL'S MOUNT (NT), Cornwall TR17 0HS
T 01736-710265 W www.stmichaelsmount.co.uk
12th-century castle with later additions, off the coast at Marazion

SANDRINGHAM, Norfolk PE35 6EN T 01553-612908
W www.sandringhamestate.co.uk
The Queen's private residence; a neo-Jacobean house built in 1870

SCARBOROUGH CASTLE (EH), Scarborough, N. Yorks YO11 1HY T 01723-372451
Remains of 12th-century keep and curtain walls

SHERBORNE CASTLE, Sherborne, Dorset DT9 3PY
T 01935-813182 W www.sherbornecastle.com
16th-century castle built by Sir Walter Raleigh set in landscaped gardens

SHUGBOROUGH ESTATE (NT), Milford, Staffs ST17 0XB
T 01889-881388 W www.shugborough.org.uk
House set in 18th-century park with monuments, temples and pavilions in the Greek Revival style; arboretum; seat of the Earls of Lichfield

SKIPTON CASTLE, Skipton, N. Yorks BD23 1AW
T 01756-792442 W www.skiptoncastle.co.uk
D-shaped castle with six round towers and inner courtyard

SMALLHYTHE PLACE (NT), Tenterden, Kent TN30 7NG
T 01580-762334
Half-timbered 16th-century house; home of Ellen Terry 1899–1928; the Barn Theatre

STONEHENGE (EH), nr Amesbury, Wilts SP4 7DE
T 0870-333 1181
Prehistoric monument consisting of concentric stone circles surrounded by a ditch and bank

STONOR PARK, Henley-on-Thames, Oxon RG9 6HF
T 01491-638587 W www.stonor.com
Medieval house with Georgian facade; centre of Roman Catholicism after the Reformation

STOURHEAD (NT), Stourton, Wilts BA12 6QD
T 01747-841152
English 18th-century Palladian mansion with famous gardens

STRATFIELD SAYE HOUSE, Hants RG7 2BZ
T 01256-882882 W www.stratfield-saye.co.uk
House built 1630–40; home of the Dukes of Wellington since 1817

STRATFORD-UPON-AVON, Warks T 01789-204016
W www.shakespeare.org.uk
Shakespeare's Birthplace Trust with Shakespeare Centre; Anne Hathaway's Cottage, home of Shakespeare's wife; Mary Arden's House, home of Shakespeare's mother; grammar school attended by Shakespeare; Holy Trinity Church, where Shakespeare is buried; Royal Shakespeare Theatre (burnt down 1926, rebuilt 1932) and Swan Theatre (opened 1986)

SUDELEY CASTLE, Winchcombe, Glos GL54 5JD
T 01242-602308 W www.sudeleycastle.co.uk
Castle built in 1442; restored in the 19th century

SULGRAVE MANOR, nr Banbury, Oxon OX17 2SD
T 01295-760205 W www.sulgravemanor.org.uk
Home of George Washington's family

SUTTON HOUSE (NT), 2 & 4 Homerton High Street, Hackney, London E9 6JQ T 020-8986 2264
Tudor house, built in 1535 by Sir Ralph Sadleir

SYON HOUSE, Brentford, Middx TW8 8JF T 020-8560 0881
W www.syonpark.co.uk
Built on the site of a former monastery; Robert Adam interior; Capability Brown park

TILBURY FORT (EH), Tilbury, Essex RM18 7NR
T 01375-858489
17th-century coastal fort

TINTAGEL CASTLE (EH), Tintagel, Cornwall PL34 0HE
T 01840-770328
13th-century cliff-top castle and Dark Age settlement site; linked with Arthurian legend

TOWER OF LONDON, London EC3N 4AB
T 0870-482 7777 W www.hrp.org.uk
Royal palace and fortress begun by William the Conqueror in 1078; houses the Crown Jewels

TRERICE (NT), nr Newquay, Cornwall TR8 4PG
T 01637-875404
Elizabethan manor house

TYNEMOUTH PRIORY AND CASTLE (EH), Tyne and Wear NE30 4BZ T 0191-257 1090
Remains of a Benedictine priory, founded *c.*1090, on Saxon monastic site

UPPARK (NT), South Harting, W. Sussex GU31 5QR
T 01730-825857
Late 17th-century house, completely restored after fire; Fetherstonhaugh art collection

WALMER CASTLE (EH), Walmer, Kent CT14 7LJ
T 01304-364288
One of Henry VIII's coastal defence castles, now the residence of the Lord Warden of the Cinque Ports

WARKWORTH CASTLE (EH), Warkworth, Northumberland NE65 0UJ T 01665-711423
14th-century keep amidst earlier ruins, with hermitage upstream

WHITBY ABBEY (EH), Whitby, N. Yorks YO22 4JT
T 01947-603568
Remains of Norman church on the site of a monastery founded in AD 657

WILTON HOUSE, nr Salisbury, Wilts SP2 0BJ
T 01722-746714 W www.wiltonhouse.co.uk
17th-century house on the site of a Tudor house and ninth-century nunnery

WINDSOR CASTLE, Windsor, Berks SL4 1NJ
T 020-7766 7304 W www.royal.gov.uk
Official residence of the Queen; oldest royal residence still in regular use; largest inhabited castle in the world. Also St George's Chapel

WOBURN ABBEY, Woburn, Beds MK17 9WA
T 01525-292148 W www.woburnabbey.co.uk
Built on the site of a Cistercian abbey; seat of the Dukes of Bedford; important art collection; antiques centre

WROXETER ROMAN CITY (EH), nr Shrewsbury, Shropshire SY5 6PH T 01743-761330
Second-century public baths and part of the forum of the Roman town of Viroconium

WALES

For more information on Cadw properties, including those listed below, the official website is www.cadw.wales.gov.uk

For more information on National Trust properties in Wales, including those listed below, the official website is www.nationaltrust.org.uk

(C) Property of Cadw: Welsh Historic Monuments
(NT) National Trust property

BEAUMARIS CASTLE (C), Anglesey LL58 8AP
T 01248-810361
Concentrically planned castle, still virtually intact

CAERLEON ROMAN BATHS AND AMPHITHEATRE (C), Newport NP18 1AE T 01633-423134
Rare example of a legionary bath-house and late first-century arena surrounded by bank for spectators

CAERNARFON CASTLE (C), Gwynedd LL55 2AY
T 01286-677617 W www.caernarfon.com
Castle built between 1283 and 1330, initially for King Edward I of England; setting for the investiture of Prince Charles in 1969

CAERPHILLY CASTLE (C), Caerphilly CF83 1JD
T 029-2088 3143
Concentrically-planned castle (*c.*1270) notable for its scale and use of water defences

CARDIFF CASTLE, Cardiff CF10 3RB T 029-2087 8100
W www.cardiffcastle.com
Castle built on the site of a Roman fort

CASTELL COCH (C), Tongwynlais, Cardiff CF15 7JS
T 029-2081 0101
'Fairytale castle' rebuilt 1875–90 on medieval foundations

CHEPSTOW CASTLE (C), Monmouthshire NP16 5EZ
T 01291-624065
Rectangular keep amid extensive fortifications; developed throughout the Middle Ages

CONWY CASTLE (C), Gwynedd LL32 8AY
T 01492-592358
Built for Edward I, 1283–7, on a narrow rocky outcrop

CRICCIETH CASTLE (C), Gwynedd LL55 0DP
T 01766-522227
Native Welsh 13th-century castle, altered by Edward I and Edward II

DENBIGH CASTLE (C), Denbighshire LL16 3NB
T 01745-813385
Remains of the castle (begun 1282), including triple-towered gatehouse

HARLECH CASTLE (C), Gwynedd LL46 2YH
T 01766-780552
Well-preserved Edwardian castle, constructed 1283–89, on an outcrop above the former shoreline

PEMBROKE CASTLE, Pembrokeshire SA71 4LA
T 01646-684585 W www.pembrokecastle.co.uk
Castle founded in 1093; Great Tower built in the late 12th century; birthplace of King Henry VII

PENRHYN CASTLE (NT), Bangor, Gwynedd LL57 4HN
T 01248-371337
Neo-Norman castle built in the 19th century; railway museum; private art collection

PORTMEIRION, Gwynedd LL48 6ER T 01766-770000
W www.portmeirion-village.com
Village in Italianate style built by Clough Williams-Ellis

POWIS CASTLE (NT), Welshpool, Powys SY21 8RF
T 01938-551944
Medieval castle with interior in variety of styles; 17th-century gardens; Clive of India museum

RAGLAN CASTLE (C), Monmouthshire NP15 2BT
T 01291-690228
Remains of 15th-century castle with moated hexagonal keep

ST DAVIDS BISHOP'S PALACE (C), Pembrokeshire SA62 6PE T 01437-720517
Remains of residence of Bishops of St Davids built 1328–47

TINTERN ABBEY (C), nr Chepstow, Monmouthshire NP16 6SE T 01291-689251
Remains of 13th-century church and conventual buildings of a 12th-century Cistercian monastery

TRETOWER COURT AND CASTLE (C), nr Crickhowell, Powys NP8 1RF T 01874-730279
Medieval house rebuilt in the 15th century, with remains of 12th-century castle nearby

SCOTLAND

For more information on Historic Scotland properties, including those listed below, the official website is www.historic-scotland.gov.uk

For more information on National Trust for Scotland properties, including those listed below, the official website is www.nts.org.uk

(HS) Historic Scotland property
(NTS) National Trust for Scotland property

ABBOTSFORD HOUSE, Melrose, Roxburghshire TD6 9BQ
T 01896-752043 W www.scottsabbotsford.co.uk
Home of Sir Walter Scott

ANTONINE WALL, between the Clyde and the Forth
Built around AD 142; consists of ditch, turf rampart, road and forts at regular intervals

BALMORAL CASTLE, Ballater, Aberdeenshire AB35 5TB
T 01339-742534 W www.balmoralcastle.com
Baronial-style castle built for Victoria and Albert; the Queen's private residence

BLACK HOUSE, ARNOL (HS), Lewis, Western Isles HS2 9DB T 01851-710395
Traditional Lewis thatched house

BLAIR CASTLE, Blair Atholl, Perthshire PH18 5TL
T 01796-481207 W www.blair-castle.co.uk
Mid-18th-century mansion with 13th-century tower; seat of the Dukes and Earls of Atholl

BONAWE IRON FURNACE (HS), Taynuilt, Argyll PA35 1JQ T 01866-822432
Charcoal fuelled ironworks founded in 1753

BOWHILL, Selkirkshire TD7 5ET T 01750-22204
Seat of the Dukes of Buccleuch and Queensberry; fine collection of paintings

BROUGH OF BIRSAY (HS), Orkney KW17 2NH
T 01856-841815
Remains of Norse and Pictish village on the tidal island of Birsay

BURNS NATIONAL HERITAGE PARK (NTS), Alloway, Ayrshire KA7 4PQ T 01292-443700
W www.burnsheritagepark.com
Contains Burns Cottage, birthplace of the poet, and a museum

CAERLAVEROCK CASTLE (HS), Glencaple, Dumfriesshire DG1 4RU T 01387-770244
Triangular 13th-century castle with classical Renaissance additions

CAIRNPAPPLE HILL (HS), Torphichen, West Lothian
T 01506-634622
Neolithic and Bronze Age ceremonial site and burial chambers

CALANAIS STANDING STONES (HS), Lewis, Western Isles HS2 9DY T 01851-621422
Standing stones in a cross-shaped setting, dating from *c.* 3000 BC

CATERTHUNS (BROWN AND WHITE) (HS), Menmuir, nr Brechin, Angus
Two large Iron Age hill forts

CAWDOR CASTLE, Nairn, Moray IV12 5RD
T 01667-404401 W www.cawdorcastle.com
14th-century keep with 15th- and 17th-century additions

CLAVA CAIRNS (HS), nr Inverness, Inverness-shire
T 01667-460232
Bronze Age cemetery complex of cairns and standing stones

CRATHES CASTLE (NTS), nr Banchory, Aberdeenshire AB31 5QJ T 08444-932166
16th-century baronial castle in woodland, fields and gardens

CULZEAN CASTLE (NTS), Maybole, Ayrshire KA19 8LE
T 08444-932149 W www.culzeanexperience.org
18th-century Robert Adam castle with oval staircase and circular saloon

DRYBURGH ABBEY (HS), nr Melrose, Roxburghshire TD6 0RQ T 01835-822381
12th-century abbey containing the tomb of Sir Walter Scott

DUNVEGAN CASTLE, Skye IV55 8WF T 01470-521206
W www.dunvegancastle.com
13th-century castle with later additions; home of the chiefs of the Clan MacLeod

EDINBURGH CASTLE (HS) EH1 2NG T 0131-225 9846
Includes the Scottish Crown Jewels, Scottish National War Memorial, Scottish United Services Museum and historic apartments

EDZELL CASTLE (HS), nr Brechin, Angus DD9 7UE
T 01356-648631
16th-century tower house on medieval foundations; walled garden

EILEAN DONAN CASTLE, Dornie, Ross and Cromarty IV40 8DX T 01599-555202 W www.eileandonancastle.com
13th-century castle with Jacobite relics at the meeting point of three sea lochs

ELGIN CATHEDRAL (HS), Moray IV30 1HU
T 01343-547171
13th-century cathedral and chapterhouse

FLOORS CASTLE, Kelso, Roxburghshire TD5 7SF
T 01573-223333 W www.floorscastle.com
Largest inhabited castle in Scotland; seat of the Dukes of Roxburghe; built 1721 by William Adam

FORT GEORGE (HS), Ardersier, Inverness-shire IV2 7TD
T 01667-460232
18th-century fort, still a working army barracks

GLAMIS CASTLE, Forfar, Angus DD8 1RJ T 01307-840393
W www.glamis-castle.co.uk
Seat of the Lyon family (later Earls of Strathmore and Kinghorne) since 1372

GLASGOW CATHEDRAL (HS), Lanarkshire G4 0QZ
T 0141-552 6891 W www.glasgowcathedral.org.uk
Medieval cathedral with elaborately vaulted crypt

GLENELG BROCHS (HS), Shielbridge, Ross and Cromarty
T 01667-460232
Two broch towers (Dun Telve and Dun Troddan) with well-preserved structural features

HOPETOUN HOUSE, South Queensferry, W. Lothian EH30 9SL T 0131-331 2451 W www.hopetounhouse.com
House designed by Sir William Bruce, enlarged by William Adam, built 1699

HUNTLY CASTLE (HS), Aberdeenshire AB54 4SH T 01466-793191
Ruin of a 16th- and 17th-century baronial residence

INVERARAY CASTLE, Argyll PA32 8XE T 01499-302203 W www.inveraray-castle.com
Gothic-style 18th-century castle; seat of the Dukes of Argyll

IONA ABBEY (HS), Iona, Inner Hebrides PA76 6SQ T 01681-700512
Monastery founded by St Columba in AD 563

JARLSHOF (HS), Sumburgh Head, Shetland ZE3 9JN T 01950-460112
Prehistoric and Norse settlement

JEDBURGH ABBEY (HS), Scottish Borders TD8 6JQ T 01835-863925
Romanesque and early Gothic church founded *c.*1138

KISIMUL CASTLE (HS), Castlebay, Barra, Western Isles HS9 5UZ T 01871-810313
Medieval home of the Clan MacNeil

LINLITHGOW PALACE (HS), Kirkgate, Linlithgow, W. Lothian EH49 7AL T 01506-842896
Ruin of royal palace in park setting; birthplace of James V and Mary, Queen of Scots

MAESHOWE (HS), Stenness, Orkney KW16 3HA T 01856-761606
Neolithic chambered tomb

MEIGLE SCULPTURED STONES (HS), Meigle, Perthshire PH12 8SB T 01828-640612
Twenty-six carved stones dating from the eighth to the 10th centuries

MELROSE ABBEY (HS), Melrose, Roxburghshire TD6 9LG T 01896-822562
Ruin of Cistercian abbey founded *c.*1136 by David I

MOUSA BROCH (HS), Island of Mousa, Shetland T 01856-841815
Finest surviving Iron Age broch tower

NEW ABBEY CORN MILL (HS), Dumfriesshire DG2 8BX T 01387-850260
Working water-powered mill; operates in summer months

PALACE OF HOLYROODHOUSE, Edinburgh EH8 8DX T 0131-556 5100 W www.royal.gov.uk
The Queen's official Scottish residence; main part of the palace built 1671–9

RING O' BRODGAR (HS), nr Stromness, Orkney T 01856-841815
Neolithic circle of upright stones with an enclosing ditch

ROSSLYN CHAPEL, Roslin, Midlothian EH25 9PU T 0131-440 2159 W www.rosslynchapel.org.uk
Historic church with unique stone carvings

RUTHWELL CROSS (HS), Ruthwell, Dumfriesshire T 01387-870249
Seventh-century Anglo-Saxon cross

ST ANDREWS CASTLE AND CATHEDRAL (HS), Fife KY16 9QL T 01334-477196 (castle); 01334-472563 (cathedral)
Ruins of 13th-century castle and remains of the largest cathedral in Scotland

SCONE PALACE, Perth, Perthshire PH2 6BD T 01738-552300 W www.scone-palace.co.uk
House built 1802–13 on the site of a medieval palace

SKARA BRAE (HS), nr Stromness, Orkney KW16 3LR T 01856-841815
Stone Age village with adjacent replica house

SMAILHOLM TOWER (HS), nr Kelso, Roxburghshire TD5 7PG T 01573-460365
Well-preserved 15th-century tower-house

STIRLING CASTLE (HS), Stirlingshire FK8 1EJ T 01786-450000
Great Hall and gatehouse of James IV, palace of James V, Chapel Royal remodelled by James VI

TANTALLON CASTLE (HS), North Berwick, E. Lothian EH39 5PN T 01620-892727
Fortification with earthwork defences; 14th-century curtain wall with towers

THREAVE CASTLE (HS), Castle Douglas, Kirkcudbrightshire DG7 1TJ T 07711-223101
Late 14th-century tower on an island; accessible only by boat

URQUHART CASTLE (HS), Drumnadrochit, Inverness-shire IV63 6XJ T 01456-450551
13th-century castle remains on the banks of Loch Ness

NORTHERN IRELAND

For the Northern Ireland Environment and Heritage Service, the official website is www.ni-environment.gov.uk
For more information on National Trust properties in Northern Ireland, including those listed below, the official website is www.nationaltrust.org.uk
(EHS) Property in the care of the Northern Ireland Environment and Heritage Service
(NT) National Trust property

CARRICKFERGUS CASTLE (EHS), Carrickfergus, Co. Antrim BT38 7BG T 028-9335 1273
Castle begun in 1180 and garrisoned until 1928

CASTLE COOLE (NT), Enniskillen, Co. Fermanagh BT74 6JY T 028-6632 2690
18th-century mansion by James Wyatt in parkland

CASTLE WARD (NT), Strangford, Co. Down BT30 7LS T 028-4488 1204
18th-century house with Classical and Gothic facades

DEVENISH ISLAND (EHS), nr Enniskillen, Co. Fermanagh T 028-9054 6518
Island monastery founded in the sixth century by St Molaise

DOWNHILL DEMESNE (NT), Castlerock, Co. Londonderry BT51 4RP T 028-2073 1582
Ruins of palatial house in landscaped estate including Mussenden Temple

DUNLUCE CASTLE (EHS), Bushmills, Co. Antrim BT57 8UY T 028-2073 1938
Ruins of 16th-century stronghold of the McDonnells

FLORENCE COURT (NT), Enniskillen, Co. Fermanagh BT92 1DB T 028-6634 8249
Mid-18th-century house with Rococo decoration

GREY ABBEY (EHS), Greyabbey, Co. Down BT22 2NQ T 028-9054 6552
Substantial remains of a Cistercian abbey founded in 1193

HILLSBOROUGH FORT (EHS), Hillsborough, Co. Down BT26 6AG T 028-9054 3095
Square keep built in 1650

MOUNT STEWART (NT), Newtownards, Co. Down BT22 2AD T 028-4278 8387
18th-century house; childhood home of Lord Castlereagh; Temple of the Winds

NENDRUM MONASTERY (EHS), Mahee Island, Co. Down T 028-9181 1491
Island monastery founded in the fifth century by St Machaoi

PATTERSON'S SPADE MILL (NT), Templepatrick, Co. Antrim BT39 0AP T 028-9443 3619
An authentic water-driven spade mill

TULLY CASTLE (EHS), Co. Fermanagh T 028-9054 6552
Fortified house and bawn built in 1613

MUSEUMS AND GALLERIES

There are approximately 2,500 museums and galleries in the United Kingdom. Around 1,860 are accredited by the Museums, Libraries and Archives Council (MLA), which indicates that they have an appropriate constitution, are soundly financed, have adequate collection management standards and public services, and have access to professional curatorial advice. Applications for accreditation are assessed by either the relevant regional agency in England; Museums Archives and Libraries Wales (CyMAL); the Scottish Museums Council or the Northern Ireland Museums Council.

The following is a selection of museums and art galleries in the United Kingdom. Opening hours and admission charges vary. Further information about museums and galleries in the UK is available from the Museums Association (W www.museumsassociation.org T 020-7426 6910).

W www.culture24.org.uk includes a database of all the museums and galleries in the UK.

ENGLAND

* England's national museums and galleries, which receive government funding directly from the DCMS. These institutions are deemed to have collections of national importance, and the government is able to call upon their staff for expert advice

BARNARD CASTLE

The Bowes Museum, Co. Durham DL12 8NP T 01833-690606 W www.thebowesmuseum.org.uk
European art from the late medieval period to the 19th century; music and costume galleries; English period rooms from Elizabeth I to Victoria; local archaeology

BATH

American Museum, Claverton Manor BA2 7BD T 01225-460503 W www.americanmuseum.org
American decorative arts from the 17th to 19th century; American heritage exhibition

Fashion Museum, Bennett Street BA1 2QH T 01225-477173 W www.museumofcostume.co.uk
Fashion from the 18th century to the present day

Roman Baths Museum, Pump Room, Stall Street BA1 1LZ T 01225-477785 W www.romanbaths.co.uk
Museum adjoins the remains of a Roman baths and temple complex

Victoria Art Gallery, Bridge Street BA2 4AT T 01225-477233 W www.victoriagal.org.uk
European Old Masters and British art since the 15th century

BEAMISH

The North of England Open Air Museum, Co. Durham DH9 0RG T 0191-370 4000 W www.beamish.org.uk
Northern town recreated in 1825 and 1913

BEAULIEU

National Motor Museum, Hants SO42 7ZN T 01590-612345 W www.beaulieu.co.uk
Displays of over 250 vehicles dating from 1895 to the present day

BIRMINGHAM

Aston Hall, Trinity Road B6 6JD T 0121-327 0062 W www.bmag.org.uk
Jacobean House containing paintings, furniture and tapestries from the 17th to 19th century

Barber Institute of Fine Arts, University of Birmingham, Edgbaston B15 2TS T 0121-414 7333 W www.barber.org.uk
Fine arts, including Old Masters

Birmingham Museum and Art Gallery, Chamberlain Square B3 3DH T 0121-303 2834 W www.bmag.org.uk
Includes notable collection of Pre-Raphaelite art

Museum of the Jewellery Quarter, Vyse Street, Hockley B18 6HA T 0121-554 3598 W www.bmag.org.uk
Built around a real jewellery workshop

BOVINGTON

Tank Museum, BH20 6JG T 01929-405096 W www.tankmuseum.co.uk
Collection of 300 tanks from the earliest days of tank warfare to the present

BRADFORD

Bradford Industrial Museum and Horses at Work, Moorside Road, Eccleshill BD2 3HP T 01274-435900 W www.bradfordmuseums.org
Engineering, textiles, transport and social history exhibits

Cartwright Hall Art Gallery, Lister Park BD9 4NS T 01274-431212 W www.bradfordmuseums.org
British 19th- and 20th-century fine art

**National Media Museum,* Princes Way BD1 1NQ T 0870-701 0200 W www.nationalmediamuseum.org.uk
Photography, film and television interactive exhibits; features the UK's first IMAX cinema and the only public Cinerama screen in the world

BRIGHTON

Booth Museum of Natural History, Dyke Road BN1 5AA T 03000-290900 W www.booth.virtualmuseum.info
Zoology, botany and geology collections; British birds in recreated habitats

Brighton Museum and Art Gallery, Royal Pavilion Gardens BN1 1EE T 03000-290900 W www.brighton.virtualmuseum.info
Includes fine art and design, fashion, non-Western art; Brighton history

BRISTOL

Arnolfini, Narrow Quay BS1 4QA T 0117-917 2300 W www.arnolfini.org.uk
Contemporary visual arts, dance, performance, music, talks and workshops

Blaise Castle House Museum, Henbury BS10 7QS T 0117-903 9818 W www.bristol-city.gov.uk/museums
Agricultural and social history collections in an 18th-century mansion

City Museum and Art Gallery, Queen's Road BS8 1RL T 0117-922 3571 W www.bristol-city.gov.uk/museums
Includes fine and decorative art, oriental art, Egyptology and Bristol ceramics and paintings

CAMBRIDGE

Fitzwilliam Museum, Trumpington Street CB2 1RB T 01223-332900 W www.fitzmuseum.cam.ac.uk

Antiquities, fine and applied arts, clocks, ceramics, manuscripts, furniture, sculpture, coins and medals

**Imperial War Museum Duxford*, Duxford CB22 4QR
T 01223-835000 W www.duxford.iwm.org.uk
Displays of military and civil aircraft, tanks, guns and naval exhibits

Sedgwick Museum of Earth Sciences, Downing Street CB2 3EQ
T 01223-333456 W www.sedgwickmuseum.org
Extensive geological collection

University Museum of Archaeology and Anthropology, Downing Street CB2 3DZ T 01223-333516
W www.maa.cam.ac.uk
Extensive global archaeological and anthropological collections

University Museum of Zoology, Downing Street CB2 3EJ
T 01223-336650 W www.zoo.cam.ac.uk/museum
Extensive zoological collection

Whipple Museum of the History of Science, Free School Lane CB2 3RH T 01223-330906 W www.hps.cam.ac.uk/whipple
Scientific instruments from the 14th century to the present

CARLISLE

Tullie House Museum and Art Gallery, Castle Street CA3 8TP
T 01228-618718 W www.tulliehouse.co.uk
Prehistoric archaeology, Hadrian's Wall, Viking and medieval Cumbria, and the social history of Carlisle

CHATHAM

The Historic Dockyard, ME4 4TZ T 01634-823800
W www.chdt.org.uk
Maritime attractions including HMS *Cavalier*, the UK's last Second World War destroyer

Royal Engineers Museum of Military Engineering, Prince Arthur Road, Gillingham ME4 4UG T 01634-822839
W www.remuseum.org.uk
Regimental history, ethnography, decorative art and photography

CHELTENHAM

Art Gallery and Museum, Clarence Street GL50 3JT
T 01242-237431 W www.cheltenhammuseum.org.uk
Paintings, arts and crafts

CHESTER

Grosvenor Museum, Grosvenor Street CH1 2DD
T 01244-402008 W www.chester.gov.uk
Roman collections, natural history, art, Chester silver, local history and costume

CHICHESTER

Weald and Downland Open Air Museum, Singleton PO18 0EU T 01243-811363 W www.wealddown.co.uk
Rebuilt vernacular buildings from south-east England; includes medieval houses, agricultural and rural craft buildings and a working watermill

COLCHESTER

Colchester Castle Museum, Castle Park CO1 1TJ
T 01206-282939 W www.colchestermuseums.org.uk
Largest Norman keep in Europe standing on foundations of the Roman Temple of Claudius; tours of the Roman vaults, castle walls and chapel

COVENTRY

Coventry Transport Museum, Hales Street CV1 1JD
T 024-7623 4270 W www.transport-museum.com
Hundreds of motor vehicles and bicycles

Herbert Art Gallery and Museum, Jordan Well CV1 5QP
T 024-7683 2386 W www.theherbert.org
Local history, archaeology and industry, and fine and decorative art

DERBY

Derby Museum and Art Gallery, The Strand DE1 1BS
T 01332-641901 W www.derby.gov.uk
Includes paintings by Joseph Wright of Derby and Derby porcelain

Pickford's House Museum, Friar Gate DE1 1DA
T 01332-255363 W www.derby.gov.uk
Georgian town house by architect Joseph Pickford; museum of Georgian life and costume

The Silk Mill, Derby's Museum of Industry and History, Full Street DE1 3AF T 01332-255308 W www.derby.gov.uk
Rolls-Royce aero engine collection and railway engineering gallery; on the site of two silk mills built in the early 1700s

DEVIZES

Wiltshire Heritage Museum, Long Street SN10 1NS
T 01380-727369 W www.wiltshireheritage.org.uk
Natural and local history; art gallery; archaeological finds from prehistoric, Roman and Saxon sites

DORCHESTER

Dorset County Museum, High West Street DT1 1XA
T 01305-262735 W www.dorsetcountymuseum.org
Includes a collection of Thomas Hardy's manuscripts, books, notebooks and drawings; local history

DOVER

Dover Museum, Market Square CT16 1PB T 01304-201066
W www.dovermuseum.co.uk
Contains the Dover Bronze Age Boat Gallery and archaeological finds from Bronze Age, Roman and Saxon sites

GATESHEAD

Baltic Centre for Contemporary Art, South Shore Road NE8 3BA T 0191-478 1810 W www.balticmill.com
Contemporary art exhibitions and events

Shipley Art Gallery, Prince Consort Road NE8 4JB
T 0191-477 1495 W www.twmuseums.org.uk/shipley
Contemporary crafts

GAYDON

Heritage Motor Centre, Banbury Road, Warks CV35 0BJ
T 01926-641188 W www.heritage-motor-centre.co.uk
History of British motor industry from 1895 to present; classic vehicles; engineering gallery; Corgi and Lucas collections

GLOUCESTER

National Waterways Museum, Gloucester Docks GL1 2EH
T 01452-318200 W www.nwm.org.uk
Two-hundred-year history of Britain's canals and inland waterways

GOSPORT

Royal Navy Submarine Museum, Haslar Jetty Road, Hants PO12 2AS T 023-9252 9217 W www.rnsubmus.co.uk
Underwater warfare, including the submarine *Alliance*; first Royal Navy submarine

GRASMERE

Dove Cottage and the *Wordsworth Museum*, Cumbria LA22 9SH T 01539-435544 W www.wordsworth.org.uk
William Wordsworth's manuscripts, home and garden

HULL

Ferens Art Gallery, Queen Victoria Square HU1 3RA
T 01482-300300 W www.hullcc.gov.uk
European art, especially Dutch 17th-century paintings, British portraits from 17th to 20th century, and marine paintings

Hull Maritime Museum, Queen Victoria Square HU1 3DX
T 01482-300300 W www.hullcc.gov.uk
Whaling, fishing and navigation exhibits

HUNTINGDON

The Cromwell Museum, Grammar School Walk PE29 3LF
T 01480-375830 W www.cambridgeshire.gov.uk/cromwell
Portraits and memorabilia relating to Oliver Cromwell

IPSWICH

Christchurch Mansion and *Wolsey Art Gallery*, Christchurch Park IP4 2BE T 01473-433554 W www.ipswich.gov.uk
Tudor house with paintings by Gainsborough, Constable and other Suffolk artists; furniture and 18th-century ceramics; temporary exhibitions

LEEDS

Armley Mills, Leeds Industrial Museum, Canal Road, Armley LS12 2QF T 0113-263 7861 W www.leeds.gov.uk/armleymills
World's largest woollen mill, now a museum for textiles, clothing and engine manufacture

Leeds City Art Gallery, The Headrow LS1 3AA T 0113-247 8256 W www.leeds.gov.uk/artgallery
Includes English watercolours; modern sculpture; Henry Moore gallery; print room

Lotherton Hall, Aberford LS25 3EB T 0113-281 3259 W www.leeds.gov.uk/lothertonhall
Costume, ceramics and furniture collections in furnished Edwardian house; deer park and bird garden

**Royal Armouries Museum*, Armouries Drive LS10 1LT T 08700-344344 W www.royalarmouries.org
National collection of arms and armour from BC to present; demonstrations of foot combat in museum's five galleries; falconry and mounted combat in the tiltyard

Temple Newsam, LS15 0AE T 0113-264 5535 W www.leeds.gov.uk/templenewsam
Old Masters and 17th- and 18th-century decorative art in furnished Jacobean/Tudor house

LEICESTER

Jewry Wall Museum, St Nicholas Circle LE1 4LB T 0116 225 4971 W www.leicester.gov.uk
Archaeology; Roman Jewry Wall and baths; mosaics

New Walk Museum and Art Gallery, New Walk LE1 7EA T 0116-255 4900 W www.leicester.gov.uk
Natural history and geology; ancient Egypt gallery; European art and decorative arts

LINCOLN

The Collection, Danes Terrace LN2 1LP T 01522-550990 W www.lincolnshire.gov.uk
Artefacts from the Stone Age to the Viking and Medieval eras; adjacent art gallery with decorative and contemporary visual arts

Museum of Lincolnshire Life, Burton Road LN1 3LY T 01522-528448 W www.lincolnshire.gov.uk
Social history and agricultural collection

LIVERPOOL

**International Slavery Museum*, Albert Dock L3 4AQ T 0151-478 4499 W www.liverpoolmuseums.org.uk
Explores historical and contemporary aspects of slavery

**Lady Lever Art Gallery*, Wirral CH62 5EQ T 0151-478 4136 W www.liverpoolmuseums.org.uk/ladylever
Paintings, furniture and porcelain

**Merseyside Maritime Museum*, Albert Dock L3 4AQ T 0151-478 4499 W www.liverpoolmuseums.org.uk/maritime
Floating exhibits, working displays and craft demonstrations; incorporates *HM Customs and Excise National Museum*

**Museum of Liverpool*, Pier Head L3 1PZ W www.liverpoolmuseums.org.uk
Due to reopen in 2010, formerly known as the *Museum of Liverpool Life*

**Sudley House*, Mossley Hill Road L18 8BX T 0151-724 3245 W www.liverpoolmuseums.org.uk/sudley
Late 18th- and 19th-century paintings in former shipowner's home

**Tate Liverpool*, Albert Dock L3 4BB T 0151-702 7400 W www.tate.org.uk/liverpool
Twentieth-century paintings and sculpture

**Walker Art Gallery*, William Brown Street L3 8EL T 0151-478 4199 W www.liverpoolmuseums.org.uk/walker
Paintings from the 14th to 20th century

**World Museum Liverpool*, William Brown Street L3 8EN T 0151-478 4393 W www.liverpoolmuseums.org.uk/wml
Includes Egyptian mummies, weapons and classical sculpture; planetarium, aquarium, vivarium and natural history centre

LONDON: GALLERIES

Barbican Art Gallery, Barbican Centre, Silk Street EC2Y 8DS T 020-7638 4141 W www.barbican.org.uk
Temporary exhibitions

Courtauld Institute of Art Gallery, Somerset House, Strand WC2R 0RN T 020-7848 2526 W www.courtauld.ac.uk
Impressionist and post-impressionist paintings

Dulwich Picture Gallery, Gallery Road, Dulwich Village SE21 7AD T 020-8693 5254 W www.dulwichpicturegallery.org.uk
England's first public art gallery; designed by Sir John Soane to house 17th- and 18th-century paintings

Hayward Gallery, Belvedere Road SE1 8XZ T 020-7960 5226 W www.southbankcentre.co.uk
Temporary exhibitions

**National Gallery*, Trafalgar Square WC2N 5DN T 020-7747 2885 W www.nationalgallery.org.uk
Western painting from the 13th to 20th century; early Renaissance collection in the Sainsbury Wing

**National Portrait Gallery*, St Martin's Place WC2H 0HE T 020-7306 0055 W www.npg.org.uk
Portraits of eminent people in British history

Percival David Foundation of Chinese Art, Gordon Square WC1H 0PD T 020-7387 3909
Chinese ceramics from 10th to 18th century

Photographers' Gallery, Great Newport Street WC2H 7HY T 0845-262 1618 W www.photonet.org.uk
Temporary exhibitions

The Queen's Gallery, Buckingham Palace SW1A 1AA T 020-7766 7301 W www.royalcollection.org.uk
Art from the Royal Collection

Royal Academy of Arts, Burlington House, Piccadilly W1J 0BD T 020-7300 8000 W www.royalacademy.org.uk
British art since 1750 and temporary exhibitions; annual Summer Exhibition

Saatchi Gallery, Sloane Square SW3 4RY T 020-7823 2363 W www.saatchi-gallery.co.uk
Contemporary art including paintings, photographs, sculpture and installations

Serpentine Gallery, Kensington Gardens W2 3XA T 020-7402 6075 W www.serpentinegallery.org
Temporary exhibitions of British and international contemporary art

**Tate Britain*, Millbank SW1P 4RG T 020-7887 8888 W www.tate.org.uk/britain
British painting and 20th-century painting and sculpture

**Tate Modern*, Bankside SE1 9TG T 020-7887 8888 W www.tate.org.uk/modern
International modern art from 1900 to the present

**Wallace Collection*, Manchester Square W1U 3BN T 020-7563 9500 W www.wallacecollection.org
Paintings and drawings, French 18th-century furniture, armour, porcelain, clocks and sculpture

Whitechapel Art Gallery, Whitechapel High Street E1 7QX T 020-7522 7888 W www.whitechapel.org
Temporary exhibitions of modern art

LONDON: MUSEUMS

Bank of England Museum, Threadneedle Street EC2R 8AH (entrance on Bartholomew Lane) T 020-7601 5545 W www.bankofengland.co.uk/museum
History of the Bank of England since 1694

**British Museum,* Great Russell Street WC1B 3DG T 020-7323 8000 W www.thebritishmuseum.org
Antiquities, coins, medals, prints and drawings; temporary exhibitions

Brunel Museum, Rotherhithe SE16 4LF T 020-7231 3840 W www.brunel-museum.org.uk
Explores the engineering achievements of Isambard Kingdom Brunel and his father, Marc Brunel

**Cabinet War Rooms,* King Charles Street SW1A 2AQ T 020-7930 6961 W cwr.iwm.org.uk
Underground rooms used by Churchill and the government during the Second World War

Design Museum, Shad Thames SE1 2YD T 0870-833 9955 W www.designmuseum.org
The development of design and the mass-production of consumer objects

Firepower, the Royal Artillery Museum, Royal Arsenal, Woolwich SE18 6ST T 020-8855 7755 W www.firepower.org.uk
The history and development of artillery over the last 700 years including the collections of the Royal Regiment of Artillery

Geffrye Museum, Kingsland Road E2 8EA T 020-7739 9893 W www.geffrye-museum.org.uk
English urban domestic interiors from 1600 to present day; also paintings, furniture, decorative arts, walled herb garden and period garden rooms

**HMS Belfast,* Morgan's Lane, Tooley Street SE1 2JH T 020-7940 6300 W www.hmsbelfast.iwm.org.uk
Life on a Second World War cruiser

Horniman Museum, London Road SE23 3PQ T 020-8699 1872 W www.horniman.ac.uk
Museum of anthropology, musical instruments and natural history; aquarium; reference library; gardens

**Imperial War Museum,* Lambeth Road SE1 6HZ T 020-7416 5320 W www.iwm.org.uk
All aspects of the two World Wars and other military operations involving Britain and the Commonwealth since 1914

London Metropolitan Archives, Northampton Road EC1R OHB T 020-7332 3820 W www.cityoflondon.gov.uk
Material on the history of London and its people dating 1067–2006

London Transport Museum, Covent Garden Piazza WC2E 7BB T 020-7379 6344 W www.ltmuseum.co.uk
Vehicles, photographs and graphic art relating to the history of transport in London

MCC Museum, Lord's, St John's Wood NW8 8QN T 020-7616 8656 W www.lords.org
Cricket museum; guided tours by appointment

**Museum of Childhood at Bethnal Green (V&A),* Cambridge Heath Road E2 9PA T 020-8983 5200 W www.museumofchildhood.org.uk
Toys, games and exhibits relating to the social history of childhood

**Museum in Docklands,* West India Quay, Hertsmere Road E14 4AL T 020-7001 9844 W www.museumindocklands.org.uk
Explores the story of London's river, port and people over 2,000 years, from Roman times through to the recent regeneration of London's Docklands

Museum of Garden History, Lambeth Palace Road SE1 7LB T 020-7401 8865 W www.museumgardenhistory.org
History and development of gardens and gardening; recreated 17th-century garden

**Museum of London,* London Wall EC2Y 5HN T 020-7001 9844 W www.museumoflondon.org.uk
History of London from prehistoric times to present day

National Archives Museum, Kew TW9 4DU T 020-8876 3444 W www.nationalarchives.gov.uk
Displays treasures from the archives, including the Domesday Book

National Army Museum, Royal Hospital Road SW3 4HT T 020-7730 0717 W www.national-army-museum.ac.uk
Five-hundred-year history of the British soldier; exhibits include model of the Battle of Waterloo and recreated First World War trench

**National Maritime Museum,* Greenwich SE10 9NF T 020-8858 4422 W www.nmm.ac.uk
Maritime history of Britain; collections include globes, clocks, telescopes and paintings; comprises the main building, the Royal Observatory and the Queen's House

**Natural History Museum,* Cromwell Road SW7 5BD T 020-7942 5000 W www.nhm.ac.uk
Natural history collections

Petrie Museum of Egyptian Archaeology, University College London, Malet Place WC1E 6BT T 020-7679 2884 W www.petrie.ucl.ac.uk
Egyptian archaeology collection

Royal Air Force Museum, Hendon NW9 5LL T 020-8205 2266 W www.rafmuseum.org.uk
Aviation from before the Wright brothers to the present-day RAF

Royal Mews, Buckingham Palace SW1A 1AA T 020-7766 7302 W www.royalcollection.org.uk
State vehicles, including the Queen's gold state coach; home to the Queen's horses

**Science Museum,* Exhibition Road SW7 2DD T 0870 870 4868 W www.sciencemuseum.org.uk
Science, technology, industry and medicine collections; children's interactive gallery; IMAX cinema

Shakespeare's Globe Exhibition, Bankside SE1 9DT T 020-7902 1400 W www.shakespeares-globe.org
Recreation of Elizabethan theatre using 16th-century techniques; includes a tour of the theatre

**Sir John Soane's Museum,* Lincoln's Inn Fields WC2A 3BP T 020-7405 2107 W www.soane.org
Art and antiquities collected by Soane throughout his lifetime; house designed by Soane

Tower Bridge Experience, SE1 2UP T 020-7403 3761 W www.towerbridge.org.uk
History of the bridge and display of Victorian steam machinery; panoramic views from walkways

**Victoria and Albert Museum,* Cromwell Road SW7 2RL T 020-7942 2000 W www.vam.ac.uk
Includes National Art Library and Print Room; fine and applied art and design; furniture, glass, textiles, theatre and dress collections

Wimbledon Lawn Tennis Museum, Church Road SW19 5AE T 020-8946 6131 W www.wimbledon.org/museum
Tennis trophies, fashion and memorabilia; view of Centre Court

MALTON

Eden Camp, N. Yorks YO17 6RT T 01653-697777 W www.edencamp.co.uk
Restored POW camp and Second World War memorabilia

MANCHESTER
**Imperial War Museum North*, Trafford Wharf, Trafford Park M17 1TZ T 0161-836 4000 W www.north.iwm.org.uk
History of war in the 20th and 21st centuries
Manchester Art Gallery, Mosley Street M2 3JL
T 0161-235 8888 W www.manchestergalleries.org
Six centuries of European fine and decorative art
Manchester Museum, Oxford Road M13 9PL T 0161-275 2634
W www.museum.manchester.ac.uk
Collections include archaeology, decorative arts, Egyptology, natural history and zoology
**Museum of Science and Industry*, Liverpool Road, Castlefield M3 4FP T 0161-832 2244 W www.mosi.org.uk
On site of world's oldest passenger railway station; galleries relating to space, energy, power, transport, aviation, textiles and social history
Whitworth Art Gallery, Oxford Road M15 6ER
T 0161-275 7450 W www.whitworth.manchester.ac.uk
Watercolours, drawings, prints, textiles, wallpapers and British art

MILTON KEYNES
Bletchley Park National Codes Centre, Bucks MK3 6EB
T 01908-640404 W www.bletchleypark.org.uk
Home of British codebreaking during the Second World War; Enigma machine; computer museum; wartime toys and memorabilia

MONKWEARMOUTH
Monkwearmouth Station Museum, North Bridge Street, Sunderland SR5 1AP T 0191-567 7075
W www.twmuseums.org.uk/monkwearmouth
Victorian train station; interactive galleries

NEWCASTLE UPON TYNE
Discovery Museum, Blandford Square NE1 4JA
T 0191-232 6789 W www.twmuseums.org.uk/discovery
Science and industry, local history, fashion; Tyneside's maritime history; *Turbinia* (first steam-driven vessel) gallery
Great North Museum: Hancock, Barras Bridge NE2 4PT
T 0191-222 6765
W www.twmuseums.org.uk/greatnorthmuseum
Natural history and ancient history
Laing Art Gallery, New Bridge Street NE1 8AG
T 0191-232 7734 W www.twmuseums.org.uk/laing
18th- and 19th-century collection; watercolour gallery

NEWMARKET
National Horseracing Museum, High Street CB8 8JH
T 01638-667333 W www.nhrm.co.uk
The story of people and horses involved in racing; temporary exhibitions

NORTH SHIELDS
Stephenson Railway Museum, Middle Engine Lane NE29 8DX
T 0191-200 7146 W www.twmuseums.org.uk/stephenson
Locomotive engines and rolling stock

NOTTINGHAM
Brewhouse Yard Museum, Castle Boulevard NG7 1FB
T 0115-915 3600 W www.nottinghamcity.gov.uk
Social history from the 17th to 20th century
Castle Museum and Art Gallery, Friar Lane NG1 6EL
T 0115-915 3700 W www.nottinghamcity.gov.uk
Paintings, ceramics, silver and glass; history of Nottingham
Industrial Museum, Wollaton Park, Wollaton NG8 2AE
T 0115-915 3900 W www.nottinghamcity.gov.uk
Lacemaking machinery, steam engines and transport exhibits
Natural History Museum, Wollaton Hall, Wollaton NG8 2AE
T 0115-915 3900 W www.nottinghamcity.gov.uk
Local natural history and wildlife dioramas

OXFORD
Ashmolean Museum, Beaumont Street OX1 2PH
T 01865-278000 W www.ashmolean.org
European and oriental fine and applied arts, archaeology, Egyptology and numismatics
Modern Art Oxford, Pembroke Street OX1 1BP
T 01865-722733 W www.modernartoxford.org.uk
Temporary exhibitions
Museum of the History of Science, Broad Street OX1 3AZ
T 01865-277280 W www.mhs.ox.ac.uk
Displays include early scientific instruments, chemical apparatus, clocks and watches
Oxford University Museum of Natural History, Parks Road OX1 3PW T 01865-272950 W www.oum.ox.ac.uk
Entomology, geology, mineralogy and zoology
Pitt Rivers Museum, South Parks Road OX1 3PP
T 01865-270927 W www.prm.ox.ac.uk
Ethnographic and archaeological artefacts

PLYMOUTH
City Museum and Art Gallery, Drake Circus PL4 8AJ
T 01752-304774 W www.plymouthmuseum.gov.uk
Local and natural history; ceramics; silver; Old Masters; temporary exhibitions

PORTSMOUTH
Charles Dickens Birthplace, Old Commercial Road PO1 4QL
T 023-9282 7261 W www.charlesdickensbirthplace.co.uk
Dickens memorabilia
D-Day Museum, Clarence Esplanade, Southsea PO5 3NT
T 023-9282 7261 W www.ddaymuseum.co.uk
Includes the Overlord embroidery
Portsmouth Historic Dockyard, HM Naval Base PO1 3LJ
T 023-9283 9766 W www.historicdockyard.co.uk
Incorporates the *Royal Naval Museum* (PO1 3NH T 023-9272 7562 W www.royalnavalmuseum.org), *HMS Victory* (PO1 3NH T 023-9286 1533 W www.hms-victory.com), *HMS Warrior* (PO1 3QX T 023-9277 8600 W www.hmswarrior.org), the *Mary Rose* (PO1 3LX T 023-9281 2931 W www.maryrose.org) and *Action Stations* (PO1 3LJ T 023-9289 3316 W www.actionstations.org)
History of the Royal Navy and of the dockyard; warships and technology spanning 500 years

PRESTON
Harris Museum and Art Gallery, Market Square PR1 2PP
T 01772-258248 W www.harrismuseum.org.uk
British art since the 18th century; ceramics, glass, costume and local history; contemporary exhibitions
National Football Museum, Sir Tom Finney Way PR1 6PA
T 01772-908442 W www.nationalfootballmuseum.com
Home to the FIFA, FA and Football League collections on long-term loan

ST ALBANS
Verulamium Museum, St Michael's Street AL3 4SW
T 01727-751810 W www.stalbansmuseums.org.uk
Remains of Iron Age settlement and the third-largest city in Roman Britain; exhibits include Roman wall plasters, jewellery, mosaics and room reconstructions

ST IVES
**Tate St Ives*, Porthmeor Beach, Cornwall TR26 1TG
T 01736-796226 W www.tate.org.uk/stives
Modern art, much by artists associated with St Ives; includes the Barbara Hepworth Museum and Sculpture Garden

SALISBURY
Salisbury & South Wiltshire Museum, The Close SP1 2EN
T 01722-332151 W www.salisburymuseum.org.uk
Archaeology collection

SHEFFIELD

Graves Art Gallery, Surrey Street S1 1XZ T 0114-278 2600 W www.museums-sheffield.org.uk
20th-century British art, Grice Collection of Chinese ivories

Millennium Galleries, Arundel Gate S1 2PP T 0114-278 2600 W www.museums-sheffield.org.uk
Incorporates four different galleries: the Special Exhibition Gallery, the Craft and Design Gallery, the Metalwork Gallery and the Ruskin Gallery, which houses John Ruskin's collection of paintings, drawings, books and medieval manuscripts

Weston Park Museum, Western Bank S10 2TP T 0114-278 2600 W www.museums-sheffield.org.uk
World history for families

SOUTHAMPTON

City Art Gallery, Commercial Road SO14 7LP T 023-8083 2277 W www.southampton.gov.uk/art
Fine art collection spanning six centuries of European art

God's House Tower Museum of Archaeology, Winkle Street SO14 2NY T 023-8063 5904 W www.southampton.gov.uk
Roman, Saxon and medieval archaeology

Maritime Museum, Town Quay Road SO14 2NY T 023-8063 5904 W www.southampton.gov.uk
Southampton maritime history

SOUTH SHIELDS

Arbeia Roman Fort, Baring Street NE33 2BB T 0191-456 1369 W www.twmuseums.org.uk/arbeia
Excavated ruins; reconstructions of original buildings

South Shields Museum and Art Gallery, Ocean Road NE33 2JA T 0191-456 8740 W www.twmuseums.org.uk/southshields
South Tyneside history; interactive art gallery

STOKE-ON-TRENT

Etruria Industrial Museum, Lower Bedford Street ST4 7AF T 01782-233144 W www.stoke.gov.uk/museums
Britain's sole surviving steam-powered potter's mill

Gladstone Pottery Museum, Longton ST3 1PQ T 01782-237777 W www.stoke.gov.uk/museums
A working Victorian pottery

Potteries Museum and Art Gallery, Hanley ST1 3DW T 01782-232323 W www.stoke.gov.uk/museums
Pottery, china and porcelain collections and a Mark XVI Spitfire

The Wedgwood Museum, Barlaston ST12 9ER T 01782-371900 W www.wedgwoodmuseum.org.uk
The story of Josiah Wedgwood and the ceramic company he founded

SUNDERLAND

Sunderland Museum & Winter Gardens, Burdon Road SR1 1PP T 0191-553 2323 W www.twmuseums.org.uk/sunderland
Fine and decorative art, local history and gardens

TELFORD

Ironbridge Gorge Museums, TF8 7DQ T 01952-884391 W www.ironbridge.org.uk
World's first iron bridge; Blists Hill (late Victorian working town); Museum of Iron; Jackfield Tile Museum; Coalport China Museum; Tar Tunnel; Broseley Pipeworks

WAKEFIELD

National Coal Mining Museum for England, Overton WF4 4RH T 01924-848806 W www.ncm.org.uk
Includes underground tours of one of Britain's oldest working mines

Yorkshire Sculpture Park, West Bretton WF4 4LG T 01924-832631 W www.ysp.co.uk
Open-air sculpture gallery including works by Moore, Hepworth, Frink and others in 202 hectares (500 acres) of parkland

WEYBRIDGE

Brooklands Museum, KT13 0QN T 01932-857381 W www.brooklandsmuseum.com
Birthplace of British motorsport; world's first purpose-built motor racing circuit

WILMSLOW

Quarry Bank Mill, Styal SK9 4LA T 01625-527468 W www.quarrybankmill.org.uk
Working mill owned by the National Trust illustrating history of cotton industry; costumed guides at restored Apprentice House

WINCHESTER

INTECH, Telegraph Way, Hampshire SO21 1HX T 01962-863791 W www.intech-uk.com
Interactive science centre and planetarium

WORCESTER

City Museum and Art Gallery, Foregate Street WR1 1DT T 01905-25371 W www.worcestercitymuseums.org.uk
Includes a military museum, 19th-century chemist shop and changing art exhibitions

Museum of Worcester Porcelain, Severn Street WR1 2NE T 01905-21247 W www.worcesterporcelainmuseum.org.uk
Worcester porcelain from 1751 to the present day

YEOVIL

Fleet Air Arm Museum, Royal Naval Air Station, Yeovilton, Somerset BA22 8HT T 01935-840565 W www.fleetairarm.com
History of naval aviation; historic aircraft, including Concorde 002

YORK

Beningbrough Hall, Beningbrough YO30 1DD T 01904-472027 W www.nationaltrust.org.uk
18th-century house with portraits from the National Portrait Gallery

Jorvik – The Viking City, Coppergate YO1 9WT T 01904-543400 W www.jorvik-viking-centre.co.uk
Reconstruction of Viking York based on archaeological evidence

**National Railway Museum,* Leeman Road YO26 4XJ T 0844-815 3139 W www.nrm.org.uk
Includes locomotives, rolling stock and carriages

York Art Gallery, Exhibition Square YO1 7EW T 01904-687687 W www.yorkartgallery.org.uk
European and British painting spanning seven centuries; modern pottery; decorative arts

York Castle Museum, Eye of York YO1 9RY T 01904-687687 W www.yorkcastlemuseum.org.uk
Reconstructed streets and rooms; costume and military collections

Yorkshire Museum & Gardens, Museum Gardens YO1 7FR T 01904-687687 W www.yorkshiremuseum.org.uk
Yorkshire life from Roman to medieval times; geology and biology; York observatory

WALES

* Members of National Museum Wales, a public body that receives its funding through grant-in-aid from the Welsh Assembly

ABERYSTWYTH

Ceredigion Museum, Terrace Road SY23 2AQ T 01970-633088 W www.ceredigion.gov.uk
Local history, housed in a restored Edwardian theatre

Llywernog Silver-Lead Mine, Ponterwyd SY23 3AB
T 01970-890620 W www.silverminetours.co.uk
Tours of an 18th-century silver mine shaft, exhibitions containing artefacts used therein
BLAENAFON
**Big Pit National Coal Museum,* Torfaen NP4 9XP
T 01495-790311 W www.museumwales.ac.uk
Colliery with underground tour
BODELWYDDAN
Bodelwyddan Castle, Denbighshire LL18 5YA T 01745-584060
W www.bodelwyddan-castle.co.uk
Portraits from the National Portrait Gallery; furniture from the Victoria and Albert Museum; sculptures from the Royal Academy
CAERLEON
**National Roman Legion Museum,* NP18 1AE
T 01633-423134 W www.museumwales.ac.uk
Material from the site of the Roman fortress of Isca and its suburbs
CARDIFF
**National Museum Cardiff,* Cathays Park CF10 3NP
T 029-2039 7951 W www.museumwales.ac.uk
Includes natural sciences, archaeology and Impressionist paintings
**St Fagans: National History Museum,* St Fagans CF5 6XB
T 029-2057 3500 W www.museumwales.ac.uk
Open-air museum with re-erected buildings, agricultural equipment and costume
TECHNIQUEST, Stuart Street CF10 5BW T 029-2047 5475
W www.techniquest.org
Interactive science exhibits, planetarium and science theatre
CRICCIETH
Lloyd George Museum, Llanystumdwy LL52 0SH
T 01766-522071 W www.gwynedd.gov.uk
Childhood home of David Lloyd George; museum commemorates his life
DRE-FACH FELINDRE
**National Wool Museum,* nr Llandysul SA44 5UP
T 01559-370929 W www.museumwales.ac.uk
Exhibitions, a working woollen mill and craft workshops
LLANBERIS
**National Slate Museum,* Gwynedd LL55 4TY
T 01286-870630 W www.museumwales.ac.uk
Former slate quarry with original machinery and plant; slate crafts demonstrations; working waterwheel
LLANDRINDOD WELLS
National Cycle Collection, Automobile Palace, Temple Street LD1 5DL T 01597-825531 W www.cyclemuseum.org.uk
Over 200 bicycles on display, from 1819–present
PRESTEIGNE
Judge's Lodging Museum, Broad Street LD8 2AD
T 01544-260650 W www.judgeslodging.org.uk
Restored apartments, courtroom, cells and servants' quarters
SWANSEA
Glynn Vivian Art Gallery, Alexandra Road SA1 5DZ
T 01792-516900 W www.swansea.gov.uk/glynnvivian
Paintings, ceramics, Swansea pottery and porcelain, clocks, glass and Welsh art
**National Waterfront Museum,* Oystermouth Road SA1 3RD
T 01792-638950 W www.museumwales.ac.uk
Wales during the Industrial Revolution
Swansea Museum, Victoria Road SA1 1SN T 01792-653763
W www.swansea.gov.uk/swanseamuseum
Archaeology, social history, Swansea pottery
TENBY
Tenby Museum and Art Gallery, Castle Hill SA70 7BP
T 01834-842809 W www.tenbymuseum.org.uk
Local archaeology, history, geology and art

SCOTLAND

* Members of National Museums of Scotland or National Galleries of Scotland, which are non-departmental public bodies funded by, and accountable to, the Scottish government

ABERDEEN
Aberdeen Art Gallery, Schoolhill AB10 1FQ T 01224-523700
W www.aagm.co.uk
Impressionists, Scottish Colourists, decorative art and modern art
Aberdeen Maritime Museum, Shiprow AB11 5BY
T 01224-337700 W www.aagm.co.uk
Maritime history, including shipbuilding and North Sea oil
DUMFRIES
National Museum of Costume, New Abbey DG2 8HQ
T 01387-850375 W www.nms.ac.uk/costume
History of fashion from the 1850s to the 1950s
EDINBURGH
Britannia, Leith EH6 6JJ T 0131-555 5566
W www.royalyachtbritannia.co.uk
Former royal yacht with royal barge and royal family picture gallery
City Art Centre, Market Street EH1 1DE T 0131-529 3993
W www.cac.org.uk
Scottish late 19th- and 20th-century art and temporary exhibitions
**Dean Gallery,* Belford Road EH4 3DS T 0131-624 6200
W www.nationalgalleries.org
Dada, Surrealism and sculpture – particularly works by Sir Eduardo Paolozzi
Museum of Childhood, High Street EH1 1TG T 0131-529 4142
W www.cac.org.uk
Toys, games, clothes and exhibits relating to the social history of childhood
Museum of Edinburgh, Canongate EH8 8DD
T 0131-529 4143 W www.cac.org.uk
Local history, silver, glass and Scottish pottery
**Museum of Flight,* East Fortune Airfield, East Lothian EH39 5LF T 01620-897240 W www.nms.ac.uk/flight
Display of aircraft
**Museum of Scotland,* Chambers Street EH1 1JF
T 0131-225 7534 W www.nms.ac.uk/scotland
Scottish history from prehistoric times to the present
**National Gallery of Scotland,* The Mound EH2 2EL
T 0131-624 6200 W www.nationalgalleries.org
Paintings, drawings and prints from the early Renaissance to the end of the 19th century
**National War Museum of Scotland,* Edinburgh Castle EH1 2NG T 0131-247 4413 W www.nms.ac.uk/war
History of Scottish military and conflicts
**Royal Museum,* Chambers Street EH1 1JF T 0131-247 4422
W www.nms.ac.uk
Decorative arts, natural history, science and industry; closed for major refurbishment until 2011
**Scottish National Gallery of Modern Art,* Belford Road EH4 3DR T 0131-624 6200 W www.nationalgalleries.org
20th-century painting, sculpture and graphic art
**Scottish National Portrait Gallery,* Queen Street EH2 1JD
T 0131-624 6200 W www.nationalgalleries.org
Portraits of eminent people in Scottish history; the national collection of photography

The Writers' Museum, Lawnmarket EH1 2PA
T 0131-529 4901 W www.cac.org.uk
Exhibitions relating to Robert Louis Stevenson, Walter Scott and Robert Burns

FORT WILLIAM

West Highland Museum, Cameron Square PH33 6AJ
T 01397-702169 W www.westhighlandmuseum.org.uk
Includes tartan collections and exhibits relating to 1745 uprising

GLASGOW

Burrell Collection, Pollokshaws Road G43 1AT
T 0141-287 2550 W www.glasgowmuseums.com
Paintings, textiles, furniture, ceramics, stained glass and silver from classical times to the 19th century

Gallery of Modern Art, Royal Exchange Square G1 3AH
T 0141-287 3050 W www.glasgowmuseums.com
Collection of contemporary Scottish and world art

Hunterian Museum & Art Gallery, University of Glasgow G12 8QQ T 0141-330 4221 W www.hunterian.gla.ac.uk
Rennie Mackintosh and Whistler collections; Old Masters; Scottish paintings; archaeology; medicine; zoology

Kelvingrove Art Gallery & Museum, Argyle Street G3 8AG
T 0141-276 9599 W www.glasgowmuseums.com
Includes Old Masters, 19th-century French paintings and armour collection

Museum of Piping, McPhater Street G4 0HW
T 0141-353 0220 W www.thepipingcentre.co.uk
The history and origins of bagpiping

**Museum of Rural Life,* East Kilbride G76 9HR
T 0131-247 4377 W www.nms.ac.uk
History of rural life and work

Museum of Transport, Bunhouse Road G3 8DP
T 0141-287 2720 W www.glasgowmuseums.com
Includes a reproduction of a 1938 Glasgow street, cars since the 1930s, trams and a Glasgow subway station

People's Palace and Winter Gardens, Glasgow Green G40 1AT
T 0141-276 0788 W www.glasgowmuseums.com
Social history of Glasgow since 1750

St Mungo Museum of Religious Life and Art, Castle Street G4 0RH T 0141-276 1625 W www.glasgowmuseums.com
Explores universal themes through objects from all the main world religions

NORTHERN IRELAND

* Members of National Museums Northern Ireland, a non-departmental public body of the Northern Ireland Office

ARMAGH

**Armagh County Museum,* The Mall East BT61 9BE
T 028-3752 3070 W www.armaghcountymuseum.org.uk
Local history; archaeology; crafts

BANGOR

North Down Museum, Castle Park Avenue BT20 4BT
T 028-9127 1200 W www.northdown.gov.uk/heritage
Presents the history of North Down, including its early-Christian monastery

BELFAST

**W5,* Odyssey, Queen's Quay BT3 9QQ T 028-9046 7700
W www.w5online.co.uk
Interactive science and technology centre

HOLYWOOD

**Ulster Folk and Transport Museum,* Cultra, Co. Down BT18 0EU T 028-9042 8428 W www.uftm.org.uk
Open-air museum with original buildings from Ulster town and rural life *c.*1900; indoor galleries including Irish rail and road transport and *Titanic* exhibitions

LONDONDERRY

The Tower Museum, Union Hall Place BT48 6LU
T 028-7137 2411 W www.derrycity.gov.uk/museums
Tells the story of Ireland through the history of Londonderry

Workhouse Museum, Glendermott Road BT48 6BG
T 028-7131 8328 W www.derrycity.gov.uk/museums
Exhibitions on the Second World War, workhouse life, 19th-century poverty and the famine

NEWTOWNARDS

The Somme Heritage Centre, Whitespots Country Park BT23 7PH T 01247-823202 W www.irishsoldier.org
Commemorates the part played by Irish forces in the First World War

OMAGH

**Ulster American Folk Park,* Castletown, Co. Tyrone BT78 5QY T 028-8224 3292 W www.folkpark.com
Open-air museum telling the story of Ulster's emigrants to America; restored or recreated dwellings and workshops; ship and dockside gallery

**Ulster Museum,* Botanic Gardens BT9 5AB T 028-9038 3000
W www.ulstermuseum.org.uk
Irish antiquities; natural and local history; fine and applied arts

SIGHTS OF LONDON

For historic buildings, museums and galleries in London, *see* the Historic Buildings and Monuments and Museums and Galleries sections.

BRIDGES

The bridges over the Thames in London, from east to west, are:

Queen Elizabeth II Bridge (2,872m/9,423ft), engineer: William Halcrow and partners, opened 1991

Tower Bridge (268m/880ft by 18m/60ft), architect: Horace Jones, engineer: John Wolfe Barry, opened 1894

London Bridge (262m/860ft by 32m/105ft), original 13th-century stone bridge rebuilt and opened 1831 (engineer: John Rennie), reconstructed in Arizona when current London Bridge opened 1973 (architect: Lord Holford, engineer: Mott, Hay and Anderson)

Cannon Street Railway Bridge (261m/855ft), engineers: John Hawkshaw and John Wolfe Barry, originally named the Alexandra Bridge, opened 1866; renovated 1979–82

Southwark Bridge (244m/800ft by 17m/55ft), engineer: John Rennie, opened 1819; rebuilt 1912–21 (architect: Ernest George, engineer: Mott, Hay and Anderson)

Millennium Bridge (325m/1,066ft by 5m/15ft), architect: Foster and Partners, engineer: Ove Arup and Partners, opened 2000; reopened after modification 2002

Blackfriars Railway Bridge (284m/933ft), engineers: John Wolfe Barry and Henri Marc Brunel, opened 1886

London, Chatham and Dover Railway Bridge (234m/933ft), engineer: Joseph Cubitt, opened in 1864; only the columns remain, the rest of the structure was removed in 1985

Blackfriars Bridge (294m/963ft by 32m/105ft), engineer: Robert Mylne, opened 1769; rebuilt 1869 (engineer: Joseph Cubitt); widened 1909

Waterloo Bridge (366m/1,200ft by 24m/80ft), engineer: John Rennie, opened 1817; rebuilt 1945 (architect: Sir Giles Gilbert Scott, engineer: Rendel, Palmer and Triton)

Golden Jubilee Bridges (325m/1,066ft by 4.7m/15ft), architect: Lifschutz Davidson, engineer: WSP Group, opened 2002; commonly known as the Hungerford Footbridges

Hungerford Railway Bridge (366m/1,200ft), engineer: Isambard Kingdom Brunel, suspension bridge opened 1845; present railway bridge opened 1864 (engineer: John Hawkshaw); widened in 1886

Westminster Bridge (228m/748ft by 26m/85ft), engineer: Charles Labelye, opened 1750; rebuilt 1862 (architect: Charles Barry, engineer: Thomas Page)

Lambeth Bridge (237m/776ft by 18m/60ft), engineer: Peter W. Barlow, original suspension bridge opened 1862; current structure opened 1932 (architect: Reginald Blomfield, engineer: George W. Humphreys)

Vauxhall Bridge (231m/759ft by 24m/80ft), engineer: James Walker, opened 1816; redesigned and opened 1906 (architect: William Edward Riley, engineers: Alexander Binnie and Maurice Fitzmaurice)

Grosvenor Railway Bridge (213m/700ft), engineer: John Fowler, opened 1860; rebuilt 1965; also known as the Victoria Railway Bridge

Chelsea Bridge (213m/698ft by 25m/83ft), original suspension bridge opened 1858 (engineer: Thomas Page); rebuilt 1937 (architects: George Topham Forrest and E. P. Wheeler, engineer: Rendel, Palmer and Triton)

Albert Bridge (216m/710ft, by 12m/40ft) engineer: Rowland M. Ordish, opened 1873; restructured 1884 (engineer: Joseph Bazalgette); strengthened 1971–3

Battersea Bridge (204m/670ft by 17m/55ft), engineer: Henry Holland, opened 1771; rebuilt 1890 (engineer: Joseph Bazalgette)

Battersea Railway Bridge (204m/670ft), engineer: William Baker, opened 1863, also known as Cremorne Bridge

Wandsworth Bridge (189m/619ft by 18m/60ft), engineer: Julian Tolmé, opened 1873; rebuilt 1940 (architect: E. P. Wheeler, engineer: T. Peirson Frank)

Putney Railway Bridge (229m/750ft), engineers: W. H. Thomas and William Jacomb and opened 1889, also known as the Fulham Railway Bridge or the Iron Bridge – it has no official name

Putney Bridge (213m/700ft by 23m/74ft), architect: Jacob Ackworth, original wooden bridge opened 1729; current granite structure completed in 1886 (engineer: Joseph Bazalgette)

Hammersmith Bridge (210m/688ft by 10m/33ft), engineer: William Tierney Clarke, the first suspension bridge in London, originally built 1827; rebuilt 1887 (engineer: Joseph Bazalgette)

Barnes Railway Bridge (also footbridge, 110m/360ft), engineer: Joseph Locke,opened 1849; rebuilt 1895 (engineers: London and South Western Railway); the original structure stands unused

Chiswick Bridge (137m/450ft by 21m/70ft), architect: Herbert Baker, engineer: Alfred Dryland, opened 1933

Kew Railway Bridge (175m/575ft), engineer: W. R. Galbraith, opened 1869

Kew Bridge (110m/360ft by 17m/56ft), engineer: Robert Tunstall, original timber bridge built 1759; replaced by a Portland stone structure in 1789 (engineer: James Paine); current granite bridge renamed King Edward VII Bridge in 1903, but still known as Kew Bridge (engineers: John Wolfe Barry and Cuthbert Brereton)

Richmond Lock (91m/300ft by 11m/36ft), engineer: F. G. M. Stoney, lock and footbridge opened 1894

Twickenham Bridge (85m/280ft by 21m/70ft), architect: Maxwell Ayrton, engineer: Alfred Dryland, opened 1933

Richmond Railway Bridge (91m/300ft), engineer: Joseph Locke, opened 1848; rebuilt 1906–8 (engineer: J. W. Jacomb-Hood)

Richmond Bridge (85m/280ft by 10m/36ft), architect: James Paine, engineer: Kenton Couse, built 1777; widened 1939

Teddington Lock (198m/650ft), engineer: G. Pooley, two footbridges opened 1889; marks the end of the tidal reach of the Thames

Kingston Railway Bridge, architects: J. E. Errington and W. R. Galbraith, engineer: Thomas Brassey, opened 1863

Kingston Bridge (116m/382ft), engineer: Edward Lapidge,

built 1825–8; widened 1911–14 (engineers: Basil Mott and David Hay) and 1999–2001

Hampton Court Bridge engineers: Samuel Stevens and Benjamin Ludgator, built 1753; replaced by iron bridge 1865; present bridge opened 1933 (architect: Edwin Lutyens, engineer: W. P. Robinson)

CEMETERIES

In 1832, in response to the overcrowding of burial grounds in London, the government authorised the establishment of seven non-denominational cemeteries that would encircle the city. These large cemeteries, known as the 'magnificent seven', were seen by many Victorian families as places in which to demonstrate their wealth and stature, and as a result there are some highly ornate graves and tombs.

THE MAGNIFICENT SEVEN

Abney Park, Stamford Hill, N16 (13ha/32 acres), established 1840; tomb of General Booth, founder of the Salvation Army, and memorials to many nonconformists and dissenters

Brompton, Old Brompton Road, SW10 (16ha/40 acres), established 1840; graves of Sir Henry Cole, Emmeline Pankhurst, John Wisden

Highgate, Swains Lane, N6 (15ha/38 acres), established 1839; graves of Douglas Adams, George Eliot, Michael Faraday, Karl Marx, Christina Rossetti and Radclyffe Hall; western side only accessible as part of a guided tour

Kensal Green, Harrow Road, W10 (31.5ha/79 acres), established 1832; tombs of William Makepeace Thackeray, Anthony Trollope, Sydney Smith, Wilkie Collins, Tom Hood, George Cruikshank, Leigh Hunt, Isambard Kingdom Brunel and Charles Kemble

Nunhead, Linden Grove, SE15 (21ha/52 acres), established 1840; closed in 1969, subsequently restored and opened for burials

Tower Hamlets, Southern Grove, E3 (11ha/27 acres), established 1841; bombed heavily during the Second World War and closed to burials in 1966; now a nature reserve

West Norwood Cemetery and Crematorium, Norwood High Street, SE27 (17ha/42 acres), established 1837; tombs of Sir Henry Bessemer, Mrs Beeton, Sir Henry Tate and Joseph Whitaker *(Whitaker's Almanack)*

OTHER CEMETERIES

Bunhill Fields, City Road, EC1 (1.6ha/4 acres), 17th-century nonconformist burial ground containing the graves of William Blake, John Bunyan and Daniel Defoe

City of London Cemetery and Crematorium, Aldersbrook Road, E12 (81ha/200 acres), established 1856

Golders Green Crematorium, Hoop Lane, NW11 (5ha/12 acres), established 1902; retains the ashes of Kingsley Amis, Peter Sellers, Marc Bolan, Sigmund Freud, Ivor Novello, Bram Stoker, H. G. Wells, Anna Pavlova and Joe Orton

Hampstead, Fortune Green Road, NW6 (10.5ha/26 acres), established 1876; graves of Kate Greenaway, Lord Lister, Marie Lloyd

MARKETS

Billingsgate (fish), a market site for over 1,000 years, with the Lower Thames Street site dating from 1876; moved to the Isle of Dogs (Trafalgar Way, E14) in 1982; owned and run by the Corporation of London

Borough, Southwark Street, SE1 (vegetables, fruit, flowers), established on present site in 1756; privately owned and run

Camden Lock, NW1 (second-hand clothing, jewellery, alternative fashion, crafts), established in 1973

Columbia Road, E2 (flowers), dates from 19th century; became dedicated flower market in the 20th century

Covent Garden, (vegetables, fruit, flowers, etc), established in 1670 under a charter of Charles II; owned and run by the Covent Garden Market Authority, whose board is appointed by DEFRA; moved in 1974 to Nine Elms, SW8

Leadenhall, Leadenhall Street, EC3 (meat, poultry, fish, etc), site of market since 14th century; present hall built 1881; owned and run by the Corporation of London

Petticoat Lane, Middlesex Street, E1, a market has existed on the site for over 500 years, now a Sunday morning market selling almost anything

Portobello Road, W11, originally for herbs and horse-trading from 1870; became famous for antiques after the closure of the Caledonian Market in 1948

Smithfield, EC1 (meat, poultry), built 1866–8, refurbished 1993–4; the site of St Bartholomew's Fair from 12th to 19th century; owned and run by the Corporation of London

New Spitalfields, E10 (vegetables, fruit, flowers), established 1682, modernised 1928, moved out of the City to Leyton in 1991

Old Spitalfields, E1, continues to trade on the original Spitalfields site on Commercial Street, selling arts, crafts, books, clothes, organic food and antiques on Sundays

MONUMENTS

CENOTAPH

Whitehall, SW1. The Cenotaph (from the Greek meaning 'empty tomb') was built to commemorate 'The Glorious Dead' and is a memorial to all ranks of the sea, land and air forces who gave their lives in the service of the Empire during the First World War. Designed by Sir Edwin Lutyens and constructed in plaster as a temporary memorial in 1919, it was replaced by a permanent structure of Portland stone and unveiled by George V on 11 November 1920, Armistice Day. An additional inscription was made in 1946 to commemorate those who gave their lives in the Second World War

FOURTH PLINTH

Trafalgar Square, WC2. The fourth plinth (1841) was designed for an equestrian statue that was never built due to lack of funds. From 1999 temporary works have been displayed on the plinth including *Ecce Homo* (Mark Wallinger), *Regardless of History* (Bill Woodrow), *Monument* (Rachel Whiteread), *Alison Lapper Pregnant* (Marc Quinn) and *Model for a Hotel* (Thomas Schütte). Antony Gormley's project *One & Other* occupied the plinth from July–October 2009, followed by *Nelson's Ship in a Bottle* by Yinka Shonibare

LONDON MONUMENT

(Commonly called the Monument), Monument Street, EC3. Built to designs by Sir Christopher Wren and Robert Hooke between 1671 and 1677, the Monument commemorates the Great Fire of London, which broke out in Pudding Lane on 2 September 1666. The fluted Doric column is 36.6m (120ft) high, the moulded cylinder above the balcony supporting a flaming vase of gilt bronze is an additional 12.8m (42ft), and the column is based on a square plinth 12.2m (40ft) high (with fine carvings on the west face), making a total height of 61.6m (202ft) – the tallest isolated stone column in the world, with views of London from a gallery at the top (311 steps)

OTHER MONUMENTS
(sculptor's name in parentheses):
7 July Memorial (Carmody Groarke), Hyde Park
Viscount Alanbrooke (Roberts-Jones), Whitehall
Albert Memorial (Scott), Kensington Gore
Battle of Britain (Day), Victoria Embankment
Beatty (Wheeler), Trafalgar Square
Belgian Gratitude (setting by Blomfield, statue by Rousseau), Victoria Embankment
Boadicea (or Boudicca), *Queen of the Iceni* (Thornycroft), Westminster Bridge
Brunel (Marochetti), Victoria Embankment
Burghers of Calais (Rodin), Victoria Tower Gardens, Westminster
Burns (Steell), Embankment Gardens
Canada Memorial (Granche), Green Park
Carlyle (Boehm), Chelsea Embankment
Cavalry (Jones), Hyde Park
Edith Cavell (Frampton), St Martin's Place
Charles I (Le Sueur), Trafalgar Square
Charles II (Gibbons), Royal Hospital, Chelsea
Churchill (Roberts-Jones), Parliament Square
Cleopatra's Needle (20.9m/68.5ft high, *c*.1500BC, erected in London in 1878; the sphinxes are Victorian), Thames Embankment
Clive (Tweed), King Charles Street
Captain Cook (Brock), The Mall
Oliver Cromwell (Thornycroft), outside Westminster Hall
Cunningham (Belsky), Trafalgar Square
Gen. Charles de Gaulle (Conner), Carlton Gardens
Diana, Princess of Wales Memorial Fountain (Gustafson Porter), Hyde Park
Disraeli, Earl of Beaconsfield (Raggi), Parliament Square
Lord Dowding (Winter), Strand
Duke of Cambridge (Jones), Whitehall
Duke of York (37.8m/124ft column, with statue by Westmacott), Carlton House Terrace
Edward VII (Mackennal), Waterloo Place
Elizabeth I (Kerwin, 1586, oldest outdoor statue in London; from Ludgate), Fleet Street
Eros (Shaftesbury Memorial) (Gilbert), Piccadilly Circus
Marechal/Marshall Foch (Mallisard, copy of one in Cassel, France), Grosvenor Gardens
Charles James Fox (Westmacott), Bloomsbury Square
George III (Cotes Wyatt), Cockspur Street
George IV (Chantrey), Trafalgar Square
George V (Reid Dick and Scott), Old Palace Yard
George VI (McMillan), Carlton Gardens
Gladstone (Thornycroft), Strand
Guards' (Crimea) (Bell), Waterloo Place
Guards Division (Ledward, figures, Bradshaw, cenotaph), Horse Guards' Parade
Haig (Hardiman), Whitehall
Sir Arthur (Bomber) Harris (Winter), Strand
Gen. Henry Havelock (Behnes), Trafalgar Square
International Brigades Memorial (Spanish Civil War) (Ian Walters), Jubilee Gardens, South Bank
Irving (Brock), north side of National Portrait Gallery
James II (Gibbons), Trafalgar Square
Jellicoe (McMillan), Trafalgar Square
Samuel Johnson (Fitzgerald), opposite St Clement Danes
Kitchener (Tweed), Horse Guards' Parade
Abraham Lincoln (Saint-Gaudens, copy of one in Chicago), Parliament Square
Mandela (Walters), Parliament Square
Milton (Montford), St Giles, Cripplegate
Mountbatten (Belsky), Foreign Office Green
Gen. Charles James Napier (Adams), Trafalgar Square
Nelson (Railton), Trafalgar Square, with Landseer's lions (cast from guns recovered from the wreck of the *Royal George*)
Florence Nightingale (Walker), Waterloo Place
Palmerston (Woolner), Parliament Square
Peel (Noble), Parliament Square
Pitt (Chantrey), Hanover Square
Portal (Nemon), Embankment Gardens
Prince Albert (Bacon), Holborn Circus
Queen Elizabeth Gate (Lund and Wynne), Hyde Park Corner
Queen Mother (Jackson), Carlton Gardens
Raleigh (McMillan), Greenwich
Richard I (Coeur de Lion) (Marochetti), Old Palace Yard
Roberts (Bates), Horse Guards' Parade
Royal Air Force (Blomfield), Victoria Embankment
Franklin D. Roosevelt (Reid Dick), Grosvenor Square
Royal Artillery (Great War) (Jagger and Pearson), Hyde Park Corner
Royal Artillery (South Africa) (Colton), The Mall; *Captain Scott* (Lady Scott), Waterloo Place; *Shackleton* (Jagger), Kensington Gore
Shakespeare (Fontana, copy of one by Scheemakers in Westminster Abbey), Leicester Square
Smuts (Epstein), Parliament Square
Sullivan (Goscombe John), Victoria Embankment
Trenchard (McMillan), Victoria Embankment
Victoria Memorial (Webb and Brock), in front of Buckingham Palace
Raoul Wallenberg (Jackson), Great Cumberland Place
George Washington (Houdon copy), Trafalgar Square
Wellington (Boehm), Hyde Park Corner
Wellington (Chantrey), outside Royal Exchange
John Wesley (Adams Acton), City Road
Westminster School (Crimea) (Scott), Broad Sanctuary
William III (Bacon), St James's Square
Wolseley (Goscombe John), Horse Guards' Parade

PARKS, GARDENS AND OPEN SPACES

CORPORATION OF LONDON OPEN SPACES
W www.cityoflondon.gov.uk
Ashtead Common (200ha/500 acres), Surrey
Burnham Beeches and *Fleet Wood* (220ha/540 acres), Bucks. Purchased by the Corporation for the benefit of the public in 1880, Fleet Wood (26ha/65 acres) being presented in 1921
Coulsdon Common (51ha/127 acres), Surrey
Epping Forest (2,428ha/6,000 acres), Essex. Purchased by the Corporation and opened to the public in 1882. The Queen Elizabeth Hunting Lodge, built for Henry VIII in the mid-16th century lies at the edge of the forest. The present forest is 19.3km (12 miles) long by around 3km (2 miles) wide, approximately one-tenth of its original area
Farthing Downs and New Hill (95ha/235 acres), Surrey
Hampstead Heath (319ha/791 acres), NW3 Including Golders Hill (15ha/36 acres) and Parliament Hill (110ha/271 acres)
Highgate Wood (28ha/70 acres), N6/N10
Kenley Common (56ha/139 acres), Surrey

Queen's Park (12ha/30 acres), NW6
Riddlesdown (43ha/107 acres), Surrey
Spring Park (21ha/51 acres), Kent
West Ham Park (31ha/77 acres), E15
West Wickham Common (10ha/26 acres), Kent
Woodredon and Warlies Park Estate (299ha/740 acres), Waltham Abbey
Also over 150 smaller open spaces within the City of London, including *Finsbury Circus* and *St Dunstan-in-the-East*

OTHER PARKS AND GARDENS
CHELSEA PHYSIC GARDEN, 66 Royal Hospital Road, SW3 4HS T 020-7352 5646 W www.chelseaphysicgarden.co.uk A garden of general botanical research and education, maintaining a wide range of rare and unusual plants; established in 1673 by the Society of Apothecaries
HAMPTON COURT PARK AND GARDENS (303.5ha/750 acres), Surrey KT8 9AU T 0844-482 7777 W www.hrp.org.uk Also known as Home Park, the park lies beyond the palace's formal gardens. It contains a herd of deer and a 1,000-year-old oak tree from the original park
THAMES BARRIER PARK (9ha/22acres), North Woolwich, E16 2HP T 020-7476 3741 W www.thamesbarrierpark.org.uk Opened in 2000, landscaped gardens with spectacular views of the Thames Barrier

ROYAL PARKS
W www.royalparks.gov.uk
Bushy Park (445ha/1,099 acres), Middx. Adjoins Hampton Court; contains avenue of horse-chestnuts enclosed in a fourfold avenue of limes planted by William III
Green Park (19ha/47 acres), W1 Between Piccadilly and St James's Park, with Constitution Hill leading to Hyde Park Corner
Greenwich Park (74ha/183 acres), SE10 Enclosed by Humphrey, Duke of Gloucester, and laid out by Charles II from the designs of Le Nôtre. On a hill in Greenwich Park is the Royal Observatory (founded 1675). Its buildings are now managed by the National Maritime Museum T 020-8858 4422 W www.nmm.ac.uk and the earliest building is named Flamsteed House, after John Flamsteed (1646–1719), the first astronomer royal
Hyde Park (142ha/350 acres), W1/W2 From Park Lane to Kensington Gardens and incorporating the Serpentine lake, Apsley House, the Achilles Statue, Rotten Row and the Ladies' Mile; fine gateway at Hyde Park Corner. To the north-east is Marble Arch, originally erected by George IV at the entrance to Buckingham Palace and re-erected in the present position in 1851
Kensington Gardens (111ha/275 acres), W2/W8 From the western boundary of Hyde Park to Kensington Palace; contains the Albert Memorial, Serpentine Gallery and Peter Pan statue
Kew, Royal Botanic Gardens (120ha/300 acres), Richmond, Surrey TW9 3AB T 020-8332 5655 W www.kew.org Officially inscribed on the UNESCO list of World Heritage Sites
Regent's Park and *Primrose Hill* (197ha/487 acres), NW1 From Marylebone Road to Primrose Hill surrounded by the Outer Circle; divided by the Broad Walk leading to the Zoological Gardens
Richmond Park (1,000ha/2,500 acres), Surrey. Designated a National Nature Reserve, a Site of Special Scientific Interest and a Special Area of Conservation
St James's Park (23ha/58 acres), SW1 From Whitehall to Buckingham Palace; ornamental lake of 4.9 ha (12 acres); the Mall leads from Admiralty Arch to Buckingham Palace, Birdcage Walk from Storey's Gate to Buckingham Palace

PLACES OF HISTORICAL AND CULTURAL INTEREST

1 Canada Square
Canary Wharf, E14 5DY T 020-7418 2000
W www.canarywharf.com
Also known as 'Canary Wharf', the steel and glass skyscraper is the tallest structure in London and the tallest habitable building in the UK

30 St Mary Axe
EC3A 8EP W www.30stmaryaxe.com
Completed in 2004 and commonly known as the 'Gherkin', it is the second-tallest building in the City of London

Alexandra Palace
Alexandra Palace Way, Wood Green, N22 7AY
T 020-8365 2121 W www.alexandrapalace.com
The Victorian palace was severely damaged by fire in 1980 but was restored, and reopened in 1988. Alexandra Palace now provides modern facilities for exhibitions, conferences, banquets and leisure activities. There is a winter ice rink, a boating lake, the Phoenix Bar and a conservation area

Barbican Centre
Silk Street, EC2Y 8DS T 020-7638 4141
W www.barbican.org.uk
Owned, funded and managed by the Corporation of London, the Barbican Centre opened in 1982 and houses the Barbican Theatre, a studio theatre called The Pit and the Barbican Hall; it is also home to the London Symphony Orchestra. There are three cinemas, seven conference rooms, two art galleries, a sculpture court, a lending library, trade and banqueting facilities, a conservatory, shops, restaurants, cafes and bars

British Library
St Pancras, 96 Euston Road, NW1 2DB T 0870-444 1500
W www.bl.uk
The largest building constructed in the UK in the 20th century with basements extending 24.5m underground. Holdings include the *Magna Carta*, the *Lindisfarne Gospels*, Mozart manuscripts and the world's earliest dated printed book, the *Diamond Sutra*. Holds temporary exhibitions on a range of topics

Central Criminal Court
Old Bailey, EC4M 7EH T 020-7248 3277
W www.cityoflondon.gov.uk
The highest criminal court in the UK, the 'Old Bailey' is located on the site of the old Newgate Prison. Trials held here have included those of Oscar Wilde, Dr Crippen and the Yorkshire Ripper. The courthouse has been rebuilt several times since 1674; Edward VII officially opened the current neo-baroque building in 1907

Charterhouse
Charterhouse Square, EC1M 6AN T 020-7253 9503
A Carthusian monastery from 1371 to 1537, purchased in 1611 by Thomas Sutton, who endowed it as a residence for aged men 'of gentle birth' and a school for poor scholars (removed to Godalming in 1872)

Cutty Sark
Greenwich, SE10 T 020-8858 2698
W www.cuttysark.org.uk
The last of the famous tea clippers, it was moved into a specially constructed dry dock in 1954 and opened to the public in 1957. Damaged by fire in 2007, the ship is closed to the public and restoration work is ongoing

Downing Street, SW1
Number 10 Downing Street is the official town residence of the Prime Minister, number 11 of the Chancellor of the Exchequer and number 12 is the office of the Government Whips. The street was named after Sir George Downing, Bt., soldier and diplomat, who was MP for Morpeth 1660–84

George Inn
Borough High Street, SE1 1NH T 020-7407 2056
W www.nationaltrust.org.uk
The last galleried inn in London, built in 1677. Now owned by the National Trust and run as an ordinary public house

Horse Guards, Whitehall, SW1
Archway and offices built about 1753. The changing of the guard takes place daily at 11am (10am on Sundays) and the inspection at 4pm. Only those with the Queen's permission may drive through the gates and archway into *Horse Guards' Parade,* where the colour is 'trooped' on the Queen's official birthday

HOUSES OF PARLIAMENT

House of Commons, Westminster, SW1A 0AA T 020-7219 4272
E hcinfo@parliament.uk W www.parliament.uk

House of Lords, Westminster, SW1A 0PW T 020-7219 3107
E hlinfo@parliament.uk W www.parliament.uk

The royal palace of Westminster, originally built by Edward the Confessor, was the normal meeting place of Parliament from about 1340. St Stephen's Chapel was used from about 1550 for the meetings of the House of Commons, which had previously been held in the Chapter House or Refectory of Westminster Abbey. The House of Lords met in an apartment of the royal palace. The fire of 1834 destroyed much of the palace, and the present Houses of Parliament were erected on the site from the designs of Sir Charles Barry and Augustus Welby Pugin between 1840 and 1867. The chamber of the House of Commons was destroyed by bombing in 1941, and a new chamber designed by Sir Giles Gilbert Scott was used for the first time in 1950. *Westminster Hall and the Crypt Chapel* was the only part of the old palace of Westminster to survive the fire of 1834. It was built by William II from 1097 to 1099 and altered by Richard II between 1394 and 1399. The hammerbeam roof of carved oak dates from 1396–8. The Hall was the scene of the trial of Charles I. *The Victoria Tower* of the House of Lords is 98.5m (323ft) high, and when Parliament is sitting, the Union flag flies by day from its flagstaff. *The Clock Tower* of the House of Commons is 96.3m (316ft) high and contains 'Big Ben', the hour bell said to be named after Sir Benjamin Hall, First Commissioner of Works when the original bell was cast in 1856. This bell, which weighed 16 tons 11 cwt, was found to be cracked in 1857. The present bell (13.5 tons) is a recasting of the original and was first brought into use in 1859. The dials of the clock are 7m (23ft) in diameter, the hands being 2.7m (9ft) and 4.3m (14ft) long (including balance piece). A light is displayed from the Clock Tower at night when parliament is sitting.

During session, tours of the Houses of Parliament are only available to UK residents who have made advance arrangements through an MP or peer. Overseas visitors are no longer provided with permits to tour the Houses of Parliament during session, although they can tour during the summer opening and attend debates for both houses in the Strangers' Galleries. During the summer recess tickets for tours of the Houses of Parliament can be booked by telephone (T 0870-906 3773) or bought on site at the ticket office on Abingdon Green opposite Parliament and the Victoria Tower Gardens. The Strangers' Gallery of the House of Commons is open to the public when the house is sitting. To acquire tickets in advance UK residents should write to their local MP and overseas visitors should apply to their embassy or high commission in the UK for a permit. If none of these arrangements has been made, visitors should join the public queue outside St Stephen's Entrance, where there is also a queue for entry to the House of Lords Gallery

INNS OF COURT

The Inns of Court are ancient unincorporated bodies of lawyers which for more than five centuries have had the power to call to the Bar those of their members who have qualified for the rank or degree of Barrister-at-Law. There are four Inns of Court as well as many lesser inns

Lincoln's Inn, Chancery Lane/Lincoln's Inn Fields, WC2A 3TL T 020-7405 1393 W www.lincolnsinn.org.uk
The most ancient of the inns with records dating back to 1422. The hall and library buildings are from 1845, although the library is first mentioned in 1474; the old hall (late 15th century) and the chapel were rebuilt *c.*1619–23

Inner Temple, King's Bench Walk, EC4Y 7HL
T 020-7797 8250 W www.innertemple.org.uk

Middle Temple, Middle Temple Lane, EC4Y 9AT
T 020-7427 4800 W www.middletemple.org.uk
Records for the Middle and Inner Temple date back to the beginning of the 16th century. The site was originally occupied by the Order of Knights Templar *c.*1160–1312. The two inns have separate halls thought to have been formed *c.*1350. The division between the two societies was formalised in 1732 with Temple Church and the Masters House remaining in common. The Inner Temple Garden is normally open to the public on weekdays between 12.30pm and 3pm

Temple Church, EC4Y 7BB T 020-7353 8559
W www.templechurch.com
The nave forms one of five remaining round churches in England

Gray's Inn, South Square, WC1R 5ET T 020-7458 7800
W www.graysinn.org.uk
Founded early 14th century; Hall 1556–8
No other 'Inns' are active, but there are remains of *Staple Inn,* a gabled front on Holborn (opposite Gray's Inn Road). *Clement's Inn* (near St Clement Danes Church), *Clifford's Inn,* Fleet Street, and *Thavies Inn,* Holborn Circus, are all rebuilt. *Serjeants' Inn,* Fleet Street, and another (demolished 1910) of the same name in Chancery Lane, were composed of Serjeants-at-Law, the last of whom died in 1922

Institute of Contemporary Arts
The Mall, SW1Y 5AH T 020-7930 3647 W www.ica.org.uk
Exhibitions of modern art in the fields of film, theatre, new media and the visual arts

Lloyd's
Lime Street, EC3M 7HA T 020-7327 1000
W www.lloyds.com
International insurance market which evolved during the 17th century from Lloyd's Coffee House. The present building was opened for business in May 1986, and houses the Lutine Bell. Underwriting is on three floors with a total area of 10,591 sq. m (114,000 sq. ft). The Lloyd's building is not open to the general public

London Central Mosque and the Islamic Cultural Centre
Park Road, NW8 7RG T 020-7724 3363 W www.iccuk.org
The focus for London's Muslims; established in 1944 but not completed until 1977, the mosque can accommodate about 5,000 worshippers; guided tours are available

London Eye
South Bank, SE1 7PB T 0870-990 8883
W www.londoneye.com
Opened in March 2000 as London's millennium landmark, this 450ft observation wheel is the capital's fourth-largest structure. The wheel provides a 30-minute ride offering panoramic views of the capital

London Zoo
Regent's Park, NW1 4RY T 020-7722 3333
W www.londonzoo.org

Madame Tussauds
Marylebone Road, NW1 5LR T 0870-999 0046
W www.madametussauds.com
Waxwork exhibition

Marlborough House
Pall Mall, SW1Y 5HX T 020-7747 6500
W www.thecommonwealth.org
Built by Wren for the first Duke of Marlborough and completed in 1711, the house reverted to the Crown in 1835. In 1863 it became the London house of the Prince of Wales and was the London home of Queen Mary until her death in 1953. In 1959 Marlborough House was given by the Queen as the headquarters for the Commonwealth Secretariat and it was opened as such in 1965. The Queen's Chapel, Marlborough Gate, was begun in 1623 from the designs of Inigo Jones for the Infanta Maria of Spain, and completed for Queen Henrietta Maria. Marlborough House is not open to the public

Mansion House
Cannon Street, EC4N 8BH T 020-7626 2500
W www.cityoflondon.gov.uk
The official residence of the Lord Mayor. Built in the 18th century in the Palladian style. Open to groups by appointment only

Neasden Temple
BAPS Shri Swaminarayan Mandir, 105–119 Brentfield Road, Neasden, NW10 8LD T 020-8965 2651 W www.mandir.org
The first and largest traditional Hindu Mandir outside of India; opened in 1995

Port of London
Port of London Authority, Bakers' Hall, 7 Harp Lane, EC3R 6LB T 01474-562200 W www.pla.co.uk
The Port of London covers the tidal section of the river Thames from Teddington to the seaward limit (the outer Tongue buoy and the Sunk light vessel), a distance of 150km. The governing body is the Port of London Authority (PLA). Cargo is handled at privately operated riverside terminals between Fulham and Canvey Island, including the enclosed dock at Tilbury, 40km below London Bridge. Passenger vessels and cruise liners can be handled at moorings at Greenwich, Tower Bridge and Tilbury

Roman Remains
The city wall of Roman *Londinium* was largely rebuilt during the medieval period but sections may be seen near the White Tower in the Tower of London; at Tower Hill; at Coopers' Row; at All Hallows, London Wall, its vestry being built on the remains of a semi-circular Roman bastion; at St Alphage, London Wall, showing a succession of building repairs from the Roman until the late medieval period; and at St Giles, Cripplegate. Sections of the great forum and basilica, more than 165 sq. m, have been encountered during excavations in the area of Leadenhall, Gracechurch Street and Lombard Street. Traces of Roman activity along the river include a massive riverside wall built in the late Roman period, and a succession of Roman timber quays along Lower and Upper Thames Street. Finds from these sites can be seen at the Museum of London.

Other major buildings are the amphitheatre at Guildhall, remains of bath-buildings in Upper and Lower Thames Street, and the temple of Mithras in Walbrook

Royal Albert Hall
Kensington Gore, SW7 2AP T 020-7589 8212
W www.royalalberthall.com
The elliptical hall, one of the largest in the world, was completed in 1871; since 1941 it has been the venue each summer for the Promenade Concerts founded in 1895 by Sir Henry Wood. Other events include pop and classical music concerts, dance, opera, sporting events, conferences and banquets

Royal Courts of Justice
Strand, WC2A 2LL T 020-7947 6000
W www.hmcourts-service.gov.uk
Victorian Gothic building that is home to the High Court. Visitors are free to watch proceedings

Royal Hospital, Chelsea
Royal Hospital Road, SW3 4SR T 020-7881 5200
W www.chelsea-pensioners.co.uk
Founded by Charles II in 1682, and built by Wren; opened in 1692 for old and disabled soldiers. The extensive grounds include the former Ranelagh Gardens and are the venue for the Chelsea Flower Show each May

Royal Naval College
Greenwich, SE10 9LW T 020-8269 4747
W www.greenwichfoundation.org.uk
The building was the Greenwich Hospital until 1869. It was built by Charles II, largely from designs by John Webb, and by Queen Mary II and William III, from designs by Wren. It stands on the site of an ancient abbey, a royal house and Greenwich Palace, which was constructed by Henry VII. Henry VIII, Mary I and Elizabeth I were born in the royal palace and Edward VI died there

Royal Opera House
Covent Garden, WC2E 9DD T 020-7240 1200
W www.roh.org.uk
Home of The Royal Ballet (1931) and The Royal Opera (1946). The Royal Opera House is the third theatre to be built on the site, opening 1858; the first was opened in 1732

St James's Palace
Pall Mall, SW1A 1BQ T 020-7930 4832
W www.royal.gov.uk
Built by Henry VIII, only the Gatehouse and Presence Chamber remain; later alterations were made by Wren

and Kent. Representatives of foreign powers are still accredited 'to the Court of St James's'. *Clarence House* (1825), the official London residence of the Prince of Wales and his sons, stands within the St James's Palace estate

St Paul's Cathedral
St Paul's Churchyard, EC4M 8AD **T** 020-7236 4128
E chapter@stpaulscathedral.org.uk **W** www.stpauls.co.uk
Built 1675–1710. The cross on the dome is 111m (365ft) above ground level, the inner cupola 66.4m (218ft) above the floor. 'Great Paul' in the south-west tower weighs nearly 17 tons. The organ by Father Smith (enlarged by Willis and rebuilt by Mander) is in a case carved by Grinling Gibbons, who also carved the choir stalls

Somerset House
Strand, WC2R 1LA **T** 020 7845 4600
W www.somersethouse.org.uk
The river facade (183m/600ft long) was built in 1776–1801 from the designs of Sir William Chambers; the eastern extension, which houses part of King's College, was built by Smirke in 1829–35. Somerset House was the property of Lord Protector Somerset, at whose attainder in 1552 the palace passed to the Crown, and it was a royal residence until 1692. Somerset House has recently undergone extensive renovation and is home to the Gilbert Collection, Embankment Galleries and the Courtauld Institute Gallery. Open-air concerts and ice-skating (Dec–Jan) are held in the courtyard

SOUTH BANK, SE1
Arts complex on the south bank of the river Thames which consists of:

The Royal Festival Hall **T** 0871-663 2500
W www.southbankcentre.co.uk
Opened in 1951 for the Festival of Britain, adjacent are the *Queen Elizabeth Hall*, the *Purcell Room*, and the *Hayward Gallery*

BFI Southbank **T** 020-7255 1444 **W** www.bfi.org.uk
Opened in 1952 and is administered by the British Film Institute, has three auditoria and an IMAX cinema. The London Film Festival is held here every November

The *Royal National Theatre*, **T** 020-7452 3000
W www.nationaltheatre.org.uk
Opened in 1976, comprises the Olivier, the Lyttelton and the Cottesloe theatres

Southwark Cathedral
London Bridge, SE1 9DA **T** 020-7367 6700
W www.cathedral.southwark.anglican.org
Mainly 13th century, but the nave is largely rebuilt. The tomb of John Gower (1330–1408) is between the Bunyan and Chaucer memorial windows in the north aisle; Shakespeare's effigy, backed by a view of Southwark and the Globe Theatre, is in the south aisle; the tomb of Bishop Andrewes (*d.*1626) is near the screen. The Lady Chapel was the scene of the consistory courts of the reign of Mary (Gardiner and Bonner) and is still used as a consistory court. John Harvard, after whom Harvard University is named, was baptised here in 1607, and the chapel by the north choir aisle is his memorial chapel

Thames Embankments
Sir Joseph Bazalgette (1819–91) constructed the *Victoria Embankment*, on the north side from Westminster to Blackfriars for the Metropolitan Board of Works, 1864–70; (the seats, of which the supports of some are a kneeling camel, laden with spicery, and of others a winged sphinx, were presented by the Grocers' Company and by W. H. Smith, MP, in 1874); the *Albert Embankment*, on the south side from Westminster Bridge to Vauxhall, 1866–9, and the Chelsea Embankment, 1871–4. The total cost exceeded £2m. Bazalgette also inaugurated the London main drainage system, 1858–65. A medallion *(Flumini vincula posuit)* has been placed on a pier of the *Victoria Embankment* to commemorate the engineer

Thames Flood Barrier
W www.environment-agency.gov.uk
Officially opened in May 1984, though first used in February 1983, the barrier consists of ten rising sector gates which span approximately 570 yards from bank to bank of the Thames at Woolwich Reach. When not in use the gates lie horizontally, allowing shipping to navigate the river normally; when the barrier is closed, the gates turn through 90 degrees to stand vertically more than 50 feet above the river bed. The barrier took eight years to complete and can be raised within about 30 minutes

Trafalgar Tavern
Park Row, Greenwich, SE10 9NW **T** 020-8858 2909
W www.trafalgartavern.co.uk
Regency-period riverside public house built in 1837. Charles Dickens and William Gladstone were patrons

Westminster Abbey
Broad Sanctuary, SW1P 3PA **T** 020-7222 5152
E info@westminster-abbey.org
W www.westminster-abbey.org
Founded as a Benedictine monastery over 1,000 years ago, the church was rebuilt by Edward the Confessor in 1065 and again by Henry III in the 13th century. The abbey is the resting place for monarchs including Edward I, Henry III, Henry V, Henry VII, Elizabeth I, Mary I and Mary Queen of Scots, and has been the setting of coronations since that of William the Conqueror in 1066. In Poets' Corner there are memorials to many literary figures, and many scientists and musicians are also remembered here. The grave of the Unknown Warrior is to be found in the nave

Westminster Cathedral
Francis Street, SW1P 1QW **T** 020-7798 9055
W www.westminstercathedral.org.uk
Roman Catholic cathedral built 1895–1903 from the designs of J. F. Bentley. The campanile is 284ft high

LONDON THEATRES

Adelphi Theatre, Strand, WC2R 0NS **T** 020 7344 0055
⊖ Charing Cross

Aldwych Theatre, Aldwych, WC2B 4DF **T** 020-7379 3367
⊖ Covent Garden/Holborn

Almeida Theatre, Almeida Street, N1 1TA **T** 020-7359 4404
⊖ Angel/Highbury & Islington

Apollo Theatre, Shaftesbury Avenue, W1D 7EZ
T 0870-890 1101 ⊖ Piccadilly Circus

Apollo Victoria Theatre, Wilton Road, SW1 1LL
T 020-7834 6318 ⊖ Victoria

Arcola Theatre, Arcola Street, E8 2DJ **T** 020-7503 1646
⊖ Highbury and Islington/Liverpool Street

Barbican Theatre, Barbican Centre, EC2Y 8DS
T 020-7638 8891 ⊖ Barbican/Moorgate

Bloomsbury Theatre, Gordon Street, WC1H 0AH
T 020-7388 8822 ⊖ Euston/Euston Square

Cambridge Theatre, Earlham Street, WC2 9HU
T 0870-890 1102 ⊖ Covent Garden/Leicester Square

Chelsea Theatre, World's End Place, SW10 0DR
T 020-7352 1967 ⊖ Sloane Square

Comedy Theatre, Panton Street, SW1Y 4DN
T 0870-060 6637 ⊖ Leicester Square/Piccadilly Circus
Criterion Theatre, Jermyn Street, SW1Y 4XA
T 020-7839 8811 ⊖ Piccadilly Circus
Dominion Theatre, Tottenham Court Road, W1T 7AQ
T 020-7927 0900 ⊖ Tottenham Court Road
Donmar Warehouse, Earlham Street, WC2H 9LX
T 0870-060 6624 ⊖ Covent Garden
Duchess Theatre, Catherine Street, WC2B 5LA
T 020-7494 5075 ⊖ Covent Garden
Duke Of York's Theatre, St Martin's Lane, WC2N 4BG
T 0870-060 6623 ⊖ Leicester Square/Piccadilly Circus
Fortune Theatre, Russell Street, WC2B 5HH T 0870-060 6626
⊖ Covent Garden
Garrick Theatre, Charing Cross Road, WC2H 0HH
T 020-7520 5690 ⊖ Charing Cross/Leicester Square
Gielgud Theatre, Shaftesbury Avenue, W1D 6AR
T 0844-482 5130 ⊖ Piccadilly Circus
Globe Theatre, New Globe Walk, SE1 9DT T 020-401 9919
⊖ Mansion House
Hackney Empire, Mare Street, E8 1EJ T 020-8985 2424
⊖ Bethnal Green
Her Majesty's Theatre, Haymarket, SW1Y 4QL
T 0844-412 2707 ⊖ Piccadilly Circus
Jermyn Street Theatre, Jermyn Street, SW1Y 6ST
T 020-7287 2875 ⊖ Piccadilly Circus
Leicester Square Theatre, Leicester Place, WC2H 7BX
T 020-7534 1740 ⊖ Leicester Square
London Coliseum, St Martin's Lane, WC2N 4ES
T 0870-145 0200 ⊖ Charing Cross
London Palladium, Argyll Street, W1F 7TF T 020-7494 5020
⊖ Oxford Circus
Lyceum Theatre, Wellington Street, WC2E 7RQ
T 0870-243 9000 ⊖ Covent Garden
Lyric Theatre, Shaftesbury Avenue, W1D 7ES
T 0870-040 0081 ⊖ Piccadilly Circus
Lyric Theatre Hammersmith, King Street, W6 0QL
T 0871-221 1729 ⊖ Hammersmith
National Theatre, South Bank, SE1 9PX T 020-7452 3000
⊖ Waterloo
New Ambassadors Theatre, West Street, WC2H 9ND
T 08448-112334 ⊖ Leicester Square
New London Theatre, Drury Lane, WC2B 5PW
T 020-7242 9802 ⊖ Holborn
Noël Coward (formerly Albery), St Martin's Lane,
WC2N 4AA T 0844-482 5141 ⊖ Leicester Square
Novello Theatre, Aldwych, WC2B 4LD T 0844-482 5120
⊖ Charing Cross
Old Vic Theatre, The Cut, SE1 8NB T 0870-060 6628
⊖ Waterloo
Palace Theatre, Shaftesbury Avenue, W1V 8AY
T 0844-755 0016 ⊖ Leicester Square/Piccadilly Circus
Phoenix Theatre, Charing Cross Road, WC2H 0JP
T 0870-060 6629 ⊖ Tottenham Court Road
Piccadilly Theatre, Denman Street, W1D 7DY
T 020-7478 8800 ⊖ Piccadilly Circus
Playhouse Theatre, Northumberland Avenue, WC2N 5DE
T 0870-060 6631 ⊖ Embankment
Prince Edward Theatre, Old Compton Street, W1D 4HS
T 0844-482 5151 ⊖ Leicester Square
Prince of Wales Theatre, Coventry Street, W1D 6AS
T 0844-482 5115 ⊖ Piccadilly Circus
Queen's Theatre, Shaftesbury Avenue, W1D 6BA
T 020-7395 5243 ⊖ Piccadilly Circus
Riverside Studios, Crisp Road, W6 9RL T 020-8237 1111
⊖ Hammersmith
Royal Albert Hall, Kensington Gore, SW7 2AP
T 020-7589 8212 ⊖ South Kensington
Royal Court Theatre, Sloane Square, SW1W 8AS
T 020-7565 5000 ⊖ Sloane Square
Royal Festival Hall, South Bank SE1 8XX T 0871-663 2500
⊖ Waterloo
Sadler's Wells, Rosebery Avenue, EC1R 4TN T 020-7863 8198
⊖ Angel
St Martin's Theatre, West Street, WC2H 9NZ
T 08444-991515 ⊖ Leicester Square
Savoy Theatre, Strand, WC2R 0ET T 0870-164 8787
⊖ Charing Cross
Shaftesbury Theatre, Shaftesbury Avenue, WC2H 8DP
T 020-7379 5399 ⊖ Holborn/Tottenham Court Road
Soho Theatre, Dean Street, W1D 3NE T 020-7287 5060
⊖ Tottenham Court Road
Southwark Playhouse, Shipwright Yard, SE1 2TF
T 0844-847 1656 ⊖ Southwark
Theatre Royal Drury Lane, Catherine Street, WC2B 5JF
T 0870-890 1109 ⊖ Covent Garden
Theatre Royal Haymarket, Haymarket, SW1Y 4HT
T 020-7930 8890 ⊖ Piccadilly Circus
Trafalgar Studios, Whitehall, SW1A 2DY
T 0871-297 5454 ⊖ Charing Cross/Embankment
Tricycle Theatre, Kilburn High Road, NW6 7JR
T 020-7372 6611 ⊖ Kilburn
Unicorn Theatre, Tooley Street SE1 2HZ T 020-7645 0560
⊖ London Bridge
Vaudeville Theatre, Strand, WC2R 0NH T 0870-890 0511
⊖ Charing Cross
Victoria Palace Theatre, Victoria Street, SW1E 5EA
T 0844-248 5000 ⊖ Victoria
Wyndham's Theatre, Charing Cross Road, WC2H 0DA
T 0844-482 5120 ⊖ Leicester Square
Young Vic, The Cut, SE1 8LZ T 020-7922 2922
⊖ Waterloo

HALLMARKS

Hallmarks are the symbols stamped on gold, silver or platinum articles to indicate that they have been tested at an official Assay Office and that they conform to one of the legal standards.The marking of gold and silver articles to identify the maker was instituted in England in 1363 under a statute of Edward III. In 1478 the Assay Office in Goldsmiths' Hall was established and all gold and silversmiths were required to bring their wares to be date-marked by the Hall, hence the term 'hallmarked'.

With certain exceptions, all gold, silver or platinum articles are required by law to be hallmarked before they are offered for sale. Current hallmarking requirements come under the UK Hallmarking Act 1973 and subsequent amendments. The act is built around the principle of description, where it is an offence for any person to apply to an unhallmarked article a description indicating that it is wholly or partly made of gold, silver or platinum. There is an exemption by weight: compulsory hallmarks are not needed on gold under 1g, silver under 7.78g and platinum under 0.5g. Also, some descriptions, such as rolled gold and gold plate, are permissible. The four assay offices at London, Birmingham, Sheffield and Edinburgh operate under the act.

COMPULSORY MARKS

Since January 1999 UK hallmarks have consisted of three compulsory symbols – the sponsor's mark, the millesimal fineness (purity) mark and the assay office mark. The distinction between UK and foreign articles has been removed, and more finenesses are now legal, reflecting the more common finenesses elsewhere in Europe.

SPONSOR'S MARK

Formerly known as the maker's mark, the sponsor's mark was instituted in England in 1363. Originally a device such as a bird or fleur-de-lis, now it consists of a combination of at least two initials (usually a shortened form of the manufacturer's name) and a shield design. The London Assay Office offers 45 standard shield designs but other designs are possible by arrangement.

MILLESIMAL FINENESS MARK

The millesimal fineness (purity) mark indicates the number of parts per thousand of pure metal in the alloy. The current finenesses allowed in the UK are:

Gold	999	
	990	
	916.6	(22 carat)
	750	(18 carat)
	585	(14 carat)
	375	(9 carat)
Silver	999	
	958.4	(Britannia)
	925	(sterling)
	800	
Platinum	999	
	950	
	900	
	850	

ASSAY OFFICE MARK

This mark identifies the particular assay office at which the article was tested and marked. The British assay offices are:

LONDON, Goldsmiths' Hall, Gutter Lane, London EC2V 8AQ T 020-7606 8971 W www.thegoldsmiths.co.uk

BIRMINGHAM, PO Box 151, Newhall Street, Birmingham B3 1SB T 0121-236 6951 W www.theassayoffice.co.uk

SHEFFIELD, Guardians' Hall, 137 Portobello Street, Sheffield S1 4DS T 0114-275 5111 W www.assayoffice.co.uk

EDINBURGH, Goldsmiths' Hall, 24a Broughton Street, Edinburgh EH1 3RH T 0131-556 1144 W www.assayofficescotland.com

Assay offices formerly existed in other towns, eg Chester, Exeter, Glasgow, Newcastle, Norwich and York, each having its own distinguishing mark.

OPTIONAL MARKS

Since 1999 traditional pictorial marks such as a crown for gold, the Britannia for 958 silver, the lion passant for 925 silver (lion rampant in Scotland) and the orb for 950 platinum may be added voluntarily to the millesimal mark.

Gold – a crown

Britannia silver

Sterling silver (England)

Sterling silver (Scotland)

Platinum – an orb

DATE LETTER

The date letter shows the year in which an article was assayed and hallmarked. Each alphabetical cycle has a distinctive style of lettering or shape of shield. The date letters were different at the various assay offices and the particular office must be established from the assay office mark before reference is made to tables of date letters. Date letter marks became voluntary from 1 January 1999.

The table which follows shows one specimen shield and letter used by the London Assay Office on silver articles for each alphabetical cycle from 1498. The same letters are found on gold articles but the surrounding shield may differ. Until 1 January 1975 two calendar years are given for each specimen date letter as the letter changed annually in May on St Dunstan's Day (the patron saint of silversmiths). Since 1 January 1975, each date letter has indicated a calendar year from January to December and each office has used the same style of date letter and shield for all articles:

LONDON (GOLDSMITHS' HALL) DATE LETTERS FROM 1498

	from	*to*
	1498–9	1517–18
	1518–19	1537–8
	1538–9	1557–8
	1558–9	1577–8
	1578–9	1597–8
	1598–9	1617–18
	1618–19	1637–8
	1638–9	1657–8
	1658–9	1677–8
	1678–9	1696–7
	1697	1715–16
	1716–17	1735–6
	1736–7	1738–9
	1739–40	1755–6
	1756–7	1775–6
	1776–7	1795–6
	1796–7	1815–16
	1816–17	1835–6
	1836–7	1855–6
	1856–7	1875–6
	1876–7 [A to M square shield, N to Z as shown]	1895–6
	1896–7	1915–16
	1916–17	1935–6
	1936–7	1955–6
	1956–7	1974
	1975	1999
	2000	

OTHER MARKS

FOREIGN GOODS

Foreign goods imported into the UK are required to be hallmarked before sale, unless they already bear a convention mark (*see* below) or a hallmark struck by an independent assay office in the European Economic Area which is deemed to be equivalent to a UK hallmark.

The following are the assay office marks used for gold imported articles until the end of 1998. For silver and platinum the symbols remain the same but the shields differ in shape.

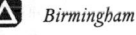

 *London*

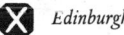

 *Sheffield*

 *Birmingham*

 *Edinburgh*

CONVENTION HALLMARKS

Special marks at authorised assay offices of the signatory countries of the International Convention on Hallmarking (Austria, the Czech Republic, Denmark, Finland, Hungary, Ireland, Latvia, Lithuania, the Netherlands, Norway, Poland, Portugal, Sweden, Switzerland, UK and Ukraine) are legally recognised in the United Kingdom as approved hallmarks. These consist of a sponsor's mark, a common control mark, a fineness mark (arabic numerals showing the standard in parts per thousand), and an assay office mark. There is no date letter.

The common control marks are:

GOLD SILVER PLATINUM

COMMEMORATIVE MARKS

There are other marks to commemorate special events: the silver jubilee of King George V and Queen Mary in 1935, the coronation of Queen Elizabeth II in 1953, and her silver jubilee in 1977. During 1999 and 2000 there was a voluntary additional Millennium Mark. A mark to commemorate the golden jubilee of Queen Elizabeth II was available during 2002.

BRITISH CURRENCY

The unit of currency is the pound sterling (£) of 100 pence. The decimal system was introduced on 15 February 1971.

COIN

Gold Coins
One hundred pounds £100*
Fifty pounds £50*
Twenty-five pounds £25*
Ten pounds £10*
Five pounds £5
Two pounds £2
Sovereign £1
Half-sovereign 50p

Silver Coins (Britannia coins)*
Two pounds £2
One pound £1
Fifty pence 50p
Twenty pence 20p

Maundy Money†
Fourpence 4p
Threepence 3p
Twopence 2p
Penny 1p

Bi-colour Coins‡
Two pounds £2

Nickel-Brass Coins
Two pounds £2 (pre-1997)§
One pound £1

Cupro-Nickel Coins
Crown £5 (since 1990)§
Fifty pence 50p
Crown 25p (pre-1990)§
Twenty pence 20p
Ten pence 10p
Five pence 5p

Bronze Coins
Two pence 2p
One penny 1p

Copper-plated Steel Coins¶
Two pence 2p
One penny 1p

* Britannia coins: gold bullion coins introduced 1987; silver coins introduced 1997
† Gifts of special money distributed by the sovereign annually on Maundy Thursday to the number of elderly men and women corresponding to the sovereign's own age
‡ Cupro-nickel centre and nickel-brass outer ring
§ Commemorative coins; not intended for general circulation
¶ Since September 1992, although in 1998 the 2p was struck in both copper-plated steel and bronze

GOLD COIN
Gold ceased to circulate during the First World War. Since then controls on buying, selling and holding gold coins have been imposed at various times but have subsequently been revoked. Under the Exchange Control (Gold Coins Exemption) Order 1979, gold coins may now be imported and exported without restriction, except gold coins which are more than 50 years old and valued at a sum in excess of £8,000; these cannot be exported without specific authorisation from the Department for Business, Innovation and Skills.

Value Added Taxation on the sale of gold coins was revoked in 2000.

SILVER COIN
Prior to 1920 silver coins were struck from sterling silver, an alloy of which 925 parts in 1,000 were silver. In 1920 the proportion of silver was reduced to 500 parts. Since 1947 all 'silver' coins, except Maundy money, have been struck from cupro-nickel, an alloy of 75 parts copper and 25 parts nickel, except for the 20p, composed of 84 parts copper, 16 parts nickel. Maundy coins continue to be struck from sterling silver.

BRONZE COIN
Bronze, introduced in 1860 to replace copper, is an alloy consisting mainly of copper with small amounts of zinc and tin. Bronze was replaced by copper-plated steel in September 1992 with the exception of 1998 when the 2p was made in both copper-plated steel and bronze.

LEGAL TENDER

Gold (dated 1838 onwards, if not below least current weight)	to any amount
£5 (Crown since 1990)*	to any amount
£2	to any amount
£1	to any amount
50p	up to £10
25p (Crown pre-1990)*	up to £10
20p	up to £10
10p	up to £5
5p	up to £5
2p	up to 20p
1p	up to 20p

* Only redeemable at the Post Office

The £1 coin was introduced in 1983 to replace the £1 note. The following coins have ceased to be legal tender:

Farthing	31 Dec 1960
Halfpenny (½d)	31 Jul 1969
Half-crown	31 Dec 1969
Threepence	31 Aug 1971
Penny (1d)	31 Aug 1971
Sixpence	30 Jun 1980
Halfpenny (½p)	31 Dec 1984
Old 5 pence	31 Dec 1990
Old 10 pence	30 Jun 1993
Old 50 pence	28 Feb 1998

The Channel Islands and the Isle of Man issue their own coinage, which is legal tender only in the island of issue.

	Metal	*Standard weight (g)*	*Standard diameter (mm)*
1p	bronze	3.56	20.3
1p	copper-plated steel	3.56	20.3
2p	bronze	7.13	25.9
2p	copper-plated steel	7.13	25.9
5p	cupro-nickel	3.25	18.0
10p	cupro-nickel	6.5	24.5
20p	cupro-nickel	5.0	21.4
25p Crown	cupro-nickel	28.28	38.6
50p	cupro-nickel	8.00	27.3
£1	nickel-brass	9.5	22.5
£2	nickel-brass	15.98	28.4
£2	cupro-nickel, nickel-brass	12.00	28.4
£5 Crown	cupro-nickel	28.28	38.6

The 'remedy' is the amount of variation from standard permitted in weight and fineness of coins when first issued from the Royal Mint.

THE TRIAL OF THE PYX

The Trial of the Pyx is the examination by a jury to ascertain that coins made by the Royal Mint, which have been set aside in the pyx (or box), are of the proper weight, diameter and composition required by law. The trial is held annually, presided over by the Queen's Remembrancer, with a jury of freemen of the Company of Goldsmiths.

BANKNOTES

Bank of England notes are currently issued in denominations of £5, £10, £20 and £50 for the amount of the fiduciary note issue, and are legal tender in England and Wales. No £1 notes have been issued since 1984 and in March 1998 the outstanding notes were written off in accordance with the provision of the Currency Act 1983.

The current E series of notes was introduced from June 1990, replacing the D series (*see* below). A new-style £20 note, the first in series F, was introduced on 13 March 2007. The historical figures portrayed in these series are:

£5	May 2002–date	Elizabeth Fry
£5	Jun 1990–2003	George Stephenson*
£10	Nov 2000–date	Charles Darwin
£10	Apr 1992–2003	Charles Dickens*
£20	Mar 2007–date	Adam Smith
£20	Jun 1999–date	Sir Edward Elgar
£20	Jun 1991–2001	Michael Faraday*
£50	Apr 1994–date	Sir John Houblon

* These notes have been withdrawn from circulation: George Stephenson on 21 Nov 2003; Charles Dickens on 31 Jul 2003; Michael Faraday on 28 Feb 2001

NOTE CIRCULATION

Note circulation is highest at the two peak spending periods of the year, around Christmas and during the summer holiday period.

The value of notes in circulation (£ million) at the end of February 2008 and 2009 was:

	2008	*2009*
£5	1,242	1,302
£10	6,115	6,304
£20	25,648	28,089
£50	7,526	8,691
Other notes*	4,447	4,222
TOTAL	44,978	48,608

* Includes higher value notes used internally in the Bank of England, eg as cover for the note issues of banks in Scotland and Northern Ireland in excess of their permitted issue

LEGAL TENDER

Banknotes which are no longer legal tender are payable when presented at the head office of the Bank of England in London.

The white notes for £10, £20, £50, £100, £500 and £1,000, which were issued until April 1943, ceased to be legal tender in May 1945, and the white £5 note in March 1946.

The white £5 note issued between October 1945 and September 1956, the £5 notes issued between 1957 and 1963 (bearing a portrait of Britannia) and the first series to bear a portrait of the Queen, issued between 1963 and 1971, ceased to be legal tender in March 1961, June 1967 and September 1973 respectively.

The series of £1 notes issued during the years 1928 to 1960 and the 10 shilling notes issued from 1928 to 1961 (those without the royal portrait) ceased to be legal tender in May and October 1962 respectively. The £1 note first issued in March 1960 (bearing on the back a representation of Britannia) and the £10 note first issued in February 1964 (bearing a lion on the back), both bearing a portrait of the Queen on the front, ceased to be legal tender in June 1979. The £1 note first issued in 1978 ceased to be legal tender on 11 March 1988. The 10 shilling note was replaced by the 50p coin in October 1969, and ceased to be legal tender on 21 November 1970.

The D series of banknotes was introduced from 1970 and ceased to be legal tender from the dates shown below. The predominant identifying feature of each note was the portrayal on the back of a prominent figure from British history:

£1	Feb 1978–Mar 1988	Sir Isaac Newton
£5	Nov 1971–Nov 1991	Duke of Wellington
£10	Feb 1975–May 1994	Florence Nightingale
£20	Jul 1970–Mar 1993	William Shakespeare
£50	Mar 1981–Sep 1996	Sir Christopher Wren

The £1 coin was introduced on 21 April 1983 to replace the £1 note.

OTHER BANKNOTES

Scotland – Banknotes are issued by three Scottish banks. The Royal Bank of Scotland issues notes for £1, £5, £10, £20, £50 and £100. Bank of Scotland and the Clydesdale Bank issue notes for £5, £10, £20, £50 and £100. Scottish notes are not legal tender in the UK but they are an authorised currency.

Northern Ireland – Banknotes are issued by four banks in Northern Ireland. The Bank of Ireland, the Northern Bank and the Ulster Bank issue notes for £5, £10, £20, £50 and £100. The First Trust Bank issues notes for £10, £20, £50 and £100. Northern Ireland notes are not legal tender in Northern Ireland but they circulate widely and enjoy a status comparable to that of Bank of England notes.

Channel Islands – The States of Guernsey issues its own currency notes and coinage. The notes are for £1, £5, £10, £20 and £50, and the coins are for 1p, 2p, 5p, 10p, 20p, 50p, £1, £2 and £5. The States of Jersey issues its own currency notes and coinage. The notes are for £1, £5, £10, £20 and £50, and the coins are for 1p, 2p, 5p, 10p, 20p, 50p, £1 and £2.

The Isle of Man – The Isle of Man government issues notes for £1, £5, £10, £20 and £50. Although these notes are only legal tender in the Isle of Man, they are accepted at face value in branches of the clearing banks in the UK. The Isle of Man issues coins for 1p, 2p, 5p, 10p, 20p, 50p, £1, £2 and £5.

Although none of the series of notes specified above is legal tender in the UK, they are generally accepted by banks irrespective of their place of issue. At one time banks made a commission charge for handling Scottish and Irish notes but this was abolished some years ago.

BANK FAMILY TREE

Includes the major retail banks operating in the UK as at April 2009. Financial results for these banks are given on the following page. Building societies are only included in instances where they demutualised to become a bank.

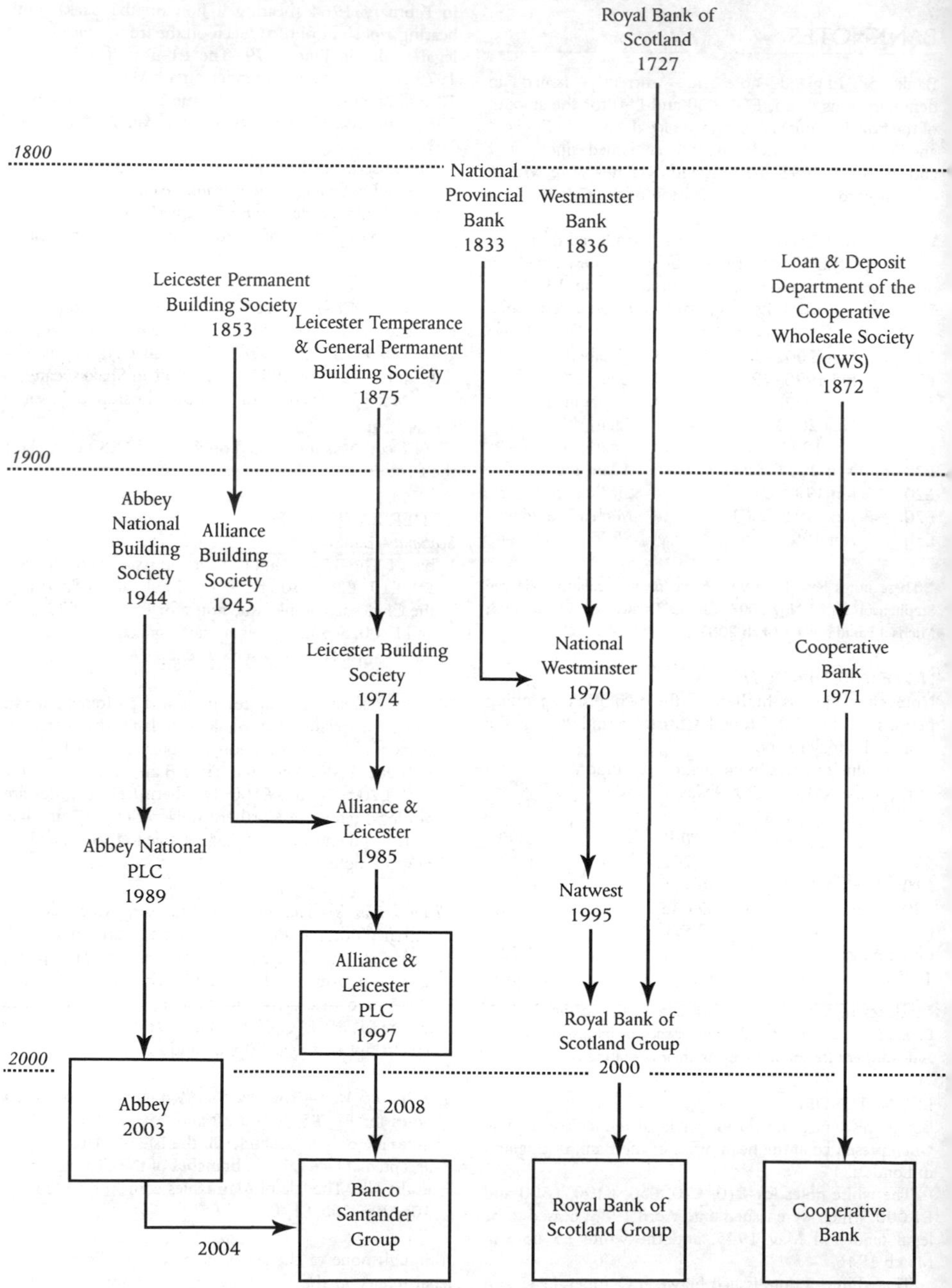

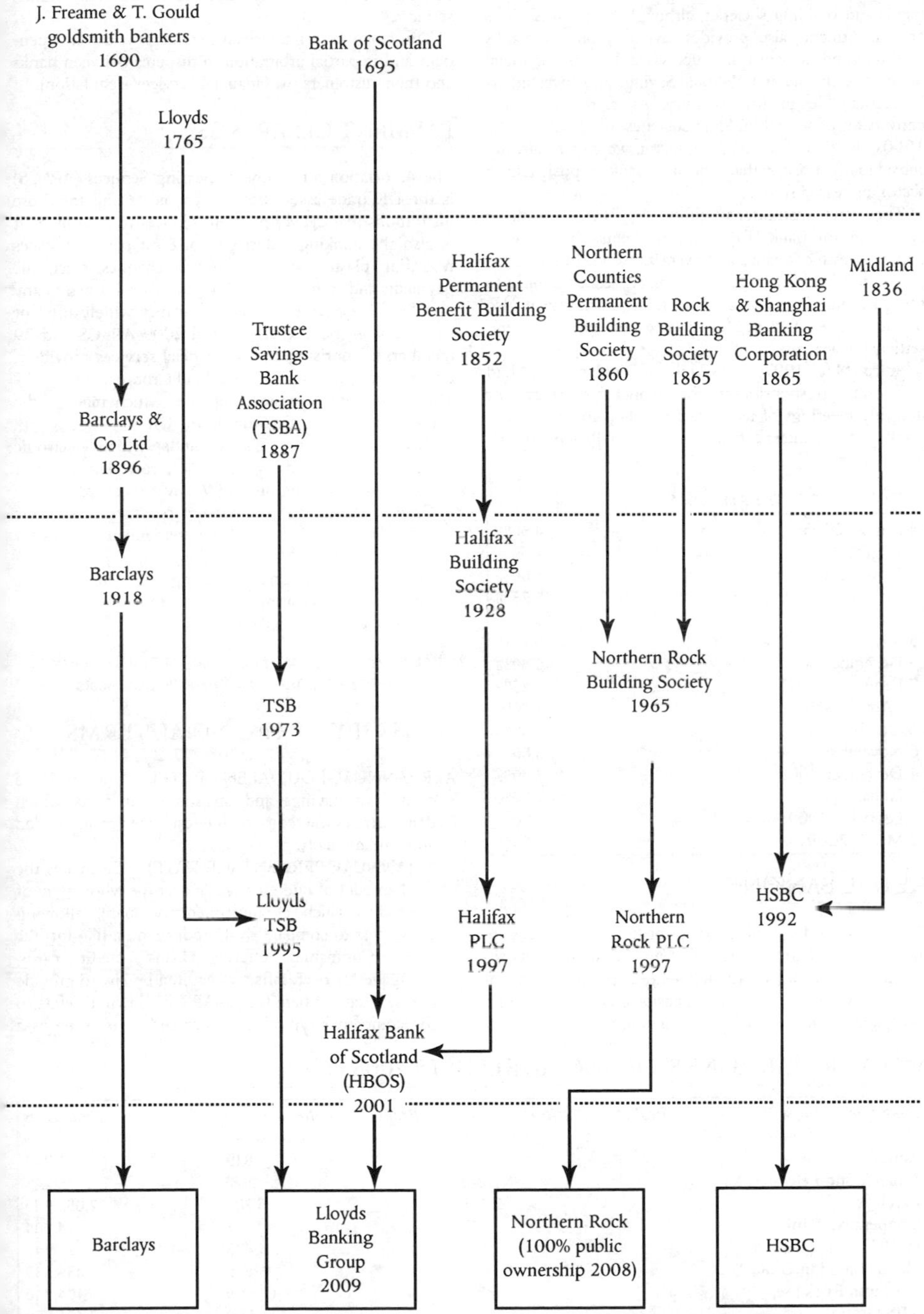
J. Freame & T. Gould goldsmith bankers 1690
Bank of Scotland 1695
Lloyds 1765
Halifax Permanent Benefit Building Society 1852
Northern Counties Permanent Building Society 1860
Rock Building Society 1865
Hong Kong & Shanghai Banking Corporation 1865
Midland 1836
Trustee Savings Bank Association (TSBA) 1887
Barclays & Co Ltd 1896
Barclays 1918
Halifax Building Society 1928
Northern Rock Building Society 1965
TSB 1973
Lloyds TSB 1995
Halifax PLC 1997
Northern Rock PLC 1997
HSBC 1992
Halifax Bank of Scotland (HBOS) 2001
Barclays
Lloyds Banking Group 2009
Northern Rock (100% public ownership 2008)
HSBC

BANKING AND PERSONAL FINANCE

There are two main types of deposit-taking institutions: banks and building societies, although National Savings and Investments also provides savings products. Banks and building societies are supervised by the Financial Services Authority and National Savings and Investments is accountable to the Treasury. As a result of the conversion of several building societies into banks in the 1990s, the size of the banking sector, which was already substantially greater than the non-bank deposit-taking sector, increased further.

The main institutions within the British banking system are the Bank of England (the central bank), retail banks, investment banks and overseas banks. In its role as the central bank, the Bank of England acts as banker to the government and as a note-issuing authority; it also oversees the efficient functioning of payment and settlement systems.

Since May 1997, the Bank of England has had operational responsibility for monetary policy. At monthly meetings of its monetary policy committee the Bank sets the interest rate at which it will lend to the money markets.

OFFICIAL INTEREST RATES 2005–9

4 August 2005	4.50%
3 August 2006	4.75%
9 November 2006	5.00%
11 January 2007	5.25%
10 May 2007	5.50%
5 July 2007	5.75%
6 December 2007	5.50%
7 February 2008	5.25%
10 April 2008	5.00%
8 October 2008	4.50%
6 November 2008	3.00%
4 December 2008	2.00%
8 January 2009	1.50%
5 February 2009	1.00%
5 March 2009	0.50%

RETAIL BANKING

Retail banks offer a wide variety of financial services to individuals and companies, including current and deposit accounts, loan and overdraft facilities, credit and debit cards, investment services, pensions, insurance and mortgages. All banks offer telephone and internet banking facilities in addition to traditional branch services.

The Financial Ombudsman Service provides independent and impartial arbitration in disputes between banks and their customers (*see* Financial Services Regulation).

PAYMENT CLEARINGS

The Association for Payment Clearing Services (APACS) is the UK trade association for payments and for those institutions that deliver payment services to customers. It is also the banking industry's voice on payment issues regarding plastic cards, card fraud, cheques, electronic payments and cash. Membership of APACS is open to any member of a payment scheme which is widely used or significant in the UK. As at April 2009 APACS had 29 members, comprising banks, financial services providers, one building society and Royal Mail Group.

There are three separate companies which manage the majority of payment clearings in the UK:

- BACS manages the schemes under which electronic payments are made, processing direct debits, direct credits and standing orders (W www.bacs.co.uk)
- CHAPS Clearing Company provides electronic same-day clearing and real-time settlement services for sterling payments (W www.chapsco.co.uk)
- The Cheque and Credit Clearing Company manages the cheque clearing system in Great Britain (W www.chequeandcredit.co.uk

APACS, Mercury House, Triton Court, 14 Finsbury Square, London EC2A 1LQ T 020-7711 6200 W www.apacs.org.uk

GLOSSARY OF FINANCIAL TERMS

AER (ANNUAL EQUIVALENT RATE) – A notional rate quoted on savings and investment products which demonstrates the return on interest, when compounded and paid annually.

APR (ANNUAL PERCENTAGE RATE) – Calculates the total amount of interest payable over the whole term of a product (such as investment or loan), allowing consumers to compare rival products on a like-for-like basis. Companies offering loans, credit cards, mortgages or overdrafts are required by law to provide the APR rate. Where typical APR is shown, it refers to the company's typical borrower and so is given as a

MAJOR RETAIL BANKS' FINANCIAL RESULTS 2008

Bank group	*Profit/(loss) before taxation*	*Profit/(loss) after taxation*	*Total assets*
	£ million	*£ million*	*£ million*
Abbey	1,094	819	231,742
Alliance and Leicester	(1,288)	(918)	75,248
Barclays	6,077	5,287	2,052,980
Cooperative Bank	23	17	14,964
HSBC	6,357	4,438	1,725,747
Lloyds Banking Group*	807	845	436,033
Northern Rock†	(1,356)	(1,310)	104,346
RBS Group	(40,667)	(34,373)	2,401,652

* Includes Lloyds TSB and Halifax Bank of Scotland (HBOS)
† In February 2008 Northern Rock was taken into temporary public ownership

best example; rate and costs may vary depending on individual circumstances.

ANNUITY – A type of insurance policy that provides regular income in exchange for a lump sum. Everyone who has a pension and has built-up a lump sum with their provider must buy an annuity by the time they reach 75. The annuity can be bought from a company other than the existing pension provider.

ASU – Accident, sickness and unemployment insurance taken out by a borrower to protect against being unable to work for these reasons. The policy will usually pay a percentage of the normal monthly mortgage repayment if the borrower is unable to work.

ATM (AUTOMATED TELLER MACHINES) – Commonly referred to as cash machines. Users can access their bank accounts using a card for simple transactions such as withdrawing and depositing cash. Some banks and independent ATM deployers charge for transactions.

BANKER'S DRAFT – A cheque drawn on a bank against a cash deposit. Considered to be a secure way of receiving money in instances where a cheque could 'bounce' or where it is not desirable to receive cash.

BASE RATE – The interest rate set by the Bank of England at which it will lend to financial institutions. This acts as a benchmark for all other interest rates.

BASIS POINT – Unit of measure (usually one-hundredth of a percentage point) used to express movements in interest rates, foreign rates or bond yields.

BUY-TO-LET – The purchase of a residential property for the sole purpose of letting to a tenant. Not all lenders provide mortgage finance for this purpose. Buy-to-let lenders assess projected rental income (typical expectations are between 125 and 130 per cent of the monthly interest payment) in addition to, or instead of, the borrower's income. Buy-to-let mortgages are available as either interest only or repayment.

CAPITAL GAIN/LOSS – Increase/decrease in the value of a capital asset when it is sold or transferred compared to its initial worth.

CAPPED RATE MORTGAGE – The interest rate applied to a loan is guaranteed not to rise above a certain rate for a set period of time; the rate can therefore fall but will not rise above the capped rate. The level at which the cap is fixed is usually higher than for a fixed rate mortgage for a comparable period of time. The lender normally imposes early redemption penalties within the first few years.

CASH CARD – Issued by banks and building societies for withdrawing cash from ATMs.

CHARGE CARD – Charge cards, eg American Express and Diners Club, can be used in a similar way to credit cards but the debt must be settled in full each month.

CHIP AND PIN CARD – A credit/debit card which incorporates an embedded chip containing unique owner details. When used with a PIN, such cards offer greater security as they are less prone to fraud. Since 14 February 2006, most card transactions in the UK have required the use of a chip and pin card.

CREDIT CARD – Normally issued with a credit limit, credit cards can be used for purchases until the limit is reached. There is normally an interest-free period on the outstanding balance of up to 56 days. Charges can be avoided if the balance is paid off in full within the interest-free period. Alternatively part of the balance can be paid and in most cases there is a minimum amount set by the issuer (normally a percentage of the outstanding balance) which must be paid on a monthly basis. Some card issuers charge an annual fee and most issuers belong to a least one major credit card network, eg Mastercard or Visa.

CREDIT RATING – Overall credit worthiness of a borrower based on information from a credit reference agency, such as Experian or Equifax, which holds details of credit agreements, payment records, county court judgements etc for all adults in the UK. This information is supplied to lenders who use it in their credit scoring or underwriting systems to calculate the risk of granting a loan to an individual and the probability that it will be repaid. Each lender sets their own criteria for credit worthiness and may accept or reject a credit application based on an individual's credit rating.

CRITICAL ILLNESS COVER – Insurance that covers borrowers against critical illnesses such as stroke, heart attack or cancer and is designed to protect mortgage or other loan payments.

DEBIT CARD – Debit cards were introduced on a large scale in the UK in the mid-1980s, replacing cash and cheques to purchase goods and services. They can be used to withdraw cash from ATMs in the UK and abroad and may also function as a cheque guarantee card. Funds are automatically withdrawn from an individual's bank account after making a purchase and no interest is charged.

DISCOUNTED MORTGAGE – Discounted mortgages guarantee an interest rate set at a margin below the standard variable rate for a period of time. The discounted rate will move up or down with the standard variable rate, but the payment rate will retain the agreed differential below the standard variable rate. The lender normally imposes early redemption penalties within the first few years.

EARLY REDEMPTION PENALTY – *see* Redemption Penalty

ENDOWMENT MORTGAGE – Only the interest on a property loan is paid back to the lender each month as long as an endowment life insurance policy is taken out for an agreed amount of time, typically 25 years. When the policy matures the lender will take repayment of the money owed on the property loan and any surplus goes to the policyholder. If the endowment policy shows a shortfall on projected returns, the policy holder must make further provision to pay off the mortgage.

EQUITY – When applied to real estate, equity is the difference between the value of a property and the amount outstanding on any loan secured against it. Negative equity occurs when the loan is greater than the market value of the property.

FIXED RATE MORTGAGE – A repayment mortgage where the interest rate on the loan is fixed for a set amount of time, normally a period of between one and ten years. The interest rate does not vary with changes to the base rate resulting in the monthly mortgage payment remaining the same for the duration of the fixed period. The lender normally imposes early redemption penalties within the first few years.

INTEREST ONLY MORTGAGE – Only interest is paid by the borrower and capital remains constant for the term of the loan. The onus is on the borrower to make provision to repay the capital at the end of the term. This is usually achieved through an investment vehicle such as an endowment policy or pension.

ISA – The individual savings account is a means by which investors can save and invest without paying any tax on the proceeds. Money can be invested across three investment elements: cash, stocks and shares and life insurance products. There are limits on the amount that can be invested during any given tax year.

LOAN TO VALUE (LTV) – This is the ratio between the size of a mortgage loan sought and the mortgage lender's valuation. On a loan of £55,000, for example, on a property valued at £100,000 the loan to value is 55 per cent. This means that there is sufficient equity in the property for the lender to be reassured that if interest or capital repayments were stopped, it could sell the property and recoup the money owed. Fewer options are available to borrowers requiring high LTV.

LONDON INTERBANK OFFERED RATE (LIBOR) – Is the interest rate that London banks charge when lending to one another on the wholesale money market. LIBOR is set by supply and demand of money as banks lend to each other in order to balance their books on a daily basis.

MIG (MORTGAGE INDEMNITY GUARANTEE) – An insurance for the lender paid by the borrower on high LTV mortgages (typically more than 90 per cent). It is a policy designed to protect the lender against loss in the event of the borrower defaulting or ceasing to repay a mortgage and is usally paid as a one-off premium or can be added to the value of the loan. It offers no protection to the borrower. Not all lenders charge MIG premiums.

ONLINE BANKING – Also known as internet banking, nearly all banking transactions can now be carried out online rather than attending a bank branch in person.

PERSONAL PENSION PLAN (PPP) – Designed for the self-employed or those in non-pensionable employment. Contributions made to a PPP are exempt from tax and the retirement age may be selected at any time from age 50 to 75. Up to 25 per cent of the pension fund may be taken as a tax-free cash sum on retirement.

PHISHING – A fraudulent attempt to obtain bank account details and security codes through an email. The email purports to come from a *bona fide* bank or building society and attempts to steer the recipient, usually under the pretext that the banking institution is updating its security arrangements, to a website which requests personal details.

PIN (PERSONAL IDENTIFICATION NUMBER) – A PIN is issued alongside a cash card to allow the user to access a bank account via an ATM. PINs are also issued with smart, credit and debit cards and, since 14 February 2006, have been requested in the majority of shops and restaurants as a further security measure when making a purchase.

PORTABLE MORTGAGE – A mortgage product that can be transferred to a different property in the event of a house move. Preferable where early redemption penalties are charged.

REDEMPTION PENALTY – A charge levied for paying off a loan, debt balance or mortgage before a date agreed with the lender.

REPAYMENT MORTGAGE – In contrast to the interest only mortgage, the monthly repayment includes an element of the capital sum borrowed in addition to the interest charged.

SELF-CERTIFICATION – Some lenders allow borrowers to self-certify their income. This type of scheme is useful to the self-employed who may not have accounts available or any other person who has difficulty proving their regular income.

SHARE – A share is a divided-up unit of the value of a company. If a company is worth £100m, and there are 50m shares in issue, then each share is worth £2 (usually listed as pence). As the overall value of the company fluctuates so does the share price.

SMART CARD – *see* chip and pin card

TELEPHONE BANKING – Banking facilities which can be accessed via the telephone.

UNIT TRUST – A 'pooled' fund of assets, usually shares, owned by a number of individuals. Managed by professional, authorised fund-management groups, unit trusts have traditionally delivered better returns than average cash deposits, but do rise and fall in value as their underlying investment varies in value.

VARIABLE RATE MORTGAGE – Repayment mortgages where the interest rate set by the lender increases or decreases in relation to the base interest rate which can result in fluctuating monthly repayments.

WITH-PROFITS – Usually applies to pensions, endowments, savings schemes or bonds. The intention is to smooth out the rises and falls in the stock market for the benefit of the investor. Actuaries working for the insurance company, or fund managers, hold back some profits in good years in order to make up the difference in years when shares perform badly.

FINANCIAL SERVICES REGULATION

FINANCIAL SERVICES AUTHORITY

The FSA has been the single regulator for financial services in the UK since 1 December 2001, when the Financial Services and Markets Act 2000 (FSMA) came into force. The FSA is required to pursue four statutory objectives:

- maintaining market confidence
- raising public awareness
- protecting consumers
- reducing financial crime

The legislation also requires the FSA to have regard to the following principles while carrying out its general functions:

- using its resources in an economic and efficient way
- the responsibilities of regulated firms' own management
- being proportionate in imposing burdens or restrictions on the industry
- facilitating innovation
- the international character of financial services and the competitive position of the UK
- not impeding or distorting competition unnecessarily

ORGANISATION AND STRUCTURE

The FSA is a company limited by guarantee and financed by levies on the industry. It receives no funds from the public purse. It is accountable to treasury ministers and, through them, to parliament. The FSA must report annually on the achievement of its statutory objectives to the Treasury, which is required to lay the report before parliament. The FSA's budgeted costs for 2009–10 are £415m.

FSA REGISTER

The FSA register is a public record of financial services firms, individuals and other bodies who come under the FSA's regulatory jurisdiction as defined in the FSMA. The register has information on all authorised firms currently doing business in the UK. It includes firms that are UK registered as well as those authorised in other European economic area states that conduct business in the UK. Each entry outlines exactly what regulated activities the firm or individual is authorised to carry out.

FINANCIAL SERVICES AUTHORITY, 25 The North Colonnade, Canary Wharf, London E14 5HS **T** 020-7066 1000
W www.fsa.gov.uk
Chair, Lord Turner of Ecchinswell
Chief Executive, Hector Sants

COMPENSATION

Created under the FSMA, the Financial Services Compensation Scheme (FSCS) is the UK's statutory fund of last resort for customers of authorised financial services firms. It provides compensation if a firm authorised by the FSA is unable, or likely to be unable, to pay claims against it. In general this is when a firm has stopped trading and has insufficient assets to meet claims, or is in insolvency. The FSCS covers deposits, insurance policies, insurance broking, investment business and mortgage advice and arranging. The FSCS is independent of the FSA, with separate staff and premises. However, the FSA appoints the board of the FSCS and sets its guidelines. The FSCS is funded by levies on authorised firms.

The Pension Protection Fund (PPF) is a statutory fund established under the Pensions Act 2004 and became operational on 6 April 2005. The fund was set up to pay compensation to members of eligible defined benefit pension schemes, where there is a qualifying insolvency event in relation to the employer and where there are insufficient assets in the pension scheme to cover PPF levels of compensation. Compulsory annual levies are charged on all eligible schemes to help fund the PPF, in addition to investment of PPF assets.

FINANCIAL SERVICES COMPENSATION SCHEME, 7th Floor, Lloyds Chambers, Portsoken Street, London E1 8BN
T 020-7892 7300 **E** enquiries@fscs.org.uk
W www.fscs.org.uk
Chair, David Hall
Chief Executive, Loretta Minghella

PENSION PROTECTION FUND, Knollys House, 17 Addiscombe Road, Croydon, Surrey CR0 6SR **T** 0845-600 2541
E information@ppf.gsi.gov.uk
W www.pensionprotectionfund.org.uk
Chair, Lawrence Churchill
Chief Executive, Alan Rubenstein

DESIGNATED PROFESSIONAL BODIES

Professional firms are exempt from requiring direct regulation by the FSA if they carry out only certain restricted activities that arise out of, or are complementary to, the provision of professional services, such as arranging the sale of shares on the instructions of executors or trustees, or providing services to small, private companies. These firms are, however, supervised by designated professional bodies (DPBs). There are a number of safeguards to protect consumers dealing with firms that do not require direct regulation. These arrangements include:

- the FSA's power to ban a specific firm from taking advantage of the exemption and to restrict the regulated activities permitted to the firms
- rules which require professional firms to ensure that their clients are aware that they are not authorised persons
- a requirement for the DPBs to supervise and regulate the firms and inform the FSA on how the professional firms carry on their regulated activities

See Professional Education section for details of the following DPBs:
Association of Chartered Certified Accountants
Council for Licensed Conveyancers
Institute of Actuaries
Institute of Chartered Accountants in England and Wales
Institute of Chartered Accountants in Ireland
Institute of Chartered Accountants of Scotland
Law Society of England and Wales

Law Society of Northern Ireland
Law Society of Scotland
Royal Institution of Chartered Surveyors

RECOGNISED INVESTMENT EXCHANGES

The FSA currently supervises seven recognised investment exchanges (RIEs) in the UK; under the FSMA, recognition confers an exemption from the need to be authorised to carry out regulated activities in the UK. The RIEs are organised markets on which member firms can trade investments such as equities and derivatives. As a regulator the FSA must focus on the impact of changes brought about by the continued growth in electronic trading by exchanges and other organisations. Issues such as how these changes affect market quality, reliability and access are important and the FSA works with the exchanges to ensure that new systems meet regulatory requirements. The RIEs are listed with their year of recognition in parentheses:

EUROPEAN DERIVATIVES EXCHANGE (EDX) LONDON (2003), 10 Paternoster Square, London EC4M 7LS **T** 020-7797 4683 **W** www.londonstockexchange.com/edx (*see also* London Stock Exchange)

INTERCONTINENTAL EXCHANGE (ICE) FUTURES EUROPE (2001), 5th Floor, Milton Gate, 60 Chiswell Street, London EC1Y 4SA **T** 020-7065 7700 **W** www.theice.com

LONDON INTERNATIONAL FINANCIAL FUTURES (LIFFE) ADMINISTRATION AND MANAGEMENT (2001), Cannon Bridge House, 1 Cousin Lane, London EC4R 3XX **T** 020-7623 0444 **W** www.liffe.com

LONDON METAL EXCHANGE (2001), 56 Leadenhall Street, London EC3A 2BJ **T** 020-7264 5555 **W** www.lme.co.uk

LONDON STOCK EXCHANGE (LSE) (2001), 10 Paternoster Square, London EC4M 7LS **T** 020-7797 1000 **W** www.londonstockexchange.com

PLUS MARKETS (2007), Standon House, 21 Mansell Street, London E1 8AA **T** 020-7553 2000 **W** www.plusmarketsgroup.com

SWISS EXCHANGE (SWX) EUROPE (2001), 34th Floor, One Canada Square, Canary Wharf, London E14 5AA **T** 020-7074 4444 **W** www.swxeurope.com

RECOGNISED CLEARING HOUSES

The FSA is also responsible for recognising and supervising recognised clearing houses (RCHs), which organise the settlement of transactions on recognised investment exchanges. There are currently four RCHs in the UK:

EUROCLEAR UK AND IRELAND (2001), Watling House, 33 Cannon Street, London EC4M 5SB **T** 020-7849 0000 **W** www.euroclear.com

EUROPEAN CENTRAL COUNTERPARTY (2008), Broadgate West, 1 Snowdon Street, London EC2A 2DQ **T** 020-7650 1401 **W** www.euroccp.co.uk

ICE CLEAR EUROPE (2008), 5th Floor, Milton Gate, 60 Chiswell Street, London EC1Y 4SA **T** 020-7265 3648 **W** www.theice.com/clear_europe

LONDON CLEARING HOUSE (LCH) CLEARNET (2001), Aldgate House, 33 Aldgate High Street, London EC3N 1EA **T** 020-7426 7000 **W** www.lchclearnet.com

OMBUDSMAN SCHEMES

The Financial Ombudsman Service was set up by the Financial Services and Markets Act 2000 to provide consumers with a free, independent service for resolving disputes with authorised financial firms. The Financial Ombudsman Service can consider complaints about most financial matters including: banking; credit cards and store cards; financial advice; hire purchase and pawnbroking; insurance; loans and credit; mortgages; pensions; savings and investments; stocks, shares, unit trusts and bonds.

Complainants must first complain to the firm involved. They do not have to accept the ombudsman's decision and are free to go to court if they wish, but if a decision is accepted, it is binding for both the complainant and the firm.

The Pensions Ombudsman can investigate and decide complaints and disputes about the way that occupational and personal pension schemes are administered and managed. The Pensions Ombudsman is also the Ombudsman for the Pension Protection Fund (PPF) and the Financial Assistance Scheme (which offers help to those who were a member of an under-funded defined benefit pension scheme that started to wind-up in specific financial circumstances between 1 January 1997 and 5 April 2005).

FINANCIAL OMBUDSMAN SERVICE, South Quay Plaza, 183 Marsh Wall, London E14 9SR
T 020-7964 1000 Helpline 0845-080 1800
E complaint.info@financial-ombudsman.org.uk
W www.financial-ombudsman.org.uk
Chief Ombudsman, Walter Merricks, CBE
Principal Ombudsmen, Tony Boorman; David Thomas

PENSIONS OMBUDSMAN, 11 Belgrave Road, London SW1V 1RB
T 020-7630 2200 **E** enquiries@pensions-ombudsman.org.uk
W www.pensions-ombudsman.org.uk
Pensions Ombudsman, Tony King
Deputy Pensions Ombudsman, Charlie Gordon

PANEL ON TAKEOVERS AND MERGERS

The Panel on Takeovers and Mergers is an independent body, established in 1968, whose main functions are to issue and administer the City code and to ensure equality of treatment and opportunity for all shareholders in takeover bids and mergers. The panel's statutory functions are set out in the Companies Act 2006.

The panel comprises up to 34 members drawn from major financial and business institutions. The chair, deputy chair and up to 20 independent members are nominated by the panel's own nomination committee. The remaining members are nominated by professional bodies representing the banking, insurance, investment, pension and accountancy industries and the CBI.

PANEL ON TAKEOVERS AND MERGERS, 10 Paternoster Square, London EC4M 7DY **T** 020-7382 9026
W www.thetakeoverpanel.org.uk
Chair, Peter Scott, QC

NATIONAL SAVINGS AND INVESTMENTS

NS&I (National Savings and Investments) is an executive agency of HM Treasury and one of the UK's largest financial providers, with 27 million customers and over £93bn invested. NS&I offers savings and investment products to personal savers and investors and the money is used to manage the national debt. When people invest in NS&I they are lending money to the government which pays them interest or prizes in return. All products are financially secure because they are guaranteed by HM Treasury.

TAX-FREE PRODUCTS

SAVINGS CERTIFICATES

Index-linked Saving Certificates
Otherwise known as inflation-beating savings, index-linked saving certificates are fixed rate investments that pay tax-free returns guaranteed to be above inflation. They are available in three- and five-year terms and are sold in issues. The minimum investment for each issue is £100 and the maximum £15,000.

Fixed Interest Saving Certificates
Fixed interest saving certificates are fixed rate investments that pay tax-free returns. They are available in two- and five-year terms and are sold in issues for which the minimum investment is £100 and the maximum £15,000.

PREMIUM BONDS

Introduced in 1956, premium bonds enable savers to enter a regular draw for tax-free prizes, while retaining the right to get their money back. A sum equivalent to interest on each bond is put into a prize fund and distributed by monthly prize draws. The prizes are drawn by ERNIE (electronic random number indicator equipment) and are free of all UK income tax and capital gains tax. A £1m jackpot is drawn each month in addition to other tax-free prizes ranging in value from £25 to £100,000.

Bonds are in units of £1, with a minimum purchase of £100; above this, purchases must be in multiples of £10, up to a maximum holding limit of £30,000 per person. Bonds become eligible for prizes once they have been held for one clear calendar month following the month of purchase. Each £1 unit can win only one prize per draw, but it will be awarded the highest for which it is drawn. Bonds remain eligible for prizes until they are repaid.

The scheme offers a facility to reinvest prize wins automatically. Upon completion of an automatic prize reinvestment mandate, holders receive new bonds which are immediately eligible for future prize draws. Bonds can only be held in the name of an individual and not by organisations.

As at March 2009, 186 million prizes totalling £11.9bn had been distributed since the first prize draw in 1957.

CHILDREN'S BONUS BONDS

Children's bonus bonds were introduced in 1991. The bonds are sold in five-year issues at multiples of £25. For each issue the minimum holding is £25 and the maximum holding is £3,000 per child. They can be bought for any child under 16, but must be held by a parent or guardian. All returns are totally exempt from UK income tax and a bonus is payable if the bond is held for the full five years.

OTHER PRODUCTS

GUARANTEED EQUITY BONDS

Guaranteed equity bonds are five-year investments where the returns are linked to the performance of the FTSE-100 index with a guarantee that the original capital invested will be returned even if the FTSE-100 index fell over the five years. They are sold in limited issues with a minimum investment of £1,000 and a maximum of £1m. The returns are subject to income tax on maturity, unless they are held in a self-invested pension plan (SIPP).

SAVINGS AND INVESTMENT ACCOUNTS

The easy access savings account was launched in January 2004 replacing the ordinary account (also known as the Post Office savings account). The easy access savings account offers access to savings via Post Office counters, an ATM card, telephone and online. It can be opened with a minimum balance of £100 and has a maximum limit of £2m (£4m jointly). The interest is paid without deduction of tax at source.

The investment account is a passbook account which pays tiered rates of interest. It can be opened with a minimum balance of £20 and has a maximum limit of £100,000. The interest is paid without deduction of tax at source.

Since April 1999 NS&I has offered cash individual savings accounts (ISAs). Its Direct ISA, launched in April 2006, can be opened and managed online and by telephone with a minimum investment of £100. Interest for the Direct ISA is calculated daily and is free of tax.

INCOME BONDS

NS&I income bonds were introduced in 1982. They are suitable for those who want to receive regular monthly payments of interest while preserving the full cash value of their capital. The bonds are sold in multiples of £500. The minimum holding is £500 and the maximum £1m (sole or joint holding). A variable rate of interest is calculated on a day-to-day basis and paid monthly. Interest is taxable but is paid without deduction of tax at source.

GUARANTEED INCOME BONDS

Guaranteed income bonds were introduced in February 2008. They are designed for those who want to receive regular monthly payments of interest while preserving the full cash value of their capital. The minimum holding is £500 and the maximum £1m, including any amount held in guaranteed growth bonds and fixed rate savings bonds (the latter was closed to new investment in 2008). A fixed rate of interest is calculated on a day-to-day basis and paid monthly on these bonds. Interest is taxable and tax is deducted at source.

GUARANTEED GROWTH BONDS

Guaranteed growth bonds were introduced in February 2008. They are suitable for those who want to receive regular monthly payments of interest while preserving the full cash value of their capital. The minimum holding is £500 and the maximum £1m, including any amount held in guaranteed income bonds and fixed rate savings bonds (the latter was closed to new investment in 2008). A fixed rate of interest is calculated on a day-to-day basis and is paid annually on the anniversary of the date of investment. Interest is taxable and tax is deducted at source.

FURTHER INFORMATION

Further information can be obtained online (W www.nsandi.com), by telephone (T 0845-964 5000) or at Post Office counters.

NATIONAL DEBT

The decision to transfer monetary policy to the Bank of England in 1997 while HM Treasury retained control of fiscal matters led to the creation of the UK Debt Management Office (DMO) as an executive agency of HM Treasury in April 1998. In April 2000 exchequer cash management was transferred to the DMO, which assumed responsibility for issuing Treasury bills (very short-dated securities) and gilts. The national debt also includes the liabilities of National Savings and Investments and other public sector debt and foreign currency. In 2002 the operations of the long-standing statutory functions of the Public Works Loan Board, which lends capital to local authorities, and the Commissioners for the Reduction of National Debt, which manages the investment portfolios of certain public funds, were integrated within the DMO. (*See also* Government Departments.)

THE LONDON STOCK EXCHANGE

The London Stock Exchange serves the needs of companies and investors by providing facilities for raising capital and a central marketplace for securities trading. This marketplace covers UK and overseas company shares and other instruments such as: exchange traded funds (ETFs) and exchange traded commodities (ETCs), Russian and Scandinavian equity derivative products (through EDX London) and both corporate and government bonds.

Over 500 member firms trading on the London Stock Exchange buy and sell securities on behalf of the public, as well as institutions such as pension funds or insurance companies.

The London Stock Exchange is a subsidiary, along with Borsa Italiana, of the London Stock Exchange Group (LSEG).

HISTORY

The London Stock Exchange is one of the world's oldest stock exchanges dating back more than 300 years when it began in the coffee houses of 17th-century London. It was formally established as a membership organisation in 1801.

RECENT DEVELOPMENTS

'BIG BANG'

What has come to be known as 'Big Bang', was a package of reforms in 1986 that transformed the Exchange and the City, liberalising the way in which banks and stock-broking firms operated and bringing in foreign investment. The Exchange ceased granting voting rights to individual members and became a private company. Big Bang also saw the start of a move towards fully electronic trading and the closure of the trading floor.

INTRODUCTION OF SETS

In October 1997, the Exchange introduced SETS, its electronic order book. The system enhanced the efficiency and transparency of trading on the Exchange, allowing trades to be executed automatically and anonymously rather than negotiated by telephone.

DEMUTALISATION AND LISTING

The London Stock Exchange became demutualised in 2000 and listed on its own main market in 2001 in order to allow further commercialisation.

EDX LONDON

In 2003 the London Stock Exchange created EDX London (European derivatives exchange), a recognised investment exchange for international equity derivatives. It now also offers trading in Russian and Scandinavian equity derivatives.

MERGER WITH BORSA ITALIANA

On 1 October 2007 the Exchange merged with the Italian stock exchange Borsa Italiana and London Stock Exchange Group PLC replaced the London Stock Exchange as the listed entity.

PRIMARY MARKETS

The London Stock Exchange enables UK and overseas companies to raise capital for development and growth through the issue of securities. For a company entering the market the Exchange offers a choice of four differently regulated markets, depending upon the size, history and requirements of the company:

- the main market enables established companies to raise capital, widen their investor base and have their shares traded on a global stock market. The market is regulated by the FSA's UK Listing Authority (UKLA). The FTSE 100 index is based on main market stocks
- the Alternative Investment Market (AIM), established in June 1995, is specially designed to meet the needs of small, young and growing companies, enabling them to raise capital, broaden their investor base and benefit from being traded on an internationally recognised market. AIM is regulated by the London Stock Exchange and quoted companies must adhere to the AIM rules and retain a Nominated Adviser (or 'Nomad') at all times, who is responsible for ensuring the company's suitability for the market. The AIM model has been extended to AIM Italia, launched in Italy at the end of 2008, and AIM Tokyo, launched in collaboration with the Tokyo Stock Exchange in spring 2009
- the Professional Securities Market (PSM), established in July 2005 and regulated by the FSA, offers international companies that wish to access an exclusively institutional investor base an option to list equity and debt securities in London on a market that offers greater flexibility in accounting standards
- the Specialist Fund Market (SFM), established in November 2007, is the Exchange's market for highly specialised investment entities, such as hedge funds or private equity funds, that wish to target institutional investors. This market is regulated by the FSA in accordance with standards set out in EU directives

At 31 December 2008 there were 3,095 companies quoted on the London Stock Exchange: 1,174 on the UK main market, with a combined market capitalisation of £1,288.1bn; 326 on the international main market, with a combined market capitalisation of £1,609.1bn; 1,550 on AIM, with a combined market capitalisation of £37.7bn; 43 on the PSM, with a combined market capitalisation of £4.7bn; and two companies listed on the SFM.

LONDON STOCK EXCHANGE, 10 Paternoster Square, London EC4M 7LS T 020-7797 1000
W www.londonstockexchange.com
Chair, Dr Christopher Gibson-Smith
Chief Executive, Xavier Rolet

ECONOMIC STATISTICS

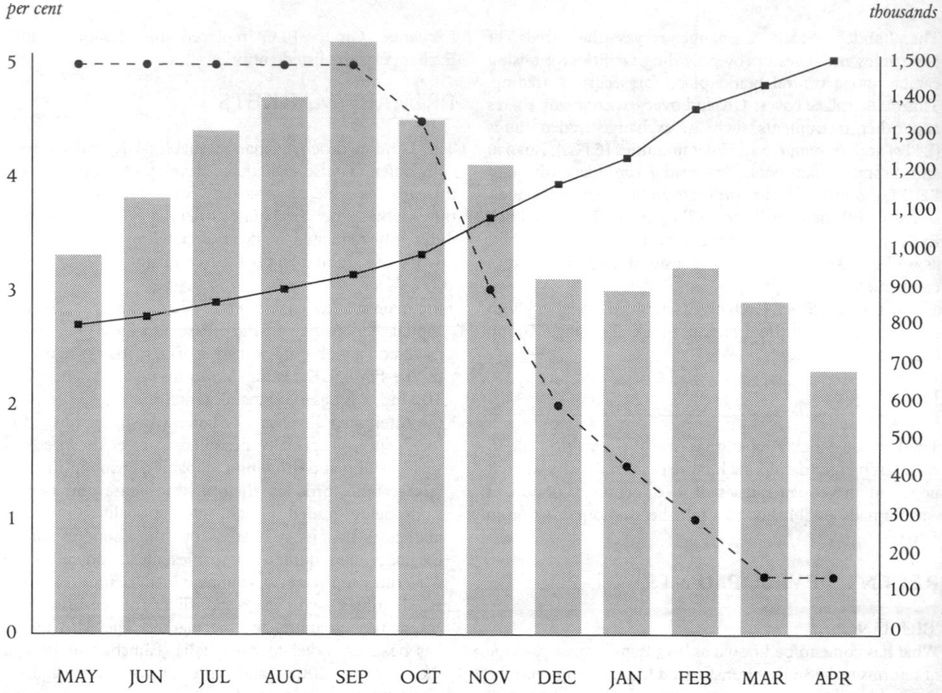

The figures in the graph above are for May 2008 – April 2009

KEY

CPI (Consumer Prices Index) Measure of Inflation – 12 monthly percentage change in the average level of prices of goods and services purchased by households in the UK (*see also* Cost of Living)

The Official Interest Rate set by the bank of England at its monthly monetary policy committee meeting (*see also* Banking and Personal Finance)

Claimant Count – the number of people in the UK claiming unemployment benefit (jobseeker's allowance) (*see also* Social Welfare)

Sources: ONS (Crown Copyright); Bank of England – Official Interest Rates

NUMBER OF UK RESIDENTIAL PROPERTY TRANSACTIONS
with a value of £40,000 or above

	England	*Wales*	*Scotland*	*Norther Ireland*	*UK*
2006	1,418,000	71,000	144,000	52,000	1,686,000
2007	1,375,000	67,000	148,000	39,000	1,628,000
2008	755,000	36,000	99,000	15,000	905,000

Source: ONS (Crown copyright)

REDUNDANCIES BY SELECTED INDUSTRIES

	Jan–Mar 2008	*Apr–Jun 2008*	*Jul–Sep 2008*	*Oct–Dec 2008*	*Jan–Mar 2009*
All redundancies	120,000	121,000	156,000	263,000	299,000
Manufacturing	29,000	24,000	26,000	60,000	67,000
Construction	17,000	13,000	31,000	48,000	49,000
Distribution, hotels and restaurants	21,000	28,000	30,000	49,000	71,000
Transport and Communication	–	12,000	13,000	20,000	23,000
Banking, finance and insurance	26,000	21,000	34,000	52,000	61,000
Education, health and public administration	11,000	11,000	12,000	14,000	11,000

Source: ONS (Crown copyright)

GDP GROWTH, QUARTER ON PREVIOUS QUARTER

per cent

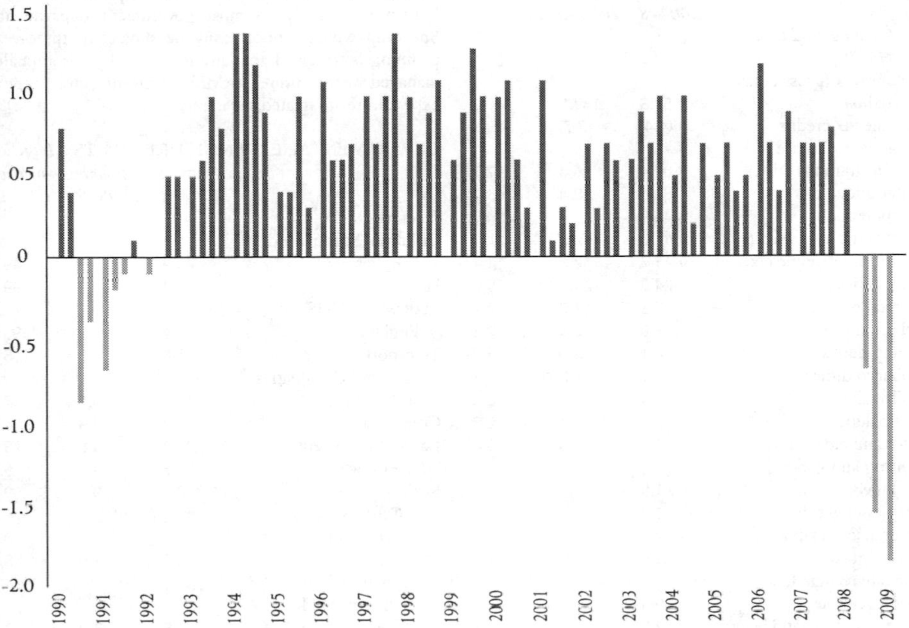

Source: ONS

There was no growth in the second quarter of 1992 and 2008

AVERAGE HOUSEHOLD INCOME

Income by source	*£ per week*	*Percentage of total*
Wages and Salaries	444.90	67
Self-employment	53.50	8
Investments	23.20	4
Annuities and pensions	47.60	7
Social security benefits*	83.30	13
Other sources	7.00	1
Total	659.40	100

* Excluding housing and council tax benefit

Source: ONS – *Annual Abstract of Statistics 2009* (Crown copyright)

AVERAGE HOUSEHOLD EXPENDITURE

Commodity or service	*£ per week*	*Percentage of total*
Housing	92.00	20
Fuel and power	17.20	4
Food and non-alcoholic drinks	71.40	16
Alcoholic drink	14.70	3
Tobacco	4.60	1
Clothing footwear	21.60	5
Household goods	34.60	8
Household services	26.50	6
Personal goods and services	17.80	4
Motoring	62.00	14
Fares and other travel costs	10.90	2
Leisure goods	20.10	4
Leisure services	61.70	13
Miscellaneous	1.90	–
Total	456.80	100

Source: ONS – *Annual Abstract of Statistics 2009* (Crown copyright)

HOUSEHOLD OWNERSHIP OF SELECTED DURABLE GOODS

Percentages

	2000–1	*2007**
Car/van	72	75
One	44	44
Two	22	25
Three+	6	6
Central heating (full or partial)	91	95
Washing machine	92	96
Tumble dryer	53	57
Fridge/freezer or deep freezer	94	97
Dishwasher	25	37
Microwave	84	91
Telephone	93	89
Mobile phone	47	78
Home computer	44	70
Video recorder	87	75
DVD player	–	86
CD player	77	86
Digital television service	40	77
Internet connection	32	61

* from 2006 the survey moved onto a calendar year basis

Source: ONS – *Annual Abstract of Statistics 2009* (Crown copyright)

THE BUDGET (2009)

GOVERNMENT RECEIPTS

£ billion	Outturn 2007–8	Estimate 2008–9	Projection 2009–10
HM Revenue and Customs (HMRC)			
Income tax (gross of tax credits)	151.8	152.5	140.5
Income tax credits	(4.4)	(5.7)	(6.2)
National insurance contributions (NIC)	100.4	96.4	97.7
Value added tax	80.6	78.4	63.7
Corporation tax[1]	46.9	43.4	34.7
Corporation tax credits[2]	(0.6)	(0.6)	(0.7)
Petroleum revenue tax	1.7	2.6	1.1
Fuel duties	24.9	24.6	26.6
Capital gains tax	5.3	7.8	2.2
Inheritance tax	3.9	2.9	2.3
Stamp duties	14.1	8.0	5.0
Tobacco duties	8.1	8.2	8.3
Spirits duties	2.4	2.4	2.6
Wine duties	2.6	2.7	2.7
Beer and cider duties	3.3	3.4	3.4
Betting and gaming duties	1.5	1.5	1.5
Air passenger duty	2.0	1.9	1.8
Insurance premium tax	2.3	2.3	2.4
Landfill tax	0.9	1.0	1.0
Climate change levy	0.7	0.7	0.7
Aggregates levy	0.3	0.3	0.3
Customs duties and levies	2.5	2.7	2.7
TOTAL HMRC	451.1	437.4	394.2
Vehicle excise duties	5.4	5.6	5.6
Business rates	21.4	22.8	23.8
Council tax[3]	23.3	24.3	24.9
Other taxes and royalties[4]	14.6	15.3	16.8
NET TAXES AND NIC[5]	515.9	505.4	465.4
Accruals adjustments on taxes	1.2	(4.4)	0.3
Less own resources contribution to European Commission (EC) budget	(5.0)	(5.2)	(4.2)
Less private company corporation tax payments	(0.3)	(0.2)	(0.2)
Tax credits adjustment[6]	0.6	0.6	0.7
Interest and dividends	8.7	7.4	5.6
Other receipts[7]	27.0	27.1	28.4
CURRENT RECEIPTS	548.0	530.7	496.1
North Sea revenues[8]	7.8	12.9	6.9

[1] National accounts measure: gross of enhanced and payable tax credits

[2] Includes enhanced company tax credits

[3] Council tax increases are projections determined annually by local authorities, not by the government

[4] Includes VAT refunds and money paid into the National Lottery Distribution Fund

[5] Includes VAT and 'traditional own resources' contributions to EC budget

[6] Tax credits which are scored as negative tax in the calculation of net taxes and NIC but expenditure in the national accounts

[7] Includes gross operating surplus, rent and business rate payments by local authorities

[8] Consists of North Sea corporation tax and petroleum revenue tax

Source: HM Treasury – *Budget 2009* (Crown copyright)

GOVERNMENT EXPENDITURE

The 1998 Economic and Fiscal Strategy Report introduced changes to the public expenditure control regime. Three-year departmental expenditure limits (DELs) now apply to most government departments. Spending which cannot easily be subject to three-year planning is reviewed annually in the budget as annually managed expenditure (AME). Current and capital expenditure are treated separately.

DEPARTMENTAL EXPENDITURE LIMITS

£ billion	Outturn 2007–8	Estimate 2008–9	Projection 2009–10
Resource DEL			
Children, Schools and Families	44.9	46.8	49.2
Health	88.4	92.5	99.9
of which NHS England	86.4	90.9	98.2
Transport	6.8	6.5	6.4
Innovation, Universities and Skills	15.5	16.7	17.2
Communities	4.2	4.3	4.5
Local Government	22.8	24.6	25.6
Home Office	8.6	8.9	9.4
Justice	8.8	9.3	9.5
Law Officers' Departments	0.7	0.7	0.7
Defence	35.7	37.9	38.7
Foreign and Commonwealth Office	1.9	2.0	2.0
International Development	4.5	4.8	5.5
Energy and Climate Change	0.6	1.0	1.1
Business, Enterprise and Regulatory Reform	1.8	1.6	1.8
Environment, Food and Rural Affairs	2.7	2.7	2.7
Culture, Media and Sport	1.6	1.6	1.7
Work and Pensions	8.1	8.1	9.1
Scotland	23.8	24.6	25.4
Wales	12.3	13.0	13.6
Northern Ireland Executive	7.6	8.1	8.4
Northern Ireland Office	1.3	1.3	1.2
Chancellor's departments	4.8	4.8	4.6
Cabinet Office	1.8	2.0	2.3
Independent bodies	0.7	0.8	0.9
Modernisation funding	0.0	0.0	0.3
Reserve	0.0	0.0	0.7
Allowance for shortfall	0.0	(0.6)	0.0
TOTAL RESOURCE DEL	309.9	324.3	342.1
Capital DEL			
Children, Schools and Families	5.2	5.6	7.2
Health	3.8	4.6	5.6
of which NHS England	3.6	4.4	5.4
Transport	7.1	7.3	8.3
Innovation, Universities and Skills	2.1	2.1	2.6
Communities	6.1	7.1	8.8
Local Government	0.0	0.1	0.1
Home Office	0.7	0.9	0.8

Justice	0.8	1.0	0.8
Law Officers' Departments	0.0	0.0	0.0
Defence	7.9	8.6	9.1
Foreign and Commonwealth Office	0.2	0.2	0.2
International Development	0.7	0.9	1.4
Energy and Climate Change	1.5	1.7	2.0
Business, Enterprise and Regulatory Reform	0.0	0.0	0.3
Environment, Food and Rural Affairs	0.6	0.6	0.7
Culture, Media and Sport	0.5	0.8	0.4
Work and Pensions	0.1	0.1	0.1
Scotland	3.6	3.3	3.7
Wales	1.5	1.6	1.7
Northern Ireland Executive	1.1	1.1	1.1
Northern Ireland Office	0.0	0.1	0.1
Chancellor's departments	0.3	0.3	1.0
Cabinet Office	0.3	0.4	0.4
Independent bodies	0.1	0.0	0.1
Reserve	0.0	0.0	1.2
Allowance for shortfall	0.0	(0.2)	0.0
TOTAL CAPITAL DEL	44.1	48.3	57.7
Less depreciation	(10.8)	(11.9)	(12.4)
TOTAL DEL	343.2	360.7	387.3

Source: HM Treasury – *Budget 2009* (Crown copyright)

ANNUALLY MANAGED EXPENDITURE *£ billion*

	Outturn 2007–8	*Estimate 2008–9*	*Projection 2009–10*
Resource AME			
Social security benefits[1]	138.7	150.1	164.7
Tax credits[1]	17.2	19.8	21.7
Net public service pensions[2]	2.3	3.1	4.1
National Lottery	0.9	0.9	0.9
BBC domestic services	3.5	3.4	3.5
Other departmental expenditure	2.7	0.8	2.5
Net expenditure transfers to EU institutions[3]	5.4	3.1	5.6
Locally-financed expenditure[4]	24.3	27.3	27.9
Central government gross debt interest	30.0	30.5	27.2
AME margin	0.0	0.0	0.9
Accounting adjustments	0.8	1.2	6.9
TOTAL RESOURCE AME	225.7	240.2	265.9
Capital AME			
National Lottery	0.7	0.6	1.0
Locally-financed expenditure[4]	4.0	4.5	4.4
Public corporations' own-financed capital expenditure	5.4	7.2	7.4
Other capital expenditure	(1.0)	0.4	1.5
AME margin	0.0	0.0	0.1
Accounting adjustments	(6.1)	(4.8)	(8.6)
TOTAL CAPITAL AME	3.0	7.9	5.8

[1] Child allowances in income support and jobseeker's allowance are included under tax credits
[2] Reported on a national accounts basis
[3] AME spending component only
[4] This expenditure is mainly financed by council tax revenues
Source: HM Treasury – *Budget 2009* (Crown copyright)

TRADE

TRADE IN GOODS

	Exports	*Imports*	*£ million Balance*
1998	164,056	185,869	(21,813)
1999	166,166	195,217	(29,051)
2000	187,936	220,912	(32,976)
2001	189,093	230,305	(41,212)
2002	186,524	234,229	(47,705)
2003	188,320	236,927	(48,607)
2004	190,874	251,774	(60,900)
2005	211,608	280,197	(68,589)
2006	243,635	319,947	(76,312)
2007	220,858	310,612	(89,754)
2008	251,088	343,964	(92,876)

Source: ONS – *Annual Abstract of Statistics 2009* (Crown copyright)

BALANCE OF PAYMENTS

Current Account	*£ million*
Trade in goods and services	
Trade in goods	(92,876)
Trade in services	48,878
Total trade in goods and services	(43,998)
Income	
Compensation of employees	(619)
Investment income	33,748
Total income	33,129
Total current transfers	(13,624)
TOTAL (CURRENT BALANCE)	(24,493)

Source: ONS – *Annual Abstract of Statistics 2009* (Crown copyright)

EMPLOYMENT

DISTRIBUTION OF THE WORKFORCE

Claimant count	902,400
Workforce jobs	31,661,000
HM forces	193,000
Self-employment jobs	4,181,000
Employees jobs	27,232,000
Government-supported trainees	54,000

Source: ONS – *Annual Abstract of Statistics 2009* (Crown copyright)

EMPLOYMENT

Age	*Male*	*Thousands Female*
16–17	260	265
18–24	1,935	1,729
25–34	3,444	2,841
35–49	5,871	5,195
50–64(m)/59(f)	3,943	2,640
65+(m)/60+(f)	443	880
All aged 16+	15,894	13,549

m = male, f = female
Source: ONS – *Annual Abstract of Statistics 2009* (Crown copyright)

UNEMPLOYMENT

		Thousands
Age	*Male*	*Female*
16–17	102	86
18–24	331	196
25–34	182	145
35–49	218	187
50–64(m)/59(f)	147	69
65+(m)/60+(f)	11	12
All aged 16+	990	695

Source: ONS – *Annual Abstract of Statistics 2009* (Crown copyright)

DURATION OF UNEMPLOYMENT

	Thousands
All unemployed	1,685
Duration of unemployment	
Less than 6 months	994
6 months–1 year	276
1 year +	415
1 year + as percentage of total	24.6

Source: ONS – *Annual Abstract of Statistics 2009* (Crown copyright)

AVERAGE EARNINGS AND HOURS OF FULL-TIME EMPLOYEES

	All	*Male*	*Female*
Average weekly earnings (£)	574.3	631.2	485.5
Average hours	39.5	40.8	37.6
Average hourly earnings (£)			
Including overtime	14.53	15.49	12.91
Excluding overtime	14.53	15.54	12.88

Source: ONS – *Annual Abstract of Statistics 2009* (Crown copyright)

NUMBER OF TAXPAYERS BY ANNUAL INCOME[1]

	Number of taxpayers (thousands)
£6,035[2]–£7,499	1,440
£7,500–£9,999	2,900
£10,000–£14,999	6,390
£15,000–£19,999	4,930
£20,000–£29,999	6,910
£30,000–£49,999	5,810
£50,000–£99,999	2,010
£100,000–£199,999	470
£200,000–£499,999	143
£500,000–£999,999	26
£1,000,000+	11
All incomes	31,000

[1] Includes investment income

[2] Basic personal tax-free allowance for 2008–9 (*see* Taxation)

Source: ONS – *Social Trends 2009* (Crown copyright)

LABOUR DISPUTES BY DURATION

Under 5 days	119
5–10 days	12
10–20 days	6
20–30 days	1
30–50 days	2
50+ days	2

Source: ONS – *Annual Abstract of Statistics 2009* (Crown copyright)

WORKING DAYS LOST THROUGH LABOUR DISPUTES BY INDUSTRY

Mining, quarrying, electricity, gas and water	–
Manufacturing	16,000
Construction	2,000
Transport, storage and communications	657,000
Public administration and defence	325,000
Education	31,000
Health and social work	5,000
Other community, social and personal services	4,000
All other industries and services	2,000

Source: ONS – *Annual Abstract of Statistics 2009* (Crown copyright)

TRADE UNIONS

Year	*No. of unions*	*Total membership*
2000–1	237	7,897,519
2001–2	226	7,779,393
2002–3	216	7,750,990
2003–4	213	7,735,983
2004–5	206	7,559,062
2005–6	193	7,473,000
2006–7	192	7,602,842
2007–8	193	7,627,693

Source: ONS – *Annual Abstract of Statistics 2009* (Crown copyright)

COST OF LIVING AND INFLATION RATES

The first cost of living index to be calculated took July 1914 as 100 and was based on the pattern of expenditure of working-class families in 1914. The cost of living index was superseded in 1947 by the general index of retail prices (RPI), although the older term is still popularly applied.

The Harmonised Index of Consumer Prices (HICP) was introduced in 1997 to enable comparisons within the European Union using an agreed methodology. In 2003 the National Statistician renamed the HICP as the Consumer Prices Index (CPI) to reflect its role as the main target measure of inflation for macroeconomic purposes. The RPI and indices based on it continue to be published alongside the CPI. Pensions, benefits and index-linked gilts continue to be calculated with reference to RPI or its derivatives.

CPI AND RPI

The CPI and RPI measure the changes month by month in the average level of prices of goods and services purchased by households in the UK. The indices are compiled using a selection of around 650 goods and services, and the prices charged for these items are collected at regular intervals at about 150 locations throughout the country. The Office for National Statistics (ONS) reviews the components of the indices once every year to reflect changes in consumer preferences and the establishment of new products. The table below shows changes made by the ONS to the CPI 'shopping basket' in 2009.

CPI excludes a number of items that are included in RPI, mainly related to housing such as council tax and a range of owner-occupier housing costs, such as mortgage payments. The CPI covers all private households, whereas RPI excludes the top 4 per cent by income and pensioner households who derive at least three-quarters of their income from state benefits. The two indices use different methodologies to combine the prices of goods and services, which means that since 1996 the CPI inflation measure is less than the RPI inflation measure.

INFLATION RATE

The 12-monthly percentage change in the 'all items' index of the RPI or CPI is referred to as the rate of inflation. As the most familiar measure of inflation, RPI is often referred to as the 'headline rate of inflation'. CPI is the main measure of inflation for macroeconomic purposes and forms the basis for the government's inflation target, which is currently 2 per cent. The percentage change in prices between any two months/years can be obtained using the following formula:

$$\frac{\text{Later date RPI/CPI} - \text{Earlier date RPI/CPI}}{\text{Earlier date RPI/CPI}} \times 100$$

CHANGES TO THE 2009 'SHOPPING BASKET' OF GOODS AND SERVICES

The table below shows changes to the 2009 CPI* basket of goods and services made by the ONS in order to reflect changes in consumer preferences and the establishment of new products:

Goods and Services Group	*Removed items*	*New items*
Alcoholic beverages	1–2 litre bottles of cider; 3 litre box of wine	500ml–750ml bottles of cider; rosé wine
Audio-visual equipment	MP3 player	blu-ray disc; freeview box; MP4 player
Food	fresh single cream; frozen imported lamb loin chops; imported Cheddar cheese; individual chilled ready-meal; large eggs; peaches; small individual yoghurt/fromage frais	chilled fish/meat/vegetable based ready-meal; fresh double cream; large free range eggs; Parmesan cheese; peaches/nectarines, plums; rotisserie-cooked hot whole chicken; small individual yoghurt
Furniture, furnishings and carpets	–	hardwood flooring
Maintenance and repair services	hire of domestic steam wallpaper stripper	–
Personal effects	watch repair, clean and service	replacement watch battery
Recreation and culture	can of cat food; DVD film rental; TV, video and DVD rentals	cat food pouch; DVD rental internet subscription; TV rentals
Tools and equipment for the house and garden	–	hire of domestic carpet shampoo/cleaner

* RPI goods and services are grouped together under different classifications

eg to find the CPI rate of inflation for 2006, using the annual averages for 2005 and 2006:

$$\frac{102.3 - 100.0}{100.0} \times 100 = 2.3$$

From 14 February 2006 the reference year for CPI was re-based to 2005=100 to improve price comparison clarity across the EU. None of the underlying data, from which the re-referenced series was calculated, was revised. Historical rates of change (such as annual inflation figures), calculated from the re-based rounded index levels, were revised due to the effect of rounding. The CPI rate of inflation figure given in the table below may differ by plus or minus 0.1 percentage points from the figure calculated by the above equation. The change of reference period and revision due to rounding does not apply to the RPI which remains unchanged.

The RPI and CPI figures are published by the Office for National Statistics on either the second or third Tuesday of each month in an Indices bulletin and electronically on the National Statistics website (W www.statistics.gov.uk).

PURCHASING POWER OF THE POUND

Changes in the internal purchasing power of the pound may be defined as the 'inverse' of changes in the level of prices: when prices go up, the amount which can be purchased with a given sum of money goes down. To find the purchasing power of the pound in one month or year, given that it was 100p in a previous month or year, the calculation would be:

$$100\text{p} \times \frac{\text{Earlier month/year RPI}}{\text{Later month/year RPI}}$$

Thus, if the purchasing power of the pound is taken to be 100p in 1975, the comparable purchasing power in 2000 would be:

$$100\text{p} \times \frac{34.2}{170.3} = 20.1\text{p}$$

For longer term comparisons, it has been the practice to use an index which has been constructed by linking together the RPI for the period 1962 to date; an index derived from the consumers expenditure deflator for the period from 1938 to 1962; and the pre-war 'cost of living' index for the period 1914 to 1938. This long-term index enables the internal purchasing power of the pound to be calculated for any year from 1914 onwards. It should be noted that these figures can only be approximate.

	Annual average RPI (1987 = 100)	*Purchasing power of £ (1998 = 1.00)*	*Annual average CPI (2005 = 100)**	*Rate of inflation (RPI/CPI)*
1914	2.8	58.18		
1915	3.5	46.54		
1920	7.0	23.27		
1925	5.0	32.58		
1930	4.5	36.20		
1935	4.0	40.72		
1938	4.4	37.02		
There are no official figures for 1939–45				
1946	7.4	22.01		
1950	9.0	18.10		
1955	11.2	14.54		
1960	12.6	12.93		
1965	14.8	11.00		
1970	18.5	8.80		
1975	34.2	4.76		
1980	66.8	2.44	18.0	
1985	94.6	1.72	6.1	
1990	126.1	1.29	71.5	9.5/7.0
1995	149.1	1.09	86.0	3.5/2.6
1998	162.9	1.00	91.1	3.4/1.6
2000	170.3	0.96	93.1	3.0/0.8
2005	192.0	0.85	100.0	2.8/2.1
2006	198.1	0.82	102.3	3.2/2.3
2007	206.6	0.79	104.7	4.3/2.3
2008	214.8	0.76	108.5	4.0/3.6

* In accordance with an EU Commission regulation all published CPI figures were re-based to 2005 = 100 with effect from 14 February 2006, replacing the 1996 = 100 series

INSURANCE

AUTHORISATION AND REGULATION OF INSURANCE COMPANIES

Since 2001, the Financial Services Authority (FSA) has been the authorising, enforcement, supervisory and rule-making body of insurers. Since 2005, this has also included insurance brokers.

The FSA's powers are primarily conferred by the Financial Services and Markets Act 2000, which unified the previous sectoral arrangements and regulators.

AUTHORISATION

The FSA's role is to ensure that firms to which it grants authorisation satisfy the necessary financial criteria, that the senior management of the company are 'fit and proper persons' and that unauthorised firms are not permitted to trade. This part of the FSA's role was previously undertaken by HM Treasury under the Insurance Companies Act 1982, which was repealed when the Financial Services and Markets Act came fully into force. At the end of 2008 there were over 1,200 insurance organisations and friendly societies with authorisation from the FSA to transact one or more classes of insurance business in the UK. However, the single European insurance market, established in 1994, gave insurers authorised in any other European Union country automatic UK authorisation without further formality. This means a potential market of over 5,000 insurers.

REGULATION

All life insurers, general insurers, re-insurers, insurance and reinsurance brokers, financial advisers and composite firms are statutorily regulated. This is achieved through the formulation (after consultation) by the FSA of rules and guidance for regulated organisations. The FSA is also responsible for consumer education and the reduction of financial crime, particularly money laundering.

FINANCIAL SERVICES AUTHORITY, 25 The North Colonnade, London E14 5HS T 020-7066 1000 W www.fsa.gov.uk

COMPLAINTS

Disputes between policyholders and insurers can be referred to the Financial Ombudsman Service (FOS). Policyholders with a complaint against their financial services provider must firstly take the matter to the highest level within the company. Thereafter, if it remains unresolved and it involves an amount below £100,000, they can refer, free of charge, to the Ombudsman Bureau, which examines the facts of a complaint and delivers a decision binding on the provider (but not the policyholder). Small businesses with a turnover of up to £1m also have access to the scheme. The Financial Ombudsman Service also covers other areas of the financial services industry including banks, building societies and investment firms. In 2008 the FOS handled 127,471 complaints about financial services companies.

FINANCIAL SERVICES OMBUDSMAN SERVICE, South Quay Plaza, 183 Marsh Wall, London E14 9SR T 020-7964 1000 F 020-7964 1002 W www.financial-ombudsman.org.uk
Chief Ombudsman, Walter Merricks, CBE

ASSOCIATION OF BRITISH INSURERS

Over 90 per cent of the domestic business of UK insurance companies is transacted by the 340 members of the Association of British Insurers (ABI). ABI is a trade association which protects and promotes the interests of all its insurance company members. Only insurers authorised in the EU are eligible for membership. Brokers, intermediaries, financial advisers and claims handlers may not join ABI but may have their own trade associations.

In May 2009 ABI Director-General Stephen Haddrill was appointed Chief Executive of the Financial Reporting Council. His replacement is expected to be appointed by the end of 2009.

ASSOCIATION OF BRITISH INSURERS (ABI), 51 Gresham Street, London EC2V 7HQ W www.abi.org.uk
Chair, Archie Kane
Director-General, vacant

BALANCE OF PAYMENTS

The financial services industry contributes 7.6 per cent to the UK's gross domestic product (GDP). In 2007 insurance companies' net exports rose to £5.5bn, a 34 per cent increase on 2006.

WORLDWIDE MARKET

The UK insurance industry is the second largest in the world behind the United States.

Market	*Premium Income ($bn)*	*Percentage of total*
United States	1,230	30
UK	464	11
Japan	425	10

TAKEOVERS AND MERGERS

The UK banking crisis saw the takeover of Halifax Bank of Scotland (HBOS) by Lloyds TSB. Both groups had substantial insurance interests and the resulting company, Lloyds Banking Group, instantly became the UK's largest insurance group with insurers as diverse as Halifax, esure, Scottish Widows and Clerical Medical.

INDUSTRY ISSUES

Because of the way they are structured and the long-term nature of their investments, insurers have coped with the effects of the recession far better than their banking counterparts. In such cases as Scottish Widows, Clerical Medical, Direct Line and Churchill, insurers are owned by banking groups but because the FSA regulations insist that their operations are kept entirely separate, there can be no cross-subsidy and there have been no insurers seeking government rescue packages. Tightening of financial regulation, after a crisis of the magnitude seen in autumn 2008, is inevitable. The difficult task for insurers will be to persuade the government, the EU authorities and the FSA not to treat the whole financial services industry as one entity and to recognise the differences between banks and insurers.

Insurers rely on investment income to offset underwriting losses but with interest rates and investment returns at a low ebb, margins will be tight. In a more favourable economic climate insurers would increase premiums to offset the loss of investment income, but the downturn necessitates exploring alternative strategies such as cuts in dividends or operational costs. Recession is traditionally accompanied by an increase in insurance fraud, the first signs of which are beginning to emerge.

GENERAL INSURANCE

After the serious flooding of the previous year, the 2008 claim figures returned to manageable levels. The total claim payments for UK weather-related incidents dropped from £2,459m in 2007 to £904m in 2008. A number of claims followed flash flooding in the West Country in May 2008, but this was minor compared to 2007. As recession took hold and the government looked for ways to cut public spending and stimulate the housing market, insurers raised concerns that the flood defence budget would be reduced. Insurers insisted that the availability of flood insurance cover is conditional on continued government maintenance of adequate flood defences. Plans to encourage more home-building might provide a stimulus to the building trade, but if the land used for such building is prone to flooding, the new houses could prove uninsurable and therefore un-sellable.

At the beginning of 2008, critical illness, income protection and non-investment life insurers agreed to change the rules on payments in cases where medical information has not been disclosed because of innocent oversight or because a client could not have known of the condition at the time. This was welcomed by policy holders, the media and the Financial Ombudsman Service because it closed a loophole associated with many consumer complaints.

The controversy over a disease known as pleural plaques – small fibrous disks on the inside of the chest – continued throughout the year. In October 2007 the House of Lords held that this condition, which insurers and the medical profession stated was symptomless and did not develop into any other asbestos-related condition, did not merit compensation. However, the Scottish Parliament published the Damages (Asbestos-related Conditions) (Scotland) Bill in June 2008 which was designed to force the payment of compensation. The Bill became law in Scotland but insurers are mounting a judicial review.

For the 14th year in succession, motor insurance recorded an underwriting loss. Premium increases are the inevitable consequence, but with more than a hundred insurers, a competitive market, low increases in parts prices, and the risk that premium increases may force policyholders to drive without insurance, the levels of increase might be less steep than predicted. The highest motor insurance premiums are paid by the oldest and youngest drivers, and for a number of years insurers have targeted these groups to try to reduce claims. The latest initiative focuses on drivers under 21, proposing a limit on passenger numbers. Motoring organisations and road safety groups welcomed the proposal, but it was met with little enthusiasm from ministers.

LONDON INSURANCE MARKET

The London Insurance Market is a unique wholesale marketplace and a distinct, separate sector of the UK insurance and reinsurance industry. It is the world's leading market for internationally traded insurance and reinsurance, its business comprising mainly overseas non-life large and high-exposure risks. The market is centred on the City of London, which provides the required financial, banking, legal and other support services. Around 52 per cent of London market business is transacted at Lloyd's of London, 42 per cent through insurance companies and the remainder through protection and indemnity clubs. In 2007 the market had a written gross premium income of over £24.5bn. Around 170 Lloyd's brokers service the market.

The trade association for the international insurers and reinsurers writing primarily non-marine insurance and all classes of reinsurance business in the London market is the International Underwriting Association (IUA).

INTERNATIONAL UNDERWRITING ASSOCIATION, London Underwriting Centre, 3 Mincing Lane, London EC3R 7DD **W** www.iua.co.uk

BRITISH INSURANCE COMPANIES

The following insurance company figures refer to members and certain non-members of the ABI.

WORLDWIDE GENERAL BUSINESS UNDERWRITING RESULTS *(£m)*

	2006			*2007*		
	UK	*Overseas*	*Total*	*UK*	*Overseas*	*Total*
Motor						
Premiums	10,277	3,289	13,566	10,527	3,435	13,962
Profit (loss)	(204)	3	(201)	(267)	3	(17)
Percentage of premiums	2.0	0.1	1.5	2.5	0.1	0.1
Non-motor						
Premiums	20,144	6,681	26,825	20,770	6,875	27,645
Profit (loss)	1,685	218	1,903	(667)	218	(206)
Percentage of premiums	8.4	3.3	7.1	3.2	3.2	0.7

CLAIMS STATISTICS *(£m)*

	2004	*2005*	*2006*	*2007*	*2008*
Theft	512	475	517	525	531
Fire	812	1,128	1,139	1,102	1,273
Weather	424	735	475	2,459	904
Domestic subsidence	199	225	302	162	137
Business interruption	108	267	168	320	193
Total	2,052	2,851	2,601	4,568	3,038

WORLDWIDE GENERAL BUSINESS TRADING RESULTS *(£m)*

	2006	*2007*
Net written premiums	41,440	43,700
Underwriting results	1,624	90
Investment income	5,118	5,374
Overall trading profit	6,742	5,464
Profit as percentage of premium income	16.3	12.5

NET PREMIUM INCOME BY SECTOR 2006 *(£m)*

	UK	*Overseas*
Motor	10,527	3,435
Non-motor	20,770	6,875
Marine, aviation and transport	639	277
Reinsurance	807	218
Total general business	32,743	10,805
Ordinary long-term	185,193	33,513
Industrial long-term	204	–
Total long-term business	185,397	33,513

LLOYD'S OF LONDON

Lloyd's of London is an international market for almost all types of general insurance. Lloyd's currently has a capacity to accept insurance premiums of around £16.1bn. Much of this business comes from outside the UK and makes a valuable contribution to the balance of payments.

A policy is underwritten at Lloyd's by a mixture of private and corporate members, corporate members having been admitted for the first time in 1992. Specialist underwriters accept insurance risks at Lloyd's on behalf of members (referred to as 'Names') grouped in syndicates. There are currently 80 syndicates of varying sizes, each managed by one of the 51 underwriting agents approved by the Council of Lloyd's.

Members divide into three categories: corporate organisations, individuals who have no limit to their liability for losses, and those who have an agreed limit (known as NameCos).

Lloyd's is incorporated by an act of parliament (Lloyd's Acts 1871 onwards) and is governed by an 18-person council, made up of six working, six external and six nominated members. The structure immediately below this changed when, in 2002, Lloyd's members voted at an extraordinary general meeting to implement a new franchise system for the market with the aim of improving profitability. The first move was the introduction of a new governance structure, replacing the Lloyd's Market Board and the Lloyd's Regulatory Board with a new 11-person Lloyd's Franchise Board. Four main committees report to this new board.

The corporation is a non-profit making body chiefly financed by its members' subscriptions. It provides the premises, administrative staff and services enabling Lloyd's underwriting syndicates to conduct their business. It does not, however, assume corporate liability for the risks accepted by its members. Individual members are responsible to the full extent of their personal means for their underwriting affairs unless they have converted to limited liability companies.

Lloyd's syndicates have no direct contact with the public. All business is transacted through insurance brokers accredited by the Corporation of Lloyd's. In addition, non-Lloyd's brokers in the UK, when guaranteed by Lloyd's brokers, are able to deal directly with Lloyd's motor syndicates, a facility which has made the Lloyd's market more accessible to the insuring public.

The FSA has ultimate responsibility for the regulation of the Lloyd's market. However, in situations where Lloyd's internal regulatory and compensation arrangements are more far-reaching – as for example with the Lloyd's Central Fund which safeguards claim payments to policyholders – the regulatory role is delegated to the Council of Lloyd's.

Lloyd's also provides the most comprehensive shipping intelligence service in the world. The shipping and other information received from Lloyd's agents, shipowners, news agencies and other sources throughout the world is collated and distributed to the media as well as to the maritime and commercial sectors in general. *Lloyd's List* is London's oldest daily newspaper and contains news of general commercial interest as well as shipping information. It has been independent of Lloyd's since a management buy-out in 1992. *Lloyd's Shipping Index,* published weekly, lists some 23,000 ocean-going merchant vessels in alphabetical order and gives the latest known report of each.

DEVELOPMENTS IN 2008

The hurricane seasons of 2006 and 2007 saw very low recorded losses in the Lloyd's market and it was inevitable this would come to an end. Hurricanes Ike and Gustav in 2008 cost Lloyd's around £1.4bn.

In other circumstances a 51 per cent drop in pre-tax profit to £1,899m might be regarded as disappointing. Seen in the context of global recession, however, it is further evidence of the difference between sectors of the financial services industry. Lloyd's, like any insurer, is not immune from lower investment returns and capital values, but optimistic commentators believe that a difficult economic climate will encourage improved underwriting and risk management. Lloyd's itself highlighted that it had better results during the Great Depression than in the boom years of the 1980s.

LLOYD'S OF LONDON, One Lime Street, London EC3M 7HA T 020-7327 1000
W www.lloydsoflondon.co.uk
Chair, Lord Levene of Portsoken
Chief Executive, Richard Ward

LLOYD'S MEMBERSHIP

	2007	*2008*
Individual	907	773
Corporate	1,155	1,238

LLOYD'S SEGMENTAL RESULTS 2008 *(£m)*

	Gross premiums written	*Net earned premium*	*Result*
Reinsurance	6,298	4,522	734
Casualty	3,762	3,005	1484
Property	3,971	3,125	148
Marine	1,334	1,041	160
Motor	939	897	3
Energy	1,150	814	(194)
Aviation	481	363	48
Life	49	28	(2)
Total from syndicate operations	17,984	13,795	1,000

LIFE AND LONG-TERM INSURANCE AND PENSIONS

Although a great deal of work and discussion was conducted in 2008, the FSA's Distribution Review remains to be completed. This is a fundamental review of the way financial services products are sold and how those who sell them should be remunerated. The FSA has delayed making its final decision on these issues until late 2009.

Publicity from a variety of organisations to persuade consumers to make provision for their retirement through savings in ISAs, life insurance and other vehicles continued throughout 2008. However the onset of recession brought historic lows in interest rates and increased unemployment, making this task harder. With the UK population living longer, the economy will struggle to provide an adequate state pension, so individuals face contributing themselves or working for longer.

During 2008 attention also turned to retirees intending to use their pension pot to buy an annuity. Pension providers attracted criticism for depriving consumers of the best annuity deals by being slow to react. In May 2008 the Association of British Insurers announced an initiative to streamline the annuity transfer process and early indications are that transfer times are falling. With 90 per cent of the pension annuity market signed up to this scheme, there's now pressure on the remainder to join.

Genetic testing has long been a controversial and emotive subject for life insurers. Some countries already prohibit the practice of forcing policy holders to disclose genetic test information. In the UK since 2001, insurers have agreed with the government to a moratorium on requesting any form of genetic data in all but the largest life-insurance policies. Even if a person has had an adverse result from a predictive genetic test, they do not need to disclose this when buying an average-sized life insurance policy. All UK life, medical and health insurers are signatories to this agreement, which has been extended until 2014.

Overall, life and pensions results for 2008 were static. In real terms, regular premium, accumulation and protection product sales showed no change year-on-year from 2007.

PAYMENTS TO POLICYHOLDERS *(£m)*

	2006	*2007*
Payments to UK policyholders	144,223	170,154
Payments to overseas policyholders	17,487	22,327
Total	161,710	192,481

WORLDWIDE LONG-TERM PREMIUM INCOME *(£m)*

	2003	*2004*	*2005*	*2006*	*2007*
UK Life Insurance					
Regular Premium	11,777	10,507	10,542	9,414	8,927
Single Premium	17,010	20,516	25,421	32,088	40,256
Total	28,787	31,023	36,032	41,502	49,183
Individual Pensions					
Regular Premium	8,059	8,973	7,910	8,628	8,714
Single Premium	14,278	12,036	11,631	24,906	24,368
Total	22,337	21,009	19,601	33,534	33,082
Other Pensions					
Regular Premium	4,239	4,183	4,761	5,752	5,687
Single Premium	29,052	25,836	34,838	59,410	93,020
Total	33,291	30,019	39,539	60,162	98,707
Other (eg Income protection, Annuities)	5,502	4,994	4,400	3,207	2,800
TOTAL UK PREMIUM INCOME	89,917	87,045	99,503	177,205	183,772
Overseas Premium Income					
Regular Premium	7,958	7,692	8,171	8,191	7,877
Single Premium	14,464	16,075	16,814	21,104	25,693
Total	22,422	23,767	24,985	21,925	33,570
TOTAL WORLDWIDE PREMIUM INCOME	112,339	110,812	124,488	146,500	217,432

PRIVATE MEDICAL INSURANCE

	2004	2005	2006	2007	2008
Number of people covered (thousand)	5,820	5,820	5,879	6,004	6,224
Corporate	4,084	4,125	4,188	4,341	4,571
Personal	1,736	1,695	1,691	1,663	1,653
Gross Earned Premiums (£m)	2,855	2,942	3,070	3,241	3,468
Corporate	1,433	1,493	1,561	1,696	1,831
Personal	1,422	1,449	1,509	1,545	1,631
Gross Claims Incurred (£m)	2,188	2,255	2,376	2,501	2,653

INVESTMENTS OF INSURANCE COMPANIES 2007

Investment of funds	*Long-term business (£m)*	*General business (£m)*
Index-linked British government securities	54,473	303
Non-index-linked British government securities	112,634	10,556
Other UK public sector debt securities	33,001	1,251
Overseas government, provincial and municipal securities	44,748	12,532
Debentures, loan shares, preference and guaranteed stocks and shares		
UK	148,619	12,919
Overseas	127,368	16,928
Ordinary stocks and shares UK	336,335	7,134
Overseas	224,021	2,918
Unit trusts		
Equities	150,866	2,311
Fixed interest	45,873	817
Loans secured on property	23,060	5,764
Real property and ground rents	75,296	1,384
Other invested assets	101,594	46,195
Total invested assets	1,477,890	121,013
NET INVESTMENT INCOME	49,799	5,372

NEW BUSINESS

	2004	2005	2006	2007	2008
New regular premiums					
Investment and savings	109	117	92	88	75
Individual protection	977	894	905	867	859
Group protection	385	387	311	318	290
Individual pension	1,864	2,127	3,024	3,273	3,363
Group pension	802	766	753	821	989
Offshore business	n/a	26	22	21	19
TOTAL REGULAR	4,136	4,319	5,107	5,388	5,594
New single premiums					
Investments and savings	20,150	24,121	30,540	38,903	23,769
Individual protection	1,606	1,698	1,634	1,266	1,019
Individual pensions	10,621	12,164	18,758	22,165	18,430
Retirement income products	9,022	9,307	12,157	14,061	13,916
Occupational pensions	4,385	6,544	10,790	10,986	12,097
Offshore business	n/a	4,804	7,150	7,594	7,777
TOTAL SINGLE	45,784	58,638	81,034	94,970	77,008

TAXATION

The government raises money to pay for public services such as education, health and the social security system through tax. Each year the Chancellor of the Exchequer's budget sets out how much it will cost to provide these services and how much tax is therefore needed to pay for them. HM Revenue and Customs (HMRC) is the government department that collects it. There are several different types of tax. The varieties that individuals may have to pay include income tax payable on earnings, pensions, state benefits, savings and investments; capital gains tax (CGT) payable on the disposal of certain assets; inheritance tax (IHT) payable on estates upon death and certain lifetime gifts; stamp duty payable when purchasing property and shares; and value added tax (VAT) payable on goods and services plus certain other duties such as fuel duty on petrol and excise duty on alcohol and tobacco. Government funds are also raised from companies and small businesses through corporation tax.

HELP AND INFORMATION ON TAXATION

For detailed information on any aspect of taxation individuals may contact their local tax office or enquiry centre. The HMRC website (W www.hmrc.gov.uk) provides wide-ranging information online. All HMRC forms, leaflets and guides are listed on, and can be downloaded from, the website or ordered by telephone. A list of all HMRC telephone helplines and order lines can also be found on the website. Those most relevant to topics covered in this section on taxation have been included at pertinent points throughout. Information on taxation is also available in the Money, Tax and Benefits section of the government's public information website for individuals W www.direct.gov.uk, and the Taxes, Returns and Payroll section of the equivalent information website for companies, W www.businesslink.gov.uk.

INCOME TAX

Income tax is a tax on different sorts of income. Not all types of income are taxable, however, and individuals are only taxed on their 'taxable income' above a certain level. Reliefs and allowances can also reduce or, in some cases, cancel out an individual's income tax bill.

An individual's taxable income is assessed each tax year, starting on 6 April one year and ending on 5 April the following year. The following information relates specifically to the year of assessment 2009–10, ending on 5 April 2010, and has only limited application to earlier years. Changes due to come into operation at a later date are briefly mentioned where information is available. Types of income that are taxable include:

- earnings from employment or self-employment
- most pensions income including state, company and personal pensions
- interest on most savings
- income (dividends) from shares
- income from property
- income received from a trust
- certain state benefits
- an individual's share of any joint income

There are certain sorts of income on which individuals never pay tax. These are ignored altogether when working out how much income tax an individual may need to pay. Types of income that are not taxable include:

- certain state benefits and tax credits such as child benefit, working tax credit, child tax credit, pension credit, attendance allowance, disability living allowance, income support, housing benefit and the first 28 weeks of incapacity benefit
- winter fuel payments
- income from tax-free National Savings and Investments, such as savings certificates
- interest and terminal bonuses under Save As You Earn schemes
- interest, dividends and other income from various tax-free investments, notably individual savings accounts (ISAs)
- premium bond, national lottery and gambling prizes

PERSONAL ALLOWANCE

Every individual resident in the UK for tax purposes has a 'personal allowance'. This is an amount of taxable income an individual is allowed to earn or receive each year tax-free. This tax year (2009–10) the basic personal allowance or tax-free amount is £6,475. Individuals may be entitled to a higher personal allowance if they are 65 or over. Income tax is only due on an individual's taxable income that is above his or her tax-free allowance. Husbands and wives are taxed separately, with each entitled to his or her personal allowance. Each spouse may obtain other allowances and reliefs where the required conditions are satisfied.

The amount of personal allowance depends on an individual's age on 5 April 2009 and, if he or she is 65 or over, the total income received from all taxable sources. There are three age-related levels of personal allowance – *see* table below. If an individual became 65 or 75 during the year to 5 April 2009, he or she is entitled to the allowance for that age group.

If an individual's income is over the 'income limit', the age-related allowance reduces by half the amount (£1 for every £2) he or she has over that limit, until the basic rate allowance is reached. For a 66-year-old with an income of £23,300 (£400 over the limit), for example, the age-related allowance would reduce by £200 to £22,700.

Individuals always receive the basic allowance, whatever the level of their income. The government has announced that the personal allowance for those aged 75 and over will increase to £10,000 in 2010–11, meaning that no pensioner aged 75 or over will pay any tax until their annual income reaches £10,000.

As in the past, throughout the tax year 2009–10, all individuals entitled to the basic personal allowance receive the same amount of tax-free income – currently £6,475. However, the government announced in the April 2009 budget that, from 6 April 2010, the value of the basic personal allowance will be restricted for individuals with gross incomes over £100,000, tapering down to zero. It is anticipated that where an individual's gross income is above the £100,000 income limit, the amount of their allowance will be reduced by £1 for every £2 above the income limit up to a maximum of the full amount of the basic personal allowance. Where an individual's gross income before personal allowances is below or equal to the £100,000 income limit, he or she will continue to be entitled to the full amount of the basic personal allowance.

LEVELS OF PERSONAL ALLOWANCE FOR 2009–10

	Personal allowance	*Income limit*
Age under 65	£6,475	none
Age 65–74	£9,490	£22,900
Age 75 and over	£9,640	£22,900

BLIND PERSON'S ALLOWANCE

If an individual is registered blind or is unable to perform any work for which eyesight is essential, he or she can claim blind person's allowance, an extra amount of tax-free income added to the personal allowance. In 2009–10 the blind person's allowance is £1,890. It is the same for everyone who can claim it, whatever his or her age or level of income. If an individual is married or in a civil partnership and cannot use all of his or her blind person's allowance because of insufficient income, the unused part of the allowance can be passed to the spouse or civil partner.

Other deductible allowances and reliefs that have the effect of reducing an income tax bill are available to taxpayers in certain circumstances and will be explained in more detail later in this section.

CALCULATING INCOME TAX DUE

Individuals' liability to pay income tax is determined by establishing their level of taxable income for the year. For married couples and civil partners income must be allocated between the couple by reference to the individual who is beneficially entitled to that income. Where income arises from jointly held assets, it is normally apportioned equally between the partners. If, however, the beneficial interests in jointly held assets are not equal, in most cases couples can make a special declaration to have income apportioned by reference to the actual interests in that income.

To work out an individual's liability for tax, his or her taxable income must be allocated between three different types: earned income (excluding income from savings and dividends); income from savings; and company dividends from shares and other equity-based investments.

After the tax-free allowance plus any deductible allowances and reliefs have been taken into account, the amount of tax an individual pays is calculated using different tax rates and a series of tax bands. The tax band applies to an individual's income after tax allowances and any reliefs have been taken into account. Individuals are not taxed on all of their income.

As part of the government's ongoing programme of reform to the UK tax and benefit system, there were some significant changes to income tax rates for 2008–9. The basic rate of income tax was reduced from 22 per cent to 20 per cent. At the same time, the 10 per cent starting rate was removed for earned income and pensions. This change created a simpler structure of two rates which persists for 2009–10: a 20 pence (in the pound) basic rate and a 40 pence (in the pound) higher rate.

The 10 per cent starting rate continues to be available for savings income only, with a limit of £2,440. If an individual's taxable non-savings income is above this £2,440 limit then the 10 per cent savings rate is not applicable.

The government has announced that from 6 April 2010 a new 50 per cent rate of income tax will apply to taxable non-savings and savings income above £150,000.

INCOME TAX RATES (PER CENT) FOR 2009–10

Band	*Earned*	*Band*	*Savings*	*Dividends*
£0–£37,400	20%	£0–£2,440*	10%	10%
£37,400+	40%	£2,440–£37,400	20%	10%
		£37,400+	40%	32.5%

*If an individual's taxable non-savings income is above £2,440 the 20 per cent tax band applies to savings income from £0–£37,400

The first calculation is applied to earned income which includes income from employment or self employment, most pension income and rental income plus the value of a wide range of employee fringe benefits such as company cars, living accommodation and private medical insurance (for more information on fringe benefits, *see* later section on payment of income tax). In working out the amount of an individual's net taxable earnings, all expenses incurred 'wholly, exclusively and necessarily' in the performance of his or her work duties, together with the cost of business travel, may be deducted. Fees and subscriptions to certain professional bodies may also be deducted. Redundancy payments and other sums paid on the termination of an employment are assessable to income tax, but the first £30,000 is normally tax-free provided the payment is not linked with the recipient's retirement or performance.

The first £37,400 of taxable income remaining after the tax-free allowance plus any deductible allowances and reliefs have been taken into account is taxed at the new basic rate of 20 per cent. Any excess over £37,400 is taxed at the higher rate of 40 per cent.

Savings and dividend income is added to an individual's other taxable income and taxed last. This means that tax on these sorts of income is based on an individual's highest income tax band.

SAVINGS INCOME

The second calculation is applied to any income from savings received by an individual. The appropriate rate at which it must be taxed is determined by adding income from savings to an individual's other taxable income, excluding dividends.

There is a 10 per cent starting rate for savings income only, with a limit of £2,440. If an individual's taxable non-savings income is above this limit then the 10 per cent savings rate is not applicable. Savings income that falls above the £2,440 band but within the £37,400 basic rate band is taxable at 20 per cent. Savings income that falls above the £37,400 band is taxable at 40 per cent. If savings income falls on both sides of a tax band, the relevant amounts are taxed at the rates for each tax band. As noted above, from 6 April 2010, the government has announced that it will introduce a new 50 per cent income tax on taxable non-savings and savings income over £150,000.

Most savings income, such as interest paid on bank and building society accounts, already has tax at a rate of 20 per cent deducted from it 'at source' – that is, before it is paid out to individuals. This is confirmed by the entry 'net interest' on bank and building society statements.

Higher rate taxpayers whose income is sufficient to pay 40 per cent tax on their savings income must let their tax office know what savings income they have received so that the extra tax they owe can be collected.

Non taxpayers – that is, individuals, including most children, whose taxable income is less than their tax allowances – can register to have their savings interest paid 'gross' without any tax being deducted from it at source. To do this, they must complete form R85, available at all banks and building societies. Parents or guardians need to fill in this form on behalf of those under 16. For individuals who are unsure whether they qualify as non taxpayers and, therefore, whether they are able to register to have their savings interest paid gross, HMRC offers an 'R85 checker' on its website at W www.hmrc.gov.uk/calcs/r85/.

Non taxpayers who have already had tax deducted from their savings interest can claim it back from HMRC by filling in form R40. For help or information about registering to get interest paid tax-free or to claim tax back on savings interest, individuals may visit W www.hmrc.gov.uk/taxon/bank.htm or call a savings helpline on T 0845-980 0645. Further information is available in the leaflet *IR111: Bank and building society interest – Are you paying tax when you don't need to?*

DIVIDEND INCOME

The third and final income tax calculation is on UK dividends, which means income from shares in UK companies and other share-based investments including unit trusts and open-ended investment companies (OEICs).

Tax on dividends is paid at different rates from tax on savings income and there are two different rates. The rate an individual pays depends on whether his or her overall taxable income (after allowances) falls within or above the basic rate income tax limit, which is £37,400 for the 2009–10 tax year. All dividend income that falls within this limit is taxable at 10 per cent while any that falls above is taxable at 32.5 per cent.

When dividends are paid, a voucher is sent that shows the dividend paid and the amount of associated 'tax credit'. Companies pay dividends out of profits on which they have already paid or are due to pay tax. The tax credit takes account of this and is available to the shareholder to offset against any income tax that may be due on their dividend income. The dividend paid represents 90 per cent of their dividend income. The remaining 10 per cent is made up of the tax credit. In other words the tax credit represents 10 per cent of the dividend income.

Individuals who pay tax at the basic rate have no tax to pay on their dividend income because the tax liability is 10 per cent – the same amount as the tax credit. Higher rate taxpayers pay a total of 32.5 per cent tax on dividend income that falls above the £37,400 basic rate income tax limit, but because the first 10 per cent of the tax due on their dividend income is already covered by the tax credit, in practice they owe only 22.5 per cent.

Non taxpayers cannot claim the 10 per cent tax credit. This is because income tax has not been deducted from the dividends paid to them. The view is that they have simply been given a 10 per cent credit against any income tax due.

The government has announced that from 6 April 2010, there will be three rates of tax for dividends. Dividends otherwise taxable at the basic rate will continue to be taxable at the 10 per cent dividend ordinary rate and dividends otherwise taxable at the higher rate will continue to be taxable at the 32.5 per cent dividend upper rate. A new 42.5 per cent rate of tax will apply to taxable dividend income over £150,000.

If there is significant change to an individual's savings or other income, whatever his or her current tax bracket, it is the individual's responsibility to contact the relevant tax office immediately, even if he or she does not normally complete a tax return. This enables the tax office to work out whether extra or less tax should be paid.

INDIVIDUAL SAVINGS ACCOUNTS (ISAS)

There is a small selection of savings and investment products that is tax-free. This means that there is no tax to pay on any income generated in the form of interest or dividends nor on any increase in the value of the capital invested. Their tax-efficient status has been granted by the government in order to give people an incentive to save more. For this reason there are usually limits and restrictions on the amount of money that an individual may invest in such savings and investments. Individual savings accounts (ISAs) are the best known among tax-efficient savings and investments. They were introduced in 1999 to replace other similar schemes called PEPs and TESSAs. Individuals can use an ISA to save cash, or invest in stocks and shares.

Changes were made to the ISA rules which took effect from April 2008. These reforms removed the distinction between what were previously known as maxi and mini ISAs and simplified an individual's options.

Since 6 April 2009 individuals have been able to save up to £7,200 each tax year in an ISA and receive all profits free of tax provided that they are UK residents and are over 18 (over 16 for cash ISAs). An ISA must be in an individual's name and cannot be held jointly with another person.

Individuals may invest in two separate ISAs each tax year: a cash ISA and a stocks and shares ISA (an umbrella term covering investments in unit trusts, company shares, bonds, investment-type life insurance and so on). Up to £3,600 of an individual's ISA allowance may be saved in one cash ISA with one provider. The remainder of the £7,200 can be invested in one stocks and shares ISA with either the same or a different provider. Alternatively an individual may open a single stocks and shares ISA and invest the full £7,200 into it. Various non-cash assets can be held in a stocks and shares ISA including unit trusts, company shares, bonds, investment-type life insurance and investment trusts.

It was announced in the April 2009 budget that the annual investment limit for ISAs would rise to £10,200, up to £5,100 of which may be saved in cash. These higher limits are already available to people aged 50 and will be available to all from 6 April 2010.

Under the simplified ISA regime, what used to be known as mini cash ISAs, TESSA-only ISAs (TOISAs) and the cash component of a maxi ISA have become cash ISAs. Similarly, mini stocks and shares ISAs, the stocks and shares component of a maxi ISA and all Personal Equity Plans (PEPs) have become stocks and shares ISAs.

ISA savers have the option to transfer some or all of the money they have saved in previous tax years in cash ISAs to their stocks and shares ISA without affecting their annual ISA investment allowance. They may also choose to transfer all the money they have saved to date in a cash ISA in the current tax year to a stocks and shares ISA. However, the rules do not allow the reverse; that is, the transfer of monies saved in a stocks and shares ISA to a cash ISA.

Further details are available via HMRC's ISA helpline on T 0845-604 1701.

DEDUCTIBLE ALLOWANCES AND RELIEF

Income taxpayers may be entitled to certain tax-deductible allowances and reliefs as well as their personal allowances. Examples include the married couple's allowance and maintenance payments relief, both of which are explained below. Unlike the tax-free allowances, these are not amounts of income that an individual can receive tax-free but amounts by which their tax bill can be reduced.

MARRIED COUPLE'S ALLOWANCE

A married couple's allowance (MCA) is available to taxpayers who are married or are in a civil partnership only where one or other partner was born before 6 April 1935. Eligible couples can start to claim the MCA from the year of marriage or civil partnership registration.

The MCA is restricted to give relief at a fixed rate of 10 per cent, which means that – unlike the personal allowance – it is not income that can be received without paying tax. Instead, it reduces an individual's tax bill by up to a fixed amount calculated as 10 per cent of the amount of the allowance to which they are entitled.

Previously there have been two different levels of MCA: a lower rate for couples where either partner was born before 6 April 1935 but was aged under 75, and a higher rate for couples where either partner was aged 75 or over. In the 2009–10 tax year, all MCA claimants in the former category will become 75 at some point during the year. Therefore in 2009–10, there is one rate of MCA for everyone. This is £6,965 at 10 per cent, worth up to £696.50 off a couple's tax bill.

The MCA is made up of two parts. There is a minimum amount (£2,670 in 2009–10) which will always be due. The remaining amount (£4,295 in 2009–10) can be reduced if the husband's income exceeds certain limits.

The husband will normally receive the allowance, but the couple can jointly decide which of them will get the minimum amount of the allowance. Alternatively, they can decide to have the minimum amount of the allowance split equally between them. They must inform their tax office of their decision before the start of the new tax year in which they want the decision to become effective. Once this is done, the change will apply until the couple decides to alter it. The remaining part of the allowance must go to the husband unless he does not have sufficient income to use it.

If an individual does not have enough income to use all his or her share of the married couple's allowance, the tax office can transfer the unused part of it to his or her spouse or civil partner.

Like the personal allowance, the MCA can be gradually reduced at the rate of £1 of the allowance for every £2 of income above the income limit (£22,900 in 2009–10). The amount of MCA can only be affected by the husband's income, and it only starts to be affected if his personal allowance has already been reduced back to the basic level for people under 65. The wife's income never affects the amount of the MCA. It does not matter whether all or part of the minimum amount of the allowance has been transferred to her. Whatever the level of the husband's income, the MCA can never be reduced below the minimum amount. In 2009–10 this is £2,670 at 10 per cent.

The same system of allowance allocation applies to civil partners based on the income of the highest earner. *See* leaflets *FS1 (MCA): Married couple's allowance restrictions* and *REV BN 28: Tax and civil partners.*

MAINTENANCE PAYMENTS RELIEF

An allowance is available to reduce an individual's tax bill for maintenance payments he or she makes to his or her ex spouse or former civil partner in certain circumstances. To be eligible one or other partner must have been born before 6 April 1935; the couple must be legally separated or divorced; the maintenance payments being made must be under a court order; and the payments must be for the maintenance of an ex spouse or former civil partner (provided he or she is not now remarried or in a new civil partnership) or for children who are under 21. For the tax year 2009–10, this allowance can reduce an individual's tax bill by:

- 10 per cent of £2,670 (maximum £267) – this applies where an individual makes maintenance payments of £2,670 or more a year
- 10 per cent of the amount the individual has actually paid – this applies where an individual makes maintenance payments of less than £2,670 a year

An individual cannot claim a tax reduction for any voluntary payments he or she makes for a child, ex spouse or former civil partner. To claim maintenance payments relief, individuals should contact their tax office.

CHARITABLE DONATIONS

A number of charitable donations qualify for tax relief. Individuals can increase the value of regular or one-off charitable gifts, however small, by using the Gift Aid scheme that allows charities or community amateur sports clubs (CASCs) to reclaim basic rate tax relief on donations they receive.

The basic rate of income tax went down from 22 per cent to 20 per cent from 6 April 2008. This was expected to result in a reduction in revenue from Gift Aid donations for charities and CASCs. With a 22 per cent rate, each £100 donated via the scheme was worth £128 to the recipient but with a 20 per cent rate, each £100 gift is worth just £125.

However, it was announced in the 2008 budget that charities and CASCs would be able to claim 'transitional relief' for at least three years (2008–9, 2009–10 and 2010–11) funded by the government, allowing them to retain the 22 per cent relief rate. It therefore remains the case that, until at least 5 April 2011, for every £10 a donor gives using the Gift Aid scheme, the charity or CASC actually receives £12.82 once it reclaims the transitional tax relief at a rate of 22 per cent.

The transitional provision means that where Gift Aid donations are made by basic rate taxpayers, the 22 per cent reclaimable is preserved without an impact on the donor. In the case of higher rate taxpayers the overall effect of the provision is beneficial. Higher rate relief continues to be given in relation to the difference between the basic and higher rates of income tax which means that from April 2008, the higher rate tax relief claimed by the donor increased from 18 per cent to 20 per cent (being the difference between the unchanged 40 per cent higher rate and the new 20 per cent basic rate). Non taxpayers should not use Gift Aid.

For employees or those in receipt of an occupational pension, a tax-efficient way of making regular donations to charities is to make them straight from a salary or pension before income tax is deducted under the Payroll Giving scheme. This effectively reduces the cost of giving for donors which may allow them to give more. For example, it costs a basic-rate taxpayer only £8 in take-home pay to give £10 to charity from their pre-tax pay and where a donor pays higher rate tax at 40 per cent that same donation of £10 costs the taxpayer just £6. Anyone who pays tax through PAYE can give to any charity of their choosing in this way, providing his or her employer or pension provider offers a payroll giving scheme, and there is no limit to the amount individuals can donate.

TAX RELIEF ON PENSION CONTRIBUTIONS

Pensions are long-term investments designed to help ensure that people have enough income in retirement. The government encourages individuals to save towards a pension by offering tax relief on their contributions. Tax relief reduces an individual's tax bill or increases their pension fund.

The way tax relief is given on pension contributions depends on whether an individual pays into a company, public service or personal pension scheme.

For employees who pay into a company or public service pension scheme, most employers take the pension contributions from the employee's pay before deducting tax which means that the individual, whether they pay income tax at the basic or higher rate, gets full tax relief straight away. Some employers, however, use the same method of paying pension contributions as that used by personal pension scheme payers described below.

Individuals who pay into a personal pension scheme make contributions from their net salary; that is, after tax has been deducted. For each pound individuals contribute to their pension from net salary, the pension provider claims tax back from the government at the basic rate of 20 per cent and reinvests it on behalf of the individual into the scheme. In practice this means that for every £80 an individual pays into their pension, they receive £100 in their pension fund.

All higher rate taxpayers currently get 40 per cent tax relief on money they put into a pension. On contributions made from net salary, the first 20 per cent is claimed back from HMRC by the pension scheme in the same way as for a lower rate taxpayer. It is then up to individuals to claim back the other 20 per cent from their tax office, either when they fill in their annual tax return or by telephone or letter.

Most providers of retirement annuities, which are a type of personal pension scheme set up before July 1988, do not offer a 'tax relief at source' scheme whereby they claim back tax at the basic rate as is the case with more modern personal pensions. In such cases, contributing individuals need to claim the tax relief they are due through their tax return or by telephoning or writing to HMRC.

Non taxpayers can still pay into a personal pension scheme and benefit from 20 per cent basic rate relief on the first £2,880 a year they contribute. In practice this means that the government tops up their £2,880 contribution to make it £3,600 which is the current universal pension allowance. Such pension contributions may be made on behalf of a non taxpayer by another individual. An individual may, for example, contribute to a pension on behalf of a husband, wife, civil partner, child or grandchild. Tax relief will be added to their contribution at the basic rate, again on up to £2,880 a year benefiting the recipient, but their own tax bill will not be affected.

In any one tax year, individuals can get tax relief on pension contributions made into any number and type of registered pension schemes of 100 per cent of their annual earnings, irrespective of age, up to a maximum 'annual allowance'. For the tax year 2009–10 the annual allowance is £245,000. Individuals pay tax at 40 per cent on any contributions they make above the annual allowance. Everyone now also has a 'lifetime allowance' (£1.75m for 2009–10) which means taxpayers can save up to a total of £1.75m in their pension fund and still get tax relief at their highest income tax rate on all their contributions.

It was announced in the April 2009 Budget that, from April 2011, tax relief on pension contributions will be restricted for individuals with incomes over £150,000 a year. From that level of income the value of pensions tax relief will be tapered down until it is 20 per cent for those on incomes over £180,000, making it worth the same for each pound of contribution to pension entitlement as for a basic rate income tax payer. In anticipation of this change, the government announced that it was also introducing legislation to prevent individuals from making substantial additional pension contributions prior to the restriction taking effect. Individuals who have never earned in excess of £150,000 are unaffected, as are those who continue with their regular pattern of contributions.

For information and leaflets on pensions and tax relief, contact the government's Pensions Service on T 0845-606 0265 or visit W www.thepensionservice.gov.uk. Another useful source of information and advice is The Pensions Advisory Service (TPAS), an independent voluntary organisation grant-aided by the Department for Work and Pensions at W www.pensionsadvisoryservice.org.uk. Its Pensions Helpline is on T 0845-601 2923.

PAYMENT OF INCOME TAX

Employees have their income tax deducted from their wages throughout the year by their employer who sends it on to HMRC. Those in receipt of a company pension have their due tax deducted in the same way by their pension provider. This system of collecting income tax is known as 'pay as you earn' (PAYE).

BENEFITS IN KIND

The PAYE system is also used to collect tax on certain fringe benefits or 'benefits in kind' that employees or directors receive from their employer but that are not included in their salary cheque or wages. These include company cars, private medical insurance paid for by the employer or cheap or free loans from the employer. Some fringe benefits are tax-free, including employer-paid contributions into an employee's pension fund, cheap or free canteen meals, works buses, in-house sports facilities, reasonable relocation expenses, provision of a mobile phone, workplace nursery places provided for the children of employees, and certain other employer-supported childcare up to £55 a week.

For taxable fringe benefits tax is paid on the 'taxable value' of the benefit. The way this is calculated depends on whether or not the benefit is given to a director or 'higher-paid' employee defined as an individual earning £8,500 gross or more per year, including the value of his or her taxable fringe benefits. Company directors normally count as higher-paid, however much they earn.

Employers submit returns for individual employees to the tax office on the form P11D, with details of any fringe benefits they have been given. Employees should get a copy of this form by 6 July following the end of the tax year and must enter the value of the fringe benefits they have received on their tax return for the relevant year, even if tax has already been paid on them under PAYE. Fringe benefits may be taxed under PAYE by being offset against personal tax allowances in an individual's PAYE code. Otherwise tax will be collected after the end of the tax year by the issue of an assessment on the fringe benefits.

SELF-ASSESSMENT

Individuals who are not on PAYE, notably the self-employed, need to complete a self assessment tax return each year, in paper form or online at the HMRC website (W www.hmrc.gov.uk), and pay any income tax owed in twice-yearly instalments. Some individuals with more complex tax affairs such as those who earn money from rents or investments above a certain level may also need to fill out a self-assessment return, even if they are on PAYE. HMRC uses the figures supplied on the tax return to work out the individual's tax bill, or they can choose to work it out themselves. It is called 'self-assessment' because individuals are responsible for making sure the details they provide are correct.

Tax returns are usually sent out in early April, following the end of the tax year to which they apply. They may also go out at other times, for example if an individual wants to claim an allowance or repayment or to register for self-assessment for the first time.

Individuals with simple tax affairs, including employees, pensioners and the self-employed with turnovers below £30,000, receive a short four-page return. Those with more complex affairs must fill out a full return that has 12 core pages plus extra pages, depending on the sorts of income received.

Central to the self-assessment system is the requirement for individuals to contact their tax office if they do not receive a self-assessment return but think they should or if their financial circumstances change. Individuals have six months from when the tax year ends to report any new income, for example. If an individual becomes self-employed, they have three months after the calendar month in which they began self-employed work to let HMRC know. This can be done by telephoning the helpline number for the newly self employed on T 0845-915 4515.

TAX RETURN FILING AND PAYMENT DEADLINES

There are also key deadlines for filing (sending in) completed tax returns and paying the tax due. Failure to do so can incur penalties, interest charges and surcharges. The deadlines are more generous for individuals who do not want to calculate the tax due themselves and file their tax return online.

KEY FILING DATES FOR SELF-ASSESSMENT RETURNS ISSUED ON OR AFTER 6 APRIL 2009

Date	*Why the deadline is important*
31 Oct	Deadline for filing paper returns for tax year ended the previous 5 April. Late filing incurs an automatic £100 penalty. This deadline applies whether the taxpayer calculates his or her own tax liability or whether he or she wants HMRC to calculate it on their behalf.
31 Jan	Deadline for online filing of returns received by the previous 31 October. Late filing incurs an automatic £100 penalty.
30 Dec	Where a taxpayer files the return online, he or she must do so by this date if HMRC is to collect tax through his or her tax code (if possible) where the amount owed is less than £2,000. Otherwise it can be filed up to 31 January.

KEY SELF-ASSESSMENT DATES

Date	*What payments or penalties are due?*
31 Jan	If a tax return was sent by the previous 31 October, this is the deadline for paying the balance of any tax owed – the 'balancing payment'. HMRC will charge daily interest after this date until it receives the payment. It is also the date by which a taxpayer must make any first 'payment on account' for the current tax year. For example on 31 January 2010 a taxpayer may have to pay both the balancing payment for the year 2008–9 and the first payment on account for 2009–10.
28 Feb	If the balancing payment is not paid by 31 January, there is an automatic 5 per cent surcharge incurred on top of the amount outstanding. This is in addition to any interest payments.
31 Jul	The deadline for making a second payment on account for tax owing for the preceding tax year. If tax is still owed that was due by the previous 31 January, there is a second automatic 5 per cent surcharge levied on top of the amount owed.

TAX CREDITS

Child tax credit and working tax credit are paid to qualifying individuals. Although the title of both credits incorporates the word 'tax', neither affects the amount of income tax payable or repayable. Both are forms of social security benefits. *See* the Social Welfare section.

CAPITAL GAINS TAX

Capital gains tax (CGT) is a tax on capital 'gains'. A gain is an increase in value. When an individual disposes of an asset – that is, something he or she owns such as shares, land or buildings – by selling it or giving it away, CGT may have to be paid on the gain or profit. An individual is potentially chargeable to CGT on gains that accrue from disposals made during a year of tax assessment.

The following information relates to the year of assessment 2009–10 ending on 5 April 2010 and incorporates these changes. It therefore has only limited relevance to earlier years.

CGT is paid by individuals who are either resident or ordinarily resident in the UK for the tax year, executors or administrators – 'personal representatives' – responsible for a deceased person's financial affairs and trustees of a settlement. Non-residents are not usually liable to CGT unless they carry on a business in the UK through a branch or agency. Special CGT rules may apply to individuals who used to live and work in the UK but have since left the country.

CAPITAL GAINS CHARGEABLE TO CGT

Typically, individuals have made a gain if they sell an asset for more than they paid for it. It is the gain that is taxed, not the amount the individual receives for the asset. For example, a man buys shares for £1,000 and later sells them for £3,000. He has made a gain of £2,000 (£3,000 less £1,000). If someone gives an asset away, the gain will be based on the difference between what the asset was worth when originally acquired compared with its worth at the time of disposal. The same is true when an asset is sold for less than its full worth in order to give away part of the value. For example, a woman buys a property for £120,000 and three years later, when the property's market value has risen to £180,000, she gives it to her son. The son may pay nothing for the property or pay less than its true worth, eg £100,000. Either way, she has made a gain of £60,000 (£180,000 less £120,000).

If an individual disposes of an asset he or she received as a gift, the gain is worked out according to the market value of the asset when it was received. For example, a man gives his sister a painting worth £8,000. She pays nothing for it. Later she sells the painting for £10,000. For CGT purposes, she is treated as making a gain of £2,000 (£10,000 less £8,000). If an individual inherits an asset, the estate of the person who died does not pay CGT at the time. If the inheritor later disposes of the asset, the gain is worked out by looking at the market value at the time of the death. For example, a woman acquires some shares for £5,000 and leaves them to her niece when she dies. No CGT is payable at the time of death when the shares are worth £8,000. Later the niece sells the shares for £10,000. She has made a gain of £2,000 (£10,000 less £8,000).

Individuals may also have to pay CGT if they dispose of part of an asset or exchange one asset for another. Similarly, CGT may be payable if an individual receives a capital sum of money from an asset without disposing of it, for example where he or she receives compensation when an asset is damaged.

Assets that may lead to a CGT charge when they are disposed of include:

- shares in a company
- units in a unit trust
- land and buildings (though not normally an individual's main home – *see* 'disposal of a home' section for details)
- higher value jewellery, paintings, antiques and other personal effects assets used in business such as goodwill

EXEMPT GAINS

Certain kinds of assets do not give rise to a chargeable gain when they are disposed of. Assets exempt from CGT include:

- an individual's private car
- an individual's main home, provided certain conditions are met
- tax-free investments such as assets held in an individual savings account (ISA)
- UK government gilts or 'bonds'
- personal belongings including jewellery, paintings, antiques individually worth £6,000 or less
- cash in sterling or foreign currency held for an individual or his/her family's own personal use
- betting, lottery or pools winnings
- personal injury compensation

DISPOSAL OF A HOME: PRIVATE RESIDENCE RELIEF

Individuals do not have to pay CGT when they sell their main home if all the following conditions are met:

- they bought it and made any expenditure on it, primarily for use as their home rather than with a view to making a profit
- the property was their only home throughout the period they owned it (ignoring the last three years of ownership)
- the property was actually used as their home all the time that they owned it and, throughout the period, it was not used for any purpose other than as a home for the individual, his or her family and no more than one lodger
- the garden and area of grounds sold with the property does not exceed 5,000 sq. m (1.24 acres) including the site of the property

Even if all these conditions are not met, individuals may still be entitled to CGT relief when they sell the home. They may, for example, qualify for relief if they lived away from home temporarily while working abroad. Married couples or couples in a civil partnership may have relief from CGT on only one home. There is a special exception, however, where the spouse or partner each had a qualifying home before marriage or civil partnership and both live together in one of these homes after marriage or civil partnership and sell the other. Provided that it is sold within three years of marriage or the civil partnership, they may not have to pay any CGT (subject to the normal rules for this relief). If they sell it after more than three years it may qualify for partial relief. There are special rules on divorce and separation.

Certain other kinds of disposal similarly do not give rise to a chargeable gain. For example, individuals who are married or in a civil partnership and who live together may sell or give assets to their spouse or civil partner without having to pay CGT. Individuals may not, however, give or sell assets cheaply to their children without having to consider CGT. There is no CGT to pay on assets given to a registered charity.

CALCULATING CGT

CGT is worked out for each tax year and is charged on the total of an individual's taxable gains after taking into account certain costs and reliefs that can reduce or defer chargeable gains, allowable losses made on assets to which CGT normally applies and an annual exempt (tax-free) amount that applies to every individual. If the total of an individual's net gains in a tax year is less than the annual exempt amount (AEA), the individual will not have to pay CGT. For the tax year 2009–10 the AEA is £10,100. If an individual's net gains are more than the AEA, they pay CGT on the excess. Should any part of the exemption remain unused, this cannot be carried forward to a future year. A smaller exemption amount (£5,050 for 2009–10) applies to most trusts.

There are certain reliefs available that may eliminate, reduce or defer CGT, though several reliefs previously available were withdrawn from April 2008 as part of the government's simplification of the CGT regime. Some reliefs are available to many people while others are available only in special circumstances. Some reliefs are given automatically while others are given only if they are claimed. Some of the costs of buying, selling and improving assets may be deducted from total gains when working out an individual's chargeable gain.

RATES OF TAX

The net gains remaining, if any, calculated after deduction of costs, taking into account all CGT reliefs and subtracting the annual exemption, incur liability to capital gains tax. The rate of CGT individuals pay used to depend on their overall income and their consequent top rate of income tax. Under the simplified CGT regime, however, introduced for disposals made on or after 6 April 2008, individuals and trustees pay a single rate of charge to CGT at 18 per cent.

CGT for 2009–10 falls due for payment in full on 31 January 2011. If payment is delayed, interest or surcharges may be imposed. A husband and wife or registered civil partners who live together are separately assessed to CGT. Each partner must independently calculate his or her gains and losses with each entitled to the AEA of £10,100 for 2009–10.

VALUATION OF ASSETS

The disposal proceeds – that is the amount received as consideration for the disposal of an asset – are the sum used to establish the gain or loss once certain allowable costs have been deducted. In most cases this is straightforward because the disposal proceeds are the amount actually received for disposing of the asset. This may include cash payable now or in the future and the value of any asset received in exchange for the asset disposed of. However, in certain circumstances, the disposal proceeds may not accurately reflect the value of the asset and the individual may be treated as disposing of an asset for an amount other than the actual amount (if any) that they received. This applies, in particular, where an asset is transferred as a gift or sold for a price known to be below market value. Disposal proceeds in such transactions are deemed to be equal to the market value of the asset at the time it was disposed of rather than the actual amount (if any) received for it.

Market value represents the price that an asset might reasonably be expected to fetch upon sale in the open market. In the case of unquoted shares or securities, it is to be assumed that the hypothetical purchaser in the open market would have available all the information that a prudent prospective purchaser of shares or securities might reasonably require if that person were proposing to purchase them from a willing vendor by private treaty and at arm's length. The market value of unquoted shares or securities will often be established following negotiations with the specialist HM Revenue and Customs Shares & Assets Valuation department. The valuation of land and interests in land in the UK is dealt with by District Valuer Services, part of the Valuation Office Agency. Special rules apply to determine the market value of shares quoted on the London Stock Exchange.

ALLOWABLE COSTS

When working out a chargeable gain, once the actual or notional disposal proceeds have been determined, five kinds of allowable costs may be deducted. There is a general rule that no costs that could be taken into account when working out income or losses for income tax purposes may be deducted. Subject to this, allowable costs are:

- acquisition costs – the actual amount spent on acquiring the asset or, in certain circumstances, the equivalent market value
- incidental costs of acquiring the asset such as fees paid for professional advice, valuation costs, stamp duty and advertising costs to find a seller
- enhancement costs – incurred for the purpose of enhancing the value of the asset (not including normal maintenance and repair costs)
- expenditure on defending or establishing a person's rights over the asset
- incidental costs of disposing of the asset such as fees paid for professional advice, valuation costs, stamp duty and advertising costs to find a buyer

If an individual disposes of part of his or her interest in an asset, or part of a holding of shares of the same class in the same company, or part of a holding of units in the same unit trust, he or she can deduct part of the allowable costs of the asset or holding when working out the chargeable gain. Allowable costs may also be reduced by some reliefs.

ENTREPRENEURS' RELIEF

In January 2008, the government announced a new relief – entrepreneurs' relief – from CGT for gains arising on the disposal of a business. The announcement came after complaints that the new 18 per cent CGT flat rate would mean small business owners paying almost twice as much tax as before when they sold their businesses and that the change could deter entrepreneurs from starting new UK businesses. The new relief took effect from 6 April 2008 alongside the CGT reform programme.

Entrepreneurs' relief is available in respect of gains made on the disposal of all or part of a business (including professions and vocations, but not including a property letting business other than furnished holiday lettings), or of gains made on disposals of assets following the cessation of a business by certain individuals who were involved in running the business. The relief also applies to gains on disposals of shares and securities in a trading company (or the holding company of a trading group) provided that the individual making the disposal has been an officer or employee of the company, or of a company in the same group of companies, and owns at least 5 per cent of the ordinary share capital of the company.

The relief reduces gains liable to CGT (at the single 18 per cent rate) by 4/9ths, resulting in an effective 10 per cent rate (5/9ths × 18 per cent). It is available for gains of up to £1m on disposals of a business by an individual. The first £1m of gains that qualify for relief are charged to CGT at the effective rate of 10 per cent. Gains in excess of £1m are charged at the normal 18 per cent rate. An individual is able to make claims for relief on more than one occasion up to a lifetime total of £1m of gains qualifying for relief.

Where an individual qualifies for entrepreneurs' relief on a disposal of shares or securities, relief is also available in respect of any 'associated disposal' of an asset which was used in the company's (or group's) business. For example, if a company director who owns the premises from which the company carries on its business sells the premises at the same time as he sells his shares in the company, the sale of the premises may count as an associated disposal and any gain may attract entrepreneurs' relief. The relief due on an associated disposal is restricted where the asset in question was not wholly in business use throughout the period it was owned. A similar rule allows relief on an associated disposal by a member of a partnership who is entitled to relief on disposal of his or her interest in the assets of the partnership.

Certain trustees may also benefit from entrepreneurs' relief on gains on assets used in a business.

BUSINESS ASSET ROLL-OVER RELIEF

A capital gain on the disposal of certain types of asset used in a person's business may be deferred or 'rolled over' if the proceeds are reinvested in new qualifying trading assets. The gain is deducted from the base cost of the new asset and only becomes chargeable to CGT on the eventual disposal of that replacement asset unless a further roll-over situation then develops. Full relief is available if all the proceeds from the original asset (the old asset) are reinvested in the qualifying replacement asset (the new asset). If only part of the proceeds is reinvested, the difference represents an immediately chargeable gain. If the amount not reinvested is greater than the gain, no roll-over relief is due.

Relief is only available if the acquisition of the new asset takes place within a period commencing 12 months before, and ending three years after, the disposal of the old asset. However, HMRC may extend this time limit at their discretion where there is a clear intention to acquire a replacement asset. The most common types of business assets that qualify for roll-over relief are land, buildings occupied and used for the purposes of trade, fixed plant and machinery. Assets used for the commercial letting of furnished holiday accommodation qualify if certain conditions are satisfied. Roll-over relief is also available where shares in a company are transferred to trustees administering an employees' share incentive plan for the benefit of persons employed by that company.

GIFTS HOLD-OVER RELIEF

The gift of an asset is treated as a disposal made for a consideration equal to market value, with a corresponding acquisition by the transferee at an identical value. In the case of gifts made by individuals and a limited range of trustees to a transferee resident in the UK, a form of hold-over relief may be available. This relief, which must be claimed, in effect enables liability for CGT to be deferred and passed to the person to whom the gift is made. Relief is limited to the transfer of certain assets including the following:

- gifts of assets used for the purposes of a business carried on by the donor or his or her personal company
- gifts of shares in trading companies that are not listed on a stock exchange
- gifts of shares or securities in the donor's personal trading company
- gifts of agricultural land and buildings that would qualify for inheritance tax agricultural property relief
- gifts that are chargeable transfers for inheritance tax purposes
- certain types of gifts that are specifically exempted from inheritance tax

Hold-over relief is automatically due on certain sorts of gifts including gifts to charities and community amateur sports clubs, and gifts of works of art where certain undertakings have been given. There are certain rules to prevent gifts hold-over relief being used for tax-avoidance purposes. For example, restrictions may apply where an individual gifts assets to trustees administering a trust in which the individual retains an interest or the assets transferred comprise a dwelling-house. Subject to these exceptions, the effect of a valid claim for hold-over relief is similar to that following a claim for roll-over relief on the disposal of business assets. Adjustments may be necessary where some consideration (less than market value) is given for a gift or where a gifted asset has not been used for business purposes throughout the period of ownership.

OTHER CGT RELIEFS

There are certain other CGT reliefs available on the disposal of property, shares and business assets. For detailed information on these reliefs and for more general guidance on CGT, see the capital gains tax pages on the HMRC website (W www.hmrc.gov.uk/cgt/index.htm).

REPORTING AND PAYING CGT

Individuals are responsible for telling HMRC about capital gains on which they they have to pay tax. Individuals who receive a self-assessment tax return may report capital gains by filling in the capital gains supplementary pages – the return explains how to obtain these pages if needed.

Individuals who do not normally complete a tax return but who need to report capital gains or losses should contact their local tax office. If an individual has CGT to pay, they must tell their tax office in writing by 5 October after the end of the tax year for which the CGT is due.

There is a time limit for claiming capital losses. The deadline is five years from 31 January after the end of the tax year in which the loss was made.

INHERITANCE TAX

Inheritance tax (IHT) is a tax on the value of a person's estate on death and on certain gifts made by an individual during his or her lifetime, usually payable within six months of death. Broadly speaking, a person's estate is everything he or she owned at the time of death including property, possessions, money and investments, less his or her debts. Not everyone pays IHT. It only applies if the taxable value of an estate is above the current inheritance tax threshold. If an estate, including any assets held in trust and gifts made within seven years of death, is less than the threshold, no IHT will be due. See table for the lower threshold limit, known as the nil rate band.

2007–8	£300,000
2008–9	£312,000
2009–10	£325,000
2010–11	£350,000

The autumn pre-budget report of October 2007 now means that a claim can be made to transfer any unused IHT nil-rate band on a person's death to the estate of their surviving spouse or civil partner. This applies where the IHT nil-rate band of the first deceased spouse or civil partner was not fully used in calculating the IHT liability of their estate. When the surviving spouse or civil partner dies, the unused amount may be added to their own nil-rate band (*see* below for details).

IHT used to be something only very wealthy individuals needed to consider. This is no longer the case. The fact that the IHT threshold has not kept pace with house price inflation in recent years means that the estates of an increasing number of 'ordinary' taxpayers, who would not consider themselves wealthy, are now becoming liable for IHT purely because of the value of their home. However, there are a number of ways that individuals – while still alive – can legally reduce the IHT bill that will apply to their estates on death. Several valuable IHT exemptions are available (explained further below) which allow individuals to pass on assets during their lifetime or in their will without any IHT being due. Detailed information on IHT is available on the HMRC website at W http://www.hmrc.gov.uk/inheritancetax/

index.htm. Further help is also available from the IHT & Probate Helpline on T 0845-302 0900.

DOMICILE

Liability to IHT depends on an individual's domicile at the time of any gift or on death. Domicile is a complex legal concept and what follows explains some of the main issues. An individual is domiciled in the country where he or she has a permanent home. Domicile is different from nationality or residence, and an individual can only have one domicile at any given time.

A 'domicile of origin' is normally acquired from the individual's father on birth, though this may not be the country in which he or she is born. For example, a child born in Germany while his or her father is working there, but whose permanent home is in the UK, will have the UK as his or her domicile of origin. Until a person legally changes his or her domicile, it will be the same as that of the person on whom they are legally dependent.

Individuals can legally acquire a new domicile – a 'domicile of choice' – from the age of 16 by leaving the current country of domicile and settling in another country and providing strong evidence of intention to live there permanently or indefinitely. Women who were married before 1974 acquired their husband's domicile and still retain it until they legally acquire a new domicile.

For IHT purposes, there is a concept of 'deemed domicile'. This means that even if a person is not domiciled in the UK under general law, he or she is treated as domiciled in the UK at the time of a transfer (ie at the time of a lifetime gift or on death) if he or she (a) was domiciled in the UK within the three years immediately before the transfer, or (b) was 'resident' in the UK in at least 17 of the 20 income tax years of assessment ending with the year in which a transfer is made. Where a person is domiciled, or treated as domiciled, in the UK at the time of a gift or on death, the location of assets is immaterial and full liability to IHT arises. A non-UK domiciled individual is also liable to IHT but only on chargeable property in the UK.

The assets of husband and wife and registered civil partners are not merged for IHT purposes, except that the IHT value of assets owned by one spouse or civil partner may be affected if the other also owns similar assets (eg shares in the same company or a share in their jointly owned house). Each spouse or partner is treated as a separate individual entitled to receive the benefit of his or her exemptions, reliefs and rates of tax.

IHT EXEMPTIONS

There are some important exemptions that allow individuals to legally pass assets on to others, both before and after their death – without being subject to IHT.

Exempt beneficiaries
Assets can be given away to certain people and organisations without any IHT having to be paid. These gifts, which are exempt whether individuals make them during their lifetime or in their will, include gifts to:

- a husband, wife or civil partner, even if the couple is legally separated (but not if they are divorced or the civil partnership has dissolved), as long as both partners have a permanent home in the UK. Note that gifts to an unmarried partner or a partner with whom the donor has not formed a civil partnership are not exempt
- UK charities
- some national institutions, including national museums, universities and the National Trust
- UK political parties

Annual exemption
The first £3,000 of gifts made each tax year by each individual is exempt from IHT. If this exemption is not used, or not wholly used in any year, the balance may be carried forward to the following year only. A couple, therefore, may give away a total of £6,000 per tax year between them or £12,000 if they haven't used their previous year's annual exemptions.

Wedding gifts/civil partnership ceremony gifts
Some gifts are exempt from IHT because of the type of gift or reason for making it. Wedding or civil partnership ceremony gifts made to either of the couple are exempt from IHT up to certain amounts:

- gifts by a parent, £5,000
- gifts by a grandparent or other relative, £2,500
- gifts by anyone else, £1,000

The gift must be made on or shortly before the date of the wedding or civil partnership ceremony. If the ceremony is called off but the gift is made, this exemption will not apply.

Small gifts
An individual can make small gifts, up to the value of £250, to any number of people in any one tax year without them being liable for IHT. However, a larger sum such as £500 cannot be given and exemption claimed for the first £250. In addition, this exemption cannot be used with any other exemption when giving to the same person. For example, a parent cannot combine a 'small gifts exemption' with a 'wedding/civil partnership ceremony gift exemption' to give a child £5,250 when he or she gets married or forms a civil partnership. Neither may an individual combine a 'small gifts exemption' with the 'annual exemption' to give someone £3,250. Note that it is possible to use the 'annual exemption' with any other exemption, such as the 'wedding/civil partnership ceremony gift exemption'. For example, if a child marries or forms a civil partnership, the parent can give him or her a total IHT-free gift of £8,000 by combining £5,000 under the wedding/civil partnership gift exemption and £3,000 under the annual exemption.

Normal expenditure
Any gifts made out of individuals' after-tax income (not capital) are exempt from IHT if they are part of their normal expenditure and do not result in a fall in their standard of living. These can include regular payments to someone, such as an allowance or gifts for Christmas or a birthday and regular premiums paid on a life insurance policy for someone else.

Maintenance gifts
An individual can make IHT-free maintenance payments to his or her spouse or registered civil partner, ex spouse or former civil partner, relatives dependent because of old age or infirmity, and children (including adopted children and step-children) who are under 18 or in full-time education.

POTENTIALLY EXEMPT TRANSFERS

If an individual makes a gift to either another individual or certain types of trust and it is not covered by one of the above exemptions, it is known as a 'potentially exempt transfer' (PET). A PET is only free of IHT on two strict conditions: (a) the gift must be made at least seven years before the donor's death. If the donor does not survive seven years after making the gift, it will be liable for IHT and (b) the gift must be made as a true gift with no strings attached (technically known as a 'gift with reservation of benefit'). This means that the donor must give up all rights to the gift and stop benefiting from it in any way.

If a gift is made and the donor does retain some benefit from it then it will still count as part of his or her estate no matter how long he or she lives after making it. For example, a father could make a lifetime gift of his home to his child. HMRC would not accept this as a true gift, however, if the father continued to live in the home (unless he paid his child a full commercial rent to do so) because he would be considered to still have a material interest in the gifted home. Its value, therefore, would still be liable for IHT.

In some circumstances a gift with strings attached might give rise to an income tax charge on the donor based on the value of the benefit he or she retains. In this case the donor can choose whether to pay the income tax or have the gift treated as a gift with reservation.

CHARGEABLE TRANSFERS

Any remaining lifetime gifts that are not (potentially or otherwise) exempt transfers are chargeable transfers or 'chargeable gifts', meaning that they incur liability to IHT. Chargeable transfers comprise mainly gifts to or from companies and gifts to particular types of trust called discretionary trusts. There is an immediate claim for IHT on chargeable gifts, and additional tax may be payable if the donor dies within seven years of making a chargeable gift.

DEATH

Immediately before the time of death an individual is deemed to make a transfer of value. This transfer will comprise the value of assets forming part of the deceased's estate after subtracting most liabilities. Any exempt transfers may be excluded such as transfers for the benefit of a surviving spouse or civil partner, and charities. Death may also trigger three additional liabilities:

- a PET made within the seven years before the death loses its potential status and becomes chargeable to IHT
- the value of gifts made with reservation may incur liability if any benefit was enjoyed within the seven years before the death
- additional tax may become payable for chargeable lifetime transfers made within the seven years before the death

The 'personal representative' (the person nominated to handle the affairs of the deceased person) arranges to value the estate and pay any IHT that is due. One or more personal representatives can be nominated in a person's will, in which case they are known as the 'executors'. If a person dies without leaving a will a court can nominate the personal representative, who is then known as the 'administrator'. Valuing the deceased person's estate is one of the first things his or her personal representative needs to do. The representative will not normally be able to take over management of the estate (called 'applying for probate') until all or some of any IHT that is due has been paid.

VALUATIONS

When valuing a deceased person's estate all assets (property, possessions and money) owned at the time of death and certain assets given away during the seven years before death must be included. The valuation must accurately reflect what those assets would reasonably fetch in the open market at the date of death. The value of all of the assets that the deceased owned should include:

- his or her share of any assets owned jointly with someone else, for example a house owned with a partner
- any assets that are held in a trust, from which the deceased had the right to benefit
- any assets given away, but in which he or she kept an interest (gifts with reservation)
- PETs given away within the last seven years

Most estate assets can be valued quite easily, for example money in bank accounts or stocks and shares. In other instances the help of a professional valuer may be needed. Advice on how to value different assets including joint or trust assets is available at W www.hmrc.gov.uk. When valuing an estate, special relief is made available for certain assets. The two main reliefs are business relief and agricultural property relief outlined below. Once all assets have been valued, the next step is to deduct from the total assets everything that the deceased person owed such as unpaid bills, outstanding mortgages and other loans plus their funeral expenses. The value of all of the assets, less the deductible debts, is their estate. IHT is only payable on any value above £325,000 for the tax year 2009–10 at the current rate of 40 per cent.

RELIEF FOR SELECTED ASSETS

Agricultural Property

Relief from IHT is available on the agricultural value of agricultural property that is transferred. Agricultural property generally includes land or pasture used in the growing of crops or intensive rearing of animals for food consumption. It can also include farmhouses and farm cottages. The agricultural property can be owner-occupied or let. Relief is only due if the transferor has owned the property and it has been occupied for agricultural purposes for a minimum period.

The chargeable value transferred, either on a lifetime gift or on death, must be determined. This value may then be reduced by a percentage. Under current rates, a 100 per cent deduction will be available if the transferor retained vacant possession or could have obtained that possession within a period of 12 months following the transfer. In other cases, notably including land let to tenants, a lower deduction of 50 per cent is usually available. However, this lower deduction may be increased to 100 per cent if the letting was made after 31 August 1995.

To qualify for the relief, the agricultural property must either have been occupied by the transferor for the purposes of agriculture throughout a two-year period ending on the date of the transfer, or have been owned by the transferor throughout a period of seven years ending on that date and also occupied for agricultural purposes.

Business Relief

Business relief is available on transfers of certain types of business and of business assets if they qualify as relevant business property and the transferor has owned them for a minimum period. The relief can be claimed for transfers made during the person's lifetime and on death and on chargeable occasions arising on relevant business property held in trust. Where the chargeable value transferred is attributable to relevant business property, the business relief reduces that value by a percentage. Business relief may be claimed on relevant business property including:

- a business or an interest in a business such as a partnership
- unquoted shares and securities
- shares or securities of a quoted company which themselves or with other listed shares or securities give the transferor control of a company
- any land, buildings, plant or machinery owned by a partner or controlling shareholder and used wholly or mainly in the business of the partnership or company immediately before the transfer; this applies only if the partnership interest or shareholding would itself, if it were transferred, qualify for business relief
- any land, buildings, machinery or plant that were used wholly or mainly for the purpose of a business carried on by the transferor

If an asset qualifies for business relief, the rates at which it is currently allowed are as follows:

A business or interest in a business	100%
A holding of shares in an unquoted company	100%
Control holding of shares in a quoted company (more than 50 per cent of the voting rights)	50%
Land, buildings or plant and machinery used in a business of which the deceased was a partner at the date of death or used by a company controlled by the deceased	50%
Land, buildings, plant and machinery held in a trust where the deceased had the right to benefit from the trust and the asset was used in a business carried on by the deceased	50%

It is a general requirement that the property must have been retained for a period of two years before the transfer or death, and restrictions may be necessary if the property has not been used wholly for business purposes. The same property cannot obtain both business property relief and the relief available for agricultural property.

CALCULATION OF TAX PAYABLE

The calculation of IHT payable adopts the use of a cumulative or 'running' total. Looking back seven years from the death the chargeable value of gifts in that period is added to the total value of the estate at death. The gifts will use up all or part of the inheritance tax threshold (the 'nil-rate band' above which IHT becomes payable) first.

Lifetime Chargeable Transfers

The value transferred by lifetime chargeable transfers must be added to the seven-year running total to calculate whether any IHT is due. If the nil-rate band is exceeded, tax will be imposed on the excess at the rate of 20 per cent. However, if the donor dies within a period of seven years from the date of the chargeable lifetime transfer, additional tax may be due. This is calculated by applying tax at the full rate of 40 per cent in substitution for the rate of 20 per cent previously used. The amount of tax is then reduced to a percentage by applying tapering relief. This percentage is governed by the number of years from the date of the lifetime gift to the date of death, as follows:

PERIOD OF YEARS BEFORE DEATH

Not more than 3	100%
More than 3 but not more than 4	80%
More than 4 but not more than 5	60%
More than 5 but not more than 6	40%
More than 6 but not more than 7	20%

Should this exercise produce liability greater than that previously paid at the 20 per cent rate on the lifetime transfer, additional tax, representing the difference, must be paid. Where the calculation shows an amount falling below tax paid on the lifetime transfer, no additional liability can arise nor will the shortfall become repayable.

Tapering relief is, of course, only available if the calculation discloses a liability to IHT. There is no liability if the lifetime transfer falls within the nil-rate band.

Potentially Exempt Transfers

Where a PET loses immunity from liability to IHT because the donor dies within seven years of making the transfer, the value transferred enters into the running total. Any liability to IHT will be calculated by applying the full rate of 40 per cent, reduced to the percentage governed by tapering relief if the original transfer occurred more than three years before death. Again, liability to IHT can only arise if the nil-rate band is exceeded.

Death

On death, IHT is due on the value of the deceased's estate plus the running total of gifts made in the seven years before death if they come to more than the nil-rate band. IHT is then charged at the full rate of 40 per cent on the amount in excess of the nil-rate band.

Settled Property and Trusts

Trusts are special legal arrangements that can be used by individuals to control how their assets are distributed to their beneficiaries and minimise their IHT liability. Complex rules apply to establish IHT liability on settled property which includes property held in trust, and individuals are advised to take expert legal advice when setting up trusts.

RATES OF TAX

Previously there were several rates of IHT that progressively increased as the value transferred grew in size. However, since 1988 there have been only three rates:

- a nil rate
- a lifetime rate of 20 per cent
- a full rate of 40 per cent

The nil-rate band usually changes on an annual basis, and for events taking place after 5 April 2009 applies to the first £325,000. Any excess over this level is taxable at 20 per cent or 40 per cent as the case may be. The IHT threshold will be increased to £350,000 for 2010–11.

TRANSFER OF NIL-RATE BAND

Transfers of property between spouses or civil partners are generally exempt from IHT. This means that someone who dies leaving some or all of their property to their spouse or civil partner may not have fully used up their nil-rate band. Under new rules introduced in autumn 2007, any nil-rate band unused on the first death can be used when the surviving spouse or civil partner dies. A transfer of unused nil-rate band from a deceased spouse or civil partner (no matter what the date of their death) may be made to the estate of their surviving spouse or civil partner who dies on or after 9 October 2007.

Where a valid claim to transfer unused nil-rate band is made, the nil-rate band that is available when the surviving spouse or civil partner dies is increased by the proportion of the nil-rate band unused on the first death. For example, if on the first death the chargeable estate is £150,000 and the nil-rate band is £300,000, 50 per cent of the nil-rate band would be unused. If the nil-rate band when the survivor dies is £325,000, then that would be increased by 50 per cent to £487,500. The amount of the nil-rate band that can be transferred does not depend on the value of the first spouse or civil partner's estate. Whatever proportion of the nil-rate band is unused on the first death is available for transfer to the survivor.

The amount of additional nil-rate band that can be accumulated by any one surviving spouse or civil partner is limited to the value of the nil-rate band in force at the time of their death. This may be relevant, for example, where a person dies having survived more than one spouse or civil partner.

Where these rules have effect, personal representatives do not have to claim for unused nil-rate band to be transferred at the time of the first death. Any claims for transfer of unused nil-rate band amounts are made by the personal representatives of the estate of the second spouse or civil partner to die when they make an IHT return.

Detailed guidance on how to transfer the nil-rate band can be found on the HMRC website.

PAYMENT OF TAX

IHT is normally due six months after the end of the month in which the death occurs or the chargeable transaction takes place. This is referred to as the 'due date'. Tax on some assets such as business property, certain shares and securities and land and buildings (including the deceased person's home) can be deferred and paid in equal instalments over ten years, though interest will be charged in most cases. If IHT is due on lifetime gifts and transfers, the person or transferee who received the gift or assets is normally liable to pay the IHT, though any IHT already paid at the time of a transfer into a trust or company will be taken into account. If tax owed is not paid by the due date, interest is charged on any unpaid IHT, no matter what caused the delay in payment.

CORPORATION TAX

Corporation tax is a tax on a company's profits, including all its income and gains. This tax is payable by UK resident companies and by non-resident companies carrying on a trade in the UK through a permanent establishment. The following comments are confined to companies resident in the UK. The word 'company' is also used to include:

- members' clubs, societies and associations
- trade associations
- housing associations
- groups of individuals carrying on a business but not as a partnership (for example, cooperatives)

A company's taxable income is charged by reference to income or gains arising in its 'accounting period', which is normally 12 months long. In some circumstances accounting periods can be shorter than 12 months, but never longer. The accounting period is also normally the period for which a company's accounts are drawn up, but the two periods do not have to coincide.

If a company is liable to pay corporation tax on its profits, several things must be done. HMRC must be informed that the company exists and is liable for tax. A self-assessment company tax return plus full accounts and calculation of tax liability must be filed by the statutory filing date, normally 12 months after the end of the accounting period. Companies have to work out their own tax liability and have to pay their tax without prior assessment by HMRC. Records of all company expenditure and income must be kept in order to work out the tax liability correctly. Companies are liable to penalties if they fail to carry out these obligations.

Measures to reform the business tax system were announced in the 2007 budget with a staged introduction over the following years. The major elements of the reform package applied from 2008–9.

Extensive corporation tax information is available on the HMRC website and companies may file their company tax returns online at the HMRC's corporation tax online service at W www.hmrc.gov.uk/ctsa/ct-online.htm.

RATE OF TAX

The rate of corporation tax is fixed for a financial year starting on 1 April and ending on the following 31 March. If a company's accounting period does not coincide with the financial year, its profits must be apportioned between the financial years and the tax rates for each financial year applied to those profits. The corporation tax liability is the total tax for both financial years.

The main rate of corporation tax for 2009–10 is 28 per cent. North Sea oil and gas ring fence activities however retain a main corporation tax rate of 30 per cent. The main rate of corporation tax applies when profits (including ring fence profits) are at a rate exceeding £1.5m, or where there is no claim to another rate, or where another rate does not apply.

SMALL COMPANIES' RATE

Where the profits of a company do not exceed stated limits, corporation tax becomes payable at the small companies' rate. It is the amount of profits and not the size of the company that governs the application of the small companies' rate.

Budget 2007 announced a staged increase in the small companies rate from 19 per cent to 20 per cent from April 2007, 21 per cent from April 2008 and 22 per cent from April 2009. However, the increase from 21 per cent to 22 per cent from April 2009 has been deferred until April 2010. This deferral was announced by the Chancellor in his November 2008 Pre-Budget Report and will apply from 1 April 2010. North Sea oil and gas ring fence activities retain a small companies' rate of 19 per cent.

A company can make profits of up to £300,000 without losing the benefit of the small companies' rate. If, however, its profits exceed £300,000 but fall below £1,500,000, then marginal small companies' rate relief applies to ease the transition. The effect of marginal relief is that the average rate of corporation tax imposed on all profits steadily increases from the lower small companies' rate of 21 per cent to the main rate of 28 per cent, with tax being imposed on profits in the margin at an increased rate. HMRC has produced an easy-to-use corporation tax marginal relief rate calculator on its website at W www.hmrc.gov.uk/calcs/mrr.htm.

Where a change in the rate of tax is introduced and the accounting period of a company overlaps 31 March, profits must be apportioned to establish the appropriate rate for each part of those profits.

The lower limit of £300,000 and the upper limit of £1,500,000 apply to a period of 12 months and must be proportionately reduced for shorter periods. Some restriction in the small companies' rate and the marginal rate may be necessary if there are two or more associated companies, namely companies under common control. From 1 April 2006 a previous corporation tax 'starting rate' of zero for very small companies and a 19 per cent non-corporate distribution rate (NCDR), which could apply to company profits distributed to persons who were not companies, were replaced with a single banding for small companies.

CORPORATION TAX ON PROFITS

£ per year	*2008–9*	*2009–10*
£0–£300,000	21%	21%
£300,001–£1,500,000	Marginal relief	Marginal relief
£1,500,001 or more	28%	28%

CAPITAL ALLOWANCES

Businesses can claim tax allowances, called capital allowances, on certain purchases or investments. This means that a proportion of these costs can be deducted from a business' taxable profits and reduce its tax bill. Capital allowances are currently available on plant and machinery, buildings and research and development. The amount of the allowance depends on what is being claimed for. As part of the staged business tax reform package announced in the 2007 budget, changes to the capital allowances regime are being introduced.

Detailed information on capital allowances is available from the Enhanced Capital Allowances website (W www.eca.gov.uk).

PAYMENT OF TAX

Corporation tax liabilities are normally due and payable in a single lump sum not later than nine months and one day after the end of the accounting period. For 'large' companies – those with profits over £1.5m which pay corporation tax at the main rate – there is a requirement to pay corporation tax in four quarterly instalments. Where a company is a member of a group, the profits of the entire group must be merged to establish whether the company is large.

CAPITAL GAINS

Chargeable gains arising to a company are calculated in a manner similar to that used for individuals. However, companies are not entitled to the CGT annual exemption of £9,600. Companies do not suffer capital gains tax on chargeable gains but incur liability to corporation tax instead. Tax is due on the full chargeable gain of an accounting period after subtracting relief for losses, if any.

GROUPS OF COMPANIES

Each company within a group is separately charged to corporation tax on profits, gains and income. However, where one group member realises a loss for which special rules apply, other than a capital loss, a claim may be made to offset the deficiency against profits of some other member of the same group. The transfer of capital assets from one member of a group to a fellow member will usually incur no liability to tax on chargeable gains.

SPORTS CLUBS

Though corporation tax is payable by unincorporated associations including most clubs, a substantial exemption from liability to corporation tax, introduced in April 2002, is available to qualifying registered community amateur sports clubs (CASCs). Sports clubs that are registered as CASCs are exempt from liability to corporation tax on:

- profits from trading where the turnover of the trade is less than £30,000 in a 12-month period
- income from letting property where the gross rental income is less than £20,000 in a 12-month period
- bank and building society interest received
- chargeable gains

All of the exemptions depend upon the club having been a registered CASC for the whole of the relevant accounting period and the income or gains being used only for qualifying purposes. If the club has only been a registered CASC for part of an accounting period the exemption amounts of £30,000 (for trading) and £20,000 (for income from property) are reduced proportionately. Only interest and gains received after the club is registered are exempted.

Among other advantages available to registered clubs is that donations may be received under the Gift Aid arrangements. Charities are also generally exempt from corporation tax where they operate through a company structure.

VALUE ADDED TAX

Value added tax (VAT) is a tax on consumer expenditure charged when an individual buys goods and services in the European Union including the UK. It is normally included in the sale price of goods and services and paid at the point of purchase. Each EU country has its own rate of VAT. From a business point of view, VAT is charged on most business transactions involving the supply of goods and services by a registered trader in the UK and Isle of Man. It is also charged on goods and some services imported from places outside the EU and on goods and some services coming into the UK from the other EU countries. VAT is administered by HM Revenue and Customs. A wide range of information on VAT, including VAT forms, is available online (W www.hmrc.gov.uk). HMRC runs a national advice service enquiry line dealing with all general queries about taxes and duties including VAT on T 0845-010 9000.

RATES OF TAX

There are three rates of VAT in the UK. The standard rate, payable on most goods and services in the UK, was reduced by the government from 17.5 per cent to 15 per cent from 1 December 2008, and will remain at this rate until 1 January 2010 when it will revert to 17.5 per cent. The government made this VAT rate change as part of a broader package of measures to give the economy a boost. It was envisaged that passing on the VAT reduction through reduced prices would stimulate consumer spending.

The reduced rate – currently 5 per cent – is payable on certain goods and services including, for example, domestic fuel and power, children's car seats, women's sanitary products, contraceptive products and the installation of energy-saving materials such as wall insulation and solar panels. Since 1 January 2008 renovations and alterations to residential properties that have been empty for at least two years have been eligible for the 5 per cent rate.

A zero, or nil, rate applies to certain items including, for example, children's clothes, books, newspapers, most food and drink, and drugs and aids for disabled people. There are numerous exceptions to the zero-rated categories however. While most food and drink is zero-rated, items including ice creams, chocolates, sweets, potato crisps and alcoholic drinks are not. Neither are drinks or items sold for consumption in a restaurant or cafe. Takeaway cold items such as sandwiches are zero-rated, while takeaway hot foods like fish and chips are not.

REGISTRATION

All traders, including professional persons and companies, must register for VAT if they are making 'taxable supplies' of a value exceeding stated limits. All goods and services that are VAT-rated are defined as 'taxable supplies' including zero-rated items which must be included when calculating the total value of a trader's taxable supplies – his or her 'taxable turnover'. The limits that govern mandatory registration are amended periodically.

From 1 April 2008, an unregistered trader must register for VAT if:

- at the end of any month the total value of his or her taxable turnover (not just profit) for the past 12 months or less is more than the current VAT threshold of £68,000 – *and*
- at any time he or she has reasonable grounds to expect that his or her taxable turnover will be more than the current registration threshold of £68,000 in the next 30 days alone

To register for VAT, form VAT 1 must be completed and sent to HMRC within 30 days of any of the above. Basic VAT registration can currently be completed online (W https://online.hmrc.gov.uk/registration/). Traders who do not register at the correct time can be fined. Traders must charge VAT on their taxable supplies from the date they first need to be registered. Traders who only supply zero-rated goods may not have to register for VAT even if their taxable turnover goes above the registration threshold. However, a trader in this position must inform HMRC first and apply to be 'exempt from registration'. A trader whose taxable turnover does not reach the mandatory registration limit may choose to register for VAT voluntarily if what he or she does counts as a business for VAT purposes. This step may be thought advisable to recover input tax (*see* below) or to compete with other registered traders. Registered traders may submit an application for deregistration if their taxable turnover subsequently falls. An application for deregistration can be made if the taxable turnover for the year beginning on the application date is not expected to exceed £66,000.

INPUT TAX

Registered traders suffer input tax when buying in goods or services for the purposes of their business. It is the VAT that traders pay out to their suppliers on goods and services coming *in* to their business. Relief can usually be obtained for input tax suffered, either by setting that tax against output tax due or by repayment. Most items of input tax can be relieved in this manner. Where a registered trader makes both exempt supplies and taxable supplies to his customers or clients, there may be some restriction in the amount of input tax that can be recovered.

OUTPUT TAX

When making a taxable supply of goods or services, registered traders must account for output tax, if any, on the value of that supply. Output tax is the term used to describe the VAT on the goods and services that they supply or sell – the VAT on supplies going *out* of the business and collected from customers on each sale made. Usually the price charged by the registered trader will be increased by adding VAT, but failure to make the required addition will not remove liability to account for output tax. The liability to account for output tax, and also relief for input tax, may be affected where a trader is using a special secondhand goods scheme.

EXEMPT SUPPLIES

VAT is not chargeable on certain goods and services because the law deems them 'exempt' from VAT. These include the provision of burial and cremation facilities, insurance, loans of money, certain types of education and training and some property transactions. The granting of a lease to occupy land or the sale of land will usually comprise an exempt supply, for example, but there are numerous exceptions. Exempt supplies do not enter into the calculation of taxable turnover that governs liability to mandatory registration (*see* above). Such supplies made by a registered trader may, however, limit the amount of input tax that can be relieved. It is for this reason that the exemption may be useful.

COLLECTION OF TAX

Registered traders submit VAT returns for accounting periods usually of three months in duration, but arrangements can be made to submit returns on a monthly basis. Very large traders must account for tax on a monthly basis, but this does not affect the three-monthly return. The return will show both the output tax due for supplies made by the trader in the accounting period and also the input tax for which relief is claimed. If the output tax exceeds input tax the balance must be remitted with the VAT return. Where input tax suffered exceeds the output tax due, the registered trader may claim recovery of the excess from HMRC.

This basis for collecting tax explains the structure of VAT. Where supplies are made between registered traders the supplier will account for an amount of tax that will usually be identical to the tax recovered by the person to whom the supply is made. However, where the supply is made to a person who is not a registered trader there can be no recovery of input tax and it is on this person that the final burden of VAT eventually falls. Where goods are acquired by a UK trader from a supplier within the EU, the trader must also account for the tax due on acquisition. There are a number of simplified arrangements to make VAT accounting easier for businesses, particularly small businesses, and there is advice on the HMRC website about how to choose the most appropriate scheme for a business:

Cash accounting

This scheme allows businesses to only pay VAT on the basis of payments received from their customers rather than on invoice dates or time of supply. It can therefore be useful for businesses with cash flow problems that cannot pay their VAT as a result. Businesses may use the cash accounting scheme if taxable turnover is under

£1,350,000. There is no need to apply for the scheme – eligible businesses may start using it at the beginning of a new tax period. If a trader opts to use this scheme, he or she can do so until the taxable turnover reaches £1,600,000.

Annual accounting
If taxable turnover is under £1,350,000 a year, the trader may join the annual accounting scheme which allows them to make nine monthly or three quarterly instalments during the year based on an estimate of their total annual VAT bill. At the end of the year they submit a single return and any balance due. The advantages of this scheme for businesses are easier budgeting and cash flow planning because fixed payments are spread regularly throughout the year. Once a trader has joined the annual accounting scheme, membership may continue until the annual taxable turnover reaches £1,600,000.

Flat rate scheme
First introduced in the 2002 budget and simplified with effect from 1 April 2009, this scheme allows small businesses with an annual taxable turnover of less than £150,000 to save on administration by paying VAT as a set flat percentage of their annual turnover instead of accounting internally for VAT on each individual 'in and out'. The percentage rate used is governed by the trade sector into which the business falls. The scheme can no longer be used once annual income exceeds £225,000.

Retail schemes
There are special schemes that offer retailers an alternative if it is impractical for them to issue invoices for a large number of supplies direct to the public. These schemes include a provision to claim relief from VAT on bad debts where goods or services are supplied to a customer who does not pay for them.

VAT FACT SUMMARY
from 1 April 2009

Standard rate	15%
Reduced rate	5%
Registration (last 12 months or next 30 days)	£68,000
Deregistration (next 12 months under)	£66,000
Cash accounting scheme – up to	£1,350,000
Flat rate scheme – up to	£150,000
Annual accounting scheme – up to	£1,350,000

STAMP DUTY

For the majority of people, contact with stamp duty arises when they buy a property. Stamp duty is payable by the buyer as a way of raising revenue for the government based on the purchase price of a property, stocks and shares. This section aims to provide a broad overview of stamp duty as it may affect the average person.

STAMP DUTY LAND TAX

Stamp duty land tax was introduced on 1 December 2003 and covers the purchase of houses, flats and other land, buildings and certain leases in the UK.

Before 1 December 2003 property purchasers had to submit documents providing all details of the purchase to the Stamp Office for 'stamping'. The purchaser's solicitor or licensed conveyancer would then send the stamped documentation to the appropriate land registry to register ownership of the property. Under stamp duty land tax, purchasers do not have to send documents for stamping. Instead, a land transaction return form SDLT1, which contains all information regarding the purchase that is relevant to HMRC, is signed by the purchaser. Buyers of property are responsible for completing the land transaction return and payment of stamp duty, though the solicitor or licensed conveyancer acting for them in a land transaction will normally complete the relevant paperwork. Once HMRC has received the completed land transaction return and the payment of any stamp duty due, a certificate will be issued that enables a solicitor or licensed conveyancer to register the property in the new owner's name at the Land Registry.

The threshold for notification of residential property went up from £1,000 to £40,000 on 12 March 2008. This means that taxpayers entering into a transaction involving residential or non-residential property where the chargeable consideration is less than £40,000 no longer need to notify HMRC about the transaction.

RATES OF STAMP DUTY LAND TAX
Stamp duty is charged at different rates and has thresholds for different types of property and different values of transaction. The tax rate and payment threshold can vary according to whether the property is in residential or non-residential use and whether it is freehold or leasehold.

Below a certain threshold, no stamp duty is payable on residential property purchases. This threshold was £125,000 (£150,000 for residential property transactions in certain designated disadvantaged areas) until September 2008 when the government announced it was raising the threshold to £175,000 for one year in order to assist first-time buyers. However, the April 2009 budget extended the 'stamp duty holiday' on residential properties sold for less than £175,000 by three months until the end of 2009.

This £175,000 threshold applies to all residential properties, including those in designated disadvantaged areas, with one exception: leasehold properties where the lease is less than 21 years. On such properties the normal thresholds of £125,000 (£150,000 if the property is in a disadvantaged area) continue to apply. The following table shows the rates of stamp duty and payment thresholds that apply on residential property purchase prices during 2009–10:

Purchase price	*Rate of tax (% of purchase price)*
£175,000 or less (until 31.12.09)*	0%
£175,001 to £250,000 (until 31.12.09)	1%
£250,001 to £500,000	3%
£500,001 or more	4%

* It is anticipated that once the temporary £175,000 threshold comes to an end on 31.12.09 this will revert to the previous threshold of £125,000 (or £150,000 for residential property transactions in certain designated disadvantaged areas, a full list of which can be found at W www.hmrc.gov.uk). For transactions of non-residential land and property, the zero per cent rate applies for purchases up to £150,000. A 1 per cent rate is payable for transactions of £150,001–£250,000; thereafter, rates are as per residential property transactions.

When assessing how much stamp duty is payable, the

entire purchase price must be taken into account so the relevant stamp duty rate is paid on the whole sum, not just on the amount over each tax threshold. For example, on a property bought for £250,000, 1 per cent (£2,500) is payable in stamp duty. On a property bought for £250,001, however, 3 per cent of the whole price (£7,500) is payable.

RELIEF FOR NEW ZERO CARBON HOMES

A new relief from stamp duty land tax was introduced on 1 October 2007 for the vast majority of new-build 'zero carbon' homes in the UK. The relief is time limited for five years and therefore expires on 30 September 2012. Qualifying criteria for the relief require zero carbon emissions from all energy use in the home over a year. To achieve this, the fabric of the home is required to reach a very high energy efficiency standard and to be able to provide onsite renewable heat and power. New homes which are liable to stamp duty land tax on the first sale are eligible to qualify. The relief provides complete removal of stamp duty liabilities for all homes up to a purchase price of £500,000. Where the purchase price is in excess of £500,000 then the stamp duty liability is reduced by £15,000. The balance of the stamp duty is due in the normal way. Relief is not available on second and subsequent sales of new-build zero carbon homes.

FIXTURES AND CHATTELS

As well as buying a property a purchaser may buy items inside the property. Some things inside a property are, in law, part of the land. These are called 'fixtures'. Examples are fitted kitchen units and bathroom suites. Because these fixtures are part of the land, any price paid for them must be taken into account for stamp duty purposes. Other things inside a property are not part of the land. These are called 'chattels'. Examples are free-standing cookers, curtains and fitted carpets. The purchase of chattels is not chargeable to stamp duty. However, where both a property and chattels are purchased, the amount shown on the land transaction return as the purchase price of the property must be a 'just and reasonable' apportionment of the total amount paid. As with other entries on the form, the purchaser is responsible for the accuracy of this information. HMRC pays especial attention to residential property purchases just below stamp duty thresholds to prevent arrangements between buyer and seller to hand over cash so that the purchase price on paper looks lower or to pay unreasonably high amounts to buy chattels.

STAMP DUTY RESERVE TAX

Stamp duty or stamp duty reserve tax (SDRT) is payable at the rate of 0.5 per cent when shares are purchased. Stamp duty is payable when the shares are transferred using a stock transfer form, whereas SDRT is payable on 'paperless' share transactions where the shares are transferred electronically without using a stock transfer form. Most share transactions nowadays are paperless and settled by stockbrokers through CREST (the electronic settlement and registration system). SDRT therefore now accounts for the majority of taxation collected on share transactions effected through the London Stock Exchange.

The flat rate of 0.5 per cent is based on the amount paid for the shares, not what they are worth. If, for example, shares are bought for £2,000, £10 SDRT is payable, whatever the value of the shares themselves. If shares are transferred for free, no SDRT is payable.

A higher rate of 1.5 per cent is payable if shares are transferred into a 'depositary receipt scheme' or a 'clearance service'. These are special arrangements where the shares are held by a third party.

CREST automatically deducts the SDRT and sends it to the HMRC. A stockbroker will settle up with CREST for the cost of the shares and the SDRT and then bill the purchaser for these and the broker's fees. If shares are not purchased through CREST, the stamp duty must be paid by the purchaser to HMRC.

UK stamp duty or SDRT is not payable on the purchase of foreign shares, though there may be foreign taxes to pay. SDRT is already accounted for in the price paid for units in unit trusts or shares in open-ended investment companies.

HELP AND INFORMATION

Further information on stamp duty land tax is available via the stamp taxes helpline on T 0845-603 0135 (open 8.30am to 5pm Monday to Friday) or the HMRC website (W www.hmrc.gov.uk), where a stamp duty calculator for both shares and land and property can be found. For buyers wishing to undertake their own conveyancing, copies of the land transaction return (SDLT1) and guidance notes (SDLT6) can be obtained by calling T 0845-302 1472.

LEGAL NOTES

These notes outline certain aspects of the law as they might affect the average person. They are intended only as a broad guideline and are by no means definitive. The law is constantly changing so expert advice should always be taken. In some cases, sources of further information are given in these notes.

It is always advisable to consult a solicitor without delay. Anyone who does not have a solicitor already can contact the following for assistance in finding one: Citizens Advice Bureau (W www.nacab.org.uk), the Community Legal Service (W www.legalservices.gov.uk), the Law Society of England and Wales. For assistance in Scotland, contact the Scottish Citizens Advice Bureau (W www.cas.org.uk) or the Law Society of Scotland.

The community legal service fund and legal aid and assistance schemes exist to make the help of a lawyer available to those who would not otherwise be able to afford one. Entitlement depends on an individual's means but a solicitor or Citizens Advice Bureau will be able to advise about entitlement.

LAW SOCIETY OF ENGLAND AND WALES
113 Chancery Lane, London WC2A 1PL T 020-7242 1222
W www.lawsociety.co.uk

LAW SOCIETY OF SCOTLAND
26 Drumsheugh Gardens, Edinburgh EH3 7YR
T 0131-226 7411 W www.lawscot.org.uk

ABORTION

Abortion is governed by the Abortion Act 1967. This act was reviewed by the Commons Select Committee on science and technology in 2007. The provisions below are accurate at the time of writing.

Under the provisions of the Abortion Act 1967, a legally induced abortion must be:

- performed by a registered medical practitioner
- carried out in an NHS hospital or other approved premises
- certified by two registered medical practitioners as justified on one or more of the following grounds:
  (a) that the pregnancy has not exceeded its 24th week and that the continuance of the pregnancy would involve risk, greater than if the pregnancy were terminated, of injury to the physical or mental health of the pregnant woman or any existing children of her family
  (b) that the termination is necessary to prevent grave permanent injury to the physical or mental health of the pregnant woman
  (c) that the continuance of the pregnancy would involve risk to the life of the pregnant woman, greater than if the pregnancy were terminated
  (d) that there is a substantial risk that if the child were born it would suffer from such physical or mental abnormalities as to be seriously handicapped.

In determining whether the continuance of a pregnancy would involve such risk of injury to health as is mentioned in grounds (a) or (b), account may be taken of the pregnant woman's actual or reasonably foreseeable environment.

The requirements relating to the opinion of two registered medical practitioners and to the performance of the abortion at an NHS hospital or other approved place cease to apply in circumstances where a registered medical practitioner is of the opinion, formed in good faith, that a termination is immediately necessary to save the life, or to prevent grave permanent injury to the physical or mental health, of the pregnant woman.

The provisions of the Abortion Act 1967 do not apply to Northern Ireland, where abortion is not legal.

Further information and advice can be obtained from:

FAMILY PLANNING ASSOCIATION (UK)
50 Featherstone Street, London EC1Y 8QU T 0845-122 8690
W www.fpa.org.uk

FAMILY PLANNING ASSOCIATION (SCOTLAND)
Unit 10, Firhill Business Centre, 76 Firhill Road, Glasgow G20 7BA T 0141-576 5088 or 0845-122 8676
W www.fpa.org.uk

FAMILY PLANNING ASSOCIATION (NORTHERN IRELAND)
3rd Floor, Ascot House, 24–31 Shaftsbury Square, Belfast BT2 7DB T 0845-122 8687 W www.fpa.org.uk
3rd Floor, 67 Carlisle Road, Derry BT48 6JJ T 028-7126 0016
W www.fpa.org.uk

BRITISH PREGNANCY ADVISORY SERVICE (BPAS)
T 0845-730 4030 W www.bpas.org

ADOPTION OF CHILDREN

The Adoption and Children Act 2002 reformed the framework for domestic and intercountry adoption in England and Wales and some parts of it extend to Scotland and Northern Ireland.

WHO MAY APPLY FOR AN ADOPTION ORDER

A couple (whether married or two people living as partners in an enduring family relationship) may apply for an adoption order where both of them are over 21 or where one is only 18 but the natural parent and the other is 21. An adoption order may be made for one applicant where that person is 21 and: a) the court is satisfied that person is the partner of a parent of the person to be adopted; or b) they are not married and are not civil partners; or c) married or in a civil partnership but they are separated from their spouse or civil partner and living apart with the separation likely to be permanent; or d) their spouse/civil partner is either unable to be found, or their spouse/civil partner is incapable by reason of ill-health of making an application. There are certain qualifying conditions an applicant must meet eg residency in the British Isles.

ARRANGING AN ADOPTION

Adoptions may generally only be arranged by an adoption agency or by way of an order from the high court; breach of the restrictions on who may arrange an adoption would constitute a criminal offence. When deciding whether a child should be placed for adoption, the court or adoption agency must consider all the factors set out in the 'welfare checklist' – the paramount consideration being the child's welfare, throughout his or her life. These factors include the child's wishes, needs, age, sex, background and any harm which the child has suffered or is likely to suffer. At all times, the court or adoption agency must bear in mind that delay is likely to prejudice a child's welfare.

ADOPTION ORDER

Once an adoption has been arranged, a court order is necessary to make it legal; this may be obtained from the high court, county court or magistrates' court (including family proceedings court). An adoption order may not be given unless the court is satisfied that the consent of the child's natural parents (or guardians) has correctly been given. Consent can be dispensed with on two grounds: where the parent or guardian cannot be found or is incapable of giving consent, or where the welfare of the child so demands.

An adoption order has the effect of extinguishing the parental responsibility that a person other than the adopters (or adopter) has for the child, although where an order is made on the application of the partner of the parent, that parent keeps parental responsibility. This means that once adopted the child has the same status as a child born to the adoptive parents and will be treated as such for the purposes of intestate succession, National Insurance, child benefit etc. In addition the child may lose rights to the estates of those losing their parental responsibility.

REGISTRATION AND CERTIFICATES

All adoption orders made in England and Wales are required to be registered in the Adopted Children Register which also contains particulars of children adopted under registrable foreign adoptions. The General Register Office keeps this register from which certificates may be obtained in a similar way to birth certificates. The General Register Office also has equivalents in Scotland and Northern Ireland.

TRACING NATURAL PARENTS OR CHILDREN WHO HAVE BEEN ADOPTED

An adult adopted person may apply to the Registrar-General to obtain a certified copy of his/her birth certificate. For those adopted before 12 November 1975 it is obligatory to receive counselling services before this information is given. In any event, adoption agencies and adoption support agencies should provide services to adopted persons to assist them in obtaining information about their adoption and facilitate contact with their relatives. There is an Adoption Contact Register which provides a safe and confidential way for birth parents and other relatives to assure an adopted person that contact would be welcome. The BAAF (*see* below) can provide addresses of organisations which offer advice, information and counselling to adopted people, adoptive parents and people who have had their children adopted.

BRITISH ASSOCIATION FOR ADOPTION AND FOSTERING (BAAF)
Saffron House, 6–10 Kirkby Street, London EC1N 8TS
T 020-7421 2600 W www.baaf.org.uk

SCOTLAND

The relevant legislation is the Adoption (Scotland) Act 1978 (as amended by the Children Act 1995 and the Adoption and Children (Scotland) Act 2007) and the provisions are similar to those described above. In Scotland, petitions for adoption are made to the sheriff court or the court of session. The 2007 Act is expected to come fully into force in September 2009. It will repeal the 1978 Act, save for Part IV and will further amend the Children (Scotland) Act 1995.

Further information can be obtained from:

BRITISH ASSOCIATION FOR ADOPTION AND FOSTERING (BAAF)
BAAF Scottish Centre, 40 Shandwick Place, Edinburgh EH2 4RT T 0131-220 4749

SCOTTISH ADOPTION ADVICE SERVICE
16 Sandyford Place, Glasgow G3 7NB T 0141-339 0772

BIRTHS (REGISTRATION)

It is the duty of the parents of a child born in England or Wales to register the birth within 42 days of the date of birth at the register office in the district in which the baby was born. If it is inconvenient to go to the district where the birth took place, the information for the registration may be given to a registrar in another district. Failure to register the birth within 42 days without reasonable cause may leave the parents liable to a penalty. If a birth has not been registered within 12 months of its occurrence it is possible for the late registration of the birth to be authorised by the Registrar-General, provided certain requirements can be met.

If the parents of the child were married to each other at the time of the birth (or conception), either the mother or the father may register the birth. If the parents were not married to each other at the time of the child's birth (or conception), the father's particulars may be entered in the register only where he attends the register office with the mother and they sign the birth register together. Where an unmarried parent is unable to attend the register office either parent may submit to the registrar a statutory declaration on Form 16 (or Form 16W for births which took place in Wales) acknowledging the father's paternity (this form may be obtained from any registrar in England or Wales or online at W www.gro.gov.uk); alternatively a parental responsibility agreement or appropriate court order may be produced to the registrar.

If the parents do not register the birth of their child the following people may do so:

- the occupier of the house or hospital where the child was born
- a person who was present at the birth
- a person who is responsible for the child

Upon registration of the birth a short certificate is issued.

BIRTHS ABROAD

There are certain countries where birth registrations may be made for British citizens overseas (for more details on British citizenship *see* below). The British consul or high commission may register the births and issue certificates which are then sent to the General Register Office. If a birth is registered by the British consul or high commission, the registration would show the person's claim to British citizenship, British overseas territories citizenship or British overseas citizenship.

SCOTLAND

In Scotland the birth of a child must be registered within 21 days at the register office of either the district in which the baby was born or the district in which the mother was resident at the time of the birth.

If the child is born, either in or out of Scotland, on a ship, aircraft or land vehicle that ends its journey at any place in Scotland, the child, in most cases, will be registered as if born in that place.

CERTIFICATES OF BIRTHS, DEATHS OR MARRIAGES

Certificates of births, deaths or marriages that have taken place in England and Wales since 1837 can be obtained from the General Register Office or the Family Records Centre.

Certificates of births, marriages and deaths may be obtained in the following ways:

- by post, telephone, fax or online (details of which may be obtained by calling T 0845-603 7788 or visiting W www.gro.gov.uk)
- locally from the register office where the event was originally registered

Marriage or death certificates may be obtained from the minister of the church in which the marriage or funeral took place. Any register office can advise about the best way to obtain certificates. The fees for certificates are:

Online application:

- full certificate of birth, marriage, death or adoption, £10.00
- full certificate of birth, marriage, death or adoption with GRO reference supplied, £7.00

By postal/phone/fax application:

- full certificate of birth, marriage, death or adoption, £11.50
- full certificate of birth, marriage, death or adoption with GRO reference supplied, £8.50
- extra copies of the same birth, marriage or death certificate issued at the same time, £7.00

A priority service is also available with certificates despatched on the working day following receipt of your application at an additional cost. Visit W www.gro.gov.uk or call T 0845-603 7788 for further information.

A complete set of the GRO indexes including births, deaths and marriages, civil partnerships, adoptions and provisional indexes for births and deaths for 2007 is available at City of Westminster Archives Centre, Greater Manchester County Record Office, Birmingham Central Library, Bridgend Reference and Information Library and Plymouth Central Library. These are also available at the National Archives at Kew. Copies of GRO indexes may also be held at some libraries, family history societies, local records offices and The Church of Jesus Christ of Latter Day Saints family history centres. Some organisations may not hold a complete record of indexes and a small fee may be charged by some of these organisations. GRO indexes are also available online (visit W www.gro.gov.uk for the full list of websites), again, a small fee may be charged by some of the websites.

The Society of Genealogists has many records of baptisms, marriages and deaths prior to 1837.

SCOTLAND

Certificates of births, deaths or marriages that have taken place in Scotland since 1855 can be obtained from the General Register Office for Scotland or from the appropriate local registrar.

Applicable fees – local registrar:

- each extract or abbreviated certificate of birth, death, marriage, civil partnership or adoption within the year of registration, £9.00
- each extract or abbreviated certificate of birth, death, marriage, civil partnership or adoption outwith the current year of registration, £14.00

A priority service for response within 24 hours is available for an additional fee.

The General Register Office for Scotland also keeps the Register of Divorces (including decrees of declaration of nullity of marriage), and holds parish registers dating from before 1855.

Applicable fees – General Register Office for Scotland:

- personal application: £11.00
- postal, telephone or fax order: £13.00

A priority service for a response within 24 hours is available for an additional fee of £10.00.

General search in the indexes to the statutory registers and parochial registers, per day or part thereof:

- full or part-day search pass: £10.00
- quarterly search pass: £440.00
- annual search pass: £1,250.00

Online searching is also available. For more information, visit W www.scotlandspeople.gov.uk Further information can be obtained from:

THE GENERAL REGISTER OFFICE
General Register Office, Trafalgar Road, Southport PR8 2HH
T 0845-603 7788 W www.gro.gov.uk

FAMILY RECORDS CENTRE
1 Myddelton Street, London EC1R 1UW

THE GENERAL REGISTER OFFICE FOR SCOTLAND
New Register House, 3 West Register Street, Edinburgh
EH1 3YT T 0131-334 0380 W www.gro-scotland.gov.uk

THE SOCIETY OF GENEALOGISTS
14 Charterhouse Buildings, Goswell Road, London EC1M 7BA
T 020-7251 8799

BRITISH NATIONALITY

Principally, there are six types of British nationality status, the most widely held being British citizenship. Almost everyone who was a citizen of the UK and colonies before 1 January 1983 and had a right of abode in the UK became a British citizen when the British Nationality Act 1981 came into force. British citizens have the right to live permanently in the UK and are free to leave and re-enter the UK at any time.

A person born on or after 1 January 1983 in the UK (including, for this purpose, the Channel Islands and the Isle of Man) is entitled to British citizenship if he/she falls into one of the following categories:

- he/she has a parent who is a British citizen
- he/she has a parent who is settled in the UK
- he/she is a newborn infant found abandoned in the UK
- his/her parents subsequently settle in the UK or become British citizens and an application is made before he/she is 18
- he/she lives in the UK for the first ten years of his/her life and is not absent for more than 90 days in each of those years
- he/she is adopted in the UK and one of the adopters is a British citizen
- the home secretary consents to his/her registration while he/she is a minor
- if he/she has always been stateless and lives in the UK for a period of five years before his/her 22nd birthday

A person born outside the UK may acquire British citizenship if he/she falls into one of the following categories:

- he/she has a parent who is a British citizen otherwise than by descent, eg a parent who was born in the UK
- he/she has a parent who is a British citizen serving the crown overseas
- the home secretary consents to his/her registration while he/she is a minor
- he/she is a British overseas territories citizen, a British

overseas citizen, a British subject or a British protected person and has been lawfully resident in the UK for five years
- he/she is a British overseas territories citizen who acquired that citizenship from a connection with Gibraltar
- he/she is adopted or naturalised

Where parents are married, the status of either may confer citizenship on their child. Where parents are not married, the status of the mother determines the child's citizenship.

Under the 1981 act, Commonwealth citizens and citizens of the Republic of Ireland were entitled to registration as British citizens before 1 January 1988. In 1983, citizens of the Falkland Islands were granted British citizenship.

Renunciation of British citizenship must be registered with the home secretary and will be revoked if no new citizenship or nationality is acquired within six months. If the renunciation was required in order to retain or acquire another citizenship or nationality, the citizenship may be reacquired only once. The secretary of state may deprive a person of a citizenship status if he or she is satisfied that the person has done anything seriously prejudicial to the vital interests of the UK, or a British overseas territory, unless making the order would have the effect of rendering a person stateless. A person may also be deprived of a citizenship status which results from his registration or naturalisation if the secretary of state is satisfied that the registration or naturalisation was obtained by means of fraud, false representation or concealment of a material fact.

BRITISH DEPENDENT TERRITORIES CITIZENSHIP

Since 26 February 2006, this category of nationality no longer exists and has been replaced by British overseas territory citizenship.

If a person had this class of nationality only by reason of a connection to the territory of Hong Kong, they lost it automatically when Hong Kong was returned to the People's Republic of China. However, if after 30 June 1997, they had no other nationality and would have become stateless, or were born after 30 June 1997 and would have been born stateless (but had a parent who was a British national (overseas) or a British overseas citizen), they became a British overseas citizen.

BRITISH OVERSEAS CITIZENSHIP

Under the 1981 act, as amended by the British Overseas Territories Act 2002, this type of citizenship was conferred on any UK and colonies citizens who did not become either a British citizen or a British overseas territories citizen on 1 January 1983 and as such is now, for most purposes, only acquired by persons who would otherwise be stateless.

BRITISH OVERSEAS TERRITORIES CITIZENSHIP

This category of nationality replaced British dependent territories citizenship. Most commonly, this form of nationality is acquired where, after 31 December 1982, a person was a citizen of the UK and colonies and did not become a British citizen, and that person, and their parents or grandparents, were born, registered or naturalised in the specified British overseas territory.

However, on 21 May 2002, people became British citizens if they had British overseas territories citizenship by connection with any British overseas territory except for the sovereign base areas of Akrotiri and Dhekelia in Cyprus.

RESIDUAL CATEGORIES

British subjects, British protected persons and British nationals (overseas) may be entitled to registration as British citizens on completion of five years' legal residence in the UK.

Citizens of the Republic of Ireland who were also British subjects before 1 January 1949 can retain that status if they fulfil certain conditions.

EUROPEAN UNION CITIZENSHIP

British citizens (including Gibraltarians who are registered as such) are also EU citizens and are entitled to travel freely to other EU countries to work, study, reside and set up a business. EU citizens have the same rights with respect to the UK.

NATURALISATION

Naturalisation is granted at the discretion of the home secretary. The basic requirements are five years' residence (three years if the applicant is married to, or is the civil partner of a British citizen), good character, adequate knowledge of the English, Welsh or Scottish Gaelic language, passing the UK citizenship test and an intention to reside permanently in the UK.

STATUS OF ALIENS

Aliens, being persons without any of the above forms of British nationality granted under the British Nationality Act 1981, may not hold public office or vote in Britain and they may not own a British ship or aircraft. Citizens of the Republic of Ireland are not deemed to be aliens. Certain provisions of the Immigration and Asylum Act 1999 make provision about immigration and asylum and about procedures in connection with marriage by superintendent registrar's certificate.

CONSUMER LAW

SALE OF GOODS

A sale of goods contract is the most common type of contract. It is governed by the Sale of Goods Act 1979 (as amended by the Sale and Supply of Goods Act 1994). The act provides protection for buyers by implying terms into every sale of goods contract. These terms include:

- an implied term that the seller will pass good title to the buyer (unless it appears from the contract or is to be inferred from the circumstances that there is an intention that the seller should transfer only such title as he has)
- where the seller sells goods by reference to a description, an implied term that the goods will match that description and, where the sale is by sample and description, it will not be sufficient that the bulk of the goods corresponds with the sample if the goods do not also correspond with the description
- where goods are sold by a business seller, an implied term that the goods will be of satisfactory quality if they meet the standard that a reasonable person would regard as satisfactory, taking into account any description of the goods, the price, and all other relevant circumstances. The quality of the goods includes their state and condition, relevant aspects being whether they are fit for all the purposes for which such goods are commonly supplied, their appearance and finish, freedom from minor defects and their safety and durability. This term will not be implied, however, if a buyer has examined the goods

(including in a sale by sample) and should have noticed the defect or if the seller specifically drew the buyer's attention to the defect
- where goods are sold by a business seller, an implied term that the goods are reasonably fit for any purpose made known to the seller by the buyer (either expressly or by implication), unless it is shown that the buyer does not rely on the seller's judgment, or it is not reasonable for him/her to do so
- where goods are sold by sample, implied terms that the bulk of the sample will correspond with the sample in quality, and that the goods are free from any defect rendering them unsatisfactory which would have been apparent on a reasonable examination of the sample

Some of the above terms can be excluded from contracts by the seller. The seller's right to do this is, however, restricted by the Unfair Contract Terms Act 1977. The act offers more protection to a buyer who 'deals as a consumer' (that is where the seller is selling in the course of a business, the goods are of a type ordinarily bought for private use and the goods are bought by a buyer who is not a business buyer, though not allowing any liability for breach of the implied terms described above to be excluded). In a sale by auction (at which individuals have the opportunity of attending the sale in person), a buyer never deals as a consumer.

HIRE-PURCHASE AGREEMENTS

Terms similar to those implied in contracts of sales of goods are implied into contracts of hire-purchase, under the Supply of Goods (Implied Terms) Act 1973. The 1977 act limits the exclusion of these implied terms as before.

SUPPLY OF GOODS AND SERVICES

Under the Supply of Goods and Services Act 1982, similar terms are also implied in other types of contract under which ownership of goods passes, and contracts for the hire of goods (though not hire-purchase agreements). These types of contracts have additional implied terms:
- that the supplier will use reasonable care and skill in carrying out the service
- that the supplier will carry out the service in a reasonable time (unless the time has been agreed)
- that the supplier will make a reasonable charge (unless the charge has already been agreed)

The 1977 act limits the exclusion of these implied terms in a similar manner as before.

UNFAIR TERMS

The Unfair Terms in Consumer Contracts Regulations 1999 apply to contracts between business sellers (or suppliers of goods and services) and consumers. Where the terms have not been individually negotiated, ie where the terms were drafted in advance so that the consumer was unable to influence those terms, there will be an unfair term where a term operates to the detriment of the consumer (ie carries a significant imbalance in the parties' rights and obligations arising under the contract). An unfair term does not bind the consumer but the contract will continue to bind the parties if it is capable of existing without the unfair term. The regulations contain a non-exhaustive list of terms that are regarded as unfair. When a term does not fall into such a category, whether it will be regarded as fair or not will depend on many factors, including the nature of the goods or services, the surrounding circumstances (such as the bargaining strength of both parties) and the other terms in the contract.

TRADE DESCRIPTIONS

It is a criminal offence under the Trade Descriptions Act 1968 for a business seller to apply a false trade description of goods or to supply or offer to supply any goods to which a false description has been applied. A 'trade description' includes descriptions of size, composition, fitness for purpose, performance, method of manufacture, and place and date of manufacture of the goods.

CONSUMER PROTECTION

Under the Consumer Protection Act 1987, producers of goods are liable for any injury, death or damage to any property exceeding £275 caused by a defect in their product (subject to certain defences).

Consumers are also afforded protection under the Consumer Protection (Distance Selling) Regulations 2000 in relation to cancellation periods, for example.

CONSUMER CREDIT

In matters relating to the provision of credit (or the supply of goods on hire or hire-purchase), consumers are also protected by the Consumer Credit Act 1974 (as amended by the Consumer Credit Act 2006). Under this act a licence, issued by the Director-General of Fair Trading, is required to conduct a consumer credit or consumer hire business or an ancillary credit business. Any 'fit' person as defined within the act may apply to the Director-General of Fair Trading for a licence, which is normally renewable after five years. A licence is not necessary if only exempt agreements are involved. The provisions of the act only apply to 'regulated' agreements. Individuals, unincorporated associations and partnerships with three or fewer partners entering consumer credit agreements for business purposes are protected when the value of the credit does not exceed £25,000. Provisions include:
- in order for a creditor to enforce a regulated agreement, the agreement must comply with certain formalities and must be properly executed. An improperly executed regulated agreement is enforceable only on an order of the court. The debtor must also be given specified information by the creditor or his/her broker or agent during the negotiations which take place before the signing of the agreement. The agreement must state certain information such as the rights and duties conferred or imposed on the debtor and the protection and remedies available to him/her under the act
- if an agreement is signed other than at the creditor's (or credit broker's or negotiator's) place of business and oral representations were made in the debtor's presence during pre-agreement discussions, the debtor has a right to cancel the agreement. Time for cancellation expires five days after the debtor receives a second copy of the agreement. The agreement must inform the debtor of his right to cancel and how to cancel
- if the debtor is in breach of the agreement, the creditor must serve a default notice before taking any action such as repossessing the goods
- if the agreement is a hire-purchase or conditional sale agreement, the creditor cannot repossess the goods without a court order if the debtor has paid one third of the total price of the goods
- in agreements where the relationship between the creditor and the debtor is unfair to the debtor, the court may alter or set aside some of the terms of the agreement. The agreement can also be reopened during enforcement proceedings by the court itself.

Where a credit reference agency has been used to check the debtor's financial standing, the creditor must give the agency's name to the debtor, who is entitled to see the agency's file on him. A fee of £1 is payable to the agency.

SCOTLAND

The legislation governing the sale and supply of goods applies to Scotland as follows:

- the Sale of Goods Act 1979 applies with some modifications and it has been amended by the Sale and Supply of Goods Act 1994
- the Supply of Goods (Implied Terms) Act 1973 applies
- the Supply of Goods and Services Act 1982 does not extend to Scotland but some of its provisions were introduced by the Sale and Supply of Goods Act 1994
- only Parts II and III of the Unfair Contract Terms Act 1977 apply
- the Trade Descriptions Act 1968 applies with minor modifications
- the Consumer Credit Act 1974 applies
- the Consumer Protection Act 1987 applies
- the General Product Safety Regulations 2005 apply
- the Unfair Terms in Consumer Contracts Regulations 1999 apply
- the Unfair Terms in Consumer Contracts (Amendment) Regulations 2001 apply
- the Consumer Protection (Distance Selling) Regulations 2000 apply
- the Sale and Supply of Goods to Consumers Regulations 2002 apply

PROCEEDINGS AGAINST THE CROWN

Until 1947, proceedings against the Crown were generally possible only by a procedure known as a petition of right, which put the private litigant at a considerable disadvantage. The Crown Proceedings Act 1947 placed the Crown (not the sovereign in his/her private capacity, but as the embodiment of the state) largely in the same position as a private individual and made proceedings in the high court involving the Crown subject to the same rules as any other case. The act did not, however, extinguish or limit the Crown's prerogative or statutory powers, and it continued the immunity of HM ships and aircraft. It also left certain Crown privileges unaffected. The act largely abolished the special procedures which previously applied to civil proceedings by and against the Crown. Civil proceedings may be initiated against the appropriate government department or if there is doubt regarding which is the appropriate department, against the attorney-general.

In Scotland proceedings against the Crown founded on breach of contract could be taken before the 1947 act and no special procedures applied. The Crown could, however, claim certain special pleas. The 1947 act applies in part to Scotland and brings the practice of the two countries as closely together as the different legal systems permit. As a result of the Scotland Act 1998 actions against government departments should be raised against the Lord Advocate or the advocate-general. Actions should be raised against the Lord Advocate where the department involved administers a devolved matter. Devolved matters include agriculture, education, housing, local government, health and justice. Actions should be raised against the advocate-general where the department is dealing with a reserved matter. Reserved matters include defence, foreign affairs and social security.

DEATHS

WHEN A DEATH OCCURS

If the death (including stillbirth) was expected, the doctor who attended the deceased during their final illness should be contacted. If the death was sudden or unexpected, the family doctor (if known) and police should be contacted. If the cause of death is quite clear the doctor will provide:

- a medical certificate that shows the cause of death
- a formal notice that states that the doctor has signed the medical certificate and that explains how to get the death registered

If the death was known to be caused by a natural illness but the doctor wishes to know more about the cause of death, he/she may ask the relatives for permission to carry out a post-mortem examination.

In England and Wales a coroner is responsible for investigating deaths occurring in the following circumstances:

- where there is no doctor who can issue a medical certificate of cause of death
- when no doctor has treated the deceased during his or her last illness or when the doctor attending the patient did not see him or her within 14 days before death, or after death
- when the death occurred during an operation or before recovery from the effect of an anaesthetic
- when the death was sudden and unexplained or attended by suspicious circumstances
- when the death might be due to an industrial injury or disease, or to accident, violence, neglect or abortion, attended by suspicious circumstances
- the death occurred in prison or in police custody

The doctor will write on the formal notice that the death has been referred to the coroner; if the post-mortem shows that death was due to natural causes, the coroner may issue a notification which gives the cause of death so that the death can be registered. If the cause of death was violent or unnatural, the coroner is obliged to hold an inquest.

In Scotland the office of coroner does not exist. The local procurator fiscal inquires into sudden or suspicious deaths. A fatal accident inquiry will be held before the sheriff where the death has resulted from an accident during the course of the employment of the person who has died, or where the person who has died was in legal custody, or where the Lord Advocate deems it in the public interest that an inquiry be held.

REGISTERING A DEATH

In England and Wales the death must be registered by the registrar of births and deaths for the district in which it occurred. Information concerning a death can be given before any registrar of births and deaths in England and Wales. The registrar will pass the relevant details to the registrar for the district where the death occurred, who will then register the death.

In England and Wales the death must normally be registered within five days; in Scotland within eight days. If the death has been referred to the coroner/local procurator fiscal it cannot be registered until the registrar has received authority from the coroner/local procurator fiscal to do so. Failure to register a death involves a penalty in England and Wales and may lead to a court decree being granted by a sheriff in Scotland.

If the death occurred at a house or hospital, the death may be registered by:

- any relative of the deceased
- any person present at the death
- the occupier or any inmate of the house or hospital if he/she knew of the occurrence of the death
- any person making the funeral arrangements
- an official from the hospital
- in Scotland, the deceased's executor or legal representative

For deaths that took place elsewhere, the death may be registered by:

- any relative of the deceased
- someone present at the death
- someone who found the body
- a person in charge of the body
- any person making the funeral arrangements

The majority of deaths are registered by a relative of the deceased. The registrar would normally allow one of the other listed persons to register the death only if there were no relatives available.

The person registering the death should take the medical certificate of the cause of death with them; it is also useful, though not essential, to take the deceased's birth and marriage/civil partnership certificates, NHS medical card, pension documentation and life assurance details. The details given to the registrar must be absolutely correct, otherwise it may be difficult to change them later. The person registering the death should check the entry carefully before it is signed. The registrar will issue a certificate for burial or cremation, a certificate of registration of death and a certificate for social security benefits – all free of charge. A death certificate is a certified copy of the entry in the death register; these can be provided on payment of a fee and may be required for the following purposes:

- the will
- bank and building society accounts
- savings bank certificates and premium bonds
- insurance policies
- pension claims

If the death occurred abroad or on a foreign ship or aircraft, the death should be registered according to the local regulations of the relevant country and a death certificate should be obtained. The death can also be registered with the British consul in that country and a record will be kept at the General Register Office. This avoids the expense of bringing the body back.

After 12 months (three months in Scotland) of death or the finding of a dead body, no death can be registered without the consent of the registrar-general.

BURIAL AND CREMATION

In most circumstances in England and Wales a certificate for burial or cremation must be obtained from the registrar before the burial or cremation can take place. If the death has been referred to the coroner, an order for burial or a certificate for cremation must be obtained. In Scotland a body may be buried (but not cremated) before the death is registered.

Funeral costs can normally be repaid out of the deceased's estate and will be given priority over any other claims. If the deceased has left a will it may contain directions concerning the funeral; however, these directions need not be followed by the executor.

The deceased's papers should also indicate whether a grave space had already been arranged. This information will be contained in a document known as a 'Deed of Grant'. Most town churchyards and many suburban churchyards are no longer open for burial because they are full. Most cemeteries are non-denominational and may be owned by local authorities or private companies; fees vary.

If the body is to be cremated, an application form, two cremation certificates (for which there is a charge) or a certificate for cremation if the death was referred to the coroner, and a certificate signed by the medical referee must be completed in addition to the certificate for burial or cremation (the form is not required if the coroner has issued a certificate for cremation). All the forms are available from the funeral director or crematorium. Most crematoria are run by local authorities; the fees usually include the medical referee's fee and the use of the chapel. Ashes may be scattered, buried in a churchyard or cemetery, or kept.

The registrar must be notified of the date, place and means of disposal of the body within 96 hours (England and Wales) or three days (Scotland).

If the death occurred abroad or on a foreign ship or aircraft, a local burial or cremation may be arranged. If the body is to be brought back to England or Wales, a death certificate from the relevant country or an authorisation for the removal of the body from the country of death from the coroner or relevant authority will be required. To arrange a funeral in England or Wales, an authenticated translation of a foreign death certificate or a death certificate issued in Scotland or Northern Ireland which must show the cause of death, is needed, together with a certificate of no liability to register from the registrar in England and Wales in whose sub-district it is intended to bury or cremate the body. If it is intended to cremate the body, a cremation order will be required from the Home Office or a certificate for cremation.

Further information can be obtained from:

THE GENERAL REGISTER OFFICE
General Register Office, Trafalgar Road, Southport PR8 2HH
T 0845-603 7788 W www.gro.gov.uk

THE GENERAL REGISTER OFFICE FOR SCOTLAND
New Register House, 3 West Register Street, Edinburgh
EH1 3YT T 0131-334 0380 W www.gro-scotland.gov.uk

DIVORCE AND RELATED MATTERS

There are three types of matrimonial suit: annulment of marriage, judicial separation and divorce. To obtain an annulment, judicial separation or divorce in England and Wales (provided a European Union court (except Denmark) has jurisdiction) the one commencing the proceedings (the petitioner) and the one defending the proceedings (the respondent) must be habitually resident in England and Wales; or the petitioner and the respondent must have last been habitually resident in England and Wales and one of them must continue to reside there; or the respondent must be habitually resident in England and Wales; or the petitioner must have been habitually resident in England and Wales throughout the period of at least one year ending with the start of proceedings; or the petitioner must be domiciled in England and Wales and must have been habitually resident in England and Wales throughout the period of at least six months, ending with the start of the proceedings; or both parties must be domiciled in England and Wales. If no European Union court (except Denmark) has jurisdiction, one or both parties must be domiciled in England and Wales. All cases are commenced in a divorce county court or in the Principal Registry in London. If a suit is defended, it may be transferred to the high court.

ANNULMENT OF MARRIAGE

Various circumstances have the potential to render a marriage void or voidable in annulment proceedings including: if there has been wilful non-consummation of the marriage; one partner has a venereal disease at the time of the marriage and the other did not know about it; the female partner was pregnant at the time of the marriage with another person's child and the male partner did not know of the pregnancy; the parties were within prohibited degrees of consanguinity, affinity or adoption; the parties were not male and female; either of the parties was already married or had entered a civil partnership; either of the parties was under the age of 16; the formalities of the marriage were defective, eg the marriage did not take place in an authorised building and both parties knew of the defect.

SEPARATION

A couple may enter into a private agreement to separate by consent without getting divorced but for the agreement to be valid it must be followed by an immediate separation; a solicitor should be contacted.

Another form of separation is judicial separation. Judicial separation does not dissolve a marriage and it is not necessary to prove that the marriage has irretrievably broken down. Either party can petition for a judicial separation at any time; the grounds listed below as grounds for divorce are also grounds for judicial separation. To petition for judicial separation, the parties do not have to prove that they have been married for 12 months or more.

A financial settlement between spouses in a separation agreement or which accompanies a judicial separation is not binding on the court and will not necessarily be upheld by the court after the commencement of divorce proceedings.

DIVORCE

Neither party can petition for divorce until at least one year after the date of the marriage. The sole ground for divorce is the irretrievable breakdown of the marriage; this must be proved on one or more of the following facts:

- the respondent has committed adultery and the petitioner finds it intolerable to live with him/her; however, the petitioner cannot rely on an act of adultery by the respondent if they have lived together as husband and wife for more than six months after the discovery of the adultery
- the respondent has behaved in such a way that the petitioner cannot reasonably be expected to continue living with him/her
- the respondent has deserted the petitioner for two years immediately before the petition
- the petitioner and the respondent have lived separately for two years immediately before the petition and the respondent consents to the divorce
- the petitioner and the respondent have lived separately for five years immediately before the petition

A total period of less than six months during which the parties have resumed living together is disregarded in determining whether the prescribed period of separation or desertion has been continuous (but may not be included as part of the period of separation).

The Matrimonial Causes Act 1973 requires the solicitor for the petitioner to certify whether the possibility of a reconciliation has been discussed with the petitioner.

THE DECREE NISI

A decree nisi does not dissolve or annul the marriage, but must be obtained before a divorce or annulment can take place.

Where the suit is undefended, the evidence normally takes the form of a sworn written statement made by the petitioner which is considered by a district judge. If the judge is satisfied that the petitioner has proved the contents of the petition, a date will be set for the pronouncement of the decree nisi in open court: neither party need attend.

If the suit is defended, the petition will be heard in open court with parties giving oral evidence.

THE DECREE ABSOLUTE

The decree nisi is capable of being made absolute on the application of the petitioner six weeks after the decree nisi. If the petitioner does not apply, the respondent must wait for a further three months before application may be made. In exceptional circumstances the granting of the decree absolute may be delayed, for example if matters regarding children are not capable of resolution. A decree absolute is unlikely to be applied for until the financial matters have been resolved. The decree absolute dissolves or annuls the marriage. Where the couple have been married in accordance with Jewish or other religious usages, the court may require them to produce a declaration that they have taken such steps as are required to dissolve the marriage in accordance with those usages before the decree absolute is issued.

MAINTENANCE

Either party may be liable to make financial payments as maintenance to a spouse or former spouse. If there are any children of the marriage, both parties have a legal responsibility to support them financially if they can afford to do so.

The courts are responsible for assessing maintenance for a spouse or former spouse, taking into account each party's income and essential outgoings and other aspects of the case. The court can also deal with any maintenance for a child that has been treated by the spouses as a child of the family, such as a step-child.

The Child Maintenance and Other Payments Act 2008 changed the law with regards to child maintenance and set up a new commission, the Child Maintenance and Enforcement Commission (CMEC). Since October 2008, all parents have been able to choose either a private or statutory maintenance arrangement, thereby removing the compulsion for benefit claimants to use the Child Support Agency (CSA).

Parents responsible for day-to-day care who are claiming benefits are now able to keep up to £20 per week of any child maintenance payments before it affects their benefits. From April 2010, child maintenance will be fully disregarded when calculating all unemployment benefits.

At the time of writing the CSA is still responsible for assessing the maintenance that non-resident parents shall pay for their natural or adopted children (whether or not a marriage has taken place). The CSA accepts applications only when all the people involved are habitually resident in the UK; the courts will continue to deal with cases where one of the individuals lives abroad (and does not work for a UK-based employer, the armed forces or the civil service).

A formula is used to work out how much child maintenance is payable under CSA jurisdiction. The basic rate formula requires the non-resident parent to pay 15 per cent net of income post-tax, national insurance and pension contributions for one child, 20 per cent for two and 25 per cent for more than two children. An earnings cap of £104,000 net a year applies. Deductions are applied for staying in contact and for further children in the non-resident parent's household. In court jurisdiction cases, the CSA formula is adopted as a guideline only.

Some cases involving unusual circumstances are treated as special cases and the assessment is modified, and in some cases the court retains jurisdiction (for educational costs and high income cases, for example). Where there is financial need (eg because of disability or continual education) maintenance may be ordered by the court for children beyond the age of 18.

Either parent can report a change of circumstances and request a review at any time but appeals must be made within one month of the letter informing the parents of the CSA's decision. There is an independent complaints examiner for the CSA.

If the non-resident parent does not pay CSA maintenance, the CSA may make an order for payments to be deducted directly from his/her salary; if all other methods fail, the CSA may take court action to enforce payment.

OTHER FINANCIAL RELIEF

Unlike in some other jurisdictions, there is no formula for division of assets on divorce. The courts must exercise their powers so as to achieve an outcome which is fair between the parties. In determining what is 'fair' the court must have regard to all the circumstances of the case, first consideration being given to the welfare of any minor child(ren) of the family. Beyond this, the court must have particular regard to a prescribed list of statutory factors:

- the income, earning capacity, property and other financial resources which each of the parties to the marriage has or is likely to have in the foreseeable future, including in the case of earning capacity, any increase in that capacity which it would, in the opinion of the court, be reasonable to expect a party to the marriage to take steps to acquire
- the financial needs, obligations and responsibilities which each of the parties to the marriage has or is likely to have in the foreseeable future
- the standard of living enjoyed by the family before the breakdown of the marriage
- the age of each party to the marriage and the duration of the marriage
- any physical or mental disability of either of the parties to the marriage
- the contribution which each of the parties has made or is likely in the foreseeable future to make to the welfare of the family, including any contribution by looking after the home or caring for the family
- the conduct of each of the parties, if that conduct is such that it would, in the opinion of the court, be inequitable to disregard it
- in the case of proceedings for divorce or nullity of marriage, the value to each of the parties to the marriage of any benefit (for example a pension) which by reason of the dissolution of the marriage that party will lose the chance of acquiring.

The court also has a duty to consider making an order which will settle once and for all the parties financial responsibilities towards each other. This is known as a financial 'clean break'. Where a clean break is not possible, the court will combine provision of capital via a lump sum and/or property adjustment order and/or pension sharing/attachment order with an ongoing income order, known as maintenance (alimony).

Maintenance can be for a 'term' (ie for a limited period only) or it can be for the joint lives of the parties. In some cases, the courts use nominal maintenance to leave a party's income claims open. It is possible for either party to apply to court to vary the amount or duration of the maintenance at a future date.

Prior to 2000, in considering the above factors, the courts considered the 'reasonable financial requirements' of the applicant, usually the wife, and treated this as determinative of the extent of the applicant's award. In the landmark case of *White v White* in 2000 the House of Lords re-evaluated the court's approach to dividing assets on divorce. The law lords enunciated three key principles. Firstly, the outcome has to be as fair as possible in all the circumstances with each party being entitled to a fair share of the available property. Secondly, in seeking to achieve a fair outcome there is no space for discriminating between the breadwinner and the homemaker in their respective roles. Thirdly, having considered all the circumstances of the case, and the statutory checklist, the judge should consider his view against the 'yardstick of equality of division'.

More recently, the law lords have offered further guidance as to how to achieve a fair division of assets on divorce in the cases of *Miller* and *McFarlane*. In determining fairness, the court must now consider three strands or principles, being each party's respective needs, the possibility of compensating the financially weaker party for any 'relationship' generated disadvantage, which will be relevant where one party has given up a career, and 'equal sharing' of family assets, which is applicable as much to short marriages as to long marriages, and which will apply unless there is good reason to the contrary.

In the recent 'huge money' divorce case of *Charman* the presumption of 50:50 in assessing financial awards on divorce emerged undamaged. Those with trust interests must be aware that the court will ignore the trust structure if it takes the view that the assets will be made available to the party on request.

In assessing whether there is a good reason to depart from the concept of equal sharing, the court will consider the nature of property and whether the property was acquired during the marriage otherwise than by inheritance or gift, known as matrimonial property, such as the matrimonial home, or other property to which the other spouse has not contributed. Whilst the yardstick of equality will apply to matrimonial assets to give full effect to the sharing entitlement, it will apply less readily to non-matrimonial assets, particularly in short marriages.

Additionally, conduct and special contributions will be relevant in assessing whether there should be a departure from equality, but only in exceptional cases, where such conduct or contribution is 'gross and obvious'.

The Law Commission's Marital Property Agreements project is due to begin in late 2009. The project will examine the status and enforceability of agreements made between spouses or civil partners (or those contemplating marriage or civil partnership) concerning their property or finances.

COHABITING COUPLES

Rights of unmarried couples are not the same as for married couples. Agreements, whether express or inferred by conduct, often determine interest in money and property. Reliance upon inferences is problematic, therefore it is advisable to consider entering into a contract, or 'cohabitation agreement', which establishes how money and property should be divided in the event of a relationship breakdown.

This area of the law is still developing. In July 2007, the Law Commission published its report to parliament, recommending a scheme to provide remedies for eligible candidates. The Cohabitation Bill was subsequently introduced to parliament in December 2008 and had its second reading in March 2009. The bill is now before a committee for further security. In the meantime, cohabitation agreements continue to be governed by the general principles of contract law.

CIVIL PARTNERSHIP
The Civil Partnership Act 2004 came into force on 5 December 2005; it has UK-wide status. Same-sex couples, by registering as civil partners, are able to gain legal recognition of their relationship and thereby obtain rights and obligations broadly equivalent to those of married couples. These rights and responsibilities include a duty to provide reasonable maintenance for your civil partner and any children of the family, equitable treatment in respect of life assurance and pension benefits, recognition under intestacy rules and domestic violence protection. In addition, inheritance tax is waived as with married couples and there is a right of succession for tenancy. A civil partnership which has irretrievably broken down may be dissolved by the court on the application of either civil partner. The irretrievable breakdown of the partnership must be proved on one of four grounds. These grounds are the same as those for divorce (*see* above), save for a civil partner may not seek dissolution of the partnership on the basis of the other's adultery.

DOMESTIC VIOLENCE
The Domestic Violence, Crime and Victims Act 2004 is intended to provide greater protection for victims of domestic violence. If one spouse has been subjected to violence at the hands of the other, it is possible to obtain an order from court to restrain further violence and if necessary to have the other spouse excluded from the home. Such orders also apply to civil partnerships and cohabiting couples (including same sex couples), and may also apply to a range of other relationships including parents and children and, to a lesser extent, non-cohabitating couples

SCOTLAND

Although some provisions are similar to those for England and Wales, there is separate legislation for Scotland covering nullity of marriage, judicial separation, divorce and ancillary matters. The principal legislation in relation to family law in Scotland is the Family Law (Scotland) Act 1985. The Family Law (Scotland) Act 2006 came in to force on 4 May 2006, and introduced reforms to various aspects of Scottish family law. The following is confined to major points on which the law in Scotland differs from that of England and Wales.

An action for judicial separation or divorce may be raised in the court of session; it may also be raised in the sheriff court if either party was resident in the sheriffdom for 40 days immediately before the date of the action or for 40 days ending not more than 40 days before the date of the action. The fee for starting a divorce petition in the sheriff court is £120.

The grounds for raising an action of divorce in Scotland have been subject to reform in terms of the 2006 act. The current grounds for divorce are:

- the defender has committed adultery. When adultery is cited as proof that the marriage has broken down irretrievably, it is not necessary in Scotland to prove that it is also intolerable for the pursuer to live with the defender
- the defender's behaviour is such that the pursuer cannot reasonably be expected to cohabit with the defender
- there has been no cohabitation between the parties for one year prior to the raising of the action for divorce, and the defender consents to the granting of decree of divorce
- there has been no cohabitation between the parties for two years prior to the raising of the action for divorce

The previously available ground of desertion was abolished by the 2006 act.

A simplified procedure for 'do-it-yourself divorce' was introduced in 1983 for certain divorces. If the action is based on one or two years' separation and will not be opposed, and if there are no children under 16 and no financial claims, and there is no sign that the applicant's spouse is unable to manage his or her affairs through mental illness or handicap, the applicant can write directly to the local sheriff court or to the court of session for the appropriate forms to enable him or her to proceed. The fee is £90, unless the applicant receives income support or legal advice and assistance, in which case there may be no fee.

Where a divorce action has been raised, it may be put on hold for a variety of reasons. In all actions for divorce an extract decree, which brings the marriage to an end, will be made available 14 days after the divorce has been granted. Unlike in England, there is no decree nisi, only a final decree of divorce. Parties must ensure that all financial issues have been resolved prior to divorce, as it is not possible to seek further financial provision after divorce has been granted.

FINANCIAL PROVISION
In relation to financial provision on divorce, the first, and most important, principle is fair sharing of the matrimonial property. In terms of Scots law matrimonial property is defined as all property acquired by either spouse from the date of marriage up to the date of separation. Property acquired before the marriage is not deemed to be matrimonial unless it was acquired for use by the parties as a family home or as furniture for that home. Property acquired after the date of separation is not matrimonial property. Any property acquired by either of the parties by way of gift or inheritance during the marriage is excluded and does not form part of the matrimonial property.

When considering whether to make an award of financial provision a court shall also take account of any economic advantage derived by either party to the marriage as a result of contributions, financial or otherwise, by the other, and of any economic disadvantage suffered by either party for the benefit of the other party. The court must also ensure that the economic burden of caring for a child under the age of 16 is shared fairly between the parties.

A court can also consider making an order requiring one party to pay the other party a periodical allowance for a certain period of time following divorce. Such an order may be appropriate in cases where there is insufficient capital to effect a fair sharing of the matrimonial property. Orders for periodical allowance are uncommon, as courts will favour a 'clean break' where possible.

CHILDREN
The court has the power to award a residence order in respect of any children of the marriage or to make an order regulating the child's contact with the non-resident parent. The court will only make such orders if it is deemed better for the child to do so than to make no order at all, and the welfare of the children is of paramount importance. The fact that a spouse has caused the breakdown of the marriage does not in itself preclude him/her from being awarded residence.

NULLITY
An action for 'declaration of nullity' can be brought if someone with a legitimate interest is able to show that the marriage is void or voidable. The action can only be brought in the court of session. Although the grounds on which a marriage may be void or voidable are similar to those on which a marriage can be declared invalid in England, there are some differences. Where a spouse is capable of sexual intercourse but refuses to consummate the marriage, this is not a ground for nullity in Scots law, though it could be a ground for divorce. Where a spouse was suffering from venereal disease at the time of marriage and the other spouse did not know, this is not a ground for nullity in Scots law, neither is the fact that a wife was pregnant by another man at the time of marriage without the knowledge of her husband.

COHABITING COUPLES
The law in Scotland now provides certain financial and property rights for cohabiting couples in terms of the Family Law (Scotland) Act 2006, or 'the 2006 act'. The relevant 2006 act provisions do not place cohabitants in Scotland on an equal footing with married couples or civil partners, but provide some rights for cohabitants in the event that the relationship is terminated by separation or death. The provisions relate to couples who cease to cohabit after 4 May 2006.

The legislation provides for a presumption that any contents of the home shared by the cohabitants are owned in equal shares. A former cohabitant can also seek financial provision on termination of the relationship in the form of a capital payment if they can successfully demonstrate that they have been financially disadvantaged, and that conversely the other cohabitant has been financially advantaged, as a consequence of contributions made (financial or otherwise). Such a claim must be made no later than one year after the day on which the cohabitants cease to cohabit.

The 2006 act also provides that a cohabitant may make a claim on their partner's estate in the event of that partner's death, providing that there is no will. A claim of this nature must be made no later than six months after the date of the partner's death.

Further information can be obtained from:

THE PRINCIPAL REGISTRY
First Avenue House, 42–49 High Holborn, London WC2V 6NP

THE COURT OF SESSION
Parliament House, Parliament Square, Edinburgh EH1 1RQ
T 0131-225 2595 W www.scotcourts.gov.uk

THE CHILD SUPPORT AGENCY
National Enquiry Line 08457-133133 W www.csa.gov.uk

EMPLOYMENT LAW

EMPLOYEES
A fundamental distinction in employment law is that drawn between an employee and someone who is self-employed. Further, there is an important, intermediate category introduced by legislation: 'workers' covers all employees but also catches some of those who are self-employed. Whether or not someone is an employee or a worker as opposed to being genuinely self-employed is an important question, for it determines that person's statutory rights and protections.

The greater the level of control that the employer has over the work carried out, the greater the depth of integration of the employee in the employer's business, and the closer the obligations to provide and perform work between the parties, the more likely it is that the parties will be employer and employee. Although there is no formal definition of a worker, broadly speaking someone will be such if they enter into or work under a contract which requires them to do or perform personally any work or services for another party whose status is not that of a client or customer.

PAY AND CONDITIONS
The Employment Rights Act 1996 consolidated the statutory provisions relating to employees' rights. Employers must give each employee employed for one month or more a written statement containing the following information:

- names of employer and employee
- date when employment began and the date on which the employee's period of *continuous* employment began (taking into account any employment with a previous employer which counts towards that period)
- the scale, rate or other method of calculating remuneration and intervals at which it will be paid
- job title or description of job
- hours and the permitted place(s) of work and, where there are several such places, the address of the employer
- holiday entitlement and holiday pay
- provisions concerning incapacity for work due to sickness and injury, including provisions for sick pay
- details of pension scheme(s)
- length of notice period that employer and employee need to give to terminate employment
- if the employment is not intended to be permanent, the period for which it is expected to continue or, if it is for a fixed term, the end date of the contract
- details of any collective agreement (including the parties to the agreement) which affects the terms of employment
- details of disciplinary and grievance procedures (including the individual to whom a complaint should be made and the process of making that complaint)
- if the employee is to work outside the UK for more than one month, the period of such work and the currency in which payment is made
- a note stating whether a contracting out certificate is in force

This must be given to the employee within two months of the start of their employment.

The Working Time Regulations 1998, the National Minimum Wage Act 1998, the Employment Rights (Dispute Resolution) Act 1998 and the Employment Relations Act 1999 now supplement the 1996 act. If the employer does not provide the written statement within two months (or a statement of any changes to these particulars within one month of the changes being made) then the employee can complain to an employment tribunal, which can specify the information that the employer should have given. The Employment Act 2002 provides that when, in the context of an employee's successful tribunal claim, the employer is also found to have been in breach of the duty to provide the written statement at the time proceedings were commenced, the tribunal must award the employee two weeks' pay, and may award four weeks' pay, unless it would be unjust or inequitable to do so.

FLEXIBLE WORKING

The Employment Act 2002 (and regulations made under it) gives employees who are responsible for the upbringing of a child the right to apply for flexible working for the purpose of caring for that child. The right has been extended to carers of adults. Whether or not an employee has this right depends on both the employee and the child/adult cared for meeting a number of criteria. If an application under the act is rejected, it is open to the employee to complain to an employment tribunal.

SICK PAY

Employees absent from work through illness or injury are entitled to receive Statutory Sick Pay (SSP) from the employer for a maximum period of 28 weeks in any three-year period.

MATERNITY AND PARENTAL RIGHTS

Under the Employment Relations Act 1999, the Employment Act 2002 and the Maternity and Parental Leave Regulations 1999 (as amended in 2002 and 2006), both men and women are entitled to take leave when they become a parent. Women are protected from discrimination, detriment or dismissal by reason of their pregnancy. Men are protected from suffering a detriment or dismissal for taking paternity or parental leave.

Any woman who needs to attend an antenatal appointment on the advice of a registered medical professional is entitled to paid leave from work to attend the appointment. All women are entitled to a maximum period of maternity leave of 52 weeks. This comprises 26 weeks' ordinary maternity leave, followed immediately by 26 weeks' additional maternity leave. A woman who takes ordinary maternity leave normally has the right to return to the job in which she was employed before her absence. If she takes additional maternity leave, she is entitled to return to the same job or, if that is not reasonably practicable, to another job that is suitable and appropriate for her to do. There is a two-week period of compulsory maternity leave, immediately following the birth of the child, wherein the employer is not permitted to allow the mother to work.

A woman will qualify for Statutory Maternity Pay (SMP), which is payable for up to 39 weeks, if she has been continuously employed for not less than 26 weeks prior to the 15th week before the expected week of childbirth. For further information *see* Social Welfare, Employers Payments.

Employees are entitled to adoption leave and adoption pay (at the same rates as SMP) subject to fulfilment of similar criteria to those in relation to maternity leave and pay. Where a couple is adopting a child, either one (but not both) of the parents may take adoption leave, and the other may take paternity leave.

Certain employees are entitled to paternity leave on the birth or adoption of a child. To be eligible, the employee must be the child's father, or the partner of the mother or adopter, and meet other conditions. These conditions are, firstly, that they must have been continuously employed for not less than 26 weeks at the beginning of the 14th week before the expected week of childbirth (or, in the case of adoptions, 26 weeks ending with the week in which notification of the adoption match is given) and, secondly, that the employee must have or expect to have responsibility for the upbringing of the child. The employee may take either one week's leave, or two consecutive weeks' leave. This leave may be taken at any time between the date of the child's birth (or placement of adoption) and 56 days later. For further information *see* Social Welfare, Employer Payments.

Any employee with one year's service who has, or expects to have, responsibility for a child may take parental leave to care for the child. Each parent is entitled to a total of 13 weeks' parental leave for each of their children (or 18 weeks if the child is disabled) but this leave must be taken (at the rate of no more than four weeks per year, and in blocks of whole weeks only) before the child's fifth birthday (or 18th birthday if the child is disabled).

SUNDAY TRADING

The Sunday Trading Act 1994 allows shops to open on Sunday for serving retail customers. The Employment Rights Act 1996 gives shop workers and betting workers the right not to be dismissed, selected for redundancy or to suffer any detriment (such as the denial of overtime, promotion or training) if they refuse to work on Sundays. This does not apply to those who, under their contracts, are employed to work on Sundays.

TERMINATION OF EMPLOYMENT

An employee may be dismissed without notice if guilty of gross misconduct but in other cases a period of notice must be given by the employer. The minimum periods of notice specified in the Employment Rights Act 1996 are:

- one week if the employee has been continuously employed for one month or more but for less than two years
- two weeks if the employee has been continuously employed for at least two years
- a week is added for every additional complete year of continuous employment up to 12 years (making the maximum statutory notice period 12 weeks after 12 years' continuous employment)
- longer periods apply if these are specified in the contract of employment

If an employee is dismissed with less notice than he/she is entitled to by statute, or under their contract if longer, he/she will have a wrongful dismissal claim (unless the employer paid the employee in lieu of notice in accordance with a contractual provision entitling it to do so). This claim for wrongful dismissal can be brought by the employee either in the court system or the employment tribunal, but if brought in the tribunal the maximum amount that can be awarded is £25,000. This claim can also be brought by an employee whose fixed-term contract has been terminated by the employer prematurely, and without justification.

REDUNDANCY

An employee dismissed because of redundancy may be entitled to redundancy pay. This applies if:

- the employee has at least two years' continuous service
- the employee is dismissed by the employer (this can include cases of voluntary redundancy)
- dismissal is due to redundancy

Redundancy can mean closure of the entire business, closure of a particular site of the business, or a reduction in the need for employees to carry out work of a particular kind.

An employee may not be entitled to a redundancy payment if offered a suitable alternative job by the same employer. The amount of statutory redundancy pay depends on the length of service, age, and their earnings, subject to a weekly maximum of (currently) £350. The maximum payment that can be awarded is £10,500. The redundancy payment is guaranteed by the government in cases where the employer becomes insolvent.

UNFAIR DISMISSAL

Complaints of unfair dismissal are dealt with by an employment tribunal. Any employee with one year's continuous service (subject to exceptions, including in relation to whistleblowers – *see* below) can make a complaint to the tribunal. At the tribunal, it is for the employer to prove that the dismissal was due to one or more potentially fair reasons: a legal restriction preventing the continuation of the employee's contract; the employee's capability or qualifications for the job he/she was employed to do; the employee's conduct; redundancy; retirement; or some other substantial reason.

If the employer succeeds in showing this, the tribunal must then decide whether the employer acted reasonably in dismissing the employee for that reason. If the employee is found to have been unfairly dismissed, the tribunal can order that he/she be reinstated, re-engaged or compensated. Any person believing that they may have been unfairly dismissed should contact their local Citizens Advice Bureau or seek legal advice. A claim must be brought within three months of the date of termination of employment.

The normal maximum compensatory award for unfair dismissal is £66,200 (as at 1 February 2009). Where an employer dismissed the employee before 6 April 2009 and failed to follow the statutory dismissal procedures which came into force on 1 October 2004, the tribunal must usually increase the compensatory award by 10 per cent and it may increase by up to 50 per cent. If the dismissal occurred after 6 April 2009 and the employer unreasonably failed to follow the new ACAS code, the tribunal may increase the employee's compensation by up to 25 per cent.

WHISTLEBLOWING

Under the whistleblowing legislation (Public Interest Disclosure Act 1998, which inserted provisions into the Employment Rights Act 1996) dismissal of an employee is automatically unfair if the reason or principal reason for the dismissal is that the employee has made a protected disclosure. The legislation also makes it unlawful to subject workers (a broad category that includes employees and certain other individuals, such as agency workers) who have made a protected disclosure to any detriment on the ground that they have done so.

For a disclosure to qualify for protection, the claimant must show that he has disclosed information, which in his reasonable belief tends to show one or more of six categories of wrongdoing: criminal offences; breach of any legal obligation; miscarriages of justice; danger to the health and safety of any individual; damage to the environment; or the deliberate concealing of information about any of the other categories. The malpractices can be past, present, prospective or merely alleged.

A qualifying disclosure will only be protected if the manner of the disclosure fulfills certain conditions, including being made in good faith and being made to a defined category of persons, which varies according to the type of disclosure.

Any whistleblower claim in the employment tribunal must normally be brought within three months of the date of dismissal or other act leading to a detriment.

An individual does not need to have been working with the employer for any particular period of time to be able to bring such a claim and compensation is uncapped (and can include an amount for injury to feelings).

DISCRIMINATION

Discrimination in employment on the grounds of sex (including gender reassignment), sexual orientation, race, colour, nationality, ethnic or national origins, religion or belief, married status, age, trade union membership or (subject to wide exceptions) disability is unlawful. Discrimination legislation generally covers direct discrimination, indirect discrimination, harassment and victimisation. Only in limited circumstances can such discrimination be justified (rendering it lawful).

An individual does not need to be employed for any particular period of time to be able to claim discrimination (discrimination can be alleged at the recruitment phase), and discrimination compensation is uncapped (and can include an amount for injury to feelings). These features distinguish the discrimination laws from, for example, the unfair dismissal laws.

The following legislation applies to those employed in Great Britain but not to employees in Northern Ireland or (subject to EC exceptions) to those who work mainly abroad:

- the Race Relations Act 1976 gives individuals the right not to be discriminated against on the grounds of race, colour, nationality, or ethnic or national origins. It applies to all aspects of employment (unless there is a genuine occupational requirement that the job be given to someone of a particular racial background)
- the Disability Discrimination Act 1995 makes discrimination against a disabled person in all aspects of employment (and against anyone working under a contract personally to do any work, ie the self-employed and independent contractors) unlawful. In certain circumstances, the employer may show that the less favourable treatment is justified and so does not constitute discrimination. The act also imposes a duty on employers to make 'reasonable adjustments' to the arrangements and physical features of the workplace if these place disabled people at a substantial disadvantage compared with those who are not disabled. The definition of a 'disabled person' is wide and includes people diagnosed with HIV, cancer and multiple sclerosis. Since early 2007 there has been a new positive duty on public bodies to promote equality of opportunity for disabled people
- the Sex Discrimination Act 1975 (as amended) makes it unlawful to discriminate on the grounds of sex or marital/civil partner status. This covers all aspects of employment (including advertising for jobs), but there are some limited exceptions, such as where the essential nature of the job requires it to be given to someone of a particular sex, or where decency and privacy requires it. The Equal Pay Act 1970 (as amended) entitles men and

women to equality of renumeration for equivalent work or work of the same value
- the Employment Equality (Religion or Belief) Regulations 2003 make discrimination against a person on the grounds of religion or belief, in all aspects of employment, unlawful
- the Employment Equality (Sexual Orientation) Regulations 2003 make discrimination against an individual on the grounds of sexual orientation, in all aspects of employment, unlawful
- The Employment Equality (Age) Regulations 2006 outlaw age discrimination in the workplace. This is having profound implications for employers' policies and practices and has required major changes to selection procedures, recruitment policies, terms and conditions, benefits, dismissals and retirements

The responsibility for monitoring equality in society rests with the Equality and Human Rights Commission. In 2008 the government announced its intention to introduce a consolidating bill into parliament to codify and streamline equality law by simplifying definitions of discrimination and harmonising the rules of each ground of discrimination. At the time of printing, the Equality bill had been introduced to the House of Commons and was before the public bill committee for scrutiny.

In Northern Ireland similar provisions exist but are contained in separate legislation (although the Disability Discrimination Act does extend to Northern Ireland).

In Northern Ireland there is one combined body working towards equality and eliminating discrimination, the Equality Commission for Northern Ireland.

WORKING TIME

The Working Time Regulations 1998 impose rules that limit working hours and provide for rest breaks and holidays. The regulations apply to workers and so cover not only employees but also other individuals who undertake to perform personally any work or services (eg freelancers). The regulations are complex and subject to various exceptions and qualifications but the basic provisions relating to adult day workers are as follows:
- No worker is permitted to work more than an average of 48 hours per week (unless they have made a genuine volutary opt-out of this limit – it is not sufficient to make it a term of the contract that the worker opts out), and a worker is entitled to, but is not required to take, the following breaks:
- 11 consecutive hours' rest in every 24-hour period
- an uninterrupted rest period of at least 24 hours in each 7-day period (in addition to the daily rest period)
- 20 minutes' rest break provided that the working day is longer than 6 hours
- 5.6 weeks' paid annual leave (28 days full-time). 5.6 weeks equates to 4 weeks plus public holidays

There are specific provisions relating to night work, young workers (ie those over school leaving age but under 18) and a variety of workers in specialised sectors (such as off-shore oil rig workers).

HUMAN RIGHTS

On 2 October 2000 the Human Rights Act 1998 came into force. This act incorporates the European Convention on Human Rights into the law of the UK. The main principles of the act are as follows:
- all legislation must be interpreted and given effect by the courts as compatible with the Convention so far as it is possible to do so. Before the second reading of a new bill the minister responsible for the bill must provide a statement regarding the compatibility of the bill with the Human Rights Act
- subordinate legislation (eg statutory instruments) which are incompatible with the Convention can be struck down by the courts
- primary legislation (eg an act of parliament) which is incompatible with the Convention cannot be struck down by a court, but the higher courts can make a declaration of incompatibility which is a signal to parliament to change the law
- all public authorities (including courts and tribunals) must not act in a way which is incompatible with the Convention
- individuals whose Convention rights have been infringed by a public authority may bring proceedings against that authority, but the act is not intended to create new rights as between individuals

The main human rights protected by the Convention are the right to life (article 2); protection from torture and inhuman or degrading treatment (article 3); protection from slavery or forced labour (article 4); the right to liberty and security of the person (article 5); the right to a fair trial (article 6); the right not to be subject to retrospective criminal offences (article 7); the right to respect for private and family life (article 8); freedom of thought, conscience and religion (article 9); freedom of expression (article 10); freedom of peaceful association and assembly (article 11); the right to marry and found a family (article 12); protection from discrimination (article 14); the right to property (article 1 protocol No.1); the right to education (article 2 protocol No.1); and the right to free elections (article 3 protocol No.1). Most of the Convention rights are subject to limitations which deem the breach of the right acceptable on the basis it is 'necessary in a democratic society'.

Human rights are also enshrined in the common law (of tort). Although this is of historical significance, the common law (for example the duty of confidentiality) remains especially important regarding violations of human rights that occur between private parties, where the Human Rights Act 1998 does not apply.

PARENTAL RESPONSIBILITY

The Children Act 1989 gives both the mother and father parental responsibility for the child if the parents are married to each other at the time of the child's birth. If the parents are not married, only the mother has parental responsibility. The father may acquire it in accordance with the provisions of section 4 of the Children Act 1989. He can do this in one of four ways: a) by being registered as the father on the child's birth certificate with the consent of the mother (only for fathers of children born after 1 December 2003, following changes to the Adoption and Children Act 2002); b) by applying to the court for a parental responsibility order; c) by entering into a parental responsibility agreement with the mother which must be in the prescribed form; or d) by obtaining a residence order from the court. Otherwise, a father can gain parental responsibility by marrying the mother of the child.

Where a child is adopted, parental responsibility will be given to the adopter of a child. However, before an order for adoption can be made, the court must be satisfied that he is free for adoption. In other words, every parent or guardian must give their agreement. The consent of a father without parental responsibility is not required, although adoption agencies and local authorities must be careful to establish, if possible, the identity of the father and satisfy themselves that any person claiming to be the father either has no intention to apply for parental responsibility or that if he did apply, the application would be likely to be refused.

In Scotland, the relevant legislation is the Children (Scotland) Act 1995, which also gives the mother parental responsibility for her child whether or not she is married to the child's father. A father who is married to the mother, either at the time of the child's conception or subsequently, will also have automatic parental rights. Section 23 of the 2006 act provides that an unmarried father will obtain automatic parental responsibilities and rights if he is registered as the father on the child's birth certificate. For unmarried fathers who are not named on the birth certificate, or whose children were born before the 2006 act came into force, it is possible to acquire parental responsibilities and rights by applying to the court or by entering into a parental responsibilities and rights agreement with the mother. The father of any child, regardless of parental rights, has a duty to aliment that child until he/she is 18 (25 if the child is still at an educational establishment).

LEGITIMATION

Under the Legitimacy Act 1976, an illegitimate person automatically becomes legitimate when his/her parents marry. This applies even where one of the parents was married to a third person at the time of the birth. In such cases it is necessary to re-register the birth of the child. In Scotland, the status of illegitimacy has finally been abolished by section 21 of the 2006 act. The Law Reform Act 1987 reformed the law so as to remove so far as possible the legal disadvantages of illegitimacy.

JURY SERVICE

In England and Wales a person charged with more serious criminal offences and more complex civil cases is entitled to be tried by jury. No such right exists in Scotland, although more serious offences are heard before a jury. In England and Wales there must be at least nine, and not more than 12 members of a jury in a criminal case and eight members in a civil case. In Scotland there are 12 members of a jury in a civil case in the court of session (the civil jury being confined to the court of session and a restricted number of actions), and 15 in a criminal trial in the high court of justiciary. Jurors are normally asked to serve for ten working days, although jurors selected for longer cases are expected to sit for the duration of the trial.

Every 'registered' parliamentary or local government elector between the ages of 18 and 70 who has lived in the UK (including, for this purpose, the Channel Islands and the Isle of Man) for any period of at least five years since reaching the age of 13 is qualified to serve on a jury unless he/she is 'mentally disordered' or disqualified. Those disqualified from jury service include:

- those who have at any time been sentenced by a court in the UK (including, for this purpose, the Channel Islands and the Isle of Man) to a term of imprisonment or youth custody of five years or more
- those who have been imprisoned for life, at Her Majesty's pleasure, for a period of at least five years, or imprisoned or detained for public protection
- those who have within the previous ten years served any part of a sentence of imprisonment, youth custody or detention, been detained in a young offenders' institution, received a suspended sentence of imprisonment or order for detention, or received a community service order
- those who are on bail in criminal proceedings

The court has the discretion to excuse a juror from service, or defer the date of service, if the juror can show there is good reason why he/she should be excused from attending or good reason why his attendance should be deferred. It is an offence to fail to attend when summoned, to serve knowing that you are disqualified from service, or to make false representations in an attempt to evade service. The defendant can object to any juror if he/she can show cause.

An individual juror (or the entire jury) can be discharged if it is shown that they or any of their number have, among other things, separated from the rest of the jury without the leave of the court; talked to any person out of court who is not a member of the jury; determined the verdict of the trial by drawing lots; been drunk, or otherwise incapacitated, while carrying out their duties as a juror; exerted improper pressure on the other members of the jury (eg harassment or bullying); declined to take part in the jury's functions; displayed actual or apparent bias (eg racism, sexism or other discriminatory or deliberate hostility); or inadvertently possessed knowledge of the bad character of a party to the proceedings which has not been adduced as evidence in the proceedings.

A jury's verdict need not be unanimous. In criminal proceedings the agreement of ten jurors will suffice when there are not less than 11people on the jury (or 9 in a jury of 10). In civil proceedings the agreement of seven jurors will suffice. However the court must be satisfied that the jury had reasonable time to consider its verdict based on the nature and complexity of the case. In criminal proceedings this must be no less than two hours.

A juror may claim travelling expenses, a subsistence allowance and an allowance for other financial loss (eg loss of earnings or benefits, fees paid to carers or child-minders) up to a stated limit. It is a contempt of court for a juror to disclose what happened in the jury room even after the trial is over.

SCOTLAND

Qualification criteria for jury service in Scotland are similar to those in England and Wales, except that the maximum age for a juror is 65, members of the judiciary are ineligible for ten years after ceasing to hold their post, and others concerned with the administration of justice are only eligible for service five years after ceasing to hold office. Certain persons who have the right to be excused include full-time members of the medical, dental, nursing, veterinary and pharmaceutical professions, full-time members of the armed forces, ministers of religion, persons who have served on a jury within the previous five years, members of the Scottish parliament, members of the Scottish government and junior Scottish ministers. Those convicted of a serious crime are automatically disqualified. Those who are incapable by reason of a mental disorder may also be excused. The maximum fine for a person serving on a jury knowing himself/herself to be ineligible is £1,000. The maximum fine for failing to attend without good cause is also £1,000.

Further information can be obtained from:

THE COURT SERVICE
Southside, 105 Victoria Street, London SW1E 6QT
T 020-7210 2266

SCOTTISH COURTS SERVICE
Courts of Session, Parliament House, Parliament Square, Edinburgh EH1 1RQ T 0131-225 2595
W www.scotcourts.gov.uk

THE CLERK OF JUSTICIARY
High Court of Justiciary, Lawnmarket, Edinburgh EH2 2NS
T 0131-240 6900

LANDLORD AND TENANT

RESIDENTIAL LETTINGS

The provisions outlined here apply only where the tenant lives in a separate dwelling from the landlord and where the dwelling is the tenant's only or main home. It does not apply to licensees such as lodgers, guests or service occupiers.

The 1996 Housing Act radically changed certain aspects of the legislation referred to below; in particular, the grant of assured and assured shorthold tenancies under the Housing Act 1988.

ASSURED SHORTHOLD TENANCIES

If a tenancy was granted on or after 15 January 1989 and before 28 February 1997, the tenant would have an assured tenancy unless the landlord served notice under section 20 in the prescribed form prior to the commencement of the tenancy, stating that the tenancy is to be an assured shorthold tenancy and the tenancy is for a minimum fixed term period of six months (*see* below). An assured tenancy gives that tenant greater security. The tenant could, for example, stay in possession of the dwelling for as long as the tenant observed the terms of the tenancy. The landlord cannot obtain possession from such a tenant unless the landlord can establish a specific ground for possession (set out in the Housing Act 1988) and obtains a court order. The rent payable is that agreed with the landlord at the start of the tenancy. The landlord has the right to increase the rent annually by serving a notice. If that happens the tenant can apply to have the rent fixed by the rent assessment committee of the local authority. The tenant or the landlord may request that the committee sets the rent in line with open market rents for that type of property.

Under the Housing Act 1996, all new lettings entered into on or after 28 February 1997 (for whatever term) will be assured shorthold tenancies unless the landlord serves a notice stating that the tenancy is not to be an assured shorthold tenancy. This means that the landlord is entitled to possession at the end of the tenancy provided he serves a notice under section 21 Housing Act 1988 and commences the proceedings in accordance with the correct procedure. The landlord must obtain a court order, however, to obtain possession if the tenant refuses to vacate at the end of the tenancy. If the tenancy is an assured shorthold tenancy, the court must grant the order. For both assured and assured shorthold tenancies, if the tenant is more than eight weeks in arrears, the landlord can serve notice and, if the tenant is still in arrears at the date of the hearing, the court must make an order for possession.

REGULATED TENANCIES

Before the Housing Act 1988 came into force on 15 January 1989 there were regulated tenancies; some are still in existence and are protected by the Rent Act 1977. Under this act it is possible for the landlord or the tenant to apply to the local rent officer to have a 'fair' rent registered. The fair rent is then the maximum rent payable.

SECURE TENANCIES

Secure tenancies are generally given to tenants of local authorities, housing associations (before 15 January 1989) and certain other bodies. This gives the tenant security of tenure unless the terms of the agreement are broken by the tenant and it is reasonable to make an order for possession. Those with secure tenancies may have the right to buy their property. In practice this right is generally only available to council tenants.

AGRICULTURAL PROPERTY

Tenancies in agricultural properties are governed by the Agricultural Holdings Act 1986, the Agricultural Tenancies Act 1995 (both amended by the Regulatory Reform (Agricultural Tenancies) (England and Wales) Order 2006), the Tribunals, Courts and Enforcement Act 2007, the Legal Services Act 2007 and the Rent (Agriculture) Act 1976, which give similar protections to those described above, eg security of tenure, right to compensation for disturbance, etc. The Agricultural Holdings (Scotland) Act 1991 along with Agricultural Holdings (Scotland) Act 2003 and the Housing (Scotland) Act 2006 apply similar provisions to Scotland.

EVICTION

The Protection from Eviction Act 1977 (as amended by the Housing Act 1988 and Nationality, Immigration and Asylum Act 2002) sets out the procedure a landlord must follow in order to obtain possession of property. It is unlawful for a landlord to evict a tenant otherwise than in accordance with the law. For common law tenancies and for Rent Act tenants a notice to quit in the prescribed form giving 28 days is required. For secure and assured tenancies a notice seeking possession must be served. It is unlawful for the landlord to evict a person by putting their belongings onto the street, by changing the locks and so on. It is also unlawful for a landlord to harass a tenant in any way in order to persuade him/her to give up the tenancy. The tenant may be able to obtain an injunction to restrain the actions of the landlord and get back into the property and be awarded damages.

LANDLORD RESPONSIBILITIES

Under the Landlord and Tenant Act 1985, where the term of the lease is less than seven years, the landlord is responsible for maintaining the structure and exterior of the property, for sanitation, for heating and hot water, and all installations for the supply of water, gas and electricity.

LEASEHOLDERS

Strictly speaking, leaseholders have bought a long lease rather than a property and in certain limited circumstances the landlord can end the tenancy. Under the Leasehold Reform Act 1967 (as amended by the Housing Acts 1969, 1974, 1980 and 1985), leaseholders of houses may have the right to buy the freehold or to take an extended lease for a term of 50 years. This applies to leases where the term of the lease is over 21 years, at a low rent, and where the leaseholder has occupied the house as his/her only or main residence for the last two years, or for a total of two years over the last ten. The tenant must give the landlord written notice of his desire to acquire the freehold or extend the leasehold.

The Leasehold Reform, Housing and Urban Development Act came into force in 1993 and allows the leaseholders of flats in certain circumstances to buy the freehold of the building in which they live.

Responsibility for maintenance of the structure,

exterior and interior of the building should be set out in the lease. Usually the upkeep of the interior of his/her part of the property is the responsibility of the leaseholder, and responsibility for the structure, exterior and common interior areas is shared between the freeholder and the leaseholder(s).

If leaseholders are dissatisfied with charges made in respect of lease extensions, they are entitled to have their situation evaluated by the Leasehold Valuation Tribunal.

The Commonhold and Leasehold Reform Act 2002 makes provision for the freehold estate in land to be registered as commonhold land and for the legal interest in the land to be vested in a 'commonhold association' ie a private limited company.

BUSINESS LETTINGS

The Landlord and Tenant acts 1927 and 1954 (as amended) give security of tenure to the tenants of most business premises. The landlord can only evict the tenant on one of the grounds laid down in the 1954 act, and in some cases where the landlord repossesses the property the tenant may be entitled to compensation.

SCOTLAND

In Scotland assured and short assured tenancies exist for lettings after 2 January 1989 and are similar to assured tenancies in England and Wales. The relevant legislation is the Housing (Scotland) Act 1988.

Most tenancies created before 2 January 1989 were regulated tenancies and the Rent (Scotland) Act 1984 still applies where these exist. The act defines, among other things, the circumstances in which a landlord can increase the rent when improvements are made to the property. The provisions of the Rent Act do not apply to tenancies where the landlord is the Crown, a local authority or a housing corporation.

The Housing (Scotland) Acts of 1987 and 2001 relate to local authority responsibilities for housing, the right to buy, and local authority secured tenancies. The provisions are broadly similar to England and Wales.

In Scotland, business premises are not controlled by statute to the same extent as in England and Wales, although the Tenancy of Shops (Scotland) Act 1949 gives some security to tenants of shops. Tenants of shops can apply to the sheriff, within 21 days of being served a notice to quit, for a renewal of tenancy if threatened with eviction. This application may be dismissed on various grounds including where the landlord has offered to sell the property to the tenant at an agreed price or, in the absence of agreement as to price, at a price fixed by a single arbiter appointed by the parties or the sheriff. The act extends to properties where the Crown or government departments are the landlords or the tenants.

Under the Leases Act 1449 the landlord's successors (either purchasers or creditors) are bound by the agreement made with any tenants so long as the following conditions are met:

- the lease, if for more than one year, must be in writing
- there must be a rent
- there must be a term of expiry
- the tenant must have entered into possession
- the subjects of the lease must be land
- the landlord, if owner, must be the proprietor with a recorded title, ie the title deeds are recorded in the Register of Sasines or registered in the Land Register

The Antisocial Behaviour (Scotland) Act 2001 provides that all landlords letting property in Scotland must register with the local authority in which the let property is situated. It is a criminal offence to fail to do this. Exceptions apply to holiday lets, owner-occupied accommodation and agricultural holdings. The act applies to partnerships, trusts and companies as well as to individuals.

LEGAL AID

The Access to Justice Act 1999 has transformed what used to be known as the Legal Aid system. The Legal Aid Board has been replaced by the Legal Services Commission, which is responsible for the development and administration of two legal funding schemes in England and Wales, namely the Criminal Defence Service and the Community Legal Service fund. The Criminal Defence Service assists people who are under police investigation or facing criminal charges. The Community Legal Service is designed to increase access to legal information and advice by involving a much wider network of funders and providers in giving publicly funded legal services. In Scotland, provision of legal aid is governed by the Legal Aid (Scotland) Act 1986 and administered by the Scottish Legal Aid Board.

LEGAL SERVICES COMMISSION
85 Gray's Inn Road, London WC1X 8TX T 020-7759 0000
W www.legalservices.gov.uk

CIVIL LEGAL AID

From 1 January 2000, only organisations (such as solicitors or Citizens Advice Bureaux) with a contract with the Legal Services Commission have been able to give initial help in any civil matter. Moreover, from that date decisions about funding were devolved from the Legal Services Commission to contracted organisations in relation to any level of publicly funded service in family and immigration cases. For other types of case, applications for public funding are made through a solicitor (or other contracted legal services providers) in much the same way as the former Legal Aid. On 1 April 2001 the so-called civil contracting scheme was extended to cover all levels of service for all types of cases.

Under the new civil funding scheme there are broadly seven levels of service available:

- legal help
- help at court
- general family help
- legal representation – either investigative help or full representation
- help with mediation
- family mediation
- such other services as authorised by specific orders

ELIGIBILITY

Eligibility for funding from the Community Legal Service depends broadly on five factors:

- the level of service sought (*see* above)
- whether the applicant qualifies financially
- the merits of the applicant's case
- a costs-benefits analysis (if the costs are likely to outweigh any benefit that might be gained from the proceedings, funding may be refused)
- whether there is any public interest in the case being litigated (ie whether the case has a wider public interest beyond that of the parties involved – for example, a human rights case)

The limits on capital and income above which a person is not entitled to public funding vary with the type of service sought.

CONTRIBUTIONS
Some of those who qualify for Community Legal Service funding will have to contribute towards their legal costs. Contributions must be paid by anyone who has a disposable income or disposable capital exceeding a prescribed amount. The rules relating to applicable contributions are complex and detailed information can be obtained from the Legal Services Commission.

STATUTORY CHARGE
A statutory charge is made if a person keeps or gains money or property in a case for which they have received legal aid. This means that the amount paid by the Community Legal Service fund on their behalf is deducted from the amount that the person receives. This does not apply if the court has ordered that the costs be paid by the other party (unless the amount paid by the other party does not cover all of the costs). In certain circumstances, the Legal Services Commission may waive or postpone payment.

CONTINGENCY OR CONDITIONAL FEES
This system was introduced by the Courts and Legal Services Act 1990. It offers legal representation on a 'no win, no fee' basis. It provides an alternative form of assistance, especially for those cases which are ineligible for funding by the Community Legal Service. The main area for such work is in the field of personal injuries.

Not all solicitors offer such a scheme and different solicitors may well have different terms. The effect of the agreement is that solicitors will not make any charges until the case is concluded successfully. If a case is won then the losing party will usually have to pay towards costs, with the winning party contributing around one third.

SCOTLAND
Civil legal aid is available for cases in the following:

- the sheriff courts
- the court of session
- the House of Lords
- the lands valuation appeal court
- the Scottish land court
- the Lands Tribunal for Scotland
- the Employment Appeal Tribunals
- the Judicial Committee of the Privy Council
- the Proscribed Organisations Appeal Commissioner
- proceedings before the Social Security Commissioners
- proceedings before the Child Support Commissioners

Civil legal aid is not available for defamation actions, small claims or simplified divorce procedures or petitions by a debtor for his own sequestration.

Eligibility for civil legal aid is assessed in a similar way to that in England and Wales, though the financial limits differ in some respects. A person shall be eligible for civil legal aid if their disposable income does not exceed £25,000 a year. A person may be refused civil aid if their disposable capital exceeds £12,429 and it appears to the Legal Aid board that they can afford to pay without legal aid. Additionally:

- if disposable income is between £3,355 and £10,995, a contribution of one third of the difference between £3,355 and the disposable income may be payable
- if disposable income is between £10,995 and £15,000, one third of the difference between £3,355 and £10,995 plus half the difference between £10,996 and the disposable income may be payable
- if disposable income is between £15,000 and £25,000, a contribution of the following: one third of the difference between £3,355 and £10,995, plus half the difference between £10,996 and £15,000, plus all the remaining disposable income between £15,001 and £25,000 – will be payable

CRIMINAL LEGAL AID

The Legal Services Commission provides defendants facing criminal charges with free legal representation if they pass a merits test and a means test.

Criminal legal aid covers the cost of preparing a case and legal representation in criminal proceedings. It is also available for appeals against verdicts or sentences in magistrates' courts, the crown court or the court of appeal. It is not available for bringing a private prosecution in a criminal court.

If granted criminal legal aid, either the person may choose their own solicitor or the court will assign one. Contributions to the legal costs may be required if the case proceeds to the crown court. The rules relating to applicable contributions are complex and detailed information can be obtained from the Legal Services Commission.

DUTY SOLICITORS
The Legal Aid Act 1988 also provides free advice and assistance to anyone questioned by the police (whether under arrest or helping the police with their enquiries). No means test or contributions are required for this.

SCOTLAND
Legal advice and assistance operates in a similar way in Scotland. A person is eligible:

- if disposable income does not exceed £234 a week. If disposable income is between £100 and £234 a week, contributions are payable
- if disposable capital does not exceed £1,639 (if the person has dependent relatives, the savings allowance is higher)
- if receiving income support or income-related job seeker's allowance they qualify automatically provided they have no savings over the limit

The procedure for application for criminal legal aid depends on the circumstances of each case. In solemn cases (more serious cases, such as murder) heard before a jury, a person is automatically entitled to criminal legal aid until they are given bail or placed in custody. Thereafter, it is for the court to decide whether to grant legal aid. The court will do this if the person accused cannot meet the expenses of the case without undue hardship on him or his dependants. In less serious cases the procedure depends on whether the person is in custody:

- anyone taken into custody has the right to free legal aid from the duty solicitor up to and including the first court appearance
- if the person is not in custody and wishes to plead guilty, they are not entitled to criminal legal aid but may be entitled to legal advice and assistance, including assistance by way of representation
- if the person is not in custody and wishes to plead not guilty, they can apply for criminal legal aid. This must be done within 14 days of the first court appearance at which they made the plea

The criteria used to assess whether or not criminal legal aid should be granted is similar to the criteria for England and Wales. When meeting with your solicitor, take evidence of your financial position such as details of savings, bank statements, pay slips, pension book or benefits book.

Further information can be obtained from:
THE SCOTTISH LEGAL AID BOARD
44 Drumsheugh Gardens, Edinburgh EH3 7SW
T 0131-226 7061 W www.slab.org.uk

MARRIAGE

Any two persons may marry provided that:
- they are at least 16 years old on the day of the marriage (in England and Wales persons under the age of 18 must generally obtain the consent of their parents; if consent is refused an appeal may be made to the high court, the county court or a court of summary jurisdiction)
- they are not related to one another in a way which would prevent their marrying
- they are unmarried (a person who has already been married must produce documentary evidence that the previous marriage has been ended by death, divorce or annulment)
- they are not of the same sex (though same sex couples can register a civil partnership instead)
- they are capable of understanding the nature of a marriage ceremony and of consenting to marriage

The parties should check the marriage will be recognised as valid in their home country if either is not a British citizen.

DEGREES OF RELATIONSHIP

A marriage between persons within the prohibited degrees of consanguinity, affinity or adoption is void.

A man may not marry his mother, daughter, grandmother, granddaughter, sister, aunt, niece, great-grandmother, adoptive mother, former adoptive mother, adopted daughter or former adopted daughter.

A woman may not marry her father, son, grandfather, grandson, brother, uncle, nephew, great-grandfather, adoptive father, former adoptive father, adopted son or former adopted son. Under the Marriage (Prohibited Degrees of Relationship) Act 1986, some exceptions to the law permit a man or a woman to marry certain step-relatives or in-laws.

ENGLAND AND WALES

TYPES OF MARRIAGE CEREMONY

It is possible to marry by either religious or civil ceremony. A religious ceremony can take place at a church or chapel of the Church of England or the Church in Wales, or at any other place of worship which has been formally registered by the Registrar-General.

A civil ceremony can take place at a register office, a registered building or any other premises approved by the local authority.

An application for an approved premises licence must be made by the owners or trustees of the building concerned; it cannot be made by the prospective marriage couple. Approved premises must be regularly open to the public so that the marriage can be witnessed; the venue must be deemed to be a permanent and immovable structure. Open-air ceremonies are prohibited.

Non-Anglican marriages may also be solemnised following the issue of a Registrar-General's licence in unregistered premises where one of the parties is seriously ill, is not expected to recover, and cannot be moved to registered premises. Detained and housebound persons may be married at their place of residence.

MARRIAGE IN THE CHURCH OF ENGLAND OR THE CHURCH IN WALES

Marriage by banns

The marriage can take place in a parish in which one of the parties lives, or in a church in another parish if it is the usual place of worship of either or both of the parties. New regulations introduced in October 2008 also allow marriages to take place in a parish where one of the parties was baptised or prepared for confirmation; a parish where one of the parties lived for six months or more; a parish where one of the parents of either of the parties lived for six months or more; in a parish where one of the parents of either of the parties has attended public worship for six months or more in the child's lifetime; or a parish where the parents or grandparents of either of the parties were married. The banns (ie the announcement of the marriage ceremony) must be called in the parish in which the marriage is to take place on three Sundays before the day of the ceremony; if either or both of the parties lives in a different parish the banns must also be called there. After three months the banns are no longer valid. The minister will not perform the marriage unless he or she is satisfied that the banns have been properly called.

Marriage by common licence

The vicar who is to conduct the marriage will arrange for a common licence to be issued by the diocesan bishop; this dispenses with the necessity for banns. One of the parties must have lived in the parish for 15 days immediately before the issuing of the licence or must usually worship at the church. Eligibility requirements vary from diocese to diocese, but it is not normally required that the parties should have been baptised. The licence is valid for three months.

Marriage by special licence

A special licence is granted by the Archbishop of Canterbury in special circumstances for the marriage to take place at any place, with or without previous residence in the parish, or at any time. Application must be made to the registrar of the Faculty Office: 1 The Sanctuary, London SW1P 3JT T 020-7222 5381.

Marriage by certificate

The marriage can be conducted on the authority of the superintendent registrar's certificate, provided that the vicar's consent is obtained (there is no obligation upon the vicar to accept the certificate). One of the parties must live in the parish or must usually worship at the church.

MARRIAGE BY OTHER RELIGIOUS CEREMONY

One of the parties must normally live in the registration district where the marriage is to take place. In addition to giving notice to the superintendent registrar it may also be necessary to book a registrar to be present at the ceremony.

CIVIL MARRIAGE

A marriage may be solemnised at any register office, registered building or approved premises in England and Wales. The superintendent registrar of the district should be contacted, and, if the marriage is to take place at approved premises, the necessary arrangements at the venue must also be made.

NOTICE OF MARRIAGE

Unless it is to take place by banns or under common or special licence in the Church of England or the Church in

Wales, a notice of the marriage must be given in person to the superintendent registrar. Notice of marriage may be given in the following ways:

- by certificate. Both parties must have lived in a registration district in England or Wales for at least seven days immediately before giving notice at the local register office. If they live in different registration districts, notice must be given in both districts. The marriage can take place in any register office or other approved premises in England and Wales no sooner than 16 days after notice has been given, when the superintendent registrar issues a certificate.
- by licence (often known as 'special licence'). One of the parties must have lived in a registration district in England or Wales for at least 15 days before giving notice at the register office; the other party need only be a resident of, or be physically in, England and Wales on the day notice is given. The marriage can take place one clear day (other than a Sunday, Christmas Day or Good Friday) after notice has been given.

A notice of marriage is valid for 12 months, unless it is for the marriage of a detained or housebound person, when it will usually only be accepted within three months of publication. Notice for marriages taking place within the Church of England or Church of Wales should also only be valid within three months of publication. It should be possible to make an advance (provisional) booking 12 months before the ceremony. In this case it is still necessary to give formal notice three months before the marriage. When giving notice of the marriage it is necessary to produce official proof, if relevant, that any previous marriage has ended in divorce or death by producing a decree absolute or death certificate; it is also necessary to provide proof of age, identity and nationality for each of the parties, for example, with a passport. If either party is under 18 years old, evidence of consent by their parent or guardian is required. There are special procedures for those wishing to get married in the UK that are subject to immigration control; the register office will be able to advise on these.

SOLEMNISATION OF THE MARRIAGE

On the day of the wedding there must be at least two other people present who are prepared to act as witnesses and sign the marriage register. A registrar of marriages must be present at a marriage in a register office or at approved premises, but an authorised person may act in the capacity of registrar in a registered building.

If the marriage takes place at approved premises, the room must be separate from any other activity on the premises at the time of the ceremony, and no food or drink can be sold or consumed in the room during the ceremony or for one hour beforehand.

The marriage must be solemnised between 8am and 6pm, with open doors. At some time during the ceremony the parties must make a declaration that they know of no legal impediment to the marriage and they must also say the contracting words; the declaratory and contracting words may vary according to the form of service. A civil marriage cannot contain any religious aspects, but it may be possible for non-religious music and/or readings to be included. It may also be possible to embellish the marriage vows taken by the couple.

CIVIL FEES

Marriage at a Register Office

By superintendent registrar's certificate, £30 per person for the notice of the marriage (which is not refundable if the marriage does not in fact take place) and £40 for the ceremony at the register office.

Marriage on Approved Premises

By superintendent registrar's certificate, £30 per person for the ceremony at the register office.

An additional fee will also be payable for the superintendent registrar's and registrar's attendance at the marriage. This is set locally by the local authority responsible. A further charge is likely to be made by the owners of the building for the use of the premises. For marriages taking place in a religious building other than the Church of England or Church of Wales, an additional fee of £47 is payable for the registrar's attendance at the marriage unless an 'Authorised Person' appointed by the trustees of the building has agreed to register the marriage. Additional fees may be charged by the trustees of the building for the wedding and by the person who performs the ceremony.

ECCLESIASTICAL FEES

(Church of England and Church in Wales*)

Marriage by banns

For publication of banns, £22

For certificate of banns issued at time of publication, £12.00

For marriage service, £254

Marriage by common licence

Fee for licence, £85

Marriage by special licence

Fee for licence, £138

* These fees are revised from 1 April each calendar year. Some may not apply to the Church in Wales

SCOTLAND

REGULAR MARRIAGES

A regular marriage is one which is celebrated by a minister of religion or authorised registrar or other celebrant. Each of the parties must complete a marriage notice form and return it to the district registrar for the area in which they are to be married, irrespective of where they live, within the three month period prior to the date of the marriage and not later than 15 days prior to that date. The district registrar must then enter the date of receipt and certain details in a marriage book kept for this purpose, and must also enter the names of the parties and the proposed date of marriage in a list which is displayed in a conspicuous place at the registration office until the date of the marriage has passed. All persons wishing to enter into a regular marriage in Scotland must follow the same preliminary procedure regardless of whether they intend to have a religious or civil ceremony. Before the marriage ceremony takes place any person may submit an objection in writing to the district registrar.

A marriage schedule, which is prepared by the registrar, will be issued to one or both of the parties in person up to seven days before a religious marriage; for a civil marriage the schedule will be available at the ceremony. The schedule must be handed to the celebrant before the ceremony starts; it must be signed immediately after the wedding and the marriage must be registered within three days.

The authority to conduct a religious marriage is deemed to be vested in the authorised celebrant rather than the building in which it takes place; open-air religious ceremonies are therefore permissible in Scotland.

From 10 June 2002 it has been possible, under the Marriage (Scotland) Act 2002, for venues or couples to apply to the local council for a licence to allow a civil ceremony to take place at a venue other than a registration office. To obtain further information, a venue or couple should contact the district registrar in the area they wish to marry. A list of licensed venues is also available on the General Registers of Scotland website (W www.gro-scotland.gov.uk).

MARRIAGE BY COHABITATION WITH HABIT AND REPUTE

Prior to the enactment of the 2006 act, if two people had lived together constantly as husband and wife and were generally held to be such by the neighbourhood and among their friends and relations, a presumption could arise from which marriage could be inferred. Before such a marriage could be registered, however, a decree of declarator of marriage had to be obtained from the court of session. Section 3 of the 2006 act provides that it will no longer be possible for a marriage to be constituted by cohabitation with habit and repute, but it will still be possible for couples whose period of cohabitation began before commencement of the 2006 act to seek a declarator under the old rule of law.

CIVIL FEES

The fee for submitting a notice of marriage to the district registrar is £28 a person. Solemnisation of a civil marriage costs £50.00, while the extract of the entry in the register of marriages attracts a fee of £9.00. The costs of religious marriage ceremonies can vary. Further information can be obtained from:

THE GENERAL REGISTER OFFICE
Trafalgar Road, Southport PR8 2HH
T 0845-603 7788 W www.gro.gov.uk

THE GENERAL REGISTER OFFICE FOR SCOTLAND
New Register House, 3 West Register Street, Edinburgh
EH1 3YT T 0131-314 4452

TOWN AND COUNTRY PLANNING

The planning system can help to protect the environment and assist individuals in assessing their land rights. There are a number of acts governing the development of land and buildings in England and Wales and advice should always be sought from a Citizens Advice Bureau or local planning authority before undertaking building works on any land or to property. If development takes place which requires planning permission without permission being given, enforcement action may take place and the situation may need to be rectified.

PLANNING PERMISSION

Planning permission is needed if the work involves:

- making a material change in use, such as dividing off part of the house or garden so that it can be used as a separate home or dividing off part of the house for commercial use, eg for a workshop
- going against the terms of the original planning permission, eg there may be a restriction on fences in front gardens on an open-plan estate
- building, engineering for mining, except for the permissions below
- new or wider access to a main road
- additions or extensions to flats or maisonettes
- work which might obstruct the view of road users

Planning permission is not needed to carry out internal alterations or work which does not affect the external appearance of the building, and are not works for making good damage or works begun after 5 December 1968 for the alteration of a building by providing additional space in it underground.

Under new regulations that came into effect on 1 October 2008, there are certain types of development for which the Secretary of State for the Environment, Food and Rural Affairs has granted general permissions (permitted development rights). These include house extensions and additions, outbuildings and garages, other ancillary garden buildings such as swimming pools or ponds, and laying patios, paths or driveways for domestic use. All developments are subject to a number of conditions (for more information, see W www.planningportal.gov.uk).

Before carrying out any of the above permitted developments you should contact your local authority to find out whether the general permission has been modified in your area.

OTHER RESTRICTIONS

It may be necessary to obtain other types of permissions before carrying out any development. These permissions are separate from planning permission and apply regardless of whether or not planning permission is needed, eg:

- building regulations will probably apply if a new building is to be erected, if an existing one is to be altered or extended, or if the work involves building over a drain or sewer. The building control department of the local authority will advise on this
- any alterations to a listed building or the grounds of a listed building must be approved by the local authority. Listing will include not only the main building but everything in the curtilage of the building
- local authority approval is necessary if a building (or, in some circumstances, gates, walls, fences or railings) in a conservation area is to be demolished; each local authority keeps a register of all local buildings that are in conservation areas
- many trees are protected by tree preservation orders and must not be pruned or taken down without local authority consent
- bats and many other species are protected, and Natural England, the Countryside Council for Wales or Scottish Natural Heritage must be notified before any work is carried out that will affect the habitat of protected species, eg timber treatment, renovation or extensions of lofts
- any development in areas designated as a national park, an AONB, a national scenic area or in the Norfolk or Suffolk Broads is subject to greater restrictions. The local planning authority will advise or refer enquirers to the relevant authority

The local authority should be contacted if planning permission is required. There may also be restriction on development contained in the title to the property which should be considered when works are planned.

VOTERS' QUALIFICATIONS

Those entitled to vote at parliamentary, and local government elections are those who, at the date of taking the pole, are:

- On the electoral roll
- Aged 18 years or older
- British citizens, Commonwealth citizens or citizens of the Irish Republic who are resident in the UK
- Those who suffer from no other legal bar to voting (eg prisoners)
- In Northern Ireland electors must have been resident in

Northern Ireland during the whole of the three-month period prior to the relevant date
- Citizens of any EU member state may vote in local elections if they meet the criteria listed above

British citizens resident abroad are entitled to vote for 15 years after leaving Britain, as overseas electors in domestic parliamentary elections in the constituency in which they were last resident if they are on the electoral roll of the relevant constituency. Members of the armed forces, Crown servants and employees of the British Council who are overseas and their spouses are entitled to vote regardless of how long they have been abroad. British citizens who had never been registered as an elector in the UK are not eligible to register as an overseas voter unless they left the UK before they were 18, providing they left the country no more than 15 years ago.

The main categories of people who are not entitled to vote at general elections are:
- sitting peers in the House of Lords
- convicted persons detained in pursuance of their sentences (though remand prisoners, unconvicted prisoners and civil prisoners can vote if on the electoral register)
- those convicted within the previous five years of corrupt or illegal election practices
- EU citizens (who may only vote in EU and local government elections)

Under the Representation of the Peoples Act 2000, several new groups of people are permitted to vote for the first time. These include: people who live on barges; people in mental health hospitals (other than those with criminal convictions) and homeless people who have made a 'declaration of local connection'.

REGISTERING TO VOTE

Voters must be entered on an electoral register. The Electoral Registration Officer (ERO) for each council area is responsible for preparing and publishing the register for his area by 1 December each year. Names may be added to the register to reflect changes in people's circumstances as they occur and each month during December to August, the ERO publishes a list of alterations to the published register.

A registration form is sent to all households in the autumn of each year and the householder is required to provide details of all occupants who are eligible to vote, including ones who will reach their 18th birthday in the year covered by the register. Anyone failing to supply information to the ERO when requested, or supplying false information, may be fined by up to £1,000. Application forms and more information are available from the Electoral Commission (W www.electoralcommision.org.uk or W www.aboutmyvote.co.uk).

VOTING

Voting is not compulsory in the UK. Those who wish to vote do so in person at the allotted polling station. Postal votes are now available to anyone on request and you do not need to give a reason for using a postal vote.

For the appointment of an indefinite or long-term proxy (whereby the voter nominates someone to vote in person on their behalf), the voter needs to specify physical employment or study reasons as to why they are making an application. With proxy votes where a particular election is specified, the voter needs to provide details of the circumstances by which they cannot reasonably be expected to go to the polling station. Overseas electors who wish to vote must do so by proxy.

Further information can be obtained from the local authority's ERO in England and Wales or the electoral registration office in Scotland, or the Chief Electoral Officer in Northern Ireland.

WILLS

A will is used to appoint executors (who will administer the estate), give directions as to the disposal of the body, appoint guardians for children and, for larger estates, can operate to reduce the level of inheritance tax. It is best to have a will drawn up by a solicitor, but if a solicitor is not employed the following points must be taken into account:
- if possible the will must not be prepared on behalf of another person by someone who is to benefit from it or who is a close relative of a major beneficiary
- the language used must be clear and unambiguous and it is better to avoid the use of legal terms where the same thing can be expressed in plain language
- it is better to rewrite the whole document if a mistake is made. If necessary, alterations can be made by striking through the words with a pen, and the signature or initials of the testator and the witnesses must be put in the margin opposite the alteration. No alteration of any kind should be made after the will has been executed
- if the person later wishes to change the will or part of it, it is better to write a new will revoking the old. The use of codicils (documents written as supplements or containing modifications to the will) should be left to a solicitor
- the will should be typed or printed, or if handwritten be legible and preferably in ink. Commercial will forms can be obtained from some stationers

The form of a will varies to suit different cases – a solicitor will be able to advise as to wording, however, 'DIY' will-writing kits can be purchased from good stationery shops and many banks offer a will-writing service.

LAPSED LEGATEES

If a person who has been left property in a will dies before the person who made the will, the gift fails and will pass to the person entitled to everything not otherwise disposed of (the residuary estate).

If the person residuary estate is to pass to someone who predeceased the person who made the will, their share will pass to the closest relative(s) of the testator under the intestacy rules, unless the will names a beneficiary such as a charity who will take as a 'long stop' if the gift is unable to take effect. It is always better to draw up a new will if a beneficiary predeceases the person who made the will.

EXECUTORS

It is usual to appoint two executors, although one is sufficient. No more than four persons can deal with the estate of the person who has died. The name and address of each executor should be given in full (the addresses are not essential but including them adds clarity to the document). Executors should be 18 years of age or over. An executor may be a beneficiary of the will.

WITNESSES

A person who is a beneficiary of a will, or the spouse of a beneficiary at the time the will is signed, must not act as a witness or else he/she will be unable to take his/her gift. Husband and wife can both act as witnesses provided neither benefits from the will.

It is better that a person does not act as an executor and as a witness, as he/she can take no benefit under a will to which he/she is witness. The identity of the witnesses should be made as explicit as possible.

EXECUTION OF A WILL

The person making the will should sign his/her name at the foot of the document, in the presence of the two witnesses. The witnesses must then sign their names while the person making the will looks on. If this procedure is not adhered to, the will will be considered invalid. There are certain exceptional circumstances where these rules are relaxed, eg where the person may be too ill to sign.

CAPACITY TO MAKE A WILL

Anyone aged 18 or over can make a will. However, if there is any suspicion that the person making the will is not, through reasons of infirmity or age, fully in command of his/her faculties, it is advisable to arrange for a medical practitioner to examine the person making the will at the time it is to be executed (to verify his/her mental capacity and to record that medical opinion in writing), and to ask the examining practitioner to act as a witness. If a person is not mentally able to make a will, the court may do this for him/her by virtue of the Mental Health Act 1983.

REVOCATION

A will may be revoked or cancelled in a number of ways:

- a later will revokes an earlier one if it says so; otherwise the earlier will is by implication revoked by the later one to the extent that it contradicts or repeats the earlier one
- a will is also revoked if the physical document on which it is written is destroyed by the person whose will it is. There must be an intention to revoke the will and it may not be sufficient to obliterate the will with a pen
- a will is revoked when the person marries or forms a civil partnership, unless it is clear from the will that the person intended the will to stand after the marriage or civil partnership
- where a marriage or civil partnership ends in divorce or dissolution or is annulled or declared void, gifts to the spouse or civil partner and the appointment of the spouse or civil partner as executor fail unless the will says that this is not to happen. A former spouse or civil partner is treated as having predeceased the testator. A separation does not change the effect of a married person's will.

PROBATE AND LETTERS OF ADMINISTRATION

Probate is granted to the executors named in a will and once granted, the executors are obliged to carry out the instructions of the will. Letters of administration are granted where no executor is named in a will or is willing or able to act or where there is no will or no valid will; this gives a person, often the next of kin, similar powers and duties to those of an executor.

Applications for probate or for letters of administration can be made to the Principal Registry of the Family Division, to a district probate registry or to a probate sub-registry. Applicants will need the following documents: the Probate Application Form; the original will (if any); a certificate of death; oath for executors or administrators; and the appropriate tax form (an 'IHT 205' if no inheritance tax is owed; otherwise an 'IHT 400'). Certain property, up to the value of £5,000, may be disposed of without a grant of probate or letters of administration.

WHERE TO FIND A PROVED WILL

Since 1858 wills which have been proved, that is wills on which probate or letters of administration have been granted, must have been proved at the Principal Registry of the Family Division or at a district probate registry. The Lord Chancellor has power to direct where the original documents are kept but most are filed where they were proved and may be inspected there and a copy obtained. The Principal Registry also holds copies of all wills proved at district probate registries and these may be inspected at First Avenue House, High Holborn. An index of all grants, both of probate and of letters of administration, is compiled by the Principal Registry and may be seen either at the Principal Registry or at a district probate registry.

It is also possible to discover when a grant of probate or letters of administration is issued by requesting a standing search. In response to a request and for a small fee, a district probate registry will supply the names and addresses of executors or administrators and the registry in which the grant was made, of any grant in the estate of a specified person made in the previous 12 months or following six months. This is useful for applicants who may be beneficiaries to a will but who have lost contact with the deceased and for creditors of the deceased.

INTESTACY

Intestacy occurs when someone dies without leaving a will or leaves a will which is invalid or which does not take effect for some reason. Intestacy can be partial, for instance, if there is a will which disposes of some but not all of the testator's property. In such cases the person's estate (property, possessions, other assets following the payment of debts) passes to certain members of the family. The relevant legislation is the Administration of Estates Act 1925, as amended by various legislation including the Intestates Estates Act 1952, the Law Reform (Succession) Act 1995, and the Trusts of Land and Appointment of Trustees Act 1996 and Orders made thereunder. Some of the provisions of this legislation are described below. If a will has been written that disposes of only part of a person's property, these rules apply to the part which is undisposed of.

If the person (intestate) leaves a spouse or a civil partner who survives for 28 days and children (legitimate, illegitimate and adopted children and other descendants), the estate is divided as follows:

- the spouse or civil partner takes the 'personal chattels' (household articles, including cars, but nothing used for business purposes), £125,000 tax-free (with interest payable at six per cent from the time of the death until payment) and a life interest in half of the rest of the estate (which can be capitalised by the spouse or civil partner if he/she wishes)
- the rest of the estate goes to the children*

If the person leaves a spouse or civil partner who survives for 28 days but no children:

- the spouse or civil partner takes the personal chattels, £200,000 tax-free (interest payable as before) and full ownership of half of the rest of the estate
- the other half of the rest of the estate goes to the parents (equally, if both alive) or, if none, to the brothers and sisters of the whole blood*
- if there are no parents or brothers or sisters of the whole blood or their children, the spouse or civil partner takes the whole estate

If there is no surviving spouse or civil partner, the estate is distributed among those who survive the intestate as follows:

- to surviving children*, but if none to

- parents (equally, if both alive), but if none to
- brothers and sisters of the whole blood* (including issue of deceased ones), but if none to
- brothers and sisters of the half blood* (including issue of deceased ones), but if none to
- grandparents (equally, if more than one), but if none to
- aunts and uncles of the whole blood*, but if none to
- aunts and uncles of the half blood*, but if none to
- the crown, Duchy of Lancaster or the Duke of Cornwall *(bona vacantia)*

* To inherit, a member of these groups must survive the intestate and attain the age of 18, or marry under that age. If they die under the age of 18 (unless married under that age), their share goes to others, if any, in the same group. If any member of these groups predeceases the intestate leaving children, their share is divided equally among their children.

In England and Wales the provisions of the Inheritance (Provision for Family and Dependants) Act 1975 may allow other people to claim provision from the deceased's assets. This act also applies to cases where a will has been made and allows a person to apply to the court if they feel that the will or rules of intestacy or both do not make adequate provision for them. The court can order payment from the deceased's assets or the transfer of property from them if the applicant's claim is accepted. The application must be made within six months of the grant of probate or letters of administration and the following people can make an application:

- the spouse or civil partner
- a former spouse or civil partner who has not remarried or formed a subsequent civil partnership
- a child of the deceased
- someone treated as a child of the deceased's family
- someone maintained by the deceased
- someone who has cohabited for two years before the death in the same household as the deceased and as the husband or wife or civil partner of the deceased

SCOTLAND

In Scotland any person over 12 and of sound mind can make a will. The person making the will can only freely dispose of the heritage and what is known as the 'dead's part' of the estate because:

- the spouse or civil partner has the right to inherit one-third of the moveable estate if there are children or other descendants, and one-half of it if there are not
- children are entitled to one-third of the moveable estate if there is a surviving spouse or civil partner, and one-half of it if there is not

The remaining portion is the dead's part, and legacies and bequests are payable from this. Debts are payable out of the whole estate before any division.

From August 1995, wills no longer needed to be 'holographed' and it is now only necessary to have one witness. The person making the will still needs to sign each page. It is better that the will is not witnessed by a beneficiary although the attestation would still be sound and the beneficiary would not have to relinquish the gift.

Subsequent marriage or civil partnership does not revoke a will but the birth of a child who is not provided for may do so. A will may be revoked by a subsequent will, either expressly or by implication, but in so far as the two can be read together both have effect. If a subsequent will is revoked, the earlier will is revived.

Wills may be registered in the sheriff court Books of the Sheriffdom in which the deceased lived or in the Books of Council and Session at the Registers of Scotland.

CONFIRMATION

Confirmation (the Scottish equivalent of probate) is obtained in the sheriff court of the sheriffdom in which the deceased was resident at the time of death. Executors are either 'nominate' (named by the deceased in the will) or 'dative' (appointed by the court in cases where no executor is named in a will or in cases of intestacy). Applicants for confirmation must first provide an inventory of the deceased's estate and a schedule of debts, with an affidavit. In estates under £30,000 gross, confirmation can be obtained under a simplified procedure at reduced fees, with no need for a solicitor. The local sheriff clerk's office can provide assistance.

Further information can be obtained from:

PRINCIPAL REGISTRY (FAMILY DIVISION)
First Avenue House, 42–49 High Holborn, London WC2V 6NP
T 020-7947 6980

REGISTERS OF SCOTLAND
Erskine House, 68 Queen Street, Edinburgh, EH2 4NF
T 0845 607 0161

INTESTACY

The rules of distribution are contained in the Succession (Scotland) Act 1964 and are extended to include civil partners by the Civil Partnership Act 2004.

A surviving spouse or civil partner is entitled to 'prior rights'. This means that the spouse or civil partner has the right to inherit:

- the matrimonial or family home up to a value of £300,000, or one matrimonial or family home if there is more than one, or, in certain circumstances, the value of the home
- the furnishings and contents of that home, up to the value of £24,000
- a cash sum of £42,000 if the deceased left children or other descendants, or £75,000 if not

These figures are increased from time to time by regulations.

Once prior rights have been satisfied legal rights are settled. Legal rights are:

- *Jus relicti(ae) and rights under the section 131 of the Civil Partnership Act 2004* – the right of a surviving spouse or civil partner to one-half of the net moveable estate, after satisfaction of prior rights, if there are no surviving children; if there are surviving children, the spouse or civil partner is entitled to one-third of the net moveable estate
- *Legitim and rights under the section 131 of the Civil Partnership Act 2004* – the right of surviving children to one-half of the net moveable estate if there is no surviving spouse or civil partner; if there is a surviving spouse or civil partner, the children are entitled to one-third of the net moveable estate after the satisfaction of prior rights

Where there is no surviving spouse, civil partner or children, half of the estate is taken by the parents and half by the brothers and sisters. Failing that, the lines of succession, in general, are:

- to descendants
- if no descendants, then to collaterals (ie brothers and sisters) and parents
- surviving spouse or civil partner
- if no collaterals, parents, spouse or civil partner, then to ascendants collaterals (ie aunts and uncles), and so on in an ascending scale
- if all lines of succession fail, the estate passes to the Crown. Relatives of the whole blood are preferred to relatives of the half blood. The right of representation, ie the right of the issue of a person who would have succeeded if he/she had survived the intestate, also applies.

INTELLECTUAL PROPERTY

Intellectual property is a broad term covering a number of legal rights provided by the government to help people protect their creative works and encourage further innovation. By using these legal rights people can own the things they create and control the way in which others use their innovations. Intellectual property owners can take legal action to stop others using their intellectual property, they can license their intellectual property to others or they can sell it on. Different types of intellectual property utilise different forms of protection including copyright, designs, patents and trademarks, which are all covered below in more detail.

COPYRIGHT

Copyright protects all original literary, dramatic, musical and artistic works (including photographs, maps and plans), published editions of works, computer programs, sound recordings, websites, films (including video and DVD) and broadcasts (including cable, radio, satellite broadcasts, and transmissions on the internet). Under copyright the creators of these works can control the various ways in which their material may be exploited, the rights broadly covering copying, adapting, issuing (including renting and lending) copies to the public, performing in public, and broadcasting the material. The transfer of copyright works to formats accessible to visually impaired persons without infringement of copyright was enacted in 2002.

Copyright protection in the United Kingdom is automatic and there is no official registration system. The creator of a work can help to protect it by including the copyright symbol (©), the name of the copyright owner, and the year in which the work was created. In addition, steps can be taken by the work's creator to provide evidence that he/she had the work at a particular time (eg by depositing a copy with a bank or solicitor). The main legislation is the Copyright, Designs and Patents Act 1988, which has been amended by other acts and by statutory instrument to take account of EU directives. As a result of an EU directive effective from January 1996, the term of copyright protection for literary, dramatic, musical and artistic works lasts for 70 years after the death of the creator. For film, copyright lasts for 70 years after the death of the last to survive of the director, authors of the screenplay and dialogue, or the composer of any music specially created for the film. Sound recordings are protected for 50 years after their publication (or their first performance if they are not published), and broadcasts for 50 years from the end of the year in which the broadcast/transmission was made. The typographical arrangement of published editions remains under copyright protection for 25 years from the end of the year in which the edition was published.

The main international treaties protecting copyright are the Berne Convention for the Protection of Literary and Artistic Works (administered by the World Intellectual Property Organisation (WIPO)), the Rome Convention for the Protection of Performers, Producers of Phonograms and Broadcasting Organisations (administered by UNESCO, the International Labour Organisation and WIPO), and the Universal Copyright Convention (developed by UNESCO); the UK is a signatory to these conventions. Copyright material created by UK nationals or residents is protected in each country that is a member of the conventions by the national law of that country. A list of participating countries may be obtained from the UK Intellectual Property Office. The World Trade Organisation's Trade-Related Aspects of Intellectual Property Rights (TRIPS) agreement, signed in 1995, may also provide copyright protection abroad.

Two treaties which strengthen and update international standards of protection, particularly in relation to new technologies, were agreed in December 1996: the WIPO copyright treaty, and the WIPO performance and phonograms treaty. In May 2001 the European Union passed a new directive (which in 2003 became law in the UK) aimed at harmonising copyright law throughout the EU to take account of the internet and other technologies. More information can be found online (W www.ipo.gov.uk).

LICENSING

Use of copyright material without seeking permission in each instance may be permitted under 'blanket' licences available from national copyright licensing agencies. The International Federation of Reproduction Rights Organisations facilitates agreements between its member licensing agencies and on behalf of its members with organisations such as WIPO, UNESCO, the European Union and the Council of Europe. More information can be found online (W www.iffro.org).

DESIGN PROTECTION

Design protection covers the outward appearance of an article and in the UK takes two forms: registered design and design right, which are not mutually exclusive. Registered design protects the aesthetic appearance of an article, including shape, configuration, pattern or ornament, although artistic works such as sculptures are excluded, being generally protected by copyright. In order to qualify for protection, a design must be new and materially different from earlier UK published designs. The owner of the design must apply to the UK Intellectual Property Office. Initial registration lasts for five years and can be extended in five-year increments to a maximum of 25 years. The current legislation is the Registered Designs Act 1949 which has been amended several times, most recently by the Regulatory Reform Order 2006.

UK applicants wishing to protect their designs in the EU can do so by applying for a Registered Community Design with the Office for Harmonisation in the Internal Market. Outside the EU separate applications must be made in each country in which protection is sought.

Design right is an automatic right which applies to the shape or configuration of articles and does not require registration. Unlike registered design, two-dimensional designs do not qualify for protection but designs of semiconductor chips (topographies) are protected by design right. Designs must be original and non-commonplace. The term of design right is ten years from first marketing of the design, or 15 years after the creation of the design, whichever is earlier. The right is effective only in the UK. After five years anyone is entitled to apply for a licence of right, which allows others to make and sell products copying the design. The current legislation is Part 3 of the Copyright, Designs and Patents Act 1988, amended on 9 December 2001 to incorporate the European designs directive, and again in 2006.

PATENTS

A patent is a document issued by the UK Intellectual Property Office relating to an invention and giving the proprietor the right for a limited period to stop others from making, using, importing or selling the invention without the inventor's permission. In return the patentee pays a fee to cover the costs of processing the patent and publicly discloses details of the invention.

To qualify for a patent an invention must be new, must be functional or technical, must exhibit an inventive step, and must be capable of industrial application. The patent is valid for a maximum of 20 years from the date on which the application was filed, subject to payment of annual fees from the end of the fourth year.

The UK Intellectual Property Office, established in 1852, is responsible for ensuring that all stages of an application comply with the Patents Act 1977, and that the invention meets the criteria for a patent.

WIPO is responsible for administering many of the international conventions on intellectual property. The Patent Cooperation Treaty allows inventors to file a single application for patent rights in some or all of the contracting states. This application is searched by an International Searching Authority and published by the International Bureau of WIPO. It may also be the subject of an (optional) international preliminary examination. Applicants must then deal directly with the patent offices in the countries where they are seeking patent rights. The European Patent Convention allows inventors to obtain patent rights in all the contracting states by filing a single application with the European Patent Office. More information can be found online (W www.ipo.gov.uk).

RESEARCH DISCLOSURES

Research disclosures are publicly disclosed details of inventions. Once published, an invention is considered no longer novel and becomes prior art. Publishing a disclosure is significantly cheaper than applying for a patent, however unlike a patent, it does not entitle the author to exclusive rights to use or license the invention. Instead, research disclosures are primarily published to ensure the inventor freedom to use the invention. This works because publishing legally prevents other parties from patenting the disclosed innovation and in the UK, patent law dictates that by disclosing, even the inventor relinquishes their right to a patent.

In theory, publishing details of an invention anywhere should be enough to make a research disclosure. However to be effective a research disclosure needs to be published in a location which patent examiners will include in their prior art searches. To ensure global legal precedent it must be included in a publication with a recognised date stamp and made publicly available across the world.

The *Research Disclosure* journal established in 1960, published by KMP Ltd, is the primary publisher of research disclosures. It is the only disclosure service recognised by the Patent Cooperation Treaty as a mandatory search resource which must be consulted by the international search authorities. More information can be found online (W www.researchdisclosure.com).

TRADE MARKS

Trade marks are a means of identification, whether words or a logo or a combination of both, which enables traders to make their goods or services readily distinguishable from those supplied by other traders. Registration prevents other traders using the same or similar trade marks for similar products or services for which the mark is registered.

In the UK trade marks are registered at the UK Intellectual Property Office. In order to qualify for registration a mark must be capable of distinguishing its proprietor's goods or services from those of other undertakings; it should be non-deceptive, should not be contrary to law or morality and should not be similar or identical to any earlier marks for the same or similar goods or services. The relevant current legislation is the Trade Marks Act 1994, most recently amended by the Trade Marks (Earlier Trade Marks) Regulations 2008.

It is possible to obtain an international trade mark registration, effective in 84 countries, under the Madrid system for the international registration of marks (consisting of the Madrid Agreement and the Madrid Protocol), to which the UK is party. British companies can obtain international trade mark registration in those countries party to the system through a single application to WIPO.

EC trade mark regulation is now in force and is administered by the Office for Harmonisation in the Internal Market (Trade Marks and Designs) in Alicante, Spain. The office registers Community trade marks, which are valid throughout the European Union. The national registration of trade marks in member states continues in parallel with EC trade mark standards.

DOMAIN NAMES

An internet domain name (eg www.acblack.com) has to be registered separately from a trade mark, and this can be done through a number of registrars which charge varying rates and compete for business. For each top-level domain name (eg .uk, .com), there is a central registry to store the unique internet names and addresses using that suffix. A list of accredited registrars can be found online (W www.icann.org).

CONTACTS

COPYRIGHT LICENSING AGENCY LTD, Saffron House, 6–10 Kirby Street, London EC1N 8TS
T 020-7400 3100 W www.cla.co.uk

EUROPEAN PATENT OFFICE, Headquarters, Erhardtstrasse 27, 80469, Munich 2, Germany
T (+49) 892 3990 W www.epo.org

THE UK INTELLECTUAL PROPERTY OFFICE, Concept House, Cardiff Road, Newport NP10 8QQ
T 0845-950 0505 W www.ipo.gov.uk

WORLD INTELLECTUAL PROPERTY ORGANISATION, 34 chemin des Colombettes, CH-1211 Geneva 20, Switzerland T (+41) 22 338 9111
W www.wipo.int

BROADCASTING

CROSS-MEDIA OWNERSHIP

The rules surrounding cross-media ownership were overhauled as part of the 2003 Communications Act. The act simplified and relaxed existing rules to encourage dispersion of ownership and new market entry while preventing the most influential media in any community being controlled by too narrow a range of interests. However, transfers and mergers are not solely subject to examination on competition grounds by the competition authorities. The secretary of state has a broad remit to decide if a transaction is permissible and can intervene on public interest grounds (relating both to newspapers and cross-media criteria, if broadcasting interests are also involved). The Office of Communications (OFCOM) has an advisory role in this context. Government and parliamentary assurances were given that any intervention into local newspaper transfers would be rare and exceptional.

REGULATION

OFCOM is the regulator for the communication industries in the UK and has responsibility for television, radio, telecommunications and wireless communications services. It replaced the Broadcasting Standards Commission, the Independent Television Commission, the Radio Authority, the Radio Communications Agency and OFTEL. OFCOM is required to report annually to parliament and exists to further the interests of consumers by balancing choice and competition with the duty to foster plurality; protect viewers and listeners and promote cultural diversity in the media; and to ensure full and fair competition between communications providers.

OFFICE OF COMMUNICATIONS (OFCOM)
Riverside House, 2A Southwark Bridge Road, London SE1 9HA
T 020-7981 3000 E enquiries@ofcom.org.uk
W www.ofcom.org.uk
Chief Executive, Ed Richards

COMPLAINTS

Under the Communications Act 2003 OFCOM's licensees are obliged to adhere to the provisions of its codes (including advertising, programme standards, fairness, privacy and sponsorship). Complainants should contact the broadcaster in the first instance (details can be found on OFCOM's website); however, if the complainant wishes the complaint to be considered by OFCOM, it will do so. Complaints should be made within a reasonable time as broadcasters are only required to keep recordings for the following periods: radio, 42 days; television, 90 days; and cable and satellite, 60 days. OFCOM can fine a broadcaster, revoke a licence or take programmes off the air.

TELEVISION

There are six major television broadcasters operating in the UK. Four of these – the BBC, ITV, Channel 4 and Five – launched as free-to-air analogue terrestrial networks. BSky B and Virgin Media Television provide satellite television services.

The BBC is the oldest broadcaster in the world. The corporation began a London-only television service from Alexandra Palace in 1936 and achieved nationwide coverage 15 years later. A second station, BBC Two, was launched in 1964. The BBC's digital services comprise BBC Three, BBC Four, BBC News 24 and BBC Parliament; the children's channels, CBeebies and CBBC; and the interactive channel BBCi. The services are funded by the licence fee. The corporation also has a commercial arm, BBC Worldwide, which was formed in 1994 and exists to maximise the value of the BBC's programme and publishing assets for the benefit of the licence payer. Its businesses include international programming distribution, magazines, other licensed products, live events and media monitoring.

The ITV (Independent Television) network was set up on a regional basis in 1955 to provide competition for the BBC. It comprised a number of independent licensees, the majority of which have now merged to form ITV plc. The network generates funds through broadcasting television advertisements. Its flagship analogue channel was renamed ITV1 in 2001 as part of a rebranding exercise to coincide with the creation of a number of digital-only channels. These now include ITV2, ITV3, ITV4, ITV Play and CiTV. ITV Network Centre is wholly owned by the ITV companies and undertakes commissioning and scheduling of programmes shown across the ITV network and, as with the other terrestrial channels, 25 per cent of programmes must come from independent producers.

Channel 4 and S4C were launched in 1982 to provide programmes with a distinctive character that appeal to interests not catered for by ITV. Although state-owned, Channel 4 receives no public funding and is financed by commercial activities, including advertising. S4C's digital service, S4C Digidol, broadcasts entirely in the Welsh language. Channel 4 has expanded to create the digital stations E4, More4, Film4 and 4Music.

Channel 5 (later renamed Five) began broadcasting in 1997. Digital stations Five USA and Five Life (later renamed Fiver) were launched in October 2006.

BSkyB was formed after the merger in 1990 of Sky Television and British Sky Broadcasting. The company operates a satellite television service and has around 40 television channels, including Sky One and the Sky Sports and Sky Movies ranges. It is part-owned by Rupert Murdoch's News Corporation. Sky Digital was launched in 1998 and offers access to over 500 channels. With the 2005 acquisition of Easynet, an internet access provider and network operator, BSkyB now offers voice over IP (VoIP) telephony, video on demand and internet-based TV. With a special box, Sky+ allows viewers to pause and rewind live TV and record up to 40 hours of programming. Virgin Television runs a similar service called Virgin On Demand.

Virgin Media Television was founded in February 2007 as the television production arm of Virgin Media. It was previously known as NTL:Telewest. It owns a number of channels available via satellite, digital and cable platforms, including Bravo, Challenge and Living and runs a single branded channel, Virgin 1.

VIEWING TRENDS, TERRESTRIAL TELEVISION

- Over a fifth of programmes watched on BBC One are UK/national news
- More than a third of BBC Two viewers (40 per cent) choose factual programmes
- On ITV, soap operas and entertainment programmes account for over a fifth of viewing
- Over a third of viewing on Channel 4 is factual and entertainment programming
- Films make up 28 per cent of programmes watched on Five

Source: OFCOM Public Service Broadcasting Annual Report 2009

THE TELEVISION LICENCE

In the United Kingdom and its dependencies, a television licence is required to receive any publicly broadcast television service, regardless of its source, including commercial, satellite and cable programming.

The TV licence is classified as a tax, thereforc non-payment is a criminal offence. A fine of up to £1,000 can be imposed on those successfully prosecuted. The Broadcasting Act 1990 made the BBC responsible for licence administration. TV Licensing is the name of the agent contracted to collect the licence fee on behalf of the BBC. Total licence fee income for 2009 was £3,493.8m. In 2009 an annual colour television licence cost £142.50 and a black and white licence £48. Concessions are available for the elderly and people with disabilities. Further details can be found at W www.tvlicensing.co.uk/information

BBC EXPENDITURE

By medium, 2008–9

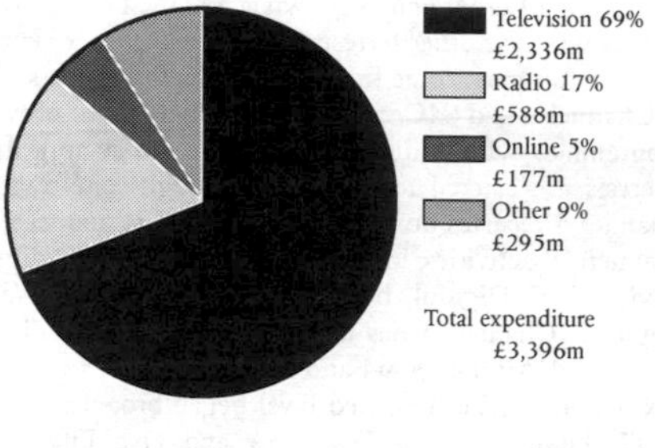

Source: BBC Annual Report 2008–9

DIGITAL TELEVISION

Digital broadcasting has dramatically increased the number and reception quality of television channels. Sound and pictures are converted into a digital format and compressed, using as few bits as possible to convey the information on a digital signal. This technique enables several television channels to be carried in the space used by the current analogue signals to carry one channel. Digital signals can be received by standard aerials using Freeview (*see* below), satellite dishes or cable. The signals are decoded and turned back into sound and pictures by either a set-top box or a decoder built into the television set (iDTV). A basic package of channels is available without charge and services are also offered by cable and satellite companies.

The Broadcasting Act 1996 provided for the licensing of 20 or more digital terrestrial television channels (on six frequency channels or 'multiplexes'). The first digital services went on air in autumn 1998.

In June 2002, following the collapse of ITV Digital, the digital terrestrial television licence was awarded to a consortium made up of the BBC, BSkyB and transmitter company Crown Castle by the Independent Television Commission. Freeview, a new digital network, was launched on 30 October 2002. Freeview offers around 30 digital channels and requires the purchase of a set-top box, but is subsequently free of charge.

At the end of March 2009, nearly 90 per cent of British homes had access to multi-channel TV. The digital channels combined have a greater share of viewing than any of the five main channels and continue to increase this lead.

DIGITAL SWITCHOVER

The digital switchover involves the turning off of the analogue terrestrial transmissions network that has been in place since the 1930s and replacing it with an all-digital terrestrial network. Viewers who receive television through an aerial will need to upgrade their sets with a set-top box (typically costing between £20 and £100) or use integrated digital television (iDTV), cable or satellite digital services. The switchover has started and is due to be completed in 2012. The old analogue frequencies are likely to be sold to mobile telephone companies. For more information, *see* W www.digitaluk.co.uk.

Region	*Expected switchover date*
Border, West Country	complete
Granada	2009
Wales	2009–10
West, STV North	2010
STV Central	2010–11
Central, Yorkshire, Anglia	2011
Meridian, London, Tyne Tees, Ulster	2012

Source: Digital UK

RECENT DEVELOPMENTS

The advent of digital television has coincided with the emergence of the internet as a viable alternative means of watching TV. Channel 4's 4oD (4 On Demand) service allows viewers to revisit and download programmes from the previous 28 days and access an archive of older footage using their PC. The BBC launched its iPlayer on Christmas Day 2007; viewers are now able to watch programmes broadcast in the previous seven days via the streaming option or download and store programmes for up to 30 days on their computer. A new integrated service, launched in June 2008, allows viewers to access BBC radio programmes in addition to televisual output. Eventually, iPlayer will be offered through Freeview and satellite. ITV has a similar service called Catch Up, and Five's service is called Demand Five. Online streaming of TV has been a major success, especially with a younger demographic. By March 2009, iPlayer alone had received over 390 million views and averages more than 400,000 visitors each day.

High Definition (HD) TV is the latest development in TV picture quality, providing more vibrant colours, greater detail and picture clarity in addition to improved sound quality. While a standard television picture is made up of 576 lines of pixels, a HD television screen uses either 720 or 1,080 lines. Sky Digital, ITV and the BBC all provide HD channels, with a growing number becoming available. To access HD channels, viewers need an 'HD ready' TV set and HD TV decoder available through satellite services or a cable connection. It is expected that up to four HD channels will become available through Freeview from late 2009.

ESTIMATED AUDIENCE SHARE
per cent

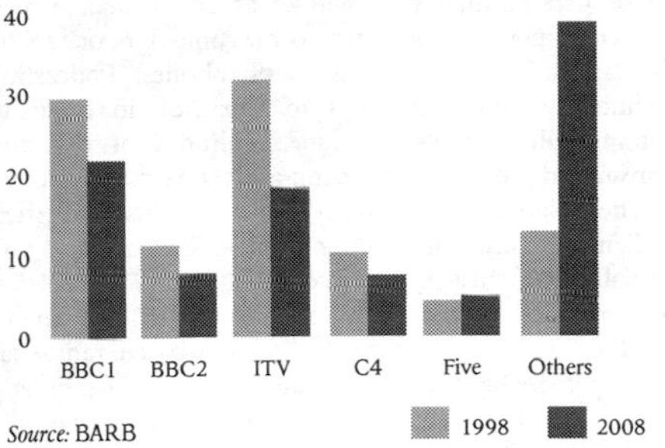

Source: BARB

CONTACTS

THE BRITISH BROADCASTING CORPORATION

BBC TV Centre, Wood Lane, London W12 7RJ T 020-8743 8000 W www.bbc.co.uk
Chair, Sir Michael Lyons

BBC Worldwide Ltd, Woodlands, 80 Wood Lane, London W12 0TT T 020-8433 2000 W www.bbcworldwide.com

INDEPENDENT TELEVISION NETWORK

ITV Network Centre/ITV Association, 200 Gray's Inn Road, London WC1V 8HF T 020-7843 8000 W www.itv.com
Chair, vacant

INDEPENDENT TELEVISION NETWORK REGIONS AND COMPANIES

Anglia (eastern England), Anglia House, Rose Lane, Norwich NR1 3JG T 01603-615151 W www.itv.com/anglia
Border (Borders and the Isle of Man), Television Centre, Carlisle CA1 3NT T 01228-525101 W www.itv.com/border
Central (east, west and south Midlands), Gas Street, Birmingham B1 2JT T 0121-643 9898 W www.itv.com/central
Channel (Channel Islands), The Television Centre, St Helier, Jersey JE1 3ZD T 01534-816816 W www.channelonline.tv
Granada (north-west England), Quay Street, Manchester M60 9EA T 0161-832 7211 W www.itv.com/granada
London (London), London Television Centre, Upper Ground, London SE1 9LT T 020-7620 1620 W www.itv.com/london
Meridian (south and south-east England), Solent Business Park, Whiteley, Hants PO15 7PA T 01489-442000 W www.itv.com/meridian
STV (Scotland), Pacific Quay, Glasgow G51 1PQ T 0141-300 3704 W www.stv.tv
Tyne Tees (north-east England), Television House, The Watermark, Gateshead, Tyne and Wear NE11 9SZ T 0191-404 8700 W www.itv.com/tynetees
Ulster (Northern Ireland), Ormeau Road, Belfast BT7 1EB T 028-9032 8122 W www.u.tv
Wales, The Television Centre, Culverhouse Cross, Cardiff CF5 6XJ T 029-2059 0590 W www.itv.com/wales
West, Television Centre, Bath Road, Bristol BS4 3HG T 0117-972 2722 W www.itv.com/west
Westcountry (south-west England), Langage Science Park, Western Wood Way, Plymouth PL7 5BG T 01752-333333 W www.itv.com/westcountry
Yorkshire (Yorkshire), 96–104 Kirkstall Road, Leeds LS3 1JS T 0113-243 8283 W www.itv.com/yorkshire

OTHER TELEVISION COMPANIES

Channel 4 Television, 124 Horseferry Road, London SW1P 2TX T 020-7396 4444 W www.channel4.com
Five Broadcasting Ltd, 22 Long Acre, London WC2E 9LY T 020-7421 7270 W www.five.tv
GMTV, The London Television Centre, Upper Ground, London SE1 9TT T 020-7827 7000 W www.gm.tv
Owned by ITV and Disney, with 75 per cent and 25 per cent respectively, GMTV provides breakfast television and sells its own advertising.
Independent Television News, 200 Gray's Inn Road, London WC1X 8XZ T 020-7833 3000 W www.itn.co.uk
Provides news programming for ITV and Channel 4.
Sianel Pedwar Cymru (S4C) , Parc Ty Glas, Llanishen, Cardiff CF14 5DU T 0870-600 4141 W www.s4c.co.uk
S4C schedules Welsh language and some Channel 4 programmes.
Teletext Ltd, Building 10, Chiswick Park, 566 Chiswick High Road, London W4 5TS T 020-8323 5000 W www.teletext.co.uk
Its analogue news service (available on commercial analogue TV channels) will close in January 2010, but Teletext Ltd will continue to offer holiday and other commercial services on digital channels.

DIRECT BROADCASTING BY SATELLITE TELEVISION

British Sky Broadcasting Group, Grant Way, Isleworth, Middx TW7 5QD T 020-7705 3000 W www.sky.com
Chief Executive, James Murdoch
Virgin Media Television, 160 Great Portland Street, London W1W 5QA T 020-7299 5000 W www.virginmediatv.co.uk
Chair, Jim Mooney

RADIO

ESTIMATED AUDIENCE SHARE

	Jan–Mar 2007	*Jan-Mar 2008*	*Jan-Mar 2009*
			Percentage
BBC Radio 1	10.1	10.0	10.3
BBC Radio 2	15.8	16.0	15.9
BBC Radio 3	1.2	1.2	1.1
BBC Radio 4	12.2	12.0	12.5
BBC Radio Five Live	4.2	4.6	4.7
Five Live Sports Extra	0.1	0.2	0.1
6 Music	0.3	0.3	0.4
BBC7	0.4	0.4	0.5
Asian Network	0.2	0.3	0.2
1Xtra	0.2	0.3	0.3
BBC Local/Regional	10.6	9.6	9.4
BBC World Service	0.7	0.7	0.8
All BBC	56.0	55.5	56.3
All independent	42.1	42.4	41.6
All national independent	10.7	11.2	10.2
All local independent	31.4	31.2	31.3
Other	1.8	2.1	2.1

Source: RAJAR / Ipsos-MORI

UK domestic radio services are broadcast across three wavebands: FM, medium wave and long wave (used by BBC Radio 4). In the UK the FM waveband extends in frequency from 87.5MHz to 108MHz and the medium waveband from 531kHz to 1602kHz. A number of radio stations are broadcast in both analogue and digital as well as a growing number in digital alone. As at March 2009, the BBC Radio network controlled just over 56 per cent of the listening market (*see* BBC Radio section), and the independent sector (*see* Independent Radio section) just under 42 per cent.

DIGITAL RADIO

DAB (Digital Audio Broadcasting) allows more services to be broadcast to a higher technical quality and provides the data facility for text and pictures. It improves the robustness of high fidelity radio services, especially compared with current FM and AM radio transmissions. It was developed in a collaborative research project under the pan-European Eureka 147 initiative and has been adopted as a world standard by the International Telecommunication Union for new digital radio systems. The frequencies allocated for terrestrial digital radio in the UK are 174 to 239MHz. More spectrum (in the 'L-Band' range: 1452–1490MHz) was introduced in 2007.

Digital radios are available as standalone portable units, hi-fi stacks, car radios and PC cards, or inbuilt within a mobile phone. Newer DAB radios allow the listener to rewind, pause and record broadcasts and can be uploaded to a computer using a USB cable. Some portable sets now combine MP3 playback with DAB. An alternative method is to listen to digital radio through television sets via Freeview, cable or satellite.

The possibility of a switchover to entirely digital radio services remains uncertain as takeup is still proportionately low. Over 20 per cent of listening is now on a digital platform. DAB accounts for 63 per cent of total digital listening, 11 per cent is on the internet and 17 per cent on digital TV. In November 2007 the government launched the Digital Radio Working Group, looking at strategies to ensure the future of digital radio. In June 2009 the government published the white paper *Digital Britain*, which recommends that all services carried on the national and local DAB multiplexes should cease broadcasting on analogue radio by 2015. The two criteria that must be met for digital migration to occur are:

- at least 50 per cent of radio listening is digital
- national DAB coverage is comparable to FM coverage, and local DAB reaches 90 per cent of the population and all major roads

LICENSING

The Broadcasting Act 1996 provided for the licensing of digital radio services (on multiplexes, where a number of stations share one frequency to transmit their services). To allocate the multiplexes, OFCOM advertises licences for which interested parties can bid. Once the licence has been awarded, the new owner seeks out services to broadcast on the multiplex. The BBC has a separate national multiplex for its services. There are local multiplexes around the country, each broadcasting an average of seven services, plus the local BBC station. There are also several regional multiplexes covering a wider area and broadcasting up to 11 services each.

INNOVATIONS

As with television, the opportunities offered by digital services and the internet have made important changes to radio. The internet offers a number of advantages compared to other digital platforms such as DAB including a higher sound quality, a greater range of channel availability and flexibility in listening opportunity. Listeners can tune in to the majority of radio stations live on the internet or listen again online for seven days after broadcast. DAB radio does not allow the same interactivity as the data is only able to travel one-way from broadcaster to listener, unlike the internet which allows a two-way flow of information.

Since 2005 increasing numbers of radio stations offer all or part of their programmes as downloadable files, known as podcasts, to listen to on computers or mobile devices such as mp3 players or phones. Podcasting technology allows listeners to subscribe in order to automatically receive the latest episodes of regularly transmitted programmes as soon as they become available.

The relationship between radio stations and their audiences is also undergoing change. The quantity and availability of music on the internet has led to the creation of shows dedicated entirely to music sent in by listeners. Another new development in internet-based radio has been personalised radio stations, such as last.fm and Spotify. Last.fm 'recommends' songs based on the favourite artists and previous choices made by the user. Spotify allows listeners access to the track, artist or genre of their choice, or to share and create playlists; either advertisements are played at set intervals or there is a subscription charge. WiFi technology is also making changes to radio-listening behaviour. WiFi internet radios and media adaptors (which plug into a hi-fi) mean that people are not limited to listening to internet radio stations, podcasts, or on-demand programmes solely when using their computer.

BBC RADIO

BBC Radio broadcasts network services to the UK, Isle of Man and the Channel Islands. There is also a tier of national services in Wales, Scotland and Northern Ireland and 40 local radio stations in England and the Channel Islands. In Wales and Scotland there are also dedicated language services in Welsh and Gaelic respectively. The frequency allocated for digital BBC broadcasts is 225.648MHz.

Broadcasting House, Portland Place, London W1A 1AA
T 020-7580 4468

BBC NETWORK RADIO STATIONS

Radio 1 (contemporary pop music and entertainment news) – 24 hours a day, *frequencies:* 97–99 FM and digital

Radio 2 (popular music, entertainment, comedy and the arts) – 24 hours a day, *frequencies:* 88–91 FM and digital

Radio 3 (classical music, classic drama, documentaries and features) – 24 hours a day, *frequencies:* 90–93 FM and digital

Radio 4 (news, documentaries, drama, entertainment and cricket on long wave in season) – 5.20am–1am daily, with BBC World Service overnight, *frequencies:* 92–95 FM and 198 LW and digital

Radio Five Live (news and sport) – 24 hours a day, *frequencies:* 693/909 MW and digital

Five Live Sports Extra (live sport) – schedule varies, digital only

6 Music (contemporary and classic pop and rock music) – 24 hours a day, digital only

BBC7 (comedy, drama and children's) – 24 hours a day, digital only

Asian Network (news, music and sport) – 24 hours a day Friday and Saturday; 5am–1am Sunday–Thursday, with Radio Five Live overnight, *frequencies:* various MW frequencies in Midlands and digital

1Xtra (urban music: drum & bass, garage, hip hop, R&B) – 24 hours a day, digital only

BBC NATIONAL RADIO STATIONS

Radio Cymru (Welsh-language), *frequencies:* digital; 93.6–96.8 FM and 103.5–105 FM

Radio Foyle, frequency: digital; 92 AM and 93.1 MW

Radio Nan Gaidheal (Gaelic service), *frequencies:* digital; 103.5–105 FM and 990 MW

Radio Scotland, frequencies: digital; 810/585 MW and 92.4–94.7 FM. Local programmes for: Highlands and Islands; North East; Borders; South West; Orkney; and Shetland

Radio Ulster, frequencies: digital; 1341 MW and 92.4–95.4 FM. Local programmes on Radio Foyle

Radio Wales, frequencies: digital; 882 MW and 93.9–95.9 FM

BBC LOCAL RADIO STATIONS

In England, BBC local radio has an average weekly reach of 7.1 million listeners. There are 40 local BBC stations serving England and the Channel Islands, all of which are available via the internet:

Berkshire, PO Box 1044, Reading RG4 8FH
T 0118-946 4200 *Frequencies:* 95.4/104.1 FM and DAB

Bristol, PO Box 194, Bristol, BS99 7QT
T 0117-974 1111 *Frequencies:* 94.9/104.6/103.6 FM and 1548 AM and DAB

Cambridgeshire, 104 Hills Road, Cambridge CB2 1LQ
T 01223-259696 *Frequencies:* 95.7/96 FM and DAB

Cornwall, Phoenix Wharf, Truro TR1 1UA
T 01872-275421 *Frequencies:* 95.2/103.9 FM and DAB

Coventry and Warwickshire, Priory Place, Coventry CV1 5SQ
T 024-7655 1000 *Frequencies:* 94.8/103.7 FM and DAB

Cumbria, Annetwell Street, Carlisle CA3 8BB
T 01228-592444 *Frequencies:* 95.6/96.1 FM

Derby, 56 St Helen's Street, Derby DE1 3HY
T 01332-361111 *Frequencies:* 95.3/96.0/104.5 FM

Devon, Broadcasting House, Seymour Road, Plymouth PL3 5BD
T 01752-229201 *Frequencies:* 95.7103.4 FM and DAB

Essex, PO Box 765, Chelmsford CM2 9XB
T 01245-616000 *Frequencies.* 95.3/103.5 FM and DAB

Gloucestershire, London Road, Gloucester GL1 1SW
T 01452-308585 *Frequencies:* 95.0/95.8/104.7 FM, 1413 AM

Guernsey, Broadcasting House, Bulwer Avenue, St Sampson's GY2 4LA
T 01481-200600 *Frequencies:* 93.2, 1116 MW

Hereford and Worcester, Hylton Road, Worcester WR2 5WW
T 01905-748485 *Frequencies:* 94.7/104.0/104.4/104.6 FM, 738 MW

Humberside, Queen's Court, Hull HU1 3RH
T 01482-323232 *Frequency:* 95.9 FM, 1485 AM and DAB

Jersey, 18 Parade Road, St Helier JE2 3PL
T 01534-870000 *Frequency:* 88.8 FM and DAB

Kent, The Great Hall, Mount Pleasant, Tunbridge Wells TN1 1QQ
T 01892-670000 *Frequencies:* 96.7/97.6/104.2 FM, 774 AM and DAB

Lancashire, 20–26 Darwen Street, Blackburn BB2 2EA
T 01254-262411 *Frequencies:* 95.5/103.9/104.5 FM and DAB

Leeds, 2 St Peter's Square, Leeds LS9 8AH
T 0113-244 2131 *Frequencies:* 92.4/95.3/102.7/103.9 FM, 774 AM and DAB

Leicester, 9 St Nicholas Place, Leicester LE1 5LB
T 0116-251 6688 *Frequency:* 104.9 FM and DAB

Lincolnshire, PO Box 219, Newport, Lincoln LN1 3XY
T 01522-511411 *Frequencies:* 94.9/104.7 FM, 1368 AM and DAB

London, PO Box 949, Marylebone High Street, London W1A 6FL
T 020-7224 2424 *Frequency:* 94.9 FM and DAB

Manchester, G100, New Broadcasting House, Oxford Road, Manchester M60 1SJ
T 0161-200 2020 *Frequencies:* 95.1 FM and DAB

Merseyside, PO Box 95.8, Liverpool L69 1ZJ
T 0151-708 5500 *Frequencies:* 95.8 FM, 1485 AM and DAB

Newcastle, Broadcasting Centre, Barrack Road, Newcastle upon Tyne NE99 1RN
T 0191-232 4141 *Frequencies:* 95.4/96.0/ /103.7/104.4 FM, 1458 AM and DAB

Norfolk, The Forum, Millennium Plain, Norwich NR2 1BH
T 01603-617411 *Frequencies:* 95.1/95.6/104.4 FM and DAB

Northampton, Broadcasting House, Abington Street, Northampton NN1 2BH
T 01604-239100 *Frequencies:* 103.6/104.2 FM

Nottingham, London Road, Nottingham NG2 4UU
T 0115-955 0500 *Frequencies:* 95.5/103.8 FM and DAB

Oxford, 269 Banbury Road, Oxford OX2 7DW
T 0845-931 1444 *Frequency:* 95.2 FM

Sheffield, 54 Shoreham Street, Sheffield S1 4RS
T 0114-273 1177 *Frequencies:* 88.6/104.1 FM and DAB

Shropshire, PO Box 96, Shrewsbury SY1 3WW
T 01743-248484 *Frequency:* 96 FM and DAB

Solent, Havelock Road, Southampton SO14 7PU
T 023-8063 1311 *Frequencies:* 96.1/103.8 FM

Somerset, Broadcasting House, Park Street, Taunton TA1 4DA
T 01823-323956 *Frequency:* 95.5 FM,1566 AM

Surrey, Broadcasting Centre, Guildford, Surrey GU2 7AP
T 01273-320400 *Frequencies:* 95.1/104/104.6 FM, 1368/1485 AM

Sussex, Broadcasting House, Queens Road, Brighton, East Sussex BN1 3XB
T 0845-957 0057 *Frequencies:* 95.3/104.5/104.8 FM and DAB

Stoke, Cheapside, Hanley, Stoke-on-Trent ST1 1JJ
T 01782-208080 *Frequencies:* 94.6/104.1 FM and DAB

Suffolk, Broadcasting House, St Matthew's Street, Ipswich IP1 3EP
T 01473-250000 *Frequencies:* 95.5/95.9/103.9/104.6 FM

Tees, Broadcasting House, Newport Road, Middlesborough TS1 5DJ
T 01642-225211 *Frequency:* 95 FM and DAB

Three Counties, 1 Hastings Street, Luton LU1 5XL
T 01582-637400 *Frequencies:* 95.5/103.8/104.5 FM

Wiltshire, Broadcasting House, 56–58 Prospect Place, Swindon SN1 3RW
T 01793-513626 *Frequencies:* 103.5/104.3/ FM and DAB

WM (West Midlands), The Mailbox,102–108 Wharfside Street, Birmingham B1 1AY
T 0121-567 6000 *Frequency:* 95.6 FM and DAB

York, 20 Bootham Row, York YO30 7BR
T 01904-641351 *Frequencies:* 95.5/103.7/104.3 FM

BBC WORLD SERVICE

The BBC World Service broadcasts to an estimated weekly audience of 188 million worldwide, in 32 languages including English, and is now available in 154 capital cities. It no longer broadcasts in Dutch, French for Europe, German, Hebrew, Italian, Japanese or Malay because it was found that most speakers of these languages preferred to listen to the English broadcasts. In

2006 services in ten languages (Bulgarian, Croatian, Czech, Greek, Hungarian, Kazakh, Polish, Slovak, Slovene and Thai) were terminated to provide funding for a new Arabic television channel, which was launched in March 2008. In August 2008 the BBC's Romanian World Service broadcasts were discontinued after 68 years. The BBC World Service website offers interactive news services in English, Arabic, Chinese, Hindi, Persian, Portuguese for Brazil, Russian, Spanish and Urdu with audiostreaming available in 32 languages.

LANGUAGES
Albanian, Arabic, Azeri, Bengali, Burmese, Caribbean-English, Chinese, French for Africa, Hausa, Hindi, Indonesian, Kinyarwanda, Kirundi, Kyrgyz, Macedonian, Mandarin, Nepali, Pashto, Persian, Portuguese, Russian, Serbian, Sinhala, Somali, Spanish, Swahili, Tamil, Turkish, Ukrainian, Urdu, Uzbek and Vietnamese.

UK frequencies: digital and 648 MW in southern England; overnight on BBC Radio 4, BBC Radio Ulster, BBC Radio Wales or the Asian Network.

BBC Learning English teaches English worldwide through radio, television and a wide range of published and online courses.

BBC Monitoring tracks the global media for the latest news reports emerging around the world.

BBC World Service Trust is a registered charity established in 1999 by BBC World Service. It promotes development through the innovative use of the media in the developing world. The trust presently works in over 40 countries worldwide, tackling health, education and good governance.

BBC WORLD SERVICE, Bush House, Strand, London WC2B 4PH T 020-7557 2462

INDEPENDENT RADIO

Until 1973, the BBC had a legal monopoly on radio broadcasting in the UK. During this time, the corporation's only competition came from pirate stations located abroad, such as Radio Luxembourg. Christopher Chataway, Minister for Post and Telecommunications in Edward Heath's government, changed this by creating the first licences for commercial radio stations. The Independent Broadcasting Authority (IBA) awarded the first of these licences to the London Broadcasting Company (LBC) to provide London's news and information service. LBC was followed by Capital Radio, to offer the city's entertainment service, Radio Clyde in Glasgow and BRMB in Birmingham.

The IBA was dissolved when the Broadcasting Act of 1990 de-regulated broadcasting, to be succeeded by the less rigid Radio Authority (RA). The RA began advertising new licences for the development of independent radio in January 1991. It awarded national and local radio, satellite and cable services licences, and long-term restricted service licences for stations serving non-commercial establishments such as hospitals and universities. The first national commercial digital multiplex licence was awarded in October 1998 and a number of local digital multiplex licences followed.

At the end of 2003 the RA was replaced by OFCOM, which now carries out the licensing administration.

The RadioCentre was formed in July 2006 as a result of the merger between the Radio Advertising Bureau (RAB) and the Commercial Radio Companies Association (CRCA), the former non-profit trade body for commercial radio companies in the United Kingdom, to operate essentially as a union for commercial radio stations. According to a 2008 audit, it is possible to listen to 93 per cent of independent radio stations online, while 48 per cent can be listened to on DAB radios.

THE RADIOCENTRE, 77 Shaftesbury Avenue, London W1D 5DU T 020-7306 2603 W www.radiocentre.org
Chief Executive, Andrew Harrison

INDEPENDENT NATIONAL RADIO STATIONS

Absolute Radio, 1 Golden Square, London W1F 9DJ T 020-7434 1215 – 24 hours a day, *Frequencies:* 105.8 FM, 1197/1215/1233/1242/1260 AM and DAB/digital

Amazing Radio, 19 Grey Street, Newcastle NE1 6EE – 24 hours a day, *Frequencies:* DAB/digital only

BFBS Radio UK, Chalfont Grove, Narcot Lane, Chalfont St Peter, Bucks SL9 8TN T 01494-878703 *Frequencies:* DAB/digital only

Classic FM, 30 Leicester Square, London WC2H 7LA T 020-7343 9000 – 24 hours a day, *Frequencies:* 100–102 FM and DAB/digital

Planet Rock, 54 Lisson Street, London NW1 5DF T 020-7453 1600 – 24 hours a day, *Frequency:* DAB/digital only

Talk Sport, 18 Hatfields, London SE1 8DJ T 020-7959 7800 – 24 hours a day, *Frequencies:* 1053/1071/1089/1107 AM and DAB/digital

INDEPENDENT LOCAL RADIO STATIONS ENGLAND

2BR, Lomeshaye Business Village, Nelson, Lancs BB9 7DR T 01282-690000 *Frequency:* 99.8 FM

3FM, 45 Victoria Street, Douglas, IOM IM1 3RS T 01624-616333 *Frequencies:* 104–106 FM

3TR FM, Riverside Studios, Warminster, Wilts BA12 9HQ T 01985-211111 *Frequency:* 107.5 FM

95.8 galaxy Radio, 30 Leicester Square, London WC2H 7LA T 020-7766 6000 *Frequency:* 95.8 FM and DAB

96 Trent FM, Maid Marian Way, Nottingham NG1 6JR T 0115-873 1500 *Frequencies:* 96.2/96.5 FM and DAB

96.2 The Revolution, Sarah Moor Studios, Henshaw Street, Oldham OL1 3JF T 0161-621 6500 *Frequency:* 96.2 FM

96.2 Touch Radio (Coventry), Holly Farm Business Park, Honiley, Kenilworth, Warks CV8 1NP T 01926-485600 *Frequency:* 96.2 FM

96.3 Radio Aire, 51 Burley Road, Leeds LS3 1LR T 0113-283 5500 *Frequency:* 96.3 FM and DAB

96.4 FM BRMB, Nine Brindleyplace, 4 Oozells Square, Birmingham B1 2DJ T 0121-566 5200 *Frequency:* 96.4 FM

96.4 Eagle Radio, Dolphin House, North Street, Guildford, Surrey GU1 4AA T 01483-300964 *Frequency:* 96.4 FM

96.9 Viking FM, The Boathouse, Commercial Road, Hull, E. Yorks HU1 2SG T 01482-325141 *Frequency:* 96.9 FM and DAB

97 FM Plymouth Sound, Earl's Acre, Plymouth PL3 4HX T 01752-275600 *Frequencies:* 96.6/97 FM and DAB

97.2 Stray FM, The Hamlet, Hornbeam Park Avenue, Harrogate HG2 8RE T 01423-522972 *Frequency:* 97.2 FM

97.4 Rock FM, PO Box 974, St. Paul's Square, Preston, Lancs PR1 1YE T 01772-477700 *Frequency:* 97.4 FM and DAB

99.9 Radio Norwich, PO Box 999, Norwich T 0845-365 6999 *Frequency:* 99.9 FM

102 Touch FM, Holly Farm Business Park, Honiley, Kenilworth, Warks CV8 1NP T 01926-485600 *Frequency:* 102 FM

102.4 Wish FM, Orrell Lodge, Orrell Road, Wigan, Lancs WN5 8HJ T 01942-761024 *Frequency:* 102.4 FM

103.2 Alpha FM, Radio House, 11 Woodland Road, Darlington, Co Durham DL3 7BJ T 01325-255552 *Frequency:* 103.2 FM

103.4 Sun FM, PO Box 1034, Sunderland, Tyne and Wear SR5 2YL T 0191-548 1034 *Frequency:* 103.4 FM

106.5 Central Radio, 9–10 Eastway Business Village, Olivers Place, Fulwood, Preston PR2 9WT T 01772-708001 *Frequency:* 106.5 FM

107 The Bee, 8 Dalton Court, Darwen, Lancs BB3 0DG T 01254-778000 *Frequency:* 107 FM

107.2 The Wyre, Foley House, 123 Stourport Road, Kidderminster DY11 7BW T 01562-641072 *Frequency:* 107.2 FM

107.4 Telford FM, c/o The Shropshire Star, Waterloo Road, Ketley TF1 5HU T 01952-280011 *Frequency:* 107.4 FM

107.4 The Quay, Media House, Tipner Wharf, Twyford Avenue, Portsmouth PO2 8PE T 023-9236 4141 *Frequency:* 107.4 FM

107.5 Sovereign Radio, 14 St Mary's Walk, Hailsham, E. Sussex BN27 1AF T 01323-442700 *Frequency:* 107.5 FM

107.6 FM Juice Liverpool, 27 Fleet Street, Liverpool L1 4AR T 0151-707 3107 *Frequency:* 107.6 FM

107.6 Touch Banbury, Unit 9A, Manor Park, Banbury, Oxfordshire OX16 3TB T 0129-566 1076 *Frequency:* 107.6

107.7 Splash FM, The Guildbourne Centre, Worthing, W. Sussex BN11 1LZ T 01903-233005 *Frequency:* 107.7 FM

107.7 The Wolf, 2nd Floor, Mander House, Wolverhampton WV1 3NB T 01902-571070 *Frequency:* 107.7 FM

107.8 Arrow FM, Priory Meadow Centre, Hastings, E. Sussex TN34 1PJ T 01424-461177 *Frequency:* 107.8 FM

107.8 Radio Jackie, 110–112 Tolworth Broadway, Surbiton, Surrey KT6 7JD T 020-8288 1300 *Frequency:* 107.8 FM

107.9 Dune FM, The Power Station, Victoria Way, Southport, Merseyside PR8 1RR T 01704-502500 *Frequency:* 107.9 FM

107.9 Pennine FM, The Old Stable Block, Lockwood Park, Huddersfield HD1 3UR T 01484-321107 *Frequency:* 107.9 FM

1548 AM Capital Gold, 30 Leicester Square, London WC2H 7LA T 020-7054 8000 *Frequency:* 1548 AM

Absolute Radio Classic Rock, 1 Golden Square, London W1F 9DJ T 020-7434 1215 *Frequency:* DAB/digital only

Absolute Radio London, 1 Golden Square, London W1F 9DJ T 020-7434 1215 *Frequency:* 105.8 FM and DAB

Absolute Radio Xtreme, 1 Golden Square, London W1F 9DJ T 020-7434 1215 *Frequency:* DAB/digital only

The Arrow, 1 The Square, 111 Broad Street, Birmingham, West Midlands B15 1AS T 0121-695 0000 *Frequency:* DAB/digital only

Asian Sound Radio, Globe House, Southall Street, Manchester M3 1LG T 0161-288 1000 *Frequencies:* 963/1377 AM and DAB

Atlantic FM, Unit 10, Wheal Kitty Workshops, St Agnes, Cornwall TR5 0RD T 01872-554400 *Frequencies:* 105/107 FM

Bath FM, Station House, Ashley Avenue, Lower Weston, Bath BA1 3DS T 01225-471571 *Frequency:* 107.9 FM

The Bay, PO Box 969, St George's Quay, Lancaster LA1 3LD T 0871-200 0747 *Frequencies:* 96.9/102.3/103.2 FM

The Beach, PO Box 1034, Lowestoft, Suffolk NR32 2TL T 0845-345 1035 *Frequencies:* 97.4/103.4 FM and DAB

Beacon Radio, 267 Tettenhall Road, Wolverhampton WV6 0DE T 01902-461300 *Frequencies:* 97.2/103.1 FM and DAB

Big L, 8 Manchester Park, Tewkesbury Road, Cheltenham GL51 9EJ T 01242-699555 *Frequency:* digital only

Bright 106.4, 11A The Market Place Shopping Centre, Burgess Hill, W. Sussex RH15 9NP T 01444-248127 *Frequency:* 106.4 FM

Brighton's Juice, 107.2, 170 North Street, Brighton BN1 1EA T 01273-386107 *Frequency:* 107.2 FM and DAB

BRMB, Nine Brindleyplace, 4 Oozells Square, Birmingham B1 2DJ T 0121-566 5200 *Frequency:* 96.4 FM and DAB

Brunel FM, Unit 4, Shivenham Hundred Business Park, Majors Road, Watchfield, Swindon SN6 8TZ T 01793-784267 *Frequency:* 107.7 FM

CFM (Carlisle and West Cumbria), PO Box 964, Carlisle, Cumbria CA1 3NG T 01228-818964 *Frequencies:* 96.4/102.5 FM (Carlisle); 102.2/103.4 FM (west Cumbria)

Chelmsford Radio 107.7, Icon Building, Western Esplanade, Southend-on-Sea, Essex SS1 1EE T 0845-365 1078 *Frequency:* 107.7 FM

Cheshire's 106.9 Silk FM, Radio House, Bridge Street, Macclesfield, Cheshire SK11 6DJ T 01625-268000 *Frequency:* 106.9 FM

Choice 96.9/107.1 FM, 30 Leicester Square, London WC2H 7LA T 020-7766 6810 *Frequency:* 96.9/107.1 FM and DAB

Club Asia, Asia House, 227–247 Gascoigne Road, Barking, Essex IG11 7LN T 020-8594 6662 *Frequencies:* 963/972 AM

Compass FM, 26A Wellowgate, Grimsby, Lincs DN32 0RA T 01472-346666 *Frequency:* 96.4 FM

Connect FM, 2nd Floor, 5 Church Street, Peterborough PE1 1XB T 0844-800 1769 *Frequencies:* 97.2/107.4 FM

County Sound Radio 1566 AM, Dolphin House, North Street, Guildford, Surrey GU1 4AA T 01483-300964 *Frequency:* 1566 AM

Dearne FM, Unit 7, Network Centre, Zenith Park, Whaley Road, Barnsley S75 1HT T 01226-321733 *Frequencies:* 97.1/102 FM

Dee 106.3, 2 Chantry Court, Chester CH1 4QN T 01244-391000 *Frequency:* 106.3 FM

Delta FM, Tindle House, High Street, Bordon, Hants GU35 0AY T 01420-473473 *Frequencies:* 97.1/101.6/101.8/102 FM

Dream 100 FM, Northgate House, St Peter's Street, Colchester, Essex CO1 1HT T 01206-764466 *Frequency:* 100.2 FM

Energy FM, 100 Market Street, Douglas, IOM IM1 2PH T 01624-611936 *Frequencies:* 91.2 FM (Laxey); 93.4 FM (north Isle of Man); 98.4 FM (Ramsey); 98.6 FM

Fire 107.6 FM, The Picture House, 307 Holden Hurst Road, Bournemouth, Dorset BH8 8BX T 01202-443600 *Frequency:* 107.6 FM

Fresh Radio, Firth Mill, Firth Street, Skipton, N. Yorks BD23 2PT T 01756-799991 *Frequencies:* 936/1413/1431 AM; 102.6/107.1/107.8 FM

Galaxy Birmingham, 1 The Square, 111 Broad Street, Birmingham, West Midlands B15 1AS T 0121-695 0000 *Frequency:* 102.2 FM and DAB

Galaxy Manchester, Suite 1.1, 4 Exchange Quay, Salford, Manchester M5 3EE T 0161-662 4700 *Frequency:* 102 FM and DAB

Galaxy North East, Kingfisher Way, Silverlink Business Park, Wallsend, Tyne and Wear NE28 9NX T 0191-444 2500 *Frequencies:* 105.3/105.6/105.8/106.4 FM and DAB

Galaxy South Coast, Segensworth West, Fareham, Hampshire PO15 5SX T 01489-587754 *Frequency:* 103.2 FM and DAB

Galaxy Yorkshire, Joseph's Well, Hanover Walk, Leeds LS3 1AB T 0113-213 0105 *Frequencies:* 105.1/105.6/105.8 FM and DAB

Gaydar Radio, 6th Floor, Queens House, 2 Holly Road, Twickenham, Middlesex TW1 4EG T 020-8744 1287 *Frequency:* digital

Gold (Berkshire and North Hampshire), The Chase, Calcot, Reading, Berks RG3 7RB T 0118-945 4400 *Frequencies:* 1431/1485 AM and DAB

Gold (Birmingham), Nine Brindleyplace, 4 Oozells Square, Birmingham B1 2DJ T 0121-245 5000 *Frequency:* 1152 AM and DAB

Gold (Bristol and Bath), PO Box 2000, One Passage Street, Bristol BS99 7SN T 0117-984 3200 *Frequency:* 1260 AM and DAB

Gold (Cambridgeshire), PO Box 225, Queensgate Centre, Peterborough, Cambridge PE1 1XJ T 01733-460460 *Frequency:* 1332 AM and DAB

Gold (Devon), Hawthorn House, Exeter Business Park, Exeter EX1 3QS T 01392-444444 *Frequencies:* 666/954 AM and DAB

Gold (Dorset and Hampshire), 5–7 Southcote Road, Bournemouth, Dorset BH1 3LR T 01202-234900 *Frequency:* 828 AM and DAB

Gold (East Midlands), Chapel Quarter, Maid Marian Way, Nottingham NG1 6JR T 01245-524549 *Frequencies:* 1359/1431 AM and DAB

Gold (Essex), 31 Glebe Road, Chelmsford, Essex CM1 1QG T 01245-524549 *Frequencies:* 1359/1431 AM and DAB

Gold (Gloucester and Cheltenham), Bridge Studios, Eastgate Centre, Gloucester GL1 1SS T 01452-572400 *Frequency:* 774 AM

Gold (Hampshire), Radio House, Whittle Avenue, Segensworth West, Farnham, Hants PO15 5SH T 01489-587610 *Frequencies:* 1170/1557 AM and DAB

Gold (Herts, Beds and Bucks), Chiltern Road, Dunstable, Beds LU6 1HQ T 01582-676200 *Frequencies:* 792/828 AM and DAB

Gold (Kent), Radio House, John Wilson Business Park, Whitstable, Kent CT5 3QX T 01227-772004 *Frequencies:* 603/1242 AM and DAB

Gold (London), 30 Leicester Square, London WC2H 7LA T 020-7054 8000 *Frequency:* 1548 AM and DAB

Gold (Manchester), Laser House, Waterfront Quays, Manchester M5 2XW T 0161-662 4700 *Frequency:* 1458 AM and DAB

Gold (Norfolk), St George's Plain, 47–49 Colegate, Norwich NR3 1DB T 01603-630621 *Frequency: 1152 AM* and DAB

Gold (Northamptonshire), 19–21 St Edmunds Road, Northampton NN1 5DY T 01604-795600 *Frequency:* 1557 AM and DAB

Gold (Plymouth), Earl's Acre, Plymouth PL3 4HX T 01752-275600 *Frequency:* 1152 AM and DAB

Gold (Suffolk), Alpha Business Park, 6–12 White House Road, Ipswich IP1 5LT T 01473-461000 *Frequency:* 1170/1251 AM

Gold (Sussex), Radio House, PO Box 2000, Brighton BN41 2SS T 01273-430111 *Frequencies:* 945/1323 AM and DAB

Gold (Sussex and Surrey), 9 The Stanley Centre, Kelvin Way, Crawley, W. Sussex RH10 9SE T 01293-519161 *Frequency:* 1521 AM and DAB

Gold (Warwickshire), Hertford Place, Coventry CV1 3TT T 024-7686 8200 *Frequency:* 1359 AM and DAB

Gold (Wiltshire), 1st Floor, Chiseldon House, Stonehill Green, Westlea, Swindon, Wilts SN5 7HB T 01793-663000 *Frequencies:* 936/1161 AM and DAB

Gold (Wolverhampton and Shropshire), 267 Tettenhall Road, Wolverhampton WV6 0DQ T 01902-461200 *Frequencies:* 990/1017 AM and DAB

Hallam FM, Radio House, 900 Herries Road, Sheffield S6 1RH T 0114-209 1000 *Frequencies:* 97.4/102.9/103.4 FM and DAB

Heart (Bath), PO Box 2000, One Passage Street, Bristol BS99 7SN T 0117-984 3200 *Frequencies:* 103 FM and DAB

Heart (Bedfordshire) 5 Abbey Court, Fraser Road, Priory Business Park, Bedford MK44 3WH T 01234-235010 *Frequency:* 96.9 FM

Heart (Berkshire and North Hampshire), PO Box 2020, Reading, Berks RG31 7FG T 0118-945 4400 *Frequencies:* 97/102.9/103.4 FM and DAB

Heart (Bristol and South Gloucester), PO Box 2000, One Passage Street, Bristol BS99 7SN T 0117-984 3200 *Frequencies:* 96.3/103 FM and DAB

Heart (Cambridgeshire), Enterprise House, The Vision Park, Chivers Way, Histon, Cambridge CB24 9ZR T 01223-235255 *Frequencies:* 97.4/103 FM and DAB

Heart (Colchester), Abbeygate Two, 9 Whitewell Road, Colchester, Essex CO2 7DE T 01206-216140 *Frequency:* 96.1 FM

Heart (Dorset and The New Forest), 5–7 Southcote Road, Bournemouth BH1 3LR T 01202-234000 *Frequency:* 102.3 FM and DAB

Heart (East Midlands), City Link, Nottingham NG2 4NG T 0115-910 6100 *Frequency:* 106 FM and DAB

Heart (Essex), Radio House, 31 Glebe Road, Chelmsford, Essex CM1 1QG T 01245-524500 *Frequencies:* 96.3102.6 FM and DAB

Heart (Exeter and East Devon), Hawthorn House, Exeter Business Park, Exeter EX1 3QS T 01392-444444 *Frequencies:* 97/103 FM and DAB

Heart (Gloucester and Cheltenham), The Mall, Gloucester GL1 1SS T 01452-572400 *Frequencies:* 102.4/103 FM

Heart (Hampshire and West Sussex), Radio House, Apple Industrial Estate, Whittle Avenue, Fareham PO15 5SX T 01489-589911 *Frequencies:* 96.7/97.5 FM and DAB

Heart (Herts, Beds and Bucks), Chiltern Road, Dunstable LU6 1HQ T 01582-676200 *Frequency:* 97.6 FM

Heart (Kent), Radio House, PO Box 100, Whitstable, Kent CT5 3QX T 01227-772004 *Frequencies:* 102.8/103.1 FM and DAB

Heart (London), 30 Leicester Square, London WC2H 7LA T 020-7766 6222 *Frequency:* 106.2 FM and DAB

Heart (Milton Keynes), 14 Vincent Avenue, Crownhill, Milton Keynes MK8 0AB, T 01908-269111 *Frequency:* 103.3 FM

Heart (Norfolk and North Suffolk), 47–49 Colegate, Norwich NR3 1DB T 01603-630621 *Frequency:* 102.4 FM and DAB

Heart (North Devon), Unit 2B, Lauder Lane, Roundswell Business Park, Barnstaple EX31 3TA T 01271-342342 *Frequencies:* 96.2/97.3 FM

Heart (Northamptonshire), 19–22 St Edmunds Road, Northampton NN1 5DY T 01604-795600 *Frequency:* 96.6 FM

Heart (Oxfordshire), Brush House, Pony Road, Oxford OX4 2XR T 01865-871000 *Frequencies:* 97.4/102.6 FM

Heart (Peterborough), Queensgate Centre, Peterborough PE1 1XJ T 01733-460460 *Frequency:* 102.7 FM and DAB

Heart (Plymouth), Earls Acre, Plymouth PL3 4HX T 01752-275600 *Frequencies:* 96.6/97 FM and DAB

Heart (Somerset), Haygrove House, Shoreditch Road, Taunton, Somerset TA3 7BT T 01823-338448 *Frequencies:* 102.6 FM

Heart (South Devon), Unit 1G, South Hams Business Park, Churchstow, Kingsbridge, Devon TQ7 3QH T 01548-854595 *Frequency:* 100.5/100.8/101.2/101.9 FM

Heart (Suffolk), Alpha Business Park, 6–12 White House Road, Ipswich, Suffolk IP1 5LT T 01473-461000 *Frequencies:* 96.4/97.1 FM

Heart (Sussex), Franklin Road, Brighton BN41 1AF T 01273-430111 *Frequencies:* 102.4/103.5 FM and DAB

Heart (Torbay and South Devon), Harbourpoint, Victoria Parade, Torquay, Devon TQ1 2RA T 01803-201444 *Frequency:* 96.4 FM

Heart (Birmingham and West Midlands), 1 The Square, 111 Broad Street, Birmingham B15 1AS T 0121-695 0000 *Frequency:* 100.7 FM and DAB

Heart (Wiltshire), Chiseldon House, Stonehill Green, Westlea,

Swindon, Wilts SN5 7HB T 01793-842600 *Frequencies:* 96.5/97.2/102.2 FM and DAB

Heart (Wirral), Pacific Road Arts Centre, Pacific Road, Birkenhead CH41 1LJ T 0151-650 1700 *Frequency:* 97.1 FM

Hertbeat FM, The Pump House, Knebworth Park, Herts SG3 6HQ T 01438-810900 *Frequencies:* 106.7/106.9 FM

Hertfordshire's Mercury, Unit 5, The Metro Centre, Dwight Road, Watford WD18 9UP T 01923-205470 *Frequency:* 96.6 FM

High Peak Radio, The Studios, Smithbrook Close, Chapel-en-le-Frith, High Peak, Derbys SK23 0QD T 01298-813144 *Frequencies:* 103.3/106.4 FM

Imagine FM, Regent House, Heaton Lane, Stockport, Cheshire, SK4 1BX T 0161-609 1400 *Frequency:* 104.9 FM

Isle of Wight Radio, Dodnor Park, Newport, IOW PO30 5XE T 01983 822557 *Frequencies:* 102/107 FM

Jack FM, 270 Woodstock Road, Oxford, Oxfordshire OX2 7NW T 01865-315980 Frequency: *106 FM*

Kerrang! 105.2 FM, Aqua House, 20 Lionel Street, Birmingham B3 1AQ T 0845-053 1052 *Frequency:* 105.2 FM and DAB

Kestrel FM, 2nd Floor, Paddington House, Festival Place, Basingstoke, Hants RG21 7LJ T 01256-694000 *Frequency:* 107.6 FM

Key 103, Castle Quay, Castlefield, Manchester M15 4PR T 0161-288 5000 *Frequency:* 103 FM and DAB

Kick FM, The Studios, 42 Bone Lane, Newbury, Berks RG14 5SD T 01635-841600 *Frequencies:* 105.6/107.4 FM

Kismat, Radio House, Bridge Road, Southall, Middx UB2 4AT T 020-8574 6666 *Frequency:* 1035 AM and DAB

Kiss 100 FM, Mappin House, 4 Winsley Street, London W1W 8HF T 020-7975 8100 *Frequency:* 100 FM and DAB

Kiss 101 FM, 26 Baldwin Street, Bristol BS1 1SE T 0117-901 0101 *Frequency:* 97.2/101 FM and DAB

Kiss FM 105-108, Reflection House, Western Way, Olding Road, Bury St Edmunds, Suffolk IP33 3TA T 01284-715300 *Frequencies:* 105.6/106.1/106.4/107.7 FM and DAB

KL.FM 96.7, 18 Blackfriars Street, King's Lynn, Norfolk PE30 1NN T 01553-772777 *Frequency:* 96.7 FM

KMFM for Ashford, 34–36 North Street, Ashford, Kent TN24 8JR T 01233-623232 *Frequency:* 107.7 FM

KMFM for Canterbury, 34–36 North Street, Ashford, Kent, TN24 8JR T 01227-623232 *Frequency:* 106 FM

KMFM for Maidstone, 6-8 Mill Street, Maidstone, Kent ME15 6XH T 01622-662500 *Frequency:* 105.5 FM

KMFM for Medway, Medway House, Ginsbury Close, Sir Thomas Longley Road, Medway City Estate, Strood, Rochester, Kent ME2 4DU T 01634-227800 *Frequencies:* 100.4/107.9 FM

KMFM for Shepway and White Cliffs Country, 93–95 Sandgate Road, Folkestone, Kent CT20 2BQ T 01303-220303 *Frequencies:* 96.4/106.8 FM

KMFM for Thanet, 183 Northdown Road, Cliftonville, Margate, Kent CT9 2TA T 01843-296969 *Frequency:* 107.2 FM

KMFM for West Kent, Medway House, Ginsbury Close, Sir Thomas Longley Road, Medway City Estate, Strood, Rochester, Kent ME2 4DU T 01634-227800 *Frequencies:* 96.2/101.6 FM

Lakeland Radio, Unit 4, Lakelands Food Park, Plumgarths, Crook Road, Kendal, Cumbria LA8 8QJ T 01539-737380 *Frequencies:* 100.1/100.8 FM

LBC 97.3 FM, 30 Leicester Square, London WC2H 7LA T 020-7314 7300 *Frequency:* 97.3 FM and DAB

LBC News 1152 AM, The Chrysalis Building, 13 Bramley Road, London W10 6SP T 020-7314 7300 *Frequency:* 1152 AM and DAB

Leicester Sound, 6 Dominus Way, Meridian Business Park, Leicester LE19 1RP T 0116-256 1300 *Frequency:* 105.4 FM and DAB

Lincs FM, Witham Park, Waterside South, Lincoln LN5 7JN T 01522-549900 *Frequencies:* 96.7/102.2/97.6 FM and DAB

Lite FM, 2nd Floor, 5 Church Street, Peterborough PE1 1XB T 01733-898106 *Frequency:* 106.8/96.4 FM

London Greek Radio, LGR House, 437 High Road, London N12 0AP T 020-8349 6969 *Frequency:* 103.3 FM

London Turkish Radio, 185B High Road, Wood Green, London N22 6BA T 020-8881 0606 *Frequency:* 1584 AM

Magic 105.4 FM, Mappin House, 4 Winsley Street, London W1W 8HF T 020-7182 8000 *Frequency:* 105.4 FM and DAB

Magic 828, 51 Burley Road, Leeds LS3 1LR T 0113-283 5500 *Frequency:* 828 AM and DAB

Magic 999, St Paul's Square, Preston, Lancs PR1 1YE T 01772-477700 *Frequency:* 999 AM and DAB

Magic 1152 (Tyne & Wear), 55 Degrees North, Pilgrim Street, Newcastle upon Tyne NE1 6BF T 0191-230 6100 *Frequency:* 1152 AM and DAB

Magic 1161 AM, Commercial Road, Hull, E. Yorks HU1 2SQ T 01482-325141 *Frequency:* 1161 AM and DAB

Magic 1170, Radio House, Yale Crescent, Thornaby, Stockton-on-Tees TS17 6AA T 01642-888222 *Frequency:* 1170 AM and DAB

Magic 1548 AM, St John's Beacon, 1 Houghton Street, Liverpool L1 1RL T 0151-472 6800 *Frequency:* 1548 AM and DAB

Magic AM, Radio House, 900 Herries Road, Sheffield S6 1RH T 0114-209 1000 *Frequencies:* 990/1305/1548 AM and DAB

Manchester's Magic 1152, Castle Quay, Castlefield, Manchester M15 4PR T 0161-288 5000 *Frequency:* 1152 AM and DAB

Mansfield 103.2 FM, The Media Suite, Brunts Business Centre, Samuel Brunts Way, Mansfield, Notts NG18 2AH T 01623-646666 *Frequency:* 103.2 FM

Manx Radio, PO Box 1368, Broadcasting House, Douglas, IOM IM99 1SW T 01624-682600 *Frequencies:* 89.0/97.2/103.7 FM, 1368 AM

Mercia FM, Hertford Place, Coventry CV1 3TT T 024-7686 8200 *Frequencies:* 97/102.9 FM and DAB

Mercury FM , 9 The Stanley Centre, Kelvin Way, Crawley, West Sussex RH10 9SE T 01293-636000 *Frequency:* 97.5/102.7 FM

Metro Radio, 55 Degrees North, Pilgrim Street, Newcastle upon Tyne NE1 6BF T 0191-230 6100 *Frequencies:* 97.1/102.6/103/103.2 FM and DAB

Midwest Radio, The Studios, Middle Street, Yeovil, Somerset BA20 1DJ T 01935-848488 *Frequencies:* 97.4/96.6 (Vale); 105.6/106.6 (Ivel)

Minster FM, PO Box 123, Dunnington, York YO1 5ZX T 01904-488888 *Frequencies:* 102.3/104.7 FM

Mix 96, Friars Square Studios, 11 Bourbon Street, Aylesbury, Bucks HP20 2PZ T 01296-399396 *Frequency:* 96.2 FM

NME, B2 Blue Fin Building, 110 Southwark Street, London SE1 0SU T 0207-922 1991 *Frequency:* DAB/digital only

North Norfolk Radio, The Studio, Breck Farm, Stody, Norfolk NR24 2ER T 01263-863988 *Frequencies:* 96.2/103.2 FM

Oak FM, 3 Martins Court, Telford Way, Coalville LE67 3HD T 01530-835107 *Frequency:* 107/107.9 FM

Original 106.5, County Gates, Ashton Road, Bristol BS3 2JH T 0117-996 1065 *Frequency:* 106.5 FM

Oxford's FM 1079, 270 Woodstock Road, Oxford OX2 7NW T 0845-444 1079 *Frequency:* 107.9 FM

Palm (105.5), Marble Court, Lymington Road, Torquay TQ1 4FB T 01803-321 055 *Frequency:* 105.5 FM

Passion Radio, PO Box 9738, Worthing, West Sussex BN11 9LR T 08707-444703 *Frequency:* digital only
Peak 107 FM, Radio House, Foxwood Road, Chesterfield, Derbys S41 9RF T 01246-267138 *Frequencies:* 102/107.4 FM
Pirate FM, Carn Brea Studios, Wilson Way, Redruth, Cornwall TR15 3XX T 01209-314400 *Frequencies:* 102.2/102.8 FM and DAB
Polish Radio London 91.8, Unit 6, King Street Cloisters, Clifton Walk, London W6 0GY T 020-8846 3619 *Frequency:* 91.8 FM and DAB
Premier Christian Radio, 22 Chapter Street, London SW1P 4NP T 020-7316 1300 *Frequencies:* 1305/1332/1413 AM and DAB
Pulse of West Yorkshire, Forster Square, Bradford, W. Yorks BD1 5NE T 01274-203040 *Frequencies:* 97.5/102.5 FM and DAB
Pulse 2, Forster Square, Bradford, W. Yorks BD1 5NE T 01274-203040 *Frequencies:* 1278/1530 AM and DAB
Quaywest 102.4 FM, Robertsacre, Bridford, Exeter EX6 7HH T 01984-634061 *Frequencies:* 100.8/102.4/107.4 FM
Radio City 96.7, St John's Beacon, 1 Houghton Street, Liverpool L1 1RL T 0151-472 6800 *Frequency:* 96.7 FM and DAB
Radio Wave 96.5 FM, 965 Mowbray Drive, Blackpool, Lancs FY3 7JR T 01253-650300 *Frequency:* 96.5 FM
Radio XL 1296 AM, KMS House, Bradford Street, Birmingham B12 0JD T 0121-753 5353 *Frequency:* 1296 AM and DAB
Ram FM, 35/36 Irongate, Derby DE1 3GA T 01332-324000 *Frequency:* 102.8 FM
Reading 107 FM, Radio House, Madejski Stadium, Reading, Berks RG2 0FN T 0118-986 2555 *Frequency:* 107 FM
Real Radio (Northeast), Marquis Court, Team Valley, Trading Estate, Gateshead NE11 0RU T 0191-440 7500 *Frequencies:* 100–102 FM
Real Radio (Northwest), Laser House, Waterfront Quays, Manchester M50 3XW T 0161-886 8800 *Frequency:* 105.4 FM
Real Radio (Yorkshire), 1 Sterling Court, Capitol Park, Leeds WF3 1EL T 0113-238 1114 *Frequencies:* 106.2/107.6/107.7 FM and DAB
Ridings FM, 2 Thornes Office Park, Monckton Road, Wakefield WF2 7AN T 01924-367177 *Frequency:* 106.8 FM and DAB
Rother FM, Aspen Court, Bessemer Way, Rotherham S60 1FB T 01709-369991 *Frequency:* 96.1 FM
Rugby FM, Holly Farm Business Park, Honiley, Kenilworth CV8 1NP T 0845-094 9780 *Frequency:* 107.1 FM
Rutland Radio, 40 Melton Road, Oakham, Rutland, Leics LE15 6AY T 01572-757868 *Frequencies:* 97.4/107.2 FM
Sabras Radio, Radio House, 63 Melton Road, Leicester LE4 6PN T 0116-261 0666 *Frequency:* 1260 AM and DAB
The Severn, Abbey Studios, 13–14 Abbey Foregate, Shrewsbury SY2 6AE T 01743-284940 *Frequencies:* 106.5/107.1 FM
Signal 1, Stoke Road, Stoke-on-Trent ST4 2SR T 01782-441300 *Frequencies:* 96.4/96.9/102.6 FM and DAB
Signal 2, Stoke Road, Stoke-on-Trent ST4 2SR T 01782-441300 *Frequency:* 1170 AM and DAB
Smooth Radio East Midlands, PO Box 1066, East Midlands, NG2 1RX T 0115-986 1066, *Frequencies:* 101.4/106.6 FM and DAB
Smooth Radio London, 26–27 Castlereagh Street, London W1H 5DL T 020-7706 4100 *Frequency:* 102.2 FM and DAB
Smooth Radio Northeast, Marquis Court, Team Valley Trading Estate, Gateshead NE11 0RU T 0191-440 7500 *Frequencies:* 95.7FM /107.7 FM and DAB
Smooth Radio Northwest, Laser House, Waterfront Quay, Salford Quays, Manchester M50 3XW T 0845-054 1005 *Frequency:* 100.4 FM and DAB
Smooth Radio West Midlands, 3rd Floor, Crown House, 123 Hagley Road, Birmingham B16 8LD T 0121-452 3222 *Frequency:* 105.7 FM and DAB
Southend Radio 105.1, Western Esplanade, Southend-on-Sea, Essex SS1 1EE T 01702-455070, *Frequency:* 105.1 FM and DAB
Spectrum Radio, 4 Ingate Place, Battersea, London SW8 3NS T 020-7627 1953 *Frequency:* 558 AM and DAB
Spire FM, City Hall Studios, Malthouse Lane, Salisbury, Wilts SP2 7QQ T 01722-416644 *Frequency:* 102 FM
Spirit FM, 9–10 Dukes Court, Bognor Road, Chichester, W. Sussex PO19 8FX T 01243-773600 *Frequencies:* 96.6/102.3/106.6 FM
Star Radio in Bristol, County Gates, Ashton Road, Bristol, BS3 2JH T 0117-966 1065 *Frequency:* 107.2 FM
Star Radio in Cambridge, 20 Mercers Row, Cambridge CB5 8HY T 01223-305107 *Frequencies:* 107.1/107.9 FM
Star Radio in Cheltenham, Cheltenham Film Studios, 1st Floor, West Suite, Arle Court, Cheltenham, Glos GL51 6PN T 01242-252333 *Frequency:* 107.5 FM
Star Radio in Somerset, 11 Beaconsfield Road, Weston-super-Mare BS23 1YE T 01934-624455 *Frequency:* 107.7 FM
Sunshine Radio, PO Box 262, Worcester, Worcs WR6 5ZE T 01905-740600 *Frequencies:* 954/1530 AM
Sunrise FM, Sunrise House, 55 Leeds Road, Little Germany, Bradford BD1 5AF T 01274-735043 *Frequency:* 103.2 FM and DAB
Sunrise Radio, Sunrise House, Sunrise Road, Southall, Middx UB2 4AT T 020-8574 6666 *Frequency:* 1458 AM and DAB
Telford FM, c/o The Shropshire Star, Waterloo Road, Ketley TF1 5HU T 01952-280011 *Frequency:* 107.4 FM
Ten 17, Latton Bush Centre, Southern Way, Harlow, Essex CM18 7BB T 01279-431017 *Frequency:* 101.7 FM
TFM, Radio House, Yale Crescent, Thornaby, Stockton-on-Tees TS17 6AA T 01642-888222 *Frequency:* 96.6 FM and DAB
Time 106.6, Radio House, Southall, Middlesex UB2 4AT T 0845-194 1066 *Frequency:* 106.6 FM
Time 107.5, 7th Floor, Lambourne House, 7 Western Road, Romford, Essex RM1 3LD T 01708-731 643 *Frequency:* 107.5 FM
Tower FM, The Mill, Brownlow Way, Bolton BL1 2RA T 01204-387000 *Frequency:* 107.4 FM
Town FM, First Floor, Radio House Prion Court, Great Blakenham, Ipswich, Suffolk IP6 OLW T 0845-365 1102 *Frequency:* 102 FM
Touch FM, 5–6 Aldergate, Tamworth, Staffordshire B79 7DJ T 01827-318000 *Frequencies:* 101.6/102.4 FM and DAB
Trax FM, 5 Sidings Court, White Rose Way, Doncaster DN4 5NU T 01302-341166 *Frequency:* 107.1/107.9 FM and DAB
Wave 105 FM, PO Box 105, Fareham, Hampshire PO15 5TH T 01489-481050 *Frequencies:* 105.2/105.8 FM and DAB
Wessex FM, Radio House, Trinity Street, Dorchester, Dorset DT1 1DJ T 01305-250333 *Frequencies:* 96/97.2 FM
Wire FM, Warrington Business Park, Long Lane, Warrington WA2 8TX T 01925-445545 *Frequency:* 107.2 FM
Wyvern FM, First Floor, Kirkham House, John Comyn Drive, Worcester WR3 7NS T 01905-545510 *Frequencies:* 96.7/97.6/102.8 FM
XFM Manchester, Suite 1.1, 4 Exchange Quay, Manchester M5 3EE T 0161-662 4700 *Frequency:* 97.7 FM and DAB
XFM UK, 30 Leicester Square, London WC2H 7LA T 020-7054 8000 *Frequency:* 104.9 FM and DAB

Yorkshire Coast Radio, Unit 2B, Newchase Business Centre, Hopper Hill Road, Scarborough, N. Yorks YO11 3YS T 01723-581700 *Frequencies:* 96.2/102.4/103.1 FM

Yorkshire Radio, PO Box 197, Elland Road, Leeds LS11 1AZ T 0113-367 6117 *Frequency:* DAB

WALES

96.4 FM The Wave, PO Box 964, Victoria Road, Gowerton, Swansea SA4 3AB T 01792-511964 *Frequency:* 96.4 FM and DAB

97.1 Radio Carmarthenshire, PO Box 971, Llanelli, Carmarthenshire SA15 1YH T 0845-890 7000 *Frequencies:* 97.1/97.5 FM

97.5 Scarlet FM, PO Box 971, Llanelli, Carmarthenshire SA15 1YH T 0845-890 7000 *Frequency:* 97.5 FM

102.5 Radio Pembrokeshire, Unit 14, The Old School Estate, Station Road, Narberth, Pembrokeshire SA67 7DU T 01834-869384 *Frequencies:* 102.5/107.5 FM

106.3 Bridge FM, PO Box 1063, Bridgend CF35 6WF T 0845-890 4000 *Frequency:* 106.3 FM

Afan FM, AquaDome, Hollywood Park, Princess Margaret Way, Port Talbot SA12 6QW T 01639-896292 *Frequency:* 97.4/107.9 FM

Gold (North Wales and Cheshire), Mold Road, Gwersyllt, Wrexham LL11 4AF T 01978-752202 *Frequency:* 1260 AM

Gold (South Wales), Red Dragon Centre, Atlantic Wharf, Cardiff CF10 4DJ T 029-2066 2066 *Frequencies:* 1305/1359 AM and DAB

Heart (Anglesey and Gwynedd), Llys-Y-Dderwen, Parc Menai, Bangor, Gwynedd LL55 4BN T 01248-673400 *Frequency:* 103 FM

Heart (Cheshire and Northeast Wales), The Studios, Mold Road, Gwersyllt, Wrexham LL11 4AF T 01978-752200 *Frequency:* 103.4 FM

Heart (North Wales Coast), PO Box 963, Bangor LL57 4ZR T 01248 [illegible] *Frequency:* 96.3 FM

Nation Radio, Newby House, Neath Abbey Business Park, Neath SA10 7DR T 0845-025 1000 *Frequencies:* 106.8/107.3 FM and DAB

Radio Ceredigion, Yr Hen Ysgol Gymraeg, Aberystwyth, Ceredigion, SY23 1LF T 01970-627999 *Frequencies:* 96.6/97.4/103.3/FM

Radio Maldwyn, The Studios, The Park, Newtown, Powys SY16 2NZ T 01686-623555 *Frequency:* 756 AM

Real Radio (Wales), Unit 1, Ty-Nant Court, Ty-Nant Road, Morganstown, Cardiff CF15 8LW T 029-2031 5100 *Frequencies:* 105.2/105.4/105.7/105.9/106/106.2 FM and DAB

Red Dragon FM, Atlantic Wharf, Cardiff CF10 4DJ T 029-2066 2066 *Frequencies:* 97.4/103.2 FM and DAB

Swansea Bay Radio Newby House, Neath Abbey Industrial Estate, Neath SA10 7DR T 0845-890 4000 *Frequency:* 102.1 FM

Swansea Sound, Victoria Road, Gowerton, Swansea SA4 3AB T 01792-511170 *Frequency:* 1170 AM and DAB

SCOTLAND

Argyll FM, 27–29 Longrow, Campbelltown, Argyll PA28 6ER T 01586-551800 *Frequencies:* 106.5/107.1/107.7 FM

Central 103.1 FM, 201–203 High Street, Falkirk FK1 1DU T 01324-611164 *Frequency:* 103.1 FM

Clyde 1, Clydebank Business Park, Clydebank, Glasgow G81 2RX T 0141-565 2200 *Frequencies:* 97/102.5/103.3 FM and DAB

Clyde 2, Clydebank Business Park, Clydebank, Glasgow G81 2RX T 0141-565 2200 *Frequency:* 1152 AM and DAB

Cuillin FM, Stormyhill Road, Portree, Isle of Skye IV51 9DY T 01478-611234 *Frequency:* 106.2 FM

Forth One, Forth House, Forth Street, Edinburgh EH1 3LE T 0131-556 9255 *Frequencies:* 97.3/97.6/102.2 FM and DAB

Forth 2, Forth House, Forth Street, Edinburgh EH1 3LE T 0131-556 9255 *Frequency:* 1548 AM and DAB

Heartland FM, 9 Alba Place, Pitlochry, Perthshire PH16 5BU T 01796-474040 *Frequency:* 97.5 FM

Isles FM, PO Box 333, Stornoway, Isle of Lewis HS1 2PU T 01851-703333 *Frequency:* 103 FM

Kingdom FM, Haig House, Haig Business Park, Balgonie Road, Markinch, Fife KY7 6AQ T 01592-753753 *Frequencies:* 95.2/96.1/96.6/105.4/106.3 FM

Lanarkshire's L107, Radio House, 69 Bothwell Road, Hamilton, Lanarkshire ML3 0DW T 01698-303420 *Frequencies:* 107.5/107.9 FM

Lochbroom FM, Radio House, Mill Street, Ullapool, Ross-shire IV26 2UN T 01854-613131 *Frequencies:* 96.8/102.2 FM

Moray Firth Radio (MFR), Scorguie Place, Inverness IV3 8UJ T 01463-224433 *Frequencies:* 97.4 FM/1107 AM and DAB

NECR, The Shed, School Road, Kintore, Iveruie, Aberdeenshire AB51 0UX T 01467-632909 *Frequencies:* 97.1/101.9/102.1/102.6/103.2/106.4 FM and DAB

Nevis Radio, Ben Nevis Estate, Claggan, Fort William PH33 6PR T 01397-700007 *Frequencies:* 96.6/97/102.3/102.4 FM

Northsound 1, Abbotswell Road, West Tullos, Aberdeen AB12 3AJ T 01224-337000 *Frequencies:* 96.9/97.6/103 FM and DAB

Northsound 2, Abbotswell Road, West Tullos, Aberdeen AB12 3AJ T 01224-337000 *Frequency:* 1035 AM and DAB

Oban FM, 132 George Street, Oban, Argyll PA34 5NT T 01631 570057 *Frequency:* 103.3 FM

Original 106, Craigshaw Road, West Tullos, Aberdeen AB12 3AR T 01224-294860 *Frequency: 106 FM*

Radio Borders, Tweedside Park, Galashiels TD1 3TD T 01896-759444 *Frequencies:* 96.8/97.5/103.1/103.4 FM

Real Radio (Scotland), Parkway Court, Glasgow Business Park, Glasgow G69 6GA T 0141-781 1011 *Frequencies:* 100.3/101.1 FM and DAB

RNA FM, Rosemount Road, Arbroath, Angus DD11 2AT T 01241-879660 *Frequencies:* 96.6/87.7 FM and DAB

Rock Radio, Unit 1130, Glasgow Business Park, Glasgow G69 6GA T 0141-4781 1011 *Frequency:* 96.3 FM and DAB

SIBC, Market Street, Lerwick, Shetland ZE1 0JN T 01595-695299 *Frequencies:* 96.2/102.2 FM

Smooth 105.2, PO Box 105, Glasgow G69 1AQ T 0141-781 1011, *Frequency:* 105.2 FM and DAB

South West Sound FM, Unit 40, The Loreburne Centre, High St, Dumfries DG1 2BD T 01387-250999 *Frequencies:* 96.5/97/103 FM

Tay AM, 6 North Isla Street, Dundee DD3 7JQ T 01382-200800 *Frequencies:* 1161/1584 AM and DAB

Tay FM, 6 North Isla Street, Dundee DD3 7JQ T 01382-200800 *Frequencies:* 96.4/102.8 FM and DAB

Two Lochs Radio, Gairloch, Ross-shire IV21 2BQ T 01445-712106 *Frequencies:* 106/106.6 FM

UCA, University Campus Ayr, Beech Grove, Ayr, S. Ayrshire KA8 0SR T 01292-886385 *Frequency:* 87.7 FM and DAB

Wave 102, 8 South Tay Street, Dundee DD1 1PA T 01382-901000 *Frequency:* 102 FM and DAB

Waves Radio, 7 Blackhouse Circle, Blackhouse Industrial Estate, Peterhead, Aberdeenshire AB42 1BN T 01779-491012 *Frequency:* 101.2 FM and DAB

West FM, Radio House, 54A Holmston Road, Ayr KA7 3BE T 01292-283662 *Frequencies:* 96.7/97.5 FM and DAB

West Sound AM, Radio House, 54A Holmston Road, Ayr KA7 3BE T 01292-283662 *Frequency:* 1035 AM and DAB

Yourradio, Pioneer Park Studios, Unit 3, 80 Castlegreen Street, Dumbarton G82 1JB T 01389-734444 *Frequencies:* 103 FM (Dumbarton), 106.9 FM (Helensburgh)

NORTHERN IRELAND

Citybeat 96.7 FM, 2nd Floor, Arena Building, 85 Ormeau Road, Belfast, Antrim BT7 1SH T 028-9023 4967 *Frequency:* 96.7 FM and DAB

Cool FM, PO Box 974, Belfast BT1 1RT T 028-9181 7181 *Frequency:* 97.4 FM and DAB

Downtown Radio, Newtownards, Co. Down BT23 4ES T 028-9181 5555 *Frequencies:* 96.4 FM (Limavady); 96.6 FM (Enniskillen); 97.1 FM (Larne); 102.3 FM (Ballymena); 102.4 FM (Londonderry) and DAB

Q97.2 FM (Causeway Coast), 24 Cloyfin Road, Coleraine, Co. Londonderry BT52 2NU T 028-7035 9100 *Frequency:* 97.2 FM

Q101.2 West FM, 42A Market Street, Omagh, Co. Tyrone BT78 1EH T 028-8224 5777 *Frequency:* 101.2 FM

Q102.9 FM Northwest, The Riverview Suite, 87 Rossdowney Road, Waterside, Londonderry BT47 5SU T 028-7134 4449/346666 *Frequency:* 102.9 FM and DAB

Seven FM, 1 Millennium Park, Woodside Industrial Estate, Woodside Road, Ballymena, Co Antrim BT42 4PT T 028-2564 8777 *Frequency:* 107 FM

Six FM, 2C Park Avenue, Cookstown, Co. Tyrone BT80 8AH T 028-8675 8696 *Frequencies:* 106/107.2 FM

U105, Ulster Television plc, Unit 105, Havelock House Ormeau Road, Belfast BT7 1EB T 028-9033 2105 *Frequency:* 105.8 FM

CHANNEL ISLANDS

Channel 103 FM, 6 Tunnell Street, St Helier, Jersey JE2 4LU T 01534-888103 *Frequency:* 103.7 FM

Island FM, 12 Westerbrook, St Sampsons, Guernsey GY2 4QQ T 01481-242000 *Frequencies:* 93.7/104.7 FM

THE PRESS

The newspaper and periodical press in the UK is large and diverse, catering for a wide variety of views and interests. There is no state control or censorship of the press; however, it is subject to the laws on publication, and the Press Complaints Commission (PCC) was set up by the industry as a means of self-regulation.

The press is not state-subsidised and receives few tax concessions. The income of most newspapers and periodicals is derived largely from sales and from advertising; the press is the largest advertising medium in Britain, although its market share is dropping as the proportion of online advertising grows.

SELF-REGULATION

The PCC was founded by the newspaper and magazine industry in January 1991 to replace the Press Council (established in 1953). It is a voluntary, non-statutory body set up to operate the press' self-regulation system following the Calcutt report in 1990 on privacy and related matters, when the industry feared that failure to regulate itself might lead to statutory regulation of the press. The performance of the PCC was reviewed after 18 months of operation (the *Calcutt Review of Press Self-Regulation,* presented to parliament in January 1993) to determine whether statutory measures were required. No proposals for replacing the self regulation system have been made to date. The commission is funded by the industry through the Press Standards Board of Finance.

COMPLAINTS

The PCC's aims are to consider, adjudicate, conciliate, and resolve complaints of unfair treatment by the press; and to ensure that the press maintains the highest professional standards and shows respect for generally recognised freedoms, including freedom of expression, the public's right to know, and the right of the press to operate free from improper pressure. The commission judges newspaper and magazine conduct by a code of practice drafted by editors, agreed by the industry and ratified by the commission.

The PCC has three classes of members: the chairman, public members and press members. Although a number of the commision's members are newspaper or magazine editors, the majority of the 17 members have no connection with the press in order to ensure that the PCC maintains independence from the newspaper industry. The PCC received 4,698 complaints in 2008, an increase of 8 per cent from 2007.

PRESS COMPLAINTS COMMISSION
Halton House, 20–23 Holborn, London EC1N 2JD
T 020-7831 0022 **E** complaints@pcc.org.uk
W www.pcc.org.uk
Chair, Baroness Peta Buscombe

NEWSPAPERS

Newspapers are mostly financially independent of any political party, though most adopt a political stance in their editorial comments, usually reflecting proprietorial influence. Ownership of the national and regional daily newspapers is concentrated in the hands of large corporations whose interests cover publishing and communications, although *The Guardian* and *The Observer* are owned by the *Scott Trust,* formed in 1936 to protect the financial and editorial independence of *The Guardian* in perpetuity. The rules on cross-media ownership, as amended by the Broadcasting Act 1996, which limited the extent to which newspaper organisations may become involved in broadcasting, have been relaxed by the Communications Act 2003: newspapers with over a 20 per cent share of national circulation may own national and/or local radio licences.

There are around 15 daily and 15 Sunday national papers and several hundred local papers that are published daily, weekly or twice-weekly. Scotland, Wales and Northern Ireland all have at least one daily and one Sunday national paper.

UK CIRCULATION

National Daily Newspapers	*June 2008*	*June 2009*
The Sun	2,884,987	2,860,159
Daily Mail	2,042,453	2,025,338
Daily Mirror	1,340,535	1,205,197
The Daily Telegraph	813,346	781,744
Daily Express	694,260	687,555
Daily Star	606,331	753,460
The Times	576,444	560,258
Daily Record	374,595	347,195
The Guardian	302,636	292,854
The Independent	176,785	152,932
Financial Times	131,807	112,111
The Herald	63,949	57,754
The Scotsman	51,361	47,559
National Sunday Newspapers	*June 2008*	*June 2009*
News of the World	2,908,392	2,796,589
The Mail on Sunday	1,947,444	1,802,623
Sunday Mirror	1,243,042	1,155,776
The Sunday Times	983,767	1,039,625
Sunday Express	625,193	595,859
The People	580,948	533,896
The Sunday Telegraph	598,493	576,219
Sunday Mail	459,465	394,437
Sunday Post	383,122	345,527
The Observer	386,140	363,431
Daily Star Sunday	304,927	319,048
The Independent on Sunday	162,832	117,498
Scotland on Sunday	66,918	62,653
Sunday Herald	45,450	37,335

Source: Audit Bureau of Circulations Ltd

Newspapers are usually published in either broadsheet or smaller, tabloid format. The 'quality' daily papers – ie those providing detailed coverage of a wide range of public matters – have traditionally been broadsheets, the more populist newspapers tabloid. In 2004 this correlation between format and content was redefined when three traditionally broadsheet newspapers, *The Times, The Independent* and *The Scotsman,* switched to tabloid-sized editions, while *The Guardian* launched a new 'Berliner' format in September 2005. In October 2005 *The Independent on Sunday* became the first Sunday broadsheet to be published in the tabloid (or 'compact') size, and *The Observer,* like its daily counterpart *The Guardian,* began publishing in the Berliner format in January 2006.

NATIONAL DAILY NEWSPAPERS

DAILY EXPRESS
Northern & Shell Building,10 Lower Thames Street, London EC4R 6EN **T** 0871-434 1010 **W** www.express.co.uk
Editor, Peter Hill

DAILY MAIL
Northcliffe House, 2 Derry Street, London W8 5TT **T** 020-7938 6000 **W** www.dailymail.co.uk
Editor, Paul Dacre

DAILY MIRROR
1 Canada Square, Canary Wharf, London E14 5AP **T** 020-7293 3000 **W** www.mirror.co.uk
Editor, Richard Wallace

DAILY RECORD
1 Central Quay, Glasgow G3 8DA **T** 0141-309 3000 **W** www.record-mail.co.uk/rm
Editor, Bruce Waddell

DAILY SPORT
19 Great Ancoats Street, Manchester M60 4BT **T** 0161-236 4466 **W** www.dailysport.co.uk
Editor, Pam McVitie

DAILY STAR
Express Newspapers, Northern & Shell Building, 10 Lower Thames Street, London EC3R 6EN **T** 0871-434 1010 **W** www.dailystar.co.uk
Editor, Dawn Neesom

THE DAILY TELEGRAPH
111 Buckingham Palace Road, London SW1W 0DT **T** 020-7931 2000 **W** www.telegraph.co.uk
Editor, William Lewis

FINANCIAL TIMES
1 Southwark Bridge, London SE1 9HL **T** 020-7873 3000 **W** www.ft.com
Editor, Lionel Barber

THE GUARDIAN
King's Place, 90 York Way, London N1 9GU **T** 020-3353 2000 **W** www.guardian.co.uk
Editor, Alan Rusbridger

THE HERALD
Herald & Times Group, 200 Renfield Street, Glasgow G2 3QB **T** 0141-302 7000 **W** www.theherald.co.uk
Editor, Charles McGhee

THE INDEPENDENT
2 Derry Street, London W8 5HF **T** 020-7005 2000 **W** www.independent.co.uk
Editor-in-Chief, Roger Alton

MORNING STAR
People's Press Printing Society Ltd, William Rust House, 52 Beachy Road, London E3 2NS **T** 020-8510 0815 **W** www.morningstaronline.co.uk
Editor, Bill Benfield

THE SCOTSMAN
Barclay House, 108 Holyrood Road, Edinburgh EH8 8AS **T** 0131-620 8620 **W** www.scotsman.com
Editor, John McLellan

THE SUN
News Group Newspapers Ltd, 1 Virginia Street, London E1 9XP **T** 020-7782 4000 **W** www.the-sun.co.uk
Editor, Dominic Mohan

THE TIMES
1 Pennington Street, London E98 1TT **T** 020-7782 5000 **W** www.timesonline.co.uk
Editor, James Harding

WEEKLY NEWSPAPERS

DAILY STAR SUNDAY
Express Newspapers, The Northern and Shell Building, 10 Lower Thames Street, London EC3R 6EN **T** 0871-520 7424 **W** www.dailystarsunday.co.uk
Editor, Michael Booker

INDEPENDENT ON SUNDAY
2 Derry Street, London W8 5HF **T** 020-7005 2000 **W** www.independent.co.uk
Editor, John Mullin

THE MAIL ON SUNDAY
Northcliffe House, 2 Derry Street, London W8 5TS **T** 020-7938 6000 **W** www.mailonsunday.co.uk
Editor, Peter Wright

NEWS OF THE WORLD
1 Virginia Street, London E98 1NW **T** 020-7782 4000 **W** www.newsoftheworld.co.uk
Editor, Neil McLeod

THE OBSERVER
Kings Place, 90 York Way, London N1 9GU **T** 020-3353 2000 **W** www.observer.co.uk
Editor, John Mulholland

THE PEOPLE
1 Canada Square, Canary Wharf, London E14 5AP **T** 020-7293 3000 **W** www.people.co.uk
Editor, Lloyd Embley

SCOTLAND ON SUNDAY
108 Holyrood Road, Edinburgh EH8 8AS **T** 0131-620 8620 **W** www.scotlandonsunday.co.uk
Editor, Les Snowdon

SUNDAY EXPRESS
Northern & Shell Building, 10 Lower Thames Street, London EC4R 6EN **T** 0871-434 1010 **W** www.express.co.uk
Editor, Martin Townsend

SUNDAY HERALD
200 Renfield Street, Glasgow G2 3QB **T** 0141-302 7800 **W** www.sundayherald.com
Editor, Richard Walker

SUNDAY MAIL
1 Central Quay, Glasgow G3 8DA **T** 0141-309 3000 **W** www.sundaymail.com
Editor, Allan Rennie

SUNDAY MIRROR
1 Canada Square, Canary Wharf, London E14 5AP **T** 020-7293 3000 **W** www.sundaymirror.co.uk
Editor, Tina Weaver

SUNDAY POST
D.C. Thomson & Co. Ltd, 144 Port Dundas Road, Glasgow G4 0HZ **T** 0141-332 9933 **W** www.sundaypost.com
Editor, David Pollington

SUNDAY TELEGRAPH
111 Buckingham Palace Road, London SW1W 0DT **T** 020-7931 2000 **W** www.telegraph.co.uk
Editor, Ian MacGregor

THE SUNDAY TIMES
1 Pennington Street, London E98 1ST **T** 020-7782 5000 **W** www.timesonline.co.uk
Editor, John Witherow

THE SUNDAY TIMES SCOTLAND
Times Newspapers Ltd, 124 Portman Street, Kinning Park, Glasgow G41 1EJ **T** 0141-420 5100 **W** www.timesonline.co.uk

WALES ON SUNDAY
6 Park Street, Cardiff CF10 1XR **T** 029-2024 3600 **W** www.icwales.co.uk
Editor, Tim Gordon

REGIONAL DAILY NEWSPAPERS

EAST ANGLIA

CAMBRIDGE EVENING NEWS
Winship Road, Milton, Cambs CB24 6PP **T** 01223-434434
W www.cambridge-news.co.uk
Editor, Murray Morse

EAST ANGLIAN DAILY TIMES
30 Lower Brook Street, Ipswich, Suffolk IP4 1AN
T 01473-230023 **W** www.eadt.co.uk
Editor, Terry Hunt

EASTERN DAILY PRESS
Prospect House, Rouen Road, Norwich NR1 1RE
T 01603-628311 **W** www.edp24.co.uk
Editor, Peter Franzen OBE

EVENING STAR
Archant Regional, Press House, 30 Lower Brook Street, Ipswich, Suffolk IP4 1AN **T** 01473-230023 **W** www.eveningstar.co.uk
Editor, Nigel Pickoner

NORWICH EVENING NEWS
Prospect House, Rouen Road, Norwich NR1 1RE
T 01603-628311 **W** www.eveningnews24.co.uk
Editor, James Foster

EAST MIDLANDS

BURTON MAIL
Burton Daily Mail Ltd, 65–68 High Street, Burton on Trent DE14 1LE **T** 01283-512345 **W** www.burtonmail.co.uk
Editor, Andy Parker

DERBY EVENING TELEGRAPH
Northcliffe House, Meadow Road, Derby DE1 2BH
T 01332-291111 **W** www.thisisderbyshire.co.uk
Editor, Steve Hall

THE LEICESTER MERCURY
St George Street, Leicester LE1 9FQ **T** 0116-251 2512
W www.thisisleicestershire.co.uk
Editor, Nick Carter

NORTHAMPTON CHRONICLE & ECHO
Northamptonshire Newspapers Ltd, Upper Mounts, Northampton NN1 3HR **T** 01604-467000
Editor, David Summers

NOTTINGHAM EVENING POST
Castle Wharf House, Nottingham NG1 7EU **T** 0115-948 2000
W www.thisisnottingham.co.uk
Editor, Malcolm Pheby

PETERBOROUGH EVENING TELEGRAPH
Telegraph House, 57 Priesgate, Peterborough PE1 1JW
T 01733 555111 **W** www.peterboroughtoday.co.uk
Editor, Mark Edwards

LONDON

LONDON EVENING STANDARD LTD
Northcliffe House, 2 Derry Street, London W8 5EE
T 020-7367 7000 **W** www.thisislondon.com
Editor, Geordie Greig

LONDON LITE
Northcliffe House, 2 Derry Street, London W8 5TT
T 020-7938 6000 **W** www.thelondonlite.co.uk
Editor, Martin Clarke

METRO
Northcliffe House, 2 Derry Street, London W8 5TT
T 020-7651 5200 **W** www.metro.co.uk
Editor, Kenny Campbell

NORTH EAST

EVENING CHRONICLE
NCJ Media Ltd, Groat Market, Newcastle upon Tyne NE1 1ED
T 0191-232 7500 **W** www.chroniclelive.co.uk
Editor, Paul Robertson

EVENING GAZETTE
Gazette Media Company Ltd, 105–111 Borough Road, Middlesbrough TS1 3AZ **T** 01642-245401
W www.gazettelive.co.uk
Editor, Sue Giles

HARTLEPOOL MAIL
Northeast Press Ltd, New Clarence House, Wesley Square, Hartlepool TS24 8BX **T** 01429-239333
W www.hartlepoolmail.co.uk, www.peterleemail.co.uk
Editor, Joy Yates

THE JOURNAL
Groat Market, Newcastle upon Tyne NE1 1ED **T** 0191-232 7500
W www.icnewcastle.co.uk
Editor, Brian Aitken

THE NORTHERN ECHO
Priestgate, Darlington, Co. Durham DL1 1NF **T** 01325-381313
W www.thenorthernecho.co.uk
Editor, Peter Barron

THE SHIELDS GAZETTE
Chapter Row, South Shields, Tyne & Wear NE33 1BL
T 0191-427 4800 **W** www.shieldsgazette.com
Editor, John Szymanski

SUNDERLAND ECHO
Echo House, Pennywell, Sunderland, Tyne & Wear SR4 9ER
T 0191-501 5800 **W** www.sunderlandecho.com
Editor, Rob Lawson

NORTH WEST

THE BLACKPOOL GAZETTE
Avroe House, Avroe Crescent, Blackpool Business Park, Squires Gate, Blackpool FY4 2DP **T** 01253-400888
W www.blackpoolgazette.co.uk
Editor, David Helliwell

THE BOLTON NEWS
Newspaper House, Churchgate, Bolton, Lancs BL1 1DE
T 01204-522345 **W** www.theboltonnews.co.uk
Editor, Ian Savage

LANCASHIRE EVENING POST
Oliver's Place, Preston PR2 9ZA **T** 01772-254841
W www.lep.co.uk
Editor, Simon Reynolds

LANCASHIRE TELEGRAPH
Newspaper House, High Street, Blackburn, Lancs BB1 1HT
T 01254 678678 **W** www.lancashiretelegraph.co.uk
Editor, Ian Singleton

LIVERPOOL DAILY POST
PO Box 48, Old Hall Street, Liverpool L69 3EB **T** 0151-227 2000
W www.liverpooldailypost.co.uk
Editor, Mark Thomas

LIVERPOOL ECHO
PO Box 48, Old Hall Street, Liverpool L69 3EB **T** 0151-227 2000
W www.liverpoolecho.co.uk
Editor, Alastair Machray

MANCHESTER EVENING NEWS
1 Scott Place, Hardman Street, Manchester M3 3RN
T 0161-832 7200 **W** www.manchestereveningnews.co.uk
Editor, Paul Horrocks

NEWS AND STAR
CN Group, Newspaper House, Dalston Road, Carlisle CA2 5UA
T 01228-612600 **W** www.news-and-star.co.uk
Editor, Neil Hodgkinson

NORTH-WEST EVENING MAIL
Newspaper House, Abbey Road, Barrow-in-Furness, Cumbria LA14 5QS T 01229-840150 W www.nwemail.co.uk
Editor, Jonathan Lee

OLDHAM EVENING CHRONICLE
PO Box 47, Union Street, Oldham, Lancs OL1 1EQ
T 0161-633 2121 W www.oldham-chronicle.co.uk
Editor, Jim Williams

SOUTH

THE ARGUS
Argus House, Crowhurst Road, Hollingbury, Brighton BN1 8AR
T 01273-544544 W www.theargus.co.uk
Editor, Michael Beard

ECHO
Newspaper House, Chester Hall Lane, Basildon, Essex SS14 3BL
T 01268-522792 W www.echo-news.co.uk
Editor, Martin McNeill

MEDWAY MESSENGER
Medway House, Ginsbury Close, Sir Thomas Longley Road, Medway City Estate, Strood, Kent ME2 4DU
T 01634-227800 W www.kentonline.co.uk
Editor, Bob Bounds

THE NEWS, PORTSMOUTH
The News Centre, London Road, Hilsea, Portsmouth PO2 9SX
T 023-9266 4488 W www.portsmouth.co.uk
Editor, Mark Waldron

OXFORD MAIL
Newspaper House, Osney Mead, Oxford OX2 0EJ
T 01865-425262 W www.oxfordmail.co.uk
Editor, Simon O'Neill

READING EVENING POST
8 Tessa Road, Reading, Berks RG1 8NS T 0118-918 3000
W www.getreading.co.uk
Editor, Andy Murrill

THE SOUTHERN DAILY ECHO
Newspaper House, Test Lane, Redbridge, Southampton SO16 9JX T 023-8042 4777 W www.dailyecho.co.uk
Editor, Ian Murray

SWINDON ADVERTISER
100 Victoria Road, Old Town, Swindon SN1 3BE
T 01793-528144 W www.swindonadvertiser.co.uk
Editor, Dave King

SOUTH WEST

BRISTOL EVENING POST
Temple Way, Old Market, Bristol BS99 7HD T 0117-934 3000
W www.thisisbristol.co.uk
Editor, Mike Norton

THE CITIZEN
1 Clarence Parade, Cheltenham GL50 3NY T 01242-271900
W www.thisisgloucestershire.co.uk
Editor, Ian Mean

DAILY ECHO
Richmond Hill, Bournemouth BH2 6HH T 01202-554601
W www.bournemouthecho.co.uk
Editor, Neal Butterworth

DORSET ECHO
Fleet House, Hampshire Road, Weymouth, Dorset DT4 9XD
T 01305-830930 W www.dorsetecho.co.uk
Editor, Toby Granville

EVENING HERALD
17 Brest Road, Derriford Business Park, Plymouth PL6 5AA
T 01752-765500 W www.thisisplymouth.co.uk
Editor, Bill Martin

EXPRESS & ECHO
Express & Echo News & Media, Heron Road, Sowton, Exeter EX2 7NF T 01392-442211 W www.thisisexeter.co.uk
Editor, Marc Astley

GLOUCESTERSHIRE ECHO
1 Clarence Parade, Cheltenham, Glos GL50 3NY
T 01242-271900 W www.thisisgloucestershire.co.uk
Editor, Kevan Blackadder

THE HERALD
17 Brest Road, Derriford Business Park, Plymouth PL6 5AA
T 01752-765500 W www.thisisplymouth.co.uk
Editor, Bill Martin

HERALD EXPRESS
Harmsworth House, Barton Hill Road, Torquay, Devon TQ2 8JN
T 01803-676000 W www.thisissouthdevon.co.uk
Editor, Andy Phelan

WESTERN DAILY PRESS
Bristol Evening Post and Press Ltd, Temple Way, Bristol BS99 7HD T 0117-934 3000
W www.westerndailypress.co.uk
Editor, Andy Wright

THE WESTERN MORNING NEWS
17 Brest Road, Derriford, Plymouth PL6 5AA T 01752-765500
W www.thisiswesternmorningnews.co.uk
Editor, Alan Qualtrough

WEST MIDLANDS

BIRMINGHAM MAIL
6th Floor, Fort Dunlop, Fort Parkway, Birmingham B24 9FF
T 0121-236 3366 W www.birminghammail.net
Editor, Steve Dyson

THE BIRMINGHAM POST
6th Floor, Fort Dunlop, Fort Parkway, Birmingham B24 9FF
T 0121-236 3366 W www.birminghampost.net
Editor, Marc Reeves

COVENTRY TELEGRAPH
Corporation Street, Coventry CV1 1FP T 024-7663 3633
W www.coventrytelegraph.net
Editor, David Brookes

EXPRESS & STAR
Queen Street, Wolverhampton WV1 1ES T 01902-313131
W www.expressandstar.com
Editor, Adrian Faber

THE SENTINEL
Staffordshire Sentinel News & Media Ltd, Sentinel House, Etruria, Stoke-on-Trent ST1 5SS T 01782-602525
W www.thisisthesentinel.co.uk
Editor, Michael Sassi

SHROPSHIRE STAR
Waterloo Road, Ketley, Telford TF1 5HU T 01952-242424
W www.shropshirestar.com
Editor, Sarah Jane Smith

WORCESTER NEWS
Berrows House, Hylton Road, Worcester WR2 5JX
T 01905-748200 W www.worcesternews.co.uk
Editor, Kevin Ward

YORKSHIRE AND HUMBERSIDE

EVENING COURIER
PO Box 19, King Cross Street, Halifax HX1 2SF T 01422-260200
W www.halifaxcourier.co.uk
Editor, John Furbisher

EVENING NEWS
17–23 Aberdeen Walk, Scarborough, North Yorkshire YO11 1BB T 01723-363636
W www.scarborougheveningnews.co.uk
Editor, Ed Asquith

GRIMSBY TELEGRAPH
80 Cleethorpe Road, Grimsby, North East Lincolnshire DN31 3EH T 01472-360360 W www.thisisgrimsby.co.uk
Editor, Michelle Lalor

THE HUDDERSFIELD DAILY EXAMINER
Trinity Mirror Huddersfield Ltd, Queen Street South, Huddersfield HD1 3DU **T** 01484-430000
W www.examiner.co.uk
Editor, Roy Wright

HULL DAILY MAIL
Blundell's Corner, Beverley Road, Hull HU3 1XS
T 01482-327111 **W** www.thisishullandeastriding.co.uk
Editor, Rick Lyon

LINCOLNSHIRE ECHO
Brayford Wharf East, Lincoln LN5 7AT **T** 01522-820000
W www.thisislincolnshire.co.uk
Editor, Jon Grubb

THE PRESS
Newsquest York, PO Box 29, 76–86 Walmgate, York YO1 9YN
T 01904-653051 **W** www.yorkpress.co.uk
Editor, Kevin Booth

THE STAR
York Street, Sheffield S1 1PU **T** 0114-276 7676
W www.thestar.co.uk
Editor, Alan Powell

TELEGRAPH & ARGUS
Hall Ings, Bradford BD1 1JR **T** 01274-729511
W www.thetelegraphandargus.co.uk
Editor, Perry Austin-Clarke

YORKSHIRE EVENING POST
PO Box 168, Wellington Street, Leeds LS1 1RF **T** 0113-243 2701
W www.yorkshireeveningpost.co.uk
Editor, Paul Napier

YORKSHIRE POST
Wellington Street, Leeds LS1 1RF **T** 0113-243 2701
W www.yorkshirepost.co.uk
Editor, Peter Charlton

SCOTLAND

THE COURIER
D.C. Thomson & Co. Ltd, 80 Kingsway East, Dundee DD4 8SL
T 01382-223131 **W** www.thecourier.co.uk
Editor, Bill Hutcheon

DUNDEE EVENING TELEGRAPH AND POST
80 Kingsway East, Dundee DD4 8SL **T** 01382-223131
W www.eveningtelegraph.co.uk
Editor, Gordon Wishart

EVENING EXPRESS
Aberdeen Journals Ltd, PO Box 43, Lang Stracht, Mastrick, Aberdeen AB15 6DF **T** 01224-690222
W www.eveningexpress.co.uk
Editor, Damian Bates

EVENING NEWS
108 Holyrood Road, Edinburgh EH8 8AS **T** 0131-620 8620
W www.edinburghnews.com
Editor, John McLellan

GLASGOW EVENING TIMES
200 Renfield Street, Glasgow G2 3QB **T** 0141-302 7000
W www.eveningtimes.co.uk
Editor, Donald Martin

INVERNESS COURIER
New Century House, Stadium Road, Inverness IV1 1FF
T 01463-233059 **W** www.inverness-courier.co.uk
Editor, Robert Taylor

PAISLEY DAILY EXPRESS
Scottish and Universal Newspapers Ltd, 14 New Street, Paisley, Renfrewshire PA1 1YA **T** 0141-887 7911
W www.paisleydailyexpress.co.uk
Editor, Anne Dalrymple

THE PRESS AND JOURNAL
Lang Stracht, Aberdeen AB15 6DF **T** 01224-690222
W www.pressandjournal.co.uk
Editor, Derek Tucker

WALES

EVENING LEADER
NWN Media Ltd, Mold Business Park, Wrexham Road, Mold, Flintshire CH7 1XY **T** 01352-707707
W www.eveningleader.co.uk
Editor, Barrie Jones

SOUTH WALES ARGUS
South Wales Argus, Cardiff Road, Maesglas, Newport, Gwent NP20 3QN **T** 01633-777219
W www.southwalesargus.co.uk
Editor, Gerry Keighley

SOUTH WALES ECHO
6 Park Street, Cardiff CF10 1XR **T** 029-2058 3622
W www.walesonline.co.uk
Editor, Mike Hill

SOUTH WALES EVENING POST
PO Box 14, Adelaide Street, Swansea SA1 1QT
T 01792-510000 **W** www.thisissouthwales.co.uk
Editor-in-Chief, Spencer Feeney

WESTERN MAIL
6 Park Street, Cardiff CF10 1XR **T** 029-2058 3583
W www.walesonline.co.uk
Editor, Alan Edmunds

NORTHERN IRELAND

BELFAST TELEGRAPH
124–144 Royal Avenue, Belfast BT1 1EB **T** 028-9026 4000
W www.belfasttelegraph.co.uk
Editor, Martin Lindsay

IRISH NEWS
113–117 Donegall Street, Belfast BT1 2GE **T** 028-9032 2226
W www.irishnews.com
Editor, Noel Doran

NEWS LETTER
2 Esky Drive, Portadown, Craigavon, Belfast BT63 5YY
T 028-3839 3939 **W** www.newsletter.co.uk
Editor, Darwin Templeton

CHANNEL ISLANDS

GUERNSEY PRESS AND STAR
PO Box 57, Braye Road, Vale, Guernsey GY1 3BW
T 01481-240240 **W** www.guernseypress.com
Editor, Richard Digard

JERSEY EVENING POST
PO Box 582, Five Oaks, St Saviour, Jersey JE4 8XQ
T 01534-611611 **W** www.thisisjersey.com
Editor, Chris Bright

PERIODICALS

ACCOUNTANCY AGE
32–34 Broadwick Street, London W1A 2HG **T** 020-7316 9000
W www.accountancyage.com
Editor, Gavin Hinks

ACCOUNTING & BUSINESS
Association of Chartered Certified Accountants, 10–11 Lincolns Inn Fields, London WC2A 3BP **T** 020-7059 5966
W www.accaglobal.com
Editor, Chris Quick

AEROPLANE MONTHLY
The Blue Fin Building, 110 Southwark Street, London SE1 0SU
T 020-3148 4100 **W** www.aeroplanemonthly.com
Editor, Michael Oakey

AESTHETICA MAGAZINE
PO Box 371, York YO23 1WL **T** 0844-568 2001
W www.aestheticamagazine.com
Editor, Cherie Federico

AFRICA CONFIDENTIAL
73 Farringdon Road, London EC1M 3JQ T 020-7831 3511
W www.africa-confidential.com
Editor, Patrick Smith

ALL OUT CRICKET
The Brit Oval, Kennington, London SE11 5SS T 020-7820 4190
W www.alloutcricket.com
Editor, Andy Afford

AMATEUR PHOTOGRAPHER
The Blue Fin Building, 110 Southwark Street, London SE1 0SU
T 020-3148 5000 W www.amateurphotographer.co.uk
Editor, Damien Demolder

AMBIT
17 Priory Gardens, London N6 5QY T 020-8340 3566
W www.ambitmagazine.co.uk
Editors, Martin Bax and Kate Pemberton

ANGLING TIMES
Bushfield House, Orton Centre, Peterborough PE2 5UW
T 01733-232600 W www.anglingtimes.co.uk
Editor, Richard Lee

THE ARCHITECTURAL REVIEW
Greater London House, Hampstead Road, London NW1 7EJ
T 020-7728 4591 W www.arplus.com
Editor-in-Chief, Kieran Long

ARCHITECTURE TODAY
161 Rosebery Avenue, London EC1R 4QX T 020-7837 0143
W www.architecturetoday.co.uk
Editor, Ian Latham

ART MONTHLY
4th Floor, 28 Charing Cross Road, London WC2H 0DB
T 020-7240 0389 W www.artmonthly.co.uk
Editor, Patricia Bickers

THE ART NEWSPAPER
70 South Lambeth Road, London SW8 1RL T 020-7735 3331
W www.theartnewspaper.com
Editor, Jane Morris

ART REVIEW
1 Sekforde Street, London EC1R 0BE T 020-7107 2760
W www.artreview.com
Editor, Mark Rappolt

ARTISTS AND ILLUSTRATORS
26–30 Old Church Street, London SW3 5BY T 020-7349 3150
W www.artistsandillustrators.co.uk
Editor, Lynn Parr

ASTRONOMY NOW
PO Box 175, Tonbridge, Kent TN10 4ZY T 01732-446110
W www.astronomynow.com
Editor, Keith Cooper

ATTITUDE
Ground Floor, 211 Old Street, London EC1V 9NR
T 020-7608 6446 W www.attitude.co.uk
Editor, Matthew Todd

THE BEANO
D.C. Thomson & Co. Ltd, 80 Kingsway East, Dundee DD4 8SL
W www.beanotown.co.uk
Editor, Alan Digby

THE BIG ISSUE
1–5 Wandsworth Road, London SW8 2LN T 020-7526 3200
W www.bigissue.com
Editor-in-Chief, John Bird

BIKE
Media House, Lynchwood, Peterborough PE2 6EA
T 01733-468181 W www.bikemagazine.co.uk
Editor, Steve Rose

BIRDWATCH
The Chocolate Factory, 5 Clarendon Road, London N22 6XJ
T 020-8881 0550 W www.birdwatch.co.uk
Editor, Dominic Mitchell

BIZARRE
30 Cleveland Street, London W1T 4JD T 020-7907 6000
W www.bizarremag.com
Editor, David McComb

BMA NEWS
British Medical Association, BMA House, Tavistock Square, London WC1H 9JP T 020-7383 6122
Editors, Caroline Winter-Jones and Carol Harris

THE BOOKSELLER
5th Floor, Endeavour House, 189 Shaftesbury Avenue, London WC2H 8TJ T 020-7420 6006 W www.thebookseller.com
Editor-in-Chief, Neill Denny

BRITISH CHESS MAGAZINE
44 Baker Street, London W1U 7RT T 020-7486 8222
W www.bcmchess.co.uk
Editor, John Saunders

THE BRITISH JOURNAL OF PHOTOGRAPHY
32–34 Broadwick Street, London W1A 2HG T 020-7316 9000
W www.bjp-online.com
Editor, Simon Bainbridge

BRITISH JOURNALISM REVIEW
Sage Publications, 1 Oliver's Yard, 55 City Road, London EC1Y 1SP T 020-7324 8500 W www.bjr.org.uk
Editor, Bill Hagerty

BRITISH MEDICAL JOURNAL
BMA House, Tavistock Square, London WC1H 9JR
T 020-7387 4499 W www.bmj.com
Editor, Dr Fiona Godlee

BRITISH PHILATELIC BULLETIN
Royal Mail, 35–50 Rathbone Place, London W1T 1HQ
W www.royalmail.com/stamps
Editor, J. R. Holman

BUILDING DESIGN
The Builder Group, Ludgate House, 245 Blackfriars Road, London SE1 9UY T 020-7921 5000 W www.bdonline.co.uk
Editor, Amanda Baillieu

CANALS & RIVERS
PO Box 618, Norwich NR7 0QT T 01603-708930
W www.canalsandrivers.co.uk
Editor, Chris Cattrall

CAR
3rd Floor, Media House, Lynchwood, Peterborough PE2 6EA
T 01733-468379 W www.carmagazine.co.uk
Editor, Phil McNamara

CARING BUSINESS
Ludgate House, 245 Blackfriars Road, London SE1 9UY
T 020-7921 5002 W www.caringbusiness.co.uk
Editor, Olufunmi Majekodunmi

CHURCH TIMES
13–17 Long Lane, London EC1A 9DJ T 020-7776 1060
W www.churchtimes.co.uk
Editor, Paul Handley

CLASSIC CARS
Media House, Lynchwood, Peterborough Business Park, Peterborough PE2 6EA T 01733-468582
W www.classiccarsmagazine.co.uk
Editor, Phil Bell

CLASSIC ROCK
30 Monmouth Street, Bath BA1 2BW T 01225-442244
W www.classicrockmagazine.com
Editor, Scott Rowley

CLASSICAL MUSIC
241 Shaftesbury Avenue, London WC2H 8TF T 020-7333 1742
W www.rhinegold.co.uk
Editor, Keith Clarke

CLIMB MAGAZINE
PO Box 21, Buxton, Derbyshire SK17 9BR T 01298-72801
W www.climbmagazine.com
Editor, Neil Pearsons

:OIN NEWS
›ken Publishing Ltd, Orchard House, Duchy Road, Heathpark, Honiton, Devon EX14 1YD **T** 01404-46972 **W** www.tokenpublishing.com
Editor, John W. Mussell

:OMMUNITY CARE
uadrant House, The Quadrant, Sutton, Surrey SM2 5AS **T** 020-8652 3500 **W** www.communitycare.co.uk
Editor, Mike Broad

:OMPUTER WEEKLY
uadrant House, The Quadrant, Sutton, Surrey SM2 5AS **T** 020-8652 8642 **W** www.computerweekly.com
Editor, Brian McKenna

:ONDÉ NAST TRAVELLER
ogue House, Hanover Square, London W1S 1JU **T** 020-7499 9080 **W** www.cntraveller.com
Editor, Sarah Miller

:ONTEMPORARY
tudio 56, 4 Montpelier Street, London SW7 1EE **T** 020-7019 6205 **W** www.contemporary-magazine.com
Editor, Brian Muller

:ONTEMPORARY REVIEW
O Box 1242, Oxford OX1 4FJ **T** 01865-201529 **W** www.contemporaryreview.co.uk
Editor, Dr Richard Mullen

:OSMOPOLITAN
lational Magazine House, 72 Broadwick Street, London W1F 9EP **T** 020-7439 5000 **W** www.cosmopolitan.co.uk
:ditor-in-Chief, Louise Court

:OUNTRY LIFE
he Blue Fin Building, 110 Southwark Street, London SE1 0SU **T** 020-3148 4428 **W** www.countrylife.co.uk
Editor, Mark Hedges

:YCLING WEEKLY
eon House, 233 High Street, Croydon CR9 1HZ **T** 020-8726 8462 **W** www.cyclingweekly.co.uk
Editor, Robert Garbutt

)ANCING TIMES
.5–47 Clerkenwell Green, London EC1R 0EB **T** 020-7250 3006 **W** www.dancing-times.co.uk
Editor, Jonathan Gray

)ARTS WORLD
1 Selwood Road, Croydon CR0 7JW **T** 020-8650 6580 **W** www.dartsworld.com
Editor, Tony Wood

)IGITAL CAMERA
0 Monmouth Street, Bath BA1 2BW **T** 01225-442244 **W** www.dcmag.co.uk
Editor, Marcus Hawkins

)ISABILITY NOW
Market Road, London N7 9PW **T** 020-7619 7323 **W** www.disabilitynow.org.uk
Acting Editor, John Pring

:ASTERN EYE
thnic Media Group, Unit 2, 65 Whitechapel Road, London E1 1DU **T** 020-7650 2000 **W** www.easterneyeonline.co.uk
Editor, Hamant Verma

THE ECOLOGIST
Jnit 102, Lana House Studios, 116–118 Commercial Street, London E1 6NF **T** 020-7422 8100 **W** www.theecologist.org
Editor, Pat Thomas

THE ECONOMIST
5 St James's Street, London SW1A 1HG **T** 020-7830 7000 **W** www.economist.com
Editor, John Micklethwait

:MPIRE
Aappin House, 4 Winsley Street, London W1W 8HF **T** 020-7182 8000 **W** www.empireonline.com
Editor, Mark Dinning

THE ENGINEER
St Giles House, 50 Poland Street, London W1F 7AX **T** 020-7970 4000 **W** www.theengineer.com
Editor, Andrew Lee

ESQUIRE
National Magazine House, 72 Broadwick Street, London W1F 9EP **T** 020-7439 5601 **W** www.esquire.co.uk
Editor, Jeremy Langmead

ESSENTIALS
The Blue Fin Building, 110 Southwark Street, London SE1 0SU **T** 020-3148 7211
Editor, Jules Barton-Breck

FAMILY TREE MAGAZINE
61 Great Whyte, Ramsey, Huntingdon, Cambs PE26 1HJ **T** 01487-814050 **W** www.family-tree.co.uk
Editor, Helen Tovey

FARMERS WEEKLY
Quadrant House, The Quadrant, Sutton, Surrey SM2 5AS **T** 020-8652 4911 **W** www.fwi.co.uk
Editor, Jane King

THE FEMINIST REVIEW
Brunel Road, Houndmills, Basingstoke, Hants RG21 6XS **T** 01256-329242 **W** www.feminist-review.com
Editors, a collective

FHM (FOR HIM MAGAZINE)
Mappin House, 4 Winsley Street, London W1W 8HF **T** 020 7182 8028 **W** www.fhm.com
Editor, Anthony Noguera

THE FIELD
The Blue Fin Building, 110 Southwark Street, London SE1 0SU **T** 020-3148 5000 **W** www.thefield.co.uk
Editor, Jonathan Young

FOLIO
2nd Floor, Bristol News and Media, Temple Way, Bristol BS99 7HD **T** 0117-942 8491 **W** www.foliomagazine.co.uk
Editor, Rachel Nott

FORTEAN TIMES
Box 2409, London NW5 4NP **T** 020-7907 6235 **W** www.forteantimes.com
Editor, David Sutton

FORTNIGHT
11 University Road, Belfast BT7 1NA **T** 028-9023 2353 **W** www.fortnight.org
Editor, Rudie Goldsmith

FOURFOURTWO
Haymarket, Teddington Studios, Broom Road, Teddington, Middlesex TW11 9BE **T** 020-8267 5061 **W** www.fourfourtwo.magazine.co.uk
Editor-in-Chief, Hugh Sleight

GAMES MASTER
30 Monmouth Street, Bath BA1 2BW **T** 01225-442244
Editor-in-Chief, Robin Alway

GAY TIMES (GT)
Spectrum House, 32–34 Gordon House Road, London NW5 1LP **T** 020-7424 7400 **W** www.gaytimes.co.uk
Editor, Joseph Galliano

GEOGRAPHICAL JOURNAL
Royal Geographical Society, 1 Kensington Gore, London SW7 2AR **T** 020-7591 3026 **W** www.rgs.org
Editor, Prof. John Briggs

GLAMOUR
6–8 Old Bond Street, London W1S 4PH **T** 020-7499 9080 **W** www.glamourmagazine.com
Editor, Jo Elvin

GOLF WORLD
Media House, Lynchwood, Peterborough Business Park, Peterborough PE2 6EA **T** 01733-468000 **W** www.todaysgolfer.co.uk/golfworld
Editor, Chris Jones

GOOD HOUSEKEEPING
National Magazine House, 72 Broadwick Street, London W1F 9EP T 020-7439 5000
W www.goodhousekeeping.co.uk
Editorial Director, Lindsay Nicholson

GQ
Vogue House, Hanover Square, London W1S 1JU
T 020-7499 9080 W www.gq-magazine.co.uk
Editor, Dylan Jones

GRANTA
12 Addison Avenue, London W11 4QR T 020-7605 1360
W www.granta.com
Editor, Alex Clark

GREEN FUTURES
Overseas House, 19–23 Ironmonger Row, London EC1V 3QN
W www.greenfutures.org.uk
Editor-in-Chief, Martin Wright

GROW YOUR OWN
25 Phoenix Court, Hawkins Road, Colchester CO2 8JY
T 01206-505979 W www.growfruitandveg.co.uk
Editor, Lucy Halsall

GUITARIST
30 Monmouth Street, Bath BA1 2BW T 01225-442244
W www.futurenet.co.uk
Editor, Michael Leonard

HARPER'S BAZAAR
National Magazine House, 72 Broadwick Street, London W1F 9EP T 020-7439 5000 W www.natmags.co.uk
Editor, Lucy Yeomans

HEALTHY
Victory House, 14 Leicester Place, London WC2H 7BZ
T 020-7306 0304 W www.healthy-magazine.co.uk
Editor, Heather Beresford

HEAT
Endeavour House, 189 Shaftesbury Avenue, London WC2H 8JG T 020-7859 8657 W www.heatworld.com
Editor, Julian Linley

HELLO!
Wellington House, 69–71 Upper Ground, London SE1 9PQ
T 020-7667 8700 W www.hellomagazine.com
Editor-in-Chief, Eduardo Sanchez Perez

HISTORY TODAY
20 Old Compton Street, London W1D 4TW T 020-7534 8000
W www.historytoday.com
Editor, Paul Lay

HOMES AND GARDENS
The Blue Fin Building, 110 Southwark Street, London SE1 0SU
T 020-3148 5000 W www.homesandgardens.com
Editor, Deborah Barker

HORSE & HOUND
9th Floor, The Blue Fin Building, 110 Southwark Street, London SE1 0SU T 020-3148 4562 W www.horseandhound.co.uk
Editor, Lucy Higginson

HOUSE & GARDEN
Vogue House, 1 Hanover Square, London W1S 1JU
T 020-7499 9080 W www.houseandgarden.co.uk
Editor, Susan Crewe

ICON MAGAZINE
Media 10, National House, High Street, Epping, Essex CM16 4BD T 01992-570030 W www.iconeye.com
Editor, Justin McGuirk

IN STYLE
9th Floor, The Blue Fin Building, 110 Southwark Street, London SE1 0SU T 020-3148 5000 W www.instyle.com
Editor, Eilidh MacAskill

INTERNATIONAL AFFAIRS
The Royal Institute of International Affairs, Chatham House, 10 St James's Square, London SW1Y 4LE T 020-7957 5728
Editor, Caroline Soper

JEWISH CHRONICLE
25 Furnival Street, London EC4A 1JT T 020-7415 1500
W www.thejc.com
Editor, Stephen Pollard

KERRANG!
Mappin House, 4 Winsley Street, London W1W 8HF
T 020-7436 1515 W www.kerrang.com
Editor, Paul Brannigan

LANCET
32 Jamestown Road, London NW1 7BY T 020-7424 4910
W www.thelancet.com
Editor, Dr Richard Horton

THE LAWYER
St Giles House, 50 Poland Street, London W1F 7AX
T 020-7970 4000 W www.thelawyer.com
Editor, Catrin Griffiths

LEGAL WEEK
32–34 Broadwick Street, London W1A 2HG T 020-7316 9000
W www.legalweek.com
Editor, Alex Novarese

THE LIST
14 High Street, Edinburgh EH1 1TE T 0131-550 3050
W www.list.co.uk
Editor, Claire Prentice

THE LITERARY REVIEW
44 Lexington Street, London W1F 0LW T 020-7437 9392
W www.literaryreview.co.uk
Editor, Nancy Sladek

THE LONDON MAGAZINE: A REVIEW OF LITERATURE AND THE ARTS
32 Addison Grove, London W4 1ER
W www.thelondonmagazine.net
Editor, Sara-Mae Tuson

LONDON REVIEW OF BOOKS
28 Little Russell Street, London WC1A 2HN T 020-7209 1101
W www.lrb.co.uk
Editor, Mary-Kay Wilmers

MACWORLD
101 Euston Road, London NW1 2RA T 020-7756 2800
W www.macworld.co.uk
Editor, Karen Haslam

MARIE CLAIRE
7th Floor, The Blue Fin Building, 110 Southwark Street, London SE1 0SU T 020-3148 7513 W www.marieclaire.co.uk
Editor, Trish Halpin

MAXIM
30 Cleveland Street, London W1T 4JD T 020-7907 6410
W www.maxim.co.uk
Editor, Ben Raworth

MEDIA WEEK
174 Hammersmith Road, London W6 7JP T 020-8267 8026
W www.mediaweek.co.uk
Editor, Steve Barrett

MEN'S HEALTH
33 Broadwick Street, London W1F 0DQ T 020-7339 4400
W www.menshealth.co.uk
Editor, Morgan Rees

MIXMAG
Development Hell Ltd, 90–92 Pentonville Road, London N1 9HS
T 020-7078-8400 W www.mixmag.net
Editor, Nick DeCosemo

MOJO
Mappin House, 4 Winsley Street, London W1W 8HF
T 020-7436 1515 W www.mojo4music.com
Editor, Phil Alexander

MONEYWISE
Standon House, 21 Mansell Street, London E1 8AA
T 020-7680 3600 W www.moneywise.co.uk
Editor, Rachel Lacey

MORE!
Endeavour House, 189 Shaftesbury Avenue, London WC2H 8JG T 020-7208 3165 W www.moremagazine.co.uk
Editor, Lisa Smosarski

MOTHER & BABY
Endeavour House, 189 Shaftsbury Avenue, London WC2H 8JG T 020-7347 1869 W www.motherandbabymagazine.com
Editor, Miranda Levy

MUSIC WEEK
CMPi, 1st Floor, Ludgate House, 245 Blackfriars Road, London SE1 9LS W www.musicweek.com
Editor, Paul Williams

THE NATIONAL TRUST MAGAZINE
Heelis, Kemble Drive, Swindon SN2 2NA T 01793-817400
W www.nationaltrust.org.uk
Editor, Sue Herdman

NATURE
The Macmillan Building, 4 Crinan Street, London N1 9XW
T 020-7833 4000 W www.nature.com/nature
Editor, Philip Campbell

NB MAGAZINE
RNIB, 105 Judd Street, London WC1H 9NE T 020-7391 2070
W www.rnib.org.uk
Editor, Ann Lee

NEW HUMANIST
1 Gower Street, London WC1E 6HD T 020-7436 1171
W www.newhumanist.org.uk
Editor, Caspar Melville

NEW INTERNATIONALIST
55 Rectory Road, Oxford OX4 1BW T 01865-811400
W www.newint.org
Editors, Vanessa Baird, Chris Brazier, Wayne Ellwood, Dinyar Godrej, Adam Ma'anit, David Ransom and Jess Worth

NEW LAW JOURNAL
Halsbury House, 35 Chancery Lane, London WC2A 1EL
T 020-7400 2500 W www.newlawjournal.co.uk
Editor, Jan Miller

NEW MUSICAL EXPRESS (NME)
The Blue Fin Building, 110 Southwark Street, London SE1 0SU
T 020-3148 5000 W www.nme.com
Editor, Conor McNicholas

NEW SCIENTIST
Lacon House, 84 Theobalds Road, London WC1X 8NS
T 020-7611 1200 W www.newscientist.com
Editor, Jeremy Webb

NEW STATESMAN
1st Floor, Boundary House, 91–93 Charterhouse Street, London EC1M 6HR T 020-7730 3444 W www.newstatesman.com
Managing Editor, Sue Matthias

THE NEWSPAPER
PO Box 400, Bridgwater TA6 9DT T 0845-094 0646
W www.thenewspaper.org.uk
Managing Editor, Phil Wood

NOW
The Blue Fin Building, 110 Southwark Street, London SE1 0SU
T 020-3148 5000 W www.nowmagazine.co.uk
Editor, Abigail Blackburn

OK!
Northern & Shell Building, 10 Lower Thames Street, London EC3R 6EN T 0871-434 1010 W www.ok.co.uk
Editor, Lisa Byrne

THE OLDIE
65 Newman Street, London W1T 3EG T 020-7436 8801
W www.theoldie.co.uk
Editor, Richard Ingrams

OPERA
36 Black Lion Lane, London W6 9BE T 020-8563 8893
W www.opera.co.uk
Editor, John Allison

PC ADVISOR
101 Euston Road, London NW1 2RA T 020-7756 2800
W www.pcadvisor.co.uk
Editor, Paul Trotter

PC PRO
30 Cleveland Street, London W1T 4JD T 020-7907 6000
W www.pcpro.co.uk
Editor, Tim Danton

PEACE NEWS
5 Caledonian Road, London N1 9DY T 020-7278 3344
W www.peacenews.info
Editors, Milan Rai and Emily Johns

THE PHOTOGRAPHER
The British Institute of Professional Photography, 18 Dove Close, Bishops Stortford CM23 4JD T 01279-503871
W www.bipp.com
Editor, Steve Hynes

POETRY LONDON
81 Lambeth Walk, London SE11 6DX T 020-7735 8880
W www.poetrylondon.co.uk
Editors, Maurice Riordan, Scott Verner, Martha Kapos, Tim Dooley

POETRY REVIEW
22 Betterton Street, London WC2H 9BX T 020-7420 9883
W www.poetrysociety.org.uk
Editor, Fiona Sampson

THE POLITICAL QUARTERLY
9600 Garsington Road, Oxford OX4 2DQ T 01865-776868
W www.politicalquarterly.com
Editors, Andrew Gamble and Tony Wright MP

PRACTICAL PARENTING
15–18 White Lion Street, Islington, London N1 9PD
T 020-7843 8800 W www.practicalparenting.co.uk
Editor, Susie Boone

PRESS GAZETTE
Brunel House, 55–57 North Wharf Road, London W2 1LA
T 020-7753 4291 W www.pressgazette.co.uk
Editor, Dominic Ponsford

PRIDE
Pride House, 55 Battersea Bridge Road, London SW11 3AX
T 020-7228 3110 W www.pridemagazine.com
Publisher, C. Cushnie

PRIVATE EYE
6 Carlisle Street, London W1D 3BN T 020-7437 4017
W www.private-eye.co.uk
Editor, Ian Hislop

PROSPECT MAGAZINE
2 Bloomsbury Place, London WC1A 2QA T 020-7255 1281
W www.prospect-magazine.co.uk
Editor, David Goodhart

PSYCHOLOGIES
64 North Row, London W1K 7LL T 020-7150 7000
W www.psychologies.co.uk
Editor, Maureen Rice

PULSE
CMP Medica Ltd, Ludgate House, 245 Blackfriars Road, London SE1 9UY **T** 020-7921 8102 **W** www.pulsetoday.co.uk
Editor, Jo Haynes

Q MAGAZINE
Mappin House, 4 Winsley Street, London W1W 8HF **T** 020-7182 8000 **W** www.q4music.com
Editor, Paul Rees

RA MAGAZINE
Royal Academy of Arts, Burlington House, Piccadilly, London W1J 0BD **T** 020-7300 5820 **W** www.ramagazine.org.uk
Editor, Sarah Greenberg

RACING POST
Floor 23, 1 Canada Square, Canary Wharf, London E14 5AP **T** 020-7293 3000 **W** www.racingpost.com
Editor, Bruce Millington

RADIO TIMES
BBC Worldwide Ltd, 201 Wood Lane, London W12 7TQ **T** 020-8433 3400 **W** www.radiotimes.com
Editor, Gill Hudson

RAILWAY MAGAZINE
The Blue Fin Building, 110 Southwark Street, London SE1 0SU **T** 020-3148 5000 **W** www.railwaymagazine.co.uk
Editor, Nick Pigott

READER'S DIGEST
11 Westferry Circus, Canary Wharf, London E14 4HE **T** 020-7715 8000 **W** www.readersdigest.co.uk
Editor-in-Chief, Gill Hudson

RED
64 North Row, London W1K 7LL **T** 020-7150 7000 **W** www.redmagazine.co.uk
Editor, Sam Baker

RED PEPPER
1B Waterlow Road, London N19 5NJ **T** 020-7281 7024 **W** www.redpepper.org.uk
Co-editor, Hilary Wainwright

RUGBY WORLD
9th Floor, The Blue Fin Building, 110 Southwark Street, London SE1 0SU **T** 020-3148 4700 **W** www.rugbyworld.com
Editor, Paul Morgan

RUNNER'S WORLD
33 Broadwick Street, London W1F 0DG **T** 020-7339 4400 **W** www.runnersworld.co.uk
Editor, Andy Dixon

RUSI JOURNAL
Whitehall, London SW1A 2ET **T** 020-7747 2600 **W** www.rusi.org
Editor, Dr Terence McNamee

SAFETY EDUCATION JOURNAL
Royal Society for the Prevention of Accidents, Edgbaston Park, 353 Bristol Road, Birmingham B5 7ST **T** 0121-248 2000 **W** www.rospa.org.uk
Editor, Janice Cave

SAGA MAGAZINE
The Saga Building, Enbrook Park, Sandgate, Folkestone, Kent CT20 3SE **T** 01303-771523 **W** www.saga.co.uk/saga-magazine
Editor, Katy Bravery

SCREEN INTERNATIONAL
Greater London House, 1 Hampstead Road, London NW1 7EJ **T** 020-7728 5000 **W** www.screendaily.com
Editor, Conor Dignam

SFX MAGAZINE
30 Monmouth Street, Bath BA1 2BW **T** 01225-442244 **W** www.sfx.co.uk
Editor, Dave Bradley

SHOOTING TIMES AND COUNTRY MAGAZINE
The Blue Fin Building, 110 Southwark Street, London SE1 0SU **T** 020-3148 4741 **W** www.shootingtimes.co.uk
Editor, Camilla Clark

SIGHT AND SOUND
BFI, 21 Stephen Street, London W1T 1LN **T** 020-7255 1444 **W** www.bfi.org.uk/sightandsound
Editor, Nick James

SNOOKER SCENE
Hayley Green Court, 130 Hagley Road, Halesowen, West Midlands B63 1DY **T** 0121-585 9188 **W** www.snookerscene.com
Editor, Clive Everton

SOLICITORS JOURNAL
6–14 Underwood Street, London N1 7JQ **T** 020-7549 8670 **W** www.solicitorsjournal.com
Editor, Jean-Yves Gilg

THE SPECTATOR
22 Old Queen Street, London SW1H 9HP **T** 020-7961 0200 **W** www.spectator.co.uk
Editor, Matthew d'Ancona

SPIRIT & DESTINY
Academic House, 24–28 Oval Road, London NW1 7DT **T** 020-7241 8000 **W** www.spiritanddestiny.co.uk
Editor, Rhiannon Powell

THE STAGE
Stage House, 47 Bermondsey Street, London SE1 3XT **T** 020-7403 1818 **W** www.thestage.co.uk
Editor, Brian Attwood

STAR TREK MAGAZINE
Titan Magazines, Titan House, 144 Southwark Street, London SE1 0UP **T** 020-7620 0200
Editor, Paul Simpson

STUFF
Haymarket Ltd, Teddington Studios, Broom Road, Teddington, Middlesex TW11 9BE **T** 020-8267 5036 **W** www.stuff.tv
Editor, Fraser Macdonald

THE TABLET
1 King Street Cloisters, Clifton Walk, London W6 0QZ **T** 020-8748 8484 **W** www.thetablet.co.uk
Editor, Catherine Pepinster

TAKE A BREAK
Academic House, 24–28 Oval Road, London NW1 7DT **T** 020-7241 8000 **W** www.bauer.com
Editor, John Dale

TATE ETC
20 John Islip Street, London SW1P 4RG **T** 020-7887 8724 **W** www.tate.org.uk/tateetc
Editor, Simon Grant

TATLER
Vogue House, Hanover Square, London W1S 1JU **T** 020-7499 9080 **W** www.tatler.co.uk
Editor, Geordie Greig

THE TEACHER
National Union of Teachers, Hamilton House, Mabledon Place, London WC1H 9BD **T** 020-7380 4708
Editor, Elyssa Campbell-Barr

TEMPO
Cambridge University Press, The Edinburgh Building, Shaftesbury Road, Cambridge CB2 8RU **W** www.journals.cambridge.org
Editor, Calum MacDonald

THE TES
26 Red Lion Square, Holborn WC1R 4HQ **T** 020-3194 3000 **W** www.tes.co.uk
Editor, Gerard Kelly

TGO (THE GREAT OUTDOORS) MAGAZINE
Newsquest, 200 Renfield Street, Glasgow G2 3QB
T 0141-302 7700 W www.tgomagazine.co.uk
Editor, Cameron McNeish

THIRD WAY
13–17 Long Lane, London EC1A 9PN T 020-7776 1071
W www.thirdway.org.uk
Editor, Simon Jones

TIME OUT
Universal House, 251 Tottenham Court Road, London W1T 7AB
T 020-7813 3000 W www.timeout.com
Acting Editor, Mark Frith

TLS (THE TIMES LITERARY SUPPLEMENT)
Times House, 1 Pennington Street, London E98 1BS
T 020-7782 5000 W www.thetls.co.uk
Editor, Peter Stothard

TODAY'S GOLFER
Media House, Lynchwood, Peterborough Business Park, Peterborough PE2 6EA T 01733-468000
W www.todaysgolfer.co.uk
Editor-in-Chief, Andy Calton

TOTAL FILM
Beauford Court, 30 Monmouth Street, Bath BA1 2BW
T 020-7042 4832 W www.totalfilm.com
Editor, Aubrey Day

TRIBUNE
9 Arkwright Road, London, NW3 6AN T 020-7433 6410
W www.tribunemagazine.co.uk
Editor, Chris McLaughlin

VANITY FAIR
Condé Nast Publications Ltd, Vogue House, Hanover Square, London W1S 1JU T 020-7499 9080
W www.vanityfair.co.uk
Editor-in-Chief, Graydon Carter

VENUE
Venue Publishing, Bristol News & Media, Temple Way, Bristol BS99 7HD T 0117-942 8491 W www.venue.co.uk
Editor, Joe Spurgeon

VIZ
Dennis Publishing, 30 Cleveland Street, London W1T 4JD
T 020-7907 6000 W www.viz.co.uk
Publisher, Russell Blackman

VOGUE
Vogue House, 1 Hanover Square, London W1S 1JU
T 020-7499 9080 W www.vogue.co.uk
Editor, Alexandra Shulman

THE VOICE
6th Floor, Northern & Shell Tower, 4 Selsdon Way, London E14 9GL T 020-7510 0340 W www.voice-online.co.uk
Editor, Steve Pope

WALK
The Ramblers' Association, 2nd Floor, Camelford House, 87–90 Albert Embankment, London SE1 7TW T 020-7339 8500
W www.walkmag.co.uk
Editor, Dominic Bates

WALLPAPER
The Blue Fin Building, 110 Southwark Street, London SE1 0SU
T 020-3148 5000 W www.wallpaper.com
Editor-in-Chief, Tony Chambers

WANDERLUST
PO Box 1832, Windsor SL4 1YT T 01753-620426
W www.wanderlust.co.uk
Editor, Dan Linstead

WATERWAYS WORLD
151 Station Street, Burton-on-Trent DE14 1BG
T 01283-742950 W www.waterwaysworld.com
Editor, Richard Fairhurst

WEDDING MAGAZINE
6th Floor, The Blue Fin Building, 110 Southwark Street, London SE1 0SU T 020-3148 7790
W www.weddingmagazine.co.uk
Editor, Catherine Westwood

THE WEEK
6th Floor, Compass House, 22 Redan Place, London W2 4SA
T 020-7907 6180 W www.theweek.co.uk
Editor-in-chief, Jeremy O'Grady

WEIGHT WATCHERS MAGAZINE
River Publishing Ltd, Victory House, 14 Leicester Place, London WC2H 7BZ T 020-7306 0304
W www.weightwatchers.co.uk
Editor, Mary Frances

WHAT CAR?
Haymarket Motoring Magazines Ltd, Teddington Studios, Broom Road, Teddington, Middlesex TW11 9BE
T 020-8267 5688 W www.whatcar.com
Group Editor, Steve Fowler

WHAT'S ON TV
6th Floor, The Blue Fin Building, 110 Southwark Street, London SE1 0SU T 020-3148 5928 W www.whatsontv.co.uk
Editor, Colin Tough

THE WISDEN CRICKETER
2nd Floor, 123 Buckingham Palace Road, London SW1W 9SL
T 020-7705 4911 W www.wisdencricketer.com
Editor, John Stern

WOMAN'S OWN
The Blue Fin Building, 110 Southwark Street, London SE1 0SU
T 020-3148 5000
Editor, Karen Livermore

WOMAN'S WEEKLY
The Blue Fin Building, 110 Southwark Street, London SE1 0SU
T 020-3148 3603
Editor, Diane Kenwood

THE WORD
Development Hell Ltd, 90–92 Pentonville Road, London N1 9HS
T 020-7078 8400 W www.wordmagazine.co.uk
Editor, Mark Ellen

WORLD SOCCER
The Blue Fin Building, 110 Southwark Street, London SE1 0SU
T 020-3148 5000 W www.worldsoccer.com
Editor, Gavin Hamilton

THE WORLD TODAY
Chatham House, 10 St James's Square, London SW1Y 4LE
T 020-7957 5712 W www.theworldtoday.org
Editor, Graham Walker

YACHTING WORLD
The Blue Fin Building, 110 Southwark Street, London SE1 0SU
T 020-3148 4848 W www.yachtingworld.com
Editor, Andrew Bray

YOGA & HEALTH
PO Box 16969, London E1W 1FY T 020-7480 5456
W www.yogaandhealthmag.co.uk
Editor, Jane Sill

ZEST
National Magazine House, 72 Broadwick Street, London W1F 9EP T 020-7439 5000 W www.zest.co.uk
Editor, Mandie Gower

ZOO
Mappin House, 4 Winsley Street, London W1W 8HF
T 020-7182 8355 W www.zootoday.co.uk
Editor, Ben Todd

INTERNET

INTERNET TRENDS

During 2008 internet usage continued to grow both in terms of the number of people accessing the web and the number of goods and services available online. A total of 16.46 million households in the UK now have internet access. This represents 65 per cent of all UK households and an increase of 1.23 million households since 2007. Nearly 19 out of 20 internet connections are via broadband, with an average speed of 4mbps, encouraging greater uptake of services such as high-quality video and television, music downloads and VOIP.

TOP 10 BROADBAND SUBSCRIBERS BY COUNTRY

Country (2007 position)	*2008*
1. China (2)	83,366,000
2. USA (1)	79,074,000
3. Japan (3)	30,325,900
4. Germany (4)	23,425,150
5. France (6)	17,503,518
6. UK (5)	17,392,800
7. South Korea (7)	15,474,931
8. Italy (8)	12,170,080
9. Canada (9)	9,633,300
10. Brazil (–)	9,386,846

Source: www.point-topic.com

UK households continue to be enamoured with social media and networking sites such as Facebook, Linkedin and Twitter. In 2008 UK internet users spent more time on Facebook than any other website: over 7 million people each spent an average of more than three hours a month on Facebook. Twitter also made an impression on the public consciousness through its microblogging platform where users post 'tweets' (status updates) on anything from breaking news to more mundane aspects of life.

Over half of UK households bought goods or services over the internet and, of those purchases available as downloads, a quarter were films or music. Online buying and selling through eBay continued to be popular, with the auction site remaining one of the top 10 UK sites.

Mobile phone internet usage grew eight times faster than computer-based access with nearly 23 per cent of the UK population relying on mobile internet. A notable 80 per cent of iPhone users accessed the internet with their phone, compared to 48 per cent of smartphone users and just 20 per cent of regular mobile phone users.

- Google remained the most popular search engine in the UK – of all those who visited a search site, 87 per cent visited Google
- The number of people who have listened to podcasts increased to 6 million in May 2008, a 40 per cent increase on the figure six months earlier, with 3.7 million listening to them every week
- The UK region with the highest proportion of household internet access in 2008 was the south-east, at 74 per cent; the north-east had the lowest level at 54 per cent

Sources: Oxford Internet Institute, OFCOM *Communications Market Report 2008*, Office of National Statistics

GLOSSARY OF TERMS

The following is a selected list of internet terms. It is by no means exhaustive but is intended to cover those that the average computer user might encounter.

AJAX: Asynchronous JavaScript and XML – a more interactive way of including content in a web page achieved by exchanging small amounts of data with the server behind the scenes, so that an entire web page does not have to be reloaded each time the user makes a change.

BANNER AD: An advertisement on a web page which links to a corresponding website when clicked.

BLOG: A blog (short for web log) is an online personal journal that is frequently updated and intended to be read by the public. Blogs are kept by 'bloggers' and are commonly available as RSS feeds.

BROWSER: Typically referring to a 'web browser' program that allows a computer user to view web page content on their computer, eg Firefox, Microsoft Explorer or Safari.

CLICK-THROUGH: The number of times a web user 'clicks-through' a paid advertisement link to the corresponding website.

COOKIE: A piece of information sent by a web server to a web browser which is then saved and sent back to the server whenever the browser makes requests from the server. Cookies contain information such as login, registration or online 'shopping cart' data, user preferences etc and are usually set to expire after a predetermined length of time.

CSS: Cascading Style Sheet – a standard for specifying the appearance of text. It provides a single 'library' of styles that are used throughout a large number of related documents. A CSS file might specify for example that all numbered lists are to appear in italics or render text differently depending if it is being viewed through a PC web browser or a mobile phone web browser.

DOMAIN: A set of words or letters, separated by dots, used to identify an internet server, eg www.whitakersalmanack.co.uk, where 'www' denotes a web (http) server, 'whitakersalmanack' denotes the organisation name, 'co' denotes that the organisation is a company and 'uk' indicates United Kingdom. (For a complete list of country suffixes *see* Internet Domain Names section.)

FTP: File Transfer Protocol – an internet protocol enabling exchange of files with a remote server.

HACKER: A person who attempts to break or 'hack' into websites in order to obtain personal information such as addresses, passwords or credit card details. Hackers may also delete code or incorporate traces of malicious code to ruin the functionality of a website.

HIT: A single request from a web browser for a single item from a web server. In order for a web browser to display a page that contains three graphics, four 'hits' would occur at the server: one for the HTML page and one for each of the three graphics. Therefore the number of hits on a website is not synonymous with the number of unique visitors.

HTML: HyperText Mark-up Language – a programming language used to denote or mark-up how an internet page should be presented to a user from an HTTP server via a web browser.

HTTP: HyperText Transfer Protocol – an internet protocol whereby a web server sends web pages, images and files to a web browser.

HYPERLINK: A piece of specially coded text that users can click on to navigate to the webpage or element of a webpage associated with that link's code. Links are typically distinguished through the use of bold, underlined, or a different coloured text.

MALWARE: A combination of the words 'malicious' and 'software'. Malware is software designed with the specific intention of hacking into a computer and damaging its system.

META TAG: A type of HTML tag that contains information not normally displayed to the user. Meta tags are typically used to include information for search engines to help them categorise a page.

MP3: A popular format for compressing audio information for transmission over the internet for later playback on personal computers, music players and other devices.

MPEG: Motion Picture Encoding Group – popular format standard for compressing video and audio information for transmission over the internet for later playback on personal computers and on hand-held devices.

OPEN CONTENT: Copyrighted information that is made available by the owner to the general public under licence terms that allow reuse of the material, often with the requirement that the reuser grant the public the same rights to the modified version. Information that is in the 'public domain' might also be considered a form of open content.

OPEN-SOURCE: A computer program that has its source-code (the instructions that make up a program) freely available for viewing and modification is said to be open-source.

P2P: Peer to peer – the act of a computer on one network communicating to a computer on a different network. The communication usually revolves around the sharing of information, content, or a file between computers.

PAGERANK: Pagerank is a link analysis algorithm used by search engines that assigns a numerical value based on a website's relevance and reputation. In general, a site with a higher pagerank has more traffic than a site with a low pagerank.

PODCASTING: A form of audio and video broadcasting using the internet. The word is a portmanteau of 'iPod' and broadcasting, though podcasting does not require the use of an iPod. A podcaster creates a list of files and makes it available in the RSS 2.0 format. The list can then be obtained using various podcast 'retriever' software which makes the files available to digital devices (including, but not limited to, iPods); users may then listen or watch at their convenience.

RSS FEED: Rich Site Summary or RDF Site Summary or Real Simple Syndication – a commonly used protocol for syndication and sharing of content, originally developed to facilitate the syndication of news articles, now widely used to share the contents of blogs.

SEO: An acronym for search engine optimisation, SEO refers to the process of optimising the content on a webpage to ensure that a website is properly set up and structured to be crawled by search engines.

SERVER: A node on a network that provides service to the terminals on the network. These computers have higher hardware specifications, ie more resources and greater speed, in order to handle large amounts of data.

SOCIAL NETWORKING: the practice of using a web-hosted service such as Facebook or MySpace to upload and share content and build friendship networks

SPAM: A term used for unsolicited, generally junk, email. Junk email is a major issue with some estimates suggesting that spam is becoming more prevalent than legitimate email. Many legislatures around the globe are taking steps to ban or regulate spam.

TRAFFIC: The number of visitors to a website and its pages.

TROLL: Someone who posts controversial, inflammatory, irrelevant or off-topic messages on a blog or other online discussion forum in order to provoke other users into an emotional response or to generally disrupt on-topic discussion.

TWITTER: An online microblogging service that allows users to stay connected through the exchange of 140-character answers (known as a 'tweet') to the simple question: What are you doing?

URL: Uniform Resource Locator – address of an internet file accessible on the internet, eg http://www.whitakersalmanack.com

USER-GENERATED CONTENT (UGC): Refers to various media content produced or primarily influenced by end-users, as opposed to traditional media producers such as licensed broadcasters and production companies. These forms of media include digital video, blogging, podcasting, mobile phone photography and wikis.

VISIBILITY: How visible a website is to search engines and browsers.

VOIP: Voice Over Internet Protocol – various technologies used to make telephone calls over IP networks, especially the internet. Just as modems allow computers to connect to the internet over regular telephone lines, VOIP technology allows telephone calls to take place over internet connections. Costs for VOIP calls are usually much lower than for traditional telephone calls.

WEB 2.0: Generally refers to a second generation of services available on the web that lets people collaborate and share information online. In contrast to the first generation, Web 2.0 gives users an experience closer to desktop applications than traditional static web pages. Web 2.0 applications often use a combination of techniques including AJAX and web syndication.

WIDGET: A widget is a piece of software that provides access to online information items or to functions that the user accesses on a regular basis.

WIKI: Software that allows users to freely create and edit web page content using any web browser. Theoretically this encourages democratic use of the internet and promotes content composition by non-technical users.

TIME AND SPACE

ASTRONOMY

TIME MEASUREMENT AND CALENDARS

TIDAL PREDICTIONS

ASTRONOMY

The following pages give astronomical data for each month of the year 2010. There are four pages of data for each month. All data are given for 0h Greenwich Mean Time (GMT), ie at the midnight at the beginning of the day named. This applies also to data for the months when British Summer Time is in operation (for dates, *see* below).

The astronomical data are given in a form suitable for observation with the naked eye or with a small telescope. These data do not attempt to replace the *Astronomical Almanac* for professional astronomers.

A fuller explanation of how to use the astronomical data is given on pages 685–8.

CALENDAR FOR EACH MONTH

The calendar for each month comprises dates of general interest plus the dates of birth or death of well-known people. For key religious, civil and legal dates *see* page 9. For details of flag-flying days *see* page 23. For royal birthdays *see* pages 23 and 24–5. Public holidays are given in italics. *See* also pages 10 and 11.

Fuller explanations of the various calendars can be found under Time Measurement and Calendars.

The zodiacal signs through which the Sun is passing during each month are illustrated. The date of transition from one sign to the next, to the nearest hour, is given under Astronomical Phenomena.

JULIAN DATE

The Julian date on 2010 January 0.0 is 2455196.5. To find the Julian date for any other date in 2010 (at 0h GMT), add the day-of-the year number on the extreme right of the calendar for each month to the Julian date for January 0.0.

SEASONS

The seasons are defined astronomically as follows:

Spring from the vernal equinox to the summer solstice
Summer from the summer solstice to the autumnal equinox
Autumn from the autumnal equinox to the winter solstice
Winter from the winter solstice to the vernal equinox

The time when seasons start in 2010 (to the nearest hour) are:

Northern Hemisphere

Vernal equinox	March 20d 18h GMT
Summer solstice	June 21d 11h GMT
Autumnal equinox	September 23d 03h GMT
Winter solstice	December 22d 00h GMT

Southern Hemisphere

Autumnal equinox	March 20d 18h GMT
Winter solstice	June 21d 11h GMT
Vernal equinox	September 23d 03h GMT
Summer solstice	December 22d 00h GMT

The longest day of the year, measured from sunrise to sunset, is at the summer solstice. The longest day in the United Kingdom will fall on 21 June in 2010.

The shortest day of the year is at the winter solstice. The shortest day in the United Kingdom will fall on 22 December in 2010.

The equinox is the point at which day and night are of equal length all over the world.

In popular parlance, the seasons in the northern hemisphere comprise the following months:

Spring	March, April, May
Summer	June, July, August
Autumn	September, October, November
Winter	December, January, February

BRITISH SUMMER TIME

British Summer Time is the legal time for general purposes during the period in which it is in operation (*see also* pages 689–90). During this period, clocks are kept one hour ahead of Greenwich Mean Time. The hour of changeover is 01h Greenwich Mean Time. The duration of Summer Time in 2010 is from March 28 01h GMT to October 31 01h GMT.

♑ JANUARY 2010 ♒

FIRST MONTH, 31 DAYS. *Janus*, god of the portal, facing two ways, past and future

1	*Friday*	British battleship HMS *Formidable* was torpedoed by a German U-boat, killing 574 people 1915	day 1
2	*Saturday*	Christian forces took control of Granada and expelled the Moors from Spain 1492	2
3	*Sunday*	General Washington's revolutionary forces defeated the British at the Battle of Princeton 1777	3
4	*Monday*	Titus Labienus' Optimates defeated Julius Caesar's Populares at the Battle of Ruspina 46 BC	week 1 day 4
5	*Tuesday*	French officer Alfred Dreyfus was convicted of treason in a secret court marshal 1894	5
6	*Wednesday*	Ferdinand von Schill, Prussian officer and rebel *b.* 1776; Theodore Roosevelt, US president *d.* 1919	6
7	*Thursday*	Vietnamese forces recaptured Phnom Penh from Pol Pot and the Khmer Rouge 1979	7
8	*Friday*	The forces of King Ethelred of Wessex defeated the Danes at the Battle of Ashdown 871	8
9	*Saturday*	Karel Bonaventura Buquoy, military commander *b.* 1571; Napoleon III, emperor of France *d.* 1873	9
10	*Sunday*	The Treaty of Versailles was ratified 1920	10
11	*Monday*	The Anglo–Zulu War began in South Africa 1879	week 2 day 11
12	*Tuesday*	Joseph Joffre, French general *b.* 1852; William Wyndham Grenville, British prime minister *d.* 1834	12
13	*Wednesday*	Emile Zola accused the military of falsifying evidence against Alfred Dreyfus 1898	13
14	*Thursday*	The Treaty of Paris was ratified by US Congress, ending the American War of Independence 1784	14
15	*Friday*	Nebuchadnezzar of Babylon laid siege to Jerusalem 588 BC	15
16	*Saturday*	The Chalpultepec peace accords ended civil war in El Salvador 1992	16
17	*Sunday*	David Lloyd George, British prime minister *b.* 1863; Walther von Reichenau, German field marshal *d.* 1942	17
18	*Monday*	Soviet forces broke the siege of Leningrad 1943	week 3 day 18
19	*Tuesday*	The British East India Company conquered Aden, Yemen 1839	19
20	*Wednesday*	The Wannsee conference set out the basis for the Nazi 'final solution' 1942	20
21	*Thursday*	The first nuclear-powered submarine, USS *Nautilus*, was launched in the USA 1954	21
22	*Friday*	Henry VIII of England and Francis I of France declared war on Holy Roman Emperor Charles V 1528	22
23	*Saturday*	The British East India company defeated the Bengali–French army at the Battle of Plassey 1757	23
24	*Sunday*	Ernst Heinkel, German aircraft designer *b.* 1888; Winston Churchill, British prime minister *d.* 1965	24
25	*Monday*	Charles François Dumouriez, French general *b.* 1739; Joseph Wheeler, American general *d.* 1906	week 4 day 25
26	*Tuesday*	The Treaty of Karlowitz ended the Austro–Ottoman War 1699	26
27	*Wednesday*	Soviet troops liberated the Auschwitz concentration camp 1945	27
28	*Thursday*	George Hamilton-Gordon, British prime minister *b.* 1784; Francis Drake, vice admiral *d.* 1596	28
29	*Friday*	France defeated Russia and Prussia at the Battle of Brienne 1814	29
30	*Saturday*	Charles I was executed on the charge of treason 1649	30
31	*Sunday*	The 100th British soldier was killed in the Iraq conflict 2006	31

ASTRONOMICAL PHENOMENA

d	*h*	
3	01	Earth at perihelion (147 million km.)
3	08	Mars in conjunction with Moon. Mars 6°N.
4	19	Mercury in inferior conjunction
5	11	Venus in conjunction with Mercury. Venus 3°S.
6	13	Saturn in conjunction with Moon. Saturn 7°N.
11	21	Venus in superior conjunction
13	16	Saturn at stationary point
13	17	Mercury in conjunction with Moon. Mercury 5°N.
15	07	Annular eclipse of Sun
15	09	Venus in conjunction with Moon. Venus 1°S.
15	17	Mercury at stationary point
18	06	Jupiter in conjunction with Moon. Jupiter 4°S.
20	04	Sun's longitude 300° ♒
27	05	Mercury at greatest elongation W. 25°
29	20	Mars at opposition
30	05	Mars in conjunction with Moon. Mars 6°N.

MINIMA OF ALGOL

d	*h*	*d*	*h*	*d*	*h*
1	19.9	13	07.2	24	18.5
4	16.7	16	04.0	27	15.3
7	13.6	19	00.8	30	12.1
10	10.4	21	21.7		

CONSTELLATIONS

The following constellations are near the meridian at

	d	*h*		*d*	*h*
December	1	24	January	16	21
December	16	23	February	1	20
January	1	22	February	15	19

Draco (below the Pole), Ursa Minor (below the Pole), Camelopardalis, Perseus, Auriga, Taurus, Orion, Eridanus and Lepus

THE MOON

Phases, Apsides and Node	*d*	*h*	*m*
☾ Last Quarter	7	10	39
● New Moon	15	07	11
☽ First Quarter	23	10	53
○ Full Moon	30	06	18
Perigee (358,672km)	1	20	39
Apogee (406,448km)	17	01	55
Perigee (356,591km)	30	09	11

Mean longitude of ascending node on January 1, 292°

THE SUN

s.d. 16′.3

Day	Right Ascension	Dec. –	Equation of time	Rise 52°	Rise 56°	Transit	Set 52°	Set 56°	Sidereal time	Transit of first point of Aries
	h m s	° ′	m s	h m	h m	h m	h m	h m	h m s	h m s
1	18 45 28	23 02	−3 18	8 08	8 31	12 04	15 59	15 36	6 42 10	17 15 00
2	18 49 53	22 57	−3 46	8 08	8 31	12 04	16 00	15 37	6 46 07	17 11 04
3	18 54 17	22 51	−4 14	8 08	8 31	12 04	16 01	15 39	6 50 03	17 07 08
4	18 58 41	22 45	−4 42	8 08	8 30	12 05	16 03	15 40	6 54 00	17 03 12
5	19 03 05	22 39	−5 09	8 07	8 30	12 05	16 04	15 41	6 57 56	16 59 16
6	19 07 28	22 32	−5 35	8 07	8 29	12 06	16 05	15 43	7 01 53	16 55 20
7	19 11 51	22 25	−6 02	8 06	8 29	12 06	16 06	15 44	7 05 49	16 51 24
8	19 16 13	22 17	−6 27	8 06	8 28	12 07	16 08	15 46	7 09 46	16 47 29
9	19 20 35	22 09	−6 53	8 05	8 27	12 07	16 09	15 47	7 13 43	16 43 33
10	19 24 57	22 00	−7 17	8 05	8 26	12 07	16 10	15 49	7 17 39	16 39 37
11	19 29 17	21 51	−7 42	8 04	8 25	12 08	16 12	15 51	7 21 36	16 35 41
12	19 33 38	21 42	−8 05	8 04	8 24	12 08	16 13	15 52	7 25 32	16 31 45
13	19 37 57	21 32	−8 28	8 03	8 24	12 09	16 15	15 54	7 29 29	16 27 49
14	19 42 16	21 22	−8 51	8 02	8 22	12 09	16 16	15 56	7 33 25	16 23 53
15	19 46 35	21 11	−9 13	8 01	8 21	12 09	16 18	15 58	7 37 22	16 19 57
16	19 50 52	21 00	−9 34	8 00	8 20	12 10	16 20	16 00	7 41 18	16 16 01
17	19 55 09	20 48	−9 54	7 59	8 19	12 10	16 21	16 02	7 45 15	16 12 05
18	19 59 26	20 36	−10 14	7 58	8 18	12 10	16 23	16 04	7 49 12	16 08 09
19	20 03 41	20 24	−10 33	7 57	8 16	12 11	16 25	16 06	7 53 08	16 04 14
20	20 07 56	20 11	−10 52	7 56	8 15	12 11	16 26	16 08	7 57 05	16 00 18
21	20 12 10	19 58	−11 09	7 55	8 14	12 11	16 28	16 10	8 01 01	15 56 22
22	20 16 24	19 45	−11 26	7 54	8 12	12 12	16 30	16 12	8 04 58	15 52 26
23	20 20 36	19 31	−11 42	7 53	8 11	12 12	16 31	16 14	8 08 54	15 48 30
24	20 24 48	19 17	−11 57	7 52	8 09	12 12	16 33	16 16	8 12 51	15 44 34
25	20 28 59	19 02	−12 11	7 50	8 07	12 12	16 35	16 18	8 16 47	15 40 38
26	20 33 09	18 48	−12 25	7 49	8 06	12 13	16 37	16 20	8 20 44	15 36 42
27	20 37 18	18 32	−12 38	7 48	8 04	12 13	16 38	16 22	8 24 41	15 32 46
28	20 41 27	18 17	−12 50	7 46	8 02	12 13	16 40	16 24	8 28 37	15 28 50
29	20 45 35	18 01	−13 01	7 45	8 01	12 13	16 42	16 26	8 32 34	15 24 54
30	20 49 41	17 45	−13 11	7 43	7 59	12 13	16 44	16 28	8 36 30	15 20 59
31	20 53 47	17 28	−13 21	7 42	7 57	12 13	16 46	16 31	8 40 27	15 17 03

DURATION OF TWILIGHT (in minutes)

Latitude	52°	56°	52°	56°	52°	56°	52°	56°
	1 January		*11 January*		*21 January*		*31 January*	
Civil	41	47	40	45	38	43	37	41
Nautical	84	96	82	93	80	90	78	87
Astronomical	125	141	123	138	120	134	117	130

THE NIGHT SKY

Mercury passes through inferior conjunction on the 4th and reaches its greatest western elongation (25 degrees) on the 27th. However it is very poorly placed for observation as a morning object. It might be glimpsed between the 14th and the 25th, low above the southeastern horizon at the beginning of morning civil twilight, when it is barely 6 degrees above the horizon. Mercury's magnitude brightens from +0.7 to −0.1 during this period. Because of its southerly declination observers in Scotland will be unlikely to see it at all.

Venus passes through superior conjunction on the 11th and is therefore unsuitably placed for observation throughout the month.

Mars is at opposition on the 29th and is therefore visible throughout the hours of darkness. It is moving slowly retrograde from the western part of the constellation of Leo into the eastern part of Cancer. During the month its magnitude brightens from −0.8 to −1.3. On the morning of the 3rd the waning gibbous Moon passes 7 degrees south of the planet. This conjunction is repeated on the 30th when the Moon is Full.

Jupiter, magnitude −2.1, is an evening object, visible low in the south-western sky for a short time in the early evening. The waxing crescent Moon passes 1 degree north of the planet on the 18th. By the end of the month it is becoming a difficult object to locate unless the sky near the horizon is very clear.

Saturn, magnitude +0.9, is a morning object, reaching its first stationary point on the 13th, in the constellation of Virgo. At the beginning of the month it becomes visible in the eastern sky shortly after midnight. The rings of Saturn are barely visible as the minor axis is only 4 seconds of arc. On the 6th to 7th the Moon, at Last Quarter, passes 8 degrees south of Saturn.

THE MOON

Day	R.A.		Dec.	Hor. Par.	Semi-diam.	Sun's Co-Long.	PA of Br. Limb	Ph.	Age	Rise				Transit		Set			
										52°		56°				52°		56°	
	h	m	°	′	′	°	°	%	d	h	m	h	m	h	m	h	m	h	m
1	6	58	+23.5	61.0	16.6	95	81	100	15.5	17	01	16	39	0	16	8	43	9	07
2	8	01	+19.8	61.1	16.7	107	104	98	16.5	18	33	18	18	1	18	9	14	9	31
3	9	01	+14.9	60.9	16.6	119	110	93	17.5	20	03	19	54	2	16	9	38	9	49
4	9	57	+9.1	60.5	16.5	131	113	86	18.5	21	30	21	27	3	10	9	56	10	02
5	10	50	+2.9	59.8	16.3	143	115	76	19.5	22	54	22	57	4	00	10	13	10	13
6	11	42	–3.3	59.0	16.1	155	115	66	20.5	—		—		4	49	10	29	10	24
7	12	32	–9.1	58.2	15.9	167	114	55	21.5	0	16	0	24	5	37	10	45	10	35
8	13	23	–14.4	57.4	15.6	180	111	44	22.5	1	36	1	50	6	26	11	04	10	49
9	14	14	–18.9	56.7	15.4	192	108	34	23.5	2	54	3	14	7	15	11	27	11	06
10	15	07	–22.3	56.0	15.3	204	103	25	24.5	4	09	4	34	8	06	11	57	11	31
11	16	01	–24.6	55.5	15.1	216	98	16	25.5	5	18	5	47	8	58	12	35	12	05
12	16	55	–25.7	55.0	15.0	228	92	10	26.5	6	16	6	48	9	50	13	24	12	53
13	17	49	–25.5	54.6	14.9	240	87	5	27.5	7	04	7	34	10	42	14	23	13	53
14	18	42	–24.2	54.4	14.8	253	82	2	28.5	7	40	8	06	11	31	15	29	15	04
15	19	33	–21.7	54.1	14.8	265	82	0	29.5	8	07	8	28	12	19	16	38	16	19
16	20	21	–18.3	54.0	14.7	277	248	0	0.7	8	28	8	44	13	03	17	49	17	34
17	21	08	–14.2	53.9	14.7	289	247	3	1.7	8	45	8	56	13	46	18	58	18	49
18	21	52	–9.6	54.0	14.7	301	245	6	2.7	8	59	9	05	14	27	20	07	20	02
19	22	36	–4.7	54.1	14.8	314	244	12	3.7	9	12	9	14	15	07	21	16	21	16
20	23	19	+0.5	54.4	14.8	326	243	19	4.7	9	24	9	22	15	47	22	25	22	30
21	0	02	+5.7	54.8	14.9	338	244	27	5.7	9	38	9	31	16	29	23	36	23	46
22	0	47	+10.8	55.4	15.1	350	245	36	6.7	9	53	9	42	17	13	—		—	
23	1	34	+15.5	56.1	15.3	2	248	46	7.7	10	12	9	55	18	00	0	50	1	05
24	2	25	+19.7	56.9	15.5	14	252	56	8.7	10	36	10	14	18	52	2	07	2	27
25	3	20	+23.0	57.8	15.8	27	257	66	9.7	11	10	10	43	19	49	3	25	3	51
26	4	20	+25.1	58.8	16.0	39	262	76	10.7	11	58	11	27	20	50	4	38	5	09
27	5	22	+25.8	59.7	16.3	51	269	85	11.7	13	02	12	32	21	53	5	43	6	13
28	6	27	+24.7	60.6	16.5	63	275	93	12.7	14	23	13	58	22	56	6	33	7	00
29	7	31	+21.8	61.2	16.7	75	279	98	13.7	15	54	15	35	23	56	7	10	7	31
30	8	33	+17.4	61.5	16.7	87	264	100	14.7	17	27	17	15	—		7	37	7	52
31	9	32	+11.8	61.4	16.7	99	123	99	15.7	18	59	18	53	0	54	7	59	8	07

MERCURY

Day	R.A.		Dec.	Diam.	Phase	Transit		5° high			
								52°		56°	
	h	m	°	″	%	h	m	h	m	h	m
1	19	21	–20.5	10	6	12	35	15	58	15	30
3	19	11	–20.2	10	2	12	16	15	42	15	15
5	19	00	–20.0	10	1	11	57	8	30	8	57
7	18	48	–19.9	10	3	11	38	8	11	8	37
9	18	38	–19.8	10	7	11	21	7	53	8	20
11	18	31	–19.9	9	14	11	06	7	39	8	06
13	18	26	–20.1	9	21	10	54	7	28	7	55
15	18	24	–20.3	9	29	10	45	7	20	7	48
17	18	24	–20.5	8	36	10	38	7	15	7	43
19	18	27	–20.8	8	42	10	33	7	12	7	41
21	18	31	–21.1	8	48	10	30	7	11	7	41
23	18	37	–21.4	7	54	10	28	7	11	7	42
25	18	44	–21.6	7	58	10	28	7	13	7	44
27	18	53	–21.8	7	62	10	28	7	14	7	46
29	19	02	–21.9	7	66	10	30	7	17	7	49
31	19	11	–21.9	6	69	10	32	7	19	7	51

VENUS

Day	R.A.		Dec.	Diam.	Phase	Transit		5° high			
								52°		56°	
	h	m	°	″	%	h	m	h	m	h	m
1	18	34	–23.6	10	100	11	53	14	51	14	13
6	19	02	–23.3	10	100	12	01	15	02	14	26
11	19	29	–22.7	10	100	12	08	15	15	14	41
16	19	56	–21.7	10	100	12	15	15	30	14	59
21	20	22	–20.6	10	100	12	22	15	47	15	19
26	20	48	–19.1	10	100	12	28	16	04	15	39
31	21	14	–17.4	10	100	12	34	16	22	16	00

MARS

Day	R.A.		Dec.	Diam.	Phase	Transit		5° high			
								52°		56°	
	h	m	°	″	%	h	m	h	m	h	m
1	9	30	+18.8	13	96	2	47	19	37	19	24
6	9	26	+19.2	13	97	2	24	19	11	18	58
11	9	22	+19.8	13	98	2	00	18	43	18	29
16	9	15	+20.4	14	99	1	34	18	14	17	59
21	9	08	+21.1	14	100	1	07	17	43	17	27
26	9	00	+21.7	14	100	0	40	17	12	16	55
31	8	52	+22.3	14	100	0	12	16	40	16	23

SUNRISE AND SUNSET

	London		*Bristol*		*Birmingham*		*Manchester*		*Newcastle*		*Glasgow*		*Belfast*	
	0° 05′	*51° 30′*	*2° 35′*	*51° 28′*	*1° 55′*	*52° 28′*	*2° 15′*	*53° 28′*	*1° 37′*	*54° 59′*	*4° 14′*	*55° 52′*	*5° 56′*	*54° 35′*
d	*h m*	*h m*	*h m*	*h m*	*h m*	*h m*	*h m*	*h m*	*h m*	*h m*	*h m*	*h m*	*h m*	*h m*
1	8 06	16 02	8 16	16 12	8 18	16 04	8 25	16 00	8 31	15 49	8 47	15 54	8 46	16 09
2	8 06	16 03	8 16	16 13	8 18	16 05	8 25	16 01	8 31	15 50	8 47	15 55	8 46	16 10
3	8 06	16 04	8 16	16 14	8 18	16 07	8 25	16 03	8 31	15 51	8 47	15 56	8 46	16 11
4	8 05	16 05	8 15	16 15	8 18	16 08	8 24	16 04	8 30	15 53	8 46	15 58	8 45	16 12
5	8 05	16 07	8 15	16 17	8 17	16 09	8 24	16 05	8 30	15 54	8 46	15 59	8 45	16 14
6	8 05	16 08	8 15	16 18	8 17	16 10	8 23	16 06	8 29	15 55	8 45	16 01	8 44	16 15
7	8 04	16 09	8 14	16 19	8 16	16 12	8 23	16 08	8 29	15 57	8 45	16 02	8 44	16 16
8	8 04	16 10	8 14	16 21	8 16	16 13	8 22	16 09	8 28	15 58	8 44	16 04	8 43	16 18
9	8 03	16 12	8 13	16 22	8 15	16 14	8 22	16 11	8 28	16 00	8 43	16 05	8 43	16 19
10	8 03	16 13	8 13	16 23	8 15	16 16	8 21	16 12	8 27	16 02	8 42	16 07	8 42	16 21
11	8 02	16 15	8 12	16 25	8 14	16 17	8 20	16 14	8 26	16 03	8 42	16 09	8 41	16 23
12	8 02	16 16	8 11	16 26	8 13	16 19	8 20	16 15	8 25	16 05	8 41	16 10	8 40	16 24
13	8 01	16 17	8 11	16 28	8 13	16 20	8 19	16 17	8 24	16 06	8 40	16 12	8 39	16 26
14	8 00	16 19	8 10	16 29	8 12	16 22	8 18	16 19	8 23	16 08	8 39	16 14	8 38	16 28
15	7 59	16 21	8 09	16 31	8 11	16 24	8 17	16 20	8 22	16 10	8 38	16 16	8 37	16 29
16	7 58	16 22	8 08	16 32	8 10	16 25	8 16	16 22	8 21	16 12	8 36	16 17	8 36	16 31
17	7 58	16 24	8 07	16 34	8 09	16 27	8 15	16 24	8 20	16 14	8 35	16 19	8 35	16 33
18	7 57	16 25	8 06	16 35	8 08	16 28	8 14	16 25	8 19	16 15	8 34	16 21	8 34	16 35
19	7 56	16 27	8 05	16 37	8 07	16 30	8 13	16 27	8 18	16 17	8 33	16 23	8 33	16 37
20	7 55	16 29	8 04	16 39	8 06	16 32	8 12	16 29	8 16	16 19	8 31	16 25	8 32	16 38
21	7 53	16 30	8 03	16 40	8 05	16 34	8 10	16 31	8 15	16 21	8 30	16 27	8 30	16 40
22	7 52	16 32	8 02	16 42	8 04	16 35	8 09	16 32	8 14	16 23	8 28	16 29	8 29	16 42
23	7 51	16 34	8 01	16 44	8 02	16 37	8 08	16 34	8 12	16 25	8 27	16 31	8 28	16 44
24	7 50	16 35	8 00	16 46	8 01	16 39	8 07	16 36	8 11	16 27	8 25	16 33	8 26	16 46
25	7 49	16 37	7 59	16 47	8 00	16 41	8 05	16 38	8 09	16 29	8 24	16 35	8 25	16 48
26	7 47	16 39	7 57	16 49	7 58	16 43	8 04	16 40	8 08	16 31	8 22	16 37	8 23	16 50
27	7 46	16 41	7 56	16 51	7 57	16 44	8 02	16 42	8 06	16 33	8 20	16 40	8 22	16 52
28	7 45	16 42	7 55	16 53	7 56	16 46	8 01	16 44	8 04	16 35	8 19	16 42	8 20	16 54
29	7 43	16 44	7 53	16 54	7 54	16 48	7 59	16 46	8 03	16 37	8 17	16 44	8 18	16 56
30	7 42	16 46	7 52	16 56	7 53	16 50	7 58	16 48	8 01	16 39	8 15	16 46	8 17	16 58
31	7 40	16 48	7 50	16 58	7 51	16 52	7 56	16 50	7 59	16 41	8 13	16 48	8 15	17 00

JUPITER

Day	*R.A.*		*Dec.*		*Transit*		*5° high*			
							52°		*56°*	
	h	*m*	°	′	*h*	*m*	*h*	*m*	*h*	*m*
1	21	55.7	−13	37	15	12	19	23	19	06
11	22	03.7	−12	53	14	40	18	56	18	40
21	22	12.2	−12	06	14	09	18	30	18	15
31	22	20.9	−11	17	13	39	18	04	17	50

Diameters – equatorial 34″ polar 32″

SATURN

Day	*R.A.*		*Dec.*		*Transit*		*5° high*			
							52°		*56°*	
	h	*m*	°	′	*h*	*m*	*h*	*m*	*h*	*m*
1	12	20.2	+0	19	5	37	0	09	0	12
11	12	20.8	+0	18	4	58	23	26	23	29
21	12	20.7	+0	21	4	19	22	47	22	50
31	12	19.9	+0	20	3	39	22	06	22	09

Diameters – equatorial 18″ polar 16″
Rings – major axis 41″ minor axis 4″

URANUS

Day	*R.A.*		*Dec.*		*Transit*		*10° high*			
							52°		*56°*	
	h	*m*	°	′	*h*	*m*	*h*	*m*	*h*	*m*
1	23	35.8	−3	26	16	51	21	26	21	16
11	23	36.9	−3	18	16	13	20	48	20	39
21	23	38.2	−3	10	15	35	20	11	20	02
31	23	39.7	−2	59	14	57	19	35	19	25

Diameter 4″

NEPTUNE

Day	*R.A.*		*Dec.*		*Transit*		*10° high*			
							52°		*56°*	
	h	*m*	°	′	*h*	*m*	*h*	*m*	*h*	*m*
1	21	48.1	−13	43	15	04	18	35	18	11
11	21	49.3	−13	37	14	25	17	57	17	34
21	21	50.6	−13	30	13	47	17	20	16	57
31	21	52.0	−13	23	13	10	16	43	16	20

Diameter 2″

♒ FEBRUARY 2010 ♓

SECOND MONTH, 28 or 29 DAYS. *Februa*, Roman festival of Purification

1	*Monday*	France declared war on Britain and the Netherlands 1793	week 5 day 32
2	*Tuesday*	The Germans surrendered at the Battle of Stalingrad 1943	33
3	*Wednesday*	The naval battle of Diu, India, took place between the Portuguese and the Ottomans 1509	34
4	*Thursday*	The 'big three' Allied leaders discussed postwar reorganisation at the Yalta conference 1945	35
5	*Friday*	Steam ship HMS *Tuscania* sank after a German torpedo attack 1918	36
6	*Saturday*	Eva Braun, mistress and wife of Adolf Hitler *b.* 1912; King George VI *d.* 1952	37
7	*Sunday*	In the Napoleonic Wars, the two-day Battle of Eylau began 1807	38
8	*Monday*	The Russo–Japanese War began 1904	week 6 day 39
9	*Tuesday*	Conscription started in Britain with the Military Service Act 1916	40
10	*Wednesday*	The British East India Company won the Battle of Sobraon in the first Anglo–Sikh War 1846	41
11	*Thursday*	Britain, the USA and the Soviet Union signed the Seabed Arms Control Treaty 1971	42
12	*Friday*	The February Uprising began in Austria 1934	43
13	*Saturday*	Allied forces bombed the German city of Dresden 1945	44
14	*Sunday*	Germany launched the 823ft battleship *Bismarck* in Hamburg 1939	45
15	*Monday*	British forces surrendered Singapore to the Japanese 1942	week 7 day 46
16	*Tuesday*	Nearly 300 British prisoners were rescued from the German prison ship the *Altmark* 1940	47
17	*Wednesday*	André Maginot, French minister of war *b.* 1877; Geronimo, Apache chief *d.* 1909	48
18	*Thursday*	Uesugi Kenshin, Japanese samurai *b.* 1530; Kublai Khan, Mongol and Chinese emperor *d.* 1294	49
19	*Friday*	US Marines invaded the Japanese island Iwo Jima 1945	50
20	*Saturday*	Lord Louis Mountbatten became the last viceroy of India 1947	51
21	*Sunday*	The Battle of Verdun, the longest battle of the First World War, began 1916	52
22	*Monday*	George Washington, first US president *b.* 1732; Christopher Snider, first martyr of the American Revolution *d.* 1770	week 8 day 53
23	*Tuesday*	The Alamo siege started in Texas, USA 1836	54
24	*Wednesday*	The Cuban War of Independence began 1895	55
25	*Thursday*	French troops surrendered in the 'last invasion of Britain' 1797	56
26	*Friday*	Coalition forces liberated Kuwait City in the Gulf War 1991	57
27	*Saturday*	Nigeria elected a civilian president, ending 15 years of military rule 1999	58
28	*Sunday*	The North Atlantic Treaty Organisation (NATO) undertook its first military action 1994	59

ASTRONOMICAL PHENOMENA

d	*h*	
2	21	Saturn in conjunction with Moon. Saturn 7°N.
12	05	Mercury in conjunction with Moon. Mercury 2°S.
14	21	Venus in conjunction with Moon. Venus 5°S.
14	23	Neptune in conjunction
15	02	Jupiter in conjunction with Moon. Jupiter 5°S.
17	02	Jupiter in conjunction with Venus. Jupiter 0°.5 N.
18	19	Sun's longitude 330° ♓
26	03	Mars in conjunction with Moon. Mars 5°N
28	11	Jupiter in conjunction

MINIMA OF ALGOL

d	*h*	*d*	*h*	*d*	*h*
2	09.0	13	20.2	25	07.5
5	05.8	16	17.1	28	04.4
8	02.6	19	13.9		
10	23.4	22	10.7		

CONSTELLATIONS

The following constellations are near the meridian at

	d	*h*		*d*	*h*
January	1	24	February	15	21
January	16	23	March	1	20
February	1	22	March	16	19

Draco (below the Pole), Camelopardalis, Auriga, Taurus, Gemini, Orion, Canis Minor, Monoceros, Lepus, Canis Major and Puppis

THE MOON

Phases, Apsides and Node	*d*	*h*	*m*
☾ Last Quarter	5	23	48
● New Moon	14	02	51
☽ First Quarter	22	00	42
○ Full Moon	28	16	38
Apogee (406,533km)	13	02	23
Perigee (357,835km)	27	21	45

Mean longitude of ascending node on February 1, 290°

THE SUN

s.d. 16′.2

Day	Right Ascension			Dec. –		Equation of time		Rise 52°		Rise 56°		Transit		Set 52°		Set 56°		Sidereal time			Transit of first point of Aries		
	h	*m*	*s*	°	′	*m*	*s*	*h*	*m*	*h*	*m*	*h*	*m*	*h*	*m*	*h*	*m*	*h*	*m*	*s*	*h*	*m*	*s*
1	20	57	53	17	11	−13	29	7	40	7	55	12	14	16	48	16	33	8	44	23	15	13	07
2	21	01	57	16	54	−13	37	7	39	7	53	12	14	16	49	16	35	8	48	20	15	09	11
3	21	06	01	16	37	−13	44	7	37	7	51	12	14	16	51	16	37	8	52	16	15	05	15
4	21	10	04	16	19	−13	51	7	35	7	49	12	14	16	53	16	39	8	56	13	15	01	19
5	21	14	06	16	01	−13	56	7	34	7	47	12	14	16	55	16	41	9	00	10	14	57	23
6	21	18	07	15	43	−14	01	7	32	7	45	12	14	16	57	16	44	9	04	06	14	53	27
7	21	22	07	15	24	−14	05	7	30	7	43	12	14	16	59	16	46	9	08	03	14	49	31
8	21	26	07	15	06	−14	08	7	28	7	41	12	14	17	01	16	48	9	11	59	14	45	35
9	21	30	06	14	47	−14	10	7	27	7	39	12	14	17	02	16	50	9	15	56	14	41	39
10	21	34	04	14	27	−14	12	7	25	7	37	12	14	17	04	16	52	9	19	52	14	37	43
11	21	38	01	14	08	−14	13	7	23	7	35	12	14	17	06	16	55	9	23	49	14	33	48
12	21	41	58	13	48	−14	13	7	21	7	32	12	14	17	08	16	57	9	27	45	14	29	52
13	21	45	54	13	28	−14	12	7	19	7	30	12	14	17	10	16	59	9	31	42	14	25	56
14	21	49	49	13	08	−14	10	7	17	7	28	12	14	17	12	17	01	9	35	39	14	22	00
15	21	53	43	12	47	−14	08	7	15	7	26	12	14	17	14	17	03	9	39	35	14	18	04
16	21	57	37	12	27	−14	05	7	13	7	23	12	14	17	16	17	06	9	43	32	14	14	08
17	22	01	30	12	06	−14	02	7	11	7	21	12	14	17	17	17	08	9	47	28	14	10	12
18	22	05	22	11	45	−13	57	7	09	7	19	12	14	17	19	17	10	9	51	25	14	06	16
19	22	09	14	11	24	−13	52	7	07	7	16	12	14	17	21	17	12	9	55	21	14	02	20
20	22	13	04	11	02	−13	46	7	05	7	14	12	14	17	23	17	14	9	59	18	13	58	24
21	22	16	54	10	41	−13	40	7	03	7	12	12	14	17	25	17	17	10	03	14	13	54	29
22	22	20	44	10	19	−13	33	7	01	7	09	12	13	17	27	17	19	10	07	11	13	50	33
23	22	24	33	9	57	−13	25	6	59	7	07	12	13	17	28	17	21	10	11	08	13	46	37
24	22	28	21	9	35	−13	17	6	57	7	04	12	13	17	30	17	23	10	15	04	13	42	41
25	22	32	09	9	13	−13	08	6	55	7	02	12	13	17	32	17	25	10	19	01	13	38	45
26	22	35	56	8	50	−12	58	6	53	6	59	12	13	17	34	17	27	10	22	57	13	34	49
27	22	39	42	8	28	−12	48	6	51	6	57	12	13	17	36	17	30	10	26	54	13	30	53
28	22	43	28	8	05	−12	37	6	48	6	54	12	13	17	38	17	32	10	30	50	13	26	57

DURATION OF TWILIGHT (in minutes)

Latitude	*52°*	*56°*	*52°*	*56°*	*52°*	*56°*	*52°*	*56°*
	1 February		*11 February*		*21 February*		*31 February*	
Civil	37	41	35	39	34	38	34	37
Nautical	77	86	75	83	74	81	73	80
Astronomical	117	130	114	126	113	124	112	124

THE NIGHT SKY

Mercury is unsuitably placed for observation throughout the month.

Venus is too close to the Sun for observation for the first half of the month but then becomes visible as an evening object, magnitude −3.9, low above the west-south-western horizon for a short while after sunset.

Mars is a conspicuous object in the evening skies and even by the end of the month can be seen low above the west-north-western horizon as late as 05h. Its magnitude fades during February from −1.3 to −0.6 as it moves retrograde in Cancer. During the early hours of the 26th the waxing Moon, nearly Full, passes 6 degrees south of the planet.

Jupiter, magnitude −2.0, may only be glimpsed with difficulty during the first ten days of the month, low above the south-western horizon at the end of evening civil twilight. Thereafter it is too close to the Sun for observation as it passes through conjunction on the last day of the month.

Saturn, in the constellation of Virgo, is rising in the eastern sky in the evenings and remains visible until the morning twilight inhibits observation. Its magnitude is +0.7. On the evening of the 2nd the waning gibbous Moon passes 8 degrees south of the planet.

Zodiacal Light. The evening cone may be observed stretching up from the western horizon, along the ecliptic, after the end of twilight, from the beginning of the month until the 15th. This faint phenomenon is only visible under good conditions and in the absence of both moonlight and artificial lighting.

THE MOON

Day	R.A.		Dec.	Hor. par.	Semi-diam.	Sun's Co-Long.	PA of Br. Limb	Ph.	Age	Rise				Transit		Set			
										52°		56°				52°		56°	
	h	*m*	°	′	′	°	°	%	*d*	*h*	*m*	*h*	*m*	*h*	*m*	*h*	*m*	*h*	*m*
1	10	28	+5.6	61.0	16.6	112	120	95	16.7	20	27	20	27	1	48	8	17	8	20
2	11	22	−0.9	60.4	16.5	124	119	89	17.7	21	53	21	59	2	39	8	34	8	31
3	12	15	−7.1	59.5	16.2	136	117	81	18.7	23	17	23	29	3	29	8	51	8	43
4	13	07	−12.8	58.6	16.0	148	115	71	19.7	—		—		4	20	9	09	8	56
5	14	00	−17.7	57.6	15.7	160	111	61	20.7	0	39	0	56	5	10	9	32	9	13
6	14	53	−21.5	56.8	15.5	172	107	50	21.7	1	57	2	20	6	02	9	59	9	35
7	15	47	−24.1	56.0	15.3	184	102	40	22.7	3	09	3	37	6	54	10	35	10	06
8	16	42	−25.5	55.3	15.1	197	96	30	23.7	4	11	4	43	7	46	11	20	10	49
9	17	36	−25.7	54.8	14.9	209	91	22	24.7	5	02	5	33	8	38	12	16	11	46
10	18	29	−24.6	54.4	14.8	221	86	14	25.7	5	41	6	09	9	28	13	20	12	53
11	19	20	−22.4	54.1	14.8	233	82	8	26.7	6	11	6	34	10	16	14	28	14	06
12	20	09	−19.3	54.0	14.7	245	80	4	27.7	6	34	6	51	11	01	15	38	15	22
13	20	56	−15.4	53.9	14.7	257	83	1	28.7	6	52	7	05	11	45	16	48	16	37
14	21	41	−10.9	54.0	14.7	270	137	0	29.7	7	07	7	15	12	26	17	57	17	51
15	22	25	−6.0	54.1	14.7	282	228	1	0.9	7	21	7	24	13	07	19	06	19	04
16	23	08	−0.9	54.3	14.8	294	236	3	1.9	7	33	7	33	13	47	20	15	20	18
17	23	51	+4.3	54.6	14.9	306	239	8	2.9	7	47	7	42	14	28	21	25	21	33
18	0	36	+9.4	55.0	15.0	318	241	13	3.9	8	01	7	52	15	11	22	38	22	51
19	1	22	+14.2	55.5	15.1	331	244	21	4.9	8	18	8	04	15	57	23	52	—	
20	2	11	+18.5	56.0	15.3	343	248	30	5.9	8	40	8	20	16	46	—		0	11
21	3	04	+22.0	56.7	15.5	355	253	39	6.9	9	09	8	44	17	39	1	08	1	32
22	4	00	+24.5	57.5	15.7	7	258	50	7.9	9	49	9	20	18	36	2	21	2	50
23	5	00	+25.6	58.4	15.9	19	265	61	8.9	10	44	10	13	19	36	3	27	3	58
24	6	01	+25.2	59.3	16.1	31	271	71	9.9	11	55	11	27	20	36	4	22	4	51
25	7	04	+23.1	60.1	16.4	44	277	81	10.9	13	18	12	56	21	36	5	04	5	27
26	8	05	+19.5	60.7	16.5	56	281	89	11.9	14	48	14	32	22	34	5	35	5	53
27	9	04	+14.5	61.1	16.7	68	282	96	12.9	16	20	16	10	23	30	5	59	6	11
28	10	02	+8.6	61.3	16.7	80	272	99	13.9	17	50	17	47	—		6	19	6	25

MERCURY

Day	R.A.		Dec.	Diam.	Phase	Transit		5° high			
								52°		56°	
	h	*m*	°	″	%	*h*	*m*	*h*	*m*	*h*	*m*
1	19	17	−22.0	6	71	10	33	7	20	7	52
3	19	27	−21.9	6	73	10	36	7	23	7	55
5	19	38	−21.8	6	76	10	39	7	25	7	56
7	19	50	−21.6	6	78	10	42	7	27	7	58
9	20	01	−21.3	6	80	10	46	7	28	7	58
11	20	13	−21.0	6	82	10	50	7	29	7	59
13	20	25	−20.5	5	84	10	55	7	30	7	58
15	20	38	−20.0	5	85	10	59	7	30	7	57
17	20	50	−19.4	5	87	11	04	7	30	7	56
19	21	03	−18.7	5	88	11	09	7	30	7	54
21	21	16	−17.9	5	90	11	14	7	29	7	52
23	21	29	−17.0	5	91	11	19	7	28	7	49
25	21	42	−16.0	5	92	11	24	7	26	7	46
27	21	55	−15.0	5	93	11	29	7	24	7	43
29	22	08	−13.8	5	95	11	34	7	22	7	39
31	22	21	−12.6	5	96	11	40	7	20	7	35

VENUS

Day	R.A.		Dec.	Diam.	Phase	Transit		5° high			
								52°		56°	
	h	*m*	°	″	%	*h*	*m*	*h*	*m*	*h*	*m*
1	21	19	−17.1	10	100	12	35	16	26	16	05
6	21	44	−15.1	10	100	12	40	16	44	16	25
11	22	08	−13.0	10	99	12	45	17	02	16	46
16	22	32	−10.8	10	99	12	49	17	19	17	06
21	22	55	−8.4	10	99	12	53	17	37	17	26
26	23	19	−6.0	10	98	12	56	17	54	17	46
31	23	41	−3.5	10	98	12	59	18	11	18	05

MARS

Day	R.A.		Dec.	Diam.	Phase	Transit		5° high			
								52°		56°	
	h	*m*	°	″	%	*h*	*m*	*h*	*m*	*h*	*m*
1	8	51	+22.4	14	100	0	06	7	33	7	50
6	8	42	+22.9	14	100	23	33	7	08	7	26
11	8	35	+23.3	14	99	23	06	6	43	7	01
16	8	28	+23.6	13	99	22	40	6	19	6	37
21	8	22	+23.8	13	98	22	15	5	55	6	13
26	8	18	+23.8	12	97	21	51	5	31	5	50
31	8	15	+23.8	12	96	21	29	5	08	5	27

SUNRISE AND SUNSET

	London				*Bristol*				*Birmingham*				*Manchester*				*Newcastle*				*Glasgow*				*Belfast*			
	0° 05′		*51° 30′*		*2° 35′*		*51° 28′*		*1° 55′*		*52° 28′*		*2° 15′*		*53° 28′*		*1° 37′*		*54° 59′*		*4° 14′*		*55° 52′*		*5° 56′*		*54° 35′*	
d	*h*	*m*	*h*	*m*	*h*	*m*	*h*	*m*	*h*	*m*	*h*	*m*	*h*	*m*	*h*	*m*	*h*	*m*	*h*	*m*	*h*	*m*	*h*	*m*	*h*	*m*	*h*	*m*
1	7	39	16	50	7	49	17	00	7	49	16	54	7	54	16	52	7	57	16	43	8	11	16	50	8	13	17	02
2	7	37	16	51	7	47	17	02	7	48	16	56	7	53	16	53	7	56	16	45	8	10	16	52	8	11	17	04
3	7	36	16	53	7	46	17	03	7	46	16	57	7	51	16	55	7	54	16	47	8	08	16	55	8	10	17	06
4	7	34	16	55	7	44	17	05	7	44	16	59	7	49	16	57	7	52	16	50	8	06	16	57	8	08	17	08
5	7	32	16	57	7	42	17	07	7	43	17	01	7	47	16	59	7	50	16	52	8	04	16	59	8	06	17	10
6	7	31	16	59	7	41	17	09	7	41	17	03	7	45	17	01	7	48	16	54	8	02	17	01	8	04	17	12
7	7	29	17	01	7	39	17	11	7	39	17	05	7	44	17	03	7	46	16	56	8	00	17	03	8	02	17	15
8	7	27	17	02	7	37	17	12	7	37	17	07	7	42	17	05	7	44	16	58	7	57	17	06	8	00	17	17
9	7	26	17	04	7	35	17	14	7	36	17	09	7	40	17	07	7	42	17	00	7	55	17	08	7	58	17	19
10	7	24	17	06	7	34	17	16	7	34	17	11	7	38	17	09	7	40	17	02	7	53	17	10	7	56	17	21
11	7	22	17	08	7	32	17	18	7	32	17	13	7	36	17	11	7	38	17	04	7	51	17	12	7	54	17	23
12	7	20	17	10	7	30	17	20	7	30	17	15	7	34	17	13	7	36	17	06	7	49	17	14	7	52	17	25
13	7	18	17	12	7	28	17	22	7	28	17	16	7	32	17	15	7	34	17	09	7	47	17	16	7	50	17	27
14	7	16	17	13	7	26	17	23	7	26	17	18	7	30	17	17	7	31	17	11	7	44	17	19	7	48	17	29
15	7	14	17	15	7	24	17	25	7	24	17	20	7	28	17	19	7	29	17	13	7	42	17	21	7	45	17	31
16	7	13	17	17	7	22	17	27	7	22	17	22	7	26	17	21	7	27	17	15	7	40	17	23	7	43	17	33
17	7	11	17	19	7	21	17	29	7	20	17	24	7	24	17	23	7	25	17	17	7	38	17	25	7	41	17	35
18	7	09	17	21	7	19	17	31	7	18	17	26	7	22	17	25	7	23	17	19	7	35	17	27	7	39	17	37
19	7	07	17	22	7	17	17	33	7	16	17	28	7	19	17	27	7	20	17	21	7	33	17	30	7	37	17	39
20	7	05	17	24	7	15	17	34	7	14	17	30	7	17	17	29	7	18	17	23	7	31	17	32	7	34	17	41
21	7	03	17	26	7	13	17	36	7	12	17	32	7	15	17	31	7	16	17	25	7	28	17	34	7	32	17	43
22	7	01	17	28	7	11	17	38	7	10	17	33	7	13	17	33	7	13	17	27	7	26	17	36	7	30	17	46
23	6	59	17	30	7	08	17	40	7	08	17	35	7	11	17	35	7	11	17	29	7	23	17	38	7	28	17	48
24	6	56	17	31	7	06	17	42	7	05	17	37	7	08	17	37	7	09	17	32	7	21	17	40	7	25	17	50
25	6	54	17	33	7	04	17	43	7	03	17	39	7	06	17	39	7	06	17	34	7	18	17	42	7	23	17	52
26	6	52	17	35	7	02	17	45	7	01	17	41	7	04	17	41	7	04	17	36	7	16	17	45	7	21	17	54
27	6	50	17	37	7	00	17	47	6	59	17	43	7	02	17	43	7	02	17	38	7	14	17	47	7	18	17	56
28	6	48	17	39	6	58	17	49	6	57	17	45	6	59	17	45	6	59	17	40	7	11	17	49	7	16	17	58

JUPITER

Day	*R.A.*		*Dec.*		*Transit*		*5° high*			
							52°		*56°*	
	h	*m*	°	′	*h*	*m*	*h*	*m*	*h*	*m*
1	22	21.8	−11	12	13	36	18	02	17	48
11	22	30.8	−10	20	13	05	17	36	17	24
21	22	39.8	−9	27	12	35	17	11	16	59
31	22	48.9	−8	33	12	05	16	46	16	35

Diameters – equatorial 33″ polar 31″

SATURN

Day	*R.A.*		*Dec.*		*Transit*		*5° high*			
							52°		*56°*	
	h	*m*	°	′	*h*	*m*	*h*	*m*	*h*	*m*
1	12	19.8	+0	30	3	35	22	02	22	04
11	12	18.4	+0	42	2	54	21	20	21	23
21	12	16.5	+0	57	2	13	20	37	20	40
31	12	14.1	+1	14	1	31	19	54	19	56

Diameters – equatorial 19″ polar 17″
Rings – major axis 43″ minor axis 3″

URANUS

Day	*R.A.*		*Dec.*		*Transit*		*10° high*			
							52°		*56°*	
	h	*m*	°	′	*h*	*m*	*h*	*m*	*h*	*m*
1	23	39.9	−2	58	14	53	19	31	19	21
11	23	41.7	−2	47	14	16	18	54	18	45
21	23	43.6	−2	34	13	38	18	18	18	09
31	23	45.6	−2	21	13	01	17	42	17	33

Diameter 4″

NEPTUNE

Day	*R.A.*		*Dec.*		*Transit*		*10° high*			
							52°		*56°*	
	h	*m*	°	′	*h*	*m*	*h*	*m*	*h*	*m*
1	21	52.2	−13	22	13	06	9	32	9	55
11	21	53.6	−13	15	12	28	8	53	9	16
21	21	55.1	−13	07	11	50	8	15	8	37
31	21	56.5	−13	00	11	12	7	36	7	58

Diameter 2″

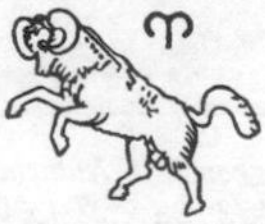

MARCH 2010

THIRD MONTH, 31 DAYS. *Mars*, Roman god of battle

1	*Monday*	Glenn Miller, wartime musician *b.* 1904; Dom Francisco de Almeida, Portuguese soldier and explorer *d.* 1510	week 9 day 60
2	*Tuesday*	Soviet troops captured Tuppura Island from Finland 1940	61
3	*Wednesday*	Russia signed the Treaty of Brest-Litovsk, marking its withdrawal from the First World War 1918	62
4	*Thursday*	King Charles II declared war on the Netherlands, starting the second Anglo-Dutch War 1665	63
5	*Friday*	Winston Churchill stated that an 'iron curtain has descended across the continent' 1946	64
6	*Saturday*	Philip Henry Sheridan, US cavalry commander *b.* 1831; Davy Crockett, US pioneer *d.* 1836	65
7	*Sunday*	Napoleon Bonaparte led France to victory against Prussian and Russian forces at Craonne 1814	66
8	*Monday*	The first US combat troops arrived in Vietnam 1965	week 10 day 67
9	*Tuesday*	Jean-Baptiste Kléber, French general *b.* 1753; William I, German emperor *d.* 1888	68
10	*Wednesday*	The French Foreign Legion was established 1831	69
11	*Thursday*	US Congress passed the Lend-Lease Bill 1941	70
12	*Friday*	Nazi Germany annexed Austria 1938	71
13	*Saturday*	The siege of Khartoum, Sudan, began 1884	72
14	*Sunday*	The German cruiser *Dresden* was scuttled to avoid capture 1915	73
15	*Monday*	German forces entered Czechoslovakia 1939	week 11 day 74
16	*Tuesday*	An Iraqi gas attack on the Kurdish town of Halabja killed 5,000 people 1988	75
17	*Wednesday*	Lachlan McIntosh, US military and political leader *b.* 1725; Ashikaga Yoshikazu, Japanese shogun *d.* 1425	76
18	*Thursday*	Wilfred Owen, soldier and poet *b.* 1893; Ivan IV, Russian tsar *d.* 1584	77
19	*Friday*	The Argentine national flag was hoisted on a dependency of the British Falkland Islands 1982	78
20	*Saturday*	The US-led invasion of Iraq began without support from the United Nations 2003	79
21	*Sunday*	The Battle of Karameh took place in Jordan between Israel and the Palestinian Fatah movement 1968	80
22	*Monday*	Powhatan Native Americans killed 350 English settlers in the Jamestown Massacre 1622	week 12 day 81
23	*Tuesday*	US President Ronald Reagan announced plans for a space-based defence system 1983	82
24	*Wednesday*	NATO launched air strikes on Serbian positions in the Yugoslavian province of Kosovo 1999	83
25	*Thursday*	Yugoslavia joined the Axis alliance in the Second World War 1941	84
26	*Friday*	The first Battle of Gaza took place between the Allies and Turkey 1917	85
27	*Saturday*	The European fighter jet made its maiden flight 1994	86
28	*Sunday*	The Spanish Civil War ended with the Republican surrender of Madrid 1939	87
29	*Monday*	The US withdrew the last of its troops from Vietnam 1973	week 13 day 88
30	*Tuesday*	French forces were defeated at the Battle of Paris 1814	89
31	*Wednesday*	Kaiser Wilhelm I's support for the Sultan of Morocco precipitated the first Moroccan Crisis 1905	90

ASTRONOMICAL PHENOMENA

d	*h*	
2	05	Saturn in conjunction with Moon. Saturn 7°N.
8	02	Jupiter in conjunction with Mercury. Jupiter 1°N.
10	17	Mars at stationary point
14	13	Mercury in superior conjunction
14	21	Jupiter in conjunction with Moon. Jupiter 5°S.
16	00	Mercury in conjunction with Moon. Mercury 6°S.
17	06	Venus in conjunction with Moon. Venus 6°S.
17	07	Uranus in conjunction
20	18	Sun's longitude 0° ♈
22	01	Saturn at opposition
25	12	Mars in conjunction with Moon. Mars 4°N.
29	12	Saturn in conjunction with Moon. Saturn 7°N.

MINIMA OF ALGOL

d	*h*	*d*	*h*	*d*	*h*
3	01.2	14	12.5	25	23.8
5	22.0	17	09.3	28	20.6
8	18.8	20	06.1	31	17.4
11	15.7	23	02.9		

CONSTELLATIONS

The following constellations are near the meridian at

	d	*h*		*d*	*h*
February	1	24	March	16	21
February	15	23	April	1	20
March	1	22	April	15	19

Cepheus (below the Pole), Camelopardalis, Lynx, Gemini, Cancer, Leo, Canis Minor, Hydra, Monoceros, Canis Major and Puppis

THE MOON

Phases, Apsides and Node	*d*	*h*	*m*
☾ Last Quarter	7	15	42
● New Moon	15	21	01
☽ First Quarter	23	11	00
○ Full Moon	30	02	25
Apogee (405,984km)	12	10	15
Perigee (361,892km)	28	05	06

Mean longitude of ascending node on March 1, 289°

THE SUN

s.d. 16′.1

Day	Right Ascension			Dec.		Equation of time		Rise 52°		Rise 56°		Transit		Set 52°		Set 56°		Sidereal time			Transit of first point of Aries		
	h	m	s	°	′	m	s	h	m	h	m	h	m	h	m	h	m	h	m	s	h	m	s
1	22	47	13	−7	43	−12	26	6	46	6	52	12	12	17	39	17	34	10	34	47	13	23	01
2	22	50	58	−7	20	−12	14	6	44	6	49	12	12	17	41	17	36	10	38	43	13	19	05
3	22	54	42	−6	57	−12	02	6	42	6	47	12	12	17	43	17	38	10	42	40	13	15	09
4	22	58	26	−6	34	−11	49	6	40	6	44	12	12	17	45	17	40	10	46	37	13	11	14
5	23	02	09	−6	11	−11	36	6	37	6	42	12	11	17	47	17	42	10	50	33	13	07	18
6	23	05	52	−5	48	−11	23	6	35	6	39	12	11	17	48	17	44	10	54	30	13	03	22
7	23	09	35	−5	24	−11	09	6	33	6	37	12	11	17	50	17	46	10	58	26	12	59	26
8	23	13	17	−5	01	−10	54	6	31	6	34	12	11	17	52	17	49	11	02	23	12	55	30
9	23	16	59	−4	38	−10	40	6	28	6	31	12	11	17	54	17	51	11	06	19	12	51	34
10	23	20	40	−4	14	−10	25	6	26	6	29	12	10	17	55	17	53	11	10	16	12	47	38
11	23	24	22	−3	51	−10	09	6	24	6	26	12	10	17	57	17	55	11	14	12	12	43	42
12	23	28	02	−3	27	−9	53	6	22	6	24	12	10	17	59	17	57	11	18	09	12	39	46
13	23	31	43	−3	03	−9	37	6	19	6	21	12	09	18	01	17	59	11	22	05	12	35	50
14	23	35	23	−2	40	−9	21	6	17	6	18	12	09	18	02	18	01	11	26	02	12	31	54
15	23	39	03	−2	16	−9	05	6	15	6	16	12	09	18	04	18	03	11	29	59	12	27	59
16	23	42	43	−1	52	−8	48	6	12	6	13	12	09	18	06	18	05	11	33	55	12	24	03
17	23	46	23	−1	29	−8	31	6	10	6	11	12	08	18	08	18	07	11	37	52	12	20	07
18	23	50	02	−1	05	−8	14	6	08	6	08	12	08	18	09	18	09	11	41	48	12	16	11
19	23	53	41	−0	41	−7	56	6	05	6	05	12	08	18	11	18	11	11	45	45	12	12	15
20	23	57	20	−0	17	−7	39	6	03	6	03	12	07	18	13	18	13	11	49	41	12	08	19
21	0	00	59	+0	06	−7	21	6	01	6	00	12	07	18	15	18	15	11	53	38	12	04	23
22	0	04	38	+0	30	−7	03	5	58	5	57	12	07	18	16	18	18	11	57	34	12	00	27
23	0	08	16	+0	54	−6	45	5	56	5	55	12	07	18	18	18	20	12	01	31	11	56	31
24	0	11	55	+1	17	−6	27	5	54	5	52	12	06	18	20	18	22	12	05	28	11	52	35
25	0	15	33	+1	41	−6	09	5	52	5	50	12	06	18	22	18	24	12	09	24	11	48	39
26	0	19	12	+2	05	−5	51	5	49	5	47	12	06	18	23	18	26	12	13	21	11	44	44
27	0	22	50	+2	28	−5	33	5	47	5	44	12	05	18	25	18	28	12	17	17	11	40	48
28	0	26	28	+2	52	−5	15	5	45	5	42	12	05	18	27	18	30	12	21	14	11	36	52
29	0	30	07	+3	15	−4	56	5	42	5	39	12	05	18	28	18	32	12	25	10	11	32	56
30	0	33	45	+3	38	−4	38	5	40	5	36	12	04	18	30	18	34	12	29	07	11	29	00
31	0	37	24	+4	02	−4	20	5	38	5	34	12	04	18	32	18	36	12	33	03	11	25	04

DURATION OF TWILIGHT (in minutes)

Latitude	52°	56°	52°	56°	52°	56°	52°	56°
	1 March		*11 March*		*21 March*		*31 March*	
Civil	34	37	34	37	34	37	34	38
Nautical	73	80	73	80	74	81	75	84
Astronomical	112	124	113	125	115	128	120	135

THE NIGHT SKY

Mercury passes through superior conjunction on the 14th. It then moves rapidly eastwards from the Sun and emerges from the evening twilight during the last few days of the month. Then it may be seen low above the western horizon about the end of evening civil twilight. Its magnitude fades slightly from −1.2 to −0.9. During the night of the 7/8th Mercury passes 1 degree south of Jupiter.

Venus, magnitude −3.9, is visible as an evening object, low in the western sky after sunset. The thin crescent Moon, only two days old, passes 5 degrees north of Venus on the evening of the 17th.

Mars continues to be visible as a conspicuous object in the night sky but will be lost to view over the west-north-western horizon after about 03h. During the month its magnitude fades from −0.6 to +0.2. The planet reaches its second stationary point on the 10th and resumes its direct motion, in the constellation of Cancer. The waxing gibbous Moon passes 5 degrees south of Mars on the 25th.

Jupiter remains too close to the Sun for observation throughout the month.

Saturn, magnitude +0.5, reaches opposition on the 22nd and thus remains visible throughout the hours of darkness. The rings of Saturn are still difficult to observe as the angular width is only three arcseconds. The waning gibbous Moon passes 8 degrees south of Saturn on the 2nd. The same event occurs again on the 29th, when the Moon is Full.

Zodiacal Light. The evening cone may be observed stretching up from the western horizon, along the ecliptic, after the end of twilight, from the 2nd until the 17th. This faint phenomenon is only visible under good conditions and in the absence of both moonlight and artificial lighting.

THE MOON

Day	R.A.		Dec.	Hor. par.	Semi-diam.	Sun's Co-Long.	PA of Br. Limb	Ph.	Age	Rise				Transit		Set			
										52°		56°				52°		56°	
	h	*m*	°	′	′	°	°	%	*d*	*h*	*m*	*h*	*m*	*h*	*m*	*h*	*m*	*h*	*m*
1	10	57	+2.2	61.1	16.6	92	156	100	14.9	19	19	19	22	0	23	6	37	6	37
2	11	51	−4.3	60.6	16.5	104	128	97	15.9	20	47	20	55	1	15	6	54	6	49
3	12	45	−10.4	59.8	16.3	117	121	92	16.9	22	12	22	27	2	07	7	13	7	02
4	13	39	−15.7	58.9	16.1	129	116	85	17.9	23	35	23	56	2	59	7	34	7	18
5	14	34	−20.1	58.0	15.8	141	111	76	18.9	—		—		3	52	8	00	7	38
6	15	30	−23.2	57.0	15.5	153	106	67	19.9	0	52	1	19	4	46	8	34	8	07
7	16	26	−25.1	56.1	15.3	165	100	57	20.9	2	01	2	31	5	40	9	17	8	46
8	17	21	−25.6	55.4	15.1	177	94	47	21.9	2	57	3	28	6	33	10	10	9	39
9	18	15	−24.8	54.8	14.9	189	88	37	22.9	3	40	4	09	7	24	11	11	10	43
10	19	07	−22.9	54.4	14.8	202	83	28	23.9	4	13	4	37	8	13	12	18	11	55
11	19	56	−20.0	54.1	14.8	214	79	20	24.9	4	39	4	58	8	59	13	27	13	09
12	20	44	−16.4	54.0	14.7	226	77	13	25.9	4	58	5	12	9	43	14	37	14	24
13	21	29	−12.1	54.0	14.7	238	76	7	26.9	5	14	5	24	10	25	15	46	15	38
14	22	13	−7.3	54.1	14.8	250	78	3	27.9	5	29	5	34	11	06	16	55	16	52
15	22	57	−2.2	54.4	14.8	263	90	1	28.9	5	42	5	43	11	46	18	05	18	06
16	23	40	+3.0	54.6	14.9	275	173	0	0.1	5	55	5	52	12	27	19	15	19	21
17	0	25	+8.1	55.0	15.0	287	226	1	1.1	6	10	6	02	13	10	20	27	20	38
18	1	11	+13.0	55.4	15.1	299	237	5	2.1	6	26	6	14	13	55	21	41	21	58
19	2	00	+17.4	55.9	15.2	312	243	10	3.1	6	47	6	29	14	43	22	56	23	18
20	2	52	+21.1	56.4	15.4	324	249	16	4.1	7	13	6	51	15	35	—		—	
21	3	47	+23.8	56.9	15.5	336	255	25	5.1	7	50	7	22	16	30	0	10	0	37
22	4	45	+25.2	57.6	15.7	348	262	34	6.1	8	38	8	08	17	27	1	17	1	47
23	5	44	+25.2	58.2	15.9	0	268	45	7.1	9	42	9	13	18	26	2	15	2	44
24	6	45	+23.7	58.9	16.0	12	274	56	8.1	10	58	10	33	19	24	3	00	3	25
25	7	44	+20.7	59.5	16.2	25	280	67	9.1	12	22	12	03	20	21	3	34	3	54
26	8	42	+16.4	60.0	16.4	37	284	78	10.1	13	49	13	37	21	15	4	00	4	14
27	9	38	+11.0	60.4	16.5	49	286	87	11.1	15	18	15	11	22	08	4	21	4	29
28	10	33	+4.9	60.6	16.5	61	285	94	12.1	16	45	16	45	23	00	4	40	4	43
29	11	27	−1.4	60.5	16.5	73	277	98	13.1	18	12	18	18	23	51	4	57	4	55
30	12	21	−7.6	60.2	16.4	85	219	100	14.1	19	39	19	51	—		5	15	5	07
31	13	15	−13.3	59.6	16.2	98	134	99	15.1	21	05	21	23	0	44	5	35	5	22

MERCURY

Day	R.A.		Dec.	Diam.	Phase	Transit		5° high			
								52°		56°	
	h	*m*	°	″	%	*h*	*m*	*h*	*m*	*h*	*m*
1	22	08	−13.8	5	95	11	34	7	22	7	39
3	22	21	−12.6	5	96	11	40	7	20	7	35
5	22	34	−11.3	5	97	11	45	7	18	7	31
7	22	48	−9.9	5	98	11	51	7	15	7	27
9	23	01	−8.4	5	99	11	57	7	12	7	23
11	23	15	−6.8	5	99	12	02	16	57	16	49
13	23	29	−5.2	5	100	12	08	17	13	17	05
15	23	43	−3.5	5	100	12	15	17	28	17	22
17	23	57	−1.7	5	100	12	21	17	44	17	40
19	0	11	+0.2	5	99	12	27	18	00	17	57
21	0	25	+2.0	5	97	12	34	18	16	18	15
23	0	40	+3.9	5	95	12	40	18	32	18	32
25	0	54	+5.8	5	91	12	46	18	48	18	50
27	1	08	+7.6	6	86	12	52	19	03	19	06
29	1	21	+9.4	6	81	12	57	19	17	19	22
31	1	34	+11.1	6	74	13	02	19	31	19	37

VENUS

Day	R.A.		Dec.	Diam.	Phase	Transit		5° high			
								52°		56°	
	h	*m*	°	″	%	*h*	*m*	*h*	*m*	*h*	*m*
1	23	32	−4.5	10	98	12	58	18	04	17	57
6	23	55	−1.9	10	98	13	01	18	20	18	16
11	0	18	+0.6	10	97	13	04	18	37	18	34
16	0	40	+3.2	10	97	13	07	18	53	18	53
21	1	03	+5.7	10	96	13	10	19	09	19	11
26	1	26	+8.2	10	95	13	13	19	25	19	29
31	1	49	+10.6	10	95	13	16	19	41	19	46

MARS

Day	R.A.		Dec.	Diam.	Phase	Transit		5° high			
								52°		56°	
	h	*m*	°	″	%	*h*	*m*	*h*	*m*	*h*	*m*
1	8	16	+23.8	12	96	21	37	5	17	5	36
6	8	14	+23.8	12	95	21	16	4	55	5	14
11	8	13	+23.6	11	94	20	56	4	34	4	53
16	8	14	+23.4	11	94	20	37	4	14	4	32
21	8	16	+23.1	10	93	20	19	3	54	4	12
26	8	19	+22.8	10	92	20	02	3	35	3	53
31	8	22	+22.4	9	92	19	47	3	17	3	34

SUNRISE AND SUNSET

	London				*Bristol*				*Birmingham*				*Manchester*				*Newcastle*				*Glasgow*				*Belfast*			
	0° 05′		*51° 30′*		*2° 35′*		*51° 28′*		*1° 55′*		*52° 28′*		*2° 15′*		*53° 28′*		*1° 37′*		*54° 59′*		*4° 14′*		*55° 52′*		*5° 56′*		*54° 35′*	
d	*h*	*m*	*h*	*m*	*h*	*m*	*h*	*m*	*h*	*m*	*h*	*m*	*h*	*m*	*h*	*m*	*h*	*m*	*h*	*m*	*h*	*m*	*h*	*m*	*h*	*m*	*h*	*m*
1	6	46	17	40	6	56	17	50	6	54	17	46	6	57	17	46	6	57	17	42	7	09	17	51	7	13	18	00
2	6	44	17	42	6	54	17	52	6	52	17	48	6	55	17	48	6	54	17	44	7	06	17	53	7	11	18	02
3	6	42	17	44	6	52	17	54	6	50	17	50	6	53	17	50	6	52	17	46	7	04	17	55	7	09	18	04
4	6	39	17	46	6	49	17	56	6	48	17	52	6	50	17	52	6	49	17	48	7	01	17	57	7	06	18	06
5	6	37	17	47	6	47	17	57	6	45	17	54	6	48	17	54	6	47	17	50	6	59	17	59	7	04	18	08
6	6	35	17	49	6	45	17	59	6	43	17	56	6	46	17	56	6	45	17	52	6	56	18	01	7	01	18	10
7	6	33	17	51	6	43	18	01	6	41	17	57	6	43	17	58	6	42	17	54	6	53	18	04	6	59	18	12
8	6	31	17	53	6	41	18	03	6	39	17	59	6	41	18	00	6	40	17	56	6	51	18	06	6	56	18	14
9	6	28	17	54	6	38	18	04	6	36	18	01	6	38	18	02	6	37	17	58	6	48	18	08	6	54	18	16
10	6	26	17	56	6	36	18	06	6	34	18	03	6	36	18	04	6	35	18	00	6	46	18	10	6	52	18	18
11	6	24	17	58	6	34	18	08	6	32	18	05	6	34	18	05	6	32	18	02	6	43	18	12	6	49	18	19
12	6	22	18	00	6	32	18	10	6	29	18	06	6	31	18	07	6	30	18	04	6	41	18	14	6	47	18	21
13	6	19	18	01	6	29	18	11	6	27	18	08	6	29	18	09	6	27	18	06	6	38	18	16	6	44	18	23
14	6	17	18	03	6	27	18	13	6	25	18	10	6	26	18	11	6	25	18	08	6	35	18	18	6	42	18	25
15	6	15	18	05	6	25	18	15	6	22	18	12	6	24	18	13	6	22	18	10	6	33	18	20	6	39	18	27
16	6	13	18	06	6	23	18	16	6	20	18	14	6	22	18	15	6	19	18	12	6	30	18	22	6	37	18	29
17	6	10	18	08	6	20	18	18	6	18	18	15	6	19	18	17	6	17	18	14	6	28	18	24	6	34	18	31
18	6	08	18	10	6	18	18	20	6	15	18	17	6	17	18	18	6	14	18	16	6	25	18	26	6	32	18	33
19	6	06	18	11	6	16	18	21	6	13	18	19	6	14	18	20	6	12	18	18	6	22	18	28	6	29	18	35
20	6	03	18	13	6	13	18	23	6	11	18	21	6	12	18	22	6	09	18	20	6	20	18	30	6	27	18	37
21	6	01	18	15	6	11	18	25	6	08	18	22	6	10	18	24	6	07	18	22	6	17	18	32	6	24	18	39
22	5	59	18	17	6	09	18	27	6	06	18	24	6	07	18	26	6	04	18	24	6	14	18	34	6	22	18	41
23	5	57	18	18	6	07	18	28	6	04	18	26	6	05	18	28	6	02	18	26	6	12	18	36	6	19	18	43
24	5	54	18	20	6	04	18	30	6	01	18	28	6	02	18	29	5	59	18	28	6	09	18	39	6	17	18	45
25	5	52	18	22	6	02	18	32	5	59	18	29	6	00	18	31	5	57	18	30	6	07	18	41	6	14	18	47
26	5	50	18	23	6	00	18	33	5	57	18	31	5	57	18	33	5	54	18	32	6	04	18	43	6	11	18	49
27	5	48	18	25	5	58	18	35	5	54	18	33	5	55	18	35	5	51	18	33	6	01	18	45	6	09	18	50
28	5	45	18	27	5	55	18	37	5	52	18	35	5	53	18	37	5	49	18	35	5	59	18	47	6	06	18	52
29	5	43	18	28	5	53	18	38	5	50	18	36	5	50	18	39	5	46	18	37	5	56	18	49	6	04	18	54
30	5	41	18	30	5	51	18	40	5	47	18	38	5	48	18	40	5	44	18	39	5	53	18	51	6	01	18	56
31	5	38	18	32	5	48	18	42	5	45	18	40	5	45	18	42	5	41	18	41	5	51	18	53	5	59	18	58

JUPITER

Day	*R.A.*		*Dec.*		*Transit*		*5° high*			
							52°		*56°*	
	h	*m*	°	′	*h*	*m*	*h*	*m*	*h*	*m*
1	22	47.1	–8	44	12	11	7	31	7	42
11	22	56.1	–7	50	11	40	6	55	7	06
21	23	05.0	–6	55	11	10	6	20	6	29
31	23	13.7	–6	01	10	39	5	44	5	53

Diameters – equatorial 33″ polar 31″

SATURN

Day	*R.A.*		*Dec.*		*Transit*		*5° high*			
							52°		*56°*	
	h	*m*	°	′	*h*	*m*	*h*	*m*	*h*	*m*
1	12	14.6	+1	11	1	40	20	03	20	05
11	12	11.9	+1	29	0	58	19	19	19	21
21	12	09.1	+1	49	0	15	18	35	18	37
31	12	06.2	+2	08	23	29	17	52	17	53

Diameters – equatorial 19″ polar 17″
Rings – major axis 44″ minor axis 3″

URANUS

Day	*R.A.*		*Dec.*		*Transit*		*10° high*			
							52°		*56°*	
	h	*m*	°	′	*h*	*m*	*h*	*m*	*h*	*m*
1	23	45.2	–2	23	13	08	8	28	8	37
11	23	47.2	–2	10	12	31	7	49	7	58
21	23	49.3	–1	56	11	54	7	11	7	19
31	23	51.4	–1	43	11	17	6	32	6	40

Diameter 4″

NEPTUNE

Day	*R.A.*		*Dec.*		*Transit*		*10° high*			
							52°		*56°*	
	h	*m*	°	′	*h*	*m*	*h*	*m*	*h*	*m*
1	21	56.2	–13	01	11	20	7	44	8	06
11	21	57.7	–12	54	10	42	7	05	7	27
21	21	59.0	–12	47	10	04	6	26	6	48
31	22	00.2	–12	40	9	26	5	47	6	09

Diameter 2″

APRIL 2010

FOURTH MONTH, 30 DAYS. *Aperire*, to open; Earth opens to receive seed.

1	*Thursday*	Otto von Bismarck, German chancellor *b.* 1815; Gabrielle Petit, Belgian resistance fighter *d.* 1916	day 91
2	*Friday*	The British fleet defeated the Danish at the Battle of Copenhagen 1801	92
3	*Saturday*	US president Harry Truman signed the Marshall Plan 1948	93
4	*Sunday*	NATO was established by 12 countries 1949	94
5	*Monday*	Mass demonstrations against the Vietnam War took place in the USA 1969	week 14 day 95
6	*Tuesday*	Germany invaded Greece and Yugoslavia 1941	96
7	*Wednesday*	US president Jimmy Carter delayed production of the neutron bomb 1978	97
8	*Thursday*	Britain and France signed the Entente Cordiale 1904	98
9	*Friday*	US tanks entered Baghdad and Saddam Hussein's statue was toppled 2003	99
10	*Saturday*	Northern Ireland peace talks culminated in the Good Friday Agreement 1998	100
11	*Sunday*	Uganda's military dictator Idi Amin was overthrown 1979	101
12	*Monday*	The American Civil War began 1861	week 15 day 102
13	*Tuesday*	Frederick North, British prime minister *b.* 1732	103
14	*Wednesday*	The House of Lancaster won the Battle of Barnet in the War of the Roses 1471	104
15	*Thursday*	The French won a decisive victory at the Battle of Formigny during the Hundred Years War 1450	105
16	*Friday*	The Hanoverians defeated Bonnie Prince Charlie and the Jacobites at the Battle of Culloden 1746	106
17	*Saturday*	The Bay of Pigs was invaded by anti-Castro Cuban exiles 1961	107
18	*Sunday*	Over 60,000 people demonstrated against the hydrogen bomb in Trafalgar Square 1960	108
19	*Monday*	The American War of Independence began in Lexington, Mass. 1775	week 16 day 109
20	*Tuesday*	Operation Little Switch freed 100 UN prisoners during the Korean War 1953	110
21	*Wednesday*	The Soviet Red Army entered the outskirts of Berlin 1945	111
22	*Thursday*	Germany used poison gas against the Allies in the second Battle of Ypres 1915	112
23	*Friday*	Exeter was bombed in the first of Germany's Baedeker air raids 1942	113
24	*Saturday*	Russia declared war on the Ottoman Empire 1877	114
25	*Sunday*	Allied operations in Gallipoli began with the landing of ANZAC soldiers 1915	115
26	*Monday*	The Luftwaffe bombed Guernica in Spain 1937	week 17 day 116
27	*Tuesday*	The army of Edward I defeated the Scottish at the Battle of Dunbar 1296	117
28	*Wednesday*	Italian partisans assassinated fascist leader Benito Mussolini 1945	118
29	*Thursday*	US troops liberated the Dachau concentration camp in Germany 1945	119
30	*Friday*	The Vietnam War ended as Saigon surrendered to North Vietnamese forces 1975	120

ASTRONOMICAL PHENOMENA

d	*h*	
7	03	Pluto at stationary point
8	23	Mercury at greatest elongation E.19°
11	17	Jupiter in conjunction with Moon. Jupiter 5°S.
15	22	Mercury in conjunction with Moon. Mercury 1°S.
16	11	Venus in conjunction with Moon. Venus 4°S.
18	04	Mercury at stationary point
20	04	Sun's longitude 30° ♉
22	07	Mars in conjunction with Moon. Mars 4°N.
25	18	Saturn in conjuction with Moon. Saturn 7°N.
28	17	Mercury in inferior conjunction

MINIMA OF ALGOL

d	*h*	*d*	*h*	*d*	*h*
3	14.2	15	01.5	26	12.8
6	11.0	17	22.3	29	09.6
9	07.9	20	19.1		
12	04.7	23	16.0		

CONSTELLATIONS

The following constellations are near the meridian at

	d	*h*		*d*	*h*
March	1	24	April	15	21
March	16	23	May	1	20
April	1	22	May	16	19

Cepheus (below the Pole), Cassiopeia (below the Pole), Ursa Major, Leo Minor, Leo., Sextans, Hydra and Crater

THE MOON

Phases, Apsides and Node	*d*	*h*	*m*
☾ Last Quarter	6	09	37
● New Moon	14	12	29
☽ First Quarter	21	18	20
○ Full Moon	28	12	18
Apogee (404, 967 km)	9	02	49
Perigee (367, 168 km)	24	21	09

Mean longitude of ascending node on April 1, 287°

THE SUN

s.d. 16′.0

Day	Right Ascension			Dec. +		Equation of time		Rise 52°		Rise 56°		Transit		Set 52°		Set 56°		Sidereal time			Transit of first point of Aries		
	h	*m*	*s*	°	′	*m*	*s*	*h*	*m*	*h*	*m*	*h*	*m*	*h*	*m*	*h*	*m*	*h*	*m*	*s*	*h*	*m*	*s*
1	0	41	02	4	25	−4	02	5	35	5	31	12	04	18	34	18	38	12	37	00	11	21	08
2	0	44	41	4	48	−3	44	5	33	5	28	12	04	18	35	18	40	12	40	57	11	17	12
3	0	48	20	5	11	−3	26	5	31	5	26	12	03	18	37	18	42	12	44	53	11	13	16
4	0	51	58	5	34	−3	09	5	28	5	23	12	03	18	39	18	44	12	48	50	11	09	20
5	0	55	38	5	57	−2	51	5	26	5	21	12	03	18	40	18	46	12	52	46	11	05	24
6	0	59	17	6	20	−2	34	5	24	5	18	12	02	18	42	18	48	12	56	43	11	01	29
7	1	02	56	6	42	−2	17	5	22	5	15	12	02	18	44	18	50	13	00	39	10	57	33
8	1	06	36	7	05	−2	00	5	19	5	13	12	02	18	45	18	52	13	04	36	10	53	37
9	1	10	16	7	27	−1	44	5	17	5	10	12	02	18	47	18	54	13	08	32	10	49	41
10	1	13	56	7	50	−1	27	5	15	5	08	12	01	18	49	18	56	13	12	29	10	45	45
11	1	17	37	8	12	−1	11	5	13	5	05	12	01	18	51	18	58	13	16	26	10	41	49
12	1	21	18	8	34	−0	56	5	10	5	03	12	01	18	52	19	00	13	20	22	10	37	53
13	1	24	59	8	56	−0	40	5	08	5	00	12	01	18	54	19	02	13	24	19	10	33	57
14	1	28	40	9	17	−0	25	5	06	4	58	12	00	18	56	19	04	13	28	15	10	30	01
15	1	32	22	9	39	−0	10	5	04	4	55	12	00	18	57	19	06	13	32	12	10	26	05
16	1	36	04	10	00	+0	04	5	02	4	52	12	00	18	59	19	09	13	36	08	10	22	09
17	1	39	47	10	22	+0	18	4	59	4	50	12	00	19	01	19	11	13	40	05	10	18	14
18	1	43	30	10	43	+0	32	4	57	4	47	11	59	19	03	19	13	13	44	01	10	14	18
19	1	47	13	11	04	+0	45	4	55	4	45	11	59	19	04	19	15	13	47	58	10	10	22
20	1	50	57	11	24	+0	58	4	53	4	43	11	59	19	06	19	17	13	51	55	10	06	26
21	1	54	41	11	45	+1	10	4	51	4	40	11	59	19	08	19	19	13	55	51	10	02	30
22	1	58	25	12	05	+1	22	4	49	4	38	11	59	19	09	19	21	13	59	48	9	58	34
23	2	02	10	12	25	+1	34	4	47	4	35	11	58	19	11	19	23	14	03	44	9	54	38
24	2	05	55	12	45	+1	45	4	45	4	33	11	58	19	13	19	25	14	07	41	9	50	42
25	2	09	41	13	05	+1	56	4	43	4	30	11	58	19	14	19	27	14	11	37	9	46	46
26	2	13	27	13	25	+2	07	4	41	4	28	11	58	19	16	19	29	14	15	34	9	42	50
27	2	17	14	13	44	+2	16	4	39	4	26	11	58	19	18	19	31	14	19	30	9	38	55
28	2	21	01	14	03	+2	26	4	37	4	23	11	57	19	20	19	33	14	23	27	9	34	59
29	2	24	49	14	22	+2	35	4	35	4	21	11	57	19	21	19	35	14	27	24	9	31	03
30	2	28	37	14	40	+2	43	4	33	4	19	11	57	19	23	19	37	14	31	20	9	27	07

DURATION OF TWILIGHT (in minutes)

Latitude	52°	56°	52°	56°	52°	56°	52°	56°
	1 April		*11 April*		*21 April*		*31 April*	
Civil	34	38	35	39	37	42	39	44
Nautical	76	84	79	89	83	96	89	106
Astronomical	120	136	127	147	137	165	152	204

THE NIGHT SKY

Mercury reaches greatest eastern elongation (19 degrees) on the 8th. It becomes visible low above the western horizon in the evenings, at the end of civil twilight, until the middle of the month. During this time its magnitude fades from −0.8 to +1.4. This evening apparition is the most suitable one of the year for observers in the British Isles. Mercury passes through inferior conjunction on the 28th.

Venus continues to be visible for a short time in the evenings, low in the western sky after sunset. Its magnitude is −3.9. The thin crescent Moon, only 2 days old, passes 3 degrees north of the planet on the evening of the 16th.

Mars, its magnitude fading from +0.2 to +0.7 during the month, continues to move eastwards in Cancer, passing just north of the open cluster known as the Beehive (Praesepe) around the middle of April. Mars will be seen high in the southern sky in the evenings, and not setting in the west until the early hours. Before setting on the morning of the 22nd, the Moon, at First Quarter, passes 5 degrees south of Mars.

Jupiter is still too close to the Sun for observation.

Saturn, magnitude +0.6, continues to be visible as an evening object and remains visible for most of the night in the south-western quadrant of the sky. On the evening of the 25th the waxing gibbous Moon passes 8 degrees south of the planet.

THE MOON

Day	R.A.		Dec.	Hor. Par.	Semi-diam.	Sun's Co-Long.	PA of Br. Limb	Ph.	Age	Rise 52°		Rise 56°		Transit		Set 52°		Set 56°	
	h	m	°	′	′	°	°	%	d	h	m	h	m	h	m	h	m	h	m
1	14	11	−18.2	58.9	16.0	110	119	95	16.1	22	27	22	51	1	37	6	00	5	41
2	15	08	−21.9	58.0	15.8	122	111	89	17.1	23	41	—		2	32	6	31	6	06
3	16	05	−24.3	57.1	15.6	134	104	82	18.1	—		0	10	3	28	7	10	6	42
4	17	02	−25.3	56.3	15.3	146	97	73	19.1	0	45	1	15	4	23	8	01	7	30
5	17	57	−24.9	55.5	15.1	158	91	64	20.1	1	34	2	04	5	16	9	00	8	31
6	18	51	−23.4	54.9	15.0	171	85	54	21.1	2	12	2	37	6	06	10	06	9	42
7	19	42	−20.8	54.5	14.9	183	80	44	22.1	2	40	3	01	6	54	11	15	10	56
8	20	30	−17.3	54.2	14.8	195	77	35	23.1	3	02	3	18	7	39	12	25	12	10
9	21	16	−13.2	54.1	14.8	207	74	26	24.1	3	20	3	31	8	21	13	34	13	24
10	22	00	−8.6	54.2	14.8	219	73	19	25.1	3	35	3	42	9	03	14	43	14	38
11	22	44	−3.6	54.4	14.8	232	73	12	26.1	3	49	3	51	9	43	15	52	15	51
12	23	27	+1.5	54.7	14.9	244	75	6	27.1	4	02	4	00	10	24	17	02	17	06
13	0	12	+6.7	55.1	15.0	256	82	3	28.1	4	17	4	10	11	07	18	13	18	23
14	0	58	+11.6	55.6	15.1	268	107	0	29.1	4	33	4	22	11	52	19	28	19	42
15	1	47	+16.2	56.1	15.3	281	209	0	0.5	4	52	4	37	12	39	20	43	21	03
16	2	39	+20.1	56.6	15.4	293	238	2	1.5	5	18	4	57	13	31	21	59	22	24
17	3	33	+23.1	57.1	15.5	305	250	7	2.5	5	51	5	26	14	25	23	09	23	38
18	4	31	+24.8	57.5	15.7	317	258	13	3.5	6	37	6	08	15	23	—		—	
19	5	31	+25.1	58.0	15.8	329	266	21	4.5	7	36	7	07	16	21	0	10	0	39
20	6	31	+23.9	58.4	15.9	342	273	31	5.5	8	48	8	22	17	19	0	58	1	24
21	7	30	+21.3	58.8	16.0	354	279	42	6.5	10	08	9	48	18	15	1	35	1	56
22	8	27	+17.4	59.2	16.1	6	284	53	7.5	11	32	11	18	19	08	2	03	2	18
23	9	22	+12.4	59.5	16.2	18	287	64	8.5	12	57	12	49	20	00	2	25	2	35
24	10	16	+6.7	59.7	16.3	30	289	75	9.5	14	22	14	19	20	50	2	44	2	49
25	11	08	+0.7	59.7	16.3	43	289	84	10.5	15	46	15	49	21	40	3	01	3	01
26	12	00	−5.4	59.6	16.2	55	286	92	11.5	17	11	17	20	22	31	3	18	3	13
27	12	54	−11.2	59.3	16.2	67	279	97	12.5	18	36	18	50	23	23	3	37	3	27
28	13	48	−16.3	58.9	16.0	79	255	99	13.5	19	59	20	20	—		4	00	3	43
29	14	44	−20.4	58.3	15.9	91	142	100	14.5	21	18	21	44	0	18	4	27	4	06
30	15	42	−23.4	57.6	15.7	104	113	97	15.5	22	27	22	57	1	13	5	03	4	37

MERCURY

Day	R.A.		Dec.	Diam.	Phase	Transit		5° high 52°		5° high 56°	
	h	m	°	″	%	h	m	h	m	h	m
1	1	40	+11.9	6	71	13	04	19	37	19	44
3	1	52	+13.4	7	63	13	08	19	48	19	56
5	2	02	+14.7	7	55	13	10	19	57	20	06
7	2	12	+15.8	7	48	13	11	20	03	20	14
9	2	20	+16.8	8	40	13	11	20	08	20	19
11	2	26	+17.5	8	33	13	09	20	09	20	21
13	2	31	+18.1	9	26	13	06	20	08	20	21
15	2	35	+18.4	9	21	13	01	20	05	20	17
17	2	37	+18.5	10	15	12	55	19	58	20	11
19	2	37	+18.3	10	11	12	47	19	49	20	01
21	2	36	+18.0	11	7	12	37	19	37	19	49
23	2	33	+17.5	11	4	12	27	19	23	19	34
25	2	30	+16.8	11	2	12	16	19	07	19	18
27	2	26	+16.0	12	0	12	04	18	50	19	00
29	2	22	+15.0	12	0	11	51	5	08	4	59
31	2	17	+14.1	12	1	11	39	5	01	4	53

VENUS

Day	R.A.		Dec.	Diam.	Phase	Transit		5° high 52°		5° high 56°	
	h	m	°	″	%	h	m	h	m	h	m
1	1	54	+11.1	11	95	13	17	19	44	19	50
6	2	17	+13.4	11	94	13	21	20	00	20	08
11	2	41	+15.5	11	93	13	25	20	15	20	25
16	3	05	+17.5	11	92	13	29	20	31	20	43
21	3	30	+19.3	11	91	13	34	20	46	21	00
26	3	55	+20.9	11	90	13	40	21	01	21	16
31	4	20	+22.3	11	89	13	46	21	15	21	32

MARS

Day	R.A.		Dec.	Diam.	Phase	Transit		5° high 52°		5° high 56°	
	h	m	°	″	%	h	m	h	m	h	m
1	8	23	+22.4	9	92	19	44	3	13	3	30
6	8	28	+21.9	9	91	19	29	2	56	3	12
11	8	34	+21.4	8	91	19	15	2	39	2	55
16	8	40	+20.9	8	90	19	02	2	23	2	38
21	8	47	+20.3	8	90	18	49	2	06	2	21
26	8	54	+19.7	8	90	18	37	1	50	2	04
31	9	02	+19.0	7	90	18	25	1	35	1	48

SUNRISE AND SUNSET

	London				*Bristol*				*Birmingham*				*Manchester*				*Newcastle*				*Glasgow*				*Belfast*			
	0° 05′		*51° 30′*		*2° 35′*		*51° 28′*		*1° 55′*		*52° 28′*		*2° 15′*		*53° 28′*		*1° 37′*		*54° 59′*		*4° 14′*		*55° 52′*		*5° 56′*		*54° 35′*	
d	*h*	*m*	*h*	*m*	*h*	*m*	*h*	*m*	*h*	*m*	*h*	*m*	*h*	*m*	*h*	*m*	*h*	*m*	*h*	*m*	*h*	*m*	*h*	*m*	*h*	*m*	*h*	*m*
1	5	36	18	33	5	46	18	43	5	43	18	42	5	43	18	44	5	39	18	43	5	48	18	55	5	56	19	00
2	5	34	18	35	5	44	18	45	5	40	18	43	5	40	18	46	5	36	18	45	5	46	18	57	5	54	19	02
3	5	32	18	37	5	42	18	47	5	38	18	45	5	38	18	48	5	34	18	47	5	43	18	59	5	51	19	04
4	5	29	18	38	5	39	18	48	5	36	18	47	5	36	18	49	5	31	18	49	5	40	19	01	5	49	19	06
5	5	27	18	40	5	37	18	50	5	33	18	49	5	33	18	51	5	29	18	51	5	38	19	03	5	46	19	08
6	5	25	18	42	5	35	18	52	5	31	18	50	5	31	18	53	5	26	18	53	5	35	19	05	5	44	19	10
7	5	23	18	43	5	33	18	53	5	29	18	52	5	28	18	55	5	24	18	55	5	33	19	07	5	41	19	11
8	5	20	18	45	5	30	18	55	5	26	18	54	5	26	18	57	5	21	18	57	5	30	19	09	5	39	19	13
9	5	18	18	47	5	28	18	57	5	24	18	56	5	24	18	59	5	19	18	59	5	27	19	11	5	37	19	15
10	5	16	18	48	5	26	18	58	5	22	18	57	5	21	19	00	5	16	19	01	5	25	19	13	5	34	19	17
11	5	14	18	50	5	24	19	00	5	19	18	59	5	19	19	02	5	14	19	03	5	22	19	15	5	32	19	19
12	5	12	18	52	5	22	19	02	5	17	19	01	5	17	19	04	5	11	19	05	5	20	19	17	5	29	19	21
13	5	09	18	53	5	19	19	03	5	15	19	03	5	14	19	06	5	09	19	07	5	17	19	19	5	27	19	23
14	5	07	18	55	5	17	19	05	5	13	19	04	5	12	19	08	5	06	19	09	5	15	19	21	5	24	19	25
15	5	05	18	57	5	15	19	07	5	11	19	06	5	10	19	10	5	04	19	10	5	12	19	23	5	22	19	27
16	5	03	18	58	5	13	19	08	5	08	19	08	5	07	19	11	5	01	19	12	5	10	19	25	5	20	19	29
17	5	01	19	00	5	11	19	10	5	06	19	10	5	05	19	13	4	59	19	14	5	07	19	27	5	17	19	31
18	4	59	19	02	5	09	19	12	5	04	19	11	5	03	19	15	4	57	19	16	5	05	19	29	5	15	19	33
19	4	57	19	03	5	07	19	13	5	02	19	13	5	01	19	17	4	54	19	18	5	02	19	31	5	13	19	34
20	4	55	19	05	5	05	19	15	5	00	19	15	4	58	19	19	4	52	19	20	5	00	19	33	5	10	19	36
21	4	52	19	07	5	02	19	17	4	57	19	17	4	56	19	20	4	50	19	22	4	57	19	35	5	08	19	38
22	4	50	19	08	5	00	19	18	4	55	19	18	4	54	19	22	4	47	19	24	4	55	19	37	5	06	19	40
23	4	48	19	10	4	58	19	20	4	53	19	20	4	52	19	24	4	45	19	26	4	53	19	39	5	03	19	42
24	4	46	19	12	4	56	19	22	4	51	19	22	4	50	19	26	4	43	19	28	4	50	19	41	5	01	19	44
25	4	44	19	13	4	54	19	23	4	49	19	23	4	47	19	28	4	40	19	30	4	48	19	43	4	59	19	46
26	4	42	19	15	4	52	19	25	4	47	19	25	4	45	19	30	4	38	19	32	4	45	19	45	4	57	19	48
27	4	40	19	17	4	50	19	27	4	45	19	27	4	43	19	31	4	36	19	34	4	43	19	47	4	54	19	50
28	4	38	19	18	4	48	19	28	4	43	19	29	4	41	19	33	4	33	19	36	4	41	19	49	4	52	19	52
29	4	36	19	20	4	46	19	30	4	41	19	30	4	39	19	35	4	31	19	38	4	38	19	51	4	50	19	54
30	4	34	19	22	4	45	19	32	4	39	19	32	4	37	19	37	4	29	19	40	4	36	19	53	4	48	19	55

JUPITER

Day	*R.A.*		*Dec.*		*Transit*		*5° high*			
							52°		*56°*	
	h	*m*	°	′	*h*	*m*	*h*	*m*	*h*	*m*
1	23	14.6	–5	56	10	36	5	41	5	49
11	23	23.0	–5	04	10	05	5	05	5	13
21	23	31.1	–4	13	9	34	4	29	4	36
31	23	38.8	–3	26	9	02	3	53	4	00

Diameters – equatorial 34″ polar 32″

SATURN

Day	*R.A.*		*Dec.*		*Transit*		*5° high*			
							52°		*56°*	
	h	*m*	°	′	*h*	*m*	*h*	*m*	*h*	*m*
1	12	06.0	+2	09	23	25	5	07	5	05
11	12	03.2	+2	27	22	43	4	26	4	25
21	12	00.8	+2	41	22	01	3	46	3	45
31	11	58.8	+2	53	21	20	3	05	3	04

Diameters – equatorial 19″ polar 17″
Rings – major axis 44″ minor axis 2″

URANUS

Day	*R.A.*		*Dec.*		*Transit*		*10° high*			
							52°		*56°*	
	h	*m*	°	′	*h*	*m*	*h*	*m*	*h*	*m*
1	23	51.6	–1	41	11	13	6	28	6	37
11	23	53.6	–1	28	10	36	5	50	5	58
21	23	55.6	–1	16	9	58	5	11	5	19
31	23	57.3	–1	05	9	21	4	33	4	40

Diameter 4″

NEPTUNE

Day	*R.A.*		*Dec.*		*Transit*		*10° high*			
							52°		*56°*	
	h	*m*	°	′	*h*	*m*	*h*	*m*	*h*	*m*
1	22	00.3	–12	40	9	22	5	43	6	05
11	22	01.4	–12	34	8	44	5	04	5	26
21	22	02.3	–12	30	8	05	4	25	4	47
31	22	03.0	–12	26	7	27	3	46	4	08

Diameter 2″

MAY 2010

FIFTH MONTH, 31 DAYS. *Maia*, goddess of growth and increase

1	*Saturday*	The US navy defeated the Spanish–Pacific fleet at the Battle of Manila Bay 1898	day 121
2	*Sunday*	A British nuclear submarine sank the Argentine cruiser *General Belgrano* 1982	122
3	*Monday*	The May Uprising took place in Dresden, Germany 1848	week 18 day 123
4	*Tuesday*	Edward, Prince of Wales, was killed at the Battle of Tewkesbury 1471	124
5	*Wednesday*	The Mexicans defeated the French at the Battle of Pueblo 1862	125
6	*Thursday*	The Mughals won the Battle of Ghagra in north-east India 1529	126
7	*Friday*	Native Americans attacked British forces at Fort Detroit 1763	127
8	*Saturday*	Winston Churchill officially announced the end of war with Germany 1945	128
9	*Sunday*	West Germany joined NATO 1955	129
10	*Monday*	A mutiny by Indian conscripts in the British army began India's first War of Independence 1857	week 19 day 130
11	*Tuesday*	Paul Nash, war artist *b.* 1889; William Pitt the Elder, British prime minister *d.* 1778	131
12	*Wednesday*	The USSR lifted its blockade on Berlin 1949	132
13	*Thursday*	Mary Queen of Scots' army was defeated at the Battle of Langside 1568	133
14	*Friday*	The Battle of Lewes, Sussex, took place between the armies of Henry III and Simon de Montfort 1264	134
15	*Saturday*	Britain tested its first hydrogen bomb over Christmas Island in the central Pacific 1957	135
16	*Sunday*	Nazi troops suppressed a Jewish uprising in the Warsaw ghetto 1943	136
17	*Monday*	The 'Dambusters' air raids (RAF Operation Chastise) began over the Ruhr valley, Germany 1943	week 20 day 137
18	*Tuesday*	The Allies were victorious at the Battle of Monte Cassino, Italy 1944	138
19	*Wednesday*	Ho Chi Minh, Vietnamese communist leader *b.* 1890; T. E. Lawrence 'of Arabia' *d.* 1935	139
20	*Thursday*	German paratroopers invaded Crete during the first fully airborne country invasion 1941	140
21	*Friday*	The US exploded the first airborne hydrogen bomb over Bikini Atoll in the central Pacific 1956	141
22	*Saturday*	Adolf Hitler and Benito Mussolini signed the 'Pact of Steel' 1939	142
23	*Sunday*	Símon Bolívar was proclaimed *El Libertador* as he entered Merida, Venezuela 1813	143
24	*Monday*	The HMS *Hood* was sunk by German battleship *Bismarck* off Greenland 1941	week 21 day 144
25	*Tuesday*	Alicante was heavily bombed by Italian planes during the Spanish Civil War 1938	145
26	*Wednesday*	The last Confederate army in the American Civil War surrendered near New Orleans 1865	146
27	*Thursday*	Henry Kissinger, US secretary of state *b.* 1923; Joseph Gallieni, French general *d.* 1916	147
28	*Friday*	Belgium surrendered to Germany 1940	148
29	*Saturday*	Ottoman Turks captured Constantinople, ending the Byzantine Empire 1453	149
30	*Sunday*	The first RAF 'thousand bomber raid' took place over Cologne, Germany 1942	150
31	*Monday*	The US Senate voted to cut off funds for the bombing of Cambodia 1973	week 22 day 151

ASTRONOMICAL PHENOMENA

d	*h*	
9	13	Jupiter in conjunction with Moon. Jupiter 6°S.
11	22	Mercury at stationary point
12	12	Mercury in conjunction with Moon. Mercury 7°S.
16	10	Venus in conjunction with Moon. Venus 0°.02S.
20	09	Mars in conjunction with Moon. Mars 5°N.
21	04	Sun's longitude 60° ♊
22	23	Saturn in conjunction with Moon. Saturn 7°N.
26	02	Mercury at greatest elongation W.25°
30	18	Saturn at stationary point
31	19	Neptune at stationary point

MINIMA OF ALGOL

Algol is inconveniently situated for observation during May

CONSTELLATIONS

The following constellations are near the meridian at

	d	*h*		*d*	*h*
April	1	24	May	16	21
April	15	23	June	1	20
May	1	22	June	15	19

Cepheus (below the Pole), Cassiopeia (below the Pole), Ursa Minor, Ursa Major, Canes Venatici, Coma Berenices, Bootes, Leo, Virgo, Crater, Corvus and Hydra

THE MOON

Phases, Apsides and Node	*d*	*h*	*m*
☾ Last Quarter	6	04	15
● New Moon	14	01	04
☽ First Quarter	20	23	43
○ Full Moon	27	23	07
Apogee (404,196 km)	6	21	54
Perigee (369,769 km)	20	08	42

Mean longitude of ascending node on May 1, 285°

THE SUN

s.d. 15′.8

Day	Right Ascension			Dec. +		Equation of time		Rise 52°		Rise 56°		Transit		Set 52°		Set 56°		Sidereal time			Transit of first point of Aries		
	h	*m*	*s*	°	′	*m*	*s*	*h*	*m*	*h*	*m*	*h*	*m*	*h*	*m*	*h*	*m*	*h*	*m*	*s*	*h*	*m*	*s*
1	2	32	26	14	59	+2	51	4	31	4	17	11	57	19	25	19	39	14	35	17	9	23	11
2	2	36	15	15	17	+2	58	4	29	4	14	11	57	19	26	19	41	14	39	13	9	19	15
3	2	40	05	15	35	+3	05	4	27	4	12	11	57	19	28	19	43	14	43	10	9	15	19
4	2	43	56	15	52	+3	11	4	25	4	10	11	57	19	30	19	45	14	47	06	9	11	23
5	2	47	47	16	10	+3	16	4	23	4	08	11	57	19	31	19	47	14	51	03	9	07	27
6	2	51	38	16	27	+3	21	4	21	4	06	11	57	19	33	19	49	14	54	59	9	03	31
7	2	55	30	16	43	+3	26	4	20	4	03	11	57	19	35	19	51	14	58	56	8	59	35
8	2	59	23	17	00	+3	30	4	18	4	01	11	56	19	36	19	53	15	02	53	8	55	40
9	3	03	16	17	16	+3	33	4	16	3	59	11	56	19	38	19	55	15	06	49	8	51	44
10	3	07	10	17	32	+3	35	4	14	3	57	11	56	19	39	19	57	15	10	46	8	47	48
11	3	11	05	17	48	+3	38	4	13	3	55	11	56	19	41	19	59	15	14	42	8	43	52
12	3	15	00	18	03	+3	39	4	11	3	53	11	56	19	43	20	01	15	18	39	8	39	56
13	3	18	55	18	18	+3	40	4	10	3	51	11	56	19	44	20	03	15	22	35	8	36	00
14	3	22	52	18	33	+3	40	4	08	3	49	11	56	19	46	20	05	15	26	32	8	32	04
15	3	26	48	18	47	+3	40	4	06	3	47	11	56	19	47	20	06	15	30	28	8	28	08
16	3	30	46	19	02	+3	39	4	05	3	46	11	56	19	49	20	08	15	34	25	8	24	12
17	3	34	44	19	15	+3	38	4	03	3	44	11	56	19	50	20	10	15	38	22	8	20	16
18	3	38	42	19	29	+3	36	4	02	3	42	11	56	19	52	20	12	15	42	18	8	16	20
19	3	42	41	19	42	+3	33	4	01	3	40	11	56	19	53	20	14	15	46	15	8	12	24
20	3	46	41	19	55	+3	30	3	59	3	39	11	57	19	55	20	16	15	50	11	8	08	29
21	3	50	41	20	07	+3	27	3	58	3	37	11	57	19	56	20	17	15	54	08	8	04	33
22	3	54	41	20	19	+3	23	3	57	3	35	11	57	19	58	20	19	15	58	04	8	00	37
23	3	58	42	20	31	+3	18	3	55	3	34	11	57	19	59	20	21	16	02	01	7	56	41
24	4	02	44	20	42	+3	13	3	54	3	32	11	57	20	00	20	22	16	05	57	7	52	45
25	4	06	46	20	53	+3	08	3	53	3	31	11	57	20	02	20	24	16	09	54	7	48	49
26	4	10	49	21	04	+3	02	3	52	3	30	11	57	20	03	20	26	16	13	51	7	44	53
27	4	14	52	21	14	+2	55	3	51	3	28	11	57	20	04	20	27	16	17	47	7	40	57
28	4	18	55	21	24	+2	48	3	50	3	27	11	57	20	05	20	29	16	21	44	7	37	01
29	4	22	59	21	34	+2	41	3	49	3	26	11	57	20	07	20	30	16	25	40	7	33	05
30	4	27	04	21	43	+2	33	3	48	3	24	11	58	20	08	20	32	16	29	37	7	29	09
31	4	31	08	21	52	+2	25	3	47	3	23	11	58	20	09	20	33	16	33	33	7	25	14

DURATION OF TWILIGHT (in minutes)

Latitude	*52°*	*56°*	*52°*	*56°*	*52°*	*56°*	*52°*	*56°*
	1 May		*11 May*		*21 May*		*31 May*	
Civil	39	44	41	48	44	53	46	57
Nautical	89	106	97	120	106	141	115	187
Astronomical	152	204	176	TAN	TAN	TAN	TAN	TAN

THE NIGHT SKY

Mercury, although reaching greatest western elongation on the 26th, remains unsuitably placed for observation throughout the month.

Venus, magnitude −4.0, is visible as a brilliant object in the western sky for almost two hours after sunset. Venus passes 6 degrees north of Aldebaran on the 4th. During the morning of the 16th there is a close conjunction of the Moon with Venus, the latter being only about 0.5 degrees above the upper edge of the Moon.

Mars is visible in the southwestern quadrant of the evening skies, its magnitude fading from +0.7 to +1.1. By the end of the month it will be too low in the west to be visible after midnight. During May the planet moves from Cancer into Leo. On the 20th the Moon, at First Quarter, passes 6 degrees south of Mars.

Jupiter, magnitude −2.2, becomes visible as a morning object early in the month, though only visible low above the south-eastern horizon for a short while before dawn. Jupiter is moving slowly eastwards in the constellation of Pisces.

Saturn, magnitude +0.8, is still visible as an evening object in the south-western sky in the evenings, though by the end of the month it will only be visible for about an hour after midnight. Saturn reaches its second stationary point on the 30th, resuming its direct motion. During the evening of the 22nd the waxing gibbous Moon passes about 8 degrees south of the planet.

THE MOON

Day	R.A.		Dec.	Hor. Par.	Semi-diam.	Sun's Co-Long.	PA of Bright Limb	Ph.	Age	Rise				Transit		Set			
										52°		56°				52°		56°	
	h	m	°	′	′	°	°	%	d	h	m	h	m	h	m	h	m	h	m
1	16	40	−24.9	56.9	15.5	116	102	93	16.5	23	24	23	53	2	09	5	50	5	20
2	17	37	−25.0	56.2	15.3	128	94	86	17.5	—		—		3	04	6	46	6	17
3	18	32	−23.8	55.5	15.1	140	87	79	18.5	0	07	0	34	3	57	7	51	7	25
4	19	24	−21.5	55.0	15.0	152	82	70	19.5	0	40	1	02	4	46	9	00	8	39
5	20	14	−18.3	54.6	14.9	164	77	61	20.5	1	04	1	22	5	33	10	10	9	54
6	21	01	−14.4	54.3	14.8	177	74	52	21.5	1	24	1	36	6	17	11	20	11	08
7	21	46	−9.9	54.2	14.8	189	71	42	22.5	1	40	1	48	6	58	12	28	12	22
8	22	29	−5.1	54.3	14.8	201	70	33	23.5	1	54	1	58	7	39	13	37	13	35
9	23	13	0.0	54.6	14.9	213	70	25	24.5	2	08	2	08	8	20	14	46	14	48
10	23	57	+5.1	55.0	15.0	226	71	17	25.5	2	22	2	17	9	01	15	56	16	04
11	0	42	+10.1	55.5	15.1	238	74	10	26.5	2	37	2	28	9	45	17	10	17	22
12	1	30	+14.8	56.1	15.3	250	79	5	27.5	2	56	2	42	10	32	18	25	18	43
13	2	22	+18.9	56.7	15.5	262	90	1	28.5	3	19	3	00	11	23	19	42	20	05
14	3	16	+22.2	57.3	15.6	274	157	0	29.5	3	50	3	26	12	17	20	56	21	23
15	4	14	+24.3	57.9	15.8	287	246	1	1.0	4	32	4	04	13	15	22	01	22	31
16	5	15	+25.0	58.4	15.9	299	261	5	2.0	5	28	4	59	14	14	22	55	23	22
17	6	16	+24.2	58.8	16.0	311	271	10	3.0	6	38	6	11	15	13	23	36	23	58
18	7	16	+21.8	59.0	16.1	323	278	18	4.0	7	57	7	35	16	11	—		—	
19	8	14	+18.1	59.2	16.1	336	284	28	5.0	9	21	9	05	17	05	0	06	0	23
20	9	10	+13.4	59.3	16.2	348	288	39	6.0	10	45	10	35	17	57	0	30	0	41
21	10	03	+7.9	59.3	16.2	0	290	50	7.0	12	09	12	04	18	46	0	49	0	56
22	10	55	+2.0	59.2	16.1	12	291	62	8.0	13	31	13	32	19	35	1	07	1	08
23	11	46	−3.9	59.0	16.1	25	291	72	9.0	14	53	15	00	20	24	1	24	1	20
24	12	38	−9.7	58.8	16.0	37	289	82	10.0	16	16	16	28	21	15	1	42	1	33
25	13	30	−14.8	58.4	15.9	49	285	90	11.0	17	38	17	56	22	07	2	02	1	48
26	14	25	−19.2	58.0	15.8	61	279	95	12.0	18	57	19	31	23	01	2	27	2	07
27	15	21	−22.5	57.5	15.7	73	267	99	13.0	20	10	20	28	23	57	2	59	2	34
28	16	19	−24.4	56.9	15.5	85	181	100	14.0	21	12	21	42	—		3	40	3	12
29	17	16	−25.0	56.4	15.4	98	103	99	15.0	22	01	22	29	0	52	4	33	4	03
30	18	12	−24.3	55.8	15.2	110	91	96	16.0	22	38	23	02	1	46	5	35	5	08
31	19	06	−22.3	55.3	15.1	122	83	91	17.0	23	06	23	25	2	38	6	43	6	20

MERCURY

Day	R.A.		Dec.	Diam.	Phase	Transit		5° high			
								52°		56°	
	h	m	°	″	%	h	m	h	m	h	m
1	2	17	+14.1	12	1	11	39	5	01	4	53
3	2	13	+13.1	12	2	11	27	4	54	4	47
5	2	10	+12.2	12	4	11	16	4	48	4	41
7	2	07	+11.4	12	6	11	06	4	41	4	35
9	2	06	+10.8	11	9	10	57	4	35	4	30
11	2	05	+10.3	11	12	10	49	4	30	4	25
13	2	06	+9.9	11	16	10	42	4	24	4	19
15	2	07	+9.8	10	19	10	36	4	19	4	14
17	2	10	+9.7	10	23	10	31	4	14	4	09
19	2	14	+9.9	10	26	10	27	4	09	4	04
21	2	18	+10.2	9	30	10	24	4	04	3	59
23	2	24	+10.6	9	33	10	22	4	00	3	54
25	2	30	+11.1	8	37	10	20	3	56	3	50
27	2	38	+11.7	8	41	10	20	3	52	3	45
29	2	46	+12.5	8	44	10	20	3	48	3	41
31	2	55	+13.3	7	48	10	22	3	45	3	37

VENUS

Day	R.A.		Dec.	Diam.	Phase	Transit		5° high			
								52°		56°	
	h	m	°	″	%	h	m	h	m	h	m
1	4	20	+22.3	11	89	13	46	21	15	21	32
6	4	46	+23.4	12	88	13	52	21	27	21	46
11	5	12	+24.2	12	87	13	58	21	39	21	59
16	5	39	+24.8	12	85	14	05	21	49	22	09
21	6	05	+25.0	12	84	14	12	21	57	22	18
26	6	31	+25.0	13	83	14	18	22	03	22	23
31	6	58	+24.6	13	81	14	25	22	07	22	27

MARS

Day	R.A.		Dec.	Diam.	Phase	Transit		5° high			
								52°		56°	
	h	m	°	″	%	h	m	h	m	h	m
1	9	02	+19.0	7	90	18	25	1	35	1	48
6	9	11	+18.3	7	90	18	14	1	19	1	32
11	9	19	+17.6	7	90	18	03	1	04	1	16
16	9	28	+16.8	7	90	17	52	0	49	0	59
21	9	37	+15.9	6	90	17	42	0	33	0	43
26	9	47	+15.0	6	90	17	31	0	18	0	27
31	9	56	+14.1	6	90	17	21	0	03	0	11

SUNRISE AND SUNSET

	London		*Bristol*		*Birmingham*		*Manchester*		*Newcastle*		*Glasgow*		*Belfast*	
	0° 05′	*51° 30′*	*2° 35′*	*51° 28′*	*1° 55′*	*52° 28′*	*2° 15′*	*53° 28′*	*1° 37′*	*54° 59′*	*4° 14′*	*55° 52′*	*5° 56′*	*54° 35′*
d	*h m*	*h m*	*h m*	*h m*	*h m*	*h m*	*h m*	*h m*	*h m*	*h m*	*h m*	*h m*	*h m*	*h m*
1	4 33	19 23	4 43	19 33	4 37	19 34	4 35	19 39	4 27	19 42	4 34	19 55	4 46	19 57
2	4 31	19 25	4 41	19 35	4 35	19 36	4 33	19 40	4 25	19 43	4 32	19 57	4 43	19 59
3	4 29	19 27	4 39	19 37	4 33	19 37	4 31	19 42	4 23	19 45	4 29	19 59	4 41	20 01
4	4 27	19 28	4 37	19 38	4 31	19 39	4 29	19 44	4 20	19 47	4 27	20 01	4 39	20 03
5	4 25	19 30	4 35	19 40	4 29	19 41	4 27	19 46	4 18	19 49	4 25	20 03	4 37	20 05
6	4 23	19 31	4 34	19 41	4 27	19 42	4 25	19 47	4 16	19 51	4 23	20 05	4 35	20 07
7	4 22	19 33	4 32	19 43	4 26	19 44	4 23	19 49	4 14	19 53	4 21	20 07	4 33	20 09
8	4 20	19 35	4 30	19 45	4 24	19 46	4 21	19 51	4 12	19 55	4 19	20 09	4 31	20 10
9	4 18	19 36	4 28	19 46	4 22	19 47	4 19	19 53	4 10	19 57	4 17	20 11	4 29	20 12
10	4 17	19 38	4 27	19 48	4 20	19 49	4 18	19 54	4 08	19 59	4 15	20 13	4 27	20 14
11	4 15	19 39	4 25	19 49	4 19	19 51	4 16	19 56	4 07	20 00	4 13	20 15	4 26	20 16
12	4 13	19 41	4 24	19 51	4 17	19 52	4 14	19 58	4 05	20 02	4 11	20 17	4 24	20 18
13	4 12	19 42	4 22	19 52	4 15	19 54	4 12	19 59	4 03	20 04	4 09	20 19	4 22	20 19
14	4 10	19 44	4 20	19 54	4 14	19 55	4 11	20 01	4 01	20 06	4 07	20 21	4 20	20 21
15	4 09	19 45	4 19	19 55	4 12	19 57	4 09	20 03	3 59	20 08	4 05	20 23	4 18	20 23
16	4 07	19 47	4 17	19 57	4 11	19 59	4 07	20 04	3 57	20 09	4 03	20 25	4 17	20 25
17	4 06	19 48	4 16	19 58	4 09	20 00	4 06	20 06	3 56	20 11	4 02	20 26	4 15	20 26
18	4 04	19 50	4 15	20 00	4 08	20 02	4 04	20 08	3 54	20 13	4 00	20 28	4 13	20 28
19	4 03	19 51	4 13	20 01	4 06	20 03	4 03	20 09	3 52	20 15	3 58	20 30	4 12	20 30
20	4 02	19 53	4 12	20 03	4 05	20 05	4 01	20 11	3 51	20 16	3 56	20 32	4 10	20 31
21	4 01	19 54	4 11	20 04	4 03	20 06	4 00	20 12	3 49	20 18	3 55	20 33	4 09	20 33
22	3 59	19 56	4 09	20 05	4 02	20 07	3 58	20 14	3 48	20 19	3 53	20 35	4 07	20 35
23	3 58	19 57	4 08	20 07	4 01	20 09	3 57	20 15	3 46	20 21	3 52	20 37	4 06	20 36
24	3 57	19 58	4 07	20 08	4 00	20 10	3 56	20 17	3 45	20 23	3 50	20 38	4 04	20 38
25	3 56	20 00	4 06	20 09	3 58	20 12	3 55	20 18	3 44	20 24	3 49	20 40	4 03	20 39
26	3 55	20 01	4 05	20 11	3 57	20 13	3 53	20 20	3 42	20 26	3 47	20 42	4 02	20 41
27	3 54	20 02	4 04	20 12	3 56	20 14	3 52	20 21	3 41	20 27	3 46	20 43	4 01	20 42
28	3 53	20 03	4 03	20 13	3 55	20 16	3 51	20 22	3 40	20 29	3 45	20 45	3 59	20 43
29	3 52	20 05	4 02	20 14	3 54	20 17	3 50	20 24	3 39	20 30	3 43	20 46	3 58	20 45
30	3 51	20 06	4 01	20 16	3 53	20 18	3 49	20 25	3 37	20 31	3 42	20 48	3 57	20 46
31	3 50	20 07	4 00	20 17	3 52	20 19	3 48	20 26	3 36	20 33	3 41	20 49	3 56	20 47

JUPITER

Day	*R.A.*		*Dec.*		*Transit*		*5° high*			
							52°		*56°*	
	h	*m*	°	′	*h*	*m*	*h*	*m*	*h*	*m*
1	23	38.8	–3	26	9	02	3	53	4	00
11	23	46.0	–2	41	8	30	3	17	3	23
21	23	52.6	–2	01	7	57	2	41	2	46
31	23	58.5	–1	24	7	24	2	05	2	09

Diameters – equatorial 36″ polar 34″

SATURN

Day	*R.A.*		*Dec*		*Transit*		*5° high*			
							52°		*56°*	
	h	*m*	°	′	*h*	*m*	*h*	*m*	*h*	*m*
1	11	58.8	+2	53	21	20	3	05	3	04
11	11	57.2	+3	01	20	39	2	25	2	24
21	11	56.3	+3	05	19	59	1	45	1	44
31	11	55.9	+3	05	19	19	1	06	1	05

Diameters – equatorial 19″ polar 17″
Rings – major axis 42″ minor axis 1″

URANUS

Day	*R.A.*		*Dec.*		*Transit*		*10° high*			
							52°		*56°*	
	h	*m*	°	′	*h*	*m*	*h*	*m*	*h*	*m*
1	23	57.3	–1	05	9	21	4	33	4	40
11	23	58.9	–0	55	8	43	3	54	4	02
21	0	00.3	–0	46	8	05	3	15	3	23
31	0	01.5	–0	39	7	27	2	37	2	44

Diameter 4″

NEPTUNE

Day	*R.A.*		*Dec.*		*Transit*		*10° high*			
							52°		*56°*	
	h	*m*	°	′	*h*	*m*	*h*	*m*	*h*	*m*
1	22	03.0	–12	26	7	27	3	46	4	08
11	22	03.6	–12	23	6	48	3	07	3	29
21	22	03.9	–12	22	6	09	2	28	2	49
31	22	04.0	–12	21	5	30	1	49	2	10

Diameter 2″

JUNE 2010

SIXTH MONTH, 30 DAYS. *Junius*, Roman *gens* (family)

1	*Tuesday*	Frank Whittle, inventor of the jet engine *b.* 1907; James Buchanan, US president *d.* 1868	day 152
2	*Wednesday*	The first Australian combat troops arrived in Vietnam 1965	153
3	*Thursday*	The Tiananmen Square massacre took place in Peking (Beijing), China 1989	154
4	*Friday*	Allied forces completed their evacuation from Dunkirk 1940	155
5	*Saturday*	HMS *Hampshire* sank off Orkney; Lord Kitchener was among the dead 1916	156
6	*Sunday*	D-day: the Allied invasion of Normandy began 1944	157
7	*Monday*	Israel launched the world's first air strike on a nuclear power plant in Iraq 1981	week 23 day 158
8	*Tuesday*	Around 50 British men were killed at Bluff Cove in the Falklands War 1982	159
9	*Wednesday*	The US launched the first submarine armed with ballistic missiles, USS *George Washington* 1959	160
10	*Thursday*	Israel ended the six-day war with neighbouring states 1967	161
11	*Friday*	James Keith, Scottish field-marshal in the Prussian army *b.* 1696; James III, king of Scotland *d.* 1488	162
12	*Saturday*	The Philippines declared independence from Spain during the Spanish–American War 1898	163
13	*Sunday*	Israeli troops pulled out of southern Lebanon 1978	164
14	*Monday*	English Civil War: parliamentarians defeated the royalists at the Battle of Naseby 1645	week 24 day 165
15	*Tuesday*	Wat Tyler, leader of the Peasants' Revolt, was beheaded 1381	166
16	*Wednesday*	The Battle of Quatre Bras, which preceded Waterloo, ended in a tactical draw 1815	167
17	*Thursday*	The English won the Battle of Bunker Hill in the American War of Independence 1775	168
18	*Friday*	Wellington defeated Napoleon at the Battle of Waterloo 1815	169
19	*Saturday*	Ethel and Julius Rosenberg were executed in New York for communist espionage 1953	170
20	*Sunday*	The nationalist Boxer Rebellion began in Peking (Beijing), China 1900	171
21	*Monday*	Allied forces defeated the French at the Battle of Vitoria 1813	week 25 day 172
22	*Tuesday*	Hitler launched a surprise German invasion of the Soviet Union 1941	173
23	*Wednesday*	Britain won the Battle of Plassey in Bengal, India 1757	174
24	*Thursday*	Robert Bruce defeated Edward II at Bannockburn, securing Scottish independence 1314	175
25	*Friday*	Sioux Native Americans defeated General Custer and his men at the Battle of Little Bighorn 1876	176
26	*Saturday*	Representatives of 50 countries signed the United Nations Charter 1945	177
27	*Sunday*	Yugoslav troops moved into Slovenia after it declared independence 1991	178
28	*Monday*	Archduke Franz Ferdinand was assassinated in Sarajevo 1914	week 26 day 179
29	*Tuesday*	US bombers attacked the Vietnamese cities of Hanoi and Haiphong 1966	180
30	*Wednesday*	The French defeated the Anglo–Dutch at the Battle of Beachy Head 1690	181

ASTRONOMICAL PHENOMENA

d	*h*	
6	06	Jupiter in conjunction with Moon. Jupiter 6°S.
11	01	Mercury in conjunction with Moon. Mercury 5°S.
15	06	Venus in conjunction with Moon. Venus 4°N.
17	15	Mars in conjunction with Moon. Mars 5°N.
19	05	Saturn in conjunction with Moon. Saturn 7°N.
21	11	Sun's longitude 90° ♋
25	19	Pluto at opposition
26	11	Partial eclipse of Moon
28	12	Mercury in superior conjunction

MINIMA OF ALGOL

Algol is inconveniently situated for observation during June

CONSTELLATIONS

The following constellations are near the meridian at

	d	*h*		*d*	*h*
May	1	24	June	15	21
May	16	23	July	1	20
June	1	22	July	16	19

Cassiopeia (below the Pole), Ursa Minor, Draco, Ursa Major, Canes Venatici, Bootes, Corona, Serpens, Virgo and Libra

THE MOON

Phases, Apsides and Node	*d*	*h*	*m*
☾ Last Quarter	4	22	13
● New Moon	12	11	15
☽ First Quarter	19	04	29
○ Full Moon	26	11	30
Apogee (404,227 km)	3	16	48
Perigee (365,957 km)	15	14	51

Mean longitude of ascending node on June 1, 284°

THE SUN

s.d. 15′.8

Day	Right Ascension			Dec. +		Equation of time		Rise 52°		Rise 56°		Transit		Set 52°		Set 56°		Sidereal time			Transit of first point of Aries		
	h	m	s	°	′	m	s	h	m	h	m	h	m	h	m	h	m	h	m	s	h	m	s
1	4	35	14	22	01	+2	16	3	46	3	22	11	58	20	10	20	34	16	37	30	7	21	18
2	4	39	19	22	09	+2	07	3	45	3	21	11	58	20	11	20	36	16	41	26	7	17	22
3	4	43	26	22	16	+1	57	3	45	3	20	11	58	20	12	20	37	16	45	23	7	13	26
4	4	47	32	22	24	+1	47	3	44	3	19	11	58	20	13	20	38	16	49	20	7	09	30
5	4	51	39	22	31	+1	37	3	43	3	18	11	58	20	14	20	39	16	53	16	7	05	34
6	4	55	46	22	37	+1	27	3	43	3	18	11	59	20	15	20	40	16	57	13	7	01	38
7	4	59	54	22	43	+1	16	3	42	3	17	11	59	20	16	20	42	17	01	09	6	57	42
8	5	04	01	22	49	+1	04	3	42	3	16	11	59	20	17	20	43	17	05	06	6	53	46
9	5	08	10	22	54	+0	53	3	41	3	15	11	59	20	18	20	44	17	09	02	6	49	50
10	5	12	18	22	59	+0	41	3	41	3	15	11	59	20	19	20	44	17	12	59	6	45	54
11	5	16	27	23	04	+0	29	3	40	3	14	12	00	20	19	20	45	17	16	55	6	41	59
12	5	20	36	23	08	+0	16	3	40	3	14	12	00	20	20	20	46	17	20	52	6	38	03
13	5	24	45	23	11	+0	04	3	40	3	14	12	00	20	21	20	47	17	24	49	6	34	07
14	5	28	54	23	15	−0	09	3	40	3	13	12	00	20	21	20	47	17	28	45	6	30	11
15	5	33	03	23	18	−0	22	3	39	3	13	12	00	20	22	20	48	17	32	42	6	26	15
16	5	37	13	23	20	−0	34	3	39	3	13	12	01	20	22	20	49	17	36	38	6	22	19
17	5	41	22	23	22	−0	47	3	39	3	13	12	01	20	23	20	49	17	40	35	6	18	23
18	5	45	32	23	24	−1	00	3	39	3	13	12	01	20	23	20	50	17	44	31	6	14	27
19	5	49	41	23	25	−1	14	3	39	3	13	12	01	20	23	20	50	17	48	28	6	10	31
20	5	53	51	23	26	−1	27	3	40	3	13	12	02	20	24	20	50	17	52	24	6	06	35
21	5	58	01	23	26	−1	40	3	40	3	13	12	02	20	24	20	50	17	56	21	6	02	39
22	6	02	10	23	26	−1	53	3	40	3	13	12	02	20	24	20	51	18	00	18	5	58	43
23	6	06	20	23	26	−2	06	3	40	3	14	12	02	20	24	20	51	18	04	14	5	54	48
24	6	10	29	23	25	−2	18	3	41	3	14	12	02	20	24	20	51	18	08	11	5	50	52
25	6	14	39	23	24	−2	31	3	41	3	14	12	03	20	24	20	51	18	12	07	5	46	56
26	6	18	48	23	22	−2	44	3	41	3	15	12	03	20	24	20	51	18	16	04	5	43	00
27	6	22	57	23	20	−2	56	3	42	3	15	12	03	20	24	20	50	18	20	00	5	39	04
28	6	27	06	23	18	−3	09	3	42	3	16	12	03	20	24	20	50	18	23	57	5	35	08
29	6	31	14	23	15	−3	21	3	43	3	17	12	03	20	24	20	50	18	27	53	5	31	12
30	6	35	23	23	11	−3	33	3	44	3	17	12	04	20	23	20	49	18	31	50	5	27	16

DURATION OF TWILIGHT (in minutes)

Latitude	52°	56°	52°	56°	52°	56°	52°	56°
	1 June		*11 June*		*21 June*		*31 June*	
Civil	46	58	48	61	49	63	48	61
Nautical	116	TAN	124	TAN	127	TAN	124	TAN
Astronomical	TAN	TAN	TAN	TAN	TAN	TAN	TAN	TAN

THE NIGHT SKY

Mercury passes through superior conjunction on the 28th and remains unsuitably placed for observation throughout the month.

Venus, magnitude −4.0, is visible as a brilliant object in the western sky in the evenings. Although it is continuing to increase its eastern elongation from the Sun, the period available for observation actually decreases slightly during the month because it is moving southwards in declination, and also because the Sun is setting about a quarter of an hour later at the end of the month than it did at the beginning. Venus passes 5 degrees south of Pollux in Gemini on the 6th. On the 15th the waxing crescent Moon passes 4 degrees south of the planet.

Mars, magnitude +1.1 to +1.3, is still visible in the evening skies, though no longer the conspicuous object it was at the beginning of the year. However, it is marginally brighter than Regulus when it passes 0.9 degrees north of that star on the 6th. The waxing crescent Moon passes 6 degrees south of Mars on the 17th.

Jupiter, magnitude −2.4, continues to be visible as a bright object in the south-eastern sky in the early hours. By the end of the month it becomes visible shortly after midnight. On the morning of the 6th the Moon, just past Last Quarter, passes 5 degrees north of Jupiter.

Saturn, magnitude +0.9, continues to be visible in the western sky in the evenings. Saturn is in the constellation of Virgo. The Moon passes 8 degrees south of the planet on the 19th.

Twilight. Reference to the section above shows that astronomical twilight lasts all night for a period around the summer solstice (ie in June and July), even in southern England. Under these conditions the sky never gets completely dark as the Sun is always less than 18 degrees below the horizon.

THE MOON

Day	*R.A.*		*Dec.*	*Hor. Par.*	*Semi-diam.*	*Sun's Co-Long.*	*PA. of Br. Limb*	*Ph.*	*Age*	*Rise*				*Transit*		*Set*			
										52°		*56°*				*52°*		*56°*	
	h	*m*	°	′	′	°	°	%	*d*	*h*	*m*	*h*	*m*	*h*	*m*	*h*	*m*	*h*	*m*
1	19	57	−19.3	54.8	14.9	134	78	84	18.0	23	27	23	42	3	26	7	54	7	36
2	20	45	−15.6	54.5	14.8	146	73	77	19.0	23	45	23	54	4	11	9	04	8	51
3	21	31	−11.3	54.3	14.8	159	70	68	20.0		—	—		4	53	10	13	10	05
4	22	15	−6.5	54.3	14.8	171	68	59	21.0	0	00	0	05	5	34	11	22	11	18
5	22	58	−1.6	54.4	14.8	183	67	49	22.0	0	13	0	15	6	15	12	30	12	30
6	23	41	+3.5	54.7	14.9	195	68	40	23.0	0	27	0	24	6	56	13	39	13	44
7	0	26	+8.5	55.2	15.0	208	69	31	24.0	0	42	0	34	7	38	14	50	15	00
8	1	12	+13.2	55.8	15.2	220	71	22	25.0	0	59	0	47	8	23	16	04	16	19
9	2	02	+17.6	56.5	15.4	232	75	14	26.0	1	19	1	03	9	11	17	20	17	41
10	2	55	+21.2	57.2	15.6	244	80	8	27.0	1	47	1	25	10	04	18	36	19	02
11	3	52	+23.7	58.0	15.8	256	88	3	28.0	2	24	1	57	11	01	19	46	20	15
12	4	53	+25.0	58.7	16.0	269	105	0	29.0	3	15	2	45	12	01	20	46	21	15
13	5	55	+24.6	59.3	16.1	281	260	0	0.5	4	21	3	52	13	02	21	33	21	57
14	6	57	+22.7	59.7	16.3	293	276	3	1.5	5	39	5	15	14	02	22	08	22	27
15	7	58	+19.2	59.9	16.3	305	283	9	2.5	7	04	6	46	14	59	22	34	22	47
16	8	55	+14.6	59.9	16.3	318	288	16	3.5	8	31	8	19	15	53	22	55	23	03
17	9	50	+9.2	59.8	16.3	330	292	26	4.5	9	56	9	50	16	44	23	14	23	16
18	10	43	+3.3	59.5	16.2	342	293	37	5.5	11	19	11	19	17	33	23	31	23	28
19	11	34	−2.7	59.1	16.1	354	294	48	6.5	12	42	12	47	18	22	23	48	23	41
20	12	25	−8.5	58.7	16.0	7	292	59	7.5	14	03	14	14	19	11		—	23	55
21	13	17	−13.8	58.2	15.9	19	290	70	8.5	15	24	15	41	20	02	0	07	—	
22	14	11	−18.3	57.7	15.7	31	286	79	9.5	16	43	17	05	20	55	0	30	0	12
23	15	06	−21.7	57.2	15.6	43	281	87	10.5	17	57	18	24	21	49	0	59	0	36
24	16	02	−24.0	56.7	15.4	55	275	94	11.5	19	02	19	32	22	44	1	36	1	09
25	16	59	−25.0	56.2	15.3	68	269	98	12.5	19	56	20	25	23	38	2	24	1	54
26	17	55	−24.6	55.7	15.2	80	258	100	13.5	20	37	21	02	—		3	22	2	53
27	18	49	−23.0	55.3	15.1	92	86	100	14.5	21	08	21	29	0	30	4	28	4	03
28	19	41	−20.3	54.9	14.9	104	77	98	15.5	21	31	21	48	1	19	5	38	5	18
29	20	30	−16.8	54.5	14.9	116	72	94	16.5	21	50	22	02	2	06	6	49	6	34
30	21	16	−12.6	54.3	14.8	129	69	89	17.5	22	06	22	13	2	49	7	59	7	49

MERCURY

Day	*R.A.*		*Dec.*	*Diam.*	*Phase*	*Transit*		*5° high*			
								52°		*56°*	
	h	*m*	°	″	%	*h*	*m*	*h*	*m*	*h*	*m*
1	2	59	+13.7	7	50	10	22	3	43	3	35
3	3	10	+14.6	7	54	10	25	3	41	3	32
5	3	20	+15.6	7	58	10	28	3	38	3	29
7	3	32	+16.6	6	62	10	32	3	37	3	26
9	3	45	+17.6	6	67	10	37	3	36	3	24
11	3	58	+18.7	6	71	10	43	3	36	3	23
13	4	13	+19.7	6	76	10	49	3	36	3	22
15	4	28	+20.6	6	80	10	57	3	38	3	23
17	4	44	+21.6	6	85	11	05	3	41	3	25
19	5	01	+22.4	5	89	11	15	3	45	3	28
21	5	19	+23.1	5	93	11	25	3	50	3	32
23	5	37	+23.7	5	96	11	35	3	57	3	38
25	5	56	+24.2	5	98	11	46	4	05	3	46
27	6	15	+24.4	5	100	11	58	4	15	3	55
29	6	34	+24.5	5	100	12	09	19	52	20	12
31	6	53	+24.4	5	99	12	20	20	02	20	22

VENUS

Day	*R.A.*		*Dec.*	*Diam.*	*Phase*	*Transit*		*5° high*			
								52°		*56°*	
	h	*m*	°	″	%	*h*	*m*	*h*	*m*	*h*	*m*
1	7	03	+24.5	13	81	14	26	22	07	22	27
6	7	29	+23.8	13	79	14	32	22	08	22	27
11	7	54	+22.9	14	78	14	38	22	08	22	25
16	8	19	+21.7	14	76	14	43	22	05	22	21
21	8	43	+20.2	15	74	14	47	22	00	22	15
26	9	06	+18.6	15	73	14	51	22	54	22	07
31	9	29	+16.8	15	71	14	54	21	47	21	57

MARS

Day	*R.A.*		*Dec.*	*Diam.*	*Phase*	*Transit*		*5° high*			
								52°		*56°*	
	h	*m*	°	″	%	*h*	*m*	*h*	*m*	*h*	*m*
1	9	58	+13.9	6	90	17	19	0	00	0	08
6	10	08	+12.9	6	90	17	09	23	42	23	49
11	10	18	+11.9	6	90	16	59	23	27	23	33
16	10	28	+10.9	6	91	16	50	23	11	23	17
21	10	38	+9.8	5	91	16	40	22	56	23	01
26	10	48	+8.7	5	91	16	31	22	41	22	45
31	10	58	+7.5	5	91	16	21	22	26	22	29

SUNRISE AND SUNSET

	London		*Bristol*		*Birmingham*		*Manchester*		*Newcastle*		*Glasgow*		*Belfast*	
	0° 05′	*51° 30′*	*2° 35′*	*51° 28′*	*1° 55′*	*52° 28′*	*2° 15′*	*53° 28′*	*1° 37′*	*54° 59′*	*4° 14′*	*55° 52′*	*5° 56′*	*54° 35′*
d	*h m*	*h m*	*h m*	*h m*	*h m*	*h m*	*h m*	*h m*	*h m*	*h m*	*h m*	*h m*	*h m*	*h m*
1	3 49	20 08	3 59	20 18	3 51	20 20	3 47	20 27	3 35	20 34	3 40	20 50	3 55	20 49
2	3 48	20 09	3 58	20 19	3 50	20 21	3 46	20 28	3 34	20 35	3 39	20 52	3 54	20 50
3	3 48	20 10	3 58	20 20	3 50	20 23	3 45	20 30	3 33	20 36	3 38	20 53	3 53	20 51
4	3 47	20 11	3 57	20 21	3 49	20 24	3 45	20 31	3 33	20 38	3 37	20 54	3 52	20 52
5	3 46	20 12	3 56	20 22	3 48	20 25	3 44	20 32	3 32	20 39	3 36	20 55	3 52	20 53
6	3 46	20 13	3 56	20 23	3 48	20 26	3 43	20 33	3 31	20 40	3 35	20 56	3 51	20 54
7	3 45	20 14	3 55	20 24	3 47	20 26	3 43	20 34	3 30	20 41	3 35	20 57	3 50	20 55
8	3 45	20 15	3 55	20 24	3 47	20 27	3 42	20 35	3 30	20 42	3 34	20 59	3 50	20 56
9	3 44	20 15	3 54	20 25	3 46	20 28	3 41	20 35	3 29	20 43	3 33	20 59	3 49	20 57
10	3 44	20 16	3 54	20 26	3 46	20 29	3 41	20 36	3 29	20 44	3 33	21 00	3 49	20 58
11	3 43	20 17	3 54	20 27	3 45	20 30	3 41	20 37	3 28	20 44	3 32	21 01	3 48	20 59
12	3 43	20 17	3 53	20 27	3 45	20 30	3 40	20 38	3 28	20 45	3 32	21 02	3 48	21 00
13	3 43	20 18	3 53	20 28	3 45	20 31	3 40	20 38	3 27	20 46	3 32	21 03	3 47	21 00
14	3 43	20 19	3 53	20 28	3 45	20 32	3 40	20 39	3 27	20 47	3 31	21 03	3 47	21 01
15	3 43	20 19	3 53	20 29	3 44	20 32	3 40	20 40	3 27	20 47	3 31	21 04	3 47	21 02
16	3 43	20 20	3 53	20 30	3 44	20 33	3 40	20 40	3 27	20 48	3 31	21 05	3 47	21 02
17	3 42	20 20	3 53	20 30	3 44	20 33	3 39	20 40	3 27	20 48	3 31	21 05	3 47	21 03
18	3 43	20 20	3 53	20 30	3 44	20 33	3 39	20 41	3 27	20 49	3 31	21 05	3 47	21 03
19	3 43	20 21	3 53	20 31	3 44	20 34	3 40	20 41	3 27	20 49	3 31	21 06	3 47	21 03
20	3 43	20 21	3 53	20 31	3 44	20 34	3 40	20 42	3 27	20 49	3 31	21 06	3 47	21 04
21	3 43	20 21	3 53	20 31	3 45	20 34	3 40	20 42	3 27	20 49	3 31	21 06	3 47	21 04
22	3 43	20 21	3 53	20 31	3 45	20 34	3 40	20 42	3 27	20 50	3 31	21 07	3 47	21 04
23	3 43	20 22	3 54	20 31	3 45	20 35	3 40	20 42	3 28	20 50	3 32	21 07	3 48	21 04
24	3 44	20 22	3 54	20 31	3 45	20 35	3 41	20 42	3 28	20 50	3 32	21 07	3 48	21 04
25	3 44	20 22	3 54	20 32	3 46	20 35	3 41	20 42	3 28	20 50	3 32	21 07	3 48	21 04
26	3 45	20 22	3 55	20 31	3 46	20 35	3 41	20 42	3 29	20 50	3 33	21 06	3 49	21 04
27	3 45	20 22	3 55	20 31	3 47	20 34	3 42	20 42	3 29	20 49	3 33	21 06	3 49	21 04
28	3 46	20 21	3 56	20 31	3 47	20 34	3 43	20 42	3 30	20 49	3 34	21 06	3 50	21 04
29	3 46	20 21	3 56	20 31	3 48	20 34	3 43	20 41	3 31	20 49	3 35	21 06	3 51	21 03
30	3 47	20 21	3 57	20 31	3 49	20 34	3 44	20 41	3 31	20 49	3 35	21 05	3 51	21 03

JUPITER

Day	*R.A.*		*Dec.*		*Transit*		*5° high*			
							52°		*56°*	
	h	*m*	°	′	*h*	*m*	*h*	*m*	*h*	*m*
1	23	59.1	−1	21	7	21	2	01	2	05
11	0	04.2	−0	51	6	46	1	24	1	28
21	0	08.3	−0	27	6	11	0	47	0	50
31	0	11.5	−0	09	5	35	0	09	0	13

Diameters equatorial 40″ polar 37″

SATURN

Day	*R.A.*		*Dec.*		*Transit*		*5° high*			
							52°		*56°*	
	h	*m*	°	′	*h*	*m*	*h*	*m*	*h*	*m*
1	11	55.9	+3	05	19	15	1	02	1	01
11	11	56.2	+3	01	18	36	0	22	0	21
21	11	57.2	+2	52	17	58	23	39	23	38
31	11	58.7	+2	40	17	20	23	00	22	59

Diameters equatorial 18″ polar 16″
Rings – major axis 40″ minor axis 1″

URANUS

Day	*R.A.*		*Dec.*		*Transit*		*10° high*			
							52°		*56°*	
	h	*m*	°	′	*h*	*m*	*h*	*m*	*h*	*m*
1	0	01.6	−0	38	7	23	2	33	2	40
11	0	02.5	−0	33	6	44	1	54	2	01
21	0	03.0	−0	29	6	06	1	15	1	22
31	0	03.3	−0	28	5	27	0	36	0	43

Diameter 4″

NEPTUNE

Day	*R.A.*		*Dec.*		*Transit*		*10° high*			
							52°		*56°*	
	h	*m*	°	′	*h*	*m*	*h*	*m*	*h*	*m*
1	22	04.0	−12	21	5	26	1	45	2	06
11	22	03.9	−12	22	4	46	1	06	1	27
21	22	03.6	−12	24	4	07	0	26	0	48
31	22	03.1	−12	27	3	27	23	43	0	08

Diameter 2″

JULY 2010

SEVENTH MONTH, 31 DAYS. *Julius* Caesar, formerly *Quintilis*, fifth month of Roman pre-Julian calendar

1	*Thursday*	The Battle of the Somme began: 21,000 men were killed in one day 1916	day 182
2	*Friday*	Russia invaded the Danubian principalities, precipitating the Crimean War 1853	183
3	*Saturday*	American Civil War: the Union army won the Battle of Gettysburg 1863	184
4	*Sunday*	Giuseppe Garibaldi, Italian military leader *b.* 1807; James Monroe, US president *d.* 1831	185
5	*Monday*	American forces defeated the British at the Battle of Chippawa 1814	week 27 day 186
6	*Tuesday*	James II was victorious at Sedgemoor, one of the last major battles fought in England 1685	187
7	*Wednesday*	Tsar Alexander I and Emperor Napoleon I signed the treaty of Tilsit 1807	188
8	*Thursday*	Russia defeated Sweden at the Battle of Poltava, Ukraine 1709	189
9	*Friday*	America defeated Japan at the Battle of Saipan 1944	190
10	*Saturday*	The Luftwaffe attacked shipping convoys off the south-east coast of Britain 1940	191
11	*Sunday*	The Battle of Passchendaele, which was to claim hundreds of thousands of lives, began 1917	192
12	*Monday*	Military conflict broke out between Lebanon and Israel 2006	week 28 day 193
13	*Tuesday*	Sir Robert Calder, British naval officer *b.* 1745; Jean-Paul Marat, French revolutionary *d.* 1793	194
14	*Wednesday*	Crowds stormed the Bastille, marking the start of the French Revolution 1789	195
15	*Thursday*	James Scott, Duke of Monmouth, was executed for leading a rebellion against James II 1685	196
16	*Friday*	The first atomic bomb was secretly detonated near Los Alamos, New Mexico 1945	197
17	*Saturday*	English forces were defeated at the Battle of Castillon, ending the Hundred Years War 1453	198
18	*Sunday*	The body of the scientist and weapons expert Dr David Kelly was discovered 2003	199
19	*Monday*	The Franco–Prussian War began 1870	week 29 day 200
20	*Tuesday*	Turkish troops invaded northern Cyprus 1974	201
21	*Wednesday*	Henry IV defeated a rebel army led by Henry Percy at the Battle of Shrewsbury 1403	202
22	*Thursday*	Peninsular War: British, Spanish and Portuguese forces defeated the French at Salamanca 1812	203
23	*Friday*	Darius N. Couch, US major-general *b.* 1822; Philippe Pétain, French Vichy leader *d.* 1951	204
24	*Saturday*	The first air raids of RAF Operation Gomorrah began over Hamburg, Germany 1943	205
25	*Sunday*	Mata Hari was sentenced to death in France, accused of spying for Germany 1917	206
26	*Monday*	Joseph I, Holy Roman Emperor *b.* 1678; Edward Mannock, wartime flying ace *d.* 1918	week 30 day 207
27	*Tuesday*	The Korean War armistice was signed 1953	208
28	*Wednesday*	Austro–Hungary declared war on Serbia, starting the First World War 1914	209
29	*Thursday*	The Spanish Armada was first sighted off the coast of Cornwall 1588	210
30	*Friday*	US settlers and Shoshoni Native Americans signed the Treaty of Box Elder, Utah 1863	211
31	*Saturday*	Britain announced a total ban on the use of landmines 1998	212

ASTRONOMICAL PHENOMENA

d	*h*	
3	19	Jupiter in conjunction with Moon. Jupiter 7°S.
5	17	Uranus at stationary point
6	11	Earth at aphelion (152 million km)
11	20	Total eclipse of Sun (*see* Eclipses)
12	23	Mercury in conjunction with Moon. Mercury 4°N.
14	21	Venus in conjunction with Moon. Venus 5°N.
16	01	Mars in conjunction with Moon. Mars 6°N.
16	14	Saturn in conjunction with Moon. Saturn 7°N.
22	22	Sun's longitude 120° ♌
23	12	Jupiter at stationary point
31	03	Jupiter in conjunction with Moon. Jupiter 7°S.
31	08	Saturn in conjunction with Mars. Saturn 2°N.

MINIMA OF ALGOL

d	*h*	*d*	*h*	*d*	*h*
1	11.5	12	22.8	24	10.0
4	08.3	15	19.6	27	06.8
7	05.2	18	16.4	30	03.6
10	02.0	21	13.2		

CONSTELLATIONS

The following constellations are near their meridian at

	d	*h*		*d*	*h*
June	1	24	July	16	21
June	15	23	August	1	20
July	1	22	August	16	19

Ursa Minor, Draco, Corona, Hercules, Lyra, Serpens, Ophiuchus, Libra, Scorpius and Sagittarius

THE MOON

Phases, Apsides and Node	*d*	*h*	*m*
☾ Last Quarter	4	14	35
● New Moon	11	19	40
☽ First Quarter	18	10	11
○ Full Moon	26	01	37
Apogee (405,003 km)	1	10	06
Perigee (361,129 km)	13	11	15
Apogee (405,934 km)	28	23	38

Mean longitude of ascending node on July 1, 282°

THE SUN

s.d. 15′.8

Day	Right Ascension			Dec. +		Equation of time		Rise 52°		Rise 56°		Transit		Set 52°		Set 56°		Sidereal time			Transit of first point of Aries		
	h	*m*	*s*	°	′	*m*	*s*	*h*	*m*	*h*	*m*	*h*	*m*	*h*	*m*	*h*	*m*	*h*	*m*	*s*	*h*	*m*	*s*
1	6	39	31	23	08	−3	45	3	44	3	18	12	04	20	23	20	49	18	35	47	5	23	20
2	6	43	39	23	04	−3	56	3	45	3	19	12	04	20	23	20	48	18	39	43	5	19	24
3	6	47	47	22	59	−4	07	3	46	3	20	12	04	20	22	20	48	18	43	40	5	15	28
4	6	51	55	22	54	−4	18	3	46	3	21	12	04	20	22	20	47	18	47	36	5	11	33
5	6	56	02	22	49	−4	29	3	47	3	22	12	05	20	21	20	47	18	51	33	5	07	37
6	7	00	09	22	43	−4	40	3	48	3	23	12	05	20	21	20	46	18	55	29	5	03	41
7	7	04	16	22	37	−4	50	3	49	3	24	12	05	20	20	20	45	18	59	26	4	59	45
8	7	08	22	22	31	−4	59	3	50	3	25	12	05	20	20	20	44	19	03	23	4	55	49
9	7	12	28	22	24	−5	09	3	51	3	26	12	05	20	19	20	43	19	07	19	4	51	53
10	7	16	33	22	16	−5	18	3	52	3	28	12	05	20	18	20	42	19	11	16	4	47	57
11	7	20	38	22	09	−5	26	3	53	3	29	12	05	20	17	20	41	19	15	12	4	44	01
12	7	24	43	22	01	−5	34	3	54	3	30	12	06	20	16	20	40	19	19	09	4	40	05
13	7	28	47	21	52	−5	42	3	55	3	32	12	06	20	15	20	39	19	23	05	4	36	09
14	7	32	51	21	43	−5	49	3	57	3	33	12	06	20	14	20	38	19	27	02	4	32	13
15	7	36	54	21	34	−5	55	3	58	3	35	12	06	20	13	20	36	19	30	58	4	28	18
16	7	40	57	21	25	−6	02	3	59	3	36	12	06	20	12	20	35	19	34	55	4	24	22
17	7	44	59	21	15	−6	07	4	00	3	38	12	06	20	11	20	34	19	38	52	4	20	26
18	7	49	00	21	05	−6	12	4	01	3	39	12	06	20	10	20	32	19	42	48	4	16	30
19	7	53	01	20	54	−6	17	4	03	3	41	12	06	20	09	20	31	19	46	45	4	12	34
20	7	57	02	20	43	−6	21	4	04	3	42	12	06	20	08	20	29	19	50	41	4	08	38
21	8	01	02	20	32	−6	24	4	05	3	44	12	06	20	07	20	28	19	54	38	4	04	42
22	8	05	01	20	20	−6	27	4	07	3	46	12	06	20	05	20	26	19	58	34	4	00	46
23	8	09	00	20	08	−6	29	4	08	3	47	12	07	20	04	20	24	20	02	31	3	56	50
24	8	12	58	19	56	−6	31	4	10	3	49	12	07	20	03	20	23	20	06	27	3	52	54
25	8	16	56	19	43	−6	32	4	11	3	51	12	07	20	01	20	21	20	10	24	3	48	58
26	8	20	53	19	30	−6	32	4	12	3	53	12	07	20	00	20	19	20	14	21	3	45	02
27	8	24	49	19	17	−6	32	4	14	3	54	12	07	19	58	20	17	20	18	17	3	41	07
28	8	28	45	19	03	−6	31	4	15	3	56	12	07	19	57	20	16	20	22	14	3	37	11
29	8	32	40	18	49	−6	30	4	17	3	58	12	06	19	55	20	14	20	26	10	3	33	15
30	8	36	34	18	35	−6	28	4	18	4	00	12	06	19	53	20	12	20	30	07	3	29	19
31	8	40	28	18	21	−6	25	4	20	4	02	12	06	19	52	20	10	20	34	03	3	25	23

DURATION OF TWILIGHT (in minutes)

Latitude	*52°*	*56°*	*52°*	*56°*	*52°*	*56°*	*52°*	*56°*
	1 July		*11 July*		*21 July*		*31 July*	
Civil	48	61	47	58	44	53	42	49
Nautical	124	TAN	117	TAN	107	146	98	123
Astronomical	TAN	TAN	TAN	TAN	TAN	TAN	182	TAN

THE NIGHT SKY

Mercury remains unsuitably placed for observation.

Venus continues to be visible as a brilliant object in the western sky after sunset. Its magnitude is −4.1. Venus passes 1 degree north of Regulus on the 10th. On the evening of the 14th the waxing crescent Moon passes 6 degrees south of the planet.

Mars, magnitude +1.4, is still an evening object, low in the western sky in the evenings. It is moving eastwards, passing from Leo into Virgo before it gets lost in the long evening twilight shortly before the end of the month. Around the 16th the crescent Moon passes 6 degrees south of Mars.

Jupiter, magnitude −2.6, continues to be visible as a morning object, in the south-eastern sky, and is now becoming visible low above the eastern horizon before midnight. The Moon, at Last Quarter, passes 6 degrees north of Jupiter on the 3rd. Again, on the last day of the month, the Moon repeats this performance. On the 23rd the planet reaches its first stationary point and commences its retrograde motion.

Saturn, magnitude +1.0, continues to be visible in the evenings, low above the western horizon, although the long evening twilight severely restricts the time available for observation before the planet sets. Around the middle of the month Mars may be seen about 3 degrees below and 7 degrees to the right of Saturn.

THE MOON

Day	R.A.		Dec.	Hor. Par.	Semi-diam.	Sun's Co-Long.	PA of Br. Limb	Ph.	Age	Rise 52°		Rise 56°		Transit		Set 52°		Set 56°	
	h	*m*	°	′	′	°	°	%	*d*	*h*	*m*	*h*	*m*	*h*	*m*	*h*	*m*	*h*	*m*
1	22	01	−8.0	54.2	14.8	141	67	82	18.5	22	20	22	23	3	31	9	07	9	02
2	22	44	−3.1	54.2	14.8	153	65	74	19.5	22	33	22	32	4	11	10	15	10	14
3	23	27	+1.9	54.3	14.8	165	65	65	20.5	22	47	22	42	4	51	11	23	11	27
4	0	11	+6.9	54.7	14.9	177	66	56	21.5	23	03	22	53	5	32	12	32	12	41
5	0	56	+11.7	55.2	15.0	190	68	46	22.5	23	21	23	07	6	15	13	44	13	57
6	1	43	+16.1	55.8	15.2	202	70	36	23.5	23	45	23	25	7	01	14	58	15	16
7	2	34	+19.9	56.6	15.4	214	74	27	24.5	—		23	52	7	51	16	13	16	36
8	3	29	+22.9	57.4	15.7	226	79	18	25.5	0	17	—		8	45	17	25	17	53
9	4	28	+24.7	58.3	15.9	239	85	10	26.5	1	00	0	32	9	44	18	31	19	00
10	5	30	+25.0	59.2	16.1	251	91	5	27.5	1	59	1	29	10	45	19	24	19	51
11	6	32	+23.6	59.9	16.3	263	95	1	28.5	3	12	2	46	11	46	20	05	20	26
12	7	35	+20.7	60.4	16.5	275	300	0	0.2	4	37	4	16	12	46	20	35	20	51
13	8	35	+16.4	60.7	16.5	288	292	2	1.2	6	06	5	52	13	43	20	59	21	09
14	9	32	+11.0	60.7	16.5	300	294	7	2.2	7	35	7	27	14	36	21	19	21	24
15	10	27	+5.1	60.4	16.5	312	296	14	3.2	9	02	8	59	15	28	21	37	21	36
16	11	20	−1.1	60.0	16.3	324	296	24	4.2	10	27	10	30	16	18	21	55	21	49
17	12	13	−7.1	59.4	16.2	337	295	34	5.2	11	50	11	59	17	08	22	13	22	03
18	13	05	−12.6	58.7	16.0	349	293	45	6.2	13	12	13	27	17	59	22	35	22	19
19	13	58	−17.3	58.0	15.8	1	290	56	7.2	14	32	14	53	18	51	23	02	22	41
20	14	53	−21.0	57.3	15.6	13	285	67	8.2	15	48	16	13	19	45	23	36	23	10
21	15	48	−23.6	56.7	15.4	26	280	76	9.2	16	56	17	25	20	39	—		23	51
22	16	45	−24.9	56.1	15.3	38	275	85	10.2	17	52	18	22	21	32	0	20	—	
23	17	40	−24.9	55.6	15.1	50	270	91	11.2	18	37	19	04	22	25	1	14	0	45
24	18	34	−23.6	55.1	15.0	62	266	96	12.2	19	10	19	33	23	15	2	17	1	51
25	19	27	−21.2	54.8	14.9	74	265	99	13.2	19	36	19	54	—		3	26	3	04
26	20	16	−17.9	54.5	14.8	87	325	100	14.2	19	56	20	10	0	02	4	36	4	19
27	21	03	−13.9	54.2	14.8	99	58	99	15.2	20	13	20	22	0	46	5	46	5	35
28	21	48	−9.4	54.1	14.7	111	61	97	16.2	20	28	20	32	1	28	6	55	6	48
29	22	32	−4.6	54.0	14.7	123	61	92	17.2	20	41	20	42	2	09	8	03	8	01
30	23	15	+0.4	54.1	14.7	135	62	87	18.2	20	55	20	51	2	49	9	11	9	13
31	23	58	+5.4	54.3	14.8	147	63	79	19.2	21	10	21	01	3	30	10	19	10	25

MERCURY

Day	R.A.		Dec.	Diam.	Phase	Transit		5° high 52°		5° high 56°	
	h	*m*	°	″	%	*h*	*m*	*h*	*m*	*h*	*m*
1	6	53	+24.4	5	99	12	20	20	02	20	22
3	7	12	+24.1	5	98	12	31	20	10	20	29
5	7	30	+23.6	5	95	12	41	20	17	20	35
7	7	48	+23.0	5	93	12	51	20	22	20	40
9	8	05	+22.2	5	90	13	00	20	26	20	42
11	8	21	+21.4	5	87	13	08	20	28	20	44
13	8	36	+20.4	5	84	13	15	20	30	20	44
15	8	51	+19.4	6	81	13	22	20	30	20	43
17	9	05	+18.3	6	78	13	28	20	29	20	41
19	9	18	+17.1	6	75	13	33	20	28	20	38
21	9	31	+15.9	6	72	13	37	20	25	20	35
23	9	42	+14.7	6	70	13	41	20	22	20	31
25	9	54	+13.4	6	67	13	44	20	19	20	26
27	10	04	+12.2	6	64	13	46	20	14	20	21
29	10	14	+11.0	7	61	13	48	20	10	20	15
31	10	23	+9.7	7	59	13	49	20	04	20	09

VENUS

Day	R.A.		Dec.	Diam.	Phase	Transit		5° high 52°		5° high 56°	
	h	*m*	°	″	%	*h*	*m*	*h*	*m*	*h*	*m*
1	9	29	+16.8	15	71	14	54	21	47	21	57
6	9	51	+14.8	16	69	14	56	21	38	21	47
11	10	13	+12.6	17	67	14	58	21	28	21	35
16	10	34	+10.4	17	65	14	59	21	17	21	22
21	10	54	+8.0	18	63	14	59	21	06	21	09
26	11	14	+5.6	19	61	14	59	20	53	20	54
31	11	33	+3.2	20	59	14	59	20	40	20	39

MARS

Day	R.A.		Dec.	Diam.	Phase	Transit		5° high 52°		5° high 56°	
	h	*m*	°	″	%	*h*	*m*	*h*	*m*	*h*	*m*
1	10	58	+7.5	5	91	16	21	22	26	22	29
6	11	09	+6.4	5	92	16	12	22	11	22	12
11	11	20	+5.2	5	92	16	03	21	56	21	56
16	11	30	+4.0	5	92	15	54	21	40	21	40
21	11	41	+2.7	5	93	15	45	21	25	21	24
26	11	52	+1.5	5	93	15	37	21	10	21	08
31	12	03	+0.2	5	93	15	28	20	55	20	51

SUNRISE AND SUNSET

	London				*Bristol*				*Birmingham*				*Manchester*				*Newcastle*				*Glasgow*				*Belfast*			
	0° 05′		*51° 30′*		*2° 35′*		*51° 28′*		*1° 55′*		*52° 28′*		*2° 15′*		*53° 28′*		*1° 37′*		*54° 59′*		*4° 14′*		*55° 52′*		*5° 56′*		*54° 35′*	
d	*h*	*m*	*h*	*m*	*h*	*m*	*h*	*m*	*h*	*m*	*h*	*m*	*h*	*m*	*h*	*m*	*h*	*m*	*h*	*m*	*h*	*m*	*h*	*m*	*h*	*m*	*h*	*m*
1	3	47	20	21	3	58	20	31	3	49	20	33	3	45	20	41	3	32	20	48	3	36	21	05	3	52	21	03
2	3	48	20	20	3	58	20	30	3	50	20	33	3	45	20	40	3	33	20	48	3	37	21	04	3	53	21	02
3	3	49	20	20	3	59	20	30	3	51	20	33	3	46	20	40	3	34	20	47	3	38	21	04	3	54	21	02
4	3	50	20	19	4	00	20	29	3	51	20	32	3	47	20	39	3	35	20	47	3	39	21	03	3	55	21	01
5	3	50	20	19	4	01	20	29	3	52	20	32	3	48	20	39	3	36	20	46	3	40	21	03	3	55	21	01
6	3	51	20	18	4	01	20	28	3	53	20	31	3	49	20	38	3	37	20	45	3	41	21	02	3	56	21	00
7	3	52	20	18	4	02	20	28	3	54	20	30	3	50	20	38	3	38	20	44	3	42	21	01	3	57	20	59
8	3	53	20	17	4	03	20	27	3	55	20	30	3	51	20	37	3	39	20	44	3	43	21	00	3	59	20	58
9	3	54	20	17	4	04	20	26	3	56	20	29	3	52	20	36	3	40	20	43	3	44	20	59	4	00	20	58
10	3	55	20	16	4	05	20	26	3	57	20	28	3	53	20	35	3	41	20	42	3	46	20	58	4	01	20	57
11	3	56	20	15	4	06	20	25	3	58	20	27	3	54	20	34	3	42	20	41	3	47	20	57	4	02	20	56
12	3	57	20	14	4	07	20	24	3	59	20	26	3	55	20	33	3	44	20	40	3	48	20	56	4	03	20	55
13	3	58	20	13	4	08	20	23	4	01	20	26	3	56	20	32	3	45	20	39	3	50	20	55	4	05	20	54
14	3	59	20	12	4	10	20	22	4	02	20	25	3	58	20	31	3	46	20	38	3	51	20	54	4	06	20	52
15	4	01	20	11	4	11	20	21	4	03	20	24	3	59	20	30	3	48	20	36	3	52	20	52	4	07	20	51
16	4	02	20	10	4	12	20	20	4	04	20	22	4	00	20	29	3	49	20	35	3	54	20	51	4	09	20	50
17	4	03	20	09	4	13	20	19	4	06	20	21	4	02	20	28	3	50	20	34	3	55	20	50	4	10	20	49
18	4	04	20	08	4	14	20	18	4	07	20	20	4	03	20	27	3	52	20	33	3	57	20	48	4	12	20	47
19	4	05	20	07	4	16	20	17	4	08	20	19	4	04	20	25	3	53	20	31	3	59	20	47	4	13	20	46
20	4	07	20	06	4	17	20	16	4	10	20	18	4	06	20	24	3	55	20	30	4	00	20	45	4	14	20	45
21	4	08	20	05	4	18	20	14	4	11	20	16	4	07	20	23	3	56	20	28	4	02	20	44	4	16	20	43
22	4	09	20	03	4	20	20	13	4	12	20	15	4	09	20	21	3	58	20	27	4	03	20	42	4	18	20	42
23	4	11	20	02	4	21	20	12	4	14	20	14	4	10	20	20	4	00	20	25	4	05	20	41	4	19	20	40
24	4	12	20	01	4	22	20	10	4	15	20	12	4	12	20	18	4	01	20	24	4	07	20	39	4	21	20	39
25	4	14	19	59	4	24	20	09	4	17	20	11	4	13	20	17	4	03	20	22	4	09	20	37	4	22	20	37
26	4	15	19	58	4	25	20	08	4	18	20	09	4	15	20	15	4	05	20	20	4	10	20	35	4	24	20	35
27	4	16	19	56	4	27	20	06	4	20	20	08	4	16	20	14	4	06	20	19	4	12	20	34	4	26	20	34
28	4	18	19	55	4	28	20	05	4	21	20	06	4	18	20	12	4	08	20	17	4	14	20	32	4	27	20	32
29	4	19	19	53	4	29	20	03	4	23	20	05	4	20	20	10	4	10	20	15	4	16	20	30	4	29	20	30
30	4	21	19	52	4	31	20	02	4	24	20	03	4	21	20	09	4	11	20	13	4	17	20	28	4	31	20	28
31	4	22	19	50	4	32	20	00	4	26	20	01	4	23	20	07	4	13	20	11	4	19	20	26	4	32	20	27

JUPITER

Day	*R.A.*		*Dec.*		*Transit*		*5° high*			
							52°		*56°*	
	h	*m*	°	′	*h*	*m*	*h*	*m*	*h*	*m*
1	0	11.5	–0	09	5	35	0	09	0	13
11	0	13.7	+0	02	4	58	23	27	23	30
21	0	14.6	+0	05	4	19	22	48	22	52
31	0	14.4	0	00	3	40	22	00	22	1[illegible]

Diameters – equatorial 44″ polar 41″

SATURN

Day	*R.A.*		*Dec.*		*Transit*		*5° high*			
							52°		*56°*	
	h	*m*	°	′	*h*	*m*	*h*	*m*	*h*	*m*
1	11	58.7	+2	40	17	20	23	00	22	59
11	12	00.8	+2	24	16	43	22	22	22	21
21	12	03.4	+2	05	16	06	21	44	21	42
31	12	06.5	+1	44	15	30	21	05	21	04

Diameters – equatorial 17″ polar 15″
Rings – major axis 38″ minor axis 2″

URANUS

Day	*R.A.*		*Dec.*		*Transit*		*10° high*			
							52°		*56°*	
	h	*m*	°	′	*h*	*m*	*h*	*m*	*h*	*m*
1	0	03.3	–0	28	5	27	0	36	0	43
11	0	03.3	–0	28	4	47	23	52	0	03
21	0	03.1	–0	30	4	08	23	13	23	20
31	0	02.5	–0	34	3	28	22	33	22	41

Diameter 4″

NEPTUNE

Day	*R.A.*		*Dec.*		*Transit*		*10° high*			
							52°		*56°*	
	h	*m*	°	′	*h*	*m*	*h*	*m*	*h*	*m*
1	22	03.1	–12	27	3	27	23	43	0	08
11	22	02.5	–12	31	2	47	23	03	23	25
21	22	01.7	12	35	2	07	22	24	22	45
31	22	00.8	–12	40	1	27	21	44	22	06

Diameter 2″

AUGUST 2010

EIGHTH MONTH, 31 DAYS. *Augustus*, formerly *Sextilis*, sixth month of Roman pre-Julian calendar

1	*Sunday*	The Warsaw uprising began in Poland 1944	day 213
2	*Monday*	Iraq invaded the Gulf state of Kuwait 1990	week 31 day 214
3	*Tuesday*	Germany and France mutually declared war 1914	215
4	*Wednesday*	President Woodrow Wilson proclaimed US neutrality from the war in Europe 1914	216
5	*Thursday*	The mobilisation of the British Expeditionary Force began 1914	217
6	*Friday*	The USA dropped an atomic bomb on Hiroshima, killing 140,000 people 1945	218
7	*Saturday*	Benjamin Netanyahu resigned as finance minister in protest at Israel's withdrawal from Gaza 2005	219
8	*Sunday*	The House of Commons passed the Defence of the Realm Act 1914	220
9	*Monday*	The USA dropped an atomic bomb on Nagasaki, killing 70,000 people 1945	week 32 day 221
10	*Tuesday*	The Treaty of Bucharest ended the second Balkan War 1913	222
11	*Wednesday*	NATO took command of peacekeeping forces in Afghanistan 2003	223
12	*Thursday*	Guy Gibson, RAF commander *b.* 1918; Viscount Castlereagh, British foreign secretary *d.* 1822	224
13	*Friday*	Anglo–Austrian forces defeated France and Bavaria at the Battle of Blenheim 1704	225
14	*Saturday*	British troops were sent into Northern Ireland to restore law and order 1969	226
15	*Sunday*	Allied nations celebrated Victory in Japan Day 1945	227
16	*Monday*	The Peterloo Massacre took place in Manchester 1819	week 33 day 228
17	*Tuesday*	Napoleon Bonaparte led France to victory against the Russians at Smolensk 1812	229
18	*Wednesday*	Franz Joseph I, Austrian emperor *b.* 1830; Genghis Khan, Mongol ruler *d.* 1272	230
19	*Thursday*	The Allies launched a beach raid on Dieppe 1942	231
20	*Friday*	Bulgaria won a decisive victory against the Byzantine empire at the Battle of Anchialus 917	232
21	*Saturday*	Soviet forces occupied Czechoslovakia, ending the 'Prague Spring' 1968	233
22	*Sunday*	The Battle of Bosworth Field concluded the War of the Roses 1485	234
23	*Monday*	Louis XVI, king of France *b.* 1754; William Wallace, Scottish resistance leader *d.* 1305	week 34 day 235
24	*Tuesday*	Graham Sutherland, war artist *b.* 1903; Charles de Téligny, French diplomat *d.* 1572	236
25	*Wednesday*	Allied forces liberated Paris after the Germans surrendered 1944	237
26	*Thursday*	The English were victorious at the Battle of Crécy in the Hundred Years War 1346	238
27	*Friday*	Napoleon Bonaparte defeated Allied forces at the Battle of Dresden 1813	239
28	*Saturday*	The first Battle of Heligoland Bight took place 1914	240
29	*Sunday*	Britain and China signed the Treaty of Nanking, ending the first Opium War 1842	241
30	*Monday*	The International War Crimes Tribunal charged Slobodan Milosevic with genocide 2001	week 35 day 242
31	*Tuesday*	The IRA announced a complete cessation of military operations 1994	243

ASTRONOMICAL PHENOMENA

d	*h*	
7	01	Mercury at greatest elongation E.27°
8	17	Saturn in conjunction with Venus. Saturn 3°N.
12	00	Mercury in conjunction with Moon. Mercury 2°N.
13	02	Saturn in conjunction with Moon. Saturn 7°N.
13	09	Venus in conjunction with Moon. Venus 4°N.
13	13	Mars in conjunction with Moon. Mars 5°N.
20	04	Venus at greatest elongation E. 46°
20	10	Neptune at opposition
20	19	Mars in conjunction with Venus. Mars 2°N.
20	20	Mercury at stationary point
23	05	Sun's longitude 150° ♍
27	06	Jupiter in conjunction with Moon. Jupiter 7°S.

MINIMA OF ALGOL

d	*h*	*d*	*h*	*d*	*h*
2	00.5	13	11.7	24	22.9
4	21.3	16	08.5	27	19.8
7	18.1	19	05.3	30	16.6
10	14.9	22	02.1		

CONSTELLATIONS

The following constellations are near their meridian at

	d	*h*		*d*	*h*
July	1	24	August	16	21
July	16	23	September	1	20
August	1	22	September	15	19

Draco, Hercules, Lyra, Cygnus, Sagitta, Ophiuchus, Serpens, Aquila and Sagittarius

THE MOON

Phases, Apsides and Node	*d*	*h*	*m*
☾ Last Quarter	3	04	59
● New Moon	10	03	08
☽ First Quarter	16	18	14
○ Full Moon	24	17	05
Perigee (357,863km)	10	17	51
Apogee (406,385km)	25	05	35

Mean longitude of ascending node on August 1, 280°

THE SUN

s.d. 15′.8

Day	Right Ascension			Dec. +		Equation of time		Rise				Transit		Set				Sidereal time			Transit of first point of Aries		
								52°		56°				52°		56°							
	h	*m*	*s*	°	′	*m*	*s*	*h*	*m*	*h*	*m*	*h*	*m*	*h*	*m*	*h*	*m*	*h*	*m*	*s*	*h*	*m*	*s*
1	8	44	22	18	06	−6	22	4	21	4	04	12	06	19	50	20	08	20	38	00	3	21	27
2	8	48	15	17	51	−6	18	4	23	4	05	12	06	19	48	20	06	20	41	56	3	17	31
3	8	52	07	17	35	−6	14	4	25	4	07	12	06	19	47	20	04	20	45	53	3	13	35
4	8	55	58	17	19	−6	09	4	26	4	09	12	06	19	45	20	02	20	49	50	3	09	39
5	8	59	49	17	03	−6	03	4	28	4	11	12	06	19	43	20	00	20	53	46	3	05	43
6	9	03	40	16	47	−5	57	4	29	4	13	12	06	19	41	19	57	20	57	43	3	01	47
7	9	07	30	16	30	−5	51	4	31	4	15	12	06	19	40	19	55	21	01	39	2	57	52
8	9	11	19	16	14	−5	43	4	32	4	17	12	06	19	38	19	53	21	05	36	2	53	56
9	9	15	08	15	57	−5	35	4	34	4	19	12	06	19	36	19	51	21	09	32	2	50	00
10	9	18	56	15	39	−5	27	4	36	4	21	12	05	19	34	19	49	21	13	29	2	46	04
11	9	22	43	15	22	−5	18	4	37	4	23	12	05	19	32	19	46	21	17	25	2	42	08
12	9	26	30	15	04	−5	08	4	39	4	25	12	05	19	30	19	44	21	21	22	2	38	12
13	9	30	17	14	46	−4	58	4	40	4	27	12	05	19	28	19	42	21	25	19	2	34	16
14	9	34	03	14	27	−4	48	4	42	4	29	12	05	19	26	19	39	21	29	15	2	30	20
15	9	37	48	14	09	−4	36	4	44	4	31	12	05	19	24	19	37	21	33	12	2	26	24
16	9	41	33	13	50	−4	24	4	45	4	32	12	04	19	22	19	35	21	37	08	2	22	28
17	9	45	17	13	31	−4	12	4	47	4	34	12	04	19	20	19	32	21	41	05	2	18	32
18	9	49	01	13	12	−3	59	4	49	4	36	12	04	19	18	19	30	21	45	01	2	14	37
19	9	52	44	12	52	−3	46	4	50	4	38	12	04	19	16	19	28	21	48	58	2	10	41
20	9	56	26	12	33	−3	32	4	52	4	40	12	03	19	14	19	25	21	52	54	2	06	45
21	10	00	08	12	13	−3	17	4	53	4	42	12	03	19	12	19	23	21	56	51	2	02	49
22	10	03	50	11	53	−3	03	4	55	4	44	12	03	19	10	19	20	22	00	48	1	58	53
23	10	07	31	11	33	−2	47	4	57	4	46	12	03	19	07	19	18	22	04	44	1	54	57
24	10	11	12	11	13	−2	31	4	58	4	48	12	02	19	05	19	15	22	08	41	1	51	01
25	10	14	52	10	52	−2	15	5	00	4	50	12	02	19	03	19	13	22	12	37	1	47	05
26	10	18	32	10	31	−1	59	5	02	4	52	12	02	19	01	19	10	22	16	34	1	43	09
27	10	22	12	10	10	−1	41	5	03	4	54	12	02	18	59	19	08	22	20	30	1	39	13
28	10	25	51	9	49	−1	24	5	05	4	56	12	01	18	57	19	05	22	24	27	1	35	17
29	10	29	30	9	28	−1	06	5	07	4	58	12	01	18	54	19	03	22	28	23	1	31	22
30	10	33	08	9	07	−0	48	5	08	5	00	12	01	18	52	19	00	22	32	20	1	27	26
31	10	36	46	8	45	−0	30	5	10	5	02	12	00	18	50	18	57	22	36	17	1	23	30

DURATION OF TWILIGHT (in minutes)

Latitude	52°	56°	52°	56°	52°	56°	52°	56°
	1 August		*11 August*		*21 August*		*31 August*	
Civil	41	49	39	45	37	42	35	40
Nautical	97	121	90	107	84	97	79	90
Astronomical	179	TAN	154	210	139	168	128	148

THE NIGHT SKY

Mercury is at greatest eastern elongation (27 degrees) on the 7th but remains unsuitably placed for observation throughout August.

Venus, magnitude −4.3, is a magnificent object, visible low in the western sky in the evenings after sunset. Although greatest eastern elongation (46 degrees) occurs on the 20th, Venus is only visible for a short while after sunset. Shortly after sunset it may be possible to detect the planet low above the west-south-western horizon and on the evening of the 13th to see the thin crescent Moon some 7 degrees to the left and 4 degrees lower in altitude. Although the Moon will be about 20 degrees to the left of Venus on the following evening, it should be possible to detect the two bodies more easily.

Mars is too close to the Sun to permit observation.

Jupiter is a brilliant object, magnitude −2.8, in the sky for most of the night, becoming visible low in the eastern sky as early as 20h by the end of the month. The waning crescent Moon is near Jupiter on the mornings of the 26th and 27th.

Saturn, even at the beginning of the month, is setting in the long evening twilight and will not be seen again until October.

Neptune is at opposition on the 20th, in the constellation of Capricornus. It is not visible to the naked eye since its magnitude is +7.9.

Meteors. The maximum of the famous Perseid meteor shower occurs on the evening of the 12th and the crescent Moon will cause minimal interference as it sets at about 20h local mean time.

THE MOON

Day	R.A.		Dec.	Hor. Par.	Semi-diam.	Sun's Co-Long.	PA of Br. Limb	Ph.	Age	Rise 52°		Rise 56°		Transit		Set 52°		Set 56°	
	h	*m*	°	′	′	°	°	%	*d*	*h*	*m*	*h*	*m*	*h*	*m*	*h*	*m*	*h*	*m*
1	0	42	+10.2	54.6	14.9	160	64	71	20.2	21	26	21	14	4	11	11	28	11	40
2	1	28	+14.7	55.1	15.0	172	67	62	21.2	21	47	21	30	4	55	12	40	12	56
3	2	17	+18.6	55.7	15.2	184	71	52	22.2	22	14	21	52	5	42	13	53	14	14
4	3	09	+21.9	56.5	15.4	196	75	42	23.2	22	51	22	24	6	33	15	05	15	31
5	4	05	+24.1	57.4	15.6	209	80	32	24.2	23	41	23	12	7	28	16	12	16	41
6	5	04	+25.0	58.3	15.9	221	86	22	25.2		—		—	8	26	17	11	17	39
7	6	06	+24.4	59.3	16.2	233	92	14	26.2	0	46	0	18	9	27	17	57	18	21
8	7	08	+22.2	60.1	16.4	245	96	7	27.2	2	05	1	41	10	27	18	32	18	51
9	8	09	+18.4	60.8	16.6	258	96	2	28.2	3	32	3	14	11	26	19	00	19	13
10	9	08	+13.4	61.2	16.7	270	50	0	29.2	5	02	4	51	12	22	19	22	19	29
11	10	05	+7.6	61.3	16.7	282	308	1	0.9	6	33	6	28	13	16	19	41	19	43
12	11	01	+1.3	61.0	16.6	294	302	5	1.9	8	01	8	02	14	09	20	00	19	56
13	11	55	−5.0	60.5	16.5	307	299	12	2.9	9	28	9	35	15	01	20	19	20	10
14	12	49	−10.8	59.8	16.3	319	297	21	3.9	10	54	11	06	15	53	20	40	20	26
15	13	43	−16.0	58.9	16.1	331	293	31	4.9	12	17	12	36	16	46	21	06	20	46
16	14	39	−20.1	58.1	15.8	343	289	42	5.9	13	36	14	00	17	40	21	38	21	13
17	15	35	−23.0	57.2	15.6	355	283	53	6.9	14	47	15	15	18	35	22	19	21	50
18	16	31	−24.6	56.5	15.4	8	278	63	7.9	15	48	16	17	19	29	23	10	22	40
19	17	27	−24.9	55.8	15.2	20	272	73	8.9	16	36	17	04	20	21		—	23	43
20	18	22	−23.9	55.2	15.0	32	267	81	9.9	17	13	17	37	21	12	0	10		—
21	19	14	−21.8	54.8	14.9	44	263	88	10.9	17	41	18	00	21	59	1	17	0	53
22	20	04	−18.8	54.4	14.8	56	261	93	11.9	18	03	18	17	22	44	2	26	2	08
23	20	51	−15.0	54.2	14.8	69	262	97	12.9	18	20	18	31	23	27	3	36	3	22
24	21	37	−10.6	54.0	14.7	81	275	99	13.9	18	36	18	42		—	4	45	4	36
25	22	21	−5.9	54.0	14.7	93	16	100	14.9	18	50	18	51	0	08	5	53	5	49
26	23	04	−1.0	54.0	14.7	105	49	98	15.9	19	04	19	01	0	49	7	01	7	01
27	23	47	+4.0	54.1	14.7	117	56	95	16.9	19	18	19	11	1	29	8	08	8	13
28	0	31	+8.9	54.3	14.8	130	60	90	17.9	19	34	19	23	2	10	9	17	9	27
29	1	16	+13.4	54.7	14.9	142	63	84	18.9	19	53	19	38	2	53	10	27	10	42
30	2	04	+17.5	55.1	15.0	154	67	76	19.9	20	18	19	57	3	38	11	39	11	58
31	2	54	+20.9	55.7	15.2	166	72	67	20.9	20	49	20	25	4	27	12	50	13	14

MERCURY

Day	R.A.		Dec.	Diam.	Phase	Transit		5° high 52°		5° high 56°	
	h	*m*	°	″	%	*h*	*m*	*h*	*m*	*h*	*m*
1	10	28	+9.1	7	57	13	50	20	02	20	05
3	10	36	+8.0	7	55	13	50	19	56	19	58
5	10	43	+6.8	7	52	13	49	19	49	19	51
7	10	50	+5.7	8	49	13	48	19	42	19	43
9	10	56	+4.7	8	45	13	46	19	35	19	35
11	11	02	+3.7	8	42	13	43	19	28	19	27
13	11	06	+2.8	8	39	13	40	19	20	19	18
15	11	10	+2.1	9	35	13	35	19	11	19	09
17	11	12	+1.4	9	31	13	29	19	02	19	00
19	11	13	+0.9	9	27	13	22	18	53	18	50
21	11	13	+0.6	10	23	13	14	18	43	18	41
23	11	12	+0.5	10	18	13	05	18	34	18	31
25	11	10	+0.5	10	14	12	54	18	23	18	21
27	11	06	+0.8	10	10	12	42	18	13	18	11
29	11	01	+1.4	11	6	12	29	18	03	18	01
31	10	55	+2.1	11	3	12	15	17	54	17	52

VENUS

Day	R.A.		Dec.	Diam.	Phase	Transit		5° high 52°		5° high 56°	
	h	*m*	°	″	%	*h*	*m*	*h*	*m*	*h*	*m*
1	11	37	+2.7	20	58	14	58	20	37	20	36
6	11	55	+0.2	21	56	14	57	20	24	20	20
11	12	13	−2.3	22	53	14	56	20	09	20	04
16	12	31	−4.7	23	51	14	53	19	54	19	46
21	12	48	−7.1	25	48	14	51	19	38	19	28
26	13	05	−9.4	26	45	14	48	19	22	19	10
31	13	20	−11.6	28	43	14	44	19	05	18	50

MARS

Day	R.A.		Dec.	Diam.	Phase	Transit		5° high 52°		5° high 56°	
	h	*m*	°	″	%	*h*	*m*	*h*	*m*	*h*	*m*
1	12	05	−0.1	5	93	15	26	20	52	20	48
6	12	16	−1.3	5	93	15	18	20	37	20	32
11	12	28	−2.6	5	94	15	09	20	21	20	16
16	12	39	−3.9	5	94	15	01	20	06	20	00
21	12	51	−5.2	4	94	14	53	19	51	19	43
26	13	03	−6.5	4	95	14	45	19	37	19	27
31	13	15	−7.8	4	95	14	37	19	22	19	11

SUNRISE AND SUNSET

	London				*Bristol*				*Birmingham*				*Manchester*				*Newcastle*				*Glasgow*				*Belfast*			
	0° 05′		*51° 30′*		*2° 35′*		*51° 28′*		*1° 55′*		*52° 28′*		*2° 15′*		*53° 28′*		*1° 37′*		*54° 59′*		*4° 14′*		*55° 52′*		*5° 56′*		*54° 35′*	
d	*h*	*m*	*h*	*m*	*h*	*m*	*h*	*m*	*h*	*m*	*h*	*m*	*h*	*m*	*h*	*m*	*h*	*m*	*h*	*m*	*h*	*m*	*h*	*m*	*h*	*m*	*h*	*m*
1	4	24	19	49	4	34	19	58	4	27	20	00	4	24	20	05	4	15	20	09	4	21	20	24	4	34	20	25
2	4	25	19	47	4	35	19	57	4	29	19	58	4	26	20	03	4	17	20	07	4	23	20	22	4	36	20	23
3	4	27	19	45	4	37	19	55	4	30	19	56	4	28	20	02	4	19	20	06	4	25	20	20	4	38	20	21
4	4	28	19	44	4	38	19	53	4	32	19	54	4	29	20	00	4	20	20	04	4	27	20	18	4	39	20	19
5	4	30	19	42	4	40	19	52	4	34	19	53	4	31	19	58	4	22	20	02	4	29	20	16	4	41	20	17
6	4	31	19	40	4	41	19	50	4	35	19	51	4	33	19	56	4	24	19	59	4	31	20	14	4	43	20	15
7	4	33	19	38	4	43	19	48	4	37	19	49	4	34	19	54	4	26	19	57	4	32	20	12	4	45	20	13
8	4	34	19	36	4	45	19	46	4	38	19	47	4	36	19	52	4	28	19	55	4	34	20	09	4	47	20	11
9	4	36	19	35	4	46	19	44	4	40	19	45	4	38	19	50	4	29	19	53	4	36	20	07	4	48	20	09
10	4	38	19	33	4	48	19	43	4	42	19	43	4	40	19	48	4	31	19	51	4	38	20	05	4	50	20	07
11	4	39	19	31	4	49	19	41	4	43	19	41	4	41	19	46	4	33	19	49	4	40	20	03	4	52	20	05
12	4	41	19	29	4	51	19	39	4	45	19	39	4	43	19	44	4	35	19	47	4	42	20	00	4	54	20	02
13	4	42	19	27	4	52	19	37	4	47	19	37	4	45	19	42	4	37	19	44	4	44	19	58	4	56	20	00
14	4	44	19	25	4	54	19	35	4	48	19	35	4	46	19	40	4	39	19	42	4	46	19	56	4	57	19	58
15	4	46	19	23	4	56	19	33	4	50	19	33	4	48	19	38	4	41	19	40	4	48	19	54	4	59	19	56
16	4	47	19	21	4	57	19	31	4	52	19	31	4	50	19	35	4	43	19	38	4	50	19	51	5	01	19	54
17	4	49	19	19	4	59	19	29	4	53	19	29	4	52	19	33	4	44	19	35	4	52	19	49	5	03	19	51
18	4	50	19	17	5	00	19	27	4	55	19	27	4	53	19	31	4	46	19	33	4	54	19	46	5	05	19	49
19	4	52	19	15	5	02	19	25	4	57	19	25	4	55	19	29	4	48	19	31	4	56	19	44	5	07	19	47
20	4	53	19	13	5	04	19	23	4	58	19	23	4	57	19	27	4	50	19	28	4	58	19	42	5	08	19	45
21	4	55	19	11	5	05	19	21	5	00	19	21	4	59	19	24	4	52	19	26	5	00	19	39	5	10	19	42
22	4	57	19	09	5	07	19	19	5	02	19	18	5	00	19	22	4	54	19	24	5	02	19	37	5	12	19	40
23	4	58	19	07	5	08	19	17	5	03	19	16	5	02	19	20	4	56	19	21	5	04	19	34	5	14	19	38
24	5	00	19	05	5	10	19	14	5	05	19	14	5	04	19	18	4	57	19	19	5	06	19	32	5	16	19	35
25	5	01	19	02	5	12	19	12	5	07	19	12	5	06	19	15	4	59	19	17	5	07	19	29	5	18	19	33
26	5	03	19	00	5	13	19	10	5	08	19	10	5	07	19	13	5	01	19	14	5	09	19	27	5	19	19	30
27	5	05	18	58	5	15	19	08	5	10	19	07	5	09	19	11	5	03	19	12	5	11	19	24	5	21	19	28
28	5	06	18	56	5	16	19	06	5	12	19	05	5	11	19	08	5	05	19	09	5	13	19	22	5	23	19	26
29	5	08	18	54	5	18	19	04	5	13	19	03	5	13	19	06	5	07	19	07	5	15	19	19	5	25	19	23
30	5	09	18	51	5	19	19	01	5	15	19	01	5	14	19	04	5	09	19	04	5	17	19	17	5	27	19	21
31	5	11	18	49	5	21	18	59	5	17	18	58	5	16	19	01	5	11	19	02	5	19	19	14	5	29	19	18

JUPITER

Day	*R.A.*		*Dec.*		*Transit*		*5° high*			
							52°		*56°*	
	h	*m*	°	′	*h*	*m*	*h*	*m*	*h*	*m*
1	0	14.3	–0	01	3	36	22	05	22	00
11	0	12.8	–0	14	2	55	21	26	21	29
21	0	10.1	–0	34	2	13	20	45	20	49
31	0	06.5	–1	00	1	30	20	05	20	09

Diameters – equatorial 48″ polar 44″

SATURN

Day	*R.A.*		*Dec.*		*Transit*		*5° high*			
							52°		*56°*	
	h	*m*	°	′	*h*	*m*	*h*	*m*	*h*	*m*
1	12	06.8	+1	42	15	26	21	02	21	00
11	12	10.3	+1	18	14	51	20	24	20	21
21	12	14.1	+0	52	14	15	19	46	19	43
31	12	18.1	+0	24	13	40	19	08	19	05

Diameters – equatorial 16″ polar 14″
Rings – major axis 36″ minor axis 3″

URANUS

Day	*R.A.*		*Dec.*		*Transit*		*10° high*			
							52°		*56°*	
	h	*m*	°	′	*h*	*m*	*h*	*m*	*h*	*m*
1	0	02.4	–0	35	3	24	22	29	22	37
11	0	01.6	–0	41	2	44	21	50	21	57
21	0	00.5	–0	48	2	03	21	10	21	18
31	23	59.2	–0	56	1	23	20	30	20	38

Diameter 4″

NEPTUNE

Day	*R.A.*		*Dec.*		*Transit*		*10° high*			
							52°		*56°*	
	h	*m*	°	′	*h*	*m*	*h*	*m*	*h*	*m*
1	22	00.7	–12	41	1	22	21	40	22	02
11	21	59.7	–12	47	0	42	21	00	21	22
21	21	58.6	–12	52	0	02	20	21	20	43
31	21	57.6	–12	58	23	17	19	41	20	03

Diameter 2″

SEPTEMBER 2010 ♎

NINTH MONTH, 30 DAYS. *Septem* (seven), seventh month of Roman pre-Julian calendar

1	*Wednesday*	Germany invaded Poland 1939	day 244
2	*Thursday*	Japan formally surrendered aboard the USS *Missouri* in Tokyo Bay 1945	245
3	*Friday*	Oliver Cromwell's parliamentarians defeated Charles II's royalists at the second Battle of Worcester 1651	246
4	*Saturday*	Apache chief Geronimo surrendered to the US army at Skeleton Creek, Arizona 1886	247
5	*Sunday*	The Treaty of Portsmouth ended the Russo–Japanese War 1905	248
6	*Monday*	Indian troops invaded west Pakistan 1965	week 36 day 249
7	*Tuesday*	Leonard Cheshire, RAF pilot *b.* 1917; A. J. P. Taylor, historian *d.* 1990	250
8	*Wednesday*	Germany launched its first long-range rocket, the V2 1944	251
9	*Thursday*	James IV of Scotland was killed at the Battle of Flodden Field 1513	252
10	*Friday*	Pablo Picasso's monumental painting, *Guernica,* was returned to Spain 1981	253
11	*Saturday*	The French army of Louis XIV was defeated at the Battle of Malplaquet 1709	254
12	*Sunday*	US president George W. Bush declared a 'war on terror' following the 9/11 attacks 2001	255
13	*Monday*	The first Israeli–Palestinian peace accord was signed in Washington DC, USA 1993	week 37 day 256
14	*Tuesday*	The military staged a coup in the west African state of Congo 1960	257
15	*Wednesday*	Battle of Britain Day: the RAF defended Britain against a massive Luftwaffe assault 1940	258
16	*Thursday*	Phalangist militias killed hundreds in Palestinian refugee camps in Lebanon 1982	259
17	*Friday*	Allied forces began airborne invasions of Holland 1944	260
18	*Saturday*	The Treaty of Belgrade ended the war between the Ottomans and the Habsburgs 1739	261
19	*Sunday*	The Soviet Union and Finland signed the Moscow Armistice 1944	262
20	*Monday*	The French defeated the Prussians at the Battle of Valmy 1792	week 38 day 263
21	*Tuesday*	Bonnie Prince Charlie and the Jacobites defeated the English at the Battle of Prestonpans 1745	264
22	*Wednesday*	War broke out between Iran and Iraq 1980	265
23	*Thursday*	The British East India Company was victorious at the Battle of Assaye, India 1803	266
24	*Friday*	The Japanese Imperial Army suppressed the Satsuma Rebellion 1877	267
25	*Saturday*	King Harold II defeated Norwegian King Harald Hardrada at the Battle of Stamford Bridge 1066	268
26	*Sunday*	Allied forces retreated from Arnhem in the Netherlands after heavy losses 1944	269
27	*Monday*	The Taliban defeated Afghan forces and gained control of Kabul, Afghanistan 1996	week 39 day 270
28	*Tuesday*	William the Conqueror landed at Pevensey in Sussex 1066	271
29	*Wednesday*	The Babi Yar massacre of nearly 34,000 Jews began in Nazi-occupied Ukraine 1941	272
30	*Thursday*	Neville Chamberlain declared 'peace for our time' after signing the Munich Agreement 1938	273

ASTRONOMICAL PHENOMENA

d	*h*	
3	13	Mercury in inferior conjunction
7	21	Mercury in conjunction with Moon. Mercury 2°N.
9	17	Saturn in conjunction with Moon. Saturn 7°N.
11	05	Mars in conjunction with Moon. Mars 5°N.
11	13	Venus in conjunction with Moon. Venus 0°.3 N.
12	23	Mercury at stationary point
14	05	Pluto at stationary point
19	17	Mercury at greatest elongation W.18°
21	12	Jupiter at opposition
21	17	Uranus at opposition
23	03	Sun's longitude 180° ♎
23	05	Jupiter in conjunction with Moon. Jupiter 7°S.
23	23	Venus at greatest brilliancy

MINIMA OF ALGOL

d	*h*	*d*	*h*	*d*	*h*
2	13.4	14	00.6	25	11.9
5	10.2	16	21.4	28	08.7
8	07.0	19	18.2		
11	03.8	22	15.0		

CONSTELLATIONS

The following constellations are near their meridian at

	d	*h*		*d*	*h*
August	1	24	September	15	21
August	16	23	October	1	20
September	1	22	October	16	19

Draco, Cepheus, Lyra, Cygnus, Vulpecula, Sagitta, Delphinus, Equuleus, Aquila, Aquarius and Capricornus

THE MOON

Phases, Apsides and Node	*d*	*h*	*m*
☾ Last Quarter	1	17	22
● New Moon	8	10	30
☽ First Quarter	15	05	50
○ Full Moon	23	09	17
Perigee (357,188 km)	8	03	52
Apogee (406,182 km)	21	07	50

Mean longitude of ascending node on September 1, 279°

THE SUN

s.d. 15′.9

Day	Right Ascension			Dec.		Equation of time		Rise 52°		Rise 56°		Transit		Set 52°		Set 56°		Sidereal time			Transit of first point of Aries		
	h	*m*	*s*	°	′	*m*	*s*	*h*	*m*	*h*	*m*	*h*	*m*	*h*	*m*	*h*	*m*	*h*	*m*	*s*	*h*	*m*	*s*
1	10	40	24	+8	24	−0	11	5	11	5	04	12	00	18	48	18	55	22	40	13	1	19	34
2	10	44	01	+8	02	+0	08	5	13	5	06	12	00	18	45	18	52	22	44	10	1	15	38
3	10	47	39	+7	40	+0	27	5	15	5	08	11	59	18	43	18	50	22	48	06	1	11	42
4	10	51	16	+7	18	+0	47	5	16	5	10	11	59	18	41	18	47	22	52	03	1	07	46
5	10	54	52	+6	56	+1	07	5	18	5	12	11	59	18	38	18	44	22	55	59	1	03	50
6	10	58	29	+6	34	+1	27	5	20	5	14	11	58	18	36	18	42	22	59	56	0	59	54
7	11	02	05	+6	11	+1	47	5	21	5	16	11	58	18	34	18	39	23	03	52	0	55	58
8	11	05	42	+5	49	+2	07	5	23	5	18	11	58	18	32	18	37	23	07	49	0	52	02
9	11	09	17	+5	26	+2	28	5	24	5	19	11	57	18	29	18	34	23	11	46	0	48	07
10	11	12	53	+5	03	+2	49	5	26	5	21	11	57	18	27	18	31	23	15	42	0	44	11
11	11	16	29	+4	41	+3	10	5	28	5	23	11	57	18	25	18	29	23	19	39	0	40	15
12	11	20	04	+4	18	+3	31	5	29	5	25	11	56	18	22	18	26	23	23	35	0	36	19
13	11	23	40	+3	55	+3	52	5	31	5	27	11	56	18	20	18	23	23	27	32	0	32	23
14	11	27	15	+3	32	+4	13	5	33	5	29	11	56	18	18	18	21	23	31	28	0	28	27
15	11	30	50	+3	09	+4	34	5	34	5	31	11	55	18	15	18	18	23	35	25	0	24	31
16	11	34	26	+2	46	+4	56	5	36	5	33	11	55	18	13	18	15	23	39	21	0	20	35
17	11	38	01	+2	23	+5	17	5	37	5	35	11	55	18	11	18	13	23	43	18	0	16	39
18	11	41	36	+2	00	+5	39	5	39	5	37	11	54	18	08	18	10	23	47	14	0	12	43
19	11	45	11	+1	36	+6	00	5	41	5	39	11	54	18	06	18	07	23	51	11	0	08	48
20	11	48	46	+1	13	+6	22	5	42	5	41	11	53	18	04	18	05	23	55	08	0	04	52
21	11	52	21	+0	50	+6	43	5	44	5	43	11	53	18	01	18	02	23	59	04	0	00	56
																					23	57	00
22	11	55	56	+0	26	+7	04	5	46	5	45	11	53	17	59	17	59	0	03	01	23	53	04
23	11	59	32	+0	03	+7	25	5	47	5	47	11	52	17	56	17	57	0	06	57	23	49	08
24	12	03	07	−0	20	+7	47	5	49	5	49	11	52	17	54	17	54	0	10	54	23	45	12
25	12	06	43	−0	44	+8	08	5	51	5	51	11	52	17	52	17	52	0	14	50	23	41	16
26	12	10	19	−1	07	+8	28	5	52	5	53	11	51	17	49	17	49	0	18	47	23	37	20
27	12	13	54	−1	30	+8	49	5	54	5	55	11	51	17	47	17	46	0	22	43	23	33	24
28	12	17	31	−1	54	+9	09	5	56	5	57	11	51	17	45	17	44	0	26	40	23	29	28
29	12	21	07	−2	17	+9	30	5	57	5	59	11	50	17	42	17	41	0	30	37	23	25	33
30	12	24	44	−2	40	+9	49	5	59	6	01	11	50	17	40	17	38	0	34	33	23	21	37

DURATION OF TWILIGHT (in minutes)

Latitude	52°	56°	52°	56°	52°	56°	52°	56°
	1 September		*11 September*		*21 September*		*31 September*	
Civil	35	39	34	38	34	37	34	37
Nautical	79	89	76	85	74	82	73	80
Astronomical	127	147	120	136	116	129	113	125

THE NIGHT SKY

Mercury is too close to the Sun to be observed at first but after the first two weeks of the month it is visible low above the eastern horizon at about the beginning of morning civil twilight, for the rest of September. This is the most favourable morning apparition of the year for observers in the northern hemisphere. During its period of visibility its magnitude brightens from +1.1 to −1.1.

Venus, magnitude −4.5, is a magnificent object in the south-western sky in the early evenings for a very short time after sunset. The planet is gradually drawing closer to the Sun and being well south of the equator is unlikely to be seen from the latitudes of the British Isles after the first week of September. Only observers much farther south will be able to see it at its greatest brilliancy on the 23rd. The thin crescent Moon passes only about 1 degree south of the planet on the 11th.

Mars is unsuitably placed for observation.

Jupiter, magnitude −2.9, reaches opposition on the 21st and thus is observable throughout the hours of darkness. The Full Moon passes 6 degrees north of Jupiter on the 23rd.

Saturn continues to be too close to the Sun for observation.

Uranus is at opposition on the 21st, in the constellation of Pisces. The planet is barely visible to the naked eye as its magnitude is +5.7, but it is readily located with only small optical aid.

Zodiacal Light. The morning cone may be observed stretching up from the eastern horizon, along the ecliptic, before the beginning of morning twilight, from the 7th to the 21st. This faint phenomenon is only visible under good conditions and in the absence of both moonlight and artificial lighting.

THE MOON

Day	R.A. h	R.A. m	Dec. °	Hor. Par. ′	Semi-diam. ′	Sun's Co-Long. °	P.A. of Br. Limb °	Ph. %	Age d	Rise 52° h	Rise 52° m	Rise 56° h	Rise 56° m	Transit h	Transit m	Set 52° h	Set 52° m	Set 56° h	Set 56° m
1	3	48	+23.3	56.4	15.4	178	77	58	21.9	21	32	21	04	5	19	13	57	14	25
2	4	44	+24.6	57.2	15.6	191	83	47	22.9	22	29	22	00	6	14	14	58	15	27
3	5	43	+24.6	58.1	15.8	203	89	37	23.9	23	39	23	13	7	12	15	48	16	14
4	6	43	+23.1	59.0	16.1	215	94	26	24.9	—		—		8	10	16	27	16	49
5	7	43	+20.1	59.9	16.3	227	99	17	25.9	1	00	0	40	9	08	16	58	17	14
6	8	42	+15.7	60.6	16.5	239	101	9	26.9	2	27	2	13	10	05	17	22	17	32
7	9	40	+10.3	61.2	16.7	252	100	3	27.9	3	57	3	49	11	00	17	43	17	48
8	10	36	+4.2	61.4	16.7	264	77	0	28.9	5	27	5	25	11	54	18	02	18	02
9	11	31	−2.2	61.3	16.7	276	324	1	0.6	6	56	7	00	12	47	18	22	18	16
10	12	27	−8.4	60.8	16.6	288	305	4	1.6	8	25	8	34	13	41	18	43	18	31
11	13	23	−14.0	60.1	16.4	301	299	10	2.6	9	52	10	07	14	35	19	07	18	50
12	14	20	−18.6	59.3	16.1	313	293	18	3.6	11	16	11	37	15	31	19	38	19	16
13	15	17	−22.0	58.3	15.9	325	287	27	4.6	12	32	12	59	16	27	20	17	19	50
14	16	15	−24.0	57.4	15.6	337	281	37	5.6	13	39	14	08	17	22	21	05	20	36
15	17	12	−24.7	56.5	15.4	350	275	48	6.6	14	32	15	00	18	16	22	03	21	35
16	18	08	−24.1	55.7	15.2	2	269	58	7.6	15	13	15	38	19	08	23	09	22	44
17	19	01	−22.2	55.1	15.0	14	264	67	8.6	15	44	16	05	19	57	—		23	57
18	19	52	−19.4	54.6	14.9	26	260	76	9.6	16	08	16	24	20	43	0	17	—	
19	20	40	−15.8	54.3	14.8	38	257	84	10.6	16	27	16	38	21	26	1	27	1	12
20	21	25	−11.7	54.1	14.7	50	256	90	11.6	16	43	16	50	22	07	2	35	2	25
21	22	10	−7.1	54.0	14.7	63	257	95	12.6	16	58	17	01	22	48	3	44	3	38
22	22	53	−2.2	54.0	14.7	75	264	98	13.6	17	12	17	11	23	28	4	51	4	50
23	23	36	+2.7	54.1	14.7	87	295	100	14.6	17	26	17	21	—		5	59	6	02
24	0	20	+7.6	54.3	14.8	99	30	99	15.6	17	42	17	33	0	09	7	07	7	15
25	1	05	+12.2	54.6	14.9	111	53	97	16.6	18	01	17	47	0	52	8	17	8	30
26	1	52	+16.4	54.9	15.0	124	61	94	17.6	18	23	18	05	1	37	9	28	9	46
27	2	42	+19.9	55.4	15.1	136	68	88	18.6	18	53	18	30	2	24	10	39	11	01
28	3	35	+22.6	55.9	15.2	148	74	81	19.6	19	31	19	05	3	15	11	47	12	14
29	4	30	+24.2	56.5	15.4	160	80	72	20.6	20	22	19	54	4	08	12	49	13	17
30	5	27	+24.5	57.2	15.6	172	86	62	21.6	21	26	20	59	5	04	13	41	14	08

MERCURY

Day	R.A. h	R.A. m	Dec. °	Diam. ″	Phase %	Transit h	Transit m	5° high 52° h	5° high 52° m	5° high 56° h	5° high 56° m
1	10	52	+2.6	11	2	12	08	17	49	17	48
3	10	45	+3.6	11	1	11	54	6	09	6	09
5	10	39	+4.7	10	1	11	40	5	49	5	49
7	10	34	+5.8	10	3	11	27	5	30	5	29
9	10	29	+6.9	10	7	11	15	5	13	5	11
11	10	27	+7.8	9	12	11	06	4	59	4	56
13	10	27	+8.5	9	19	10	58	4	48	4	44
15	10	29	+9.0	8	27	10	53	4	40	4	36
17	10	34	+9.1	8	36	10	50	4	36	4	32
19	10	40	+9.0	7	45	10	49	4	35	4	31
21	10	48	+8.7	7	54	10	50	4	38	4	34
23	10	58	+8.0	6	63	10	52	4	43	4	40
25	11	09	+7.2	6	71	10	55	4	51	4	48
27	11	21	+6.1	6	78	10	59	5	00	4	59
29	11	33	+4.9	6	83	11	04	5	11	5	11
31	11	46	+3.6	5	88	11	09	5	23	5	24

VENUS

Day	R.A. h	R.A. m	Dec. °	Diam. ″	Phase %	Transit h	Transit m	5° high 52° h	5° high 52° m	5° high 56° h	5° high 56° m
1	13	23	−12.1	28	42	14	43	19	02	18	46
6	13	38	−14.1	30	39	14	38	18	44	18	26
11	13	52	−16.1	32	35	14	32	18	25	18	05
16	14	05	−17.8	35	32	14	24	18	06	17	43
21	14	16	−19.4	38	28	14	15	17	46	17	19
26	14	24	−20.7	41	24	14	04	17	25	16	55
31	14	31	−21.8	45	19	13	50	17	03	16	31

MARS

Day	R.A. h	R.A. m	Dec. °	Diam. ″	Phase %	Transit h	Transit m	5° high 52° h	5° high 52° m	5° high 56° h	5° high 56° m
1	13	17	−8.1	4	95	14	36	19	19	19	08
6	13	29	−9.3	4	95	14	28	19	04	18	52
11	13	42	−10.6	4	96	14	21	18	50	18	36
16	13	54	−11.8	4	96	14	14	18	35	18	20
21	14	07	−13.0	4	96	14	07	18	21	18	05
26	14	20	−14.2	4	96	14	01	18	07	17	49
31	14	33	−15.3	4	97	14	54	17	54	17	34

SUNRISE AND SUNSET

	London				*Bristol*				*Birmingham*				*Manchester*				*Newcastle*				*Glasgow*				*Belfast*			
	0° 05′		*51° 30′*		*2° 35′*		*51° 28′*		*1° 55′*		*52° 28′*		*2° 15′*		*53° 28′*		*1° 37′*		*54° 59′*		*4° 14′*		*55° 52′*		*5° 56′*		*54° 35′*	
d	*h*	*m*	*h*	*m*	*h*	*m*	*h*	*m*	*h*	*m*	*h*	*m*	*h*	*m*	*h*	*m*	*h*	*m*	*h*	*m*	*h*	*m*	*h*	*m*	*h*	*m*	*h*	*m*
1	5	13	18	47	5	23	18	57	5	18	18	56	5	18	18	59	5	12	18	59	5	21	19	12	5	30	19	16
2	5	14	18	45	5	24	18	55	5	20	18	54	5	20	18	57	5	14	18	57	5	23	19	09	5	32	19	13
3	5	16	18	43	5	26	18	53	5	22	18	51	5	21	18	54	5	16	18	54	5	25	19	06	5	34	19	11
4	5	17	18	40	5	27	18	50	5	23	18	49	5	23	18	52	5	18	18	52	5	27	19	04	5	36	19	08
5	5	19	18	38	5	29	18	48	5	25	18	47	5	25	18	50	5	20	18	49	5	29	19	01	5	38	19	06
6	5	21	18	36	5	31	18	46	5	27	18	44	5	27	18	47	5	22	18	47	5	31	18	59	5	40	19	03
7	5	22	18	34	5	32	18	44	5	28	18	42	5	28	18	45	5	24	18	44	5	33	18	56	5	41	19	01
8	5	24	18	31	5	34	18	41	5	30	18	40	5	30	18	42	5	25	18	42	5	35	18	53	5	43	18	58
9	5	25	18	29	5	35	18	39	5	32	18	37	5	32	18	40	5	27	18	39	5	37	18	51	5	45	18	56
10	5	27	18	27	5	37	18	37	5	33	18	35	5	33	18	37	5	29	18	37	5	39	18	48	5	47	18	53
11	5	29	18	24	5	39	18	34	5	35	18	33	5	35	18	35	5	31	18	34	5	40	18	45	5	49	18	51
12	5	30	18	22	5	40	18	32	5	37	18	30	5	37	18	33	5	33	18	31	5	42	18	43	5	51	18	48
13	5	32	18	20	5	42	18	30	5	38	18	28	5	39	18	30	5	35	18	29	5	44	18	40	5	52	18	46
14	5	33	18	18	5	43	18	28	5	40	18	26	5	40	18	28	5	37	18	26	5	46	18	38	5	54	18	43
15	5	35	18	15	5	45	18	25	5	42	18	23	5	42	18	25	5	38	18	24	5	48	18	35	5	56	18	41
16	5	36	18	13	5	47	18	23	5	43	18	21	5	44	18	23	5	40	18	21	5	50	18	32	5	58	18	38
17	5	38	18	11	5	48	18	21	5	45	18	18	5	46	18	20	5	42	18	19	5	52	18	30	6	00	18	36
18	5	40	18	08	5	50	18	18	5	47	18	16	5	47	18	18	5	44	18	16	5	54	18	27	6	02	18	33
19	5	41	18	06	5	51	18	16	5	48	18	14	5	49	18	15	5	46	18	13	5	56	18	24	6	03	18	31
20	5	43	18	04	5	53	18	14	5	50	18	11	5	51	18	13	5	48	18	11	5	58	18	22	6	05	18	28
21	5	44	18	01	5	54	18	11	5	52	18	09	5	53	18	10	5	50	18	08	6	00	18	19	6	07	18	25
22	5	46	17	59	5	56	18	09	5	53	18	07	5	54	18	08	5	52	18	06	6	02	18	16	6	09	18	23
23	5	48	17	57	5	58	18	07	5	55	18	04	5	56	18	06	5	53	18	03	6	04	18	14	6	11	18	20
24	5	49	17	54	5	59	18	04	5	57	18	02	5	58	18	03	5	55	18	01	6	06	18	11	6	13	18	18
25	5	51	17	52	6	01	18	02	5	58	17	59	6	00	18	01	5	57	17	58	6	08	18	08	6	14	18	15
26	5	52	17	50	6	02	18	00	6	00	17	57	6	01	17	58	5	59	17	56	6	10	18	06	6	16	18	13
27	5	54	17	48	6	04	17	58	6	02	17	55	6	03	17	56	6	01	17	53	6	12	18	03	6	18	18	10
28	5	56	17	45	6	06	17	55	6	03	17	52	6	05	17	53	6	03	17	50	6	14	18	01	6	20	18	08
29	5	57	17	43	6	07	17	53	6	05	17	50	6	07	17	51	6	05	17	48	6	15	17	58	6	22	18	05
30	5	59	17	41	6	09	17	51	6	07	17	48	6	08	17	49	6	07	17	45	6	17	17	55	6	24	18	03

JUPITER

Day	*R.A.*		*Dec.*		*Transit*		*5° high*			
							52°		*56°*	
	h	*m*	°	′	*h*	*m*	*h*	*m*	*h*	*m*
1	0	06.1	–1	02	1	26	6	47	6	42
11	0	01.7	–1	33	0	42	6	00	5	56
21	23	56.9	–2	05	23	53	5	13	5	08
31	23	52.0	–2	36	23	09	4	27	4	21

Diameters – equatorial 50″ polar 47″

SATURN

Day	*R.A.*		*Dec.*		*Transit*		*5° high*			
							52°		*56°*	
	h	*m*	°	′	*h*	*m*	*h*	*m*	*h*	*m*
1	12	18.6	+0	21	13	36	19	05	19	02
11	12	22.9	–0	07	13	01	18	27	18	24
21	12	27.3	–0	36	12	26	17	50	17	46
31	12	31.9	–1	05	11	52	17	13	17	08

Diameters – equatorial 16″ polar 14″
Rings – major axis 36″ minor axis 3″

URANUS

Day	*R.A.*		*Dec.*		*Transit*		*10° high*			
							52°		*56°*	
	h	*m*	°	′	*h*	*m*	*h*	*m*	*h*	*m*
1	23	59.1	–0	57	1	19	6	07	6	00
11	23	57.7	–1	06	0	38	5	26	5	18
21	23	56.2	–1	16	23	53	4	44	4	36
31	23	54.8	–1	25	23	12	4	02	3	54

Diameter 4″

NEPTUNE

Day	*R.A.*		*Dec.*		*Transit*		*10° high*			
							52°		*56°*	
	h	*m*	°	′	*h*	*m*	*h*	*m*	*h*	*m*
1	21	57.5	–12	59	23	13	2	54	2	32
11	21	56.5	–13	04	22	33	2	13	1	50
21	21	55.6	–13	09	21	53	1	32	1	10
31	21	54.8	–13	13	21	13	0	51	0	29

Diameter 2″

OCTOBER 2010

TENTH MONTH, 31 DAYS. *Octo* (eighth), eighth month of Roman pre-Julian calendar

1	*Friday*	General Franco became Spain's head of state 1936	day 274
2	*Saturday*	Ferdinand Foch, Allied army commander *b.* 1851; Charles Lee, British-born US army general *d.* 1782	275
3	*Sunday*	The Polish Home Army surrendered to the Germans, ending the Warsaw Uprising 1944	276
4	*Monday*	Two US helicopters were shot down in Somalia, killing 19 soldiers 1993	week 40 day 277
5	*Tuesday*	US troops defeated a British and Native American coalition at the Battle of the Thames 1813	278
6	*Wednesday*	Syria and Egypt began the October War with Israel 1973	279
7	*Thursday*	The USA launched air strikes against al-Qaida and Taliban positions in Afghanistan 2001	280
8	*Friday*	The first Balkan War began between the Balkan League and the Ottoman Empire 1912	281
9	*Saturday*	Ernesto 'Che' Guevara was executed by the Bolivian army 1967	282
10	*Sunday*	Paul Kruger, South African president *b.* 1825; Granville Elliott, British military officer *d.* 1759	283
11	*Monday*	The second Boer War began 1899	week 41 day 284
12	*Tuesday*	British nurse Edith Cavell was executed for helping Allied soldiers escape from Belgium 1915	285
13	*Wednesday*	Italy declared war on Germany 1943	286
14	*Thursday*	William the Conqueror defeated King Harold II at the Battle of Hastings 1066	287
15	*Friday*	Pierre Laval, former French prime minister, was shot for collaborating with the Germans 1945	288
16	*Saturday*	Ten Nazi war criminals were executed following sentencing at the Nuremberg trials 1946	289
17	*Sunday*	British troops surrendered to American colonists at the Battle of Saratoga in New York 1777	290
18	*Monday*	The second Opium War ended as China surrendered to the occupying Franco–British forces in Peking (Beijing) 1860	week 42 day 291
19	*Tuesday*	Napoleon Bonaparte was defeated by the Allies at a major battle in Leipzig 1813	292
20	*Wednesday*	Allied squadrons destroyed the Turkish fleet at the Battle of Navarino 1805	293
21	*Thursday*	The British fleet was victorious at the Battle of Trafalgar 1805	294
22	*Friday*	President Kennedy announced a naval blockade in the Cuban Missile Crisis 1962	295
23	*Saturday*	Edgehill, the first major battle of the English Civil War, ended indecisively 1642	296
24	*Sunday*	The Treaty of Westphalia marked the end of the Thirty Years War 1648	297
25	*Monday*	The Light Brigade charged Russian guns at Balaclava during the Crimean War 1854	week 43 day 298
26	*Tuesday*	The Battle of Leyte Gulf in the Philippines ended with US victory over the Japanese 1944	299
27	*Wednesday*	Theodore Roosevelt, US president *b.* 1858; Athelstan, king of England *d.* 939	300
28	*Thursday*	Italy invaded Greece 1940	301
29	*Friday*	Joseph Goebbels, Nazi propaganda minister *b.* 1897; Walter Raleigh, naval explorer *d.* 1618	302
30	*Saturday*	The Ottoman Empire signed the Armistice of Mudros with the Allies 1918	303
31	*Sunday*	British forces in New Zealand began the invasion of the Waikato 1863	304

ASTRONOMICAL PHENOMENA

d	*h*	
1	01	Saturn in conjunction
3	22	Mars in conjunction with Venus. Mars 7°N.
7	06	Mercury in conjunction with Moon. Mercury 7°N.
7	09	Saturn in conjunction with Moon. Saturn 7°N.
8	07	Venus at stationary point
8	12	Saturn in conjunction with Mercury. Saturn 0°.5N.
9	18	Venus in conjunction with Moon. Venus 3°S.
10	00	Mars in conjunction with Moon. Mars 3°N.
17	01	Mercury in superior conjunction
20	05	Jupiter in conjunction with Moon. Jupiter 7°S.
23	13	Sun's longitude 210° ♏
25	13	Venus in conjunction with Mercury. Venus 6°S.
29	01	Venus in inferior conjunction

MINIMA OF ALGOL

d	*h*	*d*	*h*	*d*	*h*
1	05.5	12	16.7	24	04.0
4	02.3	15	13.5	27	00.8
6	23.1	18	10.4	29	21.6
9	19.9	21	07.2		

CONSTELLATIONS

The following constellations are near their meridian at

	d	*h*		*d*	*h*
September	1	24	October	16	21
September	15	23	November	1	20
October	1	22	November	15	19

Ursa Major (below the Pole), Cepheus, Cassiopeia, Cygnus, Lacerta, Andromeda, Pegasus, Capricornus, Aquarius and Piscis Austrinus

THE MOON

Phases, Apsides and Node	*d*	*h*	*m*
☾ Last Quarter	1	03	52
● New Moon	7	18	44
☽ First Quarter	14	21	27
○ Full Moon	23	01	36
☾ Last Quarter	30	12	46
Perigee (359,444 km)	6	13	32
Apogee (405,461 km)	18	18	10

Mean longitude of ascending node on October 1, 277°

THE SUN

s.d. 16′.1

Day	*Right Ascension* *h*	*m*	*s*	*Dec.* – °	′	*Equation of time* *m*	*s*	*Rise* *52°* *h*	*m*	*56°* *h*	*m*	*Transit* *h*	*m*	*Set* *52°* *h*	*m*	*56°* *h*	*m*	*Sidereal time* *h*	*m*	*s*	*Transit of first point of Aries* *h*	*m*	*s*
1	12	28	21	3	04	+10	09	6	01	6	03	11	50	17	38	17	36	0	38	30	23	17	41
2	12	31	58	3	27	+10	28	6	02	6	05	11	49	17	36	17	33	0	42	26	23	13	45
3	12	35	35	3	50	+10	47	6	04	6	07	11	49	17	33	17	30	0	46	23	23	09	49
4	12	39	13	4	13	+11	06	6	06	6	09	11	49	17	31	17	28	0	50	19	23	05	53
5	12	42	51	4	36	+11	24	6	07	6	11	11	48	17	29	17	25	0	54	16	23	01	57
6	12	46	30	5	00	+11	42	6	09	6	13	11	48	17	26	17	23	0	58	12	22	58	01
7	12	50	09	5	23	+12	00	6	11	6	15	11	48	17	24	17	20	1	02	09	22	54	05
8	12	53	48	5	46	+12	17	6	12	6	17	11	48	17	22	17	17	1	06	06	22	50	09
9	12	57	28	6	08	+12	34	6	14	6	19	11	47	17	20	17	15	1	10	02	22	46	13
10	13	01	08	6	31	+12	50	6	16	6	21	11	47	17	17	17	12	1	13	59	22	42	18
11	13	04	49	6	54	+13	06	6	17	6	23	11	47	17	15	17	10	1	17	55	22	38	22
12	13	08	30	7	17	+13	21	6	19	6	25	11	47	17	13	17	07	1	21	52	22	34	26
13	13	12	12	7	39	+13	36	6	21	6	27	11	46	17	11	17	05	1	25	48	22	30	30
14	13	15	54	8	01	+13	51	6	23	6	29	11	46	17	09	17	02	1	29	45	22	26	34
15	13	19	37	8	24	+14	05	6	24	6	31	11	46	17	06	17	00	1	33	41	22	22	38
16	13	23	20	8	46	+14	18	6	26	6	33	11	46	17	04	16	57	1	37	38	22	18	42
17	13	27	04	9	08	+14	31	6	28	6	35	11	45	17	02	16	55	1	41	35	22	14	46
18	13	30	48	9	30	+14	43	6	30	6	37	11	45	17	00	16	52	1	45	31	22	10	50
19	13	34	33	9	52	+14	55	6	31	6	39	11	45	16	58	16	50	1	49	28	22	06	54
20	13	38	19	10	13	+15	06	6	33	6	41	11	45	16	56	16	47	1	53	24	22	02	58
21	13	42	05	10	35	+15	16	6	35	6	43	11	45	16	54	16	45	1	57	21	21	59	03
22	13	45	52	10	56	+15	26	6	37	6	45	11	44	16	52	16	43	2	01	17	21	55	07
23	13	49	39	11	17	+15	35	6	38	6	48	11	44	16	49	16	40	2	05	14	21	51	11
24	13	53	27	11	38	+15	43	6	40	6	50	11	44	16	47	16	38	2	09	10	21	47	15
25	13	57	16	11	59	+15	51	6	42	6	52	11	44	16	45	16	36	2	13	07	21	43	19
26	14	01	06	12	20	+15	58	6	44	6	54	11	44	16	43	16	33	2	17	04	21	39	23
27	14	04	56	12	40	+16	04	6	46	6	56	11	44	16	41	16	31	2	21	00	21	35	27
28	14	08	47	13	00	+16	10	6	47	6	58	11	44	16	39	16	29	2	24	57	21	31	31
29	14	12	39	13	20	+16	14	6	49	7	00	11	44	16	38	16	26	2	28	53	21	27	35
30	14	16	31	13	40	+16	18	6	51	7	02	11	44	16	36	16	24	2	32	50	21	23	39
31	14	20	25	14	00	+16	21	6	53	7	04	11	44	16	34	16	22	2	36	46	21	19	44

DURATION OF TWILIGHT (in minutes)

Latitude	*52°*	*56°*	*52°*	*56°*	*52°*	*56°*	*52°*	*56°*
	1 October		*11 October*		*21 October*		*31 October*	
Civil	34	37	34	37	34	38	35	39
Nautical	73	80	73	80	74	81	75	83
Astronomical	113	125	112	124	113	124	114	126

THE NIGHT SKY

Mercury may only be visible for the first couple of days in the month, low above the eastern horizon for a short while at the beginning of morning civil twilight. Its magnitude is about −1.1. Mercury passes through superior conjunction on the 17th and thus remains too close to the Sun for the rest of the month.

Venus is unsuitably placed for observation throughout October. Although it is well over 30 degrees from the Sun at the beginning of the month, its declination of −22 degrees completely nullifies this apparently favourable elongation as seen from the latitudes of the British Isles. Venus passes rapidly through inferior conjunction on the 29th, becoming a morning object early next month.

Mars remains unsuitably placed for observation.

Jupiter, magnitude −2.9, is a brilliant object in the southern skies for the greater part of the night. By the end of the month it is lost to view over the western horizon before 02h. The waxing gibbous Moon passes 6 degrees north of the planet on the 20th.

Saturn remains too close to the Sun for observation for the first three weeks of the month but thereafter slowly becomes visible as a morning object low above the eastern horizon for a short while, before being lost in the brightening sky prior to sunrise. Saturn, magnitude +0.9, is in the constellation of Virgo.

THE MOON

Day	R.A.		Dec.	Hor. Par.	Semi-diam.	Sun's Co-Long.	P.A. of Br. Limb	Ph.	Age	Rise				Transit		Set			
										52°		56°				52°		56°	
	h	m	°	′	′	°	°	%	d	h	m	h	m	h	m	h	m	h	m
1	6	25	+23.4	57.9	15.8	184	92	52	22.6	22	40	22	18	6	00	14	23	14	47
2	7	23	+21.0	58.7	16.0	197	98	41	23.6	—		23	45	6	56	14	56	15	14
3	8	20	+17.2	59.4	16.2	209	102	30	24.6	0	02	—		7	51	15	22	15	35
4	9	17	+12.4	60.1	16.4	221	105	20	25.6	1	27	1	16	8	45	15	44	15	52
5	10	12	+6.7	60.7	16.5	233	106	11	26.6	2	54	2	49	9	38	16	04	16	06
6	11	07	+0.6	61.0	16.6	245	103	5	27.6	4	21	4	22	10	31	16	23	16	20
7	12	02	–5.6	61.0	16.6	258	89	1	28.6	5	50	5	56	11	24	16	44	16	35
8	12	58	–11.5	60.7	16.5	270	351	0	0.2	7	18	7	31	12	19	17	07	16	53
9	13	55	–16.6	60.1	16.4	282	305	2	1.2	8	45	9	04	13	15	17	35	17	16
10	14	54	–20.6	59.4	16.2	294	293	7	2.2	10	08	10	32	14	12	18	11	17	46
11	15	53	–23.2	58.5	15.9	307	285	14	3.2	11	21	11	49	15	10	18	57	18	29
12	16	52	–24.4	57.5	15.7	319	278	22	4.2	12	22	12	50	16	07	19	53	19	25
13	17	50	–24.1	56.6	15.4	331	271	32	5.2	13	09	13	35	17	01	20	57	20	32
14	18	45	–22.6	55.8	15.2	343	265	41	6.2	13	44	14	06	17	51	22	06	21	45
15	19	37	–20.1	55.2	15.0	355	261	51	7.2	14	10	14	28	18	39	23	16	22	59
16	20	26	–16.7	54.7	14.9	8	257	61	8.2	14	31	14	44	19	23	—		—	
17	21	13	–12.7	54.3	14.8	20	254	70	9.2	14	49	14	57	20	05	0	25	0	13
18	21	57	–8.2	54.1	14.7	32	253	78	10.2	15	04	15	09	20	46	1	33	1	26
19	22	41	–3.4	54.1	14.7	44	252	85	11.2	15	19	15	19	21	26	2	40	2	38
20	23	24	+1.5	54.2	14.8	56	254	91	12.2	15	33	15	29	22	07	3	48	3	50
21	0	08	+6.3	54.4	14.8	68	258	96	13.2	15	49	15	41	22	50	4	56	5	02
22	0	53	+11.0	54.7	14.9	81	269	99	14.2	16	07	15	54	23	34	6	06	6	17
23	1	40	+15.3	55.0	15.0	93	329	100	15.2	16	29	16	12	—		7	17	7	33
24	2	30	+19.0	55.5	15.1	105	51	99	16.2	16	56	16	35	0	21	8	28	8	49
25	3	22	+21.9	55.9	15.2	117	67	96	17.2	17	33	17	07	1	11	9	38	10	03
26	4	17	+23.7	56.4	15.4	129	77	91	18.2	18	20	17	52	2	04	10	43	11	10
27	5	14	+24.3	56.9	15.5	141	84	85	19.2	19	19	18	53	2	59	11	38	12	05
28	6	11	+23.6	57.4	15.6	153	91	76	20.2	20	30	20	06	3	55	12	22	12	46
29	7	09	+21.5	58.0	15.8	166	97	67	21.2	21	48	21	29	4	51	12	57	13	17
30	8	05	+18.1	58.5	15.9	178	102	56	22.2	23	09	22	56	5	45	13	25	13	39
31	9	00	+13.7	59.0	16.1	190	106	45	23.2	—		—		6	37	13	47	13	56

MERCURY

Day	R.A.		Dec.	Diam.	Phase	Transit		5° high			
								52°		56°	
	h	m	°	″	%	h	m	h	m	h	m
1	11	46	+3.6	5	88	11	09	5	23	5	24
3	11	59	+2.2	5	92	11	14	5	35	5	37
5	12	12	+0.7	5	94	11	19	5	48	5	51
7	12	25	–0.8	5	97	11	24	6	01	6	05
9	12	38	–2.3	5	98	11	29	6	14	6	20
11	12	51	–3.8	5	99	11	34	6	27	6	34
13	13	03	–5.4	5	100	11	39	6	40	6	48
15	13	16	–6.8	5	100	11	43	6	53	7	02
17	13	28	–8.3	5	100	11	48	7	06	7	17
19	13	41	–9.7	5	100	11	52	7	18	7	31
21	13	53	–11.1	5	100	11	57	7	31	7	45
23	14	05	–12.5	5	99	12	01	16	18	16	02
25	14	18	–13.8	5	99	12	06	16	14	15	57
27	14	30	–15.0	5	99	12	10	16	10	15	51
29	14	42	–16.2	5	98	12	14	16	07	15	46
31	14	54	–17.3	5	97	12	19	16	04	15	41

VENUS

Day	R.A.		Dec.	Diam.	Phase	Transit		5° high			
								52°		56°	
	h	m	°	″	%	h	m	h	m	h	m
1	14	31	–21.8	45	19	13	50	17	03	16	31
6	14	34	–22.4	48	15	13	33	16	40	16	07
11	14	33	–22.7	52	11	13	13	16	18	15	44
16	14	29	–22.4	56	6	12	48	15	57	15	24
21	14	21	–21.5	59	3	12	21	15	37	15	07
26	14	11	–20.1	61	1	11	51	15	19	14	52
31	14	00	–18.2	61	1	11	21	15	03	14	39

MARS

Day	R.A.		Dec.	Diam.	Phase	Transit		5° high			
								52°		56°	
	h	m	°	″	%	h	m	h	m	h	m
1	14	33	–15.3	4	97	13	54	17	54	17	34
6	14	47	–16.4	4	97	13	48	17	40	17	19
11	15	01	–17.5	4	97	13	42	17	27	17	05
16	15	15	–18.5	4	97	13	37	17	15	16	50
21	15	29	–19.4	4	98	13	31	17	02	16	36
26	15	44	–20.3	4	98	13	26	16	51	16	23
31	15	59	–21.1	4	98	13	22	16	40	16	10

SUNRISE AND SUNSET

	London				*Bristol*				*Birmingham*				*Manchester*				*Newcastle*				*Glasgow*				*Belfast*			
	0° 05′		*51° 30′*		*2° 35′*		*51° 28′*		*1° 55′*		*52° 28′*		*2° 15′*		*53° 28′*		*1° 37′*		*54° 59′*		*4° 14′*		*55° 52′*		*5° 56′*		*54° 35′*	
d	*h*	*m*	*h*	*m*	*h*	*m*	*h*	*m*	*h*	*m*	*h*	*m*	*h*	*m*	*h*	*m*	*h*	*m*	*h*	*m*	*h*	*m*	*h*	*m*	*h*	*m*	*h*	*m*
1	6	01	17	38	6	11	17	48	6	08	17	45	6	10	17	46	6	08	17	43	6	19	17	53	6	26	18	00
2	6	02	17	36	6	12	17	46	6	10	17	43	6	12	17	44	6	10	17	40	6	21	17	50	6	27	17	58
3	6	04	17	34	6	14	17	44	6	12	17	41	6	14	17	41	6	12	17	38	6	23	17	47	6	29	17	55
4	6	06	17	32	6	16	17	42	6	14	17	38	6	16	17	39	6	14	17	35	6	25	17	45	6	31	17	53
5	6	07	17	29	6	17	17	39	6	15	17	36	6	17	17	36	6	16	17	33	6	27	17	42	6	33	17	50
6	6	09	17	27	6	19	17	37	6	17	17	34	6	19	17	34	6	18	17	30	6	29	17	40	6	35	17	48
7	6	11	17	25	6	21	17	35	6	19	17	31	6	21	17	32	6	20	17	28	6	31	17	37	6	37	17	45
8	6	12	17	23	6	22	17	33	6	20	17	29	6	23	17	29	6	22	17	25	6	33	17	35	6	39	17	43
9	6	14	17	21	6	24	17	31	6	22	17	27	6	25	17	27	6	24	17	23	6	35	17	32	6	41	17	40
10	6	16	17	18	6	26	17	28	6	24	17	25	6	26	17	25	6	26	17	20	6	37	17	29	6	43	17	38
11	6	17	17	16	6	27	17	26	6	26	17	22	6	28	17	22	6	28	17	18	6	39	17	27	6	44	17	36
12	6	19	17	14	6	29	17	24	6	27	17	20	6	30	17	20	6	30	17	15	6	41	17	24	6	46	17	33
13	6	21	17	12	6	31	17	22	6	29	17	18	6	32	17	18	6	32	17	13	6	44	17	22	6	48	17	31
14	6	22	17	10	6	32	17	20	6	31	17	16	6	34	17	15	6	34	17	10	6	46	17	19	6	50	17	28
15	6	24	17	07	6	34	17	17	6	33	17	13	6	36	17	13	6	36	17	08	6	48	17	17	6	52	17	26
16	6	26	17	05	6	36	17	15	6	35	17	11	6	37	17	11	6	38	17	06	6	50	17	14	6	54	17	24
17	6	27	17	03	6	37	17	13	6	36	17	09	6	39	17	09	6	40	17	03	6	52	17	12	6	56	17	21
18	6	29	17	01	6	39	17	11	6	38	17	07	6	41	17	06	6	42	17	01	6	54	17	10	6	58	17	19
19	6	31	16	59	6	41	17	09	6	40	17	05	6	43	17	04	6	44	16	59	6	56	17	07	7	00	17	17
20	6	33	16	57	6	43	17	07	6	42	17	02	6	45	17	02	6	46	16	56	6	58	17	05	7	02	17	14
21	6	34	16	55	6	44	17	05	6	43	17	00	6	47	17	00	6	48	16	54	7	00	17	02	7	04	17	12
22	6	36	16	53	6	46	17	03	6	45	16	58	6	49	16	57	6	49	16	52	7	02	17	00	7	06	17	10
23	6	38	16	51	6	48	17	01	6	47	16	56	6	51	16	55	6	52	16	49	7	04	16	58	7	08	17	07
24	6	39	16	49	6	49	16	59	6	49	16	54	6	52	16	53	6	54	16	47	7	06	16	55	7	10	17	05
25	6	41	16	47	6	51	16	57	6	51	16	52	6	54	16	51	6	56	16	45	7	08	16	53	7	12	17	03
26	6	43	16	45	6	53	16	55	6	53	16	50	6	56	16	49	6	58	16	42	7	10	16	51	7	14	17	01
27	6	45	16	43	6	55	16	53	6	54	16	48	6	58	16	47	7	00	16	40	7	13	16	48	7	16	16	59
28	6	46	16	41	6	56	16	51	6	56	16	46	7	00	16	45	7	02	16	38	7	15	16	46	7	18	16	56
29	6	48	16	39	6	58	16	49	6	58	16	44	7	02	16	43	7	04	16	36	7	17	16	44	7	20	16	54
30	6	50	16	37	7	00	16	47	7	00	16	42	7	04	16	41	7	06	16	34	7	19	16	41	7	22	16	52
31	6	52	16	35	7	02	16	45	7	02	16	40	7	06	16	39	7	08	16	32	7	21	16	39	7	24	16	50

JUPITER

Day	*R.A.*		*Dec.*		*Transit*		*5° high*			
							52°		*56°*	
	h	*m*	°	′	*h*	*m*	*h*	*m*	*h*	*m*
1	23	52.0	−2	36	23	09	4	27	4	21
11	23	47.5	−3	05	22	26	3	40	3	34
21	23	43.6	−3	28	21	42	2	55	2	49
31	23	40.7	−3	45	21	00	2	11	2	05

Diameters – equatorial 49″ polar 45″

SATURN

Day	*R.A.*		*Dec.*		*Transit*		*5° high*			
							52°		*56°*	
	h	*m*	°	′	*h*	*m*	*h*	*m*	*h*	*m*
1	12	31.9	−1	05	11	52	6	31	6	35
11	12	36.4	−1	34	11	17	5	58	6	03
21	12	40.9	−2	02	10	42	5	26	5	31
31	12	45.2	−2	28	10	07	4	53	4	59

Diameters – equatorial 16″ polar 14″
Rings – major axis 36″ minor axis 5″

URANUS

Day	*R.A.*		*Dec.*		*Transit*		*10° high*			
							52°		*56°*	
	h	*m*	°	′	*h*	*m*	*h*	*m*	*h*	*m*
1	23	54.8	−1	25	23	12	4	02	3	54
11	23	53.4	−1	34	22	32	3	21	3	13
21	23	52.1	−1	43	21	51	2	40	2	31
31	23	50.9	−1	50	21	11	1	58	1	50

Diameter 4″

NEPTUNE

Day	*R.A.*		*Dec.*		*Transit*		*10° high*			
							52°		*56°*	
	h	*m*	°	′	*h*	*m*	*h*	*m*	*h*	*m*
1	21	54.8	−13	13	21	13	0	51	0	29
11	21	54.1	−13	16	20	33	0	11	23	44
21	21	53.7	−13	19	19	53	23	27	23	04
31	21	53.4	−13	20	19	14	22	47	22	25

Diameter 2″

NOVEMBER 2010

ELEVENTH MONTH, 30 DAYS. *Novem* (nine), ninth month of Roman pre-Julian calendar

1	*Monday*	The USA tested the first hydrogen bomb at Enewetak Atoll in the Pacific Ocean 1952	week 44 day 305
2	*Tuesday*	President Ngo Dinh Diem of Vietnam was executed following a military coup 1963	306
3	*Wednesday*	John Montagu, British statesman *b.* 1718; Thomas Montacute, British army commander *d.* 1428	307
4	*Thursday*	The Soviet military crushed the Hungarian uprising 1956	308
5	*Friday*	The Battle of Inkerman ended in British and French victory over Russian forces 1854	309
6	*Saturday*	Allied forces declared a ceasefire in the Suez Canal Crisis 1956	310
7	*Sunday*	The Bolsheviks seized power from the Tsarist regime in Russia 1917	311
8	*Monday*	The Battle of White Mountain ended the Bohemian period of the Thirty Years War 1620	week 45 day 312
9	*Tuesday*	*Kristallnacht* ('Night of Broken Glass'): the Nazis led a co-ordinated attack on Jewish people and their property 1938	313
10	*Wednesday*	President George W. Bush's address to the UN called for support in the 'war on terror' 2001	314
11	*Thursday*	The signing of the Armistice at 11am marked the end of the First World War 1918	315
12	*Friday*	Royal Air Force bombers sank *Tirpitz,* the last of Germany's major battleships 1944	316
13	*Saturday*	The Vietnam Veterans' Memorial was dedicated in Washington DC, USA 1982	317
14	*Sunday*	The Luftwaffe bombed Coventry, destroying much of the city 1940	318
15	*Monday*	Iraq allowed the return of UN weapons inspectors 1998	week 46 day 319
16	*Tuesday*	Protestant leader Gustavus II of Sweden was killed at the Battle of Lützen 1632	320
17	*Wednesday*	The French defeated the Austrians at the Battle of the Bridge of Arcole 1796	321
18	*Thursday*	General Douglas Haig called an end to the offensive at the Battle of the Somme 1916	322
19	*Friday*	Soviet forces began the 'Operation Uranus' counter-offensive at the Battle of Stalingrad 1942	323
20	*Saturday*	Twenty Nazi leaders went on trial in Nuremberg 1945	324
21	*Sunday*	IRA bombs destroyed two Birmingham pubs 1974	325
22	*Monday*	The US air force unveiled the Northrop B-2 stealth bomber 1988	week 47 day 326
23	*Tuesday*	The Battle of Chattanooga began in Tennessee 1863	327
24	*Wednesday*	America launched its first bombing raid over Tokyo 1944	328
25	*Thursday*	Britain withdrew the last of its soldiers from New York following the end of the American War of Independence 1783	329
26	*Friday*	Chile defeated Spain at the naval Battle of Papudo 1865	330
27	*Saturday*	In Delhi, Indian Prime Minister Jawaharlal Nehru spoke in favour of nuclear disarmament 1957	331
28	*Sunday*	Churchill, Roosevelt and Stalin met to discuss the Allied war strategy 1943	332
29	*Monday*	The US cavalry massacred Cheyenne and Arapaho Native Americans at Sand Creek, Colorado 1864	Week 48 day 333
30	*Tuesday*	The Soviet Union invaded Finland 1939	334

ASTRONOMICAL PHENOMENA

d	*h*	
4	01	Saturn in conjunction with Moon. Saturn 7°N.
5	08	Venus in conjunction with Moon. Venus 0°.2N.
7	04	Mercury in conjunction with Moon. Mercury 2°N.
7	06	Neptune at stationary point
7	22	Mars in conjunction with Moon. Mars 2°N.
16	10	Jupiter in conjunction with Moon. Jupiter 7°S.
18	17	Jupiter at stationary point
18	21	Venus at stationary point
20	19	Mars in conjunction with Mercury. Mars 2°N.
22	10	Sun's longitude 240° ♐

MINIMA OF ALGOL

d	*h*	*d*	*h*	*d*	*h*
1	18.4	13	05.7	24	17.0
4	15.2	16	02.5	27	13.8
7	12.1	18	23.3	30	10.6
10	08.9	21	20.1		

CONSTELLATIONS

The following constellations are near their meridian at

	d	*h*		*d*	*h*
October	1	24	November	15	21
October	16	23	December	1	20
November	1	22	December	16	19

Ursa Major (below the Pole), Cepheus, Cassiopeia, Andromeda, Pegasus, Pisces, Aquarius and Cetus

THE MOON

Phases, Apsides and Node	*d*	*h*	*m*
○ New Moon	6	04	52
☽ First Quarter	13	16	39
● Full Moon	21	17	27
☾ Last Quarter	28	20	36
Perigee (364,170 km)	3	17	18
Apogee (404,670 km)	15	11	43
Perigee (369,398 km)	30	18	47

Mean longitude of ascending node on November 1,276°

THE SUN

s.d. 16′.2

Day	Right Ascension (h m s)	Dec. − (° ′)	Equation of time (m s)	Rise 52° (h m)	Rise 56° (h m)	Transit (h m)	Set 52° (h m)	Set 56° (h m)	Sidereal time (h m s)	Transit of first point of Aries (h m s)
1	14 24 19	14 19	+16 24	6 55	7 07	11 44	16 32	16 20	2 40 43	21 15 48
2	14 28 14	14 39	+16 25	6 56	7 09	11 44	16 30	16 18	2 44 39	21 11 52
3	14 32 10	14 57	+16 26	6 58	7 11	11 44	16 28	16 15	2 48 36	21 07 56
4	14 36 07	15 16	+16 26	7 00	7 13	11 44	16 27	16 13	2 52 32	21 04 00
5	14 40 04	15 35	+16 25	7 02	7 15	11 44	16 25	16 11	2 56 29	21 00 04
6	14 44 02	15 53	+16 23	7 04	7 17	11 44	16 23	16 09	3 00 26	20 56 08
7	14 48 02	16 11	+16 20	7 05	7 19	11 44	16 21	16 07	3 04 22	20 52 12
8	14 52 02	16 28	+16 17	7 07	7 21	11 44	16 20	16 05	3 08 19	20 48 16
9	14 56 03	16 46	+16 13	7 09	7 24	11 44	16 18	16 03	3 12 15	20 44 20
10	15 00 04	17 03	+16 08	7 11	7 26	11 44	16 16	16 01	3 16 12	20 40 24
11	15 04 07	17 20	+16 02	7 13	7 28	11 44	16 15	16 00	3 20 08	20 36 28
12	15 08 10	17 36	+15 55	7 14	7 30	11 44	16 13	15 58	3 24 05	20 32 33
13	15 12 14	17 52	+15 47	7 16	7 32	11 44	16 12	15 56	3 28 01	20 28 37
14	15 16 19	18 08	+15 39	7 18	7 34	11 44	16 10	15 54	3 31 58	20 24 41
15	15 20 25	18 24	+15 29	7 20	7 36	11 45	16 09	15 52	3 35 55	20 20 45
16	15 24 32	18 39	+15 19	7 21	7 38	11 45	16 08	15 51	3 39 51	20 16 49
17	15 28 39	18 54	+15 08	7 23	7 40	11 45	16 06	15 49	3 43 48	20 12 53
18	15 32 48	19 09	+14 57	7 25	7 42	11 45	16 05	15 47	3 47 44	20 08 57
19	15 36 57	19 23	+14 44	7 26	7 44	11 45	16 04	15 46	3 51 41	20 05 01
20	15 41 07	19 37	+14 31	7 28	7 46	11 46	16 03	15 44	3 55 37	20 01 05
21	15 45 17	19 50	+14 17	7 30	7 48	11 46	16 01	15 43	3 59 34	19 57 09
22	15 49 29	20 03	+14 02	7 31	7 50	11 46	16 00	15 41	4 03 31	19 53 13
23	15 53 41	20 16	+13 46	7 33	7 52	11 46	15 59	15 40	4 07 27	19 49 18
24	15 57 54	20 29	+13 29	7 35	7 54	11 47	15 58	15 39	4 11 24	19 45 22
25	16 02 08	20 41	+13 12	7 36	7 56	11 47	15 57	15 37	4 15 20	19 41 26
26	16 06 23	20 52	+12 54	7 38	7 58	11 47	15 56	15 36	4 19 17	19 37 30
27	16 10 39	21 04	+12 35	7 39	8 00	11 48	15 55	15 35	4 23 13	19 33 34
28	16 14 55	21 15	+12 15	7 41	8 01	11 48	15 54	15 34	4 27 10	19 29 38
29	16 19 12	21 25	+11 55	7 42	8 03	11 48	15 54	15 33	4 31 06	19 25 42
30	16 23 29	21 35	+11 34	7 44	8 05	11 49	15 53	15 32	4 35 03	19 21 46

DURATION OF TWILIGHT (in minutes)

Latitude	52°	56°	52°	56°	52°	56°	52°	56°
	1 November		*11 November*		*21 November*		*31 November*	
Civil	36	40	37	41	38	43	40	45
Nautical	75	84	78	87	80	90	82	93
Astronomical	115	127	117	130	120	134	123	138

THE NIGHT SKY

Mercury remains unsuitably placed for observation throughout the month.

Venus becomes visible as a morning object after the first few days of the month. It is then visible above the south-eastern horizon before dawn. During this period its magnitude increases in brightness from −4.2 to −4.7. Venus is now moving rapidly away from the Sun and by the end of the month can be detected low above the horizon nearly three hours before sunrise.

Mars remains unsuitably placed for observation.

Jupiter, magnitude −2.7, is visible as a brilliant evening object in the southern and south-western skies. It reaches its second stationary point on the 18th, on the borders of Aquarius and Pisces, then resumes its direct motion eastwards. The waxing gibbous Moon passes 6 degrees north of Jupiter on the 16th. The four Galilean satellites are readily observable with a small telescope or even a good pair of binoculars.

Saturn, magnitude +1.0, is visible for a short while as a morning object, low above the east-south-eastern horizon before the increasing twilight glow, inhibits observation. Saturn is in the constellation of Virgo.

THE MOON

Day	R.A.		Dec.	Hor. Par.	Semi-diam.	Sun's Co-Long.	PA. of Br. Limb	Ph.	Age	Rise 52°		Rise 56°		Transit		Set 52°		Set 56°	
	h	m	°	′	′	°	°	%	d	h	m	h	m	h	m	h	m	h	m
1	9	54	+8.4	59.5	16.2	202	108	34	24.2	0	32	0	25	7	28	14	07	14	11
2	10	47	+2.6	59.9	16.3	214	109	23	25.2	1	56	1	54	8	19	14	26	14	25
3	11	40	−3.3	60.2	16.4	227	108	14	26.2	3	21	3	25	9	10	14	45	14	39
4	12	34	−9.2	60.2	16.4	239	105	7	27.2	4	47	4	56	10	03	15	06	14	55
5	13	30	−14.5	60.0	16.4	251	96	2	28.2	6	13	6	28	10	58	15	32	15	15
6	14	28	−18.9	59.6	16.2	263	52	0	29.2	7	38	7	59	11	55	16	04	15	42
7	15	27	−22.1	59.0	16.1	275	301	1	0.8	8	57	9	23	12	53	16	46	16	19
8	16	28	−23.9	58.3	15.9	288	284	4	1.8	10	05	10	33	13	52	17	38	17	10
9	17	27	−24.2	57.5	15.7	300	275	10	2.8	10	59	11	26	14	48	18	40	18	14
10	18	24	−23.1	56.6	15.4	312	267	17	3.8	11	40	12	03	15	42	19	49	19	26
11	19	19	−20.9	55.9	15.2	324	262	25	4.8	12	11	12	30	16	31	21	00	20	42
12	20	10	−17.7	55.2	15.0	336	257	34	5..8	12	34	12	49	17	18	22	10	21	57
13	20	58	−13.8	54.7	14.9	349	253	44	6.8	12	53	13	03	18	01	23	19	23	11
14	21	43	−9.4	54.4	14.8	1	251	53	7.8	13	09	13	15	18	42	—		—	
15	22	27	−4.8	54.2	14.8	13	250	62	8.8	13	24	13	26	19	23	0	27	0	23
16	23	10	+0.1	54.2	14.8	25	249	71	9.8	13	39	13	36	20	03	1	34	1	35
17	23	54	+4.9	54.4	14.8	37	250	79	10.8	13	54	13	48	20	45	2	42	2	47
18	0	38	+9.7	54.7	14.9	49	252	87	11.8	14	11	14	00	21	28	3	51	4	00
19	1	25	+14.1	55.1	15.0	61	256	92	12.8	14	31	14	16	22	15	5	01	5	15
20	2	14	+18.0	55.6	15.1	74	262	97	13.8	14	57	14	37	23	04	6	13	6	32
21	3	06	+21.1	56.1	15.3	86	276	99	14.8	15	31	15	07	23	57	7	25	7	48
22	4	01	+23.3	56.7	15.4	98	40	100	15.8	16	15	15	48	—		8	32	8	59
23	4	58	+24.2	57.2	15.6	110	78	98	16.8	17	12	16	45	0	53	9	32	9	59
24	5	57	+23.8	57.7	15.7	122	89	94	17.8	18	21	17	56	1	50	10	21	10	46
25	6	55	+21.9	58.1	15.8	134	97	88	18.8	19	37	19	18	2	46	10	59	11	20
26	7	53	+18.8	58.5	15.9	146	102	80	19.8	20	58	20	44	3	41	11	28	11	44
27	8	48	+14.6	58.8	16.0	159	107	71	20.8	22	20	22	11	4	34	11	52	12	03
28	9	41	+9.5	59.0	16.1	171	110	60	21.8	23	42	23	39	5	25	12	12	12	18
29	10	33	+4.0	59.2	16.1	183	112	49	22.8	—		—		6	15	12	31	12	32
30	11	25	−1.8	59.3	16.2	195	112	37	23.8	1	04	1	06	7	04	12	49	12	45

MERCURY

Day	R.A.		Dec.	Diam.	Phase	Transit		5° high 52°		5° high 56°	
	h	m	°	″	%	h	m	h	m	h	m
1	15	00	−17.9	5	97	12	21	16	02	15	38
3	15	13	−18.9	5	96	12	25	15	59	15	33
5	15	25	−19.9	5	95	12	30	15	56	15	28
7	15	37	−20.8	5	94	12	34	15	53	15	24
9	15	50	−21.7	5	93	12	39	15	51	15	19
11	16	02	−22.5	5	92	12	43	15	49	15	15
13	16	15	−23.2	5	91	12	48	15	48	15	11
15	16	27	−23.8	5	89	12	53	15	47	15	08
17	16	40	−24.4	5	87	12	57	15	46	15	05
19	16	52	−24.9	5	85	13	02	15	47	15	03
21	17	04	−25.2	6	83	13	06	15	47	15	02
23	17	16	−25.5	6	81	13	10	15	49	15	02
25	17	28	−25.7	6	77	13	14	15	51	15	03
27	17	39	−25.8	6	74	13	17	15	53	15	05
29	17	50	−25.9	6	70	13	20	15	56	15	08
31	18	00	−25.8	7	65	13	21	15	59	15	11

VENUS

Day	R.A.		Dec.	Diam.	Phase	Transit		5° high 52°		5° high 56°	
	h	m	°	″	%	h	m	h	m	h	m
1	13	58	−17.8	61	1	11	15	7	31	7	54
6	13	49	−15.8	60	3	10	46	6	49	7	08
11	13	43	−13.8	57	6	10	21	6	11	6	28
16	13	41	−12.3	54	10	9	59	5	40	5	55
21	13	42	−11.2	50	14	9	41	5	16	5	29
26	13	47	−10.6	46	19	9	27	4	57	5	11
31	13	55	−10.4	42	24	9	15	4	45	4	58

MARS

Day	R.A.		Dec.	Diam.	Phase	Transit		5° high 52°		5° high 56°	
	h	m	°	″	%	h	m	h	m	h	m
1	16	02	−21.3	4	98	13	21	16	38	16	07
6	16	17	−22.0	4	98	13	16	16	28	15	55
11	16	33	−22.6	4	99	13	12	16	18	15	44
16	16	48	−23.1	4	99	13	08	16	10	15	34
21	17	04	−23.6	4	99	13	05	16	02	15	25
26	17	21	−23.9	4	99	13	01	15	56	15	17
31	17	37	−24.1	4	99	12	58	15	50	15	11

SUNRISE AND SUNSET

	London				*Bristol*				*Birmingham*				*Manchester*				*Newcastle*				*Glasgow*				*Belfast*			
	0° 05′		*51° 30′*		*2° 35′*		*51° 28′*		*1° 55′*		*52° 28′*		*2° 15′*		*53° 28′*		*1° 37′*		*54° 59′*		*4° 14′*		*55° 52′*		*5° 56′*		*54° 35′*	
d	*h*	*m*	*h*	*m*	*h*	*m*	*h*	*m*	*h*	*m*	*h*	*m*	*h*	*m*	*h*	*m*	*h*	*m*	*h*	*m*	*h*	*m*	*h*	*m*	*h*	*m*	*h*	*m*
1	6	54	16	34	7	03	16	44	7	04	16	38	7	08	16	37	7	10	16	30	7	23	16	37	7	26	16	48
2	6	55	16	32	7	05	16	42	7	05	16	36	7	10	16	35	7	12	16	27	7	25	16	35	7	28	16	46
3	6	57	16	30	7	07	16	40	7	07	16	35	7	11	16	33	7	14	16	25	7	27	16	33	7	30	16	44
4	6	59	16	28	7	09	16	38	7	09	16	33	7	13	16	31	7	16	16	23	7	29	16	31	7	32	16	42
5	7	01	16	27	7	11	16	37	7	11	16	31	7	15	16	29	7	18	16	21	7	32	16	29	7	34	16	40
6	7	02	16	25	7	12	16	35	7	13	16	29	7	17	16	27	7	20	16	20	7	34	16	27	7	36	16	38
7	7	04	16	23	7	14	16	33	7	15	16	28	7	19	16	26	7	22	16	18	7	36	16	25	7	38	16	36
8	7	06	16	22	7	16	16	32	7	16	16	26	7	21	16	24	7	24	16	16	7	38	16	23	7	40	16	34
9	7	08	16	20	7	18	16	30	7	18	16	24	7	23	16	22	7	26	16	14	7	40	16	21	7	42	16	33
10	7	09	16	18	7	19	16	29	7	20	16	23	7	25	16	20	7	28	16	12	7	42	16	19	7	44	16	31
11	7	11	16	17	7	21	16	27	7	22	16	21	7	27	16	19	7	30	16	10	7	44	16	17	7	46	16	29
12	7	13	16	15	7	23	16	26	7	24	16	19	7	29	16	17	7	32	16	08	7	46	16	15	7	48	16	27
13	7	15	16	14	7	24	16	24	7	25	16	18	7	30	16	15	7	34	16	07	7	48	16	13	7	50	16	26
14	7	16	16	13	7	26	16	23	7	27	16	16	7	32	16	14	7	36	16	05	7	50	16	12	7	52	16	24
15	7	18	16	11	7	28	16	21	7	29	16	15	7	34	16	12	7	38	16	03	7	52	16	10	7	54	16	22
16	7	20	16	10	7	30	16	20	7	31	16	14	7	36	16	11	7	40	16	02	7	55	16	08	7	56	16	21
17	7	21	16	09	7	31	16	19	7	33	16	12	7	38	16	09	7	42	16	00	7	57	16	07	7	57	16	19
18	7	23	16	07	7	33	16	17	7	34	16	11	7	40	16	08	7	44	15	59	7	59	16	05	7	59	16	18
19	7	25	16	06	7	35	16	16	7	36	16	10	7	42	16	07	7	46	15	57	8	01	16	03	8	01	16	16
20	7	26	16	05	7	36	16	15	7	38	16	08	7	43	16	05	7	48	15	56	8	03	16	02	8	03	16	15
21	7	28	16	04	7	38	16	14	7	39	16	07	7	45	16	04	7	50	15	54	8	05	16	00	8	05	16	14
22	7	30	16	03	7	40	16	13	7	41	16	06	7	47	16	03	7	51	15	53	8	06	15	59	8	07	16	12
23	7	31	16	02	7	41	16	12	7	43	16	05	7	49	16	02	7	53	15	52	8	08	15	58	8	09	16	11
24	7	33	16	01	7	43	16	11	7	44	16	04	7	50	16	01	7	55	15	51	8	10	15	56	8	10	16	10
25	7	34	16	00	7	44	16	10	7	46	16	03	7	52	15	59	7	57	15	49	8	12	15	55	8	12	16	09
26	7	36	15	59	7	46	16	09	7	48	16	02	7	54	15	58	7	59	15	48	8	14	15	54	8	14	16	08
27	7	38	15	58	7	47	16	08	7	49	16	01	7	55	15	57	8	00	15	47	8	16	15	53	8	16	16	07
28	7	39	15	57	7	49	16	07	7	51	16	00	7	57	15	57	8	02	15	46	8	18	15	52	8	17	16	06
29	7	41	15	56	7	50	16	06	7	52	15	59	7	58	15	56	8	04	15	45	8	19	15	51	8	19	16	05
30	7	42	15	56	7	52	16	06	7	54	15	58	8	00	15	55	8	05	15	44	8	21	15	50	8	21	16	04

JUPITER

Day	*R.A.*		*Dec.*		*Transit*		*5° high*			
							52°		*56°*	
	h	*m*	°	′	*h*	*m*	*h*	*m*	*h*	*m*
1	23	40.5	−3	46	20	56	2	07	2	01
11	23	38.8	−3	54	20	15	1	25	1	19
21	23	38.4	−3	54	19	36	0	46	0	39
31	23	39.3	−3	46	18	57	0	08	0	02

Diameters – equatorial 45″ polar 42″

SATURN

Day	*R.A.*		*Dec.*		*Transit*		*5° high*			
							52°		*56°*	
	h	*m*	°	′	*h*	*m*	*h*	*m*	*h*	*m*
1	12	45.7	−2	31	10	04	4	50	4	55
11	12	49.8	−2	55	9	28	4	17	4	23
21	12	53.7	−3	18	8	53	3	43	3	50
31	12	57.2	−3	38	8	17	3	09	3	16

Diameters – equatorial 16″ polar 14″
Rings– major axis 36″ minor axis 6″

URANUS

Day	*R.A.*		*Dec.*		*Transit*		*10° high*			
							52°		*56°*	
	h	*m*	°	′	*h*	*m*	*h*	*m*	*h*	*m*
1	23	50.8	−1	50	21	07	1	54	1	46
11	23	50.0	−1	56	20	26	1	14	1	05
21	23	49.4	−1	59	19	47	0	33	0	25
31	23	49.0	−2	01	19	07	23	50	23	41

Diameter 4″

NEPTUNE

Day	*R.A.*		*Dec.*		*Transit*		*10° high*			
							52°		*56°*	
	h	*m*	°	′	*h*	*m*	*h*	*m*	*h*	*m*
1	21	53.4	−13	20	19	10	22	43	22	21
11	21	53.4	−13	20	18	30	22	04	21	41
21	21	53.5	−13	19	17	51	21	25	21	02
31	21	54.0	−13	17	17	12	20	47	20	24

Diameter 2″

DECEMBER 2010

TWELFTH MONTH, 31 DAYS. *Decem* (ten), tenth month of Roman pre-Julian calendar

1	*Wednesday*	The Locarno Treaties were formally signed 1925	day 335
2	*Thursday*	Napoleon Bonaparte led the defeat of Austro–Russian armies at Austerlitz 1805	336
3	*Friday*	The Malta summit brought the Cold War to a close 1989	337
4	*Saturday*	US president George H. W. Bush ordered US troops into Somalia 1992	338
5	*Sunday*	Chinese troops took control of Pyongyang, North Korea 1950	339
6	*Monday*	The Anglo–Irish treaty partitioned Northern Ireland from the Republic of Ireland 1921	week 49 day 340
7	*Tuesday*	The Japanese bombed Pearl Harbor in Hawaii 1941	341
8	*Wednesday*	Ronald Reagan and Mikhail Gorbachev signed the Intermediate-Range Nuclear Forces Treaty 1987	342
9	*Thursday*	China declared war on the Axis powers 1941	343
10	*Friday*	US president Woodrow Wilson won the Nobel Peace Prize 1920	344
11	*Saturday*	Russian troops entered the secessionist region of Chechnya 1994	345
12	*Sunday*	Japanese planes sunk US gunboat *Panay* during the Sino–Japanese War 1937	346
13	*Monday*	The first major naval battle of the Second World War, the Battle of the River Plate, began 1939	week 50 day 347
14	*Tuesday*	Leaders of Bosnia, Serbia and Croatia signed the Dayton Accord to end war in the Balkans 1995	348
15	*Wednesday*	British prime minister John Major and Irish prime minister Albert Reynolds signed the Joint Declaration of Peace 1993	349
16	*Thursday*	The Battle of the Bulge began with a surprise German attack 1944	350
17	*Friday*	German battleship *Admiral Graf Spee* was scuttled 1939	351
18	*Saturday*	The Battle of Verdun ended after ten months of fighting 1916	352
19	*Sunday*	The Viet Minh attacked French positions in Hanoi, starting the first Indochina War 1946	353
20	*Monday*	The USA invaded Panama 1989	week 51 day 354
21	*Tuesday*	Joseph Stalin, Soviet leader *b.* 1879; George S. Patton, US army commander *d.* 1945	355
22	*Wednesday*	The Romanian government fell in an anti-communist coup 1989	356
23	*Thursday*	British and French troops left Egypt after failing to gain control of the Suez Canal 1956	357
24	*Friday*	US General Dwight D. Eisenhower was appointed Supreme Allied Commander 1943	358
25	*Saturday*	German and Allied troops held a Christmas Day truce on the Western Front 1914	359
26	*Sunday*	France defeated Austria at the Battle of Geisberg 1793	360
27	*Monday*	Afghan president Hafizullah Amin was murdered in a Soviet-backed coup 1979	week 52 day 361
28	*Tuesday*	Woodrow Wilson, US president *b.* 1856; Victor Emmanuel III, king of Italy *d.* 1947	362
29	*Wednesday*	London experienced its worst night of bombing in the Blitz 1940	363
30	*Thursday*	Former Iraqi leader Saddam Hussein was executed by the Iraqi government 2006	364
31	*Friday*	British defenders of Quebec, Canada, defeated Patriot forces in the American Revolution 1775	365

ASTRONOMICAL PHENOMENA

d	*h*	
1	13	Saturn in conjunction with Moon. Saturn 7°N.
1	16	Mercury at greatest elongation E.21°
2	17	Venus in conjunction with Moon. Venus 6°N.
4	15	Venus at greatest brilliancy
6	02	Uranus at stationary point
6	22	Mars in conjunction with Moon. Mars 0°5 S.
7	09	Mercury in conjunction with Moon. Mercury 2°S.
10	12	Mercury at stationary point
13	20	Jupiter in conjunction with Moon. Jupiter 7°S.
14	04	Mars in conjunction with Mercury. Mars 1°S.
20	01	Mercury in inferior conjunction
21	08	Total eclipse of Moon (*see* Eclipses)
22	00	Sun's longitude 270° ♑
27	01	Pluto in conjunction
28	22	Saturn in conjunction with Moon. Saturn 8°N.
30	07	Mercury at stationary point
31	13	Venus in conjunction with Moon. Venus 7°N.

MINIMA OF ALGOL

d	*h*	*d*	*h*	*d*	*h*
3	07.4	14	18.7	26	06.0
6	04.2	17	15.5	29	02.8
9	01.0	20	12.3	31	23.6
11	21.9	23	09.1		

CONSTELLATIONS

The following constellations are near their meridian at

	d	*h*		*d*	*h*
November	1	24	December	16	21
November	15	23	January	1	20
December	1	22	January	16	19

Ursa Major (below the Pole), Ursa Minor (below the Pole), Cassiopeia, Andromeda, Perseus, Triangulum, Aries, Taurus, Cetus and Eridanus

THE MOON

Phases, Apsides and Node	*d*	*h*	*m*
● New Moon	5	17	36
☽ First Quarter	13	13	59
○ Full Moon	21	08	13
☾ Last Quarter	28	04	18
Apogee (404,447 km)	13	08	35
Perigee (368,435 km)	25	12	25

Mean longitude of ascending node on December 1, 274°

THE SUN

s.d. 16′.3

Day	Right Ascension			Dec. –		Equation of time		Rise				Transit		Set				Sidereal time			Transit of first point of Aries		
								52°		56°				52°		56°							
	h	*m*	*s*	°	′	*m*	*s*	*h*	*m*	*h*	*m*	*h*	*m*	*h*	*m*	*h*	*m*	*h*	*m*	*s*	*h*	*m*	*s*
1	16	27	48	21	45	+11	12	7	45	8	07	11	49	15	52	15	31	4	39	00	19	17	50
2	16	32	07	21	54	+10	49	7	47	8	08	11	49	15	52	15	30	4	42	56	19	13	54
3	16	36	26	22	03	+10	26	7	48	8	10	11	50	15	51	15	29	4	46	53	19	09	58
4	16	40	47	22	11	+10	02	7	49	8	11	11	50	15	51	15	29	4	50	49	19	06	03
5	16	45	08	22	19	+9	38	7	51	8	13	11	51	15	50	15	28	4	54	46	19	02	07
6	16	49	29	22	27	+9	13	7	52	8	14	11	51	15	50	15	27	4	58	42	18	58	11
7	16	53	51	22	34	+8	48	7	53	8	16	11	51	15	49	15	27	5	02	39	18	54	15
8	16	58	14	22	41	+8	22	7	54	8	17	11	52	15	49	15	26	5	06	35	18	50	19
9	17	02	37	22	47	+7	55	7	56	8	18	11	52	15	49	15	26	5	10	32	18	46	23
10	17	07	00	22	53	+7	29	7	57	8	20	11	53	15	49	15	26	5	14	29	18	42	27
11	17	11	24	22	58	+7	01	7	58	8	21	11	53	15	48	15	25	5	18	25	18	38	31
12	17	15	48	23	03	+6	34	7	59	8	22	11	54	15	48	15	25	5	22	22	18	34	35
13	17	20	13	23	07	+6	06	8	00	8	23	11	54	15	48	15	25	5	26	18	18	30	39
14	17	24	37	23	11	+5	37	8	01	8	24	11	55	15	48	15	25	5	30	15	18	26	43
15	17	29	03	23	15	+5	09	8	02	8	25	11	55	15	48	15	25	5	34	11	18	22	48
16	17	33	28	23	18	+4	40	8	02	8	26	11	56	15	49	15	25	5	38	08	18	18	52
17	17	37	54	23	20	+4	11	8	03	8	27	11	56	15	49	15	25	5	42	04	18	14	56
18	17	42	19	23	23	+3	42	8	04	8	28	11	57	15	49	15	25	5	46	01	18	11	00
19	17	46	45	23	24	+3	12	8	05	8	28	11	57	15	50	15	26	5	49	58	18	07	04
20	17	51	12	23	25	+2	43	8	05	8	29	11	58	15	50	15	26	5	53	54	18	03	08
21	17	55	38	23	26	+2	13	8	06	8	30	11	58	15	50	15	26	5	57	51	17	59	12
22	18	00	04	23	26	+1	43	8	06	8	30	11	59	15	51	15	27	6	01	47	17	55	16
23	18	04	30	23	26	+1	13	8	07	8	31	11	59	15	51	15	28	6	05	44	17	51	20
24	18	08	57	23	25	+0	44	8	07	8	31	12	00	15	52	15	28	6	09	40	17	47	24
25	18	13	23	23	24	+0	14	8	07	8	31	12	00	15	53	15	29	6	13	37	17	43	28
26	18	17	49	23	22	–0	16	8	08	8	31	12	01	15	53	15	30	6	17	33	17	39	32
27	18	22	15	23	20	–0	45	8	08	8	32	12	01	15	54	15	31	6	21	30	17	35	37
28	18	26	41	23	18	–1	15	8	08	8	32	12	01	15	55	15	31	6	25	27	17	31	41
29	18	31	07	23	15	–1	44	8	08	8	32	12	02	15	56	15	32	6	29	23	17	27	45
30	18	35	33	23	11	–2	13	8	08	8	32	12	02	15	57	15	33	6	33	20	17	23	49
31	18	39	58	23	07	–2	42	8	08	8	31	12	03	15	58	15	35	6	37	16	17	19	53

DURATION OF TWILIGHT (in minutes)

Latitude	*52°*	*56°*	*52°*	*56°*	*52°*	*56°*	*52°*	*56°*
	1 December		*11 December*		*21 December*		*31 December*	
Civil	40	45	41	47	41	47	41	47
Nautical	82	93	84	96	85	97	84	96
Astronomical	123	138	125	141	126	142	125	141

THE NIGHT SKY

Mercury is unsuitably placed for observation at first, inferior conjunction occurring on the 20th. For the last few days of the month Mercury becomes visible as a morning object low above the south-eastern horizon around the beginning of morning civil twilight. Its magnitude brightens from +0.8 to +0.3.

Venus is a magnificent object in the early mornings, attaining its greatest brilliancy (magnitude −4.7) on the 4th. It completely dominates the south-eastern sky for several hours before sunrise. The mornings of both the 1st and 31st will be suitable for using the old crescent Moon as a guide to locating Venus in daylight. On the first occasion Venus should be seen about 10 degrees above the Moon; on the second occasion Venus can be seen 8–9 degrees to the left and above the Moon.

Mars is still unsuitably placed for observation and will not be seen from the British Isles until about the middle of next year.

Jupiter continues to be visible in the evenings, magnitude −2.4, crossing the meridian about an hour after sunset, by the end of the year. The Moon, at First Quarter, will be seen passing about 6 degrees north of the planet on the evening of the 13th.

Saturn, magnitude +0.9, can now be seen in the south-eastern quadrant of the sky after about 03h at the beginning of the month and shortly after 01h by the end of the month. The old crescent Moon passes 8 degrees south of the planet on the 1st and again on the 31st.

Meteors. The maximum of the well-known Geminid meteor shower occurs in the early hours of the 14th. The Moon, at First Quarter, will provide some interference until shortly after midnight.

THE MOON

Day	R.A.		Dec.	Hor. Par.	Semi-diam.	Sun's Co-Long.	PA. of Br. Limb	Ph.	Age	Rise				Transit		Set			
										52°		56°				52°		56°	
	h	m	°	′	′	°	°	%	d	h	m	h	m	h	m	h	m	h	m
1	12	17	−7.6	59.4	16.2	207	111	26	24.8	2	26	2	34	7	55	13	09	13	00
2	13	11	−12.9	59.3	16.2	219	108	17	25.8	3	50	4	03	8	47	13	32	13	18
3	14	07	−17.5	59.1	16.1	232	104	9	26.8	5	13	5	32	9	41	14	00	13	41
4	15	04	−21.1	58.7	16.0	244	97	4	27.8	6	33	6	57	10	38	14	37	14	12
5	16	04	−23.4	58.3	15.9	256	86	1	28.8	7	46	8	13	11	36	15	24	14	56
6	17	03	−24.2	57.7	15.7	268	299	0	0.3	8	46	9	14	12	33	16	22	15	54
7	18	02	−23.7	57.0	15.5	280	271	2	1.3	9	33	9	59	13	29	17	29	17	04
8	18	58	−21.8	56.4	15.4	293	262	6	2.3	10	09	10	30	14	21	18	40	18	20
9	19	51	−18.9	55.7	15.2	305	257	11	3.3	10	36	10	52	15	09	19	52	19	37
10	20	40	−15.2	55.2	15.0	317	253	18	4.3	10	57	11	08	15	55	21	03	20	52
11	21	27	−10.9	54.7	14.9	329	250	27	5.3	11	14	11	22	16	37	22	12	22	06
12	22	12	−6.3	54.4	14.8	341	248	35	6.3	11	29	11	33	17	18	23	19	23	18
13	22	55	−1.5	54.2	14.8	353	247	45	7.3	11	44	11	43	17	58	—		—	
14	23	38	+3.4	54.3	14.8	6	247	54	8.3	11	59	11	54	18	39	0	26	0	29
15	0	22	+8.1	54.5	14.8	18	248	63	9.3	12	15	12	06	19	21	1	34	1	41
16	1	08	+12.6	54.8	14.9	30	250	72	10.3	12	34	12	20	20	06	2	43	2	55
17	1	55	+16.7	55.3	15.1	42	253	81	11.3	12	57	12	39	20	54	3	54	4	11
18	2	46	+20.1	56.0	15.2	54	257	88	12.3	13	26	13	04	21	45	5	06	5	27
19	3	40	+22.7	56.6	15.4	66	262	94	13.3	14	06	13	40	22	40	6	16	6	41
20	4	37	+24.0	57.4	15.6	78	268	98	14.3	14	58	14	31	23	38	7	20	7	47
21	5	37	+24.1	58.0	15.8	91	277	100	15.3	16	04	15	38	—		8	14	8	40
22	6	37	+22.6	58.6	16.0	103	97	99	16.3	17	20	16	58	0	36	8	57	9	20
23	7	36	+19.8	59.1	16.1	115	104	97	17.3	18	42	18	26	1	33	9	31	9	48
24	8	33	+15.8	59.4	16.2	127	109	91	18.3	20	06	19	56	2	29	9	57	10	09
25	9	28	+10.8	59.5	16.2	139	112	84	19.3	21	30	21	25	3	21	10	19	10	26
26	10	21	+5.2	59.5	16.2	151	114	74	20.3	22	52	22	53	4	12	10	38	10	40
27	11	13	−0.6	59.4	16.2	163	114	63	21.3	—		—		5	02	10	56	10	53
28	12	05	−6.3	59.2	16.1	176	114	52	22.3	0	14	0	20	5	52	11	15	11	07
29	12	58	−11.7	58.9	16.1	188	112	41	23.3	1	36	1	48	6	42	11	36	11	24
30	13	52	−16.4	58.6	16.0	200	109	30	24.3	2	58	3	15	7	35	12	02	11	44
31	14	48	−20.2	58.2	15.9	212	104	20	25.3	4	17	4	40	8	29	12	35	12	12

MERCURY

Day	R.A.		Dec.	Diam.	Phase	Transit		5° high			
								52°		56°	
	h	m	°	″	%	h	m	h	m	h	m
1	18	00	−25.8	7	65	13	21	15	59	15	11
3	18	09	−25.6	7	59	13	22	16	01	15	15
5	18	16	−25.3	7	52	13	21	16	03	15	19
7	18	22	−25.0	8	45	13	18	16	04	15	21
9	18	25	−24.6	8	37	13	13	16	03	15	22
11	18	26	−24.1	8	28	13	05	15	59	15	21
13	18	23	−23.5	9	19	12	54	15	53	15	17
15	18	18	−23.0	9	11	12	39	15	44	15	09
17	18	09	−22.3	10	4	12	22	15	31	14	59
19	17	58	−21.7	10	1	12	03	15	17	14	47
21	17	46	−21.1	10	1	11	43	8	25	8	54
23	17	35	−20.6	10	4	11	25	8	03	8	31
25	17	26	−20.2	9	10	11	09	7	44	8	11
27	17	20	−20.0	9	18	10	55	7	29	7	56
29	17	16	−20.0	9	26	10	45	7	18	7	45
31	17	16	−20.1	8	34	10	37	7	11	7	39

VENUS

Day	R.A.		Dec.	Diam.	Phase	Transit		5° high			
								52°		56°	
	h	m	°	″	%	h	m	h	m	h	m
1	13	55	−10.4	42	24	9	15	4	45	4	58
6	14	05	−10.7	39	28	9	06	4	37	4	50
11	14	18	−11.2	36	32	8	59	4	33	4	47
16	14	33	−11.9	34	36	8	54	4	33	4	47
21	14	49	−12.9	31	39	8	51	4	35	4	51
26	15	06	−13.9	29	42	8	48	4	39	4	56
31	15	24	−15.0	27	45	8	47	4	45	5	04

MARS

Day	R.A.		Dec.	Diam.	Phase	Transit		5° high			
								52°		56°	
	h	m	°	″	%	h	m	h	m	h	m
1	17	37	−24.1	4	99	12	58	15	50	15	11
6	17	53	−24.3	4	99	12	54	15	46	15	06
11	18	10	−24.3	4	99	12	51	15	43	15	03
16	18	27	−24.2	4	100	12	48	15	41	15	01
21	18	43	−24.0	4	100	12	45	15	40	15	01
26	19	00	−23.7	4	100	12	42	15	40	15	02
31	19	17	−23.3	4	100	12	39	15	41	15	05

SUNRISE AND SUNSET

	London				Bristol				Birmingham				Manchester				Newcastle				Glasgow				Belfast			
	0° 05'		51° 30'		2° 35'		51° 28'		1° 55'		52° 28'		2° 15'		53° 28'		1° 37'		54° 59'		4° 14'		55° 52'		5° 56'		54° 35'	
d	*h*	*m*	*h*	*m*	*h*	*m*	*h*	*m*	*h*	*m*	*h*	*m*	*h*	*m*	*h*	*m*	*h*	*m*	*h*	*m*	*h*	*m*	*h*	*m*	*h*	*m*	*h*	*m*
1	7	43	15	55	7	53	16	05	7	55	15	58	8	02	15	54	8	07	15	43	8	23	15	49	8	22	16	03
2	7	45	15	54	7	55	16	04	7	57	15	57	8	03	15	53	8	09	15	43	8	24	15	48	8	24	16	02
3	7	46	15	54	7	56	16	04	7	58	15	56	8	04	15	53	8	10	15	42	8	26	15	47	8	25	16	01
4	7	47	15	53	7	57	16	03	7	59	15	56	8	06	15	52	8	12	15	41	8	27	15	46	8	27	16	01
5	7	49	15	53	7	59	16	03	8	01	15	55	8	07	15	52	8	13	15	41	8	29	15	46	8	28	16	00
6	7	50	15	52	8	00	16	03	8	02	15	55	8	09	15	51	8	15	15	40	8	30	15	45	8	30	16	00
7	7	51	15	52	8	01	16	02	8	03	15	55	8	10	15	51	8	16	15	40	8	32	15	45	8	31	15	59
8	7	52	15	52	8	02	16	02	8	05	15	54	8	11	15	50	8	17	15	39	8	33	15	44	8	32	15	59
9	7	53	15	52	8	03	16	02	8	06	15	54	8	12	15	50	8	19	15	39	8	35	15	44	8	33	15	58
10	7	55	15	51	8	04	16	02	8	07	15	54	8	13	15	50	8	20	15	38	8	36	15	43	8	35	15	58
11	7	56	15	51	8	05	16	01	8	08	15	54	8	15	15	50	8	21	15	38	8	37	15	43	8	36	15	58
12	7	57	15	51	8	06	16	01	8	09	15	54	8	16	15	50	8	22	15	38	8	38	15	43	8	37	15	58
13	7	58	15	51	8	07	16	01	8	10	15	54	8	17	15	49	8	23	15	38	8	39	15	43	8	38	15	58
14	7	58	15	51	8	08	16	01	8	11	15	54	8	18	15	49	8	24	15	38	8	40	15	43	8	39	15	58
15	7	59	15	51	8	09	16	02	8	12	15	54	8	18	15	50	8	25	15	38	8	41	15	43	8	40	15	58
16	8	00	15	52	8	10	16	02	8	13	15	54	8	19	15	50	8	26	15	38	8	42	15	43	8	41	15	58
17	8	01	15	52	8	11	16	02	8	13	15	54	8	20	15	50	8	27	15	38	8	43	15	43	8	41	15	58
18	8	02	15	52	8	11	16	02	8	14	15	54	8	21	15	50	8	27	15	39	8	44	15	43	8	42	15	58
19	8	02	15	52	8	12	16	03	8	15	15	55	8	22	15	50	8	28	15	39	8	44	15	44	8	43	15	59
20	8	03	15	53	8	13	16	03	8	15	15	55	8	22	15	51	8	29	15	39	8	45	15	44	8	44	15	59
21	8	03	15	53	8	13	16	03	8	16	15	56	8	23	15	51	8	29	15	40	8	46	15	44	8	44	15	59
22	8	04	15	54	8	14	16	04	8	16	15	56	8	23	15	52	8	30	15	40	8	46	15	45	8	45	16	00
23	8	04	15	54	8	14	16	04	8	17	15	57	8	24	15	52	8	30	15	41	8	47	15	45	8	45	16	00
24	8	05	15	55	8	15	16	05	8	17	15	57	8	24	15	53	8	31	15	41	8	47	15	46	8	45	16	01
25	8	05	15	56	8	15	16	06	8	18	15	58	8	24	15	54	8	31	15	42	8	47	15	47	8	46	16	02
26	8	05	15	56	8	15	16	07	8	18	15	59	8	25	15	54	8	31	15	43	8	47	15	48	8	46	16	03
27	8	06	15	57	8	16	16	07	8	18	15	59	8	25	15	55	8	31	15	44	8	48	15	48	8	46	16	03
28	8	06	15	58	8	16	16	08	8	18	16	00	8	25	15	56	8	32	15	45	8	48	15	49	8	46	16	04
29	8	06	15	59	8	16	16	09	8	18	16	01	8	25	15	57	8	32	15	45	8	48	15	50	8	46	16	05
30	8	06	16	00	8	16	16	10	8	18	16	02	8	25	15	58	8	32	15	47	8	48	15	51	8	46	16	06
31	8	06	16	01	8	16	16	11	8	18	16	03	8	25	15	59	8	31	15	48	8	48	15	52	8	46	16	07

JUPITER

Day	*R.A.*		*Dec.*		*Transit*		*5° high*			
							52°		*56°*	
	h	*m*	°	′	*h*	*m*	*h*	*m*	*h*	*m*
1	23	39.3	−3	46	18	57	0	08	0	02
11	23	41.4	−3	29	18	20	23	29	23	23
21	23	44.6	−3	06	17	44	22	55	22	49
31	23	48.9	−2	35	17	09	22	23	22	17

Diameters – equatorial 41″ polar 38″

SATURN

Day	*R.A.*		*Dec.*		*Transit*		*5° high*			
							52°		*56°*	
	h	*m*	°	′	*h*	*m*	*h*	*m*	*h*	*m*
1	12	57.2	−3	38	8	17	3	09	3	16
11	13	00.3	−3	55	7	41	2	35	2	41
21	13	02.9	−4	09	7	04	1	59	2	06
31	13	04.9	−4	19	6	27	1	23	1	30

Diameters – equatorial 17″ polar 15″

Rings – major axis 38″ minor axis 6″

URANUS

Day	*R.A.*		*Dec.*		*Transit*		*10° high*			
							52°		*56°*	
	h	*m*	°	′	*h*	*m*	*h*	*m*	*h*	*m*
1	23	49.0	−2	01	19	07	23	50	23	41
11	23	49.0	−2	00	18	28	23	11	23	02
21	23	49.3	−1	58	17	49	22	32	22	23
31	23	49.9	−1	54	17	10	21	53	21	45

Diameter 4″

NEPTUNE

Day	*R.A.*		*Dec.*		*Transit*		*10° high*			
							52°		*56°*	
	h	*m*	°	′	*h*	*m*	*h*	*m*	*h*	*m*
1	21	54.0	−13	17	17	12	20	47	20	24
11	21	54.6	−13	14	16	34	20	08	19	46
21	21	55.4	−13	09	15	55	19	30	19	08
31	21	56.4	−13	04	15	17	18	53	18	30

Diameter 2″

RISING AND SETTING TIMES

TABLE 1. SEMI-DIURNAL ARCS (HOUR ANGLES AT RISING/SETTING)

Dec.	Latitude 0°	10°	20°	30°	40°	45°	50°	52°	54°	56°	58°	60°	Dec.
	h m	*h m*	*h m*	*h m*	*h m*	*h m*	*h m*	*h m*	*h m*	*h m*	*h m*	*h m*	
0°	6 00	6 00	6 00	6 00	6 00	6 00	6 00	6 00	6 00	6 00	6 00	6 00	0°
1°	6 00	6 01	6 01	6 02	6 03	6 04	6 05	6 05	6 06	6 06	6 06	6 07	1°
2°	6 00	6 01	6 03	6 05	6 07	6 08	6 10	6 10	6 11	6 12	6 13	6 14	2°
3°	6 00	6 02	6 04	6 07	6 10	6 12	6 14	6 15	6 17	6 18	6 19	6 21	3°
4°	6 00	6 03	6 06	6 09	6 13	6 16	6 19	6 21	6 22	6 24	6 26	6 28	4°
5°	6 00	6 04	6 07	6 12	6 17	6 20	6 24	6 26	6 28	6 30	6 32	6 35	5°
6°	6 00	6 04	6 09	6 14	6 20	6 24	6 29	6 31	6 33	6 36	6 39	6 42	6°
7°	6 00	6 05	6 10	6 16	6 24	6 28	6 34	6 36	6 39	6 42	6 45	6 49	7°
8°	6 00	6 06	6 12	6 19	6 27	6 32	6 39	6 41	6 45	6 48	6 52	6 56	8°
9°	6 00	6 06	6 13	6 21	6 31	6 36	6 44	6 47	6 50	6 54	6 59	7 04	9°
10°	6 00	6 07	6 15	6 23	6 34	6 41	6 49	6 52	6 56	7 01	7 06	7 11	10°
11°	6 00	6 08	6 16	6 26	6 38	6 45	6 54	6 58	7 02	7 07	7 12	7 19	11°
12°	6 00	6 09	6 18	6 28	6 41	6 49	6 59	7 03	7 08	7 13	7 20	7 26	12°
13°	6 00	6 09	6 19	6 31	6 45	6 53	7 04	7 09	7 14	7 20	7 27	7 34	13°
14°	6 00	6 10	6 21	6 33	6 48	6 58	7 09	7 14	7 20	7 27	7 34	7 42	14°
15°	6 00	6 11	6 22	6 36	6 52	7 02	7 14	7 20	7 27	7 34	7 42	7 51	15°
16°	6 00	6 12	6 24	6 38	6 56	7 07	7 20	7 26	7 33	7 41	7 49	7 59	16°
17°	6 00	6 12	6 26	6 41	6 59	7 11	7 25	7 32	7 40	7 48	7 57	8 08	17°
18°	6 00	6 13	6 27	6 43	7 03	7 16	7 31	7 38	7 46	7 55	8 05	8 17	18°
19°	6 00	6 14	6 29	6 46	7 07	7 21	7 37	7 45	7 53	8 03	8 14	8 26	19°
20°	6 00	6 15	6 30	6 49	7 11	7 25	7 43	7 51	8 00	8 11	8 22	8 36	20°
21°	6 00	6 16	6 32	6 51	7 15	7 30	7 49	7 58	8 08	8 19	8 32	8 47	21°
22°	6 00	6 16	6 34	6 54	7 19	7 35	7 55	8 05	8 15	8 27	8 41	8 58	22°
23°	6 00	6 17	6 36	6 57	7 23	7 40	8 02	8 12	8 23	8 36	8 51	9 09	23°
24°	6 00	6 18	6 37	7 00	7 28	7 46	8 08	8 19	8 31	8 45	9 02	9 22	24°
25°	6 00	6 19	6 39	7 02	7 32	7 51	8 15	8 27	8 40	8 55	9 13	9 35	25°
26°	6 00	6 20	6 41	7 05	7 37	7 57	8 22	8 35	8 49	9 05	9 25	9 51	26°
27°	6 00	6 21	6 43	7 08	7 41	8 03	8 30	8 43	8 58	9 16	9 39	10 08	27°
28°	6 00	6 22	6 45	7 12	7 46	8 08	8 37	8 52	9 08	9 28	9 53	10 28	28°
29°	6 00	6 22	6 47	7 15	7 51	8 15	8 45	9 01	9 19	9 41	10 10	10 55	29°
30°	6 00	6 23	6 49	7 18	7 56	8 21	8 54	9 11	9 30	9 55	10 30	12 00	30°
35°	6 00	6 28	6 59	7 35	8 24	8 58	9 46	10 15	10 58	12 00	12 00	12 00	35°
40°	6 00	6 34	7 11	7 56	8 59	9 48	12 00	12 00	12 00	12 00	12 00	12 00	40°
45°	6 00	6 41	7 25	8 21	9 48	12 00	12 00	12 00	12 00	12 00	12 00	12 00	45°
50°	6 00	6 49	7 43	8 54	12 00	12 00	12 00	12 00	12 00	12 00	12 00	12 00	50°
55°	6 00	6 58	8 05	9 42	12 00	12 00	12 00	12 00	12 00	12 00	12 00	12 00	55°
60°	6 00	7 11	8 36	12 00	12 00	12 00	12 00	12 00	12 00	12 00	12 00	12 00	60°
65°	6 00	7 29	9 25	12 00	12 00	12 00	12 00	12 00	12 00	12 00	12 00	12 00	65°
70°	6 00	7 56	12 00	12 00	12 00	12 00	12 00	12 00	12 00	12 00	12 00	12 00	70°
75°	6 00	8 45	12 00	12 00	12 00	12 00	12 00	12 00	12 00	12 00	12 00	12 00	75°
80°	6 00	12 00	12 00	12 00	12 00	12 00	12 00	12 00	12 00	12 00	12 00	12 00	80°

Note: If latitude and declination are of the same sign, take out the respondent directly. If they are of opposite signs, subtract the respondent from 12h.

Table 1 gives the complete range of declinations in case any user wishes to calculate semi-diurnal arcs for bodies other than the Sun and Moon.

Example:

Lat.	Dec.	Semi-diurnal arc
+52°	+20°	7h 51m
+52°	−20°	4h 09m

TABLE 2. CORRECTION FOR REFRACTION AND SEMI-DIAMETER

	m	*m*	*m*	*m*	*m*	*m*	*m*	*m*	*m*	*m*	*m*	*m*	*m*
0°	3	3	4	4	4	5	5	5	6	6	6	7	0°
10°	3	3	4	4	4	5	5	6	6	6	7	7	10°
20°	4	4	4	4	5	5	6	7	7	8	8	9	20°
25°	4	4	4	4	5	6	7	8	8	9	11	13	25°
30°	4	4	4	5	6	7	8	9	11	14	21	—	30°

SUNRISE AND SUNSET

The local mean time of sunrise or sunset may be found by obtaining the hour angle from Table 1 and applying it to the time of transit. The hour angle is negative for sunrise and positive for sunset. A small correction to the hour angle, which always has the effect of increasing it numerically, is necessary to allow for the Sun's semi-diameter (16′) and for refraction (34′); it is obtained from Table 2. The resulting local mean time may be converted into the standard time of the country by taking the difference between the longitude of the standard meridian of the country and that of the place, adding it to the local mean time if the place is west of the standard meridian, and subtracting it if the place is east.

Example– Required the New Zealand Mean Time (12h fast on GMT) of sunset on May 23 at Auckland, latitude 36° 50′ S. (or minus), longitude 11h 39m E. Taking the declination as +20°.6 (page 651), we find

		h	*m*
New Zealand Standard Time	+	12	00
Longitude	–	11	39
Longitudinal Correction	+	0	21
Tabular entry for Lat. 30° and Dec. 20°, opposite signs	+	5	11
Proportional part for 6° 50′ of Lat.	–		15
Proportional part for 0°.6 of Dec.	–		2
Correction (Table 2)	+		4
Hour angle		4	58
Sun transits (page 651)		11	57
Longitudinal correction	+		21
New Zealand Mean Time		17	16

MOONRISE AND MOONSET

It is possible to calculate the times of moonrise and moonset using Table 1, though the method is more complicated because the apparent motion of the Moon is much more rapid and also more variable than that of the Sun.

TABLE 3. LONGITUDE CORRECTION

X	*40m*	*45m*	*50m*	*55m*	*60m*	*65m*	*70m*
A							
h	*m*	*m*	*m*	*m*	*m*	*m*	*m*
1	2	2	2	2	3	3	3
2	3	4	4	5	5	5	6
3	5	6	6	7	8	8	9
4	7	8	8	9	10	11	12
5	8	9	10	11	13	14	15
6	10	11	13	14	15	16	18
7	12	13	15	16	18	19	20
8	13	15	17	18	20	22	23
9	15	17	19	21	23	24	26
10	17	19	21	23	25	27	29
11	18	21	23	25	28	30	32
12	20	23	25	28	30	33	35
13	22	24	27	30	33	35	38
14	23	26	29	32	35	38	41
15	25	28	31	34	38	41	44
16	27	30	33	37	40	43	47
17	28	32	35	39	43	46	50
18	30	34	38	41	45	49	53
19	32	36	40	44	48	51	55
20	33	38	42	46	50	54	58
21	35	39	44	48	53	57	61
22	37	41	46	50	55	60	64
23	38	43	48	53	58	62	67
24	40	45	50	55	60	65	70

The parallax of the Moon, about 57′, is near to the sum of the semi-diameter and refraction but has the opposite effect on these times. It is thus convenient to neglect all three quantities in the method outlined below.

Notation

ϕ	= latitude of observer
λ	= longitude of observer (measured positively towards the west)
T_{-1}	= time of transit of Moon on previous day
T_0	= time of transit of Moon on day in question
T_1	= time of transit of Moon on following day
δ_0	= approximate declination of Moon
δ_R	= declination of Moon at moonrise
δ_S	= declination of Moon at moonset
h_0	= approximate hour angle of Moon
h_R	= hour angle of Moon at moonrise
h_S	= hour angle of Moon at moonset
t_R	= time of moonrise
t_S	= time of moonset

Method

1. With arguments ϕ, δ_0 enter Table 1 on page 682 to determine h_0 where h_0 is negative for moonrise and positive for moonset.

2. Form approximate times from
$t_R = T_0 + \lambda + h_0$
$t_S = T_0 + \lambda + h_0$

3. Determine δ_R, δ_S for times t_R, t_S respectively.

4. Re-enter Table 1 (as above) with
(*a*) arguments ϕ, δ_R to determine h_R
(*b*) arguments ϕ, δ_S to determine h_S

5. Form $t_R = T_0 + \lambda + h_R + AX$
$t_S = T_0 + \lambda + h_S + AX$

where $A = (\lambda + h)$

and $X = (T_0 - T_{-1})$ if $(\lambda + h)$ is negative
$X = (T_1 - T_0)$ if $(\lambda + h)$ is positive

AX is the respondent in Table 3.

Example – To find the times (GMT) of moonrise and moonset at Vancouver (ϕ = +49°, λ = +8h 12m) on 2010 January 10. The starting data (page 636) are
T_{-1} = 7h 15m
T_0 = 8h 06m
T_1 = 8h 58m
δ_0 = –23°

1. h_0 = 4h 02m
2. Approximate values
t_R = 10d 08h 06m + 8h 12m + (–4h 02m)
= 10d 12h 16m
t_S = 10d 08h 06m + 8h 12m + (+4h 02m)
= 10d 20h 20m
3. δ_R = –23°.5
δ_S = –24°.3
4. h_R = – 3h 59m
h_S = +3h 54m
5. t_R = 10d 08h 06m + 8h 12m + (–3h 59m) + 8m
= 10d 12h 27m
t_S = 10d 08h 06m + 8h 12m + (+3h 54m) + 25m
= 10d 20h 37m

To get the LMT of the phenomenon the longitude is subtracted from the GMT thus:

Moonrise = 10d 12h 27m – 8h 12m = 10d 04h 15m
Moonset = 10d 20h 37m – 8h 12m = 10d 12h 25m

ECLIPSES 2010

ECLIPSES

During 2010 there will be four eclipses, two of the Sun and two of the Moon. (Penumbral eclipses of the Moon are not mentioned in this section as they are so difficult to observe.)

1. An annular eclipse of the Sun on January 15 is visible as a partial eclipse from Africa, eastern Europe, Asia, and the Indian Ocean. The partial phase begins at 04h 05m and ends at 10h 07m. The annular phase starts on the border between Chad and the Central African Republic. It then crosses Zaire, Uganda, and Kenya, leaving land on the border between Kenya and the Somali Republic. It then crosses the Indian Ocean, the southern tip of India, northern Sri Lanka and Burma, before ending on the eastern coast of China. Annularity begins at 05h 14m and ends at 08h 59m.

2. A partial eclipse of the Moon on June 26 is visible from the Americas (except the extreme northerly parts and the extreme east of Brazil), the Pacific Ocean, Australasia, and eastern Asia. The eclipse begins at 10h 16m and ends at 13h 00m. At maximum eclipse 54 per cent of the Moon's surface is obscured.

3. A total eclipse of the Sun on July 11 is visible as a partial eclipse from the western and southern parts of South America. The partial phase begins at 17h 10m and ends at 21h 57m. The path of totality starts in the western South Pacific Ocean and ends in the extreme south of South America. Totality begins at 18h 15m and ends at 20h 52m.

4. A total eclipse of the Moon on December 21 is visible from Europe, north and west Africa, the Americas, Australasia (except for the extreme west of Western Australia) and Asia (except India). The partial phase begins at 06h 32m and ends at 10h 02m. Totality begins at 07h 40m and ends at 08h 53m.

POSITIONS OF STARS

The positions of heavenly bodies on the celestial sphere are defined by two co-ordinates, right ascension and declination, which are analogous to longitude and latitude on the surface of the Earth. If we imagine the plane of the terrestrial equator extended indefinitely, it will cut the celestial sphere in a great circle known as the celestial equator. Similarly the plane of the Earth's orbit, when extended, cuts in the great circle called the ecliptic. The two intersections of these circles are known as the First Point of Aries and the First Point of Libra. If from any star a perpendicular is drawn to the celestial equator, the length of this perpendicular is the star's declination. The arc, measured eastwards along the equator from the First Point of Aries to the foot of this perpendicular, is the right ascension. An alternative definition of right ascension is that it is the angle at the celestial pole (where the Earth's axis, if prolonged, would meet the sphere) between the great circles to the First Point of Aries and to the star.

The plane of the Earth's equator has a slow movement, so that our reference system for right ascension and declination is not fixed. The consequent alteration in these quantities from year to year is called precession. In right ascension it is an increase of about 3 seconds a year for equatorial stars, and larger or smaller changes in either direction for stars near the poles, depending on the right ascension of the star. In declination it varies between +20″ and −20″ according to the right ascension of the star.

A star or other body crosses the meridian when the sidereal time is equal to its right ascension. The altitude is then a maximum, and may be deduced by remembering that the altitude of the elevated pole is numerically equal to the latitude, while that of the equator at its intersection with the meridian is equal to the co-latitude, or complement of the latitude.

Thus in London (lat. 51° 30′) the meridian altitude of Sirius is found as follows:

	°	′
Altitude of equator	38	30
Declination south	16	43
Difference	21	47

The altitude of Capella (Dec. +46° 00′) at lower transit is:

Altitude of pole	51	30
Polar distance of star	44	00
Difference	7	30

The brightness of a heavenly body is denoted by its magnitude. Omitting the exceptionally bright stars Sirius and Canopus, the twenty brightest stars are of the first magnitude, while the faintest stars visible to the naked eye are of the sixth magnitude. The magnitude scale is a precise one, as a difference of five magnitudes represents a ratio of 100 to 1 in brightness. Typical second magnitude stars are Polaris and the stars in the belt of Orion. The scale is most easily fixed in memory by comparing the stars with Norton's *Star Atlas*. The stars Sirius and Canopus and the planets Venus and Jupiter are so bright that their magnitudes are expressed by negative numbers. A small telescope will show stars down to the ninth or tenth magnitude, while stars fainter than the twentieth magnitude may be photographed by long exposures with the largest telescopes.

MEAN AND SIDEREAL TIME

The length of a sidereal day in mean time is 23h 56m 04s.09. Hence 1h MT = 1h+9^s.86 ST and 1h ST = 1h − 9^s.83 MT.

Acceleration

h	*m*	*s*	*m*	*s*	*s*
1	0	10	0	00	0
2	0	20	3	02	1
3	0	30	9	07	2
4	0	39	15	13	3
5	0	49	21	18	4
6	0	59	27	23	5
7	1	09	33	28	6
8	1	19	39	34	7
9	1	29	45	39	8
10	1	39	51	44	9
11	1	48	57	49	10
12	1	58	60	00	
13	2	08			
14	2	18			
15	2	28			
16	2	38			
17	2	48			
18	2	57			
19	3	07			
20	3	17			
21	3	27			
22	3	37			
23	3	47			
24	3	57			

Retardation

h	*m*	*s*	*m*	*s*	*s*
1	0	10	0	00	0
2	0	20	3	03	1
3	0	29	9	09	2
4	0	39	15	15	3
5	0	49	21	21	4
6	0	59	27	28	5
7	1	09	33	34	6
8	1	19	39	40	7
9	1	28	45	46	8
10	1	38	51	53	9
11	1	48	57	59	10
12	1	58	60	00	
13	2	08			
14	2	18			
15	2	27			
16	2	37			
17	2	47			
18	2	57			
19	3	07			
20	3	17			
21	3	26			
22	3	36			
23	3	46			
24	3	56			

To convert an interval of mean time to the corresponding interval of sidereal time, enter the acceleration table with the given mean time (taking the hours and the minutes and seconds separately) and add the acceleration obtained to the given mean time. To convert an interval of sidereal time to the corresponding interval of mean time, take out the retardation for the given sidereal time and subtract.

The columns for the minutes and seconds of the argument are in the form known as critical tables. To use these tables, find in the appropriate left-hand column the two entries between which the given number of minutes and seconds lies; the quantity in the right-hand column between these two entries is the required acceleration or retardation. Thus the acceleration for 11m 26s (which lies between the entries 9m 07s and 15m 13s) is 2s. If the given number of minutes and seconds is a tabular entry, the required acceleration or retardation is the entry in the right-hand column above the given tabular entry, eg the retardation for 45m 46s is 7s.

Example – Convert 14h 27m 35s from ST to MT

	h	*m*	*s*
Given ST	14	27	35
Retardation for 14h		2	18
Retardation for 27m 35s			5
Corresponding MT	14	25	12

EXPLANATION OF ASTRONOMICAL DATA

Positions of the heavenly bodies are given only to the degree of accuracy required by amateur astronomers for setting telescopes, or for plotting on celestial globes or star atlases. Where intermediate positions are required, linear interpolation may be employed.

Definitions of the terms used cannot be given here. They must be sought in astronomical literature and textbooks.

A special feature has been made of the times when the various heavenly bodies are visible in the British Isles. Since two columns, calculated for latitudes 52° and 56°, are devoted to risings and settings, the range 50° to 58° can be covered by interpolation and extrapolation. The times given in these columns are Greenwich Mean Times for the meridian of Greenwich. An observer west of this meridian must add his/her longitude (in time) and vice versa.

In accordance with the usual convention in astronomy, + and – indicate respectively north and south latitudes or declinations.

All data are, unless otherwise stated, for 0h Greenwich Mean Time (GMT), ie at the midnight at the beginning of the day named. Allowance must be made for British Summer Time during the period that this is in operation.

PAGE ONE OF EACH MONTH

The calendar for each month is explained on page 633.

Under the heading Astronomical Phenomena will be found particulars of the more important conjunctions of the Sun, Moon and planets with each other, and also the dates of other astronomical phenomena of special interest.

Times of Minima of Algol are approximate times of the middle of the period of diminished light.

The Constellations listed each month are those that are near the meridian at the beginning of the month at 22h local mean time. Allowance must be made for British Summer Time if necessary. The fact that any star crosses the meridian 4m earlier each night or 2h earlier each month may be used, in conjunction with the lists given each month, to find what constellations are favourably placed at any moment. The table preceding the list of constellations may be extended indefinitely at the rate just quoted.

The principal phases of the Moon are the GMTs when the difference between the longitude of the Moon and that of the Sun is 0°, 90°, 180° or 270°. The times of perigee and apogee are those when the Moon is nearest to, and farthest from, the Earth, respectively. The nodes or points of intersection of the Moon's orbit and the ecliptic make a complete retrograde circuit of the ecliptic in about 19 years. From a knowledge of the longitude of the ascending node and the inclination, whose value does not vary much from 5°, the path of the Moon among the stars may be plotted on a celestial globe or star atlas.

PAGE TWO OF EACH MONTH

The Sun's semi-diameter, in arc, is given once a month.

The right ascension and declination (Dec.) is that of the true Sun. The right ascension of the mean Sun is obtained by applying the equation of time, with the sign given, to the right ascension of the true Sun, or, more easily, by applying 12h to the Sidereal Time. The direction in which the equation of time has to be applied in different problems is a frequent source of confusion and error. Apparent Solar Time is equal to the Mean Solar Time plus the Equation of Time. For example, at 12h GMT on August 8 the Equation of Time is –5m 39s and thus at 12h Mean Time on that day the Apparent Time is 12h – 5m 39s = 11h 54m 21s.

The Greenwich Sidereal Time at 0h and the Transit of the First Point of Aries (which is really the mean time when the sidereal time is 0h) are used for converting mean time to sidereal time and vice versa.

The GMT of transit of the Sun at Greenwich may also be taken as the local mean time (LMT) of transit in any longitude. It is independent of latitude. The GMT of transit in any longitude is obtained by adding the longitude to the time given if west, and vice versa.

LIGHTING-UP TIME

The legal importance of sunrise and sunset is that the Road Vehicles Lighting Regulations 1989 (SI 1989 No. 1796) as amended, make the use of front and rear position lamps on vehicles compulsory during the period between sunset and sunrise. Headlamps on vehicles are required to be used during the hours of darkness on unlit roads, on lit roads with a speed limit exceeding 30mph, or whenever visibility is seriously reduced. The hours of darkness are defined in these regulations as the period between half an hour after sunset and half an hour before sunrise.

In all laws and regulations 'sunset' refers to the local sunset, ie the time at which the Sun sets at the place in question. This common-sense interpretation has been upheld by legal tribunals. Thus the necessity for providing for different latitudes and longitudes, as already described, is evident.

SUNRISE AND SUNSET

The times of sunrise and sunset are those when the Sun's upper limb, as affected by refraction, is on the true horizon of an observer at sea-level. Assuming the mean refraction to be 34′, and the Sun's semi-diameter to be 16′, the time given is that when the true zenith distance of the Sun's centre is 90°+34′+16′ or 90° 50′, or, in other words, when the depression of the Sun's centre below the true horizon is 50′. The upper limb is then 34′ below the true horizon, but is brought there by refraction. An observer on a ship might see the Sun for a minute or so longer, because of the dip of the horizon, while another viewing the sunset over hills or mountains would record an earlier time. Nevertheless, the moment when the true zenith distance of the Sun's centre is 90° 50′ is a precise time dependent only on the latitude and longitude of the place, and independent of its altitude above sea-level, the contour of its horizon, the vagaries of refraction or the small seasonal change in the Sun's semi-diameter; this moment is suitable in every way as a definition of sunset (or sunrise) for all statutory purposes.

TWILIGHT

Light reaches us before sunrise and continues to reach us for some time after sunset. The interval between darkness and sunrise or sunset and darkness is called twilight. Astronomically speaking, twilight is considered to begin or end when the Sun's centre is 18° below the horizon, as no light from the Sun can then reach the observer. As thus defined twilight may last several hours; in high latitudes at the summer solstice the depression of 18° is not reached, and twilight lasts from sunset to sunrise.

The need for some sub-division of twilight is met by dividing the gathering darkness into four stages.

(1) *Sunrise or Sunset,* defined as above
(2) *Civil twilight,* which begins or ends when the Sun's centre is 6° below the horizon. This marks the time when operations requiring daylight may commence or must cease. In England it varies from about 30 to 60 minutes after sunset and the same interval before sunrise
(3) *Nautical twilight,* which begins or ends when the Sun's centre is 12° below the horizon. This marks the time when it is, to all intents and purposes, completely dark
(4) *Astronomical twilight,* which begins or ends when the Sun's centre is 18° below the horizon. This marks theoretical perfect darkness. It is of little practical importance, especially if nautical twilight is tabulated

To assist observers the durations of civil, nautical and astronomical twilights are given at intervals of ten days. The beginning of a particular twilight is found by subtracting the duration from the time of sunrise, while the end is found by adding the duration to the time of sunset. Thus the beginning of astronomical twilight in latitude 52°, on the Greenwich meridian, on March 11 is found as 06h 24m – 113m = 04h 31m and similarly the end of civil twilight as 17h 57m +34m = 18h 31m. The letters TAN (twilight all night) are printed when twilight lasts all night.

Under the heading The Night Sky will be found notes describing the position and visibility of the planets and other phenomena.

PAGE THREE OF EACH MONTH

The Moon moves so rapidly among the stars that its position is given only to the degree of accuracy that permits linear interpolation. The right ascension (RA) and declination (Dec.) are geocentric, ie for an imaginary observer at the centre of the Earth. To an observer on the surface of the Earth the position is always different, as the altitude is always less on account of parallax, which may reach 1°.

The lunar terminator is the line separating the bright from the dark part of the Moon's disk. Apart from irregularities of the lunar surface, the terminator is elliptical, because it is a circle seen in projection. It becomes the full circle forming the limb, or edge, of the Moon at New and Full Moon. The selenographic longitude of the terminator is measured from the mean centre of the visible disk, which may differ from the visible centre by as much as 8°, because of libration.

Instead of the longitude of the terminator the Sun's selenographic co-longitude (Sun's co-long.) is tabulated. It is numerically equal to the selenographic longitude of the morning terminator, measured eastwards from the mean centre of the disk. Thus its value is approximately 270° at New Moon, 360° at First Quarter, 90° at Full Moon and 180° at Last Quarter.

The Position Angle (PA) of the Bright Limb is the position angle of the midpoint of the illuminated limb, measured eastwards from the north point on the disk. The Phase column shows the percentage of the area of the Moon's disk illuminated; this is also the illuminated percentage of the diameter at right angles to the line of cusps. The terminator is a semi-ellipse whose major axis is the line of cusps, and whose semi-minor axis is determined by the tabulated percentage; from New Moon to Full Moon the east limb is dark, and vice versa.

The times given as moonrise and moonset are those when the upper limb of the Moon is on the horizon of an observer at sea-level. The Sun's horizontal parallax (Hor. par.) is about 9″, and is negligible when considering sunrise and sunset, but that of the Moon averages about 57′. Hence the computed time represents the moment when the true zenith distance of the Moon is 90° 50′ (as for the Sun) minus the horizontal parallax. The time required for the Sun or Moon to rise or set is about four minutes (except in high latitudes).

See also page 683 and footnote on page 687.

The GMT of transit of the Moon over the meridian of Greenwich is given; these times are independent of latitude but must be corrected for longitude. For places in the British Isles it suffices to add the longitude if west, and vice versa. For other places a further correction is necessary because of the rapid movement of the Moon relative to the stars. The entire correction is conveniently determined by first finding the west longitude λ of the place. If the place is in west longitude, λ is the ordinary west longitude; if the place is in east longitude λ is the complement to 24h (or 360°) of the longitude and will be greater than 12h (or 180°). The correction then consists of two positive portions, namely λ and the fraction $\lambda/24$ (or $\lambda°/360$) multiplied by the difference between consecutive transits. Thus for Christchurch, New Zealand, the longitude is 11h 31m east, so λ = 12h 29m and the fraction $\lambda/24$ is 0.52. The transit on the local date 8 April 2010 is found as follows:

		d	*h*	*m*
GMT of transit at Greenwich	April	7	06	54
λ			12	29
0.52 × (3h 37m – 2h 49m)				25
GMT of transit at Christchurch		7	19	48
Corr. to NZ Standard Time			12	00
Local standard time of transit	April	8	07	48

As is evident, for any given place the quantities λ and the correction to local standard time may be combined permanently, being here 24h 29m.

Positions of Mercury are given for every second day, and those of Venus and Mars for every fifth day; they may be interpolated linearly. The diameter (Diam.) is given in seconds of arc. The phase is the illuminated percentage of the disk. In the case of the inner planets this approaches 100 at superior conjunction and 0 at inferior conjunction. When the phase is less than 50 the planet is crescent-shaped or horned; for greater phases it is gibbous. In the case of the exterior planet Mars, the phase approaches 100 at conjunction and opposition, and is a minimum at the quadratures.

Since the planets cannot be seen when on the horizon, the actual times of rising and setting are not given; instead, the time when the planet has an apparent altitude of 5° has been tabulated. If the time of transit is between 00h and 12h the time refers to an altitude of 5° above the eastern horizon; if between 12h and 24h, to the western horizon. The phenomenon tabulated is the one that occurs between sunset and sunrise. The times given may be interpolated for latitude and corrected for longitude, as in the case of the Sun and Moon.

PAGE FOUR OF EACH MONTH

The GMTs of sunrise and sunset for seven cities, whose adopted positions in longitude (W.) and latitude (N.) are given immediately below the name, may be used not only for these phenomena, but also for lighting-up times (*see* page 685 for a fuller explanation).

The particulars for the four outer planets resemble those for the planets on Page Three of each month, except that, under Uranus and Neptune, times when the planet is 10° high instead of 5° high are given; this is because of the inferior brightness of these planets. The diameters given for the rings of Saturn are those of the major axis (in the plane of the planet's equator) and the minor axis respectively. The former has a small seasonal change due to the slightly varying distance of the Earth from Saturn, but the latter varies from zero when the Earth passes through the ring plane every 15 years to its maximum opening half-way between these periods. The rings were last open at their widest extent (and Saturn at its brightest) in 2002; this will occur again in 2017. The Earth passed through the ring plane in 2009.

TIME

From the earliest ages, the natural division of time into recurring periods of day and night has provided the practical time-scale for the everyday activities of the human race. Indeed, if any alternative means of time measurement is adopted, it must be capable of adjustment so as to remain in general agreement with the natural time-scale defined by the diurnal rotation of the Earth on its axis. Ideally the rotation should be measured against a fixed frame of reference; in practice it must be measured against the background provided by the celestial bodies. If the Sun is chosen as the reference point, we obtain Apparent Solar Time, which is the time indicated by a sundial. It is not a uniform time but is subject to variations which amount to as much as a quarter of an hour in each direction. Such wide variations cannot be tolerated in a practical time-scale, and this has led to the concept of Mean Solar Time in which all the days are exactly the same length and equal to the average length of the Apparent Solar Day.

The positions of the stars in the sky are specified in relation to a fictitious reference point in the sky known as the First Point of Aries (or the Vernal Equinox). It is therefore convenient to adopt this same reference point when considering the rotation of the Earth against the background of the stars. The time-scale so obtained is known as Apparent Sidereal Time.

GREENWICH MEAN TIME

The daily rotation of the Earth on its axis causes the Sun and the other heavenly bodies to appear to cross the sky from east to west. It is convenient to represent this relative motion as if the Sun really performed a daily circuit around a fixed Earth. Noon in Apparent Solar Time may then be defined as the time at which the Sun transits across the observer's meridian. In Mean Solar Time, noon is similarly defined by the meridian transit of a fictitious Mean Sun moving uniformly in the sky with the same average speed as the true Sun. Mean Solar Time observed on the meridian of the transit circle telescope of the Royal Observatory at Greenwich is called Greenwich Mean Time (GMT). The mean solar day is divided into 24 hours and, for astronomical and other scientific purposes, these are numbered 0 to 23, commencing at midnight. Civil time is usually reckoned in two periods of 12 hours, designated am (*ante meridiem,* ie before noon) and pm (*post meridiem,* ie after noon), although the 24 hour clock is increasingly being used.

UNIVERSAL TIME

Before 1925 January 1, GMT was reckoned in 24 hours commencing at noon; since that date it has been reckoned from midnight. To avoid confusion in the use of the designation GMT before and after 1925, since 1928 astronomers have tended to use the term Universal Time (UT) or Weltzeit (WZ) to denote GMT measured from Greenwich Mean Midnight.

In precision work it is necessary to take account of small variations in Universal Time. These arise from small irregularities in the rotation of the Earth. Observed astronomical time is designated UT0. Observed time corrected for the effects of the motion of the poles (giving rise to a 'wandering' in longitude) is designated UT1. There is also a seasonal fluctuation in the rate of rotation of the Earth arising from meteorological causes, often called the annual fluctuation. UT1 corrected for this effect is designated UT2 and provides a time-scale free from short-period fluctuations. It is still subject to small secular and irregular changes.

APPARENT SOLAR TIME

As mentioned above, the time shown by a sundial is called Apparent Solar Time. It differs from Mean Solar Time by an amount known as the Equation of Time, which is the

---

SUNRISE, SUNSET, MOONRISE AND MOONSET

The tables have been constructed for the meridian of Greenwich and for latitudes 52° and 56°. They give Greenwich Mean Time (GMT) throughout the year. To obtain the GMT of the phenomenon as seen from any other latitude and longitude in the British Isles, first interpolate or extrapolate for latitude by the usual rules of proportion. To the time thus found, the longitude (expressed in time) is to be added if west (as it usually is in Great Britain) or subtracted if east. If the longitude is expressed in degrees and minutes of arc, it must be converted to time at the rate of 1° = 4m and 15′ = 1m. A method of calculating rise and set time for other places in the world is given on page 683.

The GMT at which the planet transits the Greenwich meridian is also given. The times of transit are to be corrected to local meridians in the usual way, as already described.

total effect of two causes which make the length of the apparent solar day non-uniform. One cause of variation is that the orbit of the Earth is not a circle but an ellipse, having the Sun at one focus. As a consequence, the angular speed of the Earth in its orbit is not constant; it is greatest at the beginning of January when the Earth is nearest the Sun.

The other cause is due to the obliquity of the ecliptic; the plane of the equator (which is at right angles to the axis of rotation of the Earth) does not coincide with the ecliptic (the plane defined by the apparent annual motion of the Sun around the celestial sphere) but is inclined to it at an angle of 23° 26′. As a result, the apparent solar day is shorter than average at the equinoxes and longer at the solstices. From the combined effects of the components due to obliquity and eccentricity, the equation of time reaches its maximum values in February (−14 minutes) and early November (+16 minutes). It has a zero value on four dates during the year, and it is only on these dates (approximately April 15, June 14, September 1 and December 25) that a sundial shows Mean Solar Time.

SIDEREAL TIME

A sidereal day is the duration of a complete rotation of the Earth with reference to the First Point of Aries. The term sidereal (or 'star') time is a little misleading since the time-scale so defined is not exactly the same as that which would be defined by successive transits of a selected star, as there is a small progressive motion between the stars and the First Point of Aries due to the precession of the Earth's axis. This makes the length of the sidereal day shorter than the true period of rotation by 0.008 seconds. Superimposed on this steady precessional motion are small oscillations (nutation), giving rise to fluctuations in apparent sidereal time amounting to as much as 1.2 seconds. It is therefore customary to employ Mean Sidereal Time, from which these fluctuations have been removed. The conversion of GMT to Greenwich sidereal time (GST) may be performed by adding the value of the GST at 0h on the day in question (page two of each month) to the GMT converted to sidereal time using the table on page 684.

Example – To find the GST at August 8d 02h 41m 11s GMT

	h	*m*	*s*
GST at 0h	21	05	36
GMT	2	41	11
Acceleration for 2h			20
Acceleration for 41m 11s			7
Sum = GST =	23	47	14

If the observer is not on the Greenwich meridian then his/her longitude, measured positively westwards from Greenwich, must be subtracted from the GST to obtain Local Sidereal Time (LST). Thus, in the above example, an observer 5h east of Greenwich, or 19h west, would find the LST as 4h 48m 11s.

EPHEMERIS TIME

An analysis of observations of the positions of the Sun, Moon and planets taken over an extended period is used in preparing ephemerides. (An ephemeris is a table giving the apparent position of a heavenly body at regular intervals of time, eg one day or ten days, and may be used to compare current observations with tabulated positions.) Discrepancies between the positions of heavenly bodies observed over a 300-year period and their predicted positions arose because the time-scale to which the observations were related was based on the assumption that the rate of rotation of the Earth is uniform. It is now known that this rate of rotation is variable. A revised time-scale, Ephemeris Time (ET), was devised to bring the ephemerides into agreement with the observations.

The second of ET is defined in terms of the annual motion of the Earth in its orbit around the Sun (1/31556925.9747 of the tropical year for 1900 January 0d 12h ET). The precise determination of ET from astronomical observations is a lengthy process as the requisite standard of accuracy can only be achieved by averaging over a number of years.

In 1976 the International Astronomical Union adopted Terrestrial Dynamical Time (TDT), a new dynamical time-scale for general use whose scale unit is the SI second (*see* Atomic Time, below). TDT was renamed Terrestrial Time (TT) in 1991. ET is now of little more than historical interest.

TERRESTRIAL TIME

The uniform time system used in computing the ephemerides of the solar system is Terrestrial Time (TT), which has replaced ET for this purpose. Except for the most rigorous astronomical calculations, it may be assumed to be the same as ET. During 2010 the estimated difference TT − UT is about 66 seconds.

ATOMIC TIME

The fundamental standards of time and frequency must be defined in terms of a periodic motion adequately uniform, enduring and measurable. Progress has made it possible to use natural standards, such as atomic or molecular oscillations. Continuous oscillations are generated in an electrical circuit, the frequency of which is then compared or brought into coincidence with the frequency characteristic of the absorption or emission by the atoms or molecules when they change between two selected energy levels. Since the 13th General Conference on Weights and Measures in October 1967, the unit of time, the second, has been defined in the International System of units (SI) as 'the duration of 9 192 631 770 periods of the radiation corresponding to the transition between the two hyperfine levels of the ground state of the caesium-133 atom'.

In the UK, the national time scale is maintained by the National Physical Laboratory (NPL), using an ensemble of atomic clocks based on either caesium or hydrogen atoms. In addition the NPL (along with several other national laboratories) has constructed and operates a caesium fountain primary frequency standard, which utilises the cooling of caesium atoms by laser light to determine the duration of the SI second at the highest attainable level of accuracy. Caesium fountain primary standards typically achieve an accuracy of around 1 part in 1,000 000 000 000 000, which is equivalent to one second in 30 million years.

Timekeeping worldwide is based on two closely related atomic time scales that are established through international collaboration. International Atomic Time (TAI) is formed by combining the readings of more than 250 atomic clocks located in about 55 institutes and was set close to the astronomically based Universal Time (UT) near the beginning of 1958. It was formally recognised in 1971 and since 1988 January 1 has been maintained by the International Bureau of Weights and Measures

(BIPM). Civil time in almost all countries is now based on Coordinated Universal Time (UTC), which differs from TAI by an integer number of seconds and was designed to make both atomic time and UT available with accuracy appropriate for most users. On 1 January 1972 UTC was set to be exactly 10 seconds behind TAI, and since then the UTC time-scale has been adjusted by the insertion (or, in principle, omission) of leap seconds in order to keep it within ±0.9 s of UT. These leap seconds are introduced, when necessary, at the same instant throughout the world, either at the end of December or at the end of June. The last leap second occurred immediately prior to 0h UTC on 2009 January 1 and was the 24th leap second. All leap seconds so far have been positive, with 61 seconds in the final minute of the UTC month. The time 23h 59m 60s UTC is followed one second later by 0h 0m 00s of the first day of the following month. Notices concerning the insertion of leap seconds are issued by the International Earth Rotation and Reference Systems Service (IERS).

The computation of UTC is carried out monthly by the BIPM and takes place in three stages. First, a weighted average known as Echelle Atomique Libre (EAL) is calculated from all of the contributing atomic clocks. In the second stage, TAI is generated by applying small corrections, derived from the results contributed by primary frequency standards, to the scale interval of EAL to maintain its value close to that of the SI second. Finally, UTC is formed from TAI by the addition of an integer number of seconds. The results are published monthly in the BIPM Circular T in the form of offsets at 5-day intervals between UTC and the time scales of contributing organisations.

RADIO TIME SIGNALS

UTC is made generally available through time-signals and standard frequency broadcasts such as MSF in the UK, CHU in Canada and WWV and WWVH in the USA. These are based on national time-scales that are maintained in close agreement with UTC and provide traceability to the national time-scale and to UTC. The markers of seconds in the UTC scale coincide with those of TAI.

To disseminate the national time-scale in the UK, special signals (call-sign MSF) are broadcast by the National Physical Laboratory. From 2007 April 1 the MSF service, previously broadcast from British Telecom's radio station at Rugby, has been transmitted from Anthorn radio station in Cumbria. The signals are controlled from a caesium beam atomic frequency standard and consist of a precise frequency carrier of 60 kHz which is switched off, after being on for at least half a second, to mark every second. The first second of the minute begins with a period of 500 ms with the carrier switched off, to serve as a minute marker. In the other seconds the carrier is always off for at least one tenth of a second at the start and then it carries an on-off code giving the British clock time and date, together with information identifying the start of the next minute. Changes to and from summer time are made following government announcements. Leap seconds are inserted as announced by the IERS and information provided by them on the difference between UTC and UT is also signalled. Other broadcast signals in the UK include the BBC six pips signal, the BT Timeline ('speaking clock'), the NPL telephone and internet time services for computers, and a coded time-signal on the BBC 198 kHz transmitters which is used for timing in the electricity supply industry. From 1972 January 1 the six pips on the BBC have consisted of five short pips from second 55 to second 59 (six pips in the case of a leap second) followed by one lengthened pip, the start of which indicates the exact minute. From 1990 February 5 these signals have been controlled by the BBC with seconds markers referenced to the satellite-based US navigation system GPS (Global Positioning System) and time and day referenced to the MSF transmitter. Formerly they were generated by the Royal Greenwich Observatory. The NPL telephone and internet services are directly connected to the national time scale.

Accurate timing may also be obtained from the signals of international navigation systems such as the ground-based LORAN-C, or the satellite-based American GPS or Russian GLONASS systems.

STANDARD TIME

Since 1880 the standard time in Britain has been Greenwich Mean Time (GMT); a statute that year enacted that the word 'time' when used in any legal document relating to Britain meant, unless otherwise specifically stated, the mean time of the Greenwich meridian. Greenwich was adopted as the universal meridian on 13 October 1884. A system of standard time by zones is used worldwide, standard time in each zone differing from that of the Greenwich meridian by an integral number of hours or, exceptionally, half-hours or quarter-hours, either fast or slow. The large territories of the USA and Canada are divided into zones approximately 7.5° on either side of central meridians.

Variations from the standard time of some countries occur during part of the year; they are decided annually and are usually referred to as Summer Time or Daylight Saving Time.

At the 180th meridian the time can be either 12 hours fast on Greenwich Mean Time or 12 hours slow, and a change of date occurs. The internationally recognised date or calendar line is a modification of the 180th meridian, drawn so as to include islands of any one group on the same side of the line, or for political reasons. The line is indicated by joining up the following coordinates:

Lat.	*Long.*	*Lat.*	*Long.*
90° S.	180°	48° N.	180°
51° S.	180°	53° N.	170° E.
45° S.	172.5° W.	65.5° N.	169° W.
15° S.	172.5° W.	68° N.	169° W.
5° S.	180°	90° N.	180°

Changes to the date line would require an international conference.

BRITISH SUMMER TIME

In 1916 an Act ordained that during a defined period of that year the legal time for general purposes in Great Britain should be one hour in advance of Greenwich Mean Time. The Summer Time Acts 1922 and 1925 defined the period during which Summer Time was to be in force, stabilising practice until the Second World War.

During the Second World War (1941–5) and in 1947 Double Summer Time (two hours in advance of Greenwich Mean Time) was used for the period in which ordinary Summer Time would have been in force. During these years clocks were also kept one hour in advance of Greenwich Mean Time in the winter. After the war, ordinary Summer Time was invoked each year from 1948–68.

Between 1968 October 27 and 1971 October 31

clocks were kept one hour ahead of Greenwich Mean Time throughout the year. This was known as British Standard Time.

The most recent legislation is the Summer Time Act 1972, which enacted that 'the period of summer time for the purposes of this Act is the period beginning at two o'clock, Greenwich Mean Time, in the morning of the day after the third Saturday in March or, if that day is Easter Day, the day after the second Saturday in March, and ending at two o'clock, Greenwich Mean Time, in the morning of the day after the fourth Saturday in October.'

The duration of Summer Time can be varied by Order in Council and in recent years alterations have been made to synchronise the period of Summer Time in Britain with that used in Europe. The rule for 1981–94 defined the period of Summer Time in the UK as from the last Sunday in March to the day following the fourth Saturday in October and the hour of changeover was altered to 01h Greenwich Mean Time.

There was no rule for the dates of Summer Time between 1995–7. Since 1998 the 9th European Parliament and Council Directive on Summer Time has harmonised the dates on which Summer Time begins and ends across member states as the last Sundays in March and October respectively. Under the directive Summer Time begins and ends at 01hr Greenwich Mean Time in each member state. Amendments to the Summer Time Act to implement the directive came into force in 2002.

The duration of Summer Time in 2010 is:
March 28 01h GMT to October 31 01h GMT

MEAN REFRACTION

Alt. ° ′	Ref. ′	Alt. ° ′	Ref. ′	Alt. ° ′	Ref. ′
1 20		3 12		7 54	
	21		13		6
1 30		3 34		9 27	
	20		12		5
1 41		4 00		11 39	
	19		11		4
1 52		4 30		15 00	
	18		10		3
2 05		5 06		20 42	
	17		9		2
2 19		5 50		32 20	
	16		8		1
2 35		6 44		62 17	
	15		7		0
2 52		7 54		90 00	
	14				
3 12					

The refraction table is in the form of a critical table (*see* page 684).

ASTRONOMICAL CONSTANTS

Solar parallax	8″.794
Astronomical unit	149597870 km
Precession for the year 2010	50″.291
Precession in right ascension	$3^{s}.075$
Precession in declination	20″.043
Constant of nutation	9″.202
Constant of aberration	20″.496
Mean obliquity of ecliptic (2010)	23° 26′ 17″
Moon's equatorial hor. parallax	57′ 02″.70
Velocity of light in vacuo per second	299792.5 km
Solar motion per second	20.0 km
Equatorial radius of the Earth	6378.140 km
Polar radius of the Earth	6356.755 km
North galactic pole (IAU standard)	RA 12h 49m (1950.0). Dec.+27°.4 N.
Solar apex	RA 18h 06m Dec. +30°
Length of year (in mean solar days)	
Tropical	365.24219
Sidereal	365.25636
Anomalistic (perihelion to perihelion)	365.25964
Eclipse	346.62003

Length of month (mean values)	*d*	*h*	*m*	*s*
New Moon to New	29	12	44	02.9
Sidereal	27	07	43	11.5
Anomalistic (perigee to perigee)	27	13	18	33.2

THE EARTH

The shape of the Earth is that of an oblate spheroid or solid of revolution whose meridian sections are ellipses not differing much from circles, while the sections at right angles are circles. The length of the equatorial axis is about 12,756 km, and that of the polar axis is 12,714 km. The mean density of the Earth is 5.5 times that of water, although that of the surface layer is less. The Earth and Moon revolve about their common centre of gravity in a lunar month; this centre in turn revolves round the Sun in a plane known as the ecliptic, that passes through the Sun's centre. The Earth's equator is inclined to this plane at an angle of 23.4°. This tilt is the cause of the seasons. In mid-latitudes, and when the Sun is high above the Equator, not only does the high noon altitude make the days longer, but the Sun's rays fall more directly on the Earth's surface; these effects combine to produce summer. In equatorial regions the noon altitude is large throughout the year, and there is little variation in the length of the day. In higher latitudes the noon altitude is lower, and the days in summer are appreciably longer than those in winter.

The average velocity of the Earth in its orbit is 30km a second. It makes a complete rotation on its axis in about 23h 56m of mean time, which is the sidereal day. Because of its annual revolution round the Sun, the rotation with respect to the Sun, or the solar day, is more than this by about four minutes. The extremity of the axis of rotation, or the North Pole of the Earth, is not rigidly fixed, but wanders over an area roughly 20 metres in diameter.

ELEMENTS OF THE SOLAR SYSTEM

Orb	Mean distance from Sun (Earth = 1)	Mean distance from Sun km 10^6	Sidereal period days	Synodic period days	Incl. of orbit to ecliptic °	Incl. of orbit to ecliptic ′	Diameter km	Mass (Earth = 1)	Period of rotation on axis days
Sun	—	—	—	—	—		1,392,000	332,981	25–35*
Mercury	0.39	58	88.0	116	7	00	4,879	0.0553	58.646
Venus	0.72	108	224.7	584	3	24	12,104	0.8150	243.019*r*
Earth	1.00	150	365.3	—	—		12,756*e*	1.0000	0.997
Mars	1.52	228	687.0	780	1	51	6,794*e*	0.1074	1.026
Jupiter	5.20	778	4,332.6	399	1	18	142,984*e* 133,708*p*	317.83	0.410*e*
Saturn	9.55	1429	10,759.2	378	2	29	120,536*e* 108,728*p*	95.16	0.426*e*
Uranus	19.22	2875	30,684.6	370	0	46	51,118*e*	14.54	0.718*r*
Neptune	30.11	4504	60,191.2	367	1	46	49,528*e*	17.15	0.671
Pluto †	39.80	5954	91,708.2	367	17	09	2,390	0.002	6.387

e equatorial, *p* polar, *r* retrograde, * depending on latitude, † reclassified as a dwarf planet since August 2006

THE SATELLITES

	Name	Star mag.	Mean distance from primary km	Sidereal period of revolution d
EARTH				
I	Moon	—	384,400	27.322
MARS				
I	Phobos	11	9,378	0.319
II	Deimos	12	23,459	1.262
JUPITER				
XVI	Metis	17	127,960	0.295
XV	Adrastea	19	128,980	0.298
V	Amalthea	14	181,300	0.498
XIV	Thebe	16	221,900	0.675
I	Io	5	421,600	1.769
II	Europa	5	670,900	3.551
III	Ganymede	5	1,070,000	7.155
IV	Callisto	6	1,883,000	16.689
XIII	Leda	20	11,165,000	240.92
VI	Himalia	15	11,460,000	250.57
X	Lysithea	18	11,717,000	259.22
VII	Elara	17	11,741,000	259.65
XII	Ananke	19	21,276,000	629.77*r*
XI	Carme	18	23,404,000	734.17*r*
VIII	Pasiphae	17	23,624,000	743.63*r*
IX	Sinope	18	23,939,000	758.90*r*
SATURN				
XVIII	Pan	20	133,583	0.575
XV	Atlas	18	137,640	0.602
XVI	Prometheus	16	139,353	0.613
XVII	Pandora	16	141,700	0.629
XI	Epimetheus	15	151,422	0.694
X	Janus	14	151,472	0.695
I	Mimas	13	185,520	0.942
II	Enceladus	12	238,020	1.370
III	Tethys	10	294,660	1.888
XIII	Telesto	19	294,660	1.888
XIV	Calypso	19	294,660	1.888
IV	Dione	10	377,400	2.737
XII	Helene	18	377,400	2.737
V	Rhea	10	527,040	4.518
VI	Titan	8	1,221,850	15.945
VII	Hyperion	14	1,481,000	21.277
VIII	Iapetus	11	3,561,300	79.330
IX	Phoebe	16	12,952,000	550.48*r*
URANUS				
VI	Cordelia	24	49,770	0.335
VII	Ophelia	24	53,790	0.376
VIII	Bianca	23	59,170	0.435
IX	Cressida	22	61,780	0.464
X	Desdemona	22	62,680	0.474
XI	Juliet	21	64,350	0.493
XII	Portia	21	66,090	0.513
XIII	Rosalind	22	66,940	0.558
XIV	Belinda	22	75,260	0.624
XV	Puck	20	86,010	0.762
V	Miranda	16	129,390	1.413
I	Ariel	14	191,020	2.520
II	Umbriel	15	266,300	4.144
III	Titania	14	435,910	8.706
IV	Oberon	14	583,520	13.463
XVI	Caliban	22	7,230,000	579.5*r*
XX	Stephano	24	8,002,000	676.5*r*
XVII	Sycorax	21	12,179,000	1,283.4*r*
XVIII	Prospero	23	16,418,000	1,992.8*r*
XIX	Setebos	23	17,459,000	2,202.2*r*
NEPTUNE				
III	Naiad	25	48,230	0.294
IV	Thalassa	24	50,080	0.311
V	Despina	23	52,530	0.335
VI	Galatea	22	61,950	0.429
VII	Larissa	22	73,550	0.555
VIII	Proteus	20	117,650	1.122
I	Triton	13	354,760	5.877
II	Nereid	19	5,513,400	360.136
PLUTO				
I	Charon	17	19,600	6.387

Currently the total number of satellites of the outer planets are: Jupiter 62, Saturn 60, Uranus 27, Neptune 13, Pluto 3.

TERRESTRIAL MAGNETISM

The Earth's main magnetic field corresponds approximately to that of a very strong small bar magnet near the centre of the Earth, but with appreciable smooth spatial departures. The origin of the main field is generally ascribed to electric currents associated with fluid motions in the Earth's core. As a result not only does the main field vary in strength and direction from place to place, but also with time. Superimposed on the main field are local and regional anomalies whose magnitudes may in places approach that of the main field; these are due to the influence of mineral deposits in the Earth's crust. A small proportion of the field is of external origin, mostly associated with electric currents in the ionosphere. The configuration of the external field and the ionisation of the atmosphere depend on the incident particle and radiation flux from the Sun. There are, therefore, short-term and non-periodic as well as diurnal, 27-day, seasonal and 11-year periodic changes in the magnetic field, dependent upon the position of the Sun and the degree of solar activity.

A magnetic compass points along the horizontal component of a magnetic line of force. These lines of force converge on the 'magnetic dip-poles', the places where the Earth's magnetic field is vertical. These poles move with time, and their present approximate adopted mean positions are 85.2° N., 133.2° W. and 64.4° S., 137.4° E.

There is also a 'magnetic equator', at all points of which the vertical component of the Earth's magnetic field is zero and a magnetised needle remains horizontal. This line runs between 2° and 12° north of the geographical equator in Asia and Africa, turns sharply south off the west African coast, and crosses South America through Brazil, Bolivia and Peru; it re-crosses the geographical equator in mid-Pacific.

Reference has already been made to secular changes in the Earth's field. The following table indicates the changes in magnetic declination (or variation of the compass). Declination is the angle in the horizontal plane between the direction of true north and that in which a magnetic compass points. Similar, though much smaller, changes have occurred in 'dip' or magnetic inclination. Secular changes differ throughout the world. Although the London observations suggest a cycle with a period of several hundred years, an exact repetition is unlikely.

London				*Greenwich*			
1580	11°	15′	E.	1900	16°	29′	W.
1622	5°	56′	E.	1925	13°	10′	W.
1665	1°	22′	W.	1950	9°	07′	W.
1730	13°	00′	W.	1975	6°	39′	W.
1773	21°	09′	W.	1998	3°	32′	W.
1850	22°	24′	W.				

In order that up-to-date information on declination may be available, many governments publish magnetic charts on which there are lines (isogonic lines) passing through all places at which specified values of declination will be found at the date of the chart.

In the British Isles, isogonic lines now run approximately north-east to south-west. Though there are considerable local deviations due to geological causes, a rough value of magnetic declination may be obtained by assuming that at 50° N. on the meridian of Greenwich, the value in 2010 is 1° 10′ west and allowing an increase of 11′ for each degree of latitude northwards and one of 27′ for each degree of longitude westwards. For example, at 53° N., 5° W., declination will be about 1°10′ + 33′ + 135′, ie 3° 58′ west. The average annual change at the present time is about 10′ decrease.

The number of magnetic observatories is about 180, irregularly distributed over the globe. There are three in Great Britain, run by the British Geological Survey: at Hartland, north Devon; at Eskdalemuir, Dumfries and Galloway; and at Lerwick, Shetland Islands. The following are some recent annual mean values of the magnetic elements for Hartland.

Year	*Declination West* °	′	*Dip or inclination* °	′	*Horizontal intensity nanoTesla (nT)*	*Vertical intensity nT*
1960	9	58.8	66	43.9	18707	43504
1965	9	30.1	66	34.0	18872	43540
1970	9	06.5	66	26.1	19033	43636
1975	8	32.3	66	17.0	19212	43733
1980	7	43.8	66	10.3	19330	43768
1985	6	56.1	66	07.9	19379	43796
1990	6	15.0	66	09.7	19539	43896
1995	5	33.2	66	07.3	19457	43951
2000	4	43.6	66	06.9	19508	44051
2005	3	56.4	66	06.0	19576	44177
2008	3	29.8	66	03.4	19601	44224

As well as navigation at sea, in the air and on land by compass the oil industry depends on the Earth's magnetic field as a directional reference. They use magnetic survey tools when drilling well-bores and require accurate estimates of the local magnetic field, taking into account the crustal and external fields.

MAGNETIC STORMS

Occasionally, sometimes with great suddenness, the Earth's magnetic field is subject for several hours to marked disturbance. During a severe storm in October 2003 the declination at Eskdalemuir changed by over 5° in six minutes. In many instances such disturbances are accompanied by widespread displays of aurorae, marked changes in the incidence of cosmic rays, an increase in the reception of 'noise' from the Sun at radio frequencies, and rapid changes in the ionosphere and induced electric currents within the Earth which adversely affect satellite operations, telecommunications and electric power transmission systems. The disturbances are caused by changes in the stream of ionised particles which emanates from the Sun and through which the Earth is continuously passing. Some of these changes are associated with visible eruptions on the Sun, usually in the region of sun-spots. There is a marked tendency for disturbances to recur after intervals of about 27 days, the apparent period of rotation of the Sun on its axis, which is consistent with the sources being located on particular areas of the Sun.

TIME MEASUREMENT AND CALENDARS

MEASUREMENTS OF TIME

Measurements of time are based on the time taken by the earth to rotate on its axis (day); by the moon to revolve around the earth (month); and by the earth to revolve around the sun (year). From these, which are not commensurable, certain average or mean intervals have been adopted for ordinary use.

THE DAY

The day begins at midnight and is divided into 24 hours of 60 minutes, each of 60 seconds. The hours are counted from midnight up to 12 noon (when the sun crosses the meridian), and these hours are designated am *(ante meridiem)*; and again from noon up to 12 midnight, which hours are designated pm *(post meridiem)*, except when the 24-hour reckoning is employed. The 24-hour reckoning ignores am and pm, numbering the hours 0 to 23 from midnight.

Colloquially the 24 hours are divided into day and night, day being the time while the sun is above the horizon (including the four stages of twilight defined in the Astronomy section). Day is subdivided into morning, the early part of daytime, ending at noon; afternoon, from noon to about 6pm; and evening, which may be said to extend from 6pm until midnight. Night begins at the close of astronomical twilight (*see* the Astronomy section) and extends beyond midnight to sunrise the next day.

The names of the days are derived from Old English translations or adaptations of the Roman titles.

Sunday	Sol	Sun
Monday	Luna	Moon
Tuesday	Tiw/Tyr (god of war)	Mars
Wednesday	Woden/Odin	Mercury
Thursday	Thor	Jupiter
Friday	Frigga/Freyja (goddess of love)	Venus
Saturday	Saeterne	Saturn

THE MONTH

The month in the ordinary calendar is approximately the twelfth part of a year, but the lengths of the different months vary from 28 (or 29) days to 31.

THE YEAR

The equinoctial or tropical year is the time that the earth takes to revolve around the sun from equinox to equinox, ie 365.24219 mean solar days, or 365 days 5 hours 48 minutes and 45 seconds.

The calendar year usually consists of 365 days but a year containing 366 days is called a bissextile (*see* Roman calendar) or leap year, one day being added to the month of February so that a date 'leaps over' a day of the week. In the Roman calendar the day that was repeated was the sixth day before the beginning of March, the equivalent of 24 February.

A year is a leap year if the date of the year is divisible by four without remainder, unless it is the last year of the century. The last year of a century is a leap year only if its number is divisible by 400 without remainder, eg the years 1800 and 1900 had only 365 days but the year 2000 had 366 days.

THE SOLSTICE

A solstice is the point in the tropical year at which the sun attains its greatest distance, north or south, from the Equator. In the northern hemisphere the furthest point north of the Equator marks the summer solstice and the furthest point south marks the winter solstice.

The date of the solstice varies according to locality. For example, if the summer solstice falls on 21 June late in the day by Greenwich time, that day will be the longest of the year at Greenwich though it may be by only a second, but it will fall on 22 June, local date, in Japan, and so 22 June will be the longest day there. The date of the solstice is also affected by the length of the tropical year, which is 365 days 6 hours less about 11 minutes 15 seconds. If a solstice happens late on 21 June in one year, it will be nearly 6 hours later in the next (unless the next year is a leap year), ie early on 22 June, and that will be the longest day.

This delay of the solstice does not continue because the extra day in a leap year brings it back a day in the calendar. However, because of the 11 minutes 15 seconds mentioned above, the additional day in a leap year brings the solstice back too far by 45 minutes, and the time of the solstice in the calendar is earlier, in a four-year pattern, as the century progresses. The last year of a century is in most cases not a leap year, and the omission of the extra day puts the date of the solstice later by about 6 hours. Compensation for this is made by the fourth centennial year being a leap year. The solstice has become earlier in date throughout the last century and, because the year 2000 was a leap year, the solstice will get earlier still throughout the 21st century.

The date of the winter solstice, the shortest day of the year, is affected by the same factors as the longest day.

At Greenwich the sun sets at its earliest by the clock about ten days before the shortest day. The daily change in the time of sunset is due in the first place to the sun's movement southwards at this time of the year, which diminishes the interval between the sun's transit and its setting. However, the daily decrease of the Equation of Time causes the time of apparent noon to be continuously later day by day, which to some extent counteracts the first effect. The rates of the change of these two quantities are not equal or uniform; their combination causes the date of earliest sunset to be 12 or 13 December at Greenwich. In more southerly latitudes the effect of the movement of the sun is less, and the change in the time of sunset depends on that of the Equation of Time to a greater degree, and the date of earliest sunset is earlier than it is at Greenwich, eg on the Equator it is about 1 November.

THE EQUINOX

The equinox is the point at which the sun crosses the Equator and day and night are of equal length all over the world. This occurs in March and September.

DOG DAYS

The days about the heliacal rising of the Dog Star, noted from ancient times as the hottest period of the year in the northern hemisphere, are called the Dog Days. Their incidence has been variously calculated as depending on the Greater or Lesser Dog Star (Sirius or Procyon) and their duration has been reckoned as from 30 to 54 days. A generally accepted period is from 3 July to 15 August.

CHRISTIAN CALENDAR

In the Christian chronological system the years are distinguished by cardinal numbers before or after the birth of Christ, the period being denoted by the letters BC (Before Christ) or, more rarely, AC *(Ante Christum),* and AD (*Anno Domini* – In the Year of Our Lord). The correlative dates of the epoch are the fourth year of the 194th Olympiad, the 753rd year from the foundation of Rome, AM 3761 in Jewish chronology, and the 4714th year of the Julian period. The actual date of the birth of Christ is somewhat uncertain.

The system was introduced into Italy in the sixth century. Though first used in France in the seventh century, it was not universally established there until about the eighth century. It has been said that the system was introduced into England by St Augustine (AD 596), but it was probably not generally used until some centuries later. It was ordered to be used by the bishops at the Council of Chelsea (AD 816).

THE JULIAN CALENDAR

In the Julian calendar (adopted by the Roman Empire in 45 BC) all the centennial years were leap years, and for this reason towards the close of the 16th century there was a difference of ten days between the tropical and calendar years; the equinox fell on 11 March of the calendar, whereas at the time of the Council of Nicaea (AD 325), it had fallen on 21 March. In 1582 Pope Gregory ordained that 5 October should be called 15 October and that of the end-century years only the fourth should be a leap year.

THE GREGORIAN CALENDAR

The Gregorian calendar was adopted by Italy, France, Spain and Portugal in 1582, by Prussia, the Roman Catholic German states, Switzerland, Holland and Flanders on 1 January 1583, by Poland in 1586, Hungary in 1587, the Protestant German and Netherland states and Denmark in 1700, and by Great Britain and its Dominions (including the North American colonies) in 1752, by the omission of 11 days (3 September being reckoned as 14 September). Sweden omitted the leap day in 1700 but observed leap days in 1704 and 1708, and reverted to the Julian calendar by having two leap days in 1712; the Gregorian calendar was adopted in 1753 by the omission of 11 days (18 February being reckoned as 1 March). Japan adopted the calendar in 1872, China in 1912, Bulgaria in 1915, Turkey and Soviet Russia in 1918, Yugoslavia and Romania in 1919, and Greece in 1923.

In the same year that the change was made in England from the Julian to the Gregorian calendar, the beginning of the new year was also changed from 25 March to 1 January.

THE ORTHODOX CHURCHES

Some Orthodox churches still use the Julian reckoning but the majority of Greek Orthodox churches and the Romanian Orthodox Church have adopted a modified 'New Calendar', observing the Gregorian calendar for fixed feasts and the Julian for movable feasts.

The Orthodox Church year begins on 1 September. There are four fast periods and, in addition to Pascha (Easter), twelve great feasts, as well as numerous commemorations of the saints of the Old and New Testaments throughout the year.

THE DOMINICAL LETTER

The dominical letter is one of the letters A–G which are used to denote the Sundays in successive years. If the first day of the year is a Sunday the letter is A; if the second, B; the third, C; and so on. A leap year requires two letters, the first for 1 January to 29 February, the second for 1 March to 31 December.

EPIPHANY

The feast of the Epiphany, commemorating the manifestation of Christ, later became associated with the offering of gifts by the Magi. The day was of great importance from the time of the Council of Nicaea (AD 325), as the primate of Alexandria was charged at every Epiphany feast with the announcement in a letter to the churches of the date of the forthcoming Easter. The day was also of importance in Britain as it influenced dates, ecclesiastical and lay, eg Plough Monday, when work was resumed in the fields, fell on the Monday in the first full week after Epiphany.

LENT

The Teutonic word *Lent,* which denotes the fast preceding Easter, originally meant no more than the spring season; but from Anglo-Saxon times, at least, it has been used as the equivalent of the more significant Latin term *Quadragesima,* meaning the 'forty days' or, more literally, the fortieth day. Ash Wednesday is the first day of Lent, which ends at midnight before Easter Day.

PALM SUNDAY

Palm Sunday, the Sunday before Easter and the beginning of Holy Week, commemorates the triumphal entry of Christ into Jerusalem and is celebrated in Britain (when palm is not available) by branches of willow gathered for use in the decoration of churches on that day.

MAUNDY THURSDAY

Maundy Thursday is the day before Good Friday, the name itself being a corruption of *dies mandati* (day of the mandate) when Christ washed the feet of the disciples and gave them the mandate to love one another.

EASTER DAY

Easter Day is the first Sunday after the full moon which happens on, or next after, the 21st day of March; if the full moon happens on a Sunday, Easter Day is the Sunday after.

This definition is contained in an Act of Parliament (24 Geo. II c. 23) and explanation is given in the preamble to the Act that the day of full moon depends on certain tables that have been prepared. These tables are summarised in the early pages of the Book of Common Prayer. The moon referred to is not the real moon of the heavens, but a hypothetical moon on whose 'full' the date of Easter depends, and the lunations of this 'calendar' moon consist of 29 and 30 days alternately, with certain necessary modifications to make the date of its full agree as nearly as possible with that of the real moon, which is known as the Paschal Full Moon.

A FIXED EASTER

In 1928 the House of Commons agreed to a motion for the third reading of a bill proposing that Easter Day shall, in the calendar year next but one after the commencement of the Act and in all subsequent years, be the first Sunday after the second Saturday in April. Easter would thus fall on the second or third Sunday in April, ie between 9 and 15 April (inclusive). A clause in the bill provided that before it shall come into operation, regard shall be had to any opinion expressed officially by the various Christian churches. Efforts by the World Council of Churches to secure a unanimous choice of date for Easter by its member churches have so far been unsuccessful.

ROGATION DAYS

Rogation Days are the Monday, Tuesday and Wednesday preceding Ascension Day and from the fifth century were observed as public fasts with solemn processions and supplications. The processions were discontinued as religious observances at the Reformation, but survive in the ceremony known as 'beating the parish bounds'. Rogation Sunday is the Sunday before Ascension Day.

EMBER DAYS

The Ember days occur on the Wednesday, Friday and Saturday of the same week, four times a year. Used for the ordination of clergy, these days are set aside for fasting and prayer. The weeks in which they fall are: *(a)* after the third Sunday in Advent, *(b)* before the second Sunday in Lent, *(c)* before Trinity Sunday and *(d)* after Holy Cross day.

TRINITY SUNDAY

Trinity Sunday is eight weeks after Easter Day, on the Sunday following Pentecost (Whit Sunday). Subsequent Sundays are reckoned in the Book of Common Prayer calendar of the Church of England as 'after Trinity'.

Thomas Becket (1118–70) was consecrated Archbishop of Canterbury on the Sunday after Whit Sunday and his first act was to ordain that the day of his consecration should be held as a new festival in honour of the Holy Trinity. This observance spread from Canterbury throughout the whole of Christendom.

MOVEABLE FEASTS TO THE YEAR 2035

Year	*Ash Wednesday*	*Easter*	*Ascension*	*Pentecost (Whit Sunday)*	*Advent Sunday*
2010	17 February	4 April	13 May	23 May	28 November
2011	9 March	24 April	2 June	12 June	27 November
2012	22 February	8 April	17 May	27 May	2 December
2013	13 February	31 March	9 May	19 May	1 December
2014	5 March	20 April	29 May	8 June	30 November
2015	18 February	5 April	14 May	24 May	29 November
2016	10 February	27 March	5 May	15 May	27 November
2017	1 March	16 April	25 May	4 June	3 December
2018	14 February	1 April	10 May	20 May	2 December
2019	6 March	21 April	30 May	9 June	1 December
2020	26 February	12 April	21 May	31 May	29 November
2021	17 February	4 April	13 May	23 May	28 November
2022	2 March	17 April	26 May	5 June	27 November
2023	22 February	9 April	18 May	28 May	3 December
2024	14 February	31 March	9 May	19 May	1 December
2025	5 March	20 April	29 May	8 June	30 November
2026	18 February	5 April	14 May	24 May	29 November
2027	10 February	28 March	6 May	16 May	28 November
2028	1 March	16 April	25 May	4 June	3 December
2029	14 February	1 April	10 May	20 May	2 December
2030	6 March	21 April	30 May	9 June	1 December
2031	26 February	13 April	22 May	1 June	30 November
2032	11 February	28 March	6 May	16 May	28 November
2033	2 March	17 April	26 May	5 June	27 November
2034	22 February	9 April	18 May	28 May	3 December
2035	7 February	25 March	3 May	13 May	2 December

NOTES

Ash Wednesday (first day in Lent) can fall at earliest on 4 February and at latest on 10 March

Mothering Sunday (fourth Sunday in Lent) can fall at earliest on 1 March and at latest on 4 April

Easter Day can fall at earliest on 22 March and at latest on 25 April

Ascension Day is forty days after Easter Day and can fall at earliest on 30 April and at latest on 3 June

Pentecost (Whit Sunday) is seven weeks after Easter and can fall at earliest on 10 May and at latest on 13 June

Trinity Sunday is the Sunday after Whit Sunday

Corpus Christi falls on the Thursday after Trinity Sunday

Sundays after Pentecost – there are not less than 18 and not more than 23

Advent Sunday is the Sunday nearest to 30 November

EASTER DAYS AND DOMINICAL LETTERS 1500 TO 2035

Dates up to and including 1752 are according to the Julian calendar. For dominical letters in leap years, *see* note below

		1500–1599	1600–1699	1700–1799	1800–1899	1900–1999	2000–2035
March							
d	22	1573	1668	1761	1818		
e	23	1505/16	1600	1788	1845/56	1913	2008
f	24	1611/95	1706/99	1940			
g	25	1543/54	1627/38/49	1722/33/44	1883/94	1951	2035
A	26	1559/70/81/92	1654/65/76	1749/58/69/80	1815/26/37	1967/78/89	
b	27	1502/13/24/97	1608/87/92	1785/96	1842/53/64	1910/21/32	2005/16
c	28	1529/35/40	1619/24/30	1703/14/25	1869/75/80	1937/48	2027/32
d	29	1551/62	1635/46/57	1719/30/41/52	1807/12/91	1959/64/70	
e	30	1567/78/89	1651/62/73/84	1746/55/66/77	1823/34	1902/75/86/97	
f	31	1510/21/32/83/94	1605/16/78/89	1700/71/82/93	1839/50/61/72	1907/18/29/91	2002/13/24
April							
g	1	1526/37/48	1621/32	1711/16	1804/66/77/88	1923/34/45/56	2018/29
A	2	1553/64	1643/48	1727/38	1809/20/93/99	1961/72	
b	3	1575/80/86	1659/70/81	1743/63/68/74	1825/31/36	1904/83/88/94	
c	4	1507/18/91	1602/13/75/86/97	1708/79/90	1847/58	1915/20/26/99	2010/21
d	5	1523/34/45/56	1607/18/29/40	1702/13/24/95	1801/63/74/85/96	1931/42/53	2015/26
e	6	1539/50/61/72	1634/45/56	1729/35/40/60	1806/17/28/90	1947/58/69/80	
f	7	1504/77/88	1667/72	1751/65/76	1822/33/44	1901/12/85/96	
g	8	1509/15/20/99	1604/10/83/94	1705/87/92/98	1849/55/60	1917/28	2007/12
A	9	1531/42	1615/26/37/99	1710/21/32	1871/82	1939/44/50	2023/34
b	10	1547/58/69	1631/42/53/64	1726/37/48/57	1803/14/87/98	1955/66/77	
c	11	1501/12/63/74/85/96	1658/69/80	1762/73/84	1819/30/41/52	1909/71/82/93	2004
d	12	1506/17/28	1601/12/91/96	1789	1846/57/68	1903/14/25/36/98	2009/20
e	13	1533/44	1623/28	1707/18	1800/73/79/84	1941/52	2031
f	14	1555/60/66	1639/50/61	1723/34/45/54	1805/11/16/95	1963/68/74	
g	15	1571/82/93	1655/66/77/88	1750/59/70/81	1827/38	1900/06/79/90	2001
A	16	1503/14/25/36/87/98	1609/20/82/93	1704/75/86/97	1843/54/65/76	1911/22/33/95	2006/17/28
b	17	1530/41/52	1625/36	1715/20	1808/70/81/92	1927/38/49/60	2022/33
c	18	1557/68	1647/52	1731/42/56	1802/13/24/97	1954/65/76	
d	19	1500/79/84/90	1663/74/85	1747/67/72/78	1829/35/40	1908/81/87/92	
e	20	1511/22/95	1606/17/79/90	1701/12/83/94	1851/62	1919/24/30	2003/14/25
f	21	1527/38/49	1622/33/44	1717/28	1867/78/89	1935/46/57	2019/30
g	22	1565/76	1660	1739/53/64	1810/21/32	1962/73/84	
A	23	1508	1671		1848	1905/16	2000
b	24	1519	1603/14/98	1709/91	1859		2011
c	25	1546	1641	1736	1886	1943	

No dominical letter is placed against the intercalary day 29 February, but since it is still counted as a weekday and given a name, the series of letters moves back one day every leap year after intercalation. Thus, a leap year beginning with the dominical letter C will change to a year with the dominical letter B on 1 March

HINDU CALENDAR

The Hindu calendar is a luni-solar calendar of 12 months, each containing 29 days, 12 hours. Each month is divided into a light fortnight (Shukla or Shuddha) and a dark fortnight (Krishna or Vadya) based on the waxing and waning of the moon. In most parts of India the month starts with the light fortnight, ie the day after the new moon, although in some regions it begins with the dark fortnight, ie the day after the full moon.

The new year according to the civil calendar begins in the month of Chaitra (March/April) and ends in the month of Phalgun (March). The 12 months – Chaitra, Vaishakh, Jyeshtha, Ashadh, Shravan, Bhadrapad, Ashvin, Kartik, Margashirsh, Paush, Magh and Phalgun – have Sanskrit names derived from 12 asterisms (constellations). There are regional variations to the names of the months but the Sanskrit names are understood throughout India.

Every lunar month that has a solar transit is termed pure *(shuddha)*. The lunar month without a solar transit is impure *(mala)* and called an intercalary month. An intercalary month occurs approximately every 32 lunar months, whenever the difference between the Hindu year of 360 lunar days (354 days 8 hours solar time) and the 365 days 6 hours of the solar year reaches the length of one Hindu lunar month (29 days 12 hours).

The leap month may be added at any point in the Hindu year. The name given to the month varies according to when it occurs but is taken from the month immediately following it. There is no leap month in 2010.

The days of the week are called Raviwar (Sunday), Somawar (Monday), Mangalwar (Tuesday), Budhawar (Wednesday), Guruwar (Thursday), Shukrawar (Friday) and Shaniwar (Saturday). The names are derived from the Sanskrit names of the sun, the moon and five planets, Mars, Mercury, Jupiter, Venus and Saturn.

Most fasts and festivals are based on the lunar calendar but a few are determined by the apparent movement of the sun, eg Sankranti and Pongal (in southern India), which are celebrated on 14/15 January to mark the start of the Sun's apparent journey northwards and a change of season.

Festivals celebrated throughout India are Chaitra (the New Year), Raksha-bandhan (the renewal of the kinship bond between brothers and sisters), Navaratri (a nine-night festival dedicated to the goddess Parvati), Dasara (the victory of Rama over the demon army), Diwali (a festival of lights), Makara Sankranti, Shivaratri (dedicated to Shiva), and Holi (a spring festival). British Hindus commonly celebrate the festival of Diwali as the start of the new year instead of observing it at the beginning of Chaitra.

Regional festivals are Durga-puja (dedicated to the goddess Durga (Parvati)), Sarasvati-puja (dedicated to the goddess Sarasvati), Ganesh Chaturthi (worship of Ganesh on the fourth day (Chaturthi) of the light half of Bhadrapad), Ramanavami (the birth festival of the god Rama) and Janmashtami (the birth festival of the god Krishna).

The main festivals celebrated in Britain are Navaratri, Dasara, Durga-puja, Diwali, Holi, Sarasvati-puja, Ganesh Chaturthi, Raksha-bandhan, Ramanavami and Janmashtami.

For dates of the main festivals in 2010, *see* page 9.

JEWISH CALENDAR

The story of the Flood in the Book of Genesis indicates the use of a calendar of some kind and that the writers recognised 30 days as the length of a lunation. However, after the diaspora, Jewish communities were left in considerable doubt as to the times of fasts and festivals. This led to the formation of the Jewish calendar as used today. It is said that this was done in AD 358 by Rabbi Hillel II, though some assert that it did not happen until much later.

The calendar is luni-solar, and is based on the lengths of the lunation and of the tropical year as found by Hipparchus (*c.*120 BC), which differ little from those adopted at the present day. The year AM 5770 (2009–10) is the 13th year of the 304th Metonic (Minor or Lunar) cycle of 19 years and the 2nd year of the 207th Solar (or Major) cycle of 28 years since the Era of the Creation. Jews hold that the Creation occurred at the time of the autumnal equinox in the year known in the Christian calendar as 3760 BC (954 of the Julian period). The epoch or starting point of Jewish chronology corresponds to 7 October 3761 BC. At the beginning of each solar cycle, the Tekufah of Nisan (the vernal equinox) returns to the same day and to the same hour.

The hour is divided into 1,080 minims, and the month between one new moon and the next is reckoned as 29 days 12 hours 793 minims. The normal calendar year, called a regular common year, consists of 12 months of 30 days and 29 days alternately. Since 12 months such as these comprise only 354 days, in order that each of them shall not diverge greatly from an average place in the solar year, a 13th month is occasionally added after the fifth month of the civil year (which commences on the first day of the month Tishri), or as the penultimate month of the ecclesiastical year (which commences on the first day of the month Nisan). The years when this happens are called Embolismic or leap years.

Of the 19 years that form a Metonic cycle, seven are leap years; they occur at places in the cycle indicated by the numbers 3, 6, 8, 11, 14, 17 and 19, these places being chosen so that the accumulated excesses of the solar years should be as small as possible.

A Jewish year is of one of the following six types:

Minimal common	353 days
Regular common	354 days
Full common	355 days
Minimal leap	383 days
Regular leap	384 days
Full leap	385 days

The regular year has alternate months of 30 and 29 days. In a Full year Marcheshvan, the second month of the civil year, has 30 days instead of 29; in minimal years Kislev, the third month, has 29 instead of 30. The additional month in leap years is called Adar Sheni and precedes the month called Adar Rishon; the usual Adar festivals are observed in Adar Sheni. In a leap year Adar I has 30 days, in all other years it has 29. None of the variations mentioned are allowed to change the number of days in the other months, which still follow the alternation of the normal 12.

These are the main features of the Jewish calendar, which must be considered permanent because as a Jewish law it cannot be altered except by a Great Sanhedrin.

The Jewish day begins between sunset and nightfall. The time used is that of the meridian of Jerusalem, which is 2h 21m in advance of Greenwich Mean Time. Rules for the beginning of sabbaths and festivals were laid down for the latitude of London in the 18th century and hours for nightfall are fixed annually by the Chief Rabbi.

JEWISH CALENDAR 5770–71

AM 5770 is a full common year of 12 months, 51 sabbaths and 355 days. AM 5771 is a regular leap year of 13 months, 55 sabbaths and 384 days.

Month (length)	AM 5770	AM 5771
Tishri 1 (30)	19 September 2009	9 September
Marcheshvan 1 (30)	19 October	9 October
Kislev 1 (30)	18 November	8 November
Tebet 1 (29)	18 December	8 December
Shebat 1 (30)	16 January 2010	6 January 2011
**Adar II* (30)		
†*Adar 1* (29/30)	15 February	
Nisan 1 (30)	16 March	
Iyar 1 (29)	15 April	
Sivan 1 (30)	14 May	
Tammuz 1 (29)	13 June	
Ab 1 (30)	12 July	
Elul 1 (29)	11 August	

* Additional month in leap years, known as Adar Sheni

† Known as Adar Rishon in leap years

JEWISH FASTS AND FESTIVALS

For dates of principal festivals in 2010, *see* page 9.

Tishri 1–2	Rosh Hashanah (New Year)
Tishri 3	*Fast of Gedaliah
Tishri 10	Yom Kippur (Day of Atonement)
Tishri 15–21	Succoth (Feast of Tabernacles)
Tishri 21	Hoshana Rabba
Tishri 22	Shemini Atseret (Solemn Assembly)
Tishri 23	Simchat Torah (Rejoicing of the Law)
Kislev 25	Hanukkah (Dedication of the Temple) begins
Tebet 10	Fast of Tebet
†*Adar* 13	§Fast of Esther
†*Adar* 14	Purim
†*Adar* 15	Shushan Purim
Nisan 15–22	Pesach (Passover)
Sivan 6–7	Shavuoth (Feast of Weeks)
Tammuz 17	*Fast of Tammuz
Ab 9	*Fast of Ab

* If these dates fall on the sabbath the fast is kept on the following day

† Adar Sheni in leap years

§ This fast is observed on Adar 11 (or Adar Sheni 11 in leap years) if Adar 13 falls on a sabbath

MUSLIM CALENDAR

The Muslim era is dated from the *Hijrah,* or flight of the Prophet Muhammad from Mecca to Medina, the corresponding date of which in the Julian calendar is 16 July AD 622. The lunar *hijri* calendar is used principally in Iran, Egypt, Malaysia, Pakistan, Mauritania, various Arab states and certain parts of India. Iran uses the solar hijri calendar as well as the lunar hijri calendar. The dating system was adopted about AD 639, commencing with the first day of the month Muharram.

The lunar calendar consists of 12 months containing an alternate sequence of 30 and 29 days, with the intercalation of one day at the end of the 12th month at stated intervals in each cycle of 30 years. The object of the intercalation is to reconcile the date of the first day of the month with the date of the actual new moon.

Some adherents still take the date of the evening of the first physical sighting of the crescent of the new moon as that of the first of the month. If cloud obscures the moon the present month may be extended to 30 days, after which the new month will begin automatically regardless of whether the moon has been seen. (Under religious law a month must have less than 31 days.) This means that the beginning of a new month and the date of religious festivals can vary from the published calendars.

In each cycle of 30 years, 19 years are common and contain 354 days, and 11 years are intercalary (leap years) of 355 days, the latter being called *kabisah.* The mean length of the Hijrah years is 354 days 8 hours 48 minutes and the period of mean lunation is 29 days 12 hours 44 minutes.

To ascertain if a year is common or kabisah, divide it by 30: the quotient gives the number of completed cycles and the remainder shows the place of the year in the current cycle. If the remainder is 2, 5, 7, 10, 13, 16, 18, 21, 24, 26 or 29, the year is kabisah and consists of 355 days.

MUSLIM CALENDAR 1431–32

Hijrah 1431 AH (remainder 21) is a kabisah year and 1432 (remainder 22) is a common year. Calendar dates below are estimates based on calculations of moon phases.

Month (length)	1431 AH	1432 AH
Muharram 1 (30)	28 December 2009	7 December
Safar 1 (29)	17 January 2010	6 January 2011
Rabi' I 1 (30)	15 February	
Rabi' II 1 (29)	17 March	
Jumada I 1 (30)	15 April	
Jumada II 1 (29)	15 May	
Rajab 1 (30)	13 June	
Sha'ban 1 (29)	13 July	
Ramadan 1 (30)	11 August	
Shawwal 1 (29)	10 September	
Dhu'l-Qa'da 1 (30)	9 October	
Dhu'l-Hijjah 1 (30)	8 November	

MUSLIM FESTIVALS

Ramadan is a month of fasting for all Muslims because it is the month in which the revelation of the *Qur'an* (Koran) began. During Ramadan, Muslims abstain from food, drink and sexual pleasure from dawn until after sunset throughout the month.

The two major festivals are *Eid ul-Fitr* and *Eid ul-Adha.* Eid ul-Fitr marks the end of the Ramadan fast and is celebrated on the day after the sighting of the new moon of the following month. Eid ul-Adha, the festival of sacrifice (also known as the great festival), celebrates the submission of the Prophet Ibrahim (Abraham) to God. Eid ul-Adha falls on the tenth day of Dhu'l-Hijjah, coinciding with the day when those on *hajj* (pilgrimage to Mecca) sacrifice animals.

Other days accorded special recognition are:

Muharram 1	New Year's Day
Muharram 10	Ashura (the day Prophet Noah left the Ark and Prophet Moses was saved from Pharaoh (Sunni), the death of the Prophet's grandson Husain (Shi'ite))
Rabi'u-l-Awwal (Rabi' I) 12	Mawlid ul-Nabi (birthday of the Prophet Muhammad)
Rajab 27	Laylat ul-Isra' wa'l-Mi'raj (The Night of Journey and Ascension)
*Ramadan**	Laylat ul-Qadr (Night of Power)
Dhu'l-Hijjah 10	Eid ul-Adha (Festival of Sacrifice)

* Moveable feast

For dates of the major celebrations in 2010, *see* page 9.

SIKH CALENDAR

The Sikh calendar is a lunar calendar of 365 days divided into 12 months. The length of the months varies between 29 and 32 days.

There are no prescribed feast days and no fasting periods. The main celebrations are Baisakhi Mela (the new year and the anniversary of the founding of the Khalsa), Diwali Mela (festival of light), Hola Mohalla Mela (a spring festival held in the Punjab), and the Gurpurbs (anniversaries associated with the ten Gurus).

For dates of the major celebrations in 2010, *see* page 9.

THAI CALENDAR

Thailand adopted the Suriyakati calendar, a modified version of the Gregorian calendar during the reign of King Rama V in 1888, using 1 April as the first day of the year. In 1940 the date of the new year was changed to 1 January. The years are counted from the beginning of the Buddhist era (BE), which is calculated to have commenced upon the death of the Lord Buddha, taken to have occurred in 543 BC, so AD 2010 is BE 2553. The Chinese system of associating years with one of twelve animals is also in use in Thailand. The Chantarakati lunar calendar is used to determine religious holidays; the new year begins on the first day of the waxing moon in November or, if there is a leap month, in December.

CIVIL AND LEGAL CALENDAR

THE HISTORICAL YEAR

Before 1752, two calendar systems were used in England. The civil or legal year began on 25 March and the historical year on 1 January. Thus the civil or legal date 24 March 1658 was the same day as the historical date 24 March 1659; a date in that portion of the year is written as 24 March 1658/9, the earlier date showing the civil or legal year.

THE NEW YEAR

In England in the seventh century, and as late as the 13th, the year was reckoned from Christmas Day, but in the 12th century the Church in England began the year with the feast of the Annunciation of the Blessed Virgin ('Lady Day') on 25 March, and this practice was adopted generally in the 14th century. The civil or legal year in the British dominions (exclusive of Scotland) began with

Lady Day until 1751. But in and since 1752 the civil year has begun with 1 January. New Year's Day in Scotland was changed from 25 March to 1 January in 1600.

Elsewhere in Europe, 1 January was adopted as the first day of the year by Venice in 1522, German states in 1544, Spain, Portugal and the Roman Catholic Netherlands in 1556, Prussia, Denmark and Sweden in 1559, France in 1564, Lorraine in 1579, the Protestant Netherlands in 1583, Russia in 1725, and Tuscany in 1751.

REGNAL YEARS

Regnal years are the years of a sovereign's reign and each begins on the anniversary of his or her accession, eg regnal year 59 of the present queen begins on 6 February 2010.

The system was used for dating Acts of Parliament until 1962. The Summer Time Act 1925, for example, is quoted as 15 and 16 Geo. V c. 64, because it became law in the parliamentary session which extended over part of both of these regnal years. Acts of a parliamentary session during which a sovereign died were usually given two year numbers, the regnal year of the deceased sovereign and the regnal year of his or her successor, eg those passed in 1952 were dated 16 Geo. VI and 1 Elizabeth II. Since 1962 Acts of Parliament have been dated by the calendar year.

QUARTER AND TERM DAYS

Holy days and saints days were the usual means in early times for setting the dates of future and recurrent appointments. The quarter days in England and Wales are the feast of the Nativity (25 December), the feast of the Annunciation (25 March), the feast of St John the Baptist (24 June) and the feast of St Michael and All Angels (29 September).

The term days in Scotland are Candlemas (the feast of the Purification), Whitsunday, Lammas (Loaf Mass) and Martinmas (St Martin's Day). These fell on 2 February, 15 May, 1 August and 11 November respectively. However, by the Term and Quarter Days (Scotland) Act 1990, the dates of the term days were changed to 28 February (Candlemas), 28 May (Whitsunday), 28 August (Lammas) and 28 November (Martinmas).

RED-LETTER DAYS

Red-letter days were originally the holy days and saints days indicated in early ecclesiastical calendars by letters printed in red ink. The days to be distinguished in this way were approved at the Council of Nicaea in AD 325.

These days still have a legal significance, as judges of the Queen's Bench Division wear scarlet robes on red-letter days falling during the law sittings. The days designated as red-letter days for this purpose are:

Holy and saints days

The Conversion of St Paul, the Purification, Ash Wednesday, the Annunciation, the Ascension, the feasts of St Mark, SS Philip and James, St Matthias, St Barnabas, St John the Baptist, St Peter, St Thomas, St James, St Luke, SS Simon and Jude, All Saints, St Andrew.

Civil calendar (for dates, *see* page 9)

The anniversaries of the Queen's accession, the Queen's birthday and the Queen's coronation, the Queen's official birthday, the birthday of the Duke of Edinburgh, the birthday of the Prince of Wales, St David's Day and Lord Mayor's Day.

PUBLIC HOLIDAYS

Public holidays are divided into two categories, common law and statutory. Common law holidays are holidays 'by habit and custom'; in England, Wales and Northern Ireland these are Good Friday and Christmas Day.

Statutory public holidays, known as bank holidays, were first established by the Bank Holidays Act 1871. They were, literally, days on which the banks (and other public institutions) were closed and financial obligations due on that day were payable the following day. The legislation currently governing public holidays in the UK, which is the Banking and Financial Dealings Act 1971, stipulates the days that are to be public holidays in England, Wales, Scotland and Northern Ireland.

If a public holiday falls on a Saturday or a Sunday then another day will be given in lieu, usually the following Monday. For example, Christmas Day in 2010 falls on a Saturday, so Monday 27 December will be a 'substitute' holiday. For dates of public holidays in 2010 and 2011, *see* pages 10–11. The public holidays are:

England and Wales

*New Year's Day
Good Friday
Easter Monday
*The first Monday in May
The last Monday in May
The last Monday in August
Christmas Day
Boxing Day

Scotland

New Year's Day
*2 January
Good Friday
The first Monday in May
*The last Monday in May
The first Monday in August
† St Andrew's Day
Christmas Day
Boxing Day

Northern Ireland

*New Year's Day
Good Friday
17 March
Easter Monday
*The first Monday in May
The last Monday in May
‡12 July
The last Monday in August
Christmas Day
Boxing Day

* Granted annually by royal proclamation
† Voluntary public holiday in exchange for an existing local holiday
‡ Subject to proclamation by the secretary of state for Northern Ireland

CHRONOLOGICAL CYCLES AND ERAS

SOLAR (OR MAJOR) CYCLE

The solar cycle is a period of 28 years; in any corresponding year of each cycle the days of the week recur on the same day of the month.

METONIC (LUNAR, OR MINOR) CYCLE

In 432 BC, Meton, an Athenian astronomer, found that 235 lunations are very nearly, though not exactly, equal in duration to 19 solar years and so after 19 years the phases of the Moon recur on the same days of the month (nearly). The dates of full moon in a cycle of 19 years were inscribed in figures of gold on public monuments in Athens, and the number showing the position of a year in the cycle is called the golden number of that year.

JULIAN PERIOD

The Julian period was proposed by Joseph Scaliger in 1582. The period is 7,980 Julian years, and its first year coincides with the year 4713 BC. The figure of 7980 is the product of the number of years in the solar cycle, the Metonic cycle and the cycle of the Roman indiction (28 × 19 × 15).

ROMAN INDICTION

The Roman indiction is a period of 15 years, instituted for fiscal purposes about AD 300.

EPACT

The epact is the age of the calendar Moon, diminished by one day, on 1 January, in the ecclesiastical lunar calendar.

CHINESE CALENDAR

A lunar calendar was the sole calendar in use in China until 1911, when the government adopted the new (Gregorian) calendar for official and most business activities. The Chinese tend to follow both calendars, the lunar calendar playing an important part in personal life, eg birth celebrations, festivals, marriages; and in rural villages the lunar calendar dictates the cycle of activities, denoting the change of weather and farming activities.

The lunar calendar is used in Hong Kong, Singapore, Malaysia, Tibet and elsewhere in south-east Asia. The calendar has a cycle of 60 years. The new year begins at the first new moon after the sun enters the sign of Aquarius, ie the new year falls between 21 January and 19 February in the Gregorian calendar.

Each year in the Chinese calendar is associated with one of 12 animals: the rat, the ox, the tiger, the rabbit, the dragon, the snake, the horse, the goat or sheep, the monkey, the chicken or rooster, the dog, and the pig.

The date of the Chinese new year and the astrological sign for the years 2010–13 are:

2010	14 February	Tiger
2011	3 February	Rabbit
2012	23 January	Dragon
2013	10 February	Snake

COPTIC CALENDAR

In the Coptic calendar, which is used in parts of Egypt and Ethiopia, the year is made up of 12 months of 30 days each, followed, in general, by five complementary days. Every fourth year is an intercalary or leap year and in these years there are six complementary days. The intercalary year of the Coptic calendar immediately precedes the leap year of the Julian calendar. The era is that of Diocletian or the Martyrs, the origin of which is fixed at 29 August AD 284 (Julian date).

INDIAN ERAS

In addition to the Muslim reckoning, other eras are used in India. The Saka era of southern India, dating from 3 March AD 78, was declared the national calendar of the Republic of India with effect from 22 March 1957, to be used concurrently with the Gregorian calendar. As revised, the year of the new Saka era begins at the spring equinox, with five successive months of 31 days and seven of 30 days in ordinary years, and six months of each length in leap years. The year AD 2010 is 1932 of the revised Saka era.

The year AD 2010 corresponds to the following years in other eras:

Year 2067 of the Vikram Samvat era
Year 1417 of the Bengali San era
Year 1186 of the Kollam era
Year 5111 of the Kaliyuga era
Year 2553 of the Buddha Nirvana era

JAPANESE CALENDAR

The Japanese calendar is essentially the same as the Gregorian calendar, the years, months and weeks being of the same length and beginning on the same days as those of the Gregorian calendar. The numeration of the years is different, based on a system of epochs or periods, each of which begins at the accession of an emperor or other important occurrence. The method is not unlike the British system of regnal years, except that each year of a period closes on 31 December. The Japanese chronology begins about AD 650 and the three latest epochs are defined by the reigns of emperors, whose actual names are not necessarily used:

Epoch
Taisho – 1 August 1912 to 25 December 1926
Showa – 26 December 1926 to 7 January 1989
Heisei – 8 January 1989

The year Heisei 22 begins on 1 January 2010.

The months are known as First Month, Second Month, etc, First Month being equivalent to January. The days of the week are Nichiyobi (Sun-day), Getsuyobi (Moon-day), Kayobi (Fire-day), Suiyobi (Water-day), Mokuyobi (Wood-day), Kinyobi (Metal-day) and Doyobi (Earth-day).

THE MASONIC YEAR

Two dates are quoted in warrants, dispensations, etc, issued by the United Grand Lodge of England, those for the current year being expressed as *Anno Domini* 2010 – *Anno Lucis* 6010. This *Anno Lucis* (year of light) is based on the Book of Genesis 1:3, the 4,000-year difference being derived, in modified form, from *Ussher's Notation,* published in 1654, which places the Creation of the World in 4004 BC.

OLYMPIADS

Ancient Greek chronology was reckoned in Olympiads, cycles of four years corresponding with the periodic Olympic Games held on the plain of Olympia, in Elis, once every four years. The intervening years were the first, second, etc, of the Olympiad, which received the name of the victor at the Games. The first recorded Olympiad is that of Choroebus, 776 BC.

ZOROASTRIAN CALENDAR

Zoroastrians, followers of the Iranian prophet Zarathushtra (known to the Greeks as Zoroaster) are mostly to be found in Iran and in India, where they are known as Parsees.

The Zoroastrian era dates from the coronation of the last Zoroastrian Sasanian king in AD 631. The Zoroastrian calendar is divided into 12 months, each comprising 30 days, followed by five holy days of the Gathas at the end of each year to make the year consist of 365 days.

In order to synchronise the calendar with the solar year of 365 days, an extra month was intercalated once every

120 years. However, this intercalation ceased in the 12th century and the new year, which had fallen in the spring, slipped back to August. Because intercalation ceased at different times in Iran and India, there was one month's difference between the calendar followed in Iran (Kadmi calendar) and that followed by the Parsees (Shenshai calendar). In 1906 a group of Zoroastrians decided to bring the calendar back in line with the seasons again and restore the new year to 21 March each year (Fasli calendar).

The Shenshai calendar (new year in August) is mainly used by Parsees. The Fasli calendar (new year, 21 March) is mainly used by Zoroastrians living in Iran, in the Indian subcontinent, or away from Iran.

ROMAN CALENDAR

Roman historians adopted as an epoch the foundation of Rome, which is believed to have happened in the year 753 BC. The ordinal number of the years in Roman reckoning is followed by the letters AUC *(ab urbe condita)*, so that the year 2010 is 2763 AUC (MMDCCLXII). The calendar that we know has developed from one said to have been established by Romulus using a year of 304 days divided into ten months, beginning with March. To this Numa added January and February, making the year consist of 12 months of 30 and 29 days alternately, with an additional day so that the total was 355. It is also said that Numa ordered an intercalary month of 22 or 23 days in alternate years, making 90 days in eight years, to be inserted after 23 February.

However, there is some doubt as to the origination and the details of the intercalation in the Roman calendar. It is certain that some scheme of this kind was inaugurated and not fully carried out, for in the year 46 BC Julius Caesar found that the calendar had been allowed to fall into some confusion. He sought the help of the Egyptian astronomer Sosigenes, which led to the construction and adoption (45 BC) of the Julian calendar, and, by a slight alteration, to the Gregorian calendar now in use. The year 46 BC was made to consist of 445 days and is called the Year of Confusion.

In the Roman (Julian) calendar the days of the month were counted backwards from three fixed points, or days, and an intervening day was said to be so many days before the next coming point, the first and last being counted. These three points were the Kalends, the Nones, and the Ides. Their positions in the months and the method of counting from them will be seen in the table below. The year containing 366 days was called *bissextilis annus*, as it had a doubled sixth day *(bissextus dies)* before the March Kalends on 24 February – *ante diem sextum Kalendas Martias*, or a.d. VI Kal. Mart.

Present days of the month	*March, May, July, October have thirty-one days*		*January, August, December have thirty-one days*		*April, June, September, November have thirty days*		*February has twenty-eight days, and in leap year twenty-nine*	
1	Kalendis		Kalendis		Kalendis		Kalendis	
2	VI		IV	ante	IV	ante	IV	ante
3	V	ante	III	Nonas	III	Nonas	III	Nonas
4	IV	Nonas	pridie Nonas		pridie Nonas		pridie Nonas	
5	III		Nonis		Nonis		Nonis	
6	pridie Nonas		VIII		VIII		VIII	
7	Nonis		VII		VII		VII	
8	VIII		VI	ante	VI	ante	VI	ante
9	VII		V	Idus	V	Idus	V	Idus
10	VI	ante	IV		IV		IV	
11	V	Idus	III		III		III	
12	IV		pridie Idus		pridie Idus		pridie Idus	
13	III		Idibus		Idibus		Idibus	
14	pridie Idus		XIX		XVIII		XVI	
15	Idibus		XVIII		XVII		XV	
16	XVII		XVII		XVI		XIV	
17	XVI		XVI		XV		XIII	
18	XV		XV		XIV		XII	
19	XIV		XIV		XIII		XI	
20	XIII		XIII		XII	ante Kalendas	X	ante Kalendas
21	XII		XII	ante Kalendas	XI	(of the month	IX	Martias
22	XI	ante Kalendas	XI	(of the month	X	following)	VIII	
23	X	(of the month	X	following)	IX		VII	
24	IX	following)	IX		VIII		*VI	
25	VIII		VIII		VII		V	
26	VII		VII		VI		IV	
27	VI		VI		V		III	
28	V		V		IV		pridie Kalendas Martias	
29	IV		IV		III			
30	III		III		pridie Kalendas (Maias, Quinctilis, Octobris, Decembris)			
31	pridie Kalendas (Aprilis, Iunias, Sextilis, Novembris)		pridie Kalendas (Februarias, Septembris, Ianuarias)					

* Repeated in leap year

CALENDAR FOR ANY YEAR 1780–2040

To select the correct calendar for any year between 1780 and 2040, consult the index below

*leap year

1780 N*	1813 K	1846 I	1879 G	1912 D*	1945 C	1978 A	2011 M
1781 C	1814 M	1847 K	1880 J*	1913 G	1946 E	1979 C	2012 B*
1782 E	1815 A	1848 N*	1881 M	1914 I	1947 G	1980 F*	2013 E
1783 G	1816 D*	1849 C	1882 A	1915 K	1948 J*	1981 I	2014 G
1784 J*	1817 G	1850 E	1883 C	1916 N*	1949 M	1982 K	2015 I
1785 M	1818 I	1851 G	1884 F*	1917 C	1950 A	1983 M	2016 L*
1786 A	1819 K	1852 J*	1885 I	1918 E	1951 C	1984 B*	2017 A
1787 C	1820 N*	1853 M	1886 K	1919 G	1952 F*	1985 E	2018 C
1788 F*	1821 C	1854 A	1887 M	1920 J*	1953 I	1986 G	2019 E
1789 I	1822 E	1855 C	1888 B*	1921 M	1954 K	1987 I	2020 H*
1790 K	1823 G	1856 F*	1889 E	1922 A	1955 M	1988 L*	2021 K
1791 M	1824 J*	1857 I	1890 G	1923 C	1956 B*	1989 A	2022 M
1792 B*	1825 M	1858 K	1891 I	1924 F*	1957 E	1990 C	2023 A
1793 E	1826 A	1859 M	1892 L*	1925 I	1958 G	1991 E	2024 D*
1794 G	1827 C	1860 B*	1893 A	1926 K	1959 I	1992 H*	2025 G
1795 I	1828 F*	1861 E	1894 C	1927 M	1960 L*	1993 K	2026 I
1796 L*	1829 I	1862 G	1895 E	1928 B*	1961 A	1994 M	2027 K
1797 A	1830 K	1863 I	1896 H*	1929 E	1962 C	1995 A	2028 N*
1798 C	1831 M	1864 L*	1897 K	1930 G	1963 E	1996 D*	2029 C
1799 E	1832 B*	1865 A	1898 M	1931 I	1964 H*	1997 G	2030 E
1800 G	1833 E	1866 C	1899 A	1932 L*	1965 K	1998 I	2031 G
1801 I	1834 G	1867 E	1900 C	1933 A	1966 M	1999 K	2032 J*
1802 K	1835 I	1868 H*	1901 E	1934 C	1967 A	2000 N*	2033 M
1803 M	1836 L*	1869 K	1902 G	1935 E	1968 D*	2001 C	2034 A
1804 B*	1837 A	1870 M	1903 I	1936 H*	1969 G	2002 E	2035 C
1805 E	1838 C	1871 A	1904 L*	1937 K	1970 I	2003 G	2036 F*
1806 G	1839 E	1872 D*	1905 A	1938 M	1971 K	2004 J*	2037 I
1807 I	1840 H*	1873 G	1906 C	1939 A	1972 N*	2005 M	2038 K
1808 L*	1841 K	1874 I	1907 E	1940 D*	1973 C	2006 A	2039 M
1809 A	1842 M	1875 K	1908 H*	1941 G	1974 E	2007 C	2040 B*
1810 C	1843 A	1876 N*	1909 K	1942 I	1975 G	2008 F*	
1811 E	1844 D*	1877 C	1910 M	1943 K	1976 J*	2009 I	
1812 H*	1845 G	1878 E	1911 A	1944 N*	1977 M	2010 K	

A

	January	*February*	*March*
Sun.	1 8 15 22 29	5 12 19 26	5 12 19 26
Mon.	2 9 16 23 30	6 13 20 27	6 13 20 27
Tue.	3 10 17 24 31	7 14 21 28	7 14 21 28
Wed.	4 11 18 25	1 8 15 22	1 8 15 22 29
Thur.	5 12 19 26	2 9 16 23	2 9 16 23 30
Fri.	6 13 20 27	3 10 17 24	3 10 17 24 31
Sat.	7 14 21 28	4 11 18 25	4 11 18 25

	April	*May*	*June*
Sun.	2 9 16 23 30	7 14 21 28	4 11 18 25
Mon.	3 10 17 24	1 8 15 22 29	5 12 19 26
Tue.	4 11 18 25	2 9 16 23 30	6 13 20 27
Wed.	5 12 19 26	3 10 17 24 31	7 14 21 28
Thur.	6 13 20 27	4 11 18 25	1 8 15 22 29
Fri.	7 14 21 28	5 12 19 26	2 9 16 23 30
Sat.	1 8 15 22 29	6 13 20 27	3 10 17 24

	July	*August*	*September*
Sun.	2 9 16 23 30	6 13 20 27	3 10 17 24
Mon.	3 10 17 24 31	7 14 21 28	4 11 18 25
Tue.	4 11 18 25	1 8 15 22 29	5 12 19 26
Wed.	5 12 19 26	2 9 16 23 30	6 13 20 27
Thur.	6 13 20 27	3 10 17 24 31	7 14 21 28
Fri.	7 14 21 28	4 11 18 25	1 8 15 22 29
Sat.	1 8 15 22 29	5 12 19 26	2 9 16 23 30

	October	*November*	*December*
Sun.	1 8 15 22 29	5 12 19 26	3 10 17 24 31
Mon.	2 9 16 23 30	6 13 20 27	4 11 18 25
Tue.	3 10 17 24 31	7 14 21 28	5 12 19 26
Wed.	4 11 18 25	1 8 15 22 29	6 13 20 27
Thur.	5 12 19 26	2 9 16 23 30	7 14 21 28
Fri.	6 13 20 27	3 10 17 24	1 8 15 22 29
Sat.	7 14 21 28	4 11 18 25	2 9 16 23 30

EASTER DAYS

March 26	1815, 1826, 1837, 1967, 1978, 1989
April 2	1809, 1893, 1899, 1961
April 9	1871, 1882, 1939, 1950, 2023, 2034
April 16	1786, 1797, 1843, 1854, 1865, 1911 1922, 1933, 1995, 2006, 2017
April 23	1905

B (LEAP YEAR)

	January	*February*	*March*
Sun.	1 8 15 22 29	5 12 19 26	4 11 18 25
Mon.	2 9 16 23 30	6 13 20 27	5 12 19 26
Tue.	3 10 17 24 31	7 14 21 28	6 13 20 27
Wed.	4 11 18 25	1 8 15 22 29	7 14 21 28
Thur.	5 12 19 26	2 9 16 23	1 8 15 22 29
Fri.	6 13 20 27	3 10 17 24	2 9 16 23 30
Sat.	7 14 21 28	4 11 18 25	3 10 17 24 31

	April	*May*	*June*
Sun.	1 8 15 22 29	6 13 20 27	3 10 17 24
Mon.	2 9 16 23 30	7 14 21 28	4 11 18 25
Tue.	3 10 17 24	1 8 15 22 29	5 12 19 26
Wed.	4 11 18 25	2 9 16 23 30	6 13 20 27
Thur.	5 12 19 26	3 10 17 24 31	7 14 21 28
Fri.	6 13 20 27	4 11 18 25	1 8 15 22 29
Sat.	7 14 21 28	5 12 19 26	2 9 16 23 30

	July	*August*	*September*
Sun.	1 8 15 22 29	5 12 19 26	2 9 16 23 30
Mon.	2 9 16 23 30	6 13 20 27	3 10 17 24
Tue.	3 10 17 24 31	7 14 21 28	4 11 18 25
Wed.	4 11 18 25	1 8 15 22 29	5 12 19 26
Thur.	5 12 19 26	2 9 16 23 30	6 13 20 27
Fri.	6 13 20 27	3 10 17 24 31	7 14 21 28
Sat.	7 14 21 28	4 11 18 25	1 8 15 22 29

	October	*November*	*December*
Sun.	7 14 21 28	4 11 18 25	2 9 16 23 30
Mon.	1 8 15 22 29	5 12 19 26	3 10 17 24 31
Tue.	2 9 16 23 30	6 13 20 27	4 11 18 25
Wed.	3 10 17 24 31	7 14 21 28	5 12 19 26
Thur.	4 11 18 25	1 8 15 22 29	6 13 20 27
Fri.	5 12 19 26	2 9 16 23 30	7 14 21 28
Sat.	6 13 20 27	3 10 17 24	1 8 15 22 29

EASTER DAYS

April 1	1804, 1888, 1956, 2040
April 8	1792, 1860, 1928, 2012
April 22	1832, 1984

C

	January	*February*	*March*
Sun.	7 14 21 28	4 11 18 25	4 11 18 25
Mon.	1 8 15 22 29	5 12 19 26	5 12 19 26
Tue.	2 9 16 23 30	6 13 20 27	6 13 20 27
Wed.	3 10 17 24 31	7 14 21 28	7 14 21 28
Thur.	4 11 18 25	1 8 15 22	1 8 15 22 29
Fri.	5 12 19 26	2 9 16 23	2 9 16 23 30
Sat.	6 13 20 27	3 10 17 24	3 10 17 24 31

	April	*May*	*June*
Sun.	1 8 15 22 29	6 13 20 27	3 10 17 24
Mon.	2 9 16 23 30	7 14 21 28	4 11 18 25
Tue.	3 10 17 24	1 8 15 22 29	5 12 19 26
Wed.	4 11 18 25	2 9 16 23 30	6 13 20 27
Thur.	5 12 19 26	3 10 17 24 31	7 14 21 28
Fri.	6 13 20 27	4 11 18 25	1 8 15 22 29
Sat.	7 14 21 28	5 12 19 26	2 9 16 23 30

	July	*August*	*September*
Sun.	1 8 15 22 29	5 12 19 26	2 9 16 23 30
Mon.	2 9 16 23 30	6 13 20 27	3 10 17 24
Tue.	3 10 17 24 31	7 14 21 28	4 11 18 25
Wed.	4 11 18 25	1 8 15 22 29	5 12 19 26
Thur.	5 12 19 26	2 9 16 23 30	6 13 20 27
Fri.	6 13 20 27	3 10 17 24 31	7 14 21 28
Sat.	7 14 21 28	4 11 18 25	1 8 15 22 29

	October	*November*	*December*
Sun.	7 14 21 28	4 11 18 25	2 9 16 23 30
Mon.	1 8 15 22 29	5 12 19 26	3 10 17 24 31
Tue.	2 9 16 23 30	6 13 20 27	4 11 18 25
Wed.	3 10 17 24 31	7 14 21 28	5 12 19 26
Thur.	4 11 18 25	1 8 15 22 29	6 13 20 27
Fri.	5 12 19 26	2 9 16 23 30	7 14 21 28
Sat.	6 13 20 27	3 10 17 24	1 8 15 22 29

EASTER DAYS

March 25	1883, 1894, 1951, 2035
April 1	1866, 1877, 1923, 1934, 1945, 2018, 2029
April 8	1787, 1798, 1849, 1855, 1917, 2007
April 15	1781, 1827, 1838, 1900, 1906, 1979, 1990, 2001
April 22	1810, 1821, 1962, 1973

D (LEAP YEAR)

	January	*February*	*March*
Sun.	7 14 21 28	4 11 18 25	3 10 17 24 31
Mon.	1 8 15 22 29	5 12 19 26	4 11 18 25
Tue.	2 9 16 23 30	6 13 20 27	5 12 19 26
Wed.	3 10 17 24 31	7 14 21 28	6 13 20 27
Thur.	4 11 18 25	1 8 15 22 29	7 14 21 28
Fri.	5 12 19 26	2 9 16 23	1 8 15 22 29
Sat.	6 13 20 27	3 10 17 24	2 9 16 23 30

	April	*May*	*June*
Sun.	7 14 21 28	5 12 19 26	2 9 16 23 30
Mon.	1 8 15 22 29	6 13 20 27	3 10 17 24
Tue.	2 9 16 23 30	7 14 21 28	4 11 18 25
Wed.	3 10 17 24	1 8 15 22 29	5 12 19 26
Thur.	4 11 18 25	2 9 16 23 30	6 13 20 27
Fri.	5 12 19 26	3 10 17 24 31	7 14 21 28
Sat.	6 13 20 27	4 11 18 25	1 8 15 22 29

	July	*August*	*September*
Sun.	7 14 21 28	4 11 18 25	1 8 15 22 29
Mon.	1 8 15 22 29	5 12 19 26	2 9 16 23 30
Tue.	2 9 16 23 30	6 13 20 27	3 10 17 24
Wed.	3 10 17 24 31	7 14 21 28	4 11 18 25
Thur.	4 11 18 25	1 8 15 22 29	5 12 19 26
Fri.	5 12 19 26	2 9 16 23 30	6 13 20 27
Sat.	6 13 20 27	3 10 17 24 31	7 14 21 28

	October	*November*	*December*
Sun.	6 13 20 27	3 10 17 24	1 8 15 22 29
Mon.	7 14 21 28	4 11 18 25	2 9 16 23 30
Tue.	1 8 15 22 29	5 12 19 26	3 10 17 24 31
Wed.	2 9 16 23 30	6 13 20 27	4 11 18 25
Thur.	3 10 17 24 31	7 14 21 28	5 12 19 26
Fri.	4 11 18 25	1 8 15 22 29	6 13 20 27
Sat.	5 12 19 26	2 9 16 23 30	7 14 21 28

EASTER DAYS

March 24	1940
March 31	1872, 2024
April 7	1844, 1912, 1996
April 14	1816, 1968

E

	January	*February*	*March*
Sun.	6 13 20 27	3 10 17 24	3 10 17 24 31
Mon.	7 14 21 28	4 11 18 25	4 11 18 25
Tue.	1 8 15 22 29	5 12 19 26	5 12 19 26
Wed.	2 9 16 23 30	6 13 20 27	6 13 20 27
Thur.	3 10 17 24 31	7 14 21 28	7 14 21 28
Fri.	4 11 18 25	1 8 15 22	1 8 15 22 29
Sat.	5 12 19 26	2 9 16 23	2 9 16 23 30

	April	*May*	*June*
Sun.	7 14 21 28	5 12 19 26	2 9 16 23 30
Mon.	1 8 15 22 29	6 13 20 27	3 10 17 24
Tue.	2 9 16 23 30	7 14 21 28	4 11 18 25
Wed.	3 10 17 24	1 8 15 22 29	5 12 19 26
Thur.	4 11 18 25	2 9 16 23 30	6 13 20 27
Fri.	5 12 19 26	3 10 17 24 31	7 14 21 28
Sat.	6 13 20 27	4 11 18 25	1 8 15 22 29

	July	*August*	*September*
Sun.	7 14 21 28	4 11 18 25	1 8 15 22 29
Mon.	1 8 15 22 29	5 12 19 26	2 9 16 23 30
Tue.	2 9 16 23 30	6 13 20 27	3 10 17 24
Wed.	3 10 17 24 31	7 14 21 28	4 11 18 25
Thur.	4 11 18 25	1 8 15 22 29	5 12 19 26
Fri.	5 12 19 26	2 9 16 23 30	6 13 20 27
Sat.	6 13 20 27	3 10 17 24 31	7 14 21 28

	October	*November*	*December*
Sun.	6 13 20 27	3 10 17 24	1 8 15 22 29
Mon.	7 14 21 28	4 11 18 25	2 9 16 23 30
Tue.	1 8 15 22 29	5 12 19 26	3 10 17 24 31
Wed.	2 9 16 23 30	6 13 20 27	4 11 18 25
Thur.	3 10 17 24 31	7 14 21 28	5 12 19 26
Fri.	4 11 18 25	1 8 15 22 29	6 13 20 27
Sat.	5 12 19 26	2 9 16 23 30	7 14 21 28

EASTER DAYS

March 24	1799
March 31	1782, 1793, 1839, 1850, 1861, 1907 1918, 1929, 1991, 2002, 2013
April 7	1822, 1833, 1901, 1985
April 14	1805, 1811, 1895, 1963, 1974
April 21	1867, 1878, 1889, 1935, 1946, 1957, 2019, 2030

F (LEAP YEAR)

	January	*February*	*March*
Sun.	6 13 20 27	3 10 17 24	2 9 16 23 30
Mon.	7 14 21 28	4 11 18 25	3 10 17 24 31
Tue.	1 8 15 22 29	5 12 19 26	4 11 18 25
Wed.	2 9 16 23 30	6 13 20 27	5 12 19 26
Thur.	3 10 17 24 31	7 14 21 28	6 13 20 27
Fri.	4 11 18 25	1 8 15 22 29	7 14 21 28
Sat.	5 12 19 26	2 9 16 23	1 8 15 22 29

	April	*May*	*June*
Sun.	6 13 20 27	4 11 18 25	1 8 15 22 29
Mon.	7 14 21 28	5 12 19 26	2 9 16 23 30
Tue.	1 8 15 22 29	6 13 20 27	3 10 17 24
Wed.	2 9 16 23 30	7 14 21 28	4 11 18 25
Thur.	3 10 17 24	1 8 15 22 29	5 12 19 26
Fri.	4 11 18 25	2 9 16 23 30	6 13 20 27
Sat.	5 12 19 26	3 10 17 24 31	7 14 21 28

	July	*August*	*September*
Sun.	6 13 20 27	3 10 17 24 31	7 14 21 28
Mon.	7 14 21 28	4 11 18 25	1 8 15 22 29
Tue.	1 8 15 22 29	5 12 19 26	2 9 16 23 30
Wed.	2 9 16 23 30	6 13 20 27	3 10 17 24
Thur.	3 10 17 24 31	7 14 21 28	4 11 18 25
Fri.	4 11 18 25	1 8 15 22 29	5 12 19 26
Sat.	5 12 19 26	2 9 16 23 30	6 13 20 27

	October	*November*	*December*
Sun.	5 12 19 26	2 9 16 23 30	7 14 21 28
Mon.	6 13 20 27	3 10 17 24	1 8 15 22 29
Tue.	7 14 21 28	4 11 18 25	2 9 16 23 30
Wed.	1 8 15 22 29	5 12 19 26	3 10 17 24 31
Thur.	2 9 16 23 30	6 13 20 27	4 11 18 25
Fri.	3 10 17 24 31	7 14 21 28	5 12 19 26
Sat.	4 11 18 25	1 8 15 22 29	6 13 20 27

EASTER DAYS

March 23	1788, 1856, 2008
April 6	1828, 1980
April 13	1884, 1952, 2036
April 20	1924

G

	January	*February*	*March*
Sun.	5 12 19 26	2 9 16 23	2 9 16 23 30
Mon.	6 13 20 27	3 10 17 24	3 10 17 24 31
Tue.	7 14 21 28	4 11 18 25	4 11 18 25
Wed.	1 8 15 22 29	5 12 19 26	5 12 19 26
Thur.	2 9 16 23 30	6 13 20 27	6 13 20 27
Fri.	3 10 17 24 31	7 14 21 28	7 14 21 28
Sat.	4 11 18 25	1 8 15 22	1 8 15 22 29

	April	*May*	*June*
Sun.	6 13 20 27	4 11 18 25	1 8 15 22 29
Mon.	7 14 21 28	5 12 19 26	2 9 16 23 30
Tue.	1 8 15 22 29	6 13 20 27	3 10 17 24
Wed.	2 9 16 23 30	7 14 21 28	4 11 18 25
Thur.	3 10 17 24	1 8 15 22 29	5 12 19 26
Fri.	4 11 18 25	2 9 16 23 30	6 13 20 27
Sat.	5 12 19 26	3 10 17 24 31	7 14 21 28

	July	*August*	*September*
Sun.	6 13 20 27	3 10 17 24 31	7 14 21 28
Mon.	7 14 21 28	4 11 18 25	1 8 15 22 29
Tue.	1 8 15 22 29	5 12 19 26	2 9 16 23 30
Wed.	2 9 16 23 30	6 13 20 27	3 10 17 24
Thur.	3 10 17 24 31	7 14 21 28	4 11 18 25
Fri.	4 11 18 25	1 8 15 22 29	5 12 19 26
Sat.	5 12 19 26	2 9 16 23 30	6 13 20 27

	October	*November*	*December*
Sun.	5 12 19 26	2 9 16 23 30	7 14 21 28
Mon.	6 13 20 27	3 10 17 24	1 8 15 22 29
Tue.	7 14 21 28	4 11 18 25	2 9 16 23 30
Wed.	1 8 15 22 29	5 12 19 26	3 10 17 24 31
Thur.	2 9 16 23 30	6 13 20 27	4 11 18 25
Fri.	3 10 17 24 31	7 14 21 28	5 12 19 26
Sat.	4 11 18 25	1 8 15 22 29	6 13 20 27

EASTER DAYS

March 23	1845, 1913
March 30	1823, 1834, 1902, 1975, 1986, 1997
April 6	1806, 1817, 1890, 1947, 1958, 1969
April 13	1800, 1873, 1879, 1941, 2031
April 20	1783, 1794, 1851, 1862, 1919, 1930, 2003, 2014, 2025

H (LEAP YEAR)

	January	*February*	*March*
Sun.	5 12 19 26	2 9 16 23	1 8 15 22 29
Mon.	6 13 20 27	3 10 17 24	2 9 16 23 30
Tue.	7 14 21 28	4 11 18 25	3 10 17 24 31
Wed.	1 8 15 22 29	5 12 19 26	4 11 18 25
Thur.	2 9 16 23 30	6 13 20 27	5 12 19 26
Fri.	3 10 17 24 31	7 14 21 28	6 13 20 27
Sat.	4 11 18 25	1 8 15 22 29	7 14 21 28

	April	*May*	*June*
Sun.	5 12 19 26	3 10 17 24 31	7 14 21 28
Mon.	6 13 20 27	4 11 18 25	1 8 15 22 29
Tue.	7 14 21 28	5 12 19 26	2 9 16 23 30
Wed.	1 8 15 22 29	6 13 20 27	3 10 17 24
Thur.	2 9 16 23 30	7 14 21 28	4 11 18 25
Fri.	3 10 17 24	1 8 15 22 29	5 12 19 26
Sat.	4 11 18 25	2 9 16 23 30	6 13 20 27

	July	*August*	*September*
Sun.	5 12 19 26	2 9 16 23 30	6 13 20 27
Mon.	6 13 20 27	3 10 17 24 31	7 14 21 28
Tue.	7 14 21 28	4 11 18 25	1 8 15 22 29
Wed.	1 8 15 22 29	5 12 19 26	2 9 16 23 30
Thur.	2 9 16 23 30	6 13 20 27	3 10 17 24
Fri.	3 10 17 24 31	7 14 21 28	4 11 18 25
Sat.	4 11 18 25	1 8 15 22 29	5 12 19 26

	October	*November*	*December*
Sun.	4 11 18 25	1 8 15 22 29	6 13 20 27
Mon.	5 12 19 26	2 9 16 23 30	7 14 21 28
Tue.	6 13 20 27	3 10 17 24	1 8 15 22 29
Wed.	7 14 21 28	4 11 18 25	2 9 16 23 30
Thur.	1 8 15 22 29	5 12 19 26	3 10 17 24 31
Fri.	2 9 16 23 30	6 13 20 27	4 11 18 25
Sat.	3 10 17 24 31	7 14 21 28	5 12 19 26

EASTER DAYS

March 29	1812, 1964
April 5	1896
April 12	1868, 1936, 2020
April 19	1840, 1908, 1992

I

	January	*February*	*March*
Sun.	4 11 18 25	1 8 15 22	1 8 15 22 29
Mon.	5 12 19 26	2 9 16 23	2 9 16 23 30
Tue.	6 13 20 27	3 10 17 24	3 10 17 24 31
Wed.	7 14 21 28	4 11 18 25	4 11 18 25
Thur.	1 8 15 22 29	5 12 19 26	5 12 19 26
Fri.	2 9 16 23 30	6 13 20 27	6 13 20 27
Sat.	3 10 17 24 31	7 14 21 28	7 14 21 28

	April	*May*	*June*
Sun.	5 12 19 26	3 10 17 24 31	7 14 21 28
Mon.	6 13 20 27	4 11 18 25	1 8 15 22 29
Tue.	7 14 21 28	5 12 19 26	2 9 16 23 30
Wed.	1 8 15 22 29	6 13 20 27	3 10 17 24
Thur.	2 9 16 23 30	7 14 21 28	4 11 18 25
Fri.	3 10 17 24	1 8 15 22 29	5 12 19 26
Sat.	4 11 18 25	2 9 16 23 30	6 13 20 27

	July	*August*	*September*
Sun.	5 12 19 26	2 9 16 23 30	6 13 20 27
Mon.	6 13 20 27	3 10 17 24 31	7 14 21 28
Tue.	7 14 21 28	4 11 18 25	1 8 15 22 29
Wed.	1 8 15 22 29	5 12 19 26	2 9 16 23 30
Thur.	2 9 16 23 30	6 13 20 27	3 10 17 24
Fri.	3 10 17 24 31	7 14 21 28	4 11 18 25
Sat.	4 11 18 25	1 8 15 22 29	5 12 19 26

	October	*November*	*December*
Sun.	4 11 18 25	1 8 15 22 29	6 13 20 27
Mon.	5 12 19 26	2 9 16 23 30	7 14 21 28
Tue.	6 13 20 27	3 10 17 24	1 8 15 22 29
Wed.	7 14 21 28	4 11 18 25	2 9 16 23 30
Thur.	1 8 15 22 29	5 12 19 26	3 10 17 24 31
Fri.	2 9 16 23 30	6 13 20 27	4 11 18 25
Sat.	3 10 17 24 31	7 14 21 28	5 12 19 26

EASTER DAYS

March 22	1818
March 29	1807, 1891, 1959, 1970
April 5	1795, 1801, 1863, 1874, 1885, 1931, 1942, 1953, 2015, 2026, 2037
April 12	1789, 1846, 1857, 1903, 1914, 1925, 1998, 2009
April 19	1829, 1835, 1981, 1987

J (LEAP YEAR)

	January	*February*	*March*
Sun.	4 11 18 25	1 8 15 22 29	7 14 21 28
Mon.	5 12 19 26	2 9 16 23	1 8 15 22 29
Tue.	6 13 20 27	3 10 17 24	2 9 16 23 30
Wed.	7 14 21 28	4 11 18 25	3 10 17 24 31
Thur.	1 8 15 22 29	5 12 19 26	4 11 18 25
Fri.	2 9 16 23 30	6 13 20 27	5 12 19 26
Sat.	3 10 17 24 31	7 14 21 28	6 13 20 27

	April	*May*	*June*
Sun.	4 11 18 25	2 9 16 23 30	6 13 20 27
Mon.	5 12 19 26	3 10 17 24 31	7 14 21 28
Tue.	6 13 20 27	4 11 18 25	1 8 15 22 29
Wed.	7 14 21 28	5 12 19 26	2 9 16 23 30
Thur.	1 8 15 22 29	6 13 20 27	3 10 17 24
Fri.	2 9 16 23 30	7 14 21 28	4 11 18 25
Sat.	3 10 17 24	1 8 15 22 29	5 12 19 26

	July	*August*	*September*
Sun.	4 11 18 25	1 8 15 22 29	5 12 19 26
Mon.	5 12 19 26	2 9 16 23 30	6 13 20 27
Tue.	6 13 20 27	3 10 17 24 31	7 14 21 28
Wed.	7 14 21 28	4 11 18 25	1 8 15 22 29
Thur.	1 8 15 22 29	5 12 19 26	2 9 16 23 30
Fri.	2 9 16 23 30	6 13 20 27	3 10 17 24
Sat.	3 10 17 24 31	7 14 21 28	4 11 18 25

	October	*November*	*December*
Sun.	3 10 17 24 31	7 14 21 28	5 12 19 26
Mon.	4 11 18 25	1 8 15 22 29	6 13 20 27
Tue.	5 12 19 26	2 9 16 23 30	7 14 21 28
Wed.	6 13 20 27	3 10 17 24	1 8 15 22 29
Thur.	7 14 21 28	4 11 18 25	2 9 16 23 30
Fri.	1 8 15 22 29	5 12 19 26	3 10 17 24 31
Sat.	2 9 16 23 30	6 13 20 27	4 11 18 25

EASTER DAYS

March 28	1880, 1948, 2032
April 4	1920
April 11	1784, 1852, 2004
April 18	1824, 1976

K

	January	*February*	*March*
Sun.	3 10 17 24 31	7 14 21 28	7 14 21 28
Mon.	4 11 18 25	1 8 15 22	1 8 15 22 29
Tue.	5 12 19 26	2 9 16 23	2 9 16 23 30
Wed.	6 13 20 27	3 10 17 24	3 10 17 24 31
Thur.	7 14 21 28	4 11 18 25	4 11 18 25
Fri.	1 8 15 22 29	5 12 19 26	5 12 19 26
Sat.	2 9 16 23 30	6 13 20 27	6 13 20 27

	April	*May*	*June*
Sun.	4 11 18 25	2 9 16 23 30	6 13 20 27
Mon.	5 12 19 26	3 10 17 24 31	7 14 21 28
Tue.	6 13 20 27	4 11 18 25	1 8 15 22 29
Wed.	7 14 21 28	5 12 19 26	2 9 16 23 30
Thur.	1 8 15 22 29	6 13 20 27	3 10 17 24
Fri.	2 9 16 23 30	7 14 21 28	4 11 18 25
Sat.	3 10 17 24	1 8 15 22 29	5 12 19 26

	July	*August*	*September*
Sun.	4 11 18 25	1 8 15 22 29	5 12 19 26
Mon.	5 12 19 26	2 9 16 23 30	6 13 20 27
Tue.	6 13 20 27	3 10 17 24 31	7 14 21 28
Wed.	7 14 21 28	4 11 18 25	1 8 15 22 29
Thur.	1 8 15 22 29	5 12 19 26	2 9 16 23 30
Fri.	2 9 16 23 30	6 13 20 27	3 10 17 24
Sat.	3 10 17 24 31	7 14 21 28	4 11 18 25

	October	*November*	*December*
Sun.	3 10 17 24 31	7 14 21 28	5 12 19 26
Mon.	4 11 18 25	1 8 15 22 29	6 13 20 27
Tue.	5 12 19 26	2 9 16 23 30	7 14 21 28
Wed.	6 13 20 27	3 10 17 24	1 8 15 22 29
Thur.	7 14 21 28	4 11 18 25	2 9 16 23 30
Fri.	1 8 15 22 29	5 12 19 26	3 10 17 24 31
Sat.	2 9 16 23 30	6 13 20 27	4 11 18 25

EASTER DAYS

March 28	1869, 1875, 1937, 2027
April 4	1790, 1847, 1858, 1915, 1926, 1999, 2010, 2021
April 11	1819, 1830, 1841, 1909, 1971, 1982, 1993
April 18	1802, 1813, 1897, 1954, 1965
April 25	1886, 1943, 2038

L (LEAP YEAR)

	January	*February*	*March*
Sun.	3 10 17 24 31	7 14 21 28	6 13 20 27
Mon.	4 11 18 25	1 8 15 22 29	7 14 21 28
Tue.	5 12 19 26	2 9 16 23	1 8 15 22 29
Wed.	6 13 20 27	3 10 17 24	2 9 16 23 30
Thur.	7 14 21 28	4 11 18 25	3 10 17 24 31
Fri.	1 8 15 22 29	5 12 19 26	4 11 18 25
Sat.	2 9 16 23 30	6 13 20 27	5 12 19 26

	April	*May*	*June*
Sun.	3 10 17 24	1 8 15 22 29	5 12 19 26
Mon.	4 11 18 25	2 9 16 23 30	6 13 20 27
Tue.	5 12 19 26	3 10 17 24 31	7 14 21 28
Wed.	6 13 20 27	4 11 18 25	1 8 15 22 29
Thur.	7 14 21 28	5 12 19 26	2 9 16 23 30
Fri.	1 8 15 22 29	6 13 20 27	3 10 17 24
Sat.	2 9 16 23 30	7 14 21 28	4 11 18 25

	July	*August*	*September*
Sun.	3 10 17 24 31	7 14 21 28	4 11 18 25
Mon.	4 11 18 25	1 8 15 22 29	5 12 19 26
Tue.	5 12 19 26	2 9 16 23 30	6 13 20 27
Wed.	6 13 20 27	3 10 17 24 31	7 14 21 28
Thur.	7 14 21 28	4 11 18 25	1 8 15 22 29
Fri.	1 8 15 22 29	5 12 19 26	2 9 16 23 30
Sat.	2 9 16 23 30	6 13 20 27	3 10 17 24

	October	*November*	*December*
Sun.	2 9 16 23 30	6 13 20 27	4 11 18 25
Mon.	3 10 17 24 31	7 14 21 28	5 12 19 26
Tue.	4 11 18 25	1 8 15 22 29	6 13 20 27
Wed.	5 12 19 26	2 9 16 23 30	7 14 21 28
Thur.	6 13 20 27	3 10 17 24	1 8 15 22 29
Fri.	7 14 21 28	4 11 18 25	2 9 16 23 30
Sat.	1 8 15 22 29	5 12 19 26	3 10 17 24 31

EASTER DAYS

March 27	1796, 1864, 1932, 2016
April 3	1836, 1904, 1988
April 17	1808, 1892, 1960

M

	January	*February*	*March*
Sun.	2 9 16 23 30	6 13 20 27	6 13 20 27
Mon.	3 10 17 24 31	7 14 21 28	7 14 21 28
Tue.	4 11 18 25	1 8 15 22	1 8 15 22 29
Wed.	5 12 19 26	2 9 16 23	2 9 16 23 30
Thur.	6 13 20 27	3 10 17 24	3 10 17 24 31
Fri.	7 14 21 28	4 11 18 25	4 11 18 25
Sat.	1 8 15 22 29	5 12 19 26	5 12 19 26

	April	*May*	*June*
Sun.	3 10 17 24	1 8 15 22 29	5 12 19 26
Mon.	4 11 18 25	2 9 16 23 30	6 13 20 27
Tue.	5 12 19 26	3 10 17 24 31	7 14 21 28
Wed.	6 13 20 27	4 11 18 25	1 8 15 22 29
Thur.	7 14 21 28	5 12 19 26	2 9 16 23 30
Fri.	1 8 15 22 29	6 13 20 27	3 10 17 24
Sat.	2 9 16 23 30	7 14 21 28	4 11 18 25

	July	*August*	*September*
Sun.	3 10 17 24 31	7 14 21 28	4 11 18 25
Mon.	4 11 18 25	1 8 15 22 29	5 12 19 26
Tue.	5 12 19 26	2 9 16 23 30	6 13 20 27
Wed.	6 13 20 27	3 10 17 24 31	7 14 21 28
Thur.	7 14 21 28	4 11 18 25	1 8 15 22 29
Fri.	1 8 15 22 29	5 12 19 26	2 9 16 23 30
Sat.	2 9 16 23 30	6 13 20 27	3 10 17 24

	October	*November*	*December*
Sun.	2 9 16 23 30	6 13 20 27	4 11 18 25
Mon.	3 10 17 24 31	7 14 21 28	5 12 19 26
Tue.	4 11 18 25	1 8 15 22 29	6 13 20 27
Wed.	5 12 19 26	2 9 16 23 30	7 14 21 28
Thur.	6 13 20 27	3 10 17 24	1 8 15 22 29
Fri.	7 14 21 28	4 11 18 25	2 9 16 23 30
Sat.	1 8 15 22 29	5 12 19 26	3 10 17 24 31

EASTER DAYS

March 27	1785, 1842, 1853, 1910, 1921, 2005
April 3	1825, 1831, 1983, 1994
April 10	1803, 1814, 1887, 1898, 1955, 1966, 1977, 2039
April 17	1870, 1881, 1927, 1938, 1949, 2022, 2033
April 24	1791, 1859, 2011

N (LEAP YEAR)

	January	*February*	*March*
Sun.	2 9 16 23 30	6 13 20 27	5 12 19 26
Mon.	3 10 17 24 31	7 14 21 28	6 13 20 27
Tue.	4 11 18 25	1 8 15 22 29	7 14 21 28
Wed.	5 12 19 26	2 9 16 23	1 8 15 22 29
Thur.	6 13 20 27	3 10 17 24	2 9 16 23 30
Fri.	7 14 21 28	4 11 18 25	3 10 17 24 31
Sat.	1 8 15 22 29	5 12 19 26	4 11 18 25

	April	*May*	*June*
Sun.	2 9 16 23 30	7 14 21 28	4 11 18 25
Mon.	3 10 17 24	1 8 15 22 29	5 12 19 26
Tue.	4 11 18 25	2 9 16 23 30	6 13 20 27
Wed.	5 12 19 26	3 10 17 24 31	7 14 21 28
Thur.	6 13 20 27	4 11 18 25	1 8 15 22 29
Fri.	7 14 21 28	5 12 19 26	2 9 16 23 30
Sat.	1 8 15 22 29	6 13 20 27	3 10 17 24

	July	*August*	*September*
Sun.	2 9 16 23 30	6 13 20 27	3 10 17 24
Mon.	3 10 17 24 31	7 14 21 28	4 11 18 25
Tue.	4 11 18 25	1 8 15 22 29	5 12 19 26
Wed.	5 12 19 26	2 9 16 23 30	6 13 20 27
Thur.	6 13 20 27	3 10 17 24 31	7 14 21 28
Fri.	7 14 21 28	4 11 18 25	1 8 15 22 29
Sat.	1 8 15 22 29	5 12 19 26	2 9 16 23 30

	October	*November*	*December*
Sun.	1 8 15 22 29	5 12 19 26	3 10 17 24 31
Mon.	2 9 16 23 30	6 13 20 27	4 11 18 25
Tue.	3 10 17 24 31	7 14 21 28	5 12 19 26
Wed.	4 11 18 25	1 8 15 22 29	6 13 20 27
Thur.	5 12 19 26	2 9 16 23 30	7 14 21 28
Fri.	6 13 20 27	3 10 17 24	1 8 15 22 29
Sat.	7 14 21 28	4 11 18 25	2 9 16 23 30

EASTER DAYS

March 26	1780
April 2	1820, 1972
April 9	1944
April 16	1876, 2028
April 23	1848, 1916, 2000

GEOLOGICAL TIME

The earth is thought to have come into existence approximately 4,600 million years ago, but for nearly half this time, the Archean era, it was uninhabited. Life is generally believed to have emerged in the succeeding Proterozoic era. The Archean and the Proterozoic eras are often together referred to as the Precambrian.

Although primitive forms of life, eg algae and bacteria, existed during the Proterozoic era, it is not until the strata of Palaeozoic rocks are reached that abundant fossilised remains appear. Since the Precambrian, there have been three great geological eras:

PALAEOZOIC ('ANCIENT LIFE')

*c.*542–*c.*251 million years ago

Cambrian – Mainly sandstones, slate and shales; limestones in Scotland. Shelled fossils and invertebrates, eg trilobites and brachiopods appear, as do the earliest known vertebrates (jawless fish)

Ordovician – Mainly shales and mudstones, eg in north Wales; limestones in Scotland. First fish

Silurian – Shales, mudstones and some limestones, found mostly in Wales and southern Scotland

Devonian – Old red sandstone, shale, limestone and slate, eg in south Wales and the West Country

Carboniferous – Coal-bearing rocks, millstone grit, limestone and shale. First traces of land-living creatures

Permian – Marls, sandstones and clays. First reptile fossils

There were two great phases of mountain building in the Palaeozoic era: the Caledonian, characterised in Britain by NE–SW lines of hills and valleys; and the later Hercynian, widespread in west Germany and adjacent areas, and in Britain exemplified in E–W lines of hills and valleys.

The end of the Palaeozoic era was marked by the extensive glaciations of the Permian period in the southern continents and the decline of amphibians. It was succeeded by an era of warm conditions.

MESOZOIC ('MIDDLE FORMS OF LIFE')

*c.*251–*c.*65.5 million years ago

Triassic – Mostly sandstone, eg in the West Midlands; primitive mammals appear

Jurassic – Mainly limestones and clays, typically displayed in the Jura mountains, and in England in a NE–SW belt from Lincolnshire and the Wash to the Severn and the Dorset coast

Cretaceous – Mainly chalk, clay and sands, eg in Kent and Sussex

Giant reptiles were dominant during the Mesozoic era, but it was at this time that marsupial mammals first appeared, as well as *Archaeopteryx lithographica,* the earliest known species of bird. Coniferous trees and flowering plants also developed during the era and, with the birds and the mammals, were the main species to survive into the Cenozoic era. The giant reptiles became extinct.

CENOZOIC ('RECENT LIFE')

from *c.*65.5 million years ago

Palaeocene, *Eocene* – The emergence of new forms of life, including existing species; primates appear

Oligocene – Fossils of a few still existing species

Miocene – Fossil remains show a balance of existing and extinct species

Pliocene – Fossil remains show a majority of still existing species

Pleistocene – The majority of remains are those of still existing species

Holocene – The present, post-glacial period. Existing species only, except for a few exterminated by humans

In the last 25 million years, from the Miocene through the Pliocene periods, the Alpine-Himalayan and the circum-Pacific phases of mountain building reached their climax. During the Pleistocene period ice-sheets repeatedly locked up masses of water as land ice; its weight depressed the land, but the locking-up of the water lowered the sea level by 100–200 metres. The glaciations and interglacials of the Ice Age are difficult to date and classify, but recent scientific opinion considers the Pleistocene period to have begun approximately 1.64 million years ago. The last glacial retreat, merging into the Holocene period, was *c.*10,000 years ago.

HUMAN DEVELOPMENT

Any consideration of the history of humans must start with the fact that all members of the human race belong to one species of animal, ie *Homo sapiens,* the definition of a species being in biological terms that all its members can interbreed. As a species of mammal it is possible to group humans with other similar types, known as the primates. Amongst these is found a sub-group, the apes, which includes, in addition to humans, the chimpanzees, gorillas, orang-utans and gibbons. All lack a tail, have shoulder blades at the back, and a Y-shaped chewing pattern on the surface of their molars, as well as showing the more general primate characteristics of four incisors, a thumb which is able to touch the fingers of the same hand, and finger and toe nails instead of claws. The factors available to scientific study suggest that human beings have chimpanzees and gorillas as their nearest relatives in the animal world. However, there once lived creatures, now extinct, which were closer to modern man than the chimpanzees and gorillas, and which shared with modern man the characteristics of having flat faces (ie the absence of a pronounced muzzle), being bipedal, and possessing large brains.

There are two broad groups of extinct apes recognised by specialists. The ramapithecines – the remains of which, mainly jaw fragments, have been found in east Africa, Asia and Turkey – lived about 14 to 8 million years ago, and from the evidence of their teeth it seems they chewed more in the manner of modern humans than the other presently living apes. The second group, the australopithecines, have left more numerous remains among which sub-groups may be detected, although the geographic spread is limited to south and east Africa. Living between 5 and 1.5 million years ago, they were closer relatives of modern humans to the extent that they walked upright, did not have an extensive muzzle and had similar types of pre-molars. The first australopithecine remains were recognised at Taung in South Africa in 1924 and named *Australopithecus africanus,* dating between 3.3 and 2.3 million years ago. The most impressive discovery was made at Hadar, Ethiopia, in 1974 when about half a skeleton of *Australopithecus afarensis,* known as 'Lucy', was found. Some 3.2 million years ago, 'Lucy' certainly walked upright.

Also in east Africa, especially at Olduvai Gorge in Tanzania, between *c.*2.5 and 1.8 million years ago, lived a hominid group which not only walked upright, had a flat face, and a large brain case, but also made simple pebble and flake stone tools. These early pebble tool users, because of their distinctive characteristics, have been grouped as a separate sub-species, now extinct, of the genus *Homo* and are known as *Homo habilis* or 'handy man'.

The use of fire, again a human characteristic, is associated with another group of extinct hominids whose remains, about a million years old, are found in south and east Africa, China, Indonesia, north Africa and Europe. Mastery of the techniques of making fire probably helped the colonisation of the colder northern areas and in this respect the site of Vertesszollos in Hungary is of particular importance. *Homo ergaster* in Africa and *Homo erectus* in Asia are the names given to this group of fossils and they relate to a number of famous individual discoveries, eg Solo Man, Heidelberg Man, and especially Peking Man who lived at the cave site at Choukoutien which has yielded evidence of fire and burnt bone.

The well-known group Neandertal Man, or *Homo neanderthalensis,* is an extinct form of man that lived between about 350,000 and 24,000 years ago, thus spanning the last Ice Age. Indeed, its ability to adapt to the cold climate on the edge of the ice-sheets is one of its characteristic features, the remains being found only in Europe, Asia and the Middle East. Complete neandertal skeletons were found during excavations at Tabun in Israel, together with evidence of tool-making and the use of fire. Distinguished by very large brains, it seems that neandertal man was the first to develop recognisable social customs, especially deliberate burial rites. Why the neandertals became extinct is not clear but it may be connected with the climatic changes at the end of the Ice Ages, which would have seriously affected their food supplies; possibly they became too specialised for their own good.

The shin bone of Boxgrove Man found in 1993 – *Homo heidelbergensis* – and the Swanscombe skull are the best known early human fossil remains found in England. Some specialists prefer to group Swanscombe Man (or, more probably, woman) together with the Steinheim skull from Germany, seeing both as a separate sub-species. There is too little evidence as yet on which to form a final judgement.

Modern humans – *Homo sapiens* – had evolved to our present physical condition and had colonised much of the world by about 40,000 years ago. There are many previously distinguished individual specimens, eg Cromagnon Man, which may now be grouped together as *Homo sapiens.* It was modern humans who spread to the American continent by crossing the landbridge between Siberia and Alaska and thence moved south through North America and into South America. Equally it is modern humans who over the last 40,000 years have been responsible for the major developments in technology, art and civilisation generally.

One of the problems for those studying human fossils is the lack in many cases of sufficient quantities of fossil bone for analysis. It is important that theories should be tested against evidence, rather than the evidence being made to fit the theory. The Piltdown hoax of 1912 (and not fully exposed until the 1970s) is a well-known example of 'fossils' being forged to fit what was seen in some quarters as the correct theory of human evolution.

The discovery of the structure of DNA in 1953 has come to have a profound effect upon the study of human evolution. For example, it was claimed in 1987 that a common ancestor of all human beings was a person who lived in Africa some 200,000 years ago, thus encouraging the 'out of Africa' theory of hominid migration from east Africa to the Middle East and then throughout the world. There is no doubt that the studies based on DNA have vast potential to elucidate further the course of human evolution.

CULTURAL DEVELOPMENT

The Eurocentric bias of early archaeologists meant that the search for a starting point for the development and transmission of cultural ideas, especially by migration, trade and warfare, concentrated unduly on Europe and the Near East. The Three Age system, whereby prehistory was divided into a Stone Age, a Bronze Age and an Iron Age, was devised by Christian Thomsen, curator of the National Museum of Denmark in the early 19th century, to facilitate the classification of the museum's collections. The descriptive adjectives referred to the materials from which the implements and weapons were made and came to be regarded as the dominant features of the societies to which they related. The refinement of the Three Age system once dominated archaeological thought and remains a generally accepted concept in the popular mind. However, it is now seen by archaeologists as an inadequate model for human development.

Common sense suggests that there were no complete breaks between one so-called Age and another, any more than contemporaries would have regarded 1485 as a complete break between medieval and modern English history. Nor can the Three Age system be applied universally. In some areas it is necessary to insert a Copper Age, while in Africa south of the Sahara there would seem to be no Bronze Age at all; in Australia, Old Stone Age societies survived, while in South America, New Stone Age communities existed into modern times. The civilisations in other parts of the world clearly invalidate a Eurocentric theory of human development.

The concept of the 'Neolithic revolution', associated with the domestication of plants and animals, was a development of particular importance in the human cultural pattern. It reflected change from the hunter-gatherer economies to a more settled agricultural way of life and therefore, so the argument goes, made possible the development of urban civilisation. However, it can no longer be argued that this 'revolution' took place only in one area from which all development stemmed. Though it appears that the cultivation of wheat and barley was first undertaken, together with the domestication of cattle and goats/sheep, in the Fertile Crescent (the area bounded by the rivers Tigris and Euphrates), there is evidence that rice was first deliberately planted and pigs domesticated in south-east Asia, maize first cultivated in Central America and llamas first domesticated in South America. It has been recognised in recent years that cultural changes can take place independently of each other in different parts of the world at different rates and different times. There is no need for a general diffusionist theory.

Although scholars will continue to study the particular societies which interest them, it may be possible to obtain a reliable chronological framework, in absolute terms of years, against which the cultural development of any particular area may be set. The development and refinement of radio-carbon dating and other scientific methods of producing absolute chronologies is enabling the cross-referencing of societies to be undertaken. As the techniques of dating become more rigorous in application and the number of scientifically obtained dates increases, the attainment of an absolute chronology for prehistoric societies throughout the world comes closer to being achieved.

GEOLOGICAL TIME

Era	*Period*	*Epoch*	*Dates*	*Evolutionary stages*
Cenozoic	Quaternary	Holocene	9,600 BC–present	Humans
		Pleistocene	1,808,000–9,600 BC	
	Tertiary	Pliocene	5,332,000–1,806,000	
		Miocene	23,030,000–5,332,000	
		Oligocene	34–23 Ma*	
		Eocene	55.8–33.9 Ma	
		Palaeocene	65.5–55.8 Ma	
Mesozoic	Cretaceous		145.5–65.5 Ma	
	Jurassic		199.6–145.5 Ma	First birds
	Triassic		251–199.6 Ma	First mammals
Palaeozoic	Permian		299–251 Ma	First reptiles
	Carboniferous		359.2–299 Ma	First amphibians and insects
	Devonian		416–359.2 Ma	
	Silurian		443.7–416 Ma	
	Ordovician		488.3–443.7 Ma	First fish
	Cambrian		542–488.3 Ma	First invertebrates
Precambrian	Proterozoic		2,500–542 Ma	First primitive life forms, eg algae and bacteria
	Archaean		3,800–2,500 Ma	
	Hadean		4,500–3,800 Ma	

* Ma = millions of years ago

TIDAL PREDICTIONS

CONSTANTS

The constant tidal difference may be used in conjunction with the time of high water at a standard port shown in the predictions data below to find the time of high water at any of the ports or places listed.

These tidal differences are approximate and should be used only as a guide to the time of high water at the places below. More precise local data should be obtained for navigational and other nautical purposes.

All data allow high water time to be found in Greenwich Mean Time: this applies to data for the months when British Summer Time is in operation and the hour's time difference should be added. Ports marked * are in a different time zone and the standard time zone difference also needs to be added/subtracted to give local time.

EXAMPLE

Required: time of high water at Stranraer on 2 January 2010. Appropriate time of high water at Greenock

Afternoon tide 2 January	13h 11m
Tidal difference	–00hrs 20m
High water at Stranraer	12hrs 51m

The columns headed 'Springs' and 'Neaps' show the height, in metres, of the tide above datum for mean high water springs and mean high water neaps respectively.

Port		*Diff.* *h*	*min*	*Springs* *m*	*Neaps* *m*
Aberdeen	*Leith*	–1	19	4.4	3.4
*Antwerp (Prosperpolder)	*London*	+0	50	5.8	4.8
Ardrossan	*Greenock*	–0	15	3.2	2.6
Avonmouth	*London*	–6	45	12.2	9.8
Ayr	*Greenock*	–0	25	3.0	2.5
Barrow (Docks)	*Liverpool*	0	00	9.3	7.1
Belfast	*London*	–2	47	3.5	3.0
Blackpool	*Liverpool*	–0	10	8.9	7.0
*Boulogne	*London*	–2	44	8.9	7.2
*Calais	*London*	–2	04	7.2	5.9
*Cherbourg	*London*	–6	00	6.4	5.0
Cobh	*Liverpool*	–5	55	4.2	3.2
Cowes	*London*	–2	38	4.2	3.5
Dartmouth	*London*	+4	25	4.9	3.8
*Dieppe	*London*	–3	03	9.3	7.3
Douglas, IoM	*Liverpool*	–0	04	6.9	5.4
Dover	*London*	–2	52	6.7	5.3
Dublin	*London*	–2	05	4.1	3.4
Dun Loaghaire	*London*	–2	10	4.1	3.4
*Dunkirk	*London*	–1	54	6.0	4.9
Fishguard	*Liverpool*	–4	01	4.8	3.4
Fleetwood	*Liverpool*	0	00	9.2	7.3
*Flushing	*London*	–0	15	4.7	3.9
Folkestone	*London*	–3	04	7.1	5.7
Galway	*Liverpool*	–6	08	5.1	3.9
Glasgow	*Greenock*	+0	26	4.7	4.0
Harwich	*London*	–2	06	4.0	3.4
*Le Havre	*London*	–3	55	7.9	6.6
Heysham	*Liverpool*	+0	05	9.4	7.4
Holyhead	*Liverpool*	–0	50	5.6	4.4
*Hook of Holland	*London*	–0	01	2.1	1.7
Hull (Albert Dock)	*London*	–7	40	7.5	5.8
Immingham	*London*	–8	00	7.3	5.8
Larne	*London*	–2	40	2.8	2.5
Lerwick	*Leith*	–3	48	2.2	1.6
Londonderry	*London*	–5	37	2.7	2.1
Lowestoft	*London*	–4	25	2.4	2.1
Margate	*London*	–1	53	4.8	3.9
Milford Haven	*Liverpool*	–5	08	7.0	5.2
Morecambe	*Liverpool*	+0	07	9.5	7.4
Newhaven	*London*	–2	46	6.7	5.1
Oban	*Greenock*	+5	43	4.0	2.9
*Ostend	*London*	–1	32	5.1	4.2
Plymouth	*London*	+4	05	5.5	4.4
Portland	*London*	+5	09	2.1	1.4
Portsmouth	*London*	–2	38	4.7	3.8
Ramsgate	*London*	–2	32	5.2	4.1
Richmond Lock	*London*	+1	00	4.9	3.7
Rosslare Harbour	*Liverpool*	–5	24	1.9	1.4
Rosyth	*Leith*	+0	09	5.8	4.7
*Rotterdam	*London*	+1	45	2.0	1.7
*St Helier	*London*	+4	48	11.0	8.1
*St Malo	*London*	+4	27	12.2	9.2
*St Peter Port	*London*	+4	54	9.3	7.0
Scrabster	*Leith*	–6	06	5.0	4.0
Sheerness	*London*	–1	19	5.8	4.7
Shoreham	*London*	–2	44	6.3	4.9
Southampton (1st high water)	*London*	–2	54	4.5	3.7
Spurn Head	*London*	–8	25	6.9	5.5
Stornoway	*Liverpool*	–4	16	4.8	3.7
Stranraer	*Greenock*	–0	20	3.0	2.4
Stromness	*Leith*	–5	26	3.6	2.7
Swansea	*London*	–7	35	9.5	7.2
Tees (River Entrance)	*Leith*	+1	09	5.5	4.3
Tilbury	*London*	–0	49	6.4	5.4
Tobermory	*Liverpool*	–5	11	4.4	3.3
Tyne River (North Shields)	*London*	–10	30	5.0	3.9
Ullapool	*Leith*	–7	40	5.2	3.9
Walton-on-the-Naze	*London*	–2	10	4.2	3.4
Wick	*Leith*	–3	26	3.5	2.8
*Zeebrugge	*London*	–0	55	4.8	3.9

PREDICTIONS

The following data are daily predictions of the time and height of high water at London Bridge, Liverpool, Greenock and Leith. The time of the data is Greenwich Mean Time; this applies also to data for the months when British Summer Time is in operation and the hour's time difference should be added. The datum of predictions for each port shows the difference of height, in metres from Ordnance datum (Newlyn).

 The section was compiled with the assistance of Chris Stevens.

JANUARY 2010 *High Water* GMT

	LONDON BRIDGE *Datum of Predictions 3.20m below				†LIVERPOOL *Datum of Predictions 4.93m below				GREENOCK *Datum of Predictions 1.62m below				LEITH *Datum of Predictions 2.90m below			
	hr	*ht m*	*hr*	*ht m*	*hr*	*ht m*	*hr*	*ht m*	*hr*	*ht m*	*hr*	*ht m*	*hr*	*ht m*	*hr*	*ht m*
F 1	01 41	6.7	14 00	7.1	11 10	9.5	23 38	9.5	00 19	3.4	12 25	3.7	02 28	5.6	14 48	5.7
SA 2	02 31	6.8	14 51	7.3	11 58	9.7	—	—	01 11	3.4	13 11	3.8	03 16	5.8	15 32	5.8
SU 3	03 17	6.9	15 40	7.3	00 27	9.6	12 46	9.8	02 02	3.4	13 57	3.9	04 03	5.8	16 18	5.9
M 4	04 02	7.0	16 29	7.3	01 15	9.5	13 34	9.8	02 51	3.4	14 43	3.9	04 50	5.8	17 05	5.8
TU 5	04 47	7.0	17 17	7.2	02 03	9.3	14 22	9.5	03 39	3.4	15 28	3.9	05 39	5.6	17 55	5.7
W 6	05 32	6.9	18 06	6.9	02 51	8.9	15 11	9.2	04 25	3.3	16 15	3.8	06 31	5.3	18 49	5.4
TH 7	06 19	6.7	18 57	6.6	03 41	8.5	16 04	8.7	05 12	3.2	17 03	3.6	07 26	5.0	19 51	5.2
F 8	07 12	6.5	19 50	6.4	04 36	8.1	17 04	8.2	06 01	3.1	17 54	3.4	08 27	4.8	20 58	4.9
SA 9	08 12	6.3	20 51	6.1	05 40	7.7	18 14	7.8	06 57	3.0	18 50	3.2	09 31	4.6	22 05	4.7
SU 10	09 20	6.1	22 03	5.9	06 54	7.6	19 30	7.7	08 08	2.9	20 09	3.0	10 36	4.6	23 14	4.7
M 11	10 29	6.0	23 14	5.9	08 06	7.7	20 40	7.8	09 25	3.0	21 42	3.0	11 43	4.6	—	—
TU 12	11 36	6.1	—	—	09 07	8.1	21 37	8.0	10 27	3.2	22 48	3.0	00 21	4.7	12 45	4.8
W 13	00 13	6.0	12 36	6.3	09 55	8.4	22 23	8.3	11 17	3.4	23 39	3.1	01 19	4.9	13 34	5.0
TH 14	01 04	6.2	13 25	6.5	10 36	8.7	23 01	8.5	12 00	3.5	—	—	02 05	5.0	14 15	5.1
F 15	01 46	6.4	14 07	6.6	11 12	8.9	23 35	8.6	00 22	3.1	12 39	3.6	02 44	5.1	14 51	5.2
SA 16	02 22	6.5	14 44	6.6	11 45	9.0	—	—	01 00	3.1	13 13	3.6	03 18	5.2	15 24	5.3
SU 17	02 56	6.6	15 18	6.7	00 07	8.7	12 18	9.1	01 33	3.2	13 45	3.6	03 50	5.2	15 55	5.3
M 18	03 28	6.6	15 49	6.6	00 38	8.7	12 50	9.1	02 06	3.2	14 16	3.6	04 22	5.2	16 27	5.3
TU 19	03 58	6.6	16 18	6.6	01 08	8.6	13 21	8.9	02 39	3.2	14 47	3.6	04 55	5.1	16 59	5.2
W 20	04 27	6.6	16 47	6.6	01 38	8.5	13 52	8.8	03 12	3.2	15 21	3.5	05 29	5.0	17 33	5.1
TH 21	04 57	6.5	17 19	6.4	02 09	8.3	14 24	8.5	03 46	3.2	15 56	3.4	06 06	4.9	18 08	5.0
F 22	05 29	6.4	17 55	6.3	02 43	8.1	15 01	8.2	04 22	3.2	16 35	3.3	06 45	4.7	18 48	4.8
SA 23	06 07	6.3	18 37	6.1	03 24	7.8	15 47	7.9	05 00	3.1	17 18	3.1	07 29	4.6	19 35	4.7
SU 24	06 54	6.1	19 31	5.8	04 17	7.5	16 50	7.6	05 43	3.0	18 12	3.0	08 24	4.4	20 37	4.5
M 25	07 54	5.9	20 44	5.7	05 31	7.3	18 12	7.5	06 36	2.9	19 23	2.8	09 33	4.4	21 59	4.5
TU 26	09 24	5.9	22 07	5.8	06 57	7.4	19 35	7.7	07 54	2.9	20 55	2.9	10 48	4.5	23 19	4.6
W 27	10 44	6.2	23 26	6.1	08 14	7.9	20 47	8.2	09 23	3.0	22 18	3.0	11 59	4.7	—	—
TH 28	11 52	6.6	—	—	09 17	8.5	21 47	8.7	10 31	3.2	23 20	3.2	00 29	5.0	12 59	5.1
F 29	00 33	6.4	12 55	6.9	10 10	9.1	22 40	9.2	11 25	3.4	—	—	01 27	5.3	13 48	5.4
SA 30	01 29	6.7	13 50	7.2	10 59	9.6	23 28	9.6	00 13	3.3	12 14	3.6	02 16	5.6	14 33	5.7
SU 31	02 18	7.0	14 41	7.4	11 46	10.0	—	—	01 04	3.4	13 01	3.7	03 02	5.8	15 17	6.0

FEBRUARY 2010 *High Water* GMT

	LONDON BRIDGE				†LIVERPOOL				GREENOCK				LEITH			
M 1	03 03	7.1	15 28	7.5	00 13	9.8	12 31	10.1	01 52	3.4	13 46	3.8	03 46	5.9	16 01	6.1
TU 2	03 47	7.3	16 13	7.4	00 58	9.7	13 15	10.1	02 37	3.4	14 31	3.9	04 31	5.8	16 46	6.0
W 3	04 28	7.3	16 57	7.2	01 40	9.5	13 57	9.8	03 18	3.4	15 13	3.9	05 16	5.6	17 33	5.8
TH 4	05 09	7.2	17 39	6.9	02 22	9.1	14 41	9.3	03 57	3.4	15 55	3.8	06 03	5.3	18 23	5.5
F 5	05 51	6.9	18 21	6.6	03 05	8.6	15 27	8.7	04 35	3.3	16 36	3.6	06 52	5.0	19 18	5.1
SA 6	06 36	6.6	19 06	6.2	03 53	8.1	16 21	8.0	05 14	3.1	17 19	3.3	07 47	4.7	20 22	4.7
SU 7	07 28	6.3	19 56	5.9	04 54	7.6	17 33	7.4	05 59	3.0	18 07	3.0	08 49	4.4	21 32	4.5
M 8	08 35	5.9	21 04	5.6	06 13	7.2	19 03	7.1	06 56	2.8	19 06	2.7	09 58	4.3	22 49	4.4
TU 9	09 52	5.7	22 39	5.6	07 40	7.3	20 27	7.3	08 48	2.8	21 35	2.6	11 15	4.4	—	—
W 10	11 12	5.8	23 51	5.8	08 50	7.7	21 27	7.7	10 09	3.0	22 44	2.8	00 09	4.5	12 30	4.6
TH 11	12 21	6.2	—	—	09 40	8.2	22 10	8.1	11 01	3.2	23 30	2.9	01 10	4.7	13 22	4.8
F 12	00 44	6.2	13 11	6.5	10 20	8.6	22 45	8.4	11 44	3.4	—	—	01 53	4.9	14 01	5.0
SA 13	01 27	6.4	13 50	6.6	10 54	8.9	23 16	8.6	00 09	3.0	12 22	3.5	02 28	5.1	14 35	5.2
SU 14	02 03	6.6	14 24	6.7	11 25	9.1	23 46	8.8	00 43	3.1	12 56	3.5	02 59	5.2	15 05	5.3
M 15	02 35	6.7	14 55	6.7	11 56	9.2	—	—	01 14	3.1	13 26	3.5	03 27	5.2	15 34	5.4
TU 16	03 06	6.8	15 24	6.8	00 14	8.8	12 26	9.2	01 44	3.2	13 55	3.5	03 56	5.2	16 04	5.4
W 17	03 36	6.8	15 52	6.8	00 42	8.8	12 55	9.1	02 13	3.2	14 24	3.5	04 27	5.2	16 34	5.3
TH 18	04 04	6.8	16 20	6.7	01 10	8.7	13 23	9.0	02 43	3.3	14 56	3.5	04 59	5.1	17 05	5.2
F 19	04 32	6.8	16 50	6.6	01 38	8.6	13 53	8.7	03 13	3.3	15 30	3.4	05 33	5.0	17 39	5.1
SA 20	05 04	6.7	17 24	6.4	02 09	8.4	14 28	8.5	03 46	3.3	16 06	3.3	06 09	4.9	18 18	5.0
SU 21	05 41	6.5	18 04	6.1	02 46	8.1	15 12	8.1	04 21	3.2	16 46	3.1	06 51	4.7	19 05	4.7
M 22	06 24	6.3	18 53	5.9	03 36	7.7	16 12	7.6	05 01	3.1	17 36	2.9	07 41	4.5	20 05	4.5
TU 23	07 22	6.1	20 05	5.6	04 51	7.3	17 41	7.3	05 51	2.9	18 46	2.7	08 49	4.3	21 28	4.4
W 24	08 51	5.9	21 34	5.6	06 29	7.3	19 16	7.5	07 01	2.8	20 37	2.7	10 17	4.4	22 58	4.5
TH 25	10 20	6.1	23 05	6.0	07 55	7.8	20 35	8.0	08 53	2.9	22 14	2.9	11 37	4.6	—	—
F 26	11 36	6.5	—	—	09 01	8.4	21 36	8.7	10 15	3.1	23 12	3.1	00 14	4.9	12 40	5.0
SA 27	00 17	6.4	12 43	6.9	09 55	9.1	22 26	9.3	11 10	3.4	—	—	01 11	5.3	13 30	5.5
SU 28	01 12	6.8	13 37	7.2	10 43	9.7	23 10	9.7	00 01	3.3	11 59	3.5	01 59	5.6	14 14	5.8

MARCH 2010 *High Water* GMT

	LONDON BRIDGE						†LIVERPOOL						GREENOCK						LEITH					
	*Datum of Predictions 3.20m below						*Datum of Predictions 4.93m below						*Datum of Predictions 1.62m below						*Datum of Predictions 2.90m below					
	hr		*ht m*	*hr*		*ht m*	*hr*		*ht m*	*hr*		*ht m*	*hr*		*ht m*	*hr*		*ht m*	*hr*		*ht m*	*hr*		*ht m*
M 1	01	59	7.1	14	24	7.4	11	27	10.0	23	53	9.8	00	48	3.4	12	45	3.7	02	42	5.8	14	56	6.0
TU 2	02	42	7.3	15	08	7.4	12	09	10.2	—		—	01	32	3.4	13	30	3.8	03	24	5.9	15	40	6.1
W 3	03	23	7.4	15	50	7.4	00	33	9.8	12	51	10.0	02	13	3.4	14	13	3.8	04	07	5.8	16	24	6.0
TH 4	04	03	7.4	16	30	7.2	01	13	9.6	13	31	9.7	02	50	3.4	14	53	3.8	04	50	5.6	17	10	5.8
F 5	04	43	7.3	17	08	6.9	01	51	9.2	14	11	9.2	03	25	3.4	15	32	3.6	05	34	5.3	17	58	5.4
SA 6	05	22	7.0	17	44	6.5	02	30	8.7	14	53	8.5	03	59	3.3	16	10	3.4	06	19	5.0	18	51	5.0
SU 7	06	02	6.6	18	22	6.1	03	15	8.1	15	44	7.7	04	36	3.2	16	51	3.1	07	09	4.7	19	51	4.6
M 8	06	50	6.2	19	08	5.8	04	12	7.5	16	54	7.1	05	18	3.0	17	37	2.8	08	09	4.4	20	58	4.3
TU 9	07	54	5.8	20	10	5.5	05	32	7.1	18	31	6.8	06	10	2.8	18	33	2.5	09	18	4.2	22	16	4.2
W 10	09	15	5.6	21	52	5.4	07	04	7.1	20	04	7.0	07	41	2.6	21	20	2.5	10	38	4.2	23	45	4.3
TH 11	10	42	5.7	23	17	5.7	08	20	7.5	21	04	7.5	09	42	2.8	22	24	2.7	12	00	4.4	—		—
F 12	11	55	6.1	—		—	09	12	8.0	21	45	8.0	10	35	3.1	23	05	2.9	00	47	4.6	12	55	4.7
SA 13	00	14	6.1	12	44	6.4	09	52	8.4	22	19	8.3	11	17	3.2	23	41	3.0	01	29	4.8	13	35	4.9
SU 14	00	58	6.4	13	23	6.6	10	26	8.7	22	49	8.6	11	54	3.3	—		—	02	02	5.0	14	08	5.1
M 15	01	34	6.6	13	56	6.7	10	58	9.0	23	17	8.8	00	14	3.1	12	28	3.3	02	31	5.1	14	38	5.3
TU 16	02	07	6.7	14	26	6.7	11	28	9.1	23	45	8.9	00	46	3.1	12	59	3.3	02	59	5.2	15	07	5.4
W 17	02	38	6.9	14	55	6.8	11	57	9.2	—		—	01	15	3.2	13	28	3.3	03	28	5.3	15	37	5.4
TH 18	03	08	6.9	15	24	6.8	00	13	8.9	12	27	9.1	01	43	3.3	13	59	3.4	03	58	5.3	16	08	5.4
F 19	03	38	7.0	15	54	6.8	00	42	8.9	12	57	9.0	02	12	3.3	14	32	3.4	04	30	5.2	16	41	5.3
SA 20	04	09	6.9	16	26	6.6	01	11	8.8	13	30	8.8	02	43	3.4	15	08	3.4	05	04	5.1	17	18	5.2
SU 21	04	43	6.8	17	00	6.4	01	44	8.6	14	08	8.5	03	16	3.4	15	45	3.3	05	41	5.0	17	59	5.0
M 22	05	21	6.7	17	41	6.2	02	24	8.2	14	55	8.1	03	52	3.3	16	27	3.1	06	23	4.8	18	49	4.8
TU 23	06	07	6.4	18	33	5.9	03	17	7.8	15	59	7.6	04	32	3.2	17	18	2.9	07	14	4.5	19	51	4.5
W 24	07	08	6.1	19	44	5.7	04	36	7.4	17	29	7.3	05	23	3.0	18	31	2.7	08	23	4.4	21	13	4.4
TH 25	08	37	6.0	21	12	5.7	06	12	7.4	19	01	7.5	06	34	2.8	20	36	2.7	09	55	4.4	22	41	4.6
F 26	10	02	6.2	22	45	6.0	07	35	7.9	20	18	8.1	08	30	2.8	22	01	2.9	11	14	4.7	23	54	4.9
SA 27	11	21	6.6	23	55	6.5	08	40	8.5	21	16	8.7	09	54	3.1	22	54	3.1	12	16	5.1	—		—
SU 28	12	25	7.0	—		—	09	33	9.1	22	04	9.2	10	50	3.3	23	40	3.3	00	49	5.3	13	06	5.5
M 29	00	49	6.9	13	17	7.2	10	20	9.6	22	47	9.6	11	38	3.5	—		—	01	36	5.5	13	50	5.8
TU 30	01	35	7.1	14	02	7.3	11	03	9.9	23	28	9.7	00	24	3.3	12	25	3.6	02	18	5.7	14	34	6.0
W 31	02	17	7.3	14	43	7.3	11	45	9.9	—		—	01	06	3.4	13	09	3.6	02	59	5.7	15	18	6.0

APRIL 2010 *High Water* GMT

	LONDON BRIDGE						†LIVERPOOL						GREENOCK						LEITH					
TH 1	02	57	7.4	15	23	7.2	00	07	9.7	12	26	9.7	01	44	3.4	13	51	3.6	03	42	5.7	16	03	5.9
F 2	03	37	7.4	16	01	7.1	00	46	9.5	13	06	9.4	02	19	3.4	14	31	3.6	04	24	5.5	16	50	5.6
SA 3	04	17	7.3	16	37	6.8	01	23	9.2	13	45	8.9	02	53	3.4	15	09	3.4	05	07	5.3	17	37	5.3
SU 4	04	55	6.9	17	12	6.4	02	01	8.7	14	26	8.3	03	28	3.4	15	47	3.2	05	50	5.0	18	27	4.9
M 5	05	35	6.5	17	48	6.1	02	44	8.2	15	14	7.6	04	05	3.2	16	28	3.0	06	38	4.7	19	22	4.5
TU 6	06	20	6.1	18	32	5.8	03	39	7.6	16	19	7.0	04	47	3.0	17	15	2.7	07	33	4.4	20	23	4.3
W 7	07	19	5.7	19	31	5.5	04	52	7.2	17	47	6.7	05	38	2.8	18	12	2.5	08	39	4.2	21	32	4.1
TH 8	08	36	5.5	20	56	5.4	06	17	7.1	19	17	6.9	06	51	2.6	19	57	2.4	09	52	4.2	22	53	4.2
F 9	09	55	5.6	22	27	5.6	07	32	7.3	20	21	7.3	08	52	2.7	21	37	2.6	11	09	4.3	—		—
SA 10	11	11	6.0	23	30	6.0	08	28	7.8	21	06	7.8	09	55	2.9	22	23	2.8	00	04	4.4	12	11	4.6
SU 11	12	04	6.3	—		—	09	12	8.2	21	42	8.2	10	39	3.1	23	01	3.0	00	49	4.7	12	55	4.8
M 12	00	18	6.4	12	46	6.5	09	49	8.5	22	14	8.5	11	17	3.2	23	37	3.1	01	24	4.9	13	31	5.0
TU 13	00	58	6.6	13	20	6.6	10	23	8.8	22	44	8.7	11	52	3.2	—		—	01	55	5.1	14	04	5.2
W 14	01	33	6.8	13	53	6.7	10	56	9.0	23	14	8.9	00	10	3.1	12	26	3.2	02	26	5.2	14	37	5.3
TH 15	02	07	6.9	14	26	6.8	11	28	9.0	23	44	9.0	00	42	3.2	12	59	3.2	02	58	5.3	15	10	5.3
F 16	02	40	7.0	14	59	6.8	12	01	9.1	—		—	01	12	3.3	13	34	3.3	03	30	5.3	15	45	5.4
SA 17	03	14	7.0	15	33	6.7	00	17	9.0	12	37	9.0	01	44	3.4	14	11	3.3	04	04	5.3	16	22	5.3
SU 18	03	50	7.0	16	08	6.6	00	52	8.9	13	15	8.8	02	18	3.5	14	51	3.3	04	40	5.2	17	03	5.2
M 19	04	28	6.9	16	46	6.4	01	31	8.7	13	59	8.5	02	54	3.5	15	32	3.2	05	20	5.0	17	48	5.1
TU 20	05	10	6.7	17	30	6.2	02	17	8.4	14	52	8.1	03	33	3.4	16	19	3.0	06	06	4.9	18	41	4.9
W 21	06	01	6.5	18	25	6.0	03	15	8.0	15	59	7.7	04	16	3.3	17	15	2.9	07	00	4.7	19	44	4.7
TH 22	07	08	6.3	19	35	5.9	04	32	7.7	17	20	7.6	05	09	3.1	18	33	2.7	08	10	4.5	21	02	4.6
F 23	08	27	6.2	20	56	5.9	05	55	7.8	18	42	7.7	06	25	2.9	20	20	2.7	09	35	4.6	22	20	4.7
SA 24	09	45	6.4	22	21	6.2	07	09	8.1	19	52	8.2	08	06	2.9	21	33	2.9	10	48	4.8	23	28	4.9
SU 25	11	01	6.6	23	29	6.6	08	13	8.6	20	50	8.6	09	27	3.1	22	26	3.1	11	49	5.1	—		—
M 26	12	03	6.9	—		—	09	07	9.0	21	38	9.0	10	24	3.3	23	13	3.2	00	23	5.2	12	41	5.4
TU 27	00	23	6.9	12	54	7.0	09	55	9.3	22	22	9.3	11	14	3.4	23	56	3.3	01	10	5.4	13	28	5.6
W 28	01	09	7.0	13	38	7.0	10	40	9.5	23	03	9.4	12	01	3.5	—		—	01	54	5.5	14	14	5.7
TH 29	01	52	7.2	14	19	7.0	11	23	9.5	23	43	9.4	00	37	3.4	12	46	3.5	02	36	5.6	15	00	5.7
F 30	02	33	7.3	14	59	7.0	12	04	9.3	—		—	01	16	3.4	13	29	3.4	03	19	5.5	15	46	5.6

MAY 2010 *High Water* GMT

	LONDON BRIDGE *Datum of Predictions 3.20m below						†LIVERPOOL *Datum of Predictions 4.93m below						GREENOCK *Datum of Predictions 1.62m below						LEITH *Datum of Predictions 2.90m below					
	hr		*ht m*	*hr*		*ht m*	*hr*		*ht m*	*hr*		*ht m*	*hr*		*ht m*	*hr*		*ht m*	*hr*		*ht m*	*hr*		*ht m*
SA 1	03	14	7.3	15	37	6.9	00	21	9.3	12	45	9.0	01	52	3.4	14	09	3.3	04	01	5.4	16	32	5.4
SU 2	03	55	7.1	16	12	6.7	00	59	9.0	13	24	8.6	02	27	3.4	14	48	3.2	04	43	5.2	17	18	5.1
M 3	04	34	6.8	16	47	6.4	01	38	8.7	14	04	8.1	03	02	3.4	15	27	3.1	05	26	5.0	18	05	4.9
TU 4	05	14	6.4	17	22	6.1	02	20	8.3	14	50	7.7	03	40	3.3	16	09	2.9	06	10	4.8	18	54	4.6
W 5	05	56	6.1	18	05	5.9	03	10	7.8	15	45	7.2	04	21	3.1	16	57	2.8	07	01	4.5	19	47	4.4
TH 6	06	49	5.8	18	59	5.7	04	12	7.4	16	55	6.9	05	10	2.9	17	53	2.6	07	58	4.4	20	44	4.2
F 7	07	53	5.6	20	08	5.6	05	23	7.3	18	10	6.9	06	12	2.8	19	02	2.6	09	01	4.3	21	47	4.2
SA 8	09	00	5.7	21	28	5.6	06	32	7.3	19	18	7.2	07	33	2.7	20	19	2.6	10	06	4.3	22	51	4.3
SU 9	10	08	5.8	22	37	5.9	07	32	7.6	20	12	7.5	08	54	2.8	21	23	2.8	11	08	4.4	23	47	4.5
M 10	11	10	6.1	23	31	6.2	08	23	7.9	20	55	7.9	09	49	2.9	22	13	2.9	12	01	4.6	—		—
TU 11	11	59	6.3	—		—	09	06	8.2	21	33	8.3	10	33	3.0	22	55	3.1	00	34	4.7	12	47	4.8
W 12	00	17	6.5	12	42	6.5	09	46	8.5	22	08	8.6	11	12	3.1	23	33	3.2	01	14	5.0	13	29	5.0
TH 13	00	58	6.7	13	22	6.6	10	24	8.7	22	43	8.8	11	50	3.2	—		—	01	52	5.1	14	08	5.2
F 14	01	37	6.9	14	01	6.7	11	01	8.9	23	20	9.0	00	08	3.3	12	30	3.2	02	29	5.3	14	46	5.3
SA 15	02	16	7.0	14	40	6.7	11	41	9.0	23	58	9.1	00	44	3.4	13	12	3.2	03	06	5.3	15	26	5.4
SU 16	02	56	7.1	15	20	6.7	12	23	9.0	—		—	01	21	3.5	13	55	3.3	03	44	5.3	16	07	5.4
M 17	03	37	7.1	16	00	6.6	00	40	9.1	13	08	8.9	01	59	3.6	14	40	3.2	04	24	5.3	16	52	5.4
TU 18	04	20	7.0	16	42	6.5	01	26	8.9	13	57	8.7	02	40	3.6	15	26	3.2	05	07	5.2	17	41	5.2
W 19	05	08	6.9	17	29	6.4	02	17	8.7	14	52	8.4	03	22	3.5	16	17	3.1	05	56	5.1	18	34	5.0
TH 20	06	02	6.7	18	23	6.3	03	15	8.4	15	54	8.1	04	09	3.4	17	16	2.9	06	51	4.9	19	35	4.9
F 21	07	06	6.5	19	26	6.2	04	22	8.2	17	02	7.9	05	04	3.2	18	28	2.9	07	57	4.8	20	44	4.8
SA 22	08	14	6.5	20	39	6.2	05	31	8.2	18	13	8.0	06	12	3.1	19	46	2.9	09	12	4.8	21	55	4.8
SU 23	09	24	6.5	21	54	6.4	06	39	8.3	19	20	8.1	07	35	3.1	20	55	2.9	10	21	4.9	22	59	4.9
M 24	10	35	6.6	22	59	6.6	07	44	8.5	20	20	8.4	08	54	3.1	21	53	3.0	11	23	5.1	23	56	5.0
TU 25	11	37	6.7	23	56	6.7	08	42	8.7	21	12	8.7	09	56	3.2	22	44	3.2	12	18	5.2	—		—
W 26	12	30	6.7	—		—	09	34	8.8	21	59	8.9	10	50	3.3	23	30	3.3	00	46	5.2	13	10	5.3
TH 27	00	46	6.8	13	17	6.7	10	21	8.9	22	42	9.1	11	39	3.3	—		—	01	33	5.3	13	59	5.4
F 28	01	32	6.9	14	00	6.7	11	06	8.9	23	23	9.1	00	13	3.3	12	26	3.3	02	18	5.3	14	47	5.4
SA 29	02	15	7.0	14	40	6.7	11	48	8.8	—		—	00	54	3.4	13	10	3.2	03	01	5.3	15	32	5.4
SU 30	02	58	7.0	15	18	6.7	00	02	9.1	12	29	8.7	01	31	3.4	13	51	3.1	03	43	5.3	16	16	5.2
M 31	03	40	6.9	15	55	6.6	00	41	8.9	13	07	8.5	02	06	3.4	14	30	3.1	04	24	5.2	16	59	5.1

JUNE 2010 *High Water* GMT

	LONDON BRIDGE						†LIVERPOOL						GREENOCK						LEITH					
TU 1	04	19	6.7	16	29	6.4	01	19	8.7	13	45	8.2	02	42	3.4	15	10	3.0	05	03	5.1	17	40	4.9
W 2	04	57	6.5	17	04	6.3	01	58	8.5	14	25	7.9	03	19	3.4	15	51	2.9	05	44	4.9	18	23	4.7
TH 3	05	36	6.2	17	43	6.1	02	42	8.2	15	10	7.6	03	58	3.2	16	36	2.9	06	28	4.8	19	08	4.5
F 4	06	18	6.0	18	27	6.0	03	31	7.8	16	02	7.3	04	41	3.1	17	24	2.8	07	15	4.6	19	56	4.4
SA 5	07	09	5.9	19	21	5.8	04	27	7.6	17	02	7.1	05	31	2.9	18	16	2.8	08	09	4.5	20	50	4.3
SU 6	08	05	5.8	20	26	5.7	05	29	7.4	18	06	7.1	06	29	2.8	19	13	2.8	09	07	4.4	21	47	4.3
M 7	09	06	5.8	21	38	5.8	06	30	7.5	19	07	7.3	07	34	2.8	20	14	2.8	10	07	4.4	22	45	4.5
TU 8	10	09	5.9	22	41	6.1	07	28	7.7	20	02	7.7	08	43	2.8	21	15	2.9	11	06	4.5	23	42	4.6
W 9	11	10	6.1	23	35	6.4	08	21	7.9	20	51	8.0	09	43	2.9	22	09	3.0	12	03	4.7	—		—
TH 10	12	05	6.4	—		—	09	10	8.3	21	35	8.4	10	34	3.0	22	55	3.1	00	34	4.8	12	55	4.9
F 11	00	25	6.6	12	55	6.6	09	56	8.6	22	18	8.8	11	21	3.1	23	38	3.3	01	22	5.1	13	42	5.1
SA 12	01	12	6.9	13	41	6.7	10	41	8.8	23	01	9.0	12	08	3.2	—		—	02	05	5.2	14	27	5.3
SU 13	01	58	7.0	14	27	6.7	11	27	9.0	23	46	9.2	00	20	3.4	12	56	3.2	02	46	5.4	15	11	5.5
M 14	02	44	7.1	15	11	6.8	12	13	9.2	—		—	01	02	3.5	13	44	3.2	03	28	5.5	15	56	5.6
TU 15	03	30	7.2	15	55	6.8	00	32	9.3	13	02	9.1	01	45	3.6	14	33	3.2	04	11	5.5	16	42	5.6
W 16	04	17	7.2	16	39	6.8	01	21	9.3	13	52	9.0	02	29	3.7	15	23	3.2	04	56	5.5	17	30	5.5
TH 17	05	06	7.1	17	25	6.7	02	11	9.2	14	43	8.8	03	14	3.6	16	14	3.1	05	45	5.4	18	22	5.3
F 18	05	58	7.0	18	15	6.6	03	04	8.9	15	37	8.5	04	01	3.6	17	08	3.1	06	38	5.3	19	18	5.1
SA 19	06	54	6.8	19	11	6.6	04	01	8.7	16	36	8.2	04	53	3.4	18	04	3.0	07	38	5.1	20	20	4.9
SU 20	07	52	6.6	20	14	6.5	05	02	8.4	17	40	8.0	05	50	3.3	19	05	2.9	08	46	5.0	21	25	4.8
M 21	08	56	6.5	21	22	6.4	06	07	8.2	18	47	8.0	06	56	3.1	20	11	2.9	09	54	4.9	22	29	4.8
TU 22	10	04	6.3	22	28	6.4	07	15	8.1	19	52	8.1	08	15	3.0	21	18	3.0	10	59	4.9	23	30	4.8
W 23	11	10	6.3	23	30	6.5	08	21	8.2	20	51	8.3	09	30	3.0	22	18	3.1	12	02	4.9	—		—
TH 24	12	09	6.4	—		—	09	19	8.3	21	43	8.5	10	32	3.1	23	10	3.2	00	28	4.9	13	00	5.0
F 25	00	27	6.5	13	00	6.4	10	10	8.4	22	28	8.8	11	26	3.1	23	56	3.3	01	20	5.1	13	52	5.1
SA 26	01	19	6.7	13	46	6.5	10	56	8.6	23	10	8.9	12	15	3.1	—		—	02	06	5.2	14	38	5.2
SU 27	02	05	6.8	14	27	6.6	11	36	8.6	23	48	9.0	00	38	3.4	12	59	3.0	02	49	5.2	15	20	5.2
M 28	02	48	6.8	15	04	6.6	12	14	8.6	—		—	01	16	3.4	13	38	3.0	03	28	5.3	15	59	5.2
TU 29	03	27	6.8	15	40	6.6	00	24	8.9	12	49	8.5	01	51	3.5	14	15	3.0	04	05	5.2	16	36	5.1
W 30	04	04	6.7	16	14	6.6	01	00	8.9	13	23	8.4	02	25	3.4	14	51	3.0	04	41	5.2	17	13	5.0

JULY 2010 *High Water* GMT

	LONDON BRIDGE *Datum of Predictions 3.20m below						†LIVERPOOL *Datum of Predictions 4.93m below						GREENOCK *Datum of Predictions 1.62m below						LEITH *Datum of Predictions 2.90m below					
	hr		*ht m*	*hr*		*ht m*	*hr*		*ht m*	*hr*		*ht m*	*hr*		*ht m*	*hr*		*ht m*	*hr*		*ht m*	*hr*		*ht m*
TH 1	04	38	6.6	16	46	6.5	01	35	8.7	13	57	8.2	02	59	3.4	15	28	3.0	05	17	5.1	17	50	4.9
F 2	05	11	6.4	17	19	6.4	02	12	8.5	14	34	8.0	03	33	3.3	16	07	3.0	05	55	5.0	18	29	4.7
SA 3	05	46	6.3	17	54	6.3	02	50	8.2	15	13	7.7	04	10	3.2	16	47	3.0	06	35	4.8	19	12	4.6
SU 4	06	24	6.1	18	34	6.1	03	33	7.9	15	59	7.5	04	51	3.1	17	30	2.9	07	19	4.7	19	59	4.5
M 5	07	09	5.9	19	23	5.9	04	23	7.6	16	55	7.3	05	39	2.9	18	16	2.9	08	09	4.5	20	53	4.4
TU 6	08	05	5.8	20	28	5.8	05	24	7.5	18	02	7.3	06	36	2.8	19	10	2.8	09	10	4.4	21	54	4.4
W 7	09	12	5.8	21	49	5.9	06	32	7.5	19	11	7.5	07	43	2.8	20	14	2.8	10	17	4.4	22	57	4.5
TH 8	10	24	5.9	22	56	6.2	07	39	7.7	20	14	7.8	08	57	2.8	21	22	2.9	11	23	4.6	23	59	4.7
F 9	11	32	6.2	23	55	6.6	08	41	8.0	21	09	8.3	10	05	2.9	22	23	3.1	12	26	4.8	—		—
SA 10	12	32	6.5	—		—	09	36	8.5	22	00	8.8	11	02	3.0	23	14	3.3	00	55	5.0	13	22	5.1
SU 11	00	51	6.9	13	25	6.7	10	27	8.9	22	47	9.2	11	54	3.1	—		—	01	45	5.2	14	11	5.4
M 12	01	43	7.1	14	14	6.8	11	16	9.2	23	34	9.5	00	01	3.4	12	46	3.2	02	30	5.5	14	57	5.6
TU 13	02	33	7.3	15	00	7.0	12	03	9.4	—		—	00	47	3.6	13	36	3.2	03	13	5.7	15	41	5.8
W 14	03	21	7.4	15	44	7.1	00	21	9.7	12	50	9.5	01	33	3.7	14	26	3.2	03	56	5.8	16	27	5.8
TH 15	04	08	7.4	16	27	7.1	01	08	9.8	13	37	9.4	02	18	3.7	15	13	3.2	04	41	5.8	17	14	5.7
F 16	04	55	7.3	17	11	7.1	01	55	9.6	14	23	9.1	03	03	3.8	15	59	3.2	05	28	5.7	18	02	5.5
SA 17	05	42	7.1	17	56	6.9	02	42	9.4	15	11	8.8	03	48	3.7	16	44	3.2	06	19	5.6	18	54	5.2
SU 18	06	31	6.8	18	45	6.8	03	32	8.9	16	03	8.4	04	34	3.6	17	30	3.1	07	14	5.3	19	50	4.9
M 19	07	22	6.5	19	42	6.5	04	29	8.4	17	03	8.0	05	22	3.3	18	19	3.0	08	19	5.0	20	53	4.7
TU 20	08	20	6.2	20	47	6.3	05	35	8.0	18	14	7.7	06	15	3.1	19	19	2.9	09	28	4.8	21	59	4.6
W 21	09	28	6.0	21	56	6.2	06	51	7.7	19	29	7.7	07	24	2.9	20	42	2.8	10	39	4.7	23	07	4.6
TH 22	10	42	6.0	23	07	6.2	08	08	7.7	20	37	8.0	09	11	2.8	21	58	3.0	11	51	4.7	—		—
F 23	11	49	6.1	—		—	09	12	7.9	21	32	8.3	10	27	2.8	22	56	3.1	00	14	4.8	12	55	4.8
SA 24	00	14	6.4	12	46	6.3	10	04	8.2	22	18	8.6	11	22	2.9	23	43	3.3	01	12	4.9	13	47	5.0
SU 25	01	10	6.6	13	33	6.5	10	46	8.4	22	56	8.9	12	08	3.0	—		—	01	57	5.1	14	29	5.1
M 26	01	55	6.7	14	12	6.6	11	22	8.6	23	31	9.0	00	25	3.4	12	49	3.0	02	36	5.2	15	05	5.2
TU 27	02	34	6.8	14	48	6.7	11	55	8.7	—		—	01	02	3.4	13	23	3.0	03	11	5.3	15	39	5.2
W 28	03	10	6.8	15	21	6.7	00	04	9.1	12	26	8.7	01	35	3.5	13	54	3.0	03	44	5.3	16	11	5.2
TH 29	03	43	6.8	15	52	6.8	00	37	9.0	12	57	8.6	02	05	3.5	14	25	3.1	04	16	5.3	16	43	5.1
F 30	04	13	6.7	16	23	6.7	01	08	8.9	13	27	8.5	02	35	3.4	14	58	3.1	04	49	5.3	17	17	5.0
SA 31	04	42	6.6	16	51	6.6	01	40	8.8	13	57	8.3	03	07	3.4	15	31	3.1	05	23	5.1	17	53	4.9

AUGUST 2010 *High Water* GMT

	LONDON BRIDGE						†LIVERPOOL						GREENOCK						LEITH					
SU 1	05	10	6.5	17	21	6.5	02	11	8.5	14	30	8.1	03	40	3.3	16	06	3.1	05	58	5.0	18	31	4.8
M 2	05	42	6.3	17	55	6.3	02	46	8.2	15	07	7.8	04	17	3.2	16	44	3.1	06	37	4.8	19	13	4.6
TU 3	06	19	6.0	18	36	6.1	03	28	7.9	15	55	7.5	04	58	3.0	17	27	3.0	07	22	4.6	20	03	4.5
W 4	07	07	5.8	19	31	5.9	04	25	7.5	17	02	7.3	05	49	2.9	18	18	2.9	08	19	4.5	21	06	4.4
TH 5	08	16	5.6	20	55	5.8	05	42	7.3	18	28	7.3	06	57	2.7	19	23	2.8	09	32	4.4	22	19	4.4
F 6	09	40	5.7	22	20	6.1	07	06	7.4	19	45	7.7	08	22	2.7	20	42	2.9	10	51	4.5	23	30	4.6
SA 7	11	02	6.0	23	29	6.5	08	20	7.9	20	50	8.3	09	49	2.8	21	56	3.1	12	03	4.8	—		—
SU 8	12	11	6.4	—		—	09	22	8.5	21	44	8.9	10	53	3.0	22	55	3.3	00	33	5.0	13	04	5.2
M 9	00	33	6.9	13	07	6.7	10	14	9.0	22	33	9.4	11	45	3.1	23	45	3.5	01	26	5.3	13	54	5.5
TU 10	01	29	7.2	13	57	7.0	11	02	9.5	23	18	9.9	12	35	3.2	—		—	02	10	5.7	14	38	5.8
W 11	02	10	7.4	14	42	7.2	11	47	9.7	—		—	00	32	3.6	13	23	3.3	02	53	5.9	15	22	5.9
TH 12	03	05	7.5	15	25	7.3	00	03	10.1	12	31	9.8	01	19	3.7	14	09	3.3	03	36	6.1	16	06	5.9
F 13	03	50	7.5	16	06	7.4	00	48	10.1	13	14	9.7	02	04	3.8	14	52	3.3	04	21	6.1	16	51	5.8
SA 14	04	34	7.3	16	47	7.3	01	31	9.9	13	57	9.4	02	47	3.8	15	32	3.3	05	07	5.9	17	37	5.5
SU 15	05	17	7.1	17	29	7.1	02	15	9.5	14	41	8.9	03	29	3.8	16	11	3.3	05	56	5.7	18	25	5.2
M 16	06	00	6.7	18	14	6.8	03	02	8.9	15	29	8.4	04	11	3.6	16	50	3.2	06	49	5.3	19	19	4.9
TU 17	06	45	6.4	19	06	6.5	03	55	8.2	16	27	7.9	04	54	3.3	17	34	3.0	07	53	4.9	20	21	4.6
W 18	07	37	6.0	20	11	6.1	05	04	7.6	17	43	7.5	05	41	3.0	18	28	2.9	09	04	4.6	21	30	4.5
TH 19	08	44	5.7	21	26	5.9	06	31	7.3	19	08	7.5	06	39	2.7	20	00	2.8	10	19	4.5	22	45	4.5
F 20	10	12	5.7	22	45	6.0	07	59	7.4	20	23	7.8	09	09	2.6	21	42	2.9	11	40	4.5	—		—
SA 21	11	28	5.9	—		—	09	05	7.7	21	19	8.2	10	24	2.7	22	39	3.2	00	00	4.7	12	47	4.7
SU 22	00	01	6.3	12	27	6.3	09	52	8.1	22	01	8.6	11	12	2.9	23	25	3.3	00	58	4.9	13	35	4.9
M 23	00	55	6.6	13	13	6.5	10	29	8.4	22	36	8.9	11	52	3.0	—		—	01	42	5.1	14	12	5.1
TU 24	01	37	6.8	13	51	6.7	11	01	8.7	23	08	9.1	00	05	3.4	12	27	3.0	02	17	5.3	14	44	5.2
W 25	02	13	6.8	14	24	6.8	11	30	8.8	23	39	9.2	00	41	3.5	12	57	3.1	02	49	5.4	15	13	5.3
TH 26	02	45	6.8	14	55	6.8	11	59	8.9	—		—	01	12	3.5	13	26	3.1	03	18	5.4	15	42	5.3
F 27	03	14	6.8	15	25	6.9	00	09	9.2	12	27	8.8	01	40	3.4	13	54	3.2	03	48	5.4	16	12	5.2
SA 28	03	42	6.8	15	54	6.9	00	39	9.1	12	55	8.8	02	09	3.4	14	24	3.2	04	19	5.4	16	44	5.2
SU 29	04	09	6.7	16	21	6.8	01	08	8.9	13	23	8.6	02	39	3.4	14	55	3.3	04	52	5.3	17	18	5.1
M 30	04	37	6.6	16	50	6.6	01	37	8.7	13	53	8.4	03	13	3.4	15	29	3.3	05	26	5.1	17	54	4.9
TU 31	05	07	6.4	17	24	6.5	02	10	8.4	14	28	8.1	03	48	3.3	16	05	3.3	06	05	4.9	18	34	4.7

SEPTEMBER 2010 *High Water* GMT

	LONDON BRIDGE *Datum of Predictions 3.20m below				†LIVERPOOL *Datum of Predictions 4.93m below				GREENOCK *Datum of Predictions 1.62m below				LEITH *Datum of Predictions 2.90m below			
	hr	*ht m*	*hr*	*ht m*	*hr*	*ht m*	*hr*	*ht m*	*hr*	*ht m*	*hr*	*ht m*	*hr*	*ht m*	*hr*	*ht m*
W 1	05 42	6.1	18 05	6.3	02 51	8.0	15 14	7.8	04 26	3.1	16 46	3.1	06 50	4.7	19 22	4.6
TH 2	06 27	5.9	18 56	6.1	03 47	7.6	16 22	7.4	05 14	2.9	17 36	3.0	07 46	4.5	20 25	4.4
F 3	07 32	5.6	20 15	5.9	05 09	7.3	17 57	7.3	06 22	2.7	18 42	2.9	09 00	4.4	21 46	4.4
SA 4	09 00	5.6	21 49	6.0	06 43	7.4	19 23	7.7	07 58	2.7	20 09	2.9	10 26	4.5	23 05	4.7
SU 5	10 33	5.9	23 07	6.5	08 04	7.9	20 31	8.4	09 43	2.8	21 35	3.1	11 43	4.8	—	—
M 6	11 48	6.4	—	—	09 06	8.6	21 25	9.1	10 43	3.1	22 36	3.4	00 10	5.0	12 44	5.2
TU 7	00 14	6.9	12 45	6.8	09 57	9.2	22 13	9.7	11 31	3.2	23 27	3.6	01 03	5.4	13 32	5.6
W 8	01 10	7.2	13 33	7.1	10 42	9.6	22 57	10.1	12 16	3.3	—	—	01 47	5.8	14 16	5.9
TH 9	01 58	7.4	14 17	7.3	11 25	9.9	23 41	10.2	00 14	3.7	13 01	3.4	02 29	6.1	14 58	6.0
F 10	02 43	7.5	14 59	7.5	12 07	9.9	—	—	01 01	3.8	13 43	3.4	03 13	6.2	15 41	6.0
SA 11	03 26	7.4	15 40	7.5	00 23	10.2	12 48	9.8	01 45	3.8	14 22	3.4	03 58	6.2	16 25	5.8
SU 12	04 07	7.3	16 21	7.4	01 06	9.9	13 29	9.4	02 28	3.8	15 00	3.4	04 44	6.0	17 10	5.5
M 13	04 47	7.0	17 02	7.1	01 48	9.4	14 10	9.0	03 08	3.7	15 36	3.4	05 34	5.6	17 57	5.2
TU 14	05 26	6.6	17 44	6.8	02 33	8.7	14 56	8.4	03 48	3.5	16 15	3.3	06 28	5.2	18 49	4.9
W 15	06 06	6.2	18 32	6.3	03 25	8.0	15 54	7.8	04 29	3.2	16 58	3.1	07 29	4.8	19 50	4.6
TH 16	06 53	5.8	19 37	5.9	04 35	7.3	17 12	7.4	05 15	2.9	17 50	2.9	08 39	4.5	21 01	4.4
F 17	07 56	5.5	20 54	5.7	06 07	7.0	18 41	7.4	06 13	2.6	19 14	2.8	09 54	4.4	22 17	4.4
SA 18	09 32	5.5	22 18	5.8	07 40	7.2	19 57	7.7	08 58	2.5	21 14	2.9	11 17	4.4	23 33	4.6
SU 19	10 56	5.8	23 35	6.2	08 43	7.6	20 52	8.2	10 04	2.7	22 12	3.2	12 24	4.7	—	—
M 20	11 56	6.2	—	—	09 28	8.1	21 33	8.6	10 47	2.9	22 57	3.4	00 31	4.8	13 10	4.9
TU 21	00 28	6.6	12 43	6.5	10 02	8.4	22 08	8.9	11 23	3.1	23 36	3.5	01 14	5.1	13 45	5.1
W 22	01 09	6.7	13 21	6.7	10 33	8.7	22 40	9.1	11 54	3.2	—	—	01 49	5.2	14 15	5.2
TH 23	01 43	6.8	13 53	6.8	11 01	8.9	23 10	9.2	00 10	3.5	12 24	3.2	02 20	5.4	14 43	5.3
F 24	02 13	6.8	14 24	6.9	11 29	9.0	23 40	9.2	00 42	3.5	12 53	3.3	02 50	5.4	15 11	5.3
SA 25	02 42	6.8	14 54	6.9	11 57	9.0	—	—	01 11	3.5	13 22	3.3	03 20	5.4	15 41	5.3
SU 26	03 10	6.8	15 23	6.9	00 10	9.2	12 25	8.9	01 41	3.5	13 51	3.4	03 52	5.4	16 13	5.3
M 27	03 39	6.8	15 53	6.9	00 40	9.0	12 54	8.8	02 14	3.5	14 23	3.5	04 25	5.3	16 47	5.2
TU 28	04 08	6.6	16 25	6.8	01 11	8.8	13 25	8.6	02 49	3.4	14 58	3.5	05 01	5.2	17 23	5.0
W 29	04 40	6.4	17 01	6.6	01 47	8.5	14 03	8.3	03 26	3.3	15 34	3.4	05 42	5.0	18 04	4.9
TH 30	05 16	6.2	17 43	6.4	02 31	8.1	14 52	7.9	04 06	3.2	16 15	3.3	06 30	4.8	18 53	4.7

OCTOBER 2010 *High Water* GMT

	LONDON BRIDGE				†LIVERPOOL				GREENOCK				LEITH			
F 1	06 02	5.9	18 37	6.2	03 30	7.7	16 03	7.6	04 54	3.0	17 05	3.1	07 27	4.6	19 56	4.5
SA 2	07 06	5.7	19 56	6.0	04 53	7.4	17 36	7.5	06 03	2.8	18 12	3.0	08 41	4.5	21 19	4.5
SU 3	08 30	5.6	21 24	6.1	06 25	7.5	19 00	7.9	07 46	2.7	19 42	3.0	10 05	4.6	22 40	4.8
M 4	10 04	5.9	22 43	6.5	07 43	8.1	20 07	8.5	09 27	2.9	21 11	3.2	11 20	4.9	23 44	5.1
TU 5	11 20	6.4	23 51	6.9	08 44	8.7	21 02	9.2	10 23	3.2	22 14	3.4	12 19	5.3	—	—
W 6	12 17	6.8	—	—	09 34	9.3	21 50	9.7	11 09	3.4	23 05	3.6	00 36	5.5	13 07	5.6
TH 7	00 46	7.2	13 06	7.1	10 18	9.7	22 34	10.0	11 52	3.5	23 53	3.7	01 22	5.9	13 51	5.8
F 8	01 34	7.3	13 50	7.3	11 01	9.9	23 18	10.1	12 34	3.5	—	—	02 06	6.1	14 33	5.9
SA 9	02 18	7.3	14 32	7.4	11 42	9.9	—	—	00 39	3.8	13 15	3.5	02 51	6.1	15 16	5.9
SU 10	03 00	7.3	15 14	7.5	00 00	10.0	12 22	9.7	01 24	3.8	13 53	3.6	03 37	6.1	15 59	5.7
M 11	03 40	7.1	15 56	7.3	00 43	9.6	13 03	9.4	02 07	3.7	14 30	3.6	04 25	5.8	16 44	5.5
TU 12	04 19	6.8	16 37	7.0	01 25	9.1	13 43	9.0	02 47	3.6	15 07	3.5	05 15	5.5	17 31	5.2
W 13	04 56	6.5	17 19	6.6	02 09	8.5	14 28	8.5	03 27	3.4	15 46	3.4	06 08	5.1	18 21	4.9
TH 14	05 33	6.1	18 06	6.2	02 59	7.9	15 24	7.9	04 09	3.2	16 30	3.2	07 06	4.8	19 20	4.7
F 15	06 16	5.8	19 04	5.8	04 04	7.3	16 36	7.5	04 57	2.9	17 22	3.1	08 09	4.5	20 27	4.5
SA 16	07 14	5.5	20 16	5.6	05 29	7.0	17 58	7.4	05 56	2.7	18 35	2.9	09 18	4.3	21 38	4.4
SU 17	08 37	5.4	21 34	5.7	06 56	7.1	19 12	7.6	07 46	2.6	20 23	3.0	10 33	4.4	22 49	4.5
M 18	10 07	5.6	22 53	6.0	08 04	7.5	20 10	8.0	09 19	2.8	21 32	3.1	11 42	4.6	23 49	4.7
TU 19	11 13	6.0	23 50	6.3	08 51	7.9	20 56	8.4	10 05	3.0	22 19	3.3	12 31	4.8	—	—
W 20	12 02	6.3	—	—	09 27	8.3	21 33	8.7	10 43	3.2	22 59	3.4	00 36	5.0	13 08	5.0
TH 21	00 32	6.5	12 43	6.6	09 59	8.6	22 08	8.9	11 17	3.3	23 35	3.4	01 14	5.1	13 40	5.2
F 22	01 08	6.6	13 18	6.7	10 29	8.8	22 40	9.1	11 50	3.4	—	—	01 47	5.3	14 10	5.3
SA 23	01 39	6.7	13 51	6.8	10 59	9.0	23 12	9.1	00 08	3.5	12 21	3.4	02 20	5.4	14 41	5.4
SU 24	02 10	6.8	14 23	6.9	11 29	9.1	23 44	9.1	00 42	3.5	12 52	3.5	02 54	5.4	15 13	5.4
M 25	02 42	6.8	14 56	7.0	11 59	9.1	—	—	01 16	3.5	13 24	3.6	03 28	5.4	15 47	5.4
TU 26	03 14	6.7	15 30	6.9	00 18	9.0	12 33	9.0	01 53	3.5	13 58	3.7	04 04	5.4	16 22	5.3
W 27	03 47	6.6	16 06	6.9	00 55	8.9	13 10	8.8	02 31	3.5	14 35	3.7	04 43	5.3	17 00	5.2
TH 28	04 22	6.4	16 46	6.8	01 36	8.6	13 52	8.5	03 12	3.4	15 14	3.6	05 27	5.1	17 43	5.0
F 29	05 01	6.3	17 32	6.6	02 24	8.3	14 45	8.2	03 55	3.2	15 56	3.5	06 16	5.0	18 33	4.9
SA 30	05 50	6.1	18 30	6.3	03 25	7.9	15 54	7.9	04 47	3.1	16 47	3.4	07 14	4.8	19 35	4.7
SU 31	06 53	5.9	19 44	6.2	04 41	7.7	17 16	7.9	05 54	2.9	17 53	3.2	08 24	4.7	20 54	4.7

NOVEMBER 2010 *High Water* GMT

	LONDON BRIDGE *Datum of Predictions 3.20m below						†LIVERPOOL *Datum of Predictions 4.93m below						GREENOCK *Datum of Predictions 1.62m below						LEITH *Datum of Predictions 2.90m below					
	hr		*ht m*	*hr*		*ht m*	*hr*		*ht m*	*hr*		*ht m*	*hr*		*ht m*	*hr*		*ht m*	*hr*		*ht m*	*hr*		*ht m*
M 1	08	08	5.9	21	02	6.3	06	01	7.8	18	32	8.1	07	28	2.9	19	15	3.2	09	42	4.8	22	12	4.9
TU 2	09	34	6.1	22	17	6.5	07	15	8.2	19	39	8.6	08	56	3.0	20	41	3.3	10	52	5.0	23	16	5.2
W 3	10	49	6.4	23	25	6.8	08	17	8.7	20	36	9.1	09	54	3.2	21	48	3.5	11	51	5.3	—		—
TH 4	11	48	6.7	—		—	09	09	9.1	21	26	9.4	10	42	3.4	22	42	3.6	00	10	5.5	12	42	5.5
F 5	00	21	6.9	12	39	7.0	09	55	9.4	22	13	9.7	11	27	3.5	23	31	3.7	01	00	5.7	13	27	5.7
SA 6	01	10	7.0	13	25	7.1	10	38	9.6	22	58	9.7	12	09	3.6	—		—	01	46	5.9	14	10	5.8
SU 7	01	54	7.0	14	09	7.2	11	20	9.7	23	42	9.6	00	19	3.7	12	50	3.6	02	33	5.9	14	54	5.8
M 8	02	37	7.0	14	53	7.3	12	01	9.6	—		—	01	05	3.7	13	29	3.7	03	21	5.8	15	38	5.7
TU 9	03	18	6.9	15	36	7.2	00	25	9.3	12	42	9.3	01	49	3.6	14	07	3.7	04	09	5.6	16	23	5.5
W 10	03	57	6.7	16	19	6.9	01	08	8.9	13	23	9.0	02	30	3.5	14	45	3.6	04	58	5.4	17	08	5.3
TH 11	04	33	6.4	17	00	6.5	01	50	8.4	14	06	8.6	03	11	3.3	15	25	3.5	05	47	5.1	17	55	5.0
F 12	05	09	6.2	17	43	6.2	02	36	7.9	14	55	8.2	03	54	3.2	16	08	3.4	06	38	4.8	18	47	4.8
SA 13	05	49	5.9	18	33	5.9	03	30	7.5	15	55	7.8	04	41	3.0	16	57	3.2	07	32	4.6	19	45	4.6
SU 14	06	38	5.7	19	32	5.7	04	36	7.2	17	03	7.5	05	37	2.8	17	56	3.1	08	31	4.4	20	48	4.5
M 15	07	43	5.5	20	36	5.6	05	49	7.1	18	12	7.5	06	44	2.8	19	08	3.0	09	32	4.4	21	51	4.5
TU 16	09	02	5.5	21	44	5.7	07	00	7.3	19	15	7.7	07	59	2.8	20	27	3.1	10	34	4.4	22	51	4.6
W 17	10	14	5.8	22	51	5.9	07	58	7.6	20	08	8.0	09	04	3.0	21	29	3.2	11	32	4.6	23	45	4.7
TH 18	11	12	6.1	23	44	6.2	08	43	8.0	20	54	8.3	09	55	3.2	22	16	3.3	12	19	4.8	—		—
F 19	11	59	6.3	—		—	09	22	8.3	21	34	8.6	10	38	3.3	22	58	3.3	00	32	4.9	13	00	5.0
SA 20	00	26	6.4	12	41	6.6	09	57	8.7	22	11	8.8	11	17	3.4	23	36	3.4	01	14	5.1	13	38	5.2
SU 21	01	05	6.6	13	20	6.7	10	31	8.9	22	48	9.0	11	52	3.5	—		—	01	53	5.2	14	14	5.4
M 22	01	43	6.7	13	58	6.9	11	06	9.1	23	25	9.1	00	15	3.4	12	26	3.6	02	31	5.4	14	50	5.4
TU 23	02	21	6.7	14	36	6.9	11	42	9.2	—		—	00	55	3.4	13	02	3.7	03	09	5.4	15	26	5.5
W 24	02	59	6.7	15	15	7.0	00	04	9.1	12	20	9.2	01	36	3.4	13	40	3.8	03	48	5.5	16	03	5.4
TH 25	03	36	6.6	15	56	7.0	00	46	9.0	13	02	9.1	02	18	3.4	14	19	3.8	04	30	5.4	16	44	5.4
F 26	04	15	6.5	16	39	6.9	01	31	8.8	13	48	8.9	03	02	3.4	15	01	3.8	05	16	5.3	17	29	5.3
SA 27	04	57	6.4	17	28	6.7	02	21	8.6	14	41	8.7	03	49	3.3	15	46	3.7	06	05	5.2	18	19	5.1
SU 28	05	45	6.3	18	25	6.6	03	17	8.3	15	42	8.4	04	41	3.2	16	36	3.6	07	00	5.0	19	16	5.0
M 29	06	42	6.2	19	29	6.4	04	21	8.1	16	50	8.3	05	41	3.1	17	35	3.4	08	03	4.9	20	27	4.9
TU 30	07	48	6.1	20	38	6.4	05	31	8.0	18	00	8.3	06	56	3.0	18	45	3.4	09	14	4.8	21	41	5.0

DECEMBER 2010 *High Water* GMT

	LONDON BRIDGE						†LIVERPOOL						GREENOCK						LEITH					
W 1	09	04	6.2	21	49	6.4	06	42	8.1	19	08	8.5	08	15	3.1	20	04	3.3	10	22	4.9	22	48	5.1
TU 2	10	18	6.3	22	58	6.5	07	47	8.4	20	10	8.7	09	21	3.2	21	19	3.4	11	24	5.1	23	48	5.3
F 3	11	20	6.5	23	58	6.6	08	44	8.7	21	07	8.9	10	16	3.3	22	20	3.5	12	18	5.3	—		—
SA 4	12	16	6.7	—		—	09	35	9.0	21	59	9.1	11	04	3.5	23	14	3.5	00	43	5.4	13	08	5.4
SU 5	00	50	6.6	13	06	6.8	10	22	9.3	22	46	9.2	11	50	3.6	—		—	01	34	5.5	13	55	5.5
M 6	01	37	6.7	13	53	6.9	11	06	9.4	23	31	9.2	00	04	3.5	12	33	3.7	02	23	5.6	14	39	5.6
TU 7	02	20	6.7	14	39	7.0	11	47	9.4	—		—	00	52	3.5	13	13	3.7	03	11	5.6	15	23	5.5
W 8	03	01	6.7	15	23	7.0	00	13	9.0	12	27	9.3	01	36	3.4	13	52	3.7	03	56	5.5	16	06	5.5
TH 9	03	40	6.6	16	05	6.8	00	54	8.8	13	06	9.1	02	17	3.4	14	29	3.7	04	41	5.3	16	48	5.3
F 10	04	17	6.5	16	44	6.5	01	32	8.5	13	45	8.8	02	57	3.3	15	07	3.6	05	24	5.1	17	29	5.2
SA 11	04	51	6.3	17	22	6.3	02	11	8.2	14	26	8.5	03	38	3.2	15	47	3.5	06	07	4.9	18	12	5.0
SU 12	05	26	6.2	18	01	6.1	02	53	7.9	15	13	8.1	04	21	3.1	16	30	3.4	06	51	4.7	18	59	4.8
M 13	06	06	6.0	18	46	5.9	03	41	7.5	16	06	7.8	05	07	3.0	17	16	3.3	07	39	4.5	19	51	4.6
TU 14	06	54	5.8	19	38	5.8	04	38	7.3	17	06	7.5	05	57	3.0	18	09	3.1	08	31	4.4	20	48	4.5
W 15	07	53	5.7	20	35	5.7	05	43	7.2	18	10	7.5	06	52	2.9	19	09	3.0	09	28	4.4	21	48	4.5
TH 16	09	07	5.6	21	39	5.7	06	50	7.3	19	13	7.6	07	55	3.0	20	18	3.0	10	26	4.5	22	48	4.5
F 17	10	16	5.8	22	45	5.9	07	51	7.6	20	10	7.8	09	00	3.0	21	25	3.1	11	25	4.6	23	47	4.7
SA 18	11	14	6.1	23	44	6.2	08	42	7.9	21	00	8.2	09	57	3.2	22	22	3.2	12	19	4.8	—		—
SU 19	12	05	6.4	—		—	09	27	8.4	21	46	8.5	10	45	3.3	23	10	3.3	00	40	4.9	13	08	5.1
M 20	00	35	6.4	12	53	6.6	10	08	8.7	22	29	8.8	11	26	3.5	23	55	3.3	01	29	5.1	13	51	5.3
TU 21	01	22	6.6	13	37	6.8	10	48	9.0	23	11	9.0	12	05	3.6	—		—	02	12	5.3	14	32	5.4
W 22	02	06	6.7	14	22	7.0	11	29	9.3	23	53	9.2	00	40	3.4	12	45	3.7	02	54	5.5	15	10	5.5
TH 23	02	49	6.7	15	06	7.1	12	11	9.4	—		—	01	25	3.4	13	25	3.8	03	35	5.6	15	50	5.6
F 24	03	30	6.8	15	50	7.2	00	38	9.3	12	56	9.5	02	10	3.4	14	08	3.9	04	18	5.6	16	31	5.6
SA 25	04	11	6.8	16	35	7.1	01	24	9.2	13	41	9.4	02	55	3.4	14	51	3.9	05	03	5.6	17	16	5.6
SU 26	04	52	6.7	17	22	7.0	02	11	9.0	14	30	9.2	03	41	3.3	15	36	3.8	05	50	5.4	18	03	5.5
M 27	05	37	6.7	18	13	6.8	03	01	8.7	15	21	8.9	04	28	3.3	16	23	3.7	06	40	5.2	18	56	5.3
TU 28	06	26	6.5	19	08	6.6	03	55	8.4	16	19	8.6	05	19	3.2	17	14	3.6	07	37	5.0	19	58	5.1
W 29	07	24	6.4	20	09	6.3	04	57	8.1	17	25	8.3	06	16	3.1	18	12	3.4	08	42	4.8	21	11	5.0
TH 30	08	32	6.3	21	16	6.2	06	06	7.9	18	37	8.1	07	25	3.0	19	20	3.2	09	51	4.8	22	23	4.9
F 31	09	46	6.2	—		—	07	18	8.0				08	43	3.0				10	57	4.8	—		—

† Predictions are for Gladstone Dock

INDEX

U